Fundamental Accounting Principles

Fundamental Accounting Principles

23 **rd** **edition**

John J. Wild

University of Wisconsin at Madison

Ken W. Shaw

University of Missouri at Columbia

Barbara Chiappetta

Nassau Community College

Mc Graw Hill Education

To my students and family, especially **Kimberly, Jonathan, Stephanie,** and **Trevor.**

To my wife **Linda** and children **Erin, Emily,** and **Jacob.**

To my mother, husband **Bob,** and sons **Michael** and **David.**

FUNDAMENTAL ACCOUNTING PRINCIPLES, TWENTY-THIRD EDITION

Published by McGraw-Hill Education, 2 Penn Plaza, New York, NY 10121. Copyright © 2017 by McGraw-Hill Education. All rights reserved. Printed in the United States of America. Previous editions © 2015, 2013, and 2011. No part of this publication may be reproduced or distributed in any form or by any means, or stored in a database or retrieval system, without the prior written consent of McGraw-Hill Education, including, but not limited to, in any network or other electronic storage or transmission, or broadcast for distance learning.

Some ancillaries, including electronic and print components, may not be available to customers outside the United States.

This book is printed on acid-free paper.

1 2 3 4 5 6 7 8 9 DOW 21 20 19 18 17 16

ISBN 978-1-259-53635-9 (combined edition)
MHID 1-259-53635-1 (combined edition)
ISBN 978-1-259-68774-7 (principles, chapters 1-17)
MHID 1-259-68774-0 (principles, chapters 1-17)

Chief Product Officer, SVP,
    Products & Markets: *G. Scott Virkler*
Vice President, General Manager,
    Products & Markets: *Marty Lange*
Managing Director: *Tim Vertovec*
Marketing Director: *Natalie King*
Brand Manager: *Steve Schuetz*
Director, Product Development: *Rose Koos*
Director of Digital Content: *Peggy Hussey*
Associate Director of Digital Content: *Kevin Moran*
Lead Product Developer: *Kris Tibbetts*
Product Developer: *Michael McCormick*

Marketing Manager: *Michelle Williams*
Market Development Manager: *Erin Chomat*
Digital Product Analyst: *Xin Lin*
Director, Content Design & Delivery: *Linda Avenarius*
Program Manager: *Daryl Horrocks*
Content Project Managers: *Lori Koetters, Brian Nacik*
Buyer: *Sandy Ludovissy*
Design: *Debra Kubiak*
Content Licensing Specialists: *Melissa Homer, Melisa Seegmiller*
Cover Image: *Bartosz Hadyniak/Getty Images*
Compositor: *Aptara®, Inc.*
Printer: *R.R. Donnelley*

All credits appearing on page or at the end of the book are considered to be an extension of the copyright page. Icon credits— Background for icons: © *Dizzle52/Getty Images;* Lightbulb: © *Chuhail/Getty Images;* Globe: © *nidwlw/Getty Images;* Chess piece: © *AndSim/Getty Images;* Computer mouse: © *Siede Preis/Getty Images;* Global View globe: © *McGraw-Hill Education;* Sustainability and Accounting icon: © *McGraw-Hill Education*

Library of Congress Cataloging-in-Publication Data

Names: Wild, John J., author. | Shaw, Ken W., author. | Chiappetta, Barbara, author.
Title: Fundamental accounting principles / John J. Wild, University of Wisconsin at Madison, Ken W. Shaw,
    University of Missouri at Columbia, Barbara Chiappetta, Nassau Community College.
Description: 23rd edition. | New York, NY : McGraw-Hill Education, [2017]
Identifiers: LCCN 2016021247 | ISBN 9781259536359 (alk. paper) | ISBN 1259536351 (alk. paper) | ISBN 9781259687747
    (alk. paper : chapters 1–17) | ISBN 1259687740 (alk. paper : chapters 1–17)
Subjects: LCSH: Accounting.
Classification: LCC HF5636 .W675 2017 | DDC 657—dc23 LC record available at https://lccn.loc.gov/2016021247

The Internet addresses listed in the text were accurate at the time of publication. The inclusion of a website does not indicate an endorsement by the authors or McGraw-Hill Education, and McGraw-Hill Education does not guarantee the accuracy of the information presented at these sites.

mheducation.com/highered

Adapting to Today's Students

Whether the goal is to become an accountant, a businessperson, or simply an informed consumer of accounting information, *Fundamental Accounting Principles (FAP)* has helped generations of students succeed. Its leading-edge accounting content, paired with state-of-the-art technology, supports student learning and elevates understanding of key accounting principles.

FAP excels at **engaging students** with content that shows the relevance of accounting. Its chapter-opening vignettes showcase dynamic entrepreneurial companies to highlight the **usefulness of accounting.** This edition's featured companies—**Apple, Google,** and **Samsung**—capture student interest, and their annual reports are a pathway for learning. Need-to-Know demonstrations in each chapter apply key concepts and procedures and include guided video presentations.

FAP delivers innovative technology to help student performance. **Connect** provides students a media-rich eBook version of the textbook and offers instant online grading and feedback for assignments. **Connect** takes accounting content to the next level, delivering assessment material in a **more intuitive, less restrictive** format.

Our technology features:

- **A general journal interface** that looks and feels more like that found in practice.
- **An auto-calculation** feature that allows students to focus on concepts rather than rote tasks.
- **A smart (auto-fill) drop-down design.**

The result is content that prepares students for today's world.

Connect also includes digitally based, interactive, adaptive learning tools that engage students more effectively by offering varied instructional methods and more personalized learning paths that build on different learning styles, interests, and abilities.

The revolutionary technology of **SmartBook**® is available only from McGraw-Hill Education. Based on an intelligent learning system, SmartBook uses a series of adaptive questions to pinpoint each student's knowledge gaps and then provides an optimal learning path. Students spend less time in areas they already know and more time in areas they don't. The result: Students study more efficiently, learn faster, and retain more knowledge. Valuable reports provide insights into how students are progressing through textbook content and information useful for shaping in-class time or assessment.

Interactive Presentations teach each chapter's core learning objectives in a rich, multimedia format, bringing the content to life. Your students come to class prepared when you assign Interactive Presentations. Students can also review the Interactive Presentations as they study. **Guided Examples** provide students with narrated, animated, step-by-step walkthroughs of algorithmic versions of assigned exercises. Students appreciate Guided Examples, which help them learn and complete assignments outside of class.

A **General Ledger (GL) application** offers students the ability to see how transactions post from the general journal all the way through the financial statements. It uses an intuitive, less restrictive format, and it adds critical thinking components to each GL question, to ensure understanding of the entire process.

The first and only analytics tool of its kind, **Connect Insight**® is a series of visual data displays—each framed by an intuitive question—to provide information on how your class is doing on five key dimensions.

"A great enhancement! I love the fact that GL makes the student choose from an entire chart of accounts."

—TAMMY METZKE, Milwaukee Area Technical College

About the Authors

JOHN J. WILD is a distinguished professor of accounting at the University of Wisconsin at Madison. He previously held appointments at Michigan State University and the University of Manchester in England. He received his BBA, MS, and PhD from the University of Wisconsin.

John teaches accounting courses at both the undergraduate and graduate levels. He has received numerous teaching honors, including the Mabel W. Chipman Excellence-in-Teaching Award and the departmental Excellence-in-Teaching Award, and he is a two-time recipient of the Teaching Excellence Award from business graduates at the University of Wisconsin. He also received the Beta Alpha Psi and Roland F. Salmonson Excellence-in-Teaching Award from Michigan State University. John has received several research honors, is a past KPMG Peat Marwick National Fellow, and is a recipient of fellowships from the American Accounting Association and the Ernst and Young Foundation.

John is an active member of the American Accounting Association and its sections. He has served on several committees of these organizations, including the Outstanding Accounting Educator Award, Wildman Award, National Program Advisory, Publications, and Research Committees. John is author of *Financial Accounting, Managerial Accounting,* and *College Accounting*, all published by McGraw-Hill Education.

John's research articles on accounting and analysis appear in *The Accounting Review; Journal of Accounting Research; Journal of Accounting and Economics; Contemporary Accounting Research; Journal of Accounting, Auditing and Finance; Journal of Accounting and Public Policy;* and other journals. He is past associate editor of *Contemporary Accounting Research* and has served on several editorial boards including *The Accounting Review*.

In his leisure time, John enjoys hiking, sports, boating, travel, people, and spending time with family and friends.

KEN W. SHAW is an associate professor of accounting and the KPMG/Joseph A. Silvoso Distinguished Professor of Accounting at the University of Missouri. He previously was on the faculty at the University of Maryland at College Park. He has also taught in international programs at the University of Bergamo (Italy) and the University of Alicante (Spain). He received an accounting degree from Bradley University and an MBA and PhD from the University of Wisconsin. He is a Certified Public Accountant with work experience in public accounting.

Ken teaches accounting at the undergraduate and graduate levels. He has received numerous School of Accountancy, College of Business, and university-level teaching awards. He was voted the "Most Influential Professor" by four School of Accountancy graduating classes and is a two-time recipient of the O'Brien Excellence in Teaching Award. He is the advisor to his school's chapter of the Association of Certified Fraud Examiners.

Ken is an active member of the American Accounting Association and its sections. He has served on many committees of these organizations and presented his research papers at national and regional meetings. Ken's research appears in the *Journal of Accounting Research; The Accounting Review; Contemporary Accounting Research; Journal of Financial and Quantitative Analysis; Journal of the American Taxation Association; Strategic Management Journal; Journal of Accounting, Auditing, and Finance; Journal of Financial Research;* and other journals. He has served on the editorial boards of *Issues in Accounting Education; Journal of Business Research;* and *Research in Accounting Regulation.* Ken is co-author of *Financial and Managerial Accounting, Managerial Accounting,* and *College Accounting,* all published by McGraw-Hill Education.

In his leisure time, Ken enjoys tennis, cycling, music, and coaching his children's sports teams.

BARBARA CHIAPPETTA received her BBA in Accountancy and MS in Education from Hofstra University and is an emeritus tenured full professor at Nassau Community College. For many decades, she has been an active executive board member of the Teachers of Accounting at Two-Year Colleges (TACTYC), serving 10 years as vice president and as president from 1993 through 1999. As a member of the American Accounting Association, she has served on the Northeast Regional Steering Committee, chaired the Curriculum Revision Committee of the Two-Year Section, and participated in numerous national committees.

Barbara has been inducted into the American Accounting Association Hall of Fame for the Northeast Region. She has also received the Nassau Community College dean of instruction's Faculty Distinguished Achievement Award. Barbara was honored with the State University of New York Chancellor's Award for Teaching Excellence. As a confirmed believer in the benefits of the active learning pedagogy, Barbara has authored *Student Learning Tools,* an active learning workbook for a first-year accounting course, published by McGraw-Hill Education.

In her leisure time, Barbara enjoys tennis and participates on a USTA team. She also enjoys the challenge of bridge. Her husband, Robert, is an entrepreneur in the leisure sport industry. She has two sons—Michael, a lawyer specializing in intellectual property law, and David, a composer pursuing a career in music for film. Barbara has been an important member of this book's author team, and her co-authors continue to acknowledge her substantial contributions to prior editions.

Dear Colleagues and Friends,

As we roll out the new edition of *Fundamental Accounting Principles,* we thank each of you who provided suggestions to improve the textbook and its teaching resources. This new edition reflects the advice and wisdom of many dedicated reviewers, symposium and workshop participants, students, and instructors. Throughout the revision process, we steered this textbook and its teaching tools in the manner you directed. As you'll find, the new edition offers a rich set of features—especially digital features—to improve student learning and assist instructor teaching and grading. We believe you and your students will like what you find in this new edition.

Many talented educators and professionals have worked hard to create the materials for this product, and for their efforts, we're grateful. **We extend a special thank-you to our contributing and technology supplement authors,** who have worked so diligently to support this product:

Contributing Author: Kathleen O'Donnell, *Onondaga Community College*

Accuracy Checkers: Dave Krug, *Johnson County Community College;* Mark McCarthy, *East Carolina University;* Helen Roybark, *Radford University*

LearnSmart Author: April Mohr, *Jefferson Community and Technical College, SW*

Interactive Presentations: Jeannie Folk, *College of DuPage;* April Mohr, *Jefferson Community and Technical College, SW*

PowerPoint Presentations: April Mohr, *Jefferson Community and Technical College, SW*

Instructor Resource Manual: April Mohr, *Jefferson Community and Technical College, SW*

Test Bank: Kathleen O'Donnell, *Onondaga Community College;* Anna Boulware, *St. Charles Community College;* Mark McCarthy, *East Carolina University;* Beth Woods

Digital Contributor, Connect Content, General Ledger Problems, and Exercise PowerPoints: Kathleen O'Donnell, *Onondaga Community College*

In addition to the invaluable help from the colleagues listed above, we thank the entire *FAP* 23e team at McGraw-Hill Education: Tim Vertovec, Steve Schuetz, Michelle Williams, Erin Chomat, Kris Tibbetts, Michael McCormick, Lori Koetters, Peggy Hussey, Xin Lin, Kevin Moran, Debra Kubiak, Sarah Evertson, Brian Nacik, and Daryl Horrocks. We could not have published this new edition without your efforts.

John J. Wild   *Ken W. Shaw*   *Barbara Chiappetta*

Innovative Textbook Features . . .

Using Accounting for Decisions

Whether we prepare, analyze, or apply accounting information, one skill remains essential: decision making. To help develop good decision-making habits and to illustrate the relevance of accounting, we use a learning framework to enhance decision-making in four ways. (See the four nearby examples for the different types of decision boxes, including those that relate to fraud.) **Decision Insight** provides context for business decisions. **Decision Ethics** and **Decision Maker** are role-playing scenarios that show the relevance of accounting. **Decision Analysis** provides key tools to help assess company performance.

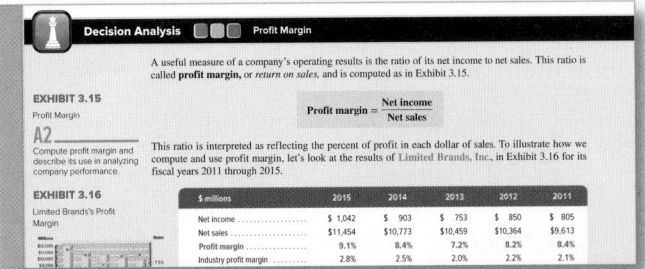

"This textbook does address many learning styles and at the same time allows for many teaching styles . . . our faculty have been very pleased with the continued revisions and supplements. I'm a 'Wild' fan!"

— **RITA HAYS, Southwestern Oklahoma State University**

Chapter Preview

Each chapter opens with a visual chapter preview. Students can begin their reading with a clear understanding of what they will learn and when. Learning objective numbers highlight the location of related content. Each "block" of content concludes with a Need-To-Know (NTK) to aid and reinforce student learning.

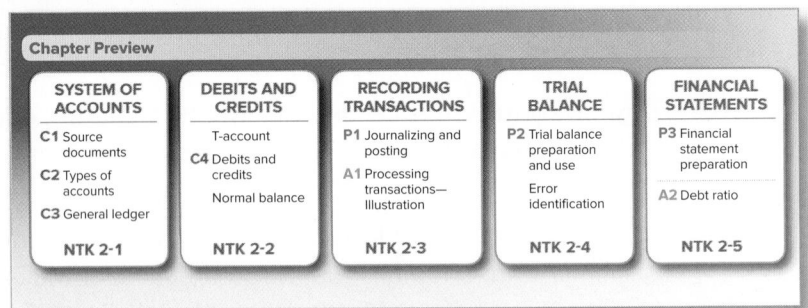

CAP Model

The Conceptual/Analytical/Procedural (CAP) model allows courses to be specially designed to meet the teaching needs of a diverse faculty. This model identifies learning objectives, textual materials, assignments, and test items by C, A, or P, allowing different instructors to teach from the same materials, yet easily customize their courses toward a conceptual, analytical, or procedural approach (or a combination thereof) based on personal preferences.

Learning Objectives

CONCEPTUAL

C1 Explain the steps in processing transactions and the role of source documents.

C2 Describe an account and its use in recording transactions.

C3 Describe a ledger and a chart of accounts.

C4 Define *debits* and *credits* and explain double-entry accounting.

ANALYTICAL

A1 Analyze the impact of transactions on accounts and financial statements.

A2 Compute the debt ratio and describe its use in analyzing financial condition.

PROCEDURAL

P1 Record transactions in a journal and post entries to a ledger.

P2 Prepare and explain the use of a trial balance.

P3 Prepare financial statements from business transactions.

Bring Accounting to Life

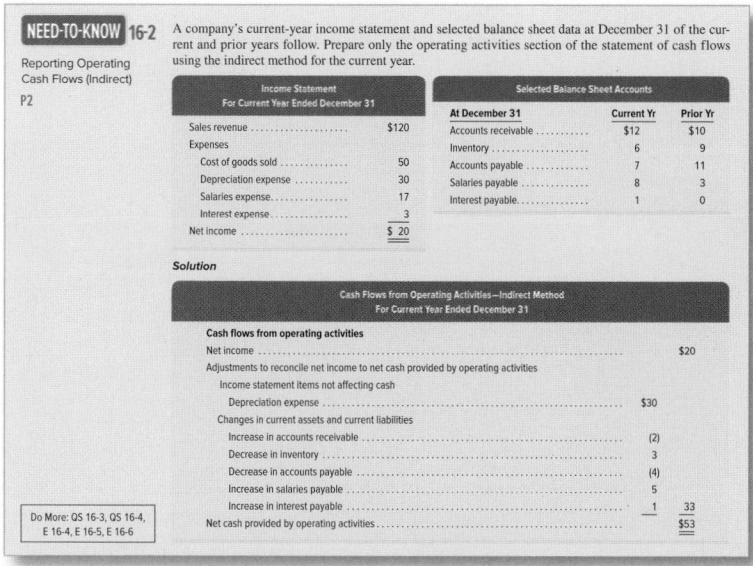

Need-to-Know Demonstrations

Need-to-Know demonstrations are located at key junctures in each chapter. These demonstrations pose questions about the material just presented—content that students "need to know" to successfully learn accounting. Accompanying solutions walk students through key procedures and analysis necessary to be successful with homework and test materials. Need-to-Know demonstrations are supplemented with narrated, animated, step-by-step walk-through videos led by an instructor and available via **Connect**.

Global View

The Global View section explains international accounting practices related to the material covered in that chapter. The aim of this section is to describe accounting practices and to identify the similarities and differences in international accounting practices versus those in the United States. The importance of student familiarity with international accounting continues to grow. This innovative section helps us begin down that path. This section is purposefully located at the very end of each chapter so that each instructor can decide what emphasis, if at all, is to be assigned to it.

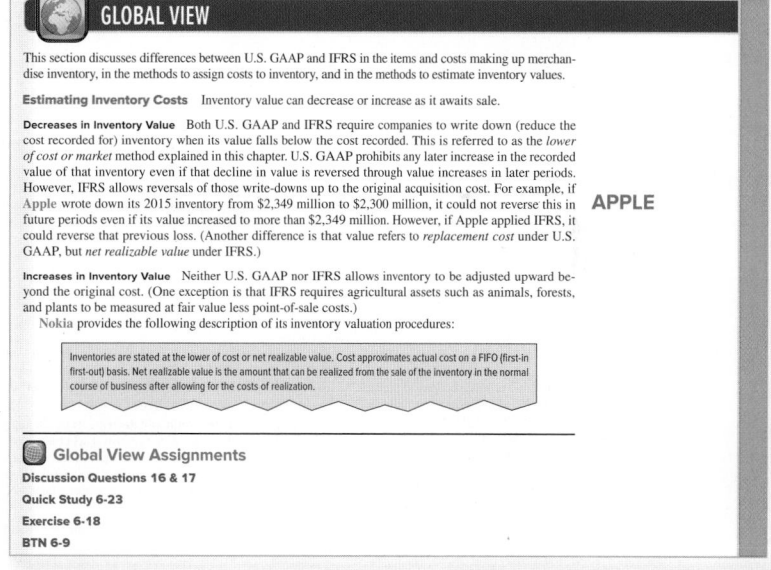

Sustainability and Accounting

This edition has brief sections that highlight the importance of sustainability within the broader context of global accounting (and accountability). Companies increasingly address sustainability in their public reporting and consider the sustainability accounting standards (from the Sustainability Accounting Standards Board) and the expectations of our global society. These sections cover different aspects of sustainability, often within the context of the chapter's featured entrepreneurial company.

Outstanding Assignment Material . . .

Once a student has finished reading the chapter, how well he or she retains the material can depend greatly on the questions, brief exercises, exercises, and problems that reinforce it. This book leads the way in comprehensive, accurate assignments.

Comprehensive Need-to-Know Problems present both a problem and a complete solution, allowing students to review the entire problem-solving process and achieve success. The problems draw on material from the entire chapter.

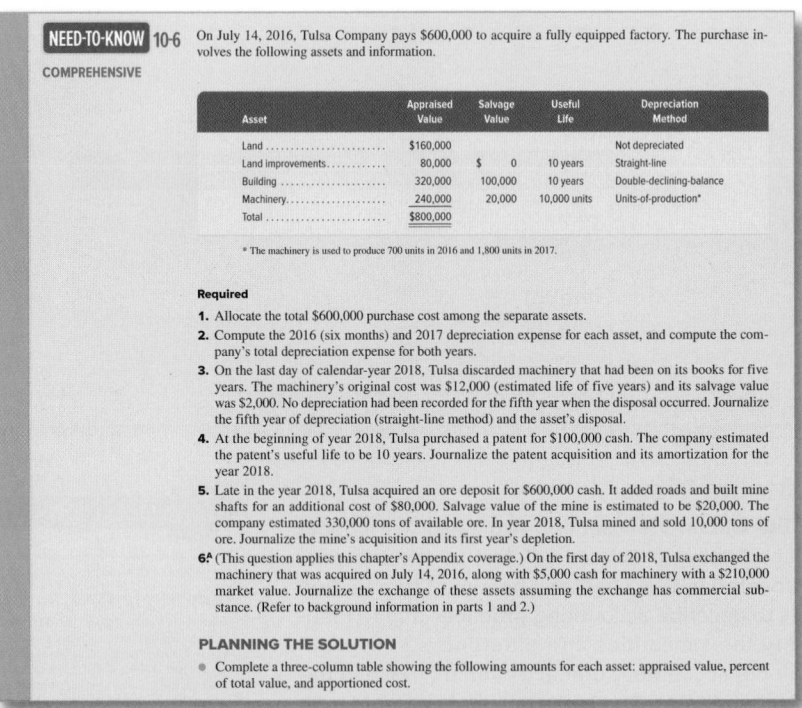

NEED-TO-KNOW 10-6

COMPREHENSIVE

On July 14, 2016, Tulsa Company pays $600,000 to acquire a fully equipped factory. The purchase involves the following assets and information.

Asset	Appraised Value	Salvage Value	Useful Life	Depreciation Method
Land	$160,000			Not depreciated
Land improvements	80,000	$ 0	10 years	Straight-line
Building	320,000	100,000	10 years	Double-declining-balance
Machinery	240,000	20,000	10,000 units	Units-of-production*
Total	$800,000			

* The machinery is used to produce 700 units in 2016 and 1,800 units in 2017.

Required

1. Allocate the total $600,000 purchase cost among the separate assets.

2. Compute the 2016 (six months) and 2017 depreciation expense for each asset, and compute the company's total depreciation expense for both years.

3. On the last day of calendar-year 2018, Tulsa discarded machinery that had been on its books for five years. The machinery's original cost was $12,000 (estimated life of five years) and its salvage value was $2,000. No depreciation had been recorded for the fifth year when the disposal occurred. Journalize the fifth year of depreciation (straight-line method) and the asset's disposal.

4. At the beginning of year 2018, Tulsa purchased a patent for $100,000 cash. The company estimated the patent's useful life to be 10 years. Journalize the patent acquisition and its amortization for the year 2018.

5. Late in the year 2018, Tulsa acquired an ore deposit for $600,000 cash. It added roads and built mine shafts for an additional cost of $80,000. Salvage value of the mine is estimated to be $20,000. The company estimated 330,000 tons of available ore. In year 2018, Tulsa mined and sold 10,000 tons of ore. Journalize the mine's acquisition and its first year's depletion.

6.ᴬ (This question applies this chapter's Appendix coverage.) On the first day of 2018, Tulsa exchanged the machinery that was acquired on July 14, 2016, along with $5,000 cash for machinery with a $210,000 market value. Journalize the exchange of these assets assuming the exchange has commercial substance. (Refer to background information in parts 1 and 2.)

PLANNING THE SOLUTION

● Complete a three-column table showing the following amounts for each asset: appraised value, percent of total value, and apportioned cost.

Summary

C1 **Explain the steps in processing transactions and the role of source documents.** Transactions and events are the starting points in the accounting process. Source documents identify and describe transactions and events and provide objective and reliable evidence. The effects of transactions and events are recorded in journals. Posting along with a trial balance helps summarize and classify these effects.

C2 **Describe an account and its use in recording transactions.** An account is a detailed record of increases and decreases in a specific asset, liability, equity, revenue, or expense. Information from accounts is analyzed, summarized, and presented in reports and financial statements.

C3 **Describe a ledger and a chart of accounts.** The ledger (or general ledger) is a record containing all accounts used by a company and their balances. It is referred to as the *books*. The chart of accounts is a list of all accounts and usually includes an identification number assigned to each account.

C4 **Define *debits* and *credits* and explain double-entry accounting.** *Debit* refers to left, and *credit* refers to right. Debits increase assets, expenses, and withdrawals while credits decrease them. Credits increase liabilities, owner capital, and

A1 **Analyze the impact of transactions on accounts and financial statements.** We analyze transactions using concepts of double-entry accounting. This analysis is performed by determining a transaction's effects on accounts.

A2 **Compute the debt ratio and describe its use in analyzing financial condition.** A company's debt ratio is computed as total liabilities divided by total assets. It reveals how much of the assets are financed by creditor (nonowner) financing. The higher this ratio, the more risk a company faces because liabilities must be repaid at specific dates.

P1 **Record transactions in a journal and post entries to a ledger.** Transactions are recorded in a journal. Each entry in a journal is posted to the accounts in the ledger. This provides information that is used to produce financial statements. Balance column accounts are widely used and include columns for debits, credits, and the account balance.

P2 **Prepare and explain the use of a trial balance.** A trial balance is a list of accounts from the ledger showing their debit or credit balances in separate columns. The trial balance is a summary of the ledger's contents and is useful in preparing financial statements and in revealing recordkeeping errors.

Chapter Summaries provide students with a review organized by learning objectives. Chapter Summaries are a component of the CAP model (as discussed in the "Innovative Textbook Features" section), which recaps each conceptual, analytical, and procedural objective.

Key Terms are bolded in the text and repeated at the end of the chapter. A complete glossary of key terms is available online through **Connect**.

Key Terms

Accounting period	Cash basis accounting	Prepaid expenses
Accrual basis accounting	Contra account	Profit margin
Accrued expenses	Depreciation	Revenue recognition principle
Accrued revenues	Expense recognition (or matching)	Straight-line depreciation method
Accumulated depreciation	principle	Time period assumption
Adjusted trial balance	Fiscal year	Unadjusted trial balance
Adjusting entry	Interim financial statements	Unearned revenues
Annual financial statements	Natural business year	
Book value	Plant assets	

Helps Students Master Key Concepts

Multiple Choice Quiz questions quickly test chapter knowledge before a student moves on to complete Quick Studies, Exercises, and Problems.

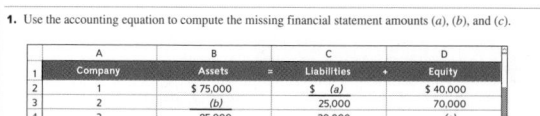

1. Use the accounting equation to compute the missing financial statement amounts (a), (b), and (c).

QS 1-8
Applying the accounting equation
A1

	A	B		C		D
1	Company	Assets	=	Liabilities	+	Equity
2	1	$ 75,000		$ (a)		$ 40,000
3	2	(b)		25,000		70,000
4	3	85,000		20,000		(c)

Quick Study assignments are short exercises that often focus on one learning objective. Most are included in **Connect**. There are at least 10–15 Quick Study assignments per chapter.

Exercises are one of this book's many strengths and a competitive advantage. There are at least 10–15 per chapter, and most are included in **Connect**.

Ford Motor Company, one of the world's largest automakers, reports the following income statement accounts for the year ended December 31, 2015 ($ in millions). Use this information to prepare Ford's income statement for the year ended December 31, 2015.

Exercise 1-20
Preparing an income statement for a global company
P2

Selling and administrative costs	$ 14,999
Cost of sales	124,041
Revenues	149,558
Other expenses	3,145

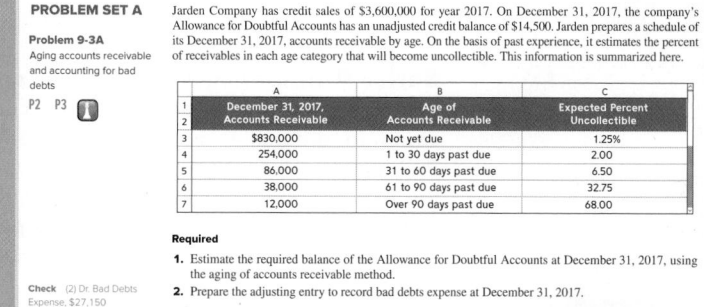

≡connect

PROBLEM SET A

Problem 9-3A
Aging accounts receivable and accounting for bad debts
P2 P3

Jarden Company has credit sales of $3,600,000 for year 2017. On December 31, 2017, the company's Allowance for Doubtful Accounts has an unadjusted credit balance of $14,500. Jarden prepares a schedule of its December 31, 2017, accounts receivable by age. On the basis of past experience, it estimates the percent of receivables in each age category that will become uncollectible. This information is summarized here.

	A	B	C
1	December 31, 2017, Accounts Receivable	Age of Accounts Receivable	Expected Percent Uncollectible
2			
3	$830,000	Not yet due	1.25%
4	254,000	1 to 30 days past due	2.00
5	86,000	31 to 60 days past due	6.50
6	38,000	61 to 90 days past due	32.75
7	12,000	Over 90 days past due	68.00

Required

1. Estimate the required balance of the Allowance for Doubtful Accounts at December 31, 2017, using the aging of accounts receivable method.
2. Prepare the adjusting entry to record bad debts expense at December 31, 2017.

Check (2) Dr. Bad Debts Expense, $27,150

Problem Sets A & B are proven problems that can be assigned as homework or for in-class projects. All problems are coded according to the CAP model (see the "Innovative Textbook Features" section), and Set A is included in **Connect**.

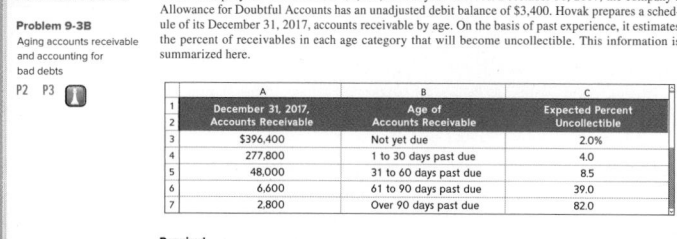

PROBLEM SET B

Problem 9-3B
Aging accounts receivable and accounting for bad debts
P2 P3

Hovak Company has credit sales of $4,500,000 for year 2017. At December 31, 2017, the company's Allowance for Doubtful Accounts has an unadjusted debit balance of $3,400. Hovak prepares a schedule of its December 31, 2017, accounts receivable by age. On the basis of past experience, it estimates the percent of receivables in each age category that will become uncollectible. This information is summarized here.

	A	B	C
1	December 31, 2017, Accounts Receivable	Age of Accounts Receivable	Expected Percent Uncollectible
2			
3	$396,400	Not yet due	2.0%
4	277,800	1 to 30 days past due	4.0
5	48,000	31 to 60 days past due	8.5
6	6,600	61 to 90 days past due	39.0
7	2,800	Over 90 days past due	82.0

Required

1. Compute the required balance of the Allowance for Doubtful Accounts at December 31, 2017, using the aging of accounts receivable method.
2. Prepare the adjusting entry to record bad debts expense at December 31, 2017.

Check (2) Dr. Bad Debts Expense, $31,390

"I like the layout of the text and the readability. The illustrations and comics in the book make the text seem less intimidating and boring for students. The PowerPoint slides are easy to understand and use, the pictorials are great, and the text has great coverage of accounting material. The addition of IFRS information and the updates to the opening stories are great. I like that the Decision Insights are about businesses the students can relate to."

—JEANNIE LIU, Chaffey College

Outstanding Assignment Material . . .

Beyond the Numbers exercises ask students to use accounting figures and understand their meaning. Students also learn how accounting applies to a variety of business situations. These creative and fun exercises are all new or updated and are divided into nine types:

- Reporting in Action
- Comparative Analysis
- Ethics Challenge
- Communicating in Practice
- Taking It to the Net
- Teamwork in Action
- Hitting the Road
- Entrepreneurial Decision
- Global Decision

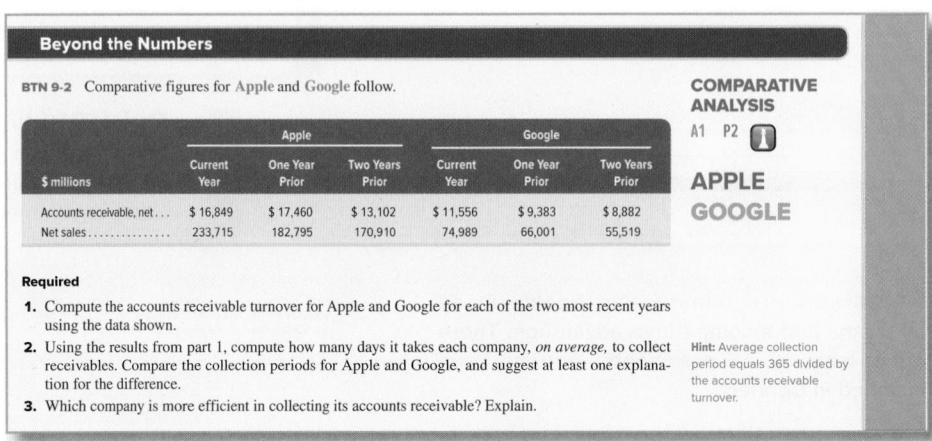

Beyond the Numbers

BTN 9-2 Comparative figures for Apple and Google follow.

COMPARATIVE ANALYSIS
A1 P2

APPLE
GOOGLE

	Apple			Google		
$ millions	Current Year	One Year Prior	Two Years Prior	Current Year	One Year Prior	Two Years Prior
Accounts receivable, net . . .	$ 16,849	$ 17,460	$ 13,102	$ 11,556	$ 9,383	$ 8,882
Net sales	233,715	182,795	170,910	74,989	66,001	55,519

Required

1. Compute the accounts receivable turnover for Apple and Google for each of the two most recent years using the data shown.
2. Using the results from part 1, compute how many days it takes each company, *on average*, to collect receivables. Compare the collection periods for Apple and Google, and suggest at least one explanation for the difference.
3. Which company is more efficient in collecting its accounts receivable? Explain.

Hint: Average collection period equals 365 divided by the accounts receivable turnover.

SERIAL PROBLEM
Business Solutions
P3

(This serial problem began in Chapter 1 and continues through most of the book. If previous chapter segments were not completed, the serial problem can begin at this point.)

SP 8 Santana Rey receives the March bank statement for **Business Solutions** on April 11, 2018. The March 31 bank statement shows an ending cash balance of $67,566. A comparison of the bank statement with the general ledger Cash account, No. 101, reveals the following.

a. S. Rey notices that the bank erroneously cleared a $500 check against her account in March that she did not issue. The check documentation included with the bank statement shows that this check was actually issued by a company named Business Systems.

b. On March 25, the bank lists a $50 charge for the safety deposit box expense that Business Solutions agreed to rent from the bank beginning March 25.

c. On March 26, the bank lists a $102 charge for printed checks that Business Solutions ordered from the bank.

d. On March 31, the bank lists $33 interest earned on Business Solutions's checking account for the month of March.

e. S. Rey notices that the check she issued for $128 on March 31, 2018, has not yet cleared the bank.

f. S. Rey verifies that all deposits made in March do appear on the March bank statement.

g. The general ledger Cash account, No. 101, shows an ending cash balance per books of $68,057 as of March 31 (prior to any reconciliation).

© Alexander Image/Shutterstock RF

Required

1. Prepare a bank reconciliation for Business Solutions for the month ended March 31, 2018.
2. Prepare any necessary adjusting entries. Use Miscellaneous Expenses, No. 677, for any bank charges. Use Interest Revenue, No. 404, for any interest earned on the checking account for the month of March.

Check (1) Adj. bank bal., $67,938

Serial Problems use a continuous running case study to illustrate chapter concepts in a familiar context. The Serial Problem can be followed continuously from the first chapter or picked up at any later point in the book; enough information is provided to ensure students can get right to work.

Helps Students Master Key Concepts

General Ledger Problems enable students to see how transactions post. Students can track an amount in any financial statement all the way back to the original journal entry. Critical thinking components then challenge students to analyze the business activities in the problem.

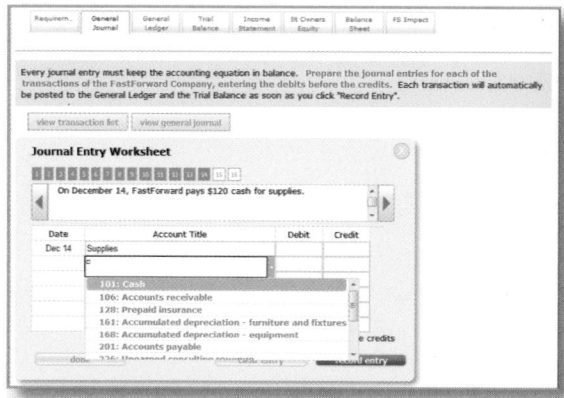

The **General Ledger** tool in Connect allows students to immediately see the financial statements as of a specific date. Each of the following questions begins with an unadjusted trial balance. Using transactions from the following assignment, prepare the necessary adjustments, and determine the impact each adjustment has on net income. The financial statements are automatically populated.

GL 3-1 Based on the FastForward illustration in this chapter

Using transactions from the following assignments, prepare the necessary adjustments, create the financial statements, and determine the impact each adjustment has on net income.

GL 3-2 Based on Problem 3-3A   **GL 3-4** Extension of Problem 2-2A

GL 3-3 Extension of Problem 2-1A   **GL 3-5** Based on Serial Problem SP 3

GL **GENERAL LEDGER PROBLEM**

Available only in Connect

connect

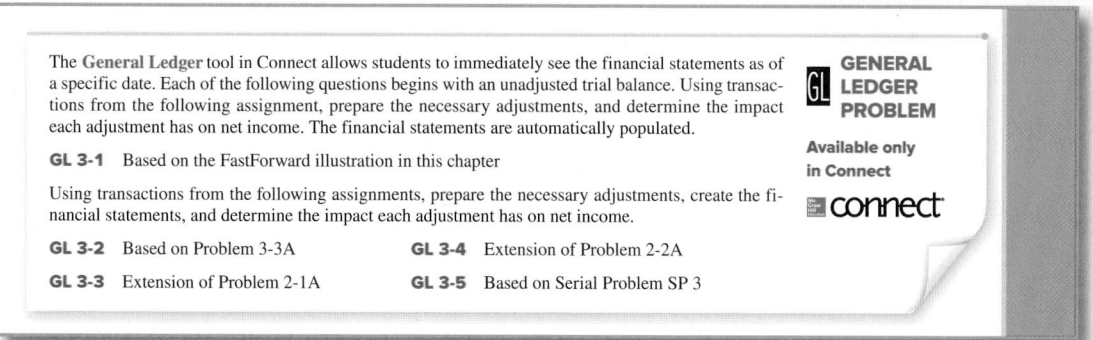

Excel Simulations allow you to practice your Excel skills, such as basic formulas and formatting, within the context of accounting. These questions feature animated, narrated Help and Show Me tutorials (when enabled by your instructor).

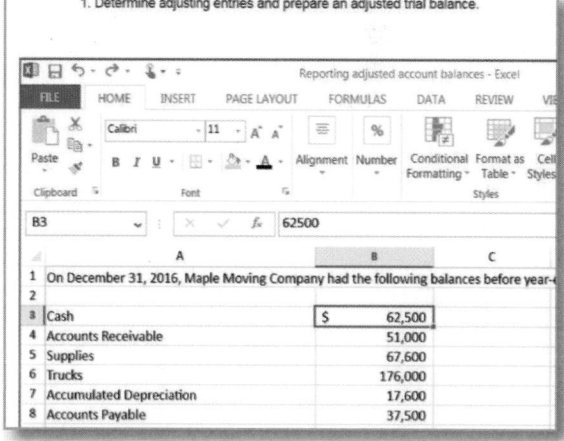

The End of the Chapter Is Only the Beginning Our valuable and proven assignments aren't just confined to the book. From problems that require technological solutions to materials found exclusively online, this book's end-of-chapter material is fully integrated with its technology package.

- Quick Studies, Exercises, and Problems available in **Connect** are marked with an icon.

 Assignments that focus on global accounting practices and companies are often identified with an icon.

 Assignments that involve ethical or fraud risk are marked with an icon.

 Assignments that involve decision analysis are identified with an icon.

 Assignments that involve sustainability issues are marked with an icon.

Content Revisions Enhance Learning

This edition's revisions are driven by feedback from instructors and students. They include:

- Many new, revised, and updated assignments throughout, including entrepreneurial and real-world assignments.
- Many Need-To-Know (NTK) demonstrations added to each chapter at key junctures to reinforce learning.
- Updated Sustainability section for each chapter, with examples linked to the chapter-opening company.
- New annual reports and comparative (BTN) assignments: Apple, Google, and Samsung.

- Revised art program, visual infographics, and text layout.
- Updated ratio/tool analysis using data from well-known firms.
- Revised General Ledger assignments for most chapters.
- New and revised entrepreneurial examples and elements.
- New technology content integrated and referenced in the book.
- Revised Global View section moved to the very end of each chapter following assignments.

Chapter 1

Updated opener—Apple and entrepreneurial assignment.
Updated salary info for accountants and for those with college degrees.
Streamlined "Fraud Triangle" section.
Updated "Cooking the Books" Fraud box.
Moved "Enforcing Ethics" section to earlier in chapter.
Streamlined the "Fundamentals of Accounting" section.
Streamlined the "International Standards" section.
Updated the revenue recognition section.
New margin point to highlight layout of statement of owner's equity.
Updated Sustainability section for Apple's renewable energy efforts, including SASB.
Updated Decision Insight box on sustainability returns.
New company, Verizon, for Decision Analysis section.
Streamlined Appendix 1A and 1B.
Added new Exercise.

Chapter 2

NEW opener—Soko and entrepreneurial assignment.
Simplified discussion on analyzing and recording process.
Streamlined discussion of classified vs. unclassified balance sheet.
Enhanced explanation of computing equity.
Enhanced Exhibit 2.4 to identify account categories.
Improved summary of transactions in the ledger.
Streamlined explanation of error correction in entries.
New accounting quality box with reference to KPMG data.
Revised Sustainability section on cost savings for small business.
Updated debt ratio analysis using Skechers.
Added two Quick Study assignments.
Updated Piaggio's (IFRS) balance sheet.

Chapter 3

NEW opener—re:char and entrepreneurial assignment.
Streamlined accrual-basis vs. cash-basis section.
New box on how accounting is used to claw back false gains.
Streamlined introduction to accounting adjustments.
Continue to emphasize 3-step adjusting process.
Simplified the "Explanation" section for each adjustment.
Enhanced Exhibit 3.12 on summary of adjustments.
Updated Sustainability section on how accounting aided funding of recycling business.
Updated profit margin analysis using Limited Brands.
Added one Quick Study and one Exercise.
Updated Piaggio's classified balance sheet.

Chapter 4

NEW opener—LuminAID and entrepreneurial assignment.
New art distinguishing between temporary vs permanent accounts.
Enhanced Exhibit 4.7 on steps of the accounting cycle.
Sustainability section on key to tracking numbers for LuminAID.
Updated current ratio analysis using Limited Brands.
Reorganized Global View section.

Chapter 5

NEW opener—Sword & Plough and entrepreneurial assignment.
Revised introduction for servicers vs. merchandisers using Liberty Tax and Nordstrom as examples.
New NTK 5-1 to aid learning of merchandising.
Reorganization of "Purchases" section to aid learning.
Enhanced entries on payment of purchases within vs. after discount period.
Simplified purchase returns illustration.
Reorganized explanation for FOB terms.

Reorganized entries for sales with vs. sales without discounts.
Enhanced entries to explain sales returns and how to account for inventory returned.
New section introducing adjusting entries for future sales discounts and sales returns and allowances—details in new Appendix 5C.
Introduced new accounts under new revenue recognition rules.
Expanded Exhibit 5.12 to cover updated merchandising transactions.
Updated "Shenanigans" box with data from KPMG.
Sustainability section on accounting for merchandising as key to Sword & Plough.
Updated acid-test ratio and gross margin analysis of JCPenney.
New Appendix 5D showing entries for gross vs. net method.
Added five Quick Study assignments and three Exercises.
Updated Volkswagen income report in Global View.

Chapter 6

NEW opener—Homegrown Sustainable Sandwich and entrepreneurial assignment.
Simplified specific identification calculations in Exhibit 6.4.
New image for each inventory method to show cost flows of goods at each sale date.
Added colored arrow lines to weighted average Exhibit 6.7 to show cost flows from purchase to sale.
Updated box on purchasing kickbacks using KPMG data.
Lower-of-cost-or-market section simplified.
Enhanced layout to explain effects of inventory errors across years.
Updated Sustainability section explains importance of perpetual inventory for organic producers.
Updated inventory turnover and days' sales in inventory analysis using Toys 'R' Us.
Appendix 6A: New images show cost flow of goods at each period end for each inventory measurement method.

Appendix 6B: Revised to be consistent with new revenue recognition rules.
Updated global accounting to remove convergence project reference.

Chapter 7

NEW opener—Box and entrepreneurial assignment.
Streamlined "System Principles" section.
Streamlined "System Components" section.
New Exhibit 7.4 to show the relation between a general ledger account and its subsidiary ledger.
Streamlined section on technology-based systems.
New image to show how Sage captures accounting basics.
Updated Sustainability section shows how Box helps nonprofits succeed.
Updated segment return analysis using Callaway Golf.

Chapter 8

NEW opener—Robinhood and entrepreneurial assignment.
New image for certificate of bond coverage.
New discussion of controls over social media with reference to Facebook's "mood" posts.
New discussion box on how fraud is detected.
New evidence on how cash is stolen from companies.
Simplified the petty cash illustration.
Simplified the bank statement for learning.
Simplified discussion of debit and credit memoranda.
New table to identify timing differences for bank reconciliation.
New pie chart on the top contributors to fraud.
Updated Sustainability section highlights cash controls as necessary for Robinhood's success.
Updated days' sales uncollected analysis using Hasbro and Mattel.
Deleted Appendix 8B (now Appendix 5D).

Chapter 9

NEW opener—ReGreen and entrepreneurial assignment.
Updated data in Exhibit 9.1.
New section for sales using store credit cards.
Simplified section for sales using bank (third-party) credit cards to show only entries for cash received at point of sale.
Revised NTK 9-1 for new credit card entries.
Reorganized section on direct write-off method.
New Exhibit 9.9 showing allowances set aside for future bad debts.
Continued 3-step process to estimate allowance for doubtful accounts.
New marginal T-account to show numbers flowing through Allowance account.
Continued Exhibit 9.13 arriving at the accounting adjustment.
New calendar graphic added as learning aid in Exhibit 9.15.
New Sustainability section on ReGreen's efforts.
Updated accounts receivable analysis using IBM and Oracle.
Added one new Exercise.

Chapter 10

NEW opener—Westland Distillery and entrepreneurial assignment.
Updated data in Exhibit 10.1.
Revised images for Exhibit 10.2.
Simplified Exhibit 10.4 for lump-sum purchases.
Enhanced Exhibit 10.7 with actual numbers.
Added margin Excel computations for Exhibit 10.12.
Added margin table to Exhibit 10.14 as learning aid.
Updated Dale Jarrett Racing asset listing.
Added table to explain additional expenditures, including examples and entries.
New simple introduction to operating and capital leases.
Added paragraph on R&D expenditures.
Updated "In Control" fraud box with new KPMG data.
Sustainability section on how Westland Distillery relies on accounting for its success.
Updated asset turnover analysis using Molson Coors and Boston Beer.
Simplified Appendix 10A by excluding exchanges without commercial substance.

Chapter 11

NEW opener—Hello Alfred and entrepreneurial assignment.
Updated data in Exhibit 11.2.
Updated payroll tax rates and explanations.

New explanation of Additional Medicare Tax.
Updated unemployment tax rate section.
New section on internal controls for payroll.
New box on payroll fraud with KPMG data.
Simplified bonus explanation and computations.
Updated NTK 11-2 and NTK 11-3.
Sustainability section explains accounting for "Alfreds."
Updated payroll reports in Appendix 11A.

Chapter 12

NEW opener—Scholly and entrepreneurial assignment.
Streamlined discussion of partnership characteristics.
New margin T-accounts for Exhibits 12.1 and 12.2.
Updated Sustainability section describes accounting for nonprofit sales of Scholly.
Added two Quick Study assignments, one Exercise, and one Problem.

Chapter 13

NEW opener—Tesla Motors and entrepreneurial assignment.
Streamlined discussion of corporate characteristics.
Updated the Target stock quote data.
Simplified section on stock dividends.
Continued 5-step process for stock dividends.
Revised Exhibit 13.8 to show dividend effects.
New reference to Apple's 7-for-1 stock split.
Streamlined section on dividend preference of preferred stock.
Updated the Apple statement of equity.
Sustainability section explains how Tesla relies on accounting data to make energy-wise decisions.
Updated PE and dividend yield ratios for Amazon and Altria.
Simplified book value per share computations.

Chapter 14

NEW opener—Uber and entrepreneurial assignment.
Simplified Exhibit 14.1 for ease of learning.
Updated the IBM stock quote data.
New bond image from Minnesota Vikings stadium bonds.
New NTK 14-1 covering bonds issued at par.
Simplified Exhibit 14.6 on discount bonds.
New T-accounts with Exhibit 14.6 to show bonds payable and the discount on bonds payable.

Simplified Exhibit 14.10 on premium bonds.
Bond pricing moved to Appendix 14A.
Simplified Exhibit 14.14 for note amortization schedule.
Updated "Missing Debt" box using new data from KPMG.
Sustainability section explains bond financing for Uber.
Updated debt-to-equity analysis using Amazon.
New margin Excel computations for bond pricing.
Added margin T-accounts for bonds in Appendix 14B.
Simplified lease example in Appendix 14C.

Chapter 15

NEW opener—Echoing Green and entrepreneurial assignment.
Updated data in Exhibit 15.1.
Continued 3-step process for fair value adjustment.
Reorganized section on securities with significant influence.
New Exhibit 15.7 to describe accounting for equity securities by ownership level.
Updated Google example for comprehensive income.
Updated Sustainability section stresses investment accounting for Echoing Green.
Updated component-returns analysis using Gap.
Investments in international operations set online in Appendix 15A.

Chapter 16

NEW opener—Amazon and entrepreneurial assignment.
Continued infographics on examples of operating, investing, and financing cash flows.
Kept 5-step process for preparing statement of cash flows.
New graphic on use of indirect vs. direct methods.
New presentation to highlight indirect adjustments to income.
Updated box comparing operating cash flows to income for companies.
Kept "Summary T-Account" for learning statement of cash flows.
New Sustainability section on Amazon's initiatives.
Updated cash flow on total assets analysis using Nike.

Chapter 17

NEW opener—Morgan Stanley and entrepreneurial assignment.
Streamlined the "Basics of Analysis" section.
Simplified computations for comparative statements.

Updated data for analysis of Apple using horizontal, vertical, and ratio analysis.
Updated comparative analysis using Google and Samsung.
New evidence on accounting ploys by CFOs.
New Sustainability section on Morgan Stanley's initiatives.
Revised "All Else Being Equal" Fraud box using KPMG data.
Revised Appendix 17A to reflect new rules that remove separate disclosure of extraordinary items.
Revised assignments for new standard on extraordinary items.

Chapter 18

NEW opener—NatureBox and entrepreneurial assignment.
Simplified discussion on purpose of managerial accounting.
Added references to more real-world companies.
Added discussion of enterprise risk management.
Revised Exhibit 18.1 to show common managerial decisions.
Simplified discussion on nature of managerial accounting.
New section on careers in managerial accounting and importance of managerial accounting for nonaccountants.
New exhibit on managerial accounting salaries.
Added example on cost of iPhone.
New section head and revised discussion for nonmanufacturing costs.
Added graphics to cost flow exhibit.
Reduced number of overhead items in exhibit for cost of goods manufactured statement.
Added section on computing cost per unit.
Updated "trends" section to include *gig economy* (Uber), triple bottom line, and ISO 9000 standards.
Expanded discussion of sustainability and SASB.
Expanded Sustainability section with Decision Insight chart and NatureBox example.
Added Discussion Question on triple bottom line.
Added two Quick Studies on raw materials activity for 3M Co.
Added Exercises on sustainability reporting for Starbucks and Hyatt.

Chapter 19

NEW opener—Neha Assar and entrepreneurial assignment.
Simplified discussion of cost accounting systems.
Simplified direct material and direct labor cost flows and entries.
Added time period information to graphic on 4-step overhead process.

Simplified discussion of recording overhead costs.
Added journal entry for depreciation expense on equipment in NTK 19-5.
Revised exhibits for posting of direct materials, direct labor, and overhead to general ledger accounts and job cost sheets.
Added section on using job cost sheet for managerial decisions.
Added entries for transfers of costs to Finished Goods Inventory and to COGS.
Expanded discussion of job order costing for service firms.
New exhibit and cost flows for service firms.
Expanded Sustainability section, including **USPS** and **Neha Assar** examples.
New NTK on using the job cost sheet.
Added new Quick Study and new Exercise on costing for service firms.

Chapter 20

NEW opener—Stance and entrepreneurial assignment.
Revised exhibit on cost flows in job order and process costing systems.
Revised exhibit on production data and physical flow of units.
Added transfer to finished goods and updated ending balance to WIP T-account for second process.
New section on using process cost summary for decisions.
Added discussion of the raw materials yield to "trends" section.
Revised exhibit and discussion of assigning cost using FIFO.
Expanded discussion of hybrid and operation costing.
Expanded Sustainability discussion, including **General Mills** and **Stance** examples.
Added Discussion Question on sustainable raw materials sourcing.

Chapter 21

NEW opener—Sweetgreen and entrepreneurial assignment.
New exhibit on building blocks of CVP analysis.
Revised discussion on uses of CVP analysis.
Revised discussion of fixed and variable costs.
Added data points to margin of fixed and variable cost exhibit.
New graphic on examples of fixed, variable, and mixed costs.
Revised discussion on step-wise and curvilinear costs.

Revised cost data for measuring cost behavior.
Reorganized break-even section into three methods.
Revised discussions of contribution margin income statement and CVP charts.
Moved margin of safety to section on applying CVP.
Added discussion of sales mix and break-even for **Amazon**.
Revised discussion of assumptions in CVP.
Revised Sustainability section with **Nike**, CVP analysis, and **Sweetgreen** example.
Expanded appendix on variable and absorption costing.
Added Discussion Question, four Quick Studies, and 1 Exercise on variable and absorption costing.
Revised Global View on **BMW**'s i3 break-even point.

Chapter 22

NEW opener—TaTa Topper and entrepreneurial assignment.
Revised discussion, with new exhibit, of budgeting as a management tool.
Revised discussion on benefits of budgeting.
Added new graphic on benefits of budgeting.
Revised discussion of budgeting and human behavior.
New Decision Insight on zero-based budgeting.
New NTK on the benefits and potential costs of budgeting.
Revised master budget process exhibit to reflect types of activities.
Added graphics showing formulas to compute direct materials requirements and direct labor cost.
Revised discussions of direct materials, direct labor, and factory overhead budgets.
Added discussion and exhibits of estimated cash receipts with alternative collection timing and uncollectible accounts.
Added T-account to cash budget exhibit.
New NTKs on the cash budget.
Added margin point on the impact of credit and debit card fees on cash receipts.
Added section with exhibit on budgeting for service companies.
New Sustainability section with discussion of **Johnson & Johnson** and exhibit and **TaTa Topper** example.
Added Discussion Question and Quick Study on sustainability and budgeting.

Added Exercise on budgeted cash payments on account.

Chapter 23

NEW opener—Riide and entrepreneurial assignment.
New exhibit on fixed versus flexible budgets.
Revised discussion of fixed versus flexible budgets.
New 3-step process to prepare a flexible budget.
Added section on formula for computing total budgeted cost in a flexible budget.
Revised discussion of setting standard costs.
Revised exhibit on cost variance formula.
Added discussion of potential causes of direct labor variances.
New 3-step process for determining standard overhead rate.
New exhibit, formula, and computation of standard overhead applied.
Revised discussion of overhead volume and controllable variances.
Added calculations of controllable variance and budgeted overhead costs.
Added discussion, exhibit, and Discussion Question of the pros and cons of standard costing.
Added discussion of the International Integrated Reporting Council.
New Sustainability section with discussion of **Intel** and executive pay and **Riide** examples.
Added two Quick Studies on sustainability and standard costs.

Chapter 24

NEW opener—Ministry of Supply and entrepreneurial assignment.
Reorganized chapter.
Revised discussion of performance evaluation and decentralization.
Revised discussion of **Kraft Heinz** responsibility centers.
Revised exhibit on responsibility accounting.
Revised discussion of responsibility accounting reports.
Added NTKs on responsibility accounting, cost allocations, and balanced scorecard.
Revised discussion of indirect expense allocations.
New exhibit and discussion of general model of expense allocation.
New exhibit on common allocation bases for indirect expenses.

Revised discussion of preparing departmental income.
New exhibit and formula for computing departmental income.
Added short section on transfer pricing to the chapter.
New Sustainability section with discussion of **General Mills**, **Target** performance reporting, and **Ministry of Supply** example.

Chapter 25

NEW opener—Simply Gum and entrepreneurial assignment.
Added exhibit and discussion of capital budgeting process.
Added exhibit and discussion of cash inflows and outflows in capital budgeting.
Added lists of strengths and weaknesses, with revised discussion, of payback period.
Added list of weaknesses of accounting rate of return method.
New art showing timeline of NPV calculation.
Added discussion of outsourcing in make or buy decisions.
Added discussion of capital rationing.
Added financial calculator and Excel steps for many calculations.
Revised discussion of relevant costs and benefits.
Revised Sustainability section on capital budgeting for solar investments and **Simply Gum** example.
Added two Quick Studies on capital budgeting for solar investments.
Added Appendix and end-of-chapter assignments on product pricing.

Appendix A

New financial statements for **Apple**, **Google**, and **Samsung**.

Appendix B

New organization with detailed subheadings.
Added Excel computation for PV and FV calculations.
Added Excel computation for PV and FV of annuity calculations.

Appendix C

New 3-step method for activity-based costing.
Revised discussion of applying activity-based costing.
Revised example and new exhibits of activity-based costing.
Added discussion of value-added activities.

McGraw-Hill Connect®
Learn Without Limits

Connect is a teaching and learning platform that is proven to deliver better results for students and instructors.

Connect empowers students by continually adapting to deliver precisely what they need, when they need it, and how they need it, so your class time is more engaging and effective.

73% of instructors who use **Connect** require it; instructor satisfaction **increases** by 28% when **Connect** is required.

Connect's Impact on Retention Rates, Pass Rates, and Average Exam Scores

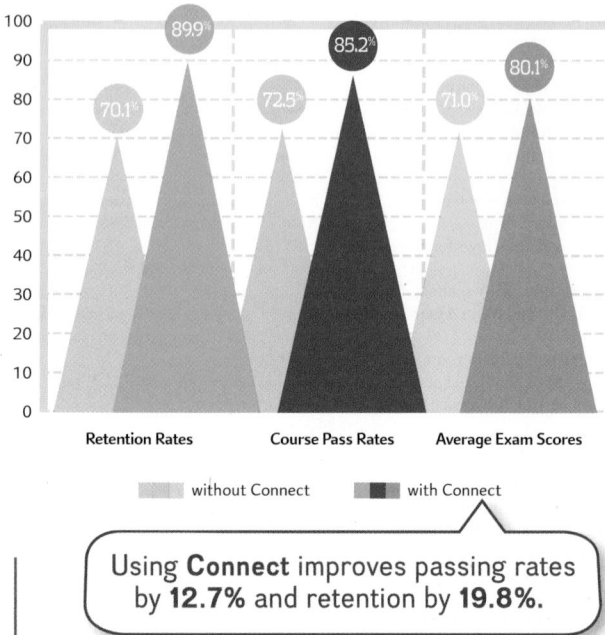

Using **Connect** improves passing rates by **12.7%** and retention by **19.8%**.

Analytics

Connect Insight®

Connect Insight is Connect's new one-of-a-kind visual analytics dashboard that provides at-a-glance information regarding student performance, which is immediately actionable. By presenting assignment, assessment, and topical performance results together with a time metric that is easily visible for aggregate or individual results, Connect Insight gives the user the ability to take a just-in-time approach to teaching and learning, which was never before available. Connect Insight presents data that helps instructors improve class performance in a way that is efficient and effective.

Impact on Final Course Grade Distribution

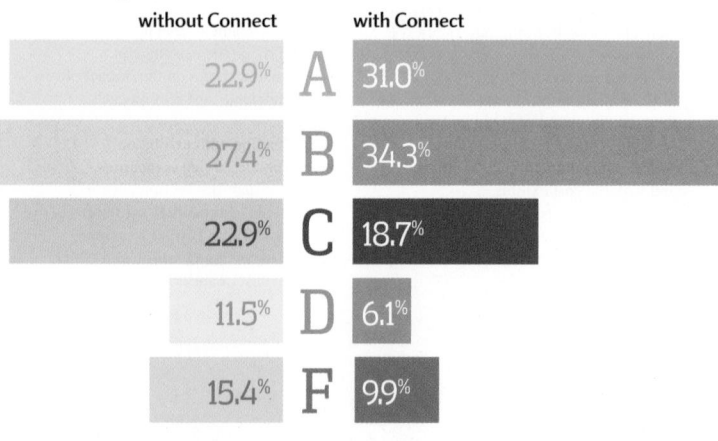

Adaptive

THE **ADAPTIVE** **READING EXPERIENCE** DESIGNED TO TRANSFORM THE WAY STUDENTS READ

More students earn **A's** and **B's** when they use McGraw-Hill Education **Adaptive** products.

SmartBook®

Proven to help students improve grades and study more efficiently, SmartBook contains the same content within the print book, but actively tailors that content to the needs of the individual. SmartBook's adaptive technology provides precise, personalized instruction on what the student should do next, guiding the student to master and remember key concepts, targeting gaps in knowledge and offering customized feedback, and driving the student toward comprehension and retention of the subject matter. Available on smartphones and tablets, SmartBook puts learning at the student's fingertips—anywhere, anytime.

Over **5.7 billion questions** have been answered, making McGraw-Hill Education products more intelligent, reliable, and precise.

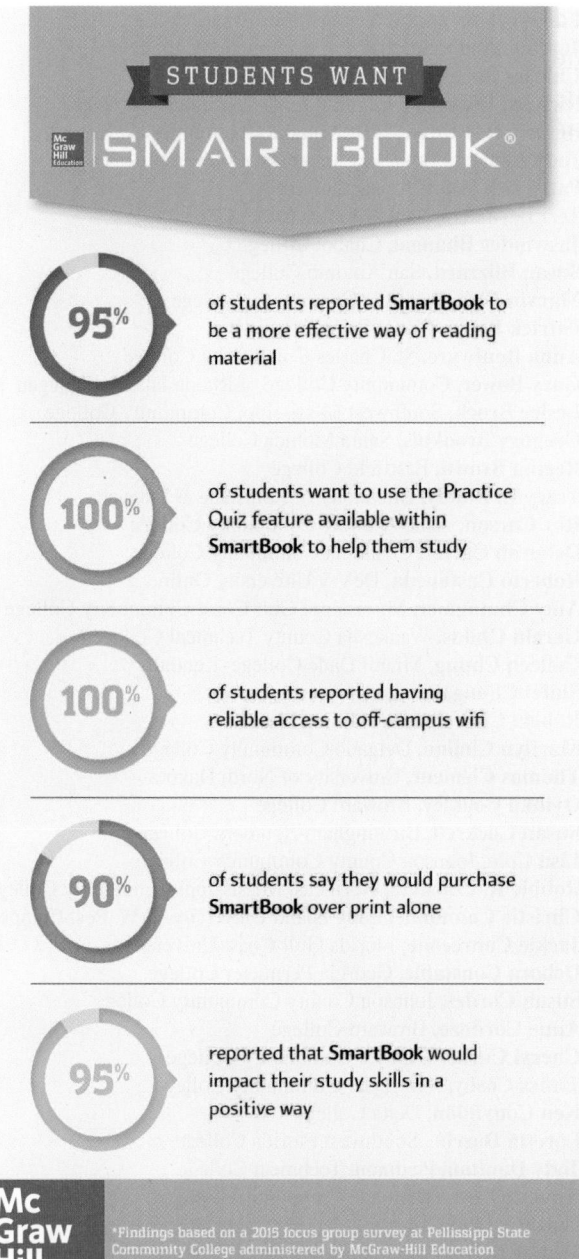

STUDENTS WANT

SMARTBOOK®

95% of students reported **SmartBook** to be a more effective way of reading material

100% of students want to use the Practice Quiz feature available within **SmartBook** to help them study

100% of students reported having reliable access to off-campus wifi

90% of students say they would purchase **SmartBook** over print alone

95% reported that **SmartBook** would impact their study skills in a positive way

*Findings based on a 2015 focus group survey at Pellissippi State Community College administered by McGraw-Hill Education

www.mheducation.com

Acknowledgments

John J. Wild, Ken W. Shaw, Barbara Chiappetta, and McGraw-Hill Education recognize the following instructors for their valuable feedback and involvement in the development of *Fundamental Accounting Principles,* 23e. We are thankful for their suggestions, counsel, and encouragement.

Khaled Abdou, Penn State University–Berks
Anne Marie Anderson, Raritan Valley Community College
Elaine Anes, Heald College–Fresno
Jerome Apple, University of Akron
Jack Aschkenazi, American Intercontinental University
Sidney Askew, Borough of Manhattan Community College
Lawrence Awopetu, University of Arkansas–Pine Bluff
Jon Backman, Spartanburg Community College
Charles Baird, University of Wisconsin–Stout
Richard Barnhart, Grand Rapids Community College
Beverly R. Beatty, Anne Arundel Community College
Judy Benish, Fox Valley Technical College
Patricia Bentley, Keiser University
Teri Bernstein, Santa Monica College
Jaswinder Bhangal, Chabot College
Susan Blizzard, San Antonio College
Marvin Blye, Wor-Wic Community College
Patrick Borja, Citrus College
Anna Boulware, St. Charles Community College
Gary Bower, Community College of Rhode Island–Flanagan
Leslee Brock, Southwest Mississippi Community College
Gregory Brookins, Santa Monica College
Regina Brown, Eastfield College
Tracy L. Bundy, University of Louisiana at Lafayette
Roy Carson, Anne Arundel Community College
Deborah Carter, Coahoma Community College
Roberto Castaneda, DeVry University Online
Amy Chataginer, Mississippi Gulf Coast Community College
Gerald Childs, Waukesha County Technical College
Colleen Chung, Miami Dade College–Kendall
Shifei Chung, Rowan University
Robert Churchman, Harding University
Marilyn Ciolino, Delgado Community College
Thomas Clement, University of North Dakota
Oyinka Coakley, Broward College
Susan Cockrell, Birmingham-Southern College
Lisa Cole, Johnson County Community College
Robbie R. Coleman, Northeast Mississippi Community College
Christie Comunale, Long Island University–C.W. Post Campus
Jackie Conrecode, Florida Gulf Coast University
Debora Constable, Georgia Perimeter College
Susan Cordes, Johnson County Community College
Anne Cordozo, Broward College
Cheryl Corke, Genesee Community College
James Cosby, John Tyler Community College
Ken Couvillion, Delta College
Loretta Darche, Southwest Florida College
Judy Daulton, Piedmont Technical College
Annette Davis, Glendale Community College
Dorothy Davis, University of Louisiana–Monroe
Walter DeAguero, Saddleback College

Mike Deschamps, MiraCosta College
Pamela Donahue, Northern Essex Community College
Steve Doster, Shawnee State University
Larry Dragosavac, Edison Community College
Samuel Duah, Bowie State University
Robert Dunlevy, Montgomery County Community College
Jerrilyn Eisenhauer, Tulsa Community College–Southeast
Ronald Elders, Virginia College
Terry Elliott, Morehead State University
Patricia Feller, Nashville State Community College
Annette Fisher, Glendale Community College
Ron Fitzgerald, Santa Monica College
David Flannery, Bryant and Stratton College
Hollie Floberg, Tennessee Wesleyan College
Linda Flowers, Houston Community College
Jeannie Folk, College of DuPage
Rebecca Foote, Middle Tennessee State University
Paul Franklin, Kaplan University
Tim Garvey, Westwood College
Barbara Gershman, Northern Virginia Community College–Woodbridge
Barbara Gershowitz, Nashville State Technical Community College
Mike Glasscock, Amarillo College
Diane Glowacki, Tarrant County College
Ernesto Gonzalez, Florida National College
Lori Grady, Bucks County Community College
Gloria Grayless, Sam Houston State University
Ann Gregory, South Plains College
Rameshwar Gupta, Jackson State University
Amy Haas, Kingsborough Community College
Pat Halliday, Santa Monica College
Keith Hallmark, Calhoun Community College
Rebecca Hancock, El Paso Community College–Valley Verde
Mechelle Harris, Bossier Parish Community College
Tracey Hawkins, University of Cincinnati–Clermont College
Thomas Hayes, University of Arkansas–Ft. Smith
Laurie Hays, Western Michigan University
Roger Hehman, University of Cincinnati–Clermont College
Cheri Hernandez, Des Moines Area Community College
Margaret Hicks, Howard University
Melanie Hicks, Liberty University
James Higgins, Holy Family University
Patricia Holmes, Des Moines Area Community College
Barbara Hopkins, Northern Virginia Community College–Manassas
Wade Hopkins, Heald College
Aileen Huang, Santa Monica College
Les Hubbard, Solano College
Deborah Hudson, Gaston College
James Hurst, National College
Constance Hylton, George Mason University
Christine Irujo, Westfield State University

Tamela Jarvais, Prince George's Community College
Fred Jex, Macomb Community College
Gina M. Jones, Aims Community College
Jeff Jones, College of Southern Nevada
Rita Jones, Columbus State University
Dmitriy Kalyagin, Chabot College
Thomas Kam, Hawaii Pacific University
Naomi Karolinski, Monroe Community College
Shirly A. Kleiner, Johnson County Community College
Kenneth A. Koerber, Bucks County Community College
Jill Kolody, Anne Arundel Community College
Tamara Kowalczyk, Appalachian State University
Anita Kroll, University of Wisconsin–Madison
David Krug, Johnson County Community College
Christopher Kwak, DeAnza College
Jeanette Landin, Empire College
Beth Lasky, Delgado Community College
Neal Leviton, Santa Monica College
Danny Litt, University of California Los Angeles
James L. Lock, Northern Virginia Community College
Steve Ludwig, Northwest Missouri State University
Debra Luna, El Paso Community College
Amado Mabul, Heald College
Lori Major, Luzerne County Community College
Jennifer Malfitano, Delaware County Community College
Maria Mari, Miami Dade College–Kendall
Thomas S. Marsh, Northern Virginia Community College–Annandale
Karen Martinson, University of Wisconsin–Stout
Brenda Mattison, Tri-County Technical College
Stacie Mayes, Rose State College
Mark McCarthy, East Carolina University
Clarice McCoy, Brookhaven College
Tammy Metzke, Milwaukee Area Technical College
Jeanine Metzler, Northampton Community College
Theresa Michalow, Moraine Valley Community College
Julie Miller, Chippewa Valley Tech College
Tim Miller, El Camino College
John Minchin, California Southern University
Edna C. Mitchell, Polk State College
Jill Mitchell, Northern Virginia Community College
April Mohr, Jefferson Community and Technical College, SW
Lynn Moore, Aiken Technical College
Angela Mott, Northeast Mississippi Community College
Andrea Murowski, Brookdale Community College
Timothy Murphy, Diablo Valley College
Kenneth F. O'Brien, Farmingdale State College
Kathleen O'Donnell, Onondaga Community College
Ahmed Omar, Burlington County College
Robert A. Pacheco, Massasoit Community College
Margaret Parilo, Cosumnes River College
Paige Paulsen, Salt Lake Community College
Yvonne Phang, Borough of Manhattan Community College
Gary Pieroni, Diablo Valley College
Debbie Porter, Tidewater Community College, Virginia Beach
Kristen Quinn, Northern Essex Community College
David Ravetch, University of California Los Angeles
Ruthie Reynolds, Howard University
Cecile Roberti, Community College of Rhode Island

Morgan Rockett, Moberly Area Community College
Patrick Rogan, Cosumnes River College
Paul Rogers, Community College of Beaver County
Brian Routh, Washington State University–Vancouver
Helen Roybark, Radford University
Alphonse Ruggiero, Suffolk County Community College
Martin Sabo, Community College of Denver
Arjan Sadhwani, South University
Gary K. Sanborn, Northwestern Michigan College
Kin Kin Sandhu, Heald College
Marcia Sandvold, Des Moines Area Community College
Gary Schader, Kean University
Darlene Schnuck, Waukesha County Technical College
Elizabeth Serapin, Columbia Southern University
Geeta Shankhar, University of Dayton
Regina Shea, Community College of Baltimore County–Essex
James Shelton, Liberty University
Jay Siegel, Union County College
Gerald Singh, New York City College of Technology
Lois Slutsky, Broward College–South
Gerald Smith, University of Northern Iowa
Kathleen Sobieralski, University of Maryland University College
Charles Spector, State University of New York at Oswego
Diane Stark, Phoenix College
Thomas Starks, Heald College
Carolyn L. Strauch, Crowder College
Latazia Stuart, Fortis University Online
Gene Sullivan, Liberty University
David Sulzen, Ferrum College
Dominique Svarc, William Rainey Harper College
Linda Sweeney, Sam Houston State University
Carl Swoboda, Southwest Tennessee Community College, Macon
Margaret Tanner, University of Arkansas–Ft. Smith
Ulysses Taylor, Fayetteville State University
Anthony Teng, Saddleback College
Paula Thomas, Middle Tennessee State University
Teresa Thompson, Chaffey Community College
Leslie Thysell, John Tyler Community College
Melanie Torborg, Globe University
Shafi Ullah, Broward College
Bob Urell, Irvine Valley College
Adam Vitalis, Georgia Tech
Patricia Walczak, Lansing Community College
Terri Walsh, Seminole State College–Oviedo
Shunda Ware, Atlanta Technical College
Dave Welch, Franklin University
Jean Wells-Jessup, Howard University
Christopher Widmer, Tidewater Community College
Andrew Williams, Edmonds Community College
Jonathan M. Wild, University of Wisconsin–Madison
Wanda Wong, Chabot College
John Woodward, Polk State College
Patricia Worsham, Norco College, Riverside Community College
Gail E. Wright, Stevenson University
Lynnette Yerbury, Salt Lake Community College
Judy Zander, Grossmont College
Mary Zenner, College of Lake County
Jane Zlojutro, Northwestern Michigan College

Brief Contents

Contents

14 Long-Term Liabilities 586

15 Investments 628

16 Reporting the Statement of Cash Flows 662

17 Analysis of Financial Statements 716

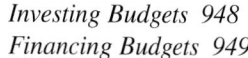

25 Capital Budgeting and Managerial Decisions 1086

Fundamental Accounting Principles

1 chapter

Accounting in Business

Chapter Preview

ACCOUNTING USES

C1 Purpose of accounting

C2 Accounting information users

Opportunities in accounting

NTK 1-1

ETHICS AND ACCOUNTING

C3 Ethics—Key concept

C4 Generally accepted accounting principles

Conceptual framework

NTK 1-2

TRANSACTION ANALYSIS

A1 Accounting equation and its components

P1 Transaction analysis—Illustrated

NTK 1-3, 1-4

FINANCIAL STATEMENTS

P2 Income statement

Statement of owner's equity

Balance sheet

Statement of cash flows

A2 Financial analysis

NTK 1-5

Chapter Preview is organized by key topics and includes learning objectives and *Need-To-Know (NTK)* guided examples

Learning Objectives are classified as conceptual, analytical, or procedural

Learning Objectives

CONCEPTUAL

C1 Explain the purpose and importance of accounting.

C2 Identify users and uses of, and opportunities in, accounting.

C3 Explain why ethics are crucial to accounting.

C4 Explain generally accepted accounting principles and define and apply several accounting principles.

C5 *Appendix 1B*—Identify and describe the three major activities of organizations.

ANALYTICAL

A1 Define and interpret the accounting equation and each of its components.

A2 Compute and interpret return on assets.

A3 *Appendix 1A*—Explain the relation between return and risk.

PROCEDURAL

P1 Analyze business transactions using the accounting equation.

P2 Identify and prepare basic financial statements and explain how they interrelate.

Apple of My Eye

*A **Decision Feature** launches each chapter showing the relevance of accounting for a real entrepreneur.
An **Entrepreneurial Decision** assignment returns to this feature with a mini-case*

CUPERTINO, CA—"When I designed the Apple stuff," says Steve Wozniak (a.k.a. the *Wizard of Woz*), "I never thought in my life I would have enough money to fly to Hawaii or make a down payment on a house." But some dreams do come true. Woz, along with Steve Jobs and Ron Wayne, founded **Apple** (**Apple.com**) when Woz was 25 and Jobs was 21.

The young entrepreneurs faced challenges, including how to read and interpret accounting data. Another challenge was how to finance the company, which they did by selling their prized possessions—Woz's Hewlett-Packard calculator and Jobs's Volkswagen van. The $1,300 raised helped them purchase the equipment Woz used to build the first Apple computer.

In setting up their company, the owners had to decide what type of entity to form—a partnership or a corporation. They decided on a partnership, and Ron "sat down at a typewriter and typed our partnership contract right out of his head," recalls Woz. "He did an etching of Newton under the apple tree for the cover of our Apple I manual."

The partnership agreement included Ron as a third partner with 10% ownership. However, a few days later, Ron had a

"The first Apple was . . . my whole life"

—Steve Wozniak

change of heart when he considered the unlimited liability of a partnership. He pulled out, leaving Woz and Jobs holding 50% each. Within nine months, Woz and Jobs identified some advantages to the corporate form, and they converted Apple to a corporation.

As their company grew, Woz and Jobs had to learn more accounting, along with details of preparing and interpreting financial statements. Important questions involving transaction analysis and financial reporting arose, and the owners took care to do things right. "Everything we did," asserts Woz, "we were setting the tone for the world."

Woz and Jobs improved their accounting system and focused it on providing information for Apple's business decisions. Today, Woz believes that Apple is integral to the language of technology, just as accounting is the language of business. In retrospect, Woz says, "Every dream I have ever had in life has come true ten times over."

Sources: *Woz website,* Woz.org, January 2017; *iWoz: From Computer Geek to Cult Icon,* W.W. Norton & Co., 2006; *Founders at Work,* Apress, 2007; *Apple website,* January 2017

IMPORTANCE OF ACCOUNTING

C1
Explain the purpose and importance of accounting.

Why is accounting so popular on campus? Why are there so many openings for accounting jobs? Why is accounting so important to companies? Why do politicians and business leaders focus on accounting regulations? The answer is that we live in an information age in which accounting information impacts us all.

Accounting is an information and measurement system that identifies, records, and communicates information about an organization's business activities. Exhibit 1.1 portrays these accounting functions.

EXHIBIT 1.1

Accounting Functions

Identifying	Recording	Communicating
Select transactions and events	Input, measure, and log	Prepare, analyze, and interpret

Our most common contact with accounting is through credit approvals, checking accounts, tax forms, and payroll. These experiences focus on **recordkeeping**, or **bookkeeping**, which is the recording of transactions and events. This is just one part of accounting. Accounting also includes the analysis and interpretation of information.

Point: Technology is only as useful as the accounting data available, and users' decisions are only as good as their understanding of accounting.

Technology is a key part of modern business and plays a major role in accounting. Technology reduces the time, effort, and cost of recordkeeping while improving accuracy. Some small organizations perform accounting tasks manually, but even they are impacted by technology. As technology makes more information available, the demand for accounting knowledge increases. Consulting, planning, and other financial services are now closely linked to accounting.

Users of Accounting Information

C2
Identify users and uses of, and opportunities in, accounting.

Accounting is called the *language of business* because all organizations set up an accounting system to communicate data that help people make better decisions. Exhibit 1.2 divides these people into two user groups, *external users* and *internal users,* and provides examples of each.

EXHIBIT 1.2

Users of Accounting Information

Infographics reinforce key concepts through visual learning

External users

- Lenders
- Shareholders
- Governments
- Consumer groups
- External auditors
- Customers

Internal users

- Executives
- Managers
- Internal auditors
- Sales staff
- Budget analysts
- Controllers

External Information Users   **External users** of accounting information do *not* directly run the organization and have limited access to its accounting information. **Financial accounting** is the area of accounting aimed at serving external users by providing them with *general-purpose financial statements*. The term *general-purpose* refers to the broad range of purposes for which external users rely on these statements. Following is a partial list of external users and decisions they make with accounting information.

- *Lenders* (creditors) loan money or other resources to an organization. Banks, savings and loans, co-ops, and mortgage and finance companies are lenders. Lenders use information to assess whether an organization will repay its loans with interest.
- *Shareholders* (*investors*) are the owners of a corporation. They use accounting reports in deciding whether to buy, hold, or sell stock.
- *Directors* are elected to a *board of directors* that oversees an organization. Directors report to shareholders and they hire top executive management.
- *External* (independent) *auditors* examine financial statements to verify that they are prepared according to generally accepted accounting principles.
- *Nonexecutive employees* and *labor unions* use financial statements to judge the fairness of wages, assess job prospects, and bargain for better wages.
- *Regulators* have legal authority over certain activities of organizations. For example, the Internal Revenue Service (IRS) requires accounting reports in computing taxes.
- *Voters, legislators,* and *government officials* use accounting information to monitor and evaluate government receipts and expenses.
- *Contributors* to nonprofit organizations use accounting information to evaluate the use and impact of their donations.
- *Suppliers* use accounting information to judge the financial health of a customer before making sales on credit.
- *Customers* use financial reports to assess the staying power of potential suppliers.

Internal Information Users   **Internal users** of accounting information directly manage and operate the organization such as the chief executive officer (CEO) and other executive or managerial-level employees. **Managerial accounting** is the area of accounting that serves the decision-making needs of internal users. Internal reports are not subject to the same rules as external reports and are designed for the unique needs of internal users. Following is a partial list of internal users and decisions they make with accounting information.

- *Research and development managers* need information about projected costs and revenues of innovations.
- *Purchasing managers* need to know what, when, and how much to purchase.
- *Human resource managers* need information about employees' payroll, benefits, performance, and compensation.
- *Production managers* depend on information to monitor costs and ensure quality.
- *Distribution managers* need reports for timely, accurate, and efficient delivery of products and services.
- *Marketing managers* use reports about sales and costs to target consumers, set prices, and monitor consumer needs, tastes, and price concerns.
- *Service managers* require information on the costs and benefits of looking after products and services.

Opportunities in Accounting

Accounting has four broad areas of opportunities: financial, managerial, taxation, and accounting-related. Exhibit 1.3 lists selected opportunities in each area.

EXHIBIT 1.3

Accounting Opportunities

Exhibit 1.4 shows that the majority of opportunities are in *private accounting,* which are employees working for businesses. *Public accounting* offers the next largest number of opportunities, which involve accounting services such as auditing and taxation. Opportunities also exist in government and not-for-profit agencies, including business regulation and investigation of law violations.

EXHIBIT 1.4

Accounting Jobs by Area

Accounting specialists are highly regarded and their professional standing is often denoted by a certificate. Certified public accountants (CPAs) must meet education and experience requirements, pass an examination, and exhibit ethical character. Many accounting specialists hold certificates in addition to or instead of the CPA. Two of the most common are the certificate in management accounting (CMA) and the certified internal auditor (CIA). Employers also look for specialists with designations such as certified bookkeeper (CB), certified payroll professional (CPP), certified fraud examiner (CFE), and certified forensic accountant (CrFA).

Point: The largest accounting firms are EY, KPMG, PwC, and Deloitte.

Point: Census Bureau reports that higher education yields higher average pay:

Master's degree	$73,738
Bachelor's degree	56,665
Associate's degree	39,771
High school degree	30,627
No high school degree	20,241

Demand for accounting specialists is strong. Exhibit 1.5 reports average annual salaries for several accounting positions. Salary variation depends on location, company size, professional designation, experience, and other factors. For example, salaries for chief financial officers (CFOs) range from under $100,000 to more than $1 million per year. Likewise, salaries for bookkeepers range from under $30,000 to more than $80,000.

EXHIBIT 1.5

Accounting Salaries for Selected Positions

Point: U.S. Bureau of Labor reports higher education is linked to a lower unemployment rate:

Bachelor's degree or more	3.2%
Associate's degree	4.5%
High school degree	6.0%
No high school degree	9.0%

Point: For more salary info:
Abbott-Langer.com
AICPA.org
Kforce.com

Field	Title (experience)	2016 Salary	2021 Estimate*
Public Accounting	Partner	$240,000	$265,000
	Manager (6–8 years)	109,500	121,000
	Senior (3–5 years)	88,000	97,000
	Junior (0–2 years)	60,500	67,000
Private Accounting	CFO	290,000	320,000
	Controller/Treasurer	180,000	199,000
	Manager (6–8 years)	98,500	109,000
	Senior (3–5 years)	81,500	90,000
	Junior (0–2 years)	58,000	64,000
Recordkeeping	Full-charge bookkeeper	60,500	67,000
	Accounts manager	58,000	64,000
	Payroll manager	59,500	65,500
	Accounting clerk (0–2 years)	39,500	43,500

*Estimates assume a 2% compounded annual increase over current levels (rounded to nearest $500).

NEED-TO-KNOWs highlight key procedures and concepts in learning accounting

Identify the following users of accounting information as either an (a) external or (b) internal user.

1. ____ Regulator   4. ____ Controller   7. ____ Production manager
2. ____ CEO   5. ____ Executive employee   8. ____ Nonexecutive employee
3. ____ Shareholder   6. ____ External auditor

NEED-TO-KNOW 1-1

Accounting Users

C1 C2 ▶

Do More: QS 1-1, QS 1-2, E 1-1, E 1-2, E 1-3

Solution

1. a   **2.** b   **3.** a   **4.** b   **5.** b   **6.** a   **7.** b   **8.** a

FUNDAMENTALS OF ACCOUNTING

Accounting is guided by principles, standards, concepts, and assumptions. This section describes several of these key fundamentals of accounting.

Ethics—A Key Concept

For information to be useful, it must be trusted. This demands ethics in accounting. **Ethics** are beliefs that distinguish right from wrong. They are accepted standards of good and bad behavior.

Identifying the ethical path is a course of action that avoids casting doubt on one's decisions. For example, accounting users are less likely to trust an auditor's report if the auditor's pay depends on that client's success. To avoid such concerns, ethics rules are often set. For example, auditors are banned from direct investment in their client and cannot accept pay that depends on figures in the client's reports. Exhibit 1.6 gives a three-step process for making ethical decisions.

C3 _____

Explain why ethics are crucial to accounting.

1. Identify ethical concerns	2. Analyze options	3. Make ethical decision

Use personal ethics to recognize an ethical concern.	Consider all good and bad consequences.	Choose best option after weighing all consequences.

EXHIBIT 1.6

Ethical Decision Making

Accountants face ethical choices as they prepare financial reports. These choices can affect the salaries and bonuses paid to workers. They can even affect the success of products and services. Misleading information can lead to a wrongful closing of a division that harms workers and the business. There is an old saying: *Good ethics are good business.*

Point: *A Code of Professional Conduct* is available at AICPA.org.

Fraud Triangle: Ethics under Attack The fraud triangle asserts that *three* factors must exist for a person to commit fraud: opportunity, pressure, and rationalization.

- *Opportunity.* A person must be able to commit fraud with a low risk of getting caught.
- *Pressure,* or incentive. A person must feel pressure or have incentive to commit fraud.
- *Rationalization,* or attitude. A person justifies the fraud and fails to see its criminal nature.

The key to dealing with fraud is to focus on prevention. It is less expensive and more effective to prevent fraud from happening than it is to detect it. By the time a fraud is discovered, the money is often gone and chances for recovery are slim.

Both internal and external users rely on internal controls to reduce the likelihood of fraud. *Internal controls* are procedures set up to protect company property and equipment, ensure reliable accounting, promote efficiency, and encourage adherence to policies. Examples are good records, physical controls (locks, passwords, guards), and independent reviews.

Financial Pressure

Point: ACFE reports 86% of fraud victims recover none or only part of their losses.

Decision Insight boxes highlight relevant items from practice

▣ Decision Insight ▶

Cooking the Books   Our economic and social welfare depends on reliable accounting. Some individuals forgot that and are now paying their dues. They include Hisao Tanaka of **Toshiba**, guilty of inflating income by $1.2 billion over five years; Tsuyoshi Kikukawa of **Olympus**, guilty of hiding $1.7 billion in losses; Bernard Ebbers of **WorldCom**, convicted of an $11 billion accounting scandal; Andrew Fastow of **Enron**, guilty of hiding debt and inflating income; and Ramalinga Raju of **Satyam Computers**, accused of overstating assets by $1.5 billion. ▪

© Craig Ruttle/AP Images

Real company names are in bold magenta

Enforcing Ethics   In response to major accounting scandals, like those at **Enron** and **WorldCom**, Congress passed the **Sarbanes-Oxley Act,** also called *SOX,* to help curb financial abuses at companies that sell their stock to the public. Compliance with SOX requires documentation and verification of internal controls and increased emphasis on internal control effectiveness. Failure to comply can yield financial penalties, stock market delisting, and criminal prosecution of executives. Management must issue a report stating that internal controls are effective. CEOs and CFOs who knowingly sign off on bogus accounting reports risk millions of dollars in fines and years in prison. **Auditors** also must verify the effectiveness of internal controls.

A listing of some of the more publicized accounting scandals in recent years follows.

Point: An **audit** examines whether financial statements are prepared using GAAP. It does *not* ensure *absolute* accuracy of the statements.

Point: *Bloomberg Businessweek* reports that external audit costs run about $35,000 for start-ups, up from $15,000 pre-SOX.

Company	Alleged Accounting Abuses
Tesco, Plc	Inflated revenues and income, and deferred expenses
WorldCom	Understated expenses to inflate income and hid debt
AOL Time Warner	Inflated revenues and income
Fannie Mae	Inflated income
Xerox	Inflated income
Bristol-Myers Squibb	Inflated revenues and income
Tyco	Hid debt and CEO evaded taxes
Global Crossing	Inflated revenues and income
Nortel Networks	Understated expenses to inflate income
Enron	Inflated income, hid debt, and bribed officials

Point: Sarbanes-Oxley Act requires a business that sells stock to disclose if it has adopted a code of ethics for its executives and the contents of that code.

Congress passed the **Dodd-Frank Wall Street Reform and Consumer Protection Act,** or *Dodd-Frank,* to (1) promote accountability and transparency, (2) put an end to the notion of "too big to fail," and (3) protect consumers from abusive financial services. Two of its notable provisions are:

● *Clawback* Mandates recovery (clawback) of excess incentive compensation.
● *Whistleblower* Requires the SEC to pay whistleblowers between 10% and 30% of any sanction exceeding $1 million.

C4 ────────

Explain generally accepted accounting principles and define and apply several accounting principles.

Point: State ethics codes require CPAs who audit financial statements to disclose areas where those statements fail to comply with GAAP. If CPAs fail to report noncompliance, they can lose their licenses and be subject to criminal and civil actions and fines.

Generally Accepted Accounting Principles

Financial accounting is governed by concepts and rules known as **generally accepted accounting principles (GAAP).** GAAP aims to make information *relevant, reliable,* and *comparable.* Relevant information affects decisions of users. Reliable information is trusted by users. Comparable information aids in contrasting organizations.

In the United States, the **Securities and Exchange Commission (SEC),** a government agency, has the legal authority to set GAAP. The SEC oversees proper use of GAAP by companies that raise money from the public through issuance of stock and debt. The SEC has largely delegated the task of setting U.S. GAAP to the **Financial Accounting Standards Board (FASB),** which is a private-sector group that sets both broad and specific principles.

International Standards

Our global economy creates demand by external users for comparability in accounting reports. To that end, the **International Accounting Standards Board (IASB),** an independent group (consisting of individuals from many countries), issues **International Financial Reporting Standards (IFRS)** that identify preferred accounting practices. These standards are in many ways similar to, but sometimes different from, U.S. GAAP. Differences between U.S. GAAP and IFRS have been decreasing in recent years as the FASB and IASB pursued a process aimed at reducing inconsistencies.

Global View section discusses international accounting relevant to each chapter—it is located after each chapter's assignments

Conceptual Framework

The FASB **conceptual framework** consists broadly of the following:

- **Objectives**—to provide information useful to investors, creditors, and others.
- **Qualitative Characteristics**—to require *relevant, reliable,* and *comparable* information.
- **Elements**—to define items that financial statements can contain.
- **Recognition and Measurement**—to set criteria for an item to be recognized as an element; and how to measure it.

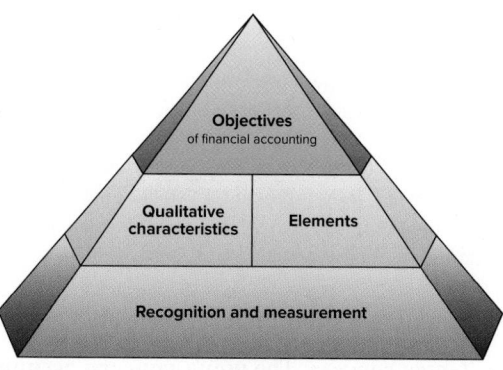

Point: For updates on the FASB and IASB conceptual framework, check FASB.org or ifrs.org.

Principles and Assumptions of Accounting Accounting principles (and assumptions) are of two types. *General principles* are the assumptions, concepts, and guidelines for preparing financial statements; these are shown in purple font with white shading in Exhibit 1.7, along with key assumptions in red font with white shading. *Specific principles* are detailed rules used in reporting business transactions and events; they often arise from rulings of authoritative groups and are described as we encounter them.

Accounting Principles General principles consist of at least four basic principles, four assumptions, and two constraints.

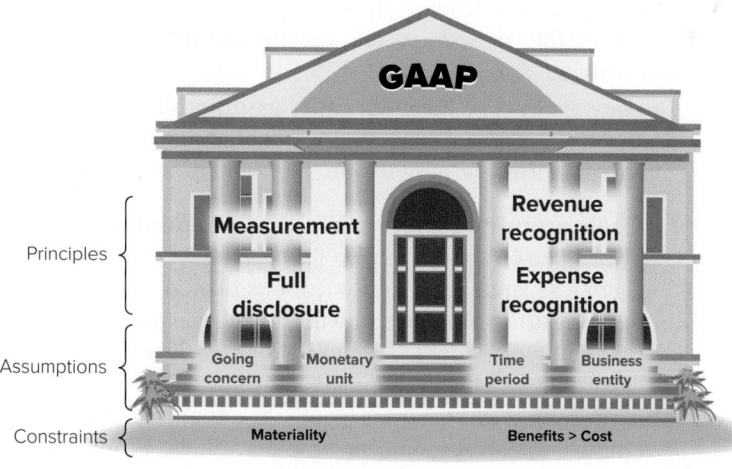

EXHIBIT 1.7

Building Blocks for GAAP

- *Measurement* The **measurement principle,** also called the **cost principle,** prescribes that accounting information is based on actual cost (with possible later adjustments to market). Cost is measured on a cash or equal-to-cash basis. This means if cash is given for a service, its cost is measured by the cash paid. If something besides cash is exchanged (such as a car traded for a truck), cost is measured as the cash value of what is given up or received. The cost principle emphasizes reliability and verifiability, and information based on cost is considered objective. *Objectivity* means that information is supported by independent, unbiased evidence; it is more than an opinion. Later chapters introduce *fair value.*

- *Revenue recognition* Revenue (sales) is the amount received from selling products and services. The **revenue recognition principle** prescribes that revenue is recognized (1) when

Point: A company pays $500 for equipment. The cost principle requires it be recorded at $500. It makes no difference if the owner thinks this equipment is worth $700.

goods or services are provided to customers and (2) at the amount expected to be received from the customer. The amount received is usually in cash, but it is also common to receive a customer's promise to pay at a future date, called credit sales. (To *recognize* means to record it.)

● *Expense recognition* The **expense recognition principle,** also called the **matching principle,** prescribes that a company record the expenses it incurred to generate the revenue reported. The principles of matching and revenue recognition are key to modern accounting.

● *Full disclosure* The **full disclosure principle** prescribes that a company report the details behind financial statements that would impact users' decisions. Those disclosures are often in footnotes to the statements.

▣ Decision Insight

Revenues for the **Carolina Panthers, Denver Broncos, Green Bay Packers**, and other professional football teams include ticket sales, television and cable broadcasts, radio rights, concessions, and advertising. Revenues from ticket sales are earned when the NFL team plays each game. Advance ticket sales are not revenues; instead, they represent a liability until the NFL team plays the game for which the ticket was sold. At that point, the liability is removed and revenues are reported. ■

© Al Bello/Getty Images

Accounting Assumptions   There are four accounting assumptions.

● *Going concern* The **going-concern assumption** means that accounting information reflects a presumption that the business will continue operating instead of being closed or sold. This implies, for example, that property is reported at cost instead of, say, liquidation value, which assumes closure.

● *Monetary unit* The **monetary unit assumption** means that we can express transactions and events in monetary, or money, units. Money is the common denominator in business. Examples of monetary units are the dollar in the United States and the peso in Mexico.

● *Time period* The **time period assumption** presumes that the life of a company can be divided into time periods, such as months and years, and that useful reports can be prepared for those periods.

● *Business entity* The **business entity assumption** means that a business is accounted for separately from other business entities, including its owner. A business entity can take one of three legal forms: *proprietorship, partnership,* or *corporation.*

1. A **sole proprietorship,** or simply **proprietorship,** is a business owned by one person and accounted for separately. However, a proprietorship is *not* a separate legal entity from its owner. This means, for example, that a court can order an owner to sell personal belongings to pay a proprietorship's debt. This *unlimited liability* of a proprietorship is a disadvantage. However, an advantage is that a proprietorship's income is not subject to a business income tax but is instead reported and taxed on the owner's personal income tax return. Proprietorship attributes are summarized in Exhibit 1.8, as well as those for partnerships and corporations.

EXHIBIT 1.8

Attributes of Businesses

Attribute Present	Proprietorship	Partnership	Corporation
One owner allowed...............	yes	no	yes
Business taxed..................	no	no	yes
Limited liability	no*	no*	yes
Business entity	yes	yes	yes
Legal entity	no	no	yes
Unlimited life	no	no	yes

*Proprietorships and partnerships that are set up as LLCs provide limited liability.

2. A **partnership** is a business owned by two or more people, called *partners,* who are jointly liable for tax and other obligations. A partnership, like a proprietorship, is *not* legally separate from its owners. This means that each partner's share of profits is reported and taxed on that partner's tax return. It also means *unlimited liability* for its partners. At least three types of partnerships limit liability: *limited partnership* (*LP*), *limited liability partnership* (*LLP*), and *limited liability company* (*LLC*). The LLC form is most popular and offers limited liability of a corporation and the tax treatment of a partnership (and proprietorship). **Most proprietorships and partnerships are now organized as LLCs.**

Point: Proprietorships and partnerships are usually managed by their owners. In a corporation, the owners (shareholders) elect a board of directors who appoint managers to run the business.

3. A **corporation,** also called a *C corporation,* is a business legally separate from its owner or owners, meaning it is responsible for its own acts and its own debts. Separate legal status means that a corporation can conduct business with the rights, duties, and responsibilities of a person. A corporation acts through its managers, who are its legal agents. Its owners, called **shareholders** (or **stockholders**), are not personally liable for corporate acts and debts. This limited liability is its main advantage. A main disadvantage is what's called *double taxation*—meaning that (1) the corporation income is taxed and (2) any distribution of income to its owners through dividends is taxed as part of the owners' personal income, usually at the individual's income tax rate. (For "qualified" dividends, the tax rate is 0%, 15%, or 20%, depending on the individual's tax bracket.) An *S corporation,* a corporation with special attributes, does not owe corporate income tax. Owners of S corporations report their share of corporate income with their personal income. Ownership of both corporate types is divided into units called **shares** or **stock.** When a corporation issues only one class of stock, we call it **common stock** (or *capital stock*).

—Decision Ethics boxes are role-playing exercises that stress ethics in accounting

 Decision Ethics ————————————————————————————

Entrepreneur   You and a friend develop a new design for in-line skates that improves speed by 25% to 30%. You plan to form a business to manufacture and market the skates. You and your friend want to minimize taxes, but your prime concern is potential lawsuits from individuals who might be injured on these skates. What form of organization do you set up? ■ [*Answer:* You should probably form the business as a corporation if potential lawsuits are the main concern. A corporate form helps protect *personal* property from lawsuits directed at the business. A downside of the corporate form is double taxation: The corporation must pay taxes on its income, and you must pay taxes on any money distributed to you. Formation as an LLC or S corp. can be explored. You must also examine the ethical and social aspects of starting a business where injuries are expected.]

Accounting Constraints   There are two basic constraints in financial reporting.

*   *Materiality* The **materiality constraint** prescribes that only information that influences decisions (such as through importance and dollar amount) need be disclosed.
*   *Benefit exceeds cost* The **cost-benefit constraint** prescribes that only information with benefits of disclosure greater than the costs of providing it need be disclosed.

Conservatism and *industry practices* are also sometimes listed as accounting constraints.

Part 1: Identify each of the following terms/phrases as either an accounting (a) principle, (b) assumption, or (c) constraint.

1. ___ Materiality	**4.** ___ Going concern	**7.** ___ Expense recognition
2. ___ Measurement	**5.** ___ Full disclosure	**8.** ___ Revenue recognition
3. ___ Business entity	**6.** ___ Time period	

NEED-TO-KNOW 1-2

Accounting Guidance

C3 C4

Solution

1. c   **2.** a   **3.** b   **4.** b   **5.** a   **6.** b   **7.** a   **8.** a

Part 2: Complete the following table with either a *yes* or a *no* regarding the attributes of a partnership and a corporation.

Attribute Present	Partnership	Corporation
Business taxed	a. _____	e. _____
Limited liability	b. _____	f. _____
Legal entity	c. _____	g. _____
Unlimited life	d. _____	h. _____

Do More: QS 1-3, QS 1-4, QS 1-5, QS 1-6, E 1-4, E 1-5, E 1-6, E 1-7

Solution

a. no   **b.** no   **c.** no   **d.** no   **e.** yes   **f.** yes   **g.** yes   **h.** yes

BUSINESS TRANSACTIONS AND ACCOUNTING

A1

Define and interpret the accounting equation and each of its components.

To understand accounting information, we need to know how an accounting system captures relevant data about transactions and then classifies, records, and reports data.

Accounting Equation

The accounting system reflects two basic aspects of a company: what it owns and what it owes. *Assets* are resources a company owns or controls. Examples are cash, supplies, equipment, and land. The claims on a company's assets—what it owes—are separated into owner and nonowner claims. *Liabilities* are what a company owes its nonowners (creditors) in future payments, products, or services. *Equity* (also called owner's equity or capital) refers to the claims of its owner(s). Together, liabilities and equity are the source of funds to acquire assets. The relation of assets, liabilities, and equity is reflected in the following **accounting equation:**

$$\textbf{Assets} = \textbf{Liabilities} + \textbf{Equity}$$

Liabilities are usually shown before equity in this equation because creditors' claims must be paid before the claims of owners. (The terms in this equation can be rearranged; for example, Assets − Liabilities = Equity.) The accounting equation applies to all transactions and events, to all companies and forms of organization, and to all points in time. Using **Apple** as an example, its assets equal $290,479, its liabilities equal $171,124, and its equity equals $119,355 ($ in millions). Let's look at the accounting equation in more detail.

Assets   Assets are resources a company owns or controls. These resources are expected to yield future benefits. Examples are web servers for an online services company, musical instruments for a rock band, and land for a vegetable grower. The term *receivable* is used to refer to an asset that promises a future inflow of resources. A company that provides a service or product on credit has an account receivable from that customer.

Liabilities   Liabilities are creditors' claims on assets. These claims reflect company obligations to provide assets, products, or services to others. The term *payable* refers to a liability that promises a future outflow of resources. Examples are wages payable to workers, accounts payable to suppliers, notes payable to banks, and taxes payable to the government.

Equity   Equity is the owner's claim on assets, and is equal to assets minus liabilities. Equity is also called *net assets* or *residual equity*.

Margin notes further enhance textual material.

Point: The phrases "on credit" and "on account" imply that cash payment will occur at a future date.

Equity increases from owner investments and from revenues. It decreases from owner withdrawals and from expenses. Equity consists of four elements.

- *Owner, Capital* **Owner investments** are inflows of resources such as cash and other net assets that an owner puts into the company; they are included under the generic title **Owner, Capital.**
- *Owner, Withdrawals* **Owner withdrawals** are outflows of resources such as cash and other assets that an owner takes from the company for personal use; they are included under the generic title **Owner, Withdrawals.**
- *Revenues* **Revenues** increase equity (via net income) from sales of products and services to customers; examples are sales of products, consulting services provided, facilities rented to others, and commissions from services.
- *Expenses* **Expenses** decrease equity (via net income) from costs of providing products and services to customers; examples are costs of employee time, use of supplies, advertising, utilities, and insurance fees.

*Key **terms** are printed in bold and defined again in the **glossary***

This breakdown of equity yields the following **expanded accounting equation:**

$$\text{Assets} = \text{Liabilities} + \underbrace{\underset{\text{Capital}}{\text{Owner,}} - \underset{\text{Withdrawals}}{\text{Owner,}} + \text{Revenues} - \text{Expenses}}_{\text{Equity}}$$

Net income occurs when revenues exceed expenses. Net income increases equity. A **net loss** occurs when expenses exceed revenues, which decreases equity.

■ Decision Insight

Big Data Most organizations offer access to large accounting databases—see Apple (**Apple.com**) as an example. The SEC keeps an online database called **EDGAR** (**sec.gov/edgar.shtml**), which has accounting information for thousands of companies that issue stock to the public. The annual report filing for most publicly traded U.S. companies is known as Form 10-K, and the quarterly filing is Form 10-Q. Information services such as **Finance.Google.com** and **Finance.Yahoo.com** offer online data and analysis. ■

© Thomas Trutschel/Photothek via Getty Images

APPLE

NEED-TO-KNOW 1-3

Accounting Equation

A1

Part 1: Use the *accounting equation* to compute the missing financial statement amounts.

Company	Assets	Liabilities	Equity
Bose	$150	$ 30	$_(a)_
Vogue	$_(b)_	$100	$300

Solution

a. $120   **b.** $400

Part 2: Use the *expanded accounting equation* to compute the missing financial statement amounts.

Company	Assets	Liabilities	Owner, Capital	Owner, Withdrawals	Revenues	Expenses
Tesla	$200	$ 80	$100	$5	_(a)_	$40
YouTube	$400	$160	$220	_(b)_	$120	$90

Solution

a. $65   **b.** $10

Do More: QS 1-7, QS 1-8, E 1-8, E 1-9

Transaction Analysis

P1

Analyze business
transactions using the
accounting equation.

Business activities can be described in terms of transactions and events. **External transactions** are exchanges of value between two entities, which yield changes in the accounting equation. An example is the sale of the *AppleCare Protection Plan* by Apple. **Internal transactions** are exchanges within an entity, which may or may not affect the accounting equation. An example is Twitter's use of its supplies, which are reported as expenses when used. **Events** refer to happenings that affect the accounting equation *and* are reliably measured. They include business events such as changes in the market value of certain assets and liabilities and natural events such as floods and fires that destroy assets and create losses.

This section uses the accounting equation to analyze 11 selected transactions and events of FastForward, a start-up consulting (service) business, in its first month of operations. Remember that each transaction and event leaves the equation in balance and that assets *always* equal the sum of liabilities and equity.

Transaction 1: Investment by Owner   On December 1, Chas Taylor forms a consulting business, named FastForward and set up as a proprietorship, that focuses on assessing the performance of footwear and accessories. Taylor owns and manages the business. The marketing plan for the business is to focus primarily on publishing online reviews and consulting with clubs, athletes, and others who place orders for footwear and accessories with manufacturers.

FASTForward

Point: There are 3 basic types of company operations: (1) **Services**—providing customer services for profit, (2) **Merchandisers**—buying products and reselling them for profit, and (3) **Manufacturers**—creating products and selling them for profit.

Taylor personally invests $30,000 cash in the new company and deposits the cash in a bank account opened under the name of FastForward. After this transaction, the cash (an asset) and the owner's equity each equals $30,000. The source of increase in equity is the owner's investment, which is included in the column titled C. Taylor, Capital. (Owner investments are always included under the title *'Owner name,' Capital*.) The effect of this transaction on FastForward is reflected in the accounting equation as follows (we label the equity entries):

	Assets	=	Liabilities	+	Equity
	Cash	=			**C. Taylor, Capital**
(1)	**+$30,000**	=			**+$30,000** Owner investment

Transaction 2: Purchase Supplies for Cash   FastForward uses $2,500 of its cash to buy supplies of brand name footwear for performance testing over the next few months. This transaction is an exchange of cash, an asset, for another kind of asset, supplies. It merely changes the form of assets from cash to supplies. The decrease in cash is exactly equal to the increase in supplies. The supplies of footwear are assets because of the expected future benefits from the test results of their performance. This transaction is reflected in the accounting equation as follows:

	Assets			=	Liabilities	+	Equity
	Cash	+	**Supplies**	=			**C. Taylor, Capital**
Old Bal.	$30,000			=			$30,000
(2)	**−2,500**	+	**$2,500**				
New Bal.	$27,500	+	$ 2,500	=			$30,000
		$30,000				$30,000	

Transaction 3: Purchase Equipment for Cash   FastForward spends $26,000 to acquire equipment for testing footwear. Like transaction 2, transaction 3 is an exchange of one asset, cash, for another asset, equipment. The equipment is an asset because of its expected future benefits from testing footwear. This purchase changes the makeup of assets but does not change the asset total. The accounting equation remains in balance.

	Assets				=	Liabilities	+	Equity
	Cash	+	Supplies	+	Equipment	=		C. Taylor, Capital
Old Bal.	$27,500	+	$2,500			=		$30,000
(3)	−26,000			+	$26,000	=		
New Bal.	$ 1,500	+	$2,500	+	$ 26,000	=		$30,000

$30,000 $30,000

Transaction 4: Purchase Supplies on Credit

Taylor decides more supplies of footwear and accessories are needed. These additional supplies total $7,100, but as we see from the accounting equation in transaction 3, FastForward has only $1,500 in cash. Taylor arranges to purchase them on credit from CalTech Supply Company. Thus, FastForward acquires supplies in exchange for a promise to pay for them later. This purchase increases assets by $7,100 in supplies, and liabilities (called *accounts payable* to CalTech Supply) increase by the same amount. The effects of this purchase follow:

Example: If FastForward pays $500 cash in transaction 4, how does this partial payment affect the liability to CalTech? *Answer:* The liability to CalTech is reduced to $6,600 and the cash balance is reduced to $1,000.

	Assets					=	Liabilities	+	Equity
	Cash	+	Supplies	+	Equipment	=	Accounts Payable	+	C. Taylor, Capital
Old Bal.	$1,500	+	$2,500	+	$26,000	=			$30,000
(4)		+	7,100				+$7,100		
New Bal.	$1,500	+	$9,600	+	$26,000	=	$ 7,100	+	$30,000

$37,100 $37,100

Transaction 5: Provide Services for Cash

FastForward plans to earn revenues by selling online ad space to manufacturers and by consulting with clients about test results on footwear and accessories. It earns net income only if its revenues are greater than its expenses incurred in earning them. In one of its first jobs, FastForward provides consulting services to a power-walking club and immediately collects $4,200 cash. The accounting equation reflects this increase in cash of $4,200 and in equity of $4,200. This increase in equity is identified in the far right column under Revenues because the cash received is earned by providing consulting services.

Point: Revenue recognition principle requires that revenue is recognized when work is performed.

	Assets					=	Liabilities	+		Equity		
	Cash	+	Supplies	+	Equipment	=	Accounts Payable	+	C. Taylor, Capital	+	Revenues
Old Bal.	$1,500	+	$9,600	+	$26,000	=	$7,100	+	$30,000		
(5)	+4,200									+	$4,200 Consulting
New Bal.	$5,700	+	$9,600	+	$26,000	=	$7,100	+	$30,000	+	$ 4,200

$41,300 $41,300

Transactions 6 and 7: Payment of Expenses in Cash

FastForward pays $1,000 rent to the landlord of the building where its facilities are located. Paying this amount allows FastForward to occupy the space for the month of December. The rental payment is reflected in the following accounting equation as transaction 6. FastForward also pays the biweekly $700 salary of the company's only employee. This is reflected in the accounting equation as transaction 7. Both transactions 6 and 7 are December expenses for FastForward. The costs of both rent and salary are expenses, as opposed to assets, because their benefits are used in December (they have no future benefits after December). These transactions also use up an asset (cash) in carrying out FastForward's operations. The accounting equation shows that both transactions reduce cash and equity. The far right column identifies these decreases as Expenses.

Point: Expense recognition principle requires that expenses are recognized when the revenue they help generate is recorded. Expenses are outflows of net assets, which decrease equity.

By definition, increases in expenses yield decreases in equity.

	Assets			=	Liabilities	+		Equity		
	Cash +	Supplies +	Equipment	=	Accounts Payable +	C. Taylor, Capital +	Revenues −	Expenses			
Old Bal.	$5,700 +	$9,600 +	$26,000	=	$7,100 +	$30,000 +	$4,200 −				
(6)	−1,000							−	$1,000 Rent		
Bal.	4,700 +	9,600 +	26,000	=	7,100 +	30,000 +	4,200 −	1,000			
(7)	− 700							−	700 Salaries		
New Bal.	$4,000 +	$9,600 +	$26,000	=	$7,100 +	$30,000 +	$4,200 −	$ 1,700			
		$39,600					$39,600				

Transaction 8: Provide Services and Facilities for Credit

Point: Transaction 8, like 5, records revenue when work is performed, not necessarily when cash is received.

FastForward provides consulting services of $1,600 and rents its test facilities for $300 to a podiatric services center. The rental involves allowing members to try recommended footwear and accessories at FastForward's testing area. The center is billed for the $1,900 total. This transaction results in a new asset, called *accounts receivable,* from this client. It also yields an increase in equity from the two revenue components reflected in the Revenues column of the accounting equation:

	Assets				=	Liabilities	+		Equity	
	Cash +	Accounts Receivable +	Supplies +	Equipment	=	Accounts Payable +	C. Taylor, Capital +	Revenues −	Expenses	
Old Bal.	$4,000 +	+	$9,600 +	$26,000	=	$7,100 +	$30,000 +	$4,200 −	$1,700	
(8)		+ $1,900						+ 1,600 Consulting		
								+ 300 Rental		
New Bal.	$4,000 +	$ 1,900 +	$9,600 +	$26,000	=	$7,100 +	$30,000 +	$6,100 −	$1,700	
		$41,500						$41,500		

Transaction 9: Receipt of Cash from Accounts Receivable

Point: Transaction 9 involved no added client work, so no added revenue is recorded.

Point: Receipt of cash is not always a revenue.

The client in transaction 8 (the podiatric center) pays $1,900 to FastForward 10 days after it is billed for consulting services. This transaction 9 does not change the total amount of assets and does not affect liabilities or equity. It converts the receivable (an asset) to cash (another asset). It does not create new revenue. Revenue was recognized when FastForward rendered the services in transaction 8, not when the cash is now collected. This emphasis on when products or services are provided instead of on cash flows is a key part of revenue recognition. The new balances follow:

	Assets				=	Liabilities	+		Equity	
	Cash +	Accounts Receivable +	Supplies +	Equipment	=	Accounts Payable +	C. Taylor, Capital +	Revenues −	Expenses	
Old Bal.	$4,000 +	$1,900 +	$9,600 +	$26,000	=	$7,100 +	$30,000 +	$6,100 −	$1,700	
(9)	+1,900 −	1,900								
New Bal.	$5,900 +	$ 0 +	$9,600 +	$26,000	=	$7,100 +	$30,000 +	$6,100 −	$1,700	
		$41,500						$41,500		

Transaction 10: Payment of Accounts Payable

FastForward pays CalTech Supply $900 cash as partial payment for its earlier $7,100 purchase of supplies (transaction 4), leaving $6,200 unpaid. The accounting equation shows that this transaction decreases FastForward's cash by $900 and decreases its liability to CalTech Supply by $900. Equity does not change. This event does not create an expense even though cash flows out of FastForward (instead the expense is recorded when FastForward derives the benefits from these supplies).

	Assets				=	Liabilities	+	Equity			
	Cash	+ Accounts Receivable	+ Supplies	+ Equipment	=	Accounts Payable	+ C. Taylor, Capital		+ Revenues	− Expenses
Old Bal.	$5,900	+ $ 0	+ $9,600	+ $26,000	=	$7,100	+ $30,000		+ $6,100	− $1,700
(10)	− 900					−900				
New Bal.	$5,000	+ $ 0	+ $9,600	+ $26,000	=	$6,200	+ $30,000		+ $6,100	− $1,700
		$40,600						$40,600		

Transaction 11: Withdrawal of Cash by Owner

The owner of FastForward withdraws $200 cash for personal use. Withdrawals (decreases in equity) are not reported as expenses because they are not part of the company's earnings process. Since withdrawals are not company expenses, they are not used in computing net income.

By definition, increases in withdrawals yield decreases in equity.

	Assets				=	Liabilities	+	Equity			
	Cash	+ Accounts Receivable	+ Supplies	+ Equipment	=	Accounts Payable	+ C. Taylor, Capital	− C. Taylor, Withdrawals	+ Revenues	− Expenses
Old Bal.	$5,000	+ $ 0	+ $9,600	+ $26,000	=	$6,200	+ $30,000		+ $6,100	− $1,700
(11)	− 200							− $200 Owner Withdrawal		
New Bal.	$4,800	+ $ 0	+ $9,600	+ $26,000	=	$6,200	+ $30,000	− $200	+ $6,100	− $1,700
		$40,400						$40,400		

Summary of Transactions

We summarize in Exhibit 1.9 the effects of these 11 transactions of FastForward using the accounting equation. We see that the accounting equation remains in balance after each transaction.

EXHIBIT 1.9

Summary of Transactions Using the Accounting Equation

	Assets				=	Liabilities	+	Equity			
	Cash	+ Accounts Receivable	+ Supplies	+ Equipment	=	Accounts Payable	+ C. Taylor, Capital	− C. Taylor, Withdrawals	+ Revenues	− Expenses
(1)	$30,000				=		$30,000			
(2)	− 2,500		+ $2,500							
Bal.	27,500		+ 2,500		=		30,000			
(3)	−26,000			+ $26,000						
Bal.	1,500		+ 2,500	+ 26,000	=		30,000			
(4)			+ 7,100		=	+$7,100				
Bal.	1,500		+ 9,600	+ 26,000	=	7,100	+ 30,000			
(5)	+ 4,200								+ $4,200	
Bal.	5,700		+ 9,600	+ 26,000	=	7,100	+ 30,000		+ 4,200	
(6)	− 1,000								+	− $1,000
Bal.	4,700		+ 9,600	+ 26,000	=	7,100	+ 30,000		+ 4,200	− 1,000
(7)	− 700									− 700
Bal.	4,000		+ 9,600	+ 26,000	=	7,100	+ 30,000		+ 4,200	− 1,700
(8)		+ $1,900							+ 1,600	
									+ 300	
Bal.	4,000	+ 1,900	+ 9,600	+ 26,000	=	7,100	+ 30,000		6,100	− 1,700
(9)	+ 1,900	− 1,900								
Bal.	5,900	+ 0	+ 9,600	+ 26,000	=	7,100	+ 30,000		+ 6,100	− 1,700
(10)	− 900					− 900				
Bal.	5,000	+ 0	+ 9,600	+ 26,000	=	6,200	+ 30,000		+ 6,100	− 1,700
(11)	− 200							− $200		
Bal.	$ 4,800	+ $ 0	+ $9,600	+ $26,000	=	$ 6,200	+ $ 30,000	− $200	+ $6,100	− $ 1,700

NEED-TO-KNOW 1-4

Transaction Analysis

P1

Do More: QS 1-10, QS 1-11,
E 1-10, E 1-11, E 1-13

Assume Tata Company began operations on January 1 and completed the following transactions during its first month of operations. Arrange the following asset, liability, and equity titles in a table like Exhibit 1.9: Cash; Accounts Receivable; Equipment; Accounts Payable; J. Tata, Capital; J. Tata, Withdrawals; Revenues; and Expenses.

Jan. 1 Jamsetji Tata invested $4,000 cash in Tata Company.
      5 The company purchased $2,000 of equipment on credit.
     14 The company provided $540 of services for a client on credit.
     21 The company paid $250 cash for an employee's salary.

Solution

	Assets				=	Liabilities	+				Equity				
	Cash	+	Accounts Receivable	+	Equipment	=	Accounts Payable	+	J. Tata, Capital	−	J. Tata, Withdrawals	+	Revenues	−	Expenses
Jan. 1	$4,000					=			$4,000						
Jan. 5					+$2,000		+$2,000								
Bal.	4,000				2,000	=	2,000		4,000						
Jan. 14			+$540										+$540		
Bal.	4,000		540		2,000	=	2,000		4,000				540		
Jan. 21	−250													−	$250
Bal.	3,750		540		2,000	=	2,000		4,000				540	−	250

$6,290	$6,290

COMMUNICATING WITH USERS

P2_____

Identify and prepare basic financial statements and explain how they interrelate.

This section introduces us to how financial statements are prepared from the analysis of business transactions. The four financial statements and their purposes are:

1. **Income statement**—describes a company's revenues and expenses along with the resulting net income or loss over a period of time.
2. **Statement of owner's equity**—explains changes in equity from net income (or loss) and from any owner investments and withdrawals over a period of time.
3. **Balance sheet**—describes a company's financial position (types and amounts of assets, liabilities, and equity) at a point in time.
4. **Statement of cash flows**—identifies cash inflows (receipts) and cash outflows (payments) over a period of time.

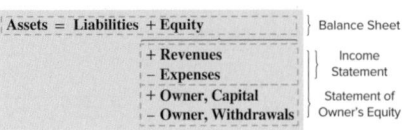

We prepare these financial statements, in the order above, using the 11 selected transactions of FastForward. (These statements are called *unadjusted*—we explain this in Chapters 2 and 3.) The graphic to the side shows that financial statements reflect different parts of the expanded accounting equation.

Income Statement

FastForward's income statement for December is shown at the top of Exhibit 1.10. Information about revenues and expenses is conveniently taken from the Equity columns of Exhibit 1.9. Revenues are reported first on the income statement. They include consulting revenues of $5,800 from transactions 5 and 8 and rental revenue of $300 from transaction 8. Expenses are reported after revenues. (For convenience in this chapter, we list larger amounts first, but we can sort expenses in different ways.) Rent and salary expenses are from transactions 6 and 7. Expenses reflect the costs to generate the revenues reported. Net income (or loss) is reported at the bottom of the statement and is the amount earned in December. Owner's investments and withdrawals are *not* part of income.

Point: Total revenues
      − Total expenses
      = Net income (or loss)

Point: Net income is sometimes called *earnings* or *profit*.

EXHIBIT 1.10

Financial Statements and
Their Links

FASTFORWARD
Income Statement
For Month Ended December 31, 2017

Revenues		
Consulting revenue ($4,200 + $1,600)	$ 5,800	
Rental revenue	300	
Total revenues		$ 6,100
Expenses		
Rent expense	1,000	
Salaries expense	700	
Total expenses		1,700
Net income		$ 4,400

Point: A statement's heading identifies the company, the statement title, and the date or time period.

FASTFORWARD
Statement of Owner's Equity
For Month Ended December 31, 2017

C. Taylor, Capital, December 1, 2017		$ 0
Plus: Investments by owner	$30,000	
Net income	4,400	34,400
		34,400
Less: Withdrawals by owner		200
C. Taylor, Capital, December 31, 2017		$34,200

Point: Arrow lines show how the statements are linked.
① Net income is used to compute equity. ② Owner capital is used to prepare the balance sheet. ③ Cash from the balance sheet is used to reconcile the statement of cash flows.

FASTFORWARD
Balance Sheet
December 31, 2017

Assets		Liabilities	
Cash	$ 4,800	Accounts payable................	$ 6,200
Supplies	9,600	Total liabilities	6,200
Equipment	26,000	**Equity**	
		C. Taylor, Capital.................	34,200
Total assets	$40,400	Total liabilities and equity	$ 40,400

Point: The income statement, the statement of owner's equity, and the statement of cash flows are prepared for a *period* of time. The balance sheet is prepared as of a *point* in time.

FASTFORWARD
Statement of Cash Flows
For Month Ended December 31, 2017

Cash flows from operating activities		
Cash received from clients ($4,200 + $1,900)	$ 6,100	
Cash paid for expenses ($2,500 + $900 + $1,000 + $700)....	(5,100)	
Net cash provided by operating activities		$ 1,000
Cash flows from investing activities		
Purchase of equipment.................................	(26,000)	
Net cash used by investing activities		(26,000)
Cash flows from financing activities		
Investments by owner.................................	30,000	
Withdrawals by owner.................................	(200)	
Net cash provided by financing activities		29,800
Net increase in cash		$ 4,800
Cash balance, December 1, 2017		0
Cash balance, December 31, 2017		$ 4,800

Point: A single ruled line denotes an addition or subtraction. Final totals are double underlined. Negative amounts may or may not be in parentheses.

Statement of Owner's Equity

Point: The statement of owner's equity is also called the *statement of changes in owner's equity.* Note:

Beginning Capital
+ Owner Investments
+ Net Income
– Withdrawals
= Ending Capital

The statement of owner's equity reports information about how equity changes over the reporting period. This statement shows beginning capital, events that increase it (owner investments and net income), and events that decrease it (withdrawals and net loss). Ending capital is computed in this statement and is carried over and reported on the balance sheet. FastForward's statement of owner's equity is the second report in Exhibit 1.10. The beginning capital balance is measured as of the start of business on December 1. It is zero because FastForward did not exist before then. An existing business reports a beginning balance equal to that as of the end of the prior reporting period (such as from November 30). FastForward's statement of owner's equity shows that Taylor's initial investment created $30,000 of equity. It also shows the $4,400 of net income for the period, which links the income statement to the statement of owner's equity (see line ①). The statement also reports Taylor's $200 cash withdrawal and FastForward's end-of-period capital balance.

Balance Sheet

FastForward's balance sheet is the third report in Exhibit 1.10. This statement refers to FastForward's financial condition at the close of business on December 31. The left side of the balance sheet lists FastForward's assets: cash, supplies, and equipment. The upper right side of the balance sheet shows that FastForward owes $6,200 to creditors. Any other liabilities (such as a bank loan) would be listed here. The equity (capital) balance is $34,200. Line ② shows the link between the ending balance of the statement of owner's equity and the equity balance on the balance sheet. (This presentation of the balance sheet is called the *account form:* assets on the left and liabilities and equity on the right. Another presentation is the *report form:* assets on top, followed by liabilities and then equity at the bottom. Either presentation is acceptable.) As always, we see the accounting equation applies: Assets of $40,400 = Liabilities of $6,200 + Equity of $34,200.

Statement of Cash Flows

Point: Payment for supplies is an operating activity because supplies are expected to be used up in short-term operations (typically less than one year).

Point: Investing activities refer to long-term asset investments by the company, *not* to owner investments.

FastForward's statement of cash flows is the final report in Exhibit 1.10. The first section reports cash flows from *operating activities.* It shows the $6,100 cash received from clients and the $5,100 cash paid for supplies, rent, and employee salaries. Outflows are in parentheses to denote subtraction. Net cash provided by operating activities for December is $1,000. The second section reports *investing activities,* which involve buying and selling assets such as land and equipment that are held for *long-term use* (typically more than one year). The only investing activity is the $26,000 purchase of equipment. The third section shows cash flows from *financing activities,* which include *long-term* borrowing and repaying of cash from lenders and the cash investments from, and withdrawals by, the owner. FastForward reports $30,000 from the owner's initial investment and a $200 cash withdrawal. The net cash effect of all financing transactions is a $29,800 cash inflow. The final part of the statement shows an increased cash balance of $4,800. The ending balance is also $4,800 as it started with no cash—see line ③.

NEED-TO-KNOW **1-5**

Financial Statements

P2 ▶

APPLE

Prepare the (a) income statement, (b) statement of owner's equity, and (c) balance sheet for **Apple** using the following *condensed* data from its fiscal year ended September 26, 2015 ($ in millions).

Accounts payable	$ 35,490		Investments and other assets	$230,039
Other liabilities	135,634		Land and equipment (net)	22,471
Cost of sales	140,089		Selling, general and other expenses	40,232
Cash	21,120		Accounts receivable	16,849
Owner, Capital, Sep. 27, 2014	111,547		Net income	53,394
Withdrawals in fiscal year 2015	45,586		Owner, Capital, Sep. 26, 2015	119,355
Revenues	233,715			

Solution ($ in millions)

APPLE Income Statement For Fiscal Year Ended September 26, 2015		
Revenues		$233,715
Expenses		
Cost of sales	$140,089	
Selling, general, and other expenses	40,232	
Total expenses		180,321
Net income		$ 53,394

APPLE Statement of Owner's Equity For Fiscal Year Ended September 26, 2015	
Owner, Capital, Sep. 27, 2014	$111,547
Plus: Net income	53,394
	164,941
Less: Withdrawals by owner	45,586
Owner, Capital, Sep. 26, 2015	$119,355

APPLE
Balance Sheet
September 26, 2015

Assets		Liabilities	
Cash	$ 21,120	Accounts payable	$ 35,490
Accounts receivable	16,849	Other liabilities	135,634
Land and equipment (net)	22,471	Total liabilities	171,124
Investments and other assets	230,039	**Equity**	
		Owner, Capital, Sep. 26, 2015	119,355
Total assets	$290,479	Total liabilities and equity	$290,479

Do More: QS 1-12, QS 1-13, QS 1-14, E 1-15, E 1-16, E 1-17

SUSTAINABILITY AND ACCOUNTING

Sustainability refers to *environmental*, *social*, and *governance* (*ESG*) aspects of a company. A company's social aspects include donations to hospitals, colleges, community programs, and law enforcement. Environmental aspects include programs to reduce pollution, increase product safety, improve worker conditions, and support "green" activities. Governance aspects include social responsibility programs, community relations, and use of sustainable materials.

The **Sustainability Accounting Standards Board (SASB)** is a nonprofit entity engaged in creating and disseminating sustainability accounting standards for use by companies. Sustainability accounting standards are intended to complement financial accounting standards. The SASB has its own *Conceptual Framework* to guide the development of sustainability standards.

Reprinted by permission of the Sustainability Accounting Standards Board (SASB)

Apple, as introduced in this chapter's opening feature, focuses on sustainability. Apple hired a Vice President of Environmental Initiatives, Lisa Jackson (in photo, and the first African-American EPA Administrator), to oversee its sustainability initiative.

Lisa sets high goals for Apple, including powering all of its facilities with 100% renewable energy and making its products 100% recyclable. "We are swinging for the fences," exclaims Lisa, which has resulted in some home runs. In Apple's sustainability report, Lisa points out that it powers data centers with 100% renewable energy and relies on renewable energy to power 80% of its corporate facilities and 50% of its retail stores.

Lisa stresses that "[sustainability] is really important at Apple." Apple is committed to reducing carbon emissions. "We would like to eliminate certain toxins," explains Lisa.

Apple's sustainability report asserts that it has markedly improved its carbon efficiency and reduced the amount of carbon dioxide produced per dollar of revenue. Lisa insists, "Leave the world better than how we found it . . . this is what really inspires people at Apple."

© Xinhua / Alamy Stock Photo

Decision Insight

Sustainability Returns Virtue is not always its own reward. Compare the S&P 500 with the iShares MSCI KLD 400 Social (DSI), which covers 400 companies that have especially good records for sustainability. We see that returns for companies with sustainable behavior are roughly on par with, or better than, those of the S&P 500 for the recent three-year period—see graph. Varying, but similar, results are evident over several recent time periods. ■

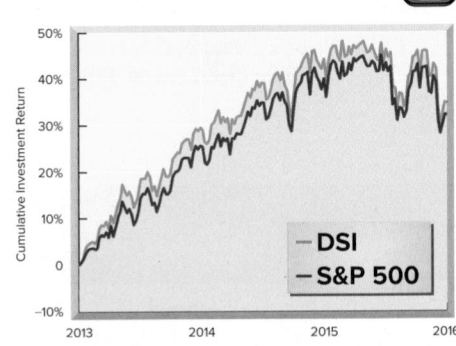

Decision Analysis (a section at the end of each chapter) introduces and explains ratios for decision making using real company data. Instructors can skip this section and cover all ratios in Chapter 17.

 Decision Analysis  Return on Assets

A2

Compute and interpret return on assets.

A *Decision Analysis* section at the end of each chapter is devoted to financial statement analysis. We organize financial statement analysis into four areas: (1) liquidity and efficiency, (2) solvency, (3) profitability, and (4) market prospects—Chapter 17 has a ratio listing with definitions and groupings by area. When analyzing ratios, we need benchmarks to identify good, bad, or average levels. Common benchmarks include the company's prior levels and those of its competitors.

This chapter presents a profitability measure: return on assets. Return on assets is useful in evaluating management, analyzing and forecasting profits, and planning activities. **Dell** has its marketing department compute return on assets for *each* order. **Return on assets (ROA),** also called *return on investment (ROI),* is defined in Exhibit 1.11.

EXHIBIT 1.11

Return on Assets

$$\text{Return on assets} = \frac{\text{Net income}}{\text{Average total assets}}$$

Net income is from the annual income statement, and average total assets is computed by adding the beginning and ending amounts for that same period and dividing by 2. To illustrate, **Verizon** reports total net income of $18,375 million for 2015. At the beginning of 2015 its total assets are $232,616 million, and at the end of 2015 they total $244,640 million. Verizon's return on assets for 2015 is:

$$\text{Return on assets} = \frac{\$18,375 \text{ million}}{(\$244,640 \text{ million} + \$232,616 \text{ million})/2} = 7.7\%$$

Is a 7.7% return on assets good or bad for Verizon? To help answer this question, we compare (benchmark) Verizon's return with its prior performance, the returns of competitors (such as AT&T, T-Mobile, and Sprint), and the returns from alternative investments. Verizon's return for each of the prior five years is in the middle column of Exhibit 1.12, which ranges from 4.5% to 9.4%.

Fiscal Year	Return on Assets	
	Verizon	Industry
2015	7.7%	4.8%
2014	4.7	4.1
2013	9.4	5.4
2012	4.6	3.3
2011	4.5	3.1

EXHIBIT 1.12

Verizon and Industry Returns

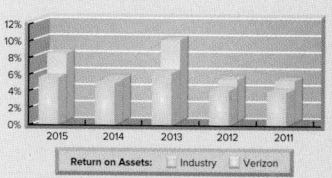

Verizon shows a fairly stable pattern of good returns that reflect its productive use of assets. There is a higher than usual return in 2013 reflecting some unusual items. We also compare Verizon's return to the normal return from its competitors (third column). We compute industry norms, which are sometimes available from services such as Dun & Bradstreet's *Industry Norms and Key Ratios* and The Risk Management Association's *Annual Statement Studies*. When compared to the industry, Verizon often performs slightly better.

*Each **Decision Analysis** section ends with a role-playing scenario to show the usefulness of ratios*

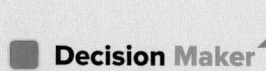 **Decision** Maker

Business Owner   You own a winter ski resort that earns a 21% return on its assets. An opportunity to purchase a winter ski equipment manufacturer is offered to you. This manufacturer earns a 14% return on its assets. The industry return for this manufacturer is 9%. Do you purchase this manufacturer? ■   [*Answer:* The 14% return on assets for the manufacturer exceeds the 9% industry return (and many others). This is positive for a potential purchase. Also, this purchase is an opportunity to spread your risk over two businesses. Still, you should hesitate to purchase a business whose 14% return is lower than your current 21% return. You might better direct efforts to increase investment in your resort if it can earn more than the 14% alternative.]

*The **Comprehensive Need-to-Know** is a review of key chapter content. The* Planning the Solution *section offers strategies in solving it*

After several months of planning, Jasmine Worthy started a haircutting business called Expressions. The following events occurred during its first month of business.

NEED-TO-KNOW 1-6

COMPREHENSIVE

a. On August 1, Worthy invested $3,000 cash and $15,000 of equipment in Expressions.

b. On August 2, Expressions paid $600 cash for furniture for the shop.

c. On August 3, Expressions paid $500 cash to rent space in a strip mall for August.

d. On August 4, it purchased $1,200 of equipment on credit for the shop (recorded as accounts payable).

e. On August 5, Expressions opened for business. Cash received from haircutting services in the first week and a half of business (ended August 15) was $825.

f. On August 15, Expressions provided $100 of haircutting services on account.

g. On August 17, Expressions received a $100 check for services previously rendered on account.

h. On August 17, Expressions paid $125 cash to an assistant for hours worked for the grand opening.

i. Cash received from services provided during the second half of August was $930.

j. On August 31, Expressions paid $400 cash toward the accounts payable entered into on August 4.

k. On August 31, Worthy made a $900 cash withdrawal from the company for personal use.

Required

1. Arrange the following asset, liability, and equity titles in a table similar to the one in Exhibit 1.9: Cash; Accounts Receivable; Furniture; Store Equipment; Accounts Payable; J. Worthy, Capital; J. Worthy, Withdrawals; Revenues; and Expenses. Show the effects of each transaction using the accounting equation.
2. Prepare an income statement for August.
3. Prepare a statement of owner's equity for August.
4. Prepare a balance sheet as of August 31.
5. Prepare a statement of cash flows for August.
6. Determine the return on assets ratio for August.

PLANNING THE SOLUTION

- Set up a table like Exhibit 1.9 with the appropriate columns for accounts.
- Analyze each transaction and show its effects as increases or decreases in the appropriate columns. Be sure the accounting equation remains in balance after each transaction.
- Prepare the income statement, and identify revenues and expenses. List those items on the statement, compute the difference, and label the result as *net income* or *net loss*.
- Use information in the Equity columns to prepare the statement of owner's equity.
- Use information in the last row of the transactions table to prepare the balance sheet.
- Prepare the statement of cash flows; include all events listed in the Cash column of the transactions table. Classify each cash flow as operating, investing, or financing.
- Calculate return on assets by dividing net income by average assets.

SOLUTION

1.

	Cash	+	Accounts Receivable	+	Furniture	+	Store Equipment	=	Accounts Payable	+	J. Worthy, Capital	−	J. Worthy, Withdrawals	+	Revenues	−	Expenses
a.	$3,000						$15,000				$18,000						
b.	− 600				+ $600												
Bal.	2,400	+			+ 600	+	15,000	=			18,000						
c.	− 500															−	$500
Bal.	1,900	+			+ 600	+	15,000	=			18,000					−	500
d.							+ 1,200		+$1,200								
Bal.	1,900	+			+ 600	+	16,200	=	1,200	+	18,000					−	500
e.	+ 825													+	$ 825		
Bal.	2,725	+			+ 600	+	16,200	=	1,200	+	18,000			+	825	−	500
f.		+	$100											+	100		
Bal.	2,725	+	100	+	600	+	16,200	=	1,200	+	18,000			+	925	−	500
g.	+ 100	−	100														
Bal.	2,825	+	0	+	600	+	16,200	=	1,200	+	18,000			+	925	−	500
h.	− 125															−	125
Bal.	2,700	+	0	+	600	+	16,200	=	1,200	+	18,000			+	925	−	625
i.	+ 930													+	930		
Bal.	3,630	+	0	+	600	+	16,200	=	1,200	+	18,000			+	1,855	−	625
j.	− 400								− 400								
Bal.	3,230	+	0	+	600	+	16,200	=	800	+	18,000			+	1,855	−	625
k.	− 900											−	$900				
Bal.	$ 2,330	+	0	+	$ 600	+	$ 16,200	=	$ 800	+	$ 18,000	−	$ 900	+	$1,855	−	$625

2.

EXPRESSIONS
Income Statement
For Month Ended August 31

Revenues		
Haircutting services revenue		$1,855
Expenses		
Rent expense	$500	
Wages expense	125	
Total expenses		625
Net income		$1,230

3.

EXPRESSIONS
Statement of Owner's Equity
For Month Ended August 31

J. Worthy, Capital, August 1*		$ 0	
Plus: Investments by owner	$18,000		
Net income	1,230	19,230	
		19,230	
Less: Withdrawals by owner		900	
J. Worthy, Capital, August 31		$18,330	

* If Expressions had been an existing business from a prior period, the beginning capital balance would equal the Capital account balance from the end of the prior period.

4.

EXPRESSIONS
Balance Sheet
August 31

Assets		Liabilities	
Cash	$ 2,330	Accounts payable	$ 800
Furniture	600	**Equity**	
Store equipment	16,200	J. Worthy, Capital	18,330
Total assets	$19,130	Total liabilities and equity	$19,130

5.

EXPRESSIONS
Statement of Cash Flows
For Month Ended August 31

Cash flows from operating activities		
Cash received from customers	$1,855	
Cash paid for expenditures ($500 + $125 + $400)	(1,025)	
Net cash provided by operating activities		$ 830
Cash flows from investing activities		
Cash paid for furniture		(600)
Cash flows from financing activities		
Cash investments by owner	3,000	
Cash withdrawals by owner	(900)	
Net cash provided by financing activities		$2,100
Net increase in cash		$2,330
Cash balance, August 1		0
Cash balance, August 31		$2,330

6. Return on assets $= \dfrac{\text{Net income}}{\text{Average assets}} = \dfrac{\$1,230}{(\$18,000^* + \$19,130)/2} = \dfrac{\$1,230}{\$18,565} = \underline{\underline{6.63\%}}$

* Uses the initial \$18,000 investment as the beginning balance for the *start-up period only*.

1A

Return and Risk

A3

Explain the relation between return and risk.

This appendix explains return and risk analysis and its role in business and accounting.

Net income is often linked to **return.** Return on assets (ROA) is stated in ratio form as income divided by assets invested. For example, banks report return from a savings account in the form of an interest return such as 4%. If we invest in a savings account or in U.S. Treasury bills, we expect a return of around 1% to 5%. We could also invest in a company's stock, or even start our own business. How do we decide among these options? The answer depends on our trade-off between return and risk.

Risk is the uncertainty about the return we will earn. All business investments involve risk, but some investments involve more risk than others. The lower the risk of an investment, the lower is our expected return. The reason that savings accounts pay such a low return is the low risk of not being repaid with interest (the government guarantees most savings accounts). If we buy a share of **eBay** or any other company, we might obtain a large return. However, we have no guarantee of any return; there is even the risk of loss.

EXHIBIT 1A.1

Average Returns for Bonds with Different Risks

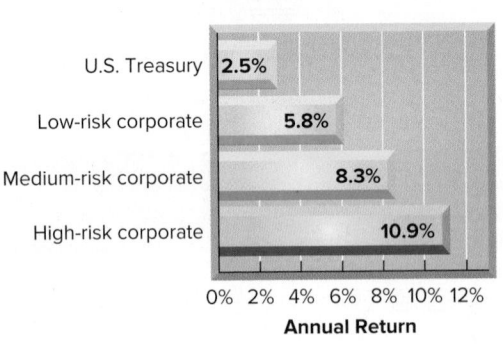

The bar graph in Exhibit 1A.1 shows recent returns for 10-year bonds with different risks. *Bonds* are written promises by organizations to repay amounts loaned with interest. U.S. Treasury bonds provide a low expected return, but they also offer low risk since they are backed by the U.S. government. High-risk corporate bonds offer a much larger potential return but with much higher risk.

The trade-off between return and risk is a normal part of business. Higher risk implies higher, but riskier, expected returns. To help us make better decisions, we use accounting information to assess both return and risk.

1B

Business Activities

C5

Identify and describe the three major activities of organizations.

This appendix explains how the accounting equation is linked to business activities. There are three major types of business activities: financing, investing, and operating. Each of these requires planning. *Planning* involves defining an organization's ideas, goals, and actions.

Financing *Financing activities* provide the means organizations use to pay for assets such as land, buildings, and equipment. The two sources of financing are owner and nonowner. *Owner financing* refers to resources contributed by the owner along with any income the owner leaves in the organization. *Nonowner* (or *creditor*) *financing* refers to resources contributed by creditors (lenders).

Investing *Investing activities* are the acquiring and disposing of assets that an organization uses to buy and sell its products or services. Some organizations require land and factories to operate. Others need only an office. Invested amounts are referred to as *assets.* Creditor and owner financing hold claims on assets. Creditors' claims are called *liabilities,* and the owner's claim is called *equity.* This yields the *accounting equation:* Assets = Liabilities + Equity.

Point: Investing (assets) and financing (liabilities plus equity) totals are *always* equal.

Operating *Operating activities* involve using resources to research, develop, purchase, produce, distribute, and market products and services. Sales and revenues are the inflow of assets from selling products and services. Costs and expenses are the outflow of assets to support operating activities.

Exhibit 1B.1 summarizes business activities. Planning is part of each activity and gives them meaning and focus. Investing (assets) and financing (liabilities and equity) are set opposite each other to stress their balance. Operating activities are below investing and financing activities to show that operating activities are the result of applying investing and financing.

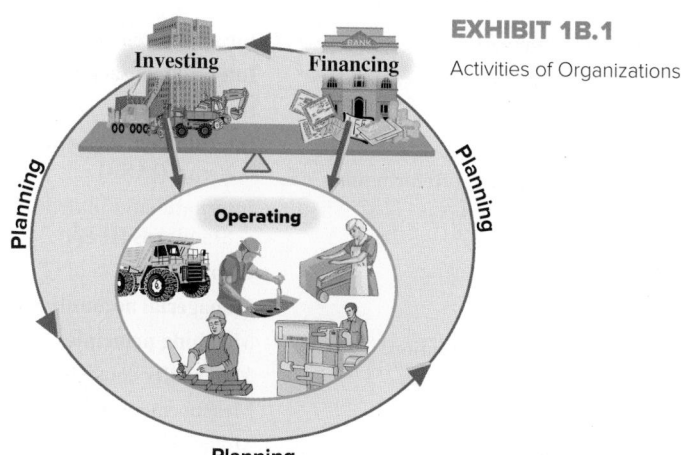

EXHIBIT 1B.1

Activities of Organizations

Summary

← *A **Summary** organized by learning objectives concludes each chapter*

C1 **Explain the purpose and importance of accounting.** Accounting is an information and measurement system that aims to identify, record, and communicate information about business activities. It helps assess opportunities, products, investments, and social and community responsibilities.

C2 **Identify users and uses of, and opportunities in, accounting.** Users of accounting are both internal and external. Some users and uses of accounting include (a) managers in controlling, monitoring, and planning; (b) lenders for measuring the risk and return of loans; (c) shareholders for assessing the return and risk of stock; (d) directors for overseeing management; and (e) employees for judging employment opportunities. Opportunities in accounting include financial, managerial, and tax accounting.

C3 **Explain why ethics are crucial to accounting.** The goal of accounting is to provide useful information for decision making. For information to be useful, it must be trusted. This demands ethical behavior in accounting.

C4 **Explain generally accepted accounting principles and define and apply several accounting principles.** Generally accepted accounting principles are a common set of standards applied by accountants. Accounting principles aid in producing relevant, reliable, and comparable information. Four principles underlying financial statements were introduced: cost, revenue recognition, expense recognition, and full disclosure. Financial statements also reflect four assumptions: going-concern, monetary unit, time period, and business entity.

C5^B **Identify and describe the three major activities of organizations.** Organizations carry out three major activities: financing, investing, and operating. Financing, from either creditors or owners, is the means used to pay for resources.

Investing refers to the buying and selling of resources such as land, buildings, and machines. Operating activities are those used in acquiring and selling products and services.

A1 **Define and interpret the accounting equation and each of its components.** The accounting equation is: Assets = Liabilities + Equity. Assets are resources owned by a company. Liabilities are creditors' claims on assets. Equity is the owner's claim on assets (*the residual*). The expanded accounting equation is: Assets = Liabilities + [Owner Capital − Owner Withdrawals + Revenues − Expenses].

A2 **Compute and interpret return on assets.** Return on assets is computed as net income divided by average assets. For example, if we have an average balance of $100 in a savings account and it earns $5 interest for the year, the return on assets is $5/$100, or 5%.

A3^A **Explain the relation between return and risk.** *Return* refers to income, and *risk* is the uncertainty about the return we hope to make. All investments involve risk. The lower the risk of an investment, the lower is its expected return. Higher risk implies higher, but riskier, expected return.

P1 **Analyze business transactions using the accounting equation.** A *transaction* is an exchange of economic consideration between two parties. Examples include exchanges of products, services, money, and rights to collect money. Transactions always have at least two effects on one or more components of the accounting equation. This equation is always in balance.

P2 **Identify and prepare basic financial statements and explain how they interrelate.** Four financial statements report on an organization's activities: balance sheet, income statement, statement of owner's equity, and statement of cash flows.

← *A list of key terms concludes each chapter (a complete glossary is also available)*

Key Terms

Accounting	Audit	Bookkeeping
Accounting equation	Auditors	Business entity assumption
Assets	Balance sheet	Common stock

Conceptual framework	Income statement	Recordkeeping
Corporation	Internal transactions	Return
Cost-benefit constraint	Internal users	Return on assets (ROA)
Cost principle	International Accounting Standards	Revenue recognition principle
Dodd-Frank Wall Street Reform and	Board (IASB)	Revenues
Consumer Protection Act	International Financial Reporting	Risk
Equity	Standards (IFRS)	Sarbanes-Oxley Act (SOX)
Ethics	Liabilities	Securities and Exchange
Events	Managerial accounting	Commission (SEC)
Expanded accounting equation	Matching principle	Shareholders
Expense recognition principle	Materiality constraint	Shares
Expenses	Measurement principle	Sole proprietorship
External transactions	Monetary unit assumption	Statement of cash flows
External users	Net income	Statement of owner's equity
Financial accounting	Net loss	Stock
Financial Accounting Standards	Owner, Capital	Stockholders
Board (FASB)	Owner, Withdrawals	Sustainability
Full disclosure principle	Owner investments	Sustainability Accounting Standards
Generally accepted accounting	Owner withdrawals	Board (SASB)
principles (GAAP)	Partnership	Time period assumption
Going-concern assumption	Proprietorship	

Multiple Choice Quiz

1. A building is offered for sale at $500,000 but is currently assessed at $400,000. The purchaser of the building believes the building is worth $475,000, but ultimately purchases the building for $450,000. The purchaser records the building at:

   a. $50,000.   **d.** $475,000.

   b. $400,000.   **e.** $500,000.

   c. $450,000.

2. On December 30 of the current year, **KPMG** signs a $150,000 contract to provide accounting services to one of its clients in *the next year*. KPMG has a December 31 year-end. Which accounting principle or assumption requires KPMG to record the accounting services revenue from this client in *the next year* and not in the current year?

   a. Business entity assumption

   b. Revenue recognition principle

   c. Monetary unit assumption

   d. Cost principle

   e. Going-concern assumption

3. If the assets of a company increase by $100,000 during the year and its liabilities increase by $35,000 during the same year, then the change in equity of the company during the year must have been:

   a. An increase of $135,000.

   b. A decrease of $135,000.

   c. A decrease of $65,000.

   d. An increase of $65,000.

   e. An increase of $100,000.

4. **Brunswick** borrows $50,000 cash from Third National Bank. How does this transaction affect the accounting equation for Brunswick?

   a. Assets increase by $50,000; liabilities increase by $50,000; no effect on equity.

   b. Assets increase by $50,000; no effect on liabilities; equity increases by $50,000.

   c. Assets increase by $50,000; liabilities decrease by $50,000; no effect on equity.

   d. No effect on assets; liabilities increase by $50,000; equity increases by $50,000.

   e. No effect on assets; liabilities increase by $50,000; equity decreases by $50,000.

5. **Geek Squad** performs services for a customer and bills the customer for $500. How would Geek Squad record this transaction?

   a. Accounts receivable increase by $500; revenues increase by $500.

   b. Cash increases by $500; revenues increase by $500.

   c. Accounts receivable increase by $500; revenues decrease by $500.

   d. Accounts receivable increase by $500; accounts payable increase by $500.

   e. Accounts payable increase by $500; revenues increase by $500.

ANSWERS TO MULTIPLE CHOICE QUIZ

1. c; $450,000 is the actual cost incurred.

2. b; revenue is recorded when earned.

3. d;

Assets	=	Liabilities	+	Equity
+$100,000	=	+$35,000	+	?

Change in equity = $100,000 − $35,000 = $65,000

4. a

5. a

$^{A(B)}$ *Superscript letter A (B) denotes assignments based on Appendix 1A (1B).*

Icon denotes assignments that involve decision making.

Discussion Questions

1. What is the purpose of accounting in society?

2. Technology is increasingly used to process accounting data. Why then must we study and understand accounting?

3. Identify four kinds of external users and describe how they use accounting information.

4. What are at least three questions business owners and managers might be able to answer by looking at accounting information?

5. Identify three actual businesses that offer services and three actual businesses that offer products.

6. Describe the internal role of accounting for organizations.

7. Identify three types of services typically offered by accounting professionals.

8. What type of accounting information might be useful to the marketing managers of a business?

9. Why is accounting described as a service activity?

10. What are some accounting-related professions?

11. How do ethics rules affect auditors' choice of clients?

12. What work do tax accounting professionals perform in addition to preparing tax returns?

13. What does the concept of *objectivity* imply for information reported in financial statements? Why?

14. A business reports its own office stationery on the balance sheet at its $400 cost, although it cannot be sold for more than $10 as scrap paper. Which accounting principle and/or assumption justifies this treatment?

15. Why is the revenue recognition principle needed? What does it demand?

16. Describe the three basic forms of business organization and their key attributes.

17. Define (*a*) *assets*, (*b*) *liabilities*, (*c*) *equity*, and (*d*) *net assets*.

18. What events or transactions change equity?

19. Identify the two main categories of accounting principles.

20. What do accountants mean by the term *revenue*?

21. Define *net income* and explain its computation.

22. Identify the four basic financial statements of a business.

23. What information is reported in an income statement?

24. Give two examples of expenses a business might incur.

25. What is the purpose of the statement of owner's equity?

26. What information is reported in a balance sheet?

27. The statement of cash flows reports on what major activities?

28. Define and explain return on assets.

29.^{A} Define return and risk. Discuss the trade-off between them.

30.^{B} Describe the three major business activities in organizations.

31.^{B} Explain why investing (assets) and financing (liabilities and equity) totals are always equal.

32. Refer to the financial statements of Google in Appendix A near the end of the book. To what level of significance are dollar amounts rounded? What time period does its income statement cover?   **GOOGLE**

33. Access the SEC EDGAR database (SEC.gov) and retrieve Apple's 2015 10-K (filed October 28, 2015). Identify its auditor. What responsibility does its independent auditor claim regarding Apple's financial statements?   **APPLE**

Connect reproduces assignments online, in static or algorithmic mode, which allows instructors to monitor, promote, and assess student learning. It can be used for practice, homework, or exams

 **connect**®

Quick Study exercises offer a brief check of key points.

QUICK STUDY

Choose from the following term or phrase *a* through *h* to best complete the statements *1* through *3*.

a. Accounting	**c.** Recording	**e.** Governmental	**g.** Language of business
b. Identifying	**d.** Communicating	**f.** Technology	**h.** Recordkeeping (bookkeeping)

1. _____ reduces the time, effort, and cost of recordkeeping while improving clerical accuracy.

2. _____ business activities requires that we keep a chronological log of transactions and events measured in dollars.

3. _____ is the recording of transactions and events, either manually or electronically.

QS 1-1

Understanding accounting

C1

QS 1-2

Identifying accounting users

C2

Identify the following users as either external users (E) or internal users (I).

_____ **a.** Customers   _____ **e.** Managers   _____ **i.** Controllers

_____ **b.** Suppliers   _____ **f.** District attorney   _____ **j.** FBI and IRS

_____ **c.** Brokers   _____ **g.** Shareholders   _____ **k.** Consumer group

_____ **d.** Business press   _____ **h.** Lenders   _____ **l.** Directors

---

QS 1-3

Identifying ethical risks

C3

This icon highlights ethics-related assignments

The fraud triangle asserts that the following *three* factors must exist for a person to commit fraud:

A. Opportunity   **B.** Pressure   **C.** Rationalization

Identify the fraud risk factor (A, B, or C) in each of the following situations:

_____ **1.** The business has no cameras or security devices at its warehouse.

_____ **2.** Managers are expected to grow business or be fired.

_____ **3.** A worker sees other employees regularly take inventory for personal use.

_____ **4.** No one matches the cash in the register to receipts when shifts end.

_____ **5.** Officers are expected to show rising income or risk dismissal.

_____ **6.** A worker feels that fellow employees are not honest.

QS 1-4

Identifying principles, assumptions, and constraints   **C4**

Identify each of the following terms or phrases as either an accounting: (a) principle, (b) assumption, or (c) constraint.

_____ **1.** Materiality   _____ **3.** Benefit exceeds cost

_____ **2.** Time period   _____ **4.** Revenue recognition

QS 1-5

Identifying attributes of businesses

C4

Complete the following table with either a *yes* or *no* regarding the attributes of a proprietorship, partnership, and corporation.

Attribute Present	Proprietorship	Partnership	Corporation
1. Business taxed	___	___	___
2. Business entity	___	___	___
3. Legal entity	___	___	___

QS 1-6

Identifying accounting principles and assumptions

C4

Identify the letter for the principle or assumption from *A* through *F* in the blank space next to each numbered situation that it best explains or justifies.

A. General accounting principle   **D.** Revenue recognition principle

B. Measurement (cost) principle   **E.** Expense recognition (matching) principle

C. Business entity assumption   **F.** Going-concern assumption

_____ **1.** In December of this year, Chavez Landscaping received a customer's order and cash prepayment to install sod at a house that would not be ready for installation until March of *next year*. Chavez should record the revenue from the customer order in March of *next year*, not in December of this year.

_____ **2.** If $51,000 cash is paid to buy land, the land is reported on the buyer's balance sheet at $51,000.

_____ **3.** Mike Derr owns both Sailing Passions and Dockside Digs. In preparing financial statements for Dockside Digs, Mike makes sure that the expense transactions of Sailing Passions are kept separate from Dockside Digs's transactions and financial statements.

QS 1-7

Applying the accounting equation   **A1**

a. Total assets of Charter Company equal $700,000 and its equity is $420,000. What is the amount of its liabilities?

b. Total assets of Martin Marine equal $500,000 and its liabilities and equity amounts are equal to each other. What is the amount of its liabilities? What is the amount of its equity?

This icon highlights assignments that enhance decision-making skills

1. Use the accounting equation to compute the missing financial statement amounts (*a*), (*b*), and (*c*).

	A	B		C		D
1	**Company**	**Assets**	**=**	**Liabilities**	**+**	**Equity**
2	1	$ 75,000		$ *(a)*		$ 40,000
3	2	*(b)*		25,000		70,000
4	3	85,000		20,000		*(c)*

QS 1-8

Applying the accounting equation

A1

2. Use the expanded accounting equation to compute the missing financial statement amounts (*a*) and (*b*).

	A	B	C	D	E	F	G
1	**Company**	**Assets**	**Liabilities**	**Owner, Capital**	**Owner, Withdrawals**	**Revenues**	**Expenses**
2							
3	1	$ 40,000	$ 16,000	$ 20,000	$ 0	*(a)*	$ 8,000
4	2	$ 80,000	$ 32,000	$ 44,000	*(b)*	$ 24,000	$ 18,000

Use Google's December 31, 2015, financial statements, in Appendix A near the end of the book, to answer the following.

a. Identify the amounts (in $ millions) of its 2015 (1) assets, (2) liabilities, and (3) equity.

b. Using amounts from part *a*, verify that Assets = Liabilities + Equity.

QS 1-9

Identifying and computing assets, liabilities, and equity

A1

GOOGLE

Create the following table similar to the one in Exhibit 1.9.

Assets			=	Liabilities	+			Equity				
Cash	+	Accounts Receivable	=	Accounts Payable	+	Owner, Capital	−	Owner, Withdrawals	+	Revenues	−	Expenses

QS 1-10

Identifying effects of transactions using accounting equation—Revenues and Expenses

P1

Then use additions and subtractions to show the dollar effects of each transaction on individual items of the accounting equation (identify each revenue and expense type, such as commissions revenue or rent expense).

a. The company completed consulting work for a client and immediately collected $5,500 cash earned.

b. The company completed commission work for a client and sent a bill for $4,000 to be received within 30 days.

c. The company paid an assistant $1,400 cash as wages for the period.

d. The company collected $1,000 cash as a partial payment for the amount owed by the client in transaction *b*.

e. The company paid $700 cash for this period's cleaning services.

Create the following table similar to the one in Exhibit 1.9.

Assets					=	Liabilities	+		Equity			
Cash	+ Supplies	+ Equipment	+ Land	=	Accounts Payable	+ A. Carr, Capital	− A. Carr, Withdrawals	+ Revenues	− Expenses

QS 1-11

Identifying effects of transactions using accounting equation—Assets and Liabilities

P1

Then use additions and subtractions to show the dollar effects of each transaction on individual items of the accounting equation.

a. The owner (Alex Carr) invested $15,000 cash in the company.

b. The company purchased supplies for $500 cash.

c. The owner (Alex Carr) invested $10,000 of equipment in the company.

d. The company purchased $200 of additional supplies on credit.

e. The company purchased land for $9,000 cash.

QS 1-12
Identifying items with financial statements
P2

Indicate in which financial statement(s) each item would most likely appear: income statement (I), balance sheet (B), statement of owner's equity (E), or statement of cash flows (CF).

_____ **a.** Assets

_____ **b.** Cash from operating activities

_____ **c.** Withdrawals

_____ **d.** Equipment

_____ **e.** Expenses

_____ **f.** Liabilities

_____ **g.** Net decrease (or increase) in cash

_____ **h.** Revenues

_____ **i.** Total liabilities and equity

QS 1-13
Identifying income and equity accounts
P2

Classify each of the following items as revenues (R), expenses (EX), or withdrawals (W).

_____ **1.** Cost of sales

_____ **2.** Service revenue

_____ **3.** Wages expense

_____ **4.** Owner withdrawal

_____ **5.** Rent expense

_____ **6.** Rental revenue

_____ **7.** Insurance expense

_____ **8.** Consulting revenue

QS 1-14
Identifying assets, liabilities, and equity
P2

Classify each of the following items as assets (A), liabilities (L), or equity (EQ).

_____ **1.** Land

_____ **2.** Owner, Capital

_____ **3.** Equipment

_____ **4.** Accounts payable

_____ **5.** Accounts receivable

_____ **6.** Supplies

QS 1-15
Computing and interpreting return on assets
A2

In a recent year's financial statements, **Home Depot** reported the following results. Compute and interpret Home Depot's return on assets (assume competitors average an 11.0% return on assets).

Sales............................	$83 billion
Net income......................	6 billion
Average total assets	40 billion

QS 1-16
Sustainability accounting
C4

This icon highlights sustainability-related assignments

Identify the letter of the term or phrase from *A* through *H* that best matches the descriptions *1* through *4*.

A. SASB

B. Principles

C. Social aspect

D. Company sustainability

E. SASB conceptual framework

F. Environmental aspect

G. Sustainability standards

H. KLD 400 Social (DSI) Index

_____ **1.** Refers to the set of environmental, social, and governance aspects of a company.

_____ **2.** A structure to help guide development of sustainability standards.

_____ **3.** An entity that creates and publishes sustainability accounting standards.

_____ **4.** Aspect of company sustainability involved with donations to hospitals, colleges, and community programs.

QS 1-17
Identifying and computing assets, liabilities, and equity
A1

Samsung

Use **Samsung**'s December 31, 2015, financial statements in Appendix A near the end of the book to answer the following.

a. Identify the amounts (in millions of Korean won) of Samsung's 2015 (1) assets, (2) liabilities, and (3) equity.

b. Using amounts from part *a*, verify that Assets = Liabilities + Equity.

■ connect

EXERCISES

Exercise 1-1
Classifying activities reflected in the accounting system
C1

Accounting is an information and measurement system that identifies, records, and communicates relevant, reliable, and comparable information about an organization's business activities. Classify the following activities as part of the identifying (I), recording (R), or communicating (C) aspects of accounting.

_____ **1.** Analyzing and interpreting reports.

_____ **2.** Presenting financial information.

_____ **3.** Keeping a log of service costs.

_____ **4.** Measuring the costs of a product.

_____ **5.** Preparing financial statements.

_____ **6.** Seeing revenues generated from a service.

_____ **7.** Observing employee tasks behind a product.

_____ **8.** Registering cash sales of products sold.

Part A. Identify the following questions as most likely to be asked by an internal (I) or an external (E) user of accounting information.

_____ **1.** What are reasonable payroll benefits and wages?

_____ **2.** Should we make a five-year loan to that business?

_____ **3.** What are the costs of our product's ingredients?

_____ **4.** Do income levels justify the current stock price?

_____ **5.** Should we spend additional money for redesign of our product?

_____ **6.** Which firm reports the highest sales and income?

_____ **7.** What are the costs of our service to customers?

Part B. Identify the following users of accounting information as either an internal (I) or an external (E) user.

_____ **1.** Research and development director

_____ **2.** Human resources director

_____ **3.** Politician

_____ **4.** Shareholder

_____ **5.** Distribution manager

_____ **6.** Creditor

_____ **7.** Production supervisor

_____ **8.** Purchasing manager

Exercise 1-2
Identifying accounting users and uses

C2

Many accounting professionals work in one of the following three areas.

A. Financial accounting   **B.** Managerial accounting   **C.** Tax accounting

Identify the area of accounting that is most involved in each of the following responsibilities.

_____ **1.** Internal auditing

_____ **2.** External auditing

_____ **3.** Cost accounting

_____ **4.** Budgeting

_____ **5.** Investigating violations of tax laws

_____ **6.** Planning transactions to minimize taxes

_____ **7.** Preparing external financial statements

_____ **8.** Reviewing reports for SEC compliance

Exercise 1-3
Describing accounting responsibilities

C2

Match each of the numbered descriptions *1* through *5* with the term or phrase it best reflects. Indicate your answer by writing the letter *A* through *H* for the term or phrase in the blank provided.

A. Audit   **C.** Ethics   **E.** SEC   **G.** Net income

B. GAAP   **D.** Tax accounting   **F.** Public accountants   **H.** IASB

_____ **1.** An examination of an organization's accounting system and its records that adds credibility to financial statements.

_____ **2.** Amount a business earns in excess of all expenses and costs associated with its sales and revenues.

_____ **3.** An accounting area that includes planning future transactions to minimize taxes paid.

_____ **4.** Accounting professionals who provide services to many clients.

_____ **5.** Principles that determine whether an action is right or wrong.

Exercise 1-4
Learning the language of business

C1 C2 C3

Match each of the numbered descriptions *1* through *9* with the term or phrase it best reflects. Indicate your answer by writing the letter *A* through *H* for the term or phrase in the blank provided.

A. Ethics   **D.** Prevention   **G.** Audit

B. Ethical path   **E.** Internal controls   **H.** Dodd-Frank Act

C. Fraud triangle   **F.** Sarbanes-Oxley Act   **I.** Clawback

_____ **1.** Recovery of excess incentive compensation.

_____ **2.** Promotes accountability and transparency, and protects consumers from abusive financial services.

_____ **3.** Examines whether financial statements are prepared using GAAP; it does not ensure absolute accuracy of the statements.

_____ **4.** Requires documentation and verification of internal controls and increases emphasis on internal control effectiveness.

_____ **5.** Procedures set up to protect company property and equipment, ensure reliable accounting, promote efficiency, and encourage adherence to policies.

_____ **6.** A less expensive and more effective means to stop fraud.

_____ **7.** Three factors must exist for a person to commit fraud: opportunity, pressure, and rationalization.

_____ **8.** Course of action that avoids casting doubt on one's decisions.

_____ **9.** Beliefs that distinguish right from wrong.

Exercise 1-5
Identifying ethical terminology

C3

Exercise 1-6

Distinguishing business organizations

C4

The following describe several different business organizations. Determine whether each description best refers to a sole proprietorship (SP), partnership (P), or corporation (C).

_____ **a.** Micah and Nancy own Financial Services, a financial services provider. Neither Micah nor Nancy has personal responsibility for the debts of Financial Services.

_____ **b.** Riley and Kay own Speedy Packages, a courier service. Both are personally liable for the debts of the business.

_____ **c.** IBC Services does not have separate legal existence apart from the one person who owns it.

_____ **d.** Trent Company is owned by Trent Malone, who is personally liable for the company's debts.

_____ **e.** Ownership of Zander Company is divided into 1,000 shares of stock.

_____ **f.** Physio Products does not pay income taxes and has one owner.

_____ **g.** AJ Company pays its own income taxes and has two owners.

Exercise 1-7

Identifying accounting principles and assumptions

C4

Enter the letter A through H for the principle or assumption in the blank space next to each numbered description that it best reflects.

A. General accounting principle

B. Cost principle

C. Business entity assumption

D. Revenue recognition principle

E. Specific accounting principle

F. Matching (expense recognition) principle

G. Going-concern assumption

H. Full disclosure principle

_____ **1.** A company reports details behind financial statements that would impact users' decisions.

_____ **2.** Financial statements reflect the assumption that the business continues operating.

_____ **3.** A company records the expenses incurred to generate the revenues reported.

_____ **4.** Derived from long-used and generally accepted accounting practices.

_____ **5.** Each business is accounted for separately from its owner or owners.

_____ **6.** Revenue is recorded when products and services are delivered.

_____ **7.** Usually created by a pronouncement from an authoritative body.

_____ **8.** Information is based on actual costs incurred in transactions.

Exercise 1-8

Using the accounting equation

A1

Determine the missing amount from each of the separate situations _a, b,_ and _c_ below.

	A		B		C
	Assets	**=**	**Liabilities**	**+**	**Equity**
1					
2	(a) $?		$ 20,000		$ 45,000
3	(b) 100,000		34,000		?
4	(c) 154,000		?		40,000

Exercise 1-9

Using the accounting equation

A1

Check   (c) Beg. equity, $60,000

Answer the following questions. (_Hint:_ Use the accounting equation.)

a. At the beginning of the year, Addison Company's assets are $300,000 and its equity is $100,000. During the year, assets increase $80,000 and liabilities increase $50,000. What is the equity at year-end?

b. Office Store has assets equal to $123,000 and liabilities equal to $47,000 at year-end. What is the equity for Office Store at year-end?

c. At the beginning of the year, Quaker Company's liabilities equal $70,000. During the year, assets increase by $60,000, and at year-end assets equal $190,000. Liabilities decrease $5,000 during the year. What are the beginning and ending amounts of equity?

Zen began a new consulting firm on January 5. Following is a financial summary, including balances, for each of the company's first five transactions (using the accounting equation form).

Exercise 1-10

Analysis using the accounting equation

P1

Transaction	Cash	+	Accounts Receivable	+	Office Supplies	+	Office Furniture	=	Accounts Payable	+	Zen, Capital	+	Revenues
___ 1.	$40,000	+	$ 0	+	$ 0	+	$ 0	=	$ 0	+	$40,000	+	$ 0
___ 2.	38,000	+	0	+	3,000	+	0	=	1,000	+	40,000	+	0
___ 3.	30,000	+	0	+	3,000	+	8,000	=	1,000	+	40,000	+	0
___ 4.	30,000	+	6,000	+	3,000	+	8,000	=	1,000	+	40,000	+	6,000
___ 5.	31,000	+	6,000	+	3,000	+	8,000	=	1,000	+	40,000	+	7,000

Identify the explanation from *a* through *j* below that best describes each transaction *1* through *5* above and enter it in the blank space in front of each numbered transaction.

a. The company purchased office furniture for $8,000 cash.

b. The company received $40,000 cash from a bank loan.

c. The owner invested $1,000 cash in the business.

d. The owner invested $40,000 cash in the business.

e. The company purchased office supplies for $3,000 by paying $2,000 cash and putting $1,000 on credit.

f. The company billed a customer $6,000 for services provided.

g. The company purchased office furniture worth $8,000 on credit.

h. The company provided services for $1,000 cash.

i. The company sold office supplies for $3,000 and received $2,000 cash and $1,000 on credit.

j. The company provided services for $6,000 cash.

The following table shows the effects of five transactions (*1* through *5*) on the assets, liabilities, and equity of Mulan's Boutique.

Exercise 1-11

Identifying effects of transactions on the accounting equation

P1

	Cash	+	Accounts Receivable	+	Office Supplies	+	Land	=	Accounts Payable	+	Mulan, Capital	+	Revenues
	$ 21,000	+	$ 0	+	$3,000	+	$19,000	=	$ 0	+	$43,000	+	$ 0
___ 1.	− 4,000					+	4,000						
___ 2.				+	1,000				+1,000				
___ 3.		+	1,900									+	1,900
___ 4.	− 1,000								− 1,000				
___ 5.	+ 1,900	−	1,900										
	$ 17,900	+	$ 0	+	$4,000	+	$23,000	=	$ 0	+	$43,000	+	$1,900

Identify the explanation from *a* through *j* below that best describes each transaction *1* through *5* above and enter it in the blank space in front of each numbered transaction.

a. The company purchased $1,000 of office supplies on credit.

b. The company collected $1,900 cash from an account receivable.

c. The company sold land for $4,000 cash.

d. The owner withdrew $1,000 cash from the business.

e. The company purchased office supplies for $1,000 cash.

f. The company purchased land for $4,000 cash.

g. The company billed a client $1,900 for services provided.

h. The company paid $1,000 cash toward an account payable.

i. The owner invested $1,900 cash in the business.

j. The company sold office supplies for $1,900 on credit.

Exercise 1-12

Identifying effects of transactions on the accounting equation

P1

For each transaction *a* through *f,* identify its impact on the accounting equation (select from *1* through 6 below).

_____ **a.** The company pays cash toward an account payable.

_____ **b.** The company purchases equipment on credit.

_____ **c.** The owner invests cash in the business.

_____ **d.** The owner withdraws cash from the business.

_____ **e.** The company purchases supplies for cash.

_____ **f.** The company workers earn wages this period but are not paid until next period.

1. Decreases an asset and decreases equity.

2. Increases an asset and increases a liability.

3. Decreases an asset and decreases a liability.

4. Increases an asset and decreases an asset.

5. Increases a liability and decreases equity.

6. Increases an asset and increases equity.

Exercise 1-13

Identifying effects of transactions using the accounting equation

P1

Ming Chen began a professional practice on June 1 and plans to prepare financial statements at the end of each month. During June, Ming Chen (the owner) completed these transactions.

a. Owner invested $60,000 cash in the company along with equipment that had a $15,000 market value.

b. The company paid $1,500 cash for rent of office space for the month.

c. The company purchased $10,000 of additional equipment on credit (payment due within 30 days).

d. The company completed work for a client and immediately collected the $2,500 cash earned.

e. The company completed work for a client and sent a bill for $8,000 to be received within 30 days.

f. The company purchased additional equipment for $6,000 cash.

g. The company paid an assistant $3,000 cash as wages for the month.

h. The company collected $5,000 cash as a partial payment for the amount owed by the client in transaction *e.*

i. The company paid $10,000 cash to settle the liability created in transaction *c.*

j. Owner withdrew $1,000 cash from the company for personal use.

Required

Create the following table similar to the one in Exhibit 1.9.

Assets			=	Liabilities	+	Equity				
Cash +	Accounts Receivable	+ Equipment	=	Accounts Payable	+	M. Chen, Capital	−	M. Chen, Withdrawals	+ Revenues	− Expenses

Check Net income, $6,000

Then use additions and subtractions to show the dollar effects of the transactions on individual items of the accounting equation. Show new balances after each transaction.

Exercise 1-14

Analysis of return on assets

A2

Swiss Group reports net income of $40,000 for 2017. At the beginning of 2017, Swiss Group had $200,000 in assets. By the end of 2017, assets had grown to $300,000. What is Swiss Group's 2017 return on assets? How would you assess its performance if competitors average an 11% return on assets?

Exercise 1-15

Preparing an income statement

P2

On October 1, Ebony Ernst organized Ernst Consulting; on October 3, the owner contributed $84,000 in assets to launch the business. On October 31, the company's records show the following items and amounts. Use this information to prepare an October income statement for the business.

Cash	$11,360	Cash withdrawals by owner.............	$ 2,000
Accounts receivable............	14,000	Consulting revenue	14,000
Office supplies	3,250	Rent expense	3,550
Land........................	46,000	Salaries expense.....................	7,000
Office equipment	18,000	Telephone expense	760
Accounts payable.............	8,500	Miscellaneous expenses	580
Owner investments	84,000		

Check Net income, $2,110

Use the information in Exercise 1-15 to prepare an October statement of owner's equity for Ernst Consulting.

Exercise 1-16
Preparing a statement of owner's equity   P2

Use the information in Exercise 1-15 to prepare an October 31 balance sheet for Ernst Consulting. *Hint*: The solution to Exercise 1-16 can help.

Exercise 1-17
Preparing a balance sheet

P2

Use the information in Exercise 1-15 to prepare an October 31 statement of cash flows for Ernst Consulting. Assume the following additional information.

a. The owner's initial investment consists of $38,000 cash and $46,000 in land.

b. The company's $18,000 equipment purchase is paid in cash.

c. The accounts payable balance of $8,500 consists of the $3,250 office supplies purchase and $5,250 in employee salaries yet to be paid.

d. The company's rent, telephone, and miscellaneous expenses are paid in cash.

e. No cash has been collected on the $14,000 consulting fees earned.

Exercise 1-18
Preparing a statement of cash flows

P2

Check   Net increase in cash, $11,360

Indicate the section (O, I, or F) where each of the following transactions *1* through *8* would appear on the statement of cash flows.

O. Cash flows from operating activity

I. Cash flows from investing activity

F. Cash flows from financing activity

_____ **1.** Cash purchase of equipment   _____ **5.** Cash paid on account payable to supplier

_____ **2.** Cash withdrawal by owner   _____ **6.** Cash received from clients

_____ **3.** Cash paid for advertising   _____ **7.** Cash investment by owner

_____ **4.** Cash paid for wages   _____ **8.** Cash paid for rent

Exercise 1-19
Identifying sections of the statement of cash flows

P2

Ford Motor Company, one of the world's largest automakers, reports the following income statement accounts for the year ended December 31, 2015 ($ in millions). Use this information to prepare Ford's income statement for the year ended December 31, 2015.

Selling and administrative costs	$ 14,999
Cost of sales	124,041
Revenues	149,558
Other expenses	3,145

Exercise 1-20
Preparing an income statement for a global company

P2

Match each transaction *a* through *e* to one of the following activities of an organization: financing activity (F), investing activity (I), or operating activity (O).

_____ **a.** An owner contributes cash to the business.

_____ **b.** An organization borrows money from a bank.

_____ **c.** An organization advertises a new product.

_____ **d.** An organization sells some of its land.

_____ **e.** An organization purchases equipment.

Exercise 1-21[B]
Identifying business activities

C5

BMW Group, one of Europe's largest manufacturers, reports the following income statement accounts for the year ended December 31, 2015 (euros in millions).

Revenues	€ 92,175
Cost of sales	74,043
Selling and administrative costs	8,633
Other expenses	3,103

Use this information to prepare BMW's income statement for the year ended December 31, 2015.

Exercise 1-22
Preparing an income statement for a global company

P2

This icon highlights IFRS-related assignments

Problem Set B, located at the end of Problem Set A, is provided for each problem to reinforce the learning process

PROBLEM SET A

Problem 1-1A

Identifying effects of transactions on financial statements

A1   P1

Identify how each of the following separate transactions *1* through *10* affects financial statements. For increases, place a "+" *and* the dollar amount in the column or columns. For decreases, place a "−" *and* the dollar amount in the column or columns. Some cells may contain both an increase (+) and a decrease (−) along with dollar amounts. The first transaction is completed as an example.

Required

a. For the balance sheet, identify how each transaction affects total assets, total liabilities, and total equity. For the income statement, identify how each transaction affects net income.

b. For the statement of cash flows, identify how each transaction affects cash flows from operating activities, cash flows from investing activities, and cash flows from financing activities.

| | | | a. | | | | b. | |
| | | Balance Sheet | | | Income Statement | Statement of Cash Flows | | |
	Transaction	Total Assets	Total Liab.	Total Equity	Net Income	Operating Activities	Investing Activities	Financing Activities
1	Owner invests $900 cash in business	+900		+900				+900
2	Receives $700 cash for services provided							
3	Pays $500 cash for employee wages							
4	Incurs $100 legal costs on credit							
5	Purchases $200 of supplies on credit							
6	Buys equipment for $300 cash							
7	Pays $200 on accounts payable							
8	Provides $400 services on credit							
9	Owner withdraws $50 cash							
10	Collects $400 cash on accounts receivable							

Problem 1-2A

Computing missing information using accounting knowledge

A1   P1

The following financial statement information is from five separate companies.

	Company A	Company B	Company C	Company D	Company E
December 31, 2016					
Assets.	$55,000	$34,000	$24,000	$60,000	$119,000
Liabilities.	24,500	21,500	9,000	40,000	?
December 31, 2017					
Assets.	58,000	40,000	?	85,000	113,000
Liabilities.	?	26,500	29,000	24,000	70,000
During year 2017					
Owner investments	6,000	1,400	9,750	?	6,500
Net income (loss)	8,500	?	8,000	14,000	20,000
Owner cash withdrawals	3,500	2,000	5,875	0	11,000

Required

1. Answer the following questions about Company A.

   a. What is the amount of equity on December 31, 2016?

   Check   *(1b)* $41,500

   b. What is the amount of equity on December 31, 2017?

   c. What is the amount of liabilities on December 31, 2017?

2. Answer the following questions about Company B.

   a. What is the amount of equity on December 31, 2016?

   b. What is the amount of equity on December 31, 2017?

   (2c) $1,600

   c. What is net income for year 2017?

Continued on next page . . .

3. Compute the amount of assets for Company C on December 31, 2017.

(3) $55,875

4. Compute the amount of owner investments for Company D during year 2017.

5. Compute the amount of liabilities for Company E on December 31, 2016.

As of December 31, 2017, Armani Company's financial records show the following items and amounts.

Problem 1-3A

Preparing an income statement

P2

Cash	$10,000
Accounts receivable	9,000
Supplies	6,000
Equipment	5,000
Accounts payable	23,000
A. Armani, Capital, Dec. 31, 2016	4,000
A. Armani, Capital, Dec. 31, 2017	7,000
A. Armani, Withdrawals	13,000
Consulting revenue	33,000
Rental revenue	22,000
Salaries expense	20,000
Rent expense	12,000
Selling and administrative expenses	8,000

Note: Early in 2017, the owner invested $1,000 cash in the business.

Required

Prepare the 2017 year-end income statement for Armani Company.

Use the information in Problem 1-3A to prepare a year-end statement of owner's equity for Armani Company. *Hint*: The owner invested $1,000 cash during the year.

Problem 1-4A

Preparing a statement of owner's equity   P2

Use the information in Problem 1-3A to prepare a year-end balance sheet for Armani Company.

Problem 1-5A

Preparing a balance sheet

P2

Following is selected financial information of Kia Company for the year ended December 31, 2017.

Problem 1-6A

Preparing a statement of cash flows

P2

Cash used by investing activities	$(2,000)
Net increase in cash	1,200
Cash used by financing activities	(2,800)
Cash from operating activities	6,000
Cash, December 31, 2016	2,300

Required

Prepare the 2017 year-end statement of cash flows for Kia Company.

Check   Cash balance, Dec. 31, 2017, $3,500

Gabi Gram started The Gram Co., a new business that began operations on May 1. The Gram Co. completed the following transactions during its first month of operations.

Problem 1-7A

Analyzing transactions and preparing financial statements

C4   P1   P2

May	1	G. Gram invested $40,000 cash in the company.
	1	The company rented a furnished office and paid $2,200 cash for May's rent.
	3	The company purchased $1,890 of office equipment on credit.
	5	The company paid $750 cash for this month's cleaning services.
	8	The company provided consulting services for a client and immediately collected $5,400 cash.
	12	The company provided $2,500 of consulting services for a client on credit.
	15	The company paid $750 cash for an assistant's salary for the first half of this month.
	20	The company received $2,500 cash payment for the services provided on May 12.
	22	The company provided $3,200 of consulting services on credit.

25 The company received $3,200 cash payment for the services provided on May 22.
26 The company paid $1,890 cash for the office equipment purchased on May 3.
27 The company purchased $80 of advertising in this month's (May) local paper on credit; cash payment is due June 1.
28 The company paid $750 cash for an assistant's salary for the second half of this month.
30 The company paid $300 cash for this month's telephone bill.
30 The company paid $280 cash for this month's utilities.

31 G. Gram withdrew $1,400 cash from the company for personal use.

Required

1. Create the following table similar to the one in Exhibit 1.9.

	Assets			=	Liabilities	+			Equity			
Date	Cash	+	Accounts Receivable	+	Office Equipment	=	Accounts Payable	+	G. Gram, Capital	−	G. Gram, Withdrawals	+ Revenues − Expenses

Check (1) Ending balances: Cash, $42,780; Expenses, $5,110

(2) Net income, $5,990; Total assets, $44,670

Enter the effects of each transaction on the accounts of the accounting equation by recording dollar increases and decreases in the appropriate columns. Do not determine new account balances after each transaction. Determine the final total for each account and verify that the equation is in balance.

2. Prepare the income statement and the statement of owner's equity for the month of May, and the balance sheet as of May 31.

3. Prepare the statement of cash flows for the month of May.

Problem 1-8A
Analyzing effects of transactions

C4 P1 P2 A1

Lita Lopez started Biz Consulting, a new business, and completed the following transactions during its first year of operations.

a. Lita Lopez invested $70,000 cash and office equipment valued at $10,000 in the company.
b. The company purchased an office suite for $40,000 cash.
c. The company purchased office equipment for $15,000 cash.
d. The company purchased $1,200 of office supplies and $1,700 of office equipment on credit.
e. The company paid a local newspaper $500 cash for printing an announcement of the office's opening.
f. The company completed a financial plan for a client and billed that client $2,800 for the service.
g. The company designed a financial plan for another client and immediately collected a $4,000 cash fee.
h. Lita Lopez withdrew $3,275 cash from the company for personal use.
i. The company received $1,800 cash as partial payment from the client described in transaction f.
j. The company made a partial payment of $700 cash on the equipment purchased in transaction d.
k. The company paid $1,800 cash for the office secretary's wages for this period.

Check (1) Ending balances: Cash, $14,525; Expenses, $2,300; Accounts Payable, $2,200

Required

1. Create the following table similar to the one in Exhibit 1.9.

	Assets							=	Liabilities	+			Equity			
Cash	+	Accounts Receivable	+	Office Supplies	+	Office Equipment	+	Office Suite	=	Accounts Payable	+	L. Lopez, Capital	−	L. Lopez, Withdrawals	+ Revenues − Expenses

(2) Net income, $4,500

Use additions and subtractions within the table to show the dollar effects of each transaction on individual items of the accounting equation. Show new balances after each transaction.

2. Determine the company's net income.

Problem 1-9A
Analyzing transactions and preparing financial statements

C4 P1 P2

Sanyu Sony started a new business and completed these transactions during December.

Dec. 1 Sanyu Sony transferred $65,000 cash from a personal savings account to a checking account in the name of Sony Electric.
       2 The company rented office space and paid $1,000 cash for the December rent.
       3 The company purchased $13,000 of electrical equipment by paying $4,800 cash and agreeing to pay the $8,200 balance in 30 days.

5 The company purchased office supplies by paying $800 cash.
6 The company completed electrical work and immediately collected $1,200 cash for these services.
8 The company purchased $2,530 of office equipment on credit.
15 The company completed electrical work on credit in the amount of $5,000.
18 The company purchased $350 of office supplies on credit.
20 The company paid $2,530 cash for the office equipment purchased on December 8.
24 The company billed a client $900 for electrical work completed; the balance is due in 30 days.
28 The company received $5,000 cash for the work completed on December 15.
29 The company paid the assistant's salary of $1,400 cash for this month.
30 The company paid $540 cash for this month's utility bill.
31 Sanyu Sony withdrew $950 cash from the company for personal use.

Required

1. Create the following table similar to the one in Exhibit 1.9.

		Assets			=	Liabilities	+			Equity		
Date	Cash +	Accounts Receivable +	Office Supplies +	Office Equipment +	Electrical Equipment =	Accounts Payable +	S. Sony, Capital −	S. Sony, Withdrawals +	Revenues −	Expenses		

Use additions and subtractions within the table to show the dollar effects of each transaction on individual items of the accounting equation. Show new balances after each transaction.

2. Prepare the income statement and the statement of owner's equity for the current month, and the balance sheet as of the end of the month.

3. Prepare the statement of cash flows for the current month.

Check (1) Ending balances: Cash, $59,180, Accounts Payable, $8,550

(2) Net income, $4,160; Total assets, $76,760

Analysis Component

4. Assume that the owner investment transaction on December 1 was $49,000 cash instead of $65,000 and that Sony Electric obtained another $16,000 in cash by borrowing it from a bank. Compute the dollar effect of this change on the month-end amounts for (a) total assets, (b) total liabilities, and (c) total equity.

Kyzera manufactures, markets, and sells cellular telephones. The average total assets for Kyzera is $250,000. In its most recent year, Kyzera reported net income of $65,000 on revenues of $475,000.

Problem 1-10A
Determining expenses, liabilities, equity, and return on assets

A1 A2

Required

1. What is Kyzera's return on assets?

2. Does return on assets seem satisfactory for Kyzera given that its competitors average a 12% return on assets?

3. What are total expenses for Kyzera in its most recent year?

4. What is the average total amount of liabilities plus equity for Kyzera?

Check (3) $410,000

(4) $250,000

Coca-Cola and PepsiCo both produce and market beverages that are direct competitors. Key financial figures (in $ millions) for these businesses for a recent year follow.

Problem 1-11A
Computing and interpreting return on assets

A2

Key Figures ($ millions)	Coca-Cola	PepsiCo
Sales	$46,542	$66,504
Net income	8,634	6,462
Average assets	76,448	70,518

Required

1. Compute return on assets for (a) Coca-Cola and (b) PepsiCo.

2. Which company is more successful in its total amount of sales to consumers?

3. Which company is more successful in returning net income from its assets invested?

Check (1a) 11.3%; (1b) 9.2%

Analysis Component

4. Write a one-paragraph memorandum explaining which company you would invest your money in and why. (Limit your explanation to the information provided.)

Problem 1-12A^A
Identifying risk and return

A3

All business decisions involve aspects of risk and return.

Required

Rank order the following investment activities from *1* through *4*, where "1" is most risky and "4" is least risky.

_____ **a.** Lowest-risk corporate bond
_____ **b.** Medium-risk corporate bond
_____ **c.** Company stock in a startup
_____ **d.** U.S. government treasury bond

Problem 1-13A^B
Describing organizational activities

C5

A start-up company often engages in the following transactions during its first year of operations. Classify those transactions in one of the three major categories of an organization's business activities.

F. Financing   **I.** Investing   **O.** Operating

_____ **1.** Owner investing land in business.   _____ **5.** Purchasing equipment.
_____ **2.** Purchasing a building.   _____ **6.** Selling and distributing products.
_____ **3.** Purchasing land.   _____ **7.** Paying for advertising.
_____ **4.** Borrowing cash from a bank.   _____ **8.** Paying employee wages.

Problem 1-14A^B
Describing organizational activities   C5

An organization undertakes various activities in pursuit of business success. Identify an organization's three major business activities, and describe each activity.

PROBLEM SET B

Problem 1-1B
Identifying effects of transactions on financial statements

A1   P1

Identify how each of the following separate transactions *1* through *10* affects financial statements. For increases, place a "+" *and* the dollar amount in the column or columns. For decreases, place a "−" *and* the dollar amount in the column or columns. Some cells may contain both an increase (+) and a decrease (−) along with dollar amounts. The first transaction is completed as an example.

Required

a. For the balance sheet, identify how each transaction affects total assets, total liabilities, and total equity. For the income statement, identify how each transaction affects net income.

b. For the statement of cash flows, identify how each transaction affects cash flows from operating activities, cash flows from investing activities, and cash flows from financing activities.

| | | a. | | | | b. | | |
| | | Balance Sheet | | | Income Statement | Statement of Cash Flows | | |
	Transaction	Total Assets	Total Liab.	Total Equity	Net Income	Operating Activities	Investing Activities	Financing Activities
1	Owner invests $800 cash in business	+800		+800				+800
2	Purchases $100 of supplies on credit							
3	Buys equipment for $400 cash							
4	Provides services for $900 cash							
5	Pays $400 cash for rent incurred							
6	Incurs $200 utilities costs on credit							
7	Pays $300 cash for wages incurred							
8	Owner withdraws $50 cash							
9	Provides $600 services on credit							
10	Collects $600 cash on accounts receivable							

The following financial statement information is from five separate companies.

Problem 1-2B
Computing missing
information using
accounting knowledge

A1   P1

	Company V	Company W	Company X	Company Y	Company Z
December 31, 2016					
Assets............................	$54,000	$ 80,000	$141,500	$92,500	$144,000
Liabilities..........................	25,000	60,000	68,500	51,500	?
December 31, 2017					
Assets............................	59,000	100,000	186,500	?	170,000
Liabilities..........................	36,000	?	65,800	42,000	42,000
During year 2017					
Owner investments	5,000	20,000	?	48,100	60,000
Net income (or loss)...............	?	40,000	18,500	24,000	32,000
Owner cash withdrawals............	5,500	2,000	0	20,000	8,000

Required

1. Answer the following questions about Company V.
   a. What is the amount of equity on December 31, 2016?
   b. What is the amount of equity on December 31, 2017?
   c. What is the net income or loss for the year 2017?
2. Answer the following questions about Company W.
   a. What is the amount of equity on December 31, 2016?
   b. What is the amount of equity on December 31, 2017?
   c. What is the amount of liabilities on December 31, 2017?
3. Compute the amount of owner investments for Company X during 2017.
4. Compute the amount of assets for Company Y on December 31, 2017.
5. Compute the amount of liabilities for Company Z on December 31, 2016.

Check   (1*b*) $23,000

(2*c*) $22,000

(4) $135,100

As of December 31, 2017, Audi Company's financial records show the following items and amounts.

Problem 1-3B
Preparing an income
statement

P2

Cash	$2,000
Accounts receivable............................	1,800
Supplies.....................................	1,200
Equipment....................................	1,000
Accounts payable..............................	4,600
A. Audi, Capital, Dec. 31, 2016...................	800
A. Audi, Capital, Dec. 31, 2017...................	1,400
A. Audi, Withdrawals	2,600
Consulting revenue	6,600
Rental revenue	4,400
Salaries expense	4,000
Rent expense	2,400
Selling and administrative expenses...............	1,600

Note: Early in 2017, the owner invested $200 cash in the business.

Required

Prepare the 2017 year-end income statement for Audi Company.

Use the information in Problem 1-3B to prepare a year-end statement of owner's equity for Audi Company.
Hint: The owner invested $200 cash during the year.

Problem 1-4B
Preparing a statement of
owner's equity   P2

Use the information in Problem 1-3B to prepare a year-end balance sheet for Audi Company.

Problem 1-5B
Preparing a balance sheet

P2

Problem 1-6B
Preparing a statement of
cash flows

P2

Selected financial information of Banji Company for the year ended December 31, 2017, follows.

Cash from investing activities	$1,600
Net increase in cash...........................	400
Cash from financing activities	1,800
Cash used by operating activities	(3,000)
Cash, December 31, 2016......................	1,300

Required

Prepare the 2017 year-end statement of cash flows for Banji Company.

Problem 1-7B
Analyzing transactions
and preparing financial
statements

C4   P1   P2

Nina Niko launched a new business, Niko's Maintenance Co., that began operations on June 1. The following transactions were completed by the company during that first month.

June 1   Nina Niko invested $130,000 cash in the company.
      2   The company rented a furnished office and paid $6,000 cash for June's rent.
      4   The company purchased $2,400 of equipment on credit.
      6   The company paid $1,150 cash for this month's advertising of the opening of the business.
      8   The company completed maintenance services for a customer and immediately collected $850
          cash.
     14   The company completed $7,500 of maintenance services for City Center on credit.
     16   The company paid $800 cash for an assistant's salary for the first half of the month.
     20   The company received $7,500 cash payment for services completed for City Center on June 14.
     21   The company completed $7,900 of maintenance services for Paula's Beauty Shop on credit.
     24   The company completed $675 of maintenance services for Build-It Coop on credit.
     25   The company received $7,900 cash payment from Paula's Beauty Shop for the work completed
          on June 21.
     26   The company made payment of $2,400 cash for equipment purchased on June 4.
     28   The company paid $800 cash for an assistant's salary for the second half of this month.
     29   Nina Niko withdrew $4,000 cash from the company for personal use.
     30   The company paid $150 cash for this month's telephone bill.
     30   The company paid $890 cash for this month's utilities.

Required

1. Create the following table similar to the one in Exhibit 1.9.

	Assets					=	Liabilities	+				Equity			
Date	Cash	+	Accounts Receivable	+	Equipment	=	Accounts Payable	+	N. Niko, Capital	−	N. Niko, Withdrawals	+	Revenues	−	Expenses

Check (1) Ending balances:
Cash, $130,060; Expenses,
$9,790

(2) Net income,
$7,135; Total assets, $133,135

Enter the effects of each transaction on the accounts of the accounting equation by recording dollar
increases and decreases in the appropriate columns. Do not determine new account balances after each
transaction. Determine the final total for each account and verify that the equation is in balance.

2. Prepare the income statement and the statement of owner's equity for the month of June, and the balance sheet as of June 30.

3. Prepare the statement of cash flows for the month of June.

Problem 1-8B
Analyzing effects of
transactions

C4   P1   P2   A1

Neva Nadal started a new business, Nadal Computing, and completed the following transactions during its
first year of operations.

a. Neva Nadal invested $90,000 cash and office equipment valued at $10,000 in the company.
b. The company purchased an office suite for $50,000 cash.
c. The company purchased office equipment for $25,000 cash.
d. The company purchased $1,200 of office supplies and $1,700 of office equipment on credit.
e. The company paid a local newspaper $750 cash for printing an announcement of the office's opening.
f. The company completed a financial plan for a client and billed that client $2,800 for the service.

g. The company designed a financial plan for another client and immediately collected a $4,000 cash fee.

h. Neva Nadal withdrew $11,500 cash from the company for personal use.

i. The company received $1,800 cash from the client described in transaction *f.*

j. The company made a payment of $700 cash on the equipment purchased in transaction *d.*

k. The company paid $2,500 cash for the office secretary's wages.

Check (1) Ending balances: Cash, $5,350; Expenses, $3,250; Accounts Payable, $2,200

Required

1. Create the following table similar to the one in Exhibit 1.9.

Assets					=	Liabilities	+	Equity				
Cash +	Accounts Receivable +	Office Supplies +	Office Equipment +	Office Suite	=	Accounts Payable	+	N. Nadal, Capital −	N. Nadal, Withdrawals	+	Revenues −	Expenses

Use additions and subtractions within the table to show the dollar effects of each transaction on individual items of the accounting equation. Show new balances after each transaction.

2. Determine the company's net income.

(2) Net income, $3,550

Rivera Roofing Company, owned by Reyna Rivera, began operations in July and completed these transactions during that first month of operations.

Problem 1-9B
Analyzing transactions and preparing financial statements

C4 P1 P2

July	1	Reyna Rivera invested $80,000 cash in the company.
	2	The company rented office space and paid $700 cash for the July rent.
	3	The company purchased roofing equipment for $5,000 by paying $1,000 cash and agreeing to pay the $4,000 balance in 30 days.
	6	The company purchased office supplies for $600 cash.
	8	The company completed work for a customer and immediately collected $7,600 cash for the work.
	10	The company purchased $2,300 of office equipment on credit.
	15	The company completed work for a customer on credit in the amount of $8,200.
	17	The company purchased $3,100 of office supplies on credit.
	23	The company paid $2,300 cash for the office equipment purchased on July 10.
	25	The company billed a customer $5,000 for work completed; the balance is due in 30 days.
	28	The company received $8,200 cash for the work completed on July 15.
	30	The company paid an assistant's salary of $1,560 cash for this month.
	31	The company paid $295 cash for this month's utility bill.
	31	Reyna Rivera withdrew $1,800 cash from the company for personal use.

Required

1. Create the following table similar to the one in Exhibit 1.9.

Assets					=	Liabilities	+	Equity				
Date Cash +	Accounts Receivable +	Office Supplies +	Office Equipment +	Roofing Equipment	=	Accounts Payable	+	R. Rivera, Capital −	R. Rivera, Withdrawals	+	Revenues −	Expenses

Use additions and subtractions within the table to show the dollar effects of each transaction on individual items of the accounting equation. Show new balances after each transaction.

2. Prepare the income statement and the statement of owner's equity for the month of July, and the balance sheet as of July 31.

3. Prepare the statement of cash flows for the month of July.

Check (1) Ending balances: Cash, $87,545; Accounts Payable, $7,100

(2) Net income, $18,245; Total assets, $103,545

Analysis Component

4. Assume that the $5,000 purchase of roofing equipment on July 3 was financed from an owner investment of another $5,000 cash in the business (instead of the purchase conditions described in the transaction above). Compute the dollar effect of this change on the month-end amounts for (a) total assets, (b) total liabilities, and (c) total equity.

Problem 1-10B

Determining expenses, liabilities, equity, and return on assets

A1   A2

Check   (3) $1,199,000

(4) $3,000,000

Ski-Doo Company manufactures, markets, and sells snowmobiles and snowmobile equipment and accessories. The average total assets for Ski-Doo is $3,000,000. In its most recent year, Ski-Doo reported net income of $201,000 on revenues of $1,400,000.

Required

1. What is Ski-Doo Company's return on assets?
2. Does return on assets seem satisfactory for Ski-Doo given that its competitors average a 9.5% return on assets?
3. What are the total expenses for Ski-Doo Company in its most recent year?
4. What is the average total amount of liabilities plus equity for Ski-Doo Company?

Problem 1-11B

Computing and interpreting return on assets

A2

AT&T and Verizon produce and market telecommunications products and are competitors. Key financial figures (in $ millions) for these businesses for a recent year follow.

Key Figures ($ millions)	AT&T	Verizon
Sales	$126,723	$110,875
Net income	4,184	10,198
Average assets	269,868	225,233

Check   (1a) 1.6%; (1b) 4.5%

Required

1. Compute return on assets for (a) AT&T and (b) Verizon.
2. Which company is more successful in the total amount of sales to consumers?
3. Which company is more successful in returning net income from its assets invested?

Analysis Component

4. Write a one-paragraph memorandum explaining which company you would invest your money in and why. (Limit your explanation to the information provided.)

Problem 1-12B[A]

Identifying risk and return

A3

All business decisions involve aspects of risk and return.

Required

Rank order the following investment activities from *1* through *4*, where "1" reflects the highest expected return and "4" the lowest expected return.

_____ **a.** Low-risk corporate bond
_____ **b.** Stock of a successful company
_____ **c.** Money stored in a fireproof vault
_____ **d.** U.S. Treasury bond

Problem 1-13B[B]

Describing organizational activities

C5

A start-up company often engages in the following activities during its first year of operations. Classify each of the following activities into one of the three major activities of an organization.

F. Financing   **I.** Investing   **O.** Operating

_____ **1.** Providing client services.
_____ **2.** Obtaining a bank loan.
_____ **3.** Purchasing machinery.
_____ **4.** Research for its products.

_____ **5.** Supervising workers.
_____ **6.** Owner investing money in business.
_____ **7.** Renting office space.
_____ **8.** Paying utilities expenses.

Problem 1-14B[B]

Describing organizational activities   C5

Identify in outline format the three major business activities of an organization. For each of these activities, identify at least two specific transactions or events normally undertaken by the business's owners or its managers.

Serial Problem starts here and continues throughout the book.

SP 1 On October 1, 2017, Santana Rey launched a computer services company, **Business Solutions**, that is organized as a proprietorship and provides consulting services, computer system installations, and custom program development. Rey adopts the calendar year for reporting purposes and expects to prepare the company's first set of financial statements on December 31, 2017.

© Alexander Image/Shutterstock RF

Required

Create a table like the one in Exhibit 1.9 using the following headings for columns: Cash; Accounts Receivable; Computer Supplies; Computer System; Office Equipment; Accounts Payable; S. Rey, Capital; S. Rey, Withdrawals; Revenues; and Expenses. Then use additions and subtractions within the table to show the dollar effects for each of the following October transactions for Business Solutions on the individual items of the accounting equation. Show new balances after each transaction.

Oct. 1 S. Rey invested $45,000 cash, a $20,000 computer system, and $8,000 of office equipment in the company.
  3 The company purchased $1,420 of computer supplies on credit from Harris Office Products.
  6 The company billed Easy Leasing $4,800 for services performed in installing a new web server.
  8 The company paid $1,420 cash for the computer supplies purchased from Harris Office Products on October 3.
  10 The company hired Lyn Addie as a part-time assistant for $125 per day, as needed.
  12 The company billed Easy Leasing another $1,400 for services performed.
  15 The company received $4,800 cash from Easy Leasing as partial payment toward its account.
  17 The company paid $805 cash to repair computer equipment damaged when moving it.
  20 The company paid $1,728 cash for advertisements published in the local newspaper.
  22 The company received $1,400 cash from Easy Leasing toward its account.
  28 The company billed IFM Company $5,208 for services performed.
  31 The company paid $875 cash for Lyn Addie's wages for seven days of work this month.
  31 S. Rey withdrew $3,600 cash from the company for personal use.

Check   Ending balances:
Cash, $42,772; Revenues,
$11,408; Expenses, $3,408

Accounting professionals apply many technology tools to aid them in their everyday tasks and decision making. The **General Ledger** tool in *Connect* automates several of the procedural steps in the accounting cycle so that the accounting professional can focus on the impacts of each transaction on the full set of financial statements. Chapter 2 is the first chapter to exploit this tool in helping students see the advantages of technology and, in particular, the power of the General Ledger tool in accounting practice, including financial analysis and "what if" scenarios.

Beyond the Numbers (BTN) is a special problem section aimed to refine communication, conceptual, analysis, and research skills. It includes many activities helpful in developing an active learning environment

Beyond the Numbers

BTN 1-1 Key financial figures for **Apple**'s fiscal year ended September 26, 2015, follow.

Key Figure	$ Millions
Liabilities + Equity	$290,479
Net income	53,394
Revenues	233,715

Required

1. What is the total amount of assets invested in Apple?
2. What is Apple's return on assets for fiscal year 2015? Its assets at September 27, 2014, equal $231,839 (in millions).
3. How much are total expenses for Apple for the year ended September 26, 2015?
4. Does Apple's return on assets for fiscal 2015 seem satisfactory if competitors average a 10% return?

Fast Forward

5. Access Apple's financial statements (Form 10-K) for years ending after September 26, 2015, from its website (**Apple.com**) or from the SEC website (**SEC.gov**) and compute its return on assets for those years. Compare the September 26, 2015, year-end return on assets to any subsequent years' returns you are able to compute, and interpret the results.

COMPARATIVE ANALYSIS

A1 A2 A3

APPLE
GOOGLE

Note: Reference to Google throughout the book sometimes refers to Alphabet Inc. as Google is a wholly owned subsidiary of Alphabet.

Check   (2b) 11.8%

BTN 1-2   Key comparative figures ($ millions) for both **Apple** and **Google** follow.

Key Figure	Apple	Google
Liabilities + Equity	$290,479	$147,461
Net income	53,394	16,348
Revenues and sales	233,715	74,989

Required

1. What is the total amount of assets invested in (*a*) Apple and (*b*) Google?
2. What is the return on assets for (*a*) Apple and (*b*) Google? Apple's beginning-year assets equal $231,839 (in millions) and Google's beginning-year assets equal $129,187 (in millions).
3. How much are expenses for (*a*) Apple and (*b*) Google?
4. Is return on assets satisfactory for (*a*) Apple and (*b*) Google? (Assume competitors average a 10% return.)
5. What can you conclude about Apple and Google from these computations?

ETHICS CHALLENGE

C3 C4

BTN 1-3   Tana Thorne works in a public accounting firm and hopes to eventually be a partner. The management of Allnet Company invites Thorne to prepare a bid to audit Allnet's financial statements. In discussing the audit fee, Allnet's management suggests a fee range in which the amount depends on the reported profit of Allnet. The higher its profit, the higher will be the audit fee paid to Thorne's firm.

Required

1. Identify the parties potentially affected by this audit and the fee plan proposed.
2. What are the ethical factors in this situation? Explain.
3. Would you recommend that Thorne accept this audit fee arrangement? Why or why not?
4. Describe some ethical considerations guiding your recommendation.

COMMUNICATING IN PRACTICE

A1 C2

APPLE

BTN 1-4   Refer to this chapter's opening feature about **Apple**. Assume that the owners, sometime during their first five years of business, desire to expand their computer product services to meet business demand regarding computing services. They eventually decide to meet with their banker to discuss a loan to allow Apple to expand and offer computing services.

Required

1. Prepare a half-page report outlining the information you would request from the owners if you were the loan officer.
2. Indicate whether the information you request and your loan decision are affected by the form of business organization for Apple.

BTN 1-5   Visit the EDGAR database at SEC.gov. Access the Form 10-K report of Rocky Mountain Chocolate Factory (ticker RMCF) filed on May 27, 2015, covering its 2015 fiscal year.

TAKING IT TO THE NET

A2

Required

1. Item 6 of the 10-K report provides comparative financial highlights of RMCF for the years 2011–2015. How would you describe the revenue trend for RMCF over this five-year period?

2. Has RMCF been profitable (see net income) over this five-year period? Support your answer.

BTN 1-6   Teamwork is important in today's business world. Successful teams schedule convenient meetings, maintain regular communications, and cooperate with and support their members. This assignment aims to establish support/learning teams, initiate discussions, and set meeting times.

TEAMWORK IN ACTION

C1

Required

1. Form teams and open a team discussion to determine a regular time and place for your team to meet between each scheduled class meeting. Notify your instructor via a memorandum or e-mail message as to when and where your team will hold regularly scheduled meetings.

2. Develop a list of telephone numbers and/or e-mail addresses of your teammates.

BTN 1-7   Refer to this chapter's opening feature about Apple. Assume that the owners decide to open a new company with an innovative mobile app devoted to microblogging for accountants and those learning accounting. This new company will be called **AccountApp**.

ENTREPRENEURIAL DECISION

A1 P1

APPLE

Required

1. AccountApp obtains a $500,000 loan and the two owners contribute $250,000 in total from their own savings in exchange for ownership of the new company.
   a. What is the new company's total amount of liabilities plus equity?
   b. What is the new company's total amount of assets?

2. If the new company earns $80,250 in net income in the first year of operation, compute its return on assets (assume average assets equal $750,000). Assess its performance if competitors average a 10% return.

Check   (2) 10.7%

BTN 1-8   You are to interview a local business owner. (This can be a friend or relative.) Opening lines of communication with members of the business community can provide personal benefits of business networking. If you do not know the owner, you should call ahead to introduce yourself and explain your position as a student and your assignment requirements. You should request a 30-minute appointment for a face-to-face or phone interview to discuss the form of organization and operations of the business. Be prepared to make a good impression.

HITTING THE ROAD

C2

Required

1. Identify and describe the main operating activities and the form of organization for this business.

2. Determine and explain why the owner(s) chose this particular form of organization.

3. Identify any special advantages and/or disadvantages the owner(s) experiences in operating with this form of business organization.

GLOBAL DECISION

A1   A2   A3

Samsung
APPLE
GOOGLE

BTN 1-9   Samsung (Samsung.com) is a leading global manufacturer, and it competes to varying degrees with both Apple and Google. Key financial figures for Samsung follow.

Key Figure*	Korean Won in Millions
Average assets	₩236,301,240
Net income	₩ 19,060,144
Revenue	₩200,653,482
Return on assets	8.1%

* Figures prepared in accordance with International Financial
Reporting Standards as adopted by the Republic of Korea.

Required

1. Identify any concerns you have in comparing Samsung's income and revenue figures to those of Apple and Google (in BTN 1-2) for purposes of making business decisions.

2. Identify any concerns you have in comparing Samsung's return on assets ratio to those of Apple and Google (computed for BTN 1-2) for purposes of making business decisions.

 **GLOBAL VIEW**

U.S. GAAP is similar, but not identical, to IFRS. We use the last section of each chapter to identify major similarities and differences between IFRS and U.S. GAAP.

Basic Principles   Both U.S. GAAP and IFRS include broad and similar guidance. However, neither system specifies particular account names nor the detail required. (A typical *chart of accounts* is shown near the end of this book.) IFRS does require certain minimum line items be reported in the balance sheet along with other minimum disclosures that U.S. GAAP does not. On the other hand, U.S. GAAP requires disclosures for the current and prior two years for the income statement, statement of cash flows, and statement of retained earnings (equity), while IFRS requires disclosures for the current and prior year only. Still, the basic principles behind these two systems are similar.*

Transaction Analysis   Both U.S. GAAP and IFRS apply transaction analysis identically as shown in this chapter. Although some variations exist in revenue and expense recognition and other principles, all of the transactions in this chapter are accounted for identically under these two systems. It is often said that U.S. GAAP is more *rules-based* whereas IFRS is more *principles-based*. Under U.S. GAAP, the approach is said to be more focused on following the accounting rules; under IFRS, the approach is more focused on a review of the situation and how accounting can best reflect it. This difference typically impacts advanced topics beyond the introductory course.

 IFRS

Like the FASB, the IASB uses a conceptual framework to aid in revising or drafting new standards. However, unlike the FASB, the IASB's conceptual framework is used as a reference when specific guidance is lacking. The IASB also requires that transactions be accounted for according to their substance (not only their legal form), and that financial statements give a fair presentation, whereas the FASB narrows that scope to fair presentation *in accordance with U.S. GAAP.* ∎

---

* The FASB and the IASB completed a joint project in 2014 to clarify the principles for recognizing revenue and to develop a common revenue standard for U.S. GAAP and IFRS. The FASB amended the FASB Accounting Standards Codification® and created a new Topic 606, *Revenue from Contracts with Customers,* and the IASB issued IFRS 15, *Revenue from Contracts with Customers.* The core principle is that "an entity should recognize revenue to depict the transfer of promised goods or services to customers in an amount that reflects the consideration to which the entity expects to be entitled in exchange for those goods or services." All discussions and presentations in this book are consistent with this new standard.

Financial Statements   Both U.S. GAAP and IFRS prepare the same four basic financial statements. To illustrate, a condensed version of Samsung's income statement follows using Korean IFRS (numbers are in thousands of U.S. dollars). Appendix A to the book has a full set of financial statements for Samsung along with those for Apple and Google.

Samsung

SAMSUNG Income Statement ($ thousands) For Year Ended December 31, 2015	
Revenues...	$177,365,404
Cost of sales	109,150,639
Cost of selling, wages, depreciation, and other expenses, net	45,266,834
Tax expense...	6,099,929
Net income (profit)	$ 16,848,002

Status of IFRS   IFRS is now adopted or accepted in over 115 countries. These countries and jurisdictions cover 97% of the global gross domestic product (GDP). For updates on global accounting, we can check with the AICPA (aicpa.org), FASB (fasb.org), and IASB (ifrs.org).

 Global View Assignments

Quick Study 1-17

Exercise 1-22

BTN 1-9

chapter 2

Analyzing and Recording Transactions

Chapter Preview

SYSTEM OF ACCOUNTS

C1 Source documents

C2 Types of accounts

C3 General ledger

NTK 2-1

DEBITS AND CREDITS

T-account

C4 Debits and credits

Normal balance

NTK 2-2

RECORDING TRANSACTIONS

P1 Journalizing and posting

A1 Processing transactions—Illustration

NTK 2-3

TRIAL BALANCE

P2 Trial balance preparation and use

Error identification

NTK 2-4

FINANCIAL STATEMENTS

P3 Financial statement preparation

A2 Debt ratio

NTK 2-5

Learning Objectives

CONCEPTUAL

C1 Explain the steps in processing transactions and the role of source documents.

C2 Describe an account and its use in recording transactions.

C3 Describe a ledger and a chart of accounts.

C4 Define *debits* and *credits* and explain double-entry accounting.

ANALYTICAL

A1 Analyze the impact of transactions on accounts and financial statements.

A2 Compute the debt ratio and describe its use in analyzing financial condition.

PROCEDURAL

P1 Record transactions in a journal and post entries to a ledger.

P2 Prepare and explain the use of a trial balance.

P3 Prepare financial statements from business transactions.

Fashioning a Better World

SAN FRANCISCO—**Soko** (shopSoko.com) is a web platform that allows "artisans in emerging economies to promote and sell their products . . . to the global marketplace," says co-founder Catherine Mahugu. Most of Soko's artisans are African women who face "many economic discriminations." Catherine explains, "we wanted to transform these micro-entrepreneurs into global entrepreneurs by giving them exposure and visibility." Jewelry crafted by her artisans is in retail stores such as **Nordstrom** and **Anthropologie**.

To date, Soko has registered more than 1,000 artisans on its web platform. Its accounting reports show over 42,000 pieces of jewelry shipped to customers. Those sales have had an enormous impact on the lives of artisans. According to Soko, the average household income for artisans grew 400% after joining Soko. "It's a brand that helps fashion a better world," says Catherine. Our artisans "should be proud of their achievements."

Catherine is committed to running a profitable business. "One has to commit a lot of his/her time to ensure sustainability of the business," explains Catherine. She relies on recordkeeping

"Never limit yourself"
—Catherine Mahugu

processes, transaction analysis, and accounting reports for business decisions. She uses the accounting system for insight into revenues and expenses that will sustain her business and that of her artisans. "I have learnt skills ranging from finance [and accounting] to government policies."

Catherine insists that accounting is crucial for her tracking of revenues and expenses, including her business investments and withdrawals. She says that her focus on accounting fundamentals keeps the dream alive for both her and her artisans. "Giving up is not an option," vows Catherine, "turn every barrier into an opportunity."

When asked about her greatest asset, Catherine responds, "Leadership is my strongest asset." Although leadership is not reported on Soko's balance sheet, it does lead to income. "When you take the risk you get the gains," insists Catherine. "I have seen the fruits of my labor!"

Sources: *Soko website,* January 2017; *Huffington Post,* October 2015; *How We Made It in Africa,* March 2014; *All Africa,* October 2015; *WMIAfrica,* September 2013; *Young African Leaders,* July 2015

SYSTEM OF ACCOUNTS

C1

Explain the steps in processing transactions and the role of source documents.

Business transactions and events are the starting points of financial statements. The process to get from transactions and events to financial statements includes the following:

- Identify each transaction and event from source documents.
- Analyze each transaction and event using the accounting equation.
- Record relevant transactions and events in a journal.
- Post journal information to ledger accounts.
- Prepare and analyze the trial balance and financial statements.

Source Documents

Point: Accounting records are informally referred to as the *accounting books,* or simply the *books.*

Source documents identify and describe transactions and events entering the accounting system. They can be in either hard copy or electronic form. Examples are sales tickets, checks, purchase orders, bills from suppliers, employee earnings records, and bank statements. For example, cash registers record information for each sale on a tape or electronic file locked inside the register. This record is a source document for recording sales in the accounting records. Source documents are objective and reliable evidence about transactions and events and their amounts.

The Account and Its Analysis

C2

Describe an account and its use in recording transactions.

EXHIBIT 2.1

Accounts Organized by the Accounting Equation

An **account** is a record of increases and decreases in a specific asset, liability, equity, revenue, or expense. The **general ledger,** or simply **ledger,** is a record of all accounts used by a company. The ledger is often in electronic form. While most companies' ledgers contain similar accounts, a company often uses one or more unique accounts because of its type of operations. An *unclassified balance sheet* broadly groups accounts into assets, liabilities, and equity. Exhibit 2.1 shows typical asset, liability, and equity accounts.

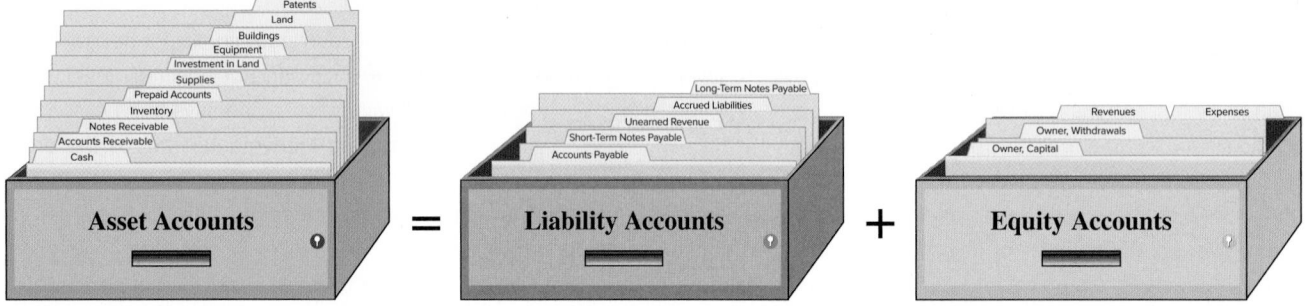

Asset Accounts   Assets are resources owned or controlled by a company, and those resources have expected future benefits. Most accounting systems include (at a minimum) separate accounts for the assets described here.

Cash   A *Cash* account reflects a company's cash balance. All increases and decreases in cash are recorded in the Cash account. It includes money and any funds that a bank accepts for deposit (coins, checks, money orders, and checking account balances).

Accounts Receivable   *Accounts receivable* are held by a seller and refer to promises of payment from customers to sellers. These transactions are often called *credit sales* or *sales on account* (or *on credit*). Accounts receivable are increased by credit sales and billings to customers but are decreased by customer payments. We record all increases and decreases in receivables in the Accounts Receivable account. When there are multiple customers, separate records are kept for each, titled Accounts Receivable—'Customer Name'.

Point: Customers and others who owe a company are called its *debtors.*

Note Receivable A *note receivable,* or promissory note, is a written promise of another entity to pay a specific sum of money on a specified future date to the holder of the note; the holder has an asset recorded in a Note (or Notes) Receivable account.

Prepaid Accounts *Prepaid accounts* (also called *prepaid expenses*) are assets that represent prepayments of future expenses (expenses expected to be incurred in one or more future accounting periods). When the expenses are later incurred, the amounts in prepaid accounts are transferred to expense accounts. Common examples of prepaid accounts include prepaid insurance, prepaid rent, and prepaid services (such as club memberships). Prepaid accounts expire with the passage of time (such as with rent) or through use (such as with prepaid meal tickets). When financial statements are prepared (1) all expired and used prepaid accounts are recorded as expenses and (2) all unexpired and unused prepaid accounts are recorded as assets (reflecting future use in future periods). To illustrate, when an insurance fee, called a *premium,* is paid in advance, the cost is typically recorded in the asset account titled Prepaid Insurance. Over time, the expiring portion of the insurance cost is removed from this asset account and reported in expenses on the income statement. Any unexpired portion remains in Prepaid Insurance and is reported on the balance sheet as an asset.

Point: A college parking pass is a prepaid account from the student's standpoint. At the beginning of the term, it is an asset that entitles a student to park on or near campus. The benefits of the parking pass expire as the term progresses. At term-end, prepaid parking (asset) equals zero as it has been entirely recorded as parking expense.

Supplies Accounts *Supplies* are assets until they are used. When they are used up, their costs are reported as expenses. The costs of unused supplies are recorded in a Supplies asset account. Supplies are often grouped by purpose—for example, office supplies and store supplies. *Office supplies* include paper, toner, and pens. *Store supplies* include packaging and cleaning materials.

Equipment Accounts *Equipment* is an asset. When equipment is used and gets worn down, its cost is gradually reported as an expense (called depreciation). Equipment is often grouped by its purpose—for example, office equipment and store equipment. *Office equipment* includes computers and desks. The *Store Equipment* account includes counters and cash registers.

Buildings Accounts *Buildings* such as stores, offices, warehouses, and factories are assets because they provide expected future benefits to those who control or own them. Their costs are recorded in a Buildings asset account. When several buildings are owned, separate accounts are sometimes kept for each of them.

Point: Some assets are described as *intangible* because they do not have physical existence or their benefits are highly uncertain. A recent balance sheet for **Coca-Cola Company** shows nearly $15 billion in intangible assets.

Land The cost of *land* owned by a business is recorded in a Land account. The cost of buildings located on the land is separately recorded in one or more building accounts.

Decision Insight

Women Entrepreneurs Sara Blakely (in photo), the billionaire entrepreneur/owner of **SPANX**, has promised to donate half of her wealth to charity. The Center for Women's Business Research reports that women-owned businesses are growing and that they:

- Total more than 11 million and employ nearly 20 million workers.
- Generate $2.5 trillion in annual sales and tend to embrace technology.
- Are philanthropic—70% of owners volunteer at least once per month.
- Are more likely funded by individual investors (73%) than venture firms (15%). ■

© Timothy A. Clary/AFP/ Getty Images

Liability Accounts Liabilities are claims (by creditors) against assets, which means they are obligations to transfer assets or provide products or services to others. **Creditors** are individuals and organizations that have rights to receive payments from a company. Common liability accounts are described here.

Point: If a company fails to pay its obligations, the law gives creditors a right to force the sale of that company's assets to obtain money to meet creditors' claims.

Accounts Payable *Accounts payable* refer to promises to pay later, which usually arise from purchases of merchandise for resale. Payables can also arise from purchases of supplies,

Point: Accounts payable are also called *trade payables*.

equipment, and services. We record all increases and decreases in payables in the Accounts Payable account. When there are multiple suppliers, separate records are kept for each, titled Accounts Payable—'Supplier Name'.

Note Payable   A *note payable* refers to a formal promise, usually indicated by the signing of a promissory note, to pay a future amount. It is recorded in either a short-term Note Payable account or a long-term Note Payable account, depending on when it must be repaid. We explain details of short- and long-term classification in the next two chapters.

Point: Two words that almost always identify liability accounts: "payable" meaning liabilities that must be paid, and "unearned" meaning liabilities that must be fulfilled.

Unearned Revenue Accounts   **Unearned revenue** refers to a liability that is settled in the future when a company delivers its products or services. When customers pay in advance for products or services (before revenue is earned), the seller considers this receipt as unearned revenue. Examples of unearned revenue include magazine subscriptions collected in advance by a publisher, rent collected in advance by a landlord, and season ticket sales by sports teams. The seller would record these in liability accounts such as Unearned Subscriptions, Unearned Rent, and Unearned Ticket Revenue. When products and services are later delivered, the earned portion of the unearned revenue is transferred to revenue accounts such as Subscription Fees Revenue, Rent Revenue, and Ticket Revenue.[1]

Accrued Liabilities   *Accrued liabilities* are amounts owed that are not yet paid. Examples are wages payable, taxes payable, and interest payable. These are often recorded in separate liability accounts by the same title. If they are not large in amount, one or more ledger accounts can be added and reported as a single amount on the balance sheet. (Financial statements often have amounts reported that are a summation of several ledger accounts.)

◼ **Decision** Insight

Unearned Revenue   The **Seattle Seahawks**, **Denver Broncos**, **New England Patriots**, and most NFL teams have over $100 million in advance ticket sales in *Unearned Revenue*. When a team plays its home games, it settles this liability to its ticket holders and then transfers the amount earned to *Ticket Revenue*. Teams in other major sports such as the National Women's Soccer League and the Women's National Basketball Association also have unearned revenue. ◼

© Mike Zarrilli/Getty Images

Equity Accounts   The owner's claim on a company's assets is called *equity* or *owner's equity*. Equity is the owner's *residual interest* in the assets of a business after deducting liabilities. Equity is impacted by four types of accounts as follows:

$$\text{Equity} = \text{Owner's capital} - \text{Owner's withdrawals} + \text{Revenues} - \text{Expenses}.$$

We show this visually in Exhibit 2.2 by expanding the accounting equation. We also organize assets and liabilities into subgroups that have similar attributes. An important subgroup for both assets and liabilities is the *current* items. Current items are usually those expected to come due (either collected or owed) within the next year. The next two chapters explain this in detail. At this point, know that a ***classified balance sheet*** groups accounts into classifications (such as land and buildings into Plant Assets) *and* it reports current assets before noncurrent assets and current liabilities before noncurrent liabilities.

Owner Capital   When an owner invests in a company, it increases both assets and equity. The increase to equity is recorded in an account titled **Owner, Capital** (where the owner's name is inserted in place of "Owner"). The account titled *C. Taylor, Capital* is used for FastForward. Any owner investments are recorded in this account.

---

[1]In practice, account titles vary. As one example, Subscription Fees Revenue is sometimes called Subscription Fees, Subscription Fees Earned, or Earned Subscription Fees. As another example, Rent Revenue is sometimes called Rent Earned, Rental Revenue, or Earned Rent Revenue. We must use good judgment when reading financial statements because titles can differ even within the same industry. For example, product sales are called *net sales* at **Apple**, *revenues* at **Google**, and *revenue* at **Samsung**. Generally, the term *revenues* or *fees* is more commonly used with service businesses, and *net sales* or *sales* with product businesses.

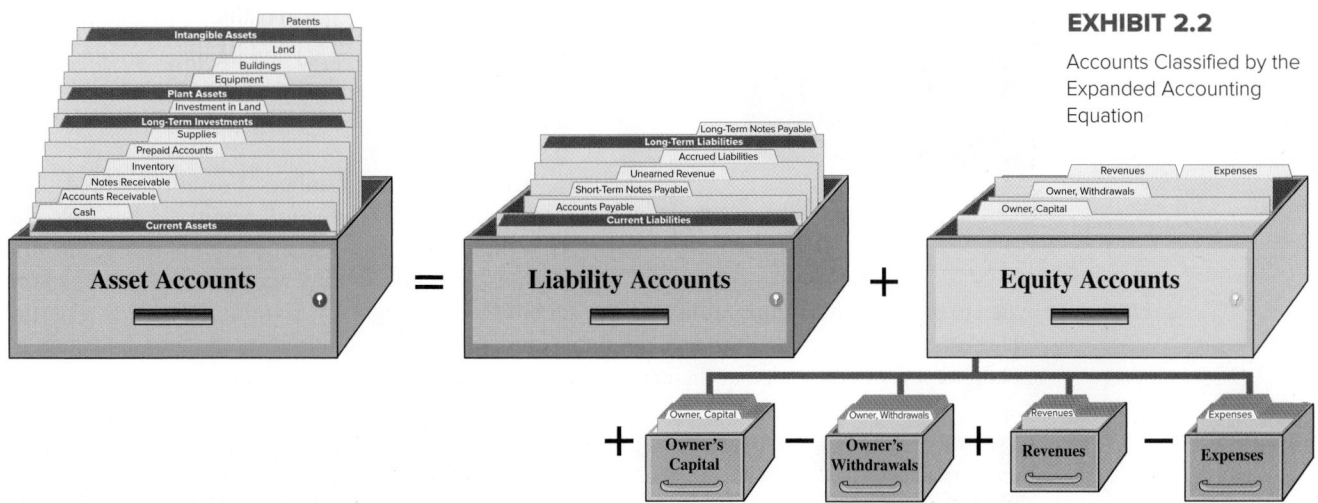

EXHIBIT 2.2

Accounts Classified by the Expanded Accounting Equation

Owner Withdrawals   When an owner withdraws assets for personal use, it decreases both company assets and total equity. The decrease to equity is recorded in an account titled Owner, Withdrawals. The account titled C. Taylor, Withdrawals is used for FastForward. Withdrawals are not expenses of the business; they are simply the opposite of owner investments. (Owners of proprietorships cannot receive company salaries because they are not legally separate from their companies; and they cannot enter into company contracts with themselves.)

Point: The Owner's Withdrawals account is a *contra equity* account because it reduces the normal balance of equity.

Point: The withdrawal of assets by the owners of a corporation is called a *dividend.*

Revenue Accounts   The inflow of net assets from providing products and services to customers increases equity through increases in revenue accounts. Examples of revenue accounts are Sales, Commissions Earned, Professional Fees Earned, Rent Revenue, and Interest Revenue. *Revenues always increase equity.*

Expense Accounts   The outflow of net assets in helping generate revenues decreases equity through increases in expense accounts. Examples of expense accounts are Advertising Expense, Store Supplies Expense, Office Salaries Expense, Office Supplies Expense, Rent Expense, Utilities Expense, and Insurance Expense. *Expenses always decrease equity.* The variety of revenues and expenses can be seen by looking at the *chart of accounts* that follows the index at the end of this book. (Different companies sometimes use different account titles than those in this book's chart of accounts. For example, some might use Interest Revenue instead of Interest Earned, or Rental Expense instead of Rent Expense. It is important only that an account title describe the item it represents.)

Decision Insight

Sporting Accounts   The **Cleveland Cavaliers**, **Boston Celtics**, **San Antonio Spurs**, **Golden State Warriors**, **Los Angeles Clippers**, and other NBA teams have the following major revenue and expense accounts:

Revenues	Expenses
Basketball ticket sales	Team salaries
TV & radio broadcast fees	Game costs
Advertising revenues	NBA franchise costs
Basketball playoff receipts	Promotional costs ■

© Frederic J. Brown/AFP/Getty Images

Ledger and Chart of Accounts

The collection of all accounts and their balances for an accounting system is called a *ledger* (or *general ledger*). A company's size and diversity of operations affect the number of accounts needed. A small company can get by with as few as 20 or 30 accounts; a large company can

C3 _____

Describe a ledger and a chart of accounts.

EXHIBIT 2.3

Typical Chart of Accounts for a Smaller Business

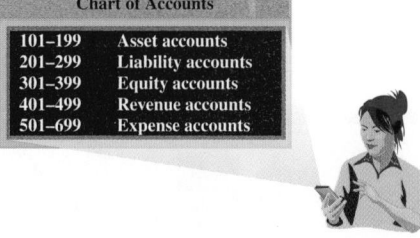

Chart of Accounts	
101–199	Asset accounts
201–299	Liability accounts
301–399	Equity accounts
401–499	Revenue accounts
501–699	Expense accounts

require several thousand. The **chart of accounts** is a list of all ledger accounts and includes an identification number assigned to each account. Exhibit 2.3 shows a common numbering system of accounts for a smaller business.

These account numbers provide a three-digit code that is useful in recordkeeping. In this case, the first digit assigned to asset accounts is a 1, the first digit assigned to liability accounts is a 2, and so on. The second and third digits relate to the accounts' subcategories. Exhibit 2.4 shows a partial chart of accounts for FastForward, the focus company of Chapter 1. (A more complete chart of accounts follows the index at the end of this book.)

EXHIBIT 2.4

Partial Chart of Accounts for FastForward

Chart of Accounts				
Assets		**Liabilities**	**Equity**	
101 Cash		201 Accounts payable	301 C. Taylor, Capital	
106 Accounts receivable		236 Unearned consulting revenue	302 C. Taylor, Withdrawals	
126 Supplies			**Revenues**	**Expenses**
128 Prepaid insurance			403 Consulting revenue	622 Salaries expense
167 Equipment			406 Rental revenue	637 Insurance expense
				640 Rent expense
				652 Supplies expense
				690 Utilities expense

NEED-TO-KNOW 2-1

Classifying Accounts

C1   C2   C3

Classify each of the following accounts as either an asset (A), liability (L), or equity (EQ).

____ **1.** Prepaid Rent   ____ **5.** Accounts Receivable   ____ **9.** Land
____ **2.** Owner, Capital   ____ **6.** Equipment   ____ **10.** Prepaid Insurance
____ **3.** Note Receivable   ____ **7.** Interest Payable   ____ **11.** Wages Payable
____ **4.** Accounts Payable   ____ **8.** Unearned Revenue   ____ **12.** Rent Payable

Solution

Do More: QS 2-2, QS 2-3

1. A   **2.** EQ   **3.** A   **4.** L   **5.** A   **6.** A   **7.** L   **8.** L   **9.** A   **10.** A   **11.** L   **12.** L

DOUBLE-ENTRY ACCOUNTING

This section explains the structure of double-entry accounting, including debits and credits.

C4 _____

Define *debits* and *credits* and explain double-entry accounting.

Debits and Credits

A **T-account** represents a ledger account and is used to depict the effects of one or more transactions. Its name comes from its shape like the letter **T**. The layout of a T-account, shown in Exhibit 2.5, is (1) the account title on top; (2) a left, or debit, side; and (3) a right, or credit, side.

EXHIBIT 2.5

The T-Account

Account Title	
(Left side)	(Right side)
Debit	*Credit*

The left side of an account is called the **debit** side, often abbreviated *Dr.* The right side is called the **credit** side, abbreviated *Cr.*[2] To enter amounts on the left side of an account is to *debit* the account. To enter amounts on

---

[2]These abbreviations are remnants of 18th-century English recordkeeping practices where the terms *debitor* and *creditor* were used instead of *debit* and *credit*. The abbreviations use the first and last letters of these terms, just as we still do for Saint (St.) and Doctor (Dr.).

the right side is to *credit* the account. The term *debit* or *credit,* by itself, does not mean increase or decrease. Whether a debit or a credit is an increase or decrease depends on the account.

The difference between total debits and total credits for an account, including any beginning balance, is the **account balance.** When the sum of debits exceeds the sum of credits, the account has a *debit balance*. It has a *credit balance* when the sum of credits exceeds the sum of debits. When the sum of debits equals the sum of credits, the account has a *zero balance*.

Point: Think of *debit* and *credit* as accounting directions for left and right.

Double-Entry System

Double-entry accounting demands the accounting equation remain in balance, which means that for each transaction:

"Total debits equal total credits for each entry."

● At least two accounts are involved, with at least one debit and one credit.
● The total amount debited must equal the total amount credited.

This means the sum of the debits for all entries must equal the sum of the credits for all entries, and the sum of debit account balances in the ledger must equal the sum of credit account balances. The system for recording debits and credits follows from the accounting equation— see Exhibit 2.6.

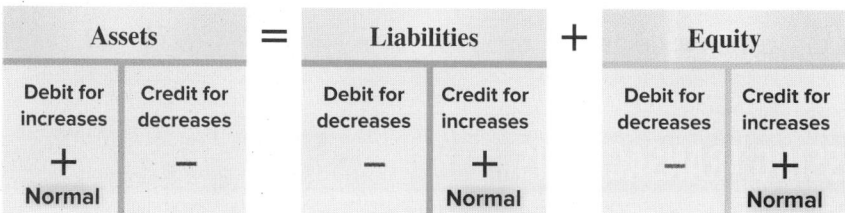

EXHIBIT 2.6

Debits and Credits in the Accounting Equation

First, net increases or decreases on one side have equal net effects on the other side. For example, a net increase in assets must be accompanied by an identical net increase on the liabilities and equity side. Recall that some transactions affect only one side of the equation, such as acquiring a land asset by giving up a cash asset, but their net effect on this one side is zero.

Second, the left side is the *normal balance* side for assets, and the right side is the *normal balance* side for liabilities and equity. This matches their layout in the accounting equation, where assets are on the left side of this equation and liabilities and equity are on the right.

Third, equity increases from revenues and owner investments and it decreases from expenses and owner withdrawals. These important equity relations are conveyed by expanding the accounting equation to include debits and credits in double-entry form as shown in Exhibit 2.7.

Point: Assets are on the left-hand side of the equation and thus increase on the left. Liabilities and Equity are on the right-hand side of the equation and thus increase on the right.

EXHIBIT 2.7

Debit and Credit Effects for Component Accounts

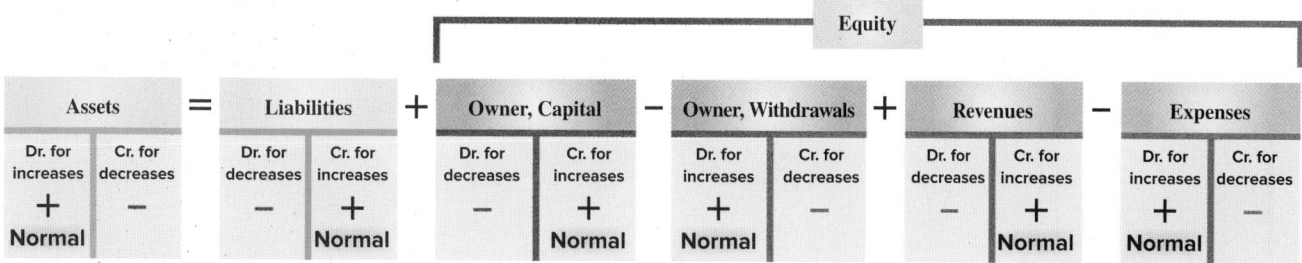

Fourth, increases (credits) to owner's capital and revenues *increase* equity; increases (debits) to withdrawals and expenses *decrease* equity. The normal balance of each account (asset, liability, capital, withdrawals, revenue, or expense) refers to the side where *increases* are recorded.

The T-account for FastForward's Cash account, reflecting its first 11 transactions (from Exhibit 1.9), is shown in Exhibit 2.8. The total increases (debits) in its Cash account are \$36,100, and the total decreases (credits) are \$31,300. Total debits exceed total credits by \$4,800, resulting in its ending debit balance of \$4,800.

Point: Debits and credits do not mean favorable or unfavorable. A debit to an asset increases it, as does a debit to an expense. A credit to a liability increases it, as does a credit to a revenue.

EXHIBIT 2.8

Computing the Balance for
a T-Account

Point: The ending balance is on
the side with the larger dollar
amount. Also, a plus (+) and
minus (–) are *not* used in a
T-account.

Cash				
Receive investment by owner	30,000	Purchase of supplies	2,500	
Consulting services revenue earned	4,200	Purchase of equipment	26,000	
Collection of account receivable	1,900	Payment of rent	1,000	
		Payment of salary	700	
		Payment of account payable	900	
		Withdrawal by owner	200	
Balance	**4,800**			

36,100

31,300

36,100 − 31,300

NEED-TO-KNOW 2-2

Normal Account Balance

C4

Do More: QS 2-4, QS 2-5,
QS 2-7, E 2-4

Identify the normal balance (debit [Dr] or credit [Cr]) for each of the following accounts.

____ **1.** Prepaid Rent	____ **5.** Accounts Receivable	____ **9.** Land
____ **2.** Owner, Capital	____ **6.** Equipment	____ **10.** Prepaid Insurance
____ **3.** Note Receivable	____ **7.** Interest Payable	____ **11.** Owner, Withdrawals
____ **4.** Accounts Payable	____ **8.** Unearned Revenue	____ **12.** Supplies

Solution

1. Dr.   **2.** Cr.   **3.** Dr.   **4.** Cr.   **5.** Dr.   **6.** Dr.   **7.** Cr.   **8.** Cr.   **9.** Dr.   **10.** Dr.   **11.** Dr.   **12.** Dr.

ANALYZING AND PROCESSING TRANSACTIONS

This section explains the analyzing, recording, and posting of transactions.

Journalizing and Posting Transactions

P1

Record transactions in
a journal and post entries
to a ledger.

EXHIBIT 2.9

Steps in Processing
Transactions

The four steps of processing transactions are depicted in Exhibit 2.9. Steps 1 and 2—involving transaction analysis and the accounting equation—were already discussed. This section extends that discussion and focuses on steps 3 and 4 of the accounting process. Step 3 is to record each transaction chronologically in a journal. A **journal** gives a complete record of each transaction in one place. It also shows debits and credits for each transaction. The process of recording transactions in a journal is called **journalizing.** Step 4 is to transfer (or *post*) entries from the journal to the ledger. The process of transferring journal entry information to the ledger is called **posting.**

Step 1: Identify transactions and source documents.

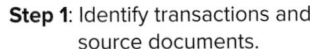

Step 2: Analyze transactions using the accounting equation.

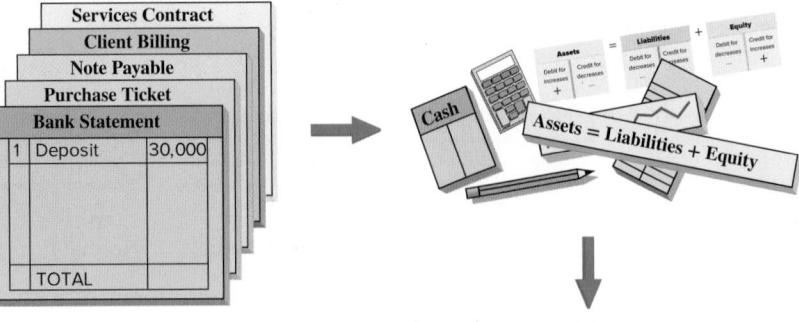

Step 3: Record journal entry.

Step 4: Post entry to ledger.

Journalizing Transactions   The process of journalizing transactions requires an understanding of a journal. While companies can use various journals, every company uses a **general journal.** It can be used to record any transaction and includes the following information about each transaction: (ⓐ) date of transaction, (ⓑ) titles of affected accounts, (ⓒ) dollar amount of each debit and credit, and (ⓓ) explanation of the transaction. Exhibit 2.10 shows how the first two transactions of FastForward are recorded in a general journal. This process is similar for manual and computerized systems. Computerized journals are often designed to look like a manual journal page and include error-checking routines that ensure debits equal credits for each entry. Shortcuts allow recordkeepers to select account names and numbers from pull-down menus.

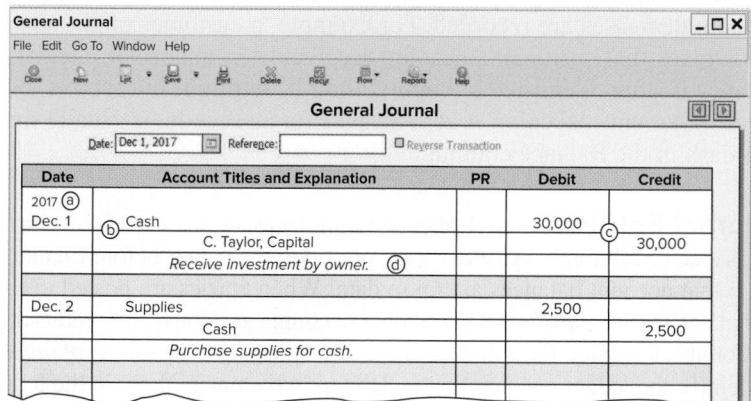

EXHIBIT 2.10

Partial General Journal for FastForward

To record entries in a general journal, apply these steps; refer to the entries in Exhibit 2.10 when reviewing these steps.

a. Date the transaction: Enter the year at the top of the first column and the month and day on the first line of each journal entry.

b. Enter titles of accounts debited and then enter amounts in the Debit column on the same line. Account titles are taken from the chart of accounts and are aligned with the left margin of the Account Titles and Explanation column.

c. Enter titles of accounts credited and then enter amounts in the Credit column on the same line. Account titles are from the chart of accounts and are indented from the left margin of the Account Titles and Explanation column to distinguish them from debited accounts.

d. Enter a brief explanation of the transaction on the line below the entry (it often references a source document). This explanation is indented about half as far as the credited account titles to avoid confusing it with accounts, and it is italicized.

Point: There are no exact rules for a journal entry explanation—it should be short yet describe why an entry is made.

A blank line is left between each journal entry for clarity. When a transaction is first recorded, the **posting reference (PR) column** is left blank (in a manual system). Later, when posting entries to the ledger, the identification numbers of the individual ledger accounts are entered in the PR column.

Balance Column Account   T-accounts are simple and direct means to show how the accounting process works. However, actual accounting systems need more structure and therefore use **balance column accounts,** such as that in Exhibit 2.11.

| General Ledger | | | | | |
| Cash | | | | | Account No. 101 |
Date	Explanation	PR	Debit	Credit	Balance
2017					
Dec. 1		G1	30,000		30,000
Dec. 2		G1		2,500	27,500
Dec. 3		G1		26,000	1,500
Dec. 10		G1	4,200		5,700

EXHIBIT 2.11

Cash Account in Balance Column Format

The balance column account format is similar to a T-account in having columns for debits and credits. It is different in including transaction date and explanation columns. It also has a column with the balance of the account after each entry is recorded. To illustrate, FastForward's Cash account in Exhibit 2.11 is debited on December 1 for the $30,000 owner investment, yielding a $30,000 debit balance. The account is credited on December 2 for $2,500, yielding a $27,500 debit balance. On December 3, it is credited again, this time for $26,000, and its debit balance is reduced to $1,500. The Cash account is debited for $4,200 on December 10, and its debit balance increases to $5,700; and so on.

The heading of the Balance column does not show whether it is a debit or credit balance. Instead, an account is assumed to have a *normal balance*. Unusual events can sometimes temporarily give an account an abnormal balance. An *abnormal balance* refers to a balance on the side where decreases are recorded. For example, a customer might mistakenly overpay a bill. This gives that customer's account receivable an abnormal (credit) balance. An abnormal balance is often identified by highlighting it, setting it in brackets, or by entering it in red or some other unusual color. A zero balance for an account is usually shown by writing zeros or a dash in the Balance column.

Point: Explanations are typically included in ledger accounts only for unusual transactions or events.

Posting Journal Entries

Step 4 of processing transactions is to post journal entries to ledger accounts (see Exhibit 2.9). All entries are posted to the ledger before financial statements are prepared so that account balances are up to date. When entries are posted to the ledger, the debits in journal entries are transferred into ledger accounts as debits, and credits are transferred into ledger accounts as credits. Exhibit 2.12 shows *four parts to the process of posting a journal entry*. First, identify the ledger account that is debited in the entry; then, in the ledger, enter the entry date, the journal and page in its PR column, the debit amount, and the new balance of the ledger account. (The letter *G* shows it came from the general journal.) Second, enter the ledger account number in the PR column of the journal. Steps 3 and 4 repeat the first two steps for

Point: A journal is often referred to as the *book of original entry.* The ledger is referred to as the *book of final entry* because financial statements are prepared from it.

EXHIBIT 2.12

Process of Posting an Entry to the Ledger

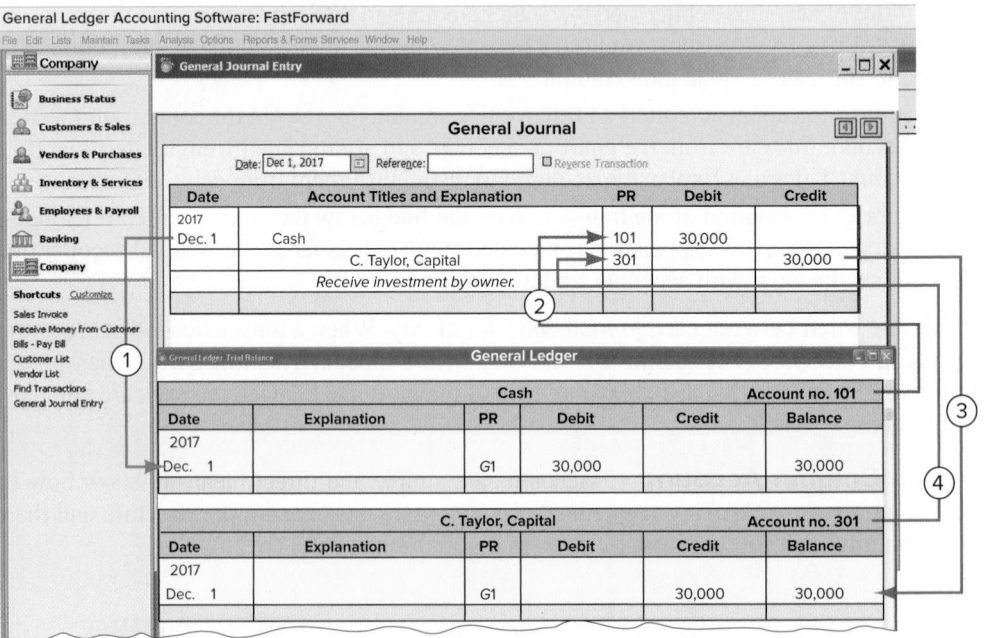

Key:
① Identify debit account in ledger: enter date, journal page, amount, and balance (in red).
② Enter the debit account number from the ledger in the PR column of the journal (in blue).
③ Identify credit account in ledger: enter date, journal page, amount, and balance (in green).
④ Enter the credit account number from the ledger in the PR column of the journal (in green).

Point: The fundamental concepts of a manual system are identical to those of a computerized information system.

credit entries and amounts. The posting process creates a link between the ledger and the journal entry. This link is a useful cross-reference for tracing an amount from one record to another.

Point: Posting is automatic with accounting software.

Processing Transactions—An Illustration

We return to the activities of FastForward to show how double-entry accounting is useful in analyzing and processing transactions. Analysis of each transaction follows the four steps of Exhibit 2.9.

A1

Analyze the impact of transactions on accounts and financial statements.

Step 1 Identify the transaction and any source documents.

Step 2 Analyze the transaction using the accounting equation.

Step 3 Record the transaction in journal entry form applying double-entry accounting.

Step 4 Post the entry (for simplicity, we use T-accounts to represent ledger accounts).

Study each transaction thoroughly before proceeding to the next. The first 11 transactions are from Chapter 1, and we analyze five additional December transactions of FastForward (numbered 12 through 16) that were omitted earlier.

Point: In Need-To-Know 2-5 we show how to use "balance column accounts" for the ledger.

1. Receive Investment by Owner

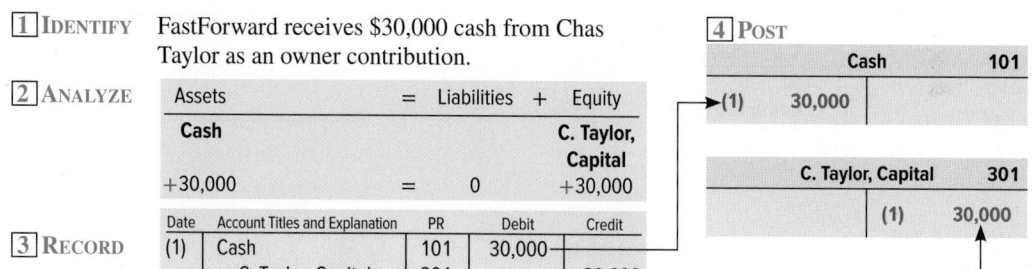

2. Purchase Supplies for Cash

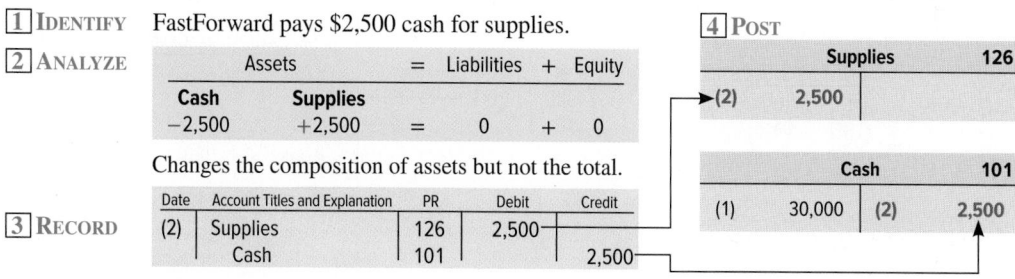

3. Purchase Equipment for Cash

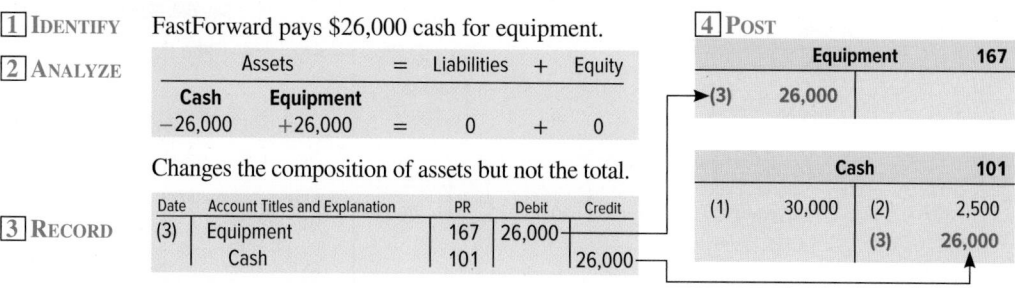

4. Purchase Supplies on Credit

1 IDENTIFY   FastForward purchases $7,100 of supplies on credit from a supplier.

2 ANALYZE

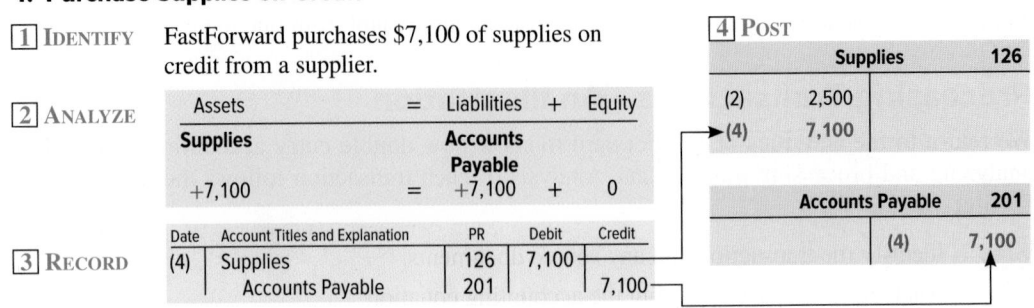

3 RECORD

5. Provide Services for Cash

1 IDENTIFY   FastForward provides consulting services and immediately collects $4,200 cash.

2 ANALYZE

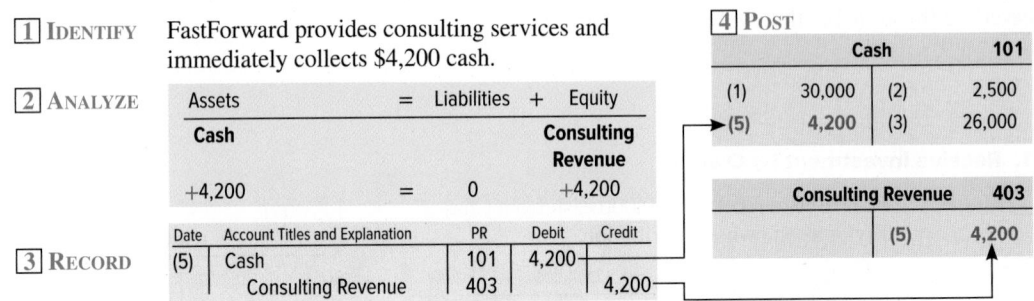

3 RECORD

6. Payment of Expense in Cash

1 IDENTIFY   FastForward pays $1,000 cash for December rent.

2 ANALYZE

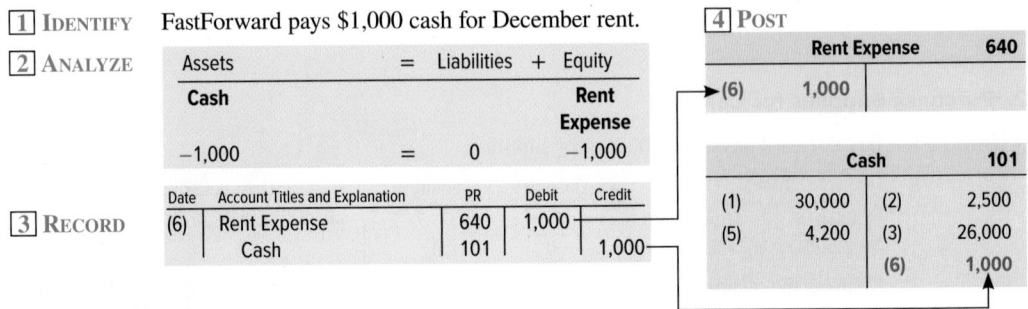

3 RECORD

7. Payment of Expense in Cash

Point: *Salary* usually refers to compensation of a fixed amount for a given time period, whereas *wages* is compensation based on time worked.

1 IDENTIFY   FastForward pays $700 cash for employee salary.

2 ANALYZE

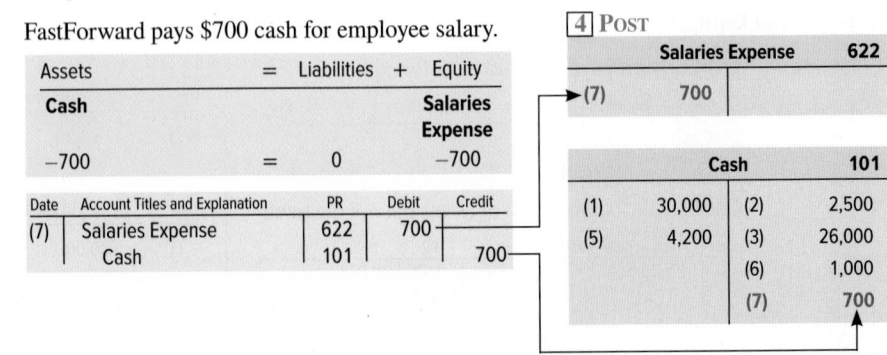

3 RECORD

8. Provide Consulting and Rental Services on Credit

1 IDENTIFY FastForward provides consulting services of $1,600 and rents its test facilities for $300. The customer is billed $1,900 for these services.

4 POST

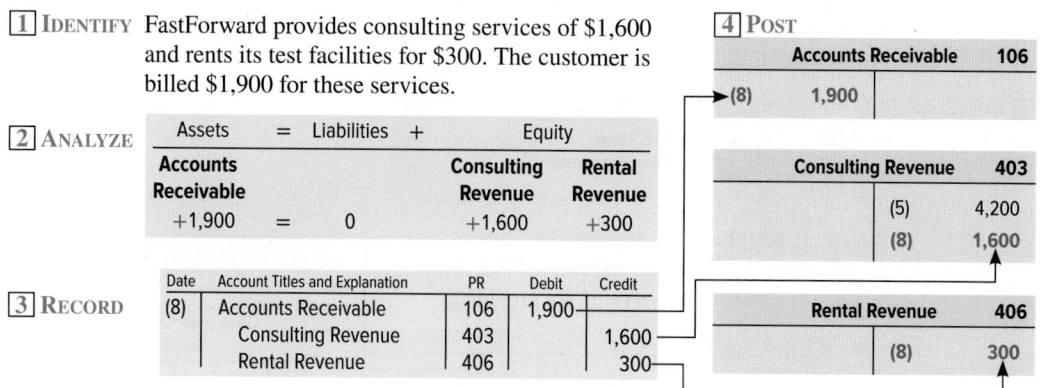

Point: The *revenue recognition principle* requires revenue to be recognized when the company provides products and services to a customer. This is not necessarily the same time that the customer pays.

Point: Transaction 8 is a compound journal entry, which is an entry that affects three or more accounts.

9. Receipt of Cash on Account

1 IDENTIFY FastForward receives $1,900 cash from the client billed in transaction 8.

4 POST

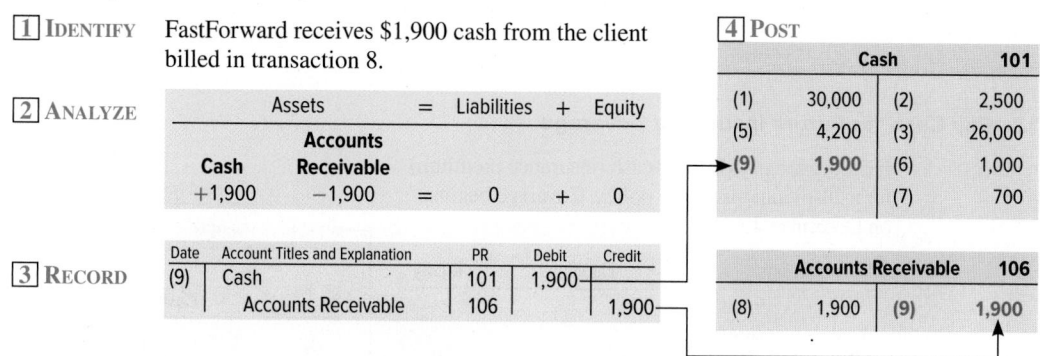

10. Partial Payment of Accounts Payable

1 IDENTIFY FastForward pays CalTech Supply $900 cash toward the payable of transaction 4.

4 POST

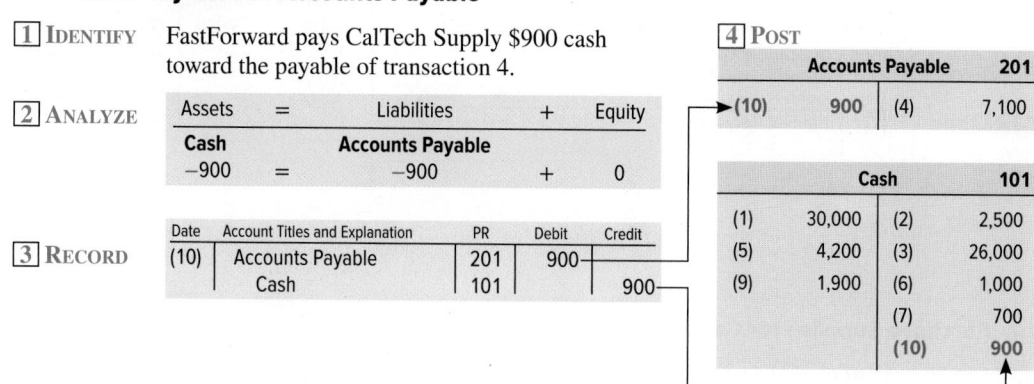

11. Withdrawal of Cash by Owner

1 IDENTIFY Chas Taylor withdraws $200 cash from FastForward for personal use.

4 POST

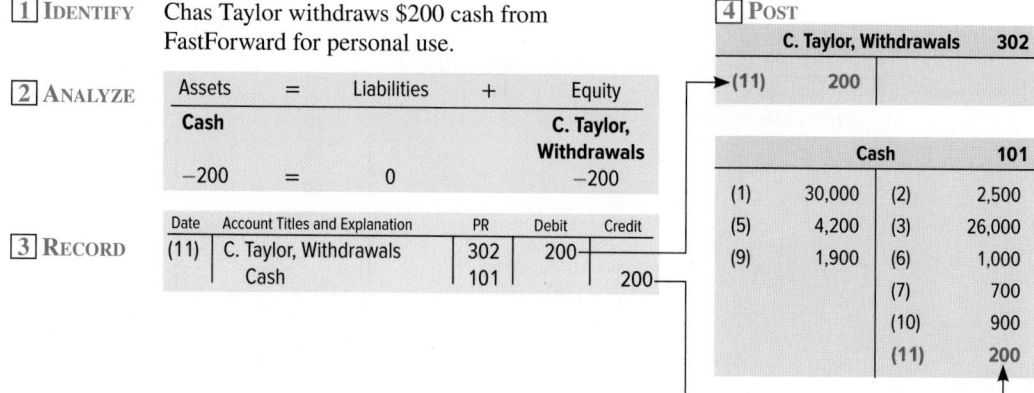

Point: Owner withdrawals always decrease equity.

12. Receipt of Cash for Future Services

Point: "Unearned" accounts are liabilities that must be fulfilled.

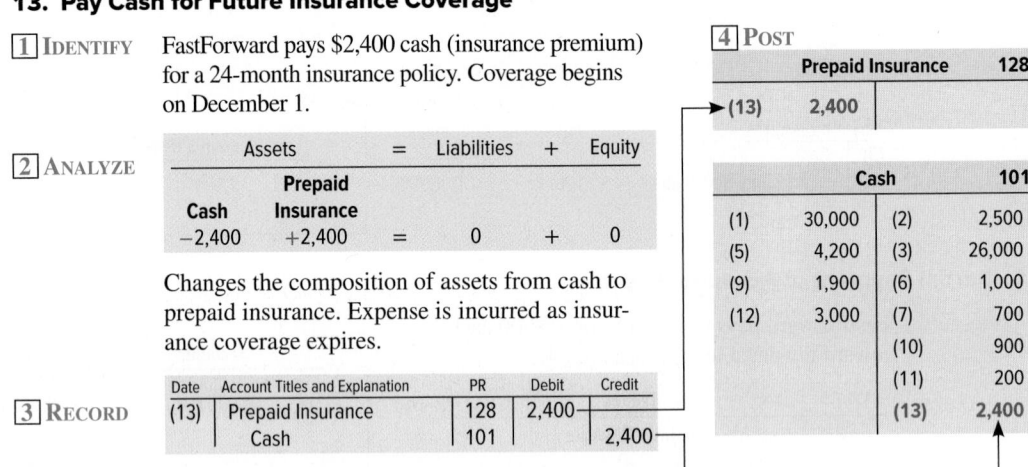

1 IDENTIFY FastForward receives $3,000 cash in advance of providing consulting services to a customer.

2 ANALYZE

Assets	=	Liabilities	+	Equity
Cash		**Unearned Consulting Revenue**		
+3,000	=	+3,000	+	0

Accepting $3,000 cash obligates FastForward to perform future services and is a liability. No revenue is earned until services are provided.

3 RECORD

Date	Account Titles and Explanation	PR	Debit	Credit
(12)	Cash	101	3,000	
	Unearned Consulting Revenue	236		3,000

4 POST

Cash			101
(1)	30,000	(2)	2,500
(5)	4,200	(3)	26,000
(9)	1,900	(6)	1,000
(12)	3,000	(7)	700
		(10)	900
		(11)	200

Unearned Consulting Revenue			236
		(12)	3,000

13. Pay Cash for Future Insurance Coverage

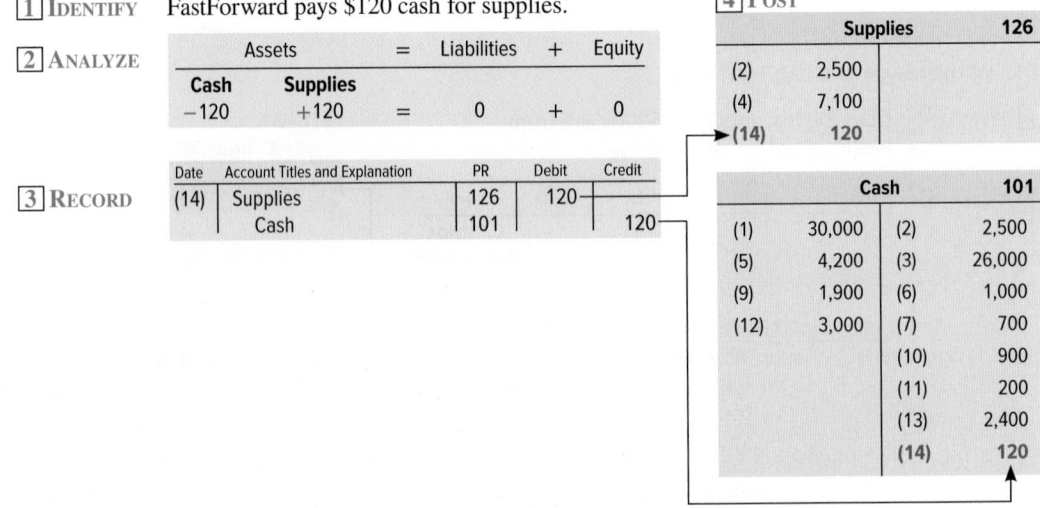

1 IDENTIFY FastForward pays $2,400 cash (insurance premium) for a 24-month insurance policy. Coverage begins on December 1.

2 ANALYZE

Assets		=	Liabilities	+	Equity
Cash	**Prepaid Insurance**				
−2,400	+2,400	=	0	+	0

Changes the composition of assets from cash to prepaid insurance. Expense is incurred as insurance coverage expires.

3 RECORD

Date	Account Titles and Explanation	PR	Debit	Credit
(13)	Prepaid Insurance	128	2,400	
	Cash	101		2,400

4 POST

Prepaid Insurance			128
(13)	2,400		

Cash			101
(1)	30,000	(2)	2,500
(5)	4,200	(3)	26,000
(9)	1,900	(6)	1,000
(12)	3,000	(7)	700
		(10)	900
		(11)	200
		(13)	2,400

14. Purchase Supplies for Cash

1 IDENTIFY FastForward pays $120 cash for supplies.

2 ANALYZE

Assets		=	Liabilities	+	Equity
Cash	**Supplies**				
−120	+120	=	0	+	0

3 RECORD

Date	Account Titles and Explanation	PR	Debit	Credit
(14)	Supplies	126	120	
	Cash	101		120

4 POST

Supplies			126
(2)	2,500		
(4)	7,100		
(14)	120		

Cash			101
(1)	30,000	(2)	2,500
(5)	4,200	(3)	26,000
(9)	1,900	(6)	1,000
(12)	3,000	(7)	700
		(10)	900
		(11)	200
		(13)	2,400
		(14)	120

Point: Luca Pacioli, a 15th-century monk and famous mathematician, is a pioneer in accounting and the first to devise double-entry accounting.

15. Payment of Expense in Cash

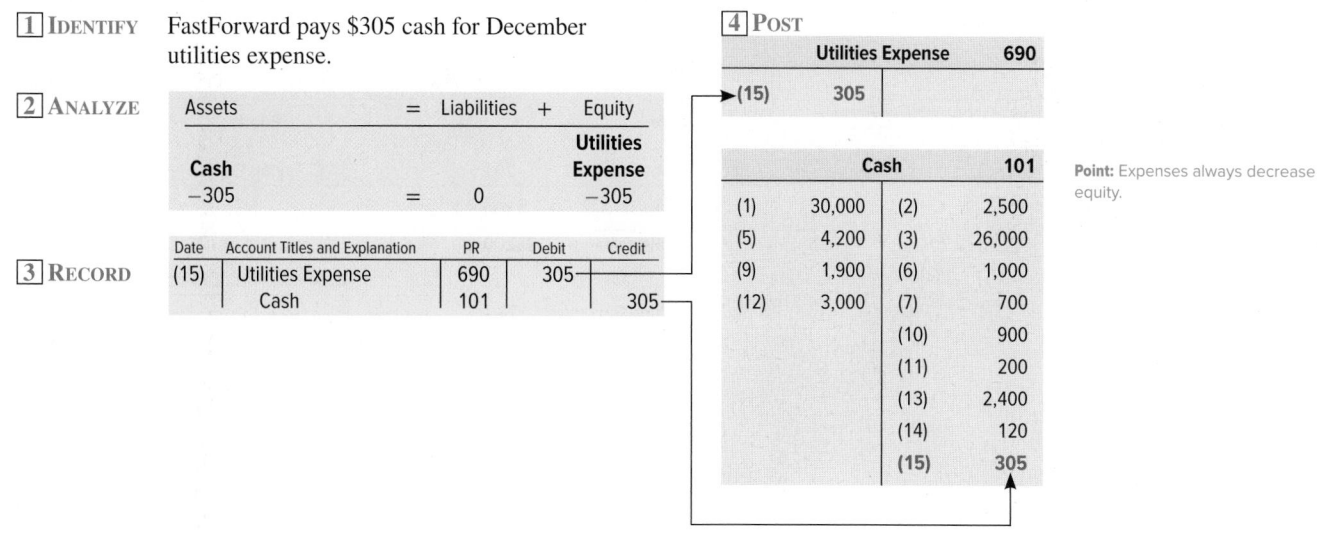

1 IDENTIFY FastForward pays $305 cash for December utilities expense.

2 ANALYZE

Assets	=	Liabilities	+	Equity
Cash				**Utilities Expense**
−305	=	0		−305

3 RECORD

Date	Account Titles and Explanation	PR	Debit	Credit
(15)	Utilities Expense	690	305	
	Cash	101		305

4 POST

Utilities Expense	690
(15) 305	

Cash		101	
(1)	30,000	(2)	2,500
(5)	4,200	(3)	26,000
(9)	1,900	(6)	1,000
(12)	3,000	(7)	700
		(10)	900
		(11)	200
		(13)	2,400
		(14)	120
		(15)	305

Point: Expenses always decrease equity.

16. Payment of Expense in Cash

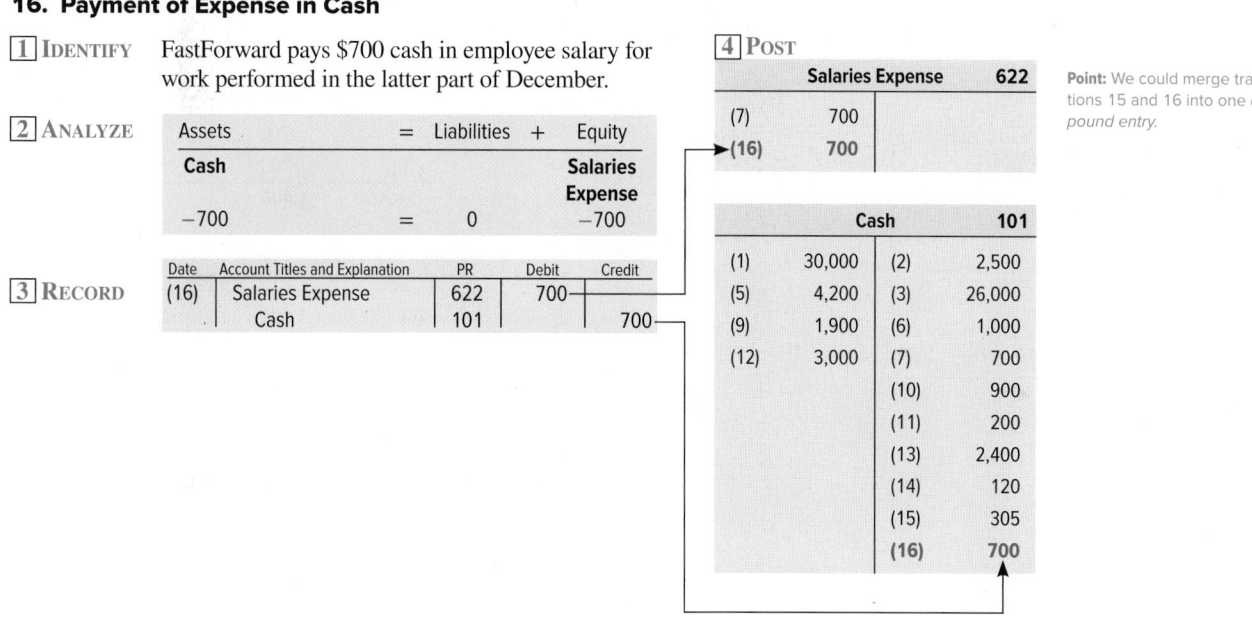

1 IDENTIFY FastForward pays $700 cash in employee salary for work performed in the latter part of December.

2 ANALYZE

Assets	=	Liabilities	+	Equity
Cash				**Salaries Expense**
−700	=	0		−700

3 RECORD

Date	Account Titles and Explanation	PR	Debit	Credit
(16)	Salaries Expense	622	700	
	Cash	101		700

4 POST

Salaries Expense	622
(7) 700	
(16) 700	

Cash		101	
(1)	30,000	(2)	2,500
(5)	4,200	(3)	26,000
(9)	1,900	(6)	1,000
(12)	3,000	(7)	700
		(10)	900
		(11)	200
		(13)	2,400
		(14)	120
		(15)	305
		(16)	700

Point: We could merge transactions 15 and 16 into one *compound entry*.

Summarizing Transactions in a Ledger

Exhibit 2.13 shows the ledger accounts (in T-account form) of FastForward after all 16 transactions are recorded and posted and the balances computed. The accounts are grouped into three columns corresponding to the accounting equation: assets, liabilities, and equity.

- Totals for the three columns obey the accounting equation: assets equal **$42,395** ($4,275 + $0 + $9,720 + $2,400 + $26,000); liabilities equal **$9,200** ($6,200 + $3,000); and equity equals **$33,195** ($30,000 − $200 + $5,800 + $300 − $1,400 − $1,000 − $305). These obey the accounting equation: $42,395 = $9,200 + $33,195.
- Capital, withdrawals, revenue, and expense accounts reflect transactions that change equity. These four accounts make up the statement of owner's equity.
- Revenue and expense account balances are summarized and reported in the income statement.

Debit and Credit Rules		
Accounts	**Increase (normal bal.)**	**Decrease**
Asset	Debit	Credit
Liability........	Credit	Debit
Capital	Credit	Debit
Withdrawals....	Debit	Credit
Revenue	Credit	Debit
Expense	Debit	Credit

EXHIBIT 2.13

Ledger for FastForward (in T-Account Form)

General Ledger			
Assets	**=**	**Liabilities**	**+ Equity**

General Ledger

Assets = **Liabilities** + **Equity**

Cash			101
(1)	30,000	(2)	2,500
(5)	4,200	(3)	26,000
(9)	1,900	(6)	1,000
(12)	3,000	(7)	700
		(10)	900
		(11)	200
		(13)	2,400
		(14)	120
		(15)	305
		(16)	700
Balance	4,275		

Accounts Receivable			106
(8)	1,900	(9)	1,900
Balance	0		

Supplies			126
(2)	2,500		
(4)	7,100		
(14)	120		
Balance	9,720		

Prepaid Insurance			128
(13)	2,400		

Equipment			167
(3)	26,000		

Accounts Payable			201
(10)	900	(4)	7,100
		Balance	6,200

Unearned Consulting Revenue			236
		(12)	3,000

C. Taylor, Capital			301
		(1)	30,000

C. Taylor, Withdrawals			302
(11)	200		

Consulting Revenue			403
		(5)	4,200
		(8)	1,600
		Balance	5,800

Rental Revenue			406
		(8)	300

Salaries Expense			622
(7)	700		
(16)	700		
Balance	1,400		

Rent Expense			640
(6)	1,000		

Utilities Expense			690
(15)	305		

Accounts in this white area are reported on the income statement.

$42,395	=	$9,200	+	$33,195

NEED-TO-KNOW 2-3

Recording Transactions

P1   A1

Assume Tata Company began operations on January 1 and completed the following transactions during its first month of operations. For each transaction, (a) analyze the transaction using the accounting equation, (b) record the transaction in journal entry form, and (c) post the entry using T-accounts to represent ledger accounts. Tata Company has the following (partial) chart of accounts—account numbers in parentheses: Cash (101); Accounts Receivable (106); Equipment (167); Accounts Payable (201); J. Tata, Capital (301); J. Tata, Withdrawals (302); Services Revenue (403); and Wages Expense (601).

Jan. 1 Jamsetji Tata invested $4,000 cash in the Tata Company.

   5 Tata Company purchased $2,000 of equipment on credit.

   14 Tata Company provided $540 of services for a client on credit.

Solution

Jan. 1 Receive Investment by Owner

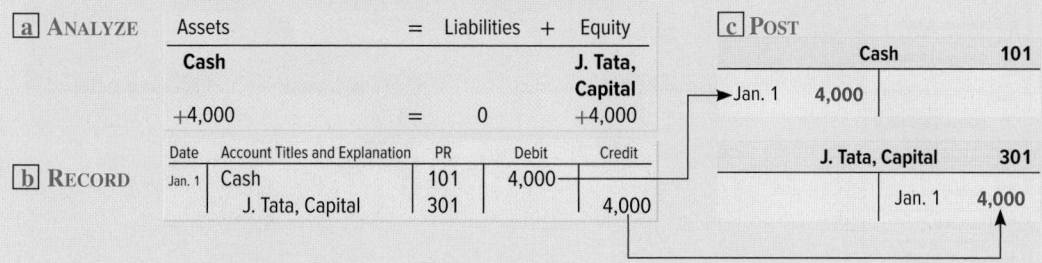

Jan. 5 Purchase Equipment on Credit

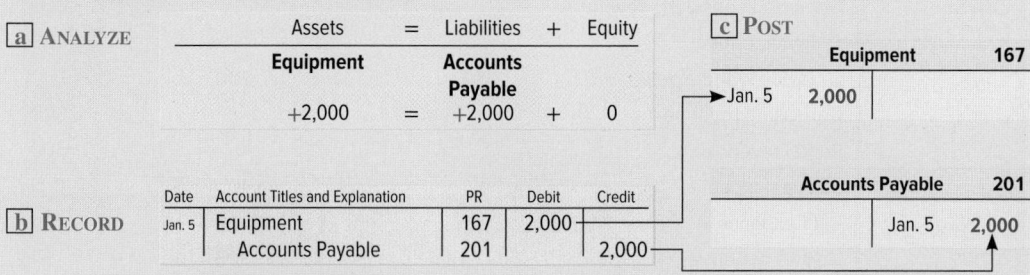

Jan. 14 Provide Services on Credit

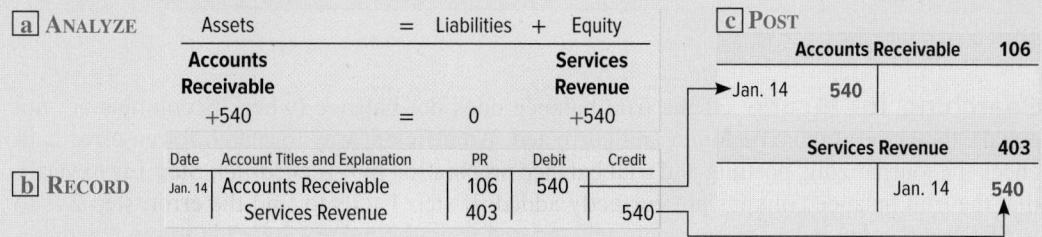

Do More: QS 2-6, E 2-7, E 2-9, E 2-11, E 2-12

TRIAL BALANCE

A **trial balance** is a list of ledger accounts and their balances (either debit or credit) at a point in time. Exhibit 2.14 shows the trial balance for FastForward after its 16 entries are posted to the ledger. (This is an *unadjusted* trial balance—Chapter 3 explains the necessary adjustments.)

P2

Prepare and explain the use of a trial balance.

Preparing a Trial Balance

Preparing a trial balance involves three steps:

1. List each account title and its amount (from ledger) in the trial balance. If an account has a zero balance, list it with a zero in its normal balance column (or omit it entirely).
2. Compute the total of debit balances and the total of credit balances.
3. Verify (*prove*) total debit balances equal total credit balances.

The total of debit balances equals the total of credit balances for the trial balance in Exhibit 2.14. Equality of these two totals does not guarantee that no errors were made. For example, the column totals will be equal when a debit or credit of a correct amount is made to a wrong account. Another error not identified with a trial balance is when equal debits and credits of an incorrect amount are entered.

Point: A trial balance is *not* a financial statement but a mechanism for checking equality of debits and credits in the ledger. Financial statements do not have debit and credit columns.

EXHIBIT 2.14

Trial Balance (Unadjusted)

FAST*Forward*

General Ledger Accounting Software: FastForward

File Edit Lists Maintain Tasks Analysis Options Reports & Forms Services Window Help

Company

Business Status
Customers & Sales
Vendors & Purchases
Inventory & Services
Employees & Payroll
Banking
Company

Shortcuts Customize
Sales Invoice
Receive Money from Customer
Bills - Pay Bill
Customer List
Vendor List
Find Transactions
General Journal Entry

FASTFORWARD
Trial Balance
December 31, 2017

	Debit	Credit
Cash	$ 4,275	
Accounts receivable	0	
Supplies	9,720	
Prepaid insurance	2,400	
Equipment	26,000	
Accounts payable		$ 6,200
Unearned consulting revenue		3,000
C. Taylor, Capital		30,000
C. Taylor, Withdrawals	200	
Consulting revenue		5,800
Rental revenue		300
Salaries expense	1,400	
Rent expense	1,000	
Utilities expense	305	
Totals	$ 45,300	$ 45,300

Point: The ordering of accounts in a trial balance follows their identification number from the chart of accounts: asset, liability, equity, revenue, and expense accounts.

Example: If a credit to Unearned Revenue was incorrectly posted from the journal as a credit to the Revenue ledger account, would the ledger still balance? Would the financial statements be correct? *Answers:* The ledger would balance, but liabilities would be understated, equity would be overstated, and income would be overstated (all because of overstated revenues).

Searching for Errors   If the trial balance does not balance (when its columns are not equal), the error(s) must be found and corrected. An efficient way to search for an error is to check the journalizing, posting, and trial balance preparation in *reverse order.* Step 1 is to verify that the trial balance columns are correctly added. If step 1 fails to find the error, step 2 is to verify that account balances are accurately entered from the ledger. Step 3 is to see whether a debit (or credit) balance is mistakenly listed in the trial balance as a credit (or debit). A clue to this error is when the difference between total debits and total credits equals twice the amount of the incorrect account balance. If the error is still undiscovered, step 4 is to recompute each account balance in the ledger. Step 5 is to verify that each journal entry is properly posted. Step 6 is to verify that the original journal entry has equal debits and credits. At this point, the errors should be uncovered.

▶ **Decision** Insight

Accounting Quality   Recording valid and accurate transactions enhances the quality of financial statements. The graph here shows the percentage of employees in information technology who report observing specific types of misconduct *and* the increased risk of such misconduct in recent years (Source: KPMG 2013). ■

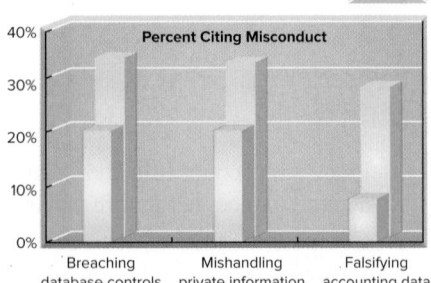

Percent Citing Misconduct

Years: ☐ 2013 ☐ 2009

Breaching database controls   Mishandling private information   Falsifying accounting data

Financial Statements Prepared from Trial Balance

Financial Statements across Time   How financial statements are linked in time is illustrated in Exhibit 2.15. A balance sheet reports on an organization's financial position at a *point in time*. The income statement, statement of owner's equity, and statement of cash flows report on financial performance over a *period of time*. The three statements in the middle column of Exhibit 2.15 explain how financial position changes from the beginning to the end of a reporting period.

Preparers and users (including regulatory agencies) determine the length of the reporting period. A one-year, or annual, reporting period is common, as are semiannual, quarterly, and monthly periods. The one-year reporting period is known as the *accounting,* or *fiscal, year.* Businesses whose accounting year begins on January 1 and ends on December 31 are known as *calendar-year* companies. **Google** is a calendar-year company. Many companies choose a fiscal year ending on a date other than December 31. **Apple** is a *noncalendar-year* company, as reflected in the headings of its September 26, 2015, year-end financial statements in Appendix A near the end of the book.

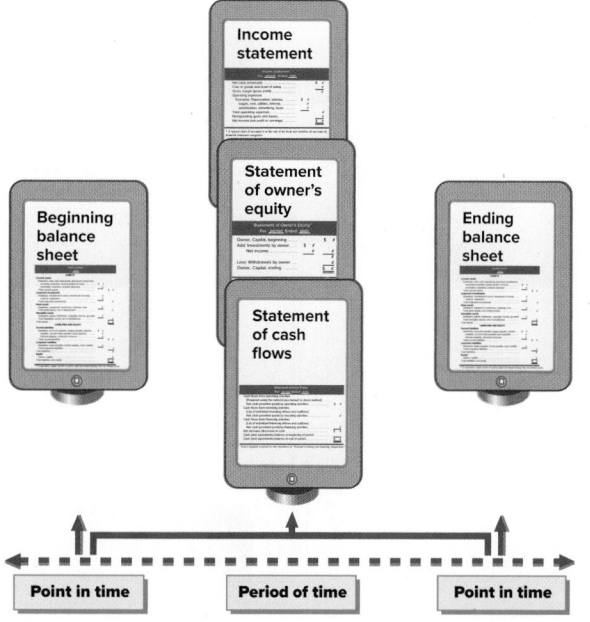

EXHIBIT 2.15

Links between Financial Statements across Time

Point: A statement's heading lists the 3 W's: **W**ho—name of organization, **W**hat—name of statement, **W**hen—statement's point in time or period of time.

Financial Statement Preparation   This section shows how to prepare *financial statements* from the trial balance. (These statements differ from those in Chapter 1 because of several additional transactions. These statements are also more precisely called *unadjusted statements* because we need to make some further accounting adjustments described in Chapter 3.)

P3

Prepare financial statements from business transactions.

Income Statement   An income statement reports revenues earned less expenses incurred by a business over a period of time. FastForward's income statement for December is shown at the top of Exhibit 2.16. Information about revenues and expenses is taken from the trial balance in Exhibit 2.14. Net income of $3,395 is reported at the bottom of the statement. Owner investments and withdrawals are *not* part of income.

Point: An income statement is also called an *earnings statement, a statement of operations,* or a *P&L* (profit and loss) *statement.* A balance sheet is also called a *statement of financial position.*

Statement of Owner's Equity   The statement of owner's equity reports how equity changes over the reporting period. FastForward's statement of owner's equity is the second report in Exhibit 2.16. It shows the $30,000 owner investment, the $3,395 of net income, the $200 withdrawal, and the $33,195 end-of-period (capital) balance. (The beginning balance in the statement of owner's equity is rarely zero; an exception is for the first period of operations. The beginning capital balance in January 2018 is $33,195, which is December 2017's ending balance.)

Point: Revenues and expenses are not reported in detail in the statement of owner's equity. Instead, their effects are reflected through net income.

Balance Sheet   The balance sheet reports the financial position of a company at a point in time, usually at the end of a month, quarter, or year. FastForward's balance sheet is the third report in Exhibit 2.16. This statement refers to financial condition at the close of business on December 31. The left side of the balance sheet lists its assets: cash, supplies, prepaid insurance, and equipment. The upper right side of the balance sheet shows that it owes $6,200 to creditors and $3,000 in services to customers who paid in advance. The equity section shows an ending balance of $33,195. Note the link between the ending balance of the statement of owner's equity and the capital balance. (Recall that this presentation of the balance sheet is called the *account form:* assets on the left and liabilities and equity on the right. Another presentation is the *report form:* assets on top, followed by liabilities and then equity. Either presentation is acceptable.)

EXHIBIT 2.16

Financial Statements Prepared from Trial Balance

FASTFORWARD
Trial Balance
December 31, 2017

	Debit	Credit
Cash	$ 4,275	
Accounts receivable	0	
Supplies	9,720	
Prepaid insurance	2,400	
Equipment	26,000	
Accounts payable		$ 6,200
Unearned consulting revenue		3,000
C. Taylor, Capital		30,000
C. Taylor, Withdrawals	200	
Consulting revenue		5,800
Rental revenue		300
Salaries expense	1,400	
Rent expense	1,000	
Utilities expense	305	
Totals	$45,300	$45,300

Each account on the trial balance is either an asset (to balance sheet), liability (to balance sheet), or equity (to income statement or to statement of equity).

FASTFORWARD
Income Statement
For Month Ended December 31, 2017

Revenues		
Consulting revenue ($4,200 + $1,600)	$ 5,800	
Rental revenue	300	
Total revenues		$ 6,100
Expenses		
Salaries expense	1,400	
Rent expense	1,000	
Utilities expense	305	
Total expenses		2,705
Net income		$ 3,395

FASTFORWARD
Statement of Owner's Equity
For Month Ended December 31, 2017

C. Taylor, Capital, December 1, 2017		$ 0
Plus: Investments by owner	$30,000	
Net income	3,395	33,395
		33,395
Less: Withdrawals by owner		200
C. Taylor, Capital, December 31, 2017		$33,195

FASTFORWARD
Balance Sheet
December 31, 2017

Assets		Liabilities	
Cash	$ 4,275	Accounts payable	$ 6,200
Supplies	9,720	Unearned consult. revenue	3,000
Prepaid insurance	2,400	Total liabilities	9,200
Equipment	26,000	**Equity**	
		C. Taylor, Capital	33,195
Total assets	$42,395	Total liabilities and equity	$ 42,395

Point: Arrow lines show how the statements are linked.

Point: To *foot* a column of numbers is to add them.

Decision Maker

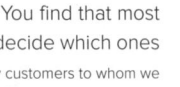

Entrepreneur   You open a wholesale business selling entertainment equipment to retail outlets. You find that most of your customers demand to buy on credit. How can you use the balance sheets of customers to decide which ones to extend credit to? ■   [*Answer:* We can use the accounting equation (Assets = Liabilities + Equity) to help us identify risky customers to whom we would likely not want to extend credit. A balance sheet provides amounts for each of these key components. The lower a customer's equity is relative to liabilities, the less likely you would be to extend credit. A low equity means the business has little value that does not already have creditor claims to it.]

Presentation Issues   Dollar signs are not used in journals and ledgers. They do appear in financial statements and other reports such as trial balances. The usual practice is to put dollar signs beside only the first and last numbers in a column. **Apple**'s financial statements in Appendix A show this. When amounts are entered in a journal, ledger, or trial balance, commas are optional to indicate thousands, millions, and so forth. However, commas are always used in financial statements. Companies also commonly round amounts in reports to the nearest dollar, or even to a higher level. Apple, like many companies, rounds its financial statement amounts to the nearest million. This decision is based on the impact of rounding for users' decisions.

Point: The terms "Debit" and "Credit" do not appear on financial statements.

IFRS

IFRS requires that companies report the following four basic financial statements with explanatory notes. IFRS does not prescribe specific formats, and comparative information is required for the preceding period only.

- Balance sheet
- Income statement
- Statement of changes in equity (or statement of recognized revenue and expense)
- Statement of cash flows ■

Prepare a trial balance for **Apple** using the following condensed data from its fiscal year ended September 26, 2015 ($ in millions).

NEED-TO-KNOW 2-4

Preparing Trial Balance

P2

APPLE

Owner, Capital	$111,547	Owner, Withdrawals	$ 45,586
Accounts payable	35,490	Investments and other assets	230,039
Other liabilities	135,634	Land and equipment	22,471
Cost of sales (and other expenses)	140,089	Selling and other expense	40,232
Cash	21,120	Accounts receivable	16,849
Revenues	233,715		

Solution ($ in millions)

APPLE Trial Balance September 26, 2015		
	Debit	**Credit**
Cash	$ 21,120	
Accounts receivable	16,849	
Land and equipment	22,471	
Investments and other assets	230,039	
Accounts payable		$ 35,490
Other liabilities		135,634
Owner, Capital		111,547
Owner, Withdrawals	45,586	
Revenues		233,715
Cost of sales and other expenses	140,089	
Selling and other expense	40,232	
Totals	$516,386	$516,386

Do More: E 2-8, E 2-10

SUSTAINABILITY AND ACCOUNTING

Catherine Mahugu, from this chapter's opening feature, uses accounting to track her revenues and expenses. She insists that accounting sustains her business by identifying and monitoring successful activities. Her business, **Soko**, partners with **Pencils of Promise** to fund childhood education in Ghana.

To sustain this partnership, Soko artisans designed a custom set of fashionable brass jewelry for an education project in Ghana. When a customer purchases this jewelry, 20% of the purchase price is accounted for separately and assigned to that project. Soko hopes to participate in similar sustainable projects in the future.

Soko's artisans create handmade goods out of locally sourced, recycled, and upcycled materials. Soko says that its accounting system helps with financial and production transparency. Further, its accounting system is set up to "connect mobile-enabled artisans from developing countries directly to brands, retailers, and online customers around the world." Soko's accounting system can work with artisans "even if they lack access to the Internet, a computer, or a bank account." This cuts logistical costs and increases artisan profits, which is sustainable.

Courtesy of Soko, Inc.

Decision Analysis    Debt Ratio

A2 _____
Compute the debt ratio and describe its use in analyzing financial condition.

An important business objective is gathering information to help assess a company's risk of failing to pay its debts. Companies finance their assets with either liabilities or equity. A company that finances a relatively large portion of its assets with liabilities is said to have higher *financial leverage*. Higher financial leverage involves greater risk because liabilities must be repaid and often require regular interest payments (equity financing does not). One measure of the risk associated with liabilities is the **debt ratio** as defined in Exhibit 2.17.

EXHIBIT 2.17

Debt Ratio

$$\text{Debt ratio} = \frac{\text{Total liabilities}}{\text{Total assets}}$$

Point: Compare the equity amount to the liability amount to assess the extent of owner versus non-owner financing.

To apply the debt ratio, let's look at **Skechers**'s liabilities and assets. Skechers designs, markets, and sells footwear for men, women, and children. Exhibit 2.18 reports the company's debt ratio at each year-end from 2011 to 2015.

EXHIBIT 2.18

Computation and Analysis of Debt Ratio

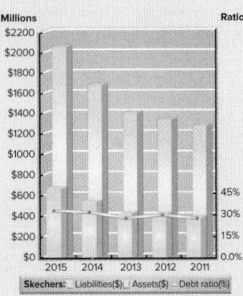

$ millions	2015	2014	2013	2012	2011
Total liabilities...............	$ 672	$ 541	$ 429	$ 421	$ 389
Total assets.................	$2,047	$1,675	$1,409	$1,340	$1,282
Debt ratio..................	0.33	0.32	0.30	0.31	0.30
Industry debt ratio	0.49	0.49	0.47	0.46	0.47

Skechers's debt ratio ranges from a low of 0.30 to a high of 0.33—also, see graph in margin. Its ratio is lower than the industry norm, suggesting a lower than average risk from financial leverage. So, is financial leverage good or bad for Skechers? The answer: If Skechers is making more money with this debt than it is paying the lenders, then it is successfully borrowing money to make more money. A company's use of debt can quickly turn unprofitable if its return from that money drops below the rate it is paying lenders.

 Decision Maker ──────────────────────────

Investor   You consider buying stock in **Converse**. As part of your analysis, you compute the company's debt ratio for 2014, 2015, and 2016 as: 0.35, 0.74, and 0.94, respectively. Based on the debt ratio, is Converse a low-risk investment? Has the risk of buying Converse stock changed over this period? (The industry debt ratio averages 0.40.) ■
[*Answer:* The debt ratio suggests that Converse's stock is of higher risk than normal and that this risk is rising. The average industry ratio of 0.40 further supports this conclusion. The 2016 debt ratio for Converse is twice the industry norm. Also, a debt ratio approaching 1.0 indicates little to no equity.]

NEED-TO-KNOW 2-5

COMPREHENSIVE

(This problem extends Need-To-Know 1-6 from Chapter 1.) After several months of planning, Jasmine Worthy started a haircutting business called Expressions. The following events occurred during its first month.

a. On August 1, Worthy invested $3,000 cash and $15,000 of equipment in Expressions.
b. On August 2, Expressions paid $600 cash for furniture for the shop.
c. On August 3, Expressions paid $500 cash to rent space in a strip mall for August.
d. On August 4, Expressions purchased $1,200 of equipment on credit for the shop (recorded as accounts payable).
e. On August 5, Expressions opened for business. Cash received from haircutting services in the first week and a half of business (ended August 15) was $825.
f. On August 15, Expressions provided $100 of haircutting services on account.
g. On August 17, Expressions received a $100 check for services previously rendered on account.
h. On August 17, Expressions paid $125 to an assistant for hours worked for the grand opening.
i. Cash received from services provided during the second half of August was $930.
j. On August 31, Expressions paid $400 cash toward the account payable entered into on August 4.
k. On August 31, Worthy made a $900 cash withdrawal from the company for personal use.

Required

1. Open the following ledger accounts in balance column format (account numbers are in parentheses): Cash (101); Accounts Receivable (102); Furniture (161); Store Equipment (165); Accounts Payable (201); J. Worthy, Capital (301); J. Worthy, Withdrawals (302); Haircutting Services Revenue (403); Wages Expense (623); and Rent Expense (640). Prepare general journal entries for the transactions.

2. Post the journal entries from part (1) to the ledger accounts.

3. Prepare a trial balance as of August 31.

4. Prepare an income statement for August.

5. Prepare a statement of owner's equity for August.

6. Prepare a balance sheet as of August 31.

7. Determine the debt ratio as of August 31.

Extended Analysis

8. In the coming months, Expressions will experience a greater variety of business transactions. Identify which accounts are debited and which are credited for the following transactions. (*Hint:* We must use some accounts not opened in part 1.)

   a. Purchase supplies with cash.

   b. Pay cash for future insurance coverage.

   c. Receive cash for services to be provided in the future.

   d. Purchase supplies on account.

PLANNING THE SOLUTION

- Analyze each transaction and use the debit and credit rules to prepare a journal entry for each.
- Post each debit and each credit from journal entries to their ledger accounts and cross-reference each amount in the posting reference (PR) columns of the journal and ledger.
- Calculate each account balance and list the accounts with their balances on a trial balance.
- Verify that total debits in the trial balance equal total credits.
- To prepare the income statement, identify revenues and expenses. List those items on the statement, compute the difference, and label the result as *net income* or *net loss*.
- Use information in the ledger to prepare the statement of owner's equity.
- Use information in the ledger to prepare the balance sheet.
- Calculate the debt ratio by dividing total liabilities by total assets.
- Analyze the future transactions to identify the accounts affected and apply debit and credit rules.

SOLUTION

1. General journal entries:

General Journal					_ □ X
					Page 1
Date	**Account Titles and Explanation**		**PR**	**Debit**	**Credit**
Aug. 1	Cash		101	3,000	
	Store Equipment		165	15,000	
	J. Worthy, Capital		301		18,000
	Owner's investment.				
2	Furniture		161	600	
	Cash		101		600
	Purchased furniture for cash.				
3	Rent Expense		640	500	
	Cash		101		500
	Paid rent for August.				
4	Store Equipment		165	1,200	
	Accounts Payable		201		1,200
	Purchased additional equipment on credit.				
15	Cash		101	825	
	Haircutting Services Revenue		403		825
	Cash receipts from first half of August.				

[continued on next page]

[continued from previous page]

15	Accounts Receivable	102	100	
	Haircutting Services Revenue	403		100
	Record revenue for services provided on account.			
17	Cash	101	100	
	Accounts Receivable....................................	102		100
	Record cash received as payment on account.			
17	Wages Expense	623	125	
	Cash..	101		125
	Paid wages to assistant.			
31	Cash	101	930	
	Haircutting Services Revenue	403		930
	Cash receipts from second half of August.			
31	Accounts Payable...	201	400	
	Cash..	101		400
	Paid cash toward accounts payable.			
31	J. Worthy, Withdrawals...................................	302	900	
	Cash..	101		900
	Cash withdrawal by owner.			

2. Post journal entries from part 1 to the ledger accounts:

General Ledger

Cash — Account No. 101

Date		PR	Debit	Credit	Balance
Aug.	1	G1	3,000		3,000
	2	G1		600	2,400
	3	G1		500	1,900
	15	G1	825		2,725
	17	G1	100		2,825
	17	G1		125	2,700
	31	G1	930		3,630
	31	G1		400	3,230
	31	G1		900	2,330

Accounts Receivable — Account No. 102

Date		PR	Debit	Credit	Balance
Aug.	15	G1	100		100
	17	G1		100	0

Furniture — Account No. 161

Date		PR	Debit	Credit	Balance
Aug.	2	G1	600		600

Store Equipment — Account No. 165

Date		PR	Debit	Credit	Balance
Aug.	1	G1	15,000		15,000
	4	G1	1,200		16,200

Accounts Payable — Account No. 201

Date		PR	Debit	Credit	Balance
Aug.	4	G1		1,200	1,200
	31	G1	400		800

J. Worthy, Capital — Account No. 301

Date		PR	Debit	Credit	Balance
Aug.	1	G1		18,000	18,000

J. Worthy, Withdrawals — Account No. 302

Date		PR	Debit	Credit	Balance
Aug.	31	G1	900		900

Haircutting Services — Revenue Account No. 403

Date		PR	Debit	Credit	Balance
Aug.	15	G1		825	825
	15	G1		100	925
	31	G1		930	1,855

Wages Expense — Account No. 623

Date		PR	Debit	Credit	Balance
Aug.	17	G1	125		125

Rent Expense — Account No. 640

Date		PR	Debit	Credit	Balance
Aug.	3	G1	500		500

3. Prepare a trial balance from the ledger:

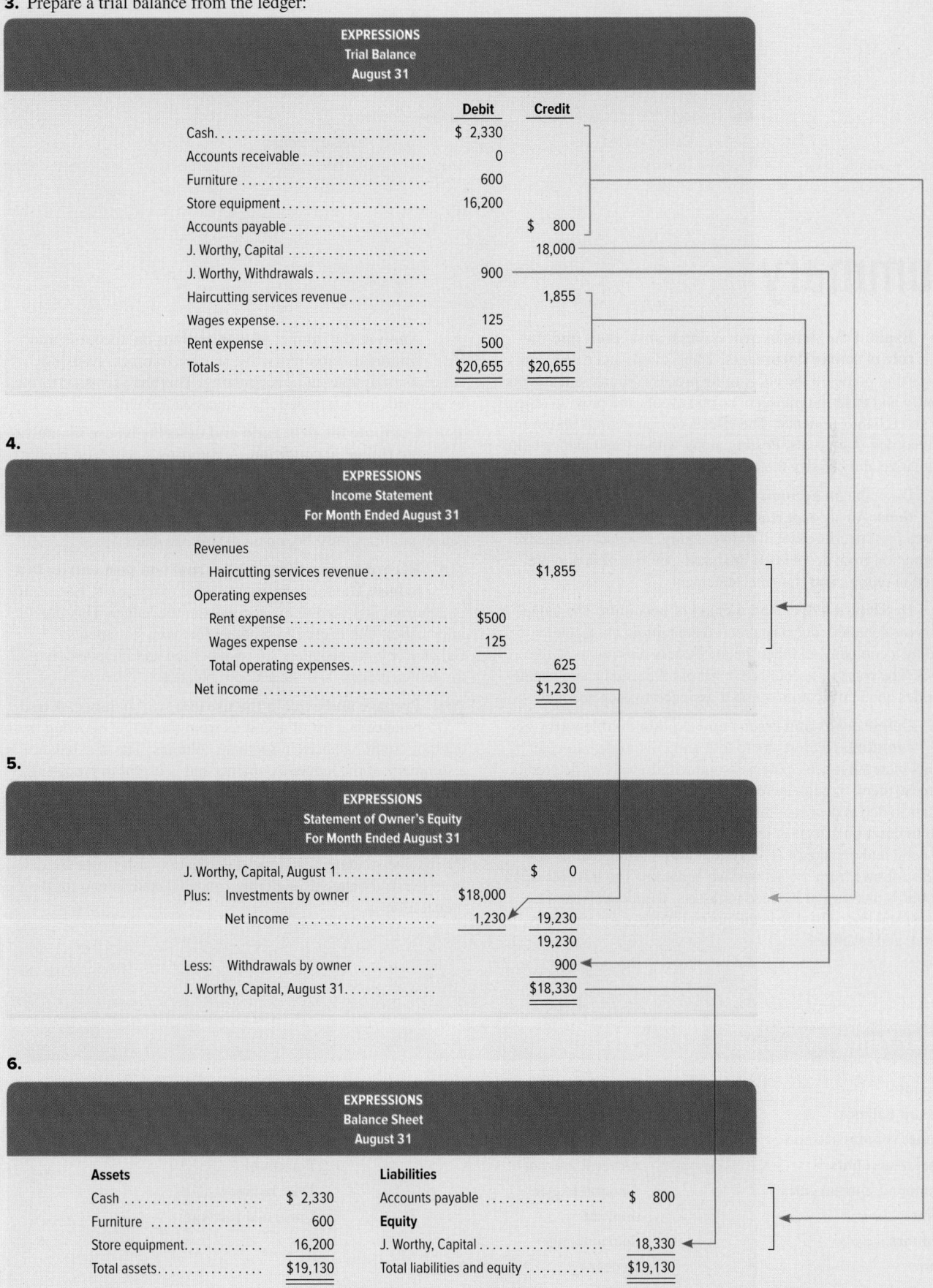

EXPRESSIONS
Trial Balance
August 31

	Debit	Credit
Cash...............................	$ 2,330	
Accounts receivable...................	0	
Furniture............................	600	
Store equipment......................	16,200	
Accounts payable....................		$ 800
J. Worthy, Capital....................		18,000
J. Worthy, Withdrawals................	900	
Haircutting services revenue...........		1,855
Wages expense......................	125	
Rent expense.......................	500	
Totals..............................	$20,655	$20,655

4.

EXPRESSIONS
Income Statement
For Month Ended August 31

Revenues		
Haircutting services revenue............		$1,855
Operating expenses		
Rent expense........................	$500	
Wages expense.....................	125	
Total operating expenses..............		625
Net income...........................		$1,230

5.

EXPRESSIONS
Statement of Owner's Equity
For Month Ended August 31

J. Worthy, Capital, August 1...............		$ 0
Plus: Investments by owner............	$18,000	
Net income.....................	1,230	19,230
		19,230
Less: Withdrawals by owner............		900
J. Worthy, Capital, August 31..............		$18,330

6.

EXPRESSIONS
Balance Sheet
August 31

Assets		Liabilities	
Cash.....................	$ 2,330	Accounts payable..................	$ 800
Furniture.................	600	**Equity**	
Store equipment...........	16,200	J. Worthy, Capital..................	18,330
Total assets...............	$19,130	Total liabilities and equity...........	$19,130

7. Debt ratio $= \dfrac{\text{Total liabilities}}{\text{Total assets}} = \dfrac{\$800}{\$19,130} = \textbf{4.18\%}$

8a. Supplies *debited*
        Cash *credited*

8b. Prepaid Insurance *debited*
        Cash *credited*

8c. Cash *debited*
        Unearned Services Revenue *credited*

8d. Supplies *debited*
        Accounts Payable *credited*

Summary

C1   **Explain the steps in processing transactions and the role of source documents.** Transactions and events are the starting points in the accounting process. Source documents identify and describe transactions and events and provide objective and reliable evidence. The effects of transactions and events are recorded in journals. Posting along with a trial balance helps summarize and classify these effects.

C2   **Describe an account and its use in recording transactions.** An account is a detailed record of increases and decreases in a specific asset, liability, equity, revenue, or expense. Information from accounts is analyzed, summarized, and presented in reports and financial statements.

C3   **Describe a ledger and a chart of accounts.** The ledger (or general ledger) is a record containing all accounts used by a company and their balances. It is referred to as the *books*. The chart of accounts is a list of all accounts and usually includes an identification number assigned to each account.

C4   **Define *debits* and *credits* and explain double-entry accounting.** *Debit* refers to left, and *credit* refers to right. Debits increase assets, expenses, and withdrawals while credits decrease them. Credits increase liabilities, owner capital, and revenues; debits decrease them. Double-entry accounting means each transaction affects at least two accounts and has at least one debit and one credit. The system for recording debits and credits follows from the accounting equation. The left side of an account is the normal balance for assets, withdrawals, and expenses, and the right side is the normal balance for liabilities, capital, and revenues.

A1   **Analyze the impact of transactions on accounts and financial statements.** We analyze transactions using concepts of double-entry accounting. This analysis is performed by determining a transaction's effects on accounts.

A2   **Compute the debt ratio and describe its use in analyzing financial condition.** A company's debt ratio is computed as total liabilities divided by total assets. It reveals how much of the assets are financed by creditor (nonowner) financing. The higher this ratio, the more risk a company faces because liabilities must be repaid at specific dates.

P1   **Record transactions in a journal and post entries to a ledger.** Transactions are recorded in a journal. Each entry in a journal is posted to the accounts in the ledger. This provides information that is used to produce financial statements. Balance column accounts are widely used and include columns for debits, credits, and the account balance.

P2   **Prepare and explain the use of a trial balance.** A trial balance is a list of accounts from the ledger showing their debit or credit balances in separate columns. The trial balance is a summary of the ledger's contents and is useful in preparing financial statements and in revealing recordkeeping errors.

P3   **Prepare financial statements from business transactions.** The balance sheet, the statement of owner's equity, the income statement, and the statement of cash flows use data from the trial balance (and other financial statements) for their preparation.

Key Terms

Account	Debt ratio	Posting
Account balance	Debtors	Posting reference (PR) column
Balance column account	Double-entry accounting	Source documents
Chart of accounts	General journal	T-account
Compound journal entry	General ledger	Trial balance
Credit	Journal	Unearned revenue
Creditors	Journalizing	
Debit	Ledger	

Multiple Choice Quiz

1. Amalia Company received its utility bill for the current period of $700 and immediately paid it. Its journal entry to record this transaction includes a
   a. Credit to Utility Expense for $700.
   b. Debit to Utility Expense for $700.
   c. Debit to Accounts Payable for $700.
   d. Debit to Cash for $700.
   e. Credit to capital for $700.

2. On May 1, Mattingly Lawn Service collected $2,500 cash from a customer in advance of five months of lawn service. Mattingly's journal entry to record this transaction includes a
   a. Credit to Unearned Lawn Service Fees for $2,500.
   b. Debit to Lawn Service Fees Earned for $2,500.
   c. Credit to Cash for $2,500.
   d. Debit to Unearned Lawn Service Fees for $2,500.
   e. Credit to capital for $2,500.

3. Liang Shue contributed $250,000 cash and land worth $500,000 to open his new business, Shue Consulting. Which of the following journal entries does Shue Consulting make to record this transaction?
   a. Cash Assets   750,000
         L. Shue, Capital   750,000
   b. L. Shue, Capital   750,000
         Assets   750,000

   c. Cash   250,000
      Land   500,000
         L. Shue, Capital   750,000
   d. L. Shue, Capital   750,000
         Cash   250,000
         Land   500,000

4. A trial balance prepared at year-end shows total credits exceed total debits by $765. This discrepancy could have been caused by
   a. An error in the general journal where a $765 increase in Accounts Payable was recorded as a $765 decrease in Accounts Payable.
   b. The ledger balance for Accounts Payable of $7,650 being entered in the trial balance as $765.
   c. A general journal error where a $765 increase in Accounts Receivable was recorded as a $765 increase in Cash.
   d. The ledger balance of $850 in Accounts Receivable was entered in the trial balance as $85.
   e. An error in recording a $765 increase in Cash as a credit.

5. Bonaventure Company has total assets of $1,000,000, liabilities of $400,000, and equity of $600,000. What is its debt ratio (rounded to a whole percent)?
   a. 250%   c. 67%   e. 40%
   b. 167%   d. 150%

ANSWERS TO MULTIPLE CHOICE QUIZ

1. b; debit Utility Expense for $700, and credit Cash for $700.
2. a; debit Cash for $2,500, and credit Unearned Lawn Service Fees for $2,500.
3. c; debit Cash for $250,000, debit Land for $500,000, and credit L. Shue, Capital for $750,000.

4. d
5. e; Debt ratio = $400,000/$1,000,000 = 40%

Ⓘ Icon denotes assignments that involve decision making.

Discussion Questions

1. Provide the names of two (a) asset accounts, (b) liability accounts, and (c) equity accounts.
2. What is the difference between a note payable and an account payable?
3. Ⓘ Discuss the steps in processing business transactions.
4. What kinds of transactions can be recorded in a general journal?
5. Are debits or credits typically listed first in general journal entries? Are the debits or the credits indented?
6. Should a transaction be recorded first in a journal or the ledger? Why?

7. If assets are valuable resources and asset accounts have debit balances, why do expense accounts also have debit balances?
8. Ⓘ Why does the recordkeeper prepare a trial balance?
9. If an incorrect amount is journalized and posted to the accounts, how should the error be corrected?
10. Identify the four financial statements of a business.
11. Ⓘ What information is reported in a balance sheet?
12. Ⓘ What information is reported in an income statement?
13. Ⓘ Why does the user of an income statement need to know the time period that it covers?

14. Define (*a*) *assets,* (*b*) *liabilities,* (*c*) *equity,* and (*d*) *net assets.*

15. Which financial statement is sometimes called the *statement of financial position?*

16. 📱 Review the **Apple** balance sheet in **APPLE** Appendix A. Identify three accounts on its balance sheet that carry debit balances and three accounts on its balance sheet that carry credit balances.

17. Review the **Google** balance sheet in Appendix A. Identify an asset with the **GOOGLE** word *receivable* in its account title and a liability with the word *payable* in its account title.

18. Review the **Samsung** balance sheet in Appendix A. Identify three current lia- **Samsung** bilities and three noncurrent liabilities in its balance sheet.

■ connect

QUICK STUDY

QS 2-1

Identifying source documents　**C1**

Identify the items from the following list that are likely to serve as source documents.

a. Sales ticket
b. Trial balance
c. Balance sheet

d. Telephone bill
e. Invoice from supplier
f. Company revenue account

g. Income statement
h. Bank statement
i. Prepaid insurance

QS 2-2

Identifying financial statement accounts

C2

Classify each of the following accounts as an asset (A), liability (L), or equity (EQ) account.

a. Cash
b. Prepaid Rent
c. Office Supplies

d. Prepaid Insurance
e. Office Equipment
f. Owner, Capital

g. Accounts Payable
h. Unearned Rent Revenue
i. Owner, Withdrawals

QS 2-3

Reading a chart of accounts

C3

A chart of accounts is a list of all ledger accounts and an identification number for each. One example of a chart of accounts is near the end of the book on pages CA and CA-1. Using that chart, identify the following accounts as either an asset (A), liability (L), equity (EQ), revenue (R), or expense (E) account, along with its identification number.

a. Advertising Expense
b. Rent Revenue
c. Rent Receivable

d. Patents
e. Rent Payable
f. Furniture

g. Notes Payable
h. Owner, Capital
i. Utilities Expense

QS 2-4

Identifying normal balance

C4

Identify the normal balance (debit or credit) for each of the following accounts.

a. Fees Earned (Revenues)
b. Office Supplies
c. Owner, Withdrawals

d. Wages Expense
e. Accounts Receivable
f. Prepaid Rent

g. Wages Payable
h. Building
i. Owner, Capital

QS 2-5

Linking debit or credit with normal balance

C4

Indicate whether a debit or credit *decreases* the normal balance of each of the following accounts.

a. Interest Payable
b. Service Revenue
c. Salaries Expense
d. Accounts Receivable

e. Owner, Capital
f. Prepaid Insurance
g. Buildings
h. Interest Revenue

i. Owner, Withdrawals
j. Unearned Revenue
k. Accounts Payable
l. Land

QS 2-6

Analyzing transactions and preparing journal entries

P1

For each transaction, (1) analyze the transaction using the accounting equation, (2) record the transaction in journal entry form, and (3) post the entry using T-accounts to represent ledger accounts. Use the following (partial) chart of accounts—account numbers in parentheses: Cash (101); Accounts Receivable (106); Office Supplies (124); Trucks (153); Equipment (167); Accounts Payable (201); Unearned Landscaping Revenue (236); D. Tyler, Capital (301); D. Tyler, Withdrawals (302); Landscaping Revenue (403); Wages Expense (601), and Landscaping Expense (696).

a. On May 15, DeShawn Tyler opens a landscaping company called Elegant Lawns by investing $7,000 in cash along with equipment having a $3,000 value.

b. On May 21, Elegant Lawns purchases office supplies on credit for $500.

c. On May 25, Elegant Lawns receives $4,000 cash for performing landscaping services.

d. On May 30, Elegant Lawns receives $1,000 cash in advance of providing landscaping services to a customer.

Identify whether a debit or credit results in the indicated change for each of the following accounts.

a. To increase Land
b. To decrease Cash
c. To increase Fees Earned (Revenues)
d. To increase Office Expense
e. To decrease Unearned Revenue

f. To decrease Prepaid Rent
g. To increase Notes Payable
h. To decrease Accounts Receivable
i. To increase Owner, Capital
j. To increase Store Equipment

QS 2-7
Analyzing debit or credit by account

A1

A trial balance has total debits of $20,000 and total credits of $24,500. Which one of the following errors would create this imbalance? Explain.

a. A $2,250 debit to Utilities Expense in a journal entry was incorrectly posted to the ledger as a $2,250 credit, leaving the Utilities Expense account with a $3,000 debit balance.

b. A $4,500 debit to Salaries Expense in a journal entry was incorrectly posted to the ledger as a $4,500 credit, leaving the Salaries Expense account with a $750 debit balance.

c. A $2,250 credit to Consulting Fees Earned (Revenues) in a journal entry was incorrectly posted to the ledger as a $2,250 debit, leaving the Consulting Fees Earned account with a $6,300 credit balance.

d. A $2,250 debit posting to Accounts Receivable was posted mistakenly to Land.

e. A $4,500 debit posting to Equipment was posted mistakenly to Cash.

f. An entry debiting Cash and crediting Accounts Payable for $4,500 was mistakenly not posted.

QS 2-8
Identifying a posting error

P2

Indicate the financial statement on which each of the following items appears. Use I for income statement, E for statement of owner's equity, and B for balance sheet.

a. Services Revenue
b. Interest Payable
c. Accounts Receivable
d. Salaries Expense

e. Equipment
f. Prepaid Insurance
g. Buildings
h. Rental Revenue

i. Owner Withdrawals
j. Office Supplies
k. Interest Expense
l. Insurance Expense

QS 2-9
Classifying accounts in financial statements

P3

Determine the ending balance of each of the following T-accounts.

QS 2-10
Computing T-account balance

C4

a.

Cash	
100	50
300	60
20	

b.

Accounts Payable	
2,000	8,000
2,700	

c.

Supplies	
10,000	3,800
1,100	

d.

Accounts Receivable	
600	150
	150
	150
	100

e.

Wages Payable	
	700
700	

f.

Cash	
11,000	4,500
800	6,000
100	1,300

Answer each of the following questions related to international accounting standards.

a. What type of journal entry system is applied when accounting follows IFRS?

b. Identify the number and usual titles of the financial statements prepared under IFRS.

c. How do differences in accounting controls and enforcement impact accounting reports prepared across different countries?

QS 2-11
International accounting standards

C4

QS 2-12

Computing and using the debt ratio   A2

In a recent year's financial statements, **Home Depot** reported the following: Total liabilities = $30,624 million and Total assets = $39,946 million. Compute and interpret Home Depot's debt ratio (assume competitors average a 60.0% debt ratio).

EXERCISES

Exercise 2-1

Steps in analyzing and recording transactions   C1

Order the following steps in the accounting process that focus on analyzing and recording transactions.

_____ **a.** Prepare and analyze the trial balance.

_____ **b.** Analyze each transaction from source documents.

_____ **c.** Record relevant transactions in a journal.

_____ **d.** Post journal information to ledger accounts.

Exercise 2-2

Identifying and classifying accounts

C2

Enter the number for the item that best completes each of the descriptions below.

1. Asset   **3.** Account   **5.** Three

2. Equity   **4.** Liability

a. Balance sheet accounts are arranged into _____ general categories.

b. Owner, Capital and Owner, Withdrawals are examples of _____ accounts.

c. Accounts Payable, Unearned Revenue, and Note Payable are examples of _____ accounts.

d. Accounts Receivable, Prepaid Accounts, Supplies, and Land are examples of _____ accounts.

e. A(n) _____ is a record of increases and decreases in a specific asset, liability, equity, revenue, or expense item.

Exercise 2-3

Identifying a ledger and chart of accounts

C3

Enter the number for the item that best completes each of the descriptions below.

1. Chart   **2.** General ledger

a. A _____ of accounts is a list of all accounts a company uses.

b. The _____ is a record containing all accounts used by a company, including account balances.

Exercise 2-4

Identifying type and normal balances of accounts

C4

For each of the following (1) identify the type of account as an asset, liability, equity, revenue, or expense; (2) identify the normal balance of the account; and (3) enter *debit* (*Dr.*) or *credit* (*Cr.*) to identify the kind of entry that would increase the account balance.

a. Land	**e.** Accounts Receivable	**i.** Fees Earned
b. Cash	**f.** Owner, Withdrawals	**j.** Equipment
c. Legal Expense	**g.** License Fee Revenue	**k.** Notes Payable
d. Prepaid Insurance	**h.** Unearned Revenue	**l.** Owner, Capital

---

Exercise 2-5

Analyzing effects of transactions on accounts

A1

Groro Co. bills a client $62,000 for services provided and agrees to accept the following three items in full payment: (1) $10,000 cash, (2) computer equipment worth $80,000, and (3) to assume responsibility for a $28,000 note payable related to the computer equipment. The entry Groro makes to record this transaction includes which one or more of the following?

a. $28,000 increase in a liability account	**d.** $62,000 increase in an asset account
b. $10,000 increase in the Cash account	**e.** $62,000 increase in a revenue account
c. $10,000 increase in a revenue account	**f.** $62,000 increase in an equity account

---

Exercise 2-6

Analyzing account entries and balances

A1

Use the information in each of the following separate cases to calculate the unknown amount.

a. Corentine Co. had $152,000 of accounts payable on September 30 and $132,500 on October 31. Total purchases on account during October were $281,000. Determine how much cash was paid on accounts payable during October.

b. On September 30, Valerian Co. had a $102,500 balance in Accounts Receivable. During October, the company collected $102,890 from its credit customers. The October 31 balance in Accounts Receivable was $89,000. Determine the amount of sales on account that occurred in October.

c. During October, Alameda Company had $102,500 of cash receipts and $103,150 of cash disbursements. The October 31 Cash balance was $18,600. Determine how much cash the company had at the close of business on September 30.

Prepare general journal entries for the following transactions of a new company called Pose-for-Pics. Use the following (partial) chart of accounts: Cash; Office Supplies; Prepaid Insurance; Photography Equipment; M. Harris, Capital; Photography Fees Earned; and Utilities Expense.

Aug. 1 Madison Harris, the owner, invested $6,500 cash and $33,500 of photography equipment in the company.
     2 The company paid $2,100 cash for an insurance policy covering the next 24 months.
     5 The company purchased office supplies for $880 cash.
    20 The company received $3,331 cash in photography fees earned.
    31 The company paid $675 cash for August utilities.

Exercise 2-7
Preparing general journal entries

P1

Use the information in Exercise 2-7 to prepare a trial balance for Pose-for-Pics. Begin by opening these T-accounts: Cash; Office Supplies; Prepaid Insurance; Photography Equipment; M. Harris, Capital; Photography Fees Earned; and Utilities Expense. Then, (1) post the general journal entries to these T-accounts (which will serve as the ledger) and (2) prepare the August 31 trial balance.

Exercise 2-8
Preparing T-accounts (ledger) and a trial balance   P2

Prepare general journal entries to record the transactions below for Spade Company by using the following accounts: Cash; Accounts Receivable; Office Supplies; Office Equipment; Accounts Payable; K. Spade, Capital; K. Spade, Withdrawals; Fees Earned; and Rent Expense. Use the letters beside each transaction to identify entries. After recording the transactions, post them to T-accounts, which serves as the general ledger for this assignment. Determine the ending balance of each T-account.

a. Kacy Spade, owner, invested $100,750 cash in the company.

b. The company purchased office supplies for $1,250 cash.

c. The company purchased $10,050 of office equipment on credit.

d. The company received $15,500 cash as fees for services provided to a customer.

e. The company paid $10,050 cash to settle the payable for the office equipment purchased in transaction *c*.

f. The company billed a customer $2,700 as fees for services provided.

g. The company paid $1,225 cash for the monthly rent.

h. The company collected $1,125 cash as partial payment for the account receivable created in transaction *f*.

i. Kacy Spade withdrew $10,000 cash from the company for personal use.

Exercise 2-9
Recording effects of transactions in T-accounts

A1

Check   Cash ending balance, $94,850

After recording the transactions of Exercise 2-9 in T-accounts and calculating the balance of each account, prepare a trial balance. Use May 31, 2017, as its report date.

Exercise 2-10
Preparing a trial balance   P2

---

1. Prepare general journal entries for the following transactions of Valdez Services.

a. The company paid $2,000 cash for payment on a 6-month-old account payable for office supplies.

b. The company paid $1,200 cash for the just completed two-week salary of the receptionist.

c. The company paid $39,000 cash for equipment purchased.

d. The company paid $800 cash for this month's utilities.

e. Owner (B. Valdez) withdrew $4,500 cash from the company for personal use.

2. Transactions *a, c,* and *e* did not record an expense. Match each transaction (*a, c,* and *e*) with one of the following reasons for not recording an expense.

_____ This transaction is a distribution of cash to the owner. Even though equity decreased, that decrease did not occur in the process of providing goods or services to customers.

_____ This transaction decreased assets in settlement of a previously existing liability (equity did not change). Cash payment does not mean the same as using up assets (expense is recorded when assets are used).

_____ This transaction involves the purchase of an asset. The form of the company's assets changed, but total assets did not (and neither did equity).

Exercise 2-11
Analyzing and journalizing transactions involving cash payments

P1

---

1. Prepare general journal entries for the following transactions of Valdez Services.

a. Brina Valdez invested $20,000 cash in the company.

b. The company provided services to a client and immediately received $900 cash.

c. The company received $10,000 cash from a client in payment for services to be provided next year.

d. The company received $3,500 cash from a client in partial payment of accounts receivable.

e. The company borrowed $5,000 cash from the bank by signing a note payable.

Exercise 2-12
Analyzing and journalizing transactions involving receipt of cash

P1

Continued on next page . . .

2. Transactions *a, c, d,* and *e* did not yield revenue. Match each transaction (*a, c, d,* and *e*) with one of the following reasons for not recording revenue.

_____ This transaction changed the form of an asset from a receivable to cash. Total assets were not increased (revenue was recognized when the services were originally provided).

_____ This transaction brought in cash (increased assets), but it also increased a liability by the same amount (no goods or services were provided to generate revenue).

_____ This transaction brought in cash, but this is an owner investment.

_____ This transaction brought in cash, but it created a liability because the services have not yet been provided to the client.

Exercise 2-13

Interpreting and describing transactions from T-accounts

A1

Assume the following T-accounts reflect Belle Co.'s general ledger and its first seven transactions *a* through *g*, which are posted to them. Identify the explanation from 1 through 7 below that best describes each transaction *a* through *g* reflected in the T-accounts, and enter that letter in the blank space in front of each numbered explanation.

Cash			
(a)	6,000	(b)	4,800
(e)	4,500	(d)	800
		(f)	900
		(g)	3,400

Supplies	
(c)	900

Prepaid Insurance	
(b)	4,800

Equipment	
(a)	7,600
(g)	3,400

Web Servers	
(a)	12,000

Accounts Payable			
(f)	900	(c)	900

D. Belle, Capital		
	(a)	25,600

Services Revenue		
	(e)	4,500

Selling Expenses	
(d)	800

_____ **1.** The company paid $4,800 cash in advance for prepaid insurance coverage.

_____ **2.** D. Belle created a new business and invested $6,000 cash, $7,600 of equipment, and $12,000 in web servers.

_____ **3.** The company purchased $900 of supplies on account.

_____ **4.** The company received $4,500 cash for services provided.

_____ **5.** The company paid $900 cash toward accounts payable.

_____ **6.** The company paid $3,400 cash for equipment.

_____ **7.** The company paid $800 cash for selling expenses.

Exercise 2-14

Preparing general journal entries   P1

Use information from the T-accounts in Exercise 2-13 to prepare the general journal entries that were made for each of the seven transactions *a* through *g*.

Exercise 2-15

Computing net income

A1

A sole proprietorship had the following assets and liabilities at the beginning and end of this year.

	Assets	Liabilities
Beginning of the year............	$ 60,000	$20,000
End of the year.................	105,000	36,000

Determine the net income earned or net loss incurred by the business during the year for each of the following *separate* cases:

a. Owner made no investments in the business, and no withdrawals were made during the year.

b. Owner made no investments in the business but withdrew $1,250 cash per month for personal use.

c. Owner made no withdrawals during the year but did invest an additional $55,000 cash.

d. Owner withdrew $1,250 cash per month for personal use and invested an additional $35,000 cash.

Carmen Camry operates a consulting firm called Help Today, which began operations on August 1. On August 31, the company's records show the following accounts and amounts for the month of August. Use this information to prepare an August income statement for the business.

Exercise 2-16
Preparing an income statement
C3 P3

Cash	$25,360	C. Camry, Withdrawals	$ 6,000
Accounts receivable	22,360	Consulting fees earned	27,000
Office supplies	5,250	Rent expense	9,550
Land	44,000	Salaries expense	5,600
Office equipment	20,000	Telephone expense	860
Accounts payable	10,500	Miscellaneous expenses	520

Check Net income, $10,470

Use the information in Exercise 2-16 to prepare an August statement of owner's equity for Help Today. The owner's capital account balance at July 31 was $0, and the owner invested $102,000 cash in the company on August 1.

Exercise 2-17
Preparing a statement of owner's equity P3

Check End. Capital, $106,470

Use the information in Exercise 2-16 to prepare an August 31 balance sheet for Help Today. (*Hint*: Compute the owner's capital account balance as of August 31.)

Exercise 2-18
Preparing a balance sheet P3

Compute the missing amount for each of the following separate companies *a* through *d*.

Exercise 2-19
Analyzing changes in a company's equity

P3

	A	B	C	D	E
1		(a)	(b)	(c)	(d)
2	Equity, December 31, 2016	$ 0	$ 0	$ 0	$ 0
3	Owner investments during the year	110,000	?	87,000	210,000
4	Owner withdrawals during the year	?	(47,000)	(10,000)	(55,000)
5	Net income (loss) for the year	22,000	90,000	(4,000)	?
6	Equity, December 31, 2017	104,000	85,000	?	110,000
7					

Posting errors are identified in the following table. In column (1), enter the amount of the difference between the two trial balance columns (debit and credit) due to the error. In column (2), identify the trial balance column (debit or credit) with the larger amount if they are not equal. In column (3), identify the account(s) affected by the error. In column (4), indicate the amount by which the account(s) in column (3) is under- or overstated. Item (a) is completed as an example.

Exercise 2-20
Identifying effects of posting errors on the trial balance
A1 P2

	Description of Posting Error	(1) Difference between Debit and Credit Columns	(2) Column with the Larger Total	(3) Identify Account(s) Incorrectly Stated	(4) Amount That Account(s) Is Over- or Understated
a.	$3,600 debit to Rent Expense is posted as a $1,340 debit.	$2,260	Credit	Rent Expense	Rent Expense understated $2,260
b.	$6,500 credit to Cash is posted twice as two credits to Cash.				
c.	$10,900 debit to the Withdrawals account is debited to Owner's Capital.				
d.	$2,050 debit to Prepaid Insurance is posted as a debit to Insurance Expense.				
e.	$38,000 debit to Machinery is posted as a debit to Accounts Payable.				
f.	$5,850 credit to Services Revenue is posted as a $585 credit.				
g.	$1,390 debit to Store Supplies is not posted.				

Exercise 2-21

Analyzing a trial balance error

P1   P2

You are told the column totals in a trial balance are not equal. After careful analysis, you discover only one error. Specifically, a correctly journalized credit purchase of an automobile for $18,950 is posted from the journal to the ledger with an $18,950 debit to Automobiles and another $18,950 debit to Accounts Payable. The Automobiles account has a debit balance of $37,100 on the trial balance. (1) Answer each of the following questions and (2) compute the dollar amount of any misstatement for parts *a* through *d*.

   a. Is the Debit column total of the trial balance overstated, understated, or correctly stated?

   b. Is the Credit column total of the trial balance overstated, understated, or correctly stated?

   c. Is the Automobiles account balance overstated, understated, or correctly stated in the trial balance?

   d. Is the Accounts Payable account balance overstated, understated, or correctly stated in the trial balance?

   e. If the Debit column total of the trial balance is $200,000 before correcting the error, what is the total of the Credit column before correction?

Exercise 2-22

Interpreting the debt ratio and return on assets

A2

   a. Calculate the debt ratio and the return on assets using the year-end information for each of the following six separate companies ($ in thousands).

	A	B	C	D	E
1	Case	Assets	Liabilities	Average Assets	Net Income
2	Company 1	$90,500	$11,765	$100,000	$20,000
3	Company 2	64,000	46,720	40,000	3,800
4	Company 3	32,500	26,650	50,000	650
5	Company 4	147,000	55,860	200,000	21,000
6	Company 5	92,000	31,280	40,000	7,520
7	Company 6	104,500	52,250	80,000	12,000

   b. Of the six companies, which business relies most heavily on creditor financing?

   c. Of the six companies, which business relies most heavily on equity financing?

   d. Which two companies indicate the greatest risk (based on the debt ratio)?

   e. Which two companies earn the highest return on assets?

   f. Which one company would investors likely prefer based on the risk-return relation?

Exercise 2-23

Preparing a balance sheet following IFRS

P3

Heineken N.V., a global brewer based in the Netherlands, reports the following balance sheet accounts for the year ended December 31, 2015 (euros in millions). Prepare the balance sheet for this company as of December 31, 2015, following the usual IFRS format.

Current liabilities	€ 8,516	Noncurrent liabilities	€14,128
Current assets	5,914	Noncurrent assets	31,800
Total equity	15,070		

PROBLEM SET A

Problem 2-1A

Preparing and posting journal entries; preparing a trial balance

C3   C4   A1   P1   P2

Karla Tanner opened a web consulting business called Linkworks and completed the following transactions in its first month of operations.

April 1   Tanner invested $80,000 cash along with office equipment valued at $26,000 in the company.
       2   The company prepaid $9,000 cash for 12 months' rent for office space. (*Hint:* Debit Prepaid Rent for $9,000.)
       3   The company made credit purchases for $8,000 in office equipment and $3,600 in office supplies. Payment is due within 10 days.
       6   The company completed services for a client and immediately received $4,000 cash.
       9   The company completed a $6,000 project for a client, who must pay within 30 days.
      13   The company paid $11,600 cash to settle the account payable created on April 3.
      19   The company paid $2,400 cash for the premium on a 12-month insurance policy. (*Hint:* Debit Prepaid Insurance for $2,400.)
      22   The company received $4,400 cash as partial payment for the work completed on April 9.
      25   The company completed work for another client for $2,890 on credit.
      28   Tanner withdrew $5,500 cash from the company for personal use.
      29   The company purchased $600 of additional office supplies on credit.
      30   The company paid $435 cash for this month's utility bill.

Required

1. Prepare general journal entries to record these transactions (use account titles listed in part 2).
2. Open the following ledger accounts—their account numbers are in parentheses (use the balance column format): Cash (101); Accounts Receivable (106); Office Supplies (124); Prepaid Insurance (128); Prepaid Rent (131); Office Equipment (163); Accounts Payable (201); K. Tanner, Capital (301); K. Tanner, Withdrawals (302); Services Revenue (403); and Utilities Expense (690). Post journal entries from part 1 to the ledger accounts and enter the balance after each posting.
3. Prepare a trial balance as of April 30.

Check (2) Ending balances: Cash, $59,465; Accounts Receivable, $4,490; Accounts Payable, $600

(3) Total debits, $119,490

Aracel Engineering completed the following transactions in the month of June.

a. Jenna Aracel, the owner, invested $100,000 cash, office equipment with a value of $5,000, and $60,000 of drafting equipment to launch the company.

b. The company purchased land worth $49,000 for an office by paying $6,300 cash and signing a long-term note payable for $42,700.

c. The company purchased a portable building with $55,000 cash and moved it onto the land acquired in *b*.

d. The company paid $3,000 cash for the premium on an 18-month insurance policy.

e. The company completed and delivered a set of plans for a client and collected $6,200 cash.

f. The company purchased $20,000 of additional drafting equipment by paying $9,500 cash and signing a long-term note payable for $10,500.

g. The company completed $14,000 of engineering services for a client. This amount is to be received in 30 days.

h. The company purchased $1,150 of additional office equipment on credit.

i. The company completed engineering services for $22,000 on credit.

j. The company received a bill for rent of equipment that was used on a recently completed job. The $1,333 rent cost must be paid within 30 days.

k. The company collected $7,000 cash in partial payment from the client described in transaction *g*.

l. The company paid $1,200 cash for wages to a drafting assistant.

m. The company paid $1,150 cash to settle the account payable created in transaction *h*.

n. The company paid $925 cash for minor maintenance of its drafting equipment.

o. Jenna Aracel withdrew $9,480 cash from the company for personal use.

p. The company paid $1,200 cash for wages to a drafting assistant.

q. The company paid $2,500 cash for advertisements on the web during June.

Problem 2-2A
Preparing and posting journal entries; preparing a trial balance

C3 C4 A1 P1 P2

Required

1. Prepare general journal entries to record these transactions (use the account titles listed in part 2).
2. Open the following ledger accounts—their account numbers are in parentheses (use the balance column format): Cash (101); Accounts Receivable (106); Prepaid Insurance (108); Office Equipment (163); Drafting Equipment (164); Building (170); Land (172); Accounts Payable (201); Notes Payable (250); J. Aracel, Capital (301); J. Aracel, Withdrawals (302); Engineering Fees Earned (402); Wages Expense (601); Equipment Rental Expense (602); Advertising Expense (603); and Repairs Expense (604). Post the journal entries from part 1 to the accounts and enter the balance after each posting.
3. Prepare a trial balance as of the end of June.

Check (2) Ending balances: Cash, $22,945; Accounts Receivable, $29,000; Accounts Payable, $1,333

(3) Trial balance totals, $261,733

Denzel Brooks opened a web consulting business called Venture Consultants and completed the following transactions in March.

March 1 Brooks invested $150,000 cash along with $22,000 in office equipment in the company.
2 The company prepaid $6,000 cash for six months' rent for an office. (*Hint:* Debit Prepaid Rent for $6,000.)
3 The company made credit purchases of office equipment for $3,000 and office supplies for $1,200. Payment is due within 10 days.
6 The company completed services for a client and immediately received $4,000 cash.
9 The company completed a $7,500 project for a client, who must pay within 30 days.
12 The company paid $4,200 cash to settle the account payable created on March 3.
19 The company paid $5,000 cash for the premium on a 12-month insurance policy. (*Hint:* Debit Prepaid Insurance for $5,000.)

Problem 2-3A
Preparing and posting journal entries; preparing a trial balance

C3 C4 A1 P1 P2

22   The company received $3,500 cash as partial payment for the work completed on March 9.
25   The company completed work for another client for $3,820 on credit.
29   Brooks withdrew $5,100 cash from the company for personal use.
30   The company purchased $600 of additional office supplies on credit.
31   The company paid $500 cash for this month's utility bill.

Required

1. Prepare general journal entries to record these transactions (use the account titles listed in part 2).

Check   (2) Ending balances: Cash, $136,700; Accounts Receivable, $7,820; Accounts Payable, $600

(3) Total debits, $187,920

2. Open the following ledger accounts—their account numbers are in parentheses (use the balance column format): Cash (101); Accounts Receivable (106); Office Supplies (124); Prepaid Insurance (128); Prepaid Rent (131); Office Equipment (163); Accounts Payable (201); D. Brooks, Capital (301); D. Brooks, Withdrawals (302); Services Revenue (403); and Utilities Expense (690). Post the journal entries from part 1 to the ledger accounts and enter the balance after each posting.

3. Prepare a trial balance as of the end of March.

Problem 2-4A

Recording transactions; posting to ledger; preparing a trial balance

C3   A1   P1   P2

Business transactions completed by Hannah Venedict during the month of September are as follows.

a. Venedict invested $60,000 cash along with office equipment valued at $25,000 in a new sole proprietorship named HV Consulting.

b. The company purchased land valued at $40,000 and a building valued at $160,000. The purchase is paid with $30,000 cash and a long-term note payable for $170,000.

c. The company purchased $2,000 of office supplies on credit.

d. Venedict invested her personal automobile in the company. The automobile has a value of $16,500 and is to be used exclusively in the business.

e. The company purchased $5,600 of additional office equipment on credit.

f. The company paid $1,800 cash salary to an assistant.

g. The company provided services to a client and collected $8,000 cash.

h. The company paid $635 cash for this month's utilities.

i. The company paid $2,000 cash to settle the account payable created in transaction c.

j. The company purchased $20,300 of new office equipment by paying $20,300 cash.

k. The company completed $6,250 of services for a client, who must pay within 30 days.

l. The company paid $1,800 cash salary to an assistant.

m. The company received $4,000 cash in partial payment on the receivable created in transaction k.

n. Venedict withdrew $2,800 cash from the company for personal use.

Required

1. Prepare general journal entries to record these transactions (use account titles listed in part 2).

Check   (2) Ending balances: Cash, $12,665; Office Equipment, $50,900

(3) Trial balance totals, $291,350

2. Open the following ledger accounts—their account numbers are in parentheses (use the balance column format): Cash (101); Accounts Receivable (106); Office Supplies (108); Office Equipment (163); Automobiles (164); Building (170); Land (172); Accounts Payable (201); Notes Payable (250); H. Venedict, Capital (301); H. Venedict, Withdrawals (302); Fees Earned (402); Salaries Expense (601); and Utilities Expense (602). Post the journal entries from part 1 to the ledger accounts and enter the balance after each posting.

3. Prepare a trial balance as of the end of September.

Problem 2-5A

Computing net income from equity analysis, preparing a balance sheet, and computing the debt ratio

C2   A1   A2   P3

The accounting records of Nettle Distribution show the following assets and liabilities as of December 31, 2016 and 2017.

December 31	2016	2017
Cash	$ 64,300	$ 15,640
Accounts receivable............	26,240	19,100
Office supplies	3,160	1,960
Office equipment	44,000	44,000
Trucks	148,000	157,000
Building.....................	0	80,000
Land	0	60,000
Accounts payable.............	3,500	33,500
Note payable	0	40,000

Required

1. Prepare balance sheets for the business as of December 31, 2016 and 2017. (*Hint:* Report only total equity on the balance sheet and remember that total equity equals the difference between assets and liabilities.)

2. Compute net income for 2017 by comparing total equity amounts for these two years and using the following information: During 2017, the owner invested $35,000 additional cash in the business and withdrew $19,000 cash for personal use.

3. Compute the 2017 year-end debt ratio (in percent and rounded to one decimal).

Check   (2) Net income, $6,000

(3) Debt ratio, 19.5%

Yi Min started an engineering firm called Min Engineering. He began operations and completed seven transactions in May, which included his initial investment of $18,000 cash. After those seven transactions, the ledger included the following accounts with normal balances.

Problem 2-6A
Analyzing account balances and reconstructing transactions

C1 C3 A1 P2

Cash	$37,600
Office supplies	890
Prepaid insurance	4,600
Office equipment	12,900
Accounts payable	12,900
Y. Min, Capital	18,000
Y. Min, Withdrawals	3,370
Engineering fees earned	36,000
Rent expense	7,540

Required

1. Prepare a trial balance for this business as of the end of May.
2. The following seven transactions produced the account balances shown above.
   a. Y. Min invested $18,000 cash in the business.
   b. Paid $7,540 cash for monthly rent expense for May.
   c. Paid $4,600 cash for this year's insurance premium beginning immediately.
   d. Purchased office supplies for $890 cash.
   e. Purchased $12,900 of office equipment on credit (with accounts payable).
   f. Received $36,000 cash for engineering services provided in May.
   g. Y. Min withdrew $3,370 cash for personal use.

   Prepare a Cash T-account, enter the cash effects (if any) of each transaction, and compute the ending Cash balance (code each entry in the T-account with one of the transaction codes *a* through *g*).

Check   (1) Trial balance totals, $66,900

(2) Ending Cash balance, $37,600

Humble Management Services opened for business and completed these transactions in September.

PROBLEM SET B

Sept. 1   Henry Humble, the owner, invested $38,000 cash along with office equipment valued at $15,000 in the company.

Problem 2-1B
Preparing and posting journal entries; preparing a trial balance

C3 C4 A1 P1 P2

2   The company prepaid $9,000 cash for 12 months' rent for office space. (*Hint:* Debit Prepaid Rent for $9,000.)
4   The company made credit purchases for $8,000 in office equipment and $2,400 in office supplies. Payment is due within 10 days.
8   The company completed work for a client and immediately received $3,280 cash.
12   The company completed a $15,400 project for a client, who must pay within 30 days.
13   The company paid $10,400 cash to settle the payable created on September 4.
19   The company paid $1,900 cash for the premium on an 18-month insurance policy. (*Hint:* Debit Prepaid Insurance for $1,900.)
22   The company received $7,700 cash as partial payment for the work completed on September 12.
24   The company completed work for another client for $2,100 on credit.
28   Henry Humble withdrew $5,300 cash from the company for personal use.
29   The company purchased $550 of additional office supplies on credit.
30   The company paid $860 cash for this month's utility bill.

Required

1. Prepare general journal entries to record these transactions (use account titles listed in part 2).

2. Open the following ledger accounts—their account numbers are in parentheses (use the balance column format): Cash (101); Accounts Receivable (106); Office Supplies (124); Prepaid Insurance (128); Prepaid Rent (131); Office Equipment (163); Accounts Payable (201); H. Humble, Capital (301); H. Humble, Withdrawals (302); Services Revenue (401); and Utilities Expense (690). Post journal entries from part 1 to the ledger accounts and enter the balance after each posting.

3. Prepare a trial balance as of the end of September.

Problem 2-2B

Preparing and posting journal entries; preparing a trial balance

C3   C4   A1   P1   P2

At the beginning of April, Bernadette Grechus launched a custom computer solutions company called Softworks. The company had the following transactions during April.

a. Bernadette Grechus invested $65,000 cash, office equipment with a value of $5,750, and $30,000 of computer equipment in the company.

b. The company purchased land worth $22,000 for an office by paying $5,000 cash and signing a long-term note payable for $17,000.

c. The company purchased a portable building with $34,500 cash and moved it onto the land acquired in *b*.

d. The company paid $5,000 cash for the premium on a two-year insurance policy.

e. The company provided services to a client and immediately collected $4,600 cash.

f. The company purchased $4,500 of additional computer equipment by paying $800 cash and signing a long-term note payable for $3,700.

g. The company completed $4,250 of services for a client. This amount is to be received within 30 days.

h. The company purchased $950 of additional office equipment on credit.

i. The company completed client services for $10,200 on credit.

j. The company received a bill for rent of a computer testing device that was used on a recently completed job. The $580 rent cost must be paid within 30 days.

k. The company collected $5,100 cash in partial payment from the client described in transaction *i*.

l. The company paid $1,800 cash for wages to an assistant.

m. The company paid $950 cash to settle the payable created in transaction *h*.

n. The company paid $608 cash for minor maintenance of the company's computer equipment.

o. B. Grechus withdrew $6,230 cash from the company for personal use.

p. The company paid $1,800 cash for wages to an assistant.

q. The company paid $750 cash for advertisements on the web during April.

Required

1. Prepare general journal entries to record these transactions (use account titles listed in part 2).

2. Open the following ledger accounts—their account numbers are in parentheses (use the balance column format): Cash (101); Accounts Receivable (106); Prepaid Insurance (108); Office Equipment (163); Computer Equipment (164); Building (170); Land (172); Accounts Payable (201); Notes Payable (250); B. Grechus, Capital (301); B. Grechus, Withdrawals (302); Fees Earned (402); Wages Expense (601); Computer Rental Expense (602); Advertising Expense (603); and Repairs Expense (604). Post the journal entries from part 1 to the accounts and enter the balance after each posting.

3. Prepare a trial balance as of the end of April.

Problem 2-3B

Preparing and posting journal entries; preparing a trial balance

C3   C4   A1   P1   P2

Zucker Management Services opened for business and completed these transactions in November.

Nov. 1   Matt Zucker, the owner, invested $30,000 cash along with $15,000 of office equipment in the company.

2   The company prepaid $4,500 cash for six months' rent for an office. (*Hint:* Debit Prepaid Rent for $4,500.)

4   The company made credit purchases of office equipment for $2,500 and of office supplies for $600. Payment is due within 10 days.

8   The company completed work for a client and immediately received $3,400 cash.

12   The company completed a $10,200 project for a client, who must pay within 30 days.

13   The company paid $3,100 cash to settle the payable created on November 4.

19   The company paid $1,800 cash for the premium on a 24-month insurance policy.

22   The company received $5,200 cash as partial payment for the work completed on November 12.

24   The company completed work for another client for $1,750 on credit.
28   M. Zucker withdrew $5,300 cash from the company for personal use.
29   The company purchased $249 of additional office supplies on credit.
30   The company paid $831 cash for this month's utility bill.

Required

1. Prepare general journal entries to record these transactions (use account titles listed in part 2).
2. Open the following ledger accounts—their account numbers are in parentheses (use the balance column format): Cash (101); Accounts Receivable (106); Office Supplies (124); Prepaid Insurance (128); Prepaid Rent (131); Office Equipment (163); Accounts Payable (201); M. Zucker, Capital (301); M. Zucker, Withdrawals (302); Services Revenue (403); and Utilities Expense (690). Post the journal entries from part 1 to the ledger accounts and enter the balance after each posting.
3. Prepare a trial balance as of the end of November.

Check   (2) Ending balances: Cash, $23,069; Accounts Receivable, $6,750; Accounts Payable, $249

(3) Total debits, $60,599

Nuncio Consulting completed the following transactions during June.

a. Armand Nuncio, the owner, invested $35,000 cash along with office equipment valued at $11,000 in the new company.

b. The company purchased land valued at $7,500 and a building valued at $40,000. The purchase is paid with $15,000 cash and a long-term note payable for $32,500.

c. The company purchased $500 of office supplies on credit.

d. A. Nuncio invested his personal automobile in the company. The automobile has a value of $8,000 and is to be used exclusively in the business.

e. The company purchased $1,200 of additional office equipment on credit.

f. The company paid $1,000 cash salary to an assistant.

g. The company provided services to a client and collected $3,200 cash.

h. The company paid $540 cash for this month's utilities.

i. The company paid $500 cash to settle the payable created in transaction *c*.

j. The company purchased $3,400 of new office equipment by paying $3,400 cash.

k. The company completed $4,200 of services for a client, who must pay within 30 days.

l. The company paid $1,000 cash salary to an assistant.

m. The company received $2,200 cash in partial payment on the receivable created in transaction *k*.

n. A. Nuncio withdrew $1,100 cash from the company for personal use.

Problem 2-4B
Recording transactions; posting to ledger; preparing a trial balance

C3   A1   P1   P2

Required

1. Prepare general journal entries to record these transactions (use account titles listed in part 2).
2. Open the following ledger accounts—their account numbers are in parentheses (use the balance column format): Cash (101); Accounts Receivable (106); Office Supplies (108); Office Equipment (163); Automobiles (164); Building (170); Land (172); Accounts Payable (201); Notes Payable (250); A. Nuncio, Capital (301); A. Nuncio, Withdrawals (302); Fees Earned (402); Salaries Expense (601); and Utilities Expense (602). Post the journal entries from part 1 to the ledger accounts and enter the balance after each posting.
3. Prepare a trial balance as of the end of June.

Check   (2) Ending balances: Cash, $17,860; Office Equipment, $15,600

(3) Trial balance totals, $95,100

The accounting records of Tama Co. show the following assets and liabilities as of December 31, 2016 and 2017.

Problem 2-5B
Computing net income from equity analysis, preparing a balance sheet, and computing the debt ratio

C2   A1   A2   P3

December 31	2016	2017
Cash	$30,000	$ 5,000
Accounts receivable............	35,000	25,000
Office supplies	8,000	13,500
Office equipment	40,000	40,000
Machinery....................	28,000	28,500
Building.....................	0	250,000
Land	0	50,000
Accounts payable.............	4,000	12,000
Note payable	0	250,000

Required

1. Prepare balance sheets for the business as of December 31, 2016 and 2017. (*Hint:* Report only total equity on the balance sheet and remember that total equity equals the difference between assets and liabilities.)

2. Compute net income for 2017 by comparing total equity amounts for these two years and using the following information: During 2017, the owner invested $5,000 additional cash in the business and withdrew $3,000 cash for personal use.

3. Compute the December 31, 2017, debt ratio (in percent and rounded to one decimal).

Problem 2-6B

Analyzing account balances and reconstructing transactions

C1 C3 A1 P2

Roshaun Gould started a web consulting firm called Gould Solutions. He began operations and completed seven transactions in April that resulted in the following accounts, which all have normal balances.

Cash	$20,000
Office supplies	750
Prepaid rent	1,800
Office equipment	12,250
Accounts payable................	12,250
R. Gould, Capital................	15,000
R. Gould, Withdrawals	5,200
Consulting fees earned	20,400
Miscellaneous expenses	7,650

Required

1. Prepare a trial balance for this business as of the end of April.

2. The following seven transactions produced the account balances shown above.

   a. Gould invested $15,000 cash in the business.

   b. Paid $1,800 cash for monthly rent expense for April.

   c. Paid $7,650 cash for miscellaneous expenses.

   d. Purchased office supplies for $750 cash.

   e. Purchased $12,250 of office equipment on credit (with accounts payable).

   f. Received $20,400 cash for consulting services provided in April.

   g. Gould withdrew $5,200 cash for personal use.

   Prepare a Cash T-account, enter the cash effects (if any) of each transaction, and compute the ending Cash balance (code each entry in the T-account with one of the transaction codes *a* through *g*).

SERIAL PROBLEM

Business Solutions

A1 P1 P2

(This serial problem started in Chapter 1 and continues through most of the chapters. If the Chapter 1 segment was not completed, the problem can begin at this point.)

SP 2 On October 1, 2017, Santana Rey launched a computer services company called **Business Solutions**, which provides consulting services, computer system installations, and custom program development. Rey adopts the calendar year for reporting purposes and expects to prepare the company's first set of financial statements on December 31, 2017. The company's initial chart of accounts follows.

Account	No.	Account	No.
Cash	101	S. Rey, Capital.........................	301
Accounts Receivable	106	S. Rey, Withdrawals	302
Computer Supplies..............	126	Computer Services Revenue.............	403
Prepaid Insurance..............	128	Wages Expense	623
Prepaid Rent...................	131	Advertising Expense....................	655
Office Equipment	163	Mileage Expense	676
Computer Equipment...........	167	Miscellaneous Expenses	677
Accounts Payable..............	201	Repairs Expense—Computer............	684

Required

1. Prepare journal entries to record each of the following transactions for Business Solutions.

Oct. 1 S. Rey invested $45,000 cash, a $20,000 computer system, and $8,000 of office equipment in the company.
2 The company paid $3,300 cash for four months' rent. (*Hint:* Debit Prepaid Rent for $3,300.)
3 The company purchased $1,420 of computer supplies on credit from Harris Office Products.
5 The company paid $2,220 cash for one year's premium on a property and liability insurance policy. (*Hint:* Debit Prepaid Insurance for $2,220.)
6 The company billed Easy Leasing $4,800 for services performed in installing a new web server.
8 The company paid $1,420 cash for the computer supplies purchased from Harris Office Products on October 3.
10 The company hired Lyn Addie as a part-time assistant for $125 per day, as needed.
12 The company billed Easy Leasing another $1,400 for services performed.
15 The company received $4,800 cash from Easy Leasing as partial payment on its account.
17 The company paid $805 cash to repair computer equipment that was damaged when moving it.
20 The company paid $1,728 cash for advertisements published in the local newspaper.
22 The company received $1,400 cash from Easy Leasing on its account.
28 The company billed IFM Company $5,208 for services performed.
31 The company paid $875 cash for Lyn Addie's wages for seven days' work.
31 S. Rey withdrew $3,600 cash from the company for personal use.
Nov. 1 The company reimbursed S. Rey in cash for business automobile mileage allowance (Rey logged 1,000 miles at $0.32 per mile).
2 The company received $4,633 cash from Liu Corporation for computer services performed.
5 The company purchased computer supplies for $1,125 cash from Harris Office Products.
8 The company billed Gomez Co. $5,668 for services performed.
13 The company received notification from Alex's Engineering Co. that Business Solutions's bid of $3,950 for an upcoming project was accepted.
18 The company received $2,208 cash from IFM Company as partial payment of the October 28 bill.
22 The company donated $250 cash to the United Way in the company's name.
24 The company completed work and sent a bill for $3,950 to Alex's Engineering Co.
25 The company sent another bill to IFM Company for the past-due amount of $3,000.
28 The company reimbursed S. Rey in cash for business automobile mileage (1,200 miles at $0.32 per mile).
30 The company paid $1,750 cash for Lyn Addie's wages for 14 days' work.
30 S. Rey withdrew $2,000 cash from the company for personal use.

2. Open ledger accounts (in balance column format) and post the journal entries from part 1 to them.
3. Prepare a trial balance as of the end of November.

Check (2) Cash, Nov. 30 bal., $38,264
(3) Trial bal. totals, $98,659

Using transactions from the following assignments along with the **General Ledger** tool, prepare journal entries for each transaction and identify the financial statement impact of each entry. The financial statements are automatically generated based on the journal entries recorded.

GL 2-1 Transactions from the FastForward illustration in this chapter

GL 2-2 Based on Exercise 2-9

GL 2-3 Based on Exercise 2-12

GL 2-4 Based on Problem 2-1A

Using transactions from the following assignments, record journal entries, create financial statements, and assess the impact of each transaction on financial statements.

GL 2-5 Based on Problem 2-2A

GL 2-6 Based on Problem 2-3A

GL 2-7 Based on Problem 2-4A

GL 2-8 Based on the Serial Problem SP 2

GENERAL LEDGER PROBLEM

Available only in Connect

Beyond the Numbers

REPORTING IN
ACTION

A1 A2

APPLE

BTN 2-1   Refer to Apple's financial statements in Appendix A for the following questions.

Required

1. What amount of total liabilities does it report for each of the fiscal years ended September 26, 2015, and September 27, 2014?
2. What amount of total assets does it report for each of the fiscal years ended September 26, 2015, and September 27, 2014?
3. Compute its debt ratio for each of the fiscal years ended September 26, 2015, and September 27, 2014. (Report ratio in percent and round it to one decimal.)
4. In which fiscal year did it employ more financial leverage: September 26, 2015, or September 27, 2014? Explain.

Fast Forward

5. Access Apple's financial statements (10-K report) for a fiscal year ending after September 26, 2015, from its website (Apple.com) or the SEC's EDGAR database (SEC.gov). Recompute its debt ratio for any subsequent year's data and compare it with the debt ratio for 2015 and 2014.

COMPARATIVE
ANALYSIS

A1 A2

APPLE
GOOGLE

BTN 2-2   Key comparative figures for Apple and Google follow.

$ millions	Apple		Google	
	Current Year	Prior Year	Current Year	Prior Year
Total liabilities..................	$171,124	$120,292	$ 27,130	$ 25,327
Total assets	290,479	231,839	147,461	129,187

1. What is the debt ratio for Apple in the current year and for the prior year?
2. What is the debt ratio for Google in the current year and for the prior year?
3. Which of the two companies has the higher degree of financial leverage? What does this imply?

ETHICS
CHALLENGE

C1

BTN 2-3   Assume that you are a cashier and your manager requires that you immediately enter each sale when it occurs. Recently, lunch hour traffic has increased and the assistant manager asks you to avoid delays by taking customers' cash and making change without entering sales. The assistant manager says she will add up cash and enter sales after lunch. She says that, in this way, customers will be happy and the register record will always match the cash amount when the manager arrives at three o'clock.

The advantage to the process proposed by the assistant manager includes improved customer service, fewer delays, and less work for you. The disadvantage is that the assistant manager could steal cash by simply recording less sales than the cash received and then pocketing the excess cash. You decide to reject her suggestion without the manager's approval and to confront her on the ethics of her suggestion.

Required

Propose and evaluate two other courses of action you might consider, and explain why.

COMMUNICATING
IN PRACTICE

C1 C2 A1 P3

BTN 2-4   Lila Corentine is an aspiring entrepreneur and your friend. She is having difficulty understanding the purposes of financial statements and how they fit together across time.

Required

Write a one-page memorandum to Corentine explaining the purposes of the four financial statements and how they are linked across time.

BTN 2-5   Access EDGAR online (SEC.gov) and locate the 2014 10-K report of Amazon.com (ticker: AMZN) filed on January 30, 2015. Review its financial statements reported for years ended 2014, 2013, and 2012 to answer the following questions.

TAKING IT TO THE NET

A1

Required

1. What are the amounts of its net income or net loss reported for each of these three years?
2. Do Amazon's operating activities provide cash or use cash for each of these three years?
3. If Amazon has a 2014 net loss of $(241) million and 2014 operating cash flows of $6,842 million, how is it possible that its cash balance at December 31, 2014, increases by only $5,899 million relative to its balance at December 31, 2013?

BTN 2-6   The expanded accounting equation consists of assets, liabilities, capital, withdrawals, revenues, and expenses. It can be used to reveal insights into changes in a company's financial position.

TEAMWORK IN ACTION

C1 C2 C4 A1

Required

1. Form *learning teams* of six (or more) members. Each team member must select one of the six components and each team must have at least one expert on each component: (*a*) assets, (*b*) liabilities, (*c*) capital, (*d*) withdrawals, (*e*) revenues, and (*f*) expenses.
2. Form *expert teams* of individuals who selected the same component in part 1. Expert teams are to draft a report that each expert will present to his or her learning team addressing the following:
    a. Identify for its component the (i) increase and decrease side of the account and (ii) normal balance side of the account.
    b. Describe a transaction, with amounts, that increases its component.
    c. Using the transaction and amounts in (b), verify the equality of the accounting equation and then explain any effects on the income statement and statement of cash flows.
    d. Describe a transaction, with amounts, that decreases its component.
    e. Using the transaction and amounts in (d), verify the equality of the accounting equation and then explain any effects on the income statement and statement of cash flows.
3. Each expert should return to his/her learning team. In rotation, each member presents his/her expert team's report to the learning team. Team discussion is encouraged.

BTN 2-7   Assume that Catherine Mahugu of Soko plans on expanding her business to accommodate more product lines. She is considering financing her expansion in one of two ways: (1) contributing more of her own funds to the business or (2) borrowing the funds from a bank.

ENTREPRENEURIAL DECISION

A1 A2 P3

Required

Identify at least two issues that Catherine should consider when trying to decide on the method for financing her expansion.

BTN 2-8   Angel Martin is a young entrepreneur who operates Martin Music Services, offering singing lessons and instruction on musical instruments. Martin wishes to expand but needs a $30,000 loan. The bank requests that Martin prepare a balance sheet and key financial ratios. Martin has not kept formal records but is able to provide the following accounts and their amounts as of December 31, 2017.

ENTREPRENEURIAL DECISION

A1 A2 P3

Cash	$ 3,600	Accounts Receivable	$ 9,600	Prepaid Insurance	$ 1,500
Prepaid Rent	9,400	Store Supplies	6,600	Equipment	50,000
Accounts Payable	2,200	Unearned Lesson Fees	15,600	Total Equity*	62,900
Annual net income	40,000				

*The total equity amount reflects all owner investments, withdrawals, revenues, and expenses as of December 31, 2017.

Required

1. Prepare a balance sheet as of December 31, 2017, for Martin Music Services. (Report only the total equity amount on the balance sheet.)
2. Compute Martin's debt ratio and its return on assets (the latter ratio is defined in Chapter 1). Assume average assets equal its ending balance.
3. Do you believe the prospects of a $30,000 bank loan are good? Why or why not?

HITTING THE ROAD

C1

BTN 2-9 Obtain a recent copy of the most prominent newspaper distributed in your area. Research the classified section and prepare a report answering the following questions (attach relevant classified clippings to your report). Alternatively, you may want to search the web for the required information. One suitable website is **CareerOneStop** (**CareerOneStop.org**). For documentation, you should print copies of websites accessed.

1. Identify the number of listings for accounting positions and the various accounting job titles.
2. Identify the number of listings for other job titles, with examples, that require or prefer accounting knowledge/experience but are not specifically accounting positions.
3. Specify the salary range for the accounting and accounting-related positions if provided.
4. Indicate the job that appeals to you, the reason for its appeal, and its requirements.

GLOBAL DECISION

A2

Samsung
APPLE
GOOGLE

BTN 2-10 Samsung (**Samsung.com**) is a market leader in high-tech electronics manufacturing and digital media, and it competes to some extent with both **Apple** and **Google**. Key financial ratios for the current fiscal year follow.

Key Figure	Samsung	Apple	Google
Return on assets............	8.1%	20.4%	11.8%
Debt ratio	26.1%	58.9%	18.4%

Required

1. Which company is most profitable according to its return on assets?
2. Which company is most risky according to the debt ratio?
3. Which company deserves increased investment based on a joint analysis of return on assets and the debt ratio? Explain.

GLOBAL VIEW

Financial accounting according to U.S. GAAP is similar, but not identical, to IFRS. This section discusses differences in analyzing and recording transactions, and with the preparation of financial statements.

Analyzing and Recording Transactions Both U.S. GAAP and IFRS include broad and similar guidance for financial accounting. Further, both U.S. GAAP and IFRS apply transaction analysis and recording as shown in this chapter—using the same debit and credit system and accrual accounting. Although some variations exist in revenue and expense recognition and other accounting principles, all of the transactions in this chapter are accounted for identically under these two systems.

Financial Statements Both U.S. GAAP and IFRS prepare the same four basic financial statements. A few differences within each statement do exist and we will discuss those throughout the book. For example, both U.S. GAAP and IFRS require balance sheets to separate current items from noncurrent items. However, while U.S. GAAP balance sheets report current items first, IFRS balance sheets normally (but are not required to) present noncurrent items first, and equity before liabilities. To illustrate, a condensed version of **Piaggio**'s balance sheet follows. Piaggio is an Italian manufacturer of scooters and compact vehicles.

PIAGGIO Balance Sheet (in thousands of euros) December 31, 2015			
Assets		**Equity and Liabilities**	
Noncurrent assets	€1,103,111	Total equity	€ 404,293
Current assets	448,439	Noncurrent liabilities	588,446
		Current liabilities	558,811
Total assets	€1,551,550	Total equity and liabilities	€1,551,550

Accounting Controls and Assurance   Accounting systems depend on control procedures that assure proper principles were applied. The passage of SOX legislation strengthened U.S. controls. However, global standards for controls are diverse and so are enforcement activities. Consequently, while global accounting standards are converging, their application in different countries can yield different outcomes depending on the quality of their auditing standards and enforcement.

 Global View Assignments

Discussion Question 18

Quick Study 2-11

Exercise 2-23

BTN 2-10

chapter 3

Adjusting Accounts for Financial Statements

Chapter Preview

PREPAID EXPENSES	UNEARNED REVENUES	ACCRUED EXPENSES	ACCRUED REVENUES	REPORTING AND ANALYSIS

C1 Timing
C2 Accrual vs. cash
C3 3-Step process
P1 Framework
    Examples
	P1 Framework
	    Examples
		P1 Framework
		    Examples
			P1 Framework
			    Examples
			A1 Summary
				P2 Adjusted trial
				    balance
				P3 Financial
				    statements
				A2 Profit margin

NTK 3-1	NTK 3-2	NTK 3-3	NTK 3-4	NTK 3-5

Learning Objectives

CONCEPTUAL

C1 Explain the importance of periodic reporting and the time period assumption.

C2 Explain accrual accounting and how it improves financial statements.

C3 Identify the types of adjustments and their purpose.

ANALYTICAL

A1 Explain how accounting adjustments link to financial statements.

A2 Compute profit margin and describe its use in analyzing company performance.

PROCEDURAL

P1 Prepare and explain adjusting entries.

P2 Explain and prepare an adjusted trial balance.

P3 Prepare financial statements from an adjusted trial balance.

P4 *Appendix 3A*—Explain the alternatives in accounting for prepaids.

BROOKLYN, NY—Jason Aramburu was working for a clean energy investor in New York when the financial crisis hit. "The investor I was working for was hit hard . . . and decided to slow down his operations," recalls Jason. "It was time to try something new." Drawing from experience he had working on soil and nutrient cycling, Jason built a device that transforms organic waste into carbon-negative charcoal used for farming, called biochar. "And **re:char** (**re-char.com**) began!" explains Jason.

The biochar device, called a rutuba kiln, is especially valuable to smaller organizations such as "one- to two-acre farms." "The kiln costs us $25 to $30 to produce and we sell it to a farmer for less than the cost of two bags of fertilizer," explains Jason. "The farmer can apply the biochar directly to his field." The re:char website claims farming with biochar can increase crop yield by 200%. Adds Jason, "biochar-rich land is worth about five times as much as the land without it."

Jason recounts how he set up an accounting system early on to account for his rapidly expanding activities. Those included asset acquisitions along with accounting for cash, revenues, and expenses. Because many of his farming customers had to buy and sell on credit, Jason needed to learn to account for the deferral and accrual of both revenues and expenses.

Jason explains that the company's cash flow numbers were a bit misleading early on when he had soaring sales but little cash to show for it. "We find that it only takes the farmer about six months to reap the savings from . . . the increased crop yield necessary to pay for the kiln." Accordingly, his accrued revenues were eventually followed by incoming cash.

Jason relied on his accounting system to properly track and record receivables and payables. "[Farmers] can purchase the kiln outright or they can pay for it over time." Tracking those customers enabled Jason to request cash payment when harvests occurred.

Jason insists on timely and accurate accounting reports. He also uses accounting data to predict future revenues

Courtesy of re:char

re:charging the Earth

"Be aggressive and don't waste any time"
—Jason Aramburu

and expenses. "We just got a grant from the Gates Foundation to test the conversion of [different types] of waste into biochar," proclaims Jason. "It's really a gold mine!"

Although re:char is a for-profit business, Jason insists on using a "triple bottom line [people, planet, profit]." Jason asserts, "I believe if you align your mission with what you're doing, you can make money and do good!"

Sources: *re:char website,* January 2017; *Fast Company*, January 2012; *Launch.org*, January 2013; *Mashable*, April 2012

TIMING AND REPORTING

This section explains the reporting of accounting information at regular intervals and its impact for recording revenues and expenses.

The Accounting Period

The value of information is often linked to its timeliness. Useful information must reach decision makers frequently and promptly. To provide timely information, accounting systems prepare reports at regular intervals. This results in an accounting process impacted by the time period (or periodicity) assumption. The **time period assumption** presumes that an organization's activities can be divided into specific time periods such as a month, a three-month quarter, a six-month interval, or a year. Exhibit 3.1 shows various **accounting,** or *reporting,* **periods.** Most organizations use a year as their primary accounting period. Reports covering a one-year period are known as **annual financial statements.** Many organizations also prepare **interim financial statements** covering one, three, or six months of activity.

"Apple announces annual income of . . ."

EXHIBIT 3.1

Accounting Periods

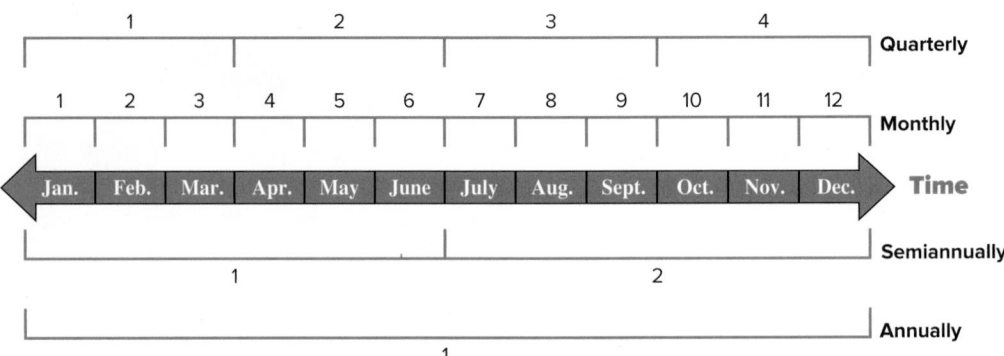

© C Flanigan/WireImage/Getty Images

The annual reporting period is not always a calendar year ending on December 31. An organization can adopt a **fiscal year** consisting of any 12 consecutive months or 52 weeks. For example, **Gap**'s fiscal year consistently ends the final week of January or the first week of February each year.

Companies with little seasonal variation in sales often choose the calendar year as their fiscal year. **Facebook, Inc.,** uses calendar-year reporting. Companies that have seasonal variations in sales often choose a **natural business year** end, which is when sales activities are at their lowest level for the year. The natural business year for retailers such as **Walmart**, **Target**, and **Macy's** usually ends around January 31, after the holiday season.

Accrual Basis versus Cash Basis

After external transactions and events are recorded, several accounts require adjustments before their balances appear in financial statements. This need arises because internal transactions and events remain unrecorded.

- **Accrual basis accounting** applies adjustments so that revenues are recognized when services and products are delivered, and expenses are recognized when incurred (matched with revenues).
- **Cash basis accounting** recognizes revenues when cash is received and records expenses when cash is paid. This means that cash basis income is the difference between cash receipts and cash payments.

Cash basis accounting is *not* consistent with generally accepted accounting principles. Most agree that accrual accounting better reflects business performance than information about cash receipts and payments. Accrual accounting also increases the *comparability* of financial statements from period to period.

Accrual Basis   To compare these two systems, let's consider FastForward's Prepaid Insurance account. FastForward paid $2,400 for 24 months of insurance coverage that began on December 1, 2017. Accrual accounting requires that $100 of insurance expense be reported each month, from December 2017 through November 2019. (This means expenses are $100 in 2017, $1,200 in 2018, and $1,100 in 2019.) Exhibit 3.2 illustrates this allocation of insurance cost across these three years. Any unexpired premium is reported as a Prepaid Insurance asset on the accrual basis balance sheet.

EXHIBIT 3.2

Accrual Accounting for Allocating Prepaid Insurance to Expense

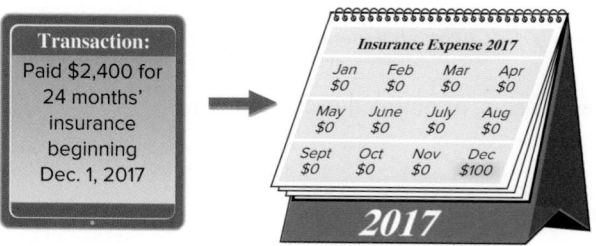

Point: Annual income statements for Exhibit 3.2 follow:

Accrual Basis	2017	2018	2019
Revenues	$ #	$ #	$ #
Insur. exp.	$100	$1,200	$1,100

Cash Basis   A *cash basis* income statement for December 2017 reports insurance expense of $2,400, as shown in Exhibit 3.3. The cash basis income statements for years 2018 and 2019 report no insurance expense. The cash basis balance sheet never reports a prepaid insurance asset because it is immediately expensed. Also, cash basis income for 2017–2019 does not match the cost of insurance with the insurance benefits received for those years and months.

EXHIBIT 3.3

Cash Accounting for Allocating Prepaid Insurance to Expense

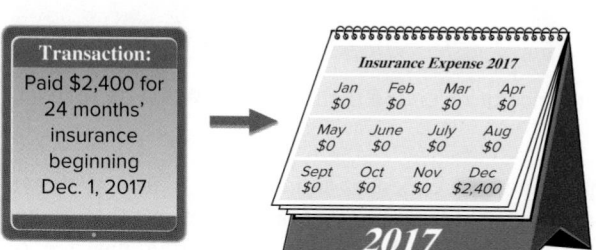

Point: Annual income statements for Exhibit 3.3 follow:

Cash Basis	2017	2018	2019
Revenues	$ #	$#	$#
Insur. exp.	$2,400	$0	$0

Recognizing Revenues and Expenses

We divide a company's activities into specific time periods, but not all activities are complete when financial statements are prepared. Thus, adjustments are required to get proper account balances.

We rely on two principles in the adjusting process: revenue recognition and expense recognition (the latter is often referred to as *matching*). *Revenue recognition principle* requires that revenue be recorded when goods or services are provided to customers and at an amount expected to be received from customers. A major goal of the adjusting process is to have revenue recognized (reported) in the time period when those services and products are delivered. The **expense recognition** (or **matching**) **principle** aims to record expenses in the same accounting period as the revenues that are recognized as a result of those expenses.

Matching expenses with revenues often requires us to predict certain events. When we use financial statements, we must understand that they require estimates. **Disney**'s annual report explains that its production costs from movies, such as *Star Wars: Episode VII* and *Frozen*, are matched to revenues based on a ratio of current revenues from the movie divided by its predicted total revenues.

Point: Recording revenue early overstates current-period revenue and income; recording it late understates current-period revenue and income.

Point: Recording expense early overstates current-period expense and understates current-period income; recording it late understates current-period expense and overstates current-period income.

■ **Decision** Insight

Clawbacks from Accounting Fraud   Former key executives at **Saba Software**, a cloud-based talent management system used by clients to hire, develop, and inspire workers, were charged with accounting fraud by the SEC when they falsified the company's revenue recognition to boost income. This alleged overstatement of income led to the reimbursement of millions of dollars to the company by the former CEO and former CFO. (For more details, see SEC release 2015-28.) ■

© Marco Marchi/Getty Images

Framework for Adjustments

C3

Identify the types of adjustments and their purpose.

Four types of adjustments are necessary for transactions and events that extend over more than one period.

⟨ **Prepaid expenses** ⟩   ⟨ **Unearned revenues** ⟩   ⟨ **Accrued expenses** ⟩   ⟨ **Accrued revenues** ⟩

Those adjustments are made using a 3-step process, as outlined in Exhibit 3.4.

EXHIBIT 3.4

Three-Step Process for Adjusting Entries

Step 1: Determine what the current account balance *equals*.

Step 2: Determine what the current account balance *should equal*.

Step 3: Record an adjusting entry to get from step 1 to step 2.

An **adjusting entry** is made at the end of an accounting period to reflect a transaction or event that is not yet recorded. Each adjusting entry affects one or more income statement accounts *and* one or more balance sheet accounts (but never the Cash account).

PREPAID (DEFERRED) EXPENSES

P1

Prepare and explain adjusting entries.

Prepaid expenses are assets *paid for* in advance of receiving their benefits. When these assets are used, their costs become expenses.

Framework   Adjusting entries for prepaids increase expenses and decrease assets, as shown in the T-accounts of Exhibit 3.5. Such adjustments reflect transactions and events that use up prepaid expenses (including passage of time). To illustrate the accounting for prepaid expenses, we look at prepaid insurance, supplies, and depreciation. In each case we decrease an asset (balance sheet) account and increase an expense (income statement) account.

EXHIBIT 3.5

Adjusting for Prepaid Expenses (decrease an asset and record an expense)

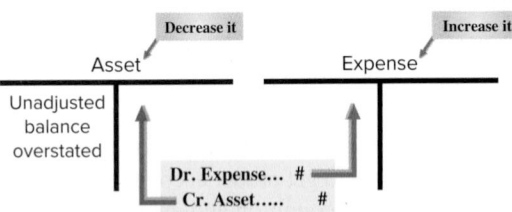

Prepaid Insurance

We use our three-step process for this and all accounting adjustments.

Step 1:   We determine that the current balance of FastForward's prepaid insurance is equal to its $2,400 payment for 24 months of insurance benefits that began on December 1, 2017.

Step 2:   As time passes, the benefits of the insurance gradually expire and a portion of the Prepaid Insurance asset becomes expense. For instance, one month's insurance coverage expires by December 31, 2017. This expense is $100, or 1/24 of $2,400, which leaves $2,300.

Insurance

Dec. 1 Pay insurance premium and record asset
    Prepaid insurance....... 2,400
      Cash...................... 2,400

Two-Year Insurance Policy
Total cost is $2,400
Monthly cost is $100

Dec. 31 Coverage expires and record expense

Step 3: The adjusting entry to record this expense and reduce the asset, along with T-account postings, follows:

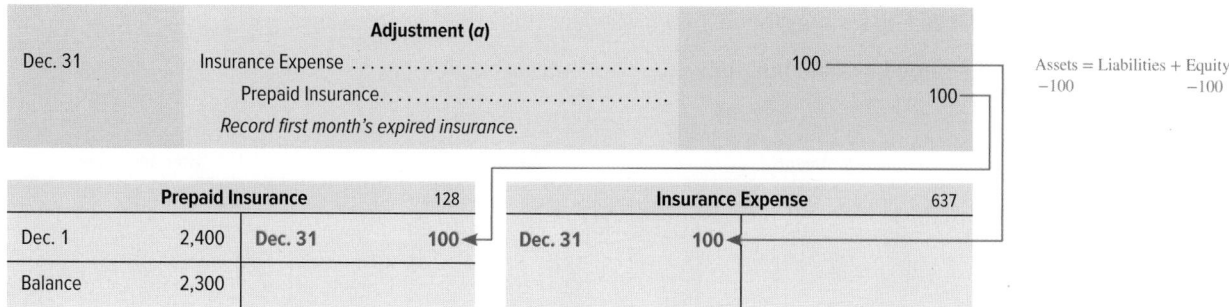

Adjustment (a)

Dec. 31	Insurance Expense	100
	Prepaid Insurance..............................	100
	Record first month's expired insurance.	

Assets = Liabilities + Equity
−100   −100

Prepaid Insurance			128
Dec. 1	2,400	Dec. 31	100
Balance	2,300		

| Insurance Expense | | 637 |
| Dec. 31 | 100 | |

Explanation After adjusting and posting, the $100 balance in Insurance Expense and the $2,300 balance in Prepaid Insurance are ready for reporting in financial statements. *Not* making the adjustment on or before December 31 would

• Understate expenses by $100 for the December income statement.
• Overstate prepaid insurance (assets) by $100 in the December 31 balance sheet.

The following table highlights the December 31, 2017, adjustment for prepaid insurance.

Before Adjustment	Adjustment	After Adjustment
Prepaid Insurance = $2,400	**Deduct $100 from Prepaid Insurance** **Add $100 to Insurance Expense**	**Prepaid Insurance = $2,300**
Reports $2,400 policy for 24 months' coverage.	Record current month's $100 insurance expense and $100 reduction in prepaid.	Reports $2,300 in coverage for remaining 23 months.

Supplies

Supplies are a prepaid expense requiring adjustment.

Step 1: FastForward purchased $9,720 of supplies in December, some of which were used during that same month. When financial statements are prepared at December 31, the cost of supplies used during December must be expensed.

Step 2: When FastForward computes (takes physical count of) its remaining unused supplies at December 31, it finds $8,670 of supplies remaining of the $9,720 total supplies. The $1,050 difference between these two amounts is December's supplies expense.

Step 3: The adjusting entry to record this expense and reduce the Supplies asset account, along with T-account postings, follows:

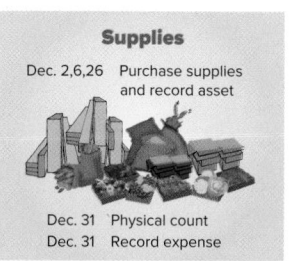

Supplies

Dec. 2,6,26 Purchase supplies and record asset

Dec. 31 Physical count
Dec. 31 Record expense

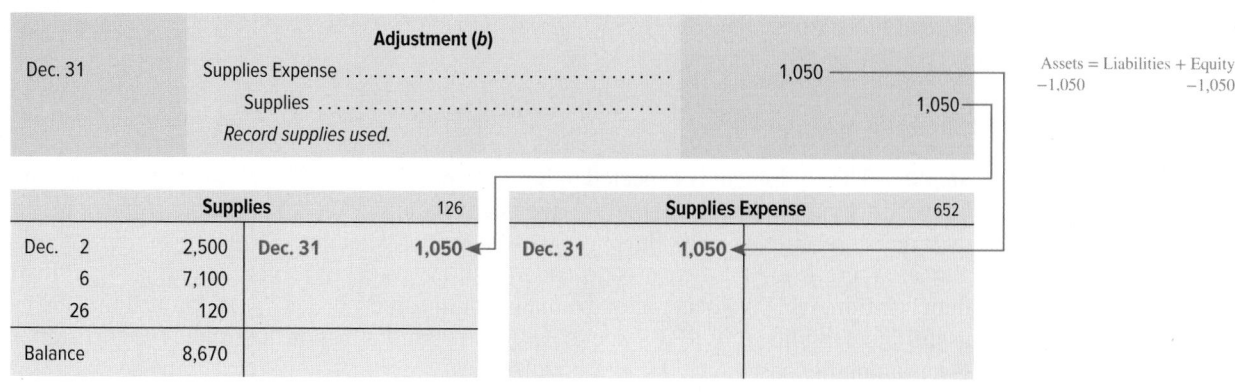

Adjustment (b)

Dec. 31	Supplies Expense	1,050
	Supplies	1,050
	Record supplies used.	

Assets = Liabilities + Equity
−1,050   −1,050

Supplies			126
Dec. 2	2,500	Dec. 31	1,050
6	7,100		
26	120		
Balance	8,670		

| Supplies Expense | | 652 |
| Dec. 31 | 1,050 | |

Explanation The balance of the Supplies account is $8,670 after posting—equaling the cost of the remaining supplies. *Not* making the adjustment on or before December 31 would

- Understate expenses by $1,050 for the December income statement.
- Overstate supplies by $1,050 in the December 31 balance sheet.

The following table highlights the adjustment for supplies.

Before Adjustment	Adjustment	After Adjustment
Supplies = $9,720	Deduct $1,050 from Supplies Add $1,050 to Supplies Expense	Supplies = $8,670
Reports $9,720 in supplies.	Record $1,050 in supplies used and $1,050 as supplies expense.	Reports $8,670 in supplies.

Other Prepaid Expenses

Other prepaid expenses, such as Prepaid Rent, Prepaid Advertising, and Prepaid Promotions, are accounted for exactly as insurance and supplies are. Some prepaid expenses are both paid for and fully used up within a single accounting period. One example is when a company pays monthly rent on the first day of each month. This payment creates a prepaid expense on the first day of each month that fully expires by the end of the month. In these special cases, we can record the cash paid with a debit to an expense account instead of an asset account. This practice is described in the appendix to the chapter.

 Decision Maker

Investor A small publishing company signs an aspiring Olympic gymnast to write a book. The company pays the gymnast $500,000 to sign plus future book royalties. A note to the company's financial statements says that "prepaid expenses include $500,000 in author signing fees to be matched against future expected sales." Is this accounting for the signing bonus acceptable? How does it affect your analysis? ■ [*Answer:* Prepaid expenses are assets paid for in advance of receiving their benefits–they are expensed as they are used up. The publishing company's treatment of the signing bonus is acceptable. As an investor, you are concerned about the risk of future book sales. The riskier the likelihood of future book sales is, the more likely your analysis is to treat the $500,000, or a portion of it, as an expense, not a prepaid expense (asset).]

Depreciation

Point: Plant assets are also called *Plant & Equipment* or *Property, Plant & Equipment.*

Point: Depreciation does not necessarily measure decline in market value.

Point: An asset's expected value at the end of its useful life is called *salvage value.*

A special category of prepaid expenses is **plant assets,** which refers to long-term tangible assets used to produce and sell products and services. Plant assets are expected to provide benefits for more than one period. Examples of plant assets are buildings, machines, vehicles, and fixtures. All plant assets, with a general exception for land, eventually wear out or decline in usefulness. The costs of these assets are gradually reported as expenses in the income statement over the assets' useful lives (benefit periods). **Depreciation** is the process of allocating the costs of these assets over their expected useful lives. Depreciation expense is recorded with an adjusting entry similar to that for other prepaid expenses.

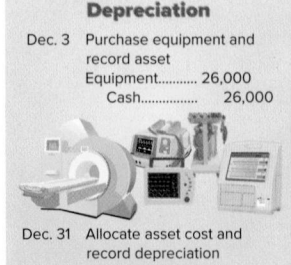

Depreciation

Dec. 3 Purchase equipment and record asset
Equipment........... 26,000
Cash................ 26,000

Dec. 31 Allocate asset cost and record depreciation

Step 1: FastForward purchased equipment for $26,000 in early December to use in earning revenue. This equipment's cost must be depreciated.

Step 2: The equipment is expected to have a useful life (benefit period) of five years and to be worth about $8,000 at the end of five years. This means the *net* cost of this equipment over its useful life is $18,000 ($26,000 − $8,000). We can use any of several methods to allocate this $18,000 net cost to expense. FastForward uses a method called **straight-line depreciation,** which allocates equal amounts of the asset's net cost to depreciation during its useful life. Dividing the $18,000 net cost by the 60 months (5 years) in the asset's useful life gives a monthly cost of $300 ($18,000/60).

Step 3:   The adjusting entry to record monthly depreciation expense, along with T-account postings, follows:

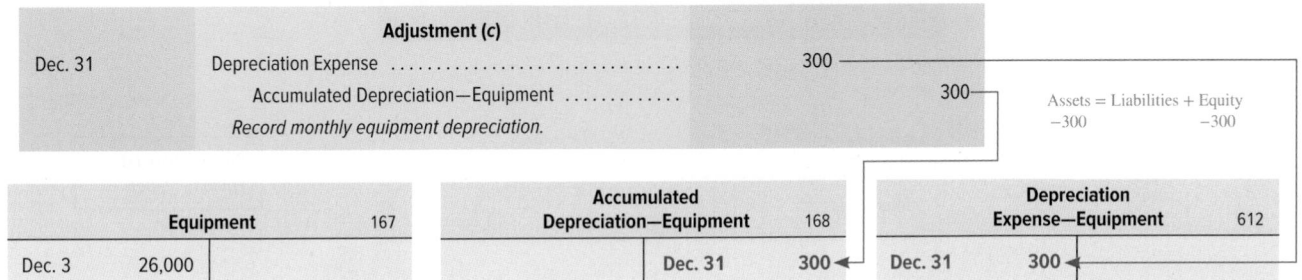

Explanation   After posting the adjustment, the Equipment account ($26,000) less its Accumulated Depreciation ($300) account equals the $25,700 net cost (made up of $17,700 for the 59 remaining months in the benefit period plus the $8,000 value at the end of that time). The $300 balance in the Depreciation Expense account is reported in the December income statement. *Not* making the adjustment at December 31 would

- Understate expenses by $300 for the December income statement.
- Overstate assets by $300 in the December 31 balance sheet.

The following table highlights the adjustment for depreciation.

Before Adjustment	Adjustment	After Adjustment
Equipment, net = $26,000	**Deduct $300 from Equipment, net Add $300 to Depreciation Expense**	**Equipment, net = $25,700**
Reports $26,000 in equipment.	Record $300 in depreciation and $300 as accumulated depreciation.	Reports $25,700 in equipment, net of accumulated depreciation.

Accumulated depreciation is kept in a separate contra account. A **contra account** is an account linked with another account, it has an opposite normal balance, and it is reported as a subtraction from that other account's balance. For instance, FastForward's contra account of Accumulated Depreciation—Equipment is subtracted from the Equipment account in the balance sheet (see Exhibit 3.7). This contra account shows users both the full costs of assets and the total depreciation.

The Accumulated Depreciation contra account includes total depreciation expense for all prior periods for which the asset was used. To illustrate, on February 28, 2018, after three months of adjusting entries, the Equipment and the Accumulated Depreciation accounts appear as in Exhibit 3.6. The $900 balance in the Accumulated Depreciation account is subtracted from its related $26,000 asset cost. The difference ($25,100) between these two balances is the cost of the asset that has not yet been depreciated. This difference is called the **book value,** or the *net amount,* which equals the asset's costs less its accumulated depreciation.

Point: Accumulated Depreciation has a normal credit balance; it decreases the asset's reported value.

Point: The net cost of equipment is also called the *depreciable basis.*

EXHIBIT 3.6

Accounts after Three Months of Depreciation Adjustments

Equipment		167
Dec. 3	26,000	

Accumulated Depreciation—Equipment		168
	Dec. 31	300
	Jan. 31	300
	Feb. 28	300
	Balance	900

These account balances are reported in the assets section of the February 28 balance sheet in Exhibit 3.7.

EXHIBIT 3.7

Equipment and Accumulated Depreciation on February 28 Balance Sheet

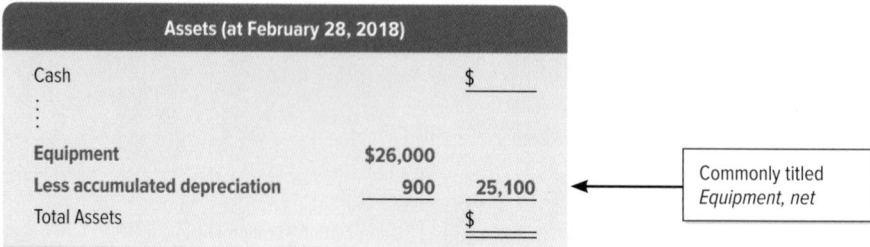

Assets (at February 28, 2018)		
Cash		$ _____
⋮		
Equipment	$26,000	
Less accumulated depreciation	900	25,100
Total Assets		$ _____

Commonly titled *Equipment, net*

NEED-TO-KNOW 3-1

Prepaid Expenses

P1

For each separate case below, follow the three-step process for adjusting the prepaid asset account at December 31. Step 1: Determine what the current account balance equals. Step 2: Determine what the current account balance should equal. Step 3: Record the December 31 adjusting entry to get from step 1 to step 2. *Assume no other adjusting entries are made during the year.*

1. **Prepaid Insurance.** The Prepaid Insurance account has a $5,000 debit balance to start the year, and no insurance payments were made during the year. A review of insurance policies and payments shows that $1,000 of unexpired insurance remains at its December 31 year-end.

2. **Prepaid Rent.** On October 1 of the current year, the company prepaid $12,000 for one year of rent for facilities being occupied from that day forward. The company debited Prepaid Rent and credited Cash for $12,000. December 31 year-end statements must be prepared.

3. **Supplies.** The Supplies account has a $1,000 debit balance to start the year. Supplies of $2,000 were purchased during the current year and debited to the Supplies account. A December 31 physical count shows $500 of supplies remaining.

4. **Accumulated Depreciation.** The company has only one fixed asset (equipment) that it purchased at the start of this year. That asset had cost $38,000, had an estimated life of 10 years, and is expected to be valued at $8,000 at the end of the 10-year life. December 31 year-end statements must be prepared.

Solution

1. Step 1: Prepaid Insurance equals $5,000 (before adjustment)

   Step 2: Prepaid Insurance should equal $1,000 (the unexpired part)

   Step 3: Adjusting entry to get from step 1 to step 2

Dec. 31	Insurance Expense..	4,000	
	Prepaid Insurance...		4,000
	Record expired insurance coverage ($5,000 – $1,000).		

2. Step 1: Prepaid Rent equals $12,000 (before adjustment)

   Step 2: Prepaid Rent should equal $9,000 (the unexpired part)*

   Step 3: Adjusting entry to get from step 1 to step 2

Dec. 31	Rent Expense	3,000	
	Prepaid Rent		3,000
	*Record expired prepaid rent. *($12,000 – $3,000 = $9,000)*		
	where $3,000 is from: ($12,000 / 12 months) × 3 months		

3. Step 1: Supplies equal $3,000 (from $1,000 + $2,000; before adjustment)

   Step 2: Supplies should equal $500 (what's left)

   Step 3: Adjusting entry to get from step 1 to step 2*

Dec. 31	Supplies Expense..	2,500	
	Supplies..		2,500
	*Record supplies used. *$1,000 + $2,000 purchased –*		
	$ ____ supplies used = $500 remaining*		

4. Step 1: Accumulated Depreciation equals $0 (before adjustment)

Step 2: Accumulated Depreciation should equal $3,000 (after current period depreciation of $3,000)*

Step 3: Adjusting entry to get from step 1 to step 2

Dec. 31	Depreciation Expense—Equipment...............................	3,000	
	Accumulated Depreciation—Equipment		3,000
	Record depreciation for period.		
	*($38,000 − $8,000)/10 years		

Do More: QS 3-5, QS 3-6, QS 3-7, QS 3-8, QS 3-9

UNEARNED (DEFERRED) REVENUES

The term **unearned revenues** refers to cash received in advance of providing products and services. Unearned revenues, also called *deferred revenues,* are liabilities. When cash is accepted, an obligation to provide products or services is accepted.

Point: To *defer* is to postpone. We postpone reporting amounts received as revenues until they are earned.

Framework As products or services are provided, the liability decreases, and the unearned revenues become *earned* revenues. Adjusting entries for unearned items decrease the unearned (balance sheet) account and increase the revenue (income statement) account, as shown in Exhibit 3.8.

An example of unearned revenues is from **Gannett Co., Inc.,** publisher of *USA TODAY,* which reports unexpired (unearned subscriptions) of $217 million: "Revenue is recognized in the period in which it is earned (as newspapers are delivered)." Unearned revenues are nearly 20% of the current liabilities for Gannett. Another example comes from the **Boston Celtics.** When the Celtics receive cash from advance ticket sales and broadcast fees, they record it in an unearned revenue account called *Deferred Game Revenues.* The Celtics recognize this unearned revenue with adjusting entries on a game-by-game basis. For a recent season, the Celtics's quarterly revenues were $0 million for July–September; $34 million for October–December; $48 million for January–March; and $17 million for April–June, which reflects the NBA season from October through April.

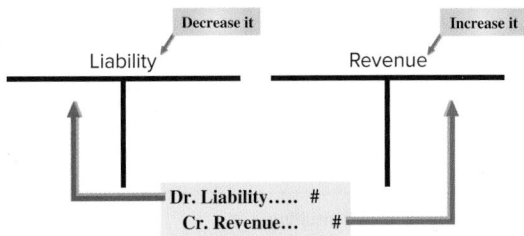

EXHIBIT 3.8

Adjusting for Unearned Revenues (decrease a liability and record revenue)

Unearned Consulting Revenue

Returning to FastForward, it has unearned revenues. The company agreed on December 26 to provide consulting services to a client for a fixed fee of $3,000 for 60 days.

Step 1: On December 26, the client paid the 60-day fee in advance, covering the period December 27 to February 24. The entry to record the cash received in advance is

Dec. 26	Cash	3,000	
	Unearned Consulting Revenue		3,000
	Received advance payment for services over the		
	next 60 days.		

Assets = Liabilities + Equity
+3,000   +3,000

Unearned Revenues

Dec. 26 Cash received in advance and record liability

Thanks for cash in advance. I'll work now through Feb. 24

Dec. 31 Provided 5 days of services and record revenue

This advance payment increases cash and creates an obligation to do consulting work over the next 60 days (5 days this year and 55 days next year).

Step 2: As time passes, FastForward earns this payment through consulting. By December 31, it has provided five days' service and earned 5/60 of the $3,000 unearned revenue. This amounts to $250 ($3,000 × 5/60). The *revenue recognition principle* implies that $250 of unearned revenue must be reported as revenue on the December income statement.

Step 3:   The adjusting entry to reduce the liability account and recognize earned revenue, along with T-account postings, follows:

Assets = Liabilities + Equity
−250   +250

Adjustment (d)		
Dec. 31 Unearned Consulting Revenue........................	250	
Consulting Revenue		250
Record earned revenue that was received in advance ($3,000 × 5/60).		

Unearned Consulting Revenue		236
Dec. 31	250	Dec. 26	3,000
		Balance	2,750

Consulting Revenue		403
	Dec. 5	4,200
	12	1,600
	31	250
	Balance	6,050

Explanation   The adjusting entry transfers $250 from unearned revenue (a liability account) to a revenue account. *Not* making the adjustment

- Understates revenue by $250 in the December income statement.
- Overstates unearned revenue by $250 on the December 31 balance sheet.

The following highlights the adjustment for unearned revenue.

Before Adjustment	Adjustment	After Adjustment
Unearned Consulting Revenue = $3,000	**Deduct $250 from Unearned Consulting Revenue Add $250 to Consulting Revenue**	**Unearned Consulting Revenue = $2,750**
Reports $3,000 in unearned revenue for consulting services promised for 60 days ($50 per day).	Record 5 days of earned consulting revenue, which is 5/60 of unearned amount.	Reports $2,750 in unearned revenue for consulting services owed over next 55 days (55 days × $50 = $2,750).

Accounting for unearned revenues is crucial to many companies. For example, the **National Retail Federation** reports that gift card sales, which are unearned revenues for sellers, exceed $20 billion annually. Gift cards are now the top selling holiday gift; roughly 60% of all gift givers planned to give at least one gift card within the next year (source: NRF website).

NEED-TO-KNOW 3-2

Unearned Revenues

P1

For each separate case below, follow the three-step process for adjusting the unearned revenue liability account at December 31. Step 1: Determine what the current account balance equals. Step 2: Determine what the current account balance should equal. Step 3: Record the December 31 adjusting entry to get from step 1 to step 2. *Assume no other adjusting entries are made during the year.*

a. Unearned Rent Revenue. The company collected $24,000 rent in advance on September 1, debiting Cash and crediting Unearned Rent Revenue. The tenant was paying 12 months' rent in advance and occupancy began September 1.

b. Unearned Services Revenue. The company charges $100 per month to spray a house for insects. A customer paid $600 on November 1 in advance for six treatments, which was recorded with a debit to Cash and a credit to Unearned Services Revenue. At year-end, the company has applied two treatments for the customer.

Solution

a. Step 1: Unearned Rent Revenue equals $24,000 (before adjustment)

Step 2: Unearned Rent Revenue should equal $16,000 (current period earned revenue is $8,000*)

Step 3: Adjusting entry to get from step 1 to step 2

Dec. 31	Unearned Rent Revenue............................	8,000	
	Rent Revenue		8,000
	Record earned portion of rent received in advance.		
	*($24,000/12 months) × 4 months' rental usage		

b. Step 1: Unearned Services Revenue equals $600 (before adjustment)

Step 2: Unearned Services Revenue should equal $400 (current period earned revenue is $200*)

Step 3: Adjusting entry to get from step 1 to step 2

Dec. 31	Unearned Services Revenue........................	200	
	Services Revenue............................		200
	Record earned portion of revenue received in advance.		
	*$100 × 2 treatments = Services revenue		

Do More: QS 3-10, QS 3-11

ACCRUED EXPENSES

Accrued expenses refer to costs that are incurred in a period but are both unpaid and unrecorded. Accrued expenses must be reported on the income statement for the period when incurred.

Point: Accrued expenses are also called *accrued liabilities.*

Framework   Adjusting entries for recording accrued expenses increase the expense (income statement) account and increase a liability (balance sheet) account, as shown in Exhibit 3.9. This adjustment recognizes expenses incurred in a period but not yet paid. Common examples of accrued expenses are salaries, interest, rent, and taxes. We use salaries and interest to show how to adjust accounts for accrued expenses.

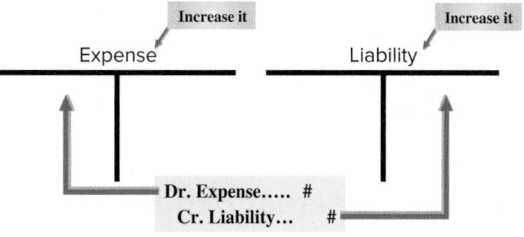

EXHIBIT 3.9

Adjusting for Accrued Expenses (increase a liability and record an expense)

Accrued Salaries Expense

FastForward's employee earns $70 per day, or $350 for a five-day workweek beginning on Monday and ending on Friday.

Step 1:   Its employee is paid every two weeks on Friday. On December 12 and 26, the wages are paid, recorded in the journal, and posted to the ledger.

Step 2:   The calendar in Exhibit 3.10 shows three working days after the December 26 payday (29, 30, and 31). This means the employee has earned three days' salary by the close of business

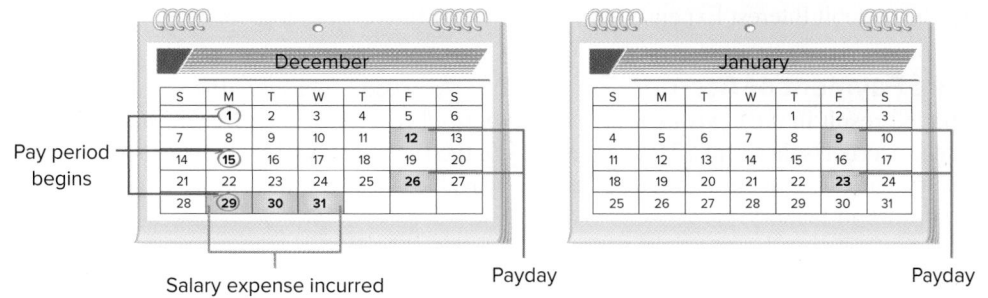

EXHIBIT 3.10

Salary Accrual and Paydays

on Wednesday, December 31, yet this salary cost has not been paid or recorded. The financial statements would be incomplete if FastForward did not report the added expense and liability for unpaid salary from December 29, 30, and 31.

Point: An employer records salaries expense and a vacation pay liability when employees earn vacation pay.

Step 3:   The adjusting entry to account for accrued salaries, along with T-account postings, follows:

Assets = Liabilities + Equity
      +210   −210

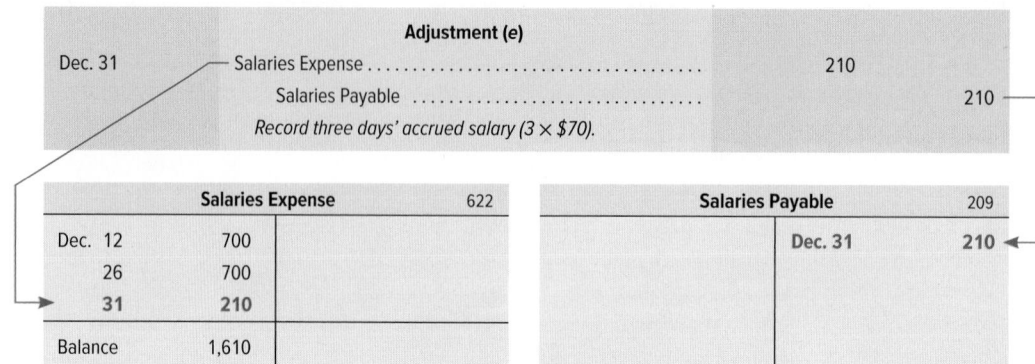

Adjustment (e)		
Dec. 31 Salaries Expense	210	
Salaries Payable		210
Record three days' accrued salary (3 × $70).		

Salaries Expense		622
Dec. 12	700	
26	700	
31	210	
Balance	1,610	

Salaries Payable		209
	Dec. 31	210

Explanation   Salaries expense of $1,610 is reported on the December income statement and $210 of salaries payable (liability) is reported in the balance sheet. *Not* making the adjustment

● Understates salaries expense by $210 in the December income statement.

● Understates salaries payable by $210 on the December 31 balance sheet.

The following highlights the adjustment for salaries incurred.

Before Adjustment	Adjustment	After Adjustment
Salaries Payable = $0	**Add $210 to Salaries Payable** **Add $210 to Salaries Expense**	**Salaries Payable = $210**
Reports $0 from employee salaries incurred but not yet paid in cash.	Record 3 days' salaries owed, but not yet paid, at $70 per day.	Reports $210 salaries payable to employee but not yet paid.

Accrued Interest Expense

Companies commonly have accrued interest expense on notes payable (loans) and other long-term liabilities at the end of a period. Interest expense is incurred as time passes. Unless interest is paid on the last day of an accounting period, we need to adjust for interest expense incurred but not yet paid. This means we must accrue interest cost from the most recent payment date up to the end of the period. The formula for computing accrued interest is:

Principal amount owed × Annual interest rate × Fraction of year since last payment date.

Point: Interest computations assume a 360-day year; known as the *bankers' rule*.

To illustrate, if a company has a $6,000 loan from a bank at 5% annual interest, then 30 days' accrued interest expense is $25—computed as $6,000 × 0.05 × 30/360. The adjusting entry would be to debit Interest Expense for $25 and credit Interest Payable for $25.

Future Payment of Accrued Expenses   Accrued expenses at the end of one accounting period result in *cash payment* in a *future period*(s). To illustrate, recall that FastForward recorded accrued salaries of $210. On January 9, the first payday of the next period, the following entry settles the accrued liability (salaries payable) and records salaries expense for seven days of work in January:

Assets = Liabilities + Equity
−700   −210   −490

Jan. 9	Salaries Payable (3 days at $70 per day)	210	
	Salaries Expense (7 days at $70 per day)	490	
	Cash		700
	Paid two weeks' salary including three days accrued.		

The $210 debit reflects the payment of the liability for the three days' salary accrued on December 31. The $490 debit records the salary for January's first seven working days (including the New Year's Day holiday) as an expense of the new accounting period. The $700 credit records the total amount of cash paid to the employee.

NEED-TO-KNOW 3-3

Accrued Expenses

P1

For each separate case below, follow the three-step process for adjusting the accrued expense account at December 31. Step 1: Determine what the current account balance equals. Step 2: Determine what the current account balance should equal. Step 3: Record the December 31 adjusting entry to get from step 1 to step 2. *Assume no other adjusting entries are made during the year.*

a. **Salaries Payable.** At year-end, salaries expense of $5,000 has been incurred by the company but is not yet paid to employees.

b. **Interest Payable.** At its December 31 year-end, the company holds a mortgage payable that has incurred $1,000 in annual interest that is neither recorded nor paid. The company intends to pay the interest on January 3 of the next year.

Solution

a. Step 1: Salaries Payable equals $0 (before adjustment)

   Step 2: Salaries Payable should equal $5,000 (not yet recorded)

   Step 3: Adjusting entry to get from step 1 to step 2

Dec. 31	Salaries Expense	5,000	
	Salaries Payable		5,000
	Record employee salaries earned but not yet paid.		

b. Step 1: Interest Payable equals $0 (before adjustment)

   Step 2: Interest Payable should equal $1,000 (not yet recorded)

   Step 3: Adjusting entry to get from step 1 to step 2

Dec. 31	Interest Expense	1,000	
	Interest Payable		1,000
	Record interest incurred but not yet paid.		

Do More: QS 3-12, QS 3-13

ACCRUED REVENUES

Accrued revenues are revenues earned in a period that are both unrecorded and not yet received in cash (or other assets). An example is a technician who bills customers after the job is done. If one-third of a job is complete by the end of a period, then the technician must record one-third of the expected billing as revenue in that period—even though there is no billing or collection.

Point: Accrued revenues are also called *accrued assets.*

Framework   The adjusting entries for accrued revenues increase a revenue (income statement) account and increase an asset (balance sheet) account, as shown in Exhibit 3.11. Accrued revenues commonly arise from services, products, interest, and rent. We use service fees and interest to show how to adjust for accrued revenues.

EXHIBIT 3.11

Adjusting for Accrued Revenues (increase an asset and record revenue)

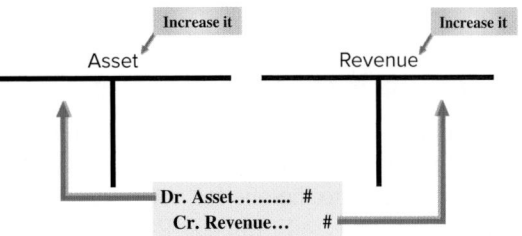

Accrued Services Revenue

Accrued revenues are recorded when adjusting entries are made at the end of the accounting period. These accrued revenues are earned but unrecorded because either the buyer has not yet paid for them or the seller has not yet billed the buyer. FastForward provides an example.

Step 1:   In the second week of December, FastForward agreed to provide 30 days of consulting services to a fitness club for a fixed fee of $2,700 (or $90 per day). FastForward will provide services from December 12, 2017, through January 10, 2018, or 30 days of service. The club agrees to pay FastForward $2,700 on January 10, 2018, when the service period is complete.

Step 2:   At December 31, 2017, 20 days of services have already been provided. Because the contracted services have not yet been entirely provided, FastForward has neither billed the club nor recorded the services already provided. Still, FastForward has earned two-thirds of the 30-day fee, or $1,800 ($2,700 × 20/30). The *revenue recognition principle* prescribes that the company report the $1,800 on the December income statement. The balance sheet reports that the club owes FastForward $1,800.

Step 3:   The year-end adjusting entry to account for accrued services revenue is

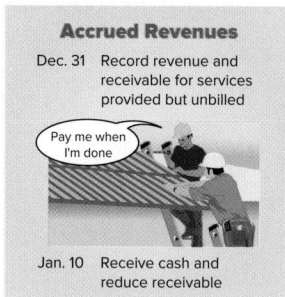

Accrued Revenues

Dec. 31   Record revenue and receivable for services provided but unbilled

Pay me when I'm done

Jan. 10   Receive cash and reduce receivable

Assets = Liabilities + Equity
+1,800   +1,800

		Adjustment (*f*)		
Dec. 31	Accounts Receivable		1,800	
	Consulting Revenue			1,800
	Record 20 days' accrued revenue.			

Accounts Receivable			106
Dec. 12	1,900	Dec. 22	1,900
31	1,800		
Balance	1,800		

Consulting Revenue		403
	Dec. 5	4,200
	12	1,600
	31	250
	31	1,800
	Balance	7,850

Explanation   Accounts receivable are reported on the balance sheet at $1,800, and the $7,850 total of consulting revenue is reported on the income statement. *Not* making the adjustment

- Understates consulting revenue by $1,800 in the December income statement.
- Understates accounts receivable by $1,800 on the December 31 balance sheet.

The following table highlights the adjustment for accrued revenue.

Example: What is the adjusting entry if the 30-day consulting period began on December 22? *Answer:* One-third of the fee is earned:
Accounts Receivable..........900
    Consulting Revenue 900

Before Adjustment	Adjustment	After Adjustment
Accounts Receivable = $0	**Add $1,800 to Accounts Receivable** **Add $1,800 to Consulting Revenue**	**Accounts Receivable = $1,800**
Reports $0 from revenue earned but not yet received in cash.	Record 20 days of earned revenue, which is 20/30 of total contract.	Reports $1,800 in accounts receivable from services provided.

Accrued Interest Revenue

If a company is holding notes or accounts receivable that produce interest revenue, we must adjust the accounts to record any earned and yet uncollected interest revenue. The adjusting entry is similar to the one for accruing services revenue. Specifically, debit Interest Receivable (asset) and credit Interest Revenue.

Future Receipt of Accrued Revenues

Accrued revenues at the end of one accounting period result in *cash receipts* in a *future period*(s). To illustrate, recall that FastForward made an adjusting entry for $1,800 to record 20 days' accrued revenue earned from its consulting contract. When FastForward receives $2,700 cash on January 10 for the entire contract amount, it makes the following entry to remove the accrued asset (accounts receivable) and recognize the revenue earned in January. The $2,700 debit reflects the cash received. The $1,800 credit reflects the removal of the receivable and the $900 credit records the revenue earned in January.

Point: Many companies record adjusting entries only at the end of each year because of the time and cost necessary.

Jan. 10	Cash...	2,700	
	Accounts Receivable (20 days at $90 per day)........		1,800
	Consulting Revenue (10 days at $90 per day)		900
	Received cash for accrued asset and recorded earned consulting revenue for January.		

Assets = Liabilities + Equity
+2,700   +900
−1,800

◾ Decision Maker

Loan Officer   The owner of a custom home theater store applies for a business loan. The store's financial statements reveal large increases in current-year revenues and income. Analysis shows that these increases are due to a promotion that let consumers buy now and pay nothing until January 1 of next year. The store recorded these sales as accrued revenue. Does your analysis raise any concerns? ◾ [*Answer:* Your concern in lending to this store arises from analysis of current-year sales. While increased revenues and income are fine, your concern is with collectibility of these promotional sales. If the owner sold products to customers with poor records of paying bills, then collectibility of these sales is low. Your analysis must assess this possibility and recognize any expected losses.]

For each separate case below, follow the three-step process for adjusting the accrued revenue account at December 31. Step 1: Determine what the current account balance equals. Step 2: Determine what the current account balance should equal. Step 3: Record the December 31 adjusting entry to get from step 1 to step 2. *Assume no other adjusting entries are made during the year.*

NEED-TO-KNOW 3-4

Accrued Revenues

P1

a. Accounts Receivable. At year-end, the company has completed services of $1,000 for a client, but the client has not yet been billed for those services.

b. Interest Receivable. At year-end, the company has earned, but not yet recorded, $500 of interest earned from its investments in government bonds.

Solution

a. Step 1: Accounts Receivable equals $0 (before adjustment)

Step 2: Accounts Receivable should equal $1,000 (not yet recorded)

Step 3: Adjusting entry to get from step 1 to step 2

Dec. 31	Accounts Receivable..................................	1,000	
	Services Revenue		1,000
	Record services revenue earned but not yet received.		

b. Step 1: Interest Receivable equals $0 (before adjustment)

Step 2: Interest Receivable should equal $500 (not yet recorded)

Step 3: Adjusting entry to get from step 1 to step 2

Dec. 31	Interest Receivable...................................	500	
	Interest Revenue		500
	Record interest earned but not yet received.		

Do More: QS 3-3, QS 3-14

Links to Financial Statements

A1

Explain how accounting adjustments link to financial statements.

Exhibit 3.12 summarizes the four types of transactions requiring adjustment. Remember that each adjusting entry affects one or more income statement (revenue or expense) accounts *and* one or more balance sheet (asset or liability) accounts, but never the Cash account. (Adjusting entries are posted like any other entry.)

EXHIBIT 3.12

Summary of Adjustments and Financial Statement Links

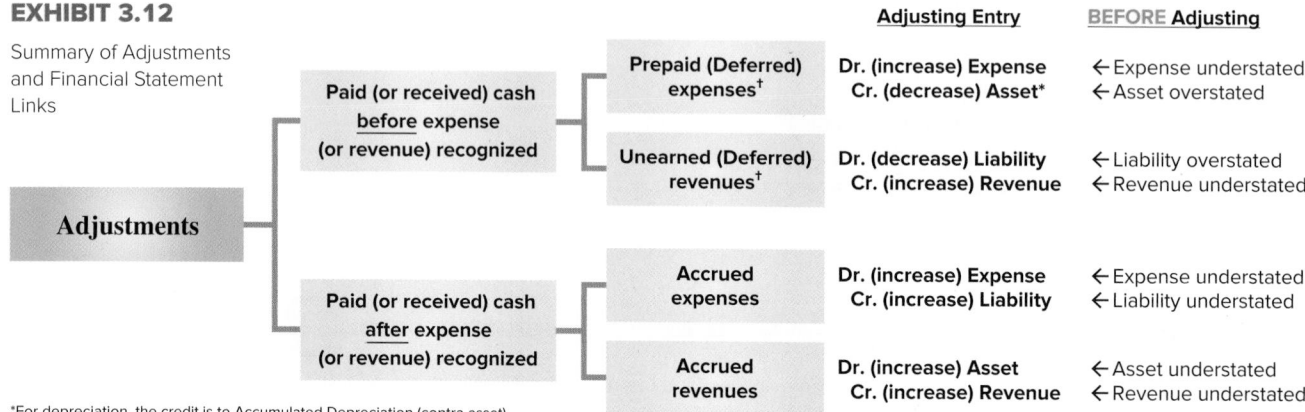

*For depreciation, the credit is to Accumulated Depreciation (contra asset).
†Exhibit assumes that prepaid expenses are initially recorded as assets and that unearned revenues are initially recorded as liabilities.

Information about some adjustments is not available until after the period-end. This means that some adjusting and closing entries are recorded later than, but dated as of, the last day of the period. One example is a company that receives a utility bill on January 10 for costs incurred for the month of December. When it receives the bill, the company records the expense and the payable as of December 31. The income statement and balance sheet reflect these adjustments even though the amounts were not actually known at period-end.

■ **Decision Ethics**

Financial Officer   At year-end, the president instructs you, the financial officer, not to record accrued expenses until next year because they will not be paid until then. The president also directs you to record in current-year sales a recent purchase order from a customer that requires merchandise to be delivered two weeks after the year-end. Your company would report a net income instead of a net loss if you carry out these instructions. What do you do? ■   [*Answer:* Omitting accrued expenses and recognizing revenue early can mislead financial statement users. One action is to request a meeting with the president so you can explain what is required. If the president persists, you might discuss the situation with legal counsel and any auditors involved. Your ethical action might cost you, but the potential pitfalls for falsification of statements, reputation and personal integrity loss, and other costs are too great.]

TRIAL BALANCE AND FINANCIAL STATEMENTS

Adjusted Trial Balance

P2

Explain and prepare an adjusted trial balance.

An **unadjusted trial balance** is a list of accounts and balances prepared *before* adjustments are recorded. An **adjusted trial balance** is a list of accounts and balances prepared *after* adjusting entries have been recorded and posted to the ledger.

Exhibit 3.13 shows both the unadjusted and the adjusted trial balances for FastForward at December 31, 2017. The order of accounts in the trial balance usually matches the order in the chart of accounts. Several new accounts usually arise from adjusting entries.

	A	B	C	D	E	F	G	H	
			**FASTFORWARD** Trial Balances December 31, 2017						
1			Unadjusted Trial Balance				Adjusted Trial Balance		
2					Adjustments				
3									
4			Dr.	Cr.	Dr.	Cr.	Dr.	Cr.	
5	Acct. No.	Account Title							
6	101	Cash	$ 4,275				$ 4,275		
7	106	Accounts receivable	0		(f) $1,800		1,800		
8	126	Supplies	9,720			(b) $1,050	8,670		
9	128	Prepaid insurance	2,400			(a) 100	2,300		
10	167	Equipment	26,000				26,000		
11	168	Accumulated depreciation—Equip.		$ 0		(c) 300		$ 300	
12	201	Accounts payable		6,200				6,200	
13	209	Salaries payable		0		(e) 210		210	
14	236	Unearned consulting revenue		3,000	(d) 250			2,750	
15	301	C. Taylor, Capital		30,000				30,000	
16	302	C. Taylor, Withdrawals	200				200		
17	403	Consulting revenue		5,800		(d) 250		7,850	
18						(f) 1,800			
19	406	Rental revenue		300				300	
20	612	Depreciation expense—Equip.	0		(c) 300		300		
21	622	Salaries expense	1,400		(e) 210		1,610		
22	637	Insurance expense	0		(a) 100		100		
23	640	Rent expense	1,000				1,000		
24	652	Supplies expense	0		(b) 1,050		1,050		
25	690	Utilities expense	305				305		
26		Totals	$45,300	$45,300	$3,710	$3,710	$47,610	$47,610	

EXHIBIT 3.13

Unadjusted and Adjusted Trial Balances

FASTForward

Each adjustment (see middle columns) is identified by a letter in parentheses that links it to an adjusting entry explained earlier. Each amount in the Adjusted Trial Balance columns is computed by taking that account's amount from the Unadjusted Trial Balance columns and adding or subtracting any adjustment(s). To illustrate, Supplies has a $9,720 Dr. balance in the unadjusted columns. Subtracting the $1,050 Cr. amount shown in the Adjustments columns yields an adjusted $8,670 Dr. balance for Supplies. An account can have more than one adjustment, such as for Consulting Revenue. Also, some accounts might not require adjustment for this period, such as Accounts Payable.

Preparing Financial Statements

We can prepare financial statements directly from information in the *adjusted* trial balance. An adjusted trial balance (see the right-most columns in Exhibit 3.13) includes all accounts and balances appearing in financial statements, and is easier to work from than the entire ledger when preparing financial statements.

Exhibit 3.14 shows how revenue and expense balances are transferred from the adjusted trial balance to the income statement (red lines). The net income and the withdrawals amounts are then used to prepare the statement of owner's equity (black lines). Asset and liability balances on the adjusted trial balance are then transferred to the balance sheet (blue lines). The ending capital is determined on the statement of owner's equity and transferred to the balance sheet (green lines).

We prepare financial statements in the following order: income statement, statement of owner's equity, and balance sheet. This order makes sense because the balance sheet uses information from the statement of owner's equity, which in turn uses information from the income statement. The statement of cash flows is usually the final statement prepared.

P3

Prepare financial statements from an adjusted trial balance.

Point: Each trial balance amount is used in only *one* financial statement and, when financial statements are completed, each account will have been used once.

EXHIBIT 3.14

Preparing Financial Statements (Adjusted Trial Balance from Exhibit 3.13)

FASTFORWARD
Adjusted Trial Balance
December 31, 2017

Acct. No.	Account Title	Debit	Credit
101	Cash	$ 4,275	
106	Accounts receivable	1,800	
126	Supplies	8,670	
128	Prepaid insurance	2,300	
167	Equipment	26,000	
168	Accumulated depreciation—Equip.		$ 300
201	Accounts payable		6,200
209	Salaries payable		210
236	Unearned consulting revenue		2,750
301	C. Taylor, Capital		30,000
302	C. Taylor, Withdrawals	200	
403	Consulting revenue		7,850
406	Rental revenue		300
612	Depreciation expense—Equip.	300	
622	Salaries expense	1,610	
637	Insurance expense	100	
640	Rent expense	1,000	
652	Supplies expense	1,050	
690	Utilities expense	305	
	Totals	$47,610	$47,610

Step 3 Prepare balance sheet

FASTFORWARD
Balance Sheet
December 31, 2017

Assets

Cash		$ 4,275
Accounts receivable		1,800
Supplies		8,670
Prepaid insurance		2,300
Equipment	$26,000	
Less accumulated depreciation	300	25,700
Total assets		$ 42,745

Liabilities

Accounts payable	$ 6,200
Salaries payable	210
Unearned consulting revenue	2,750
Total liabilities	9,160

Equity

C. Taylor, Capital	33,585
Total liabilities and equity	$ 42,745

Step 2 Prepare statement of owner's equity

FASTFORWARD
Statement of Owner's Equity
For Month Ended December 31, 2017

C. Taylor, Capital, December 1		$ 0
Plus: Investments by owner	$30,000	
Net income	3,785	
		33,785
Less: Withdrawals by owner		200
C. Taylor, Capital, December 31		$33,585

Steps to Prepare Financial Statements

Step 1	Prepare income statement using revenue and expense accounts from trial balance
Step 2	Prepare statement of owner's equity using capital and withdrawals accounts from trial balance; and pull net income from step 1
Step 3	Prepare balance sheet using asset and liability account from trial balance; and pull updated capital balance from step 2
Step 4	Prepare statement of cash flows from changes in cash flows for the period (illustrated later in the book)

Step 1 Prepare income statement

FASTFORWARD
Income Statement
For Month Ended December 31, 2017

Revenues		
Consulting revenue	$7,850	
Rental revenue	300	
Total revenues		$8,150
Expenses		
Depreciation expense—Equip.	300	
Salaries expense	1,610	
Insurance expense	100	
Rent expense	1,000	
Supplies expense	1,050	
Utilities expense	305	
Total expenses		4,365
Net income		$3,785

Use the following adjusted trial balance of Magic Company to prepare its (1) income statement, (2) statement of owner's equity, and (3) balance sheet (unclassified) for the year ended, or date of, December 31, 2017. The Magic, Capital account balance is $75,000 at December 31, 2016.

NEED-TO-KNOW 3-5

Preparing Financial Statements from a Trial Balance

P3

MAGIC COMPANY
Adjusted Trial Balance
December 31, 2017

Account Title	Debit	Credit
Cash	$ 13,000	
Accounts receivable	17,000	
Land	85,000	
Accounts payable		$ 12,000
Long-term notes payable		33,000
Magic, Capital		75,000
Magic, Withdrawals	20,000	
Fees earned		79,000
Salaries expense	56,000	
Office supplies expense	8,000	
Totals	$199,000	$199,000

Solution

Step 1

MAGIC COMPANY
Income Statement
For Year Ended December 31, 2017

Fees earned		$79,000
Expenses		
Salaries expense	$56,000	
Office supplies expense	8,000	
Total expenses		64,000
Net income		$15,000

Step 2

MAGIC COMPANY
Statement of Owner's Equity
For Year Ended December 31, 2017

Magic, Capital, December 31, 2016	$75,000
Add: Net income	15,000
	90,000
Less: Withdrawals by owner	20,000
Magic, Capital, December 31, 2017	$70,000

Step 3

MAGIC COMPANY
Balance Sheet
December 31, 2017

Assets

Cash	$ 13,000
Accounts receivable	17,000
Land	85,000
Total assets	$115,000

Liabilities

Accounts payable	$ 12,000
Long-term notes payable	33,000
Total liabilities	45,000

Equity

Magic, Capital	70,000
Total liabilities and equity	$115,000

Do More: P 3-5

SUSTAINABILITY AND ACCOUNTING

re:char, as introduced in this chapter's opening feature, is committed to improving the environment and the lives of farmers in Kenya. Jason Aramburu, the entrepreneurial founder of re:char, built the rutuba kiln to provide a sustainable solution for farmers to recycle waste into biochar. According to Jason, the "farmer takes the kiln and uses the waste they are producing—things like sugar cane waste, corn cobs, leaves, and stalks—and converts the waste into biochar." The biochar is then used to sustainably

improve the soil and increase crop yields. Adds Jason, re:char aims "to achieve a systems win: more food, more sequestered carbon, and less waste."

Recycling of waste is not the only benefit of Jason's rutuba kiln. "Biochar is unique because it's the only energy source that is actually carbon negative . . . which means that every ton of biochar produced represents carbon extracted from the air," explains Jason.

Jason also explains how an effective accounting of his operations played a role in his success. He points to the proper recording of accrued revenues to fully understand his sales growth, and the recording of accrued expenses to accurately price his rutuba kiln. If, for example, accrued expenses had been improperly recorded, Jason says he might have priced the kiln too low and not have generated sufficient money to continue operations.

Similarly, without the accrual of revenues, his cash inflows were so low that he might not have been able to obtain financing for his continuing and growing business. This is because Jason had to wait until farmers harvested their crops to receive payment on his receivables. Jason asserts that behind each great start-up is an effective accounting system.

Courtesy of Re:Char

 Decision Analysis    Profit Margin

A useful measure of a company's operating results is the ratio of its net income to net sales. This ratio is called **profit margin,** or *return on sales,* and is computed as in Exhibit 3.15.

EXHIBIT 3.15

Profit Margin

A2

Compute profit margin and describe its use in analyzing company performance.

$$\text{Profit margin} = \frac{\text{Net income}}{\text{Net sales}}$$

This ratio is interpreted as reflecting the percent of profit in each dollar of sales. To illustrate how we compute and use profit margin, let's look at the results of **Limited Brands, Inc.,** in Exhibit 3.16 for its fiscal years 2011 through 2015.

EXHIBIT 3.16

Limited Brands's Profit Margin

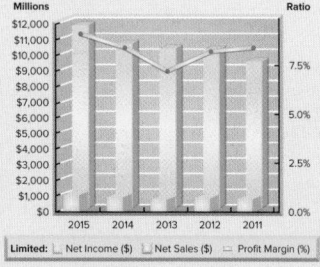

$ millions	2015	2014	2013	2012	2011
Net income	$ 1,042	$ 903	$ 753	$ 850	$ 805
Net sales	$11,454	$10,773	$10,459	$10,364	$9,613
Profit margin	9.1%	8.4%	7.2%	8.2%	8.4%
Industry profit margin	2.8%	2.5%	2.0%	2.2%	2.1%

Limited's average profit margin is 8.3% during this five-year period. This favorably compares to the average industry profit margin of 2.3%. Moreover, we see that Limited's profit margin has rebounded from the recent recessionary period and is at the 7% to 9% margin for the past five years (see margin graph). Future success depends on Limited maintaining its market share and increasing its profit margin.

Decision Maker

CFO   Your health care equipment company consistently reports a profit margin near 9%, which is similar to competitors. The treasurer argues that profit margin can be increased to near 20% if the company cuts back on marketing expenses. Do you cut those expenses? ■   [*Answer:* Cutting those expenses will increase profit margin in the short run. However, over the long run, cutting such expenses can hurt current and future sales and, potentially, put the company in financial distress. The CFO must explain that the company can cut the "fat" (expenses that do not drive sales), but should not cut those that drive sales.]

NEED-TO-KNOW 3-6

COMPREHENSIVE 1

The following information relates to Fanning's Electronics on December 31, 2017. The company, which uses the calendar year as its annual reporting period, initially records prepaid and unearned items in balance sheet accounts (assets and liabilities, respectively).

a. The company's weekly payroll is $8,750, paid each Friday for a five-day workweek. Assume December 31, 2017, falls on a Monday, but the employees will not be paid their wages until Friday, January 4, 2018.

b. Eighteen months earlier, on July 1, 2016, the company purchased equipment that cost $20,000. Its useful life is predicted to be five years, at which time the equipment is expected to be worthless (zero salvage value).

c. On October 1, 2017, the company agreed to work on a new housing development. The company is paid $120,000 on October 1 in advance of future installation of similar alarm systems in 24 new homes. That amount was credited to the Unearned Services Revenue account. Between October 1 and December 31, work on 20 homes was completed.

d. On September 1, 2017, the company purchased a 12-month insurance policy for $1,800. The transaction was recorded with an $1,800 debit to Prepaid Insurance.

e. On December 29, 2017, the company completed a $7,000 service that has not been billed or recorded as of December 31, 2017.

Required

1. Prepare any necessary adjusting entries on December 31, 2017, in relation to transactions and events *a* through *e*.

2. Prepare T-accounts for the accounts affected by adjusting entries, and post the adjusting entries. Determine the adjusted balances for the Unearned Revenue and the Prepaid Insurance accounts.

3. Complete the following table and determine the amounts and effects of your adjusting entries on the year 2017 income statement and the December 31, 2017, balance sheet. Use up (down) arrows to indicate an increase (decrease) in the Effect columns.

Entry	Amount in the Entry	Effect on Net Income	Effect on Total Assets	Effect on Total Liabilities	Effect on Total Equity

PLANNING THE SOLUTION

- Analyze each situation to determine which accounts need to be updated with an adjustment.
- Calculate the amount of each adjustment and prepare the necessary journal entries.
- Show the amount of each adjustment in the designated accounts, determine the adjusted balance, and identify the balance sheet classification of the account.
- Determine each entry's effect on net income for the year and on total assets, total liabilities, and total equity at the end of the year.

SOLUTION

1. Adjusting journal entries.

(a) Dec. 31	Wages Expense	1,750	
	Wages Payable		1,750
	Accrue wages for last day of the year ($8,750 × 1/5).		
(b) Dec. 31	Depreciation Expense—Equipment	4,000	
	Accumulated Depreciation—Equipment		4,000
	Record depreciation expense for year ($20,000/5 years = $4,000 per year).		
(c) Dec. 31	Unearned Services Revenue	100,000	
	Services Revenue		100,000
	Record services revenue earned ($120,000 × 20/24).		
(d) Dec. 31	Insurance Expense	600	
	Prepaid Insurance.		600
	Adjust for expired portion of insurance ($1,800 × 4/12).		
(e) Dec. 31	Accounts Receivable	7,000	
	Services Revenue.		7,000
	Record services revenue earned.		

2. T-accounts for adjusting journal entries *a* through *e*.

Wages Expense	
(*a*) 1,750	

Wages Payable	
	(*a*) 1,750

Depreciation Expense—Equipment	
(*b*) 4,000	

Accumulated Depreciation— Equipment	
	(*b*) 4,000

Unearned Services Revenue	
(*c*) 100,000	Unadj. Bal. 120,000
	Adj. Bal. 20,000

Services Revenue	
	(*c*) 100,000
	(*e*) 7,000
	Adj. Bal. 107,000

Insurance Expense	
(*d*) 600	

Prepaid Insurance	
Unadj. Bal. 1,800	(*d*) 600
Adj. Bal. 1,200	

Accounts Receivable	
(*e*) 7,000	

3. Financial statement effects of adjusting journal entries.

Entry	Amount in the Entry	Effect on Net Income	Effect on Total Assets	Effect on Total Liabilities	Effect on Total Equity
a	$ 1,750	$ 1,750 ↓	No effect	$ 1,750 ↑	$ 1,750 ↓
b	4,000	4,000 ↓	$4,000 ↓	No effect	4,000 ↓
c	100,000	100,000 ↑	No effect	$100,000 ↓	100,000 ↑
d	600	600 ↓	$ 600 ↓	No effect	600 ↓
e	7,000	7,000 ↑	$7,000 ↑	No effect	7,000 ↑

NEED-TO-KNOW **3-7**

COMPREHENSIVE 2

Use the following adjusted trial balance to answer questions 1–3.

CHOI COMPANY Adjusted Trial Balance December 31		
	Debit	Credit
Cash	$ 3,050	
Accounts receivable	400	
Prepaid insurance	830	
Supplies	80	
Equipment	217,200	
Accumulated depreciation—Equipment		$ 29,100
Wages payable		880
Interest payable		3,600
Unearned rent		460
Long-term notes payable		150,000
M. Choi, Capital		40,340
M. Choi, Withdrawals	21,000	
Rent earned		57,500
Wages expense	25,000	
Utilities expense	1,900	
Insurance expense	3,200	
Supplies expense	250	
Depreciation expense—Equipment	5,970	
Interest expense	3,000	
Totals	$281,880	$281,880

1. Prepare the annual income statement from the adjusted trial balance of Choi Company.

Answer:

CHOI COMPANY		
Income Statement		
For Year Ended December 31		
Revenues		
Rent earned		$57,500
Expenses		
Wages expense	$25,000	
Utilities expense	1,900	
Insurance expense	3,200	
Supplies expense	250	
Depreciation expense—Equipment	5,970	
Interest expense	3,000	
Total expenses		39,320
Net income		$18,180

2. Prepare a statement of owner's equity from the adjusted trial balance of Choi Company. Choi's capital account balance of $40,340 consists of a $30,340 balance from the prior year-end, plus a $10,000 owner investment during the current year.

Answer:

CHOI COMPANY		
Statement of Owner's Equity		
For Year Ended December 31		
M. Choi, Capital, December 31 prior year-end		$30,340
Plus: Owner investments	$10,000	
Net income	18,180	28,180
		58,520
Less: Withdrawals by owner		21,000
M. Choi, Capital, December 31 current year-end		$37,520

3. Prepare a balance sheet (unclassified) from the adjusted trial balance of Choi Company.

Answer:

CHOI COMPANY		
Balance Sheet		
December 31		
Assets		
Cash		$ 3,050
Accounts receivable		400
Prepaid insurance		830
Supplies		80
Equipment	$217,200	
Less accumulated depreciation	29,100	188,100
Total assets		$192,460
Liabilities		
Wages payable		$ 880
Interest payable		3,600
Unearned rent		460
Long-term notes payable		150,000
Total liabilities		154,940
Equity		
M. Choi, Capital		37,520
Total liabilities and equity		$192,460

3A

Alternative Accounting for Prepayments

This appendix explains an alternative in accounting for prepaid expenses and unearned revenues.

RECORDING PREPAYMENT OF EXPENSES IN EXPENSE ACCOUNTS

P4

Explain the alternatives in accounting for prepaids.

An alternative method is to record *all* prepaid expenses with debits to expense accounts. If any prepaids remain unused or unexpired at the end of an accounting period, then adjusting entries must transfer the cost of the unused portions from expense accounts to prepaid expense (asset) accounts. This alternative method is acceptable. The financial statements are identical under either method, but the adjusting entries are different. To illustrate the differences between these two methods, let's look at FastForward's cash payment on December 1 for 24 months of insurance coverage beginning on December 1. FastForward recorded that payment with a debit to an asset account, but it could have recorded a debit to an expense account. These alternatives are shown in Exhibit 3A.1.

EXHIBIT 3A.1

Alternative Initial Entries for Prepaid Expenses

			Payment Recorded as Asset		Payment Recorded as Expense	
Dec. 1	Prepaid Insurance		2,400			
	Cash			2,400		
Dec. 1	Insurance Expense				2,400	
	Cash					2,400

At the end of its accounting period on December 31, insurance protection for one month has expired. This means $100 ($2,400/24) of insurance coverage expired and is an expense for December. The adjusting entry depends on how the original payment was recorded. This is shown in Exhibit 3A.2.

EXHIBIT 3A.2

Adjusting Entry for Prepaid Expenses for the Two Alternatives

			Payment Recorded as Asset		Payment Recorded as Expense	
Dec. 31	Insurance Expense		100			
	Prepaid Insurance			100		
Dec. 31	Prepaid Insurance				2,300	
	Insurance Expense					2,300

When these entries are posted to the accounts in the ledger, we can see that these two methods give identical results. The December 31 adjusted account balances in Exhibit 3A.3 show Prepaid Insurance of $2,300 and Insurance Expense of $100 for both methods.

EXHIBIT 3A.3

Account Balances under Two Alternatives for Recording Prepaid Expenses

Payment Recorded as Asset				Payment Recorded as Expense			
Prepaid Insurance			128	**Prepaid Insurance**			128
Dec. 1	2,400	Dec. 31	100	Dec. 31	2,300		
Balance	2,300						

Payment Recorded as Asset				Payment Recorded as Expense			
Insurance Expense			637	**Insurance Expense**			637
Dec. 31	100			Dec. 1	2,400	Dec. 31	2,300
				Balance	100		

RECORDING PREPAYMENT OF REVENUES <u>IN REVENUE ACCOUNTS</u>

As with prepaid expenses, an alternative method is to record *all* unearned revenues with credits to revenue accounts. If any revenues are unearned at the end of an accounting period, then adjusting entries must transfer the unearned portions from revenue accounts to unearned revenue (liability) accounts. This alternative method is acceptable. The adjusting entries are different for these two alternatives, but the financial statements are identical. To illustrate the accounting differences between these two methods, let's look at FastForward's December 26 receipt of $3,000 for consulting services covering the period December 27 to February 24. FastForward recorded this transaction with a credit to a liability account. The alternative is to record it with a credit to a revenue account, as shown in Exhibit 3A.4.

		Receipt Recorded as Liability	Receipt Recorded as Revenue
Dec. 26	Cash	3,000	
	Unearned Consulting Revenue	3,000	
Dec. 26	Cash		3,000
	Consulting Revenue		3,000

EXHIBIT 3A.4

Alternative Initial Entries for Unearned Revenues

By the end of its accounting period on December 31, FastForward has earned $250 of this revenue. This means $250 of the liability has been satisfied. Depending on how the initial receipt is recorded, the adjusting entry is as shown in Exhibit 3A.5.

		Receipt Recorded as Liability	Receipt Recorded as Revenue
Dec. 31	Unearned Consulting Revenue	250	
	Consulting Revenue	250	
Dec. 31	Consulting Revenue		2,750
	Unearned Consulting Revenue		2,750

EXHIBIT 3A.5

Adjusting Entry for Unearned Revenues for the Two Alternatives

After adjusting entries are posted, the two alternatives give identical results. The December 31 adjusted account balances in Exhibit 3A.6 show unearned consulting revenue of $2,750 and consulting revenue of $250 for both methods.

EXHIBIT 3A.6

Account Balances under Two Alternatives for Recording Unearned Revenues

Receipt Recorded as Liability			
Unearned Consulting Revenue			236
Dec. 31	250	Dec. 26	3,000
		Balance	**2,750**

Consulting Revenue			403
		Dec. 31	**250**

Receipt Recorded as Revenue			
Unearned Consulting Revenue			236
		Dec. 31	**2,750**

Consulting Revenue			403
Dec. 31	2,750	Dec. 26	3,000
		Balance	**250**

Summary

C1 **Explain the importance of periodic reporting and the time period assumption.** The value of information is often linked to its timeliness. To provide timely information, accounting systems prepare periodic reports at regular intervals. The time period assumption presumes that an organization's activities can be divided into specific time periods for periodic reporting.

C2 **Explain accrual accounting and how it improves financial statements.** Accrual accounting recognizes revenue when earned and expenses when incurred—not necessarily when cash inflows and outflows occur. This information is valuable in assessing a company's financial position and performance.

C3 **Identify the types of adjustments and their purpose.** Adjustments can be grouped according to the timing of cash receipts and cash payments relative to when they are recognized as revenues or expenses as follows: prepaid expenses, unearned revenues, accrued expenses, and accrued revenues. Adjusting entries are necessary so that revenues, expenses, assets, and liabilities are correctly reported.

A1 **Explain how accounting adjustments link to financial statements.** Accounting adjustments bring an asset or liability account balance to its correct amount. They also update related expense or revenue accounts. Every adjusting entry affects one or more income statement accounts *and* one or more balance sheet accounts. An adjusting entry never affects the Cash account.

A2 **Compute profit margin and describe its use in analyzing company performance.** *Profit margin* is defined as the reporting period's net income divided by its net sales. Profit margin reflects on a company's earnings activities by showing how much income is in each dollar of sales.

P1 **Prepare and explain adjusting entries.** *Prepaid expenses* refer to items paid for in advance of receiving their benefits. Prepaid expenses are assets. Adjusting entries for prepaids involve increasing (debiting) expenses and decreasing (crediting) assets. *Unearned* (or *prepaid*) *revenues* refer to cash received in advance of providing products and services. Unearned revenues are liabilities. Adjusting entries for unearned revenues involve increasing (crediting) revenues and decreasing (debiting) unearned revenues. *Accrued expenses* refer to costs incurred in a period that are both unpaid and unrecorded. Adjusting entries for recording accrued expenses involve increasing (debiting) expenses and increasing (crediting) liabilities. *Accrued revenues* refer to revenues earned in a period that are both unrecorded and not yet received in cash. Adjusting entries for recording accrued revenues involve increasing (debiting) assets and increasing (crediting) revenues.

P2 **Explain and prepare an adjusted trial balance.** An adjusted trial balance is a list of accounts and balances prepared after recording and posting adjusting entries. Financial statements are often prepared from the adjusted trial balance.

P3 **Prepare financial statements from an adjusted trial balance.** Revenue and expense balances are reported on the income statement. Asset, liability, and equity balances are reported on the balance sheet. We usually prepare statements in the following order: income statement, statement of owner's equity, balance sheet, and statement of cash flows.

P4ᴬ **Explain the alternatives in accounting for prepaids.** Charging all prepaid expenses to expense accounts when they are purchased is acceptable. When this is done, adjusting entries must transfer any unexpired amounts from expense accounts to asset accounts. Crediting all unearned revenues to revenue accounts when cash is received is also acceptable. In this case, the adjusting entries must transfer any unearned amounts from revenue accounts to unearned revenue accounts.

Key Terms

Accounting period	Cash basis accounting	Prepaid expenses
Accrual basis accounting	Contra account	Profit margin
Accrued expenses	Depreciation	Revenue recognition principle
Accrued revenues	Expense recognition (or matching) principle	Straight-line depreciation method
Accumulated depreciation	Fiscal year	Time period assumption
Adjusted trial balance	Interim financial statements	Unadjusted trial balance
Adjusting entry	Natural business year	Unearned revenues
Annual financial statements	Plant assets	
Book value		

Multiple Choice Quiz

1. A company forgot to record accrued and unpaid employee wages of $350,000 at period-end. This oversight would
   a. Understate net income by $350,000.
   b. Overstate net income by $350,000.
   c. Have no effect on net income.
   d. Overstate assets by $350,000.
   e. Understate assets by $350,000.

2. Prior to recording adjusting entries, the Supplies account has a $450 debit balance. A physical count of supplies shows $125 of unused supplies still available. The required adjusting entry is:
   a. Debit Supplies $125; Credit Supplies Expense $125.
   b. Debit Supplies $325; Credit Supplies Expense $325.
   c. Debit Supplies Expense $325; Credit Supplies $325.
   d. Debit Supplies Expense $325; Credit Supplies $125.
   e. Debit Supplies Expense $125; Credit Supplies $125.

3. On May 1, 2017, a two-year insurance policy was purchased for $24,000 with coverage to begin immediately. What is the amount of insurance expense that appears on the company's income statement for the year ended December 31, 2017?

   a. $4,000   **c.** $12,000   **e.** $24,000

   b. $8,000   **d.** $20,000

4. On November 1, 2017, Stockton Co. receives $3,600 cash from Hans Co. for consulting services to be provided evenly over the period November 1, 2017, to April 30, 2018—at which time Stockton credited $3,600 to Unearned Consulting Fees. The adjusting entry on December 31, 2017 (Stockton's year-end) would include a

   a. Debit to Unearned Consulting Fees for $1,200.

   b. Debit to Unearned Consulting Fees for $2,400.

   c. Credit to Consulting Fees Earned for $2,400.

   d. Debit to Consulting Fees Earned for $1,200.

   e. Credit to Cash for $3,600.

5. If a company had $15,000 in net income for the year, and its sales were $300,000 for the same year, what is its profit margin?

   a. 20%   **c.** $285,000   **e.** 5%

   b. 2,000%   **d.** $315,000

ANSWERS TO MULTIPLE CHOICE QUIZ

1. b; the forgotten adjusting entry is: *dr.* Wages Expense, *cr.* Wages Payable.

2. c; Supplies used = $450 − $125 = $325

3. b; Insurance expense = $24,000 × (8/24) = $8,000; adjusting entry is: *dr.* Insurance Expense for $8,000, *cr.* Prepaid Insurance for $8,000.

4. a; Consulting fees earned = $3,600 × (2/6) = $1,200; adjusting entry is: *dr.* Unearned Consulting Fee for $1,200, *cr.* Consulting Fees Earned for $1,200.

5. e; Profit margin = $15,000/$300,000 = 5%

---

^A *Superscript letter A denotes assignments based on Appendix 3A.*

[I] Icon denotes assignments that involve decision making.

Discussion Questions

1. What is the difference between the cash basis and the accrual basis of accounting?

2. [I] Why is the accrual basis of accounting generally preferred over the cash basis?

3. What type of business is most likely to select a fiscal year that corresponds to its natural business year instead of the calendar year?

4. What is a prepaid expense and where is it reported in the financial statements?

5. [I] What type of assets requires adjusting entries to record depreciation?

6. [I] What contra account is used when recording and reporting the effects of depreciation? Why is it used?

7. What is an accrued revenue? Give an example.

8.^A If a company initially records prepaid expenses with debits to expense accounts, what type of account is debited in the adjusting entries for those prepaid expenses?

9. [I] Review the balance sheet of Apple in **APPLE** Appendix A. Identify one asset account that requires adjustment before annual financial statements can be prepared. What would be the effect on the income statement if this asset account were not adjusted? (Number not required, but comment on over- or understating of net income.)

10. [I] Review the balance sheet of Google **GOOGLE** in Appendix A. Identify the amount for property and equipment. What adjusting entry is necessary (no numbers required) for this account when preparing financial statements?

11. [⊞] Assume Samsung has unearned **Samsung** revenue. Explain what is unearned revenue and where is it reported in financial statements?

12. [⊞] Refer to Samsung's balance sheet **Samsung** in Appendix A. If it made an adjustment for unpaid wages at year-end, where would the accrued wages be reported on its balance sheet?

[Mc Graw Hill] **connect**

Choose from the following list of terms/phrases to best complete the statements below.

  a. Fiscal year   **d.** Accounting period   **g.** Natural business year

  b. Timeliness   **e.** Annual financial statements   **h.** Time period assumption

  c. Calendar year   **f.** Interim financial statements   **i.** Quarterly statements

1. _____ presumes that an organization's activities can be divided into specific time periods.

2. Financial reports covering a one-year period are known as _____.

3. A(n) _____ consists of any 12 consecutive months.

4. A(n) _____ consists of 12 consecutive months ending on December 31.

5. The value of information is often linked to its _____.

QUICK STUDY

QS 3-1
Periodic reporting

C1

QS 3-2

Computing accrual and cash income

C2

In its first year of operations, Roma Company reports the following:

- Earned revenues of $45,000 ($37,000 cash received from customers).
- Incurred expenses of $25,500 ($20,250 cash paid toward them).
- Prepaid $6,750 cash for costs that will not be expensed until next year.

Compute the company's first-year net income under both the cash basis *and* the accrual basis of accounting.

QS 3-3

Identifying accounting adjustments

C3

Classify the following adjusting entries as involving prepaid expenses (PE), unearned revenues (UR), accrued expenses (AE), or accrued revenues (AR).

_____ **a.** To record revenue earned that was previously received as cash in advance.

_____ **b.** To record wages expense incurred but not yet paid (nor recorded).

_____ **c.** To record revenue earned but not yet billed (nor recorded).

_____ **d.** To record expiration of prepaid insurance.

_____ **e.** To record annual depreciation expense.

QS 3-4

Concepts of adjusting entries

C3

During the year, a company recorded prepayments of expenses in asset accounts, and cash receipts of unearned revenues in liability accounts. At the end of its annual accounting period, the company must make three adjusting entries:

(1) Accrue salaries expense.   Dr. ____ Cr. ____

(2) Adjust the Unearned Services Revenue account to recognize earned revenue.   Dr. ____ Cr. ____

(3) Record services revenue earned for which cash will be received the following period.   Dr. ____ Cr. ____

For each of the adjusting entries (1), (2), and (3), indicate the account to be debited and the account to be credited—from *a* through *i* below.

a. Prepaid Salaries   **d.** Unearned Services Revenue   **g.** Accounts Receivable

b. Cash   **e.** Salaries Expense   **h.** Accounts Payable

c. Salaries Payable   **f.** Services Revenue   **i.** Equipment

---

QS 3-5

Prepaid (deferred) expenses adjustments

P1

For each separate case below, follow the three-step process for adjusting the prepaid asset account at December 31. Step 1: Determine what the current account balance equals. Step 2: Determine what the current account balance should equal. Step 3: Record the December 31 adjusting entry to get from step 1 to step 2. *Assume no other adjusting entries are made during the year.*

a. Prepaid Insurance. The Prepaid Insurance account has a $4,700 debit balance to start the year. A review of insurance policies and payments shows that $900 of unexpired insurance remains at year-end.

b. Prepaid Insurance. The Prepaid Insurance account has a $5,890 debit balance at the start of the year. A review of insurance policies and payments shows $1,040 of insurance has expired by year-end.

c. Prepaid Rent. On September 1 of the current year, the company prepaid $24,000 for two years of rent for facilities being occupied that day. The company debited Prepaid Rent and credited Cash for $24,000.

QS 3-6

Prepaid (deferred) expenses adjustments

P1

For each separate case below, follow the three-step process for adjusting the supplies asset account at December 31. Step 1: Determine what the current account balance equals. Step 2: Determine what the current account balance should equal. Step 3: Record the December 31 adjusting entry to get from step 1 to step 2. *Assume no other adjusting entries are made during the year.*

a. Supplies. The Supplies account has a $300 debit balance to start the year. No supplies were purchased during the current year. A December 31 physical count shows $110 of supplies remaining.

b. Supplies. The Supplies account has an $800 debit balance to start the year. Supplies of $2,100 were purchased during the current year and debited to the Supplies account. A December 31 physical count shows $650 of supplies remaining.

c. Supplies. The Supplies account has a $4,000 debit balance to start the year. During the current year, supplies of $9,400 were purchased and debited to the Supplies account. The inventory of supplies available at December 31 totaled $2,660.

a. On July 1, 2017, Lopez Company paid $1,200 for six months of insurance coverage. No adjustments have been made to the Prepaid Insurance account, and it is now December 31, 2017. Prepare the journal entry to reflect expiration of the insurance as of December 31, 2017.

b. Zim Company has a Supplies account balance of $5,000 on January 1, 2017. During 2017, it purchased $2,000 of supplies. As of December 31, 2017, a supplies inventory shows $800 of supplies available. Prepare the adjusting journal entry to correctly report the balance of the Supplies account and the Supplies Expense account as of December 31, 2017.

QS 3-7
Adjusting prepaid expenses

P1

For each separate case below, follow the three-step process for adjusting the accumulated depreciation account at December 31. Step 1: Determine what the current account balance equals. Step 2: Determine what the current account balance should equal. Step 3: Record the December 31 adjusting entry to get from step 1 to step 2. *Assume no other adjusting entries are made during the year.*

a. Accumulated Depreciation. The Krug Company's Accumulated Depreciation account has a $13,500 balance to start the year. A review of depreciation schedules reveals that $14,600 of depreciation expense must be recorded for the year.

b. Accumulated Depreciation. The company has only one fixed asset (truck) that it purchased at the start of this year. That asset had cost $44,000, had an estimated life of five years, and is expected to have zero value at the end of the five years.

c. Accumulated Depreciation. The company has only one fixed asset (equipment) that it purchased at the start of this year. That asset had cost $32,000, had an estimated life of seven years, and is expected to be valued at $4,000 at the end of the seven years.

QS 3-8
Accumulated depreciation adjustments

P1

---

a. Barga Company purchases $20,000 of equipment on January 1, 2017. The equipment is expected to last five years and be worth $2,000 at the end of that time. Prepare the entry to record one year's depreciation expense of $3,600 for the equipment as of December 31, 2017.

b. Welch Company purchases $10,000 of land on January 1, 2017. The land is expected to last indefinitely. What depreciation adjustment, if any, should be made with respect to the Land account as of December 31, 2017?

QS 3-9
Adjusting for depreciation

P1

For each separate case below, follow the three-step process for adjusting the unearned revenue liability account at December 31. Step 1: Determine what the current account balance equals. Step 2: Determine what the current account balance should equal. Step 3: Record the December 31 adjusting entry to get from step 1 to step 2. *Assume no other adjusting entries are made during the year.*

a. Unearned Rent Revenue. The Krug Company collected $6,000 rent in advance on November 1, debiting Cash and crediting Unearned Rent Revenue. The tenant was paying 12 months' rent in advance and occupancy began November 1.

b. Unearned Services Revenue. The company charges $75 per month to spray a house for insects. A customer paid $300 on October 1 in advance for four treatments, which was recorded with a debit to Cash and a credit to Unearned Services Revenue. At year-end, the company has applied three treatments for the customer.

c. Unearned Rent Revenue. On September 1, a client paid the company $24,000 cash for six months of rent in advance (the client leased a building and took occupancy immediately). The company recorded the cash as Unearned Rent Revenue.

QS 3-10
Unearned (deferred) revenues adjustments

P1

---

a. Tao Co. receives $10,000 cash in advance for four months of legal services on October 1, 2017, and records it by debiting Cash and crediting Unearned Revenue both for $10,000. It is now December 31, 2017, and Tao has provided legal services as planned. What adjusting entry should Tao make to account for the work performed from October 1 through December 31, 2017?

b. A. Caden started a new publication called *Contest News*. Its subscribers pay $24 to receive 12 monthly issues. With every new subscriber, Caden debits Cash and credits Unearned Subscription Revenue for the amounts received. The company has 100 new subscribers as of July 1, 2017. It sends *Contest News* to each of these subscribers every month from July through December. Assuming no changes in subscribers, prepare the journal entry that Caden must make as of December 31, 2017, to adjust the Subscription Revenue account and the Unearned Subscription Revenue account.

QS 3-11
Adjusting for unearned revenues

P1

QS 3-12
Accrued expenses adjustments
P1

For each separate case below, follow the three-step process for adjusting the accrued expense account at December 31. Step 1: Determine what the current account balance equals. Step 2: Determine what the current account balance should equal. Step 3: Record the December 31 adjusting entry to get from step 1 to step 2. *Assume no other adjusting entries are made during the year.*

a. Salaries Payable. At year-end, salaries expense of $15,500 has been incurred by the company but is not yet paid to employees.

b. Interest Payable. At its December 31 year-end, the company owes $250 of interest on a line-of-credit loan. That interest will not be paid until sometime in January of the next year.

c. Interest Payable. At its December 31 year-end, the company holds a mortgage payable that has incurred $875 in annual interest that is neither recorded nor paid. The company intends to pay the interest on January 7 of the next year.

QS 3-13
Accruing salaries
P1   A1

Molly Mocha employs one college student every summer in her coffee shop. The student works the five weekdays and is paid on the following Monday. (For example, a student who works Monday through Friday, June 1 through June 5, is paid for that work on Monday, June 8.) The coffee shop adjusts its books *monthly,* if needed, to show salaries earned but unpaid at month-end. The student works the last week of July, which is Monday, July 28, through Friday, August 1. If the student earns $100 per day, what adjusting entry must the coffee shop make on July 31 to correctly record accrued salaries expense for July?

QS 3-14
Accrued revenues adjustments
P1

For each separate case below, follow the three-step process for adjusting the accrued revenue account at December 31. Step 1: Determine what the current account balance equals. Step 2: Determine what the current account balance should equal. Step 3: Record the December 31 adjusting entry to get from step 1 to step 2. *Assume no other adjusting entries are made during the year.*

a. Accounts Receivable. At year-end, the Krug Company has completed services of $19,000 for a client, but the client has not yet been billed for those services.

b. Interest Receivable. At year-end, the company has earned, but not yet recorded, $390 of interest earned from its investments in government bonds.

c. Accounts Receivable. A painting company collects fees when jobs are complete. The work for one customer, whose job was bid at $1,300, has been completed, but the customer has not yet been billed.

QS 3-15
Recording and analyzing adjusting entries
A1

Adjusting entries affect at least one balance sheet account and at least one income statement account. For the entries below, identify the account to be debited and the account to be credited from the following accounts: Cash; Accounts Receivable; Prepaid Insurance; Equipment; Accumulated Depreciation; Wages Payable; Unearned Revenue; Revenue; Wages Expense; Insurance Expense; Depreciation Expense. Indicate which of the accounts is the income statement account and which is the balance sheet account.

a. Entry to record revenue earned that was previously received as cash in advance.

b. Entry to record wage expenses incurred but not yet paid (nor recorded).

c. Entry to record revenue earned but not yet billed (nor recorded).

d. Entry to record expiration of prepaid insurance.

e. Entry to record annual depreciation expense.

QS 3-16
Determining effects of adjusting entries
A1

In making adjusting entries at the end of its accounting period, Chao Consulting mistakenly forgot to record:

- $3,200 of insurance coverage that had expired (this $3,200 cost had been initially debited to the Prepaid Insurance account).
- $2,000 of accrued salaries expense.

As a result of these oversights, the financial statements for the reporting period will [choose one] (1) understate assets by $3,200; (2) understate expenses by $5,200; (3) understate net income by $2,000; or (4) overstate liabilities by $2,000.

The following information is taken from Camara Company's unadjusted and adjusted trial balances.

QS 3-17
Interpreting adjusting
entries
P2

	Unadjusted		Adjusted	
	Debit	Credit	Debit	Credit
Prepaid insurance...........	$4,100		$3,700	
Interest payable		$ 0		$800

Given this information, which of the following is likely included among its adjusting entries?

a. A $400 debit to Insurance Expense and an $800 debit to Interest Payable.

b. A $400 debit to Insurance Expense and an $800 debit to Interest Expense.

c. A $400 credit to Prepaid Insurance and an $800 debit to Interest Payable.

Damita Company reported net income of $48,025 and net sales of $425,000 for the current year. Calculate the company's profit margin and interpret the result. Assume that its competitors earn an average profit margin of 15%.

QS 3-18
Analyzing profit margin

A2

Garcia Company had the following selected transactions during the year. (A partial chart of accounts follows: Cash; Accounts Receivable; Prepaid Insurance; Wages Payable; Unearned Revenue; Revenue; Wages Expense; Insurance Expense; Depreciation Expense.)

QS 3-19^A
Preparing adjusting entries
P4

Jan.   1   The company paid $6,000 cash for 12 months of insurance coverage beginning immediately for the calendar year.

Aug.   1   The company received $2,400 cash in advance for 6 months of contracted services beginning on August 1 and ending on January 31.

Dec. 31   The company prepared any necessary year-end adjusting entries related to insurance coverage and services rendered.

a. Record journal entries for these transactions assuming Garcia follows the usual practice of recording a prepayment of an expense in an asset account *and* recording a prepayment of revenue received in a liability account.

b. Record journal entries for these transactions assuming Garcia follows the alternative practice of recording a prepayment of an expense in an expense account *and* recording a prepayment of revenue received in a revenue account.

Cal Consulting follows the practice that prepayments are debited to expense when paid, and unearned revenues are credited to revenue when cash is received. Given this company's accounting practices, which one of the following applies to the preparation of adjusting entries at the end of its first accounting period?

QS 3-20^A
Preparing adjusting entries
P4

a. Unearned fees (on which cash was received in advance earlier in the period) are recorded with a debit to Consulting Fees Earned of $500 and a credit to Unearned Consulting Fees of $500.

b. Unpaid salaries of $400 are recorded with a debit to Prepaid Salaries of $400 and a credit to Salaries Expense of $400.

c. Office supplies purchased for the period were $1,000. The cost of unused office supplies of $650 is recorded with a debit to Supplies Expense of $650 and a credit to Office Supplies of $650.

d. Earned but unbilled (and unrecorded) consulting fees for the period were $1,200, which are recorded with a debit to Unearned Consulting Fees of $1,200 and a credit to Consulting Fees Earned of $1,200.

Answer each of the following questions related to international accounting standards.

QS 3-21
International accounting
standards

P3

a. Do financial statements prepared under IFRS normally present assets from least liquid to most liquid or vice versa?

b. Do financial statements prepared under IFRS normally present liabilities from furthest from maturity to nearest to maturity or vice versa?

EXERCISES

Exercise 3-1

Determining assets and expenses for accrual and cash accounting

C2

On March 1, 2015, a company paid an $18,000 premium on a 36-month insurance policy for coverage beginning on that date. Refer to that policy and fill in the blanks in the following table.

	Balance Sheet Prepaid Insurance Asset Using			Insurance Expense Using		
	Accrual Basis	Cash Basis		Accrual Basis	Cash Basis
Dec. 31, 2015	$_____	$_____	2015	$_____	$_____
Dec. 31, 2016	_____	_____	2016	_____	_____
Dec. 31, 2017	_____	_____	2017	_____	_____
Dec. 31, 2018	_____	_____	2018	_____	_____
			Total	$_____	$_____

Check 2017 insurance expense: Accrual, $6,000; Cash, $0.
Dec. 31, 2017, asset: Accrual, $1,000; Cash, $0.

Exercise 3-2

Classifying adjusting entries

C3

In the blank space beside each adjusting entry, enter the letter of the explanation A through F that most closely describes the entry.

A. To record this period's depreciation expense.

B. To record accrued salaries expense.

C. To record this period's use of a prepaid expense.

D. To record accrued interest revenue.

E. To record accrued interest expense.

F. To record the earning of previously unearned income.

_____	1.	Interest Expense	2,208
		Interest Payable		2,208
_____	2.	Insurance Expense	3,180
		Prepaid Insurance		3,180
_____	3.	Unearned Professional Fees	19,250
		Professional Fees Earned		19,250
_____	4.	Interest Receivable	3,300
		Interest Revenue		3,300
_____	5.	Depreciation Expense	38,217
		Accumulated Depreciation		38,217
_____	6.	Salaries Expense	13,280
		Salaries Payable		13,280

Exercise 3-3

Adjusting and paying accrued wages

C1 P1

Pablo Management has five part-time employees, each of whom earns $250 per day. They are normally paid on Fridays for work completed Monday through Friday of the same week. Assume that December 28, 2017, was a Friday, and that they were paid in full on that day. The next week, the five employees worked only four days because New Year's Day was an unpaid holiday.

a. Assuming that December 31, 2017, was a Monday, prepare the adjusting entry for wages expense that would be recorded at the close of that day.

b. Assuming that January 4, 2018, was a Friday, prepare the journal entry that would be made to record payment of the employees' wages for that week.

Exercise 3-4

Determining cost flows through accounts

C1 A1 P1

Determine the missing amounts in each of these four separate situations *a* through *d*.

	a	b	c	d
Supplies available—prior year-end	$ 400	$1,200	$1,260	?
Supplies purchased during the current year..............	2,800	6,500	?	$3,000
Supplies available—current year-end	650	?	1,350	700
Supplies expense for the current year	?	1,200	8,400	4,588

The following three separate situations require adjusting journal entries to prepare financial statements as of April 30. For each situation, present both:

- The April 30 adjusting entry.
- The subsequent entry during May to record payment of the accrued expenses.

Exercise 3-5
Adjusting and paying accrued expenses

A1   P1

Entries can draw from the following partial chart of accounts: Cash; Accounts Receivable; Prepaid Interest; Salaries Payable; Interest Payable; Legal Services Payable; Unearned Revenue; Revenue; Salaries Expense; Interest Expense; Legal Services Expense; Depreciation Expense.

a. On April 1, the company retained an attorney for a flat monthly fee of $3,500. Payment for April legal services was made by the company on May 12.

b. A $900,000 note payable requires 12% annual interest, or $9,000, to be paid at the 20th day of each month. The interest was last paid on April 20 and the next payment is due on May 20. As of April 30, $3,000 of interest expense has accrued.

Check (b) May 20 Dr.
Interest Expense, $6,000

c. Total weekly salaries expense for all employees is $10,000. This amount is paid at the end of the day on Friday of each five-day workweek. April 30 falls on a Tuesday, which means that the employees had worked two days since the last payday. The next payday is May 3.

Prepare adjusting journal entries for the year ended (date of) December 31, 2017, for each of these separate situations. (Entries can draw from the following partial chart of accounts: Cash; Accounts Receivable; Supplies; Prepaid Insurance; Equipment; Accumulated Depreciation—Equipment; Wages Payable; Unearned Revenue; Revenue; Wages Expense; Supplies Expense; Insurance Expense; Depreciation Expense—Equipment.)

Exercise 3-6
Preparing adjusting entries

P1

a. Depreciation on the company's equipment for 2017 is computed to be $18,000.

b. The Prepaid Insurance account had a $6,000 debit balance at December 31, 2017, before adjusting for the costs of any expired coverage. An analysis of the company's insurance policies showed that $1,100 of unexpired insurance coverage remains.

c. The Office Supplies account had a $700 debit balance on December 31, 2016; and $3,480 of office supplies were purchased during the year. The December 31, 2017, physical count showed $300 of supplies available.

Check (c) Dr. Supplies
Expense, $3,880

d. Two-thirds of the work related to $15,000 of cash received in advance was performed this period.

e. The Prepaid Insurance account had a $6,800 debit balance at December 31, 2017, before adjusting for the costs of any expired coverage. An analysis of insurance policies showed that $5,800 of coverage had expired.

(e) Dr. Insurance
Expense, $5,800

f. Wage expenses of $3,200 have been incurred but are not paid as of December 31, 2017.

For each of the following separate cases, prepare adjusting entries required of financial statements for the year ended (date of) December 31, 2017. (Entries can draw from the following partial chart of accounts: Cash; Interest Receivable; Supplies; Prepaid Insurance; Equipment; Accumulated Depreciation—Equipment; Wages Payable; Interest Payable; Unearned Revenue; Interest Revenue; Wages Expense; Supplies Expense; Insurance Expense; Interest Expense; Depreciation Expense—Equipment.)

Exercise 3-7
Preparing adjusting entries

P1

a. Wages of $8,000 are earned by workers but not paid as of December 31, 2017.

b. Depreciation on the company's equipment for 2017 is $18,000.

c. The Office Supplies account had a $240 debit balance on December 31, 2016. During 2017, $5,200 of office supplies are purchased. A physical count of supplies at December 31, 2017, shows $440 of supplies available.

d. The Prepaid Insurance account had a $4,000 balance on December 31, 2016. An analysis of insurance policies shows that $1,200 of unexpired insurance benefits remain at December 31, 2017.

Check (d) Dr. Insurance
Expense, $2,800

e. The company has earned (but not recorded) $1,050 of interest from investments in CDs for the year ended December 31, 2017. The interest revenue will be received on January 10, 2018.

(e) Cr. Interest
Revenue, $1,050

f. The company has a bank loan and has incurred (but not recorded) interest expense of $2,500 for the year ended December 31, 2017. The company must pay the interest on January 2, 2018.

Exercise 3-8

Analyzing and preparing adjusting entries

A1   P1   P3

Following are two income statements for Alexis Co. for the year ended December 31. The left number column is prepared before any adjusting entries are recorded, and the right column includes the effects of adjusting entries. The middle column identifies the income statement effect of the eight adjusting entries (the balance sheet part of the entries is not shown here). Analyze the statements and prepare the eight adjusting entries *a* through *g* that likely were recorded. *Note:* Answer for *a* has two entries (i) the $7,000 adjustment for Fees Earned, 30% (or $2,100) has been earned but not billed, and (ii) the other 70% (or $4,900) has been earned by performing services that were paid for in advance.

ALEXIS CO. Income Statements For Year Ended December 31			
	Unadjusted	**Adjustments**	**Adjusted**
Revenues			
Fees earned	$18,000	a.	$25,000
Commissions earned	36,500		36,500
Total revenues	54,500		61,500
Expenses			
Depreciation expense—Computers	0	b.	1,600
Depreciation expense—Office furniture	0	c.	1,850
Salaries expense	13,500	d.	15,750
Insurance expense	0	e.	1,400
Rent expense.................................	3,800		3,800
Office supplies expense	0	f.	580
Advertising expense	2,500		2,500
Utilities expense	1,245	g.	1,335
Total expenses	21,045		28,815
Net income	$33,455		$32,685

Exercise 3-9

Preparing adjusting entries—accrued revenues and expenses

P1

Prepare year-end adjusting journal entries for M&R Company as of December 31, 2017, for each of the following separate cases. (Entries can draw from the following partial chart of accounts: Cash; Accounts Receivable; Interest Receivable; Equipment; Wages Payable; Salary Payable; Interest Payable; Lawn Services Payable; Unearned Revenue; Revenue; Interest Revenue; Wages Expense; Salary Expense; Supplies Expense; Lawn Services Expense; Interest Expense.)

a. M&R Company provided $2,000 in services to customers that are expected to pay the company sometime in January following the company's year-end.

b. Wage expenses of $1,000 have been incurred but are not paid as of December 31.

c. M&R Company has a $5,000 bank loan and has incurred (but not recorded) 8% interest expense of $400 for the year ended December 31. The company will pay the $400 interest in cash on January 2 following the company's year-end.

d. M&R Company hired a firm to provide lawn services at a monthly fee of $500 with payment occurring on the 15th of the following month. Payment for December services will occur on January 15 following the company's year-end.

e. M&R Company has earned $200 in interest revenue from investments for the year ended December 31. The interest revenue will be received on January 15 following the company's year-end.

f. Salary expenses of $900 have been earned by supervisors but not paid as of December 31.

Exercise 3-10

Computing and interpreting profit margin

A2

Use the following information to compute profit margin for each separate company *a* through *e*.

	Net Income	*Net Sales*			*Net Income*	*Net Sales*
a.	$ 4,361	$ 44,500		**d.**	$65,646	$1,458,800
b.	97,706	398,800		**e.**	80,132	435,500
c.	111,281	257,000				

Which of the five companies is the most profitable according to the profit margin ratio? Interpret the profit margin ratio for company *c*.

Ricardo Construction began operations on December 1. In setting up its accounting procedures, the company decided to debit expense accounts when it prepays its expenses and to credit revenue accounts when customers pay for services in advance. Prepare journal entries for items *a* through *d* and the adjusting entries as of its December 31 period-end for items *e* through *g*. (Entries can draw from the following partial chart of accounts: Cash; Accounts Receivable; Interest Receivable; Supplies; Prepaid Insurance; Unearned Remodeling Fees; Remodeling Fees Earned; Supplies Expense; Insurance Expense; Interest Expense.)

Exercise 3-11ᴬ
Adjusting for prepaids recorded as expenses and unearned revenues recorded as revenues
P4

a. Supplies are purchased on December 1 for $2,000 cash.

b. The company prepaid its insurance premiums for $1,540 cash on December 2.

c. On December 15, the company receives an advance payment of $13,000 cash from a customer for remodeling work.

d. On December 28, the company receives $3,700 cash from another customer for remodeling work to be performed in January.

e. A physical count on December 31 indicates that the Company has $1,840 of supplies available.

f. An analysis of the insurance policies in effect on December 31 shows that $340 of insurance coverage had expired.

Check *(f)* Cr. Insurance Expense, $1,200

g. As of December 31, only one remodeling project has been worked on and completed. The $5,570 fee for this project had been received in advance and recorded as remodeling fees earned.

(g) Dr. Remodeling Fees Earned, $11,130

Costanza Company experienced the following events and transactions during July. The company has the following partial chart of accounts: Cash; Accounts Receivable; Unearned Fees; Fees Earned.

Exercise 3-12ᴬ
Recording and reporting revenues received in advance
P4

July 1 Received $3,000 cash in advance of performing work for Vivian Solana.
     6 Received $7,500 cash in advance of performing work for Iris Haru.
    12 Completed the job for Solana.
    18 Received $8,500 cash in advance of performing work for Amina Jordan.
    27 Completed the job for Haru.
    31 None of the work for Jordan has been performed.

a. Prepare journal entries (including any adjusting entries as of the end of the month) to record these events using the procedure of initially crediting the Unearned Fees account when payment is received from a customer in advance of performing services.

b. Prepare journal entries (including any adjusting entries as of the end of the month) to record these events using the procedure of initially crediting the Fees Earned account when payment is received from a customer in advance of performing services.

Check *(c)* Fees Earned—using entries from part *b*, $10,500

c. Under each method, determine the amount of earned fees reported on the income statement for July and the amount of unearned fees reported on the balance sheet as of July 31.

---

adidas Group reported the following balance sheet accounts in a recent year (euros in millions). Prepare the balance sheet for this company, following usual IFRS practices. Assume the balance sheet is reported as of December 31, 2014.

Exercise 3-13
Preparing a balance sheet following IFRS
P3

Property, plant and equipment	€1,454	Intangible assets	€2,763
Total equity	5,617	Total current liabilities	4,378
Accounts receivable	1,946	Inventories	2,526
Total noncurrent liabilities	2,422	Total liabilities	6,800
Cash and cash equivalents	1,683	Other current assets	1,192
Total current assets	7,347	Total noncurrent assets	5,070
Other noncurrent assets	853		

▦ connect

For each of the following journal entries *1* through *12*, enter the letter of the explanation that most closely describes it in the space beside each entry. (You can use letters more than once.)

PROBLEM SET A

Problem 3-1A
Identifying adjusting entries with explanations

C3   P1

A. To record receipt of unearned revenue.

B. To record this period's earning of prior unearned revenue.

C. To record payment of an accrued expense.

D. To record receipt of an accrued revenue.

E. To record an accrued expense.

F. To record an accrued revenue.

G. To record this period's use of a prepaid expense.

H. To record payment of a prepaid expense.

I. To record this period's depreciation expense.

_____	**1.**	Interest Expense	1,000	
		Interest Payable		1,000
_____	**2.**	Depreciation Expense	4,000	
		Accumulated Depreciation		4,000
_____	**3.**	Unearned Professional Fees	3,000	
		Professional Fees Earned		3,000
_____	**4.**	Insurance Expense	4,200	
		Prepaid Insurance		4,200
_____	**5.**	Salaries Payable	1,400	
		Cash		1,400
_____	**6.**	Prepaid Rent	4,500	
		Cash		4,500
_____	**7.**	Salaries Expense	6,000	
		Salaries Payable		6,000
_____	**8.**	Interest Receivable	5,000	
		Interest Revenue		5,000
_____	**9.**	Cash	9,000	
		Accounts Receivable (from consulting)		9,000
_____	**10.**	Cash	7,500	
		Unearned Professional Fees		7,500
_____	**11.**	Cash	2,000	
		Interest Receivable		2,000
_____	**12.**	Rent Expense	2,000	
		Prepaid Rent		2,000

Problem 3-2A

Preparing adjusting and subsequent journal entries

C1   A1   P1

Arnez Company's annual accounting period ends on December 31, 2017. The following information concerns the adjusting entries to be recorded as of that date. (Entries can draw from the following partial chart of accounts: Cash; Rent Receivable; Office Supplies; Prepaid Insurance; Building; Accumulated Depreciation—Building; Salaries Payable; Unearned Rent; Rent Earned; Salaries Expense; Office Supplies Expense; Insurance Expense; Depreciation Expense—Building.)

a. The Office Supplies account started the year with a $4,000 balance. During 2017, the company purchased supplies for $13,400, which was added to the Office Supplies account. The inventory of supplies available at December 31, 2017, totaled $2,554.

b. An analysis of the company's insurance policies provided the following facts.

Policy	Date of Purchase	Months of Coverage	Cost
A	April 1, 2015	24	$14,400
B	April 1, 2016	36	12,960
C	August 1, 2017	12	2,400

The total premium for each policy was paid in full (for all months) at the purchase date, and the Prepaid Insurance account was debited for the full cost. (Year-end adjusting entries for Prepaid Insurance were properly recorded in all prior years.)

c. The company has 15 employees, who earn a total of $1,960 in salaries each working day. They are paid each Monday for their work in the five-day workweek ending on the previous Friday. Assume that December 31, 2017, is a Tuesday, and all 15 employees worked the first two days of that week. Because New Year's Day is a paid holiday, they will be paid salaries for five full days on Monday, January 6, 2018.

d. The company purchased a building on January 1, 2017. It cost $960,000 and is expected to have a $45,000 salvage value at the end of its predicted 30-year life. Annual depreciation is $30,500.

e. Since the company is not large enough to occupy the entire building it owns, it rented space to a tenant at $3,000 per month, starting on November 1, 2017. The rent was paid on time on November 1, and the amount received was credited to the Rent Earned account. However, the tenant has not paid the December rent. The company has worked out an agreement with the tenant, who has promised to pay both December and January rent in full on January 15. The tenant has agreed not to fall behind again.

f. On November 1, the company rented space to another tenant for $2,800 per month. The tenant paid five months' rent in advance on that date. The payment was recorded with a credit to the Unearned Rent account.

Required

Check (1*b*) Dr. Insurance Expense, $7,120
        (1*d*) Dr. Depreciation Expense, $30,500

1. Use the information to prepare adjusting entries as of December 31, 2017.

2. Prepare journal entries to record the first subsequent cash transaction in 2018 for parts *c* and *e*.

Wells Technical Institute (WTI), a school owned by Tristana Wells, provides training to individuals who pay tuition directly to the school. WTI also offers training to groups in off-site locations. Its unadjusted trial balance as of December 31, 2017, follows. Descriptions of items *a* through *h* that require adjusting entries on December 31, 2017, follow.

Problem 3-3A
Preparing adjusting entries, adjusted trial balance, and financial statements

A1 P1 P2 P3

Additional Information Items

a. An analysis of WTI's insurance policies shows that $2,400 of coverage has expired.

b. An inventory count shows that teaching supplies costing $2,800 are available at year-end 2017.

c. Annual depreciation on the equipment is $13,200.

d. Annual depreciation on the professional library is $7,200.

e. On November 1, WTI agreed to do a special six-month course (starting immediately) for a client. The contract calls for a monthly fee of $2,500, and the client paid the first five months' fees in advance. When the cash was received, the Unearned Training Fees account was credited. The fee for the sixth month will be recorded when it is collected in 2018.

f. On October 15, WTI agreed to teach a four-month class (beginning immediately) for an individual for $3,000 tuition per month payable at the end of the class. The class started on October 15, but no payment has yet been received. (WTI's accruals are applied to the nearest half-month; for example, October recognizes one-half month accrual.)

g. WTI's two employees are paid weekly. As of the end of the year, two days' salaries have accrued at the rate of $100 per day for each employee.

h. The balance in the Prepaid Rent account represents rent for December.

	A	B	C
1	**WELLS TECHNICAL INSTITUTE** **Unadjusted Trial Balance** **December 31, 2017**		
2		**Debit**	**Credit**
3	Cash	$ 34,000	
4	Accounts receivable	0	
5	Teaching supplies	8,000	
6	Prepaid insurance	12,000	
7	Prepaid rent	3,000	
8	Professional library	35,000	
9	Accumulated depreciation—Professional library		$ 10,000
10	Equipment	80,000	
11	Accumulated depreciation—Equipment		15,000
12	Accounts payable		26,000
13	Salaries payable		0
14	Unearned training fees		12,500
15	T. Wells, Capital		90,000
16	T. Wells, Withdrawals	50,000	
17	Tuition fees earned		123,900
18	Training fees earned		40,000
19	Depreciation expense—Professional library	0	
20	Depreciation expense—Equipment	0	
21	Salaries expense	50,000	
22	Insurance expense	0	
23	Rent expense	33,000	
24	Teaching supplies expense	0	
25	Advertising expense	6,000	
26	Utilities expense	6,400	
27	Totals	$317,400	$317,400

Required

1. Prepare T-accounts (representing the ledger) with balances from the unadjusted trial balance.

2. Prepare the necessary adjusting journal entries for items *a* through *h* and post them to the T-accounts. Assume that adjusting entries are made only at year-end.

3. Update balances in the T-accounts for the adjusting entries and prepare an adjusted trial balance.

4. Prepare Wells Technical Institute's income statement and statement of owner's equity for the year 2017 and prepare its balance sheet as of December 31, 2017.

Problem 3-4A

Interpreting unadjusted and adjusted trial balances, and preparing financial statements

C3   A1   P1   P2   P3

A six-column table for JKL Company follows. The first two columns contain the unadjusted trial balance for the company as of July 31, 2017. The last two columns contain the adjusted trial balance as of the same date.

Required

Analysis Component

1. Analyze the differences between the unadjusted and adjusted trial balances to determine the eight adjustments that likely were made. Show the results of your analysis by inserting these adjustment amounts in the table's two middle columns. Label each adjustment with a letter *a* through *h* and provide a short description of each.

Preparation Component

2. Use the information in the adjusted trial balance to prepare the company's (*a*) income statement and its statement of owner's equity for the year ended July 31, 2017 [*Note:* J. Logan, Capital at July 31, 2016, was $40,000, and the current-year withdrawals were $5,000], and (*b*) the balance sheet as of July 31, 2017.

	Unadjusted Trial Balance		Adjustments		Adjusted Trial Balance	
Cash	$ 34,000				$ 34,000	
Accounts receivable	14,000				22,000	
Office supplies	16,000				2,000	
Prepaid insurance	8,540				2,960	
Office equipment	84,000				84,000	
Accum. depreciation— Office equip.		$ 14,000				$ 20,000
Accounts payable		9,100				10,000
Interest payable		0				1,000
Salaries payable		0				7,000
Unearned consulting fees		18,000				15,000
Long-term notes payable		52,000				52,000
J. Logan, Capital		40,000				40,000
J. Logan, Withdrawals	5,000				5,000	
Consulting fees earned		123,240				134,240
Depreciation expense— Office equip.	0				6,000	
Salaries expense	67,000				74,000	
Interest expense	1,200				2,200	
Insurance expense	0				5,580	
Rent expense	14,500				14,500	
Office supplies expense	0				14,000	
Advertising expense	12,100				13,000	
Totals	$256,340	$256,340			$279,240	$279,240

The adjusted trial balance for Chiara Company as of December 31, 2017, follows.

Problem 3-5A
Preparing financial statements from the adjusted trial balance and computing profit margin

P3   A1   A2

	Debit	Credit
Cash	$ 30,000	
Accounts receivable	52,000	
Interest receivable	18,000	
Notes receivable (due in 90 days)	168,000	
Office supplies	16,000	
Automobiles	168,000	
Accumulated depreciation—Automobiles		$ 50,000
Equipment	138,000	
Accumulated depreciation—Equipment		18,000
Land	78,000	
Accounts payable		96,000
Interest payable		20,000
Salaries payable		19,000
Unearned fees		30,000
Long-term notes payable		138,000
R. Chiara, Capital		255,800
R. Chiara, Withdrawals	46,000	
Fees earned		484,000
Interest earned		24,000
Depreciation expense—Automobiles	26,000	
Depreciation expense—Equipment	18,000	
Salaries expense	188,000	
Wages expense	40,000	
Interest expense	32,000	
Office supplies expense	34,000	
Advertising expense	58,000	
Repairs expense—Automobiles	24,800	
Totals	$1,134,800	$1,134,800

Required

1. Use the information in the adjusted trial balance to prepare (*a*) the income statement for the year ended December 31, 2017; (*b*) the statement of owner's equity for the year ended December 31, 2017; and (*c*) the balance sheet as of December 31, 2017.

2. Compute the profit margin for year 2017 (use total revenues as the denominator).

Check (1) Total assets, $600,000

Gomez Co. had the following transactions in the last two months of its year ended December 31. (Entries can draw from the following partial chart of accounts: Cash; Prepaid Insurance; Prepaid Advertising; Prepaid Consulting Fees; Unearned Service Fees; Services Fees Earned; Insurance Expense; Advertising Expense; Consulting Fees Expense.)

Problem 3-6A[A]
Recording prepaid expenses and unearned revenues

P1   P4

Nov. 1   Paid $1,800 cash for future newspaper advertising.
    1   Paid $2,460 cash for 12 months of insurance through October 31 of the next year.
   30   Received $3,600 cash for future services to be provided to a customer.
Dec. 1   Paid $3,000 cash for a consultant's services to be received over the next three months.
   15   Received $7,950 cash for future services to be provided to a customer.
   31   Of the advertising paid for on November 1, $1,200 worth is not yet used.
   31   A portion of the insurance paid for on November 1 has expired. No adjustment was made in November to Prepaid Insurance.
   31   Services worth $1,500 are not yet provided to the customer who paid on November 30.
   31   One-third of the consulting services paid for on December 1 have been received.
   31   The company has performed $3,300 of services that the customer paid for on December 15.

Required

1. Prepare entries for these transactions under the method that initially records prepaid expenses as assets and records unearned revenues as liabilities. Also prepare adjusting entries at the end of the year.

2. Prepare entries for these transactions under the method that initially records prepaid expenses as expenses and records unearned revenues as revenues. Also prepare adjusting entries at the end of the year.

Analysis Component

3. Explain why the alternative sets of entries in requirements 1 and 2 do not result in different financial statement amounts.

PROBLEM SET B

Problem 3-1B

Identifying adjusting entries with explanations

C3   P1

For each of the following journal entries *1* through *12,* enter the letter of the explanation that most closely describes it in the space beside each entry. (You can use letters more than once.)

A. To record payment of a prepaid expense.

B. To record this period's use of a prepaid expense.

C. To record this period's depreciation expense.

D. To record receipt of unearned revenue.

E. To record this period's earning of prior unearned revenue.

F. To record an accrued expense.

G. To record payment of an accrued expense.

H. To record an accrued revenue.

I. To record receipt of accrued revenue.

___	1.	Interest Receivable	3,500	
		Interest Revenue		3,500
___	2.	Salaries Payable	9,000	
		Cash		9,000
___	3.	Depreciation Expense	8,000	
		Accumulated Depreciation		8,000
___	4.	Cash	9,000	
		Unearned Professional Fees		9,000
___	5.	Insurance Expense	4,000	
		Prepaid Insurance		4,000
___	6.	Interest Expense	5,000	
		Interest Payable		5,000
___	7.	Cash	1,500	
		Accounts Receivable (from services)		1,500
___	8.	Salaries Expense	7,000	
		Salaries Payable		7,000
___	9.	Cash	1,000	
		Interest Receivable		1,000
___	10.	Prepaid Rent	3,000	
		Cash		3,000
___	11.	Rent Expense	7,500	
		Prepaid Rent		7,500
___	12.	Unearned Professional Fees	6,000	
		Professional Fees Earned		6,000

Problem 3-2B

Preparing adjusting and subsequent journal entries

C1   A1   P1

Natsu Company's annual accounting period ends on October 31, 2017. The following information concerns the adjusting entries that need to be recorded as of that date. (Entries can draw from the following partial chart of accounts: Cash; Rent Receivable; Office Supplies; Prepaid Insurance; Building; Accumulated Depreciation—Building; Salaries Payable; Unearned Rent; Rent Earned; Salaries Expense; Office Supplies Expense; Insurance Expense; Depreciation Expense—Building.)

a. The Office Supplies account started the fiscal year with a $600 balance. During the fiscal year, the company purchased supplies for $4,570, which was added to the Office Supplies account. The supplies available at October 31, 2017, totaled $800.

b. An analysis of the company's insurance policies provided the following facts.

Policy	Date of Purchase	Months of Coverage	Cost
A	April 1, 2016	24	$6,000
B	April 1, 2017	36	7,200
C	August 1, 2017	12	1,320

The total premium for each policy was paid in full (for all months) at the purchase date, and the Prepaid Insurance account was debited for the full cost. (Year-end adjusting entries for Prepaid Insurance were properly recorded in all prior fiscal years.)

c. The company has four employees, who earn a total of $1,000 for each workday. They are paid each Monday for their work in the five-day workweek ending on the previous Friday. Assume that October 31, 2017, is a Monday, and all four employees worked the first day of that week. They will be paid salaries for five full days on Monday, November 7, 2017.

d. The company purchased a building on November 1, 2014, that cost $175,000 and is expected to have a $40,000 salvage value at the end of its predicted 25-year life. Annual depreciation is $5,400.

e. Since the company does not occupy the entire building it owns, it rented space to a tenant at $1,000 per month, starting on September 1, 2017. The rent was paid on time on September 1, and the amount received was credited to the Rent Earned account. However, the October rent has not been paid. The company has worked out an agreement with the tenant, who has promised to pay both October and November rent in full on November 15. The tenant has agreed not to fall behind again.

f. On September 1, the company rented space to another tenant for $725 per month. The tenant paid five months' rent in advance on that date. The payment was recorded with a credit to the Unearned Rent account.

Required

1. Use the information to prepare adjusting entries as of October 31, 2017.

2. Prepare journal entries to record the first subsequent cash transaction in November 2017 for parts *c* and *e*.

Check   (1*b*) Dr. Insurance Expense, $4,730
(1*d*) Dr. Depreciation Expense, $5,400

Following is the unadjusted trial balance for Alonzo Institute as of December 31, 2017. The Institute provides one-on-one training to individuals who pay tuition directly to the business and offers extension training to groups in off-site locations. Shown after the trial balance are items *a* through *h* that require adjusting entries as of December 31, 2017.

Problem 3-3B
Preparing adjusting entries, adjusted trial balance, and financial statements

A1   P1   P2   P3

	A	B	C
1	ALONZO INSTITUTE Unadjusted Trial Balance December 31, 2017		
2		Debit	Credit
3	Cash	$ 60,000	
4	Accounts receivable	0	
5	Teaching supplies	70,000	
6	Prepaid insurance	19,000	
7	Prepaid rent	3,800	
8	Professional library	12,000	
9	Accumulated depreciation—Professional library		$ 2,500
10	Equipment	40,000	
11	Accumulated depreciation—Equipment		20,000
12	Accounts payable		11,200
13	Salaries payable		0
14	Unearned training fees		28,600
15	C. Alonzo, Capital		71,500
16	C. Alonzo, Withdrawals	20,000	
17	Tuition fees earned		129,200
18	Training fees earned		68,000
19	Depreciation expense—Professional library	0	
20	Depreciation expense—Equipment	0	
21	Salaries expense	44,200	
22	Insurance expense	0	
23	Rent expense	29,600	
24	Teaching supplies expense	0	
25	Advertising expense	19,000	
26	Utilities expense	13,400	
27	Totals	$331,000	$331,000

Additional Information Items

a. An analysis of the Institute's insurance policies shows that $9,500 of coverage has expired.

b. An inventory count shows that teaching supplies costing $20,000 are available at year-end 2017.

c. Annual depreciation on the equipment is $5,000.

d. Annual depreciation on the professional library is $2,400.

e. On November 1, the Institute agreed to do a special five-month course (starting immediately) for a client. The contract calls for a $14,300 monthly fee, and the client paid the first two months' fees in advance. When the cash was received, the Unearned Training Fees account was credited. The last two months' fees will be recorded when collected in 2018.

f. On October 15, the Institute agreed to teach a four-month class (beginning immediately) to an individual for $2,300 tuition per month payable at the end of the class. The class started on October 15, but no payment has yet been received. (The Institute's accruals are applied to the nearest half-month; for example, October recognizes one-half month accrual.)

g. The Institute's only employee is paid weekly. As of the end of the year, three days' salaries have accrued at the rate of $150 per day.

h. The balance in the Prepaid Rent account represents rent for December.

Check (2e) Cr. Training Fees Earned, $28,600

(2f) Cr. Tuition Fees Earned, $5,750

(3) Adj. trial balance totals, $344,600

(4) Net income, $54,200; Ending C. Alonzo, Capital, $105,700

Required

1. Prepare T-accounts (representing the ledger) with balances from the unadjusted trial balance.

2. Prepare the necessary adjusting journal entries for items *a* through *h*, and post them to the T-accounts. Assume that adjusting entries are made only at year-end.

3. Update balances in the T-accounts for the adjusting entries and prepare an adjusted trial balance.

4. Prepare the company's income statement and statement of owner's equity for the year 2017, and prepare its balance sheet as of December 31, 2017.

Problem 3-4B

Interpreting unadjusted and adjusted trial balances, and preparing financial statements

C3   A1   P1   P2   P3

A six-column table for Yan Consulting Company follows. The first two columns contain the unadjusted trial balance for the company as of December 31, 2017, and the last two columns contain the adjusted trial balance as of the same date.

	Unadjusted Trial Balance		Adjustments		Adjusted Trial Balance	
Cash	$ 45,000				$ 45,000	
Accounts receivable	60,000				66,660	
Office supplies	40,000				17,000	
Prepaid insurance	8,200				3,600	
Office equipment	120,000				120,000	
Accumulated depreciation— Office equip.		$ 20,000				$ 30,000
Accounts payable		26,000				32,000
Interest payable		0				2,150
Salaries payable		0				16,000
Unearned consulting fees		40,000				27,800
Long-term notes payable		75,000				75,000
Z. Yan, Capital		80,200				80,200
Z. Yan, Withdrawals	20,000				20,000	
Consulting fees earned		234,600				253,460
Depreciation expense— Office equip.	0				10,000	
Salaries expense	112,000				128,000	
Interest expense	8,600				10,750	
Insurance expense	0				4,600	
Rent expense	20,000				20,000	
Office supplies expense	0				23,000	
Advertising expense	42,000				48,000	
Totals	$475,800	$475,800			$516,610	$516,610

Required

Analysis Component

1. Analyze the differences between the unadjusted and adjusted trial balances to determine the eight adjustments that likely were made. Show the results of your analysis by inserting these adjustment amounts in the table's two middle columns. Label each adjustment with a letter *a* through *h* and provide a short description of each.

Preparation Component

2. Use the information in the adjusted trial balance to prepare this company's (*a*) income statement and its statement of owner's equity for the year ended December 31, 2017 [*Note:* Z. Yan, Capital at December 31, 2016, was $80,200, and the current-year withdrawals were $20,000], and (*b*) the balance sheet as of December 31, 2017.

Check (2) Net income, $9,110; Z. Yan, Capital (12/31/17), $69,310; Total assets, $222,260

The adjusted trial balance for Speedy Courier as of December 31, 2017, follows.

Problem 3-5B
Preparing financial statements from the adjusted trial balance and computing profit margin

P3 A1 A2

	Debit	Credit
Cash	$ 58,000	
Accounts receivable	120,000	
Interest receivable	7,000	
Notes receivable (due in 90 days)	210,000	
Office supplies	22,000	
Trucks	134,000	
Accumulated depreciation—Trucks		$ 58,000
Equipment	270,000	
Accumulated depreciation—Equipment		200,000
Land	100,000	
Accounts payable		134,000
Interest payable		20,000
Salaries payable		28,000
Unearned delivery fees		120,000
Long-term notes payable		200,000
L. Horace, Capital		125,000
L. Horace, Withdrawals	50,000	
Delivery fees earned		611,800
Interest earned		34,000
Depreciation expense—Trucks	29,000	
Depreciation expense—Equipment	48,000	
Salaries expense	74,000	
Wages expense	300,000	
Interest expense	15,000	
Office supplies expense	31,000	
Advertising expense	27,200	
Repairs expense—Trucks	35,600	
Totals......................................	$1,530,800	$1,530,800

Required

1. Use the information in the adjusted trial balance to prepare (*a*) the income statement for the year ended December 31, 2017, (*b*) the statement of owner's equity for the year ended December 31, 2017, and (*c*) the balance sheet as of December 31, 2017.

2. Compute the profit margin for year 2017 (use total revenues as the denominator).

Check (1) Total assets, $663,000

Tremor Co. had the following transactions in the last two months of its fiscal year ended May 31. (Entries can draw from the following partial chart of accounts: Cash; Prepaid Insurance; Prepaid Advertising; Prepaid Consulting Fees; Unearned Service Fees; Services Fees Earned; Insurance Expense; Advertising Expense; Consulting Fees Expense.)

Problem 3-6B[A]
Recording prepaid expenses and unearned revenues

P1 P4

Apr. 1 Paid $2,450 cash to an accounting firm for future consulting services.
   1 Paid $3,600 cash for 12 months of insurance through March 31 of the next year.
   30 Received $8,500 cash for future services to be provided to a customer.

May 1   Paid $4,450 cash for future newspaper advertising.
     23   Received $10,450 cash for future services to be provided to a customer.
     31   Of the consulting services paid for on April 1, $2,000 worth has been performed.
     31   A portion of the insurance paid for on April 1 has expired. No adjustment was made in April to Prepaid Insurance.
     31   Services worth $4,600 are not yet provided to the customer who paid on April 30.
     31   Of the advertising paid for on May 1, $2,050 worth is not yet used.
     31   The company has performed $5,500 of services that the customer paid for on May 23.

Required

1. Prepare entries for these transactions under the method that initially records prepaid expenses and unearned revenues in balance sheet accounts. Also prepare adjusting entries at the end of the year.

2. Prepare entries for these transactions under the method that initially records prepaid expenses and unearned revenues in income statement accounts. Also prepare adjusting entries at the end of the year.

Analysis Component

3. Explain why the alternative sets of entries in parts 1 and 2 do not result in different financial statement amounts.

SERIAL PROBLEM
Business Solutions

P1   P2   P3

© Alexander Image/Shutterstock RF

This serial problem began in Chapter 1 and continues through most of the book. If previous chapter segments were not completed, the serial problem can still begin at this point.

SP 3   After the success of the company's first two months, Santana Rey continues to operate **Business Solutions**. (Transactions for the first two months are described in the Chapter 2 serial problem.) The November 30, 2017, unadjusted trial balance of Business Solutions (reflecting its transactions for October and November of 2017) follows.

No.	Account Title	Debit	Credit
101	Cash	$38,264	
106	Accounts receivable......................................	12,618	
126	Computer supplies..	2,545	
128	Prepaid insurance..	2,220	
131	Prepaid rent	3,300	
163	Office equipment	8,000	
164	Accumulated depreciation—Office equipment.................		$ 0
167	Computer equipment	20,000	
168	Accumulated depreciation—Computer equipment		0
201	Accounts payable		0
210	Wages payable		0
236	Unearned computer services revenue		0
301	S. Rey, Capital		73,000
302	S. Rey, Withdrawals	5,600	
403	Computer services revenue		25,659
612	Depreciation expense—Office equipment	0	
613	Depreciation expense—Computer equipment..................	0	
623	Wages expense	2,625	
637	Insurance expense	0	
640	Rent expense	0	
652	Computer supplies expense	0	
655	Advertising expense......................................	1,728	
676	Mileage expense	704	
677	Miscellaneous expenses	250	
684	Repairs expense—Computer	805	
	Totals	$98,659	$98,659

Business Solutions had the following transactions and events in December 2017.

Dec. 2 Paid $1,025 cash to Hillside Mall for Business Solutions's share of mall advertising costs.
      3 Paid $500 cash for minor repairs to the company's computer.
      4 Received $3,950 cash from Alex's Engineering Co. for the receivable from November.
     10 Paid cash to Lyn Addie for six days of work at the rate of $125 per day.
     14 Notified by Alex's Engineering Co. that Business Solutions's bid of $7,000 on a proposed project has been accepted. Alex's paid a $1,500 cash advance to Business Solutions.
     15 Purchased $1,100 of computer supplies on credit from Harris Office Products.
     16 Sent a reminder to Gomez Co. to pay the fee for services recorded on November 8.
     20 Completed a project for Liu Corporation and received $5,625 cash.
  22–26 Took the week off for the holidays.
     28 Received $3,000 cash from Gomez Co. on its receivable.
     29 Reimbursed S. Rey for business automobile mileage (600 miles at $0.32 per mile).
     31 S. Rey withdrew $1,500 cash from the company for personal use.

The following additional facts are collected for use in making adjusting entries prior to preparing financial statements for the company's first three months:

a. The December 31 inventory count of computer supplies shows $580 still available.

b. Three months have expired since the 12-month insurance premium was paid in advance.

c. As of December 31, Lyn Addie has not been paid for four days of work at $125 per day.

d. The computer system, acquired on October 1, is expected to have a four-year life with no salvage value.

e. The office equipment, acquired on October 1, is expected to have a five-year life with no salvage value.

f. Three of the four months' prepaid rent has expired.

Required

1. Prepare journal entries to record each of the December transactions and events for Business Solutions. Post those entries to the accounts in the ledger.

2. Prepare adjusting entries to reflect *a* through *f*. Post those entries to the accounts in the ledger.

3. Prepare an adjusted trial balance as of December 31, 2017.

4. Prepare an income statement for the three months ended December 31, 2017.

5. Prepare a statement of owner's equity for the three months ended December 31, 2017.

6. Prepare a balance sheet as of December 31, 2017.

Check (3) Adjusted trial balance totals, $109,034

(6) Total assets, $83,460

The **General Ledger** tool in Connect allows students to immediately see the financial statements as of a specific date. Each of the following questions begins with an unadjusted trial balance. Using transactions from the following assignment, prepare the necessary adjustments, and determine the impact each adjustment has on net income. The financial statements are automatically populated.

GL 3-1 Based on the FastForward illustration in this chapter

Using transactions from the following assignments, prepare the necessary adjustments, create the financial statements, and determine the impact each adjustment has on net income.

GL 3-2 Based on Problem 3-3A

GL 3-3 Extension of Problem 2-1A

GL 3-4 Extension of Problem 2-2A

GL 3-5 Based on Serial Problem SP 3

**GENERAL
LEDGER
PROBLEM**

**Available only
in Connect**

Beyond the Numbers

BTN 3-1   Refer to **Apple**'s financial statements in Appendix A to answer the following.

1. Identify and write out the revenue recognition principle as explained in the chapter.

2. Review Apple's footnotes (in Appendix A and/or from its 10-K on its website) to discover how it applies the revenue recognition principle and when it recognizes revenue. Report what you discover.

3. What is Apple's profit margin for fiscal years ended September 26, 2015, and September 27, 2014.
[Continued on next page . . .]

**REPORTING IN
ACTION**

C1 C2 A1 A2

APPLE

Fast Forward

4. Access Apple's annual report (10-K) for fiscal years ending after September 26, 2015, at its website (Apple.com) or the SEC's EDGAR database (SEC.gov). Assess and compare the September 26, 2015, fiscal year profit margin to any subsequent year's profit margin that you compute.

COMPARATIVE ANALYSIS

A2

APPLE

GOOGLE

BTN 3-2   Key figures for the recent two years of both Apple and Google follow.

	Apple		Google	
$ millions	**Current Year**	**Prior Year**	**Current Year**	**Prior Year**
Net income	$ 53,394	$ 39,510	$16,348	$14,136
Net sales	233,715	182,795	74,989	66,001

Required

1. Compute profit margins for (*a*) Apple and (*b*) Google for the two years of data shown.
2. Which company is more successful on the basis of profit margin? Explain.

ETHICS CHALLENGE

C1   C2   A1

BTN 3-3   Jessica Boland works for Sea Biscuit Co. She and Farah Smith, her manager, are preparing adjusting entries for annual financial statements. Boland computes depreciation and records it as

Depreciation Expense—Equipment	123,000	
Accumulated Depreciation—Equipment		123,000

Smith agrees with her computation but says the credit entry should be directly to the Equipment account. Smith argues that while accumulated depreciation is technically correct, "it is less hassle not to use a contra account and just credit the Equipment account directly. And besides, the balance sheet shows the same amount for total assets under either method."

Required

1. How should depreciation be recorded? Do you support Boland or Smith?
2. Evaluate the strengths and weaknesses of Smith's reasons for preferring her method.
3. Indicate whether the situation Boland faces is an ethical problem. Explain.

COMMUNICATING IN PRACTICE

C1   A2

BTN 3-4   The class should be divided into teams. Teams are to select an industry (such as automobile manufacturing, airlines, defense contractors), and each team member is to select a different company in that industry. Each team member is to acquire the annual report of the company selected. Annual reports can be downloaded from company websites or from the SEC's EDGAR database (SEC.gov).

Required

1. Use the annual report to compute the return on assets, debt ratio, and profit margin.
2. Communicate with team members via a meeting, e-mail, or telephone to discuss the meaning of the ratios, how different companies compare to each other, and the industry norm. The team must prepare a single memo reporting the ratios for each company and identifying the conclusions or consensus of opinion reached during the team's discussion. The memo is to be copied and distributed to the instructor and all classmates.

BTN 3-5   Access EDGAR online (<u>SEC.gov</u>) and locate the 10-K report of **The Gap, Inc.** (ticker: GPS), filed on March 23, 2015. Review its financial statements reported for the year ended January 31, 2015, to answer the following questions.

TAKING IT TO THE NET

C1   A2

Required

1. What are Gap's main brands?
2. When is Gap's fiscal year-end?
3. What is Gap's net sales for the period ended January 31, 2015?
4. What is Gap's net income for the period ended January 31, 2015?
5. Compute Gap's profit margin for the year ended January 31, 2015.
6. Do you believe Gap's decision to use a year-end of late January or early February relates to its natural business year? Explain.

BTN 3-6   Four types of adjustments are described in the chapter: (1) prepaid expenses, (2) unearned revenues, (3) accrued expenses, and (4) accrued revenues.

TEAMWORK IN ACTION

C3   A1   P1

Required

1. Form *learning teams* of four (or more) members. Each team member must select one of the four adjustments as an area of expertise (each team must have at least one expert in each area).
2. Form *expert teams* from the individuals who have selected the same area of expertise. Expert teams are to discuss and write a report that each expert will present to his or her learning team addressing the following:
   a. Description of the adjustment and why it's necessary.
   b. Example of a transaction or event, with dates and amounts, that requires adjustment.
   c. Adjusting entry(ies) for the example in requirement *b*.
   d. Status of the affected account(s) before and after the adjustment in requirement *c*.
   e. Effects on financial statements of not making the adjustment.
3. Each expert should return to his or her learning team. In rotation, each member should present his or her expert team's report to the learning team. Team discussion is encouraged.

BTN 3-7   Review the opening feature of this chapter dealing with **re:char** and its entrepreneurial owner, Jason Aramburu.

ENTREPRENEURIAL DECISION

A2

Required

1. Assume that re:char sells a $300 gift certificate to a customer, collecting the $300 cash in advance. Prepare the journal entry for (*a*) collection of the cash for delivery of the gift certificate to the customer and (*b*) revenue from the subsequent delivery of merchandise when the gift certificate is used.
2. How can keeping less inventory help to improve re:char's profit margin?
3. Jason Aramburu understands that many companies carry considerable inventory, and he is thinking of carrying additional inventory of merchandise for sale. Jason desires your advice on the pros and cons of carrying such inventory. Provide at least one reason for, and one reason against, carrying additional inventory.

BTN 3-8   Visit the website of a major company that interests you. Use the "Investor Relations" link at the website to obtain the toll-free telephone number of the Investor Relations Department. Call the company, ask to speak to Investor Relations, and request a copy of the company's most recent annual report (a company will sometimes send a prepackaged *investor packet,* which includes the annual report plus other relevant information). You should receive the requested report within one to two weeks. Once you have received your report, use it throughout the term to see how the principles you are learning in class are being applied in practice.

HITTING THE ROAD

C1

GLOBAL DECISION

A2 C1 C2

Samsung

APPLE

GOOGLE

BTN 3-9   **Samsung** (Samsung.com) is a leading manufacturer of consumer electronic products. The following selected information is available from Samsung's financial statements along with those from **Apple** and **Google**.

In millions	Samsung	Apple	Google
Net income	₩ 19,060,144	$ 53,394	$16,348
Net sales	200,653,482	233,715	74,989

Required

1. Compute profit margin for the current year for Samsung, Apple, and Google.
2. Which company has the higher profit margin? For that company, how much net income does it receive for each $1 or ₩1 of sales?

 **GLOBAL VIEW**

We explained that accounting under U.S. GAAP is similar, but not identical, to that under IFRS. This section discusses differences in adjusting accounts, preparing financial statements, and reporting assets and liabilities on a balance sheet.

Adjusting Accounts   Both U.S. GAAP and IFRS include broad and similar guidance for adjusting accounts. Although some variations exist in revenue and expense recognition and other principles, all of the adjustments in this chapter are accounted for identically under the two systems. In later chapters we describe how certain assets and liabilities can result in different adjusted amounts using fair value measurements.

Preparing Financial Statements   Both U.S. GAAP and IFRS prepare the same four basic financial statements following the same process discussed in this chapter. Chapter 2 explained how both U.S. GAAP and IFRS require current items to be separated from noncurrent items on the balance sheet (yielding a classified balance sheet). U.S. GAAP balance sheets report current items first. Assets are listed from most liquid to least liquid, where liquid refers to the ease of converting an asset to cash. Liabilities are listed from nearest to maturity to furthest from maturity, where maturity refers to the nearness of paying off the liability. IFRS balance sheets normally present noncurrent items first (and equity before liabilities), but this is not a requirement. Other differences with financial statements exist, which we identify in later chapters. **Piaggio** provides the following example of IFRS reporting for its assets, liabilities, and equity within the balance sheet:

Point: IASB and FASB are working to improve financial statements. One proposal would reorganize the balance sheet to show assets and liabilities classified as operating, investing, or financing.

IFRS: New revenue recognition rules by the FASB and the IASB reduce variation between U.S. GAAP and IFRS.

PIAGGIO
Balance Sheet (in thousands of euros)
December 31, 2015

Assets		Equity and Liabilities	
Noncurrent assets		Total equity	€ 404,293
Intangible assets.................	€ 673,986	Noncurrent liabilities	
Property, plant and equipment	307,608	Financial liabilities falling due after one year	520,391
Other noncurrent assets...........	121,517	Other long-term liabilities	68,055
Total noncurrent assets	1,103,111	Total noncurrent liabilities	588,446
Current assets		Current liabilities	
Trade, tax and other receivables.....	132,023	Financial liabilities falling due within one year.......	105,895
Inventories	212,812	Trade, tax and other payables....................	443,137
Cash and cash equivalents	103,604	Current portion of other long-term provisions	9,779
Total current assets	448,439	Total current liabilities	558,811
Total assets.....................	€1,551,550	Total equity and liabilities.......................	€1,551,550

IFRS

Revenue and expense recognition are key to recording accounting adjustments. IFRS tends to be more *principles-based* relative to U.S. GAAP, which is viewed as more *rules-based*. A principles-based system depends heavily on control procedures to reduce the potential for fraud or misconduct. Failure in judgment led to improper accounting adjustments at **Fannie Mae**, **WorldCom**, and others. A KPMG survey of accounting and finance employees found that more than 10% of them had witnessed falsification or manipulation of accounting data within the past year. Internal controls and governance processes are directed at curtailing such behavior. Yet, a KPMG fraud survey found that one in seven frauds was uncovered by chance, which emphasizes our need to improve internal controls and governance. ■

 Global View Assignments

Discussion Questions 11 & 12

Quick Study 3-21

Exercise 3-13

BTN 3-9

chapter 4

Completing the Accounting Cycle

Chapter Preview

WORK SHEET

P1 Benefits of a work sheet

Preparing a work sheet

Applying a work sheet

NTK 4-1

CLOSING PROCESS

C1 Temporary accounts

P2 Closing entries

P3 Post-closing trial balance

C2 Accounting cycle

NTK 4-2

CLASSIFIED BALANCE SHEET

C3 Classified balance sheet—Structure and categories

A1 Current ratio

NTK 4-3

Learning Objectives

CONCEPTUAL

C1 Explain why temporary accounts are closed each period.

C2 Identify steps in the accounting cycle.

C3 Explain and prepare a classified balance sheet.

ANALYTICAL

A1 Compute the current ratio and describe what it reveals about a company's financial condition.

PROCEDURAL

P1 Prepare a work sheet and explain its usefulness.

P2 Describe and prepare closing entries.

P3 Explain and prepare a post-closing trial balance.

P4 *Appendix 4A*—Prepare reversing entries and explain their purpose.

Courtesy of Liv Williams/LuminAID

Light Up the World

CHICAGO—Anna Stork and Andrea Sreshta found that most Haitians were lacking light. "Haiti was 80% without electricity prior to the earthquake; afterwards, it was even less," explains Anna. "We looked at what was being shipped to Haiti—they weren't shipping anything related to light." Anna and Andrea then created a solar-powered inflatable lantern that provides up to 16 hours of light and fits in your pocket, called **LuminAID** (LuminAID.com).

LuminAID has been a hit. According to their website, they have shipped tens of thousands of LuminAIDs to "more than 50 countries" in partnership with groups like **ShelterBox** and **Doctors Without Borders**. Beyond improving lives, Anna and Andrea have a profitable business. "Sales have gone from $1 million in 2014," says Andrea, "to $2 million for the first nine months of this year." With financial success, the two women secured an investment from **Shark Tank** star Mark Cuban.

The success of LuminAID was aided by Anna and Andrea's accounting system, whereby they track costs and match them with revenues. "Initially we weren't worried about the price," recounts Anna. However, as business grew and orders skyrocketed, they

"Innovation is synonymous with impact"

—Anna Stork

explain that their accounting system was key to measuring and controlling expenses. With information on expenses, along with revenues, they were able to "keep investing in new product R&D," explains Anna, "and making better, higher performing, and more useful solar lights."

Anna and Andrea point out that knowledge of the accounting cycle, and their use of work sheets and classified financial statements, enabled them to make informed decisions. For example, their accounting for expenses allowed them to identify avenues for lower expenses, thereby enabling them to produce LuminAID for $4.75 and sell it to consumers for $20 to $25.

"I definitely didn't go [to college] interested in entrepreneurship or [accounting]," explains Anna. "I was interested in sustainability and environmental design." However, she asserts that knowledge of the accounting cycle, along with a basic business sense, can open unexpected doors. "It's not a coincidence," insists Anna. "If you're solving bigger problems, you're not far from someone paying for your product."

Sources: *LuminAID website,* January 2017; *Entrepreneur,* January 2016; *The Daily Beast,* January 2014; *Business2Community,* February 2015; *SharkTank Podcast,* December 2015; *Core77,* January 2012; *Huffington Post,* September 2012

WORK SHEET AS A TOOL

A **work sheet** is a document that is used internally by companies to help with adjusting and closing accounts and with preparing financial statements.

Benefits of a Work Sheet (Spreadsheet)

P1

Prepare a work sheet and explain its usefulness.

A work sheet, which can be prepared in manual or digital form, is an internal accounting aid and is not a substitute for journals, ledgers, or financial statements. A work sheet:

- Aids the preparation of financial statements.
- Reduces the risk of errors when working with many accounts and adjustments.
- Links accounts and adjustments to their impacts in financial statements.
- Helps in preparing interim (monthly and quarterly) financial statements when journalizing adjusting entries is postponed until year-end.
- Shows the effects of proposed or "what-if" transactions.

■ **Decision** Insight

High-Tech Work Sheet   An electronic work sheet using spreadsheet software such as Excel allows us to easily change numbers, assess the impact of alternative strategies, and quickly prepare financial statements at less cost. **Google Docs** and **Microsoft Office Online** allow the sharing of a spreadsheet so that team members can work on the same work sheet simultaneously. Electronic work sheets can also increase the available time for analysis and interpretation. ■

© Dave and Les Jacobs/Blend Images LLC

Use of a Work Sheet

Point: Since a work sheet is *not a* required report or an accounting record, its format is flexible and can be modified by its user to fit his/her preferences.

When a work sheet is used to prepare financial statements, it is constructed at the end of a period before the adjusting process. The complete work sheet includes a list of the accounts, their balances and adjustments, and their sorting into financial statement columns. It provides two columns each for the unadjusted trial balance, the adjustments, the adjusted trial balance, the income statement, and the balance sheet (including the statement of owner's equity). To describe and interpret the work sheet, we use the information from FastForward. Preparing the work sheet has five important steps. Each step, 1 through 5, is color-coded and explained with reference to Exhibits 4.1 and 4.2.

① Step 1. Enter Unadjusted Trial Balance

Refer to Exhibit 4.1—green section. The first step in preparing a work sheet is to list the title of every account and its account number that appears on its financial statements. This includes all accounts in the ledger plus any new ones from adjusting entries. The unadjusted balance for each account is then entered in the appropriate Debit or Credit column of the unadjusted trial balance columns. The totals of these two columns must be equal. The light green section of Exhibit 4.1 shows FastForward's work sheet after completing this first step (dark green rows reflect accounts that arise because of the adjustments). Sometimes an account can require more than one adjustment, such as for Consulting Revenue in Exhibit 4.1. The additional adjustment can be added to a blank line below (as in Exhibit 4.1), squeezed on one line, or combined into one adjustment amount. In the unusual case when an account is not predicted, we can add a new line for such an account following the *Totals* line.

② Step 2. Enter Adjustments

Exhibit 4.1—yellow section. The second step is to enter adjustments in the Adjustments columns. The adjustments shown are the same ones shown in Exhibit 3.13. An identifying letter links the debit and credit of each adjustment. This is called *keying* the adjustments. After preparing a work sheet, **adjustments must still be entered in the journal and posted to the ledger.** The Adjustments columns provide the information for adjusting entries in the journal.

③ Step 3. Prepare Adjusted Trial Balance

Exhibit 4.1—blue section. The adjusted trial balance is prepared by combining the adjustments with the unadjusted balances for each account. As an example, the Prepaid Insurance account has a $2,400 debit balance in the Unadjusted Trial Balance columns. This $2,400 debit is combined with the $100 credit in the Adjustments columns to give Prepaid Insurance a $2,300 debit in the Adjusted Trial Balance columns. The totals of the Adjusted Trial Balance columns confirm debits and credits are equal.

④ Step 4. Sort Adjusted Trial Balance Amounts to Financial Statements

Exhibit 4.1—orange section. This step involves sorting account balances from the adjusted trial balance to their proper financial statement columns. Expenses go to the Income Statement Debit column and revenues to the Income Statement Credit column. Assets and withdrawals go to the Balance Sheet & Statement of Owner's Equity Debit column. Liabilities and owner's capital go to the Balance Sheet & Statement of Owner's Equity Credit column.

⑤ Step 5. Total Statement Columns, Compute Income or Loss, and Balance Columns

Exhibit 4.1—purple section. Each financial statement column (from step 4) is totaled. The difference between the Debit and Credit column totals of the Income Statement columns is net income or net loss. This occurs because revenues are entered in the Credit column and expenses in the Debit column. If the Credit total exceeds the Debit total, there is net income. If the Debit total exceeds the Credit total, there is a net loss. For FastForward, the Credit total exceeds the Debit total, giving a $3,785 net income.

The net income from the Income Statement columns is then entered in the Balance Sheet & Statement of Owner's Equity Credit column. Adding net income to the last Credit column implies that it is to be added to owner's capital. If a loss occurs, it is added to the Debit column. This implies that it is to be subtracted from owner's capital. **The ending balance of owner's capital does not appear in the last two columns as a single amount, but it is computed in the statement of owner's equity** using these account balances. When net income or net loss is added to the proper Balance Sheet & Statement of Owner's Equity column, the totals of the last two columns must balance. If they do not, one or more errors have occurred.

■ **Decision** Maker ━━━━━━━━━━━━━━━━━━━━━━━━━━━━━━━━━━━━

Entrepreneur   You make a printout of the electronic work sheet used to prepare financial statements. There is no depreciation adjustment, yet you own a large amount of equipment. Does the absence of depreciation adjustment concern you? ■   [*Answer:* Yes, you are concerned about the absence of a depreciation adjustment. Equipment does depreciate, and financial statements must recognize this occurrence. Its absence suggests an error or a misrepresentation (there is also the possibility that equipment is fully depreciated).]

Work Sheet Applications and Analysis

A work sheet does not substitute for financial statements. It is a tool we can use to help prepare financial statements. FastForward's financial statements are shown in Exhibit 4.2. Its income statement amounts are taken from the Income Statement columns of the work sheet. Similarly, amounts for its balance sheet and its statement of owner's equity are taken from the Balance Sheet & Statement of Owner's Equity columns of the work sheet.

Work sheets are also useful in analyzing the effects of proposed, or what-if, transactions. This is done by entering financial statement amounts in the Unadjusted (what-if) columns. Proposed transactions are then entered in the Adjustments columns. We then compute "adjusted" amounts from these proposed transactions. The extended amounts in the financial statement columns show the effects of these proposed transactions. These financial statement columns yield **pro forma financial statements** because they show the statements *as if* the proposed transactions had occurred.

EXHIBIT 4.1

Work Sheet with Five-Step Process for Completion

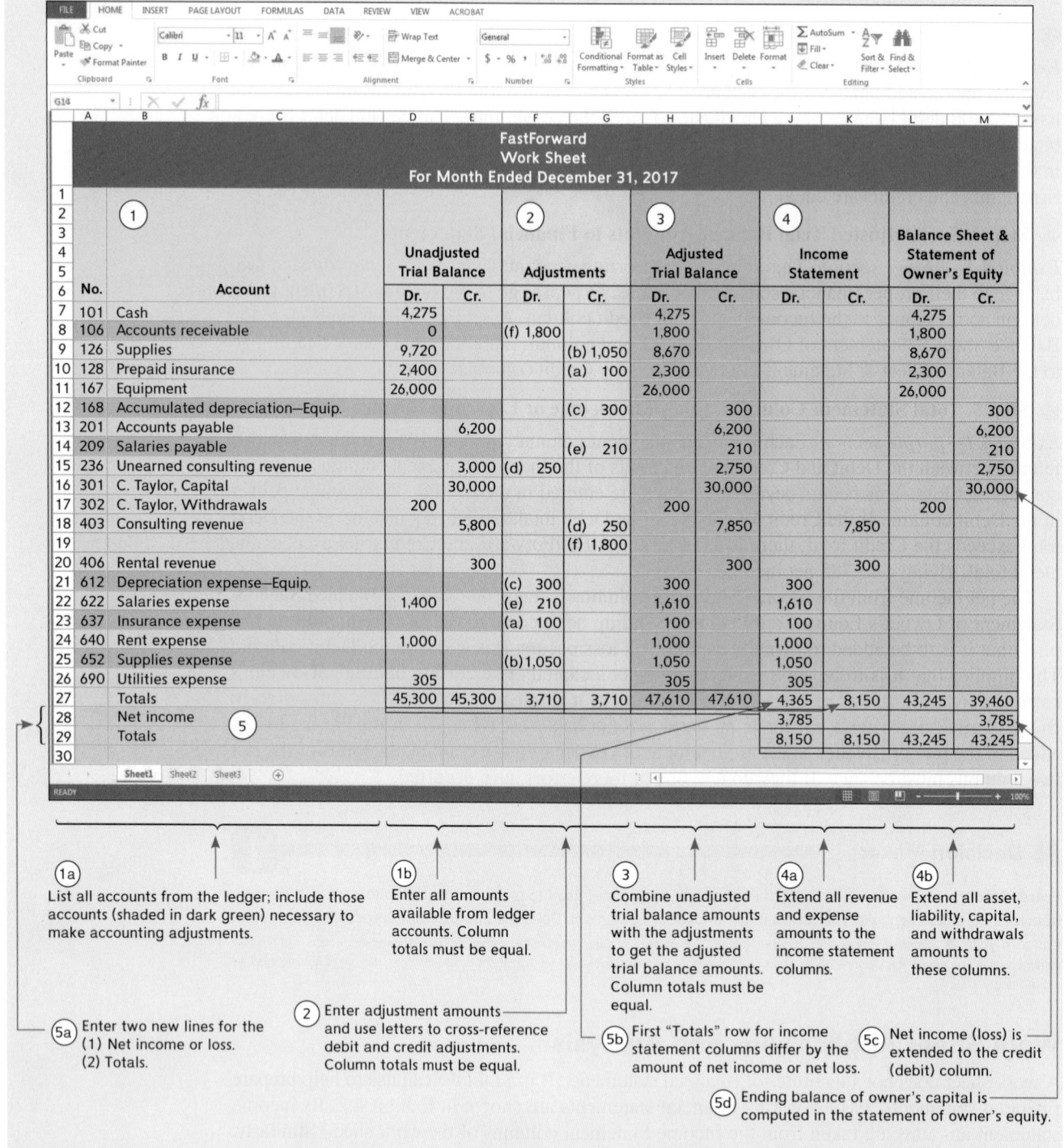

A work sheet organizes information used to prepare adjusting entries, financial statements, and closing entries.

EXHIBIT 4.2

Financial Statements
Prepared from the
Work Sheet

FAST*Forward*

FASTFORWARD		
Income Statement		
For Month Ended December 31, 2017		
Revenues		
Consulting revenue.................................	$ 7,850	
Rental revenue	300	
Total revenues.....................................		$ 8,150
Expenses		
Depreciation expense—Equipment...................	300	
Salaries expense....................................	1,610	
Insurance expense	100	
Rent expense.......................................	1,000	
Supplies expense	1,050	
Utilities expense	305	
Total expenses		4,365
Net income..		$ 3,785

FASTFORWARD		
Statement of Owner's Equity		
For Month Ended December 31, 2017		
C. Taylor, Capital, December 1		$ 0
Add: Investment by owner	$30,000	
Net income	3,785	33,785
		33,785
Less: Withdrawals by owner..........................		200
C. Taylor, Capital, December 31		$33,585

FASTFORWARD		
Balance Sheet		
December 31, 2017		
Assets		
Cash		$ 4,275
Accounts receivable		1,800
Supplies..		8,670
Prepaid insurance		2,300
Equipment	$26,000	
Accumulated depreciation—Equipment.................	(300)	25,700
Total assets		$42,745
Liabilities		
Accounts payable		$ 6,200
Salaries payable		210
Unearned consulting revenue		2,750
Total liabilities		9,160
Equity		
C. Taylor, Capital		33,585
Total liabilities and equity		$42,745

 **4-1**

Work Sheet

P1

The following 10-column work sheet contains the year-end unadjusted trial balance for Magic Company as of December 31, 2017. Complete the work sheet by entering the necessary adjustments, computing the adjusted account balances, extending the adjusted balances into the appropriate financial statement columns, and entering the amount of net income for the period. *Note:* The Magic, Capital account balance was $75,000 at December 31, 2016.

	A	B	C	D	E	F	G	H	I	J	K	L
1											Balance Sheet and	
2			Unadjusted				Adjusted		Income		Statement of	
3			Trial Balance		Adjustments		Trial Balance		Statement		Owner's Equity	
4	No.	Account Title	Dr.	Cr.	Dr.	Cr.	Dr.	Cr.	Dr.	Cr.	Dr.	Cr.
5	101	Cash	13,000									
6	106	Accounts receivable	8,000									
7	183	Land	85,000									
8	201	Accounts payable		10,000								
9	251	Long-term notes payable		33,000								
10	301	Magic, Capital		75,000								
11	302	Magic, Withdrawals	20,000									
12	401	Fees earned		70,000								
13	622	Salaries expense	54,000									
14	650	Office supplies expense	8,000									
15		Totals	188,000	188,000								
16		Net income										
17		Totals										

1. Prepare and complete the work sheet, starting with the unadjusted trial balance and including adjustments based on the following.

    a. The company has earned $9,000 in fees that were not yet recorded at year-end.

    b. The company incurred $2,000 in salary expense that was not yet recorded at year-end. (*Hint:* For simplicity, assume it records any salary not yet paid as part of accounts payable.)

    c. The long-term note payable was issued on December 31 this year. Thus, no interest has yet accrued on this loan.

2. Use information from the completed work sheet in part 1 to prepare adjusting entries.

3. Prepare the income statement and the statement of owner's equity for the year ended December 31 and the unclassified balance sheet at December 31.

Part 1 Solution

	A	B	C	D	E	F	G	H	I	J	K	L
1											Balance Sheet and	
2			Unadjusted				Adjusted		Income		Statement of	
3			Trial Balance		Adjustments		Trial Balance		Statement		Owner's Equity	
4	No.	Account Title	Dr.	Cr.	Dr.	Cr.	Dr.	Cr.	Dr.	Cr.	Dr.	Cr.
5	101	Cash	13,000				13,000				13,000	
6	106	Accounts receivable	8,000		(a)9,000		17,000				17,000	
7	183	Land	85,000				85,000				85,000	
8	201	Accounts payable		10,000		(b)2,000		12,000				12,000
9	251	Long-term notes payable		33,000				33,000				33,000
10	301	Magic, Capital		75,000				75,000				75,000
11	302	Magic, Withdrawals	20,000				20,000				20,000	
12	401	Fees earned		70,000		(a)9,000		79,000		79,000		
13	622	Salaries expense	54,000		(b)2,000		56,000		56,000			
14	650	Office supplies expense	8,000				8,000		8,000			
15		Totals	188,000	188,000	11,000	11,000	199,000	199,000	64,000	79,000	135,000	120,000
16		Net income							15,000			15,000
17		Totals							79,000	79,000	135,000	135,000

Part 2 Solution

(a) Dec. 31	Accounts Receivable..........................	9,000	
	Fees Earned		9,000
(b) Dec. 31	Salaries Expense............................	2,000	
	Accounts Payable		2,000
(c)	No entry required.		

Part 3 Solution

MAGIC COMPANY Income Statement For Year Ended December 31, 2017		
Fees earned		$79,000
Expenses		
Salaries expense	$56,000	
Office supplies expense	8,000	
Total expenses		64,000
Net income		$15,000

MAGIC COMPANY Balance Sheet December 31, 2017		
Assets		
Cash		$ 13,000
Accounts receivable		17,000
Land		85,000
Total assets		$115,000
Liabilities		
Accounts payable		$ 12,000
Long-term notes payable		33,000
Total liabilities		45,000
Equity		
Magic, Capital		70,000
Total liabilities and equity		$115,000

MAGIC COMPANY Statement of Owner's Equity For Year Ended December 31, 2017	
Magic, Capital, December 31, 2016	$75,000
Add: Net income	15,000
	90,000
Less: Withdrawals by owner	20,000
Magic, Capital, December 31, 2017	$70,000

Do More: QS 4-1, QS 4-2, QS 4-3, QS 4-4, E 4-1, E 4-2, E 4-3

CLOSING PROCESS

The **closing process** is an important step at the end of an accounting period *after* financial statements are completed. It prepares accounts for recording the transactions and events of the *next* period. In the closing process we must (1) identify accounts for closing, (2) record and post the closing entries, and (3) prepare a post-closing trial balance. The purpose of the closing process is twofold. First, it resets revenue, expense, and withdrawals account balances to zero at the end of each period (which also updates the owner's capital account for inclusion on the balance sheet). This is done so that these accounts can properly measure income and withdrawals for the next period. Second, it helps in summarizing a period's revenues and expenses. This section explains the closing process.

C1

Explain why temporary accounts are closed each period.

Temporary and Permanent Accounts

Temporary accounts relate to one accounting period. They include all income statement accounts, the owner withdrawals account, and the **Income Summary** account. They are temporary because the accounts are opened at the beginning of a period, used to record transactions and events for that period, and then closed at the end of the period. *The closing process applies only to temporary accounts.*

Permanent accounts report on activities related to one or more future accounting periods. They include asset, liability, and owner capital accounts (all balance sheet accounts). *Permanent accounts are not closed each period and carry their ending balance into future periods.*

Temporary Accounts (closed at period-end)	Permanent Accounts (not closed at period-end)
Revenues Expenses Owner, Withdrawals Income Summary	Assets Liabilities Owner, Capital

Recording Closing Entries

Closing entries transfer the end-of-period balances in revenue, expense, and withdrawals accounts to the permanent capital account. Closing entries are necessary at the end of each period after financial statements are prepared because

- Revenue, expense, and withdrawals accounts must begin each period with zero balances.
- Owner's capital must reflect prior periods' revenues, expenses, and withdrawals.

Point: If Apple did not make closing entries, prior-year revenue from Apple Watch sales would be included with current-year revenue.

An income statement reports revenues and expenses for a *specific accounting period*. The statement of owner's equity reports similar information, including withdrawals. Since revenue, expense, and withdrawals accounts record information separately for each period, they must start each period with zero balances.

To close revenue and expense accounts, we transfer their balances first to an account called Income Summary. **Income Summary is a temporary account only used for the closing process** that contains a credit for total revenues (and gains) and a debit for total expenses (and losses). Its balance equals net income or net loss and it is transferred to the capital account. Next the withdrawals account balance is transferred to the capital account. After these closing entries are posted, the revenue, expense, withdrawals, and Income Summary accounts have zero balances. These accounts are then said to be *closed* or *cleared*.

Exhibit 4.3 uses the adjusted account balances of FastForward (from the Adjusted Trial Balance columns of Exhibit 4.1 or from the left side of Exhibit 4.4) to show the four steps necessary to close its temporary accounts. We explain each step.

P2

Describe and prepare closing entries.

EXHIBIT 4.3

Four-Step Closing Process

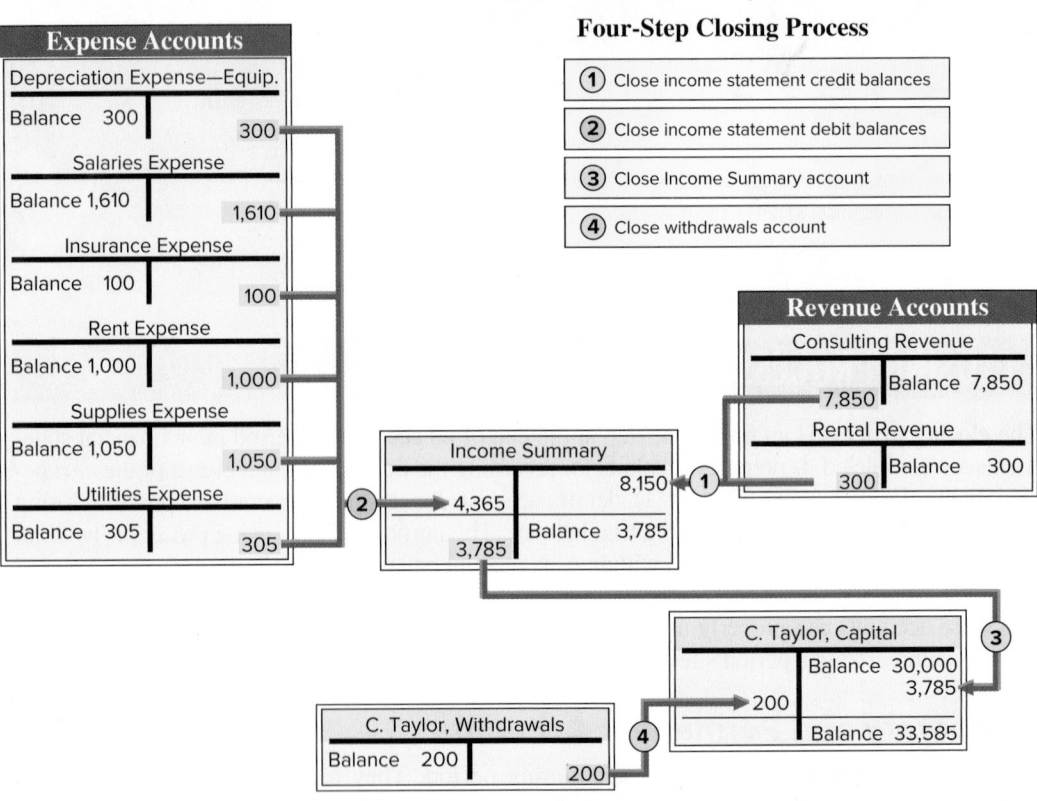

Step 1: Close Credit Balances in Revenue Accounts to Income Summary
The first closing entry transfers credit balances in revenue (and gain) accounts to the Income Summary account. We bring accounts with credit balances to zero by debiting them. For FastForward, this journal entry is step 1 in Exhibit 4.4. This entry closes revenue accounts and leaves them with zero balances. The accounts are now ready to record revenues when they occur in the next period. The $8,150 credit entry to Income Summary equals total revenues for the period.

Step 2: Close Debit Balances in Expense Accounts to Income Summary
The second closing entry transfers debit balances in expense (and loss) accounts to the Income Summary account. We bring expense accounts' debit balances to zero by crediting them. With a balance of zero, these accounts are ready to record expenses for the next period. This second closing entry for FastForward is step 2 in Exhibit 4.4. Exhibit 4.3 shows that posting this entry gives each expense account a zero balance.

Step 3: Close Income Summary to Owner's Capital
After steps 1 and 2, the balance of Income Summary is equal to December's net income of $3,785 ($8,150 credit less $4,365 debit). The third closing entry transfers the balance of the Income Summary account to

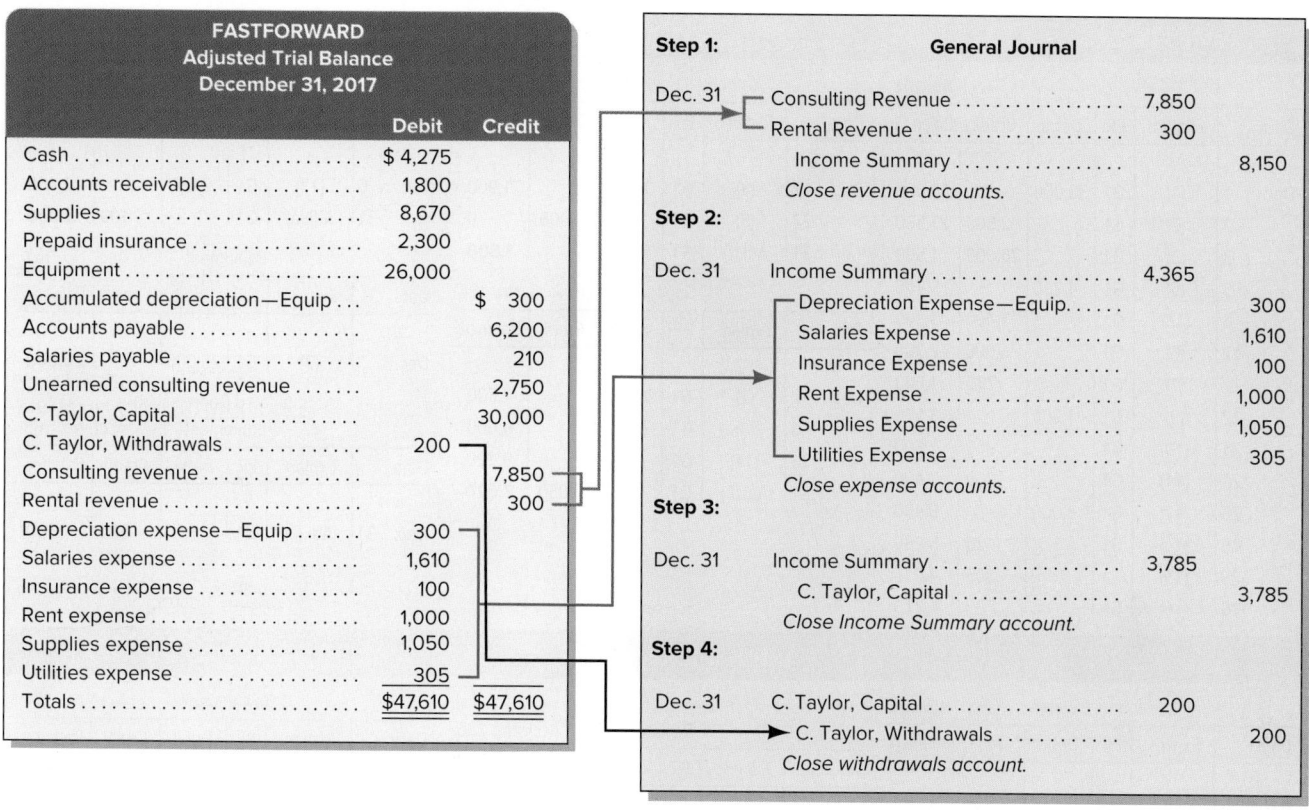

the capital account. This entry closes the Income Summary account—see step 3 in Exhibit 4.4. The Income Summary account has a zero balance after posting this entry. It continues to have a zero balance until the closing process again occurs at the end of the next period. (If a net loss occurred because expenses exceeded revenues, the third entry is reversed: debit Owner, Capital and credit Income Summary.)

Step 4: Close Withdrawals Account to Owner's Capital   The fourth closing entry transfers any debit balance in the withdrawals account to the owner's capital account—see step 4 in Exhibit 4.4. This entry gives the withdrawals account a zero balance, and the account is now ready to record next period's withdrawals. This entry also reduces the capital account balance to the $33,585 amount reported on the balance sheet.

We could also have selected the accounts and amounts needing to be closed by identifying individual revenue, expense, and withdrawals accounts in the ledger. This is illustrated in Exhibit 4.4 where we prepare closing entries using the adjusted trial balance.[1] (Information for closing entries is also in the financial statement columns of a work sheet.)

Post-Closing Trial Balance

Exhibit 4.5 shows the entire ledger of FastForward as of December 31 after adjusting and closing entries are posted. (The transaction and adjusting entries are in Chapters 2 and 3.) The temporary accounts (revenues, expenses, and withdrawals) have ending balances equal to zero.

A **post-closing trial balance** is a list of permanent accounts and their balances from the ledger after all closing entries have been journalized and posted. It lists the balances for all accounts not closed. These accounts comprise a company's assets, liabilities, and equity, which are identical to those in the balance sheet. The aim of a post-closing trial balance is to verify that (1) total debits equal total credits for permanent accounts and (2) all temporary accounts have

EXHIBIT 4.4

Preparing Closing Entries

P3

Explain and prepare a post-closing trial balance.

---

[1]The closing process has focused on proprietorships. It is identical for partnerships with the exception that each owner has separate capital and withdrawals accounts (for steps 3 and 4). The closing process for a corporation is similar with the exception that it uses a Dividend account instead of a withdrawals account, and Income Summary and Dividends are closed to a Retained Earnings account instead of a capital account.

EXHIBIT 4.5

General Ledger after the Closing Process for FastForward

Asset Accounts

Cash — Acct. No. 101

Date	Explan.	PR	Debit	Credit	Balance
2017					
Dec. 1	(1)	G1	30,000		30,000
2	(2)	G1		2,500	27,500
3	(3)	G1		26,000	1,500
5	(5)	G1	4,200		5,700
6	(13)	G1		2,400	3,300
12	(6)	G1		1,000	2,300
12	(7)	G1		700	1,600
22	(9)	G1	1,900		3,500
24	(10)	G1		900	2,600
24	(11)	G1		200	2,400
26	(12)	G1	3,000		5,400
26	(14)	G1		120	5,280
26	(15)	G1		305	4,975
26	(16)	G1		700	**4,275**

Accounts Receivable — Acct. No. 106

Date	Explan.	PR	Debit	Credit	Balance
2017					
Dec. 12	(8)	G1	1,900		1,900
22	(9)	G1		1,900	0
31	Adj.(f)	G1	1,800		**1,800**

Supplies — Acct. No. 126

Date	Explan.	PR	Debit	Credit	Balance
2017					
Dec. 2	(2)	G1	2,500		2,500
6	(4)	G1	7,100		9,600
26	(14)	G1	120		9,720
31	Adj.(b)	G1		1,050	**8,670**

Prepaid Insurance — Acct. No. 128

Date	Explan.	PR	Debit	Credit	Balance
2017					
Dec. 6	(13)	G1	2,400		2,400
31	Adj.(a)	G1		100	**2,300**

Equipment — Acct. No. 167

Date	Explan.	PR	Debit	Credit	Balance
2017					
Dec. 3	(3)	G1	26,000		**26,000**

Accumulated Depreciation—Equipment — Acct. No. 168

Date	Explan.	PR	Debit	Credit	Balance
2017					
Dec. 31	Adj.(c)	G1		300	**300**

Liability and Equity Accounts

Accounts Payable — Acct. No. 201

Date	Explan.	PR	Debit	Credit	Balance
2017					
Dec. 6	(4)	G1		7,100	7,100
24	(10)	G1	900		**6,200**

Salaries Payable — Acct. No. 209

Date	Explan.	PR	Debit	Credit	Balance
2017					
Dec. 31	Adj.(e)	G1		210	**210**

Unearned Consulting Revenue — Acct. No. 236

Date	Explan.	PR	Debit	Credit	Balance
2017					
Dec. 26	(12)	G1		3,000	3,000
31	Adj.(d)	G1	250		**2,750**

C. Taylor, Capital — Acct. No. 301

Date	Explan.	PR	Debit	Credit	Balance
2017					
Dec. 1	(1)	G1		30,000	**30,000**
31	Clos.(3)	G1		3,785	**33,785**
31	Clos.(4)	G1	200		**33,585**

C. Taylor, Withdrawals — Acct. No. 302

Date	Explan.	PR	Debit	Credit	Balance
2017					
Dec. 24	(11)	G1	200		**200**
31	Clos.(4)	G1		200	0

Revenue and Expense Accounts (Including Income Summary)

Consulting Revenue — Acct. No. 403

Date	Explan.	PR	Debit	Credit	Balance
2017					
Dec. 5	(5)	G1		4,200	4,200
12	(8)	G1		1,600	5,800
31	Adj.(d)	G1		250	6,050
31	Adj.(f)	G1		1,800	**7,850**
31	Clos.(1)	G1	7,850		0

Rental Revenue — Acct. No. 406

Date	Explan.	PR	Debit	Credit	Balance
2017					
Dec. 12	(8)	G1		300	**300**
31	Clos.(1)	G1	300		0

Depreciation Expense—Equipment — Acct. No. 612

Date	Explan.	PR	Debit	Credit	Balance
2017					
Dec. 31	Adj.(c)	G1	300		**300**
31	Clos.(2)	G1		300	0

Salaries Expense — Acct. No. 622

Date	Explan.	PR	Debit	Credit	Balance
2017					
Dec. 12	(7)	G1	700		700
26	(16)	G1	700		1,400
31	Adj.(e)	G1	210		**1,610**
31	Clos.(2)	G1		1,610	0

Insurance Expense — Acct. No. 637

Date	Explan.	PR	Debit	Credit	Balance
2017					
Dec. 31	Adj.(a)	G1	100		**100**
31	Clos.(2)	G1		100	0

Rent Expense — Acct. No. 640

Date	Explan.	PR	Debit	Credit	Balance
2017					
Dec. 12	(6)	G1	1,000		**1,000**
31	Clos.(2)	G1		1,000	0

Supplies Expense — Acct. No. 652

Date	Explan.	PR	Debit	Credit	Balance
2017					
Dec. 31	Adj.(b)	G1	1,050		**1,050**
31	Clos.(2)	G1		1,050	0

Utilities Expense — Acct. No. 690

Date	Explan.	PR	Debit	Credit	Balance
2017					
Dec. 26	(15)	G1	305		**305**
31	Clos.(2)	G1		305	0

Income Summary — Acct. No. 901

Date	Explan.	PR	Debit	Credit	Balance
2017					
Dec. 31	Clos.(1)	G1		8,150	8,150
31	Clos.(2)	G1	4,365		3,785
31	Clos.(3)	G1	3,785		0

zero balances. FastForward's post-closing trial balance is shown in Exhibit 4.6. The post-closing trial balance usually is the last step in the accounting process.

EXHIBIT 4.6

Post-Closing Trial Balance

FASTFORWARD Post-Closing Trial Balance December 31, 2017	Debit	Credit
Cash	$ 4,275	
Accounts receivable	1,800	
Supplies	8,670	
Prepaid insurance	2,300	
Equipment	26,000	
Accumulated depreciation—Equipment		$ 300
Accounts payable		6,200
Salaries payable		210
Unearned consulting revenue		2,750
C. Taylor, Capital*		33,585
Totals	$43,045	$43,045

* Computed as $30,000 + $3,785 − $200.

Point: Only balance sheet (permanent) accounts are on a post-closing trial balance.

Decision Maker

Staff Accountant   A friend shows you the post-closing trial balance she is working on. You review the statement and see a line item for rent expense. You tell your friend, "I see that you have an error." How did you conclude that an error exists? ■ [*Answer:* This error is apparent in a post-closing trial balance because rent expense is a temporary account. Post-closing trial balances only contain permanent accounts.]

ACCOUNTING CYCLE

The term **accounting cycle** refers to the steps in preparing financial statements. It is called a *cycle* because the steps are repeated each reporting period. Exhibit 4.7 shows the 10 steps in the cycle, beginning with analyzing transactions and ending with a post-closing trial balance or reversing entries. Steps 1 through 3 occur regularly as a company enters into transactions. Steps 4 through 9 are done at the end of a period. *Reversing entries* in step 10 are optional and are explained in Appendix 4A.

C2

Identify steps in the accounting cycle.

Use the adjusted trial balance solution for Magic Company from Need-To-Know 4-1 to prepare its closing entries—the accounts are also listed here for convenience.

Cash	$13,000 Dr.	Magic, Capital	$75,000 Cr.	
Accounts receivable	17,000 Dr.	Magic, Withdrawals	20,000 Dr.	
Land	85,000 Dr.	Fees earned	79,000 Cr.	
Accounts payable	12,000 Cr.	Salaries expense	56,000 Dr.	
Long-term notes payable	33,000 Cr.	Office supplies expense	8,000 Dr.	

NEED-TO-KNOW 4-2

Closing Entries

P2

Solution

Dec. 31	Fees Earned	79,000	
	Income Summary		79,000
	Close revenue account.		
Dec. 31	Income Summary	64,000	
	Salaries Expense		56,000
	Office Supplies Expense		8,000
	Close expense accounts.		
Dec. 31	Income Summary	15,000	
	Magic, Capital		15,000
	Close Income Summary.		
Dec. 31	Magic, Capital	20,000	
	Magic, Withdrawals		20,000
	Close Withdrawals account.		

Do More: QS 4-6, E 4-6, E 4-7, E 4-8, E 4-9

EXHIBIT 4.7

Steps in the Accounting Cycle*

1. Analyze transactions

	Assets				=	Liabilities	+	Equity
	Cash	+	Supplies	+	Equipment =	Accounts Payable	+	C. Taylor, Capital
Old Bal.	$1,500	+	$2,500	+	$26,000 =			$30,000
(4)		+	7,100			+$7,100		
New Bal.	$1,500	+	$9,600	+	$26,000 =	$ 7,100	+	$30,000

2. Journalize

Date	Account Titles and Explanation	PR	Debit	Credit
(4)	Supplies	126	7,100	
	Accounts Payable	201		7,100

3. Post

General Ledger

Supplies		126		Accounts Payable		201
(2)	2,500				(4)	7,100
(4)	7,100					

4. Prepare unadjusted trial balance

FASTFORWARD
Trial Balance
December 31, 2017

	Debit	Credit
Cash	$ 4,275	
Accounts receivable	0	
Supplies	9,720	
Prepaid insurance	2,400	
Equipment	26,000	
Accounts payable		$ 6,200
Unearned consulting revenue		3,000

5. Adjust and post accounts

Adjustment (b)

Dec. 31	Supplies Expense	1,050	
	Supplies		1,050
	Record supplies used.		

Supplies Expense		652		Supplies		126
Dec. 31	1,050		Dec. 2	2,500	Dec. 31	1,050
			6	7,100		
			26	120		
			Balance	8,670		

6. Prepare adjusted trial balance

FASTFORWARD
Trial Balances
December 31, 2017

Acct. No.	Account Title	Unadjusted Trial Balance Dr.	Unadjusted Trial Balance Cr.	Adjustments Dr.	Adjustments Cr.	Adjusted Trial Balance Dr.	Adjusted Trial Balance Cr.
101	Cash	$ 4,275				$ 4,275	
106	Accounts receivable	0		(f) $1,800		1,800	
126	Supplies	9,720			(b) $1,050	8,670	
128	Prepaid insurance	2,400			(a) 100	2,300	
167	Equipment	26,000				26,000	
168	Accumulated depreciation—Equip.		$ 0		(c) 300		$ 300
201	Accounts payable		6,200				6,200
209	Salaries payable		0		(e) 210		210

7. Prepare financial statements

FASTFORWARD
Statement of Owner's Equity
For Month Ended December 31, 2017

C. Taylor, Capital, December 1	$ 0
Plus:	

FASTFORWARD
Income Statement
For Month Ended December 31, 2017

Revenues	
Consulting revenue	$7,850

FASTFORWARD
Balance Sheet
December 31, 2017

Assets	
Cash	$ 4,275
Accounts receivable	1,800
Supplies	8,670
Prepaid insurance	2,300

8. Close Accounts

General Journal

Step 1:			
Dec. 31	Consulting Revenue	7,850	
	Rental Revenue	300	
	Income Summary		8,150
	Close revenue accounts.		
Step 2:			
Dec. 31	Income Summary	4,365	
	Depreciation Expense—Equip.		300
	Salaries Expense		1,610
	Insurance Expense		100
	Rent Expense		1,000
	Supplies Expense		1,050
	Utilities Expense		305
	Close expense accounts.		

9. Prepare post-closing trial balance

FASTFORWARD
Post-Closing Trial Balance
December 31, 2017

	Debit	Credit
Cash	$ 4,275	
Accounts receivable	1,800	
Supplies	8,670	
Prepaid insurance	2,300	
Equipment	26,000	
Accumulated depreciation—Equipment		$ 300
Accounts payable		6,200

10. Reverse and post (optional)

Reversing entry recorded on January 1, 2018

Salaries Payable	210	
Salaries Expense		210

Salaries Expense

Date	Expl.	Debit	Credit	Balance
2018 Jan. 1			210	(210)

Salaries Payable

Date	Expl.	Debit	Credit	Balance
2017 Dec. 31	(e)		210	210
2018 Jan. 1		210		0

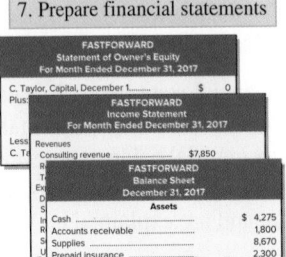

Accounting Cycle

Explanations

1. Analyze transactions	Analyze transactions to prepare for journalizing.
2. Journalize	Record accounts, including debits and credits, in a journal.
3. Post	Transfer debits and credits from the journal to the ledger.
4. Prepare unadjusted trial balance	Summarize unadjusted ledger accounts and amounts.
5. Adjust and post	Record adjustments to bring account balances up to date; journalize and post adjustments.
6. Prepare adjusted trial balance	Summarize adjusted ledger accounts and amounts.
7. Prepare financial statements	Use adjusted trial balance to prepare financial statements.
8. Close	Journalize and post entries to close temporary accounts.
9. Prepare post-closing trial balance	Test clerical accuracy of the closing procedures.
10. Reverse and post (optional step)	Reverse certain adjustments in the next period—optional step; see Appendix 4A.

* Steps 4, 6, and 9 can be done on a work sheet. A work sheet is useful in planning adjustments, but adjustments (step 5) must always be journalized and posted. Steps 3, 4, 6, and 9 are automatic with a computerized system.

CLASSIFIED BALANCE SHEET

C3

Explain and prepare a classified balance sheet.

Our discussion to this point has been limited to unclassified financial statements. This section describes a classified balance sheet. The next chapter describes a classified income statement. An **unclassified balance sheet** broadly groups accounts into assets, liabilities, and equity. One example is FastForward's balance sheet in Exhibit 4.2. A **classified balance sheet** organizes assets and liabilities into subgroups that provide more information to decision makers.

Classification Structure

A classified balance sheet has no required layout, but it usually contains the categories in Exhibit 4.8. One of the more important classifications is the separation between current and noncurrent items for both assets and liabilities. Current items are expected to come due (either collected or owed) within one year or the company's operating cycle, whichever is longer. The **operating cycle** is the time span from when *cash is used* to acquire goods and services until *cash is received* from the sale of goods and services. The length of a company's operating cycle depends on its activities. For a service company, the operating cycle is the time span between (1) paying employees who perform the services and (2) receiving cash from customers. For a merchandiser selling products, the operating cycle is the time span between (1) paying suppliers for merchandise and (2) receiving cash from customers.

Assets	Liabilities and Equity
Current assets	Current liabilities
Noncurrent assets	Noncurrent liabilities
Long-term investments	Equity
Plant assets	
Intangible assets	

EXHIBIT 4.8

Typical Categories in a Classified Balance Sheet

Most operating cycles are less than one year, which means most companies use a one-year period in deciding what assets and liabilities are current. A balance sheet lists current assets before noncurrent assets and current liabilities before noncurrent liabilities. This consistency in presentation allows users to quickly identify current assets that are most easily converted to cash and current liabilities that are shortly coming due. Items in current assets and current liabilities are listed in the order of how quickly they will be converted to, or paid in, cash.

Classification Categories

This section describes the most common categories in a classified balance sheet. The balance sheet for Snowboarding Components in Exhibit 4.9 shows the typical categories. Its assets are classified as either current or noncurrent. Its noncurrent assets include three main categories: long-term investments, plant assets, and intangible assets. Its liabilities are classified as either current or long-term. Not all companies use the same categories of assets and liabilities for their balance sheets. Jarden, a producer of snowboards and other goods, reported a balance sheet with five asset classes: current assets; property, plant, and equipment; goodwill; intangibles; and other assets.

© Purestock/SuperStock

Current Assets **Current assets** are cash and other resources that are expected to be sold, collected, or used within one year or the company's operating cycle, whichever is longer. Examples are cash, short-term investments, accounts receivable, short-term notes receivable, goods for sale (called *merchandise* or *inventory*), and prepaid expenses. The prepaid expenses in Exhibit 4.9 likely include items such as prepaid insurance, prepaid rent, office supplies, and store supplies. Prepaid expenses are usually listed last because they will not be converted to cash (instead, they are used).

Point: Current is also called *short-term,* and noncurrent is also called *long-term.*

Long-Term Investments A second major balance sheet classification is **long-term** (or *noncurrent*) **investments.** Notes receivable and investments in stocks and bonds are long-term assets when they are expected to be held for more than the longer of one year or the operating cycle. Land held for future expansion is a long-term investment because it is *not* used in operations.

Plant Assets Plant assets are tangible assets that are both *long-lived* and *used to produce or sell products and services.* Examples are equipment, machinery, buildings, and land that are used to produce or sell products and services. The order listing for plant assets is usually from most liquid to least liquid such as equipment and machinery to buildings and land.

Point: Plant assets are also called *fixed assets; property, plant and equipment (PP&E); or long-lived assets.*

EXHIBIT 4.9

Example of a Classified Balance Sheet

SNOWBOARDING COMPONENTS		
Balance Sheet		
January 31, 2017		
Assets		
Current assets		
Cash	$ 6,500	
Short-term investments	2,100	
Accounts receivable, net	4,400	
Merchandise inventory	27,500	
Prepaid expenses	2,400	
Total current assets		$ 42,900
Long-term investments		
Notes receivable (due in three years)	1,500	
Investments in stocks and bonds	18,000	
Land held for future expansion	48,000	
Total long-term investments		67,500
Plant assets		
Equipment and buildings	203,200	
Less accumulated depreciation	53,000	
Equipment and buildings, net		150,200
Land		73,200
Total plant assets		223,400
Intangible assets		10,000
Total assets		$343,800
Liabilities		
Current liabilities		
Accounts payable	$ 15,300	
Wages payable	3,200	
Notes payable (due within one year)	3,000	
Current portion of long-term liabilities	7,500	
Total current liabilities		$ 29,000
Long-term liabilities (net of current portion)		150,000
Total liabilities		179,000
Equity		
T. Hawk, Capital		164,800
Total liabilities and equity		$343,800

© Johannes Simon/Getty Images

Intangible Assets   **Intangible assets** are long-term resources that benefit business operations but lack physical form. Examples are patents, trademarks, copyrights, franchises, and goodwill. Their value comes from the privileges or rights granted to or held by the owner. **Jarden** reports intangible assets of $2,599 million, which is nearly 25% of its total assets. Its intangibles include trademarks, patents, and licensing agreements.

Current Liabilities   **Current liabilities** are obligations due to be paid or settled within one year or the operating cycle, whichever is longer. They are usually settled by paying out cash. Current liabilities often include accounts payable, notes payable, wages payable, taxes payable, interest payable, and unearned revenues. Also, any portion of a long-term liability due to be paid within one year or the operating cycle, whichever is longer, is a current liability. Unearned revenues are current liabilities when they will be settled by delivering products or services within one year or the operating cycle, whichever is longer. Current liabilities are reported in the order of those to be settled first.

Long-Term Liabilities   **Long-term liabilities** are obligations *not* due within one year or the operating cycle, whichever is longer. Notes payable, mortgages payable, bonds payable, and lease obligations are common long-term liabilities. If a company has both short- and long-term items in each of these categories, they are commonly separated into two accounts in the ledger.

Equity   Equity is the owner's claim on assets. For a proprietorship, this claim is reported in the equity section with an owner's capital account. (For a partnership, the equity section reports a capital account for each partner. For a corporation, the equity section is divided into two main subsections, contributed capital and retained earnings.)

Use the adjusted trial balance solution for Magic Company from Need-To-Know 4-1 to prepare its classified balance sheet as of December 31, 2017—the accounts are also listed here for convenience.

NEED-TO-KNOW 4-3

Classified Balance Sheet

C3

Cash	$13,000 Dr.	Magic, Capital	$75,000 Cr.
Accounts receivable	17,000 Dr.	Magic, Withdrawals	20,000 Dr.
Land	85,000 Dr.	Fees earned	79,000 Cr.
Accounts payable	12,000 Cr.	Salaries expense	56,000 Dr.
Long-term notes payable	33,000 Cr.	Office supplies expense	8,000 Dr.

Solution

MAGIC COMPANY
Balance Sheet
December 31, 2017

Assets		Liabilities	
Current assets		Current liabilities	
Cash	$ 13,000	Accounts payable	$ 12,000
Accounts receivable	17,000	Total current liabilities	12,000
Total current assets	30,000	Long-term notes payable	33,000
Plant assets		Total liabilities	45,000
Land	85,000	**Equity**	
Total plant assets	85,000	Magic, Capital*	70,000
Total assets	$115,000	Total liabilities and equity	$115,000

*Computed as $75,000 + $15,000 − $20,000.

Do More: QS 4-9, E 4-12,
P 4-3

SUSTAINABILITY AND ACCOUNTING

LuminAID, as introduced in this chapter's opening feature, puts emphasis on tracking expenses and revenues. One reason is that the owners focus on running a successful operation. Another reason is that LuminAID, through its "**Give Light, Get Light**" initiative, allows customers to buy a light for themselves and donate another to a nonprofit organization.

According to the company's website, "LuminAID has distributed over 10,000 lights in more than 50 countries." LuminAID relies on its accounting system to accurately track sales and ensure that these lights are being donated to those with the greatest need.

The company also distributes LuminAIDs with funding from several different grants (nonrepayable funds). Anna and Andrea, the two entrepreneurial founders of LuminAID, have been awarded grants of $100,000 from both the Clean Energy Trust and Chase Bank.

The two women rely on their accounting system to properly separate owner contributions from grants. This is crucial to ensure profits can be reinvested in the business and Anna and Andrea can continue their mission. According to Anna, the goal of LuminAID is to "turn one simple product into a sustainable business that can provide comfort and safety through light to people who need it most."

Courtesy of Liv Williams/LuminAID

Current Ratio  **Decision Analysis**

An important use of financial statements is to help assess a company's ability to pay its debts in the near future. Such analysis affects decisions by suppliers when allowing a company to buy on credit. It also affects decisions by creditors when lending money to a company, including loan terms such as interest rate, due date, and collateral requirements. It can also affect a manager's decisions about using cash to pay debts when they come due. The **current ratio** is one measure of a company's ability to pay its short-term obligations. It is defined in Exhibit 4.10 as current assets divided by current liabilities.

A1

Compute the current ratio and describe what it reveals about a company's financial condition.

$$\text{Current ratio} = \frac{\text{Current assets}}{\text{Current liabilities}}$$

EXHIBIT 4.10

Current Ratio

Using financial information from **Limited Brands, Inc.**, we compute its current ratio for the recent six-year period. The results are in Exhibit 4.11.

EXHIBIT 4.11

Limited Brands's Current Ratio

$ millions	2015	2014	2013	2012	2011	2010
Current assets....................	$3,232	$3,150	$2,205	$2,368	$2,592	$3,250
Current liabilities..................	$1,679	$1,826	$1,538	$1,526	$1,504	$1,322
Current ratio	**1.9**	**1.7**	**1.4**	**1.6**	**1.7**	**2.5**
Industry current ratio	1.8	1.7	1.5	1.6	1.7	1.9

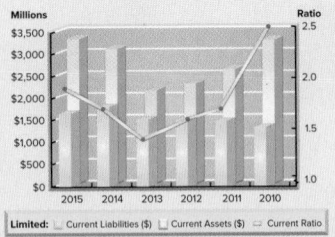

Limited Brands's current ratio averaged 1.8 for its fiscal years 2010 through 2015. The current ratio for each of these years suggests that the company's short-term obligations can be covered with its short-term assets. However, if its ratio would approach 1.0, Limited would expect to face challenges in covering liabilities. If the ratio were *less* than 1.0, current liabilities would exceed current assets, and the company's ability to pay short-term obligations could be in doubt. Limited Brands's liquidity, as evidenced by its current ratio, declined in 2011, 2012, and 2013, which roughly matches the industry decline.

■ **Decision** Maker

Analyst   You are analyzing the financial condition of a company to assess its ability to meet upcoming loan payments. You compute its current ratio as 1.2. You also find that a major portion of accounts receivable is due from one client who has not made any payments in the past 12 months. Removing this receivable from current assets lowers the current ratio to 0.7. What do you conclude? ■   [*Answer*: A current ratio of 1.2 suggests that current assets are sufficient to cover current liabilities, but it implies a minimal buffer in case of errors in measuring current assets or current liabilities. Removing the past due receivable reduces the current ratio to 0.7. You conclude that the company will have some difficulty meeting its loan payments.]

NEED-TO-KNOW 4-4

COMPREHENSIVE

The partial work sheet of Midtown Repair Company at December 31, 2017, follows.

	Adjusted Trial Balance		Income Statement		Balance Sheet and Statement of Owner's Equity	
	Debit	Credit	Debit	Credit	Debit	Credit
Cash	95,600					
Notes receivable (current)	50,000					
Prepaid insurance...........................	16,000					
Prepaid rent	4,000					
Equipment.................................	170,000					
Accumulated depreciation—Equipment		57,000				
Accounts payable...........................		52,000				
Long-term notes payable.....................		63,000				
C. Trout, Capital		178,500				
C. Trout, Withdrawals........................	30,000					
Repair services revenue......................		180,800				
Interest revenue............................		7,500				
Depreciation expense—Equipment..............	28,500					
Wages expense	85,000					
Rent expense	48,000					
Insurance expense..........................	6,000					
Interest expense............................	5,700					
Totals.....................................	538,800	538,800				

Required

1. Complete the work sheet by extending the adjusted trial balance totals to the appropriate financial statement columns.

2. Prepare closing entries for Midtown Repair Company.

3. Set up the Income Summary and the C. Trout, Capital accounts in the general ledger (in balance column format) and post the closing entries to these accounts.

4. Determine the balance of the C. Trout, Capital account to be reported on the December 31, 2017, balance sheet.

5. Prepare an income statement, statement of owner's equity, and classified balance sheet (in report form) as of December 31, 2017. The balance in C. Trout, Capital on December 31, 2016, was $178,500.

PLANNING THE SOLUTION

- Extend the adjusted trial balance account balances to the proper financial statement columns.
- Prepare entries to close the revenue accounts to Income Summary, to close the expense accounts to Income Summary, to close Income Summary to the capital account, and to close the withdrawals account to the capital account.
- Post the first and second closing entries to the Income Summary account. Examine the balance of Income Summary and verify that it agrees with the net income shown on the work sheet.
- Post the third and fourth closing entries to the capital account.
- Use the work sheet's two right-most columns and your answer in part 4 to prepare the classified balance sheet.

SOLUTION

1. Completing the work sheet.

	Adjusted Trial Balance		Income Statement		Balance Sheet and Statement of Owner's Equity	
	Debit	Credit	Debit	Credit	Debit	Credit
Cash	95,600				95,600	
Notes receivable (current)	50,000				50,000	
Prepaid insurance.........................	16,000				16,000	
Prepaid rent	4,000				4,000	
Equipment...............................	170,000				170,000	
Accumulated depreciation—Equipment		57,000				57,000
Accounts payable.........................		52,000				52,000
Long-term notes payable....................		63,000				63,000
C. Trout, Capital		178,500				178,500
C. Trout, Withdrawals......................	30,000				30,000	
Repair services revenue....................		180,800		180,800		
Interest revenue..........................		7,500		7,500		
Depreciation expense—Equipment...........	28,500		28,500			
Wages expense	85,000		85,000			
Rent expense	48,000		48,000			
Insurance expense........................	6,000		6,000			
Interest expense.........................	5,700		5,700			
Totals...................................	538,800	538,800	173,200	188,300	365,600	350,500
Net income			15,100			15,100
Totals...................................			188,300	188,300	365,600	365,600

2. Closing entries.

Dec. 31	Repair Services Revenue................................	180,800	
	Interest Revenue	7,500	
	Income Summary		188,300
	Close revenue accounts.		
Dec. 31	Income Summary......................................	173,200	
	Depreciation Expense—Equipment..................		28,500
	Wages Expense		85,000
	Rent Expense		48,000
	Insurance Expense..................................		6,000
	Interest Expense....................................		5,700
	Close expense accounts.		
Dec. 31	Income Summary......................................	15,100	
	C. Trout, Capital		15,100
	Close Income Summary account.		
Dec. 31	C. Trout, Capital.....................................	30,000	
	C. Trout, Withdrawals..............................		30,000
	Close withdrawals account.		

3. Set up the Income Summary and the capital ledger accounts and post the closing entries.

Income Summary					Account No. 901
Date	**Explanation**	**PR**	**Debit**	**Credit**	**Balance**
2017					
Jan. 1	Beginning balance......................				0
Dec. 31	Close revenue accounts			188,300	188,300
31	Close expense accounts................		173,200		15,100
31	Close Income Summary.................		15,100		0

C. Trout, Capital					Account No. 301
Date	**Explanation**	**PR**	**Debit**	**Credit**	**Balance**
2017					
Jan. 1	Beginning balance......................				178,500
Dec. 31	Close Income Summary.................			15,100	193,600
31	Close C. Trout, Withdrawals		30,000		163,600

4. The final capital balance of $163,600 (from part 3) will be reported on the December 31, 2017, balance sheet. The final capital balance reflects the increase due to the net income earned during the year and the decrease for the owner's withdrawals during the year.

5.

MIDTOWN REPAIR COMPANY
Income Statement
For Year Ended December 31, 2017

Revenues		
Repair services revenue	$180,800	
Interest revenue............................	7,500	
Total revenues		$188,300
Expenses		
Depreciation expense—Equipment..............	28,500	
Wages expense	85,000	
Rent expense	48,000	
Insurance expense...........................	6,000	
Interest expense............................	5,700	
Total expenses		173,200
Net income		$ 15,100

MIDTOWN REPAIR COMPANY
Statement of Owner's Equity
For Year Ended December 31, 2017

C. Trout, Capital, December 31, 2016		$178,500
Add: Investment by owner	$ 0	
Net income	15,100	15,100
		193,600
Less: Withdrawals by owner		30,000
C. Trout, Capital, December 31, 2017		$163,600

MIDTOWN REPAIR COMPANY
Balance Sheet
December 31, 2017

Assets

Current assets		
Cash		$ 95,600
Notes receivable		50,000
Prepaid insurance		16,000
Prepaid rent		4,000
Total current assets		165,600
Plant assets		
Equipment	$170,000	
Less: Accumulated depreciation—Equipment	(57,000)	
Total plant assets		113,000
Total assets		$278,600

Liabilities

Current liabilities		
Accounts payable		$ 52,000
Long-term liabilities		
Long-term notes payable		63,000
Total liabilities		115,000

Equity

C. Trout, Capital		163,600
Total liabilities and equity		$278,600

APPENDIX

Reversing Entries

4A

P4

Prepare reversing entries and explain their purpose.

Reversing entries are optional. They are recorded in response to accrued assets and accrued liabilities that were created by adjusting entries at the end of a reporting period. The purpose of reversing entries is to simplify a company's recordkeeping. Exhibit 4A.1 shows an example of FastForward's reversing entries. The top of the exhibit shows the adjusting entry FastForward recorded on December 31 for its employee's earned but unpaid salary. The entry recorded three days' salary of $210, which increased December's total salary expense to $1,610. The entry also recognized a liability of $210. The expense is reported on December's income statement. The expense account is then closed. The ledger on January 1, 2018, shows a $210 liability and a zero balance in the Salaries Expense account. At this point, the choice is made between using or not using reversing entries.

EXHIBIT 4A.1

Reversing Entries for an Accrued Expense

Accrue salaries expense on December 31, 2017

| Salaries Expense | .... | 210 | | |
| Salaries Payable | | | .... | 210 |

Salaries Expense

Date	Expl.	Debit	Credit	Balance
2017				
Dec. 12	(7)	700		700
26	(16)	700		1,400
31	(e)	210		1,610

Salaries Payable

Date	Expl.	Debit	Credit	Balance
2017				
Dec. 31	(e)		210	210

| **WITHOUT Reversing Entries** | — OR — | **WITH Reversing Entries** |

No reversing entry recorded on January 1, 2018

NO ENTRY

Salaries Expense

Date	Expl.	Debit	Credit	Balance
2018				

Salaries Payable

Date	Expl.	Debit	Credit	Balance
2017				
Dec. 31	(e)		210	210
2018				

Reversing entry recorded on January 1, 2018

| Salaries Payable | .... | 210 | | |
| Salaries Expense | | | .... | 210 |

Salaries Expense*

Date	Expl.	Debit	Credit	Balance
2018				
Jan. 1			210	(210)

Salaries Payable

Date	Expl.	Debit	Credit	Balance
2017				
Dec. 31	(e)		210	210
2018				
Jan. 1		210		0

Pay the accrued and current salaries on January 9, the first payday in 2018

Salaries Expense	....	490		
Salaries Payable			....	210
Cash	....			700

Salaries Expense

Date	Expl.	Debit	Credit	Balance
2018				
Jan. 9		490		490

Salaries Payable

Date	Expl.	Debit	Credit	Balance
2017				
Dec. 31	(e)		210	210
2018				
Jan. 9		210		0

| Salaries Expense | .... | 700 | | |
| Cash | .... | | | 700 |

Salaries Expense*

Date	Expl.	Debit	Credit	Balance
2018				
Jan. 1			210	(210)
Jan. 9		700		490

Salaries Payable

Date	Expl.	Debit	Credit	Balance
2017				
Dec. 31	(e)		210	210
2018				
Jan. 1		210		0

Under both approaches, the expense and liability accounts have identical balances after the cash payment on January 9.

| Salaries Expense | .... | $490 |
| Salaries Payable | .... | $ 0 |

*Circled numbers in the *Balance* column indicate abnormal balances.

Accounting *without* Reversing Entries The path down the left side of Exhibit 4A.1 is described in the chapter. To summarize here, when the next payday occurs on January 9, we record payment with a compound entry that debits both the expense and liability accounts and credits Cash. Posting that entry creates a $490 balance in the expense account and reduces the liability account balance to zero because the debt has been settled. The disadvantage of this approach is the slightly more complex entry required on January 9. Paying the accrued liability means that this entry differs from the routine entries made on all other paydays. To construct the proper entry on January 9, we must recall the effect of the December 31 adjusting entry. Reversing entries overcome this disadvantage.

Point: Firms that use reversing entries hope that this simplification will reduce errors.

Accounting *with* Reversing Entries The right side of Exhibit 4A.1 shows how a reversing entry on January 1 overcomes the disadvantage of the January 9 entry when not using reversing entries. A reversing entry is the exact opposite of an adjusting entry. For FastForward, the Salaries Payable liability account is debited for $210, meaning that this account now has a zero balance after the entry is posted. The Salaries Payable account temporarily understates the liability, but this is not a problem since financial statements are not prepared before the liability is settled on January 9. The credit to the Salaries Expense account is unusual because it gives the account an *abnormal credit balance*. We highlight an abnormal balance by circling it. Because of the reversing entry, the January 9 entry to record payment is straightforward. This entry debits the Salaries Expense account and credits Cash for the full $700 paid. It is the same as all other entries made to record 10 days' salary for the employee. Notice that after the payment entry is posted, the Salaries Expense account has a $490 balance that reflects seven days' salary of $70 per day (see the lower right side of Exhibit 4A.1). The zero balance in the Salaries Payable account is now correct. The lower section of Exhibit 4A.1 shows that the expense and liability accounts have exactly the same balances whether reversing entries are used or not. This means that both approaches yield identical results.

Point: As a general rule, adjusting entries that create new asset or liability accounts are likely candidates for reversing.

Summary

C1 Explain why temporary accounts are closed each period. Temporary accounts are closed at the end of each accounting period for two main reasons. First, the closing process updates the capital account to include the effects of all transactions and events recorded for the period. Second, it prepares revenue, expense, and withdrawals accounts for the next reporting period by giving them zero balances.

C2 Identify steps in the accounting cycle. The accounting cycle consists of 10 steps: (1) analyze transactions, (2) journalize, (3) post, (4) prepare an unadjusted trial balance, (5) adjust accounts, (6) prepare an adjusted trial balance, (7) prepare statements, (8) close, (9) prepare a post-closing trial balance, and (10) prepare (optional) reversing entries.

C3 Explain and prepare a classified balance sheet. Classified balance sheets report assets and liabilities in two categories: current and noncurrent. Noncurrent assets often include long-term investments, plant assets, and intangible assets. Owner's equity for proprietorships (and partnerships) reports the capital account balance. A corporation separates equity into common stock and retained earnings.

A1 Compute the current ratio and describe what it reveals about a company's financial condition. A company's current ratio is defined as current assets divided by current liabilities. We use it to evaluate a company's ability to pay its current liabilities out of current assets.

P1 Prepare a work sheet and explain its usefulness. A work sheet can be a useful tool in preparing and analyzing financial statements. It is helpful at the end of a period in preparing adjusting entries, an adjusted trial balance, and financial statements. A work sheet usually contains five pairs of columns: Unadjusted Trial Balance, Adjustments, Adjusted Trial Balance, Income Statement, and Balance Sheet & Statement of Owner's Equity.

P2 Describe and prepare closing entries. Closing entries involve four steps: (1) close credit balances in revenue (and gain) accounts to Income Summary, (2) close debit balances in expense (and loss) accounts to Income Summary, (3) close Income Summary to the capital account, and (4) close withdrawals account to owner's capital.

P3 Explain and prepare a post-closing trial balance. A post-closing trial balance is a list of permanent accounts and their balances after all closing entries have been journalized and posted. Its purpose is to verify that (1) total debits equal total credits for permanent accounts and (2) all temporary accounts have zero balances.

P4A Prepare reversing entries and explain their purpose. Reversing entries are an optional step. They are applied to accrued expenses and revenues. The purpose of reversing entries is to simplify subsequent journal entries. Financial statements are unaffected by the choice to use or not use reversing entries.

Key Terms

Accounting cycle
Classified balance sheet
Closing entries
Closing process
Current assets
Current liabilities
Current ratio

Income Summary
Intangible assets
Long-term investments
Long-term liabilities
Operating cycle
Permanent accounts
Post-closing trial balance

Pro forma financial statements
Reversing entries
Temporary accounts
Unclassified balance sheet
Work sheet

Multiple Choice Quiz

1. G. Venda, owner of Venda Services, withdrew $25,000 from the business during the current year. The entry to close the withdrawals account at the end of the year is:

a.	G. Venda, Withdrawals...............	25,000	
	G. Venda, Capital................		25,000
b.	Income Summary	25,000	
	G. Venda, Capital................		25,000
c.	G. Venda, Withdrawals...............	25,000	
	Cash.........................		25,000
d.	G. Venda, Capital	25,000	
	Salary Expense		25,000
e.	G. Venda, Capital	25,000	
	G. Venda, Withdrawals		25,000

2. The following information is available for the R. Kandamil Company before closing the accounts. After all of the closing entries are made, what will be the balance in the R. Kandamil, Capital account?

Total revenues..................................	$300,000
Total expenses.................................	195,000
R. Kandamil, Capital	100,000
R. Kandamil, Withdrawals.........................	45,000

    a. $360,000   **d.** $150,000
    b. $250,000   **e.** $60,000
    c. $160,000

3. Which of the following errors would cause the Balance Sheet and Statement of Owner's Equity columns of a work sheet to be out of balance?

   a. Entering a revenue amount in the Balance Sheet and Statement of Owner's Equity Debit column.

   b. Entering a liability amount in the Balance Sheet and Statement of Owner's Equity Credit column.

   c. Entering an expense amount in the Balance Sheet and Statement of Owner's Equity Debit column.

   d. Entering an asset amount in the Income Statement Debit column.

   e. Entering a liability amount in the Income Statement Credit column.

4. The temporary account used only in the closing process to hold the amounts of revenues and expenses before the net difference is added or subtracted from the owner's capital account is called the

   a. Closing account.   **d.** Balance Column account.

   b. Nominal account.   **e.** Contra account.

   c. Income Summary account.

5. Based on the following information from Repicor Company's balance sheet, what is Repicor Company's current ratio?

Current assets	$ 75,000
Investments..................	30,000
Plant assets	300,000
Current liabilities	50,000
Long-term liabilities............	60,000
D. Repicor, Capital.............	295,000

   a. 2.10   **d.** 0.95

   b. 1.50   **e.** 0.67

   c. 1.00

ANSWERS TO MULTIPLE CHOICE QUIZ

  1. e   **4.** c

  2. c   **5.** b

  3. a

[A]   *Superscript letter A denotes assignments based on Appendix 4A.*

🔲 Icon denotes assignments that involve decision making.

Discussion Questions

1. What are the steps in recording closing entries?
2. What accounts are affected by closing entries? What accounts are not affected?
3. 🔲 What two purposes are accomplished by recording closing entries?
4. What is the purpose of the Income Summary account?
5. 🔲 Explain whether an error has occurred if a post-closing trial balance includes a Depreciation Expense account.
6. What tasks are aided by a work sheet?
7. Why are the debit and credit entries in the Adjustments columns of the work sheet identified with letters?
8. What is a company's operating cycle?
9. What classes of assets and liabilities are shown on a typical classified balance sheet?
10. How is unearned revenue classified on the balance sheet?
11. What are the characteristics of plant assets?
12.[A] How do reversing entries simplify recordkeeping?
13.[A] If a company recorded accrued salaries expense of $500 at the end of its fiscal year, what reversing entry could be made? When would it be made?

14. ![] Refer to the most recent balance sheet for Apple in Appendix A. What five main non-current asset categories are used on its classified balance sheet? **APPLE**

15. Refer to Samsung's most recent balance sheet in Appendix A. Identify and list its ten current assets. **Samsung**

16. ![] Refer to Google's most recent balance sheet in Appendix A. Identify the eight accounts listed as current liabilities. **GOOGLE**

17. ![] Refer to Samsung's financial statements in Appendix A. What journal entry was likely recorded as of December 31, 2015, to close its Income Summary account? **Samsung**

---

connect

List the following steps in preparing a work sheet in their proper order by writing a number from 1 through 5 in the blank space provided.

_____ **a.** Total the statement columns, compute net income (loss), and complete the work sheet.

_____ **b.** Extend adjusted balances to appropriate financial statement columns.

_____ **c.** Prepare an unadjusted trial balance on the work sheet.

_____ **d.** Prepare an adjusted trial balance on the work sheet.

_____ **e.** Enter adjustments data on the work sheet.

QUICK STUDY

QS 4-1
Ordering work sheet steps
P1

In preparing a work sheet, indicate the financial statement Debit column to which a normal balance in the following accounts should be extended. Use IS for the Income Statement Debit column and BS for the Balance Sheet and Statement of Owner's Equity Debit column.

_____ **a.** Equipment

_____ **b.** Owner, Withdrawals

_____ **c.** Prepaid Rent

_____ **d.** Depreciation Expense—Equipment

_____ **e.** Accounts Receivable

_____ **f.** Insurance Expense

QS 4-2
Applying a work sheet
P1

The following selected information is taken from the work sheet for Warton Company at its December 31 year-end. Using this information, determine the amount for B. Warton, Capital, that should be reported on its December 31 year-end balance sheet.

QS 4-3
Interpreting a work sheet

P1 ![]

	Income Statement		Balance Sheet and Statement of Owner's Equity	
	Dr.	Cr.	Dr.	Cr.
B. Warton, Capital.................				72,000
B. Warton, Withdrawals			39,000	
Totals........................	122,000	181,000		

The ledger of Claudell Company includes the following unadjusted normal balances: Prepaid Rent $1,000, Services Revenue $55,600, and Wages Expense $5,000. Adjusting entries are required for **(a)** prepaid rent expired $200; **(b)** accrued services revenue $900; and **(c)** accrued wages expense $700. Enter these unadjusted balances and the necessary adjustments on a work sheet and complete the work sheet for these accounts. *Note:* Also include the following accounts: Accounts Receivable, Wages Payable, and Rent Expense.

QS 4-4
Preparing a partial work sheet

P1 ![]

Choose from the following list of terms/phrases to best complete the statements below.

a. Temporary   **c.** One or more   **e.** Zero balances
b. Permanent   **d.** One   **f.** Income Summary

1. _____ accounts generally consist of all balance sheet accounts, and these accounts are not closed.

2. Permanent accounts report on activities related to _____ future accounting periods, and they carry their ending balances into the next period.

3. Temporary accounts accumulate data related to _____ accounting period.

4. _____ accounts include all income statement accounts, the withdrawals account, and the Income Summary account.

QS 4-5
Explaining temporary and permanent accounts

C1

QS 4-6
Preparing closing entries
from the ledger   **P2**

The ledger of Mai Company includes the following accounts with normal balances: D. Mai, Capital $9,000; D. Mai, Withdrawals $800; Services Revenue $13,000; Wages Expense $8,400; and Rent Expense $1,600. Prepare the necessary closing entries from the available information at December 31.

QS 4-7
Identifying post-closing
accounts   **P3**

Identify which of the following accounts would be included in a post-closing trial balance.

  _____ **a.** Accounts Receivable   _____ **c.** Goodwill   _____ **e.** Income Tax Expense

  _____ **b.** Salaries Expense   _____ **d.** Land   _____ **f.** Salaries Payable

---

QS 4-8
Identifying the
accounting cycle

C2

List the following steps of the accounting cycle in their proper order.

  _____ **a.** Posting the journal entries.   _____ **f.** Preparing the financial statements.

  _____ **b.** Journalizing and posting adjusting entries.   _____ **g.** Preparing the unadjusted trial balance.

  _____ **c.** Preparing the adjusted trial balance.   _____ **h.** Journalizing transactions and events.

  _____ **d.** Journalizing and posting closing entries.   _____ **i.** Preparing the post-closing trial balance.

  _____ **e.** Analyzing transactions and events.

QS 4-9
Classifying balance
sheet items

C3

The following are common categories on a classified balance sheet.

A. Current assets   **D.** Intangible assets

B. Long-term investments   **E.** Current liabilities

C. Plant assets   **F.** Long-term liabilities

For each of the following items, select the letter that identifies the balance sheet category where the item typically would appear.

  _____ **1.** Land not currently used in operations   _____ **5.** Accounts payable

  _____ **2.** Notes payable (due in five years)   _____ **6.** Store equipment

  _____ **3.** Accounts receivable   _____ **7.** Wages payable

  _____ **4.** Trademarks   _____ **8.** Cash

QS 4-10
International accounting
standards   **P2**

Answer each of the following questions related to international accounting standards.

a. Explain how the closing process is different between accounting under IFRS versus U.S. GAAP.

b. What basic principle do U.S. GAAP and IFRS rely upon in recording the initial acquisition value for nearly all assets?

QS 4-11
Identifying current
accounts and computing
the current ratio

A1

Compute Chavez Company's current ratio using the following information.

Accounts receivable.............	$18,000	Long-term notes payable..............	$21,000
Accounts payable...............	11,000	Office supplies	2,800
Buildings......................	45,000	Prepaid insurance....................	3,560
Cash	7,000	Unearned services revenue............	3,000

QS 4-12ᴬ
Reversing entries

P4

On December 31, 2016, Yates Co. prepared an adjusting entry for $12,000 of earned but unrecorded consulting fees. On January 16, 2017, Yates received $26,700 cash in consulting fees, which included the accrued fees earned in 2016. (Assume the company uses reversing entries.)

a. Prepare the December 31, 2016, adjusting entry.

b. Prepare the January 1, 2017, reversing entry.

c. Prepare the January 16, 2017, cash receipt entry.

---

connect

EXERCISES

Exercise 4-1
Extending adjusted
account balances on a
work sheet   **P1**

These 16 accounts are from the Adjusted Trial Balance columns of a company's 10-column work sheet. In the blank space beside each account, write the letter of the appropriate financial statement column (A, B, C, or D) to which a normal account balance is extended.

A. Debit column for the Income Statement columns.

B. Credit column for the Income Statement columns.

C. Debit column for the Balance Sheet and Statement of Owner's Equity columns.

D. Credit column for the Balance Sheet and Statement of Owner's Equity columns.

_____ **1.** Interest Revenue	_____ **9.** Accounts Receivable
_____ **2.** Machinery	_____ **10.** Accumulated Depreciation
_____ **3.** Owner, Withdrawals	_____ **11.** Office Supplies
_____ **4.** Depreciation Expense	_____ **12.** Insurance Expense
_____ **5.** Accounts Payable	_____ **13.** Interest Receivable
_____ **6.** Service Fees Revenue	_____ **14.** Cash
_____ **7.** Owner, Capital	_____ **15.** Rent Expense
_____ **8.** Interest Expense	_____ **16.** Wages Payable

The Adjusted Trial Balance columns of a 10-column work sheet for Planta Company follow. Complete the work sheet by extending the account balances into the appropriate financial statement columns and by entering the amount of net income for the reporting period.

Exercise 4-2
Extending accounts in a work sheet   P1

	A	B	C	D	E	F	G	H	I	J	K	L
1											Balance Sheet and	
2			Unadjusted				Adjusted		Income		Statement of	
3			Trial Balance		Adjustments		Trial Balance		Statement		Owner's Equity	
4	No.	Account Title	Dr.	Cr.	Dr.	Cr.	Dr.	Cr.	Dr.	Cr.	Dr.	Cr.
5	101	Cash					$ 7,000					
6	106	Accounts receivable					27,200					
7	153	Trucks					42,000					
8	154	Accumulated depreciation—Trucks						$ 17,500				
9	183	Land					32,000					
10	201	Accounts payable						15,000				
11	209	Salaries payable						4,200				
12	233	Unearned fees						3,600				
13	301	F. Planta, Capital						65,500				
14	302	F. Planta, Withdrawals					15,400					
15	401	Plumbing fees earned						84,000				
16	611	Depreciation expense—Trucks					6,500					
17	622	Salaries expense					38,000					
18	640	Rent expense					13,000					
19	677	Miscellaneous expenses					8,700					
20		Totals					$189,800	$189,800				

Check   Net income, $17,800

Use the following information from the Adjustments columns of a 10-column work sheet to prepare the necessary adjusting journal entries (*a*) through (*e*).

Exercise 4-3
Preparing adjusting entries from a work sheet   P1

	A	B	C	D	E	F	G	H	I	J	K	L
1											Balance Sheet	
2			Unadjusted				Adjusted		Income		and Statement of	
3			Trial Balance		Adjustments		Trial Balance		Statement		Owner's Equity	
4	No.	Account Title	Dr.	Cr.	Dr.	Cr.	Dr.	Cr.	Dr.	Cr.	Dr.	Cr.
5	109	Interest receivable			(*d*) $ 880							
6	124	Office supplies				(*b*) $1,750						
7	128	Prepaid insurance				(*a*) 900						
8	164	Accumulated depreciation—Office equipment				(*c*) 2,200						
9	209	Salaries payable				(*e*) 560						
10	409	Interest revenue				(*d*) 880						
11	612	Depreciation expense—Office equipment			(*c*) 2,200							
12	620	Office salaries expense			(*e*) 560							
13	636	Insurance expense—Office equipment			(*a*) 332							
14	637	Insurance expense—Store equipment			(*a*) 568							
15	650	Office supplies expense			(*b*) 1,750							
16		Totals			$6,290	$6,290						

Exercise 4-4
Completing a work sheet
P1

The following data are taken from the unadjusted trial balance of the Westcott Company at December 31, 2017. Each account carries a normal balance.

Accounts Payable.	$ 6	Prepaid Insurance.	$18	W. Westcott, Withdrawals.	$ 6
Accounts Receivable	12	Revenue.	75	Unearned Revenue.	12
Accumulated Depreciation—Equip.	15	Salaries Expense.	18	Utilities Expense	12
Cash.	21	Supplies.	24		
Equipment	39	W. Westcott, Capital	42		

1. Use the data above to prepare a work sheet. Enter the accounts in proper order and enter their balances in the correct Debit or Credit column.
2. Use the following adjustment information to complete the work sheet.
   a. Depreciation on equipment, $3
   b. Accrued salaries, $6
   c. The $12 of unearned revenue has been earned
   d. Supplies available at December 31, 2017, $15
   e. Expired insurance, $15

Exercise 4-5
Determining effects of closing entries

C1

Capri Company began the current period with a $20,000 credit balance in the K. Capri, Capital account. At the end of the period, the company's adjusted account balances include the following temporary accounts with normal balances.

Service fees earned	$70,000	Interest revenue	$ 7,000
Salaries expense	38,000	K. Capri, Withdrawals	12,000
Depreciation expense	8,000	Utilities expense	4,600

1. After closing the revenue and expense accounts, what is the balance of the Income Summary account?
2. After all closing entries are journalized and posted, what is the balance of the K. Capri, Capital account?

Exercise 4-6
Completing the income statement columns and preparing closing entries
P1   P2

These partially completed Income Statement columns from a 10-column work sheet are for Brown's Bike Rental Company. (1) Use the information to determine the amount that should be entered on the net income line of the work sheet. (2) Prepare the company's closing entries. The owner, H. Brown, did not make any withdrawals this period.

Account Title	Debit	Credit
Rent earned		120,000
Salaries expense	46,300	
Insurance expense	7,400	
Office supplies expense	16,000	
Bike repair expense	4,200	
Depreciation expense—Bikes	20,500	
Totals		
Net income		
Totals		

Check   Net income, $25,600

The following unadjusted trial balance contains the accounts and balances of Dylan Delivery Company as of December 31, 2017.

Exercise 4-7
Preparing a work sheet and recording closing entries
P1   P2

1. Use the following information about the company's adjustments to complete a 10-column work sheet.

   a. Unrecorded depreciation on the trucks at the end of the year is $40,000.

   b. The total amount of accrued interest expense at year-end is $6,000.

   c. The cost of unused office supplies still available at year-end is $2,000.

2. Prepare the year-end closing entries for this company, and determine the capital amount to be reported on its year-end balance sheet.

A	B	C
	Unadjusted Trial Balance	
Account Title	**Debit**	**Credit**
Cash	$ 16,000	
Accounts receivable	34,000	
Office supplies	5,000	
Trucks	350,000	
Accumulated depreciation—Trucks		$ 80,000
Land	160,000	
Accounts payable		24,000
Interest payable		5,000
Long-term notes payable		100,000
S. Dylan, Capital		307,000
S. Dylan, Withdrawals	34,000	
Delivery fees earned		263,000
Depreciation expense—Truck	40,000	
Salaries expense	110,000	
Office supplies expense	15,000	
Interest expense	5,000	
Repairs expense—Trucks	10,000	
Totals	$779,000	$779,000

Check Adj. trial balance totals, $820,000; Net income, $39,000

Use the May 31 fiscal year-end information from the following ledger accounts (assume that all accounts have normal balances) to prepare closing journal entries and then post those entries to the appropriate ledger accounts.

Exercise 4-8
Preparing and posting closing entries
P2

General Ledger

M. Muncel, Capital — Acct. No. 301

Date	PR	Debit	Credit	Balance
May 31	G2			40,000

M. Muncel, Withdrawals — Acct. No. 302

Date	PR	Debit	Credit	Balance
May 31	G2			22,000

Services Revenue — Acct. No. 401

Date	PR	Debit	Credit	Balance
May 31	G2			76,000

Depreciation Expense — Acct. No. 603

Date	PR	Debit	Credit	Balance
May 31	G2			15,000

Salaries Expense — Acct. No. 622

Date	PR	Debit	Credit	Balance
May 31	G2			20,000

Insurance Expense — Acct. No. 637

Date	PR	Debit	Credit	Balance
May 31	G2			4,400

Rent Expense — Acct. No. 640

Date	PR	Debit	Credit	Balance
May 31	G2			8,400

Income Summary — Acct. No. 901

Date	PR	Debit	Credit	Balance

Check M. Muncel, Capital (ending balance), $46,200

Exercise 4-9

Preparing closing entries and a post-closing trial balance

P2   P3

The following adjusted trial balance contains the accounts and balances of Cruz Company as of December 31, 2017, the end of its fiscal year. (1) Prepare the December 31, 2017, closing entries for Cruz Company. Assume the account number for Income Summary is 901. (2) Prepare the December 31, 2017, post-closing trial balance for Cruz Company.

No.	Account Title	Debit	Credit
101	Cash...	$19,000	
126	Supplies..	13,000	
128	Prepaid insurance...............................	3,000	
167	Equipment......................................	24,000	
168	Accumulated depreciation—Equipment..............		$ 7,500
301	T. Cruz, Capital...............................		47,600
302	T. Cruz, Withdrawals...........................	7,000	
404	Services revenue...............................		44,000
612	Depreciation expense—Equipment.................	3,000	
622	Salaries expense...............................	22,000	
637	Insurance expense..............................	2,500	
640	Rent expense...................................	3,400	
652	Supplies expense...............................	2,200	
	Totals...	$99,100	$99,100

Check (2) T. Cruz, Capital (ending), $51,500; Total debits, $59,000

Exercise 4-10

Preparing closing entries and a post-closing trial balance P2   P3

The adjusted trial balance for Salon Marketing Co. follows. Complete the four right-most columns of the table by first entering information for the four closing entries (keyed *1* through *4*) and second by completing the post-closing trial balance.

No.	Account Title	Adjusted Trial Balance		Closing Entry Information		Post-Closing Trial Balance	
		Dr.	Cr.	Dr.	Cr.	Dr.	Cr.
101	Cash	$ 9,200					
106	Accounts receivable.............................	25,000					
153	Equipment.......................................	42,000					
154	Accumulated depreciation—Equipment..............		$ 17,500				
183	Land	31,000					
201	Accounts payable................................		15,000				
209	Salaries payable................................		4,200				
233	Unearned fees		3,600				
301	E. Salon, Capital...............................		68,500				
302	E. Salon, Withdrawals...........................	15,400					
401	Marketing fees earned...........................		80,000				
611	Depreciation expense—Equipment.................	12,000					
622	Salaries expense	32,500					
640	Rent expense	13,000					
677	Miscellaneous expenses	8,700					
901	Income summary						
	Totals..	$188,800	$188,800				

Exercise 4-11

Preparing the financial statements

C2

Use the following adjusted trial balance of Wilson Trucking Company to prepare the (1) income statement and (2) statement of owner's equity for the year ended December 31, 2017. The K. Wilson, Capital account balance is $175,000 at December 31, 2016.

Account Title	Debit	Credit
Cash	$ 8,000	
Accounts receivable	17,500	
Office supplies	3,000	
Trucks	172,000	
Accumulated depreciation—Trucks		$ 36,000
Land	85,000	
Accounts payable		12,000
Interest payable		4,000
Long-term notes payable		53,000
K. Wilson, Capital		175,000
K. Wilson, Withdrawals	20,000	
Trucking fees earned		130,000
Depreciation expense—Trucks	23,500	
Salaries expense	61,000	
Office supplies expense	8,000	
Repairs expense—Trucks	12,000	
Totals	$410,000	$410,000

Use the information in the adjusted trial balance reported in Exercise 4-11 to prepare Wilson Trucking Company's classified balance sheet as of December 31, 2017.

Exercise 4-12
Preparing a classified balance sheet   C3

Check   Total assets, $249,500; K. Wilson, Capital, $180,500 (ending)

Use the information in the adjusted trial balance reported in Exercise 4-11 to compute the current ratio as of the balance sheet date (round the ratio to two decimals). Interpret the current ratio for the Wilson Trucking Company. (Assume that the industry average for the current ratio is 1.5.)

Exercise 4-13
Computing the current ratio

A1

Following are **Nintendo**'s revenue and expense accounts for a recent March 31 fiscal year-end (yen in millions). Prepare the company's closing entries for its revenues and its expenses.

Net sales	¥549,780
Cost of sales	335,196
Advertising expense	54,834
Other expense, net	117,907

Exercise 4-14
Preparing closing entries

P2

Calculate the current ratio for each of the following companies (round the ratio to two decimals). Identify the company with the strongest liquidity position. (These companies represent competitors in the same industry.)

	Current Assets	Current Liabilities
Edison	$ 79,040	$ 32,000
MAXT	104,880	76,000
Chatter	45,080	49,000
TRU	85,680	81,600
Gleeson	61,000	100,000

Exercise 4-15
Computing and analyzing the current ratio

A1

Hawk Company records prepaid assets and unearned revenues in balance sheet accounts. The following information was used to prepare adjusting entries for the company as of August 31, the end of the company's fiscal year.

a. The company has earned $6,000 in service fees that were not yet recorded at period-end.
b. The expired portion of prepaid insurance is $3,700.
c. The company has earned $2,900 of its Unearned Service Fees account balance.
d. Depreciation expense for office equipment is $3,300.
e. Employees have earned but have not been paid salaries of $3,400.

Prepare any necessary reversing entries for the accounting adjustments *a* through *e* assuming that the company uses reversing entries in its accounting system.

Exercise 4-16[A]
Preparing reversing entries

P4

Exercise 4-17^A

Preparing reversing entries

P4

The following two events occurred for Trey Co. on October 31, 2017, the end of its fiscal year.

a. Trey rents a building from its owner for $2,800 per month. By a prearrangement, the company delayed paying October's rent until November 5. On this date, the company paid the rent for both October and November.

b. Trey rents space in a building it owns to a tenant for $850 per month. By prearrangement, the tenant delayed paying the October rent until November 8. On this date, the tenant paid the rent for both October and November.

Required

1. Prepare adjusting entries that the company must record for these events as of October 31.

2. Assuming Trey does *not* use reversing entries, prepare journal entries to record Trey's payment of rent on November 5 and the collection of the tenant's rent on November 8.

3. Assuming that the company uses reversing entries, prepare reversing entries on November 1 and the journal entries to record Trey's payment of rent on November 5 and the collection of the tenant's rent on November 8.

PROBLEM SET A

Problem 4-1A

Applying the accounting cycle

C1   C2   P2   P3

On April 1, 2017, Jiro Nozomi created a new travel agency, Adventure Travel. The following transactions occurred during the company's first month.

April 1   Nozomi invested $30,000 cash and computer equipment worth $20,000 in the company.
     2   The company rented furnished office space by paying $1,800 cash for the first month's (April) rent.
     3   The company purchased $1,000 of office supplies for cash.
    10   The company paid $2,400 cash for the premium on a 12-month insurance policy. Coverage begins on April 11.
    14   The company paid $1,600 cash for two weeks' salaries earned by employees.
    24   The company collected $8,000 cash on commissions from airlines on tickets obtained for customers.
    28   The company paid $1,600 cash for two weeks' salaries earned by employees.
    29   The company paid $350 cash for minor repairs to the company's computer.
    30   The company paid $750 cash for this month's telephone bill.
    30   Nozomi withdrew $1,500 cash from the company for personal use.

The company's chart of accounts follows:

101	Cash	405	Commissions Earned
106	Accounts Receivable	612	Depreciation Expense—Computer Equip.
124	Office Supplies	622	Salaries Expense
128	Prepaid Insurance	637	Insurance Expense
167	Computer Equipment	640	Rent Expense
168	Accumulated Depreciation—Computer Equip.	650	Office Supplies Expense
209	Salaries Payable	684	Repairs Expense
301	J. Nozomi, Capital	688	Telephone Expense
302	J. Nozomi, Withdrawals	901	Income Summary

Required

1. Use the balance column format to set up each ledger account listed in its chart of accounts.

2. Prepare journal entries to record the transactions for April and post them to the ledger accounts. The company records prepaid and unearned items in balance sheet accounts.

Check (3) Unadj. trial balance totals, $58,000

(4a) Dr. Insurance Expense, $133

3. Prepare an unadjusted trial balance as of April 30.

4. Use the following information to journalize and post adjusting entries for the month:

a. Two-thirds (or $133) of one month's insurance coverage has expired.

b. At the end of the month, $600 of office supplies are still available.

c. This month's depreciation on the computer equipment is $500.

d. Employees earned $420 of unpaid and unrecorded salaries as of month-end.

e. The company earned $1,750 of commissions that are not yet billed at month-end.

(5) Net income, $2,197; J. Nozomi, Capital (4/30/2017), $50,697; Total assets, $51,117

5. Prepare the adjusted trial balance as of April 30. Prepare the income statement and the statement of owner's equity for the month of April and the balance sheet at April 30, 2017.

6. Prepare journal entries to close the temporary accounts and post these entries to the ledger.

(7) P-C trial balance totals, $51,617

7. Prepare a post-closing trial balance.

The following unadjusted trial balance is for Ace Construction Co. as of the end of its 2017 fiscal year. The June 30, 2016, credit balance of the owner's capital account was $53,660, and the owner invested $35,000 cash in the company during the 2017 fiscal year.

Problem 4-2A

Preparing a work sheet, adjusting and closing entries, and financial statements

C3   P1   P2

	A	B	C	D
1		ACE CONSTRUCTION CO.		
2		Unadjusted Trial Balance		
3		June 30, 2017		
4	No.	Account Title	Debit	Credit
5	101	Cash	$ 18,500	
6	126	Supplies	9,900	
7	128	Prepaid insurance	7,200	
8	167	Equipment	132,000	
9	168	Accumulated depreciation—Equipment		$ 26,250
10	201	Accounts payable		6,800
11	203	Interest payable		0
12	208	Rent payable		0
13	210	Wages payable		0
14	213	Property taxes payable		0
15	251	Long-term notes payable		25,000
16	301	V. Ace, Capital		88,660
17	302	V. Ace, Withdrawals	33,000	
18	401	Construction fees earned		132,100
19	612	Depreciation expense—Equipment	0	
20	623	Wages expense	46,860	
21	633	Interest expense	2,750	
22	637	Insurance expense	0	
23	640	Rent expense	12,000	
24	652	Supplies expense	0	
25	683	Property taxes expense	7,800	
26	684	Repairs expense	2,910	
27	690	Utilities expense	5,890	
28		Totals	$278,810	$278,810

Required

1. Prepare and complete a 10-column work sheet for fiscal year 2017, starting with the unadjusted trial balance and including adjustments based on these additional facts.

   a. The supplies available at the end of fiscal year 2017 had a cost of $3,300.

   b. The cost of expired insurance for the fiscal year is $3,800.

   c. Annual depreciation on equipment is $8,400.

   d. The June utilities expense of $650 is not included in the unadjusted trial balance because the bill arrived after the trial balance was prepared. The $650 amount owed needs to be recorded.

   e. The company's employees have earned $1,800 of accrued wages at fiscal year-end.

   f. The rent expense incurred and not yet paid or recorded at fiscal year-end is $500.

   g. Additional property taxes of $1,000 have been assessed for this fiscal year but have not been paid or recorded in the accounts.

   h. The long-term note payable bears interest at 12% per year. The unadjusted Interest Expense account equals the amount paid for the first 11 months of the 2017 fiscal year. The $250 accrued interest for June has not yet been paid or recorded. (The company is required to make a $5,000 payment toward the note payable during the 2018 fiscal year.)

2. Using information from the completed 10-column work sheet in part 1, journalize the adjusting entries and the closing entries.

3. Prepare the income statement and the statement of owner's equity for the year ended June 30 and the classified balance sheet at June 30, 2017.

Check   (3) Total assets, $122,550; Current liabilities, $16,000; Net income, $30,890

Analysis Component

4. Analyze the following separate errors and describe how each would affect the 10-column work sheet. Explain whether the error is likely to be discovered in completing the work sheet and, if not, the effect of the error on the financial statements.

   a. Assume that the adjustment for supplies used consisted of a credit to Supplies and a debit to Supplies Expense for $3,300, when the correct amount was $6,600.

   b. When the adjusted trial balance in the work sheet is completed, assume that the $18,500 Cash balance is incorrectly entered in the Credit column.

Problem 4-3A

Determining balance sheet classifications

C3

In the blank space beside each numbered balance sheet item, enter the letter of its balance sheet classification. If the item should not appear on the balance sheet, enter a *Z* in the blank.

A. Current assets   **D.** Intangible assets   **F.** Long-term liabilities

B. Long-term investments   **E.** Current liabilities   **G.** Equity

C. Plant assets

_____ **1.** Long-term investment in stock

_____ **2.** Depreciation expense—Building

_____ **3.** Prepaid rent

_____ **4.** Interest receivable

_____ **5.** Taxes payable

_____ **6.** Automobiles

_____ **7.** Notes payable (due in 3 years)

_____ **8.** Accounts payable

_____ **9.** Prepaid insurance

_____ **10.** Owner, Capital

_____ **11.** Unearned services revenue

_____ **12.** Accumulated depreciation—Trucks

_____ **13.** Cash

_____ **14.** Buildings

_____ **15.** Store supplies

_____ **16.** Office equipment

_____ **17.** Land (used in operations)

_____ **18.** Repairs expense

_____ **19.** Office supplies

_____ **20.** Current portion of long-term note payable

Problem 4-4A

Preparing closing entries, financial statements, and ratios

C3   A1   P2

The adjusted trial balance for Tybalt Construction as of December 31, 2017, follows.

TYBALT CONSTRUCTION
Adjusted Trial Balance
December 31, 2017

No.	Account Title	Debit	Credit
101	Cash	$ 5,000	
104	Short-term investments	23,000	
126	Supplies	8,100	
128	Prepaid insurance	7,000	
167	Equipment	40,000	
168	Accumulated depreciation—Equipment		$ 20,000
173	Building	150,000	
174	Accumulated depreciation—Building		50,000
183	Land	55,000	
201	Accounts payable		16,500
203	Interest payable		2,500
208	Rent payable		3,500
210	Wages payable		2,500
213	Property taxes payable		900
233	Unearned professional fees		7,500
251	Long-term notes payable		67,000
301	O. Tybalt, Capital		126,400
302	O. Tybalt, Withdrawals	13,000	
401	Professional fees earned		97,000
406	Rent earned		14,000
407	Dividends earned		2,000
409	Interest earned		2,100
606	Depreciation expense—Building	11,000	
612	Depreciation expense—Equipment	6,000	
623	Wages expense	32,000	
633	Interest expense	5,100	
637	Insurance expense	10,000	
640	Rent expense	13,400	
652	Supplies expense	7,400	
682	Postage expense	4,200	
683	Property taxes expense	5,000	
684	Repairs expense	8,900	
688	Telephone expense	3,200	
690	Utilities expense	4,600	
	Totals	$411,900	$411,900

O. Tybalt invested $5,000 cash in the business during year 2017 (the December 31, 2016, credit balance of the O. Tybalt, Capital account was $121,400). Tybalt Construction is required to make a $7,000 payment on its long-term notes payable during 2018.

Required

1. Prepare the income statement and the statement of owner's equity for the calendar year 2017 and the classified balance sheet at December 31, 2017.

2. Prepare the necessary closing entries at December 31, 2017.

3. Use the information in the financial statements to compute these ratios: (*a*) return on assets (total assets at December 31, 2016, was $200,000), (*b*) debt ratio, (*c*) profit margin ratio (use total revenues as the denominator), and (*d*) current ratio. Round ratios to three decimals for parts *a* and *c,* and to two decimals for parts *b* and *d.*

Check   (1) Total assets (12/31/2017), $218,100; Net income, $4,300

The adjusted trial balance of Karise Repairs on December 31, 2017, follows.

Problem 4-5A
Preparing trial balances, closing entries, and financial statements

C3   P2   P3

No.	Account Title	Debit	Credit
	KARISE REPAIRS		
	Adjusted Trial Balance		
	December 31, 2017		
101	Cash	$ 14,000	
124	Office supplies	1,300	
128	Prepaid insurance	2,050	
167	Equipment	50,000	
168	Accumulated depreciation—Equipment		$ 5,000
201	Accounts payable.................................		14,000
210	Wages payable....................................		600
301	C. Karise, Capital		33,000
302	C. Karise, Withdrawals...........................	16,000	
401	Repair fees earned...............................		90,950
612	Depreciation expense—Equipment..................	5,000	
623	Wages expense	37,500	
637	Insurance expense................................	800	
640	Rent expense	10,600	
650	Office supplies expense..........................	3,600	
690	Utilities expense................................	2,700	
	Totals......................................	$143,550	$143,550

Required

1. Prepare an income statement and a statement of owner's equity for the year 2017, and a classified balance sheet at December 31, 2017. There are no owner investments in 2017.

2. Enter the adjusted trial balance in the first two columns of a six-column table. Use columns three and four for closing entry information and the last two columns for a post-closing trial balance. Insert an Income Summary account as the last item in the trial balance.

3. Enter closing entry information in the six-column table and prepare journal entries for it.

Check   (1) Ending capital balance, $47,750; Net income, $30,750
    (2) P-C trial balance totals, $67,350

Analysis Component

4. Assume for this part only that

   a. None of the $800 insurance expense had expired during the year. Instead, assume it is a prepayment of the next period's insurance protection.

   b. There are no earned and unpaid wages at the end of the year. (*Hint:* Reverse the $600 wages payable accrual.)

   Describe the financial statement changes that would result from these two assumptions.

Problem 4-6A^A

Preparing adjusting,
reversing, and next period
entries

P4

The following six-column table for Hawkeye Ranges includes the unadjusted trial balance as of December 31, 2017.

	A	B	C	D	E	F	G
1		HAWKEYE RANGES					
2		December 31, 2017					
3		Unadjusted				Adjusted	
4		Trial Balance		Adjustments		Trial Balance	
5	**Account Title**	Dr.	Cr.	Dr.	Cr.	Dr.	Cr.
6	Cash	$ 14,000					
7	Accounts receivable	0					
8	Supplies	6,500					
9	Equipment	135,000					
10	Accumulated depreciation—Equipment		$ 30,000				
11	Interest payable		0				
12	Salaries payable		0				
13	Unearned member fees		15,000				
14	Notes payable		75,000				
15	P. Hawkeye, Capital		50,250				
16	P. Hawkeye, Withdrawals	21,125					
17	Member fees earned		42,000				
18	Depreciation expense—Equipment	0					
19	Salaries expense	30,000					
20	Interest expense	5,625					
21	Supplies expense	0					
22	Totals	$212,250	$212,250				

Required

1. Complete the six-column table by entering adjustments that reflect the following information.

   a. As of December 31, 2017, employees had earned $1,200 of unpaid and unrecorded salaries. The next payday is January 4, at which time $1,500 of salaries will be paid.

   b. The cost of supplies still available at December 31, 2017, is $3,000.

   c. The notes payable requires an interest payment to be made every three months. The amount of unrecorded accrued interest at December 31, 2017, is $1,875. The next interest payment, at an amount of $2,250, is due on January 15, 2018.

   d. Analysis of the Unearned Member Fees account shows $5,800 remaining unearned at December 31, 2017.

   e. In addition to the member fees included in the revenue account balance, the company has earned another $9,300 in unrecorded fees that will be collected on January 31, 2018. The company is also expected to collect $10,000 on that same day for new fees earned in January 2018.

   f. Depreciation expense for the year is $15,000.

2. Prepare journal entries for the adjustments entered in the six-column table for part 1.

3. Prepare journal entries to reverse the effects of the adjusting entries that involve accruals.

4. Prepare journal entries to record the cash payments and cash collections described for January.

PROBLEM SET B

On July 1, 2017, Lula Plume created a new self-storage business, Safe Storage Co. The following transactions occurred during the company's first month.

Problem 4-1B

Applying the accounting
cycle

C1 C2 P2 P3

July	1	Plume invested $30,000 cash and buildings worth $150,000 in the company.
	2	The company rented equipment by paying $2,000 cash for the first month's (July) rent.
	5	The company purchased $2,400 of office supplies for cash.
	10	The company paid $7,200 cash for the premium on a 12-month insurance policy. Coverage begins on July 11.
	14	The company paid an employee $1,000 cash for two weeks' salary earned.
	24	The company collected $9,800 cash for storage fees from customers.
	28	The company paid $1,000 cash for two weeks' salary earned by an employee.
	29	The company paid $950 cash for minor repairs to a leaking roof.
	30	The company paid $400 cash for this month's telephone bill.
	31	Plume withdrew $2,000 cash from the company for personal use.

The company's chart of accounts follows:

101	Cash	401	Storage Fees Earned
106	Accounts Receivable	606	Depreciation Expense—Buildings
124	Office Supplies	622	Salaries Expense
128	Prepaid Insurance	637	Insurance Expense
173	Buildings	640	Rent Expense
174	Accumulated Depreciation—Buildings	650	Office Supplies Expense
209	Salaries Payable	684	Repairs Expense
301	L. Plume, Capital	688	Telephone Expense
302	L. Plume, Withdrawals	901	Income Summary

Required

1. Use the balance column format to set up each ledger account listed in its chart of accounts.
2. Prepare journal entries to record the transactions for July and post them to the ledger accounts. Record prepaid and unearned items in balance sheet accounts.
3. Prepare an unadjusted trial balance as of July 31.
4. Use the following information to journalize and post adjusting entries for the month:
   a. Two-thirds of one month's insurance coverage has expired.
   b. At the end of the month, $1,525 of office supplies are still available.
   c. This month's depreciation on the buildings is $1,500.
   d. An employee earned $100 of unpaid and unrecorded salary as of month-end.
   e. The company earned $1,150 of storage fees that are not yet billed at month-end.
5. Prepare the adjusted trial balance as of July 31. Prepare the income statement and the statement of owner's equity for the month of July and the balance sheet at July 31, 2017.
6. Prepare journal entries to close the temporary accounts and post these entries to the ledger.
7. Prepare a post-closing trial balance.

Check (3) Unadj. trial balance totals, $189,800

(4a) Dr. Insurance Expense, $400

(5) Net income, $2,725; L. Plume, Capital (7/31/2017), $180,725; Total assets, $180,825

(7) P-C trial balance totals, $182,325

The following unadjusted trial balance is for Power Demolition Company as of the end of its April 30, 2017, fiscal year. The April 30, 2016, credit balance of the owner's capital account was $46,900, and the owner invested $40,000 cash in the company during the 2017 fiscal year.

Problem 4-2B
Preparing a work sheet, adjusting and closing entries, and financial statements

C3   P1   P2

	A	B	C
1		POWER DEMOLITION COMPANY	
2		Unadjusted Trial Balance	
3		April 30, 2017	
4	No.	Account Title	Debit	Credit
5	101	Cash	$ 7,000	
6	126	Supplies	16,000	
7	128	Prepaid insurance	12,600	
8	167	Equipment	200,000	
9	168	Accumulated depreciation—Equipment		$ 14,000
10	201	Accounts payable		6,800
11	203	Interest payable		0
12	208	Rent payable		0
13	210	Wages payable		0
14	213	Property taxes payable		0
15	251	Long-term notes payable		30,000
16	301	J. Bonn, Capital		86,900
17	302	J. Bonn, Withdrawals	12,000	
18	401	Demolition fees earned		187,000
19	612	Depreciation expense—Equipment	0	
20	623	Wages expense	41,400	
21	633	Interest expense	3,300	
22	637	Insurance expense	0	
23	640	Rent expense	13,200	
24	652	Supplies expense	0	
25	683	Property taxes expense	9,700	
26	684	Repairs expense	4,700	
27	690	Utilities expense	4,800	
28		Totals	$324,700	$324,700

Required

1. Prepare and complete a 10-column work sheet for fiscal year 2017, starting with the unadjusted trial balance and including adjustments based on these additional facts.

   a. The supplies available at the end of fiscal year 2017 had a cost of $7,900.

   b. The cost of expired insurance for the fiscal year is $10,600.

   c. Annual depreciation on equipment is $7,000.

   d. The April utilities expense of $800 is not included in the unadjusted trial balance because the bill arrived after the trial balance was prepared. The $800 amount owed needs to be recorded.

   e. The company's employees have earned $2,000 of accrued wages at fiscal year-end.

   f. The rent expense incurred and not yet paid or recorded at fiscal year-end is $3,000.

   g. Additional property taxes of $550 have been assessed for this fiscal year but have not been paid or recorded in the accounts.

   h. The long-term note payable bears interest at 12% per year. The unadjusted Interest Expense account equals the amount paid for the first 11 months of the 2017 fiscal year. The $300 accrued interest for April has not yet been paid or recorded. (Note that the company is required to make a $10,000 payment toward the note payable during the 2018 fiscal year.)

2. Using information from the completed 10-column work sheet in part 1, journalize the adjusting entries and the closing entries.

Check   (3) Total assets, $195,900; Current liabilities, $23,450; Net income, $77,550

3. Prepare the income statement and the statement of owner's equity for the year ended April 30 and the classified balance sheet at April 30, 2017.

Analysis Component

4. Analyze the following separate errors and describe how each would affect the 10-column work sheet. Explain whether the error is likely to be discovered in completing the work sheet and, if not, the effect of the error on the financial statements.

   a. Assume the adjusting entry to reflect expiration of insurance coverage for the period was recorded with a $2,000 credit to Prepaid Insurance and a $2,000 debit to Insurance Expense. The adjustment should have been for $10,600.

   b. When the adjusted trial balance in the work sheet was completed, assume that the $4,700 Repairs Expense account balance is extended to the Debit column of the Balance Sheet columns.

Problem 4-3B
Determining balance sheet classifications

C3

In the blank space beside each numbered balance sheet item, enter the letter of its balance sheet classification. If the item should not appear on the balance sheet, enter a *Z* in the blank.

A. Current assets
B. Long-term investments
C. Plant assets
D. Intangible assets

E. Current liabilities
F. Long-term liabilities
G. Equity

_____ **1.** Commissions earned
_____ **2.** Interest receivable
_____ **3.** Long-term investment in stock
_____ **4.** Prepaid insurance
_____ **5.** Machinery
_____ **6.** Notes payable (due in 15 years)
_____ **7.** Copyrights
_____ **8.** Current portion of long-term note payable
_____ **9.** Accumulated depreciation—Trucks
_____ **10.** Office equipment

_____ **11.** Rent receivable
_____ **12.** Salaries payable
_____ **13.** Income taxes payable
_____ **14.** Owner, Capital
_____ **15.** Office supplies
_____ **16.** Interest payable
_____ **17.** Rent revenue
_____ **18.** Notes receivable (due in 120 days)
_____ **19.** Land (used in operations)
_____ **20.** Depreciation expense—Trucks

The adjusted trial balance for Anara Co. as of December 31, 2017, follows.

	ANARA COMPANY Adjusted Trial Balance December 31, 2017		
No.	**Account Title**	**Debit**	**Credit**
101	Cash	$ 7,400	
104	Short-term investments	11,200	
126	Supplies	4,600	
128	Prepaid insurance	1,000	
167	Equipment	24,000	
168	Accumulated depreciation—Equipment		$ 4,000
173	Building..	100,000	
174	Accumulated depreciation—Building		10,000
183	Land	30,500	
201	Accounts payable................................		3,500
203	Interest payable.................................		1,750
208	Rent payable....................................		400
210	Wages payable..................................		1,280
213	Property taxes payable		3,330
233	Unearned professional fees		750
251	Long-term notes payable..........................		40,000
301	P. Anara, Capital................................		92,800
302	P. Anara, Withdrawals	8,000	
401	Professional fees earned..........................		59,600
406	Rent earned		4,500
407	Dividends earned................................		1,000
409	Interest earned..................................		1,320
606	Depreciation expense—Building....................	2,000	
612	Depreciation expense—Equipment..................	1,000	
623	Wages expense	18,500	
633	Interest expense.................................	1,550	
637	Insurance expense...............................	1,525	
640	Rent expense	3,600	
652	Supplies expense................................	1,000	
682	Postage expense	410	
683	Property taxes expense...........................	4,825	
684	Repairs expense.................................	679	
688	Telephone expense	521	
690	Utilities expense.................................	1,920	
	Totals...	$224,230	$224,230

P. Anara invested $40,000 cash in the business during year 2017 (the December 31, 2016, credit balance of the P. Anara, Capital account was $52,800). Anara Company is required to make an $8,400 payment on its long-term notes payable during 2018.

Required

1. Prepare the income statement and the statement of owner's equity for the calendar year 2017 and the classified balance sheet at December 31, 2017.

2. Prepare the necessary closing entries at December 31, 2017.

3. Use the information in the financial statements to calculate these ratios: (*a*) return on assets (total assets at December 31, 2016, were $160,000), (*b*) debt ratio, (*c*) profit margin ratio (use total revenues as the denominator), and (*d*) current ratio. Round ratios to three decimals for parts *a* and *c*, and to two decimals for parts *b* and *d*.

Problem 4-5B
Preparing trial balances,
closing entries, and
financial statements

C3 P2 P3

Santo Company's adjusted trial balance on December 31, 2017, follows.

	SANTO COMPANY Adjusted Trial Balance December 31, 2017		
No.	**Account Title**	**Debit**	**Credit**
101	Cash	$ 14,450	
125	Store supplies.....................................	5,140	
128	Prepaid insurance	1,200	
167	Equipment	31,000	
168	Accumulated depreciation—Equipment..............		$ 8,000
201	Accounts payable.................................		1,500
210	Wages payable....................................		2,700
301	P. Santo, Capital.................................		35,650
302	P. Santo, Withdrawals............................	15,000	
401	Repair fees earned................................		54,700
612	Depreciation expense—Equipment..................	2,000	
623	Wages expense	26,400	
637	Insurance expense................................	600	
640	Rent expense	3,600	
651	Store supplies expense	1,200	
690	Utilities expense.................................	1,960	
	Totals...	$102,550	$102,550

Required

1. Prepare an income statement and a statement of owner's equity for the year 2017, and a classified balance sheet at December 31, 2017. There are no owner investments in 2017.

2. Enter the adjusted trial balance in the first two columns of a six-column table. Use the middle two columns for closing entry information and the last two columns for a post-closing trial balance. Insert an Income Summary account (No. 901) as the last item in the trial balance.

3. Enter closing entry information in the six-column table and prepare journal entries for it.

Analysis Component

4. Assume for this part only that
   a. None of the $600 insurance expense had expired during the year. Instead, assume it is a prepayment of the next period's insurance protection.
   b. There are no earned and unpaid wages at the end of the year. (*Hint:* Reverse the $2,700 wages payable accrual.)

Describe the financial statement changes that would result from these two assumptions.

The following six-column table for Solutions Co. includes the unadjusted trial balance as of December 31, 2017.

Problem 4-6B[A]

Preparing adjusting, reversing, and next period entries

P4

	A	B	C	D	E	F	G
1		SOLUTIONS COMPANY					
2		December 31, 2017					
3		Unadjusted				Adjusted	
4		Trial Balance		Adjustments		Trial Balance	
5	**Account Title**	Dr.	Cr.	Dr.	Cr.	Dr.	Cr.
6	Cash	$ 10,000					
7	Accounts receivable	0					
8	Supplies	7,600					
9	Machinery	50,000					
10	Accumulated depreciation—Machinery		$ 20,000				
11	Interest payable		0				
12	Salaries payable		0				
13	Unearned rental fees		7,200				
14	Notes payable		30,000				
15	G. Clay, Capital		14,200				
16	G. Clay, Withdrawals	9,500					
17	Rental fees earned		32,450				
18	Depreciation expense—Machinery	0					
19	Salaries expense	24,500					
20	Interest expense	2,250					
21	Supplies expense	0					
22	Totals	$103,850	$103,850				

Required

1. Complete the six-column table by entering adjustments that reflect the following information:

   a. As of December 31, 2017, employees had earned $400 of unpaid and unrecorded wages. The next payday is January 4, at which time $1,200 in wages will be paid.

   b. The cost of supplies still available at December 31, 2017, is $3,450.

   c. The notes payable requires an interest payment to be made every three months. The amount of unrecorded accrued interest at December 31, 2017, is $800. The next interest payment, at an amount of $900, is due on January 15, 2018.

   d. Analysis of the unearned rental fees shows that $3,200 remains unearned at December 31, 2017.

   e. In addition to the machinery rental fees included in the revenue account balance, the company has earned another $2,450 in unrecorded fees that will be collected on January 31, 2018. The company is also expected to collect $5,400 on that same day for new fees earned in January 2018.

   f. Depreciation expense for the year is $3,800.

2. Prepare journal entries for the adjustments entered in the six-column table for part 1.

3. Prepare journal entries to reverse the effects of the adjusting entries that involve accruals.

4. Prepare journal entries to record the cash payments and cash collections described for January.

Check   (1) Adjusted trial balance totals, $111,300

(This serial problem began in Chapter 1 and continues through most of the book. If previous chapter segments were not completed, the serial problem can begin at this point.)

SERIAL PROBLEM

Business Solutions

P2   P3

SP 4   The December 31, 2017, adjusted trial balance of **Business Solutions** (reflecting its transactions from October through December of 2017) follows.

© Alexander Image/Shutterstock RF

No.	Account Title	Debit	Credit
101	Cash..	$ 48,372	
106	Accounts receivable	5,668	
126	Computer supplies	580	
128	Prepaid insurance............................	1,665	
131	Prepaid rent..................................	825	
163	Office equipment	8,000	
164	Accumulated depreciation—Office equipment....		$ 400
167	Computer equipment..........................	20,000	
168	Accumulated depreciation—Computer equipment.		1,250
201	Accounts payable		1,100
210	Wages payable		500
236	Unearned computer services revenue		1,500
301	S. Rey, Capital...............................		73,000
302	S. Rey, Withdrawals...........................	7,100	
403	Computer services revenue....................		31,284
612	Depreciation expense—Office equipment........	400	
613	Depreciation expense—Computer equipment	1,250	
623	Wages expense...............................	3,875	
637	Insurance expense	555	
640	Rent expense	2,475	
652	Computer supplies expense....................	3,065	
655	Advertising expense..........................	2,753	
676	Mileage expense..............................	896	
677	Miscellaneous expenses	250	
684	Repairs expense—Computer	1,305	
901	Income summary..............................		0
	Totals	$109,034	$109,034

Required

1. Record and post the necessary closing entries for Business Solutions.

Check   Post-closing trial balance totals, $85,110

2. Prepare a post-closing trial balance as of December 31, 2017.

GENERAL LEDGER PROBLEM

Available only in Connect

The following **General Ledger** assignments focus on transactions related to the closing process. For each of the following questions, prepare the required closing entries, create the income statement and the classified balance sheet, and then indicate which accounts appear on the post-closing trial balance. Three options exist for displaying the trial balance: unadjusted, adjusted, or post-closing.

GL 4-1 Transactions from the FastForward illustration in this chapter

GL 4-2 Based on Problem 4-1A

GL 4-3 Based on Problem 4-2A

GL 4-4 Based on Problem 4-6A

GL 4-5 Based on Serial Problem SP 4

Beyond the Numbers

REPORTING IN ACTION

C1   P2

APPLE

BTN 4-1   Refer to **Apple**'s financial statements in Appendix A to answer the following.

1. For the fiscal year ended September 26, 2015, what amount is credited to Income Summary to summarize its revenues earned?

2. For the fiscal year ended September 26, 2015, what amount is debited to Income Summary to summarize its expenses incurred?

3. For the fiscal year ended September 26, 2015, what is the balance of its Income Summary account before it is closed?

Continued on next page . . .

Fast Forward

4. Access Apple's annual report (10-K) for fiscal years ending after September 26, 2015, at its website (Apple.com) or the SEC's EDGAR database (SEC.gov). How has the amount of net income closed to Income Summary changed in the fiscal years ending after September 26, 2015?

BTN 4-2   Key figures for the recent two years of both Apple and Google follow.

$ millions	Apple		Google	
	Current Year	Prior Year	Current Year	Prior Year
Current assets	$89,378	$68,531	$90,114	$78,656
Current liabilities	80,610	63,448	19,310	16,779

COMPARATIVE ANALYSIS

A1

APPLE

GOOGLE

Required

1. Compute the current ratio for both years for both companies.
2. Which company has the better ability to pay short-term obligations according to the current ratio?
3. Analyze and comment on each company's current ratios for the past two years.
4. How do Apple's and Google's current ratios compare to their industry (assumed) average ratio of 2.0?

BTN 4-3   On January 20, 2017, Tamira Nelson, the accountant for Picton Enterprises, is feeling pressure to complete the annual financial statements. The company president has said he needs up-to-date financial statements to share with the bank on January 21 at a dinner meeting that has been called to discuss Picton's obtaining loan financing for a special building project. Tamira knows that she will not be able to gather all the needed information in the next 24 hours to prepare the entire set of adjusting entries. Those entries must be posted before the financial statements accurately portray the company's performance and financial position for the fiscal period ended December 31, 2016. Tamira ultimately decides to estimate several expense accruals at the last minute. When deciding on estimates for the expenses, she uses low estimates because she does not want to make the financial statements look worse than they are. Tamira finishes the financial statements before the deadline and gives them to the president without mentioning that several account balances are estimates that she provided.

ETHICS CHALLENGE

C2

Required

1. Identify several courses of action that Tamira could have taken instead of the one she took.
2. If you were in Tamira's situation, what would you have done? Briefly justify your response.

BTN 4-4   Assume that one of your classmates states that a company's books should be ongoing and therefore not closed until that business is terminated. Write a half-page memo to this classmate explaining the concept of the closing process by drawing analogies between (1) a scoreboard for an athletic event and the revenue and expense accounts of a business or (2) a sports team's record book and the capital account. (*Hint:* Think about what would happen if the scoreboard were not cleared before the start of a new game.)

COMMUNICATING IN PRACTICE

C1   P2

BTN 4-5   Access Motley Fool's discussion of the current ratio at Fool.com/investing/beginning/how-to-value-stocks-how-to-read-a-balance-sheet-cu.aspx. (If the page has changed, search that site for the article "How to Read a Balance Sheet: Current and Quick Ratios".)

TAKING IT TO THE NET

A1

Required

1. What level for the current ratio is generally regarded as sufficient to meet near-term operating needs?
2. Once you have calculated the current ratio for a company, what should you compare it against?
3. What are the implications for a company that has a current ratio that is too high?

TEAMWORK IN ACTION

P1 P2 P3

BTN 4-6 The unadjusted trial balance and information for the accounting adjustments of Noseworthy Investigators follow. Each team member involved in this project is to assume one of the four responsibilities listed. After completing each of these responsibilities, the team should work together to prove the accounting equation utilizing information from teammates (1 and 4). If your equation does not balance, you are to work as a team to resolve the error. The team's goal is to complete the task as quickly and accurately as possible.

Unadjusted Trial Balance		
Account Title	Debit	Credit
Cash	$16,000	
Supplies....................................	12,000	
Prepaid insurance............................	3,000	
Equipment...................................	25,000	
Accumulated depreciation—Equipment		$ 7,000
Accounts payable.............................		3,000
D. Noseworthy, Capital........................		34,000
D. Noseworthy, Withdrawals	6,000	
Investigation fees earned		33,000
Rent expense	15,000	
Totals......................................	$77,000	$77,000

Additional Year-End Information

a. Insurance that expired in the current period amounts to $2,200.

b. Equipment depreciation for the period is $4,000.

c. Unused supplies total $5,000 at period-end.

d. Services in the amount of $800 have been provided but have not been billed or collected.

Responsibilities for Individual Team Members

1. Determine the accounts and adjusted balances to be extended to the Balance Sheet columns of the work sheet for Noseworthy. Also determine total assets and total liabilities.

2. Determine the adjusted revenue account balance and prepare the entry to close this account.

3. Determine the adjusted account balances for expenses and prepare the entry to close these accounts.

4. Prepare T-accounts for both D. Noseworthy, Capital (reflecting the unadjusted trial balance amount) and Income Summary. Prepare the third and fourth closing entries. Ask teammates assigned to parts 2 and 3 for the postings for Income Summary. Obtain amounts to complete the third closing entry and post both the third and fourth closing entries. Provide the team with the ending capital account balance.

5. The entire team should prove the accounting equation using post-closing balances.

ENTREPRENEURIAL DECISION

A1 C3 P2

BTN 4-7 Review this chapter's opening feature involving Anna Stork and Andrea Sreshta and their **LuminAID** business.

1. Explain how a classified balance sheet can help Anna and Andrea know what bills are due when, and whether they have the resources to pay those bills.

2. Why is it important for Anna and Andrea to match costs and revenues in a specific time period? How do closing entries help them in this regard?

3. What objectives are met when Anna and Andrea apply closing procedures each fiscal year-end?

HITTING THE ROAD

C2

BTN 4-8 Select a company that you can visit in person or interview on the telephone. Call ahead to the company to arrange a time when you can interview an employee (preferably an accountant) who helps prepare the annual financial statements. Inquire about the following aspects of its *accounting cycle:*

1. Does the company prepare interim financial statements? What time period(s) is used for interim statements?

2. Does the company use the cash or accrual basis of accounting?

Continued on next page . . .

3. Does the company use a work sheet in preparing financial statements? Why or why not?

4. Does the company use a spreadsheet program? If so, which software program is used?

5. How long does it take after the end of its reporting period to complete annual statements?

BTN 4-9   Samsung (Samsung.com) is a leading manufacturer of consumer electronic products. The following selected information is available from Samsung's financial statements.

GLOBAL DECISION

A1

Samsung

millions of Korean won	Current Year	Prior Year
Current assets......................	₩124,814,725	₩115,146,026
Current liabilities....................	50,502,909	52,013,913

Required

1. Compute Samsung's current ratio for both the current year and the prior year.

2. Comment on any change from the prior year to the current year for the current ratio.

 **GLOBAL VIEW**

We explained that accounting under U.S. GAAP is similar, but not identical, to that under IFRS. This section discusses differences in the closing process and in reporting assets and liabilities on a balance sheet.

Closing Process   The closing process is identical under U.S. GAAP and IFRS. Although unique accounts can arise under either system, the closing process remains the same.

Reporting Assets and Liabilities   The definition of an asset is similar under U.S. GAAP and IFRS and involves three basic criteria:

1. The company owns or controls the right to use the item.
2. The right arises from a past transaction or event.
3. The item can be reliably measured.

Both systems define the initial asset value as historical cost for nearly all assets. After acquisition, one of two asset measurement systems is applied: historical cost or fair value. Generally, U.S. GAAP defines fair value as the amount to be received in an orderly sale. IFRS defines fair value as *exchange value*—either replacement cost or selling price. We describe these differences, and the assets to which they apply, in later chapters.

The definition of a liability is similar under U.S. GAAP and IFRS and involves three basic criteria:

1. The item is a *present* obligation requiring a probable future resource outlay.
2. The obligation arises from a past transaction or event.
3. The obligation can be reliably measured.

As with assets, both systems apply one of two measurement systems to liabilities: historical cost or fair value. Later chapters discuss specific differences.

 Global View Assignments

Discussion Questions 15 & 17

Quick Study 4-10

Exercise 4-14

BTN 4-9

chapter 5

Accounting for Merchandising Operations

Learning Objectives

CONCEPTUAL

C1 Describe merchandising activities and identify income components for a merchandising company.

C2 Identify and explain the inventory asset and cost flows of a merchandising company.

ANALYTICAL

A1 Compute the acid-test ratio and explain its use to assess liquidity.

A2 Compute the gross margin ratio and explain its use to assess profitability.

PROCEDURAL

P1 Analyze and record transactions for merchandise purchases using a perpetual system.

P2 Analyze and record transactions for merchandise sales using a perpetual system.

P3 Prepare adjustments and close accounts for a merchandising company.

P4 Define and prepare multiple-step and single-step income statements.

P5 *Appendix 5A*—Record and compare merchandising transactions using both periodic and perpetual inventory systems.

P6 *Appendix 5C*—Prepare adjustments for discounts, returns, and allowances per revenue recognition rules.

P7 *Appendix 5D*—Record and compare merchandising transactions using the gross method and net method.

© Bart Young/Invision for Intuit/AP Images

Soldier On!

DENVER—Jeff Bezos founded Amazon in a garage, Mark Zuckerberg founded Facebook in a dorm room, and Lt. Emily Núñez Cavness co-founded **Sword & Plough** (**SwordandPlough.com**) while deployed in Afghanistan. "It was not the usual start-up location," recalls Emily as she describes a Skype meeting that was interrupted by mortar fire. Emily and her sister Betsy recycle military surplus materials to create totes, handbags, backpacks, and accessories. The sisters reuse materials that "would otherwise be burned or buried in a landfill," according to Emily.

To date, Emily and Betsy have recycled 30,000 pounds of surplus materials into over 7,000 bag and accessory sales. Importantly, their business success enables them to support 38 veteran jobs, one of their main goals. Emily and Betsy stress that their success is in part due to the merchandising accounting system they use for purchases and sales transactions. "We were able to pinpoint some immediate problems to solve," explains Emily, including identifying which products were selling poorly and which were unprofitable. Emily insists that the information gained from the accounting system "didn't just stay stored on my iPhone, or scrap piece of paper—we took action!"

"Whatever you dream, you can do"

—Lt. Emily Núñez Cavness

"The momentum behind Sword & Plough continues to grow," says Emily, and reliance on their merchandising accounting system grows as well. Tracking merchandising activities was necessary to set prices and to manage discounts, allowances, and returns for both sales and purchases. A perpetual inventory system enabled Emily and Betsy to stock the right kind and amount of merchandise and to avoid the costs of out-of-stock and excess inventory. "We took the idea seriously and today we can show you that the concept has become a powerful reality," asserts Emily.

Emily continues to both serve her country as a lieutenant in the Army and act as CEO of Sword & Plough. "It has been challenging at times, but the two roles complement each other," explains Emily. "I want Sword & Plough to be a leader in the field of social entrepreneurship that is able to communicate effectively the awesome skill that veterans bring to communities." Hoo-ah!

Sources: *Sword & Plough website*, January 2017; *Bloomberg Businessweek*, April 2013; *ABC News*, August 2014; *Military Times*, September 2015; *NationSwell*, January 2016; *Opportunity Lives*, October 2015; *Good Magazine*, May 2013

MERCHANDISING ACTIVITIES

C1

Describe merchandising activities and identify income components for a merchandising company.

Previous chapters emphasized the accounting activities of service companies. A merchandising company's activities differ from those of a service company. **Merchandise** consists of products, also called *goods,* that a company buys to resell to customers. A **merchandiser** earns net income by buying and selling merchandise. Merchandisers are often wholesalers or retailers. A **wholesaler** buys products from manufacturers and sells them to retailers. A **retailer** buys products from manufacturers or wholesalers and sells them to consumers.

Reporting Income for a Merchandiser

Net income for a merchandiser equals revenues from selling merchandise minus both the cost of merchandise sold to customers and other expenses for the period—see Exhibit 5.1. The usual accounting term for revenues from selling merchandise is *sales,* and the term used for the expense of buying and preparing the merchandise is **cost of goods sold.** (Some service companies use the term *sales* instead of revenues; and cost of goods sold is also called *cost of sales.*)

EXHIBIT 5.1

Computing Income for a Merchandising Company versus a Service Company

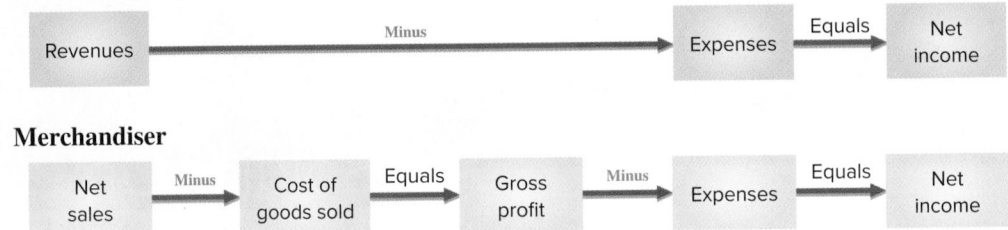

The income statements for a service company, Liberty Tax, and for a merchandiser, Nordstrom, are shown in Exhibit 5.2 ($ millions). The statement for Liberty Tax shows revenues of $173 followed by expenses of $155, which yields $18 in net income. The first two lines of the statement for Nordstrom, a merchandiser, show that products are acquired at a cost of $9,168 and sold for $14,437. The third line shows its $5,269 **gross profit,** also called **gross margin,** which equals net sales less cost of goods sold. Additional expenses of $4,669 are reported, which leaves $600 in net income.

Point: Fleming, SuperValu, and SYSCO are wholesalers. Aeropostale, Coach, Target, and Walmart are retailers.

EXHIBIT 5.2

Income Statement for a Service Company and a Merchandising Company ($ millions)

Service Company

LIBERTY TAX
Income Statement
For Year Ended April 30, 2016

Revenues	$173
Expenses	155
Net income	$ 18

Merchandising Company

NORDSTROM INC.
Income Statement
For Year Ended January 31, 2016

Net sales	$14,437
Cost of goods sold	9,168
Gross profit	5,269
Expenses	4,669
Net income	$ 600

Reporting Inventory for a Merchandiser

C2

Identify and explain the inventory asset and cost flows of a merchandising company.

A merchandiser's balance sheet includes a current asset called *merchandise inventory,* an item not on a service company's balance sheet. **Merchandise inventory,** or simply **Inventory,** refers to products that a company owns and intends to sell. The cost of this asset includes the cost incurred to buy the goods, ship them to the store, and make them ready for sale.

Operating Cycle for a Merchandiser

A merchandising company's operating cycle begins by purchasing merchandise and ends by collecting cash from selling the merchandise. The length of an operating cycle differs across the types of businesses. Department stores often have operating cycles of two to five months. Operating cycles for grocery merchants usually range from two to eight weeks. A grocer has more operating cycles in a year than clothing or electronics retailers.

Exhibit 5.3 illustrates an operating cycle for a merchandiser with credit sales. The cycle moves from (*a*) cash purchases of merchandise to (*b*) inventory for sale to (*c*) credit sales to (*d*) accounts receivable to (*e*) cash. Companies try to keep their operating cycles short because assets tied up in inventory and receivables are not productive. Cash sales shorten operating cycles.

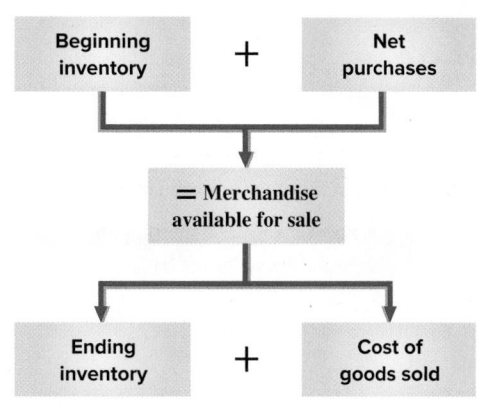

EXHIBIT 5.3

Merchandiser's Operating Cycle

Inventory Systems

Exhibit 5.4 shows that a company's merchandise available for sale consists of what it begins with (beginning inventory) and what it purchases (net purchases). The merchandise available is either sold (cost of goods sold) or kept for future sales (ending inventory).

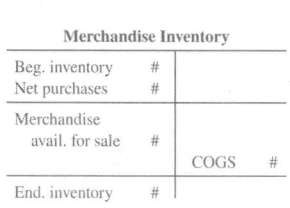

Merchandise Inventory		
Beg. inventory	#	
Net purchases	#	
Merchandise avail. for sale	#	
		COGS #
End. inventory	#	

EXHIBIT 5.4

Merchandiser's Cost Flow for a Single Time Period

Point: Mathematically, Exhibit 5.4 says

$$BI + NP = MAS,$$

where BI is beginning inventory, NP is net purchases, and MAS is merchandise available for sale. Exhibit 5.4 also says

$$MAS = EI + COGS,$$

which can be rewritten as MAS − EI = COGS or MAS − COGS = EI, where EI is ending inventory and COGS is cost of goods sold.

Companies account for inventory in one of two ways: *perpetual system* or *periodic system*.

- **Perpetual inventory system** updates accounting records for *each* purchase and sale of inventory.
- **Periodic inventory system** updates the accounting records for purchases and sales of inventory *only at the end of a period.*

Technological advances and competitive pressures have dramatically increased the use of the perpetual system. It gives managers immediate access to information on sales and inventory levels, which allows them to strategically react and increase profit. (Some companies use a *hybrid* system where the perpetual system is used for tracking units available and the periodic system is used to compute cost of sales.)

Point: Growth of superstores such as **Costco** and **Sam's Club** is fueled by efficient use of perpetual inventory.

*The following sections on purchasing, selling, and adjusting merchandise use the **perpetual system (ending with NTK 5-3)**. Appendix 5A uses the periodic system (with the perpetual results on the side). An instructor can choose to cover either one or both inventory systems. If the periodic system only is covered, then read Appendix 5A and return to the section titled "Financial Statement Formats" (after NTK 5-3).*

NEED-TO-KNOW 5-1

Merchandise Accounts
and Computations

C1 C2

Use the following information (in random order) from a merchandising company and from a service company. *Hint:* Not all information may be necessary for the solutions.

1. For the merchandiser only, compute
   a. Goods available for sale.
   b. Cost of goods sold.
   c. Gross profit.

2. Compute net income for each company.

SaveCo Merchandiser	
Supplies........................	$ 10
Beginning inventory.............	100
Ending inventory.................	50
Expenses.......................	20
Net purchases..................	80
Net sales......................	190

Hi-Tech Services	
Expenses.......................	$170
Revenues	200
Cash	10
Prepaid rent	25
Accounts payable..............	35
Supplies.......................	65

Solution

1. a. Computation of goods available for sale (SaveCo)

Beginning inventory..........	$100
Plus: Net purchases..........	80
Goods available for sale	$180

b. Computation of cost of goods sold (SaveCo)

Beginning inventory..........	$100
Plus: Net purchases..........	80
Goods available for sale	180
Less: Ending inventory........	50
Cost of goods sold...........	$130

c. Computation of gross profit (SaveCo)

Net sales...................	$190
Less: Cost of goods sold (see part b)..........	130
Gross profit................	$ 60

2. Computation of net income for each company

SaveCo Merchandiser	
Net sales...................................	$190
Less: Cost of goods sold (see part 1b)	130
Gross profit...............................	60
Less: Expenses............................	20
Net income	$ 40

Hi-Tech Services	
Revenues	$200
Less: Expenses.................	170
Net income	$ 30

Do More: QS 5-3, E 5-1, E 5-2

ACCOUNTING FOR MERCHANDISE PURCHASES

P1

Analyze and record transactions for merchandise purchases using a perpetual system.

This section explains how we record purchases under different purchase terms.

Purchases <u>without</u> Cash Discounts

Z-Mart would record a $500 cash purchase of merchandise on November 2 as follows.

Assets = Liabilities + Equity
+500
−500

Nov. 2	Merchandise Inventory	500	
	Cash		500
	Purchased goods for cash.		

If these goods were instead *purchased on credit,* and no discounts were offered for early payment, Z-Mart would make the same entry except that Accounts Payable would be credited instead of Cash.

Point: Costs recorded in Merchandise Inventory are also called *inventoriable costs.*

Trade Discounts When a manufacturer or wholesaler prepares a catalog of items it has for sale, it usually gives each item a **list price,** also called a *catalog price.* However, an item's intended *selling price* equals list price minus a given percent called a **trade discount.** The amount of trade discount usually depends on whether a buyer is a wholesaler, retailer, or final consumer. A wholesaler buying in large quantities is often granted a larger discount than a retailer buying in smaller quantities. A buyer records the net amount of list price minus trade discount. For example, a supplier of Z-Mart lists an item of merchandise in its catalog at $625 and it grants Z-Mart a 20% trade discount. This means that Z-Mart's purchase price for that item is $500, computed as $625 − (20% × $625). ■

Point: Lowe's and Home Depot offer trade discounts to construction companies and contractors. Trade discounts are not journalized; purchases are recorded based on the invoice amount.

Purchases **with** Cash Discounts

The purchase of goods on credit lists credit terms. **Credit terms** for a purchase include the amounts and timing of payments from a buyer to a seller. To illustrate, when sellers require payment within 10 days after the end of the month of the invoice date, the invoice lists credit terms as "n/10 EOM," which stands for net 10 days after end of month (**EOM**). When sellers require payment within 30 days after the invoice date, the invoice lists credit terms of "n/30," which stands for *net 30 days.*

Exhibit 5.5 portrays credit terms. The amount of time allowed before full payment is due is called the **credit period.** Sellers can grant a **cash discount** to encourage buyers to pay earlier. A buyer views a cash discount as a **purchases discount.** A seller views a cash discount as a **sales discount.** Any cash discounts are described in the credit terms on the invoice. For example, credit terms of "2/10, n/60" mean that full payment is due within a 60-day credit period, but the buyer can deduct 2% of the invoice amount if payment is made within 10 days of the invoice date. This reduced payment applies only for the **discount period.**

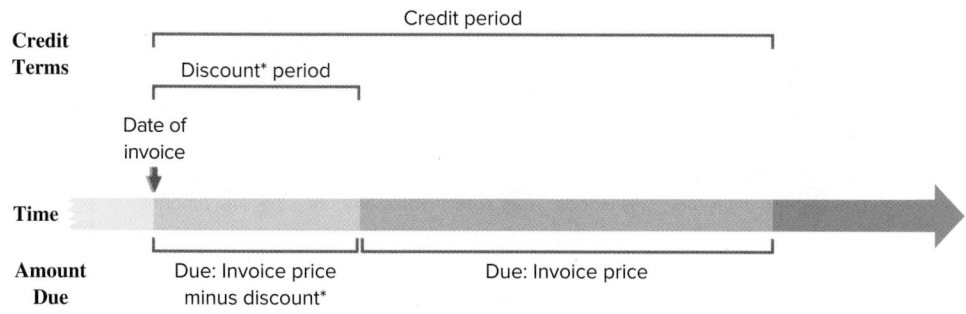

EXHIBIT 5.5

Credit Terms

To illustrate how a buyer accounts for a purchases discount, assume that on November 2, Z-Mart purchases $500 of merchandise *on credit* with terms of 2/10, n/30. The amount due, if paid on or before November 12, is $490, computed as $500 − ($500 × 2%)—or alternatively computed as $500 × (100% − 2%). Many buyers take advantage of a purchases discount because of the usually high interest rate implied by not taking it.[1] If Z-Mart does not pay within the 10-day 2% discount period, it can delay payment by 20 more days and pay $500. The *gross method* for recording purchases enters the full invoice (gross) amount for merchandise. Z-Mart's entry to record the November 2 purchase of $500 in merchandise on credit follows.

Point: Appendix 5A repeats journal entries *a* through *g* using the periodic system.

(*a*) Nov. 2	Merchandise Inventory	500	
	Accounts Payable		500
	Purchased goods, terms 2/10, n/30.		

Assets = Liabilities + Equity
+500   +500

---

[1]The *implied annual interest rate* formula is:

[365 days ÷ (Credit period − Discount period)] × Cash discount rate.

For terms of 2/10, n/30, missing the 2% discount for an additional 20 days is equal to an annual interest rate of 36.5%, computed as [365 days/(30 days − 10 days)] × 2% discount rate. *Favorable purchases discounts* are those with implied annual interest rates that exceed the purchaser's annual rate for borrowing money.

The invoice for this purchase is shown in Exhibit 5.6. This *source document* is the purchase invoice of Z-Mart (buyer) and the sales invoice for Trex (seller). The amount recorded for merchandise inventory includes its purchase cost, shipping fees, taxes, and any other costs necessary to make it ready for sale. (For recording, it can help to add the name to the payable [and receivable], such as Accounts Payable—Trex.)

EXHIBIT 5.6

Invoice

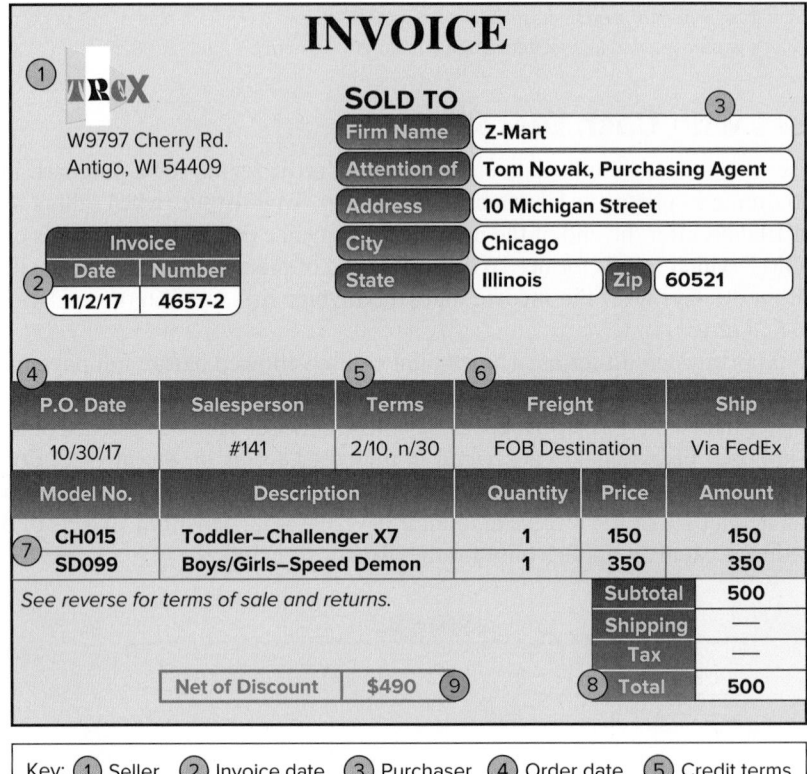

Point: The invoice date is used in setting the discount and credit periods as both buyer and seller know this date.

Payment within Discount Period

Good cash management means that invoices are not paid until the last day of the discount or credit period. This is because the buyer can use that money until payment is required. If Z-Mart pays the amount due on (or before) November 12, the entry is

Assets = Liabilities + Equity
−490   −500
− 10

(b1) Nov. 12	Accounts Payable	500	
	Merchandise Inventory..........................		10
	Cash*...		490
	Paid for goods within discount period.		
	* $500 × (100% − 2%)$		

The Merchandise Inventory account reflects the $490 net cost of purchases after these entries, and the Accounts Payable account reveals a zero balance. The relevant ledger accounts, in T-account form, follow.

Merchandise Inventory			
Nov. 2	500		
		Nov. 12	10
Bal.	**490**		

Accounts Payable			
		Nov. 2	500
Nov. 12	500		
		Bal.	0

Cash			
		Nov. 12	**490**

Payment after Discount Period   If the amount is paid *after* November 12, the discount is lost. For example, if Z-Mart pays the gross amount due on December 2 (the n/30 due date), it makes the following entry.

(b2) Dec. 2	Accounts Payable	500	
	Cash		500
	Paid for goods outside discount period.		

Assets = Liabilities + Equity
−500   −500

Entries in this chapter apply the *gross method* of accounting for purchases with discount terms. Appendix 5D shows the *net method*.

Point: Buyers sometimes make partial payments toward amounts owed. Credit terms apply to both partial and full payments.

■ **Decision** Maker

Entrepreneur   You purchase a batch of products on terms of 3/10, n/90, but your company has limited cash and you must borrow funds at an 11% annual rate if you are to pay within the discount period. Should you take the purchases discount? Explain. ■   [*Answer:* For terms of 3/10, n/90, missing the 3% discount for an additional 80 days equals an implied annual interest rate of 13.69%, computed as (365 days ÷ 80 days) × 3%. Since you can borrow funds at 11% (assuming no other costs), it is better to borrow and pay within the discount period. You save 2.69% (13.69% − 11%) in interest costs by paying early.]

Purchases with Returns and Allowances

Purchases returns are merchandise a buyer acquires but then returns to the seller. *Purchases allowances* refer to a seller granting a price reduction (allowance) to a buyer of defective or unacceptable merchandise. Buyers often keep defective goods if they can be sold and if the seller grants an acceptable allowance.

Purchases Allowances   To illustrate purchases allowances, assume that on November 5, Z-Mart (buyer) agrees to a $30 allowance from Trex for defective merchandise (assume allowance terms are $30 whether paid within discount period or not). Z-Mart's entry to update Merchandise Inventory and record the purchases allowance is

Point: When a buyer returns or takes an allowance on merchandise, the buyer issues a **debit memorandum.** This informs the seller of a debit made to the seller's account payable in the buyer's records.

(c1) Nov. 5	Accounts Payable	30	
	Merchandise Inventory...........................		30
	Allowance for defective goods.		

Assets = Liabilities + Equity
−30   −30

The buyer's allowance for defective merchandise is subtracted from the buyer's account payable balance to the seller. If cash is refunded, the Cash account is debited.

Purchases Returns   Returns are recorded at the costs charged to buyers. To illustrate the accounting for returns, suppose on June 1 that Z-Mart purchases $250 of merchandise with terms 2/10, n/60. On June 3, Z-Mart returns $50 of those goods. When Z-Mart pays on June 11, it takes the 2% discount only on the $200 remaining balance ($250 − $50). When goods are returned, a buyer takes a discount on only the remaining balance of the invoice. This means the discount is $4 (computed as $200 × 2%) and the cash payment is $196 (computed as $200 − $4). The following entries reflect this illustration.

June 1	Merchandise Inventory	250	
	Accounts Payable		250
	Purchased goods, terms 2/10, n/60.		
(c2) June 3	Accounts Payable	50	
	Merchandise Inventory...........................		50
	Returned goods to seller.		
June 11	Accounts Payable	200	
	Merchandise Inventory...........................		4
	Cash		196
	Paid for $200 of goods less $4 discount.		

Assets = Liabilities + Equity
+250   +250

Assets = Liabilities + Equity
−50   −50

Assets = Liabilities + Equity
−196   −200
−   4

For this example, the following ledger accounts, in T-account form, show the resulting $196 in inventory, the zero balance in Accounts Payable, and the $196 cash payment.

Example: Assume on June 20, Z-Mart returns all goods paid for on June 11. The return entry is

Cash.................. 196
   Merch. Inv. 196

Merchandise Inventory			
Jun. 1	250		
		Jun. 3	50
		Jun. 11	4
Bal.	196		

Accounts Payable			
		Jun. 1	250
Jun. 3	50		
Jun. 11	200		
		Bal.	0

Cash		
	Jun. 11	196

 Decision Insight

Point of No Return   Although many companies allow returns, many others do not. Buyers must be especially alert to purchase terms. Companies that often do not permit returns include those selling any of the following items: hair products such as extensions, barrettes, claws, combs, and pins; undergarments including swimsuits, leotards, and shorts; custom products such as tailored suits, pants, and shirts; and beauty and cosmetic items such as lip liners and makeup. Many of these are sold "as is," meaning returns are not allowed. ∎

Purchases and Transportation Costs

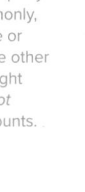

© Kirby Hamilton/iStock/Getty Images RF

The buyer and seller must agree on who is responsible for paying any freight costs and who has the risk of loss during transit for merchandising transactions. This is the same as asking at what point ownership transfers from the seller to the buyer. The point of transfer is called the **FOB** (*free on board*) point, which determines who pays transportation costs (and other costs of transit such as insurance). Whoever owns the goods in transit pays the shipping cost.

Exhibit 5.7 identifies two alternative points of transfer.

1. *FOB shipping point,* also called *FOB factory,* means the buyer accepts ownership when the goods depart the seller's place of business. The buyer pays shipping costs and has the risk of loss in transit. The goods are part of the buyer's inventory when they are in transit since ownership has transferred to the buyer. **1-800-Flowers.com**, a floral and gift merchandiser, and **Bare Escentuals**, a cosmetic manufacturer, both use FOB shipping point.

Point: When the party not responsible for shipping pays shipping cost, it either bills the other party responsible or, more commonly, adjusts its account payable or account receivable with the other party. Assume that any freight payments to carriers are *not* applied in computing discounts.

2. *FOB destination* means ownership of goods transfers to the buyer when the goods arrive at the buyer's place of business. The seller is responsible for paying shipping charges and has the risk of loss in transit. The seller does not record revenue from this sale until the goods arrive at the destination because this transaction is not complete before that point. **Kyocera**, a manufacturer, uses FOB destination.

EXHIBIT 5.7

Ownership Transfer and Transportation Costs

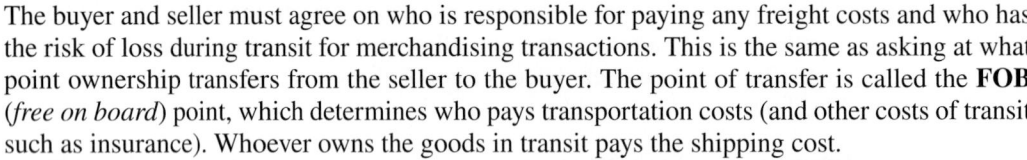

Seller   Buyer

Shipping point   Goods in transit   Destination

Shipping Terms	Ownership Transfers at	Goods in Transit Owned by	Transportation Costs Paid by	
FOB shipping point	Shipping point	Buyer	Buyer Merchandise Inventory . . . #	
			Cash	#
FOB destination	Destination	Seller	Seller Delivery Expense . . . . #	
			Cash	#

Point: If we place an order online and receive free shipping, we have terms FOB destination.

Z-Mart's $500 purchase on November 2 is on terms of FOB destination. This means Z-Mart does not pay transportation costs. When a buyer is responsible for paying transportation costs, the payment is made to a carrier or directly to the seller depending on the agreement. The cost principle requires that any transportation costs of a buyer (often called *transportation-in* or *freight-in*) be included as part of the cost of merchandise inventory. To illustrate, Z-Mart's entry to record a $75 freight charge from **UPS** for merchandise purchased FOB shipping point is

(d) Nov. 24	Merchandise Inventory	75	
	Cash		75
	Paid freight costs on goods.		

Assets = Liabilities + Equity
+75
−75

A seller records the costs of shipping goods to customers in a Delivery Expense account when the seller is responsible for these costs. Delivery expense, also called *transportation-out* or *freight-out,* is reported as a selling expense in the seller's income statement.

Point: INcoming freight costs are charged to INventory. When inventory EXits, freight costs are charged to EXpense.

Purchases and their itemized costs   In summary, purchases are recorded as debits to Merchandise Inventory (or Inventory). Any later purchases discounts, returns, and allowances are credited to (deducted from) Merchandise Inventory. Transportation-in is debited (added) to Merchandise Inventory. Z-Mart's itemized costs of merchandise purchases for year 2017 are in Exhibit 5.8.

Z-MART	
Itemized Costs of Merchandise Purchases	
For Year Ended December 31, 2017	
Invoice cost of merchandise purchases	$ 235,800
Less: Purchases discounts received	(4,200)
Purchases returns and allowances	(1,500)
Add: Costs of transportation-in	2,300
Total net cost of merchandise purchases	**$232,400**

EXHIBIT 5.8

Itemized Costs of Merchandise Purchases

The accounting system described here does not provide separate records (accounts) for total purchases, total purchases discounts, total purchases returns and allowances, and total transportation-in. Yet nearly all companies collect this information in supplementary records because managers need this information to evaluate and control each of these costs. **Supplementary records,** also called *supplemental records,* refer to information outside the usual general ledger accounts.

Point: Some companies have separate accounts for purchases discounts, returns and allowances, and transportation-in. These accounts are then transferred to Merchandise Inventory at period-end. This is a *hybrid system* of perpetual and periodic. That is, Merchandise Inventory is updated on a perpetual basis but only for purchases and cost of goods sold.

■ **Decision** Ethics

Payables Manager   As a new accounts payable manager, you are being trained by the outgoing manager. She explains that the system prepares checks for amounts net of favorable cash discounts, and the checks are dated the last day of the discount period. She also tells you that checks are not mailed until five days later, adding that "the company gets free use of cash for an extra five days, and our department looks better. When a supplier complains, we blame the computer system and the mailroom." Do you continue this payment policy? ■   [*Answer:* Your first step is to meet with your superior to find out if the late payment policy is the actual policy and, if so, its rationale. If it is the policy to pay late, you must apply your own sense of ethics. One point of view is that the late payment policy is unethical. A deliberate plan to make late payments means the company lies when it pretends to make payment within the discount period. Another view is that the late payment policy is acceptable. In some markets, attempts to take discounts through late payments are accepted as a continued phase of "price negotiation." The suppliers can bill your company for discounts not accepted because of late payments.]

Prepare journal entries to record each of the following purchases transactions of a merchandising company. Assume a perpetual inventory system using the gross method for recording purchases.

Oct. 1 Purchased $1,000 of goods. Terms of the sale are 4/10, n/30, and FOB shipping point; the invoice is dated October 1.
 3 Paid $30 cash for freight charges from UPS for the October 1 purchase.
 7 Returned $50 of the $1,000 of goods from the October 1 purchase and received full credit.
 11 Paid the amount due from the October 1 purchase (less the return on October 7).
 31 *Assume the October 11 payment was never made* and, instead, payment of the amount due, less the return on October 7, occurred on October 31.

NEED-TO-KNOW 5-2

Merchandise Purchases

P1

Solution

Oct. 1	Merchandise Inventory	1,000	
	Accounts Payable		1,000
	Purchased goods, terms 4/10, n/30.		
Oct. 3	Merchandise Inventory	30	
	Cash		30
	Paid freight on purchases FOB shipping point.		
Oct. 7	Accounts Payable	50	
	Merchandise Inventory.		50
	Returned goods.		
Oct. 11	Accounts Payable	950	
	Merchandise Inventory*		38
	Cash†		912
	Paid for goods within discount period.		
	* $950 × 4% *† $950 − ($950 × 4%)*		
Oct. 31	Accounts Payable‡	950	
	Cash		950
	Paid for goods outside discount period.		
	‡ $1,000 − $50		

Do More: QS 5-5, QS 5-6, QS 5-7, E 5-3, E 5-5

ACCOUNTING FOR MERCHANDISE SALES

P2

Analyze and record transactions for merchandise sales using a perpetual system.

Merchandising companies must account for sales, sales discounts, sales returns and allowances, and cost of goods sold. A merchandising company such as Z-Mart reflects these items in its gross profit computation, as shown in Exhibit 5.9. This shows that customers paid $314,700 for merchandise that cost Z-Mart $230,400, yielding a markup (gross profit) of $84,300.

EXHIBIT 5.9

Gross Profit Computation

Z-MART Computation of Gross Profit For Year Ended December 31, 2017	
Net sales (net of discounts, returns, and allowances)	$314,700
Cost of goods sold	230,400
Gross profit	$ 84,300

Each sale of merchandise has two parts: the revenue side and the cost side.

1. **Revenue received (and asset increased) from the customer.**
2. **Cost of goods sold incurred (and asset decreased) to the customer.**

Accounting for a sales transaction under the perpetual system requires recording information about both parts. This means that **each sales transaction for a merchandiser, whether for cash or on credit, requires** *two entries:* **one for revenue and one for cost.**

Sales without Cash Discounts

Revenue Side: Inflow of Assets   To illustrate, Z-Mart sold $1,000 of merchandise on credit terms n/60 on November 12. The revenue part of this transaction is recorded as

Assets = Liabilities + Equity
+1,000   +1,000

Nov. 12	Accounts Receivable	1,000	
	Sales		1,000
	Sold goods on credit.		

This entry reflects an increase in Z-Mart's assets in the form of accounts receivable. It also shows the increase in revenue (Sales). If the sale is for cash, the debit is to Cash instead of Accounts Receivable.

Cost Side: Outflow of Assets

The cost side of each sale requires that Merchandise Inventory decrease by that item's actual cost. For example, the cost of the merchandise Z-Mart sold on November 12 is $300, and the entry to record the cost part of this sales transaction follows.

Point: Gross profit on Nov. 12 sale:

Net sales	$1,000
Cost of goods sold	300
Gross profit	$ 700

Nov. 12	Cost of Goods Sold	300	
	Merchandise Inventory.		300
	Record cost of Nov. 12 sale.		

Assets = Liabilities + Equity
−300   −300

Decision Insight

Suppliers and Demands Large merchandising companies often bombard suppliers with demands. These include discounts for bar coding and technology support systems, and fines for shipping errors. Merchandisers' goals are to reduce inventories, shorten lead times, and eliminate errors. Many colleges now offer programs in supply chain management and logistics to train future employees to help merchandisers meet such goals. ■

© Polaris/Newscom

Sales with Cash Discounts

Sales discounts on credit sales can benefit a seller through earlier cash receipts and reduced collection efforts. Many sales discounts are favorable to the buyer, and many buyers will take advantage of them. *New revenue recognition rules **require that sellers report sales net of expected sales discounts.** These rules apply to annual periods of public entities beginning after December 15, 2017 (earlier use is permitted for periods beginning after December 15, 2016).*

The *gross method* records sales at the gross amount and records sales discounts if, and when, they are taken. The gross method requires a period-end adjusting entry to estimate future sales discounts. (The **net method** records sales at the net amount, which assumes that all discounts will be taken. If discounts are subsequently lost, the seller records those discounts lost. The net method is described in Appendix 5D.)

Sales on Credit

To illustrate, Z-Mart completes a credit sale for $1,000 on November 12 with terms of 2/10, n/45 (the cost of the merchandise sold is $300). The entry to record this sale using the gross method is

Nov. 12	Accounts Receivable	1,000	
	Sales		1,000
	Sold goods, terms 2/10, n/45.		
Nov. 12	Cost of Goods Sold	300	
	Merchandise Inventory.		300

Assets = Liabilities + Equity
+1,000   +1,000

Assets = Liabilities + Equity
−300   −300

This entry records the receivable and the revenue as if the customer will pay the gross amount. The customer has two options, however.

Buyer Pays within Discount Period

One option is for the buyer to pay $980 within the 10-day discount period ending November 22. The $20 sales discount is computed as

$1,000 \times 2\%$. Thus, if the customer pays on (or before) November 22, Z-Mart records the cash receipt as

Assets = Liabilities + Equity
+ 980   −20
−1,000

Nov. 22	Cash*	980	
	Sales Discounts	20	
	Accounts Receivable		1,000
	Received payment on Nov. 12 sale less discount.		
	* $1,000 − ($1,000 \times 2\%)$		

Sales Discounts is a **contra revenue account,** meaning the Sales Discounts account is deducted from the Sales account when computing a company's net sales. The Sales Discounts account has a *normal debit balance* because it decreases Sales, which has a normal credit balance.

Buyer Pays after Discount Period

The customer's second option is to wait 45 days until December 27 (or at least until after the discount period) and then pay $1,000. Z-Mart records that cash receipt as

Assets = Liabilities + Equity
+1,000
−1,000

Dec. 27	Cash	1,000	
	Accounts Receivable		1,000
	Received payment on Nov. 12 sale after discount period.		

Sales with Returns and Allowances

If a customer is unhappy with a purchase, many sellers allow the customer to either return the merchandise for a full refund (*sales return*) or keep the merchandise along with a partial refund (*sales allowance*). Most sellers can reliably estimate returns and allowances (abbreviated *R&A*).

Returns Received by Seller *Seller Issues Refund for Returned Goods.* When returns occur, the seller debits **Sales Returns and Allowances,** a **contra revenue account** to Sales. For example, assuming that a customer returns merchandise on November 26 that sold for $15 and cost $9, the revenue-side returns entry is

Assets = Liabilities + Equity
−15   −15

(e1) Nov. 26	Sales Returns and Allowances	15	
	Cash		15
	Goods returned from Nov. 12 sale.		

Seller Returns Goods to Inventory. When returns occur, the seller must also reduce the cost of sales. Extending the above example where the returned items sold for $15 and cost $9, the cost-side entry depends on whether the goods are defective or not.

Returned Goods Not Defective. If the merchandise returned to the seller is not defective and can be resold to another customer, the seller returns these goods to its inventory and records it as follows.

Assets = Liabilities + Equity
+9   +9

(e2) Nov. 26	Merchandise Inventory	9	
	Cost of Goods Sold.............................		9
	Returned goods are added back to inventory.		

Returned Goods Are Defective. If the merchandise returned to the seller is defective, the returned inventory is recorded at its estimated value, not its cost. For example, if the returned goods costing $9 are defective and estimated to be worth $2, the following entry is made.

Assets = Liabilities + Equity
+2   −7
                +9

Nov. 26	Merchandise Inventory	2	
	Loss from Defective Merchandise	7	
	Cost of Goods Sold.............................		9
	Returned defective goods to inventory and record loss.		

Allowances Granted by Seller   To illustrate sales allowances, assume that $40 of merchandise previously sold is defective, but the buyer decides to keep it because the seller offers a $10 price reduction paid in cash to the buyer. The seller records this allowance as follows.

(f) Nov. 24	Sales Returns and Allowances	10	
	Cash		10
	Sales allowance granted.		

Assets = Liabilities + Equity
−10   −10

Point: When a seller accepts returns or grants an allowance on merchandise, the seller issues a credit memorandum. This informs the buyer of a credit made to the buyer's account receivable in the seller's records.

If the seller has *not* yet collected cash for the goods sold, the seller could credit the buyer's Account Receivable. For example, instead of the seller sending $10 cash to the buyer in the entry above, the seller could credit Accounts Receivable for $10.

NEED-TO-KNOW 5-3

Merchandise Sales

P2

Prepare journal entries to record each of the following sales transactions of a merchandising company. Assume a perpetual inventory system and use of the gross method (beginning inventory equals $9,000).

June   1   Sold 50 units of merchandise to a customer for $150 per unit under credit terms of 2/10, n/30, FOB shipping point, and the invoice is dated June 1. The 50 units of merchandise had cost $100 per unit.

      7   The customer returns 2 units purchased on June 1 because those units did not fit its needs. The seller restores those units to its inventory (as they are not defective) and credits Accounts Receivable from the customer.

    11   The seller receives the balance due from the June 1 sale to the customer less returns and allowances.

    14   The customer discovers that 10 units have minor damage but keeps them because the seller sends a $50 cash payment allowance to compensate.

Solution

June	1	Accounts Receivable.................................	7,500	
		Sales		7,500
		Sold goods. 50 units × $150		
June	1	Cost of Goods Sold	5,000	
		Merchandise Inventory..........................		5,000
		Cost of sale. 50 units × $100		
June	7	Sales Returns and Allowances	300	
		Accounts Receivable		300
		Returns accepted. 2 units × $150		
June	7	Merchandise Inventory	200	
		Cost of Goods Sold..............................		200
		Returns added to inventory. 2 units × $100		
June	11	Cash...	7,056	
		Sales Discounts*	144	
		Accounts Receivable		7,200
		Received payment. *($7,500 − $300) × 2%		
June	14	Sales Returns and Allowances	50	
		Cash		50
		Recorded allowance on goods.		

Do More: QS 5-8, E 5-4,
E 5-6, E 5-7

ADJUSTING AND CLOSING FOR MERCHANDISERS

Exhibit 5.10 shows the flow of merchandising costs during a period and where these costs are reported at period-end. Specifically, beginning inventory plus the net cost of purchases is the merchandise available for sale. As inventory is sold, its cost is recorded in cost of goods sold on the income statement; what remains is ending inventory on the balance sheet. A period's ending inventory is the next period's beginning inventory.

EXHIBIT 5.10

Merchandising Cost Flow
in the Accounting Cycle

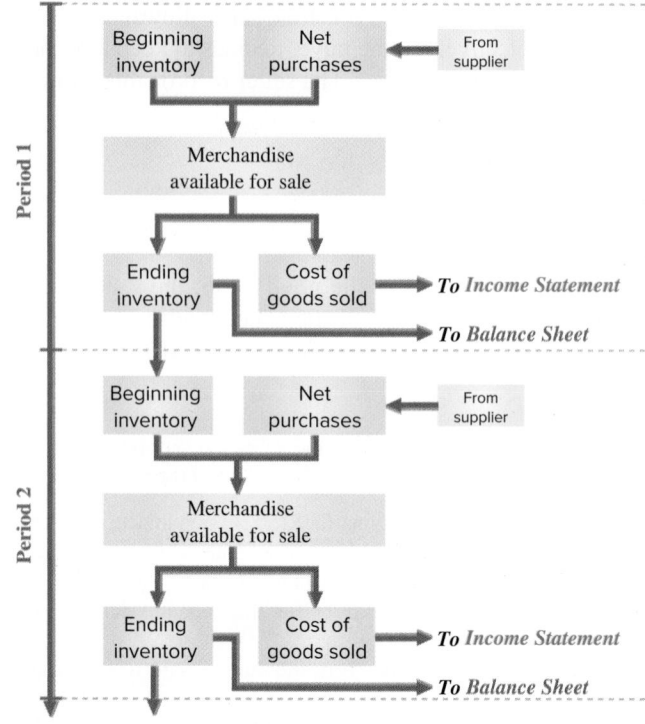

P3

Prepare adjustments and
close accounts for a
merchandising company.

Adjusting Entries for Merchandisers

Each of the steps in the accounting cycle described in the prior chapter for a service company
applies to a merchandiser. This section and the next two expand upon three steps of the accounting cycle for a merchandiser—adjustments, statement preparation, and closing.

Inventory Shrinkage—Adjusting Entry   Adjusting entries are similar for merchandising companies and service companies. However, a merchandiser using a *perpetual* inventory
system also makes an adjustment to update the Merchandise Inventory account to reflect any
loss of merchandise, including theft and deterioration. **Shrinkage** is the loss of inventory, and it
is computed by comparing a physical count of inventory with recorded amounts. A physical
count is usually performed at least once annually.

To illustrate, Z-Mart's Merchandise Inventory account at the end of year 2017 has a balance
of $21,250, but a physical count reveals that only $21,000 of inventory exists. The adjusting
entry to record this $250 shrinkage is

Assets = Liabilities + Equity
−250   −250

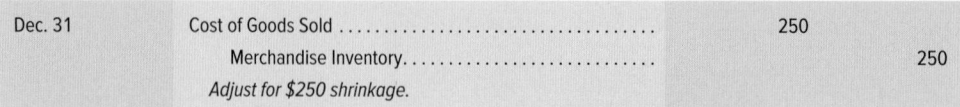

Dec. 31	Cost of Goods Sold	250	
	Merchandise Inventory.		250
	Adjust for $250 shrinkage.		

Sales Discounts, Returns, and Allowances—Adjusting Entries   Sales are to be
reported at the net amount expected, which follows new revenue recognition rules. This means
that period-end adjusting entries are commonly made for

- Expected sales discounts.
- Expected returns and allowances (revenue side).
- Expected returns and allowances (cost side).

These three adjustments produce three new accounts: Allowance for Sales Discounts, Sales
Refund Payable, and Inventory Returns Estimated. Appendix 5C explains these accounts and
the adjusting entries.

Preparing Financial Statements

The financial statements of a merchandiser, and their preparation, are similar to those for a service company described in prior chapters. The income statement mainly differs by the inclusion of *cost of goods sold* and *gross profit*. Net sales is affected by discounts, returns, and allowances, and some additional expenses such as delivery expense and loss from defective merchandise. The balance sheet differs by the inclusion of *merchandise inventory* as part of current assets. (Appendix 5C explains the presence of *inventory returns estimated* as part of current assets, and *sales refund payable* as part of current liabilities.) The statement of owner's equity is unchanged. A work sheet can be used to help prepare these statements, and one for Z-Mart is shown in Appendix 5B.

Closing Entries for Merchandisers

Closing entries are similar for service companies and merchandising companies using a perpetual system. The difference is that we close some new temporary accounts that arise from merchandising activities. Z-Mart has several temporary accounts unique to merchandisers: Sales (of goods), Sales Discounts, Sales Returns and Allowances, and Cost of Goods Sold. Their existence in the ledger means that the first two closing entries for a merchandiser are slightly different from the ones described in the prior chapter for a service company. These differences are set in **red boldface** in the closing entries of Exhibit 5.11.

Point: The Inventory account is not affected by the closing process under a perpetual system.

EXHIBIT 5.11

Closing Entries for a Merchandiser

Step 1: Close Credit Balances in Temporary Accounts to Income Summary.

Dec. 31	Sales..	321,000	
	Income Summary		321,000
	Close credit balances in temporary accounts.		

Step 2: Close Debit Balances in Temporary Accounts to Income Summary.

Dec. 31	Income Summary.....................................	308,100	
	Sales Discounts.................................		4,300
	Sales Returns and Allowances		2,000
	Cost of Goods Sold		230,400
	Depreciation Expense		3,700
	Salaries Expense		43,800
	Insurance Expense..............................		600
	Rent Expense		9,000
	Supplies Expense...............................		3,000
	Advertising Expense		11,300
	Close debit balances in temporary accounts.		

Step 3: Close Income Summary to Owner's Capital.

The third closing entry is identical for a merchandising company and a service company. The $12,900 amount is net income reported on the income statement.

Dec. 31	Income Summary....................................	12,900	
	K. Marty, Capital		12,900
	Close Income Summary account.		

Step 4: Close Withdrawals Account to Owner's Capital.

The fourth closing entry is identical for a merchandising company and a service company. It closes the Withdrawals account and adjusts the Owner's Capital account to the amount shown on the balance sheet.

Dec. 31	K. Marty, Capital	4,000	
	K. Marty, Withdrawals		4,000
	Close Withdrawals account.		

Summary of Merchandising Entries

Exhibit 5.12 summarizes the adjusting and closing entries of a merchandiser (using a perpetual inventory system). (**Need-To-Know 5-6** illustrates these entries.)

EXHIBIT 5.12

Summary of Key
Merchandising Entries
(using perpetual system
and gross method)

	Merchandising Transactions	Merchandising Entries	Dr.	Cr.
Purchases	Purchasing merchandise for resale.	Merchandise Inventory....................	#	
		Cash or Accounts Payable..............		#
	Paying freight costs on purchases; FOB shipping point.	Merchandise Inventory....................	#	
		Cash.........................		#
	Paying within discount period.	Accounts Payable.........................	#	
		Merchandise Inventory.................		#
		Cash.........................		#
	Paying outside discount period.	Accounts Payable.........................	#	
		Cash.........................		#
	Recording purchases returns or allowances.	Cash or Accounts Payable..................	#	
		Merchandise Inventory.................		#
Sales	Selling merchandise.	Cash or Accounts Receivable.............	#	
		Sales.......................		#
		Cost of Goods Sold	#	
		Merchandise Inventory.................		#
	Receiving payment within discount period.	Cash.........................	#	
		Sales Discounts.......................	#	
		Accounts Receivable..................		#
	Receiving payment outside discount period.	Cash.........................	#	
		Accounts Receivable..................		#
	Receiving sales returns of nondefective inventory.	Sales Returns and Allowances...............	#	
		Cash or Accounts Receivable...........		#
		Merchandise Inventory....................	#	
		Cost of Goods Sold..................		#
	Recognizing sales allowances.	Sales Returns and Allowances...............	#	
		Cash or Accounts Receivable...........		#
	Paying freight costs on sales; FOB destination.	Delivery Expense.........................	#	
		Cash		#

	Merchandising Events	Adjusting and Closing Entries		
Adjusting	Adjustment for shrinkage (occurs when recorded amount larger than physical inventory).	Cost of Goods Sold	#	
		Merchandise Inventory		#
	Period-end adjustment for expected sales discounts.*	Sales Discounts.........................	#	
		Allowance for Sales Discounts		#
	Period-end adjustment for expected returns—both revenue side and cost side.*	Sales Returns and Allowances...............	#	
		Sales Refund Payable		#
		Inventory Returns Estimated	#	
		Cost of Goods Sold		#
Closing	Closing temporary accounts with credit balances.	Sales	#	
		Income Summary		#
	Closing temporary accounts with debit balances.	Income Summary	#	
		Sales Returns and Allowances		#
		Sales Discounts		#
		Cost of Goods Sold		#
		Delivery Expense		#
		"Other Expenses".....................		#

Merchandise Inventory

Beginning inventory	
Purchases	Pur. returns
Freight-in (FOB shp pt)	Pur. allowances
	Pur. discounts
	Shrinkage
Goods avail. for sale	
Customer returns	COGS
Ending inventory	

* Period-end adjustments depend on unadjusted balances, which can reverse the debit and credit in the adjusting entries shown; the entries in gray are covered in Appendix 5C.

A merchandising company's ledger on May 31, its fiscal year-end, includes the following accounts that have normal balances (it uses the perpetual inventory system). A physical count of its May 31 year-end inventory reveals that the cost of the merchandise inventory still available is $656. (a) Prepare the entry to record any inventory shrinkage. (b) Prepare the four closing entries as of May 31.

Recording Shrinkage
and Closing Entries

P3

Merchandise inventory............	$ 756	Other operating expenses	$ 300
Z. Zee, Capital..................	2,300	Cost of goods sold..................	2,100
Z. Zee, Withdrawals	150	Depreciation expense.................	400
Sales	4,300	Salaries expense.....................	600
Sales discounts..................	50	Sales returns and allowances...........	250

Solution

May 31	Cost of Goods Sold	100	
	Merchandise Inventory...........................		100
	Adjust for shrinkage ($756 – $656).		
May 31	Sales..	4,300	
	Income Summary		4,300
	Close temporary accounts with credit balances.		
May 31	Income Summary......................................	3,800	
	Sales Discounts................................		50
	Sales Returns and Allowances.....................		250
	Cost of Goods Sold*		2,200
	Depreciation Expense		400
	Salaries Expense		600
	Other Operating Expenses........................		300
	Close temporary accounts with debit balances.		
	*$2,100 (Unadj. bal.) + $100 (Shrinkage)		
May 31	Income Summary......................................	500	
	Z. Zee, Capital................................		500
	Close Income Summary account.		
May 31	Z. Zee, Capital	150	
	Z. Zee, Withdrawals		150
	Close Withdrawals account.		

Do More: QS 5-9, QS 5-10,
E 5-10, E 5-12, P 5-4

MORE ON FINANCIAL STATEMENT FORMATS

Companies are not required to use any one presentation format for financial statements. This section describes two common income statement formats: multiple-step and single-step. The classified balance sheet of a merchandiser is also explained.

P4

Define and prepare
multiple-step and single-
step income statements.

Multiple-Step Income Statement

A **multiple-step income statement** shows detailed computations of net sales and other costs and expenses, and reports subtotals for various classes of items. Exhibit 5.13 shows a multiple-step income statement for Z-Mart. The statement has three main parts: (1) *gross profit*, determined by net sales less cost of goods sold; (2) *income from operations*, determined by gross profit less operating expenses; and (3) *net income*, determined by income from operations adjusted for nonoperating items.

Point: Z-Mart did not have any
nonoperating activities; however,
Exhibit 5.13 includes some for
illustrative purposes.

EXHIBIT 5.13

Multiple-Step Income
Statement

Gross profit
computation

Income from
operations
computation

Nonoperating
activities
computation

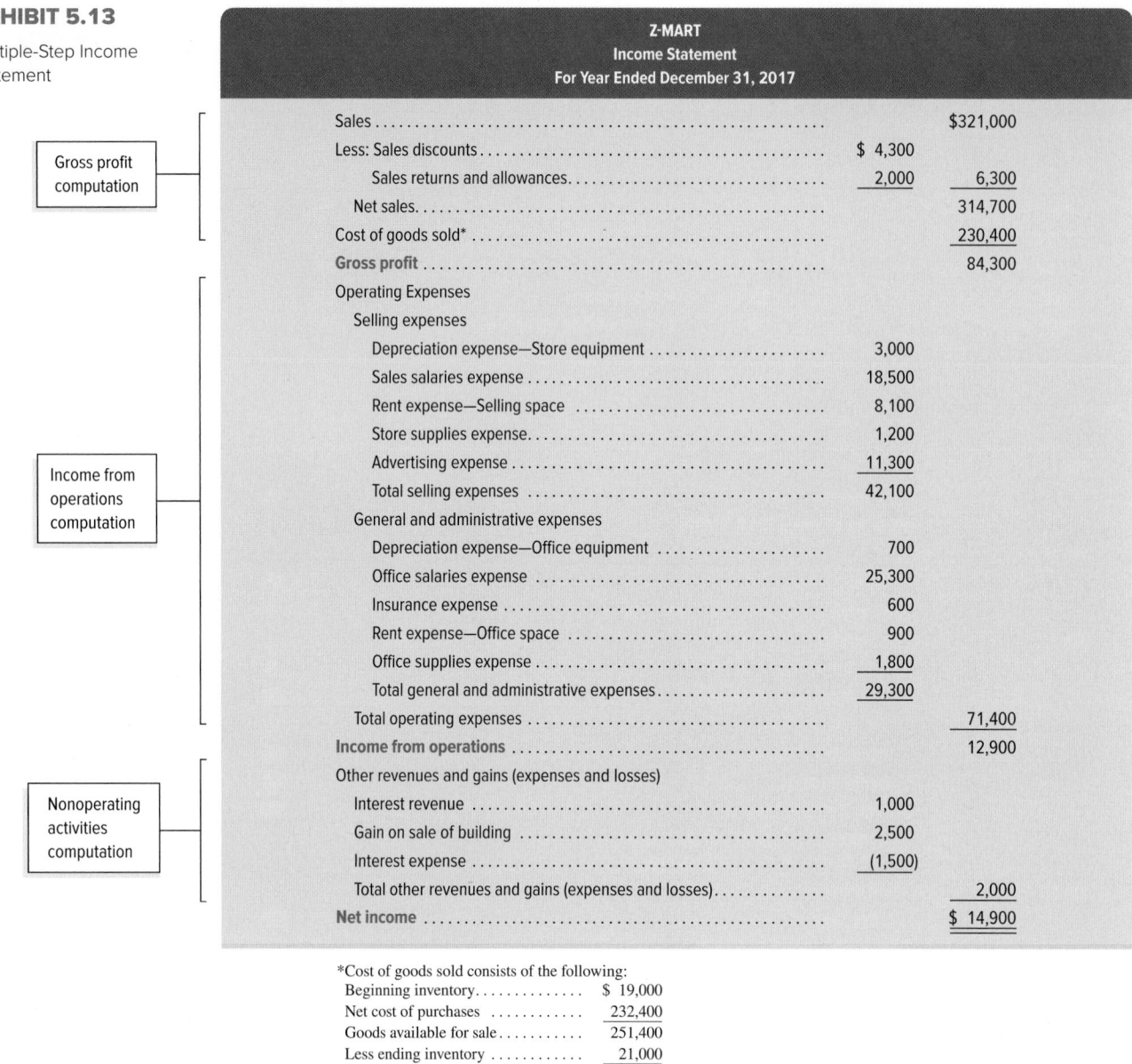

Z-MART		
Income Statement		
For Year Ended December 31, 2017		
Sales		$321,000
Less: Sales discounts	$ 4,300	
Sales returns and allowances	2,000	6,300
Net sales		314,700
Cost of goods sold*		230,400
Gross profit		84,300
Operating Expenses		
Selling expenses		
Depreciation expense—Store equipment	3,000	
Sales salaries expense	18,500	
Rent expense—Selling space	8,100	
Store supplies expense	1,200	
Advertising expense	11,300	
Total selling expenses	42,100	
General and administrative expenses		
Depreciation expense—Office equipment	700	
Office salaries expense	25,300	
Insurance expense	600	
Rent expense—Office space	900	
Office supplies expense	1,800	
Total general and administrative expenses	29,300	
Total operating expenses		71,400
Income from operations		12,900
Other revenues and gains (expenses and losses)		
Interest revenue	1,000	
Gain on sale of building	2,500	
Interest expense	(1,500)	
Total other revenues and gains (expenses and losses)		2,000
Net income		$ 14,900

*Cost of goods sold consists of the following:

Beginning inventory	$ 19,000
Net cost of purchases	232,400
Goods available for sale	251,400
Less ending inventory	21,000
Cost of goods sold	$230,400

Point: Many companies report interest expense and interest revenue in separate categories after operating income and before subtracting income tax expense. As one example, see **Samsung**'s income statement in Appendix A.

Example: Sometimes interest revenue and interest expense are reported on the income statement as *Interest, net*. To illustrate, if a company has $1,000 of interest expense and $600 of interest revenue, it might report $400 as *Interest, net*.

Operating expenses are classified into two sections. **Selling expenses** include the expenses of advertising merchandise, making sales, and delivering goods to customers. **General and administrative expenses** support a company's overall operations and include expenses related to accounting, human resource management, and financial management. Expenses are allocated between sections when they contribute to more than one. Z-Mart allocates rent expense of $9,000 from its store building between two sections: $8,100 to selling expense and $900 to general and administrative expenses.

Nonoperating activities consist of other expenses, revenues, losses, and gains that are unrelated to a company's operations. *Other revenues and gains* commonly include interest revenue, dividend revenue, rent revenue, and gains from asset disposals. *Other expenses and losses* commonly include interest expense, losses from asset disposals, and casualty losses. When a company has no reportable nonoperating activities, its income from operations is simply labeled net income.

Single-Step Income Statement

A **single-step income statement** is shown in Exhibit 5.14 for Z-Mart. It lists cost of goods sold as another expense and shows only one subtotal for total expenses. Expenses are grouped into very few, if any, categories. Many companies use formats that combine features of both single- and multiple-step statements. Provided that income statement items are shown sensibly, management can choose the format. Similar presentation options are available for the statement of owner's equity and statement of cash flows.

EXHIBIT 5.14

Single-Step Income Statement

Z-MART Income Statement For Year Ended December 31, 2017		
Revenues		
Net sales..		$314,700
Interest revenue...............................		1,000
Gain on sale of building		2,500
Total revenues		318,200
Expenses		
Cost of goods sold...........................	$230,400	
Selling expenses	42,100	
General and administrative expenses	29,300	
Interest expense	1,500	
Total expenses...............................		303,300
Net income		$ 14,900

Point: Net income is identical under the single-step and multiple-step formats.

Classified Balance Sheet

The classified balance sheet reports merchandise inventory as a current asset, usually after accounts receivable according to an asset's nearness to liquidity. Inventory is usually less liquid than accounts receivable because inventory must first be sold before cash can be received; but it is more liquid than supplies and prepaid expenses. Exhibit 5.15 shows the current asset section of Z-Mart's classified balance sheet (other sections are as shown and explained in our previous chapter; Appendix 5C explains the presence of *sales refund payable* as part of current liabilities).

Point: Appendix 5C explains *inventory returns estimated* as part of current assets, usually after accounts receivable (net of allowance for sales discounts).

EXHIBIT 5.15

Classified Balance Sheet (partial) of a Merchandiser

Z-MART Balance Sheet (partial) December 31, 2017	
Current assets	
Cash............................	$ 8,200
Accounts receivable	11,200
Merchandise inventory..............	21,000
Office supplies	550
Store supplies	250
Prepaid insurance	300
Total current assets	$41,500

Decision Insight

Shenanigans   Accurate invoices are important to both sellers and buyers. Merchandisers rely on invoices to make certain they receive all monies for products provided—no more, no less. To achieve this, controls are set up. Still, failures arise. A survey reports that 30% of employees in sales and marketing witnessed false or misleading invoices sent to customers. Another 29% observed employees violating contract terms with customers (KPMG 2013). ■

NEED-TO-KNOW 5-5

Multiple- and Single-Step
Income Statements

P4

Assume Taret's adjusted trial balance on April 30, 2017, its fiscal year-end, follows. (a) Prepare a multiple-step income statement that begins with gross sales and includes separate categories for net sales, cost of goods sold, selling expenses, and general and administrative expenses. (b) Prepare a single-step income statement that begins with net sales and includes these expense categories: cost of goods sold, selling expenses, and general and administrative expenses.

Merchandise inventory....................	$ 800	
Other (noninventory) assets..............	2,600	
Total liabilities..........................		$ 500
Taret, Capital...........................		2,100
Taret, Withdrawals	300	
Sales....................................		9,500
Sales discounts..........................	260	
Sales returns and allowances	240	
Cost of goods sold	6,500	
Sales salaries expense....................	450	
Rent expense—Selling space..............	400	
Store supplies expense	30	
Advertising expense	20	
Office salaries expense	420	
Rent expense—Office space	72	
Office supplies expense	8	
Totals..................................	$12,100	$12,100

Solution

a. Multiple-step income statement

b. Single-step income statement

TARET
Income Statement
For Year Ended April 30, 2017

Sales...		$9,500
Less: Sales discounts	$260	
Sales returns and allowances..................	240	500
Net sales		9,000
Cost of goods sold		6,500
Gross profit		2,500
Operating expenses		
Selling expenses		
Sales salaries expense.........................	450	
Rent expense—Selling space	400	
Store supplies expense	30	
Advertising expense...........................	20	
Total selling expenses		900
General and administrative expenses		
Office salaries expense	420	
Rent expense—Office space	72	
Office supplies expense	8	
Total general and administrative expenses		500
Total operating expenses		1,400
Net income		$1,100

TARET
Income Statement
For Year Ended April 30, 2017

Net sales		$ 9,000
Expenses		
Cost of goods sold	$6,500	
Selling expenses	900	
General and administrative expenses..........	500	
Total expenses		7,900
Net income		$ 1,100

Do More: QS 5-11, E 5-11,
P 5-3

SUSTAINABILITY AND ACCOUNTING

Emily Núñez Cavness and Betsy Núñez, from this chapter's opening feature, are committed to improving the lives of veterans. Their company, **Sword & Plough**, donates 10% of after-tax profits to veterans initiatives. However, the two women stress that their donation pledge would not be possible without a reliable merchandising system.

Emily and Betsy use accounting data to accurately compute their performance, including their 10% donation to veterans groups—see graphic. "I really wanted to create a product that would . . . remind [all of us] of veterans and the sacrifice that they made," explains Emily, "but also the challenges that they encounter as they transition into civilian life."

Beyond hiring and improving the lives of veterans, Emily and Betsy are committed to using military surplus materials that, explains Emily, "would otherwise be burned or buried in a landfill." The use of limited army surplus materials underscores their use of an effective inventory merchandising system.

Emily and Betsy set up their accounting system to provide accurate information on product inventory so they can plan military surplus purchases. Without this accounting system, Emily and Betsy could not achieve their goal. "What I saw wasted on a daily basis could be harnessed and turned into something beautiful," insists Emily. "Our social enterprise embodies the movement toward *Made in USA*, sustainable fashion, veteran employment, and strengthened civil-military relations."

Courtesy of Sword & Plough

We start by recycling thousands of pounds of military surplus material that would otherwise be thrown away.

...with 10% of profits going to veteran initatives; giving back to the initial users of our materials

OUR SUSTAINABLE DESIGN

Then we combine these durable fabrics with leather accents and other American-made textiles, and incorporate them into stylish designs

We source from American suppliers and work with veteran owned, operated or staffed manufacturers to create our product line.

These durable and fashionable bags and accessories are then sold...

Acid-Test and Gross Margin Ratios    **Decision Analysis**

Acid-Test Ratio

For many merchandisers, inventory makes up a large portion of current assets. Inventory must be sold and any resulting accounts receivable must be collected before cash is available. The prior chapter explained that the current ratio, defined as current assets divided by current liabilities, is useful in assessing a company's ability to pay current liabilities. Because it is sometimes unreasonable to assume that inventories are a source of payment for current liabilities, we look to other measures.

One measure of a merchandiser's ability to pay its current liabilities (referred to as its *liquidity*) is the acid-test ratio. It differs from the current ratio by excluding less liquid current assets such as inventory and prepaid expenses that take longer to be converted to cash. The **acid-test ratio,** also called *quick ratio,* is defined as *quick assets* (cash, short-term investments, and current receivables) divided by current liabilities—see Exhibit 5.16.

A1

Compute the acid-test ratio and explain its use to assess liquidity.

$$\text{Acid-test ratio} = \frac{\text{Cash and cash equivalents} + \text{Short-term investments} + \text{Current receivables}}{\text{Current liabilities}}$$

EXHIBIT 5.16

Acid-Test (Quick) Ratio

Exhibit 5.17 shows both the acid-test and current ratios of retailer **JCPenney** for fiscal years 2010 through 2015—also see the ratio graphic. JCPenney's acid-test ratio reveals an increase in 2014 and 2015 that exceeds the industry average (following a marked decline in 2012 and 2013). Further, JCPenney's current ratio shows an increase in 2014 and 2015 (again, following marked declines in 2012 and 2013). This suggests that its short-term obligations are more confidently covered with short-term assets in recent years as compared with prior years (especially versus 2013).

EXHIBIT 5.17

JCPenney's Acid-Test and Current Ratios

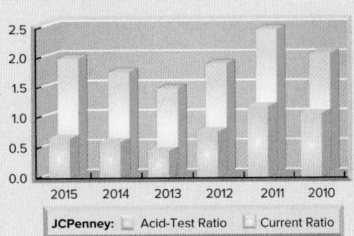

$ millions	2015	2014	2013	2012	2011	2010
Total quick assets	$1,318	$1,519	$ 987	$1,920	$2,956	$3,406
Total current assets	$4,331	$4,833	$3,683	$5,081	$6,370	$6,652
Total current liabilities	$2,241	$2,846	$2,568	$2,756	$2,647	$3,249
Acid-test ratio	**0.59**	**0.53**	**0.38**	**0.70**	**1.12**	**1.05**
Current ratio	**1.93**	**1.70**	**1.43**	**1.84**	**2.41**	**2.05**
Industry acid-test ratio	0.55	0.50	0.51	0.54	0.61	0.59
Industry current ratio	2.03	1.99	1.94	2.01	2.27	2.15

An acid-test ratio less than 1.0 means that current liabilities exceed quick assets. A rule of thumb is that the acid-test ratio should have a value near, or higher than, 1.0 to conclude that a company is unlikely to face near-term liquidity problems. A value much less than 1.0 raises liquidity concerns unless a company can generate enough cash from inventory sales or if much of its liabilities are not due until late in the next period. Similarly, a value slightly larger than 1.0 can hide a liquidity problem if payables are due shortly and receivables are not collected until late in the next period. Analysis of JCPenney shows some need for concern regarding its liquidity as its acid-test ratio is less than 1.0. However, retailers such as JCPenney pay many current liabilities from inventory sales; moreover, in all years except 2013, JCPenney's acid-test ratios exceed the industry norm (and its inventory is fairly liquid).

Point: Successful use of a just-in-time inventory system can narrow the gap between the acid-test ratio and the current ratio.

■ Decision Maker

Supplier A retailer requests to purchase supplies on credit from your company. You have no prior experience with this retailer. The retailer's current ratio is 2.1, its acid-test ratio is 0.5, and inventory makes up most of its current assets. Do you extend credit? ■ [*Answer:* A current ratio of 2.1 suggests sufficient current assets to cover current liabilities. An acid-test ratio of 0.5 suggests, however, that quick assets can cover only about one-half of current liabilities. This implies that the retailer depends on money from sales of inventory to pay current liabilities. If sales of inventory decline or profit margins decrease, the likelihood that this retailer will default on its payments increases. Your decision is probably not to extend credit. If you do extend credit, you are likely to closely monitor the retailer's financial condition. (It is better to hold unsold inventory than uncollectible receivables.)]

Gross Margin Ratio

A2
_____
Compute the gross margin ratio and explain its use to assess profitability.

The cost of goods sold makes up much of a merchandiser's expenses. Without sufficient gross profit, a merchandiser will likely fail. Users often compute the gross margin ratio to help understand this relation. It differs from the profit margin ratio in that it excludes all costs except cost of goods sold. The **gross margin ratio** (also called *gross profit ratio*) is defined as *gross margin* (net sales minus cost of goods sold) divided by net sales—see Exhibit 5.18.

EXHIBIT 5.18

Gross Margin Ratio

$$\text{Gross margin ratio} = \frac{\text{Net sales} - \text{Cost of goods sold}}{\text{Net sales}}$$

Exhibit 5.19 shows the gross margin ratio of JCPenney for fiscal years 2010 through 2015. For JCPenney, each $1 of sales in 2015 yielded about 34.8¢ in gross margin to cover all other expenses and still produce a net income. This 34.8¢ margin is up from 29.4¢ in 2014. This increase is a favorable development. Success for merchandisers such as JCPenney depends on adequate gross margin. For example, the 5.4¢ increase in the gross margin ratio, computed as 34.8¢ − 29.4¢, means that JCPenney has $662 million more in gross margin! (This is computed as net sales of $12,257 million multiplied by the 5.4% increase in gross margin.)

EXHIBIT 5.19

JCPenney's Gross Margin Ratio

$ millions	2015	2014	2013	2012	2011	2010
Gross margin....................	$ 4,261	$ 3,492	$ 4,066	$ 6,218	$ 6,960	$ 6,910
Net sales......................	$12,257	$11,859	$12,985	$17,260	$17,759	$17,556
Gross margin ratio	34.8%	29.4%	31.3%	36.0%	39.2%	39.4%

■ Decision Maker

Financial Officer Your company has a 36% gross margin ratio and a 17% net profit margin ratio. Industry averages are 44% for gross margin and 16% for net profit margin. Do these comparative results concern you? ■ [*Answer:* Your company's net profit margin is about equal to the industry average and suggests typical industry performance. However, gross margin reveals that your company is paying far more in cost of goods sold or receiving far less in sales price than competitors. Your attention must be directed to finding the problem with cost of goods sold, sales, or both. One positive note is that your company's expenses make up 19% of sales (36% − 17%). This favorably compares with competitors' expenses, which make up 28% of sales (44% − 16%).]

Use the following adjusted trial balance and additional information to complete the requirements.

NEED-TO-KNOW 5-6

COMPREHENSIVE 1

Single- and multi-step income statement, closing entries, and analysis using acid-test and gross margin

KC ANTIQUES
Adjusted Trial Balance
December 31, 2017

	Debit	Credit
Cash	$ 7,000	
Accounts receivable	13,000	
Merchandise inventory	60,000	
Store supplies	1,500	
Equipment	45,600	
Accumulated depreciation—Equipment.................		$ 16,600
Accounts payable		9,000
Salaries payable		2,000
K. Carter, Capital		79,000
K. Carter, Withdrawals	10,000	
Sales..		343,250
Sales discounts	5,000	
Sales returns and allowances.......................	6,000	
Cost of goods sold	159,900	
Depreciation expense—Store equipment	4,100	
Depreciation expense—Office equipment..............	1,600	
Sales salaries expense	30,000	
Office salaries expense	34,000	
Insurance expense	11,000	
Rent expense (70% is store, 30% is office)	24,000	
Store supplies expense	5,750	
Advertising expense	31,400	
Totals	$449,850	$449,850

KC Antiques's *supplementary records* for 2017 reveal the following itemized costs for merchandising activities:

Invoice cost of merchandise purchases	$150,000
Purchases discounts received	2,500
Purchases returns and allowances	2,700
Cost of transportation-in	5,000

Required

1. Use the supplementary records to compute the total cost of merchandise purchases for 2017.
2. Prepare a 2017 multiple-step income statement. (Inventory at December 31, 2016, is $70,100.)
3. Prepare a single-step income statement for 2017.
4. Prepare closing entries for KC Antiques at December 31, 2017.
5. Compute the acid-test ratio and the gross margin ratio. Explain the meaning of each ratio and interpret them for KC Antiques.

PLANNING THE SOLUTION

- Compute the total cost of merchandise purchases for 2017.
- To prepare the multiple-step statement, first compute net sales. Then, to compute cost of goods sold, add the net cost of merchandise purchases for the year to beginning inventory and subtract the cost of ending inventory. Subtract cost of goods sold from net sales to get gross profit. Then classify expenses as selling expenses or general and administrative expenses.
- To prepare the single-step income statement, begin with net sales. Then list and subtract the expenses.
- The first closing entry debits all temporary accounts with credit balances and opens the Income Summary account. The second closing entry credits all temporary accounts with debit balances. The

third entry closes the Income Summary account to the capital account, and the fourth entry closes the withdrawals account to the capital account.

● Identify the quick assets on the adjusted trial balance. Compute the acid-test ratio by dividing quick assets by current liabilities. Compute the gross margin ratio by dividing gross profit by net sales.

SOLUTION

1.

Invoice cost of merchandise purchases	$150,000
Less: Purchases discounts received	2,500
Purchases returns and allowances	2,700
Add: Cost of transportation-in	5,000
Total cost of merchandise purchases	$149,800

2. Multiple-step income statement

KC ANTIQUES
Income Statement
For Year Ended December 31, 2017

Sales		$343,250
Less: Sales discounts	$ 5,000	
Sales returns and allowances	6,000	11,000
Net sales..		332,250
Cost of goods sold*		159,900
Gross profit		172,350
Expenses		
Selling expenses		
Depreciation expense—Store equipment	4,100	
Sales salaries expense	30,000	
Rent expense—Selling space	16,800	
Store supplies expense	5,750	
Advertising expense	31,400	
Total selling expenses............................	88,050	
General and administrative expenses		
Depreciation expense—Office equipment..............	1,600	
Office salaries expense............................	34,000	
Insurance expense	11,000	
Rent expense—Office space........................	7,200	
Total general and administrative expenses............	53,800	
Total operating expenses		141,850
Net income		$ 30,500

> Tax expense for a corporation appears immediately before Net income in its own category.

* Cost of goods sold can also be directly computed (applying concepts from Exhibit 5.4):

Merchandise inventory, December 31, 2016	$ 70,100
Total cost of merchandise purchases (from part 1)	149,800
Goods available for sale	219,900
Merchandise inventory, December 31, 2017	60,000
Cost of goods sold	$159,900

3. Single-step income statement

KC ANTIQUES
Income Statement
For Year Ended December 31, 2017

Net sales....................................		$332,250
Expenses		
Cost of goods sold..........................	$159,900	
Selling expenses	88,050	
General and administrative expenses	53,800	
Total expenses		301,750
Net income		$ 30,500

4.

Dec. 31	Sales	343,250	
	Income Summary		343,250
	Close credit balances in temporary accounts.		
Dec. 31	Income Summary	312,750	
	Sales Discounts		5,000
	Sales Returns and Allowances		6,000
	Cost of Goods Sold		159,900
	Depreciation Expense—Store Equipment		4,100
	Depreciation Expense—Office Equipment		1,600
	Sales Salaries Expense		30,000
	Office Salaries Expense		34,000
	Insurance Expense		11,000
	Rent Expense		24,000
	Store Supplies Expense		5,750
	Advertising Expense		31,400
	Close debit balances in temporary accounts.		
Dec. 31	Income Summary	30,500	
	K. Carter, Capital		30,500
	Close Income Summary account.		
Dec. 31	K. Carter, Capital	10,000	
	K. Carter, Withdrawals		10,000
	Close Withdrawals account.		

5. Acid-test ratio = (Cash and equivalents + Short-term investments + Current receivables)/
Current liabilities

= (Cash + Accounts receivable)/(Accounts payable + Salaries payable)

= ($7,000 + $13,000)/($9,000 + $2,000) = $20,000/$11,000 = 1.82

Gross margin ratio = Gross profit/Net sales = $172,350/$332,250 = 0.52 (or 52%)

KC Antiques has a healthy acid-test ratio of 1.82. This means it has $1.82 in liquid assets to satisfy each $1.00 in current liabilities. The gross margin of 0.52 shows that KC Antiques spends 48¢ ($1.00 − $0.52) of every dollar of net sales on the costs of acquiring the merchandise it sells. This leaves 52¢ of every dollar of net sales to cover other expenses incurred in the business and to provide a net profit.

Prepare journal entries to record the following merchandising transactions for both the seller (BMX) and buyer (Sanuk).

NEED-TO-KNOW 5-7

COMPREHENSIVE 2

Recording merchandising transactions—both seller and buyer

May 4 BMX sold $1,500 of merchandise on account to Sanuk, terms FOB shipping point, n/45, invoice dated May 4. The cost of the merchandise was $900. This sale was "as is" with no returns.

6 Sanuk paid transportation charges of $30 on the May 4 purchase from BMX.

8 BMX sold $1,000 of merchandise on account to Sanuk, terms FOB destination, n/15, invoice dated May 8. The cost of the merchandise was $700. This sale permitted returns for 30 days.

10 BMX paid transportation costs of $50 for delivery of merchandise sold to Sanuk on May 8.

16 BMX issued Sanuk a $200 credit memorandum for merchandise returned. The merchandise was purchased by Sanuk on account on May 8. The cost of the merchandise returned was $140.

18 BMX received payment from Sanuk for purchase of May 8.

21 BMX sold $2,400 of merchandise on account to Sanuk, terms FOB shipping point, 2/10, n/EOM. The cost of the merchandise was $1,440. This sale permitted returns for 90 days.

31 BMX received payment from Sanuk for purchase of May 21, less discount.

Solution

	BMX (Seller)				Sanuk (Buyer)		
May 4	Accounts Receivable—Sanuk	1,500			Merchandise Inventory	1,500	
	Sales		1,500		Accounts Payable—BMX		1,500
	Cost of Goods Sold	900					
	Merchandise Inventory		900				
6	No entry.				Merchandise Inventory	30	
					Cash		30
8	Accounts Receivable—Sanuk	1,000			Merchandise Inventory	1,000	
	Sales		1,000		Accounts Payable—BMX		1,000
	Cost of Goods Sold	700					
	Merchandise Inventory		700				
10	Delivery Expense	50			No entry.		
	Cash		50				
16	Sales Returns & Allowances	200			Accounts Payable—BMX	200	
	Accounts Receivable—Sanuk		200		Merchandise Inventory		200
	Merchandise Inventory	140					
	Cost of Goods Sold		140				
18	Cash	800			Accounts Payable—BMX	800	
	Accounts Receivable—Sanuk		800		Cash		800
21	Accounts Receivable—Sanuk.	2,400			Merchandise Inventory	2,400	
	Sales		2,400		Accounts Payable—BMX		2,400
	Cost of Goods Sold	1,440					
	Merchandise Inventory		1,440				
31	Cash	2,352			Accounts Payable—BMX	2,400	
	Sales Discounts	48			Merchandise Inventory		48
	Accounts Receivable—Sanuk		2,400		Cash		2,352

APPENDIX

5A

Accounting under the Periodic System

A periodic inventory system requires updating the inventory account only at the *end of a period* to reflect the cost of both the goods available and the goods sold. Thus, during the period, the Merchandise Inventory balance remains unchanged. During the period, the cost of merchandise is recorded in a temporary *Purchases* account. When a company sells merchandise, it records revenue **but not the cost of the goods sold.** At the end of the period when a company prepares financial statements, it takes a *physical count of inventory* by counting the quantities and costs of merchandise available. The cost of goods sold is then computed by subtracting the ending inventory amount from the cost of merchandise available for sale.

P5

Record and compare merchandising transactions using both periodic and perpetual inventory systems.

Recording Merchandise Purchases   Under a periodic system, the purchases, purchases returns and allowances, purchases discounts, and transportation-in transactions are recorded in separate temporary accounts. At period-end, each of these temporary accounts is closed, which updates the Merchandise Inventory account. To illustrate, journal entries under the periodic inventory system are shown for the most common transactions (codes *a* through *d* link these transactions to those in the chapter, and we drop explanations for simplicity). For comparison, perpetual system journal entries are shown to the right of each periodic entry, where differences are highlighted.

Credit Purchases with Cash Discounts   The periodic system uses a temporary **Purchases** account that accumulates the cost of all purchase transactions during each period. The Purchases account has a normal debit balance, as it increases the cost of merchandise available for sale. Z-Mart's November 2 entry to record the purchase of merchandise for $500 on credit with terms of 2/10, n/30 is

(a)

Periodic		
Purchases	500	
Accounts Payable		500

Perpetual		
Merchandise Inventory	500	
Accounts Payable		500

Payment of Purchases   The periodic system uses a temporary **Purchases Discounts** account that accumulates discounts taken on purchase transactions during the period. If payment for transaction *a* above is made *within the discount period,* the entry is

(b1)

Periodic		
Accounts Payable	500	
Purchases Discounts*		10
Cash		490
*$500 × 2%		

Perpetual		
Accounts Payable	500	
Merchandise Inventory*		10
Cash		490
*$500 × 2%		

If payment for transaction *a* above is made *after the discount period expires,* the entry is

(b2)

Periodic		
Accounts Payable	500	
Cash		500

Perpetual		
Accounts Payable	500	
Cash		500

Purchases Allowances   The buyer and seller agree to a $30 purchases allowance for defective goods (assume allowance terms are $30 whether paid within the discount period or not). In the periodic system, the temporary **Purchases Returns and Allowances** account accumulates the cost of all returns and allowances during a period. The buyer records the $30 allowance as

(c1)

Periodic		
Accounts Payable	30	
Purchases Returns and		
Allowances		30

Perpetual		
Accounts Payable	30	
Merchandise Inventory		30

Point: Purchases Discounts <u>and</u> Purchases Returns and Allowances are contra purchases accounts *and* have normal credit balances, as they both decrease the cost of merchandise available for sale.

Purchases Returns   The buyer returns $50 of merchandise within the discount period. The entry is

(c2)

Periodic		
Accounts Payable	50	
Purchases Returns and		
Allowances		50

Perpetual		
Accounts Payable	50	
Merchandise Inventory		50

Transportation-In   The buyer paid a $75 freight charge to transport goods with terms FOB destination. In the periodic system, this cost is charged to a temporary **Transportation-In** account, which has a normal debit balance as it increases the cost of merchandise available for sale.

(d)

Periodic		
Transportation-In	75	
Cash		75

Perpetual		
Merchandise Inventory	75	
Cash		75

Recording Merchandise Sales   Journal entries under the periodic system are shown for the most common transactions (codes *e* through *h* link these transactions to those in the chapter). Perpetual system entries are shown to the right of each periodic entry, where differences are highlighted.

Credit Sales and Receipt of Payments   Both the periodic and perpetual systems record sales entries similarly, using the gross method. The same holds for entries related to payment of receivables from sales both within and after the discount period. However, under the periodic system, the cost of goods sold is *not* recorded at the time of each sale (whereas it is under the perpetual system)—we show later in this appendix how to compute cost of goods sold at period-end under the periodic system. The entries to record $1,000 in credit sales (costing $300) is

Periodic		
Accounts Receivable.	1,000	
Sales		1,000
No cost-side entry		

Perpetual		
Accounts Receivable.	1,000	
Sales		1,000
Cost of Goods Sold	300	
Merchandise Inventory		300

Returns Received by Seller   A customer returned merchandise for a cash refund. The goods sell for $15 and cost $9. (*Recall:* The periodic system records only the revenue effect, not the cost effect, for sales transactions.) The entries for the seller to restore the returned items to inventory are

	Periodic				*Perpetual*		
(e1)	Sales Returns and Allowances....	15			Sales Returns and Allowances......	15	
	Cash		15		Cash		15
(e2)					Merchandise Inventory	9	
	No entry				Cost of Goods Sold		9

Allowances Granted by Seller   A customer received an allowance in transaction *f* of $10 cash; only the revenue side is impacted as no inventory was returned and cost stays the same. The entry is identical under the periodic and perpetual systems. The seller records this allowance as

	Periodic				*Perpetual*		
(f)	Sales Returns and Allowances....	10			Sales Returns and Allowances......	10	
	Cash		10		Cash		10

EXHIBIT 5A.1

Comparison of Adjusting and Closing Entries—Periodic and Perpetual

Recording Adjusting Entries

Shrinkage—Adjusting Entry   Adjusting (and closing) entries for the two systems are shown in Exhibit 5A.1. The $250 shrinkage is only recorded under the perpetual system—see entry *z* in Exhibit 5A.1.

PERIODIC				PERPETUAL		
Adjusting Entries				**Adjusting Entries**		
(z) None			(z)	Cost of Goods Sold	250	
				Merchandise Inventory		250
(g) Sales Discounts...........................	50		(g)	Sales Discounts.........................	50	
Allowance for Sales Discounts............		50		Allowance for Sales Discounts		50
(h1) Sales Returns and Allowances	900		(h1)	Sales Returns and Allowances...........	900	
Sales Refund Payable..................		900		Sales Refund Payable		900
(h2) Inventory Returns Estimated.................	300		(h2)	Inventory Returns Estimated	300	
Purchases........................		300		Cost of Goods Sold		300

Entries in gray are covered in Appendix 5C.   Entries in gray are covered in Appendix 5C.

PERIODIC			PERPETUAL		
Closing Entries			**Closing Entries**		
(1) Sales	321,000		(1) Sales	321,000	
Merchandise Inventory (ending)	21,000				
Purchases Discounts	4,200				
Purchases Returns and Allowances	1,500				
Income Summary		347,700	Income Summary		321,000
(2) Income Summary.........................	334,800		(2) Income Summary	308,100	
Sales Discounts		4,300	Sales Discounts		4,300
Sales Returns and Allowances		2,000	Sales Returns and Allowances		2,000
Merchandise Inventory (beginning)		19,000			
Purchases		235,800	Cost of Goods Sold		230,400
Transportation-In		2,300			
Depreciation Expense		3,700	Depreciation Expense		3,700
Salaries Expense		43,800	Salaries Expense		43,800
Insurance Expense		600	Insurance Expense		600
Rent Expense		9,000	Rent Expense		9,000
Supplies Expense		3,000	Supplies Expense		3,000
Advertising Expense		11,300	Advertising Expense		11,300
(3) Income Summary	12,900		(3) Income Summary	12,900	
K. Marty, Capital		12,900	K. Marty, Capital....................		12,900
(4) K. Marty, Capital	4,000		(4) K. Marty, Capital	4,000	
K. Marty, Withdrawals..................		4,000	K. Marty, Withdrawals................		4,000

Shrinkage in cost of goods is unknown using a periodic system because inventory is not continually updated and therefore cannot be compared to the physical count.

Expected Sales Discounts—Adjusting Entry   Both the periodic and perpetual methods make a period-end adjusting entry under the gross method to estimate the $50 sales discounts arising from current period's sales that are likely to be taken in future periods. Z-Mart made the period-end adjusting entry g in Exhibit 5A.1 for expected sales discounts.

Expected Returns and Allowances—Adjusting Entry   Both the periodic and perpetual inventory systems estimate returns and allowances arising from current-period sales that will occur in future periods. The adjusting entry approach for both systems is identical for the sales side, but slightly different for the cost side. The period-end entries h1 and h2 in Exhibit 5A.1 are used to record the updates to expected sales refunds of $900 and the cost side of $300. Under both systems, the seller sets up a **Sales Refund Payable** account, which is a current liability reflecting the amount expected to be refunded to customers, and an **Inventory Returns Estimated** account, which is a current asset reflecting the inventory estimated to be returned.

Recording Closing Entries   The periodic and perpetual inventory systems have slight differences in closing entries. The period-end Merchandise Inventory balance (unadjusted) is $19,000 under the periodic system. Since the periodic system does not update the Merchandise Inventory balance during the period, the $19,000 amount is the beginning inventory. A physical count of inventory taken at the end of the period reveals $21,000 of merchandise available. The adjusting and closing entries for the two systems are shown in Exhibit 5A.1. Recording the periodic inventory balance is a two-step process. The ending inventory balance of $21,000 (which includes shrinkage) is entered by debiting the inventory account in the first closing entry. The beginning inventory balance of $19,000 is deleted by crediting the inventory account in the second closing entry.[2]

By updating Merchandise Inventory and closing Purchases, Purchases Discounts, Purchases Returns and Allowances, and Transportation-In, the periodic system transfers the cost of sales amount to Income Summary. Review the periodic side of Exhibit 5A.1 and see that the **red boldface** items affect Income Summary as follows.

Credit to Income Summary in the first closing entry includes amounts from:	
Merchandise inventory (ending)	$ 21,000
Purchases discounts	4,200
Purchases returns and allowances	1,500
Debit to Income Summary in the second closing entry includes amounts from:	
Merchandise inventory (beginning)	(19,000)
Purchases	(235,800)
Transportation-in	(2,300)
Net effect on Income Summary (net debit = cost of goods sold)	**$(230,400)**

This $230,400 effect on Income Summary is the cost of goods sold amount (which is equal to cost of goods sold reported in a perpetual inventory system). The periodic system transfers cost of goods sold to the Income Summary account but without using a Cost of Goods Sold account. Also, the periodic system does not separately measure shrinkage. Instead, it computes cost of goods available for sale, subtracts the cost of ending inventory, and defines the difference as cost of goods sold, which includes shrinkage.

Preparing Financial Statements   The financial statements of a merchandiser using the periodic system are similar to those for a service company described in prior chapters. The income statement mainly differs by the inclusion of *cost of goods sold* and *gross profit*—of course, net sales is affected by discounts, returns, and allowances. The cost of goods sold section under the periodic system follows.

---

[2]This approach is called the *closing entry method.* An alternative approach, referred to as the *adjusting entry method,* would not make any entries to Merchandise Inventory in the closing entries of Exhibit 5A.1, but instead would make two adjusting entries. Using Z-Mart data, the two adjusting entries would be: (1) Dr. Income Summary and Cr. Merchandise Inventory for $19,000 each and (2) Dr. Merchandise Inventory and Cr. Income Summary for $21,000 each. The first entry removes the beginning balance of Merchandise Inventory and the second entry records the actual ending balance.

Calculation of Cost of Goods Sold
For Year Ended December 31, 2017

Beginning inventory	$ 19,000
Net cost of purchases	232,400
Cost of goods available for sale	251,400
Less ending inventory	21,000
Cost of goods sold	$230,400

EXHIBIT 5A.2

Work Sheet for Merchandiser (using a periodic system)

The balance sheet mainly differs by the inclusion of *merchandise inventory,* inventory returns estimated, allowance for sales discounts, and sales refund payable. The work sheet in Exhibit 5A.2 can be used to help prepare these statements. The only differences under the periodic system from the work sheet illustrated in Appendix 5B using the perpetual system are highlighted as follows in blue boldface.

	A	B	C	D	E	F	G	H	I	J	K	L
			Unadjusted Trial Balance		Adjustments		Adjusted Trial Balance		Income Statement		Balance Sheet and Statement of Equity	
1												
2	No.	Account	Dr.	Cr.	Dr.	Cr.	Dr.	Cr.	Dr.	Cr.	Dr.	Cr.
3	101	Cash	8,200				8,200				8,200	
4	106	Accounts receivable	11,250				11,250				11,250	
5	108	Allowance for sales discounts		0		(e) 50		50				50
6	119	Merchandise inventory	19,000				19,000		19,000	21,000	21,000	
7	121	Inventory returns estimated	200		(h2) 300		500				500	
8	126	Supplies	3,800			(2) 3,000	800				800	
9	128	Prepaid insurance	900			(1) 600	300				300	
10	167	Equipment	34,200				34,200				34,200	
11	168	Accumulated depr.—Equip.		3,700		(3) 3,700		7,400				7,400
12	201	Accounts payable		16,000				16,000				16,000
13	209	Salaries payable				(4) 800		800				800
14	227	Sales refund payable		300		(h1) 900		1,200				1,200
15	301	K. Marty, Capital		41,900				41,900				41,900
16	302	K. Marty, Withdrawals	4,000				4,000				4,000	
17	413	Sales		321,000				321,000		321,000		
18	414	Sales returns and allowances	1,100		(h1) 900		2,000		2,000			
19	415	Sales discounts	4,250		(e) 50		4,300		4,300			
20	505	Purchases	236,100			(h2) 300	235,800		235,800			
21	506	Purchases returns & allowances		1,500				1,500		1,500		
22	507	Purchases discounts		4,200				4,200		4,200		
23	508	Transportation-in	2,300				2,300		2,300			
24	612	Depreciation expense—Equip.			(3) 3,700		3,700		3,700			
25	622	Salaries expense	43,000		(4) 800		43,800		43,800			
26	637	Insurance expense			(1) 600		600		600			
27	640	Rent expense	9,000				9,000		9,000			
28	652	Supplies expense			(2) 3,000		3,000		3,000			
29	655	Advertising expense	11,300				11,300		11,300			
30		Totals	388,600	388,600	9,350	9,350	394,050	394,050	334,800	347,700	80,250	67,350
31		Net income							12,900			12,900
32		Totals							347,700	347,700	80,250	80,250
33												

APPENDIX

5B   Work Sheet—Perpetual System

Exhibit 5B.1 shows the work sheet for preparing financial statements of a merchandiser. It differs slightly from the work sheet layout in the prior chapter—the differences are in red boldface. The adjustments in the work sheet reflect the following: (*1*) expiration of $600 of prepaid insurance, (*2*) use of $3,000 of supplies, (*3*) depreciation of $3,700 for equipment, (*4*) accrual of $800 of unpaid salaries, and (*5*) inventory shrinkage of $250. Once the adjusted amounts are extended into the financial statement columns, the information is used to develop financial statements.

EXHIBIT 5B.1

Work Sheet for Merchandiser (using a perpetual system)

	A	B	C	D	E	F	G	H	I	J	K	L
1	No.	Account	Unadjusted Trial Balance		Adjustments		Adjusted Trial Balance		Income Statement		Balance Sheet and Statement of Equity	
2			Dr.	Cr.	Dr.	Cr.	Dr.	Cr.	Dr.	Cr.	Dr.	Cr.
3	101	Cash	8,200				8,200				8,200	
4	106	Accounts receivable	11,250				11,250				11,250	
5	108	Allowance for sales discounts		0		(e) 50		50				50
6	119	Merchandise inventory	21,250			(5) 250	21,000				21,000	
7	121	Inventory returns estimated	200		(h2) 300		500				500	
8	126	Supplies	3,800			(2) 3,000	800				800	
9	128	Prepaid insurance	900			(1) 600	300				300	
10	167	Equipment	34,200				34,200				34,200	
11	168	Accumulated depr.—Equip.		3,700		(3) 3,700		7,400				7,400
12	201	Accounts payable		16,000				16,000				16,000
13	209	Salaries payable				(4) 800		800				800
14	227	Sales refund payable		300		(h1) 900		1,200				1,200
15	301	K. Marty, Capital		41,900				41,900				41,900
16	302	K. Marty, Withdrawals	4,000				4,000				4,000	
17	413	Sales		321,000				321,000		321,000		
18	414	Sales returns and allowances	1,100		(h1) 900		2,000		2,000			
19	415	Sales discounts	4,250		(e) 50		4,300		4,300			
20	502	Cost of goods sold	230,450		(5) 250	(h2) 300	230,400		230,400			
21	612	Depreciation expense—Equip.			(3) 3,700		3,700		3,700			
22	622	Salaries expense	43,000		(4) 800		43,800		43,800			
23	637	Insurance expense			(1) 600		600		600			
24	640	Rent expense	9,000				9,000		9,000			
25	652	Supplies expense			(2) 3,000		3,000		3,000			
26	655	Advertising expense	11,300				11,300		11,300			
27		Totals	382,900	382,900	9,600	9,600	388,350	388,350	308,100	321,000	80,250	67,350
28		Net income							12,900			12,900
29		Totals							321,000	321,000	80,250	80,250
30												

APPENDIX

Adjusting Entries under New Revenue Recognition Rules

5C

Expected Sales Discounts—Adjusting Entry   Sales are to be reported at the net amount expected, which follows new revenue recognition rules. This means that a period-end adjusting entry is commonly made to estimate sales discounts for current-period's sales that are expected to be taken in future periods. To illustrate, assume Z-Mart has the following unadjusted balances: Accounts Receivable, $11,250; and Allowance for Sales Discounts, $0. Of the $11,250 of receivables, $2,500 of them are within the 2% discount period, and we expect buyers to take $50 in future-period discounts (computed as $2,500 × 2%) arising from this period's sales. The adjusting entry for the $50 update to the allowance for sales discounts is

P6

Prepare adjustments for discounts, returns, and allowances per revenue recognition rules.

(g) Dec. 31	Sales Discounts	50	
	Allowance for Sales Discounts.		50
	Adjustment for future discounts.		

Assets = Liabilities + Equity
−50   −50

Allow. for Sales Discounts

Beg. bal.	0
Req. adj.	50
Est. bal.	50

Allowance for Sales Discounts is a **contra asset account** and is reported on the balance sheet as a reduction to the Accounts Receivable asset account. The Allowance for Sales Discounts account has a *normal credit balance* because it reduces Accounts Receivable, which has a normal debit balance.

This adjusting entry results in both accounts receivable and sales being reported at their net expected amounts:[3]

Balance Sheet—partial	
Accounts receivable......................	$11,250
Less allowance for sales discounts........	50
Accounts receivable, net................	$11,200

Income Statement—partial	
Sales	$321,000
Less sales discounts..............	4,300
Net sales........................	$316,700

Expected Returns and Allowances—Adjusting Entries   To avoid overstatement of sales and cost of sales, sellers estimate sales returns and allowances in the period of the sale. Estimating returns and allowances requires companies to maintain the following two balance sheet accounts that are set up with adjusting entries:

Current asset: Inventory Returns Estimated
Current liability: Sales Refund Payable

Two adjusting entries are made: one for the revenue side *and* one for the cost side.

Revenue Side for Expected R&A   When returns and allowances are expected, a seller sets up a **Sales Refund Payable** account, which is **a current liability reflecting the amount expected to be refunded to customers.** To illustrate, assume that on December 31 the company estimates future sales refunds to be $1,200. Assume also that the *unadjusted balance* in Sales Refund Payable is a $300 credit. The adjusting entry for the $900 update to Sales Refund Payable is

Assets = Liabilities + Equity
+900   −900

(h1) Dec. 31	Sales Returns and Allowances	900	
	Sales Refund Payable		900
	*Expected refund of sales.**		

Sales Refund Payable

	Beg. bal.	300
	Req. adj.	900
	Est. bal.	1,200

*This entry uses our three-step adjusting process:
Step 1: Current bal. is $300 credit for Sales Refund Payable.
Step 2: Current bal. should be $1,200 credit for Sales Refund Payable.
Step 3: Record entry to get from step 1 to step 2.

The Sales Refund Payable account is updated only during the adjusting entry process. Its balance remains unchanged during the period when actual returns and allowances are recorded.

Cost Side for Expected R&A   On the cost side, the expected returns and allowances implies that some inventory is expected to be returned, which means that cost of goods sold recorded at the time of sale is overstated due to expected returns. A seller sets up an **Inventory Returns Estimated** account, which is **a current asset reflecting the inventory estimated to be returned.** Extending the example above, assume that the company estimates future inventory returns to be $500 (which is the cost side of the $1,200 expected returns and allowances above). Assume also that the (beginning) *unadjusted balance*

---

[3]*Next Period Adjustment* The Allowance for Sales Discounts balance remains unchanged during a period except for the period-end adjusting entry. At next period-end, assume that Z-Mart computes an $80 balance for the Allowance for Sales Discounts. Using our three-step adjusting process we get:

Step 1: Current bal. is $50 credit in Allowance for Sales Discounts.

Step 2: Current bal. should be $80 credit in Allowance for Sales Discounts.

Step 3: Record entry to get from step 1 to step 2.

Sales Discounts	30	
Allowance for Sales Discounts		30

in Inventory Returns Estimated is a $200 debit. The adjusting entry for the $300 update to expected returns is

(h2) Dec. 31	Inventory Returns Estimated	300	
	Cost of Goods Sold............................		300
	*Expected return of inventory.**		

Assets = Liabilities + Equity
+300   +300

Inventory Returns Est.		
Beg. bal.	200	
Req. adj.	300	
Est. bal.	500	

*This entry uses our three-step adjusting process:
<u>Step 1:</u> Current bal. <u>is</u> $200 debit for Inventory Returns Estimated.
<u>Step 2:</u> Current bal. <u>should be</u> $500 debit for Inventory Returns Estimated.
<u>Step 3:</u> Record entry to get from step 1 to step 2.

The Inventory Returns Estimated account is updated only during the adjusting entry process. Its balance remains unchanged during the period when actual returns and allowances are recorded.

Use of expected amounts better recognizes both sales and costs in their proper periods, including the amount of sales and inventory actually sold (net of expected returns and allowances). If estimates of returns and allowances prove too high or too low, we adjust future estimates accordingly. (Advanced courses cover variations in revenue and expense recognition.)

Decision Insight

Call to Account   It is important we know these accounts:

- **Allowance for Sales Discounts** is a contra asset account and is reported in the balance sheet as a reduction to the Accounts Receivable asset account.
- **Sales Refund Payable** is a current liability account, meaning it is reported in the balance sheet.
- **Inventory Returns Estimated** is a current asset account (often as a subcategory of Inventory), meaning it is reported in the balance sheet—this asset is subject to impairment, which is explained in advanced courses. ■

At the current year-end, a company shows the following unadjusted balances for selected accounts:

NEED-TO-KNOW 5-8

Allowance for Sales Discounts..............	$ 75 credit	Sales Discounts......................	$1,850 debit	
Sales Refund Payable....................	800 credit	Sales Returns and Allowances	4,825 debit	
Inventory Returns Estimated	450 debit	Cost of Goods Sold	9,875 debit	

Estimating Discounts, Returns, and Allowances

P6

a. After an analysis of future sales discounts, the company estimates that the Allowance for Sales Discounts account should have a $275 credit balance. Prepare the current year-end adjusting journal entry for future sales discounts.

b. After an analysis of future sales returns and allowances, the company estimates that the Sales Refund Payable account should have an $870 credit balance (revenue side).

c. After an analysis of future inventory returns, the company estimates that the Inventory Returns Estimated account should have a $500 debit balance (cost side).

Solution

Dec. 31	Sales Discounts	200	
	Allowance for Sales Discounts....................		200
	Adjustment for future discounts. $275 Cr. – $75 Cr.		
Dec. 31	Sales Returns and Allowances	70	
	Sales Refund Payable............................		70
	Adjustment for future sales refund. $870 Cr. – $800 Cr.		
Dec. 31	Inventory Returns Estimated..........................	50	
	Cost of Goods Sold.............................		50
	Adjustment for future inventory returns. $500 Dr. – $450 Dr.		

Do More: QS 5-19, QS 5-20, E 5-19, E 5-20, E 5-21

5D   Accounting under the Net Method

P7

Record and compare merchandising transactions using the gross method and net method.

This chapter described entries to record the receipt and payment of an invoice for merchandise with and without cash discount terms. Those entries were prepared under the **gross method,** which initially records an invoice at its *gross* amount. The **net method** is another means of recording invoices, which initially records the invoice at its *net* amount (net of any cash discount). This appendix records merchandising transactions using the net method, where key differences with the gross method are highlighted.

When invoices are recorded at *net* amounts, any cash discounts are deducted from the balance of the Merchandise Inventory account when initially recorded. **This assumes that all cash discounts will be taken.** If any discounts are later lost, they are recorded in a **Discounts Lost** expense account reported on the income statement.

Perpetual Inventory System

PURCHASES—Perpetual   A company purchases merchandise on November 2 at a $500 invoice price ($490 net) with terms of 2/10, n/30. Its November 2 entries under the gross and net methods are

Gross Method—Perpetual			Net Method—Perpetual		
Merchandise Inventory........	500		Merchandise Inventory...........	490	
Accounts Payable........		500	Accounts Payable...........		490

If the invoice is paid on (or before) November 12 within the discount period, it records

Gross Method—Perpetual			Net Method—Perpetual		
Accounts Payable	500		Accounts Payable	490	
Merchandise Inventory ...		10			
Cash		490	Cash		490

If, instead, the invoice is *not* paid within the discount period, but is later paid on December 2 (the n/30 due date), *after the discount period,* it records

Gross Method—Perpetual			Net Method—Perpetual		
Accounts Payable	500		Accounts Payable	490	
			Discounts Lost*..................	10	
Cash		500	Cash		500

*For simplicity, we record Discounts Lost on the *payment date* when that date is after the discount period.

SALES—Perpetual   To illustrate, a company sells merchandise on November 2 at a $500 invoice price ($490 net) with terms of 2/10, n/30. The goods cost $200. Its November 2 entries under the gross and net methods are

Gross Method—Perpetual			Net Method—Perpetual		
Accounts Receivable..........	500		Accounts Receivable..............	490	
Sales.................		500	Sales.....................		490

Gross Method—Perpetual			Net Method—Perpetual		
Cost of Goods Sold	200		Cost of Goods Sold...............	200	
Merchandise Inventory ...		200	Merchandise Inventory		200

If cash is received on (or before) November 12 within the discount period, it records

Gross Method—Perpetual		
Cash......................	490	
Sales Discounts.............	10	
Accounts Receivable.....		500

Net Method—Perpetual		
Cash.........................	490	
Accounts Receivable........		490

If, instead, cash is *not* received within the discount period, but it is later received on December 2 (the n/30 due date), *after the discount period*, it records

Gross Method—Perpetual*		
Cash......................	500	
Accounts Receivable.....		500

Net Method—Perpetual*		
Cash.........................	500	
Interest Revenue............		10
Accounts Receivable........		490

*Two points: (1) An adjusting entry for expected sales discounts is common with the gross method (see Appendix 5C); also, an adjusting entry *may* be necessary with the net method if the seller expects that some future sales discounts will *not* be taken (this is explained in advanced courses). (2) Adjusting entries for sales returns and allowances are identical under the gross and net methods.

Periodic Inventory System

PURCHASES—Periodic   Under the periodic system, the balance of the Merchandise Inventory account remains unchanged during the period and is updated at period-end as part of the adjusting process. During the period, three accounts are used to record purchases of inventory: Purchases; Purchases Discounts; and Purchases Returns and Allowances. *It is helpful to see that the entries below are identical to the perpetual system except that Merchandise Inventory is substituted for each of the three purchases accounts.*

To illustrate, we apply the periodic system to purchases transactions. On November 2, a buyer purchases goods ($500 gross; $490 net) with terms of 2/10, n/30. Its November 2 entries under the gross and net methods are

Gross Method—Periodic		
Purchases..................	500	
Accounts Payable........		500

Net Method—Periodic		
Purchases.....................	490	
Accounts Payable...........		490

If the invoice is paid on (or before) November 12 within the discount period, it records

Gross Method—Periodic		
Accounts Payable............	500	
Purchases Discounts.....		10
Cash.................		490

Net Method—Periodic		
Accounts Payable................	490	
Cash.....................		490

If, instead, the invoice is *not* paid within the discount period, but it is later paid on December 2 (the n/30 due date), *after the discount period*, it records

Gross Method—Periodic		
Accounts Payable............	500	
Cash.................		500

Net Method—Periodic		
Accounts Payable................	490	
Discounts Lost...................	10	
Cash.....................		500

SALES—Periodic   For the above sales transactions, the **perpetual and periodic entries are identical except that under the periodic system the cost-side entries are *not* made at the time of each sale nor for any subsequent returns.** Instead, the cost of goods sold is computed at period-end based on a physical count of inventory. This entry is illustrated in Exhibit 5A.1.

Summary

C1 **Describe merchandising activities and identify income components for a merchandising company.** Merchandisers buy products and resell them. Examples of merchandisers include Walmart, Home Depot, The Limited, and Barnes & Noble. A merchandiser's costs on the income statement include an amount for cost of goods sold. Gross profit, or gross margin, equals sales minus cost of goods sold.

C2 **Identify and explain the inventory asset and cost flows of a merchandising company.** The current asset section of a merchandising company's balance sheet includes the cost of products held for resale as of the balance sheet date. When the merchandise is sold, its cost is transferred from the balance sheet to the income statement, where it is reported as Cost of Goods Sold.

A1 **Compute the acid-test ratio and explain its use to assess liquidity.** The acid-test ratio is computed as quick assets (cash, short-term investments, and current receivables) divided by current liabilities. It indicates a company's ability to pay its current liabilities with its existing quick assets. An acid-test ratio equal to or greater than 1.0 is often adequate.

A2 **Compute the gross margin ratio and explain its use to assess profitability.** The gross margin ratio is computed as gross margin (net sales minus cost of goods sold) divided by net sales. It indicates a company's profitability before considering other expenses.

P1 **Analyze and record transactions for merchandise purchases using a perpetual system.** For a perpetual inventory system, purchases of inventory are added to the Merchandise Inventory account. Discounts, returns, and allowances of purchases are subtracted from Merchandise Inventory, and transportation-in costs are added to Merchandise Inventory.

P2 **Analyze and record transactions for merchandise sales using a perpetual system.** A merchandiser records sales at the invoice price (using the gross method). The cost of items sold is transferred from Merchandise Inventory to Cost of Goods Sold. When cash discounts from the sales price are offered and customers pay within the discount period, the seller records this in Sales Discounts, a contra account to Sales. Refunds or credits given to customers for unsatisfactory merchandise are recorded in Sales Returns and Allowances, a contra account to Sales.

P3 **Prepare adjustments and close accounts for a merchandising company.** With a perpetual system, it is sometimes necessary to make an adjustment for inventory shrinkage, which is normally charged to Cost of Goods Sold. New revenue recognition rules require additional adjusting entries that are explained in the appendix. Temporary accounts closed to Income Summary for a merchandiser include Sales, Sales Discounts, Sales Returns and Allowances, and Cost of Goods Sold.

P4 **Define and prepare multiple-step and single-step income statements.** Multiple-step income statements include greater detail for sales and expenses than do single-step income statements. They often show details of net sales and report expenses in categories reflecting different activities, where some information is taken from supplementary records.

P5^A **Record and compare merchandising transactions using both periodic and perpetual inventory systems.** A perpetual inventory system continuously tracks the cost of goods available for sale and the cost of goods sold. A periodic system accumulates the cost of goods purchased during the period but does not tally the cost of goods sold until the end of a period. Transactions involving the sale and purchase of merchandise are recorded and analyzed under both the periodic and perpetual inventory systems. Adjusting and closing entries for both inventory systems are illustrated and explained.

P6^C **Prepare adjustments for discounts, returns, and allowances per revenue recognition rules.** New revenue recognition rules can be applied using adjusting entries. Future expected sales discounts arising from current-period sales are recorded using an adjusting entry with a debit to Sales Discounts and a credit to Allowance for Sales Discounts (a contra asset). Estimates of future sales returns and allowances are made with an adjusting entry to debit Sales Returns and Allowances and to credit Sales Refund Payable (a current liability); this results in Sales being recorded net of expected returns and allowances. Similarly, an estimate of future inventory returns is made and recorded in Inventory Returns Estimated (a current asset, debit) with a corresponding credit to Cost of Goods Sold.

P7^D **Record and compare merchandising transactions using the gross method and net method.** When invoices are recorded at gross amounts, the amount of discounts later taken is deducted from the balance of the Inventory account. When purchases are recorded at net amounts, a Discounts Lost account is brought to management's attention as an operating expense.

Key Terms

Acid-test ratio	Gross margin	Perpetual inventory system
Allowance for sales discounts	Gross margin ratio	Purchases discount
Cash discount	Gross method	Retailer
Cost of goods sold	Gross profit	Sales discount
Credit memorandum	Inventory	Sales refund payable
Credit period	Inventory returns estimated	Sales returns and allowances
Credit terms	List price	Selling expenses
Debit memorandum	Merchandise	Shrinkage
Discount period	Merchandise inventory	Single-step income statement
Discounts Lost	Merchandiser	Supplementary records
EOM	Multiple-step income statement	Trade discount
FOB	Net method	Wholesaler
General and administrative expenses	Periodic inventory system	

Multiple Choice Quiz

1. A company has $550,000 in net sales and $193,000 in gross profit. This means its cost of goods sold equals

  a. $743,000   **c.** $357,000   **e.** $(193,000)

  b. $550,000   **d.** $193,000

2. A company purchased $4,500 of merchandise on May 1 with terms of 2/10, n/30. On May 6, it returned $250 of that merchandise. On May 8, it paid the balance owed for merchandise, taking any discount it is entitled to. The cash paid on May 8 is

  a. $4,500   **c.** $4,160   **e.** $4,410

  b. $4,250   **d.** $4,165

3. A company has cash sales of $75,000, credit sales of $320,000, sales returns and allowances of $13,700, and sales discounts of $6,000. Its net sales equal

  a. $395,000   **c.** $300,300   **e.** $414,700

  b. $375,300   **d.** $339,700

4. A company's quick assets are $37,500, its current assets are $80,000, and its current liabilities are $50,000. Its acid-test ratio equals

  a. 1.600   **c.** 0.625   **e.** 0.469

  b. 0.750   **d.** 1.333

5. A company's net sales are $675,000, its cost of goods sold is $459,000, and its net income is $74,250. Its gross margin ratio equals

  a. 32%   **c.** 47%   **e.** 34%

  b. 68%   **d.** 11%

ANSWERS TO MULTIPLE CHOICE QUIZ

1. c; Gross profit = $550,000 − $193,000 = $357,000

2. d; ($4,500 − $250) × (100% − 2%) = $4,165

3. b; Net sales = $75,000 + $320,000 − $13,700 − $6,000 = $375,300

4. b; Acid-test ratio = $37,500/$50,000 = 0.750

5. a; Gross margin ratio = ($675,000 − $459,000)/$675,000 = 32%

$^{A(B,C,D)}$ *Superscript letter A (B,C,D) denotes assignments based on Appendix 5A (5B,5C,5D).*

 Icon denotes assignments that involve decision making.

Discussion Questions

1. What items appear in financial statements of merchandising companies but not in the statements of service companies?

2. In comparing the accounts of a merchandising company with those of a service company, what additional accounts would the merchandising company likely use, assuming it employs a perpetual inventory system?

3. Explain how a business can earn a positive gross profit on its sales and still have a net loss.

4. Why do companies offer a cash discount?

5. How does a company that uses a perpetual inventory system determine the amount of inventory shrinkage?

6. Distinguish between cash discounts and trade discounts for purchases. Is the amount of a trade discount on purchased merchandise recorded in the accounts?

7. What is the difference between a sales discount and a purchases discount?

8. Why would a company's manager be concerned about the quantity of its purchases returns if its suppliers allow unlimited returns?

9. Does the sender (maker) of a debit memorandum record a debit or a credit in the recipient's account? What entry (debit or credit) does the recipient record?

10. What is the difference between the single-step and multiple-step income statement formats?

11. Refer to the balance sheet and income statement for **Apple** in Appendix A. What **APPLE** does the company title its inventory account? Does the company present a detailed calculation of its cost of goods sold?

12. Refer to **Google**'s income statement in Appendix A. What title does it use for **GOOGLE** cost of goods sold?

13. Refer to the income statement for **Samsung** in Appendix A. What does **Samsung** Samsung title its cost of goods sold account?

14. Refer to the income statement of **Samsung** in Appendix A. Does its in- **Samsung** come statement report a gross profit figure? If yes, what is the amount?

15. Buyers negotiate purchase contracts with suppliers. What type of shipping terms should a buyer attempt to negotiate to minimize freight-in costs?

QUICK STUDY

QS 5-1

Applying merchandising terms

C1

Enter the letter for each term in the blank space beside the definition that it most closely matches.

A. Sales discount   **E.** FOB shipping point   **H.** Purchases discount
B. Credit period   **F.** Gross profit   **I.** Cash discount
C. Discount period   **G.** Merchandise inventory   **J.** Trade discount
D. FOB destination

———— **1.** Goods a company owns and expects to sell to its customers.

———— **2.** Time period that can pass before a customer's payment is due.

———— **3.** Seller's description of a cash discount granted to buyers in return for early payment.

———— **4.** Reduction below list or catalog price that is negotiated in setting the price of goods.

———— **5.** Ownership of goods is transferred when the seller delivers goods to the carrier.

———— **6.** Purchaser's description of a cash discount received from a supplier of goods.

———— **7.** Reduction in a receivable or payable if it is paid within the discount period.

———— **8.** Difference between net sales and the cost of goods sold.

———— **9.** Time period in which a cash discount is available.

———— **10.** Ownership of goods is transferred when delivered to the buyer's place of business.

QS 5-2

Identifying inventory costs

C2

Costs of $5,000 were incurred to acquire goods and make them ready for sale. The goods were shipped to the buyer (FOB shipping point) for a cost of $200. Additional necessary costs of $400 were incurred to acquire the goods. No other incentives or discounts were available. What is the buyer's total cost of merchandise inventory?

a. $5,000   **b.** $5,200   **c.** $5,400   **d.** $5,600

QS 5-3

Merchandise accounts and computations

C2

Use the following information (in random order) from a merchandising company and from a service company. *Hint:* Not all information may be necessary for the solutions.

a. For the merchandiser only, compute:

1. Goods available for sale.

2. Cost of goods sold.

3. Gross profit.

b. Compute net income for each company.

Kleiner Merchandising Company	
Accumulated depreciation........	$ 700
Beginning inventory.............	5,000
Ending inventory................	1,700
Expenses.......................	1,450
Net purchases..................	3,900
Net sales......................	9,500

Krug Service Company	
Expenses	$12,500
Revenues	14,000
Cash	700
Prepaid rent	800
Accounts payable..................	200
Equipment	1,300

QS 5-4

Computing net invoice amounts

P1

Compute the amount to be paid for each of the four separate invoices assuming that all invoices are paid *within* the discount period.

Merchandise (gross)	Terms	Merchandise (gross)	Terms
a. $5,000	2/10, n/60	**c.** $75,000	1/10, n/30
b. $20,000	1/15, EOM	**d.** $10,000	3/15, n/45

QS 5-5

Recording purchases, returns, and discounts taken

P1

Prepare journal entries to record each of the following transactions of a merchandising company. The company uses a perpetual inventory system and the gross method.

Nov. 5 Purchased 600 units of product at a cost of $10 per unit. Terms of the sale are 2/10, n/60; the invoice is dated November 5.

  7 Returned 25 defective units from the November 5 purchase and received full credit.

  15 Paid the amount due from the November 5 purchase, less the return on November 7.

Prepare journal entries to record each of the following transactions. The company records purchases using the gross method and a perpetual inventory system.

Aug. 1 Purchased merchandise with an invoice price of $60,000 and credit terms of 3/10, n/30.
     11 Paid supplier the amount owed from the August 1 purchase.

QS 5-6
Recording purchases and discounts taken
P1

Prepare journal entries to record each of the following transactions. The company records purchases using the gross method and a perpetual inventory system.

Sept. 15 Purchased merchandise with an invoice price of $35,000 and credit terms of 2/5, n/15.
      29 Paid supplier the amount owed on the September 15 purchase.

QS 5-7
Recording purchases and discounts missed
P1

Prepare journal entries to record each of the following sales transactions of a merchandising company. The company uses a perpetual inventory system and the gross method.

Apr. 1 Sold merchandise for $3,000, with credit terms n/30; invoice dated April 1. The cost of the merchandise is $1,800.
     4 The customer in the April 1 sale returned $300 of merchandise for full credit. The merchandise, which had cost $180, is returned to inventory.
     8 Sold merchandise for $1,000, with credit terms of 1/10, n/30; invoice dated April 8. Cost of the merchandise is $700.
    11 Received payment for the amount due from the April 1 sale less the return on April 4.

QS 5-8
Recording sales, returns, and discounts taken
P2

Nix'It Company's ledger on July 31, its fiscal year-end, includes the following selected accounts that have normal balances (Nix'It uses the perpetual inventory system).

QS 5-9
Accounting for shrinkage—perpetual system
P3

Merchandise inventory	$ 37,800	Sales returns and allowances	$ 6,500
T. Nix, Capital	115,300	Cost of goods sold	105,000
T. Nix, Withdrawals	7,000	Depreciation expense	10,300
Sales	160,200	Salaries expense	32,500
Sales discounts	4,700	Miscellaneous expenses	5,000

A physical count of its July 31 year-end inventory discloses that the cost of the merchandise inventory still available is $35,900. Prepare the entry to record any inventory shrinkage.

Refer to QS 5-9 and prepare journal entries to close the balances in temporary revenue and expense accounts. Remember to consider the entry for shrinkage that is made to solve that assignment.

QS 5-10
Closing entries   P3

For each item below, indicate whether the statement describes a multiple-step income statement or a single-step income statement.

a. Multiple-step income statement   **b.** Single-step income statement

_____ **1.** Commonly reports detailed computations of net sales and other costs and expenses.
_____ **2.** Statement limited to two main categories (revenues and expenses).
_____ **3.** Reports gross profit as a separate line item.
_____ **4.** Reports net income equal to income from operations adjusted for any nonoperating items.

QS 5-11
Multiple-step income statement
P4

Use the following information on current assets and current liabilities to compute and interpret the acid-test ratio. Explain what the acid-test ratio of a company measures.

QS 5-12
Computing and interpreting acid-test ratio

A1

Cash	$1,490	Prepaid expenses	$ 700
Accounts receivable	2,800	Accounts payable	5,750
Inventory	6,000	Other current liabilities	850

Identify similarities and differences between the acid-test ratio and the current ratio. Compare and describe how the two ratios reflect a company's ability to meet its current obligations.

QS 5-13
Contrasting liquidity ratios A1

QS 5-14

Computing and analyzing
gross margin ratio

A2

Compute net sales, gross profit, and the gross margin ratio for each separate case *a* through *d*. Interpret the
gross margin ratio for case *a*.

	a	b	c	d
Sales	$150,000	$550,000	$38,700	$255,700
Sales discounts	5,000	17,500	600	4,800
Sales returns and allowances	20,000	6,000	5,100	900
Cost of goods sold	79,750	329,589	24,453	126,500

QS 5-15

IFRS income statement
presentation

P4

Income statement information for **adidas Group**, a German footwear, apparel, and accessories manufacturer, for the year ended December 31, 2014, follows. The company applies IFRS and reports its results in
millions of euros. Prepare its calendar-year 2014 (1) multiple-step income statement and (2) single-step
income statement.

Net income	€ 564
Financial income	19
Financial expenses.	67
Operating profit	883
Cost of sales	7,610
Income taxes.	271
Income before taxes.	835
Gross profit	6,924
Royalty and commission income	102
Other operating income.	138
Other operating expenses	6,281
Net sales	14,534

QS 5-16^A

Contrasting periodic and
perpetual systems

P5

Identify whether each description best applies to a periodic or a perpetual inventory system.

_____ **a.** Updates the inventory account only at period-end.

_____ **b.** Requires an adjusting entry to record inventory shrinkage.

_____ **c.** Markedly increased in frequency and popularity in business within the past decade.

_____ **d.** Records cost of goods sold each time a sales transaction occurs.

_____ **e.** Provides more timely information to managers.

QS 5-17^A

Recording purchases,
returns, and discounts—
periodic & gross
methods   P5

Refer to QS 5-5 and prepare journal entries to record each of the merchandising transactions assuming
that the company records purchases using the *gross* method and a *periodic* inventory system.

QS 5-18^A

Recording sales, returns,
and discounts—periodic &
gross methods   P5

Refer to QS 5-8 and prepare journal entries to record each of the merchandising transactions assuming
that the company records purchases using the *gross* method and a *periodic* inventory system.

QS 5-19^C

Recording estimated
sales discounts

P6

ProBuilder has the following June 30, 2016, fiscal-year-end unadjusted balances: Allowance for Sales
Discounts, $0; and Accounts Receivable, $10,000. Of the $10,000 of receivables, $2,000 are within a 3%
discount period, meaning that it expects buyers to take $60 in future discounts arising from this period's sales.

a. Prepare the June 30, 2016, fiscal-year-end adjusting journal entry for future sales discounts.

b. Assume the same facts above *and* that there is a $10 fiscal-year-end unadjusted credit balance in the
Allowance for Sales Discounts. Prepare the June 30, 2016, fiscal-year-end adjusting journal entry for
future sales discounts.

QS 5-20^c

Recording estimated
sales returns

P6

ProBuilder reports merchandise sales of $50,000 and cost of merchandise sales of $20,000 in its first year
of operations ending June 30, 2016. It makes fiscal-year-end adjusting entries for estimated future returns
and allowances equal to 2% of sales, or $1,000, and 2% of cost of sales, or $400.

a. Prepare the June 30, 2016, fiscal-year-end adjusting journal entry for future returns and allowances
related to sales.

b. Prepare the June 30, 2016, fiscal-year-end adjusting journal entry for future returns and allowances
related to cost of sales.

Refer to QS 5-5 and prepare journal entries to record each of the merchandising transactions assuming that the company records purchases using the *net* method and a *perpetual* inventory system.

QS 5-21^D

Recording purchases, returns, and discounts—net & perpetual methods   **P7**

Refer to QS 5-8 and prepare journal entries to record each of the merchandising transactions assuming that the company records purchases using the *net* method and a *perpetual* inventory system.

QS 5-22^D

Recording sales, returns, and discounts—net & perpetual methods   **P7**

Answer each of the following questions related to international accounting standards.
  a. Explain how the accounting for merchandise purchases and sales is different between accounting under IFRS versus U.S. GAAP.
  b. Income statements prepared under IFRS usually report an item titled *finance costs*. What do finance costs refer to?
  c. U.S. GAAP prohibits alternative measures of income reported on the income statement. Does IFRS permit such alternative measures on the income statement?

QS 5-23

International accounting standards

C1

connect

Using your accounting knowledge, fill in the blanks in the following separate income statements *a* through *e*. Identify any negative amount by putting it in parentheses.

EXERCISES

Exercise 5-1
Computing revenues, expenses, and income

C1

	a	b	c	d	e
Sales	$62,000	$43,500	$46,000	$?	$25,600
Cost of goods sold					
Merchandise inventory (beginning)	8,000	17,050	7,500	8,000	4,560
Total cost of merchandise purchases	38,000	?	?	32,000	6,600
Merchandise inventory (ending)	?	(3,000)	(9,000)	(6,600)	?
Cost of goods sold	34,050	16,000	?	?	7,000
Gross profit	?	?	3,750	45,600	?
Expenses	10,000	10,650	12,150	3,600	6,000
Net income (loss)	$?	$16,850	$ (8,400)	$42,000	$?

The operating cycle of a merchandiser with credit sales includes the following five activities. Starting with merchandise acquisition, identify the chronological order of these five activities.
  _____ **a.** Prepare merchandise for sale.
  _____ **b.** Collect cash from customers on account.
  _____ **c.** Make credit sales to customers.
  _____ **d.** Purchase merchandise.
  _____ **e.** Monitor and service accounts receivable.

Exercise 5-2
Operating cycle for merchandiser

C2

Prepare journal entries to record the following transactions for a retail store. The company uses a perpetual inventory system and the gross method.

Apr. 2   Purchased $4,600 of merchandise from Lyon Company with credit terms of 2/15, n/60, invoice dated April 2, and FOB shipping point.
      3   Paid $300 cash for shipping charges on the April 2 purchase.
      4   Returned to Lyon Company unacceptable merchandise that had an invoice price of $600.
     17   Sent a check to Lyon Company for the April 2 purchase, net of the discount and the returned merchandise.
     18   Purchased $8,500 of merchandise from Frist Corp. with credit terms of 1/10, n/30, invoice dated April 18, and FOB destination.
     21   After negotiations, received from Frist a $500 allowance toward the $8,500 owed on the April 18 purchase.
     28   Sent check to Frist paying for the April 18 purchase, net of the allowance and the discount.

Exercise 5-3
Recording purchases, purchases returns, and purchases allowances

P1

Check   April 28, Cr. Cash, $7,920

Exercise 5-4

Recording sales, sales returns, and sales allowances

P2

Allied Merchandisers was organized on May 1. Macy Co. is a major customer (buyer) of Allied (seller) products. Prepare journal entries to record the following transactions for Allied assuming it uses a perpetual inventory system and the gross method. (Allied estimates returns using an adjusting entry at each year-end.)

May 3   Allied made its first and only purchase of inventory for the period on May 3 for 2,000 units at a price of $10 cash per unit (for a total cost of $20,000).

      5   Allied sold 1,500 of the units in inventory for $14 per unit (invoice total: $21,000) to Macy Co. under credit terms 2/10, n/60. The goods cost Allied $15,000.

      7   Macy returns 125 units because they did not fit the customer's needs (invoice amount: $1,750). Allied restores the units, which cost $1,250, to its inventory.

      8   Macy discovers that 200 units are scuffed but are still of use and, therefore, keeps the units. Allied sends Macy a credit memorandum for $300 toward the original invoice amount to compensate for the damage.

     15   Allied receives payment from Macy for the amount owed on the May 5 purchase; payment is net of returns, allowances, and any cash discount.

Exercise 5-5

Recording purchases, purchases returns, and purchases allowances   **P1**

Refer to Exercise 5-4 and prepare journal entries for Macy Co. to record each of the May transactions. Macy is a retailer that uses the gross method and a perpetual inventory system, and purchases these units for resale.

Exercise 5-6

Recording sales, purchases, and cash discounts—buyer *and* seller

P1   P2

Santa Fe Retailing purchased merchandise "as is" (with no returns) from Mesa Wholesalers with credit terms of 3/10, n/60 and an invoice price of $24,000. The merchandise had cost Mesa $16,000. Assume that both buyer and seller use a perpetual inventory system and the gross method.

1. Prepare entries that the *buyer* records for the (*a*) purchase, (*b*) cash payment *within* the discount period, and (*c*) cash payment *after* the discount period.

2. Prepare entries that the *seller* records for the (*a*) sale, (*b*) cash collection *within* the discount period, and (*c*) cash collection *after* the discount period.

Exercise 5-7

Recording sales, purchases, shipping, and returns—buyer *and* seller

P1   P2

Sydney Retailing (buyer) and Troy Wholesalers (seller) enter into the following transactions. Both Sydney and Troy use a perpetual inventory system and the gross method.

May 11   Sydney accepts delivery of $40,000 of merchandise it purchases for resale from Troy: invoice dated May 11; terms 3/10, n/90; FOB shipping point. The goods cost Troy $30,000. Sydney pays $345 cash to Express Shipping for delivery charges on the merchandise.

     12   Sydney returns $1,400 of the $40,000 of goods to Troy, who receives them the same day and restores them to its inventory. The returned goods had cost Troy $1,050.

     20   Sydney pays Troy for the amount owed. Troy receives the cash immediately.

Check (1) May 20, Cr. Cash, $37,442

1. Prepare journal entries that Sydney Retailing (buyer) records for these three transactions.

2. Prepare journal entries that Troy Wholesalers (seller) records for these three transactions.

Exercise 5-8

Inventory and cost of sales transactions in T-accounts

P1   P2

The following *supplementary records* summarize Tesla Company's merchandising activities for year 2017 (it uses a perpetual inventory system). Set up T-accounts for Merchandise Inventory and Cost of Goods Sold. Then record the summarized activities in those T-accounts and compute account balances.

Cost of merchandise sold to customers in sales transactions	$196,000
Merchandise inventory, December 31, 2016	25,000
Invoice cost of merchandise purchases, gross amount	192,500
Shrinkage determined on December 31, 2017	800
Cost of transportation-in	2,900
Cost of merchandise returned by customers and restored to inventory	2,100
Purchases discounts received	1,700
Purchases returns and allowances	4,000

Check Year-end Merch. Inventory, Dec. 31, $20,000

Prepare journal entries for the following merchandising transactions of Dollar Store assuming it uses a perpetual inventory system and the gross method.

Nov. 1   Dollar Store purchases merchandise for $1,500 on terms of 2/5, n/30, FOB shipping point, invoice dated November 1.

    5   Dollar Store pays cash for the November 1 purchase.

    7   Dollar Store discovers and returns $200 of defective merchandise purchased on November 1, and paid for on November 5, for a cash refund.

  10   Dollar Store pays $90 cash for transportation costs for the November 1 purchase.

  13   Dollar Store sells merchandise for $1,600 with terms n/30. The cost of the merchandise is $800.

  16   Merchandise is returned to the Dollar Store from the November 13 transaction. The returned items are priced at $160 and cost $80; the items were not damaged and were returned to inventory.

Exercise 5-9
Recording purchases, sales, returns, and shipping
P1   P2

The following list includes selected permanent accounts and all of the temporary accounts from the December 31, 2017, unadjusted trial balance of Emiko Co., a business owned by Kumi Emiko. Use these account balances along with the additional information to journalize (*a*) adjusting entries and (*b*) closing entries. Emiko Co. uses a perpetual inventory system.

Exercise 5-10
Preparing adjusting and closing entries for a merchandiser
P3

	Debit	Credit
Merchandise inventory	$ 30,000	
Prepaid selling expenses	5,600	
K. Emiko, Withdrawals	33,000	
Sales		$529,000
Sales returns and allowances	17,500	
Sales discounts	5,000	
Cost of goods sold	212,000	
Sales salaries expense	48,000	
Utilities expense	15,000	
Selling expenses	36,000	
Administrative expenses	105,000	

Additional Information

Accrued sales salaries amount to $1,700. Prepaid selling expenses of $3,000 have expired. A physical count of year-end merchandise inventory shows $28,700 of goods still available.

Check   Entry to close Income Summary: Cr. K. Emiko, Capital, $84,500

A company reports the following sales-related information. Compute and prepare the net sales portion only of this company's multiple-step income statement.

Exercise 5-11
Net sales computation for multiple-step income statement
P4

Sales, gross	$200,000	Sales returns and allowances	$16,000
Sales discounts	4,000	Sales salaries expense	10,000

A retail company recently completed a physical count of ending merchandise inventory to use in preparing adjusting entries. In determining the cost of the counted inventory, company employees failed to consider that $3,000 of incoming goods had been shipped by a supplier on December 31 under an FOB shipping point agreement. These goods had been recorded in Merchandise Inventory as a purchase, but *they were not included in the physical count because they were in transit.*

a. Explain how this overlooked fact impacts the company's balance sheet and income statement.

b. Indicate whether this overlooked fact results in an overstatement, understatement, or no effect on the following separate ratios: return on assets, debt ratio, current ratio, and acid-test ratio.

Exercise 5-12
Interpreting a physical count error as inventory shrinkage

A1

Refer to the information in Exercise 5-12 and indicate whether the failure to include in-transit inventory as part of the physical count results in an overstatement, understatement, or no effect on the following separate ratios: (*a*) gross margin ratio and (*b*) profit margin ratio.

Exercise 5-13
Physical count error and profits   A2

Exercise 5-14

Computing and analyzing acid-test and current ratios

A1

Compute the current ratio and acid-test ratio for each of the following separate cases. (Round ratios to two decimals.) Which company situation is in the best position to meet short-term obligations? Explain.

	Case X	Case Y	Case Z
Cash	$2,000	$ 110	$1,000
Short-term investments	50	0	580
Current receivables	350	470	700
Inventory......................	2,600	2,420	4,230
Prepaid expenses.................	200	500	900
Total current assets	$5,200	$3,500	$7,410
Current liabilities.................	$2,000	$1,000	$3,800

Exercise 5-15ᴬ

Recording purchases, returns, and allowances—periodic **P5**

Refer to Exercise 5-3 and prepare journal entries to record each of the merchandising transactions assuming that the buyer uses the *periodic inventory system and the gross method.*

Exercise 5-16ᴬ

Recording sales, purchases, and discounts: buyer and seller—periodic **P5**

Refer to Exercise 5-6 and prepare journal entries to record each of the merchandising transactions assuming that the *periodic inventory system and the gross method* are used by both the buyer and the seller.

Exercise 5-17ᴬ

Recording sales, purchases, shipping, and returns: buyer and seller—periodic **P5**

Refer to Exercise 5-7 and prepare journal entries to record each of the merchandising transactions assuming that the *periodic inventory system and the gross method* are used by both the buyer and the seller.

Exercise 5-18

Preparing an income statement under IFRS

P4

L'Oréal reports the following income statement accounts for the year ended December 31, 2014 (euros in millions). Prepare the income statement for this company for the year ended December 31, 2014, following usual IFRS practices.

Net profit.................	€ 4,908.6	Income tax expense...........................	€1,111.0
Finance costs	31.4	Profit before tax expense.......................	6,019.6
Net sales.................	22,532.0	Research and development expense	760.6
Gross profit..............	16,031.3	Selling, general and administrative expense	4,821.1
Other income	2,118.0	Advertising and promotion expense..............	6,558.9
Cost of sales.............	6,500.7	Finance income	42.3

Exercise 5-19ᶜ

Recording estimated sales discounts

P6

Med Labs has the following December 31, 2017, year-end unadjusted balances: Allowance for Sales Discounts, $0; and Accounts Receivable, $5,000. Of the $5,000 of receivables, $1,000 are within a 2% discount period, meaning that it expects buyers to take $20 in future-period discounts arising from this period's sales.

a. Prepare the December 31, 2017, year-end adjusting journal entry for future sales discounts.

b. Assume the same facts above *and* that there is a $5 year-end unadjusted credit balance in the Allowance for Sales Discounts. Prepare the December 31, 2017, year-end adjusting journal entry for future sales discounts.

c. Is Allowance for Sales Discounts a contra asset or a contra liability account?

Exercise 5-20ᶜ

Recording estimates of future returns

P6

Chico Company allows its customers to return merchandise within 30 days of purchase.

• At December 31, 2017, the end of its first year of operations, Chico estimates future-period merchandise returns of $60,000 (cost of $22,500) related to its 2017 sales.

• On January 3, 2018, a customer returns merchandise with a selling price of $2,000 for a cash refund; the returned merchandise cost $750 and is returned to inventory as it is not defective.

a. Prepare the December 31, 2017, year-end adjusting journal entry for estimated future sales returns and allowances (revenue side).

b. Prepare the December 31, 2017, year-end adjusting journal entry for estimated future inventory returns and allowances (cost side).

c. Prepare the January 3, 2018, journal entry(ies) to record the merchandise returned.

Lopez Company reports unadjusted first-year merchandise sales of $100,000 and cost of merchandise sales of $30,000.

a. Compute gross profit (using the unadjusted numbers above).

b. The company expects future returns and allowances equal to 5% of sales and 5% of cost of sales.

   1. Prepare the year-end adjusting entry to record the sales expected to be refunded.

   2. Prepare the year-end adjusting entry to record the cost side of sales returns and allowances.

   3. Recompute gross profit (using the adjusted numbers from parts 1 and 2).

c. Is Sales Refund Payable an asset, liability, or equity account?

d. Is Inventory Returns Estimated an asset, liability, or equity account?

Exercise 5-21ᶜ
Recording estimates of future returns
P6

Refer to Exercise 5-7 and prepare journal entries to record each of the merchandising transactions assuming that the *perpetual inventory system and the net method* are used by both the buyer and the seller.

Exercise 5-22ᴰ
Recording sales, purchases, shipping, and returns: buyer and seller—perpetual and net method   P7

Piere Imports uses the perpetual system in accounting for merchandise inventory and had the following transactions during the month of October. Prepare entries to record these transactions assuming that Piere Imports records invoices (*a*) at gross amounts and (*b*) at net amounts.

Oct. 2   Purchased merchandise at a $3,000 price ($2,940 net), invoice dated October 2, terms 2/10, n/30.

     10   Received a credit memorandum toward the return of $500 ($490 net) of merchandise that it purchased on October 2.

     17   Purchased merchandise at a $5,400 price ($5,292 net), invoice dated October 17, terms 2/10, n/30.

     27   Paid for the merchandise purchased on October 17, less the discount.

     31   Paid for the merchandise purchased on October 2. (Payment was mistakenly delayed, which caused the discount to be lost.)

Exercise 5-23ᴰ
Recording purchases, sales, returns, and discounts: buyer and seller—perpetual and both net & gross methods
P7

▉ connect

Prepare journal entries to record the following merchandising transactions of Cabela's, which uses the perpetual inventory system and the gross method. (*Hint:* It will help to identify each receivable and payable; for example, record the purchase on July 1 in Accounts Payable—Boden.)

July 1   Purchased merchandise from Boden Company for $6,000 under credit terms of 1/15, n/30, FOB shipping point, invoice dated July 1.

     2   Sold merchandise to Creek Co. for $900 under credit terms of 2/10, n/60, FOB shipping point, invoice dated July 2. The merchandise had cost $500.

     3   Paid $125 cash for freight charges on the purchase of July 1.

     8   Sold merchandise that had cost $1,300 for $1,700 cash.

     9   Purchased merchandise from Leight Co. for $2,200 under credit terms of 2/15, n/60, FOB destination, invoice dated July 9.

    11   Received a $200 credit memorandum from Leight Co. for the return of part of the merchandise purchased on July 9.

    12   Received the balance due from Creek Co. for the invoice dated July 2, net of the discount.

    16   Paid the balance due to Boden Company within the discount period.

    19   Sold merchandise that cost $800 to Art Co. for $1,200 under credit terms of 2/15, n/60, FOB shipping point, invoice dated July 19.

    21   Issued a $100 credit memorandum to Art Co. for an allowance on goods sold on July 19.

    24   Paid Leight Co. the balance due, net of discount.

    30   Received the balance due from Art Co. for the invoice dated July 19, net of discount.

    31   Sold merchandise that cost $4,800 to Creek Co. for $7,000 under credit terms of 2/10, n/60, FOB shipping point, invoice dated July 31.

PROBLEM SET A

Problem 5-1A
Preparing journal entries for merchandising activities—perpetual system
P1   P2

Check July 12, Dr. Cash, $882

July 16, Cr. Cash, $5,940

July 24, Cr. Cash, $1,960

July 30, Dr. Cash, $1,078

Problem 5-2A
Preparing journal entries for merchandising activities—perpetual system

P1 P2

Check Aug. 9, Dr. Delivery Expense, $125

Aug. 18, Cr. Cash, $4,950

Aug. 29, Dr. Cash, $4,300

Prepare journal entries to record the following merchandising transactions of Lowe's, which uses the perpetual inventory system and the gross method. (*Hint:* It will help to identify each receivable and payable; for example, record the purchase on August 1 in Accounts Payable—Aron.)

Aug. 1 Purchased merchandise from Aron Company for $7,500 under credit terms of 1/10, n/30, FOB destination, invoice dated August 1.

5 Sold merchandise to Baird Corp. for $5,200 under credit terms of 2/10, n/60, FOB destination, invoice dated August 5. The merchandise had cost $4,000.

8 Purchased merchandise from Waters Corporation for $5,400 under credit terms of 1/10, n/45, FOB shipping point, invoice dated August 8.

9 Paid $125 cash for shipping charges related to the August 5 sale to Baird Corp.

10 Baird returned merchandise from the August 5 sale that had cost Lowe's $400 and was sold for $600. The merchandise was restored to inventory.

12 After negotiations with Waters Corporation concerning problems with the purchases on August 8, Lowe's received a credit memorandum from Waters granting a price reduction of $400 off the $5,400 of goods purchased.

14 At Aron's request, Lowe's paid $200 cash for freight charges on the August 1 purchase, reducing the amount owed to Aron.

15 Received balance due from Baird Corp. for the August 5 sale less the return on August 10.

18 Paid the amount due Waters Corporation for the August 8 purchase less the price allowance from August 12.

19 Sold merchandise to Tux Co. for $4,800 under credit terms of n/10, FOB shipping point, invoice dated August 19. The merchandise had cost $2,400.

22 Tux requested a price reduction on the August 19 sale because the merchandise did not meet specifications. Lowe's sent Tux a $500 credit memorandum toward the $4,800 invoice to resolve the issue.

29 Received Tux's cash payment for the amount due from the August 19 sale less the price allowance from August 22.

30 Paid Aron Company the amount due from the August 1 purchase.

Problem 5-3A
Computing merchandising amounts and formatting income statements

C2 P4

Valley Company's adjusted trial balance on August 31, 2017, its fiscal year-end, follows.

	Debit	Credit
Merchandise inventory	$ 41,000	
Other (noninventory) assets	130,400	
Total liabilities		$ 25,000
K. Valley, Capital		104,550
K. Valley, Withdrawals	8,000	
Sales		225,600
Sales discounts	2,250	
Sales returns and allowances	12,000	
Cost of goods sold	74,500	
Sales salaries expense	32,000	
Rent expense—Selling space	8,000	
Store supplies expense	1,500	
Advertising expense	13,000	
Office salaries expense	28,500	
Rent expense—Office space	3,600	
Office supplies expense	400	
Totals	$355,150	$355,150

On August 31, 2016, merchandise inventory was $25,400. Supplementary records of merchandising activities for the year ended August 31, 2017, reveal the following itemized costs.

Invoice cost of merchandise purchases	$92,000
Purchases discounts received	2,000
Purchases returns and allowances	4,500
Costs of transportation-in	4,600

Required

1. Compute the company's net sales for the year.
2. Compute the company's total cost of merchandise purchased for the year.
3. Prepare a multiple-step income statement that includes separate categories for net sales, cost of goods sold, selling expenses, and general and administrative expenses.
4. Prepare a single-step income statement that includes these expense categories: cost of goods sold, selling expenses, and general and administrative expenses.

Check   (2) $90,100
(3) Gross profit,
$136,850; Net income,
$49,850
(4) Total expenses,
$161,500

Use the data for Valley Company in Problem 5-3A to complete the following requirements.

Problem 5-4A

Preparing closing entries and interpreting information about discounts and returns

C2   P3

Required

1. Prepare closing entries as of August 31, 2017 (the perpetual inventory system is used).

Analysis Component

2. In prior years, the company experienced a 4% returns and allowance rate on its sales, which means approximately 4% of its gross sales were eventually returned outright or caused the company to grant allowances to customers. Compute the ratio of sales returns and allowances divided by gross sales. How does this year's ratio compare to the 4% ratio in prior years?

Check   (1) $49,850 Dr. to
close Income Summary
(2) Current-year
rate, 5.3%

The following unadjusted trial balance is prepared at fiscal year-end for Nelson Company.

Problem 5-5A

Preparing adjusting entries and income statements; computing gross margin, acid-test, and current ratios

A1   A2   P3   P4

	A	B	C
	NELSON COMPANY **Unadjusted Trial Balance** **January 31, 2017**		
1		Debit	Credit
2	Cash	$ 1,000	
3	Merchandise inventory	12,500	
4	Store supplies	5,800	
5	Prepaid insurance	2,400	
6	Store equipment	42,900	
7	Accumulated depreciation—Store equipment		$ 15,250
8	Accounts payable		10,000
9	J. Nelson, Capital		32,000
10	J. Nelson, Withdrawals	2,200	
11	Sales		111,950
12	Sales discounts	2,000	
13	Sales returns and allowances	2,200	
14	Cost of goods sold	38,400	
15	Depreciation expense—Store equipment	0	
16	Salaries expense	35,000	
17	Insurance expense	0	
18	Rent expense	15,000	
19	Store supplies expense	0	
20	Advertising expense	9,800	
21	Totals	$169,200	$169,200

Rent expense and salaries expense are equally divided between selling activities and general and administrative activities. Nelson Company uses a perpetual inventory system.

Required

1. Prepare adjusting journal entries to reflect each of the following:

   a. Store supplies still available at fiscal year-end amount to $1,750.

   b. Expired insurance, an administrative expense, for the fiscal year is $1,400.

   c. Depreciation expense on store equipment, a selling expense, is $1,525 for the fiscal year.

   d. To estimate shrinkage, a physical count of ending merchandise inventory is taken. It shows $10,900 of inventory is still available at fiscal year-end.

Check   (2) Gross profit, $67,750

2. Prepare a multiple-step income statement for fiscal year 2017 that begins with gross sales and includes separate categories for net sales, cost of goods sold, selling expenses, and general and administrative expenses.

(3) Total expenses, $106,775; Net income, $975

3. Prepare a single-step income statement for fiscal year 2017.

4. Compute the current ratio, acid-test ratio, and gross margin ratio as of January 31, 2017. (Round ratios to two decimals.)

Problem 5-6A^B

Preparing a work sheet for a merchandiser

P3

Refer to the data and information in Problem 5-5A.

Required

Prepare and complete the entire 10-column work sheet for Nelson Company. Follow the structure of Exhibit 5B.1 in Appendix 5B.

PROBLEM SET B

Problem 5-1B

Preparing journal entries for merchandising activities—perpetual system

P1   P2

Prepare journal entries to record the following merchandising transactions of IKEA, which uses the perpetual inventory system and gross method. (*Hint:* It will help to identify each receivable and payable; for example, record the purchase on May 2 in Accounts Payable—Havel.)

May 2   Purchased merchandise from Havel Co. for $10,000 under credit terms of 1/15, n/30, FOB shipping point, invoice dated May 2.

      4   Sold merchandise to Rath Co. for $11,000 under credit terms of 2/10, n/60, FOB shipping point, invoice dated May 4. The merchandise had cost $5,600.

      5   Paid $250 cash for freight charges on the purchase of May 2.

      9   Sold merchandise that had cost $2,000 for $2,500 cash.

     10   Purchased merchandise from Duke Co. for $3,650 under credit terms of 2/15, n/60, FOB destination, invoice dated May 10.

     12   Received a $650 credit memorandum from Duke Co. for the return of a portion of the merchandise purchased on May 10.

Check   May 14, Dr. Cash, $10,780

     14   Received the balance due from Rath Co. for the invoice dated May 4, net of the discount.

     17   Paid the balance due to Havel Co. within the discount period.

May 17, Cr. Cash, $9,900

     20   Sold merchandise that cost $1,450 to Tamer Co. for $2,800 under credit terms of 2/15, n/60, FOB shipping point, invoice dated May 20.

     22   Issued a $300 credit memorandum to Tamer Co. for an allowance on goods sold on May 20.

     25   Paid Duke Co. the balance due, net of the discount.

May 30, Dr. Cash, $2,450

     30   Received the balance due from Tamer Co. for the invoice dated May 20, net of discount and allowance.

     31   Sold merchandise that cost $3,600 to Rath Co. for $7,200 under credit terms of 2/10, n/60, FOB shipping point, invoice dated May 31.

Problem 5-2B

Preparing journal entries for merchandising activities—perpetual system

P1   P2

Prepare journal entries to record the following merchandising transactions of Menards, which applies the perpetual inventory system and gross method. (*Hint:* It will help to identify each receivable and payable; for example, record the purchase on July 3 in Accounts Payable—OLB.)

July 3   Purchased merchandise from OLB Corp. for $15,000 under credit terms of 1/10, n/30, FOB destination, invoice dated July 3.

      7   Sold merchandise to Brill Co. for $11,500 under credit terms of 2/10, n/60, FOB destination, invoice dated July 7. The merchandise had cost $7,750.

     10   Purchased merchandise from Rupert Co. for $14,200 under credit terms of 1/10, n/45, FOB shipping point, invoice dated July 10.

     11   Paid $300 cash for shipping charges related to the July 7 sale to Brill Co.

Continued on next page . . .

12 Brill returned merchandise from the July 7 sale that had cost Menards $1,450 and been sold for $2,000. The merchandise was restored to inventory.

14 After negotiations with Rupert Co. concerning problems with the merchandise purchased on July 10, Menards received a credit memorandum from Rupert granting a price reduction of $1,200.

15 At OLB's request, Menards paid $200 cash for freight charges on the July 3 purchase, reducing the amount owed to OLB.

17 Received balance due from Brill Co. for the July 7 sale less the return on July 12.

20 Paid the amount due Rupert Co. for the July 10 purchase less the price reduction granted on July 14.

21 Sold merchandise to Brown for $11,000 under credit terms of 1/10, n/30, FOB shipping point, invoice dated July 21. The merchandise had cost $7,000.

24 Brown requested a price reduction on the July 21 sale because the merchandise did not meet specifications. Menards sent Brown a credit memorandum for $1,000 toward the $11,000 invoice to resolve the issue.

30 Received Brown's cash payment for the amount due from the July 21 sale less the price allowance from July 24.

31 Paid OLB Corp. the amount due from the July 3 purchase.

Check July 17, Dr. Cash, $9,310

July 30, Dr. Cash, $9,900

July 31, Cr. Cash, $14,800

Barkley Company's adjusted trial balance on March 31, 2017, its fiscal year-end, follows.

Problem 5-3B
Computing merchandising amounts and formatting income statements

C1   C2   P4

	Debit	Credit
Merchandise inventory..............	$ 56,500	
Other (noninventory) assets............	202,600	
Total liabilities......................		$ 42,500
C. Barkley, Capital		164,425
C. Barkley, Withdrawals	3,000	
Sales		332,650
Sales discounts......................	5,875	
Sales returns and allowances	20,000	
Cost of goods sold	115,600	
Sales salaries expense.................	44,500	
Rent expense—Selling space...........	16,000	
Store supplies expense	3,850	
Advertising expense..................	26,000	
Office salaries expense	40,750	
Rent expense—Office space	3,800	
Office supplies expense...............	1,100	
Totals............................	$539,575	$539,575

On March 31, 2016, merchandise inventory was $37,500. Supplementary records of merchandising activities for the year ended March 31, 2017, reveal the following itemized costs.

Invoice cost of merchandise purchases	$138,500
Purchases discounts received....................	2,950
Purchases returns and allowances	6,700
Costs of transportation-in	5,750

Required

1. Compute the company's net sales for the year.
2. Compute the company's total cost of merchandise purchased for the year.
3. Prepare a multiple-step income statement that includes separate categories for net sales, cost of goods sold, selling expenses, and general and administrative expenses.
4. Prepare a single-step income statement that includes these expense categories: cost of goods sold, selling expenses, and general and administrative expenses.

Check (2) $134,600
(3) Gross profit, $191,175; Net income, $55,175
(4) Total expenses, $251,600

Problem 5-4B

Preparing closing entries and interpreting information about discounts and returns

C2 P3

Check (1) $55,175 Dr. to close Income Summary

    (2) Current-year ratio, 6.0%

Use the data for Barkley Company in Problem 5-3B to complete the following requirements.

Required

1. Prepare closing entries as of March 31, 2017 (the perpetual inventory system is used).

Analysis Component

2. In prior years, the company experienced a 5% returns and allowance rate on its sales, which means approximately 5% of its gross sales were eventually returned outright or caused the company to grant allowances to customers. Compute the ratio of sales returns and allowances divided by gross sales. How does this year's ratio compare to the 5% ratio in prior years?

Problem 5-5B

Preparing adjusting entries and income statements; computing gross margin, acid-test, and current ratios

A1   A2   P3   P4

The following unadjusted trial balance is prepared at fiscal year-end for Foster Products Company.

	A	B	C
	FOSTER PRODUCTS COMPANY **Unadjusted Trial Balance** **October 31, 2017**		
1		Debit	Credit
2	Cash	$ 7,400	
3	Merchandise inventory	24,000	
4	Store supplies	9,700	
5	Prepaid insurance	6,600	
6	Store equipment	81,800	
7	Accumulated depreciation—Store equipment		$ 32,000
8	Accounts payable		18,000
9	D. Foster, Capital		43,000
10	D. Foster, Withdrawals	2,000	
11	Sales		227,100
12	Sales discounts	1,000	
13	Sales returns and allowances	5,000	
14	Cost of goods sold	75,800	
15	Depreciation expense—Store equipment	0	
16	Salaries expense	63,000	
17	Insurance expense	0	
18	Rent expense	26,000	
19	Store supplies expense	0	
20	Advertising expense	17,800	
21	Totals	$320,100	$320,100

Rent expense and salaries expense are equally divided between selling activities and general and administrative activities. Foster Products Company uses a perpetual inventory system.

Required

1. Prepare adjusting journal entries to reflect each of the following:
   a. Store supplies still available at fiscal year-end amount to $3,700.
   b. Expired insurance, an administrative expense, for the fiscal year is $2,800.
   c. Depreciation expense on store equipment, a selling expense, is $3,000 for the fiscal year.
   d. To estimate shrinkage, a physical count of ending merchandise inventory is taken. It shows $21,300 of inventory is still available at fiscal year-end.

Check (2) Gross profit, $142,600

2. Prepare a multiple-step income statement for fiscal year 2017 that begins with gross sales and includes separate categories for net sales, cost of goods sold, selling expenses, and general and administrative expenses.

3. Prepare a single-step income statement for fiscal year 2017.

   (3) Total expenses, $197,100; Net income, $24,000

4. Compute the current ratio, acid-test ratio, and gross margin ratio as of October 31, 2017. (Round ratios to two decimals.)

Refer to the data and information in Problem 5-5B.

Required

Prepare and complete the entire 10-column work sheet for Foster Products Company. Follow the structure of Exhibit 5B.1 in Appendix 5B.

Problem 5-6B[B]

Preparing a work sheet for a merchandiser

P3

(This serial problem began in Chapter 1 and continues through most of the book. If previous chapter segments were not completed, the serial problem can begin at this point.)

SERIAL PROBLEM

Business Solutions

P1   P2   P3   P4

SP 5 Santana Rey created **Business Solutions** on October 1, 2017. The company has been successful, and its list of customers has grown. To accommodate the growth, the accounting system is modified to set up separate accounts for each customer. The following chart of accounts includes the account number used for each account and any balance as of December 31, 2017. Santana Rey decided to add a fourth digit with a decimal point to the 106 account number that had been used for the single Accounts Receivable account. This change allows the company to continue using the existing chart of accounts.

No.	Account Title	Dr.	Cr.
101	Cash	$48,372	
106.1	Alex's Engineering Co.	0	
106.2	Wildcat Services	0	
106.3	Easy Leasing	0	
106.4	IFM Co.	3,000	
106.5	Liu Corp.	0	
106.6	Gomez Co.	2,668	
106.7	Delta Co.	0	
106.8	KC, Inc.	0	
106.9	Dream, Inc.	0	
119	Merchandise inventory	0	
126	Computer supplies	580	
128	Prepaid insurance	1,665	
131	Prepaid rent	825	
163	Office equipment	8,000	
164	Accumulated depreciation—Office equipment		$ 400
167	Computer equipment	20,000	
168	Accumulated depreciation—Computer equipment		1,250
201	Accounts payable		1,100

No.	Account Title	Dr.	Cr.
210	Wages payable		$ 500
236	Unearned computer services revenue		1,500
301	S. Rey, Capital		80,360
302	S. Rey, Withdrawals	$0	
403	Computer services revenue		0
413	Sales		0
414	Sales returns and allowances	0	
415	Sales discounts	0	
502	Cost of goods sold	0	
612	Depreciation expense—Office equipment	0	
613	Depreciation expense—Computer equipment	0	
623	Wages expense	0	
637	Insurance expense	0	
640	Rent expense	0	
652	Computer supplies expense	0	
655	Advertising expense	0	
676	Mileage expense	0	
677	Miscellaneous expenses	0	
684	Repairs expense—Computer	0	

In response to requests from customers, S. Rey will begin selling computer software. The company will extend credit terms of 1/10, n/30, FOB shipping point, to all customers who purchase this merchandise. However, no cash discount is available on consulting fees. Additional accounts (Nos. 119, 413, 414, 415, and 502) are added to its general ledger to accommodate the company's new merchandising activities. Also, Business Solutions does not use reversing entries and, therefore, all revenue and expense accounts have zero beginning balances as of January 1, 2018. Its transactions for January through March follow:

Jan. 4   The company paid cash to Lyn Addie for five days' work at the rate of $125 per day. Four of the five days relate to wages payable that were accrued in the prior year.
5   Santana Rey invested an additional $25,000 cash in the company.
7   The company purchased $5,800 of merchandise from Kansas Corp. with terms of 1/10, n/30, FOB shipping point, invoice dated January 7.

© Alexander Image/Shutterstock RF

Check Jan. 11, Dr.
Unearned Computer Services
Revenue, $1,500

Jan. 20, No entry to
Cost of Goods Sold

9 The company received $2,668 cash from Gomez Co. as full payment on its account.

11 The company completed a five-day project for Alex's Engineering Co. and billed it $5,500, which is the total price of $7,000 less the advance payment of $1,500.

13 The company sold merchandise with a retail value of $5,200 and a cost of $3,560 to Liu Corp., invoice dated January 13.

15 The company paid $600 cash for freight charges on the merchandise purchased on January 7.

16 The company received $4,000 cash from Delta Co. for computer services provided.

17 The company paid Kansas Corp. for the invoice dated January 7, net of the discount.

20 Liu Corp. returned $500 of defective merchandise from its invoice dated January 13. The returned merchandise, which had a $320 cost, is discarded. (The policy of Business Solutions is to leave the cost of defective products in Cost of Goods Sold.)

22 The company received the balance due from Liu Corp., net of both the discount and the credit for the returned merchandise.

24 The company returned defective merchandise to Kansas Corp. and accepted a credit against future purchases. The defective merchandise invoice cost, net of the discount, was $496.

26 The company purchased $9,000 of merchandise from Kansas Corp. with terms of 1/10, n/30, FOB destination, invoice dated January 26.

26 The company sold merchandise with a $4,640 cost for $5,800 on credit to KC, Inc., invoice dated January 26.

31 The company paid cash to Lyn Addie for 10 days' work at $125 per day.

Feb. 1 The company paid $2,475 cash to Hillside Mall for another three months' rent in advance.

3 The company paid Kansas Corp. for the balance due, net of the cash discount, less the $496 amount in the credit memorandum.

5 The company paid $600 cash to the local newspaper for an advertising insert in today's paper.

11 The company received the balance due from Alex's Engineering Co. for fees billed on January 11.

15 Santana Rey withdrew $4,800 cash from the company for personal use.

23 The company sold merchandise with a $2,660 cost for $3,220 on credit to Delta Co., invoice dated February 23.

26 The company paid cash to Lyn Addie for eight days' work at $125 per day.

27 The company reimbursed Santana Rey for business automobile mileage (600 miles at $0.32 per mile).

Mar. 8 The company purchased $2,730 of computer supplies from Harris Office Products on credit, invoice dated March 8.

9 The company received the balance due from Delta Co. for merchandise sold on February 23.

11 The company paid $960 cash for minor repairs to the company's computer.

16 The company received $5,260 cash from Dream, Inc., for computing services provided.

19 The company paid the full amount due to Harris Office Products, consisting of amounts created on December 15 (of $1,100) and March 8.

24 The company billed Easy Leasing for $9,047 of computing services provided.

25 The company sold merchandise with a $2,002 cost for $2,800 on credit to Wildcat Services, invoice dated March 25.

30 The company sold merchandise with a $1,048 cost for $2,220 on credit to IFM Company, invoice dated March 30.

31 The company reimbursed Santana Rey for business automobile mileage (400 miles at $0.32 per mile).

The following additional facts are available for preparing adjustments on March 31 prior to financial statement preparation:

a. The March 31 amount of computer supplies still available totals $2,005.

b. Three more months have expired since the company purchased its annual insurance policy at a $2,220 cost for 12 months of coverage.

c. Lyn Addie has not been paid for seven days of work at the rate of $125 per day.

d. Three months have passed since any prepaid rent has been transferred to expense. The monthly rent expense is $825.

e. Depreciation on the computer equipment for January 1 through March 31 is $1,250.

f. Depreciation on the office equipment for January 1 through March 31 is $400.

g. The March 31 amount of merchandise inventory still available totals $704.

Required

1. Prepare journal entries to record each of the January through March transactions.

2. Post the journal entries in part 1 to the accounts in the company's general ledger. (*Note:* Begin with the ledger's post-closing adjusted balances as of December 31, 2017.)

3. Prepare a partial work sheet consisting of the first six columns (similar to the one shown in Exhibit 5B.1) that includes the unadjusted trial balance, the March 31 adjustments (*a*) through (*g*), and the adjusted trial balance. Do not prepare closing entries and do not journalize the adjustments or post them to the ledger.

4. Prepare an income statement (from the adjusted trial balance in part 3) for the three months ended March 31, 2018. Use a single-step format. List all expenses without differentiating between selling expenses and general and administrative expenses.

5. Prepare a statement of owner's equity (from the adjusted trial balance in part 3) for the three months ended March 31, 2018.

6. Prepare a classified balance sheet (from the adjusted trial balance) as of March 31, 2018.

Check (2) Ending balances at March 31: Cash, $68,057; Sales, $19,240

(3) Unadj. TB totals, $151,557; Adj. TB totals, $154,082

(4) Net income, $18,833

(5) S. Rey, Capital (at March 31), $119,393

(6) Total assets, $120,268

The **General Ledger** tool in *Connect* automates several of the procedural steps in the accounting cycle so that the accounting professional can focus on the impacts of each transaction on the various financial reports. The following General Ledger questions highlight the operating cycle of a merchandising company. In each case, the trial balance is automatically updated from the journal entries recorded.

GL 5-1 Based on Problem 5-1A

GL 5-2 Based on Problem 5-2A

GL 5-3 Based on Problem 5-5A

GENERAL LEDGER PROBLEM

Available only in Connect

Beyond the Numbers

BTN 5-1 Refer to **Apple**'s financial statements in Appendix A to answer the following.

Required

1. Assume that the amounts reported for inventories and cost of sales reflect items purchased in a form ready for resale. Compute the net cost of goods purchased for the year ended September 26, 2015.

2. Compute the current ratio and acid-test ratio as of September 26, 2015, and September 27, 2014. Interpret and comment on the ratio results. How does Apple compare to the industry average of 1.5 for the current ratio and 1.25 for the acid-test ratio?

Fast Forward

3. Access Apple's financial statements (Form 10-K) for fiscal years ending after September 26, 2015, from its website (Apple.com) or the SEC's EDGAR database (SEC.gov). Recompute and interpret the current ratio and acid-test ratio for these current fiscal years.

REPORTING IN ACTION
A1
APPLE

BTN 5-2 Key comparative figures for **Apple** and **Google** follow.

COMPARATIVE ANALYSIS
A2
APPLE
GOOGLE

$ millions	Apple Current Year	Apple Prior Year	Google Current Year	Google Prior Year
Net sales	$233,715	$182,795	$74,989	$66,001
Cost of sales	140,089	112,258	28,164	25,691

Required

1. Compute the dollar amount of gross margin and the gross margin ratio for the two years shown for each of these companies.

2. Which company earns more in gross margin for each dollar of net sales? How do they compare to the industry average of 45.0%?

3. Did the gross margin ratio improve or decline for these companies?

ETHICS CHALLENGE

C1   P2

BTN 5-3   Amy Martin is a student who plans to attend approximately four professional events a year at her college. Each event necessitates a financial outlay of $100 to $200 for a new suit and accessories. After incurring a major hit to her savings for the first event, Amy developed a different approach. She buys the suit on credit the week before the event, wears it to the event, and returns it the next week to the store for a full refund on her charge card.

Required

1. Comment on the ethics exhibited by Amy and possible consequences of her actions.

2. How does the merchandising company account for the suits that Amy returns?

COMMUNICATING IN PRACTICE

C2   P3   P5

BTN 5-4   You are the financial officer for Music Plus, a retailer that sells goods for home entertainment needs. The business owner, Vic Velakturi, recently reviewed the annual financial statements you prepared and sent you an e-mail stating that he thinks you overstated net income. He explains that although he has invested a great deal in security, he is sure shoplifting and other forms of inventory shrinkage have occurred, but he does not see any deduction for shrinkage on the income statement. The store uses a perpetual inventory system.

Required

Prepare a brief memorandum that responds to the owner's concerns.

TAKING IT TO THE NET

A2   C1

BTN 5-5   Access the SEC's EDGAR database (SEC.gov) and obtain the March 17, 2015, filing of its fiscal 2015 10-K report (for year ended January 31, 2015) for **J. Crew Group, Inc.** (ticker: JCG).

Required

Prepare a table that reports the gross margin ratios for J. Crew using the revenues and cost of goods sold data from J. Crew's income statement for each of its most recent three years. Analyze and comment on the trend in its gross margin ratio.

TEAMWORK IN ACTION

C1   C2

BTN 5-6   Official Brands's general ledger and supplementary records at the end of its current period reveal the following.

Sales, gross	$600,000	Merchandise inventory (beginning of period)	$ 98,000
Sales returns & allowances	20,000	Invoice cost of merchandise purchases	360,000
Sales discounts	13,000	Purchases discounts received	9,000
Cost of transportation-in	22,000	Purchases returns and allowances	11,000
Operating expenses	50,000	Merchandise inventory (end of period)	84,000

Required

1. *Each* member of the team is to assume responsibility for computing *one* of the following items. You are not to duplicate your teammates' work. Get any necessary amounts to compute your item from the appropriate teammate. Each member is to explain his or her computation to the team in preparation for reporting to the class.

    a. Net sales   **d.** Gross profit

    b. Total cost of merchandise purchases   **e.** Net income

    c. Cost of goods sold

Continued on next page . . .

Point: In teams of four, assign the same student *a* and *e*. Rotate teams for reporting on a different computation and the analysis in step 3.

2. Check your net income with the instructor. If correct, proceed to step 3.

3. Assume that a physical inventory count finds that actual ending inventory is $76,000. Discuss how this affects previously computed amounts in step 1.

BTN 5-7   Refer to the opening feature about Sword & Plough. Assume that Emily and Betsy report current annual sales at approximately $1 million and prepare the following income statement.

SWORD & PLOUGH	
Income Statement	
For Year Ended January 31, 2016	
Net sales	$1,000,000
Cost of sales	610,000
Expenses (other than cost of sales)	200,000
Net income	$ 190,000

Emily and Betsy sell to individuals and retailers, ranging from small shops to large chains. Assume that they currently offer credit terms of 1/15, n/60, and ship FOB destination. To improve their cash flow, they are considering changing credit terms to 3/10, n/30. In addition, they propose to change shipping terms to FOB shipping point. They expect that the increase in discount rate will increase net sales by 9%, but the gross margin ratio (and ratio of cost of sales divided by net sales) is expected to remain unchanged. They also expect that delivery expenses will be zero under this proposal; thus, expenses other than cost of sales are expected to increase only 6%.

Required

1. Prepare a forecasted income statement for the year ended January 31, 2017, based on the proposal.

2. Based on the forecasted income statement alone (from your part 1 solution), do you recommend that Emily and Betsy implement the new sales policies? Explain.

3. What else should Emily and Betsy consider before deciding whether or not to implement the new policies? Explain.

BTN 5-8   Arrange an interview (in person or by phone) with the manager of a retail shop in a mall or in the downtown area of your community. Explain to the manager that you are a student studying merchandising activities and the accounting for sales returns and sales allowances. Ask the manager what the store policy is regarding returns. Also find out if sales allowances are ever negotiated with customers. Inquire whether management perceives that customers are abusing return policies and what actions management takes to counter potential abuses. Be prepared to discuss your findings in class.

BTN 5-9   Samsung (Samsung.com), Apple, and Google are competitors in the global marketplace. Key comparative figures for each company follow.

	Net Sales	Cost of Sales
Samsung*	₩200,653,482	₩123,482,118
Apple[†]	$ 233,715	$ 140,089
Google[†]	$ 74,989	$ 28,164

* Millions of Korean won for Samsung.
[†] Millions of dollars for Apple and Google.

Required

1. Rank the three companies (highest to lowest) based on the gross margin ratio.
2. Which of the companies uses a multiple-step income statement format? (These companies' income statements are in Appendix A.)

GLOBAL VIEW

This section discusses similarities and differences between U.S. GAAP and IFRS in accounting and reporting for merchandise purchases and sales, and for the income statement.

Accounting for Merchandise Purchases and Sales   Both U.S. GAAP and IFRS include broad and similar guidance for the accounting of merchandise purchases and sales. Nearly all of the transactions presented and illustrated in this chapter are accounted for identically under the two systems. The closing process for merchandisers is also similar for U.S. GAAP and IFRS.

Income Statement Presentation   We explained that net income, profit, and earnings refer to the same (*bottom line*) item. However, IFRS tends to use the term *profit* more than any other term, whereas U.S. statements tend to use *net income* more than any other term. Both U.S. GAAP and IFRS income statements begin with the net sales or net revenues (*top line*) item. For merchandisers and manufacturers, this is followed by cost of goods sold. The remaining presentation is similar with the following differences.

- U.S. GAAP offers little guidance about the presentation or order of expenses. IFRS requires separate disclosures for financing costs (interest expense), income tax expense, and some other special items.
- Both systems require separate disclosure of items when their size, nature, or frequency is important.
- IFRS permits expenses to be presented by their function or their nature. U.S. GAAP provides no direction but the SEC requires presentation by function.
- Neither U.S. GAAP nor IFRS defines *operating* income, which results in latitude in reporting.
- IFRS permits alternative income measures on the income statement; U.S. GAAP does not.

VOLKSWAGEN   Volkswagen Group provides the following example of income statement reporting. We see the separate disclosure of finance costs, taxes, and other items. We also see the unusual practice of using the minus symbol in an income statement.

VOLKSWAGEN GROUP Income Statement (in euros million) For Year Ended December 31, 2014	
Sales revenue	€ 202,458
Cost of sales	−165,934
Gross profit	36,524
Distribution expenses	−20,292
Administrative expenses	−6,841
Other operating income (net of other expenses)	3,306
Operating profit	12,697
Finance costs	−2,658
Other financial results (including equity investments)	4,755
Profit before tax	14,794
Income tax	−3,726
Profit	€ 11,068

Balance Sheet Presentation   Earlier chapters explained how both U.S. GAAP and IFRS require current items to be separated from noncurrent items on the balance sheet (yielding a *classified balance sheet*). As discussed, U.S. GAAP balance sheets report current items first. Assets are listed from most liquid to least liquid, whereas liabilities are listed from nearest to maturity to furthest from maturity. IFRS balance sheets normally present noncurrent items first (and equity before liabilities), but this is *not* a requirement, as evidenced in **Samsung**'s balance sheet in Appendix A.

 Global View Assignments

Discussion Questions 13 and 14

Quick Study 5-15

Quick Study 5-23

Exercise 5-18

BTN 5-9

6
chapter

Inventories and Cost of Sales

Learning Objectives

CONCEPTUAL

C1 Identify the items making up merchandise inventory.

C2 Identify the costs of merchandise inventory.

ANALYTICAL

A1 Analyze the effects of inventory methods for both financial and tax reporting.

A2 Analyze the effects of inventory errors on current and future financial statements.

A3 Assess inventory management using both inventory turnover and days' sales in inventory.

PROCEDURAL

P1 Compute inventory in a perpetual system using the methods of specific identification, FIFO, LIFO, and weighted average.

P2 Compute the lower of cost or market amount of inventory.

P3 *Appendix 6A*—Compute inventory in a periodic system using the methods of specific identification, FIFO, LIFO, and weighted average.

P4 *Appendix 6B*—Apply both the retail inventory and gross profit methods to estimate inventory.

SEATTLE—Brad Gillis and Ben Friedman started **Homegrown Sustainable Sandwich Shop** (**EatHomegrown.com**), a sandwich shop that uses organic produce and buys ingredients from local farmers. Brad and Ben have opened 10 shops in Seattle and, according to Ben, plan on "opening up in the Bay Area this year." Homegrown has already surpassed $5 million in annual sales.

Brad and Ben had no business experience before starting Homegrown. "At first we were a little scared . . . we wrote the business plan for Homegrown during our senior year of college," recalls Ben, and "started this business right out of college at age 22." Adds Brad, "We just jumped right in!"

The company's launch was a challenge. "Everything has been a steep learning curve!" admits Brad. The two confronted inventory production and sales planning, and had to deal with discounts and allowances. A major challenge was identifying proper inventories while controlling costs.

> *"It's not as scary if you don't know what you're doing"*
> —**Brad Gillis**

Each consumer demands a different product, explains Ben. For example, Brad's favorite sandwich is smoked ham, egg, and cheese and Ben's favorite is smoked pastrami. Brad and Ben depend on their accounting system to give them up-to-date information on inventory to avoid selling out of specific sandwiches.

Applying inventory management and old-fashioned trial and error, Ben and Brad learned to fill orders, collect money, and maintain the right level and mix of inventory. To help, they set up an inventory system to account for sales and purchases in real time.

The two owners insist that while it is important to stay on the cutting edge, business success demands sound inventory management. "It doesn't get talked about as much . . . but [accounting data] can really impact what products we carry," explains Brad. "It definitely goes into product selection."

Rachel Coward/425 Magazine

Homegrown Talent

While Brad and Ben continue to measure, monitor, and manage inventories and costs, their success and growth are moving them into new markets. "We're built to grow," insists Brad. Adds Ben, "We would love to open stores on the East Coast one day."

Ben and Brad have achieved success with Homegrown, but they have not forgotten about their sustainable roots. "We kept coming back to the environment as the cause we wanted to dedicate ourselves to," recalls Ben. "We developed the idea for Homegrown out of a drive to build a social business that effected positive change on the environment."

Sources: *Homegrown website*, January 2017; *425 Magazine*, March 2016; *Eco18*, March 2016; *Culintro*, February 2014; *Seattle Times*, August 2013

INVENTORY BASICS

This section identifies the items and costs making up merchandise inventory. It also describes the importance of internal controls in taking a physical count of inventory.

Determining Inventory Items

C1

Identify the items making up merchandise inventory.

Merchandise inventory includes all goods that a company owns and holds for sale. This is true regardless of where the goods are located when inventory is counted. Certain inventory items require special attention, including goods in transit, goods on consignment, and goods that are damaged or obsolete.

Goods in Transit   Does a purchaser's inventory include goods in transit from a supplier? The answer is that if ownership has passed to the purchaser, the goods are included in the purchaser's inventory. We determine this by reviewing the shipping terms: *FOB destination* or *FOB shipping point.* Goods purchased FOB shipping point are included in the buyer's inventory when the items are shipped. Goods purchased FOB destination are not included in the buyer's inventory until they arrive at their destination.

Goods on Consignment   Goods on consignment are goods shipped by the owner, called the **consignor,** to another party, the **consignee.** A consignee sells goods for the owner. The consignor continues to own the consigned goods and reports them in its inventory. For instance, **Upper Deck** pays sports celebrities such as Aaron Rodgers of the Green Bay Packers to sign memorabilia, which are offered to card shops on consignment. Upper Deck, the consignor, must report these items in its inventory until sold. The consignee never reports consigned goods in inventory.

Goods Damaged or Obsolete   Damaged and obsolete (and deteriorated) goods are not reported in inventory if they cannot be sold. If these goods can be sold at a reduced price, they are included in inventory at a conservative estimate of their **net realizable value.** Net realizable value is sales price minus the cost of making the sale. The period when damage or obsolescence (or deterioration) occurs is the period when the loss in value is reported.

⬜ **Decision** Insight

Managing Inventory   A wireless portable device with a two-way radio allows clerks to quickly record inventory by scanning bar codes and to instantly send and receive inventory data. It gives managers access to up-to-date information on inventory and its location. Bar codes have influenced nearly all aspects of inventory control and management. The use of bar codes makes accounting for inventory simpler, more accurate, and more efficient. ■

© moodboard/Getty Images RF

Determining Inventory Costs

C2

Identify the costs of merchandise inventory.

Merchandise inventory includes costs of expenditures necessary, directly or indirectly, to bring an item to a salable condition and location. This means that the cost of an inventory item includes its invoice cost minus any discount, plus any incidental costs necessary. Incidental costs can include shipping, storage, and insurance. The *expense recognition (matching) principle* states that inventory costs should be recorded as cost of goods sold in the period when inventory is sold.

Internal Controls and Taking a Physical Count

Fraud: Auditors observe employees as they take a physical inventory. Auditors take their own test counts to monitor the accuracy of a company's count.

Events can cause the Inventory account balance to differ from the actual inventory available. Such events include theft, loss, damage, and errors. Thus, nearly all companies take a *physical count of inventory* at least once each year—informally called *taking an inventory.* This often occurs at the end of a fiscal year or when inventory amounts are low. This physical count is used to adjust the Inventory account balance to the actual inventory available.

▤ **Decision** Insight

In Control   A company applies internal controls when taking a physical count of inventory that usually include the following to minimize fraud and to increase reliability:

- *Prenumbered inventory tickets* are distributed to *counters*—each ticket must be accounted for.
- Counters of inventory are assigned and do not include those responsible for inventory.
- Counters confirm the validity of inventory, including its existence, amount, and quality.
- A second count is taken by a different counter.
- A manager confirms that all inventories are ticketed once, and only once. ▪

Point: The Inventory account is a controlling account for the inventory subsidiary ledger. This *subsidiary ledger* contains a separate record (units and costs) for each separate product.

NEED-TO-KNOW **6-1**

Inventory Items and Costs

C1   C2

1. A master carver of wooden birds operates her business out of a garage. At the end of the current period, the carver has 17 units (carvings) in her garage, 3 of which were damaged by water and cannot be sold. The distributor also has another 5 units in her truck, ready to deliver per a customer order, terms FOB destination, and another 11 units out on consignment at several small retail stores. How many units does the carver include in the business's period-end inventory?

2. A distributor of artistic iron-based fixtures acquires a piece for $1,000, terms FOB shipping point. Additional costs in obtaining it and offering it for sale include $150 for transportation-in, $300 for import duties, $100 for insurance during shipment, $200 for advertising, a $50 voluntary gratuity to the delivery person, $75 for enhanced store lighting, and $250 for sales staff salaries. For computing inventory, what cost is assigned to this artistic piece?

Solutions

1.

Units in ending inventory	
Units in storage..........................	17 units
Less damaged (unsalable) units	(3)
Plus units in transit......................	5
Plus units on consignment.................	11
Total units in ending inventory.............	30 units

2.

Merchandise cost................	$1,000
Plus:	
Transportation-in	150
Import duties	300
Insurance	100
Total inventory cost	$1,550

Do More: QS 6-1, QS 6-2, E 6-1, E 6-2

INVENTORY COSTING UNDER A PERPETUAL SYSTEM

Accounting for inventory affects both the balance sheet and the income statement. A major goal in accounting for inventory is to properly match costs with sales. We use the *expense recognition* (or *matching*) *principle* to compute how much of the cost of the goods available for sale is expensed and how much is carried forward as inventory.

Management decisions in accounting for inventory focus on the following:

- Items included in inventory and their costs.
- Costing method (specific identification, FIFO, LIFO, or weighted average).
- Inventory system (perpetual or periodic).
- Use of market values or other estimates.

The first point was explained in the prior section. The second and third points will be addressed now. The fourth point is the focus at the end of this chapter.

An important issue in accounting for inventory is determining the per unit costs assigned to inventory items. When all units are purchased at the same unit cost, this process is simple. When identical items are purchased at different costs, we must decide which amounts to record in cost of goods sold and which amounts remain in inventory.

Four methods are used to assign costs to inventory and to cost of goods sold: (1) specific identification; (2) first-in, first-out (FIFO); (3) last-in, first-out (LIFO); and (4) weighted average. Exhibit 6.1 shows the frequency in use of these methods.

Each method assumes a particular pattern for how costs flow through inventory. The cost flow assumption does not have to match the actual physical flow of

EXHIBIT 6.1

Frequency in Use of Inventory Methods

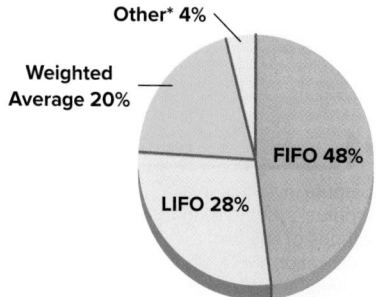

*Includes specific identification.

goods. For example, Kroger's grocery chain sells food first-in, first-out, meaning they sell the oldest food in inventory first. However, Kroger could use last-in, first-out to assign costs to food sold. With the exception of specific identification, the **physical flow and cost flow need not be the same.**

Inventory Cost Flow Assumptions

Point: Cost of goods sold is abbreviated COGS.

This section introduces inventory cost flow assumptions. For this purpose, assume that three identical units are purchased separately at the following three dates and costs: May 1 at $45, May 3 at $65, and May 6 at $70. One unit is then sold on May 7 for $100. Exhibit 6.2 shows the flow of costs to either cost of goods sold on the income statement or inventory reported on the balance sheet for FIFO, LIFO, and weighted average.

EXHIBIT 6.2

Cost Flow Assumptions

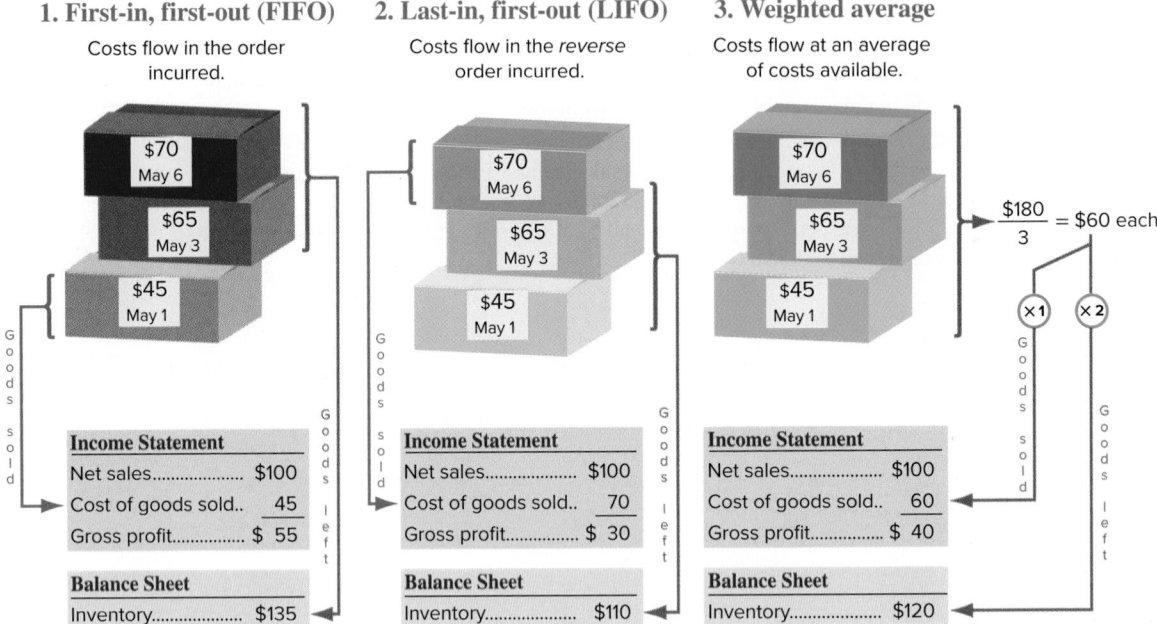

(1) *FIFO assumes costs flow in the order incurred.* The unit purchased on May 1 for $45 is the earliest cost incurred—it is sent to cost of goods sold on the income statement first. The remaining two units ($65 and $70) are reported in inventory on the balance sheet.

Point: It is helpful to recall the cost flow of inventory.

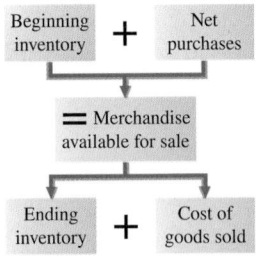

(2) *LIFO assumes costs flow in the reverse order incurred.* The unit purchased on May 6 for $70 is the most recent cost incurred—it is sent to cost of goods sold on the income statement. The remaining two units ($45 and $65) are reported in inventory on the balance sheet.

(3) *Weighted average assumes costs flow at an average of the costs available.* The units available at the May 7 sale average $60 in cost, computed as ($45 + $65 + $70)/3. One unit's $60 average cost is sent to cost of goods sold on the income statement. The remaining two units' average costs are reported in inventory at $120 on the balance sheet.

Cost flow assumptions can impact gross profit and inventory numbers. Exhibit 6.2 shows that gross profit ranges from $30 to $55 due to the cost flow assumption.

> *The following sections on inventory costing use the **perpetual system.** Appendix 6A uses the periodic system. An instructor can choose to cover either one or both systems. If the perpetual system is skipped, then read Appendix 6A and return to the Decision Maker box (ahead) titled "Cost Analyst."*

P1

Compute inventory in a perpetual system using the methods of specific identification, FIFO, LIFO, and weighted average.

Inventory Costing Illustration

This section illustrates inventory costing methods. We use information from Trekking, a sporting goods store. Among its products, Trekking carries one type of mountain bike whose sales are directed at resorts that provide inexpensive bikes for guest use. These resorts usually purchase in amounts of 10 or more bikes. We use Trekking's data from August. Its mountain bike (unit) inventory at the beginning of August and its purchases and sales during August are in Exhibit 6.3. It ends August with 12 bikes in inventory.

Date	Activity	Units Acquired at Cost	Units Sold at Retail	Unit Inventory
Aug. 1	Beginning inventory.......	10 units @ $ 91 = $ 910		10 units
Aug. 3	Purchases..............	15 units @ $106 = $ 1,590		25 units
Aug. 14	Sales..................		20 units @ $130	5 units
Aug. 17	Purchases..............	20 units @ $115 = $ 2,300		25 units
Aug. 28	Purchases..............	10 units @ $119 = $ 1,190		35 units
Aug. 30	Sales..................		23 units @ $150	**12 units**
	Totals	**55 units** → **$5,990**	**43 units**	
		Units available for sale	Goods available for sale	Units sold	Units left

EXHIBIT 6.3

Purchases and Sales of Goods

Trekking uses the **perpetual inventory system**, which means that its Merchandise Inventory account is updated for each purchase and sale of inventory. **(Appendix 6A describes the assignment of costs to inventory using a periodic system.)** Regardless of what inventory method is used, cost of goods available for sale must be allocated between cost of goods sold and ending inventory.

Specific Identification

When each item in inventory can be matched with a specific purchase and invoice, we can use **specific identification** or **SI** (also called *specific invoice inventory pricing*) to assign costs. We also need sales records that identify exactly which items were sold and when. For example, each bike's serial number could be used to track costs and compute cost of goods sold. Trekking's internal documents reveal the following specific unit sales:

August 14   Sold 8 bikes costing $91 each and 12 bikes costing $106 each
August 30   Sold 2 bikes costing $91 each, 3 bikes costing $106 each, 15 bikes costing
            $115 each, and 3 bikes costing $119 each

Applying specific identification and using the information above, we prepare Exhibit 6.4. This exhibit begins with the $5,990 in total units available for sale—this is from Exhibit 6.3. For the 20 units sold on August 14, the company specifically identified that 8 of them had cost $91 each and 12 had cost $106 each, resulting in an August 14 cost of sales of $2,000. Next, for the 23 units sold on August 30, the company specifically identified that 2 of them had cost $91 each, that 3 had cost $106 each, that 15 had cost $115 each, and that 3 had cost $119 each, resulting in an August 30 cost of sales of $2,582. The total cost of sales for the period is $4,582. We then subtract this $4,582 in cost of goods sold from the $5,990 in cost of goods available to get $1,408 in ending inventory. Study Exhibit 6.4 to see the flow of costs. Each unit, whether sold or remaining in inventory, has its own specific cost attached to it.

Merchandise Inventory (SI)		
Aug. 1	910	
Aug. 3	1,590	
		Aug. 14 2,000
Aug. 17	2,300	
Aug. 28	1,190	
		Aug. 30 2,582
Aug. 31	1,408	

Total cost of 55 units available for sale (from Exhibit 6.3)		$ 5,990
Cost of goods sold*		
Aug. 14 (8 @ $91) + (12 @ $106)...	$2,000	
Aug. 30 (2 @ $91) + (3 @ $106) + (15 @ $115) + (3 @ $119)	2,582	4,582
Ending inventory		**$1,408**

EXHIBIT 6.4

Specific Identification Computations

* Identification of items sold (and their costs) is from internal documents that track each unit from its purchase to its sale.

When using specific identification, Trekking's cost of goods sold reported on the income statement totals **$4,582**, the sum of $2,000 and $2,582 from the cost of goods sold section of Exhibit 6.4. Trekking's ending inventory reported on the balance sheet is **$1,408**, which is the final inventory balance from Exhibit 6.4. The following graphic shows this flow of costs.

Point: Specific identification is usually practical for companies with expensive or custom-made inventory. Examples include car dealerships, implement dealers, jewelers, and fashion designers.

Point: SI yields identical results under both periodic and perpetual.

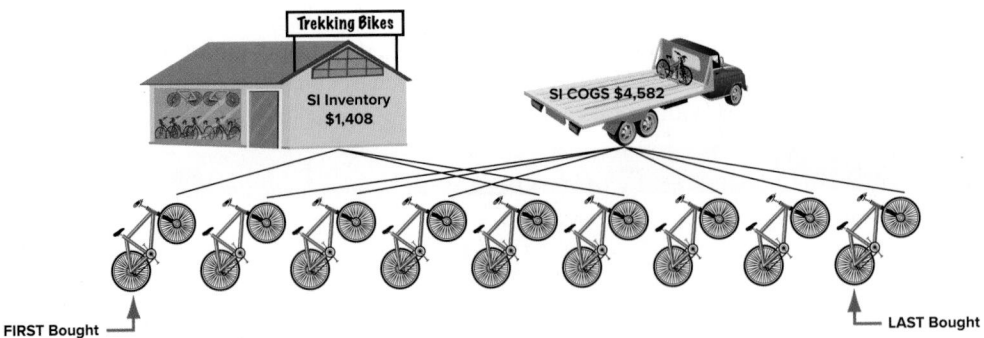

First-In, First-Out

The **first-in, first-out (FIFO)** method of assigning costs assumes that inventory items are sold in the order acquired. When sales occur, the costs of the earliest units acquired are charged to cost of goods sold. This leaves the costs from the most recent purchases in ending inventory. Use of FIFO for computing the cost of inventory and cost of goods sold is shown in Exhibit 6.5.

EXHIBIT 6.5

FIFO Computations—
Perpetual System

For the 20 units sold on Aug. 14, the first 10 sold are assigned the earliest cost of $91 (from beg. bal.). The next 10 sold are assigned the next earliest cost of $106.

Date	Goods Purchased	Cost of Goods Sold		Inventory Balance	
Aug. 1	Beginning balance			10 @ $ 91	= $ 910
Aug. 3	15 @ $106 = $1,590			10 @ $ 91 15 @ $106	= $ 2,500
Aug. 14		10 @ $ 91 = $ 910 10 @ $106 = $1,060	= $1,970	5 @ $106	= $ 530
Aug. 17	20 @ $115 = $2,300			5 @ $106 20 @ $115	= $ 2,830
Aug. 28	10 @ $119 = $1,190			5 @ $106 20 @ $115 10 @ $119	= $ 4,020
Aug. 30		5 @ $106 = $ 530 18 @ $115 = $2,070	= $2,600 $4,570	2 @ $115 10 @ $119	= $1,420

For the 23 units sold on Aug. 30, the first 5 sold are assigned the earliest available cost of $106 (from Aug. 3 purchase). The next 18 sold are assigned the next earliest cost of $115 (from Aug. 17 purchase).

Merchandise Inventory (FIFO)

Aug. 1	910		
Aug. 3	1,590		
		Aug. 14	1,970
Aug. 17	2,300		
Aug. 28	1,190		
		Aug. 30	2,600
Aug. 31	1,420		

Point: The "Goods Purchased" column is identical for all methods. Data are taken from Exhibit 6.3.

This exhibit starts with beginning inventory of 10 bikes at $91 each. On August 3, 15 more bikes costing $106 each are bought for $1,590. Inventory now consists of 10 bikes at $91 each and 15 bikes at $106 each, for a total of $2,500. On August 14, 20 bikes are sold—applying FIFO, the first 10 sold cost $91 each and the next 10 sold cost $106 each, for a total cost of $1,970. This leaves 5 bikes costing $106 each, or $530, in inventory. On August 17, 20 bikes costing $2,300 are purchased, and on August 28, another 10 bikes costing $1,190 are purchased, for a total of 35 bikes costing $4,020 in inventory. On August 30, 23 bikes are sold—applying FIFO, the first 5 bikes sold cost $530 and the next 18 sold cost $2,070, which leaves 12 bikes costing $1,420 in ending inventory.

Trekking's FIFO cost of goods sold reported on its income statement (reflecting the 43 units sold) is **$4,570** ($1,970 + $2,600), and its ending inventory reported on the balance sheet (reflecting the 12 units unsold) is **$1,420**.

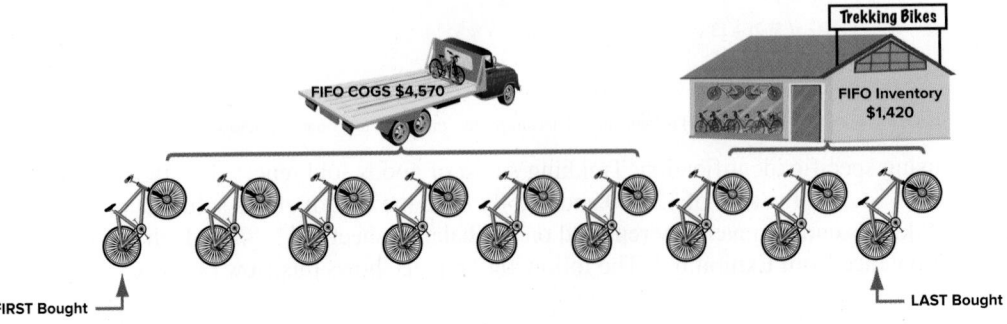

Last-In, First-Out

The **last-in, first-out (LIFO)** method of assigning costs assumes that the most recent purchases are sold first. These more recent costs are charged to the goods sold, and the costs of the earliest purchases are assigned to inventory.

Exhibit 6.6 shows the LIFO computations. It starts with beginning inventory of 10 bikes at $91 each. On August 3, 15 more bikes costing $106 each are bought for $1,590. Inventory now consists of 10 bikes at $91 each and 15 bikes at $106 each, for a total of $2,500. On August 14, 20 bikes are sold—applying LIFO, the first 15 sold are from the most recent purchase costing $106 each, and the next 5 sold are from the next most recent purchase costing $91 each, for a total cost of $2,045. This leaves 5 bikes costing $91 each, or $455, in inventory. On August 17, 20 bikes costing $2,300 are purchased, and on August 28, another 10 bikes costing $1,190 are purchased, for a total of 35 bikes costing $3,945 in inventory. On August 30, 23 bikes are sold—applying LIFO, the first 10 bikes sold are from the most recent purchase costing $1,190, and the next 13 sold are from the next most recent purchase costing $1,495, which leaves 12 bikes costing $1,260 in ending inventory.

Point: By assigning costs from the most recent purchases to cost of goods sold, LIFO comes closest to matching current costs of goods sold with revenues (compared to FIFO or weighted average).

Date	Goods Purchased	Cost of Goods Sold	Inventory Balance
Aug. 1	Beginning balance		10 @ $91 = $ 910
Aug. 3	15 @ $106 = $1,590		10 @ $ 91 15 @ $106 } = $2,500
Aug. 14		15 @ $106 = $1,590 5 @ $ 91 = $ 455 } = $2,045	5 @ $ 91 = $ 455
Aug. 17	20 @ $115 = $2,300		5 @ $ 91 20 @ $115 } = $2,755
Aug. 28	10 @ $119 = $1,190		5 @ $ 91 20 @ $115 10 @ $119 } = $3,945
Aug. 30		10 @ $119 = $1,190 13 @ $115 = $1,495 } = $2,685 $4,730	5 @ $ 91 7 @ $115 } = $1,260

EXHIBIT 6.6

LIFO Computations— Perpetual System

For the 20 units sold on Aug. 14, the first 15 sold are assigned the most recent cost of $106. The next 5 sold are assigned the next most recent cost of $91.

For the 23 units sold on Aug. 30, the first 10 sold are assigned the most recent cost of $119. The next 13 sold are assigned the next most recent cost of $115.

Merchandise Inventory (LIFO)

Aug. 1	910		
Aug. 3	1,590		
		Aug. 14	2,045
Aug. 17	2,300		
Aug. 28	1,190		
		Aug. 30	2,685
Aug. 31	1,260		

Trekking's LIFO cost of goods sold reported on the income statement is **$4,730** ($2,045 + $2,685), and its ending inventory reported on the balance sheet is **$1,260**.

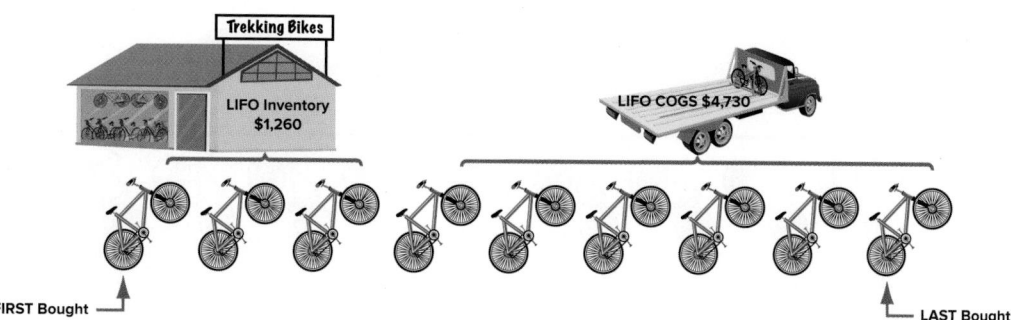

Weighted Average

The **weighted average** or **WA** (also called **average cost**) method of assigning cost requires that we use the weighted average cost per unit of inventory at the time of each sale. Weighted average cost per unit at the time of each sale equals the cost of goods available for sale

EXHIBIT 6.7

Weighted Average Computations—Perpetual System

Date	Goods Purchased	Cost of Goods Sold	Inventory Balance
Aug. 1	Beginning balance		10 @ $91 = $ 910 (10 @ $ 91 per unit)
Aug. 3	15 @ $106 = $1,590		10 @ $ 91 15 @ $106 } = $2,500 (25 @ $100 per unit)[a]
Aug. 14		20 @ $100 = $2,000	5 @ $100 = $ 500 (5 @ $100 per unit)[b]
Aug. 17	20 @ $115 = $2,300		5 @ $100 20 @ $115 } = $2,800 (25 @ $112 per unit)[c]
Aug. 28	10 @ $119 = $1,190		25 @ $112 10 @ $119 } = $3,990 (35 @ $114 per unit)[d]
Aug. 30		23 @ $114 = $2,622	12 @ $114 = $1,368 (12 @ $114 per unit)[e]
		$4,622	

For the 20 units sold on Aug. 14, the cost assigned is the $100 *average cost* per unit from the Inventory Balance column at the time of sale.

For the 23 units sold on Aug. 30, the cost assigned is the $114 *average cost* per unit from the Inventory Balance column at the time of sale.

[a] $100 per unit = ($2,500 inventory balance ÷ 25 units in inventory).
[b] $100 per unit = ($500 inventory balance ÷ 5 units in inventory).
[c] $112 per unit = ($2,800 inventory balance ÷ 25 units in inventory).
[d] $114 per unit = ($3,990 inventory balance ÷ 35 units in inventory).
[e] $114 per unit = ($1,368 inventory balance ÷ 12 units in inventory).

Merchandise Inventory (WA)

Aug. 1	910		
Aug. 3	1,590		
		Aug. 14	2,000
Aug. 17	2,300		
Aug. 28	1,190		
		Aug. 30	2,622
Aug. 31	1,368		

divided by the units available. The results using weighted average (WA) for Trekking are shown in Exhibit 6.7.

This exhibit starts with beginning inventory of 10 bikes at $91 each. On August 3, 15 more bikes costing $106 each are bought for $1,590. Inventory now consists of 10 bikes at $91 each and 15 bikes at $106 each, for a total of $2,500. The average cost per bike for that inventory is $100, computed as $2,500/(10 bikes + 15 bikes). On August 14, 20 bikes are sold—applying WA, the 20 sold are assigned the $100 average cost, for a total cost of $2,000. This leaves 5 bikes with an average cost of $100 each, or $500, in inventory. On August 17, 20 bikes costing $2,300 are purchased, and on August 28, another 10 bikes costing $1,190 are purchased, for a total of 35 bikes costing $3,990 in inventory at August 28. The average cost per bike for the August 28 inventory is $114, computed as $3,990/(5 bikes + 20 bikes + 10 bikes). On August 30, 23 bikes are sold—applying WA, the 23 sold are assigned the $114 average cost, for a total cost of $2,622. This leaves 12 bikes costing $1,368 in ending inventory.

Trekking's cost of goods sold reported on the income statement (reflecting the 43 units sold) is **$4,622** ($2,000 + $2,622), and its ending inventory reported on the balance sheet (reflecting the 12 units unsold) is **$1,368**.

Point: Cost of goods available for sale, units available for sale, and units in ending inventory are identical for all methods.

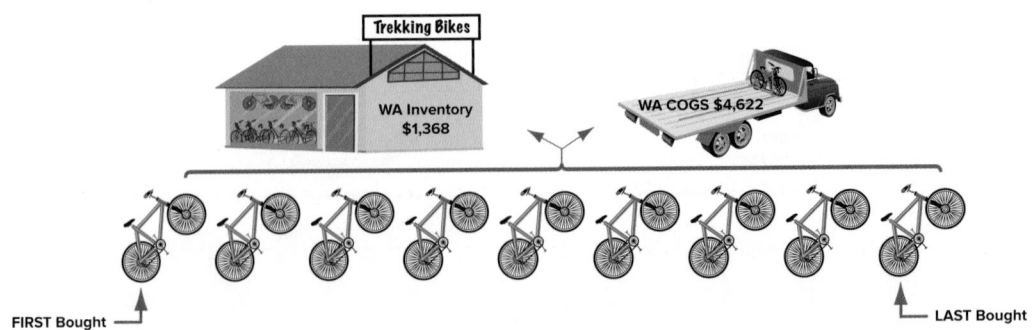

Advances in technology have greatly reduced the cost of a perpetual inventory system. Many companies now ask whether they can afford *not* to have a perpetual inventory system because timely access to inventory information is a competitive advantage and can help reduce the amount of inventory, which reduces costs.

■ **Decision** Insight

Kickbacks and Invoice Fraud   Inventory safeguards include restricted access, use of authorized requisitions, security measures, and controlled environments to prevent damage. Proper accounting includes matching inventory received with purchase order terms and quality requirements, preventing misstatements, and controlling access to inventory records. A study reports that 35% of employees in purchasing and procurement observed inappropriate kickbacks or gifts from suppliers. Another study reports that submission of fraudulent supplier invoices is not uncommon, and perpetrators are often employees (Data taken from *A Survey of Fraud, Bribery and Corruption in Australia & New Zealand, 2012,* KPMG). ■

Financial Statement Effects of Costing Methods

When purchase prices do not change, each inventory costing method assigns the same cost amounts to inventory and to cost of goods sold. When purchase prices are different, however, the methods nearly always assign different cost amounts. We show these differences in Exhibit 6.8 using Trekking's data.

A1_____

Analyze the effects of inventory methods for both financial and tax reporting.

TREKKING COMPANY For Month Ended August 31				
	Specific Identification	FIFO	LIFO	Weighted Average
Income Statement				
Sales..............................	$ 6,050	$ 6,050	$ 6,050	$ 6,050
Cost of goods sold.................	4,582	4,570	4,730	4,622
Gross profit	1,468	1,480	1,320	1,428
Expenses	450	450	450	450
Income before taxes	1,018	1,030	870	978
Income tax expense (30%)	305	309	261	293
Net income	$ 713	$ 721	$ 609	$ 685
Balance Sheet				
Inventory..........................	$1,408	$1,420	$1,260	$1,368

EXHIBIT 6.8

Financial Statement Effects of Inventory Costing Methods

This exhibit reveals two important results. First, when purchase costs *regularly rise,* as in Trekking's case, the following occurs:

● FIFO assigns the lowest amount to cost of goods sold—yielding the highest gross profit and net income.

● LIFO assigns the highest amount to cost of goods sold—yielding the lowest gross profit and net income.

● Weighted average yields results between FIFO and LIFO.

● Specific identification always yields results that depend on which units are sold.

Point: Managers prefer FIFO when costs are rising *and* incentives exist to report higher income for reasons such as bonus plans, job security, and reputation.

Second, when costs *regularly decline,* the reverse occurs for FIFO and LIFO. Namely, FIFO gives the highest cost of goods sold—yielding the lowest gross profit and income. However, LIFO then gives the lowest cost of goods sold—yielding the highest gross profit and income.

All four inventory costing methods are acceptable. However, a company must disclose the inventory method it uses in its financial statements or notes. Each method offers certain advantages, as follows:

● FIFO assigns an amount to inventory on the balance sheet that approximates its current cost; it also mimics the actual flow of goods for most businesses.

● LIFO assigns an amount to cost of goods sold on the income statement that approximates its current cost; it also better matches current costs with revenues in computing gross profit.

● Weighted average tends to smooth out erratic changes in costs.

● Specific identification exactly matches the costs of items with the revenues they generate.

Point: LIFO inventory is often less than the inventory's replacement cost because LIFO inventory is valued using the oldest inventory purchase costs.

Decision Maker

Cost Analyst   Your supervisor says she finds managing product costs easier if the balance sheet reflects inventory values that closely reflect replacement cost. Which inventory costing method do you advise adopting? ■

[*Answer:* Explain to your supervisor that FIFO results in an inventory valuation that approximates replacement cost. The most recently purchased goods are assigned to ending inventory under FIFO and are likely closer to replacement values than earlier costs that would be assigned to inventory if LIFO were used.]

Tax Effects of Costing Methods   Trekking's segment income statement in Exhibit 6.8 includes income tax expense (at a rate of 30%) because it was formed as a corporation. Since inventory costs affect net income, they have potential tax effects. Trekking gains a temporary tax advantage by using LIFO. Many companies use LIFO for this reason.

Companies can and often do use different costing methods for financial reporting and tax reporting. *The only exception is when LIFO is used for tax reporting; in this case, the IRS requires that it also be used in financial statements*—called the LIFO conformity rule.

Consistency in Costing Methods   The **consistency concept** prescribes that a company use the same accounting methods period after period so that financial statements are comparable across periods—the only exception is when a change from one method to another will improve its financial reporting. The *full-disclosure principle* prescribes that the notes to the statements report this type of change, its justification, and its effect on income.

The consistency concept does *not* require a company to use one method exclusively. For example, it can use different methods to value different categories of inventory.

Decision Ethics

Inventory Manager   Your compensation as inventory manager includes a bonus plan based on gross profit. Your superior asks your opinion on changing the inventory costing method from FIFO to LIFO. As costs are expected to continue to rise, your superior predicts that LIFO would match higher current costs against sales, thereby lowering taxable income (and gross profit). What do you recommend? ■   [*Answer:* It seems your company can save (or at least postpone) taxes by switching to LIFO, but the switch is likely to reduce bonus money that you believe you have earned and deserve. Since the U.S. tax code requires companies that use LIFO for tax reporting also use it for financial reporting, your options are further constrained. Your best decision is to tell your superior about the tax savings with LIFO. You should discuss your bonus plan and how this is likely to hurt you unfairly. You might propose to compute inventory under the LIFO method for reporting purposes but use the FIFO method for your bonus calculations. Another solution is to revise the bonus plan to reflect the company's use of the LIFO method.]

NEED-TO-KNOW 6-2

Perpetual SI, FIFO, LIFO, and WA

P1

A company reported the following December purchase and sales data for its only product.

Date	Activities	Units Acquired at Cost	Units Sold at Retail
Dec. 1	Beginning inventory	5 units @ $3.00 = $ 15.00	
Dec. 8	Purchase	10 units @ $4.50 = 45.00	
Dec. 9	Sales		8 units @ $7.00
Dec. 19	Purchase	13 units @ $5.00 = 65.00	
Dec. 24	Sales		18 units @ $8.00
Dec. 30	Purchase	8 units @ $5.30 = 42.40	
Totals	....	36 units $167.40	26 units

The company uses a *perpetual inventory system.* Determine the cost assigned to ending inventory and to cost of goods sold using (*a*) specific identification, (*b*) FIFO, (*c*) LIFO, and (*d*) weighted average. (Round per unit costs and inventory amounts to cents.) For specific identification, ending inventory consists of 10 units, where 8 are from the December 30 purchase and 2 are from the December 8 purchase.

Solutions

a. Specific identification: Ending inventory—eight units from December 30 purchase and two units from December 8 purchase.

Specific Identification	Ending Inventory	Cost of Goods Sold
(8 × $5.30) + (2 × $4.50)	$51.40	
(5 × $3.00) + (8 × $4.50) + (13 × $5.00) + (0 × $5.30)		$116.00
or $167.40 [Total Goods Available] − $51.40 [Ending Inventory]		$116.00

Merchandise Inventory (SI)

Beg. inventory	15.00		
Net purchases	152.40		
Avail. for sale	167.40		
		COGS	116.00
End. inventory	51.40		

b. FIFO—Perpetual

Date	Goods Purchased	Cost of Goods Sold	Inventory Balance
12/1			5 @ $3.00 = $15.00
12/8	10 @ $4.50		5 @ $3.00 ⎱ = $60.00 10 @ $4.50 ⎰
12/9		5 @ $3.00 ⎱ = $ 28.50 3 @ $4.50 ⎰	7 @ $4.50 = $31.50
12/19	13 @ $5.00		7 @ $4.50 ⎱ = $96.50 13 @ $5.00 ⎰
12/24		7 @ $4.50 ⎱ = $ 86.50 11 @ $5.00 ⎰	2 @ $5.00 = $10.00
12/30	8 @ $5.30		2 @ $5.00 ⎱ = $52.40 8 @ $5.30 ⎰
		$115.00	

Merchandise Inventory (FIFO)

Beg. inventory	15.00		
Net purchases	152.40		
Avail. for sale	167.40		
		COGS	115.00
End. inventory	52.40		

OR "short-cut" FIFO—Perpetual

FIFO	Ending Inventory	Cost of Goods Sold
(8 × $5.30) + (2 × $5.00)	$52.40	
(5 × $3.00) + (10 × $4.50) + (11 × $5.00)		$115.00
or $167.40 [Total Goods Available] − $52.40 [Ending Inventory]		$115.00

c. LIFO—Perpetual

Date	Goods Purchased	Cost of Goods Sold	Inventory Balance
12/1			5 @ $3.00 = $15.00
12/8	10 @ $4.50		5 @ $3.00 ⎱ = $60.00 10 @ $4.50 ⎰
12/9		8 @ $4.50 = $ 36.00	5 @ $3.00 ⎱ = $24.00 2 @ $4.50 ⎰
12/19	13 @ $5.00		5 @ $3.00 ⎱ 2 @ $4.50 ⎬ = $89.00 13 @ $5.00 ⎰
12/24		13 @ $5.00 ⎱ 2 @ $4.50 ⎬ = $ 83.00 3 @ $3.00 ⎰	2 @ $3.00 = $ 6.00
12/30	8 @ $5.30		2 @ $3.00 ⎱ = $48.40 8 @ $5.30 ⎰
		$119.00	

Merchandise Inventory (LIFO)

Beg. inventory	15.00		
Net purchases	152.40		
Avail. for sale	167.40		
		COGS	119.00
End. inventory	48.40		

d. Weighted Average—Perpetual

Date	Goods Purchased	Cost of Goods Sold	Inventory Balance
12/1			5 @ $3.00 = $15.00 (5 @ $3.00 per unit)
12/8	10 @ $4.50		5 @ $3.00 ⎫ 10 @ $4.50 ⎬ = $60.00 ($60.00/15 units = $4.00 avg. cost)
12/9		8 @ $4.00 = $ 32.00	7 @ $4.00 = $28.00 (7 @ $4.00 per unit)
12/19	13 @ $5.00		7 @ $4.00 ⎫ 13 @ $5.00 ⎬ = $93.00 ($93.00/20 units = $4.65 avg. cost)
12/24		18 @ $4.65 = $ 83.70	2 @ $4.65 = $ 9.30 (2 @ $4.65 per unit)
12/30	8 @ $5.30	$115.70	2 @ $4.65 ⎫ 8 @ $5.30 ⎬ = $51.70 ($51.70/10 units = $5.17 avg. cost)

Merchandise Inventory (WA)

Beg. inventory	15.00		
Net purchases	152.40		
Avail. for sale	167.40	COGS	115.70
End. inventory	51.70		

Do More: QS 6-4, QS 6-5, QS 6-6, QS 6-10, QS 6-11, QS 6-12, QS 6-13

VALUING INVENTORY AT LCM AND THE EFFECTS OF INVENTORY ERRORS

This section examines the role of market costs in determining inventory on the balance sheet and also the financial statement effects of inventory errors.

Lower of Cost or Market

P2

Compute the lower of cost or market amount of inventory.

After companies apply one of four costing methods (FIFO, LIFO, weighted average, or specific identification), inventory is reviewed to ensure it is reported at the **lower of cost or market (LCM).** LCM requires that *inventory be reported at the market value (cost) of replacing inventory when market value is lower than cost.*

Computing the Lower of Cost or Market   *Market* in the term *LCM* is defined as the current replacement cost of purchasing the same inventory items. A decline in replacement cost reflects a loss of value in inventory. When the recorded cost of inventory is higher than the replacement cost, a loss is recognized. When the recorded cost is lower, no adjustment is made.

Point: LCM applied to each individual item always yields the lowest inventory.

LCM is applied in one of three ways: (1) to each individual item separately, (2) to major categories of items, or (3) to the whole of inventory. With the increasing application of technology and inventory tracking, companies increasingly apply LCM to each individual item separately. Accordingly, we show that method only; however, advanced courses cover the other two methods. To illustrate LCM, we apply it to the ending inventory of a motorsports retailer in Exhibit 6.9.

EXHIBIT 6.9

Lower of Cost or Market Computations

$140,000 is the lower of $170,000 or $140,000.

The amount of $190,000 is lower than the $220,000 recorded cost.

Inventory Items	Units	Per Unit Cost	Per Unit Market	Total Cost	Total Market	LCM Applied to Items
Roadster.............	20	$8,500	$7,000	$170,000	$140,000	$ 140,000
Sprint	10	5,000	6,000	50,000	60,000	50,000
Totals				$220,000		$190,000

When LCM is applied to individual *items* of inventory, the number of comparisons equals the number of items. For Roadster, $140,000 is the lower of the $170,000 cost and the $140,000 market. For Sprint, $50,000 is the lower of the $50,000 cost and the $60,000 market. This yields a $190,000 reported inventory, computed from $140,000 for Roadster plus $50,000 for Sprint.

The retailer **The Buckle** applies LCM and reports that its "inventory is stated at the lower of cost or market. Cost is determined using the average cost method."

Recording the Lower of Cost or Market

Inventory must be adjusted downward when market is less than cost. To illustrate, if LCM is applied to the individual items of inventory in Exhibit 6.9, the Merchandise Inventory account must be adjusted from the $220,000 recorded cost down to the $190,000 market amount as follows.

Point: Conservatism principle prescribes that when choosing between two options, the one with the less favorable outcome is chosen.

Cost of Goods Sold.............................	30,000	
Merchandise Inventory		30,000
Adjust inventory cost to market.		

NEED-TO-KNOW 6-3

LCM Method

P2

A company has the following products in its ending inventory, along with cost and market values. (a) Compute the lower of cost or market for its inventory when applied *separately to each product*. (b) If the market amount is less than the recorded cost of the inventory, then record the December 31 LCM adjustment to the Merchandise Inventory account.

		Per Unit	
	Units	Cost	Market
Road bikes	5	$1,000	$800
Mountain bikes...........	4	500	600
Town bikes	10	400	450

Solution

a.

Inventory Items	Units	Per Unit Cost	Per Unit Market	Total Cost	Total Market	LCM Items
Road bikes	5	$1,000	$800	$ 5,000	$4,000	$ 4,000
Mountain bikes.........	4	500	600	2,000	2,400	2,000
Town bikes	10	400	450	4,000	4,500	4,000
				$11,000		$ 10,000
LCM applied to each product.............						$10,000

b.

Dec. 31	Cost of Goods Sold	1,000	
	Merchandise Inventory		1,000
	Adjust inventory cost to market ($11,000 – $10,000).		

Do More: QS 6-19, E 6-10

Financial Statement Effects of Inventory Errors

An inventory error causes misstatements in cost of goods sold, gross profit, net income, current assets, and equity. It also causes misstatements in the next period's statements because ending inventory of one period is the beginning inventory of the next. As we consider the financial statement effects in this section, it is helpful if we recall the following *inventory relation*.

A2

Analyze the effects of inventory errors on current and future financial statements.

Beginning inventory **+** Net purchases **−** Ending inventory **=** Cost of goods sold

Income Statement Effects   Exhibit 6.10 shows the effects of inventory errors on key amounts in the current and next periods' income statements. Let's look at row 1 and year 1. We see that understating ending inventory overstates cost of goods sold. This is clear from the inventory relation where we subtract a smaller ending inventory amount in computing cost of goods sold. Then a higher cost of goods sold yields a lower income.

To understand year 2 of row 1, remember that an understated ending inventory for year 1 becomes an understated beginning inventory for year 2. Using the inventory relation, we see that if beginning inventory is understated, then cost of goods sold is understated (because we are starting with a smaller amount). A lower cost of goods sold yields a higher income.

Turning to overstatements, let's look at row 2 and year 1. If ending inventory is overstated, we use the inventory relation to see that cost of goods sold is understated. A lower cost of goods sold yields a higher income.

For year 2 of row 2, recall that an overstated ending inventory for year 1 becomes an overstated beginning inventory for year 2. If beginning inventory is overstated, we use the inventory relation to see that cost of goods sold is overstated. A higher cost of goods sold yields a lower income.

EXHIBIT 6.10

Effects of Inventory Errors on the Income Statement

	Year 1			Year 2	
Ending Inventory	**Cost of Goods Sold**	**Net Income**		**Cost of Goods Sold**	**Net Income**
Understated ⬇	Overstated ⬆	Understated ⬇		Understated ⬇	Overstated ⬆
Overstated ⬆	Understated ⬇	Overstated ⬆		Overstated ⬆	Understated ⬇

To illustrate, consider an inventory error for a company with $100,000 in sales for each of the years 2015, 2016, and 2017. If this company maintains a steady $20,000 inventory level during this period and makes $60,000 in purchases in each of these years, its cost of goods sold is $60,000 and its gross profit is $40,000 each year.

Year 1 Effects from Year 1 Understated Ending Inventory   Assume that this company errs in computing its 2015 ending inventory and reports $16,000 instead of the correct amount of $20,000. The effects of this error are shown in Exhibit 6.11. The $4,000 understatement of 2015 ending inventory causes a $4,000 overstatement in 2015 cost of goods sold and a $4,000 understatement in both gross profit and net income for 2015. We see that these effects match the effects predicted in Exhibit 6.10.

Example: If 2015 ending inventory in Exhibit 6.11 is overstated by $3,000 (not understated by $4,000), what is the effect on cost of goods sold, gross profit, assets, and equity? *Answer:* Cost of goods sold is understated by $3,000 in 2015 and overstated by $3,000 in 2016. Gross profit and net income are overstated in 2015 and understated in 2016. Assets and equity are overstated in 2015.

EXHIBIT 6.11

Effects of Inventory Errors on Three Periods' Income Statements

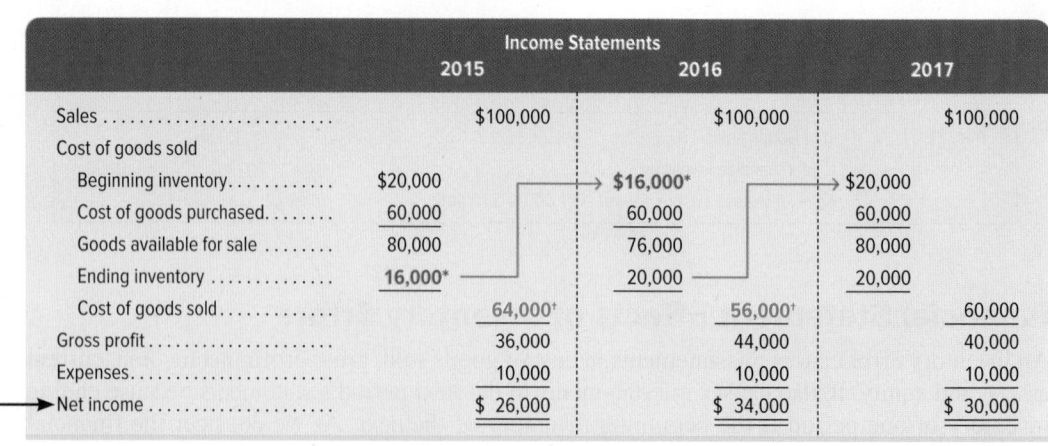

		Income Statements		
		2015	**2016**	**2017**
Sales		$100,000	$100,000	$100,000
Cost of goods sold				
Beginning inventory...........	$20,000		→ $16,000*	→ $20,000
Cost of goods purchased........	60,000		60,000	60,000
Goods available for sale	80,000		76,000	80,000
Ending inventory	16,000*		20,000	20,000
Cost of goods sold.............		64,000†	56,000†	60,000
Gross profit		36,000	44,000	40,000
Expenses......................		10,000	10,000	10,000
Net income		$ 26,000	$ 34,000	$ 30,000

Correct income is $30,000 for each year.

* Correct amount is $20,000.   † Correct amount is $60,000.

Year 2 Effects from Year 1 Understated Ending Inventory   The 2015 understated ending inventory becomes the 2016 understated beginning inventory. We see in Exhibit 6.11 that this error causes an understatement in 2016 cost of goods sold and a $4,000 overstatement in both gross profit and net income for 2016.

Year 3 Effects from Year 1 Understated Ending Inventory   Exhibit 6.11 shows that the 2015 ending inventory error affects only that period and the next. It does not affect 2017 results or any period thereafter. An inventory error is said to be self-correcting because it always yields an offsetting error in the next period. This does not reduce the severity of inventory errors.

Balance Sheet Effects   Balance sheet effects of an inventory error can be seen by considering the accounting equation: Assets = Liabilities + Equity. For example, understating ending inventory understates both current and total assets. An understatement in ending inventory also yields an understatement in equity because of the understatement in net income. Exhibit 6.12 shows the effects of inventory errors on the current period's balance sheet amounts. Errors in beginning inventory do not yield misstatements in the end-of-period balance sheet, but they do affect that current period's income statement.

Point: A former internal auditor at Coca-Cola alleges that just before midnight at a prior calendar year-end, fully loaded Coke trucks were ordered to drive about 2 feet away from the loading dock so that Coke could record millions of dollars in extra sales.

Ending Inventory		Assets	Equity
Understated⬇	....	Understated⬇	Understated⬇
Overstated⬆	....	Overstated⬆	Overstated⬆

EXHIBIT 6.12

Effects of Inventory Errors on Current Period's Balance Sheet

NEED-TO-KNOW 6-4

Effects of Inventory Errors

A2

A company had $10,000 of sales in each of three consecutive years, 2015–2017, and it purchased merchandise costing $7,000 in each of those years. It also maintained a $2,000 physical inventory from the beginning to the end of that three-year period. In accounting for inventory, it made an error at the end of year 2015 that caused its year-end 2015 inventory to appear on its statements as $1,600 rather than the correct $2,000. (a) Determine the correct amount of the company's gross profit in each of the years 2015–2017. (b) Prepare comparative income statements as in Exhibit 6.11 to show the effect of this error on the company's cost of goods sold and gross profit for each of the years 2015–2017.

Solution

a. Correct gross profit = $10,000 − $7,000 = $3,000 (for each year).

b. Cost of goods sold and gross profit figures follow:

	Year 2015		Year 2016		Year 2017	
Sales		$10,000		$10,000		$10,000
Cost of goods sold						
Beginning inventory.............	$2,000		→$1,600		→$2,000	
Cost of purchases	7,000		7,000		7,000	
Goods available for sale	9,000		8,600		9,000	
Ending inventory	1,600		2,000		2,000	
Cost of goods sold.............		7,400		6,600		7,000
Gross profit......................		$ 2,600		$ 3,400		$ 3,000

See that combined income for the 3 years is $9,000 ($2,600 + $3,400 + $3,000), which is correct, meaning the inventory error is "self-correcting" (even though individual years' inventory amounts are in error).

Do More: QS 6-20, E 6-12

SUSTAINABILITY AND ACCOUNTING

Homegrown Sustainable Sandwich Shop co-founders Brad Gillis and Ben Friedman are committed to sustainable practices and the use of accounting data to achieve "sandwich environmentalism." Homegrown prides itself on using "100% organic produce" and on buying as many ingredients as possible from local farmers, according to its website. "Our mission from day one has been to effect positive change on the food system," explains Ben.

Both Brad and Ben recognize that exclusively using organic produce in sandwiches and buying from local farmers requires an effective inventory system. That system enables Brad and Ben to manage ingredients inventory and to predict inventory shortages and stock-outs. That system also enables Brad and Ben to use organic produce to serve their dedicated customers.

© littleny/shutterstock

The two founders are committed to the environment and to their use of clean energy. "We now offset 100% of our electrical power with clean wind energy," Ben proudly asserts. Brad and Ben's decision to use clean energy required a review of their financial statements. They had to ensure the presence of adequate cash flows and income levels to sustain the added cost of using clean energy. Their financial analysis showed that both cash flows and income were sufficient to offset added energy costs.

Brad and Ben regularly apply financial analysis for business decisions, and they assert that this has helped them achieve their dream of opening up "farm-to-table fine dining" sandwich shops across the country. "It's a big dream," admits Brad, "but we couldn't be more excited about what we're doing."

 **Decision Analysis**  Inventory Turnover and Days' Sales in Inventory

A3

Assess inventory management using both inventory turnover and days' sales in inventory.

Inventory Turnover

Earlier chapters described two important ratios useful in evaluating a company's short-term liquidity: current ratio and acid-test ratio. A merchandiser's ability to pay its short-term obligations also depends on how quickly it sells its merchandise inventory. **Inventory turnover,** also called *merchandise inventory turnover* or, simply, *turns,* is one ratio used to assess this and is defined in Exhibit 6.13.

EXHIBIT 6.13

Inventory Turnover

$$\text{Inventory turnover} = \frac{\text{Cost of goods sold}}{\text{Average inventory}}$$

Point: We must take care when comparing turnover ratios across companies that use different costing methods (such as FIFO and LIFO).

Point: Companies with low inventory turnover can be susceptible to losses due to obsolescence and trend changes.

This ratio reveals how many *times* a company turns over (sells) its inventory during a period. If a company's inventory greatly varies within a year, average inventory amounts can be computed from interim periods such as quarters or months.

Users apply inventory turnover to help analyze short-term liquidity and to assess whether management is doing a good job controlling the amount of inventory available. A low ratio compared to that of competitors suggests inefficient use of assets. The company may be holding more inventory than it needs to support its sales volume. Similarly, a very high ratio compared to that of competitors suggests inventory might be too low. This can cause lost sales if customers must back-order merchandise. Inventory turnover has no simple rule except to say *a high ratio is preferable provided inventory is adequate to meet demand.*

Days' Sales in Inventory

Point: Inventory turnover is higher and days' sales in inventory is lower for industries such as foods and other perishable products. The reverse holds for nonperishable product industries.

To better interpret inventory turnover, many users measure the adequacy of inventory to meet sales demand. **Days' sales in inventory,** also called *days' stock on hand,* is a ratio that reveals how much inventory is available in terms of the number of days' sales. It can be interpreted as the number of days one can sell from inventory if no new items are purchased. This ratio is often viewed as a measure of the buffer against out-of-stock inventory and is useful in evaluating liquidity of inventory. It is defined in Exhibit 6.14.

EXHIBIT 6.14

Days' Sales in Inventory

$$\text{Days' sales in inventory} = \frac{\text{Ending inventory}}{\text{Cost of goods sold}} \times 365$$

Days' sales in inventory focuses on ending inventory and estimates how many days it will take to convert inventory at the end of a period into accounts receivable or cash. Days' sales in inventory focuses on *ending* inventory, whereas inventory turnover focuses on *average* inventory.

Analysis of Inventory Management

Inventory management is a major emphasis for merchandisers. They must both plan and control inventory purchases and sales. **Toys "R" Us** is one of those merchandisers. Its inventory at fiscal year-end 2016 was $2,270 million. This inventory constituted 69% of its current assets and 33% of its total assets. We apply the analysis tools in this section to Toys "R" Us, as shown in Exhibit 6.15—also see margin graph.

$ millions	2016	2015	2014	2013	2012	2011
Cost of goods sold	$7,576	$7,931	$8,154	$8,592	$8,939	$8,939
Ending inventory	$2,270	$2,064	$2,171	$2,229	$2,232	$2,104
Inventory turnover	**3.5** times	**3.7** times	**3.7** times	**3.9** times	**4.1** times	**4.6** times
Industry inventory turnover	3.3 times	3.3 times	3.4 times	3.2 times	3.4 times	3.3 times
Days' sales in inventory.	**109** days	**95** days	**97** days	**95** days	**91** days	**86** days
Industry days' sales in inventory	130 days	126 days	129 days	132 days	128 days	132 days

EXHIBIT 6.15

Inventory Turnover and Days' Sales in Inventory for Toys "R" Us

Its 2016 inventory turnover of 3.5 times means that Toys "R" Us turns over its inventory 3.5 times per year, or once every 104 days (365 days ÷ 3.5). We prefer inventory turnover to be high provided inventory is not out of stock and the company is not losing customers. The second metric computed, the 2016 days' sales in inventory of 109 days, reveals that it is carrying 109 days of sales in inventory. This inventory buffer seems more than adequate. The increase in days' sales in inventory suggests that Toys "R" Us management needs to increase inventory turnover and to especially reduce inventory levels.

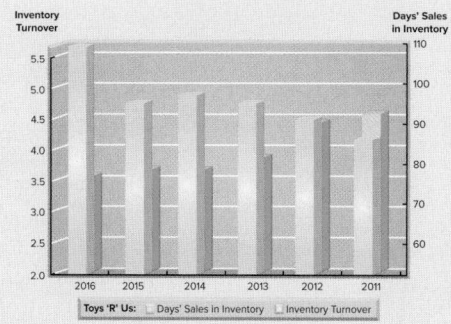

■ **Decision Maker**

Entrepreneur   Analysis of your retail store yields an inventory turnover of 5.0 and a days' sales in inventory of 73 days. The industry norm for inventory turnover is 4.4 and for days' sales in inventory is 74 days. What is your assessment of inventory management? ■ [*Answer:* Your inventory turnover is markedly higher than the norm, whereas days' sales in inventory approximates the norm. Since your turnover is already 14% better than average, you are probably best served by directing attention to days' sales in inventory. You should see whether you can reduce the level of inventory while maintaining service to customers. Given your higher turnover, you should be able to hold less inventory.]

Craig Company buys and sells one product. Its beginning inventory, purchases, and sales during calendar-year 2017 follow.

NEED-TO-KNOW 6-5

COMPREHENSIVE 1

Perpetual Method

Date	Activity	Units Acquired at Cost	Units Sold at Retail	Unit Inventory
Jan. 1	Beg. inventory	400 units @ $14 = $ 5,600		400 units
Jan. 15	Sale		200 units @ $30	200 units
Mar. 10	Purchase	200 units @ $15 = $ 3,000		400 units
Apr. 1	Sale		200 units @ $30	200 units
May 9	Purchase	300 units @ $16 = $ 4,800		500 units
Sept. 22	Purchase	250 units @ $20 = $ 5,000		750 units
Nov. 1	Sale		300 units @ $35	450 units
Nov. 28	Purchase	100 units @ $21 = $ 2,100		550 units
	Totals.	1,250 units $20,500	700 units	

Additional tracking data for specific identification: (1) January 15 sale—200 units @ $14, (2) April 1 sale—200 units @ $15, and (3) November 1 sale—200 units @ $14 and 100 units @ $20.

Required

1. Compute the cost of goods available for sale.

2. Apply the four different methods of inventory costing (FIFO, LIFO, weighted average, and specific identification) to compute ending inventory and cost of goods sold under each method using the *perpetual system*.

3. Compute gross profit earned by the company for each of the four costing methods in part 2. Also, report the inventory amount reported on the balance sheet for each of the four methods.

4. In preparing financial statements for year 2017, the financial officer was instructed to use FIFO but failed to do so and instead computed cost of goods sold according to LIFO, which led to a $1,400 overstatement in cost of goods sold from using LIFO. Determine the impact on year 2017's income from the error. Also determine the effect of this error on year 2018's income. Assume no income taxes.

5. Management wants a report that shows how changing from FIFO to another method would change net income. Prepare a table showing (1) the cost of goods sold amount under each of the four methods, (2) the amount by which each cost of goods sold total is different from the FIFO cost of goods sold, and (3) the effect on net income if another method is used instead of FIFO.

PLANNING THE SOLUTION

- Compute cost of goods available for sale by multiplying the units of beginning inventory and each purchase by their unit costs to determine the total cost of goods available for sale.

- Prepare a perpetual FIFO table starting with beginning inventory and showing how inventory changes after each purchase and after each sale (see Exhibit 6.5).

- Prepare a perpetual LIFO table starting with beginning inventory and showing how inventory changes after each purchase and after each sale (see Exhibit 6.6).

- Make a table of purchases and sales recalculating the average cost of inventory prior to each sale to arrive at the weighted average cost of ending inventory. Total the average costs associated with each sale to determine cost of goods sold (see Exhibit 6.7).

- Prepare a table showing the computation of cost of goods sold and ending inventory using the specific identification method (see Exhibit 6.4).

- Compare the year-end 2017 inventory amounts under FIFO and LIFO to determine the misstatement of year 2017 income that results from using LIFO. The errors for years 2017 and 2018 are equal in amount but opposite in effect.

- Create a table showing cost of goods sold under each method and how net income would differ from FIFO net income if an alternate method were adopted.

SOLUTION

1. Cost of goods available for sale (this amount is the same for all methods).

Date		Units	Unit Cost	Cost
Jan. 1	Beg. inventory	400	$14	$ 5,600
Mar. 10	Purchase.................	200	15	3,000
May 9	Purchase.................	300	16	4,800
Sept. 22	Purchase.................	250	20	5,000
Nov. 28	Purchase.................	100	21	2,100
Total goods available for sale		1,250		$20,500

2a. FIFO perpetual method.

Date	Goods Purchased	Cost of Goods Sold	Inventory Balance	
Jan. 1	Beginning balance		400 @ $14	= $ 5,600
Jan. 15		200 @ $14 = $2,800	200 @ $14	= $ 2,800
Mar. 10	200 @ $15 = $3,000		200 @ $14 ⎱ 200 @ $15 ⎰	= $ 5,800
Apr. 1		200 @ $14 = $2,800	200 @ $15	= $ 3,000
May 9	300 @ $16 = $4,800		200 @ $15 ⎱ 300 @ $16 ⎰	= $ 7,800
Sept. 22	250 @ $20 = $5,000		200 @ $15 ⎱ 300 @ $16 ⎰ 250 @ $20	= $ 12,800
Nov. 1		200 @ $15 = $3,000 100 @ $16 = $1,600	200 @ $16 ⎱ 250 @ $20 ⎰	= $ 8,200
Nov. 28	100 @ $21 = $2,100		200 @ $16 ⎱ 250 @ $20 ⎰ 100 @ $21	= $10,300
Total cost of goods sold		**$10,200**		

Note: **In a classroom situation,** once we compute cost of goods available for sale, we can compute the amount for either cost of goods sold or ending inventory—it is a matter of preference. **In practice,** the costs of items sold are identified as sales are made and immediately transferred from the Inventory account to the Cost of Goods Sold account. The previous solution showing the line-by-line approach illustrates actual application in practice. The following alternate solutions illustrate that, once the concepts are understood, other solution approaches are available. Although this is only shown for FIFO, it could be shown for all methods.

Alternate Methods to Compute FIFO Perpetual Numbers

[FIFO Alternate No. 1: Computing ending inventory first]

Cost of goods available for sale (from part 1).			$ 20,500
Ending inventory*			
Nov. 28	Purchase (100 @ $21)	$2,100	
Sept. 22	Purchase (250 @ $20)	5,000	
May 9	Purchase (200 @ $16)	3,200	
Ending inventory.			10,300
Cost of goods sold			**$10,200**

* FIFO assumes that the earlier costs are the first to flow out; thus, we determine ending inventory by assigning the most recent costs to the remaining items.

[FIFO Alternate No. 2: Computing cost of goods sold first]

Cost of goods available for sale (from part 1).			$ 20,500
Cost of goods sold			
Jan. 15	Sold (200 @ $14)	$2,800	
Apr. 1	Sold (200 @ $14)	2,800	
Nov. 1	Sold (200 @ $15 and 100 @ $16).	4,600	10,200
Ending inventory.			**$10,300**

2b. LIFO perpetual method.

Date	Goods Purchased	Cost of Goods Sold	Inventory Balance	
Jan. 1	Beginning balance		400 @ $14	= $ 5,600
Jan. 15		200 @ $14 = $2,800	200 @ $14	= $ 2,800
Mar. 10	200 @ $15 = $3,000		200 @ $14 200 @ $15	= $ 5,800
Apr. 1		200 @ $15 = $3,000	200 @ $14	= $ 2,800
May 9	300 @ $16 = $4,800		200 @ $14 300 @ $16	= $ 7,600
Sept. 22	250 @ $20 = $5,000		200 @ $14 300 @ $16 250 @ $20	= $12,600
Nov. 1		250 @ $20 = $5,000 50 @ $16 = $ 800	200 @ $14 250 @ $16	= $ 6,800
Nov. 28	100 @ $21 = $2,100		200 @ $14 250 @ $16 100 @ $21	= $ 8,900
Total cost of goods sold		**$11,600**		

2c. Weighted average perpetual method.

Date	Goods Purchased	Cost of Goods Sold	Inventory Balance	
Jan. 1	Beginning balance		400 @ $14.00 ($5,600/400 units	= $ 5,600 = $14.00 avg. cost)
Jan. 15		200 @ $14.00 = $ 2,800	200 @ $14.00	= $ 2,800
Mar. 10	200 @ $15.00 = $3,000		200 @ $14.00 200 @ $15.00 ($5,800/400 units	= $ 5,800 = $14.50 avg. cost)
Apr. 1		200 @ $14.50 = $ 2,900	200 @ $14.50	= $ 2,900
May 9	300 @ $16.00 = $4,800		200 @ $14.50 300 @ $16.00 ($7,700/500 units	= $ 7,700 = $15.40 avg. cost)
Sept. 22	250 @ $20.00 = $5,000		500 @ $15.40 250 @ $20.00 ($12,700/750 units	= $ 12,700 = $16.93[†] avg. cost)
Nov. 1		300 @ $16.93 = $ 5,079	450 @ $16.93	= $ 7,618.50
Nov. 28	100 @ $21.00 = $2,100		450 @ $16.93 100 @ $21.00 ($9,718.50/550 units	= $9,718.50 = $17.67 avg. cost)
Total cost of goods sold*		**$10,779**		

* Cost of goods sold ($10,779) plus ending inventory ($9,718.50) is $2.50 less than the cost of goods available for sale ($20,500) due to rounding.

[†] Rounded to 2 decimal places.

2d. Specific identification method.

Cost of goods available for sale (from part 1).		$ 20,500
Ending inventory*		
May 9 Purchase (300 @ $16)	$4,800	
Sept. 22 Purchase (150 @ $20)	3,000	
Nov. 28 Purchase (100 @ $21)	2,100	
Ending inventory.		9,900
Cost of goods sold		$10,600

* The additional tracking data provided are used to identify the items in ending inventory.

3.

	FIFO	LIFO	Weighted Average	Specific Identification
Income Statement				
Sales*	$ 22,500	$22,500	$ 22,500	$22,500
Cost of goods sold	10,200	11,600	10,779	10,600
Gross profit.	$ 12,300	$10,900	$ 11,721	$11,900
Balance Sheet				
Inventory	$10,300	$ 8,900	$9,718.50	$ 9,900

* Sales = (200 units × $30) + (200 units × $30) + (300 units × $35) = $22,500

4. Mistakenly using LIFO when FIFO should have been used overstates cost of goods sold in year 2017 by $1,400, which is the difference between the FIFO and LIFO amounts of ending inventory. It understates income in 2017 by $1,400. In year 2018, income is overstated by $1,400 because of the understatement in beginning inventory.

5. Analysis of the effects of alternative inventory methods.

	Cost of Goods Sold	Difference from FIFO Cost of Goods Sold	Effect on Net Income If Adopted Instead of FIFO
FIFO	$10,200	—	—
LIFO	11,600	+$1,400	$1,400 lower
Weighted average	10,779	+ 579	579 lower
Specific identification	10,600	+ 400	400 lower

Craig Company buys and sells one product. Its beginning inventory, purchases, and sales during calendar-year 2017 follow.

NEED-TO-KNOW 6-6

COMPREHENSIVE 2

Periodic Method

Date	Activity	Units Acquired at Cost	Units Sold at Retail	Unit Inventory
Jan. 1	Beg. inventory	400 units @ $14 = $ 5,600		400 units
Jan. 15	Sale		200 units @ $30	200 units
Mar. 10	Purchase.	200 units @ $15 = $ 3,000		400 units
Apr. 1	Sale		200 units @ $30	200 units
May 9	Purchase.	300 units @ $16 = $ 4,800		500 units
Sept. 22	Purchase.	250 units @ $20 = $ 5,000		750 units
Nov. 1	Sale		300 units @ $35	450 units
Nov. 28	Purchase.	100 units @ $21 = $ 2,100		550 units
	Totals.	1,250 units $20,500	700 units	

Additional tracking data for specific identification: (1) January 15 sale—200 units @ $14, (2) April 1 sale—200 units @ $15, and (3) November 1 sale—200 units @ $14 and 100 units @ $20.

Required

1. Compute the cost of goods available for sale.

2. Apply the four different methods of inventory costing (FIFO, LIFO, weighted average, and specific identification) to compute ending inventory and cost of goods sold under each method using the *periodic system*.

3. Compute gross profit earned by the company for each of the four costing methods in part 2. Also, report the inventory amount reported on the balance sheet for each of the four methods.

4. In preparing financial statements for year 2017, the financial officer was instructed to use FIFO but failed to do so and instead computed cost of goods sold according to LIFO. Determine the impact of the error on year 2017's income. Also determine the effect of this error on year 2018's income. Assume no income taxes.

PLANNING THE SOLUTION

- Compute cost of goods available for sale by multiplying the units of beginning inventory and each purchase by their unit costs to determine the total cost of goods available for sale.

- Prepare a periodic FIFO computation starting with cost of units available and subtracting FIFO ending inventory amounts to obtain FIFO cost of goods sold (see Exhibit 6A.3).

- Prepare a periodic LIFO computation starting with cost of units available and subtracting LIFO ending inventory amounts to obtain LIFO cost of goods sold (see Exhibit 6A.4).

- Compute weighted average ending inventory and cost of goods sold using the three-step process illustrated in Exhibits 6A.5a and 6A.5b.

- Prepare a table showing the computation of cost of goods sold and ending inventory using the specific identification method (see Exhibit 6A.2).

- Compare the year-end 2017 inventory amounts under FIFO and LIFO to determine the misstatement of year 2017 income that results from using LIFO. The errors for year 2017 and 2018 are equal in amount but opposite in effect.

SOLUTION

1. Cost of goods available for sale (this amount is the same for all methods).

Date		Units	Unit Cost	Cost
Jan. 1	Beg. inventory	400	$14	$ 5,600
Mar. 10	Purchase.................	200	15	3,000
May 9	Purchase.................	300	16	4,800
Sept. 22	Purchase.................	250	20	5,000
Nov. 28	Purchase.................	100	21	2,100
Total goods available for sale		1,250		$20,500

2a. FIFO **periodic** method (FIFO under periodic and perpetual yields identical results).

Cost of goods available for sale (from part 1)................			$ 20,500
Ending inventory*			
Nov. 28	Purchase (100 @ $21)	$2,100	
Sept. 22	Purchase (250 @ $20)	5,000	
May 9	Purchase (200 @ $16)	3,200	
Ending inventory......................................			10,300
Cost of goods sold			$10,200

* FIFO assumes that the earlier costs are the first to flow out; thus, we determine ending
   inventory by assigning the most recent costs to the remaining items.

2b. LIFO **periodic** method.

Cost of goods available for sale (from part 1)...............		$ 20,500
Ending inventory*		
January 1 Beg. inventory (400 @ $14)	$5,600	
March 10 Purchase (150 @ $15)....................	2,250	
Ending inventory.......................................		7,850
Cost of goods sold		$12,650

> * LIFO assumes that the most recent (newest) costs are the first to flow out; thus, we determine
> ending inventory by assigning the earliest (oldest) costs to the remaining items.

2c. Weighted average **periodic** method.

Step 1:	400 units @ $14 = $ 5,600	
	200 units @ $15 = 3,000	
	300 units @ $16 = 4,800	
	250 units @ $20 = 5,000	
	100 units @ $21 = 2,100	
	1,250 units $20,500	
Step 2:	$20,500/1,250 units = **$16.40** weighted average cost per unit	
Step 3:	Total cost of 1,250 units available for sale	$ 20,500
	Less **ending inventory** priced on a weighted average	
	cost basis: 550 units at $16.40 each......................	9,020
	Cost of goods sold (700 units at $16.40 each)............	**$11,480**

2d. Specific identification method.

Cost of goods available for sale (from part 1)..............		$ 20,500
Ending inventory*		
May 9 Purchase (300 @ $16)...................	$4,800	
Sept. 22 Purchase (150 @ $20)...................	3,000	
Nov. 28 Purchase (100 @ $21)...................	2,100	
Ending inventory.......................................		9,900
Cost of goods sold		$10,600

> * The additional tracking data provided are used to identify the items in ending inventory.

3.

	FIFO	LIFO	Weighted Average	Specific Identification
Income Statement				
Sales*	$ 22,500	$22,500	$ 22,500	$22,500
Cost of goods sold	10,200	12,650	11,480	10,600
Gross profit.....................	$ 12,300	$ 9,850	$ 11,020	$11,900
Balance Sheet				
Inventory	$10,300	$ 7,850	$ 9,020	$ 9,900

> * Sales = (200 units × $30) + (200 units × $30) + (300 units × $35) = $22,500

4. Mistakenly using LIFO, when FIFO should have been used, overstates cost of goods sold in year 2017 by $2,450, which is the difference between the FIFO and LIFO amounts of ending inventory. It understates income in 2017 by $2,450. In year 2018, income is overstated by $2,450 because of the understatement in beginning inventory.

6A

Inventory Costing under a Periodic System

P3

Compute inventory in a periodic system using the methods of specific identification, FIFO, LIFO, and weighted average.

EXHIBIT 6A.1

Purchases and Sales of Goods

This section illustrates inventory costing methods. We use information from Trekking, a sporting goods store. Among its many products, Trekking carries one type of mountain bike whose sales are directed at resorts that provide inexpensive bikes for guest use. We use Trekking's data from August. Its mountain bike (unit) inventory at the beginning of August and its purchases and sales during August are shown in Exhibit 6A.1. It ends August with 12 bikes remaining in inventory.

Date	Activity	Units Acquired at Cost	Units Sold at Retail	Unit Inventory
Aug. 1	Beginning inventory.......	10 units @ $ 91 = $ 910		10 units
Aug. 3	Purchases..............	15 units @ $106 = $ 1,590		25 units
Aug. 14	Sales...................		20 units @ $130	5 units
Aug. 17	Purchases..............	20 units @ $115 = $ 2,300		25 units
Aug. 28	Purchases..............	10 units @ $119 = $ 1,190		35 units
Aug. 30	Sales..................		23 units @ $150	12 units
	Totals	55 units $5,990	43 units	
		Units available for sale / Goods available for sale	Units sold	Units left

Trekking uses the periodic inventory system, which means that its Merchandise Inventory account is updated at the end of each period (monthly for Trekking) to reflect purchases and sales. Regardless of what inventory method is used, cost of goods available for sale must be allocated between cost of goods sold and ending inventory.

Point: Three key variables determine the value assigned to ending inventory: (1) inventory quantity, (2) unit costs of inventory, and (3) cost flow assumption.

Specific Identification When each item in inventory can be matched with a specific purchase and invoice, we can use **specific identification** or **SI** (also called *specific invoice inventory pricing*) to assign costs. We also need sales records that identify exactly which items were sold and when. Trekking's internal documents reveal the following specific unit sales:

August 14 Sold 8 bikes costing $91 each and 12 bikes costing $106 each
August 30 Sold 2 bikes costing $91 each, 3 bikes costing $106 each, 15 bikes costing $115 each, and 3 bikes costing $119 each

Applying specific identification, and using the information above and from Exhibit 6A.1, we prepare Exhibit 6A.2. This exhibit begins with the $5,990 in total units available for sale—this is from Exhibit 6A.1. For the 20 units sold on August 14, the company specifically identified that 8 of them had cost $91 each and 12 had cost $106 each, resulting in an August 14 cost of sales of $2,000. Next, for the 23 units sold on August 30, the company specifically identified that 2 of them had cost $91 each, 3 had cost $106 each, 15 had cost $115 each, and 3 had cost $119 each, resulting in an August 30 cost of sales of $2,582. The total cost of sales for the period is $4,582. We then subtract this $4,582 in cost of goods sold from the $5,990 in cost of goods available to get $1,408 in ending inventory. Carefully study this exhibit and the explanations to see the flow of costs. Each unit, whether sold or remaining in inventory, has its own specific cost attached to it.

EXHIBIT 6A.2

Specific Identification Computations

Total cost of 55 units available for sale (from Exhibit 6A.1).........................			$ 5,990
Cost of goods sold*			
Aug. 14 (8 @ $91) + (12 @ $106)...		$2,000	
Aug. 30 (2 @ $91) + (3 @ $106) + (15 @ $115) + (3 @ $119)		2,582	4,582
Ending inventory			**$1,408**

* Identification of items sold (and their costs) is obtained from internal documents that track each unit from its purchase to its sale.

When using specific identification, Trekking's cost of goods sold reported on the income statement totals **$4,582**, the sum of $2,000 and $2,582 from the cost of goods sold section of Exhibit 6A.2. Trekking's ending inventory reported on the balance sheet is **$1,408**, which is the final inventory balance from Exhibit 6A.2. The following graphic visually reflects computations under specific identification.

Point: Specific identification is usually practical for companies with expensive or custom-made inventory. Examples include car dealerships, implement dealers, jewelers, and fashion designers.

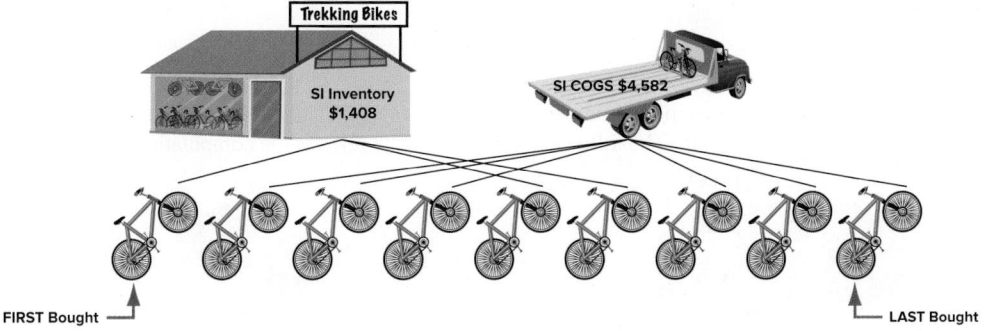

First-In, First-Out   The **first-in, first-out (FIFO)** method of assigning costs assumes that inventory items are sold in the order acquired. When sales occur, the costs of the earliest units acquired are charged to cost of goods sold. This leaves the costs from the most recent purchases in ending inventory. Use of FIFO for computing the cost of inventory and cost of goods sold is shown in Exhibit 6A.3.

This exhibit starts with computing $5,990 in total units available for sale—this is from Exhibit 6A.1. Applying FIFO, we know that the 12 units in ending inventory will be reported at the cost of the most recent 12 purchases. Reviewing purchases in reverse order, we assign costs to the 12 bikes in ending inventory as follows: $119 cost to 10 bikes and $115 cost to 2 bikes. This yields 12 bikes costing $1,420 in ending inventory. We then subtract this $1,420 in ending inventory from $5,990 in cost of goods available to get $4,570 in cost of goods sold.

Point: The assignment of costs to goods sold and to inventory using FIFO is the same for both the periodic and perpetual systems.

EXHIBIT 6A.3

FIFO Computations—Periodic System

Total cost of 55 units available for sale (from Exhibit 6A.1)	$ 5,990
Less ending inventory priced using FIFO	
10 units from August 28 purchase at $119 each	$1,190
2 units from August 17 purchase at $115 each	230
Ending inventory	1,420
Cost of goods sold	$4,570

Exhibit 6A.1 shows that the 12 units in ending inventory consist of 10 units from the latest purchase on Aug. 28 and 2 units from the next latest purchase on Aug. 17.

Trekking's ending inventory reported on the balance sheet is **$1,420**, and its cost of goods sold reported on the income statement is **$4,570**. The following graphic visually reflects computations under FIFO.

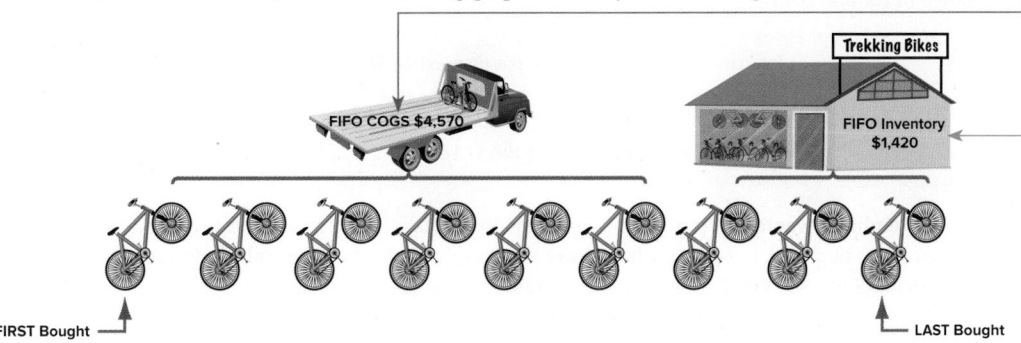

Last-In, First-Out   The **last-in, first-out (LIFO)** method of assigning costs assumes that the most recent purchases are sold first. These more recent costs are charged to goods sold, and the costs of the earliest purchases are assigned to inventory. Use of LIFO for computing cost of inventory and cost of goods sold is shown in Exhibit 6A.4.

This exhibit starts with computing $5,990 in total units available for sale—this is from Exhibit 6A.1. Applying LIFO, we know that the 12 units in ending inventory will be reported at the cost of the earliest 12 purchases. Reviewing the earliest purchases in order, we assign costs to the 12 bikes in ending inventory as follows: $91 cost to 10 bikes and $106 cost to 2 bikes. This yields 12 bikes costing $1,122 in ending inventory. We then subtract this $1,122 in ending inventory from $5,990 in cost of goods available to get $4,868 in cost of goods sold.

Point: By assigning costs from the most recent purchases to cost of goods sold, LIFO comes closest to matching current costs of goods sold with revenues (compared to FIFO or weighted average).

EXHIBIT 6A.4

LIFO Computations—
Periodic System

Exhibit 6A.1 shows that the 12
units in ending inventory
consist of 10 units from the
earliest purchase (beg. inv.)
and 2 units from the next
earliest purchase on Aug. 3.

Total cost of 55 units available for sale (from Exhibit 6A.1).		$ 5,990
Less ending inventory priced using LIFO		
10 units in beginning inventory at $91 each	$910	
2 units from August 3 purchase at $106 each.	212	
Ending inventory		1,122
Cost of goods sold		$4,868

Trekking's ending inventory reported on the balance sheet is $1,122, and its cost of goods sold reported on the income statement is $4,868. The following graphic visually reflects the computations under LIFO.

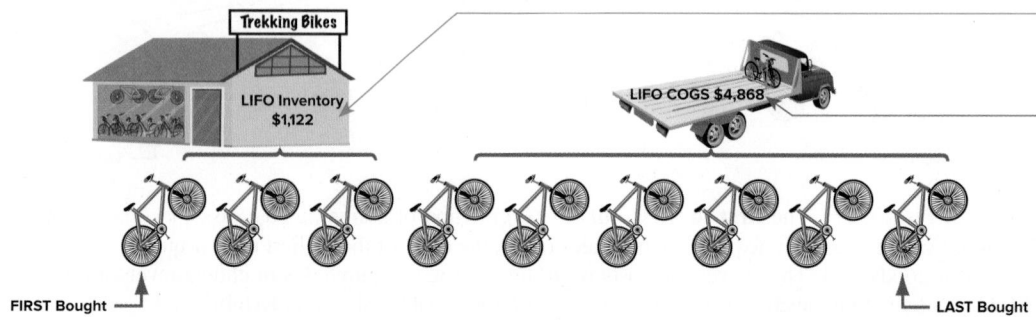

Weighted Average

The **weighted average** or **WA** (also called **average cost**) method of assigning cost requires that we use the average cost per unit of inventory at the end of the period. Weighted average cost per unit equals the cost of goods available for sale divided by the units available. The weighted average method of assigning cost involves three important steps. The first two steps are shown in Exhibit 6A.5a. First, multiply the per unit cost for beginning inventory and each particular purchase by the corresponding number of units (from Exhibit 6A.1). Second, add these amounts and divide by the total number of units available for sale to find the weighted average cost per unit.

EXHIBIT 6A.5a

Weighted Average Cost
per Unit

Example: In Exhibit 6A.5a, if 5
more units had been purchased
at $120 each, what would be the
weighted average cost per unit?
Answer: $109.83 ($6,590/60)

Step 1:	10 units @ $ 91 = $ 910	
	15 units @ $106 = 1,590	
	20 units @ $115 = 2,300	
	10 units @ $119 = 1,190	
	55 $5,990	
Step 2:	$5,990/55 units = **$108.91** weighted average cost per unit	

The third step is to use the weighted average cost per unit to assign costs to inventory and to the units sold, as shown in Exhibit 6A.5b.

EXHIBIT 6A.5b

Weighted Average
Computations—Periodic

Step 3:	Total cost of 55 units available for sale (from Exhibit 6A.1)	$ 5,990
	Less ending inventory priced on a weighted average	
	cost basis: 12 units at $108.91 each (from Exhibit 6A.5a).	1,307
	Cost of goods sold (43 units at $108.91 each).	$4,683

Trekking's ending inventory reported on the balance sheet is $1,307, and its cost of goods sold reported on the income statement is $4,683 when using the weighted average (periodic) method. The following graphic visually reflects computations under weighted average.

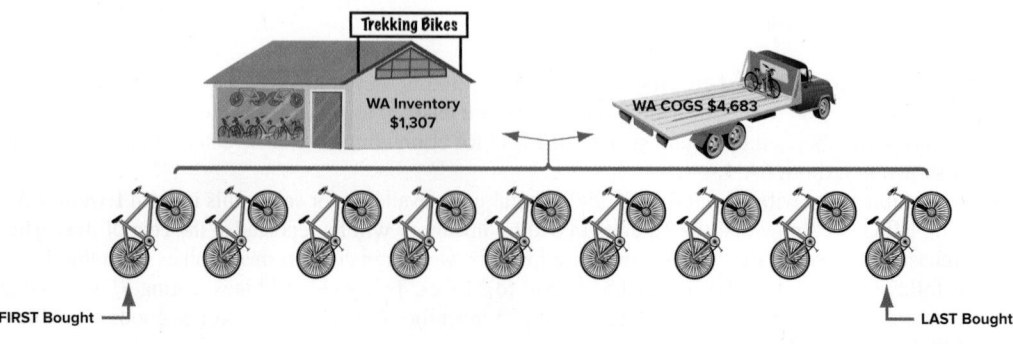

Financial Statement Effects of Costing Methods   When purchase prices do not change, each inventory costing method assigns the same cost amounts to inventory and to cost of goods sold. When purchase prices are different, however, the methods nearly always assign different cost amounts. We show these differences in Exhibit 6A.6 using Trekking's data.

A1_____

Analyze the effects of inventory methods for both financial and tax reporting.

EXHIBIT 6A.6

Financial Statement Effects of Inventory Costing Methods

TREKKING COMPANY For Month Ended August 31				
	Specific Identification	FIFO	LIFO	Weighted Average
Income Statement				
Sales	$ 6,050	$ 6,050	$ 6,050	$ 6,050
Cost of goods sold....................	4,582	4,570	4,868	4,683
Gross profit	1,468	1,480	1,182	1,367
Expenses...........................	450	450	450	450
Income before taxes...................	1,018	1,030	732	917
Income tax expense (30%)..............	305	309	220	275
Net income.........................	$ 713	$ 721	$ 512	$ 642
Balance Sheet				
Inventory	$1,408	$1,420	$1,122	$1,307

This exhibit reveals two important results. First, when purchase costs *regularly rise,* as in Trekking's case, observe the following:

- FIFO assigns the lowest amount to cost of goods sold—yielding the highest gross profit and net income.
- LIFO assigns the highest amount to cost of goods sold—yielding the lowest gross profit and net income.
- Weighted average yields results between FIFO and LIFO.
- Specific identification always yields results that depend on which units are sold.

Point: Managers prefer FIFO when costs are rising *and* incentives exist to report higher income.

Second, when costs *regularly decline,* the reverse occurs for FIFO and LIFO. FIFO gives the highest cost of goods sold—yielding the lowest gross profit and income. And LIFO gives the lowest cost of goods sold—yielding the highest gross profit and income.

All four inventory costing methods are acceptable in practice. A company must disclose the inventory method it uses. Each method offers certain advantages as follows:

- FIFO assigns an amount to inventory on the balance sheet that approximates its current cost; it also mimics the actual flow of goods for most businesses.
- LIFO assigns an amount to cost of goods sold on the income statement that approximates its current cost; it also better matches current costs with revenues in computing gross profit.
- Weighted average tends to smooth out erratic changes in costs.
- Specific identification exactly matches the costs of items with the revenues they generate.

Point: LIFO inventory is often less than the inventory's replacement cost because LIFO inventory is valued using the oldest inventory purchase costs.

A company reported the following December purchases and sales data for its only product.

NEED-TO-KNOW 6-7

Periodic SI, FIFO, LIFO, and WA

P3

Date	Activities	Units Acquired at Cost	Units Sold at Retail
Dec. 1	Beginning inventory	5 units @ $3.00 = $ 15.00	
Dec. 8	Purchase	10 units @ $4.50 = 45.00	
Dec. 9	Sales		8 units @ $7.00
Dec. 19	Purchase	13 units @ $5.00 = 65.00	
Dec. 24	Sales		18 units @ $8.00
Dec. 30	Purchase	8 units @ $5.30 = 42.40	
Totals	....	36 units $167.40	26 units

The company uses a *periodic inventory system.* Determine the cost assigned to ending inventory and to cost of goods sold using (*a*) specific identification, (*b*) FIFO, (*c*) LIFO, and (*d*) weighted average. (Round per unit costs and inventory amounts to cents.) For specific identification, ending inventory consists of 10 units, where 8 are from the December 30 purchase and 2 are from the December 8 purchase.

Solutions

a. Specific identification: Ending inventory—eight units from December 30 purchase and two units from December 8 purchase

Specific Identification	Ending Inventory	Cost of Goods Sold
(8 × $5.30) + (2 × $4.50)	$51.40	
(5 × $3.00) + (8 × $4.50) + (13 × $5.00) + (0 × $5.30)		$116.00
or $167.40 [Total Goods Available] − $51.40 [Ending Inventory]		$116.00

b. FIFO—Periodic

FIFO	Ending Inventory	Cost of Goods Sold
(8 × $5.30) + (2 × $5.00)	$52.40	
(5 × $3.00) + (10 × $4.50) + (11 × $5.00)		$115.00
or $167.40 [Total Goods Available] − $52.40 [Ending Inventory]		$115.00

c. LIFO—Periodic

LIFO	Ending Inventory	Cost of Goods Sold
(5 × $3.00) + (5 × $4.50)	$37.50	
(8 × $5.30) + (13 × $5.00) + (5 × $4.50)		$129.90
or $167.40 [Total Goods Available] − $37.50 [Ending Inventory]		$129.90

d. WA—Periodic

WA	Ending Inventory	Cost of Goods Sold
10 × $4.65 (computed from $167.40/36)	$46.50	
26 × $4.65 (computed from $167.40/36)		$120.90
or $167.40 [Total Goods Available] − $46.50 [Ending Inventory]		$120.90

Do More: QS 6-7, QS 6-8, QS 6-9, QS 6-14, QS 6-15, QS 6-16, QS 6-17

APPENDIX

6B

Inventory Estimation Methods

P4

Apply both the retail inventory and gross profit methods to estimate inventory.

Inventory sometimes requires estimation for two reasons. First, companies often require **interim statements** (financial statements prepared for periods of less than one year), but they only annually take a physical count of inventory. Second, companies may require an inventory estimate if some casualty such as fire or flood makes taking a physical count impossible. Estimates are usually only required for companies that use the periodic system. Companies using a perpetual system would presumably have updated inventory data.

This appendix describes two methods to estimate inventory.

Retail Inventory Method   To avoid the time-consuming and expensive process of taking a physical inventory each month or quarter, some companies use the **retail inventory method** to estimate cost of goods sold and ending inventory. Some companies even use the retail inventory method to prepare the annual statements. Home Depot, for instance, says in its annual report: "Inventories are stated at the lower of cost (first-in, first-out) or market, as determined by the retail inventory method." A company may also estimate inventory for audit purposes or when inventory is damaged or destroyed.

The retail inventory method uses a three-step process to estimate ending inventory. We need to know the amount of inventory a company had at the beginning of the period in both *cost* and *retail* amounts. We already explained how to compute the cost of inventory. The *retail amount of inventory* refers to its dollar amount measured using selling prices of inventory items. We also need to know the net amount of goods purchased (minus returns, allowances, and discounts) in the period, both at cost and at retail. The amount of net sales at retail is also needed. The process is shown in Exhibit 6B.1.

Point: When a retailer takes a physical inventory, it can restate the retail value of inventory to a cost basis by applying the cost-to-retail ratio. It can also estimate the amount of shrinkage by comparing the inventory computed with the amount from a physical inventory.

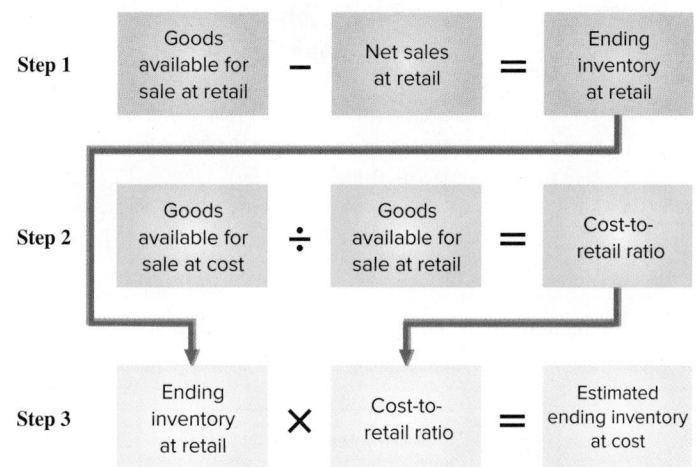

EXHIBIT 6B.1

Retail Inventory Method of Inventory Estimation

The reasoning behind the retail inventory method is that if we can get a good estimate of the cost-to-retail ratio, we can multiply ending inventory at retail by this ratio to estimate ending inventory at cost. We show in Exhibit 6B.2 how these steps are applied to estimate ending inventory for a typical company. First, we find that $100,000 of goods (at retail selling prices) were available for sale. We see that $70,000 of these goods were sold, leaving $30,000 (retail value) of merchandise in ending inventory. Second, the cost of these goods is 60% of the $100,000 retail value. Third, since cost for these goods is 60% of retail, the estimated cost of ending inventory is $18,000.

Example: What is the cost of ending inventory in Exhibit 6B.2 if the cost of beginning inventory is $22,500 and its retail value is $34,500? *Answer:* $30,000 × 62% = $18,600

		At Cost	At Retail
Goods available for sale			
	Beginning inventory	$ 20,500	$ 34,500
	Cost of goods purchased	39,500	65,500
Step 1:	Goods available for sale	60,000	100,000
	Deduct net sales at retail		70,000
	Ending inventory at retail		$ 30,000
Step 2:	Cost-to-retail ratio: ($60,000 ÷ $100,000) = 60%		
Step 3:	Estimated ending inventory at cost ($30,000 × 60%)	$18,000	

EXHIBIT 6B.2

Estimated Inventory Using the Retail Inventory Method

Gross Profit Method   The **gross profit method** estimates the cost of ending inventory by applying the gross profit ratio to net sales (at retail). This type of estimate often is needed when inventory is destroyed, lost, or stolen. These cases require an inventory estimate so that a company can file a claim with its insurer. Users also apply this method to see whether inventory amounts from a physical count are reasonable. This method uses the historical relation between cost of goods sold and net sales to estimate the proportion of cost of goods sold making up current sales. This cost of goods sold estimate is then subtracted from cost of goods available for sale to estimate the ending inventory at cost. These two steps are shown in Exhibit 6B.3.

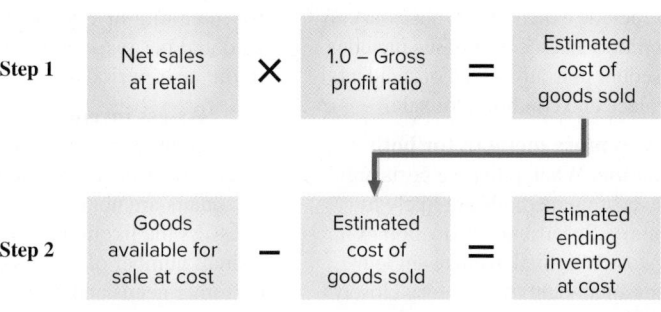

EXHIBIT 6B.3

Gross Profit Method of Inventory Estimation

Point: Reliability of the gross profit method depends on an accurate and stable estimate of the gross profit ratio.

To illustrate, assume that a company's inventory is destroyed by fire in March 2017. When the fire occurs, the company's accounts show the following balances for January through March: Net Sales, $30,000; Inventory, $12,000 (at January 1, 2017); and Cost of Goods Purchased, $20,500. If this company's gross profit ratio is 30%, then 30% of each net sales dollar is gross profit and 70% is cost of goods sold. We show in Exhibit 6B.4 how this 70% is used to estimate lost inventory of $11,500. To understand this exhibit, think of subtracting the cost of goods sold from the goods available for sale to get the ending inventory.

EXHIBIT 6B.4

Estimated Inventory Using the Gross Profit Method

Goods available for sale		
Inventory, January 1, 2017		$12,000
Cost of goods purchased		20,500
Goods available for sale (at cost)		32,500
Net sales at retail		$30,000
Step 1: Estimated cost of goods sold ($30,000 × 70%)		(21,000) ← × 0.70
Step 2: Estimated March inventory at cost		$11,500

NEED-TO-KNOW 6-8

Using the retail method and the following data, estimate the cost of ending inventory.

Retail Inventory Estimation

P4

	Cost	Retail
Beginning inventory	$324,000	$530,000
Cost of goods purchased	195,000	335,000
Net sales		320,000

Solution

Estimated ending inventory (at cost) is $327,000. It is computed as follows:

Step 1: ($530,000 + $335,000) − $320,000 = $545,000

Step 2: $\dfrac{\$324,000 + \$195,000}{\$530,000 + \$335,000} = 60\%$

Step 3: $545,000 × 60\% = \underline{\$327,000}$

Do More: QS 6-22, E 6-16, E 6-17

Summary

C1 Identify the items making up merchandise inventory. Merchandise inventory refers to goods owned by a company and held for resale. Three special cases merit our attention. Goods in transit are reported in inventory of the company that holds ownership rights. Goods on consignment are reported in the consignor's inventory. Goods damaged or obsolete are reported in inventory at their net realizable value.

C2 Identify the costs of merchandise inventory. Costs of merchandise inventory include expenditures necessary to bring an item to a salable condition and location. This includes its invoice cost minus any discount plus any added or incidental costs necessary to put it in a place and condition for sale.

A1 Analyze the effects of inventory methods for both financial and tax reporting. When purchase costs are rising or falling, the inventory costing methods are likely to assign different costs to inventory. Specific identification exactly matches costs and revenues. Weighted average smooths out cost changes. FIFO assigns an amount to inventory closely

approximating current replacement cost. LIFO assigns the most recent costs incurred to cost of goods sold and likely better matches current costs with revenues.

A2 Analyze the effects of inventory errors on current and future financial statements. An error in the amount of ending inventory affects assets (inventory), net income (cost of goods sold), and equity for that period. Since ending inventory is next period's beginning inventory, an error in ending inventory affects next period's cost of goods sold and net income. Inventory errors in one period are offset in the next period.

A3 Assess inventory management using both inventory turnover and days' sales in inventory. We prefer a high inventory turnover, provided that goods are not out of stock and customers are not turned away. We use days' sales in inventory to assess the likelihood of goods being out of stock. We prefer a small number of days' sales in inventory if we can serve customer needs and provide a buffer for uncertainties.

P1 **Compute inventory in a perpetual system using the methods of specific identification, FIFO, LIFO, and weighted average.** Costs are assigned to the Cost of Goods Sold account *each time* a sale occurs in a perpetual system. Specific identification assigns a cost to each item sold by referring to its actual cost (for example, its net invoice cost). Weighted average assigns a cost to items sold by dividing the current balance in the Inventory account by the total items available for sale to determine cost per unit. We then multiply the number of units sold by this cost per unit to get the cost of each sale. FIFO assigns cost to items sold assuming that the earliest units purchased are the first units sold. LIFO assigns cost to items sold assuming that the most recent units purchased are the first units sold.

P2 **Compute the lower of cost or market amount of inventory.** Inventory is reported at market cost when market is *lower* than recorded cost, called the *lower of cost or market (LCM) inventory.* Market is typically measured as replacement cost. Lower of cost or market can be applied separately to each item, to major categories of items, or to the entire inventory.

P3ᴬ **Compute inventory in a periodic system using the methods of specific identification, FIFO, LIFO, and weighted average.** Periodic inventory systems allocate the cost of goods available for sale between cost of goods sold and ending inventory *at the end of a period.* Specific identification and FIFO give identical results whether the periodic or perpetual system is used. LIFO assigns costs to cost of goods sold assuming the last units purchased for the period are the first units sold. The weighted average cost per unit is computed by dividing the total cost of beginning inventory and net purchases for the period by the total number of units available. Then, it multiplies cost per unit by the number of units sold to give cost of goods sold.

P4ᴮ **Apply both the retail inventory and gross profit methods to estimate inventory.** The retail inventory method involves three steps: (1) goods available at retail minus net sales at retail equals ending inventory at retail, (2) goods available at cost divided by goods available at retail equals the cost-to-retail ratio, and (3) ending inventory at retail multiplied by the cost-to-retail ratio equals estimated ending inventory at cost. The gross profit method involves two steps: (1) net sales at retail multiplied by 1 minus the gross profit ratio equals estimated cost of goods sold and (2) goods available at cost minus estimated cost of goods sold equals estimated ending inventory at cost.

Key Terms

Average cost	Gross profit method	Net realizable value
Consignee	Interim statements (interim financial statements)	Retail inventory method
Consignor		Specific identification (SI)
Consistency concept	Inventory turnover	Weighted average (WA)
Days' sales in inventory	Last-in, first-out (LIFO)	
First-in, first-out (FIFO)	Lower of cost or market (LCM)	

Multiple Choice Quiz

Use the following information from Marvel Company for the month of July to answer questions 1 through 4.

July 1	Beginning inventory............	75 units @ $25 each
July 3	Purchase....................	348 units @ $27 each
July 8	Sale........................	300 units
July 15	Purchase....................	257 units @ $28 each
July 23	Sale........................	275 units

1. **Perpetual:** Assume that Marvel uses a *perpetual* FIFO inventory system. What is the dollar value of its ending inventory?

   a. $2,940   **d.** $2,852
   b. $2,685   **e.** $2,705
   c. $2,625

2. **Perpetual:** Assume that Marvel uses a *perpetual* LIFO inventory system. What is the dollar value of its ending inventory?

   a. $2,940   **d.** $2,852
   b. $2,685   **e.** $2,705
   c. $2,625

3. **Perpetual and Periodic:** Assume that Marvel uses a specific identification inventory system. Its ending inventory consists of 20 units from beginning inventory, 40 units from the July 3 purchase, and 45 units from the July 15 purchase. What is the dollar value of its ending inventory?

   a. $2,940   **d.** $2,852
   b. $2,685   **e.** $2,840
   c. $2,625

4.ᴬ **Periodic:** Assume that Marvel uses a *periodic* FIFO inventory system. What is the dollar value of its ending inventory?

   a. $2,940   **d.** $2,852
   b. $2,685   **e.** $2,705
   c. $2,625

5.ᴬ **Periodic:** A company reports the following beginning inventory and purchases, and it ends the period with 30 units in inventory.

Beginning inventory.........	100 units at $10 cost per unit
Purchase 1	40 units at $12 cost per unit
Purchase 2	20 units at $14 cost per unit

i) Compute ending inventory using the FIFO *periodic* system.

   a. $400   **b.** $1,460   **c.** $1,360   **d.** $300

ii) Compute cost of goods sold using the LIFO *periodic* system.

   a. $400   **b.** $1,460   **c.** $1,360   **d.** $300

6. A company has cost of goods sold of $85,000 and ending inventory of $18,000. Its days' sales in inventory equals:

   a. 49.32 days   **d.** 77.29 days

   b. 0.21 day   **e.** 1,723.61 days

   c. 4.72 days

ANSWERS TO MULTIPLE CHOICE QUIZ

1. a; FIFO perpetual

Date	Goods Purchased	Cost of Goods Sold	Inventory Balance
July 1			75 units @ $25 = $ 1,875
July 3	348 units @ $27 = $9,396		75 units @ $25 ⎱ 348 units @ $27 ⎰ = $11,271
July 8		75 units @ $25 ⎱ 225 units @ $27 ⎰ = $ 7,950	123 units @ $27 = $ 3,321
July 15	257 units @ $28 = $7,196		123 units @ $27 ⎱ 257 units @ $28 ⎰ = $10,517
July 23		123 units @ $27 ⎱ 152 units @ $28 ⎰ = $ 7,577	105 units @ $28 = **$2,940**
		$15,527	

2. b; LIFO perpetual

Date	Goods Purchased	Cost of Goods Sold	Inventory Balance
July 1			75 units @ $25 = $ 1,875
July 3	348 units @ $27 = $9,396		75 units @ $25 ⎱ 348 units @ $27 ⎰ = $11,271
July 8		300 units @ $27 = $ 8,100	75 units @ $25 ⎱ 48 units @ $27 ⎰ = $ 3,171
July 15	257 units @ $28 = $7,196		75 units @ $25 ⎱ 48 units @ $27 ⎱ 257 units @ $28 ⎰ = $10,367
July 23		257 units @ $28 ⎱ 18 units @ $27 ⎰ = $ 7,682	75 units @ $25 ⎱ 30 units @ $27 ⎰ = **$ 2,685**
		$15,782	

3. e; Specific identification (perpetual and periodic are identical for specific identification)—Ending inventory computation:

20 units @ $25	$ 500	
40 units @ $27	1,080	
45 units @ $28	1,260	
105 units	$2,840	

4.ᴬ a; FIFO periodic. Ending inventory computation: 105 units @ $28 each = $2,940. (*Hint:* FIFO periodic inventory computation is identical to the FIFO perpetual inventory computation—see question 1.)

5.ᴬ i) a; FIFO periodic inventory $= (20 \times \$14) + (10 \times \$12)$
$$= \$400$$

ii) b; LIFO periodic cost of goods sold $= (20 \times \$14) + (40 \times \$12)$
$$+ (70 \times \$10) = \$1,460$$

6. d; Days' sales in inventory = (Ending inventory/Cost of goods sold)
$$\times 365 = (\$18,000/\$85,000) \times 365$$
$$= \underline{77.29 \text{ days}}$$

A(B) *Superscript letter A(B) denotes assignments based on Appendix 6A (6B).*

🔲 Icon denotes assignments that involve decision making.

Discussion Questions

1. Describe how costs flow from inventory to cost of goods sold for the following methods: (*a*) FIFO and (*b*) LIFO.

2. Where is the amount of merchandise inventory disclosed in the financial statements?

3. Why are incidental costs sometimes ignored in inventory costing? Under what accounting constraint is this permitted?

4. 🔲 If costs are declining, will the LIFO or FIFO method of inventory valuation yield the lower cost of goods sold? Why?

5. What does the full disclosure principle prescribe if a company changes from one acceptable accounting method to another?

6. Can a company change its inventory method each accounting period? Explain.

7. 🔲 Does the accounting concept of consistency preclude any changes from one accounting method to another?

8. 🔲 If inventory errors are said to correct themselves, why are accounting users concerned when such errors are made?

9. Explain the following statement: "Inventory errors correct themselves."

10. What is the meaning of *market* as it is used in determining the lower of cost or market for inventory?

11. 🔲 What guidance does the accounting constraint of conservatism offer?

12. What factors contribute to (or cause) inventory shrinkage?

13.ᴮ When preparing interim financial statements, what two methods can companies utilize to estimate cost of goods sold and ending inventory?

14. Refer to **Apple**'s financial statements in Appendix A. On September 26, 2015, what percent of current assets is represented by inventory? **APPLE**

15. Refer to **Apple**'s financial statements in Appendix A and compute its cost of goods available for sale for the year ended September 26, 2015. **APPLE**

16. Refer to **Samsung**'s financial statements in Appendix A. Compute its cost of goods available for sale for the year ended December 31, 2015. **Samsung**

17. Refer to **Samsung**'s financial statements in Appendix A. What percent of its current assets is inventory as of December 31, 2015 and 2014? **Samsung**

---

connect

Homestead Crafts, a distributor of handmade gifts, operates out of owner Emma Finn's house. At the end of the current period, Emma looks over her inventory and finds that she has:

- 1,300 units (products) in her basement, 20 of which were damaged by water and cannot be sold.
- 350 units in her van, ready to deliver per a customer order, terms FOB destination.
- 80 units out on consignment to a friend who owns a retail store.

How many units should Emma include in her company's period-end inventory?

QUICK STUDY

QS 6-1
Inventory ownership
C1

A car dealer acquires a used car for $14,000, with terms FOB shipping point. Additional costs in obtaining and offering the car for sale include:

- $250 for transportation-in.
- $300 for insurance during shipment.
- $900 for import duties.
- $150 for advertising.
- $1,250 for sales staff salaries.

For computing inventory, what cost is assigned to the used car?

QS 6-2
Inventory costs
C2

Wattan Company reports beginning inventory of 10 units at $60 each. Every week for four weeks it purchases an additional 10 units at respective costs of $61, $62, $65, and $70 per unit for weeks 1 through 4. Compute the cost of goods available for sale and the units available for sale for this four-week period. Assume that no sales occur during those four weeks.

QS 6-3
Computing goods available for sale   P1

QS 6-4
Perpetual: Inventory costing with FIFO
P1

A company reports the following beginning inventory and two purchases for the month of January. On January 26, the company sells 350 units. Ending inventory at January 31 totals 150 units.

	Units	Unit Cost
Beginning inventory on January 1.............	320	$3.00
Purchase on January 9.....................	80	3.20
Purchase on January 25	100	3.34

Required

Assume the perpetual inventory system is used and then determine the costs assigned to ending inventory when costs are assigned based on the FIFO method. (Round per unit costs and inventory amounts to cents.)

QS 6-5
Perpetual: Inventory costing with LIFO   **P1**

Refer to the information in QS 6-4 and assume the perpetual inventory system is used. Determine the costs assigned to ending inventory when costs are assigned based on LIFO. (Round per unit costs and inventory amounts to cents.)

QS 6-6
Perpetual: Inventory costing with weighted average   **P1**
Check End. inv., $465

Refer to the information in QS 6-4 and assume the perpetual inventory system is used. Determine the costs assigned to ending inventory when costs are assigned based on the weighted average method. (Round per unit costs and inventory amounts to cents.)

QS 6-7^A
Periodic: Inventory costing with FIFO   **P3**

Refer to the information in QS 6-4 and assume the periodic inventory system is used. Determine the costs assigned to ending inventory when costs are assigned based on the FIFO method. (Round per unit costs and inventory amounts to cents.)

QS 6-8^A
Periodic: Inventory costing with LIFO   **P3**

Refer to the information in QS 6-4 and assume the periodic inventory system is used. Determine the costs assigned to ending inventory when costs are assigned based on the LIFO method. (Round per unit costs and inventory amounts to cents.)

QS 6-9^A
Periodic: Inventory costing with weighted average   **P3**

Refer to the information in QS 6-4 and assume the periodic inventory system is used. Determine the costs assigned to ending inventory when costs are assigned based on the weighted average method. (Round per unit costs and inventory amounts to cents.)

QS 6-10
Perpetual: Assigning costs with FIFO
P1

Trey Monson starts a merchandising business on December 1 and enters into the following three inventory purchases. Also, on December 15, Monson sells 15 units for $20 each.

Purchases on December 7	10 units @ $ 6.00 cost
Purchases on December 14	20 units @ $12.00 cost
Purchases on December 21	15 units @ $14.00 cost

Required

Monson uses a perpetual inventory system. Determine the costs assigned to the December 31 ending inventory based on the FIFO method. (Round per unit costs and inventory amounts to cents.)

QS 6-11
Perpetual: Inventory costing with LIFO   **P1**

Refer to the information in QS 6-10 and assume the perpetual inventory system is used. Determine the costs assigned to ending inventory when costs are assigned based on the LIFO method. (Round per unit costs and inventory amounts to cents.)

Refer to the information in QS 6-10 and assume the perpetual inventory system is used. Determine the costs assigned to ending inventory when costs are assigned based on the weighted average method. (Round per unit costs and inventory amounts to cents.)

QS 6-12
Perpetual: Inventory costing with weighted average   **P1**

Check   End. inv., $360

Refer to the information in QS 6-10 and assume the perpetual inventory system is used. Determine the costs assigned to ending inventory when costs are assigned based on specific identification. Of the units sold, eight are from the December 7 purchase and seven are from the December 14 purchase. (Round per unit costs and inventory amounts to cents.)

QS 6-13
Perpetual: Inventory costing with specific identification   **P1**

Refer to the information in QS 6-10 and assume the periodic inventory system is used. Determine the costs assigned to ending inventory when costs are assigned based on the FIFO method. (Round per unit costs and inventory amounts to cents.)

QS 6-14[A]
Periodic: Inventory costing with FIFO   **P3**

Refer to the information in QS 6-10 and assume the periodic inventory system is used. Determine the costs assigned to ending inventory when costs are assigned based on the LIFO method. (Round per unit costs and inventory amounts to cents.)

QS 6-15[A]
Periodic: Inventory costing with LIFO   **P3**

Refer to the information in QS 6-10 and assume the periodic inventory system is used. Determine the costs assigned to ending inventory when costs are assigned based on the weighted average method. (Round per unit costs and inventory amounts to cents.)

QS 6-16[A]
Periodic: Inventory costing with weighted average   **P3**

Refer to the information in QS 6-10 and assume the periodic inventory system is used. Determine the costs assigned to ending inventory when costs are assigned based on specific identification. Of the units sold, eight are from the December 7 purchase and seven are from the December 14 purchase. (Round per unit costs and inventory amounts to cents.)

QS 6-17[A]
Periodic: Inventory costing with specific identification   **P3**

Identify the inventory costing method best described by each of the following separate statements. Assume a period of increasing costs.

_____ **1.** Yields a balance sheet inventory amount often markedly less than its replacement cost.
_____ **2.** Results in a balance sheet inventory amount approximating replacement cost.
_____ **3.** Provides a tax advantage (deferral) to a corporation when costs are rising.
_____ **4.** Recognizes (matches) recent costs against net sales.
_____ **5.** The preferred method when each unit of product has unique features that markedly affect cost.

QS 6-18
Contrasting inventory costing methods

A1 ♟

Ames Trading Co. has the following products in its ending inventory. Compute lower of cost or market for inventory applied separately to each product.

QS 6-19
Applying LCM to inventories

P2

Product	Quantity	Cost per Unit	Market per Unit
Mountain bikes...........	11	$600	$550
Skateboards	13	350	425
Gliders.................	26	800	700

In taking a physical inventory at the end of year 2017, Grant Company forgot to count certain units. Explain how this error affects the following: (*a*) 2017 cost of goods sold, (*b*) 2017 gross profit, (*c*) 2017 net income, (*d*) 2018 net income, (*e*) the combined two-year income, and (*f*) income for years after 2018.

QS 6-20
Inventory errors

A2 ♟

Endor Company begins the year with $140,000 of goods in inventory. At year-end, the amount in inventory has increased to $180,000. Cost of goods sold for the year is $1,200,000. Compute Endor's inventory turnover and days' sales in inventory. Assume that there are 365 days in the year.

QS 6-21
Analyzing inventory   A3

QS 6-22ᴮ
Estimating inventories—
gross profit method

P4

Confucius Bookstore's inventory is destroyed by a fire on September 5, 2017. The following data for year 2017 are available from the accounting records. Estimate the cost of the inventory destroyed.

Jan. 1 inventory	$190,000
Jan. 1 through Sept. 5 purchases (net).............	$352,000
Jan. 1 through Sept. 5 sales (net)	$685,000
Year 2017 estimated gross profit rate	44%

QS 6-23
International accounting
standards

C1   C2   P2

Answer each of the following questions related to international accounting standards.

a. Explain how the accounting for items and costs making up merchandise inventory is different between IFRS and U.S. GAAP.

b. Can companies reporting under IFRS apply a cost flow assumption in assigning costs to inventory? If yes, identify at least two acceptable cost flow assumptions.

c. Both IFRS and U.S. GAAP apply the lower of cost or market method for reporting inventory values. If inventory is written down from applying the lower of cost or market method, explain in general terms how IFRS and U.S. GAAP differ in accounting for any subsequent period reversal of that reported decline in inventory value.

EXERCISES

Exercise 6-1
Inventory ownership   **C1**

1. At year-end, Harris Co. had shipped $12,500 of merchandise FOB destination to Harlow Co. Which company should include the $12,500 of merchandise in transit as part of its year-end inventory?

2. Harris Company has shipped $20,000 of goods to Harlow Co., and Harlow Co. has arranged to sell the goods for Harris. Identify the consignor and the consignee. Which company should include any unsold goods as part of its inventory?

Exercise 6-2
Inventory costs

C2

Walberg Associates, antique dealers, purchased the contents of an estate for $75,000. Terms of the purchase were FOB shipping point, and the cost of transporting the goods to Walberg Associates's warehouse was $2,400. Walberg Associates insured the shipment at a cost of $300. Prior to putting the goods up for sale, they cleaned and refurbished them at a cost of $980. Determine the cost of the inventory acquired from the estate.

Exercise 6-3
Perpetual: Inventory
costing methods

P1

Laker Company reported the following January purchases and sales data for its only product.

Date	Activities	Units Acquired at Cost	Units Sold at Retail
Jan. 1	Beginning inventory	140 units @ $6.00 = $ 840	
Jan. 10	Sales		100 units @ $15
Jan. 20	Purchase	60 units @ $5.00 = 300	
Jan. 25	Sales		80 units @ $15
Jan. 30	Purchase	180 units @ $4.50 = 810	
	Totals	380 units $1,950	180 units

Required

The company uses a perpetual inventory system. Determine the cost assigned to ending inventory and to cost of goods sold using (*a*) specific identification, (*b*) weighted average, (*c*) FIFO, and (*d*) LIFO. (Round per unit costs and inventory amounts to cents.) For specific identification, ending inventory consists of 200 units, where 180 are from the January 30 purchase, 5 are from the January 20 purchase, and 15 are from beginning inventory.

Check   Ending inventory:
LIFO, $930; WA, $918

Exercise 6-4
Perpetual: Income effects
of inventory methods

A1

Use the data in Exercise 6-3 to prepare comparative income statements for the month of January for Laker Company similar to those shown in Exhibit 6.8 for the four inventory methods. Assume expenses are $1,250, and that the applicable income tax rate is 40%. (Round amounts to cents.)

1. Which method yields the highest net income?

2. Does net income using weighted average fall above, between, or below that using FIFO and LIFO?

3. If costs were rising instead of falling, which method would yield the highest net income?

Refer to the information in Exercise 6-3 and assume the periodic inventory system is used. Determine the costs assigned to ending inventory and to cost of goods sold using (a) specific identification, (b) weighted average, (c) FIFO, and (d) LIFO. (Round per unit costs and inventory amounts to cents.) For specific identification, ending inventory consists of 200 units, where 180 are from the January 30 purchase, 5 are from the January 20 purchase, and 15 are from beginning inventory.

Exercise 6-5^A → **Exercise 6-5**[A]
Periodic: Inventory costing
P3

Use the data and results from Exercise 6-5 to prepare comparative income statements for the month of January for the company similar to those shown in Exhibit 6.8 for the four inventory methods. Assume expenses are $1,250, and that the applicable income tax rate is 40%. (Round amounts to cents.)

Exercise 6-6[A]
Periodic: Income effects of inventory methods

A1

Required

1. Which method yields the highest net income?
2. Does net income using weighted average fall above, between, or below that using FIFO and LIFO?
3. If costs were rising instead of falling, which method would yield the highest net income?

Hemming Co. reported the following current-year purchases and sales for its only product.

Exercise 6-7
Perpetual: Inventory costing methods—FIFO and LIFO

P1

Date	Activities	Units Acquired at Cost	Units Sold at Retail
Jan. 1	Beginning inventory	200 units @ $10 = $ 2,000	
Jan. 10	Sales.		150 units @ $40
Mar. 14	Purchase	350 units @ $15 = 5,250	
Mar. 15	Sales.		300 units @ $40
July 30	Purchase	450 units @ $20 = 9,000	
Oct. 5	Sales.		430 units @ $40
Oct. 26	Purchase	100 units @ $25 = 2,500	
	Totals	1,100 units $18,750	880 units

Required

Hemming uses a perpetual inventory system. Determine the costs assigned to ending inventory and to cost of goods sold using (a) FIFO and (b) LIFO. Compute the gross margin for each method. (Round amounts to cents.)

Check   Ending inventory:
LIFO, $4,150

Refer to the information in Exercise 6-7. Ending inventory consists of 45 units from the March 14 purchase, 75 units from the July 30 purchase, and all 100 units from the October 26 purchase. Using the specific identification method, compute (a) the cost of goods sold and (b) the gross profit. (Round amounts to cents.)

Exercise 6-8
Specific identification   P1

Refer to the information in Exercise 6-7 and assume the periodic inventory system is used. Determine the costs assigned to ending inventory and to cost of goods sold using (a) FIFO and (b) LIFO. Then (c) compute the gross margin for each method.

Exercise 6-9[A]
Periodic: Inventory costing   P3

Martinez Company's ending inventory includes the following items. Compute the lower of cost or market for ending inventory applied separately to each product.

Exercise 6-10
Lower of cost or market

P2

Product	Units	Cost per Unit	Market per Unit
Helmets.	24	$50	$54
Bats	17	78	72
Shoes.	38	95	91
Uniforms	42	36	36

Check   LCM = $7,394

Exercise 6-11

Comparing LIFO numbers
to FIFO numbers; ratio
analysis

A1   A3

Cruz Company uses LIFO for inventory costing and reports the following financial data. It also recomputed inventory and cost of goods sold using FIFO for comparison purposes.

	2017	2016
LIFO inventory.	$160	$110
LIFO cost of goods sold	740	680
FIFO inventory	240	110
FIFO cost of goods sold	660	645
Current assets (using LIFO)	220	180
Current liabilities.	200	170

Check   (1) FIFO: Current
ratio, 1.5; Inventory turnover,
3.8 times

1. Compute its current ratio, inventory turnover, and days' sales in inventory for 2017 using (*a*) LIFO numbers and (*b*) FIFO numbers. (Round answers to one decimal.)

2. Comment on and interpret the results of part 1.

Exercise 6-12

Analysis of inventory errors

A2

Check   2016 reported gross
profit, $330,000

Vibrant Company had $850,000 of sales in each of three consecutive years 2016–2018, and it purchased merchandise costing $500,000 in each of those years. It also maintained a $250,000 physical inventory from the beginning to the end of that three-year period. In accounting for inventory, it made an error at the end of year 2016 that caused its year-end 2016 inventory to appear on its statements as $230,000 rather than the correct $250,000.

1. Determine the correct amount of the company's gross profit in each of the years 2016–2018.

2. Prepare comparative income statements as in Exhibit 6.11 to show the effect of this error on the company's cost of goods sold and gross profit for each of the years 2016–2018.

Exercise 6-13

Inventory turnover and
days' sales in inventory

A3

Use the following information for Palmer Co. to compute inventory turnover for 2017 and 2016, and its days' sales in inventory at December 31, 2017 and 2016. (Round answers to one decimal.) Comment on Palmer's efficiency in using its assets to increase sales from 2016 to 2017.

	2017	2016	2015
Cost of goods sold	$643,825	$426,650	$391,300
Ending inventory.	97,400	87,750	92,500

Exercise 6-14ᴬ
Periodic: Cost flow
assumptions

P3

Lopez Company reported the following current-year data for its only product. The company uses a periodic inventory system, and its ending inventory consists of 150 units—50 from each of the last three purchases. Determine the cost assigned to ending inventory and to cost of goods sold using (*a*) specific identification, (*b*) weighted average, (*c*) FIFO, and (*d*) LIFO. (Round per unit costs and inventory amounts to cents.) Which method yields the highest net income?

Jan.	1	Beginning inventory	96 units @ $2.00 =	$ 192
Mar.	7	Purchase	220 units @ $2.25 =	495
July	28	Purchase	544 units @ $2.50 =	1,360
Oct.	3	Purchase	480 units @ $2.80 =	1,344
Dec.	19	Purchase	160 units @ $2.90 =	464
		Totals	1,500 units	$3,855

Check   Inventory; LIFO,
$313.50; FIFO, $435.00

Exercise 6-15ᴬ
Periodic: Cost flow
assumptions

P3

Flora's Gifts reported the following current-month data for its only product. The company uses a periodic inventory system, and its ending inventory consists of 60 units—50 units from the January 6 purchase and 10 units from the January 25 purchase. Determine the cost assigned to ending inventory and to cost of goods sold using (*a*) specific identification, (*b*) weighted average, (*c*) FIFO, and (*d*) LIFO. (Round per unit costs and inventory amounts to cents.) Which method yields the lowest net income?

Jan.	1	Beginning inventory	138 units @ $3.00 = $ 414
Jan.	6	Purchase	300 units @ $2.80 = 840
Jan.	17	Purchase	540 units @ $2.30 = 1,242
Jan.	25	Purchase	22 units @ $2.00 = 44
		Totals	1,000 units $2,540

Check Inventory: LIFO, $180.00; FIFO, $131.40

In 2017, Dakota Company had net sales (at retail) of $260,000. The following additional information is available from its records at the end of 2017. Use the retail inventory method to estimate Dakota's 2017 ending inventory at cost.

	At Cost	At Retail
Beginning inventory................	$ 63,800	$128,400
Cost of goods purchased............	115,060	196,800

Exercise 6-16[B]
Estimating ending inventory—retail method
P4

Check End. inventory at cost, $35,860

On January 1, JKR Shop had $225,000 of inventory at cost. In the first quarter of the year, it purchased $795,000 of merchandise, returned $11,550, and paid freight charges of $18,800 on purchased merchandise, terms FOB shipping point. The company's gross profit averages 30%, and the store had $1,000,000 of net sales (at retail) in the first quarter of the year. Use the gross profit method to estimate its cost of inventory at the end of the first quarter.

Exercise 6-17[B]
Estimating ending inventory—gross profit method **P4**

Samsung Electronics reports the following regarding its accounting for inventories.

> Inventories are stated at the lower of cost or net realizable value. Cost is determined using the average cost method, except for materials-in-transit. Inventories are reduced for the estimated losses arising from excess, obsolescence, and the decline in value. This reduction is determined by estimating market value based on future customer demand. The losses on inventory obsolescence are recorded as a part of cost of sales.

Exercise 6-18
Accounting for inventory following IFRS

P2

1. What cost flow assumption(s) does Samsung apply in assigning costs to its inventories?
2. If at year-end 2016 there was an increase in the value of its inventories such that there was a reversal of ₩550 (₩ is Korean won) million for the 2015 write-down, how would Samsung account for this under IFRS? Would Samsung's accounting be different for this reversal if it reported under U.S. GAAP? Explain.

---

connect

Warnerwoods Company uses a perpetual inventory system. It entered into the following purchases and sales transactions for March. (For specific identification, the March 9 sale consisted of 80 units from beginning inventory and 340 units from the March 5 purchase; the March 29 sale consisted of 40 units from the March 18 purchase and 120 units from the March 25 purchase.)

PROBLEM SET A

Problem 6-1A
Perpetual: Alternative cost flows
P1

Date	Activities	Units Acquired at Cost	Units Sold at Retail
Mar. 1	Beginning inventory.............	100 units @ $50.00 per unit	
Mar. 5	Purchase.....................	400 units @ $55.00 per unit	
Mar. 9	Sales		420 units @ $85.00 per unit
Mar. 18	Purchase.....................	120 units @ $60.00 per unit	
Mar. 25	Purchase.....................	200 units @ $62.00 per unit	
Mar. 29	Sales		160 units @ $95.00 per unit
	Totals........................	820 units	580 units

Required

1. Compute cost of goods available for sale and the number of units available for sale.
2. Compute the number of units in ending inventory.
3. Compute the cost assigned to ending inventory using (*a*) FIFO, (*b*) LIFO, (*c*) weighted average, and (*d*) specific identification. (Round all amounts to cents.)
4. Compute gross profit earned by the company for each of the four costing methods in part 3.

Check (3) Ending inventory: FIFO, $14,800; LIFO, $13,680; WA, $14,352

(4) LIFO gross profit, $17,980

Problem 6-2A^A

Periodic: Alternative cost flows

P3

Refer to the information in Problem 6-1A and assume the periodic inventory system is used.

Required

1. Compute cost of goods available for sale and the number of units available for sale.
2. Compute the number of units in ending inventory.
3. Compute the cost assigned to ending inventory using (*a*) FIFO, (*b*) LIFO, (*c*) weighted average, and (*d*) specific identification. (Round all amounts to cents.)
4. Compute gross profit earned by the company for each of the four costing methods in part 3.

Problem 6-3A

Perpetual: Alternative cost flows

P1

Montoure Company uses a perpetual inventory system. It entered into the following calendar-year purchases and sales transactions. (For specific identification, units sold consist of 600 units from beginning inventory, 300 from the February 10 purchase, 200 from the March 13 purchase, 50 from the August 21 purchase, and 250 from the September 5 purchase.)

Date	Activities	Units Acquired at Cost	Units Sold at Retail
Jan. 1	Beginning inventory.............	600 units @ $45.00 per unit	
Feb. 10	Purchase......................	400 units @ $42.00 per unit	
Mar. 13	Purchase......................	200 units @ $27.00 per unit	
Mar. 15	Sales........................		800 units @ $75.00 per unit
Aug. 21	Purchase......................	100 units @ $50.00 per unit	
Sept. 5	Purchase......................	500 units @ $46.00 per unit	
Sept. 10	Sales........................		600 units @ $75.00 per unit
	Totals.......................	1,800 units	1,400 units

Required

1. Compute cost of goods available for sale and the number of units available for sale.
2. Compute the number of units in ending inventory.
3. Compute the cost assigned to ending inventory using (*a*) FIFO, (*b*) LIFO, (*c*) weighted average, and (*d*) specific identification. (Round all amounts to cents.)
4. Compute gross profit earned by the company for each of the four costing methods in part 3.

Check (3) Ending inventory: FIFO, $18,400; LIFO, $18,000; WA, $17,760

(4) LIFO gross profit, $45,800

Analysis Component

5. If the company's manager earns a bonus based on a percent of gross profit, which method of inventory costing will the manager likely prefer?

Problem 6-4A^A

Periodic: Alternative cost flows

P3

Refer to the information in Problem 6-3A and assume the periodic inventory system is used.

Required

1. Compute cost of goods available for sale and the number of units available for sale.
2. Compute the number of units in ending inventory.
3. Compute the cost assigned to ending inventory using (*a*) FIFO, (*b*) LIFO, (*c*) weighted average, and (*d*) specific identification. (Round all amounts to cents.)
4. Compute gross profit earned by the company for each of the four costing methods in part 3.

Analysis Component

5. If the company's manager earns a bonus based on a percentage of gross profit, which method of inventory costing will the manager likely prefer?

Problem 6-5A

Lower of cost or market   P2

A physical inventory of Liverpool Company taken at December 31 reveals the following.

	A	B	C	D
1 / 2	**Item**	**Units**	**Cost per Unit**	**Market per Unit**
3	Car audio equipment			
4	Speakers	345	$ 90	$ 98
5	Stereos	260	111	100
6	Amplifiers	326	86	95
7	Subwoofers	204	52	41
8	Security equipment			
9	Alarms	480	150	125
10	Locks	291	93	84
11	Cameras	212	310	322
12	Binocular equipment			
13	Tripods	185	70	84
14	Stabilizers	170	97	105

Required

1. Compute the lower of cost or market for the inventory applied separately to each item.

2. If the market amount is less than the recorded cost of the inventory, then record the LCM adjustment to the Merchandise Inventory account.

Check   (1) $273,054

Navajo Company's financial statements show the following. The company recently discovered that in making physical counts of inventory, it had made the following errors: Inventory on December 31, 2016, is understated by $56,000 and inventory on December 31, 2017, is overstated by $20,000.

Problem 6-6A
Analysis of inventory errors

A2

For Year Ended December 31		2016	2017	2018
(a)	Cost of goods sold	$ 615,000	$ 957,000	$ 780,000
(b)	Net income	230,000	285,000	241,000
(c)	Total current assets	1,255,000	1,365,000	1,200,000
(d)	Total equity	1,387,000	1,530,000	1,242,000

Required

1. For each key financial statement figure—(a), (b), (c), and (d) above—prepare a table similar to the following to show the adjustments necessary to correct the reported amounts.

Figure: _____	2016	2017	2018
Reported amount	_____	_____	_____
Adjustments for: 12/31/2016 error	_____	_____	_____
12/31/2017 error	_____	_____	_____
Corrected amount	_____	_____	_____

Check   (1) Corrected net income: 2016, $286,000; 2017, $209,000; 2018, $261,000

Analysis Component

2. What is the error in total net income for the combined three-year period resulting from the inventory errors? Explain.

3. Explain why the understatement of inventory by $56,000 at the end of 2016 results in an understatement of equity by the same amount in that year.

Seminole Company began year 2017 with 23,000 units of product in its January 1 inventory costing $15 each. It made successive purchases of its product in year 2017 as follows. The company uses a periodic inventory system. On December 31, 2017, a physical count reveals that 40,000 units of its product remain in inventory.

Problem 6-7A^A
Periodic: Alternative cost flows   **P3**

Mar. 7	30,000 units @ $18.00 each
May 25	39,000 units @ $20.00 each
Aug. 1	23,000 units @ $25.00 each
Nov. 10	35,000 units @ $26.00 each

Required

1. Compute the number and total cost of the units available for sale in year 2017.

2. Compute the amounts assigned to the 2017 ending inventory and the cost of goods sold using (*a*) FIFO, (*b*) LIFO, and (*c*) weighted average. (Round all amounts to cents.)

Problem 6-8A[A]
Periodic: Income comparisons and cost flows

A1   P3

QP Corp. sold 4,000 units of its product at $50 per unit in year 2017 and incurred operating expenses of $5 per unit in selling the units. It began the year with 700 units in inventory and made successive purchases of its product as follows.

Jan. 1	Beginning inventory	....	700 units @ $18.00 per unit
Feb. 20	Purchase	....	1,700 units @ $19.00 per unit
May 16	Purchase	....	800 units @ $20.00 per unit
Oct. 3	Purchase	....	500 units @ $21.00 per unit
Dec. 11	Purchase	....	2,300 units @ $22.00 per unit
	Total	....	6,000 units

Required

1. Prepare comparative income statements similar to Exhibit 6.8 for the three inventory costing methods of FIFO, LIFO, and weighted average. (Round all amounts to cents.) Include a detailed cost of goods sold section as part of each statement. The company uses a periodic inventory system, and its income tax rate is 40%.

2. How would the financial results from using the three alternative inventory costing methods change if the company had been experiencing *declining* costs in its purchases of inventory?

3. What advantages and disadvantages are offered by using (*a*) LIFO and (*b*) FIFO? Assume the continuing trend of *increasing* costs.

Problem 6-9A[B]
Retail inventory method

P4

The records of Alaska Company provide the following information for the year ended December 31.

	At Cost	At Retail
January 1 beginning inventory	$ 469,010	$ 928,950
Cost of goods purchased................	3,376,050	6,381,050
Sales		5,595,800
Sales returns.........................		42,800

Required

1. Use the retail inventory method to estimate the company's year-end inventory at cost.

2. A year-end physical inventory at retail prices yields a total inventory of $1,686,900. Prepare a calculation showing the company's loss from shrinkage at cost and at retail.

Problem 6-10A[B]
Gross profit method   P4

Wayward Company wants to prepare interim financial statements for the first quarter. The company wishes to avoid making a physical count of inventory. Wayward's gross profit rate averages 34%. The following information for the first quarter is available from its records.

January 1 beginning inventory	$ 302,580
Cost of goods purchased................	941,040
Sales	1,211,160
Sales returns.........................	8,410

Required

Use the gross profit method to estimate the company's first-quarter ending inventory.

Ming Company uses a perpetual inventory system. It entered into the following purchases and sales transactions for April. (For specific identification, the April 9 sale consisted of 8 units from beginning inventory and 27 units from the April 6 purchase; the April 30 sale consisted of 12 units from beginning inventory, 3 units from the April 6 purchase, and 10 units from the April 25 purchase.)

Date	Activities	Units Acquired at Cost	Units Sold at Retail
Apr. 1	Beginning inventory.............	20 units @ $3,000.00 per unit	
Apr. 6	Purchase......................	30 units @ $3,500.00 per unit	
Apr. 9	Sales		35 units @ $12,000.00 per unit
Apr. 17	Purchase......................	5 units @ $4,500.00 per unit	
Apr. 25	Purchase......................	10 units @ $4,800.00 per unit	
Apr. 30	Sales		25 units @ $14,000.00 per unit
	Total.........................	65 units	60 units

Required

1. Compute cost of goods available for sale and the number of units available for sale.
2. Compute the number of units in ending inventory.
3. Compute the cost assigned to ending inventory using (*a*) FIFO, (*b*) LIFO, (*c*) weighted average, and (*d*) specific identification. (Round all amounts to cents.)
4. Compute gross profit earned by the company for each of the four costing methods in part 3.

Refer to the information in Problem 6-1B and assume the periodic inventory system is used.

Required

1. Compute cost of goods available for sale and the number of units available for sale.
2. Compute the number of units in ending inventory.
3. Compute the cost assigned to ending inventory using (*a*) FIFO, (*b*) LIFO, (*c*) weighted average, and (*d*) specific identification. (Round all amounts to cents.)
4. Compute gross profit earned by the company for each of the four costing methods in part 3.

Aloha Company uses a perpetual inventory system. It entered into the following calendar-year purchases and sales transactions. (For specific identification, the May 9 sale consisted of 80 units from beginning inventory and 100 units from the May 6 purchase; the May 30 sale consisted of 200 units from the May 6 purchase and 100 units from the May 25 purchase.)

Date	Activities	Units Acquired at Cost	Units Sold at Retail
May 1	Beginning inventory.............	150 units @ $300.00 per unit	
May 6	Purchase......................	350 units @ $350.00 per unit	
May 9	Sales		180 units @ $1,200.00 per unit
May 17	Purchase......................	80 units @ $450.00 per unit	
May 25	Purchase......................	100 units @ $458.00 per unit	
May 30	Sales		300 units @ $1,400.00 per unit
	Total.........................	680 units	480 units

Required

1. Compute cost of goods available for sale and the number of units available for sale.
2. Compute the number of units in ending inventory.
3. Compute the cost assigned to ending inventory using (*a*) FIFO, (*b*) LIFO, (*c*) weighted average, and (*d*) specific identification. (Round all amounts to cents.)
4. Compute gross profit earned by the company for each of the four costing methods in part 3.

Analysis Component

5. If the company's manager earns a bonus based on a percent of gross profit, which method of inventory costing will the manager likely prefer?

PROBLEM SET B

Problem 6-1B
Perpetual: Alternative cost flows

P1

Check (3) Ending inventory: FIFO, $24,000; LIFO, $15,000; WA, $20,000
(4) LIFO gross profit, $549,500

Problem 6-2B[A]
Periodic: Alternative cost flows

P3

Problem 6-3B
Perpetual: Alternative cost flows

P1

Check (3) Ending inventory: FIFO, $88,800; LIFO, $62,500; WA, $75,600
(4) LIFO gross profit, $449,200

Problem 6-4B[A]

Periodic: Alternative
cost flows

P3

Refer to the information in Problem 6-3B and assume the periodic inventory system is used.

Required

1. Compute cost of goods available for sale and the number of units available for sale.
2. Compute the number of units in ending inventory.
3. Compute the cost assigned to ending inventory using (*a*) FIFO, (*b*) LIFO, (*c*) weighted average, and (*d*) specific identification. (Round all amounts to cents.)
4. Compute gross profit earned by the company for each of the four costing methods in part 3.

Analysis Component

5. If the company's manager earns a bonus based on a percentage of gross profit, which method of inventory costing will the manager likely prefer?

Problem 6-5B

Lower of cost or market

P2

A physical inventory of Office Necessities Company taken at December 31 reveals the following.

	A	B	C	D
1	**Item**	**Units**	**Cost per Unit**	**Market per Unit**
2				
3	Office furniture			
4	Desks	536	$261	$305
5	Chairs	395	227	256
6	Mats	687	49	43
7	Bookshelves	421	93	82
8	Filing cabinets			
9	Two-drawer	114	81	70
10	Four-drawer	298	135	122
11	Lateral	75	104	118
12	Office equipment			
13	Projectors	370	168	200
14	Copiers	475	317	288
15	Phones	302	125	117

Required

Check (1) $580,054

1. Compute the lower of cost or market for the inventory applied separately to each item.
2. If the market amount is less than the recorded cost of the inventory, then record the LCM adjustment to the Merchandise Inventory account.

Problem 6-6B

Analysis of inventory errors

A2

Hallam Company's financial statements show the following. The company recently discovered that in making physical counts of inventory, it had made the following errors: Inventory on December 31, 2016, is overstated by $18,000 and inventory on December 31, 2017, is understated by $26,000.

For Year Ended December 31	2016	2017	2018
(*a*) Cost of goods sold	$207,200	$213,800	$197,030
(*b*) Net income	175,800	212,270	184,910
(*c*) Total current assets	276,000	277,500	272,950
(*d*) Total equity	314,000	315,000	346,000

Required

1. For each key financial statement figure—(*a*), (*b*), (*c*), and (*d*) above—prepare a table similar to the following to show the adjustments necessary to correct the reported amounts.

Figure: _____	2016	2017	2018
Reported amount	_____	_____	_____
Adjustments for: 12/31/2016 error	_____	_____	_____
12/31/2017 error	_____	_____	_____
Corrected amount	_____	_____	_____

Check (1) Corrected net income: 2016, $157,800; 2017, $256,270; 2018, $158,910

Continued on next page . . .

Analysis Component

2. What is the error in total net income for the combined three-year period resulting from the inventory errors? Explain.

3. Explain why the overstatement of inventory by $18,000 at the end of 2016 results in an overstatement of equity by the same amount in that year.

Seneca Co. began year 2017 with 6,500 units of product in its January 1 inventory costing $35 each. It made successive purchases of its product in year 2017 as follows. The company uses a periodic inventory system. On December 31, 2017, a physical count reveals that 8,500 units of its product remain in inventory.

Jan.	4	. . . .	11,500 units @ $33 each
May	18	. . . .	13,400 units @ $32 each
July	9	. . . .	11,000 units @ $29 each
Nov.	21	. . . .	7,600 units @ $27 each

Problem 6-7B[A]
Periodic: Alternative cost flows
P3

Required

1. Compute the number and total cost of the units available for sale in year 2017.

2. Compute the amounts assigned to the 2017 ending inventory and the cost of goods sold using (*a*) FIFO, (*b*) LIFO, and (*c*) weighted average. (Round all amounts to cents.)

Check (2) Cost of goods sold: FIFO, $1,328,700; LIFO, $1,266,500; WA, $1,294,800

Shepard Company sold 4,000 units of its product at $100 per unit in year 2017 and incurred operating expenses of $15 per unit in selling the units. It began the year with 840 units in inventory and made successive purchases of its product as follows.

Jan.	1	Beginning inventory	840 units @ $58 per unit
Apr.	2	Purchase	600 units @ $59 per unit
June	14	Purchase	1,205 units @ $61 per unit
Aug.	29	Purchase	700 units @ $64 per unit
Nov.	18	Purchase	1,655 units @ $65 per unit
		Total	5,000 units

Problem 6-8B[A]
Periodic: Income comparisons and cost flows
A1   P3

Required

1. Prepare comparative income statements similar to Exhibit 6.8 for the three inventory costing methods of FIFO, LIFO, and weighted average. (Round all amounts to cents.) Include a detailed cost of goods sold section as part of each statement. The company uses a periodic inventory system, and its income tax rate is 40%.

2. How would the financial results from using the three alternative inventory costing methods change if the company had been experiencing decreasing prices in its purchases of inventory?

3. What advantages and disadvantages are offered by using (*a*) LIFO and (*b*) FIFO? Assume the continuing trend of increasing costs.

Check (1) Net income: LIFO, $52,896; FIFO, $57,000; WA, $55,200

The records of Macklin Co. provide the following information for the year ended December 31.

	At Cost	At Retail
January 1 beginning inventory	$ 90,022	$115,610
Cost of goods purchased.	502,250	761,830
Sales		782,300
Sales returns.		3,460

Problem 6-9B[B]
Retail inventory method
P4

Required

1. Use the retail inventory method to estimate the company's year-end inventory.

2. A year-end physical inventory at retail prices yields a total inventory of $80,450. Prepare a calculation showing the company's loss from shrinkage at cost and at retail.

Check (1) Inventory, $66,555 cost
(2) Inventory shortage at cost, $12,251.25

Problem 6-10B[B]

Gross profit method

P4

Otingo Equipment Co. wants to prepare interim financial statements for the first quarter. The company wishes to avoid making a physical count of inventory. Otingo's gross profit rate averages 35%. The following information for the first quarter is available from its records.

January 1 beginning inventory	$ 802,880
Cost of goods purchased...............	2,209,636
Sales	3,760,260
Sales returns.........................	79,300

Check Est. ending inventory, $619,892

Required

Use the gross profit method to estimate the company's first-quarter ending inventory.

SERIAL PROBLEM

Business Solutions

P2 A3

© Alexander Image/Shutterstock RF

(This serial problem began in Chapter 1 and continues through most of the book. If previous chapter segments were not completed, the serial problem can begin at this point.)

SP 6

Part A

Santana Rey of **Business Solutions** is evaluating her inventory to determine whether it must be adjusted based on lower of cost or market rules. Business Solutions has three different types of software in its inventory, and the following information is available for each.

Inventory Items	Units	Cost per Unit	Market per Unit
Office productivity	3	$ 76	$ 74
Desktop publishing...........	2	103	100
Accounting	3	90	96

Required

1. Compute the lower of cost or market for ending inventory assuming Rey applies the lower of cost or market rule to inventory as a whole. Must Rey adjust the reported inventory value? Explain.

2. Assume that Rey had instead applied the lower of cost or market rule to each product in inventory. Under this assumption, must Rey adjust the reported inventory value? Explain.

Part B

Selected accounts and balances for the three months ended March 31, 2018, for Business Solutions follow.

January 1 beginning inventory	$ 0
Cost of goods sold	14,052
March 31 ending inventory	704

Required

1. Compute inventory turnover and days' sales in inventory for the three months ended March 31, 2018.

2. Assess the company's performance if competitors average 15 times for inventory turnover and 25 days for days' sales in inventory.

Beyond the Numbers

REPORTING IN ACTION

C2 A3

APPLE

BTN 6-1   Refer to **Apple**'s financial statements in Appendix A to answer the following.

Required

1. What amount of inventories did Apple report as a current asset on September 26, 2015? On September 27, 2014?

2. Inventories represent what percent of total assets on September 26, 2015? On September 27, 2014?

3. Comment on the relative size of Apple's inventories compared to its other types of assets.

4. What accounting method did Apple use to compute inventory amounts on its balance sheet?

5. Compute inventory turnover for fiscal year ended September 26, 2015, and days' sales in inventory as of September 26, 2015.

Continued on next page . . .

Fast Forward

6. Access Apple's financial statements for fiscal years ended after September 26, 2015, from its website (<u>Apple.com</u>) or the SEC's EDGAR database (<u>SEC.gov</u>). Answer questions 1 through 5 using the current Apple information and compare results to those prior years.

BTN 6-2   Comparative figures for Apple and Microsoft follow.

COMPARATIVE ANALYSIS

A3

APPLE

$ millions	Apple			Microsoft		
	Current Year	One Year Prior	Two Years Prior	Current Year	One Year Prior	Two Years Prior
Inventory..............	$ 2,349	$ 2,111	$ 1,764	$ 2,902	$ 2,660	$ 1,938
Cost of sales...........	140,089	112,258	106,606	33,038	27,078	20,385

Required

1. Compute inventory turnover for each company for the most recent two years shown.

2. Compute days' sales in inventory for each company for the three years shown.

3. Comment on and interpret your findings from parts 1 and 2. Assume an industry average for inventory turnover of 15.

BTN 6-3   Golf Challenge Corp. is a retail sports store carrying golf apparel and equipment. The store is at the end of its second year of operation and is struggling. A major problem is that its cost of inventory has continually increased in the past two years. In the first year of operations, the store assigned inventory costs using LIFO. A loan agreement the store has with its bank, its prime source of financing, requires the store to maintain a certain profit margin and current ratio. The store's owner is currently looking over Golf Challenge's preliminary financial statements for its second year. The numbers are not favorable. The only way the store can meet the required financial ratios agreed on with the bank is to change from LIFO to FIFO. The store originally decided on LIFO because of its tax advantages. The owner recalculates ending inventory using FIFO and submits those numbers and statements to the loan officer at the bank for the required bank review. The owner thankfully reflects on the available latitude in choosing the inventory costing method.

ETHICS CHALLENGE

A1

Required

1. How does Golf Challenge's use of FIFO improve its net profit margin and current ratio?

2. Is the action by Golf Challenge's owner ethical? Explain.

BTN 6-4   You are a financial adviser with a client in the wholesale produce business that just completed its first year of operations. Due to weather conditions, the cost of acquiring produce to resell has escalated during the later part of this period. Your client, Javonte Gish, mentions that because her business sells perishable goods, she has striven to maintain a FIFO flow of goods. Although sales are good, the increasing cost of inventory has put the business in a tight cash position. Gish has expressed concern regarding the ability of the business to meet income tax obligations.

COMMUNICATING IN PRACTICE

A1

Required

Prepare a memorandum that identifies, explains, and justifies the inventory method you recommend your client, Ms. Gish, adopt.

BTN 6-5   Access the September 26, 2015, 10-K report for Apple, Inc. (ticker: AAPL), filed on October 28, 2015, from the EDGAR filings at <u>SEC.gov</u>.

TAKING IT TO THE NET

A3

APPLE

Required

1. What products are manufactured by Apple?

2. What inventory method does Apple use? (*Hint:* See the Note 1 to its financial statements.)

3. Compute its gross margin and gross margin ratio for the 2015 fiscal year. Comment on your computations—assume an industry average of 40% for the gross margin ratio.

4. Compute its inventory turnover and days' sales in inventory for the year ended September 26, 2015. Comment on your computations—assume an industry average of 15 for inventory turnover and 9 for days' sales in inventory.

TEAMWORK IN ACTION

A1 P1

Point: Step 1 allows four choices or areas for expertise. Larger teams will have some duplication of choice, but the specific identification method should not be duplicated.

BTN 6-6 Each team member has the responsibility to become an expert on an inventory method. This expertise will be used to facilitate teammates' understanding of the concepts relevant to that method.

1. Each learning team member should select an area for expertise by choosing one of the following inventory methods: specific identification, LIFO, FIFO, or weighted average.

2. Form expert teams made up of students who have selected the same area of expertise. The instructor will identify where each expert team will meet.

3. Using the following data, each expert team must collaborate to develop a presentation that illustrates the relevant concepts and procedures for its inventory method. Each team member must write the presentation in a format that can be shown to the learning team.

Data

The company uses a *perpetual* inventory system. It had the following beginning inventory and current-year purchases of its product.

Jan. 1	Beginning inventory	50 units @ $100 = $ 5,000
Jan. 14	Purchase	150 units @ $120 = 18,000
Apr. 30	Purchase	200 units @ $150 = 30,000
Sept.26	Purchase	300 units @ $200 = 60,000

The company transacted sales on the following dates at a $350 per unit sales price.

Jan. 10	30 units	(specific cost: 30 @ $100)
Feb. 15	100 units	(specific cost: 100 @ $120)
Oct. 5	350 units	(specific cost: 100 @ $150 and 250 @ $200)

Concepts and Procedures to Illustrate in Expert Presentation

a. Identify and compute the costs to assign to the units sold. (Round per unit costs to three decimals.)
b. Identify and compute the costs to assign to the units in ending inventory. (Round inventory balances to the dollar.)
c. How likely is it that this inventory costing method will reflect the actual physical flow of goods? How relevant is that factor in determining whether this is an acceptable method to use?
d. What is the impact of this method versus others in determining net income and income taxes?
e. How closely does the ending inventory amount reflect replacement cost?

4. Re-form learning teams. In rotation, each expert is to present to the team the presentation developed in part 3. Experts are to encourage and respond to questions.

ENTREPRENEURIAL DECISION

A3

BTN 6-7 Review the chapter's opening feature highlighting Brad Gillis and Ben Friedman and their company, **Homegrown Sustainable Sandwich Shop**. Assume that Homegrown consistently maintains an inventory level of $30,000, meaning that its average and ending inventory levels are the same. Also assume its annual cost of sales is $120,000. To cut costs, Brad and Ben propose to slash inventory to a constant level of $15,000 with no impact on cost of sales. They plan to work with suppliers to get quicker deliveries and to order smaller quantities more often.

Required

1. Compute the company's inventory turnover and its days' sales in inventory under (a) current conditions and (b) proposed conditions.
2. Evaluate and comment on the merits of their proposal given your analysis for part 1. Identify any concerns you might have about the proposal.

HITTING THE ROAD

C1 C2

BTN 6-8 Visit four retail stores with another classmate. In each store, identify whether the store uses a bar coding system to help manage its inventory. Try to find at least one store that does not use bar coding. If a store does not use bar coding, ask the store's manager or clerk whether he or she knows which type of inventory method the store employs. Create a table that shows columns for the name of store visited, type of merchandise sold, use or nonuse of bar coding, and the inventory method used if bar coding is not employed. You might also inquire as to what the store's inventory turnover is and how often physical inventory is taken.

BTN 6-9   Following are key figures (in millions of Korean won) for **Samsung** (**Samsung.com**), which is a leading manufacturer of consumer electronics products.

GLOBAL DECISION

A3

Samsung

APPLE

₩ in millions	Current Year	One Year Prior	Two Years Prior
Inventory..............	₩ 18,811,794	₩ 17,317,504	₩ 19,134,868
Cost of sales...........	123,482,118	128,278,800	137,696,309

Required

1. Use these data and those from BTN 6-2 to compute (*a*) inventory turnover and (*b*) days' sales in inventory for the most recent two years shown for **Samsung**, **Apple**, and **Microsoft**.

2. Comment on and interpret your findings from part 1.

GLOBAL VIEW

This section discusses differences between U.S. GAAP and IFRS in the items and costs making up merchandise inventory, in the methods to assign costs to inventory, and in the methods to estimate inventory values.

Items and Costs Making Up Inventory   Both U.S. GAAP and IFRS include broad and similar guidance for the items and costs making up merchandise inventory. Specifically, under both accounting systems, merchandise inventory includes all items that a company owns and holds for sale. Further, merchandise inventory includes costs of expenditures necessary, directly or indirectly, to bring those items to a salable condition and location.

Assigning Costs to Inventory   Both U.S. GAAP and IFRS allow companies to use specific identification in assigning costs to inventory. Further, both systems allow companies to apply a *cost flow assumption*. The usual cost flow assumptions are FIFO, weighted average, and LIFO. However, IFRS does not allow use of LIFO.

Global: IFRS requires that LCM be applied to individual items.

Estimating Inventory Costs   Inventory value can decrease or increase as it awaits sale.

Decreases in Inventory Value   Both U.S. GAAP and IFRS require companies to write down (reduce the cost recorded for) inventory when its value falls below the cost recorded. This is referred to as the *lower of cost or market* method explained in this chapter. U.S. GAAP prohibits any later increase in the recorded value of that inventory even if that decline in value is reversed through value increases in later periods. However, IFRS allows reversals of those write-downs up to the original acquisition cost. For example, if **Apple** wrote down its 2015 inventory from $2,349 million to $2,300 million, it could not reverse this in future periods even if its value increased to more than $2,349 million. However, if Apple applied IFRS, it could reverse that previous loss. (Another difference is that value refers to *replacement cost* under U.S. GAAP, but *net realizable value* under IFRS.)

APPLE

Increases in Inventory Value   Neither U.S. GAAP nor IFRS allows inventory to be adjusted upward beyond the original cost. (One exception is that IFRS requires agricultural assets such as animals, forests, and plants to be measured at fair value less point-of-sale costs.)

   Nokia provides the following description of its inventory valuation procedures:

> Inventories are stated at the lower of cost or net realizable value. Cost approximates actual cost on a FIFO (first-in first-out) basis. Net realizable value is the amount that can be realized from the sale of the inventory in the normal course of business after allowing for the costs of realization.

 Global View Assignments

Discussion Questions 16 & 17

Quick Study 6-23

Exercise 6-18

BTN 6-9

7

chapter

Accounting Information Systems

Learning Objectives

CONCEPTUAL

C1 Identify the principles and components of accounting information systems.

C2 Explain the goals and uses of special journals.

C3 Describe the use of controlling accounts and subsidiary ledgers.

ANALYTICAL

A1 Compute segment return on assets and use it to evaluate segment performance.

PROCEDURAL

P1 Journalize and post transactions using special journals.

P2 Prepare and prove the accuracy of subsidiary ledgers.

© Paul Chinn/Corbis News/Getty Images

BOX Office Success

LOS ALTOS, CA—Aaron Levie, Dylan Smith, Jeff Queisser, and Sam Ghods met in high school. "[Aaron] was a magician, and I was very much a hard core nerd," recalls Jeff. Beyond magic and nerdiness, the four friends were interested in information systems. "Aaron and I were always bouncing ideas off of each other," recalls Dylan. Then, Aaron pitched his idea of a company. Although initially reluctant, the three friends joined Aaron and they launched **Box** (**Box.com**), a cloud storage solution.

An immediate concern was how to obtain money to launch the business. "We had a lot of unsuccessful pitches," explains Dylan. "A couple of 19- and 20-year-olds starting a business isn't that old school." Then a surprise occurred. As a result of a cold e-mail to Mark Cuban, the *Shark Tank* TV star, the founders received an investment of $350,000, which helped legitimize their company.

"Nothing more exciting than . . . creation of great products"

—Aaron Levie

As the number of businesses and individuals using their service skyrocketed, the owners realized they needed to get their accounting system in order. This included setting up internal controls to guard against errors and fraud, and creating special journals and accounting ledgers. Aaron insists that reliable accounting "platforms not only offer agility and productivity, but also an opportunity for better security."

Box now maintains special journals for sales, cash receipts, purchases, and cash disbursements. Because Box has many customers paying to use its services, Box maintains subsidiary accounts receivable ledgers for each customer. The owners insist that even more growth is in the future, and that an effective accounting system is crucial to achieving that growth.

Aaron knows that effective management of their own information system is key to future success. To help, the owners regularly review the cash disbursements journal to know where cash is spent, and they examine the cash receipts journal for growth strategies. They place controls over all special journals to secure their reliability and reduce fraud.

The larger message of Box according to Aaron is, "Take the stodgiest, oldest, slowest moving industry you can find. And build amazing software for it."

Sources: *Box website,* January 2017; *Yahoo Finance,* January 2016; *Inc.,* October 2012; *BBC,* May 2013; *TechRepublic,* March 2014; *CrunchBase.com,* 2016

SYSTEM PRINCIPLES

C1_____

Identify the principles and components of accounting information systems.

Accounting information systems collect and process data from transactions and events, organize them in reports, and communicate results to decision makers. Knowledge of accounting systems gives decision makers a competitive edge as they gain a better understanding of information constraints, measurement limitations, and potential applications. It allows them to make more informed decisions and to better balance the risks and returns of different strategies. This section explains five principles of accounting information systems, shown in Exhibit 7.1.

EXHIBIT 7.1

System Principles

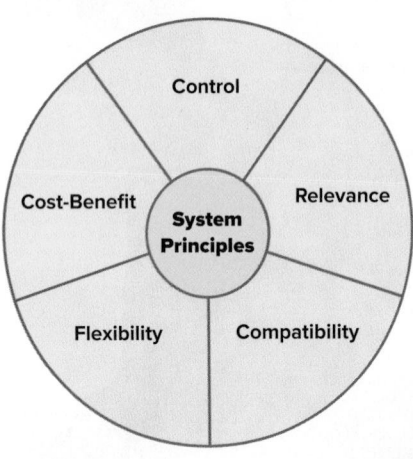

Control Principle

The **control principle** prescribes that an accounting information system has internal controls. **Internal controls** are methods and procedures allowing managers to control and monitor business activities. They include policies to protect company assets and achieve compliance with laws and regulations.

Relevance Principle

The **relevance principle** prescribes that an accounting information system report useful, understandable, timely, and pertinent information for effective decision making. The system must be designed to capture and produce relevant information for all decision makers.

Compatibility Principle

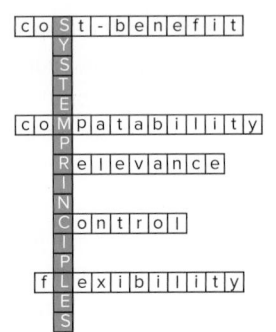

The **compatibility principle** prescribes that an accounting information system conform with a company's activities, personnel, and structure. It also must adapt to a company's unique characteristics. Most start-up entrepreneurs require only a simple information system. **Starbucks**, on the other hand, demands a more advanced system to manage multiple divisions of its business.

Flexibility Principle

The **flexibility principle** prescribes that an accounting information system be able to adapt to changes in the company, business environment, and needs of decision makers. Technological advances, competitive pressures, consumer tastes, regulations, and company activities constantly evolve. A system must be designed to adapt to these changes.

Cost-Benefit Principle

Point: Hackers stole 45 million debit and credit card numbers from **T.J. Maxx**. The security breach is estimated to have cost the company $100 per card, or $4.5 billion.

The **cost-benefit principle** prescribes that the benefits from an activity in an accounting information system outweigh the costs of that activity. For example, the benefits of producing a specific report must outweigh the costs of time and effort to produce that report. Decisions regarding other system principles (control, relevance, compatibility, and flexibility) are also affected by the cost-benefit principle.

 Decision Insight ━━━━━━━━━━━━━━━━━━━━━━━━━━

Digitals Are Forever E-communications have helped bring down many employees, including the former CEO of **Boeing**. To comply with Sarbanes-Oxley, more and more companies now archive and monitor e-mails, instant messages, blog postings, and web-based phone calls. Using natural-language software, companies sift through digital communications in milliseconds, checking for trade secrets, bad language, porn, and pirated files. ■

SYSTEM COMPONENTS

The five **components of accounting systems** are source documents, input devices, information processors, information storage, and output devices. These components apply whether a system is heavily computerized or manual.

Exhibit 7.2 shows these components as a series of steps, yet we know multi-level communications occur between many of these components. We briefly describe each of these components.

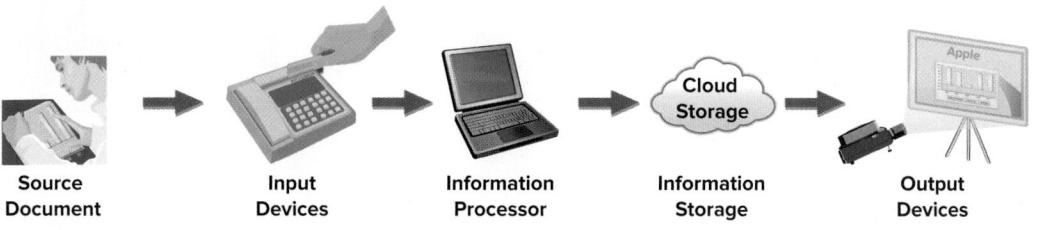

| Source Document | Input Devices | Information Processor | Information Storage | Output Devices |

EXHIBIT 7.2

Accounting System Components

Source Documents

Source documents provide the information processed by an accounting system. Examples of source documents include bank statements and checks, invoices from suppliers, billings to customers, cash register files, and employee earnings records. Source documents can be paper, but normally take the form of electronic files and web communications. Accurate source documents are crucial to accounting information systems. Input of wrong information damages the reliability of the information system.

Input Devices

Input devices capture information from source documents and transfer it to the information processing component. These devices convert data on source documents to a form usable for the system. Journal entries, both electronic and paper based, are a type of input device. Keyboards and scanners are the most common input devices in business. For example, bar code readers capture code numbers and transfer them to the organization's computer for processing.

© Vstock LLC/Getty Images RF

Information Processors

Information processors transform and summarize information for use in analysis and reporting. An information processor includes journals, ledgers, working papers, and posting procedures. Each assists in transforming raw data to useful information. Increasingly, technology is assisting manual information processors and is enabling accounting professionals to take on increased analysis, interpretive, and managerial roles.

Information Storage

Information storage keeps data accessible to information processors. After being input and processed, data are stored for use in future analyses and reports. Auditors rely on this database when they audit both financial statements and a company's controls. Older systems relied on paper documents, but modern systems depend on electronic storage devices or, increasingly, cloud storage.

Output Devices

Output devices take information out of an accounting system and make it available to users. Common output devices are printers, monitors, projectors, and web communications. Output devices provide users a variety of items including bills to customers, checks to suppliers, employee paychecks, financial statements, and internal reports. When requests for output occur, an information processor takes the needed data from a database and prepares the necessary report, which is then sent to an output device. One example is the transfer of payroll from the company's bank account to its employees' bank accounts.

■ Decision Insight

Virtual Output   A screenless computer display, called *virtual retinal display* (VRD), scans rows of pixels directly onto the user's retina by means of a laser. VRDs can simulate three-dimensional virtual worlds, including 3D financial graphics. VRDs have a control advantage as only the intended user can see the image displayed. ■

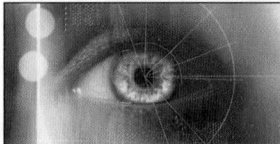

©Colin Anderson/Stockbyte/Getty Images

NEED-TO-KNOW 7-1

System Principles and Components

C1

Match each of the numbered descriptions with the principle, component, or descriptor that it best reflects. Indicate your answer by entering the letter *A* through *J* in the blank provided.

A. Control principle
B. Relevance principle
C. Compatibility principle
D. Flexibility principle
E. Cost-benefit principle
F. Source documents
G. Input devices
H. Information processors
I. Information storage
J. Output devices

_____ **1.** Capture information from source documents and enable its transfer to information processing.
_____ **2.** Keeps data accessible to information processors.
_____ **3.** Systems that transform and summarize information for use.
_____ **4.** Means to take information out of an accounting system and make it available to users.
_____ **5.** Information for entries that can be in either electronic or paper form.
_____ **6.** Prescribes that benefits from an activity in a system outweigh the costs.
_____ **7.** Prescribes that a system be adaptable to changes in the company, environment, and user needs.
_____ **8.** Prescribes that a system conform with a company's activities, personnel, and structure.
_____ **9.** Prescribes that a system report useful, understandable, timely, and pertinent information.
_____ **10.** Prescribes that a system have internal controls.

Do More: QS 7-1, QS 7-2

Solution

1. G   **2.** I   **3.** H   **4.** J   **5.** F   **6.** E   **7.** D   **8.** C   **9.** B   **10.** A

SPECIAL JOURNALS IN ACCOUNTING

C2

Explain the goals and uses of special journals.

This section focuses on special journals and subsidiary ledgers. We describe how special journals are used to capture transactions, and we explain how subsidiary ledgers are set up to capture details of accounts. This section uses a *perpetual* inventory system, and the special journals are set up using this system. A note at the bottom of each special journal explains the change required if a company uses a periodic system.

Basics of Special Journals

A **general journal** is an all-purpose journal in which we can record any transaction. Use of a general journal for all transactions is usually more costly for a business *and* is a less effective control procedure. Moreover, for less technologically advanced systems, use of a general journal requires that each debit and each credit entered be individually posted to its respective ledger account. To enhance internal control and reduce costs, transactions are organized into common groups. A **special journal** is used to record and post transactions of similar type. Most transactions of a merchandiser, for instance, can be categorized into the journals shown in Exhibit 7.3. This section assumes the use of these four special journals along with the general journal. The general journal continues to be used for transactions not covered by special journals and for adjusting, closing, and correcting entries. We show in the following discussion that special journals are *efficient tools in helping journalize and post transactions.* This is done, for instance, by accumulating debits and credits of similar transactions, which allows posting of amounts as column *totals* rather than as individual amounts. The advantage of this system increases as the number of transactions increases. Special journals allow an *efficient division of labor,* which is also an effective control procedure.

Point: Companies can use as many special journals as necessary given their unique business activities.

Point: A specific transaction is recorded in only *one* journal.

EXHIBIT 7.3

Using Special Journals with a General Journal

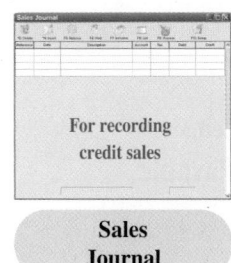

For recording credit sales

Sales Journal

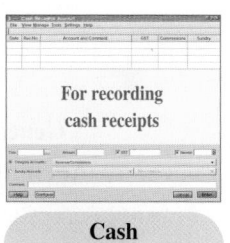

For recording cash receipts

Cash Receipts Journal

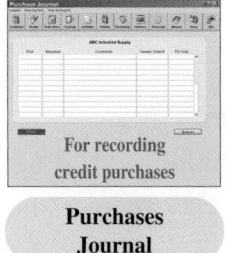

For recording credit purchases

Purchases Journal

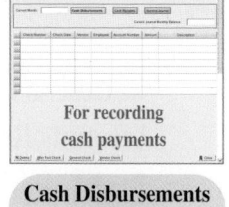

For recording cash payments

Cash Disbursements Journal

For transactions not in special journals

General Journal

It is important to note that special journals and subsidiary ledgers *are designed in a manner that is best suited for each business.* A business typically creates special journals for its most recurring transactions, such as sales, cash receipts, purchases, and cash disbursements. However, good systems design for a business could involve collapsing sales and cash receipts in one journal, or purchases and cash disbursements in another. It could also involve adding more special journals or additional subsidiary ledgers for other recurring transactions. This design decision extends to journal and ledger format. That is, the selection on number of columns, column headings, and so forth is based on what is best suited for each business. Thus, read the following sections as one example of a common systems design, but not the only design. (Proprietary software is internally developed by companies to meet system needs not met by off-the-shelf accounting software.)

Subsidiary Ledgers

To understand special journals, it is necessary to understand a **subsidiary ledger,** which is a list of individual accounts with a common characteristic. A subsidiary ledger contains detailed information on specific accounts in the general ledger. Information systems often include several subsidiary ledgers. Two of the most important are:

- **Accounts receivable ledger**—stores transaction data of individual customers.
- **Accounts payable ledger**—stores transaction data of individual suppliers.

Individual accounts in subsidiary ledgers are often arranged alphabetically, which is the approach taken here.

Accounts Receivable Ledger   When we recorded credit sales in prior chapters, we debited (increased) Accounts Receivable. When a company has more than one credit customer, the accounts receivable records must show how much *each* customer purchased, paid, and has yet to pay. This information is collected by keeping a separate account receivable for each credit

C3

Describe the use of controlling accounts and subsidiary ledgers.

customer. A separate account for each customer *could* be kept in the general ledger with the other financial statement accounts, but this is uncommon. Instead, the general ledger usually has a single Accounts Receivable account, and a *subsidiary ledger* is set up to keep a separate account for each customer. This subsidiary ledger is called the **accounts receivable ledger** (also called *accounts receivable subsidiary ledger* or *customers ledger*), and it can exist in electronic or paper form.

Exhibit 7.4 shows the relation between the Accounts Receivable account and its individual accounts in the subsidiary ledger. After all items are posted, the balance in the Accounts Receivable account must equal the sum of all balances of its customers' accounts. The Accounts Receivable account is said to control the accounts receivable ledger and is called a **controlling account.** Since the accounts receivable ledger is a supplementary record controlled by an account in the general ledger, it is called a *subsidiary* ledger.

Point: When a general ledger account has a subsidiary ledger, any transaction that impacts one of them also impacts the other—some refer to this as *general and subsidiary ledgers kept in tandem.*

EXHIBIT 7.4

Controlling Accounts and Subsidiary Ledgers

General Ledger

Subsidiary Ledgers

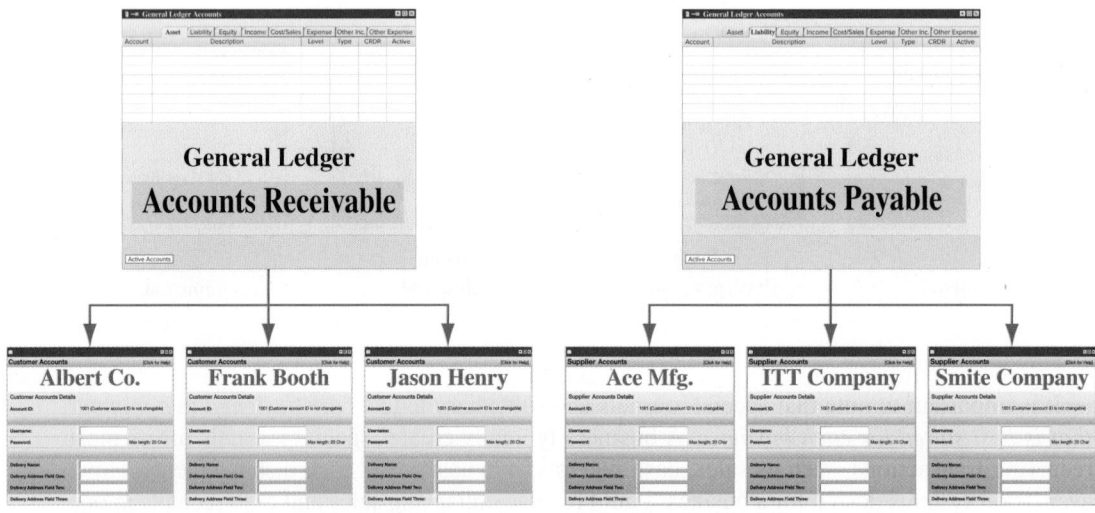

Point: A *control account* refers to any general ledger account that summarizes subsidiary ledger data.
Point: Controlling account balance = Sum of subsidiary account balances.

Accounts Payable Ledger   There are other controlling accounts and subsidiary ledgers. We know, for example, that many companies buy on credit from several suppliers. This means that companies must keep a separate account for each supplier by keeping an Accounts Payable controlling account in the general ledger and a separate account for each supplier (creditor) in an **accounts payable ledger** (also called *accounts payable subsidiary ledger* or *creditors ledger*)—see Exhibit 7.4.

Other Subsidiary Ledgers   Subsidiary ledgers are common for several other accounts. For example, a company might keep only one Equipment account in its general ledger, but its Equipment account subsidiary ledger could record each class of equipment in a separate account. Similar treatment is common for investments, inventory, and any accounts needing separate detailed records. **Genmar Holdings**, which manufactures boats by Glastron, Champion, Four Winns, and Larson, reports sales information by product line in its report. Yet its accounting system keeps much more detailed sales records. Genmar Holdings, for instance, sells hundreds of different products and must be able to analyze the sales performance of each. This detail can be captured by many different general ledger sales accounts but is instead captured by using supplementary records that function like subsidiary ledgers.

Subsidiary ledgers have at least four benefits:

- Removal of excessive details, and detailed accounts, from the general ledger.
- Up-to-date information readily available on specific customers and suppliers.
- Aid in error identification for specific accounts.
- Potential efficiencies in recordkeeping through division of labor in posting.

Match each of the numbered descriptions with the term, title, or phrase that it best reflects. Indicate your answer by entering the letter A through J in the blank provided.

NEED-TO-KNOW 7-2

Journals and Ledgers

C2   C3

A. General journal
E. Accounts payable ledger
I. Purchases journal

B. Special journal
F. Controlling account
J. Cash disbursements journal

C. Subsidiary ledger
G. Sales journal

D. Accounts receivable ledger
H. Cash receipts journal

_____ **1.** Used to record all cash payments.
_____ **2.** Used to record all credit purchases.
_____ **3.** Used to record all receipts of cash.
_____ **4.** Used to record sales of inventory on credit.
_____ **5.** Stores transaction data of individual customers.
_____ **6.** Stores transaction data of individual suppliers.
_____ **7.** Account that is said to control a specific subsidiary ledger.
_____ **8.** Contains detailed information on a specific account from the general ledger.
_____ **9.** Used to record and post transactions of similar type.
_____ **10.** All-purpose journal in which any transaction can be recorded.

Solution

1. J   **2.** I   **3.** H   **4.** G   **5.** D   **6.** E   **7.** F   **8.** C   **9.** B   **10.** A

Do More: QS 7-3, QS 7-4, QS 7-5, QS 7-7, QS 7-10, E 7-2, E 7-4, E 7-5, E 7-7

Sales Journal

A **sales journal** is used to record sales of inventory *on credit*. Sales of inventory for cash are not recorded in a sales journal but in a cash receipts journal. Sales of noninventory assets on credit are recorded in the general journal.

P1_____

Journalize and post transactions using special journals.

Journalizing   Credit sale transactions are recorded with information about each sale entered separately in a sales journal. This information is often taken from a copy of the sales ticket or invoice prepared at the time of sale. The top portion of Exhibit 7.5 shows a typical sales journal from a merchandiser. It has columns for recording the date, customer's name, invoice number, posting reference, and the sales and cost amounts of each credit sale. The sales journal in this exhibit is called a **columnar journal,** which is any journal with more than one column.

Each transaction recorded in the sales journal yields an entry in the Accounts Receivable Dr., Sales Cr. column. We usually need only one column for these two accounts. (An exception is when managers need more information about taxes, returns, and other sales details.) Each transaction in the sales journal also yields an entry in the Cost of Goods Sold Dr., Inventory Cr. column. This entry reflects the perpetual inventory system of tracking costs with each sale. To illustrate, on February 2, this company sold merchandise on account to Jason Henry for $450. The invoice number is 307, and the cost of this merchandise is $315. This information is captured on one line in the sales journal. No further explanations or entries are necessary, saving time and effort. Moreover, this sales journal is consistent with most inventory systems that use bar codes to record both sales and costs with each sale transaction. The Posting Reference (PR) column is not used when entering transactions but instead is used when posting.

Point: Continuously updated customer accounts provide timely information for customer inquiries on those accounts and on current amounts owed.

Posting   A sales journal is posted as reflected in the arrow lines of Exhibit 7.5. Two types of posting can be identified: (1) posting to the subsidiary ledger(s) and (2) posting to the general ledger.

Posting to subsidiary ledger.   Individual transactions in the sales journal are posted regularly to customer accounts in the accounts receivable ledger. These postings keep customer accounts up to date, which is important for the person granting credit to customers. When sales recorded in the sales journal are individually posted to customer accounts in the accounts

EXHIBIT 7.5

Sales Journal with Posting*

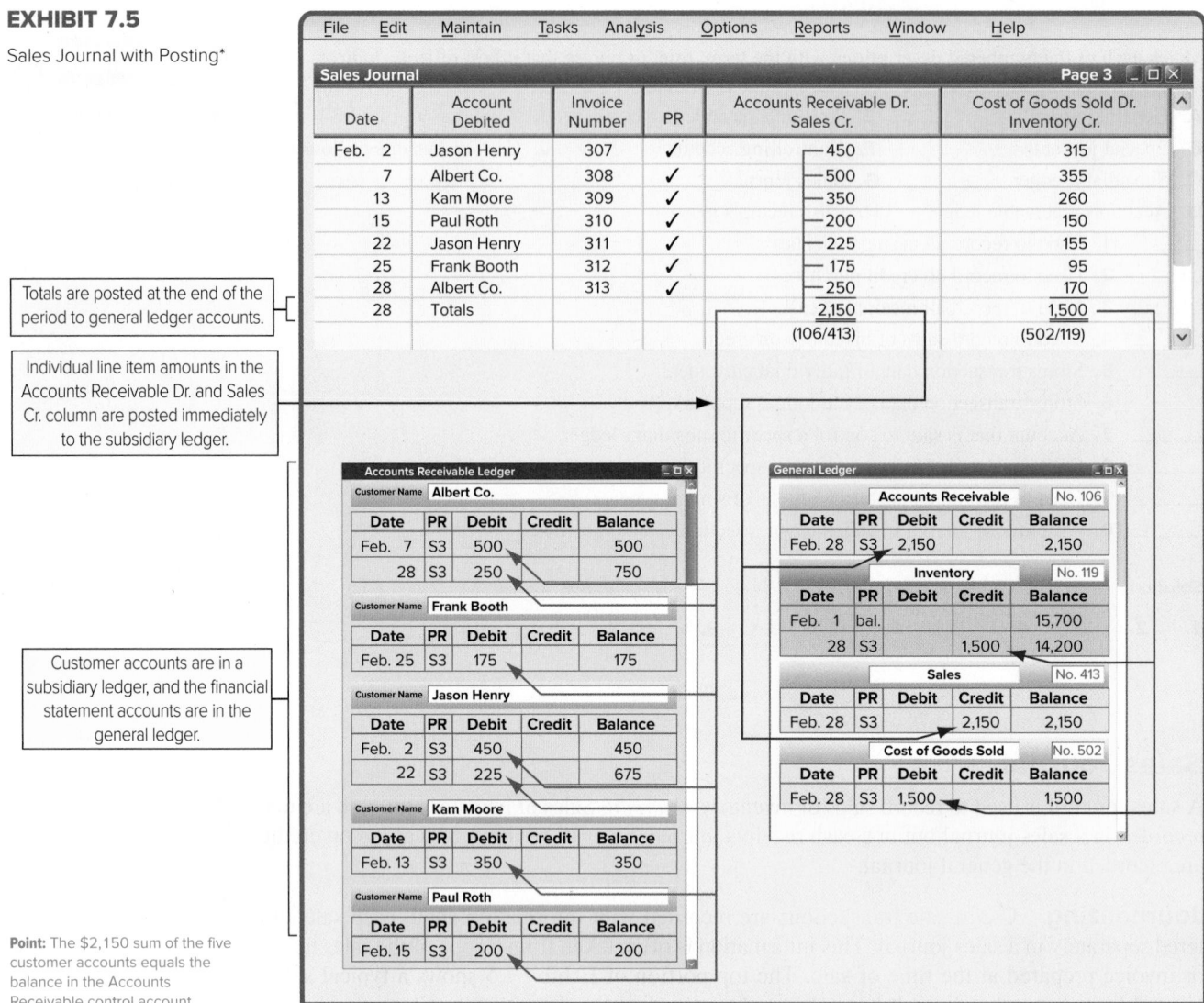

Totals are posted at the end of the period to general ledger accounts.

Individual line item amounts in the Accounts Receivable Dr. and Sales Cr. column are posted immediately to the subsidiary ledger.

Customer accounts are in a subsidiary ledger, and the financial statement accounts are in the general ledger.

Point: The $2,150 sum of the five customer accounts equals the balance in the Accounts Receivable control account.

*The sales journal in a *periodic* system excludes the column on the far right titled "Cost of Goods Sold Dr., Inventory Cr."

Point: The PR column is only checked *after* the amount(s) is posted.

receivable ledger, check marks are entered in the sales journal's PR column. Check marks are used rather than account numbers because customer accounts usually are arranged alphabetically in the accounts receivable ledger. Posting debits to Accounts Receivable twice—once to Accounts Receivable and once to the customer's subsidiary account—does not violate the accounting equation of debits equal credits. The equality of debits and credits is always maintained in the general ledger.

Posting to general ledger.   The sales journal's account columns are totaled at the end of each period (the month of February in this case). For the "sales" column, the $2,150 total is debited to Accounts Receivable and credited to Sales in the general ledger (see Exhibit 7.5). For the "cost" column, the $1,500 total is debited to Cost of Goods Sold and credited to Inventory in the general ledger. When totals are posted to accounts in the general ledger, the account numbers are entered below the column total in the sales journal for tracking. For example, we enter (106/413) below the total in the sales column after this amount is posted to account number 106 (Accounts Receivable) and account number 413 (Sales).

Point: Postings are automatic in a computerized system.

A company identifies in the PR column of its subsidiary ledgers the journal and page number from which an amount is taken. We identify a journal by using an initial. Items posted from the sales journal have the initial **S** before their journal page numbers in a PR column. Likewise, items from the cash receipts journal have the initial **R**; items from the cash disbursements journal have the initial **D**; items from the purchases journal have the initial **P**; and items from the general journal have the initial **G**.

Proving the Ledgers Account balances in the general ledger and subsidiary ledgers are periodically proved (or reviewed) for accuracy after posting. To do this, we first prepare a trial balance of the general ledger to confirm that debits equal credits. Second, we test a subsidiary ledger by preparing a *schedule* of individual accounts and amounts. A **schedule of accounts receivable** lists each customer and the balance owed. If this total equals the balance of the Accounts Receivable controlling account, the accounts in the accounts receivable ledger are assumed correct. Exhibit 7.6 shows a schedule of accounts receivable drawn from the accounts receivable ledger of Exhibit 7.5.

P2

Prepare and prove the accuracy of subsidiary ledgers.

Schedule of Accounts Receivable February 28	
Albert Co.	$ 750
Frank Booth	175
Jason Henry	675
Kam Moore	350
Paul Roth.	200
Total accounts receivable.	$2,150

EXHIBIT 7.6

Schedule of Accounts Receivable

Point: The expression "tie out" is used when confirming the balance of the Accounts Receivable control account matches the total balance on the subsidiary listing of accounts receivable.

Additional Issues We consider three additional issues with the sales journal: (1) recording sales taxes, (2) recording sales returns and allowances, and (3) using actual sales invoices as a journal.

Point: In accounting, *schedule* generally means a list.

Sales taxes. State and city governments require sellers to collect sales taxes from customers and send these taxes to the appropriate agency. When using a columnar sales journal, we can keep a record of taxes collected by adding a Sales Taxes Payable column as follows.

File	Edit	Maintain	Tasks	Analysis	Options	Reports	Window	Help		

Sales Journal							Page 3
Date	Account Debited	Invoice Number	PR	Accounts Receivable Dr.	Sales Taxes Payable Cr.	Sales Cr.	Cost of Goods Sold Dr. Inventory Cr.
Dec. 1	Favre Co.	7-1698		103	3	100	75

Individual amounts in the Accounts Receivable column would continue to be posted immediately to customer accounts in the accounts receivable ledger. Individual amounts in the Sales Taxes Payable and Sales columns are not posted. Column totals would continue to be posted as usual. (A company that collects sales taxes on its cash sales can also use a Sales Taxes Payable column in its cash receipts journal.)

Sales returns and allowances. A company with only a few sales returns and allowances can record them in a general journal with an entry such as the following:

May 17	Sales Returns and Allowances	414	175	
	Accounts Receivable—Ray Ball	106/✓		175
	Customer returned merchandise.			

Assets = Liabilities + Equity
−175 −175

The debit in this entry is posted to the Sales Returns and Allowances account (no. 414). The credit is posted to both the Accounts Receivable controlling account (no. 106) and to the customer's account. When we enter the account number and the check mark, 106/✓, in the PR column on the credit line, this means both the Accounts Receivable controlling account in the general ledger and the Ray Ball account in the accounts receivable ledger are credited for $175. [*Note:* If the returned goods can be resold to another customer, the company would debit (increase) the Inventory account and credit (decrease) the Cost of Goods Sold account. If the returned goods are defective, the returned inventory is recorded at its estimated value, not its cost; for example, if defective goods costing $60 are returned and estimated to be worth $20, the seller debits Inventory for $20, debits Loss from Defective Inventory for $40, and credits Cost of Goods Sold for $60 (see Chapter 5).] A company with a large number of sales returns and allowances can save time by recording them in a separate sales returns and allowances journal.

Sales invoices as a sales journal.   To save costs, some small companies avoid using a sales journal for credit sales and instead post each sales invoice amount directly to the customer's account in the accounts receivable ledger. They then put copies of invoices in a file. At the end of the period, they total all invoices for that period and make a general journal entry to debit Accounts Receivable and credit Sales for the total amount. The file of invoice copies acts as a sales journal. This is called *direct posting of sales invoices.*

NEED-TO-KNOW 7-3

Sales Journal

P1

Do More: E 7-1

Prepare headings for a sales journal like the one in Exhibit 7.5 and then record the following sales transactions.

July   7   Sold merchandise costing $400 to J. Dahl for $600, terms 2/10, n/30, invoice no. 704.
    12   Sold merchandise costing $100 to R. Lim for $150, terms n/30, invoice no. 705.

Solution

Sales Journal					Page 3
Date	Account Debited	Invoice Number	PR	Accounts Receivable Dr. Sales Cr.	Cost of Goods Sold Dr. Inventory Cr.
July 7	J. Dahl	704		600	400
12	R. Lim	705		150	100

Cash Receipts Journal

A **cash receipts journal** is typically used to record all receipts of cash (all transactions that include a debit to Cash). Exhibit 7.7 shows one common form of the cash receipts journal.

Journalizing and Posting   Cash receipts can be separated into one of three types: (1) cash from credit customers in payment of their accounts, (2) cash from cash sales, and (3) cash from other sources. The cash receipts journal in Exhibit 7.7 has a separate credit column for each of these three sources. We describe how to journalize transactions from each of these three sources. (An Explanation column is included in the cash receipts journal to identify the source.)

Cash from credit customers.   *Journalizing.* To record cash received in payment of a customer's account, the customer's name is first entered in the Account Credited column—see transactions dated February 12, 17, 23, and 25. Then the amounts debited to both Cash and Sales Discount (if any) are entered in their respective columns, and the amount credited to the customer's account is entered in the Accounts Receivable Cr. column.

    Posting. Individual amounts in the Accounts Receivable Cr. column are posted immediately to customer accounts in the subsidiary accounts receivable ledger. The $1,500 column total is posted at the end of the period (month in this case) as a credit to the Accounts Receivable controlling account in the general ledger.

Cash sales.   *Journalizing.* The amount for each cash sale is entered in the Cash Dr. column and the Sales Cr. column. The February 7, 14, 21, and 28 transactions are examples. Each cash sale also yields an entry to Cost of Goods Sold Dr. and Inventory Cr. for the cost of merchandise—see the far right column.

Point: Cash sales are usually journalized daily or at point of sale, but are journalized weekly in Exhibit 7.7 for brevity.

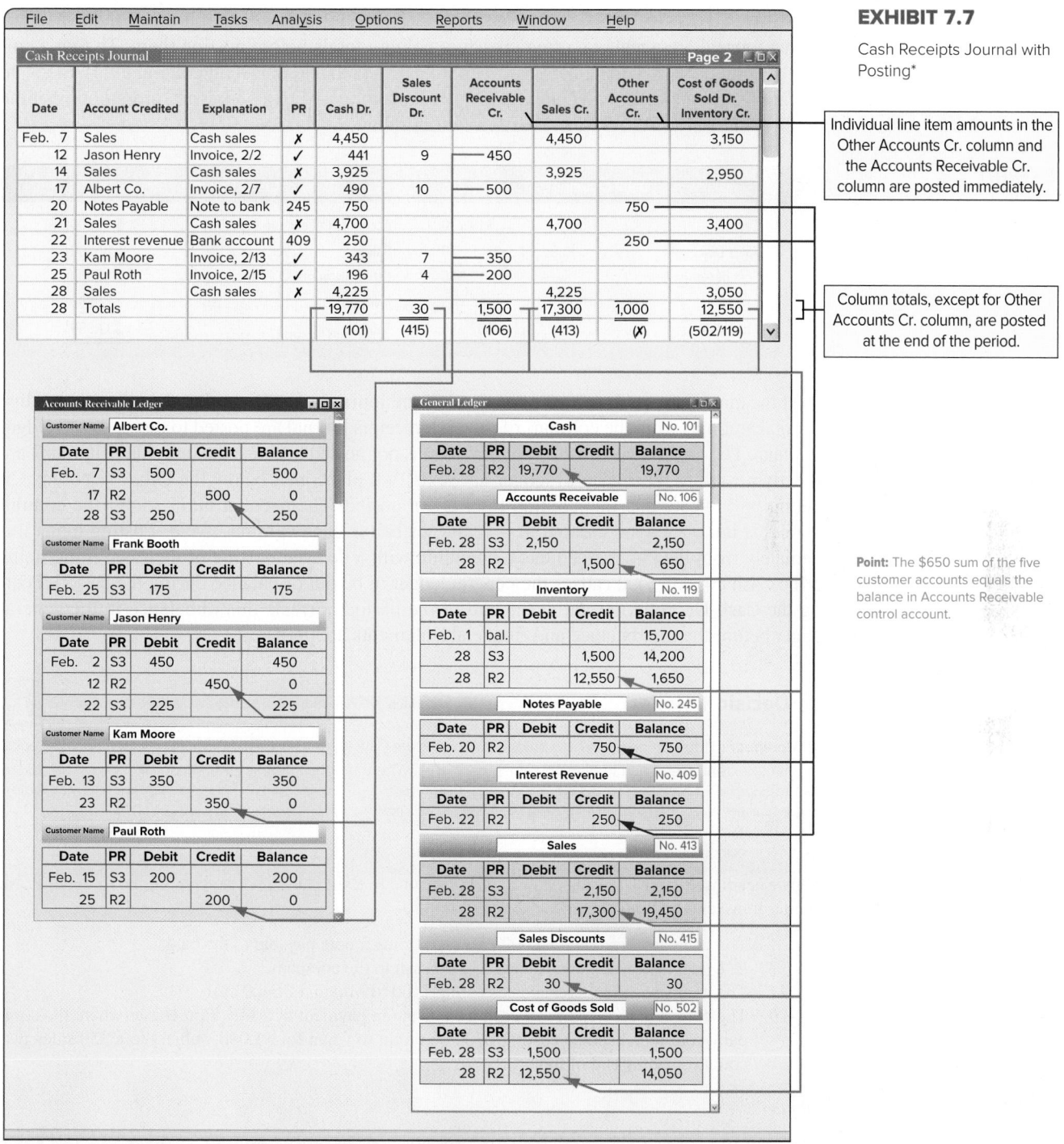

EXHIBIT 7.7

Cash Receipts Journal with Posting*

Individual line item amounts in the Other Accounts Cr. column and the Accounts Receivable Cr. column are posted immediately.

Column totals, except for Other Accounts Cr. column, are posted at the end of the period.

Point: The $650 sum of the five customer accounts equals the balance in Accounts Receivable control account.

*The cash receipts journal in a *periodic* system excludes the column on the far right titled "Cost of Goods Dr., Inventory Cr."

Posting. For cash sales, we place an *x* in the PR column to indicate that its amount is not individually posted. We do post the $17,300 Sales Cr. total and the $12,550 total from the "cost" column.

Cash from other sources.   *Journalizing.* Examples of cash from other sources are money borrowed from a bank, cash interest received on account, and cash sale of noninventory assets. The transactions of February 20 and 22 are illustrative. The Other Accounts Cr. column is used for these transactions.

Posting. Amounts from these transactions are immediately posted to their general ledger accounts, and the PR column identifies those accounts.

Example: Record in the cash receipts journal a $700 cash sale of land when the land carries a $700 original cost. *Answer:* Debit the Cash column for $700, and credit the Other Accounts column for $700 (the account credited is Land).

Point: Subsidiary ledgers and their controlling accounts are *in balance* only after all posting is complete.

Footing, Crossfooting, and Posting

To be sure that total debits and credits in a columnar journal are equal, we often crossfoot column totals before posting them. To *foot* a column of numbers is to add it. To *crossfoot* in this case is to add the Debit column totals, then add the Credit column totals, and compare the two sums for equality. Footing and crossfooting of the numbers in Exhibit 7.7 result in the report in Exhibit 7.8.

EXHIBIT 7.8

Footing and Crossfooting Journal Totals

Debit Columns		Credit Columns	
Cash	$19,770	Accounts Receivable	$ 1,500
Sales Discounts	30	Sales	17,300
Cost of Goods Sold.................	12,550	Other Accounts....................	1,000
		Inventory........................	12,550
Total............................	$32,350	Total	$32,350

At the end of the period, after crossfooting the journal to confirm that debits equal credits, the total amounts from the columns of the cash receipts journal are posted to their general ledger accounts. The Other Accounts Cr. column total is not posted because the individual amounts are directly posted to their general ledger accounts. We place an *x* below the Other Accounts Cr. column to indicate that this column total is not posted. The account numbers for the column totals that are posted are entered in parentheses below each column. (*Note:* Posting items immediately from the Other Accounts Cr. column with a delayed posting of their offsetting items in the Cash column total causes the general ledger to be out of balance during the period. Posting the Cash Dr. column total at the end of the period corrects this imbalance in the general ledger before the trial balance and financial statements are prepared.)

 Decision Maker ━━━━━━━━━━━━━━━━━━━━━━━━━━━━━━━━━

Entrepreneur   You want to know how quickly customers are paying their bills. This information can help you decide whether to extend credit and to plan your cash payments. Where do you find this information? ■   [*Answer:* The accounts receivable ledger has much of the needed information. It lists detailed information for each customer's account, including the amounts, dates of transactions, and dates of payments. It can be reorganized into an "aging schedule" to show how long customers wait before paying their bills.]

 **7-4**

Cash Receipts Journal

P1

Prepare headings for a cash receipts journal like the one in Exhibit 7.7 and then record the following cash receipts transactions.

July 1   The company borrowed $5,000 cash by signing a note payable to the bank.
    2   C. Ming, the owner, contributed $1,000 cash to the company.
    11   The company sold merchandise costing $100 to Mulan for $400 cash.
    29   The company received $950 cash from Chan in payment of a July 7 purchase (where the company sold merchandise costing $700 on credit to Chan for $1,000, subject to a $50 sales discount if paid by end of month).

Solution

Cash Receipts Journal									Page 2 □✕
Date	Account Credited	Explanation	PR	Cash Dr.	Sales Discount Dr.	Accounts Receivable Cr.	Sales Cr.	Other Accounts Cr.	Cost of Goods Sold Dr. Inventory Cr.
July 1	Notes Payable	Note to bank		5,000				5,000	
2	C. Ming, Capital	Contribution		1,000				1,000	
11	Sales	Cash sale		400			400		100
29	Chan	Invoice, 7/7		950	50	1,000			

Do More: E 7-3

Purchases Journal

A **purchases journal** is used to record all credit purchases, including those for inventory. Purchases for cash are recorded in the cash disbursements journal.

Journalizing   Entries in the purchases journal in Exhibit 7.9 reflect purchase invoices or other source documents. We use the invoice date and terms to compute the date when payment for each purchase is due. The Accounts Payable Cr. column is used to record the amounts owed to each creditor. Inventory purchases are recorded in the Inventory Dr. column.

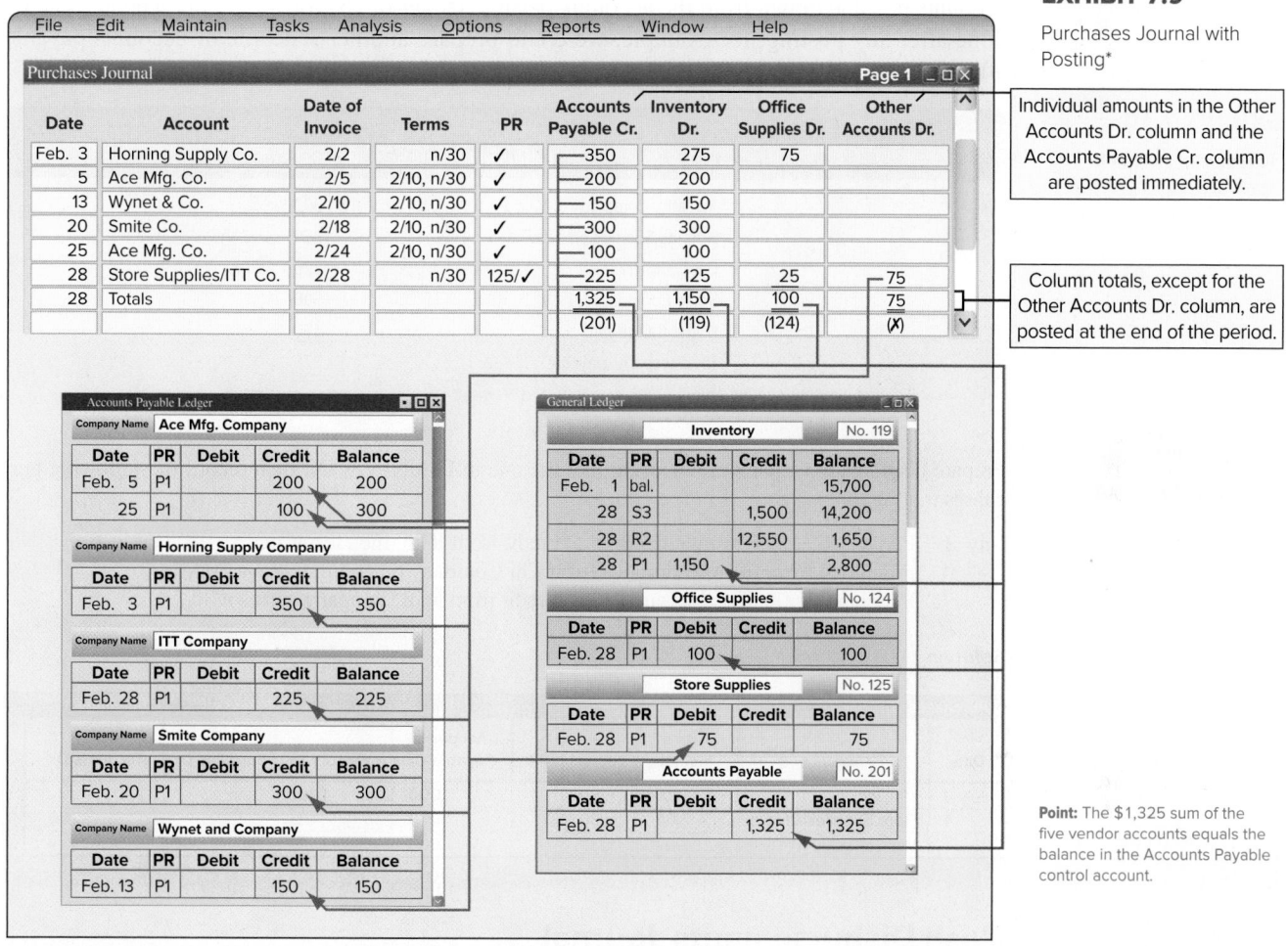

EXHIBIT 7.9

Purchases Journal with Posting*

Individual amounts in the Other Accounts Dr. column and the Accounts Payable Cr. column are posted immediately.

Column totals, except for the Other Accounts Dr. column, are posted at the end of the period.

Point: The $1,325 sum of the five vendor accounts equals the balance in the Accounts Payable control account.

*The purchases journal in a *periodic* system replaces "Inventory Dr." with "Purchases Dr."

To illustrate, inventory costing $200 is purchased from Ace Manufacturing on February 5. The creditor's name (Ace) is entered in the Account column, the invoice date is entered in the Date of Invoice column, the purchase terms are entered in the Terms column, and the $200 amount is entered in the Accounts Payable Cr. and the Inventory Dr. columns. When a purchase involves an amount recorded in the Other Accounts Dr. column, we use the Account column to identify the general ledger account debited. For example, the February 28 transaction involves purchases of inventory, office supplies, and store supplies from ITT. The journal has no column for store supplies, so the Other Accounts Dr. column is used. In this case, Store Supplies is entered in the Account column along with the creditor's name (ITT). This purchases journal also includes a separate column for credit purchases of office supplies. A separate column such as this is useful when several transactions involve debits to the same account. Each company decides the number of separate columns necessary.

Point: Each transaction in the purchases journal has a credit to Accounts Payable. Debit accounts will vary.

Point: The Other Accounts Dr. column allows the purchases journal to be used for any purchase on credit.

Posting   The amounts in the Accounts Payable Cr. column are immediately posted to individual creditor accounts in the accounts payable subsidiary ledger. Individual amounts in the Other Accounts Dr. column are immediately posted to their general ledger accounts. At the end of the period, all column totals except the Other Accounts Dr. column are posted to their general ledger accounts.

Proving the Ledger   Accounts payable balances in the subsidiary ledger are proved after posting. We prove the subsidiary ledger by preparing a **schedule of accounts payable,** which is a list of accounts from the accounts payable ledger with their balances and the total. If the total of the individual balances equals the balance of the Accounts Payable controlling account, the accounts in the accounts payable ledger are assumed correct. Exhibit 7.10 shows a schedule of accounts payable drawn from the accounts payable ledger of Exhibit 7.9. (This schedule can be done after any posting; for example, we could prepare another schedule of accounts payable after the postings in Exhibit 7.11.)

Point: The balance in the Accounts Payable controlling account must equal the sum of the individual account balances in the accounts payable subsidiary ledger after posting.

EXHIBIT 7.10

Schedule of Accounts Payable

Schedule of Accounts Payable February 28	
Ace Mfg. Company	$ 300
Horning Supply Company	350
ITT Company	225
Smite Company	300
Wynet & Company	150
Total accounts payable	$1,325

NEED-TO-KNOW 7-5

Purchases Journal

P1

Prepare headings for a purchases journal like the one in Exhibit 7.9 and then record the following purchases transactions.

July	1	Purchased $1,000 of merchandise on credit from Kim, Inc., terms n/60.
	4	Purchased $200 of store supplies from Chi Company on credit, terms n/30.
	7	Purchased $600 of office supplies on credit from Min Company, terms n/30.

Solution

Purchases Journal								Page 1
Date	Account	Date of Invoice	Terms	PR	Accounts Payable Cr.	Inventory Dr.	Office Supplies Dr.	Other Accounts Dr.
July 1	Kim, Inc.	7/01	n/60		1,000	1,000		
4	Store Supplies/Chi Co.	7/04	n/30		200			200
7	Min Company	7/07	n/30		600		600	

Do More: QS 7-6, E 7-8

Cash Disbursements Journal

A **cash disbursements journal,** also called a *cash payments journal,* is used to record all cash payments (all transactions with a credit to Cash).

Journalizing   The cash disbursements journal shown in Exhibit 7.11 illustrates repetitive entries to the Cash Cr. column of this journal (reflecting cash payments). Also note the frequent credits to Inventory (which reflect purchase discounts) and the debits to Accounts Payable. For example, on February 15, the company pays Ace on account (credit terms of 2/10, n/30—see February 5 transaction in Exhibit 7.9). Since payment occurs in the discount period, the company pays $196 ($200 invoice less $4 discount). The $4 discount is credited to Inventory. Note that when this company purchases inventory for cash, it is recorded using the Other Accounts Dr. column and the Cash Cr. column as illustrated in the February 3 and 12 transactions. Generally, the Other Accounts column is used to record cash payments on items for which no column exists. For example, on February 15, the company pays salaries expense of $250. The title of the account debited (Salaries Expense) is entered in the Account Debited column.

The cash disbursements journal has a column titled Ck. No. (check number). For control over cash disbursements, all payments except for those of small amounts are made by check. Checks should be prenumbered and each check's number entered in the journal in numerical order in the column headed Ck. No. This makes it possible to search the numbers in the column for omitted checks. When a cash disbursements journal has a column for check numbers, it is sometimes called a **check register.**

EXHIBIT 7.11

Cash Disbursements
Journal with Posting*

Cash Disbursements Journal   Page 2

	Date	Ck. No.	Payee	Account Debited	PR	Cash Cr.	Inventory Cr.	Other Accounts Dr.	Accounts Payable Dr.
	Feb.3	105	L. & N. Railroad	Inventory	119	15		15	
	12	106	East Sales Co.	Inventory	119	25		25	
	15	107	Ace Mfg. Co.	Ace Mfg. Co.	✓	196	4		200
	15	108	Jerry Hale	Salaries Expense	622	250		250	
	20	109	Wynet & Co.	Wynet & Co.	✓	147	3		150
	28	110	Smite Co.	Smite Co.	✓	294	6		300
	28		Totals			927	13	290	650
						(101)	(119)	(X)	(201)

Individual amounts in the Other Accounts Dr. column and the Accounts Payable Dr. column are posted immediately.

Column totals, except for the Other Accounts column, are posted at the end of the period.

General Ledger

Cash   No. 101

Date	PR	Debit	Credit	Balance
Feb. 28	R2	19,770		19,770
28	D2		927	18,843

Inventory   No. 119

Date	PR	Debit	Credit	Balance
Feb. 1	bal.			15,700
3	D2	15		15,715
12	D2	25		15,740
28	S3		1,500	14,240
28	R2		12,550	1,690
28	P1	1,150		2,840
28	D2		13	2,827

Accounts Payable   No. 201

Date	PR	Debit	Credit	Balance
Feb. 28	P1		1,325	1,325
28	D2	650		675

Salaries Expense   No. 622

Date	PR	Debit	Credit	Balance
Feb. 15	D2	250		250

Accounts Payable Ledger

Company Name   Ace Mfg. Company

Date	PR	Debit	Credit	Balance
Feb. 5	P1		200	200
15	D2	200		0
25	P1		100	100

Company Name   Horning Supply Company

Date	PR	Debit	Credit	Balance
Feb. 3	P1		350	350

Company Name   ITT Company

Date	PR	Debit	Credit	Balance
Feb. 28	P1		225	225

Company Name   Smite Company

Date	PR	Debit	Credit	Balance
Feb. 20	P1		300	300
28	D2	300		0

Company Name   Wynet & Company

Date	PR	Debit	Credit	Balance
Feb. 13	P1		150	150
20	D2	150		0

Point: The $675 sum of the five vendor accounts equals the balance in the Accounts Payable control account.

*The cash disbursements journal in a *periodic* system replaces "Inventory Cr." with "Purchases Discounts Cr."

Posting   Individual amounts in the Other Accounts Dr. column of a cash disbursements journal are immediately posted to their general ledger accounts. Individual amounts in the Accounts Payable Dr. column are also immediately posted to creditors' accounts in the subsidiary accounts payable ledger. At the end of the period, we crossfoot column totals and post the Accounts Payable Dr. column total to the Accounts Payable controlling account. Also, the Inventory Cr. column total is posted to the Inventory account, and the Cash Cr. column total is posted to the Cash account.

■ **Decision** Maker

Controller   You wish to analyze your company's cash payments to suppliers and its purchases discounts. Where do you find this information? ■   [*Answer:* Much of the needed information is in the accounts payable ledger. It contains information for each supplier, the amounts due, and when payments are made. This subsidiary ledger, along with information on credit terms, provides the data for analyses.]

General Journal Transactions

When special journals are used, we still need a general journal for adjusting, closing, and any other transactions for which no special journal has been set up. Examples of these other transactions might include purchases returns and allowances, purchases of plant assets by issuing a note payable, sales returns if a sales returns and allowances journal is not used, and receipt of a note receivable from a customer.

NEED-TO-KNOW 7-6

Cash Disbursements
Journal

P1

Prepare headings for a cash disbursements journal like the one in Exhibit 7.11 and then record the following cash payments transactions.

July 5   Issued Check No. 910 to Kam Corp. to buy store supplies for $500.
    13   Issued Check No. 911 for $4,000 to pay off a note payable to China Bank.
    24   Issued Check No. 912 to Lim to pay the amount due from a July 16 purchase less the discount (it purchased merchandise for $1,000 on credit from Lim, terms 2/10, n/30).
    29   Paid salary of $700 to B. Tung by issuing Check No. 913.

Solution

Cash Disbursements Journal Page 2

Date	Ck. No.	Payee	Account Debited	PR	Cash Cr.	Inventory Cr.	Other Accounts Dr.	Accounts Payable Dr.
July 5	910	Kam Corp.	Store Supplies		500		500	
13	911	China Bank	Notes Payable		4,000		4,000	
24	912	Lim	Lim		980	20		1,000
29	913	B. Tung	Salaries Expense		700		700	

Do More: E 7-6, E 7-9

TECHNOLOGY-BASED ACCOUNTING SYSTEMS

This section describes the impact of computer technology, how data processing works with accounting data, and the role of computer networks.

Computer Technology in Accounting

Computer technology provides accuracy, speed, efficiency, and convenience in performing accounting tasks. A program can be written, for instance, to process customers' merchandise orders. Multipurpose off-the-shelf software applications exist for a variety of business operations. These include familiar accounting programs such as **Sage 50** (formerly known as Peachtree®) and **QuickBooks®**. Off-the-shelf programs are menu driven, and many operate more efficiently as *integrated* systems. In an integrated system, actions taken in one part of the system automatically affect related parts. When a credit sale is recorded in an integrated system, for instance, several parts of the system are automatically updated, such as posting.

Less effort spent on recordkeeping means more time for accounting professionals to concentrate on analysis and managerial decision making. These advances have created a greater demand for accounting professionals who understand financial reports and can draw insights and information from mountains of processed data. Accounting professionals have expertise in determining relevant and reliable information for decision making. They also can assess the effects of transactions and events on a company and its financial statements.

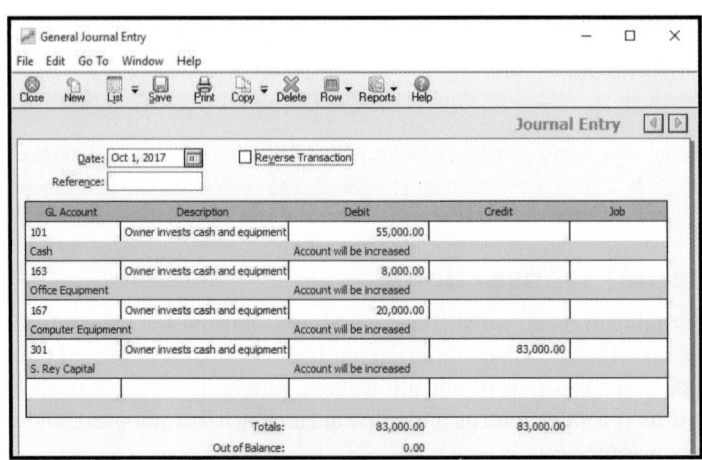

Middleware is software allowing different computer programs in a company or across companies to work together. It allows transfer of purchase orders, invoices, and other electronic documents between accounting systems. For example, suppliers can monitor inventory levels of their buyers for production and shipping purposes. ■

© Lawrence Lawry/Getty Images RF

Data Processing in Accounting

Accounting systems differ with regard to how input is entered and processed.

- **Online processing** enters and processes data as soon as source documents are available. This means that databases are immediately updated.
- **Batch processing** accumulates source documents for a period of time and then processes them all at once such as daily, weekly, or monthly.

The advantage of online processing is timeliness. The advantage of batch processing is that it requires only periodic updating of databases. Records used to send bills to customers, for instance, might require updating only once a month. The disadvantage of batch processing is the lack of updated databases for management to use when making business decisions.

Computer Networks in Accounting

Networking, or linking computers with each other, can create information advantages (and cost efficiencies). **Computer networks** are links among computers giving different users and different computers access to common databases, programs, and hardware. The network setups by **UPS** and **FedEx** allow multiple users to connect to a common database to track packages and bill customers.

Enterprise Resource Planning Software

Enterprise resource planning (ERP) software includes the programs that manage a company's operations. They extend from order taking to manufacturing to accounting. (Your college likely relies on ERP software to track its budget and student records information.) When working properly, these integrated programs can speed decision making, identify costs for reduction, and give managers control over operations with the click of a mouse. For many managers, ERP software allows them to scrutinize business, identify where inventories are piling up, and see what plants are most efficient.

Several companies offer ERP software. **SAP** leads the market, with **Oracle** a distant second (*AMR Research*). SAP software is used by more than half of the world's 500 largest companies.

ERP is increasingly used by small business. One-third of Oracle's sales in North America are to companies with less than $500 million in annual revenue. Worldwide, small and midsize companies are 25% to 30% of Oracle's sales.

Total ERP Market: About $30 Billion

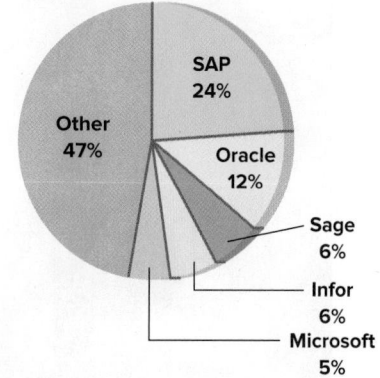

SAP 24%
Oracle 12%
Other 47%
Sage 6%
Infor 6%
Microsoft 5%

A new generation of accounting support is available. With the touch of a key, users can create real-time inventory reports showing all payments, charges, and credit limits at any point in the accounting cycle. Many services also include "alert signals" notifying the company when, for example, a large order exceeds a customer's credit limit or when purchases need to be made or when a bank balance is running low. ■

Cloud Computing

Cloud computing is the delivery of computing as a service rather than a product. Cloud computing uses applications via the web instead of installing them on individual computers. This means that companies lease, rather than purchase, those applications.

When a company transfers computing applications to a provider, users and their clients can access the same applications and share data. Accountants, lawyers, and analysts can similarly access data for quicker and easier processing and analysis. For example, all invoices could be offloaded to a web-based bill management system, where documentation, disbursement, and recordkeeping could all be handled in the cloud. However, the user does lose some control over the data and is dependent on the provider's control system.

Cloud computing has enormous potential for greater efficiency and effectiveness with information systems applications. Users should consider the following factors when looking at providers of cloud computing:

- Provider's knowledge of user's business.
- Security of provider's cloud, including firewalls.
- Provider's history, reputation, and references.
- Service level agreement for hardware and software.
- Provider's cloud compatibility with user's system.

SUSTAINABILITY AND ACCOUNTING

Box, the company from this chapter's opening feature, provides nonprofit organizations with a way to store content, share files, and collaborate on key ideas. Box runs a special website, **Box.org**, that is solely committed to helping nonprofit organizations be more productive and collaborative in achieving their missions.

This is important to Box because, as the owners point out, 87% of nonprofits are without a dedicated IT department. Box's cloud solutions and ease of use lessen the need for an IT department.

Over 1,000 nonprofits have teamed with Box and utilize its services. These nonprofits include **Teach for America**, **Boys & Girls Clubs**, and **Livestrong Foundation**. Box proclaims: "At Box, we believe that those committed to doing good should have the best tools available to them."

Kathryn Scott Osler/The Denver Post via Getty Images

Segment Return on Assets **Decision Analysis**

Good accounting information systems collect financial data for a company's various segments. A *segment* refers to a part of a company that is separately identified by its products or services, or by the geographic market it serves. Callaway Golf Company reports that it operates in two business segments: (1) golf clubs and (2) golf balls. Users of financial statements are especially interested in segment information to better understand a company's activities because segments often vary on profitability, risk, and growth.

Companies must report segment information, including their sales, operating income, identifiable assets, capital expenditures, and depreciation. However, managers are reluctant to release information that can harm competitive position. Exhibit 7.12 shows survey results on the number of companies with different (reported) segments.

A1_____

Compute segment return on assets and use it to evaluate segment performance.

*Total exceeds 100% because companies can report more than one segment.

EXHIBIT 7.12

Companies Reporting Operations by Types of Segments*

One measure of success for business segments is the **segment return on assets** ratio defined as follows.

$$\text{Segment return on assets} = \frac{\text{Segment operating income}}{\text{Segment average assets}}$$

This ratio reflects on the profitability of a segment. Exhibit 7.13 shows the segments' pretax income, average assets, and return on assets for Callaway Golf Company.

EXHIBIT 7.13

Callaway Golf's Segment Return on Assets

Golf Segment* ($ thousands)	2015		2014	
	Clubs	Balls	Clubs	Balls
Net sales..........................	$700,649	$143,145	$749,956	$136,989
Operating income...................	$ 52,999	$ 17,724	$ 50,891	$ 15,222
Average assets....................	$316,395	$ 37,420	$345,592	$ 43,353
Segment return on assets	16.8%	47.4%	14.7%	35.1%

* A segment's operating income is usually measured as pretax income, and assets is usually measured as identifiable assets.

Callaway's performance has been improving over the past few years. Years 2014 and 2015 were good for Callaway, as both its golf club and golf ball segments generated positive income. Both segments' return on assets improved from 2014 to 2015. However, net sales for clubs declined in 2015. Callaway must work to improve its net sales for clubs while maintaining its return on assets if it wishes to achieve sustained success. Callaway might also consider making greater investments in its golf ball segment. If additional golf ball assets can generate a similar 47.4% return versus a return of 16.8% for golf club assets, Callaway should make additional asset investments in the golf ball segment. This analysis can be extended to geographical segments and any other segments that companies report.

▇ Decision Maker

Banker A soccer equipment merchandiser requests a loan from you to expand operations. Its net income is $220,000, reflecting a 10% increase over the prior year. You ask about segment results. The owner reports that $160,000 of net income is from Cuban operations, reflecting a 60% increase over the prior year. The remaining $60,000 of net income is from U.S. operations, reflecting a 40% decrease. Does this segment information impact your loan decision? ▇ [*Answer:* This merchandiser's segment information is likely to greatly impact your loan decision. The risks associated with the company's two sources of net income are quite different. While net income is up by 10%, U.S. operations are performing poorly and Cuban operations are subject to many uncertainties. These uncertainties depend on political events, legal issues, business relationships, Cuban economic conditions, and a host of other risks. Overall, income results suggest a low-risk loan opportunity, but segment data reveal more risk.]

NEED-TO-KNOW 7-7

COMPREHENSIVE

Using special journals for recording transactions (Perpetual System)

Pepper Company completed the following selected transactions and events during March of this year. (Terms of all credit sales for the company are 2/10, n/30.)

Mar. 4	Sold merchandise on credit to Jennifer Nelson, Invoice No. 954, for $16,800 (cost is $12,200).
6	Purchased $1,220 of office supplies on credit from Mack Company. Invoice dated March 3, terms n/30.
6	Sold merchandise on credit to Dennie Hoskins, Invoice No. 955, for $10,200 (cost is $8,100).
11	Purchased $52,600 of merchandise, invoice dated March 6, terms 2/10, n/30, from Defore Industries.
12	Borrowed $26,000 cash by giving Commerce Bank a long-term promissory note payable.
14	Received cash payment from Jennifer Nelson for the March 4 sale less the discount (Invoice No. 954).
16	Received a $200 credit memorandum from Defore Industries for unsatisfactory merchandise Pepper purchased on March 11 and later returned.
16	Received cash payment from Dennie Hoskins for the March 6 sale less the discount (Invoice No. 955).
18	Purchased $22,850 of store equipment on credit from Schmidt Supply, invoice dated March 15, terms n/30.
20	Sold merchandise on credit to Marjorie Allen, Invoice No. 956, for $5,600 (cost is $3,800).
21	Sent Defore Industries Check No. 516 in payment of its March 6 dated invoice less the return and the discount.
22	Purchased $41,625 of merchandise, invoice dated March 18, terms 2/10, n/30, from Welch Company.
26	Issued a $600 credit memorandum to Marjorie Allen for defective merchandise Pepper sold on March 20 and Allen later returned.
31	Issued Check No. 517, payable to Payroll, in payment of $15,900 sales salaries for the month. Cashed the check and paid the employees.
31	Cash sales for the month are $134,680 (cost is $67,340). (Cash sales are recorded daily but are recorded only once here to reduce repetitive entries.)

Required

1. Open the following selected general ledger accounts: Cash (101), Accounts Receivable (106), Inventory (119), Office Supplies (124), Store Equipment (165), Accounts Payable (201), Long-Term Notes Payable (251), Sales (413), Sales Returns and Allowances (414), Sales Discounts (415), Cost of Goods Sold (502), and Sales Salaries Expense (621). Open the following accounts receivable ledger accounts: Marjorie Allen, Dennie Hoskins, and Jennifer Nelson. Open the following accounts payable ledger accounts: Defore Industries, Mack Company, Schmidt Supply, and Welch Company.

2. Enter the transactions using a sales journal, a purchases journal, a cash receipts journal, a cash disbursements journal, and a general journal similar to the ones illustrated in the chapter. Regularly post to the individual customer and creditor accounts. Also, post any amounts that should be posted as individual amounts to general ledger accounts. Foot and crossfoot the journals and make the month-end postings. *Pepper Co. uses the perpetual inventory system.*

3. Prepare a trial balance for the selected general ledger accounts in part 1 and prove the accuracy of subsidiary ledgers by preparing schedules of accounts receivable and accounts payable.

PLANNING THE SOLUTION

- Set up the required general ledger, the subsidiary ledger accounts, and the five required journals as illustrated in the chapter.
- Read and analyze each transaction and decide in which special journal (or general journal) the transaction is recorded.

- Record each transaction in the proper journal (and post the appropriate individual amounts).
- Once you have recorded all transactions, total the journal columns. Post from each journal to the appropriate ledger accounts.
- Prepare a trial balance (covering the selected transactions for this problem only) to prove the equality of the debit and credit balances in your general ledger.
- Prepare schedules of accounts receivable and accounts payable. Compare the totals of these schedules to the Accounts Receivable and Accounts Payable controlling account balances, making sure that they agree.

SOLUTION

Sales Journal — Page 2

Date	Account Debited	Invoice Number	PR	Accounts Receivable Dr. Sales Cr.	Cost of Goods Sold Dr. Inventory Cr.
Mar. 4	Jennifer Nelson	954	✓	16,800	12,200
6	Dennie Hoskins	955	✓	10,200	8,100
20	Marjorie Allen	956	✓	5,600	3,800
31	Totals			32,600	24,100
				(106/413)	(502/119)

Cash Receipts Journal — Page 3

Date	Account Credited	Explanation	PR	Cash Dr.	Sales Discount Dr.	Accounts Receivable Cr.	Sales Cr.	Other Accounts Cr.	Cost of Goods Sold Dr. Inventory Cr.
Mar. 12	L.T. Notes Payable	Note to bank	251	26,000				26,000	
14	Jennifer Nelson	Invoice 954, 3/4	✓	16,464	336	16,800			
16	Dennie Hoskins	Invoice 955, 3/6	✓	9,996	204	10,200			
31	Sales	Cash sales	x	134,680			134,680		67,340
31	Totals			187,140	540	27,000	134,680	26,000	67,340
				(101)	(415)	(106)	(413)	(x)	(502/119)

Purchases Journal — Page 3

Date	Account	Date of Invoice	Terms	PR	Accounts Payable Cr.	Inventory Dr.	Office Supplies Dr.	Other Accounts Dr.
Mar. 6	Office Supplies/Mack Co	3/3	n/30	✓	1,220		1,220	
11	Defore Industries	3/6	2/10, n/30	✓	52,600	52,600		
18	Store Equipment/Schmidt Supp	3/15	n/30	165/✓	22,850			22,850
22	Welch Company	3/18	2/10, n/30	✓	41,625	41,625		
31	Totals				118,295	94,225	1,220	22,850
					(201)	(119)	(124)	(x)

Cash Disbursements Journal — Page 3

Date	Ck. No.	Payee	Account Debited	PR	Cash Cr.	Inventory Cr.	Other Accounts Dr.	Accounts Payable Dr.
Mar. 21	516	Defore Industries	Defore Industries	✓	51,352	1,048		52,400
31	517	Payroll	Sales Salaries Expense	621	15,900		15,900	
31		Totals			67,252	1,048	15,900	52,400
					(101)	(119)	(x)	(201)

General Journal — Page 2

Mar. 16	Accounts Payable—Defore Industries	201/✓	200	
	Inventory	119		200
	Record credit memorandum received.			
26	Sales Returns and Allowances	414	600	
	Accounts Receivable—Marjorie Allen	106/✓		600
	Record credit memorandum issued.			

Accounts Receivable Ledger

Marjorie Allen

Date	PR	Debit	Credit	Balance
Mar. 20	S2	5,600		5,600
26	G2		600	5,000

Dennie Hoskins

Date	PR	Debit	Credit	Balance
Mar. 6	S2	10,200		10,200
16	R3		10,200	0

Jennifer Nelson

Date	PR	Debit	Credit	Balance
Mar. 4	S2	16,800		16,800
14	R3		16,800	0

Accounts Payable Ledger

Defore Industries

Date	PR	Debit	Credit	Balance
Mar. 11	P3		52,600	52,600
16	G2	200		52,400
21	D3	52,400		0

Mack Company

Date	PR	Debit	Credit	Balance
Mar. 6	P3		1,220	1,220

Schmidt Supply

Date	PR	Debit	Credit	Balance
Mar. 18	P3		22,850	22,850

Welch Company

Date	PR	Debit	Credit	Balance
Mar. 22	P3		41,625	41,625

General Ledger (covering transactions provided)

Cash   Acct. No. 101

Date	PR	Debit	Credit	Balance
Mar. 31	R3	187,140		187,140
31	D3		67,252	119,888

Accounts Receivable   Acct. No. 106

Date	PR	Debit	Credit	Balance
Mar. 26	G2		600	(600)
31	S2	32,600		32,000
31	R3		27,000	5,000

Inventory   Acct. No. 119

Date	PR	Debit	Credit	Balance
Mar. 16	G2		200	(200)
21	D3		1,048	(1,248)
31	P3	94,225		92,977
31	S2		24,100	68,877
31	R3		67,340	1,537

Office Supplies   Acct. No. 124

Date	PR	Debit	Credit	Balance
Mar. 31	P3	1,220		1,220

Store Equipment   Acct. No. 165

Date	PR	Debit	Credit	Balance
Mar. 18	P3	22,850		22,850

Accounts Payable   Acct. No. 201

Date	PR	Debit	Credit	Balance
Mar. 16	G2	200		(200)
31	P3		118,295	118,095
31	D3	52,400		65,695

Long-Term Notes Payable   Acct. No. 251

Date	PR	Debit	Credit	Balance
Mar. 12	R3		26,000	26,000

Sales   Acct. No. 413

Date	PR	Debit	Credit	Balance
Mar. 31	S2		32,600	32,600
31	R3		134,680	167,280

Sales Returns and Allowances   Acct. No. 414

Date	PR	Debit	Credit	Balance
Mar. 26	G2	600		600

Sales Discounts   Acct. No. 415

Date	PR	Debit	Credit	Balance
Mar. 31	R3	540		540

Cost of Goods Sold   Acct. No. 502

Date	PR	Debit	Credit	Balance
Mar. 31	R3	67,340		67,340
31	S2	24,100		91,440

Sales Salaries Expense   Acct. No. 621

Date	PR	Debit	Credit	Balance
Mar. 31	D3	15,900		15,900

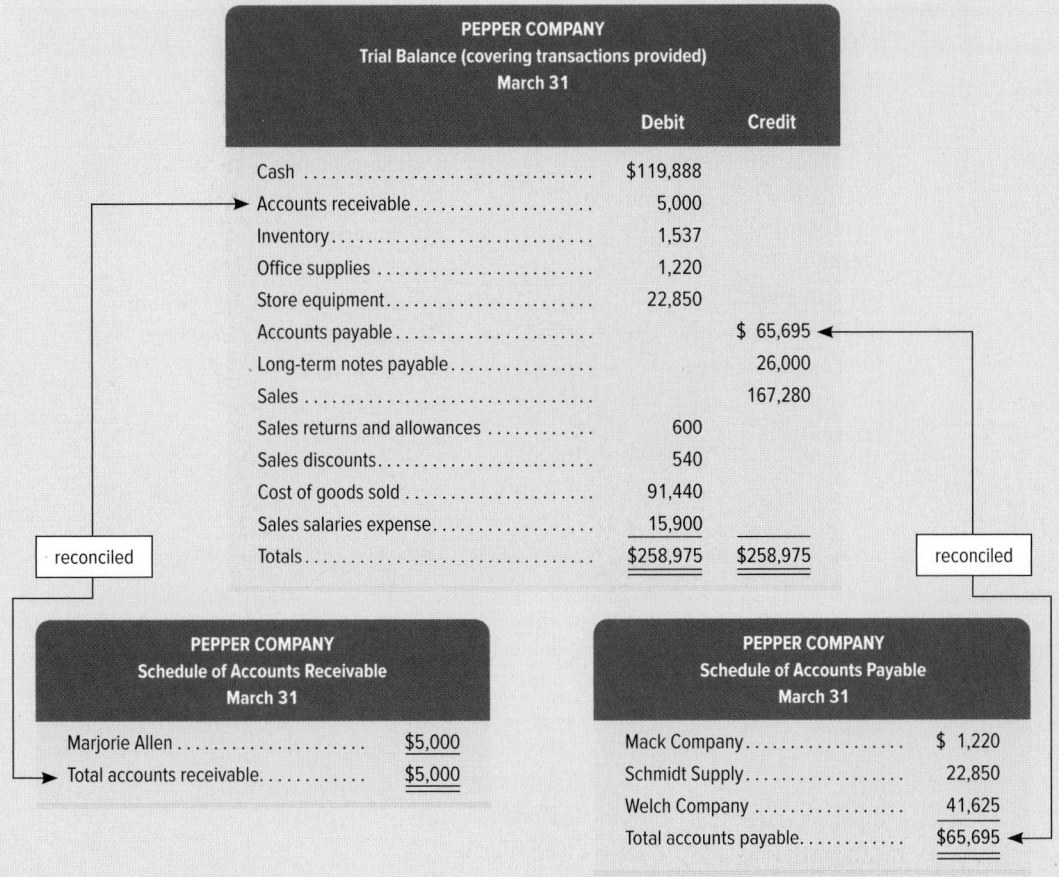

PEPPER COMPANY Trial Balance (covering transactions provided) March 31	Debit	Credit
Cash	$119,888	
Accounts receivable	5,000	
Inventory	1,537	
Office supplies	1,220	
Store equipment	22,850	
Accounts payable		$ 65,695
Long-term notes payable		26,000
Sales		167,280
Sales returns and allowances	600	
Sales discounts	540	
Cost of goods sold	91,440	
Sales salaries expense	15,900	
Totals	$258,975	$258,975

reconciled

reconciled

PEPPER COMPANY Schedule of Accounts Receivable March 31	
Marjorie Allen	$5,000
Total accounts receivable	$5,000

PEPPER COMPANY Schedule of Accounts Payable March 31	
Mack Company	$ 1,220
Schmidt Supply	22,850
Welch Company	41,625
Total accounts payable	$65,695

Summary

C1 Identify the principles and components of accounting information systems. Accounting information systems are governed by five fundamental principles: control, relevance, compatibility, flexibility, and cost-benefit. The five basic components of an accounting information system are source documents, input devices, information processors, information storage, and output devices.

C2 Explain the goals and uses of special journals. Special journals are used for recording transactions of similar type, each meant to cover one kind of transaction. Four of the most common special journals are the sales journal, cash receipts journal, purchases journal, and cash disbursements journal. Special journals are efficient and cost-effective tools in the journalizing and posting processes.

C3 Describe the use of controlling accounts and subsidiary ledgers. A general ledger keeps controlling accounts such as Accounts Receivable and Accounts Payable, but details on individual accounts making up the controlling account are kept in subsidiary ledgers (such as an accounts receivable ledger). The balance in a controlling account must equal the sum of its subsidiary account balances after posting is complete.

A1 Compute segment return on assets and use it to evaluate segment performance. A business segment is a part of a company that is separately identified by its products or

services or by the geographic market it serves. Analysis of a company's segments is aided by the segment return on assets (segment operating income divided by segment average assets).

P1 Journalize and post transactions using special journals. Each special journal is devoted to similar kinds of transactions. Transactions are journalized on one line of a special journal, with columns devoted to specific accounts, dates, names, posting references, explanations, and other necessary information. Posting is threefold: (1) individual amounts in the Other Accounts column are posted to their general ledger accounts on a regular (daily) basis, (2) individual amounts in a column whose total is *not* posted to a controlling account at the end of a period (month) are posted regularly (daily) to their general ledger accounts, and (3) total amounts for all columns except the Other Accounts column are posted at the end of a period (month) to their column's account title in the general ledger.

P2 Prepare and prove the accuracy of subsidiary ledgers. Account balances in the general ledger and its subsidiary ledgers are tested for accuracy after posting is complete. This procedure is twofold: (1) prepare a trial balance of the general ledger to confirm that debits equal credits and (2) prepare a schedule to confirm that the controlling account's balance equals the subsidiary ledger's balance.

Key Terms

Accounting information system	Control principle	Online processing
Accounts payable ledger	Controlling account	Output devices
Accounts receivable ledger	Cost-benefit principle	Purchases journal
Batch processing	Enterprise resource planning (ERP)	Relevance principle
Cash disbursements journal	software	Sales journal
Cash receipts journal	Flexibility principle	Schedule of accounts payable
Check register	General journal	Schedule of accounts receivable
Columnar journal	Information processor	Segment return on assets
Compatibility principle	Information storage	Special journal
Components of accounting systems	Input device	Subsidiary ledger
Computer network	Internal controls	

Multiple Choice Quiz

1. The sales journal is used to record
   a. Credit sales.
   b. Cash sales.
   c. Cash receipts.
   d. Cash purchases.
   e. Credit purchases.

2. The purchases journal is used to record
   a. Credit sales.
   b. Cash sales.
   c. Cash receipts.
   d. Cash purchases.
   e. Credit purchases.

3. The ledger that contains the financial statement accounts of a company is the
   a. General journal.
   b. Column balance journal.
   c. Special ledger.
   d. General ledger.
   e. Special journal.

4. A subsidiary ledger that contains a separate account for each supplier (creditor) to the company is the
   a. Controlling account.
   b. Accounts payable ledger.
   c. Accounts receivable ledger.
   d. General ledger.
   e. Special journal.

5. Enterprise resource planning software
   a. Refers to programs that help manage company operations.
   b. Is another name for spreadsheet programs.
   c. Uses batch processing of business information.
   d. Is substantially declining in use.
   e. Is another name for database programs.

ANSWERS TO MULTIPLE CHOICE QUIZ

1. a
2. e
3. d

4. b
5. a

🛈 Icon denotes assignments that involve decision making.

Discussion Questions

1. What are five basic components of an accounting system?
2. What are source documents? Give two examples.
3. What are the five fundamental principles of accounting information systems?
4. What is the purpose of an input device? Give examples of input devices for computer systems.
5. What is the difference between data that are stored off-line and data that are stored online?
6. What purpose is served by the output devices of an accounting system?

7. When special journals are used, they are usually used to record each of four different types of transactions. What are these four types of transactions?
8. What notations are entered into the Posting Reference column of a ledger account?
9. 🛈 When a general journal entry is used to record sales returns, the credit of the entry must be posted twice. Does this cause the trial balance to be out of balance? Explain.
10. Describe the procedures involving the use of copies of a company's sales invoices as a sales journal.

11. Credits to customer accounts and credits to Other Accounts are individually posted from a cash receipts journal such as the one in Exhibit 7.7. Why not put both types of credits in the same column and save journal space?

12. 🔲 Why should sales to and receipts of cash from credit customers be recorded and posted immediately?

13. Locate "Note 11," which reports Apple's segments from its September 26, 2015, annual **APPLE** report on its website (Apple.com). Identify its segments and list the net sales for each.

14. Locate "Note 16," which reports Google's geographical segments from its 2015 annual report (sec.gov/Archives/edgar/data/1288776/000165204416000012/goog10-k2015.htm). Identify its geographical segments and list the revenues for each. **GOOGLE**

15. Locate "Note 11," which reports Apple's segments from its September 26, 2015, annual **APPLE** report on its website (Apple.com). Compute the ratio "Operating income/Net sales" for each segment. Comment on the results.

■ connect

Identify the most likely role in an accounting system played by each of the numbered items 1 through 10 by assigning a letter from the list A through E on the left.

A. Source documents
B. Input devices
C. Information processors
D. Information storage
E. Output devices

_____ **1.** Computer keyboard
_____ **2.** Computer printer
_____ **3.** Computer monitor
_____ **4.** Bank statement
_____ **5.** Computer software
_____ **6.** Bar code reader
_____ **7.** Digital camera
_____ **8.** Invoice from a supplier
_____ **9.** Computer scanner
_____ **10.** Filing cabinet

QUICK STUDY

QS 7-1
Accounting information system components
C1

Enter the letter of each system principle in the blank next to its best description.

A. Control principle
B. Relevance principle
C. Compatibility principle
D. Flexibility principle
E. Cost-benefit principle

_____ **1.** The principle prescribes the accounting information system to help monitor activities.
_____ **2.** The principle prescribes the accounting information system to adapt to the unique characteristics of the company.
_____ **3.** The principle prescribes the accounting information system to change in response to technological advances and competitive pressures.
_____ **4.** The principle that affects all other accounting information system principles.
_____ **5.** The principle prescribes the accounting information system to provide timely information for effective decision making.

QS 7-2
Accounting information system principles
C1

Wilcox Electronics uses a sales journal, a purchases journal, a cash receipts journal, a cash disbursements journal, and a general journal as illustrated in this chapter. Wilcox recently completed the following transactions a through h. Identify the journal in which each transaction should be recorded.

_____ **a.** Sold merchandise on credit.
_____ **b.** Purchased shop supplies on credit.
_____ **c.** Paid an employee's salary in cash.
_____ **d.** Borrowed cash from the bank.
_____ **e.** Sold merchandise for cash.
_____ **f.** Purchased merchandise on credit.
_____ **g.** Purchased inventory for cash.
_____ **h.** Paid cash to a creditor.

QS 7-3
Identifying the special journal of entry
C2 🔲

Biloxi Gifts uses a sales journal, a purchases journal, a cash receipts journal, a cash disbursements journal, and a general journal as illustrated in this chapter. Journalize its November transactions that should be recorded in the general journal. For those not recorded in the general journal, identify the special journal where each should be recorded.

Nov. 2 The company purchased $2,600 of merchandise on credit from the Midland Co., terms 2/10, n/30.
  12 The owner, T. Biloxi, contributed an automobile worth $17,000 to the company.
  16 The company sold $1,200 of merchandise (cost is $800) on credit to K. Myer, terms n/30.
  19 K. Myer returned $175 of (worthless) merchandise originally purchased on November 16 to the company (assume the cost of this merchandise is left in cost of goods sold).

QS 7-4
Entries in the general journal
C2

QS 7-5
Controlling accounts and subsidiary ledgers
C3

Following is information from Fredrickson Company for its initial month of business.

1. Identify the balances listed in the accounts receivable subsidiary ledger.
2. Identify the Accounts Receivable balance listed in the general ledger at month's end.

Credit Sales			Cash Collections		
Jan. 10	Stern Company...............	$4,000	Jan. 20	Stern Company...............	$2,000
19	Diaz Brothers	1,600	28	Diaz Brothers.................	1,600
23	Rex Company	2,500	31	Rex Company	1,300

QS 7-6
Purchases journal—perpetual
P1

Peachtree Company uses a sales journal, a purchases journal, a cash receipts journal, a cash disbursements journal, and a general journal. The following transactions occur in the month of May.

May 1 Purchased $10,100 of merchandise on credit from Krause, Inc., terms n/30.
    8 Sold merchandise costing $900 on credit to G. Seles for $1,500 subject to a $30 sales discount if paid by the end of the month.
  14 Purchased $240 of store supplies from Chang Company on credit, terms n/30.
  17 Purchased $260 of office supplies on credit from Monder Company, terms n/30.
  24 Sold merchandise costing $400 to D. Air for $650 cash.
  28 Purchased store supplies from Porter's for $90 cash.
  29 Paid Krause, Inc., $10,100 cash for the merchandise purchased on May 1.

Prepare headings for a purchases journal like the one in Exhibit 7.9. Journalize the May transactions that should be recorded in the purchases journal.

QS 7-7
Identifying journal of entry C2

Refer to QS 7-6 and for each of the May transactions identify the journal in which it would be recorded. Assume the company uses a sales journal, purchases journal, cash receipts journal, cash disbursements journal, and general journal as illustrated in this chapter.

QS 7-8
Accounts receivable ledger; posting from sales journal
P2

Warton Company posts its sales invoices directly and then binds them into a sales journal. The company had the following credit sales to these customers during July.

July	2	Mary Mack...............	$ 8,600
	8	Eric Horner...............	11,100
	10	Troy Wilson	13,400
	14	Hong Jiang................	20,500
	20	Troy Wilson	11,200
	29	Mary Mack...............	7,300
		Total credit sales	$72,100

1. Open an accounts receivable subsidiary ledger having a T-account for each customer. Post the invoices to the subsidiary ledger.
2. Open an Accounts Receivable controlling T-account and a Sales T-account to reflect general ledger accounts. Post the end-of-month total from the sales journal to these accounts.
3. Prepare a schedule of accounts receivable and prove that its total equals the Accounts Receivable controlling account balance.

QS 7-9
Analyzing segment reports

A1

APPLE

Apple reports the following net sales by product segment. Compute the percentage of total sales for each of its five product segments. Comment on the relative contributions of each product segment.

$ millions	iPhone	iPad	Mac	Services	Other	Total
Sales	$155,041	$23,227	$25,471	$19,909	$10,067	$233,715

Nestlé, a Switzerland-based company, uses a sales journal, a purchases journal, a cash receipts journal, a cash disbursements journal, and a general journal in a manner similar to that explained in this chapter. Journalize the following summary transactions of Nestlé transactions that should be recorded in the general journal. For those not recorded in the general journal, identify only the special journal where each should be recorded. (All amounts in millions of Swiss franc, CHF.)

1. Assume Nestlé purchased CHF 17,000 of merchandise on credit from suppliers.

2. Assume Nestlé sold CHF 94,000 of merchandise (cost is CHF 42,300) on credit to customers.

3. Assume a key customer returned CHF 2,400 of (worthless) merchandise to Nestlé (assume the cost of this merchandise is left in cost of goods sold).

QS 7-10
International accounting and special journals

C2

connect

Finer Company uses a sales journal, a purchases journal, a cash receipts journal, a cash disbursements journal, and a general journal. The following transactions occur in the month of May.

May 2   Sold merchandise costing $300 to B. Facer for $450 cash, Invoice No. 5703.
    5   Purchased $2,400 of merchandise on credit from Marchant Corp.
    7   Sold merchandise costing $800 to J. Dryer for $1,250, terms 2/10, n/30, Invoice No. 5704.
    8   Borrowed $9,000 cash by signing a note payable to the bank.
   12   Sold merchandise costing $200 to R. Lamb for $340, terms n/30, Invoice No. 5705.
   16   Received $1,225 cash from J. Dryer to pay for the purchase of May 7.
   19   Sold used store equipment for $900 cash to Golf, Inc.
   25   Sold merchandise costing $500 to T. Taylor for $750, terms n/30, Invoice No. 5706.

Prepare headings for a sales journal like the one in Exhibit 7.5. Journalize the May transactions that should be recorded in the sales journal.

EXERCISES

Exercise 7-1
Sales journal—perpetual

P1

Refer to Exercise 7-1 and for each of the May transactions identify the journal in which it would be recorded. Assume the company uses a sales journal, purchases journal, cash receipts journal, cash disbursements journal, and general journal as illustrated in this chapter.

Exercise 7-2
Identifying journal of entry C2

Ali Co. uses a sales journal, a purchases journal, a cash receipts journal, a cash disbursements journal, and a general journal. The following transactions occur in the month of November.

Nov. 3   The company purchased $3,200 of merchandise on credit from Hart Co., terms n/20.
     7   The company sold merchandise costing $840 on credit to J. Than for $1,000, subject to a $20 sales discount if paid by the end of the month.
     9   The company borrowed $3,750 cash by signing a note payable to the bank.
    13   J. Ali, the owner, contributed $5,000 cash to the company.
    18   The company sold merchandise costing $250 to B. Cox for $330 cash.
    22   The company paid Hart Co. $3,200 cash for the merchandise purchased on November 3.
    27   The company received $980 cash from J. Than in payment of the November 7 purchase.
    30   The company paid salaries of $1,650 in cash.

Prepare headings for a cash receipts journal like the one in Exhibit 7.7. Journalize the November transactions that should be recorded in the cash receipts journal.

Exercise 7-3
Cash receipts journal—perpetual

P1

Refer to Exercise 7-3 and for each of the November transactions identify the journal in which it would be recorded. Assume the company uses a sales journal, purchases journal, cash receipts journal, cash disbursements journal, and general journal as illustrated in this chapter.

Exercise 7-4
Identifying journal of entry C2

Following is information from Jesper Company for its initial month of business.

1. Identify the balances listed in the accounts payable subsidiary ledger.

2. Identify the Accounts Payable balance listed in the general ledger at month's end.

Exercise 7-5
Controlling accounts and subsidiary ledgers

C3

Credit Purchases			Cash Paid		
Jan. 9	Bailey Company	$14,000	Jan. 19	Bailey Company	$10,100
18	Johnson Brothers	6,600	27	Johnson Brothers	6,600
22	Preston Company	6,200	31	Preston Company	5,400

Exercise 7-6

Cash disbursements journal—perpetual

P1

Marx Supply uses a sales journal, a purchases journal, a cash receipts journal, a cash disbursements journal, and a general journal. The following transactions occur in the month of April.

Apr. 3   Purchased merchandise for $2,950 on credit from Seth, Inc., terms 2/10, n/30.
      9   Issued Check No. 210 to Kitt Corp. to buy store supplies for $650.
     12   Sold merchandise costing $500 on credit to C. Myrs for $770, terms n/30.
     17   Issued Check No. 211 for $1,400 to pay off a note payable to City Bank.
     20   Purchased merchandise for $4,500 on credit from Lite, terms 2/10, n/30.
     28   Issued Check No. 212 to Lite to pay the amount due for the purchase of April 20 less the discount.
     29   Paid salary of $1,800 to B. Dock by issuing Check No. 213.
     30   Issued Check No. 214 to Seth, Inc., to pay the amount due for the purchase of April 3.

Prepare headings for a cash disbursements journal like the one in Exhibit 7.11. Journalize the April transactions that should be recorded in the cash disbursements journal.

Exercise 7-7

Identifying journal of entry C2

Refer to Exercise 7-6 and for each of the April transactions identify the journal in which it would be recorded. Assume the company uses a sales journal, purchases journal, cash receipts journal, cash disbursements journal, and general journal as illustrated in this chapter.

Exercise 7-8

Purchases journal and error identification

P1

A company that records credit purchases in a purchases journal and records purchases returns in a general journal made the following errors. Enter A, B, or C indicating when each error should be discovered.

A. When preparing the schedule of accounts payable.

B. When crossfooting the purchases journal.

C. When preparing the trial balance.

_____ **1.** Made an addition error in totaling the Office Supplies column of the purchases journal.

_____ **2.** Made an addition error in determining the balance of a creditor's subsidiary account.

_____ **3.** Posted a purchases return to the Accounts Payable account and to the creditor's subsidiary account but did not post the purchases return to the Inventory account.

_____ **4.** Correctly recorded an $8,000 purchase in the purchases journal but posted it to the creditor's subsidiary account as an $800 purchase.

_____ **5.** Posted a purchases return to the Inventory account and to the Accounts Payable account but did not post to the creditor's subsidiary account.

Exercise 7-9

Special journal transactions and error discovery

P1

Post Pharmacy uses the following journals: sales journal, purchases journal, cash receipts journal, cash disbursements journal, and general journal. The following two transactions were processed.

June 5   Post Pharmacy purchased merchandise priced at $14,000, subject to credit terms of 2/10, n/30.
June 14   Post Pharmacy paid the net amount due for the merchandise purchased on June 5.

In journalizing the June 14 payment, the pharmacy debited Accounts Payable for $14,000 but failed to record the cash discount on the purchase. Cash was properly credited for the actual $13,720 paid.

a. In what journals would the June 5 and June 14 transactions be recorded?

b. What procedure is likely to discover the error in journalizing the June 14 transaction?

Exercise 7-10

Posting to subsidiary ledger accounts; preparing a schedule of accounts receivable

P2

At the end of May, the sales journal of Mountain View appears as follows.

Sales Journal					Page 2
Date	Account Debited	Invoice Number	PR	Accounts Receivable Dr. Sales Cr.	Cost of Goods Sold Dr. Inventory Cr.
May 6	Aaron Reckers	190		3,880	3,120
10	Sara Reed	191		2,940	2,325
17	Anna Page	192		1,850	1,480
25	Sara Reed	193		1,340	1,075
31	Totals			10,010	8,000

Mountain View also recorded the return of defective merchandise with the following entry.

May 20	Sales Returns and Allowances	350	
	Accounts Receivable—Anna Page...................		350
	Customer returned (worthless) merchandise.		

Required

1. Open an accounts receivable subsidiary ledger that has a T-account for each customer listed in the sales journal. Post to the customer accounts the entries in the sales journal and any portion of the general journal entry that affects a customer's account.

2. Open a general ledger that has T-accounts for Accounts Receivable, Inventory, Sales, Sales Returns and Allowances, and Cost of Goods Sold. Post the sales journal and any portion of the general journal entry that affects these accounts.

3. Prepare a schedule of accounts receivable and prove that its total equals the balance in the Accounts Receivable controlling account.

Check (3) Ending Accounts Receivable, $9,660

Complete the following segment return on assets table for Teton Company (round ratios to three decimals, or one decimal if shown in percent form). Analyze your findings and identify the segment with the highest, and that with the lowest, segment return on assets.

Exercise 7-11
Computing and analyzing segment return on assets

A1

Segment	Segment Operating Income (in $ mil.)		Segment Assets (in $ mil.)		Segment Return on Assets
	2017	**2016**	**2017**	**2016**	**2017**
Specialty					
Skiing Group.................	$ 72	$ 68	$ 591	$ 450	
Skating Group...............	19	16	63	52	
Specialty Footwear	32	29	165	146	
Other Specialty..............	21	14	47	34	
Subtotal	144	127	866	682	
General Merchandise					
South America	42	46	315	284	
United States	17	18	62	45	
Europe	15	13	24	22	
Subtotal	74	77	401	351	
Total.......................	$218	$204	$1,267	$1,033	

Check Europe segment return, 65.2%

▨ connect

Church Company completes these transactions and events during March of the current year (terms for all its credit sales are 2/10, n/30).

PROBLEM SET A

Problem 7-1A
Special journals, subsidiary ledgers, trial balance—perpetual

C3 P1 P2

Mar. 1 Purchased $43,600 of merchandise from Van Industries, invoice dated March 1, terms 2/15, n/30.
  2 Sold merchandise on credit to Min Cho, Invoice No. 854, for $16,800 (cost is $8,400).
  3 Purchased $1,230 of office supplies on credit from Gabel Company, invoice dated March 3, terms n/10 EOM.
  3 Sold merchandise on credit to Linda Witt, Invoice No. 855, for $10,200 (cost is $5,800).
  6 Borrowed $82,000 cash from Federal Bank by signing a long-term note payable.
  9 Purchased $21,850 of office equipment on credit from Spell Supply, invoice dated March 9, terms n/10 EOM.
  10 Sold merchandise on credit to Jovita Albany, Invoice No. 856, for $5,600 (cost is $2,900).
  12 Received payment from Min Cho for the March 2 sale less the discount.
  13 Sent Van Industries Check No. 416 in payment of the March 1 invoice less the discount.
  13 Received payment from Linda Witt for the March 3 sale less the discount.

14   Purchased $32,625 of merchandise from the CD Company, invoice dated March 13, terms 2/10, n/30.

15   Issued Check No. 417, payable to Payroll, in payment of sales salaries expense for the first half of the month, $18,300. Cashed the check and paid the employees.

15   Cash sales for the first half of the month are $34,680 (cost is $20,210). (Cash sales are recorded daily but are recorded only twice here to reduce repetitive entries.)

16   Purchased $1,770 of store supplies on credit from Gabel Company, invoice dated March 16, terms n/10 EOM.

17   Received a $2,425 credit memorandum from CD Company for the return of unsatisfactory merchandise purchased on March 14.

19   Received a $630 credit memorandum from Spell Supply for office equipment received on March 9 and returned for credit.

20   Received payment from Jovita Albany for the sale of March 10 less the discount.

23   Issued Check No. 418 to CD Company in payment of the invoice of March 13 less the March 17 return and the discount.

27   Sold merchandise on credit to Jovita Albany, Invoice No. 857, for $14,910 (cost is $7,220).

28   Sold merchandise on credit to Linda Witt, Invoice No. 858, for $4,315 (cost is $3,280).

31   Issued Check No. 419, payable to Payroll, in payment of sales salaries expense for the last half of the month, $18,300. Cashed the check and paid the employees.

31   Cash sales for the last half of the month are $30,180 (cost is $16,820).

31   Verify that amounts impacting customer and creditor accounts were posted and that any amounts that should have been posted as individual amounts to the general ledger accounts were posted. Foot and crossfoot the journals and make the month-end postings.

Required

1. Open the following general ledger accounts: Cash; Accounts Receivable; Inventory (March 1 beg. bal. is $10,000); Office Supplies; Store Supplies; Office Equipment; Accounts Payable; Long-Term Notes Payable; Z. Church, Capital (March 1 beg. bal. is $10,000); Sales; Sales Discounts; Cost of Goods Sold; and Sales Salaries Expense. Open the following accounts receivable subsidiary ledger accounts: Jovita Albany, Min Cho, and Linda Witt. Open the following accounts payable subsidiary ledger accounts: Gabel Company, Van Industries, Spell Supply, and CD Company.

2. Enter these transactions in a sales journal like Exhibit 7.5, a purchases journal like Exhibit 7.9, a cash receipts journal like Exhibit 7.7, a cash disbursements journal like Exhibit 7.11, or a general journal. Number all journal pages as page 2.

Check   Trial balance totals, $232,905

3. Prepare a trial balance of the general ledger and prove the accuracy of the subsidiary ledgers by preparing schedules of both accounts receivable and accounts payable.

Problem 7-2A

Special journals, subsidiary ledgers, and schedule of accounts receivable—perpetual

C3   P1   P2

Wiset Company completes these transactions during April of the current year (the terms of all its credit sales are 2/10, n/30).

Apr.   2   Purchased $14,300 of merchandise on credit from Noth Company, invoice dated April 2, terms 2/10, n/60.

3   Sold merchandise on credit to Page Alistair, Invoice No. 760, for $4,000 (cost is $3,000).

3   Purchased $1,480 of office supplies on credit from Custer, Inc. Invoice dated April 2, terms n/10 EOM.

4   Issued Check No. 587 to *World View* for advertising expense, $899.

5   Sold merchandise on credit to Paula Kohr, Invoice No. 761, for $8,000 (cost is $6,500).

6   Received an $80 credit memorandum from Custer, Inc., for the return of some of the office supplies received on April 3.

9   Purchased $12,125 of store equipment on credit from Hal's Supply, invoice dated April 9, terms n/10 EOM.

11   Sold merchandise on credit to Nic Nelson, Invoice No. 762, for $10,500 (cost is $7,000).

12   Issued Check No. 588 to Noth Company in payment of its April 2 invoice less the discount.

13   Received payment from Page Alistair for the April 3 sale less the discount.

13   Sold $5,100 of merchandise on credit to Page Alistair (cost is $3,600), Invoice No. 763.

14   Received payment from Paula Kohr for the April 5 sale less the discount.

16   Issued Check No. 589, payable to Payroll, in payment of sales salaries expense for the first half of the month, $10,750. Cashed the check and paid employees.

16   Cash sales for the first half of the month are $52,840 (cost is $35,880). (Cash sales are recorded daily from cash register data but are recorded only twice in this problem to reduce repetitive entries.)

17   Purchased $13,750 of merchandise on credit from Grant Company, invoice dated April 17, terms 2/10, n/30.

18   Borrowed $60,000 cash from First State Bank by signing a long-term note payable.

20   Received payment from Nic Nelson for the April 11 sale less the discount.

20   Purchased $830 of store supplies on credit from Hal's Supply, invoice dated April 19, terms n/10 EOM.

23   Received a $750 credit memorandum from Grant Company for the return of defective merchandise received on April 17.

23   Received payment from Page Alistair for the April 13 sale less the discount.

25   Purchased $11,375 of merchandise on credit from Noth Company, invoice dated April 24, terms 2/10, n/60.

26   Issued Check No. 590 to Grant Company in payment of its April 17 invoice less the return and the discount.

27   Sold $3,170 of merchandise on credit to Paula Kohr, Invoice No. 764 (cost is $2,520).

27   Sold $6,700 of merchandise on credit to Nic Nelson, Invoice No. 765 (cost is $4,305).

30   Issued Check No. 591, payable to Payroll, in payment of the sales salaries expense for the last half of the month, $10,750.

30   Cash sales for the last half of the month are $73,975 (cost is $58,900).

Required

1. Prepare a sales journal like that in Exhibit 7.5 and a cash receipts journal like that in Exhibit 7.7. Number both journal pages as page 3. Then review the transactions of Wiset Company and enter those that should be journalized in the sales journal and those that should be journalized in the cash receipts journal. Ignore any transactions that should be journalized in a purchases journal, a cash disbursements journal, or a general journal.

2. Open the following general ledger accounts: Cash; Accounts Receivable; Inventory; Long-Term Notes Payable; B. Wiset, Capital; Sales; Sales Discounts; and Cost of Goods Sold. Enter the March 31 balances for Cash ($85,000), Inventory ($125,000), Long-Term Notes Payable ($110,000), and B. Wiset, Capital ($100,000). Also open accounts receivable subsidiary ledger accounts for Paula Kohr, Page Alistair, and Nic Nelson.

3. Verify that amounts that should be posted as individual amounts from the journals have been posted. (Such items are immediately posted.) Foot and crossfoot the journals and make the month-end postings.

4. Prepare a trial balance of the general ledger accounts opened as required for part 2; then prove the accuracy of the subsidiary ledger by preparing a schedule of accounts receivable.

Check   Trial balance totals, $434,285

Analysis Component

5. Assume that the total for the schedule of accounts receivable does not equal the balance of the controlling account in the general ledger. Describe steps you would take to discover the error(s).

The April transactions of Wiset Company are described in Problem 7-2A.

Required

1. Prepare a general journal, a purchases journal like that in Exhibit 7.9, and a cash disbursements journal like that in Exhibit 7.11. Number all journal pages as page 3. Review the April transactions of Wiset Company and enter those transactions that should be journalized in the general journal, the purchases journal, or the cash disbursements journal. Ignore any transactions that should be journalized in a sales journal or cash receipts journal.

2. Open the following general ledger accounts: Cash; Inventory; Office Supplies; Store Supplies; Store Equipment; Accounts Payable; Long-Term Notes Payable; B. Wiset, Capital; Sales Salaries Expense; and Advertising Expense. Enter the March 31 balances of Cash ($85,000), Inventory ($125,000), Long-Term Notes Payable ($110,000), and B. Wiset, Capital ($100,000). Also open accounts payable subsidiary ledger accounts for Hal's Supply, Noth Company, Grant Company, and Custer, Inc.

3. Verify that amounts that should be posted as individual amounts from the journals have been posted. (Such items are immediately posted.) Foot and crossfoot the journals and make the month-end postings.

4. Prepare a trial balance of the general ledger accounts opened as required for part 2; then prepare a schedule of accounts payable.

Problem 7-3A
Special journals, subsidiary ledgers, and schedule of accounts payable—perpetual

C3   P1   P2

Check   Trial balance totals, $235,730

PROBLEM SET B

Problem 7-1B

Special journals, subsidiary ledgers, trial balance—perpetual

C3   P2   P3

Grassley Company completes these transactions during November of the current year (terms for all its credit sales are 2/10, n/30).

Nov. 1   Purchased $5,058 of office equipment on credit from Brun Supply, invoice dated November 1, terms n/10 EOM.

2   Borrowed $88,500 cash from Wisconsin Bank by signing a long-term note payable.

4   Purchased $33,500 of merchandise from BLR Industries, invoice dated November 3, terms 2/10, n/30.

5   Purchased $1,040 of store supplies on credit from Grebe Company, invoice dated November 5, terms n/10 EOM.

8   Sold merchandise on credit to Cyd Rounder, Invoice No. 439, for $6,550 (cost is $3,910).

10   Sold merchandise on credit to Carlos Mantel, Invoice No. 440, for $13,500 (cost is $8,500).

11   Purchased $2,557 of merchandise from Lo Company, invoice dated November 10, terms 2/10, n/30.

12   Sent BLR Industries Check No. 633 in payment of its November 3 invoice less the discount.

15   Issued Check No. 634, payable to Payroll, in payment of sales salaries expense for the first half of the month, $6,585. Cashed the check and paid the employees.

15   Cash sales for the first half of the month are $18,170 (cost is $9,000). (Cash sales are recorded daily but are recorded only twice in this problem to reduce repetitive entries.)

15   Sold merchandise on credit to Tori Tripp, Invoice No. 441, for $5,250 (cost is $2,450).

16   Purchased $459 of office supplies on credit from Grebe Company, invoice dated November 16, terms n/10 EOM.

17   Received a $557 credit memorandum from Lo Company for the return of unsatisfactory merchandise purchased on November 11.

18   Received payment from Cyd Rounder for the November 8 sale less the discount.

19   Received payment from Carlos Mantel for the November 10 sale less the discount.

19   Issued Check No. 635 to Lo Company in payment of its invoice of November 10 less the return and the discount.

22   Sold merchandise on credit to Carlos Mantel, Invoice No. 442, for $3,695 (cost is $2,060).

24   Sold merchandise on credit to Tori Tripp, Invoice No. 443, for $4,280 (cost is $2,130).

25   Received payment from Tori Tripp for the sale of November 15 less the discount.

26   Received a $922 credit memorandum from Brun Supply for the return of office equipment purchased on November 1.

30   Issued Check No. 636, payable to Payroll, in payment of sales salaries expense for the last half of the month, $6,585. Cashed the check and paid the employees.

30   Cash sales for the last half of the month are $16,703 (cost is $10,200).

30   Verify that amounts impacting customer and creditor accounts were posted and that any amounts that should have been posted as individual amounts to the general ledger accounts were posted. Foot and crossfoot the journals and make the month-end postings.

Required

1. Open the following general ledger accounts: Cash; Accounts Receivable; Inventory (Nov. 1 beg. bal. is $40,000); Office Supplies; Store Supplies; Office Equipment; Accounts Payable; Long-Term Notes Payable; C. Grassley, Capital (Nov. 1 beg. bal. is $40,000); Sales; Sales Discounts; Cost of Goods Sold; and Sales Salaries Expense. Open the following accounts receivable subsidiary ledger accounts: Carlos Mantel, Tori Tripp, and Cyd Rounder. Open the following accounts payable subsidiary ledger accounts: Grebe Company, BLR Industries, Brun Supply, and Lo Company.

2. Enter these transactions in a sales journal like that in Exhibit 7.5, a purchases journal like that in Exhibit 7.9, a cash receipts journal like that in Exhibit 7.7, a cash disbursements journal like that in Exhibit 7.11, or a general journal. Number all journal pages as page 2.

Check Trial balance totals, $202,283

3. Prepare a trial balance of the general ledger and prove the accuracy of the subsidiary ledgers by preparing schedules of both accounts receivable and accounts payable.

Problem 7-2B

Special journals, subsidiary ledgers, schedule of accounts receivable—perpetual

C3   P1   P2

Acorn Industries completes these transactions during July of the current year (the terms of all its credit sales are 2/10, n/30).

July 1   Purchased $6,500 of merchandise on credit from Teton Company, invoice dated June 30, terms 2/10, n/30.

3   Issued Check No. 300 to *The Weekly* for advertising expense, $625.

5   Sold merchandise on credit to Kim Nettle, Invoice No. 918, for $19,200 (cost is $10,500).

6   Sold merchandise on credit to Ruth Blake, Invoice No. 919, for $7,500 (cost is $4,300).

7   Purchased $1,250 of store supplies on credit from Plaine, Inc., invoice dated July 7, terms n/10 EOM.

8   Received a $250 credit memorandum from Plaine, Inc., for the return of store supplies received on July 7.

9   Purchased $38,220 of store equipment on credit from Charm's Supply, invoice dated July 8, terms n/10 EOM.

10   Issued Check No. 301 to Teton Company in payment of its June 30 invoice less the discount.

13   Sold merchandise on credit to Ashton Moore, Invoice No. 920, for $8,550 (cost is $5,230).

14   Sold merchandise on credit to Kim Nettle, Invoice No. 921, for $5,100 (cost is $3,800).

15   Received payment from Kim Nettle for the July 5 sale less the discount.

15   Issued Check No. 302, payable to Payroll, in payment of sales salaries expense for the first half of the month, $31,850. Cashed the check and paid employees.

15   Cash sales for the first half of the month are $118,350 (cost is $76,330). (Cash sales are recorded daily using data from the cash registers but are recorded only twice in this problem to reduce repetitive entries.)

16   Received payment from Ruth Blake for the July 6 sale less the discount.

17   Purchased $7,200 of merchandise on credit from Drake Company, invoice dated July 17, terms 2/10, n/30.

20   Purchased $650 of office supplies on credit from Charm's Supply, invoice dated July 19, terms n/10 EOM.

21   Borrowed $15,000 cash from College Bank by signing a long-term note payable.

23   Received payment from Ashton Moore for the July 13 sale less the discount.

24   Received payment from Kim Nettle for the July 14 sale less the discount.

24   Received a $2,400 credit memorandum from Drake Company for the return of defective merchandise received on July 17.

26   Purchased $9,770 of merchandise on credit from Teton Company, invoice dated July 26, terms 2/10, n/30.

27   Issued Check No. 303 to Drake Company in payment of its July 17 invoice less the return and the discount.

29   Sold merchandise on credit to Ruth Blake, Invoice No. 922, for $17,500 (cost is $10,850).

30   Sold merchandise on credit to Ashton Moore, Invoice No. 923, for $16,820 (cost is $9,840).

31   Issued Check No. 304, payable to Payroll, in payment of the sales salaries expense for the last half of the month, $31,850.

31   Cash sales for the last half of the month are $80,244 (cost is $53,855).

Required

1. Prepare a sales journal like that in Exhibit 7.5 and a cash receipts journal like that in Exhibit 7.7. Number both journals as page 3. Then review the transactions of Acorn Industries and enter those transactions that should be journalized in the sales journal and those that should be journalized in the cash receipts journal. Ignore any transactions that should be journalized in a purchases journal, a cash disbursements journal, or a general journal.

2. Open the following general ledger accounts: Cash; Accounts Receivable; Inventory; Long-Term Notes Payable; R. Acorn, Capital; Sales; Sales Discounts; and Cost of Goods Sold. Enter the June 30 balances for Cash ($100,000), Inventory ($200,000), Long-Term Notes Payable ($200,000), and R. Acorn, Capital ($100,000). Also open accounts receivable subsidiary ledger accounts for Kim Nettle, Ashton Moore, and Ruth Blake.

3. Verify that amounts that should be posted as individual amounts from the journals have been posted. (Such items are immediately posted.) Foot and crossfoot the journals and make the month-end postings.

4. Prepare a trial balance of the general ledger accounts opened as required for part 2; then prove the accuracy of the subsidiary ledger by preparing a schedule of accounts receivable.

Check   Trial balance totals, $588,264

Analysis Component

5. Assume that the total for the schedule of accounts receivable does not equal the balance of the controlling account in the general ledger. Describe steps you would take to discover the error(s).

Problem 7-3B
Special journals, subsidiary ledgers, and schedule of accounts payable—perpetual

C3   **P1**   **P2**

The July transactions of Acorn Industries are described in Problem 7-2B.

Required

1. Prepare a general journal, a purchases journal like that in Exhibit 7.9, and a cash disbursements journal like that in Exhibit 7.11. Number all journal pages as page 3. Review the July transactions of Acorn Industries and enter those transactions that should be journalized in the general journal, the purchases journal, or the cash disbursements journal. Ignore any transactions that should be journalized in a sales journal or cash receipts journal.

2. Open the following general ledger accounts: Cash; Inventory; Office Supplies; Store Supplies; Store Equipment; Accounts Payable; Long-Term Notes Payable; R. Acorn, Capital; Sales Salaries Expense; and Advertising Expense. Enter the June 30 balances of Cash ($100,000), Inventory ($200,000), Long-Term Notes Payable ($200,000), and R. Acorn, Capital ($100,000). Also open accounts payable subsidiary ledger accounts for Charm's Supply, Teton Company, Drake Company, and Plaine, Inc.

3. Verify that amounts that should be posted as individual amounts from the journals have been posted. (Such items are immediately posted.) Foot and crossfoot the journals and make the month-end postings.

Check   Trial balance totals, $349,640

4. Prepare a trial balance of the general ledger accounts opened as required for part 2; then prepare a schedule of accounts payable.

SERIAL PROBLEM
Business Solutions

P1

© Alexander Image/Shutterstock RF

(This serial problem began in Chapter 1 and continues through most of the book. If previous chapter segments were not completed, the serial problem can begin at this point.)

SP 7   Assume that Santana Rey expands **Business Solutions**'s accounting system to include special journals.

Required

1. Locate the transactions related to January through March 2018 for Business Solutions in Chapter 5.

2. Enter the Business Solutions transactions for January through March in a sales journal like that in Exhibit 7.5 (insert "n/a" in the Invoice column), a cash receipts journal like that in Exhibit 7.7, a purchases journal like that in Exhibit 7.9 (use Computer Supplies heading instead of Office Supplies), and a cash disbursements journal like that in Exhibit 7.11 (insert "n/a" in the Check Number column), or a general journal. Number journal pages as page 2. If the transaction does not specify the name of the payee, state "not specified" in the Payee column of the cash disbursements journal.

3. The transactions on the following dates should be journalized in the general journal: January 5, 11, 20, and 24 and March 24. Do not record and post the adjusting entries for the end of March.

COMPREHENSIVE PROBLEM

(If the Working Papers that accompany this book are not available, omit this comprehensive problem.)
Assume it is Monday, May 1, the first business day of the month, and you have just been hired as the accountant for Colo Company, which operates with monthly accounting periods. All of the company's accounting work is completed through the end of April, and its ledgers show April 30 balances. During your first month on the job, the company experiences the following transactions and events (terms for all its credit sales are 2/10, n/30 unless stated differently):

May   1   Issued Check No. 3410 to S&P Management Co. in payment of the May rent, $3,710. (Use two lines to record the transaction. Charge 80% of the rent to Rent Expense—Selling Space and the balance to Rent Expense—Office Space.)

      2   Sold merchandise on credit to Hensel Company, Invoice No. 8785, for $6,100 (cost is $4,100).

      2   Issued a $175 credit memorandum to Knox Co. for defective (worthless) merchandise sold on April 28 and returned for credit. The total selling price (gross) was $4,725.

      3   Received a $798 credit memorandum from Peyton Products for the return of merchandise purchased on April 29.

4   Purchased the following on credit from Gear Supply Co.: merchandise, $37,072; store supplies, $574; and office supplies, $83. Invoice dated May 4, terms n/10 EOM.

5   Received payment from Knox Co. for the balance from the April 28 sale less the May 2 return and the discount.

8   Issued Check No. 3411 to Peyton Products to pay for the $7,098 of merchandise purchased on April 29 less the May 3 return and a 2% discount.

9   Sold store supplies to the merchant next door at their cost of $350 cash.

10   Purchased $4,074 of office equipment on credit from Gear Supply Co., invoice dated May 10, terms n/10 EOM.

11   Received payment from Hensel Company for the May 2 sale less the discount.

11   Purchased $8,800 of merchandise from Garcia, Inc., invoice dated May 10, terms 2/10, n/30.

12   Received an $854 credit memorandum from Gear Supply Co. for the return of defective office equipment received on May 10.

15   Issued Check No. 3412, payable to Payroll, in payment of sales salaries, $5,320, and office salaries, $3,150. Cashed the check and paid the employees.

15   Cash sales for the first half of the month are $59,220 (cost is $38,200). (Cash sales are recorded daily but are recorded only twice here to reduce repetitive entries.)

15   Post to the customer and creditor accounts. Also post individual items that are not included in column totals at the end of the month to the general ledger accounts. (Such items are posted daily but are posted only twice each month because they are few in number.)

16   Sold merchandise on credit to Hensel Company, Invoice No. 8786, for $3,990 (cost is $1,890).

17   Purchased $13,650 of merchandise from Fink Corp., invoice dated May 14, terms 2/10, n/60.

19   Issued Check No. 3413 to Garcia, Inc., in payment of its May 10 invoice less the discount.

22   Sold merchandise to Lee Services, Invoice No. 8787, for $6,850 (cost is $4,990), terms 2/10, n/60.

23   Issued Check No. 3414 to Fink Corp. in payment of its May 14 invoice less the discount.

24   Purchased the following on credit from Gear Supply Co.: merchandise, $8,120; store supplies, $630; and office supplies, $280. Invoice dated May 24, terms n/10 EOM.

25   Purchased $3,080 of merchandise from Peyton Products, invoice dated May 23, terms 2/10, n/30.

26   Sold merchandise on credit to Crane Corp., Invoice No. 8788, for $14,210 (cost is $8,230).

26   Issued Check No. 3415 to Perennial Power in payment of the May electric bill, $1,283.

29   The owner of Colo Company, Jenny Colo, used Check No. 3416 to withdraw $7,000 cash from the business for personal use.

30   Received payment from Lee Services for the May 22 sale less the discount.

30   Issued Check No. 3417, payable to Payroll, in payment of sales salaries, $5,320, and office salaries, $3,150. Cashed the check and paid the employees.

31   Cash sales for the last half of the month are $66,052 (cost is $42,500).

31   Post to the customer and creditor accounts. Also post individual items that are not included in column totals at the end of the month to the general ledger accounts. Foot and crossfoot the journals and make the month-end postings.

Required

1. Enter these transactions in a sales journal, a purchases journal, a cash receipts journal, a cash disbursements journal, or a general journal as illustrated in this chapter (number all journal pages as page 2). Post when instructed to do so. Assume a perpetual inventory system.

2. Prepare a trial balance in the Trial Balance columns of the work sheet form provided with the working papers. Complete the work sheet using the following information for accounting adjustments.

Check (2) Unadjusted trial balance totals, $545,020; Adjustments column totals, $2,407

    a. Expired insurance, $553.

    b. Ending store supplies inventory, $2,632.

    c. Ending office supplies inventory, $504.

    d. Depreciation of store equipment, $567.

    e. Depreciation of office equipment, $329.

Prepare and post adjusting and closing entries.

3. Prepare a May 2017 multiple-step income statement, a May 2017 statement of owner's equity, and a May 31, 2017, classified balance sheet.

(3) Net income, $31,647; Total assets, $385,791

4. Prepare a post-closing trial balance. Also prove the accuracy of subsidiary ledgers by preparing schedules of both accounts receivable and accounts payable.

GENERAL LEDGER PROBLEM

Available only in Connect

The **General Ledger** tool in *Connect* automates several of the procedural steps in the accounting cycle so that the accounting professional can focus on the impacts of each transaction on the various financial reports.

GL 7-1   General Ledger assignment GL 7-1, based on Problem 7-1A, highlights the relation between the subsidiary ledgers and the control accounts. Prepare journal entries for a merchandiser, both purchase and sale transactions.

Beyond the Numbers

REPORTING IN ACTION

A1

APPLE

BTN 7-1   Refer to Apple's financial statements in Appendix A to answer parts 1 and 2.

1. Identify the note that reports on Apple's business segments.
2. Describe the focus and activities of each of Apple's business segments.
3. In a recent year, Apple reported the following operating income and average segment assets (which exclude shared corporate assets) for its geographic segments. Compute Apple's return on assets for each of its geographic segments. Assess the relative performance of the five segments shown here.

$ millions	Americas	Europe	Greater China	Japan	Rest of Asia Pacific
Operating income..............	$22,817	$13,025	$8,541	$6,819	$3,753
Average assets................	5,589	3,115	2,132	2,315	918

Fast Forward

4. Access Apple's annual report for fiscal years ending after September 26, 2015, from its website (Apple.com) or the SEC's EDGAR database (SEC.gov). Has Apple changed its reporting policy regarding segment information? Explain.

COMPARATIVE ANALYSIS

A1

APPLE

GOOGLE

BTN 7-2   Key figures for Apple and Google follow ($ millions).

Apple Segment	Current Year		One Year Prior	
	Segment Revenue	Segment Assets	Segment Revenue	Segment Assets
Domestic..................	$ 81,732	$12,022	$ 68,909	$ 9,108
International	151,983	11,762	113,886	12,394

Google Segment	Current Year		One Year Prior	
	Segment Revenue	Segment Assets	Segment Revenue	Segment Assets
Domestic..................	$34,810	$43,686	$29,482	$37,421
International	40,179	13,661	36,519	13,110

Required

1. Compute the ratio of segment revenue divided by segment assets for each of the segments of Apple and Google for the most recent year shown.
2. Interpret and comment on your results from part 1.

BTN 7-3 Erica Gray, CPA, is a sole practitioner. She has been practicing as an auditor for 10 years. Recently a long-standing audit client asked Gray to design and implement an integrated computer-based accounting information system. The fees associated with this additional engagement with the client are very attractive. However, Gray wonders if she can remain objective on subsequent audits in her evaluation of the client's accounting system and its records if she was responsible for its design and implementation. Gray knows that professional auditing standards require her to remain independent in fact and appearance from her auditing clients.

ETHICS CHALLENGE

C1

Required

1. What do you believe auditing standards are mainly concerned with when they require independence in fact? In appearance?

2. Why is it important that auditors remain independent of their clients?

3. Do you think Gray can accept this engagement and remain independent? Justify your response.

BTN 7-4 Your friend, Wendy Geiger, owns a small retail store that sells candies and nuts. Geiger acquires her goods from a few select vendors. She generally makes purchase orders by phone and on credit. Sales are primarily for cash. Geiger keeps her own manual accounting system using a general journal and a general ledger. At the end of each business day, she records one summary entry for cash sales. Geiger recently began offering items in creative gift packages. This has increased sales substantially, and she is now receiving orders from corporate and other clients who order large quantities and prefer to buy on credit. As a result of increased credit transactions in both purchases and sales, keeping the accounting records has become extremely time-consuming. Geiger wants to continue to maintain her own manual system and calls you for advice. Write a memo to her advising how she might modify her current manual accounting system to accommodate the expanded business activities. Geiger is accustomed to checking her ledger by using a trial balance. Your memo should explain the advantages of what you propose and of any other verification techniques you recommend.

COMMUNICATING IN PRACTICE

C2 C3

BTN 7-5 Access the December 16, 2015, filing of the fiscal 2015 10-K report for **HP** (ticker: HPQ) at SEC.gov. Read its Note 2, which details HP's segment information, and answer the following.

1. HP's operations are divided among which seven business segments?

2. In fiscal year 2015, which segment had the largest dollar amount of operating income (titled "Earnings from operations")? Which segment had the largest amount of assets?

3. Compute the return on assets for each segment for fiscal year 2015. Use operating income and average total assets by segment for your calculation. Which segment has the highest return on assets?

TAKING IT TO THE NET

A1

BTN 7-6 Each member of the team is to assume responsibility for one of the following tasks:

a. Journalizing in the purchases journal.

b. Journalizing in the cash disbursements journal.

c. Maintaining and verifying the accounts payable ledger.

d. Journalizing in the sales journal and the general journal.

e. Journalizing in the cash receipts journal.

f. Maintaining and verifying the accounts receivable ledger.

The team should abide by the following procedures in carrying out responsibilities.

TEAMWORK IN ACTION

C3 P1 P2

Required

1. After tasks *a–f* are assigned, each team member is to quickly read the list of transactions in Problem 7-1A, identifying with initials the journal in which each transaction is to be recorded. Upon completion, the team leader is to read transaction dates, and the appropriate team member is to vocalize responsibility. Any disagreement between teammates must be resolved.

Continued on next page . . .

2. Journalize and continually update subsidiary ledgers. Journal recorders should alert teammates assigned to subsidiary ledgers when an entry must be posted to their subsidiary ledger.

3. Team members responsible for tasks *a*, *b*, *d*, and *e* are to summarize and prove journals; members responsible for tasks *c* and *f* are to prepare both payables and receivables schedules.

4. The team leader is to take charge of the general ledger, rotating team members to obtain amounts to be posted. The person responsible for a journal must complete posting references in that journal. Other team members should verify the accuracy of account balance computations. To avoid any abnormal account balances, post in the following order: P, S, G, R, D. (*Note:* Posting any necessary individual general ledger amounts is also done at this time.)

5. The team leader is to read out general ledger account balances while another team member fills in the trial balance form. Concurrently, one member should keep a running balance of debit account balance totals and another credit account balance totals. Verify the final total of the trial balance and the schedules. If necessary, the team must resolve any errors. Turn in the trial balance and schedules to the instructor.

ENTREPRENEURIAL DECISION

P1

BTN 7-7   Refer to the chapter's opening feature about Aaron, Dylan, Jeff, and Sam and their company, Box. Their company deals with numerous suppliers and customers, and their cloud storage needs.

Required

1. Identify the special journals that Box would be likely to use in its operations. Also identify any subsidiary ledgers that it would likely use.

2. Box hopes to double yearly sales within five years from its current $10 million annual assumed amount. Also assume that its sales growth projections are as follows.

Year	One Year Hence	Two Years Hence	Three Years Hence	Four Years Hence	Five Years Hence
Projected growth in sales (from the preceding year)	0%	20%	15%	25%	20%

Estimate Box's projected sales for each year (round to the nearest dollar). If this pattern of sales growth holds, will Box achieve its goal of doubling sales in five years?

GLOBAL DECISION

A1

Samsung

BTN 7-8   Access and refer to the December 31, 2015, annual report for Samsung at samsung.com/us/aboutsamsung/investor_relations/financial_information/financial_statement.html.

Required

1. Identify its footnote #33 to its financial statements on segment information and locate its part (B), titled "Regional information." List its five regional segments.

2. What two items of accounting information does it disclose for each of its regional segments? (Answers need only list titles for the accounting line items, not numbers, disclosed for each segment.)

GLOBAL VIEW

This section discusses similarities and differences between U.S. GAAP and IFRS regarding system principles and components, and special journals.

System Principles and Components   Both U.S. GAAP and IFRS aim for high-quality financial reporting. That aim implies that sound information system principles and components are applied worldwide. However, while system principles and components are fundamentally similar across the globe, culture and other realities often mean different emphases are placed on the mix of system controls. BMW provides the following description of its system controls:

> The internal control system ensures that all the information needed to achieve the objectives set for the internal control system is made available to those responsible in an appropriate and timely manner. Controls are carried out with the aid of the IT applications, thus reducing the incidence of process risks.

Special Journals   Accounting systems for recording sales, purchases, cash receipts, and cash disbursements are similar worldwide. Although the exact structure of special journals is unique to each company, the basic structure is identical. Companies desire to apply accounting in an efficient manner. Accordingly, systems that employ special journals are applied worldwide.

 Global View Assignments

Discussion Question 14

Quick Study 7-10

BTN 7-8

chapter 8

Cash, Fraud, and Internal Controls

Chapter Preview

FRAUD AND INTERNAL CONTROL

C1 Purpose and principles of controls

Technology and controls

Limitations of controls

NTK 8-1

CONTROL OF CASH

C2 Definition and reporting of cash

P1 Control of cash receipts and cash disbursements

NTK 8-2

TOOLS OF CONTROL AND ANALYSIS

P2 Control of petty cash

P3 Bank reconciliation as a control tool

A1 Assessing liquidity

NTK 8-3, 8-4

Learning Objectives

CONCEPTUAL

C1 Define internal control and identify its purpose and principles.

C2 Define cash and cash equivalents and explain how to report them.

ANALYTICAL

A1 Compute the days' sales uncollected ratio and use it to assess liquidity.

PROCEDURAL

P1 Apply internal control to cash receipts and disbursements.

P2 Explain and record petty cash fund transactions.

P3 Prepare a bank reconciliation.

P4 *Appendix 8A*—Describe use of documentation and verification to control cash disbursements.

© Andy Buchanan/AFP/Getty Images

Free For All

PALO ALTO, CA—How do you get one million people to sign up on an app waitlist? Well, you offer something for free! Former college roommates Vlad Tenev and Baiju Bhatt offer commission-free stock trades through their app, **Robinhood** (**Robinhood.com**). "We view this as a revolution," explains Vlad. "We saw an opportunity to provide a product that makes investing easy, is mobile first, and dramatically reduces cost."

If Robinhood does not charge fees for trading stocks, and it has no minimum balance, how does it make money? According to Vlad, "if you have cash in your Robinhood account, we can put it into certain products that earn low interest rates." He adds, we also "offer premium trading services like margin lending."

To date, over $500 million worth of transactions have been executed using the Robinhood app. As the number of transactions grew, Vlad and Baiju set up internal controls to protect against errors and fraud. "This part hasn't been easy," laments Vlad.

The two co-founders learned the value of internal controls the hard way. On the app's launch day, customers signed up for accounts on Robinhood. One of the internal controls was to have customers confirm e-mail addresses. Unfortunately, as Vlad recalls, "the e-mails weren't working and nobody was getting a confirmation."

Robinhood resolved the e-mail issue, but the crisis served as a lesson for Vlad and Baiju to focus more on internal controls. "Without [internal controls], we wouldn't have been able to run our business," insists Vlad, "and since that point, we've been fortunate."

Vlad and Baiju also focus on cash controls. With millions of dollars in Robinhood's customer cash accounts, cash controls are crucial. "The margin for error is nonexistent," insists Baiju. These include controls over cash receipts, cash disbursements, and petty cash. The use of bank reconciliations helps with Robinhood's management of cash. Adds Baiju, "I think that [control of cash] is the biggest challenge at the early stage of a business."

The average age of Robinhood users is 26. Explains Vlad, "we're making investing accessible to young people."

> *"Keep experimenting until you find something that works"*
> **—Vlad Tenev**

Sources: *Robinhood website,* January 2017; *Huffington Post,* August 2015; *Bloomberg,* March 2015; *Tech Crunch,* September 2014

FRAUD AND INTERNAL CONTROL

C1_____

Define internal control and
identify its purpose and
principles.

This section describes internal control and its fundamental principles. We also discuss the impact of technology on internal control and the limitations of control procedures.

Purpose of Internal Control

Managers (or owners) of small businesses often control the entire operation. They know from personal contact and observation whether the business is actually receiving the assets and services paid for. Most companies cannot maintain personal supervision and must delegate responsibilities and rely on formal procedures in controlling business activities.

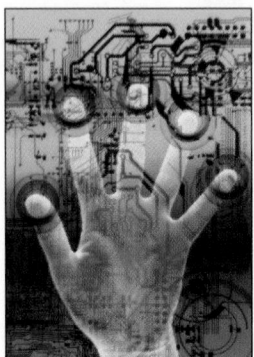

© Victor Habbick Visions/Corbis

Internal Control System   Managers use an internal control system to monitor and control business activities. An **internal control system** consists of the policies and procedures managers use to

- Protect assets.
- Ensure reliable accounting.
- Promote efficient operations.
- Uphold company policies.

Managers value internal control systems because they can prevent avoidable losses, help managers plan operations, and monitor company and employee performance. For example, internal controls for health care must protect patient records and privacy. Internal controls do not provide guarantees, but they lower the risk of loss.

Sarbanes-Oxley Act (SOX)   The **Sarbanes-Oxley Act (SOX)** requires managers and auditors of companies whose stock is traded on an exchange (called *public companies*) to document and certify the system of internal controls. Following are some of the specific requirements:

- Executives and boards of directors must install effective internal controls.
- Auditors must evaluate internal controls.
- Violators receive harsh penalties—up to 25 years in prison with severe fines.
- Auditors' work overseen by the *Public Company Accounting Oversight Board* (PCAOB).

SOX has greatly impacted companies, and the costs of its implementation are high. Importantly, SOX requires that managers document and assess the effectiveness of all internal control processes that can impact financial reporting. SOX also requires that auditors provide an opinion on managers' documentation and assessment. The benefits include greater confidence in accounting systems and their related reports. However, the public continues to debate the costs versus the benefits of SOX. Costs of complying with SOX are reported to average $4 million per company (Financial Executives Institute).

Principles of Internal Control

Internal control policies and procedures vary from company to company based on the nature and size of the business. Certain fundamental internal control principles apply to all companies. The **principles of internal control** are to

1. Establish responsibilities.
2. Maintain adequate records.
3. Insure assets and bond key employees.
4. Separate recordkeeping from custody of assets.
5. Divide responsibility for related transactions.
6. Apply technological controls.
7. Perform regular and independent reviews.

...a control system
is only as strong
as its weakest link

This section explains these seven principles and describes how internal control procedures minimize the risk of fraud and theft. These procedures also increase the reliability and accuracy of accounting records. A framework for how these seven principles improve the quality of financial reporting is provided by the **Committee of Sponsoring Organizations (COSO)** (COSO.org). Specifically, these principles link to five aspects of internal control: control activities, control environment, risk assessment, monitoring, and communication.

Point: Sarbanes-Oxley Act (SOX) requires that each annual report contain an *internal control report*, which must: (1) state managers' responsibility for establishing and maintaining adequate internal controls for financial reporting and (2) assess the effectiveness of those controls.

Establish Responsibilities Proper internal control means that responsibility for a task is clearly established and assigned to one person. When a problem occurs in a company where responsibility is not established, determining who is at fault is difficult. For instance, if two salesclerks share the same cash register and there is a cash shortage, neither clerk can be held accountable. To prevent this problem, one clerk might be given responsibility for handling all cash sales. Alternately, a company can use a register with separate cash drawers for each clerk.

Point: Many companies have a mandatory vacation policy for employees who handle cash. When another employee must cover for the one on vacation, it is more difficult to hide cash frauds.

Maintain Adequate Records Good recordkeeping helps protect assets and ensures that employees use prescribed procedures. Reliable records are also a source of information that managers use to monitor company activities. When detailed records of equipment are kept, for instance, items are unlikely to be lost or stolen without detection. Similarly, transactions are less likely to be entered in wrong accounts if a chart of accounts is set up and carefully used. Preprinted forms and internal documents are also designed for use in a good internal control system. When sales slips are properly designed, for instance, sales personnel can record information efficiently with less chance of errors or delays to customers. When sales slips are prenumbered and controlled, each one issued is the responsibility of one salesperson, preventing the salesperson from pocketing cash by making a sale and destroying the sales slip. Computerized point-of-sale systems achieve the same control results.

Commercial Law League of America
Commercial Collection Agency
Association
Certificate of Bond Coverage
This is to certify that
«Company»

A member of the Commercial Collection Agency Association of the Commercial Law League of America has in place for the benefit of its customer's indemnity bond coverage totaling 500,000. The insurance afforded is subject to all terms, exclusions and conditions of such policies. Copies of the original bonds and the current status of the bonds can be obtained by writing:

Jeff Henderson
Executive Vice President
Commercial Law League of America
1000 N. Rand Rd., Suite 214
Wauconda, IL 60084

Jeff Henderson, EVP

Policy effective dates:
August 1, 2015 - July 31, 2016

Certificate Number: 982

Courtesy of Commercial Collection Agency Association of the Commercial Law League of America

Insure Assets and Bond Key Employees Good internal control means that assets are adequately insured against casualty and that employees handling large amounts of cash and easily transferable assets are bonded. An employee is *bonded* when a company purchases an insurance policy, or a bond, against losses from theft by that employee. Bonding reduces the risk of loss. It also discourages theft because bonded employees know the bonding company will investigate reported theft.

Decision Insight

Asset Theft Control A technique exists for marking physical assets. It involves embedding a less than one-inch-square tag of fibers that creates a unique optical signature recordable by scanners. Manufacturers hope to embed tags in everything from smartphones and credit cards to designer clothes for purposes of internal control and efficiency. ■

© Ingram Publishing

Separate Recordkeeping from Custody of Assets A person who controls or has access to an asset must not have access to that asset's accounting records. This principle reduces the risk of theft or waste of an asset because the person with control over it knows that another person keeps its records. Also, a recordkeeper who does not have access to the asset has no reason to falsify records. This means that to steal an asset and hide the theft from the records, two or more people must *collude*—or agree in secret to commit the fraud.

Point: The Association of Certified Fraud Examiners (acfe.com) estimates that employee fraud costs companies more than $150,000 per incident.

Divide Responsibility for Related Transactions

Good internal control divides responsibility for a transaction or a series of related transactions between two or more individuals or departments. This is to ensure that the work of one individual acts as a check on the other to prevent fraud and errors. This principle, called *separation of duties,* does not mean duplication of work. Each employee or department should perform unduplicated effort. For example, when a company orders inventory, the task should be split among several employees. One employee submits a request to purchase inventory, a second employee approves the request, a third employee makes the payment, and a fourth employee records the transaction in the accounting system.

Apply Technological Controls

Cash registers, time clocks, and personal identification scanners are examples of devices that can improve internal control. A cash register with a locked-in tape or electronic file makes a record of each cash sale. A time clock registers the exact time an employee both arrives at and departs from the job. Mechanical change and currency counters quickly and accurately count amounts, and personal scanners limit access to only authorized individuals. Technological controls are an effective part of internal control systems.

Point: There's a new security device—a person's ECG (electrocardiogram) reading—that is as unique as a fingerprint and a lot harder to lose or steal than a PIN. ECGs can be read through fingertip touches. An ECG also shows that a living person is actually there, whereas fingerprint and facial recognition software can be fooled.

Decision Insight

Face to Face   Face recognition software snaps a digital picture of the face and converts key facial features—say, the distance between the eyes—into a series of numerical values. These can be stored on an ID or ATM card as a simple bar code to prohibit unauthorized access. ■

© Photoshot

Perform Regular and Independent Reviews

Changes in personnel, stress of time pressures, and technological advances present opportunities for shortcuts and lapses. To counter these factors, regular reviews of internal control systems are needed to ensure that procedures are followed. These reviews are preferably done by internal auditors not directly involved in the activities. Their impartial perspective encourages an evaluation of the efficiency as well as the effectiveness of the internal control system. Many companies also pay for audits by independent, external auditors. These external auditors test the company's financial records and evaluate the effectiveness of the internal control system.

Decision Maker

Entrepreneur   As owner of a start-up information services company, you hire a systems analyst. The analyst sees that your company employs only two workers. She recommends you improve controls and says that as owner you must serve as a compensating control. What does the analyst mean? ■   [*Answer:* To achieve proper separation of duties, a minimum of three employees is required. Transaction authorization, recording, and asset custody are ideally handled by three employees. Many small businesses do not employ three workers. In such cases, an owner must exercise more oversight to make sure that the lack of separation of duties does not result in fraudulent transactions.]

Technology, Fraud, and Internal Control

The fundamental principles of internal control are relevant no matter what the technological state of the accounting system, from purely manual to fully automated systems. Technology allows us quicker access to information and improves managers' abilities to monitor and control business activities. This section describes technological impacts we must be alert to.

Reduced Processing Errors

Technologically advanced systems reduce, but do not eliminate, errors in processing information. Less human involvement can cause data entry errors to go undiscovered. Moreover, errors in software can produce consistent but inaccurate processing of transactions.

Point: Evidence of any internal control failure for a company reduces user confidence in its financial statements.

More Extensive Testing of Records   A review of electronic records can include broader testing when information is easily accessible. When accounting records are kept manually, only small samples of data are usually tested. When data are accessible with technology, large samples or even the entire database can quickly be tested.

Limited Evidence of Processing   Many data processing steps are increasingly done by computer. Accordingly, fewer hard-copy items of documentary evidence are available for review. Yet technologically advanced systems can provide new evidence. They can, for instance, record who made the entries, the date and time, the source of the entry, and so on. Technology can also be designed to require the use of passwords or other identification before access to the system is granted. This means that internal control depends more on the design and operation of the information system and less on the analysis of its resulting documents.

Separation of Duties   A company with a smaller workforce risks losing separation of duties. For instance, the person who designs and programs the information system should not operate it. The company must also separate control over programs and files from the activities related to cash receipts and disbursements. For instance, a computer operator should not control check-writing activities.

Increased E-Commerce   **Amazon** and **eBay** are examples of successful e-commerce companies. Most companies have some e-commerce transactions. All such transactions involve at least three risks. (1) *Credit card number theft* is a risk of using, transmitting, and storing such data online. This increases the cost of e-commerce. (2) *Computer viruses* are malicious programs that attach themselves to innocent files for purposes of infecting and harming other files and programs. (3) *Impersonation* online can result in charges of sales to bogus accounts, purchases of inappropriate materials, and the unknowing giving up of confidential information to hackers. Companies use both firewalls and encryption to combat some of these risks— firewalls are points of entry to a system that require passwords to continue and encryption is a mathematical process to rearrange contents that cannot be read without the process code. Nearly 5% of Americans already report being victims of identity theft, and roughly 10 million say their privacy has been compromised.

"Worst case of identity theft I've ever seen!"

Copyright 2004 by Randy Glasbergen. www.glasbergen.com

Decision Insight

Controls and Social Media   Should controls extend to social media? What controls exist for a company's social media strategy? Controls over social media might have impacted **Facebook**'s decision to experiment with the "mood" of posts to see if it affected the happiness of the content posted by those users. **OKCupid** later acknowledged its own experiments on members. Given the potential financial impacts of such activities, can companies afford not to adopt control systems over social media? ■

Limitations of Internal Control

Internal control policies and procedures have limitations from either (1) the human element or (2) the cost-benefit principle.

Internal control policies and procedures are applied by people. This human element creates limitations that we can categorize as either (1) human error or (2) human fraud. *Human error* occurs from carelessness, misjudgment, or confusion. *Human fraud* is people intentionally defeating internal controls, such as *management override,* for personal gain. Human fraud is driven by the *triple threat* of fraud:

- **Opportunity**—refers to internal control weaknesses in a business.
- **Pressure**—refers to financial, family, society, and other stresses to succeed.
- **Rationalization**—refers to employees justifying fraudulent behavior.

Financial Pressure

The second limitation on internal control is the *cost-benefit principle,* which says that the costs of internal controls must not exceed their benefits. Analysis of costs and benefits must consider all factors, including the impact on morale. Most companies, for instance, have a legal right to read employees' e-mails, yet companies rarely do unless there is evidence of potential harm to the company.

Hacker's Guide to Cyberspace

Pharming Viruses attached to e-mails and websites load software onto your PC that monitors keystrokes; when you sign on to financial websites, it steals your passwords.

Phishing Hackers send e-mails to you posing as banks; you are asked for information using fake websites where they reel in your passwords and personal data.

Wi-Phishing Cybercrooks set up wireless networks hoping you will use them to connect to the web; your passwords and data are stolen as you use their network.

Bot-Networking Hackers send remote-control programs to your PC that take control to send out spam and viruses; they even rent your bot to other cybercrooks.

Typo-Squatting Hackers set up websites with addresses similar to legit outfits; when you make a typo and hit their sites, they infect your PC with viruses or take them over as bots.

Hackers also have their own self-identification system:
- *Hackers,* or *external attackers,* crack systems and take data for illicit gains (as unauthorized users).
- *Rogue insiders,* or *internal attackers,* crack systems and take data for illicit gains or revenge (as authorized users).
- *Ethical hackers,* or *good-guys* or *white-hat hackers,* crack systems and reveal vulnerabilities to enhance controls.
- *Crackers,* or *criminal hackers,* crack systems illegally for illicit gains, fame, or revenge.

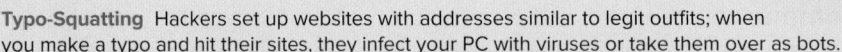

Decision Insight

Fraud Discovery The Association of Certified Fraud Examiners (ACFE) reports that 43% of frauds are detected from a "tip," which is much higher than the next three detection sources (13% from management review, 17% from internal audit, and 6% by accident). The top source for a tip is an employee, followed by a customer and a vendor—see graph. [Source: 2016 Report to the Nations, ACFE (acfe.com).] ■

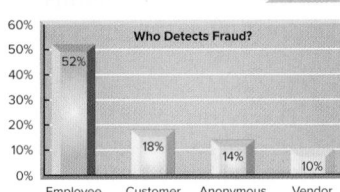

NEED-TO-KNOW   **8-1**

Internal Controls

C1

Identify the following phrases/terms as best associated with the (a) purposes of an internal control system, (b) principles of internal control, or (c) limitations of internal control.

1. ____ Protect assets
2. ____ Establish responsibilities
3. ____ Human error
4. ____ Maintain adequate records
5. ____ Apply technological controls
6. ____ Ensure reliable accounting
7. ____ Insure assets and bond key employees

8. ____ Human fraud
9. ____ Separate recordkeeping from custody of assets
10. ____ Divide responsibility for related transactions
11. ____ Cost-benefit principle
12. ____ Promote efficient operations
13. ____ Perform regular and independent reviews
14. ____ Uphold company policies

Do More: QS 8-1, E 8-1, E 8-2, P 8-1

Solution

1. a **2.** b **3.** c **4.** b **5.** b **6.** a **7.** b **8.** c **9.** b **10.** b **11.** c **12.** a **13.** b **14.** a

CONTROL OF CASH

Cash is the most liquid of all assets and easily hidden and moved. An effective system of internal controls protects cash assets and it should meet three basic guidelines:

1. Handling cash is separate from recordkeeping of cash.
2. Cash receipts are promptly deposited in a bank.
3. Cash disbursements are made by check (or electronic funds transfer, EFT).

The first guideline applies separation of duties to minimize errors and fraud. When duties are separated, two or more people must collude to steal cash and conceal this action in the accounting records. The second guideline uses immediate (say, daily) deposits of all cash receipts to produce a timely independent record of the cash received. It also reduces the likelihood of cash theft (or loss). The third guideline uses payments by check to develop an independent bank record of cash disbursements. This guideline also reduces the risk of cash theft (or loss).

Cash, Cash Equivalents, and Liquidity

Good accounting systems help in managing the amount of cash and controlling who has access to it. **Liquidity** refers to a company's ability to pay for its near-term obligations. Cash and similar assets are called **liquid assets** because they can be readily used to settle obligations.

    Cash includes currency, coins, and deposits in bank accounts, checking accounts, and savings accounts. Cash also includes items that are acceptable for deposit in these accounts such as customer checks, cashier's checks, certified checks, and money orders. **Cash equivalents** are short-term, highly liquid investment assets meeting two criteria: (1) readily convertible to a known cash amount and (2) sufficiently close to their due date so that their market value is not sensitive to interest rate changes. Only investments purchased within three months of their due date usually satisfy these criteria. Examples of cash equivalents are short-term investments in assets such as U.S. Treasury bills and money market funds. Most companies combine cash equivalents with cash as a single item on the balance sheet.

C2

Define cash and cash equivalents and explain how to report them.

Point: The most liquid assets are usually reported first on a balance sheet; the least liquid assets are reported last.

Point: Companies invest idle cash in cash equivalents to increase income.

Cash Management

One of the most common reasons companies fail is inability to manage cash. Companies must plan both cash receipts and cash payments. The goals of cash management are:

1. Plan cash receipts to meet cash payments when due.
2. Keep a minimum level of cash necessary to operate.

The *treasurer* of the company is responsible for cash management. Effective cash management involves applying the following cash management principles.

- **Encourage collection of receivables.** The more quickly customers and others pay the company, the more quickly that company can use the money. Some companies offer discounts for payments received early.
- **Delay payment of liabilities.** The more delayed a company is in paying others, the more time it has to use the money. Companies regularly wait to pay bills until the last possible day allowed.
- **Keep only necessary assets.** The less money a company has tied up in unused assets, the more money it has to invest in productive assets. Some companies lease warehouse space or rent equipment as needed instead of buying it.
- **Plan expenditures.** Companies must look at seasonal and business cycles to plan expenditures when money is available.
- **Invest excess cash.** Excess cash earns no return and should be invested. Excess cash from seasonal cycles can be placed in a short-term investment for interest. Excess cash beyond what's needed for regular business should be invested in productive assets like factories and inventories.

Days' Cash Expense Coverage The ratio of *cash (and cash equivalents) to average daily cash expenses* indicates the number of days a company can operate without additional cash inflows. It reflects on company liquidity and on the potential of excess cash. ∎

Control of Cash Receipts

P1

Apply internal control to cash receipts and disbursements.

Internal control of cash receipts ensures that cash received is properly recorded and deposited. Cash receipts can arise from transactions such as cash sales, collections of customer accounts, receipts of interest earned, bank loans, sales of assets, and owner investments. This section explains internal control over two important types of cash receipts: over-the-counter and by mail.

Over-the-Counter Cash Receipts For purposes of internal control, over-the-counter cash receipts from sales should be recorded on a cash register at the time of each sale. To help ensure that correct amounts are entered, each register should be located so customers can read the amounts entered. Clerks also should be required to enter each sale before wrapping merchandise and to give the customer a receipt for each sale. The design of each cash register should provide a permanent, locked-in record of each transaction. In many systems, the register is directly linked with computing and accounting services. Less advanced registers record each transaction on a paper tape or electronic file locked inside the register.

Point: Convenience stores sometimes display a sign: *Cashier has no access to cash in safe.* Such signs help deter theft and holdups.

Custody over cash should be separate from recordkeeping. For over-the-counter cash receipts, this separation begins with the cash sale. The clerk who has access to cash in the register should not have access to its record. At the end of the clerk's work period, the clerk should count the cash in the register, record the amount, and turn over the cash and a record of its amount to the company cashier. The cashier, like the clerk, has access to the cash but should not have access to accounting records (or the register tape or file). A third employee, often a supervisor, compares the record of total register transactions (or the register tape or file) with the cash receipts reported by the cashier. This record is the basis for a journal entry recording over-the-counter cash receipts. The third employee has access to the records for cash but not to the actual cash. The clerk and the cashier have access to cash but not to the accounting records. None of them can make a mistake or divert cash without the difference being revealed (see the following diagram).

Point: Many businesses have signs that read: If you receive no receipt, your purchase is free! This helps ensure that clerks ring up all transactions on registers.

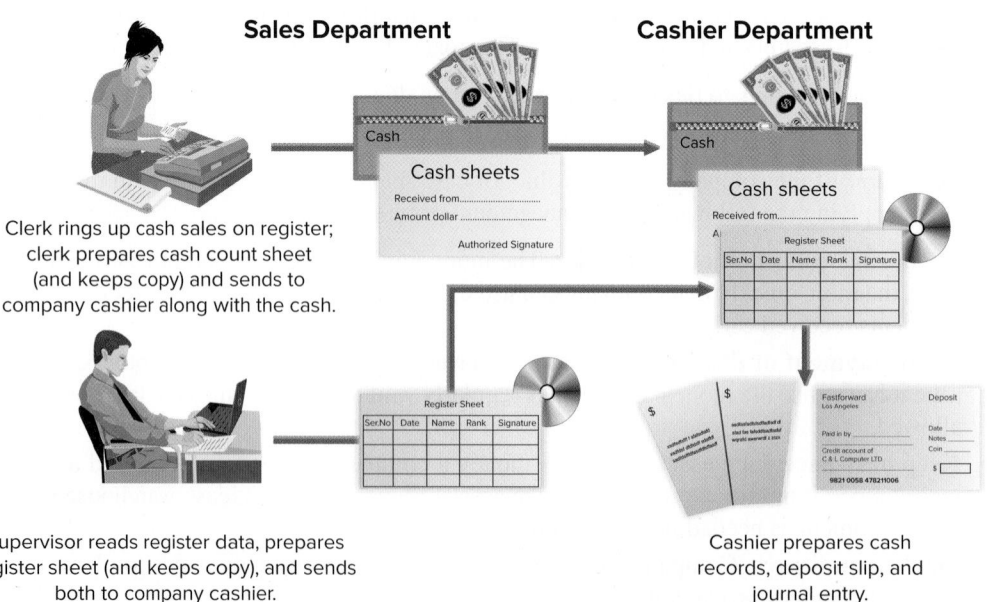

Sales Department

Clerk rings up cash sales on register; clerk prepares cash count sheet (and keeps copy) and sends to company cashier along with the cash.

Supervisor reads register data, prepares register sheet (and keeps copy), and sends both to company cashier.

Cashier Department

Cashier prepares cash records, deposit slip, and journal entry.

Point: Retailers often require cashiers to restrictively endorse checks immediately on receipt by stamping them "For deposit only."

Cash Over and Short Sometimes errors in making change are discovered from differences between the cash in a cash register and the record of the amount of cash receipts. One or more customers can be given too much or too little change. This means that at the end of a work period, the cash in a cash register might not equal the record of cash receipts. This difference is reported in the **Cash Over and Short** account, also called *Cash Short and Over,* which is an income statement account recording the income effects of cash overages and cash shortages. To illustrate, if a cash register's record shows $550 but the count of cash in the register is $555, the entry to record cash sales and its overage is

Cash..	555	
Cash Over and Short............................		5
Sales...		550
Record cash sales and a cash overage.		

Assets = Liabilities + Equity
+555   + 5
                    +550

Alternatively, if a cash register's record shows $625 but the count of cash in the register is $621, the entry to record cash sales and its shortage is

Cash..	621	
Cash Over and Short................................	4	
Sales...		625
Record cash sales and a cash shortage.		

Assets = Liabilities + Equity
+621   − 4
                    +625

Because customers are more likely to dispute being shortchanged than being given too much change, the Cash Over and Short account usually has a debit balance. A debit balance reflects an expense. It is reported on the income statement as part of selling, general, and administrative expenses. (Since the amount is usually small, it is often combined with other small expenses and reported as part of *miscellaneous expenses*—or as part of *miscellaneous revenues* if it has a credit balance.)

Point: Merchants begin a business day with a *change fund* in their cash register. The accounting for a change fund is similar to that for petty cash, including that for cash shortages or overages.

Cash Receipts by Mail   Control of cash receipts that arrive through the mail starts with the person who opens the mail. Preferably, two people are assigned the task of, and are present for, opening the mail. In this case, theft of cash receipts by mail requires collusion between these two employees. Specifically, the person(s) opening the mail enters a list (in triplicate) of money received. This list should contain a record of each sender's name, the amount, and an explanation of why the money was sent. The first copy is sent with the money to the cashier. A second copy is sent to the recordkeeper in the accounting area. A third copy is kept by the clerk(s) who opened the mail. The cashier deposits the money in a bank, and the recordkeeper records the amounts received in the accounting records.

This process reflects good internal control. That is, when the bank balance is reconciled by another person (explained later in the chapter), errors or acts of fraud by the mail clerks, the cashier, or the recordkeeper are revealed. They are revealed because the bank's record of cash deposited must agree with the records from each of the three. Moreover, if the mail clerks do not report all receipts correctly, customers will question their account balances. If the cashier does not deposit all receipts, the bank balance does not agree with the recordkeeper's cash balance. The recordkeeper and the person who reconciles the bank balance do not have access to cash and therefore have no opportunity to steal cash. This system makes errors and fraud highly unlikely. The exception is employee collusion.

 **Decision** Insight

Rapid Receipts   Walmart uses a network of information links with its point-of-sale cash registers to coordinate sales, purchases, and distribution. Its stores ring up tens of thousands of separate sales on heavy days. By using cash register information, the company can fix pricing mistakes quickly and capitalize on sales trends. Interestingly, Sam Walton, the founder, was a self-described distruster of computers. ■

Control of Cash Disbursements

Control of cash disbursements is especially important as most large thefts occur from payment of fictitious invoices. One key to controlling cash disbursements is to require all expenditures to be made by check. The only exception is small payments made from petty cash. Another key is to deny access to the accounting records to anyone other than the owner who has the authority to sign checks. A small-business owner often signs checks and knows from personal contact that the items being paid for are actually received. This arrangement is impossible in large businesses. Instead, internal control procedures must be substituted for personal contact. Such procedures are designed to assure the check signer that the obligations recorded are properly incurred and should be paid. This section describes these and other internal control procedures, including the voucher system and petty cash system.

Cash Budget   Projected cash receipts and cash disbursements are often summarized in a *cash budget.* Provided that sufficient cash exists for effective operations, companies wish to minimize the cash they hold because of its risk of theft and its low return versus investment opportunities.

Decision Insight

Lockbox   Some companies do not receive cash in the mail but, instead, elect to have customers send deposits directly to the bank using a *lockbox* system. Bank employees are charged with receipting the cash and depositing it in the correct business bank account. ■

Voucher System of Control

A **voucher system** is a set of procedures and approvals designed to control cash disbursements and the acceptance of obligations. The voucher system of control establishes procedures for

- Verifying, approving, and recording obligations for eventual cash disbursement.
- Issuing checks for payment of verified, approved, and recorded obligations.

A reliable voucher system follows standard procedures for every transaction. This applies even when multiple purchases are made from the same supplier.

A voucher system's control over cash disbursements begins when a company incurs an obligation that will result in payment of cash. A key factor in this system is that only approved departments and individuals are authorized to incur such obligations. The system limits the type of obligations that a department or individual can incur. In a large retail store, for instance, only a purchasing department should be authorized to incur obligations for merchandise inventory. Another key factor is that procedures for purchasing, receiving, and paying for merchandise are divided among several departments (or individuals). These departments include the one requesting the purchase, the purchasing department, the receiving department, and the accounting department. To coordinate and control responsibilities of these departments, a company uses several different business documents. Exhibit 8.1 shows how documents are accumulated in a **voucher,** which is an internal document (or file) used to accumulate information to control cash

Point: MCI, formerly WorldCom, paid a whopping $500 million in SEC fines for accounting fraud. Among the charges were that it inflated earnings by as much as $10 billion. Its CEO, Bernard Ebbers, was sentenced to 25 years.

EXHIBIT 8.1

Document Flow in a Voucher System

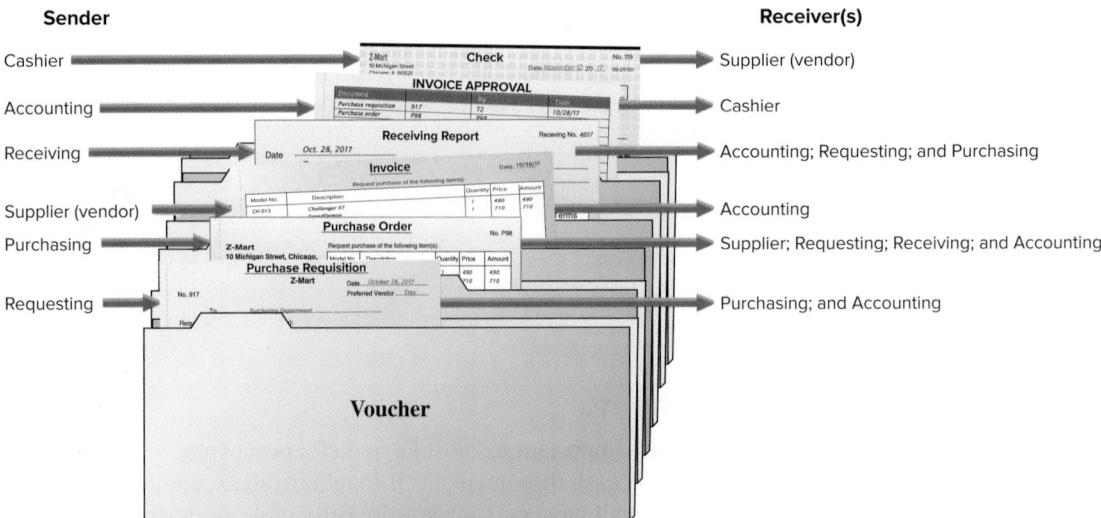

disbursements and to ensure that a transaction is properly recorded. This specific example begins with a *purchase requisition* and concludes with a *check* drawn against cash. Appendix 8A describes the documentation and verification necessary for a voucher system of control. It also describes the internal control objective served by each document.

A voucher system should be applied not only to purchases of inventory but to all expenditures. To illustrate, when a company receives a monthly telephone bill, it should review and verify the charges, prepare a voucher (file), and insert the bill. This transaction is then recorded with a journal entry. If the amount is currently due, a check is issued. If not, the voucher is filed for payment on its due date. If no voucher is prepared, verifying the invoice and its amount after several days or weeks can be difficult. Also, without records, a dishonest employee could collude with a dishonest supplier to get more than one payment for an obligation, payment for excessive amounts, or payment for goods and services not received. An effective voucher system helps prevent such frauds.

▨ Decision Insight

At Risk   The Association of Certified Fraud Examiners (ACFE) reports that 87% of fraud is from asset theft. Of those asset thefts, the graph here shows a few that stand out—in both frequency and median loss. Namely, cash is most frequently stolen through billing (22%) and theft (20%). However, losses are largest through check tampering ($158,000) and billing ($100,000). [Source: 2016 Report to the Nations, ACFE (acfe.com).] ▨

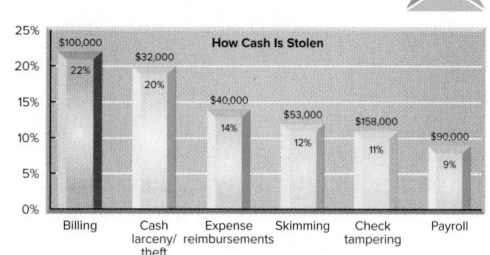

A good system of internal control for cash provides adequate procedures for protecting both cash receipts and cash disbursements. Which of the following statements are true regarding the control of cash receipts and cash disbursements?

_____ **1.** Over-the-counter cash receipts from sales should be recorded on a cash register at the time of each sale.

_____ **2.** Custody over cash should be separate from the recordkeeping of cash.

_____ **3.** For control of cash receipts that arrive through the mail, two people should be assigned the task of, and be present for, opening that mail.

_____ **4.** One key to controlling cash disbursements is to require that no expenditures be made by check; instead, all expenditures should be made from petty cash.

_____ **5.** A voucher system of control should be applied only to purchases of inventory and never to other expenditures.

Solution

1. True   **2.** True   **3.** True   **4.** False   **5.** False

NEED-TO-KNOW 8-2

Control of Cash Receipts and Payments

P1   C2

Do More: QS 8-3, E 8-3, E 8-4

Petty Cash System of Control   A basic principle for controlling cash disbursements is that all payments must be made by check. An exception to this rule is made for *petty cash disbursements,* which are the small payments required for items such as postage, courier fees, minor repairs, and low-cost supplies. To avoid the time and cost of writing checks for small amounts, a company sets up a petty cash fund to make small payments. (**Petty cash** activities are part of an *imprest system,* which designates advance money to establish the fund, to withdraw from the fund, and to reimburse the fund.)

Operating a Petty Cash Fund   Establishing a petty cash fund requires estimating the total amount of small payments likely to be made during a short period such as a week or month. A check is then drawn by the company cashier for an amount slightly in excess of this estimate. This check is recorded with a debit to the Petty Cash account (an asset) and a credit to Cash. The check is cashed and given to an employee designated as the *petty cashier* or *petty cash custodian.*

P2 _____

Explain and record petty cash fund transactions.

The petty cashier is responsible for keeping this cash safe, making payments from the fund, and keeping records of it in a secure place called the *petty cashbox*.

When each cash disbursement is made, the person receiving payment should sign a prenumbered *petty cash receipt,* also called *petty cash ticket*—see Exhibit 8.2. The petty cash receipt is then placed in the petty cashbox with the remaining money. Under this system, the sum of all receipts plus the remaining cash equals the total fund amount. A $100 petty cash fund, for instance, contains any combination of cash and petty cash receipts that totals $100 (examples are $80 cash plus $20 in receipts, or $10 cash plus $90 in receipts). Each disbursement reduces cash and increases the amount of receipts in the petty cashbox.

Point: A petty cash fund is used only for business expenses.

EXHIBIT 8.2

Petty Cash Receipt

Z-Mart	No. 9
PETTY CASH RECEIPT	
For *Freight charges*	
Date *November 5, 2017*	Approved by *fb Gull*
Charge to *Merchandise Inventory*	
Amount *$15.05*	Received by *Dk Fbb*

Point: Petty cash receipts with either no signature or a forged signature usually indicate misuse of petty cash. Companies respond with surprise petty cash counts for verification.

The petty cash fund should be reimbursed when it is nearing zero and at the end of an accounting period when financial statements are prepared. For this purpose, the petty cashier sorts the paid receipts by the type of expense or account and then totals the receipts. The petty cashier presents all paid receipts to the company cashier, who stamps all receipts *paid* so they cannot be reused, files them for recordkeeping, and gives the petty cashier a check for their sum. When this check is cashed and the money placed in the cashbox, the total money in the cashbox is restored to its original amount. The fund is now ready for a new cycle of petty cash payments.

Illustrating a Petty Cash Fund   To illustrate, assume Z-Mart establishes a petty cash fund on November 1 and designates one of its office employees as the petty cashier. A $75 check is drawn, cashed, and the proceeds given to the petty cashier. The entry to record the setup of this petty cash fund is

Assets = Liabilities + Equity
+75
−75

Nov. 1	Petty Cash	75	
	Cash		75
	Establish a petty cash fund.		

After the petty cash fund is established, the Petty Cash account is not debited or credited again unless the amount of the fund is changed.

Next, assume that Z-Mart's petty cashier makes several November payments from petty cash. Each person who receives payment is required to sign a receipt. On November 27, after making a $46.50 cash payment for tile cleaning, only $3.70 cash remains in the fund. The petty cashier then summarizes and totals the petty cash receipts as shown in Exhibit 8.3.

Point: Although *individual* petty cash disbursements are not evidenced by a check, the initial petty cash fund is evidenced by a check, and later petty cash expenditures are evidenced by a check to replenish them *in total*.

EXHIBIT 8.3

Petty Cash Payments Report

Z-MART	
Petty Cash Payments Report	
Miscellaneous Expense	
Nov. 27 Tile cleaning	$ 46.50
Merchandise Inventory (transportation-in)	
Nov. 5 Transport of merchandise purchased	15.05
Delivery Expense	
Nov. 18 Customer's package delivered	5.00
Office Supplies Expense	
Nov. 15 Purchase of office supplies immediately used	4.75
Total	$71.30

Point: This report can also include receipt number and names of those who approved and received cash payment (see Need-To-Know 8-3).

The petty cash payments report and all receipts are given to the company cashier in exchange for a $71.30 check to reimburse the fund. The petty cashier cashes the check and puts the $71.30 cash in the petty cashbox. The company records this reimbursement as follows.

Nov. 27	Miscellaneous Expenses.....................................	46.50	
	Merchandise Inventory.....................................	15.05	
	Delivery Expense..	5.00	
	Office Supplies Expense...................................	4.75	
	Cash*...		71.30
	*Reimburse petty cash. *$75 fund bal. − $3.70 cash remaining.*		

Assets = Liabilities + Equity
−71.30   −46.50
+15.05   − 5.00
                − 4.75

A petty cash fund is usually reimbursed at the end of an accounting period so that expenses are recorded in the proper period, even if the fund is not low on money. If the fund is not reimbursed at the end of a period, the financial statements would show both an overstated cash asset and understated expenses (or assets) that were paid out of petty cash. Some companies do not reimburse the petty cash fund at the end of each period if this amount is immaterial to users of financial statements.

Point: To avoid errors in recording petty cash reimbursement, follow these steps: (1) prepare payments report, (2) compute cash needed by subtracting cash remaining from total fund amount, (3) record entry, and (4) check "Dr. = Cr." in entry. Any difference is Cash Over and Short.

Increasing or Decreasing a Petty Cash Fund   A decision to increase or decrease a petty cash fund is often made when reimbursing it. To illustrate, assume Z-Mart decides to *increase* its petty cash fund from $75 to $100 on November 27 when it reimburses the fund. The entries required are to (1) reimburse the fund as usual (see the preceding November 27 entry) and (2) increase the fund amount as follows.

Nov. 27	Petty Cash	25	
	Cash		25
	Increase the petty cash fund amount from $75 to $100.		

Alternatively, if Z-Mart *decreases* the petty cash fund from $75 to $55 on November 27, the entry is

Nov. 27	Cash...	20	
	Petty Cash...		20
	Decrease the petty cash fund amount from $75 to $55.		

Cash Over and Short   Sometimes a petty cashier fails to get a receipt for payment or overpays for the amount due. When this occurs and the fund is later reimbursed, the petty cash payments report plus the cash remaining will not total to the fund balance. This mistake causes the fund to be *short*. This shortage is recorded as an expense in the reimbursing entry with a debit to the Cash Over and Short account. (An overage in the petty cash fund is recorded with a credit to Cash Over and Short in the reimbursing entry.)

To illustrate, prepare the June 1 entry to reimburse a $200 petty cash fund when its payments report shows $178 in miscellaneous expenses and $15 cash remains.

Summary of Petty Cash Accounting

Event	Petty Cash	Cash	Expenses
Set up fund........	Dr.	Cr.	—
Reimburse fund.....	—	Cr.	Dr.
Increase fund	Dr.	Cr.	—
Decrease fund......	Cr.	Dr.	—

$200 Petty Cash Fund

$15 Cash $7 Short $178 Receipts

June 1	Miscellaneous Expenses.....................................	178	
	Cash Over and Short.....................................	7	
	Cash*...		185
	*Reimburse petty cash. *$200 fund bal. − $15 cash remaining.*		

Decision Insight

Have a Clue   There are clues to fraudulent activities. Clues from accounting include (1) an increase in customer refunds—could be fake, (2) missing documents—could be used for fraud, (3) differences between bank deposits and cash receipts—could be cash embezzled, and (4) delayed recording—could reflect fraudulent records. Clues from employees include (1) lifestyle change—could be embezzlement, (2) too close with suppliers—could signal fraudulent transactions, and (3) failure to leave job, even for vacations—could conceal fraudulent activities. ■

NEED-TO-KNOW 8-3

Petty Cash System

P2

Bacardi Company established a $150 petty cash fund with Eminem as the petty cashier. When the fund balance reached $19 cash, Eminem prepared a petty cash payments report, which follows.

Petty Cash Payments Report

Receipt No.	Account Charged		Approved by	Received by
12	Delivery Expense..............	$ 29	Eminem	A. Smirnoff
13	Merchandise Inventory	18	Eminem	J. Daniels
15	(Omitted)	32	Eminem	C. Carlsberg
16	Miscellaneous Expense..........	41	(Omitted)	J. Walker
	Total	$120		

Required

1. Identify four internal control weaknesses from the petty cash payments report.
2. Prepare general journal entries to record:
   a. Establishment of the petty cash fund.
   b. Reimbursement of the fund. (Assume for this part only that petty cash Receipt No. 15 was issued for miscellaneous expenses.)
3. What is the Petty Cash account balance immediately before reimbursement? Immediately after reimbursement?

Solution

1. Four internal control weaknesses that are apparent from the payments report include:
   a. Petty cash Receipt No. 14 is missing. Its omission raises questions about the petty cashier's management of the fund.
   b. The $19 cash balance means that $131 has been withdrawn ($150 − $19 = $131). However, the total amount of the petty cash receipts is only $120 ($29 + $18 + $32 + $41). The fund is $11 short of cash ($131 − $120 = $11). Was petty cash Receipt No. 14 issued for $11? Management should investigate.
   c. The petty cashier (Eminem) did not sign petty cash Receipt No. 16. This omission could have been an oversight on his part or he might not have authorized the payment. Management should investigate.
   d. Petty cash Receipt No. 15 does not indicate which account to charge. This omission could have been an oversight on the petty cashier's part. Management could check with C. Carlsberg and the petty cashier (Eminem) about the transaction. Without further information, debit Miscellaneous Expense.

2. Petty cash general journal entries.
   a. Entry to establish the petty cash fund.

Petty Cash	150	
Cash..........................		150

   b. Entry to reimburse the fund.

Delivery Expense............................	29	
Merchandise Inventory	18	
Miscellaneous Expense ($41 + $32)	73	
Cash Over and Short	11	
Cash ($150 fund bal. − $19 cash rem.)		131

3. The Petty Cash account balance *always* equals its fund balance, in this case $150. This account balance does not change unless the fund is increased or decreased.

Do More: QS 8-4, E 8-5, E 8-6, P 8-2

BANKING ACTIVITIES AS CONTROLS

Banks help companies control cash. Banks safeguard cash, provide detailed and independent records of cash transactions, and are a source of cash financing. This section describes these services and the documents provided by banking activities that increase managers' control over cash.

Basic Bank Services

This section explains basic bank services—such as the bank account, the bank deposit, and checking—that help control of cash.

Bank Account, Deposit, and Check

A *bank account* is a record set up by a bank for a customer. It permits a customer to deposit money for safekeeping and helps control withdrawals. To limit access to a bank account, all persons authorized to write checks on the account must sign a **signature card,** which bank employees use to verify signatures on checks.

Point: Firms often have multiple bank accounts for different needs and for specific transactions such as payroll.

Each bank deposit is supported by a **deposit ticket,** which lists items such as currency, coins, and checks deposited along with their corresponding dollar amounts. The bank gives the customer a copy of the deposit ticket or a deposit receipt as proof of the deposit. Exhibit 8.4 shows one type of deposit ticket.

EXHIBIT 8.4

Deposit Ticket

Front

Back

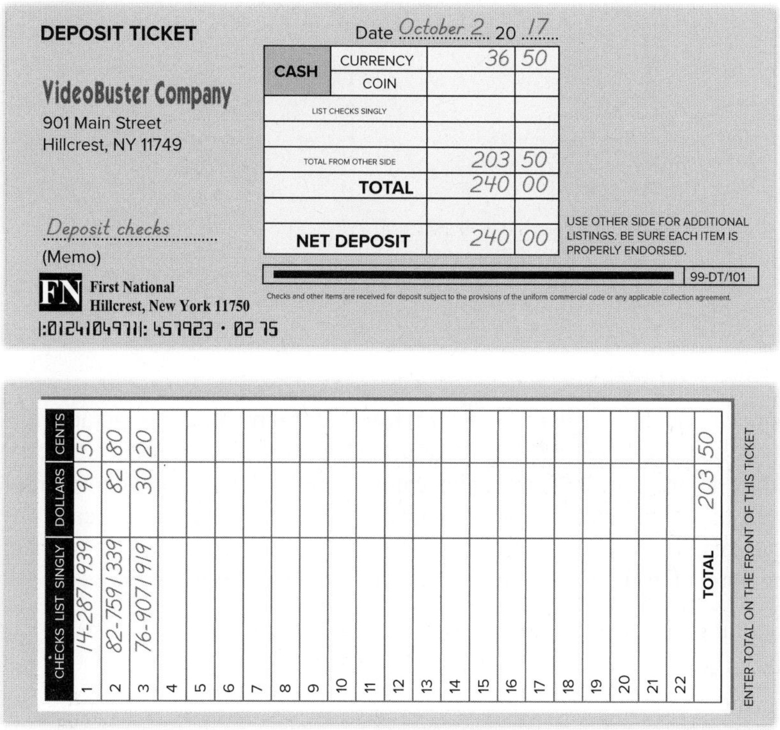
DEPOSIT TICKET

Date October 2 20 17

VideoBuster Company
901 Main Street
Hillcrest, NY 11749

CASH	CURRENCY	36	50
	COIN		
LIST CHECKS SINGLY			
TOTAL FROM OTHER SIDE		203	50
TOTAL		240	00
NET DEPOSIT		240	00

USE OTHER SIDE FOR ADDITIONAL LISTINGS. BE SURE EACH ITEM IS PROPERLY ENDORSED.

Deposit checks
(Memo)

99-DT/101

FN First National
Hillcrest, New York 11750

Checks and other items are received for deposit subject to the provisions of the uniform commercial code or any applicable collection agreement.

|:012410497|: 457923 • 02 75

	CHECKS LIST SINGLY	DOLLARS	CENTS
1	14-287/939	90	50
2	82-759/339	82	80
3	76-907/919	30	20
4			
5			
6			
7			
8			
9			
10			
11			
12			
13			
14			
15			
16			
17			
18			
19			
20			
21			
22			
	TOTAL	203	50

ENTER TOTAL ON THE FRONT OF THIS TICKET

To withdraw money from an account, the depositor can use a **check,** which is a document signed by the depositor instructing the bank to pay a specified amount of money to a designated recipient. A check involves three parties: a *maker* who signs the check, a *payee* who is the recipient, and a *bank* (or *payer*) on which the check is drawn. The bank provides a depositor the checks, which are serially numbered and imprinted with the name and address of both the depositor and bank. Exhibit 8.5 shows one type of check. It is attached to an optional *remittance advice* explaining the payment. The *memo* line is often used for a brief explanation.

Electronic Funds Transfer

Electronic funds transfer (EFT) is the electronic transfer of cash from one party to another. Companies are increasingly using EFT because of its convenience and low cost. We now commonly see items such as payroll, rent, utilities, insurance, and interest payments being handled by EFT. The bank statement lists cash withdrawals by EFT with the checks and other deductions. Cash receipts by EFT are listed with deposits and other additions.

EXHIBIT 8.5

Check with Remittance
Advice

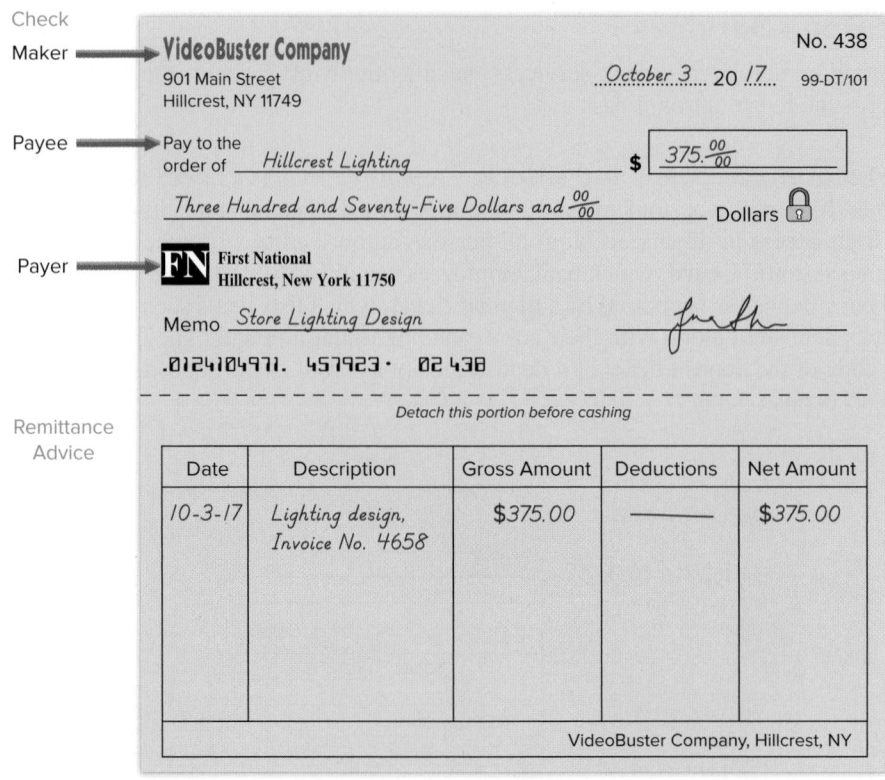

Check
Maker

Payee

Payer

Remittance
Advice

Bank Statement

Usually once a month, the bank sends a **bank statement** showing the activity in the account. Although a monthly statement is common, companies often regularly access information on their banking transactions. (Companies can choose to record any accounting adjustments required from the bank statement immediately or later, say, at the end of each day, week, month, or when reconciling a bank statement.) Different banks use different formats for their bank statements, but all of them include the following items of information:

1. Beginning-of-period balance of the depositor's account.
2. Checks and other debits decreasing the account during the period.
3. Deposits and other credits increasing the account during the period.
4. End-of-period balance of the depositor's account.

Exhibit 8.6 shows one type of bank statement. Part Ⓐ of Exhibit 8.6 summarizes changes in the account. Part Ⓑ lists paid checks along with other debits. Part Ⓒ lists deposits and credits to the account.

Enclosed with a bank statement is a list of the depositor's canceled checks (or the actual canceled checks) along with any debit or credit memoranda affecting the account. Banks usually show canceled checks electronically via online access to accounts. **Canceled checks** are checks the bank has paid and deducted from the customer's account during the period. We say such checks have *cleared the bank.* Other deductions that can appear on a bank statement include (1) service charges and fees assessed by the bank, (2) checks deposited that are uncollectible, (3) corrections of previous errors, (4) withdrawals through automated teller machines (ATMs), and (5) periodic payments arranged in advance by a depositor. (Most company checking accounts do not allow ATM withdrawals because of the company's desire to make all disbursements by check.) Except for service charges, the bank notifies the depositor of each deduction with a debit memorandum when the bank reduces the balance.

Transactions that increase the depositor's account include amounts the bank collects on behalf of the depositor and the corrections of previous errors. Credit memoranda notify the

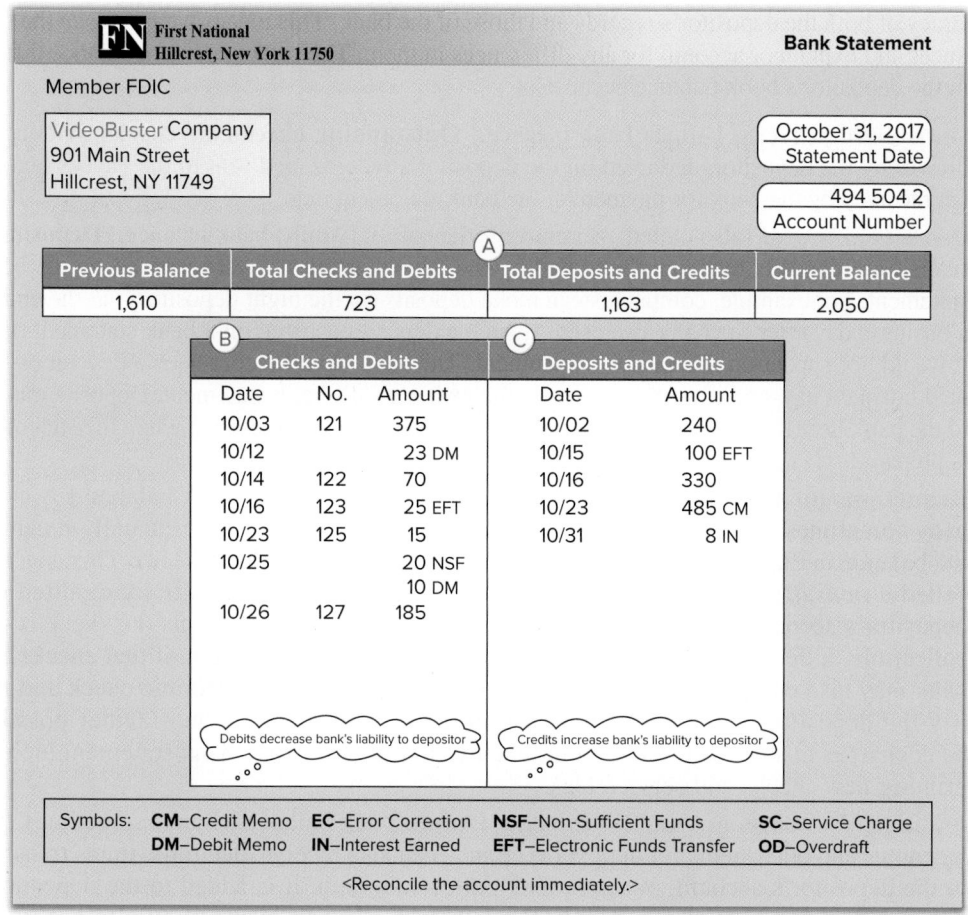

EXHIBIT 8.6

Bank Statement

Point: Debit memos (DM) from the bank produce credits on the depositor's books. Credit memos (CM) from the bank produce debits on the depositor's books.

Point: Many banks separately report other debits and credits apart from checks and deposits.

depositor of all increases when they are recorded. Banks that pay interest on checking accounts often compute the amount of interest earned on the average cash balance and credit it to the depositor's account each period. In Exhibit 8.6, the bank credits $8 of interest to the account.

Bank Reconciliation

When a company deposits all cash receipts and makes all cash payments (except petty cash) by check, it can use the bank statement to prove the accuracy of its cash records. This is done using a **bank reconciliation,** which is a report explaining any differences between the checking account balance according to the depositor's records and the balance reported on the bank statement. The figure below reflects this process, which we describe in the following sections.

P3

Prepare a bank reconciliation.

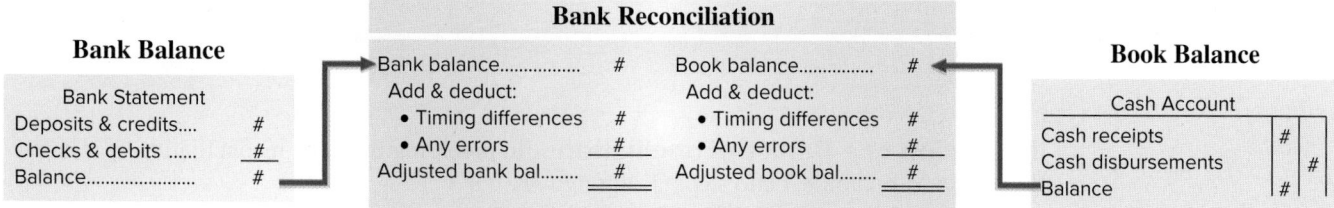

Purpose of Bank Reconciliation   The balance of a checking account reported on the bank statement rarely equals the balance in the depositor's accounting records. This is usually due to information that one party has that the other does not. We must therefore prove the accuracy of both the depositor's records and those of the bank. This means we *reconcile* the two balances and explain or account for any differences in them. The bank statement balance differs from the depositor's book balance because of:

- **Outstanding checks.** [Adjust bank balance.] **Outstanding checks** are checks written (or drawn) by the depositor, deducted on the depositor's records, and sent to the payees but not yet received by the bank for payment at the bank statement date.

- **Deposits in transit** (also called **outstanding deposits**). [Adjust bank balance.] **Deposits in transit** are deposits made and recorded by the depositor but not yet recorded on the bank statement. For example, companies can make deposits (in the night depository) at the end of a business day after the bank is closed. If such a deposit occurred on a bank statement date, it would not appear on this period's statement. The bank would record such a deposit on the next business day, and it would appear on the next period's bank statement. Deposits mailed to the bank near the end of a period also can be in transit and unrecorded when the statement is prepared.

- **Deductions for uncollectible items and for services.** [Adjust book balance.] A company sometimes deposits another party's check that is uncollectible (usually meaning the balance in that party's account is not large enough to cover the check). This check is called a *nonsufficient funds (NSF)* check. The bank would have initially credited the depositor's account for the amount of the check. When the bank learns the check is uncollectible, it debits (reduces) the depositor's account for the amount of that check. The bank may also charge the depositor a fee for processing an uncollectible check and notify the depositor of the deduction by sending a debit memorandum. Other possible bank charges to a depositor's account that are first reported on a bank statement include printing new checks and service fees.

- **Additions for collections and for interest.** [Adjust book balance.] Banks sometimes collect notes and other items for depositors. Banks can also receive electronic funds transfers to the depositor's account. When a bank collects an item, it is added to the depositor's account, less any service fee. The bank also sends a credit memorandum to notify the depositor of the transaction. The bank statement also includes a credit for any interest earned.

- **Errors.** [Adjust bank or book balance.] Both banks and depositors can make errors. Bank errors might not be discovered until the depositor prepares the bank reconciliation. Also, depositor errors are sometimes discovered when the bank balance is reconciled. Error testing includes: (a) comparing deposits on the bank statement with deposits in the accounting records and (b) comparing canceled checks on the bank statement with checks recorded in the accounting records.

Timing Differences   Following is a summary of the common timing differences. Each of these items has already been recorded by either the bank or the company, but not both.

Bank Balance Adjustments	Book Balance Adjustments
Add deposits in transit.	Add interest earned and unrecorded cash receipts.
Subtract outstanding checks.	Subtract bank fees and NSF checks.
Add or subtract corrections of bank errors.	Add or subtract corrections of book errors.

Illustration of a Bank Reconciliation   In preparing the bank reconciliation, it is helpful to refer to Exhibit 8.7 and steps ❶ through ❾.

❶ Identify the bank statement balance of the Cash account (*balance per bank*). VideoBuster's bank balance is $2,050.

❷ Identify and list any unrecorded deposits and any bank errors understating the bank balance. Add them to the bank balance. VideoBuster's $145 deposit placed in the bank's night depository on October 31 is not recorded on its bank statement.

Point: The person preparing the bank reconciliation should not be responsible for processing cash receipts, managing checks, or maintaining cash records.

Point: Businesses with few employees often allow recordkeepers to both write checks and keep the general ledger. If this is done, the owner must do the bank reconciliation.

EXHIBIT 8.7

Bank Reconciliation

VIDEOBUSTER
Bank Reconciliation
October 31, 2017

①	Bank statement balance............		$ 2,050	⑤	Book balance	$ 1,405
②	Add			⑥	Add	
	Deposit of Oct. 31 in transit......		145		Collect $500 note less $15 fee....	$485
			2,195		Interest earned.................	8 493
③	Deduct					1,898
	Outstanding checks			⑦	Deduct	
	No. 124....................	$150			Check printing charge...........	23
	No. 126....................	200	350		NSF check plus service fee.......	30 53
④	**Adjusted bank balance...........**		**$1,845**	⑧	**Adjusted book balance ....**	**$1,845**

⑨ Balances are equal (reconciled)

3 Identify and list any outstanding checks and any bank errors overstating the bank balance. Subtract them from the bank balance. VideoBuster's comparison of canceled checks with its books shows two checks outstanding: No. 124 for $150 and No. 126 for $200.

4 Compute the *adjusted bank balance,* also called the *corrected* or *reconciled balance.*

5 Identify the company's book balance of the Cash account (*balance per book*). VideoBuster's book balance is $1,405.

6 Identify and list any unrecorded credit memoranda from the bank, any interest earned, and errors understating the book balance. Add them to the book balance. VideoBuster's bank statement includes a credit memorandum showing the bank collected a note receivable for the company on October 23. The note's proceeds of $500 (minus a $15 collection fee) are credited to the company's account. VideoBuster's bank statement also shows a credit of $8 for interest earned on the average cash balance. There was no prior notification of this item, and it is not yet recorded.

7 Identify and list any unrecorded debit memoranda from the bank, any service charges, and errors overstating the book balance. Deduct them from the book balance. Debits on VideoBuster's bank statement that are not yet recorded include (a) a $23 charge for check printing and (b) an NSF check for $20 plus a related $10 processing fee. (The NSF check is dated October 16 and was included in the book balance.)

8 Compute the *adjusted book balance,* also called *corrected* or *reconciled balance.*

9 Verify that the two adjusted balances from steps 4 and 8 are equal. If so, they are reconciled. If not, check for accuracy and missing data to achieve reconciliation.

Point: Outstanding checks are identified by comparing canceled checks on the bank statement with checks recorded. This includes identifying any outstanding checks listed on the *previous* period's bank reconciliation that are not included in the canceled checks on this period's bank statement.

Adjusting Entries from a Bank Reconciliation A bank reconciliation often identifies unrecorded items that need recording by the company. In VideoBuster's reconciliation, the adjusted balance of $1,845 is the correct balance as of October 31. But the company's accounting records show a $1,405 balance. We must prepare journal entries to adjust the book balance to the correct balance. **Only items reconciling the *book balance* require adjustment.** A review of Exhibit 8.7 indicates that four entries are required.

Collection of Note The first entry is to record the proceeds of its note receivable collected by the bank less the expense of having the bank perform that service.

Oct. 31	Cash..	485	
	Collection Expense	15	
	Notes Receivable		500
	Record collection fee and proceeds		
	for a note collected by the bank.		

Assets = Liabilities + Equity
+485   −15
−500

Interest Earned The second entry records interest credited to its account by the bank.

Assets = Liabilities + Equity
+8   +8

Oct. 31	Cash	8	
	Interest Revenue		8
	Record interest earned on the cash		
	balance in checking account.		

Check Printing The third entry records expenses for the check printing charge.

Assets = Liabilities + Equity
−23   −23

Oct. 31	Miscellaneous Expenses.............................	23	
	Cash		23
	Check printing charge.		

NSF Check The fourth entry records the NSF check that is returned as uncollectible. The $20 check was originally received from T. Woods in payment of his account and then deposited. The bank charged $10 for handling the NSF check and deducted $30 total from VideoBuster's account. This means the entry must reverse the effects of the original entry made when the check was received and must record (add) the $10 bank fee.

Point: The company will try to collect the entire NSF amount of $30 from the customer.

Assets = Liabilities + Equity
+30
−30

Oct. 31	Accounts Receivable—T. Woods........................	30	
	Cash		30
	Charge Woods' account for $20 NSF check		
	and $10 bank fee.		

Point: Need-To-Know 8-4 shows an adjusting entry for an error correction.

After these four entries are recorded, the book balance of cash is adjusted to the correct amount of $1,845 (the adjusted book balance). The Cash T-account to the side shows the same computation, where entries are keyed to the numerical codes in Exhibit 8.7.

Cash			
Unadj. bal.	1,405		
⑥	485	⑦	23
⑥	8	⑦	30
Adj. bal.	1,845		

Decision Insight

Weakest Link The Association of Certified Fraud Examiners (ACFE) reports that the primary factor contributing to frauds is the lack of internal controls (29%), including the override of existing controls (20%). Together, this highlights the importance of internal controls (49%), including controls over cash. The chart shows the top five factors contributing to frauds. [Source: 2016 Report to the Nations, ACFE (acfe.com).] ■

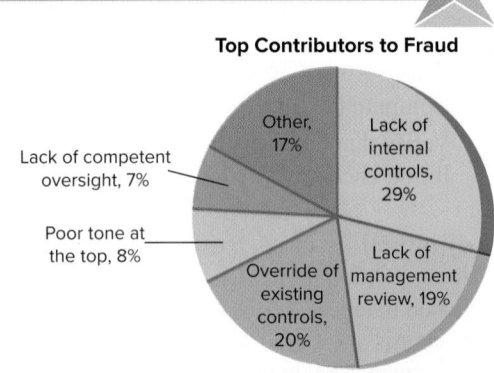

Top Contributors to Fraud

Lack of internal controls, 29%
Other, 17%
Lack of competent oversight, 7%
Poor tone at the top, 8%
Override of existing controls, 20%
Lack of management review, 19%

NEED-TO-KNOW 8-4

Bank Reconciliation

P3

The following information is available to reconcile Gucci's book balance of cash with its bank statement cash balance as of December 31, 2017.

a. The December 31 cash balance according to the accounting records is $1,610, and the bank statement cash balance for that date is $1,900.

b. Gucci's December 31 daily cash receipts of $800 were placed in the bank's night depository on December 31 but do not appear on the December 31 bank statement.

c. Check No. 6273 for $400 and Check No. 6282 for $100, both written and entered in the accounting records in December, are not among the canceled checks. Two checks, No. 6231 for $2,000 and No. 6242 for $200, were outstanding on the most recent November 30 reconciliation. Check No. 6231 is listed with the December canceled checks, but Check No. 6242 is not.

d. When the December checks are compared with entries in the accounting records, it is found that Check No. 6267 had been correctly drawn for $340 to pay for office supplies but was erroneously entered in the accounting records as $430.

e. A credit memorandum indicates that the bank collected $500 cash on a note receivable for the company, deducted a $30 collection fee, and credited the balance to the company's Cash account. Gucci had not recorded this transaction before receiving the statement.

f. Two debit memoranda are enclosed with the statement and are unrecorded at the time of the reconciliation. One debit memorandum is for $150 and dealt with an NSF check for $140 received from a customer, Prada Inc., in payment of its account. The bank assessed a $10 fee for processing it. The second debit memorandum is a $20 charge for check printing. Gucci had not recorded these transactions before receiving the statement.

Required

1. Prepare the bank reconciliation for this company as of December 31, 2017.

2. Prepare the journal entries necessary to bring Gucci's book balance of cash into conformity with the reconciled cash balance as of December 31, 2017.

Solutions

Part 1

GUCCI Bank Reconciliation December 31, 2017					
Bank statement balance		$1,900	Book balance		$1,610
Add			Add		
Deposit of Dec. 31..............		800	Error (Ck. 6267)..........	$ 90	
		2,700	Proceeds of note		
			less $30 fee...........	470	560
					2,170
Deduct			Deduct		
Outstanding Checks No. 6242	$200		NSF check	$150	
6273....	400		Printing fee	20	
6282....	100	700			170
Adjusted bank balance.............		$2,000	Adjusted book balance		$2,000

Part 2

Dec. 31	Cash	90	
	Office Supplies		90
	Correct an entry error.		
Dec. 31	Cash	470	
	Collection Expense	30	
	Notes Receivable		500
	Record note collection less fees.		
Dec. 31	Accounts Receivable—Prada Inc........................	150	
	Cash		150
	Charge account for NSF check plus fees.		
Dec. 31	Miscellaneous Expenses..............................	20	
	Cash		20
	Record check printing charge.		

> Do More: QS 8-5, QS 8-6, QS 8-7, E 8-8, E 8-9, E 8-10, E 8-11

SUSTAINABILITY AND ACCOUNTING

Vlad Tenev and Baiju Bhatt, and their company **Robinhood**, help lower-income and younger people invest in the stock market. Their company makes investing accessible by not charging fees for trading or requiring a minimum balance to open an account. "People expected more from us," explains Baiju. Competitors charge fees in the range of $7 to $15 each time a customer wants to make an investment. Most competitors also require at least a $1,000 minimum balance to invest.

"There are a lot of people in our age group who have lost faith in the system," claims Tenev. In response, Baiju and Tenev aim to restore the idea that anyone can invest and that you do not need "millions of dollars to invest." Further, Robinhood's social network is intended to be like the "Merry Men" from the legend. Members share ideas on the future and areas to bet on. Members who perform best rise to the top.

Vlad and Baiju explain that zero-fee investing is not possible without effective cash controls. Because Robinhood does not charge to invest, Vlad and Baiju must run a lean business operation. Robinhood does not have a budget for a full-time treasurer to manage cash and monitor bank balances. Instead, Vlad and Baiju set up internal controls for the safekeeping of company assets. The two also perform bank reconciliations to identify errors or fraud. These control tools allow Vlad and Baiju to keep operating costs low and permit commission-free investing. "We view this as a revolution in the financial sector," proclaims Vlad. A sustainable revolution in trading stocks.

Source: Effinger, Anthony, "Robinhood app offers zero-commission trading" March 19, 2015, Bloomberg News.

© Ian Horrocks/Getty Images for LTA

 **Decision Analysis**  Days' Sales Uncollected

A1

Compute the days' sales uncollected ratio and use it to assess liquidity.

An important part of cash management is monitoring the receipt of cash from receivables. If customers and others who owe money to a company are delayed in payment, then that company can find it difficult to pay its obligations when they are due. A company's customers are crucial partners in its cash management. Many companies attract customers by selling to them on credit. This means that cash receipts from customers are delayed until accounts receivable are collected.

One measure of how quickly a company can convert its accounts receivable into cash is the **days' sales uncollected,** also called *days' sales in receivables*. This measure is computed by dividing the current balance of receivables by net credit sales over the year just completed and then multiplying by 365 (number of days in a year). Since net credit sales usually are not reported to external users, the net sales (or revenues) figure is commonly used in the computation as in Exhibit 8.8.

EXHIBIT 8.8

Days' Sales Uncollected

$$\text{Days' sales uncollected} = \frac{\text{Accounts receivable}}{\text{Net sales}} \times 365$$

We use days' sales uncollected to estimate how much time is likely to pass before the current amount of accounts receivable is received in cash. For evaluation purposes, we compare this estimate to that for other companies in the same industry. We also make comparisons between current and prior periods.

To illustrate, we select data from the annual reports of two toy manufacturers, Hasbro and Mattel. Their days' sales uncollected figures are shown in Exhibit 8.9.

EXHIBIT 8.9

Analysis Using Days' Sales Uncollected

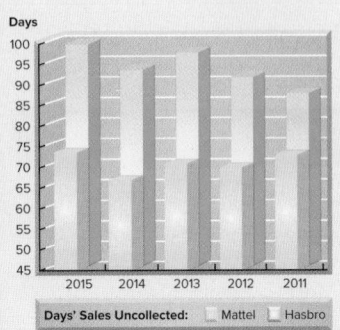

Days' Sales Uncollected: Mattel Hasbro

Company	Figure ($ millions)	2015	2014	2013	2012	2011
Hasbro	Accounts receivable	$1,218	$1,095	$1,094	$1,030	$1,035
	Net sales	$4,448	$4,277	$4,082	$4,089	$4,286
	Days' sales uncollected	100 days	93 days	98 days	92 days	88 days
Mattel	Accounts receivable	$1,145	$1,094	$1,260	$1,227	$1,247
	Net sales	$5,703	$6,024	$6,485	$6,421	$6,266
	Days' sales uncollected	73 days	66 days	71 days	70 days	73 days

Days' sales uncollected for Hasbro in 2015 is computed as ($1,218/$4,448) × 365 days = 100 days. This means that it will take about 100 days to collect cash from ending accounts receivable. This number reflects one or more of the following factors: a company's ability to collect receivables, customer financial health, customer payment strategies, and discount terms. To further assess days' sales uncollected for Hasbro, we compare it to its own four prior years and to those of Mattel. We see that Hasbro's days' sales uncollected worsened in 2015 as it took longer to collect its receivables relative to 2014. In comparison, Mattel's performance worsened in 2015 as its days' sales uncollected increased by 7 days. For all years, Mattel is superior to Hasbro on this measure of cash management. The less time that money is tied up in receivables often translates into increased profitability.

■ Decision Maker

Sales Representative   The sales staff are told to take action to help reduce days' sales uncollected for cash management purposes. What can you, a salesperson, do to reduce days' sales uncollected? ■   [*Answer:* A salesperson can (1) decrease the ratio of sales on account to total sales by encouraging more cash sales, (2) identify customers most delayed in their payments and encourage earlier payments or cash sales, and (3) apply stricter credit policies to eliminate credit sales to customers that never pay.]

NEED-TO-KNOW 8-5

COMPREHENSIVE

Prepare a bank reconciliation for Jamboree Enterprises for the month ended November 30, 2017. The following information is available to reconcile Jamboree Enterprises's book balance of cash with its bank statement balance as of November 30, 2017:

a. After all posting is complete on November 30, the company's book balance of cash has a $16,380 debit balance, but its bank statement shows a $38,520 balance.

b. Checks No. 2024 for $4,810 and No. 2026 for $5,000 are outstanding.

c. In comparing the canceled checks on the bank statement with the entries in the accounting records, it is found that Check No. 2025 in payment of rent is correctly drawn for $1,000 but is erroneously entered in the accounting records as $880.

d. The November 30 deposit of $17,150 was placed in the night depository after banking hours on that date, and this amount does not appear on the bank statement.

e. In reviewing the bank statement, a check written by Jumbo Enterprises in the amount of $160 was erroneously drawn against Jamboree's account.

f. A credit memorandum enclosed with the bank statement indicates that the bank collected a $30,000 note and $900 of related interest on Jamboree's behalf. This transaction was not recorded by Jamboree prior to receiving the statement.

g. A debit memorandum for $1,100 lists a $1,100 NSF check received from a customer, Marilyn Welch. Jamboree had not recorded the return of this check before receiving the statement.

h. Bank service charges for November total $40. These charges were not recorded by Jamboree before receiving the statement.

Point: Generally, the party that is not the initial recorder of an item, but is later informed, includes that item on its "book" of the bank reconciliation. For example, the bank records an NSF check and then informs the company. The company, as not the initial recorder of the item, reports it on the book side of its reconciliation.

PLANNING THE SOLUTION

● Set up a bank reconciliation with a bank side and a book side (as in Exhibit 8.7). Leave room to both add and deduct items. Each column will result in a reconciled, equal balance.

● Examine each item *a* through *h* to determine whether it affects the book or the bank balance and whether it should be added or deducted from the bank or book balance.

● After all items are analyzed, complete the reconciliation and arrive at a reconciled balance between the bank side and the book side.

● For each reconciling item on the book side, prepare an adjusting entry. Additions to the book side require an adjusting entry that debits Cash. Deductions on the book side require an adjusting entry that credits Cash.

SOLUTION

JAMBOREE ENTERPRISES Bank Reconciliation November 30, 2017					
Bank statement balance		$ 38,520	Book balance		$ 16,380
Add			Add		
Deposit of Nov. 30	$17,150		Collection of note	$30,000	
Bank error (Jumbo)	160	17,310	Interest earned	900	30,900
		55,830			47,280
Deduct			Deduct		
Outstanding checks			NSF check (M. Welch)	1,100	
No. 2024	4,810		Recording error (# 2025)	120	
No. 2026	5,000	9,810	Service charge	40	1,260
Adjusted bank balance		**$46,020**	**Adjusted book balance**		**$46,020**

Required Adjusting Entries for Jamboree

Nov. 30	Cash...	30,900	
	Notes Receivable...............................		30,000
	Interest Earned..................................		900
	Record collection of note with interest.		
Nov. 30	Accounts Receivable—M. Welch......................	1,100	
	Cash..		1,100
	Reinstate account due from an NSF check.		
Nov. 30	Rent Expense.....................................	120	
	Cash..		120
	Correct recording error on Check No. 2025.		
Nov. 30	Bank Service Charges................................	40	
	Cash..		40
	Record bank service charges.		

Point: Error correction can alternatively involve (1) reversing the erroneous entry and (2) recording the correct entry. Auditors prefer this alternative.

APPENDIX

8A Documentation and Verification

P4

Describe use of documentation and verification to control cash disbursements.

This appendix describes the important business documents of a voucher system of control.

Purchase Requisition Department managers are usually not allowed to place orders directly with suppliers for control purposes. Instead, a department manager must inform the purchasing department of its needs by preparing and signing a **purchase requisition,** which lists the merchandise needed and requests that it be purchased—see Exhibit 8A.1. Two copies of the purchase requisition are sent to the purchasing department, which then sends one copy to the accounting department. When the accounting department receives a purchase requisition, it creates and maintains a voucher for this transaction. The requesting department keeps the third copy.

EXHIBIT 8A.1

Purchase Requisition

Z-Mart

PURCHASE REQUISITION No. 917

From Sporting Goods Department

To Purchasing Department

Date October 28, 2017

Preferred Vendor Trex

Request purchase of the following item(s):

MODEL NO.	DESCRIPTION	QUANTITY
CH 015	Toddler—Challenger X7	1
SD 099	Boys/Girls—Speed Demon	1

Reason for Request Replenish inventory

Approval for Request T.Z.

For Purchasing Department use only: Order Date 10-30-17 P.O. No. P98

Purchase Order A **purchase order** is a document the purchasing department uses to place an order with a **vendor** (seller or supplier). A purchase order authorizes a vendor to ship ordered merchandise at the stated price and terms—see Exhibit 8A.2. When the purchasing department receives a purchase requisition, it prepares at least five copies of a purchase order. The copies are distributed as follows: *copy 1* to the vendor as a purchase request and as authority to ship merchandise; *copy 2,* along with a copy of the purchase requisition, to the accounting department, where it is entered in the voucher and used in approving payment of the invoice; *copy 3* to the requesting department to inform its manager that action is being taken; *copy 4* to the receiving department without order quantity so it can compare with goods received and provide an independent count of goods received; and *copy 5* retained on file by the purchasing department.

Point: This appendix is one example of a common voucher system design, but *not* the only design.

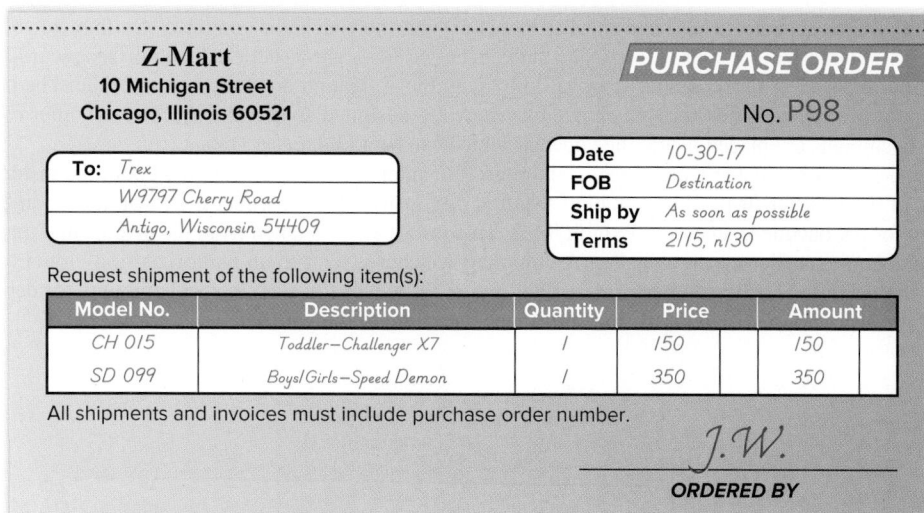

EXHIBIT 8A.2

Purchase Order

Point: Shipping terms and credit terms are shown on the purchase order.

Invoice   An **invoice** is an itemized statement of goods prepared by the vendor listing the customer's name, items sold, sales prices, and terms of sale. An invoice is also a bill sent to the buyer from the supplier. From the vendor's point of view, it is a *sales invoice*. The buyer, or **vendee**, treats it as a *purchase invoice*. When receiving a purchase order, the vendor ships the ordered merchandise to the buyer and includes or mails a copy of the invoice covering the shipment to the buyer. The invoice is sent to the buyer's accounting department, where it is placed in the voucher. (Refer back to Exhibit 5.6, which shows Z-Mart's purchase invoice.)

Receiving Report   Many companies maintain a separate department to receive all merchandise and purchased assets. When each shipment arrives, this receiving department counts the goods and checks them for damage and agreement with the purchase order. It then prepares four or more copies of a **receiving report,** which is used within the company to notify the appropriate persons that ordered goods have been received and to describe the quantities and condition of the goods. One copy is sent to accounting and placed in the voucher. Copies are also sent to the requesting department and the purchasing department to notify them that the goods have arrived. The receiving department retains a copy in its files.

Invoice Approval   When a receiving report arrives, the accounting department should have copies of the following documents in the voucher: purchase requisition, purchase order, and invoice. With the information in these documents, the accounting department can record the purchase and approve its payment. In approving an invoice for payment, it checks and compares information across all documents. To facilitate this checking and to ensure that no step is omitted, it often uses an **invoice approval,** also called *check authorization*—see Exhibit 8A.3. An invoice approval is a checklist of steps necessary for approving an invoice for recording and payment. It is a separate document either filed in the voucher or preprinted (or stamped) on the voucher.

EXHIBIT 8A.3

Invoice Approval

INVOICE APPROVAL				
DOCUMENT			**BY**	**DATE**
Purchase requisition		917	TZ	10-28-17
Purchase order		P98	JW	10-30-17
Receiving report		R85	SK	11-03-17
Invoice:		4657		11-12-17
Price			JK	11-12-17
Calculations			JK	11-12-17
Terms			JK	11-12-17
Approved for payment			BC	

As each step in the checklist is approved, the person initials the invoice approval and records the current date. Final approval implies the following steps have occurred:

1. **Requisition check:** Items on invoice are requested per purchase requisition.
2. **Purchase order check:** Items on invoice are ordered per purchase order.
3. **Receiving report check:** Items on invoice are received per receiving report.
4. **Invoice check: Price:** Invoice prices are as agreed with the vendor.

    Calculations: Invoice has no mathematical errors.

    Terms: Terms are as agreed with the vendor.

Point: Recording a purchase is initiated by an invoice approval, not an invoice. An invoice approval verifies that the amount is consistent with that requested, ordered, and received. This controls and verifies purchases and related liabilities.

Point: Auditors, when auditing inventory, check a sampling of purchases by reviewing the purchase order, receiving report, and invoice.

Voucher Once an invoice has been checked and approved, the voucher is complete. A complete voucher is a record summarizing a transaction. Once the voucher certifies a transaction, it authorizes recording an obligation. A voucher also contains approval for paying the obligation on an appropriate date. The physical form of a voucher varies across companies. Many are designed so that the invoice and other related source documents are placed inside the voucher, which can be a folder.

Completion of a voucher usually requires a person to enter certain information on both the inside and outside of the voucher. Typical information required on the inside of a voucher is shown in Exhibit 8A.4, and that for the outside is shown in Exhibit 8A.5. This information is taken from the invoice and the supporting documents filed in the voucher. A complete voucher is sent to an authorized individual (often called an *auditor*). This person performs a final review, approves the accounts and amounts for debiting (called the *accounting distribution*), and authorizes recording of the voucher.

EXHIBIT 8A.4

Inside of a Voucher

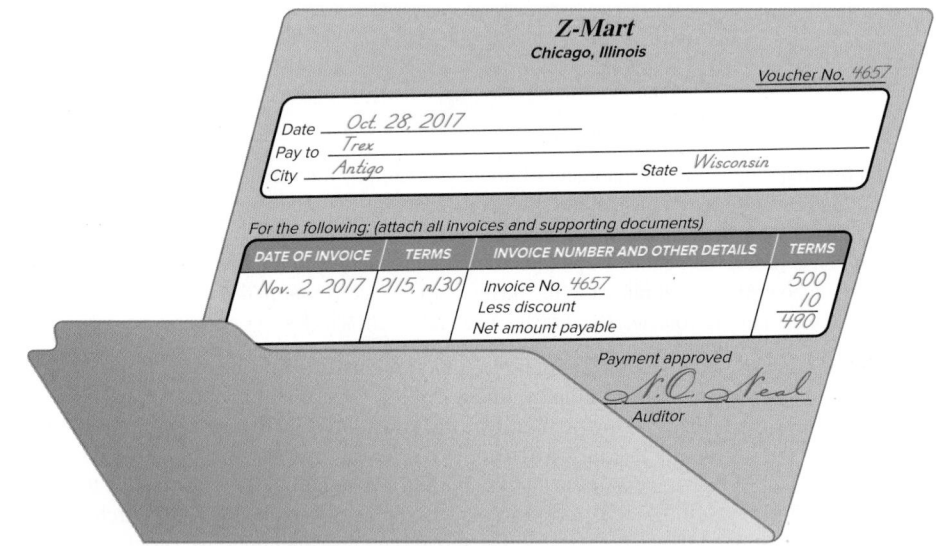

EXHIBIT 8A.5

Outside of a Voucher

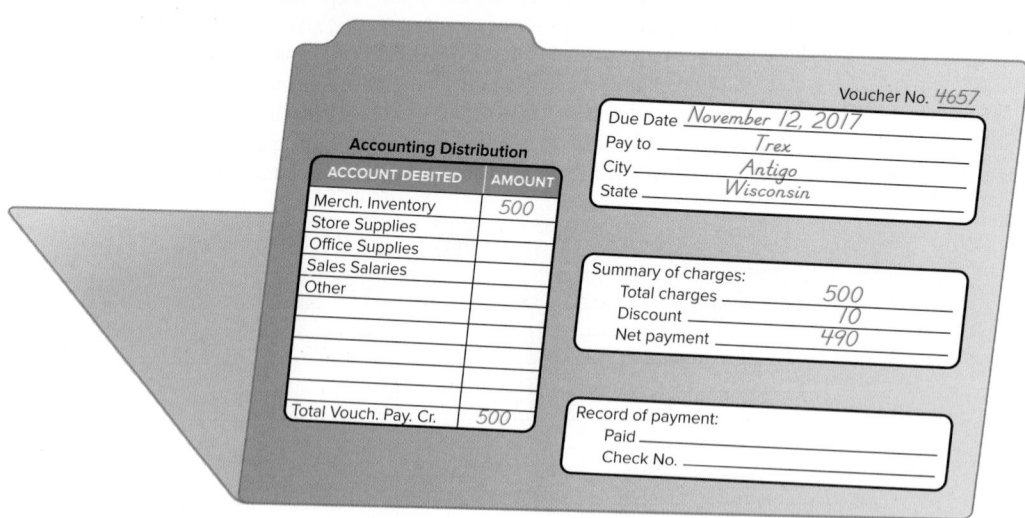

After a voucher is approved and recorded (in a journal called a **voucher register**), it is filed by its due date. A check is then sent on the payment date from the cashier, the voucher is marked "paid," and the voucher is sent to the accounting department and recorded (in a journal called the **check register**). The person issuing checks relies on the approved voucher and its signed supporting documents as proof that an obligation has been incurred and must be paid. The purchase requisition and purchase order confirm the purchase was authorized. The receiving report shows that items have been received, and the invoice approval form verifies that the invoice has been checked for errors. There is little chance for error and even less chance for fraud without collusion unless all the documents and signatures are forged.

Summary

C1 **Define internal control and identify its purpose and principles.** An internal control system consists of the policies and procedures managers use to protect assets, ensure reliable accounting, promote efficient operations, and uphold company policies. It can prevent avoidable losses and help managers both plan operations and monitor company and human performance. Principles of good internal control include establishing responsibilities, maintaining adequate records, insuring assets and bonding employees, separating recordkeeping from custody of assets, dividing responsibilities for related transactions, applying technological controls, and performing regular independent reviews.

C2 **Define cash and cash equivalents and explain how to report them.** Cash includes currency, coins, and amounts on (or acceptable for) deposit in checking and savings accounts. Cash equivalents are short-term, highly liquid investment assets readily convertible to a known cash amount and sufficiently close to their maturity date so that market value is not sensitive to interest rate changes. Cash and cash equivalents are liquid assets because they are readily converted into other assets or can be used to pay for goods, services, or liabilities.

A1 **Compute the days' sales uncollected ratio and use it to assess liquidity.** Many companies attract customers by selling to them on credit. This means that cash receipts from customers are delayed until accounts receivable are collected. Users want to know how quickly a company can convert its accounts receivable into cash. The days' sales uncollected ratio, one measure reflecting company liquidity, is computed by dividing the ending balance of receivables by annual net sales, and then multiplying by 365.

P1 **Apply internal control to cash receipts and disbursements.** Internal control of cash receipts ensures that all cash received is properly recorded and deposited. Attention focuses on two important types of cash receipts: over-the-counter and by mail. Good internal control for over-the-counter cash receipts includes use of a cash register, customer review, use of receipts, a permanent transaction record, and separation of the custody of cash from its recordkeeping. Good internal control for cash receipts by mail includes at least two people assigned to open mail and a listing of each sender's name, amount, and explanation. (Banks offer several services that promote the control and safeguarding of cash.)

P2 **Explain and record petty cash fund transactions.** Petty cash disbursements are payments of small amounts for items such as postage, courier fees, minor repairs, and supplies. A company usually sets up one or more petty cash funds. A petty cash fund cashier is responsible for safekeeping the cash, making payments from this fund, and keeping receipts and records. A Petty Cash account is debited only when the fund is established or increased in amount. When the fund is replenished, petty cash disbursements are recorded with debits to expense (or asset) accounts and a credit to Cash.

P3 **Prepare a bank reconciliation.** A bank reconciliation proves the accuracy of the depositor's and the bank's records. The bank statement balance is adjusted for items such as outstanding checks and unrecorded deposits made on or before the bank statement date but not reflected on the statement. The book balance is adjusted for items such as service charges, bank collections for the depositor, and interest earned on the account.

P4[A] **Describe use of documentation and verification to control cash disbursements.** A voucher system is a set of procedures and approvals designed to control cash disbursements and acceptance of obligations. The voucher system of control relies on several important documents, including the voucher and its supporting files. A key factor in this system is that only approved departments and individuals are authorized to incur certain obligations.

Key Terms

Bank reconciliation	Deposit ticket	Purchase order
Bank statement	Deposits in transit	Purchase requisition
Canceled checks	Electronic funds transfer (EFT)	Receiving report
Cash	Internal control system	Sarbanes-Oxley Act (SOX)
Cash equivalents	Invoice	Signature card
Cash Over and Short	Invoice approval	Vendee
Check	Liquid assets	Vendor
Check register	Liquidity	Voucher
Committee of Sponsoring Organizations (COSO)	Outstanding checks	Voucher register
Days' sales uncollected	Petty cash	Voucher system
	Principles of internal control	

Multiple Choice Quiz

1. A company needs to replenish its $500 petty cash fund. Its petty cashbox has $75 cash and petty cash receipts of $420. The journal entry to replenish the fund includes
   a. A debit to Cash for $75.
   b. A credit to Cash for $75.
   c. A credit to Petty Cash for $420.
   d. A credit to Cash Over and Short for $5.
   e. A debit to Cash Over and Short for $5.

2. The following information is available for Hapley Company:
   • The November 30 bank statement shows a $1,895 balance.
   • The general ledger shows a $1,742 balance at November 30.
   • A $795 deposit placed in the bank's night depository on November 30 does not appear on the November 30 bank statement.
   • Outstanding checks amount to $638 at November 30.
   • A customer's $335 note was collected by the bank in November. A collection fee of $15 was deducted by the bank and the difference deposited in Hapley's account.
   • A bank service charge of $10 is deducted by the bank and appears on the November 30 bank statement.

How will the customer's note appear on Hapley's November 30 bank reconciliation?
   a. $320 appears as an addition to the book balance of cash.
   b. $320 appears as a deduction from the book balance of cash.
   c. $320 appears as an addition to the bank balance of cash.
   d. $320 appears as a deduction from the bank balance of cash.
   e. $335 appears as an addition to the bank balance of cash.

3. Using the information from question 2, what is the reconciled balance on Hapley's November 30 bank reconciliation?
   a. $2,052   c. $1,742   e. $1,184
   b. $1,895   d. $2,201

4. A company had net sales of $84,000 and accounts receivable of $6,720. Its days' sales uncollected is
   a. 3.2 days   c. 230.0 days   e. 12.5 days
   b. 18.4 days   d. 29.2 days

ANSWERS TO MULTIPLE CHOICE QUIZ

1. e; The entry follows.

Debits to expenses (or assets)	420	
Cash Over and Short.	5	
Cash		425

2. a; recognizes cash collection of note by bank.

3. a; the bank reconciliation follows.

Bank Reconciliation November 30			
Balance per bank statement. . . .	$1,895	Balance per books	$1,742
Add: Deposit in transit.	795	Add: Note collected less fee. . .	320
Deduct: Outstanding checks. . . .	(638)	Deduct: Service charge.	(10)
Reconciled balance.	$2,052	Reconciled balance.	$2,052

4. d; ($6,720/$84,000) × 365 = 29.2 days

---

^A *Superscript letter A denotes assignments based on Appendix 8A.*

🔢 Icon denotes assignments that involve decision making.

Discussion Questions

1. List the seven broad principles of internal control.
2. 🔢 Internal control procedures are important in every business, but at what stage in the development of a business do they become especially critical?
3. 🔢 Why should responsibility for related transactions be divided among different departments or individuals?
4. 🔢 Why should the person who keeps the records of an asset not be the person responsible for its custody?
5. 🔢 When a store purchases merchandise, why are individual departments not allowed to directly deal with suppliers?
6. What are the limitations of internal controls?
7. Which of the following assets—inventory, building, accounts receivable, or cash—is most liquid? Which is least liquid?
8. What is a petty cash receipt? Who should sign it?
9. Why should cash receipts be deposited on the day of receipt?

10. Apple's statement of cash flows in Appendix A describes changes in cash and cash equivalents for the year ended September 26, 2015. What total amount is provided (used) by investing activities? What amount is provided (used) by financing activities?

APPLE

11. Refer to Google's financial statements in Appendix A. Identify Google's net earnings (income) for the year ended December 31, 2015. Is its net earnings equal to the change in cash and cash equivalents for the year? Explain the difference between net earnings and the change in cash and cash equivalents.

GOOGLE

12. Refer to Samsung's balance sheet in Appendix A. How does its cash (titled "Cash and cash equivalents") compare with its other current assets (in both amount and percent) as of December 31, 2015? Compare and assess its cash at December 31, 2015, with its cash at December 31, 2014.

Samsung

13. Samsung's statement of cash flows in Appendix A reports the change in cash and equivalents for the year ended December 31, 2015. Identify the cash generated (or used) by operating activities, by investing activities, and by financing activities.

Samsung

connect

An internal control system consists of all policies and procedures used to protect assets, ensure reliable accounting, promote efficient operations, and urge adherence to company policies. Evaluate each of the following statements and indicate which are true and which are false regarding the objectives of an internal control system.

QUICK STUDY

QS 8-1
Internal control objectives

C1

_____ **1.** Separation of recordkeeping for assets from the custody over assets is intended to reduce theft and fraud.

_____ **2.** The primary objective of internal control procedures is to safeguard the business against theft from government agencies.

_____ **3.** The main objective of internal control procedures is best accomplished by designing an operational system with managerial policies that protect the assets from waste, fraud, and theft.

_____ **4.** Separating the responsibility for a transaction between two or more individuals or departments will not help prevent someone from creating a fictitious invoice and paying the money to herself or himself.

Choose from the following list of terms/phrases to best complete the following statements.

QS 8-2
Cash and equivalents

C2

a. Cash   **c.** Outstanding check   **e.** Bank reconciliation

b. Cash equivalents   **d.** Liquidity   **f.** Current assets

_____ **1.** The _____ category includes currency and coins along with amounts on deposit in bank accounts, checking accounts, and savings accounts.

_____ **2.** The term _____ refers to a company's ability to pay for its near-term obligations.

_____ **3.** The _____ category includes short-term, highly liquid investment assets that are readily convertible to a known cash amount and sufficiently close to their due dates so that their market value is not sensitive to interest rate changes.

A good system of internal control for cash provides adequate procedures for protecting both cash receipts and cash disbursements. Identify each of the following statements as either true or false regarding this protection.

QS 8-3
Internal control for cash

P1

_____ **a.** A basic guideline for safeguarding cash is that all cash receipts be deposited weekly or monthly.

_____ **b.** A voucher system of control is a control system exclusively for cash receipts.

_____ **c.** A basic guideline for safeguarding cash is to separate the duties of those who have custody of cash from those who keep cash records.

_____ **d.** A petty cash system is not a control procedure for safeguarding cash.

1. The petty cash fund of the Brooks Agency is established at $150. At the end of the current period, the fund contained $28 and had the following receipts: entertainment, $70; postage, $30; and printing, $22. Prepare journal entries to record (*a*) establishment of the fund and (*b*) reimbursement of the fund at the end of the current period.

QS 8-4
Petty cash accounting

P2

2. Identify the two events from the following that cause a Petty Cash account to be credited in a journal entry.

_____ **a.** Fund amount is being reduced.   _____ **c.** Fund is being eliminated.

_____ **b.** Fund amount is being increased.   _____ **d.** Fund is being established.

QS 8-5
Bank reconciliation
P3

For each of the following items *a* through *g*, indicate whether its amount (1) affects the bank or book side of a bank reconciliation, (2) represents an addition or a subtraction in a bank reconciliation, and (3) requires an adjusting journal entry.

	Bank or Book Side	Add or Subtract	Adj. Entry or Not
a. Interest on cash balance	_____	_____	_____
b. Bank service charges	_____	_____	_____
c. Minimum balance charge...............	_____	_____	_____
d. Outstanding checks	_____	_____	_____
e. Credit memo on collection of note.........	_____	_____	_____
f. NSF checks	_____	_____	_____
g. Outstanding deposits	_____	_____	_____

QS 8-6
Bank reconciliation
P3

Nolan Company deposits all cash receipts on the day when they are received and it makes all cash payments by check. At the close of business on June 30, 2017, its Cash account shows a $22,352 debit balance. Nolan's June 30 bank statement shows $21,332 on deposit in the bank. Prepare a bank reconciliation for the company using the following information.

a. Outstanding checks as of June 30 total $3,713.

b. The June 30 bank statement lists $41 in bank service charges; the company has not yet recorded the cost of these services.

c. In reviewing the bank statement, a $90 check written by the company was mistakenly recorded in the company's books at $99.

d. June 30 cash receipts of $4,724 were placed in the bank's night depository after banking hours and were not recorded on the June 30 bank statement.

e. The bank statement included a $23 credit for interest earned on the company's cash in the bank.

QS 8-7
Reviewing bank statements
P3

An entrepreneur commented that a bank reconciliation may not be necessary as she regularly reviews her online bank statement for any unusual items and errors.

a. Describe how a bank reconciliation and an online review (or reading) of the bank statement are not equivalent.

b. Identify and explain at least two frauds or errors that would be uncovered through a bank reconciliation and that would *not* be uncovered through an online review of the bank statement.

QS 8-8
Days' sales uncollected
A1

The following annual account balances are taken from Armour Sports at December 31.

	2017	2016
Accounts receivable............	$ 100,000	$ 85,000
Net sales....................	2,500,000	2,000,000

What is the change in the number of days' sales uncollected between years 2016 and 2017? (Round the number of days to one decimal.) According to this analysis, is the company's collection of receivables improving? Explain.

QS 8-9ᴬ
Documents in a voucher system   P4

Management uses a voucher system to help control and monitor cash disbursements. Which one or more of the four documents listed below are prepared as part of a voucher system of control?

_____ **a.** Purchase order   _____ **b.** Outstanding check   _____ **c.** Invoice   _____ **d.** Voucher

QS 8-10
International accounting and internal controls

C1   P1

Answer each of the following related to international accounting standards.

a. Explain how the purposes and principles of internal controls are different between accounting systems reporting under IFRS versus U.S. GAAP.

b. Cash presents special internal control challenges. How do internal controls for cash differ for accounting systems reporting under IFRS versus U.S. GAAP? How do the procedures applied differ across those two accounting systems?

≡ connect

Franco Company is a rapidly growing start-up business. Its recordkeeper, who was hired six months ago, left town after the company's manager discovered that a large sum of money had disappeared over the past three months. An audit disclosed that the recordkeeper had written and signed several checks made payable to her fiancé and then recorded the checks as salaries expense. The fiancé, who cashed the checks but never worked for the company, left town with the recordkeeper. As a result, the company incurred an uninsured loss of $184,000.

Evaluate Franco's internal control system and indicate which principles of internal control appear to have been ignored.

EXERCISES

Exercise 8-1
Analyzing internal control

C1

What internal control procedures would you recommend in each of the following situations?

1. A concession company has one employee who sells towels, coolers, and sunglasses at the beach. Each day, the employee is given enough towels, coolers, and sunglasses to last through the day and enough cash to make change. The money is kept in a box at the stand.

2. An antique store has one employee who is given cash and sent to garage sales each weekend. The employee pays cash for any merchandise acquired that the antique store resells.

Exercise 8-2
Internal control recommendations

C1

Good accounting systems help with the management and control of cash and cash equivalents.

1. Define and contrast the terms *liquid asset* and *cash equivalent.*

2. Why would companies invest their idle cash in cash equivalents?

3. Identify five principles of effective cash management.

Exercise 8-3
Cash, liquidity, and return

C2

Some of Crown Company's cash receipts from customers are received by the company with the regular mail. The company's recordkeeper opens these letters and deposits the cash received each day.

a. Identify any internal control problem(s) in this arrangement.

b. What changes to its internal control system do you recommend?

Exercise 8-4
Control of cash receipts by mail   P1

Waupaca Company establishes a $350 petty cash fund on September 9. On September 30, the fund shows $104 in cash along with receipts for the following expenditures: transportation-in, $40; postage expenses, $123; and miscellaneous expenses, $80. The petty cashier could not account for a $3 shortage in the fund.

The company uses the perpetual system in accounting for merchandise inventory. Prepare (1) the September 9 entry to establish the fund, (2) the September 30 entry to reimburse the fund, and (3) an October 1 entry to increase the fund to $400.

Exercise 8-5
Petty cash fund with a shortage   P2

Check (2) Cr. Cash, $246 and (3) Cr. Cash, $50

Palmona Co. establishes a $200 petty cash fund on January 1. On January 8, the fund shows $38 in cash along with receipts for the following expenditures: postage, $74; transportation-in, $29; delivery expenses, $16; and miscellaneous expenses, $43.

Palmona uses the perpetual system in accounting for merchandise inventory. Prepare journal entries to (1) establish the fund on January 1, (2) reimburse it on January 8, and (3) both reimburse the fund and increase it to $450 on January 8, assuming no entry in part 2. (*Hint*: Make two separate entries for part 3.)

Exercise 8-6
Petty cash fund accounting

P2

Check (3) Cr. Cash, $162 & $250

The voucher system of control is designed to control cash disbursements and the acceptance of obligations.

1. The voucher system of control establishes procedures for what two processes?

2. What types of expenditures should be overseen by a voucher system of control?

3. When is the voucher initially prepared? Explain.

Exercise 8-7
Voucher system

P1

Prepare a table with the following headings for a monthly bank reconciliation dated September 30.

Exercise 8-8
Bank reconciliation and adjusting entries

P3

Bank Balance		Book Balance			Not Shown on the Reconciliation
Add	Deduct	Add	Deduct	Adjust	

For each item 1 through 12, place an *x* in the appropriate column to indicate whether the item should be added to or deducted from the book or bank balance, or whether it should not appear on the reconciliation. If the book balance is to be adjusted, place a *Dr.* or *Cr.* in the Adjust column to indicate whether the Cash balance should be debited or credited. At the left side of your table, number the items to correspond to the following list.

1. NSF check from customer is returned on September 25 but not yet recorded by this company.
2. Interest earned on the September cash balance in the bank.
3. Deposit made on September 5 and processed by the bank on September 6.
4. Checks written by another depositor but charged against this company's account.
5. Bank service charge for September.
6. Checks outstanding on August 31 that cleared the bank in September.
7. Check written against the company's account and cleared by the bank; erroneously not recorded by the company's recordkeeper.
8. Principal and interest on a note receivable to this company is collected by the bank but not yet recorded by the company.
9. Checks written and mailed to payees on October 2.
10. Checks written by the company and mailed to payees on September 30.
11. Night deposit made on September 30 after the bank closed.
12. Special bank charge for collection of note in part 8 on this company's behalf.

Exercise 8-9

Bank reconciliation

P3

Del Gato Clinic deposits all cash receipts on the day when they are received and it makes all cash payments by check. At the close of business on June 30, 2017, its Cash account shows an $11,589 debit balance. Del Gato Clinic's June 30 bank statement shows $10,555 on deposit in the bank. Prepare a bank reconciliation for Del Gato Clinic using the following information:

a. Outstanding checks as of June 30 total $1,829.
b. The June 30 bank statement lists a $16 bank service charge.
c. Check No. 919, listed with the canceled checks, was correctly drawn for $467 in payment of a utility bill on June 15. Del Gato Clinic mistakenly recorded it with a debit to Utilities Expense and a credit to Cash in the amount of $476.

Check Reconciled bal., $11,582

d. The June 30 cash receipts of $2,856 were placed in the bank's night depository after banking hours and were not recorded on the June 30 bank statement.

Exercise 8-10

Adjusting entries from bank reconciliation **P3**

Prepare the adjusting journal entries that Del Gato Clinic must record as a result of preparing the bank reconciliation in Exercise 8-9.

Exercise 8-11

Bank reconciliation

P3

Wright Company deposits all cash receipts on the day when they are received and it makes all cash payments by check. At the close of business on May 31, 2017, its Cash account shows a $27,500 debit balance. The company's May 31 bank statement shows $25,800 on deposit in the bank. Prepare a bank reconciliation for the company using the following information.

a. The May 31 bank statement lists $100 in bank service charges; the company has not yet recorded the cost of these services.
b. Outstanding checks as of May 31 total $5,600.
c. May 31 cash receipts of $6,200 were placed in the bank's night depository after banking hours and were not recorded on the May 31 bank statement.
d. In reviewing the bank statement, a $400 check written by Smith Company was mistakenly drawn against Wright's account.

Check Reconciled bal., $26,800

e. The bank statement shows a $600 NSF check from a customer; the company has not yet recorded this NSF check.

Exercise 8-12

Liquid assets and accounts receivable

A1

Barga Co. reported net sales for 2016 and 2017 of $730,000 and $1,095,000, respectively. Its year-end balances of accounts receivable follow: December 31, 2016, $65,000; and December 31, 2017, $123,000.

a. Compute its days' sales uncollected at the end of each year. Round the number of days to one decimal.
b. Evaluate and comment on any changes in the amount of liquid assets tied up in receivables.

Match each document in a voucher system in column one with its description in column two.

Exercise 8-13ᴬ

Documents in a voucher system

P4

Document	Description
1. Purchase requisition	____ **A.** An itemized statement of goods prepared by the vendor listing the customer's name, items sold, sales prices, and terms of sale.
2. Purchase order	
3. Invoice	____ **B.** An internal file used to store documents and information to control cash disbursements and to ensure that a transaction is properly authorized and recorded.
4. Receiving report	
5. Invoice approval	____ **C.** A document used to place an order with a vendor that authorizes the vendor to ship ordered merchandise at the stated price and terms.
6. Voucher	

____ **D.** A checklist of steps necessary for the approval of an invoice for recording and payment; also known as a check authorization.

____ **E.** A document used by department managers to inform the purchasing department to place an order with a vendor.

____ **F.** A document used to notify the appropriate persons that ordered goods have arrived, including a description of the quantities and condition of goods.

connect

For each of these five separate cases, identify the principle(s) of internal control that is violated. Recommend what the business should do to ensure adherence to principles of internal control.

PROBLEM SET A

Problem 8-1A

Analyzing internal control

C1

1. Chi Han records all incoming customer cash receipts for her employer and posts the customer payments to their respective accounts.

2. At Tico Company, Julia and Trevor alternate lunch hours. Julia is the petty cash custodian, but if someone needs petty cash when she is at lunch, Trevor fills in as custodian.

3. Nori Nozumi posts all patient charges and payments at the Hopeville Medical Clinic. Each night Nori backs up the computerized accounting system to a drive and stores it in a locked file at her desk.

4. Ben Shales prides himself on hiring quality workers who require little supervision. As office manager, Ben gives his employees full discretion over their tasks and for years has seen no reason to perform independent reviews of their work.

5. Carla Farah's manager has told her to reduce costs. Carla decides to raise the deductible on the plant's property insurance from $5,000 to $10,000. This cuts the property insurance premium in half. In a related move, she decides that bonding the plant's employees is a waste of money since the company has not experienced any losses due to employee theft. Carla saves the entire amount of the bonding insurance premium by dropping the bonding insurance.

Kiona Co. set up a petty cash fund for payments of small amounts. The following transactions involving the petty cash fund occurred in May (the last month of the company's fiscal year).

Problem 8-2A

Establishing, reimbursing, and adjusting petty cash

P2

May 1   Prepared a company check for $300 to establish the petty cash fund.
  15   Prepared a company check to replenish the fund for the following expenditures made since May 1.
    a.   Paid $88 for janitorial expenses.
    b.   Paid $53.68 for miscellaneous expenses.
    c.   Paid postage expenses of $53.50.
    d.   Paid $47.15 to *The County Gazette* (the local newspaper) for advertising expense.
    e.   Counted $62.15 remaining in the petty cashbox.
  16   Prepared a company check for $200 to increase the fund to $500.
  31   The petty cashier reports that $288.20 cash remains in the fund. A company check is drawn to replenish the fund for the following expenditures made since May 15.
    f.   Paid postage expenses of $147.36.
    g.   Reimbursed the office manager for mileage expense, $23.50.
    h.   Paid $34.75 in delivery expense for products to a customer, terms FOB destination.
  31   The company decides that the May 16 increase in the fund was too large. It reduces the fund by $100, leaving a total of $400.

Required

1. Prepare journal entries (in dollars and cents) to establish the fund on May 1, to replenish it on May 15 and on May 31, and to reflect any increase or decrease in the fund balance on May 16 and May 31.

Check   (1) Cr. to Cash: May 15, $237.85; May 16, $200.00

Analysis Component

2. Explain how the company's financial statements are affected if the petty cash fund is not replenished and no entry is made on May 31.

Problem 8-3A

Establishing, reimbursing, and increasing petty cash

P2

Nakashima Gallery had the following petty cash transactions in February of the current year.

Feb. 2   Wrote a $400 check, cashed it, and gave the proceeds and the petty cashbox to Chloe Addison, the petty cashier.
     5   Purchased paper for the copier for $14.15 that is immediately used.
     9   Paid $32.50 COD shipping charges on merchandise purchased for resale, terms FOB shipping point. Nakashima uses the perpetual system to account for merchandise inventory.
    12   Paid $7.95 postage to deliver a contract to a client.
    14   Reimbursed Adina Sharon, the manager, $68 for mileage on her car.
    20   Purchased stationery for $67.77 that is immediately used.
    23   Paid a courier $20 to deliver merchandise sold to a customer, terms FOB destination.
    25   Paid $13.10 COD shipping charges on merchandise purchased for resale, terms FOB shipping point.
    27   Paid $54 for postage expenses.
    28   The fund had $120.42 remaining in the petty cashbox. Sorted the petty cash receipts by accounts affected and exchanged them for a check to reimburse the fund for expenditures.
    28   The petty cash fund amount is increased by $100 to a total of $500.

Required

1. Prepare the journal entry to establish the petty cash fund.

2. Prepare a petty cash payments report for February with these categories: delivery expense, mileage expense, postage expense, merchandise inventory (for transportation-in), and office supplies expense. Sort the payments into the appropriate categories and total the expenditures in each category.

Check   Cash credit: (3a) $279.58; (3b) $100.00

3. Prepare the journal entries (in dollars and cents) for part 2 to both (a) reimburse and (b) increase the fund amount.

Problem 8-4A

Preparing a bank reconciliation and recording adjustments

P3

The following information is available to reconcile Branch Company's book balance of cash with its bank statement cash balance as of July 31, 2017.

a. On July 31, the company's Cash account has a $27,497 debit balance, but its July bank statement shows a $27,233 cash balance.

b. Check No. 3031 for $1,482 and Check No. 3040 for $558 were outstanding on the June 30 bank reconciliation. Check No. 3040 is listed with the July canceled checks, but Check No. 3031 is not. Also, Check No. 3065 for $382 and Check No. 3069 for $2,281, both written in July, are not among the canceled checks on the July 31 statement.

c. In comparing the canceled checks on the bank statement with the entries in the accounting records, it is found that Check No. 3056 for July rent expense was correctly written and drawn for $1,270 but was erroneously entered in the accounting records as $1,250.

d. The July bank statement shows the bank collected $8,000 cash on a noninterest-bearing note for Branch, deducted a $45 collection expense, and credited the remainder to its account. Branch had not recorded this event before receiving the statement.

e. The bank statement shows an $805 charge for a $795 NSF check plus a $10 NSF charge. The check had been received from a customer, Evan Shaw. Branch has not yet recorded this check as NSF.

f. The July statement shows a $25 bank service charge. It has not yet been recorded in miscellaneous expenses because no previous notification had been received.

g. Branch's July 31 daily cash receipts of $11,514 were placed in the bank's night depository on that date but do not appear on the July 31 bank statement.

Required

Check   (1) Reconciled balance, $34,602; (2) Cr. Notes Receivable, $8,000

1. Prepare the bank reconciliation for this company as of July 31, 2017.

2. Prepare the journal entries necessary to bring the company's book balance of cash into conformity with the reconciled cash balance as of July 31, 2017.

Analysis Component

3. Assume that the July 31, 2017, bank reconciliation for this company is prepared and some items are treated incorrectly. For each of the following errors, explain the effect of the error on (i) the adjusted bank statement cash balance and (ii) the adjusted Cash account book balance.

a. The company's unadjusted Cash account balance of $27,497 is listed on the reconciliation as $27,947.

b. The bank's collection of the $8,000 note less the $45 collection fee is added to the bank statement cash balance on the reconciliation.

Chavez Company most recently reconciled its bank statement and book balances of cash on August 31 and it reported two checks outstanding, No. 5888 for $1,028.05 and No. 5893 for $494.25. The following information is available for its September 30, 2017, reconciliation.

Problem 8-5A
Preparing a bank reconciliation and recording adjustments
P3

From the September 30 Bank Statement

PREVIOUS BALANCE	TOTAL CHECKS AND DEBITS	TOTAL DEPOSITS AND CREDITS	CURRENT BALANCE
16,800.45	9,620.05	11,272.85	18,453.25

CHECKS AND DEBITS			DEPOSITS AND CREDITS	
Date	No.	Amount	Date	Amount
09/03	5888	1,028.05	09/05	1,103.75
09/04	5902	719.90	09/12	2,226.90
09/07	5901	1,824.25	09/21	4,093.00
09/17		600.25 NSF	09/25	2,351.70
09/20	5905	937.00	09/30	12.50 IN
09/22	5903	399.10	09/30	1,485.00 CM
09/22	5904	2,090.00		
09/28	5907	213.85		
09/29	5909	1,807.65		

From Chavez Company's Accounting Records

Cash Receipts Deposited			Cash Disbursements		
Date		Cash Debit	Check No.		Cash Credit
Sept. 5		1,103.75	5901		1,824.25
12		2,226.90	5902		719.90
21		4,093.00	5903		399.10
25		2,351.70	5904		2,060.00
30		1,682.75	5905		937.00
		11,458.10	5906		982.30
			5907		213.85
			5908		388.00
			5909		1,807.65
					9,332.05

Cash						Acct. No. 101
Date		Explanation	PR	Debit	Credit	Balance
Aug.	31	Balance				15,278.15
Sept.	30	Total receipts	R12	11,458.10		26,736.25
	30	Total disbursements	D23		9,332.05	17,404.20

Additional Information

Check No. 5904 is correctly drawn for $2,090 to pay for computer equipment; however, the recordkeeper misread the amount and entered it in the accounting records with a debit to Computer Equipment and a credit to Cash of $2,060. The NSF check shown in the statement was originally received from a customer, S. Nilson, in payment of her account. Its return has not yet been recorded by the company. The credit memorandum (CM) is from the collection of a $1,500 note for Chavez Company by the bank. The bank deducted a $15 collection expense. The collection and fee are not yet recorded.

Required

1. Prepare the September 30, 2017, bank reconciliation for this company.
2. Prepare the journal entries (in dollars and cents) to adjust the book balance of cash to the reconciled balance.

Analysis Component

3. The bank statement reveals that some of the prenumbered checks in the sequence are missing. Describe three situations that could explain this.

PROBLEM SET B

Problem 8-1B

Analyzing internal control

C1

For each of these five separate cases, identify the principle(s) of internal control that is violated. Recommend what the business should do to ensure adherence to principles of internal control.

1. Latisha Tally is the company's computer specialist and oversees its computerized payroll system. Her boss recently asked her to put password protection on all office computers. Latisha has put a password in place that allows only the boss access to the file where pay rates are changed and personnel are added or deleted from the payroll.
2. Marker Theater has a computerized order-taking system for its tickets. The system is active all week and backed up every Friday night.
3. Sutton Company has two employees handling acquisitions of inventory. One employee places purchase orders and pays vendors. The second employee receives the merchandise.
4. The owner of Super Pharmacy uses a check software/printer to prepare checks, making it difficult for anyone to alter the amount of a check. The check software/printer, which is not password protected, is on the owner's desk in an office that contains company checks and is normally unlocked.
5. Lavina Company is a small business that has separated the duties of cash receipts and cash disbursements. The employee responsible for cash disbursements reconciles the bank account monthly.

Problem 8-2B

Establishing, reimbursing, and adjusting petty cash

P2

Moya Co. establishes a petty cash fund for payments of small amounts. The following transactions involving the petty cash fund occurred in January (the last month of the company's fiscal year).

Jan. 3 A company check for $150 is written and made payable to the petty cashier to establish the petty cash fund.

14 A company check is written to replenish the fund for the following expenditures made since January 3.
   a. Purchased office supplies for $14.29 that are immediately used up.
   b. Paid $19.60 COD shipping charges on merchandise purchased for resale, terms FOB shipping point. Moya uses the perpetual system to account for inventory.
   c. Paid $38.57 to All-Tech for repairs expense to a computer.
   d. Paid $12.82 for items classified as miscellaneous expenses.
   e. Counted $62.28 remaining in the petty cashbox.

15 Prepared a company check for $50 to increase the fund to $200.

31 The petty cashier reports that $17.35 remains in the fund. A company check is written to replenish the fund for the following expenditures made since January 14.
   f. Paid $50 to *The Smart Shopper* in advertising expense for January's newsletter.
   g. Paid $48.19 for postage expenses.
   h. Paid $78 to Smooth Delivery for delivery expense of merchandise, terms FOB destination.

31 The company decides that the January 15 increase in the fund was too little. It increases the fund by another $50, leaving a total of $250.

Required

1. Prepare journal entries (in dollars and cents) to establish the fund on January 3, to replenish it on January 14 and January 31, and to reflect any increase or decrease in the fund balance on January 15 and 31.

Analysis Component

2. Explain how the company's financial statements are affected if the petty cash fund is not replenished and no entry is made on January 31.

Blues Music Center had the following petty cash transactions in March of the current year.

March   5   Wrote a $250 check, cashed it, and gave the proceeds and the petty cashbox to Jen Rouse, the petty cashier.

      6   Paid $12.50 COD shipping charges on merchandise purchased for resale, terms FOB shipping point. Blues uses the perpetual system to account for merchandise inventory.

   11   Paid $10.75 in delivery expense on merchandise sold to a customer, terms FOB destination.

   12   Purchased office file folders for $14.13 that are immediately used.

   14   Reimbursed Bob Geldof, the manager, $11.65 for office supplies purchased and used.

   18   Purchased office printer paper for $20.54 that is immediately used.

   27   Paid $45.10 COD shipping charges on merchandise purchased for resale, terms FOB shipping point.

   28   Paid postage expense of $18.

   30   Reimbursed Geldof $56.80 for mileage expense.

   31   Cash of $61.53 remained in the fund. Sorted the petty cash receipts by accounts affected and exchanged them for a check to reimburse the fund for expenditures.

   31   The petty cash fund amount is increased by $50 to a total of $300.

Required

1. Prepare the journal entry to establish the petty cash fund.

2. Prepare a petty cash payments report for March with these categories: delivery expense, mileage expense, postage expense, merchandise inventory (for transportation-in), and office supplies expense. Sort the payments into the appropriate categories and total the expenses in each category.

3. Prepare the journal entries (in dollars and cents) for part 2 to both (*a*) reimburse and (*b*) increase the fund amount.

Problem 8-3B

Establishing, reimbursing, and increasing petty cash

P2

Check   (2) Total expenses, $189.47

(3*a* & 3*b*) Total Cr. to Cash, $238.47

The following information is available to reconcile Severino Co.'s book balance of cash with its bank statement cash balance as of December 31, 2017.

a. The December 31 cash balance according to the accounting records is $32,878.30, and the bank statement cash balance for that date is $46,822.40.

b. Check No. 1273 for $4,589.30 and Check No. 1282 for $400, both written and entered in the accounting records in December, are not among the canceled checks. Two checks, No. 1231 for $2,289 and No. 1242 for $410.40, were outstanding on the most recent November 30 reconciliation. Check No. 1231 is listed with the December canceled checks, but Check No. 1242 is not.

c. When the December checks are compared with entries in the accounting records, it is found that Check No. 1267 had been correctly drawn for $3,456 to pay for office supplies but was erroneously entered in the accounting records as $3,465.

d. Two memoranda are enclosed with the statement and are unrecorded at the time of the reconciliation. The first is for a $762.50 charge that dealt with an NSF check for $745 received from a customer, Titus Industries, in payment of its account. The bank assessed a $17.50 fee for processing it. The second is $99 in miscellaneous expenses for check printing.

e. The bank statement shows that the bank collected $19,000 cash on a note receivable for the company, deducted a $20 collection expense, and credited the balance to the company's Cash account. Severino did not record this transaction before receiving the statement.

f. Severino's December 31 daily cash receipts of $9,583.10 were placed in the bank's night depository on that date but do not appear on the December 31 bank statement.

Problem 8-4B

Preparing a bank reconciliation and recording adjustments

P3

Required

1. Prepare the bank reconciliation for this company as of December 31, 2017.

2. Prepare the journal entries (in dollars and cents) necessary to bring the company's book balance of cash into conformity with the reconciled cash balance as of December 31, 2017.

Check   (1) Reconciled balance, $51,005.80; (2) Cr. Notes Receivable, $19,000.00

Analysis Component

3. Explain the nature of the communications conveyed by a bank when the bank sends the depositor (*a*) a debit memorandum and (*b*) a credit memorandum.

Problem 8-5B
Preparing a bank
reconciliation and
recording adjustments

P3

Shamara Systems most recently reconciled its bank balance on April 30 and reported two checks outstanding at that time, No. 1771 for $781 and No. 1780 for $1,425.90. The following information is available for its May 31, 2017, reconciliation.

From the May 31 Bank Statement

PREVIOUS BALANCE	TOTAL CHECKS AND DEBITS	TOTAL DEPOSITS AND CREDITS	CURRENT BALANCE
18,290.70	13,094.80	16,566.80	21,762.70

CHECKS AND DEBITS			DEPOSITS AND CREDITS	
Date	No.	Amount	Date	Amount
05/01	1771	781.00	05/04	2,438.00
05/02	1783	382.50	05/14	2,898.00
05/04	1782	1,285.50	05/22	1,801.80
05/11	1784	1,449.60	05/25	7,350.00 CM
05/18		431.80 NSF	05/26	2,079.00
05/25	1787	8,032.50		
05/26	1785	63.90		
05/29	1788	654.00		
05/31		14.00 SC		

From Shamara Systems's Accounting Records

Cash Receipts Deposited			
Date			Cash Debit
May	4		2,438.00
	14		2,898.00
	22		1,801.80
	26		2,079.00
	31		2,727.30
			11,944.10

Cash Disbursements		
Check No.		Cash Credit
1782		1,285.50
1783		382.50
1784		1,449.60
1785		63.90
1786		353.10
1787		8,032.50
1788		644.00
1789		639.50
		12,850.60

Cash						Acct. No. 101
Date		Explanation	PR	Debit	Credit	Balance
Apr.	30	Balance				16,083.80
May	31	Total receipts	R7	11,944.10		28,027.90
	31	Total disbursements	D8		12,850.60	15,177.30

Additional Information

Check No. 1788 is correctly drawn for $654 to pay for May utilities; however, the recordkeeper misread the amount and entered it in the accounting records with a debit to Utilities Expense and a credit to Cash for $644. The bank paid and deducted the correct amount. The NSF check shown in the statement was originally received from a customer, W. Sox, in payment of her account. The company has not yet recorded its return. The credit memorandum (CM) is from a $7,400 note that the bank collected for the company. The bank deducted a $50 collection expense and deposited the remainder in the company's account. The collection and expense have not yet been recorded.

Required

1. Prepare the May 31, 2017, bank reconciliation for Shamara Systems.
2. Prepare the journal entries (in dollars and cents) to adjust the book balance of cash to the reconciled balance.

Analysis Component

3. The bank statement reveals that some of the prenumbered checks in the sequence are missing. Describe three possible situations to explain this.

Check   (1) Reconciled balance, $22,071.50; (2) Cr. Notes Receivable, $7,400.00

(This serial problem began in Chapter 1 and continues through most of the book. If previous chapter segments were not completed, the serial problem can begin at this point.)

SERIAL PROBLEM
Business Solutions

P3

SP 8   Santana Rey receives the March bank statement for **Business Solutions** on April 11, 2018. The March 31 bank statement shows an ending cash balance of $67,566. A comparison of the bank statement with the general ledger Cash account, No. 101, reveals the following.

a. S. Rey notices that the bank erroneously cleared a $500 check against her account in March that she did not issue. The check documentation included with the bank statement shows that this check was actually issued by a company named Business Systems.

b. On March 25, the bank lists a $50 charge for the safety deposit box expense that Business Solutions agreed to rent from the bank beginning March 25.

c. On March 26, the bank lists a $102 charge for printed checks that Business Solutions ordered from the bank.

d. On March 31, the bank lists $33 interest earned on Business Solutions's checking account for the month of March.

e. S. Rey notices that the check she issued for $128 on March 31, 2018, has not yet cleared the bank.

f. S. Rey verifies that all deposits made in March do appear on the March bank statement.

g. The general ledger Cash account, No. 101, shows an ending cash balance per books of $68,057 as of March 31 (prior to any reconciliation).

© Alexander Image/Shutterstock RF

Required

1. Prepare a bank reconciliation for Business Solutions for the month ended March 31, 2018.
2. Prepare any necessary adjusting entries. Use Miscellaneous Expenses, No. 677, for any bank charges. Use Interest Revenue, No. 404, for any interest earned on the checking account for the month of March.

Check   (1) Adj. bank bal., $67,938

The **General Ledger** tool in *Connect* automates several of the procedural steps in the accounting cycle so that the financial professional can focus on the impacts of each transaction on the various financial reports.

GENERAL LEDGER PROBLEM

GL 8-1   General Ledger assignment GL 8-1, based on Problem 8-2A, focuses on transactions related to the petty cash fund and highlights the impact each transaction has on net income, if any. Prepare the journal entries related to the petty cash fund and assess the impact of each transaction on the company's net income, if any.

Available only in Connect

Beyond the Numbers

REPORTING IN
ACTION

C2   A1

APPLE

BTN 8-1   Refer to Apple's financial statements in Appendix A to answer the following.

1. For both fiscal years ended September 26, 2015, and September 27, 2014, identify the total amount of cash and cash equivalents. Determine the percent (rounded to one decimal) that this amount represents of total current assets, total current liabilities, total shareholders' equity, and total assets for both years. Comment on any trends.

2. For fiscal years ended September 26, 2015, and September 27, 2014, use the information in the statement of cash flows to determine the percent change (rounded to one decimal) between the beginning and ending year amounts of cash and cash equivalents.

3. Compute the days' sales uncollected (rounded to two decimals) as of September 26, 2015, and September 27, 2014. Has the collection of receivables improved? Are accounts receivable an important asset for Apple? Explain.

Fast Forward

4. Access Apple's financial statements for fiscal years ending after September 26, 2015, from its website (Apple.com) or the SEC's EDGAR database (SEC.gov). Recompute its days' sales uncollected for years ending after September 26, 2015. Compare this to the days' sales uncollected for fiscal years ended September 26, 2015, and September 27, 2014.

COMPARATIVE
ANALYSIS

A1

APPLE
GOOGLE

BTN 8-2   Key comparative figures for Apple and Google follow.

$ millions	Apple		Google	
	Current Year	Prior Year	Current Year	Prior Year
Accounts receivable	$ 16,849	$ 17,460	$11,556	$ 9,383
Net sales	233,715	182,795	74,989	66,001

Required

Compute days' sales uncollected (rounded to two decimals) for these companies for each of the two years shown. Comment on any trends for the companies. Which company has the largest percent change (rounded to two decimals) in days' sales uncollected?

ETHICS
CHALLENGE

C1

BTN 8-3   Harriet Knox, Ralph Patton, and Marcia Diamond work for a family physician, Dr. Gwen Conrad, who is in private practice. Dr. Conrad is knowledgeable about office management practices and has segregated the cash receipt duties as follows. Knox opens the mail and prepares a triplicate list of money received. She sends one copy of the list to Patton, the cashier, who deposits the receipts daily in the bank. Diamond, the recordkeeper, receives a copy of the list and posts payments to patients' accounts. About once a month the office clerks have an expensive lunch they pay for as follows. First, Patton endorses a patient's check in Dr. Conrad's name and cashes it at the bank. Knox then destroys the remittance advice accompanying the check. Finally, Diamond posts payment to the customer's account as a miscellaneous credit. The three justify their actions by their relatively low pay and knowledge that Dr. Conrad will likely never miss the money.

Required

1. Who is the best person in Dr. Conrad's office to reconcile the bank statement?
2. Would a bank reconciliation uncover this office fraud?
3. What are some procedures to detect this type of fraud?
4. Suggest additional internal controls that Dr. Conrad could implement.

BTN 8-4   Assume you are a business consultant. The owner of a company sends you an e-mail expressing concern that the company is not taking advantage of its discounts offered by vendors. The company currently uses the gross method of recording purchases. The owner is considering a review of all invoices and payments from the previous period. Due to the volume of purchases, however, the owner recognizes that this is time-consuming and costly. The owner *seeks your advice about monitoring purchase discounts* in the future. Provide a response in memorandum form. (*Hint:* It will help to review the recording of purchase discounts in Appendix 5D.)

COMMUNICATING IN PRACTICE

P4

BTN 8-5   Visit the Association of Certified Fraud Examiners website and open the "2016 Report to the Nation" (s3-us-west-2.amazonaws.com/acfepublic/2016-report-to-the-nations.pdf). Read the two-page Executive Summary and fill in the following blanks.

TAKING IT TO THE NET

C1 P1

1. The median loss for all cases in our study was _____, with _____ of cases causing losses of $1 million or more.
2. The typical organization loses _____ of revenues in a given year as a result of fraud.
3. The median duration—the amount of time from when the fraud commenced until it was detected—for the fraud cases reported to us was _____.
4. Asset misappropriation was by far the most common form of occupational fraud, occurring in more than _____ of cases, but causing the smallest median loss of _____.
5. Financial statement fraud was on the other end of the spectrum, occurring in less than 10% of cases but causing a median loss of _____. Corruption cases fell in the middle, with _____ of cases and a median loss of _____.
6. The most common detection method in our study was _____ (39.1% of cases).
7. Approximately _____ of the cases reported to us targeted privately held or publicly owned companies. These for-profit organizations suffered the largest median losses among the types of organizations analyzed, at _____ and _____, respectively.

BTN 8-6   Organize the class into teams. Each team must prepare a list of 10 internal controls a consumer could observe in a typical retail department store. When called upon, the team's spokesperson must be prepared to share controls identified by the team that have not been shared by another team's spokesperson.

TEAMWORK IN ACTION

C1

BTN 8-7   Review the opening feature of this chapter that highlights Vlad Tenev and Baiju Bhatt and their company **Robinhood**. Their company plans to open a kiosk in the Ferry Building in San Francisco to sell Robinhood shirts, hats, and other merchandise. Other retail outlets and expansion plans may be in the works.

ENTREPRENEURIAL DECISION

C1 P1

Required

1. List the seven principles of internal control and explain how a retail outlet might implement each of the principles in its store.
2. Do you believe that a retail outlet will need to add controls to the business as it expands? Explain.

BTN 8-8   Visit an area of your college that serves the student community with either products or services. Some examples are food services, libraries, and bookstores. Identify and describe between four and eight internal controls being implemented.

HITTING THE ROAD

C1

GLOBAL DECISION

C2 A1

Samsung

BTN 8-9 The following information is from Samsung (Samsung.com or its financial statements in Appendix A), which is a leading manufacturer of consumer electronic products.

₩ in millions	Current Year	Prior Year
Cash	₩ 22,636,744	₩ 16,840,766
Accounts receivable	28,520,689	28,234,485
Current assets	124,814,725	115,146,026
Total assets	242,179,521	230,422,958
Current liabilities	50,502,909	52,013,913
Shareholders' equity	179,059,805	168,088,188
Net sales	200,653,482	206,205,987

Required

1. For each year, compute the percentage (rounded to one decimal) that cash represents of current assets, total assets, current liabilities, and shareholders' equity. Comment on any trends in these percentages.
2. Determine the percentage change (rounded to one decimal) between the current and prior year cash balances.
3. Compute the days' sales uncollected (rounded to one decimal) at the end of both the current year and the prior year. Has the collection of receivables improved? Explain.

GLOBAL VIEW

This section discusses similarities and differences between U.S. GAAP and IFRS regarding internal controls and in the accounting and reporting of cash.

Internal Control Purposes, Principles, and Procedures   Both U.S. GAAP and IFRS aim for high-quality financial reporting. The purposes and principles of internal control systems are fundamentally the same across the globe. However, culture and other realities suggest different emphases on the mix of control procedures, and some sensitivity to different customs and environments when establishing that mix. Nokia provides the following description of its control activities.

> Nokia has an internal audit function that acts as an independent appraisal function by examining and evaluating the adequacy and effectiveness of the company's system of internal control.

Global: If cash is in more than one currency, a company usually translates these amounts into U.S. dollars using the exchange rate as of the balance sheet date. Also, a company must disclose any restrictions on cash accounts located outside the United States.

Control of Cash   Accounting definitions for cash are similar for U.S. GAAP and IFRS. The need for control of cash is universal. This means that companies worldwide desire to apply cash management procedures as explained in this chapter and aim to control both cash receipts and disbursements. Accordingly, systems that employ tools such as cash monitoring mechanisms, verification of documents, and petty cash processes are applied worldwide. The basic techniques of this chapter are part of those control procedures.

Banking Activities as Controls   There is a global demand for banking services, bank statements, and bank reconciliations. To the extent feasible, companies utilize banking services as part of their effective control procedures. Further, bank statements are similarly used along with bank reconciliations to control and monitor cash.

IFRS

Internal controls are crucial to companies that convert from U.S. GAAP to IFRS. Major risks include misstatement of financial information and fraud. Other risks are ineffective communication of the impact of this change for investors, creditors, and others, and management's inability to certify the effectiveness of controls over financial reporting. ∎

 Global View Assignments

Discussion Questions 12 & 13

Quick Study 8-10

BTN 8-9

chapter 9

Accounting for Receivables

Learning Objectives

CONCEPTUAL

C1 Describe accounts receivable and how they occur and are recorded.

C2 Describe a note receivable, the computation of its maturity date, and the recording of its existence.

C3 Explain how receivables can be converted to cash before maturity.

ANALYTICAL

A1 Compute accounts receivable turnover and use it to help assess financial condition.

PROCEDURAL

P1 Apply the direct write-off method to accounts receivable.

P2 Apply the allowance method to accounts receivable.

P3 Estimate uncollectibles based on sales and accounts receivable.

P4 Record the honoring and dishonoring of a note and adjustments for interest.

© sanjeri/E+/Getty Images

Think ReGreen

LOS ANGELES—Sean Neman, Kevin Refoua, and David Duel founded **ReGreen Corporation** (**ReGreenCorp.com**), a company that helps clients "go green" *and* make it profitable. "Most companies don't have the in-house expertise to understand how to integrate [green] technologies," explains David. "We thought it was important to emphasize the cost and energy savings." The three promise to offset and reduce clients' energy bills.

The founders are so confident that they offer customers *guaranteed* payback on the cost of their work within two years. David claims that in some cases, ReGreen helps customers "achieve significant energy cost savings . . . with *zero* up-front costs to them!"

ReGreen's success is being noticed. It now has over 100 full-time employees and has worked with more than a thousand clients.

David insists that the road to success had its challenges, especially with managing its receivables. He recalls that early on, ReGreen had a problem with collecting an accounts receivable from a major client. Namely, the client failed to pay for $900,000 in services. This was a devastating blow. David explains that

"Emphasize the cost and energy savings"

—David Duel

they laid off 45 of 52 employees. During this crisis, David was quoted explaining that "in every sense, we've had to downsize our company . . . we're just trying to survive."

ReGreen has more than survived. It learned a crucial lesson in managing receivables and the importance of an effective accounting system. The entrepreneurs now regularly monitor receivables, including decisions on credit sales and policies for extending credit. They ensure credit sales are only extended to customers with good credit standing.

ReGreen knows its clients well. This includes cash payment patterns that allow it to estimate uncollectibles and minimize bad debts. "We're pleased to have met those challenges," explains David.

Success has not caused them to lose sight of their mission. "We've had such a positive response from our clients," proclaims David. We continually raise "awareness of the economic and environmental benefits" of sustainable energy.

Sources: *ReGreen website,* January 2017; *Forbes,* January 2014; *Bloomberg,* September 2011; *Market Wired,* August 2011; *PRLog,* February 2010; *L.A. Times,* July 2009

VALUING ACCOUNTS RECEIVABLE

C1

Describe accounts receivable and how they occur and are recorded.

A *receivable* is an amount due from another party. The two most common receivables are accounts receivable and notes receivable. Other receivables include interest receivable, rent receivable, tax refund receivable, and receivables from employees. **Accounts receivable** are amounts due from customers for credit sales. This section begins by describing how accounts receivable occur. It includes receivables that occur when customers use credit cards and when a company gives credit directly to customers.

Exhibit 9.1 shows recent dollar amounts of receivables and their percent of total assets for some well-known companies.

EXHIBIT 9.1

Accounts Receivable for Selected Companies

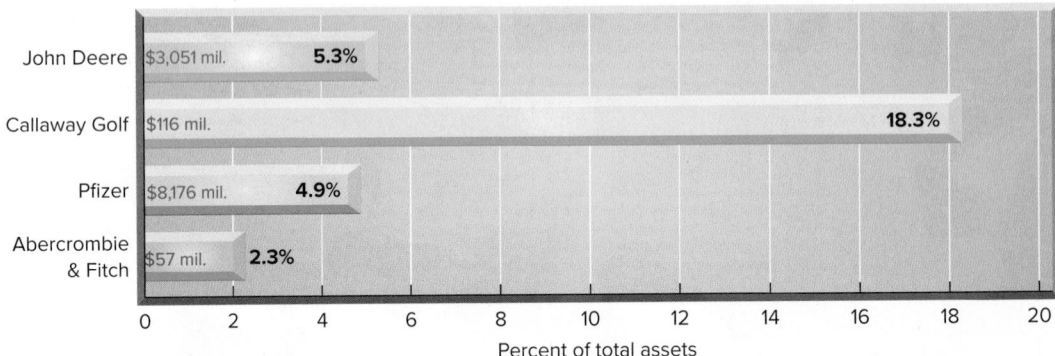

Sales on Credit   Credit sales are recorded by increasing (debiting) Accounts Receivable. A company also maintains a separate account for each customer that tracks how much that customer purchases, has already paid, and still owes. The general ledger continues to have a single Accounts Receivable account (called a *control* account). A supplementary record maintains a separate account for each customer and is called the *accounts receivable ledger* (or *accounts receivable subsidiary ledger*).

Exhibit 9.2 shows the relation between the Accounts Receivable account in the general ledger and its individual customer accounts in the accounts receivable ledger for TechCom, a small electronics wholesaler. This exhibit reports a $3,000 ending balance of TechCom's accounts receivable for June 30. TechCom has two major credit customers: CompStore and RDA Electronics. Its *schedule of accounts receivable* shows that the $3,000 balance of the Accounts Receivable account in the general ledger equals the total of its two customers' balances in the accounts receivable ledger.

EXHIBIT 9.2

General Ledger and the Accounts Receivable Ledger (before July 1 transactions)

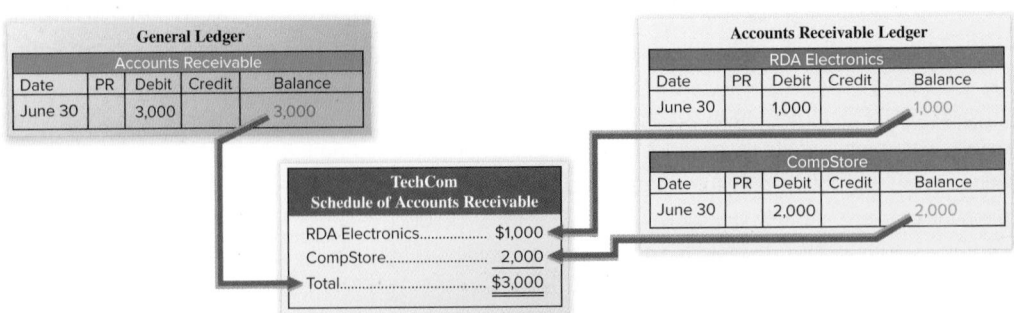

To see how accounts receivable from credit sales are recognized in the accounting records, we look at two transactions on July 1 between TechCom and its credit customers—see Exhibit 9.3.

The first is a credit sale of $950 to CompStore. The second transaction is a collection of $720 from RDA Electronics from a prior credit sale.

EXHIBIT 9.3

Accounts Receivable Transactions

July 1	Accounts Receivable—CompStore	950	
	Sales		950
	*Record credit sales.**		
July 1	Cash	720	
	Accounts Receivable—RDA Electronics.		720
	Record collection of credit sales.		

Assets = Liabilities + Equity
+950 +950

Assets = Liabilities + Equity
+720
−720

* We omit the entry to Dr. Cost of Sales and Cr. Merchandise Inventory to focus on sales and receivables; no sales returns and allowances are expected.

Exhibit 9.4 shows the general ledger and the accounts receivable ledger after recording the two July 1 transactions. The general ledger shows the effects of the sale, the collection, and the resulting balance of $3,230. These events are also reflected in the individual customer accounts: RDA Electronics has an ending balance of $280 and CompStore's ending balance is $2,950. The $3,230 sum of the individual accounts equals the debit balance of the Accounts Receivable account in the general ledger.

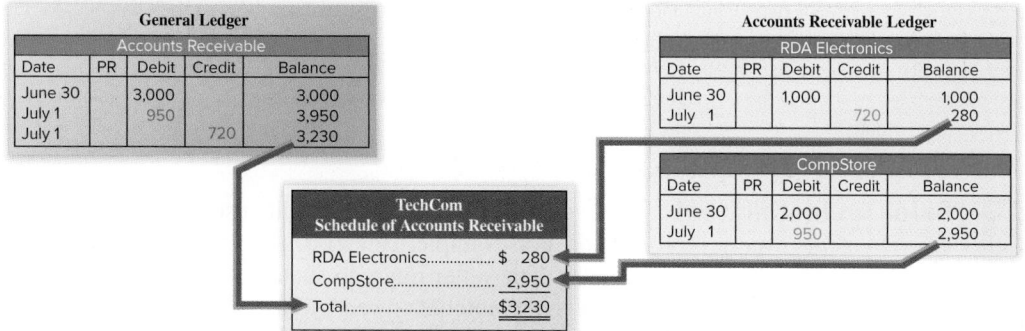

EXHIBIT 9.4

General Ledger and the Accounts Receivable Ledger (after July 1 transactions)

Sales on Store Credit Cards   Like TechCom, many large retailers such as **Home Depot** sell on credit. Many also maintain their own credit cards to grant credit to approved customers and to earn interest on any balance past due. The entries in this case are the same as those for TechCom except for added interest revenue as follows.

Nov. 1	Accounts Receivable	1,000	
	Sales		1,000
	Record sales on store credit card.		
Dec. 31	Accounts Receivable	15	
	Interest Revenue		15
	Interest of 1.5% earned on store card sales past due.		

Assets = Liabilities + Equity
+1,000 +1,000

Assets = Liabilities + Equity
+15 +15

Sales on Bank Credit Cards   Most companies allow customers to pay for products and services using bank (or third-party) credit cards such as **Visa**, **MasterCard**, or **American Express** and debit cards. Sellers allow customers to use credit cards and debit cards instead of granting credit directly for several reasons. First, the seller does not have to decide who gets credit and how much. Second, the seller avoids the risk of customers not paying (this risk is transferred to the card company). Third, the seller typically receives cash from the card company sooner than had it granted credit directly to customers. Fourth, more credit options for customers can lead to more sales.

Assets = Liabilities + Equity
+96   +100
                        −4

The seller pays a fee for services provided by the card company, often ranging from 1% to 5% of card sales. This fee reduces the cash received by the seller. To illustrate, if TechCom has $100 of credit card sales with a 4% fee, the entry is

July 15	Cash	96	
	Credit Card Expense	4	
	Sales		100
	*Record credit card sales less a 4% credit card expense.**		

* We omit the entry to Dr. Cost of Sales and Cr. Merchandise Inventory to focus on credit card expense.

Some sellers report credit card expense in the income statement as a discount subtracted from sales to get net sales. Other sellers classify it as a selling expense or an administrative expense. Arguments can be made for each approach. In this book we classify credit card expense as a selling expense.

◼ Decision Insight

Debit Card vs. Credit Card A buyer's debit card purchase reduces the buyer's cash account balance at the card company, which is often a bank. Since the buyer's cash account balance is a liability (with a credit balance) for the card company to the buyer, the card company would debit that account for a buyer's purchase—hence, the term *debit card*. A credit card reflects authorization by the card company of a line of credit for the buyer with preset interest rates and payment terms—hence, the term *credit card*. Most card companies waive interest charges if the buyer pays its balance each month. ◼

© Justin Sullivan/Getty Images

Sales on Installment Many companies allow their credit customers to make periodic payments over several months. For example, **Harley-Davidson** reports more than $2 billion in installment receivables. The seller refers to such assets as *installment accounts* (or *finance*) *receivable*, which are amounts owed by customers from credit sales for which payment is required in periodic amounts over an extended time period. Most of these receivables require interest payments, and they can be either current or noncurrent assets depending on the length of repayment.

◼ Decision Maker

Entrepreneur As a small retailer, you are considering allowing customers to buy merchandise using credit cards. Until now, your store accepted only cash and checks. What analysis do you use to make this decision? ◼ [*Answer:* This analysis must weigh benefits versus costs. The main benefit is the potential to increase sales by attracting customers who prefer the convenience of credit cards. The main cost is the fee charged by the credit card company. We must estimate the expected increase in sales from allowing credit cards and then subtract (1) normal costs and expenses and (2) card fees associated with the expected sales increase. If analysis shows an increase in profit, the store should probably accept credit cards.]

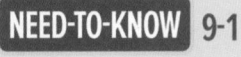 **9-1**

Credit Card Sales

C1

A small retailer allows customers to use two different credit cards in charging purchases. The AA Bank Card assesses a 5% service charge for credit card sales. The VIZA Card assesses a 3% charge on sales for using its card. This retailer also has its own store credit card. As of January 31 month-end, the retailer earned $75 in net interest revenue on its own card. Prepare journal entries to record the following selected credit card transactions for the retailer. (The retailer uses the perpetual inventory system for recording sales.)

Jan. 2   Sold merchandise for $1,000 (that had cost $600) and accepted the customer's AA Bank Card.

6   Sold merchandise for $400 (that had cost $300) and accepted the customer's VIZA Card.

31   Recognized the $75 interest revenue earned on its store credit card for January.

Solution

Jan. 2	Cash..	950	
	Credit Card Expense*.....................................	50	
	Sales...		1,000
	*Record credit card sales less 5% fee. *($1,000 × 0.05)*		
Jan. 2	Cost of Goods Sold......................................	600	
	Merchandise Inventory		600
	Record cost of sales.		
Jan. 6	Cash..	388	
	Credit Card Expense*.....................................	12	
	Sales...		400
	*Record credit card sales less 3% fee. *($400 × 0.03)*		
Jan. 6	Cost of Goods Sold......................................	300	
	Merchandise Inventory		300
	Record cost of sales.		
Jan. 31	Accounts Receivable	75	
	Interest Revenue		75
	Record interest earned from store credit card.		

Do More: QS 9-1, E 9-2, E 9-3

DIRECT WRITE-OFF METHOD

When a company directly grants credit to its customers, it expects that some customers will not pay what they promised. The accounts of these customers are *uncollectible accounts,* commonly called **bad debts.** The total amount of uncollectible accounts is an expense of selling on credit. Why do companies sell on credit if they expect some accounts to be uncollectible? The answer is that companies believe that granting credit will increase total sales and net income enough to offset bad debts. Companies use two methods to account for uncollectible accounts: (1) direct write-off method and (2) allowance method.

P1

Apply the direct write-off method to accounts receivable.

Recording and Writing Off Bad Debts   The **direct write-off method** of accounting for bad debts records the loss from an uncollectible account receivable when it is determined to be uncollectible. No attempt is made to predict bad debts expense. To illustrate, if TechCom determines on January 23 that it cannot collect $520 owed to it by its customer J. Kent, it recognizes the loss using the direct write-off method as follows.

Point: Managers realize that some portion of credit sales will be uncollectible, but which credit sales are uncollectible is unknown.

Jan. 23	Bad Debts Expense...................................	520	
	Accounts Receivable—J. Kent		520
	Write off an uncollectible account.		

Assets = Liabilities + Equity
−520   −520

The debit in this entry charges the uncollectible amount directly to the current period's Bad Debts Expense account. The credit removes its balance from the Accounts Receivable account in the general ledger (and its subsidiary ledger).

Recovering a Bad Debt   Sometimes an account written off is later collected. If the account of J. Kent that was written off directly to Bad Debts Expense is later collected in full, the following two entries record this recovery.

Point: Recovery of a bad debt always requires two journal entries.

Mar. 11	Accounts Receivable—J. Kent..........................	520	
	Bad Debts Expense		520
	Reinstate account previously written off.		
Mar. 11	Cash...	520	
	Accounts Receivable—J. Kent		520
	Record full payment of account.		

Assets = Liabilities + Equity
+520   +520

Assets = Liabilities + Equity
+520
−520

Assessing the Direct Write-Off Method   Many publicly traded companies and thousands of privately held companies use the direct write-off method; they include **Rand Medical Billing, Gateway Distributors, First Industrial Realty, New Frontier Energy, Globalink, Solar3D,** and **Sub Surface Waste Management.** The following disclosure by **Pharma-Bio Serv** is the usual justification for this method: Bad debts are accounted for using the direct write-off method whereby an expense is recognized only when a specific account is determined to be uncollectible. The effect of using this method approximates that of the allowance method. Companies weigh at least two concepts when considering use of the direct write-off method: (1) expense recognition and (2) materiality.

Expense Recognition Applied to Bad Debts   The **expense recognition principle** requires expenses to be reported in the same period as the sales they helped produce. This means that if extending credit to customers helped produce sales, the bad debts expense linked to those sales is matched and reported in the same period. The direct write-off method usually does *not* best match sales and expenses because bad debts expense is not recorded until an account becomes uncollectible, which often occurs in a period after that of the credit sale.

Materiality Applied to Bad Debts   The **materiality constraint** states that an amount can be ignored if its effect on the financial statements is unimportant to users' business decisions. The materiality constraint permits use of the direct write-off method when its results are similar to using the allowance method.

NEED-TO-KNOW 9-2

Entries under Direct Write-Off Method

P1

A retailer applies the direct write-off method in accounting for uncollectible accounts. Prepare journal entries to record the following selected transactions.

Feb. 14   The retailer determines that it cannot collect $400 of its accounts receivable from a customer named ZZZ Company.

Apr. 1   ZZZ Company unexpectedly pays its account in full to the retailer, which then records its recovery of this bad debt.

Solution

Feb. 14	Bad Debts Expense..	400	
	Accounts Receivable—ZZZ Co............................		400
	Write off an account.		
Apr. 1	Accounts Receivable—ZZZ Co.	400	
	Bad Debts Expense		400
	Reinstate an account previously written off.		
Apr. 1	Cash...	400	
	Accounts Receivable—ZZZ Co............................		400
	Record cash received on account.		

Do More: QS 9-2, QS 9-3, E 9-4

ALLOWANCE METHOD

P2

Apply the allowance method to accounts receivable.

The **allowance method** of accounting for bad debts matches the *estimated* loss from uncollectible accounts receivable against the sales they helped produce. We must use estimated losses because when sales occur, sellers do not know which customers will not pay their bills. This means that at the end of each period, the allowance method requires an estimate of the total bad debts expected from that period's sales. This method has two advantages over the direct write-off method: (1) it records estimated bad debts expense in the period when the related sales are recorded and (2) it reports accounts receivable on the balance sheet at the estimated amount of cash to be collected.

Recording Bad Debts Expense   The allowance method estimates bad debts expense at the end of each accounting period and records it with an adjusting entry. TechCom, for instance, had credit sales of $300,000 during its first year of operations. At the end of the first year, $20,000 of credit sales remained uncollected. Based on the experience of similar businesses, TechCom estimated that $1,500 of its accounts receivable would be uncollectible and made the following adjusting entry.

Method	Bad Debts Expense Recognized
Direct write-off...	*In future* when account deemed uncollectible.
Allowance.......	*Currently,* yielding realizable Accts. Rec. bal.

Dec. 31	Bad Debts Expense...................................	1,500	
	Allowance for Doubtful Accounts		1,500
	Record estimated bad debts.		

Assets = Liabilities + Equity
−1,500   −1,500

The estimated bad debts expense of $1,500 is reported on the income statement (as either a selling expense or an administrative expense). The **Allowance for Doubtful Accounts** is a contra asset account. A contra account is used instead of reducing accounts receivable directly because at the time of the adjusting entry, the company does not know which customers will not pay. TechCom's account balances (in T-account form) for Accounts Receivable and its Allowance for Doubtful Accounts are as shown in Exhibit 9.5.

Allowance method

Advantages:
- Receivables fairly stated
- Bad debts expense matched with sales
- Writing off bad debt does not affect net receivables or income

Disadvantages:
- Estimates needed

Accounts Receivable		
Dec. 31	20,000	

Allowance for Doubtful Accounts		
	Dec. 31	1,500

EXHIBIT 9.5

Ledger after Bad Debts Adjusting Entry

The Allowance for Doubtful Accounts credit balance of $1,500 reduces accounts receivable to its **realizable value,** which is the amount expected to be received. Although credit customers owe $20,000 to TechCom, only $18,500 is expected in cash collections from these customers. (TechCom continues to bill its customers a total of $20,000.) In the balance sheet, the Allowance for Doubtful Accounts is subtracted from Accounts Receivable and is often reported as shown in Exhibit 9.6.

Current assets		
Accounts receivable......................................	$20,000	
Less allowance for doubtful accounts......................	1,500	$18,500

EXHIBIT 9.6

Balance Sheet for the Allowance for Doubtful Accounts

Sometimes the Allowance for Doubtful Accounts is not reported separately. This alternative presentation is shown in Exhibit 9.7 (also see Appendix A).

Current assets	
Accounts receivable (net of $1,500 doubtful accounts).....................	$18,500

EXHIBIT 9.7

Alternative Presentation of the Allowance for Doubtful Accounts

Writing Off a Bad Debt   When specific accounts are identified as uncollectible, they are written off against the Allowance for Doubtful Accounts. To illustrate, TechCom decides that J. Kent's $520 account is uncollectible and makes the following entry to write it off.

Jan. 23	Allowance for Doubtful Accounts	520	
	Accounts Receivable—J. Kent		520
	Write off an uncollectible account.		

Assets = Liabilities + Equity
+520
−520

Posting this write-off entry to the Accounts Receivable account removes the amount of the bad debt from the general ledger (it is also posted to the accounts receivable subsidiary

Point: Bad Debts Expense is not debited in the write-off because it was recorded in the period when sales occurred.

ledger). The general ledger accounts now appear as follows (assuming no other transactions affect these accounts).

Accounts Receivable					Allowance for Doubtful Accounts				
Dec. 31	20,000								
		Jan. 23	520		Jan. 23	520			
							Dec. 31	1,500	

Point: In posting a write-off, the ledger's Explanation column indicates the reason for this credit so it is not misinterpreted as payment in full.

The write-off does *not* affect the realizable value of accounts receivable, as shown in Exhibit 9.8. Neither total assets nor net income is affected by the write-off of a specific account. Instead, both assets and net income are affected in the period when bad debts expense is predicted and recorded with an adjusting entry.

EXHIBIT 9.8

Realizable Value before and after Write-Off of a Bad Debt

	Before Write-Off	After Write-Off
Accounts receivable	$ 20,000	$ 19,480
Less allowance for doubtful accounts	1,500	980
Realizable value of accounts receivable	**$18,500**	**$18,500**

Exhibit 9.9 portrays the allowance method. It shows the creation of the allowance to reflect future write-offs—which some managers view like creating a cookie jar reserve. It also shows the decrease of the allowance through write-offs—which some managers view like eating down the cookie jar reserve.

EXHIBIT 9.9

Increases and Decreases to the Allowance for Doubtful Accounts

Adjusting entries add to allowance for doubtful accounts.

Bad debt write-offs subtract from allowance for doubtful accounts.

Recovering a Bad Debt   When a customer fails to pay and the account is written off as uncollectible, his or her credit standing declines. To help restore credit standing, a customer sometimes volunteers to pay all or part of the amount owed. Two entries are required when collecting an account previously written off by the allowance method. The first is to reverse the write-off and reinstate the customer's account. The second is to record the collection of the reinstated account. To illustrate, if on March 11 Kent pays in full his account previously written off, the entries are

Assets = Liabilities + Equity
+520
−520

Mar. 11	Accounts Receivable—J. Kent.	520	
	Allowance for Doubtful Accounts		520
	Reinstate account previously written off.		

Assets = Liabilities + Equity
+520
−520

Mar. 11	Cash	520	
	Accounts Receivable—J. Kent		520
	Record full payment of account.		

In this illustration, Kent paid the entire amount previously written off, but sometimes a customer pays only a portion of the amount owed. If we believe this customer will later pay in full, we return the entire amount owed to accounts receivable, but if we expect no further collection, we return only the amount paid.

A retailer applies the allowance method in accounting for uncollectible accounts. Prepare journal entries to record the following selected transactions.

NEED-TO-KNOW 9-3

Entries under Allowance Method

P2

2016
Dec. 31   The retailer estimates $3,000 of its accounts receivable are uncollectible.

2017
Feb. 14   The retailer determines that it cannot collect $400 of its accounts receivable from a customer named ZZZ Company.
Apr. 1   ZZZ Company unexpectedly pays its account in full to the retailer, which then records its recovery of this bad debt.

Solution

2016			
Dec. 31	Bad Debts Expense.....................................	3,000	
	Allowance for Doubtful Accounts		3,000
	Record estimated bad debts.		
2017			
Feb. 14	Allowance for Doubtful Accounts............................	400	
	Accounts Receivable—ZZZ Co.............................		400
	Write off an account.		
Apr. 1	Accounts Receivable—ZZZ Co.	400	
	Allowance for Doubtful Accounts		400
	Reinstate an account previously written off.		
Apr. 1	Cash...	400	
	Accounts Receivable—ZZZ Co.............................		400
	Record cash received on account.		

Do More: QS 9-5, E 9-9

ESTIMATING BAD DEBTS

Under the *allowance method only* do we estimate bad debts expense to prepare an adjusting entry at the end of each accounting period. There are two common methods. One is based on the income statement relation between bad debts expense and sales. The second is based on the balance sheet relation between accounts receivable and the allowance for doubtful accounts.

P3
Estimate uncollectibles based on sales and accounts receivable.

Percent of Sales Method

The *percent of sales method,* also called the *income statement method,* is based on the idea that a percent of a company's credit sales for the period is uncollectible. To illustrate, assume that Musicland has credit sales of $400,000 in year 2017. Based on past experience, Musicland estimates 0.6% of credit sales to be uncollectible. This implies that Musicland expects $2,400 of bad debts expense from its sales (computed as $400,000 × 0.006). The adjusting entry to record this estimated expense is

Point: Focus is on *credit* sales because cash sales do not produce bad debts.

Dec. 31*	Bad Debts Expense	2,400	
	Allowance for Doubtful Accounts		2,400
	Record estimated bad debts.		

* The adjusting entry above applies our three-step adjusting entry process:
Step 1: Current balance for Bad Debts Expense <u>is</u> $0 debit (as the expense account was closed in prior period).
Step 2: Current balance for Bad Debts Expense <u>should be</u> $2,400 debit.
Step 3: Record entry to get from step 1 to step 2.

Assets = Liabilities + Equity
−2,400   −2,400

Bad Debts Expense	
Unadj. bal. 0	
Adj. (% sales) 2,400	
Est. bal. 2,400	

The allowance account ending balance on the balance sheet for this method would rarely equal the bad debts expense on the income statement. This is because unless a company is in its first period of operations, its allowance account has a zero balance only if the prior amounts written

Point: When using the *percent of sales method* for estimating uncollectibles, and because the "Unadj. bal." in Bad Debts Expense is always $0, the adjusting entry amount always equals the % of sales.

off as uncollectible *exactly* equal the prior estimated bad debts expenses. (When computing bad debts expense as a percent of sales, managers monitor and adjust the percent so it is not too high or too low.)

Percent of Receivables Method

The *accounts receivable methods,* also called *balance sheet methods,* use balance sheet relations to estimate bad debts—mainly the relation between accounts receivable and the allowance amount. The goal of the bad debts adjusting entry for these methods is to make the Allowance for Doubtful Accounts balance equal to the portion of accounts receivable that is estimated to be uncollectible. The estimated balance for the allowance account is obtained in one of two ways: (1) computing the percent uncollectible from the total accounts receivable or (2) aging accounts receivable.

Point: When using an accounts receivable method for estimating uncollectibles, the allowance account balance is adjusted to equal the estimate of uncollectibles.

The *percent of accounts receivable method* assumes that a percent of a company's receivables is uncollectible. This percent is based on past experience and is impacted by current conditions such as economic trends and customer difficulties. The total dollar amount of all receivables is multiplied by this percent to get the estimated dollar amount of uncollectible accounts—reported in the balance sheet as the Allowance for Doubtful Accounts.

To illustrate, assume that Musicland has $50,000 of accounts receivable on December 31, 2017. Experience suggests 5% of its receivables is uncollectible. This means that *after* the adjusting entry is posted, we want the Allowance for Doubtful Accounts to show a $2,500 credit balance (5% of $50,000). We are also told that its beginning balance is $2,200, which is 5% of the $44,000 accounts receivable on December 31, 2016—see Exhibit 9.10.

EXHIBIT 9.10

Allowance for Doubtful Accounts after Bad Debts Adjusting Entry

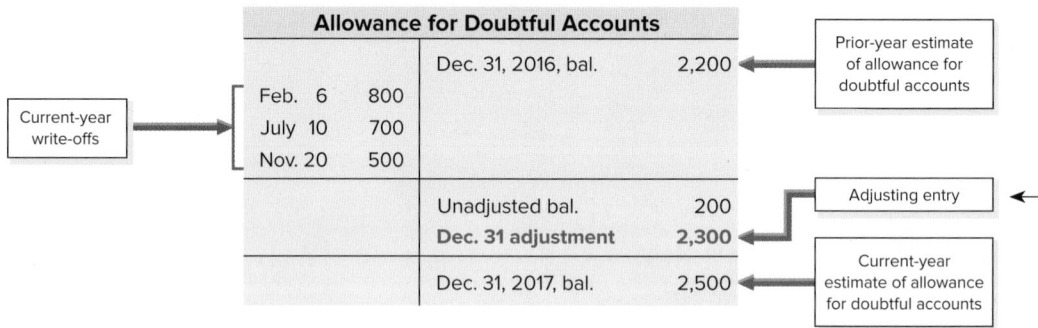

During 2017, accounts of customers are written off on February 6, July 10, and November 20. Thus, the account has a $200 credit balance *before* the December 31, 2017, adjustment. The adjusting entry to give the allowance account the estimated $2,500 balance is

Assets = Liabilities + Equity
−2,300   −2,300

Dec. 31*	Bad Debts Expense	2,300	
	Allowance for Doubtful Accounts		2,300
	Record estimated bad debts.		

* The adjusting entry above applies our three-step adjusting entry process:
Step 1: Current balance for Allowance account is $200 credit.
Step 2: Current balance for Allowance account should be $2,500 credit.
Step 3: Record entry to get from step 1 to step 2.

■ **Decision** Insight

Come of Age   Unlike wine, accounts receivable do not improve with age. The longer a receivable is past due, the less likely it is to be collected. An *aging schedule* uses this knowledge to estimate bad debts. The chart here is from a survey that reported estimates of bad debts for receivables grouped by how long they were past their due dates. Each company sets its own estimates based on its customers and its experiences with those customers' payment patterns. ■

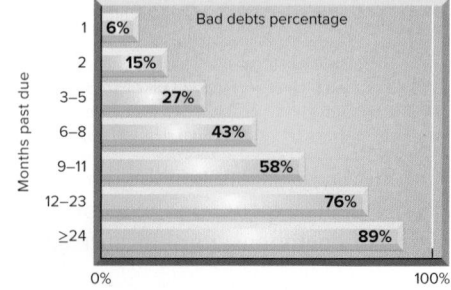

Aging of Receivables Method

The **aging of accounts receivable** method uses both past and current receivables information to estimate the allowance amount. Specifically, each receivable is classified by how long it is past its due date. Then estimates of uncollectible amounts are made assuming that the longer an amount is past due, the more likely it is to be uncollectible. Classifications are often based on 30-day periods. After the amounts are classified (or aged), experience is used to estimate the percent of each uncollectible class. These percents are applied to the amounts in each class and then totaled to get the estimated balance of the Allowance for Doubtful Accounts. This computation is performed by setting up a schedule such as Exhibit 9.11.

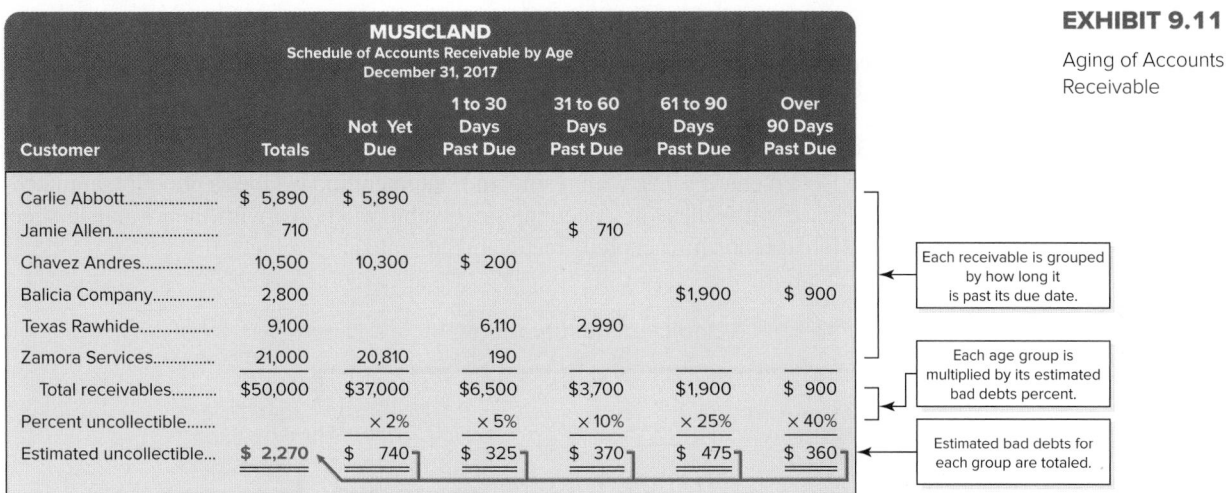

EXHIBIT 9.11

Aging of Accounts Receivable

Exhibit 9.11 lists each customer's individual balances assigned to one of five classes based on its days past due. The amounts in each class are totaled and multiplied by the estimated percent of uncollectible accounts for each class. The percents used are regularly reviewed to reflect changes in the company and economy.

To explain, Musicland has $3,700 in accounts receivable that are 31 to 60 days past due. Its management estimates 10% of the amounts in this age class are uncollectible, or a total of $370 ($3,700 × 10%). Similar analysis is done for each of the other four classes. The final total of $2,270 ($740 + $325 + $370 + $475 + $360) shown in the first column is the estimated balance for the Allowance for Doubtful Accounts. Exhibit 9.12 shows that because the allowance account

EXHIBIT 9.12

Computation of the Required Adjustment for the Accounts Receivable Method

Step 1:	Current account balance equals	Unadjusted balance	$ 200 credit
Step 2:	Determine what account balance should be	Estimated balance................	2,270 credit
Step 3:	Make adjustment to get from step 1 to step 2	**Required adjustment**	**$2,070 credit**

has an unadjusted credit balance of $200, the required adjustment to the Allowance for Doubtful Accounts is $2,070. (We could also use a T-account for this analysis as shown to the side.) This analysis yields the following end-of-period adjusting entry.

Allowance for Doubtful Accounts		
	Unadj. bal.	200
	Req. adj.	**2,070**
	Est. bal.	2,270

Dec. 31	Bad Debts Expense.....................................	2,070	
	Allowance for Doubtful Accounts		2,070
	Record estimated bad debts.		

Assets = Liabilities + Equity
−2,070   −2,070

Alternatively, if the allowance account had an unadjusted *debit* balance of $500 (instead of the $200 credit balance), its required adjustment would be computed as follows. (Again, a T-account can be used for this analysis as shown to the side.)

Point: A debit balance implies that write-offs for that period exceed the total allowance.

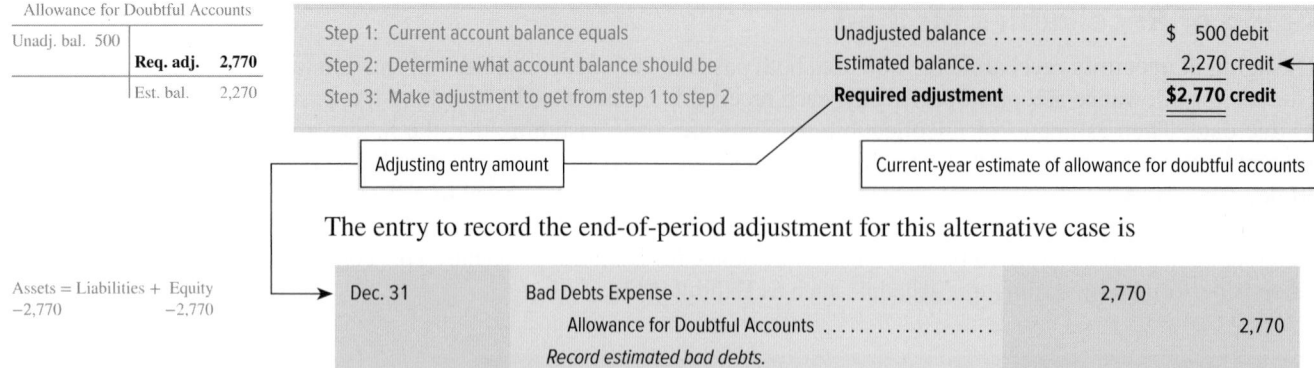

Allowance for Doubtful Accounts		
Unadj. bal. 500		
	Req. adj.	2,770
	Est. bal.	2,270

Step 1: Current account balance equals
Step 2: Determine what account balance should be
Step 3: Make adjustment to get from step 1 to step 2

Unadjusted balance	$ 500 debit
Estimated balance................	2,270 credit
Required adjustment	**$2,770 credit**

Adjusting entry amount

Current-year estimate of allowance for doubtful accounts

The entry to record the end-of-period adjustment for this alternative case is

Assets = Liabilities + Equity
−2,770　　　　　　 −2,770

Dec. 31	Bad Debts Expense	2,770	
	Allowance for Doubtful Accounts		2,770
	Record estimated bad debts.		

Point: Credit approval is usually not assigned to the selling dept. because its goal is to increase sales, and it may approve customers at the cost of increased bad debts. Instead, approval is assigned to a separate credit-granting or administrative dept.

The aging of accounts receivable method focuses on specific accounts and is usually the most reliable of the estimation methods.

Estimating Bad Debts—Summary of Methods　　Exhibit 9.13 summarizes the three estimation methods. Percent of sales, with its income statement focus, does a good job at matching bad debts expense with sales. The accounts receivable methods, with their balance sheet focus, do a better job at reporting accounts receivable at realizable value.

EXHIBIT 9.13

Methods to Estimate Bad Debts under the Allowance Method

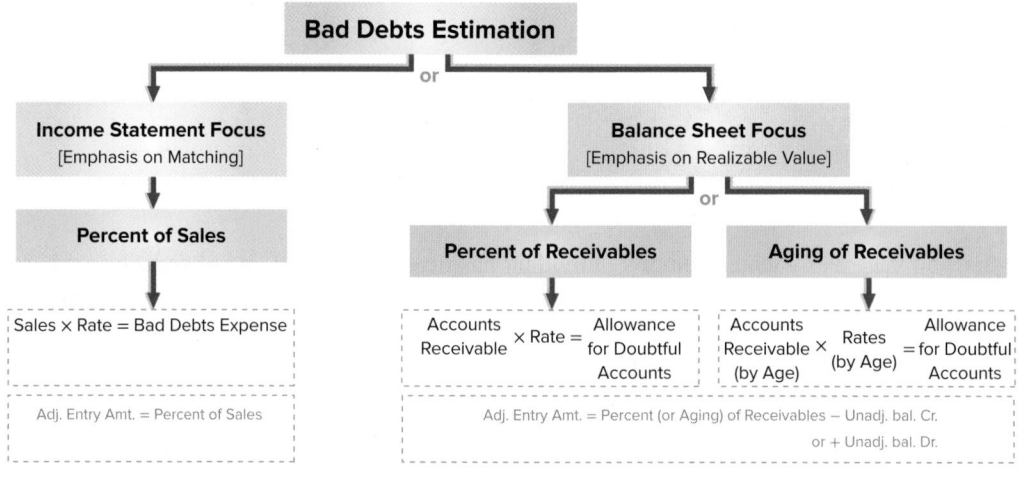

Decision Maker

Labor Union Chief　　One week prior to labor contract negotiations, financial statements are released showing no income growth. A 10% growth was predicted. Your analysis finds that the company increased its allowance for uncollectibles from 1.5% to 4.5% of receivables. Without this change, income would show a 9% growth. Does this analysis impact negotiations? ■　[*Answer:* Yes, this information is likely to impact negotiations. The obvious question is why the company greatly increased this allowance. The large increase in this allowance means a substantial increase in bad debts expense and a decrease in earnings. This change (coming prior to labor negotiations) also raises concerns since it reduces labor's bargaining power. We want to ask management for documentation justifying this increase. We also want data for two or three prior years and data from competitors. These data should give us some sense of whether the change in the allowance is justified.]

 **9-4**

Estimating Bad Debts

P3

At its December 31 year-end, a company estimates uncollectible accounts using the allowance method.
1. It prepared the following aging of receivables analysis. (a) Estimate the balance of the Allowance for Doubtful Accounts using the aging of accounts receivable method. (b) Prepare the adjusting entry to record bad debts expense using the estimate from part *a*. Assume the unadjusted balance in the Allowance for Doubtful Accounts is a $10 debit.

		Days Past Due				
	Total	0	1 to 30	31 to 60	61 to 90	Over 90
Accounts receivable	$2,600	$2,000	$300	$80	$100	$120
Percent uncollectible		1%	2%	5%	7%	10%

2. Refer to the data in part *1*. (a) Estimate the balance of the Allowance for Doubtful Accounts assuming the company uses 2% of total accounts receivable to estimate uncollectibles instead of the aging of receivables method in part *1*. (b) Prepare the adjusting entry to record bad debts expense using the estimate from part *2a*. Assume the unadjusted balance in the Allowance for Doubtful Accounts is a $4 credit.

3. Refer to the data in part *1*. (a) Estimate the balance of the uncollectibles assuming the company uses 0.5% of annual credit sales (annual credit sales were $10,000). (b) Prepare the adjusting entry to record bad debts expense using the estimate from part *3a*. Assume the unadjusted balance in the Allowance for Doubtful Accounts is a $4 credit.

Do More: QS 9-6, QS 9-7, E 9-5, E 9-6, E 9-7, E 9-8, E 9-10

Solutions

1a. Computation of the estimated balance of the allowance for uncollectibles:

Not due:	$2,000 × 0.01 =	$20
1 to 30:	300 × 0.02 =	6
31 to 60:	80 × 0.05 =	4
61 to 90:	100 × 0.07 =	7
Over 90:	120 × 0.10 =	12
		$49 credit

1b.

Dec. 31	Bad Debts Expense	59	
	Allowance for Doubtful Accounts		59
	*Record estimated bad debts.**		

Allowance for Doubtful Accounts			
Unadj. Dec. 31 10			
		Adj. Dec. 31	59
		Est. bal. Dec. 31	49

Step 1:	Current account balance equals	*Unadjusted balance	$10 debit
Step 2:	Determine what account balance should be	Estimated balance	49 credit
Step 3:	Make adjustment to get from step 1 to step 2	Required adjustment	$59 credit

2a. Computation of the estimated balance of the allowance for uncollectibles:

$2,600 × 0.02 = $52 credit

2b.

Dec. 31	Bad Debts Expense	48	
	Allowance for Doubtful Accounts		48
	*Record estimated bad debts.**		

Allowance for Doubtful Accounts			
		Unadj. Dec. 31	4
		Adj. Dec. 31	48
		Est. bal. Dec. 31	52

Step 1: Current account balance equals	*Unadjusted balance	$ 4 credit
Step 2: Determine what account balance should be	Estimated balance	52 credit
Step 3: Make adjustment to get from step 1 to step 2	Required adjustment	$48 credit

3a. Computation of the estimated balance of the bad debts expense:

$10,000 × 0.005 = $50 credit

3b.

Dec. 31	Bad Debts Expense	50	
	Allowance for Doubtful Accounts		50
	Record estimated bad debts.		

Bad Debts Expense		
Unadj. Dec. 31	0	
Adj. Dec. 31	50	
Est. bal. Dec. 31	50	

NOTES RECEIVABLE

A **promissory note** is a written promise to pay a specified amount of money, usually with interest, either on demand or at a stated future date. Promissory notes are used in many transactions, including paying for products and services, and lending and borrowing money. Sellers sometimes ask for a note to replace an account receivable when a customer requests additional time to pay a past-due account. For legal reasons, sellers generally prefer to receive notes when the credit period is long and when the receivable is for a large amount. If a lawsuit is needed to collect from a customer, a note is the buyer's written acknowledgment of the debt, its amount, and its terms.

C2

Describe a note receivable, the computation of its maturity date, and the recording of its existence.

Exhibit 9.14 shows a promissory note dated July 10, 2017. For this note, Julia Browne promises to pay TechCom or to its order (according to TechCom's instructions) a specified amount of money ($1,000), called the **principal of a note,** at a stated future date (October 8, 2017). As the one who signed the note and promised to pay it at maturity, Browne is the **maker of the note.** As the person to whom the note is payable, TechCom is the **payee of the note.** To Browne, the note is a liability called a *note payable.* To TechCom, the same note is an asset called a *note receivable.* This note bears interest at 12%, as written on the note. **Interest** is the charge for using the money until its due date. To a borrower, interest is an expense. To a lender, it is revenue.

EXHIBIT 9.14

Promissory Note

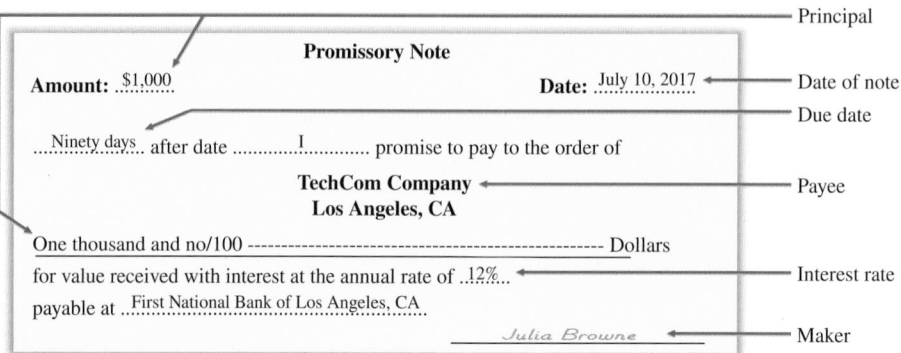

Computing Maturity and Interest

This section describes key computations for notes including the determination of maturity date, period covered, and interest computation.

Maturity Date and Period The **maturity date of a note** is the day the note (principal and interest) must be repaid. The *period* of a note is the time from the note's (contract) date to its maturity date. Many notes mature in less than a full year, and the period they cover is often expressed in days. When the time of a note is expressed in days, its maturity date is the stated number of days after the note's date. As an example, a five-day note dated June 15 matures and is due on June 20. A 90-day note dated July 10 matures on October 8. This October 8 due date is computed as shown in Exhibit 9.15. The period of a note is sometimes expressed in months or years. When months are used, the note matures and is payable in the month of its maturity on the *same day of the month* as its original date. A nine-month note dated July 10, for instance, is payable on April 10. The same analysis applies when years are used.

EXHIBIT 9.15

Maturity Date Computation

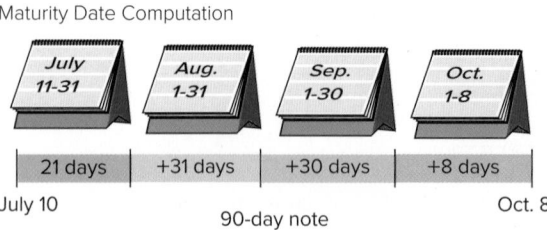

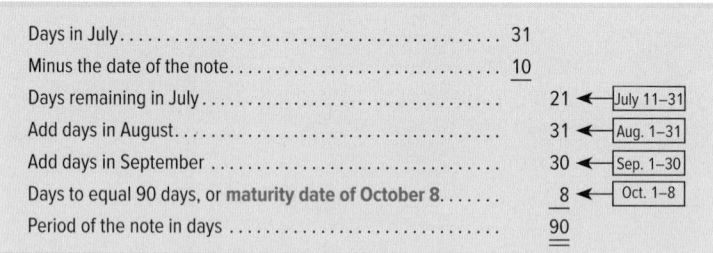

Interest Computation *Interest* is the cost of borrowing money for the borrower or, alternatively, the profit from lending money for the lender. Unless otherwise stated, the rate of interest on a note is the rate charged for the use of the principal for one year. The formula for computing interest on a note is shown in Exhibit 9.16.

EXHIBIT 9.16

Computation of Interest Formula

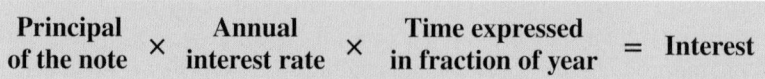

To simplify interest computations, a year is commonly treated as having 360 days (called the *banker's rule* in the business world and widely used in commercial transactions). **We treat a**

year as having 360 days for interest computations in the examples and assignments. Using the promissory note in Exhibit 9.14 where we have a 90-day, 12%, $1,000 note, the total interest is computed as follows.

$$\$1,000 \times 12\% \times \frac{90}{360} = \$1,000 \times 0.12 \times 0.25 = \$30$$

Point: If the *banker's rule* is <u>not</u> followed, interest is computed as:

$1,000 × 12% × 90/365 = $29.589041

The *banker's rule* would yield $30, which is easier to account for than $29.589041.

Recording Notes Receivable

Notes receivable are usually recorded in a single Notes Receivable account to simplify record-keeping. To illustrate the recording for the receipt of a note, we use the $1,000, 90-day, 12% promissory note in Exhibit 9.14. TechCom received this note at the time of a product sale to Julia Browne. This transaction is recorded as

July 10*	Notes Receivable..................................	1,000	
	Sales		1,000
	Sold goods in exchange for a 90-day, 12% note.		

Assets = Liabilities + Equity
+1,000   +1,000

* We omit the entry to Dr. Cost of Sales and Cr. Merchandise Inventory to focus on sales and receivables.

When a seller accepts a note from an overdue customer to grant a time extension on a past-due account receivable, it will often collect part of the past-due balance in cash. To illustrate, assume that TechCom agreed to accept $232 in cash along with a $600, 60-day, 15% note from Jo Cook to settle her $832 past-due account. TechCom made the following entry to record receipt of this cash and note.

Oct. 5	Cash..	232	
	Notes Receivable..................................	600	
	Accounts Receivable—J. Cook.....................		832
	Received cash and note to settle account.		

Assets = Liabilities + Equity
+232
+600
−832

Valuing and Settling Notes

Recording an Honored Note
The principal and interest of a note are due on its maturity date. The maker of the note usually *honors* the note and pays it in full. To illustrate, when J. Cook pays the note above on its due date, TechCom records it as follows.

Dec. 4	Cash..	615	
	Notes Receivable		600
	Interest Revenue		15
	Collect note with interest of $600 × 15% × 60/360.		

P4_____

Record the honoring and dishonoring of a note and adjustments for interest.

Assets = Liabilities + Equity
+615   +15
−600

Interest revenue, also called *interest earned,* is reported on the income statement.

Recording a Dishonored Note
When a note's maker does not pay at maturity, the note is *dishonored.* Dishonoring a note does not relieve the maker of the obligation to pay. The payee continues to attempt to collect. How do companies report this event? The balance of the Notes Receivable account should include only those notes that have not matured. Thus, when a note is dishonored, we remove the amount of this note from the Notes Receivable account and charge it back to an account receivable from its maker. To illustrate, assume that J. Cook dishonors the note above at maturity. The journal entry to record the dishonoring of the note follows.

Point: When posting a dishonored note to a customer's account, an explanation is included so as not to misinterpret the debit as a sale on account.

Dec. 4	Accounts Receivable—J. Cook........................	615	
	Interest Revenue		15
	Notes Receivable		600
	Charge account of J. Cook for a dishonored note and interest of $600 × 15% × 60/360.		

Assets = Liabilities + Equity
+615   +15
−600

Point: Reporting the details of notes is consistent with the *full disclosure principle,* which requires financial statements (including footnotes) to report all relevant information.

Charging a dishonored note back to the account of its maker serves two purposes. First, it removes the amount of the note from the Notes Receivable account and records the dishonored note in the maker's account. Second, and more important, if the maker of the dishonored note applies for credit in the future, his or her account will reveal all past dealings, including the dishonored note. Restoring the account also reminds the company to continue collection efforts from Cook for both principal and interest.

Recording End-of-Period Interest Adjustment

When notes receivable are outstanding at the end of a period, any accrued interest earned is recorded. To illustrate, on December 16, TechCom accepts a $3,000, 60-day, 12% note from a customer. When TechCom's accounting period ends on December 31, $15 of interest has accrued on this note ($3,000 × 12% × 15/360). The following adjusting entry records this revenue.

Assets = Liabilities + Equity
+15   +15

Dec. 31	Interest Receivable	15	
	Interest Revenue		15
	Record accrued interest earned.		

Point: Assume reversing entries are not made unless otherwise stated.

Interest revenue appears on the income statement, and interest receivable appears on the balance sheet as a current asset. When the December 16 note is collected on February 14, TechCom's entry to record the cash receipt is

Assets = Liabilities + Equity
+3,060   +45
  −15
−3,000

Feb. 14	Cash	3,060	
	Interest Revenue		45
	Interest Receivable.		15
	Notes Receivable		3,000
	Received payment of note and its interest.		

Total interest earned on the 60-day note is $60 ($3,000 × 12% × 60/360). The $15 credit to Interest Receivable on February 14 reflects the collection of the interest accrued from the December 31 adjusting entry. The $45 interest earned reflects TechCom's revenue from holding the note from January 1 to February 14 of the current period.

NEED-TO-KNOW 9-5

Honoring and
Dishonoring Notes

C2   P4

a. AA Company purchases $1,400 of merchandise from ZZ on December 16, 2016. ZZ accepts AA's $1,400, 90-day, 12% note as payment. ZZ's accounting period ends on December 31. Prepare entries for ZZ on December 16, 2016, and December 31, 2016. (Assume reversing entries are not made.)

b. Using the information in part *a,* prepare ZZ's March 16, 2017, entry if AA dishonors the note.

c. Instead of the facts in part *b,* prepare ZZ's March 16, 2017, entry if AA honors the note.

d. Assume the facts in part *b* above (AA dishonors the note). Then, on March 31, ZZ decides to write off the receivable from AA Company. Prepare that write-off entry assuming that ZZ uses the allowance method.

Solution

a.

Dec. 16	Note Receivable—AA.	1,400	
	Sales		1,400
Dec. 31	Interest Receivable	7	
	Interest Revenue *($1,400 × 12% × 15/360)*.		7

b.

Mar. 16	Accounts Receivable—AA	1,442	
	Interest Revenue *($1,400 × 12% × 75/360)*.		35
	Interest Receivable.		7
	Notes Receivable—AA		1,400

c.

Mar. 16	Cash	1,442	
	Interest Revenue		35
	Interest Receivable.		7
	Notes Receivable—AA		1,400

d.

Mar. 31	Allowance for Doubtful Accounts	1,442	
	Accounts Receivable—AA		1,442

> Do More: QS 9-8, QS 9-9,
> QS 9-10, E 9-11, E 9-12,
> E 9-13, E 9-14

Disposal of Receivables

Companies can convert receivables to cash before they are due if they need cash or do not want to be involved in collection activities. Converting receivables is usually done by (1) selling them or (2) using them as security for a loan.

C3

Explain how receivables can be converted to cash before maturity.

Selling Receivables   A company can sell its receivables to a finance company or bank. The buyer, called a *factor,* charges the seller a *factoring fee,* and then the buyer takes ownership of the receivables and receives cash when they come due. By incurring a factoring fee, the seller receives cash earlier and can pass the risk of bad debts to the factor. The seller also avoids costs of billing and accounting for the receivables. To illustrate, if TechCom sells $20,000 of its accounts receivable and is charged a 4% factoring fee, it records this sale as

Aug. 15	Cash	19,200	
	Factoring Fee Expense	800	
	Accounts Receivable		20,000
	Sold accounts receivable for cash less 4% fee.		

Assets = Liabilities + Equity
+19,200   −800
−20,000

The accounting for sales of notes receivable is similar to that for accounts receivable. The entries are covered in advanced courses.

Point: A seller of receivables always receives less cash than the amount of receivables sold due to factoring fees.

Pledging Receivables   A company can borrow money by *pledging* its receivables as security for the loan. Pledging receivables does not transfer the risk of bad debts to the lender because the borrower retains ownership of the receivables. If the borrower defaults on the loan, the lender has a right to be paid from the cash receipts of the receivable when collected. To illustrate, when TechCom borrows $35,000 and pledges its receivables as security, it records this transaction as

Aug. 20	Cash	35,000	
	Notes Payable.		35,000
	Borrow with a note secured by pledging receivables.		

Assets = Liabilities + Equity
+35,000 +35,000

Since pledged receivables are committed as security for a specific loan, the borrower's financial statements disclose the pledging of them. TechCom, for instance, includes the following note with its statements: Accounts receivable of $40,000 are pledged as security for a $35,000 note payable.

 **Decision Maker**

Analyst/Auditor   You are reviewing accounts receivable. Over the past five years, the allowance account as a percentage of gross accounts receivable shows a steady downward trend. What does this finding suggest? ■   [*Answer:* The downward trend suggests the company is reducing the relative amount charged to bad debts expense each year. This may reflect the company's desire to increase net income. On the other hand, it might be that collections have improved and the lower provision for bad debts is justified. If this is not the case, the lower allowances might be insufficient for bad debts.]

SUSTAINABILITY AND ACCOUNTING

© Helen H. Richardson/The Denver Post via Getty Images

ReGreen Corporation, featured in this chapter's opening story, is committed to improving the environment by helping businesses apply sustainable solutions. ReGreen's website touts its mission: "to improve the health of our planet and economy through the implementation of profitable energy solutions."

So far, ReGreen has been able to reduce their clients' energy consumption and water costs by an average of 60%. It offers customers guaranteed payback on sustainable investments within two years. "We're pleased to have met those challenges," proclaims co-founder David Duel.

David explains that the two-year payback guarantee on sustainable investments requires use of a reliable accounting system. ReGreen uses its accounting system to track investments in assets and the cost savings associated with these assets. This information is used to make sure ReGreen can meet its two-year payback guarantee. Without such a guarantee, businesses may be less willing to invest in sustainable solutions.

ReGreen also uses accounting data to track clients' progress on sustainability initiatives. ReGreen reviews its customers' accounting systems to analyze energy and water expenses. The entrepreneurs use these data to make recommendations on how ReGreen's customers can "achieve significant energy cost savings" and reduce their impact on the environment, explains David.

Decision Analysis **Accounts Receivable Turnover**

A1
_____
Compute accounts
receivable turnover and
use it to help assess
financial condition.

For a company selling on credit, we want to assess both the quality and liquidity of its accounts receivable. _Quality_ of receivables refers to the likelihood of collection without loss. Experience shows that the longer receivables are outstanding beyond their due date, the lower the likelihood of collection. _Liquidity_ of receivables refers to the speed of collection. **Accounts receivable turnover** is a measure of both the quality and liquidity of accounts receivable. It indicates how often, on average, receivables are received and collected during the period. The formula for this ratio is shown in Exhibit 9.17.

EXHIBIT 9.17

Accounts Receivable
Turnover

$$\text{Accounts receivable turnover} = \frac{\text{Net sales}}{\text{Average accounts receivable, net}}$$

We prefer to use net _credit_ sales in the numerator because cash sales do not create receivables. However, because financial statements rarely report net credit sales, our analysis uses net sales. The denominator is the _average_ accounts receivable balance, computed as (Beginning balance + Ending balance) ÷ 2. TechCom has an accounts receivable turnover of 5.1. This indicates its average accounts receivable balance is converted into cash 5.1 times during the period. Exhibit 9.18 shows graphically this turnover activity for TechCom.

EXHIBIT 9.18

Rate of Accounts
Receivable Turnover
for TechCom

5.1 times per year

| ① | ② | ③ | ④ | ⑤ |

| Jan. | Feb. | March | Apr. | May | June | July | Aug. | Sep. | Oct. | Nov. | Dec. |

Accounts receivable turnover also reflects how well management is doing in granting credit to customers in a desire to increase sales. A high turnover in comparison with competitors suggests that management should consider using more liberal credit terms to increase sales. A low turnover suggests management should consider stricter credit terms and more aggressive collection efforts to avoid having its resources tied up in accounts receivable.

To illustrate, we take fiscal year data from two competitors: **IBM** and **Oracle** (ticker: ORCL). Exhibit 9.19 shows accounts receivable turnover for both companies.

Point: Credit risk ratio is computed by dividing the Allowance for Doubtful Accounts by Accounts Receivable. The higher this ratio, the higher is credit risk.

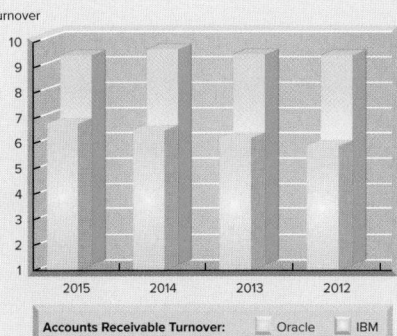

EXHIBIT 9.19

Analysis Using Accounts Receivable Turnover

Company	Figure ($ millions)	2015	2014	2013	2012
IBM	Net sales..........................	$81,741	$92,793	$98,367	$102,874
	Average accounts receivable, net.......	$ 8,712	$ 9,778	$10,566	$ 10,923
	Accounts receivable turnover.........	9.4	9.5	9.3	9.4
Oracle	Net sales..........................	$38,226	$38,275	$37,180	$ 37,121
	Average accounts receivable, net.......	$ 5,618	$ 6,068	$ 6,213	$ 6,503
	Accounts receivable turnover.........	6.8	6.3	6.0	5.7

IBM's 2015 turnover is 9.4, computed as $81,741/$8,712 ($ millions). This means that IBM's average accounts receivable balance was converted into cash 9.4 times in 2015. Its turnover slightly decreased in 2015 (9.4) compared with 2014 (9.5). However, IBM's turnover exceeds that for Oracle in each of the years shown here. Both IBM and Oracle seem to be doing an adequate job of managing receivables.[1]

Accounts Receivable Turnover: ☐ Oracle ☐ IBM

■ Decision Maker

Family Physician Your medical practice is barely profitable, so you hire a health care analyst. The analyst highlights several points including the following: *"Accounts receivable turnover is too low. Tighter credit policies are recommended along with discontinuing service to those most delayed in payments."* How do you interpret these recommendations? What actions do you take? ■ [*Answer:* First, the analyst suggests more stringent screening of patients' credit standing. Second, the analyst suggests dropping patients who are most overdue. We are likely bothered by both suggestions. They are probably financially wise recommendations, but we are likely troubled by eliminating services to those less able to pay. One alternative is to follow the recommendations while implementing a care program directed at patients less able to pay for services. This allows you to continue services to patients less able to pay and to discontinue services to patients able but unwilling to pay.]

NEED-TO-KNOW 9-6

COMPREHENSIVE

Clayco Company completes the following selected transactions during year 2017.

July 14   Writes off a $750 account receivable arising from a sale to Briggs Company that dates to 10 months ago. (Clayco Company uses the allowance method.)

30   Clayco Company receives a $1,000, 90-day, 10% note in exchange for merchandise sold to Sumrell Company (the merchandise cost $600).

Aug. 15   Receives $2,000 cash plus a $10,000 note from JT Co. in exchange for merchandise that sells for $12,000 (its cost is $8,000). The note is dated August 15, bears 12% interest, and matures in 120 days.

Nov. 1   Completes a $200 credit card sale with a 4% fee (the cost of sales is $150). The cash is transferred immediately from the credit card company.

3   Sumrell Company refuses to pay the note that was due to Clayco Company on October 28. Prepare the journal entry to charge the dishonored note plus accrued interest to Sumrell Company's accounts receivable.

5   Completes a $500 credit card sale with a 5% fee (the cost of sales is $300). The cash is transferred immediately from the credit card company.

15   Receives the full amount of $750 from Briggs Company that was previously written off on July 14. Record the bad debts recovery.

Dec. 13   Receives payment of principal plus interest from JT for the August 15 note.

Required

1. Prepare journal entries to record these transactions on Clayco Company's books.

2. Prepare an adjusting journal entry as of December 31, 2017, assuming the following:

a. Bad debts are estimated to be $20,400 by aging accounts receivable. The unadjusted balance of the Allowance for Doubtful Accounts is a $1,000 debit.

b. Alternatively, assume that bad debts are estimated using the percent of sales method. The Allowance for Doubtful Accounts had a $1,000 debit balance before adjustment, and the company estimates bad debts to be 1% of its credit sales of $2,000,000.

---

[1] As an estimate of *average days' sales uncollected*, we compute how many days (*on average*) it takes to collect receivables as follows: 365 days ÷ Accounts receivable turnover. An increase in this *average collection period* can signal a decline in customers' financial condition.

PLANNING THE SOLUTION

- Examine each transaction to determine the accounts affected, and then record the entries.
- For the year-end adjustment, record the bad debts expense for the two approaches.

SOLUTION

1.

July 14	Allowance for Doubtful Accounts	750	
	Accounts Receivable—Briggs Co.		750
	Wrote off an uncollectible account.		
July 30	Notes Receivable—Sumrell Co.	1,000	
	Sales		1,000
	Sold merchandise for a 90-day, 10% note.		
July 30	Cost of Goods Sold	600	
	Merchandise Inventory............................		600
	Record the cost of July 30 sale.		
Aug. 15	Cash	2,000	
	Notes Receivable—JT Co.	10,000	
	Sales		12,000
	Sold merchandise to customer for $2,000 cash *and $10,000 note.*		
Aug. 15	Cost of Goods Sold	8,000	
	Merchandise Inventory............................		8,000
	Record the cost of Aug. 15 sale.		
Nov. 1	Cash	192	
	Credit Card Expense	8	
	Sales		200
	Record credit card sale less a 4% credit card expense.		
Nov. 1	Cost of Goods Sold	150	
	Merchandise Inventory		150
	Record the cost of Nov. 1 sale.		
Nov. 3	Accounts Receivable—Sumrell Co.	1,025	
	Interest Revenue		25
	Notes Receivable—Sumrell Co.		1,000
	Charge account of Sumrell Company for *a $1,000 dishonored note and interest of* *$1,000 × 10% × 90/360.*		
Nov. 5	Cash	475	
	Credit Card Expense	25	
	Sales		500
	Record credit card sale less a 5% credit card expense.		
Nov. 5	Cost of Goods Sold	300	
	Merchandise Inventory............................		300
	Record the cost of Nov. 5 sale.		
Nov. 15	Accounts Receivable—Briggs Co.	750	
	Allowance for Doubtful Accounts		750
	Reinstate account of Briggs Company *previously written off.*		
Nov. 15	Cash	750	
	Accounts Receivable—Briggs Co.		750
	Cash received in full payment of account.		
Dec. 13	Cash	10,400	
	Interest Revenue		400
	Note Receivable—JT Co.		10,000
	Collect note with interest of $10,000 × 12% × 120/360.		

2a. Aging of accounts receivable method.

Dec. 31	Bad Debts Expense	21,400	
	Allowance for Doubtful Accounts		21,400
	Adjust allowance account from a $1,000 debit		
	balance to a $20,400 credit balance.		

2b. Percent of sales method.*

Dec. 31	Bad Debts Expense	20,000	
	Allowance for Doubtful Accounts		20,000
	Record bad debts expense as 1% × $2,000,000		
	of credit sales.		

* For the income statement approach, which requires estimating bad debts as a percent of sales or credit sales, the Allowance for Doubtful Accounts balance is *not* considered when making the adjusting entry.

Summary

C1 Describe accounts receivable and how they occur and are recorded. Accounts receivable are amounts due from customers for credit sales. A subsidiary ledger lists amounts owed by each customer. Credit sales arise from at least two sources: (1) sales on credit and (2) store credit card sales. *Sales on credit* refers to a company's granting credit directly to customers. Store credit card sales involve customers' use of store credit cards.

C2 Describe a note receivable, the computation of its maturity date, and the recording of its existence. A note receivable is a written promise to pay a specified amount of money at a stated future date. The maturity date is the day the note (principal and interest) must be repaid. Interest rates are normally stated in annual terms. The amount of interest on the note is computed by expressing time as a fraction of one year and multiplying the note's principal by this fraction and the annual interest rate. A note received is recorded at its principal amount by debiting the Notes Receivable account. The credit amount is to the asset, product, or service provided in return for the note.

C3 Explain how receivables can be converted to cash before maturity. Receivables can be converted to cash before maturity in at least two ways. First, a company can sell accounts receivable to a factor, who charges a factoring fee. Second, a company can borrow money by signing a note payable that is secured by pledging the accounts receivable.

A1 Compute accounts receivable turnover and use it to help assess financial condition. Accounts receivable turnover is a measure of both the quality and liquidity of accounts receivable. The accounts receivable turnover measure indicates how often, on average, receivables are received and collected during the period. Accounts receivable turnover is computed as net sales divided by average accounts receivable.

P1 Apply the direct write-off method to accounts receivable. The direct write-off method charges Bad Debts Expense when accounts are written off as uncollectible. This method is acceptable only when the amount of bad debts expense is immaterial.

P2 Apply the allowance method to accounts receivable. Under the allowance method, bad debts expense is recorded with an adjustment at the end of each accounting period that debits the Bad Debts Expense account and credits the Allowance for Doubtful Accounts. The uncollectible accounts are later written off with a debit to the Allowance for Doubtful Accounts.

P3 Estimate uncollectibles based on sales and accounts receivable. Uncollectibles are estimated by focusing on either (1) the income statement relation between bad debts expense and credit sales or (2) the balance sheet relation between accounts receivable and the allowance for doubtful accounts. The first approach emphasizes the matching principle using the income statement. The second approach emphasizes realizable value of accounts receivable using the balance sheet.

P4 Record the honoring and dishonoring of a note and adjustments for interest. When a note is honored, the payee debits the money received and credits both Notes Receivable and Interest Revenue. Dishonored notes are credited to Notes Receivable and debited to Accounts Receivable (to the account of the maker in an attempt to collect), and Interest Revenue is recorded for interest earned for the time the note is held.

Key Terms

Accounts receivable	Allowance for Doubtful Accounts	Credit risk ratio
Accounts receivable turnover	Allowance method	Direct write-off method
Aging of accounts receivable	Bad debts	Expense recognition principle

Interest	Maturity date of a note	Promissory note (or note)
Maker of the note	Payee of the note	Realizable value
Materiality constraint	Principal of a note	

Multiple Choice Quiz

1. A company's Accounts Receivable balance at its December 31 year-end is $125,650, and its Allowance for Doubtful Accounts has a credit balance of $328 before year-end adjustment. Its net sales are $572,300. It estimates that 4% of outstanding accounts receivable are uncollectible. What amount of bad debts expense is recorded at December 31?

  a. $5,354   **c.** $5,026   **e.** $34,338
  b. $328   **d.** $4,698

2. A company's Accounts Receivable balance at its December 31 year-end is $489,300, and its Allowance for Doubtful Accounts has a debit balance of $554 before year-end adjustment. Its net sales are $1,300,000. It estimates that 6% of outstanding accounts receivable are uncollectible. What amount of bad debts expense is recorded at December 31?

  a. $29,912   **c.** $78,000   **e.** $554
  b. $28,804   **d.** $29,358

3. Total interest to be earned on a $7,500, 5%, 90-day note is

  a. $93.75   **c.** $1,125.00   **e.** $125.00
  b. $375.00 **d.** $31.25

4. A company receives a $9,000, 8%, 60-day note. The maturity value of the note is

  a. $120   **c.** $9,120   **e.** $9,720
  b. $9,000   **d.** $720

5. A company has net sales of $489,600 and average accounts receivable of $40,800. What is its accounts receivable turnover?

  a. 0.08   **c.** 1,341.00   **e.** 111.78
  b. 30.41   **d.** 12.00

ANSWERS TO MULTIPLE CHOICE QUIZ

1. d; Desired balance in Allowance for Doubtful Accounts = $ 5,026 cr.
  ($125,650 × 0.04)
  Current balance in Allowance for Doubtful Accounts = (328) cr.
  Bad debts expense to be recorded = $ 4,698

2. a; Desired balance in Allowance for Doubtful Accounts = $ 29,358 cr.
  ($489,300 × 0.06)
  Current balance in Allowance for Doubtful Accounts = 554 dr.
  Bad debts expense to be recorded = $29,912

3. a; $7,500 × 0.05 × 90/360 = $93.75

4. c; Principal amount $9,000
  Interest accrued . . . . 120 ($9,000 × 0.08 × 60/360)
  Maturity value $9,120

5. d; $489,600/$40,800 = 12

---

[i] Icon denotes assignments that involve decision making.

Discussion Questions

1. [i] How do sellers benefit from allowing their customers to use credit cards?

2. [i] Why does the direct write-off method of accounting for bad debts usually fail to match revenues and expenses?

3. Explain the accounting constraint of materiality.

4. Why might a business prefer a note receivable to an account receivable?

5. Explain why writing off a bad debt against the Allowance for Doubtful Accounts does not reduce the estimated realizable value of a company's accounts receivable.

6. [i] Why does the Bad Debts Expense account usually not have the same adjusted balance as the Allowance for Doubtful Accounts?

7. [i] Refer to the financial statements and notes of **Apple** in Appendix A. In its presentation of accounts receivable on the balance sheet, how **APPLE** does it title accounts receivable? What does it report for its allowance as of September 26, 2015?

8. [i] Refer to the balance sheet of **Google** in Appendix A. Does it use the direct **GOOGLE** write-off method or allowance method in accounting for its accounts receivable? What is the realizable value of its receivables balance as of December 31, 2015?

9. Refer to the financial statements of **Samsung** in Appendix A. What is the **Samsung** amount of Samsung's accounts receivable, titled as "Trade Receivables," on its December 31, 2015, balance sheet?

10. Refer to the December 31, 2015, financial statements of **Samsung** in **Samsung** Appendix A. Does Samsung report its accounts receivable, titled as "Trade Receivables," as a current or noncurrent asset?

■ connect

Prepare journal entries for the following credit card sales transactions (the company uses the perpetual inventory system).

1. Sold $20,000 of merchandise, which cost $15,000, on MasterCard credit cards. MasterCard charges a 5% fee.

2. Sold $5,000 of merchandise, which cost $3,000, on an assortment of bank credit cards. These cards charge a 4% fee.

Solstice Company determines on October 1 that it cannot collect $50,000 of its accounts receivable from its customer P. Moore. Apply the direct write-off method to record this loss as of October 1.

Solstice Company determines on October 1 that it cannot collect $50,000 of its accounts receivable from its customer P. Moore. It uses the direct write-off method to record this loss as of October 1. On October 30, P. Moore unexpectedly paid his account in full to Solstice Company. Record Solstice's entry(ies) to reflect recovery of this bad debt.

The following list describes aspects of either the allowance method or the direct write-off method to account for bad debts. For each item listed, indicate if the statement best describes either the allowance (A) method or the direct write-off (DW) method.

_____ **1.** No attempt is made to predict bad debts expense.

_____ **2.** Accounts receivable on the balance sheet is reported at net realizable value.

_____ **3.** The write-off of a specific account does not affect net income.

_____ **4.** When an account is written off, the debit is to Bad Debts Expense.

_____ **5.** Sales and any bad debt expense are usually not recorded in the same period; thus, proper matching (of revenue and expense recognition) does not consistently occur.

_____ **6.** Requires a company to estimate bad debts expense related to the sales recorded in that period.

Gomez Corp. uses the allowance method to account for uncollectibles. On January 31, it wrote off an $800 account of a customer, C. Green. On March 9, it receives a $300 payment from Green.

1. Prepare the journal entry or entries for January 31.

2. Prepare the journal entry or entries for March 9; assume no additional money is expected from Green.

Warner Company's year-end unadjusted trial balance shows accounts receivable of $99,000, allowance for doubtful accounts of $600 (credit), and sales of $280,000. Uncollectibles are estimated to be 1.5% of accounts receivable.

1. Prepare the December 31 year-end adjusting entry for uncollectibles.

2. What amount would have been used in the year-end adjusting entry if the allowance account had a year-end unadjusted debit balance of $300?

Warner Company's year-end unadjusted trial balance shows accounts receivable of $99,000, allowance for doubtful accounts of $600 (credit), and sales of $280,000. Uncollectibles are estimated to be 0.5% of sales. Prepare the December 31 year-end adjusting entry for uncollectibles.

On August 2, Jun Co. receives a $6,000, 90-day, 12% note from customer Ryan Albany as payment on his $6,000 account. (1) Compute the maturity date for this note. (2) Prepare Jun's journal entry for August 2.

On August 2, Jun Co. receives a $6,000, 90-day, 12% note from customer Ryan Albany as payment on his $6,000 account. Prepare Jun's journal entry assuming the note is honored by the customer on October 31 of that same year.

QS 9-10

Note receivable interest and maturity **P4**

Daw Company's December 31 year-end unadjusted trial balance shows a $10,000 balance in Notes Receivable. This balance is from one 6% note dated December 1, with a period of 45 days. Prepare any necessary journal entries for December 31 *and* for the note's maturity date assuming it is honored.

QS 9-11

Factoring receivables **C3**

Record the sale by Balus Company of $125,000 in accounts receivable on May 1. Balus is charged a 2.5% factoring fee.

QS 9-12

Accounts receivable turnover

A1

The following data are taken from the comparative balance sheets of Ruggers Company. Compute and interpret its accounts receivable turnover for year 2017 (competitors average a turnover of 7.5).

	2017	2016
Accounts receivable, net	$153,400	$138,500
Net sales	861,105	910,600

QS 9-13

International accounting standards

C1

Answer each of the following related to international accounting standards.

a. Explain (in general terms) how the accounting for recognition of receivables is different between IFRS and U.S. GAAP.

b. Explain (in general terms) how the accounting for valuation of receivables is different between IFRS and U.S. GAAP.

EXERCISES

Vail Company recorded the following selected transactions during November 2017.

Exercise 9-1

Accounts receivable subsidiary ledger; schedule of accounts receivable

C1

Nov. 5	Accounts Receivable—Ski Shop	4,615	
	Sales		4,615
10	Accounts Receivable—Welcome Enterprises..............	1,350	
	Sales		1,350
13	Accounts Receivable—Zia Natara......................	832	
	Sales		832
21	Sales Returns and Allowances	209	
	Accounts Receivable—Zia Natara		209
30	Accounts Receivable—Ski Shop	2,713	
	Sales		2,713

1. Open a general ledger having T-accounts for Accounts Receivable, Sales, and Sales Returns and Allowances. Also open an accounts receivable subsidiary ledger having a T-account for each of its three customers. Post these entries to both the general ledger and the accounts receivable ledger.

Check Accounts Receivable ending balance, $9,301

2. Prepare a schedule of accounts receivable (see Exhibit 9.4) and compare its total with the balance of the Accounts Receivable controlling account as of November 30.

Exercise 9-2

Accounting for credit card sales

C1

Levine Company uses the perpetual inventory system and allows customers to use two credit cards in charging purchases. With the Suntrust Bank Card, a 4% service charge for credit card sales is assessed. The second credit card that Levine accepts is the Continental Card. Continental assesses a 2.5% charge on sales for using its card. Prepare journal entries to record the following selected credit card transactions of Levine Company.

Apr. 8 Sold merchandise for $8,400 (that had cost $6,000) and accepted the customer's Suntrust Bank Card.

12 Sold merchandise for $5,600 (that had cost $3,500) and accepted the customer's Continental Card.

Z-Mart uses the perpetual inventory system and allows customers to use the Z-Mart store credit card in charging purchases. Z-Mart assesses a per-month interest fee for any unpaid balance on its store credit card at each month-end.

Apr. 30   Z-Mart sold merchandise for $1,000 (that had cost $650) and accepted the customer's Z-Mart store credit card.

May 31   Z-Mart recorded $4 of interest earned from its store credit card as of this month-end.

Exercise 9-3
Sales on store credit card
C1

Dexter Company applies the direct write-off method in accounting for uncollectible accounts. Prepare journal entries to record the following selected transactions of Dexter.

Mar. 11   Dexter determines that it cannot collect $45,000 of its accounts receivable from its customer Leer Company.

  29   Leer Company unexpectedly pays its account in full to Dexter Company. Dexter records its recovery of this bad debt.

Exercise 9-4
Direct write-off method
P1

At year-end (December 31), Chan Company estimates its bad debts as 0.5% of its annual credit sales of $975,000. Chan records its bad debts expense for that estimate. On the following February 1, Chan decides that the $580 account of P. Park is uncollectible and writes it off as a bad debt. On June 5, Park unexpectedly pays the amount previously written off.

Prepare the journal entries of Chan to record these transactions and events of December 31, February 1, and June 5.

Exercise 9-5
Percent of sales method; write-off
P3

At each calendar year-end, Mazie Supply Co. uses the percent of accounts receivable method to estimate bad debts. On December 31, 2017, it has outstanding accounts receivable of $55,000, and it estimates that 2% will be uncollectible.

Prepare the adjusting entry to record bad debts expense for year 2017 under the assumption that the Allowance for Doubtful Accounts has (a) a $415 credit balance before the adjustment and (b) a $291 debit balance before the adjustment.

Exercise 9-6
Percent of accounts receivable method
P3

Daley Company estimates uncollectible accounts using the allowance method at December 31. It prepared the following aging of receivables analysis.

Exercise 9-7
Aging of receivables method
P3

			Days Past Due			
	Total	0	1 to 30	31 to 60	61 to 90	Over 90
Accounts receivable............	$570,000	$396,000	$90,000	$36,000	$18,000	$30,000
Percent uncollectible		1%	2%	5%	7%	10%

a. Estimate the balance of the Allowance for Doubtful Accounts using the aging of accounts receivable method.

b. Prepare the adjusting entry to record bad debts expense using the estimate from part a. Assume the unadjusted balance in the Allowance for Doubtful Accounts is a $3,600 credit.

c. Prepare the adjusting entry to record bad debts expense using the estimate from part a. Assume the unadjusted balance in the Allowance for Doubtful Accounts is a $100 debit.

Refer to the information in Exercise 9-7 to complete the following requirements.

a. Estimate the balance of the Allowance for Doubtful Accounts assuming the company uses 4.5% of total accounts receivable to estimate uncollectibles, instead of the aging of receivables method.

b. Prepare the adjusting entry to record bad debts expense using the estimate from part a. Assume the unadjusted balance in the Allowance for Doubtful Accounts is a $12,000 credit.

c. Prepare the adjusting entry to record bad debts expense using the estimate from part a. Assume the unadjusted balance in the Allowance for Doubtful Accounts is a $1,000 debit.

Exercise 9-8
Percent of receivables method
P3

Exercise 9-9
Writing off receivables
P2

Refer to the information in Exercise 9-7 to complete the following requirements.

a. On February 1 of the next period, the company determined that $6,800 in customer accounts was uncollectible; specifically, $900 for Oakley Co. and $5,900 for Brookes Co. Prepare the journal entry to write off those two accounts.

b. On June 5 of that next period, the company unexpectedly received a $900 payment on a customer account, Oakley Company, that had previously been written off in part *a*. Prepare the entries necessary to reinstate the account and to record the cash received.

Exercise 9-10
Estimating bad debts
P3

At December 31, Folgeys Coffee Company reports the following results for its calendar year.

Cash sales	$900,000
Credit sales	300,000

Its year-end unadjusted trial balance includes the following items.

Accounts receivable	$125,000 debit
Allowance for doubtful accounts	5,000 debit

Check Dr. Bad Debts
Expense: (*a*) $9,000

a. Prepare the adjusting entry to record bad debts expense assuming uncollectibles are estimated to be 3% of credit sales.

b. Prepare the adjusting entry to record bad debts expense assuming uncollectibles are estimated to be 1% of total sales.

(*c*) $12,500

c. Prepare the adjusting entry to record bad debts expense assuming uncollectibles are estimated to be 6% of year-end accounts receivable.

Exercise 9-11
Notes receivable
transactions
C2

Prepare journal entries for the following selected transactions of Danica Company for 2016.

2016

Dec. 13   Accepted a $9,500, 45-day, 8% note dated December 13 in granting Miranda Lee a time extension on her past-due account receivable.

Check Dec. 31, Cr. Interest
Revenue, $38

      31   Prepared an adjusting entry to record the accrued interest on the Lee note.

Exercise 9-12
Notes receivable
transactions P4

Refer to the information in Exercise 9-11 and prepare the journal entries for the following selected transactions of Danica Company for 2017.

2017

Check Jan. 27, Dr. Cash,
$9,595

Jan. 27   Received Lee's payment for principal and interest on the note dated December 13.

Mar. 3   Accepted a $5,000, 10%, 90-day note dated March 3 in granting a time extension on the past-due account receivable of Tomas Company.

      17   Accepted a $2,000, 30-day, 9% note dated March 17 in granting H. Cheng a time extension on his past-due account receivable.

Apr. 16   Cheng dishonored his note when presented for payment.

May   1   Wrote off the Cheng account against the Allowance for Doubtful Accounts.

June 1, Dr. Cash,

June   1   Received the Tomas payment for principal and interest on the note dated March 3.

$5,125

Exercise 9-13
Honoring a note
P4

Prepare journal entries to record these selected transactions for Vitalo Company (assume that no reversing entries are recorded).

Nov. 1   Accepted a $6,000, 180-day, 8% note dated November 1 from Kelly White in granting a time extension on her past-due account receivable.

Dec. 31   Adjusted the year-end accounts for the accrued interest earned on the White note.

Apr. 30   White honored her note when presented for payment; February has 28 days for the current year.

Prepare journal entries to record the following selected transactions of Ridge Company.

Mar. 21   Accepted a $9,500, 180-day, 8% note dated March 21 from Tamara Jackson in granting a time extension on her past-due account receivable.
Sep. 17   Jackson dishonored her note when it is presented for payment.
Dec. 31   After exhausting all legal means of collection, Ridge Company wrote off Jackson's account against the Allowance for Doubtful Accounts.

Exercise 9-14
Dishonoring a note
P4

On June 30, Petrov Co. has $128,700 of accounts receivable. Prepare journal entries to record the following selected July transactions. Also prepare any footnotes to the July 31 financial statements that result from these transactions. (The company uses the perpetual inventory system.)

July   4   Sold $7,245 of merchandise (that had cost $5,000) to customers on credit.
        9   Sold $20,000 of accounts receivable to Main Bank. Main charges a 4% factoring fee.
       17   Received $5,859 cash from customers in payment on their accounts.
       27   Borrowed $10,000 cash from Main Bank, pledging $12,500 of accounts receivable as security for the loan.

Exercise 9-15
Selling and pledging
accounts receivable
C3

The following information is from the annual financial statements of Raheem Company. Compute its accounts receivable turnover for 2016 and 2017. Compare the two years' results and give a possible explanation for any change (competitors average a turnover of 11).

Exercise 9-16
Accounts receivable
turnover

A1

	2017	2016	2015
Net sales..................................	$405,140	$335,280	$388,000
Accounts receivable, net (year-end)	44,800	41,400	34,800

Hitachi, Ltd., reports total revenues of ¥9,616,202 million for its current fiscal year, and its current fiscal year-end unadjusted trial balance reports a debit balance for trade receivables (gross) of ¥2,797,935 million.

a. Prepare the adjusting entry to record its bad debts expense assuming uncollectibles are estimated to be 0.4% of total revenues and its unadjusted trial balance reports a credit balance of ¥10,000 million for the Allowance for Doubtful Accounts.

b. Prepare the adjusting entry to record bad debts expense assuming uncollectibles are estimated to be 2.0% of year-end trade receivables (gross) and its unadjusted trial balance reports a credit balance of ¥10,000 million for the Allowance for Doubtful Accounts.

Exercise 9-17
Accounting for bad debts
following IFRS

P2

---

connect

PROBLEM SET A

Mayfair Co. allows select customers to make purchases on credit. Its other customers can use either of two credit cards: Zisa or Access. Zisa deducts a 3% service charge for sales on its credit card. Access deducts a 2% service charge for sales on its card. Mayfair completes the following transactions in June.

Problem 9-1A
Sales on account and credit
card sales
C1

June   4   Sold $650 of merchandise on credit (that had cost $400) to Natara Morris.
        5   Sold $6,900 of merchandise (that had cost $4,200) to customers who used their Zisa cards.
        6   Sold $5,850 of merchandise (that had cost $3,800) to customers who used their Access cards.
        8   Sold $4,350 of merchandise (that had cost $2,900) to customers who used their Access cards.
       13   Wrote off the account of Abigail McKee against the Allowance for Doubtful Accounts. The $429 balance in McKee's account stemmed from a credit sale in October of last year.
       18   Received Morris's check in full payment for the purchase of June 4.

Check   June 18, Dr. Cash,
$650

Required

Prepare journal entries to record the preceding transactions and events. (The company uses the perpetual inventory system. Round amounts to the nearest dollar.)

Problem 9-2A

Estimating and reporting
bad debts

P2   P3

At December 31, 2017, Hawke Company reports the following results for its calendar year.

Cash sales.....................................	$1,905,000
Credit sales....................................	5,682,000

In addition, its unadjusted trial balance includes the following items.

Accounts receivable......................	$1,270,100 debit
Allowance for doubtful accounts............	16,580 debit

Required

1. Prepare the adjusting entry for this company to recognize bad debts under each of the following independent assumptions.

   a. Bad debts are estimated to be 1.5% of credit sales.

   b. Bad debts are estimated to be 1% of total sales.

Check Bad Debts Expense:
(1a) $85,230, (1c) $80,085

   c. An aging analysis estimates that 5% of year-end accounts receivable are uncollectible.

2. Show how Accounts Receivable and the Allowance for Doubtful Accounts appear on its December 31,
2017, balance sheet given the facts in part 1a.

3. Show how Accounts Receivable and the Allowance for Doubtful Accounts appear on its December 31,
2017, balance sheet given the facts in part 1c.

Problem 9-3A

Aging accounts receivable
and accounting for bad
debts

P2   P3

Jarden Company has credit sales of $3,600,000 for year 2017. On December 31, 2017, the company's
Allowance for Doubtful Accounts has an unadjusted credit balance of $14,500. Jarden prepares a schedule of
its December 31, 2017, accounts receivable by age. On the basis of past experience, it estimates the percent
of receivables in each age category that will become uncollectible. This information is summarized here.

	A	B	C
1	**December 31, 2017,**	**Age of**	**Expected Percent**
2	**Accounts Receivable**	**Accounts Receivable**	**Uncollectible**
3	$830,000	Not yet due	1.25%
4	254,000	1 to 30 days past due	2.00
5	86,000	31 to 60 days past due	6.50
6	38,000	61 to 90 days past due	32.75
7	12,000	Over 90 days past due	68.00

Required

1. Estimate the required balance of the Allowance for Doubtful Accounts at December 31, 2017, using
the aging of accounts receivable method.

Check (2) Dr. Bad Debts
Expense, $27,150

2. Prepare the adjusting entry to record bad debts expense at December 31, 2017.

Analysis Component

3. On June 30, 2018, Jarden Company concludes that a customer's $4,750 receivable (created in 2017) is
uncollectible and that the account should be written off. What effect will this action have on Jarden's
2018 net income? Explain.

Problem 9-4A

Accounts receivable
transactions and bad
debts adjustments

C1   P2   P3

Liang Company began operations on January 1, 2016. During its first two years, the company completed
a number of transactions involving sales on credit, accounts receivable collections, and bad debts. These
transactions are summarized as follows:

2016

   a. Sold $1,345,434 of merchandise (that had cost $975,000) on credit, terms n/30.

   b. Wrote off $18,300 of uncollectible accounts receivable.

   c. Received $669,200 cash in payment of accounts receivable.

Check (d) Dr. Bad Debts
Expense, $28,169

   d. In adjusting the accounts on December 31, the company estimated that 1.5% of accounts receivable
will be uncollectible.

2017

e. Sold $1,525,634 of merchandise on credit (that had cost $1,250,000), terms n/30.

f. Wrote off $27,800 of uncollectible accounts receivable.

g. Received $1,204,600 cash in payment of accounts receivable.

h. In adjusting the accounts on December 31, the company estimated that 1.5% of accounts receivable will be uncollectible.

(h) Dr. Bad Debts Expense, $32,199

Required

Prepare journal entries to record Liang's 2016 and 2017 summarized transactions and its year-end adjustments to record bad debts expense. (The company uses the perpetual inventory system and it applies the allowance method for its accounts receivable. Round amounts to the nearest dollar.)

The following selected transactions are from Ohlm Company.

2016

Dec. 16   Accepted a $10,800, 60-day, 8% note dated this day in granting Danny Todd a time extension on his past-due account receivable.

    31   Made an adjusting entry to record the accrued interest on the Todd note.

2017

Feb. 14   Received Todd's payment of principal and interest on the note dated December 16.

Mar. 2   Accepted a $6,100, 8%, 90-day note dated this day in granting a time extension on the past-due account receivable from Midnight Co.

    17   Accepted a $2,400, 30-day, 7% note dated this day in granting Ava Privet a time extension on her past-due account receivable.

Apr. 16   Privet dishonored her note when presented for payment.

May 31   Midnight Co. refused to pay the note that was due to Ohlm Co. on May 31. Prepare the journal entry to charge the dishonored note plus accrued interest to Midnight Co.'s accounts receivable.

July 16   Received payment from Midnight Co. for the maturity value of its dishonored note plus interest for 46 days beyond maturity at 8%.

Aug. 7   Accepted a $7,450, 90-day, 10% note dated this day in granting a time extension on the past-due account receivable of Mulan Co.

Sep. 3   Accepted a $2,100, 60-day, 10% note dated this day in granting Noah Carson a time extension on his past-due account receivable.

Nov. 2   Received payment of principal plus interest from Carson for the September 3 note.

Nov. 5   Received payment of principal plus interest from Mulan for the August 7 note.

Dec. 1   Wrote off the Privet account against the Allowance for Doubtful Accounts.

Problem 9-5A
Analyzing and journalizing notes receivable transactions

C2   C3   P4

Check   Feb. 14, Cr. Interest Revenue, $108

May 31, Cr. Interest Revenue, $122

Nov. 2, Cr. Interest Revenue, $35

Required

1. Prepare journal entries to record these transactions and events. (Round amounts to the nearest dollar.)

Analysis Component

2. What reporting is necessary when a business pledges receivables as security for a loan and the loan is still outstanding at the end of the period? Explain the reason for this requirement and the accounting principle being satisfied.

Archer Co. allows select customers to make purchases on credit. Its other customers can use either of two credit cards: Commerce Bank or Goldman. Commerce Bank deducts a 3% service charge for sales on its credit card. When customers use the Goldman card, a 2% service charge is deducted from sales on its card. Archer completed the following transactions in August.

Aug. 4   Sold $3,700 of merchandise on credit (that had cost $2,000) to McKenzie Carpenter.

    10   Sold $5,200 of merchandise (that had cost $2,800) to customers who used their Commerce Bank credit cards.

    11   Sold $1,250 of merchandise (that had cost $900) to customers who used their Goldman cards.

PROBLEM SET B

Problem 9-1B
Sales on account and credit card sales

C1

Check Aug. 14, Dr. Cash, $3,700

14 Received Carpenter's check in full payment for the purchase of August 4.
15 Sold $3,250 of merchandise (that had cost $1,758) to customers who used their Goldman cards.
22 Wrote off the account of Craw Co. against the Allowance for Doubtful Accounts. The $498 balance in Craw Co.'s account stemmed from a credit sale in November of last year.

Required

Prepare journal entries to record the preceding transactions and events. (The company uses the perpetual inventory system. Round amounts to the nearest dollar.)

Problem 9-2B
Estimating and reporting bad debts

P2   P3

At December 31, 2017, Ingleton Company reports the following results for the year:

Cash sales.....................................	$1,025,000
Credit sales....................................	1,342,000

In addition, its unadjusted trial balance includes the following items:

Accounts receivable.......................	$575,000 debit
Allowance for doubtful accounts.............	7,500 credit

Required

1. Prepare the adjusting entry for Ingleton Co. to recognize bad debts under each of the following independent assumptions.
   a. Bad debts are estimated to be 2.5% of credit sales.
   b. Bad debts are estimated to be 1.5% of total sales.
   c. An aging analysis estimates that 6% of year-end accounts receivable are uncollectible.

Check Dr. Bad Debts Expense: (1b) $35,505, (1c) $27,000

2. Show how Accounts Receivable and the Allowance for Doubtful Accounts appear on its December 31, 2017, balance sheet given the facts in part 1a.
3. Show how Accounts Receivable and the Allowance for Doubtful Accounts appear on its December 31, 2017, balance sheet given the facts in part 1c.

Problem 9-3B
Aging accounts receivable and accounting for bad debts

P2   P3

Hovak Company has credit sales of $4,500,000 for year 2017. At December 31, 2017, the company's Allowance for Doubtful Accounts has an unadjusted debit balance of $3,400. Hovak prepares a schedule of its December 31, 2017, accounts receivable by age. On the basis of past experience, it estimates the percent of receivables in each age category that will become uncollectible. This information is summarized here.

	A	B	C
1	**December 31, 2017,**	**Age of**	**Expected Percent**
2	**Accounts Receivable**	**Accounts Receivable**	**Uncollectible**
3	$396,400	Not yet due	2.0%
4	277,800	1 to 30 days past due	4.0
5	48,000	31 to 60 days past due	8.5
6	6,600	61 to 90 days past due	39.0
7	2,800	Over 90 days past due	82.0

Required

1. Compute the required balance of the Allowance for Doubtful Accounts at December 31, 2017, using the aging of accounts receivable method.

Check (2) Dr. Bad Debts Expense, $31,390

2. Prepare the adjusting entry to record bad debts expense at December 31, 2017.

Analysis Component

3. On July 31, 2018, Hovak concludes that a customer's $3,455 receivable (created in 2017) is uncollectible and that the account should be written off. What effect will this action have on Hovak's 2018 net income? Explain.

Sherman Co. began operations on January 1, 2016, and completed several transactions during 2016 and 2017 that involved sales on credit, accounts receivable collections, and bad debts. These transactions are summarized as follows.

Problem 9-4B
Accounts receivable transactions and bad debts adjustments

C1 P2 P3

2016

a. Sold $685,350 of merchandise on credit (that had cost $500,000), terms n/30.

b. Received $482,300 cash in payment of accounts receivable.

c. Wrote off $9,350 of uncollectible accounts receivable.

d. In adjusting the accounts on December 31, the company estimated that 1% of accounts receivable will be uncollectible.

Check (*d*) Dr. Bad Debts Expense, $11,287

2017

e. Sold $870,220 of merchandise on credit (that had cost $650,000), terms n/30.

f. Received $990,800 cash in payment of accounts receivable.

g. Wrote off $11,090 of uncollectible accounts receivable.

h. In adjusting the accounts on December 31, the company estimated that 1% of accounts receivable will be uncollectible.

(*h*) Dr. Bad Debts Expense, $9,773

Required

Prepare journal entries to record Sherman's 2016 and 2017 summarized transactions and its year-end adjusting entry to record bad debts expense. (The company uses the perpetual inventory system and it applies the allowance method for its accounts receivable. Round amounts to the nearest dollar.)

The following selected transactions are from Springer Company.

Problem 9-5B
Analyzing and journalizing notes receivable transactions

C2 C3 P4

2016

Nov. 1   Accepted a $4,800, 90-day, 8% note dated this day in granting Steve Julian a time extension on his past-due account receivable.

Dec. 31   Made an adjusting entry to record the accrued interest on the Julian note.

2017

Jan. 30   Received Julian's payment for principal and interest on the note dated November 1.

Feb. 28   Accepted a $12,600, 30-day, 8% note dated this day in granting a time extension on the past-due account receivable from King Co.

Mar. 1   Accepted a $6,200, 60-day, 12% note dated this day in granting Myron Shelley a time extension on his past-due account receivable.

     30   The King Co. dishonored its note when presented for payment.

Apr. 30   Received payment of principal plus interest from M. Shelley for the March 1 note.

June 15   Accepted a $2,000, 72-day, 8% note dated this day in granting a time extension on the past-due account receivable of Ryder Solon.

     21   Accepted a $9,500, 90-day, 8% note dated this day in granting J. Felton a time extension on his past-due account receivable.

Aug. 26   Received payment of principal plus interest from R. Solon for the note of June 15.

Sep. 19   Received payment of principal plus interest from J. Felton for the June 21 note.

Nov. 30   Wrote off King's account against Allowance for Doubtful Accounts.

Check Jan. 30, Cr. Interest Revenue, $32

Apr. 30, Cr. Interest Revenue, $124

Sep. 19, Cr. Interest Revenue, $190

Required

1. Prepare journal entries to record these transactions and events. (Round amounts to the nearest dollar.)

Analysis Component

2. What reporting is necessary when a business pledges receivables as security for a loan and the loan is still outstanding at the end of the period? Explain the reason for this requirement and the accounting principle being satisfied.

SERIAL PROBLEM
Business Solutions

P1 P2

© Alexander Image/Shutterstock RF

Check (2) Dr. Bad Debts Expense, $48

(This serial problem began in Chapter 1 and continues through most of the book. If previous chapter segments were not completed, the serial problem can begin at this point.)

SP 9 Santana Rey, owner of **Business Solutions**, realizes that she needs to begin accounting for bad debts expense. Assume that Business Solutions has total revenues of $44,000 during the first three months of 2018 and that the Accounts Receivable balance on March 31, 2018, is $22,867.

Required

1. Prepare the adjusting entry needed for Business Solutions to recognize bad debts expense on March 31, 2018, under each of the following independent assumptions (assume a zero unadjusted balance in the Allowance for Doubtful Accounts at March 31).

    a. Bad debts are estimated to be 1% of total revenues. (Round amounts to the dollar.)

    b. Bad debts are estimated to be 2% of accounts receivable. (Round amounts to the dollar.)

2. Assume that Business Solutions's Accounts Receivable balance at June 30, 2018, is $20,250 and that one account of $100 has been written off against the Allowance for Doubtful Accounts since March 31, 2018. If S. Rey uses the method prescribed in part 1*b*, what adjusting journal entry must be made to recognize bad debts expense on June 30, 2018?

3. Should S. Rey consider adopting the direct write-off method of accounting for bad debts expense rather than one of the allowance methods considered in part 1? Explain.

 **GENERAL LEDGER PROBLEM**

Available only in Connect

The **General Ledger** tool in *Connect* automates several of the procedural steps in accounting so that the financial professional can focus on the impacts of each transaction on various financial reports and performance measures.

GL 9-1 General Ledger assignment GL 9-1, based on Problem 9-5A, focuses on transactions related to accounts and notes receivable and highlights the impact each transaction has on interest revenue, if any. Prepare the journal entries related to accounts and notes receivable; the schedules of accounts receivable and notes receivable are automatically completed using the General Ledger tool. Next, compute both the amount and timing of interest revenue for each note receivable.

Beyond the Numbers

REPORTING IN ACTION

A1

APPLE

BTN 9-1 Refer to **Apple**'s financial statements in Appendix A to answer the following.

1. What is the amount of Apple's accounts receivable as of September 26, 2015?

2. Compute Apple's accounts receivable turnover as of September 26, 2015.

3. How long does it take, *on average,* for the company to collect receivables?

4. Apple's most liquid assets include (*a*) cash and cash equivalents, (*b*) short-term marketable securities, (*c*) receivables, and (*d*) inventory. Compute the percentage that these liquid assets make up of current liabilities as of September 26, 2015. Do the same computations for September 27, 2014. Comment on the company's ability to satisfy its current liabilities as of its fiscal 2015 year-end compared to its fiscal 2014 year-end.

5. What criteria did Apple use to classify items as cash equivalents? (*Hint:* Refer to Apple's footnotes describing cash equivalents in Appendix A.)

Fast Forward

6. Access Apple's financial statements for fiscal years after September 26, 2015, at its website (Apple.com) or the SEC's EDGAR database (SEC.gov). Recompute parts 2 and 4 and comment on any changes since September 26, 2015.

BTN 9-2   Comparative figures for Apple and Google follow.

COMPARATIVE ANALYSIS

A1   P2

APPLE

GOOGLE

$ millions	Apple			Google		
	Current Year	One Year Prior	Two Years Prior	Current Year	One Year Prior	Two Years Prior
Accounts receivable, net . . .	$ 16,849	$ 17,460	$ 13,102	$ 11,556	$ 9,383	$ 8,882
Net sales	233,715	182,795	170,910	74,989	66,001	55,519

Required

1. Compute the accounts receivable turnover for Apple and Google for each of the two most recent years using the data shown.

2. Using the results from part 1, compute how many days it takes each company, *on average,* to collect receivables. Compare the collection periods for Apple and Google, and suggest at least one explanation for the difference.

3. Which company is more efficient in collecting its accounts receivable? Explain.

Hint: Average collection period equals 365 divided by the accounts receivable turnover.

BTN 9-3   Anton Blair is the manager of a medium-size company. A few years ago, Blair persuaded the owner to base a part of his compensation on the net income the company earns each year. Each December he estimates year-end financial figures in anticipation of the bonus he will receive. If the bonus is not as high as he would like, he offers several recommendations to the accountant for year-end adjustments. One of his favorite recommendations is for the controller to reduce the estimate of doubtful accounts.

ETHICS CHALLENGE

P2   P3

Required

1. What effect does lowering the estimate for doubtful accounts have on the income statement and balance sheet?

2. Do you believe Blair's recommendation to adjust the allowance for doubtful accounts is within his rights as manager, or do you believe this action is an ethics violation? Justify your response.

3. What type of internal control(s) might be useful for this company in overseeing the manager's recommendations for accounting changes?

BTN 9-4   As the accountant for Pure-Air Distributing, you attend a sales managers' meeting devoted to a discussion of credit policies. At the meeting, you report that bad debts expense is estimated to be $59,000 and accounts receivable at year-end amount to $1,750,000 less a $43,000 allowance for doubtful accounts. Sid Omar, a sales manager, expresses confusion over why bad debts expense and the allowance for doubtful accounts are different amounts. Write a one-page memorandum to him explaining why a difference in bad debts expense and the allowance for doubtful accounts is not unusual. The company estimates bad debts expense as 2% of sales.

COMMUNICATING IN PRACTICE

P2   P3

BTN 9-5   Access eBay's February 1, 2016, filing of its 10-K report for the year ended December 31, 2015, at SEC.gov.

TAKING IT TO THE NET

C1   P3

Required

1. What is the amount of eBay's net accounts receivable at December 31, 2015, and at December 31, 2014?

2. "Financial Statement Schedule II" of its 10-K report lists eBay's allowance for doubtful accounts (including authorized credits). For the two years ended December 31, 2015 and 2014, identify its allowance for doubtful accounts (including authorized credits), and then compute it as a percent of gross accounts receivable.

3. Do you believe that these percentages are reasonable based on what you know about eBay? Explain.

**TEAMWORK IN
ACTION**

P2   P3

BTN 9-6   Each member of a team is to participate in estimating uncollectibles using the aging schedule and percents shown in Problem 9-3A. The division of labor is up to the team. Your goal is to accurately complete this task as soon as possible. After estimating uncollectibles, check your estimate with the instructor. If the estimate is correct, the team then should prepare the adjusting entry and the presentation of accounts receivable (net) for the December 31, 2017, balance sheet.

**ENTREPRENEURIAL
DECISION**

C1

BTN 9-7   The cofounders of **ReGreen Corporation** are introduced in the chapter's opening feature. Assume that they are considering two new selling options.

Plan A. ReGreen would begin selling instruction videos on reducing water usage online directly to customers. The new online customers would use their credit cards. The company has the capability of selling instructional videos through its website with no additional investment in hardware or software. Annual credit sales are expected to increase by $250,000.

   Costs associated with Plan A: Cost of these new sales is $135,500; credit card fees will be 4.75% of sales; and additional recordkeeping and shipping costs will be 6% of sales. Instructional video sales will reduce consulting sales for ReGreen by $35,000 annually because some customers will now only purchase instructional videos—assume that consulting sales for ReGreen have a 25% gross margin percentage.

Plan B. ReGreen would expand to more cities. It would make additional annual credit sales of $500,000 to customers in those new cities.

   Costs associated with Plan B: Cost of these new sales is $375,000; additional recordkeeping and shipping costs will be 4% of sales; and uncollectible accounts will be 6.2% of sales.

Required

Check   (1*b*) Additional net income, $74,000

1. Compute the additional annual net income or loss expected under (a) Plan A and (b) Plan B.
2. Should the company pursue either plan? Discuss both the financial and nonfinancial factors relevant to this decision.

**HITTING THE
ROAD**

C1

BTN 9-8   Many commercials include comments similar to the following: "We accept **VISA**" or "We do not accept **American Express**." Conduct your own research by contacting at least five companies via interviews, phone calls, or the Internet to determine the reason(s) companies discriminate in their use of credit cards. Collect information on the fees charged by the different cards for the companies contacted. (The instructor can assign this as a team activity.)

GLOBAL DECISION

C1   A1

Samsung

APPLE

GOOGLE

BTN 9-9   Key information from **Samsung** (**Samsung.com**), which is a leading manufacturer of consumer electronic products, follows.

₩ in millions	Current Year	One Year Prior	Two Years Prior
Accounts receivable, net*	₩ 25,168,026	₩ 24,694,610	₩ 24,988,532
Sales	200,653,482	206,205,987	228,692,667

* Samsung refers to this as "**Trade receivables, net**" in its footnotes.

1. Compute its accounts receivable turnover for the current year.
2. How long does it take on average for Samsung to collect receivables?
3. Refer to BTN 9-2. How does Samsung compare to **Apple** and **Google** in terms of its accounts receivable turnover and its collection period?

GLOBAL VIEW

This section discusses similarities and differences between U.S. GAAP and IFRS regarding the recognition, measurement, and disposition of receivables.

Recognition of Receivables Both U.S. GAAP and IFRS have similar asset criteria that apply to recognition of receivables. Further, receivables that arise from revenue-generating activities are subject to broadly similar criteria for U.S. GAAP and IFRS. Specifically, both refer to the realization principle and an earnings process. The realization principle under U.S. GAAP implies an *arm's-length transaction* occurs, whereas under IFRS this notion is applied in terms of reliable measurement and likelihood of economic benefits. Regarding U.S. GAAP's reference to an earnings process, IFRS instead refers to risk transfer and ownership reward. While these criteria are broadly similar, differences do exist, and they arise mainly from industry-specific guidance under U.S. GAAP, which is very limited under IFRS.

Valuation of Receivables Both U.S. GAAP and IFRS require that receivables be reported net of estimated uncollectibles. Further, both systems require that the expense for estimated uncollectibles be recorded in the same period when any revenues from those receivables are recorded. This means that for accounts receivable, both U.S. GAAP and IFRS require the allowance method for uncollectibles (unless uncollectibles are immaterial). The allowance method using percent of sales, percent of receivables, and aging was explained in this chapter. **Nokia** reports the following for its allowance for uncollectibles:

> Management specifically analyzes accounts receivables and historical bad debt, customer concentrations, customer creditworthiness, current economic trends and changes in our customer payment terms when evaluating the adequacy of the allowance.

The valuation of receivables with a large financing component, such as many notes receivable, is a bit different under IFRS. Namely, uncollectible accounts are estimated based on expected losses over the next 12 months for long-term financing receivables that have declined in quality since issuance.

Disposition of Receivables Both U.S. GAAP and IFRS apply broadly similar rules in recording disposition of receivables. Those rules are discussed in this chapter. We should be aware of an important difference in terminology. Companies reporting under U.S. GAAP disclose Bad Debts Expense, which is also referred to as *Provision for Bad Debts* or the *Provision for Uncollectible Accounts*. For U.S. GAAP, *provision* here refers to expense. Under IFRS, the term *provision* usually refers to a contra asset (or liability) whose amount or timing (or both) is uncertain.

 Global View Assignments

Discussion Questions 9 & 10

Quick Study 9-13

Exercise 9-17

BTN 9-9

10

chapter

Plant Assets, Natural Resources, and Intangibles

Learning Objectives

CONCEPTUAL

C1 Explain the cost principle for computing the cost of plant assets.

C2 Explain depreciation for partial years and changes in estimates.

C3 Distinguish between revenue and capital expenditures, and account for them.

ANALYTICAL

A1 Compute total asset turnover and apply it to analyze a company's use of assets.

PROCEDURAL

P1 Compute and record depreciation using the straight-line, units-of-production, and declining-balance methods.

P2 Account for asset disposal through discarding or selling an asset.

P3 Account for natural resource assets and their depletion.

P4 Account for intangible assets.

P5 *Appendix 10A*—Account for asset exchanges.

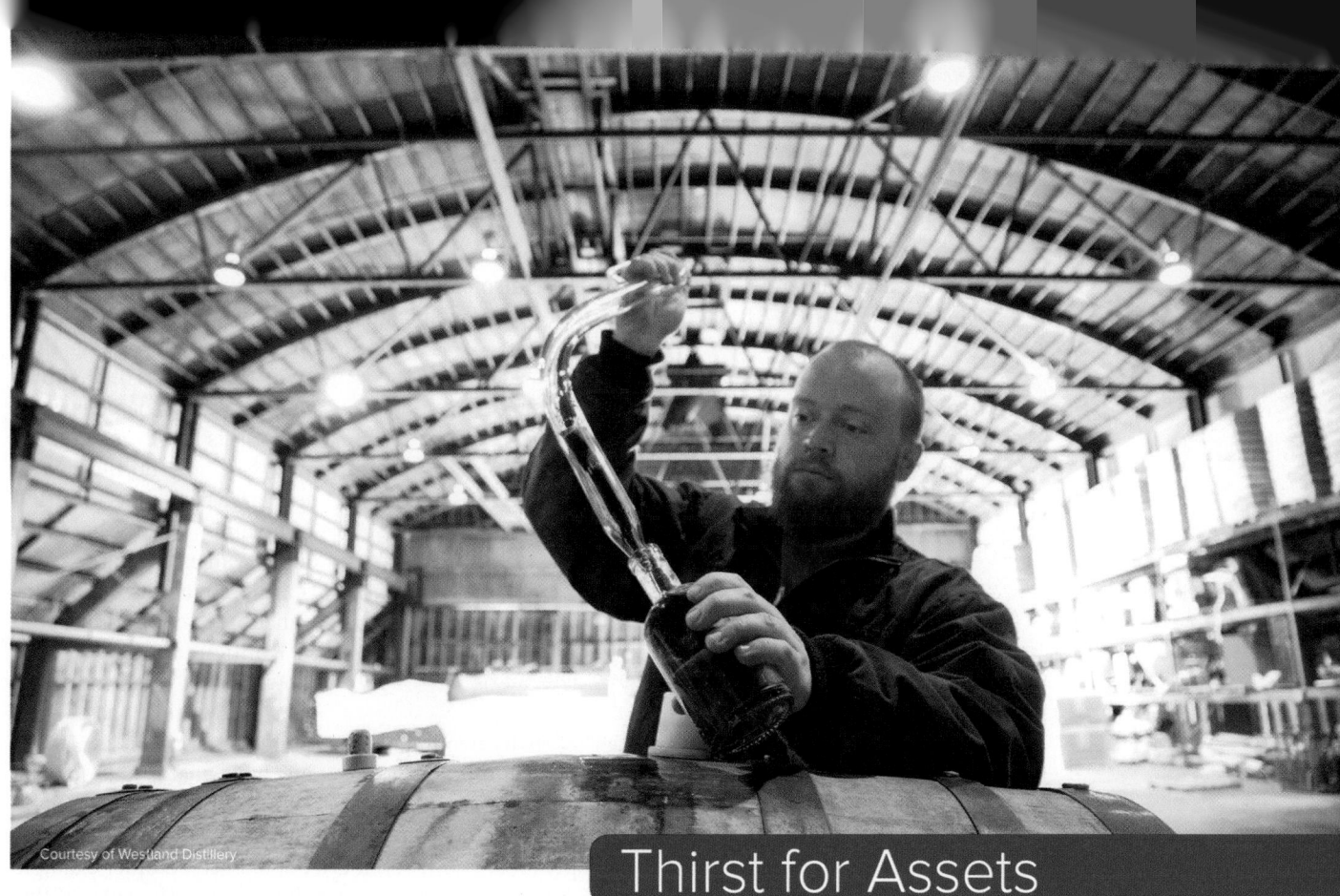

Courtesy of Westland Distillery

Thirst for Assets

SEATTLE—Matt Hofmann crafted a business plan to distill malt whiskey. Although he was barely old enough to drink, that did not stop Matt from pursuing his dream. Matt went off to attend Heriot-Watt University in Scotland to pursue a postgraduate diploma in distilling. Soon after, he launched **Westland Distillery** (**WestlandDistillery.com**).

"The goal for Westland Distillery is to be the leader for American single malt," explains Matt. For quality reasons, Matt invested in specially crafted buildings and distilling equipment—titled "Plant Assets" on his balance sheet. Matt insists that finding the proper building and equipment was crucial to his aim of becoming a "world-class malt whiskey distillery."

To achieve his goal, Matt brushed up on accounting for assets. He learned how to invest in the right kind and amount of assets to meet growing demand, maintain a commitment to quality, and reach the necessary level of profitability. "Never assume you have everything figured out," insists Matt.

Success depends on continued monitoring and control of the types and costs of long-term assets, explains Matt. "There

"Always be curious"

—Matt Hofmann

just aren't that many distilling resources," says Matt, in explaining his focus on long-term assets. He now has nearly $4 million in such assets, making his malt whiskey distillery one of the largest on the West Coast.

Matt proudly proclaims that he produces over 60,000 gallons of product per year. "All . . . are produced by us right here in Seattle," adds Matt. His products sell across the United States and in numerous overseas markets.

Interestingly, although Matt focuses on tangible assets such as equipment, machinery, and buildings, his trademark is quickly emerging as a valuable intangible asset. So too are the company's secret ingredients and distilling processes. Matt explains that protecting and managing intangible assets is one of "the most important things I do." With his success in acquiring and applying both tangible and intangible assets, Matt is able to focus on product quality.

Sources: *Westland Distillery website,* January 2017; *Star Chefs,* November 2015; *Crosscut,* March 2015; *Cool Hunting,* July 2014; *Seattle Magazine,* March 2014

Section 1—Plant Assets

Plant assets are tangible assets used in a company's operations that have a useful life of more than one accounting period. Plant assets are also called *plant and equipment; property, plant and equipment (PP&E);* or *fixed assets.* For many companies, plant assets make up the single largest class of assets they own. Exhibit 10.1 shows plant assets as a percentage of total assets for several companies. Not only do they make up a large percentage of many companies' assets, but their dollar values are large. **McDonald's** plant assets, for instance, are reported at about $23 billion, while **Walmart** reports plant assets of more than $116 billion.

EXHIBIT 10.1

Plant Assets of Selected Companies

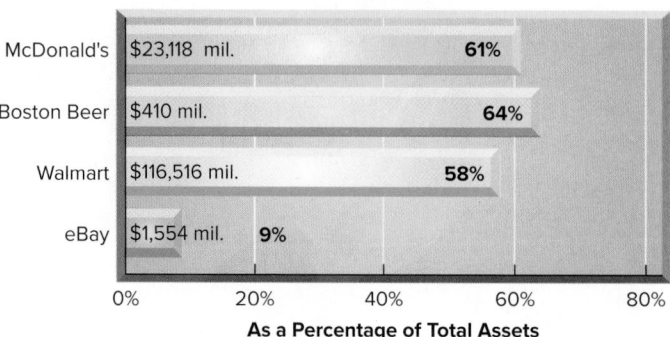

As a Percentage of Total Assets

McDonald's	$23,118 mil.	61%
Boston Beer	$410 mil.	64%
Walmart	$116,516 mil.	58%
eBay	$1,554 mil.	9%

Plant assets are set apart from other assets by two important features. First, *plant assets are used in operations.* This makes them different from, for instance, inventory that is held for sale and not used in operations. The distinctive feature here is use, not type of asset. A company that purchases a computer to resell it reports it on the balance sheet as inventory. If the same company purchases this computer to use in operations, however, it is a plant asset. Another example is land held for future expansion, which is reported as a long-term investment. However, if this land holds a factory used in operations, the land is part of plant assets.

Point: *Capital-intensive* refers to companies with large amounts of plant assets.

The second important feature is that *plant assets have useful lives extending over more than one accounting period.* This makes plant assets different from current assets such as supplies that are normally consumed in a short time period after they are placed in use.

Accordingly, because plant assets are used in operations, we match their costs against the revenues they generate. Because their useful lives extend over several periods, our matching of costs and revenues must extend over several periods. Specifically, we value plant assets (balance sheet effect) and then allocate their costs to periods benefiting from their use (income statement effect). An important exception is land; land cost is not allocated to expense when we expect it to have an indefinite life.

Exhibit 10.2 shows four main issues in accounting for plant assets: (1) computing the costs of plant assets, (2) allocating the costs of plant assets (less any salvage amounts) against revenues for the periods they benefit, (3) accounting for expenditures such as repairs and improvements to plant assets, and (4) recording the disposal of plant assets. The following sections discuss these issues.

EXHIBIT 10.2

Issues in Accounting for Plant Assets

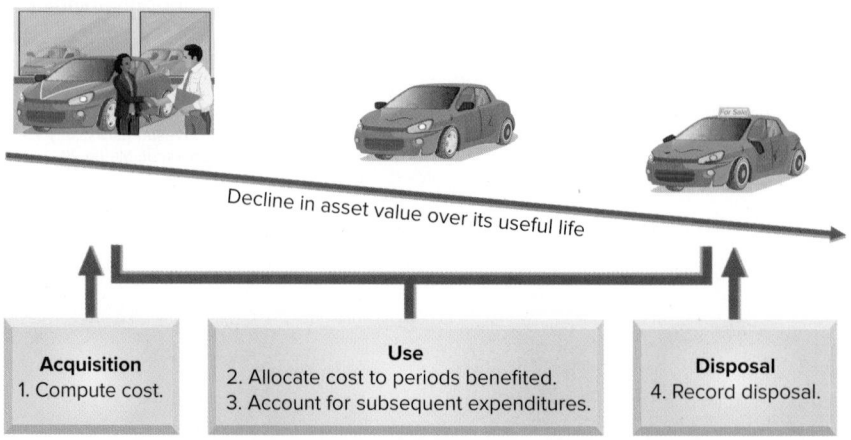

Decline in asset value over its useful life

Acquisition
1. Compute cost.

Use
2. Allocate cost to periods benefited.
3. Account for subsequent expenditures.

Disposal
4. Record disposal.

COST DETERMINATION

Plant assets are recorded at cost when acquired. This is consistent with the *cost principle*. **Cost** includes all normal and reasonable expenditures necessary to get the asset in place and ready for its intended use. The cost of a factory machine, for instance, includes its invoice cost less any discount, plus any necessary freight, unpacking, assembling, installing, and testing costs. Examples are the costs of building a base for a machine, providing electrical hookups, and testing the asset before using it in operations.

To be recorded as part of the cost of a plant asset, an expenditure must be normal, reasonable, and necessary in preparing it for its intended use. If an asset is damaged during unpacking, the repairs are not added to its cost. Instead, they are charged to an expense account. Nor is a paid traffic fine for moving heavy machinery without a proper permit part of the machinery's cost; but payment for a proper permit is included in the cost of machinery. Charges to modify or customize a new plant asset are added to the asset's cost. We explain in this section how to determine the cost of plant assets for each of its four major classes.

C1

Explain the cost principle for computing the cost of plant assets.

Machinery and Equipment

The costs of machinery and equipment consist of all costs normal and necessary to purchase them and prepare them for their intended use. These include the purchase price, taxes, transportation charges, insurance while in transit, and the installing, assembling, and testing of the machinery and equipment.

Buildings

A Building account is charged for the costs of purchasing or constructing a building that is used in operations. When purchased, a building's costs usually include its purchase price, brokerage fees, taxes, title fees, and attorney fees. Its costs also include all expenditures to ready it for its intended use, including any necessary repairs or renovations such as wiring, lighting, flooring, and wall coverings. When a company such as **Apple** (see photo of its new campus) constructs a building or any plant asset for its own use, its costs include materials and labor plus a reasonable amount of indirect overhead cost. Overhead includes the costs of items such as heat, lighting, power, and depreciation on machinery used to construct the asset. Costs of construction also include design fees, building permits, and insurance during construction. However, costs such as insurance to cover the asset *after* it is placed in use are operating expenses.

© Hans Blossey/Alamy Stock Photo

Land Improvements

Land improvements are additions to land and have limited useful lives. Examples are parking lot surfaces, driveways, walkways, fences, landscaping, and sprinkling and lighting systems. Costs of land improvements include expenditures necessary to make those improvements ready for their intended use. While the costs of these improvements increase the usefulness of the land, they are charged to a separate Land Improvement account so that their costs can be allocated to the periods they benefit.

Point: Entry for cash purchase of land improvements:
Land Improvements . . . . . .   #
   Cash . . . .   #

Land

Land is the earth's surface and has an indefinite (unlimited) life. Costs of land include expenditures necessary to make that property ready for its intended use. When land is purchased for a building site, its cost includes the total amount paid for the land, including any real estate commissions, title insurance fees, legal fees, and any accrued property taxes paid by the purchaser.

Payments for surveying, clearing, grading, and draining also are included in the cost of land. Other costs include government assessments, whether incurred at the time of purchase or later, for items such as public roadways, sewers, and sidewalks. These assessments are included because they permanently add to the land's value. Land purchased as a building site sometimes includes structures that must be removed. In such cases, the cost of removing the structures, less any amounts recovered through sale of salvaged materials, is charged to the Land account. To illustrate, assume that **Starbucks** paid $167,000 cash to acquire land for a retail store. This land had an old service garage that was removed at a net cost of $13,000 ($15,000 in costs less $2,000 proceeds from salvaged materials). Additional closing costs total $10,000, consisting of brokerage fees ($8,000), legal fees ($1,500), and title costs ($500). The cost of this land to Starbucks is $190,000 and is computed as shown in Exhibit 10.3.

Point: Entry for cash purchase of land:

Land.   190,000
　Cash   190,000

EXHIBIT 10.3

Computing Cost of Land

Cash price of land.	$ 167,000
Net cost of garage removal	13,000
Closing costs.	10,000
Cost of land	**$190,000**

Lump-Sum Purchase

Plant assets sometimes are purchased as a group in a single transaction for a lump-sum price. This transaction is called a *lump-sum purchase,* or *group, bulk,* or *basket purchase.* When this occurs, we allocate the cost of the purchase among the different types of assets acquired based on their *relative market values,* which is estimated by appraisal or by using the tax-assessed valuations of the assets. To illustrate, assume **CarMax** paid $90,000 cash to acquire a group of items consisting of a building appraised at $60,000 and land appraised at $40,000. The $90,000 cost is allocated based on appraised values as shown in Exhibit 10.4.

Point: Entry for lump-sum cash purchase:

Bldg.   54,000
Land.   36,000
　Cash   90,000

EXHIBIT 10.4

Computing Costs in a Lump-Sum Purchase

	Appraised Value	Percent of Total	Apportioned Cost
Building.	$ 60,000	60% ($60,000/$100,000)	**$54,000** ($90,000 × 60%)
Land.	40,000	40 ($40,000/$100,000)	**36,000** ($90,000 × 40%)
Totals.	$100,000	100%	$ 90,000

NEED-TO-KNOW 10-1

Cost Determination

C1

Do More: QS 10-1, QS 10-2, E 10-1, E 10-2, E 10-3

Compute the amount recorded as the cost of a new machine given the following payments related to its purchase: gross purchase price, $700,000; sales tax, $49,000; purchase discount taken, $21,000; freight cost—terms FOB shipping point, $3,500; normal assembly costs, $3,000; cost of necessary machine platform, $2,500; cost of parts used in maintaining machine, $4,200.

Solution

$737,000 = $700,000 + $49,000 − $21,000 + $3,500 + $3,000 + $2,500

DEPRECIATION

Depreciation is the process of allocating the cost of a plant asset to expense in the accounting periods benefiting from its use. Depreciation does not measure the decline in the asset's market value each period, nor does it measure the asset's physical deterioration. Because depreciation reflects the cost of using a plant asset, depreciation charges are only recorded when the asset is actually in service. This section describes the factors we consider in computing depreciation, the depreciation methods used, revisions in depreciation, and depreciation for partial periods.

Factors in Computing Depreciation

Factors that determine depreciation are (1) cost, (2) salvage value, and (3) useful life.

Cost   The cost of a plant asset consists of all necessary and reasonable expenditures to acquire it and to prepare it for its intended use.

Salvage Value   The **salvage value,** also called *residual value* or *scrap value,* is an estimate of the asset's value at the end of its benefit period. This is the amount the owner expects to receive from disposing of the asset at the end of its benefit period. If the asset is expected to be traded in on a new asset, its salvage value is the expected trade-in value.

Useful Life   The **useful life** of a plant asset is the length of time it is productively used in a company's operations. Useful life, also called *service life,* might not be as long as the asset's total productive life. For example, the productive life of a computer can be eight years or more. Some companies, however, trade in old computers for new ones every two years. In this case, these computers have a two-year useful life, meaning the cost of these computers (less their expected trade-in values) is charged to depreciation expense over a two-year period.

The useful life of a plant asset is difficult to predict due to wear and tear from use in operations, along with inadequacy and obsolescence. **Inadequacy** refers to the insufficient capacity of a company's plant assets to meet its demands. **Obsolescence** refers to the condition of a plant asset that is no longer useful in producing goods or services with a competitive advantage because of innovations.

A company is often able to better predict a new asset's useful life when it has past experience with a similar asset. In note 1 of its annual report, **Tootsie Roll**, a snack food manufacturer, reports the following useful lives:

Buildings	20–35 years
Machinery and Equipment	5–20 years

Decision Insight

Good Life   Life expectancy of plant assets is often in the eye of the beholder. For instance, **Hershey Foods** and **Tootsie Roll** are competitors and apply similar manufacturing processes, yet their equipment's life expectancies are different. Hershey depreciates equipment over 3 to 15 years, but Tootsie Roll depreciates them over 5 to 20 years. Such differences greatly impact financial statements. ■

© Sergey Lavrentev/iStock/360/
Getty Images

Depreciation Methods

Depreciation methods are used to allocate a plant asset's cost over the accounting periods in its useful life. The most frequently used method of depreciation is the straight-line method. Other common depreciation methods include units-of-production and double-declining method. We explain all three methods in this section.

The computations in this section use information about a machine that inspects athletic shoes before packaging. Manufacturers such as **Converse**, **Reebok**, **Adidas**, and **Fila** use this machine. Data for this machine are in Exhibit 10.5.

Cost............................	$10,000	Useful life:	
Salvage value....................	1,000	Accounting periods..............	5 years
Depreciable cost..................	$ 9,000	Units inspected	36,000 shoes

Straight-Line Method

Straight-line depreciation charges the same amount of expense to each period of the asset's useful life. A two-step process is used. We first compute the *depreciable cost* of the asset, also called the *cost to be depreciated.* It is computed by subtracting the asset's salvage value from its total cost. Second, depreciable cost is divided by the number of accounting periods in the asset's useful life. The formula for straight-line depreciation, along with its computation for the inspection machine, is shown in Exhibit 10.6.

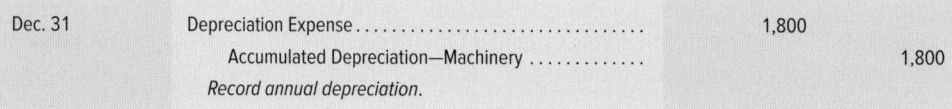

$$\frac{\text{Cost} - \text{Salvage value}}{\text{Useful life in periods}} = \frac{\$10,000 - \$1,000}{5 \text{ years}} = \$1,800 \text{ per year}$$

Point: Excel for SLN.

	A	B
1	Cost	$10,000
2	Salvage	$1,000
3	Life	5
4	SLN Depr	

=SLN(B1,B2,B3) = $1,800

Assets = Liabilities + Equity
−1,800   −1,800

If this machine is purchased on December 31, 2016, and used throughout its predicted useful life of five years, the straight-line method allocates an equal amount of depreciation to each of the years 2017 through 2021. We make the following adjusting entry at the end of each of the five years to record straight-line depreciation of this machine.

Dec. 31	Depreciation Expense................................	1,800	
	Accumulated Depreciation—Machinery		1,800
	Record annual depreciation.		

The $1,800 Depreciation Expense is reported on the income statement. The $1,800 Accumulated Depreciation is a contra asset account to the Machinery account in the balance sheet. The graph on the left in Exhibit 10.7 shows the $1,800 per year expenses reported in each of the five years. The graph on the right shows the amounts reported on each of the six December 31 balance sheets.

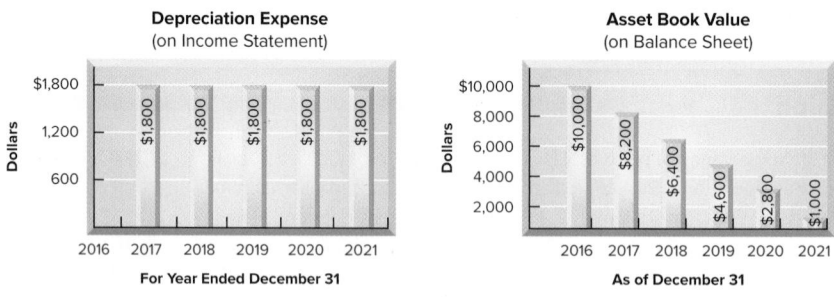

Book value = Cost − Accumulated depreciation

The net balance sheet amount is the **asset book value,** or simply *book value,* and is computed as the asset's total cost less its accumulated depreciation. For example, at the end of year 2 (December 31, 2018), its book value is $6,400, which is $10,000 less $3,600 (2 years × $1,800), and is reported in the balance sheet as follows:

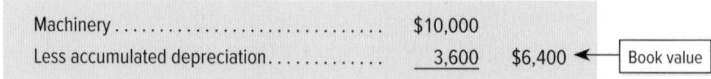

| Machinery............................. | $10,000 | |
| Less accumulated depreciation............ | 3,600 | $6,400 ← Book value |

The book value of this machine declines by $1,800 each year due to depreciation. The left-side graphic in Exhibit 10.7 reveals why this method is called straight-line.

We also can compute the *straight-line depreciation rate,* defined as 100% divided by the number of periods in the asset's useful life. For the inspection machine, this rate is 20% (100% ÷ 5 years, or 20% per period). We use this rate, along with other information, to compute the machine's *straight-line depreciation schedule* shown in Exhibit 10.8. Note three points in this exhibit. First, depreciation expense is the same each period. Second, accumulated depreciation is the sum of current and prior periods' depreciation expense. Third, book value declines each period until it equals salvage value at the end of the machine's useful life.

Point: Once an asset's book value equals its salvage value, depreciation stops.

Example: If salvage value of the machine is $2,500, what is the annual depreciation? *Answer:* ($10,000 − $2,500)/ 5 years = $1,500 per year

EXHIBIT 10.8

Straight-Line Depreciation Schedule

| | Depreciation for the Period | | | End of Period | |
Annual Period	Depreciable Cost*	Depreciation Rate	Depreciation Expense	Accumulated Depreciation	Book Value†
2016	—	—	—	—	$10,000
2017	$9,000	20%	$1,800	$1,800	8,200
2018	9,000	20	1,800	3,600	6,400
2019	9,000	20	1,800	5,400	4,600
2020	9,000	20	1,800	7,200	2,800
2021	9,000	20	1,800	9,000	**1,000**
			$9,000		

Salvage value is not depreciated.

$10,000 cost − $1,000 salvage

* $10,000 − $1,000.   † Book value is total cost minus accumulated depreciation.

Units-of-Production Method

The use of some plant assets varies greatly from one period to the next. A builder, for instance, might use a piece of construction equipment for a month and then not use it again for several months. When equipment use varies from period to period, the units-of-production depreciation method can better match expenses with revenues. **Units-of-production depreciation** charges a varying amount to expense for each period of an asset's useful life depending on its *usage.*

A two-step process is used to compute units-of-production depreciation. We first compute *depreciation per unit* by subtracting the asset's salvage value from its total cost and then dividing by the total number of units expected to be produced during its useful life. Units of production can be expressed in product or other units such as hours used or miles driven. The second step is to compute depreciation expense for the period by multiplying the units produced in the period by the depreciation per unit. The formula for units-of-production depreciation, along with its computation for the machine described in Exhibit 10.5, is shown in Exhibit 10.9. (*Note:* 7,000 shoes are inspected and sold in its first year.)

EXHIBIT 10.9

Units-of-Production Depreciation Formula and Example

Step 1

$$\text{Depreciation per unit} = \frac{\text{Cost} - \text{Salvage value}}{\text{Total units of production}} = \frac{\$10,000 - \$1,000}{36,000 \text{ shoes}} = \$0.25 \text{ per shoe}$$

Step 2

Depreciation expense = Depreciation per unit × Units produced in period

$$\$0.25 \text{ per shoe} \times 7,000 \text{ shoes} = \$1,750$$

Using data on the number of shoes inspected by the machine, we can compute the *units-of-production depreciation schedule* shown in Exhibit 10.10. For example, depreciation for the first year is $1,750 (7,000 shoes at $0.25 per shoe). Depreciation for the second year is $2,000 (8,000 shoes at $0.25 per shoe). Other years are similarly computed. Exhibit 10.10 shows that (1) depreciation expense depends on unit output, (2) accumulated depreciation is the sum of current and prior periods' depreciation expense, and (3) book value declines each period until it

Example: Refer to Exhibit 10.10. If the number of shoes inspected in 2021 is 5,500, what is depreciation for 2021? *Answer:* $1,250 (never depreciate below salvage value)

equals salvage value at the end of the asset's useful life. **Deltic Timber** is one of many companies using the units-of-production depreciation method. It reports that depreciation "is calculated over the estimated useful lives of the assets by using the units of production method for machinery and equipment."

EXHIBIT 10.10

Units-of-Production Depreciation Schedule

Annual Period	Depreciation for the Period			End of Period	
	Number of Units	Depreciation per Unit	Depreciation Expense	Accumulated Depreciation	Book Value
2016	—	—	—	—	$10,000
2017	7,000	$0.25	$1,750	$1,750	8,250
2018	8,000	0.25	2,000	3,750	6,250
2019	9,000	0.25	2,250	6,000	4,000
2020	7,000	0.25	1,750	7,750	2,250
2021	5,000	0.25	1,250	9,000	1,000
	36,000 units		$9,000		

$10,000 cost − $1,000 salvage

Salvage value is not depreciated.

Declining-Balance Method

An **accelerated depreciation method** yields larger depreciation expenses in the early years of an asset's life and less depreciation in later years. The most common accelerated method is the **declining-balance method** of depreciation, which uses a depreciation rate that is a multiple of the straight-line rate and applies it to the asset's beginning-of-period book value. The amount of depreciation declines each period because book value declines each period.

A common depreciation rate for the declining-balance method is double the straight-line rate. This is called the *double-declining-balance (DDB)* method. This method is applied in three steps:

1. Compute the asset's straight-line depreciation rate.
2. Double the straight-line rate.
3. Compute depreciation by multiplying this rate by the asset's beginning-of-period book value.

Point: In the DDB method, *double* refers to the rate and *declining balance* refers to book value. The rate is applied to beginning book value each period.

$$\text{SL rate} = \frac{100\%}{\text{Useful life}}$$

$$\text{DDB rate} = \frac{200\%}{\text{Useful life}}$$

To illustrate, let's return to the machine in Exhibit 10.5 and apply the double-declining-balance method to compute depreciation expense. Exhibit 10.11 shows the first-year depreciation computation for the machine. The three-step process is to (1) divide 100% by five years to determine the straight-line rate of 20%, or 1/5, per year; (2) double this 20% rate to get the declining-balance rate of 40%, or 2/5, per year; and (3) compute depreciation expense as 40%, or 2/5, multiplied by the beginning-of-period book value.

EXHIBIT 10.11

Double-Declining-Balance Depreciation Formula*

Step 1
Straight-line rate = 100% ÷ Useful life = 100% ÷ 5 years = 20%

Step 2
Double-declining-balance rate = 2 × Straight-line rate = 2 × 20% = 40%

Step 3
Depreciation expense = Double-declining-balance rate × Beginning-period book value
40% × $10,000 = $4,000 (for 2017)

* In simple form: DDB depreciation = (2 × Beginning-period book value)/Useful life.

Point: Excel for DDB.

	A	B
1	Cost	$10,000
2	Salvage	$1,000
3	Life	5
4	DDB Depr	
5	1	
6	2	
7	etc	

=DDB(B1,B2,B3,A5) = $4,000
=DDB(B1,B2,B3,A6) = $2,400

The *double-declining-balance depreciation schedule* is shown in Exhibit 10.12. The schedule follows the formula except for year 2021, when depreciation expense is $296. This $296 is not equal to 40% × $1,296, or $518.40. If we had used the $518.40 for depreciation expense in 2021, the ending book value would equal $777.60, which is less than the $1,000 salvage value. Instead,

EXHIBIT 10.12

Double-Declining-Balance
Depreciation Schedule

| Annual Period | Depreciation for the Period | | | End of Period | |
	Beginning of Period Book Value	Depreciation Rate	Depreciation Expense	Accumulated Depreciation	Book Value
2016	—	—	—	—	$10,000
2017	$10,000	40%	$4,000	$4,000	6,000
2018	6,000	40	2,400	6,400	3,600
2019	3,600	40	1,440	7,840	2,160
2020	2,160	40	864	8,704	1,296
2021	1,296	40	296*	9,000	**1,000**
			$9,000		

Salvage value is not depreciated.

$10,000 cost – $1,000 salvage

* Year 2021 depreciation is $1,296 – $1,000 = $296 (never depreciate book value below salvage value).

the $296 is computed by subtracting the $1,000 salvage value from the $1,296 book value at the beginning of the fifth year (the year when DDB depreciation cuts into salvage value).

Example: What is the DDB depreciation in year 2020 if salvage value is $2,000? *Answer:* $2,160 – $2,000 = $160

Comparing Depreciation Methods Exhibit 10.13 shows depreciation expense for each year of the machine's useful life under each of the three depreciation methods. While depreciation expense per period differs for different methods, total depreciation expense of $9,000 is the same over the machine's useful life.

EXHIBIT 10.13

Depreciation Expense for the Different Methods

	A	B	C	D
1	**Period**	**Straight-Line**	**Units-of-Production**	**Double-Declining-Balance**
2	2017	$1,800	$1,750	$4,000
3	2018	1,800	2,000	2,400
4	2019	1,800	2,250	1,440
5	2020	1,800	1,750	864
6	2021	1,800	1,250	296
7	Totals	$9,000	$9,000	$9,000

Each method starts with a total cost of $10,000 and ends with a salvage value of $1,000. The difference is the pattern in depreciation expense over the useful life. The book value of the asset when using straight-line is always greater than the book value from using double-declining-balance, except at the beginning and end of the asset's useful life, when it is the same.

Decision Insight

Survey Says About 85% of companies use straight-line depreciation for plant assets, 5% use units-of-production, and 4% use declining-balance. Another 6% use an unspecified accelerated method—most likely declining-balance. ■

Straight-line, 85%

Accelerated and other, 6%

Declining-balance, 4%

Units-of-production, 5%

Depreciation for Tax Reporting The records a company keeps for financial accounting purposes are usually separate from the records it keeps for tax accounting purposes. This is because financial accounting aims to report useful information on financial performance and position, whereas tax accounting reflects government objectives in raising revenues. Differences between these two accounting systems are normal and expected. Depreciation is a common example of how the records differ. For example, many companies use accelerated depreciation in computing taxable income. Reporting higher depreciation expense in the early years of an asset's life reduces the company's taxable income in those years and increases it in later years, when the depreciation expense is lower. The company's goal here is to *postpone* its tax payments.

Point: Rules for MACRS are available from IRS.gov.

The U.S. federal income tax law has rules for depreciating assets. These rules include the **Modified Accelerated Cost Recovery System (MACRS),** which allows straight-line depreciation for some assets but requires accelerated depreciation for most kinds of assets. MACRS separates depreciable assets into different classes and defines the depreciable life and rate for each class. MACRS is *not* acceptable for financial reporting because it often allocates costs over an arbitrary period that is less than the asset's useful life and it fails to estimate salvage value. Details of MACRS are covered in tax accounting courses.

Partial-Year Depreciation

C2

Explain depreciation for partial years and changes in estimates.

Point: Assets purchased on days 1 through 15 of a month are usually recorded as purchased on the 1st of that month. Assets purchased on days 16 to the month-end are recorded as if purchased on the 1st of the next month. The same applies to asset sales.

When an asset is purchased (or sold) at a time other than the beginning or end of an accounting period, depreciation is recorded for part of a year.

Mid-Period Asset Purchase   To illustrate, assume that the machine in Exhibit 10.5 is purchased and placed in service on October 8, 2016, and the annual accounting period ends on December 31. Because this machine is purchased and used for nearly three months in 2016, the calendar-year income statement should report depreciation expense on the machine for that part of the year. Normally, depreciation assumes that the asset is purchased on the first day of the month nearest the actual date of purchase. In this case, because the purchase occurred on October 8, we assume an October 1 purchase date. This means that three months' depreciation is recorded in 2016. Using straight-line depreciation, we compute three months' depreciation of $450 as follows.

$$\frac{\$10,000 - \$1,000}{5 \text{ years}} \times \frac{3}{12} = \$450$$

Example: If the machine's salvage value is zero and purchase occurs on Oct. 8, 2016, how much depreciation is recorded at Dec. 31, 2016? *Answer:* $10,000/5 × 3/12 = $500

Mid-Period Asset Sale   A similar computation is made when an asset sale occurs during a period. To illustrate, assume that the machine above is sold on June 24, 2021. Depreciation is recorded for the period January 1 through July 1 (assumes sale date to the nearest whole month) as follows:

$$\frac{\$10,000 - \$1,000}{5 \text{ years}} \times \frac{6}{12} = \$900$$

Change in Estimates for Depreciation

Depreciation is based on estimates of salvage value and useful life. During the useful life of an asset, if our estimate of an asset's useful life and/or salvage value changes, what should we do? The answer is to use the new estimate to compute depreciation for current and future periods. This means that we revise the depreciation expense computation by spreading the cost yet to be depreciated over the remaining useful life. This approach is used for all depreciation methods.

Point: Remaining depreciable cost equals book value less revised salvage value at the point of revision.

Let's return to the machine described in Exhibit 10.8 using straight-line depreciation. At the beginning of this asset's third year, its book value is $6,400, computed as $10,000 minus $3,600. Assume that at the beginning of its third year, the estimated number of years remaining in its useful life changes from three to four years *and* its estimate of salvage value changes from $1,000 to $400. Straight-line depreciation for each of the four remaining years is computed as shown in Exhibit 10.14.

EXHIBIT 10.14

Computing Revised Straight-Line Depreciation

$$\frac{\text{Book value} - \text{Revised salvage value}}{\text{Revised remaining useful life}} = \frac{\$6,400 - \$400}{4 \text{ years}} = \$1,500 \text{ per year}$$

Annual Period	Original Depreciation	Revised Depreciation
2016	—	—
2017	$1,800	$1,800
2018	1,800	1,800
2019	1,800	1,500
2020	1,800	1,500
2021	1,800	1,500
2022	—	1,500
	$9,000	$9,600

Thus, $1,500 of depreciation expense is recorded for the machine at the end of the third through sixth years—each year of its remaining useful life. Because this asset was depreciated at $1,800 per year for the first two years, it is tempting to conclude that depreciation expense was overstated in the first two years. However, these expenses reflected the best information available at that time. We do not go back and restate prior years' financial statements. Instead, we adjust the current and future periods' statements to reflect this new information. Revising an estimate of the useful life or salvage value of a plant asset is referred to as a **change in an accounting esti-mate** and is reflected in current and future financial statements, not in prior statements.

Reporting Depreciation

Both the cost and accumulated depreciation of plant assets are reported on the balance sheet or in its notes. **Dale Jarrett Racing Adventure**, for instance, reports the following.

Race vehicles and other..................................	$ 778,704
Furniture, software, DJ Graphics, and equipment..............	105,032
Shop and track equipment..................................	173,739
Property and equipment, gross...........................	1,057,475
Less accumulated depreciation............................	884,772
Property and equipment, net	$ 172,703

© Chris Trotman/NASCAR/Getty Images

Apple and many other companies show plant assets on one line with the net amount of cost less accumulated depreciation. When this is done, the amount of accumulated depreciation is disclosed in a note.

Reporting both the cost and accumulated depreciation of plant assets helps users compare the assets of different companies. For example, a company holding assets costing $50,000 and accumulated depreciation of $40,000 is likely in a situation different from a company with new assets costing $10,000. While the net undepreciated cost of $10,000 is the same in both cases, the first company may have more productive capacity available but likely is facing the need to replace older assets. These insights are not provided if the two balance sheets report only the $10,000 book values.

Users must remember that plant assets are reported on a balance sheet at their undepreciated costs (book value), not at fair (market) values. An exception is when there is a *permanent decline* in the fair value of an asset relative to its book value, called an asset **impairment.** In this case the company writes the asset down to this fair value (details on impairment loss are in advanced courses).

Accumulated Depreciation is a contra asset account with a normal credit balance. It does *not* reflect funds accumulated to buy new assets when the assets currently owned are replaced.

Point: A company usually keeps records (in a subsidiary ledger) for each asset showing its cost and depreciation to date.

Example: Assume equipment carries a book value of $800 ($900 cost less $100 accumulated depreciation) and a fair (market) value of $750, *and* this $50 decline in value meets the impairment test. The entry to record this impairment is:
Impairment Loss 50
   Accum. Depr.–Equip.   50

■ **Decision Ethics**

Controller   You are the controller for a struggling company. Its operations require regular investments in equipment, and depreciation is its largest expense. Its competitors frequently replace equipment—often depreciated over three years. The company president instructs you to revise useful lives of equipment from three to six years and to use a six-year life on all new equipment. What actions do you take? ■   [*Answer:* The president's instructions may reflect an honest and reasonable prediction of the future. Because the company is struggling financially, the president may feel that the usual pattern of replacing assets every three years cannot continue. However, if you believe the president's decision is unprincipled, you might confront the president with your opinion that it is unethical to change the estimate to increase income. The statements must be based on reasonable estimates.]

NEED-TO-KNOW 10-2

Depreciation Computations

P1   C2

Part 1. A machine costing $22,000 with a five-year life and an estimated $2,000 salvage value is installed on January 1. The manager estimates the machine will produce 1,000 units of product during its life. It actually produces the following units: 200 in 1st year, 400 in 2nd year, 300 in 3rd year, 80 in 4th year, 30 in 5th year. The total units produced by the end of year 5 exceed the original estimate—this difference was not predicted. (The machine must not be depreciated below its estimated salvage value.) Prepare a table with the following column headings—Year, Straight-Line, Units-of-Production, Double-Declining-Balance—and then compute depreciation expense for each year (and total depreciation for all years combined) under each method.

Part 2. In early January 2015, a company acquires equipment for $3,800. The company estimates this equipment to have a useful life of three years and a salvage value of $200. Early in 2017, the company changes its estimates to a total four-year useful life and zero salvage value. Using the straight-line method, what is depreciation expense for the year ended 2017?

Solution—Part 1

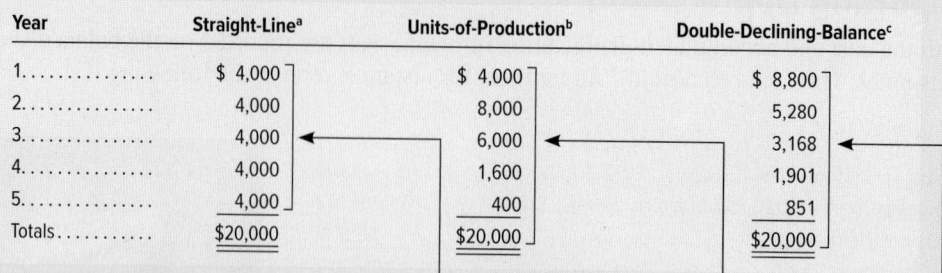

Year	Straight-Line[a]	Units-of-Production[b]	Double-Declining-Balance[c]
1.	$ 4,000	$ 4,000	$ 8,800
2.	4,000	8,000	5,280
3.	4,000	6,000	3,168
4.	4,000	1,600	1,901
5.	4,000	400	851
Totals.	$20,000	$20,000	$20,000

[a]Straight-line: Cost per year = ($22,000 − $2,000)/5 years = $4,000 per year
[b]Units-of-production: Cost per unit = ($22,000 − $2,000)/1,000 units = $20 per unit

Year	Units	Depreciation per Unit	Depreciation
1.	200	$20	$ 4,000
2.	400	20	8,000
3.	300	20	6,000
4.	80	20	1,600
5.	30	20	400*
Total			$20,000

* Set depreciation in year 5 to reduce book value to the $20,000 salvage value; namely, instead of $600 (30 × $20), we use the maximum of $400 ($20,000 − $19,600 accum. depr.).
[c]Double-declining-balance: (100%/5) × 2 = 40% depreciation rate

Year	Beginning Book Value	Annual Depreciation (40% of Book Value)	Accumulated Depreciation at the End of the Year	Ending Book Value ($22,000 Cost Less Accumulated Depreciation)
1.	$22,000	$ 8,800	$ 8,800	$13,200
2.	13,200	5,280	14,080	7,920
3.	7,920	3,168	17,248	4,752
4.	4,752	1,901*	19,149	2,851
5.	2,851	851**	20,000	2,000
Total		$20,000		

* Rounded to the nearest dollar.
** Set depreciation in year 5 to reduce book value to the $20,000 salvage value; namely, instead of $1,140 ($2,851 × 40%), we use the maximum of $851 ($2,851 − $2,000).

Solution—Part 2

($3,800 − $200)/3 years = $1,200 (original depreciation per year)

$1,200 × 2 years = $2,400 (accumulated depreciation at date of change in estimate)

($3,800 − $2,400)/2 years = **$700** (revised depreciation)

Do More: QS 10-3 through QS 10-6, E 10-4 through E 10-13

ADDITIONAL EXPENDITURES

C3

Distinguish between revenue and capital expenditures, and account for them.

After a company acquires a plant asset and puts it into service, it often makes additional expenditures for that asset's operation, maintenance, repair, and improvement. In recording these expenditures, it must decide whether to capitalize or expense them (to capitalize an expenditure is to debit the asset account). The issue is whether these expenditures are reported as current-period expenses or added to the plant asset's cost and depreciated over its remaining useful life.

Revenue expenditures, also called *income statement expenditures,* are additional costs of plant assets that do not materially increase the asset's life or productive capabilities. They are recorded as expenses and deducted from revenues in the current period's income statement.

Capital expenditures, also called *balance sheet expenditures,* are additional costs of plant assets that provide benefits extending beyond the current period. They are debited to asset accounts and reported on the balance sheet.

 **Decision Maker**

Entrepreneur Your start-up Internet services company needs cash, and you are preparing financial statements to apply for a short-term loan. A friend suggests that you treat as many expenses as possible as capital expenditures. What are the impacts on financial statements of this suggestion? What do you think is the aim of this suggestion? ■
[*Answer:* Treating an expense as a capital expenditure means that expenses are lower and income higher in the short run. This is so because a capital expenditure is not expensed immediately but is spread over the asset's useful life. It also means that asset and equity totals are reported at higher amounts in the short run. This continues until the asset is fully depreciated. Thus, the friend's suggestion is misguided. Only an expenditure benefiting future periods is a capital expenditure.]

Ordinary Repairs

Ordinary repairs are expenditures to keep an asset in normal, good operating condition. Ordinary repairs do not extend an asset's useful life beyond its original estimate or increase its productivity beyond original expectations. Examples are normal costs of cleaning, lubricating, adjusting, oil changing, and replacing small parts of a machine. Ordinary repairs are treated as *revenue expenditures.* This means their costs are reported as expenses on the current-period income statement. Following this rule, **Brunswick** reports that "maintenance and repair costs are expensed as incurred." If Brunswick's current-year repair costs are $9,500, it makes the following entry.

Dec. 31	Repairs Expense	9,500	
	Cash		9,500
	Record ordinary repairs of equipment.		

Assets = Liabilities + Equity
−9,500   −9,500

Betterments and Extraordinary Repairs

Accounting for betterments and extraordinary repairs is similar—both are treated as *capital expenditures.*

Additional Expenditures	Examples	Expense Timing	Entry
Ordinary repairs	• Cleaning • Lubricating • Adjusting • Repainting	Expensed currently	Repairs Expense..... # Cash............. #
Betterments and extraordinary repairs	• Replacing main parts • Major asset expansions • Major asset overhauls	Expensed in future	Asset (such as Equip) # Cash............. #

Betterments (Improvements) **Betterments,** also called *improvements,* are expenditures that make a plant asset more efficient or productive. A betterment often involves adding a component to an asset or replacing one of its old components with a better one and does not always increase an asset's useful life. An example is replacing manual controls on a machine with automatic controls. One special type of betterment is an *addition,* such as adding a new wing or dock to a warehouse. Because a betterment benefits future periods, it is debited to the asset account as a capital expenditure. The new book value (less salvage value) is then depreciated over the asset's remaining useful life. To illustrate, suppose a company pays $8,000 for a machine with an eight-year useful life and no salvage value. After three years and $3,000 of depreciation, it adds an automated control system to the machine at a cost of $1,800. The cost of the betterment is added to the Machinery account with this entry.

Example: Assume a firm owns a web server. Identify each cost as a revenue or capital expenditure: (1) purchase price, (2) necessary wiring, (3) platform for operation, (4) circuits to increase capacity, (5) cleaning after each month of use, (6) repair of a faulty switch, and (7) replacement of a worn fan. *Answer:* Capital expenditures: 1, 2, 3, 4; revenue expenditures: 5, 6, 7.

Jan. 2	Machinery	1,800	
	Cash		1,800
	Record installation of automated system.		

Assets = Liabilities + Equity
+1,800
−1,800

After the betterment is recorded, the remaining cost to be depreciated is $6,800, computed as $8,000 − $3,000 + $1,800. Depreciation expense for the remaining five years is $1,360 per year, computed as $6,800/5 years.

Point: Both extraordinary repairs and betterments require revising future depreciation.

Extraordinary Repairs (Replacements)

Extraordinary repairs are expenditures extending the asset's useful life beyond its original estimate. Extraordinary repairs are *capital expenditures* because they benefit future periods. Their costs are debited to the asset account (or to Accumulated Depreciation). For example, **Delta Air Lines** reports, "modifications that . . . extend the useful lives of airframes or engines are capitalized and amortized [depreciated] over the remaining estimated useful life of the asset."

▌ **Decision** Insight

Far Out   If we owned a 20-year-old truck and planned to use it in our work for another 40 years, we would expect some extraordinary repairs in future years. A similar situation confronts Whiteman Air Force Base, home to the B-2 stealth bomber, which rolled out of a **Northrop Grumman** hangar in the 1980s. The plan is to keep those bat-winged bombers flying until 2058. The Pentagon is moving forward with a $2 billion, 10-year effort to modernize the bombers' defensive capabilities. ▪

© Purestock/Superstock

DISPOSALS OF PLANT ASSETS

P2 _____

Account for asset disposal through discarding or selling an asset.

Disposal of plant assets occurs in one of three basic ways: discarding, sale, or exchange. Discarding and selling are covered here; Appendix 10A covers exchanging assets. The general steps in accounting for a disposal of plant assets are described in Exhibit 10.15.

EXHIBIT 10.15

Accounting for Disposals of Plant Assets

1. Record depreciation up to the date of disposal—this also updates Accumulated Depreciation.
2. Record the removal of the disposed asset's account balances—including its Accumulated Depreciation.
3. Record any cash (and/or other assets) received or paid in the disposal.
4. Record any gain or loss—computed by comparing the disposed asset's book value with the market value of any assets received.

Discarding Plant Assets

A plant asset is *discarded* when it is no longer useful to the company and it has no market value. To illustrate, assume that a machine costing $9,000 with accumulated depreciation of $9,000 is discarded. When accumulated depreciation equals the asset's cost, it is said to be *fully depreciated* (zero book value). The entry to record the discarding of this asset is

Assets = Liabilities + Equity
+9,000
−9,000

June 5	Accumulated Depreciation—Machinery.................	9,000	
	Machinery......................................		9,000
	Discarding of fully depreciated machinery.		

This entry reflects all four steps of Exhibit 10.15. Step 1 is unnecessary because the machine is fully depreciated. Step 2 is reflected in the debit to Accumulated Depreciation and credit to Machinery. Because no other asset is involved, step 3 is irrelevant. Finally, because book value is zero and no other asset is involved, no gain or loss is recorded in step 4.

How do we account for discarding an asset that is not fully depreciated or one whose depreciation is not up-to-date? To answer this, consider equipment costing $8,000 with accumulated depreciation of $6,000 on December 31 of the prior fiscal year-end. This equipment is being depreciated using the straight-line method over eight years with zero salvage. On July 1 of the current year it is discarded. Step 1 is to bring depreciation up-to-date.

Point: Recording depreciation expense up-to-date gives an up-to-date book value for determining gain or loss.

Assets = Liabilities + Equity
−500   −500

July 1	Depreciation Expense............................	500	
	Accumulated Depreciation—Equipment............		500
	Record 6 months' depreciation ($1,000 × 6/12).		

Steps 2 through 4 of Exhibit 10.15 are reflected in the second (and final) entry.

July 1	Accumulated Depreciation—Equipment	6,500	
	Loss on Disposal of Equipment.........................	1,500	
	Equipment.......................................		8,000
	Discarding equipment with a $1,500 book value.		

Assets = Liabilities + Equity
+6,500   −1,500
−8,000

This loss is computed by comparing the equipment's $1,500 book value ($8,000 − $6,000 − $500) with the zero net cash proceeds. The loss is reported in the Other Expenses and Losses section of the income statement. Discarding an asset can sometimes require a cash payment that would increase the loss.

Point: Gain or loss is determined by comparing "value given" (book value) to "value received."

Selling Plant Assets

To illustrate the accounting for selling plant assets, we consider BTO's March 31 sale of equipment that cost $16,000 and has accumulated depreciation of $12,000 at December 31 of the prior calendar year-end. Annual depreciation on this equipment is $4,000 computed using straight-line depreciation. Step 1 of this sale is to record depreciation expense and update accumulated depreciation to March 31 of the current year.

March 31	Depreciation Expense...............................	1,000	
	Accumulated Depreciation—Equipment............		1,000
	Record 3 months' depreciation ($4,000 × 3/12).		

Assets = Liabilities + Equity
−1,000   −1,000

Steps 2 through 4 of Exhibit 10.15 can be reflected in one final entry that depends on the amount received from the asset's sale. We consider three different possibilities.

Sale at Book Value   If BTO receives $3,000 cash, an amount equal to the equipment's book value as of March 31 (book value = $16,000 − $12,000 − $1,000), no gain or loss occurs on disposal. The entry is

Sale price = Book value → No gain or loss

March 31	Cash..	3,000	
	Accumulated Depreciation—Equipment	13,000	
	Equipment.......................................		16,000
	Record sale of equipment for no gain or loss.		

Assets = Liabilities + Equity
+3,000
+13,000
−16,000

Sale above Book Value   If BTO receives $7,000, an amount that is $4,000 above the equipment's $3,000 book value as of March 31, a gain on disposal occurs. The entry is

Sale price > Book value → Gain

March 31	Cash..	7,000	
	Accumulated Depreciation—Equipment	13,000	
	Gain on Disposal of Equipment		4,000
	Equipment.......................................		16,000
	Record sale of equipment for a $4,000 gain.		

Assets = Liabilities + Equity
+7,000   +4,000
+13,000
−16,000

Sale below Book Value   If BTO receives $2,500, an amount that is $500 below the equipment's $3,000 book value as of March 31, a loss on disposal occurs. The entry is

Sale price < Book value → Loss

March 31	Cash..	2,500	
	Loss on Disposal of Equipment.......................	500	
	Accumulated Depreciation—Equipment	13,000	
	Equipment.......................................		16,000
	Record sale of equipment for a $500 loss.		

Assets = Liabilities + Equity
+2,500   −500
+13,000
−16,000

NEED-TO-KNOW 10-3

Additional Expenditures and Asset Disposals

C3   P2

Part 1. A company pays $1,000 for equipment expected to last four years and have a $200 salvage value. Prepare journal entries to record the following costs related to the equipment.

a. During the second year of the equipment's life, $400 cash is paid for a new component expected to increase the equipment's productivity by 20% per year.

b. During the third year, $250 cash is paid for normal repairs necessary to keep the equipment in good working order.

c. During the fourth year, $500 is paid for repairs expected to increase the useful life of the equipment from four to five years.

Part 2. A company owns a machine that cost $500 and has accumulated depreciation of $400. Prepare the entry to record the disposal of the machine on January 2 under each of the following independent situations.

a. The machine needed extensive repairs, and it was not worth repairing. The company disposed of the machine, receiving nothing in return.

b. The company sold the machine for $80 cash.

c. The company sold the machine for $100 cash.

d. The company sold the machine for $110 cash.

Solution—Part 1

a.

Year 2	Equipment	400	
	Cash		400
	Record betterment.		

b.

Year 3	Repairs Expense	250	
	Cash		250
	Record ordinary repairs.		

c.

Year 4	Equipment	500	
	Cash		500
	Record extraordinary repairs.		

Solution—Part 2   [Note: Book value of machine = $500 − $400 = $100]

a. Disposed of at no value

Jan. 2	Loss on Disposal of Machine	100	
	Accumulated Depreciation—Machine	400	
	Machine.....................................		500
	Record disposal of machine.		

b. Sold for $80 cash

Jan. 2	Cash...	80	
	Loss on Sale of Machine	20	
	Accumulated Depreciation—Machine	400	
	Machine.....................................		500
	Record cash sale of machine (below book value).		

c. Sold for $100 cash

Jan. 2	Cash...	100	
	Accumulated Depreciation—Machine	400	
	Machine.....................................		500
	Record cash sale of machine (at book value).		

d. Sold for $110 cash

Jan. 2	Cash...	110	
	Accumulated Depreciation—Machine	400	
	Gain on Sale of Machine		10
	Machine.....................................		500
	Record cash sale of machine (above book value).		

Do More: QS 10-8, QS 10-9, E 10-14, E 10-15, E 10-16, E 10-17

Section 2—Natural Resources

Natural resources are assets that are physically consumed when used. Examples are standing timber, mineral deposits, and oil and gas fields. Because they are consumed when used, they are often called *wasting assets*. These assets represent soon-to-be inventories of raw materials that will be converted into one or more products by cutting, mining, or pumping. Until that conversion takes place, they are noncurrent assets and are shown in a balance sheet using titles such as *Timberlands, Mineral deposits,* or *Oil reserves*. Natural resources are reported under either plant assets or their own separate category. **Alcoa**, for instance, reports its natural resources under the balance sheet title *Properties, plants and equipment.* In a note to its financial statements, Alcoa reports a separate amount for *Land and land rights, including mines.* **Weyerhaeuser**, on the other hand, reports its timber holdings in a separate balance sheet category titled *Timber and timberlands.*

P3

Account for natural resource assets and their depletion.

Cost Determination and Depletion

Natural resources are recorded at cost, which includes all expenditures necessary to acquire the resource and prepare it for its intended use. **Depletion** is the process of allocating the cost of a natural resource to the period when it is consumed. Natural resources are reported on the balance sheet at cost less *accumulated depletion.* The depletion expense per period is usually based on units extracted from cutting, mining, or pumping. This is similar to units-of-production depreciation. **ExxonMobil** uses this approach to amortize the costs of discovering and operating its oil wells.

© Digital Vision/Getty Images

To illustrate depletion of natural resources, let's consider a mineral deposit with an estimated 250,000 tons of available ore. It is purchased for $500,000, and we expect zero salvage value. The depletion charge per ton of ore mined is $2, computed as $500,000 ÷ 250,000 tons. If 85,000 tons are mined and sold in the first year, the depletion charge for that year is $170,000. These computations are detailed in Exhibit 10.16.

Step 1

$$\text{Depletion per unit} = \frac{\text{Cost} - \text{Salvage value}}{\text{Total units of capacity}} = \frac{\$500,000 - \$0}{250,000 \text{ tons}} = \$2 \text{ per ton}$$

Step 2

Depletion expense = Depletion per unit × Units extracted and sold in period
$$= \$2 \times 85,000 = \$170,000$$

EXHIBIT 10.16

Depletion Formula and Example

Depletion expense for the first year is recorded as follows.

Dec. 31	Depletion Expense—Mineral Deposit.	170,000	
	Accumulated Depletion—Mineral Deposit		170,000
	Record depletion of the mineral deposit.		

Assets = Liabilities + Equity
−170,000   −170,000

The period-end balance sheet reports the mineral deposit as shown in Exhibit 10.17.

EXHIBIT 10.17

Balance Sheet Presentation of Natural Resources

| Mineral deposit . . . . | $500,000 | |
| Less accumulated depletion . . . . | 170,000 | $330,000 |

Because all 85,000 tons of the mined ore are sold during the year, the entire $170,000 of depletion is reported on the income statement. If some of the ore remains unsold at year-end, however, the depletion related to the unsold ore is carried forward on the balance sheet and reported as Ore Inventory, a current asset. To illustrate, and altering our example, assume that of the 85,000 tons mined the first year, only 70,000 tons are sold. We record depletion of $140,000 (70,000 tons × $2 depletion per unit) and the remaining Ore Inventory of $30,000 (15,000 tons × $2 depletion per unit) as follows.

Assets = Liabilities + Equity
−170,000   −140,000
+30,000

Dec. 31	Depletion Expense—Mineral Deposit....................	140,000	
	Ore Inventory..	30,000	
	Accumulated Depletion—Mineral Deposit		170,000
	Record depletion and inventory of mineral deposit.		

Plant Assets Tied into Extracting

The conversion of natural resources by mining, cutting, or pumping requires machinery, equipment, and buildings. When the usefulness of these plant assets is directly related to the depletion of a natural resource, their costs are depreciated using the units-of-production method in proportion to the depletion of the natural resource. For example, if a machine is permanently installed in a mine and 10% of the ore is mined and sold in the period, then 10% of the machine's cost (less any salvage value) is allocated to depreciation expense. The same procedure is used when a machine is abandoned once resources have been extracted. If, however, a machine will be moved to and used at another site when extraction is complete, the machine is depreciated over its own useful life.

 Decision Insight

In Control   Long-term assets must be safeguarded against theft, misuse, and other damages. Controls take many forms depending on the asset, including use of security tags, the legal monitoring of rights infringements, and approvals of all asset disposals. A study reports that 43% of employees in operations and service areas witnessed the wasting, mismanaging, or abusing of assets in the past year (KPMG 2013). ■

 10-4

Depletion Accounting

P3

A company acquires a zinc mine at a cost of $750,000 on January 1. At that same time it incurs additional costs of $100,000 to access the mine, which is estimated to hold 200,000 tons of zinc. The estimated value of the land after the zinc is removed is $50,000.

1. Prepare the January 1 entry(ies) to record the cost of the zinc mine.

2. Prepare the December 31 year-end adjusting entry if 50,000 tons of zinc are mined, but only 40,000 tons are sold the first year.

Solution

1.

Jan. 1	Zinc Mine	850,000	
	Cash		850,000
	Record cost of zinc mine.		

2. Depletion per unit = ($750,000 + $100,000 − $50,000)/200,000 tons = $4.00 per ton

Dec. 31	Depletion Expense—Zinc Mine......................	160,000	
	Zinc Inventory	40,000	
	Accumulated Depletion—Zinc Mine		200,000
	Record depletion of zinc mine (50,000 × $4.00).		

Do More: QS 10-10, E 10-18

Section 3—Intangible Assets

P4

Account for intangible assets.

Intangible assets are nonphysical assets (used in operations) that give companies long-term rights, privileges, or competitive advantages. Examples are patents, copyrights, licenses, leaseholds, franchises, goodwill, and trademarks. Lack of physical substance does not necessarily imply an intangible asset. Notes and accounts receivable, for instance, lack physical substance, but they are not intangibles. This section identifies common types of intangible assets and explains the accounting for them.

Cost Determination and Amortization

An intangible asset is recorded at cost when purchased. Intangibles are then separated into those with limited lives or indefinite lives. If an intangible has a **limited life,** its cost is expensed over its estimated useful life through the process of **amortization.** If an intangible asset has an **indefinite life**—meaning that no legal, regulatory, contractual, competitive, economic, or other factors limit its useful life—it should not be amortized. (If an intangible with an indefinite life is later judged to have a limited life, it is amortized over that limited life.)

Amortization of intangible assets is similar to depreciation and depletion in that it is a process of cost allocation. However, only the straight-line method is used for amortizing intangibles *unless* the company can show that another method is preferred. The effects of amortization are recorded in a contra account (Accumulated Amortization). The gross acquisition cost of intangible assets is to be disclosed along with the accumulated amortization. The disposal of an intangible asset involves removing its book value, recording any other asset(s) received or given up, and recognizing any gain or loss for the difference.

Many intangibles have limited lives due to laws, contracts, or other asset characteristics. Examples are patents, copyrights, and leaseholds. The cost of intangible assets is amortized over the periods expected to benefit by their use, but in no case can this period be longer than the asset's legal existence. Other intangibles such as trademarks and trade names have lives that can continue indefinitely and are not amortized. An intangible asset that is not amortized is tested annually for **impairment**—if necessary, an impairment loss is recorded. (Details for this test are in advanced courses.)

Point: Goodwill is not amortized; instead, it is annually tested for impairment.

Intangible assets are often shown in a separate section of the balance sheet immediately after plant assets. Callaway Golf, for instance, follows this approach in reporting nearly $90 million of intangible assets in its balance sheet, plus nearly $30 million in goodwill. Companies usually disclose their amortization periods for intangibles. The remainder of our discussion focuses on accounting for specific types of intangible assets.

© Scott Halleran/Getty Images

Types of Intangibles

Patents   The federal government grants patents to encourage the invention of new technology, mechanical devices, and production processes. A **patent** is an exclusive right granted to its owner to manufacture and sell a patented item or to use a process for 20 years. When patent rights are purchased, the cost to acquire the rights is debited to an account called Patents. If the owner engages in lawsuits to successfully defend a patent, the cost of lawsuits is debited to the Patents account; if the defense is unsuccessful, the book value of the patent is expensed. However, the costs of research and development leading to a new patent are expensed when incurred.

A patent's cost is amortized over its estimated useful life (not to exceed 20 years). If we purchase a patent costing $25,000 with a useful life of 10 years, we make the following adjusting entry at the end of each of the 10 years to amortize one-tenth of its cost.

Dec. 31	Amortization Expense—Patents	2,500	
	Accumulated Amortization—Patents		2,500
	Amortize patent costs over its useful life.		

Assets = Liabilities + Equity
−2,500   −2,500

The $2,500 debit to Amortization Expense appears on the income statement as a cost of the product or service provided under protection of the patent. The Accumulated Amortization—Patents account is a contra asset account to Patents.

Decision Insight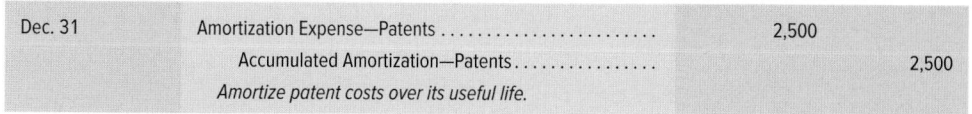

Meds   Mention "drug war" and most people think of illegal drug trade. But another drug war is under way: Brand-name drugmakers are fighting to stop generic copies of their products from hitting the market once patents expire. Delaying a generic rival can yield millions in extra sales. One way drugmakers fight patent expirations is to alter *drug delivery*. The first patent might require a patient to take a pill 4×/day. When that patent expires, the drugmaker can "improve" the drug's delivery release system to 2×/day, and then 1×/day, and so forth. ■

Prescriptions That Specify Generics

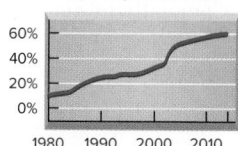
60%
40%
20%
0%
1980 1990 2000 2010

Copyrights   A **copyright** gives its owner the exclusive right to publish and sell a musical, literary, or artistic work during the life of the creator plus 70 years, although the useful life of most copyrights is much shorter. The costs of a copyright are amortized over its useful life. The only identifiable cost of many copyrights is the fee paid to the Copyright Office of the federal government or international agency granting the copyright. Identifiable costs of a copyright are capitalized (recorded in an asset account) and periodically amortized by debiting an account called Amortization Expense—Copyrights.

Decision Insight

Mickey Mouse Protection Act   The Walt Disney Company successfully lobbied Congress to extend copyright protection from the life of the creator plus 50 years to the life of the creator plus 70 years. This extension allows the company to protect its characters for 20 additional years before the right to use them enters the public domain. Mickey Mouse is now protected by copyright law until 2023. The law is officially termed the Copyright Term Extension Act (CTEA), but it is also known as the Mickey Mouse Protection Act. ∎

© Yoshikazu Tsuno/AFP/Getty Images

Franchises and Licenses   **Franchises** and **licenses** are rights that a company or government grants an entity to deliver a product or service under specified conditions. Many organizations grant franchise and license rights—**Anytime Fitness**, **Firehouse Subs**, and **Major League Baseball** are just a few examples. The costs of franchises and licenses are debited to a Franchises and Licenses asset account and are amortized over the life of the agreement. If an agreement is for an indefinite or perpetual period, those costs are not amortized.

Trademarks and Trade Names   Companies often use unique symbols or select unique names and brands in marketing their products. A **trademark** or **trade (brand) name** is a symbol, name, phrase, or jingle identified with a company, product, or service. Examples are Nike swoosh, Marlboro Man, Big Mac, Coca-Cola, and Corvette. Ownership and exclusive right to use a trademark or trade name are often established by showing that one company used it before another. Ownership is best established by registering a trademark or trade name with the government's Patent Office. The cost of developing, maintaining, or enhancing the value of a trademark or trade name (such as advertising) is charged to expense when incurred. If a trademark or trade name is purchased, however, its cost is debited to an asset account and then amortized over its expected life. If the company plans to renew indefinitely its right to the trademark or trade name, the cost is not amortized.

Point: McDonald's "golden arches" are one of the world's most valuable trademarks, yet this asset is not shown on McDonald's balance sheet.

Goodwill   **Goodwill** has a specific meaning in accounting. Goodwill is the amount by which a company's value exceeds the value of its individual assets and liabilities. This implies that the company as a whole has certain valuable attributes not measured among its individual assets and liabilities. These can include superior management, skilled workforce, good supplier or customer relations, quality products or services, good location, or other competitive advantages.

Goodwill is not recorded unless an entire company or business segment is purchased. Purchased goodwill is measured by taking the purchase price of the company and subtracting the market value of its individual net assets (excluding goodwill). For instance, **Google** paid $1.19 billion to acquire **YouTube**; about $1.13 of the $1.19 billion was for goodwill. Goodwill was also a major portion of the $19 billion that **Facebook** paid to acquire **WhatsApp**.

Goodwill is measured as the excess of the cost of an acquired entity over the value of the acquired net assets. Goodwill is recorded as an asset, and it is *not* amortized. Instead, goodwill is annually tested for impairment. (Details on impairment testing are in advanced courses.)

Point: Amortization of goodwill is different for financial accounting and tax accounting. The IRS requires the amortization of goodwill over 15 years.

Example: Assume goodwill carries a book value of $500 and has an implied fair value of $475, *and* this $25 decline in value meets the impairment test. The entry to record this impairment is:
Impairment Loss 25
  Goodwill   25

Leaseholds   Property is rented under a contract called a **lease.** The property's owner, called the **lessor,** grants the lease. The one who secures the right to possess and use the property is called the **lessee. A leasehold** refers to the rights the lessor grants to the lessee under the terms of the lease. A leasehold is an intangible asset for the lessee.

Lease or Buy   The advantages of leasing an asset versus buying it include:

- Little or no down payment normally required (making it more affordable).
- Lease terms often allow exchanges to better leased assets (reducing obsolescence).
- Lessor receives the asset's tax deduction (meaning lessee may get a better deal).

Operating Lease or Capital Lease   An *operating lease* is accounted for as a rental. This means that periodic (such as monthly) rent payments are debited to a Rent Expense account. If a lease requires the lessee to pay the final period's rent in advance when the lease is signed, the lessee records this advance payment with a debit to the Leasehold account. Because the advance payment is not used until the final period, the Leasehold account balance remains on the balance sheet until that final period, when its amount is transferred to Rent Expense. Alternatively, some long-term leases give the lessee essentially the same rights as a purchaser. This results in a tangible asset and a liability reported by the lessee. This is called a *capital lease* and is explained in the chapter on long-term liabilities.

Sublease   A long-term lease can increase in value when current rental rates for similar property rise while payments under the lease remain constant. This increase in value of a lease is not reported on the lessee's balance sheet. However, if the property is subleased and the new tenant makes a cash payment to the original lessee for the rights under the old lease, the new tenant debits this payment to a Leasehold account, which is amortized to Rent Expense over the remaining life of the lease.

Point: A Leasehold account implies existence of future benefits that the lessee controls because of a prepayment. It also meets the definition of an asset.

Leasehold Improvements

A lessee sometimes pays for alterations or improvements to the leased property such as partitions, painting, and storefronts. These alterations and improvements are called **leasehold improvements,** and the lessee debits these costs to a Leasehold Improvements account. The lessee amortizes these costs over the life of the lease or the life of the improvements, whichever is shorter. The amortization entry *debits* Amortization Expense—Leasehold Improvements and *credits* Accumulated Amortization—Leasehold Improvements.

Research and Development

Research and development costs are expenditures aimed at discovering new products, new processes, or knowledge. Creating patents, copyrights, and innovative products and services requires research and development costs. The costs of research and development are expensed when incurred because it is difficult to predict the future benefits from research and development.

Other Intangibles

There are other types of intangible assets such as *software, noncompete covenants, customer lists,* and so forth. Our accounting for them is the same. First, we record the intangible asset's costs. Second, we determine whether the asset has a limited or indefinite life. If limited, we allocate its costs over that period. If indefinite, its costs are not amortized.

Decision Insight

Into Hiding   Most people view fraud involving long-term assets as low risk. Yet, opportunity for fraud in a one-time transaction is a higher risk and requires scrutiny. Theft involving concealment of an asset can include recording it as scrap, obsolete, donated, or destroyed—for example:

- Recording an asset disposal as a customer adjustment, as a no-charge item, or as promotion.
- Recording false counts or altering records after a physical count.
- Recording false receiving reports as to asset quantity.
- Nonbilling of an asset sale.
- Write-off of an asset. ■

NEED-TO-KNOW 10-5

Accounting for
Intangibles

P4

Part 1. A publisher purchases the copyright on a book for $1,000 on January 1 of this year. The copyright legally protects its owner for five more years. The company plans to market and sell prints of the original for seven years. Prepare entries to record the purchase of the copyright on January 1 of this year and its annual amortization on December 31 of this year.

Part 2. On January 3 of this year, a retailer incurs a $9,000 cost to modernize its store. Improvements include lighting, partitions, and sound system. These improvements are estimated to yield benefits for five years. The retailer leases its store and has three years remaining on its lease. Prepare the entry to record (a) the cost of modernization and (b) amortization at the end of this current year.

Part 3. On January 6 of this year, a company pays $6,000 for a patent with a remaining 12-year legal life to produce a supplement expected to be marketable for 3 years. Prepare entries to record its acquisition and the December 31 amortization entry for this current year.

Solution—Part 1

Jan. 1	Copyright...	1,000	
	Cash		1,000
	Record purchase of copyright.		
Dec. 31	Amortization Expense—Copyright........................	200	
	Accumulated Amortization—Copyright....................		200
	Record amortization of copyright [$1,000/5 years].		

Solution—Part 2

a.

Jan. 3	Leasehold Improvements................................	9,000	
	Cash		9,000
	Record leasehold improvements.		

b.

Dec. 31	Amortization Expense–Leasehold Improvements	3,000	
	Accumulated Amortization—Leasehold Improvements		3,000
	Record amortization of leasehold over remaining lease life.*		

*Amortization = $9,000/3-year lease term = $3,000 per year

Solution—Part 3

Jan. 6	Patents...	6,000	
	Cash		6,000
	Record purchase of patent.		
Dec. 31	Amortization Expense*.................................	2,000	
	Accumulated Amortization—Patents.....................		2,000
	Record amortization of patent. *$6,000/3 years = $2,000		

Do More: QS 10-12, E 10-19,
E 10-20

SUSTAINABILITY AND ACCOUNTING

Matt Hofmann is committed to distilling on a local level. Matt's company, **Westland Distillery**, supports farmers in the Seattle area by using locally sourced ingredients. "Seattle is a natural place to make single malt whiskey," explains Matt. "We have some of the best barley-growing regions in the world and water quality that is tough to match."

Matt laments that many of his "friends in the industry" do not have the same commitment to locally sourced ingredients. "I'd love to help change that in my lifetime," admits Matt. Matt explains that accounting is one key to using local ingredients. He describes how his accounting system is continually used to check on the viability of using locally sourced ingredients and to negotiate with local providers to make it happen.

Matt explains that he references accounting information to ensure assets are not tied up in unproductive long-term assets. If assets are not managed properly and are tied up in nonproducing assets like plant, property, and equipment, his profits will suffer. This would impact his ability to purchase more expensive, locally sourced ingredients, which could have a profound impact on the quality of the product and break his quality commitment.

Matt refuses to go down the path of cutting quality. "What I love about any product, really, is the connection to place," explains Matt. He is equally committed to sustainability. Matt explains, "we want to take these [sustainable initiatives] and push them in a new direction." This includes "sourcing the right ingredients," insists Matt, and "having people involved at all steps who care."

Courtesy of Westland Distillery

Total Asset Turnover   **Decision Analysis**

A company's assets are important in determining its ability to generate sales and earn income. Managers devote much attention to deciding what assets a company acquires, how much it invests in assets, and how to use assets most efficiently and effectively. One important measure of a company's ability to use its assets is **total asset turnover,** defined in Exhibit 10.18.

A1
Compute total asset turnover and apply it to analyze a company's use of assets.

$$\text{Total asset turnover} = \frac{\text{Net sales}}{\text{Average total assets}}$$

EXHIBIT 10.18

Total Asset Turnover

The numerator reflects the net amounts earned from the sale of products and services. The denominator reflects the average total resources devoted to operating the company and generating sales.

To illustrate, let's look at total asset turnover in Exhibit 10.19 for two competing companies: Molson Coors and Boston Beer.

Company	Figure ($ millions)	2015	2014	2013	2012	2011
Molson Coors	Net sales..................	$ 3,567.5	$ 4,146.3	$ 4,206.1	$ 3,916.5	$ 3,515.7
	Average total assets..........	$13,128.2	$14,780.1	$15,896.2	$14,318.0	$12,560.7
	Total asset turnover.........	0.27	0.28	0.26	0.27	0.28
Boston Beer	Net sales..................	$ 959.9	$ 903.0	$ 739.1	$ 580.2	$ 513.0
	Average total assets..........	$ 625.3	$ 524.6	$ 401.8	$ 316.0	$ 265.5
	Total asset turnover.........	1.54	1.72	1.84	1.84	1.93

EXHIBIT 10.19

Analysis Using Total Asset Turnover

To show how we use total asset turnover, let's look at Molson Coors. We express Molson Coors's use of assets in generating net sales by saying "it turned its assets over 0.27 times during 2015." This means that each $1.00 of assets produced $0.27 of net sales.

Is a total asset turnover of 0.27 good or bad? It is safe to say that all companies desire a high total asset turnover. Like many ratio analyses, however, a company's total asset turnover must be interpreted in comparison with those of prior years and of its competitors. Interpreting the total asset turnover also requires an understanding of the company's operations. Some operations are capital-intensive, meaning that a relatively large amount is invested in assets to generate sales. This suggests a relatively lower total asset turnover. Other companies' operations are labor-intensive, meaning that they generate sales more by the efforts of people than the use of assets. In that case, we expect a higher total asset turnover.

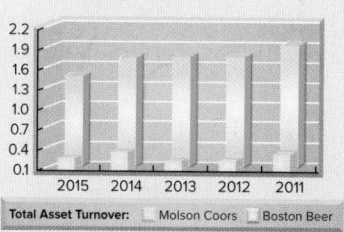

Companies with low total asset turnover require higher profit margins (examples are hotels and real estate); companies with high total asset turnover can succeed with lower profit margins (examples are

Point: An estimate of **plant asset useful life** equals the plant asset cost divided by depreciation expense.

food stores and toy merchandisers). Molson Coors's turnover is much lower than that for Boston Beer and many other competitors. Total asset turnover for Molson Coors's competitors, available in industry publications, is generally in the range of 0.5 to 1.0 over this same period. Overall, Molson Coors must improve relative to its competitors on total asset turnover.

■ Decision Maker

Environmentalist   A paper manufacturer claims it cannot afford more environmental controls. It points to its low total asset turnover of 1.9 and argues that it cannot compete with companies whose total asset turnover is much higher. Examples cited are food stores (5.5) and auto dealers (3.8). How do you respond? ■   [*Answer:* The paper manufacturer's comparison of its total asset turnover with food stores and auto dealers is misdirected. These other industries' turnovers are higher because their profit margins are lower (about 2%). Profit margins for the paper industry are usually 3% to 3.5%. You need to collect data from competitors in the paper industry to show that a 1.9 total asset turnover is about the norm for this industry. You might also want to collect data on this company's revenues and expenses, along with compensation data for its high-ranking officers and employees.]

NEED-TO-KNOW 10-6

COMPREHENSIVE

On July 14, 2016, Tulsa Company pays $600,000 to acquire a fully equipped factory. The purchase involves the following assets and information.

Asset	Appraised Value	Salvage Value	Useful Life	Depreciation Method
Land	$160,000			Not depreciated
Land improvements............	80,000	$ 0	10 years	Straight-line
Building	320,000	100,000	10 years	Double-declining-balance
Machinery....................	240,000	20,000	10,000 units	Units-of-production*
Total	$800,000			

* The machinery is used to produce 700 units in 2016 and 1,800 units in 2017.

Required

1. Allocate the total $600,000 purchase cost among the separate assets.

2. Compute the 2016 (six months) and 2017 depreciation expense for each asset, and compute the company's total depreciation expense for both years.

3. On the last day of calendar-year 2018, Tulsa discarded machinery that had been on its books for five years. The machinery's original cost was $12,000 (estimated life of five years) and its salvage value was $2,000. No depreciation had been recorded for the fifth year when the disposal occurred. Journalize the fifth year of depreciation (straight-line method) and the asset's disposal.

4. At the beginning of year 2018, Tulsa purchased a patent for $100,000 cash. The company estimated the patent's useful life to be 10 years. Journalize the patent acquisition and its amortization for the year 2018.

5. Late in the year 2018, Tulsa acquired an ore deposit for $600,000 cash. It added roads and built mine shafts for an additional cost of $80,000. Salvage value of the mine is estimated to be $20,000. The company estimated 330,000 tons of available ore. In year 2018, Tulsa mined and sold 10,000 tons of ore. Journalize the mine's acquisition and its first year's depletion.

6.^A (This question applies this chapter's Appendix coverage.) On the first day of 2018, Tulsa exchanged the machinery that was acquired on July 14, 2016, along with $5,000 cash for machinery with a $210,000 market value. Journalize the exchange of these assets assuming the exchange has commercial substance. (Refer to background information in parts 1 and 2.)

PLANNING THE SOLUTION

● Complete a three-column table showing the following amounts for each asset: appraised value, percent of total value, and apportioned cost.

- Using allocated costs, compute depreciation for 2016 (only one-half year) and 2017 (full year) for each asset. Summarize those computations in a table showing total depreciation for each year.
- Depreciation must be recorded up-to-date before discarding an asset. Calculate and record depreciation expense for the fifth year using the straight-line method. Because salvage value is not received at the end of a discarded asset's life, the salvage value becomes a loss on disposal. Record the loss on the disposal as well as the removal of the discarded asset and its related accumulated depreciation.
- Record the patent (an intangible asset) at its purchase price. Use straight-line amortization over its useful life to calculate amortization expense.
- Record the ore deposit (a natural resource asset) at its cost, including any added costs to ready the mine for use. Calculate depletion per ton using the depletion formula. Multiply the depletion per ton by the amount of tons mined and sold to calculate depletion expense for the year.
- Gains and losses on asset exchanges that have commercial substance are recognized. Make a journal entry to add the acquired machinery to the books and to remove the old machinery, along with its accumulated depreciation, and to record the cash given in the exchange.

SOLUTION

1. Allocation of the total cost of $600,000 among the separate assets.

Asset	Appraised Value	Percent of Total Value	Apportioned Cost
Land....................	$160,000	20%	$120,000 ($600,000 × 20%)
Land improvements	80,000	10	60,000 ($600,000 × 10%)
Building....................	320,000	40	240,000 ($600,000 × 40%)
Machinery..................	240,000	30	180,000 ($600,000 × 30%)
Total.......................	$800,000	100%	$ 600,000

2. Depreciation for each asset. (Land is not depreciated.)

Land Improvements

Cost...	$ 60,000
Salvage value...	0
Depreciable cost	$ 60,000
Useful life	10 years
Annual depreciation expense ($60,000/10 years).................	$ 6,000
2016 depreciation ($6,000 × 6/12)	$ 3,000
2017 depreciation	$ 6,000

Building

Straight-line rate = 100%/10 years = 10%
Double-declining-balance rate = 10% × 2 = 20%

2016 depreciation ($240,000 × 20% × 6/12)	$ 24,000
2017 depreciation [($240,000 − $24,000) × 20%]	$ 43,200

Machinery

Cost...	$180,000
Salvage value...	20,000
Depreciable cost	$160,000
Total expected units of production	10,000 units
Depreciation per unit ($160,000/10,000 units)	$ 16
2016 depreciation ($16 × 700 units)..........................	$ 11,200
2017 depreciation ($16 × 1,800 units)	$ 28,800

Total depreciation expense for each year:

	2016	2017
Land improvements	$ 3,000	$ 6,000
Building	24,000	43,200
Machinery	11,200	28,800
Total	$38,200	$78,000

3. Record the depreciation up-to-date on the discarded asset.

Depreciation Expense—Machinery	2,000	
Accumulated Depreciation—Machinery		2,000
Record depreciation on date of disposal: ($12,000 − $2,000)/5		

Record the removal of the discarded asset and its loss on disposal.

Accumulated Depreciation—Machinery	10,000	
Loss on Disposal of Machinery	2,000	
Machinery		12,000
Record the discarding of machinery with a $2,000 book value.		

4.

Patent	100,000	
Cash		100,000
Record patent acquisition.		

Amortization Expense—Patent	10,000	
Accumulated Amortization—Patent		10,000
Record amortization expense: $100,000/10 years = $10,000.		

5.

Ore Deposit	680,000	
Cash		680,000
Record ore deposit acquisition and its related costs.		

Depletion Expense—Ore Deposit	20,000	
Accumulated Depletion—Ore Deposit		20,000
Record depletion expense: ($680,000 − $20,000)/330,000 tons = $2 per ton.		
10,000 tons mined and sold × $2 = $20,000 depletion.		

6. Record the asset exchange: The book value on the exchange date is $180,000 (cost) − $40,000 (accumulated depreciation). The book value of the machinery given up in the exchange ($140,000) plus the $5,000 cash paid is less than the $210,000 value of the machine acquired. The entry to record this exchange of assets that has commercial substance and recognizes the $65,000 gain ($210,000 − $140,000 − $5,000) is:

Machinery (new)	210,000	
Accumulated Depreciation—Machinery (old)	40,000	
Machinery (old)		180,000
Cash		5,000
Gain on Exchange of Assets		65,000
Record exchange with commercial substance of old equipment		
plus cash for new equipment.		

Exchanging Plant Assets

10A

P5

Account for asset exchanges.

Many plant assets such as machinery, automobiles, and equipment are disposed of by exchanging them for newer assets. In a typical exchange of plant assets, a *trade-in allowance* is received on the old asset and the balance is paid in cash. Accounting for the exchange of assets depends on whether the transaction has *commercial substance*. An exchange has commercial substance if the company's future cash flows change as a result of the exchange of one asset for another asset. If an asset exchange has commercial substance, a gain or loss is recorded based on the difference between the book value of the asset(s) given up and the market value of the asset(s) received. Because most exchanges have commercial substance, we cover gains and losses for only that situation. Advanced courses cover exchanges without commercial substance.

Exchange with Commercial Substance: A Loss   A company acquires $42,000 in new equipment. In exchange, the company pays $33,000 cash and trades in old equipment. The old equipment originally cost $36,000 and has accumulated depreciation of $20,000, which implies a $16,000 book value at the time of exchange. We are told this exchange has commercial substance and that the old equipment has a trade-in allowance of $9,000. This exchange yields a loss as computed in the middle (Loss) columns of Exhibit 10A.1; the loss is computed as Asset received − Assets given = $42,000 − $49,000 = $(7,000). We can also compute the loss as Trade-in allowance − Book value of assets given = $9,000 − $16,000 = $(7,000).

Asset Exchange Has Commercial Substance	Loss		Gain	
Market value of asset received		$42,000		$42,000
Book value of assets given:				
Equipment ($36,000 − $20,000)	$16,000		$16,000	
Cash	33,000	49,000	23,000	39,000
Gain (loss) on exchange		$(7,000)		$ 3,000

EXHIBIT 10A.1

Computing Gain or Loss on Asset Exchange with Commercial Substance

The entry to record this asset exchange is

Jan. 3	Equipment (**new**)	42,000	
	Loss on Exchange of Assets	7,000	
	Accumulated Depreciation—Equipment (**old**)	20,000	
	Equipment (**old**)		36,000
	Cash		33,000
	Record exchange (with commercial substance) of old equipment and cash for new equipment.		

Assets = Liabilities + Equity
+42,000   −7,000
+20,000
−36,000
−33,000

Point: Parenthetical notes to "new" and "old" equipment are for illustration only. Both the debit and credit are to the same Equipment account.

Exchange with Commercial Substance: A Gain   Let's assume the same facts as in the preceding asset exchange *except that the company pays $23,000 cash, not $33,000, with the trade-in.* We are told that this exchange has commercial substance and that the old equipment has a trade-in allowance of $19,000. This exchange yields a gain as computed in the right-most (Gain) columns of Exhibit 10A.1; the gain is computed as Asset received − Assets given = $42,000 − $39,000 = $3,000. We can also compute the gain as Trade-in allowance − Book value of assets given = $19,000 − $16,000 = $3,000. The entry to record this asset exchange is

Jan. 3	Equipment (**new**)	42,000	
	Accumulated Depreciation—Equipment (**old**)	20,000	
	Equipment (**old**)		36,000
	Cash		23,000
	Gain on Exchange of Assets.		3,000
	Record exchange (with commercial substance) of old equipment and cash for new equipment.		

Assets = Liabilities + Equity
+42,000   +3,000
+20,000
−36,000
−23,000

NEED-TO-KNOW **10-7**

Asset Exchange

P5

A company acquires $45,000 in new web servers. In exchange, the company trades in old web servers along with a cash payment. The old servers originally cost $30,000 and had accumulated depreciation of $23,400 at the time of the trade. Prepare entries to record the trade under two different assumptions where (*a*) the exchange has commercial substance and the old servers have a trade-in allowance of $3,000 and (*b*) the exchange has commercial substance and the old servers have a trade-in allowance of $7,000.

Solution

(*a*) Equipment (new)...	45,000	
Loss on Exchange of Assets.....................................	3,600	
Accumulated Depreciation—Equipment (old)............................	23,400	
Equipment (old)...		30,000
Cash ($45,000 − $3,000)..		42,000

(*b*) Equipment (new)...	45,000	
Accumulated Depreciation—Equipment (old)............................	23,400	
Equipment (old)...		30,000
Cash ($45,000 − $7,000)..		38,000
Gain on Exchange of Assets.......................................		400

Do More: QS 10-14, E 10-23, E 10-24

Summary

C1 **Explain the cost principle for computing the cost of plant assets.** Plant assets are set apart from other tangible assets by two important features: use in operations and useful lives longer than one period. Plant assets are recorded at cost when purchased. Cost includes all normal and reasonable expenditures necessary to get the asset in place and ready for its intended use. The cost of a lump-sum purchase is allocated among its individual assets.

C2 **Explain depreciation for partial years and changes in estimates.** Partial-year depreciation is often required because assets are bought and sold throughout the year. Depreciation is revised when changes in estimates such as salvage value and useful life occur. If the useful life of a plant asset changes, for instance, the remaining cost to be depreciated is spread over the remaining (revised) useful life of the asset.

C3 **Distinguish between revenue and capital expenditures, and account for them.** Revenue expenditures expire in the current period and are debited to expense accounts and matched with current revenues. Ordinary repairs are an example of revenue expenditures. Capital expenditures benefit future periods and are debited to asset accounts. Examples of capital expenditures are extraordinary repairs and betterments.

A1 **Compute total asset turnover and apply it to analyze a company's use of assets.** Total asset turnover measures a company's ability to use its assets to generate sales. It is defined as net sales divided by average total assets. While all companies desire a high total asset turnover, it must be interpreted in comparison with those for prior years and its competitors.

P1 **Compute and record depreciation using the straight-line, units-of-production, and declining-balance methods.** *Depreciation* is the process of allocating to expense the cost of a plant asset over the accounting periods that benefit from its use. Depreciation does not measure the decline in a plant asset's market value or its physical deterioration. Three factors determine depreciation: cost, salvage value, and useful life. Salvage value is an estimate of the asset's value at the end of its benefit period. Useful (service) life is the length of time an asset is productively used. The straight-line method divides cost less salvage value by the asset's useful life to determine depreciation expense per period. The units-of-production method divides cost less salvage value by the estimated number of units the asset will produce over its life to determine depreciation per unit. The declining-balance method multiplies the asset's beginning-of-period book value by a factor that is often double the straight-line rate.

P2 **Account for asset disposal through discarding or selling an asset.** When a plant asset is discarded or sold, its cost and accumulated depreciation are removed from the accounts. Any cash proceeds from discarding or selling an asset are recorded and compared to the asset's book value to determine gain or loss.

P3 **Account for natural resource assets and their depletion.** The cost of a natural resource is recorded in a noncurrent asset account. Depletion of a natural resource is recorded by allocating its cost to depletion expense using the units-of-production method. Depletion is credited to an Accumulated Depletion account.

P4   **Account for intangible assets.** An intangible asset is recorded at the cost incurred to purchase it. The cost of an intangible asset with a definite useful life is allocated to expense using the straight-line method and is called *amortization*. Intangible assets with an indefinite useful life are not amortized— they are annually tested for impairment. Intangible assets include patents, copyrights, leaseholds, goodwill, and trademarks.

P5ᴬ   **Account for asset exchanges.** For an asset exchange with commercial substance, a gain or loss is recorded based on the difference between the book value of the asset given up and the market value of the asset received.

Key Terms

Accelerated depreciation method

Amortization

Asset book value

Betterments

Capital expenditures

Change in an accounting estimate

Copyright

Cost

Declining-balance method

Depletion

Depreciation

Extraordinary repairs

Franchises

Goodwill

Impairment

Inadequacy

Indefinite life

Intangible assets

Land improvements

Lease

Leasehold

Leasehold improvements

Lessee

Lessor

Licenses

Limited life

Modified Accelerated Cost Recovery System (MACRS)

Natural resources

Obsolescence

Ordinary repairs

Patent

Plant asset age

Plant asset useful life

Plant assets

Research and development costs

Revenue expenditures

Salvage value

Straight-line depreciation

Total asset turnover

Trademark or trade (brand) name

Units-of-production depreciation

Useful life

Multiple Choice Quiz

1. A company paid $326,000 for property that included land, land improvements, and a building. The land was appraised at $175,000, the land improvements were appraised at $70,000, and the building was appraised at $105,000. What is the allocation of property costs to the three assets purchased?

   a. Land, $150,000; Land Improvements, $60,000; Building, $90,000

   b. Land, $163,000; Land Improvements, $65,200; Building, $97,800

   c. Land, $150,000; Land Improvements, $61,600; Building, $92,400

   d. Land, $159,000; Land Improvements, $65,200; Building, $95,400

   e. Land, $175,000; Land Improvements, $70,000; Building, $105,000

2. A company purchased a truck for $35,000 on January 1, 2017. The truck is estimated to have a useful life of four years and an estimated salvage value of $1,000. Assuming that the company uses straight-line depreciation, what is the depreciation expense on the truck for the year ended December 31, 2018?

   a. $8,750   c. $8,500   e. $25,500

   b. $17,500   d. $17,000

3. A company purchased machinery for $10,800,000 on January 1, 2017. The machinery has a useful life of 10 years and an estimated salvage value of $800,000. What is the depreciation expense on the machinery for the year ended December 31, 2018, assuming that the double-declining-balance method is used?

   a. $2,160,000   c. $1,728,000   e. $1,600,000

   b. $3,888,000   d. $2,000,000

4. A company sold a machine that originally cost $250,000 for $120,000 when accumulated depreciation on the machine was $100,000. The gain or loss recorded on the sale of this machine is

   a. $0 gain or loss.   d. $30,000 gain.

   b. $120,000 gain.   e. $150,000 loss.

   c. $30,000 loss.

5. A company had average total assets of $500,000, gross sales of $575,000, and net sales of $550,000. The company's total asset turnover is

   a. 1.15   d. 0.87

   b. 1.10   e. 1.05

   c. 0.91

ANSWERS TO MULTIPLE CHOICE QUIZ

1. b;

	Appraisal Value	%	Total Cost	Allocated
Land.	$175,000	50%	$326,000	$163,000
Land improvements	70,000	20	326,000	65,200
Building.	105,000	30	326,000	97,800
Totals.	$350,000			$326,000

4. c;

Cost of machine	$250,000
Accumulated depreciation.	100,000
Book value	150,000
Cash received.	120,000
Loss on sale	$ 30,000

2. c; ($35,000 − $1,000)/4 years = $8,500 per year

3. c; 2017: $10,800,000 × (2 × 10%) = $2,160,000
2018: ($10,800,000 − $2,160,000) × (2 × 10%) = $1,728,000

5. b; $550,000/$500,000 = 1.10

---

^{A} *Superscript letter A denotes assignments based on Appendix 10A.*

[I] Icon denotes assignments that involve decision making.

Discussion Questions

1. [I] What characteristics of a plant asset make it different from other assets?

2. What is the general rule for cost inclusion for plant assets?

3. What is different between land and land improvements?

4. Why is the cost of a lump-sum purchase allocated to the individual assets acquired?

5. [I] Does the balance in the Accumulated Depreciation—Machinery account represent funds to replace the machinery when it wears out? If not, what does it represent?

6. Why is the Modified Accelerated Cost Recovery System not generally accepted for financial accounting purposes?

7. [I] What accounting concept justifies charging low-cost plant asset purchases immediately to an expense account?

8. What is the difference between ordinary repairs and extraordinary repairs? How should each be recorded?

9. [I] Identify events that might lead to disposal of a plant asset.

10. What is the process of allocating the cost of natural resources to expense as they are used?

11. Is the declining-balance method an acceptable way to compute depletion of natural resources? Explain.

12. What are the characteristics of an intangible asset?

13. What general procedures are applied in accounting for the acquisition and potential cost allocation of intangible assets?

14. [I] When do we know that a company has goodwill? When can goodwill appear in a company's balance sheet?

15. [I] Assume that a company buys another business and pays for its goodwill. If the company plans to incur costs each year to maintain the value of the goodwill, must it also amortize this goodwill?

16. [I] How is total asset turnover computed? Why would a financial statement user be interested in total asset turnover?

17. On its recent balance sheet in Appendix A, **Apple** lists its plant assets as "Property, plant and equipment, net." What does "net" mean in this title?   **APPLE**

18. Refer to **Google**'s recent balance sheet in Appendix A. What is the book value of its total net property, plant, and equipment assets at December 31, 2015?   **GOOGLE**

19. [I] Refer to **Samsung**'s balance sheet in Appendix A. What does it title its plant assets? What is the book value of its plant assets at December 31, 2015?   **Samsung**

20. Refer to the December 31, 2015, balance sheet of **Samsung** in Appendix A. What long-term assets discussed in this chapter are reported by the company?   **Samsung**

21. Identify the main difference between (a) plant assets and current assets, (b) plant assets and inventory, and (c) plant assets and long-term investments.

Mc Graw Hill Education **connect**

QUICK STUDY

QS 10-1

Cost of plant assets

C1 [I]

Kegler Bowling installs automatic scorekeeping equipment with an invoice cost of $190,000. The electrical work required for the installation costs $20,000. Additional costs are $4,000 for delivery and $13,700 for sales tax. During the installation, a component of the equipment is carelessly left on a lane and hit by the automatic lane-cleaning machine. The cost of repairing the component is $1,850.

What is the total recorded cost of the automatic scorekeeping equipment?

Listed below are certain costs (or discounts) incurred in the purchase or construction of new plant assets. (1) Indicate whether the costs should be *expensed* or *capitalized* (meaning they are included in the cost of the plant assets on the balance sheet). (2) For costs that should be included in plant assets, indicate in which category of plant assets (Equipment, Building, or Land) the related costs should be recorded on the balance sheet.

QS 10-2
Assigning costs to plant assets

C1

Expensed or Capitalized	Asset Category	
_____	_____	**1.** Charges incurred to train employees to use new equipment
_____	_____	**2.** Invoice cost to purchase new equipment
_____	_____	**3.** Deduction for an early payment discount taken on the purchase of new equipment
_____	_____	**4.** Real estate commissions incurred on land purchased for a new plant
_____	_____	**5.** Property taxes on land incurred after it was purchased
_____	_____	**6.** Costs of tune-up for the truck used to deliver new equipment
_____	_____	**7.** Costs to lay foundation for a new building
_____	_____	**8.** Insurance on a new building during the construction phase

On January 2, 2017, the Matthews Band acquires sound equipment for concert performances at a cost of $65,800. The band estimates it will use this equipment for four years, during which time it anticipates performing about 200 concerts. It estimates that after four years it can sell the equipment for $2,000. During year 2017, the band performs 45 concerts.
   Compute the year 2017 depreciation using the straight-line method.

QS 10-3
Straight-line depreciation

P1

On January 2, 2017, the Matthews Band acquires sound equipment for concert performances at a cost of $65,800. The band estimates it will use this equipment for four years, during which time it anticipates performing about 200 concerts. It estimates that after four years it can sell the equipment for $2,000. During year 2017, the band performs 45 concerts.
   Compute the year 2017 depreciation using the units-of-production method.

QS 10-4
Units-of-production depreciation   P1

On January 2, 2017, the Matthews Band acquires sound equipment for concert performances at a cost of $65,800. The band estimates it will use this equipment for four years. It estimates that after four years it can sell the equipment for $2,000. Matthews Band uses straight-line depreciation but realizes at the start of the second year that due to concert bookings beyond expectations, this equipment will last only a total of three years. The salvage value remains unchanged.
   Compute the revised depreciation for both the second and third years.

QS 10-5
Computing revised depreciation   C2

A fleet of refrigerated delivery trucks is acquired on January 5, 2017, at a cost of $830,000 with an estimated useful life of eight years and an estimated salvage value of $75,000. Compute the depreciation expense for the first three years using the double-declining-balance method.

QS 10-6
Double-declining-balance method   P1

Assume a company's equipment carries a book value of $16,000 ($16,500 cost less $500 accumulated depreciation) and a fair value of $14,750, *and* that the $1,250 decline in fair value in comparison to the book value meets the impairment test. Prepare the entry to record this $1,250 impairment.

QS 10-7
Recording plant asset impairment   C2

1. Classify the following as either a revenue expenditure (RE) or a capital expenditure (CE).
   ____ **a.** Paid $40,000 cash to replace a compressor on a refrigeration system that extends its useful life by four years.
   ____ **b.** Paid $200 cash per truck for the cost of their annual tune-ups.
   ____ **c.** Paid $175 for the monthly cost of replacement filters on an air-conditioning system.
   ____ **d.** Completed an addition to an office building for $225,000 cash.
2. Prepare the journal entries to record transactions *a* and *d* of part 1.

QS 10-8
Revenue and capital expenditures

C3

Garcia Co. owns equipment that cost $76,800, with accumulated depreciation of $40,800. Garcia sells the equipment for cash. Record the sale of the equipment under the following three separate cases assuming Garcia sells the equipment for (1) $47,000 cash, (2) $36,000 cash, and (3) $31,000 cash.

QS 10-9
Disposal of assets   P2

QS 10-10
Natural resources and depletion
P3

Perez Company acquires an ore mine at a cost of $1,400,000. It incurs additional costs of $400,000 to access the mine, which is estimated to hold 1,000,000 tons of ore. The estimated value of the land after the ore is removed is $200,000.

1. Prepare the entry(ies) to record the cost of the ore mine.

2. Prepare the year-end adjusting entry if 180,000 tons of ore are mined and sold the first year.

QS 10-11
Classifying assets
P3   P4

Identify the following assets *a* through *i* as reported on the balance sheet as intangible assets (IA), natural resources (NR), or other (O).

____ **a.** Oil well	____ **d.** Gold mine	____ **g.** Franchise
____ **b.** Trademark	____ **e.** Building	____ **h.** Timberland
____ **c.** Leasehold	____ **f.** Copyright	____ **i.** Salt mine

---

QS 10-12
Intangible assets and amortization   P4

On January 4 of this year, Diaz Boutique incurs a $105,000 cost to modernize its store. Improvements include new floors, ceilings, wiring, and wall coverings. These improvements are estimated to yield benefits for 10 years. Diaz leases its store and has eight years remaining on the lease. Prepare the entry to record (1) the cost of modernization and (2) amortization at the end of this current year.

QS 10-13
Computing total asset turnover   A1

Aneko Company reports the following ($000s): net sales of $14,800 for 2017 and $13,990 for 2016; end-of-year total assets of $19,100 for 2017 and $17,900 for 2016. Compute its total asset turnover for 2017, and assess its level if competitors average a total asset turnover of 2.0 times.

QS 10-14ᴬ
Asset exchange
P5

Caleb Co. owns a machine that costs $42,400 with accumulated depreciation of $18,400. Caleb exchanges the machine for a newer model that has a market value of $52,000.

1. Record the exchange assuming Caleb paid $30,000 cash and the exchange has commercial substance.

2. Record the exchange assuming Caleb paid $22,000 cash and the exchange has commercial substance.

QS 10-15
International accounting standards
C1   C3

Answer each of the following related to international accounting standards.

a. Accounting for plant assets involves cost determination, depreciation, additional expenditures, and disposals. Is plant asset accounting broadly similar or dissimilar between IFRS and U.S. GAAP? Identify one notable difference between IFRS and U.S. GAAP in accounting for plant assets.

b. Describe how IFRS and U.S. GAAP treat increases in the value of plant assets subsequent to their acquisition (but before their disposition).

Ⓜ connect

EXERCISES

Exercise 10-1
Cost of plant assets
C1

Rizio Co. purchases a machine for $12,500, terms 2/10, n/60, FOB shipping point. The seller prepaid the $360 freight charges, adding the amount to the invoice and bringing its total to $12,860. The machine requires special steel mounting and power connections costing $895. Another $475 is paid to assemble the machine and get it into operation. In moving the machine to its steel mounting, $180 in damages occurred. Materials costing $40 are used in adjusting the machine to produce a satisfactory product. The adjustments are normal for this machine and are not the result of the damages. Compute the cost recorded for this machine. (Rizio pays for this machine within the cash discount period.)

Exercise 10-2
Recording costs of assets
C1

Cala Manufacturing purchases a large lot on which an old building is located as part of its plans to build a new plant. The negotiated purchase price is $280,000 for the lot plus $110,000 for the old building. The company pays $33,500 to tear down the old building and $47,000 to fill and level the lot. It also pays a total of $1,540,000 in construction costs—this amount consists of $1,452,200 for the new building and $87,800 for lighting and paving a parking area next to the building. Prepare a single journal entry to record these costs incurred by Cala, all of which are paid in cash.

Exercise 10-3
Lump-sum purchase of plant assets   C1

Rodriguez Company pays $375,280 for real estate plus $20,100 in closing costs. The real estate consists of land appraised at $157,040; land improvements appraised at $58,890; and a building appraised at $176,670. Allocate the total cost among the three purchased assets and prepare the journal entry to record the purchase.

Ramirez Company installs a computerized manufacturing machine in its factory at the beginning of the year at a cost of $43,500. The machine's useful life is estimated at 10 years, or 385,000 units of product, with a $5,000 salvage value. During its second year, the machine produces 32,500 units of product. Determine the machine's second-year depreciation under the straight-line method.

Exercise 10-4
Straight-line depreciation
P1

Ramirez Company installs a computerized manufacturing machine in its factory at the beginning of the year at a cost of $43,500. The machine's useful life is estimated at 10 years, or 385,000 units of product, with a $5,000 salvage value. During its second year, the machine produces 32,500 units of product. Determine the machine's second-year depreciation using the units-of-production method.

Exercise 10-5
Units-of-production
depreciation P1

Ramirez Company installs a computerized manufacturing machine in its factory at the beginning of the year at a cost of $43,500. The machine's useful life is estimated at 10 years, or 385,000 units of product, with a $5,000 salvage value. During its second year, the machine produces 32,500 units of product. Determine the machine's second-year depreciation using the double-declining-balance method.

Exercise 10-6
Double-declining-balance
depreciation P1

In early January 2017, NewTech purchases computer equipment for $154,000 to use in operating activities for the next four years. It estimates the equipment's salvage value at $25,000. Prepare a table showing depreciation and book value for each of the four years assuming straight-line depreciation.

Exercise 10-7
Straight-line depreciation
P1

In early January 2017, NewTech purchases computer equipment for $154,000 to use in operating activities for the next four years. It estimates the equipment's salvage value at $25,000. Prepare a table showing depreciation and book value for each of the four years assuming double-declining-balance depreciation.

Exercise 10-8
Double-declining-balance
depreciation P1

Tory Enterprises pays $238,400 for equipment that will last five years and have a $43,600 salvage value. By using the equipment in its operations for five years, the company expects to earn $88,500 annually, after deducting all expenses except depreciation. Prepare a table showing income before depreciation, depreciation expense, and net (pretax) income for each year and for the total five-year period, assuming straight-line depreciation.

Exercise 10-9
Straight-line depreciation
and income effects

P1

Tory Enterprises pays $238,400 for equipment that will last five years and have a $43,600 salvage value. By using the equipment in its operations for five years, the company expects to earn $88,500 annually, after deducting all expenses except depreciation. Prepare a table showing income before depreciation, depreciation expense, and net (pretax) income for each year and for the total five-year period, assuming double-declining-balance depreciation is used.

Exercise 10-10
Double-declining-balance
depreciation P1

Check Year 3 NI, $54,170

On April 1, 2016, Cyclone's Backhoe Co. purchases a trencher for $280,000. The machine is expected to last five years and have a salvage value of $40,000. Compute depreciation expense for both 2016 and 2017 assuming the company uses the straight-line method.

Exercise 10-11
Straight-line, partial-year
depreciation C2

On April 1, 2016, Cyclone's Backhoe Co. purchases a trencher for $280,000. The machine is expected to last five years and have a salvage value of $40,000. Compute depreciation expense for both 2016 and 2017 assuming the company uses the double-declining-balance method.

Exercise 10-12
Double-declining-
balance, partial-year
depreciation C2

Apex Fitness Club uses straight-line depreciation for a machine costing $23,860, with an estimated four-year life and a $2,400 salvage value. At the beginning of the third year, Apex determines that the machine has three more years of remaining useful life, after which it will have an estimated $2,000 salvage value. Compute (1) the machine's book value at the end of its second year and (2) the amount of depreciation for each of the final three years given the revised estimates.

Exercise 10-13
Revising depreciation

C2

Check (2) $3,710

Oki Company pays $264,000 for equipment expected to last four years and have a $29,000 salvage value. Prepare journal entries to record the following costs related to the equipment.

1. During the second year of the equipment's life, $22,000 cash is paid for a new component expected to increase the equipment's productivity by 10% a year.

2. During the third year, $6,250 cash is paid for normal repairs necessary to keep the equipment in good working order.

3. During the fourth year, $14,870 is paid for repairs expected to increase the useful life of the equipment from four to five years.

Exercise 10-14
Ordinary repairs,
extraordinary repairs,
and betterments

C3

Exercise 10-15
Extraordinary repairs;
plant asset age

C3

Check   (3) $211,350

Martinez Company owns a building that appears on its prior year-end balance sheet at its original $572,000 cost less $429,000 accumulated depreciation. The building is depreciated on a straight-line basis assuming a 20-year life and no salvage value. During the first week in January of the current calendar year, major structural repairs are completed on the building at a $68,350 cost. The repairs extend its useful life for 5 years beyond the 20 years originally estimated.

1. Determine the building's age (plant asset age) as of the prior year-end balance sheet date.

2. Prepare the entry to record the cost of the structural repairs that are paid in cash.

3. Determine the book value of the building immediately after the repairs are recorded.

4. Prepare the entry to record the current calendar year's depreciation.

Exercise 10-16
Disposal of assets

P2

Diaz Company owns a milling machine that cost $250,000 and has accumulated depreciation of $182,000. Prepare the entry to record the disposal of the milling machine on January 3 under each of the following independent situations.

1. The machine needed extensive repairs, and it was not worth repairing. Diaz disposed of the machine, receiving nothing in return.

2. Diaz sold the machine for $35,000 cash.

3. Diaz sold the machine for $68,000 cash.

4. Diaz sold the machine for $80,000 cash.

Exercise 10-17
Partial-year depreciation;
disposal of plant asset

P2

Rayya Co. purchases and installs a machine on January 1, 2017, at a total cost of $105,000. Straight-line depreciation is taken each year for four years assuming a seven-year life and no salvage value. The machine is disposed of on July 1, 2021, during its fifth year of service. Prepare entries to record the partial year's depreciation on July 1, 2021, and to record the disposal under the following separate assumptions:

1. The machine is sold for $45,500 cash.

2. An insurance settlement of $25,000 is received due to the machine's total destruction in a fire.

Exercise 10-18
Depletion of natural
resources

P1   P3

On April 2, 2017, Montana Mining Co. pays $3,721,000 for an ore deposit containing 1,525,000 tons. The company installs machinery in the mine costing $213,500, with an estimated seven-year life and no salvage value. The machinery will be abandoned when the ore is completely mined. Montana begins mining on May 1, 2017, and mines and sells 166,200 tons of ore during the remaining eight months of 2017. Prepare the December 31, 2017, entries to record both the ore deposit depletion and the mining machinery depreciation. Mining machinery depreciation should be in proportion to the mine's depletion.

Exercise 10-19
Amortization of
intangible assets   P4

Milano Gallery purchases the copyright on an oil painting for $418,000 on January 1, 2017. The copyright legally protects its owner for 10 more years. The company plans to market and sell prints of the original for 11 years. Prepare entries to record the purchase of the copyright on January 1, 2017, and its annual amortization on December 31, 2017.

Exercise 10-20
Goodwill

P4

On January 1, 2017, Robinson Company purchased Franklin Company at a price of $2,500,000. The fair market value of the net assets purchased equals $1,800,000.

1. What is the amount of goodwill that Robinson records at the purchase date?

2. Explain how Robinson would determine the amount of goodwill amortization for the year ended December 31, 2017.

3. Robinson Company believes that its employees provide superior customer service, and through their efforts, Robinson Company believes it has created $900,000 of goodwill. How would Robinson Company record this goodwill?

Exercise 10-21
Cash flows related
to assets

C1

GOOGLE

Refer to the statement of cash flows for Google in Appendix A for the fiscal year ended December 31, 2015, to answer the following.

1. What amount of cash is used to purchase property and equipment?

2. How much depreciation and impairment of property and equipment are recorded?

3. What total amount of net cash is used in investing activities?

Exercise 10-22
Evaluating efficient use
of assets   A1

Lok Co. reports net sales of $5,856,480 for 2016 and $8,679,690 for 2017. End-of-year balances for total assets are 2015, $1,686,000; 2016, $1,800,000; and 2017, $1,982,000. (*a*) Compute Lok's total asset turnover for 2016 and 2017. (*b*) Comment on Lok's efficiency in using its assets if its competitors average a total asset turnover of 3.0.

Gilly Construction trades in an old tractor for a new tractor, receiving a $29,000 trade-in allowance and paying the remaining $83,000 in cash. The old tractor had cost $96,000, and straight-line accumulated depreciation of $52,500 had been recorded to date under the assumption that it would last eight years and have a $12,000 salvage value. Answer the following questions assuming the exchange has commercial substance.

1. What is the book value of the old tractor at the time of exchange?
2. What is the loss on this asset exchange?
3. What amount should be recorded (debited) in the asset account for the new tractor?

Exercise 10-23ᴬ
Exchanging assets

P5

Check (2) $14,500

On January 2, 2017, Bering Co. disposes of a machine costing $44,000 with accumulated depreciation of $24,625. Prepare the entries to record the disposal under each of the following separate assumptions.

1. The machine is sold for $18,250 cash.
2. The machine is traded in for a newer machine having a $60,200 cash price. A $25,000 trade-in allowance is received, and the balance is paid in cash. Assume the asset exchange has commercial substance.
3. The machine is traded in for a newer machine having a $60,200 cash price. A $15,000 trade-in allowance is received, and the balance is paid in cash. Assume the asset exchange has commercial substance.

Exercise 10-24ᴬ
Recording plant asset disposals P2   P5

Check (3) Dr. Loss on Exchange, $4,375

Volkswagen Group reported the following information for property, plant, and equipment, along with additions, disposals, depreciation, and impairments, for a recent year-end (euros in millions).

Exercise 10-25
Accounting for plant assets under IFRS

C2   P1   P2

Property, plant, and equipment, net	€46,169
Additions to property, plant, and equipment	11,560
Disposals of property, plant, and equipment	2,430
Depreciation on property, plant, and equipment	7,509
Impairments to property, plant, and equipment	143

1. Prepare Volkswagen's journal entry to record depreciation.
2. Prepare Volkswagen's journal entry to record additions assuming they are paid in cash and are treated as "betterments (improvements)" to the assets.
3. Prepare Volkswagen's journal entry to record €2,430 in disposals assuming it receives €720 cash in return and the accumulated depreciation on the disposed assets totals €1,195.
4. Volkswagen reports €143 of impairments. Do these impairments increase or decrease the Property, Plant, and Equipment account? By what amount?

⬛ connect

Timberly Construction negotiates a lump-sum purchase of several assets from a company that is going out of business. The purchase is completed on January 1, 2017, at a total cash price of $900,000 for a building, land, land improvements, and four vehicles. The estimated market values of the assets are building, $508,800; land, $297,600; land improvements, $28,800; and four vehicles, $124,800. The company's fiscal year ends on December 31.

PROBLEM SET A

Problem 10-1A
Plant asset costs; depreciation methods

C1   P1

Required

1. Prepare a table to allocate the lump-sum purchase price to the separate assets purchased (round percents to the nearest 1%). Prepare the journal entry to record the purchase.
2. Compute the depreciation expense for year 2017 on the building using the straight-line method, assuming a 15-year life and a $27,000 salvage value.
3. Compute the depreciation expense for year 2017 on the land improvements assuming a five-year life and double-declining-balance depreciation.

Check (2) $30,000

(3) $10,800

Analysis Component

4. Defend or refute this statement: Accelerated depreciation results in payment of less taxes over the asset's life.

Problem 10-2A

Depreciation methods

P1

A machine costing $257,500 with a four-year life and an estimated $20,000 salvage value is installed in Luther Company's factory on January 1. The factory manager estimates the machine will produce 475,000 units of product during its life. It actually produces the following units: 220,000 in 1st year, 124,600 in 2nd year, 121,800 in 3rd year, 15,200 in 4th year. The total number of units produced by the end of year 4 exceeds the original estimate—this difference was not predicted. (The machine must not be depreciated below its estimated salvage value.)

Required

Prepare a table with the following column headings and compute depreciation for each year (and total depreciation of all years combined) for the machine under each depreciation method.

Check Year 4: units-of-production depreciation, $4,300; DDB depreciation, $12,187

Year	Straight-Line	Units-of-Production	Double-Declining-Balance

---

Problem 10-3A

Asset cost allocation; straight-line depreciation

C1 P1

In January 2017, Mitzu Co. pays $2,600,000 for a tract of land with two buildings on it. It plans to demolish Building 1 and build a new store in its place. Building 2 will be a company office; it is appraised at $644,000, with a useful life of 20 years and a $60,000 salvage value. A lighted parking lot near Building 1 has improvements (Land Improvements 1) valued at $420,000 that are expected to last another 12 years with no salvage value. Without the buildings and improvements, the tract of land is valued at $1,736,000. The company also incurs the following additional costs:

Cost to demolish Building 1...	$ 328,400
Cost of additional land grading.....................................	175,400
Cost to construct new building (Building 3), having a useful life of 25 years and a $392,000 salvage value	2,202,000
Cost of new land improvements (Land Improvements 2) near Building 2 having a 20-year useful life and no salvage value.....................	164,000

Required

Check (1) Land costs, $2,115,800; Building 2 costs, $598,000

1. Prepare a table with the following column headings: Land, Building 2, Building 3, Land Improvements 1, and Land Improvements 2. Allocate the costs incurred by Mitzu to the appropriate columns and total each column (round percents to the nearest 1%).

2. Prepare a single journal entry to record all the incurred costs assuming they are paid in cash on January 1, 2017.

(3) Depr.—Land Improv. 1 and 2, $32,500 and $8,200

3. Using the straight-line method, prepare the December 31 adjusting entries to record depreciation for the 12 months of 2017 when these assets were in use.

Problem 10-4A

Computing and revising depreciation; revenue and capital expenditures

C1 C2 C3

Champion Contractors completed the following transactions and events involving the purchase and operation of equipment in its business.

2016

Jan.   1   Paid $287,600 cash plus $11,500 in sales tax and $1,500 in transportation (FOB shipping point) for a new loader. The loader is estimated to have a four-year life and a $20,600 salvage value. Loader costs are recorded in the Equipment account.

        3   Paid $4,800 to enclose the cab and install air-conditioning in the loader to enable operations under harsher conditions. This increased the estimated salvage value of the loader by another $1,400.

Check Dec. 31, 2016, Dr. Depr. Expense—Equip., $70,850

Dec. 31   Recorded annual straight-line depreciation on the loader.

2017

Jan.   1   Paid $5,400 to overhaul the loader's engine, which increased the loader's estimated useful life by two years.

Feb. 17   Paid $820 to repair the loader after the operator backed it into a tree.

Dec. 31, 2017, Dr. Depr. Expense—Equip., $43,590

Dec. 31   Recorded annual straight-line depreciation on the loader.

Required

Prepare journal entries to record these transactions and events.

Yoshi Company completed the following transactions and events involving its delivery trucks.

2016

Jan. 1   Paid $20,515 cash plus $1,485 in sales tax for a new delivery truck estimated to have a five-year life and a $2,000 salvage value. Delivery truck costs are recorded in the Trucks account.

Dec. 31   Recorded annual straight-line depreciation on the truck.

2017

Dec. 31   Due to new information obtained earlier in the year, the truck's estimated useful life was changed from five to four years, and the estimated salvage value was increased to $2,400. Recorded annual straight-line depreciation on the truck.

Check Dec. 31, 2017,
Dr. Depr. Expense—Trucks,
$5,200

2018

Dec. 31   Recorded annual straight-line depreciation on the truck.
    31   Sold the truck for $5,300 cash.

Dec. 31, 2018,
Dr. Loss on Disposal of
Trucks, $2,300

Required

Prepare journal entries to record these transactions and events.

Onslow Co. purchases a used machine for $178,000 cash on January 2 and readies it for use the next day at a $2,840 cost. On January 3, it is installed on a required operating platform costing $1,160, and it is further readied for operations. The company predicts the machine will be used for six years and have a $14,000 salvage value. Depreciation is to be charged on a straight-line basis. On December 31, at the end of its fifth year in operations, it is disposed of.

Required

1. Prepare journal entries to record the machine's purchase and the costs to ready and install it. Cash is paid for all costs incurred.

2. Prepare journal entries to record depreciation of the machine at December 31 of (*a*) its first year in operations and (*b*) the year of its disposal.

Check (2*b*) Depr. Exp.,
$28,000

3. Prepare journal entries to record the machine's disposal under each of the following separate assumptions: (*a*) it is sold for $15,000 cash; (*b*) it is sold for $50,000 cash; and (*c*) it is destroyed in a fire and the insurance company pays $30,000 cash to settle the loss claim.

(3*c*) Dr. Loss from
Fire, $12,000

On July 23 of the current year, Dakota Mining Co. pays $4,715,000 for land estimated to contain 5,125,000 tons of recoverable ore. It installs machinery costing $410,000 that has a 10-year life and no salvage value and is capable of mining the ore deposit in 8 years. The machinery is paid for on July 25, seven days before mining operations begin. The company removes and sells 480,000 tons of ore during its first five months of operations ending on December 31. Depreciation of the machinery is in proportion to the mine's depletion as the machinery will be abandoned after the ore is mined.

Required

Prepare entries to record (*a*) the purchase of the land, (*b*) the cost and installation of machinery, (*c*) the first five months' depletion assuming the land has a net salvage value of zero after the ore is mined, and (*d*) the first five months' depreciation on the machinery.

Check (*c*) Depletion,
$441,600

(*d*) Depreciation,
$38,400

Analysis Component

Describe both the similarities and differences in amortization, depletion, and depreciation.

On July 1, 2012, Falk Company signed a contract to lease space in a building for 15 years. The lease contract calls for annual (prepaid) rental payments of $80,000 on each July 1 throughout the life of the lease and for the lessee to pay for all additions and improvements to the leased property. On June 25, 2017, Falk decides to sublease the space to Ryan & Associates for the remaining 10 years of the lease—Ryan pays $200,000 to Falk for the right to sublease and it agrees to assume the obligation to pay the $80,000 annual rent to the building owner beginning July 1, 2017. After taking possession of the leased space, Ryan pays for improving the office portion of the leased space at a $130,000 cost. The improvements are paid for by Ryan on July 5, 2017, and are estimated to have a useful life equal to the 16 years remaining in the life of the building.

Required

1. Prepare entries for Ryan to record (*a*) its payment to Falk for the right to sublease the building space, (*b*) its payment of the 2017 annual rent to the building owner, and (*c*) its payment for the office improvements.

Check Dr. Rent Expense: (2*a*) $10,000, (2*c*) $40,000

2. Prepare Ryan's year-end adjusting entries required at December 31, 2017, to (*a*) amortize the $200,000 cost of the sublease, (*b*) amortize the office improvements, and (*c*) record rent expense.

PROBLEM SET B

Problem 10-1B

Plant asset costs; depreciation methods

C1 P1

Check (2) $65,000

(3) $50,400

Nagy Company negotiates a lump-sum purchase of several assets from a contractor who is relocating. The purchase is completed on January 1, 2017, at a total cash price of $1,800,000 for a building, land, land improvements, and five trucks. The estimated market values of the assets are building, $890,000; land, $427,200; land improvements, $249,200; and five trucks, $213,600. The company's fiscal year ends on December 31.

Required

1. Prepare a table to allocate the lump-sum purchase price to the separate assets purchased (round percents to the nearest 1%). Prepare the journal entry to record the purchase.

2. Compute the depreciation expense for year 2017 on the building using the straight-line method, assuming a 12-year life and a $120,000 salvage value.

3. Compute the depreciation expense for year 2017 on the land improvements assuming a 10-year life and double-declining-balance depreciation.

Analysis Component

4. Defend or refute this statement: Accelerated depreciation results in payment of more taxes over the asset's life.

Problem 10-2B

Depreciation methods

P1

On January 2, Manning Co. purchases and installs a new machine costing $324,000 with a five-year life and an estimated $30,000 salvage value. Management estimates the machine will produce 1,470,000 units of product during its life. Actual production of units is as follows: 355,600 in 1st year, 320,400 in 2nd year, 317,000 in 3rd year, 343,600 in 4th year, 138,500 in 5th year. The total number of units produced by the end of year 5 exceeds the original estimate—this difference was not predicted. (The machine must not be depreciated below its estimated salvage value.)

Required

Prepare a table with the following column headings and compute depreciation for each year (and total depreciation of all years combined) for the machine under each depreciation method.

Check DDB Depreciation, year 3, $46,656; U-of-P Depreciation, year 4, $68,720

Year	Straight-Line	Units-of-Production	Double-Declining-Balance

---

Problem 10-3B

Asset cost allocation; straight-line depreciation

C1 P1

In January 2017, ProTech Co. pays $1,550,000 for a tract of land with two buildings. It plans to demolish Building A and build a new shop in its place. Building B will be a company office; it is appraised at $482,800, with a useful life of 15 years and a $99,500 salvage value. A lighted parking lot near Building B has improvements (Land Improvements B) valued at $142,000 that are expected to last another five years with no salvage value. Without the buildings and improvements, the tract of land is valued at $795,200. The company also incurs the following additional costs.

Cost to demolish Building A.	$ 122,000
Cost of additional land grading	174,500
Cost to construct new building (Building C), having a useful life of 20 years and a $258,000 salvage value	1,458,000
Cost of new land improvements (Land Improvements C) near Building C, having a 10-year useful life and no salvage value	103,500

Required

Check (1) Land costs, $1,164,500; Building B costs, $527,000

1. Prepare a table with the following column headings: Land, Building B, Building C, Land Improvements B, and Land Improvements C. Allocate the costs incurred by ProTech to the appropriate columns and total each column (round percents to the nearest 1%).

2. Prepare a single journal entry to record all incurred costs assuming they are paid in cash on January 1, 2017.

(3) Depr.—Land Improv. B and C, $31,000 and $10,350

3. Using the straight-line method, prepare the December 31 adjusting entries to record depreciation for the 12 months of 2017 when these assets were in use.

Mercury Delivery Service completed the following transactions and events involving the purchase and operation of equipment for its business.

Problem 10-4B
Computing and revising depreciation; revenue and capital expenditures

C1   C2   C3

2016

Jan. 1   Paid $25,860 cash plus $1,810 in sales tax for a new delivery van that was estimated to have a five-year life and a $3,670 salvage value. Van costs are recorded in the Equipment account.

     3   Paid $1,850 to install sorting racks in the van for more accurate and quicker delivery of packages. This increases the estimated salvage value of the van by another $230.

Dec. 31   Recorded annual straight-line depreciation on the van.

Check Dec. 31, 2016,
Dr. Depr. Expense—Equip.,
$5,124

2017

Jan. 1   Paid $2,064 to overhaul the van's engine, which increased the van's estimated useful life by two years.

May 10   Paid $800 to repair the van after the driver backed it into a loading dock.

Dec. 31   Record annual straight-line depreciation on the van. (Round to the nearest dollar.)

Dec. 31, 2017,
Dr. Depr. Expense—Equip.,
$3,760

Required

Prepare journal entries to record these transactions and events.

York Instruments completed the following transactions and events involving its machinery.

Problem 10-5B
Computing and revising depreciation; selling plant assets

C2   P1   P2

2016

Jan. 1   Paid $107,800 cash plus $6,470 in sales tax for a new machine. The machine is estimated to have a six-year life and a $9,720 salvage value.

Dec. 31   Recorded annual straight-line depreciation on the machinery.

2017

Dec. 31   Due to new information obtained earlier in the year, the machine's estimated useful life was changed from six to four years, and the estimated salvage value was increased to $14,345. Recorded annual straight-line depreciation on the machinery.

Check Dec. 31, 2017,
Dr. Depr. Expense—
Machinery, $27,500

2018

Dec. 31   Recorded annual straight-line depreciation on the machinery.

     31   Sold the machine for $25,240 cash.

Dec. 31, 2018,
Dr. Loss on Disposal of
Machinery, $16,605

Required

Prepare journal entries to record these transactions and events.

On January 1, Walker purchases a used machine for $150,000 and readies it for use the next day at a cost of $3,510. On January 4, it is mounted on a required operating platform costing $4,600, and it is further readied for operations. Management estimates the machine will be used for seven years and have an $18,110 salvage value. Depreciation is to be charged on a straight-line basis. On December 31, at the end of its sixth year of use, the machine is disposed of.

Problem 10-6B
Disposal of plant assets

C1   P1   P2

Required

1. Prepare journal entries to record the machine's purchase and the costs to ready and install it. Cash is paid for all costs incurred.

2. Prepare journal entries to record depreciation of the machine at December 31 of (*a*) its first year in operations and (*b*) the year of its disposal.

Check (2b) Depr. Exp.,
$20,000

3. Prepare journal entries to record the machine's disposal under each of the following separate assumptions: (*a*) it is sold for $28,000 cash; (*b*) it is sold for $52,000 cash; and (*c*) it is destroyed in a fire and the insurance company pays $25,000 cash to settle the loss claim.

(3c) Dr. Loss from
Fire, $13,110

On February 19 of the current year, Quartzite Co. pays $5,400,000 for land estimated to contain 4 million tons of recoverable ore. It installs machinery costing $400,000 that has a 16-year life and no salvage value and is capable of mining the ore deposit in 12 years. The machinery is paid for on March 21, eleven days before mining operations begin. The company removes and sells 254,000 tons of ore during its first nine months of operations ending on December 31. Depreciation of the machinery is in proportion to the mine's depletion as the machinery will be abandoned after the ore is mined.

Problem 10-7B
Natural resources

P3

Required

Prepare entries to record (*a*) the purchase of the land, (*b*) the cost and installation of the machinery, (*c*) the first nine months' depletion assuming the land has a net salvage value of zero after the ore is mined, and (*d*) the first nine months' depreciation on the machinery.

Analysis Component

Describe both the similarities and differences in amortization, depletion, and depreciation.

Problem 10-8B

Intangible assets—lease and sublease

P4

On January 1, 2010, Mason Co. entered into a 12-year lease on a building. The lease contract requires (1) annual (prepaid) rental payments of $36,000 each January 1 throughout the life of the lease and (2) for the lessee to pay for all additions and improvements to the leased property. On January 1, 2017, Mason decides to sublease the space to Stewart Co. for the remaining five years of the lease—Stewart pays $40,000 to Mason for the right to sublease and agrees to assume the obligation to pay the $36,000 annual rent to the building owner beginning January 1, 2017. After taking possession of the leased space, Stewart pays for improving the office portion of the leased space at a $20,000 cost. The improvements are paid for by Stewart on January 3, 2017, and are estimated to have a useful life equal to the 13 years remaining in the life of the building.

Required

1. Prepare entries for Stewart to record (*a*) its payment to Mason for the right to sublease the building space, (*b*) its payment of the 2017 annual rent to the building owner, and (*c*) its payment for the office improvements.

2. Prepare Stewart's year-end adjusting entries required on December 31, 2017, to (*a*) amortize the $40,000 cost of the sublease, (*b*) amortize the office improvements, and (*c*) record rent expense.

SERIAL PROBLEM

Business Solutions

P1   A1

(This serial problem began in Chapter 1 and continues through most of the book. If previous chapter segments were not completed, the serial problem can begin at this point.)

SP 10   Selected ledger account balances for **Business Solutions** follow.

	For Three Months Ended December 31, 2017	For Three Months Ended March 31, 2018
Office equipment	$ 8,000	$ 8,000
Accumulated depreciation—Office equipment.........	400	800
Computer equipment............................	20,000	20,000
Accumulated depreciation—Computer equipment	1,250	2,500
Total revenue	31,284	44,000
Total assets..................................	83,460	120,268

Required

1. Assume that Business Solutions does not acquire additional office equipment or computer equipment in 2018. Compute amounts for *the year ended* December 31, 2018, for Depreciation Expense—Office Equipment and for Depreciation Expense—Computer Equipment (assume use of the straight-line method).

2. Given the assumptions in part 1, what is the book value of both the office equipment and the computer equipment as of December 31, 2018?

3. Compute the three-month total asset turnover for Business Solutions as of March 31, 2018. Use total revenue for the numerator and average the December 31, 2017, total assets and the March 31, 2018, total assets for the denominator. Interpret its total asset turnover if competitors average 2.5 for annual periods. (Round turnover to two decimals.)

Beyond the Numbers

REPORTING IN ACTION

A1   **APPLE**

BTN 10-1   Refer to the financial statements of **Apple** in Appendix A to answer the following.

1. What percent of the original cost of Apple's property and equipment remains to be depreciated as of September 26, 2015, and September 27, 2014? Assume these assets have no salvage value. (Note: Accumulated Depreciation is listed under "Property, Plant and Equipment" in the notes to Apple's financial statements in Appendix A.)

2. Over what length(s) of time is Apple depreciating its major categories of buildings and equipment?

Continued on next page . . .

3. What is the change in total property, plant, and equipment (before accumulated depreciation) for the year ended September 26, 2015? What is the amount of cash provided (used) by investing activities for property and equipment for the year ended September 26, 2015? What is one possible explanation for the difference between these two amounts?

4. Compute Apple's total asset turnover for the year ended September 26, 2015, and the year ended September 27, 2014. Assume total assets at September 28, 2013, are $207,000 ($ millions).

Fast Forward

5. Access Apple's financial statements for fiscal years ending after September 26, 2015, at its website (Apple.com) or the SEC's EDGAR database (SEC.gov). Recompute Apple's total asset turnover for the additional years' data you collect. Comment on any differences relative to the turnover computed in part 4.

BTN 10-2   Comparative figures for Apple and Google follow.

$ millions	Apple			Google		
	Current Year	One Year Prior	Two Years Prior	Current Year	One Year Prior	Two Years Prior
Total assets	$290,479	$231,839	$207,000	$147,461	$129,187	$110,920
Net sales	233,715	182,795	170,910	74,989	66,001	55,519

COMPARATIVE ANALYSIS

A1

APPLE

GOOGLE

Required

1. Compute total asset turnover for the most recent two years for Apple and Google using the data shown.

2. Which company is more efficient in generating net sales given the total assets it employs? Assume an industry average of 1.0 for asset turnover.

BTN 10-3   Flo Choi owns a small business and manages its accounting. Her company just finished a year in which a large amount of borrowed funds was invested in a new building addition as well as in equipment and fixture additions. Choi's banker requires her to submit semiannual financial statements so he can monitor the financial health of her business. He has warned her that if profit margins erode, he might raise the interest rate on the borrowed funds to reflect the increased loan risk from the bank's point of view. Choi knows profit margin is likely to decline this year. As she prepares year-end adjusting entries, she decides to apply the following depreciation rule: All asset additions are considered to be in use on the first day of the following month. (The previous rule assumed assets are in use on the first day of the month nearest to the purchase date.)

ETHICS CHALLENGE

C1

Required

1. Identify decisions that managers like Choi must make in applying depreciation methods.

2. Is Choi's rule an ethical violation, or is it a legitimate decision in computing depreciation?

3. How will Choi's new depreciation rule affect the profit margin of her business?

BTN 10-4   Teams are to select an industry, and each team member is to select a different company in that industry. Each team member is to acquire the financial statements (Form 10-K) of the company selected— see the company's website or the SEC's EDGAR database (SEC.gov). Use the financial statements to compute total asset turnover. Communicate with teammates via a meeting, e-mail, or telephone to discuss the meaning of this ratio, how different companies compare to each other, and the industry norm. The team must prepare a one-page report that describes the ratios for each company and identifies the conclusions reached during the team's discussion.

COMMUNICATING IN PRACTICE

A1

BTN 10-5   Access the Yahoo! (ticker: YHOO) 10-K report for the year ended December 31, 2015, filed on February 29, 2016, at SEC.gov.

TAKING IT TO THE NET

P4

Required

1. What amount of goodwill is reported on Yahoo!'s balance sheet? What percentage of total assets does its goodwill represent? Is goodwill a major asset for Yahoo!? Explain.

2. Locate Note 5 to its financial statements. Identify the change in goodwill from December 31, 2014, to December 31, 2015. Comment on the change in goodwill over this period.

Continued on next page . . .

3. Locate Note 6 to its financial statements. What are the three categories of intangible assets that Yahoo! reports at December 31, 2015? What proportion of total assets do the intangibles represent?

4. What does Yahoo! indicate is the life of "Tradenames, trademarks, and domain names" according to its Note 6?

TEAMWORK IN ACTION

P1

BTN 10-6 Each team member is to become an expert on one depreciation method to facilitate teammates' understanding of that method. Follow these procedures:

a. Each team member is to select an area of expertise from one of the following depreciation methods: straight-line, units-of-production, or double-declining-balance.

b. Expert teams are to be formed from those who have selected the same area of expertise. The instructor will identify the location where each expert team meets.

c. Using the following data, expert teams are to collaborate and develop a presentation answering the requirements. Expert team members must write the presentation in a format they can show to their learning teams.

Data and Requirements On January 8, 2015, Whitewater Riders purchases a van to transport rafters back to the point of departure at the conclusion of the rafting adventures they operate. The cost of the van is $44,000. It has an estimated salvage value of $2,000 and is expected to be used for four years and driven 60,000 miles. The van is driven 12,000 miles in 2015; 18,000 miles in 2016; 21,000 in 2017; and 10,000 in 2018.

1. Compute the annual depreciation expense for each year of the van's estimated useful life.

2. Explain when and how annual depreciation is recorded.

3. Explain the impact on income of this depreciation method versus others over the van's life.

4. Identify the van's book value for each year of its life and illustrate the reporting of this amount for any one year.

d. Re-form original learning teams. In rotation, experts are to present to their teams the results from part c. Experts are to encourage and respond to questions.

Point: This activity can follow an overview of each method. Step 1 allows for three areas of expertise. Larger teams will have some duplication of areas, but the straight-line choice should not be duplicated. Expert teams can use the book and consult with the instructor.

ENTREPRENEURIAL DECISION

A1

BTN 10-7 Review the chapter's opening feature involving Matt Hofmann and his company, Westland Distillery. Assume that the company currently has net sales of $8,000,000 and that it is planning an expansion that will increase net sales by $4,000,000. To accomplish this expansion, Westland Distillery must increase its average total assets from $2,500,000 to $3,000,000.

Required

1. Compute the company's total asset turnover under (a) current conditions and (b) proposed conditions.

2. Evaluate and comment on the merits of the proposal given your analysis in part 1. Identify any concerns you would express about the proposal.

HITTING THE ROAD

P3 P4

BTN 10-8 Team up with one or more classmates for this activity. Identify companies in your community or area that must account for at least one of the following assets: natural resource; patent; lease; leasehold improvement; copyright; trademark; or goodwill. You might find a company that has more than one type of asset. Once you identify a company with a specific asset, describe the accounting this company uses to allocate the cost of that asset to the periods that benefit from its use.

GLOBAL DECISION

A1

BTN 10-9 Samsung (Samsung.com), Apple, and Google are all competitors in the global marketplace. Comparative figures for these companies' recent annual accounting periods follow.

In millions, except turnover	Samsung			Apple		Google	
	Current Year	Prior Year	Two Years Prior	Current Year	Prior Year	Current Year	Prior Year
Total assets.............	₩242,179,521	₩230,422,958	₩214,075,018	$290,479	$231,839	$147,461	$129,187
Net sales...............	200,653,482	206,205,987	228,692,667	233,715	182,795	74,989	66,001
Total asset turnover	?	?	—	0.89	0.83	0.54	0.55

Samsung
APPLE
GOOGLE

Required

1. Compute total asset turnover for the most recent two years for Samsung using the data shown.

2. Which company is most efficient in generating net sales given the total assets it employs?

GLOBAL VIEW

This section discusses similarities and differences between U.S. GAAP and IFRS in accounting and reporting for plant assets and intangible assets.

Accounting for Plant Assets   Issues involving cost determination, depreciation, additional expenditures, and disposals of plant assets are subject to broadly similar guidance for both U.S. GAAP and IFRS. Although differences exist, the similarities vastly outweigh the differences. Nokia describes its accounting for plant assets as follows:

> Property, plant and equipment are stated at cost less accumulated depreciation. Depreciation is recorded on a straight-line basis over the expected useful lives of the assets. Maintenance, repairs and renewals are generally charged to expense during the financial period in which they are incurred. However, major renovations are capitalized and included in the carrying amount of the asset . . . Major renovations are depreciated over the remaining useful life of the related asset.

One area where notable differences exist is in accounting for changes in the value of plant assets (between the time they are acquired and when they are disposed of). Namely, how do IFRS and U.S. GAAP treat decreases and increases in the value of plant assets subsequent to acquisition?

Decreases in the Value of Plant Assets   When the value of plant assets declines after acquisition, but before disposition, both U.S. GAAP and IFRS require companies to record those decreases as *impairment losses*. While the *test for impairment* uses a different base between U.S. GAAP and IFRS, a more fundamental difference is that U.S. GAAP revalues impaired plant assets to *fair value* whereas IFRS revalues them to a *recoverable amount* (defined as fair value less costs to sell).

Increases in the Value of Plant Assets   U.S. GAAP prohibits companies from recording increases in the value of plant assets. However, IFRS permits upward *asset revaluations*. Namely, under IFRS, if an impairment was previously recorded, a company would reverse that impairment to the extent necessary and record that increase in income. If the increase is beyond the original cost, that increase is recorded in comprehensive income.

Accounting for Intangible Assets   For intangible assets, the accounting for cost determination, amortization, additional expenditures, and disposals is subject to broadly similar guidance for U.S. GAAP and IFRS. Although differences exist, the similarities vastly outweigh differences. Again, and consistent with the accounting for plant assets, U.S. GAAP and IFRS handle decreases and increases in the value of intangible assets differently. However, IFRS requirements for recording increases in the value of intangible assets are so restrictive that such increases are rare. Nokia describes its accounting for intangible assets as follows:

> [Intangible assets] are capitalized and amortized using the straight-line method over their useful lives. Where an indication of impairment exists, the carrying amount of the related intangible asset is assessed for recoverability. Any resulting impairment losses are recognized immediately in the income statement.

 IFRS

Life Changing   Unlike U.S. GAAP, IFRS requires an annual review of useful life and salvage value estimates. IFRS also permits revaluation of plant assets to market if market value is reliably determined. ∎

 Global View Assignments

Discussion Questions 19 & 20

Quick Study 10-15

Exercise 10-25

BTN 10-9

11

chapter

Current Liabilities and Payroll Accounting

Chapter Preview

KNOWN LIABILITIES

C1 Reporting liabilities

C2 Sales taxes payable

Unearned revenues

P1 Short-term notes

NTK 11-1

PAYROLL LIABILITIES

P2 Employee payroll and deductions

P3 Employer payroll taxes

Multi-period liabilities

NTK 11-2

ESTIMATED LIABILITIES

P4 Reporting for:

Health and pension

Vacation benefits

Bonus plans

Warranty liabilities

NTK 11-3

CONTINGENCIES AND ANALYSIS

C3 Accounting for contingencies:

Probable

Possible

Remote

A1 Times interest earned

NTK 11-4

Learning Objectives

CONCEPTUAL

C1 Describe current and long-term liabilities and their characteristics.

C2 Identify and describe known current liabilities.

C3 Explain how to account for contingent liabilities.

ANALYTICAL

A1 Compute the times interest earned ratio and use it to analyze liabilities.

PROCEDURAL

P1 Prepare entries to account for short-term notes payable.

P2 Compute and record *employee* payroll deductions and liabilities.

P3 Compute and record *employer* payroll expenses and liabilities.

P4 Account for estimated liabilities, including warranties and bonuses.

P5 *Appendix 11A*—Identify and describe the details of payroll reports, records, and procedures.

Courtesy of Hello Alfred

So Help Me

New York—"I was in my studio working all of the time," admits Marcela Sapone, "and coming back to an apartment that was a total mess." Her friend, Jessica Beck, said the same.

The two decided to take action. They hired a woman from craigslist to do their laundry and buy groceries. Their friends learned of the new hire and asked Marcela and Jessica to set them up with help. Within months, Marcela and Jessica launched **Hello Alfred** (**HelloAlfred.com**), a tech-savvy "butler service" that does people's errands.

"It was a little bit of an accident," insists Marcela. "We built the product for ourselves, and over time people in our apartment building said, 'Hey, can I get in on that?'" They launched the service in New York at a price of $99 per week. Hello Alfred now has more than "10,000 sign-ups" in New York and has expanded into six cities.

Part of Jessica and Marcela's growth strategy is investment in their accounting system. Customers pay Hello Alfred in advance of their errands being done. Jessica and Marcela must record and track unearned revenues, which is a current liability. When the errands are performed, Jessica and Marcela's

accounting system removes the liability and records revenue. "We did a lot of our prep work," explains Marcela.

Beyond tracking unearned revenues, Hello Alfred's system tracks payroll liabilities. Unlike services such as **Uber** and **Lyft**, Hello Alfred employees are not contractors and are instead on the payroll. "We believe that if we treat the 'Alfred' as a customer," explains Marcela, "then our end users are going to be happy."

As the "Alfreds" are employees of Hello Alfred, the accounting system must record FICA taxes payable, medical insurance payable, federal income taxes payable, pension benefits, vacation benefits, and many other business liabilities. "We wanted to have the best possible relationship with the most important people in our business," insists Marcela in referring to her workers.

Marcela and Jessica encourage others to pursue their dreams. "What we're doing is really meaningful," exclaims Marcela, "and is going to change how people live."

"Help busy people to get access to affordable help"

—Marcela Sapone

Sources: *Hello Alfred website,* January 2017; *Tip Magazine,* February 2016; *Forbes,* January 2016; *CBS News,* August 2015; *Business Insider,* June 2015

KNOWN LIABILITIES

Known liabilities arise from agreements, contracts, or laws and they are measurable. Known liabilities include accounts payable, notes payable, payroll obligations, sales taxes, unearned revenues, and leases.

Characteristics of Liabilities

C1
_____

Describe current and long-term liabilities and their characteristics.

This section discusses characteristics of liabilities and how liabilities are classified.

Defining Liabilities   A *liability* is a probable future payment of assets or services that a company is presently obligated to make as a result of past transactions or events. This definition includes three crucial elements:

1. A past transaction or event.
2. A present obligation.
3. A future payment of assets or services.

These three elements are portrayed visually in Exhibit 11.1. Liabilities reported in financial statements exhibit those characteristics. No liability is reported when one or more of those characteristics are absent. For example, companies expect to pay wages in future years, but these future payments are *not* liabilities because no past event such as employee work resulted in a present obligation. Instead, liabilities are recorded when employees perform work and earn wages.

EXHIBIT 11.1

Characteristics of a Liability

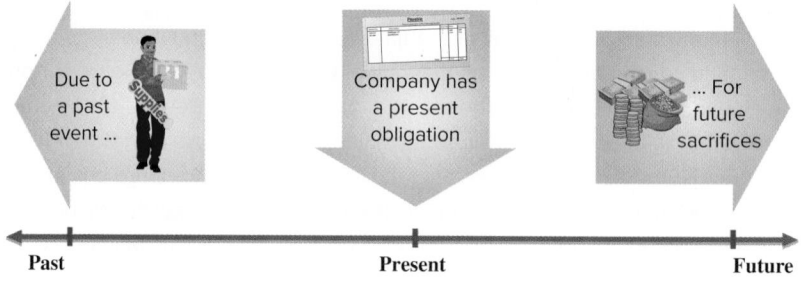

Point: Account titles using "payable" and "unearned" refer to liabilities. Unearned accounts are liabilities that must be fulfilled rather than repaid.

Classifying Liabilities   Information about liabilities is more useful when the balance sheet identifies them as either current or long term.

Current Liabilities   **Current liabilities,** also called *short-term liabilities,* **are obligations due *within* one year or the company's operating cycle, whichever is longer.** They are expected to be paid using current assets or by creating other current liabilities. Common examples are accounts payable, short-term notes payable, wages payable, warranty liabilities, lease liabilities, taxes payable, and unearned revenues.

Current liabilities differ across companies because they depend on the type of company operations. **MGM Resorts,** for instance, reported the following current liabilities related to its gaming, hospitality, and entertainment operations ($000s):

Advance deposits and ticket sales	$104,461	Casino front money deposits	$127,947
Casino outstanding chip liability	282,810	Other gaming-related accruals	91,318

Harley-Davidson reports a much different set of current liabilities. It reports items such as warranty, recall, and dealer incentive liabilities.

Long-Term Liabilities   **Long-term liabilities are obligations due *after* one year or the company's operating cycle, whichever is longer.** They include long-term notes payable, warranty liabilities, lease liabilities, and bonds payable.

Domino's Pizza, for instance, reports long-term liabilities of $2,224 million. They are reported after current liabilities. A single liability can be divided between the current and noncurrent sections if a company expects to make payments toward it in both the short and long term. Domino's reports long-term debt, $2,181 million; and current portion of long-term debt, $59 million. The second item is reported in current liabilities. We sometimes see liabilities that do not have a fixed due date but instead are payable on the creditor's demand. These are reported as current liabilities because of the possibility of payment in the near term. Exhibit 11.2 shows amounts of current liabilities and as a percentage of total liabilities for selected companies.

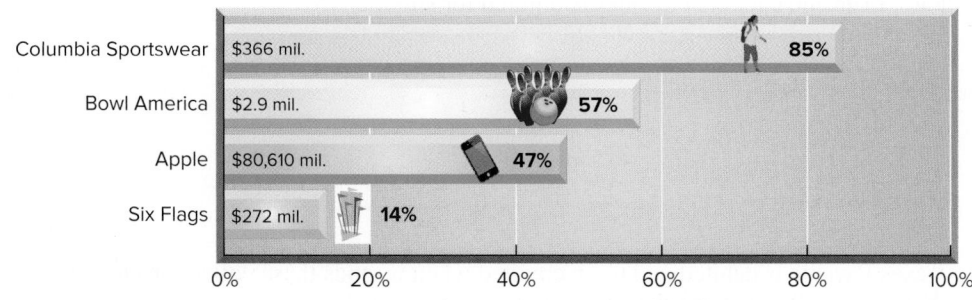

EXHIBIT 11.2

Current Liabilities of Selected Companies

Uncertainty in Liabilities   Accounting for liabilities involves addressing three important questions: Whom to pay? When to pay? How much to pay? Answers to these questions are often decided when a liability is incurred. For example, if a company has a $100 account payable to a specific individual, payable on March 15, the answers are clear. However, answers to one or more of these three questions are uncertain for some liabilities.

Uncertainty in Whom to Pay   Liabilities can involve uncertainty in whom to pay. For instance, a company can create a liability with a known amount when issuing a note that is payable to its holder. In this case, a specific amount is payable to the note's holder at a specified date, but the company does not know who the holder is until that date. Despite this uncertainty, the company reports this liability on its balance sheet.

Uncertainty in When to Pay   A company can have an obligation of a known amount to a known creditor but not know when it must be paid. For example, a legal services firm can accept fees in advance from a client who plans to use the firm's services in the future. This means that the firm has a liability that it settles by providing services at an unknown future date. Although this uncertainty exists, the legal firm's balance sheet must report this liability. These types of obligations are reported as current liabilities because they are likely to be settled in the short term.

Uncertainty in How Much to Pay   A company can be aware of an obligation, but not know how much will be required to settle it. For example, a company using electrical power is billed only after the meter has  been read. This cost is incurred and the liability created before a bill is received. A liability to the power company is reported as an estimated amount if the balance sheet is prepared before a bill arrives.

Accounts Payable

Accounts payable, or trade accounts payable, are amounts owed to suppliers, also called *vendors,* for products or services purchased on credit. Accounting for accounts payable is explained and illustrated in our chapter on merchandising activities.

Sales Taxes Payable

C2

Identify and describe known current liabilities.

Nearly all states and many cities levy taxes on retail sales. Sales taxes are stated as a percent of selling prices. The seller collects sales taxes from customers when sales occur and sends these collections to the government. Since sellers currently owe these collections to the government, this amount is a current liability. **Home Depot**, for instance, reports sales taxes payable of $476 million in its recent annual report. To illustrate, if Home Depot sells materials on August 31 for $6,000 cash that are subject to a 5% sales tax, the revenue portion of this transaction is recorded as follows. (The entry for cost of sales is omitted for simplicity.)

Assets = Liabilities + Equity
+6,300   +300   +6,000

Aug. 31	Cash	6,300	
	Sales		6,000
	Sales Taxes Payable ($6,000 × 0.05)		300
	Record cash sales and 5% sales tax.		

Sales Taxes Payable is debited and Cash credited when it sends these collections to the government. Sales Taxes Payable is not an expense.[1]

© Cameron Spencer/Getty Images

Unearned Revenues

Unearned revenues (also called *deferred revenues, collections in advance,* and *prepayments*) are amounts received in advance from customers for future products or services. Advance ticket sales for sporting events or music concerts are examples. **Rihanna**, for instance, has "deferred revenues" from advance ticket sales. To illustrate, assume that Rihanna sells $5 million in tickets for eight concerts; the entry is:

Point: To *defer* a revenue means to postpone recognition of a revenue collected in advance until it is earned.

Assets = Liabilities + Equity
+5,000,000   +5,000,000

June 30	Cash	5,000,000	
	Unearned Ticket Revenue		5,000,000
	Record sale of concert tickets.		

When a concert is played, Rihanna would record revenue for the portion earned.

Assets = Liabilities + Equity
        −625,000   +625,000

Oct. 31	Unearned Ticket Revenue	625,000	
	Ticket Revenue		625,000
	Record concert ticket revenues earned. *$5,000,000 × 1/8*		

Unearned Ticket Revenue is reported as a current liability. Unearned revenues also arise with airline ticket sales, magazine subscriptions, construction projects, hotel reservations, gift card sales, and custom orders.

---

[1] Sales taxes can be computed from total sales receipts when sales taxes are not separately listed on the register. To illustrate, assume a 5% sales tax and $420 in total sales receipts (which includes sales taxes). Sales are computed as:

$$\text{Sales} = \text{Total sales receipts}/(1 + \text{Sales tax percentage}) = \$420/1.05 = \$400$$

The sales tax amount equals total sales receipts minus sales, or $420 − $400 = $20.

Short-Term Notes Payable

A **short-term note payable** is a written promise to pay a specified amount on a stated future date within one year or the company's operating cycle, whichever is longer. Promissory notes can be sold or transferred from party to party. Most notes payable bear interest. The written documentation provided by notes is helpful in resolving legal disputes. We describe two transactions that create notes payable.

Note Given to Extend Credit Period A company can replace an account payable with a note payable. A common example is a creditor that requires the substitution of an interest-bearing note for an overdue account payable.

To illustrate, let's assume that on August 23, Brady Company asks to extend its past-due $600 account payable to McGraw. After negotiations, McGraw agrees to accept $100 cash and a 60-day, 12%, $500 note payable to replace the account payable. Brady records the transaction with this entry:

Aug. 23	Accounts Payable—McGraw............................	600	
	Cash...		100
	Notes Payable—McGraw.........................		500
	Sent $100 cash and a 60-day, 12% note for payment on account.		

Signing the note changes Brady's debt from an account payable to a note payable. McGraw prefers the note payable over the account payable because it earns interest and it is written documentation of the debt's existence, term, and amount. When the note comes due, Brady pays the note and interest by giving McGraw a check for $510. Brady records that payment with this entry:

Oct. 22	Notes Payable—McGraw............................	500	
	Interest Expense.................................	10	
	Cash...		510
	Paid note with interest ($500 × 12% × 60/360).		

Interest expense is computed by multiplying the principal of the note ($500) by the annual interest rate (12%) for the fraction of the year the note is outstanding (60 days/360 days).

Note Given to Borrow from Bank A bank requires a borrower to sign a promissory note when making a loan. When the note comes due, the borrower repays the note with an amount larger than the amount borrowed. The difference between the amount borrowed and the amount repaid is *interest*. Consider a type of note whose signer promises to pay *principal* (the amount borrowed) plus interest. In this case, the *face value* of the note equals the principal. Face value is the value shown on the face (front) of the note.

To illustrate, assume that a company borrows $2,000 from a bank at 12% annual interest. The loan is made on September 30, 2017, and is due in 60 days. The note states: *"I promise to pay $2,000 plus interest at 12% within 60 days after September 30."* The borrower records its receipt of cash and the new liability with this entry:

Sep. 30	Cash...	2,000	
	Notes Payable		2,000
	Borrowed $2,000 cash with a 60-day, 12%, $2,000 note.		

When principal and interest are paid, the borrower records payment with this entry:

Nov. 29	Notes Payable	2,000	
	Interest Expense.................................	40	
	Cash...		2,040
	Paid note with interest ($2,000 × 12% × 60/360).		

P1

Prepare entries to account for short-term notes payable.

Point: Required characteristics of a note: (1) unconditional promise, (2) in writing, (3) specific amount, and (4) stated due date.

Assets = Liabilities + Equity
−100   −600
         +500

Assets = Liabilities + Equity
−510   −500   −10

Point: Companies commonly compute interest using a 360-day year. This is known as the *banker's rule.*

Point: When a bank loans money, the loan is reported as an asset (receivable) on the bank's balance sheet.

Assets = Liabilities + Equity
+2,000   +2,000

Assets = Liabilities + Equity
−2,040   −2,000   −40

When Note Extends over Two Periods   When a note is issued in one period but paid in the next, interest expense is recorded in each period based on the number of days the note extends over each period. To illustrate, return to the above note payable but assume that the company borrows $2,000 cash on December 16, 2017, instead of September 30. This 60-day note matures on February 14, 2018, and the company's fiscal year ends on December 31. This means 15 of the 60 days are in 2017 and 45 of the 60 days are in 2018. Interest for these two periods is:

- 12/16/2017 to 12/31/2017 = 15 days. Interest expense = $2,000 × 12% × 15/360 = $10.
- 12/31/2017 to 02/14/2018 = 45 days. Interest expense = $2,000 × 12% × 45/360 = $30.

The borrower records the 2017 expense with the following adjusting entry:

Assets = Liabilities + Equity
    +10   −10

2017			
Dec. 31	Interest Expense	10	
	Interest Payable		10
	Record accrued interest ($2,000 × 12% × 15/360).		

Point: Feb. 14 entry assumes no reversing entry was made.

When this note matures on February 14, the borrower records 45 days of interest expense in 2018 and removes the balances of the two liability accounts:

Assets = Liabilities + Equity
−2,040   −10   −30
      −2,000

2018			
Feb. 14	Interest Expense*	30	
	Interest Payable.....................................	10	
	Notes Payable	2,000	
	Cash		2,040
	*Paid note with interest. *$2,000 × 12% × 45/360*		

Decision Insight

Sweet Notes   Many franchisors, such as **Baskin-Robbins**, **Planet Smoothie**, and **Cold Stone Creamery**, use notes to help entrepreneurs acquire their own franchises, including using notes to pay for the franchise fee and any equipment. Payments on these notes are usually collected monthly and often are secured by the franchisees' assets. For example, a **McDonald's** franchise can cost from under $200,000 to over $2 million, depending on the type selected; see **FranchiseFoundations.com**. ■

© Adam Gault/OJO Images/Getty Images

NEED-TO-KNOW 11-1

Accounting for Known Liabilities

P1   C2

Part 1. A retailer sells merchandise for $500 cash on June 30 (cost of merchandise is $300). The sales tax law requires the retailer to collect 7% sales tax. Record the entry for the $500 sale and its applicable sales tax. Also record the entry that shows the remittance of the 7% tax on this sale to the state government on July 15.

Part 2. A ticket agency receives $40,000 cash in advance ticket sales for a four-date tour of Haim. Record the advance ticket sales on April 30. Record the revenue earned for the first concert date of May 15, assuming it represents one-fourth of the advance ticket sales.

Part 3. On November 25 of the current year, a company borrows $8,000 cash by signing a 90-day, 5% note payable with a face value of $8,000. (a) Compute the accrued interest payable on December 31 of the current year, (b) prepare the journal entry to record the accrued interest expense at December 31 of the current year, and (c) prepare the journal entry to record payment of the note at maturity.

Solution—Part 1

June 30	Cash	535	
	Sales		500
	Sales Taxes Payable		35
	Record cash sales and 7% sales tax.		
June 30	Cost of Goods Sold	300	
	Merchandise Inventory.		300
	Record cost of June 30 sales.		
July 15	Sales Taxes Payable	35	
	Cash		35
	Record remittance of sales taxes to govt.		

Solution—Part 2

Apr. 30	Cash	40,000	
	Unearned Ticket Revenue		40,000
	Record sales in advance of concerts.		
May 15	Unearned Ticket Revenue.	10,000	
	Earned Ticket Revenue		10,000
	Record concert revenues earned ($40,000 × 1/4).		

Solution—Part 3

a.

Computation of interest payable at December 31:	
Days from November 25 to December 31.	36 days
Accrued interest (5% × $8,000 × 36/360).	<u>$40</u>

b.

Dec. 31	Interest Expense	40	
	Interest Payable		40
	Record accrued interest (5% × $8,000 × 36/360).		

c.

Feb. 23	Interest Expense	60	
	Interest Payable.	40	
	Notes Payable	8,000	
	Cash		8,100
	Record payment of note plus interest		
	(5% × $8,000 × 90/360 = $100 total interest)		
	(5% × $8,000 × 54/360 = $60 interest expense).		

Point: Feb. 23 entry assumes no reversing entry was made.

Do More: QS 11-2, QS 11-3, QS 11-4, E 11-2, E 11-3, E 11-4

PAYROLL LIABILITIES

Payroll liabilities are an important part of *known liabilities* and arise from salaries and wages earned, from employee benefits, and from payroll taxes levied on the employer. **Boston Beer**, for instance, reports payroll-related current liabilities of more than $12.367 million from accrued "employee wages, benefits and reimbursements." We discuss payroll liabilities and related accounts in this section. Appendix 11A describes details about payroll reports, records, and procedures.

P2 _____

Compute and record *employee* payroll deductions and liabilities.

Employee Payroll and Deductions

Gross pay is the total compensation an employee earns including wages, salaries, commissions, bonuses, and any compensation earned before deductions such as taxes. (*Wages* usually refer to payments to employees at an hourly rate. *Salaries* usually refer to payments to employees at a monthly or yearly rate.) **Net pay,** also called *take-home pay,* is gross pay less all deductions. **Payroll deductions,** commonly called *withholdings,* are amounts withheld from an employee's gross pay, either required or voluntary. Required deductions result from laws and include income taxes and Social Security taxes. Voluntary deductions, at an employee's option, include pension and health contributions, health and life insurance premiums, union dues, and charitable giving.

Exhibit 11.3 shows typical payroll deductions of an employee. The employer withholds payroll deductions from employees' pay and is obligated to send this money to the designated group or government. The employer records payroll deductions as current liabilities until these amounts are transmitted. This section discusses major payroll deductions.

Point: Deductions at some companies, such as those for insurance coverage, are "required" under labor contracts.

EXHIBIT 11.3

Payroll Deductions

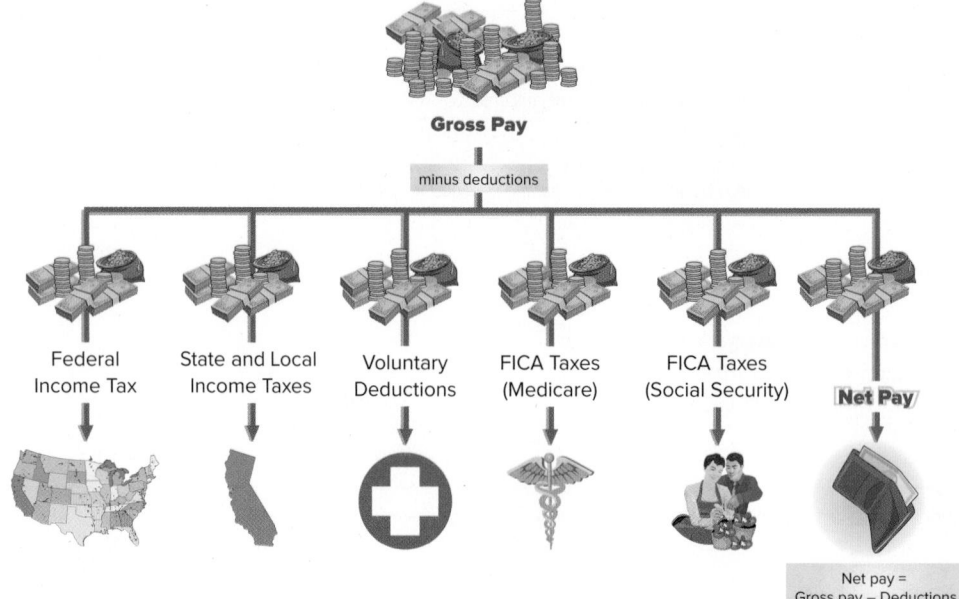

Employee FICA Taxes   The federal Social Security system provides retirement, disability, survivorship, and medical benefits to qualified workers. Laws *require* employers to withhold **Federal Insurance Contributions Act (FICA) taxes** from employees' pay to cover costs of the system. Employers separate FICA taxes into two groups: (1) retirement, disability, and survivorship and (2) medical. For the first group, the Social Security system makes payments to those who qualify. Taxes related to this group are often called *Social Security taxes.* For the second group, the system makes payments to those who qualify, and taxes related to this group are commonly called *Medicare taxes.*

Taxes for Social Security and Medicare are computed separately. For 2016, the amount withheld from each employee's pay for Social Security tax was 6.2% of the first $118,500 the employee earns in the calendar year. The Medicare tax is 1.45% of *all* amounts the employee earns; there is no maximum limit to Medicare tax. A 0.9% *Additional Medicare Tax* is imposed on the employee for pay in excess of $200,000 (this additional tax is *not* imposed on the employer, whereas the others are).

Employers must pay withheld taxes to the Internal Revenue Service (IRS) on specific filing dates during the year. Until all the taxes are sent to the IRS, they are included in employers' current liabilities. For any changes in rates or with the maximum earnings level, check the IRS website at IRS.gov or the SSA website at SSA.gov.

Point: Sources of U.S. tax receipts:
50% Personal income tax
35 FICA and FUTA taxes
10 Corporate income tax
5 Other taxes

Employee Income Tax   Most employers are required to withhold federal income tax from each employee's paycheck. The amount withheld is computed using tables published by the IRS. The amount depends on the employee's annual earnings rate and the number of *with-holding allowances* the employee claims. Allowances reduce the amount of taxes one owes the government. The more allowances one claims, the less tax the employer will withhold. Employees can claim allowances for themselves and their dependents. Until the government is paid, withholdings are reported as a current liability on the employer's balance sheet.

Point: IRS withholding tables are based on projecting weekly (or other period) pay into an annual figure.

Employee Voluntary Deductions   Voluntary deduction withholdings arise from employee requests, contracts, unions, or other agreements. They can include amounts for charitable giving, medical and life insurance premiums, pension contributions, and union dues. Until they are paid, such withholdings are reported as part of employers' current liabilities.

Employee Payroll Recording   Employers accrue payroll expenses and liabilities at the end of each pay period. To illustrate, assume that an employee earns a salary of $2,000 per month. At the end of January, the employer's entry to accrue payroll expenses and liabilities for this employee is

Jan. 31	Salaries Expense	2,000	
	FICA—Social Security Taxes Payable (6.2%)		124
	FICA—Medicare Taxes Payable (1.45%)		29
	Employee Federal Income Taxes Payable*		213
	Employee Medical Insurance Payable*		85
	Employee Union Dues Payable*		25
	Salaries Payable		1,524
	Record accrued payroll for January.		

Assets = Liabilities + Equity
+124   −2,000
+29
+213
+85
+25
+1,524

* Amounts taken from employer's accounting records.

Salaries Expense (debit) shows that the employee earns a gross salary of $2,000. The first five payables (credits) show the liabilities the employer owes on behalf of this employee to cover FICA taxes, income taxes, medical insurance, and union dues. The Salaries Payable account (credit) records the $1,524 net pay the employee receives from the $2,000 gross pay earned. The February 1 entry to record cash payment to this employee is

| Feb. 1 | Salaries Payable .... | 1,524 | |
| | Cash .... | | 1,524 |

▮ Decision Insight

Eyes of the Law   "Failure to pay employment taxes is stealing from the employees of the business," alleges former IRS Commissioner Mark W. Everson. "The IRS pursues business owners who don't follow the law, and those who embrace these schemes face civil or criminal sanctions." There are many reasons employers do not withhold or pay employment taxes. Some attempt to use the government as a "bank to borrow money for a short time," some collect the taxes and keep them, and others object to U.S. tax laws. Regardless, federal law requires employment tax withholding and payment by employers (**IRS.gov/newsroom**). ▮

Employer Payroll Taxes

Employers must pay payroll taxes in addition to those required of employees. Employer taxes include FICA and unemployment taxes.

Employer FICA Tax   Employers must pay FICA taxes on their payroll. For 2016, the employer must pay Social Security tax of 6.2% on the first $118,500 earned by each employee and 1.45% Medicare tax on all earnings of each employee. An employer's tax is credited to the same FICA Taxes Payable accounts used to record the Social Security and Medicare taxes withheld from employees.

P3_____

Compute and record *employer* payroll expenses and liabilities.

Point: A self-employed person must pay both the employee and employer FICA taxes.

Federal and State Unemployment Taxes   The federal government participates with states in a joint federal and state unemployment insurance program. Each state administers its program. These programs provide unemployment benefits to qualified workers.

Federal Unemployment Tax Act (FUTA).   Employers are subject to a federal unemployment tax on wages and salaries paid to their employees. For the recent year, employers were required to pay FUTA taxes of as much as 6.0% of the first $7,000 earned by each employee. This federal tax can be reduced by a credit of up to 5.4% for taxes paid to a state program. As a result, the net federal unemployment tax is often only 0.6%.

State Unemployment Tax Act (SUTA).   All states support their unemployment insurance programs by placing a payroll tax on employers. (A few states require employees to make a contribution. In the book's assignments, we assume this tax is only levied on the employer.) In most states, the base rate for SUTA taxes is 5.4% of the first $7,000 paid each employee. This base rate is adjusted according to an employer's merit rating. The state assigns a **merit rating** that reflects a company's stability or instability in employing workers. A good rating reflects stability in employment and means an employer can pay less than the 5.4% base rate. A low rating reflects high turnover or seasonal hirings and layoffs.

Recording Employer Payroll Taxes   Employer payroll taxes are an added expense beyond the wages and salaries earned by employees. These taxes are often recorded in an entry separate from the one recording payroll expenses and deductions. To illustrate, assume that the $2,000 recorded salaries expense from the previous example is earned by an employee whose earnings have not yet reached $5,000 for the year. This means the entire salaries expense for this period is subject to tax because year-to-date pay is under $7,000. Consequently, the FICA portion of the employer's tax is $153, computed by multiplying both the 6.2% and 1.45% by the $2,000 gross pay. Assume that the federal unemployment tax rate is 0.6% and the state unemployment tax rate is 5.4%. This means state unemployment (SUTA) taxes are $108 (5.4% of the $2,000 gross pay) and federal unemployment (FUTA) taxes are $12 (0.6% of $2,000). The entry to record the employer's payroll tax expense and related liabilities is

Example: If the employer's merit rating in this example reduces its SUTA rate to 2.9%, what is its SUTA liability? *Answer:* SUTA payable = $2,000 × 2.9% = $58

Assets = Liabilities + Equity
+124   −273
+29
+108
+12

Jan. 31	Payroll Taxes Expense	273	
	FICA—Social Security Taxes Payable (6.2%)..........		124
	FICA—Medicare Taxes Payable (1.45%)		29
	State Unemployment Taxes Payable		108
	Federal Unemployment Taxes Payable..............		12
	Record employer payroll taxes.		

Internal Control of Payroll

Internal controls are crucial for payroll because of a high risk of fraud and error. Exhibit 11.4 identifies and explains four key areas of payroll activities that we aim to *separate and monitor*.

EXHIBIT 11.4

Internal Control of Payroll

Employee Hiring   **Payroll Preparation**   **Timekeeping**   **Payroll Payment**

Duty: Authorize, hire, and fire.
Aim: Keep fake workers off payroll.

Duty: Verify tax rates and payroll amounts.
Aim: Rates updated and amounts accurate.

Duty: Track and verify time worked.
Aim: Paid for time worked only.

Duty: Sign and issue prenumbered checks.
Aim: Checks valid, secured, and correct.

■ **Decision** Insight

Payroll Fraud   Probably the greatest number of frauds involve payroll. Controls include proper approvals and processes for employee additions, deletions, and pay rate changes. A common fraud is a manager adding a fictitious employee to the payroll and then cashing the fictitious employee's check. A study reports that 42% of employees in operations and service areas witnessed violations of employee wage, overtime, or benefit rules in the past year (KPMG 2013). Another 33% observed falsifying of time and expense reports. ■

Ceridian Connection reports: **8.5%** of fraud is tied to payroll; **$72,000** is the median loss per payroll fraud; and **24 months** is the median time to uncover payroll fraud.

Multi-Period Known Liabilities

Many known liabilities extend over multiple periods. These often include unearned revenues and notes payable. For example, if **Sports Illustrated** sells a three-year digital magazine subscription, it records amounts received for this subscription in an Unearned Subscription Revenues account. Amounts in this account are liabilities, but are they current or long term? They are *both*. The portion of the Unearned Subscription Revenues account that will be fulfilled in the next year is reported as a current liability. The remaining portion is reported as a long-term liability.

The same analysis applies to notes payable. For example, a borrower reports a three-year note payable as a long-term liability in the first two years it is outstanding. In the third year, the borrower reclassifies this note as a current liability since it is due within one year or the operating cycle, whichever is longer. The **current portion of long-term debt** refers to that part of long-term debt due within one year or the operating cycle, whichever is longer. Long-term debt is reported under long-term liabilities, but the *current portion due* is reported under current liabilities. To illustrate, assume that a $7,500 debt is paid in installments of $1,500 per year for five years. The $1,500 due within the year is reported as a current liability. No journal entry is necessary for this reclassification. Instead, we simply classify the amounts for debt as either current or long term when the balance sheet is prepared.

Point: Some accounting systems make an entry to transfer the current amount due out of Long-Term Debt and into the Current Portion of Long-Term Debt as follows:

Long-Term Debt 1,500
   Current Portion
      of L-T Debt   1,500

■ **Decision** Ethics

Web Designer   You take a summer job working for a family friend who runs a small IT service. On your first payday, the owner slaps you on the back, gives you full payment in cash, winks, and adds: "No need to pay those high taxes, eh." What action, if any, do you take? ■   [*Answer:* You wish to avoid being an accomplice to unlawful payroll activities. Not paying federal and state taxes on wages is illegal and unethical. One action is to request payment by check. If this fails, you must consider quitting.]

A company's first weekly pay period of the year ends on January 8. On that date, the column totals in its payroll register show that sales employees earned $30,000 and office employees earned $20,000 in salaries. The employees are to have withheld from their salaries FICA Social Security taxes at the rate of 6.2%, FICA Medicare taxes at the rate of 1.45%, $9,000 of federal income taxes, $2,000 of medical insurance deductions, and $1,000 of pension contributions. No employee earned more than $7,000 in the first pay period.

NEED-TO-KNOW 11-2

Payroll Liabilities

P2   P3

Part 1. Compute FICA Social Security taxes payable and FICA Medicare taxes payable. Prepare the journal entry to record the company's January 8 (employee) payroll expenses and liabilities. (Round amounts to cents.)

Part 2. Prepare the journal entry to record the company's (employer) payroll taxes resulting from the January 8 payroll. Its merit rating reduces its state unemployment tax rate to 3.4% of the first $7,000 paid to each employee. The federal unemployment tax rate is 0.6%. (Round amounts to cents.)

Solution—Part 1

Jan. 8	Sales Salaries Expense	30,000.00	
	Office Salaries Expense.	20,000.00	
	FICA—Social Security Taxes Payable*		3,100.00
	FICA—Medicare Taxes Payable†		725.00
	Employee Fed. Income Taxes Payable		9,000.00
	Employee Med. Insurance Payable		2,000.00
	Employee Pensions Payable		1,000.00
	Salaries Payable		34,175.00
	Record payroll for period.		

* $50,000 × 6.2% = $3,100   †$50,000 × 1.45% = $725

Solution—Part 2

Jan. 8	Payroll Taxes Expense.................................	5,825.00	
	FICA—Social Security Taxes Payable		3,100.00
	FICA—Medicare Taxes Payable		725.00
	State Unemployment Taxes Payable*		1,700.00
	Federal Unemployment Taxes Payable†		300.00
	Record employer payroll taxes.		

Do More: QS 11-5, QS 11-6,
E 11-5, E 11-6, E 11-7,
E 11-8, E 11-9

* $50,000 \times 3.4\% = \$1,700$ †$50,000 \times 0.6\% = \$300$

ESTIMATED LIABILITIES

P4

Account for estimated liabilities, including warranties and bonuses.

An **estimated liability** is a known obligation that is of an uncertain amount but that can be reasonably estimated. Common examples are employee benefits such as pensions, health care, and vacation pay, and warranties offered by a seller. We discuss each of these in this section.

Health and Pension Benefits

Many companies provide **employee benefits** beyond salaries and wages. An employer often pays all or part of medical, dental, life, and disability insurance. Many employers also contribute to *pension plans,* which are agreements by employers to provide benefits (payments) to employees after retirement. Many companies also provide medical care and insurance benefits to their retirees. When payroll taxes and charges for employee benefits are totaled, payroll cost often exceeds employees' gross earnings by 25% or more.

To illustrate, assume that an employer agrees to (1) pay an amount for medical insurance equal to $8,000 and (2) contribute an additional 10% of the employees' $120,000 gross salaries to a retirement program. The entry to record these accrued benefits is

Assets = Liabilities + Equity
+8,000   −20,000
+12,000

Dec. 31	Employee Benefits Expense	20,000	
	Employee Medical Insurance Payable		8,000
	Employee Retirement Program Payable		12,000
	Record costs of employee benefits.		

Decision Insight

Win-Win   Major League Baseball was the first pro sport to set up a pension, originally up to $100 per month depending on years played. Many former players now take home six-figure pensions. Cal Ripken Jr.'s pension when he reaches 62 is estimated at $180,000 per year (he played 21 seasons). The same applies to Hank Aaron, who played 23 seasons—see photo. The requirement is 43 games for a full pension and just one game for full medical benefits for life. ■

© Focus on Sport/Getty Images

Vacation Benefits

Many employers offer paid vacation benefits, also called *paid absences* or *compensated absences.* To illustrate, assume that salaried employees earn 2 weeks' vacation per year. This benefit increases employers' payroll expenses because employees are paid for 52 weeks but work for only 50 weeks. Total annual salary is the same, but the cost per week worked is greater than the amount paid per week. For example, if an employee is paid $20,800 for 52 weeks but works only 50 weeks, the total weekly expense to the employer is $416 ($20,800/50 weeks)

Point: An *accrued expense* is an unpaid expense and is also called an *accrued liability.*

instead of the $400 cash paid weekly to the employee ($20,800/52 weeks). The $16 difference between these two amounts is recorded weekly as follows:

Vacation Benefits Expense................................	16	
Vacation Benefits Payable...........................		16
Record vacation benefits accrued.		

Assets = Liabilities + Equity
+16 −16

Vacation Benefits Expense is an operating expense, and Vacation Benefits Payable is a current liability. When the employee takes a one-week vacation, the employer reduces (debits) Vacation Benefits Payable and credits Cash (with no other expense recorded) for the employer's $416 total weekly expense.

Vacation Benefits Payable...........................	416	
Cash..		416
Record vacation benefits taken.		

Assets = Liabilities + Equity
−416 −416

Bonus Plans

Many companies offer bonuses to employees, and many of the bonuses depend on net income. To illustrate, assume that an employer offers a bonus to its employees based on the company's annual net income (to be equally shared by all). The year-end adjusting entry to record a $10,000 bonus is

Dec. 31	Employee Bonus Expense............................	10,000	
	Bonus Payable..................................		10,000
	Record expected bonus costs.		

Assets = Liabilities + Equity
+10,000 −10,000

Warranty Liabilities

A **warranty** is a seller's obligation to replace or correct a product (or service) that fails to perform as expected within a specified period. Most new cars, for instance, are sold with a warranty covering parts for a specified period of time. **Ford Motor Company** reported nearly $11 billion in "dealer and dealers' customer allowances and claims" in its annual report. The seller reports the expected warranty expense in the period when revenue from the sale of the product or service is reported. The seller reports this warranty obligation as a liability, although the existence, amount, payee, and date of future sacrifices are uncertain. This is because such warranty costs are probable and the amount can be estimated using, for instance, past experience with warranties.

To illustrate, a dealer sells a used car for $16,000 on December 1, 2017, with a one-year or 12,000-mile warranty covering parts. Experience shows that warranty expense averages about 4% of a car's selling price, or $640 in this case ($16,000 × 4%). The dealer records the estimated expense and liability related to this sale with this entry:

Dec. 1	Warranty Expense.................................	640	
	Estimated Warranty Liability		640
	Record estimated warranty expense.		

Assets = Liabilities + Equity
+640 −640

This entry alternatively could be made as part of end-of-period adjustments. Either way, the estimated warranty expense is reported on the 2017 income statement and the warranty liability on the 2017 balance sheet. Continuing this example, suppose the customer returns the car for warranty repairs on January 9, 2018. The dealer performs this work by replacing parts costing $200. The entry to record partial settlement of the estimated warranty liability is

Jan. 9	Estimated Warranty Liability........................	200	
	Auto Parts Inventory		200
	Record costs of warranty repairs.		

Assets = Liabilities + Equity
−200 −200

This entry reduces the balance of the Estimated Warranty Liability account. Warranty expense was previously recorded in 2017, the year the car was sold with the warranty. Finally, what happens if total warranty expenses are more or less than the estimated 4%, or $640? The answer is that management should monitor actual warranty expenses to see whether the 4% rate is accurate. If experience reveals a large difference from the estimate, the rate for current and future sales should be changed. Differences are expected, but they should be small.

Decision Insight

Turn a Profit When we purchase a new laptop at **Best Buy**, a sales clerk commonly asks: *"Do you want the Geek Squad Protection Plan?"* Best Buy earns about a 60% profit margin on such warranty contracts, and those contracts are a large part of its profit—see table here (*BusinessWeek*). ■

Warranty contracts as a percentage of sales.	4%
Warranty contracts as a percentage of operating profit.	45%
Profit margin on warranty contracts.	60%

Multi-Period Estimated Liabilities

Estimated liabilities can be both current and long term. For example, pension liabilities to employees are long term to workers who will not retire within the next period. For employees who are retired or will retire within the next period, a portion of pension liabilities is current. Other examples include employee health benefits and warranties. Specifically, many warranties are for 30 or 60 days in length. Estimated costs under these warranties are properly reported in current liabilities. Many other automobile warranties are for three years or 36,000 miles. A portion of these warranties is reported as long term.

Estimated Liabilities

P4

Part 1. A company's salaried employees earn two weeks' vacation per year. It pays $208,000 in total employee salaries for 52 weeks, but its employees work only 50 weeks. This means its total weekly expense is $4,160 ($208,000/50 weeks) instead of the $4,000 cash paid weekly to the employees ($208,000/52 weeks). Record the company's regular weekly vacation benefits expense.

Part 2. For the current year ended December 31, a company has implemented an employee bonus program based on its net income, which employees share equally. Its bonus expense is $40,000. (a) Prepare the journal entry at December 31 of the current year to record the bonus due. (b) Prepare the journal entry at January 20 of the following year to record payment of that bonus to employees.

Part 3. On June 11 of the current year, a retailer sells a trimmer for $400 with a one-year warranty that covers parts. Warranty expense is estimated at 5% of sales. On March 24 of the next year, the trimmer is brought in for repairs covered under the warranty requiring $15 in materials taken from the Repair Parts Inventory. Prepare the (a) June 11 entry to record the trimmer sale—ignore the cost of sales part of this sales entry—and (b) March 24 entry to record warranty repairs.

Solution—Part 1

Weekly	Vacation Benefits Expense*	160	
	Vacation Benefits Payable		160
	*Record vacation benefits accrued. *$4,160 − $4,000*		

Solution—Part 2

a.

Dec. 31	Employee Bonus Expense	40,000	
	Bonus Payable		40,000
	Record expected bonus costs.		

b.

Jan. 20	Bonus Payable	40,000	
	Cash		40,000
	Record payment of bonus.		

Solution—Part 3

June 11	Cash	400	
	Sales		400
	Record trimmer sales.		
June 11	Warranty Expense	20	
	Estimated Warranty Liability		20
	Record estimated warranty expense ($400 × 5%).		
Mar. 24	Estimated Warranty Liability	15	
	Repair Parts Inventory		15
	Record cost of warranty repairs.		

Do More: QS 11-7, QS 11-8, QS 11-9, E 11-10, E 11-11, E 11-12

CONTINGENT LIABILITIES

A **contingent liability** is a potential obligation that depends on a future event arising from a past transaction or event. An example is a pending lawsuit. Here, a past transaction or event leads to a lawsuit whose financial outcome depends on the result of the suit.

C3

Explain how to account for contingent liabilities.

Accounting for Contingent Liabilities

Accounting for contingent liabilities depends on the likelihood that a future event will occur and the ability to estimate the future amount owed if this event occurs. Three different possibilities are identified in Exhibit 11.5: record liability, disclose in notes, or no disclosure.

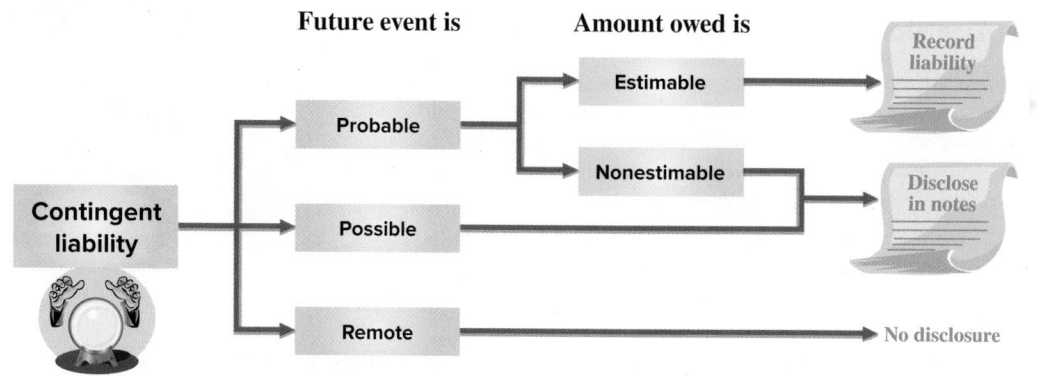

EXHIBIT 11.5

Accounting for Contingent Liabilities

The conditions that determine each of these three possibilities follow:

1. The future event is *probable* (likely) and the amount owed can be *reasonably estimated*. We then record this amount as a liability. Examples are the estimated liabilities described earlier such as warranties, vacation pay, and income taxes.

2. The future event is *reasonably possible* (could occur). We disclose information about this type of contingent liability in notes to the financial statements.

3. The future event is *remote* (unlikely). We do not record or disclose information on remote contingent liabilities.

Point: A contingency is an *if.* Namely, *if* a future event occurs, then financial consequences are likely for the entity.

Applying Rules of Contingent Liabilities

This section demonstrates how accounting rules are applied to common contingent liabilities.

Potential Legal Claims   Many companies are sued or at risk of being sued. The accounting issue is whether the defendant should recognize a liability on its balance sheet or disclose a contingent liability in its notes while a lawsuit is outstanding and not yet settled. The answer is

Point: A sale of a note receivable "with recourse" is a contingent liability. It becomes a liability if the original signer of the note fails to pay it at maturity.

that a potential claim is recorded *only* if payment for damages is probable and the amount can be reasonably estimated. If the potential claim cannot be reasonably estimated but is reasonably possible, it is disclosed. **Ford Motor Company**, for example, includes the following note in its annual report: "Various legal actions, proceedings, and claims are pending . . . arising out of alleged defects in our products."

Debt Guarantees Sometimes a company guarantees the payment of debt owed by a supplier, customer, or another company. The guarantor usually discloses the guarantee in its financial statement notes as a contingent liability. If it is probable that the debtor will default, the guarantor needs to record and report the guarantee in its financial statements as a liability. The **Boston Celtics** report a unique guarantee when it comes to coaches and players: "Certain of the contracts provide for guaranteed payments which must be paid even if the employee [player] is injured or terminated."

Other Contingencies Other examples of contingencies include environmental damages, possible tax assessments, insurance losses, and government investigations. **Chevron**, for instance, reports that it "is subject to loss contingencies pursuant to laws, regulations, private claims and legal proceedings related to environmental matters that are subject to legal settlements or that in the future may require the company to take action to correct or ameliorate the effects on the environment of prior release of chemicals or petroleum substances. . . . Such contingencies may exist for various sites. . . . The amount of additional future costs are not fully determinable." Many of Chevron's contingencies are revealed only in notes.

Uncertainties That Are Not Contingencies

All organizations face uncertainties from future events such as natural disasters and the development of new competing products or services. These uncertainties are not contingent liabilities because they are future events *not* arising from past transactions. Accordingly, they are not disclosed.

 Decision Insight

At What Price? What's it worth to see from one side of the Grand Canyon to the other? What's the cost when Gulf Coast beaches are closed due to an oil well disaster? A method to measure environmental liabilities is *contingent valuation,* by which people answer such questions. Regulators use their answers to levy fines and assess punitive damages. ■

Courtesy of JJW Images

NEED-TO-KNOW 11-4

Contingent Liabilities

C3

The following legal claims exist for a company. Identify the accounting treatment for each claim as either (i) a liability that is recorded or (ii) an item described in notes to its financial statements. If an item is to be recorded, prepare the entry (date any entry Dec. 31).

a. The company (defendant) estimates that a pending lawsuit could result in damages of $500,000; it is reasonably possible that the plaintiff will win the case.

b. The company faces a probable loss on a pending lawsuit; the amount is not reasonably estimable.

c. The company estimates environmental damages in a pending case at $900,000 with a high probability of losing the case.

Solution

a. (ii); reason—is reasonably estimated but not a probable loss.

b. (ii); reason—probable loss but cannot be reasonably estimated.

c. (i); reason—can be reasonably estimated and loss is probable. The journal entry follows:

Dec. 31	Environmental Contingent Expense......................	900,000	
	Environmental Contingent Liability		900,000
	Record environmental contingent liability.		

Do More: QS 11-10, E 11-13

SUSTAINABILITY AND ACCOUNTING

Marcela Sapone and Jessica Beck's company, **Hello Alfred**, engages in sustainable practices by providing employees with paid time off and health insurance benefits. Employees of Hello Alfred are provided with benefits like health insurance and paid family leave. In discussing her employees, Marcela says, "we wanted to have the best possible relationship with the most important people in our business."

To provide employee benefits, Marcela and Jessica set up an accounting system to track benefit expenses to ensure employees receive what they are promised. This includes expenditures on employee health and vacation benefits each period. Although employee benefits are costly, Marcela insists "they are worth it."

Hello Alfred ensures its customers that they receive the best care from carefully screened "Alfreds." The company guarantees that its personal butlers, whom customers allow into their homes, have clean backgrounds. "They're literally inside people's homes," admits Marcela, "we wanted to make sure we trained them, and that we were able to do background and credit check them on a repetitive basis."

These practices keep customers and their belongings in the care of honest workers. Such practices reduce the risk of legal claims. Any such measurable and likely claims must be disclosed in the company's financial statements. As of yet, Hello Alfred has not had to and does not expect to disclose such claims. "We integrated these concepts into a scalable and sustainable business model," insists Marcela, "that we want to share with as many people as possible."

Courtesy of Hello Alfred

Times Interest Earned Ratio  **Decision Analysis**

A company incurs interest expense on many of its current and long-term liabilities. Examples extend from its short-term notes and the current portion of long-term liabilities to its long-term notes and bonds. Interest expense is often viewed as a *fixed expense* because the amount of these liabilities is likely to remain in one form or another for a substantial period of time. This means that the amount of interest is unlikely to vary due to changes in sales or other operating activities. While fixed expenses can be advantageous when a company is growing, they create risk. This risk stems from the possibility that a company might be unable to pay fixed expenses if sales decline. To illustrate, consider Diego Co.'s results for 2017 and two possible outcomes for year 2018 in Exhibit 11.6.

A1

Compute the times interest earned ratio and use it to analyze liabilities.

| $ millions | 2017 | 2018 Projections | |
		Sales Increase	Sales Decrease
Sales	$600	$900	$300
Expenses (75% of sales)	450	675	225
Income before interest	150	225	75
Interest expense (fixed)	60	60	60
Net income.....................	$ 90	$165	$ 15

EXHIBIT 11.6

Actual and Projected Results

Expenses excluding interest are at, and expected to remain at, 75% of sales. Expenses such as these that change with sales volume are called *variable expenses.* However, interest expense is at, and expected to remain at, $60 million per year due to its fixed nature.

The middle numerical column of Exhibit 11.6 shows that Diego's income increases by 83% to $165 million if sales increase by 50% to $900 million. In contrast, the far right column shows that income decreases by 83% if sales decline by 50%. These results reveal that the amount of fixed interest expense affects a company's risk of its ability to pay interest, which is numerically reflected in the **times interest earned** ratio in Exhibit 11.7.

$$\text{Times interest earned} = \frac{\text{Income before interest expense and income taxes}}{\text{Interest expense}}$$

EXHIBIT 11.7

Times Interest Earned

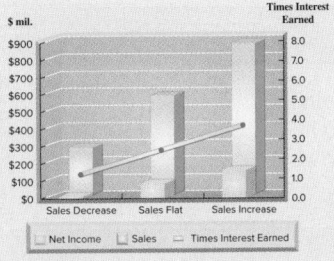

For 2017, Diego's times interest earned is computed as $150 mil./$60 mil., or 2.5 times. This ratio suggests that Diego faces low to moderate risk because its sales must decline sharply before it would be unable to cover its interest expenses. (Diego is an LLC and does not pay income taxes.)

Experience shows that when times interest earned falls below 1.5 to 2.0 and remains at that level or lower for several periods, the default rate on liabilities increases sharply. This reflects increased risk for companies and their creditors. We also must interpret the times interest earned ratio in light of information about the variability of a company's income before interest. If income is stable from year to year or if it is growing, the company can afford to take on added risk by borrowing. If its income greatly varies from year to year, fixed interest expense can increase the risk that it will not earn enough income to pay interest.

■ Decision Maker

Entrepreneur You wish to invest in a franchise for either one of two national chains. Each franchise has an expected annual net income *after* interest and taxes of $100,000. Net income for the first franchise includes a regular fixed interest charge of $200,000. The fixed interest charge for the second franchise is $40,000. Which franchise is riskier to you if sales forecasts are not met? Does your decision change if the first franchise has more variability in its income stream? ■ [*Answer:* Risk is partly reflected by times interest earned. This ratio for the first franchise is 1.5 [($100,000 + $200,000)/$200,000], whereas it is 3.5 for the second [($100,000 + $40,000)/$40,000]. This shows the first franchise is more at risk of incurring a loss if its sales decline. The second question asks about income variability. If income greatly varies, this increases the risk of not earning sufficient income to cover interest. Because the first franchise has greater variability, it is a riskier investment.]

NEED-TO-KNOW 11-5

COMPREHENSIVE

The following transactions and events took place at Kern Company during its recent calendar-year reporting period (Kern does *not* use reversing entries).

a. In September 2017, Kern sold $140,000 of merchandise covered by a 180-day warranty. Prior experience shows that costs of the warranty equal 5% of sales. Compute September's warranty expense and prepare the adjusting journal entry for the warranty liability as recorded at September 30. Also prepare the journal entry on October 8 to record a $300 cash expenditure to provide warranty service on an item sold in September.

b. On October 12, 2017, Kern arranged with a supplier to replace Kern's overdue $10,000 account payable by paying $2,500 cash and signing a note for the remainder. The note matures in 90 days and has a 12% interest rate. Prepare the entries recorded on October 12, December 31, and January 10, 2018, related to this transaction.

c. In late December, Kern learns it is facing a product liability suit filed by an unhappy customer. Kern's lawyer advises that although it will probably suffer a loss from the lawsuit, it is not possible to estimate the amount of damages at this time.

d. Sally Bline works for Kern. For the pay period ended November 30, her gross earnings are $3,000. Bline has $800 deducted for federal income taxes and $200 for state income taxes from each paycheck. Additionally, a $35 premium for her health care insurance and a $10 donation to the United Way are deducted. Bline pays FICA Social Security taxes at a rate of 6.2% and FICA Medicare taxes at a rate of 1.45%. She has not earned enough this year to be exempt from any FICA taxes. Journalize the accrual of salaries expense of Bline's wages by Kern.

e. On November 1, Kern borrows $5,000 cash from a bank in return for a 60-day, 12%, $5,000 note. Record the note's issuance on November 1 and its repayment with interest on December 31.

f.^B *(Part f covers Appendix 11B.)* Kern has estimated and recorded its quarterly income tax payments. In reviewing its year-end tax adjustments, it identifies an additional $5,000 of income tax expense that should be recorded. A portion of this additional expense, $1,000, is deferred to future years. Record this year-end income taxes expense adjusting entry.

g. For this calendar year, Kern's net income is $1,000,000, its interest expense is $275,000, and its income taxes expense is $225,000. Compute Kern's times interest earned ratio.

PLANNING THE SOLUTION

- For *a,* compute the warranty expense for September and record it with an estimated liability. Record the October expenditure as a decrease in the liability.

- For *b,* eliminate the liability for the account payable and create the liability for the note payable. Compute interest expense for the 80 days that the note is outstanding in 2017 and record it as an additional liability. Record the payment of the note, being sure to include the interest for the 10 days in 2018.

- For *c*, decide whether the company's contingent liability needs to be disclosed or accrued (recorded) according to the two necessary criteria: probable loss and reasonably estimable.
- For *d*, set up payable accounts for all items in Bline's paycheck that require deductions. After deducting all necessary items, credit the remaining amount to Salaries Payable.
- For *e*, record the issuance of the note. Compute 60 days' interest due using the 360-day convention in the interest formula.
- For *f*, determine how much of the income taxes expense is payable in the current year and how much needs to be deferred.
- For *g*, apply and compute times interest earned.

SOLUTION

a. Warranty expense = 5% × $140,000 = **$7,000**

Sep. 30	Warranty Expense	7,000	
	Estimated Warranty Liability.		7,000
	Record warranty expense for month.		
Oct. 8	Estimated Warranty Liability	300	
	Cash		300
	Record cost of warranty service.		

b. Interest expense for 2017 = 12% × $7,500 × 80/360 = $200
Interest expense for 2018 = 12% × $7,500 × 10/360 = $25

Oct. 12	Accounts Payable	10,000	
	Notes Payable.		7,500
	Cash		2,500
	Paid $2,500 cash and gave a 90-day, 12% note *to extend due date on the account.*		
Dec. 31	Interest Expense	200	
	Interest Payable		200
	Accrue interest on note payable.		
Jan. 10	Interest Expense	25	
	Interest Payable.	200	
	Notes Payable	7,500	
	Cash		7,725
	Paid note with interest, including accrued interest payable.		

c. Disclose the pending lawsuit in the financial statement notes. Although the loss is probable, no liability can be accrued since the loss cannot be reasonably estimated.

d.

Nov. 30	Salaries Expense	3,000.00	
	FICA—Social Security Taxes Payable (6.2%)		186.00
	FICA—Medicare Taxes Payable (1.45%)		43.50
	Employee Federal Income Taxes Payable		800.00
	Employee State Income Taxes Payable		200.00
	Employee Medical Insurance Payable		35.00
	Employee United Way Payable		10.00
	Salaries Payable		1,725.50
	Record Bline's accrued payroll.		

e.

Nov. 1	Cash	5,000	
	Notes Payable.		5,000
	Borrowed cash with a 60-day, 12% note.		

When the note and interest are paid 60 days later, Kern Company records this entry:

Dec. 31	Notes Payable	5,000	
	Interest Expense	100	
	Cash		5,100
	Paid note with interest ($5,000 × 12% × 60/360).		

f.^B

Dec. 31	Income Taxes Expense	5,000	
	Income Taxes Payable		4,000
	Deferred Income Tax Liability		1,000
	Record added income taxes expense and the deferred tax liability.		

g. Times interest earned = $\dfrac{\$1,000,000 + \$275,000 + \$225,000}{\$275,000} = \underline{\underline{5.45 \text{ times}}}$

APPENDIX

11A

Payroll Reports, Records, and Procedures

Understanding payroll procedures and keeping adequate payroll reports and records are essential. This appendix focuses on payroll accounting and its reports, records, and procedures.

P5

Identify and describe the details of payroll reports, records, and procedures.

Payroll Reports   Most employees and employers are required to pay local, state, and federal payroll taxes. Payroll expenses involve liabilities to individual employees, to federal and state governments, and to other organizations such as insurance companies. Beyond paying these liabilities, employers are required to prepare and submit reports explaining how they computed these payments.

Reporting FICA Taxes and Income Taxes   The Federal Insurance Contributions Act (FICA) requires each employer to file an Internal Revenue Service (IRS) **Form 941,** the *Employer's Quarterly Federal Tax Return,* within one month after the end of each calendar quarter. A sample Form 941 is shown in Exhibit 11A.1 for Phoenix Sales & Service, a landscape design company. Accounting information and software are helpful in tracking payroll transactions and reporting the accumulated information on Form 941. Specifically, the employer reports total wages subject to income tax withholding on line 2 of Form 941. (For simplicity, this appendix uses *wages* to refer to both wages and salaries.) The income tax withheld is reported on line 3. The combined amount of employee and employer FICA (Social Security) taxes for Phoenix Sales & Service is reported on line 5a (taxable Social Security wages, $36,599 × 12.4% = $4,538.28). The 12.4% is the sum of the Social Security tax withheld, computed as 6.2% tax withheld from the employee wages for the quarter, plus the 6.2% tax levied on the employer. The combined amount of employee Medicare wages is reported on line 5c. The 2.9% is the sum of 1.45% withheld from employee wages for the quarter plus 1.45% tax levied on the employer. Total FICA taxes are reported on line 5d and are added to the total income taxes withheld of $3,056.47 to yield a total of $8,656.12. For this year, assume that income up to $118,500 is subject to Social Security tax. There is no income limit on amounts subject to Medicare tax. Congress sets rates owed for Social Security tax (and it typically changes each year).

Federal depository banks are authorized to accept deposits of amounts payable to the federal government. Deposit requirements depend on the amount of tax owed. For example, when the sum of FICA taxes plus the employee income taxes is less than $2,500 for a quarter, the taxes can be paid when Form 941 is filed.

Point: Deposits for federal payroll taxes must be made by electronic funds transfer (EFT).

Form **941**

Employer's QUARTERLY Federal Tax Return

Department of the Treasury — Internal Revenue Service

(EIN)
Employer identification number   8 6 – 3 2 1 4 5 8 7

Name (not your trade name)   Phoenix Sales & Service

Trade name (if any)

Address   1214   Mill Road
Number   Street   Suite or room number

Phoenix   AZ   85621
City   State   ZIP code

Report for this Quarter ...
(Check one.)

☐ **1:** January, February, March
☐ **2:** April, May, June
☐ **3:** July, August, September
☒ **4:** October, November, December

Part 1: Answer these questions for this quarter.

1 Number of employees who received wages, tips, or other compensation for the pay period including: *Mar. 12* (Quarter 1), *June 12* (Quarter 2), *Sept. 12* (Quarter 3), *Dec. 12* (Quarter 4)	1	2
2 Wages, tips, and other compensation	2	36,599.00
3 Total income tax withheld from wages, tips, and other compensation	3	3,056.47

4 If no wages, tips, and other compensation are subject to social security or Medicare tax. ☐ Check and go to line 6.

5 Taxable social security and Medicare wages and tips:

	Column 1		Column 2
5a Taxable social security wages	36,599.00	× .124 =	4,538.28
5b Taxable social security tips		× .124 =	
5c Taxable Medicare wages & tips	36,599.00	× .029 =	1,061.37

5d Total social security and Medicare taxes (*Column 2*, lines 5a + 5b + 5c = line 5d)	5d	5,599.65
6 Total taxes before adjustments (lines 3 + 5d = line 6)	6	8,656.12

7 **TAX ADJUSTMENTS** (Read the instructions for line 7 before completing lines 7a through 7h.):

7a Current quarter's fractions of cents	.
7b Current quarter's sick pay	.
7c Current quarter's adjustments for tips and group-term life insurance	.
7d Current year's income tax withholding (attach Form 941c)	.
7e Prior quarters' social security and Medicare taxes (attach Form 941c)	.
7f Special additions to federal income tax (attach Form 941c)	.
7g Special additions to social security and Medicare (attach Form 941c)	.

7h **TOTAL ADJUSTMENTS** (Combine all amounts: lines 7a through 7g.)	7h	0.00
8 Total taxes after adjustments (Combine lines 6 and 7h.)	8	8,656.12
9 Advance earned income credit (EIC) payments made to employees	9	
10 Total taxes after adjustment for advance EIC (lines 8 – line 9 = line 10)	10	8,656.12
11 Total deposits for this quarter, including overpayment applied from a prior quarter.	11	8,656.12
12 Balance due (If line 10 is more than line 11, write the difference here.) Make checks payable to *United States Treasury*.	12	0.00

13 Overpayment (If line 11 is more than line 10, write the difference here.)   0.00   Check one ☐ Apply to next return.
☐ Send a refund.

Part 2: Tell us about your deposit schedule and tax liability for this quarter.

If you are unsure about whether you are a monthly schedule depositor or a semiweekly schedule depositor, see *Pub. 15 (Circular E)*, section 11.

14   A Z   Write the state abbreviation for the state where you made your deposits OR write "MU" if you made your deposits in *multiple* states.

15 Check one: ☐ Line 10 is less than $2,500. Go to Part 3.

☒ You were a monthly schedule depositor for the entire quarter. Fill out your tax liability for each month. Then go to Part 3.

Tax liability:	Month 1	3,079.11	
	Month 2	2,049.77	
	Month 3	3,527.24	
	Total liability for quarter	8,656.12	Total must equal line 10.

☐ You were a semiweekly schedule depositor for any part of this quarter. Fill out *Schedule B (Form 941): Report of Tax Liability for Semiweekly Schedule Depositors*, and attach it to this form.

Part 3: Tell us about your business. If a question does NOT apply to your business, leave it blank.

16 If your business has closed or you stopped paying wages . . . . ☐ Check here, and

enter the final date you paid wages   /   /

17 If you are a seasonal employer and you do not have to file a return for every quarter of the year . . . ☐ Check here.

Part 4: May we speak with your third-party designee?

Do you want to allow an employee, a paid tax preparer, or another person to discuss this return with the IRS? See the instructions for details.

☐ Yes. Designee's name

Phone ( )   –   Personal Identification Number (PIN) ☐☐☐☐☐

☒ No.

Part 5: Sign here. You MUST fill out both sides of this form and SIGN it.

Under penalties of perjury, I declare that I have examined this return, including accompanying schedules and statements, and to the best of my knowledge and belief, it is true, correct, and complete.

✗ Sign your name here

Print name and title

Date   /   /   Phone ( )   –

Point: Line 5a shows the matching nature of FICA tax as 6.2% × 2, or 12.4%; which is shown as 0.124.

Point: Auditors rely on the four 941 forms filed during a year when auditing a company's annual wages and salaries expense account.

Reporting FUTA Taxes and SUTA Taxes   An employer's federal unemployment taxes (FUTA) are reported on an annual basis by filing an *Annual Federal Unemployment Tax Return,* IRS **Form 940.** It must be mailed on or before January 31 following the end of each tax year. Ten more days are allowed if all required tax deposits are filed on a timely basis and the full amount of tax is paid on or before January 31. FUTA payments are made quarterly to a federal depository bank if the total amount due exceeds $500. If $500 or less is due, the taxes are remitted annually. Requirements for paying and reporting state unemployment taxes (SUTA) vary depending on the laws of each state. Most states require quarterly payments and reports.

Reporting Wages and Salaries   Employers are required to give each employee an annual report of his or her wages subject to FICA and federal income taxes along with the amounts of these taxes withheld. This report is called a *Wage and Tax Statement,* or **Form W-2.** It must be given to employees before January 31 following the year covered by the report. Exhibit 11A.2 shows Form W-2 for one of the employees at Phoenix Sales & Service. Copies of Form W-2 must be sent to the Social Security Administration, where the amount of the employee's wages subject to FICA taxes and FICA taxes withheld are posted to each employee's Social Security account. These posted amounts become the basis for determining an employee's retirement and survivors' benefits. The Social Security Administration also transmits to the IRS the amount of each employee's wages subject to federal income taxes and the amount of taxes withheld.

EXHIBIT 11A.2

Form W-2

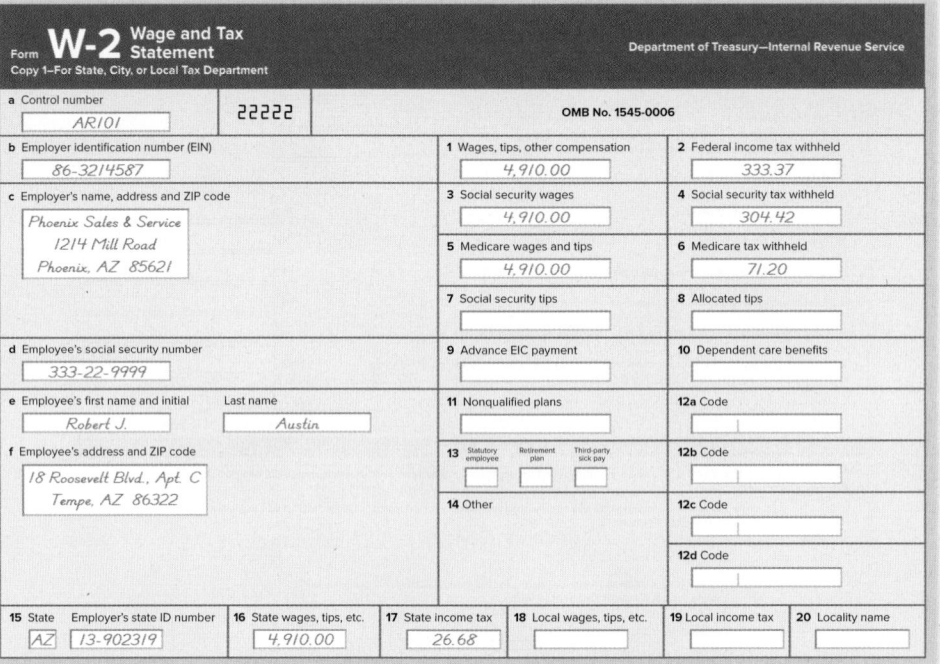

Payroll Records   Employers must keep payroll records in addition to reporting and paying taxes. These records usually include a payroll register and an individual earnings report for each employee.

Payroll Register   A **payroll register** usually shows the pay period dates, hours worked, gross pay, deductions, and net pay of each employee for each pay period. Exhibit 11A.3 shows a payroll register for Phoenix Sales & Service. It is organized into nine columns:

Col. A   Employee identification (ID); Employee name; Social Security number (SS No.); Reference (check number); and Date (date check issued)
Col. B   Pay Type (regular and overtime)
Col. C   Pay Hours (number of hours worked as regular and overtime)
Col. D   Gross Pay (amount of gross pay)[2]

---

[2] The Gross Pay column shows regular hours worked on the first line multiplied by the regular pay rate—this equals regular pay. Overtime hours multiplied by the overtime premium rate equals overtime premium pay reported on the second line. If employers are engaged in interstate commerce, federal law sets a minimum overtime rate of pay to employees. For this company, workers earn 150% of their regular rate for hours in excess of 40 per week.

EXHIBIT 11A.3

Payroll Register

	A	B	C	D	E	F	G	H	I
1				Phoenix Sales & Service					
2				Payroll Register					
3				For Week Ended Jan. 8, 2017					
4	Employee ID	Gross Pay			FIT	SIT	FICA-SS_EE	FICA-Med_EE	
5	Employee				[blank]	[blank]	[blank]	[blank]	Net
6	SS No.	Pay	Pay	Gross					Pay
7	Refer., Date	Type	Hours	Pay	FUTA	SUTA	FICA-SS_ER	FICA-Med_ER	
8	AR101	Regular	40.00	400.00	−28.99	−2.32	−24.80	−5.80	338.09
9	Robert Austin	Overtime	0.00	0.00					
10	333-22-9999			400.00	−2.40	−10.80	−24.80	−5.80	
11	9001, 1/8/17								
12	CJ102	Regular	40.00	560.00	−52.97	−4.24	−36.02	−8.42	479.35
13	Judy Cross	Overtime	1.00	21.00					
14	299-11-9201			581.00	−3.49	−15.69	−36.02	−8.42	
15	9002, 1/8/17								
16	DJ103	Regular	40.00	560.00	−48.33	−3.87	−37.32	−8.73	503.75
17	John Diaz	Overtime	2.00	42.00					
18	444-11-9090			602.00	−3.61	−16.25	−37.32	−8.73	
19	9003, 1/8/17								
20	KK104	Regular	40.00	560.00	−68.57	−5.49	−34.72	−8.12	443.10
21	Kay Keife	Overtime	0.00	0.00					
22	909-11-3344			560.00	−3.36	−15.12	−34.72	−8.12	
23	9004, 1/8/17								
24	ML105	Regular	40.00	560.00	−34.24	−2.74	−34.72	−8.12	480.18
25	Lee Miller	Overtime	0.00	0.00					
26	444-56-3211			560.00	−3.36	−15.12	−34.72	−8.12	
27	9005, 1/8/17								
28	SD106	Regular	40.00	560.00	−68.57	−5.49	−34.72	−8.12	443.10
29	Dale Sears	Overtime	0.00	0.00					
30	909-33-1234			560.00	−3.36	−15.12	−34.72	−8.12	
31	9006, 1/8/17								
32	Totals	Regular	240.00	3,200.00	−301.67	−24.15	−202.30	−47.31	2,687.57
33		Overtime	3.00	63.00					
34				3,263.00	−19.58	−88.10	−202.30	−47.31	

Col. E FIT (federal income taxes withheld); FUTA (federal unemployment taxes)

Col. F SIT (state income taxes withheld); SUTA (state unemployment taxes)

Col. G FICA-SS_EE (Social Security taxes withheld, employee); FICA-SS_ER (Social Security taxes, employer)

Col. H FICA-Med_EE (Medicare tax withheld, employee); FICA-Med_ER (Medicare tax, employer)

Col. I Net Pay (gross pay less amounts withheld from employees)

Net pay for each employee is computed as gross pay minus the items on the first line of columns E through H. The employer's payroll tax for each employee is computed as the sum of items on the third line of columns E through H. A payroll register includes all data necessary to record payroll. In some software programs the entries to record payroll are made in a special *payroll journal*.

Payroll Check Payment of payroll is usually done by check or electronic funds transfer. Exhibit 11A.4 shows a *payroll check* for a Phoenix employee. This check is accompanied with a detachable *statement of earnings* (at top) showing gross pay, deductions, and net pay.

Employee Earnings Report An **employee earnings report** is a cumulative record of an employee's hours worked, gross earnings, deductions, and net pay. Payroll information on this report is taken from the payroll register. The employee earnings report for R. Austin at Phoenix Sales & Service is shown in Exhibit 11A.5. An employee earnings report accumulates information that can show when an employee's earnings reach the tax-exempt points for FICA, FUTA, and SUTA taxes. It also gives data an employer needs to prepare Form W-2.

Payroll Procedures Employers must be able to compute federal income tax for payroll purposes. This section explains how we compute this tax and how to use a payroll bank account.

Computing Federal Income Taxes To compute the amount of taxes withheld from each employee's wages, we need to determine both the employee's wages earned and the employee's number of *withholding*

EXHIBIT 11A.4

Check and Statement of Earnings

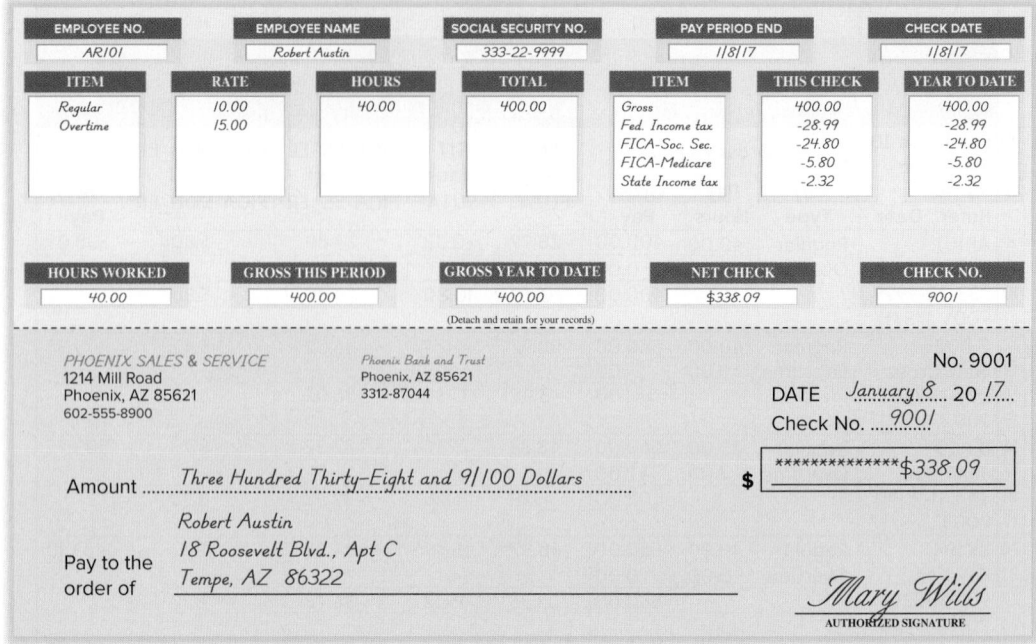

EXHIBIT 11A.5

Employee Earnings Report

	A	B	C	D	E	F	G	H
1			**Phoenix Sales & Service**					
2			**Employee Earnings Report**					
3			**For Month Ended Dec. 31, 2017**					
4	**Employee ID**			**FIT**	**SIT**	**FICA-SS_EE**	**FICA-Med_EE**	
5	**Employee**	**Date**	**Gross**	[blank]	[blank]	[blank]	[blank]	**Net**
6	**SS No.**	**Reference**	**Pay**	**FUTA**	**SUTA**	**FICA-SS_ER**	**FICA-Med_ER**	**Pay**
7	Beginning	11/26/17	2,910.00	−188.42	−15.08	−180.42	−42.20	2,483.88
8	balance for	(balance)						
9	Robert Austin			−17.46	−78.57	−180.42	−42.20	
10	AR101	12/03/17	400.00	−28.99	−2.32	−24.80	−5.80	338.09
11	Robert Austin	9049						
12	333-22-9999			−2.40	−10.80	−24.80	−5.80	
13	AR101	12/10/17	400.00	−28.99	−2.32	−24.80	−5.80	338.09
14	Robert Austin	9055						
15	333-22-9999			−2.40	−10.80	−24.80	−5.80	
16	AR101	12/17/17	400.00	−28.99	−2.32	−24.80	−5.80	338.09
17	Robert Austin	9061						
18	333-22-9999			−2.40	−10.80	−24.80	−5.80	
19	AR101	12/24/17	400.00	−28.99	−2.32	−24.80	−5.80	338.09
20	Robert Austin	9067						
21	333-22-9999			−2.40	−10.80	−24.80	−5.80	
22	AR101	12/31/17	400.00	−28.99	−2.32	−24.80	−5.80	338.09
23	Robert Austin	9073						
24	333-22-9999			−2.40	−10.80	−24.80	−5.80	
25	Total 5-wk month		2,000.00	−144.95	−11.60	−124.00	−29.00	1,690.45
26	thru 12/31/17							
27				−12.00	−54.00	−124.00	−29.00	
28	Year-to-date	12/31/17	4,910.00	−333.37	−26.68	−304.42	−71.20	4,174.33
29	total for Robert	(balance)						
30	Austin			−29.46	−132.57	−304.42	−71.20	

Point: Year-end balances agree with W-2.

allowances. Each employee records the number of withholding allowances claimed on a withholding allowance certificate, **Form W-4,** filed with the employer. When the number of withholding allowances increases, the amount of income taxes withheld decreases.

Employers often use a **wage bracket withholding table** similar to the one shown in Exhibit 11A.6 to compute the **federal income taxes withheld** from each employee's gross pay. The table in Exhibit 11A.6 is for a single employee paid weekly. Tables are also provided for married employees and for biweekly, semimonthly, and monthly pay periods (most payroll software includes these tables). When using a wage bracket withholding table to compute federal income tax withheld from an employee's gross wages, we need to locate an employee's wage bracket within the first two columns. We then find the amount withheld by looking in the withholding allowance column for that employee.

EXHIBIT 11A.6

Wage Bracket
Withholding Table

SINGLE Persons—WEEKLY Payroll Period												
If the wages are—		And the number of withholding allowances claimed is—										
At least	But less than	0	1	2	3	4	5	6	7	8	9	10
		The amount of income tax to be withheld is—										
$600	$610	$76	$67	$58	$49	$39	$30	$21	$12	$6	$0	$0
610	620	79	69	59	50	41	32	22	13	7	1	0
620	630	81	70	61	52	42	33	24	15	8	2	0
630	640	84	72	62	53	44	35	25	16	9	3	0
640	650	86	73	64	55	45	36	27	18	10	4	0
650	660	89	75	65	56	47	38	28	19	11	5	0
660	670	91	76	67	58	48	39	30	21	12	6	0
670	680	94	78	68	59	50	41	31	22	13	7	1
680	690	96	81	70	61	51	42	33	24	14	8	2
690	700	99	83	71	62	53	44	34	25	16	9	3
700	710	101	86	73	64	54	45	35	27	17	10	4
710	720	104	88	74	65	56	47	37	28	19	11	5
720	730	106	91	76	67	57	48	39	30	20	12	6
730	740	109	93	78	68	59	50	40	31	22	13	7
740	750	111	96	80	70	60	51	42	33	23	14	8

Payroll Bank Account   Companies with few employees often pay them with checks drawn on the company's regular bank account. Companies with many employees often use a special **payroll bank account** to pay employees. When this account is used, a company either (1) draws one check for total payroll on the regular bank account and deposits it in the payroll bank account or (2) executes an *electronic funds transfer* to the payroll bank account. Individual payroll checks are then drawn on this payroll bank account. Since only one check for the total payroll is drawn on the regular bank account each payday, use of a special payroll bank account helps with internal control. It also helps in reconciling the regular bank account. When companies use a payroll bank account, they usually include check numbers in the payroll register. The payroll register in Exhibit 11A.3 shows check numbers in column 1. For instance, Check No. 9001 is issued to Robert Austin. With this information, the payroll register serves as a supplementary record of wages earned by and paid to employees.

Who Pays What Payroll Taxes and Benefits   We conclude this appendix with the following table identifying who pays which payroll taxes and which common employee benefits such as medical, disability, pension, charitable, and union costs. Who pays which employee benefits, and what portion, is subject to agreements between companies and their workers. Also, self-employed workers must pay both the employer and employee FICA taxes for Social Security and Medicare.

Employer Payroll Taxes and Costs	Employee Payroll Deductions
• FICA—Social Security taxes	• FICA—Social Security taxes
• FICA—Medicare taxes	• FICA—Medicare taxes
• FUTA (federal unemployment taxes)	• Federal income taxes
• SUTA (state unemployment taxes)	• State and local income taxes
• Share of medical coverage, if any	• Share of medical coverage, if any
• Share of pension coverage, if any	• Share of pension coverage, if any
• Share of other benefits, if any	• Share of other benefits, if any

Point: IRS *Statistics of Income Bulletin* (Winter 2012) reports the following average (effective) income tax rate for different categories of U.S. income earners:

Top 1%.	24%
Top 5%.	20%
Top 10%	18%
Bottom 50%	1.85%

11B

Corporate Income Taxes

This appendix explains current liabilities involving income taxes for C corporations. Income tax on sole proprietorships, partnerships, S corporations, and limited liability companies (LLCs) is computed on their owner's tax filings and is not covered here.

Income Tax Liabilities   Corporations are subject to income taxes and must estimate their income tax liability when preparing financial statements. Since income tax expense is created by earning income, a liability is incurred when income is earned. This tax must be paid quarterly under federal regulations. To illustrate, consider a corporation that prepares monthly financial statements. Based on its income in January 2017, this corporation estimates that it owes income taxes of $12,100. The following adjusting entry records this estimate:

Assets = Liabilities + Equity
+12,100   −12,100

Jan. 31	Income Taxes Expense	12,100	
	Income Taxes Payable		12,100
	Accrue January income taxes.		

The tax liability is recorded each month until the first quarterly payment is made. If the company's estimated taxes for this first quarter total $30,000, the entry to record its payment is

Assets = Liabilities + Equity
−30,000   −30,000

Apr. 10	Income Taxes Payable	30,000	
	Cash		30,000
	Paid estimated quarterly income taxes based on		
	first-quarter income.		

This process of accruing and then paying estimated income taxes continues through the year. When annual financial statements are prepared at year-end, the corporation knows its actual total income and the actual amount of income taxes it must pay. This information allows it to properly record income taxes expense for the fourth quarter so that the total of the four quarters' expense amounts equals the actual taxes paid to the government.

Deferred Income Tax Liabilities   An income tax liability for corporations can arise when the amount of income before taxes that the corporation reports on its income statement is not the same as the amount of income reported on its income tax return. This difference occurs because income tax laws and GAAP measure income differently. (Differences between tax laws and GAAP arise because Congress uses tax laws to generate receipts, stimulate the economy, and influence behavior, whereas GAAP is intended to provide financial information useful for business decisions. Also, tax accounting often follows the cash basis, whereas GAAP follows the accrual basis.)

Some differences between tax laws and GAAP are temporary. *Temporary differences* arise when the tax return and the income statement report a revenue or expense in different years. As an example, companies are often able to deduct higher amounts of depreciation in the early years of an asset's life and smaller amounts in later years for tax reporting in comparison to GAAP. This means that in the early years, depreciation for tax reporting is often more than depreciation on the income statement. In later years, depreciation for tax reporting is often less than depreciation on the income statement. When temporary differences exist between taxable income on the tax return and the income before taxes on the income statement, corporations compute income taxes expense based on the income reported on the income statement. The result is that income taxes expense reported in the income statement is often different from the amount of income taxes payable to the government. This difference is the **deferred income tax liability.**

To illustrate, assume that in recording its usual quarterly income tax payments, a corporation computes $25,000 of income taxes expense. It also determines that only $21,000 is currently due and $4,000 is deferred to future years (a timing difference). The entry to record this end-of-period adjustment is

Assets = Liabilities + Equity
+21,000   −25,000
+4,000

Dec. 31	Income Taxes Expense	25,000	
	Income Taxes Payable		21,000
	Deferred Income Tax Liability		4,000
	Record tax expense and deferred tax liability.		

The credit to Income Taxes Payable reflects the amount currently due to be paid. The credit to Deferred Income Tax Liability reflects tax payments deferred until future years when the temporary difference reverses.

Temporary differences also can cause a company to pay income taxes *before* they are reported on the income statement as expense. If so, the company reports a *Deferred Income Tax Asset* on its balance sheet.

Summary

C1 **Describe current and long-term liabilities and their characteristics.** Liabilities are probable future payments of assets or services that past transactions or events obligate an entity to make. Current liabilities are due within one year or the operating cycle, whichever is longer. All other liabilities are long term.

C2 **Identify and describe known current liabilities.** Known (determinable) current liabilities are set by agreements or laws and are measurable with little uncertainty. They include accounts payable, sales taxes payable, unearned revenues, notes payable, payroll liabilities, and the current portion of long-term debt.

C3 **Explain how to account for contingent liabilities.** If an uncertain future payment depends on a probable future event and the amount can be reasonably estimated, the payment is recorded as a liability. The uncertain future payment is reported as a contingent liability (in the notes) if (*a*) the future event is reasonably possible but not probable or (*b*) the event is probable but the payment amount cannot be reasonably estimated.

A1 **Compute the times interest earned ratio and use it to analyze liabilities.** Times interest earned is computed by dividing a company's net income before interest expense and income taxes by the amount of interest expense. The times interest earned ratio reflects a company's ability to pay interest obligations.

P1 **Prepare entries to account for short-term notes payable.** Short-term notes payable are current liabilities; most bear interest. When a short-term note's face value equals the amount borrowed, it identifies a rate of interest to be paid at maturity.

P2 **Compute and record *employee* payroll deductions and liabilities.** Employee payroll deductions include FICA taxes, income taxes, and voluntary deductions such as for pensions and charities. They make up the difference between gross and net pay.

P3 **Compute and record *employer* payroll expenses and liabilities.** An employer's payroll expenses include employees' gross earnings, any employee benefits, and the payroll taxes levied on the employer. Payroll liabilities include employees' net pay amounts, withholdings from employee wages, any employer-promised benefits, and the employer's payroll taxes.

P4 **Account for estimated liabilities, including warranties and bonuses.** Liabilities for health and pension benefits, warranties, and bonuses are recorded with estimated amounts. These items are recognized as expenses when incurred and matched with revenues generated.

P5^A **Identify and describe the details of payroll reports, records, and procedures.** Employers report FICA taxes and federal income tax withholdings using Form 941. FUTA taxes are reported on Form 940. Earnings and deductions are reported to each employee and the federal government on Form W-2. An employer's payroll records often include a payroll register for each pay period, payroll checks and statements of earnings, and individual employee earnings reports.

Key Terms

Contingent liability	Federal Insurance Contributions Act (FICA) taxes	Merit rating
Current liabilities		Net pay
Current portion of long-term debt	Federal Unemployment Tax Act (FUTA)	Payroll bank account
Deferred income tax liability	Form 940	Payroll deductions
Employee benefits	Form 941	Payroll register
Employee earnings report	Form W-2	Short-term note payable
Estimated liability	Form W-4	State Unemployment Tax Act (SUTA)
Federal depository bank	Gross pay	Times interest earned
Federal income taxes withheld	Known liabilities	Wage bracket withholding table
	Long-term liabilities	Warranty

Multiple Choice Quiz

1. On December 1, a company signed a $6,000, 90-day, 5% note payable, with principal plus interest due on March 1 of the following year. What amount of interest expense should be accrued at December 31 on the note?

   a. $300   c. $100   e. $0

   b. $25   d. $75

2. An employee earned $50,000 during the year. FICA tax for Social Security is 6.2% and FICA tax for Medicare is 1.45%. The employer's share of FICA taxes is

   a. Zero, since the employee's pay exceeds the FICA limit.

   b. Zero, since FICA is not an employer tax.

   c. $3,100

   d. $725

   e. $3,825

3. Assume the FUTA tax rate is 0.6% and the SUTA tax rate is 5.4%. Both taxes are applied to the first $7,000 of an employee's pay. What is the total unemployment tax an employer must pay on an employee's annual wages of $40,000?

   a. $2,400

   b. $420

   c. $42

   d. $378

   e. Zero; the employee's wages exceed the $7,000 maximum.

4. A company sells big-screen televisions for $3,000 each. Each television has a two-year warranty that covers the replacement of defective parts. It is estimated that 1% of all televisions sold will be returned under warranty at an average cost of $250 each. During July, the company sold 10,000 big-screen televisions, and 80 were serviced under the warranty during July at a total cost of $18,000. The credit balance in the Estimated Warranty Liability account at July 1 was $26,000. What is the company's warranty expense for the month of July?

   a. $51,000   c. $25,000   e. $18,000

   b. $1,000   d. $33,000

5. Employees earn vacation pay at the rate of one day per month. During October, 150 employees qualify for one vacation day each. Their average daily wage is $175 per day. What is the amount of vacation benefit expense for October?

   a. $26,250   c. $2,100   e. $150

   b. $175   d. $63,875

ANSWERS TO MULTIPLE CHOICE QUIZ

1. b; $6,000 × 0.05 × 30/360 = $25
2. e; $50,000 × (0.062 + 0.0145) = $3,825
3. b; $7,000 × (0.006 + 0.054) = $420
4. c; 10,000 television sets × 0.01 × $250 = $25,000
5. a; 150 employees × $175 per day × 1 vacation day earned = $26,250

$^{A(B)}$ *Superscript letter A (B) denotes assignments based on Appendix 11A (11B).*

🔲 Icon denotes assignments that involve decision making.

Discussion Questions

1. 🔲 What is the difference between a current and a long-term liability?

2. What is an estimated liability?

3. 🔲 What are the three important questions concerning the uncertainty of liabilities?

4. If $988 is the total of a sale that includes sales tax of 4%, what is the selling price of the item only?

5. What is the combined amount (in percent) of the employee and employer Social Security tax rate? (Assume wages do not exceed $118,500 per year.)

6. What is the current Medicare tax rate? This rate is applied to what maximum level of salary and wages?

7. Which payroll taxes are the employee's responsibility and which are the employer's responsibility?

8. What determines the amount deducted from an employee's wages for federal income taxes?

9. What is an employer's unemployment merit rating? How are these ratings assigned to employers?

10. 🔲 Why are warranty liabilities usually recognized on the balance sheet as liabilities even when they are uncertain?

11. 🔲 Suppose a company has a facility located where disastrous weather conditions often occur. Should it report a probable loss from a future disaster as a liability on its balance sheet? Explain.

12.^{A} What is a wage bracket withholding table?

13.^{A} What amount of income tax is withheld from the salary of an employee who is single with two withholding allowances and earns $725 per week? What if the employee earns $625 and has no withholding allowances? (Use Exhibit 11A.6.)

14. Refer to **Apple**'s balance sheet in Appendix A. What is the amount of Apple's accounts payable as of September 26, 2015?   **APPLE**

15. 🔲 Refer to **Google**'s balance sheet in Appendix A. What "accrued" expenses (liabilities) does Google report at December 31, 2015?   **GOOGLE**

16. 🌐 Refer to **Samsung**'s balance sheet in Appendix A. List Samsung's current liabilities as of December 31, 2015.   **Samsung**

17. 🌐 Refer to **Samsung**'s recent balance sheet in Appendix A. What current liabilities related to income taxes are on its balance sheet? Explain the meaning of each income tax account identified.   **Samsung**

connect

Which of the following items are normally classified as current liabilities for a company that has a 15-month operating cycle?

_____ **1.** Portion of long-term note due in 15 months.

_____ **2.** Note payable maturing in 2 years.

_____ **3.** Note payable due in 18 months.

_____ **4.** Note payable due in 11 months.

_____ **5.** FICA taxes payable.

_____ **6.** Salaries payable.

QUICK STUDY

QS 11-1

Classifying liabilities

C1 🏛

Dextra Computing sells merchandise for $6,000 cash on September 30 (cost of merchandise is $3,900). The sales tax law requires Dextra to collect 5% sales tax on every dollar of merchandise sold. (1) Record the entry for the $6,000 sale and its applicable sales tax. (2) Record the entry that shows the payment of 5% tax on this sale to the state government on October 15.

QS 11-2

Accounting for sales taxes

C2

Ticketsales, Inc., receives $5,000,000 cash in advance ticket sales for a four-date tour of Bon Jovi. Record the advance ticket sales on October 31. Record the revenue earned for the first concert date of November 5, assuming it represents one-fourth of the advance ticket sales.

QS 11-3

Unearned revenue   **C2**

On November 7, 2017, Mura Company borrows $160,000 cash by signing a 90-day, 8% note payable with a face value of $160,000. (1) Compute the accrued interest payable on December 31, 2017, (2) prepare the journal entry to record the accrued interest expense at December 31, 2017, and (3) prepare the journal entry to record payment of the note at maturity.

QS 11-4

Interest-bearing note transactions   **P1**

On January 15, the end of the first biweekly pay period of the year, North Company's payroll register showed that its employees earned $35,000 of sales salaries. Withholdings from the employees' salaries include FICA Social Security taxes at the rate of 6.2%, FICA Medicare taxes at the rate of 1.45%, $6,500 of federal income taxes, $772.50 of medical insurance deductions, and $120 of union dues. No employee earned more than $7,000 in this first period. Prepare the journal entry to record North Company's January 15 (employee) payroll expenses and liabilities. (Round amounts to cents.)

QS 11-5

Recording employee payroll taxes

P2

Merger Co. has 10 employees, each of whom earns $2,000 per month and has been employed since January 1. FICA Social Security taxes are 6.2% of the first $118,500 paid to each employee, and FICA Medicare taxes are 1.45% of gross pay. FUTA taxes are 0.6% and SUTA taxes are 5.4% of the first $7,000 paid to each employee. Prepare the March 31 journal entry to record the March payroll taxes expenses. (Round amounts to cents.)

QS 11-6

Recording employer payroll taxes

P3

Noura Company offers an annual bonus to employees if the company meets certain net income goals. Prepare the journal entry to record a $15,000 bonus owed to its workers (to be shared equally) at calendar year-end.

QS 11-7

Accounting for bonuses

P4

Chavez Co.'s salaried employees earn four weeks' vacation per year. It pays $312,000 in total employee salaries for 52 weeks, but its employees work only 48 weeks. This means Chavez's total weekly expense is $6,500 ($312,000/48 weeks) instead of the $6,000 cash paid weekly to the employees ($312,000/52 weeks). Record Chavez's weekly vacation benefits expense.

QS 11-8

Accounting for vacations

P4

On September 11, 2016, Home Store sells a mower (that costs $200) for $500 with a one-year warranty that covers parts. Warranty expense is estimated at 8% of sales. On July 24, 2017, the mower is brought in for repairs covered under the warranty requiring $35 in materials taken from the Repair Parts Inventory. Prepare the September 11, 2016, entry to record the mower sale (and cost of sale), and the July 24, 2017, entry to record the warranty repairs.

QS 11-9

Recording warranty repairs   **P4**

The following legal claims exist for Huprey Co. Identify the accounting treatment for each claim as either (*a*) a liability that is recorded or (*b*) an item described in notes to its financial statements.

_____ **1.** Huprey (defendant) estimates that a pending lawsuit could result in damages of $1,250,000; it is reasonably possible that the plaintiff will win the case.

_____ **2.** Huprey faces a probable loss on a pending lawsuit; the amount is not reasonably estimable.

_____ **3.** Huprey estimates damages in a case at $3,500,000 with a high probability of losing the case.

QS 11-10

Accounting for contingent liabilities

C3 🏛

QS 11-11
Times interest earned
A1

Compute the times interest earned for Park Company, which reports income before interest expense and income taxes of $1,885,000 and interest expense of $145,000. Interpret its times interest earned (assume that its competitors average a times interest earned of 4.0).

QS 11-12ᴬ
Net pay and tax computations
P5

The payroll records of Speedy Software show the following information about Marsha Gottschalk, an employee, for the weekly pay period ending September 30, 2017. Gottschalk is single and claims one allowance. Compute her Social Security tax (6.2%), Medicare tax (1.45%), federal income tax withholding, state income tax (1.0%), and net pay for the current pay period. (Use the withholding table in Exhibit 11A.6 and round tax amounts to the nearest cent.)

Total (gross) earnings for current pay period	$ 740
Cumulative earnings of previous pay periods	$9,700

Check Net pay, $579.99

QS 11-13ᴮ
Recording deferred income tax liability   P4

Sera Corporation has made and recorded its quarterly income tax payments. After a final review of taxes for the year, the company identifies an additional $40,000 of income tax expense that should be recorded. A portion of this additional expense, $6,000, is deferred for payment in future years. Record Sera's year-end adjusting entry for income tax expense.

QS 11-14
International accounting standards
C1   C2

Answer each of the following related to international accounting standards.
a. In general, how similar or different are the definitions and characteristics of current liabilities between IFRS and U.S. GAAP?
b. Companies reporting under IFRS often reference a set of current liabilities with the title *financial liabilities*. Identify two current liabilities that would be classified under financial liabilities per IFRS. (*Hint:* **Samsung** offers examples in its Appendix A financial statements.)

EXERCISES

Exercise 11-1
Classifying liabilities
C1

The following items appear on the balance sheet of a company with a two-month operating cycle. Identify the proper classification of each item as follows: *C* if it is a current liability, *L* if it is a long-term liability, or *N* if it is not a liability.

_____ **1.** Notes payable (due in 13 to 24 months).	_____ **6.** FUTA taxes payable.
_____ **2.** Notes payable (due in 6 to 12 months).	_____ **7.** Accounts receivable.
_____ **3.** Notes payable (mature in five years).	_____ **8.** Sales taxes payable.
_____ **4.** Current portion of long-term debt.	_____ **9.** Salaries payable.
_____ **5.** Notes payable (due in 120 days).	_____**10.** Wages payable.

Exercise 11-2
Recording known current liabilities
C2

Prepare any necessary adjusting entries at December 31, 2017, for Piper Company's year-end financial statements for each of the following separate transactions and events.
1. Piper Company records a year-end entry for $10,000 of previously unrecorded cash sales (costing $5,000) and its sales taxes at a rate of 4%.
2. The company earned $50,000 of $125,000 previously received in advance and originally recorded as unearned services revenue.

Exercise 11-3
Accounting for note payable   P1

Check (2b) Interest expense, $2,200

Sylvestor Systems borrows $110,000 cash on May 15, 2017, by signing a 60-day, 12% note.
1. On what date does this note mature?
2. Suppose the face value of the note equals $110,000, the principal of the loan. Prepare the journal entries to record (*a*) issuance of the note and (*b*) payment of the note at maturity.

Exercise 11-4
Interest-bearing notes payable with year-end adjustments   P1

Check (2) $3,000
(3) $1,500

Keesha Co. borrows $200,000 cash on November 1, 2017, by signing a 90-day, 9% note with a face value of $200,000.
1. On what date does this note mature?
2. How much interest expense results from this note in 2017? (Assume a 360-day year.)
3. How much interest expense results from this note in 2018? (Assume a 360-day year.)
4. Prepare journal entries to record (*a*) issuance of the note, (*b*) accrual of interest at the end of 2017, and (*c*) payment of the note at maturity. (Assume no reversing entries are made.)

BMX Company has one employee. FICA Social Security taxes are 6.2% of the first $118,500 paid to its employee, and FICA Medicare taxes are 1.45% of gross pay. For BMX, its FUTA taxes are 0.6% and SUTA taxes are 2.9% of the first $7,000 paid to its employee. Compute BMX's amounts for each of these four taxes as applied to the employee's gross earnings for September under each of three separate situations (*a*), (*b*), and (*c*). (Round amounts to cents.)

Exercise 11-5

Computing payroll taxes

P2   P3

	Gross Pay through August	Gross Pay for September
a.	$ 6,400	$ 800
b.	18,200	2,100
c.	112,200	8,000

Check   (*a*) FUTA, $3.60;
SUTA, $17.40

Using the data in *situation a* of Exercise 11-5, prepare the employer's September 30 journal entries to record salary expense and its related payroll liabilities for this employee. The employee's federal income taxes withheld by the employer are $80 for this pay period. (Round amounts to cents.)

Exercise 11-6

Payroll-related
journal entries

P2

Using the data in *situation a* of Exercise 11-5, prepare the employer's September 30 journal entries to record the *employer's* payroll taxes expense and its related liabilities. (Round amounts to cents.)

Exercise 11-7

Payroll-related
journal entries

P3

The following monthly data are taken from Ramirez Company at July 31: sales salaries, $200,000; office salaries, $160,000; federal income taxes withheld, $90,000; state income taxes withheld, $20,000; Social Security taxes withheld, $22,320; Medicare taxes withheld, $5,220; medical insurance premiums, $7,000; life insurance premiums, $4,000; union dues deducted, $1,000; and salaries subject to unemployment taxes, $50,000. The employee pays 40% of medical and life insurance premiums.

Prepare journal entries to record: (1) accrued payroll, including employee deductions, for July; (2) cash payment of the net payroll (salaries payable) for July; (3) accrued employer payroll taxes, and other related employment expenses, for July—assume that FICA taxes are identical to those on employees and that SUTA taxes are 5.4% and FUTA taxes are 0.6%; and (4) cash payment of all liabilities related to the July payroll.

Exercise 11-8

Recording payroll

P2   P3

Mest Company has 9 employees. FICA Social Security taxes are 6.2% of the first $118,500 paid to each employee, and FICA Medicare taxes are 1.45% of gross pay. FUTA taxes are 0.6% and SUTA taxes are 5.4% of the first $7,000 paid to each employee. Cumulative pay for the current year for each of its employees follows.

Exercise 11-9

Computing payroll taxes

P2   P3

Employee	Cumulative Pay	Employee	Cumulative Pay	Employee	Cumulative Pay
Ken S.	$ 6,000	Michael M.	$143,500	Lori K.	$121,000
Tim V.	60,200	Erin C.	106,900	Kitty O.	36,900
Steve S.	87,000	Kyle B.	118,500	John W.	4,000

a. Prepare a table with the following six column headings. Compute the amounts in this table for each employee and then total the numerical columns.

Employee	Cumulative Pay	Pay Subject to FICA Social Security	Pay Subject to FICA Medicare	Pay Subject to FUTA Taxes	Pay Subject to SUTA Taxes

b. For the company, compute each total for: FICA Social Security taxes, FICA Medicare taxes, FUTA taxes, and SUTA taxes. (*Hint:* Remember to include in those totals any employee share of taxes that the company must collect.) (Round amounts to cents.)

Exercise 11-10
Warranty expense and
liability computations
and entries   P4

Hitzu Co. sold a copier costing $4,800 with a two-year parts warranty to a customer on August 16, 2017, for $6,000 cash. Hitzu uses the perpetual inventory system. On November 22, 2018, the copier requires on-site repairs that are completed the same day. The repairs cost $209 for materials taken from the repair parts inventory. These are the only repairs required in 2018 for this copier. Based on experience, Hitzu expects to incur warranty costs equal to 4% of dollar sales. It records warranty expense with an adjusting entry at the end of each year.

Check   (1) $240

1. How much warranty expense does the company report in 2017 for this copier?
2. How much is the estimated warranty liability for this copier as of December 31, 2017?
3. How much warranty expense does the company report in 2018 for this copier?

(4) $31

4. How much is the estimated warranty liability for this copier as of December 31, 2018?
5. Prepare journal entries to record (*a*) the copier's sale; (*b*) the adjustment on December 31, 2017, to recognize the warranty expense; and (*c*) the repairs that occur in November 2018.

Exercise 11-11
Recording bonuses
P4

For the year ended December 31, 2017, Lopez Company has implemented an employee bonus program based on Lopez's net income, which employees will share equally. Lopez's bonus expense is computed as $14,563.

1. Prepare the journal entry at December 31, 2017, to record the bonus due the employees.
2. Prepare the journal entry at January 19, 2018, to record payment of the bonus to employees.

Exercise 11-12
Accounting for
estimated liabilities
P4

Prepare any necessary adjusting entries at December 31, 2017, for Maxum Company's year-end financial statements for each of the following separate transactions and events.

1. Employees earn vacation pay at a rate of one day per month. During December, 20 employees qualify for one vacation day each. Their average daily wage is $160 per employee.
2. During December, Maxum Company sold 12,000 units of a product that carries a 60-day warranty. December sales for this product total $460,000. The company expects 10% of the units to need warranty repairs, and it estimates the average repair cost per unit will be $15.

Exercise 11-13
Accounting for
contingent liabilities
C3

Prepare any necessary adjusting entries at December 31, 2017, for Melbourn Company's year-end financial statements for each of the following separate transactions and events.

1. Melbourn Company guarantees the $100,000 debt of a supplier. It is not probable that the supplier will default on the debt.
2. A disgruntled employee is suing Melbourn Company. Legal advisers believe that the company will probably need to pay damages, but the amount cannot be reasonably estimated.

Exercise 11-14
Computing and
interpreting times
interest earned   A1

Use the following information from separate companies *a* through *f* to compute times interest earned. Which company indicates the strongest ability to pay interest expense as it comes due? (Round ratios to two decimals.)

	Net Income (Loss)	Interest Expense	Income Taxes
a.	$115,000	$44,000	$ 35,000
b.	110,000	16,000	50,000
c.	100,000	12,000	70,000
d.	235,000	14,000	130,000
e.	59,000	14,000	30,000
f.	(5,000)	10,000	0

Check (b) 11.00

Exercise 11-15^B
Accounting for
income taxes
P4

Nishi Corporation prepares financial statements for each month-end. As part of its accounting process, estimated income taxes are accrued each month for 30% of the current month's net income. The income taxes are paid in the first month of each quarter for the amount accrued for the prior quarter. The following information is available for the fourth quarter of year 2017. When tax computations are completed on January 20, 2018, Nishi determines that the quarter's Income Taxes Payable account balance should be $28,300 on December 31, 2017 (its unadjusted balance is $24,690).

October 2017 net income	$28,600
November 2017 net income	19,100
December 2017 net income	34,600

1. Determine the amount of the accounting adjustment (dated as of December 31, 2017) to produce the proper ending balance in the Income Taxes Payable account.

Check (1) $3,610

2. Prepare journal entries to record (*a*) the December 31, 2017, adjustment to the Income Taxes Payable account and (*b*) the January 20, 2018, payment of the fourth-quarter taxes.

Lenny Florita, an unmarried employee, works 48 hours in the week ended January 12. His pay rate is $14 per hour, and his wages are subject to no deductions other than FICA Social Security, FICA Medicare, and federal income taxes. He claims two withholding allowances.

Exercise 11-16[A]
Gross and net pay computation

P5

Compute his regular pay, overtime pay (this company's workers earn 150% of their regular rate for hours in excess of 40 per week), and gross pay. Then compute his FICA tax deduction (6.2% for the Social Security portion and 1.45% for the Medicare portion), income tax deduction (use the wage bracket withholding table from Exhibit 11A.6), total deductions, and net pay. (Round tax amounts to the nearest cent.)

Check Net pay, $596.30

Stark Company has five employees. Employees paid by the hour receive a $10 per hour pay rate for the regular 40-hour workweek plus one and one-half times the hourly rate for each overtime hour beyond the 40 hours per week. Hourly employees are paid every two weeks, but salaried employees are paid monthly on the last biweekly payday of each month. FICA Social Security taxes are 6.2% of the first $118,500 paid to each employee, and FICA Medicare taxes are 1.45% of gross pay. FUTA taxes are 0.6% and SUTA taxes are 5.4% of the first $7,000 paid to each employee. The company has a benefits plan that includes medical insurance, life insurance, and retirement funding for employees. Under this plan, employees must contribute 5 percent of their gross income as a payroll withholding, which the company matches with *double* the amount. Following is the partially completed payroll register for the biweekly period ending August 31, which is the last payday of August.

Exercise 11-17[A]
Preparing payroll register and related entries

P5

| Employee | Cumulative Pay (Excludes Current Period) | Current Period Gross Pay | | | FIT | FUTA | FICA-SS_EE | FICA-Med_EE | EE-Ben_Plan Withholding | Employee Net Pay |
		Pay Type	Pay Hours	Gross Pay	SIT	SUTA	FICA-SS_ER	FICA-Med_ER	ER-Ben_Plan Expense	(Current Period)
Kathleen	$116,700.00	Salary	---	$7,000.00	$2,000.00					
					300.00					
Anthony	6,800.00	Salary	---	500.00	80.00				25.00	
					20.00				50.00	
Nichole	15,000.00	Regular	80		110.00					
		Overtime	8		25.00					
Zoey	6,500.00	Regular	80		100.00					
		Overtime	4		22.00					
Gracie	5,000.00	Regular	74	740.00	90.00					
		Overtime	0	0.00	21.00					
Totals	$150,000.00				2,380.00					
					388.00					

* Table abbreviations follow those in Exhibit 11A.3; "Ben_Plan" refers to employee (EE) withholding or the employer (ER) expense for the benefits plan.

a. Complete this payroll register by filling in all cells for the pay period ended August 31. *Hint:* See Exhibit 11A.5 for guidance. (Round amounts to cents.)

b. Prepare the August 31 journal entry to record the accrued biweekly payroll and related liabilities for deductions.

c. Prepare the August 31 journal entry to record the employer's cash payment of the net payroll of part *b.*

d. Prepare the August 31 journal entry to record the employer's payroll taxes including the contribution to the benefits plan.

e. Prepare the August 31 journal entry to pay all liabilities (except for the net payroll in part *c*) for this biweekly period.

Volvo Group reports the following information for its product warranty costs as of December 31, 2014, along with provisions and utilizations of warranty liabilities for the year ended December 31, 2014 (SEK in millions).

Exercise 11-18
Accounting for current liabilities under IFRS

P4

Provision for product warranty   Warranty provisions are estimated with consideration of historical claims statistics, the warranty period, the average time-lag between faults occurring and claims to the company and anticipated changes in quality indexes. Estimated costs for product warranties are recognized as cost of sales when the products are sold . . . Differences between actual warranty claims and the estimated final claims cost generally affect the recognized expense and provisions in future periods. Refunds from suppliers, that decrease the Volvo Group's warranty costs, are recognized to the extent these are considered to be certain. As of December 31, 2014 (2013), warranty cost provisions amount to 10,583 (9,881).

Product warranty liabilities, December 31, 2013.....................	SEK 9,881
Additional provisions to product warranty liabilities	7,836
Utilizations and reductions of product warranty liabilities..............	(7,134)
Product warranty liabilities, December 31, 2014.....................	SEK 10,583

1. Prepare Volvo's journal entry to record its estimated warranty liabilities (provisions) for 2014.

2. Prepare Volvo's journal entry to record its costs (utilizations) related to its warranty program for 2014. Assume those costs involve replacements taken out of inventory, with no cash involved.

3. How much warranty expense does Volvo report for 2014?

■■ connect

PROBLEM SET A

Problem 11-1A
Short-term notes payable transactions and entries

P1

Tyrell Co. entered into the following transactions involving short-term liabilities in 2016 and 2017.

2016

Apr. 20   Purchased $40,250 of merchandise on credit from Locust, terms n/30. Tyrell uses the perpetual inventory system.

May 19   Replaced the April 20 account payable to Locust with a 90-day, $35,000 note bearing 10% annual interest along with paying $5,250 in cash.

July   8   Borrowed $80,000 cash from NBR Bank by signing a 120-day, 9% interest-bearing note with a face value of $80,000.

____?____   Paid the amount due on the note to Locust at the maturity date.

____?____   Paid the amount due on the note to NBR Bank at the maturity date.

Nov. 28   Borrowed $42,000 cash from Fargo Bank by signing a 60-day, 8% interest-bearing note with a face value of $42,000.

Dec. 31   Recorded an adjusting entry for accrued interest on the note to Fargo Bank.

2017

____?____   Paid the amount due on the note to Fargo Bank at the maturity date.

Required

1. Determine the maturity date for each of the three notes described.

2. Determine the interest due at maturity for each of the three notes. (Assume a 360-day year.)

3. Determine the interest expense to be recorded in the adjusting entry at the end of 2016.

4. Determine the interest expense to be recorded in 2017.

5. Prepare journal entries for all the preceding transactions and events for years 2016 and 2017.

Problem 11-2A
Entries for payroll transactions

P2   P3

On January 8, the end of the first weekly pay period of the year, Regis Company's payroll register showed that its employees earned $22,760 of office salaries and $65,840 of sales salaries. Withholdings from the employees' salaries include FICA Social Security taxes at the rate of 6.2%, FICA Medicare taxes at the rate of 1.45%, $12,860 of federal income taxes, $1,340 of medical insurance deductions, and $840 of union dues. No employee earned more than $7,000 in this first period.

Required

1. Calculate FICA Social Security taxes payable and FICA Medicare taxes payable. Prepare the journal entry to record Regis Company's January 8 (employee) payroll expenses and liabilities. (Round amounts to cents.)

2. Prepare the journal entry to record Regis's (employer) payroll taxes resulting from the January 8 payroll. Regis's merit rating reduces its state unemployment tax rate to 4% of the first $7,000 paid each employee. The federal unemployment tax rate is 0.6%. (Round amounts to cents.)

Paloma Co. has four employees. FICA Social Security taxes are 6.2% of the first $118,500 paid to each employee, and FICA Medicare taxes are 1.45% of gross pay. Also, for the first $7,000 paid to each employee, the company's FUTA taxes are 0.6% and SUTA taxes are 2.15%. The company is preparing its payroll calculations for the week ended August 25. Payroll records show the following information for the company's four employees.

Problem 11-3A
Payroll expenses,
withholdings, and taxes

P2   P3

	A	B	C	D
1		Gross Pay	Current Week	
2	Name	through Aug. 18	Gross Pay	Income Tax Withholding
3	Dali	$117,400	$2,000	$284
4	Trey	117,600	900	145
5	Kiesha	6,900	450	39
6	Chee	1,250	400	30

In addition to gross pay, the company must pay two-thirds of the $60 per employee weekly health insurance; each employee pays the remaining one-third. The company also contributes an extra 8% of each employee's gross pay (at no cost to employees) to a pension fund.

Required

Compute the following for the week ended August 25 (round amounts to the nearest cent):

1. Each employee's FICA withholdings for Social Security.

2. Each employee's FICA withholdings for Medicare.

3. Employer's FICA taxes for Social Security.

4. Employer's FICA taxes for Medicare.

5. Employer's FUTA taxes.

6. Employer's SUTA taxes.

7. Each employee's net (take-home) pay.

8. Employer's total payroll-related expense for each employee.

Check   (3) $176.70

(4) $54.38

(5) $3.00

(7) Total net pay,
$2,940.92

On October 29, 2016, Lobo Co. began operations by purchasing razors for resale. Lobo uses the perpetual inventory method. The razors have a 90-day warranty that requires the company to replace any nonworking razor. When a razor is returned, the company discards it and mails a new one from merchandise inventory to the customer. The company's cost per new razor is $20 and its retail selling price is $75 in both 2016 and 2017. The manufacturer has advised the company to expect warranty costs to equal 8% of dollar sales. The following transactions and events occurred.

Problem 11-4A
Warranty expense and
liability estimation

P4

2016

Nov.	11	Sold 105 razors for $7,875 cash.
	30	Recognized warranty expense related to November sales with an adjusting entry.
Dec.	9	Replaced 15 razors that were returned under the warranty.
	16	Sold 220 razors for $16,500 cash.
	29	Replaced 30 razors that were returned under the warranty.
	31	Recognized warranty expense related to December sales with an adjusting entry.

2017

Jan.	5	Sold 150 razors for $11,250 cash.
	17	Replaced 50 razors that were returned under the warranty.
	31	Recognized warranty expense related to January sales with an adjusting entry.

Required

1. Prepare journal entries to record these transactions and adjustments for 2016 and 2017.

2. How much warranty expense is reported for November 2016 and for December 2016?

3. How much warranty expense is reported for January 2017?

4. What is the balance of the Estimated Warranty Liability account as of December 31, 2016?

5. What is the balance of the Estimated Warranty Liability account as of January 31, 2017?

Check   (3) $900

(4) $1,050 Cr.

(5) $950 Cr.

Problem 11-5A
Computing and analyzing
times interest earned

A1

Shown here are condensed income statements for two different companies (both are organized as LLCs and pay no income taxes).

Miller Company	
Sales	$1,000,000
Variable expenses (80%)	800,000
Income before interest.	200,000
Interest expense (fixed)	60,000
Net income	$ 140,000

Weaver Company	
Sales	$1,000,000
Variable expenses (60%)	600,000
Income before interest.	400,000
Interest expense (fixed)	260,000
Net income	$ 140,000

Required

1. Compute times interest earned for Miller Company.
2. Compute times interest earned for Weaver Company.

Check   (3) Miller net income, $200,000 (43% increase)

3. What happens to each company's net income if sales increase by 30%?
4. What happens to each company's net income if sales increase by 50%?
5. What happens to each company's net income if sales increase by 80%?
6. What happens to each company's net income if sales decrease by 10%?

(6) Weaver net income, $100,000 (29% decrease)

7. What happens to each company's net income if sales decrease by 20%?
8. What happens to each company's net income if sales decrease by 40%?

Analysis Component

9. Comment on the results from parts 3 through 8 in relation to the fixed-cost strategies of the two companies and the ratio values you computed in parts 1 and 2.

Problem 11-6Aᴬ
Entries for payroll
transactions

P2   P3   P5

Francisco Company has 10 employees, each of whom earns $2,800 per month and is paid on the last day of each month. All 10 have been employed continuously at this amount since January 1. On March 1, the following accounts and balances exist in its general ledger:

a. FICA—Social Security Taxes Payable, $3,472; FICA—Medicare Taxes Payable, $812. (The balances of these accounts represent total liabilities for *both* the employer's and employees' FICA taxes for the February payroll only.)

b. Employees' Federal Income Taxes Payable, $4,000 (liability for February only).

c. Federal Unemployment Taxes Payable, $336 (liability for January and February together).

d. State Unemployment Taxes Payable, $2,240 (liability for January and February together).

During March and April, the company had the following payroll transactions.

Mar. 15   Issued check payable to Swift Bank, a federal depository bank authorized to accept employers' payments of FICA taxes and employee income tax withholdings. The $8,284 check is in payment of the February FICA and employee income taxes.

Check   March 31: Salaries Payable, $21,858

31   Recorded the journal entry for the March salaries payable. Then recorded the cash payment of the March payroll (the company issued checks payable to each employee in payment of the March payroll). The payroll register shows the following summary totals for the March pay period.

Salaries				Federal	
Office Salaries	Shop Salaries	Gross Pay	FICA Taxes*	Income Taxes	Net Pay
$11,200	$16,800	$28,000	$1,736	$4,000	$21,858
			$ 406		

* FICA taxes are Social Security and Medicare, respectively.

March 31: Dr. Payroll Taxes Expenses, $2,786

31   Recorded the employer's payroll taxes resulting from the March payroll. The company has a merit rating that reduces its state unemployment tax rate to 4.0% of the first $7,000 paid each employee. The federal rate is 0.6%.

April 15: Cr. Cash, $8,284 (Swift Bank)

Apr. 15   Issued check to Swift Bank in payment of the March FICA and employee income taxes.

15   Issued check to the State Tax Commission for the January, February, and March state unemployment taxes. Filed the check and the first-quarter tax return with the Commission.

30   Issued check payable to Swift Bank in payment of the employer's FUTA taxes for the first quarter of the year.

30 Filed Form 941 with the IRS, reporting the FICA taxes and the employees' federal income tax withholdings for the first quarter.

Required

Prepare journal entries to record the transactions and events for both March and April.

Warner Co. entered into the following transactions involving short-term liabilities in 2016 and 2017.

2016

Apr. 22 Purchased $5,000 of merchandise on credit from Fox-Pro, terms n/30. Warner uses the perpetual inventory system.

May 23 Replaced the April 22 account payable to Fox-Pro with a 60-day, $4,600 note bearing 15% annual interest along with paying $400 in cash.

July 15 Borrowed $12,000 cash from Spring Bank by signing a 120-day, 10% interest-bearing note with a face value of $12,000.

___?___ Paid the amount due on the note to Fox-Pro at maturity.

___?___ Paid the amount due on the note to Spring Bank at maturity.

Dec. 6 Borrowed $8,000 cash from City Bank by signing a 45-day, 9% interest-bearing note with a face value of $8,000.

31 Recorded an adjusting entry for accrued interest on the note to City Bank.

2017

___?___ Paid the amount due on the note to City Bank at maturity.

Required

1. Determine the maturity date for each of the three notes described.
2. Determine the interest due at maturity for each of the three notes. (Assume a 360-day year.)
3. Determine the interest expense to be recorded in the adjusting entry at the end of 2016.
4. Determine the interest expense to be recorded in 2017.
5. Prepare journal entries for all the preceding transactions and events for years 2016 and 2017.

PROBLEM SET B

Problem 11-1B
Short-term notes payable transactions and entries

P1

Check (2) Fox-Pro, $115
(3) $50
(4) $40

Tavella Company's first weekly pay period of the year ends on January 8. On that date, the column totals in Tavella's payroll register indicate its sales employees earned $34,745, its office employees earned $21,225, and its delivery employees earned $1,030 in salaries. The employees are to have withheld from their salaries FICA Social Security taxes at the rate of 6.2%, FICA Medicare taxes at the rate of 1.45%, $8,625 of federal income taxes, $1,160 of medical insurance deductions, and $138 of union dues. No employee earned more than $7,000 in the first pay period.

Required

1. Calculate FICA Social Security taxes payable and FICA Medicare taxes payable. Prepare the journal entry to record Tavella Company's January 8 (employee) payroll expenses and liabilities. (Round amounts to cents.)

2. Prepare the journal entry to record Tavella's (employer) payroll taxes resulting from the January 8 payroll. Tavella's merit rating reduces its state unemployment tax rate to 3.4% of the first $7,000 paid each employee. The federal unemployment tax rate is 0.6%. (Round amounts to cents.)

Problem 11-2B
Entries for payroll transactions

P2 P3

Check (1) Cr. Salaries Payable, $42,716.50

(2) Dr. Payroll Taxes Expense, $6,640.50

Fishing Guides Co. has four employees. FICA Social Security taxes are 6.2% of the first $118,500 paid to each employee, and FICA Medicare taxes are 1.45% of gross pay. Also, for the first $7,000 paid to each employee, the company's FUTA taxes are 0.6% and SUTA taxes are 1.75%. The company is preparing its payroll calculations for the week ended September 30. Payroll records show the following information for the company's four employees.

Problem 11-3B
Payroll expenses, withholdings, and taxes

P2 P3

	A	B	C	D
1		**Gross Pay**	**Current Week**	
2	**Name**	**through Sept. 23**	**Gross Pay**	**Income Tax Withholding**
3	Ahmed	$116,900	$2,500	$198
4	Carlos	116,985	1,515	182
5	Jun	6,650	475	32
6	Marie	23,700	1,000	68

In addition to gross pay, the company must pay 60% of the $50 per employee weekly health insurance; each employee pays the remaining 40%. The company also contributes an extra 5% of each employee's gross pay (at no cost to employees) to a pension fund.

Required

Compute the following for the week ended September 30 (round amounts to the nearest cent):

1. Each employee's FICA withholdings for Social Security.

2. Each employee's FICA withholdings for Medicare.

3. Employer's FICA taxes for Social Security.

4. Employer's FICA taxes for Medicare.

5. Employer's FUTA taxes.

6. Employer's SUTA taxes.

7. Each employee's net (take-home) pay.

8. Employer's total payroll-related expense for each employee.

Check   (3) $284.58

(4) $79.61

(5) $2.10

(7) Total net pay, $4,565.81

Problem 11-4B
Warranty expense and liability estimation

P4

On November 10, 2016, Lee Co. began operations by purchasing coffee grinders for resale. Lee uses the perpetual inventory method. The grinders have a 60-day warranty that requires the company to replace any nonworking grinder. When a grinder is returned, the company discards it and mails a new one from Merchandise Inventory to the customer. The company's cost per new grinder is $24 and its retail selling price is $50 in both 2016 and 2017. The manufacturer has advised the company to expect warranty costs to equal 10% of dollar sales. The following transactions and events occurred.

2016

Nov. 16	Sold 50 grinders for $2,500 cash.
30	Recognized warranty expense related to November sales with an adjusting entry.
Dec. 12	Replaced six grinders that were returned under the warranty.
18	Sold 200 grinders for $10,000 cash.
28	Replaced 17 grinders that were returned under the warranty.
31	Recognized warranty expense related to December sales with an adjusting entry.

2017

Jan. 7	Sold 40 grinders for $2,000 cash.
21	Replaced 36 grinders that were returned under the warranty.
31	Recognized warranty expense related to January sales with an adjusting entry.

Required

1. Prepare journal entries to record these transactions and adjustments for 2016 and 2017.

2. How much warranty expense is reported for November 2016 and for December 2016?

3. How much warranty expense is reported for January 2017?

4. What is the balance of the Estimated Warranty Liability account as of December 31, 2016?

5. What is the balance of the Estimated Warranty Liability account as of January 31, 2017?

Check   (3) $200

(4) $698 Cr.

(5) $34 Cr.

Problem 11-5B
Computing and analyzing times interest earned

A1

Shown here are condensed income statements for two different companies (both are organized as LLCs and pay no income taxes).

Ellis Company	
Sales	$240,000
Variable expenses (50%)	120,000
Income before interest.	120,000
Interest expense (fixed)	90,000
Net income	$ 30,000

Seidel Company	
Sales	$240,000
Variable expenses (75%)	180,000
Income before interest.	60,000
Interest expense (fixed)	30,000
Net income	$ 30,000

Required

1. Compute times interest earned for Ellis Company.

2. Compute times interest earned for Seidel Company.

3. What happens to each company's net income if sales increase by 10%?

4. What happens to each company's net income if sales increase by 40%?

5. What happens to each company's net income if sales increase by 90%?

6. What happens to each company's net income if sales decrease by 20%?

7. What happens to each company's net income if sales decrease by 50%?

8. What happens to each company's net income if sales decrease by 80%?

Check (4) Ellis net income, $78,000 (160% increase)

(6) Seidel net income, $18,000 (40% decrease)

Analysis Component

9. Comment on the results from parts 3 through 8 in relation to the fixed-cost strategies of the two companies and the ratio values you computed in parts 1 and 2.

MLS Company has five employees, each of whom earns $1,600 per month and is paid on the last day of each month. All five have been employed continuously at this amount since January 1. On June 1, the following accounts and balances exist in its general ledger:

a. FICA—Social Security Taxes Payable, $992; FICA—Medicare Taxes Payable, $232. (The balances of these accounts represent total liabilities for *both* the employer's and employees' FICA taxes for the May payroll only.)

b. Employees' Federal Income Taxes Payable, $1,050 (liability for May only).

c. Federal Unemployment Taxes Payable, $66 (liability for April and May together).

d. State Unemployment Taxes Payable, $440 (liability for April and May together).

During June and July, the company had the following payroll transactions.

June 15 Issued check payable to Security Bank, a federal depository bank authorized to accept employers' payments of FICA taxes and employee income tax withholdings. The $2,274 check is in payment of the May FICA and employee income taxes.

30 Recorded the journal entry for the June salaries payable. Then recorded the cash payment of the June payroll (the company issued checks payable to each employee in payment of the June payroll). The payroll register shows the following summary totals for the June pay period.

Problem 11-6B[A]
Entries for payroll transactions

P2 P3 P5

Check June 30: Cr. Salaries Payable, $6,338

Salaries				Federal	
Office Salaries	Shop Salaries	Gross Pay	FICA Taxes*	Income Taxes	Net Pay
$3,800	$4,200	$8,000	$496	$1,050	$6,338
			$116		

* FICA taxes are Social Security and Medicare, respectively.

30 Recorded the employer's payroll taxes resulting from the June payroll. The company has a merit rating that reduces its state unemployment tax rate to 4.0% of the first $7,000 paid each employee. The federal rate is 0.6%.

July 15 Issued check payable to Security Bank in payment of the June FICA and employee income taxes.

15 Issued check to the State Tax Commission for the April, May, and June state unemployment taxes. Filed the check and the second-quarter tax return with the State Tax Commission.

31 Issued check payable to Security Bank in payment of the employer's FUTA taxes for the first quarter of the year.

31 Filed Form 941 with the IRS, reporting the FICA taxes and the employees' federal income tax withholdings for the second quarter.

Check June 30: Dr. Payroll Taxes Expenses, $612

July 15: Cr. Cash, $2,274 (Security Bank)

Required

Prepare journal entries to record the transactions and events for both June and July.

SERIAL PROBLEM

Business Solutions

P2   P3   C2

© Alexander Image/Shutterstock RF

(This serial problem began in Chapter 1 and continues through most of the book. If previous chapter segments were not completed, the serial problem can begin at this point.)

SP 11   Review the February 26 and March 25 transactions for **Business Solutions** (SP 5) from Chapter 5.

Required

1. Assume that Lyn Addie is an unmarried employee. Her $1,000 of wages are subject to no deductions other than FICA Social Security taxes, FICA Medicare taxes, and federal income taxes. Her federal income taxes for this pay period total $159. Compute her net pay for the eight days' work paid on February 26. (Round amounts to the nearest cent.)

2. Record the journal entry to reflect the payroll payment to Lyn Addie as computed in part 1.

3. Record the journal entry to reflect the (employer) payroll tax expenses for the February 26 payroll payment. Assume Lyn Addie has not met earnings limits for FUTA and SUTA (the FUTA rate is 0.6% and the SUTA rate is 4% for the company. (Round amounts to the nearest cent.)

4. Record the entry(ies) for the merchandise sold on March 25 if a 4% sales tax rate applies.

COMPREHENSIVE PROBLEM

Bug-Off Exterminators

(Review of Chapters 1–11)

CP 11   **Bug-Off Exterminators** provides pest control services and sells extermination products manufactured by other companies. The following six-column table contains the company's unadjusted trial balance as of December 31, 2017.

	BUG-OFF EXTERMINATORS December 31, 2017				
	Unadjusted Trial Balance		Adjustments	Adjusted Trial Balance	
Cash..................................	$ 17,000				
Accounts receivable	4,000				
Allowance for doubtful accounts		$ 828			
Merchandise inventory	11,700				
Trucks.................................	32,000				
Accum. depreciation—Trucks.............		0			
Equipment	45,000				
Accum. depreciation—Equipment		12,200			
Accounts payable		5,000			
Estimated warranty liability...............		1,400			
Unearned services revenue		0			
Interest payable........................		0			
Long-term notes payable		15,000			
D. Buggs, Capital.......................		59,700			
D. Buggs, Withdrawals	10,000				
Extermination services revenue...........		60,000			
Interest revenue		872			
Sales (of merchandise)		71,026			
Cost of goods sold	46,300				
Depreciation expense—Trucks............	0				
Depreciation expense—Equipment	0				
Wages expense........................	35,000				
Interest expense	0				
Rent expense..........................	9,000				
Bad debts expense	0				
Miscellaneous expense..................	1,226				
Repairs expense	8,000				
Utilities expense	6,800				
Warranty expense	0				
Totals	$226,026	$226,026			

The following information in *a* through *h* applies to the company at the end of the current year.

a. The bank reconciliation as of December 31, 2017, includes the following facts.

Cash balance per bank	$15,100
Cash balance per books..................................	17,000
Outstanding checks	1,800
Deposit in transit	2,450
Interest earned (on bank account)	52
Bank service charges (miscellaneous expense).............	15

Reported on the bank statement is a canceled check that the company failed to record. (Information from the bank reconciliation allows you to determine the amount of this check, which is a payment on an account payable.)

b. An examination of customers' accounts shows that accounts totaling $679 should be written off as uncollectible. Using an aging of receivables, the company determines that the ending balance of the Allowance for Doubtful Accounts should be $700.

c. A truck is purchased and placed in service on January 1, 2017. Its cost is being depreciated with the straight-line method using the following facts and estimates.

Original cost	$32,000
Expected salvage value	8,000
Useful life (years)	4

d. Two items of equipment (a sprayer and an injector) were purchased and put into service in early January 2015. They are being depreciated with the straight-line method using these facts and estimates.

	Sprayer	Injector
Original cost	$27,000	$18,000
Expected salvage value	3,000	2,500
Useful life (years)	8	5

e. On August 1, 2017, the company is paid $3,840 cash in advance to provide monthly service for an apartment complex for one year. The company began providing the services in August. When the cash was received, the full amount was credited to the Extermination Services Revenue account.

f. The company offers a warranty for the services it sells. The expected cost of providing warranty service is 2.5% of the extermination services revenue of $57,760 for 2017. No warranty expense has been recorded for 2017. All costs of servicing warranties in 2017 were properly debited to the Estimated Warranty Liability account.

g. The $15,000 long-term note is an 8%, five-year, interest-bearing note with interest payable annually on December 31. The note was signed with First National Bank on December 31, 2017.

h. The ending inventory of merchandise is counted and determined to have a cost of $11,700. Bug-Off uses a perpetual inventory system.

Required

1. Use the preceding information to determine amounts for the following items.

   a. Correct (reconciled) ending balance of Cash, and the amount of the omitted check.

   b. Adjustment needed to obtain the correct ending balance of the Allowance for Doubtful Accounts.

   c. Depreciation expense for the truck used during year 2017.

   d. Depreciation expense for the two items of equipment used during year 2017.

   e. The adjusted 2017 ending balances of the Extermination Services Revenue and Unearned Services Revenue accounts.

   f. The adjusted 2017 ending balances of the Warranty Expense and the Estimated Warranty Liability accounts.

   g. The adjusted 2017 ending balances of the Interest Expense and the Interest Payable accounts. (Round amounts to nearest whole dollar.)

Check (1*a*) Reconciled cash bal. $15,750

(1*b*) $551 credit

(1*f*) Estimated Warranty Liability, $2,844 Cr.

Continued on next page . . .

(2) Adjusted trial balance totals, $238,207

2. Use the results of part 1 to complete the six-column table by first entering the appropriate adjustments for items *a* through *g* and then completing the Adjusted Trial Balance columns. (*Hint:* Item *b* requires two adjustments.)

3. Prepare journal entries to record the adjustments entered on the six-column table. Assume Bug-Off's adjusted balance for Merchandise Inventory matches the year-end physical count.

(4) Net income, $9,274; Total assets, $82,771

4. Prepare a single-step income statement, a statement of owner's equity (cash withdrawals during 2017 were $10,000), and a classified balance sheet.

GENERAL LEDGER PROBLEM

Available only in Connect

GL 11-1   General Ledger assignment GL 11-1, based on Problem 11-1A, focuses on transactions related to accounts and notes payable and highlights the impact each transaction has on interest expense, if any. Prepare the journal entries related to accounts and notes payable; the schedules for accounts payable and notes payable are automatically completed using the **General Ledger** tool. Compute both the amount and timing of interest expense for each note. Prepare the subsequent period journal entries related to accrued interest.

Beyond the Numbers

REPORTING IN ACTION

A1   P4

APPLE

BTN 11-1   Refer to the financial statements of Apple in Appendix A to answer the following.

1. Compute times interest earned for the fiscal years ended 2015, 2014, and 2013. Apple reports that in 2015 interest expense was $733 million, in 2014 interest expense was $384 million, and in 2013 interest expense was $136 million. Comment on Apple's ability to cover its interest expense for this period. Assume an industry average of 10 for times interest earned.

2. Identify Apple's total accrued expenses.

Fast Forward

3. Access Apple's financial statements for fiscal years ending after September 26, 2015, at its website (Apple.com) or the SEC's EDGAR database (SEC.gov). Compute its times interest earned for years ending after September 26, 2015, and compare your results to those in part 1.

COMPARATIVE ANALYSIS

A1

APPLE

GOOGLE

BTN 11-2   Key figures for Apple and Google follow.

	Apple			Google		
$ millions	Current Year	One Year Prior	Two Years Prior	Current Year	One Year Prior	Two Years Prior
Net income	$53,394	$39,510	$37,037	$16,348	$14,136	$12,733
Income taxes	19,121	13,973	13,118	3,303	3,639	2,739
Interest expense	733	384	136	104	101	81

Required

1. Compute times interest earned for the three years' data shown for each company.

2. Comment on which company appears stronger in its ability to pay interest obligations. Assume an industry average of 10.

BTN 11-3 Cameron Bly is a sales manager for an automobile dealership. He earns a bonus each year based on revenue from the number of autos sold in the year less related warranty expenses. Actual warranty expenses have varied over the prior 10 years from a low of 3% of an automobile's selling price to a high of 10%. In the past, Bly has tended to estimate warranty expenses on the high end to be conservative. He must work with the dealership's accountant at year-end to arrive at the warranty expense accrual for cars sold each year.

ETHICS CHALLENGE

P4

1. Does the warranty accrual decision create any ethical dilemma for Bly?
2. Since warranty expenses vary, what percent do you think Bly should choose for the current year? Justify your response.

BTN 11-4 Dusty Johnson is the accounting and finance manager for a manufacturer. At year-end, he must determine how to account for the company's contingencies. His manager, Tom Pretti, objects to Johnson's proposal to recognize an expense and a liability for warranty service on units of a new product introduced in the fourth quarter. Pretti comments, "There's no way we can estimate this warranty cost. We don't owe anyone anything until a product fails and it is returned. Let's report an expense if and when we do any warranty work."

COMMUNICATING IN PRACTICE

C3

Required

Prepare a one-page memorandum for Johnson to send to Pretti defending his proposal.

BTN 11-5 Access the February 25, 2016, filing of the December 31, 2015, annual 10-K report of McDonald's Corporation (ticker: MCD), which is available from SEC.gov.

TAKING IT TO THE NET

C1   A1

Required

1. Identify the current liabilities on McDonald's balance sheet as of December 31, 2015.
2. What portion (in percent) of McDonald's long-term debt matures within the next 12 months?
3. Use the consolidated statement of income for the year ended December 31, 2015, to compute McDonald's times interest earned ratio. Comment on the result. Assume an industry average of 15.0.

BTN 11-6 Assume that your team is in business and you must borrow $6,000 cash for short-term needs. You have been shopping banks for a loan, and you have the following two options.

A. Sign a $6,000, 90-day, 10% interest-bearing note dated June 1.
B. Sign a $6,000, 120-day, 8% interest-bearing note dated June 1.

TEAMWORK IN ACTION

C2   P1

Required

1. Discuss these two options and determine the best choice. Ensure that all teammates concur with the decision and understand the rationale.
2. Each member of the team is to prepare *one* of the following journal entries.
   a. Option A—at date of issuance.
   b. Option B—at date of issuance.
   c. Option A—at maturity date.
   d. Option B—at maturity date.
3. In rotation, each member is to explain the entry he or she prepared in part 2 to the team. Ensure that all team members concur with and understand the entries.
4. Assume that the funds are borrowed on December 1 (instead of June 1) and your business operates on a calendar-year reporting period. Each member of the team is to prepare *one* of the following entries.
   a. Option A—the year-end adjustment.
   b. Option B—the year-end adjustment.
   c. Option A—at maturity date.
   d. Option B—at maturity date.
5. In rotation, each member is to explain the entry he or she prepared in part 4 to the team. Ensure that all team members concur with and understand the entries.

ENTREPRENEURIAL DECISION

A1

BTN 11-7 Review the chapter's opening feature about Marcela Sapone and Jessica Beck and the business they founded, Hello Alfred. Assume that they are considering expanding the business to Europe and that the current abbreviated income statement appears as follows.

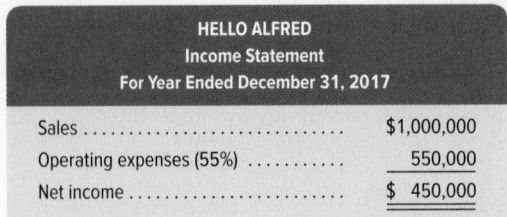

HELLO ALFRED Income Statement For Year Ended December 31, 2017	
Sales	$1,000,000
Operating expenses (55%)	550,000
Net income	$ 450,000

Assume also that Hello Alfred currently has no interest-bearing debt. If it expands to Europe, it will require a $300,000 loan. Hello Alfred has found a bank that will loan it the money on a 7% note payable. The company believes that, at least for the first few years, sales in Europe will equal $250,000 and that all expenses at both locations will continue to equal 55% of sales.

Required

1. Prepare an income statement (showing three separate columns for current operations, European, and total) for the company assuming that it borrows the funds and expands to Europe. Annual revenues for current operations are expected to remain at $1,000,000.

2. Compute the company's times interest earned under the expansion assumptions in part 1.

3. Assume sales in Europe are $400,000. Prepare an income statement (with columns for current operations, European, and total) for the company and compute times interest earned.

4. Assume sales in Europe are $100,000. Prepare an income statement (with columns for current operations, European, and total) for the company and compute times interest earned.

5. Comment on your results from parts 1 through 4.

HITTING THE ROAD

P2

BTN 11-8 Check the Social Security Administration website (SSA.gov) to locate the Social Security office near you. Visit the office to request a personal earnings and estimate form. Fill out the form and mail according to the instructions. You will receive a statement from the Social Security Administration regarding your earnings history and future Social Security benefits you can receive. (Formerly the request could be made online. The online service has been discontinued and is now under review by the Social Security Administration due to security concerns; however, it might once again be available online.) It is good to request an earnings and benefit statement every 5 to 10 years to make sure you have received credit for all wages earned and for which you and your employer have paid taxes into the system.

GLOBAL DECISION

A1

Samsung
APPLE
GOOGLE

BTN 11-9 Samsung, Apple, and Google are all competitors in the global marketplace. Comparative figures for Samsung (Samsung.com), along with selected figures from Apple and Google, follow.

Key Figures	Samsung (₩ millions)		Apple		Google	
	Current Year	Prior Year	Current Year	Prior Year	Current Year	Prior Year
Net income	₩19,060,144	₩23,394,358	—	—	—	—
Income taxes	6,900,851	4,480,676	—	—	—	—
Interest expense	776,511	592,940	—	—	—	—
Times interest earned	?	?	99.93	140.28	189.95	176.99

Required

1. Compute the times interest earned ratio for the most recent two years for Samsung using the data shown.

2. Which company of the three presented provides the best coverage of interest expense? Explain.

GLOBAL VIEW

This section discusses similarities and differences between U.S. GAAP and IFRS in accounting and reporting for current liabilities.

Characteristics of Liabilities   The definitions and characteristics of current liabilities are broadly similar for both U.S. GAAP and IFRS. Although differences exist, the similarities vastly outweigh any differences. Remembering that "provision" is typically used under IFRS to refer to what is titled "liability" under U.S. GAAP, Nokia describes its recognition of liabilities as follows:

> Provisions are recognized when the Group has a present legal or constructive obligation as a result of past events, it is probable that an outflow of resources will be required to settle the obligation and a reliable estimate of the amount can be made.

Known (Determinable) Liabilities   When there is little uncertainty surrounding current liabilities, both U.S. GAAP and IFRS require companies to record them in a similar manner. This correspondence in accounting applies to accounts payable, sales taxes payable, unearned revenues, short-term notes, and payroll liabilities. Of course, tax regulatory systems of countries are different, which implies use of different rates and levels. Still, the basic approach is the same.

Estimated Liabilities   When there is a known current obligation that involves an uncertain amount, but one that can be reasonably estimated, both U.S. GAAP and IFRS require similar treatment. This treatment extends to many obligations such as those arising from vacations, warranties, restructurings, pensions, and health care. Both accounting systems require that companies record estimated expenses related to these obligations when they can reasonably estimate the amounts. In a recent year, Nokia reported wages, salaries, and bonuses of €3,215 million. It also reported pension expenses of €207 million.

 IFRS ──

IFRS records a contingent liability when an obligation exists from a past event if there is a "probable" outflow of resources and the amount can be estimated reliably. However, IFRS defines probable as "more likely than not" while U.S. GAAP defines it as "likely to occur." ■

 ## Global View Assignments

Discussion Questions 16 & 17

Quick Study 11-14

Exercise 11-18

BTN 11-9

12

chapter

Accounting for Partnerships

Chapter Preview

PARTNERSHIP FORMATION

C1 Characteristics

Partnership form

P1 Start-up accounting

NTK 12-1

PARTNERSHIP INCOME OR LOSS

P2 Allocation on:

Ratios

Capital

Services, capital & ratios

Partners' equity

NTK 12-2

PARTNER ADMISSION

P3 Purchase interest

Invest assets

Partner bonus

NTK 12-3

PARTNER WITHDRAWAL

P4 No bonus

Bonus

Death

NTK 12-4

PARTNERSHIP LIQUIDATION

P5 No capital deficiency

Capital deficiency

A1 Partner return on equity

NTK 12-5

Learning Objectives

CONCEPTUAL

C1 Identify characteristics of partnerships and similar organizations.

ANALYTICAL

A1 Compute partner return on equity and use it to evaluate partnership performance.

PROCEDURAL

P1 Prepare entries for partnership formation.

P2 Allocate and record income and loss among partners.

P3 Account for the admission of partners.

P4 Account for the withdrawal of partners.

P5 Prepare entries for partnership liquidation.

Courtesy of Scholly

Smart Money

PHILADELPHIA—"I was born and raised in Birmingham, Alabama, to a single mom and two younger siblings. Although I came from a low-income background . . . I was determined to go to college," insists Chris Gray. "I spent long and laborious hours searching and applying for scholarships," says Chris. "The process was agonizing . . . and took me months. I knew there had to be an easier way to match students with scholarships." This is how Chris and fellow co-founders Bryson Alef and Nick Pirollo got the idea to start **Scholly** (**MyScholly.com**), an app that helps students find scholarship money.

"In less than two years, the app has helped students win over $20 million in scholarship funds," exclaims Chris. Scholly now has over "600,000 users" and was "ranked the #1 app in the iPhone and Android store for three weeks."

Chris, Bryson, and Nick set up a partnership arrangement for Scholly. Chris describes how they organized as a limited liability company (LLC), which is a partnership with some protection against liability claims. They also decided how to allocate income and how capital is computed.

"Scholarships instead of loans"

—Chris Gray

Forming their partnership as an LLC allowed them to readily add more partners, including *Shark Tank* stars Daymond John and Lori Greiner, who invested $40,000 for a 15% interest. To ensure that income is allocated correctly among the partners, they rely on their accounting system. This "is extremely important," explains Chris.

In addition to selling ownership interest, they raised "a lot of free capital," says Chris. This capital, according to Chris, includes their winnings from "competitions . . . [where] I won around $130,000 dollars for Scholly." He explains that "free capital" did not require them to give up equity. Chris relies on accounting to separate ownership capital from free capital. Otherwise, bonuses and withdrawals would not be allocated correctly.

"Helping students who can't pay for college" is Chris's social mission. "Knowing that what we're doing is helping a lot of people is something we are very proud of."

Sources: *Scholly website,* January 2017; *Huffington Post,* February 2016; *The Young Businessmen,* January 2016; *Forbes,* May 2015; *Drexel University,* February 2015

PARTNERSHIP FORMATION

C1_____

Identify characteristics of partnerships and similar organizations.

A **partnership** is an unincorporated association of two or more people to pursue a business for profit as co-owners. Partnerships are common in small retail and service businesses. Many professional practitioners, including physicians, lawyers, investors, and accountants, organize as partnerships.

Characteristics of Partnerships

Partnerships offer certain advantages with unique characteristics. We describe these characteristics in this section.

AP Images/Sal Veder

Voluntary Association   A partnership is a voluntary association between partners. Joining a partnership increases the risk to one's personal financial position. Some courts have ruled that partnerships are created by the actions of individuals even when there is no *express agreement* to form one. Steve Jobs, Steve Wozniak, and Ron Wayne were partners who voluntarily created **Apple.**

Point: When a new partner is admitted, all parties usually must agree to the admission.

Partnership Agreement   Forming a partnership requires that two or more people agree to be partners. Their agreement becomes a **partnership contract,** also called *articles of copartnership.* Although it should be in writing, the contract is binding even if it is only expressed verbally. Partnership agreements normally include partners' (1) names and contributions, (2) rights and duties, (3) sharing of income and losses, (4) withdrawal arrangement, (5) dispute procedures, (6) admission and withdrawal procedures, and (7) rights and duties in the event a partner dies.

Point: The end of a partnership is referred to as its *dissolution.*

Limited Life   The life of a partnership is limited. Death, bankruptcy, or any event taking away the ability of a partner to enter into or fulfill a contract ends a partnership. Any one partner can terminate a partnership at will.

Point: Partnership income is reported to the IRS on Form 1065. Partners receive a "K-1" form each year showing their share of income.

Taxation   A partnership is not subject to taxes on its income. The income or loss of a partnership is allocated to the partners and is used in determining the taxable income for each partner's tax return. Partnership income or loss is allocated each year whether or not cash is distributed to partners.

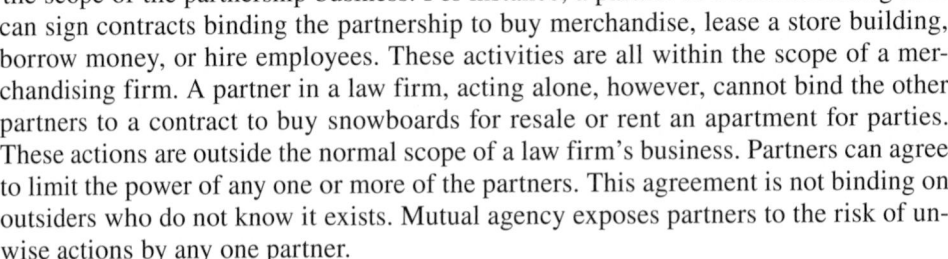

Mutual Agency   **Mutual agency** implies that each partner is a fully authorized agent of the partnership. As its agent, a partner can commit or bind the partnership to any contract within the scope of the partnership business. For instance, a partner in a merchandising firm can sign contracts binding the partnership to buy merchandise, lease a store building, borrow money, or hire employees. These activities are all within the scope of a merchandising firm. A partner in a law firm, acting alone, however, cannot bind the other partners to a contract to buy snowboards for resale or rent an apartment for parties. These actions are outside the normal scope of a law firm's business. Partners can agree to limit the power of any one or more of the partners. This agreement is not binding on outsiders who do not know it exists. Mutual agency exposes partners to the risk of unwise actions by any one partner.

Unlimited Liability   **Unlimited liability** implies that each partner can be required to pay a partnership's debts. When a partnership cannot pay its debts, creditors usually can apply claims to partners' *personal* assets. If a partner does not have enough assets to settle his or her share of the partnership debt, creditors can apply claims to the assets of the other partners. A partnership in which all partners have *mutual agency* and *unlimited liability* is called a **general partnership.** Mutual agency and unlimited liability are two main reasons that most general partnerships have only a few members.

Co-Ownership of Property   Partnership assets are owned jointly by all partners. Any investment by a partner becomes the joint property of all partners. Partners have a claim on partnership assets based on their capital account and the partnership contract.

Organizations with Partnership Characteristics

We next describe organizations that combine certain partnership characteristics.

Limited Partnerships   Individuals who want to invest in a partnership, but do not want the risk of unlimited liability, form a **limited partnership.** This type of organization is identified in its name with the words "Limited Partnership" or "Ltd." or "LP." A limited partnership has two classes of partners, general and limited. At least one partner must be a **general partner,** who has management duties and unlimited liability for the debts of the partnership. The **limited partners** have no personal liability beyond the amounts they invest in the partnership. Limited partners have no active role except as specified in the partnership agreement. A limited partnership agreement often specifies unique procedures for allocating income and losses between general and limited partners. Accounting is similar for both limited and general partnerships.

Limited Liability Partnerships   A **limited liability partnership** is designed to protect innocent partners from malpractice or negligence claims resulting from the acts of another partner. This is identified in its name with the words "Limited Liability Partnership" or "LLP." When a partner provides service resulting in a malpractice claim, that partner has personal liability for the claim. The remaining partners who were not responsible for the actions resulting in the claim are not personally liable for it. Accounting for a limited liability partnership is the same as for a general partnership.

Point: Many accounting, law, consulting, and architectural firms are set up as LLPs.

S Corporations   Certain corporations with 100 or fewer owners can elect to be treated as a partnership for income tax purposes. These corporations are called *Subchapter S* or **S corporations.** This distinguishes them from other corporations, called *Subchapter C* or **C corporations.** S corporations provide owners the same limited liability feature that C corporations do. The advantage of an S corporation is that it does not pay corporate income taxes. If owners work for an S corporation, their salaries are treated as expenses of the corporation. The remaining income or loss of the corporation is allocated to owners and included on their personal tax returns. Except for C corporations having to account for income tax expenses and liabilities, accounting is the same for both S and C corporations.

Limited Liability Companies   A **limited liability company** has features similar to a corporation and others similar to a limited partnership. The names of these businesses usually include the words "Limited Liability Company" or "LLC." The owners, who are called *members,* are protected with the same limited liability feature as owners of corporations. While limited partners cannot actively participate in the management of a limited partnership, the members of a limited liability company can have an active management role. For income tax purposes, a limited liability company is typically treated as a partnership.

Point: The majority of businesses organized today are set up as LLCs.

Point: Accounting for LLCs is similar to that for partnerships (and proprietorships). One difference is that Owner (Partner), Capital is usually called *Members, Capital* for LLCs.

Decision Insight

Chief Partners   Most states allow any business to form as a limited liability partnership (LLP); however, some states only allow approved professional service companies to form them. Of the four largest CPA firms in the United States (**KPMG, Deloitte, PwC,** and **EY**), all are set up as LLPs. ■

Choosing a Business Form

Choosing the proper business form is crucial. Many factors should be considered, including taxes, liability risk, tax and fiscal year-end, ownership structure, estate planning, business risks, and earnings and property distributions. The following table summarizes several important characteristics of different business entities.

	Proprietorship	Partnership	LLP	LLC	S Corp.	Corporation
Legal entity	No	No	No	Yes	Yes	Yes
Limited liability	No	No	Limited*	Yes	Yes	Yes
Business taxed	No	No	No	No	No	Yes
One owner allowed	Yes	No	No	Yes	Yes	Yes

* A partner's personal liability for LLP debts is limited. Most LLPs carry insurance to protect against malpractice.

Accounting for Partnership Formation

Because ownership rights in a partnership are divided among partners, partnership accounting

- Uses a capital account for each partner.
- Uses a withdrawals account for each partner.
- Allocates net income or loss to partners according to the partnership agreement.

P1

Prepare entries for partnership formation.

This section describes accounting for organizing a partnership.

When partners invest in a partnership, their capital accounts are credited for the invested amounts. Partners can invest both assets and liabilities. Each partner's investment is recorded at an agreed-on value, normally the market values of the contributed assets and liabilities at the date of contribution.

To illustrate, Kayla Zayn and Hector Perez organize a partnership on January 11 called BOARDS that offers year-round facilities for skateboarding and snowboarding. Zayn's initial net investment in BOARDS is $30,000, made up of cash ($7,000), boarding facilities ($33,000), and a note payable reflecting a bank loan for the new business ($10,000). Perez's initial investment is cash of $10,000. These amounts are the values agreed on by both partners. The entries to record these investments follow.

Assets = Liabilities + Equity
+7,000   +10,000   +30,000
+33,000

K. Zayn, Capital

	30,000

Zayn's Investment

Jan. 11	Cash	7,000	
	Boarding facilities	33,000	
	Note payable		10,000
	K. Zayn, Capital		30,000
	Record investment of Zayn.		

Assets = Liabilities + Equity
+10,000   +10,000

H. Perez, Capital

	10,000

Perez's Investment

Jan. 11	Cash	10,000	
	H. Perez, Capital		10,000
	Record investment of Perez.		

Point: Both equity and cash are reduced when a partner withdraws cash from a partnership.

Separate capital and withdrawals accounts are kept for each partner. Partnership accounting includes the following: (1) Partners' withdrawals are debited to their own separate withdrawals accounts. (2) Partners' capital accounts are credited (or debited) for their shares of net income (or net loss) when closing the accounts at the end of a period. (3) Each partner's withdrawals account is closed to that partner's capital account.

 **Decision** Insight

Star Gazing   **Starz, LLC** is a limited liability company, which is a type of partnership. Starz is a leading global media and entertainment company that competes with services such as **HBO**, **Showtime**, and **EPIX**. For a recent year, its income was roughly $250 million from a total revenue base of almost $1,800 million. In comparison, HBO, with series such as *Game of Thrones*, currently earns about $2 billion in annual income. ■

© WENN US / Alamy Stock Photo

LeBron and Durant organize a partnership on January 1. LeBron's initial net investment is $1,500, consisting of cash ($350), equipment ($1,650), and a note payable reflecting a bank loan for the new business ($500). Durant's initial investment is cash of $800. These amounts are the values agreed on by both partners. Prepare journal entries to record (1) LeBron's investment and (2) Durant's investment.

NEED-TO-KNOW 12-1

Partnership Formation
P1

Solution

1.

Jan. 1	Cash	350	
	Equipment	1,650	
	Note Payable...............................		500
	LeBron, Capital............................		1,500
	Record investment of LeBron.		

2.

Jan. 1	Cash	800	
	Durant, Capital............................		800
	Record investment of Durant.		

Do More: QS 12-3, E 12-3, E 12-4, P 12-1

DIVIDING PARTNERSHIP INCOME OR LOSS

Partners are not employees of the partnership but are its owners. If partners devote their time and services to their partnership, they are understood to do so for profit, not for salary. This means there are no salaries to partners that are reported as expenses on the partnership income statement. However, when net income or loss of a partnership is allocated among partners, the partners can agree to allocate "salary allowances" reflecting the relative value of services provided. Partners also can agree to allocate "interest allowances" based on the amount invested. For instance, since Zayn contributes three times the investment of Perez, it is only fair that this be considered when allocating income between them. Salary allowances and interest allowances are not expenses on the income statement.

P2

Allocate and record income and loss among partners.

Partners can agree to any method of dividing income or loss. In the absence of an agreement, the law says that the partners share income or loss of a partnership equally. If partners agree on how to share income but say nothing about losses, they share losses the same way they share income. Three common methods to divide income or loss use (1) a stated ratio basis, (2) the ratio of capital balances, or (3) salary and interest allowances and any remainder according to a fixed ratio. We explain each of these methods.

Point: Partners can agree on a ratio to divide income and another ratio to divide a loss.

Allocation on Stated Ratios   The *stated ratio* (also called the *income-and-loss-sharing ratio,* the *profit and loss ratio,* or the *P&L ratio*) method of allocating partnership income or loss gives each partner a fraction of the total. Partners must agree on the fractional share each receives. To illustrate, assume the partnership agreement of K. Zayn and H. Perez says Zayn receives two-thirds and Perez one-third of partnership income and loss. If their partnership's net income is $60,000, it is allocated to the partners when the Income Summary account is closed as follows.

Point: The fractional basis can be stated as a proportion, ratio, or percent. For example, a 3:2 basis is the same as $3/5$ and $2/5$, or 60% and 40%.

Dec. 31	Income Summary.....................................	60,000	
	K. Zayn, Capital (2/3 × $60,000)		40,000
	H. Perez, Capital (1/3 × $60,000)		20,000
	Allocate income and close Income Summary.		

Assets = Liabilities + Equity
$\quad\quad\quad\quad\quad\quad$ −60,000
$\quad\quad\quad\quad\quad\quad$ +40,000
$\quad\quad\quad\quad\quad\quad$ +20,000

Allocation on Capital Balances   The *capital balances* method of allocating partnership income or loss assigns an amount based on the ratio of each partner's relative capital balance. If Zayn and Perez agree to share income and loss on the ratio of their beginning capital balances—Zayn's $30,000 and Perez's $10,000—Zayn receives three-fourths of any income or loss ($30,000/$40,000) and Perez receives one-fourth ($10,000/$40,000). The journal entry follows the same format as that using stated ratios (see the previous entry).

Point: To determine the percent of income received by each partner, divide an individual partner's share by total net income.

Allocation on Services, Capital, and Stated Ratios   The *services, capital, and stated ratio* method of allocating partnership income or loss recognizes that service and capital contributions of partners often are not equal. Salary allowances can make up for differences in service contributions. Interest allowances can make up for unequal capital contributions. Also, the allocation of income and loss can include *both* salary and interest allowances. To illustrate, assume that the partnership agreement of K. Zayn and H. Perez reflects differences in service and capital contributions as follows: (1) annual salary allowances of $36,000 to Zayn and $24,000 to Perez, (2) annual interest allowances of 10% of a partner's beginning-year capital balance, and (3) equal share of any remaining balance of income or loss. These salary and interest allowances are *not* reported as expenses on the income statement. They are simply a means of dividing partnership income or loss. The remainder of this section provides two examples using this three-point allocation agreement.

When Income Exceeds Allowance If BOARDS has first-year net income of $70,000, and Zayn and Perez apply the three-point partnership agreement described in the prior paragraph, income is allocated as shown in Exhibit 12.1. Zayn gets $42,000 and Perez gets $28,000 of the $70,000 total.

EXHIBIT 12.1

Dividing Income When Income Exceeds Allowances

	Zayn	Perez	Total
Net income			**$70,000**
Salary allowances			
Zayn	$ 36,000		
Perez		$ 24,000	
Interest allowances			
Zayn (10% × $30,000)............	3,000		
Perez (10% × $10,000)		1,000	
Total salaries and interest	39,000	25,000	64,000
Balance of income			6,000
Balance allocated equally			
Zayn	3,000 ←		
Perez		3,000 ←	
Total allocated			6,000
Balance of income			$ 0
Income of each partner	**$42,000**	**$28,000**	

K. Zayn, Capital

Beg. bal. 30,000	
Allocated **42,000**	

H. Perez, Capital

Beg. bal. 10,000	
Allocated **28,000**	

Point: When allowances exceed income, the amount of this negative balance often is referred to as a *sharing agreement loss* or *deficit.*

When Allowances Exceed Income The sharing agreement between Zayn and Perez must be followed even if net income is less than the total of the allowances. For example, if BOARDS's first-year net income is $50,000 instead of $70,000, it is allocated to the partners as shown in Exhibit 12.2. Computations for salaries and interest are identical to those in Exhibit 12.1.

EXHIBIT 12.2

Dividing Income When Allowances Exceed Income

Point: See that total salary and interest allowances remain the same for Exh. 12.1 and 12.2, regardless of net income (loss).

	Zayn	Perez	Total
Net income			**$50,000**
Salary allowances			
Zayn	$ 36,000		
Perez		$24,000	
Interest allowances			
Zayn (10% × $30,000)	3,000		
Perez (10% × $10,000)		1,000	
Total salaries and interest	39,000	25,000	64,000
Balance of income			(14,000)
Balance allocated equally			
Zayn	(7,000) ←		
Perez		(7,000) ←	
Total allocated			(14,000)
Balance of income			$ 0
Income of each partner	**$32,000**	**$18,000**	

K. Zayn, Capital

Beg. bal. 30,000	
Allocated **32,000**	

H. Perez, Capital

Beg. bal. 10,000	
Allocated **18,000**	

However, when we apply the total allowances against income, the balance of income is negative. This $(14,000) negative balance is allocated equally to the partners per their sharing agreement. This means that a negative $(7,000) is allocated to each partner. In this case, Zayn ends up with $32,000 and Perez with $18,000. If BOARDS had experienced a net loss, Zayn and Perez would share it in the same manner as the $50,000 income. The only difference is that they would have begun with a negative amount because of the loss. The partners would still have been allocated their salary and interest allowances, further adding to the negative balance of the loss. This *total* negative balance *after* salary and interest allowances would have been allocated equally between the partners.

Point: Make sure the sum of the dollar amounts allocated to each partner equals net income or loss.

Point: When a loss occurs, it is possible for a specific partner's capital to increase (when closing Income Summary) if that partner's allowance is in excess of his or her share of the negative balance. This implies that decreases to the capital balances of other partners exceed the partnership's loss amount.

Partnership Financial Statements

Partnership financial statements are similar to those of other organizations. The **statement of partners' equity,** also called *statement of partners' capital,* is one exception. It shows *each* partner's beginning capital balance, additional investments, allocated income or loss, withdrawals, and ending capital balance. To illustrate, Exhibit 12.3 shows the statement of partners' equity for BOARDS prepared using the sharing agreement of Exhibit 12.1. Recall that BOARDS's income was $70,000; also, assume that Zayn withdrew $20,000 and Perez $12,000 at year-end.

EXHIBIT 12.3

Statement of Partners' Equity

BOARDS Statement of Partners' Equity For Year Ended December 31, 2017					
	Zayn		**Perez**		**Total**
Beginning capital balances		$ 0		$ 0	$ 0
Plus					
Investments by owners		30,000		10,000	40,000
Net income					
Salary allowances	$36,000		$24,000		
Interest allowances	3,000		1,000		
Balance allocated	3,000		3,000		
Total net income		42,000		28,000	70,000
		72,000		38,000	110,000
Less partners' withdrawals		(20,000)		(12,000)	(32,000)
Ending capital balances.		$52,000		$26,000	$78,000

K. Zayn, Capital

	Beg. bal.	30,000
	Allocated	42,000
With. 20,000		
	End. bal.	**52,000**

H. Perez, Capital

	Beg. bal.	10,000
	Allocated	28,000
With. 12,000		
	End. bal.	**26,000**

The equity section of the balance sheet of a partnership usually shows the separate capital account balance of each partner. In the case of BOARDS, both K. Zayn, Capital, and H. Perez, Capital, are listed in the equity section along with their balances of $52,000 and $26,000, respectively.

■ **Decision** Insight

Double Draw   Partnerships sometimes use two accounts to reflect a partner's withdrawal of cash from a partnership. For example, a "Drawing" account might be used for regular withdrawals such as a monthly salary allowance. A second "Withdrawals" account might be used for infrequent or personal draws such as for a daughter/son's wedding or a personal water craft. ■

© Vincent Ricardel/The Image Bank/Getty Images

Merkel and Putin began a partnership by investing $6,000 and $4,000, respectively. During its first year, the partnership earned $80,000. Prepare calculations showing how the $80,000 income is allocated to the partners under each of the following three separate plans for sharing income and loss: (1) the partners did not agree on a method to share income; (2) the partners agreed to share income and loss in proportion to their initial investments; and (3) the partners agreed to share income by granting a $35,000-per-year salary allowance to Merkel, a $13,000-per-year salary allowance to Putin, 20% interest on their initial capital investments, and any remaining balance shared 70% to Merkel and 30% to Putin.

NEED-TO-KNOW 12-2

Dividing Income or Loss

P2

Solution

	Merkel	Putin	Total
Plan (1) $80,000 × 1/2	**$40,000**	**$40,000**	**$80,000**
Plan (2) ($6,000/$10,000) × $80,000	$ 48,000		$48,000
($4,000/$10,000) × $80,000		$ 32,000	32,000
	$48,000	**$32,000**	**$80,000**
Plan (3) Net income			$80,000
Salary allowances.	$ 35,000	$ 13,000	48,000
Interest allowances			
($6,000 × 20%)	1,200		1,200
($4,000 × 20%)		800	800
Total salary and interest			50,000
Balance of income ($80,000 − $50,000)			30,000
Balance allocated:			
70% Merkel; 30% Putin	21,000	9,000	30,000
Balance of income			$ 0
Shares of each partner.	**$57,200**	**$22,800**	

> **Do More:** QS 12-4, QS 12-5, E 12-5, E 12-6, E 12-7

PARTNER ADMISSION

P3
Account for the admission of partners.

When a partner is admitted or withdraws, the present partnership ends. The business can continue to operate as a *new* partnership consisting of the remaining partners.

A new partner is admitted in one of two ways: by purchasing an interest from one or more current partners or by investing cash or other assets in the partnership.

Purchase of Partnership Interest

The purchase of partnership interest is a *personal transaction between one or more current partners and the new partner.* To become a partner, the current partners must accept the purchaser. Accounting for the purchase of partnership interest involves reallocating current partners' capital to reflect the transaction. To illustrate, at the end of BOARDS's first year, H. Perez sells one-half of his partnership interest to Tyrell Rasheed for $18,000. This means that Perez gives up a $13,000 recorded interest ($26,000 × 1/2) in the partnership (see the ending capital balance in Exhibit 12.3). The partnership records this January 4 transaction as follows.

Assets = Liabilities + Equity
       −13,000
       +13,000

Jan. 4	H. Perez, Capital	13,000	
	T. Rasheed, Capital.		13,000
	Record admission of Rasheed by purchase.		

After this entry is posted, BOARDS's equity shows K. Zayn, Capital; H. Perez, Capital; and T. Rasheed, Capital; and their respective balances of $52,000, $13,000, and $13,000.

Two aspects of this transaction are important. First, the partnership does *not* record the $18,000 Rasheed paid Perez. The partnership's assets, liabilities, and *total equity* are unaffected by this transaction among partners. Second, Zayn and Perez must agree that Rasheed is to become a partner. If they agree to accept Rasheed, a new partnership is formed and a new contract with a new income-and-loss-sharing agreement is prepared. If Zayn or Perez refuses to accept Rasheed as a partner, then (under the Uniform Partnership Act) Rasheed gets Perez's sold share of partnership income and loss. If the partnership is liquidated, Rasheed gets Perez's sold share of partnership assets. Rasheed gets no voice in managing the company unless Rasheed is admitted as a partner.

Point: Partners' withdrawals are not constrained by the partnership's annual income or loss.

Investing Assets in a Partnership

Admitting a partner by accepting assets is a *transaction between the new partner and the partnership*. The invested assets become partnership property. To illustrate, if Zayn (with a $52,000 interest) and Perez (with a $26,000 interest) agree to accept Rasheed as a partner in BOARDS after an investment of $22,000 cash, this is recorded as follows.

Jan. 4	Cash	22,000	
	T. Rasheed, Capital............................		22,000
	Record admission of Rasheed by investment.		

Assets = Liabilities + Equity
+22,000   +22,000

After this entry is posted, both assets (Cash) and equity (T. Rasheed, Capital) increase by $22,000. Rasheed now has a 22% equity in the assets of the business, computed as $22,000 divided by the entire partnership equity ($52,000 + $26,000 + $22,000). Rasheed does not necessarily have a right to 22% of income. Dividing income and loss is a separate matter on which partners must agree.

Bonus to Old Partners   When the current value of a partnership is greater than the recorded amounts of equity, the partners usually require a new partner to pay a bonus for the privilege of joining. When the balance in the new partner's capital account does not equal the amount of net assets invested, the difference is called a *bonus* either to or from the current partners. To illustrate, assume that Zayn and Perez agree to accept Rasheed as a partner with a 25% interest in BOARDS if Rasheed invests $42,000. Recall that the partnership's accounting records show that Zayn's recorded equity in the business is $52,000 and Perez's recorded equity is $26,000 (see Exhibit 12.3). Rasheed's equity is determined as follows.

Equities of existing partners ($52,000 + $26,000)	$ 78,000
Investment of new partner	42,000
Total partnership equity	$120,000
Equity of Rasheed (25% × $120,000)	$ 30,000

K. Zayn, Capital

	52,000
	6,000
	58,000

H. Perez, Capital

	26,000
	6,000
	32,000

T. Rasheed, Capital

| | 30,000 |
| | 30,000 |

→ **Total Capital = $120,000**

Although Rasheed invests $42,000, the equity attributed to Rasheed in the new partnership is only $30,000. The $12,000 difference is called a *bonus* and is allocated to existing partners (Zayn and Perez) according to their income-and-loss-sharing agreement. A bonus is shared in this way because it is viewed as reflecting a higher value of the partnership that is not yet reflected in income. The entry to record this transaction follows.

Jan. 4	Cash	42,000	
	T. Rasheed, Capital............................		30,000
	K. Zayn, Capital ($12,000 × ½)		6,000
	H. Perez, Capital ($12,000 × ½)		6,000
	Record admission of Rasheed and bonus.		

Assets = Liabilities + Equity
+42,000   +30,000
                         +6,000
                         +6,000

Bonus to New Partner   Alternatively, existing partners can grant a bonus to a new partner. This usually occurs when they need additional cash or the new partner has exceptional talents. The bonus to the new partner is in the form of a larger share of equity than the amount invested. To illustrate, assume that Zayn and Perez agree to accept Rasheed as a partner with a 25% interest in the partnership, but they require Rasheed to invest only $18,000. Rasheed's equity is determined as follows.

Equities of existing partners ($52,000 + $26,000)	$78,000
Investment of new partner	18,000
Total partnership equity	$96,000
Equity of Rasheed (25% × $96,000)	$24,000

K. Zayn, Capital

	52,000
3,000	
	49,000

H. Perez, Capital

	26,000
3,000	
	23,000

T. Rasheed, Capital

| | 24,000 |
| | 24,000 |

→ **Total Capital = $96,000**

The old partners contribute the $6,000 bonus (computed as $24,000 minus $18,000) to Rasheed according to their income-and-loss-sharing ratio. Moreover, Rasheed's 25% equity does not necessarily entitle Rasheed to 25% of future income or loss. This is a separate matter for agreement by the partners. The entry to record the admission and investment of Rasheed is

Assets	=	Liabilities	+	Equity
+18,000				−3,000
				−3,000
				+24,000

Jan. 4	Cash..	18,000	
	K. Zayn, Capital ($6,000 × ½).......................	3,000	
	H. Perez, Capital ($6,000 × ½).......................	3,000	
	T. Rasheed, Capital.............................		24,000
	Record Rasheed's admission and bonus.		

NEED-TO-KNOW 12-3

Partner Admission

P3

Anne, Portia, and Hedison are partners and share income and losses in a 2:3:5 ratio. The partnership's capital balances are as follows: Anne, $300; Portia, $150; and Hedison, $450. Ellen is admitted to the partnership on May 1 with a 25% equity. Prepare journal entries to record Ellen's entry into the partnership under each of the following separate assumptions: Ellen invests (a) $300; (b) $100; and (c) $700.

Solution

a.

May 1	Cash..	300	
	Ellen, Capital*.................................		300
	Record admission of Ellen, with no bonus.		

* ($900 + $300) × 25% = $300

b.

May 1	Cash..	100	
	Anne, Capital ([$250 − $100] × 2/10).................	30	
	Portia, Capital ([$250 − $100] × 3/10).................	45	
	Hedison, Capital ([$250 − $100] × 5/10)...............	75	
	Ellen, Capital ([$900 + $100] × 0.25)..............		250
	Record Ellen's admission, with bonus to new partner.		

c.

May 1	Cash..	700	
	Anne, Capital ([$700 − $400] × 2/10).................		60
	Portia, Capital ([$700 − $400] × 3/10).............		90
	Hedison, Capital ([$700 − $400] × 5/10)...........		150
	Ellen, Capital ([$900 + $700] × 0.25)..............		400
	Record admission of Ellen, with bonus to old partners.		

Do More: QS 12-6, QS 12-7, E 12-9

PARTNER WITHDRAWAL

P4

Account for the withdrawal of partners.

A partner generally withdraws from a partnership in one of two ways. (1) First, the withdrawing partner can sell his or her interest to another person who pays for it in cash or other assets. For this, we debit the withdrawing partner's capital account and credit the new partner's capital account. (2) The second case is when cash or other assets of the partnership are distributed to the withdrawing partner in settlement of his or her interest. To illustrate these cases, assume that Perez withdraws from the partnership of BOARDS in some future period. The partnership shows the following capital balances at the date of Perez's withdrawal: K. Zayn, $84,000; H. Perez, $38,000; and T. Rasheed, $38,000. The partners (Zayn, Perez, and Rasheed) share income and loss equally. Accounting for Perez's withdrawal depends on whether a bonus is paid. We describe three possibilities.

No Bonus

If Perez withdraws and takes cash equal to Perez's capital balance, the entry is

Oct. 31	H. Perez, Capital	38,000	
	Cash		38,000
	Record withdrawal of Perez with no bonus.		

Assets = Liabilities + Equity
−38,000   −38,000

Perez can take any combination of assets to which the partners agree to settle Perez's equity.

Bonus to Remaining Partners

A withdrawing partner is sometimes willing to take less than the recorded value of his or her equity to get out of the partnership or because the recorded value is overstated. Whatever the reason, when this occurs, the withdrawing partner in effect gives the remaining partners a bonus equal to the equity left behind. The remaining partners share this unwithdrawn equity (bonus) according to their income-and-loss-sharing ratio. To illustrate, if Perez withdraws and agrees to take $34,000 cash in settlement of Perez's capital balance, the entry is

Oct. 31	H. Perez, Capital	38,000	
	Cash		34,000
	K. Zayn, Capital.................................		2,000
	T. Rasheed, Capital............................		2,000
	Record withdrawal of Perez and bonus to remaining partners.		

Assets = Liabilities + Equity
−34,000   −38,000
                       +2,000
                       +2,000

Perez withdraws $4,000 less than Perez's recorded equity of $38,000. This $4,000 is divided between Zayn and Rasheed according to their income-and-loss-sharing ratio.

Bonus to Withdrawing Partner

A withdrawing partner may be able to receive more than his or her recorded equity for at least two reasons. First, the recorded equity may be understated. Second, the remaining partners may agree to remove this partner by giving assets of greater value than this partner's recorded equity. In either case, the withdrawing partner receives a bonus. The remaining partners reduce their equity by the amount of this bonus according to their income-and-loss-sharing ratio. To illustrate, if Perez withdraws and receives $40,000 cash in settlement of Perez's capital balance, the entry is

Oct. 31	H. Perez, Capital	38,000	
	K. Zayn, Capital	1,000	
	T. Rasheed, Capital	1,000	
	Cash		40,000
	Record Perez's withdrawal with a bonus to Perez.		

Assets = Liabilities + Equity
−40,000   −38,000
                       −1,000
                       −1,000

Falcon Cable Communications set up a partnership withdrawal agreement. Falcon owns and operates cable television systems and had two managing general partners. The partnership agreement stated that either partner "can offer to sell to the other partner the offering partner's entire partnership interest . . . for a negotiated price. If the partner receiving such an offer rejects it, the offering partner may elect to cause [the partnership] . . . to be liquidated and dissolved."

Death of a Partner

A partner's death dissolves a partnership. A deceased partner's estate is entitled to receive his or her equity. The partnership contract should contain provisions for settlement in this case. These provisions usually require (1) closing the books to determine income or loss since the end of the previous period and (2) determining and recording current market values for both assets and liabilities. The remaining partners and the deceased partner's estate then must agree to a settlement of the deceased partner's equity. This can involve selling the equity to remaining partners or to an outsider, or it can involve withdrawing assets.

Decision Ethics

Financial Planner The partnership agreement states that a deceased partner's estate is entitled to a "share of partnership assets equal to the partner's relative equity balance" (partners' equity balances are equal). The estate argues that it is entitled to one-third of the current value of partnership assets. The remaining partners say the distribution should use asset book values, which are 75% of current value. They also point to partnership liabilities, which equal 40% of total asset book value and 30% of current value. How would you resolve this? ∎   [*Answer:* The agreement apparently fails to mention liabilities or use the term *net assets*. To give the estate one-third of total assets is not fair to the remaining partners because if the partner had lived and the partners had decided to liquidate, the liabilities must be paid out of assets before any liquidation. Also, a settlement based on the deceased partner's recorded equity would fail to recognize excess of current value over book value. A fair settlement would seem to be a payment to the estate for the balance of the deceased partner's equity based on the current value of net assets.]

NEED-TO-KNOW 12-4

Partner Withdrawal

P4

Fluffy, Anjelah, and Lopez are partners and share income and losses in a 2:3:5 ratio. The partnership's capital balances are as follows: Fluffy, $330; Anjelah, $270; and Lopez, $400. Lopez decides to withdraw from the partnership, and the partners agree not to revalue the assets upon Lopez's retirement. Prepare journal entries to record Lopez's May 1 withdrawal from the partnership under each of the following separate assumptions:

a. Lopez sells his interest to Mencia for $500 after Fluffy and Anjelah approve the entry of Mencia as a partner.

b. Lopez gives his interest to a son-in-law, Madrigal, and thereafter Fluffy and Anjelah accept Madrigal as a partner.

c. Lopez is paid $400 in partnership cash for his equity.

d. Lopez is paid $600 in partnership cash for his equity.

e. Lopez is paid $70 in partnership cash plus equipment recorded on the partnership books at $40 less its accumulated depreciation of $10.

Solution

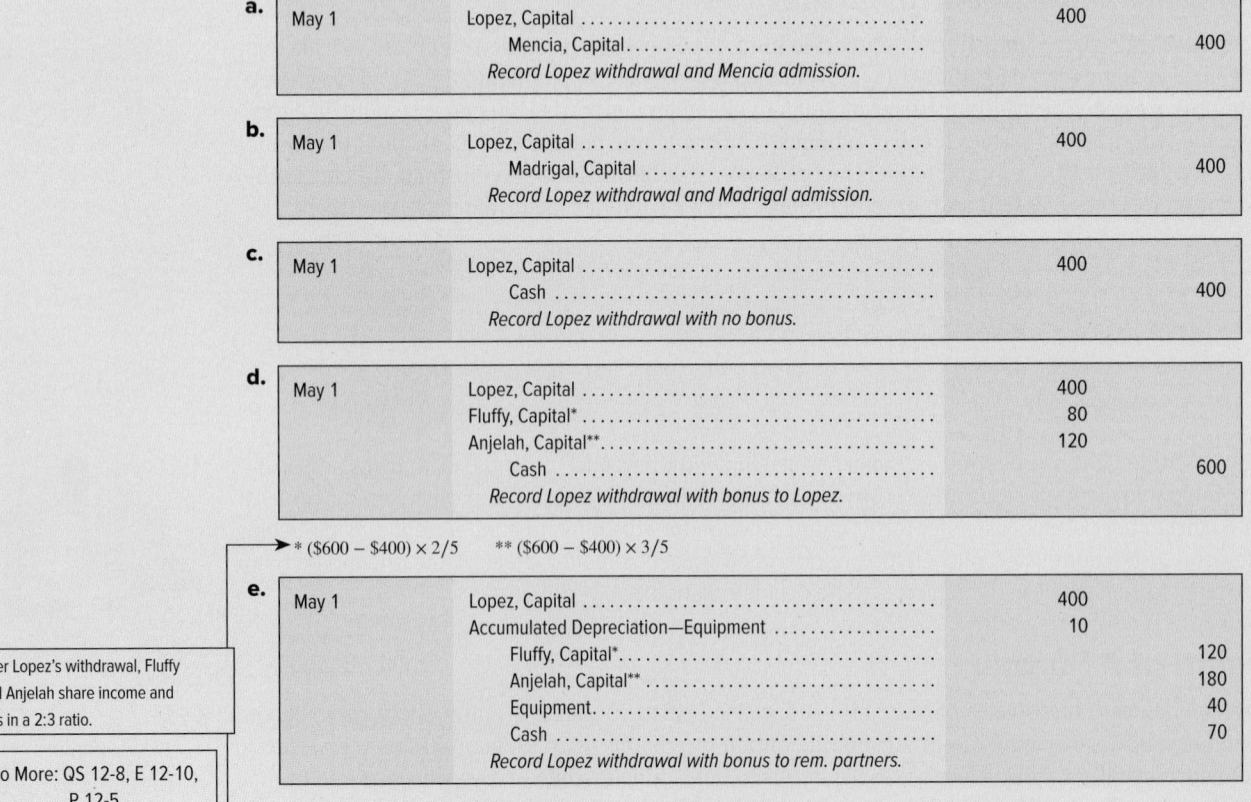

a.

May 1	Lopez, Capital	400	
	Mencia, Capital..............................		400
	Record Lopez withdrawal and Mencia admission.		

b.

May 1	Lopez, Capital	400	
	Madrigal, Capital		400
	Record Lopez withdrawal and Madrigal admission.		

c.

May 1	Lopez, Capital	400	
	Cash		400
	Record Lopez withdrawal with no bonus.		

d.

May 1	Lopez, Capital	400	
	Fluffy, Capital*	80	
	Anjelah, Capital**	120	
	Cash		600
	Record Lopez withdrawal with bonus to Lopez.		

➤ * ($600 − $400) × 2/5   ** ($600 − $400) × 3/5

e.

May 1	Lopez, Capital	400	
	Accumulated Depreciation—Equipment	10	
	Fluffy, Capital*................................		120
	Anjelah, Capital**		180
	Equipment..................................		40
	Cash		70
	Record Lopez withdrawal with bonus to rem. partners.		

After Lopez's withdrawal, Fluffy and Anjelah share income and loss in a 2:3 ratio.

Do More: QS 12-8, E 12-10, P 12-5

➤ * [$400 − ($40 − $10 + $70)] × 2/5   ** [$400 − ($40 − $10 + $70)] × 3/5

LIQUIDATION OF A PARTNERSHIP

When a partnership is liquidated, its business ends and three concluding steps are required.

1. Record the sale of noncash assets for cash, and any gain or loss from liquidation is allocated to partners *using their income-and-loss-sharing agreement.*
2. Pay or settle all partner liabilities.
3. Distribute any remaining cash to partners *based on their capital balances.*

Partnership liquidation usually falls into one of two cases, as described in this section.

P5 _____

Prepare entries for partnership liquidation.

© Kristoffer Tripplaar / Alamy Stock Photo

No Capital Deficiency

No capital deficiency means that all partners have a zero or credit balance in their capital accounts for final distribution of cash. To illustrate, assume that Zayn, Perez, and Rasheed operate their partnership in BOARDS for several years, sharing income and loss equally. The partners then decide to liquidate. On the liquidation date, the current period's income or loss is transferred to the partners' capital accounts according to the sharing agreement. After that transfer, assume the partners' recorded account balances (immediately prior to liquidation) are:

Cash.........	$178,000	Accounts Payable	$20,000	H. Perez, Capital	$66,000
Land.........	40,000	K. Zayn, Capital	70,000	T. Rasheed, Capital	62,000

We apply three steps for liquidation. ① *The partnership sells its noncash assets, and any losses or gains from liquidation are shared among partners according to their income-and-loss-sharing agreement* (equal for these partners). Assume that BOARDS sells its noncash assets consisting of $40,000 in land for $46,000 cash, yielding a net gain of $6,000. In a liquidation, gains or losses usually result from the sale of noncash assets, which are called *losses and gains from liquidation.* The entry to sell its assets for $46,000 follows.

Jan. 15	Cash	46,000	
	Land...		40,000
	Gain from Liquidation...........................		6,000
	Sold noncash assets at a gain.		

Assets = Liabilities + Equity
−40,000   +6,000
+46,000

Allocation of the gain from liquidation per the partners' income-and-loss-sharing agreement follows.

Jan. 15	Gain from Liquidation	6,000	
	K. Zayn, Capital.................................		2,000
	H. Perez, Capital................................		2,000
	T. Rasheed, Capital.............................		2,000
	Allocate liquidation gain to partners.		

Assets = Liabilities + Equity
                        −6,000
                        +2,000
                        +2,000
                        +2,000

② *The partnership pays its liabilities, and any losses or gains from liquidation of liabilities are shared among partners according to their income-and-loss-sharing agreement.* BOARDS's only liability is $20,000 in accounts payable, and no gain or loss occurred.

Jan. 15	Accounts Payable	20,000	
	Cash		20,000
	Pay claims of creditors.		

Assets = Liabilities + Equity
−20,000   −20,000

After step 2, we have the following capital balances along with the remaining cash balance.

K. Zayn		
	Bal.	70,000
	(b)	2,000
	Bal.	72,000

H. Perez, Capital		
	Bal.	66,000
	(b)	2,000
	Bal.	68,000

T. Rasheed, Capital		
	Bal.	62,000
	(b)	2,000
	Bal.	64,000

Cash				
Bal.	178,000	(c)	20,000
(a)	46,000		
Bal.	204,000		

③ *Any remaining cash is divided among the partners **according to their capital account balances.*** The entry to record the final distribution of cash to partners follows.

Assets = Liabilities + Equity
−204,000   −72,000
                            −68,000
                            −64,000

Jan. 15	K. Zayn, Capital	72,000	
	H. Perez, Capital	68,000	
	T. Rasheed, Capital	64,000	
	Cash		204,000
	Distribute remaining cash to partners.		

It is important to remember that the final cash payment is distributed to partners according to their capital account balances, whereas gains and losses from liquidation are allocated according to the income-and-loss-sharing ratio. The following *statement of liquidation* summarizes the three steps in this section.

Statement of Liquidation	Cash	Noncash Assets	=	Liabilities	K. Zayn, Capital	H. Perez, Capital	T. Rasheed, Capital
Balances prior to liquidation	$ 178,000	$ 40,000		$ 20,000	$ 70,000	$ 66,000	$ 62,000
① Sale of noncash assets	46,000	(40,000)			2,000	2,000	2,000
② Payment of liabilities	(20,000)			(20,000)	0	0	0
Balances for distribution	204,000	$ 0		$ 0	72,000	68,000	64,000
③ Distribution of cash to partners....	(204,000)				(72,000)	(68,000)	(64,000)
	$ 0				$ 0	$ 0	$ 0

Capital Deficiency

Capital deficiency means that at least one partner has a debit balance in his or her capital account at the point of final cash distribution (during step ③ as explained in the prior section). This can arise from liquidation losses, excessive withdrawals before liquidation, or recurring losses in prior periods. A partner with a capital deficiency must, if possible, cover the deficit by paying cash into the partnership.

To illustrate, assume that Zayn, Perez, and Rasheed operate their partnership in BOARDS for several years, sharing income and losses equally. The partners then decide to liquidate. Immediately prior to the final distribution of cash, the partners' recorded capital balances are Zayn, $19,000; Perez, $8,000; and Rasheed, $(3,000). Rasheed's capital deficiency means that Rasheed owes the partnership $3,000. Both Zayn and Perez have a legal claim against Rasheed's personal assets. The final distribution of cash in this case depends on how this capital deficiency is handled. Two possibilities exist: the partner pays the deficiency or the partner cannot pay the deficiency.

Partner Pays Deficiency   Rasheed is obligated to pay $3,000 into the partnership to cover the deficiency. If Rasheed is able to pay, the entry to record receipt of payment from Rasheed follows.

K. Zayn, Capital	
	19,000
	19,000

H. Perez, Capital	
	8,000
	8,000

T. Rasheed, Capital	
3,000	
	3,000
	0

Assets = Liabilities + Equity
+3,000   +3,000

Jan. 15	Cash	3,000	
	T. Rasheed, Capital............................		3,000
	Record payment of deficiency by Rasheed.		

After the $3,000 payment, the partners' capital balances are Zayn, $19,000; Perez, $8,000; and Rasheed, $0. The entry to record the final cash distributions to partners is

Jan. 15	K. Zayn, Capital	19,000	
	H. Perez, Capital	8,000	
	Cash		27,000
	Distribute remaining cash to partners.		

Assets =	Liabilities +	Equity
−27,000		−19,000
		−8,000

K. Zayn, Capital

	19,000
1,500	
	17,500

H. Perez, Capital

	8,000
1,500	
	6,500

T. Rasheed, Capital

3,000	
	3,000
	0

Partner Cannot Pay Deficiency The remaining partners with credit balances absorb any partner's unpaid deficiency according to their income-and-loss-sharing ratio. To illustrate, if Rasheed is unable to pay the $3,000 deficiency, Zayn and Perez absorb it. Since they share income and loss equally, Zayn and Perez each absorb $1,500 of the deficiency. This is recorded as follows.

Jan. 15	K. Zayn, Capital	1,500	
	H. Perez, Capital	1,500	
	T. Rasheed, Capital............................		3,000
	Transfer Rasheed deficiency to Zayn and Perez.		

Assets =	Liabilities +	Equity
		−1,500
		−1,500
		+3,000

After Zayn and Perez absorb Rasheed's deficiency, the capital accounts of the partners are Zayn, $17,500; Perez, $6,500; and Rasheed, $0. The entry to record the final cash distribution to the partners is

Jan. 15	K. Zayn, Capital	17,500	
	H. Perez, Capital	6,500	
	Cash		24,000
	Distribute remaining cash to partners.		

Assets =	Liabilities +	Equity
−24,000		−17,500
		−6,500

Rasheed's nonpayment of this deficiency does not relieve Rasheed of the liability. If Rasheed becomes able to pay at a future date, Zayn and Perez can each collect $1,500 from Rasheed.

The Danica, Gaga & Oprah partnership was begun with investments by the partners as follows: Danica, $190; Gaga, $340; and Oprah, $550. Danica, Gaga, and Oprah share income and losses in a 1:1:2 ratio. The operations did not go well, and the partners eventually decided to liquidate the partnership. On July 31, after all assets were converted to cash and all creditors were paid, only $80 in partnership cash remained.

NEED-TO-KNOW 12-5

Partnership Liquidation

P5

1. Compute the capital account balance of each partner after the liquidation of assets and the payment of creditors.

2. Assume that any partner with a deficit agrees to pay cash to the partnership to cover the deficit. Prepare the journal entries on July 31 to record (*a*) the cash receipt from the deficient partner(s) and (*b*) the final disbursement of cash to the partners.

3. Assume that any partner with a deficit is not able to reimburse the partnership. Prepare journal entries (*a*) to transfer the deficit of any deficient partners to the other partners and (*b*) to record the final disbursement of cash to the partners.

Solution

1.

	Danica	Gaga	Oprah	Total
Initial investments......................	$ 190	$ 340	$ 550	$ 1,080
Allocation of liquidation share:				
($1,080 − $80) using 1:1:2.............	(250)	(250)	(500)	(1,000)
Capital balances........................	$ (60)	$ 90	$ 50	$ 80

2. a.

July 31	Cash	60	
	Danica, Capital		60
	Record payment of deficiency.		

b.

July 31	Gaga, Capital	90	
	Oprah, Capital	50	
	Cash		140
	Distribute remaining cash.		

3. a.

July 31	Gaga, Capital ($60 × 1/3)	20	
	Oprah, Capital ($60 × 2/3)..........................	40	
	Danica, Capital		60
	Transfer deficiency to other partners (1:2).		

b.

July 31	Gaga, Capital	70	
	Oprah, Capital	10	
	Cash		80
	Distribute remaining cash.		

Do More: QS 12-9, E 12-11, E 12-12, P 12-6

SUSTAINABILITY AND ACCOUNTING

© Brad Barket/Getty Images

Scholly, introduced as this chapter's opening feature, is dedicated to helping students pay for college. Co-founder Chris Gray wants to help students "avoid the crushing student debt that is so prevalent today" by making it easier to find scholarships. In addition to offering the app for a price of $2.99 in the App Store, Scholly is partnering with "organizations and companies to provide Scholly to large populations of students . . . with our *Give: Scholly* initiative," explains Chris. "It allows organizations and companies to purchase their own branded access code to Scholly, which they can then distribute to as many selected constituents as they wish."

Chris also partners with the nonprofit *My Brother's Keeper Alliance* to provide free access to Scholly for 275,000 students. "This is the biggest deal we've ever done," says Chris.

Chris admits, however, that these sustainable initiatives would not be possible without an effective accounting system. Sales in the App Store and sales to large nonprofit organizations must be accounted for differently. Revenue per app sold is not the same amount in both of these situations. Chris relies on his accounting system to track these transactions and ensure revenue is properly recorded.

With an effective accounting system in place, Chris is able to devote much of his time to "helping students who can't pay for college . . . find scholarships." His main goal is give students who "come from a low-income background" like his the chance to "build a great company and even end up on the *Forbes* 30 Under 30 list."

 **Decision Analysis**    **Partner Return on Equity**

A1 _____

Compute partner return on equity and use it to evaluate partnership performance.

An important role of partnership financial statements is to aid current and potential partners in evaluating partnership success compared with other opportunities. One measure of this success is the **partner return on equity** ratio:

$$\text{Partner return on equity} = \frac{\text{Partner net income}}{\text{Average partner equity}}$$

This measure is separately computed for each partner. To illustrate, Exhibit 12.4 reports selected data from the **Boston Celtics LP**. The return on equity for the *total* partnership is computed as $216/[($85 + $253)/2] = 127.8%. However, return on equity is quite different across the partners. For example, the **Boston Celtics LP I** partner return on equity is computed as $44/[($122 + $166)/2] = 30.6%, whereas the **Celtics LP** partner

EXHIBIT 12.4

Selected Data from Boston Celtics LP

$ thousands	Total*	Boston Celtics LP I	Boston Celtics LP II	Celtics LP
Beginning-year balance	$ 85	$122	$(307)	$270
Net income (loss) for year	216	44	61	111
Cash distribution	(48)	—	—	(48)
Ending-year balance	$253	$166	$(246)	$333
Partner return on equity	127.8%	30.6%	n.a.	36.8%

* Totals may not add up due to rounding.

return on equity is computed as $111/[($270 + $333)/2] = 36.8\%$. Partner return on equity provides *each* partner an assessment of its return on its equity invested in the partnership. A specific partner often uses this return to decide whether additional investment or withdrawal of resources is best for that partner. Exhibit 12.4 reveals that the year shown produced good returns for all partners (the Boston Celtics LP II return is not computed because its average equity is negative due to an unusual and large distribution in the prior year).

NEED-TO-KNOW 12-6

COMPREHENSIVE

The following transactions and events affect the partners' capital accounts in several successive partnerships. Prepare a table with six columns, one for each of the five partners along with a total column to show the effects of the following events on the five partners' capital accounts.

Part 1

4/13/2014   Ries and Bax create R&B Company. Each invests $10,000, and they agree to share income and losses equally.

12/31/2014   R&B Co. earns $15,000 in income for its first year. Ries withdraws $4,000 from the partnership, and Bax withdraws $7,000.

1/1/2015   Royce is accepted as a partner in RB&R Company after contributing $12,000 cash. The partners agree that a 10% interest allowance will be given on each partner's beginning-year capital balance. In addition, Bax and Royce are to receive $5,000 salary allowances. The remainder of the income or loss is to be divided evenly.

12/31/2015   The partnership's income for the year is $40,000, and withdrawals at year-end are Ries, $5,000; Bax, $12,500; and Royce, $11,000.

1/1/2016   Ries sells her interest for $20,000 to Murdock, whom Bax and Royce accept as a partner in the new BR&M Co. Income or loss is to be shared equally after Bax and Royce receive $25,000 salary allowances.

12/31/2016   The partnership's income for the year is $35,000, and year-end withdrawals are Bax, $2,500, and Royce, $2,000.

1/1/2017   Elway is admitted as a partner after investing $60,000 cash in the new Elway & Associates partnership. He is given a 50% interest in capital after the other partners transfer $3,000 to his account from each of theirs. A 20% interest allowance (on the beginning-year capital balances) will be used in sharing any income or loss, there will be no salary allowances, and Elway will receive 40% of the remaining balance—the other three partners will each get 20%.

12/31/2017   Elway & Associates earns $127,600 in income for the year, and year-end withdrawals are Bax, $25,000; Royce, $27,000; Murdock, $15,000; and Elway, $40,000.

1/1/2018   Elway buys out Bax and Royce for the balances of their capital accounts after a revaluation of the partnership assets. The revaluation gain is $50,000, which is divided using a 1:1:1:2 ratio (Bax:Royce:Murdock:Elway). Elway pays the others from personal funds. Murdock and Elway will share income on a 1:9 ratio.

2/28/2018   The partnership earns $10,000 of income since the beginning of the year. Murdock retires and receives partnership cash equal to her capital balance. Elway takes possession of the partnership assets in his own name, and the partnership is dissolved.

Part 2

Journalize the events affecting the partnership for the year ended December 31, 2015.

PLANNING THE SOLUTION

- Evaluate each transaction's effects on the capital accounts of the partners.
- Each time a new partner is admitted or a partner withdraws, allocate any bonus based on the income-or-loss-sharing agreement.

- Each time a new partner is admitted or a partner withdraws, allocate subsequent net income or loss in accordance with the new partnership agreement.
- Prepare entries to (1) record Royce's initial investment; (2) record the allocation of interest, salaries, and remainder; (3) show the cash withdrawals from the partnership; and (4) close the withdrawal accounts on December 31, 2015.

SOLUTION

Part 1

Event	Ries	Bax	Royce	Murdock	Elway	Total
4/13/2014						
Initial investment	$10,000	$10,000				$ 20,000
12/31/2014						
Income (equal)	7,500	7,500				15,000
Withdrawals	(4,000)	(7,000)				(11,000)
Ending balance...............	$13,500	$10,500				$ 24,000
1/1/2015						
New investment..............			$12,000			$ 12,000
12/31/2015						
10% interest.................	1,350	1,050	1,200			3,600
Salaries.....................		5,000	5,000			10,000
Remainder (equal)	8,800	8,800	8,800			26,400
Withdrawals	(5,000)	(12,500)	(11,000)			(28,500)
Ending balance...............	$18,650	$12,850	$16,000			$ 47,500
1/1/2016						
Transfer interest..............	(18,650)			$18,650		$ 0
12/31/2016						
Salaries.....................		25,000	25,000			50,000
Remainder (equal)		(5,000)	(5,000)	(5,000)		(15,000)
Withdrawals		(2,500)	(2,000)			(4,500)
Ending balance...............	$ 0	$30,350	$34,000	$13,650		$ 78,000
1/1/2017						
New investment..............					$ 60,000	60,000
Bonuses to Elway............		(3,000)	(3,000)	(3,000)	9,000	0
Adjusted balance		$27,350	$31,000	$10,650	$ 69,000	$138,000
12/31/2017						
20% interest.................		5,470	6,200	2,130	13,800	27,600
Remainder (1:1:1:2)...........		20,000	20,000	20,000	40,000	100,000
Withdrawals		(25,000)	(27,000)	(15,000)	(40,000)	(107,000)
Ending balance...............		$27,820	$30,200	$17,780	$ 82,800	$158,600
1/1/2018						
Gain (1:1:1:2)		10,000	10,000	10,000	20,000	50,000
Adjusted balance		$37,820	$40,200	$27,780	$102,800	$208,600
Transfer interests		(37,820)	(40,200)		78,020	0
Adjusted balance		$ 0	$ 0	$27,780	$180,820	$208,600
2/28/2018						
Income (1:9).................				1,000	9,000	10,000
Adjusted balance				$28,780	$189,820	$218,600
Settlements				(28,780)	(189,820)	(218,600)
Final balance				$ 0	$ 0	$ 0

Part 2

2015			
Jan. 1	Cash	12,000	
	Royce, Capital		12,000
	Record investment of Royce.		
Dec. 31	Income Summary	40,000	
	Ries, Capital		10,150
	Bax, Capital		14,850
	Royce, Capital		15,000
	Allocate interest, salaries, and remainders.		
Dec. 31	Ries, Withdrawals	5,000	
	Bax, Withdrawals	12,500	
	Royce, Withdrawals	11,000	
	Cash		28,500
	Record cash withdrawals by partners.		
Dec. 31	Ries, Capital	5,000	
	Bax, Capital	12,500	
	Royce, Capital	11,000	
	Ries, Withdrawals		5,000
	Bax, Withdrawals		12,500
	Royce, Withdrawals		11,000
	Close withdrawal accounts.		

Summary

C1 **Identify characteristics of partnerships and similar organizations.** Partnerships are voluntary associations, involve partnership agreements, have limited life, are not subject to corporate income tax, include mutual agency, and have unlimited liability. Organizations that combine selected characteristics of partnerships and corporations include limited partnerships, limited liability partnerships, S corporations, and limited liability companies.

A1 **Compute partner return on equity and use it to evaluate partnership performance.** Partner return on equity provides each partner an assessment of his or her return on equity invested in the partnership.

P1 **Prepare entries for partnership formation.** A partner's initial investment is recorded at the market value of the assets contributed to the partnership.

P2 **Allocate and record income and loss among partners.** A partnership agreement should specify how to allocate partnership income or loss among partners. Allocation can be based on a stated ratio, capital balances, or salary and interest allowances to compensate partners for differences in their service and capital contributions.

P3 **Account for the admission of partners.** When a new partner buys a partnership interest directly from one or more existing partners, the amount of cash paid from one partner to another does not affect the partnership total recorded equity. When a new partner purchases equity by investing additional assets in the partnership, the new partner's investment can yield a bonus either to existing partners or to the new partner.

P4 **Account for the withdrawal of partners.** The entry to record a withdrawal can involve payment from either (1) the existing partners' personal assets or (2) partnership assets. The latter can yield a bonus to either the withdrawing or remaining partners.

P5 **Prepare entries for partnership liquidation.** When a partnership is liquidated, losses and gains from selling partnership assets are allocated to the partners according to their income-and-loss-sharing ratio. If a partner's capital account has a deficiency that the partner cannot pay, the other partners share the deficit according to their relative income-and-loss-sharing ratio.

Key Terms

C corporation	Limited partners	Partnership contract
General partner	Limited partnership	Partnership liquidation
General partnership	Mutual agency	S corporation
Limited liability company (LLC)	Partner return on equity	Statement of partners' equity
Limited liability partnership	Partnership	Unlimited liability

Multiple Choice Quiz

1. Stokely and Leder are forming a partnership. Stokely invests in a building that has a market value of $250,000; and the partnership assumes responsibility for a $50,000 note secured by a mortgage on that building. Leder invests $100,000 cash. For the partnership, the amounts recorded for the building and for Stokely's capital account are these:

   a. Building, $250,000; Stokely, Capital, $250,000.

   b. Building, $200,000; Stokely, Capital, $200,000.

   c. Building, $200,000; Stokely, Capital, $100,000.

   d. Building, $200,000; Stokely, Capital, $250,000.

   e. Building, $250,000; Stokely, Capital, $200,000.

2. Katherine, Alliah, and Paulina form a partnership. Katherine contributes $150,000, Alliah contributes $150,000, and Paulina contributes $100,000. Their partnership agreement calls for the income or loss division to be based on the ratio of capital invested. If the partnership reports income of $90,000 for its first year of operations, what amount of income is credited to Paulina's capital account?

   a. $22,500   c. $45,000   e. $90,000

   b. $25,000   d. $30,000

3. Jamison and Blue form a partnership with capital contributions of $600,000 and $800,000, respectively. Their partnership agreement calls for Jamison to receive $120,000 per year in salary. Also, each partner is to receive an interest allowance equal to 10% of the partner's beginning capital contributions, with any remaining income or loss divided equally. If net income for its initial year is $270,000, then Jamison's and Blue's respective shares are

   a. $135,000; $135,000.   d. $185,000; $85,000.

   b. $154,286; $115,714.   e. $85,000; $185,000.

   c. $120,000; $150,000.

4. Hansen and Fleming are partners and share equally in income or loss. Hansen's current capital balance in the partnership is $125,000 and Fleming's is $124,000. Hansen and Fleming agree to accept Black with a 20% interest. Black invests $75,000 in the partnership. The bonus granted to Hansen and Fleming equals

   a. $13,000 each.

   b. $5,100 each.

   c. $4,000 each.

   d. $5,285 to Hansen; $4,915 to Fleming.

   e. $0; Hansen and Fleming grant a bonus to Black.

5. Mee Su is a partner in Hartford Partners, LLC. Her partnership capital balance at the beginning of the current year was $110,000, and her ending balance was $124,000. Her share of the partnership income is $10,500. What is her partner return on equity?

   a. 8.97%   d. 1047.00%

   b. 1060.00%   e. 8.47%

   c. 9.54%

ANSWERS TO MULTIPLE CHOICE QUIZ

1. e; Capital = $250,000 − $50,000

2. a; $90,000 × [$100,000/($150,000 + $150,000 + $100,000)] = $22,500

3. d;

	Jamison	Blue	Total
Net income.			$ 270,000
Salary allowance	$120,000		(120,000)
Interest allowance	60,000	$80,000	(140,000)
Balance of income.			10,000
Balance divided equally	5,000	5,000	(10,000)
Totals	$185,000	$85,000	$ 0

4. b; Total partnership equity = $125,000 + $124,000 + $75,000 = $324,000

   Equity of Black = $324,000 × 20% = $64,800

   Bonus to old partners = $75,000 − $64,800 = $10,200, split equally

5. a; $10,500/[($110,000 + $124,000)/2] = 8.97%

🔘 Icon denotes assignments that involve decision making.

Discussion Questions

1. 🔘 If a partnership contract does not state the period of time the partnership is to exist, when does the partnership end?

2. **Apple** began as a partnership. What does the term *mutual agency* mean when applied to a partnership?

   APPLE

3. How does a general partnership differ from a limited partnership?

4. 🔘 Can partners limit the right of a partner to commit their partnership to contracts? Would such an agreement be binding (a) on the partners and (b) on outsiders?

5. 🔘 Assume that Amey and Lacey are partners. Lacey dies, and her son claims the right to take his mother's place in the partnership. Does he have this right? Why or why not?

6. Assume that the Barnes and Ardmore partnership agreement provides for a two-third/one-third sharing of income but says nothing about losses. The first year of partnership operation resulted in a loss, and Barnes argues that the loss should be shared equally because the partnership agreement said nothing about sharing losses. Is Barnes correct? Explain.

7. Allocation of partnership income among the partners appears on what financial statement?

8. What does the term *unlimited liability* mean when it is applied to partnership members?

9. George, Burton, and Dillman have been partners for three years. The partnership is being dissolved. George is leaving the firm, but Burton and Dillman plan to carry on the business. In the final settlement, George places a $75,000 salary claim against the partnership. He contends that he has a claim for a salary of $25,000 for each year because he devoted all of his time for three years to the affairs of the partnership. Is his claim valid? Why or why not?

10. Kay, Kat, and Kim are partners. In a liquidation, Kay's share of partnership losses exceeds her capital account balance. Moreover, she is unable to meet the deficit from her personal assets, and her partners share the excess losses. Does this relieve Kay of liability?

11. After all partnership assets have been converted to cash and all liabilities paid, the remaining cash should equal the sum of the balances of the partners' capital accounts. Why?

12. Assume a partner withdraws from a partnership and receives assets of greater value than the book value of his equity. Should the remaining partners share the resulting reduction in their equities in the ratio of their relative capital balances or according to their income-and-loss-sharing ratio?

connect

QUICK STUDY

Amy and Lester are partners in operating a store. Without consulting Amy, Lester enters into a contract to purchase merchandise for the store. Amy contends that she did not authorize the order and refuses to pay for it. The vendor sues the partners for the contract price of the merchandise.

a. Must the partnership pay for the merchandise? Why?

b. Does your answer to part *a* differ if Amy and Lester are partners in a public accounting firm? Explain.

QS 12-1
Partnership liability
C1

Fancher organized a limited partnership and is the only general partner. Carley invested $20,000 in the partnership and was admitted as a limited partner with the understanding that she would receive 10% of the profits. After two unprofitable years, the partnership ceased doing business. At that point, partnership liabilities were $85,000 larger than partnership assets. How much money can the partnership's creditors obtain from Carley's personal assets to satisfy the unpaid partnership debts?

QS 12-2
Liability in limited partnerships
C1

Dave Krug contributed $1,000 cash along with inventory and land to a new partnership. The inventory had a book value of $800 and a market value of $2,000. The land had a book value of $1,400 and a market value of $5,000. The partnership also accepted a $3,000 note payable owed by Krug to a creditor. Prepare the partnership's journal entry to record Krug's investment.

QS 12-3
Partnership formation
P1

Ann Stolton and Susie Bright are partners in a business they started two years ago. The partnership agreement states that Stolton should receive a salary allowance of $15,000 and that Bright should receive a $20,000 salary allowance. Any remaining income or loss is to be shared equally. Determine each partner's share of the current year's net income of $52,000.

QS 12-4
Partnership income allocation
P2

Blake and Matthew are partners who agree that Blake will receive a $100,000 salary allowance and that any remaining income or loss will be shared equally. If Matthew's capital account is credited for $2,000 as his share of the net income in a given period, how much net income did the partnership earn in that period?

QS 12-5
Partnership income allocation P2

Jules and Johnson are partners, each with $40,000 in their partnership capital accounts. Kwon is admitted to the partnership by investing $40,000 cash. Make the entry to show Kwon's admission to the partnership.

QS 12-6
Admission of a partner
P3

QS 12-7

Partner admission through
purchase of interest **P3**

Stein agrees to pay Choi and Amal $10,000 each for a one-third (33⅓%) interest in the Choi and Amal partnership. Immediately prior to Stein's admission, each partner had a $30,000 capital balance. Make the journal entry to record Stein's purchase of the partners' interest.

QS 12-8

Partner withdrawal

P4

Lopez, Cruz, and Perez are partners and share net income and loss in a 6:4:1 ratio. On December 31, Perez withdraws from the partnership when the equities of the partners are: Lopez, $3,000; Cruz, $1,800; and Perez, $1,200. Prepare journal entries to record Perez's withdrawal under each of the following separate situations: Perez is paid for her equity using partnership cash of (1) $1,200; (2) $1,600; and (3) $700.

QS 12-9

Liquidation of partnership

P5

Check (1) Field, $(3,750)

The Field, Brown & Snow partnership was begun with investments by the partners as follows: Field, $131,250; Brown, $165,000; and Snow, $153,750. The operations did not go well, and the partners eventually decided to liquidate the partnership, sharing all losses equally. On May 31, after all assets were converted to cash and all creditors were paid, only $45,000 in partnership cash remained.

1. Compute the capital account balance of each partner after the liquidation of assets and the payment of creditors.

2. Assume that any partner with a deficit agrees to pay cash to the partnership to cover the deficit. Present the journal entries on May 31 to record (*a*) the cash receipt from the deficient partner(s) and (*b*) the final disbursement of cash to the partners.

3. Assume that any partner with a deficit is not able to reimburse the partnership. Present journal entries (*a*) to transfer the deficit of any deficient partners to the other partners and (*b*) to record the final disbursement of cash to the partners.

QS 12-10

Partner return on equity

A1

Howe and Duley's company is organized as a partnership. At the prior year-end, partnership equity totaled $150,000 ($100,000 from Howe and $50,000 from Duley). For the current year, partnership net income is $24,990 ($20,040 allocated to Howe and $4,950 allocated to Duley), and year-end total partnership equity is $200,000 ($140,000 from Howe and $60,000 from Duley). Compute the total partnership return on equity *and* the individual partner return on equity ratios.

EXERCISES

Exercise 12-1

Characteristics of partnerships

C1

In the blank next to each partnership characteristic *1* through *8*, enter the letter of the description that best relates to it for a general partnership.

____ **1.** Duration of life	**a.** Requires an agreement only
____ **2.** Owners' liability	**b.** Income taxed on partners' returns
____ **3.** Legal status	**c.** Not separate entity from partners
____ **4.** Tax status of income	**d.** Difficult to transfer
____ **5.** Owners' authority and authorization	**e.** Mutual agency
____ **6.** Ease of formation	**f.** Low ability
____ **7.** Transferability of ownership	**g.** Unlimited
____ **8.** Ability to raise large capital amounts	**h.** Limited

---

Exercise 12-2

Forms of organization

C1

For each of the following separate cases:

• Recommend a form of business organization.

• Describe how income of the recommended form of organization will be taxed.

• List at least one advantage that owners will enjoy from the recommended form of organization.

a. Sharif, Henry, and Korb are recent college graduates in computer science. They want to start a website development company. They all have college debts and currently do not own any substantial computer equipment needed to get the company started.

b. Dr. Ward and Dr. Liu are recent graduates from medical residency programs. Both are family practice physicians and would like to open a clinic in an underserved rural area. Although neither has any funds to bring to the new venture, an investor has expressed interest in making a loan to provide start-up funds for their practice.

c. Munson has been out of school for about five years and has become quite knowledgeable about the residential real estate market. He would like to organize a company that buys and sells real estate. Munson believes he has the expertise to manage the company but needs funds to invest in residential property.

Angela Moss and Autumn Barber organize a partnership on January 1. Moss's initial net investment is $75,000, consisting of cash ($17,500), equipment ($82,500), and a note payable reflecting a bank loan for the new business ($25,000). Barber's initial investment is cash of $31,250. These amounts are the values agreed on by both partners. Prepare journal entries to record (1) Moss's investment and (2) Barber's investment.

Exercise 12-3
Journalizing partnership formation
P1

Steffi Derr and Leigh Finger form a partnership by combining assets of their separate businesses. Derr contributes the following: cash, $1,000; supplies that cost $2,400; inventory that cost $3,500; and machinery that cost $9,900, along with its accumulated depreciation of $5,000. The partners agree that $2,000 is a good estimate of supplies, that inventory has a market value of $3,000, and that machinery is worth $4,000. Prepare the partnership's journal entry to record Derr's investment.

Exercise 12-4
Recording partnership formation
P1

Ramer and Knox began a partnership by investing $60,000 and $80,000, respectively. During its first year, the partnership earned $160,000. Prepare calculations showing how the $160,000 income should be allocated to the partners under each of the following three separate plans for sharing income and loss:

1. The partners failed to agree on a method to share income.
2. The partners agreed to share income and loss in proportion to their initial investments (round amounts to the nearest dollar).
3. The partners agreed to share income by granting a $50,000 per year salary allowance to Ramer, a $40,000 per year salary allowance to Knox, 10% interest on their initial capital investments, and the remaining balance shared equally.

Exercise 12-5
Income allocation in a partnership
P2

Check Plan 3, Ramer, $84,000

Ramer and Knox began a partnership by investing $60,000 and $80,000, respectively. The partners agreed to share net income and loss by granting annual salary allowances of $50,000 to Ramer and $40,000 to Knox, 10% interest allowances on their investments, and any remaining balance shared equally.

1. Determine the partners' shares of Ramer and Knox given a first-year net income of $98,800.
2. Determine the partners' shares of Ramer and Knox given a first-year net loss of $16,800.

Exercise 12-6
Income allocation in a partnership P2

Check (2) Ramer, $(4,400)

On March 1, 2017, Eckert and Kelley formed a partnership. Eckert contributed $82,500 cash, and Kelley contributed land valued at $60,000 and a building valued at $100,000. The partnership also assumed responsibility for Kelley's $92,500 long-term note payable associated with the land and building. The partners agreed to share income as follows: Eckert is to receive an annual salary allowance of $25,000, both are to receive an annual interest allowance of 10% of their beginning-year capital investment, and any remaining income or loss is to be shared equally. On October 20, 2017, Eckert withdrew $34,000 cash and Kelley withdrew $20,000 cash. After the adjusting and closing entries are made to the revenue and expense accounts at December 31, 2017, the Income Summary account had a credit balance of $90,000.

1. Prepare journal entries to record (*a*) the partners' initial capital investments, (*b*) their cash withdrawals, and (*c*) the December 31 closing of both the Withdrawals and Income Summary accounts.
2. Determine the balances of the partners' capital accounts as of December 31, 2017.

Exercise 12-7
Journalizing partnership transactions
P2

Check (2) Kelley, $79,250

The partners in the Biz Partnership have agreed that partner Mandy may sell her $100,000 equity in the partnership to Brittney, for which Brittney will pay Mandy $85,000. Present the partnership's journal entry to record the sale of Mandy's interest to Brittney on September 30.

Exercise 12-8
Sale of partnership interest
P3

The Struter Partnership has total partners' equity of $510,000, which is made up of Main, Capital, $400,000, and Frist, Capital, $110,000. The partners share net income and loss in a ratio of 80% to Main and 20% to Frist. On November 1, Adison is admitted to the partnership and given a 15% interest in equity and a 15% share in any income and loss. Prepare the journal entry to record the admission of Adison under each of the following separate assumptions: Adison invests cash of (1) $90,000; (2) $120,000; and (3) $80,000.

Exercise 12-9
Admission of new partner
P3

Exercise 12-10 Retirement of partner P4	Hunter, Folgers, and Tulip have been partners while sharing net income and loss in a 5:3:2 ratio. On January 31, the date Tulip retires from the partnership, the equities of the partners are Hunter, $150,000; Folgers, $90,000; and Tulip, $60,000. Present journal entries to record Tulip's retirement under each of the following separate assumptions: Tulip is paid for her equity using partnership cash of (1) $60,000; (2) $80,000; and (3) $30,000.

Exercise 12-11 Liquidation of partnership P5	Turner, Roth, and Lowe are partners who share income and loss in a 1:4:5 ratio. After lengthy disagreements among the partners and several unprofitable periods, the partners decide to liquidate the partnership. Immediately before liquidation, the partnership balance sheet shows total assets, $126,000; total liabilities, $78,000; Turner, Capital, $2,500; Roth, Capital, $14,000; and Lowe, Capital, $31,500. The cash proceeds from selling the assets were sufficient to repay all but $28,000 to the creditors.
Check (b) Lowe, Capital after allocation, $(6,500)	**a.** Calculate the loss from selling the assets. **b.** Allocate the loss from part *a* to the partners. **c.** Determine how much, if any, each partner should contribute to the partnership to cover any remaining capital deficiency.

Exercise 12-12 Liquidation of limited partnership P5	Assume that the Turner, Roth, and Lowe partnership of Exercise 12-11 is a limited partnership. Turner and Roth are general partners and Lowe is a limited partner. Determine how much, if any, each partner should contribute to the partnership to cover any remaining capital deficiency. (Round amounts to the nearest dollar.)

Exercise 12-13 Partner return on equity A1	Rugged Sports Enterprises LP is organized as a limited partnership consisting of two individual partners: Hockey LP and Football LP. Both partners separately operate a minor league hockey team and a semipro football team. Compute partner return on equity for each limited partnership (and the total) for the year ended June 30, 2017, using the following selected data on partner capital balances from Rugged Sports Enterprises LP.

	Hockey LP	Football LP	Total
Balance at 6/30/2016	$189,000	$ 758,000	$ 947,000
Annual net income	22,208	445,473	467,681
Cash distribution	—	(50,000)	(50,000)
Balance at 6/30/2017	$211,208	$1,153,473	$1,364,681

connect

PROBLEM SET A	Mike Derr and Mark Finger form a partnership by combining assets of their separate businesses. The following balance sheet information is provided by Derr from his sole proprietorship.

Problem 12-1A Recording partnership formation P1	

	A	B	C	D	E	F
1	Cash		$ 1,000		Accounts payable	$ 4,500
2	Supplies		3,000		Notes payable	3,100
3	Equipment	$11,000			Total liabilities	7,600
4	Less: Accumulated depreciation—Equip.	9,000	2,000			
5	Land		4,000		M. Derr, Capital	2,400
6	Total assets		$10,000		Total liabilities and equity	$10,000

The new partners obtain appraised values and agree to accept the book values for Derr's assets and liabilities except for the following: Equipment is valued at $5,000, and land is worth $8,000.

Required

Prepare the partnership's journal entry to record Derr's investment.

Irene Watts and John Lyon are forming a partnership to which Watts will devote one-half time and Lyon will devote full time. They have discussed the following alternative plans for sharing income and loss: (*a*) in the ratio of their initial capital investments, which they have agreed will be $42,000 for Watts and $63,000 for Lyon; (*b*) in proportion to the time devoted to the business; (*c*) a salary allowance of $6,000 per month to Lyon and the balance in accordance with the ratio of their initial capital investments; or (*d*) a salary allowance of $6,000 per month to Lyon, 10% interest on their initial capital investments, and the balance shared equally. The partners expect the business to perform as follows: year 1, $36,000 net loss; year 2, $90,000 net income; and year 3, $150,000 net income.

Problem 12-2A
Allocating partnership
income and loss;
sequential years
P2

Required

Prepare three tables with the following column headings.

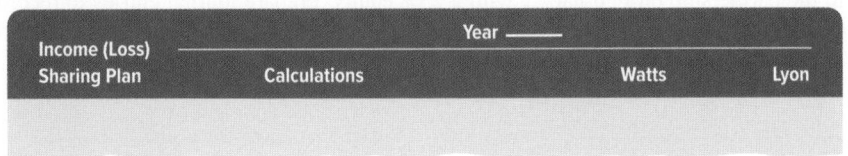

Income (Loss) Sharing Plan	Calculations	Year ――――		
			Watts	Lyon

Complete the tables, one for each of the first three years, by showing how to allocate partnership income or loss to the partners under each of the four plans being considered. (Round answers to the nearest whole dollar.)

Check Plan *d*, year 1, Lyon's
share, $19,050

Kara Ries, Tammy Bax, and Joe Thomas invested $80,000, $112,000, and $128,000, respectively, in a partnership. During its first calendar year, the firm earned $249,000.

Problem 12-3A
Allocating partnership
income
P2

Required

Prepare the entry to close the firm's Income Summary account as of its December 31 year-end and to allocate the $249,000 net income to the partners under each of the following separate assumptions:

1. The partners have no agreement on the method of sharing income and loss.

2. The partners agreed to share income and loss in the ratio of their beginning capital investments.

3. The partners agreed to share income and loss by providing annual salary allowances of $66,000 to Ries, $56,000 to Bax, and $80,000 to Thomas; granting 10% interest on the partners' beginning capital investments; and sharing the remainder equally.

Check (3) Thomas, Capital,
$97,800

Mo Meek, Lu Ling, and Barb Beck formed the MLB Partnership by making capital contributions of $67,500, $262,500, and $420,000, respectively. They predict annual partnership net income of $450,000 and are considering the following alternative plans of sharing income and loss: (*a*) equally; (*b*) in the ratio of their initial capital investments; or (*c*) salary allowances of $80,000 to Mo, $60,000 to Lu, and $90,000 to Barb; interest allowances of 10% on their initial capital investments; and the balance shared as follows: 20% to Mo, 40% to Lu, and 40% to Barb.

Problem 12-4A
Partnership income
allocation, statement of
partners' equity, and
closing entries
P2

Required

1. Prepare a table with the following column headings.

Income (Loss) Sharing Plan	Calculations	Mo	Lu	Barb	Total

Use the table to show how to distribute net income of $450,000 for the calendar year under each of the alternative plans being considered. (Round answers to the nearest whole dollar.)

2. Prepare a statement of partners' equity showing the allocation of income to the partners assuming they agree to use plan (*c*), that income earned is $209,000, and that Mo, Lu, and Barb withdraw $34,000, $48,000, and $64,000, respectively, at year-end.

3. Prepare the December 31 journal entry to close Income Summary assuming they agree to use plan (*c*) and that net income is $209,000. Also close the withdrawals accounts.

Check (2) Barb, Ending
Capital, $449,600

Problem 12-5A

Partner withdrawal and admission

P3 P4

Part 1. Meir, Benson, and Lau are partners and share income and loss in a 3:2:5 ratio. The partnership's capital balances are as follows: Meir, $168,000; Benson, $138,000; and Lau, $294,000. Benson decides to withdraw from the partnership, and the partners agree not to have the assets revalued upon Benson's retirement. Prepare journal entries to record Benson's February 1 withdrawal from the partnership under each of the following separate assumptions: Benson (*a*) sells her interest to North for $160,000 after Meir and Lau approve the entry of North as a partner; (*b*) gives her interest to a son-in-law, Schmidt, and thereafter Meir and Lau accept Schmidt as a partner; (*c*) is paid $138,000 in partnership cash for her equity; (*d*) is paid $214,000 in partnership cash for her equity; and (*e*) is paid $30,000 in partnership cash plus equipment recorded on the partnership books at $70,000 less its accumulated depreciation of $23,200.

Part 2. Assume that Benson does not retire from the partnership described in part 1. Instead, Rhode is admitted to the partnership on February 1 with a 25% equity. Prepare journal entries to record Rhode's entry into the partnership under each of the following separate assumptions: Rhode invests (*a*) $200,000; (*b*) $145,000; and (*c*) $262,000.

Problem 12-6A

Liquidation of a partnership

P5

Kendra, Cogley, and Mei share income and loss in a 3:2:1 ratio. The partners have decided to liquidate their partnership. On the day of liquidation, their balance sheet appears as follows.

KENDRA, COGLEY, AND MEI			
Balance Sheet			
May 31			
Assets		**Liabilities and Equity**	
Cash	$180,800	Accounts payable	$245,500
Inventory	537,200	Kendra, Capital	93,000
		Cogley, Capital	212,500
		Mei, Capital	167,000
Total assets	$718,000	Total liabilities and equity	$718,000

Required

Prepare journal entries for (*a*) the sale of inventory, (*b*) the allocation of its gain or loss, (*c*) the payment of liabilities at book value, and (*d*) the distribution of cash in each of the following separate cases: Inventory is sold for (1) $600,000; (2) $500,000; (3) $320,000 and any partners with capital deficits pay in the amount of their deficits; and (4) $250,000 and the partners have no assets other than those invested in the partnership. (Round to the nearest dollar.)

PROBLEM SET B

Jen Novinska and Jeff Quinlan form a partnership by combining assets of their separate businesses. The following balance sheet information is provided by Novinska from her sole proprietorship.

Problem 12-1B

Recording partnership formation

P1

	A	B	C	D	E	F
1	Cash		$ 200		Accounts payable	$ 100
2	Supplies		600		Notes payable	1,500
3	Equipment	$2,200			Total liabilities	1,600
4	Less: Accumulated depreciation—Equip.	1,800	400			
5	Land		800		J. Novinska, Capital	400
6	Total assets		$2,000		Total liabilities and equity	$2,000

The new partners obtain appraised values and agree to accept the book values for Novinska's assets and liabilities except for the following: Equipment is valued at $1,000, and land is worth $1,600.

Required

Prepare the partnership's journal entry to record Novinska's investment.

Bria Bell and Gil Green are forming a partnership to which Bell will devote one-third time and Green will devote full time. They have discussed the following alternative plans for sharing income and loss: (*a*) in the ratio of their initial capital investments, which they have agreed will be $104,000 for Bell and $156,000 for Green; (*b*) in proportion to the time devoted to the business; (*c*) a salary allowance of $4,000 per month to Green and the balance in accordance with the ratio of their initial capital investments; or (*d*) a salary allowance of $4,000 per month to Green, 10% interest on their initial capital investments, and the balance shared equally. The partners expect the business to perform as follows: year 1, $36,000 net loss; year 2, $76,000 net income; and year 3, $188,000 net income.

Problem 12-2B
Allocating partnership income and loss; sequential years
P2

Required

Prepare three tables with the following column headings.

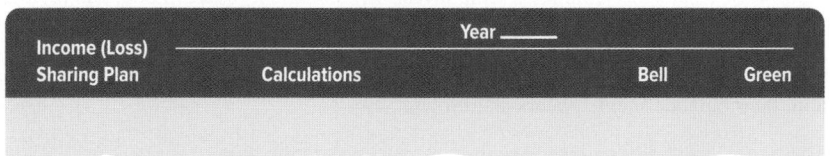

Complete the tables, one for each of the first three years, by showing how to allocate partnership income or loss to the partners under each of the four plans being considered. (Round answers to the nearest whole dollar.)

Check Plan *d*, year 1, Green's share, $8,600

Andy Albin, Paris Peters, and Ram Ramsey invested $164,000, $98,400, and $65,600, respectively, in a partnership. During its first calendar year, the firm earned $270,000.

Problem 12-3B
Allocating partnership income
P2

Required

Prepare the entry to close the firm's Income Summary account as of its December 31 year-end and to allocate the $270,000 net income to the partners under each of the following separate assumptions. (Round answers to whole dollars.)

1. The partners have no agreement on the method of sharing income and loss.
2. The partners agreed to share income and loss in the ratio of their beginning capital investments.
3. The partners agreed to share income and loss by providing annual salary allowances of $96,000 to Albin, $72,000 to Peters, and $50,000 to Ramsey; granting 10% interest on the partners' beginning capital investments; and sharing the remainder equally.

Check (3) Ramsey, Capital, $62,960

Sally Cook, Lin Jing, and Ken Schwartz formed the CJS Partnership by making capital contributions of $144,000, $216,000, and $120,000, respectively. They predict annual partnership net income of $240,000 and are considering the following alternative plans of sharing income and loss: (*a*) equally; (*b*) in the ratio of their initial capital investments; or (*c*) salary allowances of $40,000 to Cook, $30,000 to Jing, and $80,000 to Schwartz; interest allowances of 12% on their initial capital investments; and the balance shared equally.

Problem 12-4B
Partnership income allocation, statement of partners' equity, and closing entries
P2

Required

1. Prepare a table with the following column headings.

Use the table to show how to distribute net income of $240,000 for the calendar year under each of the alternative plans being considered. (Round answers to the nearest whole dollar.)

2. Prepare a statement of partners' equity showing the allocation of income to the partners assuming they agree to use plan (*c*), that income earned is $87,600, and that Cook, Jing, and Schwartz withdraw $18,000, $38,000, and $24,000, respectively, at year-end.
3. Prepare the December 31 journal entry to close Income Summary assuming they agree to use plan (*c*) and that net income is $87,600. Also close the withdrawals accounts.

Check (2) Schwartz, Ending Capital, $150,400

Problem 12-5B
Partner withdrawal and
admission

P3   P4

Check (1e) Cr. Chan,
Capital, $163,200

(2c) Cr. Hook,
Capital, $10,080

Part 1. Gibbs, Hook, and Chan are partners and share income and loss in a 5:1:4 ratio. The partnership's capital balances are as follows: Gibbs, $606,000; Hook, $148,000; and Chan, $446,000. Gibbs decides to withdraw from the partnership, and the partners agree not to have the assets revalued upon Gibbs's retirement. Prepare journal entries to record Gibbs's April 30 withdrawal from the partnership under each of the following separate assumptions: Gibbs (*a*) sells her interest to Brady for $250,000 after Hook and Chan approve the entry of Brady as a partner; (*b*) gives her interest to a daughter-in-law, Kannon, and thereafter Hook and Chan accept Kannon as a partner; (*c*) is paid $606,000 in partnership cash for her equity; (*d*) is paid $350,000 in partnership cash for her equity; and (*e*) is paid $200,000 in partnership cash plus manufacturing equipment recorded on the partnership books at $538,000 less its accumulated depreciation of $336,000.

Part 2. Assume that Gibbs does not retire from the partnership described in part 1. Instead, Chip is admitted to the partnership on April 30 with a 20% equity. Prepare journal entries to record the entry of Chip under each of the following separate assumptions: Chip invests (*a*) $300,000; (*b*) $196,000; and (*c*) $426,000.

Problem 12-6B
Liquidation of a partnership

P5

Lasu, Ramirez, and Toney, who share income and loss in a 2:1:2 ratio, plan to liquidate their partnership. At liquidation, their balance sheet appears as follows.

LASU, RAMIREZ, AND TONEY			
Balance Sheet			
January 18			
Assets		**Liabilities and Equity**	
Cash	$348,600	Accounts payable	$342,600
Equipment	617,200	Lasu, Capital	300,400
		Ramirez, Capital	195,800
		Toney, Capital	127,000
Total assets	$965,800	Total liabilities and equity	$965,800

Required

Check (4) Cash distribution:
Lasu, $73,600

Prepare journal entries for (*a*) the sale of equipment, (*b*) the allocation of its gain or loss, (*c*) the payment of liabilities at book value, and (*d*) the distribution of cash in each of the following separate cases: Equipment is sold for (1) $650,000; (2) $530,000; (3) $200,000 and any partners with capital deficits pay in the amount of their deficits; and (4) $150,000 and the partners have no assets other than those invested in the partnership. (Round amounts to the nearest dollar.)

SERIAL PROBLEM
Business Solutions

P3

© Alexander Image/Shutterstock RF

(This serial problem began in Chapter 1 and continues through most of the book. If previous chapter segments were not completed, the serial problem can begin at this point.)

SP 12   At the start of 2016, Santana Rey is considering adding a partner to her business. She envisions the new partner taking the lead in generating sales of both services and merchandise for **Business Solutions**. S. Rey's equity in Business Solutions as of January 1, 2016, is reflected in the following capital balance.

S. Rey, Capital	$80,360

Required

1. S. Rey is evaluating whether the prospective partner should be an equal partner with respect to capital investment and profit sharing (1:1) or whether the agreement should be 4:1 with Rey retaining four-fifths interest with rights to four-fifths of the net income or loss. What factors should she consider in deciding which partnership agreement to offer?

2. Prepare the January 1, 2016, journal entry(ies) necessary to admit a new partner to Business Solutions through the purchase of a partnership interest for each of the following two separate cases: (*a*) 1:1 sharing agreement and (*b*) 4:1 sharing agreement.

3. Prepare the January 1, 2016, journal entry(ies) required to admit a new partner if the new partner invests cash of $20,090.

4. After posting the entry in part 3, what would be the new partner's equity percentage?

Beyond the Numbers

BTN 12-1 Take a step back in time and imagine **Apple** in its infancy as a company. The year is 1976, and Steve Wozniak, Steve Jobs, and Ron Wayne are the organizing partners.

Required

1. Read the history of Apple from 1976 to 1980 at **en.wikipedia.org/wiki/Apple_Inc**. Identify the founders of the company. The Apple 1 went on sale in July 1976 at what price?

2. Apple was originally organized as a partnership, but was later incorporated on January 3, 1977. Its income statement in Appendix A varies in several key ways from what it would look like for a partnership. Identify at least two ways in which the Apple corporate income statement differs from a partnership income statement. (Apple's original partnership agreement is available at **apple2online.com/web_documents/apple_partnership_agreement.pdf**.)

3. Compare the Apple balance sheet in Appendix A to what a partnership balance sheet would have shown. Identify at least two accounts in the Apple corporate balance sheet that would not appear in a partnership balance sheet.

REPORTING IN ACTION

C1

APPLE

BTN 12-2 Over the years, **Apple** and **Google** have evolved into large corporations. Today it is difficult to imagine them as fledgling start-ups. Research each company's history online.

Required

1. In what year was each company first organized/started as a business?
2. In what years did each company have its first public offering of stock?
3. Which stock exchange is each company listed under?
4. What is the total equity for each company?

COMPARATIVE ANALYSIS

C1

APPLE

GOOGLE

BTN 12-3 Doctors Mobey, Oak, and Chesterfield have been in a group practice for several years. Mobey and Oak are family practice physicians, and Chesterfield is a general surgeon. Chesterfield receives many referrals for surgery from his family practice partners. Upon the partnership's original formation, the three doctors agreed to a two-part formula to share income. Every month, each doctor receives a salary allowance of $3,000. Additional income is divided according to a percent of patient charges the doctors generate for the month. In the current month, Mobey generated 10% of the billings, Oak 30%, and Chesterfield 60%. The group's income for this month is $50,000. Chesterfield has expressed dissatisfaction with the income-sharing formula and asks that income be split entirely on patient charge percents.

Required

1. Compute the income allocation for the current month using the original agreement.
2. Compute the income allocation for the current month using Chesterfield's proposed agreement.
3. Identify the ethical components of this partnership decision for the doctors.

ETHICS CHALLENGE

P2

BTN 12-4 Assume that you are studying for an upcoming accounting exam with a good friend. Your friend says that she has a solid understanding of general partnerships but is less sure that she understands organizations that combine certain characteristics of partnerships with other forms of business organization. You offer to make some study notes for your friend to help her learn about limited partnerships, limited liability partnerships, S corporations, and limited liability companies. Prepare a one-page set of well-organized, complete study notes on these four forms of business organization.

COMMUNICATING IN PRACTICE

C1

TAKING IT TO THE NET

P1   P2

BTN 12-5   Access the 2015 10-K of **Advanced BioEnergy, LLC** (look for the *unconsolidated statements,* on pages 60–62 of the 10-K filing). This company's business consists of producing ethanol and co-products, including wet, modified, and dried distillers grains and corn oil.

1. Locate its September 30, 2015, balance sheet and list the account titles reported in the equity section of that balance sheet.
2. Locate the members' (partners') equity section of its balance sheet. How many units of partnership are issued and outstanding at September 30, 2015?
3. What is the partnership's largest asset and its amount at September 30, 2015?

TEAMWORK IN ACTION

P2

BTN 12-6   This activity requires teamwork to reinforce understanding of accounting for partnerships.

Required

1. Assume that Baker, Warner, and Rice form the BWR Partnership by making capital contributions of $200,000, $300,000, and $500,000, respectively. BWR predicts annual partnership net income of $450,000. The partners are considering various plans for sharing income and loss. Assign a different team member to compute how the projected $450,000 income would be shared under each of the following separate plans:
   a. Shared equally.
   b. In the ratio of the partners' initial capital investments.
   c. Salary allowances of $50,000 to Baker, $60,000 to Warner, and $70,000 to Rice, with the remaining balance shared equally.
   d. Interest allowances of 10% on the partners' initial capital investments, with the remaining balance shared equally.
2. In sequence, each member is to present his or her income-sharing calculations with the team.
3. As a team, identify and discuss at least one other possible way that income could be shared.

ENTREPRENEURIAL DECISION

C1

BTN 12-7   Chris Gray, Bryson Alef, and Nick Pirollo are founding partners of their company, **Scholly**. Assume that Chris, Bryson, and Nick decide to expand their business with the help of general partners.

Required

1. What *details* should Chris, Bryson, Nick, and their future partners specify in the general partnership agreements?
2. What *advantages* should Chris, Bryson, Nick, and their future partners be aware of with respect to organizing as a general partnership?
3. What *disadvantages* should Chris, Bryson, Nick, and their future partners be aware of with respect to organizing as a general partnership?

GLOBAL DECISION

C1

Samsung

BTN 12-8   Access Samsung's website **samsung.com/us/aboutsamsung/corporateprofile/history06.html** and research the company's history. Also, review its 1938 to 1970 history at **en.wikipedia.org/wiki/Samsung**.

1. Byung-Chull Lee, the founder, organized/started the company in what year? What was the original name?
2. What was the original company's operating focus?
3. Samsung lists its affiliated companies on its website and groups them into four areas. List those four areas.

GLOBAL VIEW

Partnership accounting according to U.S. GAAP is similar, but not identical, to that under IFRS. This section discusses broad differences in partnership accounting, organization, admission, withdrawal, and liquidation.

Both U.S. GAAP and IFRS include broad and similar guidance for partnership accounting. Further, partnership organization is similar worldwide; however, different legal and tax systems dictate different implications and motivations for how a partnership is effectively set up.

The accounting for partnership admission, withdrawal, and liquidation is likewise similar worldwide. Specifically, procedures for admission, withdrawal, and liquidation depend on the partnership agreements constructed by all parties involved. However, different legal and tax systems impact those agreements and their implications to the parties.

 Global View Assignments

BTN 12-8

Accounting for Corporations

Chapter Preview

COMMON STOCK	DIVIDENDS	PREFERRED STOCK	TREASURY STOCK	REPORTING AND ANALYSIS
C1 Stock basics	**P2** Cash dividends	**C2** Issuance	**P3** Purchasing treasury stock	**C3** Retained earnings and equity
P1 Stock issuance:	Stock dividends	Dividend preferences	Reissuing treasury stock	
Par value	Stock splits	Rationale		**A1** EPS
No-par value				**A2** PE ratio
Stated value				**A3** Dividend yield
Noncash assets				**A4** Book value
NTK 13-1	**NTK 13-2**	**NTK 13-3**	**NTK 13-4**	

Learning Objectives

CONCEPTUAL

C1 Identify characteristics of corporations and their organization.

C2 Explain characteristics of, and distribute dividends between, common and preferred stock.

C3 Explain the items reported in retained earnings.

ANALYTICAL

A1 Compute earnings per share and describe its use.

A2 Compute price-earnings ratio and describe its use in analysis.

A3 Compute dividend yield and explain its use in analysis.

A4 Compute book value and explain its use in analysis.

PROCEDURAL

P1 Record the issuance of corporate stock.

P2 Record transactions involving cash dividends, stock dividends, and stock splits.

P3 Record purchases and sales of treasury stock.

© Peter DaSilva/The New York Times/Redux

One for the Road

PALO ALTO, CA—During college, when he would go on a first date, Elon Musk would ask, "Do you ever think about electric cars?" Today, Elon admits that discussing dreams of electric cars with first dates "was not a winning combination!" However, Elon's dreams have evolved into **Tesla Motors, Inc.** (**TeslaMotors.com**), a maker of electric vehicles.

Tesla was launched as a corporate-type entity. Elon's plan was to make a high-end electric sports car and later an electric sedan for the masses. "We really wanted to break the mold," insists Elon. The first Tesla sports car, the Roadster, traveled almost 250 miles on a single charge and earned terrific reviews. "Great companies are built on great products," explains Elon. Work is under way to launch an affordable electric sedan, the Model 3, which Elon hopes will greatly increase sales.

Success of Tesla depends on good decisions regarding creditor versus equity financing. On the creditor side, Elon must decide what amount and type of debt to carry. On the equity side, he must deal with corporate formation, equity issuance, stock types, retaining earnings, and dividend policies. He set up an accounting system to track common stock, additional paid-in capital, and other equity items. He set up the Tesla common stock with a $0.001 par value. "I spend my time solving manufacturing [and accounting] problems," claims Elon. "I don't spend my time pontificating about high-concept things."

As company head, Elon must decide whether or not to pay dividends to shareholders. Elon has chosen not to pay owners any dividends. "I don't think that's a good idea," says Elon. He points to a sales growth strategy and the need to reinvest any and all income back into Tesla.

Elon wants to revolutionize the automobile industry much like Henry Ford did with the Model T. "When Henry Ford made cheap, reliable cars, people said, 'Nah, what's wrong with a horse?'" laughs Elon. "That was a huge bet he made, and it worked."

"When something is important enough, you do it"
—Elon Musk

Sources: *Tesla Motors website,* January 2017; *Biography.com,* January 2016; *CleanTechnica,* December 2014; *CNN Money,* September 2014; *Bloomberg,* July 2013; *TED,* March 2013; *CBS,* March 2012; *L.A. Times,* April 2003

CORPORATE FORM OF ORGANIZATION

C1
Identify characteristics of corporations and their organization.

A **corporation** is an entity that is separate from its owners. By law, it has many of the same rights and privileges as individuals. Owners of corporations are called *stockholders* or *shareholders*. Corporations are separated into two types. A *privately held* (or *closely held*) corporation does not offer its stock for public sale and usually has few stockholders. A *publicly held* corporation offers its stock for public sale and can have thousands of stockholders. *Public sale* refers to selling and trading stock on an organized stock market.

Characteristics of Corporations

Corporations have unique characteristics that offer advantages and disadvantages.

Advantages of Corporate Form

- **Separate legal entity:** A corporation operates with the same rights, duties, and responsibilities of a person. It takes actions through its agents, who are its officers and managers.
- **Limited liability of stockholders:** Stockholders are not liable for corporate actions or debt.
- **Transferable ownership rights:** The transfer of shares from one stockholder to another usually has no effect on the corporation or its operations except when this causes a change in the directors who oversee the corporation.
- **Continuous life:** A corporation's life continues indefinitely because it is not tied to the physical lives of its owners.
- **Lack of mutual agency for stockholders:** A corporation acts through its agents, who are its officers and managers. Stockholders, who are not officers and managers, do not have power to bind the corporation to contracts—referred to as *lack of mutual agency.*
- **Ease of capital accumulation:** Buying stock is attractive to investors because (1) stockholders are not liable for the corporation's acts and debts, (2) stocks usually are transferred easily, (3) the life of the corporation is unlimited, and (4) stockholders are not corporate agents. These advantages enable corporations to collect large sums of capital from many stockholders.

Disadvantages of Corporate Form

- **Government regulation:** A corporation must meet requirements of a state's incorporation laws. Proprietorships and partnerships avoid many of these.
- **Corporate taxation:** Corporations pay the same property and payroll taxes as proprietorships and partnerships plus *additional* taxes. The most burdensome are federal and state corporate income taxes that together can take 40% or more of pretax income. Moreover, corporate income is usually taxed a second time as part of stockholders' personal income when they receive cash dividends. This is called *double taxation.*

Point: Proprietorships and partnerships are not subject to corporate income taxes. Their income is taxed as the personal income of their owners.

Point: Double taxation is less severe when a corporation's owner-manager collects a salary that is taxed only once as part of his or her personal income. At year-end, many small corporations distribute *bonuses* to owner-managers equal to the corporation's income. This reduces corporate income to $0 and avoids double taxation.

■ **Decision** Insight

Dorm-Corp   Mark Zuckerberg took his company, **Facebook**, public by issuing its first shares on the Nasdaq exchange. The initial public offering (IPO) of Facebook shares raised billions in equity financing. It also raised the importance of accounting reports versus market hype. The IPO of Facebook shares came eight years after the company was founded by Zuckerberg in his college dorm. Fast-forward to today: Zuckerberg vows to donate 99% of his Facebook shares, worth about $45 billion, toward charitable causes. ■

Corporate Organization and Management

This section describes the incorporation, costs, and management of corporate organizations.

Incorporation   A corporation is created by obtaining a charter from a state government. A charter application is signed by the prospective stockholders called *incorporators* or *promoters* and then filed with the state. When the application process is complete and fees paid, the charter is issued and the corporation is formed. Investors then purchase the corporation's stock, meet as stockholders, and elect a board of directors.

Point: A corporation is not required to have an office in its state of incorporation. Delaware has favorable corporate laws, and about half of all corporations listed on the NYSE are incorporated there.

Organization Expenses   **Organization expenses** (also called *organization costs*) are the costs to organize a corporation; they include legal fees, promoters' fees, and payments to obtain a charter. The corporation records (debits) these costs to an expense account called *Organization Expenses*. Organization costs are expensed as incurred.

Management of a Corporation   Stockholders control a corporation by electing a *board of directors,* or *directors*. Each stockholder usually has one vote for each share of stock owned. This control relation is shown in Exhibit 13.1. Directors are responsible for overseeing corporate activities. A board acts as a collective group and usually limits its actions to setting general policy.

A corporation usually holds a stockholder meeting at least once a year to elect directors and transact business as its bylaws require. Stockholders who do not attend stockholders' meetings have an opportunity to delegate their voting rights to an agent by signing a **proxy,** a document that gives a designated agent the right to vote the stock.

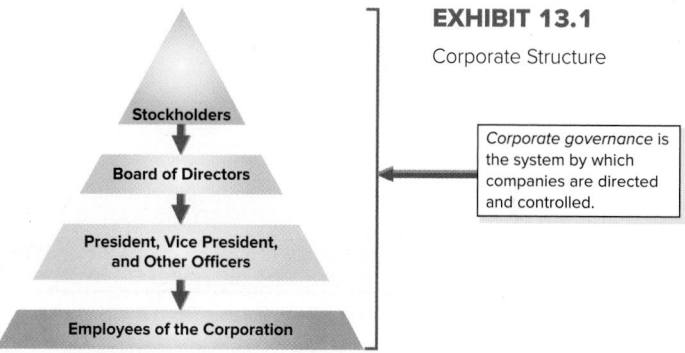

EXHIBIT 13.1

Corporate Structure

Corporate governance is the system by which companies are directed and controlled.

Executive officers are appointed by the board of directors to manage day-to-day operations. A corporation's chief executive officer (CEO) is often its president. Several vice presidents are commonly assigned specific areas of management responsibility such as finance, production, and marketing.

Point: *Bylaws* are guidelines that govern the behavior of individuals employed by and managing the corporation.

Decision Insight

Angel $s   Sources for start-up money include (1) "angel" investors such as family, friends, or anyone who believes in a company; (2) employees, investors, and even suppliers who can be paid with stock; and (3) venture capitalists (investors) who have a record of entrepreneurial success. See the National Venture Capital Association (**NVCA.org**) for information. ■

Global: Some corporate labels are:

Country	Label
United States	Inc.
France	SA
United Kingdom	
Public	PLC
Private	Ltd.
Germany & Austria	
Public	AG
Private	GmbH

Stockholders of Corporations

This section explains stockholder rights, stock purchases and sales, and the role of registrars and transfer agents.

Rights of Stockholders   When investors buy stock, they acquire all *specific* rights the corporation's charter grants to stockholders. They also acquire *general* rights granted to stockholders by the laws of the state where incorporated. When a corporation has only one class of stock, it is identified as **common stock.** State laws vary, but common stockholders usually have the general right to

- Vote at stockholders' meetings (or register proxy votes).
- Sell or dispose of their stock.
- Purchase their proportional share of any common stock later issued. This **preemptive right** protects stockholders' proportionate interest in the corporation. For example, a stockholder who owns 25% of a corporation's common stock has the first opportunity to buy 25% of any new common stock issued.

- Receive the same dividend, if any, on each common share.
- Share in any assets remaining after creditors and preferred stockholders are paid if the corporation is liquidated. Each common share receives the same amount.

Stockholders also have the right to receive timely financial reports.

Stock Certificates and Transfer   Investors who buy a corporation's stock sometimes receive a *stock certificate* as proof of share ownership. A certificate can be for any number of shares. Exhibit 13.2 shows a stock certificate issued by the **Green Bay Packers**. A certificate shows the company name, stockholder name, number of shares, and other information. Issuance of paper certificates is becoming less common.

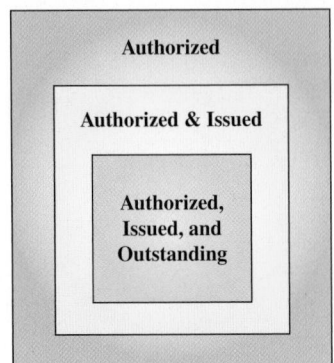

Courtesy JJW Images

Registrar and Transfer Agents   If a corporation's stock is traded on a major stock exchange, the corporation must have a registrar and a transfer agent. A *registrar* keeps stockholder records and prepares official lists of stockholders for stockholder meetings and dividend payments. A *transfer agent* assists with purchases and sales of shares by receiving and issuing certificates as necessary. Registrars and transfer agents are usually large banks or trust companies.

Decision Insight

First Call   A prospectus accompanies a stock's initial public offering (IPO), giving financial information about the company issuing the stock. A prospectus should help answer these questions to price an IPO: (1) Is the underwriter reliable? (2) Is there growth in revenues, profits, and cash flows? (3) What is management's view of operations? (4) Are current owners selling? (5) What are the risks? ■

Basics of Capital Stock

Capital stock refers to shares issued to obtain capital (owner financing). This section introduces terminology and accounting for capital stock.

Subcategories of Authorized Stock

Authorized Stock   **Authorized stock** is the number of shares that a corporation's charter allows it to sell. The number of authorized shares usually exceeds the number of shares issued (and outstanding) by a large amount. (*Outstanding stock* refers to issued stock held by stockholders.) No journal entry is required for stock authorization. A corporation discloses the number of shares authorized in the equity section of its balance sheet or notes. **Apple**'s balance sheet reports 12.6 billion common shares authorized.

Selling (Issuing) Stock   A corporation can sell stock directly or indirectly. To *sell directly,* it offers its stock to buyers. This type of sale is common with privately held corporations. To *sell indirectly,* a corporation pays a brokerage house (investment banker) to sell its stock. Some brokerage houses *underwrite* stock, meaning they buy the stock from the corporation and resell it to investors.

The innermost box shows that shares issued decline if a company buys back its previously issued stock.

Market Value of Stock   **Market value per share** is the price at which a stock is bought and sold. Expected future earnings, dividends, growth, and other company and economic factors influence market value. The current market value of previously issued shares (for example, the price of stock in trades between investors) does not impact the issuing corporation's stockholders' equity.

Classes of Stock   When all authorized shares have the same rights and characteristics, the stock is called *common stock*. A corporation sometimes issues more than one class of stock, including preferred stock and different classes of common stock. **American Greetings**, for instance, has two types of common stock: Class A stock has 1 vote per share and Class B stock has 10 votes per share.

Par Value Stock   **Par value stock** is stock that has a **par value,** which is an amount assigned per share by the corporation in its charter. For example, **Monster Worldwide, Inc.**'s common stock has a par value of $0.001. Other commonly assigned par values are $5, $1 and $0.01. There is no restriction on assigned par value. In many states, the par value of a stock establishes **minimum legal capital,** which refers to the least amount that the buyers of stock must contribute to the corporation or be subject to paying at a future date. For example, if a corporation issues 1,000 shares of $10 par value stock, the corporation's minimum legal capital in these states would be $10,000. Since creditors cannot demand payment from stockholders' personal assets, their claims are limited to the corporation's assets and any minimum legal capital.

Point: Managers are motivated to set a low par value when minimum legal capital or state issuance taxes are based on par.

Point: Minimum legal capital was intended to protect creditors by requiring a minimum level of net assets.

No-Par Value Stock   **No-par value stock,** or simply *no-par stock,* is stock *not* assigned a value per share by the corporate charter. Its advantage is that it can be issued at any price without the possibility of a minimum legal capital deficiency.

Point: Par, no-par, and stated value do *not* set the stock's market value.

Stated Value Stock   **Stated value stock** is no-par stock to which the directors assign a "stated" value per share. Stated value per share becomes the minimum legal capital per share in this case.

Stockholders' Equity   A corporation's equity is known as **stockholders' equity,** also called *shareholders' equity* or *corporate capital*. Stockholders' equity consists of (1) paid-in (or contributed) capital and (2) retained earnings; see Exhibit 13.3. **Paid-in capital** is the total amount of cash and other assets the corporation receives from its stockholders in exchange for its stock. **Retained earnings** is the cumulative net income (and loss) not distributed as dividends to its stockholders.

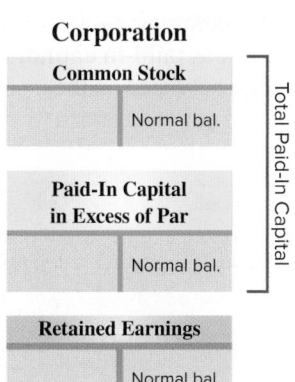

EXHIBIT 13.3

Equity Composition

Point: Paid-in capital comes from stock-related transactions, whereas retained earnings come from operations.

■ **Decision** Insight

Price Quote   The **Target** stock quote is interpreted as (left to right): **Hi,** highest price in past 52 weeks; **Lo,** lowest price in past 52 weeks; **Sym,** company exchange symbol;

52 Weeks									
Hi	**Lo**	**Sym**	**Div**	**Yld %**	**PE**	**Hi**	**Lo**	**Close**	**Net Chg**
85.81	66.46	TGT	2.24	2.67	15.6	83.63	82.50	82.75	−0.12

Div, dividends paid per share in past year; **Yld %,** dividend divided by closing price; **PE,** stock price per share divided by earnings per share; **Hi,** highest price for the day; **Lo,** lowest price for the day; **Close,** closing price for the day; **Net Chg,** change in closing price from prior day. ■

COMMON STOCK

Accounting for the issuance of common stock affects only paid-in (contributed) capital accounts; retained earnings is not affected.

P1_____

Record the issuance of corporate stock.

Issuing Par Value Stock

Par value stock can be issued at par, at a premium (above par), or at a discount (below par). Cash or noncash assets are received in exchange for stock.

Issuing Par Value Stock at Par   When common stock is issued at par value, we record both the asset(s) received and the par value stock issued. To illustrate, the entry to record Dillon's issuance of 30,000 shares of $10 par value stock for $300,000 cash on June 5, 2017, follows.

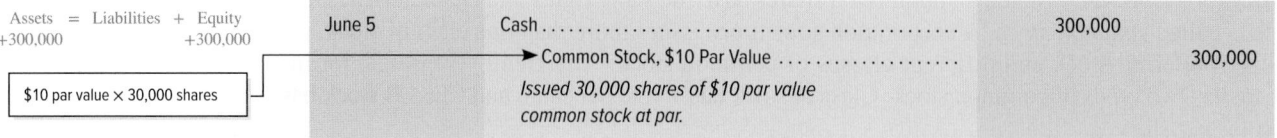

Assets = Liabilities + Equity
+300,000   +300,000

$10 par value × 30,000 shares

June 5	Cash..	300,000	
	Common Stock, $10 Par Value		300,000
	Issued 30,000 shares of $10 par value		
	common stock at par.		

Exhibit 13.4 shows stockholders' equity of Dillon at year-end 2017 (its first year of operations) with income of $65,000 and no dividend payments.

EXHIBIT 13.4

Stockholders' Equity for Stock Issued at Par

Stockholders' Equity	
Common stock—$10 par value; 50,000 shares authorized;	
30,000 shares issued and outstanding........................	$300,000
Retained earnings...	65,000
Total stockholders' equity...................................	$365,000

Issuing Par Value Stock at a Premium   A **premium on stock** occurs when a corporation sells its stock for more than par (or stated) value. To illustrate, if Dillon issues its $10 par value common stock at $12 per share, its stock is sold at a $2 per share premium. The premium, known as **paid-in capital in excess of par value,** is reported as part of equity; it is not revenue and is not listed on the income statement. The entry to record Dillon's issuance of 30,000 shares of $10 par value stock for $12 per share on June 5 follows.

Point: Paid-In Capital in Excess of Par Value is also called *Additional Paid-In Capital.*

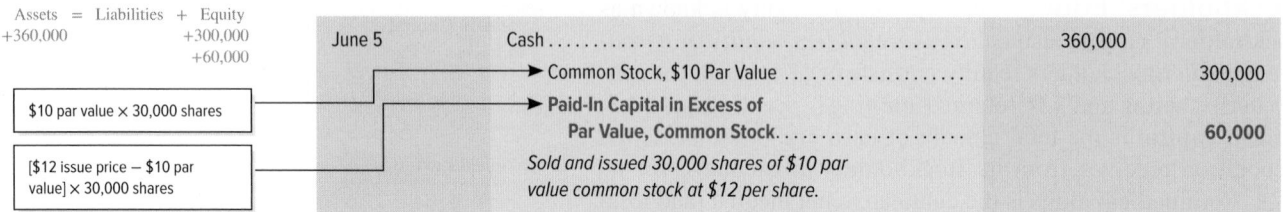

Assets = Liabilities + Equity
+360,000   +300,000
                      +60,000

$10 par value × 30,000 shares

[$12 issue price − $10 par value] × 30,000 shares

June 5	Cash..	360,000	
	Common Stock, $10 Par Value		300,000
	Paid-In Capital in Excess of		
	Par Value, Common Stock.....................		60,000
	Sold and issued 30,000 shares of $10 par		
	value common stock at $12 per share.		

Point: The phrase *paid-in capital* is interchangeable with *contributed capital.*

The Paid-In Capital in Excess of Par Value account is added to the par value of the stock in the equity section of the balance sheet as shown in Exhibit 13.5.

EXHIBIT 13.5

Stockholders' Equity for Stock Issued at a Premium

Stockholders' Equity	
Common stock—$10 par value; 50,000 shares authorized;	
30,000 shares issued and outstanding........................	$300,000
Paid-in capital in excess of par value, common stock	60,000
Retained earnings...	65,000
Total stockholders' equity...................................	$425,000

Issuing Par Value Stock at a Discount   A **discount on stock** occurs when it is sold for less than par value. Most states prohibit this. If stock is issued at a discount, the amount by which issue price is less than par is debited to a *Discount on Common Stock* account, a contra to the Common Stock account, and its balance is subtracted from the par value of stock.

Issuing No-Par Value Stock

When no-par stock is issued and is not assigned a stated value, the amount the corporation receives becomes legal capital and is recorded as common stock. This means that the entire proceeds are credited to a no-par stock account. To illustrate, a corporation records its October 20 issuance of 1,000 shares of no-par stock for $40 cash per share as follows.

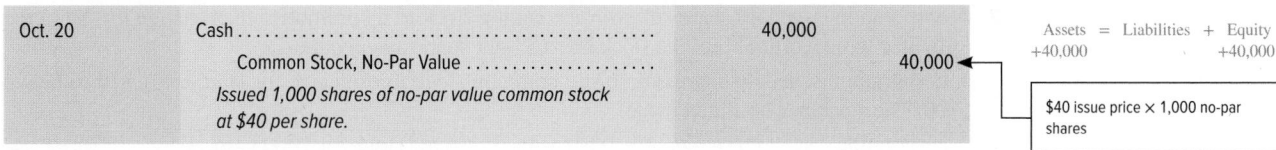

Oct. 20	Cash	40,000	
	Common Stock, No-Par Value		40,000
	Issued 1,000 shares of no-par value common stock at $40 per share.		

Assets = Liabilities + Equity
+40,000   +40,000

$40 issue price × 1,000 no-par shares

Issuing Stated Value Stock

When no-par stock is issued and assigned a stated value, its stated value becomes legal capital and is credited to a stated value stock account. Assuming that stated value stock is issued at an amount in excess of stated value (the usual case), the excess is credited to Paid-In Capital in Excess of Stated Value, Common Stock, which is reported in the stock-holders' equity section. To illustrate, a corporation that issues 1,000 shares of no-par common stock having a stated value of $40 per share in return for $50 cash per share records this as follows.

Frequency of Stock Types

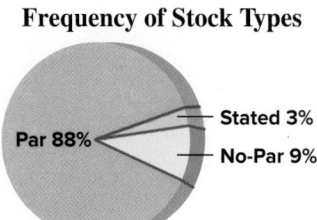

Par 88%
Stated 3%
No-Par 9%

Oct. 20	Cash	50,000	
	Common Stock, $40 Stated Value		40,000
	Paid-In Capital in Excess of Stated Value, Common Stock		10,000
	Issued 1,000 shares of $40 per share stated value stock at $50 per share.		

Assets = Liabilities + Equity
+50,000   +40,000
                      +10,000

$40 stated value × 1,000 shares

[$50 issue price − $40 stated value] × 1,000 shares

Issuing Stock for Noncash Assets

A corporation can receive assets other than cash in exchange for its stock. (It can also assume liabilities on the assets received such as a mortgage on property received.) The corporation re-cords the assets received at their market values as of the date of the transaction. The stock given in exchange is recorded at its par (or stated) value with any excess recorded in the Paid-In Capi-tal in Excess of Par (or Stated) Value account. (If no-par stock is issued, the stock is recorded at the assets' market value.) To illustrate, the entry to record receipt of land valued at $105,000 in return for issuance of 4,000 shares of $20 par value common stock on June 10 is

Point: Stock issued for noncash assets is recorded at the market value of either the stock or the noncash assets, whichever is more determinable.

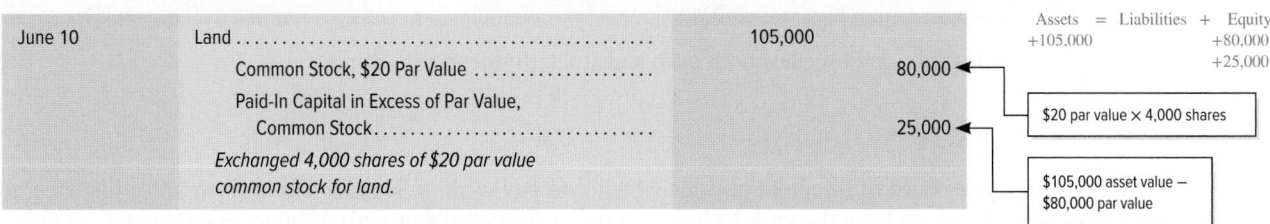

June 10	Land	105,000	
	Common Stock, $20 Par Value		80,000
	Paid-In Capital in Excess of Par Value, Common Stock		25,000
	Exchanged 4,000 shares of $20 par value common stock for land.		

Assets = Liabilities + Equity
+105,000   +80,000
                        +25,000

$20 par value × 4,000 shares

$105,000 asset value − $80,000 par value

A corporation sometimes gives shares of its stock to promoters in exchange for their services in organizing the corporation, which it records as organization expenses. The entry to record receipt of services valued at $12,000 in organizing the corporation in return for 600 shares of $15 par value common stock on June 5 is

Point: Any type of stock can be issued for noncash assets.

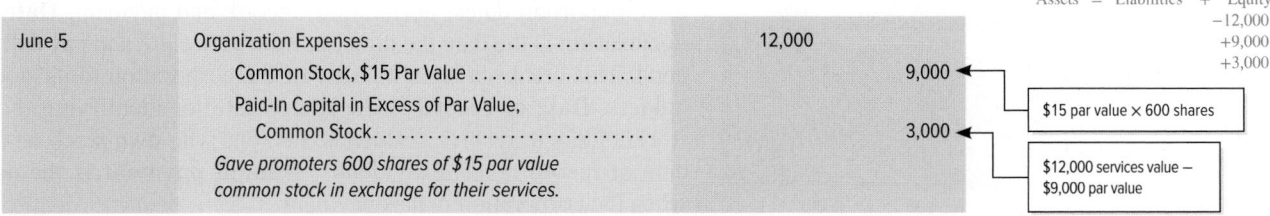

June 5	Organization Expenses	12,000	
	Common Stock, $15 Par Value		9,000
	Paid-In Capital in Excess of Par Value, Common Stock		3,000
	Gave promoters 600 shares of $15 par value common stock in exchange for their services.		

Assets = Liabilities + Equity
                        −12,000
                          +9,000
                          +3,000

$15 par value × 600 shares

$12,000 services value − $9,000 par value

NEED-TO-KNOW 13-1

Recording Stock
Issuance

P1

Prepare journal entries to record the following four separate (independent) issuances of stock.

1. A corporation issued 80 shares of $5 par value common stock for $700 cash.

2. A corporation issued 40 shares of no-par common stock to its promoters in exchange for their efforts, estimated to be worth $800. The stock has a $1 per share stated value.

3. A corporation issued 40 shares of no-par common stock in exchange for land, estimated to be worth $800. The stock has no stated value.

4. A corporation issued 20 shares of $30 par value preferred stock for $900 cash.

Solution

1.

Cash	700	
Common Stock, $5 Par Value*		400
Paid-In Capital in Excess of Par Value, Common Stock**		300
Issued common stock for cash.		

    *80 shares × $5 per share = $400   **$700 − $400 = $300

2.

Organization Expenses	800	
Common Stock, $1 Stated Value		40
Paid-In Capital in Excess of Stated Value, Common Stock		760
Issued stock to promoters.		

3.

Land	800	
Common Stock, No-Par Value.		800
Issued stock in exchange for land.		

4.

Cash	900	
Preferred Stock, $30 Par Value*.		600
Paid-In Capital in Excess of Par Value, Preferred Stock**		300
Issued preferred stock for cash.		

    *20 shares × $30 per share = $600   **$900 − $600 = $300

Do More: QS 13-2, QS 13-3, QS 13-4, QS 13-5, E 13-2, E 13-3, E 13-4

DIVIDENDS

P2

Record transactions involving cash dividends, stock dividends, and stock splits.

This section describes both cash and stock dividend transactions.

Cash Dividends

The board of directors decides whether to pay cash dividends. The directors, for instance, may decide to keep the cash to invest in the corporation's growth, to meet emergencies, to take advantage of unexpected opportunities, or to pay off debt. Alternatively, many corporations pay cash dividends to their stockholders at regular dates. These cash flows provide a return to investors and almost always affect the stock's market value.

Point: Amazon has never declared a cash dividend.

Percent of Corporations Paying Dividends

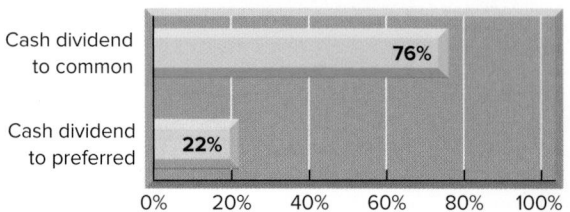

Accounting for Cash Dividends   Dividend payment has three important dates: declaration, record, and payment. **Date of declaration** is the date the directors vote to declare and pay a dividend. This creates a legal liability of the corporation to its stockholders. **Date of record** is the future date for identifying those stockholders to receive dividends. Persons who own stock on the date of record receive dividends. **Date of payment** is the date when the corporation makes payment.

To illustrate, the entry to record a January 9 *declaration* of a $1 per share cash dividend by the directors of Z-Tech, Inc., with 5,000 outstanding shares is

Date of Declaration

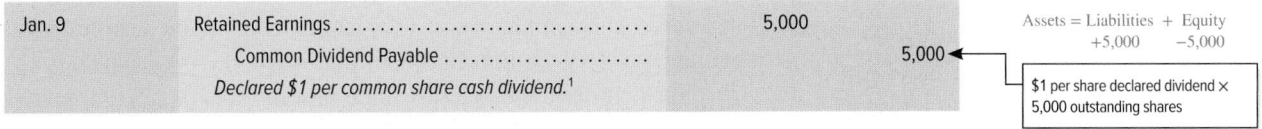

Jan. 9	Retained Earnings	5,000	
	Common Dividend Payable		5,000
	Declared $1 per common share cash dividend.[1]		

Assets = Liabilities + Equity
+5,000   −5,000

$1 per share declared dividend ×
5,000 outstanding shares

Common Dividend Payable is a current liability. The *date of record* for the Z-Tech dividend is January 22. ***No journal entry is needed on the date of record.***

The February 1 *date of payment* requires an entry to remove the liability and reduce cash.

Date of Payment

Feb. 1	Common Dividend Payable..........................	5,000	
	Cash		5,000
	Paid $1 per common share cash dividend.		

Assets = Liabilities + Equity
−5,000   −5,000

Deficits and Cash Dividends   A corporation with a debit (abnormal) balance for Retained Earnings has a **retained earnings deficit,** which occurs when a company has cumulative losses and/or pays more dividends than total earnings from current and prior years. A deficit is reported as a deduction on the balance sheet, as shown in Exhibit 13.6. Most states prohibit a corporation with a deficit from paying a cash dividend. This restriction protects creditors by preventing distributions to stockholders when the company is in financial difficulty.

Point: The Retained Earnings Deficit account is also called *Accumulated Deficit.*

Point: Pandora Media had an accumulated deficit of $367 million at the start of 2016.

Common stock—$10 par value, 5,000 shares authorized, issued, and outstanding	$50,000
Retained earnings deficit...	(6,000)
Total stockholders' equity...	$44,000

EXHIBIT 13.6

Stockholders' Equity with a Deficit

Some state laws allow cash dividends by returning a portion of the capital contributed. This type of dividend is called a **liquidating cash dividend,** or simply *liquidating dividend,* because it returns a part of the investment back to stockholders. This requires a debit entry to contributed capital accounts instead of Retained Earnings at declaration.

Stock Dividends

A **stock dividend,** declared by a corporation's directors, is a distribution of additional shares of its own stock to its stockholders without any payment in return. Stock dividends and cash dividends are different. A stock dividend does not reduce assets and equity but instead transfers a portion of equity from retained earnings to contributed capital.

Reasons for Stock Dividends   Stock dividends exist for at least two reasons. First, directors use stock dividends to keep the market price of the stock affordable. When a corporation has a stock dividend, it increases the number of outstanding shares, which lowers the per share stock price. Another reason for a stock dividend is to show management's confidence that the company is doing well and will continue to do well.

---

[1] An alternative entry is to debit Dividends instead of Retained Earnings. The period-end balance in Dividends must then be closed to Retained Earnings at period-end. The effect is the same: Retained Earnings is decreased and a Dividend Payable is increased. For simplicity, all assignments in this chapter use the Retained Earnings account to record dividend declarations.

Accounting for Stock Dividends A stock dividend transfers part of retained earnings to contributed capital accounts, sometimes described as *capitalizing* retained earnings. Accounting for a stock dividend depends on whether it is a small or large stock dividend.

> *Hint:* Five Steps to Record Stock Dividends
>
> **Step 1:** Identify number of shares outstanding.
> **Step 2:** Identify the stock dividend percentage.
> **Step 3:** Compute number of new shares (step 1 × step 2).
> **Step 4:** Value new shares at market (small stock dividend) *or* par (large stock dividend).
> **Step 5:** Determine debit (reduction) to Retained Earnings (step 3 × step 4).

- A **small stock dividend** is a distribution of 25% or less of previously outstanding shares. It is recorded by capitalizing retained earnings for an amount equal to the *market value* of the shares to be distributed.
- A **large stock dividend** is a distribution of more than 25% of previously outstanding shares. A large stock dividend is recorded by capitalizing retained earnings for the minimum amount required by state law—which is nearly always equal to the *par or stated value* of the stock.

To illustrate stock dividends, we use the equity section of Quest's balance sheet shown in Exhibit 13.7 just *before* its declaration of a stock dividend on December 31.

EXHIBIT 13.7

Stockholders' Equity *before* a Stock Dividend

Stockholders' Equity	Before Dividend
Common stock—$10 par value, 15,000 shares authorized,	
10,000 shares issued and outstanding..	$100,000
Paid-in capital in excess of par value, common stock	8,000
Retained earnings..	35,000
Total stockholders' equity..	$143,000

Small Stock Dividend Assume that Quest's directors declare a 10% stock dividend on December 31. This stock dividend of 1,000 shares, computed as 10% of its 10,000 outstanding shares, is to be distributed on January 20 to the stockholders of record on January 15. Since the market price of Quest's stock on December 31 is $15 per share, this small stock dividend declaration is recorded as follows:

Assets = Liabilities + Equity
            −15,000
            +10,000
            + 5,000

10% dividend × 10,000 outstanding shares × $10 par value

10% dividend × 10,000 outstanding shares × [$15 market price − $10 par value]

Date of Declaration—Small Stock Dividend

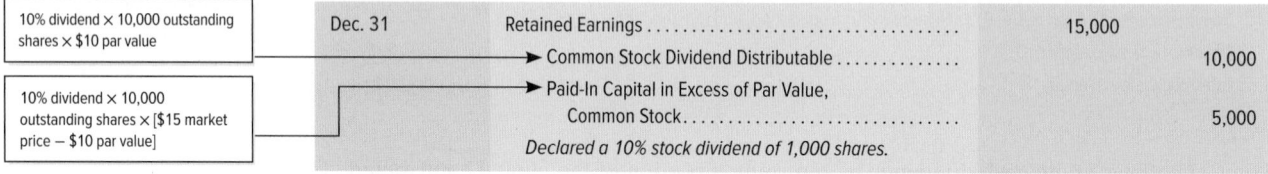

Dec. 31	Retained Earnings	15,000	
	Common Stock Dividend Distributable		10,000
	Paid-In Capital in Excess of Par Value,		
	Common Stock..		5,000
	Declared a 10% stock dividend of 1,000 shares.		

The balance sheet changes in three ways when a small stock dividend is declared.

- Common Stock Dividend Distributable, an equity account that exists only until the shares are issued, increases by $10,000. This causes combined common stock to go from $100,000 to $110,000 for 1,000 additional declared shares.
- Paid-in capital in excess of par increases by $5,000, which is the excess of market value over par value for the declared shares.
- Retained earnings decreases by $15,000, reflecting the transfer of amounts to both common stock and paid-in capital in excess of par.

Point: The term *distributable* (not *payable*) is used for stock dividends. A stock dividend is never a liability because it never reduces assets.

Point: The credit to Paid-In Capital in Excess of Par Value is recorded when the stock dividend is declared. This account is not affected when stock is later distributed.

The impacts on stockholders' equity from the 10% stock dividend are shown in Exhibit 13.8. The December 31 effects of the dividend declaration only are shown in the "Declaration" column.

EXHIBIT 13.8

Stockholders' Equity before, during, and after a Stock Dividend

Stockholders' Equity	Before Dividend	Date of Declaration	Date of Payment	After Dividend
Common stock—$10 par value, 15,000 shares				
authorized, 10,000 shares issued and outstanding	$100,000	$ —	$ 10,000	$110,000
Common stock dividend distributable—1,000 shares...........	—	10,000	(10,000)	0
Paid-in capital in excess of par value, common stock	8,000	5,000	—	13,000
Retained earnings	35,000	(15,000)	—	20,000
Total stockholders' equity	$143,000	$ 0	$ 0	$143,000

No entry is made on the date of record for a stock dividend. However, on January 20, the date of payment, Quest distributes the new shares to stockholders and records this entry (which is reflected in the "Payment" column of Exhibit 13.8):

Date of Payment—Small Stock Dividend

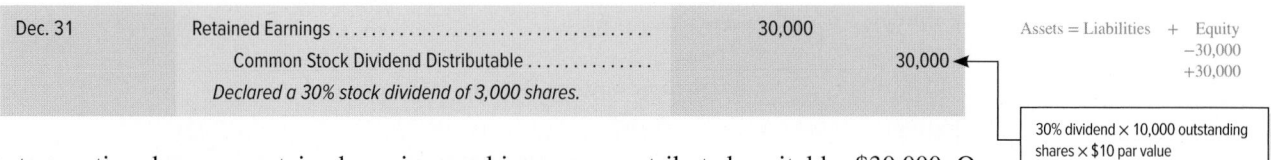

Jan. 20	Common Stock Dividend Distributable.................	10,000	
	Common Stock, $10 Par Value		10,000
	Record issuance of common stock dividend.		

Assets = Liabilities + Equity
                                −10,000
                                +10,000

The combined effect of these stock dividend entries is to transfer (or capitalize) $15,000 of retained earnings to paid-in capital accounts (see far right column of Exhibit 13.8). The capitalized retained earnings equals the market value of the 1,000 issued shares ($15 × 1,000 shares). A stock dividend has no effect on the ownership percentage of individual stockholders.

Point: A stock dividend does not affect total assets or total equity.

Large Stock Dividend   A corporation capitalizes retained earnings equal to the minimum amount required by state law for a large stock dividend—which is nearly always the par or stated value of the newly issued shares. To illustrate, suppose Quest's board declares a stock dividend of 30% instead of 10% on December 31. Since this dividend is more than 25%, it is treated as a large stock dividend. This means the par value of the 3,000 (computed as 10,000 outstanding shares × 30%) dividend shares is capitalized at the date of declaration with this entry:

Date of Declaration—Large Stock Dividend

Dec. 31	Retained Earnings	30,000	
	Common Stock Dividend Distributable		30,000
	Declared a 30% stock dividend of 3,000 shares.		

Assets = Liabilities + Equity
                                −30,000
                                +30,000

30% dividend × 10,000 outstanding shares × $10 par value

This transaction decreases retained earnings and increases contributed capital by $30,000. On the date of payment, the company debits Common Stock Dividend Distributable and credits Common Stock for $30,000.

Stock Splits

A **stock split** is the distribution of additional shares to stockholders according to their percent ownership. When a stock split occurs, the corporation "calls in" its outstanding shares and issues more than one new share in exchange for each old share. Splits can be done in any ratio, including 2-for-1, 3-for-1, or higher. Recently, **Apple** directors approved a 7-for-1 stock split. Stock splits reduce the par or stated value per share. The reasons for stock splits are similar to those for stock dividends.

Before 5:1 Split: 1 share, $50 par

To illustrate, CompTec has 100,000 outstanding shares of $20 par value common stock with a current market value of $88 per share. A 2-for-1 stock split cuts par value in half as it replaces 100,000 shares of $20 par value stock with 200,000 shares of $10 par value stock. Market value is reduced from $88 per share to about $44 per share. The split does not affect any equity amounts reported on the balance sheet or any individual stockholder's percent ownership. *No journal entry is made.* The only effect on the accounts is a change in the stock account description. CompTec's 2-for-1 split on its $20 par value stock means that after the split, it changes its stock account title to *Common Stock, $10 Par Value.* The stock's description on the balance sheet also changes to reflect the additional authorized, issued, and outstanding shares and the new par value.

After 5:1 Split: 5 shares, $10 par

■ **Decision** Maker

Entrepreneur   A company you co-founded and own stock in announces a 50% stock dividend. Has the value of your stock investment increased, decreased, or remained the same? Would it make a difference if it was a 3-for-2 stock split executed in the form of a dividend? ■   [*Answer:* The 50% stock dividend provides you no direct income. A stock dividend can reveal positive expectations and also improve a stock's marketability by making it more affordable. This means a stock dividend typically reveals good news, which usually increases (slightly) the stock's market value. The same answer applies to the 3-for-2 stock split.]

Point: A reverse stock split is the opposite of a stock split and results in fewer shares. It increases both the market value per share and the par or stated value per share.

NEED-TO-KNOW 13-2

Recording Dividends

P2

A company began the current year with the following balances in its stockholders' equity accounts.

Common stock—$10 par, 500 shares authorized, 200 shares issued and outstanding	$2,000
Paid-in capital in excess of par, common stock	1,000
Retained earnings	5,000
Total	$8,000

All outstanding common stock was issued for $15 per share when the company was created. Prepare journal entries to account for the following transactions during the current year.

Jan. 10 The board declared a $0.10 cash dividend per share to shareholders of record on January 28.
Feb. 15 Paid the cash dividend declared on January 10.
Mar. 31 Declared a 20% stock dividend when the market value of the stock was $18 per share.
May 1 Distributed the stock dividend declared on March 31.
Dec. 1 Declared a 40% stock dividend when the market value of the stock was $25 per share.
Dec. 31 Distributed the stock dividend declared on December 1.

Jan. 10	Retained Earnings[a]	20	
	Common Dividend Payable		20
	Declared a $0.10 per share cash dividend.		
	[a] 200 outstanding shares × $0.10		
Feb. 15	Common Dividend Payable	20	
	Cash		20
	Paid $0.10 per share cash dividend.		
Mar. 31	Retained Earnings[b]	720	
	Common Stock Dividend Distributable[c]		400
	Paid-In Capital in Excess of Par Value, Common Stock		320
	Declared a small stock dividend of 20% or 40 shares; market value is $18 per share.		
	[b] 200 outstanding shares × 20% × $18 market		
	[c] 40 new shares × $10 par		
May 1	Common Stock Dividend Distributable	400	
	Common Stock		400
	Distributed 40 shares of common stock.		
Dec. 1	Retained Earnings[d]	960	
	Common Stock Dividend Distributable		960
	Declared a large stock dividend of 40% or 96 shares (40% × [200 + 40]); par value is $10 per share.		
	[d] 240 outstanding shares × 40% × $10 par		
Dec. 31	Common Stock Dividend Distributable	960	
	Common Stock		960
	Distributed 96 shares of common stock.		

Do More: QS 13-6, QS 13-7, QS 13-8, E 13-5, E 13-6

PREFERRED STOCK

C2

Explain characteristics of, and distribute dividends between, common and preferred stock.

A corporation can issue two basic kinds of stock, common and preferred. **Preferred stock** has special rights that give it priority (or senior status) over common stock in one or more areas. Special rights typically include a preference for receiving dividends and for the distribution of assets if the corporation is liquidated. Preferred stock carries all rights of common stock unless the corporate charter excludes them. Most preferred stock, for instance, excludes the right to vote. Exhibit 13.9 shows that preferred stock is issued by about one out of four corporations. All corporations issue common stock.

Issuance of Preferred Stock

Preferred stock usually has a par value. Like common stock, it can be sold at a price different from par. Preferred stock is recorded in its own separate capital accounts. To illustrate, if Dillon issues 50 shares of $100 par value preferred stock for $6,000 cash on July 1, 2017, the entry is

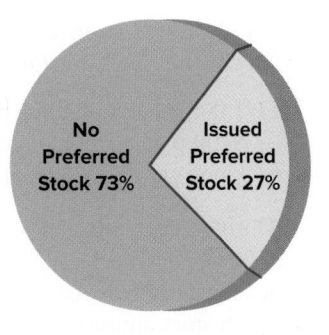

EXHIBIT 13.9

Corporations and Preferred Stock

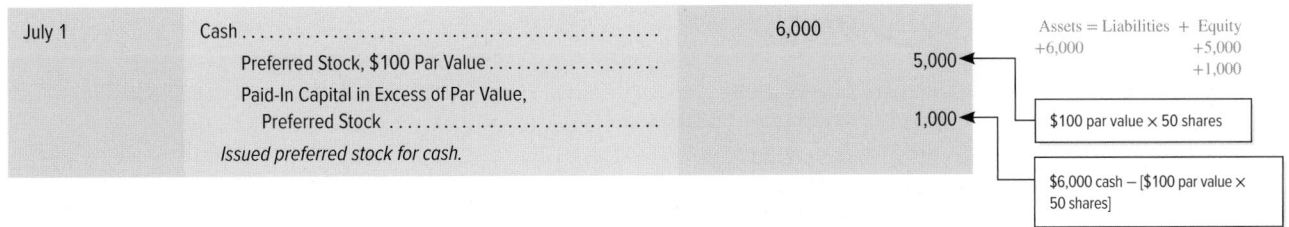

July 1	Cash...	6,000	
	Preferred Stock, $100 Par Value..................		5,000
	Paid-In Capital in Excess of Par Value,		
	Preferred Stock		1,000
	Issued preferred stock for cash.		

Assets = Liabilities + Equity
+6,000   +5,000
                                    +1,000

$100 par value × 50 shares

$6,000 cash − [$100 par value × 50 shares]

The equity section of the year-end balance sheet for Dillon, including preferred stock, is shown in Exhibit 13.10. This exhibit assumes that common stock was issued at par. (The entry for issuing no-par preferred stock is similar to issuing no-par common stock. Also, the entry for issuing preferred stock for noncash assets is similar to that for common stock.)

EXHIBIT 13.10

Stockholders' Equity with Common and Preferred Stock

Stockholders' Equity	
Common stock—$10 par value; 50,000 shares authorized;	
30,000 shares issued and outstanding	$300,000
Preferred stock—$100 par value; 1,000 shares authorized;	
50 shares issued and outstanding	5,000
Paid-in capital in excess of par value, preferred stock........................	1,000
Retained earnings	65,000
Total stockholders' equity...	$371,000

Dividend Preference of Preferred Stock

Preferred stock usually carries a preference for dividends, meaning that preferred stockholders are paid their dividends before any dividends are paid to common stockholders. The dividends paid to preferred stockholders are usually expressed as a dollar amount per share or a percent applied to par value. A preference for dividends does *not* ensure dividends. If the directors do not declare a dividend, neither the preferred nor the common stockholders receive one.

Cumulative or Noncumulative Dividend   Most preferred stocks carry a cumulative dividend right.

● **Cumulative preferred stock** gives its owners a right to be paid both the current and all prior periods' unpaid dividends before any dividend is paid to common stockholders. When preferred stock is cumulative and the directors either do not declare a dividend to preferred stockholders or declare one that does not cover the total amount of cumulative dividend, the unpaid dividend amount is called **dividend in arrears.** Accumulation of dividends in arrears on cumulative preferred stock does not guarantee they will be paid.

● **Noncumulative preferred stock** offers no right to prior periods' unpaid dividends if they were not declared in those prior periods.

Point: Dividend preference does not imply that preferred stock-holders receive more dividends than common stockholders, nor does it guarantee a dividend.

To illustrate the difference between cumulative and noncumulative preferred stock, assume that a corporation's outstanding stock includes:

(1) 1,000 shares of $100 par, 9% preferred stock—yielding $9,000 per year (1,000 shares × $100 par × 9%) in potential dividends.

(2) 4,000 shares of $50 par value common stock.

During 2016, the first year of operations, the directors declare cash dividends of $5,000. In year 2017, they declare cash dividends of $42,000. See Exhibit 13.11 for the allocation of dividends for these two years. Year 2017 dividends depend on whether the preferred stock is cumulative or noncumulative. If the preferred stock is cumulative, the $4,000 in arrears is paid in 2017 before any other dividends are paid. With noncumulative preferred, the preferred stockholders never receive the $4,000 skipped in 2016.

EXHIBIT 13.11

Allocation of Dividends (Cumulative vs. Noncumulative Preferred)

	Preferred	Common
Preferred Stock Is Cumulative		
Year 2016...	$ 5,000	$ 0
Year 2017		
Step 1: Dividend in arrears..........................	$ 4,000	
Step 2: Current year's preferred dividend..............	9,000	
Step 3: Remainder to common........................		$29,000
Totals for year 2017	$13,000	$29,000
Totals for 2016–2017	$18,000	$29,000
Preferred Stock Is Noncumulative		
Year 2016...	$ 5,000	$ 0
Year 2017		
Step 1: Current year's preferred dividend..............	$ 9,000	
Step 2: Remainder to common........................		$33,000
Totals for 2016–2017	$14,000	$33,000

A liability for a dividend does not exist until the directors declare a dividend. If a preferred dividend date passes and the corporation's board fails to declare the dividend on cumulative preferred stock, the dividend in arrears is not a liability. The *full disclosure principle* requires a corporation to report (usually in a note) the preferred dividends in arrears.

Participating or Nonparticipating Dividend   Some preferred stock carry a participating dividend right—although it is not common.

- **Nonparticipating preferred stock** limits dividends to a maximum amount each year. Once preferred stockholders receive the stated amount, the common stockholders receive any and all additional dividends.
- **Participating preferred stock** allows preferred stockholders to share with common stockholders any dividends paid in excess of the amount stated on the preferred stock. This participation feature does not apply until common stockholders receive dividends equal to the preferred stock's dividend percent.

Reasons for Issuing Preferred Stock

Preferred stock is issued for several reasons. One is to raise capital without sacrificing control. For example, suppose a company's organizers have $100,000 cash but need $200,000 of capital to start. If they issue $100,000 worth of common stock to themselves and sell outsiders $100,000 worth of common stock, they will have only 50% control and will need to negotiate extensively with other stockholders in making policy. However, if they issue $100,000 worth of common stock to themselves and sell outsiders $100,000 of 8%, cumulative preferred stock with no voting rights, they retain control.

A second reason to issue preferred stock is to boost the return earned by common stockholders. To illustrate, suppose a corporation's organizers expect to earn an annual after-tax income of $24,000 on an investment of $200,000. If they sell and issue $200,000 worth of common stock, the $24,000 income produces a 12% return on the $200,000 of common stockholders' equity. However, if they issue $100,000 of 8% preferred stock to outsiders and $100,000 of common stock to themselves, their own return increases to 16% per year, as shown in Exhibit 13.12.

Net (after-tax) income	$24,000
Less preferred dividends at 8%.................................	(8,000)
Balance to common stockholders...............................	$16,000
Return to common stockholders ($16,000/$100,000)...............	**16%**

EXHIBIT 13.12

Return to Common Stockholders When Preferred Stock Is Issued

Common stockholders earn 16% instead of 12% because assets contributed by preferred stockholders are invested to earn $12,000 while the preferred dividend is only $8,000. Use of preferred stock to increase return to common stockholders is an example of **financial leverage** (also called *trading on the equity*). As a general rule, when the dividend rate on preferred stock is less than the rate the corporation earns on its assets, the effect of issuing preferred stock is to increase (or *lever*) the rate earned by common stockholders.

Other reasons for issuing preferred stock include its appeal to some investors who believe that the corporation's common stock is too risky or that the expected return on common stock is too low.

■ **Decision** Maker

Concert Organizer   Assume that you alter your business strategy from organizing concerts targeted at under 1,000 people to those targeted at between 5,000 and 20,000 people. You also incorporate because of an increased risk of lawsuits and a desire to issue stock for financing. It is important that you control the company for decisions on whom to schedule. What types of stock do you offer? ■   [*Answer:* You have two options: (1) different classes of common stock or (2) common and preferred stock. Your aim is to own stock that has all or a majority of voting power. The other class of stock, whether common or preferred, would carry limited or no voting rights. In this way, you keep control and are able to raise money.]

A company's outstanding stock consists of 80 shares of *noncumulative* 5% preferred stock with a $5 par value and also 200 shares of common stock with a $1 par value. During its first three years of operation, the corporation declared and paid the following total cash dividends:

NEED-TO-KNOW 13-3

Allocating Cash Dividends

C2

2016 total cash dividends	$ 15
2017 total cash dividends	5
2018 total cash dividends	200

Part 1. Determine the amount of dividends paid each year to each of the two classes of stockholders: preferred and common. Also compute the total dividends paid to each class for the three years combined.

Part 2. Determine the amount of dividends paid each year to each of the two classes of stockholders assuming that the preferred stock is *cumulative.* Also determine the total dividends paid to each class for the three years combined.

Solution—Part 1

	Noncumulative Preferred	Common
2016 ($15 paid)		
Preferred*......................	$15	
Common—remainder..............	___	$ 0
Total for the year..................	$15	$ 0
2017 ($5 paid)		
Preferred*......................	$ 5	
Common—remainder..............	___	$ 0
Total for the year..................	$ 5	$ 0
2018 ($200 paid)		
Preferred*......................	$20	
Common—remainder..............	___	$180
Total for the year..................	$20	$180
2016–2018 (combined $220 paid)		
Total for three years..............	$40	$180

* Holders of noncumulative preferred stock are entitled to no more than $20 of dividends in any one year (5% × $5 × 80 shares).

Solution—Part 2

	Cumulative Preferred	Common
2016 ($15 paid)		
Preferred*..	$15	
Common—remainder.......................................	___	$ 0
Total for the year	$15	$ 0
(Note: $5 in preferred dividends in arrears; ($20 × 1 yr) − $15 paid.)		
2017 ($5 paid)		
Preferred—arrears from 2016.............................	$ 5	
Preferred*..	0	
Common—remainder.......................................	___	$ 0
Total for the year	$ 5	$ 0
(Note: $20 in preferred dividends in arrears; ($20 × 2 yrs) − $15 paid − $5 paid.)		
2018 ($200 paid)		
Preferred—arrears from 2017.............................	$20	
Preferred*..	20	
Common—remainder.......................................	___	$160
Total for the year	$40	$160
(Note: $0 in preferred dividends in arrears; ($20 × 3 yrs) − $15 paid − $5 paid − $40 paid.)		
2016–2018 (combined $220 paid)		
Total for three years.....................................	$60	$160

Do More: QS 13-9, QS 13-10, E 13-7, E 13-8, E 13-9

* Holders of cumulative preferred stock are entitled to $20 of dividends declared in any year (5% × $5 × 80 shares) plus any dividends in arrears.

TREASURY STOCK

Corporations acquire shares of their own stock for several reasons: (1) to use their shares to acquire another corporation, (2) to purchase shares to avoid a hostile takeover of the company, (3) to reissue them to employees as compensation, and (4) to maintain a strong market for their stock or to show management confidence in the current price.

A corporation's reacquired shares are called **treasury stock,** which is similar to unissued stock in several ways: (1) neither treasury stock nor unissued stock is an asset, (2) neither receives cash dividends or stock dividends, and (3) neither can exercise voting rights.

P3

Record purchases and sales of treasury stock.

Corporations and Treasury Stock

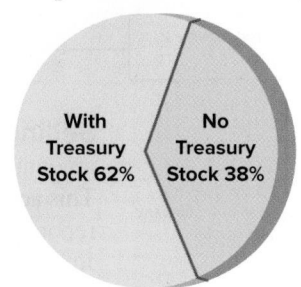

Purchasing Treasury Stock

Purchasing treasury stock reduces the corporation's assets and equity by equal amounts. We describe the *cost method* of accounting for treasury stock, which is the most widely used method. (The *par value* method is explained in advanced courses.) To illustrate, Exhibit 13.13 shows Cyber Corporation's account balances *before* any treasury stock purchase (Cyber has no liabilities).

Assets		Stockholders' Equity	
Cash	$ 30,000	Common stock—$10 par; 10,000 shares authorized, issued, and outstanding.	$100,000
Other assets	95,000	Retained earnings.	25,000
Total assets	$125,000	Total stockholders' equity.	$125,000

EXHIBIT 13.13

Account Balances *before* Purchasing Treasury Stock

Cyber then purchases 1,000 of its own shares for $11,500 on May 1, which is recorded as:

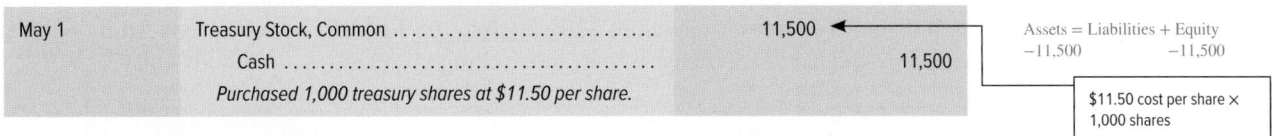

May 1	Treasury Stock, Common	11,500	
	Cash		11,500
	Purchased 1,000 treasury shares at $11.50 per share.		

Assets = Liabilities + Equity
−11,500   −11,500

$11.50 cost per share × 1,000 shares

This entry reduces equity through the debit to the Treasury Stock account, which is a contra equity account. Exhibit 13.14 shows account balances *after* this transaction.

Assets		Stockholders' Equity	
Cash	$ 18,500	Common stock—$10 par; 10,000 shares authorized and issued; 1,000 shares in treasury.	$100,000
Other assets	95,000	Retained earnings, $11,500 restricted by treasury stock purchase.	25,000
		Less cost of treasury stock	**(11,500)**
Total assets	$113,500	Total stockholders' equity.	$113,500

EXHIBIT 13.14

Account Balances *after* Purchasing Treasury Stock

The treasury stock purchase reduces Cyber's cash, total assets, and total equity by $11,500 but does not reduce the balance of either the Common Stock or the Retained Earnings account. The equity reduction is reported by deducting the cost of treasury stock in the equity section. Also, two disclosures are evident. First, the stock description reveals that 1,000 issued shares are in treasury, leaving only 9,000 shares still outstanding. Second, the description for retained earnings reveals that it is partly restricted.

Point: Treasury stock is *not* an asset. Treasury stock does not carry voting or dividend rights.

Point: A treasury stock purchase is also called a *stock buyback.*

Reissuing Treasury Stock

Treasury stock can be reissued by selling it at cost, above cost, or below cost.

Selling Treasury Stock at Cost   If treasury stock is reissued at cost, the entry is the reverse of the one made to record the purchase. For instance, if on May 21 Cyber reissues 100 of the treasury shares purchased on May 1 at the same $11.50 per share cost, the entry is

Assets = Liabilities + Equity
+1,150   +1,150

$11.50 cost per share ×
100 shares

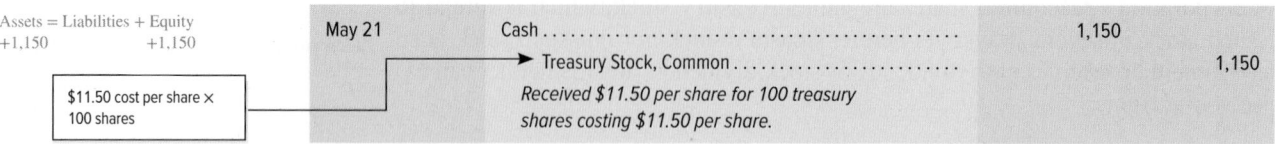

May 21	Cash	1,150	
	→ Treasury Stock, Common		1,150
	Received $11.50 per share for 100 treasury		
	shares costing $11.50 per share.		

Selling Treasury Stock *above* Cost   If treasury stock is sold for more than cost, the amount received in excess of cost is credited to the Paid-In Capital, Treasury Stock account. This account is reported as a separate item in the stockholders' equity section. No "gain" is ever reported from the sale of treasury stock. To illustrate, if Cyber receives $12 cash per share on June 3 for 400 treasury shares costing $11.50 per share, the entry is

Point: Treasury stock does not represent ownership. A company cannot own a part of itself.

Assets = Liabilities + Equity
+4,800   +4,600
                      +200

$11.50 cost per share ×
400 shares

[$12 issue price − $11.50 cost per share] × 400 shares

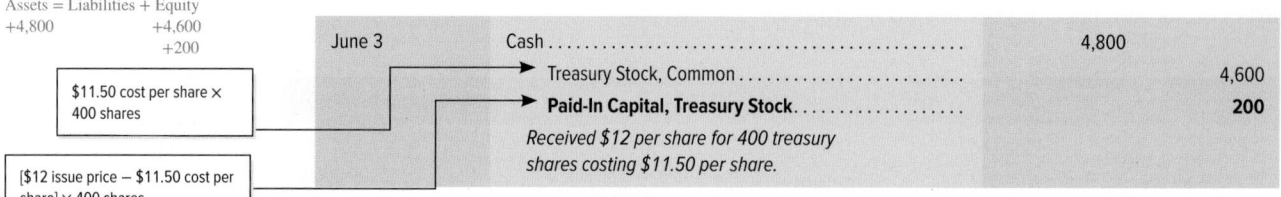

June 3	Cash	4,800	
	→ Treasury Stock, Common		4,600
	→ **Paid-In Capital, Treasury Stock**		**200**
	Received $12 per share for 400 treasury		
	shares costing $11.50 per share.		

Selling Treasury Stock *below* Cost   When treasury stock is sold below cost, the entry to record the sale depends on whether the Paid-In Capital, Treasury Stock account has a credit balance. If it has a zero balance, the excess of cost over the sales price is debited to Retained Earnings. If the Paid-In Capital, Treasury Stock account has a credit balance, it is debited for the excess of the cost over the selling price but not to exceed the balance in this account. When the credit balance in this paid-in capital account is eliminated, any remaining difference between the cost and selling price is debited to Retained Earnings. To illustrate, if Cyber sells its remaining 500 shares of treasury stock at $10 per share on July 10, equity is reduced by $750 (500 shares × $1.50 per share excess of cost over selling price), as shown in this entry:

Point: The Paid-In Capital, Treasury Stock account can have a zero or credit balance but never a debit balance.

Assets = Liabilities + Equity
+5,000   −200
                      −550
                      +5,750

[$10 issue price − $11.50 cost per share] × 500 shares; not to exceed $200

For any amount exceeding $200 PIC from TS

$11.50 cost per share ×
500 shares

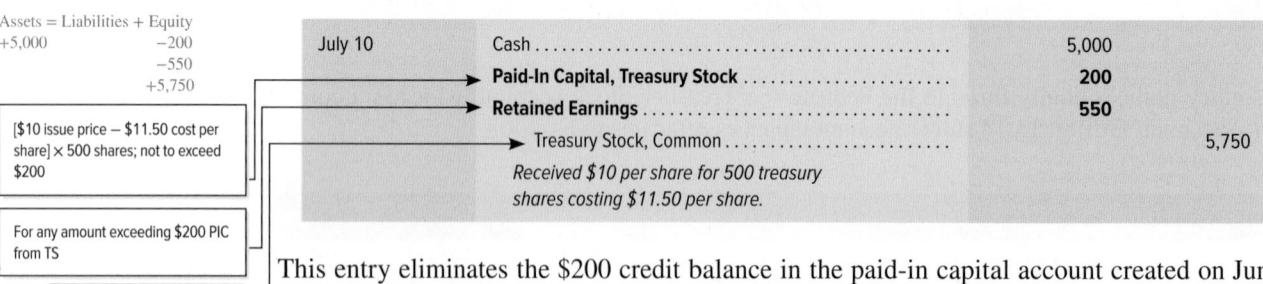

July 10	Cash	5,000	
	Paid-In Capital, Treasury Stock	**200**	
	Retained Earnings	**550**	
	→ Treasury Stock, Common		5,750
	Received $10 per share for 500 treasury		
	shares costing $11.50 per share.		

This entry eliminates the $200 credit balance in the paid-in capital account created on June 3 and then reduces the Retained Earnings balance by the remaining $550 excess of cost over selling price. A company never reports a "loss" from the sale of treasury stock.

NEED-TO-KNOW **13-4**

Recording Treasury Stock

P3

A company began the current year with the following balances in its stockholders' equity accounts.

Common stock—$10 par, 500 shares authorized, 200 shares issued and outstanding	$2,000
Paid-in capital in excess of par, common stock	1,000
Retained earnings	5,000
Total..	$8,000

All outstanding common stock was issued for $15 per share when the company was created. Prepare journal entries to account for the following transactions during the current year.

July 1   Purchased 30 shares of treasury stock at $20 per share.
Sep. 1   Sold 20 treasury shares at $26 cash per share.
Dec. 1   Sold the remaining 10 shares of treasury stock at $7 cash per share.

July 1	Treasury Stock, Common[a]	600	
	Cash		600
	Purchased 30 common shares at $20 per share.		
	[a]30 shares × $20 cost		
Sep. 1	Cash[b]	520	
	Treasury Stock, Common[c]		400
	Paid-In Capital, Treasury Stock		120
	Sold 20 treasury shares at $26 per share.		
	[b]20 shares × $26 reissue price [c]20 shares × $20 cost		
Dec. 1	Cash[d]	70	
	Paid-In Capital, Treasury Stock[e]	120	
	Retained Earnings	10	
	Treasury Stock, Common[f]		200
	Sold 10 treasury shares at $7 per share.		
	[d]10 shares × $7 reissue price		
	[e]Not to exceed existing balance [f]10 shares × $20 cost		

Do More: QS 13-11, E 13-10

REPORTING OF EQUITY

Statement of Retained Earnings

C3

Explain the items reported in retained earnings.

Retained earnings generally consist of a company's cumulative net income less any net losses and dividends declared since its inception. Retained earnings are part of stockholders' claims on the company's net assets, but this does *not* imply that a certain amount of cash or other assets is available to pay stockholders. For example, **Abercrombie & Fitch** has $2,530,196 thousand in retained earnings, but only $588,578 thousand in cash. This section describes events and transactions affecting retained earnings and how retained earnings are reported.

Restrictions and Appropriations   The term **restricted retained earnings** refers to statutory and contractual restrictions. A common *statutory* (or *legal*) *restriction* is to limit treasury stock purchases to the amount of retained earnings. The balance sheet in Exhibit 13.14 provides an example. A common *contractual restriction* involves loan agreements that restrict paying dividends beyond a specified amount or percent of retained earnings. Restrictions are usually described in the notes. The term **appropriated retained earnings** refers to a voluntary transfer of amounts from the Retained Earnings account to the Appropriated Retained Earnings account to inform users of special activities that require funds.

Prior Period Adjustments   **Prior period adjustments** are corrections of material errors in prior period financial statements. These errors include arithmetic mistakes, unacceptable accounting, and missed facts. Prior period adjustments are reported in the *statement of retained earnings* (or the statement of stockholders' equity), net of any income tax effects. Prior period adjustments result in changing the beginning balance of retained earnings for *events occurring prior to the earliest period reported in the current set of financial statements.* To illustrate,

EXHIBIT 13.15

Statement of Retained Earnings with a Prior Period Adjustment

ComUS Statement of Retained Earnings For Year Ended December 31, 2017	
Retained earnings, Dec. 31, 2016, as previously reported	$4,745,000
Prior period adjustment	
Cost of land incorrectly expensed (net of $63,000 of income tax benefit)	**147,000**
Retained earnings, Dec. 31, 2016, as adjusted	4,892,000
Plus net income	1,224,300
Less cash dividends declared	(301,800)
Retained earnings, Dec. 31, 2017.	$5,814,500

assume that ComUS makes an error in a 2015 journal entry for the purchase of land by incorrectly debiting an expense account. When this is discovered in 2017, the statement of retained earnings includes a prior period adjustment, as shown in Exhibit 13.15. This exhibit also shows the usual format of the statement of retained earnings.

Many items reported in financial statements are based on estimates. Future events reveal that some estimates were inaccurate even when based on the best data available at the time. These inaccuracies are *not* considered errors and are *not* reported as prior period adjustments. Instead, they are identified as **changes in accounting estimates** and are accounted for in current and future periods. To illustrate, we know that depreciation is based on estimated useful lives and salvage values. As time passes and new information becomes available, managers may need to change these estimates and the resulting depreciation expense for current and future periods.

Statement of Stockholders' Equity

Companies commonly report a statement of stockholders' equity that includes changes in retained earnings. A **statement of stockholders' equity** lists the beginning and ending balances of key equity accounts and describes the changes that occur during the period. Exhibit 13.16 shows a condensed statement for **Apple**.

EXHIBIT 13.16

Statement of Stockholders' Equity

APPLE

APPLE Statement of Stockholders' Equity					
$ millions, shares in thousands	Common Stock Shares	Common Stock Amount	Retained Earnings	Accumulated Other	Total Equity
Balance, Sept. 27, 2014	5,866,161	$23,313	$87,152	$1,082	$111,547
Net income	—	—	53,394	—	53,394
Issuance of common stock	37,624	(231)	(609)	—	(840)
Repurchase of common stock & other	(325,032)	4,334	(36,026)	(1,427)	(33,119)
Cash dividends	—	—	(11,627)	—	(11,627)
Balance, Sept. 26, 2015	5,578,753	$27,416	$92,284	$ (345)	$119,355

 **Decision** Insight

Pump 'n Dump Fraudulent information can be used to pump up stock price and cause naïve investors to acquire the stock and drive up its price. After that, those who released fraudulent information dump the stock at an inflated price. When later information reveals that the stock is overvalued, its price declines and investors still holding the stock lose value. This scheme is called *pump 'n dump*. A 15-year-old allegedly made about $1 million in one of the most infamous cases of pump 'n dump. (SEC Release No. 7891) ∎

SUSTAINABILITY AND ACCOUNTING

Tesla Motors, as introduced in this chapter's opening feature, is built on the idea of sustainability and preserving the environment. Tesla produces sustainable electric vehicles that are not powered by gasoline or diesel fossil fuels. Tesla vehicles do not emit harmful toxins and create no greenhouse gases.

"When I was in college, I wanted to be involved in things that would change the world," Elon Musk, co-founder and CEO of Tesla, proclaims. "I think the biggest problem that humanity faces is one of sustainable energy. If we don't solve that problem this century, independent of any environmental concerns, we will face economic collapse."

Elon admits that building an affordable electric car, the Model 3, would not have been possible without accurate and timely accounting data. He explains that early on, when Tesla did not have hundreds of thousands of reservations for its cars, management of cash was crucial. The company had few sales and thus had very little cash inflow.

Elon describes how he used cash flow reports to strategically plan and manage cash outflows. This included his decision not to pay dividends, a cash outflow, to owners—a policy that continues to this day.

Reliance on accounting data, along with management of cash flows, remains important to Elon. Today, Tesla invests much of its cash into its Gigafactory, one of the largest battery plants in the world that runs exclusively on renewable energy. No doubt, Tesla puts all its money on its sustainability dream. Explains Elon, "it's okay to have your eggs in one basket as long as you control what happens to that basket."

© Kevork Djansezian/Getty Images

Earnings per Share, Price-Earnings Ratio, Dividend Yield, and Book Value per Share   ■■■ **Decision Analysis**

Earnings per Share

The income statement reports **earnings per share,** also called *EPS* or *net income per share,* which is the amount of income earned per share of a company's outstanding common stock. The **basic earnings per share** formula is shown in Exhibit 13.17. When a company has no preferred stock, then preferred dividends are zero. The weighted-average common shares outstanding is measured over the income reporting period; its computation is explained in advanced courses.

A1

Compute earnings per share and describe its use.

$$\text{Basic earnings per share} = \frac{\text{Net income} - \text{Preferred dividends}}{\text{Weighted-average common shares outstanding}}$$

EXHIBIT 13.17

Basic Earnings per Share

To illustrate, assume that Quantum Co. earns $40,000 net income in 2017 and declares dividends of $7,500 on its noncumulative preferred stock. (If preferred stock is *non*cumulative, the income available [numerator] is the current-period net income less any preferred dividends *declared* in that same period. If preferred stock is cumulative, the income available [numerator] is the current-period net income less the preferred dividends whether declared or not.) Quantum has 5,000 weighted-average common shares outstanding during 2017. Its basic EPS is

$$\text{Basic earnings per share} = \frac{\$40,000 - \$7,500}{5,000 \text{ shares}} = \$6.50$$

Point: Diluted EPS is another EPS measure covered in advanced courses.

Price-Earnings Ratio

A stock's market value is determined by its *expected* future cash flows. A comparison of a company's EPS and its market value per share reveals information about market expectations. This comparison is traditionally made using a **price-earnings** (or **PE) ratio,** expressed also as *price earnings, price to earnings,* or *PE.* Some analysts interpret this ratio as what price the market is willing to pay for a company's current earnings stream. Price-earnings ratios can differ across companies that have similar earnings because of either higher or lower expectations of future earnings. The price-earnings ratio is defined in Exhibit 13.18.

A2

Compute price-earnings ratio and describe its use in analysis.

Point: The average PE ratio of stocks in the 1950–2017 period is about 14.

$$\text{Price-earnings ratio} = \frac{\text{Market value (price) per share}}{\text{Earnings per share}}$$

EXHIBIT 13.18

Price-Earnings Ratio

This ratio is often computed using EPS from the most recent period. However, many users compute this ratio using *expected* EPS for the next period.

Some analysts view stocks with high PE ratios (higher than 20 to 25) as more likely to be overpriced and stocks with low PE ratios (less than 5 to 8) as more likely to be underpriced. These investors prefer to sell or avoid buying stocks with high PE ratios and to buy or hold stocks with low PE ratios. However, investment decision making is rarely so simple as to rely on a single ratio. For instance, a stock with a high PE ratio can prove to be a good investment if its earnings continue to increase beyond current expectations. Similarly, a stock with a low PE ratio can prove to be a poor investment if its earnings decline below expectations.

■ Decision Maker

Money Manager You plan to invest in one of two companies identified as having identical future prospects. One has a PE of 19 and the other a PE of 25. Which do you invest in? Does it matter if your *estimate* of PE for both companies is 29 as opposed to 22? ■ [*Answer:* Because one company requires a payment of $19 for each $1 of earnings, and the other requires $25, you prefer the stock with a PE of 19; it is a better deal given identical prospects. Second, your PE *estimates* do matter. A PE of 29 means you expect both companies to exceed their market expectations of 19 and 25. If your PE *estimates* are 22, then you would not invest in the company with a market PE of 25.]

Dividend Yield

A3

Compute dividend yield and explain its use in analysis.

Investors buy company stock in anticipation of receiving a return from either or both cash dividends and stock price increases. Stocks that pay large dividends on a regular basis, called *income stocks,* are attractive to investors who want recurring cash flows from their investments. In contrast, some stocks pay little or no dividends but are still attractive to investors because of their expected stock price increases. The stocks of companies that distribute little or no cash but use their cash to finance expansion are called *growth stocks*. One way to help identify whether a stock is an income stock or a growth stock is to analyze its dividend yield. **Dividend yield,** defined in Exhibit 13.19, shows the annual amount of cash dividends distributed to common shares relative to their market value.

EXHIBIT 13.19

Dividend Yield

$$\text{Dividend yield} = \frac{\text{Annual cash dividends per share}}{\text{Market value per share}}$$

Dividend yield can be computed for current and prior periods using actual dividends and stock prices and for future periods using expected values. Exhibit 13.20 shows recent dividend and stock price data for **Amazon** and **Altria Group** to compute dividend yield.

Dividend yield is zero for Amazon, implying it is a growth stock. An investor in Amazon expects increases in stock prices (and eventual cash from the sale of stock). Altria has a dividend yield of 3.8%, implying it is an income stock for which dividends are important in assessing its value.

EXHIBIT 13.20

Dividend and Stock Price Information

Company	Cash Dividends per Share	Market Value per Share	Dividend Yield
Amazon	$0.00	$631	0.0%
Altria Group	$2.26	$ 60	3.8%

Book Value per Share

A4

Compute book value and explain its use in analysis.

Book value per common share, defined in Exhibit 13.21, reflects the amount of equity applicable to *common* shares on a per share basis.

EXHIBIT 13.21

Book Value per Common Share

$$\text{Book value per common share} = \frac{\text{Stockholders' equity applicable to common shares}}{\text{Number of common shares outstanding}}$$

To illustrate, consider LTD's equity in Exhibit 13.22. This year's dividends on preferred stock have been paid, but two years of preferred dividends are in arrears.

Stockholders' Equity	
Preferred stock—$100 par value, 7% cumulative, 2,000 shares authorized, 1,000 shares issued and outstanding	$100,000
Common stock—$25 par value, 12,000 shares authorized, 10,000 shares issued and outstanding	250,000
Paid-in capital in excess of par value, common stock	15,000
Retained earnings.	82,000
Total stockholders' equity	$447,000

EXHIBIT 13.22

Stockholders' Equity with Preferred and Common Stock

The book value computations are in Exhibit 13.23. Equity allocated to any preferred shares is removed before the book value of common shares is computed.

Total stockholders' equity		$447,000
Less equity applicable to preferred shares		
Par value (1,000 shares × $100)	$100,000	
Dividends in arrears ($100,000 × 7% × 2 years)	14,000	(114,000)
Equity applicable to common shares		$333,000
Book value per common share ($333,000 / 10,000 shares)		**$ 33.30**

EXHIBIT 13.23

Computing Book Value per Common Share

Book value per share reflects the value per share if a company is liquidated at balance sheet amounts. Book value is also the starting point in many stock valuation models, merger negotiations, price setting for public utilities, and loan contracts. The main limitation in using book value is the potential difference between recorded value and market value for assets and liabilities. Investors often adjust their analysis for estimates of these differences.

■ **Decision** Maker

Investor   You are considering investing in BMX, whose book value per common share is $4 and price per common share on the stock exchange is $7. From this information, are BMX's net assets priced higher or lower than its recorded value? ■   [*Answer:* Book value reflects recorded values. BMX's book value is $4 per common share. Stock price reflects the market's value of net assets (both tangible and intangible). BMX's market value is $7 per common share. Comparing these figures ($7 versus $4) suggests BMX's market value is higher than its recorded value.]

Barton Corporation began operations on January 1, 2016. The following transactions relating to stockholders' equity occurred in the first two years of the company's operations.

NEED-TO-KNOW 13-5

COMPREHENSIVE

2016

Jan.   1   Authorized the issuance of 2 million shares of $5 par value common stock and 100,000 shares of $100 par value, 10% cumulative, preferred stock.
    2   Issued 200,000 shares of common stock for $12 cash per share.
    3   Issued 100,000 shares of common stock in exchange for a building valued at $820,000 and merchandise inventory valued at $380,000.
    4   Paid $10,000 cash to the company's founders for organization activities.
    5   Issued 12,000 shares of preferred stock for $110 cash per share.

2017

June   4   Issued 100,000 shares of common stock for $15 cash per share.

Required

1. Prepare journal entries to record these transactions.

2. Prepare the stockholders' equity section of the balance sheet as of December 31, 2016, and December 31, 2017, based on these transactions.

3. Prepare a table showing dividend allocations and dividends per share for 2016 and 2017 assuming Barton declares the following cash dividends: 2016, $50,000, and 2017, $300,000.

4. Prepare the January 2, 2016, journal entry for Barton's issuance of 200,000 shares of common stock for $12 cash per share assuming

a. Common stock is no-par stock without a stated value.

b. Common stock is no-par stock with a stated value of $10 per share.

PLANNING THE SOLUTION

- Record journal entries for the transactions for 2016 and 2017.
- Determine the balances for the 2016 and 2017 equity accounts for the balance sheet.
- Prepare the contributed capital portion of the 2016 and 2017 balance sheets.
- Prepare a table similar to Exhibit 13.11 showing dividend allocations for 2016 and 2017.
- Record the issuance of common stock under both specifications of no-par stock.

SOLUTION

1. Journal entries.

2016			
Jan. 2	Cash...	2,400,000	
	Common Stock, $5 Par Value		1,000,000
	Paid-In Capital in Excess of Par Value,		
	Common Stock...............................		1,400,000
	Issued 200,000 shares of common stock.		
Jan. 3	Building	820,000	
	Merchandise Inventory	380,000	
	Common Stock, $5 Par Value		500,000
	Paid-In Capital in Excess of Par Value,		
	Common Stock...............................		700,000
	Issued 100,000 shares of common stock.		
Jan. 4	Organization Expenses	10,000	
	Cash		10,000
	Paid founders for organization costs.		
Jan. 5	Cash..	1,320,000	
	Preferred Stock, $100 Par Value..................		1,200,000
	Paid-In Capital in Excess of Par Value,		
	Preferred Stock		120,000
	Issued 12,000 shares of preferred stock.		
2017			
June 4	Cash..	1,500,000	
	Common Stock, $5 Par Value		500,000
	Paid-In Capital in Excess of Par Value,		
	Common Stock...............................		1,000,000
	Issued 100,000 shares of common stock.		

2. Balance sheet presentations (at December 31 year-end).

	2017	2016
Stockholders' Equity		
Preferred stock—$100 par value, 10% cumulative, 100,000 shares authorized, 12,000 shares issued and outstanding.....................	$1,200,000	$1,200,000
Paid-in capital in excess of par value, preferred stock...........................	120,000	120,000
Total paid-in capital by preferred stockholders................................	1,320,000	1,320,000
Common stock—$5 par value, 2,000,000 shares authorized, 300,000 shares issued and outstanding in 2016, and 400,000 shares issued and outstanding in 2017	2,000,000	1,500,000
Paid-in capital in excess of par value, common stock	3,100,000	2,100,000
Total paid-in capital by common stockholders	5,100,000	3,600,000
Total paid-in capital...	$6,420,000	$4,920,000

3. Dividend allocation table.

	Common	Preferred
2016 ($50,000)		
Preferred—current year (12,000 shares × $10 = $120,000)	$ 0	$ 50,000
Common—remainder (300,000 shares outstanding)	0	0
Total for the year...	$ 0	$ 50,000
2017 ($300,000)		
Preferred—dividend in arrears from 2016 ($120,000 − $50,000)	$ 0	$ 70,000
Preferred—current year	0	120,000
Common—remainder (400,000 shares outstanding)	110,000	0
Total for the year...	$110,000	$190,000
Dividends per share		
2016	$ 0.00	$ 4.17
2017	$ 0.28	$ 15.83

4. Journal entries.

a. For 2016 (no-par stock without a stated value):

Jan. 2	Cash	2,400,000	
	Common Stock, No-Par Value		2,400,000
	Issued 200,000 shares of no-par common stock at $12 per share.		

b. For 2016 (no-par stock with a stated value):

Jan. 2	Cash	2,400,000	
	Common Stock, $10 Stated Value..................		2,000,000
	Paid-In Capital in Excess of Stated Value, Common Stock...............................		400,000
	Issued 200,000 shares of $10 stated value common stock at $12 per share.		

Summary

C1 Identify characteristics of corporations and their organization. Corporations are legal entities whose stockholders are not liable for its debts. Stock is easily transferred, and the life of a corporation does not end with the incapacity of a stockholder. A corporation acts through its agents, who are its officers and managers. Corporations are regulated and subject to corporate income taxes. Authorized stock is the stock that a corporation's charter authorizes it to sell. Issued stock is the portion of authorized shares sold. Par value stock is a value per share assigned by the charter. No-par value stock is stock *not* assigned a value per share by the charter. Stated value stock is no-par stock to which the directors assign a value per share.

C2 Explain characteristics of, and distribute dividends between, common and preferred stock. Preferred stock has a priority (or senior status) relative to common stock in (1) dividends and (2) assets in case of liquidation. Preferred stock usually excludes voting rights. Preferred stockholders usually hold the right to dividend distributions before common stockholders. When preferred stock is cumulative and in arrears, the amount in arrears must be distributed to preferred stockholders before any dividends are distributed to common stockholders.

C3 Explain the items reported in retained earnings. Stockholders' equity is made up of (1) paid-in capital and (2) retained earnings. Paid-in capital consists of funds raised by stock issuances. Retained earnings consists of cumulative net income (losses) not distributed. Many companies face statutory and contractual restrictions on retained earnings. Corporations can voluntarily appropriate retained earnings. Prior period adjustments are corrections of errors in prior financial statements.

A1 Compute earnings per share and describe its use. A company with a simple capital structure computes basic EPS by dividing net income less any preferred dividends by the weighted-average number of outstanding common shares.

A2 Compute price-earnings ratio and describe its use in analysis. A common stock's price-earnings (PE) ratio is computed by dividing the stock's market value (price) per share by its EPS. A stock's PE is based on expectations that can prove to be better or worse than eventual performance.

A3 **Compute dividend yield and explain its use in analysis.** Dividend yield is the ratio of a stock's annual cash dividends per share to its market value (price) per share. Dividend yield can be compared with the yield of other companies to determine whether the stock is expected to be an income or growth stock.

A4 **Compute book value and explain its use in analysis.** Book value per common share is equity applicable to common shares divided by the number of outstanding common shares.

P1 **Record the issuance of corporate stock.** When stock is issued, its par or stated value is credited to the stock account and any excess is credited to a separate contributed capital account. If a stock has neither par nor stated value, the entire proceeds are credited to the stock account.

P2 **Record transactions involving cash dividends, stock dividends, and stock splits.** Cash dividends involve three events. On the date of declaration, the directors bind the company to pay the dividend. A dividend declaration reduces retained earnings and creates a current liability. On the date of record, recipients of the dividend are identified. On the date of

payment, cash is paid to stockholders and the current liability is removed. Neither a stock dividend nor a stock split alters the value of the company. However, the value of each share is less due to the distribution of additional shares. The distribution of additional shares is according to individual stockholders' ownership percentage. Small stock dividends ($\leq 25\%$) are recorded by capitalizing retained earnings equal to the market value of distributed shares. Large stock dividends ($>25\%$) are recorded by capitalizing retained earnings equal to the par or stated value of distributed shares. Stock splits do not require journal entries but do require changes in the description of stock.

P3 **Record purchases and sales of treasury stock.** When a corporation purchases its own previously issued stock, it debits the cost of these shares to Treasury Stock. Treasury stock is subtracted from equity in the balance sheet. If treasury stock is reissued, any proceeds in excess of cost are credited to Paid-In Capital, Treasury Stock. If the proceeds are less than cost, they are debited to Paid-In Capital, Treasury Stock to the extent a credit balance exists. Any remaining amount is debited to Retained Earnings.

Key Terms

Appropriated retained earnings	Earnings per share (EPS)	Preferred stock
Authorized stock	Financial leverage	Premium on stock
Basic earnings per share	Large stock dividend	Price-earnings (PE) ratio
Book value per common share	Liquidating cash dividend	Prior period adjustment
Capital stock	Market value per share	Proxy
Change in an accounting estimate	Minimum legal capital	Restricted retained earnings
Common stock	Noncumulative preferred stock	Retained earnings
Corporation	Nonparticipating preferred stock	Retained earnings deficit
Cumulative preferred stock	No-par value stock	Reverse stock split
Date of declaration	Organization expenses (costs)	Small stock dividend
Date of payment	Paid-in capital	Stated value stock
Date of record	Paid-in capital in excess of par value	Statement of stockholders' equity
Diluted earnings per share	Par value	Stock dividend
Discount on stock	Par value stock	Stock split
Dividend in arrears	Participating preferred stock	Stockholders' equity
Dividend yield	Preemptive right	Treasury stock

Multiple Choice Quiz

1. A corporation issues 6,000 shares of $5 par value common stock for $8 cash per share. The entry to record this transaction includes

   a. A debit to Paid-In Capital in Excess of Par Value for $18,000.

   b. A credit to Common Stock for $48,000.

   c. A credit to Paid-In Capital in Excess of Par Value for $30,000.

   d. A credit to Cash for $48,000.

   e. A credit to Common Stock for $30,000.

2. A company reports net income of $75,000. Its weighted-average common shares outstanding is 19,000. It has no other stock outstanding. Its earnings per share is

   a. $4.69.   c. $3.75.   e. $4.41.

   b. $3.95.   d. $2.08.

3. A company has 5,000 shares of $100 par preferred stock and 50,000 shares of $10 par common stock outstanding. Its total stockholders' equity is $2,000,000. Its book value per common share is

   a. $100.00.   c. $40.00.   e. $36.36.

   b. $10.00.   d. $30.00.

4. A company paid cash dividends of $0.81 per share. Its earnings per share is $6.95 and its market price per share is $45.00. Its dividend yield is

   a. 1.8%.   **c.** 15.4%.   **e.** 8.6%.

   b. 11.7%.   **d.** 55.6%.

5. A company's shares have a market value of $85 per share. Its net income is $3,500,000, and its weighted-average common shares outstanding is 700,000. Its price-earnings ratio is

   a. 5.9.   **c.** 17.0.   **e.** 41.2.

   b. 425.0.   **d.** 10.4.

ANSWERS TO MULTIPLE CHOICE QUIZ

1. e; Entry to record this stock issuance is:

Cash (6,000 × $8)	48,000	
Common Stock (6,000 × $5)..............		30,000
Paid-In Capital in Excess of Par Value,		
Common Stock		18,000

2. b; $75,000/19,000 shares = $3.95 per share

3. d; Preferred stock = 5,000 × $100 = $500,000
    Book value per share = ($2,000,000 − $500,000)/
    50,000 shares = $30 per common share

4. a; $0.81/$45.00 = 1.8%

5. c; Earnings per share = $3,500,000/700,000 shares = $5 per share; PE ratio = $85/$5 = 17.0

🎲 Icon denotes assignments that involve decision making.

Discussion Questions

1. What are organization expenses? Provide examples.

2. How are organization expenses reported?

3. 🎲 Who is responsible for directing a corporation's affairs?

4. What is the difference between authorized shares and outstanding shares?

5. What is the preemptive right of common stockholders?

6. List the general rights of common stockholders.

7. What is the difference between the market value per share and the par value per share?

8. Identify and explain the importance of the three dates relevant to corporate dividends.

9. Why is the term *liquidating dividend* used to describe cash dividends debited against paid-in capital accounts?

10. 🎲 How does declaring a stock dividend affect the corporation's assets, liabilities, and total equity? What are the effects of the eventual distribution of that stock?

11. 🎲 What is the difference between a stock dividend and a stock split?

12. 🎲 Courts have ruled that a stock dividend is not taxable income to stockholders. What justifies this decision?

13. How does the purchase of treasury stock affect the purchaser's assets and total equity?

14. 🎲 Why do laws place limits on treasury stock purchases?

15. How are EPS results computed for a corporation with a simple capital structure?

16. How is book value per share computed for a corporation with no preferred stock? What is the main limitation of using book value per share to value a corporation?

17. Refer to **Apple**'s fiscal 2015 balance sheet in Appendix A. How many shares of common **APPLE** stock are authorized? How many shares of common stock are issued?

18. 🎲 Refer to the 2015 balance sheet for **Google** in Appendix A. What is the par **GOOGLE** value per share of its preferred stock? Suggest a rationale for the amount of par value it assigned.

19. 🎲 Refer to the financial statements for **Samsung** in Appendix A. How **Samsung** much were its cash payments for treasury stock acquisitions and cash receipts from treasury stock disposals for the year ended December 31, 2015?

Mc Graw Hill Education **connect**

Of the following statements, which are true for the corporate form of organization?

_____ **1.** Ownership rights cannot be easily transferred.

_____ **2.** Owners have unlimited liability for corporate debts.

_____ **3.** Capital is more easily accumulated than with most other forms of organization.

_____ **4.** Corporate income that is distributed to shareholders is usually taxed twice.

_____ **5.** It is a separate legal entity.

_____ **6.** It has a limited life.

_____ **7.** Owners are not agents of the corporation.

QUICK STUDY

QS 13-1
Characteristics of corporations

C1

QS 13-2

Issuance of common stock

P1

Prepare the journal entry to record Zende Company's issuance of 75,000 shares of $5 par value common stock assuming the shares sell for:

a. $5 cash per share.

b. $6 cash per share.

QS 13-3

Issuance of par and stated value common stock

P1

Prepare the journal entry to record Jevonte Company's issuance of 36,000 shares of its common stock assuming the shares have a:

a. $2 par value and sell for $18 cash per share.

b. $2 stated value and sell for $18 cash per share.

QS 13-4

Issuance of no-par common stock

P1

Prepare the journal entry to record Autumn Company's issuance of 63,000 shares of no-par value common stock assuming the shares:

a. Sell for $29 cash per share.

b. Are exchanged for land valued at $1,827,000.

QS 13-5

Issuance of common stock

P1

Prepare the issuer's journal entry for each of the following separate transactions.

a. On March 1, Atlantic Co. issues 42,500 shares of $4 par value common stock for $297,500 cash.

b. On April 1, OP Co. issues no-par value common stock for $70,000 cash.

c. On April 6, MPG issues 2,000 shares of $25 par value common stock for $45,000 of inventory, $145,000 of machinery, and acceptance of a $94,000 note payable.

QS 13-6

Accounting for cash dividends

P2

Prepare journal entries to record the following transactions for Emerson Corporation.

July 15   Declared a cash dividend payable to common stockholders of $165,000.
Aug. 15   Date of record is August 15 for the cash dividend declared on July 15.
Aug. 31   Paid the dividend declared on July 15.

QS 13-7

Accounting for small stock dividend

P2

The stockholders' equity section of Jun Company's balance sheet as of April 1 follows. On April 2, Jun declares and distributes a 10% stock dividend. The stock's per share market value on April 2 is $20 (prior to the dividend). Prepare the stockholders' equity section immediately after the stock dividend.

Common stock—$5 par value, 375,000 shares authorized, 200,000 shares issued and outstanding	$1,000,000
Paid-in capital in excess of par value, common stock	600,000
Retained earnings	833,000
Total stockholders' equity	$2,433,000

QS 13-8

Accounting for dividends

P2

For each of the following statements regarding dividends, indicate whether it is true or false.

_____ **1.** Cash and stock dividends reduce retained earnings.

_____ **2.** Dividends payable is recorded at the time a cash dividend is declared.

_____ **3.** The date of record refers to the date a cash dividend is paid to stockholders.

_____ **4.** Stock dividends are a mechanism to keep the market price of stock affordable.

QS 13-9

Preferred stock issuance and dividends   C2

1. Prepare the journal entry to record Tamas Company's issuance of 5,000 shares of $100 par value, 7% cumulative preferred stock for $102 cash per share.

2. Assuming the facts in part 1, if Tamas declares a year-end cash dividend, what is the amount of dividend paid to preferred shareholders? (Assume no dividends in arrears.)

QS 13-10

Dividend allocation between classes of shareholders   C2

Stockholders' equity of Ernst Company consists of 80,000 shares of $5 par value, 8% cumulative preferred stock and 250,000 shares of $1 par value common stock. Both classes of stock have been outstanding since the company's inception. Ernst did not declare any dividends in the prior year, but it now declares and pays a $110,000 cash dividend at the current year-end. Determine the amount distributed to each class of stockholders for this two-year-old company.

On May 3, Zirbal Corporation purchased 4,000 shares of its own stock for $36,000 cash. On November 4, Zirbal reissued 850 shares of this treasury stock for $8,500. Prepare the May 3 and November 4 journal entries to record Zirbal's purchase and reissuance of treasury stock.

QS 13-11
Purchase and sale of treasury stock   **P3**

Listed below are various transactions that a company incurred during the current year. Indicate the impact on total stockholders' equity for each scenario. Identify whether stockholders' equity would increase (I), decrease (D), or have no effect (NE) as a result of each transaction listed below. Consider each transaction independently.

_____ **1.** A stock dividend equal to 30% of the previously outstanding shares is declared.

_____ **2.** New shares of common stock are issued for cash.

_____ **3.** Treasury shares of common stock are purchased (assume the cost method).

_____ **4.** Cash dividends are paid to shareholders.

QS 13-12
Impacts of stock issuances, dividends, splits, and treasury transactions

P2   P3

Answer the following questions related to a company's activities for the current year:

1. A review of the notes payable files discovers that three years ago the company reported the entire amount of a payment (principal and interest) on an installment note payable as interest expense. This mistake had a material effect on the amount of income in that year. How should the correction be reported in the current-year financial statements?

2. After using an expected useful life of seven years and no salvage value to depreciate its office equipment over the preceding three years, the company decided early this year that the equipment will last only two more years. How should the effects of this decision be reported in the current-year financial statements?

QS 13-13
Accounting for changes in estimates; error adjustments

C3

Murray Company reports net income of $770,000 for the year. It has no preferred stock, and its weighted-average common shares outstanding is 280,000 shares. Compute its basic earnings per share.

QS 13-14
Basic earnings per share   **A1**

Epic Company earned net income of $900,000 this year. The number of common shares outstanding during the entire year was 400,000, and preferred shareholders received a $20,000 cash dividend. Compute Epic Company's basic earnings per share.

QS 13-15
Basic earnings per share   **A1**

Compute Topp Company's price-earnings ratio if its common stock has a market value of $20.54 per share and its EPS is $3.95. Would an analyst likely consider this stock potentially overpriced, underpriced, or neither? Explain.

QS 13-16
Price-earnings ratio

A2

Foxburo Company expects to pay a $2.34 per share cash dividend this year on its common stock. The current market value of Foxburo stock is $32.50 per share. Compute the expected dividend yield on the Foxburo stock. Would you classify the Foxburo stock as a growth or an income stock? Explain.

QS 13-17
Dividend yield   **A3**

The stockholders' equity section of Montel Company's balance sheet follows. This year's dividends on preferred stock have been paid and no preferred dividends are in arrears. Determine the book value per share of the common stock.

QS 13-18
Book value per common share

A4

Preferred stock—5% cumulative, $10 par value,	
20,000 shares authorized, issued, and outstanding	$ 200,000
Common stock—$5 par value, 200,000 shares	
authorized, 150,000 shares issued and outstanding	750,000
Retained earnings	900,000
Total stockholders' equity	$1,850,000

Air France-KLM reported the following equity information in a recent year (euros in millions). Prepare its journal entry, using its account titles, to record the issuance of capital stock assuming that its entire par value stock was issued on March 31 for cash.

QS 13-19
International equity disclosures

P1

March 31	
Issued capital	€ 300
Additional paid-in capital	2,971

EXERCISES

Exercise 13-1

Characteristics of corporations

C1

In the blank next to each corporate characteristic *1* through *8*, enter the letter of the description that best relates to it.

____ **1.** Owner authority and control
____ **2.** Ease of formation
____ **3.** Transferability of ownership
____ **4.** Ability to raise large capital amounts
____ **5.** Duration of life
____ **6.** Owner liability
____ **7.** Legal status
____ **8.** Tax status of income

a. Requires government approval
b. Corporate income is taxed
c. Separate legal entity
d. Readily transferred
e. One vote per share
f. High ability
g. Unlimited
h. Limited

Exercise 13-2

Accounting for par, stated, and no-par stock issuances

P1

Rodriguez Corporation issues 19,000 shares of its common stock for $152,000 cash on February 20. Prepare journal entries to record this event under each of the following separate situations.

1. The stock has a $2 par value.
2. The stock has neither par nor stated value.
3. The stock has a $5 stated value.

Exercise 13-3

Recording stock issuances

P1

Prepare journal entries to record each of the following four separate issuances of stock.

1. A corporation issued 4,000 shares of $5 par value common stock for $35,000 cash.
2. A corporation issued 2,000 shares of no-par common stock to its promoters in exchange for their efforts, estimated to be worth $40,000. The stock has a $1 per share stated value.
3. A corporation issued 2,000 shares of no-par common stock to its promoters in exchange for their efforts, estimated to be worth $40,000. The stock has no stated value.
4. A corporation issued 1,000 shares of $50 par value preferred stock for $60,000 cash.

Exercise 13-4

Stock issuance for noncash assets   **P1**

Sudoku Company issues 7,000 shares of $7 par value common stock in exchange for land and a building. The land is valued at $45,000 and the building at $85,000. Prepare the journal entry to record issuance of the stock in exchange for the land and building.

Exercise 13-5

Stock dividends and splits

P2

On June 30, 2017, Sharper Corporation's common stock is priced at $62 per share before any stock dividend or split, and the stockholders' equity section of its balance sheet appears as follows.

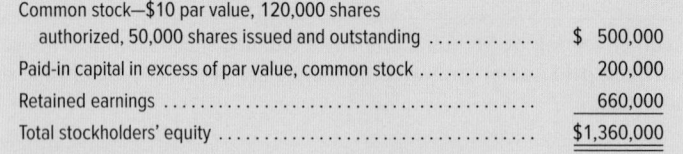

Common stock—$10 par value, 120,000 shares authorized, 50,000 shares issued and outstanding	$ 500,000
Paid-in capital in excess of par value, common stock	200,000
Retained earnings	660,000
Total stockholders' equity	$1,360,000

1. Assume that the company declares and immediately distributes a 50% stock dividend. This event is recorded by capitalizing retained earnings equal to the stock's par value. Answer these questions about stockholders' equity as it exists *after* issuing the new shares.
  a. What is the retained earnings balance?
  b. What is the amount of total stockholders' equity?
  c. How many shares are outstanding?

2. Assume that the company implements a 3-for-2 stock split instead of the stock dividend in part 1. Answer these questions about stockholders' equity as it exists *after* issuing the new shares.
  a. What is the retained earnings balance?
  b. What is the amount of total stockholders' equity?
  c. How many shares are outstanding?

3. Explain the difference, if any, to a stockholder from receiving new shares distributed under a large stock dividend versus a stock split.

Check (1*b*) $1,360,000

(2*a*) $660,000

The stockholders' equity of TVX Company at the beginning of the day on February 5 follows:

Common stock—$10 par value, 150,000 shares	
authorized, 60,000 shares issued and outstanding	$ 600,000
Paid-in capital in excess of par value, common stock	425,000
Retained earnings	550,000
Total stockholders' equity	$1,575,000

On February 5, the directors declare a 20% stock dividend distributable on February 28 to the February 15 stockholders of record. The stock's market value is $40 per share on February 5 before the stock dividend. The stock's market value is $33.40 per share on February 28.

1. Prepare entries to record both the dividend declaration and its distribution.

2. One stockholder owned 800 shares on February 5 before the dividend. Compute the book value per share and total book value of this stockholder's shares immediately before *and* after the stock dividend of February 5.

3. Compute the total market value of the investor's shares in part 2 as of February 5 and February 28.

Exercise 13-6
Stock dividends and per share book values
P2

Check   (2) Book value per share: before, $26.250; after, $21.875

Match each description 1 through 4 with the characteristic of preferred stock that it best describes by writing the letter of that characteristic in the blank next to each description.

A. Cumulative   **B.** Noncumulative   **C.** Nonparticipating   **D.** Participating

_____ **1.** Holders of the stock are entitled to receive current and all past dividends before common stockholders receive any dividends.

_____ **2.** Holders of the stock can receive dividends exceeding the stated rate under certain conditions.

_____ **3.** Holders of the stock are not entitled to receive dividends in excess of the stated rate.

_____ **4.** Holders of the stock lose any dividends that are not declared in the current year.

Exercise 13-7
Identifying characteristics of preferred stock
C2

York's outstanding stock consists of 80,000 shares of *noncumulative* 7.5% preferred stock with a $5 par value and also 200,000 shares of common stock with a $1 par value. During its first four years of operation, the corporation declared and paid the following total cash dividends:

2015 total cash dividends	$ 20,000
2016 total cash dividends	28,000
2017 total cash dividends	200,000
2018 total cash dividends	350,000

Determine the amount of dividends paid each year to each of the two classes of stockholders: preferred and common. Also compute the total dividends paid to each class for the four years combined.

Exercise 13-8
Dividends on common and noncumulative preferred stock
C2

Check   4-year total paid to preferred, $108,000

Use the data in Exercise 13-8 to determine the amount of dividends paid each year to each of the two classes of stockholders assuming that the preferred stock is *cumulative*. Also determine the total dividends paid to each class for the four years combined.

Exercise 13-9
Dividends on common and cumulative preferred stock   C2

On October 10, the stockholders' equity of Sherman Systems appears as follows:

Common stock—$10 par value, 72,000 shares	
authorized, issued, and outstanding	$ 720,000
Paid-in capital in excess of par value, common stock	216,000
Retained earnings	864,000
Total stockholders' equity	$1,800,000

Exercise 13-10
Recording and reporting treasury stock transactions
P3

1. Prepare journal entries to record the following transactions for Sherman Systems.

   a. Purchased 5,000 shares of its own common stock at $25 per share on October 11.

   b. Sold 1,000 treasury shares on November 1 for $31 cash per share.

   c. Sold all remaining treasury shares on November 25 for $20 cash per share.

Check (1c) Dr. Retained
Earnings, $14,000

2. Explain how the company's equity section changes after the October 11 treasury stock purchase, and prepare the revised equity section of its balance sheet at that date.

Exercise 13-11

Preparing a statement of retained earnings

C3

The following information is available for Amos Company for the year ended December 31, 2017.

a. Balance of retained earnings, December 31, 2016, prior to discovery of error, $1,375,000.

b. Cash dividends declared and paid during 2017, $43,000.

c. It forgot to record 2015 depreciation expense of $55,500, which is net of $4,500 in tax benefits.

d. The company earned $126,000 in 2017 net income.

Prepare a 2017 statement of retained earnings for Amos Company.

Exercise 13-12

Earnings per share

A1

Check (2) $3.41

Ecker Company reports $2,700,000 of net income for 2017 and declares $388,020 of cash dividends on its preferred stock for 2017. At the end of 2017, the company had 678,000 weighted-average shares of common stock.

1. What amount of net income is available to common stockholders for 2017?

2. What is the company's basic EPS for 2017?

Exercise 13-13

Earnings per share

A1

Check (2) $2.10

Kelley Company reports $960,000 of net income for 2017 and declares $120,000 of cash dividends on its preferred stock for 2017. At the end of 2017, the company had 400,000 weighted-average shares of common stock.

1. What amount of net income is available to common stockholders for 2017?

2. What is the company's basic EPS for 2017? Round your answer to the nearest whole cent.

Exercise 13-14

Price-earnings ratio computation and interpretation

A2

Compute the price-earnings ratio for each of these four separate companies. Which stock might an analyst likely investigate as being potentially undervalued by the market? Explain.

	A	B	C
1		Earnings	Market Value
2	Company	per Share	per Share
3	1	$12.00	$176.40
4	2	10.00	96.00
5	3	7.50	93.75
6	4	50.00	250.00

Exercise 13-15

Dividend yield computation and interpretation

A3

Compute the dividend yield for each of these four separate companies. Which company's stock would probably *not* be classified as an income stock? Explain.

	A	B	C
1		Annual Cash	Market Value
2	Company	Dividend per Share	per Share
3	1	$16.06	$220.00
4	2	13.86	132.00
5	3	3.96	72.00
6	4	0.48	80.00

Exercise 13-16

Book value per share

A4

The equity section of Cyril Corporation's balance sheet shows the following:

Preferred stock—6% cumulative, $25 par value, 10,000 shares issued and outstanding	$ 250,000
Common stock—$8 par value, 100,000 shares issued and outstanding.......................................	800,000
Retained earnings	535,000
Total stockholders' equity	$1,585,000

This year's dividends on preferred stock have been paid. Determine the book value per share of common stock under two separate situations.

1. No preferred dividends are in arrears.

2. Three years of preferred dividends are in arrears.

Check   (1) Book value of common, $13.35 per share

Unilever Group reports the following equity information for the years ended December 31, 2015 and 2014 (euros in millions).

December 31	2015	2014
Share capital..................	€ 484	€ 484
Share premium................	152	145
Other reserves	(7,816)	(7,538)
Retained profit	22,619	20,560
Shareholders' equity	€15,439	€13,651

Exercise 13-17
Accounting for equity under IFRS

C3   P1

1. Match each of the three account titles—*Share capital, Share premium,* and *Retained profit*—with the usual account title applied under U.S. GAAP from the following options:

_____ **a.** Paid-in capital in excess of par value, common stock

_____ **b.** Retained earnings

_____ **c.** Common stock, par value

2. Prepare Unilever's journal entry, using its account titles, to record the issuance of capital stock assuming that its entire par value stock was issued on December 31, 2014, for cash.

3. What were Unilever's 2015 dividends assuming that only dividends and income impacted retained profit for 2015 and that its 2015 income totaled €5,259?

Alexander Corporation reports the following components of stockholders' equity on December 31, 2016:

Common stock—$25 par value, 50,000 shares authorized, 30,000 shares issued and outstanding	$ 750,000
Paid-in capital in excess of par value, common stock	50,000
Retained earnings	340,000
Total stockholders' equity	$1,140,000

Exercise 13-18
Cash dividends, treasury stock, and statement of retained earnings

C3   P2   P3

In year 2017, the following transactions affected its stockholders' equity accounts.

Jan. 2   Purchased 3,000 shares of its own stock at $25 cash per share.
Jan. 7   Directors declared a $1.50 per share cash dividend payable on February 28 to the February 9 stockholders of record.
Feb. 28   Paid the dividend declared on January 7.
July 9   Sold 1,200 of its treasury shares at $30 cash per share.
Aug. 27   Sold 1,500 of its treasury shares at $20 cash per share.
Sep. 9   Directors declared a $2 per share cash dividend payable on October 22 to the September 23 stockholders of record.
Oct. 22   Paid the dividend declared on September 9.
Dec. 31   Closed the $52,000 credit balance (from net income) in the Income Summary account to Retained Earnings.

Required

1. Prepare journal entries to record each of these transactions for 2017.

2. Prepare a statement of retained earnings for the year ended December 31, 2017.

3. Prepare the stockholders' equity section of the company's balance sheet as of December 31, 2017.

PROBLEM SET A

Problem 13-1A
Stockholders' equity
transactions and analysis

C2   P1

Kinkaid Co. is incorporated at the beginning of this year and engages in a number of transactions. The
following journal entries impacted its stockholders' equity during its first year of operations.

a.	Cash	300,000	
	Common Stock, $25 Par Value........................		250,000
	Paid-In Capital in Excess of		
	Par Value, Common Stock		50,000
b.	Organization Expenses	150,000	
	Common Stock, $25 Par Value........................		125,000
	Paid-In Capital in Excess of		
	Par Value, Common Stock		25,000
c.	Cash	43,000	
	Accounts Receivable	15,000	
	Building	81,500	
	Notes Payable.......................................		59,500
	Common Stock, $25 Par Value........................		50,000
	Paid-In Capital in Excess of		
	Par Value, Common Stock		30,000
d.	Cash	120,000	
	Common Stock, $25 Par Value........................		75,000
	Paid-In Capital in Excess of		
	Par Value, Common Stock		45,000

Required

Check   (2) 20,000 shares

       (3) $500,000

       (4) $650,000

1. Explain the transaction(s) underlying each journal entry (*a*) through (*d*).
2. How many shares of common stock are outstanding at year-end?
3. What is the amount of minimum legal capital (based on par value) at year-end?
4. What is the total paid-in capital at year-end?
5. What is the book value per share of the common stock at year-end if total paid-in capital plus retained
   earnings equals $695,000?

Problem 13-2A
Cash dividends, treasury
stock, and statement of
retained earnings

C3   P2   P3

Kohler Corporation reports the following components of stockholders' equity on December 31, 2016:

Common stock—$10 par value, 100,000 shares authorized,	
40,000 shares issued and outstanding	$400,000
Paid-in capital in excess of par value, common stock	60,000
Retained earnings	270,000
Total stockholders' equity	$730,000

In year 2017, the following transactions affected its stockholders' equity accounts.

Jan.	1	Purchased 4,000 shares of its own stock at $20 cash per share.
Jan.	5	Directors declared a $2 per share cash dividend payable on February 28 to the February 5 stockholders of record.
Feb.	28	Paid the dividend declared on January 5.
July	6	Sold 1,500 of its treasury shares at $24 cash per share.
Aug.	22	Sold 2,500 of its treasury shares at $17 cash per share.
Sep.	5	Directors declared a $2 per share cash dividend payable on October 28 to the September 25 stockholders of record.
Oct.	28	Paid the dividend declared on September 5.
Dec.	31	Closed the $388,000 credit balance (from net income) in the Income Summary account to Retained Earnings.

Required

1. Prepare journal entries to record each of these transactions for 2017.
2. Prepare a statement of retained earnings for the year ended December 31, 2017.
3. Prepare the stockholders' equity section of the company's balance sheet as of December 31, 2017.

Check (2) Retained earnings, Dec. 31, 2017, $504,500

At September 30, the end of Beijing Company's third quarter, the following stockholders' equity accounts are reported.

Problem 13-3A
Equity analysis—journal entries and account balances

P2

Common stock, $12 par value..............................	$360,000
Paid-in capital in excess of par value, common stock	90,000
Retained earnings	320,000

In the fourth quarter, the following entries related to its equity are recorded:

Oct. 2	Retained Earnings	60,000	
	Common Dividend Payable		60,000
Oct. 25	Common Dividend Payable............................	60,000	
	Cash		60,000
Oct. 31	Retained Earnings	75,000	
	Common Stock Dividend Distributable		36,000
	Paid-In Capital in Excess of Par Value,		
	Common Stock................................		39,000
Nov. 5	Common Stock Dividend Distributable..................	36,000	
	Common Stock, $12 Par Value		36,000
Dec. 1	Memo—Change the title of the Common Stock		
	account to reflect the new par value of $4.		
Dec. 31	Income Summary......................................	210,000	
	Retained Earnings.............................		210,000

Required

1. Explain the transaction(s) underlying each journal entry.
2. Complete the following table showing the equity account balances at each indicated date (take into account the beginning balances from September 30).

	Sep. 30	Oct. 2	Oct. 25	Oct. 31	Nov. 5	Dec. 1	Dec. 31
Common stock	$ 360,000	$ ____	$ ____	$ ____	$ ____	$ ____	$ ____
Common stock dividend distributable	0	____	____	____	____	____	____
Paid-in capital in excess of par, common stock	90,000	____	____	____	____	____	____
Retained earnings	320,000	____	____	____	____	____	____
Total equity	$ 770,000	$ ____	$ ____	$ ____	$ ____	$ ____	$ ____

Check Total equity: Oct. 2, $710,000; Dec. 31, $920,000

The equity sections from Atticus Group's 2016 and 2017 year-end balance sheets follow.

Problem 13-4A
Analysis of changes in stockholders' equity accounts

C3   P2   P3

Stockholders' Equity (December 31, 2016)	
Common stock—$4 par value, 100,000 shares	
authorized, 40,000 shares issued and outstanding	$160,000
Paid-in capital in excess of par value, common stock	120,000
Retained earnings	320,000
Total stockholders' equity	$600,000

Stockholders' Equity (December 31, 2017)	
Common stock—$4 par value, 100,000 shares	
authorized, 47,400 shares issued, 3,000 shares in treasury	$189,600
Paid-in capital in excess of par value, common stock	179,200
Retained earnings ($30,000 restricted by treasury stock).	400,000
	768,800
Less cost of treasury stock	(30,000)
Total stockholders' equity	$738,800

The following transactions and events affected its equity during year 2017.

Jan.	5	Declared a $0.50 per share cash dividend, date of record January 10.
Mar.	20	Purchased treasury stock for cash.
Apr.	5	Declared a $0.50 per share cash dividend, date of record April 10.
July	5	Declared a $0.50 per share cash dividend, date of record July 10.
July	31	Declared a 20% stock dividend when the stock's market value was $12 per share.
Aug.	14	Issued the stock dividend that was declared on July 31.
Oct.	5	Declared a $0.50 per share cash dividend, date of record October 10.

Required

1. How many common shares are outstanding on each cash dividend date?
2. What is the total dollar amount for each of the four cash dividends?
3. What is the amount of the capitalization of retained earnings for the stock dividend?
4. What is the per share cost of the treasury stock purchased?
5. How much net income did the company earn during year 2017?

Check (3) $88,800

(4) $10

(5) $248,000

Problem 13-5A
Computation of book values and dividend allocations

C2   A4

Raphael Corporation's common stock is currently selling on a stock exchange at $85 per share, and its current balance sheet shows the following stockholders' equity section:

Preferred stock—5% cumulative, $___ par value, 1,000 shares	
authorized, issued, and outstanding	$ 50,000
Common stock—$___ par value, 4,000 shares authorized, issued,	
and outstanding.	80,000
Retained earnings	150,000
Total stockholders' equity	$280,000

Required

1. What is the current market value (price) of this corporation's common stock?
2. What are the par values of the corporation's preferred stock and its common stock?
3. If no dividends are in arrears, what is the book value per share of common stock? (Round per share value to the nearest cent.)
4. If two years' preferred dividends are in arrears, what is the book value per share of common stock? (Round per share value to the nearest cent.)
5. If two years' preferred dividends are in arrears and the board of directors declares cash dividends of $11,500, what total amount will be paid to the preferred and to the common shareholders? What is the amount of dividends per share for the common stock? (Round per share value to the nearest cent.)

Check (4) Book value of common, $56.25

(5) Dividends per common share, $1.00

Analysis Component

6. What are some factors that can contribute to a difference between the book value of common stock and its market value (price)?

Weiss Company is incorporated at the beginning of this year and engages in a number of transactions. The following journal entries impacted its stockholders' equity during its first year of operations.

PROBLEM SET B

Problem 13-1B
Stockholders' equity transactions and analysis

C2   P1

a.	Cash	120,000	
	Common Stock, $1 Par Value		3,000
	Paid-In Capital in Excess of		
	Par Value, Common Stock		117,000
b.	Organization Expenses	40,000	
	Common Stock, $1 Par Value		1,000
	Paid-In Capital in Excess of		
	Par Value, Common Stock		39,000
c.	Cash	13,300	
	Accounts Receivable	8,000	
	Building	37,000	
	Notes Payable		18,300
	Common Stock, $1 Par Value		800
	Paid-In Capital in Excess of		
	Par Value, Common Stock		39,200
d.	Cash	60,000	
	Common Stock, $1 Par Value		1,200
	Paid-In Capital in Excess of		
	Par Value, Common Stock		58,800

Required

1. Explain the transaction(s) underlying each journal entry (*a*) through (*d*).
2. How many shares of common stock are outstanding at year-end?
3. What is the amount of minimum legal capital (based on par value) at year-end?
4. What is the total paid-in capital at year-end?
5. What is the book value per share of the common stock at year-end if total paid-in capital plus retained earnings equals $283,200?

Check   (2) 6,000 shares
(3) $6,000
(4) $260,000

Balthus Corp. reports the following components of stockholders' equity on December 31, 2016:

Problem 13-2B
Cash dividends, treasury stock, and statement of retained earnings

C3   P2   P3

Common stock—$1 par value, 320,000 shares authorized,	
200,000 shares issued and outstanding	$ 200,000
Paid-in capital in excess of par value, common stock	1,400,000
Retained earnings	2,160,000
Total stockholders' equity	$3,760,000

It completed the following transactions related to stockholders' equity in year 2017:

Jan. 10   Purchased 40,000 shares of its own stock at $12 cash per share.
Mar. 2   Directors declared a $1.50 per share cash dividend payable on March 31 to the March 15 stockholders of record.
Mar. 31   Paid the dividend declared on March 2.
Nov. 11   Sold 24,000 of its treasury shares at $13 cash per share.
Nov. 25   Sold 16,000 of its treasury shares at $9.50 cash per share.
Dec. 1   Directors declared a $2.50 per share cash dividend payable on January 2 to the December 10 stockholders of record.
Dec. 31   Closed the $1,072,000 credit balance (from net income) in the Income Summary account to Retained Earnings.

Required

1. Prepare journal entries to record each of these transactions for 2017.
2. Prepare a statement of retained earnings for the year ended December 31, 2017.
3. Prepare the stockholders' equity section of the company's balance sheet as of December 31, 2017.

Check   (2) Retained earnings,
Dec. 31, 2017, $2,476,000

Problem 13-3B

Equity analysis—journal entries and account balances

P2

At December 31, the end of Chilton Communication's third quarter, the following stockholders' equity accounts are reported:

Common stock, $10 par value......................................	$ 960,000
Paid-in capital in excess of par value, common stock	384,000
Retained earnings	1,600,000

In the fourth quarter, the following entries related to its equity are recorded:

Jan. 17	Retained Earnings	96,000	
	Common Dividend Payable		96,000
Feb. 5	Common Dividend Payable...........................	96,000	
	Cash		96,000
Feb. 28	Retained Earnings	252,000	
	Common Stock Dividend Distributable		120,000
	Paid-In Capital in Excess of Par Value,		
	Common Stock.............................		132,000
Mar. 14	Common Stock Dividend Distributable..................	120,000	
	Common Stock, $10 Par Value		120,000
Mar. 25	Memo—Change the title of the Common Stock		
	account to reflect the new par value of $5.		
Mar. 31	Income Summary.....................................	720,000	
	Retained Earnings..............................		720,000

Required

1. Explain the transaction(s) underlying each journal entry.
2. Complete the following table showing the equity account balances at each indicated date (take into account the beginning balances from December 31).

	Dec. 31	Jan. 17	Feb. 5	Feb. 28	Mar. 14	Mar. 25	Mar. 31
Common stock	$ 960,000	$_____	$_____	$_____	$_____	$_____	$_____
Common stock dividend distributable	0	_____	_____	_____	_____	_____	_____
Paid-in capital in excess of par, common stock	384,000	_____	_____	_____	_____	_____	_____
Retained earnings	1,600,000	_____	_____	_____	_____	_____	_____
Total equity	$ 2,944,000	$_____	$_____	$_____	$_____	$_____	$_____

Check Total equity: Jan. 17, $2,848,000; Mar. 31, $3,568,000

Problem 13-4B

Analysis of changes in stockholders' equity accounts

C3 P2 P3

The equity sections from Hovo Corporation's 2016 and 2017 balance sheets follow.

Stockholders' Equity (December 31, 2016)	
Common stock—$20 par value, 30,000 shares authorized,	
17,000 shares issued and outstanding	$340,000
Paid-in capital in excess of par value, common stock	60,000
Retained earnings	270,000
Total stockholders' equity	$670,000

Stockholders' Equity (December 31, 2017)	
Common stock—$20 par value, 30,000 shares authorized, 19,000 shares issued, 1,000 shares in treasury	$380,000
Paid-in capital in excess of par value, common stock	104,000
Retained earnings ($40,000 restricted by treasury stock).	295,200
	779,200
Less cost of treasury stock.	(40,000)
Total stockholders' equity	$739,200

The following transactions and events affected its equity during year 2017.

Feb. 15   Declared a $0.40 per share cash dividend, date of record five days later.
Mar. 2   Purchased treasury stock for cash.
May 15   Declared a $0.40 per share cash dividend, date of record five days later.
Aug. 15   Declared a $0.40 per share cash dividend, date of record five days later.
Oct.   4   Declared a 12.5% stock dividend when the stock's market value is $42 per share.
Oct. 20   Issued the stock dividend that was declared on October 4.
Nov. 15   Declared a $0.40 per share cash dividend, date of record five days later.

Required

1. How many common shares are outstanding on each cash dividend date?
2. What is the total dollar amount for each of the four cash dividends?
3. What is the amount of the capitalization of retained earnings for the stock dividend?
4. What is the per share cost of the treasury stock purchased?
5. How much net income did the company earn during year 2017?

Check   (3) $84,000
(4) $40
(5) $136,000

Soltech Company's common stock is currently selling on a stock exchange at $90 per share, and its current balance sheet shows the following stockholders' equity section.

Problem 13-5B
Computation of book values and dividend allocations

C2   A4

Preferred stock—8% cumulative, $___ par value, 1,500 shares authorized, issued, and outstanding	$ 375,000
Common stock—$___ par value, 18,000 shares authorized, issued, and outstanding	900,000
Retained earnings	1,125,000
Total stockholders' equity	$2,400,000

Required

1. What is the current market value (price) of this corporation's common stock?
2. What are the par values of the corporation's preferred stock and its common stock?
3. If no dividends are in arrears, what is the book value per share of common stock? (Round per share value to the nearest cent.)
4. If two years' preferred dividends are in arrears, what is the book value per share of common stock? (Round per share value to the nearest cent.)
5. If two years' preferred dividends are in arrears and the board of directors declares cash dividends of $100,000, what total amount will be paid to the preferred and to the common shareholders? What is the amount of dividends per share for the common stock? (Round per share value to the nearest cent.)

Check   (4) Book value of common, $109.17

(5) Dividends per common share, $0.56

Analysis Component

6. Discuss why the book value of common stock is not always a good estimate of its market value.

SERIAL PROBLEM
Business Solutions

P1 C1 C2

© Alexander Image/Shutterstock RF

(This serial problem began in Chapter 1 and continues through most of the book. If previous chapter segments were not completed, the serial problem can begin at this point.)

SP 13 Santana Rey created **Business Solutions** on October 1, 2017. The company has been successful, and Santana plans to expand her business. She believes that an additional $86,000 is needed and is investigating three funding sources.

a. Santana's sister Cicely is willing to invest $86,000 in the business as a common shareholder. Since Santana currently has about $129,000 invested in the business, Cicely's investment will mean that Santana will maintain about 60% ownership and Cicely will have 40% ownership of Business Solutions.

b. Santana's uncle Marcello is willing to invest $86,000 in the business as a preferred shareholder. Marcello would purchase 860 shares of $100 par value, 7% preferred stock.

c. Santana's banker is willing to lend her $86,000 on a 7%, 10-year note payable. She would make monthly payments of $1,000 per month for 10 years.

Required

1. Prepare the journal entry to reflect the initial $86,000 investment under each of the options (*a*), (*b*), and (*c*).

2. Evaluate the three proposals for expansion, providing the pros and cons of each option.

3. Which option do you recommend Santana adopt? Explain.

GENERAL LEDGER PROBLEM

Available only in Connect

The following **General Ledger** assignments highlight the impact, or lack thereof, on financial statements from equity-based transactions.

GL 13-1 General Ledger assignment 13-1 is adapted from Problem 13-2A, including beginning equity balances. Prepare journal entries related to treasury stock, cash dividends, and net income. Then, prepare the statement of retained earnings and the stockholders' equity section of the balance sheet.

GL 13-2 General Ledger assignment 13-2 is adapted from Problem 13-4A, including beginning and ending equity balances. Prepare journal entries related to cash dividends and stock dividends. Calculate the number of shares outstanding, the amount of net income, and the amount of retained earnings to be capitalized as a result of the stock dividend, if any.

Beyond the Numbers

REPORTING IN ACTION

C2 A1 A4

APPLE

BTN 13-1 Refer to **Apple**'s financial statements in Appendix A to answer the following.

1. How many shares of common stock are issued and outstanding at September 26, 2015, and September 27, 2014? How do these numbers compare with the basic weighted-average common shares outstanding at September 26, 2015, and September 27, 2014?

2. What is the book value of its entire common stock at September 26, 2015?

3. What is the total amount of cash dividends paid to common stockholders for the years ended September 26, 2015, and September 27, 2014?

4. Identify and compare basic EPS amounts across fiscal years 2015, 2014, and 2013. Identify and comment on any notable changes.

5. How many shares does Apple hold in treasury stock, if any, as of September 26, 2015, and September 27, 2014?

Fast Forward

6. Access Apple's financial statements for fiscal years ending after September 26, 2015, from its website (Apple.com) or the SEC's EDGAR database (SEC.gov). Has the number of common shares outstanding increased since that date? Has the company increased the total amount of cash dividends paid compared to the total amount for fiscal year 2015?

BTN 13-2 Use the following comparative figures for Apple and Google.

Key Figures	Apple	Google
Net income (in millions)	$ 53,394	$ 16,348
Cash dividends declared per common share	$ 1.98	$ —
Common shares outstanding (in millions)	5,578.753	687.348
Weighted-average common shares outstanding (in millions)	5,753.421	684.626
Market value (price) per share	$ 107.00	$ 775.10
Equity applicable to common shares (in millions)	$ 119,355	$120,331

COMPARATIVE ANALYSIS

A1 A2 A3 A4

APPLE
GOOGLE

Required

1. Compute the book value per common share for each company using these data.
2. Compute the basic EPS for each company using these data.
3. Compute the dividend yield for each company using these data. Does the dividend yield of either of the companies characterize it as an income or growth stock? Explain.
4. Compute, compare, and interpret the price-earnings ratio for each company using these data.

BTN 13-3 Harriet Moore is an accountant for New World Pharmaceuticals. Her duties include tracking research and development spending in the new product development division. Over the course of the past six months, Harriet has noticed that a great deal of funds have been spent on a particular project for a new drug. She hears "through the grapevine" that the company is about to patent the drug and expects it to be a major advance in antibiotics. Harriet believes that this new drug will greatly improve company performance and will cause the company's stock to increase in value. Harriet decides to purchase shares of New World in order to benefit from this expected increase.

ETHICS CHALLENGE

C3

Required

What are Harriet's ethical responsibilities, if any, with respect to the information she has learned through her duties as an accountant for New World Pharmaceuticals? What are the implications of her planned purchase of New World shares?

BTN 13-4 Teams are to select an industry, and each team member is to select a different company in that industry. Each team member then is to acquire the selected company's financial statements (or Form 10-K) from the SEC site (SEC.gov). Use these data to identify basic EPS. Use the financial press (or finance.yahoo.com) to determine the market price of this stock, and then compute the price-earnings ratio. Communicate with teammates via a meeting, e-mail, or telephone to discuss the meaning of this ratio, how companies compare, and the industry norm. The team must prepare a single memorandum reporting the ratio for each company and identifying the team conclusions or consensus of opinion. The memorandum is to be duplicated and distributed to the instructor and teammates.

COMMUNICATING IN PRACTICE

A1 A2

Hint: Make a slide of each team's memo for a class discussion.

BTN 13-5 Access the February 25, 2016, filing of the 2015 calendar-year 10-K report of McDonald's (ticker: MCD) from SEC.gov.

TAKING IT TO THE NET

C1 C3

Required

1. Review McDonald's balance sheet and identify how many classes of stock it has issued.
2. What are the par values, number of authorized shares, and number of issued shares of the classes of stock you identified in part 1?
3. Review its statement of cash flows and identify what total amount of cash it paid in 2015 to purchase treasury stock.
4. What amount did McDonald's pay out in common stock cash dividends for 2015?

TEAMWORK IN ACTION

P3

Hint: Instructor must be sure each team accurately completes part 1 before proceeding.

BTN 13-6   This activity requires teamwork to reinforce understanding of accounting for treasury stock.

1. Write a brief team statement (*a*) generalizing what happens to a corporation's financial position when it engages in a stock buyback and (*b*) identifying reasons why a corporation would engage in this activity.

2. Assume that an entity acquires 100 shares of its $100 par value common stock at a cost of $134 cash per share. Discuss the entry to record this acquisition. Next, assign *each* team member to prepare *one* of the following entries (assume each entry applies to all shares):

    a. Reissue treasury shares at cost.

    b. Reissue treasury shares at $150 per share.

    c. Reissue treasury shares at $120 per share; assume the paid-in capital account from treasury shares has a $1,500 balance.

    d. Reissue treasury shares at $120 per share; assume the paid-in capital account from treasury shares has a $1,000 balance.

    e. Reissue treasury shares at $120 per share; assume the paid-in capital account from treasury shares has a zero balance.

3. In sequence, each member is to present his/her entry to the team and explain the *similarities* and *differences* between that entry and the previous entry.

ENTREPRENEURIAL DECISION

C2   P2

BTN 13-7   Assume that Tesla decides to launch a new website to market discount bookkeeping services to consumers. This chain, named Aladin, requires $500,000 of start-up capital. The founder contributes $375,000 of personal assets in return for 15,000 shares of common stock, but he must raise another $125,000 in cash. There are two alternative plans for raising the additional cash.

- *Plan A* is to sell 3,750 shares of common stock to one or more investors for $125,000 cash.
- *Plan B* is to sell 1,250 shares of cumulative preferred stock to one or more investors for $125,000 cash (this preferred stock would have a $100 par value, an annual 8% dividend rate, and be issued at par).

1. If the new business is expected to earn $72,000 of after-tax net income in the first year, what rate of return on beginning equity will the founder earn under each alternative plan? Which plan will provide the higher expected return?

2. If the new business is expected to earn $16,800 of after-tax net income in the first year, what rate of return on beginning equity will the founder earn under each alternative plan? Which plan will provide the higher expected return?

3. Analyze and interpret the differences between the results for parts 1 and 2.

HITTING THE ROAD

A1   A2   A3

BTN 13-8   Review 30 to 60 minutes of financial news programming on television. Take notes on companies that are catching analysts' attention. You might hear reference to over- and undervaluation of firms and to reports about PE ratios, dividend yields, and earnings per share. Be prepared to give a brief description to the class of your observations.

GLOBAL DECISION

A1   C3

Samsung

BTN 13-9   Use the following financial information for Samsung (Samsung.com).

Net income less dividends available to preferred shares (in millions)	₩ 16,317,275
Cash dividends declared for common stock (in millions)	₩ 2,677,250
Cash dividends declared per common share	₩ 21,015
Number of common shares outstanding (in millions)	127.397
Weighted-average common shares outstanding (in millions)	129.190
Equity applicable to common shares (in millions)	₩178,940,338

Required

1. Compute book value per share for Samsung.

2. Compute earnings per share (EPS) for Samsung.

3. Compare Samsung's dividends per share with its EPS. Is Samsung paying out a large or small amount of its income as dividends? Explain.

GLOBAL VIEW

This section discusses similarities and differences between U.S. GAAP and IFRS in accounting and reporting for equity.

Accounting for Common Stock   The accounting for and reporting of common stock under U.S. GAAP and IFRS are similar. Specifically, procedures for issuing common stock at par, at a premium, at a discount, and for noncash assets are similar across the two systems. However, we must be aware of legal and cultural differences across the world that can impact the rights and responsibilities of common shareholders. Samsung's terminology is a bit different as it uses the phrase "share premium" in reference to what U.S. GAAP would title "paid-in capital in excess of par value" (see Appendix A).

Samsung

Accounting for Dividends   Accounting for and reporting of dividends under U.S. GAAP and IFRS are consistent. This applies to cash dividends, stock dividends, and stock splits. Samsung "declared cash dividends to shareholders of common stock and preferred stock as interim dividends for the six-month periods . . . and as year-end dividends." Samsung, like many other companies, follows a dividend policy set by management and its board.

Accounting for Preferred Stock   Accounting and reporting for preferred stock are similar for U.S. GAAP and IFRS. Preferred stock that is redeemable at the option of the preferred stockholders is reported *between* liabilities and equity in U.S. GAAP balance sheets. However, that same stock is reported as a liability in IFRS balance sheets.

Accounting for Treasury Stock   Both U.S. GAAP and IFRS apply the principle that companies do not record gains or losses on transactions involving their own stock. This applies to purchases, reissuances, and retirements of treasury stock. Consequently, the accounting for treasury stock explained in this chapter is consistent with that under IFRS. However, IFRS in this area is less detailed than U.S. GAAP.

 IFRS

Like U.S. GAAP, IFRS requires that preferred stocks be classified as debt or equity based on analysis of the stock's contractual terms. However, IFRS uses different criteria for such classification. ■

 Global View Assignments

Discussion Question 19

Quick Study 13-19

Exercise 13-17

BTN 13-9

14 chapter

Long-Term Liabilities

Chapter Preview

BOND BASICS

A1 Bond financing

Bond trading

P1 Par bonds

NTK 14-1

DISCOUNT BONDS

Discount or premium

P2 Bond payments

Amortize discount

Straight-line

NTK 14-2

PREMIUM BONDS

P3 Bond payments

Amortize premium

Straight-line

P4 Bond retirement

NTK 14-3

LONG-TERM NOTES

C1 Recording notes

DEBT ANALYSIS

A2 Debt features

A3 Debt-to-equity

NTK 14-4

Learning Objectives

CONCEPTUAL

C1 Explain the types of notes and prepare entries to account for notes.

C2 *Appendix 14A*—Explain and compute bond pricing.

C3 *Appendix 14C*—Describe accounting for leases and pensions.

ANALYTICAL

A1 Compare bond financing with stock financing.

A2 Assess debt features and their implications.

A3 Compute the debt-to-equity ratio and explain its use.

PROCEDURAL

P1 Prepare entries to record bond issuance and interest expense.

P2 Compute and record amortization of a bond discount using the straight-line method.

P3 Compute and record amortization of a bond premium using the straight-line method.

P4 Record the retirement of bonds.

P5 *Appendix 14B*—Compute and record amortization of a bond discount using the effective interest method.

P6 *Appendix 14B*—Compute and record amortization of a bond premium using the effective interest method.

Hitch a Ride

SAN FRANCISCO—Garrett Camp and Travis Kalanick were in Paris and tried to hail a cab. "I would wait 30–40 minutes for a cab that never showed up," explains Garrett. He recalls looking at his friend Travis and saying, "I just want to push a button and get a ride." Travis perked up, "I'm like, 'That's pretty good.'" That's how **Uber** (**Uber.com**) got started.

Uber is an app that connects consumers with drivers through GPS location services. "Our mission is transportation as reliable as running water," exclaims Travis, "everywhere for everyone!"

To translate their idea into action, Garrett and Travis needed to finance the business. They decided on a mix of debt and equity financing. "Our strategy is to make sure that we are raising as much as our competitors are," explains Travis, "that our balance sheet is as healthy as theirs is."

Debt financing is key for Garrett and Travis. Debt financing enables them to keep more control and reap more of the upside of Uber's success. The two owners raised over a billion dollars in debt financing.

Garrett and Travis explain that getting their accounting system in order was crucial in raising and tracking such large issuances of bonds and notes payable. This included bond issuance procedures, including how to account for and price bonds issued at a discount or premium.

The owners discovered the usefulness of convertible bonds and issued them as one part of their financing efforts. They also had to deal with accounting rules for convertible bonds. "It takes a little time to get a system up and running," explains Garrett, and he insists the reporting system is "very important" to their success.

"Push the limits"

—Travis Kalanick

Creditors give Uber a thumbs-up for its management of debt and equity. Uber broke the U.S. record (previously held by **Facebook**) for most equity financing before offering stock to the public.

Garrett and Travis successfully navigated the waters of debt and equity financing. Yet their greatest financing challenge might still lie ahead: an Uber IPO (initial public offering) of equity. "I'm going to make sure it happens," proclaims Travis. "I want to build something that endures."

Sources: *Uber website,* January 2017; *CNBC,* March 2016; *Wall Street Journal,* January 2015; *99u,* May 2014; *Wall Street Journal,* January 2013

BASICS OF BONDS

This section explains bonds and reasons for issuing them. Both for-profit and nonprofit companies, as well as governmental units, such as nations, states, cities, and schools, issue bonds.

Bond Financing

A1
Compare bond financing with stock financing.

Projects that demand large amounts of money often are funded from bond issuances. A **bond** is its issuer's written promise to pay an amount equaling the par value of the bond with interest. The **par value of a bond,** also called the *face amount* or *face value,* is paid at a stated future date known as the bond's *maturity date.* Most bonds require the issuer to make semiannual interest payments. Interest paid each period is computed by multiplying the par value of the bond by the bond's contract rate.

Advantages of Bonds   There are three main advantages of bond financing:

1. *Bonds do not affect owner control.* Equity financing reflects ownership in a company, but bond financing does not. A person who contributes $1,000 of a company's $10,000 equity financing typically controls one-tenth of owner decisions. A person who owns a $1,000, 11%, 20-year bond has no ownership right.

2. *Interest on bonds is tax deductible.* Bond interest payments are tax deductible for the issuer, but distributions to owners are not. To illustrate, assume that a corporation with no bond financing earns $15,000 in income *before* paying taxes at a 40% tax rate, which amounts to $6,000 ($15,000 × 40%) in taxes. If a portion of its financing is in bonds, however, the resulting bond interest is deducted in computing taxable income. This means if bond interest expense is $10,000, then taxes owed would be $2,000 ([$15,000 − $10,000] × 40%), which is less than the $6,000 owed with no bond financing.

3. *Bonds can increase return on equity.* A company that earns a higher return with borrowed funds than it pays in interest on those funds increases its return on equity. This process is called *financial leverage* or *trading on the equity.*

Point: Financial leverage refers to issuance of bonds, notes, and preferred stock.

To illustrate the third point, consider Magnum Co., which has $1,000 million in equity and is planning a $500 million expansion to meet increasing demand for its product. Magnum predicts the $500 million expansion will yield $125 million in additional income before paying interest. It currently earns $100 million per year and has no interest expense. Magnum is considering three plans. Plan A is to not expand. Plan B is to expand and raise $500 million from equity financing. Plan C is to expand and issue $500 million of bonds that pay 10% annual interest ($50 mil.). Exhibit 14.1 shows how these three plans affect Magnum's net income, equity, and return on equity (net income/equity). Magnum earns a higher return on equity under Plan C to issue bonds. Income under Plan C ($175 mil.) is smaller than under Plan B ($225 mil.), but the return on equity is larger because of less equity investment. Plan C has another advantage if income is taxable. This illustration reflects a general rule: *Return on equity increases when the expected rate of return from the new assets is higher than the rate of interest expense on debt financing.*

Example: Compute return on equity for all three plans if Magnum is subject to a 40% income tax. *Answer* ($ mil.):

A = 6.0% ($100[1 − 0.4]/$1,000)

B = 9.0% ($225[1 − 0.4]/$1,500)

C = 10.5% ($175[1 − 0.4]/$1,000)

EXHIBIT 14.1

Financing with Bonds versus Equity

$ millions	Plan A: Do Not Expand	Plan B: Equity Financing	Plan C: Bond Financing
Income before interest expense............	$ 100	$ 225	$ 225
Interest expense	—	—	(50)
Net income	**$ 100**	**$ 225**	**$ 175**
Equity.................................	$1,000	$1,500	$1,000
Return on equity.......................	**10.0%**	**15.0%**	**17.5%**

Disadvantages of Bonds   The two main disadvantages of bond financing are:

1. *Bonds can decrease return on equity.* When a company earns a lower return with the borrowed funds than it pays in interest, it decreases return on equity. This downside of financial leverage is more likely when a company has periods of low income or net losses.

2. *Bonds require payment of both periodic interest and the par value at maturity.* Bond payments are a burden when income and cash flow are low. Equity financing does not require payments because withdrawals (dividends) are paid at the will of the owner (or board).

> **Point:** There are nearly 5 million individual U.S. bond issues, ranging from huge treasuries to tiny municipalities. This compares to about 12,000 individual U.S. stocks that are traded.

Bond Trading

Bonds can be bought and sold. A bond *issue* consists of a number of bonds, usually in denominations of $1,000 or $5,000, and is sold to many different lenders. After bonds are issued, they often are bought and sold among investors, meaning that a bond probably has a number of owners before it matures. When bonds are bought and sold in the market, they have a market value (price). Bond market values are expressed as a percent of par (face) value. For example, a bond trading at 103½ is bought or sold for 103.5% of par value. A bond trading at 95 is bought or sold at 95% of par value.

> **Point:** A bond with a par value of $1,000 trading at 103½ sells for $1,035 ($1,000 × 1.035).

▥ Decision Insight

Quotes   The **IBM** bond quote here is interpreted (left to right) as **Bonds,** issuer name; **Rate,** contract interest rate (4%); **Mat,** matures in year 2042 when principal is paid; **Yld,** yield rate (3.81%) of bond at current price; **Vol,** dollar worth ($110,000) of trades (in 1,000s); **Close,** closing price (103.08) for the day as percentage of par value; **Chg,** change (+0.73%) in closing price from prior day's close. ▪

Bonds	Rate	Mat	Yld	Vol	Close	Chg
IBM	4	42	3.81	110	103.08	+0.73%

> **Point:** Two of the largest bond issuances in history were:
>
> Verizon . . . . $49 billion
> Apple. . . . . $17 billion

Bond-Issuing Procedures

Authorization of bond issuances includes the number of bonds authorized, their par value, and the contract interest rate. The legal document describing the rights and obligations of both the bondholders and the issuer is called the **bond indenture,** which is the legal contract between the issuer and the bondholders (and specifies when interest is paid). A bondholder may also receive a bond certificate as evidence of the company's debt. A **bond certificate,** such as in Exhibit 14.2, includes the issuer's name, the par value, the contract interest rate, and the maturity date.[1]

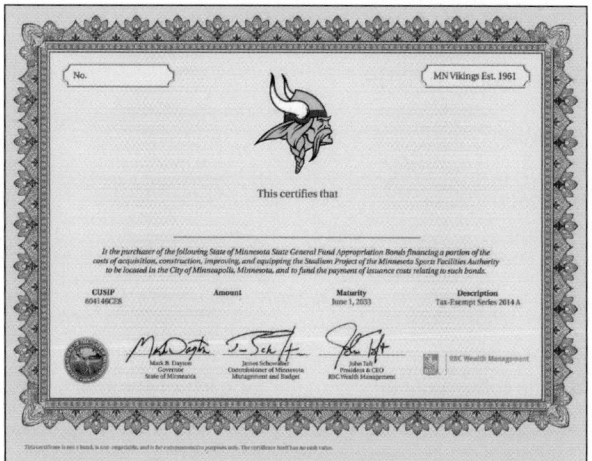

Courtesy of RBC Wealth Management

EXHIBIT 14.2

Bond Certificate

> **Point:** *Indenture* refers to a bond's legal contract; *debenture* refers to an unsecured bond.

---

[1] The issuing company normally sells its bonds to an investment firm called an *underwriter,* which resells them to the public. An issuing company can also sell bonds directly to investors. When an underwriter sells bonds to a large number of investors, a *trustee* represents and protects the bondholders' interests. The trustee monitors the issuer to ensure that it complies with the obligations in the bond indenture. Most trustees are large banks or trust companies. The trustee writes and accepts the terms of a bond indenture before it is issued. When bonds are offered to the public, called *floating an issue,* they must be registered with the Securities and Exchange Commission (SEC). SEC registration requires the issuer to file certain financial information. Most company bonds are issued in par value units of $1,000 or $5,000. *A baby bond* has a par value of less than $1,000, such as $100.

PAR BONDS

P1

Prepare entries to record bond issuance and interest expense.

Bonds issued at par value are called **par bonds**. To illustrate, suppose Nike issues $100,000 of 8%, 2-year bonds dated December 31, 2017, that mature on December 31, 2019, and pay interest semiannually each June 30 and December 31. If all bonds are sold at par value, Nike records the sale as follows—increasing Nike's cash and long-term liabilities.

Assets = Liabilities + Equity
+100,000   +100,000

2017			
Dec. 31	Cash...	100,000	
	Bonds Payable		100,000
	Sold bonds at par.		

Nike records the first semiannual interest payment as follows—the same entry is made *every* six months including the maturity date.

Assets = Liabilities + Equity
−4,000   −4,000

2018			
June 30	Bond Interest Expense	4,000	
	Cash.......................................		4,000
	Paid semiannual interest (8% × $100,000 × ½ year).		

When the bonds mature, Nike records its payment of principal as follows.

Assets = Liabilities + Equity
−100,000   −100,000

2019			
Dec. 31	Bonds Payable.......................................	100,000	
	Cash.......................................		100,000
	Paid bond principal at maturity.		

NEED-TO-KNOW 14-1

Recording Par Value Bonds

P1

A company issues 8%, two-year bonds on December 31, 2017, with a par value of $7,000 and semiannual interest payments. On the issue date, the annual market rate for these bonds is 8%, which implies a selling price of $7,000. Prepare journal entries to record (*a*) the issuance of bonds on December 31, 2017; (*b*) the first through fourth interest payments on each June 30 and December 31; and (*c*) the maturity of the bond on December 31, 2019.

Solution

a.

2017			
Dec. 31	Cash...	7,000	
	Bonds Payable		7,000
	Sold bonds at par.		

b. The following entry is made for each of the four interest payments of June 30 and December 31 for both 2018 and 2019.

	Bond Interest Expense	280	
	Cash.......................................		280
	Pay semiannual interest. $7,000 × 8% × 1/2		

c.

2019			
Dec. 31	Bonds Payable.......................................	7,000	
	Cash.......................................		7,000
	Record maturity and payment of bonds.		

Do More: QS 14-16, E 14-1, E 14-16

DISCOUNT BONDS

This section explains accounting for bond issuances *below par,* called **discount bonds**.

Bond Discount or Premium

The bond issuer pays the interest rate specified in the indenture, the **contract rate,** also called the *coupon rate, stated rate,* or *nominal rate.* The annual interest paid is computed by multiplying the bond par value by the contract rate. The contract rate is usually stated on an annual basis, even if interest is paid semiannually. For example, if a company issues a $1,000, 8% bond paying interest semiannually, it pays annual interest of $80 (8% × $1,000) in two semiannual payments of $40 each.

The contract rate sets the interest the issuer pays in *cash,* which is not necessarily the *bond interest expense* for the issuer. Bond interest expense depends on the bond's market value at issuance, which is determined by market expectations of the risk of lending to the issuer. The bond's **market rate** of interest is the rate that borrowers are willing to pay and lenders are willing to accept for a bond and its risk level. As risk increases, the market rate increases to compensate purchasers for the bonds' increased risk. Also, the market rate is usually higher when the time until the bond matures is longer due to the risk of bad events over a longer time period.

When the contract rate and market rate are equal, a bond sells at par value. If they are not equal, it is sold at a *premium* above par value or at a *discount* below par value. Exhibit 14.3 shows the relation between the contract rate, the market rate, and a bond's issue price.

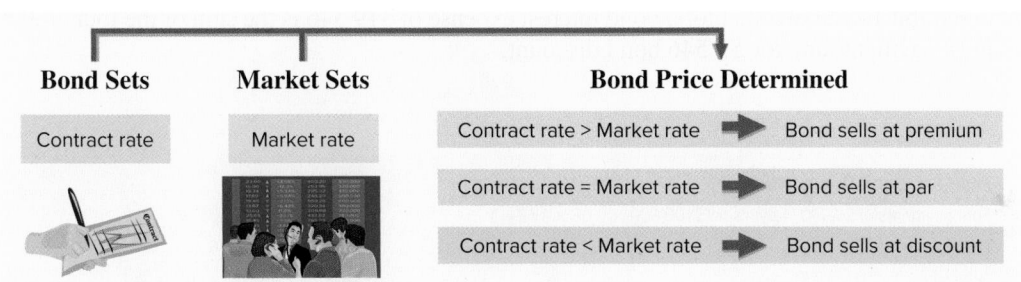

EXHIBIT 14.3

Relation between Bond Issue Price, Contract Rate, and Market Rate

Issuing Bonds at a Discount

A **discount on bonds payable** occurs when a company issues bonds with a contract rate less than the market rate. This means the issue price is less than par value—the issuer gets less money at issuance than what the issuer must pay back at maturity. To illustrate, assume that **Fila** issues bonds with a $100,000 par value, an 8% annual contract rate (paid semiannually), and a two-year life. Also assume that the market rate for Fila bonds is 10%. These bonds sell at a discount because the contract rate is less than the market rate. The exact issue price is stated as 96.454 (implying 96.454% of par value, or $96,454); we show how to compute this issue price in Appendix 14A.

P2

Compute and record amortization of a bond discount using the straight-line method.

Cash Payments with Discount Bonds   These bonds require Fila to pay:

1. Par value of $100,000 cash at the end of the bonds' two-year life.
2. Cash interest payments of $4,000 ($100,000 × 8% × 1/2 year) at the end of each semiannual period.

The pattern of cash receipts and payments for Fila bonds is shown in Exhibit 14.4.

Point: The difference between the contract rate and the market rate of interest on a new bond issue is usually a fraction of a percent. We use a difference of 2% to emphasize the effects.

EXHIBIT 14.4

Discount Bond Cash Receipts and Payments

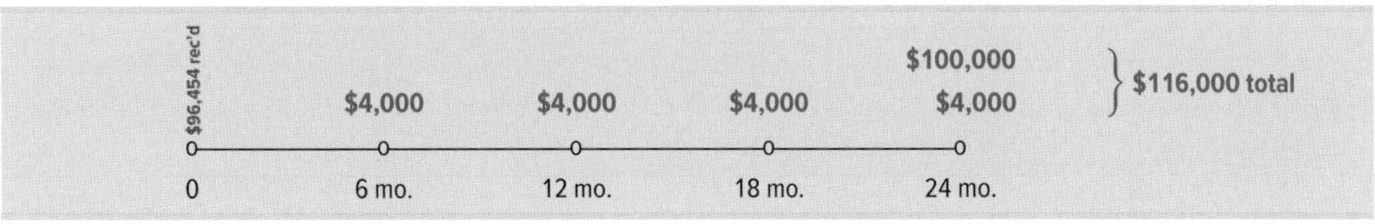

Recording Issuance of Discount Bonds   When Fila accepts $96,454 cash for its bonds on the issue date of December 31, 2017, it records the sale as follows.

Assets = Liabilities + Equity
+96,454   +100,000
             −3,546

Dec. 31	Cash	96,454	
	Discount on Bonds Payable	3,546	
	Bonds Payable		100,000
	Sold bonds at a discount on their issue date.		

Point: Book value at issuance always equals the issuer's cash borrowed.

Bonds payable are reported in the long-term liability section of Fila's December 31, 2017, balance sheet as shown in Exhibit 14.5. A discount is deducted from par value to compute the **carrying (book) value of bonds.** Discount on Bonds Payable is a contra liability account.

EXHIBIT 14.5

Balance Sheet Presentation of Bond Discount

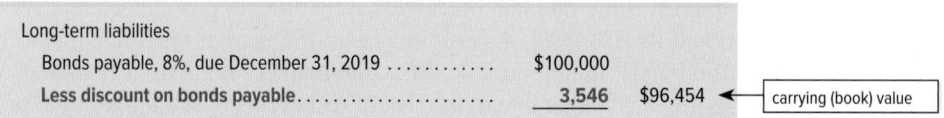

Long-term liabilities		
Bonds payable, 8%, due December 31, 2019	$100,000	
Less discount on bonds payable.....................	3,546	$96,454 ◄── carrying (book) value

Amortizing Discount Bonds   Fila receives $96,454 for its bonds; in return it must pay bondholders $100,000 when it matures in two years (plus interest). The upper portion of panel A in Exhibit 14.6 shows that total bond interest expense of $19,546 is the sum of the four $4,000 interest payments and the $3,546 bond discount.

EXHIBIT 14.6

Interest Computation and Entry for Discount Bonds

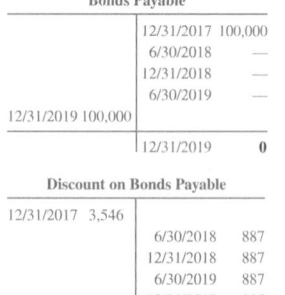

Bonds Payable		
	12/31/2017	100,000
	6/30/2018	—
	12/31/2018	—
	6/30/2019	—
12/31/2019 100,000	12/31/2019	0

Discount on Bonds Payable		
12/31/2017 3,546		
	6/30/2018	887
	12/31/2018	887
	6/30/2019	887
	12/31/2019	885
	12/31/2019	0

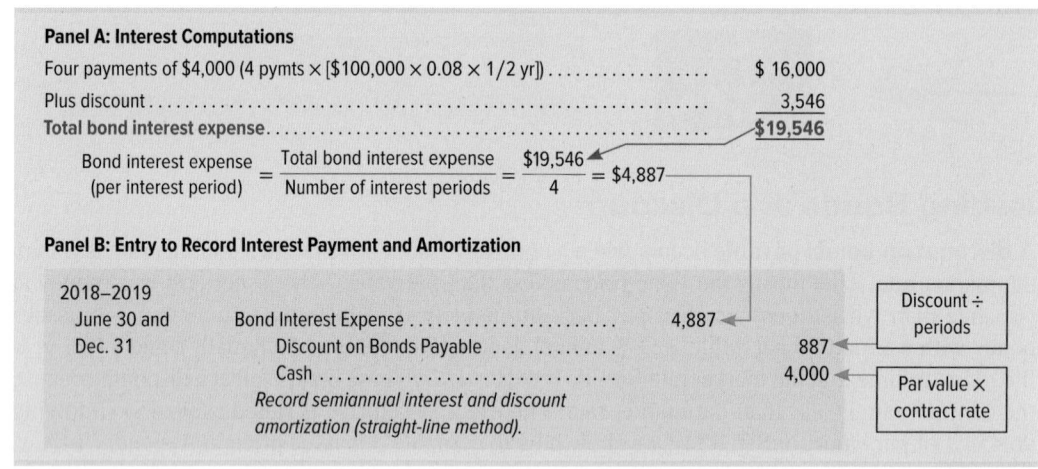

Panel A: Interest Computations

Four payments of $4,000 (4 pymts × [$100,000 × 0.08 × 1/2 yr])	$ 16,000
Plus discount	3,546
Total bond interest expense.	$19,546

$$\text{Bond interest expense (per interest period)} = \frac{\text{Total bond interest expense}}{\text{Number of interest periods}} = \frac{\$19,546}{4} = \$4,887$$

Panel B: Entry to Record Interest Payment and Amortization

2018–2019 June 30 and Dec. 31	Bond Interest Expense	4,887 ◄	
	Discount on Bonds Payable		887 ◄
	Cash		4,000 ◄
	Record semiannual interest and discount amortization (straight-line method).		

Discount ÷ periods

Par value × contract rate

The total $19,546 bond interest expense is allocated over the four semiannual periods in the bonds' life, and the bonds' carrying value is updated at each balance sheet date. This is accomplished using the straight-line method (or the effective interest method in Appendix 14B). Both methods reduce the bond discount to zero over the bond life. This process is called *amortizing a bond discount.*

> *The following section on discount amortization uses the straight-line method. Appendix 14B uses the effective interest method. An instructor can choose to cover either one or both methods. If the straight-line method is skipped, then move forward to the section titled "Premium Bonds."*

Straight-Line Method   The **straight-line bond amortization** method allocates an equal portion of the total bond interest expense to each interest period. We divide the total bond interest expense of $19,546 by 4 (the number of semiannual periods in the bonds' life). This gives a bond interest expense of $4,887 per period, which is $4,886.5 rounded to the nearest dollar per period—all computations, including those for assignments, are rounded to the nearest whole dollar. Panel B of Exhibit 14.6 shows how the issuer records bond interest expense and updates the balance of the bond liability account at the end of *each* of the four semiannual interest periods (June 30, 2018, through December 31, 2019).

Point: Another way to compute bond interest expense: 1. Divide the $3,546 discount by 4 periods to get $887 amortized each period. 2. Add $887 to the $4,000 cash payment to get bond interest expense of $4,887 per period.

Exhibit 14.7 shows the pattern of decreases in the Discount on Bonds Payable account and the pattern of increases in the bonds' carrying value. Three points summarize the discount bonds' straight-line amortization:

EXHIBIT 14.7

Straight-Line Amortization of Bond Discount

Semiannual Period-End	Unamortized Discount*	Carrying Value†
(0) 12/31/2017..........	$3,546	$ 96,454
(1) 6/30/2018..........	2,659	97,341
(2) 12/31/2018	1,772	98,228
(3) 6/30/2019..........	885	99,115
(4) **12/31/2019**..........	0‡	**100,000**

1. At issuance, the $100,000 par value consists of the $96,454 cash received by the issuer plus the $3,546 discount.

The columns always sum to par value for discount bonds.

* Total bond discount of $3,546 less accumulated periodic amortization of $887 per semiannual interest period.

† Bond par value of $100,000 less unamortized discount.

‡ Adjusted for rounding.

2. During the bonds' life, the (unamortized) discount decreases each period by the $887 amortization ($3,546/4), and carrying value (par value less unamortized discount) increases each period by $887.

3. At maturity, unamortized discount equals zero, and carrying value equals the $100,000 par value that the issuer pays the holder.

Point: Amortization always results in the carrying value of a bond moving closer to its par value.

Decision Insight

Ratings Game   Many bond buyers rely on rating services to assess bond risk. The best known are **Standard & Poor's**, **Moody's**, and **Fitch**. These services analyze the issuer's financial statements and other factors in setting ratings. Standard & Poor's ratings, from best quality to default, are AAA, AA, A, BBB, BB, B, CCC, CC, C, and D. Ratings can include a plus (+) or minus (−) to show relative standing within a category. Bonds rated in the A and B range are referred to as *investment grade;* lower-rated bonds are considered riskier. ■

A company issues 8%, two-year bonds on December 31, 2017, with a par value of $7,000 and semiannual interest payments. On the issue date, the annual market rate for these bonds is 10%, which implies a selling price of 96.46 or $6,752. (*a*) Prepare an amortization table like Exhibit 14.7 for these bonds; use the straight-line method to amortize the discount. Then, prepare journal entries to record (*b*) the issuance of bonds on December 31, 2017; (*c*) the first through fourth interest payments on each June 30 and December 31; and (*d*) the maturity of the bond on December 31, 2019.

NEED-TO-KNOW 14-2

Recording Discount Bonds

P1   P2

Solution

a.

Semiannual Period-End	Unamortized Discount	Carrying Value
(0) 12/31/2017..............	$248	$6,752
(1) 6/30/2018..............	186	6,814
(2) 12/31/2018..............	124	6,876
(3) 6/30/2019..............	62	6,938
(4) 12/31/2019	0	7,000

Interest computations for solutions *a, b,* and *c*

Four interest payments of $280	
[4 pymts × ($7,000 × 0.08 × 1/2 yr)]	$1,120
Plus discount	248
Total bond interest expense	$1,368
Divided by number of periods...................	÷ 4
Bond interest expense per period................	$ 342

b.

2017			
Dec. 31	Cash	6,752	
	Discount on Bonds Payable	248	
	Bonds Payable		7,000
	Sold bonds at discount.		

c.

2018			
June 30	Bond Interest Expense	342	
	Discount on Bonds Payable*...........................		62
	Cash†		280
	Pay semiannual interest and record amortization.		
2018			
Dec. 31	Bond Interest Expense	342	
	Discount on Bonds Payable*...........................		62
	Cash†		280
	Pay semiannual interest and record amortization.		
2019			
June 30	Bond Interest Expense	342	
	Discount on Bonds Payable*...........................		62
	Cash†		280
	Pay semiannual interest and record amortization.		
2019			
Dec. 31	Bond Interest Expense	342	
	Discount on Bonds Payable*...........................		62
	Cash†		280
	Pay semiannual interest and record amortization.		

* $248/4   † $7,000 × 8% × 1/2

d.

2019			
Dec. 31	Bonds Payable	7,000	
	Cash		7,000
	Record maturity and payment of bonds.		

Bonds Payable

	12/31/2017	7,000
	6/30/2018	—
	12/31/2018	—
	6/30/2019	—
12/31/2019 7,000		
	12/31/2019	**0**

Discount on Bonds Payable

12/31/2017 248		
	6/30/2018	62
	12/31/2018	62
	6/30/2019	62
	12/31/2019	62
	12/31/2019	**0**

Do More: QS 14-2, QS 14-6, QS 14-7, E 14-1, E 14-2, E 14-4, E 14-5

PREMIUM BONDS

This section explains accounting for bond issuances *above par,* called **premium bonds.**

Issuing Bonds at a Premium

P3

Compute and record amortization of a bond premium using the straight-line method.

When the contract rate of bonds is higher than the market rate, the bonds sell at a price higher than par value—the issuer gets more money at issuance than what the issuer must pay back at maturity. The amount by which the bond price exceeds par value is the **premium on bonds.** To illustrate, assume that **Adidas** issues bonds with a $100,000 par value, a 12% annual contract rate, semiannual interest payments, and a two-year life. Also assume the market rate for Adidas bonds is 10% on the issue date. The Adidas bonds sell at a premium because the contract rate is higher than the market rate. The issue price is stated as 103.546 (implying 103.546% of par value, or $103,546); we show how to compute this issue price in Appendix 14A.

Cash Payments with Premium Bonds   These bonds require Adidas to pay:

1. Par value of $100,000 cash at the end of the bonds' two-year life.
2. Cash interest payments of $6,000 ($100,000 × 12% × 1/2 year) at the end of each semiannual period.

Point: Contract rate *yields* Cash interest payment. And, **Market** rate *yields* interest expense.

The pattern of cash receipts and payments for Adidas bonds is shown in Exhibit 14.8.

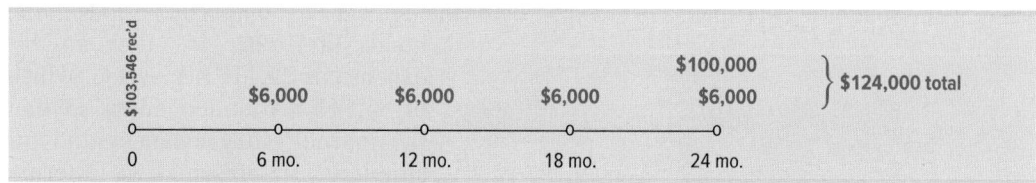

EXHIBIT 14.8

Premium Bond Cash
Receipts and Payments

Recording Issuance of Premium Bonds

When Adidas receives $103,546 cash for its bonds on the issue date of December 31, 2017, it records this as follows.

Dec. 31	Cash..	103,546	
	Premium on Bonds Payable.....................		3,546
	Bonds Payable		100,000
	Sold bonds at a premium on their issue date.		

Assets = Liabilities + Equity
+103,546   +100,000
                   +3,546

Bonds payable are reported in the long-term liability section of Adidas's December 31, 2017, balance sheet as shown in Exhibit 14.9. A premium is added to par value to compute the carrying (book) value of bonds. Premium on Bonds Payable is an adjunct ("add-on") liability account.

Long-term liabilities		
Bonds payable, 12%, due December 31, 2019	$100,000	
Plus premium on bonds payable.......................	3,546	$103,546

EXHIBIT 14.9

Balance Sheet Presentation
of Bond Premium

Amortizing Premium Bonds

Adidas receives $103,546 for its bonds; in return, it pays bondholders $100,000 after two years (plus interest). The upper portion of panel A of Exhibit 14.10 shows that total bond interest expense of $20,454 is the sum of the four $6,000 interest payments minus the $3,546 bond premium. The premium is subtracted because it reduces the issuer's cost. Total bond interest expense is allocated over the four semiannual periods using the straight-line method (or the effective interest method in Appendix 14B).

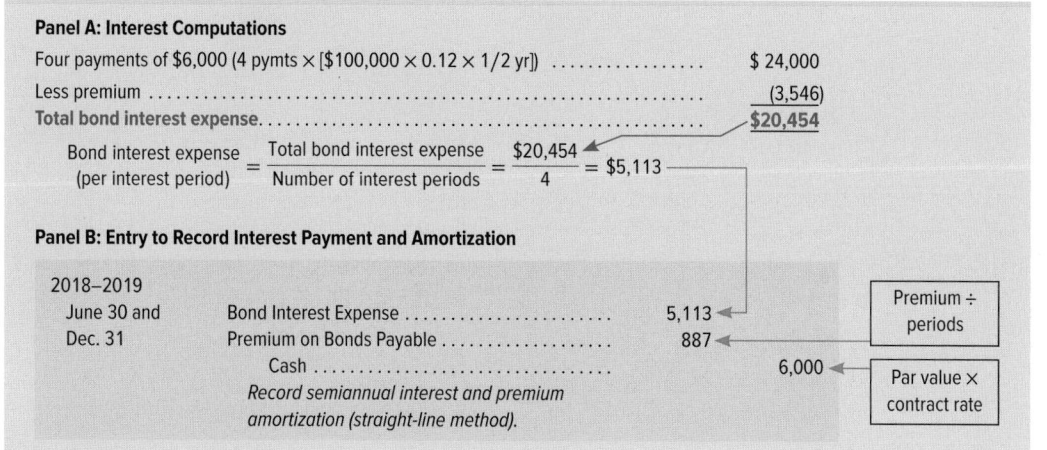

EXHIBIT 14.10

Interest Computation and
Entry for Premium Bonds

The following section on premium amortization uses the straight-line method. Appendix 14B uses the effective interest method. An instructor can choose to cover either one or both methods. If the straight-line method is skipped, then move forward to the section titled "Bond Retirement."

Straight-Line Method

The straight-line method allocates an equal portion of total bond interest expense to each of the bonds' semiannual interest periods. We divide the two years' total bond interest expense of $20,454 by 4 (the number of semiannual periods in the bonds' life). This gives bond interest expense of $5,113 per period, which is $5,113.5 rounded down so that the journal entry balances and for simplicity in presentation (alternatively, one could carry cents). Panel B of Exhibit 14.10 shows how Adidas records bond interest expense and updates the balance of the bond liability account for *each* semiannual period (June 30, 2018, through December 31, 2019).

EXHIBIT 14.11

Straight-Line Amortization
of Bond Premium

Semiannual Period-End	Unamortized Premium*	Carrying Value†
(0) 12/31/2017	$3,546	$103,546
(1) 6/30/2018	2,659	102,659
(2) 12/31/2018	1,772	101,772
(3) 6/30/2019	885	100,885
(4) 12/31/2019	0‡	**100,000**

> During the bond life, carrying value is adjusted to par and the amortized premium to zero.

* Total bond premium of $3,546 less accumulated periodic amortization of $887 per semiannual interest period.

† Bond par value of $100,000 plus unamortized premium.

‡ Adjusted for rounding.

Exhibit 14.11 shows the pattern of decreases in the unamortized Premium on Bonds Payable account and in the bonds' carrying value. Three points summarize straight-line amortization of premium bonds:

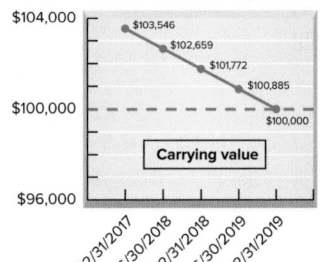

1. At issuance, the $100,000 par value plus the $3,546 premium equals the $103,546 cash received by the issuer.

2. During the bonds' life, the (unamortized) premium decreases each period by the $887 amortization ($3,546/4), and carrying value decreases each period by the same $887.

3. At maturity, unamortized premium equals zero, and carrying value equals the $100,000 par value that the issuer pays the holder.

NEED-TO-KNOW 14-3

Recording Premium
Bonds

P3

A company issues 8%, two-year bonds on December 31, 2017, with a par value of $7,000 and semiannual interest payments. On the issue date, the annual market rate for these bonds is 6%, which implies a selling price of 103.71 or $7,260. (*a*) Prepare an amortization table like Exhibit 14.11 for these bonds; use the straight-line method to amortize the premium. Then, prepare journal entries to record (*b*) the issuance of bonds on December 31, 2017; (*c*) the first through fourth interest payments on each June 30 and December 31; and (*d*) the maturity of the bond on December 31, 2019.

Solution

a.

Semiannual Period-End	Unamortized Premium	Carrying Value
(0) 12/31/2017..............	$260	$7,260
(1) 6/30/2018..............	195	7,195
(2) 12/31/2018..............	130	7,130
(3) 6/30/2019..............	65	7,065
(4) 12/31/2019..............	0	7,000

Interest computations for solutions *a, b,* and *c*

Four interest payments of $280	
[4 pymts × ($7,000 × 0.08 × 1/2 yr)]	$1,120
Less premium	260
Total bond interest expense	$ 860
Divided by number of periods	÷ 4
Bond interest expense per period................	$ 215

b.

2017			
Dec. 31	Cash..	7,260	
	Premium on Bonds Payable		260
	Bonds Payable......................................		7,000
	Sold bonds at premium.		

c.

2018			
June 30	Bond Interest Expense	215	
	Premium on Bonds Payable*	65	
	Cash†		280
	Pay semiannual interest and record amortization.		
2018			
Dec. 31	Bond Interest Expense	215	
	Premium on Bonds Payable*	65	
	Cash†		280
	Pay semiannual interest and record amortization.		
2019			
June 30	Bond Interest Expense	215	
	Premium on Bonds Payable*	65	
	Cash†		280
	Pay semiannual interest and record amortization.		
2019			
Dec. 31	Bond Interest Expense	215	
	Premium on Bonds Payable*	65	
	Cash†		280
	Pay semiannual interest and record amortization.		

* $260/4   †$7,000 × 8% × ½

Bonds Payable

		12/31/2017	7,000
		6/30/2018	—
		12/31/2018	—
		6/30/2019	—
12/31/2019	7,000		
		12/31/2019	**0**

Discount on Bonds Payable

		12/31/2017	260
6/30/2018	65		
12/31/2018	65		
6/30/2019	65		
12/31/2019	65		
		12/31/2019	**0**

d.

2019			
Dec. 31	Bonds Payable	7,000	
	Cash		7,000
	Record maturity and payment of bonds.		

> **Do More:** QS 14-8, E 14-6, E 14-7, P 14-3, P 14-4

Bond Retirement

This section describes the retirement of bonds (1) at maturity, (2) before maturity, and (3) by conversion to stock.

Bond Retirement at Maturity   The carrying value of bonds at maturity always equals par value. For example, both Exhibits 14.7 (a discount) and 14.11 (a premium) show that the carrying value of bonds at maturity equals par value ($100,000). The retirement of these bonds at maturity, assuming interest is already paid and entered, is recorded as follows.

P4

Record the retirement of bonds.

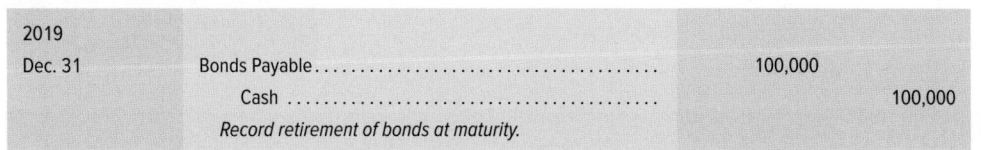

2019			
Dec. 31	Bonds Payable	100,000	
	Cash		100,000
	Record retirement of bonds at maturity.		

Assets = Liabilities + Equity
−100,000   −100,000

Bond Retirement before Maturity   Issuers sometimes retire some or all of their bonds before maturity. For instance, if interest rates decline, an issuer may want to replace high-interest-paying bonds with new low-interest bonds. Two common ways to retire bonds before maturity are:

Point: Bond retirement is also referred to as *bond redemption.*

- Exercise a call option. An issuer can reserve the right to retire bonds early by issuing *callable bonds.* The bond indenture can give the issuer an option to *call* the bonds before they mature by paying the par value plus a *call premium* to bondholders.
- Purchase them on the open market. The issuer can repurchase them from bondholders at their current price.

Whether bonds are called or repurchased, the issuer is unlikely to pay a price that equals their carrying value. When a difference exists between the bonds' carrying value and the amount paid, the issuer records a gain or loss equal to the difference.

To illustrate, assume that a company issued callable bonds with a par value of $100,000. The call option requires the issuer to pay a call premium of $3,000 to bondholders plus the par value. Next, assume that after the June 30, 2017, interest payment, the bonds have a carrying value of $104,500. Then on July 1, 2017, the issuer calls these bonds and pays $103,000 to bondholders. The issuer recognizes a $1,500 gain from the difference between the bonds' carrying value of $104,500 and the retirement price of $103,000. The issuer records this bond retirement as follows.

Assets = Liabilities + Equity
−103,000   −100,000   +1,500
            −4,500

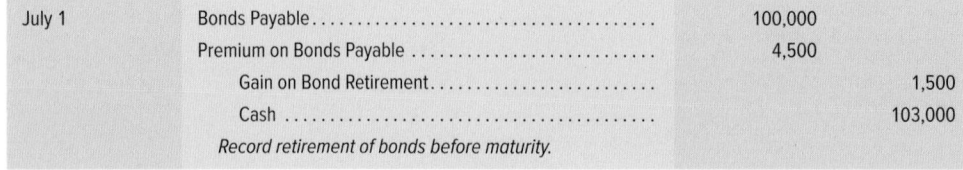

July 1	Bonds Payable.....................................	100,000	
	Premium on Bonds Payable	4,500	
	Gain on Bond Retirement........................		1,500
	Cash		103,000
	Record retirement of bonds before maturity.		

Bond Retirement by Conversion

Convertible Bond

Holders of convertible bonds have the right to convert their bonds to stock. When conversion occurs, the bonds' carrying value is transferred to equity accounts and no gain or loss is recorded. (We further describe convertible bonds in the Decision Analysis section of this chapter.)

To illustrate, assume that on January 1 the $100,000 par value bonds of **Converse**, with a carrying value of $100,000, are converted to 15,000 shares of $2 par value common stock. The entry to record this conversion follows (the market prices of the bonds and stock are *not* relevant to this entry).

Assets = Liabilities + Equity
        −100,000   +30,000
                   +70,000

Jan. 1	Bonds Payable.....................................	100,000	
	Common Stock...................................		30,000
	Paid-In Capital in Excess of Par Value		70,000
	Record retirement of bonds by conversion.		

⬛ **Decision** Insight

Junk Bonds   Junk bonds are company bonds with low credit ratings due to a higher-than-average likelihood of nonpayment. On the upside, the high risk of junk bonds can yield high returns if the issuer repays its debt. Investors in junk bonds identify and buy bonds with low credit ratings when they believe those bonds will survive and pay off their obligations. Financial statements are used to identify junk bonds that are better than what their ratings would suggest. ∎

LONG-TERM NOTES PAYABLE

C1
_____

Explain the types of notes and prepare entries to account for notes.

Point: Carrying value is also computed as the present value of all remaining payments, discounted using the market rate at issuance.

Like bonds, notes are issued to obtain assets such as cash. Unlike bonds, notes are typically transacted with a *single* lender such as a bank. An issuer initially records a note at its selling price—that is, the note's face value minus any discount or plus any premium. Over the note's life, the amount of interest expense allocated to each period is computed by multiplying the market rate (at issuance of the note) by the beginning-of-period note balance. The note's carrying (book) value at any time equals its face value minus any unamortized discount or plus any unamortized premium.

Installment Notes

An **installment note** is an obligation requiring a series of payments to the lender. Installment notes are common for franchises and other businesses when lenders and borrowers agree to spread payments over several periods.

Issuance of Notes   To illustrate, assume that Foghog borrows $60,000 from a bank to purchase equipment. It signs an 8% installment note requiring three annual payments of principal plus interest. Foghog records the note's issuance at January 1, 2017, as follows.

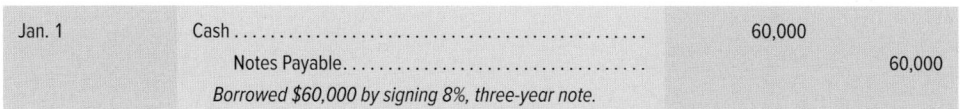

Jan. 1	Cash..	60,000	
	Notes Payable................................		60,000
	Borrowed $60,000 by signing 8%, three-year note.		

Assets = Liabilities + Equity
+60,000   +60,000

Payments of Principal and Interest   Payments on an installment note normally include accrued interest expense plus a portion of the amount borrowed (the *principal*). This section describes an installment note with equal payments.

The equal total payments pattern consists of changing amounts of both interest and principal. To illustrate, assume that Foghog borrows $60,000 by signing a $60,000 note that requires three *equal payments* of $23,282 at the end of each year. (The present value of an annuity of three annual payments of $23,282, discounted at 8%, equals $60,000; this computation is in footnote 2.) The $23,282 includes both interest and principal, the amounts of which change with each payment. Exhibit 14.12 shows the pattern of equal total payments and its two parts, interest and principal. Column A shows the note's beginning balance. Column B shows accrued interest for each year at 8% of the beginning note balance. Column C shows the portion of payment going to the principal owed, which equals the difference between the total payment in column D and the interest expense in column B. Column E shows the note's year-end balance.

Years
2017 2018 2019

Point: Most consumer notes are installment notes that require equal total payments.

EXHIBIT 14.12

Installment Note:
Equal Total Payments
Amortization Schedule

		Payments			
	(A)	**(B)** **Debit** Interest	**(C)** **Debit** Notes	**(D)** **Credit**	**(E)**
Period Ending Date	**Beginning Balance**	**Expense 8% × (A)**	+ **Payable (D) − (B)**	= **Cash (computed)**	**Ending Balance (A) − (C)**
(1) **12/31/2017**	**$60,000**	**$4,800**	**$ 18,482**	**$23,282**	**$41,518**
(2) 12/31/2018	41,518	3,321	19,961	23,282	21,557
(3) 12/31/2019	21,557	1,725	21,557	23,282	0
		$9,846	**$60,000**	**$69,846**	

☐ Interest ☐ Principal

Decreasing
Accrued
Interest
↓

Increasing
Principal
Component
↓

Equal
Total
Payments
↓

End of Year

2017	$4,800	$18,482
2018	$3,321	$19,961
2019	$1,725	$21,557

0      $5,000 $10,000 $15,000 $20,000 $25,000
Cash Payment Pattern

Although the three cash payments are equal, accrued interest decreases each year because the principal balance of the note declines. As the amount of interest decreases each year, the portion of each payment applied to principal increases. This pattern is graphed in the lower part of Exhibit 14.12. Foghog uses the amounts in Exhibit 14.12 to record its first two payments (for years 2017 and 2018) as follows:

Assets = Liabilities + Equity
−23,282 −18,482 −4,800

2017			
Dec. 31	Interest Expense	4,800	
	Notes Payable	18,482	
	Cash		23,282
	Record first installment payment.		

Assets = Liabilities + Equity
−23,282 −19,961 −3,321

2018			
Dec. 31	Interest Expense	3,321	
	Notes Payable	19,961	
	Cash		23,282
	Record second installment payment.		

Foghog records a similar entry but with different amounts for the last payment. After three years, the Notes Payable account balance is zero.[2]

 Decision Insight

Lurking Debt A study reports that 29% of employees in finance and accounting witnessed the falsifying or manipulating of accounting information in the past year (KPMG 2013). This includes nondisclosure of some long-term liabilities. Another study reports that most people committing fraud (36%) work in the finance function of their firm (KPMG 2011). ■

Mortgage Notes and Bonds

A **mortgage** is a legal agreement that helps protect a lender if a borrower fails to make required payments on notes or bonds. A mortgage gives the lender a right to be paid from the cash proceeds of the sale of a borrower's assets identified in the mortgage. A legal document, called a *mortgage contract,* describes the mortgage terms.

    Mortgage notes carry a mortgage contract pledging title to specific assets as security for the note. Mortgage notes are popular in the purchase of homes and the acquisition of plant assets. Less common *mortgage bonds* are backed by the issuer's assets. Accounting for mortgage notes and bonds is similar to that for unsecured notes and bonds, except that the mortgage agreement must be disclosed. For example, **TIBCO Software** reports that its "mortgage note payable . . . is collateralized by the commercial real property acquired [corporate headquarters]."

Point: The Truth in Lending Act requires lenders to provide information about loan costs including finance charges and interest rate.

 Decision Maker

Entrepreneur You are a retailer planning a sale on a home theater system that requires no payments for two years. At the end of two years, buyers must pay the full amount. The system's suggested retail price is $4,100, but you are willing to sell it today for $3,000 cash. What is your sale price if payment will not occur for two years and the market interest rate is 10%? ■ [*Answer:* This is a present value question. The interest rate (10%) and present value ($3,000) are known, but the payment required two years later is unknown. The two-year-later price of $3,630 is computed as $3,000 × 1.10 × 1.10. The $3,630 two years from today is equivalent to $3,000 today.]

---

[2] Table B.3 in Appendix B is used to compute the dollar amount of three payments that equal the initial note balance of $60,000 at 8% interest. We go to Table B.3, row 3, and across to the 8% column, where the present value factor is 2.5771. The dollar amount is then computed by solving this equation:

Table	Present Value Factor		Dollar Amount		Present Value
B.3	2.5771	×	?	=	$60,000

The dollar amount is computed by dividing $60,000 by 2.5771, yielding $23,282.

On January 1, 2017, a company borrows $1,000 cash by signing a four-year, 5% installment note. The note requires four equal payments of $282, consisting of accrued interest and principal on December 31 of each year from 2017 through 2020.

NEED-TO-KNOW 14-4

Recording Installment Note

C1   P5

1. Prepare an amortization table for this installment note like the one in Exhibit 14.12.

2. Prepare journal entries to record the loan on January 1, 2017, and the four payments from December 31, 2017, through December 31, 2020.

Solution

1. Amortization table for loan.

	(A)	Payments			(E)
		(B) Debit	(C) Debit	(D) Credit	
Period Ending Date	Beginning Balance [Prior (E)]	Interest Expense [5% × (A)] +	Notes Payable [(D) − (B)] =	Cash [computed]	Ending Balance [(A) − (C)]
2017...............	$1,000	$ 50	$ 232	$ 282†	$768
2018...............	768	38	244	282	524
2019...............	524	26	256	282	268
2020...............	268	14*	268	282	0
		$128	$1,000	$1,128	

* Adjusted for rounding.

† Amount of each payment = Initial note balance/PV of annuity (from Table B.3)

$$= \$1,000/3.5460 = \underline{\$282} \text{ (rounded)}$$

2.

2017			
Jan. 1	Cash...	1,000	
	Notes Payable		1,000
	Borrowed $1,000 by signing a 5% note.		
2017			
Dec. 31	Interest Expense..	50	
	Notes Payable.......................................	232	
	Cash		282
	Record first installment payment.		
2018			
Dec. 31	Interest Expense..	38	
	Notes Payable.......................................	244	
	Cash		282
	Record second installment payment.		
2019			
Dec. 31	Interest Expense..	26	
	Notes Payable.......................................	256	
	Cash		282
	Record third installment payment.		
2020			
Dec. 31	Interest Expense..	14	
	Notes Payable.......................................	268	
	Cash		282
	Record fourth installment payment.		

Do More: QS 14-11, E 14-10, E 14-11

SUSTAINABILITY AND ACCOUNTING

Garrett Camp and Travis Kalanick are committed to making their company, **Uber**, more sustainable and environmentally friendly. One sustainable initiative that they are pushing is called **UberPOOL**. When using the Uber app, customers are given the opportunity to "carpool" with other Uber riders. This greatly cuts the cost of the ride for the customers, and it is beneficial for the environment.

Three or four customers riding in the same car to similar destinations can reduce the amount of cars on the road and the costs on the environment by 75%. "We're going to take hundreds of thousands of cars off the road, which is going to make pollution in the air much better and save people time. That's just fundamentally good," explains Travis. "The change is so positive and so straightforward."

Over the first three months of 2016, "UberPOOL has eliminated 21 million auto miles. That's about 400,000 gallons of gas and 3,800 metric tons of carbon dioxide emissions," exclaims the Uber website. Travis and Garrett admit, however, that UberPOOL demands a good accounting system. Importantly, the owners depend on their system to sort customers who take an UberPOOL and those who take a regular Uber. If the system were unable to do this without errors, Uber would be unable to accurately bill customers. Then the cost incentive for customers to take UberPOOL would disappear and the carbon emission savings would be lost. "For me it's all about solving a problem," insists Garrett. Further, the solution to the problem, according to Garrett, "has to be sustainable."

© Kevork Djansezian/Getty Images

Decision Analysis ■ ■ ■   Debt Features and the Debt-to-Equity Ratio

A2
Assess debt features and their implications.

Collateral agreements can reduce the risk of loss for both bonds and notes. Unsecured bonds and notes are riskier because the issuer's obligation to pay interest and principal has the same priority as all other unsecured liabilities in the event of bankruptcy. If a company is unable to pay its debts in full, the unsecured creditors (including the holders of debentures) lose all or a portion of their balances. These types of legal agreements and other characteristics of long-term liabilities are crucial for effective business decisions. The first part of this section describes the different types of features sometimes included with bonds and notes. The second part explains and applies the debt-to-equity ratio.

Features of Bonds and Notes

This section describes common features of debt securities.

Secured Debt

Unsecured Debt

Secured or Unsecured   **Secured bonds** (and notes) have specific assets of the issuer pledged (or *mortgaged*) as collateral. This arrangement gives holders added protection against the issuer's default. If the issuer fails to pay interest or par value, the secured holders can demand that the collateral be sold and the proceeds used to pay the obligation. **Unsecured bonds** (and notes), also called *debentures,* are backed by the issuer's general credit standing. Unsecured debt is riskier than secured debt. *Subordinated debentures* are liabilities that are not repaid until the claims of the more senior unsecured (and secured) liabilities are settled.

Term or Serial   **Term bonds** (and notes) are scheduled for maturity on one specified date. **Serial bonds** (and notes) mature at more than one date (often in series) and thus are usually repaid over a number of periods. For instance, $100,000 of serial bonds might mature at the rate of $10,000 each year from 6 to 15 years after they are issued. Many bonds are **sinking fund bonds,** which, to reduce the holder's risk, require the issuer to create a *sinking fund* of assets set aside at specified amounts and dates to repay the bonds.

Registered or Bearer   Bonds issued in the names and addresses of their holders are **registered bonds.** The issuer makes bond payments by sending checks (or cash transfers) to registered holders. A registered holder must notify the issuer of any ownership change. Registered bonds offer the issuer the practical advantage of not having to actually issue bond certificates. Bonds payable to whoever holds them (the *bearer*) are called **bearer bonds** or *unregistered bonds*. Sales or exchanges might not be recorded, so the holder of a bearer bond is presumed to be its rightful owner. As a result, lost bearer bonds are difficult to replace. Many bearer bonds are also **coupon bonds.** This term reflects interest coupons that are attached to the bonds. When each coupon matures, the holder presents it to a bank or broker for collection. At maturity, the holder follows the same process and presents the bond certificate for collection. Issuers of coupon bonds cannot deduct the related interest expense for taxable income. This is to prevent abuse by taxpayers who own coupon bonds but fail to report interest income on their tax returns.

Convertible and/or Callable   **Convertible bonds** (and notes) can be exchanged for a fixed number of shares of the issuing corporation's common stock. Convertible debt offers holders the potential to profit from future increases in stock price. Holders still receive periodic interest while the debt is held and the par value if they hold the debt to maturity. In most cases, the holders decide whether and when to convert debt to stock. **Callable bonds** (and notes) have an option exercisable by the issuer to retire them at a stated dollar amount before maturity.

Convertible Debt   **Callable Debt**

 Decision Insight

Collateral   Lenders prefer that liquid assets serve as collateral for loans. These usually are current assets such as accounts receivable or inventory. The reason is if borrowers default and collateral must be seized, then lenders desire assets that are easily sold to recover losses. ■

Debt-to-Equity Ratio

Beyond assessing different characteristics of debt as just described, we want to know the level of debt, especially in relation to total equity. Such knowledge helps us assess the risk of a company's financing structure. A company financed mainly with debt is more risky because liabilities must be repaid—usually with periodic interest—whereas equity financing does not. A measure to assess the risk of a company's financing structure is the **debt-to-equity ratio** (see Exhibit 14.13).

A3

Compute the debt-to-equity ratio and explain its use.

$$\text{Debt-to-equity} = \frac{\text{Total liabilities}}{\text{Total equity}}$$

EXHIBIT 14.13

Debt-to-Equity Ratio

The debt-to-equity ratio varies across companies and industries. To apply the debt-to-equity ratio, let's look at this measure for **Amazon** in Exhibit 14.14.

$ millions	2015	2014	2013	2012
Total liabilities	$52,060	$43,764	$30,413	$24,363
Total equity	$13,384	$10,741	$ 9,746	$ 8,192
Debt-to-equity	3.9	4.1	3.1	3.0
Industry debt-to-equity	1.7	1.8	1.6	1.5

EXHIBIT 14.14

Amazon's Debt-to-Equity Ratio

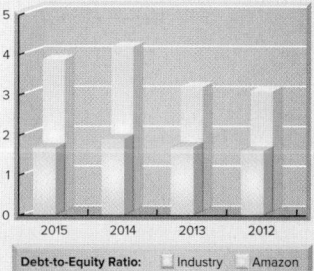

Amazon's 2015 debt-to-equity ratio is 3.9, meaning that debtholders contributed $3.90 for each $1 contributed by equity holders. This implies a riskier-than-usual financing structure for Amazon. A similar interpretation is drawn from a comparison of Amazon with its competitors, where the 2015 industry ratio is 1.7. Analysis across the years shows that Amazon's financing structure has risen to a riskier level in the recent two years. Given its growth in revenues and innovative past, investors have been patient in waiting for income. However, debtholders will grow increasingly concerned if income fails to rise in the near future.

 Decision Maker

Bond Investor   You plan to purchase debenture bonds from one of two companies in the same industry that are similar in size and performance. The first company has $350,000 in total liabilities and $1,750,000 in equity. The second company has $1,200,000 in total liabilities and $1,000,000 in equity. Which company's debenture bonds are less risky based on the debt-to-equity ratio? ■   [*Answer:* The debt-to-equity ratio for the first company is 0.2 ($350,000/$1,750,000) and for the second is 1.2 ($1,200,000/$1,000,000), suggesting that financing for the second company is more risky than that for the first. As a buyer of unsecured debenture bonds, you prefer the first company (all else equal).]

COMPREHENSIVE

Accounting for Bonds
and Notes

Water Sports Company (WSC) patented and successfully test-marketed a new product. To expand its ability to produce and market the new product, WSC needs to raise $800,000 of financing. On January 1, 2017, the company obtained the money in two ways:

a. WSC signed a $400,000, 10% installment note to be repaid with five equal annual installments of $105,519 to be made on December 31 of 2017 through 2021.

b. WSC issued five-year bonds with a par value of $400,000 for $430,881 cash on January 1, 2017. The bonds have a 12% annual contract rate and pay interest on June 30 and December 31. The bonds' annual market rate is 10%.

Required

1. For the installment note, (*a*) prepare an amortization table similar to Exhibit 14.12, and (*b*) prepare the journal entry for the first payment.

2. For the bonds, (*a*) prepare the January 1, 2017, journal entry to record their issuance; (*b*) prepare an amortization table using the straight-line method; (*c*) prepare the June 30, 2017, journal entry to record the first interest payment; and (*d*) prepare a journal entry to record retiring the bonds at a $416,000 call price on January 1, 2019.

3.[B] Using Appendix 14B, redo parts 2(*c*), 2(*d*), and 2(*e*) assuming the bonds are amortized using the effective interest method.

PLANNING THE SOLUTION

- For the installment note, divide the borrowed amount by the annuity factor (from Table B.3) using the 10% rate and five payments to compute the amount of each payment. Prepare a table similar to Exhibit 14.12 and use the numbers in the table's first line for the journal entry.

- For the bonds, compute the bonds' issue price by using the market rate to find the present value of their cash flows (use tables found in Appendix B). Then use this result to record the bonds' issuance. Next, prepare an amortization table like Exhibit 14.11 (and Exhibit 14B.2) and use it to get the numbers needed for the journal entry. Also use the table to find the carrying value as of the date of the bonds' retirement that you need for the journal entry.

SOLUTION

Part 1: Installment Note

a. An amortization table for the long-term note payable follows.

	A	B	C	D	E	F	G	H
1			**Payments**					
2		**(a)**	**(b)**		**(c)**		**(d)**	**(e)**
3			**Debit**		**Debit**		**Credit**	
3	**Annual**		**Interest**		**Notes**			**Ending**
4	**Period**	**Beginning**	**Expense**	**+**	**Payable**	**=**	**Cash**	**Balance**
5	**Ending**	**Balance**	**10% × (a)**		**(d) − (b)**		**(computed)**	**(a) − (c)**
6	(1) 12/31/2017	$400,000	$40,000		$ 65,519		$105,519*	$334,481
7	(2) 12/31/2018	334,481	33,448		72,071		105,519	262,410
8	(3) 12/31/2019	262,410	26,241		79,278		105,519	183,132
9	(4) 12/31/2020	183,132	18,313		87,206		105,519	95,926
10	(5) 12/31/2021	95,926	9,593		95,926		105,519	0
11			$127,595		$400,000		$527,595	

* Annual payment = Note balance/PV annuity factor = $400,000/3.7908 = $105,519
(The present value annuity factor is for five payments and a rate of 10%.)

b. Journal entry for December 31, 2017, payment.

Dec. 31	Interest Expense	40,000	
	Notes Payable	65,519	
	Cash		105,519
	Record first installment payment.		

Part 2: Bonds (Straight-Line Amortization)

a. Journal entry for January 1, 2017, issuance.

Jan. 1	Cash*	430,881	
	Premium on Bonds Payable.......................		30,881
	Bonds Payable		400,000
	Sold bonds at a premium.		

* Compute the bonds' issue price using Appendix 14A.

Cash Flow	Table	Present Value Factor†	Amount	Present Value
Par (maturity) value	B.1 in App. B (PV of 1)	0.6139	× 400,000 =	$245,560
Interest payments	B.3 in App. B (PV of annuity)	7.7217	× 24,000 =	185,321
Price of bond				$430,881

† Present value factors are for 10 payments using a semiannual market rate of 5%.

b. The straight-line amortization table for premium bonds follows. The semiannual discount amortization is $3,088, computed as $30,881/10 periods.

	A	B	C
1	**Semiannual**	**Unamortized**	**Carrying**
2	**Period-End**	**Discount**	**Value**
3	(0) 1/1/2017	$ 30,881	$ 430,881
4	(1) 6/30/2017	27,793	427,793
5	(2) 12/31/2017	24,705	424,705
6	(3) 6/30/2018	21,617	421,617
7	(4) 12/31/2018	18,529	418,529
8	(5) 6/30/2019	15,441	415,441
9	(6) 12/31/2019	12,353	412,353
10	(7) 6/30/2020	9,265	409,265
11	(8) 12/31/2020	6,177	406,177
12	(9) 6/30/2021	3,089	403,089
13	(10) 12/31/2021	0*	400,000

* Adjusted for rounding.

c. Journal entry for June 30, 2017, bond payment.

June 30	Bond Interest Expense	20,912	
	Premium on Bonds Payable	3,088	
	Cash		24,000
	Paid semiannual interest on bonds.		

d. Journal entry for January 1, 2019, bond retirement.

Jan. 1	Bonds Payable......................................	400,000	
	Premium on Bonds Payable	18,529	
	Cash		416,000
	Gain on Retirement of Bonds......................		2,529
	Record bond retirement (carrying value at		
	Dec. 31, 2018).		

Part 3: Bonds (Effective Interest Amortization)—Using Appendix 14B

c. The effective interest amortization table for premium bonds.

	Semiannual Interest Period	(A) Cash Interest Paid 6% × $400,000	(B) Interest Expense 5% × Prior (E)	(C) Premium Amortization (A) – (B)	(D) Unamortized Premium Prior (D) – (C)	(E) Carrying Value $400,000 + (D)
(0)	1/1/2017				$30,881	$430,881
(1)	6/30/2017	$ 24,000	$ 21,544	$ 2,456	28,425	428,425
(2)	12/31/2017	24,000	21,421	2,579	25,846	425,846
(3)	6/30/2018	24,000	21,292	2,708	23,138	423,138
(4)	12/31/2018	24,000	21,157	2,843	20,295	420,295
(5)	6/30/2019	24,000	21,015	2,985	17,310	417,310
(6)	12/31/2019	24,000	20,866	3,134	14,176	414,176
(7)	6/30/2020	24,000	20,709	3,291	10,885	410,885
(8)	12/31/2020	24,000	20,544	3,456	7,429	407,429
(9)	6/30/2021	24,000	20,371	3,629	3,800	403,800
(10)	12/31/2021	24,000	20,200*	3,800	0	400,000
		$240,000	$209,119	$30,881		

* Adjusted for rounding.

d. Journal entry for June 30, 2017, bond payment.

June 30	Bond Interest Expense	21,544	
	Premium on Bonds Payable	2,456	
	Cash		24,000
	Paid semiannual interest on bonds.		

e. Journal entry for January 1, 2019, bond retirement.

Jan. 1	Bonds Payable.......................................	400,000	
	Premium on Bonds Payable	20,295	
	Cash		416,000
	Gain on Retirement of Bonds.....................		4,295
	Record bond retirement (carrying value at Dec. 31, 2018).		

14A

Bond Pricing

C2

Explain and compute bond pricing.

Prices for bonds traded on an organized exchange are published online. This information includes the bond price (called *quote*), its contract rate, and its current market (called *yield*) rate. However, a fraction of bonds are traded on organized exchanges. To compute the price of a bond, we apply present value concepts. This section explains how to use *present value concepts* to price the **Fila** discount bond and the **Adidas** premium bond described earlier.

Present Value of Discount Bonds   The issue price of bonds is found by computing the present value of the bonds' cash payments, discounted at the bonds' market rate. When computing the present value of the Fila bonds, we use *semiannual* compounding periods because this is the time between interest payments; the annual market rate of 10% is considered a semiannual rate of 5%. Also, the two-year bond life is viewed as four semiannual periods. The price computation has two parts:

1. Find the present value of the $100,000 par value paid at maturity.
2. Find the present value of the series of four semiannual payments of $4,000 each; see Exhibit 14.4.

These present values can be found by using *present value tables*. Appendix B at the end of this book shows present value tables and describes their use. Table B.1 in Appendix B is used for the single $100,000 maturity payment, and Table B.3 in Appendix B is used for the $4,000 series of interest payments. Specifically, we go to Table B.1, row 4, and across to the 5% column to identify the present value factor of 0.8227 for the maturity payment. Next, we go to Table B.3, row 4, and across to the 5% column, where the present value factor is 3.5460 for the series of interest payments. We compute the bond price by multiplying the cash flow payments by their corresponding present value factors and adding them together; see Exhibit 14A.1.

Cash Flow	Table	Present Value Factor		Amount		Present Value
$100,000 par (maturity) value.............	B.1 (PV of 1)	0.8227	×	$100,000	=	$ 82,270
$4,000 interest payments	B.3 (PV of ann.)	3.5460	×	4,000	=	14,184
Price of bond..........................						$96,454

Present Value of Premium Bonds   We compute the issue price of the Adidas bonds by using the market rate to compute the present value of the bonds' future cash flows. When computing the present value of these bonds, we again use *semiannual* compounding periods because this is the time between interest payments. The annual 10% market rate is applied as a semiannual rate of 5%, and the two-year bond life is viewed as four semiannual periods. The computation has two parts:

1. Find the present value of the $100,000 par value paid at maturity.
2. Find the present value of the series of four payments of $6,000 each; see Exhibit 14.8.

These present values can be found by using present value tables. First, go to Table B.1, row 4, and across to the 5% column where the present value factor is 0.8227 for the maturity payment. Second, go to Table B.3, row 4, and across to the 5% column, where the present value factor is 3.5460 for the series of interest payments. The bonds' price is computed by multiplying the cash flow payments by their corresponding present value factors and adding them together; see Exhibit 14A.2.

Cash Flow	Table	Present Value Factor		Amount		Present Value
$100,000 par (maturity) value.............	B.1 (PV of 1)	0.8227	×	$100,000	=	$ 82,270
$6,000 interest payments	B.3 (PV of ann.)	3.5460	×	6,000	=	21,276
Price of bond..........................						$103,546

Point: Bond issue price equals present value of its future cash payments discounted at bond's market rate.

Point: Excel for bond pricing.

	A	B
1	Annual contract rate	8%
2	Annual market rate	10%
3	Payments within yr	2
4	Years to maturity	2
5	Par (face) value	$100,000
6	Issue price	

=PV(B2/B3,B3*B4,B5*B1/B3,B5)
=$96,454

EXHIBIT 14A.1

Computing Issue Price for Fila Discount Bonds

Calculator	
N = 4	PMT = 4,000
I/Yr = 5	FV = 100,000
	PV = 96,454

Point: Calculator inputs defined:
N   Number of semiannual periods
I/Yr   Market rate per semiannual period
FV   Future (maturity) value
PMT   Payment (interest) per semiannual period
PV   Price (present value)

Point: Excel for bond pricing.

	A	B
1	Annual contract rate	12%
2	Annual market rate	10%
3	Payments within yr	2
4	Years to maturity	2
5	Par (face) value	$100,000
6	Issue price	

=PV(B2/B3,B3*B4,B5*B1/B3,B5)
=$103,546

EXHIBIT 14A.2

Computing Issue Price for Adidas Premium Bonds

Calculator	
N = 4	PMT = 6,000
I/Yr = 5	FV = 100,000
	PV = 103,546

■ **Decision** Insight

Equivalent Payments Concept   Business decisions frequently involve concepts using the time value of money. To help in those decisions, the present value factors can be thought of as *equivalent payments*. For example, using the data in Exhibit 14A.1, one payment of $100,000 scheduled two years from today is the *equivalent* of a 0.8227 payment of $100,000 today (assuming a market with 10% return). Similarly, four semiannual payments of $4,000 over the next two years are the equivalent of 3.5460 payments of $4,000 today (again, assuming a 10% return). ■

14B Effective Interest Amortization

P5

Compute and record amortization of a bond discount using the effective interest method.

Effective Interest Amortization of Discount Bonds Accounting standards allow use of the straight-line method when the effect of using it approximates that of the effective interest method. The **effective interest method,** or simply *interest method,* allocates total bond interest expense over the bonds' life in a way that yields a constant rate of interest. This constant rate of interest is the market rate at the issue date. Thus, bond interest expense for a period equals the carrying value of the bond at the beginning of that period multiplied by the market rate when issued.

Exhibit 14B.1 shows an effective interest amortization table for Fila bonds (as described in Exhibit 14.4). The key difference between the effective interest and straight-line methods is computing bond interest expense. Instead of assigning an equal amount of bond interest expense to each period, the effective interest method assigns a bond interest expense amount that increases over the life of a discount bond. **Both methods allocate the *same* $19,546 of total bond interest expense over the bonds' life, but in different patterns.** Specifically, the amortization table in Exhibit 14B.1 shows that the balance of the discount (column D) is amortized until it reaches zero. Also, the bonds' carrying value (column E) changes each period until it equals par value at maturity. Compare columns D and E to the corresponding columns in Exhibit 14.7 to see the amortization patterns. Total bond interest expense is $19,546, consisting of $16,000 of semiannual cash payments and $3,546 of the original bond discount, the same for both methods.

Point: Contract rate determines cash interest paid, but the market rate determines the actual interest expense.

EXHIBIT 14B.1

Effective Interest Amortization of Bond Discount

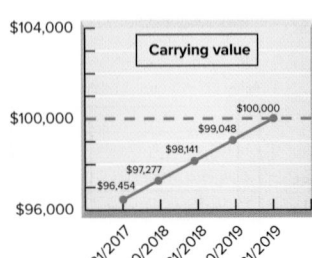

	A	B	C	D	E	F
1	Bonds: $100,000 Par Value, Semiannual Interest Payments, Two-Year Life,					
2	4% Semiannual Contract Rate, 5% Semiannual Market Rate					
3		**(A)**	**(B)**	**(C)**	**(D)**	**(E)**
4		**Cash**	**Bond**			
5	**Semiannual**	**Interest**	**Interest**	**Discount**	**Unamortized**	**Carrying**
5	**Interest**	**Paid**	**Expense**	**Amortization**	**Discount**	**Value**
6	**Period-End**	4% × $100,000	5% × Prior (E)	(B) – (A)	Prior (D) – (C)	$100,000 – (D)
7	(0) 12/31/2017				$3,546	$ 96,454
8	(1) 6/30/2018	$ 4,000	$ 4,823	$ 823	2,723	97,277
9	(2) 12/31/2018	4,000	4,864	864	1,859	98,141
10	(3) 6/30/2019	4,000	4,907	907	952	99,048
11	(4) 12/31/2019	4,000	4,952	952	0	100,000
12		$16,000	$19,546	$3,546		

Column **(A)** is the par value ($100,000) multiplied by the semiannual contract rate (4%).
Column **(B)** is the prior period's carrying value multiplied by the semiannual market rate (5%).
Column **(C)** is the difference between interest paid and bond interest expense, or [(B) – (A)].
Column **(D)** is the prior period's unamortized discount less the current period's discount amortization.
Column **(E)** is the par value less unamortized discount, or [$100,000 – (D)].

Bonds Payable

	12/31/2017	100,000
	6/30/2018	—
	12/31/2018	—
	6/30/2019	—
12/31/2019 100,000		
	12/31/2019	**0**

Except for differences in amounts, journal entries recording the expense and updating the liability balance are the same under the effective interest method and the straight-line method. We can use the numbers in Exhibit 14B.1 to record each semiannual entry during the bonds' two-year life (June 30, 2018, through December 31, 2019). For instance, we record the interest payment at the end of the first semiannual period as follows.

Discount on Bonds Payable

12/31/2017	3,546		
		6/30/2018	823
		12/31/2018	864
		6/30/2019	907
		12/31/2019	952
12/31/2019	**0**		

Assets = Liabilities + Equity
−4,000   +823   −4,823

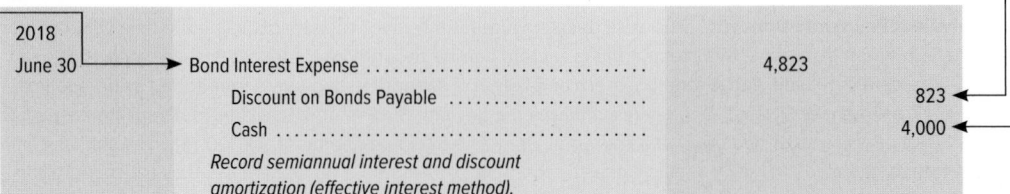

2018			
June 30	Bond Interest Expense	4,823	
	Discount on Bonds Payable		823
	Cash		4,000

Record semiannual interest and discount amortization (effective interest method).

Effective Interest Amortization of Premium Bonds   Exhibit 14B.2 shows the amortization table using the effective interest method for Adidas bonds (as described in Exhibit 14.8). Column A lists the semiannual cash payments. Column B shows the amount of bond interest expense, computed as the 5% semiannual market rate at issuance multiplied by the beginning-of-period carrying value. The amount of cash paid in column A is larger than the bond interest expense because the cash payment is based on the higher 6% semiannual contract rate. The excess cash payment over the interest expense reduces the principal. These amounts are shown in column C. Column E shows the carrying value after deducting the amortized premium in column C from the prior period's carrying value. Column D shows the premium's reduction by periodic amortization.

P6

Compute and record amortization of a bond premium using the effective interest method.

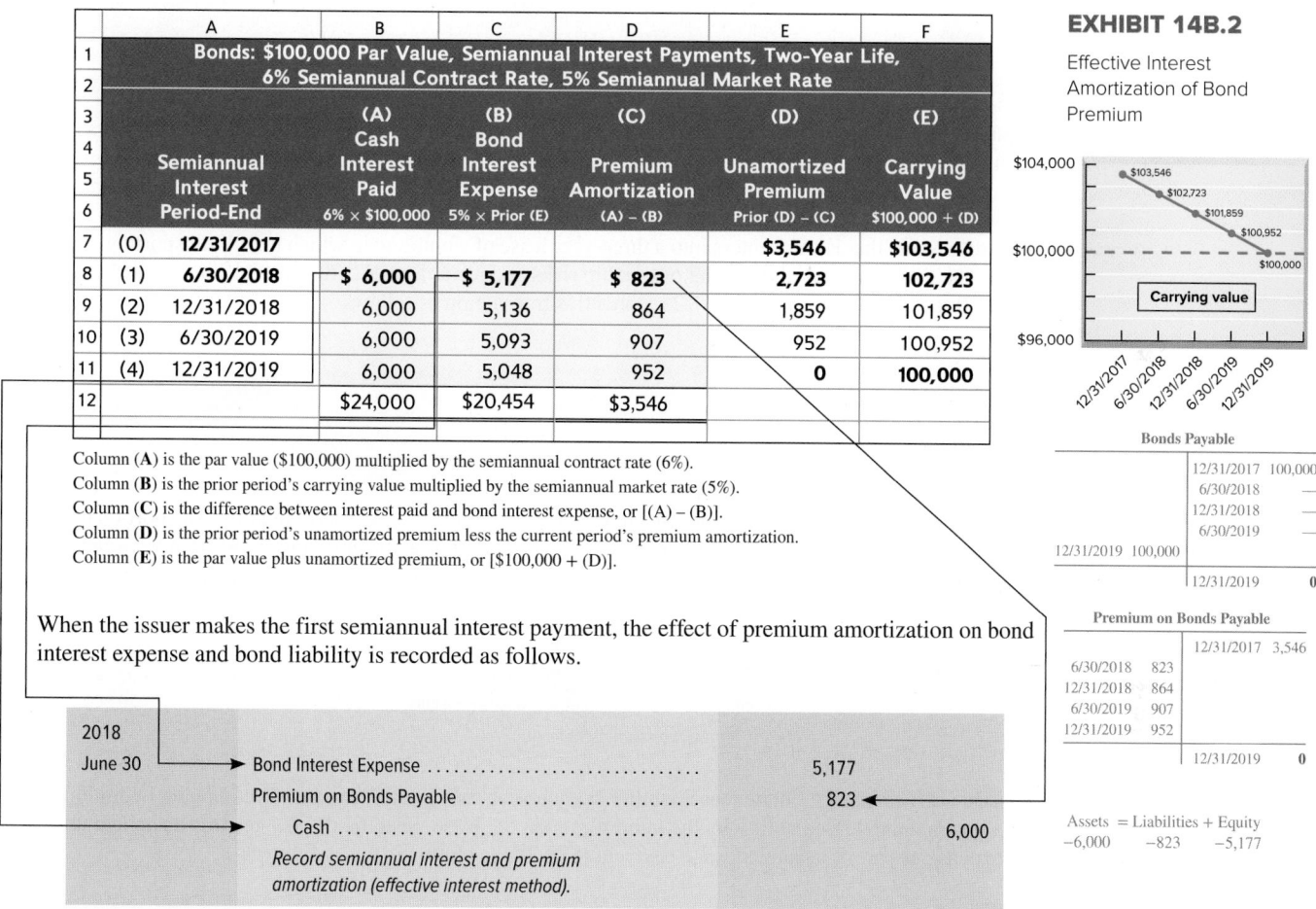

EXHIBIT 14B.2

Effective Interest Amortization of Bond Premium

	A	B	C	D	E	F
1 2	**Bonds: $100,000 Par Value, Semiannual Interest Payments, Two-Year Life, 6% Semiannual Contract Rate, 5% Semiannual Market Rate**					
3 4 5 6	**Semiannual Interest Period-End**	**(A) Cash Interest Paid** 6% × $100,000	**(B) Bond Interest Expense** 5% × Prior (E)	**(C) Premium Amortization** (A) – (B)	**(D) Unamortized Premium** Prior (D) – (C)	**(E) Carrying Value** $100,000 + (D)
7	(0) 12/31/2017				$3,546	$103,546
8	(1) 6/30/2018	$ 6,000	$ 5,177	$ 823	2,723	102,723
9	(2) 12/31/2018	6,000	5,136	864	1,859	101,859
10	(3) 6/30/2019	6,000	5,093	907	952	100,952
11	(4) 12/31/2019	6,000	5,048	952	0	100,000
12		$24,000	$20,454	$3,546		

Column (**A**) is the par value ($100,000) multiplied by the semiannual contract rate (6%).
Column (**B**) is the prior period's carrying value multiplied by the semiannual market rate (5%).
Column (**C**) is the difference between interest paid and bond interest expense, or [(A) – (B)].
Column (**D**) is the prior period's unamortized premium less the current period's premium amortization.
Column (**E**) is the par value plus unamortized premium, or [$100,000 + (D)].

When the issuer makes the first semiannual interest payment, the effect of premium amortization on bond interest expense and bond liability is recorded as follows.

2018 June 30	Bond Interest Expense	5,177	
	Premium on Bonds Payable	823	
	Cash		6,000
	Record semiannual interest and premium amortization (effective interest method).		

Bonds Payable

		12/31/2017	100,000
		6/30/2018	—
		12/31/2018	—
		6/30/2019	—
12/31/2019	100,000		
		12/31/2019	**0**

Premium on Bonds Payable

		12/31/2017	3,546
6/30/2018	823		
12/31/2018	864		
6/30/2019	907		
12/31/2019	952		
		12/31/2019	**0**

Assets = Liabilities + Equity
−6,000   −823   −5,177

Similar entries with different amounts are recorded at each payment date until the bond matures at the end of 2019. The effective interest method yields decreasing amounts of bond interest expense and increasing amounts of premium amortization over the bonds' life.

APPENDIX

Leases and Pensions

14C

This appendix briefly explains the accounting for both leases and pensions.

C3

Describe accounting for leases and pensions.

Lease Liabilities   A **lease** is a contractual agreement between a *lessor* (asset owner) and a *lessee* (asset renter or tenant) that grants the lessee the right to use the asset for a period of time in return for cash (rent) payments. Nearly one-fourth of all equipment purchases are financed with leases. The advantages of lease financing include the lack of an immediate large cash payment and the potential to deduct rental payments in computing taxable income. From an accounting perspective, leases can be classified as either operating or capital leases. (*Lease accounting is changing, whereby nearly all long-term operating leases are accounted for similar to capital leases . . . stay tuned!*)

Operating Leases **Operating leases** are short-term (or cancelable) leases in which the lessor retains the risks and rewards of ownership. Examples include most car and apartment rental agreements. The lessee records such lease payments as expenses; the lessor records them as revenue. The lessee does not report the leased item as an asset or a liability (it is the lessor's asset). To illustrate, if an employee of **Amazon** leases a car for $300 at an airport while on company business, Amazon (lessee) records this cost as follows:

Assets = Liabilities + Equity
−300   −300

July 4	Rental Expense	300	
	Cash		300
	Record lease rental payment.		

Capital Leases **Capital leases** are long-term (or noncancelable) leases by which the lessor transfers substantially all risks and rewards of ownership to the lessee. Examples include most leases of airplanes and department store buildings. The lessee records the leased item as its own asset along with a lease liability at the start of the lease term; the amount recorded equals the present value of all lease payments. To illustrate, assume that K2 Co. enters into a three-year lease of a building in which it will sell sporting equipment. The lease transfers all building ownership risks and rewards to K2 (the present value of its $23,282 annual lease payments is $60,000). K2 records this transaction as follows:

Assets = Liabilities + Equity
+60,000   +60,000

2017			
Jan. 1	Leased Asset—Building...............................	60,000	
	Lease Liability.......................................		60,000
	Record leased asset and lease liability.		

K2 reports the leased asset as a plant asset and the lease liability as a long-term liability. The portion of the lease liability expected to be paid in the next year is reported as a current liability. At each year-end, K2 records depreciation on the leased asset (assume straight-line depreciation, three-year lease term, no bargain purchase option, and no salvage value) as follows:

Assets = Liabilities + Equity
−20,000   −20,000

Dec. 31	Depreciation Expense—Leased Asset, Building	20,000	
	Accumulated Depreciation—Leased Asset, Building		20,000
	Record depreciation on leased asset.		

K2 also accrues interest on the lease liability at each year-end. Interest expense is computed by multiplying the remaining lease liability by the interest rate on the lease. Specifically, K2 records its annual interest expense as part of its annual lease payment ($23,282) as follows (for its first year):

Assets = Liabilities + Equity
−23,282   −18,482   −4,800

2017			
Dec. 31	Interest Expense	4,800	
	Lease Liability	18,482	
	Cash		23,282
	*Record first annual lease payment.**		

* These numbers are computed from a *lease payment schedule*. For simplicity, we use the same numbers from Exhibit 14.12 for this lease payment schedule—with different headings as follows:

	(A)	(B) Debit	(C) Debit	(D) Credit	(E)
				Payments	
Period Ending Date	Beginning Balance of Lease Liability	Interest on Lease Liability 8% × (A)	+ Lease Liability (D) − (B)	= Cash Lease Payment	Ending Balance of Lease Liability (A) − (C)
12/31/2017	$60,000	$4,800	$18,482	$23,282	$41,518
12/31/2018	41,518	3,321	19,961	23,282	21,557
12/31/2019	21,557	1,725	21,557	23,282	0
		$9,846	$60,000	$69,846	

Pension Liabilities A **pension plan** is a contractual agreement between an employer and its employees for the employer to provide benefits (payments) to employees after they retire. Most employers pay the full cost of the pension, but sometimes employees pay part of the cost. An employer records its payment into a pension plan with a debit to Pension Expense and a credit to Cash. A *plan administrator* receives payments from the employer, invests them in pension assets, and makes benefit payments to *pension recipients* (retired employees). Insurance and trust companies often serve as pension plan administrators.

Many pensions are known as *defined benefit plans* that define future benefits; the employer's contributions vary, depending on assumptions about future pension assets and liabilities. Several disclosures are necessary in this case. Specifically, a pension liability is reported when the accumulated benefit obligation is *more than* the plan assets, a so-called *underfunded plan*. The accumulated benefit obligation is the present value of promised future pension payments to retirees. *Plan assets* refer to the market value of assets the plan administrator holds. A pension asset is reported when the accumulated benefit obligation is *less than* the plan assets, a so-called *overfunded plan*. An employer reports pension expense when it receives the benefits from the employees' services, which is sometimes decades before it pays pension benefits to employees. (*Other Postretirement Benefits* refer to nonpension benefits such as health care and life insurance benefits. Similar to a pension, costs of these benefits are estimated and liabilities accrued when the employees earn them.)

Point: Fringe benefits are often 40% or more of salaries and wages, and pension benefits make up nearly 15% of fringe benefits.

Point: Two types of pension plans are (1) *defined benefit plan*—the retirement benefit is defined and the employer estimates the contribution necessary to pay these benefits—and (2) *defined contribution plan*—the pension contribution is defined and the employer and/or employee contribute amounts specified in the pension agreement.

Summary

C1 Explain the types of notes and prepare entries to account for notes. Notes repaid over a period of time are called *installment notes* and usually follow one of two payment patterns: (1) decreasing payments of interest plus equal amounts of principal or (2) equal total payments. Mortgage notes also are common. Interest is allocated to each period in a note's life by multiplying its beginning-period carrying value by its market rate at issuance. If a note is repaid with equal payments, the payment amount is computed by dividing the borrowed amount by the present value of an annuity factor (taken from a present value table) using the market rate and the number of payments.

C2ᴬ Explain and compute bond pricing. The basic concept of present value is that an amount of cash to be paid or received in the future is worth less than the same amount of cash to be paid or received today. An annuity is a series of equal payments occurring at equal time intervals. An annuity's present value can be computed using the present value table for an annuity (or a calculator or Excel).

C3ᶜ Describe accounting for leases and pensions. A lease is a rental agreement between the lessor and the lessee. When the lessor retains the risks and rewards of asset ownership (an *operating lease*), the lessee debits Rent Expense and credits Cash for its lease payments. When the lessor substantially transfers the risks and rewards of asset ownership to the lessee (a *capital lease*), the lessee capitalizes the leased asset and records a lease liability. Pension agreements can result in either pension assets or pension liabilities.

A1 Compare bond financing with stock financing. Bond financing is used to fund business activities. Advantages of bond financing versus stock include (1) no effect on owner control, (2) tax savings, and (3) increased earnings due to financial leverage. Disadvantages include (1) interest and principal payments and (2) amplification of poor performance.

A2 Assess debt features and their implications. Certain bonds are secured by the issuer's assets; other bonds, called *debentures,* are unsecured. Serial bonds mature at different points in time; term bonds mature at one time. Registered bonds have each bondholder's name recorded by the issuer; bearer bonds are payable to the holder. Convertible bonds are exchangeable for shares of the issuer's stock. Callable bonds can be retired by the issuer at a set price. Debt features alter the risk of loss for creditors.

A3 Compute the debt-to-equity ratio and explain its use. Both creditors and equity holders are concerned about the relation between the amount of liabilities and the amount of equity. A company's financing structure is at less risk when the debt-to-equity ratio is lower, as liabilities must be paid and usually with periodic interest.

P1 Prepare entries to record bond issuance and interest expense. When bonds are issued at par, Cash is debited and Bonds Payable is credited for the bonds' par value. At bond interest payment dates (usually semiannual), Bond Interest Expense is debited and Cash credited—the latter for an amount equal to the bond par value multiplied by the bond contract rate.

P2 Compute and record amortization of a bond discount using the straight-line method. Bonds are issued at a discount when the contract rate is less than the market rate, making the issue (selling) price less than par. When this occurs, the issuer records a credit to Bonds Payable (at par) and debits both Discount on Bonds Payable and Cash. The amount of bond interest expense assigned to each period is computed using the straight-line method.

P3 Compute and record amortization of a bond premium using the straight-line method. Bonds are issued at a premium when the contract rate is higher than the market rate, making the issue (selling) price greater than par. When this occurs, the issuer records a debit to Cash and credits both Premium on Bonds Payable and Bonds Payable (at par). The amount of bond interest expense assigned to each period is computed using the straight-line method. The Premium on Bonds Payable is allocated to reduce bond interest expense over the life of the bonds.

P4 Record the retirement of bonds. Bonds are retired at maturity with a debit to Bonds Payable and a credit to Cash at par value. The issuer can retire the bonds early by exercising a call option or purchasing them in the market. Bondholders can also retire bonds early by exercising a conversion feature on convertible bonds. The issuer recognizes a gain or loss for the difference between the amount paid and the bond carrying value.

P5ᴮ Compute and record amortization of a bond discount using the effective interest method. Bonds are issued at a discount when the contract rate is less than the market rate, making the issue (selling) price less than par. The amount of bond

interest expense assigned to each period, including amortization of the discount, is computed using the effective interest method.

P6ᴮ Compute and record amortization of a bond premium using the effective interest method. Bonds are issued at a premium when the contract rate is higher than the market rate, making the issue (selling) price greater than par. The amount of bond interest expense assigned to each period, including amortization of the premium, is computed using the effective interest method.

Key Terms

Annuity
Bearer bonds
Bond
Bond certificate
Bond indenture
Callable bonds
Capital lease
Carrying (book) value of bonds
Contract rate
Convertible bonds

Coupon bonds
Debt-to-equity ratio
Discount on bonds payable
Effective interest method
Fair value option
Installment note
Lease
Market rate
Mortgage
Operating lease

Par value of a bond
Pension plan
Premium on bonds
Registered bonds
Secured bonds
Serial bonds
Sinking fund bonds
Straight-line bond amortization
Term bonds
Unsecured bonds

Multiple Choice Quiz

1. A bond traded at 97½ means that
   a. The bond pays 97½% interest.
   b. The bond trades at $975 per $1,000 bond.
   c. The market rate of interest is below the contract rate of interest for the bond.
   d. The bonds can be retired at $975 each.
   e. The bond's interest rate is 2½%.

2. A bondholder that owns a $1,000, 6%, 15-year (term) bond has
   a. The right to receive $1,000 at maturity.
   b. Ownership rights in the bond-issuing entity.
   c. The right to receive $60 per month until maturity.
   d. The right to receive $1,900 at maturity.
   e. The right to receive $600 per year until maturity.

3. A company issues 8%, 20-year bonds with a par value of $500,000. The current market rate for the bonds is 8%. The

amount of interest owed to the bondholders for each semi-annual interest payment is
   a. $40,000.   c. $20,000.   e. $400,000.
   b. $0.   d. $800,000.

4. A company issued five-year, 5% bonds with a par value of $100,000. The company received $95,735 for the bonds. Using the straight-line method, the company's interest expense for the first semiannual interest period is
   a. $2,926.50.   c. $2,500.00.   e. $9,573.50.
   b. $5,853.00.   d. $5,000.00.

5. A company issued eight-year, 5% bonds with a par value of $350,000. The company received proceeds of $373,745. Interest is payable semiannually. The amount of premium amortized for the first semiannual interest period, assuming straight-line bond amortization, is
   a. $2,698.   c. $8,750.   e. $1,484.
   b. $23,745.   d. $9,344.

ANSWERS TO MULTIPLE CHOICE QUIZ

1. b
2. a
3. c; $500,000 × 0.08 × ½ year = $20,000

4. a; Cash interest paid = $100,000 × 5% × ½ year = $2,500
   Discount amortization = ($100,000 − $95,735)/10 periods = $426.50
   Interest expense = $2,500.00 + $426.50 = $2,926.50
5. e; ($373,745 − $350,000)/16 periods = $1,484

^B(C) *Superscript letter B(C) denotes assignments based on Appendix 14B(14C).*

🎲 Icon denotes assignments that involve decision making.

Discussion Questions

1. What is the main difference between notes payable and bonds payable?

2. What is the main difference between a bond and a share of stock?

3. 🎲 What is the advantage of issuing bonds instead of obtaining financing from the company's owners?

4. What is a bond indenture? What provisions are usually included in it?

5. What are the duties of a trustee for bondholders?

6. What are the *contract* rate and the *market* rate for bonds?

7. 🎲 What factors affect the market rates for bonds?

8^B 🎲 Does the straight-line or effective interest method produce an interest expense allocation that yields a constant rate of interest over a bond's life? Explain.

9. Explain the concept of accrued interest on bonds at the end of an accounting period.

10. 🎲 If you know the par value of bonds, the contract rate, and the market rate, how do you compute the bonds' price?

11. What is the issue price of a $2,000 bond sold at 98¼? What is the issue price of a $6,000 bond sold at 101½?

12. Describe the debt-to-equity ratio and explain how creditors and owners would use this ratio to evaluate a company's risk.

13. 🎲 What obligation does an entrepreneur (owner) have to investors that purchase bonds to finance the business?

14. Refer to Apple's annual report in Appendix A. Is there any indication that Apple has issued **APPLE** long-term debt?

15. Refer to the statements for Samsung in Appendix A. By what amount did **Samsung** Samsung's long-term borrowings increase or decrease in 2015?

16. Refer to the statement of cash flows for Samsung in Appendix A. For the year **Samsung** ended December 31, 2015, what was the amount for repayment of long-term borrowings and debentures?

17. Refer to the statements for Google in Appendix A. For the year ended December **GOOGLE** 31, 2015, what was its debt-to-equity ratio? What does this ratio tell us?

18.^C When can a lease create both an asset and a liability for the lessee?

19.^C Compare and contrast an operating lease with a capital lease.

20.^C Describe the two basic types of pension plans.

🔗 connect

> *Round dollar amounts to the nearest whole dollar.*

Identify the following as either an advantage (A) or a disadvantage (D) of bond financing.

_____ **a.** Bonds do not affect owner control.

_____ **b.** A company earns a lower return with borrowed funds than it pays in interest.

_____ **c.** A company earns a higher return with borrowed funds than it pays in interest.

_____ **d.** Bonds require payment of periodic interest.

_____ **e.** Interest on bonds is tax deductible.

_____ **f.** Bonds require payment of par value at maturity.

QUICK STUDY

QS 14-1
Bond financing
A1

Enviro Company issues 8%, 10-year bonds with a par value of $250,000 and semiannual interest payments. On the issue date, the annual market rate for these bonds is 10%, which implies a selling price of 87½. Prepare the journal entries for the issuance of the bonds. Assume the bonds are issued for cash on January 1, 2017.

QS 14-2
Journalizing bond issuance
P1

Using the bond details in QS 14-2, confirm that the bonds' selling price is approximately correct (within $100). Use present value tables B.1 and B.3 in Appendix B.

QS 14-3^A
Computing bond price
C2

Garcia Company issues 10%, 15-year bonds with a par value of $240,000 and semiannual interest payments. On the issue date, the annual market rate for these bonds is 8%, which implies a selling price of 117¼. Prepare the journal entry for the issuance of these bonds. Assume the bonds are issued for cash on January 1, 2017.

QS 14-4
Journalizing bond issuance
P1

QS 14-5^A
Computing bond price **C2**

Using the bond details in QS 14-4, confirm that the bonds' selling price is approximately correct (within $100). Use present value tables B.1 and B.3 in Appendix B.

QS 14-6
Straight-Line:
Bond computations
P2

Enviro Company issues 8%, 10-year bonds with a par value of $250,000 and semiannual interest payments. On the issue date, the annual market rate for these bonds is 10%, which implies a selling price of 87½. The straight-line method is used to allocate interest expense.

1. What are the issuer's cash proceeds from issuance of these bonds?
2. What total amount of bond interest expense will be recognized over the life of these bonds?
3. What is the amount of bond interest expense recorded on the first interest payment date?

QS 14-7
Recording bond issuance
and discount amortization
P1   P2

Sylvestor Company issues 10%, five-year bonds, on December 31, 2016, with a par value of $100,000 and semiannual interest payments. Use the following bond amortization table and prepare journal entries to record (*a*) the issuance of bonds on December 31, 2016; (*b*) the first interest payment on June 30, 2017; and (*c*) the second interest payment on December 31, 2017.

Semiannual Period-End	Unamortized Discount	Carrying Value
(0) 12/31/2016..............	$7,360	$92,640
(1) 6/30/2017..............	6,624	93,376
(2) 12/31/2017..............	5,888	94,112

QS 14-8
Straight-Line:
Bond computations   **P3**

Enviro Company issues 8%, 10-year bonds with a par value of $250,000 and semiannual interest payments. On the issue date, the annual market rate for these bonds is 5%, which implies a selling price of 123⅜. The straight-line method is used to allocate interest expense.

1. What are the issuer's cash proceeds from issuance of these bonds?
2. What total amount of bond interest expense will be recognized over the life of these bonds?
3. What is the amount of bond interest expense recorded on the first interest payment date?

QS 14-9
Bond retirement by
call option   **P4**

On July 1, 2017, Advocate Company exercises an $8,000 call option (plus par value) on its outstanding bonds that have a carrying value of $416,000 and par value of $400,000. The company exercises the call option after the semiannual interest is paid on June 30, 2017. Record the entry to retire the bonds.

QS 14-10
Bond retirement by stock
conversion   **P4**

On January 1, 2017, the $2,000,000 par value bonds of Spitz Company with a carrying value of $2,000,000 are converted to 1,000,000 shares of $1.00 par value common stock. Record the entry for the conversion of the bonds.

QS 14-11
Issuance and interest for
installment note   **C1**

On January 1, 2017, MM Co. borrows $340,000 cash from a bank and in return signs an 8% installment note for five annual payments of $85,155 each, with the first payment due one year after the note is signed.

1. Prepare the journal entry to record issuance of the note.
2. For the first $85,155 annual payment at December 31, 2017, what amount goes toward interest expense? What amount goes toward principal reduction of the note?

QS 14-12
Bond features and
terminology
A2

Enter the letter of the description *A* through *H* that best fits each term or phrase 1 through 8.

A. Records and tracks the bondholders' names.
B. Is unsecured; backed only by the issuer's credit standing.
C. Has varying maturity dates for amounts owed.
D. Identifies rights and responsibilities of the issuer and the bondholders.
E. Can be exchanged for shares of the issuer's stock.
F. Is unregistered; interest is paid to whoever possesses them.
G. Maintains a separate asset account from which bondholders are paid at maturity.
H. Pledges specific assets of the issuer as collateral.

_____ **1.** Registered bond   _____ **5.** Convertible bond
_____ **2.** Serial bond   _____ **6.** Bond indenture
_____ **3.** Secured bond   _____ **7.** Sinking fund bond
_____ **4.** Bearer bond   _____ **8.** Debenture

Compute the debt-to-equity ratio for each of the following companies. Which company appears to have a riskier financing structure? Explain.

QS 14-13
Debt-to-equity ratio

A3

	Atlanta Company	Spokane Company
Total liabilities	$429,000	$ 549,000
Total equity	572,000	1,830,000

Garcia Company issues 10%, 15-year bonds with a par value of $240,000 and semiannual interest payments. On the issue date, the annual market rate for these bonds is 14%, which implies a selling price of 75¼. The effective interest method is used to allocate interest expense.
1. What are the issuer's cash proceeds from issuance of these bonds?
2. What total amount of bond interest expense will be recognized over the life of these bonds?
3. What amount of bond interest expense is recorded on the first interest payment date?

QS 14-14^B
Effective Interest:
Bond discount computations

P5

Garcia Company issues 10%, 15-year bonds with a par value of $240,000 and semiannual interest payments. On the issue date, the annual market rate for these bonds is 8%, which implies a selling price of 117¼. The effective interest method is used to allocate interest expense.
1. What are the issuer's cash proceeds from issuance of these bonds?
2. What total amount of bond interest expense will be recognized over the life of these bonds?
3. What amount of bond interest expense is recorded on the first interest payment date?

QS 14-15^B
Effective Interest:
Bond premium computations

P6

Madrid Company plans to issue 8% bonds on January 1, 2017, with a par value of $4,000,000. The company sells $3,600,000 of the bonds at par on January 1, 2017. The remaining $400,000 sells at par on July 1, 2017. The bonds pay interest semiannually as of June 30 and December 31.
1. Record the entry for the first interest payment on June 30, 2017.
2. Record the entry for the July 1 cash sale of bonds.

QS 14-16
Issuing bonds at par

P1

Jin Li, an employee of ETrain.com, leases a car at O'Hare airport for a three-day business trip. The rental cost is $250. Prepare the entry by ETrain.com to record Jin Li's short-term car lease cost.

QS 14-17^C
Recording operating leases   C3

Algoma, Inc., signs a five-year lease for office equipment with Office Solutions. The present value of the lease payments is $15,499. Prepare the journal entry that Algoma records at the inception of this capital lease.

QS 14-18^C
Recording capital leases

C3

Vodafone Group Plc reports the following information among its bonds payable as of March 31, 2015 (pounds in millions).

QS 14-19
International liabilities disclosures

P1

Financial Long-Term Liabilities Measured at Amortized Cost			
£ millions	Nominal (par) Value	Carrying Value	Fair Value
4.625% (US dollar 500 million) bond due July 2018	£337	£375	£367

a. What is the par value of the 4.625% bond issuance? What is its book (carrying) value?
b. Was the 4.625% bond sold at a discount or a premium? Explain.

Refer to the information in QS 14-19 for Vodafone Group Plc. The following price quotes relate to its bonds payable. The price quote indicates that the 4.625% bonds have a market price of 111.67 (111.67% of par value), resulting in a yield to maturity of 1.710%.

QS 14-20
International liabilities disclosures and interpretations

P1

Price	Contract Rate (coupon)	Maturity Date	Market Rate (YTM)
111.67	4.625%	15-Jul-2018	1.710%

a. Assuming that the 4.625% bonds were originally issued at par value, what does the market price reveal about interest rate changes since bond issuance? (Assume that Vodafone's credit rating has remained the same.)

b. Does the change in market rates since the issuance of these bonds affect the amount of interest expense reported on Vodafone's income statement? Explain.

c. How much cash would Vodafone need to pay to repurchase the 4.625% bonds at the quoted market price of 111.67? (Assume no interest is owed when the bonds are repurchased.)

d. Assuming that the 4.625% bonds remain outstanding until maturity, at what market price will the bonds sell on the due date in 2018?

■ connect

EXERCISES

Round dollar amounts to the nearest whole dollar. Assume no reversing entries are used.

Exercise 14-1

Recording bond issuance and interest

P1

On January 1, 2017, Boston Enterprises issues bonds that have a $3,400,000 par value, mature in 20 years, and pay 9% interest semiannually on June 30 and December 31. The bonds are sold at par.

1. How much interest will Boston pay (in cash) to the bondholders every six months?

2. Prepare journal entries to record (*a*) the issuance of bonds on January 1, 2017; (*b*) the first interest payment on June 30, 2017; and (*c*) the second interest payment on December 31, 2017.

3. Prepare the journal entry for issuance assuming the bonds are issued at (*a*) 98 and (*b*) 102.

Exercise 14-2

Straight-Line:

Amortization of bond discount

P2

Tano issues bonds with a par value of $180,000 on January 1, 2017. The bonds' annual contract rate is 8%, and interest is paid semiannually on June 30 and December 31. The bonds mature in three years. The annual market rate at the date of issuance is 10%, and the bonds are sold for $170,862.

1. What is the amount of the discount on these bonds at issuance?

2. How much total bond interest expense will be recognized over the life of these bonds?

3. Prepare an amortization table like the one in Exhibit 14.7 for these bonds; use the straight-line method to amortize the discount.

Exercise 14-3[A]

Computing bond interest and price; recording bond issuance

C2

Check (4) $691,287

Bringham Company issues bonds with a par value of $800,000 on their stated issue date. The bonds mature in 10 years and pay 6% annual interest in semiannual payments. On the issue date, the annual market rate for the bonds is 8%.

1. What is the amount of each semiannual interest payment for these bonds?

2. How many semiannual interest payments will be made on these bonds over their life?

3. Use the interest rates given to determine whether the bonds are issued at par, at a discount, or at a premium.

4. Compute the price of the bonds as of their issue date.

5. Prepare the journal entry to record the bonds' issuance.

Exercise 14-4

Straight-Line:

Recording bond issuance and discount amortization

P1   P2

Paulson Company issues 6%, four-year bonds, on December 31, 2017, with a par value of $200,000 and semiannual interest payments. Use the following bond amortization table and prepare journal entries to record (*a*) the issuance of bonds on December 31, 2017; (*b*) the first interest payment on June 30, 2018; and (*c*) the second interest payment on December 31, 2018.

Semiannual Period-End	Unamortized Discount	Carrying Value
(0) 12/31/2017	$13,466	$186,534
(1) 6/30/2018	11,782	188,218
(2) 12/31/2018	10,098	189,902

Exercise 14-5

Straight-Line: Recording bond issuance and discount amortization

P1   P2

Dobbs Company issues 5%, two-year bonds, on December 31, 2017, with a par value of $200,000 and semiannual interest payments. Use the following bond amortization table and prepare journal entries to record (*a*) the issuance of bonds on December 31, 2017; (*b*) the first through fourth interest payments on each June 30 and December 31; and (*c*) the maturity of the bonds on December 31, 2019.

Semiannual Period-End	Unamortized Discount	Carrying Value
(0) 12/31/2017	$12,000	$188,000
(1) 6/30/2018	9,000	191,000
(2) 12/31/2018	6,000	194,000
(3) 6/30/2019	3,000	197,000
(4) 12/31/2019	0	200,000

Woodwick Company issues 10%, five-year bonds, on December 31, 2016, with a par value of $200,000 and semiannual interest payments. Use the following bond amortization table and prepare journal entries to record (*a*) the issuance of bonds on December 31, 2016; (*b*) the first interest payment on June 30, 2017; and (*c*) the second interest payment on December 31, 2017.

Exercise 14-6
Straight-Line:
Recording bond issuance and premium amortization

P1   P3

Semiannual Period-End	Unamortized Premium	Carrying Value
(0) 12/31/2016	$16,222	$216,222
(1) 6/30/2017	14,600	214,600
(2) 12/31/2017	12,978	212,978

Quatro Co. issues bonds dated January 1, 2017, with a par value of $400,000. The bonds' annual contract rate is 13%, and interest is paid semiannually on June 30 and December 31. The bonds mature in three years. The annual market rate at the date of issuance is 12%, and the bonds are sold for $409,850.

1. What is the amount of the premium on these bonds at issuance?

2. How much total bond interest expense will be recognized over the life of these bonds?

3. Prepare an amortization table like the one in Exhibit 14.11 for these bonds; use the straight-line method to amortize the premium.

Exercise 14-7
Straight-Line:
Amortization of bond premium

P3

Citywide Company issues bonds with a par value of $150,000 on their stated issue date. The bonds mature in five years and pay 10% annual interest in semiannual payments. On the issue date, the annual market rate for the bonds is 8%.

1. What is the amount of each semiannual interest payment for these bonds?

2. How many semiannual interest payments will be made on these bonds over their life?

3. Use the interest rates given to determine whether the bonds are issued at par, at a discount, or at a premium.

4. Compute the price of the bonds as of their issue date.

5. Prepare the journal entry to record the bonds' issuance.

Exercise 14-8[A]
Computing bond interest and price; recording bond issuance

P3   C2

Check (4) $162,172

On January 1, 2017, Shay issues $700,000 of 10%, 15-year bonds at a price of 97¾. Six years later, on January 1, 2023, Shay retires 20% of these bonds by buying them on the open market at 104½. All interest is accounted for and paid through December 31, 2022, the day before the purchase. The straight-line method is used to amortize any bond discount.

1. How much does the company receive when it issues the bonds on January 1, 2017?

2. What is the amount of the discount on the bonds at January 1, 2017?

3. How much amortization of the discount is recorded on the bonds for the entire period from January 1, 2017, through December 31, 2022?

4. What is the carrying (book) value of the bonds as of the close of business on December 31, 2022? What is the carrying value of the 20% soon-to-be-retired bonds on this same date?

5. How much did the company pay on January 1, 2023, to purchase the bonds that it retired?

6. What is the amount of the recorded gain or loss from retiring the bonds?

7. Prepare the journal entry to record the bond retirement at January 1, 2023.

Exercise 14-9
Straight-Line: Bond computations, amortization, and bond retirement

P2   P4

Check (6) $8,190 loss

On January 1, 2017, Eagle borrows $100,000 cash by signing a four-year, 7% installment note. The note requires four equal payments of $29,523, consisting of accrued interest and principal on December 31 of each year from 2017 through 2020. Prepare an amortization table for this installment note like the one in Exhibit 14.12.

Exercise 14-10
Installment note amortization table   C1

Exercise 14-11
Installment note entries
C1

Use the information in Exercise 14-10 to prepare the journal entries for Eagle to record the loan on January 1, 2017, and each of the four payments from December 31, 2017, through December 31, 2020.

Exercise 14-12
Applying debt-to-equity ratio
A3

Montclair Company is considering a project that will require a $500,000 loan. It presently has total liabilities of $220,000 and total assets of $620,000.

1. Compute Montclair's (a) present debt-to-equity ratio and (b) the debt-to-equity ratio assuming it borrows $500,000 to fund the project.
2. Evaluate and discuss the level of risk involved if Montclair borrows the funds to pursue the project.

Exercise 14-13ᴮ
Effective Interest:
Amortization of
bond discount
P5

Stanford issues bonds dated January 1, 2017, with a par value of $500,000. The bonds' annual contract rate is 9%, and interest is paid semiannually on June 30 and December 31. The bonds mature in three years. The annual market rate at the date of issuance is 12%, and the bonds are sold for $463,140.

1. What is the amount of the discount on these bonds at issuance?
2. How much total bond interest expense will be recognized over the life of these bonds?
3. Prepare an amortization table like the one in Exhibit 14B.1 for these bonds; use the effective interest method to amortize the discount.

Exercise 14-14ᴮ
Effective Interest:
Amortization of
bond premium
P6

Quatro Co. issues bonds dated January 1, 2017, with a par value of $400,000. The bonds' annual contract rate is 13%, and interest is paid semiannually on June 30 and December 31. The bonds mature in three years. The annual market rate at the date of issuance is 12%, and the bonds are sold for $409,850.

1. What is the amount of the premium on these bonds at issuance?
2. How much total bond interest expense will be recognized over the life of these bonds?
3. Prepare an amortization table like the one in Exhibit 14B.2 for these bonds; use the effective interest method to amortize the premium.

Exercise 14-15
Straight-Line:
Amortization table and
bond interest expense
P2

Duval Co. issues four-year bonds with a $100,000 par value on January 1, 2017, at a price of $95,952. The annual contract rate is 7%, and interest is paid semiannually on June 30 and December 31.

1. Prepare an amortization table like the one in Exhibit 14.7 for these bonds. Use the straight-line method of interest amortization.
2. Prepare journal entries to record the first two interest payments.
3. Prepare the journal entry for maturity of the bonds on December 31, 2020 (assume semiannual interest is already recorded).

Exercise 14-16
Recording bond issuance
at par, interest payments,
and bond maturity
P1

On January 1, 2017, Brussels Enterprises issues bonds at par dated January 1, 2017, that have a $3,400,000 par value, mature in 4 years, and pay 9% interest semiannually on June 30 and December 31.

1. Record the entry for the issuance of bonds for cash on January 1, 2017.
2. Record the entry for the first semiannual interest payment on June 30, 2017.
3. Record the entry for the second semiannual interest payment on December 31, 2017.
4. Record the entry for the maturity of the bonds on December 31, 2020 (assume semiannual interest is already recorded).

Exercise 14-17ᶜ
Identifying capital and
operating leases
C3

Indicate whether the company in each separate case 1 through 3 has entered into an operating lease or a capital lease.

1. The lessor retains title to the asset, and the lease term is three years on an asset that has a five-year useful life.
2. The title is transferred to the lessee, the lessee can purchase the asset for $1 at the end of the lease, and the lease term is five years. The leased asset has an expected useful life of six years.
3. The present value of the lease payments is 95% of the leased asset's market value, and the lease term is 70% of the leased asset's useful life.

Exercise 14-18ᶜ
Accounting for
capital lease
C3

Harbor (lessee) signs a five-year capital lease for office equipment with a $10,000 annual lease payment. The present value of the five annual lease payments is $41,000, based on a 7% interest rate.

1. Prepare the journal entry Harbor will record at inception of the lease.
2. If the leased asset has a five-year useful life with no salvage value, prepare the journal entry Harbor will record each year to recognize depreciation expense related to the leased asset.

General Motors advertised three alternatives for a 25-month lease on a new Tahoe: (1) zero dollars down and a lease payment of $1,750 per month for 25 months, (2) $5,000 down and $1,500 per month for 25 months, or (3) $38,500 down and no payments for 25 months. Use the present value Table B.3 in Appendix B to determine which is the best alternative for the customer (assume you have enough cash to accept any alternative and the annual interest rate is 12% compounded monthly).

Exercise 14-19ᶜ
Analyzing lease options
C3

Heineken N.V. reports the following information for its loans and borrowings as of December 31, 2015, including proceeds and repayments for the year ended December 31, 2015 (euros in millions).

Exercise 14-20
Accounting for long-term liabilities under IFRS
C1

Loans and borrowings (noncurrent liabilities)	
Loans and borrowings, December 31, 2015	€ 10,658
Proceeds (cash) from issuances of loans and borrowings.	1,888
Repayments (in cash) of loans and borrowings	(1,753)

1. Prepare Heineken's journal entry to record its cash proceeds from issuances of its loans and borrowings for 2015. Assume that the par value of these issuances is €1,900.
2. Prepare Heineken's journal entry to record its cash repayments of its loans and borrowings for 2015. Assume that the par value of these issuances is €1,700, and the premium on them is €24.
3. Compute the discount or premium on its loans and borrowings as of December 31, 2015, assuming that the par value of these liabilities is €10,000.
4. Given the facts in part 3 and viewing the entirety of loans and borrowings as one issuance, was the contract rate on these loans and borrowings higher or lower than the market rate at the time of issuance? Explain. (Assume that Heineken's credit rating has remained the same.)

▦ connect

> *Round dollar amounts to the nearest whole dollar. Assume no reversing entries are used.*

PROBLEM SET A

Hartford Research issues bonds dated January 1, 2017, that pay interest semiannually on June 30 and December 31. The bonds have a $40,000 par value and an annual contract rate of 10%, and they mature in 10 years.

Problem 14-1Aᴬ
Computing bond price and recording issuance

C2   P1

Required

For each of the following three separate situations, (*a*) determine the bonds' issue price on January 1, 2017, and (*b*) prepare the journal entry to record their issuance.
1. The market rate at the date of issuance is 8%.
2. The market rate at the date of issuance is 10%.
3. The market rate at the date of issuance is 12%.

Check (1) Premium, $5,437

(3) Discount, $4,588

Hillside issues $4,000,000 of 6%, 15-year bonds dated January 1, 2017, that pay interest semiannually on June 30 and December 31. The bonds are issued at a price of $3,456,448.

Problem 14-2A
Straight-Line:
Amortization of bond discount

P1   P2

Required

1. Prepare the January 1, 2017, journal entry to record the bonds' issuance.
2. For each semiannual period, compute (*a*) the cash payment, (*b*) the straight-line discount amortization, and (*c*) the bond interest expense.
3. Determine the total bond interest expense to be recognized over the bonds' life.
4. Prepare the first two years of an amortization table like Exhibit 14.7 using the straight-line method.
5. Prepare the journal entries to record the first two interest payments.

Check (3) $4,143,552

(4) 12/31/2018 carrying value, $3,528,920

Refer to the bond details in Problem 14-2A, *except* assume that the bonds are issued at a price of $4,895,980.

Problem 14-3A
Straight Line:
Amortization of bond premium

P1   P3

Required

1. Prepare the January 1, 2017, journal entry to record the bonds' issuance.
2. For each semiannual period, compute (*a*) the cash payment, (*b*) the straight-line premium amortization, and (*c*) the bond interest expense.

Continued on next page . . .

3. Determine the total bond interest expense to be recognized over the bonds' life.
4. Prepare the first two years of an amortization table like Exhibit 14.11 using the straight-line method.
5. Prepare the journal entries to record the first two interest payments.

Problem 14-4A
Straight-Line: Amortization of bond premium
P1 P3

Ellis issues 6.5%, five-year bonds dated January 1, 2017, with a $250,000 par value. The bonds pay interest on June 30 and December 31 and are issued at a price of $255,333. The annual market rate is 6% on the issue date.

Required

1. Calculate the total bond interest expense over the bonds' life.

2. Prepare a straight-line amortization table like Exhibit 14.11 for the bonds' life.
3. Prepare the journal entries to record the first two interest payments.

Problem 14-5A
Straight-Line: Amortization of bond premium and discount
P1 P2 P3

Legacy issues $325,000 of 5%, four-year bonds dated January 1, 2017, that pay interest semiannually on June 30 and December 31. They are issued at $292,181, and their market rate is 8% at the issue date.

Required

1. Prepare the January 1, 2017, journal entry to record the bonds' issuance.

2. Determine the total bond interest expense to be recognized over the bonds' life.
3. Prepare a straight-line amortization table like the one in Exhibit 14.7 for the bonds' first two years.
4. Prepare the journal entries to record the first two interest payments.

Analysis Component

5. Assume the market rate on January 1, 2017, is 4% instead of 8%. Without providing numbers, describe how this change affects the amounts reported on Legacy's financial statements.

Problem 14-6A
Installment notes
C1

On November 1, 2017, Norwood borrows $200,000 cash from a bank by signing a five-year installment note bearing 8% interest. The note requires equal payments of $50,091 each year on October 31.

Required

1. Complete an amortization table for this installment note similar to the one in Exhibit 14.12.
2. Prepare the journal entries in which Norwood records (*a*) accrued interest as of December 31, 2017 (the end of its annual reporting period) and (*b*) the first annual payment on the note.

Problem 14-7A
Applying the debt-to-equity ratio
A3

At the end of the current year, the following information is available for both Pulaski Company and Scott Company.

	Pulaski Company	Scott Company
Total assets	$860,000	$440,000
Total liabilities	360,000	240,000
Total equity	500,000	200,000

Required

1. Compute the debt-to-equity ratios for both companies.
2. Comment on your results and discuss the riskiness of each company's financing structure.

Problem 14-8A[B]
Effective Interest:
Amortization of bond discount **P1 P5**

Refer to the bond details in Problem 14-5A.

Required

1. Prepare the January 1, 2017, journal entry to record the bonds' issuance.
2. Determine the total bond interest expense to be recognized over the bonds' life.

3. Prepare an effective interest amortization table like the one in Exhibit 14B.1 for the bonds' first two years.
4. Prepare the journal entries to record the first two interest payments.

Refer to the bond details in Problem 14-4A.

Required

1. Compute the total bond interest expense over the bonds' life.
2. Prepare an effective interest amortization table like the one in Exhibit 14B.2 for the bonds' life.
3. Prepare the journal entries to record the first two interest payments.
4. Use the market rate at issuance to compute the present value of the remaining cash flows for these bonds as of December 31, 2019. Compare your answer with the amount shown on the amortization table as the balance for that date (from part 2) and explain your findings.

Problem 14-9A^B
Effective Interest: Amortization of bond premium; computing bond price **P1 P6**

Check (2) 6/30/2019 carrying value, $252,865

(4) $252,326

Ike issues $180,000 of 11%, three-year bonds dated January 1, 2017, that pay interest semiannually on June 30 and December 31. They are issued at $184,566. Their market rate is 10% at the issue date.

Required

1. Prepare the January 1, 2017, journal entry to record the bonds' issuance.
2. Determine the total bond interest expense to be recognized over the bonds' life.
3. Prepare an effective interest amortization table like Exhibit 14B.2 for the bonds' first two years.
4. Prepare the journal entries to record the first two interest payments.
5. Prepare the journal entry to record the bonds' retirement on January 1, 2019, at 98.

Analysis Component

6. Assume that the market rate on January 1, 2017, is 12% instead of 10%. Without presenting numbers, describe how this change affects the amounts reported on Ike's financial statements.

Problem 14-10A^B
Effective Interest: Amortization of bond; retiring bonds

P1 P4 P5 P6

Check (3) 6/30/2018 carrying value, $182,448

(5) $5,270 gain

Rogers Company signs a five-year capital lease with Packer Company for office equipment. The annual year-end lease payment is $10,000, and the interest rate is 8%.

Required

1. Compute the present value of Rogers's five-year lease payments.
2. Prepare the journal entry to record Rogers's capital lease at its inception.
3. Complete a lease payment schedule for the five years of the lease with the following headings. Assume that the beginning balance of the lease liability (present value of lease payments) is $39,927. (*Hint:* To find the amount allocated to interest in year 1, multiply the interest rate by the beginning-of-year lease liability. The amount of the annual lease payment not allocated to interest is allocated to principal. Reduce the lease liability by the amount allocated to principal to update the lease liability at each year-end.)

Problem 14-11A^C
Capital lease accounting

C3

Check (1) $39,927

(3) Year 3 ending balance, $17,833

Period Ending Date	Beginning Balance of Lease Liability	Interest on Lease Liability	Reduction of Lease Liability	Cash Lease Payment	Ending Balance of Lease Liability

4. Use straight-line depreciation and prepare the journal entry to depreciate the leased asset at the end of year 1. Assume zero salvage value and a five-year life for the office equipment.

connect

Round dollar amounts to the nearest whole dollar. Assume no reversing entries are used.

Flagstaff Systems issues bonds dated January 1, 2017, that pay interest semiannually on June 30 and December 31. The bonds have a $90,000 par value and an annual contract rate of 12%, and they mature in five years.

Required

For each of the following three separate situations, (*a*) determine the bonds' issue price on January 1, 2017, and (*b*) prepare the journal entry to record their issuance.

1. The market rate at the date of issuance is 10%.
2. The market rate at the date of issuance is 12%.
3. The market rate at the date of issuance is 14%.

PROBLEM SET B

Problem 14-1B^A
Computing bond price and recording issuance

C2 P1

Check (1) Premium, $6,948

(3) Discount, $6,326

Problem 14-2B
Straight-Line: Amortization of bond discount

P1 P2

Check (3) $3,790,000
(4) 6/30/2018 carrying value, $3,068,500

Romero issues $3,400,000 of 10%, 10-year bonds dated January 1, 2017, that pay interest semiannually on June 30 and December 31. The bonds are issued at a price of $3,010,000.

Required

1. Prepare the January 1, 2017, journal entry to record the bonds' issuance.
2. For each semiannual period, compute (*a*) the cash payment, (*b*) the straight-line discount amortization, and (*c*) the bond interest expense.
3. Determine the total bond interest expense to be recognized over the bonds' life.
4. Prepare the first two years of an amortization table like Exhibit 14.7 using the straight-line method.
5. Prepare the journal entries to record the first two interest payments.

Problem 14-3B
Straight-Line: Amortization of bond premium

P1 P3

Check (3) $2,607,068
(4) 6/30/2018 carrying value, 4,073,991

Refer to the bond details in Problem 14-2B, *except* assume that the bonds are issued at a price of $4,192,932.

Required

1. Prepare the January 1, 2017, journal entry to record the bonds' issuance.
2. For each semiannual period, compute (*a*) the cash payment, (*b*) the straight-line premium amortization, and (*c*) the bond interest expense.
3. Determine the total bond interest expense to be recognized over the bonds' life.
4. Prepare the first two years of an amortization table like Exhibit 14.11 using the straight-line method.
5. Prepare the journal entries to record the first two interest payments.

Problem 14-4B
Straight-Line: Amortization of bond premium

P1 P3

Check (2) 6/30/2019 carrying value, $326,493

Ripkin Company issues 9%, five-year bonds dated January 1, 2017, with a $320,000 par value. The bonds pay interest on June 30 and December 31 and are issued at a price of $332,988. Their annual market rate is 8% on the issue date.

Required

1. Calculate the total bond interest expense over the bonds' life.
2. Prepare a straight-line amortization table like Exhibit 14.11 for the bonds' life.
3. Prepare the journal entries to record the first two interest payments.

Problem 14-5B
Straight-Line: Amortization of bond discount

P1 P2

Check (2) $257,506
(3) 6/30/2018 carrying value, $202,646

Gomez issues $240,000 of 6%, 15-year bonds dated January 1, 2017, that pay interest semiannually on June 30 and December 31. They are issued at $198,494, and their market rate is 8% at the issue date.

Required

1. Prepare the January 1, 2017, journal entry to record the bonds' issuance.
2. Determine the total bond interest expense to be recognized over the life of the bonds.
3. Prepare a straight-line amortization table like the one in Exhibit 14.7 for the bonds' first two years.
4. Prepare the journal entries to record the first two interest payments.

Problem 14-6B
Installment notes

C1

Check (1) 9/30/2019 ending balance, $54,836

On October 1, 2017, Gordon borrows $150,000 cash from a bank by signing a three-year installment note bearing 10% interest. The note requires equal payments of $60,316 each year on September 30.

Required

1. Complete an amortization table for this installment note similar to the one in Exhibit 14.12.
2. Prepare the journal entries to record (*a*) accrued interest as of December 31, 2017 (the end of its annual reporting period) and (*b*) the first annual payment on the note.

Problem 14-7B
Applying the debt-to-equity ratio

A3

At the end of the current year, the following information is available for both Atlas Company and Bryan Company.

	Atlas Company	Bryan Company
Total assets	$180,000	$750,000
Total liabilities	80,000	562,500
Total equity	100,000	187,500

Required

1. Compute the debt-to-equity ratios for both companies.
2. Comment on your results and discuss what they imply about the relative riskiness of these companies.

Refer to the bond details in Problem 14-5B.

Required

1. Prepare the January 1, 2017, journal entry to record the bonds' issuance.
2. Determine the total bond interest expense to be recognized over the bonds' life.
3. Prepare an effective interest amortization table like the one in Exhibit 14B.1 for the bonds' first two years.
4. Prepare the journal entries to record the first two interest payments.

Problem 14-8B[B]
Effective Interest:
Amortization of bond
discount **P1 P5**

Check (2) $257,506
(3) 6/30/2018
carrying value, $200,803

Refer to the bond details in Problem 14-4B.

Required

1. Compute the total bond interest expense over the bonds' life.
2. Prepare an effective interest amortization table like the one in Exhibit 14B.2 for the bonds' life.
3. Prepare the journal entries to record the first two interest payments.
4. Use the market rate at issuance to compute the present value of the remaining cash flows for these bonds as of December 31, 2019. Compare your answer with the amount shown on the amortization table as the balance for that date (from part 2) and explain your findings.

Problem 14-9B[B]
Effective Interest:
Amortization of bond
premium; computing
bond price **P1 P6**

Check (2) 6/30/2019
carrying value, $327,136
(4) $325,807

Valdez issues $450,000 of 13%, four-year bonds dated January 1, 2017, that pay interest semiannually on June 30 and December 31. They are issued at $493,608, and their market rate is 10% at the issue date.

Required

1. Prepare the January 1, 2017, journal entry to record the bonds' issuance.
2. Determine the total bond interest expense to be recognized over the bonds' life.
3. Prepare an effective interest amortization table like the one in Exhibit 14B.2 for the bonds' first two years.
4. Prepare the journal entries to record the first two interest payments.
5. Prepare the journal entry to record the bonds' retirement on January 1, 2019, at 106.

Analysis Component

6. Assume that the market rate on January 1, 2017, is 14% instead of 10%. Without presenting numbers, describe how this change affects the amounts reported on Valdez's financial statements.

Problem 14-10B[B]
Effective Interest:
Amortization of bond;
retiring bonds

P1 P4 P5 P6

Check (3) 6/30/2018
carrying value, $479,202

(5) $3,088 loss

Braun Company signs a five-year capital lease with Verdi Company for office equipment. The annual year-end lease payment is $20,000, and the interest rate is 10%.

Required

1. Compute the present value of Braun's lease payments.
2. Prepare the journal entry to record Braun's capital lease at its inception.
3. Complete a lease payment schedule for the five years of the lease with the following headings. Assume that the beginning balance of the lease liability (present value of lease payments) is $75,816. (*Hint:* To find the amount allocated to interest in year 1, multiply the interest rate by the beginning-of-year lease liability. The amount of the annual lease payment not allocated to interest is allocated to principal. Reduce the lease liability by the amount allocated to principal to update the lease liability at each year-end.)

Problem 14-11B[C]
Capital lease accounting

C3

Check (1) $75,816

(3) Year 3 ending
balance, $34,712

Period Ending Date	Beginning Balance of Lease Liability	Interest on Lease Liability	Reduction of Lease Liability	Cash Lease Payment	Ending Balance of Lease Liability

4. Use straight-line depreciation and prepare the journal entry to depreciate the leased asset at the end of year 1. Assume zero salvage value and a five-year life for the office equipment.

SERIAL PROBLEM
Business Solutions

A1   A3

© Alexander Image/Shutterstock RF

Check   (1) $94,639

(This serial problem began in Chapter 1 and continues through most of the book. If previous chapter segments were not completed, the serial problem can begin at this point.)

SP 14   Santana Rey has consulted with her local banker and is considering financing an expansion of her business by obtaining a long-term bank loan. Selected account balances at March 31, 2018, for **Business Solutions** follow.

Total assets	$120,268	Total liabilities	$875	Total equity	$119,393

Required

1. The bank has offered a long-term secured note to Business Solutions. The bank's loan procedures require that a client's debt-to-equity ratio not exceed 0.8. As of March 31, 2018, what is the maximum amount that Business Solutions could borrow from this bank (rounded to the nearest dollar)?
2. If Business Solutions borrows the maximum amount allowed from the bank, what percentage of assets would be financed (*a*) by debt and (*b*) by equity?
3. What are some factors Santana Rey should consider before borrowing the funds?

Beyond the Numbers

REPORTING IN ACTION

A1   A2

APPLE

BTN 14-1   Refer to **Apple**'s financial statements in Appendix A to answer the following.
1. Identify the items, if any, that make up Apple's long-term debt as reported on its balance sheet at September 26, 2015.
2. Assume that Apple has $100 million in convertible debentures that carry a 4.25% contract rate of interest. How much annual cash interest must be paid on those convertible debentures?
3. Assume that the convertible bonds discussed in part 2 are convertible into 20,000 shares of Apple's stock. If the carrying value of these bonds is $100 million, what is the entry recorded by Apple upon conversion?

Fast Forward

4. Access Apple's financial statements for the years ending after September 26, 2015, from its website (Apple.com) or the SEC's EDGAR database (SEC.gov). Has it issued additional long-term debt since the year-end September 26, 2015? If yes, identify the amount(s).

COMPARATIVE ANALYSIS

A3

APPLE
GOOGLE

BTN 14-2   Key figures for **Apple** and **Google** follow.

$ millions	Apple Current Year	Apple Prior Year	Google Current Year	Google Prior Year
Total assets	$290,479	$231,839	$147,461	$129,187
Total liabilities	171,124	120,292	27,130	25,327
Total equity	119,355	111,547	120,331	103,860

Required

1. Compute the debt-to-equity ratios for Apple and Google for both the current year and the prior year.
2. Use the ratios you computed in part 1 to determine which company's financing structure is least risky. Assume an industry average of 0.44 for debt-to-equity.

ETHICS CHALLENGE

C3   A1

BTN 14-3   Traverse County needs a new county government building that would cost $10 million. The politicians feel that voters will not approve a municipal bond issue to fund the building since it would increase taxes. They opt to have a state bank issue $10 million of tax-exempt securities to pay for the building construction. The county then will make yearly lease payments (of principal and interest) to repay the obligation. Unlike conventional municipal bonds, the lease payments are not binding obligations on the county and, therefore, require no voter approval.

Required

1. Do you think the actions of the politicians and the bankers in this situation are ethical?

2. In terms of risk, how do the tax-exempt securities used to pay for the building compare to a conventional municipal bond issued by Traverse County?

BTN 14-4 Your business associate mentions that she is considering investing in corporate bonds currently selling at a premium. She says that since the bonds are selling at a premium, they are highly valued and her investment will yield more than the going rate of return for the risk involved. Reply with a memorandum to confirm or correct your associate's interpretation of premium bonds.

COMMUNICATING IN PRACTICE

P3

BTN 14-5 Access the March 24, 2016, filing of the 10-K report of **Home Depot** for the year ended January 31, 2016, from **SEC.gov** (ticker: HD). Refer to Home Depot's balance sheet, including its note 6 (on debt).

TAKING IT TO THE NET

A2

Required

1. Identify Home Depot's long-term liabilities and the amounts for those liabilities from Home Depot's balance sheet at January 31, 2016.

2. Review Home Depot's note 6. The note reports that as of January 31, 2016, it had $2.964 billion of "5.875% Senior Notes; due December 16, 2036; interest payable semiannually on June 16 and December 16." These notes have a face value of $3.0 billion and were originally issued at $2.958 billion.

   a. Why would Home Depot issue $3.0 billion of its notes for only $2.958 billion?

   b. How much cash interest must Home Depot pay each June 16 and December 16 on these notes?

BTN 14-6ᴮ Break into teams and complete the following requirements related to *effective interest* amortization for a premium bond.

TEAMWORK IN ACTION

P5 P6

1. Each team member is to independently prepare a blank table with proper headings for amortization of a bond premium. When all have finished, compare tables and ensure that all are in agreement.

Parts 2 and 3 require use of these facts: On January 1, 2017, McElroy issues $100,000, 9%, five-year bonds at 104.1. The market rate at issuance is 8%. McElroy pays interest semiannually on June 30 and December 31.

2. In rotation, *each* team member must explain how to complete *one* line of the bond amortization table, including all computations for his or her line. (Round amounts to the nearest dollar.) All members are to fill in their tables during this process. You need not finish the table; stop after all members have explained a line.

3. In rotation, *each* team member is to identify a separate column of the table and indicate what the final number in that column will be and explain the reasoning.

4. Reach a team consensus as to what the total bond interest expense on this bond issue will be if the bond is not retired before maturity.

5. As a team, prepare a list of similarities and differences between the amortization table just prepared and the amortization table if the bond had been issued at a discount.

Hint: Rotate teams to report on parts 4 and 5. Consider requiring entries for issuance and interest payments.

BTN 14-7 Garrett Camp and Travis Kalanick are the founders of **Uber**. Assume that the company currently has $250,000 in equity and is considering a $100,000 expansion to meet increased demand. The $100,000 expansion would yield $16,000 in additional annual income before interest expense. Assume that the business currently earns $40,000 annual income before interest expense of $10,000, yielding a return on equity of 12% ($30,000/$250,000). To fund the expansion, the company is considering the issuance of a 10-year, $100,000 note with annual interest payments (the principal due at the end of 10 years).

ENTREPRENEURIAL DECISION

A1

Required

1. Using return on equity as the decision criterion, show computations to support or reject the expansion if interest on the $100,000 note is (*a*) 10%, (*b*) 15%, (*c*) 16%, (*d*) 17%, and (*e*) 20%.

2. What general rule do the results in part 1 illustrate?

HITTING THE ROAD

A1

BTN 14-8 Visit your city or county library. Ask the librarian to help you locate the most recent financial records of your city or county government. Examine those records.

Required

1. Determine the amount of long-term bonds and notes currently outstanding.
2. Read the supporting information to your municipality's financial statements and record
   a. The market interest rate(s) when the bonds and/or notes were issued.
   b. The date(s) when the bonds and/or notes will mature.
   c. Any rating(s) on the bonds and/or notes received from **Moody's Investors Service, Standard & Poor's Ratings Services, Fitch Ratings**, or another rating agency.

GLOBAL DECISION

A3

Samsung

APPLE

GOOGLE

BTN 14-9 **Samsung** (Samsung.com), **Apple**, and **Google** are competitors in the global marketplace. Selected results from these companies follow.

Key Figures (in millions, except ratio)	Samsung		Apple		Google	
	Current Year	Prior Year	Current Year	Prior Year	Current Year	Prior Year
Total assets	₩242,179,521	₩230,422,958	$290,479	$231,839	$147,461	$129,187
Total liabilities	63,119,716	62,334,770	171,124	120,292	27,130	25,327
Total equity	179,059,805	168,088,188	119,355	111,547	120,331	103,860
Debt-to-equity ratio	?	?	1.43	1.08	0.23	0.24

Required

1. Compute Samsung's debt-to-equity ratio for the current year and the prior year.
2. Use the data provided and the ratios computed in part 1 to determine which company's financing structure is least risky.

GLOBAL VIEW

This section discusses similarities and differences between U.S. GAAP and IFRS in accounting for long-term liabilities such as bonds and notes.

Accounting for Bonds and Notes   The definitions and characteristics of bonds and notes are broadly similar for both U.S. GAAP and IFRS. Although slight differences exist, accounting for bonds and notes under U.S. GAAP and IFRS is similar. Specifically, the accounting for issuances (including recording discounts and premiums), market pricing, and retirement of both bonds and notes follows the procedures in this chapter. **Nokia** describes its accounting for bonds, which follows the amortized cost approach explained in this chapter (and in Appendix 14B), as follows: Loans payable [bonds] are recognized initially at fair value, net of transaction costs incurred. In the subsequent periods, loans payable are measured at amortized cost using the effective interest method.

    Both U.S. GAAP and IFRS allow companies to account for bonds and notes using fair value (different from the amortized value described in this chapter). This method is referred to as the **fair value option.** This method is similar to that applied in measuring and accounting for debt and equity securities. *Fair value* is the amount a company would receive if it settled a liability (or sold an asset) in an orderly transaction as of the balance sheet date. Companies can use several sources of inputs to determine fair value, and those inputs fall into the following three classes (ranked in order of preference). The procedures for marking liabilities to fair value at each balance sheet date are in advanced courses.

Level 1: Observable quoted market prices in active markets for identical items.
Level 2: Observable inputs other than those in Level 1 such as prices from inactive markets or from similar, but not identical, items.
Level 3: Unobservable inputs reflecting a company's assumptions about value.

 IFRS

Global Interest   Unlike U.S. GAAP, IFRS requires that interest expense be computed using the effective interest method with *no* exceptions. ■

Accounting for Leases and Pensions   Both U.S. GAAP and IFRS require companies to distinguish between operating leases and capital leases; the latter are referred to as *finance leases* under IFRS. The accounting and reporting for leases are broadly similar for both U.S. GAAP and IFRS. The main difference is the criteria for identifying a lease as a capital lease are more general under IFRS. However, the basic approach applies.

For pensions, both U.S. GAAP and IFRS require companies to record costs of retirement benefits as employees work and earn them. The basic methods are similar in accounting and reporting for pensions.

 Global View Assignments

Discussion Question 15

Discussion Question 16

Quick Study 14-19

Quick Study 14-20

Exercise 14-20

BTN 14-9

15

chapter

Investments

Chapter Preview

BASICS OF INVESTMENTS

C1 Short- vs. long-term

Recording debt securities

Recording equity securities

TRADING SECURITIES

P1 Debt and equity

Recording

Reporting

Selling

NTK 15-1

HELD-TO-MATURITY SECURITIES

P2 Debt securities

Recording

Reporting

NTK 15-2

AVAILABLE-FOR-SALE SECURITIES

P3 Classification

Reporting

Selling

NTK 15-3

EQUITY METHOD SECURITIES

P4 Significant influence

C2 Controlling influence

A1 Return on assets components

NTK 15-4

Learning Objectives

CONCEPTUAL

C1 Distinguish between debt and equity securities and between short-term and long-term investments.

C2 Describe how to report equity securities with controlling influence.

C3 *Appendix 15A (online only)*—Explain foreign exchange rates and record transactions listed in a foreign currency.

ANALYTICAL

A1 Compute and analyze the components of return on total assets.

PROCEDURAL

P1 Account for trading securities.

P2 Account for held-to-maturity securities.

P3 Account for available-for-sale securities.

P4 Account for equity securities with significant influence.

© Godong/Getty Images

Giving Green

NEW YORK—"I received an Echoing Green Fellowship," explains Cheryl Dorsey. "We started a program that Echoing Green funded called the Family Van. It's a mobile health unit that travels through inner-city Boston providing medical services." Cheryl is now president of **Echoing Green** (**EchoingGreen.org**).

"We are angel investors in the social sector, providing seed capital and support to some of the world's best emerging social entrepreneurs," proclaims Cheryl. "Our mission is to unleash next-generation talent to solve the world's toughest social problems." To date, Echoing Green has invested in over 700 entrepreneurs in 70 countries.

Echoing Green invests in both nonprofit and for-profit organizations. According to Echoing Green's website, "in 2006, only 15 percent of our fellowship applications had elements of for-profit business models; in 2015, they had increased to 50 percent." Cheryl explains, "we've seen an explosion in the number of young people starting for-profit social enterprises."

This change brings unique accounting challenges for Echoing Green. "While nonprofit organizations are awarded grants as their fellowship stipend," explains the Echoing Green website, "we have provided for-profit companies with recoverable grants." These two types of investments must be tracked and accounted for differently.

A grant to a nonprofit is given with no expectation of repayment. After the grant is paid, it is permanently removed from Echoing Green's financial statements. However, a "recoverable grant" investment made to for-profit entrepreneurs has the potential for repayment. "As Fellows' businesses achieve certain financial thresholds, it triggers payback," explains the website, "if the business does not hit the thresholds, then they do not pay us back."

"Build a social capital market"

—Cheryl Dorsey

Given the potential for repayment and future benefit, Echoing Green must track such investments in their financial records. Such an investment could be recorded as a held-to-maturity investment or another type of short- or long-term investment.

Cheryl encourages people to start businesses even if they do not have revolutionary ideas or aims. She claims that solving a problem—rather than "starting something new"—is key. "Invest in the right person, who has an important idea for social change," asserts Cheryl, "that's a winning strategy."

Sources: *Echoing Green website,* January 2017; *ZDNet,* June 2012; *Change Makers,* March 2011

BASICS OF INVESTMENTS

C1

Distinguish between debt and equity securities and between short-term and long-term investments.

In prior chapters we discussed the reporting of both equity (common and preferred stock) and debt (bonds and notes) from the seller's (also called *issuer* or *investee*) standpoint. **This chapter explains the reporting of both equity and debt from the buyer's (also called *investor*) standpoint.** The first section of this chapter describes the purpose of investments, the distinction between short- and long-term investments, and the different classes of investments.

Purposes and Types of Investments

Companies make investments for at least three reasons. First, companies invest *extra cash* to earn more income. Second, some entities, such as mutual funds and pension funds, are set up to earn income from investments. Third, companies make investments for strategic reasons. Examples are investments in competitors, suppliers, and even customers. Exhibit 15.1 shows short-term (S-T) and long-term (L-T) investments as a percent of total assets for several companies.

EXHIBIT 15.1

Investments of Selected Companies

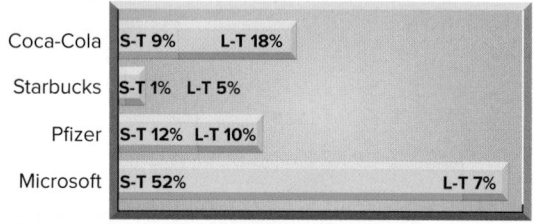

Percent of total assets

Short-Term Investments Cash equivalents are investments that are readily converted to known amounts of cash and mature within three months. Many investments, however, mature between 3 and 12 months. These investments are **short-term investments,** also called *temporary investments* and *marketable securities*. Specifically, short-term investments are securities that (1) management intends to convert to cash within one year or the operating cycle, whichever is longer, and (2) are readily convertible to cash. Short-term investments are current assets.

Long-Term Investments   **Long-term investments** are securities that are not readily convertible to cash or are not intended to be converted into cash in the short term. Long-term investments also include funds designated for a special purpose, such as investments in land or other assets not used in the company's operations. Long-term investments are noncurrent assets, often titled *Long-Term Investments*.

Investee's Balance Sheet	Investor's Balance Sheet
Liabilities	Assets
Notes Payable	
Bonds Payable	→ Investment in Debt Securities
Equity	
Common Stock	
Preferred Stock	→ Investment in Equity Securities

Debt Securities versus Equity Securities   Investments in securities include both debt and equity securities. *Debt securities* reflect a creditor relationship such as investments in notes, bonds, and certificates of deposit; they are issued by governments, companies, and individuals. *Equity securities* reflect an owner relationship such as shares of stock issued by companies.

© Scott Olson/Getty Images

Classification and Reporting

Accounting for investments in securities depends on three factors: (1) security type, either debt or equity; (2) the company's intent to hold the security either short term or long term; and (3) the company's (investor's) percentage of ownership in the other company's (investee's) equity securities. Exhibit 15.2 identifies five classes of securities using these three factors. We describe each of these five classes of securities and the reporting required under each.

Debt Securities: Accounting Basics

This section explains the accounting basics for **debt securities,** including that for acquisition, sale, and any interest.

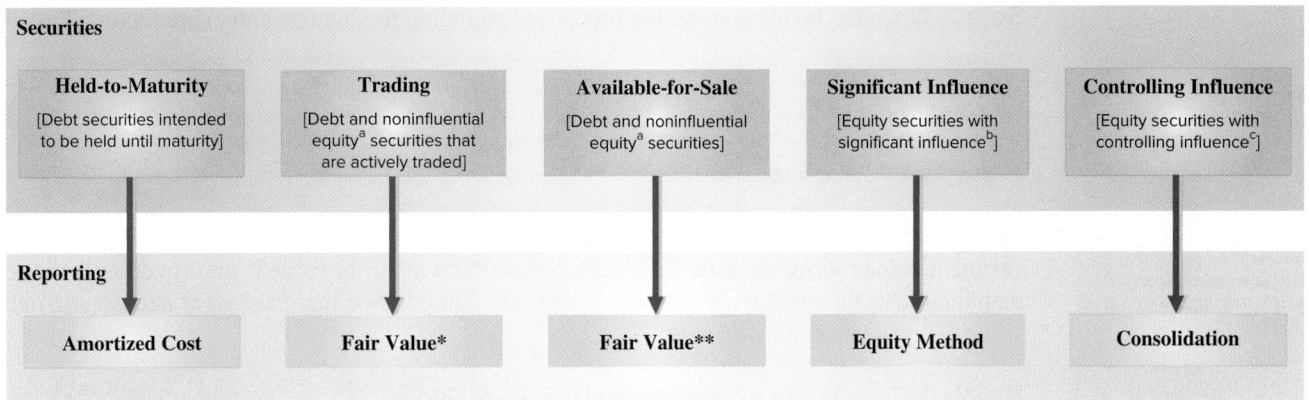

EXHIBIT 15.2

Investments in Securities

Acquisition   Debt securities are recorded at cost when purchased. To illustrate, assume that Music City paid $29,500 plus a $500 brokerage fee on June 30, 2016, to buy Dell's 7%, two-year bonds payable with a $30,000 par value. The bonds pay interest semiannually on January 1 and July 1. Music City intends to hold the bonds until they mature on June 30, 2018; consequently, they are classified as held-to-maturity (HTM). The entry to record this purchase follows. (If instead the maturity of the securities was short term, then they would be recorded in the Short-Term Investments—HTM account.)

2016			
June 30	Long-Term Investments—HTM (Dell)	30,000	
	Cash		30,000
	Purchased bonds to be held to maturity.		

Assets = Liabilities + Equity
+30,000
−30,000

Interest Earned   Interest revenue for investments in debt securities is recorded when earned. To illustrate, on December 31, 2016, at the end of its accounting period, Music City accrues interest receivable as follows.

Dec. 31	Interest Receivable	1,050	
	Interest Revenue		1,050
	Accrued interest earned ($30,000 × 7% × ⁶/₁₂).		

Assets = Liabilities + Equity
+1,050   +1,050

The $1,050 interest earned from June 30 to December 31 is computed as "Principal × Annual rate × Fraction of year."

Reporting   Music City's financial statements at December 31, 2016, report the interest revenue and the investment as shown in Exhibit 15.3.

On the income statement for year 2016:	
Interest revenue	**$ 1,050**
On the December 31, 2016, balance sheet:	
Long-term investments—Held-to-maturity securities (at amortized cost)	**$30,000**

EXHIBIT 15.3

Financial Statement Presentation of Debt Securities

On January 1, 2017, Music City records the cash receipt of semiannual interest (accrued above).

Jan. 1	Cash	1,050	
	Interest Receivable............................		1,050
	Received six months' interest on Dell bonds.		

Assets = Liabilities + Equity
+1,050
−1,050

Sale When the bonds mature, the proceeds (excluding the interest entry) are recorded as:

Assets = Liabilities + Equity
+30,000
−30,000

2018			
June 30	Cash	30,000	
	Long-Term Investments—HTM (Dell)		30,000
	Received cash from matured bonds.		

Example: What is cost per share? *Answer:* Cost per share is the total cost of acquisition, including broker fees, divided by number of shares acquired.

The cost of a debt security can be either higher or lower than its maturity value. When the investment is long term, the difference between cost and maturity value is amortized over the remaining life of the security. We assume for ease of computation that the cost of a long-term debt security equals its maturity value.

Equity Securities: Accounting Basics

This section explains the accounting basics for **equity securities**, including that for acquisition, dividends, and sale.

Acquisition Equity securities are recorded at cost when acquired, including commissions and brokerage fees paid. To illustrate, assume that Music City purchases 1,000 shares of Intex common stock at par value for $86,000 on October 10, 2016. It records this purchase of available-for-sale (AFS) securities as follows.

Assets = Liabilities + Equity
+86,000
−86,000

Oct. 10	Long-Term Investments—AFS (Intex)	86,000	
	Cash		86,000
	Purchased 1,000 shares of Intex.		

Dividend Earned Any cash dividends received are credited to Dividend Revenue and reported in the income statement. To illustrate, on November 2, Music City receives a $1,720 quarterly cash dividend on the Intex shares, which it records as:

Assets = Liabilities + Equity
+1,720   +1,720

Nov. 2	Cash	1,720	
	Dividend Revenue		1,720
	Received dividend of $1.72 per share.		

Sale When the securities are sold, sale proceeds are compared with the cost, and any gain or loss is recorded. To illustrate, on December 20, Music City sells 500 of the Intex shares for $45,000 cash and records this sale as:

Assets = Liabilities + Equity
+45,000   +2,000
−43,000

Dec. 20	Cash	45,000	
	Long-Term Investments—AFS (Intex)...............		43,000
	Gain on Sale of Long-Term Investments		2,000
	Sold 500 Intex shares ($86,000 × 500/1,000).		

TRADING SECURITIES

P1

Account for trading securities.

Trading securities are *debt and equity securities* that the company intends to actively trade for profit. Frequent purchases and sales are made to earn profits on short-term price changes. **Trading securities are *always* current assets.**

The entire portfolio of trading securities is reported at fair value; this requires a "fair value adjustment" from the cost of the portfolio. The term *portfolio* refers to a group of securities. **Any unrealized gain (or loss) from a change in the fair value of the portfolio of trading securities is reported on the income statement.**

Point: *Unrealized gain (or loss)* refers to a change in fair value that is not yet realized through actual sale.

Recording Fair Value To illustrate, TechCom's portfolio of trading securities had a total cost of $11,500 and a fair value of $13,000 on December 31, 2016, the first year it held trading securities. The difference between the $11,500 cost and the $13,000 fair value reflects a $1,500 gain. It is an **unrealized gain** because it is not yet confirmed by actual sales. The fair value adjustment for trading securities is recorded with an adjusting entry at the end of each period to equal the difference between the portfolio's cost and its fair value. TechCom records this gain as follows.

Point: Fair Value Adj. is a balance sheet account with either a debit balance (Fair value > Cost) or credit balance (Fair value < Cost).

Dec. 31	Fair Value Adjustment—Trading	1,500	
	Unrealized Gain—Income.		1,500
	Record an unrealized gain in fair values of trading securities.		

Assets = Liabilities + Equity
+1,500   +1,500

This adjustment can be computed using our three-step adjusting process.

Step 1:	Determine what unadjusted balance equals: Fair Value Adj.—Trading = $0.
Step 2:	Determine what adjusted balance should equal: Fair Value Adj.—Trading = $1,500 Dr.
	Explanation: $13,000 fair value > $11,500 cost; thus Fair Value Adj.—Trading requires a $1,500 debit to be at fair value.
Step 3:	Record the $1,500 adjusting entry to get from step 1 to step 2.
	Explanation: This means a $1,500 debit to Fair Value Adj.—Trading; and a $1,500 credit to Unrealized Gain.

Unadj. bal. is rarely $0; it is $0 here because it's the first year.

Reporting Fair Value

The **unrealized gain (or loss)** is reported in the Other Revenues and Gains (or Expenses and Losses) section on the income statement. Unrealized Gain (or Loss)—Income is a *temporary* account that is closed to Income Summary at the end of each period. Fair Value Adjustment—Trading is a *permanent* asset account that adjusts the reported value of the trading securities portfolio from its prior period fair value to the current period fair value. The total cost of the trading securities portfolio is maintained in one account, and the fair value adjustment is recorded in a separate account. For example, TechCom's investment in trading securities is reported in the current assets section of its balance sheet as follows.

Example: If TechCom's trading securities have a cost of $14,800 and a fair value of $16,100 at Dec. 31, 2017, its adjusting entry is

Unreal. Loss—Income . . .200
  FV Adj.—Trading. 200

This is computed as:

$1,500 Beg. Dr. bal. + $200 Cr. = $1,300 End. Dr. bal.

Current Assets		
Short-term investments—Trading (at cost)	$11,500	
Fair value adjustment—Trading.	1,500	
Short-term investments—Trading (at fair value)		$13,000
or simply		
Short-term investments—Trading (at fair value; cost is $11,500)		$13,000

ST Investments–Trading

1/1/2016	0	
Purch.	11,500	
12/31/2016	11,500	

Fair Value Adj.–Trading

1/1/2016	0	
Adj.	**1,500**	
12/31/2016	1,500	

Selling Trading Securities

When individual trading securities are sold, the difference between the net proceeds (sale price less fees) and the cost of the individual trading securities that are sold is recorded as a gain or a loss. **Any prior period fair value adjustment to the portfolio is *not* used to compute the gain or loss from the sale of individual trading securities.** This is because the balance in the Fair Value Adjustment account is for the entire portfolio, not individual securities. For example, if TechCom sold some of its trading securities that had cost $1,000 for $1,200 cash on January 9, 2017, it would record the following.

Jan. 9	Cash.	1,200	
	Short-Term Investments—Trading		1,000
	Gain on Sale of Short-Term Investments.		200
	Sold trading securities costing $1,000 for $1,200 cash.		

Assets = Liabilities + Equity
+1,200   +200
−1,000

A gain is reported in the Other Revenues and Gains section on the income statement and a loss is reported in Other Expenses and Losses. When the period-end fair value adjustment for the portfolio of trading securities is computed, it excludes the cost and fair value of any securities sold.

Point: This is a *realized* $200 gain—realized by actual sale.

NEED-TO-KNOW 15-1

Trading Securities

P1

Berkshire Co. purchases investments in trading securities at a cost of $130 on December 15, 2017. (This is its first and only purchase of such securities.) On December 28, Berkshire received a $15 cash dividend from the stock purchased on December 15. At December 31, 2017, the trading securities had a fair value of $140.

a. Prepare the December 15 acquisition entry for the trading securities' portfolio.

b. Prepare the December 28 receipt of cash dividends entry for the trading securities' portfolio.

c. Prepare the December 31 year-end adjusting entry for the trading securities' portfolio.

d. Explain how each account in entry *c* is reported in financial statements.

e. Prepare the January 3, 2018, entry when a portion of its trading securities (that had originally cost $33) is sold for $36.

Solution

a.

Dec. 15	Short-Term Investments—Trading....................	130	
	Cash		130
	Record purchase of trading securities.		

b.

Dec. 28	Cash	15	
	Dividend Revenue		15
	Record dividend received on trading securities.		

c.

Fair Value Adj.–Trading

Unadj. bal.	0	
Adj.	10	
12/31/2017	10	

Dec. 31	Fair Value Adjustment—Trading	10	
	Unrealized Gain—Income......................		10
	Record unrealized gain in fair value of trading securities.		

d. (i) The $10 debit in the Fair Value Adjustment—Trading account is an adjunct asset account in the balance sheet. It increases the $130 balance of the Short-Term Investment—Trading account to its $140 fair value.

(ii) The $10 credit for Unrealized Gain is reported in the Other Revenues and Gains section of the income statement.

e.

Jan. 3	Cash..	36	
	Gain on Sale of Short-Term Investments..........		3
	Short-Term Investments—Trading		33
	Record sale of trading securities.		

Do More: QS 15-3, QS 15-4, QS 15-5, E 15-2, E 15-3

HELD-TO-MATURITY SECURITIES

P2

Account for held-to-maturity securities.

Held-to-maturity (HTM) securities are *debt* securities a company intends and is able to hold until maturity. They are reported in current assets if their maturity dates are within one year or the operating cycle, whichever is longer. HTM securities are reported in long-term assets when the maturity dates extend beyond one year or the operating cycle, whichever is longer. The basics of accounting for HTM securities were described earlier in this chapter.

Recording Acquisition and Interest   All HTM securities are recorded at cost when purchased, and interest revenue is recorded when earned—see earlier entries.

Reporting HTM Securities at Cost   The portfolio of HTM securities is usually reported at (amortized) cost, which is explained in advanced courses. There is no fair value adjustment to the portfolio of HTM securities—neither to the short-term nor long-term portfolios.

Point: Only debt securities can be classified as *held-to-maturity;* equity securities have no maturity date.

■ **Decision** Maker

Money Manager   You expect interest rates to fall within a few weeks and remain at this lower rate. What is your strategy for holding investments in fixed-rate bonds and notes? ■   [*Answer:* When interest rates fall, the value of investments in fixed-rate bonds and notes increases because the bonds and notes held continue to pay the same (high) rate while the market demands a new lower rate. Your strategy before the rates fall is to continue holding or increase your investments in bonds and notes.]

Prepare journal entries to record the following transactions involving short-term investments.

a. On May 15, paid $100 cash to purchase Muni's 120-day short-term debt securities ($100 principal), dated May 15, that pay 6% interest (categorized as held-to-maturity securities).

b. On September 13, received a check from Muni in payment of the principal and 120 days' interest on the debt securities purchased in transaction *a*.

NEED-TO-KNOW **15-2**

Held-to-Maturity Securities

P2

Solution

a.

May 15	Short-Term Investments—HTM (Muni)	100	
	Cash		100
	Purchased 120-day, 6% debt securities.		

b.

Sep. 13	Cash	102	
	Short-Term Investments—HTM (Muni).		100
	Interest Revenue		2
	Collected $100 principal plus interest of $100 × 6% × 120/360.		

Do More: QS 15-6, E 15-4

AVAILABLE-FOR-SALE SECURITIES

Available-for-sale (AFS) securities are *debt and equity securities* not classified as trading or held-to-maturity securities. AFS securities are purchased to earn interest, dividends, or increases in fair value. If the intent is to sell AFS securities within the longer of one year or the operating cycle, they are classified as short-term investments. Otherwise, they are classified as long-term investments.

Companies adjust the cost of the portfolio of AFS securities to reflect changes in fair value. This is done with a fair value adjustment to its total portfolio cost. **Any unrealized gain or loss for the portfolio of AFS securities is *not* reported on the income statement. It is reported in the equity section of the balance sheet** (and is part of *comprehensive income,* explained later).

P3

Account for available-for-sale securities.

Recording Fair Value   To illustrate, assume that Music City had no prior investments in available-for-sale securities other than those purchased in the current period. Exhibit 15.4 shows both the cost and fair value of those investments on December 31, 2016, the end of its reporting period.

	Cost	Fair Value	Unrealized Gain (Loss)
Improv bonds.	$30,000	$29,050	$ (950)
Intex common stock, 500 shares	43,000	45,500	2,500
Total	$73,000	$74,550	**$1,550**

EXHIBIT 15.4

Cost and Fair Value of Available-for-Sale Securities

Example: If fair value in Exhibit 15.4 is $70,000 (instead of $74,550), what entry is made? *Answer:* Unreal. Loss—Equity . . . 3,000 FV Adj.—AFS.   3,000

The year-end adjusting entry to record the fair value of these investments follows.

Dec. 31	Fair Value Adjustment—Available-for-Sale (LT)	1,550	
	Unrealized Gain—Equity.		1,550
	Record adjustment to fair value of		
	available-for-sale securities.		

Assets = Liabilities + Equity
+1,550   +1,550

Point: Unrealized Loss—Equity and Unrealized Gain—Equity are *permanent* (balance sheet) equity accounts.

Reporting Fair Value

Exhibit 15.5 shows the December 31, 2016, balance sheet presentation—it assumes these investments are long term, but they can also be short term. It is also common to combine the cost of investments with the balance in the Fair Value Adjustment account and report the net as a single amount.

EXHIBIT 15.5

Balance Sheet Presentation of Available-for-Sale Securities

LT Investments–AFS	
1/1/2016	0
Purch.	73,000
12/31/2016	73,000

Fair Value Adj.–AFS (LT)	
1/1/2016	0
Adj.	**1,550**
12/31/2016	1,550

Assets

Long-term investments—Available-for-sale (at cost)	$73,000	
Fair value adjustment—Available-for-sale	1,550	
Long-term investments—Available-for-sale (at fair value)		$74,550

or simply

Long-term investments—Available-for-sale (at fair value; cost is $73,000)	$74,550

Equity

Add unrealized gain on available-for-sale securities*	$ 1,550

(Reconciled)

* Often included under the caption Accumulated Other Comprehensive Income.

Point: Income is increased by selling AFS securities with unrealized gains; income is reduced by selling those with unrealized losses.

Reporting for Next Year

Let's extend this illustration and assume that at the end of its next calendar year (December 31, 2017), Music City's portfolio of long-term AFS securities has an $81,000 cost and an $82,000 fair value. It records the adjustment to fair value as follows.

Assets = Liabilities + Equity
−550   −550

Dec. 31	Unrealized Gain—Equity	550	
	Fair Value Adjustment—Available-for-Sale (LT).		550
	Record adjustment to fair value of available-for-sale securities.		

The effects of the 2016 and 2017 securities transactions are reflected in the following T-accounts.

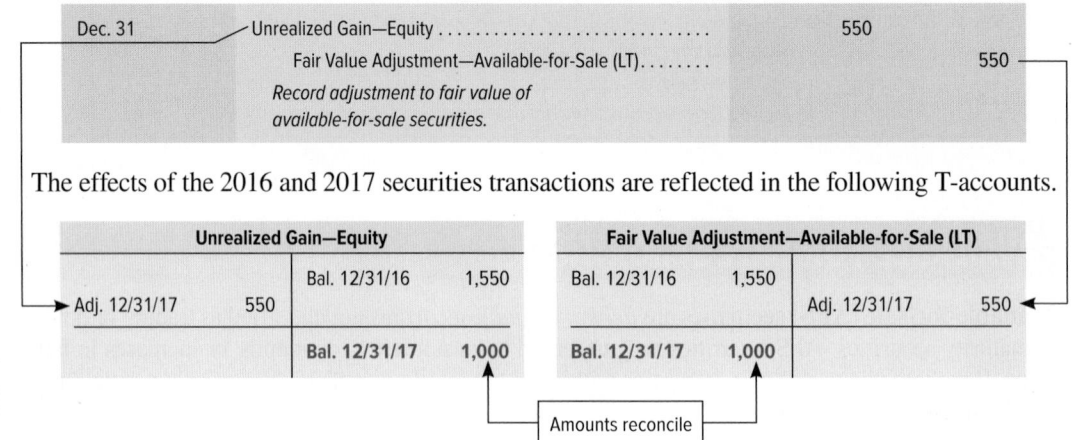

Unrealized Gain—Equity			
		Bal. 12/31/16	1,550
Adj. 12/31/17	550		
		Bal. 12/31/17	1,000

Fair Value Adjustment—Available-for-Sale (LT)			
Bal. 12/31/16	1,550		
		Adj. 12/31/17	550
Bal. 12/31/17	1,000		

Amounts reconcile

Example: If cost is $83,000 and fair value is $82,000 at Dec. 31, 2017, it records the following adjustment:
Unreal. Gain—Equity 1,550
Unreal. Loss—Equity 1,000
  FV Adj.—AFS   2,550

This adjustment can be computed using our three-step adjusting process.

Step 1:	Determine what unadjusted balance equals: Fair Value Adj.—AFS = $1,550 Dr.
Step 2:	Determine what adjusted balance should equal: Fair Value Adj.—AFS = $1,000 Dr.
	Explanation: $82,000 fair value > $81,000 cost; thus Fair Value Adj.—AFS must have a $1,000 Dr. bal. so securities are at fair value.
Step 3:	Record the $550 adjusting entry to get from step 1 to step 2.
	Explanation: This implies a $550 credit to Fair Value Adj.—AFS (and a $550 debit to Unrealized Gain).

Point: Fair Value Adj.—AFS is a permanent account, shown as a deduction or addition to the investment account.

Selling AFS Securities

Accounting for the sale of individual AFS securities is identical to accounting for the sale of trading securities. When individual AFS securities are sold, the difference between the cost of the individual securities sold and the net proceeds (sale price less fees) is recognized as a gain or loss.

Alert: Both U.S. GAAP (and IFRS) permit companies to use fair value in reporting financial assets (referred to as the fair value option). This option allows companies to report any financial asset at fair value and recognize value changes in income. This method was previously reserved only for trading securities, but is now an option for available-for-sale and held-to-maturity securities (and other "financial assets and liabilities" such as accounts and notes receivable, accounts and notes payable, and bonds). U.S. standards also set a three-level system to determine fair value:
—Level 1: Use quoted market values.
—Level 2: Use observable values from related assets or liabilities.
—Level 3: Use unobservable values from estimates or assumptions.
To date, a fairly small set of companies has chosen to broadly apply the fair value option—but we continue to monitor its use.

Gard Company completes the following selected transactions related to its short-term investments.

May 8   Purchased 300 shares of FedEx stock as a short-term investment in available-for-sale securities at $40 per share plus $975 in broker fees.
Sep. 2   Sold 100 shares of its investment in FedEx stock at $47 per share and held the remaining 200 shares; broker's commission was $225.
Oct. 2   Purchased 400 shares of Ajay stock for $60 per share plus $1,600 in commissions. The stock is held as a short-term investment in available-for-sale securities.

Required

1. Prepare journal entries for the above transactions.

2. Prepare a year-end adjusting journal entry as of December 31 if the fair values of the equity securities held by Gard are $48 per share for FedEx and $55 per share for Ajay. (This year is the first year Gard Company acquired short-term investments.)

Solution

1.

May 8	Short-Term Investments—AFS (FedEx)................	12,975	
	Cash		12,975
	Purchased FedEx stock; (300 sh. × $40) + $975.		
Sep. 2	Cash ([100 sh. × $47] − $225)......................	4,475	
	Gain on Sale of Short-Term Investment............		150
	Short-Term Investments—AFS (FedEx)		4,325
	Sold FedEx shares; original cost is ($12,975 × 100/300).		
Oct. 2	Short-Term Investments—AFS (Ajay)	25,600	
	Cash		25,600
	Purchased Ajay shares; (400 sh. × $60) + $1,600.		

2. Computation of unrealized gain or loss follows.

Short-Term Investments in Available-for-Sale Securities	Shares	Cost per Share	Total Cost	Fair Value per Share	Total Fair Value	Unrealized Gain (Loss)
FedEx.............................	200	$43.25	$ 8,650	$48.00	$ 9,600	
Ajay	400	64.00	25,600	55.00	22,000	
Totals.............................			$34,250		$31,600	$(2,650)

ST Investments–AFS

Jan. 1	0		
May 8	12,975		
		Sep. 2	4,325
Oct. 2	25,600		
Dec. 31 bal.	34,250		

Fair Value Adj.–AFS (ST)

Jan. 1	0		
		Dec. 31 adj.	2,650
		Dec. 31 bal.	2,650

The adjusting entry follows:

Dec. 31	Unrealized Loss—Equity	2,650	
	Fair Value Adjustment—Available-for-Sale (ST)		2,650
	Record an unrealized loss in fair values.		

Do More: QS 15-7, QS 15-8, QS 15-9, QS 15-10, E 15-5, E 15-7, E 15-8, E 15-10

EQUITY METHOD INVESTMENTS

Investment in Securities with Significant Influence

A long-term investment classified as **equity securities with significant influence** implies that the investor has significant influence over the investee. An investor that owns between 20% and 50% of a company's voting stock is usually presumed to have a significant influence over the investee. The **equity method** of accounting is used for long-term investments in equity securities with significant influence, which is explained in this section.

P4
Account for equity securities with significant influence.

Recording Acquisition   Long-term investments in equity securities with significant influence are recorded at cost when acquired. To illustrate, Micron Co. records the purchase of 3,000 shares (30%) of Star Co. common stock at a total cost of $70,650 on January 1, 2016, as follows.

Assets = Liabilities + Equity
+70,650
−70,650

Jan. 1	Long-Term Investments—Star.............................	70,650	
	Cash		70,650
	Record purchase of 3,000 Star shares.		

Recording Share of Earnings   The investee's (Star) earnings increase both its net assets and the claim of the investor (Micron) on the investee's net assets. When the investee reports its earnings, the investor records its share of those earnings in its investment account. To illustrate, assume that Star reports net income of $20,000 for 2016. Micron records its 30% share of those earnings as follows.

Assets = Liabilities + Equity
+6,000   +6,000

Dec. 31	Long-Term Investments—Star.............................	6,000	
	Earnings from Long-Term Investment		6,000
	Record 30% equity in investee earnings.		

The debit increases Micron's equity in Star. The credit reflects 30% of Star's net income. Earnings from Long-Term Investment is a *temporary* account (closed to Income Summary at each period-end) and is reported on the investor's (Micron's) income statement. If the investee incurs a net loss instead of a net income, the investor records its share of the loss and reduces (credits) its investment account.

Recording Share of Dividends   The receipt of cash dividends is not revenue under the equity method because the investor has already recorded its share of the investee's earnings. Instead, cash dividends received by an investor from an investee are viewed as a conversion of one asset to another; that is, dividends reduce the balance of the investment account. To illustrate, Star declares and pays $10,000 in cash dividends on its common stock. Micron records its 30% share of these dividends received on January 9, 2017, as:

Assets = Liabilities + Equity
+3,000
−3,000

Jan. 9	Cash...	3,000	
	Long-Term Investments—Star		3,000
	Record share of dividend paid by Star.		

Reporting Investments with Significant Influence   The book value of an investment under the equity method equals the cost of the investment plus the investor's share of earnings, minus its share of dividends, of the investee. Once Micron records these transactions, its Long-Term Investment account appears as in Exhibit 15.6.

EXHIBIT 15.6

Investment in Star Common Stock (ledger T-account)

Long-Term Investment—Star			
1/1/2016 Investment acquisition	70,650		
12/31/2016 Share of earnings	6,000		
12/31/2016 Balance	76,650		
		1/9/2017 Share of dividend	3,000
1/9/2017 Balance	73,650		

Micron's account balance on January 9, 2017, for its investment in Star is $73,650. This is the investment's cost *plus* Micron's equity in Star's earnings *less* Micron's equity in Star's cash dividends.

Selling Investments with Significant Influence   When an investment in equity securities is sold, the gain or loss is computed by comparing proceeds from the sale with the book value of the investment on the date of sale. If Micron sells its Star stock for $80,000 on January 10, 2017, it records the sale as:

Jan. 10	Cash..	80,000	
	Long-Term Investments—Star		73,650
	Gain on Sale of Investment		6,350
	Sold 3,000 shares of stock for $80,000.		

Assets = Liabilities + Equity
+80,000   +6,350
−73,650

Investment in Securities with Controlling Influence

A long-term investment classified as **equity securities with controlling influence** implies that the investor has a controlling influence over the investee. An investor who owns more than 50% of a company's voting stock has control over the investee. This investor can dominate all other shareholders in electing the corporation's board of directors and has control over the investee's management. Exhibit 15.7 summarizes the accounting for investments in equity securities based on an investor's ownership in the stock.

C2

Describe how to report equity securities with controlling influence.

Fair value method (under 20%)	Equity method (20% to 50%)	Equity method with consolidation (more than 50%)

0%   20%   50%   100%

Investor's percent ownership of a company's stock

EXHIBIT 15.7

Accounting for Equity Investments by Percent of Ownership

The *equity method with consolidation* is used to account for long-term investments in equity securities with controlling influence. The investor reports *consolidated financial statements* when owning such securities. The controlling investor is called the **parent,** and the investee is called the **subsidiary.** Many companies are parents with subsidiaries. Examples are (1) **Gap Inc.**, the parent of Gap, Old Navy, and Banana Republic; and (2) **Whole Foods Market, Inc.**, the parent of Allegro Coffee, Mrs. Gooch's Natural Food Markets, and other subsidiaries. When a company operates as a parent with subsidiaries, each entity maintains separate accounting records. The parent and each subsidiary are separate entities with all rights, duties, and responsibilities of individual companies.

© Tim Greenway/Portland Press Herald/Getty Images

Consolidated financial statements show the financial position, results of operations, and cash flows of all entities under the parent's control, including all subsidiaries. These statements are prepared as if the business were organized as one entity. The parent uses the equity method in its accounts, but the investment account is *not* reported on the parent's financial statements. Instead, the individual assets and liabilities of the parent and its subsidiaries are combined on one balance sheet. Their revenues and expenses also are combined on one income statement, and their cash flows are combined on one statement of cash flows. The procedures for preparing consolidated financial statements are in advanced courses.

Accounting Summary for Investments in Securities

Exhibit 15.8 summarizes accounting for investments in securities. Recall that investment securities are classified as either short term or long term depending on management's intent and ability to convert them in the future.

Comprehensive Income   **Comprehensive income** is defined as all changes in equity during a period except those from owners' investments and dividends. Specifically,

EXHIBIT 15.8

Accounting for Investments in Securities

Classification	Accounting
Short-Term Investment in Securities	
Held-to-maturity (debt) securities	**Cost** (without any discount or premium amortization)
Trading (debt and equity) securities	**Fair value** (with fair value adjustment to income)
Available-for-sale (debt and equity) securities.	**Fair value** (with fair value adjustment to equity)
Long-Term Investment in Securities	
Held-to-maturity (debt) securities	**Cost** (with any discount or premium amortization)
Available-for-sale (debt and equity) securities.	**Fair value** (with fair value adjustment to equity)
Equity securities with significant influence.	Equity method
Equity securities with controlling influence	Equity method (with consolidation)

comprehensive income is computed by adding or subtracting *other comprehensive income* to net income:

Net income	$ #
Other comprehensive income	#
Comprehensive income	$ #

Other comprehensive income includes **unrealized** gains and losses on available-for-sale securities, foreign currency translation adjustments, and certain other adjustments. (*Accumulated other comprehensive income* is defined as the cumulative impact of *other comprehensive income.*)

Comprehensive income is reported in financial statements in one of two ways (which reflects new FASB guidance):

1. On a separate *statement of comprehensive income* that immediately follows the income statement.
2. On the lower section of the income statement (as a single continuous *statement of income and comprehensive income*).

GOOGLE

Option 1 is the most common. Google, for example, reports a statement of comprehensive income following its income statement. Shown here is an abbreviated version of the Google statement:

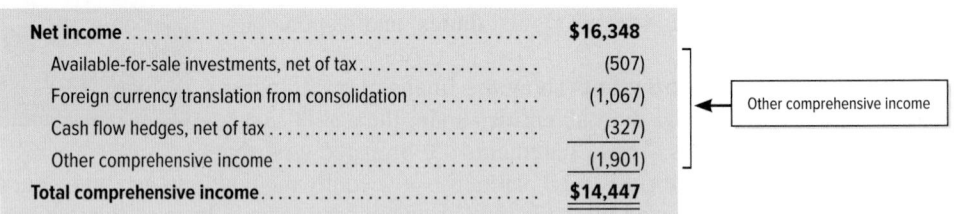

Option 2 adds the components of other comprehensive income to net income on the bottom of the income statement to compute a continuous statement of income and comprehensive income. There is no difference in the numbers; it is simply a matter of how those numbers are presented.

NEED-TO-KNOW 15-4

Equity Method Securities

P4

Prepare entries to record the following transactions of Garcia Company.

2016

Jan. 1   Purchased 400 shares of Lopez Co. common stock for $3,000 cash. Lopez has 1,000 shares of common stock outstanding, and its policies will be significantly influenced by Garcia.

Aug. 1   Lopez declared and paid a cash dividend of $2 per share.

Dec. 31   Lopez announced that net income for the year is $2,500.

2017

Aug. 1   Lopez declared and paid a cash dividend of $2.25 per share.
Dec. 31   Lopez announced that net income for the year is $2,750.

2018

Jan. 1   Garcia sold 100 shares of Lopez for $1,300 cash.

Solution

2016			
Jan. 1	Long-Term Investments—Lopez	3,000	
	Cash		3,000
	*Record purchase of investment.**		

* Garcia's investment is 40% of Lopez's stock (400/1,000). Garcia uses the equity method.

Aug. 1	Cash	800	
	Long-Term Investments—Lopez...................		800
	Record receipt of cash dividend (400 × $2).		
Dec. 31	Long-Term Investments—Lopez	1,000	
	Earnings from Long-Term Investment		1,000
	Record equity in investee earnings ($2,500 × 40%).		

2017			
Aug. 1	Cash	900	
	Long-Term Investments—Lopez...................		900
	Record receipt of cash dividend (400 × $2.25).		
Dec. 31	Long-Term Investments—Lopez	1,100	
	Earnings from Long-Term Investment		1,100
	Record equity in investee earnings ($2,750 × 40%).		

2018			
Jan. 1	Cash	1,300	
	Gain on Sale of Investments		450
	Long-Term Investments—Lopez*..................		850
	Record sale of investment.		

* Book value (Lopez stock) at 1/1/2018:

Original cost..	$3,000
Less 2016 dividends...	(800)
Plus share of 2016 earnings	1,000
Less 2017 dividends...	(900)
Plus share of 2017 earnings	1,100
Book value at date of sale......................................	$3,400
Book value of shares sold ($3,400 × [100/400])	$ 850

> **Do More:** QS 15-11, E 15-12

 ## SUSTAINABILITY AND ACCOUNTING

Echoing Green, and its president Cheryl Dorsey, invest in entrepreneurs who want to have a social impact. "These entrepreneurs are building what we think will be the sustainable business models of tomorrow," explains Cheryl. Before making investment decisions, Cheryl reviews the entrepreneur's proposed plan and accompanying financial statements and financial projections. "You're using your gut," insists Cheryl. "But you're also using hard [accounting] data."

Cheryl expects entrepreneurs applying for funding to have a good understanding of accounting and financial reports. "You can be a terrific leader with a great idea," cautions Cheryl, "but if you can't generate resources to drive toward the solutions it's for naught."

© Per-Anders Pettersson/Getty Images

In addition to expecting financial reports when budding entrepreneurs apply for funding, Cheryl wants to see timely financial reports after the business is running. According to the Echoing Green website, when "businesses achieve certain financial thresholds, it triggers payback."

Those financial thresholds are based on accounting results such as revenue and net income. Cheryl reviews the organization's financial data to determine if a payback of the grant has been triggered. "Echoing Green then recycles that money to fund future Fellows," explains Echoing Green's website.

Without an understanding of accounting investments, Cheryl would be unable to assess current projects or invest in future social entrepreneurs. The excitement of future Fellows depends on it.

 **Decision Analysis**    **Components of Return on Total Assets**

A1

Compute and analyze the components of return on total assets.

A company's **return on total assets** (or simply *return on assets*) is important in assessing financial performance. The return on total assets can be separated into two components, profit margin and total asset turnover, for additional analyses. Exhibit 15.9 shows how these two components determine return on total assets.

EXHIBIT 15.9

Components of Return on Total Assets

$$\text{Return on total assets} = \text{Profit margin} \times \text{Total asset turnover}$$

$$\frac{\text{Net income}}{\text{Average total assets}} = \frac{\text{Net income}}{\text{Net sales}} \times \frac{\text{Net sales}}{\text{Average total assets}}$$

Profit margin reflects the percent of net income in each dollar of net sales. Total asset turnover reflects a company's ability to produce net sales from total assets. All companies want a high return on total assets. By considering these two components, we can often discover strengths and weaknesses not revealed by return on total assets alone. This improves our ability to assess future performance and company strategy.

To illustrate, consider return on total assets and its components for **Gap Inc.** in Exhibit 15.10.

EXHIBIT 15.10

Gap's Components of Return on Total Assets

Fiscal Year	Return on Total Assets	=	Profit Margin	×	Total Asset Turnover
2016	12.1%	=	5.8%	×	2.08
2015	16.3	=	7.7	×	2.12
2014	16.7	=	7.9	×	2.11
2013*	15.0	=	7.3	×	2.06
2012	11.5	=	5.7	×	2.01

* 2013 sales and income data scaled by 52/53 due to the 53-week year.

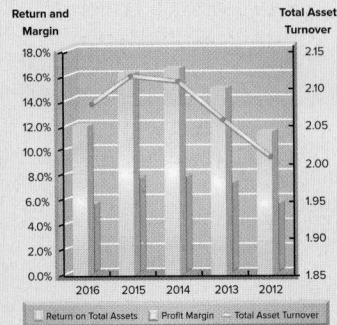

At least three findings emerge. First, Gap's return on total assets decreased (worsened) from 16.3% in 2015 to 12.1% in 2016. This ended a three-year period in which Gap's return on assets was at least 15%. Second, asset turnover decreased (worsened) from 2.12 in 2015 to 2.08 in 2016. Third, Gap's profit margin dipped in 2016 to 5.8%. Profit margin has not been this low since 2012. These components reveal the dual role of profit margin and asset turnover in determining return on total assets. They also reveal that the main driver of Gap's recent decline in return on total assets is profit margin.

Generally, if a company is to maintain or improve its return on total assets, it must meet any decline in either profit margin or total asset turnover with an increase in the other. If not, return on assets suffers. Companies consider these components in planning strategies. A component analysis can also reveal where a company is weak and where changes are needed, especially in a competitor analysis. If asset turnover is lower than the industry norm, for instance, a company should focus on raising asset turnover at least to the norm. The same applies to profit margin.

■ **Decision Maker**

Retailer   You are an entrepreneur and owner of a retail store. The store's recent annual performance reveals (industry norms in parentheses): return on total assets = 11% (11.2%); profit margin = 4.4% (3.5%); and total asset turnover = 2.5 (3.2). What does your analysis reveal? ■   [*Answer:* The store's 11% return on assets is similar to the 11.2% industry norm. However, disaggregation of return on assets reveals that the store's 4.4% profit margin is much higher than the 3.5% norm, but the 2.5 asset turnover is much lower than the 3.2 norm. The poor turnover suggests that this store is less efficient in using assets. It must focus on increasing sales or reducing assets. One might reduce prices to increase sales, provided such a strategy does not reduce return on assets. For instance, the store might reduce profit margin to 4% to increase sales. If total asset turnover increases to more than 2.75, overall return on assets is improved.]

The following transactions relate to Brown Company's long-term investments. Brown did not own any long-term investments prior to these transactions. Show (1) the necessary journal entries and (2) the relevant portions of each year's balance sheet and income statement that reflect these transactions for both years.

2016

Sep. 9   Purchased 1,000 shares of Packard, Inc., common stock for $80,000 cash. These shares represent 30% of Packard's outstanding shares.

Oct. 2   Purchased 2,000 shares of AT&T common stock for $60,000 cash as a long-term investment. These shares represent less than a 1% ownership in AT&T.

17   Purchased as a long-term investment 1,000 shares of Apple common stock for $40,000 cash. These shares are less than 1% of Apple's outstanding shares.

Nov. 1   Received $5,000 cash dividend from Packard.

30   Received $3,000 cash dividend from AT&T.

Dec. 15   Received $1,400 cash dividend from Apple.

31   Packard's net income for this year is $70,000.

31   Fair values for the investments in equity securities are Packard, $84,000; AT&T, $48,000; and Apple, $45,000.

31   For preparing financial statements, note the following post-closing account balances: Common Stock, $500,000, and Retained Earnings, $350,000.

2017

Jan. 1   Sold Packard, Inc., shares for $108,000 cash.

May 30   Received $3,100 cash dividend from AT&T.

June 15   Received $1,600 cash dividend from Apple.

Aug. 17   Sold the AT&T stock for $52,000 cash.

19   Purchased 2,000 shares of Coca-Cola common stock for $50,000 cash as a long-term investment. The stock represents less than a 5% ownership in Coca-Cola.

Dec. 15   Received $1,800 cash dividend from Apple.

31   Fair values of the investments in equity securities are Apple, $39,000, and Coca-Cola, $48,000.

31   For preparing financial statements, note the following post-closing account balances: Common Stock, $500,000, and Retained Earnings, $410,000.

PLANNING THE SOLUTION

● Account for the investment in Packard under the equity method.

● Account for the investments in AT&T, Apple, and Coca-Cola as long-term investments in available-for-sale securities.

● Prepare the information for the two years' balance sheets by including the relevant asset and equity accounts, and the two years' income statements by identifying the relevant revenues, earnings, gains, and losses.

SOLUTION

1. Journal entries for 2016.

Sep. 9	Long-Term Investments—Packard		80,000	
	Cash			80,000
	Acquired 1,000 shares, representing a 30% equity in Packard.			
Oct. 2	Long-Term Investments—AFS (AT&T)		60,000	
	Cash			60,000
	Acquired 2,000 shares as a long-term investment in available-for-sale securities.			
Oct. 17	Long-Term Investments—AFS (Apple)		40,000	
	Cash			40,000
	Acquired 1,000 shares as a long-term investment in available-for-sale securities.			
Nov. 1	Cash		5,000	
	Long-Term Investments—Packard.................			5,000
	Received dividend from Packard.			
Nov. 30	Cash		3,000	
	Dividend Revenue			3,000
	Received dividend from AT&T.			
Dec. 15	Cash		1,400	
	Dividend Revenue			1,400
	Received dividend from Apple.			
Dec. 31	Long-Term Investments—Packard		21,000	
	Earnings from Investment (Packard)			21,000
	Record 30% share of Packard's annual earnings of $70,000.			
Dec. 31	Unrealized Loss—Equity		7,000	
	Fair Value Adjustment—Available-for-Sale (LT)*			7,000
	Record change in fair value of long-term available-for-sale securities.			

LT Investments–AFS

12/31/2015	0
10/2/2016	60,000
10/17/2016	40,000
12/31/2016	100,000

Fair Value Adj.–AFS (LT)

12/31/2015	0	
Adj.	**7,000**	
12/31/2016	7,000	

* Fair value adjustment computations:

	Cost	Fair Value	Unrealized Gain (Loss)
AT&T	$ 60,000	$48,000	$(12,000)
Apple	40,000	45,000	5,000
Total	$100,000	$93,000	$ (7,000)

Required balance of the Fair Value Adjustment—Available-for-Sale (LT) account (credit)	$(7,000)
Existing balance..................	0
Necessary adjustment (credit)	$(7,000)

2. The December 31, 2016, selected balance sheet items follow.

Assets	
Long-term investments	
Available-for-sale securities (at fair value; cost is $100,000)	$ 93,000
Investment in equity securities.....................................	96,000
Total long-term investments	189,000
Stockholders' Equity	
Common stock..	500,000
Retained earnings	350,000
Unrealized loss—Equity..	(7,000)

The relevant income statement items for the year ended December 31, 2016, follow.

Dividend revenue...	$ 4,400
Earnings from investment	21,000

1. Journal entries for 2017.

Jan. 1	Cash	108,000	
	Long-Term Investments—Packard..............		96,000
	Gain on Sale of Long-Term Investments		12,000
	Sold 1,000 shares for cash.		
May 30	Cash	3,100	
	Dividend Revenue		3,100
	Received dividend from AT&T.		
June 15	Cash	1,600	
	Dividend Revenue		1,600
	Received dividend from Apple.		
Aug. 17	Cash	52,000	
	Loss on Sale of Long-Term Investments..............	8,000	
	Long-Term Investments—AFS (AT&T)............		60,000
	Sold 2,000 shares for cash.		
Aug. 19	Long-Term Investments—AFS (Coca-Cola)............	50,000	
	Cash		50,000
	Acquired 2,000 shares as a long-term investment in available-for-sale securities.		
Dec. 15	Cash	1,800	
	Dividend Revenue		1,800
	Received dividend from Apple.		
Dec. 31	Fair Value Adjustment—Available-for-Sale (LT)*	4,000	
	Unrealized Loss—Equity......................		4,000
	Record change in fair value of long-term available-for-sale securities.		

LT Investments–AFS

12/31/2016	100,000		
		8/17/2017	60,000
8/19/2017	50,000		
12/31/2017	90,000		

Fair Value Adj.–AFS (LT)

		12/31/2016	7,000
Adj.	**4,000**		
		12/31/2017	3,000

* Fair value adjustment computations:

	Cost	Fair Value	Unrealized Gain (Loss)
Apple	$40,000	$39,000	$(1,000)
Coca-Cola	50,000	48,000	(2,000)
Total	$90,000	$87,000	$(3,000)

Required balance of the Fair Value Adjustment—Available-for-Sale (LT) account (credit)	$(3,000)
Existing balance (credit)	(7,000)
Necessary adjustment (debit)........	$ 4,000

2. The December 31, 2017, balance sheet items follow.

Assets

Long-term investments	
Available-for-sale securities (at fair value; cost is $90,000)	$ 87,000

Stockholders' Equity

Common stock	500,000
Retained earnings	410,000
Unrealized loss—Equity..	(3,000)

The relevant income statement items for the year ended December 31, 2017, follow.

Dividend revenue	$ 6,500
Gain on sale of long-term investments	12,000
Loss on sale of long-term investments	(8,000)

Summary

C1 **Distinguish between debt and equity securities and between short-term and long-term investments.** *Debt securities* reflect a creditor relationship and include investments in notes, bonds, and certificates of deposit. *Equity securities* reflect an owner relationship and include shares of stock issued by other companies. Short-term investments in securities are current assets that meet two criteria: (1) They are expected to be converted into cash within one year or the current operating cycle of the business, whichever is longer, and (2) they are readily convertible to cash, or *marketable*. All other investments in securities are long term. Long-term investments also include assets not used in operations and those held for special purposes, such as land for expansion. Investments in securities are classified into one of five groups: (1) trading securities, which are always short term; (2) debt securities held-to-maturity; (3) debt and equity securities available-for-sale; (4) equity securities in which an investor has a significant influence over the investee; and (5) equity securities in which an investor has a controlling influence over the investee.

C2 **Describe how to report equity securities with controlling influence.** If an investor owns more than 50% of another company's voting stock and controls the investee, the investor's financial reports are prepared on a consolidated basis. These reports are prepared as if the company were organized as one entity.

A1 **Compute and analyze the components of return on total assets.** Return on total assets has two components: profit margin and total asset turnover. A decline in one component must be met with an increase in another if return on assets is to be maintained. Component analysis is helpful in assessing company performance compared to that of competitors and its own past.

P1 **Account for trading securities.** Investments are initially recorded at cost, and any dividend or interest from these investments is recorded in the income statement. Investments classified as trading securities are reported at fair value. Unrealized gains and losses on trading securities are reported in income. When investments are sold, the difference between the net proceeds from the sale and the cost of the securities is recognized as a gain or loss.

P2 **Account for held-to-maturity securities.** Debt securities held-to-maturity are reported at cost when purchased. Interest revenue is recorded as it accrues. The cost of long-term held-to-maturity securities is adjusted for the amortization of any difference between cost and maturity value.

P3 **Account for available-for-sale securities.** Debt and equity securities available-for-sale are recorded at cost when purchased. Available-for-sale securities are reported at their fair values on the balance sheet with unrealized gains or losses shown in the equity section. Gains and losses realized on the sale of these investments are reported in the income statement.

P4 **Account for equity securities with significant influence.** The equity method is used when an investor has a significant influence over an investee. This usually exists when an investor owns 20% or more of the investee's voting stock but not more than 50%. The equity method means an investor records its share of investee earnings with a debit to the investment account and a credit to a revenue account. Dividends received reduce the investment account balance.

Key Terms

Available-for-sale (AFS) securities	Equity securities with significant influence	Parent
Comprehensive income	Foreign exchange rate	Return on total assets
Consolidated financial statements	Held-to-maturity (HTM) securities	Short-term investments
Equity method	Long-term investments	Subsidiary
Equity securities with controlling influence	Multinational	Trading securities
	Other comprehensive income	Unrealized gain (loss)

Multiple Choice Quiz

1. A company purchased $30,000 of 5% bonds for investment purposes on May 1. The bonds pay interest on February 1 and August 1. The amount of interest revenue accrued at December 31 (the company's year-end) is
   - **a.** $1,500.
   - **b.** $1,375.
   - **c.** $1,000.
   - **d.** $625.
   - **e.** $300.

2. Earlier this period, Amadeus Co. purchased its only available-for-sale investment in the stock of Bach Co. for $83,000. The period-end fair value of this stock is $84,500. Amadeus records a
   - **a.** Credit to Unrealized Gain—Equity for $1,500.
   - **b.** Debit to Unrealized Loss—Equity for $1,500.
   - **c.** Debit to Investment Revenue for $1,500.
   - **d.** Credit to Fair Value Adjustment—Available-for-Sale for $3,500.
   - **e.** Credit to Cash for $1,500.

3. Mozart Co. owns 35% of Melody Inc. Melody pays $50,000 in cash dividends to its shareholders for the period. Mozart's entry to record the Melody dividend includes a

   a. Credit to Investment Revenue for $50,000.

   b. Credit to Long-Term Investments for $17,500.

   c. Credit to Cash for $17,500.

   d. Debit to Long-Term Investments for $17,500.

   e. Debit to Cash for $50,000.

4. A company has net income of $300,000, net sales of $2,500,000, and total assets of $2,000,000. Its return on total assets equals

   a. 6.7%.   **c.** 8.3%.   **e.** 15.0%.

   b. 12.0%.   **d.** 80.0%.

5. A company had net income of $80,000, net sales of $600,000, and total assets of $400,000. Its profit margin and total asset turnover are

	Profit Margin	Total Asset Turnover
a.	1.5%	13.3
b.	13.3%	1.5
c.	13.3%	0.7
d.	7.0%	13.3
e.	10.0%	26.7

ANSWERS TO MULTIPLE CHOICE QUIZ

1. d; $30,000 \times 5\% \times 5/12 = \$625$

2. a; Unrealized gain = $84,500 - $83,000 = $1,500

3. b; $50,000 \times 35\% = \$17,500$

4. e; $300,000/$2,000,000 = 15%

5. b; Profit margin = $80,000/$600,000 = 13.3%
      Total asset turnover = $600,000/$400,000 = 1.5

[i] Icon denotes assignments that involve decision making.

Discussion Questions

1. Under what two conditions should investments be classified as current assets?

2. [i] On a balance sheet, what valuation must be reported for short-term investments in trading securities?

3. If a short-term investment in available-for-sale securities costs $10,000 and is sold for $12,000, how should the difference between these two amounts be recorded?

4. Identify the three classes of noninfluential and two classes of influential investments in securities.

5. Under what conditions should investments be classified as current assets? As long-term assets?

6. For investments in available-for-sale securities, how are unrealized (holding) gains and losses reported?

7. If a company purchases its only long-term investments in available-for-sale debt securities this period and their fair value is below cost at the balance sheet date, what entry is required to recognize this unrealized loss?

8. On a balance sheet, what valuation must be reported for debt securities classified as available-for-sale?

9. Under what circumstances are long-term investments in debt securities reported at cost and adjusted for amortization of any difference between cost and maturity value?

10. In accounting for investments in equity securities, when should the equity method be used?

11. Under what circumstances does a company prepare consolidated financial statements?

12. [i] Refer to **Apple**'s statement of comprehensive income in Appendix A. What is the **APPLE** amount of *change in foreign currency translation, net of tax effects,* for the year ended September 26, 2015? Is this change an unrealized gain or an unrealized loss?

13. Refer to **Google**'s statement of comprehensive income in Appendix A. What **GOOGLE** was the amount of its 2015 *change in net unrealized gains (losses)* for its AFS investments?

14. [i] Refer to the income statement of **Samsung** in Appendix A. How can **Samsung** you tell that it uses the consolidated method of accounting?

---

connect

Which of the following statements *a* through *g* are true of long-term investments?

_____ **a.** They are held as an investment of cash available for current operations.

_____ **b.** They can include funds earmarked for a special purpose, such as bond sinking funds.

_____ **c.** They can include investments in trading securities.

_____ **d.** They can include debt securities held-to-maturity.

_____ **e.** They are always easily sold and therefore qualify as being marketable.

_____ **f.** They can include debt and equity securities available-for-sale.

_____ **g.** They can include bonds and stocks not intended to serve as a ready source of cash.

QUICK STUDY

QS 15-1

Distinguishing between short- and long-term investments

C1

QS 15-2

Distinguishing between debt and equity securities

C1

A solar company invests in the following securities. Identify those investments as either an investment in debt (D) securities or equity (E) securities.

_____ **a.** U.S. treasury bonds   _____ **e.** IBM corporate notes   _____ **i.** Chicago municipal bonds

_____ **b.** Google stock   _____ **f.** German government bonds   _____ **j.** Apple stock

_____ **c.** Certificate of deposit   _____ **g.** Amazon stock   _____ **k.** David Bowie bonds

_____ **d.** Apple bonds   _____ **h.** Costco corporate notes   _____ **l.** Facebook stock

---

QS 15-3

Short-term equity investments   **P1**

On April 18, Riley Co. made a short-term investment in 300 common shares of XLT Co. The purchase price is $42 per share and the broker's fee is $250. The intent is to actively manage these shares for profit. On May 30, Riley Co. receives $1 per share from XLT in dividends. Prepare the April 18 and May 30 journal entries to record these transactions.

QS 15-4

Recording trading securities

P1

Prepare Hertog Company's journal entries to record the following transactions for the current year.

May   7   Purchases 200 shares of Kraft stock as a short-term investment in trading securities at a cost of $50 per share plus $300 in broker fees.

June 6   Sells 200 shares of its investment in Kraft stock at $56 per share. The broker's commission on this sale is $150.

QS 15-5

Multiyear fair value adjustments to trading securities

P1

Kitty Company began operations in 2016 and maintains short-term investments in trading securities. The year-end cost and fair values for its portfolio of these investments follow. Prepare journal entries to record each December 31 year-end fair value adjustment for these securities.

Portfolio of Trading Securities	Cost	Fair Value
December 31, 2016........................	$37	$35
December 31, 2017........................	42	46
December 31, 2018........................	60	69
December 31, 2019........................	56	55

QS 15-6

Debt securities transactions   **P2**

On January 1, 2017, Garzon purchased 6% bonds (held-to-maturity) issued by PBS Utilities at a cost of $40,000, which is their par value. The bonds pay interest semiannually on July 1 and January 1. For 2017, prepare entries to record Garzon's July 1 receipt of interest and its December 31 year-end interest accrual.

QS 15-7

Available-for-sale securities

P3

Journ Co. purchased short-term investments in available-for-sale securities at a cost of $50,000 cash on November 25, 2017. At December 31, 2017, these securities had a fair value of $47,000. This is the first and only time the company has purchased such securities.

1. Prepare the November 25, 2017, entry to record the purchase of securities.

2. Prepare the December 31, 2017, year-end adjusting entry for the securities' portfolio.

3. For each account in the entry for part 2, explain how it is reported in financial statements.

4. Prepare the April 6, 2018, entry when Journ sells one-half of these securities for $26,000.

QS 15-8

Available-for-sale securities

P3

Hiker Company completes the following transactions during the current year. Prepare the May 9 and June 2 journal entries and the December 31 adjusting entry. This is the first and only time the company purchased such securities.

May   9   Purchases 200 shares of Higo stock as a short-term investment in available-for-sale securities at a cost of $25 per share plus $150 in broker fees.

June 2   Sells 100 shares of its investment in Higo stock at $28 per share. The broker's commission on this sale is $90.

Dec. 31   The closing market price (fair value) of the Higo stock is $23 per share.

QS 15-9

Recording fair value adjustment for securities

P3

During the current year, Reed Consulting Group acquired long-term available-for-sale securities at a $70,000 cost. At its December 31 year-end, these securities had a fair value of $58,000. This is the first and only time the company purchased such securities.

1. Prepare the necessary year-end adjusting entry related to these securities.

2. Explain how each account used in part 1 is reported in the financial statements.

On May 20, 2017, Montero Co. paid $1,000,000 to acquire 25,000 shares (10%) of ORD Corp. as a long-term available-for-sale investment. On August 5, 2018, Montero sold one-half of these shares for $625,000.

1. Should the fair value or cost method be used to account for this investment on the balance sheet?

2. Prepare entries to record both (*a*) the acquisition and (*b*) the sale of these shares.

QS 15-10
Recording long-term equity securities
P3

Montero Co. holds 100,000 common shares (40%) of ORD Corp. as a long-term investment. ORD Corp. paid a $100,000 dividend on November 1, 2017, and reported a net income of $700,000 for 2017. Prepare Montero's entries to record (1) the receipt of the dividend and (2) the December 31, 2017, year-end adjustment required for the investment account.

QS 15-11
Equity method transactions
P4

Complete the following descriptions by filling in the blanks using the terms or phrases *a* through *f*.

a. subsidiary **b.** parent **c.** interest revenue **d.** current **e.** fair value **f.** equity method

1. Equity securities that give an investor significant influence are accounted for using the ＿＿＿ ＿＿＿.

2. Available-for-sale debt securities are reported on the balance sheet at ＿＿＿ ＿＿＿.

3. Trading securities are classified as ＿＿＿ assets.

4. Accrual of interest on bonds held as long-term investments requires a credit to ＿＿＿ ＿＿＿.

5. The controlling investor (more than 50% ownership) is called the ＿＿＿, and the investee company is called the ＿＿＿.

QS 15-12
Describing investments in securities
C2

Complete the following descriptions by filling in the blanks using the terms or phrases *a* through *c*.

a. subsidiary **b.** parent **c.** controlling

1. The controlling investor is called the ＿＿＿, and the investee is called the ＿＿＿.

2. A long-term investment classified as equity securities with controlling influence implies that the investor can exert a ＿＿＿ influence over the investee.

QS 15-13
Equity securities with controlling influence
C2

The return on total assets is the focus of analysts, creditors, and other users of financial statements.

1. How is the return on total assets computed?

2. What does this important ratio reflect?

QS 15-14
Return on total assets
A1

Return on total assets can be separated into two important components.

1. Write the formula to separate the return on total assets into its two basic components.

2. Explain how these components of the return on total assets are helpful to financial statement users for business decisions.

QS 15-15
Component return on total assets A1

The **Carrefour Group** reported the following description of its trading securities.

> These are financial assets held by the Group in order to make a short-term profit on the sale. These assets are valued at their fair value with variations in value recognized in the income statement.

In a recent year, Carrefour's financial statements reported €7 million in unrealized gains and €26 million in unrealized losses, both included in the fair value of those financial assets held for trading. What amount of these unrealized gains and unrealized losses, if any, is reported in its income statement? Explain.

QS 15-16
International accounting for investments
P1

---

connect

Complete the following descriptions by filling in the blanks using the terms or phrases *a* through *g*.

a. not intended **b.** not readily **c.** cash **d.** operating cycle **e.** one year **f.** owner **g.** creditor

1. Debt securities reflect a ＿＿＿ relationship such as investments in notes, bonds, and certificates of deposit.

2. Equity securities reflect a(n) ＿＿＿ relationship such as shares of stock issued by companies.

3. Short-term investments are securities that (1) management intends to convert to cash within ＿＿＿ ＿＿＿ or the ＿＿＿ ＿＿＿, whichever is longer, and (2) are readily convertible to ＿＿＿.

4. Long-term investments in securities are defined as those securities that are ＿＿＿ ＿＿＿ convertible to cash or are ＿＿＿ ＿＿＿ to be converted into cash in the short term.

EXERCISES

Exercise 15-1
Debt and equity securities and short- and long-term investments
C1

Exercise 15-2

Accounting for short-term trading securities

P1

(c) Dr. Cash $7,450

Prepare journal entries to record the following transactions involving the short-term securities investments of Duke Co., all of which occurred during year 2017.

  a. On March 22, purchased 1,000 shares of RIP Company stock at $10 per share plus an $80 brokerage fee. These shares are categorized as trading securities.

  b. On September 1, received a $1.00 per share cash dividend on the RIP Company stock purchased in transaction *a*.

  c. On October 8, sold 500 shares of RIP Co. stock for $15 per share, less a $50 brokerage fee.

Exercise 15-3

Accounting for trading securities

P1

Check   (3) Gain, $2,000

Brooks Co. purchases various investments in trading securities at a cost of $66,000 on December 27, 2017. (This is its first and only purchase of such securities.) At December 31, 2017, these securities had a fair value of $72,000.

  1. Prepare the December 31, 2017, year-end adjusting entry for the trading securities' portfolio.

  2. Explain how each account in the entry of part 1 is reported in financial statements.

  3. Prepare the January 3, 2018, entry when Brooks sells a portion of its trading securities (that had originally cost $33,000) for $35,000.

Exercise 15-4

Accounting for short-term held-to-maturity securities

P2

Prepare journal entries to record the following transactions involving the short-term securities investments of Natura Co., all of which occurred during year 2017.

  a. On June 15, paid $1,000,000 cash to purchase Remedy's 90-day short-term debt securities ($1,000,000 principal), dated June 15, that pay 10% interest (categorized as held-to-maturity securities).

  b. On September 16, received a check from Remedy in payment of the principal and 90 days' interest on the debt securities purchased in transaction *a*.

Exercise 15-5

Accounting for short-term available-for-sale securities

P3

Prepare journal entries to record the following transactions involving the short-term securities investments of Krum Co., all of which occurred during year 2017.

  a. On August 1, paid $450,000 cash to purchase Houtte's 9% debt securities ($450,000 principal), dated July 30, 2017, and maturing January 30, 2018 (categorized as available-for-sale securities).

  b. On October 30, received a check from Houtte for 90 days' interest on the debt securities purchased in transaction *a*.

Exercise 15-6

Transactions in short-term and long-term investments

P1   P2   P3

Prepare journal entries to record the following transactions involving both the short-term and long-term investments of Cancun Corp., all of which occurred during calendar-year 2017. Use the account Short-Term Investments for any transactions that you determine are short term.

  a. On February 15, paid $160,000 cash to purchase American General's 90-day short-term notes at par, which are dated February 15 and pay 10% interest (classified as held-to-maturity).

  b. On March 22, bought 700 shares of Fran Industries common stock at $51 cash per share plus a $150 brokerage fee (classified as long-term available-for-sale securities).

  c. On May 15, received a check from American General in payment of the principal and 90 days' interest on the notes purchased in transaction *a*.

  d. On July 30, paid $100,000 cash to purchase MP3 Electronics's 8% notes at par, dated July 30, 2017, and maturing on January 30, 2018 (classified as trading securities).

  e. On September 1, received a $1.00 per share cash dividend on the Fran Industries common stock purchased in transaction *b*.

  f. On October 8, sold 350 shares of Fran Industries common stock for $64 cash per share, less a $125 brokerage fee.

  g. On October 30, received a check from MP3 Electronics for three months' interest on the notes purchased in transaction *d*.

Exercise 15-7

Adjusting available-for-sale securities to fair value

P3

Check   Unrealized loss, $9,100

On December 31, 2017, Reggit Company held the following short-term investments in its portfolio of available-for-sale securities. Reggit had no short-term investments in its prior accounting periods. Prepare the December 31, 2017, adjusting entry to report these investments at fair value.

Available-for-Sale Securities	Cost	Fair Value
Verrizano Corporation bonds payable	$89,600	$91,600
Preble Corporation notes payable	70,600	62,900
Lucerne Company common stock.................	86,500	83,100

On December 31, 2017, Lujack Co. held the following short-term available-for-sale securities. Lujack had no short-term investments prior to the current period. Prepare the December 31, 2017, year-end adjusting entry to record the fair value adjustment for these securities.

Exercise 15-8
Fair value adjustment to available-for-sale securities

P3

Available-for-Sale Securities	Cost	Fair Value
Nintendo Co. common stock	$44,450	$48,900
Atlantic bonds payable	49,000	47,000
Kellogg Co. notes payable	25,000	23,200
McDonald's Corp. common stock	46,300	44,800

Prescrip Co. began operations in 2016. The cost and fair values for its long-term investments portfolio in available-for-sale securities are shown below. Prepare the December 31, 2017, adjusting entry to reflect any necessary fair value adjustment for these investments.

Exercise 15-9
Fair value adjustment to available-for-sale securities

P3

Portfolio of Available-for-Sale Securities	Cost	Fair Value
December 31, 2016	$120,483	$118,556
December 31, 2017	60,120	90,271

Ticker Services began operations in 2015 and maintains long-term investments in available-for-sale securities. The year-end cost and fair values for its portfolio of these investments follow. Prepare journal entries to record each year-end fair value adjustment for these securities.

Exercise 15-10
Multiyear fair value adjustments to available-for-sale securities

P3

Portfolio of Available-for-Sale Securities	Cost	Fair Value
December 31, 2015	$372,000	$360,860
December 31, 2016	428,500	455,800
December 31, 2017	600,200	700,500
December 31, 2018	876,900	780,200

Information regarding Carperk Company's individual investments in securities during its calendar-year 2017, along with the December 31, 2017, fair values, follows.

a. Investment in Brava Company bonds: $420,500 cost; $457,000 fair value. Carperk intends to hold these bonds until they mature in 2022.

b. Investment in Baybridge common stock: 29,500 shares; $362,450 cost; $391,375 fair value. Carperk owns 32% of Baybridge's voting stock and has a significant influence over Baybridge.

c. Investment in Buffa common stock: 12,000 shares; $165,500 cost; $178,000 fair value. This investment amounts to 3% of Buffa's outstanding shares, and Carperk's goal with this investment is to earn dividends over the next few years.

d. Investment in Newton common stock: 3,500 shares; $90,300 cost; $88,625 fair value. Carperk's goal with this investment is to reap an increase in fair value of the stock over the next three to five years. Newton has 30,000 common shares outstanding.

e. Investment in Farmers common stock: 16,300 shares; $100,860 cost; $111,210 fair value. This stock is marketable and is held as an investment of cash available for operations.

Exercise 15-11
Classifying investments in securities; recording fair values

C1   P2   P3   P4

Required

1. Identify whether each investment *a* through *e* should be classified as a short-term or long-term investment. For each long-term investment, indicate in which of the long-term investment classifications it should be placed.

2. Prepare a journal entry dated December 31, 2017, to record the fair value adjustment of the long-term investments in available-for-sale securities. Carperk had no long-term investments prior to year 2017.

Check (2) Unrealized gain, $10,825

Exercise 15-12

Securities transactions; equity method

P4

Prepare journal entries to record the following transactions and events of Kodax Company.

2017

Jan.   2   Purchased 30,000 shares of Grecco Co. common stock for $408,000 cash plus a broker's fee of $3,000 cash. Grecco has 90,000 shares of common stock outstanding, and its policies will be significantly influenced by Kodax.
Sep.   1   Grecco declared and paid a cash dividend of $1.50 per share.
Dec. 31   Grecco announced that net income for the year is $486,900.

2018

June   1   Grecco declared and paid a cash dividend of $2.10 per share.
Dec. 31   Grecco announced that net income for the year is $702,750.
Dec. 31   Kodax sold 10,000 shares of Grecco for $320,000 cash.

Exercise 15-13

Equity securities with controlling influence

C2

Complete the following descriptions by filling in the blanks using the terms or phrases *a* through *d*.

a. trial balances   **b.** reconciliation   **c.** consolidation   **d.** financial statements

1. Consolidated _____ _____ show the financial position, results of operations, and cash flows of all entities under the parent's control, including all subsidiaries.

2. The equity method with _____ is used to account for long-term investments in equity securities with controlling influence.

Exercise 15-14

Return on total assets

A1

The following information is available from the financial statements of Regae Industries. Compute Regae's return on total assets for 2017 and 2018. (Round returns to one-tenth of a percent.) Comment on the company's efficiency in using its assets in 2017 and 2018.

	A	B	C	D
1		**2016**	**2017**	**2018**
2	Total assets, December 31	$210,000	$340,000	$770,000
3	Net income	30,200	38,400	60,300

Exercise 15-15

International accounting for investments

P3

The **Carrefour Group** reported the following description of its financial assets available-for-sale.

> Assets available for sale are . . . valued at fair value. Unrealized . . . gains or losses are recorded as shareholders' equity until they are sold.

In a recent year, Carrefour's financial statements reported €18 million in *net* unrealized losses (net of unrealized gains), which are included in the fair value of its available-for-sale securities reported on the balance sheet.

1. What amount of the €18 million net unrealized losses, if any, is reported in the income statement? Explain.

2. If the €18 million net unrealized losses are not reported in the income statement, in which statement are they reported, if any? Explain.

---

connect

PROBLEM SET A

Problem 15-1A

Recording transactions and fair value adjustments for trading securities

P1

Carlsville Company, which began operations in 2017, invests its idle cash in trading securities. The following transactions are from its short-term investments in trading securities.

2017

Jan. 20   Purchased 800 shares of Ford Motor Co. at $26 per share plus a $125 commission.
Feb.   9   Purchased 2,200 shares of Lucent at $44.25 per share plus a $578 commission.
Oct. 12   Purchased 750 shares of Z-Seven at $7.50 per share plus a $200 commission.
Dec. 31   Fair value of the short-term investments in trading securities is $130,000.

2018

Apr. 15   Sold 800 shares of Ford Motor Co. at $29 per share less a $285 commission.
July   5   Sold 750 shares of Z-Seven at $10.25 per share less a $102.50 commission.
July 22   Purchased 1,600 shares of Hunt Corp. at $30 per share plus a $444 commission.
Aug. 19   Purchased 1,800 shares of Donna Karan at $18.25 per share plus a $290 commission.
Dec. 31   Fair value of the short-term investments in trading securities is $160,000.

2019

Feb. 27   Purchased 3,400 shares of HCA at $34 per share plus a $420 commission.
Mar.   3   Sold 1,600 shares of Hunt at $25 per share less a $250 commission.
June 21   Sold 2,200 shares of Lucent at $42 per share less a $420 commission.
June 30   Purchased 1,200 shares of Black & Decker at $47.50 per share plus a $595 commission.
Nov.   1   Sold 1,800 shares of Donna Karan at $18.25 per share less a $309 commission.
Dec. 31   Fair value of the short-term investments in trading securities is $180,000.

Required

Prepare journal entries to record these short-term investment activities for the years shown. On December 31 of each year, prepare the adjusting entry to record any necessary fair value adjustment for the portfolio of trading securities.

Rose Company had no short-term investments prior to year 2017. It had the following transactions involving short-term investments in available-for-sale securities during 2017.

Apr. 16   Purchased 4,000 shares of Gem Co. stock at $24.25 per share plus a $180 brokerage fee.
May   1   Paid $100,000 to buy 3-month U.S. Treasury bills (debt securities): $100,000 principal amount, 6% interest, securities mature on July 31.
July   7   Purchased 2,000 shares of PepsiCo stock at $49.25 per share plus a $175 brokerage fee.
        20   Purchased 1,000 shares of Xerox stock at $16.75 per share plus a $205 brokerage fee.
Aug.   1   Received a check for principal and accrued interest on the U.S. Treasury bills that matured on July 31.
        15   Received an $0.85 per share cash dividend on the Gem Co. stock.
        28   Sold 2,000 shares of Gem Co. stock at $30 per share less a $225 brokerage fee.
Oct.   1   Received a $1.90 per share cash dividend on the PepsiCo shares.
Dec. 15   Received a $1.05 per share cash dividend on the remaining Gem Co. shares.
        31   Received a $1.30 per share cash dividend on the PepsiCo shares.

Problem 15-2A
Recording, adjusting, and reporting short-term available-for-sale securities

P3

Required

1. Prepare journal entries to record the preceding transactions and events.
2. Prepare a table to compare the year-end cost and fair values of Rose's short-term investments in available-for-sale securities. The year-end fair values per share are: Gem Co., $26.50; PepsiCo, $46.50; and Xerox, $13.75.
3. Prepare an adjusting entry, if necessary, to record the year-end fair value adjustment for the portfolio of short-term investments in available-for-sale securities.

Check   (2) Cost = $164,220

(3) Dr. Unrealized Loss—Equity, $4,470

Analysis Component

4. Explain the balance sheet presentation of the fair value adjustment for Rose's short-term investments.
5. How do these short-term investments affect Rose's (*a*) income statement for year 2017 and (*b*) the equity section of its balance sheet at year-end 2017?

Grass Security, which began operations in 2017, invests in long-term available-for-sale securities. Following is a series of transactions and events determining its long-term investment activity.

Problem 15-3A
Recording, adjusting, and reporting long-term available-for-sale securities

P3

2017

Jan. 20   Purchased 1,000 shares of Johnson & Johnson at $20.50 per share plus a $240 commission.
Feb.   9   Purchased 1,200 shares of Sony at $46.20 per share plus a $225 commission.
June 12   Purchased 1,500 shares of Mattel at $27.00 per share plus a $195 commission.
Dec. 31   Per share fair values for stocks in the portfolio are Johnson & Johnson, $21.50; Mattel, $30.90; and Sony, $38.

2018

Apr. 15   Sold 1,000 shares of Johnson & Johnson at $23.50 per share less a $525 commission.
July   5   Sold 1,500 shares of Mattel at $23.90 per share less a $235 commission.
July 22   Purchased 600 shares of Sara Lee at $22.50 per share plus a $480 commission.
Aug. 19   Purchased 900 shares of Eastman Kodak at $17 per share plus a $198 commission.
Dec. 31   Per share fair values for stocks in the portfolio are: Kodak, $19.25; Sara Lee, $20.00; and Sony, $35.00.

2019

Feb. 27 Purchased 2,400 shares of Microsoft at $67.00 per share plus a $525 commission.
June 21 Sold 1,200 shares of Sony at $48.00 per share less an $880 commission.
June 30 Purchased 1,400 shares of Black & Decker at $36.00 per share plus a $435 commission.
Aug. 3 Sold 600 shares of Sara Lee at $16.25 per share less a $435 commission.
Nov. 1 Sold 900 shares of Eastman Kodak at $22.75 per share less a $625 commission.
Dec. 31 Per share fair values for stocks in the portfolio are: Black & Decker, $39.00; and Microsoft, $69.00.

Required

1. Prepare journal entries to record these transactions and events and any year-end fair value adjustments to the portfolio of long-term available-for-sale securities.

Check (2*b*) Fair Value Adj. bal.: 12/31/17, $3,650 Cr.; 12/31/18, $13,818 Cr.

(3*b*) Unrealized Gain at 12/31/2019, $8,040

2. Prepare a table that summarizes the (*a*) total cost, (*b*) total fair value adjustment, and (*c*) total fair value of the portfolio of long-term available-for-sale securities at each year-end.

3. Prepare a table that summarizes (*a*) the realized gains and losses and (*b*) the unrealized gains or losses for the portfolio of long-term available-for-sale securities at each year-end.

Problem 15-4A
Accounting for long-term investments in securities; with and without significant influence

P3 P4

Selk Steel Co., which began operations on January 4, 2017, had the following subsequent transactions and events in its long-term investments.

2017

Jan.   5 Selk purchased 60,000 shares (20% of total) of Kildaire's common stock for $1,560,000.
Oct. 23 Kildaire declared and paid a cash dividend of $3.20 per share.
Dec. 31 Kildaire's net income for 2017 is $1,164,000, and the fair value of its stock at December 31 is $30.00 per share.

2018

Oct. 15 Kildaire declared and paid a cash dividend of $2.60 per share.
Dec. 31 Kildaire's net income for 2018 is $1,476,000, and the fair value of its stock at December 31 is $32.00 per share.

2019

Jan.   2 Selk sold all of its investment in Kildaire for $1,894,000 cash.

Part 1

Assume that Selk has a significant influence over Kildaire with its 20% share of stock.

Required

1. Prepare journal entries to record these transactions and events for Selk.

Check (2) Carrying value per share, $29

2. Compute the carrying (book) value per share of Selk's investment in Kildaire common stock as reflected in the investment account on January 1, 2019.

3. Compute the net increase or decrease in Selk's equity from January 5, 2017, through January 2, 2019, resulting from its investment in Kildaire.

Part 2

Assume that although Selk owns 20% of Kildaire's outstanding stock, circumstances indicate that it does *not* have a significant influence over the investee and that it is classified as an available-for-sale security investment.

Required

(1) 1/2/2019 Dr. Unrealized Gain—Equity, $360,000

1. Prepare journal entries to record the preceding transactions and events for Selk. Also prepare an entry dated January 2, 2019, to remove any balance related to the fair value adjustment.

2. Compute the cost per share of Selk's investment in Kildaire common stock as reflected in the investment account on January 1, 2019.

(3) Net increase, $682,000

3. Compute the net increase or decrease in Selk's equity from January 5, 2017, through January 2, 2019, resulting from its investment in Kildaire.

Stoll Co.'s long-term available-for-sale portfolio at December 31, 2016, consists of the following.

Problem 15-5A
Long-term investment
transactions; unrealized
and realized gains
and losses

C2 P3 P4

Available-for-Sale Securities	Cost	Fair Value
40,000 shares of Company A common stock...............	$535,300	$490,000
7,000 shares of Company B common stock................	159,380	154,000
17,500 shares of Company C common stock..............	662,750	640,938

Stoll enters into the following long-term investment transactions during year 2017.

Jan. 29 Sold 3,500 shares of Company B common stock for $79,188 less a brokerage fee of $1,500.

Apr. 17 Purchased 10,000 shares of Company W common stock for $197,500 plus a brokerage fee of $2,400. The shares represent a 30% ownership in Company W.

July 6 Purchased 4,500 shares of Company X common stock for $126,562 plus a brokerage fee of $1,750. The shares represent a 10% ownership in Company X.

Aug. 22 Purchased 50,000 shares of Company Y common stock for $375,000 plus a brokerage fee of $1,200. The shares represent a 51% ownership in Company Y.

Nov. 13 Purchased 8,500 shares of Company Z common stock for $267,900 plus a brokerage fee of $2,450. The shares represent a 5% ownership in Company Z.

Dec. 9 Sold 40,000 shares of Company A common stock for $515,000 less a brokerage fee of $4,100.

The fair values of its investments at December 31, 2017, are: B, $81,375; C, $610,312; W, $191,250; X, $118,125; Y, $531,250; and Z, $278,800.

Required

1. Determine the amount Stoll should report on its December 31, 2017, balance sheet for its long-term investments in available-for-sale securities.

2. Prepare any necessary December 31, 2017, adjusting entry to record the fair value adjustment for the long-term investments in available-for-sale securities.

Check (2) Cr. Unrealized
Loss—Equity, $20,002

3. What amount of gains or losses on transactions relating to long-term investments in available-for-sale securities should Stoll report on its December 31, 2017, income statement?

Harris Company, which began operations in 2017, invests its idle cash in trading securities. The following transactions relate to its short-term investments in its trading securities.

PROBLEM SET B

Problem 15-1B
Recording transactions and
fair value adjustments for
trading securities

P1

2017

Mar. 10 Purchased 2,400 shares of AOL at $59.15 per share plus a $1,545 commission.
May 7 Purchased 5,000 shares of MTV at $36.25 per share plus a $2,855 commission.
Sep. 1 Purchased 1,200 shares of UPS at $57.25 per share plus a $1,250 commission.
Dec. 31 Fair value of the short-term investments in trading securities is $380,000.

2018

Apr. 26 Sold 5,000 shares of MTV at $34.50 per share less a $2,050 commission.
Apr. 27 Sold 1,200 shares of UPS at $60.50 per share less a $1,788 commission.
June 2 Purchased 3,600 shares of SPW at $172 per share plus a $3,250 commission.
June 14 Purchased 900 shares of Wal-Mart at $50.25 per share plus a $1,082 commission.
Dec. 31 Fair value of the short-term investments in trading securities is $828,000.

Check Dec. 31, 2018,
Dr. Fair Value Adjustment—
Trading, $33,298

2019

Jan. 28 Purchased 2,000 shares of PepsiCo at $43 per share plus a $2,890 commission.
Jan. 31 Sold 3,600 shares of SPW at $168 per share less a $2,040 commission.
Aug. 22 Sold 2,400 shares of AOL at $56.75 per share less a $2,480 commission.
Sep. 3 Purchased 1,500 shares of Vodaphone at $40.50 per share plus a $1,680 commission.
Oct. 9 Sold 900 shares of Wal-Mart at $53.75 per share less a $1,220 commission.
Dec. 31 Fair value of the short-term investments in trading securities is $140,000.

Required

Prepare journal entries to record these short-term investment activities for the years shown. On December 31 of each year, prepare the adjusting entry to record any necessary fair value adjustment for the portfolio of trading securities.

Problem 15-2B

Recording, adjusting, and reporting short-term available-for-sale securities

P3

Slip Systems had no short-term investments prior to 2017. It had the following transactions involving short-term investments in available-for-sale securities during 2017.

Feb.	6	Purchased 3,400 shares of Nokia stock at $41.25 per share plus a $3,000 brokerage fee.
	15	Paid $20,000 to buy six-month U.S. Treasury bills (debt securities): $20,000 principal amount, 6% interest, securities dated February 15.
Apr.	7	Purchased 1,200 shares of Dell Co. stock at $39.50 per share plus a $1,255 brokerage fee.
June	2	Purchased 2,500 shares of Merck stock at $72.50 per share plus a $2,890 brokerage fee.
	30	Received a $0.19 per share cash dividend on the Nokia shares.
Aug.	11	Sold 850 shares of Nokia stock at $46 per share less a $1,050 brokerage fee.
	16	Received a check for principal and accrued interest on the U.S. Treasury bills purchased February 15.
	24	Received a $0.10 per share cash dividend on the Dell shares.
Nov.	9	Received a $0.20 per share cash dividend on the remaining Nokia shares.
Dec.	18	Received a $0.15 per share cash dividend on the Dell shares.

Required

1. Prepare journal entries to record the preceding transactions and events.

Check (2) Cost = $340,232

2. Prepare a table to compare the year-end cost and fair values of the short-term investments in available-for-sale securities. The year-end fair values per share are: Nokia, $40.25; Dell, $40.50; and Merck, $59.00.

(3) Dr. Unrealized Loss—Equity, $41,494

3. Prepare an adjusting entry, if necessary, to record the year-end fair value adjustment for the portfolio of short-term investments in available-for-sale securities.

Analysis Component

4. Explain the balance sheet presentation of the fair value adjustment to Slip's short-term investments.

5. How do these short-term investments affect (*a*) its income statement for year 2017 and (*b*) the equity section of its balance sheet at the 2017 year-end?

Problem 15-3B

Recording, adjusting, and reporting long-term available-for-sale securities

P3

Paris Enterprises, which began operations in 2017, invests in long-term available-for-sale securities. Following is a series of transactions and events involving its long-term investment activity.

2017

Mar.	10	Purchased 1,200 shares of Apple at $25.50 per share plus $800 commission.
Apr.	7	Purchased 2,500 shares of Ford at $22.50 per share plus $1,033 commission.
Sep.	1	Purchased 600 shares of Polaroid at $47.00 per share plus $890 commission.
Dec.	31	Per share fair values for stocks in the portfolio are: Apple, $27.50; Ford, $21.00; and Polaroid, $49.00.

2018

Apr.	26	Sold 2,500 shares of Ford at $20.50 per share less a $1,207 commission.
June	2	Purchased 1,800 shares of Duracell at $19.25 per share plus a $1,050 commission.
June	14	Purchased 1,200 shares of Sears at $21 per share plus a $280 commission.
Nov.	27	Sold 600 shares of Polaroid at $51 per share less an $845 commission.
Dec.	31	Per share fair values for stocks in the portfolio are: Apple, $29.00; Duracell, $18.00; and Sears, $23.00.

2019

Jan.	28	Purchased 1,000 shares of Coca-Cola Co. at $40 per share plus a $1,480 commission.
Aug.	22	Sold 1,200 shares of Apple at $21.50 per share less a $1,850 commission.
Sep.	3	Purchased 3,000 shares of Motorola at $28 per share plus a $780 commission.
Oct.	9	Sold 1,200 shares of Sears at $24.00 per share less a $599 commission.
Oct.	31	Sold 1,800 shares of Duracell at $15.00 per share less an $898 commission.
Dec.	31	Per share fair values for stocks in the portfolio are: Coca-Cola, $48.00; and Motorola, $24.00.

Required

1. Prepare journal entries to record these transactions and events and any year-end fair value adjustments to the portfolio of long-term available-for-sale securities.

Check (2*b*) Fair Value Adj. bal.: 12/31/17, $2,873 Cr.; 12/31/18, $2,220 Dr.

2. Prepare a table that summarizes the (*a*) total cost, (*b*) total fair value adjustment, and (*c*) total fair value for the portfolio of long-term available-for-sale securities at each year-end.

(3*b*) Unrealized Loss at 12/31/2019, $6,260

3. Prepare a table that summarizes (*a*) the realized gains and losses and (*b*) the unrealized gains or losses for the portfolio of long-term available-for-sale securities at each year-end.

Brinkley Company, which began operations on January 3, 2017, had the following transactions and events in its long-term investments.

2017

Jan.   5   Brinkley purchased 20,000 shares (25% of total) of Bloch's common stock for $200,500.
Aug.   1   Bloch declared and paid a cash dividend of $1.05 per share.
Dec. 31   Bloch's net income for 2017 is $82,000, and the fair value of its stock is $11.90 per share.

2018

Aug.   1   Bloch declared and paid a cash dividend of $1.35 per share.
Dec. 31   Bloch's net income for 2018 is $78,000, and the fair value of its stock is $13.65 per share.

2019

Jan.   8   Brinkley sold all of its investment in Bloch for $375,000 cash.

Part 1

Assume that Brinkley has a significant influence over Bloch with its 25% share.

Required

1. Prepare journal entries to record these transactions and events for Brinkley.
2. Compute the carrying (book) value per share of Brinkley's investment in Bloch common stock as reflected in the investment account on January 7, 2019.
3. Compute the net increase or decrease in Brinkley's equity from January 5, 2017, through January 8, 2019, resulting from its investment in Bloch.

Part 2

Assume that although Brinkley owns 25% of Bloch's outstanding stock, circumstances indicate that it does *not* have a significant influence over the investee and that it is classified as an available-for-sale security investment.

Required

1. Prepare journal entries to record these transactions and events for Brinkley. Also prepare an entry dated January 8, 2019, to remove any balance related to the fair value adjustment.
2. Compute the cost per share of Brinkley's investment in Bloch common stock as reflected in the investment account on January 7, 2019.
3. Compute the net increase or decrease in Brinkley's equity from January 5, 2017, through January 8, 2019, resulting from its investment in Bloch.

Problem 15-4B
Accounting for long-term investments in securities; with and without significant influence
P3   P4

Check   (2) Carrying value per share, $9.63

(1) 1/8/2019 Dr. Unrealized Gain—Equity, $72,500

(3) Net increase, $222,500

Troyer's long-term available-for-sale portfolio at December 31, 2016, consists of the following.

Available-for-Sale Securities	Cost	Fair Value
27,500 shares of Company R common stock..............	$559,125	$599,063
8,500 shares of Company S common stock...............	308,380	293,250
11,000 shares of Company T common stock..............	147,295	151,800

Troyer enters into the following long-term investment transactions during year 2017.

Jan. 13   Sold 2,125 shares of Company S stock for $72,250 less a brokerage fee of $1,195.
Mar. 24   Purchased 15,500 shares of Company U common stock for $282,875 plus a brokerage fee of $1,980. The shares represent a 62% ownership interest in Company U.
Apr.   5   Purchased 42,500 shares of Company V common stock for $133,875 plus a brokerage fee of $1,125. The shares represent a 10% ownership in Company V.
Sep.   2   Sold 11,000 shares of Company T common stock for $156,750 less a brokerage fee of $2,700.
Sep. 27   Purchased 2,500 shares of Company W common stock for $50,500 plus a brokerage fee of $1,050. The shares represent a 25% ownership interest in Company W.
Oct. 30   Purchased 5,000 shares of Company X common stock for $48,750 plus a brokerage fee of $1,170. The shares represent a 13% ownership interest in Company X.

The fair values of its investments at December 31, 2017, are: R, $568,125; S, $210,375; U, $272,800; V, $134,938; W, $54,689; and X, $45,625.

Problem 15-5B
Long-term investment transactions; unrealized and realized gains and losses
C2   P3   P4

Required

1. Determine the amount Troyer should report on its December 31, 2017, balance sheet for its long-term investments in available-for-sale securities.

2. Prepare any necessary December 31, 2017, adjusting entry to record the fair value adjustment of the long-term investments in available-for-sale securities.

3. What amount of gains or losses on transactions relating to long-term investments in available-for-sale securities should Troyer report on its December 31, 2017, income statement?

SERIAL PROBLEM
Business Solutions

P1

© Alexander Image/Shutterstock RF

(This serial problem began in Chapter 1 and continues through most of the book. If previous chapter segments were not completed, the serial problem can begin at this point.)

SP 15   While reviewing the March 31, 2018, balance sheet of **Business Solutions**, Santana Rey notes that the business has built a large cash balance of $68,057. Its most recent bank money market statement shows that the funds are earning an annualized return of 0.75%. S. Rey decides to make several investments with the desire to earn a higher return on the idle cash balance. Accordingly, in April 2018, Business Solutions makes the following investments in trading securities:

Apr. 16   Purchases 400 shares of Johnson & Johnson stock at $50 per share plus a $300 commission.
Apr. 30   Purchases 200 shares of Starbucks Corporation at $22 per share plus a $250 commission.

On June 30, 2018, the per share market price (fair value) of the Johnson & Johnson shares is $55 and the Starbucks shares is $19.

Required

1. Prepare journal entries to record the April purchases of trading securities by Business Solutions.

2. On June 30, 2018, prepare the adjusting entry to record any necessary fair value adjustment to its portfolio of trading securities.

**GENERAL
LEDGER
PROBLEM**

**Available only
in Connect**

The following **General Ledger** assignments focus on the account for investments in available-for-sale securities and equity method investments.

GL 15-1   General Ledger assignment 15-1 is adapted from Problem 15-2A. Prepare journal entries related to short-term investments in available-for-sale securities, including the adjustment to fair value, if necessary.

GL 15-2   General Ledger assignment 15-2 is adapted from Problem 15-5A. Prepare journal entries related to long-term investments transactions and the related realized and unrealized gains.

Beyond the Numbers

**REPORTING IN
ACTION**

A1

APPLE

BTN 15-1   Refer to **Apple**'s financial statements in Appendix A to answer the following.

1. Are its financial statements consolidated? How can you tell?

2. What is the amount of *other comprehensive income (loss)* for the year ended September 26, 2015?

3. Does it have any foreign operations? How can you tell?

4. Compute its return on total assets for the year ended September 26, 2015.

Fast Forward

5. Access Apple's annual report for a fiscal year ending after September 26, 2015, from either its website (Apple.com) or the SEC's database (SEC.gov). Recompute its return on total assets for the years subsequent to September 26, 2015.

BTN 15-2 Key figures for Apple and Google follow.

$ millions	Apple			Google		
	Current Year	1 Year Prior	2 Years Prior	Current Year	1 Year Prior	2 Years Prior
Net income	$ 53,394	$ 39,510	$ 37,037	$ 16,348	$ 14,136	$ 12,733
Net sales	233,715	182,795	170,910	74,989	66,001	55,519
Total assets	290,479	231,839	207,000	147,461	129,187	109,050

Required

1. Compute return on total assets for Apple and Google for the two most recent years.

2. Separate the return on total assets computed in part 1 into its components for both companies and both years according to the formula in Exhibit 15.9.

3. Which company has the highest total return on assets? The highest profit margin? The highest total asset turnover? What does this comparative analysis reveal? (Assume an industry average of 10.0% for return on assets.)

BTN 15-3 Kasey Hartman is the controller for Wholemart Company, which has numerous long-term investments in debt securities. Wholemart's investments are mainly in five-year bonds. Hartman is preparing its year-end financial statements. In accounting for long-term debt securities, she knows that each long-term investment must be designated as a held-to-maturity or an available-for-sale security. Interest rates rose sharply this past year, causing the portfolio's fair value to substantially decline. The company does not intend to hold the bonds for the entire five years. Hartman also earns a bonus each year, which is computed as a percent of net income.

Required

1. Will Hartman's bonus depend in any way on the classification of the debt securities? Explain.

2. What criteria must Hartman use to classify the securities as held-to-maturity or available-for-sale?

3. Is there likely any company oversight of Hartman's classification of the securities? Explain.

BTN 15-4 Assume that you are Jolee Company's accountant. Company owner Mary Jolee has reviewed the 2017 financial statements you prepared and questions the $6,000 loss reported on the sale of its investment in Kemper Co. common stock. Jolee acquired 50,000 shares of Kemper's common stock on December 31, 2015, at a cost of $500,000. This stock purchase represented a 40% interest in Kemper. The 2016 income statement reported that earnings from all investments were $126,000. On January 3, 2017, Jolee Company sold the Kemper stock for $575,000. Kemper did not pay any dividends during 2016 but reported a net income of $202,500 for that year. Mary Jolee believes that because the Kemper stock purchase price was $500,000 and was sold for $575,000, the 2017 income statement should report a $75,000 gain on the sale.

Required

Draft a half-page memorandum to Mary Jolee explaining why the $6,000 loss on sale of Kemper stock is correctly reported.

BTN 15-5 Access the July 31, 2015, 10-K filing (for year-end June 30, 2015) of Microsoft (ticker: MSFT) at SEC.gov. Review its note 4, "Investments."

Required

1. How does the "cost-basis" total amount for its investments as of June 30, 2015, compare to the prior year-end amount?

2. Identify at least eight types of short-term investments held by Microsoft as of June 30, 2015.

3. What were Microsoft's unrealized gains and its unrealized losses from its investments for 2015?

4. Was the cost or fair value ("recorded basis") of the investments higher as of June 30, 2015?

TEAMWORK IN ACTION

C1 C2 P1 P2 P3 P4

BTN 15-6 Each team member is to become an expert on a specific classification of long-term investments. This expertise will be used to facilitate other teammates' understanding of the concepts and procedures relevant to the classification chosen.

1. Each team member must select an area for expertise by choosing one of the following classifications of long-term investments.

   a. Held-to-maturity debt securities
   b. Available-for-sale debt and equity securities
   c. Equity securities with significant influence
   d. Equity securities with controlling influence

2. Learning teams are to disburse and expert teams are to be formed. Expert teams are made up of those who select the same area of expertise. The instructor will identify the location where each expert team will meet.

3. Expert teams will collaborate to develop a presentation based on the following requirements. Students must write the presentation in a format they can show to their learning teams in part 4.

   Requirements for Expert Presentation

   a. Write a transaction for the acquisition of this type of investment security. The transaction description is to include all necessary data to reflect the chosen classification.

   b. Prepare the journal entry to record the acquisition.

   [*Note:* The expert team on equity securities with controlling influence will substitute requirements (*d*) and (*e*) with a discussion of the reporting of these investments.]

   c. Identify information necessary to complete the end-of-period adjustment for this investment.

   d. Assuming that this is the only investment owned, prepare any necessary year-end entries.

   e. Present the relevant balance sheet section(s).

4. Re-form learning teams. In rotation, experts are to present to their teams the presentations they developed in part 3. Experts are to encourage and respond to questions.

ENTREPRENEURIAL DECISION

P4

BTN 15-7 Assume that Echoing Green, featured in this chapter's opener, makes an investment in Sustain Inc., a sustainability consulting firm. The company purchases 200 shares of Sustain stock for $15,000 cash plus a broker's fee of $500 cash. Sustain has 500 shares of common stock outstanding, and Echoing Green will be able to significantly influence its policies.

Required

1. Prepare the journal entry to record the investment in Sustain on January 1.

2. Sustain declares and pays a dividend of $1,000. Prepare the journal entry to record Echoing Green's receipt of its share of the dividend on July 1.

3. Sustain reports net income of $5,000. Prepare the journal entry to record Echoing Green's share of those earnings on December 31.

HITTING THE ROAD

C2

BTN 15-8 Review financial news sources such as Yahoo! Finance (finance.yahoo.com) and Google Finance (google.com/finance). Identify a company that has recently purchased 50% or more of another company's outstanding shares and will report consolidated financial statements.

Required

1. Identify whether the acquired company is a supplier, customer, competitor, or unrelated company relative to the purchasing company.

2. What does the purchasing company hope to accomplish with the investment? What is its strategy?

GLOBAL DECISION

A1

Samsung
APPLE
GOOGLE

BTN 15-9 Samsung, Apple, and Google are competitors in the global marketplace. Following are selected data from each company.

Key Figure	Samsung (Korean won millions)			Apple		Google	
	Current Year	One Year Prior	Two Years Prior	Current Year	Prior Year	Current Year	Prior Year
Net income	₩ 19,060,144	₩ 23,394,358	₩ 30,474,764	—	—	—	—
Net sales	200,653,482	206,205,987	228,692,667	—	—	—	—
Total assets	242,179,521	230,422,958	214,075,018	—	—	—	—
Profit margin	?	?	—	22.8%	21.6%	21.8%	21.4%
Total asset turnover	?	?	—	0.89	0.83	0.54	0.55

Required

1. Compute Samsung's return on total assets, and its components of profit margin and total asset turnover, for the most recent two years using the data provided.

2. Which of these three companies has the highest return on total assets? Highest profit margin? Highest total asset turnover? Interpret these results for the (*a*) current year and (*b*) prior year.

GLOBAL VIEW

This section discusses similarities and differences for the accounting and reporting of investments when financial statements are prepared under U.S. GAAP vis-à-vis IFRS.

Accounting for Noninfluential Securities   The accounting for noninfluential securities is broadly similar between U.S. GAAP and IFRS. *Trading securities* are accounted for using fair values with unrealized gains and losses reported in net income as fair values change. *Available-for-sale securities* are accounted for using fair values with unrealized gains and losses reported in other comprehensive income as fair values change (and later in net income when realized). *Held-to-maturity securities* are accounted for using amortized cost. Similarly, companies have the option under both systems to apply the fair value option for available-for-sale and held-to-maturity securities. Also, both systems review held-to-maturity securities for impairment.

There are some differences in terminology under IFRS: (1) trading securities are commonly referred to as *financial assets at fair value through profit and loss,* and (2) available-for-sale securities are commonly referred to as *available-for-sale financial assets.* NOKIA reports the following categories for noninfluential securities: (1) *financial assets at fair value through profit or loss,* consisting of financial assets held for trading and financial assets designated upon initial recognition as at fair value through profit or loss, and (2) *available-for-sale financial assets,* which are measured at fair value.

Accounting for Influential Securities   The accounting for influential securities is broadly similar across U.S. GAAP and IFRS. Specifically, under the *equity method,* the share of investee's net income is reported in the investor's income in the same period the investee earns that income; also, the investment account equals the acquisition cost plus the share of investee income less the share of investee dividends (minus amortization of excess on purchase price above fair value of identifiable, limited-life assets). Under the *consolidation method,* investee and investor revenues and expenses are combined, absent intercompany transactions, and subtracting noncontrolling interests. Also, nonintercompany assets and liabilities are similarly combined (eliminating the need for an investment account), and noncontrolling interests are subtracted from equity.

There are some differences in terminology: (1) U.S. GAAP companies commonly refer to earnings from long-term investments as *equity in earnings of affiliates,* whereas IFRS companies commonly use *equity in earnings of associated (or associate) companies;* and (2) U.S. GAAP companies commonly refer to noncontrolling interests in consolidated subsidiaries as *minority interests,* whereas IFRS companies commonly use *noncontrolling interests.*

 IFRS

Global Uniformity   Unlike U.S. GAAP, IFRS requires uniform accounting policies be used throughout the group of consolidated subsidiaries. Also, unlike U.S. GAAP, IFRS offers no detailed guidance on valuation procedures. ■

 Global View Assignments

Discussion Question 14

Quick Study 15-16

Exercise 15-15

BTN 15-9

16 Reporting the Statement of Cash Flows

chapter

Chapter Preview

BASICS OF CASH FLOW REPORTING

C1 Purpose, measurement, and classification

Noncash activities

P1 Format and preparation

NTK 16-1

CASH FLOWS FROM OPERATING

P2 Indirect and direct methods

Illustration of indirect method

Summary of indirect method adjustments

NTK 16-2

CASH FLOWS FROM INVESTING

P3 Three-stage process of analysis

Analyzing noncurrent assets

Analyzing other assets

NTK 16-3

CASH FLOWS FROM FINANCING

P3 Three-stage process of analysis

Analyzing noncurrent liabilities

Analyzing equity

Summary using T-accounts

A1 Analyzing cash

NTK 16-4

Learning Objectives

CONCEPTUAL

C1 Distinguish between operating, investing, and financing activities, and describe how noncash investing and financing activities are disclosed.

ANALYTICAL

A1 Analyze the statement of cash flows and apply the cash flow on total assets ratio.

PROCEDURAL

P1 Prepare a statement of cash flows.

P2 Compute cash flows from operating activities using the indirect method.

P3 Determine cash flows from both investing and financing activities.

P4 *Appendix 16A*—Illustrate use of a spreadsheet to prepare a statement of cash flows.

P5 *Appendix 16B*—Compute cash flows from operating activities using the direct method.

© Manjunath Kiran/AFP/Getty Images

Keeping Amazon above Water

SEATTLE—Market gurus warn us of companies with losses and rising debt. One of those companies, however, is **Amazon.com** (**Amazon.com**), the largest U.S. Internet retailer. Jeff Bezos, founder and CEO of Amazon, started the company in his garage. "The first initial start-up capital for Amazon.com came primarily from my parents, and they invested a large fraction of their life savings," recalls Jeff. "My dad's first question was, 'What's the Internet?' . . . He wasn't making a bet on this company or this concept. He was making a bet on his son."

Jeff has grown Amazon from an online bookstore into one of the world's largest online retail stores to compete with the likes of Walmart and Target. Interestingly, although Amazon reports negative income and rising debt, the market sees the company in a positive light.

Forbes named Amazon the sixth "Most Innovative Company in the World" and ranked it as the thirteenth "World's Most Valuable Brand." Given Amazon's losses and debt levels, is the market failing to fully reflect the accounting information? Is there something else that the market is focusing on?

"Your margin is my opportunity"

—Jeff Bezos

Let's dig a bit deeper. Amazon's financial statements reveal rising sales, nearly doubling over the past four years. Although costs exceeded sales in two of the recent four years, the growth in revenues foretells a positive future.

Amazon's cash flows are equally revealing. The key here is its operating cash flows, which have increased 185% over the past four years . . . an impressive result! In addition, its large investing cash outflows are what we expect from a growth company. Its relatively small financing cash inflows reveal that much of its expansion is self-funded—a good situation.

Analysis of Amazon requires examination of its cash flows. While only the future can reveal if the positive cash flow trend will lead to positive income, it is clear the market uses cash flow numbers in predicting Amazon's future. "We earn trust with customers over time," insists Jeff. "And that actually does maximize free cash flow over the long term."

Sources: *Amazon website,* January 2017; *Biography.com,* January 2016; *GreenBiz,* August 2014; *Fundable,* June 2015; *Inc.com,* May 2014; *Bloomberg,* January 2013; *Wall Street Journal,* October 2011

BASICS OF CASH FLOW REPORTING

This section describes the basics of cash flow reporting, including its purpose, measurement, classification, format, and preparation.

Purpose of the Statement of Cash Flows

The purpose of the **statement of cash flows** is to report cash receipts (inflows) and cash payments (outflows) during a period. This includes separately identifying the cash flows related to operating, investing, and financing activities. It is the detailed disclosure of individual sources and uses of cash that makes this statement useful. The statement of cash flows helps users answer questions such as:

Point: Internal users use the statement of cash flows to make investing and financing decisions. External users use this statement to assess the amount and timing of a company's cash flows.

- What explains the change in the cash balance?
- Where does a company spend its cash?
- How does a company receive its cash?

- Why do income and cash flows differ?
- How much is paid in dividends?
- Is there a cash shortage?

Importance of Cash Flows

Information about cash flows influences decisions. For instance, we prefer a company to pay expenses with cash from operations rather than by selling assets. Information about cash flows helps users decide whether a company has enough cash to pay its debts. It also helps evaluate a company's ability to pay unexpected obligations and pursue unexpected opportunities. Managers use cash flow information to plan day-to-day operations and make long-term investment decisions.

Source: Boston Public Library

The case of **W. T. Grant Co.** is a classic example of the importance of cash flows. Grant reported net income of more than $40 million per year for three consecutive years. At that same time, it was experiencing an alarming decrease in cash from its operations. For instance, net cash outflow was more than $90 million by the end of that three-year period. Grant soon went bankrupt. Users who relied solely on Grant's income numbers were unpleasantly surprised. This reminds us that cash flows as well as income statement and balance sheet information are crucial in business decisions.

■ Decision Insight ▬▬▬▬▬▬▬▬▬▬▬▬▬▬▬▬▬▬▬▬▬▬▬▬▬▬▬▬▬▬

Know Cash Flows   "A lender must have a complete understanding of a borrower's cash flows to assess both the borrowing needs and repayment sources. This requires information about the major types of cash inflows and outflows. I have seen many companies, whose financial statements indicate good profitability, experience severe financial problems because the owners or managers lacked a good understanding of cash flows."—Mary E. Garza, **Bank of America** ■

Measurement of Cash Flows

Cash flows include both *cash* and *cash equivalents*. The statement of cash flows explains the difference between the beginning and ending balances of cash and cash equivalents. We continue to use the phrases *cash flows* and the *statement of cash flows,* but remember that both phrases refer to cash *and* cash equivalents.

A cash equivalent has two criteria: (1) be readily convertible to a known amount of cash and (2) be sufficiently close to its maturity so its market value is unaffected by interest rate changes. **American Express** defines its cash equivalents as including "highly liquid investments with original maturities of 90 days or less."

Classification of Cash Flows

Because cash and cash equivalents are combined, the statement of cash flows does not report transactions *between* cash and cash equivalents, such as cash paid to purchase cash equivalents

Cash Equivalents

and cash received from selling cash equivalents. However, all other cash receipts and cash payments are classified on the statement in one of three categories—operating, investing, or financing activities. Individual cash receipts and payments for each of these three categories are labeled to identify their originating transactions or events. A net cash inflow (source) occurs when the receipts in a category exceed the payments. A net cash outflow (use) occurs when the payments in a category exceed the receipts.

C1_____

Distinguish between operating, investing, and financing activities, and describe how noncash investing and financing activities are disclosed.

Operating Activities   **Operating activities** include those transactions and events that determine net income. Examples are the production and purchase of inventory, the sale of goods and services to customers, and the expenditures to operate the business. Not all items in income, such as unusual gains and losses, are operating activities (we discuss these exceptions later). Exhibit 16.1 lists common cash inflows and outflows from operating activities.

EXHIBIT 16.1

Cash Flows from Operating Activities

Point: *Cash dividends received* and *cash interest received* are reported as operating activities.

Investing Activities   **Investing activities** generally include those transactions and events that affect long-term assets—namely, the purchase and sale of long-term assets. They also include (1) the purchase and sale of short-term investments, *except* trading securities, and (2) lending and collecting money for notes receivable. Exhibit 16.2 lists examples of cash flows from investing activities. Cash from collecting the principal amounts of notes is classified as investing. However, the collection of interest on notes is reported as an operating activity; also, if a note results from sales to customers, it is classified as operating.

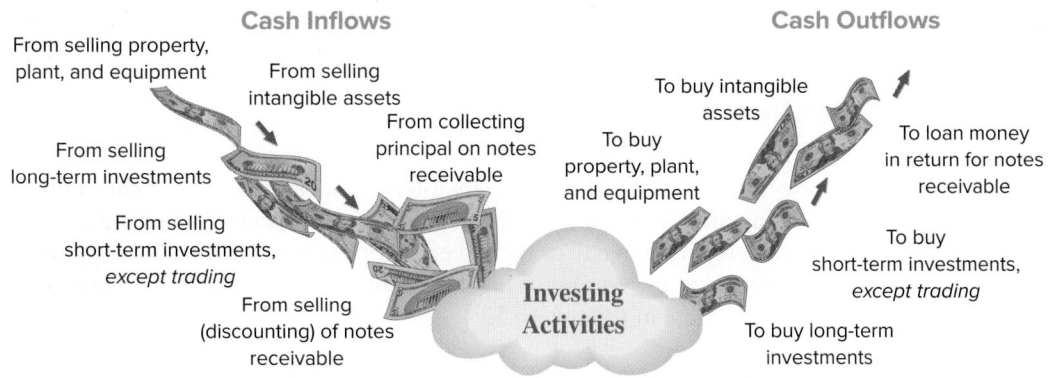

EXHIBIT 16.2

Cash Flows from Investing Activities

Financing Activities   **Financing activities** include those transactions and events that affect long-term liabilities and equity. Examples are (1) obtaining cash from issuing debt and repaying the amounts borrowed and (2) receiving cash from or distributing cash to owners. These activities involve transactions with a company's owners and creditors. Borrowing and repaying principal amounts relating to both short- and long-term debt are financing activities. However, payments of interest expense are classified as operating activities. Exhibit 16.3 lists examples of cash flows from financing activities.

EXHIBIT 16.3

Cash Flows from
Financing Activities

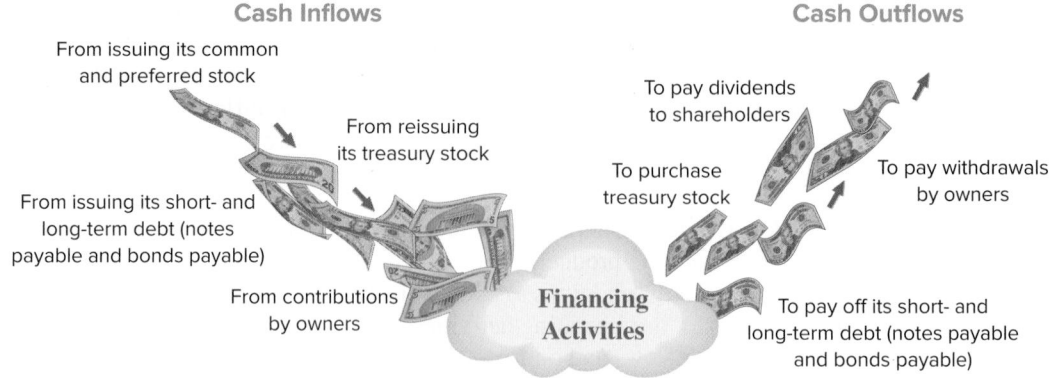

Cash Inflows — Cash Outflows

From issuing its common and preferred stock

From reissuing its treasury stock

From issuing its short- and long-term debt (notes payable and bonds payable)

From contributions by owners

To pay dividends to shareholders

To purchase treasury stock

To pay withdrawals by owners

To pay off its short- and long-term debt (notes payable and bonds payable)

Financing Activities

Link between Classification of Cash Flows and the Balance Sheet Operating, investing, and financing activities are loosely linked to different parts of the balance sheet. Operating activities are affected by changes in current assets and current liabilities (and the income statement). Investing activities are affected by changes in long-term assets. Financing activities are affected by changes in long-term liabilities and equity. These links are shown in Exhibit 16.4. Exceptions to these links include (1) current assets *unrelated* to operations—such as short-term notes receivable from noncustomers and marketable (not trading) securities, which are considered investing activities, and (2) current liabilities *unrelated* to operations—such as short-term notes payable and dividends payable, which are considered financing activities.

EXHIBIT 16.4

Linkage of Cash Flow
Classifications to the
Balance Sheet

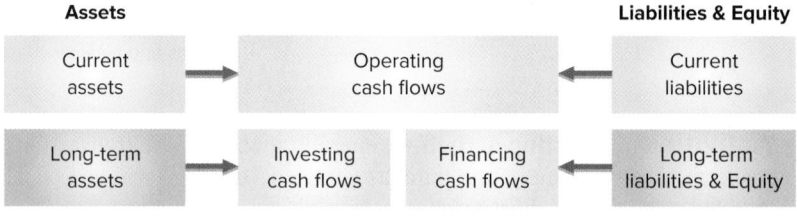

Assets — Liabilities & Equity

| Current assets | → | Operating cash flows | ← | Current liabilities |

| Long-term assets | → | Investing cash flows | Financing cash flows | ← | Long-term liabilities & Equity |

 **Decision** Insight

Where in the Statement Are Cash Flows? Cash flows can be delayed or accelerated at the end of a period to improve or reduce current period cash flows. Also, cash flows can be misclassified. Cash outflows reported under operating activities are interpreted as expense payments. However, cash outflows reported under investing activities are interpreted as a positive sign of growth potential. Thus, managers face incentives to misclassify cash flows. For these reasons, cash flow reporting requires scrutiny. ■

Noncash Investing and Financing

Some important investing and financing activities do not affect cash receipts or payments. One example is the purchase of long-term assets using a long-term note payable (loan). This transaction involves both investing and financing activities but does not affect any immediate cash inflow or outflow, so it is not reported in any of the three sections of the statement of cash flows. Such transactions are reported at the bottom of the statement of cash flows or in a note to the statement—common examples are in Exhibit 16.5.

EXHIBIT 16.5

Examples of Noncash
Investing and Financing
Activities

- Retirement of debt by issuing equity stock.
- Conversion of preferred stock to common stock.
- Lease of assets in a capital lease transaction.
- Purchase of long-term assets by issuing a note or bond.
- Exchange of noncash assets for other noncash assets.
- Purchase of noncash assets by issuing equity or debt.

Format of the Statement of Cash Flows

P1

Prepare a statement of
cash flows.

A statement of cash flows reports information about a company's cash receipts and cash payments during the period. Exhibit 16.6 shows the usual format. A company reports cash flows from three activities: operating, investing, and financing. The statement then shows

EXHIBIT 16.6

Format of the Statement
of Cash Flows

COMPANY NAME
Statement of Cash Flows
For *period* Ended *date*

Cash flows from operating activities

  [Compute operating cash flows using indirect or direct method]

  Net cash provided (used) by operating activities . . . . $ #

Cash flows from investing activities

  [List of individual inflows and outflows]

  Net cash provided (used) by investing activities. . . . .   #

Cash flows from financing activities

  [List of individual inflows and outflows]

  Net cash provided (used) by financing activities. . . . .   #

Net increase (decrease) in cash. . . . . $ #

Cash (and equivalents) balance at prior period-end . . . .   #

Cash (and equivalents) balance at current period-end . . . . $ #

Separate schedule or note disclosure of any noncash investing and financing transactions is required.

Point: Positive cash flows for
a section are titled net cash
"provided by" or "from." Negative
cash flows are labeled as net
cash "used by" or "for."

the net increase or decrease from those activities. Finally, it explains how transactions and events impact the prior period-end cash balance to produce its current period-end balance. Any noncash investing and financing transactions are disclosed in a note disclosure or separate schedule.

■ **Decision** Maker

Entrepreneur   You are considering purchasing a start-up business that recently reported a $110,000 annual net loss and a $225,000 annual net cash inflow. How are these results possible? ■ [*Answer:* Several factors can explain an increase in net cash flows when a net loss is reported, including (1) early recognition of expenses relative to revenues generated (such as research and development), (2) cash advances on long-term sales contracts not yet recognized in income, (3) issuances of debt or equity for cash to finance expansion, (4) cash sale of assets, (5) delay of cash payments, and (6) cash prepayment on sales.]

Preparing the Statement of Cash Flows

Preparing a statement of cash flows involves five steps shown in Exhibit 16.7.

Step 1 Compute net increase or decrease in cash.

Step 2 Compute net cash from or for operating activities.

Step 3 Compute net cash from or for investing activities.

EXHIBIT 16.7

Five Steps in Preparing the
Statement of Cash Flows

Step 4 Compute net cash from or for financing activities.

Step 5 Compute net cash from all sources; then *prove* it by adding it to beginning cash to get ending cash.

Computing the net increase or net decrease in cash is a simple but crucial computation. It equals the current period's cash balance minus the prior period's cash balance. This is the *bottom-line* figure for the statement of cash flows and is a check on accuracy.

Point: View the change in cash as
a *target* number (or check figure)
that we will fully explain and prove
in the statement of cash flows.

Analyzing the Cash Account

A company's cash receipts and cash payments are recorded in the Cash account in its general ledger. The Cash account is therefore a place to look for information about cash flows. To illustrate, see the summarized Cash T-account of Genesis, Inc., in Exhibit 16.8.

EXHIBIT 16.8

Summarized Cash Account

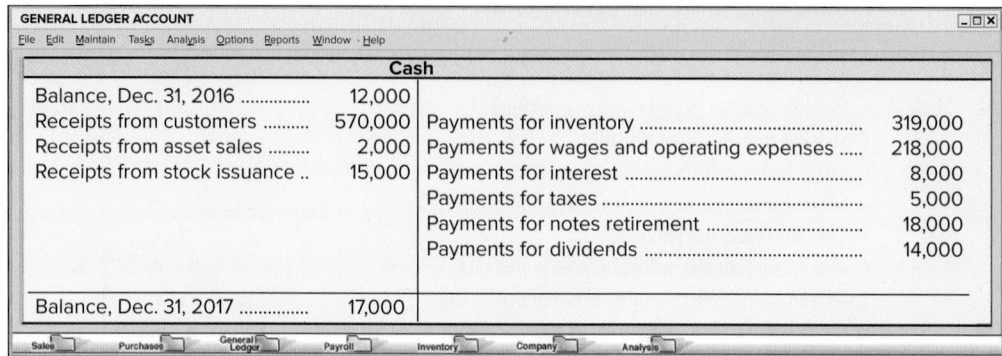

The statement of cash flows summarizes and classifies the transactions that led to the $5,000 increase in the Cash account. Preparing a statement of cash flows from Exhibit 16.8 requires determining whether an individual cash inflow or outflow is an operating, investing, or financing activity, and then listing each by activity. (We return to this approach in Exhibit 16.14.)

Analyzing Noncash Accounts

A second approach to preparing the statement of cash flows is analyzing noncash accounts. This approach uses the fact that when a company records cash inflows and outflows with debits and credits to the Cash account (see Exhibit 16.8), it also records credits and debits in noncash accounts (reflecting double-entry accounting). Many of these noncash accounts are balance sheet accounts—for instance, from the sale of land for cash. Others are revenue and expense accounts that are closed to equity. For instance, the sale of services for cash yields a credit to Services Revenue that is closed to Retained Earnings for a corporation. *All cash transactions eventually affect noncash balance sheet accounts.* Thus, we can determine cash inflows and outflows by analyzing changes in noncash balance sheet accounts.

Exhibit 16.9 uses the accounting equation to show the relation between the Cash account and the noncash balance sheet accounts. This exhibit starts with the accounting equation (at the top). It is then expanded in line (2) to separate cash from noncash asset accounts. To isolate cash on one side of the equation, line (3) shows noncash asset accounts being subtracted from both sides of the equation. Cash now equals the sum of the liability and equity accounts *minus* the noncash asset accounts. Line (4) points out that *changes* on one side of the accounting equation equal *changes* on the other side. It shows that we can explain changes in cash by

EXHIBIT 16.9

Relation between Cash and Noncash Accounts

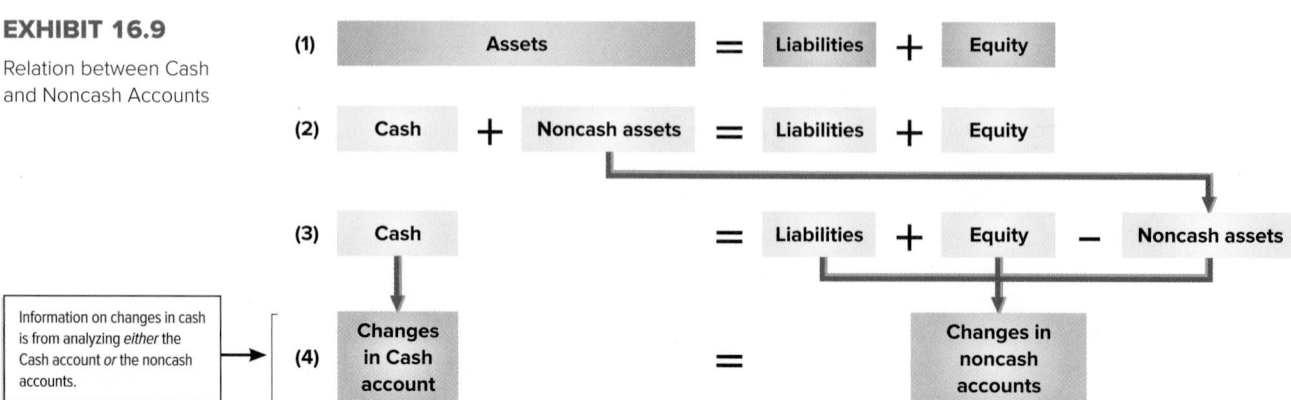

Information on changes in cash is from analyzing *either* the Cash account *or* the noncash accounts.

analyzing changes in the noncash accounts consisting of liability accounts, equity accounts, and noncash asset accounts. By analyzing noncash balance sheet accounts and any related income statement accounts, we can prepare a statement of cash flows.

Information to Prepare the Statement Information to prepare the statement of cash flows usually comes from three sources: (1) comparative balance sheets, (2) the current income statement, and (3) additional information. Comparative balance sheets are used to compute changes in noncash accounts from the beginning to the end of the period. The current income statement is used to help compute cash flows from operating activities. Additional information often includes details on transactions and events that help explain both the cash flows and non-cash investing and financing activities.

Classify each of the following cash flows as operating, investing, or financing activities.

_____ **a.** Purchase equipment for cash

_____ **b.** Cash payment of wages

_____ **c.** Issuance of stock for cash

_____ **d.** Receipt of cash dividends from investments

_____ **e.** Cash collections from customers

_____ **f.** Note payable issued for cash

_____ **g.** Cash paid for utilities

_____ **h.** Cash paid to acquire investments

_____ **i.** Cash paid to retire debt

_____ **j.** Cash received as interest on investments

_____ **k.** Cash received from selling investments

_____ **l.** Cash received from a bank loan

NEED-TO-KNOW 16-1

Classifying Cash Flows

C1

Solution

a. Investing   **c.** Financing   **e.** Operating   **g.** Operating   **i.** Financing   **k.** Investing

b. Operating   **d.** Operating   **f.** Financing   **h.** Investing   **j.** Operating   **l.** Financing

Do More: QS 16-1, QS 16-2, E 16-1

CASH FLOWS FROM OPERATING

Indirect and Direct Methods of Reporting

Cash flows provided (used) by operating activities are reported in one of two ways: the *direct method* or the *indirect method.* **These two different methods apply only to the operating activities section.**

- The **direct method** separately lists each major item of operating cash receipts (such as cash received from customers) and each major item of operating cash payments (such as cash paid for inventory). The cash payments are subtracted from cash receipts to determine the net cash provided (used) by operating activities.

- The **indirect method** reports net income and then adjusts it to obtain net cash provided or used by operating activities. It does *not* report individual items of cash inflows and cash outflows from operating activities. Instead, the indirect method reports the necessary adjustments to reconcile net income to net cash provided or used by operating activities.

The net cash amount provided by operating activities is *identical* under both the direct and indirect methods. The difference in these methods is with the computation and presentation. The indirect method is arguably easier to compute. Nearly all companies report operating cash flows using the indirect method (see margin graphic from recent survey), including **Apple**, **Google**, and **Samsung** in Appendix A.

To illustrate, we prepare the operating activities section of the statement of cash flows for Genesis. Exhibit 16.10 shows the December 31, 2016 and 2017, balance sheets of

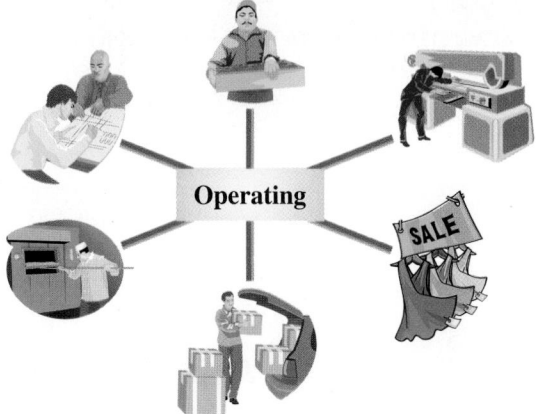

Firms Using Indirect vs. Direct

Indirect 99%   Direct 1%

Genesis along with its 2017 income statement. We use this information to prepare a statement of cash flows that explains the $5,000 increase in cash for 2017 as highlighted in its balance sheets. This $5,000 is computed as Cash of $17,000 at the end of 2017 minus Cash of $12,000 at the end of 2016.

EXHIBIT 16.10

Financial Statements

GENESIS		
Income Statement		
For Year Ended December 31, 2017		
Sales		$590,000
Cost of goods sold	$300,000	
Wages and other operating expenses	216,000	
Interest expense.	7,000	
Depreciation expense	24,000	(547,000)
		43,000
Other gains (losses)		
Loss on sale of plant assets	(6,000)	
Gain on retirement of notes	16,000	10,000
Income before taxes		53,000
Income taxes expense		(15,000)
Net income		$ 38,000

GENESIS			
Balance Sheets			
December 31, 2017 and 2016			
	2017	**2016**	**Change**
Assets			
Current assets			
Cash	$ 17,000	$ 12,000	$ 5,000 Increase
Accounts receivable	60,000	40,000	20,000 Increase
Inventory	84,000	70,000	14,000 Increase
Prepaid expenses	6,000	4,000	2,000 Increase
Total current assets	167,000	126,000	
Long-term assets			
Plant assets	250,000	210,000	40,000 Increase
Accumulated depreciation	(60,000)	(48,000)	12,000 Increase
Total assets.	$357,000	$288,000	
Liabilities			
Current liabilities			
Accounts payable	$ 35,000	$ 40,000	$ 5,000 Decrease
Interest payable.	3,000	4,000	1,000 Decrease
Income taxes payable	22,000	12,000	10,000 Increase
Total current liabilities	60,000	56,000	
Long-term notes payable.	90,000	64,000	26,000 Increase
Total liabilities.	150,000	120,000	
Equity			
Common stock, $5 par.	95,000	80,000	15,000 Increase
Retained earnings	112,000	88,000	24,000 Increase
Total equity	207,000	168,000	
Total liabilities and equity	$357,000	$288,000	

Additional information for 2017

a. The accounts payable balances result from inventory purchases.

b. Purchased $60,000 in plant assets by issuing $60,000 of notes payable.

c. Sold plant assets with a book value of $8,000 (original cost of $20,000 and accumulated depreciation of $12,000) for $2,000 cash, yielding a $6,000 loss.

d. Received $15,000 cash from issuing 3,000 shares of common stock.

e. Paid $18,000 cash to retire notes with a $34,000 book value, yielding a $16,000 gain.

f. Declared and paid cash dividends of $14,000.

> *The next section describes the indirect method. Appendix 16B describes the direct method. An instructor can choose to cover either one or both methods. Neither section depends on the other. If the indirect method is skipped, then read Appendix 16B and return to the section titled "Cash Flows from Investing."*

Applying the Indirect Method

P2

Compute cash flows from operating activities using the indirect method.

Net income is computed using accrual accounting. Revenues and expenses do not necessarily reflect the receipt and payment of cash. The indirect method adjusts the net income figure to obtain the net cash provided or used by operating activities. This includes subtracting noncash increases from net income and adding noncash charges back to net income.

To illustrate, the indirect method begins with Genesis's net income of $38,000 and adjusts it to obtain net cash provided by operating activities of $20,000—see Exhibit 16.11. There are two types of adjustments. There are ① adjustments to income statement items that neither provide nor use cash and ② adjustments to reflect changes in balance sheet current assets and current liabilities (linked to operating activities). Nearly all companies group adjustments into these two types, including Apple, Google, and Samsung in Appendix A. This section describes these two adjustments.

EXHIBIT 16.11

Operating Activities
Section—Indirect Method

GENESIS Statement of Cash Flows—Operating Section under Indirect Method For Year Ended December 31, 2017	
Cash flows from operating activities	
Net income	$ 38,000
Adjustments to reconcile net income to net cash provided by operating activities	
Income statement items not affecting cash	
Depreciation expense	24,000
Loss on sale of plant assets	6,000
Gain on retirement of notes	(16,000)
Changes in current assets and liabilities	
Increase in accounts receivable	(20,000)
Increase in inventory	(14,000)
Increase in prepaid expenses	(2,000)
Decrease in accounts payable	(5,000)
Decrease in interest payable	(1,000)
Increase in income taxes payable	10,000
Net cash provided by operating activities	**$20,000**

① **Adjustments for Income Statement Items Not Affecting Cash**   The income statement usually includes some expenses and losses that do not reflect cash outflows. Examples are depreciation, amortization, depletion, bad debts expense, loss from an asset sale, and loss from retirement of notes payable. When there are expenses and losses that do not reflect cash outflows, the indirect method for reporting operating cash flows requires the following adjustment:

Expenses and losses with no cash outflows are added back to net income.

To see the logic of this adjustment, recall that expenses such as depreciation, amortization, and depletion have *no* cash effect, and adding them back cancels their deductions. To see the logic for losses, consider that items such as a plant asset sale and a notes retirement are usually recorded by recognizing the cash, removing all plant asset or notes accounts, and recording any loss or gain. The cash received or paid is part of either investing or financing cash flows; but because *no* operating cash flow effect occurs, we add the loss back to income to reverse the deduction.

Similarly, when net income includes revenues and gains that do not reflect cash inflows, the indirect method for reporting operating cash flows requires the following adjustment:

Revenues and gains with no cash inflows are subtracted from net income.

We apply these adjustments to the income statement items in Exhibit 16.10 that do not affect cash.

Depreciation   Depreciation expense is Genesis's only operating item that has no effect on cash flows. We must add back the $24,000 depreciation expense to net income when computing cash provided by operating activities because depreciation is not a cash outflow.

Loss on Sale of Plant Assets   Genesis reports a $6,000 loss on sale of plant assets that reduces income but has no effect on cash flows. This $6,000 loss is added back to net income because it is not a cash outflow.

Gain on Retirement of Debt   A $16,000 gain on retirement of debt increases income but has no effect on cash flows. This means the $16,000 gain is subtracted from income because it is not a cash inflow.

Point: An income statement reports revenues, gains, expenses, and losses on an accrual basis. The statement of cash flows reports cash received and cash paid for operating, financing, and investing activities.

These three adjustments to net income for "items not affecting cash" are shown as follows:

Net income		$ 38,000
Adjustments to reconcile net income to net cash provided by operating activities		
Income statement items not affecting cash		
①	Depreciation expense.	24,000
	Loss on sale of plant assets	6,000
	Gain on retirement of notes	(16,000)

② Adjustments for Changes in Current Assets and Current Liabilities This section describes adjustments for changes in current assets and current liabilities.

Adjustments for Changes in Current Assets Decreases in current assets require the following adjustment:

> **Decreases in current assets are added to net income.**

Increases in current assets require the following adjustment:

> **Increases in current assets are subtracted from net income.**

Adjustments for Changes in Current Liabilities Increases in current liabilities require the following adjustment:

> **Increases in current liabilities are added to net income.**

Decreases in current liabilities require the following adjustment:

> **Decreases in current liabilities are subtracted from net income.**

To illustrate, we apply these adjustment rules to the three noncash current assets and three current liabilities in Exhibit 16.10, which are then reported as follows.

Net income		$ 38,000
Adjustments to reconcile net income to net cash provided by operating activities		
	Increase in accounts receivable	(20,000)
	Increase in inventory	(14,000)
	Increase in prepaid expenses	(2,000)
②	Decrease in accounts payable	(5,000)
	Decrease in interest payable.	(1,000)
	Increase in income taxes payable.	10,000

Following is an explanation, including T-account analysis, for how these adjustments result in cash receipts and cash payments.

Accounts Receivable Following the rule above, the $20,000 increase in the current asset of accounts receivable is subtracted from income. This increase implies that Genesis collects less cash than is reported in sales. To see this, it is helpful to use *account analysis*. This involves setting up a T-account and reconstructing its major entries to compute cash receipts or payments as follows. We see that sales are $20,000 greater than cash receipts. This $20,000—reflected in the increase in Accounts Receivable—is subtracted from net income when computing cash provided by operating activities.

	Accounts Receivable			
Numbers in black are taken from Exhibit 16.10. The red number is the computed (plug) figure.	Bal., Dec. 31, 2016	40,000		
	Sales	590,000	Cash receipts =	570,000
	Bal., Dec. 31, 2017	60,000		

Inventory   The $14,000 increase in inventory is subtracted from income. This increase implies that Genesis had greater cash purchases than cost of goods sold, as shown here:

Inventory			
Bal., Dec. 31, 2016	70,000		
Purchases =	314,000	Cost of goods sold	300,000
Bal., Dec. 31, 2017	84,000		

Prepaid Expenses   The $2,000 increase in prepaid expenses is subtracted from income, implying that Genesis's cash payments exceed its recorded prepaid expenses, as shown here:

Prepaid Expenses			
Bal., Dec. 31, 2016	4,000		
Cash payments =	218,000	Wages and other operating exp.	216,000
Bal., Dec. 31, 2017	6,000		

Accounts Payable   The $5,000 decrease in the current liability for accounts payable is subtracted from income. This decrease implies that cash payments to suppliers exceed purchases, which is shown here:

Accounts Payable			
		Bal., Dec. 31, 2016	40,000
Cash payments =	319,000	Purchases	314,000
		Bal., Dec. 31, 2017	35,000

Interest Payable   The $1,000 decrease in interest payable is subtracted from income. This decrease indicates that cash paid for interest exceeds interest expense, which is shown here:

Interest Payable			
		Bal., Dec. 31, 2016	4,000
Cash paid for interest =	8,000	Interest expense	7,000
		Bal., Dec. 31, 2017	3,000

Income Taxes Payable   The $10,000 increase in income taxes payable is added to income. This increase implies that reported income taxes exceed the cash paid for taxes, which is shown here:

Income Taxes Payable			
		Bal., Dec. 31, 2016	12,000
Cash paid for taxes =	5,000	Income taxes expense	15,000
		Bal., Dec. 31, 2017	22,000

Summary Adjustments for Indirect Method

Exhibit 16.12 summarizes the adjustments to net income when computing net cash provided or used by operating activities under the indirect method.

EXHIBIT 16.12

Summary of Adjustments for Operating Activities—Indirect Method

---

Net Income (or Loss)

① Adjustments for operating items not providing or using cash

+ Noncash expenses and losses

Examples: Expenses for depreciation, depletion, and amortization; losses from disposal of long-term assets and from retirement of debt

− Noncash revenues and gains

Examples: Gains from disposal of long-term assets and from retirement of debt

② Adjustments for changes in current assets and current liabilities

+ Decrease in noncash current operating asset

− Increase in noncash current operating asset

+ Increase in current operating liability

− Decrease in current operating liability

Net cash provided (used) by operating activities

Decision Insight

How Much Cash in Income?   The difference between net income and operating cash flows can be large and sometimes reflects on the quality of earnings. This bar chart shows the net income and operating cash flows of three companies. Operating cash flows can be either higher or lower than net income. ■

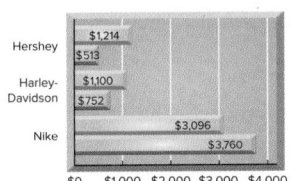
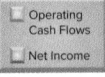

NEED-TO-KNOW 16-2

Reporting Operating Cash Flows (Indirect)

P2

A company's current-year income statement and selected balance sheet data at December 31 of the current and prior years follow. Prepare only the operating activities section of the statement of cash flows using the indirect method for the current year.

Income Statement For Current Year Ended December 31	
Sales revenue	$120
Expenses	
Cost of goods sold	50
Depreciation expense	30
Salaries expense...............	17
Interest expense...............	3
Net income	$ 20

Selected Balance Sheet Accounts		
At December 31	Current Yr	Prior Yr
Accounts receivable	$12	$10
Inventory	6	9
Accounts payable	7	11
Salaries payable	8	3
Interest payable..............	1	0

Solution

Cash Flows from Operating Activities—Indirect Method For Current Year Ended December 31		
Cash flows from operating activities		
Net income		$20
Adjustments to reconcile net income to net cash provided by operating activities		
Income statement items not affecting cash		
Depreciation expense	$30	
Changes in current assets and current liabilities		
Increase in accounts receivable	(2)	
Decrease in inventory	3	
Decrease in accounts payable	(4)	
Increase in salaries payable	5	
Increase in interest payable	1	33
Net cash provided by operating activities......................................		$53

Do More: QS 16-3, QS 16-4, E 16-4, E 16-5, E 16-6

CASH FLOWS FROM INVESTING

The third step in preparing the statement of cash flows is to compute and report cash flows from investing activities. We do this by identifying changes in (1) all noncurrent asset accounts and (2) the current accounts for both notes receivable and investments in securities (excluding trading securities). We then analyze changes in these accounts to determine their effect, if any, on cash and report the cash flow effects in the investing activities section of the statement of cash flows. **Reporting of investing activities is identical under the direct method and indirect method.**

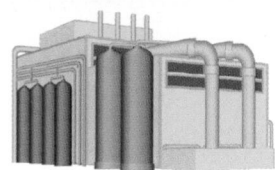

Three-Stage Process of Analysis

Information to compute cash flows from investing activities is usually taken from beginning and ending balance sheets and the income statement. We use a three-stage process to determine cash provided or used by investing activities: (1) identify changes in investing-related accounts, (2) explain these changes using reconstruction analysis, and (3) report their cash flow effects.

P3

Determine cash flows from both investing and financing activities.

Analyzing Noncurrent Assets

Genesis both purchased and sold plant assets during the period. Both transactions are investing activities and are analyzed for their cash flow effects in this section.

Plant Asset Transactions   The *first stage* in analyzing the Plant Assets account and its related Accumulated Depreciation account is to identify any changes in these accounts from comparative balance sheets in Exhibit 16.10. This analysis reveals a $40,000 increase in plant assets from $210,000 to $250,000 and a $12,000 increase in accumulated depreciation from $48,000 to $60,000.

Point: Investing activities include (1) purchasing and selling long-term assets, (2) lending and collecting on notes receivable, and (3) purchasing and selling short-term investments other than cash equivalents and trading securities.

The *second stage* is to explain these changes. Items *b* and *c* of the additional information in Exhibit 16.10 affect plant assets. Recall that the Plant Assets account is affected by both asset purchases and sales; its Accumulated Depreciation account is normally increased from depreciation and decreased from the removal of accumulated depreciation in asset sales. To explain changes in these accounts and to identify their cash flow effects, we prepare *reconstructed entries* from prior transactions; *they are not the actual entries by the preparer.*

To illustrate, item *b* reports that Genesis purchased plant assets of $60,000 by issuing $60,000 in notes payable to the seller. The reconstructed entry for analysis of item *b* follows.

Reconstruction	Plant Assets	60,000	
	Notes Payable..................................		60,000

Next, item *c* reports that Genesis sold plant assets costing $20,000 (with $12,000 of accumulated depreciation) for $2,000 cash, resulting in a $6,000 loss. The reconstructed entry for analysis of item *c* follows.

Reconstruction	Cash...	2,000	
	Accumulated Depreciation	12,000	
	Loss on Sale of Plant Assets	6,000	
	Plant Assets....................................		20,000

We also reconstruct the entry for Depreciation Expense from the income statement. Depreciation expense results in no cash flow effect.

Reconstruction	Depreciation Expense	24,000	
	Accumulated Depreciation......................		24,000

These three reconstructed entries are reflected in the following plant asset and related T-accounts.

Plant Assets					Accumulated Depreciation—Plant Assets			
Bal., Dec. 31, 2016	210,000						Bal., Dec. 31, 2016	48,000
Purchase	60,000	Sale	20,000		Sale	12,000	Depr. expense	24,000
Bal., Dec. 31, 2017	250,000						Bal., Dec. 31, 2017	60,000

This reconstruction analysis is complete in that the change in plant assets from $210,000 to $250,000 is fully explained by the $60,000 purchase and the $20,000 sale. Also, the change in accumulated depreciation from $48,000 to $60,000 is fully explained by depreciation expense of $24,000 and the removal of $12,000 in accumulated depreciation from the asset sale.

The *third stage* in analyzing the Plant Assets account looks back at the reconstructed entries to identify any cash flows. The identified cash flow effect is reported in the investing section of the statement as follows:

Cash flows from investing activities	
Cash received from sale of plant assets	$2,000

The $60,000 purchase described in item *b* and financed by issuing notes is a noncash investing and financing activity. It is reported in a note or in a separate schedule to the statement as follows:

Noncash investing and financing activity	
Purchased plant assets with issuance of notes	$60,000

Example: If a plant asset costing $40,000 with $37,000 of accumulated depreciation is sold at a $1,000 loss, what is the cash flow? What is the cash flow if this asset is sold at a gain of $3,000?
Answers: +$2,000; +$6,000

Analyzing Additional Assets

Genesis did not have any additional noncurrent assets (or nonoperating current assets) and, therefore, we have no additional investing transactions to analyze. If other investing assets did exist, we would identify and report the investing cash flows using the same three-stage process illustrated for plant assets.

NEED-TO-KNOW 16-3

Reporting Investing Cash Flows

P3

Use the following information to determine this company's cash flows from investing activities.
a. A factory with a book value of $100 and an original cost of $800 was sold at a loss of $10.
b. Paid $70 cash for new equipment.
c. Long-term stock investments were sold for $20 cash, yielding a loss of $4.
d. Sold land costing $175 for $160 cash, yielding a loss of $15.

Solution

Cash flows from investing activities	
Cash received from sale of factory (from *a**)	$ 90
Cash paid for new equipment (from *b*)	(70)
Cash received from sale of long-term investments (from *c*)	20
Cash received from sale of land (from *d*)	160
Net cash provided by investing activities	$200

* Cash received from sale of factory = Book value − Loss = $100 − $10 = $90

Do More: QS 16-5, QS 16-6, QS 16-8, E 16-7

CASH FLOWS FROM FINANCING

The fourth step in preparing the statement of cash flows is to compute and report cash flows from financing activities. We do this by identifying changes in all noncurrent liability accounts (including the current portion of any notes and bonds) and the equity accounts. These accounts include long-term debt, notes payable, bonds payable, common stock, and retained earnings. Changes in these accounts are then analyzed to determine their effect, if any, on cash. Results are reported in the financing activities section of the statement. **Reporting of financing activities is identical under the direct method and indirect method.**

Three-Stage Process of Analysis

We use a three-stage process to determine cash provided or used by financing activities: (1) identify changes in financing-related accounts, (2) explain these changes using reconstruction analysis, and (3) report their cash flow effects.

Analyzing Noncurrent Liabilities

Genesis had two transactions involving noncurrent liabilities. We analyzed one of those, the $60,000 issuance of notes payable to purchase plant assets. This transaction is reported as a significant noncash investing and financing activity in a footnote or a separate schedule to the statement of cash flows. The other remaining transaction involving noncurrent liabilities is the cash settlement of notes payable.

Point: Examples of financing activities are (1) receiving cash from issuing debt or repaying amounts borrowed and (2) receiving cash from or distributing cash to owners.

Notes Payable Transactions   The *first stage* in analysis of notes is to review the comparative balance sheets from Exhibit 16.10. This analysis reveals an increase in notes payable from $64,000 to $90,000.

The *second stage* explains this change. Item *e* of the additional information in Exhibit 16.10 reports that notes with a carrying value of $34,000 are retired for $18,000 cash, resulting in a $16,000 gain. The reconstructed entry for analysis of item *e* follows:

Reconstruction			
Notes Payable	34,000	
Gain on retirement of debt.		16,000
Cash		18,000

This entry reveals an $18,000 cash outflow for retirement of notes and a $16,000 gain from comparing the notes payable carrying value to the cash received. This gain does not reflect any cash inflow or outflow. Also, item *b* of the additional information reports that Genesis purchased plant assets costing $60,000 by issuing $60,000 in notes payable to the seller. We reconstructed this entry when analyzing investing activities: It showed a $60,000 increase to notes payable that is reported as a noncash investing and financing transaction. The Notes Payable account is explained by these reconstructed entries as follows:

		Notes Payable	
		Bal., Dec. 31, 2016	64,000
Retired notes	**34,000**	**Issued notes**	**60,000**
		Bal., Dec. 31, 2017	90,000

The *third stage* is to report the cash flow effect of the notes retirement in the financing section of the statement as follows:

Cash flows from financing activities	
Cash paid to retire notes.	$(18,000)

Analyzing Equity

Genesis had two transactions involving equity accounts. The first is the issuance of common stock for cash. The second is the declaration and payment of cash dividends. We analyze both.

Common Stock Transactions   The *first stage* in analyzing common stock is to review the comparative balance sheets from Exhibit 16.10, which reveal an increase in common stock from $80,000 to $95,000.

The *second stage* explains this change. Item *d* of the additional information in Exhibit 16.10 reports that 3,000 shares of common stock are issued at par for $5 per share. The reconstructed entry for analysis of item *d* follows:

Reconstruction			
Cash.	15,000	
Common Stock		15,000

This entry reveals a $15,000 cash inflow from stock issuance and is reflected in (and explains) the Common Stock account as follows:

Common Stock		
	Bal., Dec. 31, 2016	80,000
	Issued stock	**15,000**
	Bal., Dec. 31, 2017	95,000

The *third stage* reports the cash flow effect from stock issuance in the financing section of the statement as follows:

Cash flows from financing activities	
Cash received from issuing stock	$15,000

Retained Earnings Transactions

The *first stage* in analyzing the Retained Earnings account is to review the comparative balance sheets from Exhibit 16.10. This reveals an increase in retained earnings from $88,000 to $112,000.

The *second stage* explains this change. Item *f* of the additional information in Exhibit 16.10 reports that cash dividends of $14,000 are paid. The reconstructed entry follows:

Reconstruction	Retained Earnings	14,000	
	Cash		14,000

This entry reveals a $14,000 cash outflow for cash dividends. Also see that the Retained Earnings account is impacted by net income of $38,000. (Net income was analyzed under the operating section of the statement of cash flows.) The reconstructed Retained Earnings account follows:

Retained Earnings			
		Bal., Dec. 31, 2016	88,000
Cash dividend	**14,000**	**Net income**	**38,000**
		Bal., Dec. 31, 2017	112,000

Point: Financing activities not affecting cash flow include *declaration* of a cash dividend, *declaration* of a stock dividend, issuance of a stock dividend, and a stock split.

The *third stage* reports the cash flow effect from the cash dividend in the financing section of the statement as follows:

Cash flows from financing activities	
Cash paid for dividends.	$(14,000)

We now have identified and explained all of the Genesis cash inflows and cash outflows and one noncash investing and financing transaction.

Proving Cash Balances

The final step in preparing the statement is to report the beginning and ending cash balances and prove that the *net change in cash* is explained by operating, investing, and financing cash flows. This step is shown here for Genesis.

Net cash provided by operating activities.	$ 20,000
Net cash provided by investing activities	2,000
Net cash used in financing activities.	(17,000)
Net increase in cash.	**$ 5,000**
Cash balance at 2016 year-end	12,000
Cash balance at 2017 year-end	$ 17,000

The preceding table shows that the $5,000 net increase in cash, from $12,000 at the beginning of the period to $17,000 at the end, is reconciled by net cash flows from operating ($20,000 inflow), investing ($2,000 inflow), and financing ($17,000 outflow) activities. This is reported at the bottom of the statement of cash flows as shown in Exhibit 16.13.

GENESIS Statement of Cash Flows (Indirect Method) For Year Ended December 31, 2017		
Cash flows from operating activities		
Net income	$ 38,000	
Adjustments to reconcile net income to net cash provided by operating activities		
Income statement items not affecting cash		
Depreciation expense	24,000	
Loss on sale of plant assets	6,000	
Gain on retirement of notes	(16,000)	
Changes in current assets and liabilities		
Increase in accounts receivable	(20,000)	
Increase in inventory	(14,000)	
Increase in prepaid expenses	(2,000)	
Decrease in accounts payable	(5,000)	
Decrease in interest payable	(1,000)	
Increase in income taxes payable	10,000	
Net cash provided by operating activities		$20,000
Cash flows from investing activities		
Cash received from sale of plant assets	2,000	
Net cash provided by investing activities		2,000
Cash flows from financing activities		
Cash received from issuing stock	15,000	
Cash paid to retire notes	(18,000)	
Cash paid for dividends	(14,000)	
Net cash used in financing activities		(17,000)
Net increase in cash		$ 5,000
Cash balance at prior year-end		12,000
Cash balance at current year-end		$17,000

EXHIBIT 16.13

Complete Statement of Cash Flows—Indirect Method

Point: Refer to Exhibit 16.10 and identify the $5,000 change in cash. This change is what the statement of cash flows explains; it serves as a check.

Point: The statement of cash flows is usually the last of the four financial statements to be prepared.

■ **Decision** Maker

Reporter Management is in labor contract negotiations and grants you an interview. It highlights a recent $600,000 net loss that involves a $930,000 unusual loss and a total net cash outflow of $550,000 (which includes net cash outflows of $850,000 for investing activities and $350,000 for financing activities). What is your assessment of this company? ■ [*Answer:* An initial reaction from the $600,000 loss and a $550,000 decrease in net cash is not positive. However, closer scrutiny reveals a more positive picture. Cash flow from operations is $650,000, computed as [?] − $850,000 − $350,000 = $(550,000). We also see that net income before the unusual loss is $330,000, computed as [?] − $930,000 = $(600,000).]

Use the following information to determine this company's cash flows from financing activities.
a. Issued common stock for $40 cash.
b. Paid $70 cash to retire a note payable at its $70 maturity value.
c. Paid cash dividend of $15.
d. Paid $5 cash to acquire its treasury stock.

NEED-TO-KNOW 16-4

Reporting Financing Cash Flows

P3

Solution

Cash flows from financing activities	
Cash received from issuance of common stock (from *a*)	$ 40
Cash paid to settle note payable (from *b*)	(70)
Cash paid for dividend (from *c*)	(15)
Cash paid to acquire treasury stock (from *d*)	(5)
Net cash used by financing activities	$(50)

Do More: QS 16-9, QS 16-10, QS 16-13, E 16-8

SUMMARY USING T-ACCOUNTS

Exhibit 16.14 uses T-accounts to summarize how changes in Genesis's noncash balance sheet accounts affect its cash inflows and outflows (dollar amounts in thousands). The top of the exhibit shows the company's Cash T-account, and the lower part shows T-accounts for its remaining balance sheet accounts. We see that the $20,000 net cash provided by operating activities and the $5,000 net increase in cash shown in the Cash T-account agree with the same figures in the statement of cash flows in Exhibit 16.13. We explain Exhibit 16.14 in five parts:

a. Entry (1) records $38 net income on the credit side of the Retained Earnings account and the debit side of the Cash account. This $38 net income in the Cash T-account is adjusted until it reflects the $5 net increase in cash.

b. Entries (2) through (4) add the $24 depreciation and $6 loss on asset sale to net income and subtract the $16 gain on retirement of notes.

c. Entries (5) through (10) adjust net income for changes in current asset and current liability accounts.

d. Entry (11) records the noncash investing and financing transaction involving a $60 purchase of assets by issuing $60 of notes.

e. Entries (12) and (13) record the $15 stock issuance and the $14 dividend.

EXHIBIT 16.14

Balance Sheet T-Accounts to Explain the Change in Cash ($ thousands)

SUSTAINABILITY AND ACCOUNTING

Amazon.com seeks to reduce its environmental impact through a number of sustainability initiatives. One is frustration-free packaging. This multiyear initiative is "designed to make it easier for customers to liberate products from their packages."

Not only does this initiative lead to higher customer satisfaction, it also reduces waste and the use of plastic. According to Amazon's website, the frustration-free packaging is "100% recyclable" and eliminates "hard plastic clamshell cases and plastic-coated ties." Moreover, Amazon's packaging is made up of 50% recycled content.

Amazon supports charitable and nonprofit organizations through a program called *AmazonSmile*. According to its website, "AmazonSmile is a simple and automatic way for you to support your favorite charitable organization every time you shop, at no cost to you." AmazonSmile donates 0.5% of the purchase price of certain products to the charity or non-profit organization of your choice.

To ensure AmazonSmile sales are correctly tracked, Amazon relies on its accounting system to record separately its eligible and ineligible sales. The accounting system both records AmazonSmile sales and computes the amount to be donated.

Amazon sets up an accounts payable account for each charity that will receive a donation. At a future date, Amazon donates the cash to the charity and settles the accounts payable. Because of Amazon's charitable program and effective accounting system, programs such as the **American Red Cross** and **Doctors Without Borders** receive thousands in additional donations each year.

© Hardy Mueller/laif/Redux

Cash Flow Analysis      **Decision Analysis**

Analyzing Cash Sources and Uses

Most managers stress the importance of understanding and predicting cash flows for business decisions. Creditors evaluate a company's ability to generate cash before deciding whether to lend money. Investors also assess cash inflows and outflows before buying and selling stock. Information in the statement of cash flows helps address questions such as (1) How much cash is generated from or used in operations? (2) What expenditures are made with cash from operations? (3) What is the source of cash for debt payments? (4) What is the source of cash for distributions to owners? (5) How is the increase in investing activities financed? (6) What is the source of cash for new plant assets? (7) Why is cash flow from operations different from income? (8) How is cash from financing used?

To effectively answer these questions, it is important to separately analyze investing, financing, and operating activities. To illustrate, consider data from three different companies in Exhibit 16.15. These companies operate in the same industry and have been in business for several years.

A1 _____

Analyze the statement of cash flows and apply the cash flow on total assets ratio.

EXHIBIT 16.15

Cash Flows of Competing Companies

$ thousands	BMX	ATV	Trex
Cash provided (used) by operating activities	$90,000	$ 40,000	$(24,000)
Cash provided (used) by investing activities			
Proceeds from sale of plant assets....................			26,000
Purchase of plant assets	(48,000)	(25,000)	
Cash provided (used) by financing activities			
Proceeds from issuance of debt.....................			13,000
Repayment of debt	(27,000)		
Net increase (decrease) in cash	$15,000	$ 15,000	$ 15,000

Each company generates an identical $15,000 net increase in cash, but its sources and uses of cash flows are very different. BMX's operating activities provide net cash flows of $90,000, allowing it to purchase plant assets of $48,000 and repay $27,000 of its debt. ATV's operating activities provide $40,000 of cash flows, limiting its purchase of plant assets to $25,000. Trex's $15,000 net cash increase is due to selling plant assets and incurring additional debt. Its operating activities yield a net cash outflow of $24,000. Overall, analysis of these cash flows reveals that BMX is more capable of generating future cash flows than is ATV or Trex.

■ Decision Insight

Point: CFO (cash flow from operations)

Less: Capital expenditures

Less: Debt repayments

= FCF (free cash flows)

Free Cash Flows   Many investors use cash flows to value company stock. However, cash-based valuation models often yield different stock values due to differences in measurement of cash flows. Most models require cash flows that are "free" for distribution to shareholders. These *free cash flows* are defined as cash flows available to shareholders after operating asset reinvestments and debt payments. Knowledge of the statement of cash flows is key to proper computation of free cash flows. A company's growth and financial flexibility depend on adequate free cash flows. ■

Cash Flow on Total Assets

Cash flow information has limitations, but it can help measure a company's ability to meet its obligations, pay dividends, expand operations, and obtain financing. Users often compute and analyze a cash-based ratio similar to return on total assets except that its numerator is net cash flow from operating activities. The **cash flow on total assets** ratio is shown in Exhibit 16.16.

EXHIBIT 16.16

Cash Flow on Total Assets

$$\text{Cash flow on total assets} = \frac{\text{Cash flow from operations}}{\text{Average total assets}}$$

This ratio reflects actual cash flows and is not affected by accounting income recognition and measurement. It can help business decision makers estimate the amount and timing of cash flows when planning and analyzing operating activities.

To illustrate, the 2015 cash flow on total assets ratio for Nike is 23.3%—see Exhibit 16.17. Is a 23.3% ratio good or bad? To answer this question, we compare this ratio with the ratios of prior years (we could also compare its ratio with those of its competitors and the market). Nike's cash flow on total assets ratio for several prior years is in the second (middle) column of Exhibit 16.17. Results show that its 23.3% return is its highest return over the past five years.

EXHIBIT 16.17

Nike's Cash Flow on Total Assets

Year	Cash Flow on Total Assets	Return on Total Assets
2015	23.3%	16.3%
2014	16.6	14.9
2013	18.3	15.0
2012	12.5	14.6
2011	12.3	14.5

As an indicator of *earnings quality,* some analysts compare the cash flow on total assets ratio to the return on total assets ratio. Nike's return on total assets is provided in the third column of Exhibit 16.17. Nike's cash flow on total assets ratio exceeds its return on total assets in three of the past five years, leading some analysts to infer that Nike's earnings quality is not as good for that period because much of its earnings are not being realized in the form of cash.

■ Decision Insight

Point: The following ratio helps assess whether operating cash flow is adequate to meet long-term obligations:

Cash coverage of debt =
Cash flow from operations ÷
Noncurrent liabilities.

A low ratio suggests a higher risk of insolvency; a high ratio suggests a greater ability to meet long-term obligations.

Cash Flow Ratios   Analysts use various other cash-based ratios, including the following two:

(1) $$\text{Cash coverage of growth} = \frac{\text{Operating cash flow}}{\text{Cash outflow for plant assets}}$$

where a low ratio (less than 1) implies cash inadequacy to meet asset growth, whereas a high ratio implies cash adequacy for asset growth.

(2) $$\text{Operating cash flow to sales} = \frac{\text{Operating cash flow}}{\text{Net sales}}$$

When this ratio substantially and consistently differs from the operating income to net sales ratio, the risk of accounting improprieties increases. ■

Comparative balance sheets, income statement, and additional information follow.

NEED-TO-KNOW 16-5

COMPREHENSIVE

Preparing Statement of
Cash Flows—Indirect
and Direct Methods

UMA COMPANY Balance Sheets December 31, 2017 and 2016		
	2017	**2016**
Assets		
Cash	$ 43,050	$ 23,925
Accounts receivable	34,125	39,825
Inventory	156,000	146,475
Prepaid expenses	3,600	1,650
Total current assets	236,775	211,875
Equipment	135,825	146,700
Accum. depreciation—Equipment	(61,950)	(47,550)
Total assets	$310,650	$311,025
Liabilities		
Accounts payable	$ 28,800	$ 33,750
Income taxes payable	5,100	4,425
Dividends payable	0	4,500
Total current liabilities	33,900	42,675
Bonds payable	0	37,500
Total liabilities	33,900	80,175
Equity		
Common stock, $10 par	168,750	168,750
Retained earnings	108,000	62,100
Total liabilities and equity	$310,650	$311,025

UMA COMPANY Income Statement For Year Ended December 31, 2017		
Sales		$446,100
Cost of goods sold	$222,300	
Other operating expenses	120,300	
Depreciation expense	25,500	(368,100)
		78,000
Other gains (losses)		
Loss on sale of equipment	3,300	
Loss on retirement of bonds	825	(4,125)
Income before taxes		73,875
Income taxes expense		(13,725)
Net income		$ 60,150

Additional Information

a. Equipment costing $21,375 with accumulated depreciation of $11,100 is sold for cash.
b. Equipment purchases are for cash.
c. Accumulated Depreciation is affected by depreciation expense and the sale of equipment.
d. The balance of Retained Earnings is affected by dividend declarations and net income.
e. All sales are made on credit.
f. All inventory purchases are on credit.
g. Accounts Payable balances result from inventory purchases.
h. Prepaid expenses relate to "other operating expenses."

Required

1. Prepare a statement of cash flows using the indirect method for year 2017.
2.ᴮ Prepare a statement of cash flows using the direct method for year 2017.

PLANNING THE SOLUTION

- Prepare two blank statements of cash flows with sections for operating, investing, and financing activities using the (1) indirect method format and (2) direct method format.
- Compute the cash paid for equipment and the cash received from the sale of equipment using the additional information provided along with the amount for depreciation expense and the change in the balances of Equipment and Accumulated Depreciation. Use T-accounts to help chart the effects of the sale and purchase of equipment on the balances of the Equipment account and the Accumulated Depreciation account.

- Compute the effect of net income on the change in the Retained Earnings account balance. Assign the difference between the change in retained earnings and the amount of net income to dividends declared. Adjust the dividends declared amount for the change in the Dividends Payable balance.
- Compute cash received from customers, cash paid for inventory, cash paid for other operating expenses, and cash paid for taxes as illustrated in the chapter.
- Enter the cash effects of reconstruction entries to the appropriate section(s) of the statement.
- Total each section of the statement, determine the total net change in cash, and add it to the beginning balance to get the ending balance of cash.

SOLUTION

Supporting computations for cash receipts and cash payments.

(1)	*Cost of equipment sold	$ 21,375
	Accumulated depreciation of equipment sold	(11,100)
	Book value of equipment sold	10,275
	Loss on sale of equipment	(3,300)
	Cash received from sale of equipment	$ 6,975
	Cost of equipment sold	$ 21,375
	Less decrease in the Equipment account balance	(10,875)
	Cash paid for new equipment	$ 10,500
(2)	Loss on retirement of bonds	$ 825
	Carrying value of bonds retired	37,500
	Cash paid to retire bonds	$ 38,325
(3)	Net income	$ 60,150
	Less increase in retained earnings	45,900
	Dividends declared	14,250
	Plus decrease in dividends payable	4,500
	Cash paid for dividends	$ 18,750
(4)B	Sales	$ 446,100
	Add decrease in accounts receivable	5,700
	Cash received from customers	$451,800
(5)B	Cost of goods sold	$ 222,300
	Plus increase in inventory	9,525
	Purchases	231,825
	Plus decrease in accounts payable	4,950
	Cash paid for inventory	$236,775
(6)B	Other operating expenses	$ 120,300
	Plus increase in prepaid expenses	1,950
	Cash paid for other operating expenses	$122,250
(7)B	Income taxes expense	$ 13,725
	Less increase in income taxes payable	(675)
	Cash paid for income taxes	$ 13,050

* Supporting T-account analysis for part 1 follows.

Equipment					Accumulated Depreciation—Equipment			
Bal., Dec. 31, 2016	146,700						Bal., Dec. 31, 2016	47,550
Cash purchase	10,500	Sale	21,375		Sale	11,100	Depr. expense	25,500
Bal., Dec. 31, 2017	135,825						Bal., Dec. 31, 2017	61,950

1. Indirect method:

UMA COMPANY Statement of Cash Flows (Indirect Method) For Year Ended December 31, 2017		
Cash flows from operating activities		
Net income		$ 60,150
Adjustments to reconcile net income to net cash provided by operating activities		
Income statement items not affecting cash		
Depreciation expense	25,500	
Loss on sale of plant assets	3,300	
Loss on retirement of bonds	825	
Changes in current assets and current liabilities		
Decrease in accounts receivable	5,700	
Increase in inventory	(9,525)	
Increase in prepaid expenses	(1,950)	
Decrease in accounts payable	(4,950)	
Increase in income taxes payable	675	
Net cash provided by operating activities		$79,725
Cash flows from investing activities		
Cash received from sale of equipment	6,975	
Cash paid for equipment	(10,500)	
Net cash used in investing activities		(3,525)
Cash flows from financing activities		
Cash paid to retire bonds payable	(38,325)	
Cash paid for dividends	(18,750)	
Net cash used in financing activities		(57,075)
Net increase in cash		$19,125
Cash balance at prior year-end		23,925
Cash balance at current year-end		$43,050

2.[B] Direct method (Appendix 16B):

UMA COMPANY Statement of Cash Flows (Direct Method) For Year Ended December 31, 2017		
Cash flows from operating activities		
Cash received from customers	$ 451,800	
Cash paid for inventory	(236,775)	
Cash paid for other operating expenses	(122,250)	
Cash paid for income taxes	(13,050)	
Net cash provided by operating activities		$ 79,725
Cash flows from investing activities		
Cash received from sale of equipment	6,975	
Cash paid for equipment	(10,500)	
Net cash used in investing activities		(3,525)
Cash flows from financing activities		
Cash paid to retire bonds payable	(38,325)	
Cash paid for dividends	(18,750)	
Net cash used in financing activities		(57,075)
Net increase in cash		$ 19,125
Cash balance at prior year-end		23,925
Cash balance at current year-end		$ 43,050

16A
Spreadsheet Preparation of the Statement of Cash Flows

This appendix explains how to use a spreadsheet (work sheet) to prepare the statement of cash flows under the indirect method.

P4

Illustrate use of a spreadsheet to prepare a statement of cash flows.

Preparing the Indirect Method Spreadsheet   Analyzing noncash accounts can be challenging when a company has a large number of accounts and many operating, investing, and financing transactions. A *spreadsheet,* also called *work sheet* or *working paper,* can help us organize the information needed to prepare a statement of cash flows. A spreadsheet also makes it easier to check the accuracy of our work. To illustrate, we return to the comparative balance sheets and income statement shown in Exhibit 16.10. We use the following identifying letters *a* through *g* to code changes in accounts, and letters *h* through *m* for additional information, to prepare the statement of cash flows:

- **a.** Net income is $38,000.
- **b.** Accounts receivable increase by $20,000.
- **c.** Inventory increases by $14,000.
- **d.** Prepaid expenses increase by $2,000.
- **e.** Accounts payable decrease by $5,000.
- **f.** Interest payable decreases by $1,000.
- **g.** Income taxes payable increase by $10,000.
- **h.** Depreciation expense is $24,000.
- **i.** Plant assets costing $20,000 with accumulated depreciation of $12,000 are sold for $2,000 cash. This yields a loss on sale of assets of $6,000.
- **j.** Notes with a book value of $34,000 are retired with a cash payment of $18,000, yielding a $16,000 gain on retirement.
- **k.** Plant assets costing $60,000 are purchased with an issuance of notes payable for $60,000.
- **l.** Issued 3,000 shares of common stock for $15,000 cash.
- **m.** Paid cash dividends of $14,000.

Exhibit 16A.1 shows the indirect method spreadsheet for Genesis. We enter both beginning and ending balance sheet amounts on the spreadsheet. We also enter information in the Analysis of Changes columns (keyed to the additional information items *a* through *m*) to explain changes in the accounts and determine the cash flows for operating, investing, and financing activities. Information about noncash investing and financing activities is reported near the bottom.

Entering the Analysis of Changes on the Spreadsheet   The following sequence of procedures is used to complete the spreadsheet after the beginning and ending balances of the balance sheet accounts are entered:

① Enter net income as the first item in the statement of cash flows section for computing operating cash inflow (debit) and as a credit to Retained Earnings.

② In the statement of cash flows section, adjustments to net income are entered as debits if they increase cash flows and as credits if they decrease cash flows. Applying this same rule, adjust net income for the change in each noncash current asset and current liability account related to operating activities. For each adjustment to net income, the offsetting debit or credit must help reconcile the beginning and ending balances of a current asset or current liability account.

③ Enter adjustments to net income for income statement items not providing or using cash in the period. For each adjustment, the offsetting debit or credit must help reconcile a noncash balance sheet account.

④ Adjust net income to eliminate any gains or losses from investing and financing activities. Because the cash from a gain must be excluded from operating activities, the gain is entered as a credit in the operating activities section. Losses are entered as debits. For each adjustment, the related debit and/or credit must help reconcile balance sheet accounts and involve reconstructed entries to show the cash flow from investing or financing activities.

Point: Analysis of the changes on the spreadsheet are summarized here:

1. Cash flows from operating activities generally affect net income, current assets, and current liabilities.
2. Cash flows from investing activities generally affect noncurrent asset accounts.
3. Cash flows from financing activities generally affect noncurrent liability and equity accounts.

	A	B	C	D	E	F	G
1		GENESIS					
2		Spreadsheet for Statement of Cash Flows—Indirect Method					
3		For Year Ended December 31, 2017					
4		Dec. 31,		Analysis of Changes			Dec. 31,
5		2016		Debit		Credit	2017
6	**Balance Sheet—Debit Bal. Accounts**						
7	Cash	$ 12,000					$ 17,000
8	Accounts receivable	40,000	(b)	$ 20,000			60,000
9	Inventory	70,000	(c)	14,000			84,000
10	Prepaid expenses	4,000	(d)	2,000			6,000
11	Plant assets	210,000	(k1)	60,000	(i)	$ 20,000	250,000
12		$336,000					$417,000
13	**Balance Sheet—Credit Bal. Accounts**						
14	Accumulated depreciation	$ 48,000	(i)	12,000	(h)	24,000	$ 60,000
15	Accounts payable	40,000	(e)	5,000			35,000
16	Interest payable	4,000	(f)	1,000			3,000
17	Income taxes payable	12,000			(g)	10,000	22,000
18	Notes payable	64,000	(j)	34,000	(k2)	60,000	90,000
19	Common stock, $5 par value	80,000			(l)	15,000	95,000
20	Retained earnings	88,000	(m)	14,000	(a)	38,000	112,000
21		$336,000					$417,000
22	**Statement of Cash Flows**						
23	Operating activities						
24	Net income		(a)	38,000			
25	Increase in accounts receivable				(b)	20,000	
26	Increase in inventory				(c)	14,000	
27	Increase in prepaid expenses				(d)	2,000	
28	Decrease in accounts payable				(e)	5,000	
29	Decrease in interest payable				(f)	1,000	
30	Increase in income taxes payable		(g)	10,000			
31	Depreciation expense		(h)	24,000			
32	Loss on sale of plant assets		(i)	6,000			
33	Gain on retirement of notes				(j)	16,000	
34	Investing activities						
35	Receipts from sale of plant assets		(i)	2,000			
36	Financing activities						
37	Payment to retire notes				(j)	18,000	
38	Receipts from issuing stock		(l)	15,000			
39	Payment of cash dividends				(m)	14,000	
40							
41	**Noncash Investing and Financing Activities**						
42	Purchase of plant assets with notes		(k2)	60,000	(k1)	60,000	
				$317,000		$317,000	

EXHIBIT 16A.1

Spreadsheet for Preparing Statement of Cash Flows—Indirect Method

⑤ After reviewing any unreconciled balance sheet accounts and related information, enter the remaining reconciling entries for investing and financing activities. Examples are purchases of plant assets, issuances of long-term debt, stock issuances, and dividend payments. Some of these may require entries in the noncash investing and financing section of the spreadsheet (reconciled).

⑥ Check accuracy by totaling the Analysis of Changes columns and by determining that the change in each balance sheet account has been explained (reconciled).

We illustrate these steps in Exhibit 16A.1 for Genesis:

Step	Entries
①..........	(a)
②..........	(b) through (g)
③..........	(h)
④..........	(i) through (j)
⑤..........	(k) through (m)

Since adjustments *i, j,* and *k* are more challenging, we show them in the following debit and credit format. These entries are for purposes of our understanding; they are *not* the entries actually made in the journals. Changes in the Cash account are identified as sources or uses of cash.

i.	Cash—Receipt from sale of plant assets **(source of cash)**	2,000	
	Loss from sale of plant assets	6,000	
	Accumulated depreciation	12,000	
	Plant assets		20,000
	Describe sale of plant assets.		
j.	Notes payable	34,000	
	Cash—Payments to retire notes **(use of cash)**		18,000
	Gain on retirement of notes		16,000
	Describe retirement of notes.		
k1.	Plant assets	60,000	
	Cash—Purchase of plant assets financed by notes		60,000
	Describe purchase of plant assets.		
k2.	Cash—Purchase of plant assets financed by notes	60,000	
	Notes payable		60,000
	Issue notes for purchase of assets.		

APPENDIX

Direct Method of Reporting Operating Cash Flows

16B

P5

Compute cash flows from operating activities using the direct method.

We compute cash flows from operating activities under the direct method by adjusting accrual-based income statement items to the cash basis. The usual approach is to adjust income statement accounts related to operating activities for changes in their related balance sheet accounts as follows:

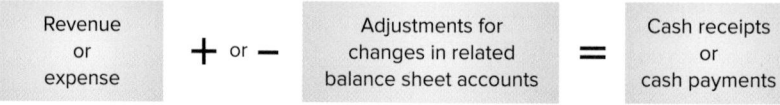

The framework for reporting cash receipts and cash payments for the operating section of the cash flow statement under the direct method is presented in Exhibit 16B.1. We consider cash receipts first and then cash payments.

EXHIBIT 16B.1

Major Classes of Operating Cash Flows

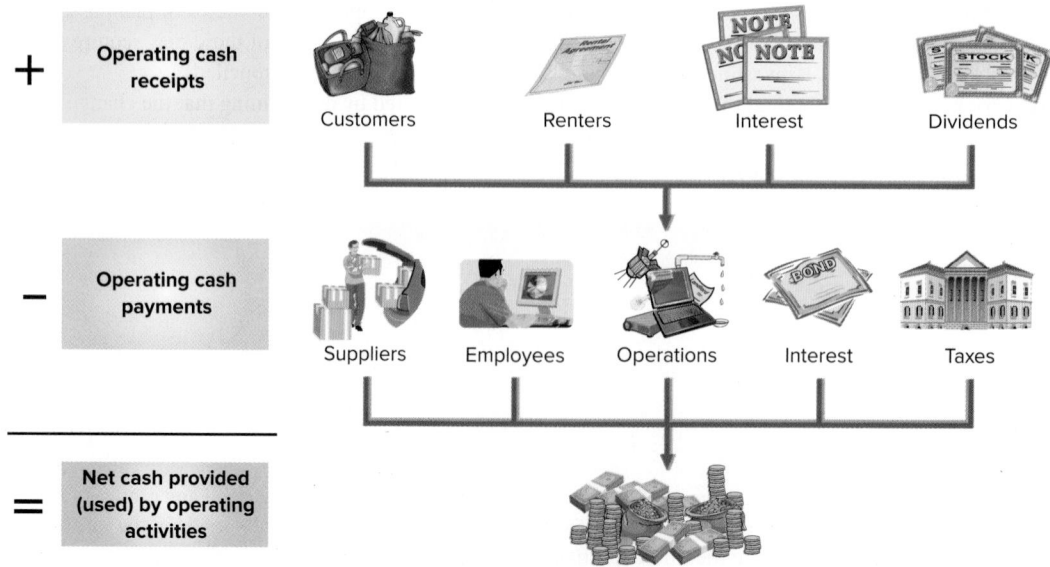

Operating Cash Receipts   A review of Exhibit 16.10 and the additional information reported by Genesis suggests only one potential cash receipt: sales to customers. This section, therefore, starts with sales to customers as reported on the income statement and then adjusts it as necessary to obtain cash received from customers to report on the statement of cash flows.

Cash Received from Customers   If all sales are for cash, the amount received from customers equals the sales reported on the income statement. When some or all sales are on account, however, we must adjust the amount of sales for the change in Accounts Receivable. It is often helpful to use *account analysis* to do this. This usually involves setting up a T-account and reconstructing its major entries, with emphasis on cash receipts and payments.

To illustrate, we use a T-account that includes accounts receivable balances for Genesis on December 31, 2016 and 2017. The beginning balance is $40,000 and the ending balance is $60,000. Next, the income statement shows sales of $590,000, which we enter on the debit side of this account. We now can reconstruct the Accounts Receivable account to determine the amount of cash received from customers as follows:

Point: An accounts receivable increase implies that cash received from customers is less than sales (the converse is also true).

Accounts Receivable			
Bal., Dec. 31, 2016	40,000		
Sales	590,000	Cash receipts =	570,000
Bal., Dec. 31, 2017	60,000		

Reconstructed Entry

Cash..........	570,000
Accts Recble....	20,000
Sales	590,000

This T-account shows that the Accounts Receivable balance begins at $40,000 and increases to $630,000 from sales of $590,000, yet its ending balance is only $60,000. This implies that cash receipts from customers are $570,000, computed as $40,000 + $590,000 − [?] = $60,000. This computation can be rearranged to express cash received as equal to sales of $590,000 minus a $20,000 increase in accounts receivable. This computation is summarized as a general rule in Exhibit 16B.2. Genesis reports the $570,000 cash received from customers as a cash inflow from operating activities.

Example: If the ending balance of Accounts Receivable is $20,000 (instead of $60,000), what is cash received from customers? *Answer:* $610,000

$$\text{Cash received from customers} = \text{Sales} \quad \begin{array}{l} + \textbf{Decrease in accounts receivable} \\ \text{or} \\ - \textbf{Increase in accounts receivable} \end{array}$$

EXHIBIT 16B.2

Formula to Compute Cash Received from Customers—Direct Method

Other Cash Receipts   While Genesis's cash receipts are limited to collections from customers, we often see other types of cash receipts, most commonly cash receipts involving rent, interest, and dividends. We compute cash received from these items by subtracting an increase in their respective receivable or adding a decrease. For instance, if rent receivable increases in the period, cash received from renters is less than rent revenue reported on the income statement. If rent receivable decreases, cash received is more than reported rent revenue. The same logic applies to interest and dividends. The formulas for these computations are summarized later in this appendix.

Point: Net income is measured using accrual accounting. Cash flows from operations are measured using cash basis accounting.

Operating Cash Payments   A review of Exhibit 16.10 and the additional Genesis information shows four operating expenses: cost of goods sold; wages and other operating expenses; interest expense; and taxes expense. We analyze each expense to compute its cash amounts for the statement of cash flows. (We then examine depreciation and the other losses and gains.)

Cash Paid for Inventory   We compute cash paid for inventory by analyzing both cost of goods sold and inventory. If all inventory purchases are for cash and the ending balance of Inventory is unchanged from the beginning balance, the amount of cash paid for inventory equals cost of goods sold—an uncommon situation. Instead, there normally is some change in the Inventory balance. Also, some or all purchases are often made on credit, and this yields changes in the Accounts Payable balance. When the balances of both Inventory and Accounts Payable change, we must adjust the cost of goods sold for changes in both accounts to compute cash paid for inventory. This is a two-step adjustment.

First, we use the change in the account balance of Inventory, along with the cost of goods sold amount, to compute cost of purchases for the period. An increase in inventory implies that we bought more than we sold, and we add this inventory increase to cost of goods sold to compute cost of purchases. A decrease in inventory implies that we bought less than we sold, and we subtract the inventory decrease from cost of goods sold to compute purchases. We illustrate the *first step* by reconstructing the Inventory account.

Inventory			
Bal., Dec. 31, 2016	70,000		
Purchases =	**314,000**	Cost of goods sold	300,000
Bal., Dec. 31, 2017	84,000		

The beginning balance is $70,000, and the ending balance is $84,000. The income statement shows that cost of goods sold is $300,000, which we enter on the credit side of this account. With this information, we determine the amount for cost of purchases to be $314,000. This computation can be rearranged to express cost of purchases as equal to cost of goods sold of $300,000 plus the $14,000 increase in inventory.

The second step uses the change in the balance of Accounts Payable, and the amount of cost of purchases, to compute cash paid for inventory. A decrease in accounts payable implies that we paid for more goods than we acquired this period, and we would then add the accounts payable decrease to cost of purchases to compute cash paid for inventory. An increase in accounts payable implies that we paid for less than the amount of goods acquired, and we would subtract the accounts payable increase from purchases to compute cash paid for inventory. The *second step* is applied to Genesis by reconstructing its Accounts Payable account.

Accounts Payable			
		Bal., Dec. 31, 2016	40,000
Cash payments =	**319,000**	Purchases	314,000
		Bal., Dec. 31, 2017	35,000

Example: If the ending balances of Inventory and Accounts Payable are $60,000 and $50,000, respectively (instead of $84,000 and $35,000), what is cash paid for inventory? *Answer:* $280,000

Its beginning balance of $40,000 plus purchases of $314,000 minus an ending balance of $35,000 yields cash paid of $319,000 (or $40,000 + $314,000 − [?] = $35,000). Alternatively, we can express cash paid for inventory as equal to purchases of $314,000 plus the $5,000 decrease in accounts payable. The $319,000 cash paid for inventory is reported on the statement of cash flows as a cash outflow under operating activities.

We summarize this two-step adjustment to cost of goods sold to compute cash paid for inventory in Exhibit 16B.3.

EXHIBIT 16B.3

Two Steps to Compute Cash Paid for Inventory—Direct Method

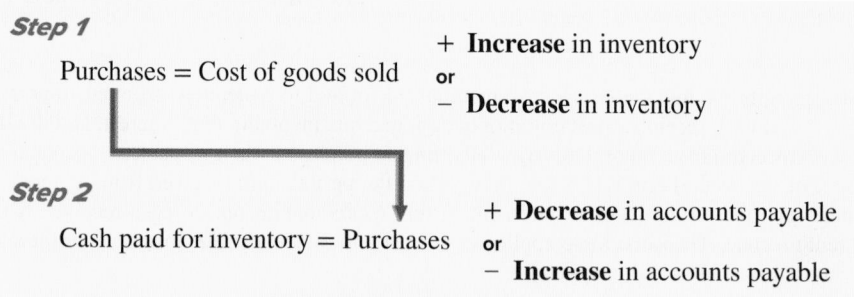

Cash Paid for Wages and Operating Expenses (Excluding Depreciation)   The income statement of Genesis shows wages and other operating expenses of $216,000 (see Exhibit 16.10). To compute cash paid for wages and other operating expenses, we adjust this amount for any changes in their related balance sheet accounts. We begin by looking for any prepaid expenses and accrued liabilities related to wages and other operating expenses in the balance sheets of Genesis in Exhibit 16.10. The balance sheets show prepaid expenses but no accrued liabilities. Thus, the adjustment is limited to the change in prepaid expenses. The amount of adjustment is computed by assuming that all cash paid for wages and other operating expenses is initially debited to Prepaid Expenses. This assumption allows us to reconstruct the Prepaid Expenses account as follows:

Prepaid Expenses			
Bal., Dec. 31, 2016	4,000		
Cash payments =	**218,000**	Wages and other operating exp.	216,000
Bal., Dec. 31, 2017	6,000		

Prepaid expenses increase by $2,000 in the period, meaning that cash paid for wages and other operating expenses exceeds the reported expense by $2,000. Alternatively, we can express cash paid for wages and other operating expenses as equal to its reported expenses of $216,000 plus the $2,000 increase in prepaid expenses.[1]

Exhibit 16B.4 summarizes the adjustments to wages (including salaries) and other operating expenses. The Genesis balance sheet did not report accrued liabilities, but we include them in the formula to explain the adjustment to cash when they do exist. A decrease in accrued liabilities implies that we paid cash for more goods or services than received this period, so we add the decrease in accrued liabilities to the expense amount to obtain cash paid for these goods or services. An increase in accrued liabilities implies that we paid cash for less than what was acquired, so we subtract this increase in accrued liabilities from the expense amount to get cash paid.

Point: A decrease in prepaid expenses implies that reported expenses include an amount(s) that did not require a cash outflow in the period.

Cash paid for wages and other operating expenses	=	Wages and other operating expenses	+ **Increase** in prepaid expenses or − **Decrease** in prepaid expenses	+ **Decrease** in accrued liabilities or − **Increase** in accrued liabilities

EXHIBIT 16B.4

Formula to Compute Cash Paid for Wages and Operating Expenses—Direct Method

Cash Paid for Interest and Income Taxes   Computing operating cash flows for interest and taxes is similar to that for operating expenses. Both require adjustments to their amounts reported on the income statement for changes in their related balance sheet accounts. We begin with the Genesis income statement showing interest expense of $7,000 and income taxes expense of $15,000. To compute the cash paid, we adjust interest expense for the change in interest payable and then the income taxes expense for the change in income taxes payable. These computations involve reconstructing both liability accounts.

Interest Payable		
	Bal., Dec. 31, 2016	4,000
Cash paid for interest = 8,000	Interest expense	7,000
	Bal., Dec. 31, 2017	3,000

Reconstructed Entry
Int. Expense	7,000	
Int. Payable	1,000	
Cash		8,000

Income Taxes Payable		
	Bal., Dec. 31, 2016	12,000
Cash paid for taxes = 5,000	Income taxes expense	15,000
	Bal., Dec. 31, 2017	22,000

Reconstructed Entry
Inc. Tax Exp.	15,000	
Inc. Tax Pay.		10,000
Cash		5,000

These T-accounts reveal cash paid for interest of $8,000 and cash paid for income taxes of $5,000. The formulas to compute these amounts are in Exhibit 16B.5. Both of these cash payments are reported as operating cash outflows on the statement of cash flows.

Cash paid for interest	=	Interest expense	+ **Decrease** in interest payable or − **Increase** in interest payable
Cash paid for taxes	=	Income taxes expense	+ **Decrease** in income taxes payable or − **Increase** in income taxes payable

EXHIBIT 16B.5

Formulas to Compute Cash Paid for Both Interest and Taxes—Direct Method

---

[1] The assumption that all cash payments for wages and operating expenses are initially debited to Prepaid Expenses is not necessary for our analysis to hold. If cash payments are debited directly to the expense account, the total amount of cash paid for wages and other operating expenses still equals the $216,000 expense plus the $2,000 increase in prepaid expenses (which arise from end-of-period adjusting entries).

Analyzing Additional Expenses, Gains, and Losses   Genesis has three additional items reported on its income statement: depreciation, loss on sale of assets, and gain on retirement of debt. We must consider each for its potential cash effects.

Depreciation Expense   Depreciation expense is $24,000. It is often called a *noncash expense* because depreciation has no cash flows. Depreciation expense is an allocation of an asset's depreciable cost. The cash outflow with a plant asset is reported as part of investing activities when it is paid for. Thus, depreciation expense is *never* reported on a statement of cash flows using the direct method; nor is depletion or amortization expense.

Loss on Sale of Assets   Sales of assets frequently result in gains and losses reported as part of net income, but the amount of recorded gain or loss does *not* reflect any cash flows in these transactions. Asset sales result in cash inflow equal to the cash amount received, regardless of whether the asset was sold at a gain or a loss. This cash inflow is reported under investing activities. Thus, the loss or gain on a sale of assets is *never* reported on a statement of cash flows using the direct method.

Point: The direct method is usually viewed as *user friendly* because less accounting knowledge is required to understand and use it.

Gain on Retirement of Debt   Retirement of debt usually yields a gain or loss reported as part of net income, but that gain or loss does *not* reflect cash flow in this transaction. Debt retirement results in cash outflow equal to the cash paid to settle the debt, regardless of whether the debt is retired at a gain or loss. This cash outflow is reported under financing activities; the loss or gain from retirement of debt is *never* reported on a statement of cash flows using the direct method.

Summary of Adjustments for Direct Method   Exhibit 16B.6 summarizes common adjustments for net income to yield net cash provided (used) by operating activities under the direct method.

EXHIBIT 16B.6

Summary of Selected Adjustments for Direct Method

Item	From Income Statement	Adjustments to Obtain Cash Flow Numbers	
Receipts			
From sales	Sales Revenue	+ Decrease in Accounts Receivable – Increase in Accounts Receivable	
From rent	Rent Revenue	+ Decrease in Rent Receivable – Increase in Rent Receivable	
From interest	Interest Revenue	+ Decrease in Interest Receivable – Increase in Interest Receivable	
From dividends	Dividend Revenue	+ Decrease in Dividends Receivable – Increase in Dividends Receivable	
Payments			
To suppliers	Cost of Goods Sold	+ Increase in Inventory – Decrease in Inventory	+ Decrease in Accounts Payable – Increase in Accounts Payable
For operations	Operating Expense	+ Increase in Prepaids – Decrease in Prepaids	+ Decrease in Accrued Liabilities – Increase in Accrued Liabilities
To employees	Wages (Salaries) Expense	+ Decrease in Wages (Salaries) Payable – Increase in Wages (Salaries) Payable	
For interest	Interest Expense	+ Decrease in Interest Payable – Increase in Interest Payable	
For taxes	Income Tax Expense	+ Decrease in Income Tax Payable – Increase in Income Tax Payable	

Direct Method Format of Operating Activities Section   Exhibit 16B.7 shows the Genesis statement of cash flows using the direct method. Major items of cash inflows and cash outflows are listed separately in the operating activities section. The format requires that operating cash outflows be subtracted from operating cash inflows to get net cash provided (used) by operating activities.

The FASB recommends that the operating activities section of the statement of cash flows be reported using the direct method. *However, the FASB requires a reconciliation of net income to net cash provided (used) by operating activities when the direct method is used* (which can be reported in the notes). This reconciliation follows the preparation of the operating activities section of the statement of cash flows using the indirect method.

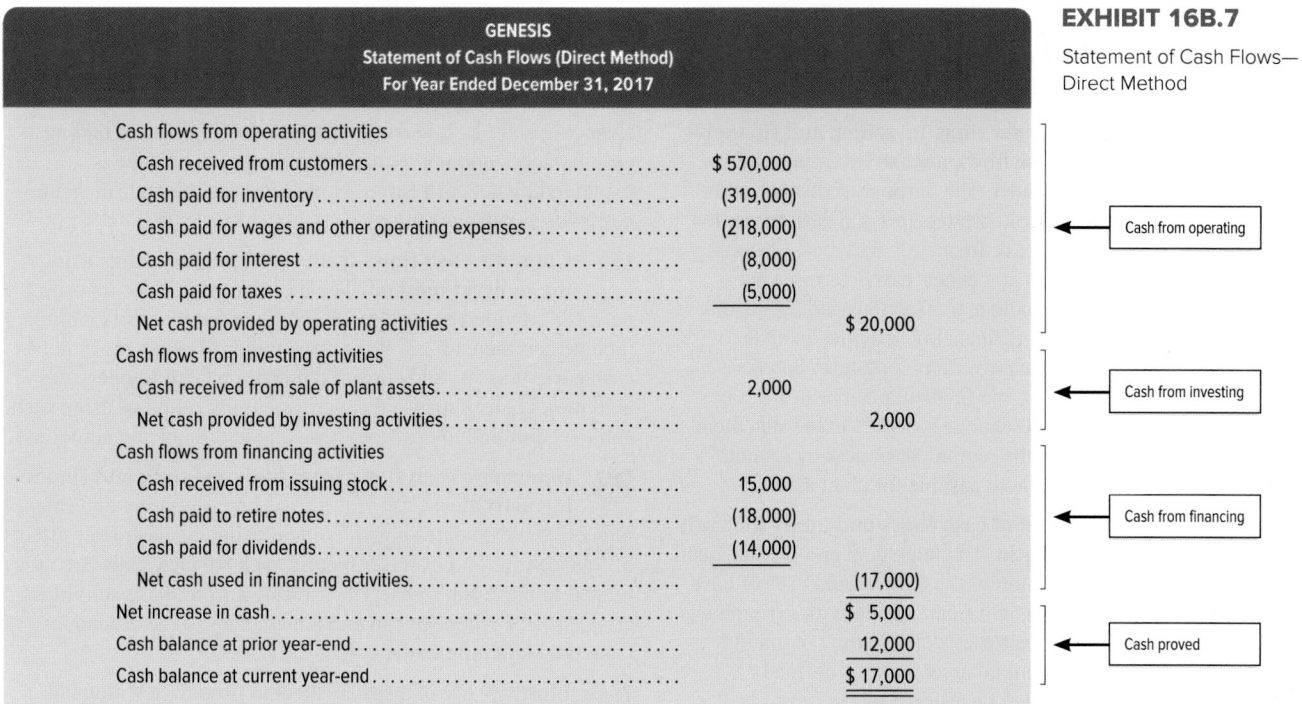

EXHIBIT 16B.7

Statement of Cash Flows—
Direct Method

GENESIS Statement of Cash Flows (Direct Method) For Year Ended December 31, 2017		
Cash flows from operating activities		
Cash received from customers	$ 570,000	
Cash paid for inventory	(319,000)	
Cash paid for wages and other operating expenses.	(218,000)	
Cash paid for interest	(8,000)	
Cash paid for taxes	(5,000)	
Net cash provided by operating activities		$ 20,000
Cash flows from investing activities		
Cash received from sale of plant assets.	2,000	
Net cash provided by investing activities.		2,000
Cash flows from financing activities		
Cash received from issuing stock	15,000	
Cash paid to retire notes.	(18,000)	
Cash paid for dividends.	(14,000)	
Net cash used in financing activities.		(17,000)
Net increase in cash.		$ 5,000
Cash balance at prior year-end		12,000
Cash balance at current year-end		$ 17,000

Cash from operating

Cash from investing

Cash from financing

Cash proved

A company's current-year income statement and selected balance sheet data at December 31 of the current and prior years follow. Prepare only the operating activities section of the statement of cash flows using the direct method for the current year.

NEED-TO-KNOW 16-6

Reporting Operating
Cash Flows (Direct)

P5

Income Statement For Current Year Ended December 31	
Sales revenue	$120
Expenses	
Cost of goods sold	50
Depreciation expense	30
Salaries expense.	17
Interest expense	3
Net income	$ 20

Selected Balance Sheet Accounts		
At December 31	Current Yr	Prior Yr
Accounts receivable	$12	$10
Inventory	6	9
Accounts payable	7	11
Salaries payable	8	3
Interest payable.	1	0

Solution

Cash Flows from Operating Activities—Direct Method For Current Year Ended December 31		
Cash flows from operating activities*		
Cash received from customers	$118	
Cash paid for inventory	(51)	
Cash paid for salaries	(12)	
Cash paid for interest	(2)	
Net cash provided by operating activities.		$53

* Supporting computations:
Cash received from customers = Sales of $120 − Accounts Receivable increase of $2.
Cash paid for inventory = COGS of $50 − Inventory decrease of $3 + Accounts Payable decrease of $4.
Cash paid for salaries = Salaries Expense of $17 − Salaries Payable increase of $5.
Cash paid for interest = Interest Expense of $3 − Interest Payable increase of $1.

Do More: QS 16-14, QS 16-15,
QS 16-16, E 16-12, E 16-14,
E 16-15, E 16-16

Summary

C1 **Distinguish between operating, investing, and financing activities, and describe how noncash investing and financing activities are disclosed.** The purpose of the statement of cash flows is to report major cash receipts and cash payments related to operating, investing, or financing activities. Operating activities include transactions and events that determine net income. Investing activities include transactions and events that mainly affect long-term assets. Financing activities include transactions and events that mainly affect long-term liabilities and equity. Noncash investing and financing activities must be disclosed in either a note or a separate schedule to the statement of cash flows. Examples are the retirement of debt by issuing equity and the exchange of a note payable for plant assets.

A1 **Analyze the statement of cash flows and apply the cash flow on total assets ratio.** To understand and predict cash flows, users stress identification of the sources and uses of cash flows by operating, investing, and financing activities. Emphasis is on operating cash flows since they derive from continuing operations. The cash flow on total assets ratio is defined as operating cash flows divided by average total assets. Analysis of current and past values for this ratio can reflect a company's ability to yield regular and positive cash flows. It is also viewed as a measure of earnings quality.

P1 **Prepare a statement of cash flows.** Preparation of a statement of cash flows involves five steps: (1) Compute the net increase or decrease in cash; (2) compute net cash provided or used by operating activities (*using either the direct or indirect method*); (3) compute net cash provided or used by investing activities; (4) compute net cash provided or used by

financing activities; and (5) report the beginning and ending cash balances and prove that the ending cash balance is explained by net cash flows. Noncash investing and financing activities are also disclosed.

P2 **Compute cash flows from operating activities using the indirect method.** The indirect method for reporting net cash provided or used by operating activities starts with net income and then adjusts it for three items: (1) changes in non-cash current assets and current liabilities related to operating activities, (2) revenues and expenses not providing or using cash, and (3) gains and losses from investing and financing activities.

P3 **Determine cash flows from both investing and financing activities.** Cash flows from both investing and financing activities are determined by identifying the cash flow effects of transactions and events affecting each balance sheet account related to these activities. All cash flows from these activities are identified when we can explain changes in these accounts from the beginning to the end of the period.

P4^A **Illustrate use of a spreadsheet to prepare a statement of cash flows.** A spreadsheet is a useful tool in preparing a statement of cash flows. Six key steps (see Appendix 16A) are applied when using the spreadsheet to prepare the statement.

P5^B **Compute cash flows from operating activities using the direct method.** The direct method for reporting net cash provided or used by operating activities lists major operating cash inflows less cash outflows to yield net cash inflow or outflow from operations.

Key Terms

Cash flow on total assets	Indirect method	Operating activities
Direct method	Investing activities	Statement of cash flows
Financing activities		

Multiple Choice Quiz

1. A company uses the indirect method to determine its cash flows from operating activities. Use the following information to determine its net cash provided or used by operating activities.

Net income	$15,200
Depreciation expense	10,000
Cash payment on note payable.............	8,000
Gain on sale of land	3,000
Increase in inventory	1,500
Increase in accounts payable	2,850

   a. $23,550 used by operating activities
   b. $23,550 provided by operating activities
   c. $15,550 provided by operating activities

   d. $42,400 provided by operating activities
   e. $20,850 provided by operating activities

2. A machine with a cost of $175,000 and accumulated depreciation of $94,000 is sold for $87,000 cash. The amount reported as a source of cash under cash flows from investing activities is
   a. $81,000.
   b. $6,000.
   c. $87,000.
   d. Zero; this is a financing activity.
   e. Zero; this is an operating activity.

3. A company settles a long-term note payable plus interest by paying $68,000 cash toward the principal amount and

$5,440 cash for interest. The amount reported as a use of cash under cash flows from financing activities is

a. Zero; this is an investing activity.

b. Zero; this is an operating activity.

c. $73,440.

d. $68,000.

e. $5,440.

4. The following information is available regarding a company's annual salaries and wages. What amount of cash is paid for salaries and wages?

Salaries and wages expense	$255,000
Salaries and wages payable, prior year-end	8,200
Salaries and wages payable, current year-end	10,900

ANSWERS TO MULTIPLE CHOICE QUIZ

1. b;

Net income	$15,200
Depreciation expense	10,000
Gain on sale of land	(3,000)
Increase in inventory	(1,500)
Increase in accounts payable	2,850
Net cash provided by operations.	$23,550

a. $252,300   c. $255,000   e. $235,900

b. $257,700   d. $274,100

5. The following information is available for a company. What amount of cash is paid for inventory for the current year?

Cost of goods sold	$545,000
Inventory, prior year-end	105,000
Inventory, current year-end	112,000
Accounts payable, prior year-end	98,500
Accounts payable, current year-end	101,300

a. $545,000   c. $540,800   e. $549,200

b. $554,800   d. $535,200

2. c; Cash received from sale of machine is reported as an investing activity.

3. d; FASB requires cash interest paid to be reported under operating.

4. a; Cash paid for salaries and wages = $255,000 + $8,200 − $10,900 = $252,300

5. e; Increase in inventory = $112,000 − $105,000 = $7,000

Increase in accounts payable = $101,300 − $98,500 = $2,800

Cash paid for inventory = $545,000 + $7,000 − $2,800 = $549,200

A(B) *Superscript letter A (B) denotes assignments based on Appendix 16A (16B).*

[I] Icon denotes assignments that involve decision making.

Discussion Questions

1. What is the reporting purpose of the statement of cash flows? Identify at least two questions that this statement can answer.

2. What are some investing activities reported on the statement of cash flows?

3. What are some financing activities reported on the statement of cash flows?

4.^B Describe the direct method of reporting cash flows from operating activities.

5. When a statement of cash flows is prepared using the direct method, what are some of the operating cash flows?

6. Describe the indirect method of reporting cash flows from operating activities.

7. Where on the statement of cash flows is the payment of cash dividends reported?

8. [I] Assume that a company purchases land for $1,000,000, paying $400,000 cash and borrowing the remainder with a long-term note payable. How should this transaction be reported on a statement of cash flows?

9. [I] On June 3, a company borrows $200,000 cash by giving its bank a 90-day, interest-bearing note. On the statement of cash flows, where should this be reported?

10. [I] If a company reports positive net income for the year, can it also show a net cash outflow from operating activities? Explain.

11. [I] Is depreciation a source of cash flow?

12. [I] Refer to Apple's statement of cash flows in Appendix A. (*a*) Which method is used to **APPLE** compute its net cash provided by operating activities? (*b*) Its balance sheet shows a decrease in accounts receivable from September 27, 2014, to September 26, 2015; why is this decrease in accounts receivable added when computing net cash provided by operating activities for the fiscal year ended September 26, 2015?

13. [I] Refer to Google's statement of cash flows in Appendix A. What are its cash **GOOGLE** flows from financing activities for the year ended December 31, 2015? List the items and amounts.

14. [I] Refer to Samsung's 2015 statement of cash flows in Appendix A. List **Samsung** its cash flows from operating activities, investing activities, and financing activities.

15. [I] Refer to Samsung's statement of cash flows in Appendix A. What in- **Samsung** vesting activities result in cash outflows for the year ended December 31, 2015? List items and amounts.

QUICK STUDY

QS 16-1

Transaction classification by activity

C1

Classify the following cash flows as either operating (O), investing (I), or financing (F) activities.

_____ **1.** Sold long-term investments for cash.

_____ **2.** Received cash payments from customers.

_____ **3.** Paid cash for wages and salaries.

_____ **4.** Purchased inventories for cash.

_____ **5.** Paid cash dividends.

_____ **6.** Issued common stock for cash.

_____ **7.** Received cash interest on a note.

_____ **8.** Paid cash interest on outstanding notes.

_____ **9.** Received cash from sale of land at a loss.

_____ **10.** Paid cash for property taxes on building.

QS 16-2

Statement of cash flows

P1

Label the following headings, line items, and notes with the numbers _1_ through _13_ according to their sequential order (from top to bottom) for presentation of the statement of cash flows.

_____ **a.** "Cash flows from investing activities" title

_____ **b.** "For _period_ Ended _date_" heading

_____ **c.** "Cash flows from operating activities" title

_____ **d.** Company name

_____ **e.** Schedule or note disclosure of noncash investing and financing transactions

_____ **f.** "Statement of Cash Flows" heading

_____ **g.** Net increase (decrease) in cash . . . . $ #

_____ **h.** Net cash provided (used) by operating activities . . . . $ #

_____ **i.** Cash (and equivalents) balance at prior period-end . . . . $ #

_____ **j.** Net cash provided (used) by financing activities . . . . $ #

_____ **k.** "Cash flows from financing activities" title

_____ **l.** Net cash provided (used) by investing activities. . . . . $ #

_____ **m.** Cash (and equivalents) balance at current period-end . . . . $ #

QS 16-3

Indirect: Computing cash flows from operations

P2

For each of the following three separate cases X, Y, and Z, compute cash flows from operations using the _indirect method._ The list includes all balance sheet accounts related to cash from operating activities.

	Case X	Case Y	Case Z
Net income	$ 4,000	$100,000	$72,000
Depreciation expense	30,000	8,000	24,000
Accounts receivable increase (decrease)	40,000	20,000	(4,000)
Inventory increase (decrease)	(20,000)	(10,000)	10,000
Accounts payable increase (decrease)	24,000	(22,000)	14,000
Accrued liabilities increase (decrease)	(44,000)	12,000	(8,000)

QS 16-4

Indirect: Computing cash from operations   **P2**

Use the following information to determine this company's cash flows from operating activities using the _indirect method._

MOSS COMPANY
Selected Balance Sheet Information
December 31, 2017 and 2016

	2017	2016
Current assets		
Cash	$84,650	$26,800
Accounts receivable.	25,000	32,000
Inventory.	60,000	54,100
Current liabilities		
Accounts payable.	30,400	25,700
Income taxes payable	2,050	2,200

MOSS COMPANY
Income Statement
For Year Ended December 31, 2017

Sales		$515,000
Cost of goods sold		331,600
Gross profit		183,400
Operating expenses		
Depreciation expense	$ 36,000	
Other expenses	121,500	157,500
Income before taxes.		25,900
Income taxes expense		7,700
Net income		$ 18,200

The plant assets section of the comparative balance sheets of Anders Company is reported below.

QS 16-5
Indirect: Computing investing cash flows
P2

ANDERS COMPANY Comparative Balance Sheets		
	2017	**2016**
Plant assets		
Equipment	$ 180,000	$270,000
Accum. depr.—Equipment............	(100,000)	(210,000)
Equipment, net......................	$ 80,000	$ 60,000
Buildings...........................	$ 380,000	$400,000
Accum. depr.—Buildings	(100,000)	(285,000)
Buildings, net	$ 280,000	$115,000

Refer to the balance sheet data above from Anders Company. During 2017, equipment with a book value of $40,000 and an original cost of $210,000 was sold at a loss of $3,000.

1. How much cash did Anders receive from the sale of equipment?

2. How much depreciation expense was recorded on equipment during 2017?

3. What was the cost of new equipment purchased by Anders during 2017?

Refer to the balance sheet data in QS 16-5 from Anders Company. During 2017, a building with a book value of $70,000 and an original cost of $300,000 was sold at a gain of $60,000.

QS 16-6
Indirect: Computing investing cash flows
P2

1. How much cash did Anders receive from the sale of the building?

2. How much depreciation expense was recorded on buildings during 2017?

3. What was the cost of buildings purchased by Anders during 2017?

The following selected information is from Ellerby Company's comparative balance sheets.

QS 16-7
Computing cash from asset sales
P3

At December 31	2017	2016
Furniture	$132,000	$ 184,500
Accumulated depreciation—Furniture......	(88,700)	(110,700)

The income statement reports depreciation expense for the year of $18,000. Also, furniture costing $52,500 was sold for its book value. Compute the cash received from the sale of furniture.

Compute cash flows from investing activities using the following company information.

QS 16-8
Computing cash flows from investing
P3

Sale of short-term investments	$ 6,000
Cash collections from customers.........................	16,000
Purchase of used equipment...........................	5,000
Depreciation expense	2,000

The following selected information is from Princeton Company's comparative balance sheets.

QS 16-9
Computing financing cash flows
P3

At December 31	2017	2016
Common stock, $10 par value............	$105,000	$100,000
Paid-in capital in excess of par	567,000	342,000
Retained earnings	313,500	287,500

The company's net income for the year ended December 31, 2017, was $48,000.

1. Compute the cash received from the sale of its common stock during 2017.

2. Compute the cash paid for dividends during 2017.

QS 16-10

Computing cash flows from financing

P3

Compute cash flows from financing activities using the following company information.

Additional short-term borrowings	$20,000
Purchase of short-term investments	5,000
Cash dividends paid	16,000
Interest paid	8,000

QS 16-11

Indirect: Computing cash from operations **P2**

CRUZ, INC.
Comparative Balance Sheets
December 31, 2017

	2017	2016
Assets		
Cash	$ 94,800	$ 24,000
Accounts receivable, net	41,000	51,000
Inventory	85,800	95,800
Prepaid expenses	5,400	4,200
Total current assets	227,000	175,000
Furniture	109,000	119,000
Accum. depreciation—Furniture	(17,000)	(9,000)
Total assets	$319,000	$285,000
Liabilities and Equity		
Accounts payable	$ 15,000	$ 21,000
Wages payable	9,000	5,000
Income taxes payable	1,400	2,600
Total current liabilities	25,400	28,600
Notes payable (long-term)	29,000	69,000
Total liabilities	54,400	97,600
Equity		
Common stock, $5 par value	229,000	179,000
Retained earnings	35,600	8,400
Total liabilities and equity	$319,000	$285,000

CRUZ, INC.
Income Statement
For Year Ended December 31, 2017

Sales		$488,000
Cost of goods sold		314,000
Gross profit		174,000
Operating expenses		
Depreciation expense	$37,600	
Other expenses	89,100	126,700
Income before taxes		47,300
Income taxes expense		17,300
Net income		$ 30,000

Required

Use the *indirect method* to prepare the cash provided or used from operating activities section only of the statement of cash flows for this company.

QS 16-12

Computing cash from asset sales **P3**

Refer to the data in QS 16-11.
Furniture costing $55,000 is sold at its book value in 2017. Acquisitions of furniture total $45,000 cash, on which no depreciation is necessary because it is acquired at year-end. What is the cash inflow related to the sale of furniture?

QS 16-13

Computing financing cash outflows **P3**

Refer to the data in QS 16-11.
1. Assume that all common stock is issued for cash. What amount of cash dividends is paid during 2017?
2. Assume that no additional notes payable are issued in 2017. What cash amount is paid to reduce the notes payable balance in 2017?

QS 16-14^B

Direct: Computing cash received from customers

P5

Refer to the data in QS 16-11.
1. How much cash is received from sales to customers for year 2017?
2. What is the net increase or decrease in cash for year 2017?

QS 16-15^B

Direct: Computing operating cash outflows **P5**

Refer to the data in QS 16-11.
1. How much cash is paid to acquire inventory during year 2017?
2. How much cash is paid for "other expenses" during year 2017? (*Hint:* Examine prepaid expenses and wages payable.)

Refer to the data in QS 16-11.
Use the *direct method* to prepare the cash provided or used from operating activities section only of the
statement of cash flows for this company.

Financial data from three competitors in the same industry follow.
1. Which of the three competitors is in the strongest position as shown by its statement of cash flows?
2. Analyze and compare the strength of Moore's cash flow on total assets ratio to that of Sykes.

	A	B	C	D
1	**$ thousands**	**Moore**	**Sykes**	**Kritch**
2	Cash provided (used) by operating activities	$ 70,000	$ 60,000	$ (24,000)
3	Cash provided (used) by investing activities			
4	Proceeds from sale of operating assets			26,000
5	Purchase of operating assets	(28,000)	(34,000)	
6	Cash provided (used) by financing activities			
7	Proceeds from issuance of debt			23,000
8	Repayment of debt	(6,000)		
9	Net increase (decrease) in cash	$ 36,000	$ 26,000	$ 25,000
10				
11	Average total assets	$790,000	$625,000	$300,000

When a spreadsheet for a statement of cash flows is prepared, all changes in noncash balance sheet accounts are fully explained on the spreadsheet. Explain how these noncash balance sheet accounts are used
to fully account for cash flows on a spreadsheet.

Use the following financial statements and additional information to (1) prepare a statement of cash flows
for the year ended December 31, 2018, using the *indirect method,* and (2) analyze and briefly discuss the
statement prepared in part 1 with special attention to operating activities and to the company's cash level.

MONTGOMERY INC.
Comparative Balance Sheets
December 31, 2018 and 2017

	2018	2017
Assets		
Cash	$ 30,400	$ 30,550
Accounts receivable, net	10,050	12,150
Inventory	90,100	70,150
Total current assets	130,550	112,850
Equipment	49,900	41,500
Accum. depreciation—Equipment	(22,500)	(15,300)
Total assets	$157,950	$139,050
Liabilities and Equity		
Accounts payable	$ 23,900	$ 25,400
Salaries payable	500	600
Total current liabilities	24,400	26,000
Equity		
Common stock, no par value	110,000	100,000
Retained earnings	23,550	13,050
Total liabilities and equity	$157,950	$139,050

MONTGOMERY INC.
Income Statement
For Year Ended December 31, 2018

Sales		$45,575
Cost of goods sold		(18,950)
Gross profit		26,625
Operating expenses		
Depreciation expense	$7,200	
Other expenses	5,550	
Total operating expense		12,750
Income before taxes		13,875
Income tax expense		3,375
Net income		$10,500

Additional Information
a. No dividends are declared or paid in 2018.
b. Issued additional stock for $10,000 cash in 2018.
c. Purchased equipment for cash in 2018; no equipment was sold in 2018.

QS 16-20
International cash
flow disclosures

C1

Answer each of the following questions related to international accounting standards.

1. Which method, indirect or direct, is acceptable for reporting operating cash flows under IFRS?

2. For each of the following four cash flows, identify whether it is reported under the operating, investing, or financing section (or some combination) within the indirect format of the statement of cash flows reported under IFRS and under U.S. GAAP.

Cash Flow Source	US GAAP Reporting	IFRS Reporting
a. Interest paid		
b. Dividends paid		
c. Interest received		
d. Dividends received		

EXERCISES

Exercise 16-1
Indirect: Cash flow
classification   C1

The following transactions and events occurred during the year. Assuming that this company uses the *indirect method* to report cash provided by operating activities, indicate where each item would appear on its statement of cash flows by placing an *x* in the appropriate column.

	Operating Activities	Investing Activities	Financing Activities	Noncash Investing and Financing Activities	Not Reported on Statement or in Notes
	Statement of Cash Flows				
a. Declared and paid a cash dividend	___	___	___	___	___
b. Recorded depreciation expense	___	___	___	___	___
c. Paid cash to settle long-term note payable.	___	___	___	___	___
d. Prepaid expenses increased in the year	___	___	___	___	___
e. Accounts receivable decreased in the year	___	___	___	___	___
f. Purchased land by issuing common stock	___	___	___	___	___
g. Inventory increased in the year	___	___	___	___	___
h. Sold equipment for cash, yielding a loss	___	___	___	___	___
i. Accounts payable decreased in the year	___	___	___	___	___
j. Income taxes payable increased in the year	___	___	___	___	___

Exercise 16-2
Indirect: Reporting cash
flows from operations

P2

Hampton Company reports the following information for its recent calendar year. Prepare the operating activities section of the statement of cash flows for Hampton Company using the *indirect method.*

Income Statement Data		Selected Year-End Balance Sheet Data	
Sales.	$160,000	Accounts receivable increase.	$10,000
Expenses		Inventory decrease	16,000
Cost of goods sold	100,000	Salaries payable increase.	1,000
Salaries expense.	24,000		
Depreciation expense	12,000		
Net income	$ 24,000		

Exercise 16-3
Indirect: Reporting and
interpreting cash flows
from operations

P2

Arundel Company disclosed the following information for its recent calendar year.

Income Statement Data		Selected Year-End Balance Sheet Data	
Revenues.	$100,000	Accounts receivable decrease	$24,000
Expenses		Purchased a machine for cash	10,000
Salaries expense.	84,000	Salaries payable increase.	18,000
Utilities expense	14,000	Other accrued liabilities decrease	8,000
Depreciation expense	14,600		
Other expenses.	3,400		
Net loss	$ (16,000)		

Required

1. Prepare the operating activities section of the statement of cash flows using the *indirect method.*

2. What were the major reasons that this company was able to report a net loss but positive cash flow from operations?

3. Of the potential causes of differences between cash flow from operations and net income, which are the most important to investors?

The following income statement and information about changes in noncash current assets and current liabilities are reported.

Exercise 16-4

Indirect: Cash flows from operating activities

P2

SONAD COMPANY
Income Statement
For Year Ended December 31, 2017

Sales		$1,828,000
Cost of goods sold		991,000
Gross profit		837,000
Operating expenses		
Salaries expense	$245,535	
Depreciation expense	44,200	
Rent expense	49,600	
Amortization expense—Patents	4,200	
Utilities expense	18,125	361,660
		475,340
Gain on sale of equipment		6,200
Net income		$ 481,540

Changes in current asset and current liability accounts for the year that relate to operations follow.

Accounts receivable	$30,500 increase	Accounts payable	$12,500 decrease
Inventory	25,000 increase	Salaries payable	3,500 decrease

Required

Prepare only the cash flows from operating activities section of the statement of cash flows using the *indirect method.*

Fitz Company reports the following information. Use the *indirect method* to prepare only the operating activities section of its statement of cash flows for the year ended December 31, 2017.

Exercise 16-5

Indirect: Cash flows from operating activities

P2

Selected 2017 Income Statement Data		Selected Year-End 2017 Balance Sheet Data	
Net income	$374,000	Accounts receivable decrease	$17,100
Depreciation expense	44,000	Inventory decrease	42,000
Amortization expense	7,200	Prepaid expenses increase	4,700
Gain on sale of plant assets	6,000	Accounts payable decrease	8,200
		Salaries payable increase	1,200

Salud Company reports the following information. Use the *indirect method* to prepare only the operating activities section of its statement of cash flows for the year ended December 31, 2017.

Exercise 16-6

Indirect: Cash flow from operations

P2

Selected 2017 Income Statement Data		Selected Year-End 2017 Balance Sheet Data	
Net income	$400,000	Accounts receivable increase	$40,000
Depreciation expense	80,000	Prepaid expenses decrease	12,000
Gain on sale of machinery	20,000	Accounts payable increase	6,000
		Wages payable decrease	2,000

Use the following information to determine this company's cash flows from investing activities.

a. Equipment with a book value of $65,300 and an original cost of $133,000 was sold at a loss of $14,000.

b. Paid $89,000 cash for a new truck.

c. Sold land costing $154,000 for $198,000 cash, yielding a gain of $44,000.

d. Long-term investments in stock were sold for $60,800 cash, yielding a gain of $4,150.

Exercise 16-7

Cash flows from investing activities

P3

Exercise 16-8

Cash flows from
financing activities

P3

Use the following information to determine this company's cash flows from financing activities.

a. Net income was $35,000.

b. Issued common stock for $64,000 cash.

c. Paid cash dividend of $14,600.

d. Paid $50,000 cash to settle a note payable at its $50,000 maturity value.

e. Paid $12,000 cash to acquire its treasury stock.

f. Purchased equipment for $39,000 cash.

Exercise 16-9

Indirect: Statement of
cash flows under IFRS

P1

Peugeot S.A. reports the following financial information for the year ended December 31, 2014 (euros in millions). Prepare its statement of cash flows under the *indirect method.* (*Hint:* Each line item below is titled, and any necessary parentheses added, as it is reported in the statement of cash flows.)

Net income (loss).	€ (822)	Cash from issuances of shares.	€ 2,961
Depreciation, amortization, and impairment. . . .	2,530	Cash paid for other financing activities	(1,891)
Losses on disposals and other	42	Cash from disposal of plant assets &	
Net decrease in current operating		intangibles.	206
assets & other	2,314	Cash paid for plant assets, intangibles & other.	(2,542)
Cash paid for dividends	(58)	Cash and cash equivalents, December 31, 2013	8,162

Exercise 16-10

Analyzing cash flow
on total assets

A1

A company reported average total assets of $1,240,000 in 2016 and $1,510,000 in 2017. Its net operating cash flow was $102,920 in 2016 and $138,920 in 2017. Calculate its cash flow on total assets ratio for both years. Comment on the results and any change in performance.

Exercise 16-11

Indirect: Preparing
statement of cash flows

P1   P2   P3   A1

The following financial statements and additional information are reported.

IKIBAN INC.
Comparative Balance Sheets
June 30, 2017 and 2016

	2017	2016
Assets		
Cash	$ 87,500	$ 44,000
Accounts receivable, net	65,000	51,000
Inventory.	63,800	86,500
Prepaid expenses.	4,400	5,400
Total current assets	220,700	186,900
Equipment.	124,000	115,000
Accum. depreciation—Equipment.	(27,000)	(9,000)
Total assets.	$317,700	$292,900
Liabilities and Equity		
Accounts payable.	$ 25,000	$ 30,000
Wages payable.	6,000	15,000
Income taxes payable	3,400	3,800
Total current liabilities	34,400	48,800
Notes payable (long term)	30,000	60,000
Total liabilities.	64,400	108,800
Equity		
Common stock, $5 par value.	220,000	160,000
Retained earnings	33,300	24,100
Total liabilities and equity.	$317,700	$292,900

IKIBAN INC.
Income Statement
For Year Ended June 30, 2017

Sales		$678,000
Cost of goods sold		411,000
Gross profit		267,000
Operating expenses		
Depreciation expense	$58,600	
Other expenses	67,000	
Total operating expenses.		125,600
		141,400
Other gains (losses)		
Gain on sale of equipment		2,000
Income before taxes.		143,400
Income taxes expense		43,890
Net income		$ 99,510

Additional Information

a. A $30,000 note payable is retired at its $30,000 carrying (book) value in exchange for cash.

b. The only changes affecting retained earnings are net income and cash dividends paid.

c. New equipment is acquired for $57,600 cash.

d. Received cash for the sale of equipment that had cost $48,600, yielding a $2,000 gain.

e. Prepaid Expenses and Wages Payable relate to Other Expenses on the income statement.

f. All purchases and sales of inventory are on credit.

Check   (1*b*) Cash paid for dividends, $90,310

(1*d*) Cash received from equip. sale, $10,000

Required

1. Prepare a statement of cash flows for the year ended June 30, 2017, using the *indirect method.*

2. Compute the company's cash flow on total assets ratio for its fiscal year 2017.

Refer to the information in Exercise 16-11. Using the *direct method,* prepare the statement of cash flows for the year ended June 30, 2017.

Exercise 16-12[B]

Direct: Preparing statement of cash flows

P1   P3   P5

Complete the following spreadsheet in preparation of the statement of cash flows. (The statement of cash flows is not required.) Prepare the spreadsheet as in Exhibit 16A.1; report operating activities under the *indirect method.* Identify the debits and credits in the Analysis of Changes columns with letters that correspond to the following transactions and events *a* through *h*.

Exercise 16-13

Indirect: Cash flows spreadsheet

P4

a. Net income for the year was $100,000.

b. Dividends of $80,000 cash were declared and paid.

c. Scoreteck's only noncash expense was $70,000 of depreciation.

d. The company purchased plant assets for $70,000 cash.

e. Notes payable of $20,000 were issued for $20,000 cash.

f. Change in accounts receivable.

g. Change in inventory.

h. Change in accounts payable.

	A	B	C	D	E	F	G
1	SCORETECK CORPORATION						
2	Spreadsheet for Statement of Cash Flows—Indirect Method						
3	For Year Ended December 31, 2017						
4				Analysis of Changes			
5		Dec. 31, 2016		Debit		Credit	Dec. 31, 2017
6	**Balance Sheet—Debit Bal. Accounts**						
7	Cash	$ 80,000					$ 60,000
8	Accounts receivable	120,000					190,000
9	Inventory	250,000					230,000
10	Plant assets	600,000					670,000
11		$1,050,000					$1,150,000
12	**Balance Sheet—Credit Bal. Accounts**						
13	Accumulated depreciation	$ 100,000					$ 170,000
14	Accounts payable	150,000					140,000
15	Notes payable	370,000					390,000
16	Common stock	200,000					200,000
17	Retained earnings	230,000					250,000
18		$1,050,000					$1,150,000
19	**Statement of Cash Flows**						
20	Operating activities						
21	Net income						
22	Increase in accounts receivable						
23	Decrease in inventory						
24	Decrease in accounts payable						
25	Depreciation expense						
26	Investing activities						
27	Cash paid to purchase plant assets						
28	Financing activities						
29	Cash paid for dividends						
30	Cash from issuance of notes						

Exercise 16-14^B

Direct: Cash flow classification

C1   P5

The following transactions and events occurred during the year. Assuming that this company uses the *direct method* to report cash provided by operating activities, indicate where each item would appear on the statement of cash flows by placing an *x* in the appropriate column.

	Statement of Cash Flows			Noncash Investing and Financing Activities	Not Reported on Statement or in Notes
	Operating Activities	Investing Activities	Financing Activities		
a. Retired long-term notes payable by issuing common stock	____	____	____	____	____
b. Paid cash toward accounts payable	____	____	____	____	____
c. Sold inventory for cash	____	____	____	____	____
d. Paid cash dividend that was declared in a prior period	____	____	____	____	____
e. Accepted six-month note receivable in exchange for plant assets	____	____	____	____	____
f. Recorded depreciation expense	____	____	____	____	____
g. Paid cash to acquire treasury stock	____	____	____	____	____
h. Collected cash from sales	____	____	____	____	____
i. Borrowed cash from bank by signing a nine-month note payable.	____	____	____	____	____
j. Paid cash to purchase a patent	____	____	____	____	____

Exercise 16-15^B

Direct: Computing cash flows

P5

For each of the following three separate cases, use the information provided about the calendar-year 2018 operations of Sahim Company to compute the required cash flow information.

Case X: Compute cash received from customers:	
Sales	$515,000
Accounts receivable, December 31, 2017	27,200
Accounts receivable, December 31, 2018	33,600
Case Y: Compute cash paid for rent:	
Rent expense.	$139,800
Rent payable, December 31, 2017	7,800
Rent payable, December 31, 2018	6,200
Case Z: Compute cash paid for inventory:	
Cost of goods sold	$525,000
Inventory, December 31, 2017	158,600
Accounts payable, December 31, 2017	66,700
Inventory, December 31, 2018	130,400
Accounts payable, December 31, 2018	82,000

Exercise 16-16^B

Direct: Cash flows from operating activities   P5

Refer to the information about Sonad Company in Exercise 16-4. Use the *direct method* to prepare only the cash provided or used by operating activities section of the statement of cash flows for this company.

Exercise 16-17^B

Direct: Preparing statement of cash flows and supporting note

P1   P3   P5

Use the following information about the cash flows of Ferron Company to prepare a complete statement of cash flows (*direct method*) for the year ended December 31, 2017. Use a note disclosure for any non-cash investing and financing activities.

Cash and cash equivalents balance, December 31, 2016.	$ 40,000
Cash and cash equivalents balance, December 31, 2017.	148,000
Cash received as interest	3,500
Cash paid for salaries	76,500

[continued on next page]

[continued from previous page]

Bonds payable retired by issuing common stock (no gain or loss on retirement).................	$185,500
Cash paid to retire long-term notes payable...	100,000
Cash received from sale of equipment	60,250
Cash received in exchange for six-month note payable................................	35,000
Land purchased by issuing long-term note payable....................................	105,250
Cash paid for store equipment..	24,750
Cash dividends paid	10,000
Cash paid for other expenses...	20,000
Cash received from customers...	495,000
Cash paid for inventory..	254,500

The following summarized Cash T-account reflects the total debits and total credits to the Cash account of Thomas Corporation for calendar-year 2017.

1. Use this information to prepare a complete statement of cash flows for year 2017. The cash provided or used by operating activities should be reported using the *direct method.*

2. Refer to the statement of cash flows prepared for part 1 to answer the following questions *a* through *d*: (*a*) Which section—operating, investing, or financing—shows the largest cash (i) inflow and (ii) outflow? (*b*) What is the largest individual item among the investing cash outflows? (*c*) Are the cash proceeds larger from issuing notes or issuing stock? (*d*) Does the company have a net cash inflow or outflow from borrowing activities?

Exercise 16-18[B]

Direct: Preparing statement of cash flows from Cash T-account

P1   P3   P5

GENERAL LEDGER ACCOUNT   `_□×`

File Edit Maintain Tasks Analysis Options Reports Window Help

Cash			
Balance, Dec. 31, 2016	333,000		
Receipts from customers	5,000,000	Payments for inventory	2,590,000
Receipts from dividends	208,400	Payments for wages	550,000
Receipts from land sale	220,000	Payments for rent	320,000
Receipts from machinery sale	710,000	Payments for interest	218,000
Receipts from issuing stock	1,540,000	Payments for taxes	450,000
Receipts from borrowing	3,600,000	Payments for machinery	2,236,000
		Payments for long-term investments	1,260,000
		Payments for note payable	386,000
		Payments for dividends	500,000
		Payments for treasury stock	218,000
Balance, Dec. 31, 2017	$?		

Sales   Purchases   General Ledger   Payroll   Inventory   Company   Analysis

---

connect

Lansing Company's 2017 income statement and selected balance sheet data (for current assets and current liabilities) at December 31, 2016 and 2017, follow.

PROBLEM SET A

Problem 16-1A

Indirect: Computing cash flows from operations

P2

LANSING COMPANY
Income Statement
For Year Ended December 31, 2017

Sales revenue	$97,200
Expenses	
Cost of goods sold	42,000
Depreciation expense	12,000
Salaries expense................	18,000
Rent expense	9,000
Insurance expense..............	3,800
Interest expense................	3,600
Utilities expense................	2,800
Net income	$ 6,000

LANSING COMPANY
Selected Balance Sheet Accounts

At December 31	2017	2016
Accounts receivable........	$5,600	$5,800
Inventory.................	1,980	1,540
Accounts payable..........	4,400	4,600
Salaries payable...........	880	700
Utilities payable	220	160
Prepaid insurance..........	260	280
Prepaid rent	220	180

Required

Prepare the cash flows from operating activities section only of the company's 2017 statement of cash flows using the *indirect method.*

Check   Cash from operating activities, $17,780

Problem 16-2A[B]

Direct: Computing cash flows from operations

P5

Refer to the information in Problem 16-1A.

Required

Prepare the cash flows from operating activities section only of the company's 2017 statement of cash flows using the *direct method.*

Problem 16-3A

Indirect: Statement of cash flows

A1   P1   P2   P3

Forten Company, a merchandiser, recently completed its calendar-year 2017 operations. For the year, (1) all sales are credit sales, (2) all credits to Accounts Receivable reflect cash receipts from customers, (3) all purchases of inventory are on credit, (4) all debits to Accounts Payable reflect cash payments for inventory, and (5) Other Expenses are paid in advance and are initially debited to Prepaid Expenses. The company's income statement and balance sheets follow.

FORTEN COMPANY
Comparative Balance Sheets
December 31, 2017 and 2016

	2017	2016
Assets		
Cash	$ 49,800	$ 73,500
Accounts receivable	65,810	50,625
Inventory	275,656	251,800
Prepaid expenses	1,250	1,875
Total current assets	392,516	377,800
Equipment	157,500	108,000
Accum. depreciation—Equipment	(36,625)	(46,000)
Total assets	$513,391	$439,800
Liabilities and Equity		
Accounts payable	$ 53,141	$114,675
Short-term notes payable	10,000	6,000
Total current liabilities	63,141	120,675
Long-term notes payable	65,000	48,750
Total liabilities	128,141	169,425
Equity		
Common stock, $5 par value	162,750	150,250
Paid-in capital in excess of par, common stock	37,500	0
Retained earnings	185,000	120,125
Total liabilities and equity	$513,391	$439,800

FORTEN COMPANY
Income Statement
For Year Ended December 31, 2017

Sales		$582,500
Cost of goods sold		285,000
Gross profit		297,500
Operating expenses		
Depreciation expense	$ 20,750	
Other expenses	132,400	153,150
Other gains (losses)		
Loss on sale of equipment		(5,125)
Income before taxes		139,225
Income taxes expense		24,250
Net income		$114,975

Additional Information on Year 2017 Transactions

  a. The loss on the cash sale of equipment was $5,125 (details in *b*).

  b. Sold equipment costing $46,875, with accumulated depreciation of $30,125, for $11,625 cash.

  c. Purchased equipment costing $96,375 by paying $30,000 cash and signing a long-term note payable for the balance.

  d. Borrowed $4,000 cash by signing a short-term note payable.

  e. Paid $50,125 cash to reduce the long-term notes payable.

  f. Issued 2,500 shares of common stock for $20 cash per share.

  g. Declared and paid cash dividends of $50,100.

Required

Check Cash from operating activities, $40,900

1. Prepare a complete statement of cash flows; report its operating activities using the *indirect method.* Disclose any noncash investing and financing activities in a note.

Analysis Component

2. Analyze and discuss the statement of cash flows prepared in part 1, giving special attention to the wisdom of the cash dividend payment.

Refer to the information reported about Forten Company in Problem 16-3A.

Required

Prepare a complete statement of cash flows using a spreadsheet as in Exhibit 16A.1; report its operating activities using the *indirect method*. Identify the debits and credits in the Analysis of Changes columns with letters that correspond to the following list of transactions and events.

a. Net income was $114,975.

b. Accounts receivable increased.

c. Inventory increased.

d. Prepaid expenses decreased.

e. Accounts payable decreased.

f. Depreciation expense was $20,750.

g. Sold equipment costing $46,875, with accumulated depreciation of $30,125, for $11,625 cash. This yielded a loss of $5,125.

h. Purchased equipment costing $96,375 by paying $30,000 cash and **(i.)** by signing a long-term note payable for the balance.

j. Borrowed $4,000 cash by signing a short-term note payable.

k. Paid $50,125 cash to reduce the long-term notes payable.

l. Issued 2,500 shares of common stock for $20 cash per share.

m. Declared and paid cash dividends of $50,100.

Problem 16-4A[A]
Indirect: Cash flows spreadsheet

P1   P2   P3   P4

Check   Analysis of Changes column totals, $600,775

Refer to Forten Company's financial statements and related information in Problem 16-3A.

Required

Prepare a complete statement of cash flows; report its operating activities according to the *direct method*. Disclose any noncash investing and financing activities in a note.

Problem 16-5A[B]
Direct: Statement of cash flows   P1   P3   P5

Check   Cash used in financing activities, $(46,225)

Golden Corp., a merchandiser, recently completed its 2017 operations. For the year, (1) all sales are credit sales, (2) all credits to Accounts Receivable reflect cash receipts from customers, (3) all purchases of inventory are on credit, (4) all debits to Accounts Payable reflect cash payments for inventory, (5) Other Expenses are all cash expenses, and (6) any change in Income Taxes Payable reflects the accrual and cash payment of taxes. The company's balance sheets and income statement follow.

Problem 16-6A
Indirect: Statement of cash flows

P1   P2   P3

GOLDEN CORPORATION
Comparative Balance Sheets
December 31, 2017 and 2016

	2017	2016
Assets		
Cash	$ 164,000	$107,000
Accounts receivable	83,000	71,000
Inventory	601,000	526,000
Total current assets	848,000	704,000
Equipment	335,000	299,000
Accum. depreciation—Equipment	(158,000)	(104,000)
Total assets	$1,025,000	$899,000
Liabilities and Equity		
Accounts payable	$ 87,000	$ 71,000
Income taxes payable	28,000	25,000
Total current liabilities	115,000	96,000
Equity		
Common stock, $2 par value	592,000	568,000
Paid-in capital in excess		
of par value, common stock	196,000	160,000
Retained earnings	122,000	75,000
Total liabilities and equity	$1,025,000	$899,000

GOLDEN CORPORATION
Income Statement
For Year Ended December 31, 2017

Sales		$1,792,000
Cost of goods sold		1,086,000
Gross profit		706,000
Operating expenses		
Depreciation expense	$ 54,000	
Other expenses	494,000	548,000
Income before taxes		158,000
Income taxes expense		22,000
Net income		$ 136,000

Additional Information on Year 2017 Transactions

a. Purchased equipment for $36,000 cash.

b. Issued 12,000 shares of common stock for $5 cash per share.

c. Declared and paid $89,000 in cash dividends.

Required

Check Cash from operating activities, $122,000

Prepare a complete statement of cash flows; report its cash inflows and cash outflows from operating activities according to the *indirect method*.

Problem 16-7A[A]

Indirect: Cash flows spreadsheet

P1 P2 P3 P4

Refer to the information reported about Golden Corporation in Problem 16-6A.

Required

Prepare a complete statement of cash flows using a spreadsheet as in Exhibit 16A.1; report operating activities under the *indirect method*. Identify the debits and credits in the Analysis of Changes columns with letters that correspond to the following list of transactions and events.

a. Net income was $136,000.

b. Accounts receivable increased.

c. Inventory increased.

d. Accounts payable increased.

e. Income taxes payable increased.

f. Depreciation expense was $54,000.

g. Purchased equipment for $36,000 cash.

h. Issued 12,000 shares at $5 cash per share.

i. Declared and paid $89,000 of cash dividends.

Check Analysis of Changes column totals, $481,000

Problem 16-8A[B]

Direct: Statement of cash flows

P1 P3 P5

Refer to Golden Corporation's financial statements and related information in Problem 16-6A.

Required

Prepare a complete statement of cash flows; report its cash flows from operating activities according to the *direct method*.

Check Cash used in financing activities, $(29,000)

PROBLEM SET B

Problem 16-1B

Indirect: Computing cash flows from operations

P2

Salt Lake Company's 2017 income statement and selected balance sheet data (for current assets and current liabilities) at December 31, 2016 and 2017, follow.

SALT LAKE COMPANY
Income Statement
For Year Ended December 31, 2017

Sales revenue	$156,000
Expenses	
Cost of goods sold	72,000
Depreciation expense	32,000
Salaries expense	20,000
Rent expense	5,000
Insurance expense	2,600
Interest expense	2,400
Utilities expense	2,000
Net income	$ 20,000

SALT LAKE COMPANY
Selected Balance Sheet Accounts

At December 31	2017	2016
Accounts receivable	$3,600	$3,000
Inventory	860	980
Accounts payable	2,400	2,600
Salaries payable	900	600
Utilities payable	200	0
Prepaid insurance	140	180
Prepaid rent	100	200

Required

Prepare the cash flows from operating activities section only of the company's 2017 statement of cash flows using the *indirect method*.

Check Cash from operating activities, $51,960

Refer to the information in Problem 16-1B.

Required

Prepare the cash flows from operating activities section only of the company's 2017 statement of cash flows using the *direct method*.

Problem 16-2B[B]
Direct: Computing cash flows from operations

P5

Gazelle Corporation, a merchandiser, recently completed its calendar-year 2017 operations. For the year, (1) all sales are credit sales, (2) all credits to Accounts Receivable reflect cash receipts from customers, (3) all purchases of inventory are on credit, (4) all debits to Accounts Payable reflect cash payments for inventory, and (5) Other Expenses are paid in advance and are initially debited to Prepaid Expenses. The company's balance sheets and income statement follow.

Problem 16-3B
Indirect: Statement of cash flows

A1 P1 P2 P3

GAZELLE CORPORATION
Comparative Balance Sheets
December 31, 2017 and 2016

	2017	2016
Assets		
Cash	$123,450	$ 61,550
Accounts receivable	77,100	80,750
Inventory	240,600	250,700
Prepaid expenses	15,100	17,000
Total current assets	456,250	410,000
Equipment	262,250	200,000
Accum. depreciation—Equipment	(110,750)	(95,000)
Total assets	$607,750	$515,000
Liabilities and Equity		
Accounts payable	$ 17,750	$102,000
Short-term notes payable	15,000	10,000
Total current liabilities	32,750	112,000
Long-term notes payable	100,000	77,500
Total liabilities	132,750	189,500
Equity		
Common stock, $5 par	215,000	200,000
Paid-in capital in excess of par, common stock	30,000	0
Retained earnings	230,000	125,500
Total liabilities and equity	$607,750	$515,000

GAZELLE CORPORATION
Income Statement
For Year Ended December 31, 2017

Sales		$1,185,000
Cost of goods sold		595,000
Gross profit		590,000
Operating expenses		
Depreciation expense	$ 38,600	
Other expenses	362,850	
Total operating expenses		401,450
		188,550
Other gains (losses)		
Loss on sale of equipment		(2,100)
Income before taxes		186,450
Income taxes expense		28,350
Net income		$ 158,100

Additional Information on Year 2017 Transactions

a. The loss on the cash sale of equipment was $2,100 (details in *b*).

b. Sold equipment costing $51,000, with accumulated depreciation of $22,850, for $26,050 cash.

c. Purchased equipment costing $113,250 by paying $43,250 cash and signing a long-term note payable for the balance.

d. Borrowed $5,000 cash by signing a short-term note payable.

e. Paid $47,500 cash to reduce the long-term notes payable.

f. Issued 3,000 shares of common stock for $15 cash per share.

g. Declared and paid cash dividends of $53,600.

Required

1. Prepare a complete statement of cash flows; report its operating activities using the *indirect method.* Disclose any noncash investing and financing activities in a note.

Analysis Component

2. Analyze and discuss the statement of cash flows prepared in part 1, giving special attention to the wisdom of the cash dividend payment.

Problem 16-4B[A]

Indirect: Cash flows
spreadsheet

P1   P2   P3   P4

Refer to the information reported about Gazelle Corporation in Problem 16-3B.

Required

Prepare a complete statement of cash flows using a spreadsheet as in Exhibit 16A.1; report its operating activities using the *indirect method.* Identify the debits and credits in the Analysis of Changes columns with letters that correspond to the following list of transactions and events.

a. Net income was $158,100.
b. Accounts receivable decreased.
c. Inventory decreased.
d. Prepaid expenses decreased.
e. Accounts payable decreased.
f. Depreciation expense was $38,600.
g. Sold equipment costing $51,000, with accumulated depreciation of $22,850, for $26,050 cash. This yielded a loss of $2,100.
h. Purchased equipment costing $113,250 by paying $43,250 cash and **(i.)** by signing a long-term note payable for the balance.
j. Borrowed $5,000 cash by signing a short-term note payable.
k. Paid $47,500 cash to reduce the long-term notes payable.
l. Issued 3,000 shares of common stock for $15 cash per share.

m. Declared and paid cash dividends of $53,600.

Problem 16-5B[B]

Direct: Statement of
cash flows

P1   P3   P5

Refer to Gazelle Corporation's financial statements and related information in Problem 16-3B.

Required

Prepare a complete statement of cash flows; report its operating activities according to the *direct method.* Disclose any noncash investing and financing activities in a note.

Problem 16-6B

Indirect: Statement of
cash flows

P1   P2   P3

Satu Company, a merchandiser, recently completed its 2017 operations. For the year, (1) all sales are credit sales, (2) all credits to Accounts Receivable reflect cash receipts from customers, (3) all purchases of inventory are on credit, (4) all debits to Accounts Payable reflect cash payments for inventory, (5) Other Expenses are cash expenses, and (6) any change in Income Taxes Payable reflects the accrual and cash payment of taxes. The company's balance sheets and income statement follow.

SATU COMPANY Comparative Balance Sheets December 31, 2017 and 2016		
	2017	**2016**
Assets		
Cash..................................	$ 58,750	$ 28,400
Accounts receivable	20,222	25,860
Total current assets......................	78,972	54,260
Inventory	165,667	140,320
Equipment	107,750	77,500
Accum. depreciation—Equipment	(46,700)	(31,000)
Total assets	$305,689	$241,080
Liabilities and Equity		
Accounts payable	$ 20,372	$157,530
Income taxes payable....................	2,100	6,100
Total current liabilities...................	22,472	163,630
Equity		
Common stock, $5 par value	40,000	25,000
Paid-in capital in excess		
of par, common stock..................	68,000	20,000
Retained earnings......................	175,217	32,450
Total liabilities and equity.................	$305,689	$241,080

SATU COMPANY Income Statement For Year Ended December 31, 2017		
Sales		$750,800
Cost of goods sold		269,200
Gross profit.......................		481,600
Operating expenses		
Depreciation expense	$ 15,700	
Other expenses	173,933	189,633
Income before taxes................		291,967
Income taxes expense		89,200
Net income		$202,767

Additional Information on Year 2017 Transactions

a. Purchased equipment for $30,250 cash.

b. Issued 3,000 shares of common stock for $21 cash per share.

c. Declared and paid $60,000 of cash dividends.

Required

Prepare a complete statement of cash flows; report its cash inflows and cash outflows from operating activities according to the *indirect method*.

Check Cash from operating activities, $57,600

Refer to the information reported about Satu Company in Problem 16-6B.

Required

Prepare a complete statement of cash flows using a spreadsheet as in Exhibit 16A.1; report operating activities under the *indirect method*. Identify the debits and credits in the Analysis of Changes columns with letters that correspond to the following list of transactions and events.

a. Net income was $202,767.

b. Accounts receivable decreased.

c. Inventory increased.

d. Accounts payable decreased.

e. Income taxes payable decreased.

f. Depreciation expense was $15,700.

g. Purchased equipment for $30,250 cash.

h. Issued 3,000 shares at $21 cash per share.

i. Declared and paid $60,000 of cash dividends.

Problem 16-7B[A]
Indirect: Cash flows spreadsheet

P1 P2 P3 P4

Check Analysis of Changes column totals, $543,860

Refer to Satu Company's financial statements and related information in Problem 16-6B.

Required

Prepare a complete statement of cash flows; report its cash flows from operating activities according to the *direct method*.

Problem 16-8B[B]
Direct: Statement of cash flows

P1 P3 P5

Check Cash provided by financing activities, $3,000

SERIAL PROBLEM

Business Solutions **(Indirect)**

P1 P2 P3

© Alexander Image/Shutterstock RF

(This serial problem began in Chapter 1 and continues through most of the book. If previous chapter segments were not completed, the serial problem can begin at this point.)

SP 16 Santana Rey, owner of **Business Solutions**, decides to prepare a statement of cash flows for her business. (Although the serial problem allowed for various ownership changes in earlier chapters, we will prepare the statement of cash flows using the following financial data.)

BUSINESS SOLUTIONS Income Statement For Three Months Ended March 31, 2018		
Computer services revenue.		$25,307
Net sales		18,693
Total revenue		44,000
Cost of goods sold	$14,052	
Depreciation expense— Office equipment.	400	
Depreciation expense— Computer equipment.	1,250	
Wages expense	3,250	
Insurance expense	555	
Rent expense	2,475	
Computer supplies expense	1,305	
Advertising expense.	600	
Mileage expense	320	
Repairs expense—Computer	960	
Total expenses		25,167
Net income		$18,833

BUSINESS SOLUTIONS Comparative Balance Sheets December 31, 2017, and March 31, 2018		
	Mar. 31, 2018	**Dec. 31, 2017**
Assets		
Cash	$ 68,057	$48,372
Accounts receivable.	22,867	5,668
Inventory.	704	0
Computer supplies	2,005	580
Prepaid insurance.	1,110	1,665
Prepaid rent	825	825
Total current assets	95,568	57,110
Office equipment	8,000	8,000
Accumulated depreciation—Office equipment	(800)	(400)
Computer equipment.	20,000	20,000
Accumulated depreciation— Computer equipment.	(2,500)	(1,250)
Total assets.	$120,268	$83,460
Liabilities and Equity		
Accounts payable	$ 0	$ 1,100
Wages payable	875	500
Unearned computer service revenue	0	1,500
Total current liabilities	875	3,100
Equity		
Common stock	98,000	73,000
Retained earnings	21,393	7,360
Total liabilities and equity.	$120,268	$83,460

Required

Check Cash flows used by operations: $(515)

Prepare a statement of cash flows for Business Solutions using the *indirect method* for the three months ended March 31, 2018. Recall that owner Santana Rey contributed $25,000 to the business in exchange for additional stock in the first quarter of 2018 and has received $4,800 in cash dividends.

GENERAL LEDGER PROBLEM

Available only in Connect

The following **General Ledger** assignments highlight the impact, or lack thereof, on the statement of cash flows from summary journal entries derived from consecutive trial balances. Prepare summary journal entries reflecting changes in consecutive trial balances. Then prepare the statement of cash flows (direct method) from those entries. Finally, prepare the reconciliation to the indirect method for net cash provided (used) by operating activities.

GL 16-1 General Ledger assignment based on Exercise 16-11

GL 16-2 General Ledger assignment based on Problem 16-1

GL 16-3 General Ledger assignment based on Problem 16-6

Beyond the Numbers

BTN 16-1   Refer to Apple's financial statements in Appendix A to answer the following.

1. Is Apple's statement of cash flows prepared under the direct method or the indirect method? How do you know?

2. For each fiscal year 2015, 2014, and 2013, is the amount of cash provided by operating activities more or less than the cash paid for dividends?

3. What is the largest amount in reconciling the difference between net income and cash flow from operating activities in fiscal 2015? In fiscal 2014? In fiscal 2013?

4. Identify the largest cash inflow and cash outflow for investing *and* for financing activities in fiscal 2015 and in fiscal 2014.

Fast Forward

5. Obtain Apple's financial statements for a fiscal year ending after September 27, 2015, from either its website (Apple.com) or the SEC's database (SEC.gov). Since September 27, 2015, what are Apple's largest cash outflows and cash inflows in the investing and in the financing sections of its statement of cash flows?

REPORTING IN ACTION

A1

APPLE

BTN 16-2   Key figures for Apple and Google follow.

$ millions	Apple			Google		
	Current Year	1 Year Prior	2 Years Prior	Current Year	1 Year Prior	2 Years Prior
Operating cash flows	$ 81,266	$ 59,713	$ 53,666	$ 26,024	$ 22,376	$ 18,659
Total assets......................	290,479	231,839	207,000	147,461	129,187	109,050

COMPARATIVE ANALYSIS

A1

APPLE
GOOGLE

Required

1. Compute the recent two years' cash flow on total assets ratios for Apple and Google.

2. What does the cash flow on total assets ratio measure?

3. Which company has the highest cash flow on total assets ratio for the periods shown?

4. Does the cash flow on total assets ratio reflect on the quality of earnings? Explain.

BTN 16-3   Katie Murphy is preparing for a meeting with her banker. Her business is finishing its fourth year of operations. In the first year, it had negative cash flows from operations. In the second and third years, cash flows from operations were positive. However, inventory costs rose significantly in year 4, and cash flows from operations will probably be down 25%. Murphy wants to secure a line of credit from her banker as a financing buffer. From experience, she knows the banker will scrutinize operating cash flows for years 1 through 4 and will want a projected number for year 5. Murphy knows that a steady progression upward in operating cash flows for years 1 through 4 will help her case. She decides to use her discretion as owner and considers several business actions that will turn her operating cash flow in year 4 from a decrease to an increase.

ETHICS CHALLENGE

C1 A1

Required

1. Identify two business actions Murphy might take to improve cash flows from operations.

2. Comment on the ethics and possible consequences of Murphy's decision to pursue these actions.

BTN 16-4   Your friend, Diana Wood, recently completed the second year of her business and just received annual financial statements from her accountant. Wood finds the income statement and balance sheet informative but does not understand the statement of cash flows. She says the first section is especially confusing because it contains a lot of additions and subtractions that do not make sense to her. Wood adds, "The income statement tells me the business is more profitable than last year and that's most important. If I want to know how cash changes, I can look at comparative balance sheets."

COMMUNICATING IN PRACTICE

C1

Required

Write a half-page memorandum to your friend explaining the purpose of the statement of cash flows. Speculate as to why the first section is so confusing and how it might be rectified.

TAKING IT TO THE NET

A1

BTN 16-5   Access the April 14, 2016, filing of the 10-K report (for year ending December 31, 2015) of **Mendocino Brewing Company, Inc.** (ticker: MENB), at **SEC.gov**.

Required

1. Does Mendocino Brewing use the direct or indirect method to construct its consolidated statement of cash flows?

2. For the year ended December 31, 2015, what is the largest item in reconciling the net income (or loss) to net cash provided by operating activities?

3. In the recent two years, has the company been more successful in generating operating cash flows or in generating net income? Identify the figures to support the answer.

4. In the year ended December 31, 2015, what was the largest cash outflow for investing activities *and* for financing activities?

5. What item(s) does the company report as supplemental cash flow information?

6. Does the company report any noncash financing activities for 2015? Identify them, if any.

TEAMWORK IN ACTION

C1 A1 P2 P5

BTN 16-6   Team members are to coordinate and independently answer one question within each of the following three sections. Team members should then report to the team and confirm or correct teammates' answers.

1. Answer *one* of the following questions about the statement of cash flows.
   a. What are this statement's reporting objectives?
   b. What two methods are used to prepare it? Identify similarities and differences between them.
   c. What steps are followed to prepare the statement?
   d. What types of analyses are often made from this statement's information?

2. Identify and explain the adjustment from net income to obtain cash flows from operating activities using the indirect method for *one* of the following items.
   a. Noncash operating revenues and expenses.
   b. Nonoperating gains and losses.
   c. Increases and decreases in noncash current assets.
   d. Increases and decreases in current liabilities.

3.[B] Identify and explain the formula for computing cash flows from operating activities using the direct method for *one* of the following items.
   a. Cash receipts from sales to customers.
   b. Cash paid for inventory.
   c. Cash paid for wages and operating expenses.
   d. Cash paid for interest and taxes.

Note: For teams of more than four, some pairing within teams is necessary. Use as an in-class activity or as an assignment. If used in class, specify a time limit on each part. Conclude with reports to the entire class, using team rotation. Each team can prepare responses on a transparency.

ENTREPRENEURIAL DECISION

C1 A1

BTN 16-7   Review the chapter's opener involving **Amazon.com** and its founder, Jeff Bezos.

Required

1. In a business such as Amazon, monitoring cash flow is always a priority. Even though Amazon now has billions in annual sales and sometimes earns a positive net income, explain how cash flow can lag behind net income.

2. Amazon is a publicly traded corporation. What are potential sources of financing for its future expansion?

ENTREPRENEURIAL DECISION

C1 A1

BTN 16-8   Jenna and Matt Wilder are completing their second year operating Mountain High, a downhill ski area and resort. Mountain High reports a net loss of $(10,000) for its second year, which includes an $85,000 unusual loss from fire. This past year also involved major purchases of plant assets for renovation and expansion, yielding a year-end total asset amount of $800,000. Mountain High's net cash outflow for its second year is $(5,000); a summarized version of its statement of cash flows follows.

Net cash flow provided by operating activities..............	$ 295,000
Net cash flow used by investing activities..................	(310,000)
Net cash flow provided by financing activities	10,000

Required

Write a one-page memorandum to the Wilders evaluating Mountain High's current performance and assessing its future. Give special emphasis to cash flow data and their interpretation.

BTN 16-9 Visit The Motley Fool's website (Fool.com). Enter the *Fool's School* (at *Fool.com/School*). Identify and select the link "How to Value Stocks." (This site might ask you to register with your e-mail address; registration had been free and did grant access to articles.)

HITTING THE ROAD

C1

Required

1. Click on "Introduction to Valuation Methods," and then "Cash-Flow Based Valuations." How does the Fool's School define cash flow? What is the school's reasoning for this definition?

2. Per the school's instruction, why do analysts focus on earnings before interest and taxes (EBIT)?

3. Visit other links at this website that interest you such as "How to Read a Balance Sheet," or find out what the "Fool's Ratio" is. Write a half-page report on what you find.

BTN 16-10 Key comparative information for Samsung (Samsung.com), a leading manufacturer of electronic consumer products, follows.

GLOBAL DECISION

C1

Samsung
APPLE
GOOGLE

₩ in millions	Current Year	1 Year Prior	2 Years Prior
Operating cash flows	₩ 40,061,761	₩ 36,975,389	₩ 46,707,440
Total assets	242,179,521	230,422,958	214,075,018

Required

1. Compute the recent two years' cash flow on total assets ratio for Samsung.

2. How does Samsung's ratio compare to Apple's and Google's ratios from BTN 16-2?

 **GLOBAL VIEW**

The statement of cash flows, which explains changes in cash (including cash equivalents) from period to period, is required under both U.S. GAAP and IFRS. This section discusses similarities and differences between U.S. GAAP and IFRS in reporting that statement.

Reporting Cash Flows from Operating Both U.S. GAAP and IFRS permit the reporting of cash flows from operating activities using either the direct or indirect method. Basic requirements underlying the application of both methods are fairly consistent across U.S. GAAP and IFRS. Appendix A shows that Samsung reports its cash flows from operating activities using the indirect method, and in a manner similar to that explained in this chapter. Further, the definition of cash and cash equivalents is roughly similar for U.S. GAAP and IFRS.

There are some differences between U.S. GAAP and IFRS in reporting operating cash flows. We mention two of the more notable. First, U.S. GAAP requires that cash inflows from interest revenue and dividend revenue be classified as operating, whereas IFRS permits classification under operating or investing provided that this classification is consistently applied. Samsung reports its cash from interest received under operating, consistent with U.S. GAAP. Second, U.S. GAAP requires cash outflows for interest expense be classified as operating, whereas IFRS again permits classification under operating or financing provided that it is consistently applied. (Some believe that interest payments, like dividend payments, are better classified as financing because they represent payments to financiers.) Samsung reports cash outflows for interest under operating, which is consistent with U.S. GAAP and acceptable under IFRS.

Samsung

Global: There are no requirements to separate domestic and international cash flows, leading some users to ask, "Where in the world is cash flow?"

Reporting Cash Flows from Investing and Financing U.S. GAAP and IFRS are broadly similar in computing and classifying cash flows from investing and financing activities. A quick review of these two sections for Samsung's statement of cash flows shows a structure similar to that explained in this chapter. One notable exception is that U.S. GAAP requires that cash outflows for income tax be classified as operating, whereas IFRS permits the splitting of those cash flows among operating, investing, and financing depending on the sources of that tax. Samsung reports its cash outflows for income tax under operating, which is similar to U.S. GAAP.

 Global View Assignments

Discussion Questions 14 and 15

Quick Study 16-20

Exercise 16-9

BTN 16-10

17 chapter

Analysis of Financial Statements

Chapter Preview

BASICS OF ANALYSIS

C1 Analysis purpose

Building blocks

C2 Standards for comparisons

Analysis tools

HORIZONTAL ANALYSIS

P1 Application of:

Comparative balance sheets

Comparative income statements

Trend analysis

NTK 17-1

VERTICAL ANALYSIS

P2 Application of:

Common-size balance sheet

Common-size income statement

Common-size graphics

NTK 17-2

RATIO ANALYSIS AND REPORTING

P3 Liquidity and efficiency

Solvency

Profitability

Market prospects

A1 Analysis reports

NTK 17-3

Learning Objectives

CONCEPTUAL

C1 Explain the purpose and identify the building blocks of analysis.

C2 Describe standards for comparisons in analysis.

ANALYTICAL

A1 Summarize and report results of analysis.

A2 *Appendix 17A*—Explain the form and assess the content of a complete income statement.

PROCEDURAL

P1 Explain and apply methods of horizontal analysis.

P2 Describe and apply methods of vertical analysis.

P3 Define and apply ratio analysis.

CARLA HARRIS
MORGAN STANLEY, VICE CHAIRMAN, WEALTH MANAGEMENT, MANAGING DIRECTOR & SENIOR CLIENT ADVISOR

© Alberto E. Rodriguez/Getty Images

Numbers Rule

NEW YORK—"I grew up as an only child in a no-nonsense, no-excuses household," recalls Carla Harris. "My parents gave me the sense that I was supposed to do well." Fast-forward and Carla is now vice chairman of **Morgan Stanley**'s (**MorganStanley.com**) prized global wealth-management division and past-chair of the Morgan Stanley Foundation.

Carla Harris and her colleagues at Morgan Stanley analyze financial statements for profit. Their success in analyzing financial statements is well documented.

One of Morgan Stanley's key tools for analysis is *ModelWare*. ModelWare is a framework to analyze the nuts and bolts of companies' financial statements, and then to compare those companies head-to-head. One of its key aims is to provide comparable information that focuses on sustainable performance. To do this, it works with the underlying accounting numbers and footnotes.

Morgan Stanley uses the accounting numbers in financial statements to produce comparable metrics using techniques such as horizontal and vertical analysis. It also computes financial ratios for

"Expect to win!"
—Carla Harris

analysis and interpretation. Those ratios include return on equity, return on assets, asset turnover, profit margin, price-to-earnings, and many other accounting measures. The focus is to uncover the drivers of profitability and to predict future levels of those drivers.

Carla has experienced much success through analyzing financial statements. As Carla likes to say, "I'm tough and analytical!" She says that people do not take full advantage of information available in financial statements. Accordingly, those with accounting know-how continue to earn profits from financial statement analysis and interpretation.

Carla and Morgan Stanley are proud to play by the rules. *Fortune* writes, "Morgan Stanley has earned some bragging rights. It's the only major bank that hasn't paid a federal fine related to the financial crisis. [It] hasn't even been accused of breaking the law." Carla is proud of such praise and adds: "always start from a place of doing the right thing."

Sources: *Morgan Stanley website,* January 2017; *MorganStanleyIQ,* November 2007; *Alumni.HBS.edu/Stories,* September 2006; *Fortune,* August 2013 and March 2016

BASICS OF ANALYSIS

C1
_____

Explain the purpose and identify the building blocks of analysis.

Financial statement analysis applies analytical tools to financial statements and related data for making business decisions. This section describes the purpose of financial statement analysis, its information sources, the use of comparisons, and issues in computation.

Purpose of Analysis

Internal users of accounting information manage and operate the company. They include managers, officers, and internal auditors. The purpose of financial statement analysis for internal users is to provide strategic information to improve company efficiency and effectiveness.

External users of accounting information are _not_ directly involved in running the company. External users rely on financial statement analysis in pursuing their own goals. Shareholders and creditors assess company prospects to make investing and lending decisions. A board of directors analyzes financial statements in monitoring management's decisions. Suppliers use financial statement information in establishing credit terms. Auditors use financial statements in assessing the "fair presentation" of financial results. Analyst services such as **Moody's** and **Standard & Poor's** use financial statements in making buy-sell recommendations and in setting credit ratings.

Point: Financial statement analysis is a topic on the CPA, CMA, CIA, and CFA exams.

The common goal of these users is to evaluate company performance and financial condition. This includes evaluating (1) past and current performance, (2) current financial position, and (3) future performance and risk.

Building Blocks of Analysis

Financial statement analysis focuses on one or more elements of a company's financial condition or performance. We emphasize four _building blocks_ of financial statement analysis:

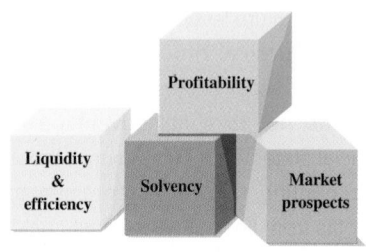

- **Liquidity** and **efficiency**—ability to meet short-term obligations and to efficiently generate revenues.
- **Solvency**—ability to generate future revenues and meet long-term obligations.
- **Profitability**—ability to provide financial rewards to attract and retain financing.
- **Market prospects**—ability to generate positive market expectations.

The four building blocks highlight different aspects of financial condition or performance, yet they are interrelated.

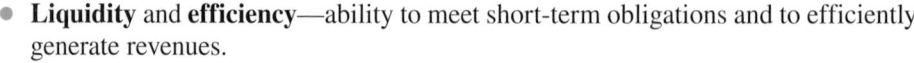 **Decision** Insight

Chips and Brokers   The phrase _blue chips_ refers to stock of big, profitable companies. The phrase comes from poker, where the most valuable chips are blue. The term _brokers_ refers to those who execute orders to buy or sell stock. The term comes from wine retailers—individuals who broach (break) wine casks. ∎

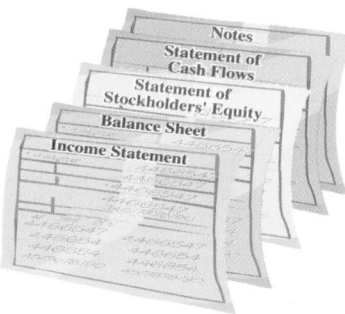

Information for Analysis

Financial analysis uses **general-purpose financial statements** that include the (1) income statement, (2) balance sheet, (3) statement of stockholders' equity (or statement of retained earnings), (4) statement of cash flows, and (5) notes to these statements.

Financial reporting is the communication of financial information useful for making investment, credit, and other business decisions. Financial reporting includes general-purpose financial statements, information from SEC 10-K and other filings, press releases, shareholders' meetings, forecasts, management letters, and auditors' reports.

Management's Discussion and Analysis (MD&A) is one example of useful information outside usual financial statements. **Apple**'s MD&A (available at <u>Investor.Apple.com</u> and "Item 7" in the annual report) begins with an overview, followed by critical accounting policies and estimates. It then discusses operating results followed by financial condition (liquidity, capital resources, and cash flows). The final few parts discuss legal proceedings, market risk of financial instruments, and risks from interest rate and foreign currency fluctuations. The MD&A is an excellent starting point in understanding a company's business.

Standards for Comparisons

When interpreting financial statements, we use standards (benchmarks) for comparisons that include:

C2
Describe standards for comparisons in analysis.

- *Intracompany*—The company's current performance is compared to its prior performance and its relations between financial items. Apple's current net income, for instance, can be compared with its prior years' net income and in relation to its revenues or total assets.
- *Competitor*—Competitors provide standards for comparisons. **Coca-Cola**'s profit margin, for instance, can be compared with **PepsiCo**'s profit margin.
- *Industry*—Industry statistics provide standards of comparisons. **Intel**'s profit margin can be compared with the industry's profit margin.
- *Guidelines (rules of thumb)*—Standards of comparisons can develop from experience. Examples are the 2:1 level for the current ratio or 1:1 level for the acid-test ratio.

Benchmarks from a selected competitor or group of competitors are often best. Intracompany and industry measures are also good. Guidelines can be applied, but only if they seem reasonable given recent experience.

Point: Each chapter's *Reporting in Action* problems engage students in *intracompany* analysis, whereas *Comparative Analysis* problems require competitor analysis (**Apple** vs. **Google** vs. **Samsung**).

Tools of Analysis

Three tools of financial statement analysis are

1. **Horizontal analysis**—comparison of a company's financial condition and performance across time.
2. **Vertical analysis**—comparison of a company's financial condition and performance to a base amount.
3. **Ratio analysis**—measurement of key relations between financial statement items.

The remainder of this chapter describes these analysis tools and how to apply them.

■ Decision Insight ⟶

Busting Frauds Horizontal, vertical, and ratio analysis tools can uncover fraud by identifying amounts out of line with expectations. One can then follow up and ask questions that can either identify a logical reason for such results or confirm/raise suspicions of fraud. Many past fraud schemes could have been identified much earlier had people applied these tools and pressured management for explanations. ■

HORIZONTAL ANALYSIS

Horizontal analysis refers to examination of financial statement data *across time*. (The term *horizontal analysis* comes from the left-to-right [or right-to-left] movement of our eyes as we review comparative financial statements across time.)

P1
Explain and apply methods of horizontal analysis.

Comparative Statements

Comparative financial statements show financial amounts in side-by-side columns on a single statement, called a *comparative format*. Using **Apple**'s financial statements, this section explains how to compute dollar changes and percent changes for comparative statements.

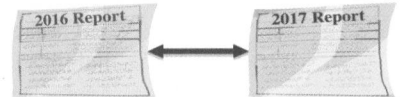

Dollar Changes and Percent Changes

Comparing financial statements over short time periods—two to three years—is often done by analyzing changes in line items. A change analysis includes analyzing dollar amount changes and percent changes. Both analyses are relevant because small dollar changes can yield large percent changes inconsistent with their importance. For instance, a 50% change from a base figure of $100 is less important than a 50% change from a base amount of $100,000. Reference to dollar amounts helps keep a perspective on the importance of changes. We compute the *dollar change* for a financial statement item as follows:

$$\text{Dollar change} = \text{Analysis period amount} - \text{Base period amount}$$

Analysis period is the point or period of time for the financial statements under analysis, and *base period* is the point or period of time for the financial statements used for comparison purposes. The prior year is commonly used as a base period. We compute the *percent change* by dividing the dollar change by the base period amount and then multiplying this quantity by 100 as follows:

$$\text{Percent change (\%)} = \frac{\text{Analysis period amount} - \text{Base period amount}}{\text{Base period amount}} \times 100$$

We must know a few rules in working with percent changes. To illustrate, look at four separate cases in this chart:

Case	Analysis Period	Base Period	Change Analysis Dollar	Percent
A	$ 1,500	$(4,500)	$ 6,000	—
B	(1,000)	2,000	(3,000)	—
C	8,000	—	8,000	—
D	0	10,000	(10,000)	(100%)

- **Cases A and B:** When a negative amount is in the base period and a positive amount in the analysis period (or vice versa), we cannot compute a meaningful percent change.
- **Case C:** When no amount is in the base period, no percent change is computable.
- **Case D:** When an item has an amount in the base period and zero in the analysis period, the decrease is 100 percent.

Comparative Balance Sheets

Comparative balance sheets consist of amounts from two or more dates arranged side by side. This method of analysis is improved by showing each item's dollar change and percent change to highlight large changes.

Analysis of comparative financial statements begins by focusing on large dollar and percent changes. We then identify the reasons for these changes and determine whether they are favorable or unfavorable. We also follow up on items with small changes when we expected the changes to be large.

APPLE

Exhibit 17.1 shows comparative balance sheets for **Apple Inc.** (ticker: AAPL). A few items stand out on the asset side. Apple's cash and cash equivalents increased by 52.6%, and short-term marketable securities increased by 82.3%. This is a substantial increase in liquid assets. In response, Apple raised its 2016 dividend 9.6% and increased its share repurchase plan by 25%. Dividends and share repurchase plans are likely to slow Apple's growth of cash and short-term securities. Other notable increases occur with (1) other noncurrent assets, partially related to derivatives; (2) vendor nontrade receivables; and (3) especially long-term marketable securities. Interestingly, accounts receivable decreased by 3.5% while sales increased by 27.9%. This suggests Apple is improving its collection of receivables, a positive trend.

On Apple's financing side, we see its overall 25.3% increase is driven by a 42.3% increase in liabilities; equity increased only 7.0%. The largest increase is due to long-term debt, which increased by $24,476 million, or 84.4%. Much of this increase results from bond offerings by

EXHIBIT 17.1

Comparative Balance Sheets

APPLE

APPLE INC. Comparative Balance Sheets September 26, 2015, and September 27, 2014				
$ millions	2015	2014	Dollar Change	Percent Change
Assets				
Cash and cash equivalents	$ 21,120	$ 13,844	$ 7,276	52.6%
Short-term marketable securities	20,481	11,233	9,248	82.3
Accounts receivable, net	16,849	17,460	(611)	(3.5)
Inventories	2,349	2,111	238	11.3
Deferred tax assets	5,546	4,318	1,228	28.4
Vendor non-trade receivables	13,494	9,759	3,735	38.3
Other current assets.	9,539	9,806	(267)	(2.7)
Total current assets	89,378	68,531	20,847	30.4
Long-term marketable securities.	164,065	130,162	33,903	26.0
Property, plant and equipment, net.	22,471	20,624	1,847	9.0
Goodwill	5,116	4,616	500	10.8
Acquired intangible assets, net	3,893	4,142	(249)	(6.0)
Other assets	5,556	3,764	1,792	47.6
Total assets.	$290,479	$231,839	$ 58,640	25.3
Liabilities				
Accounts payable	$ 35,490	$ 30,196	$ 5,294	17.5%
Accrued expenses	25,181	18,453	6,728	36.5
Deferred revenue	8,940	8,491	449	5.3
Commercial paper	8,499	6,308	2,191	34.7
Current portion of long-term debt	2,500	0	2,500	—
Total current liabilities	80,610	63,448	17,162	27.0
Deferred revenue—noncurrent	3,624	3,031	593	19.6
Long-term debt.	53,463	28,987	24,476	84.4
Other noncurrent liabilities	33,427	24,826	8,601	34.6
Total liabilities.	171,124	120,292	50,832	42.3
Stockholders' Equity				
Common stock	27,416	23,313	4,103	17.6
Retained earnings	92,284	87,152	5,132	5.9
Accumulated other comprehensive income	(345)	1,082	(1,427)	—
Total stockholders' equity	119,355	111,547	7,808	7.0
Total liabilities and stockholders' equity	$290,479	$231,839	$ 58,640	25.3

Apple to take advantage of low interest rates. We also see a modest increase of 5.9% ($5,132) in retained earnings, which consists of a strong income of $53,394 that is reduced by cash dividends and stock repurchases.

Comparative Income Statements   Exhibit 17.2 shows Apple's comparative income statements prepared similarly to comparative balance sheets. Amounts for two periods are placed side by side, with additional columns for dollar and percent changes.

Apple reports substantial sales growth of 27.9% in 2015. This finding helps support management's 25.3% growth in assets as reflected in comparative balance sheets. The 24.8% growth in cost of sales is less that its 27.9% sales increase, which suggests good control over its main costs. Additionally, the 24.2% increase in operating expenses is less than the 27.9% sales growth, which again is good news. Much of the 24.2% increase in operating expenses is driven by greater research and development costs, from which management/investors hope to reap future income. Apple currently reports an increase of 35.1% in income, which is mainly driven by its $23,089 million growth in gross margin.

EXHIBIT 17.2

Comparative Income
Statements

APPLE

APPLE INC. Comparative Income Statements For Years Ended September 26, 2015, and September 27, 2014				
$ millions, except per share	**2015**	**2014**	**Dollar Change**	**Percent Change**
Net sales	$233,715	$182,795	$50,920	27.9%
Cost of sales	140,089	112,258	27,831	24.8
Gross margin.	93,626	70,537	23,089	32.7
Research and development	8,067	6,041	2,026	33.5
Selling, general and administrative	14,329	11,993	2,336	19.5
Total operating expenses.	22,396	18,034	4,362	24.2
Operating income.	71,230	52,503	18,727	35.7
Other income, net.	1,285	980	305	31.1
Income before provision for income taxes	72,515	53,483	19,032	35.6
Provision for income taxes.	19,121	13,973	5,148	36.8
Net income	$ 53,394	$ 39,510	13,884	35.1
Basic earnings per share	$ 9.28	$ 6.49	$ 2.79	43.0
Diluted earnings per share.	$ 9.22	$ 6.45	$ 2.77	42.9

Point: Percent change can also be computed by dividing the current period by the prior period and subtracting 1.0. For example, the 27.9% sales increase in Exhibit 17.2 is computed as: ($233,715/$182,795) − 1.

Point: *Index* refers to the comparison of the analysis period to the base period. Percents determined for each period are called *index numbers*.

Trend Analysis

Trend analysis, also called *trend percent analysis* or *index number trend analysis,* is a form of horizontal analysis that can reveal patterns in data across successive periods. It involves computing trend percents for a series of financial numbers and is a variation on the use of percent changes. The difference is that trend analysis does not subtract the base period amount in the numerator. To compute trend percents, we do the following:

1. Select a *base period* and assign each item in the base period a weight of 100%.
2. Express financial numbers as a percent of their base period number.

Specifically, a *trend percent,* also called an *index number,* is computed as follows:

$$\text{Trend percent (\%)} = \frac{\text{Analysis period amount}}{\text{Base period amount}} \times 100$$

To illustrate trend analysis, we use the Apple data shown in Exhibit 17.3. These data are from Apple's current and prior financial statements.

EXHIBIT 17.3

Sales and Expenses

$ millions	2015	2014	2013	2012	2011
Net sales.	$233,715	$182,795	$170,910	$156,508	$108,249
Cost of sales.	140,089	112,258	106,606	87,846	64,431
Operating expenses.	22,396	18,034	15,305	13,421	10,028

Point: Trend analysis expresses a percent of base, not a percent of change.

The trend percents—using the data from Exhibit 17.3—are shown in Exhibit 17.4. The base period is 2011, and the trend percent is computed in each subsequent year by dividing that year's amount by its 2011 amount. For instance, the revenue trend percent for 2015 is 215.9%, computed as $233,715/$108,249.

EXHIBIT 17.4

Trend Percents for Sales and Expenses

In trend percent	2015	2014	2013	2012	2011
Net sales.	215.9%	168.9%	157.9%	144.6%	100.0%
Cost of sales.	217.4	174.2	165.5	136.3	100.0
Operating expenses.	223.3	179.8	152.6	133.8	100.0

Graphical depictions often aid analysis of trend percents. Exhibit 17.5 shows the trend percents from Exhibit 17.4 in a *line graph*, which helps us identify trends and detect changes in direction or magnitude. It reveals that the trend line for net sales has been exceeded by both cost of sales and operating expenses in 2014 and 2015. In years prior to 2013,

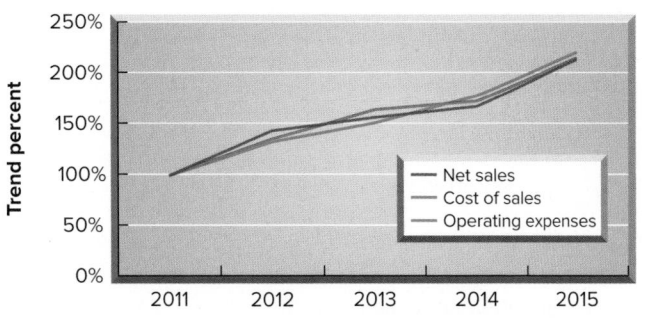

EXHIBIT 17.5

Trend Percent Lines for Sales and Expenses of Apple

the net sales trend line exceeded both cost of sales and operating expenses. The marked increase for cost of sales in 2013 is concerning, with a reduction in the difference in trend lines for 2014 and 2015. Long-run profitability will suffer if those costs are not controlled. By 2015, the difference in trend lines is reduced and net sales is nearly on par with cost of sales.

Exhibit 17.6 compares Apple's revenue trend line to those of **Google** and **Samsung**. Apple and Google were both able to grow revenue in each year relative to the base year. In this respect, Apple and Google have outperformed their competitor Samsung. We can say from these data that Apple and Google products and services have been met with consumer acceptance.

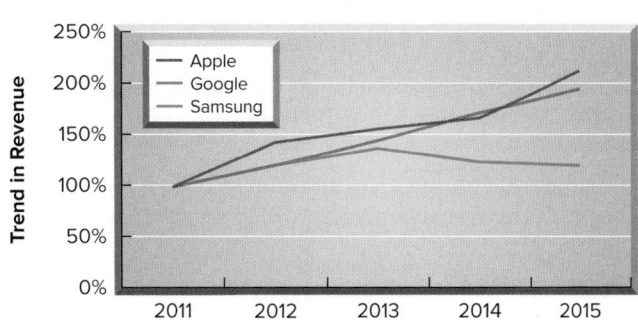

EXHIBIT 17.6

Revenue Trend Percent Lines—Apple, Google, and Samsung

APPLE

GOOGLE

Samsung

Trend analysis of financial statement items can include comparisons of relations between items on different financial statements. For instance, Exhibit 17.7 compares Apple's revenue and total assets. The increase in total assets (149.6%) exceeds the increase in net sales (115.9%) since 2011. Is this result favorable or not? One interpretation is that Apple was *less* efficient in using its assets in 2015 versus 2011. This means that management has not generated net sales sufficient to compensate for the asset growth.

EXHIBIT 17.7

Sales and Asset Data for Apple

$ millions	2015	2011	Change (2015 vs. 2011)
Net sales	$233,715	$108,249	115.9%
Total assets	290,479	116,371	149.6%

■ Decision Maker ═══════════════════════════════════

Auditor   Your tests reveal a 3% increase in sales from $200,000 to $206,000 and a 4% decrease in expenses from $190,000 to $182,400. Both changes are within your "reasonableness" criterion of ±5%, and thus you don't pursue additional tests. The audit partner in charge questions your lack of follow-up and mentions the *joint relation* between sales and expenses. To what is the partner referring? ■   *Answer:* Both *individual* accounts (sales and expenses) yield percent changes within the ±5% acceptable range. However, a *joint analysis* reveals an increase in sales and a decrease in expenses producing a more than 5% increase in income. This client's profit margin is 11.46% (($206,000 − $182,400)/$206,000) for the current year compared with 5.0% (($200,000 − $190,000)/$200,000) for the prior year—a 129% increase! This is what concerns the partner, and it suggests expanding audit tests of the client's numbers.

Compute trend percents for the following accounts, using 2014 as the base year (round percents to whole numbers). State whether the situation as revealed by the trends appears to be favorable or unfavorable for each account.

NEED-TO-KNOW 17-1

Horizontal Analysis

P1

$ millions	2017	2016	2015	2014
Sales	$500	$350	$250	$200
Cost of goods sold	400	175	100	50

Solution

$ millions	2017	2016	2015	2014
Sales	250%	175%	125%	100%
	($500/$200)	($350/$200)	($250/$200)	($200/$200)
Cost of goods sold	800%	350%	200%	100%
	($400/$50)	($175/$50)	($100/$50)	($50/$50)

Analysis: The trend in sales is favorable; however, we need more information about economic conditions such as inflation rates and competitors' performances to better assess it. Cost of sales is also rising (as expected with increasing sales); however, cost of sales is rising faster than the increase in sales, which is unfavorable and bad news. A quick analysis of the gross margin percentage would highlight this concern.

> Do More: QS 17-3, QS 17-4, E 17-3

VERTICAL ANALYSIS

P2 _____

Describe and apply methods of vertical analysis.

Vertical analysis is a tool to evaluate individual financial statement items or a group of items in terms of a specific base amount. We usually define a key aggregate figure as the base, which for an income statement is usually revenue and for a balance sheet is usually total assets. This section explains vertical analysis and applies it to **Apple**. (The term *vertical analysis* comes from the up-down [or down-up] movement of our eyes as we review common-size financial statements. Vertical analysis is also called *common-size analysis*.)

Common-Size Statements

> **Income Statement**
>
> Sales   10,000
> Expenses   6,000
> Income   4,000

The comparative statements in Exhibits 17.1 and 17.2 show the change in each item over time, but they do not show the relative importance of each item. We use **common-size financial statements** to show changes in the relative importance of each financial statement item. All individual amounts in common-size statements are redefined in terms of common-size percents. A *common-size percent* is measured by dividing each individual financial statement amount under analysis by its base amount:

$$\text{Common-size percent (\%)} = \frac{\text{Analysis amount}}{\text{Base amount}} \times 100$$

Common-Size Balance Sheets   Common-size statements show each item as a percent of a *base amount,* which for a common-size balance sheet is usually total assets. The base amount is assigned a value of 100%. (This implies that the total amount of liabilities plus equity equals 100% since this amount equals total assets.) We then compute a common-size percent for each asset, liability, and equity item using total assets as the base amount. When we present a company's successive balance sheets in this way, changes in the mixture of assets, liabilities, and equity are highlighted.

Point: The *base* amount in common-size analysis is an *aggregate* amount from that period's financial statement.

Exhibit 17.8 shows common-size comparative balance sheets for Apple. Two results that stand out on both a magnitude and percentage basis include (1) issuance of long-term debt—a 5.9% increase from 12.5% to 18.4%, the largest of any liability, and (2) a 5.8% decrease from 37.6% to 31.8% in retained earnings—likely the result of dividends and share repurchases. The absence of other substantial changes in Apple's balance sheet suggests a mature company, but with some lack of focus as evidenced by the large and increasing amounts for short-term and especially long-term securities. This buildup in securities is a concern as the return on securities is historically smaller than the return on operating assets. Time will tell whether Apple can continue to generate sufficient revenue and income from its expanding asset base.

Point: Common-size statements often are used to compare two or more companies in the same industry.

Point: Common-size statements are also useful in comparing firms that report in different currencies.

Common-Size Income Statements   Analysis also involves the use of a common-size income statement. Revenue is usually the base amount, which is assigned a value of 100%. Each common-size income statement item is shown as a percent of revenue. If we think of the 100%

EXHIBIT 17.8

Common-Size Comparative
Balance Sheets

APPLE

APPLE INC. Common-Size Comparative Balance Sheets September 26, 2015, and September 27, 2014			Common-Size Percents*	
$ millions	2015	2014	2015	2014
Assets				
Cash and cash equivalents	$ 21,120	$ 13,844	7.3%	6.0%
Short-term marketable securities	20,481	11,233	7.1	4.8
Accounts receivable, net	16,849	17,460	5.8	7.5
Inventories	2,349	2,111	0.8	0.9
Deferred tax assets	5,546	4,318	1.9	1.9
Vendor non-trade receivables	13,494	9,759	4.6	4.2
Other current assets	9,539	9,806	3.3	4.2
Total current assets	89,378	68,531	30.8	29.6
Long-term marketable securities	164,065	130,162	56.5	56.1
Property, plant and equipment, net	22,471	20,624	7.7	8.9
Goodwill	5,116	4,616	1.8	2.0
Acquired intangible assets, net	3,893	4,142	1.3	1.8
Other assets	5,556	3,764	1.9	1.6
Total assets	$290,479	$231,839	100.0%	100.0%
Liabilities				
Accounts payable	$ 35,490	$ 30,196	12.2%	13.0%
Accrued expenses	25,181	18,453	8.7	8.0
Deferred revenue	8,940	8,491	3.1	3.7
Commercial paper	8,499	6,308	2.9	2.7
Current portion of long-term debt	2,500	0	0.9	0.0
Total current liabilities	80,610	63,448	27.8	27.4
Deferred revenue—noncurrent	3,624	3,031	1.2	1.3
Long-term debt	53,463	28,987	18.4	12.5
Other noncurrent liabilities	33,427	24,826	11.5	10.7
Total liabilities	171,124	120,292	58.9	51.9
Stockholders' Equity				
Common stock	27,416	23,313	9.4	10.1
Retained earnings	92,284	87,152	31.8	37.6
Accumulated other comprehensive income	(345)	1,082	(0.1)	0.5
Total stockholders' equity	119,355	111,547	41.1	48.1
Total liabilities and stockholders' equity	$290,479	$231,839	100.0%	100.0%

* Percents are rounded to tenths and thus may not exactly sum to totals and subtotals.

revenue amount as representing one sales dollar, the remaining items show how each revenue dollar is distributed among costs, expenses, and income.

Exhibit 17.9 shows common-size comparative income statements for each dollar of Apple's net sales. The past two years' common-size numbers are similar with two exceptions. One is the decrease of 1.5 cents in the cost of sales, which is a positive development. Another is the decrease of 0.3 cent in total operating expenses. This was achieved in spite of an increase of 0.2 cent in research and development costs (an operating expense). In sum, analysis of common-size percents for successive income statements uncovered key changes in cost management.

Common-Size Graphics

Two tools of common-size analysis are trend analysis of common-size statements and graphical analysis. The trend analysis of common-size statements is similar to that of comparative

EXHIBIT 17.9

Common-Size Comparative
Income Statements

APPLE

$ millions	2015	2014	Common-Size Percents* 2015	Common-Size Percents* 2014
APPLE INC. Common-Size Comparative Income Statements For Years Ended September 26, 2015, and September 27, 2014				
Net sales	$233,715	$182,795	100.0%	100.0%
Cost of sales	140,089	112,258	59.9	61.4
Gross margin.	93,626	70,537	40.1	38.6
Research and development.	8,067	6,041	3.5	3.3
Selling, general and administrative.	14,329	11,993	6.1	6.6
Total operating expenses.	22,396	18,034	9.6	9.9
Operating income.	71,230	52,503	30.5	28.7
Other income, net.	1,285	980	0.5	0.5
Income before provision for income taxes	72,515	53,483	31.0	29.3
Provision for income taxes.	19,121	13,973	8.2	7.6
Net income	$ 53,394	$ 39,510	22.8%	21.6%

* Percents are rounded to tenths and thus may not exactly sum to totals and subtotals.

EXHIBIT 17.10

Common-Size Graphic of
Income Statement

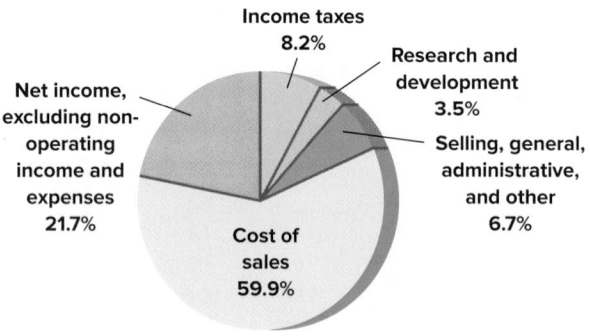

statements discussed under vertical analysis. It is not illustrated here because the only difference is the substitution of common-size percents for trend percents. Instead, this section discusses graphical analysis of common-size statements.

Exhibit 17.10 shows Apple's 2015 common-size income statement in graphical form. This pie chart highlights the contribution of each cost component of net sales for net income (for this graph, "other income, net" is included in selling, general, and administrative costs).

Exhibit 17.11 previews more complex graphical analyses and the insights provided. The data for this exhibit are taken from Apple's *Segments* footnote. Apple reports five operating segments for 2015: (1) Americas, (2) Europe, (3) China, (4) Japan, and (5) Asia Pacific.

EXHIBIT 17.11

Sales and Operating
Income Margin Breakdown
by Segment

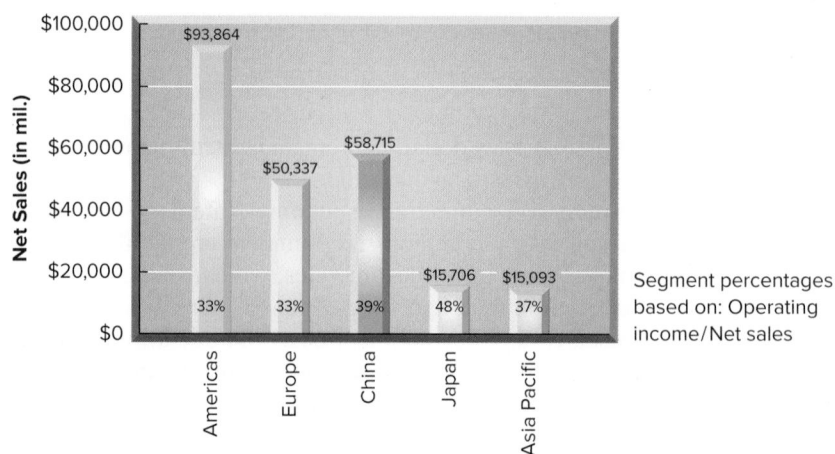

The bars in Exhibit 17.11 show the level of net sales for each of Apple's five operating segments. Its Americas segment generates $93,864 million net sales, which is roughly 40% of its total sales. The four other bars show sales generated from each of the other international segments. Within each bar is that segment's operating income margin, defined as segment operating income divided by segment net sales. The Americas segment has a 33% operating income margin. This type of graphic can raise questions about the profitability of each segment and discussion of further expansions into more lucrative segments. For example, the Japan segment has an operating margin of 48%. A natural question for management is what potential is there to further expand sales into the Japan segment and maintain a similar operating margin? This type of analysis can help in determining strategic plans and actions.

Graphical analysis is also used to identify (1) sources of financing, including the distribution among current liabilities, noncurrent liabilities, and equity capital, and (2) focuses of investing activities, including the distribution among current and noncurrent assets. To illustrate, Exhibit 17.12 shows a common-size graphical display of Apple's assets. Common-size balance sheet analysis can be extended to examine the composition of these subgroups. For instance, in assessing liquidity of current assets, knowing what proportion of *current* assets consists of inventories is usually important, and not simply what proportion inventories are of *total* assets.

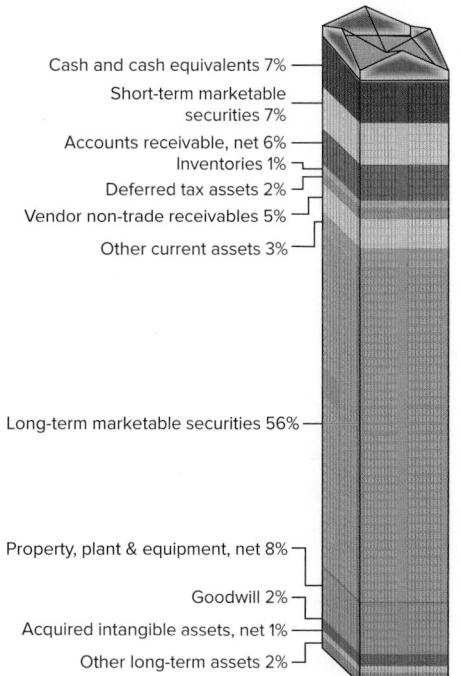

EXHIBIT 17.12

Common-Size Graphic of Asset Components

Common-size financial statements are also useful in comparing companies. Exhibit 17.13 shows common-size graphics of Apple, Google, and Samsung on financing sources. This graphic highlights the larger percent of equity financing for Google versus Apple and Samsung. It also highlights the larger noncurrent (debt) financing of Apple versus Google and Samsung. Comparison of a company's common-size statements with competitors' or industry common-size statistics alerts us to differences in the structure or distribution of its financial statements but not to their dollar magnitude.

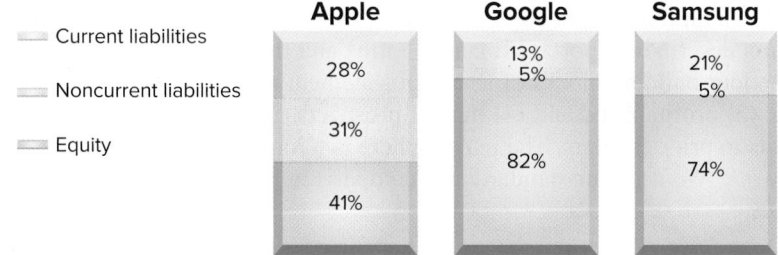

EXHIBIT 17.13

Common-Size Graphic of Financing Sources— Competitor Analysis

APPLE

GOOGLE

Samsung

■ Decision Insight

Seeing Truth In a survey of nearly 200 CFOs of large companies, roughly 20% say that firms, based on their experience, use accounting ploys to report earnings that do not fully reflect the firms' underlying operations. One goal of financial analysis is to see through such ploys. The top five reasons CFOs gave for this behavior are shown here (*Wall Street Journal,* October 2012). ■

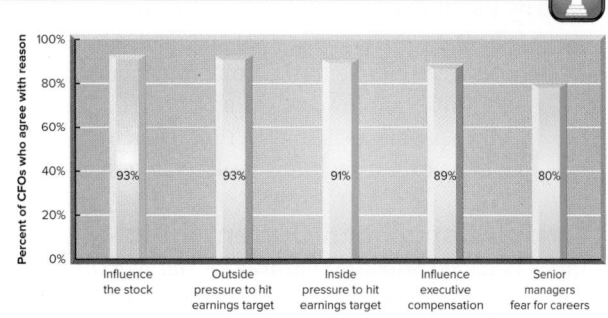

NEED-TO-KNOW 17-2

Vertical Analysis

P2

Express the following comparative income statements in common-size percents and assess whether or not this company's situation has improved in the most recent year (round percents to whole numbers).

Comparative Income Statements For Years Ended December 31, 2017 and 2016	2017	2016
Sales	$800	$500
Total expenses	560	400
Net income	$240	$100

Solution

	2017	2016
Sales	100% ($800/$800)	100% ($500/$500)
Total expenses	70% ($560/$800)	80% ($400/$500)
Net income	30%	20%

Do More: QS 17-5, E 17-4, E 17-6

Analysis: This company's situation has improved. This is evident from its substantial increase in net income as a percent of sales for 2017 (30%) relative to 2016 (20%). Further, the company's sales increased from $500 in 2016 to $800 in 2017 (while expenses declined as a percent of sales from 80% to 70%).

RATIO ANALYSIS

P3

Define and apply ratio analysis.

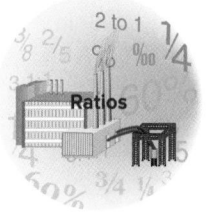

Ratios are widely used in financial analysis because they help us uncover conditions and trends difficult to detect by looking at individual amounts.

A ratio expresses a relation between two quantities. It can be expressed as a percent, rate, or proportion. For instance, a change in an account balance from $100 to $250 can be expressed as (1) 150% increase, (2) 2.5 times, or (3) 2.5 to 1 (or 2.5:1). To be meaningful, a ratio must refer to an economically important relation. For example, a ratio of cost of goods sold to sales is meaningful, but a ratio of freight costs to patents is not.

This section describes important financial ratios and their application. The ratios are organized into the four building blocks of financial statement analysis: (1) liquidity and efficiency, (2) solvency, (3) profitability, and (4) market prospects. All of these ratios were explained at relevant points in prior chapters. The purpose here is to organize and apply them under a summary framework. We use four standards for comparison: intracompany, competitor, industry, and guidelines.

Liquidity and Efficiency

Liquidity refers to the availability of resources to meet short-term cash requirements. It is affected by the timing of cash inflows and outflows along with prospects for future performance. *Efficiency* refers to how productive a company is in using its assets. Efficiency is usually measured relative to how much revenue is generated from assets. A lack of liquidity is often linked to lower profitability. To creditors, lack of liquidity can yield delays in collecting payments. Moreover, inefficient use of assets can cause liquidity problems. This section covers key ratios used to assess liquidity and efficiency.

Working Capital and Current Ratio   The amount of current assets minus current liabilities is called **working capital,** or *net working capital.* A company needs enough working capital to meet current debts, to carry sufficient inventories, and to take advantage of cash discounts. A company that runs low on working capital is less likely to meet current obligations or to continue operating. When evaluating a company's working capital, we must look at the dollar amount of current assets minus current liabilities *and* at their ratio. The *current ratio* is defined as follows (see Chapter 4 for additional explanation).

$$\text{Current ratio} = \frac{\text{Current assets}}{\text{Current liabilities}}$$

Using information in Exhibit 17.1, Apple's working capital and current ratio for both 2015 and 2014 are shown in Exhibit 17.14. Also, Google (4.67), Samsung (2.47), and the industry's current ratio (2.5) are shown in the margin. Apple's 2015 ratio (1.11) is lower than competitors' ratios, but it is not in danger of defaulting on loan payments. A high

EXHIBIT 17.14

Apple's Working Capital and Current Ratio

$ millions	2015	2014
Current assets..............	$89,378	$68,531
Current liabilities...........	80,610	63,448
Working capital...........	$ 8,768	$ 5,083
Current ratio		
$89,378/$80,610 =	1.11 to 1	
$68,531/$63,448 =		1.08 to 1

Current ratio
Google = 4.67
Samsung = 2.47
Industry = 2.5

current ratio suggests a strong liquidity position and an ability to meet current obligations. An excessively high current ratio means that the company has invested too much in current assets compared to its current obligations. An excessive investment in current assets is not an efficient use of funds because current assets normally generate a low return on investment (compared with long-term assets).

Many users apply a guideline of 2:1 (or 1.5:1) for the current ratio. A 2:1 or higher ratio is judged a good credit risk in the short run. Any analysis of the current ratio must recognize at least three additional factors: (1) type of business, (2) composition of current assets, and (3) turnover rate of current asset components.

Type of Business   A service company that grants little or no credit and carries few inventories can probably operate on a current ratio of less than 1:1 if its revenues generate enough cash to pay its current liabilities. On the other hand, a company selling high-priced clothing or furniture requires a higher ratio because of difficulties in judging customer demand and cash receipts. For instance, if demand falls, inventory may not generate as much cash as expected. Accordingly, analysis of the current ratio should include a comparison with competitors.

Composition of Current Assets   The composition of a company's current assets is important to an evaluation of short-term liquidity. For instance, cash, cash equivalents, and short-term investments are more liquid than accounts and notes receivable. An excessive amount of receivables and inventory weakens a company's ability to pay current liabilities. The acid-test ratio (covered next) can help with this assessment.

Global: Ratio analysis helps overcome currency translation problems, but it does *not* overcome differences in accounting principles.

Turnover Rate of Assets   Asset turnover measures a company's efficiency in using its assets. One relevant measure of asset efficiency is the revenue generated. A measure of total asset turnover is revenues divided by total assets, but evaluation of turnover for individual assets is also useful. We discuss both receivables turnover and inventory turnover next.

■ **Decision** Maker

Banker   A company requests a one-year, $200,000 loan for expansion. This company's current ratio is 4:1, with current assets of $160,000. Key competitors carry a current ratio of about 1.9:1. Using this information, do you approve the loan? Does your decision change if the application is for a 10-year loan? ■   [*Answer:* The loan application is likely approved for at least two reasons. First, the current ratio suggests an ability to meet short-term obligations. Second, current assets of $160,000 and a current ratio of 4:1 imply current liabilities of $40,000 (one-fourth of current assets) and a working capital excess of $120,000. The working capital excess is 60% of the loan. Finally, if the application is for a 10-year loan, a decision is less clear as the high current ratio and working capital suggest some inefficiency—for example, a 4:1 current ratio is more than double that of its peers.]

Acid-Test Ratio   Quick assets are cash, short-term investments, and current receivables. These are the most liquid types of current assets. The *acid-test ratio,* also called *quick ratio* and introduced in Chapter 5, reflects a company's short-term liquidity.

$$\text{Acid-test ratio} = \frac{\text{Cash + Short-term investments + Current receivables}}{\text{Current liabilities}}$$

Apple's acid-test ratio is computed in Exhibit 17.15. Apple's 2015 acid-test ratio (0.73) is lower than those for Google (4.41) and Samsung (1.98), as well as lower than the 1:1 common guideline for an acceptable acid-test ratio. The ratio for Apple is also less than the 0.9 industry norm; thus, it raises some concern. As with analysis of the current ratio, we need to consider other factors. For instance, the frequency with which a company converts its current assets into cash affects its working capital requirements. This implies that analysis of short-term liquidity should also include an analysis of receivables and inventories, which we consider next.

EXHIBIT 17.15

Acid-Test Ratio

$ millions	2015	2014
Cash and equivalents	$21,120	$13,844
Short-term securities.	20,481	11,233
Current receivables	16,849	17,460
Total quick assets.	$58,450	$42,537
Current liabilities	$80,610	$63,448
Acid-test ratio		
$58,450/$80,610	0.73 to 1	
$42,537/$63,448.		0.67 to 1

Acid-test ratio
Google = 4.41
Samsung = 1.98
Industry = 0.9

Accounts Receivable Turnover   We can measure how frequently a company converts its receivables into cash by computing the *accounts receivable turnover.* This ratio is defined as follows (see Chapter 9 for additional explanation).

$$\text{Accounts receivable turnover} = \frac{\text{Net sales}}{\text{Average accounts receivable, net}}$$

Point: Some users prefer using gross accounts receivable (before subtracting the allowance for doubtful accounts) to avoid the influence of a manager's bad debts estimate.

Short-term receivables from customers are often included in the denominator along with accounts receivable. Also, accounts receivable turnover is more precise if credit sales are used for the numerator, but external users generally use net sales (or net revenues) because information about credit sales is typically not reported. Apple's 2015 accounts receivable turnover is computed as follows ($ millions).

$$\frac{\$233,715}{(\$17,460 + \$16,849)/2} = 13.6 \text{ times}$$

Accounts receivable turnover
Google = 7.2
Samsung = 7.1
Industry = 5.0

Apple's turnover of 13.6 exceeds Google's 7.2 and Samsung's 7.1 turnover. Accounts receivable turnover is high when accounts receivable are quickly collected. A high turnover is favorable because it means the company need not commit large amounts of funds to accounts receivable. However, an accounts receivable turnover can be too high; this can occur when credit terms are so restrictive that they decrease sales.

Inventory Turnover   How long a company holds inventory before selling it will affect working capital. One measure of this effect is *inventory turnover,* also called *merchandise turnover* or *merchandise inventory turnover,* which is defined as follows (see Chapter 6 for additional explanation).

$$\text{Inventory turnover} = \frac{\text{Cost of goods sold}}{\text{Average inventory}}$$

Using Apple's cost of goods sold and inventories information, we compute its inventory turnover for 2015 as follows.

$$\frac{\$140,089}{(\$2,111 + \$2,349)/2} = 62.82 \text{ times}$$

Inventory turnover
Samsung = 6.84
Industry = 7.0

Apple's inventory turnover of 62.82 is higher than Samsung's 6.84 and the industry's 7.0. A company with a high turnover requires a smaller investment in inventory than one producing the same sales with a lower turnover. Inventory turnover can be too high, however, if inventory is so small and sales decrease due to stock-outs.

Days' Sales Uncollected
Accounts receivable turnover expresses how frequently a company collects its accounts. Days' sales uncollected is one measure of this activity, which is defined as follows (Chapter 8 provides additional explanation).

$$\textbf{Days' sales uncollected} = \frac{\textbf{Accounts receivable, net}}{\textbf{Net sales}} \times \textbf{365}$$

ChinaFotoPress/ChinaFotoPress via Getty Images

Any short-term notes receivable from customers are normally included in the numerator. Apple's 2015 days' sales uncollected follows.

$$\frac{\$16,849}{\$233,715} \times 365 = 26.3 \text{ days}$$

Days' sales uncollected
Google = 56.2
Samsung = 51.9

Both Google's days' sales uncollected of 56.2 days and Samsung's 51.9 days are more than the 26.3 days for Apple. Days' sales uncollected is more meaningful if we know company credit terms. A rough guideline states that days' sales uncollected should not exceed $1\frac{1}{3}$ times the days in its (1) credit period, *if* discounts are not offered, or (2) discount period, *if* favorable discounts are offered.

Days' Sales in Inventory
Days' sales in inventory is a useful measure in evaluating inventory liquidity. We compute days' sales in inventory as follows (Chapter 6 provides additional explanation).

$$\textbf{Days' sales in inventory} = \frac{\textbf{Ending inventory}}{\textbf{Cost of goods sold}} \times \textbf{365}$$

Apple's days' sales in inventory for 2015 follows.

$$\frac{\$2,349}{\$140,089} \times 365 = 6.1 \text{ days}$$

Days' sales in inventory
Samsung = 55.6
Industry = 35

If the products in Apple's inventory are in demand by customers, this formula estimates that its inventory will be converted into receivables (or cash) in 6.1 days. If all of Apple's sales were credit sales, the conversion of inventory to receivables in 6.1 days *plus* the conversion of receivables to cash in 26.3 days implies that inventory will be converted to cash in about 32.4 days (6.1 + 26.3).

Point: *Average collection period* is estimated by dividing 365 by the accounts receivable turnover ratio. For example, 365 divided by an accounts receivable turnover of 6.1 indicates a 60-day average collection period.

Total Asset Turnover
Total asset turnover reflects a company's ability to use its assets to generate sales and is an important measure of operating efficiency. The definition of this ratio follows (Chapter 10 offers additional explanation).

$$\textbf{Total asset turnover} = \frac{\textbf{Net sales}}{\textbf{Average total assets}}$$

Apple's total asset turnover of 0.89 for 2015 follows, which is greater than that for Google (0.54) and Samsung (0.85).

$$\frac{\$233{,}715}{(\$290{,}479 + \$231{,}839)/2} = 0.89 \text{ times}$$

Solvency

Solvency refers to a company's long-run financial viability and its ability to meet long-term obligations. Analysis of solvency is long term and uses broader measures than liquidity. An important component of solvency analysis is a company's capital structure. *Capital structure* refers to a company's makeup of equity and debt financing. Our analysis here focuses on a company's ability to both meet its obligations and provide security to its creditors *over the long run.*

Debt and Equity Ratios One part of solvency analysis is to assess the portion of a company's assets contributed by its owners and the portion contributed by creditors. This relation is reflected in the debt ratio (also described in Chapter 2). The *debt ratio* expresses total liabilities as a percent of total assets. The **equity ratio** expresses total equity as a percent of total assets. **Apple**'s debt and equity ratios follow.

$ millions	2015	Ratios	
Total liabilities.....................	$171,124	58.9%	[Debt ratio]
Total equity	119,355	41.1	[Equity ratio]
Total liabilities and equity............	$290,479	100.0%	

Apple's financial statements reveal slightly more debt than equity. A company is considered less risky if its capital structure (equity plus long-term debt) contains more equity. One risk factor is the required payment for interest and principal when debt is outstanding. Stockholders cannot require payment from the company. From the stockholders' point of view, if a company earns a return on borrowed capital that is higher than the cost of borrowing, the difference represents increased income to stockholders. The inclusion of debt is described as *financial leverage* because debt can have the effect of increasing the return to stockholders.

Debt-to-Equity Ratio The ratio of total liabilities to equity is another measure of solvency. We compute the ratio as follows (Chapter 14 offers additional explanation).

$$\text{Debt-to-equity ratio} = \frac{\textbf{Total liabilities}}{\textbf{Total equity}}$$

Apple's debt-to-equity ratio for 2015 is

$$\$171{,}124/\$119{,}355 = 1.43$$

Apple's 1.43 debt-to-equity ratio is higher than those of Samsung (0.35) and Google (0.23), and greater than the industry ratio of 0.6. Consistent with our inferences from the debt ratio, Apple's capital structure has more debt than equity. Recall that debt must be repaid with interest, while equity does not. Debt requirements can be burdensome when the industry and/or the economy experience a downturn. A larger debt-to-equity ratio also implies less opportunity to expand through use of additional debt financing.

Times Interest Earned

The amount of income before deductions for interest expense and income taxes is the amount available to pay interest expense. The following *times interest earned* ratio reflects the creditors' risk of loan repayments with interest (see Chapter 11 for additional explanation).

Point: The times interest earned ratio and the debt and equity ratios are of special interest to bank lending officers.

$$\text{Times interest earned} = \frac{\text{Income before interest expense and income taxes}}{\text{Interest expense}}$$

The larger this ratio, the less risky is the company for creditors. One guideline says that creditors are reasonably safe if the company earns its fixed interest expense two or more times each year. Apple's times interest earned ratio follows. Apple's 99.9 result suggests that its creditors have little risk of nonrepayment.

$$\frac{\$53,394 + \$733 + \$19,121}{\$733} = 99.9 \text{ times}$$

Times interest earned
Google = 190.0
Samsung = 34.4

 **Decision** Insight

Bears and Bulls A *bear market* is a declining market. The phrase comes from bear-skin jobbers who often sold the skins before the bears were caught. The term *bear* was then used to describe investors who sold shares they did not own in anticipation of a price decline. A *bull market* is a rising market. This phrase comes from the once popular sport of bear and bull baiting. The term *bull* came to mean the opposite of *bear.* ∎

Profitability

Profitability refers to a company's ability to earn an adequate return on invested capital. Return is judged by assessing earnings relative to the level and sources of financing. This section covers key profitability measures.

Profit Margin

A company's operating efficiency and profitability can be expressed by two measures. The first is *profit margin,* which reflects a company's ability to earn net income from sales (Chapter 3 offers additional explanation). It is measured by expressing net income as a percent of sales (*sales* and *revenues* are similar terms). Apple's profit margin follows.

$$\text{Profit margin} = \frac{\text{Net income}}{\text{Net sales}} = \frac{\$53,394}{\$233,715} = 22.8\%$$

Profit margin
Google = 21.8%
Samsung = 9.5%
Industry = 11%

To evaluate profit margin, we must consider the industry. For instance, an appliance company might require a profit margin between 10% and 15%, whereas a retail supermarket might require a profit margin of 1% or 2%. Apple's 22.8% profit margin is better than Google's 21.8%, Samsung's 9.5%, and the industry's 11% margin.

Return on Total Assets

Return on total assets is defined as follows.

$$\text{Return on total assets} = \frac{\text{Net income}}{\text{Average total assets}}$$

Apple's 2015 return on total assets is

$$\frac{\$53,394}{(\$290,479 + \$231,839)/2} = 20.4\%$$

Return on total assets
Google = 11.8%
Samsung = 8.1%
Industry = 9%

Apple's 20.4% return on total assets is higher than that for many businesses and is higher than Google's 11.8%, Samsung's 8.1%, and the industry's 9% returns. We also should evaluate any trend in the rate of return.

The following equation shows the important relation between profit margin, total asset turnover, and return on total assets.

$$\textbf{Profit margin} \times \textbf{Total asset turnover} = \textbf{Return on total assets}$$

or

$$\frac{\textbf{Net income}}{\textbf{Net sales}} \times \frac{\textbf{Net sales}}{\textbf{Average total assets}} = \frac{\textbf{Net income}}{\textbf{Average total assets}}$$

Both profit margin and total asset turnover contribute to overall operating efficiency, as measured by return on total assets. If we apply this formula to Apple, we get

Google: 21.8% × 0.54 ≈ 11.8%
Samsung: 9.5% × 0.85 ≈ 8.1%
(with rounding)

$$22.8\% \times 0.89 = 20.3\% \text{ (with rounding)}$$

This analysis shows that Apple's superior return on assets versus that of both Google and Samsung is driven by its higher profit margin and better asset turnover.

Return on Common Stockholders' Equity

The most important goal in operating a company is to earn income for its owner(s). *Return on common stockholders' equity* measures a company's success in reaching this goal and is defined as follows.

$$\textbf{Return on common stockholders' equity} = \frac{\textbf{Net income} - \textbf{Preferred dividends}}{\textbf{Average common stockholders' equity}}$$

Apple's 2015 return on common stockholders' equity is computed as follows.

Return on common equity
Google = 14.6%
Samsung = 10.8%
Industry = 15%

$$\frac{\$53,394 - \$0}{(\$111,547 + \$119,355)/2} = 46.2\%$$

The denominator in this computation is the book value of common equity (noncontrolling interest is often included in common equity for this ratio). To compute common stockholders' equity, the dividends on cumulative preferred stock are subtracted whether they are declared or are in arrears. If preferred stock is noncumulative, its dividends are subtracted only if declared. Apple's 46.2% return on common stockholders' equity is superior to Google's 14.6% and Samsung's 10.8%.

 Decision Insight

Wall Street   *Wall Street* is synonymous with financial markets, but its name comes from the street location of the original New York Stock Exchange. The street's name derives from stockades built by early settlers to protect New York from pirate attacks. ∎

Market Prospects

Market measures are useful for analyzing corporations with publicly traded stock. These market measures use stock price, which reflects the market's (public's) expectations for the company. This includes market expectations of both company return and risk.

Price-Earnings Ratio   Computation of the *price-earnings ratio* follows (Chapter 13 provides additional explanation).

$$\text{Price-earnings ratio} = \frac{\text{Market price per common share}}{\text{Earnings per share}}$$

Predicted earnings per share for the next period is often used in the denominator of this computation. Reported earnings per share for the most recent period is also commonly used. In both cases, the ratio is used as an indicator of market's expectations for future growth and risk of a company's earnings.

Point: High expected risk suggests a lower PE ratio. High expected growth suggests a higher PE ratio.

The market price of Apple's common stock at the start of fiscal year 2016 was $116.44. Using Apple's $9.28 basic earnings per share, we compute its price-earnings ratio as follows.

$$\frac{\$116.44}{\$9.28} = 12.5$$

PE (year-end)
Google = 33.7
Samsung = 10.0
Industry = 11

Apple's price-earnings ratio is less than that for Google, but it is higher than that for Samsung and near the industry norm for this period.

Point: Some investors avoid stocks with high PE ratios, believing they are "overpriced."

Dividend Yield   *Dividend yield* is used to compare the dividend-paying performance of different companies. We compute dividend yield as follows (Chapter 13 offers additional explanation).

$$\text{Dividend yield} = \frac{\text{Annual cash dividends per share}}{\text{Market price per share}}$$

Apple's dividend yield, based on its fiscal year-end market price per share of $116.44 and its $1.98 cash dividends per share, is computed as follows.

$$\frac{\$1.98}{\$116.44} = 1.7\%$$

Dividend yield
Google = 0.0%
Samsung = 1.6%

Some companies, such as Google, do not pay dividends because they reinvest the cash to grow their businesses in the hope of generating greater future earnings and dividends.

Summary of Ratios

Exhibit 17.16 summarizes the ratios illustrated in this chapter and throughout the book.

 Decision Insight

Ticker Prices   *Ticker prices* refer to a band of moving data on a monitor carrying up-to-the-minute stock prices. The phrase comes from *ticker tape,* a 1-inch-wide strip of paper spewing stock prices from a printer that ticked as it ran. Most of today's investors have never seen actual ticker tape, but the phrase survives. ∎

© Comstock Images/Jupiter Images

EXHIBIT 17.16

Financial Statement Analysis Ratios*

Ratio	Formula	Measure of
Liquidity and Efficiency		
Current ratio	$= \dfrac{\text{Current assets}}{\text{Current liabilities}}$	Short-term debt-paying ability
Acid-test ratio	$= \dfrac{\text{Cash + Short-term investments + Current receivables}}{\text{Current liabilities}}$	Immediate short-term debt-paying ability
Accounts receivable turnover	$= \dfrac{\text{Net sales}}{\text{Average accounts receivable, net}}$	Efficiency of collection
Inventory turnover	$= \dfrac{\text{Cost of goods sold}}{\text{Average inventory}}$	Efficiency of inventory management
Days' sales uncollected	$= \dfrac{\text{Accounts receivable, net}}{\text{Net sales}} \times 365$	Liquidity of receivables
Days' sales in inventory	$= \dfrac{\text{Ending inventory}}{\text{Cost of goods sold}} \times 365$	Liquidity of inventory
Total asset turnover	$= \dfrac{\text{Net sales}}{\text{Average total assets}}$	Efficiency of assets in producing sales
Solvency		
Debt ratio	$= \dfrac{\text{Total liabilities}}{\text{Total assets}}$	Creditor financing and leverage
Equity ratio	$= \dfrac{\text{Total equity}}{\text{Total assets}}$	Owner financing
Debt-to-equity ratio	$= \dfrac{\text{Total liabilities}}{\text{Total equity}}$	Debt versus equity financing
Times interest earned	$= \dfrac{\text{Income before interest expense and income taxes}}{\text{Interest expense}}$	Protection in meeting interest payments
Profitability		
Profit margin ratio	$= \dfrac{\text{Net income}}{\text{Net sales}}$	Net income in each sales dollar
Gross margin ratio	$= \dfrac{\text{Net sales} - \text{Cost of goods sold}}{\text{Net sales}}$	Gross margin in each sales dollar
Return on total assets	$= \dfrac{\text{Net income}}{\text{Average total assets}}$	Overall profitability of assets
Return on common stockholders' equity	$= \dfrac{\text{Net income} - \text{Preferred dividends}}{\text{Average common stockholders' equity}}$	Profitability of owner investment
Book value per common share	$= \dfrac{\text{Shareholders' equity applicable to common shares}}{\text{Number of common shares outstanding}}$	Liquidation at reported amounts
Basic earnings per share	$= \dfrac{\text{Net income} - \text{Preferred dividends}}{\text{Weighted-average common shares outstanding}}$	Net income per common share
Market Prospects		
Price-earnings ratio	$= \dfrac{\text{Market price per common share}}{\text{Earnings per share}}$	Market value relative to earnings
Dividend yield	$= \dfrac{\text{Annual cash dividends per share}}{\text{Market price per share}}$	Cash return per common share

* Additional ratios examined in previous chapters included credit risk ratio; plant asset useful life; plant asset age; days' cash expense coverage; cash coverage of growth; cash coverage of debt; free cash flow; cash flow on total assets; and payout ratio.

For each ratio listed, identify whether the change in ratio value from 2016 to 2017 is regarded as favorable or unfavorable.

NEED-TO-KNOW 17-3

Ratio Analysis

P3

Ratio	2017	2016
1. Profit margin	6%	8%
2. Debt ratio.	50%	70%
3. Gross margin	40%	36%
4. Accounts receivable turnover.	8.8	9.4
5. Basic earnings per share	$2.10	$2.00
6. Inventory turnover.	3.6	4.0

Solution

Ratio	2017	2016	Change
1. Profit margin ratio.	6%	8%	Unfavorable
2. Debt ratio.	50%	70%	Favorable
3. Gross margin ratio.	40%	36%	Favorable
4. Accounts receivable turnover.	8.8	9.4	Unfavorable
5. Basic earnings per share	$2.10	$2.00	Favorable
6. Inventory turnover.	3.6	4.0	Unfavorable

Do More: QS 17-6, E 17-7,
E 17-8, E 17-9, E 17-10,
E 17-11, P 17-4

SUSTAINABILITY AND ACCOUNTING

Morgan Stanley's sustainability initiative is focused on reducing its environmental impact and investing in sustainable projects. Carla Harris, of Morgan Stanley, explains that reducing the company's carbon footprint is a priority. She points out that Morgan Stanley has set a goal of cutting the greenhouse gas intensity of its building operations by 15%.

Morgan Stanley's sustainability report says the company has earned several awards for its work on sustainability. This includes being one of three finalists for Sustainable Global Bank of the Year, S&P 500 Carbon Performance Leadership, and Global 500 Carbon Performance Leadership.

Morgan Stanley is also a leader in sustainable investments. It launched the *Morgan Stanley Institute for Sustainable Investing*. Morgan Stanley's Sustainability Report outlines three core initiatives for the Institute:

- Setting a $10 billion goal for client assets in the Investing with Impact Platform, to consist of investments that deliver positive environmental or social impact.

- Investing $1 billion in a sustainable communities initiative to provide rapid access to capital for low- and moderate-income households.

- Establishing a Sustainable Investing Fellowship with Columbia Business School to develop a cadre of emerging leaders in sustainable finance.

© Andrew Harrer/Bloomberg via Getty Images

Carla proudly believes that Morgan Stanley safeguards scarce resources and invests wisely for the future.

Decision Insight

All Else Being Equal Financial regulation has several goals. Two of them are to ensure adequate accounting disclosure and to strengthen corporate governance. For disclosure purposes, companies must now provide details of related-party transactions and material off-balance-sheet agreements. This is motivated by several major frauds. For corporate governance, the CEO and CFO must now certify the fairness of financial statements and the effectiveness of internal controls. Yet, concerns remain. A study reports that 30% of management and administrative employees observed activities that posed a conflict of interest in the past year (KPMG 2013). Another 24% witnessed the falsifying or manipulating of accounting information. The bottom line: All financial statements are *not* of equal quality. ■

Decision Analysis ▫▫▫ **Analysis Reporting**

A1
_____

Summarize and report results of analysis.

Understanding the purpose of financial statement analysis is crucial to the usefulness of any analysis. This understanding leads to efficiency of effort, effectiveness in application, and relevance in focus. The purpose of most financial statement analyses is to reduce uncertainty in business decisions through a rigorous and sound evaluation. A *financial statement analysis report* helps by directly addressing the building blocks of analysis and by identifying weaknesses in inference by requiring explanation: It forces us to organize our reasoning and to verify its flow and logic. A report also serves as a communication link with readers, and the writing process reinforces our judgments and vice versa. Finally, the report helps us (re)evaluate evidence and refine conclusions on key building blocks. A good analysis report usually consists of six sections:

1. **Executive summary**—brief focus on important analysis results and conclusions.
2. **Analysis overview**—background on the company, its industry, and its economic setting.
3. **Evidential matter**—financial statements and information used in the analysis, including ratios, trends, comparisons, statistics, and all analytical measures assembled; often organized under the building blocks of analysis.
4. **Assumptions**—identification of important assumptions regarding a company's industry and economic environment, and other important assumptions for estimates.
5. **Key factors**—list of important favorable and unfavorable factors, both quantitative and qualitative, for company performance; usually organized by areas of analysis.
6. **Inferences**—forecasts, estimates, interpretations, and conclusions drawing on all sections of the report.

Point: WikiLeaks includes thousands of analysis reports and valuation reports on its website.

We must remember that the user dictates relevance, meaning that the analysis report should include a brief table of contents to help readers focus on those areas most relevant to their decisions. All irrelevant matter must be eliminated. For example, decades-old details of obscure transactions and detailed miscues of the analysis are irrelevant. Ambiguities and qualifications to avoid responsibility or hedging inferences must be eliminated. Finally, writing is important. Mistakes in grammar and errors of fact compromise the report's credibility.

Decision Insight

Short Selling *Short selling* refers to selling stock before you buy it. Here's an example: You borrow 100 shares of Nike stock, sell them at $40 each, and receive money from their sale. You then wait. You hope that Nike's stock price falls to, say, $35 each and you can replace the borrowed stock for less than you sold it, reaping a profit of $5 each less any transaction costs. ■

NEED-TO-KNOW 17-4

COMPREHENSIVE

Use the following financial statements of Precision Co. to complete these requirements.

1. Prepare comparative income statements showing the percent increase or decrease for year 2017 in comparison to year 2016.
2. Prepare common-size comparative balance sheets for years 2017 and 2016.

3. Compute the following ratios as of December 31, 2017, or for the year ended December 31, 2017, and identify its building block category for financial statement analysis.

a. Current ratio	**g.** Debt-to-equity ratio
b. Acid-test ratio	**h.** Times interest earned
c. Accounts receivable turnover	**i.** Profit margin ratio
d. Days' sales uncollected	**j.** Total asset turnover
e. Inventory turnover	**k.** Return on total assets
f. Debt ratio	**l.** Return on common stockholders' equity

PRECISION COMPANY Comparative Income Statements For Years Ended December 31, 2017 and 2016	2017	2016
Sales	$2,486,000	$2,075,000
Cost of goods sold	1,523,000	1,222,000
Gross profit	963,000	853,000
Operating expenses		
Advertising expense	145,000	100,000
Sales salaries expense	240,000	280,000
Office salaries expense	165,000	200,000
Insurance expense.................	100,000	45,000
Supplies expense..................	26,000	35,000
Depreciation expense	85,000	75,000
Miscellaneous expenses	17,000	15,000
Total operating expenses	778,000	750,000
Operating income....................	185,000	103,000
Interest expense.....................	44,000	46,000
Income before taxes..................	141,000	57,000
Income taxes........................	47,000	19,000
Net income	$ 94,000	$ 38,000
Earnings per share	$ 0.99	$ 0.40

PRECISION COMPANY Comparative Balance Sheets December 31, 2017 and 2016		2017		2016
Assets				
Current assets				
Cash	$	79,000	$	42,000
Short-term investments..............		65,000		96,000
Accounts receivable, net.............		120,000		100,000
Merchandise inventory		250,000		265,000
Total current assets		514,000		503,000
Plant assets				
Store equipment, net.................		400,000		350,000
Office equipment, net		45,000		50,000
Buildings, net......................		625,000		675,000
Land		100,000		100,000
Total plant assets		1,170,000		1,175,000
Total assets........................		$1,684,000		$1,678,000
Liabilities				
Current liabilities				
Accounts payable....................	$	164,000	$	190,000
Short-term notes payable		75,000		90,000
Taxes payable......................		26,000		12,000
Total current liabilities		265,000		292,000
Long-term liabilities				
Notes payable (secured by mortgage on buildings).............		400,000		420,000
Total liabilities.....................		665,000		712,000
Stockholders' Equity				
Common stock, $5 par value..........		475,000		475,000
Retained earnings		544,000		491,000
Total stockholders' equity		1,019,000		966,000
Total liabilities and equity...........		$1,684,000		$1,678,000

PLANNING THE SOLUTION

- Set up a four-column income statement; enter the 2017 and 2016 amounts in the first two columns and then enter the dollar change in the third column and the percent change from 2016 in the fourth column.
- Set up a four-column balance sheet; enter the 2017 and 2016 year-end amounts in the first two columns and then compute and enter the amount of each item as a percent of total assets.
- Compute the required ratios using the data provided. Use the average of beginning and ending amounts when appropriate (see Exhibit 17.16 for definitions).

SOLUTION

1.

PRECISION COMPANY Comparative Income Statements For Years Ended December 31, 2017 and 2016			Increase (Decrease) in 2017	
	2017	2016	Amount	Percent
Sales..............................	$2,486,000	$2,075,000	$411,000	19.8%
Cost of goods sold...................	1,523,000	1,222,000	301,000	24.6
Gross profit........................	963,000	853,000	110,000	12.9
Operating expenses				
Advertising expense...............	145,000	100,000	45,000	45.0
Sales salaries expense.............	240,000	280,000	(40,000)	(14.3)
Office salaries expense.............	165,000	200,000	(35,000)	(17.5)
Insurance expense................	100,000	45,000	55,000	122.2
Supplies expense	26,000	35,000	(9,000)	(25.7)
Depreciation expense..............	85,000	75,000	10,000	13.3
Miscellaneous expenses............	17,000	15,000	2,000	13.3
Total operating expenses...........	778,000	750,000	28,000	3.7
Operating income	185,000	103,000	82,000	79.6
Interest expense	44,000	46,000	(2,000)	(4.3)
Income before taxes	141,000	57,000	84,000	147.4
Income taxes	47,000	19,000	28,000	147.4
Net income.........................	$ 94,000	$ 38,000	$ 56,000	147.4
Earnings per share...................	$ 0.99	$ 0.40	$ 0.59	147.5

2.

PRECISION COMPANY Common-Size Comparative Balance Sheets December 31, 2017 and 2016	December 31		Common-Size Percents	
	2017	2016	2017*	2016*
Assets				
Current assets				
Cash	$ 79,000	$ 42,000	4.7%	2.5%
Short-term investments..............	65,000	96,000	3.9	5.7
Accounts receivable, net.............	120,000	100,000	7.1	6.0
Merchandise inventory	250,000	265,000	14.8	15.8
Total current assets.................	514,000	503,000	30.5	30.0
Plant assets				
Store equipment, net................	400,000	350,000	23.8	20.9
Office equipment, net	45,000	50,000	2.7	3.0
Buildings, net......................	625,000	675,000	37.1	40.2
Land	100,000	100,000	5.9	6.0
Total plant assets...................	1,170,000	1,175,000	69.5	70.0
Total assets........................	$1,684,000	$1,678,000	100.0	100.0
Liabilities				
Current liabilities				
Accounts payable	$ 164,000	$ 190,000	9.7%	11.3%
Short-term notes payable	75,000	90,000	4.5	5.4
Taxes payable	26,000	12,000	1.5	0.7
Total current liabilities..............	265,000	292,000	15.7	17.4
Long-term liabilities				
Notes payable (secured by				
mortgage on buildings).............	400,000	420,000	23.8	25.0
Total liabilities.....................	665,000	712,000	39.5	42.4
Stockholders' Equity				
Common stock, $5 par value............	475,000	475,000	28.2	28.3
Retained earnings	544,000	491,000	32.3	29.3
Total stockholders' equity	1,019,000	966,000	60.5	57.6
Total liabilities and equity	$1,684,000	$1,678,000	100.0	100.0

* Columns do not always exactly add to 100 due to rounding.

3. Ratios for 2017:

a. Current ratio: $514,000/$265,000 = 1.9:1 (liquidity and efficiency)

b. Acid-test ratio: ($79,000 + $65,000 + $120,000)/$265,000 = 1.0:1 (liquidity and efficiency)

c. Average receivables: ($120,000 + $100,000)/2 = $110,000

  Accounts receivable turnover: $2,486,000/$110,000 = 22.6 times (liquidity and efficiency)

d. Days' sales uncollected: ($120,000/$2,486,000) × 365 = 17.6 days (liquidity and efficiency)

e. Average inventory: ($250,000 + $265,000)/2 = $257,500

  Inventory turnover: $1,523,000/$257,500 = 5.9 times (liquidity and efficiency)

f. Debt ratio: $665,000/$1,684,000 = 39.5% (solvency)

g. Debt-to-equity ratio: $665,000/$1,019,000 = 0.65 (solvency)

h. Times interest earned: $185,000/$44,000 = 4.2 times (solvency)

i. Profit margin ratio: $94,000/$2,486,000 = 3.8% (profitability)

j. Average total assets: ($1,684,000 + $1,678,000)/2 = $1,681,000

  Total asset turnover: $2,486,000/$1,681,000 = 1.48 times (liquidity and efficiency)

k. Return on total assets: $94,000/$1,681,000 = 5.6% or 3.8% × 1.48 = 5.6% (profitability)

l. Average total common equity: ($1,019,000 + $966,000)/2 = $992,500

  Return on common stockholders' equity: $94,000/$992,500 = 9.5% (profitability)

APPENDIX

Sustainable Income

17A

When a company's revenue and expense transactions are from normal, continuing operations, a simple income statement is usually adequate. When a company's activities include income-related events not part of its normal, continuing operations, it must disclose information to help users understand these events and predict future performance. To meet these objectives, companies separate the income statement into continuing operations, discontinued segments, comprehensive income, and earnings per share. For illustration, Exhibit 17A.1 shows

A2 _____

Explain the form and assess the content of a complete income statement.

EXHIBIT 17A.1

Income Statement (all-inclusive) for a Corporation

ComUS Income Statement For Year Ended December 31, 2016		
Net sales		$ 8,478,000
Operating expenses		
Cost of goods sold	$5,950,000	
Depreciation expense	35,000	
Other selling, general, and administrative expenses.	515,000	
Interest expense.	20,000	
① Total operating expenses.		(6,520,000)
Other unusual and/or infrequent gains (losses)		
Loss on plant relocation.		(45,000)
Gain on sale of surplus land		72,000
Income from continuing operations before taxes.		1,985,000
Income taxes expense		(595,500)
Income from continuing operations.		1,389,500
Discontinued segment		
② Income from operating Division A (net of $180,000 taxes)	420,000	
Loss on disposal of Division A (net of $66,000 tax benefit).	(154,000)	266,000
Net income		1,655,500
Earnings per common share (200,000 outstanding shares)		
③ Income from continuing operations		$ 6.95
Discontinued operations		1.33
Net income (basic earnings per share)		$ 8.28

such an income statement for ComUS. These separate distinctions help us measure *sustainable income,* which is the income level most likely to continue into the future. Sustainable income is commonly used in PE ratios and other market-based measures of performance.

① **Continuing Operations**   The first major section (①) shows the revenues, expenses, and income from continuing operations. Users especially rely on this information to predict future operations and view this section as the most important. Earlier chapters explained the items comprising income from continuing operations.

Gains and losses that are neither unusual nor infrequent are reported as part of continuing operations. Gains and losses that are either unusual and/or infrequent are reported as part of continuing operations *but after* the normal revenues and expenses. Items typically considered unusual and/or infrequent include (1) expropriation (taking away) of property by a foreign government, (2) condemning of property by a domestic government body, (3) prohibition against using an asset by a newly enacted law, (4) losses and gains from an unusual and infrequent calamity ("act of God"), and (5) financial effects of labor strikes. (At one time, the FASB identified *extraordinary items*; that is no longer the case.)

② **Discontinued Segments**   A **business segment** is a part of a company's operations that serves a particular line of business or class of customers. A segment has assets, liabilities, and financial results of operations that can be distinguished from those of other parts of the company. A company's gain or loss from selling or closing down a segment is separately reported. Section ② of Exhibit 17A.1 reports both (1) income from operating the discontinued segment for the current period prior to its disposal and (2) the loss from disposing of the segment's net assets. The income tax effects of each are reported separately from the income taxes expense in section ①.

■ **Decision Maker**

Small Business Owner   You own an orange grove near Jacksonville, Florida. A bad frost destroys about one-half of your oranges. You are currently preparing an income statement for a bank loan. Where on the income statement do you report the loss of oranges? ■   [*Answer:* The frost loss is likely unusual, meaning it is reported in the nonrecurring section of continuing operations. Managers would highlight this loss apart from ongoing, normal results so that the bank views it separately from normal operations.]

③ **Earnings per Share**   The final section ③ of the income statement in Exhibit 17A.1 reports earnings per share for each of the two subcategories of income (continuing operations and discontinued segments) when they both exist. Earnings per share is discussed in Chapter 13.

Changes in Accounting Principles · The *consistency concept* directs a company to apply the same accounting principles across periods. Yet a company can change from one acceptable accounting principle (such as FIFO, LIFO, or weighted-average) to another as long as the change improves the usefulness of information in its financial statements. A footnote would describe the accounting change and why it is an improvement.

Point: Changes in principles are sometimes required when new accounting standards are issued.

Changes in accounting principles require retrospective application to prior periods' financial statements. *Retrospective application* involves applying a different accounting principle to prior periods as if that principle had always been used. Retrospective application enhances the consistency of financial information between periods, which improves the usefulness of information, especially with comparative analyses. Accounting standards also require that *a change in depreciation, amortization, or depletion method for long-term operating assets is accounted for as a change in accounting estimate*—that is, prospectively over current and future periods. This reflects the notion that an entity should change its depreciation, amortization, or depletion method only with changes in estimated asset benefits, the pattern of benefit usage, or information about those benefits.

Summary

C1 **Explain the purpose and identify the building blocks of analysis.** The purpose of financial statement analysis is to help users make better business decisions. Internal users want information to improve company efficiency and effectiveness. External users want information to make better and more informed decisions in pursuing their goals. The common goals of all users are to evaluate a company's (1) past and current performance, (2) current financial position, and (3) future performance and risk. Financial statement analysis focuses on four "building blocks" of analysis: (1) liquidity and efficiency—ability to meet short-term obligations and efficiently generate revenues; (2) solvency—ability to generate future revenues and meet long-term obligations; (3) profitability—ability to provide financial rewards sufficient to attract and retain financing; and (4) market prospects—ability to generate positive market expectations.

C2 **Describe standards for comparisons in analysis.** Standards for comparisons include (1) intracompany—prior performance and relations between financial items for the company under analysis; (2) competitor—one or more direct competitors of the company; (3) industry—industry statistics; and (4) guidelines (rules of thumb)—general standards developed from past experiences and personal judgments.

A1 **Summarize and report results of analysis.** A financial statement analysis report is often organized around the building blocks of analysis. A good report separates interpretations and conclusions of analysis from the information underlying them. An analysis report often consists of six sections: (1) executive summary, (2) analysis overview, (3) evidential matter, (4) assumptions, (5) key factors, and (6) inferences.

A2ᴬ **Explain the form and assess the content of a complete income statement.** An income statement has three sections: (1) continuing operations, (2) discontinued segments—provided any exist, and (3) earnings per share.

P1 **Explain and apply methods of horizontal analysis.** Horizontal analysis is a tool to evaluate changes in data across time. Two important tools of horizontal analysis are comparative statements and trend analysis. Comparative statements show amounts for two or more successive periods, often with changes disclosed in both absolute and percent terms. Trend analysis is used to reveal important changes occurring from one period to the next.

P2 **Describe and apply methods of vertical analysis.** Vertical analysis is a tool to evaluate each financial statement item or group of items in terms of a base amount. Two tools of vertical analysis are common-size statements and graphical analyses. Each item in common-size statements is expressed as a percent of a base amount. For the balance sheet, the base amount is usually total assets, and for the income statement, it is usually sales.

P3 **Define and apply ratio analysis.** Ratio analysis provides clues to and symptoms of underlying conditions. Ratios, properly interpreted, identify areas requiring further investigation. A ratio expresses a relation between two quantities such as a percent, rate, or proportion. Ratios can be organized into the building blocks of analysis: (1) liquidity and efficiency, (2) solvency, (3) profitability, and (4) market prospects.

Key Terms

Business segment

Common-size financial statement

Comparative financial statement

Efficiency

Equity ratio

Financial reporting

Financial statement analysis

General-purpose financial statements

Horizontal analysis

Liquidity

Market prospects

Profitability

Ratio analysis

Solvency

Vertical analysis

Working capital

Multiple Choice Quiz

1. A company's sales in 2016 were $300,000 and in 2017 were $351,000. Using 2016 as the base year, the sales trend percent for 2017 is:

  a. 17%.

  b. 85%.

  c. 100%.

  d. 117%.

  e. 48%.

Use the following information for questions 2 through 5.

ELLA COMPANY	
Balance Sheet	
December 31, 2017	
Assets	
Cash	$ 86,000
Accounts receivable	76,000
Merchandise inventory	122,000
Prepaid insurance	12,000
Long-term investments	98,000
Plant assets, net	436,000
Total assets	$830,000
Liabilities and Equity	
Current liabilities	$124,000
Long-term liabilities	90,000
Common stock	300,000
Retained earnings	316,000
Total liabilities and equity	$830,000

2. What is Ella Company's current ratio?

  a. 0.69

  b. 1.31

  c. 3.88

  d. 6.69

  e. 2.39

3. What is Ella Company's acid-test ratio?

  a. 2.39

  b. 0.69

  c. 1.31

  d. 6.69

  e. 3.88

4. What is Ella Company's debt ratio?

  a. 25.78%

  b. 100.00%

  c. 74.22%

  d. 137.78%

  e. 34.74%

5. What is Ella Company's equity ratio?

  a. 25.78%

  b. 100.00%

  c. 34.74%

  d. 74.22%

  e. 137.78%

ANSWERS TO MULTIPLE CHOICE QUIZ

1. d; ($351,000/$300,000) × 100 = 117%
2. e; ($86,000 + $76,000 + $122,000 + $12,000)/$124,000 = 2.39
3. c; ($86,000 + $76,000)/$124,000 = 1.31
4. a; ($124,000 + $90,000)/$830,000 = 25.78%
5. d; ($300,000 + $316,000)/$830,000 = 74.22%

^A *Superscript letter A denotes assignments based on Appendix 17A.*

 Icon denotes assignments that involve decision making.

Discussion Questions

1. Explain the difference between financial reporting and financial statements.
2. What is the difference between comparative financial statements and common-size comparative statements?
3. Which items are usually assigned a 100% value on (*a*) a common-size balance sheet and (*b*) a common-size income statement?
4. What three factors would influence your evaluation as to whether a company's current ratio is good or bad?
5. Suggest several reasons why a 2:1 current ratio might not be adequate for a particular company.
6. Why is working capital given special attention in the process of analyzing balance sheets?
7. What does the number of days' sales uncollected indicate?
8. What does a relatively high accounts receivable turnover indicate about a company's short-term liquidity?
9. Why is a company's capital structure, as measured by debt and equity ratios, important to financial statement analysts?
10. How does inventory turnover provide information about a company's short-term liquidity?
11. What ratios would you compute to evaluate management performance?
12. Why would a company's return on total assets be different from its return on common stockholders' equity?
13. Where on the income statement does a company report an unusual gain not expected to occur more often than once every two years or so?
14. Refer to **Apple**'s financial statements in Appendix A. Compute its profit margin for the years ended September 26, 2015, and September 27, 2014.   **APPLE**
15. Refer to **Google**'s financial statements in Appendix A to compute its equity ratio as of December 31, 2015, and December 31, 2014.   **GOOGLE**
16. Refer to **Samsung**'s financial statements in Appendix A. Compute its debt ratio as of December 31, 2015, and December 31, 2014.   **Samsung**
17. Use **Samsung**'s financial statements in Appendix A to compute its return on total assets for fiscal year ended December 31, 2015.   **Samsung**

Mc Graw Hill Education **connect**

QUICK STUDY

Which of the following items *a* through *i* are part of financial reporting but are *not* included as part of general-purpose financial statements?

QS 17-1

Financial reporting

C1

___ **a.** Income statement
___ **b.** Balance sheet
___ **c.** Prospectus
___ **d.** Financial statement notes
___ **e.** Company news releases
___ **f.** Statement of cash flows
___ **g.** Stock price information and analysis
___ **h.** Statement of shareholders' equity
___ **i.** Management discussion and analysis of financial performance

QS 17-2

Standard of comparison

C2

Identify which standard of comparison, (*a*) intracompany, (*b*) competitor, (*c*) industry, or (*d*) guidelines, is best described by each of the following.

___ **1.** Is often viewed as the best standard of comparison.
___ **2.** Rules of thumb developed from past experiences.
___ **3.** Provides analysis based on a company's prior performance.
___ **4.** Compares a company against industry statistics.

Compute the annual dollar changes and percent changes for each of the following accounts.

QS 17-3
Horizontal analysis
P1

	2017	2016
Short-term investments	$374,634	$234,000
Accounts receivable	97,364	101,000
Notes payable	0	88,000

Use the following information for Tide Corporation to determine the 2016 and 2017 trend percents for net sales using 2016 as the base year.

QS 17-4
Trend percents
P1

$ thousands	2017	2016
Net sales	$801,810	$453,000
Cost of goods sold	392,887	134,088

Refer to the information in QS 17-4. Use that information for Tide Corporation to determine the 2016 and 2017 common-size percents for cost of goods sold using net sales as the base.

QS 17-5
Common-size analysis   P2

For each ratio listed, identify whether the change in ratio value from 2016 to 2017 is usually regarded as favorable or unfavorable.

QS 17-6
Ratio interpretation

P3

Ratio	2017	2016	Ratio	2017	2016
___ 1. Profit margin	9%	8%	___ 5. Accounts receivable turnover	5.5	6.7
___ 2. Debt ratio	47%	42%	___ 6. Basic earnings per share	$1.25	$1.10
___ 3. Gross margin	34%	46%	___ 7. Inventory turnover	3.6	3.4
___ 4. Acid-test ratio	1.00	1.15	___ 8. Dividend yield	2.0%	1.2%

The following information is available for Morgan Company and Parker Company, similar firms operating in the same industry. Write a half-page report comparing Morgan and Parker using the available information. Your discussion should include their ability to meet current obligations and to use current assets efficiently.

QS 17-7
Analysis of short-term financial condition

A1

	A	B	C	D	E	F	G	H
1		Morgan				Parker		
2		2017	2016	2015		2017	2016	2015
3	Current ratio	1.7	1.6	2.1		3.2	2.7	1.9
4	Acid-test ratio	1.0	1.1	1.2		2.8	2.5	1.6
5	Accounts receivable turnover	30.5	25.2	29.2		16.4	15.2	16.0
6	Merchandise inventory turnover	24.2	21.9	17.1		14.5	13.0	12.6
7	Working capital	$70,000	$58,000	$52,000		$131,000	$103,000	$78,000

Team Project: Assume that the two companies apply for a one-year loan from the team. Identify additional information the companies must provide before the team can make a loan decision.

A review of the notes payable files discovers that three years ago the company reported the entire $1,000 cash payment (consisting of $800 principal and $200 interest) toward an installment note payable as interest expense. This mistake had a material effect on the amount of income in that year. How should the correction be reported in the current-year financial statements?

QS 17-8^A
Error adjustments

A2

Answer each of the following related to international accounting and analysis.

a. Identify a limitation to using ratio analysis when examining companies reporting under different accounting systems such as IFRS versus U.S. GAAP.

b. Identify an advantage to using horizontal and vertical analyses when examining companies reporting under different currencies.

QS 17-9
International ratio analysis

C2

connect

EXERCISES

Exercise 17-1

Building blocks of analysis

C1

Match the ratio to the building block of financial statement analysis to which it best relates.

A. Liquidity and efficiency   **B.** Solvency   **C.** Profitability   **D.** Market prospects

_____ **1.** Equity ratio

_____ **2.** Return on total assets

_____ **3.** Dividend yield

_____ **4.** Book value per common share

_____ **5.** Days' sales in inventory

_____ **6.** Accounts receivable turnover

_____ **7.** Debt-to-equity ratio

_____ **8.** Times interest earned

_____ **9.** Gross margin ratio

_____ **10.** Acid-test ratio

Exercise 17-2

Identifying financial ratios

C2

Identify which of the following six metrics *a* through *f* best completes questions 1 through 3 below.

a. Days' sales uncollected

b. Accounts receivable turnover

c. Working capital

d. Return on total assets

e. Total asset turnover

f. Profit margin

1. Which two ratios are key components in measuring a company's operating efficiency? _____ _____ Which ratio summarizes these two components? _____

2. What measure reflects the difference between current assets and current liabilities? _____

3. Which two short-term liquidity ratios measure how frequently a company collects its accounts? _____ _____

Exercise 17-3

Computation and analysis of trend percents

P1

Compute trend percents for the following accounts, using 2013 as the base year (round the percents to whole numbers). State whether the situation as revealed by the trends appears to be favorable or unfavorable for each account.

	2017	2016	2015	2014	2013
Sales	$282,880	$270,800	$252,600	$234,560	$150,000
Cost of goods sold	128,200	122,080	115,280	106,440	67,000
Accounts receivable............	18,100	17,300	16,400	15,200	9,000

Exercise 17-4

Common-size percent computation and interpretation

P2

Express the following comparative income statements in common-size percents and assess whether or not this company's situation has improved in the most recent year (round the percents to one decimal).

GOMEZ CORPORATION Comparative Income Statements For Years Ended December 31, 2017 and 2016		
	2017	**2016**
Sales	$740,000	$625,000
Cost of goods sold	560,300	290,800
Gross profit	179,700	334,200
Operating expenses...........	128,200	218,500
Net income	$ 51,500	$115,700

Exercise 17-5

Determination of income effects from common-size and trend percents

P1   P2

Common-size and trend percents for Rustynail Company's sales, cost of goods sold, and expenses follow. Determine whether net income increased, decreased, or remained unchanged in this three-year period.

	Common-Size Percents			Trend Percents		
	2017	**2016**	**2015**	**2017**	**2016**	**2015**
Sales......................	100.0%	100.0%	100.0%	105.4%	104.2%	100.0%
Cost of goods sold............	63.4	61.9	59.1	113.1	109.1	100.0
Total expenses...............	15.3	14.8	15.1	106.8	102.1	100.0

Simon Company's year-end balance sheets follow. Express the balance sheets in common-size percents. Round amounts to the nearest one-tenth of a percent. Analyze and comment on the results.

Exercise 17-6
Common-size percents

P2

At December 31	2017	2016	2015
Assets			
Cash	$ 31,800	$ 35,625	$ 37,800
Accounts receivable, net	89,500	62,500	50,200
Merchandise inventory.........................	112,500	82,500	54,000
Prepaid expenses............................	10,700	9,375	5,000
Plant assets, net............................	278,500	255,000	230,500
Total assets..................................	$523,000	$445,000	$377,500
Liabilities and Equity			
Accounts payable............................	$129,900	$ 75,250	$ 51,250
Long-term notes payable secured by mortgages on plant assets	98,500	101,500	83,500
Common stock, $10 par value..................	163,500	163,500	163,500
Retained earnings	131,100	104,750	79,250
Total liabilities and equity.....................	$523,000	$445,000	$377,500

Refer to Simon Company's balance sheets in Exercise 17-6. Analyze its year-end short-term liquidity position at the end of 2017, 2016, and 2015 by computing (1) the current ratio and (2) the acid-test ratio. Comment on the ratio results. (Round ratio amounts to two decimals.)

Exercise 17-7
Liquidity analysis

P3

Refer to the Simon Company information in Exercise 17-6. The company's income statements for the years ended December 31, 2017 and 2016, follow. Assume that all sales are on credit and then compute: (1) days' sales uncollected, (2) accounts receivable turnover, (3) inventory turnover, and (4) days' sales in inventory. Comment on the changes in the ratios from 2016 to 2017. (Round amounts to one decimal.)

Exercise 17-8
Liquidity analysis and interpretation

P3

For Year Ended December 31	2017		2016	
Sales		$673,500		$532,000
Cost of goods sold	$411,225		$345,500	
Other operating expenses............	209,550		134,980	
Interest expense....................	12,100		13,300	
Income taxes.......................	9,525		8,845	
Total costs and expenses.............		642,400		502,625
Net income		$ 31,100		$ 29,375
Earnings per share..................		$ 1.90		$ 1.80

Refer to the Simon Company information in Exercises 17-6 and 17-8. Compare the company's long-term risk and capital structure positions at the end of 2017 and 2016 by computing these ratios: (1) debt and equity ratios—percent rounded to one decimal, (2) debt-to-equity ratio—rounded to two decimals, and (3) times interest earned—rounded to one decimal. Comment on these ratio results.

Exercise 17-9
Risk and capital structure analysis

P3

Refer to Simon Company's financial information in Exercises 17-6 and 17-8. Evaluate the company's efficiency and profitability by computing the following for 2017 and 2016: (1) profit margin ratio—percent rounded to one decimal, (2) total asset turnover—rounded to one decimal, and (3) return on total assets—percent rounded to one decimal. Comment on these ratio results.

Exercise 17-10
Efficiency and profitability analysis

P3

Exercise 17-11

Profitability analysis

P3

Refer to Simon Company's financial information in Exercises 17-6 and 17-8. Additional information about the company follows. To help evaluate the company's profitability, compute and interpret the following ratios for 2017 and 2016: (1) return on common stockholders' equity—percent rounded to one decimal, (2) price-earnings ratio on December 31—rounded to one decimal, and (3) dividend yield—percent rounded to one decimal.

Common stock market price, December 31, 2017	$30.00
Common stock market price, December 31, 2016	28.00
Annual cash dividends per share in 2017.	0.29
Annual cash dividends per share in 2016.	0.24

Exercise 17-12

Analysis of efficiency and financial leverage

A1

Roak Company and Clay Company are similar firms that operate in the same industry. Clay began operations in 2015 and Roak in 2012. In 2017, both companies pay 7% interest on their debt to creditors. The following additional information is available.

	Roak Company			Clay Company		
	2017	**2016**	**2015**	**2017**	**2016**	**2015**
Total asset turnover	3.1	2.8	3.0	1.7	1.5	1.1
Return on total assets	9.0%	9.6%	8.8%	5.9%	5.6%	5.3%
Profit margin ratio	2.4%	2.5%	2.3%	2.8%	3.0%	2.9%
Sales	$410,000	$380,000	$396,000	$210,000	$170,000	$110,000

Write a half-page report comparing Roak and Clay using the available information. Your analysis should include their ability to use assets efficiently to produce profits. Also comment on their success in employing financial leverage in 2017.

Exercise 17-13^A

Income statement categories

A2

In 2017, Randa Merchandising, Inc., sold its interest in a chain of wholesale outlets, taking the company completely out of the wholesaling business. The company still operates its retail outlets. A listing of the major sections of an income statement follows:

A. Net sales less operating expense section

B. Other unusual and/or infrequent gains (losses)

C. Taxes reported on income (loss) from continuing operations

D. Income (loss) from operating a discontinued segment, or gain (loss) from its disposal

Indicate where each of the following income-related items for this company appears on its 2017 income statement by writing the letter of the appropriate section in the blank beside each item.

Section	Item	Debit	Credit
_____	1. Net sales.		$2,900,000
_____	2. Gain on state's condemnation of company property, net of tax.		230,000
_____	3. Cost of goods sold	$1,480,000	
_____	4. Income taxes expense	217,000	
_____	5. Depreciation expense	232,000	
_____	6. Gain on sale of wholesale business segment, net of tax.		775,000
_____	7. Loss from operating wholesale business segment, net of tax.	444,000	
_____	8. Loss of assets from meteor strike, net of tax	640,000	

Exercise 17-14^A

Income statement presentation   A2

Use the financial data for Randa Merchandising, Inc., in Exercise 17-13 to prepare its income statement for calendar-year 2017. (Ignore the earnings per share section.)

Nintendo Company, Ltd., reports the following financial information as of, or for the year ended, March 31, 2015. Nintendo reports its financial statements in both Japanese yen and U.S. dollars as shown (amounts in millions).

Exercise 17-15
Ratio analysis under different currencies

P3

Current assets.	¥1,097,597	$ 9,110
Total assets	1,352,944	11,229
Current liabilities.	144,232	1,197
Net sales	549,780	4,562
Net income	41,843	347

1. Compute Nintendo's current ratio, net profit margin, and sales-to-total-assets ratio using the financial information reported in (*a*) yen and (*b*) dollars. Round amounts to two decimals.
2. What can we conclude from a review of the results for part 1?

connect

Selected comparative financial statements of Haroun Company follow.

PROBLEM SET A

Problem 17-1A
Calculation and analysis of trend percents

A1   P1

HAROUN COMPANY Comparative Income Statements For Years Ended December 31, 2017–2011							
$ thousands	2017	2016	2015	2014	2013	2012	2011
Sales	$1,694	$1,496	$1,370	$1,264	$1,186	$1,110	$928
Cost of goods sold	1,246	1,032	902	802	752	710	586
Gross profit	448	464	468	462	434	400	342
Operating expenses.	330	256	234	170	146	144	118
Net income	$ 118	$ 208	$ 234	$ 292	$ 288	$ 256	$224

HAROUN COMPANY Comparative Balance Sheets December 31, 2017–2011							
$ thousands	2017	2016	2015	2014	2013	2012	2011
Assets							
Cash	$ 58	$ 78	$ 82	$ 84	$ 88	$ 86	$ 89
Accounts receivable, net	490	514	466	360	318	302	216
Merchandise inventory.	1,838	1,364	1,204	1,032	936	810	615
Other current assets.	36	32	14	34	28	28	9
Long-term investments	0	0	0	146	146	146	146
Plant assets, net	2,020	2,014	1,752	944	978	860	725
Total assets	$4,442	$4,002	$3,518	$2,600	$2,494	$2,232	$1,800
Liabilities and Equity							
Current liabilities.	$1,220	$1,042	$ 718	$ 614	$ 546	$ 522	$ 282
Long-term liabilities	1,294	1,140	1,112	570	580	620	400
Common stock	1,000	1,000	1,000	850	850	650	650
Other paid-in capital.	250	250	250	170	170	150	150
Retained earnings	678	570	438	396	348	290	318
Total liabilities and equity.	$4,442	$4,002	$3,518	$2,600	$2,494	$2,232	$1,800

Required

1. Compute trend percents for all components of both statements using 2011 as the base year. (Round percents to one decimal.)

Check (1) 2017, Total assets trend, 246.8%

Analysis Component

2. Analyze and comment on the financial statements and trend percents from part 1.

Problem 17-2A

Ratios, common-size statements, and trend percents

P1   P2   P3

Selected comparative financial statements of Korbin Company follow.

KORBIN COMPANY			
Comparative Income Statements			
For Years Ended December 31, 2017, 2016, and 2015			
	2017	2016	2015
Sales	$555,000	$340,000	$278,000
Cost of goods sold	283,500	212,500	153,900
Gross profit	271,500	127,500	124,100
Selling expenses.	102,900	46,920	50,800
Administrative expenses	50,668	29,920	22,800
Total expenses	153,568	76,840	73,600
Income before taxes.	117,932	50,660	50,500
Income taxes.	40,800	10,370	15,670
Net income	$ 77,132	$ 40,290	$ 34,830

KORBIN COMPANY			
Comparative Balance Sheets			
December 31, 2017, 2016, and 2015			
	2017	2016	2015
Assets			
Current assets.	$ 52,390	$ 37,924	$ 51,748
Long-term investments	0	500	3,950
Plant assets, net	100,000	96,000	60,000
Total assets	$152,390	$134,424	$115,698
Liabilities and Equity			
Current liabilities.	$ 22,800	$ 19,960	$ 20,300
Common stock	72,000	72,000	60,000
Other paid-in capital.	9,000	9,000	6,000
Retained earnings	48,590	33,464	29,398
Total liabilities and equity.	$152,390	$134,424	$115,698

Required

1. Compute each year's current ratio. (Round ratio amounts to one decimal.)
2. Express the income statement data in common-size percents. (Round percents to two decimals.)

Check   (3) 2017, Total assets trend, 131.71%

3. Express the balance sheet data in trend percents with 2015 as the base year. (Round percents to two decimals.)

Analysis Component

4. Comment on any significant relations revealed by the ratios and percents computed.

Problem 17-3A

Transactions, working capital, and liquidity ratios

P3

Plum Corporation began the month of May with $700,000 of current assets, a current ratio of 2.50:1, and an acid-test ratio of 1.10:1. During the month, it completed the following transactions (the company uses a perpetual inventory system).

May	2	Purchased $50,000 of merchandise inventory on credit.
	8	Sold merchandise inventory that cost $55,000 for $110,000 cash.
	10	Collected $20,000 cash on an account receivable.
	15	Paid $22,000 cash to settle an account payable.
	17	Wrote off a $5,000 bad debt against the Allowance for Doubtful Accounts account.
	22	Declared a $1 per share cash dividend on its 50,000 shares of outstanding common stock.
	26	Paid the dividend declared on May 22.
	27	Borrowed $100,000 cash by giving the bank a 30-day, 10% note.
	28	Borrowed $80,000 cash by signing a long-term secured note.
	29	Used the $180,000 cash proceeds from the notes to buy new machinery.

Check   May 22: Current ratio, 2.19; Acid-test ratio, 1.11

May 29: Current ratio, 1.80; Working capital, $325,000

Required

Prepare a table, *similar to the following,* showing Plum's (1) current ratio, (2) acid-test ratio, and (3) working capital after each transaction. Round ratios to two decimals.

	A	B	C	D	E	F	G
1		Current	Quick	Current	Current	Acid-Test	Working
2	Transaction	Assets	Assets	Liabilities	Ratio	Ratio	Capital
3	Beginning	$700,000	—	—	2.50	1.10	—

Selected year-end financial statements of Cabot Corporation follow. (All sales were on credit; selected balance sheet amounts at December 31, 2016, were inventory, $48,900; total assets, $189,400; common stock, $90,000; and retained earnings, $22,748.)

Problem 17-4A
Calculation of financial statement ratios

P3

CABOT CORPORATION Income Statement For Year Ended December 31, 2017	
Sales	$448,600
Cost of goods sold	297,250
Gross profit	151,350
Operating expenses	98,600
Interest expense	4,100
Income before taxes	48,650
Income taxes	19,598
Net income	$ 29,052

CABOT CORPORATION
Balance Sheet
December 31, 2017

Assets		Liabilities and Equity	
Cash	$ 10,000	Accounts payable	$ 17,500
Short-term investments	8,400	Accrued wages payable	3,200
Accounts receivable, net	29,200	Income taxes payable	3,300
Notes receivable (trade)*	4,500	Long-term note payable, secured	
Merchandise inventory	32,150	by mortgage on plant assets	63,400
Prepaid expenses	2,650	Common stock	90,000
Plant assets, net	153,300	Retained earnings	62,800
Total assets	$240,200	Total liabilities and equity	$240,200

*These are short-term notes receivable arising from customer (trade) sales.

Required

Compute the following: (1) current ratio, (2) acid-test ratio, (3) days' sales uncollected, (4) inventory turnover, (5) days' sales in inventory, (6) debt-to-equity ratio, (7) times interest earned, (8) profit margin ratio, (9) total asset turnover, (10) return on total assets, and (11) return on common stockholders' equity. Round to one decimal place; for part 6, round to two decimals.

Check Acid-test ratio, 2.2 to 1; Inventory turnover, 7.3

Summary information from the financial statements of two companies competing in the same industry follows.

Problem 17-5A
Comparative ratio analysis

A1   P3

	Barco Company	Kyan Company		Barco Company	Kyan Company
Data from the current year-end balance sheets			**Data from the current year's income statement**		
Assets			Sales	$770,000	$880,200
Cash	$ 19,500	$ 34,000	Cost of goods sold	585,100	632,500
Accounts receivable, net	37,400	57,400	Interest expense	7,900	13,000
Current notes receivable (trade)	9,100	7,200	Income tax expense	14,800	24,300
Merchandise inventory	84,440	132,500	Net income	162,200	210,400
Prepaid expenses	5,000	6,950	Basic earnings per share	4.51	5.11
Plant assets, net	290,000	304,400	Cash dividends per share	3.81	3.93
Total assets	$445,440	$542,450			
			Beginning-of-year balance sheet data		
Liabilities and Equity			Accounts receivable, net	$ 29,800	$ 54,200
Current liabilities	$ 61,340	$ 93,300	Current notes receivable (trade)	0	0
Long-term notes payable	80,800	101,000	Merchandise inventory	55,600	107,400
Common stock, $5 par value	180,000	206,000	Total assets	398,000	382,500
Retained earnings	123,300	142,150	Common stock, $5 par value	180,000	206,000
Total liabilities and equity	$445,440	$542,450	Retained earnings	98,300	93,600

Required

1. For both companies compute the (a) current ratio, (b) acid-test ratio, (c) accounts (including notes) receivable turnover, (d) inventory turnover, (e) days' sales in inventory, and (f) days' sales uncollected. Identify the company you consider to be the better short-term credit risk and explain why. Round to one decimal place.

2. For both companies compute the (a) profit margin ratio, (b) total asset turnover, (c) return on total assets, and (d) return on common stockholders' equity. Assuming that each company's stock can be purchased at $75 per share, compute their (e) price-earnings ratios and (f) dividend yields. Round to one decimal place. Identify which company's stock you would recommend as the better investment and explain why.

Problem 17-6A^A
Income statement
computations and format

A2

Selected account balances from the adjusted trial balance for Olinda Corporation as of its calendar year-end December 31, 2017, follow.

	Debit	Credit
a. Interest revenue.		$ 14,000
b. Depreciation expense—Equipment.	$ 34,000	
c. Loss on sale of equipment.	25,850	
d. Accounts payable.		44,000
e. Other operating expenses.	106,400	
f. Accumulated depreciation—Equipment		71,600
g. Gain from settlement of lawsuit		44,000
h. Accumulated depreciation—Buildings		174,500
i. Loss from operating a discontinued segment (pretax).	18,250	
j. Gain on insurance recovery of tornado damage		20,000
k. Net sales.		998,000
l. Depreciation expense—Buildings.	52,000	
m. Correction of overstatement of prior year's sales (pretax)	16,000	
n. Gain on sale of discontinued segment's assets (pretax)		34,000
o. Loss from settlement of lawsuit.	23,250	
p. Income taxes expense	?	
q. Cost of goods sold	482,500	

Required

Answer each of the following questions by providing supporting computations.

1. Assume that the company's income tax rate is 30% for all items. Identify the tax effects and after-tax amounts of the three items labeled pretax.

2. Compute the amount of income from continuing operations before income taxes. What is the amount of the income taxes expense? What is the amount of income from continuing operations?

3. What is the total amount of after-tax income (loss) associated with the discontinued segment?

4. What is the amount of net income for the year?

PROBLEM SET B

Selected comparative financial statements of Tripoly Company follow.

Problem 17-1B
Calculation and analysis of
trend percents

A1   P1

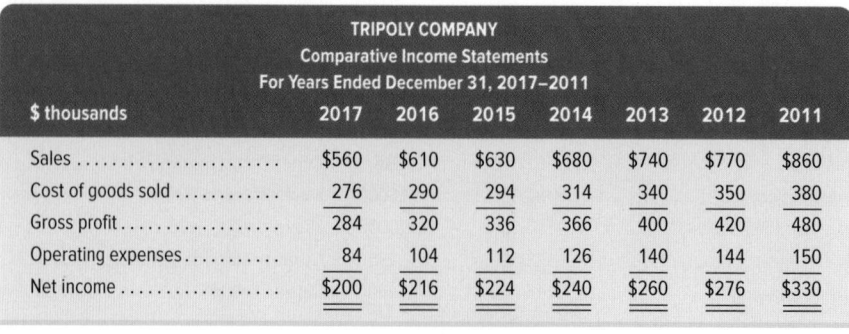

$ thousands	2017	2016	2015	2014	2013	2012	2011
Sales	$560	$610	$630	$680	$740	$770	$860
Cost of goods sold	276	290	294	314	340	350	380
Gross profit.	284	320	336	366	400	420	480
Operating expenses.	84	104	112	126	140	144	150
Net income	$200	$216	$224	$240	$260	$276	$330

TRIPOLY COMPANY
Comparative Income Statements
For Years Ended December 31, 2017–2011

TRIPOLY COMPANY Comparative Balance Sheets December 31, 2017–2011							
$ thousands	2017	2016	2015	2014	2013	2012	2011
Assets							
Cash	$ 44	$ 46	$ 52	$ 54	$ 60	$ 62	$ 68
Accounts receivable, net	130	136	140	144	150	154	160
Merchandise inventory	166	172	178	180	186	190	208
Other current assets	34	34	36	38	38	40	40
Long-term investments	36	30	26	110	110	110	110
Plant assets, net	510	514	520	412	420	428	454
Total assets	$920	$932	$952	$938	$964	$984	$1,040
Liabilities and Equity							
Current liabilities	$148	$156	$186	$190	$210	$260	$ 280
Long-term liabilities	92	120	142	148	194	214	260
Common stock	160	160	160	160	160	160	160
Other paid-in capital	70	70	70	70	70	70	70
Retained earnings	450	426	394	370	330	280	270
Total liabilities and equity	$920	$932	$952	$938	$964	$984	$1,040

Required

1. Compute trend percents for all components of both statements using 2011 as the base year. (Round percents to one decimal.)

Check (1) 2017, Total assets trend, 88.5%

Analysis Component

2. Analyze and comment on the financial statements and trend percents from part 1.

Selected comparative financial statement information of Bluegrass Corporation follows.

Problem 17-2B
Ratios, common-size statements, and trend percents

P1   P2   P3

BLUEGRASS CORPORATION Comparative Balance Sheets December 31, 2017, 2016, and 2015			
	2017	2016	2015
Assets			
Current assets	$ 54,860	$ 32,660	$ 36,300
Long-term investments	0	1,700	10,600
Plant assets, net	112,810	113,660	79,000
Total assets	$167,670	$148,020	$125,900
Liabilities and Equity			
Current liabilities	$ 22,370	$ 19,180	$ 16,500
Common stock	46,500	46,500	37,000
Other paid-in capital	13,850	13,850	11,300
Retained earnings	84,950	68,490	61,100
Total liabilities and equity	$167,670	$148,020	$125,900

BLUEGRASS CORPORATION Comparative Income Statements For Years Ended December 31, 2017, 2016, and 2015			
	2017	2016	2015
Sales	$198,800	$166,000	$143,800
Cost of goods sold	108,890	86,175	66,200
Gross profit	89,910	79,825	77,600
Selling expenses	22,680	19,790	18,000
Administrative expenses	16,760	14,610	15,700
Total expenses	39,440	34,400	33,700
Income before taxes	50,470	45,425	43,900
Income taxes	6,050	5,910	5,300
Net income	$ 44,420	$ 39,515	$ 38,600

Required

1. Compute each year's current ratio. (Round ratio amounts to one decimal.)
2. Express the income statement data in common-size percents. (Round percents to two decimals.)
3. Express the balance sheet data in trend percents with 2015 as the base year. (Round percents to two decimals.)

Check (3) 2017, Total assets trend, 133.18%

Analysis Component

4. Comment on any significant relations revealed by the ratios and percents computed.

Problem 17-3B

Transactions, working capital, and liquidity ratios P3

Koto Corporation began the month of June with $300,000 of current assets, a current ratio of 2.5:1, and an acid-test ratio of 1.4:1. During the month, it completed the following transactions (the company uses a perpetual inventory system).

June   1   Sold merchandise inventory that cost $75,000 for $120,000 cash.
         3   Collected $88,000 cash on an account receivable.
         5   Purchased $150,000 of merchandise inventory on credit.
         7   Borrowed $100,000 cash by giving the bank a 60-day, 10% note.
       10   Borrowed $120,000 cash by signing a long-term secured note.
       12   Purchased machinery for $275,000 cash.
       15   Declared a $1 per share cash dividend on its 80,000 shares of outstanding common stock.
       19   Wrote off a $5,000 bad debt against the Allowance for Doubtful Accounts account.
       22   Paid $12,000 cash to settle an account payable.
       30   Paid the dividend declared on June 15.

Required

Prepare a table, similar to the following, showing the company's (1) current ratio, (2) acid-test ratio, and (3) working capital after each transaction. Round ratios to two decimals.

	A	B	C	D	E	F	G
1		Current	Quick	Current	Current	Acid-Test	Working
2	Transaction	Assets	Assets	Liabilities	Ratio	Ratio	Capital
3	Beginning	$300,000	—	—	2.50	1.40	—

Problem 17-4B

Calculation of financial statement ratios

P3

Selected year-end financial statements of Overton Corporation follow. (All sales were on credit; selected balance sheet amounts at December 31, 2016, were inventory, $17,400; total assets, $94,900; common stock, $35,500; and retained earnings, $18,800.)

OVERTON CORPORATION
Income Statement
For Year Ended December 31, 2017

Sales	$315,500
Cost of goods sold	236,100
Gross profit	79,400
Operating expenses	49,200
Interest expense	2,200
Income before taxes	28,000
Income taxes	4,200
Net income	$ 23,800

OVERTON CORPORATION
Balance Sheet
December 31, 2017

Assets		Liabilities and Equity	
Cash	$ 6,100	Accounts payable	$ 11,500
Short-term investments	6,900	Accrued wages payable	3,300
Accounts receivable, net	12,100	Income taxes payable	2,600
Notes receivable (trade)*	3,000	Long-term note payable, secured	
Merchandise inventory	13,500	by mortgage on plant assets	30,000
Prepaid expenses	2,000	Common stock, $5 par value	35,000
Plant assets, net	73,900	Retained earnings	35,100
Total assets	$117,500	Total liabilities and equity	$117,500

* These are short-term notes receivable arising from customer (trade) sales.

Required

Compute the following: (1) current ratio, (2) acid-test ratio, (3) days' sales uncollected, (4) inventory turnover, (5) days' sales in inventory, (6) debt-to-equity ratio, (7) times interest earned, (8) profit margin ratio, (9) total asset turnover, (10) return on total assets, and (11) return on common stockholders' equity. Round to one decimal place; for part 6, round to two decimals.

Problem 17-5B

Comparative ratio analysis A1 P3

Summary information from the financial statements of two companies competing in the same industry follows.

	Fargo Company	Ball Company		Fargo Company	Ball Company
Data from the current year-end balance sheets			**Data from the current year's income statement**		
Assets			Sales	$393,600	$667,500
Cash	$ 20,000	$ 36,500	Cost of goods sold	290,600	480,000
Accounts receivable, net	77,100	70,500	Interest expense.....................	5,900	12,300
Current notes receivable (trade)	11,600	9,000	Income tax expense	5,700	12,300
Merchandise inventory................	86,800	82,000	Net income	33,850	61,700
Prepaid expenses....................	9,700	10,100	Basic earnings per share	1.27	2.19
Plant assets, net	176,900	252,300			
Total assets........................	$382,100	$460,400			
			Beginning-of-year balance sheet data		
Liabilities and Equity			Accounts receivable, net	$ 72,200	$ 73,300
Current liabilities.....................	$ 90,500	$ 97,000	Current notes receivable (trade)	0	0
Long-term notes payable..............	93,000	93,300	Merchandise inventory...............	105,100	80,500
Common stock, $5 par value...........	133,000	141,000	Total assets........................	383,400	443,000
Retained earnings	65,600	129,100	Common stock, $5 par value	133,000	141,000
Total liabilities and equity.............	$382,100	$460,400	Retained earnings..................	49,100	109,700

Required

Check (1) Fargo: Accounts receivable turnover, 4.9; Inventory turnover, 3.0

(2) Ball: Profit margin, 9.2%; PE, 11.4

1. For both companies compute the (*a*) current ratio, (*b*) acid-test ratio, (*c*) accounts (including notes) receivable turnover, (*d*) inventory turnover, (*e*) days' sales in inventory, and (*f*) days' sales uncollected. Identify the company you consider to be the better short-term credit risk and explain why. Round to one decimal place.

2. For both companies compute the (*a*) profit margin ratio, (*b*) total asset turnover, (*c*) return on total assets, and (*d*) return on common stockholders' equity. Assuming that each company paid cash dividends of $1.50 per share and each company's stock can be purchased at $25 per share, compute their (*e*) price-earnings ratios and (*f*) dividend yields. Round to one decimal place; for part b, round to two decimals. Identify which company's stock you would recommend as the better investment and explain why.

Selected account balances from the adjusted trial balance for Harbor Corp. as of its calendar year-end December 31, 2017, follow.

Problem 17-6B^A

Income statement computations and format

A2

	Debit	Credit
a. Accumulated depreciation—Buildings		$ 400,000
b. Interest revenue..		20,000
c. Net sales..		2,640,000
d. Income taxes expense...	$?	
e. Loss on hurricane damage	48,000	
f. Accumulated depreciation—Equipment.....................................		220,000
g. Other operating expenses...	328,000	
h. Depreciation expense—Equipment	100,000	
i. Loss from settlement of lawsuit	36,000	
j. Gain from settlement of lawsuit		68,000
k. Loss on sale of equipment..	24,000	
l. Loss from operating a discontinued segment (pretax)	120,000	
m. Depreciation expense—Buildings...	156,000	
n. Correction of overstatement of prior year's expense (pretax)		48,000
o. Cost of goods sold...	1,040,000	
p. Loss on sale of discontinued segment's assets (pretax)	180,000	
q. Accounts payable..		132,000

Required

Answer each of the following questions by providing supporting computations.

1. Assume that the company's income tax rate is 25% for all items. Identify the tax effects and after-tax amounts of the three items labeled pretax.
2. What is the amount of income from continuing operations before income taxes? What is the amount of income taxes expense? What is the amount of income from continuing operations?
3. What is the total amount of after-tax income (loss) associated with the discontinued segment?
4. What is the amount of net income for the year?

Check   (3) $(225,000)

(4) $522,000

SERIAL PROBLEM
Business Solutions

P3

© Alexander Image/Shutterstock RF

(This serial problem began in Chapter 1 and continues through most of the book. If previous chapter segments were not completed, the serial problem can begin at this point.)

SP 17   Use the following selected data from **Business Solutions**'s income statement for the three months ended March 31, 2018, and from its March 31, 2018, balance sheet to complete the requirements below: computer services revenue, $25,307; net sales (of goods), $18,693; total sales and revenue, $44,000; cost of goods sold, $14,052; net income, $18,833; quick assets, $90,924; current assets, $95,568; total assets, $120,268; current liabilities, $875; total liabilities, $875; and total equity, $119,393.

Required

1. Compute the gross margin ratio (both with and without services revenue) and net profit margin ratio (round the percent to one decimal).
2. Compute the current ratio and acid-test ratio (round to one decimal).
3. Compute the debt ratio and equity ratio (round the percent to one decimal).
4. What percent of its assets are current? What percent are long term? (Round the percents to one decimal.)

Beyond the Numbers

REPORTING IN ACTION

A1 P1 P2

APPLE

BTN 17-1   Refer to **Apple**'s financial statements in Appendix A to answer the following.

1. Using fiscal 2013 as the base year, compute trend percents for fiscal years 2013, 2014, and 2015 for net sales, cost of sales, operating income, other income (expense) net, provision for income taxes, and net income. (Round percents to one decimal.)
2. Compute common-size percents for fiscal years 2014 and 2015 for the following categories of assets: (*a*) total current assets; (*b*) property, plant and equipment, net; and (*c*) goodwill plus acquired intangible assets, net. (Round percents to one decimal.)
3. Comment on any notable changes across the years for the income statement trends computed in part 1 and the balance sheet percents computed in part 2.

Fast Forward

4. Access Apple's financial statements for fiscal years ending after September 26, 2015, from its website (Apple.com) or the SEC database (SEC.gov). Update your work for parts 1, 2, and 3 using the new information accessed.

COMPARATIVE ANALYSIS

C2 P2

APPLE

GOOGLE

BTN 17-2   Key figures for **Apple** and **Google** follow.

$ millions	Apple	Google
Cash and equivalents................	$ 21,120	$ 16,549
Accounts receivable, net	16,849	11,556
Inventories	2,349	0
Retained earnings	92,284	90,892
Cost of sales.....................	140,089	28,164
Revenues	233,715	74,989
Total assets......................	290,479	147,461

Required

1. Compute common-size percents for each of the companies using the data provided. (Round percents to one decimal.)
2. Which company retains a higher portion of cumulative net income in the company?
3. Which company has a higher gross margin ratio on sales?
4. Which company holds a higher percent of its total assets as inventory?

BTN 17-3   As Beacon Company controller, you are responsible for informing the board of directors about its financial activities. At the board meeting, you present the following information.

ETHICS CHALLENGE

A1

	2017	2016	2015
Sales trend percent	147.0%	135.0%	100.0%
Selling expenses to sales.................	10.1%	14.0%	15.6%
Sales to plant assets ratio	3.8 to 1	3.6 to 1	3.3 to 1
Current ratio	2.9 to 1	2.7 to 1	2.4 to 1
Acid-test ratio	1.1 to 1	1.4 to 1	1.5 to 1
Inventory turnover	7.8 times	9.0 times	10.2 times
Accounts receivable turnover	7.0 times	7.7 times	8.5 times
Total asset turnover	2.9 times	2.9 times	3.3 times
Return on total assets....................	10.4%	11.0%	13.2%
Return on stockholders' equity	10.7%	11.5%	14.1%
Profit margin ratio.......................	3.6%	3.8%	4.0%

After the meeting, the company's CEO holds a press conference with analysts in which she mentions the following ratios.

	2017	2016	2015
Sales trend percent	147.0%	135.0%	100.0%
Selling expenses to sales.................	10.1%	14.0%	15.6%
Sales to plant assets ratio	3.8 to 1	3.6 to 1	3.3 to 1
Current ratio	2.9 to 1	2.7 to 1	2.4 to 1

Required

1. Why do you think the CEO decided to report 4 ratios instead of the 11 prepared?
2. Comment on the possible consequences of the CEO's reporting of the ratios selected.

BTN 17-4   Each team is to select a different industry, and each team member is to select a different company in that industry and acquire its financial statements. Use those statements to analyze the company, including at least one ratio from each of the four building blocks of analysis. When necessary, use the financial press to determine the market price of its stock. Communicate with teammates via a meeting, e-mail, or telephone to discuss how different companies compare to each other and to industry norms. The team is to prepare a single one-page memorandum reporting on its analysis and the conclusions reached.

COMMUNICATING IN PRACTICE

A1   P3

BTN 17-5   Access the February 26, 2016, filing of the December 31, 2015, 10-K report of The Hershey Company (ticker: HSY) at SEC.gov and complete the following requirements.

TAKING IT TO THE NET

P3

Required

Compute or identify the following profitability ratios of Hershey for its years ending December 31, 2015, *and* December 31, 2014. Interpret its profitability using the results obtained for these two years.

1. Profit margin ratio (round the percent to one decimal).
2. Gross profit ratio (round the percent to one decimal).

Continued on next page . . .

3. Return on total assets (round the percent to one decimal). (Total assets at year-end 2013 were $5,349,724 in thousands.)

4. Return on common stockholders' equity (round the percent to one decimal). (Total shareholders' equity at year-end 2013 was $1,616,052 in thousands.)

5. Basic net income per common share (round to the nearest cent).

TEAMWORK IN ACTION

P1 P2 P3

BTN 17-6   A team approach to learning financial statement analysis is often useful.

Required

1. Each team should write a description of horizontal and vertical analysis that all team members agree with and understand. Illustrate each description with an example.

2. *Each* member of the team is to select *one* of the following categories of ratio analysis. Explain what the ratios in that category measure. Choose one ratio from the category selected, present its formula, and explain what it measures.

   a. Liquidity and efficiency   **c.** Profitability

   b. Solvency   **d.** Market prospects

3. Each team member is to present his or her notes from part 2 to teammates. Team members are to confirm or correct other teammates' presentations.

Hint: Pairing within teams may be necessary for part 2. Use as an in-class activity or as an assignment. Consider presentations to the entire class using team rotation with slides.

ENTREPRENEURIAL DECISION

A1 P1 P2 P3

BTN 17-7   Assume that Carla Harris of Morgan Stanley (MorganStanley.com) has impressed you with the company's success and its commitment to ethical behavior. You learn of a staff opening at Morgan Stanley and decide to apply for it. Your resume is successfully screened from the thousands received and you advance to the interview process. You learn that the interview consists of analyzing the following financial facts and answering analysis questions below. (The data are taken from a small merchandiser in outdoor recreational equipment.)

	2017	2016	2015
Sales trend percents	137.0%	125.0%	100.0%
Selling expenses to sales	9.8%	13.7%	15.3%
Sales to plant assets ratio	3.5 to 1	3.3 to 1	3.0 to 1
Current ratio	2.6 to 1	2.4 to 1	2.1 to 1
Acid-test ratio	0.8 to 1	1.1 to 1	1.2 to 1
Merchandise inventory turnover	7.5 times	8.7 times	9.9 times
Accounts receivable turnover	6.7 times	7.4 times	8.2 times
Total asset turnover	2.6 times	2.6 times	3.0 times
Return on total assets	8.8%	9.4%	11.1%
Return on equity	9.75%	11.50%	12.25%
Profit margin ratio	3.3%	3.5%	3.7%

Required

Use these data to answer each of the following questions with explanations.

1. Is it becoming easier for the company to meet its current liabilities on time and to take advantage of any available cash discounts? Explain.

2. Is the company collecting its accounts receivable more rapidly? Explain.

3. Is the company's investment in accounts receivable decreasing? Explain.

4. Is the company's investment in plant assets increasing? Explain.

5. Is the owner's investment becoming more profitable? Explain.

6. Did the dollar amount of selling expenses decrease during the three-year period? Explain.

HITTING THE ROAD

C1 P3

BTN 17-8   You are to devise an investment strategy to enable you to accumulate $1,000,000 by age 65. Start by making some assumptions about your salary. Next compute the percent of your salary that you will be able to save each year. If you will receive any lump-sum monies, include those amounts in your calculations. Historically, stocks have delivered average annual returns of around 10%. Given this history, you should probably not assume that you will earn above 10% on the money you invest. It is not necessary to specify exactly what types of assets you will buy for your investments; just assume a rate you expect to earn. Use the future value tables in Appendix B to calculate how your savings will grow. Experiment a bit with your figures to see how much less you have to save if you start at, for example, age 25 versus age 35 or 40. (For this assignment, do not include inflation in your calculations.)

BTN 17-9 Samsung (Samsung.com), a leading manufacturer of consumer electronic products, along with Apple and Google, are competitors in the global marketplace. Key figures for Samsung follow (in KRW millions).

GLOBAL DECISION

A1

Samsung

APPLE

GOOGLE

Cash and equivalents	₩ 22,636,744	Cost of sales	₩123,482,118
Accounts receivable, net	28,520,689	Revenues	200,653,482
Inventories	18,811,794	Total assets	242,179,521
Retained earnings	185,132,014		

Required

1. Compute common-size percents for Samsung using the data provided. (Round percents to one decimal.)
2. Compare the results with Apple and Google from BTN 17-2.

GLOBAL VIEW

The analysis and interpretation of financial statements are, of course, impacted by the accounting system in effect. This section discusses similarities and differences for analysis of financial statements when prepared under U.S. GAAP vis-à-vis IFRS.

Horizontal and Vertical Analyses   Horizontal and vertical analyses help eliminate many differences between U.S. GAAP and IFRS when analyzing and interpreting financial statements. Financial numbers are converted to percentages that are, in the best-case scenario, consistently applied across and within periods. This enables users to effectively compare companies across reporting regimes. However, when fundamental differences in reporting regimes impact financial statements, such as with certain recognition rule differences, the user must exercise caution when drawing conclusions. Some users will reformulate one set of numbers to be more consistent with the other system to enable comparative analysis. This reformulation process is covered in advanced courses. The important point is that horizontal and vertical analyses help strip away differences between the reporting regimes, but several key differences sometimes remain and require adjustment of the numbers.

Ratio Analysis   Ratio analysis of financial statement numbers has many of the advantages and disadvantages of horizontal and vertical analyses discussed above. Importantly, ratio analysis is useful for business decisions, with some possible changes in interpretation depending on what is and what is not included in accounting measures across U.S. GAAP and IFRS. Still, we must take care in drawing inferences from a comparison of ratios across reporting regimes because what a number measures can differ across regimes. Piaggio, which manufactures two-, three-, and four-wheel vehicles and is Europe's leading manufacturer of motorcycles and scooters, offers the following example of its own ratio analysis applied to its financing objectives: "The object of capital management . . . , [and] consistent with others in the industry, the Company monitors capital on the basis of a total liabilities to equity ratio. This ratio is calculated as total liabilities divided by equity."

 Global View Assignments

Discussion Questions 16 & 17

Quick Study 17-9

Exercise 17-15

BTN 17-9

18 chapter

Managerial Accounting Concepts and Principles

Chapter Preview

MANAGERIAL ACCOUNTING BASICS

C1 Purpose and nature of managerial accounting

Managerial decisions

Fraud and ethics

Career paths

NTK 18-1

MANAGERIAL COST CONCEPTS

C2 Types of cost classifications

C3 Identification of cost classifications

Cost concepts for service companies

NTK 18-2

MANAGERIAL REPORTING

C4 Manufacturing costs

Nonmanufacturing costs

Balance sheet

P1 Income statement

NTK 18-3

COST FLOWS

C5 Flow of activities

P2 Schedule of cost of goods manufactured

C6 Trends

A1 Inventory analysis

NTK 18-4

Learning Objectives

CONCEPTUAL

C1 Explain the purpose and nature of, and the role of ethics in, managerial accounting.

C2 Describe accounting concepts useful in classifying costs.

C3 Define product and period costs and explain how they impact financial statements.

C4 Explain how balance sheets and income statements for manufacturing, merchandising, and service companies differ.

C5 Explain manufacturing activities and the flow of manufacturing costs.

C6 Describe trends in managerial accounting.

ANALYTICAL

A1 Assess raw materials inventory management using raw materials inventory turnover and days' sales in raw materials inventory.

PROCEDURAL

P1 Compute cost of goods sold for a manufacturer and for a merchandiser.

P2 Prepare a schedule of cost of goods manufactured and explain its purpose and links to financial statements.

Courtesy of NatureBox

Out of the Box

REDWOOD CITY, CA—After losing 70 pounds by learning to eat better, Gautam Gupta developed a keen interest in foods. Gautam's college friend Ken Chen grew up working in his parents' restaurant. Together, they believed they could help people eat healthier snacks. "Everyone snacks," says Gautam, "and they tend to eat what is available." The result was **NatureBox** (**NatureBox.com**), Gautam and Ken's direct-to-consumer business selling healthy snacks. "We thought we could provide value by creating an online experience to personalize a basket of natural food items."

Gautam and Ken found success by creating a niche. "We believe if we know more about you as a customer—what foods you like and don't like," explains Gautam, "we can give you a very unique experience and tailor the products to your needs." NatureBox subscribers indicate how many snacks they wish to receive and how frequently they wish to receive them. Subscribers choose from over 120 snacks.

NatureBox reflects a data-driven relationship: Subscribers identify and adjust their choices based on snacks they like or dislike, and NatureBox's accounting system develops a profile for each customer's preferences. "Think of us as the **Netflix** of food," says Gautam. "We want to understand our customers' needs better than anyone else." The use of accounting analytics is a growing trend.

"We're passionate about using data to change how people eat"

—Gautam Gupta

Gautam and Ken point out that knowing basic managerial principles, cost classifications, and cost flows was crucial to setting up operations. Gautam explains that they use only all-natural ingredients, and offer vegan, gluten-free, nut-free, and non-GMO choices. This wide array of direct materials required that Gautam and Ken set up a managerial accounting system to monitor costs. Their accounting system now captures such information, including data on materials, labor, and overhead costs.

So far, NatureBox's recipes are winning customers. The company is one of the fastest-growing snack food brands, having delivered 50,000 snack boxes in their first year of business. They estimate sales of more than 3 million boxes this year. While expanding sales and profits is crucial, Gautam says he and his co-workers "want to make an impact." Beyond helping snackers eat better, NatureBox donates one meal to end childhood hunger for each box sold.

Gautam offers this advice: "A start-up is a journey. It's a roller-coaster ride. Focus on one thing at a time and do it really well."

Sources: *NatureBox.com website,* January 2017; *CBS MoneyWatch,* August 13, 2014; *USA Today,* April 14, 2014; *FastCompany.com,* June 4, 2014; *TheSurge. com,* December 23, 2014; *Inc.com,* December 11, 2012, and April 25, 2015

MANAGERIAL ACCOUNTING BASICS

Managerial accounting provides financial and nonfinancial information to an organization's managers. Managers include, for example, employees in charge of a company's divisions; the heads of marketing, information technology, and human resources; and top-level managers such as the chief executive officer (CEO) and chief financial officer (CFO). This section explains the purpose of managerial accounting (also called *management accounting*) and compares it with financial accounting.

Purpose of Managerial Accounting

The purpose of managerial accounting is to provide useful information to aid in three key managerial tasks:

C1

Explain the purpose and nature of, and the role of ethics in, managerial accounting.

- Determining the costs of an organization's products and services.
- Planning future activities.
- Comparing actual results to planned results.

For example, managerial accounting information can help the marketing manager decide whether to advertise on social media such as Twitter; it also can help Google's information technology manager decide whether to buy new computers.

The remainder of this book looks carefully at how managerial accounting information is gathered and used. We begin by showing how the managerial accounting system collects cost information and assigns it to an organization's products and services. Cost information is important for many decisions that managers make, such as product pricing, profitability analysis, and whether to make or buy a product or component. More generally, much of managerial accounting involves gathering information about costs for planning and control decisions.

Point: Costs are important to managers because they impact both the financial position and profitability of a business. Managerial accounting assists in analysis, planning, and control of costs.

Point: Planning involves risk. Enterprise risk management (ERM) includes the systems and processes companies use to minimize risks such as data breaches, fraud, and loss of assets.

Planning is the process of setting goals and making plans to achieve them. Companies make long-term strategic plans that usually span a 5- to 10-year horizon. Short-term plans then translate the strategic plan into actions, which are more concrete and consist of better-defined goals. A short-term plan often covers a one-year period that, when translated into monetary terms, is known as a budget.

Control is the process of monitoring planning decisions and evaluating an organization's activities and employees. Feedback provided by the control function allows managers to revise their plans. Measurement of actions and processes allows managers to take corrective actions to obtain better outcomes. For example, managers periodically compare actual results with planned results. Exhibit 18.1 portrays the important management functions of planning and control and the types of questions they seek to answer.

EXHIBIT 18.1

Planning and Control (including monitoring and feedback)

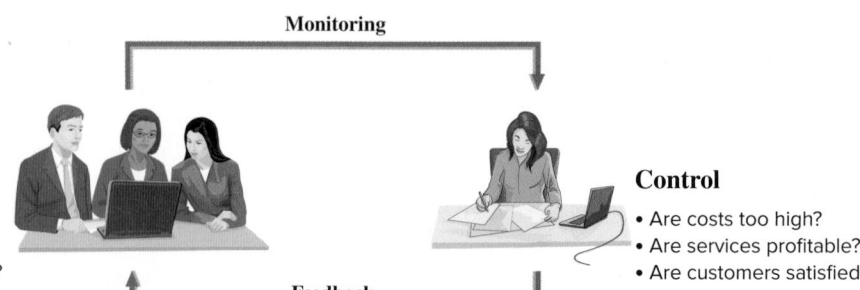

Monitoring

Planning
- Build a new factory?
- Develop new products?
- Expand into new markets?

Control
- Are costs too high?
- Are services profitable?
- Are customers satisfied?

Feedback

Nature of Managerial Accounting

Managerial accounting differs from financial accounting. We discuss seven key differences in this section, as summarized in Exhibit 18.2.

EXHIBIT 18.2

Key Differences between Managerial Accounting and Financial Accounting

	Financial Accounting	Managerial Accounting
1. Users and decision makers	External: Investors, creditors, and others outside of the organization's managers	Internal: Managers, employees, and decision makers inside the organization
2. Purpose of information	Help external users make investment, credit, and other decisions	Help managers make planning and control decisions
3. Flexibility of reporting	Structured and often controlled by GAAP	Relatively flexible (no GAAP constraints)
4. Timeliness of information	Often available only after an audit is complete	Available quickly without the need to wait for an audit
5. Time dimension	The past; historical information with some predictions	The future; many projections and estimates, with some historical information
6. Focus of information	The whole organization	An organization's projects, processes, and divisions
7. Nature of information	Monetary information	Mostly monetary; but also nonmonetary information

Users and Decision Makers   Companies report to different groups of decision makers. Financial accounting information is provided primarily to external users including investors, creditors, and regulators. External users do not manage a company's daily activities. Managerial accounting information is provided primarily to internal managers and employees who make and implement decisions about a company's business activities.

Purpose of Information   External users of financial accounting information must often decide whether to invest in or lend to a company. Internal decision makers must plan a company's future to take advantage of opportunities or to overcome obstacles. They also try to control activities.

Flexibility of Reporting   An extensive set of rules, or GAAP, aims to protect external users from false or misleading information in financial reports. Managers are responsible for preventing and detecting fraudulent activities in their companies, including their financial reports. Managerial accounting does not rely on extensive rules. Instead, companies determine what information they need to make planning and control decisions, and then they decide how that information is best collected and reported.

Point: It is desirable to accumulate information for management reports in a database separate from financial accounting records.

Timeliness of Information   Formal financial statements are not immediately available to outside users. Independent certified public accountants often must *audit* a company's financial statements before providing them to external users. As audits often take several weeks to complete, financial reports to outsiders usually are not available until well after the period-end. However, managers can quickly obtain managerial accounting information. External auditors need not review it. Estimates and projections are acceptable. To get information quickly, managers often accept less precision in reports. As an example, an early internal report to management prepared right after the year-end could estimate net income for the year between $4.2 and $4.5 million. An audited income statement could later show net income for the year at $4.4 million. The internal report is not precise, but its information can be more useful because it is available earlier.

Point: *Internal auditing* in managerial accounting evaluates information reliability not only inside but outside the company.

EXHIBIT 18.3

Focus of External and Internal Reports

Reports to external users focus on the company as a whole.

Reports to internal users focus on company units and divisions.

Time Dimension   External financial reports deal primarily with results of past activities and current conditions. While some predictions such as service lives and salvage values of plant assets are necessary, financial accounting avoids predictions whenever possible. In contrast, managerial accounting regularly includes predictions. As an example, one important managerial accounting report is a budget, which predicts revenues, expenses, and other items. Making predictions, and evaluating those predictions, are important skills for managers.

Focus of Information   Companies often organize into divisions and departments, but external investors own shares in or make loans to the entire company. Financial accounting focuses primarily on a company as a whole as depicted in the top part of Exhibit 18.3.

The focus of managerial accounting is different. While the CEO manages the whole company, most other managers are responsible for much smaller sets of activities. These middle-level and lower-level managers need managerial accounting reports dealing with their specific activities. For instance, division sales managers focus on information about results in their division. This information includes the level of success achieved by each individual, product, or department in each division of the whole company as depicted in the bottom part of Exhibit 18.3.

Nature of Information   Both financial and managerial accounting systems report monetary information. Managerial accounting systems also report considerable *nonmonetary* information. Common examples of nonmonetary information include customer and employee satisfaction data, percentage of on-time deliveries, product defect rates, energy from renewable sources, and employee diversity.

Managerial Decision Making

© James Startt/Agence Zoom/Getty Images

Although financial and managerial accounting differ, the two are not entirely separate. Some information is useful to both external and internal users. For instance, information about costs of manufacturing products is useful to all users in making decisions. Also, both financial and managerial accounting affect people's actions. For example, Trek's sales compensation plan affects the behavior of its sales force when selling its manufactured bikes. Trek also must estimate the effects of promotions on buying patterns of customers. These estimates impact the equipment purchase decisions for manufacturing and can affect the supplier selection criteria established by purchasing. Thus, financial and managerial accounting systems do more than measure; they affect people's decisions and actions.

Fraud and Ethics in Managerial Accounting

Fraud, and the role of ethics in reducing fraud, are important factors in running business operations. Fraud involves the use of one's job for personal gain through the deliberate misuse of the employer's assets. Examples include theft of the employer's cash or other assets, overstating reimbursable expenses, payroll schemes, and financial statement fraud. Three factors must exist for a person to commit fraud: opportunity, financial pressure, and rationalization. This is known as the *fraud triangle*. Fraud affects all business and it is costly: The 2016 *Report to the Nations* from the Association of Certified Fraud Examiners (ACFE) estimates the average U.S. business loses 5% of its annual revenues to fraud.

The most common type of fraud, where employees steal or misuse the employer's resources, results in an average loss of $130,000 per occurrence. For example, in a billing fraud, an employee sets up a bogus supplier. The employee then prepares bills from the supplier and pays these bills from the employer's checking account. The employee cashes the checks sent to the bogus supplier and uses them for his or her own personal benefit. An organization's best chance to minimize fraud is through reducing opportunities for employees to commit fraud.

Financial Pressure

Implications of Fraud for Managerial Accounting   Fraud increases a business's costs and hurts information reliability. Left undetected, inaccurate costs can result in poor pricing decisions, an improper product mix, and faulty performance evaluations. All of these can lead to poor results for the company. Managers rely on a reliable **internal control system** to monitor and control business activities. An internal control system is the policies and procedures managers use to:

- Ensure reliable accounting.
- Protect assets.

- Uphold company policies.
- Promote efficient operations.

Combating fraud requires ethics in accounting. **Ethics** are beliefs that distinguish right from wrong. They are accepted standards of good and bad behavior. Identifying the ethical path can be difficult. The **Institute of Management Accountants (IMA),** the professional association for management accountants, has issued a code of ethics to help accountants solve ethical dilemmas. The IMA's Statement of Ethical Professional Practice requires that management accountants be competent, maintain confidentiality, act with integrity, and communicate information in a fair and credible manner.

The IMA provides a "road map" for resolving ethical conflicts. It suggests that an employee follow the company's policies on how to resolve such conflicts. If the conflict remains unresolved, an employee should contact the next level of management (such as the immediate supervisor) who is not involved in the ethical conflict.

Point: The IMA issues the Certified Management Accountant (CMA) and the Certified Financial Manager (CFM) certifications.

Point: The Sarbanes-Oxley Act requires each issuer of securities to disclose whether it has adopted a code of ethics for its senior officers and the content of that code.

■ **Decision Ethics** ━━━━━━━━━━━━━━━━━━━━━━━━━━━━━━━━━

Production Manager   Three friends go to a restaurant. David, a self-employed entrepreneur, says, "I'll pay and deduct it as a business expense." Denise, a salesperson, takes the check and says, "I'll put this on my company's credit card. It won't cost us anything." Derek, a factory manager, laughs and says, "Neither of you understands. I'll use my company's credit card and call it overhead on a cost-plus contract with a client." (*A cost-plus contract means the company receives its costs plus a percent of those costs.*) Adds Derek, "That way, my company pays for dinner *and* makes a profit." Who should pay the bill? Why? ■   [*Answer:* All three friends want to pay the bill with someone else's money. David is using money belonging to the tax authorities, Denise is taking money from her company, and Derek is defrauding the client. To prevent such practices, companies have internal controls. Some entertainment expenses are justifiable and even encouraged. For example, the tax law allows certain deductions for entertainment that have a business purpose. Corporate policies sometimes allow and encourage reimbursable spending for social activities, and contracts can include entertainment as allowable costs. Nevertheless, without further details, this bill should be paid from personal accounts.]

Careers in Managerial Accounting

Managerial accountants are highly regarded and in high demand. Managerial accountants must have strong communication skills, understand how businesses work, and be team players. They must be able to analyze information and think critically, and they are often considered to be important business advisors.

Exhibit 18.4 shows estimated annual salaries from recent surveys. Salary variation depends on management level, company size, geographic location, professional designation, experience, and other factors. Employees with the Certified Management Accountant (CMA) or Certified Financial Manager (CFM) certifications typically earn higher salaries than those without.

Point: Managerial accounting knowledge is useful for all of us. For example, marketers use managerial accounting data to decide which products to promote and to evaluate sales force performance.

Management Level	Title	Annual Salary
Top level	Chief financial officer (CFO)	$290,000
	Controller/Treasurer	180,000
Senior management	Division controller	130,000
	General manager	105,000
Middle management	Financial analyst	85,000
	Senior accountant	85,000
Entry level	Staff accountant	60,000

EXHIBIT 18.4

Average Annual Salaries for Selected Management Levels

Sources include: AICPA.org, Kforce.com, Abbott-Langer.com, and IMA Salary Survey.

NEED-TO-KNOW 18-1

Managerial Accounting Basics

C1

Following are aspects of accounting information. Classify each as pertaining more to financial accounting or to managerial accounting.

1. Primary users are external
2. Includes more nonmonetary information
3. Focuses more on the future
4. Uses many estimates and projections

5. Controlled by GAAP
6. Used in managers' planning decisions
7. Focuses on the whole organization
8. Not constrained by GAAP

Solution

	Financial	Managerial
1. Primary users are external	X	
2. Includes more nonmonetary information		X
3. Focuses more on the future		X
4. Uses many estimates and projections		X
5. Controlled by GAAP.	X	
6. Used in managers' planning decisions		X
7. Focuses on the whole organization.	X	
8. Not constrained by GAAP		X

Do More: QS 18-1, E 18-1

MANAGERIAL COST CONCEPTS

C2

Describe accounting concepts useful in classifying costs.

Because managers use costs for many different purposes, organizations classify costs in different ways. This section explains three common ways to classify costs and links them to managerial decisions. We illustrate these cost classifications with Rocky Mountain Bikes, a manufacturer of bicycles.

Types of Cost Classifications

Fixed versus Variable   A cost can be classified by how it behaves with changes in the volume of activity.

- **Fixed costs** do not change with changes in the volume of activity (within a range of activity known as an activity's *relevant range*). For example, straight-line depreciation on equipment is a fixed cost.
- **Variable costs** change in proportion to changes in the volume of activity. Sales commissions computed as a percent of sales revenue are variable costs.

Additional examples of fixed and variable costs for a bike manufacturer are provided in Exhibit 18.5. Classifying costs as fixed or variable helps in cost-volume-profit analyses and short-term decision making.

EXHIBIT 18.5

Fixed and Variable Costs

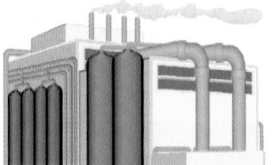

Fixed Cost: Rent for Rocky Mountain Bikes' building is $22,000, and it doesn't change with the number of bikes produced.

Variable Cost: Cost of bicycle tires is variable with the number of bikes produced—this cost is $15 per pair.

Direct versus Indirect   A cost is often traced to a **cost object,** which is a product, process, department, or customer to which costs are assigned.

- **Direct costs** are traceable to a single cost object.
- **Indirect costs** cannot be easily and cost-beneficially traced to a single cost object.

Assuming the cost object is a bicycle, Rocky Mountain Bikes will identify the costs that can be directly traced to bicycles. The direct costs traceable to a bicycle include direct material and direct labor costs used in its production. Such direct costs include wheels, brakes, chains, and seat, plus the wages and benefits of the employees who work directly on making the bike.

What are indirect costs associated with bicycles? One example is the salary of the supervisor. She monitors the production process and other factory activities, but she does not actually make bikes. Thus, her salary cannot be directly traced to bikes. Likewise, depreciation (other than the units-of-production method) on manufacturing warehouses cannot be traced to individual bikes. Another example is a maintenance department that provides services to two or more departments of a company making bicycles and strollers. If the cost object is the bicycle, the wages of the maintenance department employees who clean the factory area are indirect costs. Exhibit 18.6 identifies examples of direct and indirect costs when the cost object is a bicycle.

EXHIBIT 18.6

Direct and Indirect Costs for a Bicycle

Direct Costs (for bicycle)		Indirect Costs (for bicycle)	
• Tires	• Frames	• Factory accounting	• Factory light and heat
• Seats	• Chains	• Factory administration	• Factory intranet
• Handlebars	• Brakes	• Factory rent	• Insurance on factory
• Cables	• Pedals	• Factory manager's	• Factory equipment
• Bike maker wages	• Bike maker benefits	salary	depreciation*

* For all depreciation methods other than units-of-production.

■ Decision Maker

Entrepreneur   You wish to trace as many of your assembly department's direct costs as possible. You can trace 90% of them in an economical manner. To trace the other 10%, you need sophisticated and costly accounting software. Do you purchase this software? ■   [*Answer:* Tracing all costs directly to cost objects is always desirable, but you need to be able to do so in an economically feasible manner. In this case, you are able to trace 90% of the assembly department's direct costs. It may not be economical to spend more money on a new software to trace the final 10% of costs. You need to make a cost-benefit trade-off. If the software offers benefits beyond tracing the remaining 10% of the assembly department's costs, your decision should consider this.]

Product versus Period Costs

C3

Define product and period costs and explain how they impact financial statements.

- **Product costs** are those costs necessary to create a product and consist of: direct materials, direct labor, and factory overhead. Overhead refers to production costs other than direct materials and direct labor. Product costs are capitalized as inventory during and after completion of products; they are recorded as cost of goods sold when those products are sold.

- **Period costs** are nonproduction costs and are usually associated more with activities linked to a time period than with completed products. Common examples of period costs include salaries of the sales staff, wages of maintenance workers, advertising expenses, and depreciation on office furniture and equipment. Period costs are expensed in the period when incurred either as selling expenses or as general and administrative expenses.

Period costs are expensed when incurred and reported on the income statement. Product costs are capitalized as inventory on the balance sheet until that inventory is sold. An ability to understand and identify product costs and period costs is crucial to using and interpreting a *schedule of cost of goods manufactured,* described later in this chapter.

EXHIBIT 18.7

Period and Product Costs
in Financial Statements

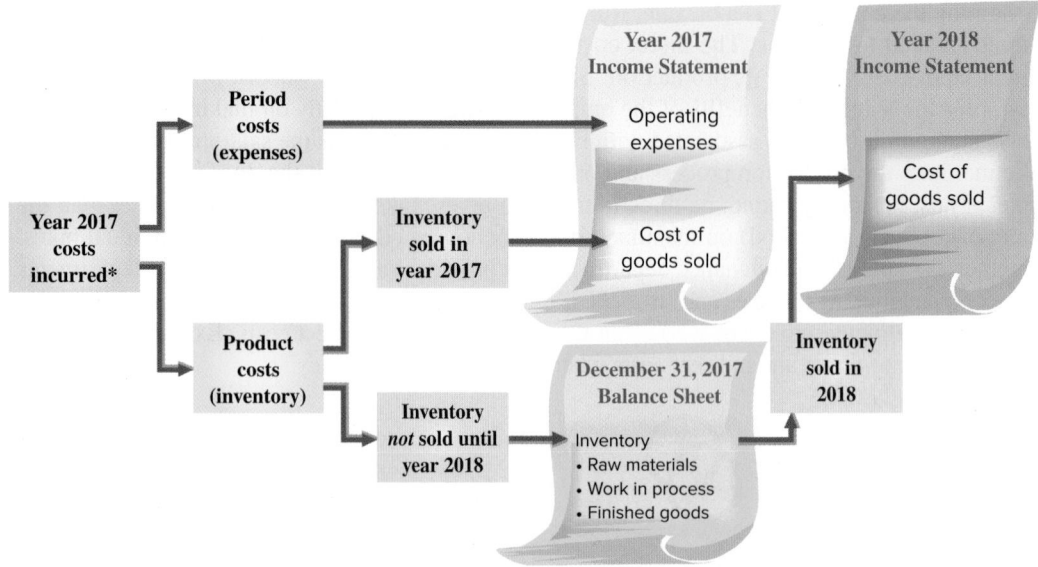

* This diagram excludes costs to acquire assets other than inventory.

Point: Product costs are either in the income statement as part of cost of goods sold or in the balance sheet as inventory. Period costs appear only on the income statement under operating expenses.

Exhibit 18.7 shows the different effects of product and period costs. Period costs flow directly to the current income statement as expenses. They are not reported as assets. Product costs are first assigned to inventory. Their final treatment depends on when inventory is sold or disposed of. Product costs assigned to finished goods that are sold in year 2017 are reported on the 2017 income statement as cost of goods sold. Product costs assigned to unsold inventory are carried forward on the balance sheet at the end of year 2017. If this inventory is sold in year 2018, product costs assigned to it are reported as cost of goods sold in that year's income statement.

Exhibit 18.8 summarizes typical managerial decisions for common cost classifications.

EXHIBIT 18.8

Summary of Cost
Classifications and Example
Managerial Decisions

Costs Classified As	Example Managerial Decision
Variable or Fixed.............	How many units must we sell to break even?
	What will profit be if we raise selling price?
	Should we add a new line of business?
Direct or Indirect.............	How well did our departments perform?
Product or Period	What is the cost of our inventory?
	Are selling expenses too high?

Point: Later chapters discuss more ways to classify costs.

Identification of Cost Classifications

It is important to understand that a cost can be classified using any one (or combination) of the three different means described here. Understanding how to classify costs in several different ways enables managers to use cost information for a variety of decisions. Factory rent, for instance, is classified as a *product* cost; it is also *fixed* with respect to the number of units produced, and it is *indirect* with respect to the product. Potential multiple classifications are shown in Exhibit 18.9

EXHIBIT 18.9

Examples of Multiple Cost
Classifications

Cost Item	Fixed or Variable	Direct or Indirect	Product or Period
Bicycle tires and wheels......................	Variable	Direct	Product
Wages of assembly worker*	Variable	Direct	Product
Advertising	Fixed	Indirect	Period
Production manager's salary..................	Fixed	Indirect	Product
Office depreciation.........................	Fixed	Indirect	Period
Factory depreciation (straight-line)	Fixed	Indirect	Product
Oil and grease applied to gears/chains**	Variable	Indirect	Product
Sales commissions..........................	Variable	Indirect	Period

*In some cases wages can be classified as fixed costs. For example, union contracts might limit an employer's ability to adjust its labor force in response to changes in demand. In this book, unless told otherwise, assume that factory wages are variable costs.
**Oil and grease are indirect costs as it is not practical to track how much of each is applied to each bike.

using different cost items incurred in manufacturing mountain bikes. The finished bike is the cost object.

Cost Concepts for Service Companies

The cost concepts described also apply to service organizations. For example, consider Southwest Airlines, and assume the cost object is a flight. The airline's cost of beverages for passengers is a variable cost based on number of flights. The monthly cost of leasing an aircraft is fixed with respect to number of flights. We can trace a flight crew's salary to a specific flight, whereas we likely cannot trace wages for the ground crew to a specific flight. Classification as product versus period costs is not relevant to service companies because services are not inventoried. Instead, costs incurred by a service firm are expensed in the reporting period when incurred.

To be effective, managers in service companies must understand and apply cost concepts. For example, an airline manager must often decide between canceling or rerouting flights. The manager must be able to estimate costs saved by canceling a flight versus rerouting. Knowledge of fixed costs is equally important. We explain more about the cost requirements for these and other managerial decisions later in this book.

© Justin Sullivan/Getty Images

Service Costs

• Beverages and snacks
• Cleaning fees
• Pilot and copilot salaries
• Attendant salaries
• Fuel and oil costs
• Travel agent fees
• Ground crew salaries

Following are selected costs of a company that manufactures computer chips. Classify each as either a product cost or a period cost. Then classify each of the product costs as direct material, direct labor, or overhead.

1. Plastic boards used to mount chips

2. Advertising costs

3. Factory maintenance workers' salaries

4. Real estate taxes paid on the sales office

5. Real estate taxes paid on the factory

6. Factory supervisor salary

7. Depreciation on factory equipment

8. Assembly worker hourly pay to make chips

NEED-TO-KNOW 18-2

Cost Classification

C2   C3

Solution

	Product Costs			Period Cost
	Direct Material	Direct Labor	Overhead	
1. Plastic boards used to mount chips	X			
2. Advertising costs........................				X
3. Factory maintenance workers' salaries.......			X	
4. Real estate taxes paid on the sales office.....				X
5. Real estate taxes paid on the factory.........			X	
6. Factory supervisor salary			X	
7. Depreciation on factory equipment..........			X	
8. Assembly worker hourly pay to make chips ...		X		

Do More: QS 18-4, QS 18-5,
E 18-5

REPORTING OF COSTS

Companies with manufacturing activities differ from both merchandising and service companies. The main difference between merchandising and manufacturing companies is that merchandisers buy goods ready for sale while manufacturers produce goods from materials and labor. Amazon is an example of a merchandising company. It buys and sells goods without physically changing them. Adidas is primarily a manufacturer of shoes, apparel, and accessories. It purchases materials such as leather, cloth, dye, plastic, rubber, glue, and laces and then uses employees' labor to convert these materials to products. Southwest Airlines is a service company that transports people and items. Some companies have several types of activities. For example, Best Buy is a merchandiser that also provides services via its Geek Squad.

Manufacturing companies like Dell, PepsiCo, and Intel separate their costs into manufacturing and nonmanufacturing costs. We discuss the reporting of activities for manufacturing, merchandising, and service companies. As these types of organizations have different kinds of costs and they classify costs in different ways, their accounting reports differ in some respects.

Manufacturing Costs

Direct Materials   **Direct materials** are tangible components of a finished product. **Direct material costs** are the expenditures for direct materials that are separately and readily traced through the manufacturing process to finished goods.

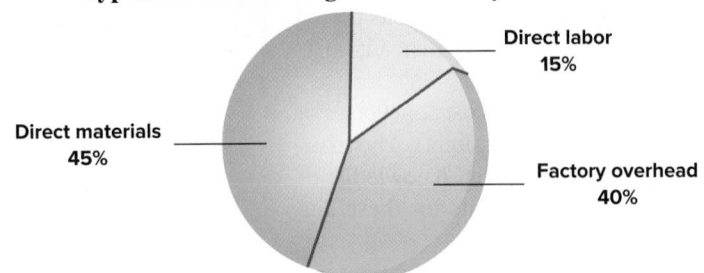

Typical Manufacturing Costs in Today's Products

Direct labor
15%

Direct materials
45%

Factory overhead
40%

Examples of direct materials in manufacturing a mountain bike include its tires, seat, frame, pedals, brakes, cables, gears, and handlebars. The pie chart here shows that direct materials make up about 45% of manufacturing costs in today's products, but this amount varies across products; for example, direct materials are estimated to comprise almost 98% of the cost of an Apple iPhone 6S.

Direct Labor   **Direct labor** refers to the efforts of employees who physically convert materials to finished product. **Direct labor costs** are the wages and salaries for direct labor that are separately and readily traced through the manufacturing process to finished goods. Examples of direct labor in manufacturing a mountain bike include operators directly involved in converting raw materials into finished products (welding, painting, forming) and assembly workers who attach materials such as tires, seats, pedals, and brakes.

Factory Overhead   **Factory overhead,** also called *manufacturing overhead,* consists of all manufacturing costs that are not direct materials or direct labor. **Factory overhead costs** cannot be separately or readily traced to finished goods. Factory overhead costs include maintenance of the mountain bike factory, supervision of its employees, repairing manufacturing equipment, factory utilities (water, gas, electricity), factory manager's salary, factory rent, depreciation on factory buildings and equipment, factory insurance, property taxes on factory buildings and equipment, and factory accounting and legal services. All factory overhead costs are considered indirect costs. These costs include indirect materials, indirect labor, and other costs not directly traceable to the product.

Point: When overhead costs vary with production, they are called *variable overhead.* When overhead costs don't vary with production, they are called *fixed overhead.*

- **Indirect materials** are components used in manufacturing the product, but they are *not* clearly identified with specific product units. Direct materials are often classified as indirect materials when their costs are low. Examples include screws and nuts used in assembling mountain bikes, and staples and glue used in manufacturing shoes. Applying the *materiality principle,* it is not cost-beneficial to trace costs of each of these materials to individual products.

- **Indirect labor** are workers who assist or supervise in manufacturing the product, but they are *not* clearly identified with specific product units. **Indirect labor costs** refer to the costs of workers who assist in or supervise manufacturing. Examples include costs for employees who maintain manufacturing equipment and salaries of production supervisors. Those workers do not assemble products, though they are indirectly related to production. Overtime premiums paid to direct laborers are also included in overhead because overtime is due to delays, interruptions, or constraints not necessarily identifiable to a specific product or batches of product.

Nonmanufacturing Costs

Factory overhead does *not* include selling and administrative expenses because they are not incurred in manufacturing products. These expenses are *period costs,* and they are recorded as expenses on the income statement when incurred. For a manufacturing company, such costs are also called *nonmanufacturing costs.* Examples of nonmanufacturing costs include office worker salaries, depreciation on office equipment, and advertising expenses.

Prime and Conversion Costs

We can classify product costs into prime or conversion costs. Direct material costs and direct labor costs are **prime costs**—expenditures directly associated with the manufacture of finished goods. Direct labor costs and overhead costs are **conversion costs**—expenditures incurred in the process of converting raw materials to finished goods. Direct labor costs are considered *both* prime costs and conversion costs. Exhibit 18.10 conveys the relation between prime and conversion costs and their components of direct material, direct labor, and factory overhead. Classification into conversion costs is useful for process costing, as we show in a later chapter.

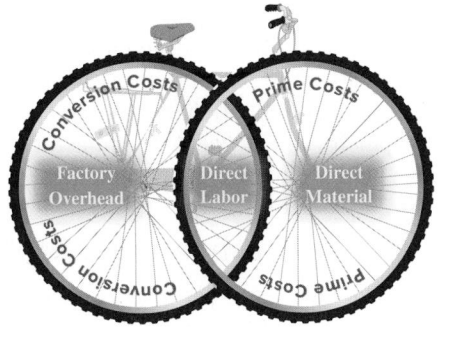

EXHIBIT 18.10

Prime and Conversion Costs and Their Makeup

Prime costs =
Direct materials + Direct labor.

Conversion costs =
Direct labor + Factory overhead.

Costs and the Balance Sheet

Manufacturers have three inventories instead of the single inventory that merchandisers carry. The three inventories are raw materials, work in process, and finished goods.

Raw Materials Inventory **Raw materials inventory** is the goods a company acquires to use in making products. Companies use raw materials in two ways: directly and indirectly. Raw materials that are possible and practical to trace to a product are called *direct materials;* they are included in raw materials inventory. Raw materials that are either impossible or impractical to trace to a product are classified as indirect materials (such as solder used for welding); they often come from factory supplies or raw materials inventory.

Work in Process Inventory **Work in process inventory,** also called *goods in process inventory,* consists of products in the process of being manufactured but not yet complete. The amount of work in process inventory depends on the type of production process. For example, work in process inventory is less for a computer maker such as **Dell** than for an airplane maker such as **Boeing**.

Finished Goods Inventory **Finished goods inventory,** which consists of completed products ready for sale, is similar to merchandise inventory owned by a merchandising company.

Balance Sheets for Manufacturers, Merchandisers, and Servicers The current assets section of the balance sheet is different for merchandising and service companies as compared to manufacturing companies. A merchandiser reports only merchandise inventory rather than the three types of inventory reported by a manufacturer. A service company's balance sheet does not have any inventory held for sale. Exhibit 18.11 shows the current assets

C4

Explain how balance sheets and income statements for manufacturing, merchandising, and service companies differ.

© Marco Prosch/Getty Images

EXHIBIT 18.11

Balance Sheets for Manufacturer, Merchandiser, and Service Provider

ROCKY MOUNTAIN BIKES Balance Sheet (partial) December 31, 2017	
Assets	
Current assets	
Cash	$11,000
Accounts receivable, net	30,150
Raw materials inventory	9,000
Work in process inventory	7,500
Finished goods inventory	10,300
Factory supplies	350
Prepaid insurance	300
Total current assets	$68,600

TELE-MART (Merchandiser) Balance Sheet (partial) December 31, 2017	
Assets	
Current assets	
Cash	$11,000
Accounts receivable, net	30,150
Merchandise inventory	21,000
Supplies	350
Prepaid insurance	300
Total current assets	$62,800

NORTHEAST AIR (Service Provider) Balance Sheet (partial) December 31, 2017	
Assets	
Current assets	
Cash	$11,000
Accounts receivable, net	30,150
Supplies	350
Prepaid insurance	300
Total current assets	$41,800

section of the balance sheet for a manufacturer, a merchandiser, and a service company. The manufacturer, Rocky Mountain Bikes, shows three different inventories. The merchandiser, Tele-Mart, shows one inventory, and the service provider, Northeast Air, shows no inventory.

Manufacturers often own unique plant assets such as small tools, factory buildings, factory equipment, and patents to manufacture products. Merchandisers and service providers typically own plant assets, including buildings, delivery vehicles, and airplanes.

Costs and the Income Statement

P1
Compute cost of goods sold for a manufacturer and for a merchandiser.

The main difference between the income statement of a manufacturer and that of a merchandiser involves the items making up cost of goods sold. In this section, we look at how manufacturers and merchandisers determine and report cost of goods sold.

Cost of Goods Sold   Exhibit 18.12 compares the components of cost of goods sold for a merchandiser with those for a manufacturer.

- *Merchandisers* add cost of goods purchased to beginning merchandise inventory and then subtract ending merchandise inventory to get cost of goods sold.
- *Manufacturers* add cost of goods manufactured to beginning finished goods inventory and then subtract ending finished goods inventory to get cost of goods sold.

EXHIBIT 18.12

Cost of Goods Sold Computation

In computing cost of goods sold, a merchandiser uses *merchandise* inventory, whereas a manufacturer uses *finished goods* inventory. A manufacturer's inventories of raw materials and work in process are not included in finished goods because they are not available for sale. A manufacturer also shows cost of goods *manufactured* instead of cost of goods *purchased*. This difference occurs because a manufacturer produces its goods instead of purchasing them ready for sale. The Cost of Goods Sold sections for both a merchandiser (Tele-Mart) and a manufacturer (Rocky Mountain Bikes) are shown in Exhibit 18.13 to highlight these differences. The remaining income statement sections are similar for merchandisers and manufacturers.

EXHIBIT 18.13

Cost of Goods Sold for a Merchandiser and Manufacturer

Merchandising Company (Tele-Mart)		Manufacturing Company (Rocky Mtn. Bikes)	
Cost of goods sold		Cost of goods sold	
Beginning *merchandise* inventory	$ 14,200	**Beginning *finished goods* inventory**	$ 11,200
Cost of merchandise *purchased*	234,150	**Cost of goods *manufactured***	170,500
Goods available for sale	248,350	Goods available for sale	181,700
Less ending *merchandise* inventory	12,100	**Less ending *finished goods* inventory**	10,300
Cost of goods sold	$236,250	Cost of goods sold	$171,400

*Cost of goods manufactured is in the income statement of Exhibit 18.14.

A merchandiser's cost of goods purchased is the cost of buying products to be sold. A manufacturer's cost of goods manufactured is the sum of direct materials, direct labor, and factory overhead costs incurred in making products.

Income Statement for Service Company Since a service provider does not make or buy inventory to be sold, it does not report cost of goods manufactured or cost of goods sold. Instead, its operating expenses include all of the costs it incurs in providing its service. Southwest Airlines, for example, reports large operating expenses for employee pay and benefits, fuel and oil, and depreciation. Southwest's operating expenses also include selling expenses and general and administrative expenses.

Income Statements for Manufacturers, Merchandisers, and Servicers
Exhibit 18.14 shows the income statement for Rocky Mountain Bikes. Its operating expenses include selling expenses and general and administrative expenses, which include salaries for those business functions as well as depreciation for related equipment. Operating expenses do not include manufacturing costs such as factory workers' wages and depreciation of production

EXHIBIT 18.14

Income Statements for Manufacturer, Merchandiser, and Service Provider

ROCKY MOUNTAIN BIKES (Manufacturer)
Income Statement
For Year Ended December 31, 2017

Sales		$310,000
Cost of goods sold		
Finished goods inventory, Dec. 31, 2016	$ 11,200	
Cost of goods manufactured (from Exhibit 18.13)	170,500	
Goods available for sale	181,700	
Less finished goods inventory, Dec. 31, 2017	10,300	
Cost of goods sold		171,400
Gross profit		138,600
Operating expenses		
Selling expenses	38,150	
General and administrative expenses	21,750	
Total operating expenses		59,900
Income before income taxes		78,700
Income tax expense		32,600
Net income		$ 46,100

TELE-MART (Merchandiser)
Income Statement
For Year Ended December 31, 2017

Sales		$345,000
Cost of goods sold		
Merchandise inventory, Dec. 31, 2016	$ 14,200	
Cost of merchandise purchased	234,150	
Goods available for sale	248,350	
Merchandise inventory, Dec. 31, 2017	12,100	
Cost of goods sold		236,250
Gross profit		108,750
Operating expenses		
Selling expenses	43,150	
General and administrative expenses	26,750	
Total operating expenses		69,900
Income before income taxes		38,850
Income tax expense		16,084
Net income		$ 22,766

NORTHEAST AIR (Service Provider)
Income Statement
For Year Ended December 31, 2017

Service revenue		$425,000
Operating expenses		
Salaries and wages	$127,750	
Fuel and oil	159,375	
Maintenance and repairs	29,750	
Rent	42,500	
Depreciation	14,000	
General and admin. expenses	20,000	
Total operating expenses		393,375
Income before income taxes		31,625
Income tax expense		13,100
Net income		$ 18,525

equipment and the factory buildings. These manufacturing costs are reported as part of cost of goods manufactured and included in cost of goods sold. This exhibit also shows the income statement for Tele-Mart (merchandiser) and Northeast Air (service provider). Tele-Mart reports *cost of merchandise purchased* instead of cost of goods manufactured. Tele-Mart reports its operating expenses like those of the manufacturing company. The income statement for Northeast Air shows only operating expenses.

NEED-TO-KNOW 18-3

Costs and Inventories for Different Businesses

C4

Indicate whether the following financial statement items apply to a manufacturer, a merchandiser, or a service provider. Some items apply to more than one type of organization.

_____ **1.** Merchandise inventory
_____ **2.** Finished goods inventory
_____ **3.** Cost of goods sold
_____ **4.** Selling expenses
_____ **5.** Operating expenses
_____ **6.** Cost of goods manufactured
_____ **7.** Supplies inventory
_____ **8.** Raw materials inventory

Solution

	Manufacturer	Merchandiser	Service Provider
1. Merchandise inventory		✓	
2. Finished goods inventory	✓		
3. Cost of goods sold	✓	✓	
4. Selling expenses	✓	✓	✓
5. Operating expenses	✓	✓	✓
6. Cost of goods manufactured	✓		
7. Supplies inventory	✓	✓	✓
8. Raw materials inventory	✓		

Do More: E 18-7

COST FLOW AND COST OF GOODS MANUFACTURED

Flow of Manufacturing Activities

C5

Explain manufacturing activities and the flow of manufacturing costs.

In addition to income statements and balance sheets, manufacturing companies prepare additional reports for planning and control. To understand these reports, we must know the flow of manufacturing activities and costs. Exhibit 18.15 shows the flow of manufacturing activities and their cost flows. Looking across the top row, the activities flow consists of *materials activity* followed by *production activity* followed by *sales activity*. The boxes below those activities show the costs for each activity and how costs flow across the three activities.

Materials Activity The left side of Exhibit 18.15 shows the flow of raw materials. Manufacturers usually start a period with some beginning raw materials inventory left over from the previous period. The company then acquires additional raw materials in the current period. Adding these purchases to beginning inventory gives *total raw materials available for use* in production. These raw materials are then either used in production in the current period or remain in raw materials inventory at the end of the period for use in future periods.

Production Activity The middle section of Exhibit 18.15 describes production activity. Four factors come together in production: beginning work in process inventory, raw materials, direct labor, and overhead. *Beginning work in process inventory* consists of partially complete products from the previous period. To the beginning work in process inventory are added the costs of direct materials, direct labor, and overhead.

The production activity that takes place in the period results in products that are either finished or not finished at the end of the period. The cost of finished products makes up the **cost of goods manufactured** for the current period. The cost of goods manufactured is the total cost of making and finishing products in the period. That amount is included on the income statement in the computation of cost of goods sold, as we showed in Exhibit 18.14. Unfinished products

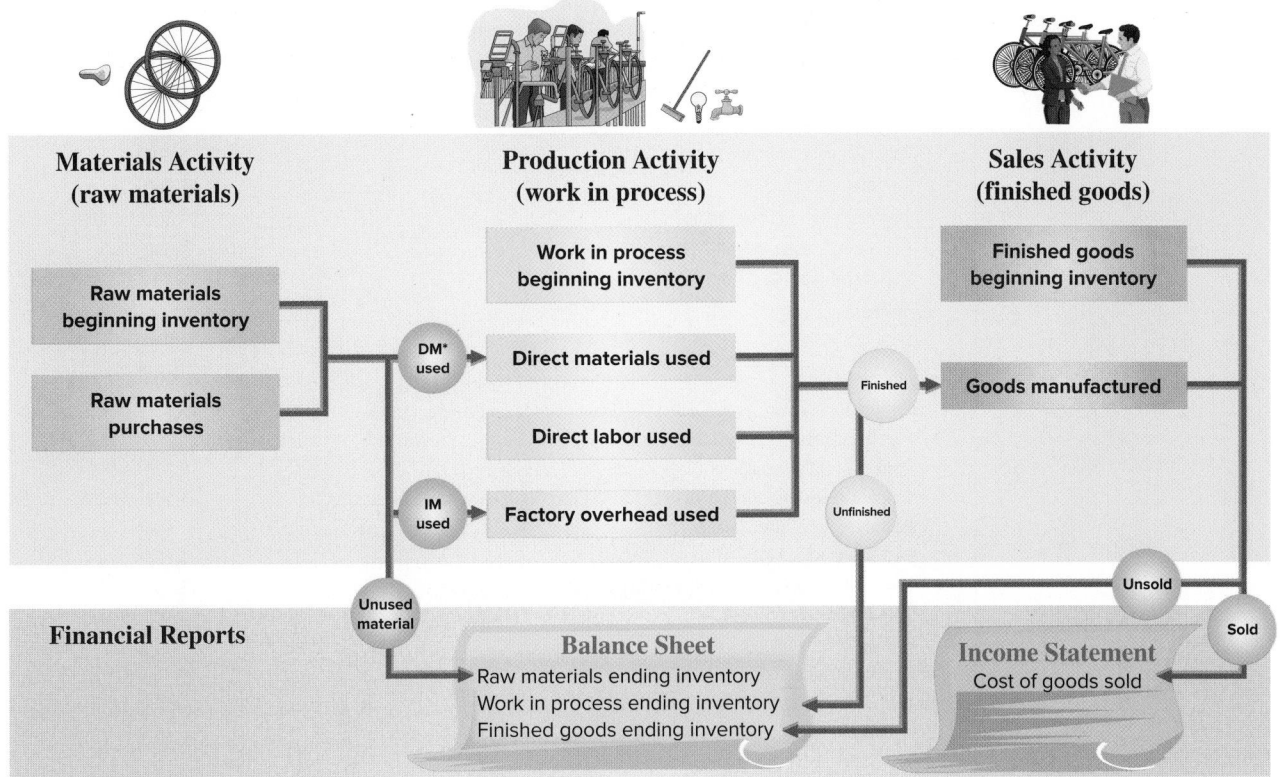

EXHIBIT 18.15

Activities and Cost Flows in Manufacturing

are identified as *ending work in process inventory*. The cost of unfinished products consists of raw materials, direct labor, and factory overhead, and is reported on the current period's balance sheet. The costs of both finished goods manufactured and work in process are *product costs*.

Sales Activity   The far right side of Exhibit 18.15 shows what happens to the finished goods: The company adds the cost of the beginning inventory of finished goods and the cost of the newly completed units (goods manufactured). Together, they make up *total finished goods available for sale* in the current period. As they are sold, the cost of finished products sold is reported on the income statement as cost of goods sold. The cost of any finished products not sold in the period is reported as a current asset, *finished goods inventory,* on the current period's balance sheet.

Schedule of Cost of Goods Manufactured

Managers of manufacturing firms analyze product costs in detail. Those managers aim to make better decisions about materials, labor, and overhead to reduce the cost of goods manufactured and improve income. A company's manufacturing activities are described in a report called a **schedule of cost of goods manufactured** (also called a *manufacturing statement* or a *statement of cost of goods manufactured*). The schedule of cost of goods manufactured summarizes the types and amounts of costs incurred in the manufacturing process. Exhibit 18.16 shows the schedule of cost of goods manufactured for Rocky Mountain Bikes. The schedule is divided into four parts: *direct materials, direct labor, overhead,* and *computation of cost of goods manufactured.*

P2

Prepare a schedule of cost of goods manufactured and explain its purpose and links to financial statements.

① **Compute direct materials used.** Add the beginning raw materials inventory of $8,000 to the current period's purchases of $86,500. This yields $94,500 of total raw materials available for use. A physical count of inventory shows $9,000 of ending raw materials inventory. If $94,500 of materials were available for use, and $9,000 of materials remains in inventory, then $85,500 of materials were used in the period.

Raw Materials Inventory			
Beg. bal.	8,000		
Purch.	86,500		
		Mtls. used	85,500
End. bal.	9,000		

EXHIBIT 18.16

Schedule of Cost of Goods
Manufactured

ROCKY MOUNTAIN BIKES			
Schedule of Cost of Goods Manufactured			
For Year Ended December 31, 2017			
Direct materials			
Raw materials inventory, Dec. 31, 2016		$ 8,000	
Raw materials purchases.		86,500	
Raw materials available for use		94,500	
Less raw materials inventory, Dec. 31, 2017		9,000	
Direct materials used.			$ 85,500
Direct labor			60,000
Factory overhead			
Indirect labor		9,000	
Factory supervision		6,000	
Factory utilities.		2,600	
Repairs—Factory equipment		2,500	
Property taxes—Factory building		1,900	
Factory supplies used (indirect materials)		600	
Factory insurance expired		1,100	
Depreciation expense—Factory assets		5,500	
Amortization expense—Patents (on factory equipment)		800	
Total factory overhead			30,000
Total manufacturing costs			$175,500
Add work in process inventory, Dec. 31, 2016			2,500
Total cost of work in process			178,000
Less work in process inventory, Dec. 31, 2017			7,500
Cost of goods manufactured.			$170,500

The ① bracket spans Direct materials. The ② bracket spans Direct labor. The ③ bracket spans Factory overhead. The ④ bracket spans Total manufacturing costs through Cost of goods manufactured.

② **Compute direct labor costs used.** Rocky Mountain Bikes had total direct labor costs of $60,000 for the period. This amount includes payroll taxes and fringe benefits.

③ **Compute total factory overhead costs used.** The statement lists each important factory overhead item and its cost. All of these costs are *indirectly* related to manufacturing activities. (Period expenses, such as selling expenses and other costs not related to manufacturing activities, are *not* reported on this statement.) Total factory overhead cost is $30,000. Some companies report only *total* factory overhead on the schedule of cost of goods manufactured and attach a separate schedule listing individual overhead costs.

④ **Compute cost of goods manufactured.** Total manufacturing costs for the period are $175,500 ($85,500 + $60,000 + $30,000), the sum of direct materials, direct labor, and overhead costs incurred. This amount is added to beginning work in process inventory, which gives the total work in process during the period of $178,000 ($175,500 + $2,500). A physical count shows $7,500 of work in process inventory remains at the end of the period. We then compute the current period's cost of goods manufactured of $170,500 by taking the $178,000 total work in process and subtracting the $7,500 cost of ending work in process inventory. The cost of goods manufactured amount is also called *net cost of goods manufactured* or *cost of goods completed.*

Point: Manufacturers sometimes report variable and fixed overhead separately in the schedule of cost of goods manufactured to provide more information to managers about cost behavior.

Work in Process Inventory			
Beg. bal.	2,500		
Mfg. costs	175,500		
		COG Mfg.	170,500
End. bal.	7,500		

Using the Schedule of Cost of Goods Manufactured   Management uses information in the schedule of cost of goods manufactured to plan and control manufacturing activities. To provide timely information for decision making, the schedule is often prepared monthly, weekly, or even daily. In anticipation of release of its much-hyped tablet, **Microsoft** grew its inventory of critical components and its finished goods inventory. The schedule of cost of goods manufactured contains information useful to external users, but it is rarely published because managers view this information as proprietary and harmful if released to competitors.

© Joe Amon/The Denver Post via Getty Images

Estimating Cost per Unit Managers use the schedule of cost of goods manufactured to make rough estimates of per unit costs. For example, if Rocky Mountain Bikes makes 1,000 bikes during the year, the average manufacturing cost per unit is $170.50 (computed as $170,500/1,000). Average cost per unit is not always an appropriate cost for managerial decisions. We show in the next two chapters how to compute more reliable unit costs for managerial decisions.

Manufacturing Cost Flows across Accounting Reports

Cost information is also used to complete financial statements at the end of an accounting period. Exhibit 18.17 summarizes how product costs flow through the accounting system. Direct materials, direct labor, and overhead costs are summarized in the schedule of cost of goods manufactured; then the amount of cost of goods manufactured from that statement is used to compute cost of goods sold on the income statement. Physical counts determine the dollar amounts of ending raw materials inventory and work in process inventory, and those amounts are included on the end-of-period balance sheet. (*Note:* This exhibit shows only partial reports.)

EXHIBIT 18.17

Manufacturing Cost Flows across Accounting Reports

ROCKY MOUNTAIN BIKES Schedule of Cost of Goods Manufactured For Year Ended December 31, 2017	
Direct materials used*	$ 85,500
Direct labor used	60,000
Factory overhead**	30,000
Total manuf. costs	175,500
Beg. work in process	2,500
Total work in process	178,000
End. work in process	(7,500)
Cost of goods manuf.	$170,500

ROCKY MOUNTAIN BIKES Income Statement For Year Ended December 31, 2017		
Sales		$310,000
Cost of goods sold		
Beg. finished goods	11,200	
Cost of goods manuf.	170,500	
End. finished goods	(10,300)	
Cost of goods sold		171,400
Gross profit		138,600
Operating expenses		59,900
Income before tax		$ 78,700

ROCKY MOUNTAIN BIKES Balance Sheet–PARTIAL December 31, 2017	
Cash	$11,000
Accounts receivable, net	30,150
Raw materials inventory	9,000
Work in process inventory	7,500
Finished goods inventory	10,300
Factory supplies	350
Prepaid insurance	300
Total current assets	$68,600

*Direct materials used is computed in Exhibit 18.16.

** Overhead items are listed in Exhibit 18.16.

Part A: Compute the following three cost measures using the information below.

_____ **1.** Cost of materials used

_____ **2.** Cost of goods manufactured

_____ **3.** Cost of goods sold

Beginning raw materials inventory	$15,500	Ending raw materials inventory	$10,600
Beginning work in process inventory	29,000	Ending work in process inventory	44,000
Beginning finished goods inventory	24,000	Ending finished goods inventory	37,400
Raw materials purchased	66,000	Direct labor used	38,000
Total factory overhead used	80,000		

Solution

1. $70,900   **2.** $173,900   **3.** $160,500

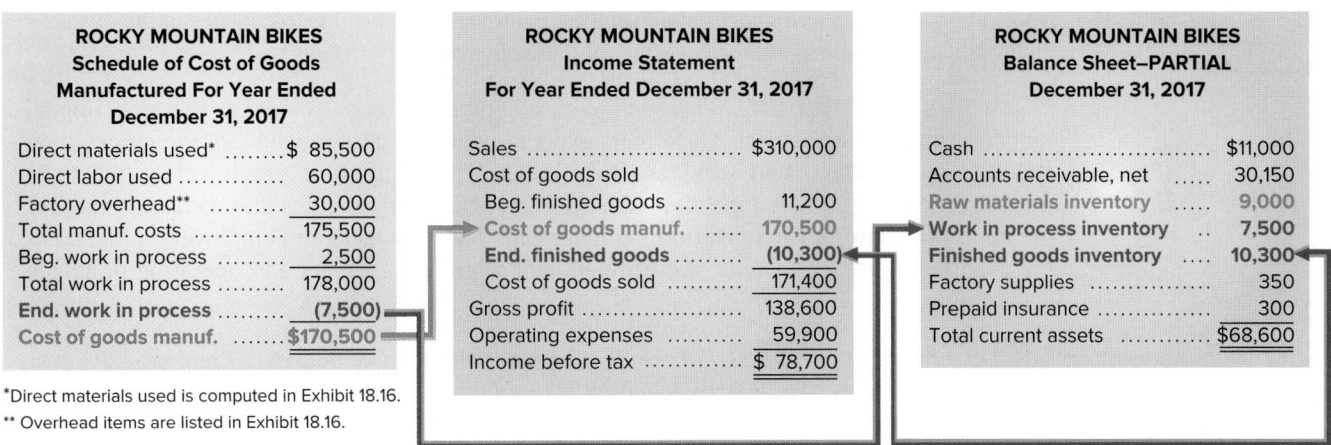

Raw Materials Inventory				Work in Process Inventory				Finished Goods Inventory			
Begin. inv.	15,500			Begin. inv.	29,000			Begin. inv.	24,000		
				Matls used	70,900						
				Labor	38,000						
Purchases	66,000			Overhead	80,000			Cost of goods	173,900		
Avail. for use	81,500				217,900			Avail. for sale	197,900		
		Matls used	70,900			Cost of goods mfg	173,900			Cost of goods sold	160,500
End. inv.	10,600			End. inv.	44,000			End. inv.	37,400		

Part B: Refer to the nine cost items listed above with their dollar amounts and indicate in which section of the schedule of cost of goods manufactured it appears as shown in Exhibit 18.16. Section *1* refers to direct materials; *2* refers to direct labor; *3* refers to factory overhead; and *4* refers to computation of cost of goods manufactured. Write *X* for any item that does not appear on the schedule of cost of goods manufactured.

Solution

__1__	Beginning raw materials inventory	__1__	Ending raw materials inventory
__4__	Beginning work in process inventory	__4__	Ending work in process inventory
__X__	Beginning finished goods inventory	__X__	Ending finished goods inventory
__1__	Raw materials purchased	__2__	Direct labor used
__3__	Total factory overhead used		

Do More: QS 18-8, QS 18-9, QS 18-10, E 18-8, E 18-11

Trends in Managerial Accounting

C6
Describe trends in managerial accounting.

Tools and techniques of managerial accounting continue to evolve due to changes in the business environment. This section describes some of these changes.

Customer Orientation   There is increased emphasis on *customers* as the most important constituent of a business. Customers expect to derive a certain value for the money they spend to buy products and services. Buyers expect that suppliers provide them the right service (or product) at the right time and the right price. This implies that companies accept the notion of **customer orientation,** which means that managers and employees understand the changing needs and wants of customers and align management and operating practices accordingly.

Global Economy   Our *global economy* expands competitive boundaries and provides customers more choices. The global economy also produces changes in business activities. One notable case that reflects these changes in customer demand and global competition is auto manufacturing. The top three Japanese auto manufacturers (**Honda**, **Nissan**, and **Toyota**) once controlled more than 40% of the U.S. auto market. Customers perceived that Japanese auto manufacturers provided value not available from other manufacturers. Many European and North American auto manufacturers responded to this challenge and regained much of the lost market share.

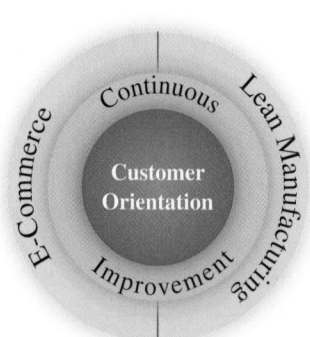

E-Commerce   People have become increasingly interconnected via smartphones, text messaging, and other electronic applications. Consumers expect and demand to be able to buy items electronically, whenever and wherever they want. Many businesses allow for online transactions. Online sales make up about 6% of total retail sales. Some companies such as **BucketFeet**, a footwear retailer, only sell online to keep costs lower.

Service Economy   Businesses that provide services, such as telecommunications and health care, constitute an ever-growing part of our economy. Many service companies, such as **Uber**, employ part-time workers. This "gig economy" changes companies' cost structures and the nature of competition. In developed economies, service businesses typically account for over 60% of total economic activity.

Lean Practices   Many companies have adopted the **lean business model,** whose goal is to *eliminate waste* while "satisfying the customer" and "providing a positive return" to the company. This is often paired with continuous improvement. **Continuous improvement** rejects the notions of "good enough" or "acceptable" and challenges employees and managers to continuously experiment with new and improved business practices. This has led companies to adopt

Point: Goals of a TQM process include reduced waste, better inventory control, fewer defects, and continuous improvement. JIT concepts have similar aims.

practices such as total quality management (TQM) and just-in-time (JIT) manufacturing. Continuous improvement underlies both practices; the difference is in the focus.

- **Total quality management** focuses on quality improvement to business activities. Managers and employees seek to uncover waste in business activities, including accounting activities such as payroll and disbursements. To encourage an emphasis on quality, the U.S. Congress established the Malcolm Baldrige National Quality Award (MBNQA). Entrants must conduct a thorough analysis and evaluation of their business using guidelines from the Baldrige committee. **Ritz Carlton Hotel** is a recipient of the Baldrige award in the service category. The company applies a core set of values, collectively called *The Gold Standards,* to improve customer service.

- **Just-in-time manufacturing** is a system that acquires inventory and produces only when needed. An important aspect of JIT is that companies manufacture products only after they receive an order (a *demand-pull* system) and then deliver the customer's requirements on time. This means that processes must be aligned to eliminate delays and inefficiencies including inferior inputs and outputs. Companies must also establish good communications with their suppliers. On the downside, JIT is more susceptible to disruption than traditional systems. As one example, several **General Motors** plants were temporarily shut down due to a strike at a supplier that provided components *just in time* to the assembly division.

Point: Quality control standards include those developed by the International Organization for Standardization (ISO). To be certified under **ISO 9000 standards,** a company must use a quality control system and document that it achieves the desired quality level.

Point: The time between buying raw materials and selling finished goods is called *throughput time.*

Value Chain   The **value chain** refers to the series of activities that add value to a company's products or services. Exhibit 18.18 illustrates a possible value chain for a retail cookie company. Companies can use lean practices across the value chain to increase efficiency and profits.

Acquire raw materials   Baking   Sales   Service

EXHIBIT 18.18

Typical Value Chain (cookie retailer)

How Lean Practices Impact the Value Chain   Adopting lean practices can be challenging because systems and procedures that a company follows must be realigned. Managerial accounting has an important role in providing accurate cost and performance information. Developing such a system is important to measuring the "value" provided to customers. The price that customers pay for acquiring goods and services is a key determinant of value. In turn, the costs a company incurs are key determinants of price.

Corporate Social Responsibility   In addition to maximizing shareholder value, corporations must consider the demands of other stakeholders, including employees, suppliers, and society in general. **Corporate social responsibility (CSR)** is a concept that goes beyond following the law. For example, to reduce its impact on the environment, **Three Twins Ice Cream** uses only cups and spoons made from organic ingredients. **United By Blue,** an apparel and jewelry company, removes one pound of trash from waterways for every product sold. Many companies extend the concept of CSR to include sustainability, which considers future generations when making business decisions.

Point: Companies like **Microsoft, Google,** and **Walt Disney,** ranked at the top of large multinational companies in terms of CSR, disclose CSR results on their websites.

Triple Bottom Line   **Triple bottom line** focuses on three measures: financial ("profits"), social ("people"), and environmental ("planet"). Adopting a triple bottom line impacts how businesses report. In response to a growing trend of such reporting, the **Sustainability Accounting Standards Board (SASB)** was established to develop reporting standards for businesses' sustainability activities. Some of the business sectors for which the SASB has developed reporting standards include health care, nonrenewable resources, and renewable resources and alternative energy.

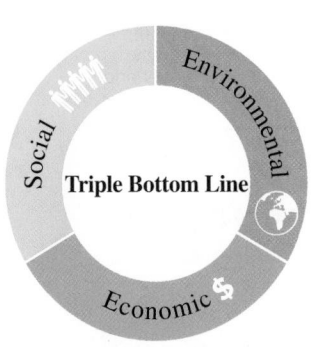

■ **Decision** Insight

Balanced Scorecard   The *balanced scorecard* aids continuous improvement by augmenting financial measures with information on the "drivers" (indicators) of future financial performance along four dimensions: **(1)** *financial*—profitability and risk, **(2)** *customer*—value creation and product and service differentiation, **(3)** *internal business processes*—business activities that create customer and owner satisfaction, and **(4)** *learning and growth*—organizational change, innovation, and growth. ■

SUSTAINABILITY AND ACCOUNTING

In creating sustainability accounting standards, the Sustainability Accounting Standards Board (SASB) has created reporting guidelines. The SASB considers sustainability information as *material* if its disclosure would affect the views of equity investors on a company's financial condition or operating performance.

Courtesy of NatureBox

Material information can vary across industries; for example, while environmental ("planet") issues such as air quality, wastewater management, and biodiversity impacts are important for investments in companies in the nonrenewable resources sectors, such issues are likely not as important for investments in banks. In contrast, "people" issues such as diversity and inclusion, fair labor practices, and employee health are considered material for most sectors, particularly those that use considerable direct labor.

NatureBox, this chapter's feature company, focuses on sustainability. The company insists on all-natural ingredients in its snack mixes. Founders Gautam Gupta and Ken Chen partner with organizations like **Feeding America** to reduce childhood hunger. Donating one meal for every snack box delivered, the company expects to donate over 1 million meals per year.

"Our company mission is to provide healthier eating choices, and the basic right to have enough food on your plate is fundamental," says NatureBox co-founder and CEO Gautam Gupta. "We're just scratching the surface of what's possible." This is one example of the triple bottom line in action.

■ **Decision** Insight

Sustainability Returns   A recent study shows the value of investing in material sustainability issues. Companies with good ratings on material sustainability issues perform better than companies with poor ratings. The chart here shows that high sustainability firms have 4% higher stock returns and almost 7% higher return on sales than low sustainability firms. (Source: hbswk.hbs.edu/item /corporate-sustainability-first-evidence-on-materiality). ■

High Sustainability Firms vs. Low Sustainability Firms

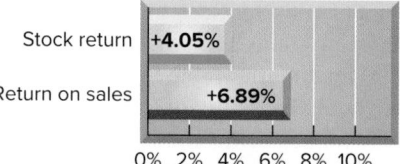

Decision Analysis ■■■   Raw Materials Inventory Turnover and Days' Sales in Raw Materials Inventory

A1
___

Assess raw materials inventory management using raw materials inventory turnover and days' sales in raw materials inventory.

Managerial accounting information helps managers perform analyses that are not readily available to external users of accounting information. Inventory management is one example. Using publicly available financial statements, an external user can compute the *inventory turnover* ratio. However, a managerial accountant can go much further.

Raw Materials Inventory Turnover

A manager can assess how effectively a company manages its *raw materials* inventory by computing the **raw materials inventory turnover** ratio as shown in Exhibit 18.19.

EXHIBIT 18.19

Raw Materials Inventory Turnover

> **Raw materials inventory turnover = Raw materials used/Average raw materials inventory**

This ratio reveals how many times a company turns over (uses in production) its raw materials inventory during a period. Generally, a high ratio of raw materials inventory turnover is preferred, as long as raw materials inventory levels are adequate to meet demand. To illustrate, Rocky Mountain Bikes reports direct (raw) materials used of $85,500 for the year, with a beginning raw materials inventory of $8,000 and an ending raw materials inventory of $9,000 (see Exhibit 18.16). Raw materials inventory turnover for Rocky Mountain Bikes for that year is computed as in Exhibit 18.20.

Raw materials inventory turnover = $85,500/[($8,000 + $9,000)/2] = 10.06 (rounded)

EXHIBIT 18.20

Raw Materials Inventory Turnover Computed

Days' Sales in Raw Materials Inventory

To further assess raw materials inventory management, a manager can measure the adequacy of raw materials inventory to meet production demand. **Days' sales in raw materials inventory** reveals how much raw materials inventory is available in terms of the number of days' sales. It is a measure of how long it takes raw materials to be used in production. It is defined and computed for Rocky Mountain Bikes in Exhibit 18.21.

Days' sales in raw materials inventory = (Ending raw materials inventory/Raw materials used) × 365
= $9,000/$85,500 × 365 = 38.4 days (rounded)

EXHIBIT 18.21

Days' Sales in Raw Materials Inventory Turnover

This computation suggests that it will take 38 days for Rocky Mountain Bikes's raw materials inventory to be used in production. Assuming production needs can be met, companies usually prefer a *lower* number of days' sales in raw materials inventory. Just-in-time manufacturing techniques can be useful in lowering days' sales in raw materials inventory; for example, Dell keeps less than seven days of production needs in raw materials inventory for most of its computer components.

■ **Decision Maker**

CFO   Your company regularly reports days' sales in raw materials of 20 days, which is similar to competitors. A manager argues that profit can be increased if the company applies just-in-time principles and cuts it down to 2 days. Do you drop it to 2 days? ■ [*Answer:* Cutting days' sales in raw materials to 2 days *might* increase profits. Having less money tied up in inventory is a positive. However, if the company loses customers over out-of-stock inventory or if production is delayed (with costs), then the increase in profit might be outweighed by the increase in costs.]

"My boss wants us to appeal to a younger and hipper crowd. So, I'd like to get a tattoo that says-- 'Accounting rules!'"

Copyright © Jerry King, www.artizans.com

The following account balances and other information are from SUNN Corporation's accounting records for year-end December 31, 2017. Use this information to prepare (1) a table listing factory overhead costs, (2) a schedule of cost of goods manufactured (show only the total factory overhead cost), and (3) an income statement.

NEED-TO-KNOW 18-5

COMPREHENSIVE

Advertising expense	$ 85,000	Work in process inventory, Dec. 31, 2016	$ 8,000
Amortization expense—Factory patents	16,000	Work in process inventory, Dec. 31, 2017	9,000
Bad debts expense	28,000	Income taxes	53,400
Depreciation expense—Office equipment	37,000	Indirect labor	26,000
Depreciation expense—Factory building	133,000	Interest expense	25,000
Depreciation expense—Factory equipment	78,000	Miscellaneous expense	55,000
Direct labor	250,000	Property taxes on factory equipment	14,000
Factory insurance used up	62,000	Raw materials inventory, Dec. 31, 2016	60,000
Factory supervisor salary	74,000	Raw materials inventory, Dec. 31, 2017	78,000
Factory supplies used	21,000	Raw materials purchases	313,000
Factory utilities	115,000	Repairs expense—Factory equipment	31,000
Finished goods inventory, Dec. 31, 2016	15,000	Salaries expense	150,000
Finished goods inventory, Dec. 31, 2017	12,500	Sales	1,630,000

PLANNING THE SOLUTION

● Analyze the account balances and select those that are part of factory overhead costs.

● Arrange these costs in a table that lists factory overhead costs for the year.

- Analyze the remaining costs and select those related to production activity for the year; selected costs should include the materials and work in process inventories and direct labor.
- Prepare a schedule of cost of goods manufactured for the year showing the calculation of the cost of materials used in production, the cost of direct labor, and the total factory overhead cost. When presenting overhead cost on this statement, report only total overhead cost from the table of overhead costs for the year. Show the costs of beginning and ending work in process inventory to determine cost of goods manufactured.
- Organize the remaining revenue and expense items into the income statement for the year. Combine cost of goods manufactured from the schedule of cost of goods manufactured with the finished goods inventory amounts to compute cost of goods sold for the year.

SOLUTION

SUNN CORPORATION
Factory Overhead Costs
For Year Ended December 31, 2017

Amortization expense—Factory patents	$ 16,000
Depreciation expense—Factory building	133,000
Depreciation expense—Factory equipment	78,000
Factory insurance used up	62,000
Factory supervisor salary	74,000
Factory supplies used	21,000
Factory utilities	115,000
Indirect labor	26,000
Property taxes on factory equipment	14,000
Repairs expense—Factory equipment	31,000
Total factory overhead	$570,000

SUNN CORPORATION
Schedule of Cost of Goods Manufactured
For Year Ended December 31, 2017

Direct materials		
Raw materials inventory, Dec. 31, 2016	$ 60,000	
Raw materials purchase	313,000	
Raw materials available for use	373,000	
Less raw materials inventory, Dec. 31, 2017	78,000	
Direct materials used		295,000
Direct labor		250,000
Factory overhead		570,000
Total manufacturing costs		1,115,000
Add work in process inventory, Dec. 31, 2016		8,000
Total cost of work in process		1,123,000
Less work in process inventory, Dec. 31, 2017		9,000
Cost of goods manufactured		$1,114,000

SUNN CORPORATION
Income Statement
For Year Ended December 31, 2017

Sales		$1,630,000
Cost of goods sold		
Finished goods inventory, Dec. 31, 2016	$ 15,000	
Cost of goods manufactured	1,114,000	
Goods available for sale	1,129,000	
Less finished goods inventory, Dec. 31, 2017	12,500	
Cost of goods sold		1,116,500
Gross profit		513,500
Operating expenses		
Advertising expense	85,000	
Bad debts expense	28,000	
Depreciation expense—Office equipment	37,000	
Interest expense	25,000	
Miscellaneous expense	55,000	
Salaries expense	150,000	
Total operating expenses		380,000
Income before income taxes		133,500
Income taxes		53,400
Net income		$ 80,100

Raw Materials Inventory

12/31/2016	60,000		
Purch.	313,000		
Avail.	373,000		
		Dir. Mtls. Used	295,000
12/31/2017	78,000		

Work in Process Inventory

12/31/2016	8,000		
Dir. Mtls. Used	295,000		
Dir. Labor	250,000		
FOH	570,000		
Avail.	1,123,000		
		COGM	1,114,000
12/31/2017	9,000		

Finished Goods Inventory

12/31/2016	15,000		
COGM	1,114,000		
Avail.	1,129,000		
		COGS	1,116,500
12/31/2017	12,500		

Summary

C1 **Explain the purpose and nature of, and the role of ethics in, managerial accounting.** The purpose of managerial accounting is to provide useful information to management and other internal decision makers. It does this by collecting, managing, and reporting both monetary and nonmonetary information in a manner useful to internal users. Major characteristics of managerial accounting include (1) focus on internal decision makers, (2) emphasis on planning and control, (3) flexibility, (4) timeliness, (5) reliance on forecasts and estimates, (6) focus on segments and projects, and (7) reporting both monetary and nonmonetary information. Ethics are beliefs that distinguish right from wrong. Ethics can be important in reducing fraud in business operations.

C2 **Describe accounting concepts useful in classifying costs.** We can classify costs as (1) fixed vs. variable, (2) direct vs. indirect, and (3) product vs. period. A cost can be classified in more than one way, depending on the purpose for which the cost is being determined. These classifications help us understand cost patterns, analyze performance, and plan operations.

C3 **Define product and period costs and explain how they impact financial statements.** Costs that are capitalized because they are expected to have future value are called *product costs;* costs that are expensed are called *period costs.* This classification is important because it affects the amount of costs expensed in the income statement and the amount of costs assigned to inventory on the balance sheet. Product costs are commonly made up of direct materials, direct labor, and overhead. Period costs include selling and administrative expenses.

C4 **Explain how balance sheets and income statements for manufacturing, merchandising, and service companies differ.** The main difference is that manufacturers usually carry three inventories on their balance sheets—raw materials, work in process, and finished goods—instead of one inventory that merchandisers carry. Service company balance sheets do not include inventories of items for sale. The main difference between income statements of manufacturers and merchandisers is the items making up cost of goods sold. A merchandiser uses merchandise inventory and the cost of goods purchased to compute cost of goods sold; a manufacturer uses finished goods inventory and the cost of goods manufactured to compute cost of goods sold. A service company's income statement does not include cost of goods sold.

C5 **Explain manufacturing activities and the flow of manufacturing costs.** Manufacturing activities consist of materials, production, and sales activities. The materials activity consists of the purchase and issuance of materials to production. The production activity consists of converting materials into finished goods. At this stage in the process, the materials, labor, and overhead costs have been incurred and the schedule of cost of goods manufactured is prepared. The sales activity consists of selling some or all of finished goods available for sale. At this stage, the cost of goods sold is determined.

C6 **Describe trends in managerial accounting.** Important trends in managerial accounting include an increased focus on satisfying customers, the impact of a global economy, and the growing presence of e-commerce and service-based businesses. The lean business model, designed to eliminate waste and satisfy customers, can be useful in responding to recent trends. Concepts such as total quality management, just-in-time production, and the value chain often aid in application of the lean business model. Trends in corporate social responsibility and sustainability activities further change how businesses report information.

A1 **Assess raw materials inventory management using raw materials inventory turnover and days' sales in raw materials inventory.** A high raw materials inventory turnover suggests a business is more effective in managing its raw materials inventory. We use days' sales in raw materials inventory to assess the likelihood of production being delayed due to inadequate levels of raw materials. We prefer a high raw materials inventory turnover ratio and a small number of days' sales in raw materials inventory, provided that raw materials inventory levels are adequate to keep production steady.

P1 **Compute cost of goods sold for a manufacturer and for a merchandiser.** A manufacturer adds beginning finished goods inventory to cost of goods manufactured and then subtracts ending finished goods inventory to get cost of goods sold. A merchandiser adds beginning merchandise inventory to cost of goods purchased and then subtracts ending merchandise inventory to get cost of goods sold.

P2 **Prepare a schedule of cost of goods manufactured and explain its purpose and links to financial statements.** This schedule reports the computation of cost of goods manufactured for the period. It begins by showing the period's costs for direct materials, direct labor, and overhead and then adjusts these numbers for the beginning and ending inventories of the work in process to yield cost of goods manufactured.

Key Terms

Continuous improvement	Customer orientation	Direct material costs
Control	Days' sales in raw materials inventory	Enterprise risk management (ERM)
Conversion costs	Direct costs	Ethics
Corporate social responsibility (CSR)	Direct labor	Factory overhead
Cost object	Direct labor costs	Factory overhead costs
Cost of goods manufactured	Direct materials	Finished goods inventory

Fixed cost	Just-in-time (JIT) manufacturing	Schedule of cost of goods manufactured
Indirect costs	Lean business model	
Indirect labor	Managerial accounting	Sustainability Accounting Standards Board (SASB)
Indirect labor costs	Period costs	
Indirect materials	Planning	Total quality management (TQM)
Institute of Management Accountants (IMA)	Prime costs	Triple bottom line
	Product costs	Value chain
Internal control system	Raw materials inventory	Variable cost
ISO 9000 standards	Raw materials inventory turnover	Work in process inventory

Multiple Choice Quiz

1. Continuous improvement
  a. Is used to reduce inventory levels.
  b. Is applicable only in service businesses.
  c. Rejects the notion of "good enough."
  d. Is used to reduce ordering costs.
  e. Is applicable only in manufacturing businesses.

2. A direct cost is one that is
  a. Variable with respect to the cost object.
  b. Traceable to the cost object.
  c. Fixed with respect to the cost object.
  d. Allocated to the cost object.
  e. A period cost.

3. Costs that are incurred as part of the manufacturing process, but are not clearly traceable to the specific unit of product or batches of product, are called
  a. Period costs.   **d.** Operating expenses.
  b. Factory overhead.   **e.** Fixed costs.
  c. Variable costs.

4. The three major cost components of manufacturing a product are
  a. Direct materials, direct labor, and factory overhead.
  b. Period costs, product costs, and conversion costs.
  c. Indirect labor, indirect materials, and fixed expenses.
  d. Variable costs, fixed costs, and period costs.
  e. Overhead costs, fixed costs, and direct costs.

5. A company reports the following for the current year.

Finished goods inventory, beginning of year	$6,000
Finished goods inventory, ending of year	3,200
Cost of goods sold	7,500

Its cost of goods manufactured for the current year is
  a. $1,500.   **d.** $2,800.
  b. $1,700.   **e.** $4,700.
  c. $7,500.

ANSWERS TO MULTIPLE CHOICE QUIZ

1. c
2. b
3. b
4. a

5. e; Beginning finished goods + Cost of goods manufactured (COGM) − Ending finished goods = Cost of goods sold
$6,000 + COGM − $3,200 = $7,500
COGM = $4,700

🅘 Icon denotes assignments that involve decision making.

Discussion Questions

1. Describe the managerial accountant's role in business planning, control, and decision making.

2. Distinguish between managerial and financial accounting on
  a. Users and decision makers.   **d.** Time dimension.
  b. Purpose of information.   **e.** Focus of information.
  c. Flexibility of practice.   **f.** Nature of information.

3. 🅘 Identify the usual changes that a company must make when it adopts a customer orientation.

4. Distinguish between direct labor and indirect labor.

5. Distinguish between (a) factory overhead and (b) selling and administrative overhead.

6. Distinguish between direct material and indirect material.

7. What product cost is both a prime cost and a conversion cost?

8. 📖 Assume that we tour **Apple**'s factory **APPLE** where it makes iPhones. List three direct costs and three indirect costs that we are likely to see.

9. 📖 Should we evaluate a production manager's performance on the basis of operating expenses? Why?

10. 📖 Explain why knowledge of cost behavior is useful in product performance evaluation.

11. Explain why product costs are capitalized but period costs are expensed in the current accounting period.

12. 📖 Explain how business activities and inventories for a manufacturing company, a merchandising company, and a service company differ.

13. 📖 Why does managerial accounting often involve working with numerous predictions and estimates?

14. How do an income statement and a balance sheet for a manufacturing company and a merchandising company differ?

15. Besides inventories, what other assets often appear on manufacturers' balance sheets but not on merchandisers' balance sheets?

16. Why does a manufacturing company require three different inventory categories?

17. Manufacturing activities of a company are described in the _____. This schedule summarizes the types and amounts of costs incurred in its manufacturing _____.

18. What are the three categories of manufacturing costs?

19. List several examples of factory overhead.

20. 📖 List the four components of a schedule of cost of goods manufactured and provide specific examples of each for **Apple**. **APPLE**

21. 📖 Prepare a proper title for the annual schedule of cost of goods manufactured **GOOGLE** of **Google**. Does the date match the balance sheet or income statement? Why?

22. 📖 Describe the relations among the income statement, the schedule of cost of goods manufactured, and a detailed listing of factory overhead costs.

23. 📖 Define and describe two measures to assess raw materials inventory management.

24. 📖 The triple bottom line includes what three main dimensions?

25. Access **3M Co.**'s annual report (10-K) for the fiscal year ended December 31, 2014, at the SEC's EDGAR database (**SEC.gov**) or its website (**3M.com**). From its balance sheet, identify the titles and amounts of its inventory components.

connect

Identify whether each description most likely applies to managerial (M) or financial (F) accounting.

_____ **1.** Its primary users are company managers.

_____ **2.** Its information is often available only after an audit is complete.

_____ **3.** Its primary focus is on the organization as a whole.

_____ **4.** Its principles and practices are very flexible.

_____ **5.** It focuses mainly on past results.

QUICK STUDY

QS 18-1
Managerial accounting versus financial accounting
C1

A cell phone company offers two different plans. Plan A costs $80 per month for unlimited talk and text. Plan B costs $0.20 per minute plus $0.10 per text message sent. You need to purchase a plan for your 14-year-old sister. Your sister currently uses 1,700 minutes and sends 1,600 texts each month.

1. What is your sister's total cost under each of the two plans?

2. Suppose your sister doubles her monthly usage to 3,400 minutes and sends 3,200 texts. What is your sister's total cost under each of the two plans?

QS 18-2
Fixed and variable costs
C2

Listed below are product costs for production of footballs. Classify each cost as either variable (V) or fixed (F).

_____ **1.** Leather covers for footballs

_____ **2.** Machinery depreciation (straight-line)

_____ **3.** Wages of assembly workers

_____ **4.** Lace to hold footballs together

_____ **5.** Insurance premium on building

_____ **6.** Factory supervisor salary

QS 18-3
Fixed and variable costs
C2

Diez Company produces sporting equipment, including leather footballs. Identify each of the following costs as direct (D) or indirect (I). The cost object is a football produced by Diez.

_____ **1.** Electricity used in the production plant

_____ **2.** Labor used on the football production line

_____ **3.** Salary of manager who supervises the entire plant

_____ **4.** Depreciation on equipment used to produce footballs

_____ **5.** Leather used to produce footballs

QS 18-4
Direct and indirect costs
C2

QS18-5
Classifying product costs
C2

Identify each of the following costs as either direct materials (DM), direct labor (DL), or factory overhead (FO). The company manufactures tennis balls.

_____ **1.** Rubber used to form the cores   _____ **4.** Glue used in binding rubber cores to felt covers

_____ **2.** Factory maintenance   _____ **5.** Depreciation—Factory equipment

_____ **3.** Wages paid to assembly workers   _____ **6.** Cans to package the balls

---

QS 18-6
Product and period costs
C3

Identify each of the following costs as either a product cost (PROD) or a period cost (PER).

_____ **1.** Factory maintenance   _____ **5.** Rent on factory building

_____ **2.** Sales commissions   _____ **6.** Interest expense

_____ **3.** Depreciation—Factory equipment   _____ **7.** Office manager salary

_____ **4.** Depreciation—Office equipment   _____ **8.** Indirect materials used in making goods

---

QS 18-7
Inventory reporting for manufacturers
C4

Compute ending work in process inventory for a manufacturer with the following information.

Raw materials purchased..............	$124,800	Total factory overhead	$ 95,700
Direct materials used	74,300	Work in process inventory, beginning of year	26,500
Direct labor used	55,000	Cost of goods manufactured	221,800

QS 18-8
Manufacturing cost flows
C5

Compute the total manufacturing cost for a manufacturer with the following information for the month.

Raw materials purchased..............	$32,400	Salesperson commissions	$6,200
Direct materials used	53,750	Depreciation expense—Factory building...........	3,500
Direct labor used	12,000	Depreciation expense—Delivery equipment.........	2,200
Factory supervisor salary..............	8,000	Indirect materials................................	1,250

QS 18-9
Cost of goods sold
P1

Compute cost of goods sold using the following information:

Finished goods inventory, beginning	$ 500
Cost of goods manufactured	4,000
Finished goods inventory, ending	750

QS 18-10
Cost of goods sold
P1

Compute cost of goods sold for 2017 using the following information.

Finished goods inventory, Dec. 31, 2016	$345,000
Work in process inventory, Dec. 31, 2016	83,500
Work in process inventory, Dec. 31, 2017	72,300
Cost of goods manufactured, 2017	918,700
Finished goods inventory, Dec. 31, 2017	283,600

QS 18-11
Cost of goods manufactured
P2

Prepare the 2017 schedule of cost of goods manufactured for Barton Company using the following information.

Direct materials	$190,500
Direct labor..	63,150
Factory overhead costs	24,000
Work in process, Dec. 31, 2016	157,600
Work in process, Dec. 31, 2017	142,750

Use the following information to compute the cost of direct materials used for the current year.

QS 18-12
Direct materials used
P2

	January 1	December 31
Inventories		
Raw materials inventory	$ 6,000	$7,500
Work in process inventory	12,000	9,000
Finished goods inventory	8,500	5,500
Activity during current year		
Materials purchased		$123,500
Direct labor.		94,000
Factory overhead.		39,000

Match each concept with its best description by entering its letter A through E in the blank.

QS 18-13
Trends in managerial
accounting
C6

_____ **1.** Just-in-time manufacturing

_____ **2.** Continuous improvement

_____ **3.** Customer orientation

_____ **4.** Total quality management

_____ **5.** Triple bottom line

A. Focuses on quality throughout the production process.

B. Flexible product designs can be modified to accommodate customer choices.

C. Every manager and employee constantly looks for ways to improve company operations.

D. Reports on financial, social, and environmental performance.

E. Inventory is acquired or produced only as needed.

3M Co. reports beginning raw materials inventory of $902 million and ending raw materials inventory of $855 million. If 3M purchased $3,646 million of raw materials during the year, what is the amount of raw materials it used during the year?

QS 18-14
Direct materials used   C5

3M Co. reports beginning raw materials inventory of $902 million and ending raw materials inventory of $855 million. Assume 3M purchased $3,646 million of raw materials and used $3,692 million of raw materials during the year. Compute raw materials inventory turnover and the number of days' sales in raw materials inventory.

QS 18-15
Raw materials inventory
management   A1

Nestlé reports beginning raw materials inventory of 3,815 and ending raw materials inventory of 3,499 (both numbers in millions of Swiss francs). If Nestlé purchased 13,860 (in millions of Swiss francs) of raw materials during the year, what is the amount of raw materials it used during the year?

QS 18-16
Direct materials used
C5

Nestlé reports beginning raw materials inventory of 3,815 and ending raw materials inventory of 3,499 (both numbers in millions of Swiss francs). Assume Nestlé purchased 13,860 and used 14,176 (both amounts in millions of Swiss francs) in raw materials during the year. Compute raw materials inventory turnover and the number of days' sales in raw materials inventory.

QS 18-17
Raw materials inventory
management
A1

connect

Indicate in the following chart the most likely source of information for each business decision. Use *M* for managerial accounting information and *F* for financial accounting information.

EXERCISES

Exercise 18-1
Sources of accounting
information
C1

Business Decision	Primary Information Source
1. Determine whether to lend to a company.	_____
2. Evaluate a purchasing department's performance.	_____
3. Report financial performance to board of directors	_____
4. Estimate product cost for a new line of shoes	_____
5. Plan the budget for next quarter	_____
6. Measure profitability of an individual store.	_____
7. Prepare financial reports according to GAAP	_____
8. Determine location and size for a new plant.	_____

Exercise 18-2

Cost classification

C2

Listed here are product costs for the production of soccer balls. Classify each cost (*a*) as either variable (V) or fixed (F) and (*b*) as either direct (D) or indirect (I). What patterns do you see regarding the relation between costs classified in these two ways?

Product Cost	a. Variable or Fixed	b. Direct or Indirect
1. Leather covers for soccer balls	_____	_____
2. Annual flat fee paid for office security	_____	_____
3. Coolants for machinery........................	_____	_____
4. Wages of assembly workers.......................	_____	_____
5. Lace to hold leather together......................	_____	_____
6. Taxes on factory...............................	_____	_____
7. Machinery depreciation (straight-line)	_____	_____

Exercise 18-3

Cost classifications for a service provider

C2

TechPro offers instructional courses in e-commerce website design. The company holds classes in a building that it owns. Classify each of TechPro's costs below as (*a*) variable (V) or fixed (F), and (*b*) direct (D) or indirect (I). Assume the cost object is an individual class.

<u>a.</u> <u>b.</u>

___ ___ **1.** Depreciation on classroom building

___ ___ **2.** Monthly Internet connection cost

___ ___ **3.** Instructional manuals for students

<u>a.</u> <u>b.</u>

___ ___ **4.** Travel expenses for salesperson

___ ___ **5.** Depreciation on computers used for classes

___ ___ **6.** Instructor wage (per class)

Exercise 18-4

Cost classifications for a service company

C2

Listed below are costs of providing an airline service. Classify each cost as (*a*) either variable (V) or fixed (F), and (*b*) either direct (D) or indirect (I). Consider the cost object to be a flight. Flight attendants and pilots are paid based on hours of flight time.

Cost	a. Variable or Fixed	b. Direct or Indirect
1. Advertising......................................	_____	_____
2. Beverages and snacks	_____	_____
3. Regional vice president salary	_____	_____
4. Depreciation (straight-line) on ground equipment	_____	_____
5. Fuel and oil used in planes.......................	_____	_____
6. Flight attendant wages...........................	_____	_____
7. Pilot wages	_____	_____
8. Aircraft maintenance manager salary	_____	_____
9. Customer service salaries........................	_____	_____

Exercise 18-5

Classifying manufacturing costs

C3

Selected costs related to **Apple**'s iPad are listed below. Classify each cost as either direct materials (DM), direct labor (DL), factory overhead (FO), selling expenses (S), or general and administrative (GA) expenses.

_____ **1.** Display screen

_____ **2.** Assembly-line supervisor salary

_____ **3.** Wages for assembly workers

_____ **4.** Salary of the chief executive officer

_____ **5.** Glue to hold iPad cases together

_____ **6.** Uniforms provided for each factory worker

_____ **7.** Wages for retail store worker

_____ **8.** Depreciation (straight-line) on robotic equipment used in assembly

Exercise 18-6

Cost classification

C3

Georgia Pacific, a manufacturer, incurs the following costs. (1) Classify each cost as either a product (PROD) or period (PER) cost. If a product cost, identify it as direct materials (DM), direct labor (DL), or factory overhead (FO), and then as a prime (PR) or conversion (CONV) cost. (2) Classify each product cost as either a direct cost (DIR) or an indirect cost (IND) using the product as the cost object.

Cost	Direct or Indirect	Product or Period	If Product Cost, Then: Direct Materials, Direct Labor, or Factory Overhead	If Product Cost, Then: Prime or Conversion
1. Factory utilities	_____	_____	_____	_____
2. Advertising	_____	_____	_____	_____
3. Amortization of patents on factory machine	_____	_____	_____	_____
4. State and federal income taxes	_____	_____	_____	_____
5. Office supplies used	_____	_____	_____	_____
6. Insurance on factory building	_____	_____	_____	_____
7. Wages to assembly workers	_____	_____	_____	_____

Current assets for two different companies at fiscal year-end 2017 are listed here. One is a manufacturer, Rayzer Skis Mfg., and the other, Sunrise Foods, is a grocery distribution company.

Exercise 18-7
Balance sheet identification and preparation

C4

1. Identify which set of numbers relates to the manufacturer and which to the merchandiser.
2. Prepare the current asset section for each company from this information. Discuss why the current asset section for these two companies is different.

Account	Company 1	Company 2
Cash	$ 7,000	$ 5,000
Raw materials inventory	—	42,000
Merchandise inventory	45,000	—
Work in process inventory	—	30,000
Finished goods inventory	—	50,000
Accounts receivable, net	62,000	75,000
Prepaid expenses	1,500	900

Using the following data from both Garcon Company and Pepper Company for the year ended December 31, 2017, compute (1) the cost of goods manufactured, and (2) the cost of goods sold.

Exercise 18-8
Cost of goods manufactured and cost of goods sold computation

P1 P2

	Garcon Company	Pepper Company
Beginning finished goods inventory	$ 12,000	$ 16,450
Beginning work in process inventory	14,500	19,950
Beginning raw materials inventory	7,250	9,000
Rental cost on factory equipment	27,000	22,750
Direct labor	19,000	35,000
Ending finished goods inventory	17,650	13,300
Ending work in process inventory	22,000	16,000
Ending raw materials inventory...................	5,300	7,200
Factory utilities	9,000	12,000
Factory supplies used	8,200	3,200
General and administrative expenses	21,000	43,000
Indirect labor...................................	1,250	7,660
Repairs—Factory equipment	4,780	1,500
Raw materials purchases	33,000	52,000
Selling expenses	50,000	46,000
Sales	195,030	290,010
Cash	20,000	15,700
Factory equipment, net	212,500	115,825
Accounts receivable, net	13,200	19,450

Check Garcon COGS, $91,030

Exercise 18-9
Preparing financial
statements for a
manufacturer **C4** **P2**

Refer to the data in Exercise 18-8. For each company, prepare (1) an income statement, and (2) the current assets section of the balance sheet. Ignore income taxes.

Exercise 18-10
Cost classification **C2**

Refer to the data in Exercise 18-8. For each company, compute the total (1) prime costs, and (2) conversion costs.

Exercise 18-11
Cost of goods sold
computation

P1

Compute cost of goods sold for each of these two companies for the year ended December 31, 2017.

	A	B	C
1			Precision
2		Unimart	Manufacturing
3	Beginning inventory		
4	Merchandise	$275,000	
5	Finished goods		$450,000
6	Cost of purchases	500,000	
7	Cost of goods manufactured		900,000
8	Ending inventory		
9	Merchandise	115,000	
10	Finished goods		375,000

Check Unimart COGS,
$660,000

Exercise 18-12
Components of accounting
reports

P2

For each of the following accounts for a manufacturing company, place a ✓ in the appropriate column indicating that it appears on the balance sheet, the income statement, the schedule of cost of goods manufactured, and/or a detailed listing of factory overhead costs. Assume that the income statement shows the calculation of cost of goods sold *and* the schedule of cost of goods manufactured shows only the total amount (not detailed listing) of factory overhead. An account can appear on more than one report.

	A	B	C	D	E
1		Balance	Income	Sched. of Cost	Overhead
2	Account	Sheet	Statement	of Goods Manuf'd.	Report
3	Accounts receivable				
4	Computer supplies used (office)				
5	Beginning finished goods inventory				
6	Beginning work in process inventory				
7	Cash				
8	Depreciation expense—Factory building				
9	Depreciation expense—Office building				
10	Direct labor				
11	Ending work in process inventory				
12	Ending raw materials inventory				
13	Factory maintenance wages				
14	Income taxes				
15	Insurance on factory building				
16	Property taxes on factory building				
17	Raw materials purchases				
18	Sales				

Exercise 18-13
Preparation of schedule
of cost of goods
manufactured

P2

Given the following selected account balances of Delray Mfg., prepare its schedule of cost of goods manufactured for the year ended December 31, 2017. Include a listing of the individual overhead account balances in this schedule.

Sales	$1,250,000	Repairs—Factory equipment	$ 5,250
Raw materials inventory, Dec. 31, 2016	37,000	Rent cost of factory building	57,000
Work in process inventory, Dec. 31, 2016	53,900	Advertising expense	94,000
Finished goods inventory, Dec. 31, 2016	62,750	General and administrative expenses	129,300
Raw materials purchases	175,600	Raw materials inventory, Dec. 31, 2017	42,700
Direct labor	225,000	Work in process inventory, Dec. 31, 2017	41,500
Factory computer supplies used	17,840	Finished goods inventory, Dec. 31, 2017	67,300
Indirect labor	47,000		

Check Cost of goods
manufactured, $534,390

Refer to the information in Exercise 18-13 to prepare an income statement for Delray Mfg. (a manufacturer). Assume that its cost of goods manufactured is $534,390.

Exercise 18-14
Income statement
preparation P2

Beck Manufacturing reports the account information below for 2017. Using this information:

1. Prepare the schedule of cost of goods manufactured for the year.

2. Compute cost of goods sold for the year.

Exercise 18-15
Schedule of cost of goods
manufactured and cost of
goods sold P1   P2

Raw Materials Inventory				Work in Process Inventory				Finished Goods Inventory		
Begin. inv.	10,000			Begin. inv.	14,000			Begin. inv.	16,000	
				DM used	46,500					
				Direct labor	27,500					
Purchases	45,000			Overhead	55,000			Cost of goods mfg.	131,000	
Avail. for use	55,000			Avail. for mfg.	143,000			Avail. for sale	147,000	
		DM used	46,500			Cost of goods mfg.	131,000			Cost of goods sold	129,000
End. inv.	8,500			End. inv.	12,000			End. inv.	18,000	

The following chart shows how costs flow through a business as a product is manufactured. Not all boxes in the chart show cost amounts. Compute the cost amounts for the boxes that contain question marks.

Exercise 18-16
Cost flows in manufacturing
C5

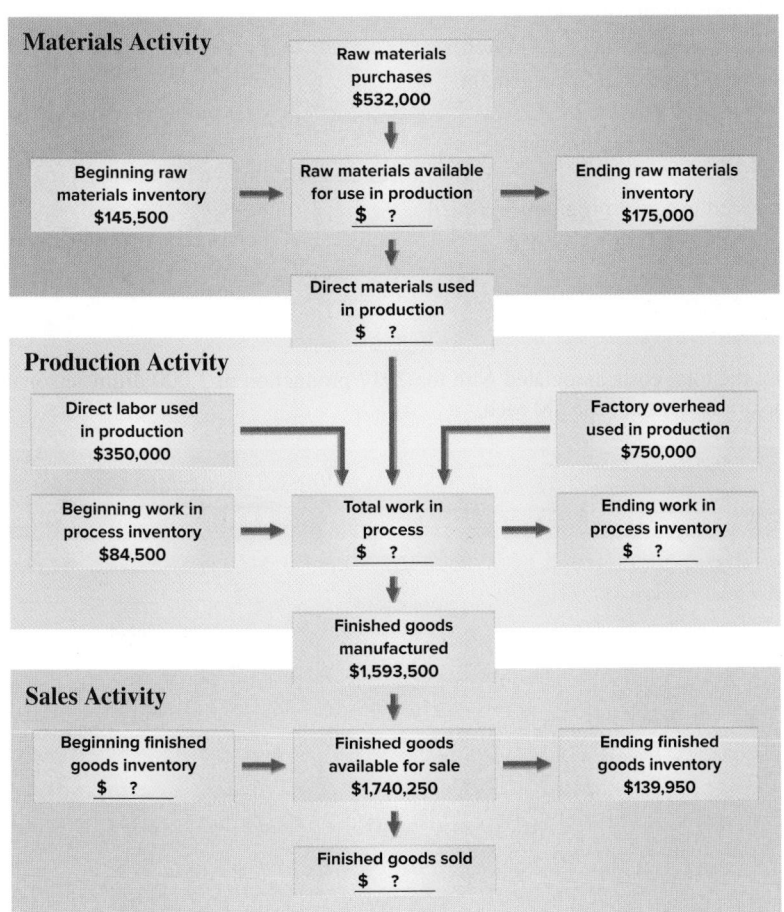

Many fast-food restaurants compete on lean business practices. Match each of the following activities at a fast-food restaurant with one of the three lean business practices *a*, *b*, or *c* that it strives to achieve. Some activities might relate to more than one lean business practice.

_____ **1.** Courteous employees

_____ **2.** Food produced to order

_____ **3.** Clean tables and floors

_____ **4.** Orders filled within three minutes

_____ **5.** Standardized food-making processes

_____ **6.** New product development

a. Just-in-time (JIT)

b. Continuous improvement (CI)

c. Total quality management (TQM)

Exercise 18-17
Lean business practice
C6

Exercise 18-18
Triple bottom line

C6

In its recent annual report and related *Global Responsibility Report,* **Starbucks** provides information on company performance on several dimensions. Indicate whether the following items best fit into the financial (label your answer "Profit"), social (label your answer "People"), or environmental (label your answer "Planet") aspects of triple bottom line reporting.

_____ **1.** Sales revenue totaled $16.5 billion.

_____ **2.** 96% of coffee was purchased from suppliers certified for responsible farming and ethics.

_____ **3.** Reduced water consumption by 4%.

_____ **4.** Reduced energy consumption.

_____ **5.** Operating income totaled $119.2 million.

_____ **6.** Increased purchases of energy from renewable sources.

_____ **7.** All new stores are built using certified green building techniques.

_____ **8.** Decreased amounts of packaging materials.

_____ **9.** Discontinued working with factories that did not meet standards for their working conditions.

Exercise 18-19
Triple bottom line

C6

In its recent annual report and related *Corporate Responsibility Report,* **Hyatt** provides information on company performance on several dimensions. Indicate whether the following items below best fit into the financial (label your answer "Profit"), social (label your answer "People"), or environmental (label your answer "Planet") aspects of triple bottom line reporting.

_____ **1.** Sales revenue totaled $4.4 billion.

_____ **2.** Increased women in management positions by 8%.

_____ **3.** Reduced water consumption at its hotels.

_____ **4.** Invested in career programs in Brazil.

_____ **5.** Operating cash flows totaled $473 million.

_____ **6.** Earned awards for best LGBT workplace.

_____ **7.** 84% of hotels recycle at least one waste stream.

_____ **8.** Invested in reading programs for young students.

_____ **9.** Focused on maximizing long-term shareholder value.

connect

PROBLEM SET A

Problem 18-1A
Cost computation, classification, and analysis

C2   C3

Listed here are the total costs associated with the 2017 production of 1,000 drum sets manufactured by TrueBeat. The drum sets sell for $500 each.

Costs	Variable or Fixed		Product or Period	
	Variable	Fixed	Product	Period
1. Plastic for casing—$17,000	$17,000	___	$17,000	___
2. Wages of assembly workers—$82,000..........................	___	___	___	___
3. Property taxes on factory—$5,000	___	___	___	___
4. Accounting staff salaries—$35,000............................	___	___	___	___
5. Drum stands (1,000 stands purchased)—$26,000.............	___	___	___	___
6. Rent cost of equipment for sales staff—$10,000..................	___	___	___	___
7. Upper management salaries—$125,000	___	___	___	___
8. Annual flat fee for factory maintenance service—$10,000	___	___	___	___
9. Sales commissions—$15 per unit	___	___	___	___
10. Machinery depreciation, straight-line—$40,000	___	___	___	___

Required

1. Classify each cost and its amount as (*a*) either variable or fixed and (*b*) either product or period. (The first cost is completed as an example.)

2. Compute the manufacturing cost per drum set.

Analysis Component

3. Assume that 1,200 drum sets are produced in the next year. What do you predict will be the total cost of plastic for the casings and the per unit cost of the plastic for the casings? Explain.

4. Assume that 1,200 drum sets are produced in the next year. What do you predict will be the total cost of property taxes and the per unit cost of the property taxes? Explain.

Check   (1) Total variable production cost, $125,000

The following calendar year-end information is taken from the December 31, 2017, adjusted trial balance and other records of Leone Company.

Advertising expense	$ 28,750	Miscellaneous production costs	$ 8,425
Depreciation expense—Office equipment	7,250	Office salaries expense	63,000
Depreciation expense—Selling equipment	8,600	Raw materials purchases	925,000
Depreciation expense—Factory equipment	33,550	Rent expense—Office space	22,000
Factory supervision	102,600	Rent expense—Selling space	26,100
Factory supplies used	7,350	Rent expense—Factory building	76,800
Factory utilities	33,000	Maintenance expense—Factory equipment	35,400
Direct labor	675,480	Sales	4,462,500
Indirect labor	56,875	Sales salaries expense	392,560

Required

1. Classify each cost as either a product or period cost.
2. Classify each product cost as either direct materials, direct labor, or factory overhead.
3. Classify each period cost as either selling expenses or general and administrative expenses.

Using the data from Problem 18-2A and the following additional inventory information for Leone Company, complete the requirements below. Assume income tax expense is $233,725 for the year.

Inventories	
Raw materials, December 31, 2016	$166,850
Raw materials, December 31, 2017	182,000
Work in process, December 31, 2016	15,700
Work in process, December 31, 2017	19,380
Finished goods, December 31, 2016	167,350
Finished goods, December 31, 2017	136,490

Required

1. Prepare the company's 2017 schedule of cost of goods manufactured.
2. Prepare the company's 2017 income statement that reports separate categories for (*a*) selling expenses and (*b*) general and administrative expenses.

Check   (1) Cost of goods manufactured, $1,935,650

Analysis Component

3. Compute the (*a*) inventory turnover, defined as cost of goods sold divided by average inventory, and (*b*) days' sales in inventory, defined as 365 times ending inventory divided by cost of goods sold, for both its raw materials inventory and its finished goods inventory. (To compute turnover and days' sales in inventory for raw materials, use raw materials used rather than cost of goods sold.) Discuss some possible reasons for differences between these ratios for the two types of inventories. Round answers to one decimal place.

Nazaro's Boot Company makes specialty boots for the rodeo circuit. On December 31, 2016, the company had (*a*) 300 pairs of boots in finished goods inventory and (*b*) 1,200 heels at a cost of $8 each in raw materials inventory. During 2017, the company purchased 35,000 additional heels at $8 each and manufactured 16,600 pairs of boots.

Required

1. Determine the unit and dollar amounts of raw materials inventory in heels at December 31, 2017.

Check   (1) Ending (heel) inventory, 3,000 units; $24,000

Analysis Component

2. Write a half-page memorandum to the production manager explaining why a just-in-time inventory system for heels should be considered. Include the amount of working capital that can be reduced at December 31, 2017, if the ending heel raw material inventory is cut by half.

Problem 18-5A
Inventory computation and reporting

C4   P1

Shown here are annual financial data at December 31, 2017, taken from two different companies.

	Music World Retail	Wave-Board Manufacturing
Beginning inventory		
Merchandise	$200,000	
Finished goods.		$500,000
Cost of purchases.	300,000	
Cost of goods manufactured		875,000
Ending inventory		
Merchandise	175,000	
Finished goods.		225,000

Required

Check (1) Wave-Board's cost of goods sold, $1,150,000

1. Compute the cost of goods sold section of the income statement at December 31, 2017, for each company. Include the proper title and format in the solution.

2. Write a half-page memorandum to your instructor (*a*) identifying the inventory accounts and (*b*) describing where each is reported on the income statement and balance sheet for both companies.

PROBLEM SET B

Problem 18-1B
Cost computation, classification, and analysis

C2   C3

Listed here are the total costs associated with the 2017 production of 15,000 Blu-ray Discs (BDs) manufactured by Maxwell. The BDs sell for $18 each.

Costs	Variable or Fixed		Product or Period	
	Variable	Fixed	Product	Period
1. Plastic for BDs—$1,500	$1,500	——	$1,500	——
2. Wages of assembly workers—$30,000	——	——	——	——
3. Cost of factory rent—$6,750	——	——	——	——
4. Systems staff salaries—$15,000	——	——	——	——
5. Labeling—$0.25 per BD	——	——	——	——
6. Cost of office equipment rent—$1,050	——	——	——	——
7. Upper management salaries—$120,000	——	——	——	——
8. Annual fixed fee for cleaning service—$4,520	——	——	——	——
9. Sales commissions—$0.50 per BD	——	——	——	——
10. Machinery depreciation, straight-line—$18,000	——	——	——	——

Required

1. Classify each cost and its amount as (*a*) either variable or fixed and (*b*) either product or period. (The first cost is completed as an example.)

Check (2) Total variable production cost, $35,250

2. Compute the manufacturing cost per BD.

Analysis Component

3. Assume that 10,000 BDs are produced in the next year. What do you predict will be the total cost of plastic for the BDs and the per unit cost of the plastic for the BDs? Explain.

4. Assume that 10,000 BDs are produced in the next year. What do you predict will be the total cost of factory rent and the per unit cost of the factory rent? Explain.

Problem 18-2B
Classifying costs

C2   C3

The following calendar year-end information is taken from the December 31, 2017, adjusted trial balance and other records of Best Bikes.

Advertising expense	$ 20,250	Miscellaneous production costs	$ 8,440
Depreciation expense—Office equipment	8,440	Office salaries expense	70,875
Depreciation expense—Selling equipment	10,125	Raw materials purchases	894,375
Depreciation expense—Factory equipment	35,400	Rent expense—Office space	23,625
Factory supervision	121,500	Rent expense—Selling space	27,000
Factory supplies used	6,060	Rent expense—Factory building	93,500
Factory utilities	37,500	Maintenance expense—Factory equipment	30,375
Direct labor	562,500	Sales	4,942,625
Indirect labor	59,000	Sales salaries expense	295,300

Required

1. Classify each cost as either a product or period cost.
2. Classify each product cost as either direct materials, direct labor, or factory overhead.
3. Classify each period cost as either selling expenses or general and administrative expenses.

Using the information from Problem 18-2B and the following additional inventory information for Best Bikes, complete the requirements below. Assume income tax expense is $136,700 for the year.

Inventories	
Raw materials, December 31, 2016	$ 40,375
Raw materials, December 31, 2017	70,430
Work in process, December 31, 2016	12,500
Work in process, December 31, 2017	14,100
Finished goods, December 31, 2016	177,200
Finished goods, December 31, 2017	141,750

Problem 18-3B
Schedule of cost of goods manufactured and income statement; analysis of inventories

P2 A1

Required

1. Prepare the company's 2017 schedule of cost of goods manufactured.
2. Prepare the company's 2017 income statement that reports separate categories for (*a*) selling expenses and (*b*) general and administrative expenses.

Check (1) Cost of goods manufactured, $1,816,995

Analysis Component

3. Compute the (*a*) inventory turnover, defined as cost of goods sold divided by average inventory, and (*b*) days' sales in inventory, defined as 365 times ending inventory divided by cost of goods sold, for both its raw materials inventory and its finished goods inventory. (To compute turnover and days' sales in inventory for raw materials, use raw materials used rather than cost of goods sold.) Discuss some possible reasons for differences between these ratios for the two types of inventories. Round answers to one decimal place.

Racer's Edge makes specialty skates for the ice skating circuit. On December 31, 2016, the company had (*a*) 1,500 skates in finished goods inventory and (*b*) 2,500 blades at a cost of $20 each in raw materials inventory. During 2017, Racer's Edge purchased 45,000 additional blades at $20 each and manufactured 20,750 pairs of skates.

Problem 18-4B
Ending inventory computation and evaluation

C4

Required

1. Determine the unit and dollar amounts of raw materials inventory in blades at December 31, 2017.

Check (1) Ending (blade) inventory, 6,000 units; $120,000

Analysis Component

2. Write a half-page memorandum to the production manager explaining why a just-in-time inventory system for blades should be considered. Include the amount of working capital that can be reduced at December 31, 2017, if the ending blade raw materials inventory is cut in half.

Problem 18-5B
Inventory computation and reporting

C4   P1

Shown here are annual financial data at December 31, 2017, taken from two different companies.

	TeeMart (Retail)	Aim Labs (Manufacturing)
Beginning inventory		
Merchandise	$100,000	
Finished goods		$300,000
Cost of purchases......................	250,000	
Cost of goods manufactured		586,000
Ending inventory		
Merchandise	150,000	
Finished goods		200,000

Required

Check (1) TeeMart cost of goods sold, $200,000

1. Compute the cost of goods sold section of the income statement at December 31, 2017, for each company. Include the proper title and format in the solution.

2. Write a half-page memorandum to your instructor (a) identifying the inventory accounts and (b) identifying where each is reported on the income statement and balance sheet for both companies.

SERIAL PROBLEM
Business Solutions

C2   C4   P2

© Alexander Image/Shutterstock RF

(This serial problem begins in Chapter 1 and continues through most of the book. If previous chapter segments were not completed, the serial problem can begin at this point.)

SP 18   Santana Rey, owner of **Business Solutions**, decides to diversify her business by also manufacturing computer workstation furniture.

Required

1. Classify the following manufacturing costs of Business Solutions as either (a) variable (V) or fixed (F), and (b) direct (D) or indirect (I).

Manufacturing Costs	a. Variable or Fixed	b. Direct or Indirect
1. Monthly flat fee to clean workshop	_____	_____
2. Laminate coverings for desktops....................	_____	_____
3. Taxes on assembly workshop.......................	_____	_____
4. Glue to assemble workstation component parts........	_____	_____
5. Wages of desk assembler..........................	_____	_____
6. Electricity for workshop	_____	_____
7. Depreciation on manufacturing tools................	_____	_____

2. Prepare a schedule of cost of goods manufactured for Business Solutions for the month ended January 31, 2018. Assume the following manufacturing costs:

Direct materials: $2,200

Factory overhead: $490

Direct labor: $900

Beginning work in process: none (December 31, 2017)

Ending work in process: $540 (January 31, 2018)

Beginning finished goods inventory: none (December 31, 2017)

Ending finished goods inventory: $350 (January 31, 2018)

Check (3) COGS, $2,700

3. Prepare the cost of goods sold section of a partial income statement for Business Solutions for the month ended January 31, 2018.

Beyond the Numbers

BTN 18-1 Managerial accounting is more than recording, maintaining, and reporting financial results. Managerial accountants must provide managers with both financial and nonfinancial information including estimates, projections, and forecasts. An important estimate for **Apple** is its reserve for warranty claims, and the company must provide shareholders information on these estimates.

REPORTING IN ACTION

C1

APPLE

Required

1. Access Apple's 2015 10-K report, filed with the SEC on October 28, 2015, and find Note 10—*Commitments and Contingencies*. What amount of warranty expense did Apple record for 2015?
2. What amount of warranty claims did Apple pay during 2015?
3. What is Apple's accrued warranty liability at the end of 2015?

Fast Forward

4. Access **Apple**'s annual report for a fiscal year ending after September 26, 2015, from either its website (**Apple.com**) or the SEC's EDGAR database (**SEC.gov**). Answer the questions in parts 1, 2, and 3 after reading the current Note 10. Identify any major changes.

BTN 18-2 Both **Apple** and **Google** (**Alphabet**) have audit committees as part of their boards of directors. Access each company's website (**investor.Apple.com** or **abc.xyz/investor/**) and read about the purpose of the audit committee.

COMPARATIVE ANALYSIS

C2

APPLE
GOOGLE

Required

1. From Apple's website, select Leadership & Governance, Committee Charters, and Audit and Finance Committee. What is the purpose of Apple's audit committee?
2. From Google's website, select Board, then Audit Committee. What is the purpose of its audit committee?
3. Based on your answers to parts 1 and 2, how would management accountants be involved in assisting the audit committee in carrying out its responsibilities?

BTN 18-3 Assume that you are the managerial accountant at Infostore, a manufacturer of hard drives, CDs, and DVDs. Its reporting year-end is December 31. The chief financial officer is concerned about having enough cash to pay the expected income tax bill because of poor cash flow management. On November 15, the purchasing department purchased excess inventory of CD raw materials in anticipation of rapid growth of this product beginning in January. To decrease the company's tax liability, the chief financial officer tells you to record the purchase of this inventory as part of supplies and expense it in the current year; this would decrease the company's tax liability by increasing expenses.

ETHICS CHALLENGE

C1 C3

Required

1. In which account should the purchase of CD raw materials be recorded?
2. How should you respond to this request by the chief financial officer?

BTN 18-4 Write a one-page memorandum to a prospective college student about salary expectations for graduates in business. Compare and contrast the expected salaries for accounting (including different subfields such as public, corporate, tax, audit, and so forth), marketing, management, and finance majors. Prepare a graph showing average starting salaries (and those for experienced professionals in those fields if available). To get this information, stop by your school's career services office; libraries also have this information. The website **JobStar.org** (click on "Salary Info") also can get you started.

COMMUNICATING IN PRACTICE

C6

BTN 18-5 Managerial accounting professionals follow a code of ethics. As a member of the Institute of Management Accountants, the managerial accountant must comply with standards of ethical conduct.

TAKING IT TO THE NET

C1

Required

1. Identify, print, and read the *Statement of Ethical Professional Practice* posted at **IMAnet.org**. (Under "Resources and Publications" select "Ethics Center," and then select "IMA Statement of Ethical Professional Practice.")
2. What four overarching ethical principles underlie the IMA's statement?
3. Describe the courses of action the IMA recommends in resolving ethical conflicts.

TEAMWORK IN ACTION

C5 P2

BTN 18-6 The following calendar-year information is taken from the December 31, 2017, adjusted trial balance and other records of Dahlia Company.

Advertising expense	$ 19,125	Direct labor		$ 650,750
Depreciation expense—Office equipment	8,750	Indirect labor		60,000
Depreciation expense—Selling equipment	10,000	Miscellaneous production costs		8,500
Depreciation expense—Factory equipment	32,500	Office salaries expense		100,875
Factory supervision	122,500	Raw materials purchases		872,500
Factory supplies used	15,750	Rent expense—Office space		21,125
Factory utilities	36,250	Rent expense—Selling space		25,750
Inventories		Rent expense—Factory building		79,750
Raw materials, December 31, 2016	177,500	Maintenance expense—Factory equipment		27,875
Raw materials, December 31, 2017	168,125	Sales		3,275,000
Work in process, December 31, 2016	15,875	Sales discounts		57,500
Work in process, December 31, 2017	14,000	Sales salaries expense		286,250
Finished goods, December 31, 2016	164,375			
Finished goods, December 31, 2017	129,000			

Required

1. *Each* team member is to be responsible for computing **one** of the following amounts. You are not to duplicate your teammates' work. Get any necessary amounts from teammates. Each member is to explain the computation to the team in preparation for reporting to class.

   a. Materials used   **d.** Total cost of work in process

   b. Factory overhead   **e.** Cost of goods manufactured

   c. Total manufacturing costs

2. Check your cost of goods manufactured with the instructor. If it is correct, proceed to part 3.

3. *Each* team member is to be responsible for computing **one** of the following amounts. You are not to duplicate your teammates' work. Get any necessary amounts from teammates. Each member is to explain the computation to the team in preparation for reporting to class.

   a. Net sales   **d.** Total operating expenses

   b. Cost of goods sold   **e.** Net income or loss before taxes

   c. Gross profit

ENTREPRENEURIAL DECISION

C1 C2 C6

BTN 18-7 Gautam Gupta and Ken Chen of NatureBox must understand manufacturing costs to effectively operate and succeed as a profitable and efficient business.

Required

1. What are the three main categories of manufacturing costs Gautam and Ken must monitor and control? Provide examples of each.

2. What are four goals of a total quality management process? (*Hint:* The goals are listed in a margin "Point.") How can NatureBox use TQM to improve its business activities?

HITTING THE ROAD

C1 C2

BTN 18-8 Visit your favorite fast-food restaurant. Observe its business operations.

Required

1. Describe all business activities from the time a customer arrives to the time that customer departs.

2. List all costs you can identify with the separate activities described in part 1.

3. Classify each cost from part 2 as fixed or variable, and explain your classification.

BTN 18-9 Access Samsung's 2015 annual report from its website (Samsung.com). Like Apple, Samsung offers warranties on its products.

GLOBAL DECISION

C1

Samsung

APPLE

Required

1. Access and read footnote 18, "Provisions," included in Samsung's 2015 annual report. What amount of warranty expense did Samsung record during 2015? What amount of warranty claims did Samsung pay in 2015?

2. Access and read information on Apple's accrued warranty in footnote 10 of its 2015 annual report. What amount of warranty expense did Apple record during 2015? What amount of warranty claims did Apple pay in 2015?

3. Using your answers from parts 1 and 2, which company was more accurate in estimating warranty claims for 2015?

 **GLOBAL VIEW**

Managerial accounting is more flexible than financial accounting and does not follow a set of strict rules. However, many international businesses use the managerial accounting concepts and principles described in this chapter.

Customer Focus Nestlé, one of the world's leading nutrition and wellness companies, adopts a customer focus and strives to understand its customers' tastes. For example, Nestlé employees spent three days living with people in Lima, Peru, to understand their motivations, routines, buying habits, and everyday lives. This allowed Nestlé to adjust its products to suit local tastes.

Reporting Manufacturing Activities Nestlé must classify and report costs. In reporting inventory, Nestlé includes direct production costs, production overhead, and factory depreciation. A recent Nestlé annual report shows the following:

Swiss francs in millions	Ending Inventory	Beginning Inventory
Raw materials, work in progress, and sundry supplies	SFr. 3,499	SFr. 3,815
Finished goods	5,138	5,302

Nestlé managers use this information, along with the more detailed information found in a schedule of cost of goods manufactured, to plan and control manufacturing activities. Nestlé seeks to increase shareholder value by reducing water usage, improving farmers' operations, and enhancing children's nutrition in developing countries.

 Global View Assignments

Discussion Question 2

Quick Study 18-16

Quick Study 18-17

BTN 18-9

Job Order Costing

Learning Objectives

CONCEPTUAL

C1 Describe important features of job order production.

C2 Explain job cost sheets and how they are used in job order costing.

ANALYTICAL

A1 Apply job order costing in pricing services.

PROCEDURAL

P1 Describe and record the flow of materials costs in job order costing.

P2 Describe and record the flow of labor costs in job order costing.

P3 Describe and record the flow of overhead costs in job order costing.

P4 Determine adjustments for overapplied and underapplied factory overhead.

© Annie Tritt Photography

Drawing Interest

LOS ANGELES—In many cultures, mehndi, temporary "tattoo-like" skin adornment, is part of wedding celebrations. The intricate designs, hand-drawn by mehndi artists with henna paste and often augmented with rhinestones and glitter, are signs of prosperity and happiness. Neha Assar, sole proprietor of **Neha Assar** (**NehaAssar.com**), explains that drawing mehndi enables her to use "creativity, experience and passion. My designs are never copied from books, they are never repeated, and they are always exclusive." Accounting for customized services and products, such as Neha's, involves *job order costing*.

Neha uses direct labor (her own). She draws freehand and estimates that each job takes between four and eight hours. Neha's main raw material is henna paste, made from henna leaves and natural oils. Neha's overhead costs are low—all of her materials and tools fit into one cosmetics toolbox.

Neha applies job order costing in pricing her services. "Each bride has her own unique ideas about how extensive and how intricate they want their designs," explains Neha. "These preferences affect how long it will take me."

"Quality is everything"

—Neha Assar

Large mehndi parties require Neha to hire several assistants. Understanding what services her clients want, and the costs required, enables Neha to properly price her services and hire assistants as needed. Job order costing enables Neha to make informed decisions about costs and selling prices.

Job order costing is also important for manufacturers. Custom home builders, for example, track costs to control those costs. Whether for service providers or manufacturers, job order costing enables entrepreneurs to control and monitor the types of costs that are often the downfall of start-ups.

Neha delivers about 100 mehndi events each year. She recently worked Hollywood Oscar parties, L.A. Fashion Week events, and parties for hip-hop artists. "I still get a little starstruck," Neha says. "I'm a 35-year-old mom, and I'm sitting at this rapper's party in Malibu!"

Neha encourages entrepreneurs to be creative. "Avoid formula and routine," she insists. "Believe in yourself."

Sources: *Neha Assar website,* January 2017; *Wall Street Journal,* December 2, 2015; *YouTube.com/watch?v=IMqFRYfwFxk,* May 11, 2015

JOB ORDER COSTING

This section describes a cost accounting system, job order production and costing, and contrasts job order production with process operations.

Cost Accounting System

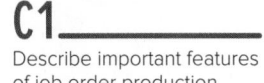

C1
Describe important features of job order production.

A **cost accounting system** accumulates production costs and then assigns them to products and services. Timely information about inventories and costs is especially helpful in managers' efforts to control costs and determine selling prices.

The two basic types of cost accounting systems are *job order costing* and *process costing*. We describe job order costing in this chapter and process costing in the next chapter.

Job Order Production

Many companies produce products individually designed to meet the needs of a specific customer. Each customized product is manufactured separately and its production is called **job order production,** or *job order manufacturing* (also called *customized production,* which is the production of products in response to special orders). Examples of such products or services include special-order machines, a factory building, custom jewelry, wedding invitations, tattoos, and audits by an accounting firm.

Courtesy JJW Images

The production activities for a customized product represent a **job.** A key feature of job order production is the diversity, often called *heterogeneity,* of the products produced. Each customer order differs from another customer order in some important respect. These differences can be large or small. For example, Nike allows custom orders over the Internet, enabling customers to select materials and colors and to personalize their shoes with letters and numbers.

When a job involves producing more than one unit of a custom product, it is often called a **job lot.** Products produced as job lots could include benches for a park, imprinted T-shirts for a 10K race or company picnic, or advertising signs for a chain of stores. Although these orders involve more than one unit, the volume of production is typically low, such as 50 benches, 200 T-shirts, or 100 signs.

Job Order vs. Process Operations

Point: Many professional examinations, including the CPA and CMA exams, require knowledge of job order and process costing.

Process operations, also called *process manufacturing* or *process production,* is the mass production of products in a continuous flow of steps. Unlike job order production, where every product differs depending on customer needs, process operations are designed to mass-produce large quantities of identical products. For example, each year Penn makes millions of tennis balls, and The Hershey Company produces over a billion pounds of chocolate.

Exhibit 19.1 lists important features of job order and process operations. Movies made by Walt Disney and financial audits done by KPMG are examples of job order service operations. Order processing in large mail-order firms like L.L. Bean is an example of a process service operation.

EXHIBIT 19.1

Comparing Job Order and Process Operations

Job Order Operations	Process Operations
• Custom orders	• Repetitive procedures
• Heterogeneous products and services	• Homogeneous products and services
• Low production volume	• High production volume
• High product flexibility	• Low product flexibility
• Low to medium standardization	• High standardization

Production Activities in Job Order Costing

An overview of job order production activity and cost flows is shown in Exhibit 19.2. This exhibit shows the March production activity of Road Warriors, which installs entertainment systems and security devices in cars and trucks. The company customizes any vehicle by adding speakers, amplifiers, video systems, alarms, and reinforced exteriors.

EXHIBIT 19.2

Job Order Production
Activities and Cost Flows

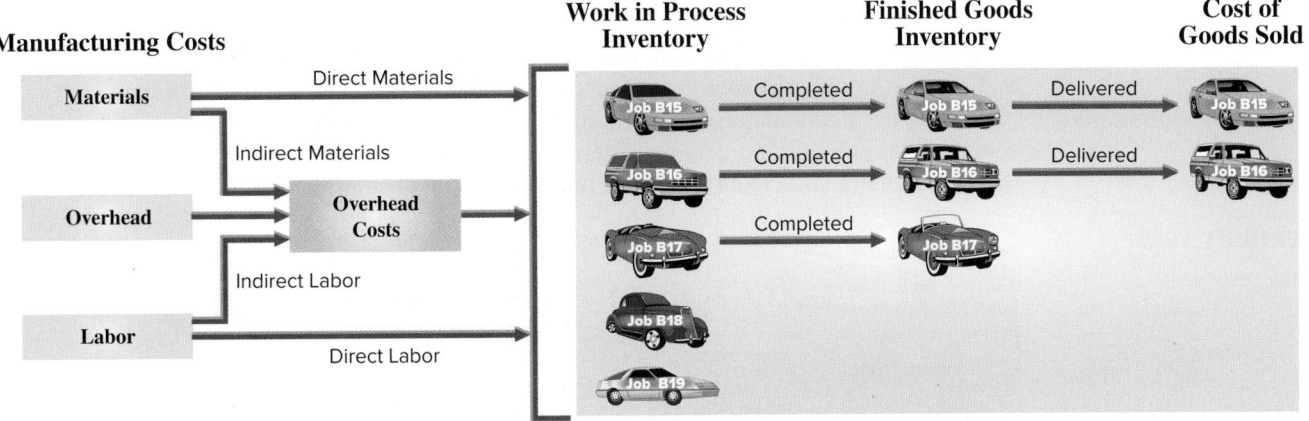

Job order production for Road Warriors requires materials, labor, and overhead costs. Direct materials are used in manufacturing and can be clearly identified with a particular job. Direct labor is effort devoted to a particular job. Overhead costs support production of more than one job. Common overhead items are depreciation on factory buildings and equipment, factory supplies (indirect materials), supervision and maintenance (indirect labor), factory insurance and property taxes, cleaning, and utilities.

Exhibit 19.2 shows that materials, labor, and overhead are added to five jobs started during the month (March). Alarm systems are added to Jobs B15 and B16; Job B17 receives a high-end audio and video entertainment system. Road Warriors completed Jobs B15, B16, and B17 in March and delivered Jobs B15 and B16 to customers. At the end of March, Jobs B18 and B19 remain in work in process inventory and Job B17 is in finished goods inventory.

■ **Decision** Insight

Target Costing   Many producers determine a **target cost** for their jobs. Target cost is determined as follows: Expected selling price − Desired profit = Target cost. If the projected target cost of the job as determined by job costing is too high, the producer can apply *value engineering,* which is a method of determining ways to reduce job cost until the target cost is met. ■

Cost Flows

Manufacturing costs flow through inventory accounts (Raw Materials Inventory, Work in Process Inventory, and Finished Goods Inventory) until the related goods are sold. While a job is being produced, its accumulated costs are kept in **Work in Process Inventory.** When a job is finished, its accumulated costs are transferred from Work in Process Inventory to **Finished Goods Inventory.** When a finished job is delivered to a customer, its accumulated costs are transferred from Finished Goods Inventory to Cost of Goods Sold.

These general ledger inventory accounts, however, do not provide enough cost detail for managers of job order operations to plan and control production activities. Managers need to know the costs of each individual job (or job lot). Subsidiary records store this information about the costs for each individual job. The next section describes the use of these subsidiary records and how they relate to general ledger accounts.

Point: Raw Materials Inventory, Work in Process Inventory, Finished Goods Inventory, and Cost of Goods Sold are general ledger accounts.

Job Cost Sheet

C2

Explain job cost sheets and how they are used in job order costing.

A major aim of a **job order costing system** is to determine the cost of producing each job or job lot. In the case of a job lot, the system also computes the cost per unit. The accounting system must include separate records for each job or job lot to accomplish this.

A **job cost sheet** is a cost record maintained for each job. Exhibit 19.3 shows a job cost sheet for Road Warriors. This job cost sheet identifies the customer, the job number, the costs, and key dates. Only product costs are recorded on job cost sheets. Direct materials and direct labor costs incurred on the job are recorded on this sheet. For Job B15, the direct materials and direct labor costs total $600 and $1,000, respectively. *Estimated* overhead costs are included on job cost sheets, through a process we discuss later in the chapter. For Job B15, estimated overhead costs are $1,600, computed as $1,000 of actual direct labor costs × 160%. When each job is complete, the supervisor enters the completion date and signs the sheet. Managers use job cost sheets to monitor costs incurred to date and to predict and control costs for each job.

Point: Documents (electronic and paper) are crucial in a job order system. The job cost sheet is the cornerstone. It aids in grasping concepts of capitalizing product costs and product cost flow.

EXHIBIT 19.3

Job Cost Sheet

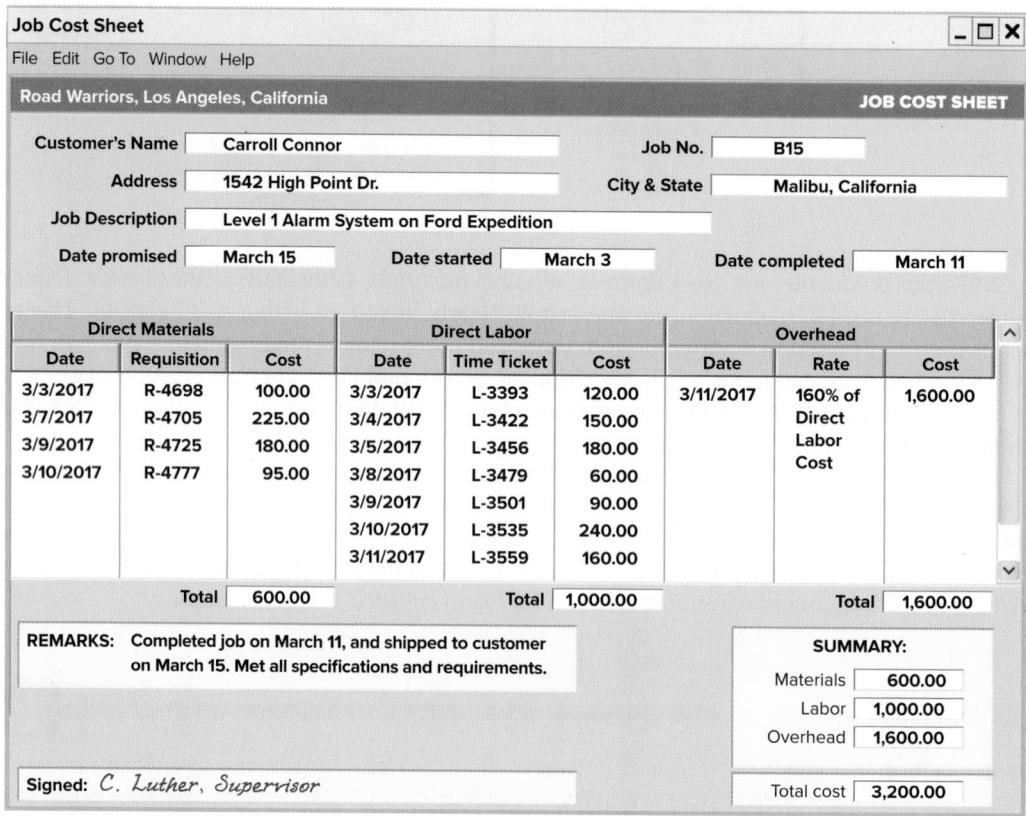

Linking Job Cost Sheets with General Ledger Accounts   The balance in the Work in Process Inventory account at any point in time is the sum of the costs on job cost sheets for all jobs that are not yet complete. The balance in the Finished Goods Inventory account at any point in time is the sum of the costs on job cost sheets for all jobs that *are* complete and awaiting sale. The balance in Cost of Goods Sold is the sum of all costs on job cost sheets for jobs that have been sold and delivered to the customer during that period.

NEED-TO-KNOW 19-1

Job Cost Sheet

C2

A manufacturer's job cost sheet reports direct materials of $1,200 and direct labor of $250 for printing 200 T-shirts for a bikers' reunion. Estimated overhead is computed as 140% of direct labor costs.

1. What is the estimated overhead cost for this job?

2. What is the total cost per T-shirt for this job?

3. What journal entry does the manufacturer make upon completion of this job to transfer costs from work in process to finished goods?

Solution

1. Estimated overhead = $250 × 140% = $350

2. Cost per T-shirt = Total cost/Total number in job lot = $1,800/200 = $9 per shirt

3.

Finished Goods Inventory	1,800	
Work in Process Inventory.		1,800
Transfer cost of completed job.		

Do More: QS 19-7, E 19-2

MATERIALS AND LABOR COST FLOWS

We look at job order costing in more detail, including the source documents for each cost flow.

Materials Cost Flows and Documents

Continuing our example, assume that Road Warriors begins the month (March) with $1,000 in Raw Materials Inventory and $0 balances in the Work in Process Inventory and Finished Goods Inventory accounts. We begin with analysis of the flow of materials costs in Exhibit 19.4. When materials are first received from suppliers, employees count and inspect them and record the items' quantity and cost on a receiving report. The **receiving report** serves as the *source document* for recording materials received in both a materials ledger card and in the general ledger. In nearly all job order cost systems, **materials ledger cards** (or digital files) are perpetual records that are updated each time materials are purchased and each time materials are issued for use in production.

Materials

P1_____

Describe and record the flow of materials costs in job order costing.

Point: Some companies certify certain suppliers based on the quality of their materials. Goods received from these suppliers are not always inspected by the purchaser to save costs.

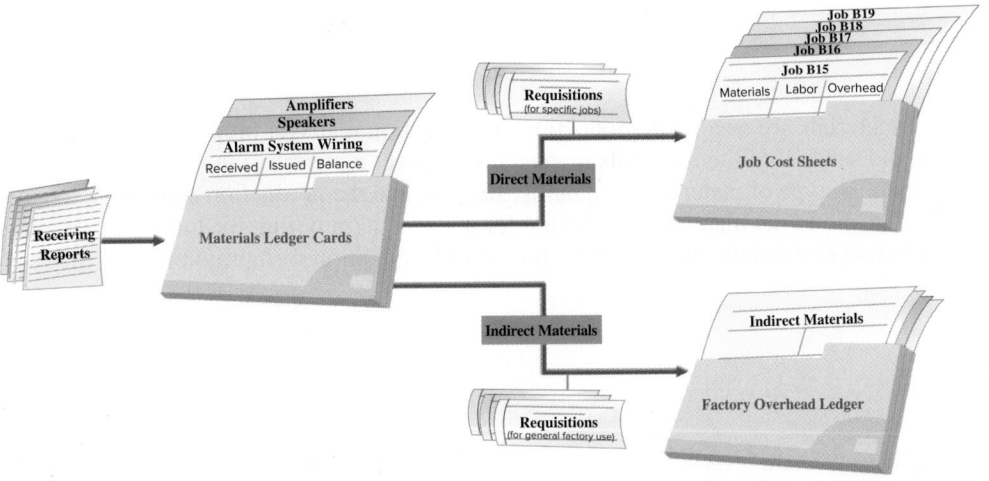

EXHIBIT 19.4

Materials Cost Flows

Materials Purchases   Road Warriors bought $2,750 of materials on credit on March 4, 2017. These include both direct and indirect materials. This purchase is recorded below. Each individual materials ledger card is updated to reflect the added materials.

Mar. 4	Raw Materials Inventory	2,750	
	Accounts Payable.		2,750
	Record purchase of materials for production.		

Assets = Liabilities + Equity
+2,750   +2,750

Materials Use (Requisitions)   Exhibit 19.4 shows that materials can be requisitioned for use either on a specific job (direct materials) or as overhead (indirect materials). Direct materials include costs, such as alarm system wiring, that are easily traced to individual jobs. Indirect materials include costs, such as those for screws, that are not easily traced to jobs. Direct materials costs flow to job cost sheets. Indirect materials costs flow to the Indirect Materials account in the factory overhead ledger, which is a subsidiary ledger controlled by the Factory Overhead account in the general ledger. The factory overhead ledger includes all of the individual overhead costs.

Exhibit 19.5 shows a materials ledger card for one type of material received and issued by Road Warriors. The card identifies the item as alarm system wiring and shows the item's stock number, its location in the storeroom, information about the maximum and minimum quantities that should be available, and the reorder quantity. For example, two units of alarm system wiring were purchased on March 4, 2017, as evidenced by receiving report C-7117. After this purchase the company has three units of alarm system wiring in inventory.

EXHIBIT 19.5

Materials Ledger Card

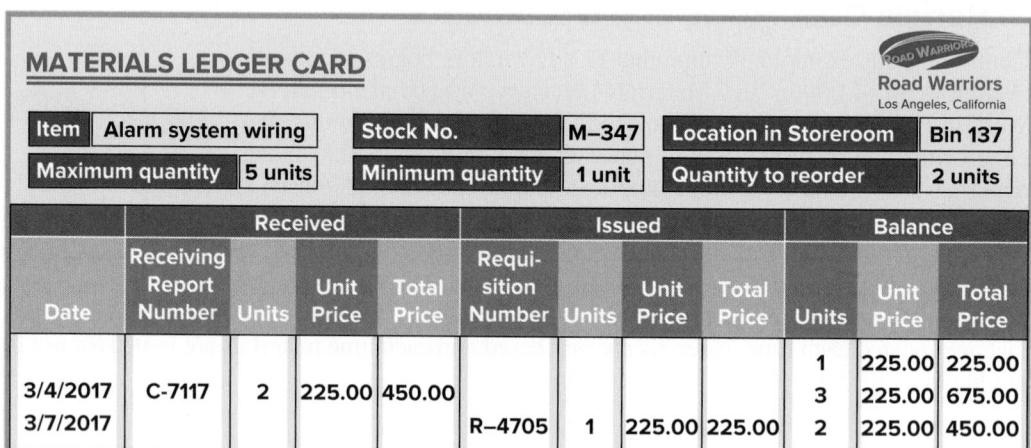

When materials are needed in production, a production manager prepares a **materials requisition** and sends it to the materials manager. For direct materials, the requisition shows the job number, the type of material, the quantity needed, and the production manager's signature. Exhibit 19.6 shows the materials requisition for alarm system wiring for Job B15. For requisitions of indirect materials, the "Job No." line in the requisition form might read "For General Factory Use."

EXHIBIT 19.6

Materials Requisition

	MATERIALS REQUISITION	No. R–4705
Road Warriors Los Angeles, California		
Job No. B15	Date 3/7/2017	
Material Stock No. M–347	Material Description Alarm system wiring	
Quantity Requested 1	Requested By C. Luther	
Quantity Provided 1	Date Provided 3/7/2017	
Filled By M. Bateman	Material Received By C. Luther	
Remarks		

Requisitions are often accumulated by job and recorded in one journal entry. The frequency of entries depends on the job, the industry, and management procedures. In this example, Road Warriors records materials requisitions at the end of each week. The total amounts of materials requisitions are shown below.

Point: Companies can use LIFO, FIFO, or the weighted-average method in computing the cost of materials requisitions.

Direct materials—requisitioned for specific jobs	
Job B15	$ 600
Job B16	300
Job B17	500
Job B18	150
Job B19	250
Total direct materials	**$1,800**
Indirect materials—requisitioned for general factory use	550
Total materials requisitions	$ 2,350

The use of direct materials for the week (including alarm system wiring for Job B15) yields the following entry.

Mar. 7	Work in Process Inventory.............................	1,800	
	Raw Materials Inventory...........................		1,800
	Record use of direct materials.		

Assets = Liabilities + Equity
+1,800
−1,800

This entry is posted both to general ledger accounts and to subsidiary records. Exhibit 19.7 shows the postings to general ledger accounts (Work in Process Inventory and Raw Materials Inventory) and to the job cost sheets (subsidiary records). The exhibit shows summary job cost sheets for all five jobs, and it shows a detailed partial job cost sheet (excerpted from Exhibit 19.3) for Job B15.

Point: Posting to subsidiary records includes debits to job cost sheets and credits to materials ledger cards.

The Raw Materials Inventory account began the month with $1,000 of beginning inventory; it was increased for the March 4 purchase of $2,750. The $1,800 cost of materials used reduces Raw Materials Inventory and increases Work in Process Inventory. The total amount of direct materials used so far ($1,800) is also reflected in the job cost sheets. Later we show the accounting for indirect materials. At this point, it is important to know that requisitions of indirect materials do not directly impact Work in Process Inventory.

EXHIBIT 19.7

Posting Direct Materials Used to the General Ledger and Job Cost Sheets

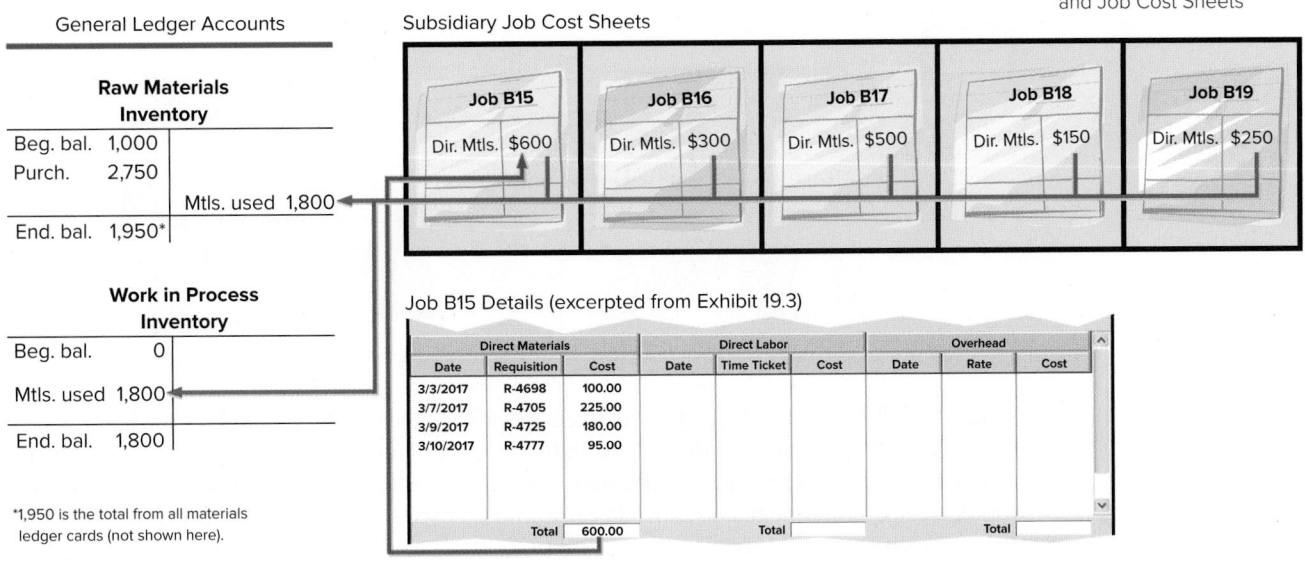

*1,950 is the total from all materials ledger cards (not shown here).

NEED-TO-KNOW 19-2

Recording Direct
Materials

P1

Do More: QS 19-4, E 19-8

Prepare journal entries to record the following two transactions.

1. A manufacturing company purchased $1,200 of materials (on account) for use in production.

2. The company used $200 of direct materials on Job 1 and $350 of direct materials on Job 2.

Solution

Raw Materials Inventory	1,200	
Accounts Payable		1,200
Record purchase of materials on account.		
Work in Process Inventory...	550	
Raw Materials Inventory		550
Record use of direct materials in production.		

P2

Describe and record the
flow of labor costs in job
order costing.

Point: Many employee fraud
schemes involve payroll, including
overstated hours on time tickets.

Labor

Labor Cost Flows and Documents

Exhibit 19.8 shows that labor costs are classified as either direct or indirect. Direct labor costs flow to job cost sheets. To assign direct labor costs to individual jobs, companies use **time tickets** to track how each employee's time is used and to record how much time they spent on each job. This process is often automated: Employees swipe electronic identification badges, and a computer system assigns employees' hours worked to individual jobs. An employee who works on several jobs during a day completes separate time tickets for each job. In all cases, supervisors check and approve the accuracy of time tickets.

EXHIBIT 19.8

Labor Cost Flows

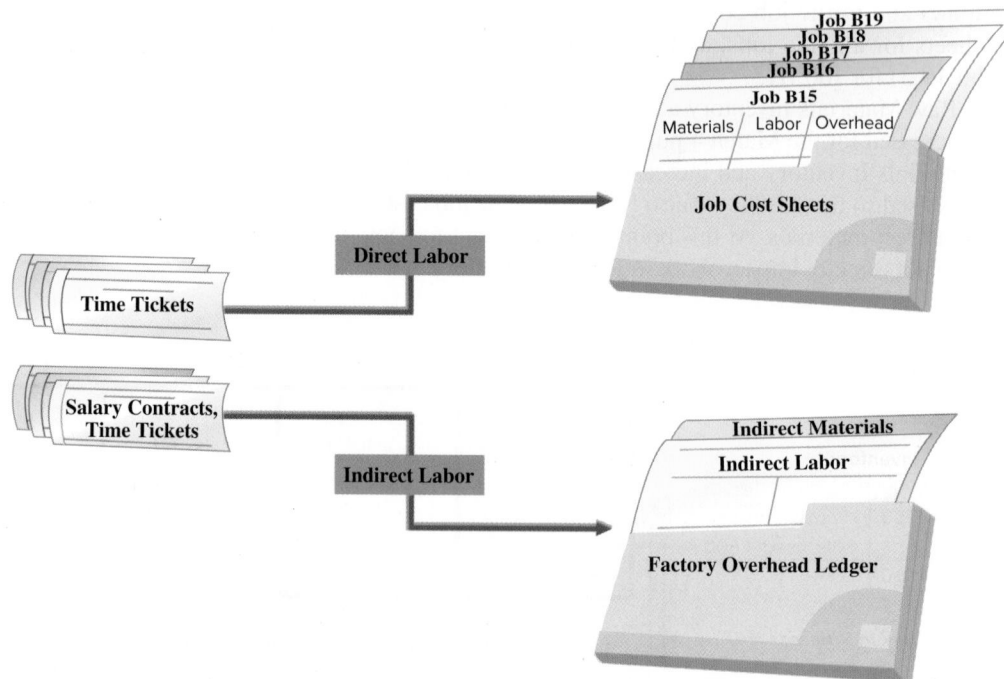

Indirect labor includes factory costs like supervisor salaries and maintenance worker wages. These costs are not assigned directly to individual jobs. Instead, the company determines the amounts of supervisor salaries from their salary contracts and the amounts of maintenance worker wages from time tickets, and classifies those costs as overhead. Indirect labor costs flow to the factory overhead ledger.

Exhibit 19.9 shows a time ticket reporting the time a Road Warrior employee spent working on Job B15. The employee's supervisor signed the ticket to confirm its accuracy. The hourly rate and total labor cost are recorded after the time ticket is turned in.

EXHIBIT 19.9

Time Ticket

Road Warriors
Los Angeles, California

TIME TICKET   No. L–3479

Date March 8 20 17

Employee Name	Employee Number	Job No.
T. Zeller	3969	B15

TIME AND RATE INFORMATION:

Start Time	Finish Time	Elapsed Time	Hourly Rate
9:00	12:00	3.0	$20.00

Remarks

Approved By C. Luther   Total Cost $60.00

Time tickets are often accumulated and recorded in one journal entry. The frequency of these entries varies across companies. In this example, Road Warriors journalizes direct labor monthly. During March, Road Warriors's factory payroll costs total $5,300. Of this amount, $4,200 can be traced directly to jobs, and the remaining $1,100 is classified as indirect labor, as shown below.

Direct labor—traceable to specific jobs

Job B15	$ 1,000
Job B16	800
Job B17	1,100
Job B18	700
Job B19	600
Total direct labor	$4,200
Indirect labor—general factory use	1,100
Total labor cost	$ 5,300

The following entry records direct labor based on all the direct labor time tickets for the month.

Mar. 31	Work in Process Inventory	4,200	
	Factory Wages Payable		4,200
	Record direct labor used for the month.		

Assets = Liabilities + Equity
+4,200   +4,200

This entry is posted to the general ledger accounts, Work in Process Inventory and Factory Wages Payable (or Cash, if paid), and to individual job cost sheets. Exhibit 19.10 shows these postings. The exhibit shows summary job cost sheets for all five jobs, and it shows a partial job cost sheet (excerpted from Exhibit 19.3) for Job B15.

Time tickets are used to determine how much of the monthly direct labor cost ($4,200) to assign to specific jobs. This total matches the amount of direct labor posted to the Work in Process Inventory general ledger account. After this entry is posted, the balance in Work in Process Inventory is $6,000, consisting of $1,800 of direct materials and $4,200 of direct labor. Later we show the accounting for indirect labor, which does not impact Work in Process Inventory.

EXHIBIT 19.10

Posting Direct Labor to General Ledger and Job Cost Sheets

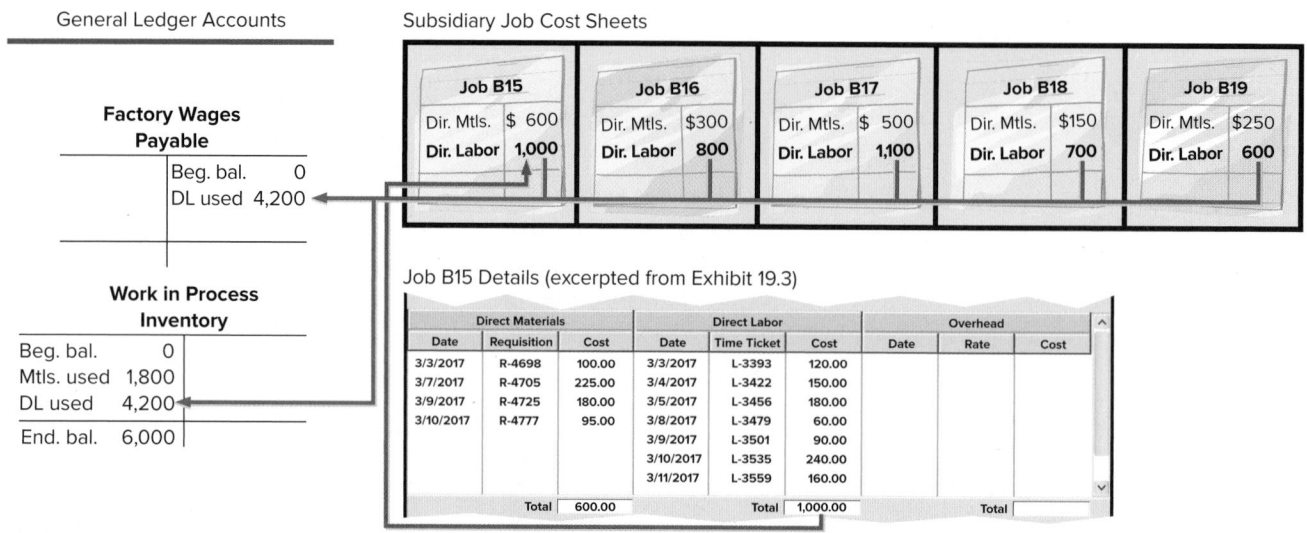

NEED-TO-KNOW 19-3

Recording Direct Labor

P2

A manufacturing company used $5,400 of direct labor in production activities in May. Of this amount, $3,100 of direct labor was used on Job A1 and $2,300 of direct labor was used on Job A2. Prepare the journal entry to record direct labor used.

Solution

Do More: QS 19-5, E 19-9

Work in Process Inventory...	5,400	
Factory Wages Payable...		5,400
Record direct labor used in production.		

OVERHEAD COST FLOWS

P3

Describe and record the flow of overhead costs in job order costing.

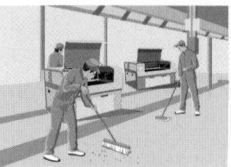

Overhead

Unlike direct materials and direct labor, overhead costs are not traced directly to individual jobs. Still, each job's total cost must include *estimated* overhead costs.

Overhead Process   The accounting for overhead costs follows the four-step process shown in Exhibit 19.11. Overhead accounting requires managers to first estimate what total overhead costs will be for the coming period. We cannot wait until the end of a period to apply overhead to jobs because managers' decisions require up-to-date costs. Overhead cost, even if it

EXHIBIT 19.11

Four-Step Process for Overhead

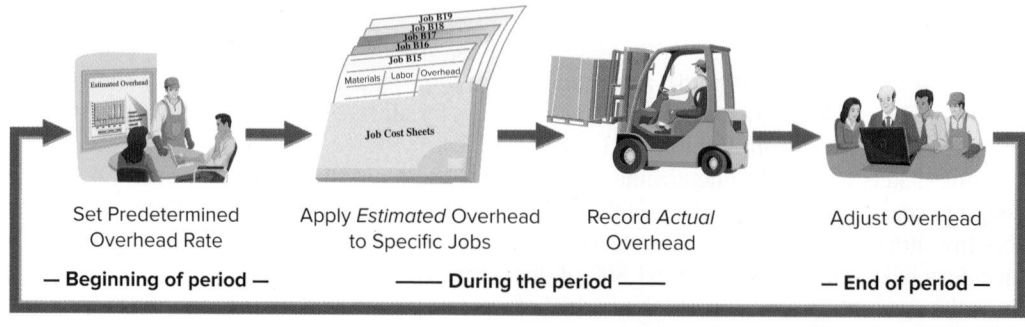

is not exactly precise, is needed to estimate a job's total costs before its completion. Such estimated costs are useful in setting prices and identifying costs that are out of control. At the end of the year, the company adjusts its estimated overhead to the actual amount of overhead incurred for that year, and then considers whether to change its predetermined overhead rate for the next year. We discuss each of these steps.

Set Predetermined Overhead Rate

Estimating overhead in advance requires a **predetermined overhead rate,** also called *predetermined overhead allocation* (or *application*) *rate.* This rate requires an estimate of total overhead cost and an activity base such as total direct labor cost *before* the start of the period. Exhibit 19.12 shows the formula for computing a predetermined overhead rate (estimates are commonly based on annual amounts). This rate is used during the period to apply estimated overhead to jobs, based on each job's *actual* usage of the activity. Some companies use multiple predetermined overhead rates for different types of products and services.

Point: Predetermined overhead rates can be estimated using mathematical equations, statistical analysis, or professional experience.

$$\text{Predetermined overhead rate} = \frac{\text{Estimated overhead costs}}{\text{Estimated activity base}}$$

EXHIBIT 19.12

Predetermined Overhead Rate Formula

Overhead Activity Base   We apply overhead by linking it to another factor used in production, such as direct labor or machine hours. The factor to which overhead costs are linked is known as the *activity* (or *allocation*) *base.* There should be a "cause and effect" relation between the base and overhead costs. A manager must think carefully about how many and which activity bases to use. This managerial decision influences the accuracy with which overhead costs are applied to individual jobs, which might impact a manager's decisions for pricing or performance evaluation.

© Royalty-Free/Corbis

Apply Estimated Overhead

Road Warriors applies (also termed *allocates, assigns,* or *charges*) overhead by linking it to direct labor costs. At the start of the current year, management estimates total direct labor costs of $125,000 and total overhead costs of $200,000. Using these estimates, management computes its predetermined overhead rate as 160% of direct labor cost ($200,000 ÷ $125,000). Earlier we showed that Road Warriors used $4,200 of direct labor in March. We now apply the predetermined overhead rate of 160% to get $6,720 (equal to $4,200 × 1.60) of estimated overhead for March. The entry is:

Point: Factory Overhead is a temporary account that holds costs. The Factory Overhead account is closed to zero at the end of the year.

Mar. 31	Work in Process Inventory............................	6,720	
	Factory Overhead................................		6,720
	Apply overhead at 160% of direct labor.		

The $6,720 of overhead is then applied to each individual job based on the amount of the activity base that job used (in this example, direct labor). Exhibit 19.13 shows these calculations for March's production activity.

EXHIBIT 19.13

Applying Estimated Overhead to Specific Jobs

Job	Direct Labor Cost	Predetermined Overhead Rate*	Applied Overhead
B15	$1,000	1.6	$1,600
B16	800	1.6	1,280
B17	1,100	1.6	1,760
B18	700	1.6	1,120
B19	600	1.6	960
Total............	$4,200		$6,720

*160% of direct labor cost

After the applied overhead is recorded and the amounts of overhead applied to each job are determined (Exhibit 19.13), postings to general ledger accounts and to individual job cost sheets follow, as in Exhibit 19.14. For all five jobs, summary job cost sheets are presented first, and then a more detailed partial job cost sheet (excerpted from Exhibit 19.3) is shown for Job B15. (Compare the partial job cost sheet for Job B15 in this exhibit to the complete version in Exhibit 19.3.)

EXHIBIT 19.14

Posting Overhead to General Ledger and Job Cost Sheets

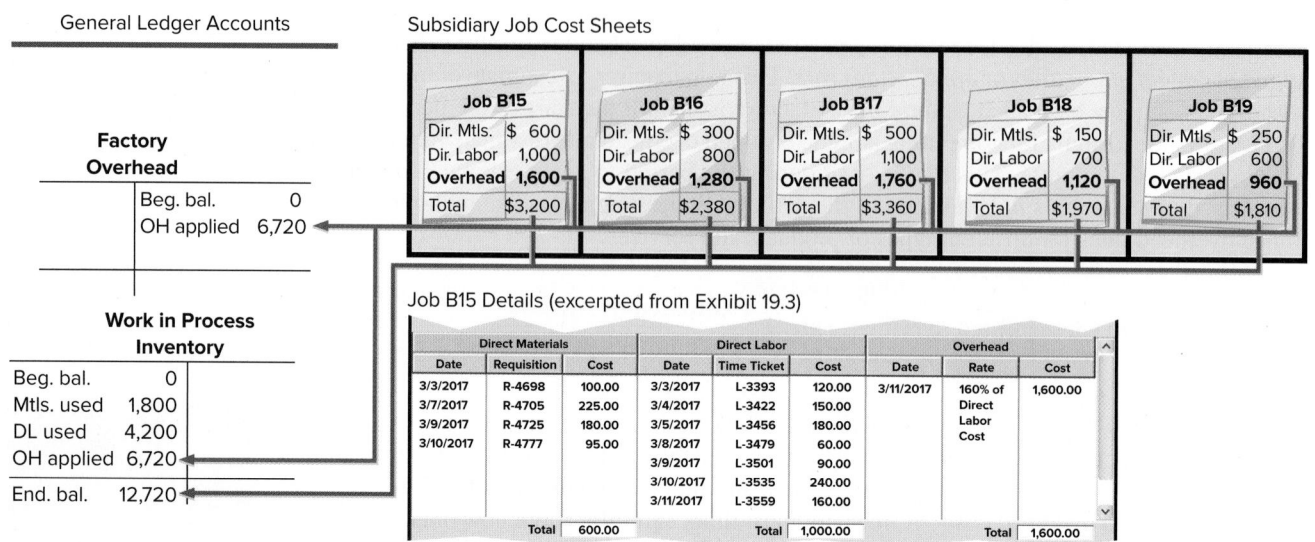

At this point, $6,720 of estimated overhead has been posted to general ledger accounts and to individual job cost sheets. In addition, the ending balance in the Work in Process Inventory account ($12,720) equals the sum of the ending balances in the job cost sheets. In the next section we discuss how to record *actual* overhead.

 **19-4**

Recording Applied Overhead

P3

A manufacturing company estimates it will incur $240,000 of overhead costs in the next year. The company applies overhead using machine hours and estimates it will use 1,600 machine hours in the next year. During the month of June, the company used 80 machine hours on Job 1 and 70 machine hours on Job 2.

1. Compute the predetermined overhead rate to be used to apply overhead during the year.

2. Determine how much overhead should be applied to Job 1 and to Job 2 for June.

3. Prepare the journal entry to record overhead applied for June.

Solution

1. $240,000/1,600 = $150 per machine hour

2. 80 × $150 = $12,000 applied to Job 1; 70 × $150 = $10,500 applied to Job 2

3.

Work in Process Inventory	22,500	
Factory Overhead		22,500
Record applied overhead.		

Do More: QS 19-6, QS 19-7, QS 19-8, E 19-10

Record Actual Overhead

Having shown how estimated overhead costs are accounted for and included in job cost sheets, we now show the accounting for actual overhead costs. Factory overhead includes all factory costs other than direct materials and direct labor. Two major sources of overhead costs are *indirect* materials and *indirect* labor. These costs are recorded from materials requisition forms for indirect materials and from salary contracts or time tickets for indirect labor. Other sources of information on overhead costs include (1) vouchers authorizing payment for factory items such as supplies or utilities and (2) adjusting journal entries for costs such as depreciation on factory assets.

Factory overhead costs are recorded with debits to the Factory Overhead general ledger account and with credits to various accounts. While journal entries for different types of overhead costs might be recorded with varying frequency, in our example we assume these entries are made at the end of the month.

Point: Companies also incur *non-manufacturing* costs, such as advertising, salespersons' salaries, and depreciation on assets not used in production. These types of costs are not considered overhead, but instead are treated as period costs and charged directly to the income statement.

Record Indirect Materials Used

During March, Road Warriors incurred $550 of actual indirect materials costs, as supported by materials requisitions. The use of these indirect materials yields the following entry.

Mar. 31	Factory Overhead	550	
	Raw Materials Inventory..........................		550
	Record indirect materials used during the month.		

This entry is posted to the general ledger accounts, Factory Overhead and Raw Materials Inventory, and is posted to Indirect Materials in the subsidiary factory overhead ledger. Unlike the recording of *direct* materials, actual *indirect* materials costs incurred are *not* recorded in Work in Process Inventory and are not posted to job cost sheets.

Record Indirect Labor Used

During March, Road Warriors incurred $1,100 of actual indirect labor costs. These costs might be supported by time tickets for maintenance workers or by salary contracts for production supervisors. The use of this indirect labor yields the following entry.

Mar. 31	Factory Overhead	1,100	
	Factory Wages Payable		1,100
	Record indirect labor used during the month.		

This entry is posted to the general ledger accounts, Factory Overhead and Factory Wages Payable, and is posted to Indirect Labor in the subsidiary factory overhead ledger. Unlike the recording of *direct* labor, actual *indirect* labor costs incurred are *not* recorded in Work in Process Inventory and are not posted to job cost sheets.

Record Other Overhead Costs

During March, Road Warriors incurred $5,270 of actual other overhead costs. These costs could include items such as factory building rent, depreciation on the factory building, factory utilities, and other costs indirectly related to production activities. These costs are recorded with debits to Factory Overhead and credits to other accounts such as Cash, Accounts Payable, Utilities Payable, and Accumulated Depreciation—Factory Equipment. The entry to record these other overhead costs for March is as follows.

Mar. 31	Factory Overhead	5,270	
	Accumulated Depreciation—Factory Equipment		2,400
	Rent Payable....................................		1,620
	Utilities Payable		250
	Prepaid Insurance...............................		1,000
	Record actual overhead costs for the month.		

This entry is posted to the general ledger account, Factory Overhead, and is posted to separate accounts for each of the overhead items in the subsidiary factory overhead ledger. These actual overhead costs are *not* recorded in Work in Process Inventory and are not posted to job cost sheets. Only estimated overhead is recorded in Work in Process Inventory and posted to job cost sheets.

NEED-TO-KNOW 19-5

Recording Actual
Overhead

P3

A manufacturing company used $400 of indirect materials and $2,000 of indirect labor during the month. The company also incurred $1,200 for depreciation on general-use factory equipment, $500 for depreciation on office equipment, and $300 for factory utilities. Prepare the necessary journal entries.

Solution

Factory Overhead...	3,900	
Raw Materials Inventory..		400
Factory Wages Payable...		2,000
Accumulated Depreciation—Factory Equipment*..........................		1,200
Utilities Payable...		300
Record actual overhead costs used in production.		
Depreciation Expense	500	
Accumulated Depreciation—Office Equipment...........................		500
Record depreciation on office equipment.		

Do More: E 19-6, E 19-10

*Depreciation on office equipment is a period cost and is excluded from factory overhead.

Summary of Cost Flows

EXHIBIT 19.15

Cost Flows and Reports

In this section we summarize the flow of costs. Exhibit 19.15 shows how costs for a manufacturing company flow to its financial statements.

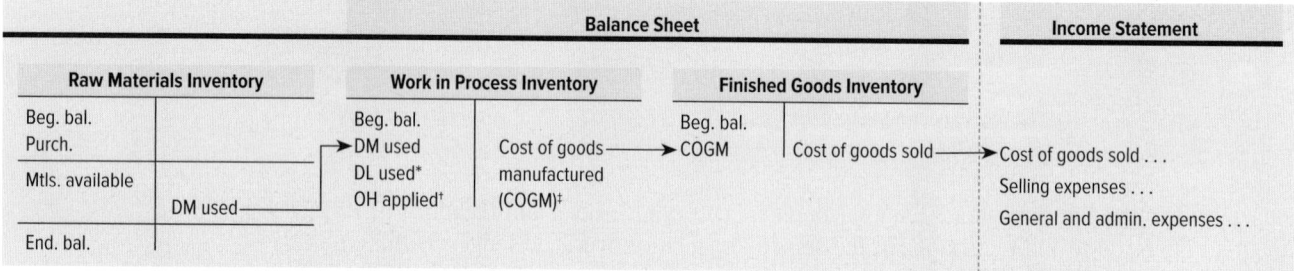

* From time tickets.   † Predetermined overhead rate × Actual amount of activity base used.   ‡ Reported on schedule of cost of goods manufactured.

Exhibit 19.15 shows that direct materials used, direct labor used, and factory overhead applied flow through the Work in Process Inventory and Finished Goods balance sheet accounts. The cost of goods manufactured (COGM) is computed and shown on the schedule of cost of goods manufactured. When goods are sold, their costs are transferred from Finished Goods Inventory to the income statement as cost of goods sold. For Road Warriors, the journal entries to record the flow of costs from Work in Process Inventory to Finished Goods Inventory, and from Finished Goods Inventory to Cost of Goods Sold, are:

Point: Sales revenue is also recorded (see Exhibit 19.17).

Mar. 31			
	Finished Goods Inventory...............................	8,940	
	Work in Process Inventory...........................		8,940
	Transfer cost of goods manufactured.		
	Cost of Goods Sold	5,580	
	Finished Goods Inventory		5,580
	Record cost of goods sold.		

Period costs (selling expenses and general and administrative expenses) do not impact inventory accounts. As a result, they do not impact cost of goods sold, and they are not reported on the schedule of cost of goods manufactured. They are reported on the income statement as operating expenses.

Cost Flows—Road Warriors We next show the flow of costs and their reporting for our Road Warriors example. The upper part of Exhibit 19.16 shows the flow of Road Warriors's product costs through general ledger accounts. Arrow lines are numbered to show the flows of costs for March. Each numbered cost flow reflects journal entries made in March. The lower part of Exhibit 19.16 shows summarized job cost sheets at the end of March. The sum of costs assigned to the two jobs in process ($1,970 + $1,810) equals the $3,780 balance in Work in Process Inventory. Costs assigned to the completed Job B17 equal the $3,360 balance in Finished Goods Inventory. These balances in Work in Process Inventory and Finished Goods Inventory are reported on the end-of-period balance sheet. The sum of costs assigned to the sold Jobs B15 and B16 ($3,200 + $2,380) equals the $5,580 balance in Cost of Goods Sold. This amount is reported on the income statement for the period.

Point: Ending balances on job cost sheets must equal ending balances in general ledger accounts.

EXHIBIT 19.16

Job Order Cost Flows and Ending Job Cost Sheets

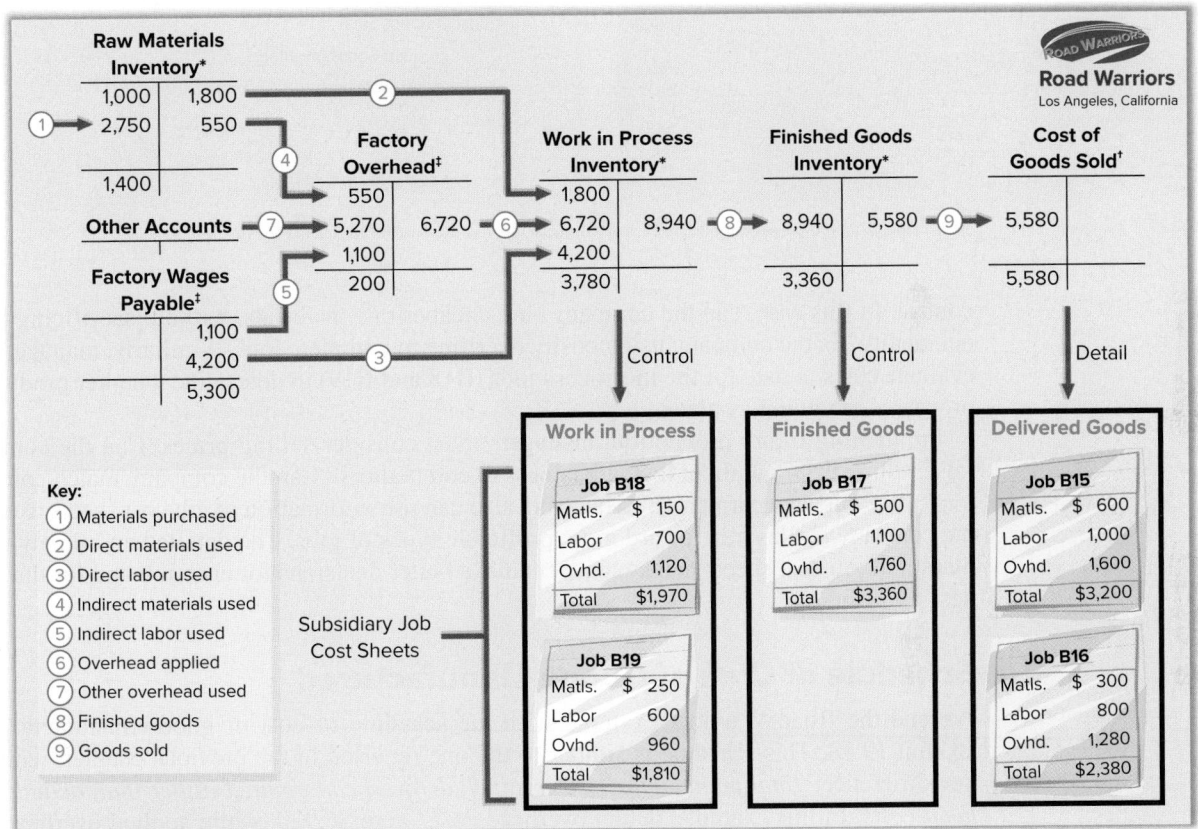

* The ending balances in the inventory accounts are reported on the balance sheet.

† The Cost of Goods Sold balance is reported on the income statement.

‡ Factory Overhead is considered a temporary account; when these costs are applied to jobs, its balance is reduced.

Exhibit 19.17 shows the journal entries made in March. Each entry is numbered to link with the arrow lines in Exhibit 19.16. In addition, Exhibit 19.17 concludes with the summary journal entry to record the sales (on account) of Jobs B15 and B16.

Using Job Cost Sheets for Managerial Decisions

Managers' decisions depend on timely information in job cost sheets. In *controlling* operations, managers must assess the profitability of the company's products or services. Road Warriors completed and sold two jobs (B15 and B16) and earned a total gross profit of $2,280 ($7,780 selling price − $5,580 cost of goods sold). If this gross profit is higher than expected, managers will try to determine if there are production efficiencies that can be applied to future jobs. For example, has the business found a way to reduce the amount of direct labor? If gross profit is less than expected, managers will determine if costs are out of

EXHIBIT 19.17

Entries for Job Order Costing*

①	Raw Materials Inventory	2,750		⑥	Work in Process Inventory	6,720	
	Accounts Payable		2,750		Factory Overhead		6,720
	Acquired raw materials.				*Apply overhead at 160% of direct labor.*		
②	Work in Process Inventory	1,800		⑦	Factory Overhead	5,270	
	Raw Materials Inventory		1,800		Cash (and other accounts)		5,270
	Assign costs of direct materials used.				*Record factory overhead costs such as*		
③	Work in Process Inventory	4,200			*insurance, utilities, rent, and depreciation.*		
	Factory Wages Payable		4,200	⑧	Finished Goods Inventory	8,940	
	Assign costs of direct labor used.				Work in Process Inventory		8,940
④	Factory Overhead	550			*Record completion of Jobs B15, B16, and B17.*		
	Raw Materials Inventory		550	⑨	Cost of Goods Sold	5,580	
	Record use of indirect materials.				Finished Goods Inventory		5,580
⑤	Factory Overhead	1,100			*Record cost of goods sold for Jobs B15 and B16.*		
	Factory Wages Payable		1,100	⑩	Accounts Receivable	7,780	
	Record indirect labor costs.				Sales		7,780
					Record sale of Jobs B15 and B16.		

* Exhibit 19.17 provides summary journal entries. *Actual* overhead is debited to Factory Overhead. *Applied* overhead is credited to Factory Overhead.

control. In this case, can the company find cheaper raw materials, without sacrificing product quality? Is the company using costly overtime to complete jobs? Similarly, managers can evaluate costs to date for the in-process jobs (B18 and B19) to determine whether production processes are going as planned.

In *planning* future production, managers must consider selling prices. Can the company raise selling prices without losing business to competitors? Can the company match competitors' price cuts and earn profit? Managers also can use information in job cost sheets to adjust the company's sales mix toward more profitable types of jobs. The detailed and timely information in job cost sheets helps managers make better decisions for each job and for the business as a whole.

Schedule of Cost of Goods Manufactured

Work in Process Inventory		
Beg. bal.	0	
DM. used	1,800	
DL used	4,200	
OH applied	6,720	
Ttl mfg. costs	12,720	
		COGM 8,940
End. bal.	3,780	

We end the Road Warriors example with the schedule of cost of goods manufactured in Exhibit 19.18. This schedule is similar to the one reported in the previous chapter, with one key difference: *Total manufacturing costs include overhead applied rather than actual overhead costs.* In this example, actual overhead costs were $6,920, while applied overhead was $6,720. We discuss how to account for the difference between applied and actual overhead in the next section.

EXHIBIT 19.18

Schedule of Cost of Goods Manufactured

ROAD WARRIORS
Road Warriors
Los Angeles, California
Schedule of Cost of Goods Manufactured
For the Month of March, 2017

Direct materials used	$ 1,800
Direct labor used	4,200
Factory overhead applied*	6,720
Total manufacturing costs	$12,720
Add: Work in process, March 1, 2017	0
Total cost of work in process	12,720
Less: Work in process, March 31, 2017	3,780
Cost of goods manufactured	$ 8,940

Point: Companies sometimes use more detailed schedules of cost of goods manufactured, as seen in the previous chapter.

* Actual overhead = $6,920. Overhead is $200 underapplied.

ADJUSTING OVERHEAD

Refer to the debits in the Factory Overhead account in Exhibit 19.16 (or Exhibit 19.17). The total cost of actual factory overhead incurred during March is $6,920 ($550 + $5,270 + $1,100). The $6,920 of actual overhead costs does not equal the $6,720 of overhead applied to work in process inventory (see ⑥). This leaves a debit balance of $200 in the Factory Overhead account. Because it is hard to precisely forecast future costs, actual overhead rarely equals applied overhead. Companies usually wait until the end of the year to adjust the Factory Overhead account for differences between actual and applied overhead. We show how this is done in the next section.

Factory Overhead Account

Exhibit 19.19 shows a Factory Overhead account. The company applies overhead (credits the Factory Overhead account) using a predetermined rate estimated at the beginning of the year. During the year, the company records actual overhead costs with debits to the Factory Overhead account. At year-end we determine whether the applied overhead is more or less than actual overhead:

EXHIBIT 19.19

Factory Overhead T-account

Factory Overhead	
Actual amounts	Applied amounts

- When *less* overhead is applied than is actually incurred, the remaining debit balance in the Factory Overhead account is called **underapplied overhead.**
- When *more* overhead is applied than is actually incurred, the resulting credit balance in the Factory Overhead account is called **overapplied overhead.**

When overhead is underapplied, it means that individual jobs have not been charged enough overhead during the year, and cost of goods sold for the year is too low. When overhead is overapplied, it means that jobs have been charged too much overhead during the year, and cost of goods sold is too high. In either case, a journal entry is needed to adjust Factory Overhead and Cost of Goods Sold. Exhibit 19.20 summarizes this entry, assuming the difference between applied and actual overhead is not material.

Example: If we do not adjust for underapplied overhead, will net income be overstated or understated? *Answer:* Overstated.

EXHIBIT 19.20

Adjusting Factory Overhead

Overhead Costs	Factory Overhead Balance	Overhead Is	Adjusting Journal Entry Required	
Actual > Applied	Debit	Underapplied	Cost of Goods Sold.	#
			Factory Overhead	#
Actual < Applied	Credit	Overapplied	Factory Overhead.	#
			Cost of Goods Sold	#

Adjust Underapplied or Overapplied Overhead

To illustrate, assume that Road Warriors applied $200,000 of overhead to jobs during 2017, which is the amount of overhead estimated in advance for the year. We further assume that Road Warriors incurred a total of $200,480 of actual overhead costs during 2017. This means, at the end of the year, the Factory Overhead account has a debit balance of $480. This amount is the difference between estimated (applied) and actual overhead costs for the year.

The $480 debit balance reflects manufacturing costs not assigned to jobs. This means the balances in Work in Process Inventory, Finished Goods Inventory, and Cost of Goods Sold do not include all production costs incurred. However, the difference between applied and actual overhead in this case is immaterial, and it is closed to Cost of Goods Sold with the following adjusting entry.

P4

Determine adjustments for overapplied and underapplied factory overhead.

Point: When the underapplied or overapplied overhead is material, the amount is normally allocated to the cost of goods sold, finished goods inventory, and work in process inventory accounts. This process is covered in advanced courses.

Dec. 31	Cost of Goods Sold	480	
	Factory Overhead.		480
	Adjust for underapplied overhead costs.		

The $480 debit (increase) to Cost of Goods Sold reduces income by $480. After this entry, the Factory Overhead account has a zero balance. Also, Cost of Goods Sold reflects actual overhead costs for the period. If instead we had overapplied overhead at the end of the period, we would debit Factory Overhead and credit Cost of Goods Sold for the amount.

NEED-TO-KNOW 19-6

Adjusting Overhead

P4

A manufacturing company applied $300,000 of overhead to its jobs during the year. For the independent scenarios below, prepare the journal entry to adjust over- or underapplied overhead. Assume the adjustment amounts are not material.

1. Actual overhead costs incurred during the year equal $305,000.

2. Actual overhead costs incurred during the year equal $298,500.

Solution

1.

Cost of Goods Sold..	5,000	
Factory Overhead		5,000
Close underapplied overhead to Cost of Goods Sold.		

2.

Factory Overhead..	1,500	
Cost of Goods Sold		1,500
Close overapplied overhead to Cost of Goods Sold.		

Do More: QS 19-11, QS 19-12, E 19-13, E 19-14

Job Order Costing of Services

Job order costing also applies to service companies. Most service companies meet customers' needs by performing a custom service for a specific customer. Examples include an accountant auditing a client's financial statements, an interior designer remodeling an office, a wedding consultant planning and supervising a reception, and a lawyer defending a client.

Job order costing has some important differences for service firms:

- Most service firms have neither raw materials inventory nor finished goods inventory. They do, however, have inventories of supplies, and they can have work in process inventory. Often these supplies are immaterial and are considered overhead costs.

- Direct labor is often used to apply overhead because service firms do not use direct materials.

- Service firms typically use different account titles, for example **Services in Process Inventory** and **Services Overhead.**

Exhibit 19.21 shows the flow of costs for a service firm called AdWorld, a developer of advertising materials. During the month, AdWorld worked on custom advertising campaigns for clients that wanted ads for three different platforms: mobile devices, television, and radio. In the following Decision Analysis section, we show an example of using job order costing to price advertising services for AdWorld.

EXHIBIT 19.21

Flow of Costs for Service Firms

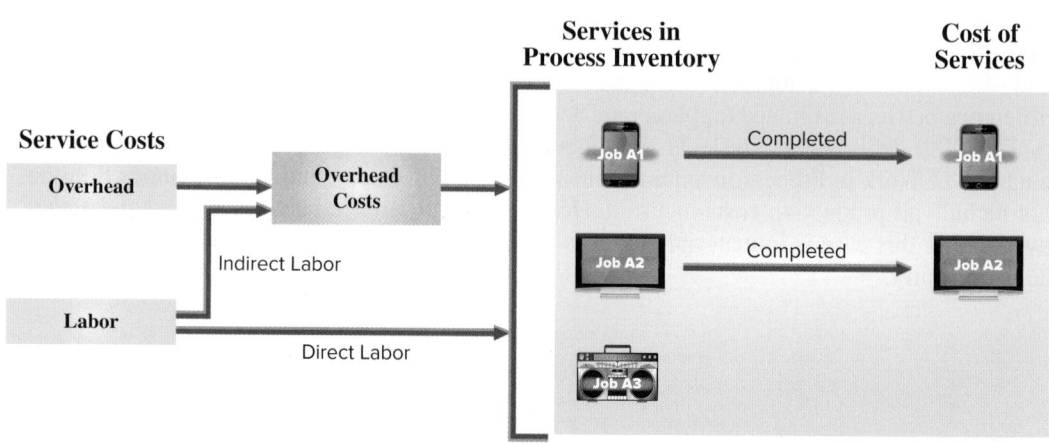

Decision Maker

Management Consultant   One of your tasks is to control and manage costs for a consulting company. At the end of a recent month, you find that three consulting jobs were completed and two are 60% complete. Each unfinished job is estimated to cost $10,000 and to earn a revenue of $12,000. You are unsure how to recognize work in process inventory and record costs and revenues. Do you recognize any inventory? If so, how much? How much revenue is recorded for unfinished jobs this month? ■ [*Answer:* Service companies (such as this consulting firm) do not recognize work in process inventory or finished goods inventory. For the two jobs that are 60% complete, you could recognize revenues and costs at 60% of the total expected amounts. This means you could recognize revenue of $7,200 (0.60 × $12,000) and costs of $6,000 (0.60 × $10,000), yielding net income of $1,200 from each job.]

SUSTAINABILITY AND ACCOUNTING

Professional service firms in accounting, consulting, law, and financial services compete for highly talented employees with strong technical skills. In addition, a more diverse workforce is likely to lead to different points of view that can arguably produce even better services and ultimately more profit for the company. Enhancing workforce diversity can also help attract and retain talented people.

Although workforce diversity is typically not recorded on job cost sheets, many companies measure and report it. Along these lines, the Sustainability Accounting Standards Board has developed suggested reporting guidelines for professional service firms. The SASB recommends that companies disclose information on gender and ethnicity for both senior management employees and all other employees.

Consistent with SASB guidelines, the United States Postal Service (USPS), a leading employer of women and minorities, discloses that women comprise roughly 40% and minorities comprise roughly 40% of its overall workforce. Moreover, roughly 21% of USPS's employees are black, 8% Hispanic, and 8% Asian.

Neha Assar, the focus of this chapter's opening feature, focuses her sustainability efforts on raw materials. Neha uses only 100% natural and organic products and does *not* use any chemicals or dyes. This enables her to offer services that are completely nontoxic and safe—a very sustainable combination of raw materials.

Courtesy of Neha Assar

Pricing for Services      **Decision Analysis**

A1
Apply job order costing in pricing services.

The chapter described job order costing mainly within a manufacturing setting. However, service providers also use job order costing. Consider AdWorld, an advertising agency that develops web-based ads (and ads for other types of media). Each of its customers has unique requirements, so costs for each individual job must be tracked separately.

AdWorld uses two types of labor: web designers ($65 per hour) and computer staff ($50 per hour). It also incurs overhead costs that it assigns using two different predetermined overhead allocation rates: $125 per designer hour and $96 per staff hour. For each job, AdWorld must estimate the number of designer and staff hours needed. Then, total costs of each job are determined using the procedures in the chapter.

To illustrate, a chip manufacturer requested a quote from AdWorld for an advertising engagement. AdWorld estimates that the job will require 43 designer hours and 61 staff hours, with the following total estimated cost for this job.

AdWorld Estimated Job Cost—Advertising Services		
Direct Labor		
Designers (43 hours × $65).....................	$2,795	
Staff (61 hours × $50).........................	3,050	
Total direct labor............................		$ 5,845
Overhead		
Designer related (43 hours × $125).............	5,375	
Staff related (61 hours × $96).................	5,856	
Total overhead		11,231
Total estimated job cost......................		$17,076

AdWorld can use this cost information to help determine the price quote for the job (see *Decision Maker,* **Sales Manager,** below).

Another source of information that AdWorld must consider is the market, that is, how much competitors will quote for this job. Competitor information is often unavailable; therefore, AdWorld's managers must use estimates based on their assessment of the competitive environment.

 Decision Maker

Sales Manager   As AdWorld's sales manager, assume that you estimate costs pertaining to a proposed job as $17,076. Your normal pricing policy is to apply a markup of 18% from total costs. However, you learn that three other agencies are likely to bid for the same job, and that their quotes will range from $16,500 to $22,000. What price should you quote? What factors other than cost must you consider? ■   [*Answer:* The price based on AdWorld's normal pricing policy is $20,150 ($17,076 × 1.18), which is within the price range offered by competitors. One option is to apply normal pricing policy and quote a price of $20,150. It is, however, useful to assess competitor pricing, especially in terms of service quality and other benefits. Although price is an input customers use to select suppliers, factors such as quality and timeliness (responsiveness) of suppliers are important. Accordingly, the price can reflect such factors.]

NEED-TO-KNOW 19-7

COMPREHENSIVE

The following information reflects Walczak Company's job order production activities for May.

Raw materials purchases..............	$16,000
Factory payroll cost	15,400
Overhead costs incurred	
Indirect materials..................	5,000
Indirect labor	3,500
Other factory overhead	9,500

Walczak's predetermined overhead rate is 150% of direct labor cost. Costs are applied to the three jobs worked on during May as follows.

	Job 401	Job 402	Job 403
Work in process inventory, April 30			
Direct materials	$3,600		
Direct labor...........................	1,700		
Applied overhead	2,550		
Costs during May			
Direct materials	3,550	$3,500	$1,400
Direct labor...........................	5,100	6,000	800
Applied overhead......................	?	?	?
Status on May 31	**Finished (sold)**	**Finished (unsold)**	**In process**

Required

1. Determine the total cost of:

   a. The April 30 inventory of jobs in process.

   b. Materials (direct and indirect) used during May.

   c. Labor (direct and indirect) used during May.

   d. Factory overhead incurred and applied during May and the amount of any over- or underapplied overhead on May 31.

   e. The total cost of each job as of May 31, the May 31 inventories of both work in process and finished goods, and the cost of goods sold during May.

2. Prepare summarized journal entries for the month to record:

   a. Materials purchases (on credit), direct materials used in production, direct labor used in production, and overhead applied.

   b. Actual overhead costs, including indirect materials, indirect labor, and other overhead costs.

   c. Transfer of each completed job to the Finished Goods Inventory account.

   d. Cost of goods sold.

   e. The sale (on account) of Job 401 for $35,000.

   f. Removal of any underapplied or overapplied overhead from the Factory Overhead account. (Assume the amount is not material.)

3. Prepare a schedule of cost of goods manufactured for May.

PLANNING THE SOLUTION

- Determine the cost of the April 30 work in process inventory by totaling the materials, labor, and applied overhead costs for Job 401.
- Compute the cost of materials used and labor by totaling the amounts assigned to jobs and to overhead.
- Compute the total overhead incurred by summing the amounts for the three components. Compute the amount of applied overhead by multiplying the total direct labor cost by the predetermined overhead rate. Compute the underapplied or overapplied amount as the difference between the actual cost and the applied cost.
- Determine the total cost charged to each job by adding the costs incurred in April (if any) to the cost of materials, labor, and overhead applied during May.
- Group the costs of the jobs according to their completion status.
- Record the direct materials costs assigned to the three jobs.
- Transfer costs of Jobs 401 and 402 from Work in Process Inventory to Finished Goods.
- Record the costs of Job 401 as cost of goods sold.
- Record the sale (on account) of Job 401 for $35,000.
- On the schedule of cost of goods manufactured, remember to include the beginning and ending work in process inventories and to use applied rather than actual overhead.

SOLUTION

1. Total cost of

a. April 30 inventory of jobs in process (Job 401).

Direct materials	$3,600
Direct labor	1,700
Applied overhead	2,550
Total cost.................	$7,850

b. Materials used during May.

Direct materials	
Job 401	$ 3,550
Job 402	3,500
Job 403	1,400
Total direct materials	8,450
Indirect materials	5,000
Total materials used	$13,450

c. Labor used during May.

Direct labor	
Job 401	$ 5,100
Job 402	6,000
Job 403	800
Total direct labor...........	11,900
Indirect labor..............	3,500
Total labor used	$15,400

d. Factory overhead incurred in May.

Actual overhead	
Indirect materials...........................	$ 5,000
Indirect labor	3,500
Other factory overhead	9,500
Total actual overhead.........................	18,000
Overhead applied (150% × $11,900).............	17,850
Underapplied overhead........................	$ 150

e. Total cost of each job.

	401	402	403
Work in process, April 30			
Direct materials	$ 3,600		
Direct labor......................	1,700		
Applied overhead*................	2,550		
Cost incurred in May			
Direct materials (from part b)	3,550	$ 3,500	$1,400
Direct labor......................	5,100	6,000	800
Applied overhead*................	7,650	9,000	1,200
Total costs.........................	$24,150	$18,500	$3,400

* Equals 150% of that job's direct labor cost.

Total cost of the May 31 inventory of work in process (Job 403) = $3,400

Total cost of the May 31 inventory of finished goods (Job 402) = $18,500

Total cost of goods sold during May (Job 401) = $24,150

2. Journal entries.

a. Record raw materials purchases, direct materials used, direct labor used, and overhead applied.

Raw Materials Inventory	16,000	
Accounts Payable		16,000
Record materials purchases.		
Work in Process Inventory	8,450	
Raw Materials Inventory		8,450
Assign direct materials to jobs.		
Work in Process Inventory	11,900	
Factory Wages Payable		11,900
Assign direct labor to jobs.		
Work in Process Inventory	17,850	
Factory Overhead		17,850
Apply overhead to jobs.		

b. Record actual overhead costs.

Factory Overhead	5,000	
Raw Materials Inventory		5,000
Record indirect materials.		
Factory Overhead	3,500	
Factory Wages Payable		3,500
Record indirect labor.		
Factory Overhead	9,500	
Cash		9,500
Record other actual factory overhead.		

c. Transfer cost of completed jobs to Finished Goods Inventory.

Finished Goods Inventory	42,650	
Work in Process Inventory		42,650
Record completion of jobs		
($24,150 for Job 401 + $18,500 for Job 402).		

d. Record cost of job sold.

Cost of Goods Sold	24,150	
Finished Goods Inventory		24,150
Record costs for sale of Job 401.		

e. Record sales for job sold.

Accounts Receivable	35,000	
Sales		35,000
Record sale of Job 401.		

f. Close underapplied overhead to cost of goods sold.

Cost of Goods Sold	150	
Factory Overhead		150
Assign underapplied overhead to Cost of Goods Sold.		

3.

WALCZAK COMPANY Schedule of Cost of Goods Manufactured For Month Ended May 31	
Direct materials	$ 8,450
Direct labor..................................	11,900
Factory overhead applied*.....................	17,850
Total manufacturing costs	38,200
Add: Work in process, April 30..................	7,850
Total cost of work in process...................	46,050
Less: Work in process, May 31	3,400
Cost of goods manufactured	$42,650

* Actual overhead = $18,000. Overhead is $150 underapplied.

Summary

C1 **Describe important features of job order production.** Certain companies called *job order manufacturers* produce custom-made products for customers. These customized products are produced in response to customers' orders. A job order manufacturer produces products that usually are different and, typically, produced in low volumes. The production systems of job order companies are flexible and are not highly standardized.

C2 **Explain job cost sheets and how they are used in job order costing.** In a job order costing system, the costs of producing each job are accumulated on a separate job cost sheet. Costs of direct materials, direct labor, and overhead applied are accumulated separately on the job cost sheet and then added to determine the total cost of a job. Job cost sheets for jobs in process, finished jobs, and jobs sold make up subsidiary records controlled by general ledger accounts.

A1 **Apply job order costing in pricing services.** Job order costing can usefully be applied to a service setting. The resulting job cost estimate can then be used to help determine a price for services.

P1 **Describe and record the flow of materials costs in job order costing.** Costs of direct materials flow to the Work in Process Inventory account and to job cost sheets. Costs of indirect materials flow to the Factory Overhead account and to the factory overhead subsidiary ledger. Receiving reports evidence the purchase of raw materials, and requisition forms evidence the use of materials in production.

P2 **Describe and record the flow of labor costs in job order costing.** Costs of direct labor flow to the Work in Process Inventory account and to job cost sheets. Costs of indirect labor flow to the Factory Overhead account and to the factory overhead subsidiary ledger. Time tickets document the use of labor.

P3 **Describe and record the flow of overhead costs in job order costing.** Overhead costs are charged to jobs using a predetermined overhead rate. Actual overhead costs incurred are accumulated in the Factory Overhead account that controls the subsidiary factory overhead ledger.

P4 **Determine adjustments for overapplied and underapplied factory overhead.** At the end of each year, the Factory Overhead account usually has a residual debit (underapplied overhead) or credit (overapplied overhead) balance. Assuming the balance is not material, it is transferred to Cost of Goods Sold, and the Factory Overhead account is closed.

Key Terms

Cost accounting system	Materials ledger card	Services Overhead
Finished Goods Inventory	Materials requisition	Target cost
Job	Overapplied overhead	Time ticket
Job cost sheet	Predetermined overhead rate	Underapplied overhead
Job lot	Process operations	Work in Process Inventory
Job order costing system	Receiving report	
Job order production	Services in Process Inventory	

Multiple Choice Quiz

1. A company's predetermined overhead rate is 150% of its direct labor costs. How much overhead is applied to a job that requires total direct labor costs of $30,000?
   a. $15,000   d. $60,000
   b. $30,000   e. $75,000
   c. $45,000

2. A company uses direct labor costs to apply overhead. Its production costs for the period are: direct materials, $45,000; direct labor, $35,000; and overhead applied, $38,500. What is its predetermined overhead rate?
   a. 10%   d. 91%
   b. 110%   e. 117%
   c. 86%

3. A company's ending inventory of finished goods has a total cost of $10,000 and consists of 500 units. If the overhead applied to these goods is $4,000, and the predetermined overhead rate is 80% of direct labor costs, how much direct materials cost was incurred in producing these 500 units?
   a. $10,000   d. $5,000
   b. $6,000   e. $1,000
   c. $4,000

4. A company's Work in Process Inventory T-account follows.

Work in Process Inventory			
Beginning balance	9,000		
Direct materials	94,200		
Direct labor	59,200	Cost of goods	
Overhead applied	31,600	manufactured	?
Ending balance	17,800		

The cost of goods manufactured is
   a. $193,000.   c. $185,000.   e. $176,200.
   b. $211,800.   d. $144,600.

5. At the end of its current year, a company learned that its overhead was underapplied by $1,500 and that this amount is not considered material. Based on this information, the company should
   a. Credit the $1,500 to Finished Goods Inventory.
   b. Credit the $1,500 to Cost of Goods Sold.
   c. Debit the $1,500 to Cost of Goods Sold.
   d. Do nothing about the $1,500 because it is not material and it is likely that overhead will be overapplied by the same amount next year.
   e. Include the $1,500 on the income statement as "Other Expense."

ANSWERS TO MULTIPLE CHOICE QUIZ

1. c; $30,000 × 150% = $45,000
2. b; $38,500/$35,000 = 110%
3. e; Direct materials + Direct labor + Overhead = Total cost;
   Direct materials + ($4,000/0.80) + $4,000 = $10,000
   Direct materials = $1,000

4. e; $9,000 + $94,200 + $59,200 + $31,600 − Finished goods
   = $17,800
   Thus, finished goods = $176,200
5. b

[I] Icon denotes assignments that involve decision making.

Discussion Questions

1. Why must a company estimate the amount of factory overhead assigned to individual jobs or job lots?

2. [I] Some companies use labor cost to apply factory overhead to jobs. Identify another factor (or base) a company might reasonably use to apply overhead costs.

3. [I] What information is recorded on a job cost sheet? How do management and employees use job cost sheets?

4. In a job order costing system, what records serve as a subsidiary ledger for Work in Process Inventory? For Finished Goods Inventory?

5. What journal entry is recorded when a materials manager receives a materials requisition and then issues materials (both direct and indirect) for use in the factory?

6. [I] How does the materials requisition help safeguard a company's assets?

7. Google uses a "time ticket" for some employees. How are time tickets used in job order costing? GOOGLE

8. What events cause debits to be recorded in the Factory Overhead account? What events cause credits to be recorded in the Factory Overhead account?

9. Google applies overhead to product costs. What account(s) is(are) used to eliminate GOOGLE overapplied or underapplied overhead from the Factory Overhead account, assuming the amount is not material?

10. [I] Assume that Apple produces a batch of 1,000 iPhones. Does it account for this as 1,000 APPLE individual jobs or as a job lot? Explain (consider costs and benefits).

11. Why must a company use predetermined overhead rates when using job order costing?

12. 🛈 How would a hospital apply job order costing? Explain.

13. 🛈 **Harley-Davidson** manufactures 30 custom-made, luxury-model motorcycles. Does it account for these motorcycles as 30 individual jobs or as a job lot? Explain.

14. Assume **Sprint** will install and service a server to link all of a customer's employees' smartphones to a centralized company server for an up-front flat price. How can Sprint use a job order costing system?

---

connect

Determine which of the following are most likely to be considered as a job and which as a job lot.

_____ **1.** Hats imprinted with company logo

_____ **2.** Little League trophies

_____ **3.** A handcrafted table

_____ **4.** A 90-foot motor yacht

_____ **5.** Wedding dresses for a chain of stores

_____ **6.** A custom-designed home

QUICK STUDY

QS 19-1

Jobs and job lots **C1** 🛈

Clemens Cars's job cost sheet for Job A40 shows that the cost to add security features to a car was $10,500. The car was delivered to the customer, who paid $14,900 in cash for the added features. What journal entries should Clemens record for the completion and delivery of Job A40?

QS 19-2

Job cost sheets **C2**

The left column lists the titles of documents and accounts used in job order costing. The right column presents short descriptions of the purposes of the documents. Match each document in the left column to its numbered description in the right column.

A. Time ticket

B. Materials ledger card

C. Voucher

D. Factory Overhead account

E. Materials requisition

_____ **1.** Shows amount of time an employee works on a job.

_____ **2.** Accumulates the cost of incurred overhead and the overhead cost assigned to specific jobs.

_____ **3.** Perpetual inventory record of raw materials received, used, and available for use.

_____ **4.** Shows amount approved for payment of an overhead or other cost.

_____ **5.** Communicates the need for materials to complete a job.

QS 19-3

Documents in job order costing

P1   P2   P3

During the current month, a company that uses job order costing purchases $50,000 in raw materials for cash. It then uses $12,000 of raw materials indirectly as factory supplies and uses $32,000 of raw materials as direct materials. Prepare journal entries to record these three transactions.

QS 19-4

Raw materials journal entries **P1**

During the current month, a company that uses job order costing incurred a monthly factory payroll of $180,000. Of this amount, $40,000 is classified as indirect labor and the remainder as direct. Prepare journal entries to record these transactions.

QS 19-5

Labor journal entries **P2**

A company incurred the following manufacturing costs this period: direct labor, $468,000; direct materials, $390,000; and factory overhead, $117,000. Compute its overhead cost as a percent of (1) direct labor and (2) direct materials. Express your answers as percents, rounded to the nearest whole number.

QS 19-6

Factory overhead rates

P3

At the beginning of the year, a company predicts total overhead costs of $560,000. The company applies overhead using machine hours and estimates it will use 1,400 machine hours during the year. What amount of overhead should be applied to Job 65A if that job uses 13 machine hours during January?

QS 19-7

Applying overhead **P3**

At the beginning of a year, a company predicts total direct materials costs of $900,000 and total overhead costs of $1,170,000. If the company uses direct materials costs as its activity base to apply overhead, what is the predetermined overhead rate it should use during the year?

QS 19-8

Predetermined overhead rate **P3**

QS 19-9
Applying overhead
P3

On March 1 a dressmaker starts work on three custom-designed wedding dresses. The company uses job order costing and applies overhead to each job (dress) at the rate of 40% of direct materials costs. During the month, the jobs used direct materials as shown below. Compute the amount of overhead applied to each of the three jobs.

	Job 1	Job 2	Job 3
Direct materials used	$5,000	$7,000	$1,500

QS 19-10
Manufacturing cost flows
P1   P2   P3

Refer to the information in QS 19-9. During the month, the jobs used direct labor as shown below. Jobs 1 and 3 are not finished by the end of March, and Job 2 is finished but not sold by the end of March. (1) Determine the amounts of direct materials, direct labor, and factory overhead applied that would be reported on job cost sheets for each of the three jobs for March. (2) Determine the total dollar amount of Work in Process Inventory at the end of March. (3) Determine the total dollar amount of Finished Goods Inventory at the end of March. Assume the company has no beginning Work in Process or Finished Goods inventories.

	Job 1	Job 2	Job 3
Direct labor used.	$9,000	$4,000	$3,000

QS 19-11
Entry for over- or underapplied overhead
P4

A company applies overhead at a rate of 150% of direct labor cost. Actual overhead cost for the current period is $950,000, and direct labor cost is $600,000. Prepare the journal entry to close over- or underapplied overhead to Cost of Goods Sold.

QS 19-12
Entry for over- or underapplied overhead
P4

A company's Factory Overhead account shows total debits of $624,000 and total credits of $646,000 at the end of the year. Prepare the journal entry to close the balance in the Factory Overhead account to Cost of Goods Sold.

QS 19-13
Job order costing of services   **A1**

An advertising agency is estimating costs for advertising a music festival. The job will require 200 direct labor hours at a cost of $50 per hour. Overhead costs are applied at a rate of $65 per direct labor hour. What is the total estimated cost for this job?

QS 19-14
Job order costing of services   **A1**

An advertising agency used 65 hours of direct labor in creating advertising for a music festival. Direct labor costs $50 per hour. The agency applies overhead at a rate of $40 per direct labor hour. Prepare journal entries to record the agency's direct labor *and* the applied overhead costs for this job.

QS 19-15
Job order production

C1

Refer to this chapter's Global View. **Porsche AG** is the manufacturer of the Porsche automobile line. Does Porsche produce in jobs or in job lots? Explain.

 connect

EXERCISES

Exercise 19-1
Job order production

C1

Match each of the terms/phrases numbered 1 through 5 with the best definition *a* through *e*.

_____ **1.** Cost accounting system
_____ **2.** Target cost
_____ **3.** Job lot
_____ **4.** Job
_____ **5.** Job order production

a. Production of products in response to customer orders.
b. Production activities for a customized product.
c. A system that records manufacturing costs.
d. The expected selling price of a job minus its desired profit.
e. Production of more than one unit of a custom product.

The following information is from the materials requisitions and time tickets for Job 9-1005 completed by Great Bay Boats. The requisitions are identified by code numbers starting with the letter Q, and the time tickets start with W. At the start of the year, management estimated that overhead cost would equal 110% of direct labor cost for each job. Determine the total cost on the job cost sheet for Job 9-1005.

Exercise 19-2
Job cost computation
C2

Date	Document	Amount
7/1/2017....................	Q-4698	$1,250
7/1/2017....................	W-3393	600
7/5/2017....................	Q-4725	1,000
7/5/2017....................	W-3479	450
7/10/2017...................	W-3559	300

As of the end of June, the job cost sheets at Racing Wheels, Inc., show the following total costs accumulated on three custom jobs.

Exercise 19-3
Analysis of cost flows
C2

	Job 102	Job 103	Job 104
Direct materials	$15,000	$33,000	$27,000
Direct labor...............	8,000	14,200	21,000
Overhead applied..........	4,000	7,100	10,500

Job 102 was started in production in May, and the following costs were assigned to it in May: direct materials, $6,000; direct labor, $1,800; and overhead, $900. Jobs 103 and 104 were started in June. Overhead cost is applied with a predetermined rate based on direct labor cost. Jobs 102 and 103 were finished in June, and Job 104 is expected to be finished in July. No raw materials were used indirectly in June. Using this information, answer the following questions. (Assume this company's predetermined overhead rate did not change across these months.)

1. What was the cost of the raw materials requisitioned in June for each of the three jobs?
2. How much direct labor cost was incurred during June for each of the three jobs?
3. What predetermined overhead rate is used during June?
4. How much total cost is transferred to finished goods during June?

Check   (4) $81,300

Starr Company reports the following information for August.

Exercise 19-4
Recording product costs
P1   P2   P3

Raw materials purchased on account.............	$76,200
Direct materials used in production	$48,000
Factory wages earned (direct labor)..............	$15,350
Overhead rate................................	120% of direct labor cost

Prepare journal entries to record the following events.
1. Raw materials purchased.
2. Direct materials used in production.
3. Direct labor used in production.
4. Applied overhead.

Custom Cabinetry has one job in process (Job 120) as of June 30; at that time, its job cost sheet reports direct materials of $6,000, direct labor of $2,800, and applied overhead of $2,240. Custom Cabinetry applies overhead at the rate of 80% of direct labor cost. During July, Job 120 is sold (on account) for $22,000, Job 121 is started and completed, and Job 122 is started and still in process at the end of the month. Custom Cabinetry incurs the following costs during July.

Exercise 19-5
Manufacturing cost flows
P1   P2   P3

July Product Costs	Job 120	Job 121	Job 122	Total
Direct materials	$1,000	$6,000	$2,500	$9,500
Direct labor...............	2,200	3,700	2,100	8,000
Overhead applied...........	?	?	?	?

1. Prepare journal entries for the following transactions and events *a* through *e* in July.
   a. Direct materials used in production.
   d. The sale of Job 120.
   b. Direct labor used in production.
   e. Cost of goods sold for Job 120.
   c. Overhead applied.

2. Compute the July 31 balances of the Work in Process Inventory and the Finished Goods Inventory accounts. (Assume there are no jobs in Finished Goods Inventory as of June 30.)

Exercise 19-6

Recording events in job order costing

P1   P2   P3   P4

Using Exhibit 19.15 as a guide, prepare summary journal entries to record the following transactions and events *a* through *g* for a company in its first month of operations.

a. Raw materials purchased on account, $90,000.

b. Direct materials used in production, $36,500. Indirect materials used in production, $19,200.

c. Paid cash for factory payroll, $50,000. Of this total, $38,000 is for direct labor and $12,000 is for indirect labor.

d. Paid cash for other actual overhead costs, $11,475.

e. Applied overhead at the rate of 125% of direct labor cost.

f. Transferred cost of jobs completed to finished goods, $56,800.

g. Sold jobs on account for $82,000. The jobs had a cost of $56,800.

Exercise 19-7

Cost flows in a job order costing system

P1   P2   P3   P4

The following information is available for Lock-Tite Company, which produces special-order security products and uses a job order costing system.

	April 30	May 31
Inventories		
Raw materials..	$43,000	$ 52,000
Work in process	10,200	21,300
Finished goods..	63,000	35,600
Activities and information for May		
Raw materials purchases (paid with cash)		210,000
Factory payroll (paid with cash)		345,000
Factory overhead		
Indirect materials...		15,000
Indirect labor		80,000
Other overhead costs		120,000
Sales (received in cash)...		1,400,000
Predetermined overhead rate based on direct labor cost		70%

Compute the following amounts for the month of May.

1. Cost of direct materials used.
4. Cost of goods sold.*

   *Do not consider any underapplied or overapplied overhead.

2. Cost of direct labor used.
5. Gross profit.

Check   (3) $625,400

3. Cost of goods manufactured.
6. Overapplied or underapplied overhead.

Exercise 19-8

Journal entries for materials

P1

Use information in Exercise 19-7 to prepare journal entries for the following events for the month of May.

1. Raw materials purchases for cash.
3. Indirect materials usage.

2. Direct materials usage.

Exercise 19-9

Journal entries for labor

P2

Use information in Exercise 19-7 to prepare journal entries for the following events for the month of May.

1. Direct labor usage.
3. Total payroll paid in cash.

2. Indirect labor usage.

Exercise 19-10

Journal entries for overhead   P3

Use information in Exercise 19-7 to prepare journal entries for the following events for the month of May.

1. Incurred other overhead costs (record credit to Other Accounts).

2. Applied overhead to work in process.

In December 2016, Shire Computer's management establishes the 2017 predetermined overhead rate based on direct labor cost. The information used in setting this rate includes estimates that the company will incur $747,500 of overhead costs and $575,000 of direct labor cost in year 2017. During March 2017, Shire began and completed Job 13-56.

1. What is the predetermined overhead rate for 2017?

2. Use the information on the following job cost sheet to determine the total cost of the job.

Exercise 19-11
Overhead rate; costs assigned to jobs
P3

Check (2) $22,710

JOB COST SHEET

| Customer's Name | Keiser Co. | | Job No. | 13-56 |

Job Description   5 plasma monitors—61 inch

Date	Direct Materials Requisition No.	Amount	Direct Labor Time-Ticket No.	Amount	Overhead Costs Applied Rate	Amount
Mar. 8	4-129	$5,000	T-306	$ 700		
Mar. 11	4-142	7,020	T-432	1,250		
Mar. 18	4-167	3,330	T-456	1,250		
Totals						

Lorenzo Company uses a job order costing system that charges overhead to jobs on the basis of direct materials cost. At year-end, the Work in Process Inventory account shows the following.

Exercise 19-12
Analysis of costs assigned to work in process
P3

	A	B	C	D	E
1		Work in Process Inventory			
2		Acct. No. 121			
3	Date	Explanation	Debit	Credit	Balance
4	2017				
5	Dec. 31	Direct materials cost	1,500,000		1,500,000
6	31	Direct labor cost	300,000		1,800,000
7	31	Overhead applied	600,000		2,400,000
8	31	To finished goods		2,350,000	50,000

1. Determine the predetermined overhead rate used (based on direct materials cost).

2. Only one job remained in work in process inventory at December 31, 2017. Its direct materials cost is $30,000. How much direct labor cost and overhead cost are assigned to this job?

Check (2) Direct labor cost, $8,000

Refer to information in Exercise 19-7. Prepare the journal entry to close overapplied or underapplied overhead to Cost of Goods Sold.

Exercise 19-13
Adjusting factory overhead P4

Record the journal entry to close over- or underapplied factory overhead to Cost of Goods Sold for each of the two companies below.

Exercise 19-14
Adjusting factory overhead
P4

	Storm Concert Promotions	Valle Home Builders
Actual indirect materials costs.	$22,000	$ 12,500
Actual indirect labor costs	46,000	46,500
Other overhead costs.	17,000	47,000
Overhead applied.	88,200	105,200

Exercise 19-15

Factory overhead computed, applied, and adjusted

P3   P4

In December 2016, Custom Mfg. established its predetermined overhead rate for jobs produced during 2017 by using the following cost predictions: overhead costs, $750,000, and direct materials costs, $625,000. At year-end 2017, the company's records show that actual overhead costs for the year are $830,000. Actual direct materials cost had been assigned to jobs as follows.

Jobs completed and sold.....................	$513,750
Jobs in finished goods inventory...............	102,750
Jobs in work in process inventory.............	68,500
Total actual direct materials cost..............	$685,000

1. Determine the predetermined overhead rate, using predicted direct materials costs, for 2017.

2. Set up a T-account for Factory Overhead and enter the overhead costs incurred and the amounts applied to jobs during the year using the predetermined overhead rate.

Check (3) $8,000 underapplied

3. Determine whether overhead is overapplied or underapplied (and the amount) during the year.

4. Prepare the adjusting entry to allocate any over- or underapplied overhead to Cost of Goods Sold.

Exercise 19-16

Factory overhead computed, applied, and adjusted

P3   P4

In December 2016, Infodeo established its predetermined overhead rate for movies produced during 2017 by using the following cost predictions: overhead costs, $1,680,000, and direct labor costs, $480,000. At year-end 2017, the company's records show that actual overhead costs for the year are $1,652,000. Actual direct labor cost had been assigned to jobs as follows.

Movies completed and released...............	$425,000
Movies still in production....................	50,000
Total actual direct labor cost	$475,000

1. Determine the predetermined overhead rate for 2017.

2. Set up a T-account for overhead and enter the overhead costs incurred and the amounts applied to movies during the year using the predetermined overhead rate.

Check (3) $10,500 overapplied

3. Determine whether overhead is overapplied or underapplied (and the amount) during the year.

4. Prepare the adjusting entry to allocate any over- or underapplied overhead to Cost of Goods Sold.

Exercise 19-17

Overhead rate calculation, allocation, and analysis

P3

Moonrise Bakery applies factory overhead based on direct labor costs. The company incurred the following costs during 2017: direct materials costs, $650,000; direct labor costs, $3,000,000; and factory overhead costs applied, $1,800,000.

1. Determine the company's predetermined overhead rate for 2017.

2. Assuming that the company's $71,000 ending Work in Process Inventory account for 2017 had $20,000 of direct labor costs, determine the inventory's direct materials costs.

Check (3) $90,000 overhead costs

3. Assuming that the company's $490,000 ending Finished Goods Inventory account for 2017 had $250,000 of direct materials costs, determine the inventory's direct labor costs and its overhead costs.

Exercise 19-18

Job order costing for services

A1

Hansel Corporation has requested bids from several architects to design its new corporate headquarters. Frey Architects is one of the firms bidding on the job. Frey estimates that the job will require the following direct labor.

	A	B	C
1	**Labor**	**Estimated Hours**	**Hourly Rate**
2	Architects	150	$300
3	Staff	300	75
4	Clerical	500	20

Frey applies overhead to jobs at 175% of direct labor cost. Frey would like to earn at least $80,000 profit on the architectural job. Based on past experience and market research, it estimates that the competition will bid between $285,000 and $350,000 for the job.

Check (1) $213,125

1. What is Frey's estimated cost of the architectural job?

2. What bid would you suggest that Frey submit?

Diaz and Associates incurred the following costs in completing a tax return for a large company. Diaz applies overhead at 50% of direct labor cost.

Exercise 19-19
Job order costing
of services
A1

Labor	Hours Used	Hourly Rate
Partner...................	5	$500
Senior manager	12	200
Staff accountants	100	50

1. Prepare journal entries to record direct labor *and* the overhead applied.

2. Prepare the journal entry to record the cost of services provided. Assume the beginning Services in Process Inventory account has a zero balance.

A recent balance sheet for **Porsche AG** shows beginning raw materials inventory of €83 million and ending raw materials inventory of €85 million. Assume the company purchased raw materials (on account) for €3,108 million during the year. (1) Prepare journal entries to record (a) the purchase of raw materials and (b) the use of raw materials in production. (2) What do you notice about the € amounts in your journal entries?

Exercise 19-20
Direct materials journal
entries   P1

connect

Marcelino Co.'s March 31 inventory of raw materials is $80,000. Raw materials purchases in April are $500,000, and factory payroll cost in April is $363,000. Overhead costs incurred in April are: indirect materials, $50,000; indirect labor, $23,000; factory rent, $32,000; factory utilities, $19,000; and factory equipment depreciation, $51,000. The predetermined overhead rate is 50% of direct labor cost. Job 306 is sold for $635,000 cash in April. Costs of the three jobs worked on in April follow.

PROBLEM SET A

Problem 19-1A
Production costs
computed and recorded;
reports prepared

C2   P1   P2   P3   P4

	Job 306	Job 307	Job 308
Balances on March 31			
Direct materials	$ 29,000	$ 35,000	
Direct labor.................	20,000	18,000	
Applied overhead.............	10,000	9,000	
Costs during April			
Direct materials	135,000	220,000	$100,000
Direct labor.................	85,000	150,000	105,000
Applied overhead.............	?	?	?
Status on April 30	Finished (sold)	Finished (unsold)	In process

Required

1. Determine the total of each production cost incurred for April (direct labor, direct materials, and applied overhead) and the total cost assigned to each job (including the balances from March 31).

2. Prepare journal entries for the month of April to record the following.

   a. Materials purchases (on credit).

   b. Direct materials used in production.

   c. Direct labor paid and assigned to Work in Process Inventory.

   d. Indirect labor paid and assigned to Factory Overhead.

   e. Overhead costs applied to Work in Process Inventory.

   f. Actual overhead costs incurred, including indirect materials. (Factory rent and utilities are paid in cash.)

   g. Transfer of Jobs 306 and 307 to Finished Goods Inventory.

   h. Cost of goods sold for Job 306.

   i. Revenue from the sale of Job 306.

   j. Assignment of any underapplied or overapplied overhead to the Cost of Goods Sold account. (The amount is not material.)

Check   (2*j*) $5,000
underapplied

(3) Cost of goods
manufactured, $828,500

3. Prepare a schedule of cost of goods manufactured.

4. Compute gross profit for April. Show how to present the inventories on the April 30 balance sheet.

Analysis Component

5. The over- or underapplied overhead is closed to Cost of Goods Sold. Discuss how this adjustment impacts business decision making regarding individual jobs or batches of jobs.

Problem 19-2A

Source documents, journal entries, overhead, and financial reports

P1   P2   P3   P4

Bergamo Bay's computer system generated the following trial balance on December 31, 2017. The company's manager knows something is wrong with the trial balance because it does not show any balance for Work in Process Inventory but does show a balance for the Factory Overhead account. In addition, the accrued factory payroll (Factory Wages Payable) has not been recorded.

	Debit	Credit
Cash	$170,000	
Accounts receivable	75,000	
Raw materials inventory...............	80,000	
Work in process inventory	0	
Finished goods inventory	15,000	
Prepaid rent	3,000	
Accounts payable		$ 17,000
Notes payable......................		25,000
Common stock		50,000
Retained earnings		271,000
Sales		373,000
Cost of goods sold	218,000	
Factory overhead	115,000	
Operating expenses	60,000	
Totals	$736,000	$736,000

After examining various files, the manager identifies the following six source documents that need to be processed to bring the accounting records up to date.

Materials requisition 21-3010:	$10,200 direct materials to Job 402
Materials requisition 21-3011:	$18,600 direct materials to Job 404
Materials requisition 21-3012:	$5,600 indirect materials
Labor time ticket 6052:	$36,000 direct labor to Job 402
Labor time ticket 6053:	$23,800 direct labor to Job 404
Labor time ticket 6054:	$8,200 indirect labor

Jobs 402 and 404 are the only units in process at year-end. The predetermined overhead rate is 200% of direct labor cost.

Required

1. Use information on the six source documents to prepare journal entries to assign the following costs.
   a. Direct materials costs to Work in Process Inventory.
   b. Direct labor costs to Work in Process Inventory.
   c. Overhead costs to Work in Process Inventory.
   d. Indirect materials costs to the Factory Overhead account.
   e. Indirect labor costs to the Factory Overhead account.

Check (2) $9,200 underapplied overhead

(3) T. B. totals, $804,000

(4) Net income, $85,800

2. Determine the revised balance of the Factory Overhead account after making the entries in part 1. Determine whether there is any under- or overapplied overhead for the year. Prepare the adjusting entry to allocate any over- or underapplied overhead to Cost of Goods Sold, assuming the amount is not material.
3. Prepare a revised trial balance.
4. Prepare an income statement for 2017 and a balance sheet as of December 31, 2017.

Analysis Component

5. Assume that the $5,600 on materials requisition 21-3012 should have been direct materials charged to Job 404. Without providing specific calculations, describe the impact of this error on the income statement for 2017 and the balance sheet at December 31, 2017.

Widmer Watercraft's predetermined overhead rate for 2017 is 200% of direct labor. Information on the company's production activities during May 2017 follows.

a. Purchased raw materials on credit, $200,000.

b. Materials requisitions record use of the following materials for the month.

Job 136......................................	$ 48,000
Job 137......................................	32,000
Job 138......................................	19,200
Job 139......................................	22,400
Job 140......................................	6,400
Total direct materials	128,000
Indirect materials	19,500
Total materials used.........................	$147,500

c. Paid $15,000 cash to a computer consultant to reprogram factory equipment.

d. Time tickets record use of the following labor for the month. These wages were paid in cash.

Job 136	$ 12,000
Job 137	10,500
Job 138	37,500
Job 139	39,000
Job 140	3,000
Total direct labor	102,000
Indirect labor..............................	24,000
Total	$126,000

e. Applied overhead to Jobs 136, 138, and 139.

f. Transferred Jobs 136, 138, and 139 to Finished Goods.

g. Sold Jobs 136 and 138 on credit at a total price of $525,000.

h. The company incurred the following overhead costs during the month (credit Prepaid Insurance for expired factory insurance).

Depreciation of factory building	$68,000
Depreciation of factory equipment	36,500
Expired factory insurance	10,000
Accrued property taxes payable	35,000

i. Applied overhead at month-end to the Work in Process Inventory account (Jobs 137 and 140) using the predetermined overhead rate of 200% of direct labor cost.

Required

1. Prepare a job cost sheet for each job worked on during the month. Use the following simplified form.

Job No. _____	
Materials...........	$ _____
Labor..............	_____
Overhead	_____
Total cost	$ _____

2. Prepare journal entries to record the events and transactions *a* through *i*.

3. Set up T-accounts for each of the following general ledger accounts, each of which started the month with a zero balance: Raw Materials Inventory; Work in Process Inventory; Finished Goods Inventory; Factory Overhead; Cost of Goods Sold. Then post the journal entries to these T-accounts and determine the balance of each account.

4. Prepare a report showing the total cost of each job in process and prove that the sum of their costs equals the Work in Process Inventory account balance. Prepare similar reports for Finished Goods Inventory and Cost of Goods Sold.

Problem 19-3A
Source documents, journal entries, and accounts in job order costing

P1 P2 P3

Check   (2e) Cr. Factory Overhead, $177,000

Check   (4) Finished Goods Inventory, $139,400

Problem 19-4A

Overhead allocation and adjustment using a predetermined overhead rate

P3 P4

In December 2016, Learer Company's manager estimated next year's total direct labor cost assuming 50 persons working an average of 2,000 hours each at an average wage rate of $25 per hour. The manager also estimated the following manufacturing overhead costs for 2017.

Indirect labor.................................	$ 319,200
Factory supervision............................	240,000
Rent on factory building	140,000
Factory utilities	88,000
Factory insurance expired	68,000
Depreciation—Factory equipment.................	480,000
Repairs expense—Factory equipment	60,000
Factory supplies used	68,800
Miscellaneous production costs	36,000
Total estimated overhead costs	$1,500,000

At the end of 2017, records show the company incurred $1,520,000 of actual overhead costs. It completed and sold five jobs with the following direct labor costs: Job 201, $604,000; Job 202, $563,000; Job 203, $298,000; Job 204, $716,000; and Job 205, $314,000. In addition, Job 206 is in process at the end of 2017 and had been charged $17,000 for direct labor. No jobs were in process at the end of 2016. The company's predetermined overhead rate is based on direct labor cost.

Required

1. Determine the following.
   a. Predetermined overhead rate for 2017.
   b. Total overhead cost applied to each of the six jobs during 2017.
   c. Over- or underapplied overhead at year-end 2017.

Check (1c) 12,800 underapplied
        (2) Cr. Factory Overhead, $12,800

2. Assuming that any over- or underapplied overhead is not material, prepare the adjusting entry to allocate any over- or underapplied overhead to Cost of Goods Sold at the end of 2017.

Problem 19-5A

Production transactions, subsidiary records, and source documents

P1 P2 P3 P4

Sager Company manufactures variations of its product, a technopress, in response to custom orders from its customers. On May 1, the company had no inventories of work in process or finished goods but held the following raw materials.

Material M......................	200 units @ $250 =	$50,000
Material R	95 units @ 180 =	17,100
Paint	55 units @ 75 =	4,125
Total cost......................		$71,225

On May 4, the company began working on two technopresses: Job 102 for Worldwide Company and Job 103 for Reuben Company.

Required

Using Exhibit 19.3 as a guide, prepare job cost sheets for Jobs 102 and 103. Using Exhibit 19.5 as a guide, prepare materials ledger cards for Material M, Material R, and paint. Enter the beginning raw materials inventory dollar amounts for each of these materials on their respective ledger cards. Then, follow the instructions in this list of activities.

a. Purchased raw materials on credit and recorded the following information from receiving reports and invoices.

> Receiving Report No. 426, Material M, 250 units at $250 each.
> Receiving Report No. 427, Material R, 90 units at $180 each.

Instructions: Record these purchases with a single journal entry. Enter the receiving report information on the materials ledger cards.

b. Requisitioned the following raw materials for production.

> Requisition No. 35, for Job 102, 135 units of Material M.
>
> Requisition No. 36, for Job 102, 72 units of Material R.
>
> Requisition No. 37, for Job 103, 70 units of Material M.
>
> Requisition No. 38, for Job 103, 38 units of Material R.
>
> Requisition No. 39, for 15 units of paint.

Instructions: Enter amounts for direct materials requisitions on the materials ledger cards and the job cost sheets. Enter the indirect materials amount on the materials ledger card. Do not record a journal entry at this time.

c. Received the following employee time tickets for work in May.

> Time tickets Nos. 1 to 10 for direct labor on Job 102, $90,000.
>
> Time tickets Nos. 11 to 30 for direct labor on Job 103, $65,000.
>
> Time tickets Nos. 31 to 36 for equipment repairs, $19,250.

Instructions: Record direct labor from the time tickets on the job cost sheets. Do not record a journal entry at this time.

d. Paid cash for the following items during the month: factory payroll, $174,250, and miscellaneous overhead items, $102,000. Use the time tickets to record the total direct and indirect labor costs.

Instructions: Record these payments with journal entries.

e. Finished Job 102 and transferred it to the warehouse. The company assigns overhead to each job with a predetermined overhead rate equal to 80% of direct labor cost.

Instructions: Enter the applied overhead on the cost sheet for Job 102, fill in the cost summary section of the cost sheet, and then mark the cost sheet "Finished." Prepare a journal entry to record the job's completion and its transfer to Finished Goods.

f. Delivered Job 102 and accepted the customer's promise to pay $400,000 within 30 days.

Instructions: Prepare journal entries to record the sale of Job 102 and the cost of goods sold.

g. Applied overhead cost to Job 103 based on the job's direct labor to date.

Instructions: Enter overhead on the job cost sheet but do not make a journal entry at this time.

h. Recorded the total direct and indirect materials costs as reported on all the requisitions for the month.

Instructions: Prepare a journal entry to record these costs.

i. Recorded the total overhead costs applied to jobs.

Instructions: Prepare a journal entry to record the allocation of these overhead costs.

j. Compute the balance in the Factory Overhead account as of the end of May.

Check   (*h*) Dr. Work in Process Inventory, $71,050

(*j*) Balance in Factory Overhead, $1,625 Cr., overapplied

Perez Mfg.'s August 31 inventory of raw materials is $150,000. Raw materials purchases in September are $400,000, and factory payroll cost in September is $232,000. Overhead costs incurred in September are: indirect materials, $30,000; indirect labor, $14,000; factory rent, $20,000; factory utilities, $12,000; and factory equipment depreciation, $30,000. The predetermined overhead rate is 50% of direct labor cost. Job 114 is sold for $380,000 cash in September. Costs for the three jobs worked on in September follow.

PROBLEM SET B

Problem 19-1B
Production costs computed and recorded; reports prepared

C2   P1   P2   P3   P4

	Job 114	Job 115	Job 116
Balances on August 31			
Direct materials	$ 14,000	$ 18,000	
Direct labor.	18,000	16,000	
Applied overhead.	9,000	8,000	
Costs during September			
Direct materials	100,000	170,000	$ 80,000
Direct labor.	30,000	68,000	120,000
Applied overhead.	?	?	?
Status on September 30	Finished (sold)	Finished (unsold)	In process

Required

1. Determine the total of each production cost incurred for September (direct labor, direct materials, and applied overhead) and the total cost assigned to each job (including the balances from August 31).

2. Prepare journal entries for the month of September to record the following.

   a. Materials purchases (on credit).

   b. Direct materials used in production.

   c. Direct labor paid and assigned to Work in Process Inventory.

   d. Indirect labor paid and assigned to Factory Overhead.

   e. Overhead costs applied to Work in Process Inventory.

   f. Actual overhead costs incurred, including indirect materials. (Factory rent and utilities are paid in cash.)

   g. Transfer of Jobs 114 and 115 to the Finished Goods Inventory.

   h. Cost of Job 114 in the Cost of Goods Sold account.

   i. Revenue from the sale of Job 114.

Check   (2*j*) $3,000 overapplied

(3) Cost of goods manufactured, $500,000

   j. Assignment of any underapplied or overapplied overhead to the Cost of Goods Sold account. (The amount is not material.)

3. Prepare a schedule of cost of goods manufactured.

4. Compute gross profit for September. Show how to present the inventories on the September 30 balance sheet.

Analysis Component

5. The over- or underapplied overhead adjustment is closed to Cost of Goods Sold. Discuss how this adjustment impacts business decision making regarding individual jobs or batches of jobs.

Problem 19-2B
Source documents, journal entries, overhead, and financial reports

P1   P2   P3   P4

Cavallo Mfg.'s computer system generated the following trial balance on December 31, 2017. The company's manager knows that the trial balance is wrong because it does not show any balance for Work in Process Inventory but does show a balance for the Factory Overhead account. In addition, the accrued factory payroll (Factory Wages Payable) has not been recorded.

	Debit	Credit
Cash	$ 64,000	
Accounts receivable	42,000	
Raw materials inventory.................	26,000	
Work in process inventory	0	
Finished goods inventory	9,000	
Prepaid rent	3,000	
Accounts payable		$ 10,500
Notes payable.........................		13,500
Common stock		30,000
Retained earnings		87,000
Sales		180,000
Cost of goods sold	105,000	
Factory overhead	27,000	
Operating expenses	45,000	
Totals..............................	$321,000	$321,000

After examining various files, the manager identifies the following six source documents that need to be processed to bring the accounting records up to date.

Materials requisition 94-231:	$4,600 direct materials to Job 603
Materials requisition 94-232:	$7,600 direct materials to Job 604
Materials requisition 94-233:	$2,100 indirect materials
Labor time ticket 765:	$5,000 direct labor to Job 603
Labor time ticket 766:	$8,000 direct labor to Job 604
Labor time ticket 777:	$3,000 indirect labor

Jobs 603 and 604 are the only units in process at year-end. The predetermined overhead rate is 200% of direct labor cost.

Required

1. Use information on the six source documents to prepare journal entries to assign the following costs.
   a. Direct materials costs to Work in Process Inventory.
   b. Direct labor costs to Work in Process Inventory.
   c. Overhead costs to Work in Process Inventory.
   d. Indirect materials costs to the Factory Overhead account.
   e. Indirect labor costs to the Factory Overhead account.

2. Determine the revised balance of the Factory Overhead account after making the entries in part 1. Determine whether there is under- or overapplied overhead for the year. Prepare the adjusting entry to allocate any over- or underapplied overhead to Cost of Goods Sold, assuming the amount is not material.

3. Prepare a revised trial balance.

4. Prepare an income statement for 2017 and a balance sheet as of December 31, 2017.

Analysis Component

5. Assume that the $2,100 indirect materials on materials requisition 94-233 should have been direct materials charged to Job 604. Without providing specific calculations, describe the impact of this error on the income statement for 2017 and the balance sheet at December 31, 2017.

Check (2) $6,100 underapplied overhead

(3) T. B. totals, $337,000

(4) Net income, $23,900

Starr Mfg.'s predetermined overhead rate is 200% of direct labor. Information on the company's production activities during September 2017 follows.

a. Purchased raw materials on credit, $125,000.

b. Materials requisitions record use of the following materials for the month.

Job 487	$30,000
Job 488	20,000
Job 489	12,000
Job 490	14,000
Job 491	4,000
Total direct materials	80,000
Indirect materials	12,000
Total materials used	$92,000

Problem 19-3B

Source documents, journal entries, and accounts in job order costing

P1 P2 P3

c. Paid $11,000 cash for miscellaneous factory overhead costs.

d. Time tickets record use of the following labor for the month. These wages are paid in cash.

Job 487	$ 8,000
Job 488	7,000
Job 489	25,000
Job 490	26,000
Job 491	2,000
Total direct labor	68,000
Indirect labor	16,000
Total	$84,000

e. Applied overhead to Jobs 487, 489, and 490.

f. Transferred Jobs 487, 489, and 490 to Finished Goods.

g. Sold Jobs 487 and 489 on credit for a total price of $340,000.

h. The company incurred the following overhead costs during the month (credit Prepaid Insurance for expired factory insurance).

Depreciation of factory building...................	$37,000
Depreciation of factory equipment	21,000
Expired factory insurance........................	7,000
Accrued property taxes payable...................	31,000

i. Applied overhead at month-end to the Work in Process Inventory account (Jobs 488 and 491) using the predetermined overhead rate of 200% of direct labor cost.

Required

1. Prepare a job cost sheet for each job worked on in the month. Use the following simplified form.

Job No. _____	
Materials............	$ _____
Labor..............	_____
Overhead	_____
Total cost	$ _____

Check   (2e) Cr. Factory
Overhead, $118,000
        (3) Finished Goods
Inventory, $92,000 bal.

2. Prepare journal entries to record the events and transactions *a* through *i*.

3. Set up T-accounts for each of the following general ledger accounts, each of which started the month with a zero balance: Raw Materials Inventory, Work in Process Inventory, Finished Goods Inventory, Factory Overhead, Cost of Goods Sold. Then post the journal entries to these T-accounts and determine the balance of each account.

4. Prepare a report showing the total cost of each job in process and prove that the sum of their costs equals the Work in Process Inventory account balance. Prepare similar reports for Finished Goods Inventory and Cost of Goods Sold.

Problem 19-4B

Overhead allocation and adjustment using a predetermined overhead rate

P3   P4

In December 2016, Pavelka Company's manager estimated next year's total direct labor cost assuming 50 persons working an average of 2,000 hours each at an average wage rate of $15 per hour. The manager also estimated the following manufacturing overhead costs for 2017.

Indirect labor.....................................	$159,600
Factory supervision.............................	120,000
Rent on factory building	70,000
Factory utilities	44,000
Factory insurance expired	34,000
Depreciation—Factory equipment.................	240,000
Repairs expense—Factory equipment	30,000
Factory supplies used	34,400
Miscellaneous production costs	18,000
Total estimated overhead costs..................	$750,000

At the end of 2017, records show the company incurred $725,000 of actual overhead costs. It completed and sold five jobs with the following direct labor costs: Job 625, $354,000; Job 626, $330,000; Job 627, $175,000; Job 628, $420,000; and Job 629, $184,000. In addition, Job 630 is in process at the end of 2017 and had been charged $10,000 for direct labor. No jobs were in process at the end of 2016. The company's predetermined overhead rate is based on direct labor cost.

Required

1. Determine the following.

   a. Predetermined overhead rate for 2017.

   b. Total overhead cost applied to each of the six jobs during 2017.

   c. Over- or underapplied overhead at year-end 2017.

2. Assuming that any over- or underapplied overhead is not material, prepare the adjusting entry to allocate any over- or underapplied overhead to Cost of Goods Sold at the end of year 2017.

Check (1c) $11,500 overapplied

(2) Dr. Factory Overhead, $11,500

King Company produces variations of its product, a megatron, in response to custom orders from its customers. On June 1, the company had no inventories of work in process or finished goods but held the following raw materials.

Problem 19-5B
Production transactions, subsidiary records, and source documents

P1   P2   P3   P4

```
Material M......................  120 units @ $200 = $24,000
Material R .....................    80 units @  160 =  12,800
Paint .........................     44 units @   72 =   3,168
Total cost.....................                       $39,968
```

On June 3, the company began working on two megatrons: Job 450 for Encinita Company and Job 451 for Fargo, Inc.

Required

Using Exhibit 19.3 as a guide, prepare job cost sheets for Jobs 450 and 451. Using Exhibit 19.5 as a guide, prepare materials ledger cards for Material M, Material R, and paint. Enter the beginning raw materials inventory dollar amounts for each of these materials on their respective ledger cards. Then, follow instructions in this list of activities.

a. Purchased raw materials on credit and recorded the following information from receiving reports and invoices.

```
Receiving Report No. 20, Material M, 150 units at $200 each.
Receiving Report No. 21, Material R, 70 units at $160 each.
```

Instructions: Record these purchases with a single journal entry. Enter the receiving report information on the materials ledger cards.

b. Requisitioned the following raw materials for production.

```
Requisition No. 223, for Job 450, 80 units of Material M.
Requisition No. 224, for Job 450, 60 units of Material R.
Requisition No. 225, for Job 451, 40 units of Material M.
Requisition No. 226, for Job 451, 30 units of Material R.
Requisition No. 227, for 12 units of paint.
```

Instructions: Enter amounts for direct materials requisitions on the materials ledger cards and the job cost sheets. Enter the indirect materials amount on the materials ledger card. Do not record a journal entry at this time.

c. Received the following employee time tickets for work in June.

```
Time tickets Nos. 1 to 10 for direct labor on Job 450, $40,000.
Time tickets Nos. 11 to 20 for direct labor on Job 451, $32,000.
Time tickets Nos. 21 to 24 for equipment repairs, $12,000.
```

Instructions: Record direct labor from the time tickets on the job cost sheets. Do not record a journal entry at this time.

d. Paid cash for the following items during the month: factory payroll, $84,000, and miscellaneous overhead items, $36,800. Use the time tickets to record the total direct and indirect labor costs.

Instructions: Record these payments with journal entries.

e. Finished Job 450 and transferred it to the warehouse. The company assigns overhead to each job with a predetermined overhead rate equal to 70% of direct labor cost.

Instructions: Enter the applied overhead on the cost sheet for Job 450, fill in the cost summary section of the cost sheet, and then mark the cost sheet "Finished." Prepare a journal entry to record the job's completion and its transfer to Finished Goods.

f. Delivered Job 450 and accepted the customer's promise to pay $290,000 within 30 days.

Instructions: Prepare journal entries to record the sale of Job 450 and the cost of goods sold.

g. Applied overhead cost to Job 451 based on the job's direct labor used to date.

Instructions: Enter overhead on the job cost sheet but do not make a journal entry at this time.

Check (*h*) Dr. Work in Process Inventory, $38,400

h. Recorded the total direct and indirect materials costs as reported on all the requisitions for the month.

Instructions: Prepare a journal entry to record these.

(*j*) Balance in Factory Overhead, $736 Cr., overapplied

i. Recorded the total overhead costs applied to jobs.

Instructions: Prepare a journal entry to record the allocation of these overhead costs.

j. Compute the balance in the Factory Overhead account as of the end of June.

SERIAL PROBLEM
Business Solutions

P1   P2   P3

© Alexander Image/Shutterstock RF

(This serial problem began in Chapter 1 and continues through most of the book. If previous chapter segments were not completed, the serial problem can begin at this point.)

SP 19   The computer workstation furniture manufacturing that Santana Rey started in January is progressing well. As of the end of June, **Business Solutions**'s job cost sheets show the following total costs accumulated on three furniture jobs.

	Job 602	Job 603	Job 604
Direct materials	$1,500	$3,300	$2,700
Direct labor	800	1,420	2,100
Overhead	400	710	1,050

Job 602 was started in production in May, and these costs were assigned to it in May: direct materials, $600; direct labor, $180; and overhead, $90. Jobs 603 and 604 were started in June. Overhead cost is applied with a predetermined rate based on direct labor costs. Jobs 602 and 603 are finished in June, and Job 604 is expected to be finished in July. No raw materials are used indirectly in June. (Assume this company's predetermined overhead rate did not change over these months.)

Required

Check (1) Total materials, $6,900

(3) 50%

1. What is the cost of the raw materials used in June for each of the three jobs and in total?
2. How much total direct labor cost is incurred in June?
3. What predetermined overhead rate is used in June?
4. How much cost is transferred to Finished Goods Inventory in June?

GL **GENERAL LEDGER PROBLEM**

Available only in Connect

The **General Ledger** tool in *Connect* automates several of the procedural steps in accounting so that the financial professional can focus on the impacts of each transaction on various reports and performance measures.

GL 19-1   General Ledger assignment GL 19-1, based on Problem 19-1A, focuses on transactions related to job order costing. Prepare summary journal entries to record the cost of jobs and their flow through the manufacturing environment. Then prepare a schedule of cost of goods manufactured and a partial income statement.

Beyond the Numbers

BTN 19-1   Manufacturers and merchandisers can apply just-in-time (JIT) to their inventory management. Apple wants to know the impact of a JIT inventory system on operating cash flows. Review Apple's statement of cash flows in Appendix A to answer the following.

Required

1. Identify the impact on operating cash flows (increase or decrease) for changes in inventory levels (increase or decrease) for each of the three most recent years.
2. What impact would a JIT inventory system have on Apple's operating income? Link the answer to your response for part 1.
3. Would the move to a JIT system have a one-time or recurring impact on operating cash flow?

REPORTING IN ACTION

P1

APPLE

BTN 19-2   Apple's and Google's income statements in Appendix A both show increasing sales and cost of sales. The gross margin ratio can be used to analyze how well companies control costs as sales increase.

Required

1. Compute the gross margin ratio for Apple for each of the three most recent years.
2. Compute the gross margin ratio for Google for each of the three most recent years.
3. Do your computed gross margin ratios indicate good cost control for each company? Explain.

COMPARATIVE ANALYSIS

P1

APPLE

GOOGLE

BTN 19-3   Assume that your company sells portable housing to both general contractors and the government. It sells jobs to contractors on a bid basis. A contractor asks for three bids from different manufacturers. The combination of low bid and high quality wins the job. However, jobs sold to the government are bid on a cost-plus basis. This means price is determined by adding all costs plus a profit based on cost at a specified percent, such as 10%. You observe that the amount of overhead applied to government jobs is higher than that applied to contract jobs. These allocations concern you.

Required

Write a half-page memo to your company's chief financial officer outlining your concerns with overhead allocation.

ETHICS CHALLENGE

P3

Point: Students could compare responses and discuss differences in concerns with allocating overhead.

BTN 19-4   Assume that you are preparing for a second interview with a manufacturing company. The company is impressed with your credentials, but it has several qualified applicants. You anticipate that in this second interview, you must show what you offer over other candidates. You learn the company is not satisfied with the timeliness of its information and its inventory management. The company manufactures custom-order holiday decorations and display items. To show your abilities, you plan to recommend that the company use a job order accounting system.

Required

In preparation for the interview, prepare notes outlining the following:

1. Your recommendation and why it is suitable for this company.
2. A general description of the documents that the proposed system requires.
3. How the documents in part 2 facilitate the operation of the job order accounting system.

COMMUNICATING IN PRACTICE

C1   C2

Point: Have students present a mock interview, one assuming the role of the president of the company and the other the applicant.

TAKING IT TO THE NET

C1

BTN 19-5   Many contractors work on custom jobs that require a job order costing system.

Required

Access the website AMSI.com; click on "Construction Management Software," and then on "StarBuilder." Prepare a one-page memorandum for the CEO of a construction company providing information about the job order costing software this company offers. Would you recommend that the company purchase this software?

TEAMWORK IN ACTION

C1

BTN 19-6   Consider the activities undertaken by a medical clinic in your area.

Required

1. Is a job order costing system appropriate for the clinic? Explain.
2. Identify as many factors as possible to lead you to conclude that the clinic uses a job order system.

ENTREPRENEURIAL DECISION

C1   C2

BTN 19-7   Refer to the chapter opener regarding Neha Assar and her company, Neha Assar. All successful businesses track their costs, and it is especially important for start-up businesses to monitor and control costs.

Required

1. Assume that Neha Assar uses a job order costing system. For the basic cost category of direct materials, explain how Neha's job cost sheet would differ from a job cost sheet for a manufacturing company.
2. For the basic cost categories of direct labor and overhead, provide examples of the types of costs that would fall into each category for Neha Assar.

HITTING THE ROAD

C2   P1   P2   P3

BTN 19-8   Home builders often use job order costing.

Required

1. You (or your team) are to prepare a job cost sheet for a single-family home under construction. List four items of both direct materials and direct labor. Explain how you think overhead should be applied.
2. Contact a builder and compare your job cost sheet to this builder's job cost sheet. If possible, speak to that company's accountant. Write your findings in a short report.

GLOBAL DECISION

P1

APPLE

Samsung

BTN 19-9   Apple and Samsung are competitors in the global marketplace. Apple's and Samsung's financial statements are in Appendix A.

Required

1. Determine the change in Apple's and Samsung's inventories for the most recent year reported. Then identify the impact on net resources generated by operating activities (increase or decrease) for the change in inventory level (increase or decrease) for Apple and Samsung for that same year.
2. How would the move to a just-in-time (JIT) system likely impact future operating cash flows and operating income?
3. Would a move to a JIT system likely impact Apple more than it would Samsung? Explain.

GLOBAL VIEW

Porsche AG manufactures high-performance cars. Each car is built according to individual customer specifications. Customers can use the Internet to place orders for their dream cars.

Porsche employs just-in-time inventory techniques to ensure a flexible production process that can respond rapidly to customer orders. At one of its plants, the company receives parts less than one hour before they are needed in production.

Porsche's sustainability efforts extend beyond its manufacturing operations to event management. Each year when the company sponsors a professional tennis tournament, it

© Sean Gallup/Getty Images

uses a Porsche Cayenne Hybrid to shuttle players to and from the venue. In addition, the company sells event tickets that include public transportation, thus reducing the number of distinct journeys to the venue by about 30%.

 Global View Assignments

Quick Study 19-15

Exercise 19-20

BTN 19-9

20 chapter

Process Costing

Chapter Preview

PROCESS OPERATIONS

C1 Organization of process operations

A1 Process cost vs. job order systems

C2 Equivalent units (EUP)

NTK 20-1

PROCESS COSTING ILLUSTRATION

C3 Overview of GenX

Physical flow of units

Computing EUP

Cost per EUP

Cost reconciliation

Process cost summary

NTK 20-2, 20-3

ACCOUNTING AND REPORTING

P1 Accounting for materials

P2 Accounting for labor

P3 Accounting for overhead

P4 Accounting for transfers

A2 Hybrid costing system

C4 *Appendix:* FIFO method

NTK 20-4

Learning Objectives

CONCEPTUAL

C1 Explain process operations and the way they differ from job order operations.

C2 Define and compute equivalent units and explain their use in process costing.

C3 Describe accounting for production activity and preparation of a process cost summary using weighted average.

C4 *Appendix 20A—*Describe accounting for production activity and preparation of a process cost summary using FIFO.

ANALYTICAL

A1 Compare process costing and job order costing.

A2 Explain and illustrate a hybrid costing system.

PROCEDURAL

P1 Record the flow of materials costs in process costing.

P2 Record the flow of labor costs in process costing.

P3 Record the flow of factory overhead costs in process costing.

P4 Record the transfer of goods across departments, to Finished Goods Inventory, and to Cost of Goods Sold.

Uncommon Threads

San Clemente, CA—Strolling the aisles of retailers, serial entrepreneur Jeff Kearl found generic, boring products. "For many products, there's nothing really cool about it, no brand, nothing that sticks out," insists Jeff. Jeff (now CEO), along with co-founders John Wilson (now president), Ryan Kingman, Taylor Shupe, and Aaron Hennings, decided to be different. They came up with socks, but not dull ones. Instead, they imprinted socks with edgy designs, basketball legends, and *Star Wars* characters. The result is **Stance** (**Stance.com**), the official sock provider to the **National Basketball Association** and a favorite of artists and musicians.

Socks are made in process operations and produced in large volumes. This requires production managers to track costs using a *process costing system*. Explains Jeff, "we start with the highest-grade polyester-nylon fabric we can find." Clarke Miyasaki, head of business development, adds, "Quality is critical. We make the best for the best players in the world."

As with many process operations, Stance uses machinery, automation, and continuous improvement of its processes.

"There's always room for innovation"

—Jeff Kearl

Stance's "innovation lab" houses state-of-the-art Italian knitting machines, and a patented process that enables it to print faithful reproductions of NBA stars on its socks. "Not only does our sock-drying process enable us to create better pictures, it also allows us to manufacture socks without seams," says chief product officer Taylor Shupe. In addition to overhead costs of machines, Stance invests in product design and testing. In process costing, overhead costs are allocated to individual processes. The *process cost summary* is a report that managers of process operations use to monitor and control costs.

Stance is profitable and has increased sales by more than 100 percent in each of its first five years. "There's a lot of growth left for socks," insists Jeff. A recent move into women's socks was wildly successful, which now accounts for 20 percent of its sales. Jeff advises aspiring entrepreneurs to "enjoy what you do and work hard."

Sources: *Stance website,* January 2017; *Transworld Business,* July 23, 2012; *Fast Company,* July 9, 2015; *Dick's Sporting Goods* blog, July 3, 2015; Rovell, Darren, "NBA agrees to licensing deal with Stance as league's official sock," *ESPN.com,* April 27, 2015

PROCESS OPERATIONS

C1

Explain process operations and the way they differ from job order operations.

We previously described differences in job order and process operations. Job order operations involve customized jobs. **Process operations** involve the mass production of similar products in a continuous flow of sequential processes. Process operations require a high level of standardization to produce large volumes of products. Thus, process operations use a standardized process to make similar products; job order operations use a customized process to make unique products.

Penn makes tennis balls in a process operation. Tennis players want every tennis ball to be identical in terms of bounce, playability, and durability. This uniformity requires Penn to use a production process that can repeatedly make large volumes of tennis balls to the same specifications. Process operations also extend to services, such as mail sorting in large post offices and order processing in retailers like **Amazon**. Other companies using process operations include:

Company	Product	Company	Product
General Mills	Cereals	Heinz	Ketchup
Pfizer	Pharmaceuticals	Kar's.....................	Trail mix
Procter & Gamble	Household products	Hershey	Chocolate
Coca-Cola	Soft drinks	Suja	Organic juice

Organization of Process Operations

Each of the above products is made in a series of repetitive *processes,* or steps. A production operation that makes tennis balls, for instance, might include the three steps shown in Exhibit 20.1. Understanding such processes is crucial for measuring product costs. Increasingly, process operations use machines and automation to control product quality and reduce manufacturing costs.

EXHIBIT 20.1

Process Operations: Making of Tennis Balls*

* For a virtual tour of a process operation, visit PennRacquet.com/video.html (tennis balls).

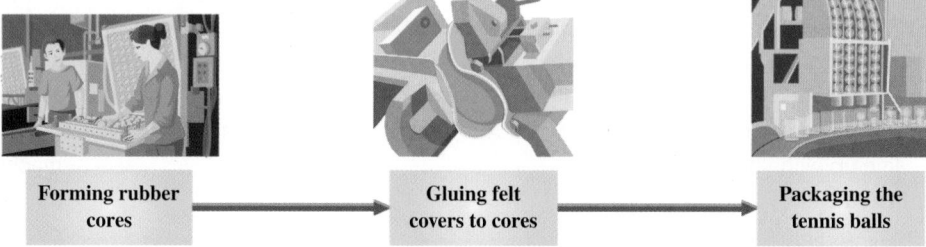

| Forming rubber cores | Gluing felt covers to cores | Packaging the tennis balls |

In a process operation, each process is a separate *production department, workstation,* or *work center.* Except for the first process or department, each receives the output from the prior department as a partially processed product. Each process applies direct labor, overhead, and, perhaps, additional direct materials to move the product toward completion. Only the final process or department in the series produces finished goods ready for sale to customers.

In Exhibit 20.1, the first step in tennis ball production involves cutting rubber into pellets and forming the core of each ball. These rubber cores are passed to the second department, where felt is cut into covers and glued to the rubber cores. The completed tennis balls are then passed to the final department for quality checks and packaging.

We must often track costs for several related departments. Because process costing procedures are applied to *the activity of each department or process separately,* we examine only one process at a time. This simplifies procedures. In addition, many of the journal entries in a process costing system are like those in job order costing.

Comparing Process and Job Order Costing Systems

A1

Compare process costing and job order costing.

Both job order costing systems and process costing systems track direct materials, direct labor, and overhead costs. The measurement focus in a job order costing system is on the individual job or batch, whereas in a process costing system it is on the individual process. Regardless of the measurement focus, we aim to compute the cost per unit of product (or service) resulting from either system. While both measure costs per unit, these two accounting systems differ in terms of how they do so.

- A **job order costing system** measures cost per unit upon completion of a job by dividing the total cost for that job by the number of units in that job. Job cost sheets accumulate the costs for each job. In a job order system, the cost object is a job.

- A **process costing system** measures unit costs at the end of a period (for example, a month) by combining the costs per equivalent unit (explained in the next section) from each separate department. In process costing, the cost object is the process.

Differences in the way these two systems apply materials, labor, and overhead costs are highlighted in Exhibit 20.2.

Point: The cost object in a job order system is the specific job; the cost object in a process costing system is the process.

EXHIBIT 20.2

Cost Flows: Comparing Job Order and Process Costing Systems

Job Order System

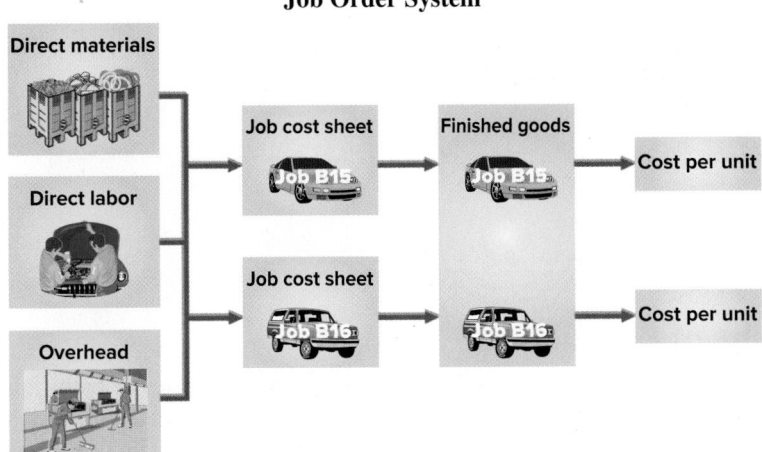

Process System

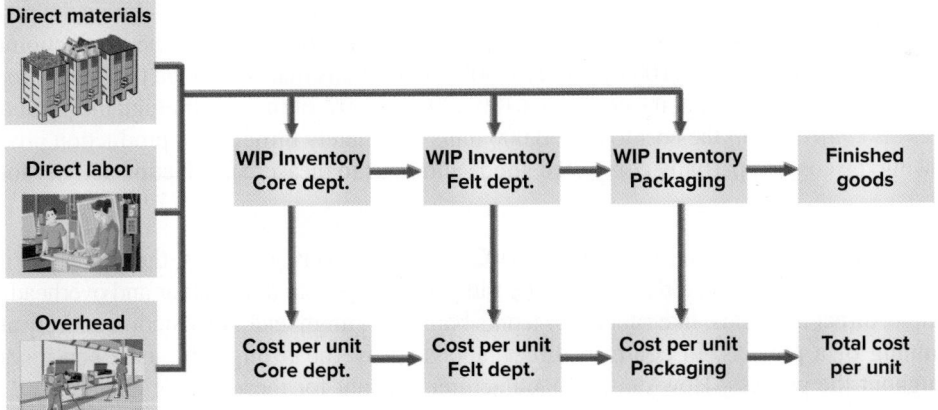

Transferring Costs across Departments   A key difference between job order and process costing arises with respect to work in process inventory:

- Job order costing often uses *only one* Work in Process Inventory account; the balance in this account agrees with the accumulated balances across all the job cost sheets for the jobs still in process.

- Process costing uses *separate* Work in Process Inventory accounts for each department. After production is complete, the completed goods and their accumulated costs are transferred from the Work in Process Inventory account for the final department in the series of processes to the Finished Goods Inventory account.

Exhibit 20.3 summarizes the journal entries to capture this flow of costs for a tennis ball manufacturer—to Ⓐ, to Ⓑ, to Ⓒ.

EXHIBIT 20.3

Flow of Costs through
Separate Work in
Process Accounts

(A)   Work in Process Inventory—Felt department ....   #
            Work in Process Inventory—Core department ....   #
        Transfer costs of partially completed goods to next department.

(B)   Work in Process Inventory—Packaging department ....   #
            Work in Process Inventory—Felt department ....   #
        Transfer costs of partially completed goods to next department.

(C)   Finished Goods Inventory ....   #
            Work in Process Inventory—Packaging department ....   #
        Transfer costs of completed products to finished goods.

NEED-TO-KNOW 20-1

Job Order vs. Process
Costing Systems

C1   A1

Do More: QS 20-1, QS 20-2,
E 20-1, E 20-2

Complete the following table with either a *yes* or *no* regarding the attributes of job order and process costing systems.

	Job Order	Process
Uses direct materials, direct labor, and overhead costs	a. _____	e. _____
Uses job cost sheets to accumulate costs	b. _____	f. _____
Typically uses several Work in Process Inventory accounts	c. _____	g. _____
Yields a cost per unit of product	d. _____	h. _____

Solution

a. yes   **b.** yes   **c.** no   **d.** yes   **e.** yes   **f.** no   **g.** yes   **h.** yes

---

Equivalent Units of Production

C2 _____

Define and compute
equivalent units and explain
their use in process costing.

Companies with process operations typically end each period with inventories of both finished goods and work in process. For example, a maker of tennis balls ends each period with both completed tennis balls and partially completed tennis balls in inventory. How does a process manufacturer measure its production activity when it has some partially completed goods at the end of a period? A key idea in process costing is **equivalent units of production (EUP),** which is the number of units that *could have been* started and completed given the costs incurred during the period.

EUP is explained as follows: 100,000 tennis balls that are 60% through the production process is *equivalent to* 60,000 (100,000 units × 60%) tennis balls that completed the entire production process. This means that the cost to put 100,000 units 60% of the way through the production process is *equivalent to* the cost to put 60,000 units completely through the production process. Knowing the costs of partially completed goods allows us to measure production activity for the period.

EUP for Materials and Conversion Costs   In many processes, the equivalent units of production for direct materials are not the same with respect to direct labor and overhead. For example, direct materials, like rubber for tennis ball cores, might enter production entirely at the beginning of a process. In contrast, direct labor and overhead might be used continuously throughout the process. How does a manufacturer account for these timing differences? The solution is by measuring equivalent units of production. For example, if all of the direct materials to produce 10,000 units have entered the production process, but those units have received only 20% of their direct labor and overhead costs, equivalent units would be computed as:

EUP: Physical unit #s × Complete %
EUP for direct materials = 10,000 × 100% = 10,000
EUP for direct labor = 10,000 × 20% = 2,000
EUP for overhead = 10,000 × 20% = 2,000

Point: When overhead is applied based on direct labor cost, the percentage of completion for direct labor and overhead will be the same.

Direct labor and factory overhead are often classified as *conversion costs*—that is, as costs of converting direct materials into finished products. Many businesses with process operations compute **conversion cost per equivalent unit,** which is the combined costs of direct labor and factory overhead per equivalent unit. If direct labor and overhead enter the production process at about the same rate, it is convenient to combine them, together, as conversion costs.

Weighted Average versus FIFO   There are different ways to compute the number of equivalent units. These methods make different assumptions about how costs flow. The **weighted-average method** combines units and costs *across two periods* in computing equivalent units. The **FIFO method** computes equivalent units based only on production activity in the *current period*. The objectives, concepts, and journal entries (but not amounts) are the same under the weighted-average and FIFO methods; the computations of equivalent units differ. While the FIFO method is generally more precise than the weighted-average method, it requires more calculations. Often, the differences between the two methods are not large. When using a just-in-time inventory system, these different methods will yield very similar results because inventories are immaterial. **In this chapter we assume the weighted-average method for inventory costs; we illustrate the FIFO method in the appendix.**

PROCESS COSTING ILLUSTRATION

We provide a step-by-step illustration of process costing. Each process (or department) in a process operation follows these steps:

1. Determine the physical flow of units.
2. Compute equivalent units of production.
3. Compute cost per equivalent unit of production.
4. Assign and reconcile costs.

We next show these steps for the first of two sequential processes used by a company to produce one of its products.

C3_____

Describe accounting for production activity and preparation of a process cost summary using weighted average.

Overview of GenX Company's Process Operation

The GenX Company produces an organic trail mix called FitMix. Its target customers are active people who are interested in fitness and the environment. GenX sells FitMix to wholesale distributors, who in turn sell it to retailers. FitMix is manufactured in a continuous, two-process operation (roasting and blending), shown in Exhibit 20.4.

EXHIBIT 20.4

GenX's Process Operation

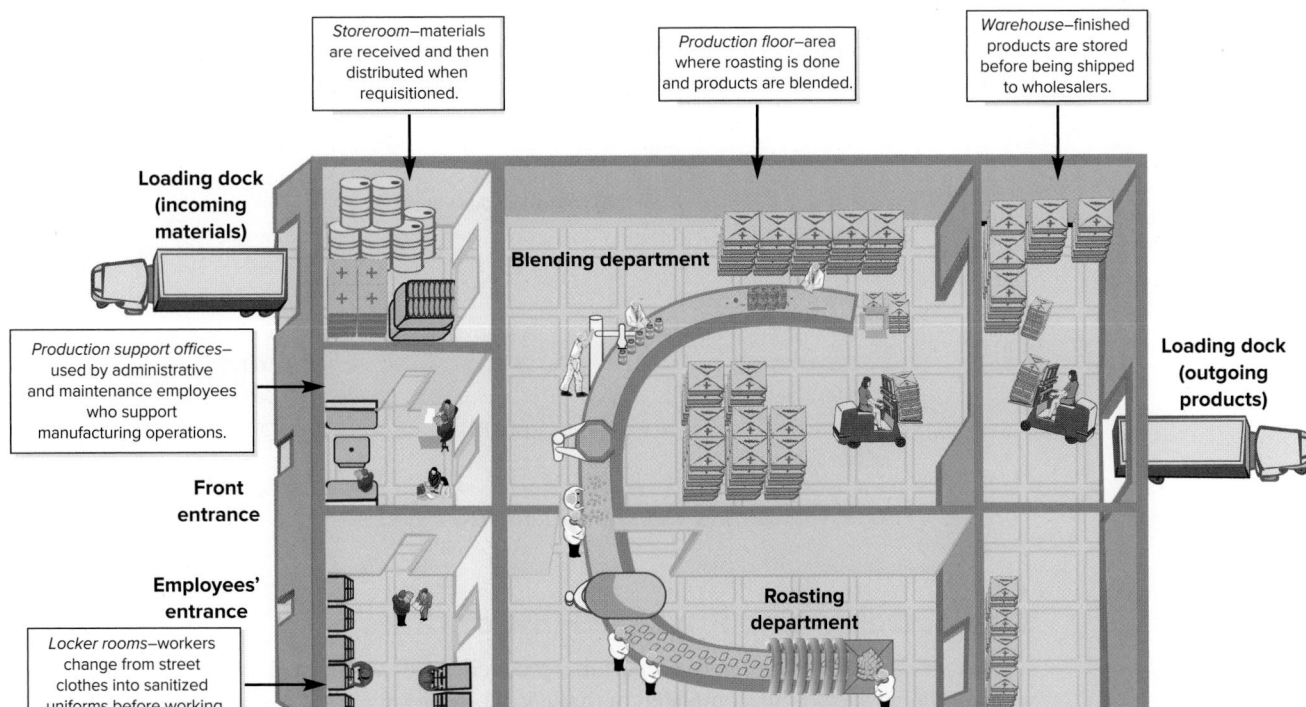

Storeroom—materials are received and then distributed when requisitioned.

Production floor—area where roasting is done and products are blended.

Warehouse—finished products are stored before being shipped to wholesalers.

Loading dock (incoming materials)

Blending department

Loading dock (outgoing products)

Production support offices—used by administrative and maintenance employees who support manufacturing operations.

Front entrance

Employees' entrance

Locker rooms—workers change from street clothes into sanitized uniforms before working in the factory.

Roasting department

In the first process (roasting department), GenX roasts, oils, and salts organically grown peanuts. These peanuts are then passed to the blending department, the second process. In the
blending department, machines blend organic chocolate pieces and organic dried fruits with the
peanuts from the first process. The blended mix is then inspected and packaged for delivery. In
both departments, direct materials enter production at the beginning of the process, while conversion costs occur continuously throughout each department's processing.

Exhibit 20.5 presents production data (in units) for GenX's roasting department. This exhibit
includes the percentage of completion for both materials and conversion; beginning work in
process inventory is 100% complete with respect to materials but only 65% complete with respect to conversion. Ending work in process inventory is 100% complete with respect to materials but only 25% complete with respect to conversion. Units completed and transferred to the
blending department are 100% complete with respect to both materials and conversion.

EXHIBIT 20.5

Production Data (in units)
for Roasting Department

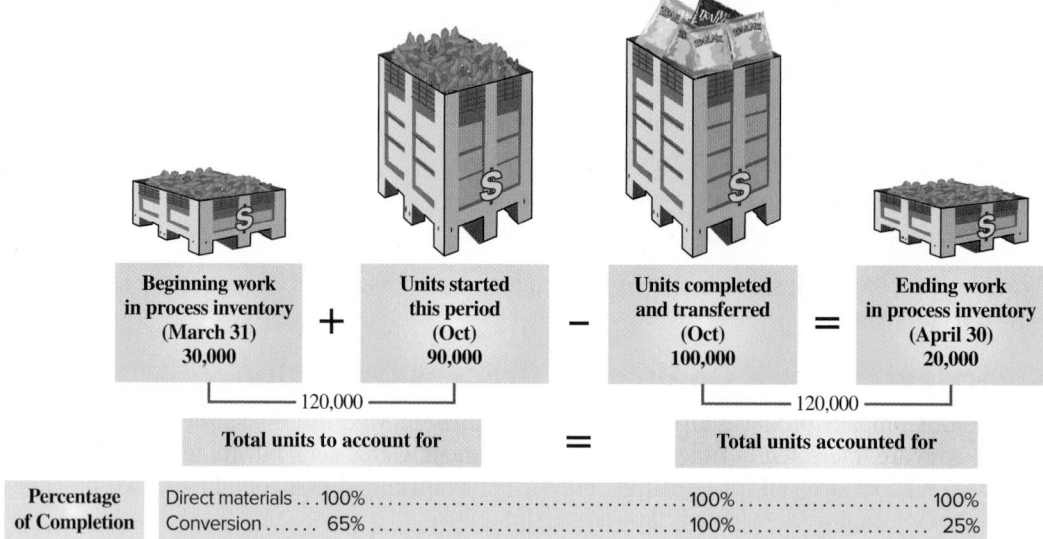

	Beginning work in process inventory (March 31) 30,000	+	Units started this period (Oct) 90,000	−	Units completed and transferred (Oct) 100,000	=	Ending work in process inventory (April 30) 20,000

└────── 120,000 ──────┘   └────── 120,000 ──────┘

Total units to account for	=	Total units accounted for

Percentage of Completion	Direct materials ...100% ....100% 100%
	Conversion ...... 65% ....100% 25%

Exhibit 20.6 presents production cost data for GenX's roasting department. We use the data
in Exhibits 20.5 and 20.6 to illustrate the four-step approach to process costing.

EXHIBIT 20.6

Roasting Department
Production Cost Data

GenX—Roasting Department		
Beginning work in process inventory (March 31)		
Direct materials costs	$ 81,000	
Conversion costs	108,900	$ 189,900
Costs during the current period (April)		
Direct materials costs	279,000	
Direct labor costs*	171,000	
Factory overhead costs applied (120% of direct labor)*	205,200	655,200
Total production costs		$845,100

*Total conversion costs for the month equal $376,200 ($171,000 + $205,200).

Step 1: Determine Physical Flow of Units

A *physical flow reconciliation* is a report that reconciles (1) the physical units started in a period
with (2) the physical units completed in that period. A physical flow reconciliation for GenX's
roasting department for April is shown in Exhibit 20.7.

GenX—Roasting Department			
Units to Account For		**Units Accounted For**	
Beginning work in process inventory.............	30,000 units	Units completed and transferred out.......................	100,000 units
Units started this period..........	90,000 units	Ending work in process inventory..........	20,000 units
Total units to account for	**120,000 units**	Total units accounted for.................	**120,000 units**

reconciled

WIP–Roasting (in units)			
Beg. inv.	30,000		
Started	90,000		
To acct. for	120,000		
		100,000	Tr. out
End. inv.	20,000		

Step 2: Compute Equivalent Units of Production

The second step is to compute *equivalent units of production* for direct materials and conversion costs for April. Since direct materials and conversion costs typically enter a process at different rates, departments must compute equivalent units separately for direct materials and conversion costs. Exhibit 20.8 shows the formula to compute equivalent units under the weighted-average method for both direct materials and conversion costs.

$$\text{Equivalent units of production (EUP)} = \text{Number of whole units completed and transferred out* } + \text{ Number of equivalent units in ending work in process}$$

*Transferred to next department or finished goods inventory.

For GenX's roasting department, we convert the 120,000 physical units to *equivalent units* based on how each input has been used. The roasting department fully completed its work on 100,000 units and partially completed its work on 20,000 units (from Exhibit 20.5). Equivalent units are computed by multiplying the number of units accounted for (from step 1) by the percentage of completion for each input—see Exhibit 20.9.

GenX—Roasting Department		
Equivalent Units of Production	**Direct Materials**	**Conversion**
Equivalent units completed and transferred out (100,000 × 100%)	100,000 EUP	100,000 EUP
Equivalent units for ending work in process		
Direct materials (20,000 × 100%)	20,000 EUP	
Conversion (20,000 × 25%)		5,000 EUP
Equivalent units of production...	120,000 EUP	105,000 EUP

The first row of Exhibit 20.9 reflects units transferred out in April. The roasting department entirely completed its work on the 100,000 units transferred out. These units have 100% of the materials and conversion required, or 100,000 equivalent units of each input (100,000 × 100%).

Rows two, three, and four refer to the 20,000 partially completed units. For direct materials, the units in ending work in process inventory include all materials required, so there are 20,000 equivalent units (20,000 × 100%) of materials in the unfinished physical units. For conversion, the units in ending work in process inventory include 25% of the conversion required, which implies 5,000 equivalent units of conversion (20,000 × 25%).

The final row reflects the total equivalent units of production, which is whole units of product that could have been manufactured with the amount of inputs used to create some complete and some incomplete units. The amount of inputs used to produce 100,000 complete units and to start 20,000 additional units is equivalent to the amount of direct materials in 120,000 whole units and the amount of conversion in 105,000 whole units.

© Ken Whitmore/Stone/Getty Images

NEED-TO-KNOW 20-2

EUP—Direct Materials
and Conversion
(Weighted Average)

C2

Do More: QS 20-5, QS 20-10,
E 20-4, E 20-8

A department began the month with 8,000 units in work in process inventory. These units were 100% complete with respect to direct materials and 40% complete with respect to conversion.

During the current month, the department started 56,000 units and completed 58,000 units. Ending work in process inventory includes 6,000 units, 80% complete with respect to direct materials and 70% complete with respect to conversion. Use the weighted-average method of process costing to:

1. Compute the department's equivalent units of production for the month for direct materials.
2. Compute the department's equivalent units of production for the month for conversion.

Solution—see supporting account computations to the side

1. EUP for materials = 58,000 + (6,000 × 80%) = 62,800 EUP
2. EUP for conversion = 58,000 + (6,000 × 70%) = 62,200 EUP

WIP (in units)			
Beg. inv.	8,000		
Started	56,000		
To acct. for	64,000		
		58,000	Tr. out
End. inv.	6,000		

Step 3: Compute Cost per Equivalent Unit

Point: Managers can examine changes in monthly costs per equivalent unit to help control production.

Under the weighted-average method, computation of EUP does not separate the units in beginning inventory from those started this period. Similarly, the weighted-average method combines the costs of beginning work in process inventory with the costs incurred in the current period. Total cost is then divided by the equivalent units of production (from step 2) to compute the average **cost per equivalent unit**. This process is illustrated in Exhibit 20.10. For direct materials, the cost averages $3.00 per EUP. For conversion, the cost per equivalent unit averages $4.62 per unit.

EXHIBIT 20.10

Cost per Equivalent Unit of Production—Weighted Average

GenX—Roasting Department		
Cost per Equivalent Unit of Production	**Direct Materials**	**Conversion**
Costs of beginning work in process inventory*..................	$ 81,000	$108,900
Costs incurred this period*................................	279,000	376,200**
Total costs...	$360,000	$485,100
÷ Equivalent units of production (from step 2)...................	120,000 EUP	105,000 EUP
= Cost per equivalent unit of production	$3.00 per EUP†	$4.62 per EUP‡

*From Exhibit 20.6   **$171,000 + $205,200   †$360,000 ÷ 120,000 EUP   ‡$485,100 ÷ 105,000 EUP

Step 4: Assign and Reconcile Costs

The EUP from step 2 and the cost per EUP from step 3 are used in step 4 to assign costs to (a) the 100,000 units that the roasting department completed and transferred to the blending department, and (b) the 20,000 units that remain in process in the roasting department. This is illustrated in Exhibit 20.11.

EXHIBIT 20.11

Report of Costs Accounted For—Weighted Average

GenX—Roasting Department		
Cost of units completed and transferred to Blending dept.		
Direct materials (100,000 EUP × $3.00 per EUP).................	$300,000	
Conversion (100,000 EUP × $4.62 per EUP).....................	462,000	
Cost of units completed this period		$762,000
Cost of ending work in process inventory		
Direct materials (20,000 EUP × $3.00 per EUP)..................	60,000	
Conversion (5,000 EUP × $4.62 per EUP).......................	23,100	
Cost of ending work in process inventory		83,100
Total costs accounted for		$845,100

Cost of Units Completed and Transferred

The 100,000 units completed and transferred to the blending department required 100,000 EUP of direct materials and 100,000 EUP of conversion. We assign $300,000 (100,000 EUP × $3.00 per EUP) of direct materials cost to those units. We also assign $462,000 (100,000 EUP × $4.62 per EUP) of conversion cost to those units. Total cost of the 100,000 completed and transferred units is $762,000 ($300,000 + $462,000), and the average cost per unit is $7.62 ($762,000 ÷ 100,000 units).

Cost of Units in Ending Work in Process Inventory

There are 20,000 incomplete units in work in process inventory at period-end. For direct materials, those units have 20,000 EUP of material (from step 2) at a cost of $3.00 per EUP (from step 3), which yields the materials cost of work in process inventory of $60,000 (20,000 EUP × $3.00 per EUP). For conversion, the in-process units reflect 5,000 EUP (from step 2). Using the $4.62 conversion cost per EUP (from step 3), we obtain conversion costs for in-process inventory of $23,100 (5,000 EUP × $4.62 per EUP). Total cost of work in process inventory at period-end is $83,100 ($60,000 + $23,100).

Reconciliation

Management verifies that total costs assigned to units completed and transferred plus the costs of units in process (from Exhibit 20.11) equal the costs incurred by production. Exhibit 20.12 shows the costs incurred by production this period. We then reconcile the *costs accounted for* in Exhibit 20.11 with the *costs to account for* in Exhibit 20.12.

EXHIBIT 20.12

Report of Costs to Account For—Weighted Average

GenX—Roasting Department		
Cost of beginning work in process inventory		
Direct materials..	$ 81,000	
Conversion	108,900	$ 189,900
Cost incurred this period		
Direct materials..	279,000	
Conversion	376,200	655,200
Total costs to account for		$845,100

The roasting department manager is responsible for $845,100 in costs: $189,000 from beginning work in process plus $655,200 of materials and conversion incurred in the period. At period-end, that manager must show where these costs are assigned. The roasting department manager reports that $83,100 is assigned to units in process and $762,000 is assigned to units completed and transferred out to the blending department (per Exhibit 20.11). The sum of these amounts equals $845,100. Thus, the total *costs to account for* equal the total *costs accounted for* (minor differences sometimes occur from rounding).

A department began the month with conversion costs of $65,000 in its beginning work in process inventory. During the current month, the department incurred $55,000 of conversion costs. Equivalent units of production for conversion for the month was 15,000 units. The department completed and transferred 12,000 units to the next department. The department uses the weighted-average method of process costing.

1. Compute the department's cost per equivalent unit for conversion for the month.
2. Compute the department's conversion cost of units transferred to the next department for the month.

NEED-TO-KNOW 20-3

Cost per EUP— Conversion, with Transfer

C3

Solution

1. ($65,000 + $55,000)/15,000 units = $8.00 per EUP for conversion

2. 12,000 units × $8.00 = $96,000 conversion cost transferred to next department

Do More: QS 20-11, QS 20-13, E 20-6

Process Cost Summary

An important managerial accounting report for a process costing system is the **process cost summary** (also called *production report*), which is prepared separately for each process or production department. Three reasons for the summary are to (1) help department managers control and

Point: The key report in a job order costing system is a job cost sheet, which reports manufacturing costs per job. A process cost summary reports manufacturing costs per equivalent unit of a process or department.

monitor their departments, (2) help factory managers evaluate department managers' performance, and (3) provide cost information for financial statements. A process cost summary achieves these purposes by describing the costs charged to each department, reporting the equivalent units of production achieved by each department, and determining the costs assigned to each department's output. It is prepared using a combination of Exhibits 20.7, 20.9, 20.10, 20.11, and 20.12.

The process cost summary for the roasting department is shown in Exhibit 20.13. The report is divided into three sections.

① This section lists the total costs charged to the department, including direct materials and conversion costs incurred, as well as the cost of the beginning work in process inventory.

② This section describes the equivalent units of production for the department. Equivalent units for materials and conversion are in separate columns. It also reports direct materials and conversion costs per equivalent unit.

③ This section allocates total costs among units worked on in the period. The $762,000 is the total cost of the 100,000 units transferred out of the roasting department to the blending department. The $83,100 is the cost of the 20,000 partially completed units in ending inventory in the

EXHIBIT 20.13

Process Cost Summary (Weighted Average)

GenX COMPANY—ROASTING DEPARTMENT
Process Cost Summary (Weighted-Average Method)
For Month Ended April 30, 2017

Costs Charged to Production

Costs of beginning work in process

Direct materials	$ 81,000	
Conversion	108,900	$ 189,900

① Costs incurred this period

Direct materials	279,000	
Conversion	376,200	655,200
Total costs to account for		$845,100

Unit Information

Units to account for:		Units accounted for:	
Beginning work in process	30,000	Completed and transferred out	100,000
Units started this period	90,000	Ending work in process	20,000
Total units to account for	120,000	Total units accounted for	120,000

Equivalent Units of Production (EUP)	**Direct Materials**	**Conversion**
Units completed and transferred out (100,000 × 100%)	100,000 EUP	100,000 EUP
Units of ending work in process		
Direct materials (20,000 × 100%)	20,000 EUP	
Conversion (20,000 × 25%)		5,000 EUP
Equivalent units of production	120,000 EUP	105,000 EUP

②

Cost per EUP	**Direct Materials**	**Conversion**
Costs of beginning work in process	$ 81,000	$108,900
Costs incurred this period	279,000	376,200
Total costs	$360,000	$485,100
÷EUP	120,000 EUP	105,000 EUP
Cost per EUP	$3.00 per EUP	$4.62 per EUP

Cost Assignment and Reconciliation

Costs transferred out (cost of goods manufactured)

Direct materials (100,000 EUP × $3.00 per EUP)	$300,000	
Conversion (100,000 EUP × $4.62 per EUP)	462,000	$ 762,000

③ Costs of ending work in process

Direct materials (20,000 EUP × $3.00 per EUP)	60,000	
Conversion (5,000 EUP × $4.62 per EUP)	23,100	83,100
Total costs accounted for		$845,100

reconciled

WIP–Roasting (in $)

Beg. inv.	189,900		
Incurred	655,200		
Subtotal	845,100		
		762,000	Tr. out
End. inv.	83,100		

roasting department. The assigned costs are then added to show that the total $845,100 cost charged to the roasting department in section ◇1◇ is now assigned to the units in section ◇3◇.

Using the Process Cost Summary   Managers use information in the process cost summary. For example, the roasting department's costs per equivalent unit are $3.00 for direct materials and $4.62 for conversion. Are the unit costs higher or lower than management expected? Are the unit costs higher or lower than prior months' unit costs? Such analyses can help managers find ways to improve production processes and to reduce future costs.

ACCOUNTING AND REPORTING FOR PROCESS COSTING

In this section we illustrate the journal entries to account for a process manufacturer. Exhibit 20.14 illustrates the flow of costs for GenX Company's roasting department. Materials, labor, and overhead costs flow into the manufacturing processes. GenX keeps separate Work in Process Inventory accounts for the roasting and blending departments; when goods are packaged and ready for sale, their costs are transferred to the Finished Goods Inventory account.

As in job order costing, a process costing system uses source documents. For example, *materials requisitions* signal the use of direct and indirect materials. *Time tickets* record the use of direct and indirect labor. While some companies might combine direct labor and overhead into conversion costs when computing costs per equivalent unit (as we showed), labor and overhead costs are accounted for separately within the company's accounts. Also, because overhead costs typically cannot be tied to individual processes, but rather benefit all processes or departments, most companies use a single Factory Overhead account to accumulate actual and applied overhead costs.

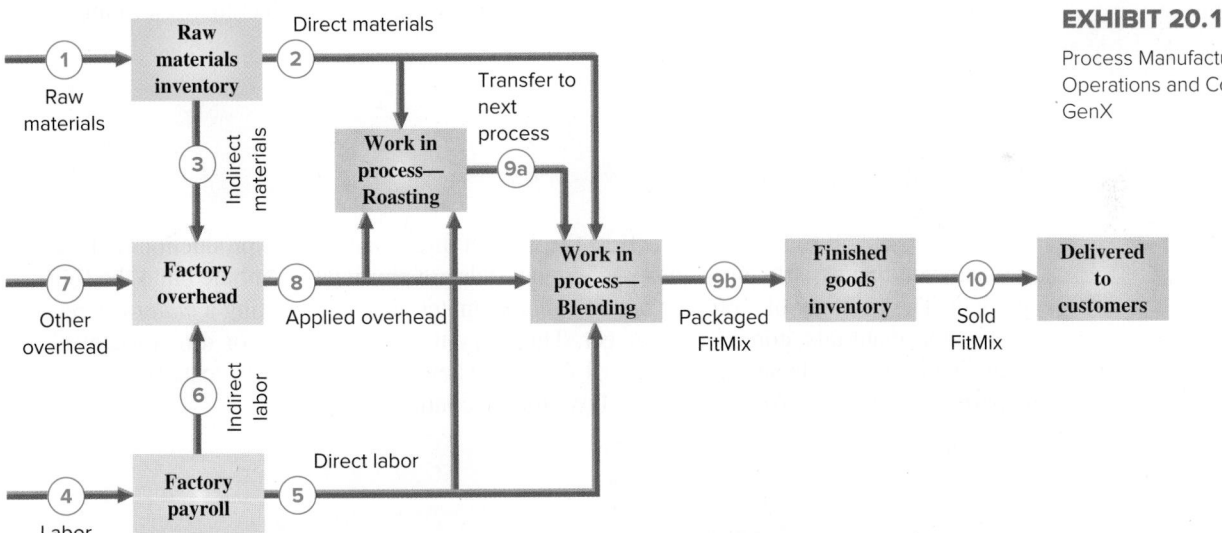

EXHIBIT 20.14

Process Manufacturing Operations and Costs: GenX

As with job order costing, process manufacturers must allocate, or apply, overhead to processes. This requires companies to find good *allocation bases,* such as direct labor hours or machine hours used. With increasing automation, companies with process operations use fewer direct labor hours and thus are more likely to use machine hours to allocate overhead.

Sometimes a single allocation base will not provide good overhead allocations. For example, direct labor cost might be a good allocation base for GenX's roasting department, but not for its blending department. As a result, a process manufacturer can use different overhead allocation rates for different production departments. However, all applied overhead is credited to a single Factory Overhead account.

Exhibit 20.15 presents cost data for GenX. Roasting department costs are from Exhibit 20.6. We use these data to show the journal entries in a process costing system.

Point: Actual overhead is debited to Factory Overhead.

EXHIBIT 20.15

Cost Data—GenX (Weighted Average)

GenX—Cost Data for Month Ending April 30	
Raw materials inventory (March 31)...........................	$100,000
Beginning work in process inventories (March 31)	
Work in process—Roasting..............................	$189,900
Work in process—Blending..............................	151,688
Materials purchased (on account)	$400,000
Materials requisitions during April	
Direct materials—Roasting.............................	$279,000
Direct materials—Blending.............................	102,000
Indirect materials	71,250
Factory payroll for April	
Direct labor—Roasting	$171,000
Direct labor—Blending	183,160
Indirect labor...	78,350
Other actual overhead costs during April	
Insurance expense—Factory	$ 11,930
Utilities payable—Factory..............................	7,945
Depreciation expense—Factory equipment	220,650
Other (paid in cash)....................................	21,875

P1

Record the flow of materials costs in process costing.

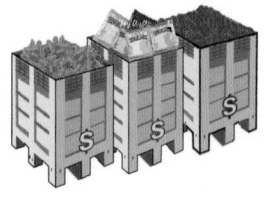

Assets = Liabilities + Equity
+400,000   +400,000

Accounting for Materials Costs

In Exhibit 20.14, arrow line ① reflects the arrival of materials at GenX's factory. These materials include organic peanuts, chocolate pieces, dried fruits, oil, salt, and packaging. They also include supplies for the production support office. GenX uses a perpetual inventory system and makes all purchases on credit. The summary entry for receipt of raw materials in April follows (dates in journal entries are omitted because they are summary entries, often reflecting two or more transactions or events).

①	Raw Materials Inventory	400,000	
	Accounts Payable..............................		400,000
	Acquired materials on credit for factory use.		

Arrow line ② in Exhibit 20.14 reflects the flow of direct materials to production in the roasting and blending departments. These direct materials are physically combined into the finished product. The manager of a process usually obtains materials by submitting a *materials requisition* to the materials storeroom manager. The entry to record the use of direct materials by GenX's production departments in April follows. These direct materials costs flow into each department's separate Work in Process Inventory account.

Assets = Liabilities + Equity
+279,000
+102,000
−381,000

②	Work in Process—Roasting	279,000	
	Work in Process—Blending............................	102,000	
	Raw Materials Inventory..........................		381,000
	Assign costs of direct materials used in production.		

In Exhibit 20.14, arrow line ③ reflects the flow of indirect materials from the storeroom to factory overhead. These materials are not clearly linked with any specific production process or department but are used to support overall production activity. As these costs cannot be linked directly to either the roasting or blending departments, they are recorded in GenX's single Factory Overhead account. The following entry records the cost of indirect materials used by GenX in April.

Example: What types of materials might the flow of arrow line ③ in Exhibit 20.14 reflect? *Answer:* Goggles, gloves, protective clothing, oil, salt, and cleaning supplies.

③	Factory Overhead	71,250	
	Raw Materials Inventory..........................		71,250
	Record indirect materials used in April.		

Accounting for Labor Costs

Exhibit 20.14 shows GenX's factory payroll costs as reflected in arrow line ④. Exhibit 20.15 shows costs of $171,000 for roasting department direct labor, $183,160 for blending department direct labor, and $78,350 for indirect labor. This total payroll of $432,510 is a product cost, and it is allocated to either Work in Process Inventory or Factory Overhead.

P2

Record the flow of labor costs in process costing.

Time reports from the production departments and the production support office trigger payroll entries. (For simplicity, we do not separately identify withholdings and additional payroll taxes for employees.) In a process operation, the direct labor of a production department includes all labor used exclusively by that department. This is the case even if labor is not applied to the product itself. If a production department in a process operation, for instance, has a full-time manager and a full-time maintenance worker, their salaries are *direct* labor costs of that process and are not factory overhead.

Arrow line ⑤ in Exhibit 20.14 shows GenX's use of direct labor. The following entry then records direct labor used. These direct labor costs flow into each department's separate Work in Process Inventory account.

⑤	Work in Process Inventory—Roasting...............	171,000	
	Work in Process Inventory—Blending	183,160	
	Factory Wages Payable		354,160
	Record direct labor used in production.		

Assets = Liabilities + Equity
+171,000   +354,160
+183,160

Arrow line ⑥ in Exhibit 20.14 reflects GenX's indirect labor costs. These employees provide clerical, maintenance, and other services that help production in both the roasting and blending departments. For example, they order materials, deliver them to the factory floor, repair equipment, operate and program computers used in production, keep payroll and other production records, clean up, and move goods across departments. The following entry records these indirect labor costs.

Point: A department's indirect labor cost might include an allocated portion of wages of a manager who supervises two or more departments. Allocation of costs between departments is discussed in a later chapter.

⑥	Factory Overhead	78,350	
	Factory Wages Payable		78,350
	Record indirect labor as overhead.		

After GenX posts these entries for direct and indirect labor, the Factory Wages Payable account has a balance of $432,510 ($354,160 + $78,350). The entry below shows the payment of this total payroll. After this entry, the Factory Wages Payable account has a zero balance.

④	Factory Wages Payable...........................	432,510	
	Cash		432,510
	Record factory wages for April.		

Assets = Liabilities + Equity
−432,510   −432,510

Accounting for Factory Overhead

Overhead costs other than indirect materials and indirect labor are reflected by arrow line ⑦ in Exhibit 20.14. These overhead items include the costs of insuring production assets, renting the factory building, using factory utilities, and depreciating factory equipment not directly related to a specific process. The following entry records these other overhead costs for April.

P3

Record the flow of factory overhead costs in process costing.

⑦	Factory Overhead	262,400	
	Prepaid Insurance.............................		11,930
	Utilities Payable		7,945
	Cash		21,875
	Accumulated Depreciation—Factory Equipment		220,650
	Record other overhead costs incurred in April.		

Point: The time it takes to process (cycle) products through a process is sometimes used to allocate costs.

Applying Overhead to Work in Process   Companies use *predetermined overhead rates* to apply overhead. These rates are estimated at the beginning of a period and used to apply overhead during the period. This allows managers to obtain up-to-date estimates of the costs of their processes during the period. This is important for process costing, where goods are transferred across departments before the entire production process is complete.

Arrow line ⑧ in Exhibit 20.14 reflects the application of factory overhead to the two production departments. Factory overhead is applied to processes by relating overhead cost to another variable such as direct labor hours or machine hours used. In many situations, a single allocation basis such as direct labor hours (or a single rate for the entire plant) fails to provide useful allocations. As a result, management may use different rates for different production departments. In our example, GenX applies overhead on the basis of direct labor cost as shown in Exhibit 20.16.

EXHIBIT 20.16

Applying Factory Overhead

Production Department	Direct Labor Cost	Predetermined Rate	Overhead Applied
Roasting...........	$171,000	120%	$205,200
Blending...........	183,160	120	219,792
Total			$424,992

GenX records its applied overhead with the following entry.

⑧	Work in Process Inventory—Roasting....................	205,200	
	Work in Process Inventory—Blending	219,792	
	Factory Overhead...............................		424,992
	Applied overhead costs to production departments at 120% of direct labor cost.		

■ Decision Ethics

Budget Officer   You are classifying costs of a new processing department as either direct or indirect. This department's manager instructs you to classify most of the costs as indirect so it will be charged a lower amount of overhead (because this department uses less labor, which is the overhead allocation base). This would penalize other departments with higher allocations and cause the ratings of managers in other departments to suffer. What action do you take? ■   [*Answer:* By classifing costs as indirect, the manager is passing some of his department's costs to a common overhead pool that other departments will partially absorb. Because overhead costs are allocated on direct labor for this company and the new department has a low direct labor cost, the new department is assigned less overhead. Such action suggests unethical behavior. You must object to such reclassification. If this manager refuses to comply, you must inform someone in a more senior position.]

NEED-TO-KNOW 20-4

Overhead Rate and Costs

P1   P2   P3

Tower Mfg. estimates it will incur $200,000 of total overhead costs during 2017. Tower allocates overhead based on machine hours; it estimates it will use a total of 10,000 machine hours during 2017. During February 2017, the assembly department of Tower Mfg. uses 375 machine hours. In addition, Tower incurred actual overhead costs as follows during February: indirect materials, $1,800; indirect labor, $5,700; depreciation on factory equipment, $8,000; factory utilities, $500.

1. Compute the company's predetermined overhead rate for 2017.

2. Prepare journal entries to record (a) overhead applied for the assembly department for the month and (b) actual overhead costs used during the month.

Solution

1. Predetermined overhead rate = Estimated overhead costs ÷ Estimated activity base
$$= \$200,000/10,000 \text{ machine hours} = \$20 \text{ per machine hour}$$

2a.

Work in Process Inventory—Assembly.................	7,500	
Factory Overhead..............................		7,500
Record applied overhead (375 hours × $20 per hour).		

2b.

Factory Overhead	16,000	
Raw Materials Inventory.........................		1,800
Factory Wages Payable		5,700
Accumulated Depreciation—Factory Equipment		8,000
Utilities Payable		500
Record actual overhead.		

Do More: QS 20-25, E 20-23, E 20-25

Accounting for Transfers

Transfers across Departments   Arrow line ⑨ⓐ in Exhibit 20.14 reflects the transfer of units from the roasting department to the blending department. The process cost summary for the roasting department (Exhibit 20.13) shows that the 100,000 units transferred to the blending department are assigned a cost of $762,000. The entry to record this transfer follows.

P4

Record the transfer of goods across departments, to Finished Goods Inventory, and to Cost of Goods Sold.

⑨ⓐ	Work in Process Inventory—Blending	762,000	
	Work in Process Inventory—Roasting		762,000
	Record transfer of 100,000 units from		
	roasting department to blending department.		

Assets = Liabilities + Equity
+762,000
−762,000

Units and costs *transferred out* of the roasting department are *transferred into* the blending department. Exhibit 20.17 shows this transfer using T-accounts for the separate Work in Process Inventory accounts (first in units and then in dollars).

EXHIBIT 20.17

Production and Cost Activity—Transfer to Blending Department

Roasting Department—Units		
Beg. inv.	30,000 units	
Started	90,000 units	
Total	120,000 units	
		100,000 units transferred out
End. inv.	20,000 units	

Blending Department—Units		
Beg. inv.	12,000 units	
Transferred in	100,000 units	
Total	112,000 units	
		97,000 units transferred to Finished Goods
End. inv.	15,000 units	

WIP Inventory—Roasting Dept.		
Beg. inv.*	189,900	
DM	279,000	
Conv.	376,200	
Total	845,100	
		762,000 Transferred out
End. inv.	83,100	

WIP Inventory—Blending Dept.		
Beg. inv.†	151,688	
Transferred in	762,000	
DM	102,000	
Conv.	402,952	
Total	1,418,640	1,262,940 Transferred to FG
End. inv.	155,700	

*$81,000 direct materials + $108,900 conversion

†$91,440 transferred in + $10,000 DM + $50,248 conversion

As Exhibit 20.17 shows, the blending department began the month with 12,000 units in beginning inventory, with a related cost of $151,688. In computing its production activity and costs, the blending department must also consider the units and costs transferred in from the roasting department, as shown in Exhibit 20.17. The 100,000 units transferred in from the roasting department, and their related costs of $762,000, are added to the blending department's number of units and separate Work in Process (WIP) Inventory account.

The blending department adds additional direct materials and conversion costs. The blending department incurred direct materials costs of $102,000 and conversion costs of $402,952 during the month. (Although not illustrated here, the concepts and methods used in this second department would be similar to those we showed in detail for the first department. The units and costs transferred in are considered separately from the materials and conversion added in the second department.)

Accounting for Transfer to Finished Goods   Arrow line ⑨b in Exhibit 20.14 reflects the transfer of units and their related costs from the blending department to finished goods inventory. At the end of the month, the blending department transferred 97,000 completed units, with a related cost of $1,262,940, to finished goods. The entry to record this transfer follows.

Assets   =   Liabilities + Equity
+1,262,940
−1,262,940

⑨b	Finished Goods Inventory	1,262,940	
	Work in Process Inventory—Blending		1,262,940
	Record transfer of completed goods.		

Accounting for Transfer to Cost of Goods Sold   Arrow line ⑩ reflects the sale of finished goods. Assume that GenX sold 106,000 units of FitMix this period, and that its beginning finished goods inventory was 26,000 units with a cost of $338,520. Also assume that its ending finished goods inventory consists of 20,000 units at a cost of $260,400. Using this information, cost of goods sold is computed as in Exhibit 20.18.

Finished Goods Inventory

Beg. bal.	338,520		
COGM	1,262,940		
Avail.	1,601,460		
		COGS	1,341,060
End. bal.	260,400		

EXHIBIT 20.18

Cost of Goods Sold

GenX—Cost of Goods Sold	
Beginning finished goods inventory	$ 338,520
+ Cost of goods manufactured this period	1,262,940
= Cost of goods available for sale	1,601,460
− Ending finished goods inventory	260,400
= Cost of goods sold	$1,341,060

The summary entry to record cost of goods sold for this period follows:

Assets   =   Liabilities + Equity
−1,341,060   −1,341,060

⑩	Cost of Goods Sold	1,341,060	
	Finished Goods Inventory		1,341,060
	Record cost of goods sold for April.		

Trends in Process Operations

Some recent trends in process operations are discussed next.

Process Design   Management concerns with production efficiency can lead companies to entirely reorganize production processes. For example, instead of producing different types of computers in a series of departments, a separate work center for each computer can be established in one department. The process cost system is then changed to account for each work center's costs.

Just-in-Time Production   Companies are increasingly adopting just-in-time techniques. With a just-in-time inventory system, inventory levels can be minimal. If raw materials are not ordered or received until needed, a Raw Materials Inventory account might be unnecessary. Instead, materials cost is immediately debited to the Work in Process Inventory account. Similarly, a Finished Goods Inventory account may not be needed. Instead, cost of finished goods may be immediately debited to the Cost of Goods Sold account.

Automation   Companies are increasingly automating their production processes and using robots. For example, manufacturers use robots on tasks that are hard for humans to perform. This automation results in reduced direct labor costs and a healthier workforce.

Continuous Processing   In some companies, like **Pepsi Bottling**, materials move continuously through the manufacturing process. In these cases, a **materials consumption report** summarizes the materials used and replaces materials requisitions.

© Natalia Kolesnikova/AFP/Getty Images

Services   Service-based businesses are increasingly prevalent. For routine, standardized services like oil changes and simple tax returns, computing costs based on the process is simpler and more useful than a cost per individual job. More complex service companies use process departments to perform specific tasks for consumers. Hospitals, for example, have radiology and physical therapy facilities, each with special equipment and trained employees. When patients need services, they are processed through departments to receive prescribed care.

Customer Orientation   Focus on customer orientation also leads to improved processes. A manufacturer of control devices improved quality and reduced production time by forming teams to study processes and suggest improvements. An ice cream maker studied customer tastes to develop a more pleasing ice cream texture.

Yield   Many process operations convert large amounts of raw materials into finished goods. In addition to information in process cost summaries, managers often measure **yield**, which is the amount of material output relative to the amount of material input. For example, assume a maker of trail mix started 10,000 pounds (units) of peanuts into its production process and ended with finished goods of 9,650 pounds. The yield is computed as: 9,650/10,000 = 96.5%. Yield might be less than 100% due to lost or stolen peanuts, roasting issues that burned peanuts, or other production problems. When yields are lower than expected, managers usually ask why and then take corrective action.

SUSTAINABILITY AND ACCOUNTING

Food processor **General Mills** needs a steady supply of high-quality corn, oats, and sugarcane. These agricultural inputs face risks due to water scarcity and climate change that could disrupt General Mills's process operations and hurt profits.

Buying from suppliers that follow sustainable principles reduces risk of reputational damage. The Sustainability Accounting Standards Board (SASB) recommends that food processors disclose information on *priority food ingredients* (those that are essential to the company's products), including details on the company's strategies to address strategic risks.

Consistent with SASB guidelines, General Mills disclosed the following information in its recent *Global Responsibility Report*.

General Mills Performance Dashboard (partial)			
Ingredient	**Primary Challenges**	**Target***	**Progress**
Vanilla	Smallholder farmer incomes, quality of ingredients	100%	45%
Oats	Declining supply due to profitability versus other crops	100	35
Sugarcane	Child and forced labor, working conditions	100	42
Palm oil	Deforestation, indigenous peoples' rights	100	83

*Target and progress amounts are the percent of the ingredient sourced sustainably.

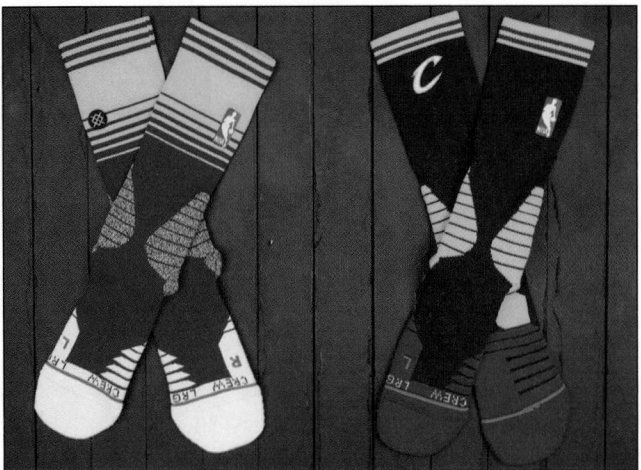

In addition to making continuous process improvements to reduce materials waste, creative companies such as **Stance** consider the sustainability of its workforce. Stance's headquarters are designed to encourage interaction and teamwork between employees.

Stance's founder, Jeff Kearl, believes that allowing his team to live more balanced lives helps in recruiting and retaining good employees, and helps them be more creative in their work. A basketball court, gym, skate bowl, and volleyball court build fun and teamwork into the workday.

Courtesy of Stance

Decision Analysis ■ ■ ■   **Hybrid Costing System**

A2

Explain and illustrate a hybrid costing system.

Many organizations use a **hybrid costing system** that contains features of both process and job order operations. A recent survey of manufacturers revealed that a majority use hybrid systems (also called **operation costing systems**).

To illustrate, consider a car manufacturer's assembly line. The line resembles a process operation in that the assembly steps for each car are nearly identical. But, the specifications of most cars have several important differences. At the **Ford** Mustang plant, each car assembled can be different from the previous car and the next car. This means that the costs of materials (subassemblies or components) for each car can differ. Accordingly, while the conversion costs (direct labor and overhead) can be accounted for using a process costing system, the component costs (direct materials) are accounted for using a job order system (separately for each car or type of car).

A hybrid system of processes requires a *hybrid costing system* to properly cost products or services. In the Ford plant, the assembly costs per car are readily determined using process costing. The costs of additional components can then be added to the assembly costs to determine each car's total cost (as in job order costing). To illustrate, consider the following information for a daily assembly process at Ford.

Assembly process costs	
Direct materials	$10.6 million
Conversion costs	$12.0 million
Number of cars assembled	1,000
Costs of three different types of wheels	$240, $330, $480
Costs of three different types of sound systems	$620, $840, $1,360

The assembly process costs $22,600 per car. Depending on the type of wheels and sound systems the customer requests, the cost of a car can range from $23,460 to $24,440 (a $980 difference).

Today companies are increasingly trying to standardize processes while attempting to meet individual customer needs. For example, **Lightning Wear** makes custom team uniforms, which are the same except for the team logo and colors added in the final process. The **Planters Company** packages peanuts in different sizes and types of packaging for different retailers. To the extent that differences among individual customers' requests are large, understanding the costs to satisfy those requests is important. Thus, monitoring and controlling both process and job order costs are important.

■ **Decision Ethics**

Entrepreneur   Your company makes similar products for three different customers. One customer demands 100% quality inspection of products at your location before shipping. The added costs of that inspection are spread across all three customers. If you charge the customer the costs of 100% quality inspection, you could lose that customer and experience a loss. Moreover, your other two customers do not question the amounts they pay. What actions (if any) do you take? ■   [*Answer:* By spreading the added quality-related costs across three customers, the price you charge is lower for the customer that demands the 100% quality inspection. You recover much of the added costs from the other two customers. This act likely breaches the trust placed by the other two customers. Your costing system should be changed, and you should consider renegotiating the pricing and/or quality test agreement with this one customer (at the risk of losing this customer).]

Pennsylvania Company produces a product that passes through two processes: grinding and mixing. Information related to its grinding department manufacturing activities for July follows. The company uses the weighted-average method of process costing.

COMPREHENSIVE 1

Weighted-Average Method

Grinding Department

Raw Materials

Beginning inventory.........................	$100,000
Raw materials purchased on credit	211,400
Direct materials used.......................	(190,000)
Indirect materials used	(51,400)
Ending inventory	$ 70,000

Factory Payroll

Direct labor incurred	$ 55,500
Indirect labor incurred.....................	50,625
Total payroll	$106,125

Factory Overhead

Indirect materials used	$ 51,400
Indirect labor used........................	50,625
Other overhead costs	71,725
Total factory overhead incurred	$173,750

Factory Overhead Applied

Overhead applied (200% of direct labor)	$111,000

Grinding Department

Beginning work in process inventory (units)	5,000
Percentage completed—Materials..............	100%
Percentage completed—Conversion............	70%
Beginning work in process inventory (costs)	
Direct materials used	$20,000
Direct labor incurred.........................	9,600
Overhead applied (200% of direct labor)	19,200
Total costs of beginning work in process	$48,800
Units started this period	20,000
Units transferred to mixing this period	17,000
Ending work in process inventory (units)	8,000
Percentage completed—Materials..............	100%
Percentage completed—Conversion............	20%

Required

Complete the requirements below for the grinding department.

1. Prepare a physical flow reconciliation for July.

2. Compute the equivalent units of production in July for direct materials and conversion.

3. Compute the costs per equivalent unit of production in July for direct materials and conversion.

4. Prepare a report of costs accounted for and a report of costs to account for.

PLANNING THE SOLUTION

- Track the physical flow to determine the number of units completed in July.
- Compute the equivalent units of production for direct materials and conversion.
- Compute the costs per equivalent unit of production with respect to direct materials and conversion, and determine the cost per unit for each.
- Compute the total cost of the goods transferred to mixing by using the equivalent units and unit costs. Determine (a) the cost of the beginning work in process inventory, (b) the materials and conversion costs added to the beginning work in process inventory, and (c) the materials and conversion costs added to the units started and completed in the month.

SOLUTION

1. Physical flow reconciliation.

Units to Account For		Units Accounted For	
Beginning work in process inventory............	5,000 units	Units completed and transferred out.......................	17,000 units
Units started this period.........	20,000 units	Ending work in process inventory..........	8,000 units
Total units to account for	**25,000 units**	Total units accounted for.................	**25,000 units**

reconciled

2. Equivalent units of production (weighted average).

Equivalent Units of Production	Direct Materials	Conversion
Equivalent units completed and transferred out	17,000 EUP	17,000 EUP
Equivalent units in ending work in process		
Direct materials (8,000 × 100%)...................	8,000 EUP	
Conversion (8,000 × 20%)		1,600 EUP
Equivalent units of production.......................	25,000 EUP	18,600 EUP

3. Costs per equivalent unit of production (weighted average).

Costs per Equivalent Unit of Production	Direct Materials	Conversion
Costs of beginning work in process	$ 20,000	$ 28,800
Costs incurred this period	190,000	166,500*
Total costs	$210,000	$195,300
÷ Equivalent units of production (from part 2)..........	25,000 EUP	18,600 EUP
= Costs per equivalent unit of production	$8.40 per EUP	$10.50 per EUP

*Direct labor of $55,500 + overhead applied of $111,000

4. Reports of costs accounted for and of costs to account for (weighted average).

Report of Costs Accounted For		
Cost of units transferred out (cost of goods manufactured)		
Direct materials ($8.40 per EUP × 17,000 EUP)	$142,800	
Conversion ($10.50 per EUP × 17,000 EUP)....................................	178,500	
Cost of units completed this period		$ 321,300
Cost of ending work in process inventory		
Direct materials ($8.40 per EUP × 8,000 EUP)	67,200	
Conversion ($10.50 per EUP × 1,600 EUP)....................................	16,800	
Cost of ending work in process inventory		84,000
Total costs accounted for		**$405,300**

Report of Costs to Account For		
Cost of beginning work in process inventory		
Direct materials	$ 20,000	
Conversion...	28,800	$ 48,800
Cost incurred this period		
Direct materials	190,000	
Conversion...	166,500	356,500
Total costs to account for		**$405,300**

reconciled

Refer to the information in Need-To-Know 20-5. For the grinding department, complete requirements 1 through 4 using the FIFO method. (Round the cost per equivalent unit of conversion to two decimal places.)

SOLUTION

1. Physical flow reconciliation (FIFO).

Units to Account For		Units Accounted For	
Beginning work in process inventory............	5,000 units	Units completed and transferred out........................	17,000 units
Units started this period.........	20,000 units	Ending work in process inventory..........	8,000 units
Total units to account for........	**25,000 units**	Total units accounted for.................	**25,000 units**

reconciled

2. Equivalent units of production (FIFO).

Equivalent Units of Production	Direct Materials	Conversion
(a) Equivalent units complete beginning work in process		
Direct materials (5,000 × 0%)	0 EUP	
Conversion (5,000 × 30%)		1,500 EUP
(b) Equivalent units started and completed..........................	12,000 EUP	12,000 EUP
(c) Equivalent units in ending work in process		
Direct materials (8,000 × 100%)	8,000 EUP	
Conversion (8,000 × 20%)		1,600 EUP
Equivalent units of production.....................................	20,000 EUP	15,100 EUP

3. Costs per equivalent unit of production (FIFO).

Costs per Equivalent Unit of Production	Direct Materials	Conversion
Costs incurred this period	$190,000	$ 166,500*
÷ Equivalent units of production (from part 2)................	20,000 EUP	15,100 EUP
= Costs per equivalent unit of production	$9.50 per EUP	$11.03 per EUP**

*Direct labor of $55,500 plus overhead applied of $111,000   **Rounded

4. Reports of costs accounted for and of costs to account for (FIFO).

Report of Costs Accounted For		
Cost of units transferred out (cost of goods manufactured)		
Cost of beginning work in process inventory.....................................		$ 48,800
Cost to complete beginning work in process		
Direct materials ($9.50 per EUP × 0 EUP)	$ 0	
Conversion ($11.03 per EUP × 1,500 EUP).................................	16,545	16,545
Cost of units started and completed this period		
Direct materials ($9.50 per EUP × 12,000 EUP)	114,000	
Conversion ($11.03 per EUP × 12,000 EUP).................................	132,360	246,360
Total cost of units finished this period		311,705
Cost of ending work in process inventory		
Direct materials ($9.50 per EUP × 8,000 EUP)	76,000	
Conversion ($11.03 per EUP × 1,600 EUP).................................	17,648	
Total cost of ending work in process inventory		93,648
Total costs accounted for.....................................		**$405,353**
Report of Costs to Account For		
Cost of beginning work in process inventory		
Direct materials	$ 20,000	
Conversion	28,800	$ 48,800
Costs incurred this period		
Direct materials	190,000	
Conversion	166,500	356,500
Total costs to account for.....................................		**$405,300**

reconciled (with $53 rounding difference)

NEED-TO-KNOW 20-7

COMPREHENSIVE 3

Journal Entries for Process Costing

Garcia Manufacturing produces a product that passes through a molding process and then through an assembly process. Partial information related to its manufacturing activities for July follows.

Direct materials

Raw materials purchased on credit	$400,000
Direct materials used—Molding	190,000
Direct materials used—Assembly	88,600

Direct Labor

Direct labor—Molding	$ 42,000
Direct labor—Assembly	55,375

Factory Overhead (Actual costs)

Indirect materials used	$ 51,400
Indirect labor used	50,625
Other overhead costs	71,725
Total factory overhead incurred	$173,750

Factory Overhead Applied

Molding (150% of direct labor)	$ 63,000
Assembly (200% of direct labor)	110,750
Total factory overhead applied	$173,750

Cost Transfers

From molding to assembly	$277,200
From assembly to finished goods	578,400
From finished goods to cost of goods sold	506,100

Required

Prepare summary journal entries to record the transactions and events of July for: (a) raw materials purchases, (b) direct materials usage, (c) indirect materials usage, (d) direct labor usage, (e) indirect labor usage, (f) other overhead costs (credit Other Accounts), (g) application of overhead to the two departments, (h) transfer of partially completed goods from molding to assembly, (i) transfer of finished goods out of assembly, and (j) the cost of goods sold.

SOLUTION

Summary journal entries for the transactions and events in July.

a. Raw Materials Inventory	400,000	
Accounts Payable		400,000
Record raw materials purchases.		
b. Work in Process Inventory—Molding	190,000	
Work in Process Inventory—Assembly	88,600	
Raw Materials Inventory		278,600
Record direct materials usage.		
c. Factory Overhead	51,400	
Raw Materials Inventory		51,400
Record indirect materials usage.		
d. Work in Process Inventory—Molding	42,000	
Work in Process Inventory—Assembly	55,375	
Factory Wages Payable		97,375
Record direct labor usage.		
e. Factory Overhead	50,625	
Factory Wages Payable		50,625
Record indirect labor usage.		

f. Factory Overhead	71,725	
Other Accounts		71,725
Record other overhead costs.		
g. Work in Process Inventory—Molding	63,000	
Work in Process Inventory—Assembly	110,750	
Factory Overhead		173,750
Record application of overhead.		
h. Work in Process Inventory—Assembly	277,200	
Work in Process Inventory—Molding		277,200
Record transfer of partially completed goods from molding to assembly.		
i. Finished Goods Inventory	578,400	
Work in Process Inventory—Assembly		578,400
Record transfer of finished goods out of assembly.		
j. Cost of Goods Sold	506,100	
Finished Goods Inventory		506,100
Record cost of goods sold.		

APPENDIX

20A   FIFO Method of Process Costing

The FIFO method of process costing assigns costs to units assuming a first-in, first-out flow of product. The key difference between the FIFO and weighted-average methods lies in the treatment of beginning work in process inventory. Under the weighted-average method, the number of units and the costs in beginning work in process inventory are combined with production activity in the current period to compute costs per equivalent unit. Thus, the weighted-average method combines production activity across two periods.

The FIFO method, in contrast, focuses on production activity *in the current period only*. The FIFO method assumes that the units that were in process at the beginning of the period are completed during the current period. Thus, under the FIFO method equivalent units of production are computed as shown in Exhibit 20A.1.

C4 _____

Describe accounting for production activity and preparation of a process cost summary using FIFO.

Equivalent units of production (EUP)	=	Number of equivalent units needed to complete beginning work in process	+	Number of whole units started, completed, and transferred out*	+	Number of equivalent units in ending work in process

EXHIBIT 20A.1

Computing EUP—FIFO Method

*Transferred to next department or finished goods inventory.

In computing cost per equivalent unit, the FIFO method ignores the cost of beginning work in process inventory. Instead, FIFO uses *only the costs incurred in the current period*, as shown in Exhibit 20A.2.

$$\text{Cost per EUP (FIFO)} = \frac{\text{Manufacturing costs added during current period}}{\text{Equivalent units of production during current period}}$$

EXHIBIT 20A.2

Cost per EUP—FIFO Method

We use the data in Exhibit 20A.3 to illustrate the FIFO method for GenX's roasting department.

EXHIBIT 20A.3

Production Data—Roasting Department (FIFO method)

GenX—Roasting Department	
Beginning work in process inventory (March 31)	
Units of product	30,000 units
Percentage of completion—Direct materials	100%
Percentage of completion—Conversion costs	65%
Direct materials costs.	$ 81,000
Conversion costs	$108,900
Production activity during the current period (April)	
Units started this period.	90,000 units
Units transferred out (completed)	100,000 units
Direct materials costs.	$279,000
Direct labor costs	$171,000
Factory overhead costs applied (120% of direct labor)	$205,200
Ending work in process inventory (April 30)	
Units of product	20,000 units
Percentage of completion—Direct materials	100%
Percentage of completion—Conversion	25%

Exhibit 20A.3 shows selected information from GenX's roasting department for the month of April. Accounting for a department's activity for a period includes four steps: (1) determine physical flow, (2) compute equivalent units, (3) compute cost per equivalent unit, and (4) determine cost assignment and reconciliation. This appendix describes each of these steps using the FIFO method for process costing.

Step 1: Determine Physical Flow of Units   A *physical flow reconciliation* is a report that reconciles (1) the physical units started in a period with (2) the physical units completed in that period. The physical flow reconciliation for GenX's roasting department for April is shown in Exhibit 20A.4.

EXHIBIT 20A.4

Physical Flow Reconciliation

GenX—Roasting Department			
Units to Account For		**Units Accounted For**	
Beginning work in process inventory.	30,000 units	Units completed and transferred out.	100,000 units
Units started this period.	90,000 units	Ending work in process inventory.	20,000 units
Total units to account for	**120,000 units**	Total units accounted for	**120,000 units**

reconciled

Point: Step 1 is exactly the same under the weighted-average method.

Step 2: Compute Equivalent Units of Production—FIFO Exhibit 20A.4 shows that the roasting department completed 100,000 units during the month. The FIFO method assumes that the units in beginning inventory were the first units completed during the month. Thus, FIFO assumes that of the 100,000 completed units, 30,000 consist of units in beginning work in process inventory that were completed during the month. This means that 70,000 (100,000 − 30,000) units were both started and completed during the month. This also means that 20,000 units were started but not completed during the month (90,000 units started − 70,000 units started and completed). Exhibit 20A.5 shows how units flowed through the roasting department, assuming FIFO.

EXHIBIT 20A.5

FIFO—Flow of Units

Roasting Department—Units			
Beg. inv.	30,000	30,000 Completed and transferred out	
Started	90,000	70,000 Started and completed	
To account for	120,000	100,000 Transferred out	
End. inv.	20,000		

In computing equivalent units of production, the roasting department must consider these three distinct groups of units:

- Units in beginning work in process inventory (30,000).
- Units started and completed during the month (70,000).
- Units in ending work in process inventory (20,000).

GenX's roasting department then computes equivalent units of production under FIFO as shown in Exhibit 20A.6. We compute EUP for each of the three distinct groups of units, and sum them to find total EUP.

EXHIBIT 20A.6

Equivalent Units of Production—FIFO

Point: EUP = Number of physical units × Percent of work completed this period.

GenX—Roasting Department		
Equivalent Units of Production	**Direct Materials**	**Conversion**
(a) Equivalent units to complete beginning work in process		
Direct materials (30,000 × 0%)	0 EUP	
Conversion (30,000 × 35%).................................		10,500 EUP
(b) Equivalent units started and completed (70,000 × 100%)*	70,000 EUP	70,000 EUP
(c) Equivalent units in ending work in process		
Direct materials (20,000 × 100%)...........................	20,000 EUP	
Conversion (20,000 × 25%).................................		5,000 EUP
Equivalent units of production	90,000 EUP	85,500 EUP

*Units completed this period.................... 100,000 units
Less units in beginning work in process .... 30,000 units
Units started and completed this period........... 70,000 units

Direct Materials To calculate the equivalent units of production for direct materials, we start with the equivalent units in beginning work in process inventory. We see that beginning work in process inventory was 100% complete with respect to materials; no materials were needed to complete these units. Thus, this group of units required 0 EUP during the month. Next, we consider the units started and completed during the month. In terms of direct materials, the 70,000 units started and completed during the month received 100% of their materials during the month. Thus, EUP for this group is 70,000 units (70,000 × 100%). Finally, we consider the units in ending work in process inventory. The roasting department started but *did not* complete 20,000 units during the month. This group received all of its materials during the month. Thus, EUP for this group is 20,000 units (20,000 × 100%). The sum of the EUP for these three distinct groups of units is 90,000 (computed as 0 + 70,000 + 20,000), which is the total number of equivalent units of production for direct materials during the month.

Conversion To calculate the equivalent units of production for conversion, we start by determining the percentage of conversion costs needed to complete the beginning work in process inventory. As Exhibit 20A.3 shows, the beginning work in process inventory of 30,000 units was 65% complete with respect to conversion. Thus, this group of units required an additional 35% of conversion costs during the period to complete those units (100% − 65%), or 10,500 EUP (30,000 × 35%). Next, we consider the units started and completed during the month. The units started and completed during the month incurred 100% of their conversion costs during the month. Thus, EUP for this group is 70,000 units (70,000 × 100%). Finally, we consider the units in ending work in process inventory. The ending work in process inventory incurred 25% of its conversion costs (see Exhibit 20A.3) during the month. Thus, EUP for this group is 5,000 units (20,000 × 25%). The sum of the EUP for these three distinct groups of units is 85,500 (computed as 10,500 + 70,000 + 5,000). Thus, the roasting department's equivalent units of production for conversion for the month is 85,500 units.

NEED-TO-KNOW 20-8

EUP—Direct Materials and Conversion (FIFO)

C4

A department began the month with 50,000 units in work in process inventory. These units were 90% complete with respect to direct materials and 40% complete with respect to conversion. During the month, the department started 286,000 units; 220,000 of these units were completed during the month. The remaining 66,000 units are in ending work in process inventory, 80% complete with respect to direct materials and 30% complete with respect to conversion. Use the FIFO method of process costing to:

1. Compute the department's equivalent units of production for the month for direct materials.
2. Compute the department's equivalent units of production for the month for conversion.

		Materials		Conversion	
	Units	Current Month %	EUP	Current Month %	EUP
Finish Bl	50,000	10%	5,000	60%	30,000
Start & Finish	220,000	100%	220,000	100%	220,000
Start El	66,000	80%	52,800	30%	19,800
			277,800		269,800

Solution—computations to the side show another way to get solutions

1. EUP for materials = (50,000 × 10%) + (220,000 × 100%) + (66,000 × 80%) = 277,800 EUP
2. EUP for conversion = (50,000 × 60%) + (220,000 × 100%) + (66,000 × 30%) = 269,800 EUP

Do More: QS 20-14, QS 20-15, E 20-5, E 20-10

Step 3: Compute Cost per Equivalent Unit—FIFO To compute cost per equivalent unit, we take the direct materials and conversion costs added in April and divide by the equivalent units of production from step 2. Exhibit 20A.7 illustrates these computations.

EXHIBIT 20A.7

Cost per Equivalent Unit of Production—FIFO

GenX—Roasting Department		
Cost per Equivalent Unit of Production	Direct Materials	Conversion
Costs incurred this period (from Exhibit 20A.3)...........	$279,000	$376,200
÷ Equivalent units of production (from step 2)	90,000 EUP	85,500 EUP
Cost per equivalent unit of production..................	$3.10 per EUP	$4.40 per EUP

It is essential to compute costs per equivalent unit for *each* input because production inputs are added at different times in the process. The FIFO method computes the cost per equivalent unit based solely on this period's EUP and costs (unlike the weighted-average method, which adds in the costs of the beginning work in process inventory).

NEED-TO-KNOW 20-9

Cost per EUP—Direct Materials and Conversion (FIFO)

C4

A department started the month with beginning work in process inventory of $130,000 ($90,000 for direct materials and $40,000 for conversion). During the month, the department incurred additional direct materials costs of $700,000 and conversion costs of $500,000. Assume that equivalent units for the month were computed as 250,000 for materials and 200,000 for conversion.

1. Compute the department's cost per equivalent unit of production for the month for direct materials.
2. Compute the department's cost per equivalent unit of production for the month for conversion.

Solution

1. Cost per EUP of materials = $700,000/250,000 = $2.80
2. Cost per EUP of conversion = $500,000/200,000 = $2.50

Do More: QS 20-15, QS 20-17, E 20-7

Step 4: Assign and Reconcile Costs The equivalent units determined in step 2 and the cost per equivalent unit computed in step 3 are both used to assign costs (1) to units that the production department completed and transferred to the blending department and (2) to units that remain in process at period-end.

As it did in computing equivalent units in step 2, the roasting department now must compute costs for three distinct groups of units:

- Costs to complete the beginning work in process inventory.
- Costs to complete the units started and completed during the month.
- Costs of ending work in process inventory.

In the first section of Exhibit 20A.8, we see that the cost of units completed in April includes the $189,900 cost carried over from March for work already applied to the 30,000 units that make up beginning work in process inventory, plus the $46,200 incurred in April to complete those units. The next section includes the $525,000 of cost assigned to the 70,000 units started and completed this period. Thus, the total cost of goods manufactured in April is $761,100. The average cost per unit for goods completed in April is $7.611 ($761,100 ÷ 100,000 completed units).

EXHIBIT 20A.8

Report of Costs Accounted For—FIFO

GenX—Roasting Department		
Cost of beginning work in process inventory		$ 189,900
Cost to complete beginning work in process		
Direct materials ($3.10 per EUP × 0 EUP)	$ 0	
Conversion ($4.40 per EUP × 10,500 EUP)	46,200	46,200
Cost of units started and completed this period		
Direct materials ($3.10 per EUP × 70,000 EUP)	217,000	
Conversion ($4.40 per EUP × 70,000 EUP)	308,000	525,000
Total cost of units finished and transferred out this period		761,100
Cost of ending work in process inventory		
Direct materials ($3.10 per EUP × 20,000 EUP)	62,000	
Conversion ($4.40 per EUP × 5,000 EUP)	22,000	
Total cost of ending work in process inventory		84,000
Total costs accounted for		**$845,100**

The computation for cost of ending work in process inventory is in the final section of Exhibit 20A.8. That cost of $84,000 ($62,000 + $22,000) also is the ending balance for the Work in Process Inventory—Roasting account.

The roasting department manager verifies that the total costs assigned to units transferred out and units still in process equal the total costs incurred by production. We reconcile the costs accounted for (in Exhibit 20A.8) to the costs that production was charged for as shown in Exhibit 20A.9.

EXHIBIT 20A.9

Report of Costs to Account For—FIFO

Cost of beginning work in process inventory		
Direct materials	$ 81,000	
Conversion	108,900	$ 189,900
Costs incurred this period		
Direct materials	279,000	
Conversion	376,200	655,200
Total costs to account for.		**$845,100**

The roasting department production manager is responsible for $845,100 in costs: $189,900 that had been assigned to the department's work in process inventory as of April 1 plus $655,200 of costs the department incurred in April. At period-end, the manager must identify where those costs were assigned. The production manager can report that $761,100 of cost was assigned to units completed in April and $84,000 was assigned to units still in process at period-end.

Process Cost Summary The final report is the process cost summary, which summarizes key information from previous exhibits. Reasons for the summary are to (1) help managers control and monitor costs, (2) help upper management assess department manager performance, and (3) provide cost information for financial reporting. The process cost summary, using FIFO, for GenX's roasting department is in Exhibit 20A.10.

① This section lists the total costs charged to the department, including direct materials and conversion costs incurred, as well as the cost of the beginning work in process inventory.

② This section describes the equivalent units of production for the department. Equivalent units for conversion are in separate columns. It also reports direct materials and conversion costs per equivalent unit.

③ This section allocates total costs among units worked on in the period.

GenX COMPANY— ROASTING DEPARTMENT
Process Cost Summary (FIFO Method)
For Month Ended April 30, 2017

Costs charged to production

Costs of beginning work in process inventory

Direct materials	$ 81,000	
Conversion	108,900	$ 189,900

Costs incurred this period

Direct materials	279,000	
Conversion	376,200	655,200
Total costs to account for		$845,100

Unit information

Units to account for		Units accounted for	
Beginning work in process	30,000	Transferred out	100,000
Units started this period	90,000	Ending work in process	20,000
Total units to account for	120,000	Total units accounted for	120,000

Equivalent units of production	**Direct Materials**	**Conversion**
Equivalent units to complete beginning work in process		
Direct materials (30,000 × 0%)	0 EUP	
Conversion (30,000 × 35%)		10,500 EUP
Equivalent units started and completed	70,000 EUP	70,000 EUP
Equivalent units in ending work in process		
Direct materials (20,000 × 100%)	20,000 EUP	
Conversion (20,000 × 25%)		5,000 EUP
Equivalent units of production	90,000 EUP	85,500 EUP

Cost per equivalent unit of production	**Direct Materials**	**Conversion**
Costs incurred this period	$279,000	$376,200
÷ Equivalent units of production	90,000 EUP	85,500 EUP
Cost per equivalent unit of production	$3.10 per EUP	$4.40 per EUP

reconciled

Cost assignment and reconciliation

(cost of units completed and transferred out)

Cost of beginning work in process		$ 189,900
Cost to complete beginning work in process		
Direct materials ($3.10 per EUP × 0 EUP)	$ 0	
Conversion ($4.40 per EUP × 10,500 EUP)	46,200	46,200
Cost of units started and completed this period		
Direct materials ($3.10 per EUP × 70,000 EUP)	217,000	
Conversion ($4.40 per EUP × 70,000 EUP)	308,000	525,000
Total cost of units finished this period		761,100

Cost of ending work in process

Direct materials ($3.10 per EUP × 20,000 EUP)	62,000	
Conversion ($4.40 per EUP × 5,000 EUP)	22,000	
Total cost of ending work in process		84,000
Total costs accounted for		$845,100

①
②
③

■ **Decision Maker**

Cost Manager   As cost manager for an electronics manufacturer, you apply a process costing system using FIFO. Your company plans to adopt a just-in-time system and eliminate inventories. What is the impact of the use of FIFO (versus the weighted-average method) given these plans? ■   [*Answer:* Differences between the FIFO and weighted-average methods are greatest when large work in process inventories exist and when costs fluctuate. The method used if inventories are eliminated does not matter; both produce identical costs.]

Summary

C1 **Explain process operations and the way they differ from job order operations.** Process operations produce large quantities of similar products or services by passing them through a series of processes, or steps, in production. Like job order operations, they combine direct materials, direct labor, and overhead in the operations. Unlike job order operations that assign the responsibility for each *job* to a manager, process operations assign the responsibility for each *process* to a manager.

C2 **Define and compute equivalent units and explain their use in process costing.** Equivalent units of production measure the activity of a process as the number of units that would be completed in a period if all effort had been applied to units that were started and finished. This measure of production activity is used to compute the cost per equivalent unit and to assign costs to finished goods and work in process inventory. To compute equivalent units, determine the number of units that would have been finished if all materials (or conversion) had been used to produce units that were started and completed during the period. The costs incurred by a process are divided by its equivalent units to yield cost per equivalent unit.

C3 **Describe accounting for production activity and preparation of a process cost summary using weighted average.** A process cost summary reports on the activities of a production process or department for a period. It describes the costs charged to the department, the equivalent units of production for the department, and the costs assigned to the output. The report aims to (1) help managers control their departments, (2) help factory managers evaluate department managers' performance, and (3) provide cost information for financial statements. A process cost summary includes the physical flow of units, equivalent units of production, costs per equivalent unit, and a cost reconciliation. It reports the units and costs to account for during the period and how they were accounted for during the period. In terms of units, the summary includes the beginning work in process inventory and the units started during the month. These units are accounted for in terms of the goods completed and transferred out, and the ending work in process inventory. With respect to costs, the summary includes materials and conversion costs assigned to the process during the period. It shows how these costs are assigned to goods completed and transferred out, and to ending work in process inventory.

C4^A **Describe accounting for production activity and preparation of a process cost summary using FIFO.** The FIFO method for process costing is applied and illustrated to (1) report the physical flow of units, (2) compute the equivalent units of production, (3) compute the cost per equivalent unit of production, and (4) assign and reconcile costs.

A1 **Compare process costing and job order costing.** Process and job order manufacturing operations are similar in that both combine materials and conversion to produce products or services. They differ in the way they are organized and managed. In job order operations, the job order costing system assigns product costs to specific jobs. In process operations, the process costing system assigns product costs to specific processes. The total costs associated with each process are then divided by the number of units passing through that process to get cost per equivalent unit. The costs per equivalent unit for all processes are added to determine the total cost per unit of a product or service.

A2 **Explain and illustrate a hybrid costing system.** A hybrid costing system contains features of both job order and process costing systems. Generally, certain direct materials are accounted for by individual products as in job order costing, but direct labor and overhead costs are accounted for similar to process costing.

P1 **Record the flow of materials costs in process costing.** Materials purchased are debited to a Raw Materials Inventory account. As direct materials are issued to processes, they are separately accumulated in a Work in Process Inventory account for that process. As indirect materials are used, their costs are debited to Factory Overhead.

P2 **Record the flow of labor costs in process costing.** Direct labor costs are assigned to the Work in Process Inventory account pertaining to each process. As indirect labor is used, its cost is debited to Factory Overhead.

P3 **Record the flow of factory overhead costs in process costing.** Actual overhead costs are recorded as debits to the Factory Overhead account. Estimated overhead costs are allocated, using a predetermined overhead rate, to the different processes. This allocated amount is credited to the Factory Overhead account and debited to the Work in Process Inventory account for each separate process.

P4 **Record the transfer of goods across departments, to Finished Goods Inventory, and to Cost of Goods Sold.** As units are passed through processes, their accumulated costs are transferred across separate Work in Process Inventory accounts for each process. As units complete the final process and are eventually sold, their accumulated cost is transferred to Finished Goods Inventory and finally to Cost of Goods Sold.

Key Terms

Conversion cost per equivalent unit	Job order costing system	Process costing system
Equivalent units of production (EUP)	Materials consumption report	Process operations
FIFO method	Operation costing system	Weighted-average method
Hybrid costing system	Process cost summary	

Multiple Choice Quiz

1. Equivalent units of production are equal to
   a. Physical units that were completed this period from all effort being applied to them.
   b. The number of units introduced into the process this period.
   c. The number of finished units actually completed this period.
   d. The number of units that could have been started and completed given the cost incurred.
   e. The number of units in the process at the end of the period.

2. Recording the cost of raw materials purchased for use in a process costing system includes a
   a. Credit to Raw Materials Inventory.
   b. Debit to Work in Process Inventory.
   c. Debit to Factory Overhead.
   d. Credit to Factory Overhead.
   e. Debit to Raw Materials Inventory.

3. The production department started the month with a beginning work in process inventory of $20,000. During the month, it was assigned the following costs: direct materials, $152,000; direct labor, $45,000; overhead applied at the rate of 40% of direct labor cost. Inventory with a cost of $218,000 was transferred to finished goods. The ending balance of Work in Process Inventory is

   a. $330,000.   d. $112,000.
   b. $ 17,000.   e. $118,000.
   c. $220,000.

4. A company's beginning work in process inventory consists of 10,000 units that are 20% complete with respect to conversion costs. A total of 40,000 units are completed this period. There are 15,000 units in work in process, one-third complete for conversion, at period-end. The equivalent units of production (EUP) with respect to conversion at period-end, assuming the weighted-average method, are
   a. 45,000 EUP.   d. 37,000 EUP.
   b. 40,000 EUP.   e. 43,000 EUP.
   c. 5,000 EUP.

5. Assume the same information as in question 4. Also assume that beginning work in process had $6,000 in conversion cost and that $84,000 in conversion is added during this period. What is the cost per EUP for conversion?
   a. $0.50 per EUP   d. $2.10 per EUP
   b. $1.87 per EUP   e. $2.25 per EUP
   c. $2.00 per EUP

ANSWERS TO MULTIPLE CHOICE QUIZ

1. d
2. e
3. b; $20,000 + $152,000 + $45,000 + $18,000 − $218,000 = $17,000

4. a; 40,000 + (15,000 × 1/3) = 45,000 EUP
5. c; ($6,000 + $84,000) ÷ 45,000 EUP = $2 per EUP

[A]   *Superscript letter A denotes assignments based on Appendix 20A.*

🅘 Icon denotes assignments that involve decision making.

Discussion Questions

1. 🅘 What is the main factor for a company in choosing between the job order costing and process costing systems? Give two likely applications of each system.

2. The focus in a job order costing system is the job or batch. Identify the main focus in process costing.

3. 🅘 Can services be delivered by means of process operations? Support your answer with an example.

4. Are the journal entries that match cost flows to product flows in process costing primarily the same or much different than those in job order costing? Explain.

5. Identify the control document for materials flow when a materials requisition slip is not used.

6. 🅘 Explain in simple terms the notion of equivalent units of production (EUP). Why is it necessary to use EUP in process costing?

7. 🅘 What are the two main inventory methods used in process costing? What are the differences between these methods?

8. 🅘 Why is it possible for direct labor in process operations to include the labor of employees who do not work directly on products or services?

9. Assume that a company produces a single product by processing it first through a single production department. Direct labor costs flow through what accounts in this company's process cost system?

10. At the end of a period, what balance should remain in the Factory Overhead account?

11. 🅘 Is it possible to have under- or overapplied overhead costs in a process costing system? Explain.

12. Explain why equivalent units of production for both direct labor and overhead can be the same as, and why they can be different from, equivalent units for direct materials.

13. List the four steps in accounting for production activity in a reporting period (for process operations).

14. Companies such as **Apple** commonly prepare a process cost summary. What purposes does a process cost summary serve? **APPLE**

15. 🔲 Are there situations where **Google** can use process costing? Identify at least one and explain it. **GOOGLE**

16. 🔲 **Samsung** produces digital televisions with a multiple process production line. Identify and list some of its production processing steps and departments. **Samsung**

17. 🔲 **General Mills** needs a steady supply of ingredients for processing. What are some risks the company faces regarding its ingredients?

🔲 **connect**

QUICK STUDY

QS 20-1

Process vs. job order operations C1

For each of the following products and services, indicate whether it is more likely produced in a process operation (P) or in a job order operation (J).

_____ **1.** Tennis courts

_____ **2.** Organic juice

_____ **3.** Audit of financial statements

_____ **4.** Luxury yachts

_____ **5.** Vanilla ice cream

_____ **6.** Tennis balls

QS 20-2

Process vs. job order costing A1

Label each statement below as either true (T) or false (F).

_____ **1.** The cost per equivalent unit is computed as the total costs of a process divided by the number of equivalent units passing through that process.

_____ **2.** Service companies are not able to use process costing.

_____ **3.** Costs per job are computed in both job order and process costing systems.

_____ **4.** Job order and process operations both combine materials, labor, and overhead in producing products or services.

QS 20-3

Process vs. job order operations

C1

For each of the following products and services, indicate whether it is more likely produced in a process operation (P) or a job order operation (J).

_____ **1.** Beach toys

_____ **2.** Concrete swimming pool

_____ **3.** iPhones

_____ **4.** Wedding reception

_____ **5.** Custom suits

_____ **6.** Juice

_____ **7.** Tattoos

_____ **8.** Guitar picks

QS 20-4

Physical flow reconciliation

C2

The following refers to units processed in Sunflower Printing's binding department in March. Prepare a physical flow reconciliation.

	Units of Product	Percent of Conversion Added
Beginning work in process..............	150,000	80%
Goods started........................	310,000	100
Goods completed.....................	340,000	100
Ending work in process	120,000	25

QS 20-5

Weighted average:
Computing equivalent units of production C2

Refer to QS 20-4. Compute the total equivalent units of production with respect to conversion for March using the weighted-average method.

QS 20-6[A]

FIFO: Computing equivalent units C4

Refer to QS 20-4. Compute the total equivalent units of production with respect to conversion for March using the FIFO method.

A production department's beginning inventory cost includes $394,900 of conversion costs. This department incurs an additional $907,500 in conversion costs in the month of March. Equivalent units of production for conversion total 740,000 for March. Calculate the cost per equivalent unit of conversion using the weighted-average method.

QS 20-7
Weighted average:
Cost per EUP **C3**

The following refers to units processed by an ice cream maker in July. Compute the total equivalent units of production with respect to conversion for July using the weighted-average method.

QS 20-8
Weighted average:
Computing equivalent units of production **C2**

	Gallons of Product	Percent of Conversion Added
Beginning work in process	320,000	25%
Goods started	620,000	100
Goods completed	680,000	100
Ending work in process	260,000	75

Refer to QS 20-8 and compute the total equivalent units of production with respect to conversion for July using the FIFO method.

QS 20-9^A
FIFO: Computing equivalent units **C4**

The following information applies to QS 20-10 through QS 20-17.

The Carlberg Company has two manufacturing departments, assembly and painting. The assembly department started 10,000 units during November. The following production activity unit and cost information refers to the assembly department's November production activities.

QS 20-10
Weighted average:
Equivalent units of production **C2**

Assembly Department	Units	Percent of Direct Materials Added	Percent of Conversion Added
Beginning work in process.............	2,000	60%	40%
Units transferred out	9,000	100	100
Ending work in process	3,000	80	30

Beginning work in process inventory—Assembly dept.	$1,581 (includes $996 for direct materials and $585 for conversion)
Costs added during the month:	
Direct materials	$10,404
Conversion	$12,285

Required

Calculate the assembly department's equivalent units of production for materials and for conversion for November. Use the weighted-average method.

Refer to the information in QS 20-10. Calculate the assembly department's cost per equivalent unit of production for materials and for conversion for November. Use the weighted-average method.

QS 20-11
Weighted average:
Cost per EUP **C2**

Refer to the information in QS 20-10. Assign costs to the assembly department's output—specifically, the units transferred out to the painting department and the units that remain in process in the assembly department at month-end. Use the weighted-average method.

QS 20-12
Weighted average:
Assigning costs to output
C3

Refer to the information in QS 20-10. Prepare the November 30 journal entry to record the transfer of units (and costs) from the assembly department to the painting department. Use the weighted-average method.

QS 20-13
Weighted average:
Journal entry to transfer costs **P4**

QS 20-14ᴬ **FIFO:** Equivalent units of production C4	Refer to the information in QS 20-10. Calculate the assembly department's equivalent units of production for materials and for conversion for November. Use the FIFO method.
QS 20-15ᴬ **FIFO:** Cost per EUP C4	Refer to the information in QS 20-10. Calculate the assembly department's cost per equivalent unit of production for materials and for conversion for November. Use the FIFO method.
QS 20-16ᴬ **FIFO:** Assigning costs to output C4	Refer to the information in QS 20-10. Assign costs to the assembly department's output—specifically, the units transferred out to the painting department and the units that remain in process in the assembly department at month-end. Use the FIFO method.
QS 20-17ᴬ **FIFO:** Journal entry to transfer costs P4	Refer to the information in QS 20-10. Prepare the November 30 journal entry to record the transfer of units (and costs) from the assembly department to the painting department. Use the FIFO method.

QS 20-18

Weighted average: Computing equivalent units and cost per EUP (direct materials)

C2   C3

The Plastic Flowerpots Company has two manufacturing departments, molding and packaging. At the beginning of the month, the molding department has 2,000 units in inventory, 70% complete as to materials. During the month, the molding department started 18,000 units. At the end of the month, the molding department had 3,000 units in ending inventory, 80% complete as to materials. Units completed in the molding department are transferred into the packaging department.

Cost information for the molding department for the month follows:

Beginning work in process inventory (direct materials)........	$ 1,200
Direct materials added during the month..................	27,900

Using the weighted-average method, compute the molding department's (a) equivalent units of production for materials and (b) cost per equivalent unit of production for materials for the month. (Round to two decimal places.)

QS 20-19

Weighted average: Assigning costs to output

C3

Refer to information in QS 20-18. Using the weighted-average method, assign direct materials costs to the molding department's output—specifically, the units transferred out to the packaging department and the units that remain in process in the molding department at month-end.

QS 20-20

Transfer of costs; ending WIP balances

C3

Azule Co. manufactures in two sequential processes, cutting and binding. The two departments report the information below for a recent month. Determine the ending balances in the Work in Process Inventory accounts of each department.

	Cutting	Binding
Beginning work in process		
Transferred in from cutting dept.		$ 1,200
Direct materials	$ 845	1,926
Conversion	2,600	3,300
Costs added during March		
Direct materials	$ 8,240	$ 6,356
Conversion	11,100	18,575
Transferred in from cutting dept.		15,685
Transferred to finished goods		30,000

BOGO Inc. has two sequential processing departments, roasting and mixing. At the beginning of the month, the roasting department has 2,000 units in inventory, 70% complete as to materials. During the month, the roasting department started 18,000 units. At the end of the month, the roasting department had 3,000 units in ending inventory, 80% complete as to materials.

Cost information for the roasting department for the month is as follows:

Beginning work in process inventory (direct materials).............	$ 2,170
Direct materials added during the month........................	27,900

Using the FIFO method, compute the roasting department's (a) equivalent units of production for materials and (b) cost per equivalent unit of production for materials for the month.

QS 20-21ᴬ
FIFO: Computing equivalent units and cost per EUP (direct materials)
C4

Refer to QS 20-21. Using the FIFO method, assign direct materials costs to the roasting department's output—specifically, the units transferred out to the mixing department and the units that remain in process in the roasting department at month-end.

QS 20-22ᴬ
FIFO: Assigning costs to output   **C4**

Hotwax makes surfboard wax in a single operation. This period, Hotwax purchased $62,000 in raw materials. Its production department requisitioned $50,000 of those materials for use in production. Prepare journal entries to record its (1) purchase of raw materials and (2) requisition of direct materials.

QS 20-23
Recording costs of materials   **P1**

Prepare journal entries to record the following production activities for Hotwax.
1. Incurred direct labor of $125,000 (credit Factory Wages Payable).
2. Incurred indirect labor of $10,000 (credit Factory Wages Payable).
3. Total factory payroll of $135,000 was paid in cash.

QS 20-24
Recording costs of labor
P2

Prepare journal entries to record the following production activities for Hotwax.
1. Requisitioned $9,000 of indirect materials for use in production of surfboard wax.
2. Incurred $156,000 overhead costs (credit Other Accounts).
3. Applied overhead at the rate of 140% of direct labor costs. Direct labor costs were $125,000.

QS 20-25
Recording costs of factory overhead
P1   P3

Hotwax completed products costing $275,000 and transferred them to finished goods. Prepare its journal entry to record the transfer of units from production to finished goods inventory.

QS 20-26
Recording transfer of costs to finished goods
P4

Anheuser-Busch InBev is attempting to reduce its water usage. How could a company manager use a process cost summary to determine if the program to reduce water usage is successful?

QS 20-27
Process cost summary
C3

connect

For each of the following products and services, indicate whether it is more likely produced in a process operation (P) or in a job order operation (J).

____ **1.** Beach towels   ____ **5.** Designed patio   ____ **9.** Concrete swimming pools

____ **2.** Bolts and nuts   ____ **6.** Door hardware   ____ **10.** Custom tailored dresses

____ **3.** Lawn chairs   ____ **7.** Cut flower arrangements   ____ **11.** Grand pianos

____ **4.** Headphones   ____ **8.** House paints   ____ **12.** Table lamps

EXERCISES

Exercise 20-1
Process vs. job order operations

C1

Exercise 20-2

Comparing process and job order operations

C1

Label each item *a* through *h* below as a feature of either a job order (J) or process (P) operation.

_____ **a.** Heterogeneous products and services

_____ **b.** Custom orders

_____ **c.** Low production volume

_____ **d.** Routine, repetitive procedures

_____ **e.** Focus on individual batch

_____ **f.** Low product standardization

_____ **g.** Low product flexibility

_____ **h.** Focus on standardized units

Exercise 20-3

Terminology in process costing

C1   A1

Match each of the following items *A* through *G* with the best numbered description of its purpose.

A. Factory Overhead account   **E.** Raw Materials Inventory account

B. Process cost summary   **F.** Materials requisition

C. Equivalent units of production   **G.** Finished Goods Inventory account

D. Work in Process Inventory account

_____ **1.** Notifies the materials manager to send materials to a production department.

_____ **2.** Holds costs of indirect materials, indirect labor, and similar costs until assigned to production.

_____ **3.** Holds costs of direct materials, direct labor, and applied overhead until products are transferred from production to finished goods (or another department).

_____ **4.** Standardizes partially completed units into equivalent completed units.

_____ **5.** Holds costs of finished products until sold to customers.

_____ **6.** Describes the activity and output of a production department for a period.

_____ **7.** Holds costs of materials until they are used in production or as factory overhead.

Exercise 20-4

Weighted average:

Computing equivalent units

C2

The production department in a process manufacturing system completed 80,000 units of product and transferred them to finished goods during a recent period. Of these units, 24,000 were in process at the beginning of the period. The other 56,000 units were started and completed during the period. At period-end, 16,000 units were in process. Compute the department's equivalent units of production with respect to direct materials under each of three separate assumptions using the weighted-average method:

1. All direct materials are added to products when processing begins.

2. Beginning inventory is 40% complete as to materials and conversion costs. Ending inventory is 75% complete as to materials and conversion costs.

Check   (3) EUP for
materials, 84,800

3. Beginning inventory is 60% complete as to materials and 40% complete as to conversion costs. Ending inventory is 30% complete as to materials and 60% complete as to conversion costs.

Exercise 20-5^A

FIFO: Computing
equivalent units   **C4**

Check   (3) EUP for
materials, 70,400

Refer to the information in Exercise 20-4 and complete the requirements for each of the three separate assumptions using the FIFO method for process costing.

Exercise 20-6

Weighted average:

Cost per EUP and costs assigned to output

C2

The Fields Company has two manufacturing departments, forming and painting. The company uses the weighted-average method of process costing. At the beginning of the month, the forming department has 25,000 units in inventory, 60% complete as to materials and 40% complete as to conversion costs. The beginning inventory cost of $60,100 consisted of $44,800 of direct materials costs and $15,300 of conversion costs.

During the month, the forming department started 300,000 units. At the end of the month, the forming department had 30,000 units in ending inventory, 80% complete as to materials and 30% complete as to conversion. Units completed in the forming department are transferred to the painting department.

Cost information for the forming department is as follows:

Beginning work in process inventory	$ 60,100
Direct materials added during the month	1,231,200
Conversion added during the month	896,700

1. Calculate the equivalent units of production for the forming department.
2. Calculate the costs per equivalent unit of production for the forming department.
3. Using the weighted-average method, assign costs to the forming department's output—specifically, its units transferred to painting and its ending work in process inventory.

Refer to the information in Exercise 20-6. Assume that Fields uses the FIFO method of process costing.
1. Calculate the equivalent units of production for the forming department.
2. Calculate the costs per equivalent unit of production for the forming department.

Exercise 20-7[A]
FIFO: Costs per EUP

C4

During April, the production department of a process manufacturing system completed a number of units of a product and transferred them to finished goods. Of these transferred units, 60,000 were in process in the production department at the beginning of April and 240,000 were started and completed in April. April's beginning inventory units were 60% complete with respect to materials and 40% complete with respect to conversion. At the end of April, 82,000 additional units were in process in the production department and were 80% complete with respect to materials and 30% complete with respect to conversion.
1. Compute the number of units transferred to finished goods.
2. Compute the number of equivalent units with respect to both materials used and conversion used in the production department for April using the weighted-average method.

Exercise 20-8
Weighted average:
Computing equivalent units of production

C2

Check   (2) EUP for materials, 365,600

The production department described in Exercise 20-8 had $850,368 of direct materials and $649,296 of conversion costs charged to it during April. Also, its beginning inventory of $167,066 consists of $118,472 of direct materials cost and $48,594 of conversion costs.
1. Compute the direct materials cost and the conversion cost per equivalent unit for the department.
2. Using the weighted-average method, assign April's costs to the department's output—specifically, its units transferred to finished goods and its ending work in process inventory.

Exercise 20-9
Weighted average:
Costs assigned to output and inventories

C2

Check   (1) $2.65 per EUP of direct materials

Refer to the information in Exercise 20-8 to compute the number of equivalent units with respect to both materials used and conversion costs in the production department for April using the FIFO method.

Exercise 20-10[A]
FIFO: Computing equivalent units of production   **C4**

Refer to the information in Exercise 20-9 and complete its parts 1 and 2 using the FIFO method.

Exercise 20-11[A]
FIFO: Costs assigned to output   **C4**   **P4**

The following partially completed process cost summary describes the July production activities of Ashad Company. Its production output is sent to its warehouse for shipping. All direct materials are added to products when processing begins. Beginning work in process inventory is 20% complete with respect to conversion. Prepare its process cost summary using the weighted-average method.

Exercise 20-12
Weighted average:
Completing a process cost summary   **C3**

Equivalent Units of Production	Direct Materials	Conversion
Units transferred out	32,000 EUP	32,000 EUP
Units of ending work in process	2,500 EUP	1,500 EUP
Equivalent units of production.............................	34,500 EUP	33,500 EUP

Costs per EUP	Direct Materials	Conversion
Costs of beginning work in process	$ 18,550	$ 2,280
Costs incurred this period	357,500	188,670
Total costs.....................................	$376,050	$190,950

Units in beginning work in process (all completed during July)	2,000
Units started this period.......................................	32,500
Units completed and transferred out	32,000
Units in ending work in process	2,500

Exercise 20-13ᴬ
FIFO: Completing a process cost summary

C3   C4

Refer to the information in Exercise 20-12. Prepare a process cost summary using the FIFO method. (Round cost per equivalent unit calculations to two decimal places.)

Exercise 20-14
Production cost flow and measurement; journal entries

P4

Pro-Weave manufactures stadium blankets by passing the products through a weaving department and a sewing department. The following information is available regarding its June inventories:

	Beginning Inventory	Ending Inventory
Raw materials inventory..................................	$ 120,000	$ 185,000
Work in process inventory—Weaving	300,000	330,000
Work in process inventory—Sewing	570,000	700,000
Finished goods inventory................................	1,266,000	1,206,000

The following additional information describes the company's manufacturing activities for June:

Raw materials purchases (on credit)..	$ 500,000
Factory payroll cost (paid in cash)...	3,060,000
Other factory overhead cost (Other Accounts credited)........................	156,000
Materials used	
Direct—Weaving...	$ 240,000
Direct—Sewing...	75,000
Indirect..	120,000
Labor used	
Direct—Weaving...	$1,200,000
Direct—Sewing...	360,000
Indirect..	1,500,000
Overhead rates as a percent of direct labor	
Weaving	80%
Sewing	150%
Sales (on credit)	$4,000,000

Required

1. Compute the (a) cost of products transferred from weaving to sewing, (b) cost of products transferred from sewing to finished goods, and (c) cost of goods sold.

2. Prepare journal entries dated June 30 to record (a) goods transferred from weaving to sewing, (b) goods transferred from sewing to finished goods, and (c) sale of finished goods.

Check (1c) Cost of goods sold, $3,275,000

Refer to the information in Exercise 20-14. Prepare journal entries dated June 30 to record: (a) raw materials purchases, (b) direct materials usage, (c) indirect materials usage, (d) direct labor usage, (e) indirect labor usage, (f) other overhead costs, (g) overhead applied, and (h) payment of total payroll costs.

Exercise 20-15
Recording product costs
P1 P2 P3

Elliott Company produces large quantities of a standardized product. The following information is available for its production activities for March.

Exercise 20-16
Weighted average:
Process cost summary C3

Units		Costs		
Beginning work in process inventory.............	2,000	Beginning work in process inventory		
Started..	20,000	Direct materials.........................	$2,500	
Ending work in process inventory	5,000	Conversion	6,360	$ 8,860
		Direct materials added		168,000
Status of ending work in process inventory		Direct labor added..........................		199,850
Materials—Percent complete...................	100%	Overhead applied (140% of direct labor)........		279,790
Conversion—Percent complete	35%	Total costs to account for		$656,500
		Ending work in process inventory		$ 84,110

Prepare a process cost summary report for this company showing costs charged to production, unit cost information, equivalent units of production, cost per EUP, and its cost assignment and reconciliation. Use the weighted-average method.

Check Cost per equivalent unit: materials, $7.75; conversion, $25.92

Oslo Company produces large quantities of a standardized product. The following information is available for its production activities for May.

Exercise 20-17
Weighted average:
Process cost summary C3

Units		Costs		
Beginning work in process inventory	4,000	Beginning work in process inventory		
Started..	12,000	Direct materials........................	$2,880	
Ending work in process inventory................	3,000	Conversion............................	5,358	$ 8,238
		Direct materials added		197,120
Status of ending work in process inventory		Direct labor added.......................		123,680
Materials—Percent complete	100%	Overhead applied (90% of direct labor)........		111,312
Conversion—Percent complete.................	25%	Total costs to account for..................		$440,350
		Ending work in process inventory............		$ 50,610

Prepare a process cost summary report for this company showing costs charged to production, unit cost information, equivalent units of production, cost per EUP, and its cost assignment and reconciliation. Use the weighted-average method.

Check Cost per equivalent unit: materials, $12.50; conversion, $17.48

RSTN Co. produces its product through two sequential processing departments. Direct materials and conversion are added to the product evenly throughout the process. The company uses monthly reporting periods for its process costing system.

During October, the company finished and transferred 150,000 units of its product to Department 2. Of these units, 30,000 were in process at the beginning of the month and 120,000 were started and completed during the month. The beginning work in process inventory was 30% complete. At the end of the month, the work in process inventory consisted of 20,000 units that were 80% complete.

Compute the number of equivalent units of production for October. Use the FIFO method.

Exercise 20-18^A
FIFO: Equivalent units
C4 P4

Check 157,000 EUP

Exercise 20-19

Production cost flows

P1   P2   P3   P4

The flowchart below shows the August production activity of the punching and bending departments of Wire Box Company. Use the amounts shown on the flowchart to compute the missing numbers identified by question marks.

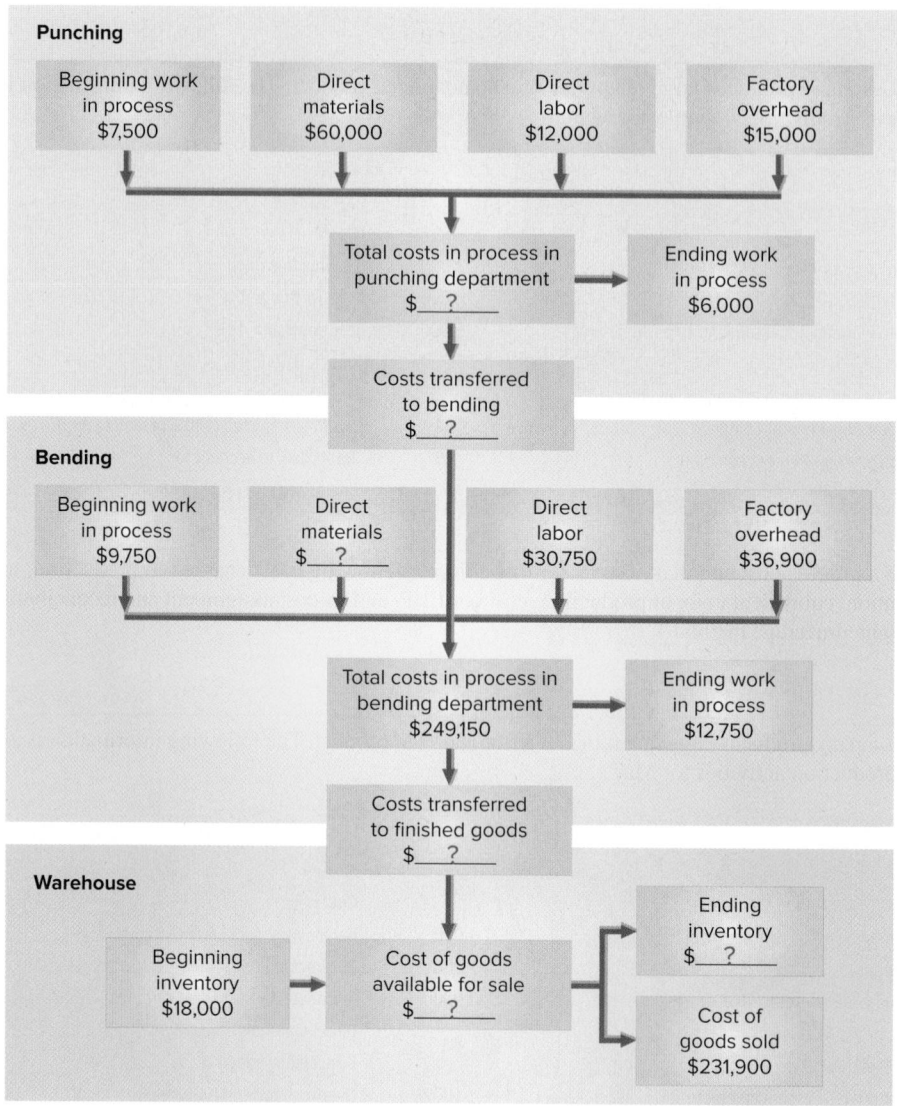

Exercise 20-20

Weighted average:

Process cost summary

C3

Hi-Test Company uses the weighted-average method of process costing to assign production costs to its products. Information for September follows. Assume that all materials are added at the beginning of its production process, and that conversion costs are added uniformly throughout the process.

Work in process inventory, September 1 (2,000 units, 100% complete with respect to direct materials, 80% complete with respect to direct labor and overhead; includes $45,000 of direct materials cost, $25,600 in direct labor cost, $30,720 overhead cost).	$101,320
Units started in September	28,000
Units completed and transferred to finished goods inventory	23,000
Work in process inventory, September 30 (? units, 100% complete with respect to direct materials, 40% complete with respect to direct labor and overhead)	$?
Costs incurred in September	
Direct materials	$375,000
Conversion	$341,000

Compute each of the following, assuming Hi-Test uses the weighted-average method of process costing.

1. The number of physical units that were transferred out and the number that are in ending work in process inventory.
2. The number of equivalent units for materials for the month.
3. The number of equivalent units for conversion for the month.
4. The cost per equivalent unit of materials for the month.
5. The cost per equivalent unit for conversion for the month.
6. The total cost of goods transferred out.
7. The total cost of ending work in process inventory.

Prepare journal entries to record the following production activities.

1. Purchased $80,000 of raw materials on credit.
2. Used $42,000 of direct materials in production.
3. Used $22,500 of indirect materials in production.

Exercise 20-21
Recording costs of materials

P1

Prepare journal entries to record the following production activities.

1. Incurred $75,000 of direct labor in production (credit Factory Wages Payable).
2. Incurred $20,000 of indirect labor in production (credit Factory Wages Payable).
3. Paid factory payroll.

Exercise 20-22
Recording costs of labor

P2

Prepare journal entries to record the following production activities.

1. Paid overhead costs (other than indirect materials and indirect labor) of $38,750.
2. Applied overhead at 110% of direct labor costs. Direct labor costs were $75,000.

Exercise 20-23
Recording overhead costs

P3

Prepare journal entries to record the following production activities.

1. Transferred completed goods from the Assembly department to finished goods inventory. The goods cost $135,600.
2. Sold $315,000 of goods on credit. Their cost is $175,000.

Exercise 20-24
Recording cost of completed goods

P4

Laffer Lumber produces bagged bark for use in landscaping. Production involves packaging bark chips in plastic bags in a bagging department. The following information describes production operations for October.

Exercise 20-25
Recording cost flows in a process cost system

P1   P2   P3   P4

	A	B
1		**Bagging**
2		**Department**
3	Direct materials used	$ 522,000
4	Direct labor used	$ 130,000
5	Predetermined overhead rate (based on direct labor)	175%
6	Goods transferred from bagging to finished goods	$(595,000)

The company's revenue for the month totaled $950,000 from credit sales, and its cost of goods sold for the month is $540,000. Prepare summary journal entries dated October 31 to record its October production activities for (1) direct materials usage, (2) direct labor incurred (3) overhead allocation, (4) goods transfer from production to finished goods, and (5) credit sales.

Check   (3) Cr. Factory Overhead, $227,500

Exercise 20-26
Interpretation of journal entries in process costing

P1   P2   P3   P4

The following journal entries are recorded in Kiesha Co.'s process costing system. Kiesha produces apparel and accessories. Overhead is applied to production based on direct labor cost for the period. Prepare a brief explanation (including any overhead rates applied) for each journal entry *a* through *k*.

a.	Raw Materials Inventory	52,000	
	Accounts Payable		52,000
b.	Work in Process Inventory	42,000	
	Raw Materials Inventory		42,000
c.	Work in Process Inventory	32,000	
	Factory Wages Payable		32,000
d.	Factory Overhead	6,000	
	Factory Wages Payable		6,000
e.	Factory Overhead	12,000	
	Cash		12,000
f.	Factory Overhead	10,000	
	Raw Materials Inventory		10,000

g.	Factory Wages Payable	38,000	
	Cash		38,000
h.	Work in Process Inventory	33,600	
	Factory Overhead		33,600
i.	Finished Goods Inventory	88,000	
	Work in Process Inventory		88,000
j.	Accounts Receivable	250,000	
	Sales		250,000
k.	Cost of Goods Sold	100,000	
	Finished Goods Inventory		100,000

Exercise 20-27
Hybrid costing system   A2

Explain a hybrid costing system. Identify a product or service operation that might well fit a hybrid costing system.

■■ connect

PROBLEM SET A

Problem 20-1A
Production cost flow and measurement; journal entries

P1   P2   P3   P4

Sierra Company manufactures woven blankets and accounts for product costs using process costing. The company uses a single processing department. The following information is available regarding its May inventories.

	Beginning Inventory	Ending Inventory
Raw materials inventory	$ 60,000	$ 92,500
Work in process inventory	435,000	515,000
Finished goods inventory	633,000	605,000

The following additional information describes the company's production activities for May.

Raw materials purchases (on credit)	$ 250,000
Factory payroll cost (paid in cash)	1,530,000
Other overhead cost (Other Accounts credited)	87,000
Materials used	
Direct	$ 157,500
Indirect	60,000
Labor used	
Direct	$ 780,000
Indirect	750,000
Overhead rate as a percent of direct labor	115%
Sales (on credit)	$2,500,000

Required

Check (1*b*) Cost of goods sold, $1,782,500

1. Compute the cost of (a) products transferred from production to finished goods and (b) goods sold.
2. Prepare summary journal entries dated May 31 to record the following production activities during May: (a) raw materials purchases, (b) direct materials usage, (c) indirect materials usage, (d) direct labor costs incurred, (e) indirect labor costs incurred, (f) payment of factory payroll, (g) other overhead costs, (h) overhead applied, (i) goods transferred from production to finished goods, and (j) sale of finished goods.

Victory Company uses weighted-average process costing to account for its production costs. Conversion cost is added evenly throughout the process. Direct materials are added at the beginning of the process. During November, the company transferred 700,000 units of product to finished goods. At the end of November, the work in process inventory consists of 180,000 units that are 30% complete with respect to conversion. Beginning inventory had $420,000 of direct materials and $139,000 of conversion cost. The direct material cost added in November is $2,220,000, and the conversion cost added is $3,254,000. Beginning work in process consisted of 60,000 units that were 100% complete with respect to direct materials and 80% complete with respect to conversion. Of the units completed, 60,000 were from beginning work in process and 640,000 units were started and completed during the period.

Problem 20-2A
Weighted average:
Cost per equivalent unit; costs assigned to products

C2   C3

Required

1. Determine the equivalent units of production with respect to (a) direct materials and (b) conversion.
2. Compute both the direct material cost and the conversion cost per equivalent unit.
3. Compute the direct material cost and the conversion cost assigned to (a) units completed and transferred out and (b) ending work in process inventory.

Check   (2) Conversion cost per equivalent unit, $4.50
(3b) $783,000

Analysis Component

4. The company sells and ships all units to customers as soon as they are completed. Assume that an error is made in determining the percentage of completion for units in ending inventory. Instead of being 30% complete with respect to labor, they are actually 60% complete. Write a one-page memo to the plant manager describing how this error affects its November financial statements.

Fast Co. produces its product through a single processing department. Direct materials are added at the start of production, and conversion costs are added evenly throughout the process. The company uses monthly reporting periods for its weighted-average process costing system. The Work in Process Inventory account has a balance of $84,300 as of October 1, which consists of $17,100 of direct materials and $67,200 of conversion costs.
   During the month, the company incurred the following costs:

Problem 20-3A
Weighted average:
Process cost summary; equivalent units

C2   C3   P4

Direct materials	$144,400
Conversion	862,400

During October, the company started 140,000 units and transferred 150,000 units to finished goods. At the end of the month, the work in process inventory consisted of 20,000 units that were 80% complete with respect to conversion costs.

Required

1. Prepare the company's process cost summary for October using the weighted-average method.
2. Prepare the journal entry dated October 31 to transfer the cost of the completed units to finished goods inventory.

Check   (1) Costs transferred out to finished goods, $982,500

Tamar Co. manufactures a single product in one department. All direct materials are added at the beginning of the manufacturing process. Conversion costs are added evenly throughout the process. During May, the company completed and transferred 22,200 units of product to finished goods inventory. Its 3,000 units of beginning work in process consisted of $19,800 of direct materials and $221,940 of conversion costs. It has 2,400 units (100% complete with respect to direct materials and 80% complete with respect to conversion) in process at month-end. During the month, $496,800 of direct material costs and $2,165,940 of conversion costs were charged to production.

Problem 20-4A
Weighted average:
Process cost summary, equivalent units, cost estimates

C2   C3   P4

Required

1. Prepare the company's process cost summary for May using the weighted-average method.
2. Prepare the journal entry dated May 31 to transfer the cost of completed units to finished goods inventory.

Check   (1) EUP for conversion, 24,120
(2) Cost transferred out to finished goods, $2,664,000

Analysis Component

3. The costing process depends on numerous estimates.
   a. Identify two major estimates that determine the cost per equivalent unit.
   b. In what direction might you anticipate a bias from management for each estimate in part 3a (assume that management compensation is based on maintaining low inventory amounts)? Explain your answer.

Problem 20-5A^A

FIFO: Process cost summary; equivalent units; cost estimates

C3 C4 P4

Refer to the data in Problem 20-4A. Assume that Tamar uses the FIFO method to account for its process costing system. The following additional information is available:

- Beginning work in process consisted of 3,000 units that were 100% complete with respect to direct materials and 40% complete with respect to conversion.
- Of the 22,200 units completed, 3,000 were from beginning work in process. The remaining 19,200 were units started and completed during May.

Required

1. Prepare the company's process cost summary for May using FIFO.

2. Prepare the journal entry dated May 31 to transfer the cost of completed units to finished goods inventory.

Problem 20-6A^A

FIFO: Costs per equivalent unit; costs assigned to products

C2 C4

During May, the production department of a process manufacturing system completed a number of units of a product and transferred them to finished goods. Of these transferred units, 37,500 were in process in the production department at the beginning of May and 150,000 were started and completed in May. May's beginning inventory units were 60% complete with respect to materials and 40% complete with respect to conversion. At the end of May, 51,250 additional units were in process in the production department and were 60% complete with respect to materials and 20% complete with respect to conversion. The production department had $505,035 of direct materials and $396,568 of conversion cost charged to it during May. Its beginning inventory included $74,075 of direct materials cost and $28,493 of conversion cost.

1. Compute the number of units transferred to finished goods.

2. Compute the number of equivalent units with respect to both materials used and conversion used in the production department for May using the FIFO method.

3. Compute the direct materials cost and the conversion cost per equivalent unit for the department.

4. Using the FIFO method, assign May's costs to the units transferred to finished goods and assign costs to its ending work in process inventory.

Problem 20-7A^A

FIFO: Process cost summary, equivalent units, cost estimates

C2 C3 C4 P4

Dengo Co. makes a trail mix in two departments: roasting and blending. Direct materials are added at the beginning of each process, and conversion costs are added evenly throughout each process. The company uses the FIFO method of process costing. During October, the roasting department completed and transferred 22,200 units to the blending department. Of the units completed, 3,000 were from beginning inventory and the remaining 19,200 were started and completed during the month. Beginning work in process was 100% complete with respect to direct materials and 40% complete with respect to conversion. The company has 2,400 units (100% complete with respect to direct materials and 80% complete with respect to conversion) in process at month-end. Information on the roasting department's costs of beginning work in process inventory and costs added during the month follows.

Cost	Direct Materials	Conversion
Of beginning work in process inventory.............	$ 9,900	$ 110,970
Added during the month	248,400	1,082,970

Required

1. Prepare the roasting department's process cost summary for October using the FIFO method.

2. Prepare the journal entry dated October 31 to transfer the cost of completed units to the blending department.

Analysis Component

3. The company provides incentives to department managers by paying monthly bonuses based on their success in controlling costs per equivalent unit of production. Assume that a production department underestimates the percentage of completion for units in ending inventory with the result that its equivalent units of production for October are understated. What impact does this error have on the October bonuses paid to that department's managers? What impact, if any, does this error have on November bonuses?

Dream Toys Company manufactures video game consoles and accounts for product costs using process costing. The company uses a single processing department. The following information is available regarding its June inventories.

	Beginning Inventory	Ending Inventory
Raw materials inventory...............	$ 72,000	$110,000
Work in process inventory	156,000	250,000
Finished goods inventory..............	160,000	198,000

The following additional information describes the company's production activities for June.

Raw materials purchases (on credit).....................	$ 200,000
Factory payroll cost (paid in cash)......................	400,000
Other overhead cost (Other Accounts credited)...........	170,500
Materials used	
Direct	$ 120,000
Indirect	42,000
Labor used	
Direct	$ 350,000
Indirect	50,000
Overhead rate as a percent of direct labor...............	75%
Sales (on credit)	$1,000,000

Required

1. Compute the cost of (a) products transferred from production to finished goods and (b) goods sold.
2. Prepare journal entries dated June 30 to record the following production activities during June: (a) raw materials purchases, (b) direct materials usage, (c) indirect materials usage, (d) direct labor costs, (e) indirect labor costs, (f) payment of factory payroll, (g) other overhead costs, (h) overhead applied, (i) goods transferred from production to finished goods, and (j) sale of finished goods.

Abraham Company uses process costing to account for its production costs. Conversion is added evenly throughout the process. Direct materials are added at the beginning of the process. During September, the production department transferred 80,000 units of product to finished goods. Beginning work in process consisted of 2,000 units that were 100% complete with respect to direct materials and 85% complete with respect to conversion. Of the units completed, 2,000 were from beginning work in process and 78,000 units were started and completed during the period. Beginning work in process had $58,000 of direct materials and $86,400 of conversion cost. At the end of September, the work in process inventory consists of 8,000 units that are 25% complete with respect to conversion. The direct materials cost added in September is $712,000, and conversion cost added is $1,980,000. The company uses the weighted-average method.

Required

1. Determine the equivalent units of production with respect to (a) conversion and (b) direct materials.
2. Compute both the conversion cost and the direct materials cost per equivalent unit.
3. Compute both conversion cost and direct materials cost assigned to (a) units completed and transferred out and (b) ending work in process inventory.

Analysis Component

4. The company sells and ships all units to customers as soon as they are completed. Assume that an error is made in determining the percentage of completion for units in ending inventory. Instead of being 25% complete with respect to conversion, they are actually 75% complete. Write a one-page memo to the plant manager describing how this error affects its September financial statements.

Problem 20-3B
Weighted average:
Process cost summary;
equivalent units

C2   C3   P4

Braun Company produces its product through a single processing department. Direct materials are added at the beginning of the process. Conversion costs are added to the product evenly throughout the process. The company uses monthly reporting periods for its weighted-average process costing. The Work in Process Inventory account had a balance of $21,300 on November 1, which consisted of $6,800 of direct materials and $14,500 of conversion costs.

During the month, the company incurred the following costs:

Direct materials	$ 116,400
Conversion	1,067,000

During November, the company finished and transferred 100,000 units of its product to finished goods. At the end of the month, the work in process inventory consisted of 12,000 units that were 100% complete with respect to direct materials and 25% complete with respect to conversion.

Required

Check (1) Cost transferred out to finished goods, $1,160,000

1. Prepare the company's process cost summary for November using the weighted-average method.
2. Prepare the journal entry dated November 30 to transfer the cost of the completed units to finished goods inventory.

Problem 20-4B
Weighted average:
Process cost summary;
equivalent units;
cost estimates

C2   C3   P4

Switch Co. manufactures a single product in one department. Direct labor and overhead are added evenly throughout the process. Direct materials are added as needed. The company uses monthly reporting periods for its weighted-average process costing. During January, Switch completed and transferred 220,000 units of product to finished goods inventory. Its 10,000 units of beginning work in process consisted of $7,500 of direct materials and $49,850 of conversion. In process at month-end are 40,000 units (50% complete with respect to direct materials and 30% complete with respect to conversion). During the month, the company used direct materials of $112,500 in production and incurred conversion costs of $616,000.

Required

Check (1) EUP for conversion, 232,000

(2) Cost transferred out to finished goods, $741,400

1. Prepare the company's process cost summary for January using the weighted-average method.
2. Prepare the journal entry dated January 31 to transfer the cost of completed units to finished goods inventory.

Analysis Component

3. The cost accounting process depends on several estimates.
   a. Identify two major estimates that affect the cost per equivalent unit.
   b. In what direction might you anticipate a bias from management for each estimate in part 3a (assume that management compensation is based on maintaining low inventory amounts)? Explain your answer.

Problem 20-5B[A]
FIFO: Process cost
summary; equivalent
units; cost estimates

C3   C4   P4

Refer to the information in Problem 20-4B. Assume that Switch uses the FIFO method to account for its process costing system. The following additional information is available.

• Beginning work in process consists of 10,000 units that were 75% complete with respect to direct materials and 60% complete with respect to conversion.
• Of the 220,000 units completed, 10,000 were from beginning work in process; the remaining 210,000 were units started and completed during January.

Required

Check (1) Conversion EUP, 226,000

(2) Cost transferred out, $743,554

1. Prepare the company's process cost summary for January using FIFO. Round cost per EUP to three decimal places.
2. Prepare the journal entry dated January 31 to transfer the cost of completed units to finished goods inventory.

During May, the production department of a process manufacturing system completed a number of units of a product and transferred them to finished goods. Of these transferred units, 62,500 were in process in the production department at the beginning of May and 175,000 were started and completed in May. May's beginning inventory units were 40% complete with respect to materials and 80% complete with respect to conversion. At the end of May, 76,250 additional units were in process in the production department and were 80% complete with respect to materials and 20% complete with respect to conversion. The production department had $683,750 of direct materials and $446,050 of conversion cost charged to it during May. Its beginning inventory included $99,075 of direct materials cost and $53,493 of conversion cost.

1. Compute the number of units transferred to finished goods.
2. Compute the number of equivalent units with respect to both materials used and conversion used in the production department for May using the FIFO method.
3. Compute the direct materials cost and the conversion cost per equivalent unit for the department.
4. Using the FIFO method, assign May's costs to the units transferred to finished goods and assign costs to its ending work in process inventory.

Problem 20-6B[A]

FIFO: Costs per equivalent unit; costs assigned to products

C2   C4

Check   (2) EUP for materials, 273,500

Belda Co. makes organic juice in two departments: cutting and blending. Direct materials are added at the beginning of each process, and conversion costs are added evenly throughout each process. The company uses the FIFO method of process costing. During March, the cutting department completed and transferred 220,000 units to the blending department. Of the units completed, 10,000 were from beginning inventory and the remaining 210,000 were started and completed during the month. Beginning work in process was 75% complete with respect to direct materials and 60% complete with respect to conversion. The company has 40,000 units (50% complete with respect to direct materials and 30% complete with respect to conversion) in process at month-end. Information on the cutting department's costs of beginning work in process inventory and costs added during the month follows.

Problem 20-7B[A]

FIFO: Process cost summary, equivalent units, cost estimates

C2   C3   C4   P4

Cost	Direct Materials	Conversion
Of beginning work in process inventory	$ 16,800	$ 97,720
Added during the month	223,200	1,233,960

Required

1. Prepare the cutting department's process cost summary for March using the FIFO method.
2. Prepare the journal entry dated March 31 to transfer the cost of completed units to the blending department.

Check   (1) EUP for conversion, 226,000
(2) Cost transferred out, $1,486,960

Analysis Component

3. The company provides incentives to department managers by paying monthly bonuses based on their success in controlling costs per equivalent unit of production. Assume that the production department overestimates the percentage of completion for units in ending inventory with the result that its equivalent units of production for March are overstated. What impact does this error have on bonuses paid to the managers of the production department? What impact, if any, does this error have on these managers' April bonuses?

(This serial problem began in Chapter 1 and continues through most of the book. If previous chapter segments were not completed, the serial problem can begin at this point.)

SERIAL PROBLEM
Business Solutions

C1   A1

SP 20   The computer workstation furniture manufacturing that Santana Rey started for **Business Solutions** is progressing well. Santana uses a job order costing system to account for the production costs of this product line. Santana is wondering whether process costing might be a better method for her to keep track of and monitor her production costs.

Required

1. What are the features that distinguish job order costing from process costing?
2. Should Santana continue to use job order costing or switch to process costing for her workstation furniture manufacturing? Explain.

© Alexander Image/Shutterstock RF

**COMPREHENSIVE
PROBLEM**

**Major League Bat
Company**

Weighted average:

Review of

Chapters 2, 5, 18, 20

CP 20   Major League Bat Company manufactures baseball bats. In addition to its work in process inventories, the company maintains inventories of raw materials and finished goods. It uses raw materials as direct materials in production and as indirect materials. Its factory payroll costs include direct labor for production and indirect labor. All materials are added at the beginning of the process, and conversion costs are applied uniformly throughout the production process.

Required

You are to maintain records and produce measures of inventories to reflect the July events of this company. Set up the following general ledger accounts and enter the June 30 balances: Raw Materials Inventory, $25,000; Work in Process Inventory, $8,135 ($2,660 of direct materials and $5,475 of conversion); Finished Goods Inventory, $110,000; Sales, $0; Cost of Goods Sold, $0; Factory Wages Payable, $0; and Factory Overhead, $0.

1. Prepare journal entries to record the following July transactions and events.

    a. Purchased raw materials for $125,000 cash (the company uses a perpetual inventory system).

    b. Used raw materials as follows: direct materials, $52,440; and indirect materials, $10,000.

    c. Recorded factory wages payable costs as follows: direct labor, $202,250; and indirect labor, $25,000.

    d. Paid factory payroll cost of $227,250 with cash (ignore taxes).

    e. Incurred additional factory overhead costs of $80,000 paid in cash.

Check (1*f*) Cr. Factory
Overhead, $101,125

    f. Allocated factory overhead to production at 50% of direct labor costs.

Check (2) EUP for
conversion, 14,200

2. Information about the July inventories follows. Use this information with that from part 1 to prepare a process cost summary, assuming the weighted-average method is used.

Units	
Beginning inventory...................................	5,000 units
Started	14,000 units
Ending inventory	8,000 units
Beginning inventory	
Materials—Percent complete	100%
Conversion—Percent complete........................	75%
Ending inventory	
Materials—Percent complete	100%
Conversion—Percent complete........................	40%

3. Using the results from part 2 and the available information, make computations and prepare journal entries to record the following:

(3*g*) $271,150

    g. Total costs transferred to finished goods for July (label this entry *g*).

    h. Sale of finished goods costing $265,700 for $625,000 in cash (label this entry *h*).

4. Post entries from parts 1 and 3 to the ledger accounts set up at the beginning of the problem.

5. Compute the amount of gross profit from the sales in July. (*Note:* Add any underapplied overhead to, or deduct any overapplied overhead from, the cost of goods sold. Ignore the corresponding journal entry.)

GL **GENERAL
LEDGER
PROBLEM**

**Available only in
Connect**

The **General Ledger** tool in *Connect* automates several of the procedural steps in accounting so that the financial professional can focus on the impacts of each transaction on various reports and performance measures.

GL 20-1   General Ledger assignment GL 20-1, based on Problem 20-1A, focuses on transactions related to process costing. Prepare summary journal entries to record the cost of units manufactured and their flow through the manufacturing environment. Then prepare a schedule of cost of goods manufactured and a partial income statement.

Beyond the Numbers

BTN 20-1   Apple reports in notes to its financial statements that, in addition to its products sold, it includes the following costs (among others) in cost of sales: customer shipping and handling expenses and warranty expenses.

REPORTING IN ACTION

C2

APPLE

Required

1. Why do you believe Apple includes these costs in its cost of sales?

2. What effect does this cost accounting policy for its cost of sales have on Apple's financial statements and any analysis of those statements? Explain.

Fast Forward

3. Access Apple's financial statements for the years after September 26, 2015, from its website (Apple.com) or the SEC's EDGAR website (SEC.gov). Review its footnote relating to Summary of Significant Accounting Policies. Has Apple changed its policy with respect to what costs are included in the cost of sales? Explain.

BTN 20-2   Apple and **Google** work to maintain high-quality and low-cost operations. One ratio routinely computed for this assessment is the cost of goods sold divided by total expenses. A decline in this ratio can mean that the company is spending too much on selling and administrative activities. An increase in this ratio beyond a reasonable level can mean that the company is not spending enough on selling activities. (Assume for this analysis that total expenses equal the cost of goods sold plus total operating expenses.)

COMPARATIVE ANALYSIS

C1

APPLE
GOOGLE

Required

1. For Apple and Google, refer to Appendix A and compute the ratios of cost of goods sold to total expenses for their two most recent fiscal years. (Record answers as percents, rounded to one decimal.)

2. Comment on the similarities or differences in the ratio results across both years between the companies.

BTN 20-3   Many accounting and accounting-related professionals are skilled in financial analysis, but most are not skilled in manufacturing. This is especially the case for process manufacturing environments (for example, a bottling plant or chemical factory). To provide professional accounting and financial services, one must understand the industry, product, and processes. We have an ethical responsibility to develop this understanding before offering services to clients in these areas.

ETHICS CHALLENGE

C1

Required

Write a one-page action plan, in memorandum format, discussing how you would obtain an understanding of key business processes of a company that hires you to provide financial services. The memorandum should specify an industry, a product, and one selected process and should draw on at least one reference, such as a professional journal or industry magazine.

BTN 20-4   You hire a new assistant production manager whose prior experience is with a company that produced goods to order. Your company engages in continuous production of homogeneous products that go through various production processes. Your new assistant e-mails you questioning some cost classifications on an internal report—specifically why the costs of some materials that do not actually become part of the finished product, including some labor costs not directly associated with producing the product, are classified as direct costs. Respond to this concern via memorandum.

COMMUNICATING IN PRACTICE

A1   C1   P1   P2

BTN 20-5   Many companies acquire software to help them monitor and control their costs and as an aid to their accounting systems. One company that supplies such software is **proDacapo** (prodacapo.com). There are many other such vendors. Access proDacapo's website, click on "Products," then click on "Prodacapo Process Management," and review the information displayed.

TAKING IT TO THE NET

C1

Required

How is process management software helpful to businesses? Explain with reference to costs, efficiency, and examples, if possible.

TEAMWORK IN ACTION

C1 P1 P2 P3 P4

BTN 20-6   The purpose of this team activity is to ensure that each team member understands process operations and the related accounting entries. Find the activities and flows identified in Exhibit 20.14 with numbers ① through ⑩. Pick a member of the team to start by describing activity number ① in this exhibit, then verbalizing the related journal entry, and describing how the amounts in the entry are computed. The other members of the team are to agree or disagree; discussion is to continue until all members express understanding. Rotate to the next numbered activity and next team member until all activities and entries have been discussed. If at any point a team member is uncertain about an answer, the team member may pass and get back in the rotation when he or she can contribute to the team's discussion.

ENTREPRENEURIAL DECISION

C3 A2

BTN 20-7   This chapter's opener featured Jeff Kearl and his company **Stance**.

Required

1. Sock makers like Stance typically use several different processes, including knitting, design imprinting, washing and drying, inspection, and packaging/shipping. What are some benefits of using separate process cost summary reports for each process?

2. Jeff tries to order raw materials just-in-time for their use in production. How does holding raw materials inventories increase costs? If the items are not used in production, how can they impact profits? Explain.

3. How can companies like Stance use *yield* to improve their production processes?

HITTING THE ROAD

C2

Point: The class can compare and discuss the different processes studied and the answers provided.

BTN 20-8   In process costing, the process is analyzed first, and then a unit measure is computed in the form of equivalent units for direct materials, conversion (direct labor and overhead), and both types of costs combined. The same analysis applies to both manufacturing and service processes.

Required

Visit your local **U.S. Postal Service** office. Look into the back room, and you will see several ongoing processes. Select one process, such as sorting, and list the costs associated with this process. Your list should include materials, labor, and overhead; be specific. Classify each cost as fixed or variable. At the bottom of your list, outline how overhead should be assigned to your identified process. The following format (with an example) is suggested.

Cost Description	Direct Material	Conversion		Variable Cost	Fixed Cost
		Direct Labor	Overhead		
Manual sorting		X		X	
⋮					
Overhead allocation suggestions:					

GLOBAL DECISION

C1

Samsung

APPLE

GOOGLE

BTN 20-9   **Samsung**, **Apple**, and **Google** are competitors in the global marketplace. Selected data for Samsung follow.

Korean won in billions	Current Year	Prior Year
Cost of goods sold	₩123,482.1	₩128,278.8
Operating expenses	50,757.9	52,902.1
Total expenses	₩174,240.0	₩181,180.9

Required

1. Review the discussion of the importance of the cost of goods sold divided by total expenses ratio in BTN 20-2. (Assume for this analysis that total expenses equal cost of goods sold plus operating expenses.) Compute the cost of goods sold to total expenses ratio for Samsung for the two years of data provided. (Record answers as percents, rounded to one decimal.)

2. Comment on the similarities or differences in the ratio results calculated in part 1 and in BTN 20-2 across years and companies. (Record answers as percents, rounded to one decimal.)

GLOBAL VIEW

As part of a series of global environmental goals, **Anheuser-Busch InBev** set targets to reduce its water usage. The company uses massive amounts of water in beer production and in its cleaning and cooling processes.

To meet these goals, the company followed recent trends in process operations. These included extensive redesign of production processes and the use of advanced technology to increase efficiency at wastewater treatment plants.

As a result, water usage decreased by almost 37 percent in its global operations. The effects of such process improvements will also result in lower costs per equivalent unit of materials and increased profits.

 Global View Assignments

Discussion Question 16

Quick Study 20-27

BTN 20-9

21 chapter

Cost-Volume-Profit Analysis

Chapter Preview

IDENTIFYING COST BEHAVIOR

C1 Fixed costs

Variable costs

Graphing costs

Mixed costs

Step-wise costs

Curvilinear costs

NTK 21-1

MEASURING COST BEHAVIOR

P1 Scatter diagrams

High-low method

Regression

Comparing cost estimation methods

NTK 21-2

CONTRIBUTION MARGIN AND BREAK-EVEN

A1 Contribution margin

P2 Break-even

P3 Cost-volume-profit chart

Impact of estimates on break-even

NTK 21-3

APPLYING COST-VOLUME-PROFIT ANALYSIS

C2 Margin of safety

Income from sales and costs

Sales for target income

Strategizing

P4 Sales mix

A2 Operating leverage

NTK 21-4, 21-5

Learning Objectives

CONCEPTUAL

C1 Describe different types of cost behavior in relation to production and sales volume.

C2 Describe several applications of cost-volume-profit analysis.

ANALYTICAL

A1 Compute the contribution margin and describe what it reveals about a company's cost structure.

A2 Analyze changes in sales using the degree of operating leverage.

PROCEDURAL

P1 Determine cost estimates using the scatter diagram, high-low, and regression methods of estimating costs.

P2 Compute the break-even point for a single product company.

P3 Graph costs and sales for a single product company.

P4 Compute the break-even point for a multiproduct company.

P5 *Appendix 21B*—Compute unit cost and income under both absorption and variable costing.

© Joshua Bright/The New York Times/Redux

Sweet Green

WASHINGTON, DC—Nearing graduation, Nicolas (Nic) Jammet, Jonathan (Jon) Neman, and Nathaniel (Nate) Ru knew they wanted to start their own business. Explains Nic, "standard job choices didn't appeal to us." And they were "sick of the food options in the area," recalls Jon. The trio's idea—to open a salad shop that sourced local, organic ingredients—evolved into a national company, **Sweetgreen** (Sweetgreen.com). Sweetgreen posted revenues of $50 million in 2014. "We want to feed people better food," insists Nate, "it's a lifestyle choice for better living."

The owners must understand and control costs. They say accounting is the key. "I met Nate the first day of Accounting 101," proclaims Jon. All three explain that they apply concepts of fixed and variable costs and how to control costs to break even and make profits.

Sweetgreen relies on small, local suppliers, which increases variable costs. The result is a better salad that customers will pay more for. Using cost-volume-profit analysis enables the owners to see how changes in selling prices, variable costs, and fixed costs impact profits.

"We're making healthy eating cool"

—Nathaniel Ru

As Sweetgreen grows, the owners face new decisions, such as where to open new stores. "It's complicated," insists Jon, as costs vary by location. The trio uses contribution margin income statements, including forecasted costs for potential new locations.

The owners have expanded beyond salad into Sweetgreen clothing. With diverse products, sales mix and multiproduct break-even points are important—which they analyze using accounting data.

The owners are building a national brand that follows sustainable practices. "One of our five core values is to think sustainably," insists Nic, "and make decisions that will last longer." By understanding costs and using cost-volume-profit analysis, the trio pursue sustainability initiatives.

Jon recalls that they started by "trying to solve a problem [and] . . . to change the way people live, starting with how they think about food." He advises entrepreneurs to pursue their dreams and "make it happen!"

Sources: *Sweetgreen website,* January 2017; *Business Insider,* June 6, 2014; *CBS This Morning* video, July 7, 2015; *Huffington Post,* May 2, 2013; *Bloomberg,* October 12, 2015; *The New Potato,* January 7, 2015; *Fortune,* February 18, 2016

IDENTIFYING COST BEHAVIOR

Planning a company's future activities is crucial to successful management. Managers use **cost-volume-profit (CVP) analysis** to predict how changes in costs and sales levels affect profit. CVP analysis requires four inputs, as shown in Exhibit 21.1.

EXHIBIT 21.1

Inputs for CVP analysis

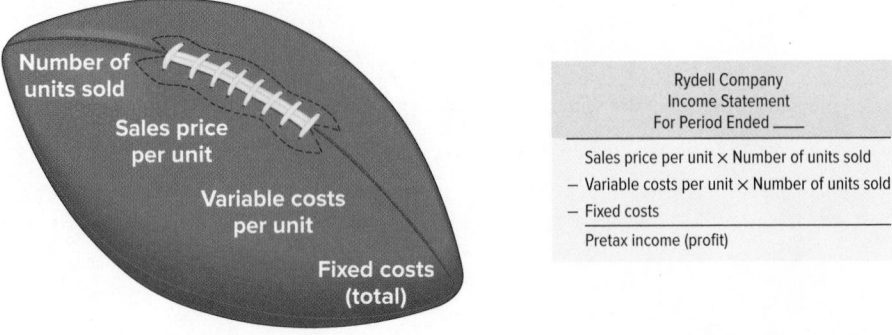

Number of units sold
Sales price per unit
Variable costs per unit
Fixed costs (total)

Rydell Company
Income Statement
For Period Ended _____

Sales price per unit × Number of units sold
− Variable costs per unit × Number of units sold
− Fixed costs
Pretax income (profit)

Using these four inputs, managers apply CVP analysis to answer questions such as:

- How many units must we sell to break even?
- How much will income increase if we install a new machine to reduce labor costs?
- What is the change in income if selling prices decline and sales volume increases?
- How will income change if we change the sales mix of our products or services?
- What sales volume is needed to earn a target income?

This chapter uses Rydell, a football manufacturer, to explain CVP analysis. We first review cost classifications like fixed and variable costs, and then we show methods for measuring these costs.

The concept of *relevant range* is important to classifying costs for CVP analysis. The **relevant range of operations** is the normal operating range for a business. Except for unusually good or bad times, management plans for operations within a range of volume neither close to zero nor at maximum capacity. The relevant range excludes extremely high or low operating levels that are unlikely to occur. CVP analysis requires management to classify costs as either *fixed* or *variable* with respect to production or sales volume, within the relevant range of operations. The remainder of this section discusses concepts of cost behavior.

Fixed Costs

C1

Describe different types of cost behavior in relation to production and sales volume.

Fixed costs do not change when the volume of activity changes (within a relevant range). For example, $32,000 in monthly rent paid for a factory building remains the same whether the factory operates with a single eight-hour shift or around the clock with three shifts. This means that rent cost is the same each month at any level of output from zero to the plant's full productive capacity.

Though the *total* amount of fixed cost does not change as volume changes, fixed cost *per unit* of output decreases as volume increases. For instance, if 200 units are produced when monthly rent is $32,000, the average rent cost per unit is $160 (computed as $32,000/200 units). When production increases to 1,000 units per month, the average rent cost per unit decreases to $32 (computed as $32,000/1,000 units).

Variable Costs

Variable costs change in proportion to changes in volume of activity. Direct materials cost is one example of a variable cost. If one unit of product requires materials costing

$20, total materials costs are $200 when 10 units are manufactured, $400 for 20 units, and so on. While the *total* amount of variable cost changes with the level of production, variable cost *per unit* remains constant as volume changes.

Graph of Costs to Volume

When production volume and costs are graphed, units of product are usually plotted on the *horizontal axis* and dollars of cost are plotted on the *vertical axis.* The upper graph in Exhibit 21.2 shows the relation between total fixed costs and volume, and the relation between total variable costs and volume. Total fixed costs of $32,000 remain the same at all production levels up to the company's monthly capacity of 2,000 units. Total variable costs increase by $20 per unit for each additional unit produced. When variable costs are plotted on a graph of cost and volume, they appear as an upward-sloping straight line starting at the zero cost level.

© gerenme/Vetta/Getty Images

The lower graph in Exhibit 21.2 shows that fixed costs *per unit* decrease as production increases. This drop in per unit costs as production increases is known as *economies of scale.* This lower graph also shows that variable costs per unit remain constant as production levels change.

Point: Fixed costs stay constant in total but decrease per unit as more units are produced. Variable costs vary in total but are fixed per unit as production changes.

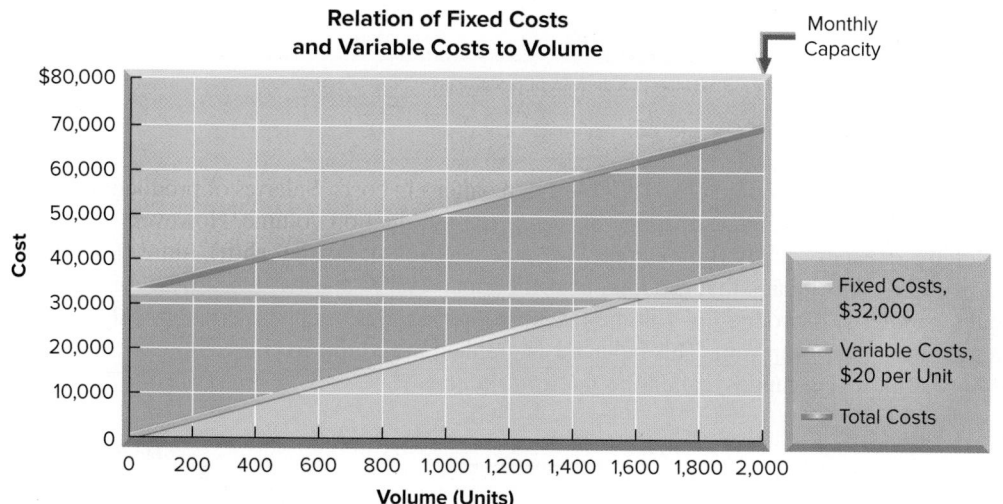

EXHIBIT 21.2

Relations of Total and Per Unit Costs to Volume

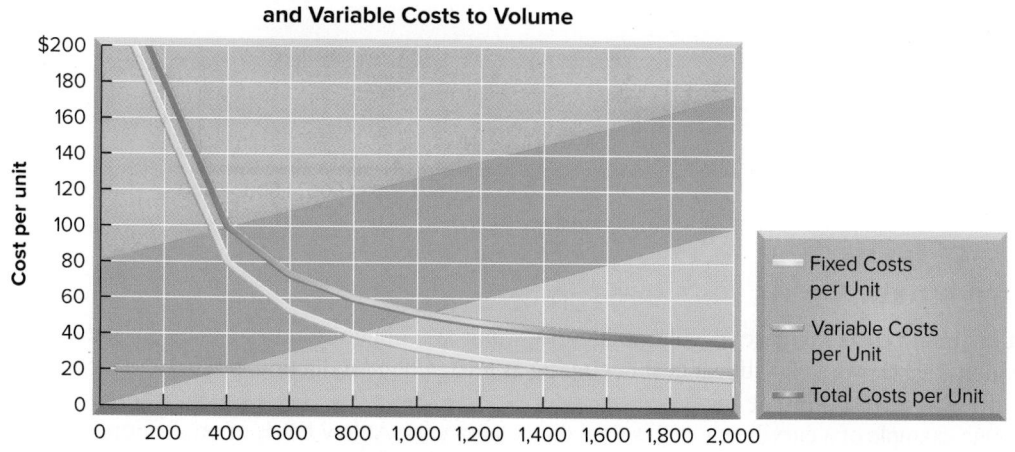

Mixed Costs

Are all costs either fixed or variable? No. **Mixed costs** include both fixed and variable cost components. For example, compensation for sales representatives often includes a fixed monthly salary and a variable commission based on sales. Utilities can also be considered a mixed cost; even if no units are produced, it is not likely a manufacturing plant will use no electricity or water. Like a fixed cost, a mixed cost is greater than zero when volume is zero; but unlike a fixed cost, it increases steadily in proportion to increases in volume.

The total cost line in the top graph in Exhibit 21.2 starts on the vertical axis at the $32,000 fixed cost point. At the zero volume level, total cost equals the fixed costs. As the volume of activity increases, the total cost line increases at an amount equal to the variable cost per unit. This total cost line is a "mixed cost"—and it is highest when the volume of activity is at 2,000 units (the end point of the relevant range). In CVP analysis, mixed costs should be separated into fixed and variable components. The fixed component is added to other fixed costs, and the variable component is added to other variable costs. We show how to separate costs later in this chapter.

Shown below are examples of fixed, variable, and mixed costs for a manufacturer of footballs.

Fixed Costs	Variable Costs	Mixed Costs
• Rent	• Direct materials	• Electricity
• Depreciation*	• Direct labor	• Water
• Property taxes	• Shipping	• Sales rep (salary plus commission)
• Supervisor salaries	• Packaging	• Natural gas
• Office salaries	• Indirect materials	• Maintenance

*Computed using a method other than the units-of-production.

Step-wise Costs

A **step-wise cost** (or *stair-step cost*) reflects a step pattern in costs. Salaries of production supervisors are fixed within a *relevant range* of the current production volume. However, if production volume expands greatly (for example, with the addition of another shift), more supervisors must be hired. This means that the total cost for supervisory salaries steps up by a lump-sum amount. Similarly, if production volume takes another large step up, supervisory salaries will increase by another lump sum. This behavior is graphed in Exhibit 21.3. See how the step-wise cost line is flat within ranges, called the *relevant range*.

EXHIBIT 21.3

Step-wise and Curvilinear Costs

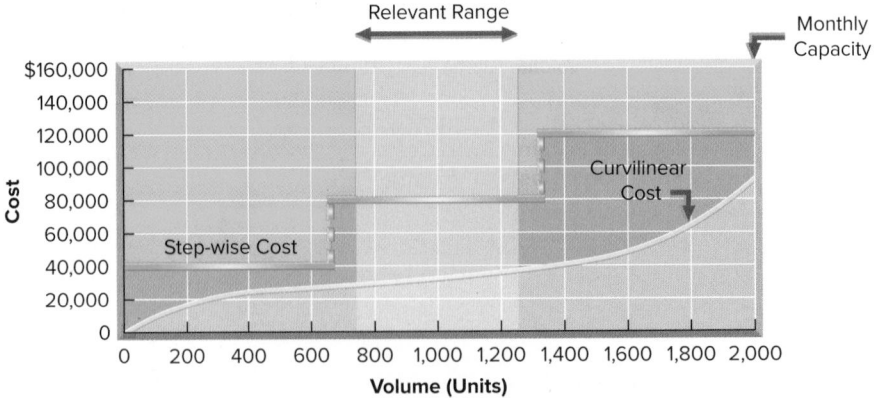

Curvilinear Costs

Curvilinear costs increase as volume increases, but at a nonconstant rate. The curved line in Exhibit 21.3 shows a curvilinear cost beginning at zero (when production is zero) and increasing at different rates as volume increases.

One example of a curvilinear cost is total direct labor cost. At low levels of production, employees can specialize in certain tasks. This efficiency results in a flatter slope in the curvilinear cost graph at lower levels of production in Exhibit 21.3. At some point, adding more employees creates inefficiencies (they get in each other's way or do not have special skills). This inefficiency is reflected in a steeper slope at higher levels of production in the curvilinear cost graph in Exhibit 21.3.

In CVP analysis, step-wise costs are usually treated as either fixed or variable costs. Likewise, curvilinear costs are typically treated as variable costs, and thus remain constant per unit. These treatments involve manager judgment and depend on the width of the relevant range and the expected volume.

NEED-TO-KNOW 21-1

Classifying Costs

C1

Determine whether each of the following is best described as a fixed, variable, mixed, step-wise, or curvilinear cost as the number of product units changes.

	Type of Cost
Rubber used to manufacture tennis balls............................	a. _____
Depreciation (straight-line method)................................	b. _____
Electricity usage..	c. _____
Supervisory salaries...	d. _____
A salesperson's commission is 7% for sales of up to $100,000, and 10% of sales for sales above $100,000............	e. _____

Solution

a. variable **b.** fixed **c.** mixed **d.** fixed* **e.** curvilinear

_____

*If more shifts are added, then supervisory salaries behave like a step-wise cost with respect to the number of shifts.

Do More: QS 21-1, QS 21-2, E 21-1, E 21-2, E 21-3

MEASURING COST BEHAVIOR

Identifying and measuring cost behavior requires analysis and judgment. A key part of this process is to classify costs as either fixed or variable, which often requires analysis of past cost behavior. A goal of classifying costs is to develop a *cost equation*. The cost equation expresses total costs as a function of total fixed costs plus variable cost per unit. Three methods are commonly used:

- Scatter diagram
- High-low method
- Regression

Each method is explained using the unit and cost data shown in Exhibit 21.4, which are from a start-up company that uses units produced as the activity base in estimating cost behavior.

P1_____

Determine cost estimates using the scatter diagram, high-low, and regression methods of estimating costs.

EXHIBIT 21.4

Data for Estimating Cost Behavior

Month	Units Produced	Total Cost
January.............	27,500	$21,500
February............	22,500	20,500
March	25,000	25,000
April...............	35,000	21,500
May	47,500	25,500
June................	17,500	18,500
July	30,000	23,500
August.............	52,500	28,500
September	37,500	26,000
October............	62,500	29,000
November...........	67,500	31,000
December...........	57,500	26,000

Scatter Diagram

A **scatter diagram** is a graph of unit volume and cost data. Units are plotted on the horizontal axis and costs are plotted on the vertical axis. Each point on a scatter diagram reflects the cost and number of units for a prior period. In Exhibit 21.5a, the prior 12 months' costs and units are graphed. Each point reflects total costs incurred and units produced in that month. For instance, the point labeled March had units produced of 25,000 and costs of $25,000.

EXHIBIT 21.5a

Scatter Diagram

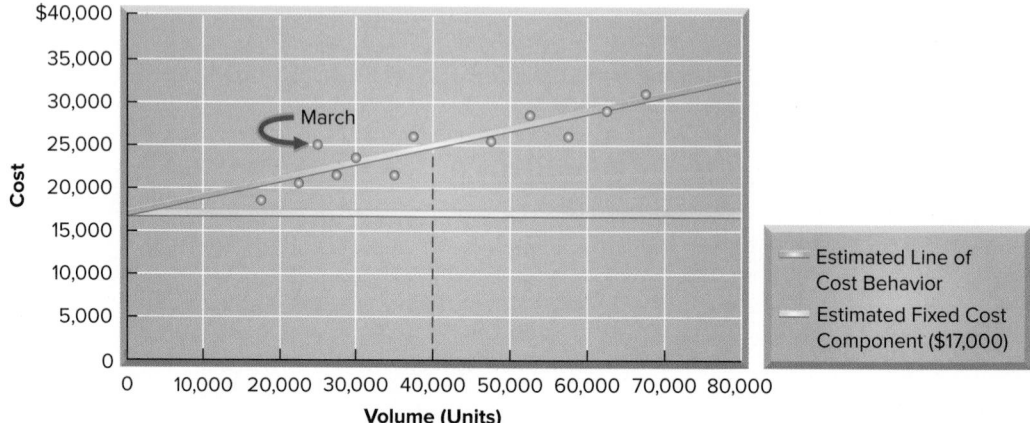

The **estimated line of cost behavior** is drawn on a scatter diagram to reflect the relation between cost and unit volume. This line best visually "fits" the points in a scatter diagram. Fitting this line demands judgment, or can be done with spreadsheet software, as we illustrate in Appendix 21A. The line drawn in Exhibit 21.5a intersects the vertical axis at approximately $17,000, which reflects fixed cost. To compute variable cost per unit, follow three steps:

Step 1: Select any two levels of units produced, say 0 and 25,000.

Step 2: Identify total costs at those production levels (at zero units of output, total costs equal fixed costs of $17,000; at 25,000 units of output, total costs equal $25,000).

Step 3: Compute the *slope* of the line, which is the change in cost divided by the change in units. This is the estimated variable cost per unit.

This computation is shown in Exhibit 21.5b.

EXHIBIT 21.5b

Variable Cost per Unit—
Scatter Diagram

Example: If units are projected at 30,000, what is the predicted cost? *Answer:* Approximately $26,600.

$$\frac{\text{Change in cost}}{\text{Change in units}} = \frac{\$25,000 - \$17,000}{25,000 - 0} = \frac{\$8,000}{25,000} = \$0.32 \text{ per unit}$$

Variable cost is $0.32 per unit. Thus, the cost equation that management will use to estimate costs for different unit levels is **$17,000 plus $0.32 per unit produced.**

High-Low Method

The **high-low method** is a way to estimate the cost equation using just two points: the highest and lowest *volume* levels. The high-low method follows three steps:

Step 1: Identify the highest and lowest volume levels. These might not be the highest or lowest levels of *costs*.

Step 2: Compute the slope (variable cost per unit) using the high and low volume levels.

Step 3: Compute the total fixed costs by computing the total variable cost at either the high or low volume level, and then subtracting that amount from the total cost at that volume level.

We illustrate the high-low method next.

Step 1: In our case, the lowest number of units is 17,500 and the highest is 67,500. The costs corresponding to these unit volumes are $18,500 and $31,000, respectively (see the data in Exhibit 21.4).

Step 2: The variable cost per unit is calculated using a simple formula: change in cost divided by the change in units. Using the data from the high and low unit volumes, this results in a slope, or variable cost per unit, of $0.25 as computed in Exhibit 21.6.

$$\frac{\textbf{Change in cost}}{\textbf{Change in units}} = \frac{\$31,000 - \$18,500}{67,500 - 17,500} = \frac{\$12,500}{50,000} = \$0.25 \text{ per unit}$$

EXHIBIT 21.6

Variable Cost per Unit— High-Low Method

Step 3: To estimate the fixed cost for the high-low method, we use the knowledge that total cost equals fixed cost plus variable cost per unit times the number of units. Then we pick either the high or low point (based on volume) to determine the fixed cost. This computation is shown in Exhibit 21.7—where we use the high point (67,500 units) in determining the fixed cost of $14,125. (Use of the low point yields the same fixed cost estimate.)

Total cost = Fixed cost + (Variable cost per unit × Units)

$31,000 = Fixed cost + ($0.25 per unit × 67,500 units)

$31,000 = Fixed cost + $16,875

$14,125 = Fixed cost

EXHIBIT 21.7

Determining Fixed Costs— High-Low Method

Thus, the cost equation from the high-low method is **$14,125 plus $0.25 per unit produced**. This cost equation differs from that determined from the scatter diagram method. A weakness of the high-low method is that it ignores all data points except the highest and lowest volume levels.

Example: Using information from Exhibit 21.7, what is the amount of fixed cost at the low level of volume? *Answer:* $14,125, computed as $18,500 − ($0.25 × 17,500 units).

Regression

Least-squares regression, or simply *regression*, is a statistical method for identifying cost behavior. We use the cost equation estimated from this method but leave the computational details for advanced courses. Computations for least-squares regression are readily done using most spreadsheet programs or calculators. We illustrate this using Excel in Appendix A of this chapter. Using least-squares regression, the cost equation for the data presented in Exhibit 21.4 is **$16,688 plus $0.20 per unit produced**; that is, the fixed cost is estimated as $16,688 and the variable cost at $0.20 per unit.

Comparing Cost Estimation Methods

The three cost estimation methods result in different estimates of fixed and variable costs, as summarized in Exhibit 21.8. Estimates from the scatter diagram, unless done with spreadsheet software, are based on a visual fit of the cost line and are subject to interpretation. Estimates from the high-low method use only two sets of values corresponding to the lowest and highest unit volumes. Sometimes these two extreme activity levels do not reflect the more usual conditions likely to recur. Estimates from least-squares regression use a statistical technique and all available data points.

Estimation Method	Fixed Cost	Variable Cost
Scatter diagram	$17,000	$0.32 per unit
High-low method	14,125	0.25 per unit
Regression	16,688	0.20 per unit

EXHIBIT 21.8

Comparison of Cost Estimation Methods

All three methods use *past data.* Thus, cost estimates resulting from these methods are only as good as the data used. Managers must establish that the data are reliable. If the data are reliable, the use of more data points, as in the regression or scatter diagram methods, should yield more accurate estimates than the high-low method. However, the high-low method is easier to apply and thus might be useful for obtaining a quick cost equation estimate.

NEED-TO-KNOW 21-2

High-Low Method

P1

Using the information below, apply the high-low method to determine the *cost equation* (total fixed costs plus variable costs per unit).

Volume	Units Produced	Total Cost
Lowest............	1,600	$ 9,800
Highest	4,000	17,000

Solution

The variable cost per unit is computed as: [$17,000 − $9,800]/[4,000 units − 1,600 units] = $3 per unit. Total fixed costs using the lowest activity level are computed from the following equation: $9,800 = Fixed costs + ($3 × 1,600 units); thus, fixed costs = $5,000. This implies the cost equation is **$5,000 plus $3 per unit produced.** We can prove the accuracy of this cost equation at either the highest or lowest point shown here.

Highest point:
Total cost = $5,000 + ($3 per unit × 4,000 units)
= $5,000 + $12,000
= $17,000

Lowest point:
Total cost = $5,000 + ($3 per unit × 1,600 units)
= $5,000 + $4,800
= $9,800

Do More: QS 21-3, E 21-6

CONTRIBUTION MARGIN AND BREAK-EVEN ANALYSIS

This section explains *contribution margin,* a key measure in CVP analysis. We also discuss break-even analysis, an important special case of CVP analysis.

Contribution Margin and Its Measures

A1

Compute the contribution margin and describe what it reveals about a company's cost structure.

After classifying costs as fixed or variable, we can compute **contribution margin,** which equals total sales minus total variable costs. Contribution margin contributes to covering fixed costs and generating profits. **Contribution margin per unit,** or *unit contribution margin,* is the amount by which a product's unit selling price exceeds its variable cost per unit. Exhibit 21.9 shows the formula for contribution margin per unit.

EXHIBIT 21.9

Contribution Margin per Unit

$$\text{Contribution margin per unit} = \text{Selling price per unit} - \text{Total variable cost per unit}$$

Contribution margin ratio is the percent of a unit's selling price that exceeds total unit variable cost. It is interpreted as the percent of each sales dollar that remains after deducting the unit variable cost. Exhibit 21.10 shows the formula for contribution margin ratio.

EXHIBIT 21.10

Contribution Margin Ratio

$$\text{Contribution margin ratio} = \frac{\text{Contribution margin per unit}}{\text{Selling price per unit}}$$

To illustrate contribution margin, consider Rydell, which sells footballs for $100 each and incurs variable costs of $70 per football sold. Its fixed costs are $24,000 per month with monthly capacity of 1,800 units (footballs). Rydell's contribution margin per unit is $30, which is computed as follows.

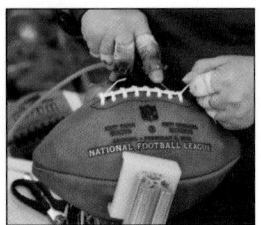

AP Images/Skip Peterson

Selling price per unit	$100
Variable cost per unit	70
Contribution margin per unit	$ 30

This means at a selling price of $100 per football, Rydell covers its per unit variable costs and makes $30 per unit to contribute to fixed costs and profit. Rydell's contribution margin ratio is 30%, computed as $30/$100. A contribution margin ratio of 30% implies that for each $1 in sales, Rydell has $0.30 that contributes to fixed cost and profit. Next we show how to use these contribution margin measures in break-even analysis.

■ **Decision** Maker

Sales Manager   You can accept only one of two customer orders due to limited capacity. The first order is for 100 units with a contribution margin ratio of 60% and a selling price of $1,000 per unit. The second order is for 500 units with a contribution margin ratio of 20% and a selling price of $800 per unit. Incremental fixed costs are the same for both orders. Which order do you accept? ■   [*Answer:* The contribution margin per unit for the first order is $600 (60% of $1,000); the contribution margin per unit for the second order is $160 (20% of $800). You are likely tempted to accept the first order based on its higher contribution margin per unit, but you must compute the *total* contribution margin for each order. Total contribution margin is $60,000 ($600 per unit × 100 units) and $80,000 ($160 per unit × 500 units) for the two orders, respectively. The second order provides the largest return in absolute dollars and is the order you would accept. Another factor to consider in your selection is the potential for a long-term relationship with these customers including repeat sales and growth.]

Break-Even Point

The **break-even point** is the sales level at which total sales equal total costs and a company neither earns a profit nor incurs a loss. Break-even applies to nearly all organizations, activities, and events. A key concern when launching a project is whether it will break even—that is, whether sales will at least cover total costs. The break-even point can be expressed in either units or dollars of sales. To illustrate break-even analysis, let's again look at Rydell, which sells footballs for $100 per unit and incurs $70 of variable costs per unit sold. Its fixed costs are $24,000 per month. Three different methods are used to find the break-even point.

- Formula method
- Contribution margin income statement
- Cost-volume-profit chart

P2

Compute the break-even point for a single product company.

Formula Method   We compute the break-even point using the formula in Exhibit 21.11. This formula uses the contribution margin per unit (calculated above), which for Rydell is $30 ($100 − $70). The break-even sales volume in units is:

Point: Selling prices and variable costs are usually expressed in per unit amounts. Fixed costs are usually expressed in total amounts.

EXHIBIT 21.11

Formula for Computing Break-Even Sales (in Units)

$$\text{Break-even point in units} = \frac{\text{Fixed costs}}{\text{Contribution margin per unit}}$$
$$= \$24{,}000/\$30$$
$$= 800 \text{ units per month}$$

If Rydell sells 800 units, its profit will be zero. Profit increases or decreases by $30 for every unit sold above or below that break-even point; if Rydell sells 801 units, profit will equal $30. We also can calculate the break-even point in dollars. Also called *break-even sales dollars,* it uses the contribution margin ratio to determine the required sales dollars needed for the company to break even. Exhibit 21.12 shows the formula and Rydell's break-even point in dollars:

Point: Even if a company operates at a level above its break-even point, management may decide to stop operating because it is not earning a reasonable return on investment.

EXHIBIT 21.12

Formula for Computing Break-Even Sales (in Dollars)

$$\text{Break-even point in dollars} = \frac{\text{Fixed costs}}{\text{Contribution margin ratio}}$$
$$= \$24{,}000/30\%$$
$$= \$24{,}000/0.30$$
$$= \$80{,}000 \text{ of monthly sales}$$

EXHIBIT 21.13

Contribution Margin
Income Statement for
Break-Even Sales

Income Statement (Traditional)	
Sales......................	$#
Cost of sales..............	#
Gross profit...............	#
Selling and admin..........	#
Income (pretax)............	$#

COMPANY Contribution Margin Income Statement Format
Sales
– Variable costs
Contribution margin
– Fixed costs
Income (pretax)

RYDELL COMPANY Contribution Margin Income Statement (at Break-Even) For Month Ended January 31, 2017	
Sales (800 units at $100 each)................	$80,000
Variable costs (800 units at $70 each)..........	56,000
Contribution margin (800 units at $30 each) ...	24,000
Fixed costs	24,000
Income (pretax).............................	$ 0

Contribution Margin Income Statement Method   The left side of Exhibit 21.13 shows the general format of a *contribution margin income statement*. It differs in format from a traditional income statement in two ways. First, it separately classifies costs and expenses as variable or fixed. Second, it reports contribution margin (sales − variable costs).

The right side of Exhibit 21.13 uses this format to find the break-even point for Rydell. To use this method, set income equal to zero and work up the income statement to find sales. Rydell's contribution margin must exactly equal its fixed costs of $24,000. For Rydell's contribution margin to equal $24,000, it must sell 800 units ($24,000/$30). The resulting contribution margin income statement shows that the $80,000 revenue from sales of 800 units exactly equals the sum of variable and fixed costs.

NEED-TO-KNOW 21-3

Contribution Margin and
Break-Even Point

A1   P2

Hudson Co. predicts fixed costs of $400,000 for 2017. Its one product sells for $170 per unit, and it incurs variable costs of $150 per unit. The company predicts total sales of 25,000 units for the next year.

1. Compute the contribution margin per unit.

2. Compute the break-even point (in units) using the formula method.

3. Prepare a contribution margin income statement at the break-even point.

Solution

1. Contribution margin per unit = $170 − $150 = $20

2. Break-even point = $400,000/$20 = 20,000 units

3.

HUDSON CO. Contribution Margin Income Statement (at Break-Even) For Year Ended December 31, 2017	
Sales (20,000 units at $170 each).............	$3,400,000
Variable costs (20,000 units at $150 each)	3,000,000
Contribution margin (20,000 units at $20 each) ...	400,000
Fixed costs	400,000
Income (pretax)............................	$ 0

Do More: QS 21-5, QS 21-6,
QS 21-10, E 21-8, E 21-9,
E 21-16

P3 _____

Graph costs and sales for a
single product company.

Point: CVP charts can also be
drawn with computer programs.

Cost-Volume-Profit Chart

A third way to find the break-even point is to make a **cost-volume-profit (CVP) chart** (*break-even chart*). Exhibit 21.14 shows Rydell's CVP chart. In a CVP chart, the horizontal axis is the number of units produced and sold, and the vertical axis is dollars of sales and costs. The lines in the chart show both sales and costs at different output levels.

We follow three steps to prepare a CVP chart:

① **Plot fixed costs on the vertical axis** ($24,000 for Rydell). Draw a horizontal line at this level to show that fixed costs remain unchanged regardless of output volume (drawing this fixed cost line is not essential to the chart).

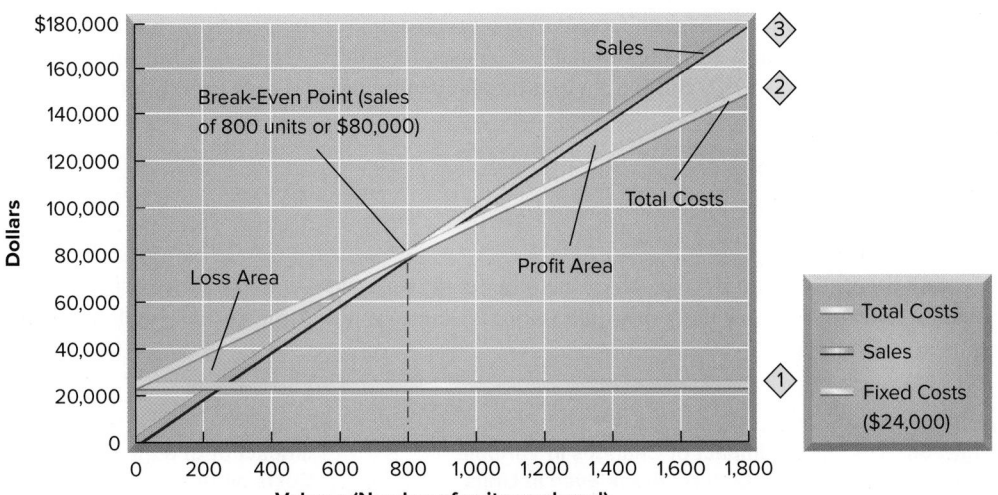

EXHIBIT 21.14

Cost-Volume-Profit Chart

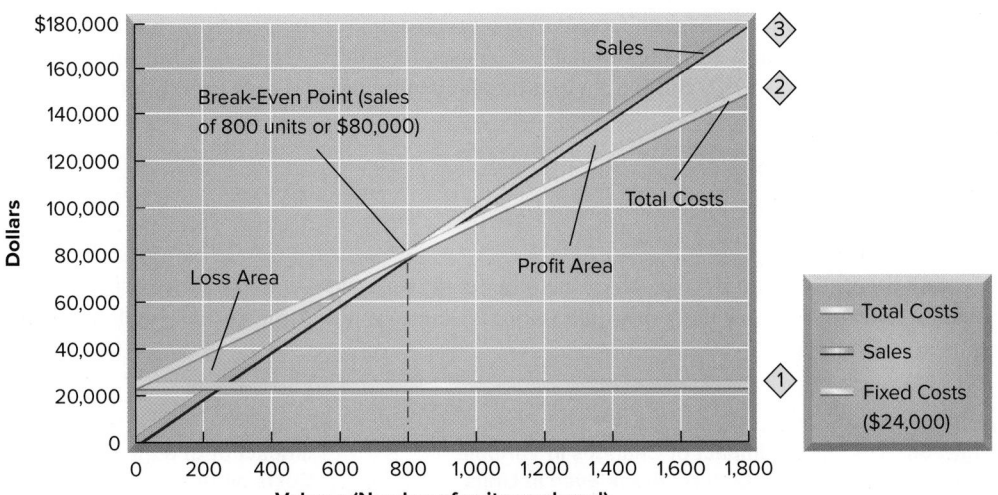

② **Draw the total (variable plus fixed) cost line for a relevant range of volume levels.** This line starts at the fixed costs level on the vertical axis because total costs equal fixed costs at zero volume. The slope of the total cost line equals the variable cost per unit ($70). To draw the line, compute the total costs for any volume level and connect this point with the vertical axis intercept ($24,000). For example, if 1,800 units are produced and sold, then total costs are $150,000. Do not draw this line beyond the productive capacity for the planning period (1,800 units for Rydell).

③ **Draw the sales line.** Start at the origin (zero units and zero dollars of sales) and make the slope of this line equal to the selling price per unit ($100). To draw the line, compute dollar sales for any volume level and connect this point with the origin. For example, if 1,800 units are sold, then total sales are $180,000. Do not extend this line beyond the productive capacity. Total sales will be highest at maximum capacity.

The total cost line and the sales line intersect at 800 units in Exhibit 21.14, which is the break-even point—the point where total dollar sales of $80,000 equals the sum of both fixed and variable costs ($80,000). (The 800 units is the same result from the formula in Exhibit 21.11 and from the contribution margin income statement in Exhibit 21.13.)

On either side of the break-even point, the vertical distance between the sales line and the total cost line at any specific volume is the profit or loss expected at that point. At volume levels to the left of the break-even point, this vertical distance is the amount of the expected loss because the total costs line is above the total sales line. At volume levels to the right of the break-even point, this vertical distance is the expected profit because the total sales line is above the total cost line.

Point: CVP analysis is often based on *sales volume,* using either units sold or dollar sales. Other output measures, such as the number of units produced, can also be used.

Example: In Exhibit 21.14, the sales line intersects the total cost line at 800 units. At what point would the two lines intersect if selling price per unit is increased by 20% to $120 per unit? *Answer:* $24,000/($120 − $70) = 480 units

Changes in Estimates   CVP analysis uses estimates, and knowing how changes in those estimates impact break-even is useful. For example, a manager might form three estimates for each of the inputs of break-even: optimistic, most likely, and pessimistic. Then ranges of break-even points in units can be computed, using any of the three methods shown above. To illustrate, assume Rydell's managers provide the estimates in Exhibit 21.15.

EXHIBIT 21.15

Alternative Estimates for Break-Even Analysis

	Selling Price per Unit	Variable Cost per Unit	Total Fixed Costs
Optimistic...........	$105	$68	$21,000
Most likely...........	100	70	24,000
Pessimistic...........	95	72	27,000

If, for example, Rydell's managers believe they can raise the selling price of a football to $105, without any change in unit variable or total fixed costs, then the revised contribution margin per football is $35 ($105 − $70), and the revised break-even in units follows in Exhibit 21.16.

EXHIBIT 21.16

Revised Break-Even in Units

$$\text{Revised break-even point in units} = \frac{\$24,000}{\$35} = 686 \text{ units (rounded)}$$

EXHIBIT 21.17

Break-Even Points for Alternative Estimates

Repeating this calculation using each of the other eight separate estimates above (keeping other estimates unchanged from their original amounts), and graphing the results, yields the three graphs in Exhibit 21.17.

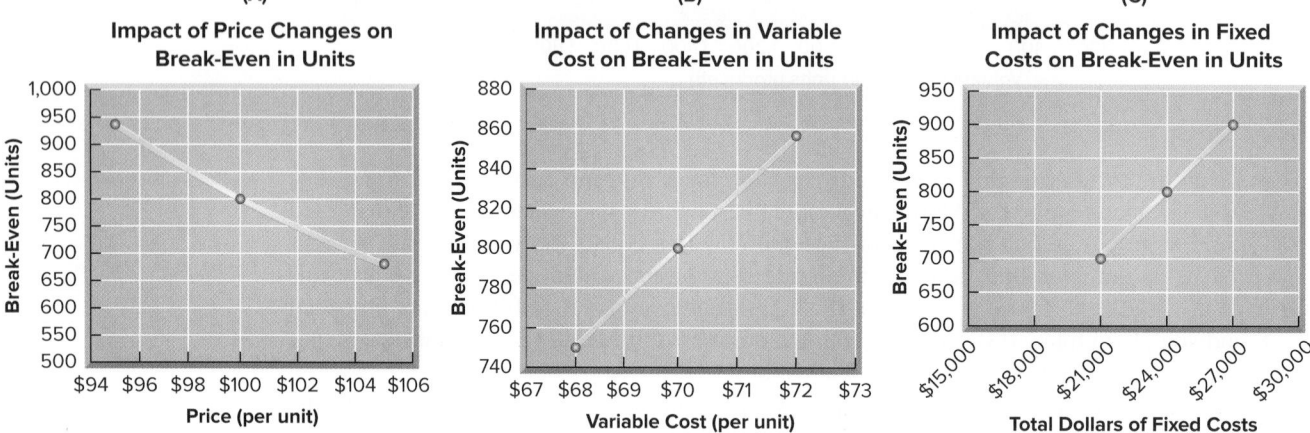

These graphs show how changes in selling prices, variable costs, and fixed costs impact break-even. When selling prices can be increased without impacting unit variable costs or total fixed costs, break-even decreases (graph A). When competition reduces selling prices, and the company cannot reduce costs, break-even increases (graph A). Increases in either variable (graph B) or fixed costs (graph C), if they cannot be passed on to customers via higher selling prices, will increase break-even. If costs can be reduced and selling prices held constant, the break-even point decreases.

Point: This analysis changed only one estimate at a time; managers can examine how combinations of changes in estimates impact break-even.

■ **Decision Ethics**

Supervisor   Your team is conducting a CVP analysis for a new product. Different sales projections have different incomes. One member suggests picking numbers yielding favorable income because any estimate is "as good as any other." Another member suggests dropping unfavorable data points for cost estimation. What do you do? ■   [*Answer:* Your dilemma is whether to go along with the suggestions to "manage" the numbers to make the project look like it will achieve sufficient profits. You should not succumb to these suggestions. Many people will likely be affected negatively if you manage the predicted numbers and the project eventually is unprofitable. Moreover, if it does fail, an investigation would likely reveal that data in the proposal were "fixed" to make the proposal look good. One way to deal with this dilemma is to prepare several analyses showing results under different assumptions and then let senior management make the decision.]

APPLYING COST-VOLUME-PROFIT ANALYSIS

Managers consider a variety of strategies in planning business operations. Cost-volume-profit analysis is useful in helping managers evaluate the likely effects of these strategies.

Margin of Safety

C2
_____

Describe several applications of cost-volume-profit analysis.

All companies wish to do more than break even. The excess of expected sales over the break-even sales level is called **margin of safety,** the amount that sales can drop before the company incurs a loss. It is often expressed in dollars or as a percent of the expected sales level.

To illustrate, Rydell's break-even point in dollars is $80,000. If its expected sales are $100,000, the margin of safety is $20,000 ($100,000 − $80,000). As a percent, the margin of safety is 20% of expected sales, as shown in Exhibit 21.18.

$$\text{Margin of safety (in percent)} = \frac{\text{Expected sales} - \text{Break-even sales}}{\text{Expected sales}}$$

$$= \frac{\$100,000 - \$80,000}{\$100,000}$$

$$= \$20,000/\$100,000$$

$$= 20\%$$

EXHIBIT 21.18

Computing Margin of Safety (in Percent)

Management must assess whether the margin of safety is adequate in light of factors such as sales variability, competition, consumer tastes, and economic conditions.

Computing Income from Sales and Costs

Managers often use contribution margin income statements to forecast future sales or income. Exhibit 21.19 shows the key variables in CVP analysis—sales, variable costs, contribution margin, and fixed costs, and their relations to income (pretax). To answer the question "What is the predicted income from a predicted level of sales?" we work our way down this income statement to compute income.

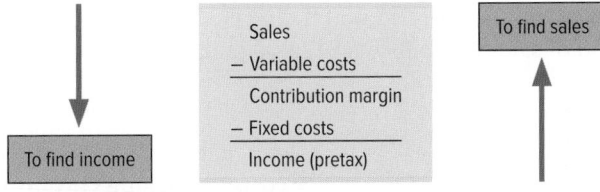

EXHIBIT 21.19

Income Relations in CVP Analysis

To illustrate, assume Rydell's management expects to sell 1,500 units in January 2017. What is the amount of income if this sales level is achieved? We first compute dollar sales, and then use the format in Exhibit 21.19 to compute Rydell's expected income in Exhibit 21.20. This $21,000 income amount can also be computed as (units sold × contribution margin per unit) − fixed costs, or (1,500 × $30) − $24,000. The $21,000 income is pretax.

Point: 1,500 units of sales is 700 units above Rydell's break-even point. Income can also be computed as 700 units × $30 contribution margin per unit.

EXHIBIT 21.20

Computing Expected Pretax Income from Expected Sales

RYDELL COMPANY	
Contribution Margin Income Statement (Pretax)	
For Month Ended January 31, 2017	
Sales (1,500 units at $100 each)	$150,000
Variable costs (1,500 units at $70 each)	105,000
Contribution margin (1,500 units at $30 each)	45,000
Fixed costs	24,000
Income (pretax)	$ 21,000

Computing After-Tax Income   To find the amount of *after-tax* income from selling 1,500 units, management uses the tax rate. Assume that the tax rate is 25%. Then we can prepare a projected after-tax income statement, shown in Exhibit 21.21. After-tax income can also be computed as: pretax income × (1 − tax rate).

EXHIBIT 21.21

Computing Expected
After-Tax Income from
Expected Sales

RYDELL COMPANY	
Contribution Margin Income Statement (After-Tax)	
For Month Ended January 31, 2017	
Sales (1,500 units at $100 each)	$150,000
Variable costs (1,500 units at $70 each)	105,000
Contribution margin (1,500 units at $30 each)	45,000
Fixed costs	24,000
Pretax income	21,000
Income taxes ($21,000 × 25%)	5,250
Net income (after tax)	$ 15,750

Point: Pretax income
= $15,750/(1 − 0.25), or $21,000.

"How many
units must we sell
to earn $50,000?"

Management then assesses whether this income is an adequate return on assets invested. Management will also consider whether sales and income can be increased by raising or lowering prices. CVP analysis is good for addressing these kinds of "what-if" questions.

Computing Sales for a Target Income

Many companies' annual plans are based on income targets (sometimes called *budgets*). Rydell's goal for this year is to increase income by 10% over the prior year. CVP analysis helps to determine the sales level needed to achieve the target income. Planning for the year is then based on this level.

We use the formula in Exhibit 21.22 to compute sales for a target income (pretax). To illustrate, Rydell has monthly fixed costs of $24,000 and a 30% contribution margin ratio. Assume that it sets a target monthly income of $12,000. Using the formula in Exhibit 21.22, we find that Rydell needs $120,000 of sales to produce a $12,000 pretax target income.

EXHIBIT 21.22

Computing Sales (Dollars)
for a Target Income

$$\text{Dollar sales at target income} = \frac{\text{Fixed costs} + \text{Target income (pretax)}}{\text{Contribution margin ratio}}$$

$$= \frac{\$24,000 + \$12,000}{30\%} = \$120,000$$

Point: Break-even is a special case of the formulas in Exhibits 21.22 and 21.23; simply set target income to $0, and the formulas reduce to those in Exhibits 21.11 and 21.12.

Alternatively, we can compute *unit sales* instead of dollar sales. To do this, use *contribution margin per unit*. Exhibit 21.23 illustrates this for Rydell. The two computations in Exhibits 21.22 and 21.23 are equivalent because sales of 1,200 units at $100 per unit equal $120,000 of sales.

EXHIBIT 21.23

Computing Sales (Units) for
a Target Income

$$\text{Unit sales at target income} = \frac{\text{Fixed costs} + \text{Target income (pretax)}}{\text{Contribution margin per unit}}$$

$$= \frac{\$24,000 + \$12,000}{\$30} = 1,200 \text{ units}$$

We can also use the contribution margin income statement approach to compute sales for a target income in two steps.

Step 1: Insert the fixed costs ($24,000) and the target profit level ($12,000) into a contribution margin income statement, as shown in Exhibit 21.24. To cover its fixed costs of $24,000 and yield target income of $12,000, Rydell must generate a contribution margin of $36,000 (computed as $24,000 plus $12,000).

Step 2: Enter $36,000 in the contribution margin row as step 2. With a contribution margin ratio of 30%, sales must be $120,000, computed as $36,000/0.30, to yield a contribution margin of $36,000. We enter $120,000 in the sales row of the contribution margin income statement and solve for variable costs of $84,000 (computed as $120,000 − $36,000). At a selling price of $100 per unit, Rydell must sell 1,200 units ($120,000/$100) to earn a target income of $12,000.

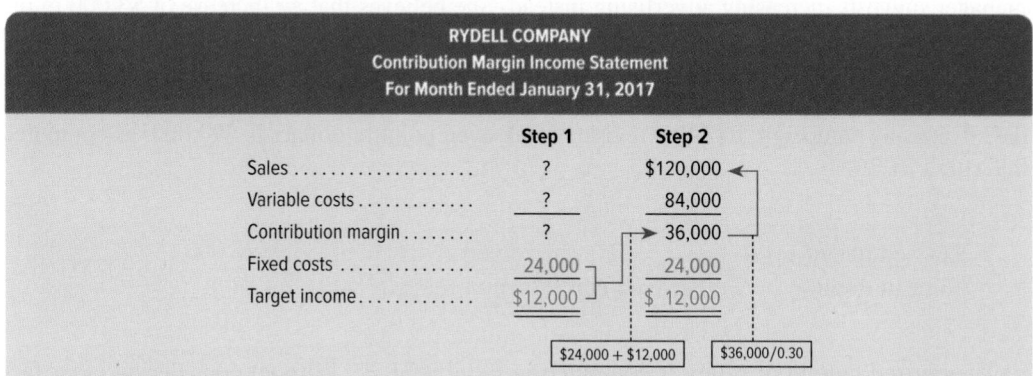

EXHIBIT 21.24

Using the Contribution Margin Income Statement to Find Target Sales

A manufacturer predicts fixed costs of $502,000 for the next year. Its one product sells for $180 per unit, and it incurs variable costs of $126 per unit. Its target (pretax) income is $200,000.

Contribution Margin, Target Income, and Margin of Safety

1. Compute the contribution margin ratio.

2. Compute the dollar sales needed to yield the target income.

3. Compute the unit sales needed to yield the target income.

4. Assume break-even sales of 9,296 units. Compute the margin of safety (in dollars) if the company expects to sell 10,000 units.

A1   C2

Solution

1. Contribution margin ratio = [$180 − $126]/$180 = 30%

2. Dollar sales at target income = [$502,000 + $200,000]/0.30 = $2,340,000

3. Unit sales at target income = [$502,000 + $200,000]/[$180 − $126] = 13,000 units

4. Margin of safety = (10,000 × $180) − (9,296 × $180) = $126,720

Do More: QS 21-9, QS 21-11, QS 21-13, E 21-12, E 21-17

Evaluating Strategies

Earlier we showed how changing one of the estimates in a CVP analysis impacts break-even. We can examine strategies that impact several estimates in the CVP analysis. For instance, we might want to know what happens to income if we automate a currently manual process. We can use *sensitivity analysis* to predict income if we can describe how these changes affect a company's fixed costs, variable costs, selling price, and volume. CVP analyses based on different estimates can be useful to management in planning business strategy. We provide some examples.

Buy a Productive Asset   Assume Rydell is considering buying a new machine that would increase monthly fixed costs from $24,000 to $30,000 and would decrease variable costs by $10 per unit (from $70 per unit to $60 per unit). Rydell's break-even point in dollars is currently $80,000. How would the new machine affect Rydell's break-even point in dollars? If Rydell maintains its selling price of $100 per unit, its contribution margin per unit will increase to $40—computed as the sales price of $100 per unit minus the (new) variable costs of $60 per unit. With this new machine, the revised contribution margin ratio per unit is 40% (computed as $40/$100). Rydell's revised break-even point in dollars would be $75,000, as computed in Exhibit 21.25. The new machine would lower Rydell's break-even point by $5,000, or 50 units, per month. The revised margin of safety increases to 25%, computed as ($100,000 − $75,000)/$100,000.

EXHIBIT 21.25

Revised Break-Even

$$\text{Revised break-even point in dollars} = \frac{\text{Revised fixed costs}}{\text{Revised contribution margin ratio}} = \frac{\$30,000}{40\%} = \$75,000$$

Increase Operating Expense   Instead of buying a new machine, Rydell's advertising manager suggests increasing advertising instead. She believes that an increase of $3,000 in the monthly advertising budget will increase sales by $25,000 per month (at a selling price of $100 per unit). The contribution margin will continue to be $30 per unit. Exhibit 21.8 showed the company's margin of safety was 20% when Rydell's expected sales level was $100,000. With the advertising campaign, Rydell's revised break-even point in dollars is $90,000, as computed in Exhibit 21.26.

EXHIBIT 21.26

Revised Break-Even
(in dollars)

$$\text{Revised break-even point in dollars} = \frac{\text{Revised fixed costs}}{\text{Revised contribution margin ratio}} = \frac{\$27,000}{30\%} = \$90,000$$

The revised margin of safety is computed in Exhibit 21.27. Without considering other factors, the advertising campaign would increase Rydell's margin of safety from 20% to 28%.

EXHIBIT 21.27

Revised Margin of Safety
(in percent)

$$\text{Revised margin of safety (in percent)} = \frac{\text{Expected sales} - \text{Break-even sales}}{\text{Expected sales}}$$
$$= \frac{\$125,000 - \$90,000}{\$125,000} = 28\%$$

Sales Mix and Break-Even

P4

Compute the break-even point for a multiproduct company.

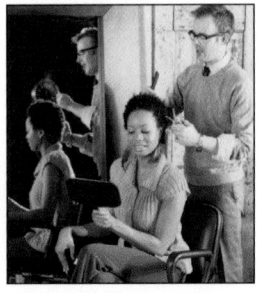

© Kali9/E+/Getty Images

So far we have looked only at cases where the company sells a single product or service. However, many companies sell multiple products or services, and we can modify the CVP analysis for these cases. An important assumption in a multiproduct setting is that the sales mix of different products is known and remains constant during the planning period. **Sales mix** is the ratio (proportion) of the sales volumes for the various products. For instance, if a company normally sells 10,000 footballs, 5,000 softballs, and 4,000 basketballs per month, its sales mix can be expressed as 10:5:4 for footballs, softballs, and basketballs.

When companies sell more than one product or service, we estimate the break-even point by using a **composite unit,** which summarizes the sales mix and contribution margins of each product. Multiproduct CVP analysis treats this composite unit as a single product. To illustrate, let's look at Hair-Today, a styling salon that offers three cuts: basic, ultra, and budget in the ratio of 4 basic cuts to 2 ultra cuts to 1 budget cut (expressed as 4:2:1). Management wants to estimate its break-even point for next year. Unit selling prices for these three cuts are basic, $20; ultra, $32; and budget, $16. Unit variable costs for these three cuts are basic, $13; ultra, $18; and budget, $8. Using the 4:2:1 sales mix, the selling price and variable costs of a composite unit of the three products are computed as follows.

Selling price per composite unit	
4 units of basic @ $20 per unit	$ 80
2 units of ultra @ $32 per unit	64
1 unit of budget @ $16 per unit	16
Selling price of a composite unit	**$160**

Variable costs per composite unit	
4 units of basic @ $13 per unit	$52
2 units of ultra @ $18 per unit	36
1 unit of budget @ $8 per unit	8
Variable costs of a composite unit.	**$96**

We compute the contribution margin for a *composite unit* using essentially the same formula used earlier (see Exhibit 21.9), as shown in Exhibit 21.28:

EXHIBIT 21.28

Contribution Margin per Composite Unit

Contribution margin per composite unit	=	Selling price per composite unit	−	Variable cost per composite unit
$64	=	$160	−	$96

Assuming Hair-Today's fixed costs are $192,000 per year, we compute its break-even point in composite units in Exhibit 21.29.

EXHIBIT 21.29

Break-Even Point in Composite Units

$$\text{Break-even point in composite units} = \frac{\text{Fixed costs}}{\text{Contribution margin per composite unit}}$$
$$= \frac{\$192,000}{\$64} = 3,000 \text{ composite units}$$

This computation implies that Hair-Today breaks even when it sells 3,000 *composite* units. Each composite unit represents seven haircuts. To determine how many units of each product it must sell to break even, we use the expected sales mix of 4:2:1 and multiply the number of units of each product in the composite by 3,000, as follows.

Point: The break-even point in dollars for Exhibit 21.29 is $192,000/($64/$160) = $480,000.

Basic:	4 × 3,000	12,000 units
Ultra:	2 × 3,000	6,000 units
Budget:	1 × 3,000	3,000 units
	7 × 3,000	21,000 units

Exhibit 21.30 verifies that with this sales mix and unit sales computed above, Hair-Today would break even.

EXHIBIT 21.30

Multiproduct Break-Even Income

	Basic	Ultra	Budget	Total
Contribution margin				
Basic (12,000 @ $7)	$84,000			
Ultra (6,000 @ $14)		$84,000		
Budget (3,000 @ $8)			$24,000	
Total contribution margin				$192,000
Fixed costs				192,000
Net income				$ 0

If the sales mix changes, the break-even point will likely change. For example, if Hair-Today sells more ultra cuts and fewer basic cuts, its break-even point will decrease. We can vary the sales mix to see what happens under alternative strategies.

For companies that sell many different products, multiproduct break-even computations can become hard. **Amazon**, for example, sells over 200 million different products. In such cases, managers can group these products into departments (such as clothing, sporting goods, music) and compute department contribution margins. The department contribution margins and the sales mix can be used as we illustrate in this section.

Point: Enterprise resource planning (ERP) systems can quickly generate multiproduct break-even analyses.

Decision Maker

Entrepreneur   CVP analysis indicates that your start-up will break even with the current sales mix and price levels. You have a target income in mind. What analysis might you perform to assess the likelihood of achieving this income? ■ [*Answer:* First compute the level of sales to achieve the desired net income. Then conduct sensitivity analysis by varying the price, sales mix, and cost estimates to assess the possibility of reaching the target sales level. For instance, you might have to pursue aggressive marketing strategies to push the high-margin products, you might have to cut prices to increase sales and profits, or another strategy might emerge.]

 **21-5**

Contribution Margin and
Break-Even Point,
Composite Units

P4

The sales mix of a company's two products, X and Y, is 2:1. Unit variable costs for both products are $2, and unit selling prices are $5 for X and $4 for Y. The company has $640,000 of fixed costs.

1. What is the contribution margin per composite unit?
2. What is the break-even point in composite units?
3. How many units of X and how many units of Y will be sold at the break-even point?

Solution

1.

Selling price of a composite unit			**Variable costs of a composite unit**	
2 units of X @ $5 per unit.	$10		2 units of X @ $2 per unit.	$4
1 unit of Y @ $4 per unit.	4		1 unit of Y @ $2 per unit.	2
Selling price of a composite unit.	$14		Variable costs of a composite unit	$6

Therefore, the contribution margin per composite unit is $8.

> Do More: QS 21-14, E 21-22, E 21-23

2. The break-even point in composite units = $640,000/$8 = 80,000 units.
3. At break-even, the company will sell 160,000 units (80,000 × 2) of X and 80,000 units of Y (80,000 × 1).

Assumptions in Cost-Volume-Profit Analysis

CVP analysis relies on several assumptions:

- Costs can be classified as variable or fixed.
- Costs are linear within the relevant range.
- All units produced are sold (inventory levels do not change).
- Sales mix is constant.

If costs and sales differ from these assumptions, the results of CVP analysis can be less useful. Managers understand that CVP analysis gives approximate answers to questions and enables them to make rough estimates about the future.

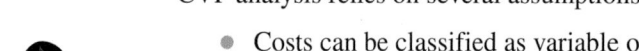

SUSTAINABILITY AND ACCOUNTING

Manufacturers try to increase the sustainability of their materials and packaging. **Nike** recently reengineered its shoeboxes to use 30% less material. These lighter shoeboxes can be shipped in cartons that are 20% lighter.

Nike also now uses recycled polyester in much of its clothing. The company estimates it has reused the equivalent of 2 billion plastic bottles since 2010.

These and other sustainability initiatives impact both variable and fixed costs, and CVP analysis. Consider Rydell, the football manufacturer illustrated in this chapter. Rydell expects to sell 1,500 footballs per month, at a price of $100 per unit. Variable costs are $70 per unit and monthly fixed costs are $24,000. Rydell is considering using some recycled materials. This would add $1,160 in fixed costs per month and reduce variable costs by $4 per unit. Management wants to know how this initiative would impact the company's break-even point, margin of safety, and forecasted income. Relevant calculations follow.

$$\text{Revised break-even point in units} = \frac{\text{Revised fixed costs}}{\text{Revised contribution margin}} = \frac{\$25,160}{\$34} = 740 \text{ units}$$

$$\text{Revised margin of safety} = \frac{\text{Expected sales} - \text{Break-even sales}}{\text{Expected sales}} = \frac{\$150,000 - \$74,000}{\$150,000} = 50.7\%$$

$$\text{Revised forecasted income} = (\text{Units sold} \times \text{Contribution margin per unit}) - \text{Fixed costs}$$

$$= (1,500 \times \$34) - \$25,160 = \$25,840$$

Sweetgreen, this chapter's opening company, is devoted to sustainability. In addition to sourcing organic ingredients from local farmers, the tables in the company's restaurants (see photo here) are made from reclaimed wood and old bowling lanes.

Once a customer orders $100 of food through the company's app, Sweetgreen donates a percentage of future purchases to FoodCorps, a nonprofit organization devoted to providing healthy food for underprivileged students. "It takes a little more work and a little more money," explains Jon Neman, one of the company's founders, "but it's worth it!"

© Joshua Bright/The New York Times/Redux

Degree of Operating Leverage      **Decision Analysis**

CVP analysis is especially useful when management begins the planning process and wishes to predict outcomes of alternative strategies. These strategies can involve changes in selling prices, fixed costs, variable costs, sales volume, and product mix. Managers are interested in seeing the effects of changes in some or all of these factors.

One goal of all managers is to get maximum benefits from their fixed costs. Managers would like to use 100% of their output capacity so that fixed costs are spread over the largest number of units. This would decrease fixed cost per unit and increase income. The extent, or relative size, of fixed costs in the total cost structure is known as **operating leverage.** Companies having a higher proportion of fixed costs in their total cost structure are said to have higher operating leverage. An example of this is a company that chooses to automate its processes instead of using direct labor, increasing its fixed costs and lowering its variable costs.

A useful managerial measure to help assess the effect of changes in the level of sales on income is the **degree of operating leverage (DOL),** calculated as shown in Exhibit 21.31.

A2

Analyze changes in sales using the degree of operating leverage.

$$\text{DOL} = \text{Total contribution margin (in dollars)}/\text{Pretax income}$$

EXHIBIT 21.31

Degree of Operating Leverage

To illustrate, assume Rydell Company sells 1,200 footballs. At this sales level, its contribution margin (in dollars) and pretax income are computed as:

Rydell Company	
Sales (1,200 × $100)..................	$120,000
Variable costs (1,200 × $70)...........	84,000
Contribution margin..................	36,000
Fixed costs	24,000
Income (pretax).....................	$ 12,000

Rydell's degree of operating leverage (DOL) is then computed as shown in Exhibit 21.32.

$$\text{DOL} = \text{Total contribution margin (in dollars)}/\text{Pretax income}$$
$$\text{DOL} = \$36,000/\$12,000 = 3.0$$

EXHIBIT 21.32

Rydell's Degree of Operating Leverage

We then can use DOL to measure the effect of changes in the level of sales on pretax income. For example, if Rydell expects sales can either increase or decrease by 10%, and these changes would be within Rydell's relevant range, we can compute the change in pretax income using DOL, as shown in Exhibit 21.33.

$$\text{Change in income (\%)} = \text{DOL} \times \text{Change in sales (\%)}$$
$$= 3.0 \times 10\%$$
$$= 30\%$$

EXHIBIT 21.33

Impact of Change in Sales on Income

Thus, if Rydell's sales *increase* by 10%, its income will increase by $3,600 (computed as $12,000 × 30%), to $15,600. If, instead, Rydell's sales decrease by 10%, its net income will decrease by $3,600, to $8,400. We can prove these results with contribution margin income statements, as shown below.

	Current	Sales Increase by 10%	Sales Decrease by 10%
Sales........................	$120,000	$132,000	$108,000
Variable costs	84,000	92,400	75,600
Contribution margin	$ 36,000	$ 39,600	$ 32,400
Fixed costs.....................	24,000	24,000	24,000
Target (pretax) income	$ 12,000	$ 15,600	$ 8,400

COMPREHENSIVE

Sport Caps Co. manufactures and sells caps for different sporting events. The fixed costs of operating the company are $150,000 per month, and variable costs are $5 per cap. The caps are sold for $8 per unit. The production capacity is 100,000 caps per month.

Required

1. Use the formulas in the chapter to compute the following:

  a. Contribution margin per cap.

  b. Break-even point in terms of the number of caps produced and sold.

  c. Amount of income at 30,000 caps sold per month (ignore taxes).

  d. Amount of income at 85,000 caps sold per month (ignore taxes).

  e. Number of caps to be produced and sold to provide $60,000 of income (pretax).

2. Draw a CVP chart for the company, showing cap output on the horizontal axis. Identify (*a*) the break-even point and (*b*) the amount of pretax income when the level of cap production is 70,000. (Omit the fixed cost line.)

3. Use the formulas in the chapter to compute the

  a. Contribution margin ratio.

  b. Break-even point in terms of sales dollars.

  c. Amount of income at $250,000 of sales per month (ignore taxes).

  d. Amount of income at $600,000 of sales per month (ignore taxes).

  e. Dollars of sales needed to provide $60,000 of pretax income.

PLANNING THE SOLUTION

- Identify the formulas in the chapter for the required items expressed in units and solve them using the data given in the problem.
- Draw a CVP chart that reflects the facts in the problem. The horizontal axis should plot the volume in units up to 100,000, and the vertical axis should plot the total dollars up to $800,000. Plot the total cost line as upward sloping, starting at the fixed cost level ($150,000) on the vertical axis and increasing until it reaches $650,000 at the maximum volume of 100,000 units. Verify that the break-even point (where the two lines cross) equals the amount you computed in part 1.
- Identify the formulas in the chapter for the required items expressed in dollars and solve them using the data given in the problem.

SOLUTION

1. a. Contribution margin per cap   = Selling price per unit − Variable cost per unit

                                      = $8 − $5 = $3

  b. Break-even point in caps $= \dfrac{\text{Fixed costs}}{\text{Contribution margin per cap}} = \dfrac{\$150,000}{\$3} = 50,000 \text{ caps}$

c. Income at 30,000 caps sold $\quad= (\text{Units} \times \text{Contribution margin per unit}) - \text{Fixed costs}$
$= (30,000 \times \$3) - \$150,000 = \underline{\$(60,000) \text{ loss}}$

d. Income at 85,000 caps sold $\quad= (\text{Units} \times \text{Contribution margin per unit}) - \text{Fixed costs}$
$= (85,000 \times \$3) - \$150,000 = \underline{\$105,000 \text{ profit}}$

e. Units needed for \$60,000 income $= \dfrac{\text{Fixed costs} + \text{Target income}}{\text{Contribution margin per cap}}$

$= \dfrac{\$150,000 + \$60,000}{\$3} = \underline{70,000 \text{ caps}}$

2. CVP chart.

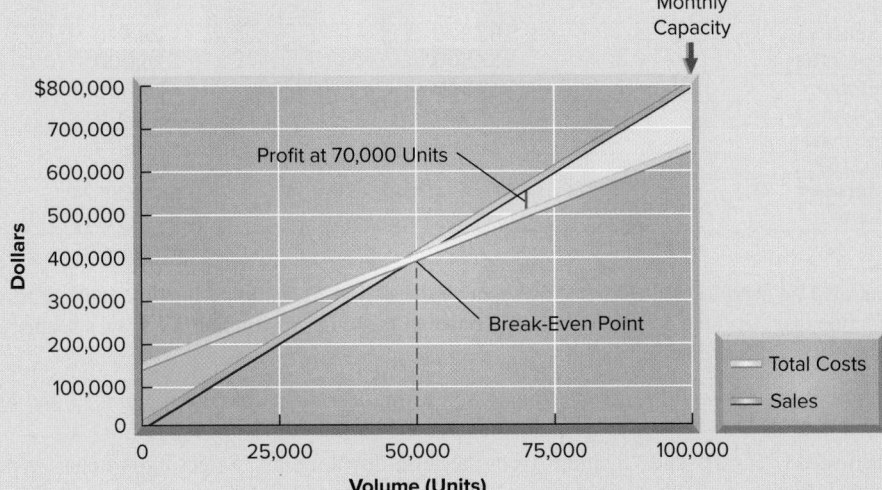

3. a. Contribution margin ratio $\quad= \dfrac{\text{Contribution margin per unit}}{\text{Selling price per unit}} = \dfrac{\$3}{\$8} = \underline{0.375 \text{ or } 37.5\%}$

b. Break-even point in dollars $\quad= \dfrac{\text{Fixed costs}}{\text{Contribution margin ratio}} = \dfrac{\$150,000}{37.5\%} = \underline{\$400,000}$

c. Income at sales of \$250,000 $\quad= (\text{Sales} \times \text{Contribution margin ratio}) - \text{Fixed costs}$
$= (\$250,000 \times 37.5\%) - \$150,000 = \underline{\$(56,250) \text{ loss}}$

d. Income at sales of \$600,000 $\quad= (\text{Sales} \times \text{Contribution margin ratio}) - \text{Fixed costs}$
$= (\$600,000 \times 37.5\%) - \$150,000 = \underline{\$75,000 \text{ income}}$

e. Dollars of sales to yield \$60,000 pretax income $= \dfrac{\text{Fixed costs} + \text{Target pretax income}}{\text{Contribution margin ratio}}$

$= \dfrac{\$150,000 + \$60,000}{37.5\%} = \underline{\$560,000}$

APPENDIX

Using Excel to Estimate Least-Squares Regression

21A

Microsoft Excel® and other spreadsheet software can be used to perform least-squares regressions to identify cost behavior. In Excel, the INTERCEPT and SLOPE functions are used. The following screen shot reports the data from Exhibit 21.4 in cells Al through C13 and shows the cell contents to find the intercept (cell B15) and slope (cell B16). Cell B15 uses Excel to find the intercept from a least-squares regression of total cost (shown as C2:C13 in cell B15) on units produced (shown as B2:B13 in cell B15). Spreadsheet software is useful in understanding cost behavior when many data points (such as monthly total costs and units produced) are available.

	A	B	C
1	**Month**	**Units Produced**	**Total Cost**
2	January	27,500	$21,500
3	February	22,500	20,500
4	March	25,000	25,000
5	April	35,000	21,500
6	May	47,500	25,500
7	June	17,500	18,500
8	July	30,000	23,500
9	August	52,500	28,500
10	September	37,500	26,000
11	October	62,500	29,000
12	November	67,500	31,000
13	December	57,500	26,000
14			**Result**
15	**Intercept**	=INTERCEPT(C2:C13, B2:B13)	$16,688.24
16	**Slope**	=SLOPE(C2:C13, B2:B13)	$ 0.1995

Point: The intercept function solves for total fixed costs. The slope function solves for the variable cost per unit.

Excel can also be used to create scatter diagrams such as that in Exhibit 21.5a. In contrast to visually drawing a line that "fits" the data, Excel more precisely fits the regression line. To draw a scatter diagram with a line of fit, follow these steps:

1. Highlight the data cells you wish to diagram; in this example, start from cell C13 and highlight through cell B2.

2. Then select "Insert" and "Scatter" from the drop-down menus. Selecting the chart type in the upper left corner of the choices under "Scatter" will produce a diagram that looks like that in Exhibit 21.5a, without a line of fit.

3. To add a line of fit (also called a trend line), select "Design," "Add Chart Element," "Trendline," and "Linear" from the drop-down menus. This will produce a diagram that looks like that in Exhibit 21.5a, including the line of fit.

APPENDIX

21B

Variable Costing and Performance Reporting

P5

Compute unit cost and income under both absorption and variable costing.

This chapter showed the usefulness of *contribution margin,* or selling price minus variable costs, in CVP analysis. The contribution margin income statement introduced in this chapter is also known as a **variable costing income statement.** In **variable costing,** only costs that change in total with changes in production levels are included in product costs. These costs include direct materials, direct labor, and *variable* overhead costs. Thus, under variable costing, *fixed* overhead costs are excluded from product costs and instead are expensed in the period incurred. As we showed in this chapter, a variable costing approach can be useful in many managerial analyses and decisions.

The variable costing method is not allowed, however, for external financial reporting. Instead, GAAP requires **absorption costing.** Under absorption costing, product costs include direct materials, direct labor, *and all overhead,* both variable and fixed. Thus, under absorption costing, fixed overhead costs are expensed when the goods are sold. Managers can use variable costing information for internal decision making, but they must use absorption costing for external reporting purposes.

Computing Unit Cost   To illustrate the difference between absorption costing and variable costing, let's consider the product cost data in Exhibit 21B.1 from IceAge, a skate manufacturer.

EXHIBIT 21B.1

Summary Product Cost Data

Direct materials cost	$4 per unit
Direct labor cost	$8 per unit
Overhead cost	
Variable overhead cost.	$180,000
Fixed overhead cost	600,000
Total overhead cost	$780,000
Expected units produced	60,000 units

Using the product cost data, Exhibit 21B.2 shows the product cost per unit computations for both absorption and variable costing. These computations are shown both in a tabular format (left side of exhibit) and a visual format (right side of exhibit). For absorption costing, the product cost per unit is $25, which consists of $4 in direct materials, $8 in direct labor, $3 in variable overhead ($180,000/60,000 units), and $10 in fixed overhead ($600,000/60,000 units).

For variable costing, the product cost per unit is $15, which consists of $4 in direct materials, $8 in direct labor, and $3 in variable overhead. Fixed overhead costs of $600,000 are treated as a period cost and are recorded as expense in the period incurred. *The difference between the two costing methods is the exclusion of fixed overhead from product costs for variable costing.*

EXHIBIT 21B.2

Unit Cost Computation

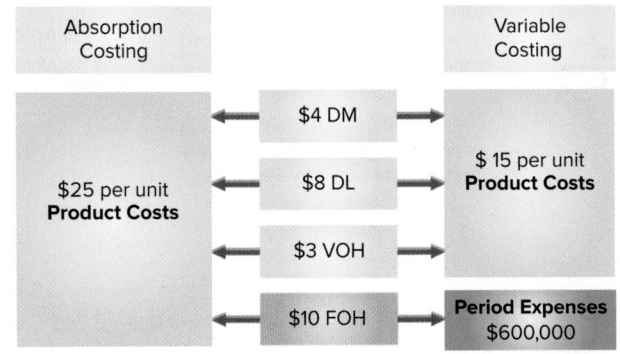

	Product Cost per Unit	
	Absorption Costing	**Variable Costing**
Direct materials	$ 4	$ 4
Direct labor	8	8
Overhead costs		
Variable overhead	3	3
Fixed overhead	**10**	—
Total product cost per unit . . .	$25	$15

A manufacturer reports the following data.

NEED-TO-KNOW 21-7**

Computing Product Cost per Unit

P1

Direct materials cost.	$6 per unit	Variable overhead	$220,000 per year
Direct labor cost	$14 per unit	Fixed overhead.	$680,000 per year
Expected units produced	20,000 units		

1. Compute the total product cost per unit under absorption costing.
2. Compute the total product cost per unit under variable costing.

Solution

Per Unit Costs	(1) Absorption Costing	(2) Variable Costing
Direct materials	$ 6	$ 6
Direct labor	14	14
Variable overhead ($220,000/20,000)	11	11
Fixed overhead ($680,000/20,000)*	34	—
Total product cost per unit	$65	$31

*Not included in product costs under variable costing.

Do More: QS 21-17, QS 21-18, QS 21-19, QS 21-20, E 21-26

Income Reporting   The prior section showed how the different treatment of fixed overhead costs leads to different product costs per unit under absorption and variable costing. This section shows the implications of this difference for income reporting.

To illustrate the income reporting implications, we return to IceAge Company. Below are the manufacturing cost data for IceAge as well as additional data on selling and administrative expenses. Assume that IceAge began year 2017 with no units in inventory. During 2017, IceAge produced 60,000 units and sold 40,000 units at $40 each, leaving 20,000 units in ending inventory.

Using the information above, we next prepare income statements for IceAge both under absorption costing and under variable costing. Under variable costing, expenses are grouped according to cost behavior—variable or fixed, and production or nonproduction. Under the traditional format of absorption costing, expenses are grouped by function but not separated into variable and fixed components.

Units Produced Exceed Units Sold   Exhibit 21B.3 shows absorption costing and variable costing income statements for 2017. In 2017, 60,000 units were produced, but only 40,000 units were sold, which means 20,000 units remain in ending inventory.

EXHIBIT 21B.3

Income under Absorption or Variable Costing

ICEAGE COMPANY Income Statement (Absorption Costing) For Year Ended December 31, 2017		
Sales* (40,000 × $40).................		$1,600,000
Cost of goods sold (40,000 × $25**)......		1,000,000
Gross margin		600,000
Selling and administrative expenses [$200,000 + (40,000 × $2)]		280,000
Net income.........................		$ 320,000

* Units produced equal 60,000; units sold equal 40,000.
** $4 DM + $8 DL + $3 VOH + $10 FOH.
† $4 DM + $8 DL + $3 VOH.

ICEAGE COMPANY Income Statement (Variable Costing) For Year Ended December 31, 2017		
Sales* (40,000 × $40)..........		$1,600,000
Variable expenses		
Variable production costs (40,000 × $15†)	$600,000	
Variable selling and administrative expenses (40,000 × $2)	80,000	680,000
Contribution margin.............		920,000
Fixed expenses		
Fixed overhead	600,000	
Fixed selling and administrative expense	200,000	800,000
Net income...................		$ 120,000

The income statements reveal that for 2017, income is $320,000 under absorption costing. Under variable costing, income is $120,000, which is $200,000 less than under absorption costing. This $200,000 difference is due to the different treatment of fixed overhead under the two costing methods. Because variable costing expenses fixed manufacturing overhead (FOH) based on the number of units produced (60,000 × $10), and absorption costing expenses FOH based on the number of units sold (40,000 × $10), net income is lower under variable costing by $200,000 (20,000 units × $10).

Under variable costing, the entire $600,000 fixed overhead cost is treated as an expense in computing 2017 income. Under absorption costing, the fixed overhead cost is allocated to each unit of product at the rate of $10 per unit (from Exhibit 21B.2). When production exceeds sales by 20,000 units (60,000 versus 40,000), the $200,000 ($10 × 20,000 units) of fixed overhead cost allocated to these 20,000 units is included in the cost of ending inventory. This means that $200,000 of fixed overhead cost incurred in 2017 is not expensed until future years under absorption costing, when it is reported in cost of goods sold as those products are sold. Consequently, income for 2017 under absorption costing is $200,000 higher than income under variable costing. Even though sales (of 40,000 units) and the number of units produced (totaling 60,000) are the same under both costing methods, net income differs greatly due to the treatment of fixed overhead.

©TOSHIFUMI KITAMURA/AFP/ Getty Images

Converting Income under Variable Costing to Income under Absorption Costing   In 2017, IceAge produced 20,000 more units than it sold. Those 20,000 units remaining in ending inventory will be sold in future years. When those units are sold, the $200,000 of fixed overhead costs attached to them will be expensed, resulting in lower income under the absorption costing method. This leads to a simple way to convert income under variable costing to income under absorption costing:

$$\text{Income under absorption costing} = \text{Income under variable costing} + \text{Fixed overhead cost in ending inventory} - \text{Fixed overhead cost in beginning inventory}$$

For example, assume IceAge produces 60,000 units and sells 80,000 units in 2018, and reports income under variable costing of $1,040,000. Income under absorption costing is then computed as:

$$\text{Income under absorption costing} = \$1,040,000 + \$0 - \$200,000 = \$840,000$$

Summary

C1 **Describe different types of cost behavior in relation to production and sales volume.** Cost behavior is described in terms of how its amount changes in relation to changes in volume of activity within a relevant range. Fixed costs remain constant to changes in volume. Total variable costs change in direct proportion to volume changes. Mixed costs display the effects of both fixed and variable components. Step-wise costs remain constant over a small volume range, then change by a lump sum and remain constant over another volume range, and so on. Curvilinear costs change in a nonlinear relation to volume changes.

C2 **Describe several applications of cost-volume-profit analysis.** Cost-volume-profit analysis can be used to predict what can happen under alternative strategies concerning sales volume, selling prices, variable costs, or fixed costs. Applications include "what-if" analysis, computing sales for a target income, and break-even analysis.

A1 **Compute the contribution margin and describe what it reveals about a company's cost structure.** Contribution margin per unit is a product's selling price less its total variable costs. Contribution margin ratio is a product's contribution margin per unit divided by its selling price. Unit contribution margin is the amount received from each sale that contributes to fixed costs and income. The contribution margin ratio reveals what portion of each sales dollar is available as contribution to fixed costs and income.

A2 **Analyze changes in sales using the degree of operating leverage.** The extent, or relative size, of fixed costs in a company's total cost structure is known as *operating leverage*. One tool useful in assessing the effect of changes in sales on income is the degree of operating leverage, or DOL. DOL is the ratio of the contribution margin divided by pretax income. This ratio can be used to determine the expected percent change in income given a percent change in sales.

P1 **Determine cost estimates using the scatter diagram, high-low, and regression methods of estimating costs.** Three different methods used to estimate costs are the scatter diagram, the high-low method, and least-squares regression. All three methods use past data to estimate costs. Cost estimates from a scatter diagram are based on a visual fit of the cost line. Estimates from the high-low method are based only on costs corresponding to the lowest and highest sales. The least-squares regression method is a statistical technique and uses all data points.

P2 **Compute the break-even point for a single product company.** A company's break-even point for a period is the sales volume at which total revenues equal total costs. To compute a break-even point in terms of sales units, we divide total fixed costs by the contribution margin per unit. To compute a break-even point in terms of sales dollars, divide total fixed costs by the contribution margin ratio.

P3 **Graph costs and sales for a single product company.** The costs and sales for a company can be graphically illustrated using a CVP chart. In this chart, the horizontal axis represents the number of units sold and the vertical axis represents dollars of sales or costs. Straight lines are used to depict both costs and sales on the CVP chart.

P4 **Compute the break-even point for a multiproduct company.** CVP analysis can be applied to a multiproduct company by expressing sales volume in terms of composite units. A composite unit consists of a specific number of units of each product in proportion to their expected sales mix. Multiproduct CVP analysis treats this composite unit as a single product.

P5^B **Compute unit cost and income under both absorption and variable costing.** Absorption cost per unit includes direct materials, direct labor, and *all* overhead, whereas variable cost per unit includes direct materials, direct labor, and only *variable* overhead. Absorption costing income is equal to variable costing income plus the fixed overhead cost in ending inventory minus the fixed overhead cost in beginning inventory.

Key Terms

Absorption costing	Curvilinear cost	Relevant range of operations
Break-even point	Degree of operating leverage (DOL)	Sales mix
Composite unit	Estimated line of cost behavior	Scatter diagram
Contribution margin	High-low method	Step-wise cost
Contribution margin per unit	Least-squares regression	Variable costing
Contribution margin ratio	Margin of safety	Variable costing income statement
Cost-volume-profit (CVP) analysis	Mixed cost	
Cost-volume-profit (CVP) chart	Operating leverage	

Multiple Choice Quiz

1. A company's only product sells for $150 per unit. Its variable costs per unit are $100, and its fixed costs total $75,000. What is its contribution margin per unit?
   - **a.** $50
   - **b.** $250
   - **c.** $100
   - **d.** $150
   - **e.** $25

2. Using information from question 1, what is the company's contribution margin ratio?
   - **a.** 66⅔%
   - **b.** 100%
   - **c.** 50%
   - **d.** 0%
   - **e.** 33⅓%

3. Using information from question 1, what is the company's break-even point in units?
   - **a.** 500 units
   - **b.** 750 units
   - **c.** 1,500 units
   - **d.** 3,000 units
   - **e.** 1,000 units

4. A company's forecasted sales are $300,000 and its sales at break-even are $180,000. Its margin of safety in dollars is
   - **a.** $180,000.
   - **b.** $120,000.
   - **c.** $480,000.
   - **d.** $60,000.
   - **e.** $300,000.

5. A product sells for $400 per unit and its variable costs per unit are $260. The company's fixed costs are $840,000. If the company desires $70,000 pretax income, what is the required dollar sales?
   - **a.** $2,400,000
   - **b.** $200,000
   - **c.** $2,600,000
   - **d.** $2,275,000
   - **e.** $1,400,000

ANSWERS TO MULTIPLE CHOICE QUIZ

1. a; $150 − $100 = $50
2. e; ($150 − $100)/$150 = 33⅓%
3. c; $75,000/$50 CM per unit = 1,500 units
4. b; $300,000 − $180,000 = $120,000
5. c; Contribution margin ratio = ($400 − $260)/$400 = 0.35
   Targeted sales = ($840,000 + $70,000)/0.35 = $2,600,000

A,B *Superscript letter A(B) denotes assignments based on Appendix 21A (21B).*

🎟 Icon denotes assignments that involve decision making.

Discussion Questions

1. What is a variable cost? Identify two variable costs.
2. 🎟 When output volume increases, do variable costs per unit increase, decrease, or stay the same within the relevant range of activity? Explain.
3. 🎟 When output volume increases, do fixed costs per unit increase, decrease, or stay the same within the relevant range of activity? Explain.
4. 🎟 How is cost-volume-profit analysis useful?
5. How do step-wise costs and curvilinear costs differ?
6. Describe the contribution margin ratio in layperson's terms.
7. Define and explain the *contribution margin ratio*.
8. Define and describe *contribution margin per unit*.
9. In performing CVP analysis for a manufacturing company, what simplifying assumption is usually made about the volume of production and the volume of sales?
10. What two arguments tend to justify classifying all costs as either fixed or variable even though individual costs might not behave exactly as classified?
11. 🎟 How does assuming that operating activity occurs within a relevant range affect cost-volume-profit analysis?
12. List three methods to measure cost behavior.
13. How is a scatter diagram used to identify and measure the behavior of a company's costs?
14. In cost-volume-profit analysis, what is the estimated profit at the break-even point?
15. 🎟 Assume that a straight line on a CVP chart intersects the vertical axis at the level of fixed costs and has a positive slope that rises with each additional unit of volume by the amount of the variable costs per unit. What does this line represent?

16. **Google** has both fixed and variable costs. Why are fixed costs depicted as a horizontal line on a CVP chart? **GOOGLE**

17. 🎟 Each of two similar companies has sales of $20,000 and total costs of $15,000 for a month. Company A's total costs include $10,000 of variable costs and $5,000 of fixed costs. If Company B's total costs include $4,000 of variable costs and $11,000 of fixed costs, which company will enjoy more profit if sales double?

18. _____ of _____ reflects expected sales in excess of the level of break-even sales.

19. 🎟 **Apple** produces tablet computers for sale. Identify some of the variable and fixed product costs associated with that production. [*Hint:* Limit costs to product costs.] **APPLE**

20. 🎟 Should **Apple** use single product or multiproduct break-even analysis? Explain. **APPLE**

21. 🎟 **Samsung** is thinking of expanding sales of its most popular smartphone model by 65%. Should we expect its variable and fixed costs for this model to stay within the relevant range? Explain. **Samsung**

22.B **Google** uses variable costing for several business decisions. How can variable costing income be converted to absorption costing income? **GOOGLE**

≋connect

Listed here are four series of separate costs measured at various volume levels. Examine each series and identify whether it is best described as a fixed, variable, step-wise, or curvilinear cost. (It can help to graph each cost series.)

Volume (Units)	Series 1	Series 2	Series 3	Series 4
0............	$ 0	$450	$ 800	$100
100...........	800	450	800	105
200...........	1,600	450	800	120
300...........	2,400	450	1,600	145
400...........	3,200	450	1,600	190
500...........	4,000	450	2,400	250
600...........	4,800	450	2,400	320

QUICK STUDY

QS 21-1
Cost behavior identification

C1

Determine whether each of the following is best described as a fixed, variable, or mixed cost with respect to product units.

_____ **1.** Rubber used to manufacture athletic shoes.

_____ **2.** Maintenance of factory machinery.

_____ **3.** Packaging expense.

_____ **4.** Wages of an assembly-line worker paid on the basis of acceptable units produced.

_____ **5.** Factory supervisor's salary.

_____ **6.** Taxes on factory building.

_____ **7.** Depreciation expense of warehouse.

QS 21-2
Cost behavior identification

C1

The following information is available for a company's maintenance cost over the last seven months. Using the high-low method, estimate both the fixed and variable components of its maintenance cost.

Month	Maintenance Hours	Maintenance Cost
June................	9	$5,450
July	18	6,900
August..............	12	5,100
September	15	6,000
October.............	21	6,900
November...........	24	8,100
December...........	6	3,600

QS 21-3
Cost behavior estimation—high-low method

P1

This scatter diagram reflects past maintenance hours and their corresponding maintenance costs.

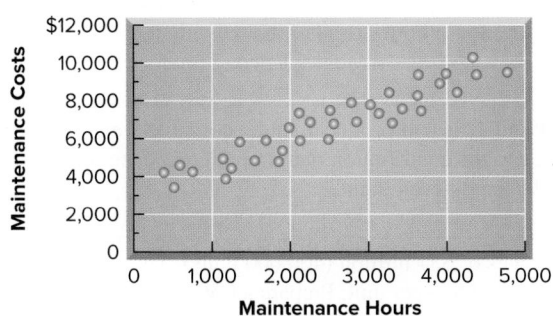

1. Draw an estimated line of cost behavior.

2. Estimate the fixed and variable components of maintenance costs.

QS 21-4
Cost behavior estimation—scatter diagram

P1

Compute and interpret the contribution margin ratio using the following data: sales, $5,000; total variable cost, $3,000.

QS 21-5
Contribution margin ratio A1

QS 21-6 Contribution margin per unit and break-even units **P2**	SBD Phone Company sells its waterproof phone case for $90 per unit. Fixed costs total $162,000, and variable costs are $36 per unit. Determine the (1) contribution margin per unit and (2) break-even point in units.
QS 21-7 Assumptions in CVP analysis **C2**	SBD Phone Company sells its waterproof phone case for $90 per unit. Fixed costs total $162,000, and variable costs are $36 per unit. How will the break-even point in units change in response to each of the following independent changes in selling price per unit, variable cost per unit, or total fixed costs? Use I for increase and D for decrease. (It is not necessary to compute new break-even points.)

Change	Break-Even in Units will _____
1. Total fixed costs to $190,000	_____
2. Variable costs to $34 per unit	_____
3. Selling price per unit to $80	_____
4. Variable costs to $67 per unit	_____
5. Total fixed costs to $150,000	_____
6. Selling price per unit to $120	_____

QS 21-8 Contribution margin ratio and break-even dollars **P2**	SBD Phone Company sells its waterproof phone case for $90 per unit. Fixed costs total $162,000, and variable costs are $36 per unit. Determine the (1) contribution margin ratio and (2) break-even point in dollars.
QS 21-9 CVP analysis and target income **P2**	SBD Phone Company sells its waterproof phone case for $90 per unit. Fixed costs total $162,000, and variable costs are $36 per unit. Compute the units of product that must be sold to earn pretax income of $200,000. (Round to the nearest whole unit.)
QS 21-10 Computing break-even **P2**	Zhao Co. has fixed costs of $354,000. Its single product sells for $175 per unit, and variable costs are $116 per unit. Determine the break-even point in units.
QS 21-11 Margin of safety **C2**	Zhao Co. has fixed costs of $354,000. Its single product sells for $175 per unit, and variable costs are $116 per unit. If the company expects sales of 10,000 units, compute its margin of safety (a) in dollars and (b) as a percent of expected sales.
QS 21-12 Contribution margin income statement **P2**	Zhao Co. has fixed costs of $354,000. Its single product sells for $175 per unit, and variable costs are $116 per unit. The company expects sales of 10,000 units. Prepare a contribution margin income statement for the year ended December 31, 2017.
QS 21-13 Target income **C2**	Zhao Co. has fixed costs of $354,000. Its single product sells for $175 per unit, and variable costs are $116 per unit. Compute the level of sales in units needed to produce a target (pretax) income of $118,000.
QS 21-14 Sales mix and break-even **P4**	US-Mobile manufactures and sells two products, tablet computers and smartphones, in the ratio of 5:3. Fixed costs are $105,000, and the contribution margin per composite unit is $125. What number of each type of product is sold at the break-even point?
QS 21-15 CVP chart **P3**	Corme Company expects sales of $34 million (400,000 units). The company's total fixed costs are $17.5 million and its variable costs are $35 per unit. Prepare a CVP chart from this information.
QS 21-16 Operating leverage analysis **A2**	Singh Co. reports a contribution margin of $960,000 and fixed costs of $720,000. (1) Compute the company's degree of operating leverage. (2) If sales increase by 15%, what amount of income will Singh Co. report?
QS 21-17[B] Computing unit cost under absorption costing **P5**	Vijay Company reports the following information regarding its production costs. Compute its product cost per unit under absorption costing.

Direct materials	$10 per unit
Direct labor.................................	$20 per unit
Overhead costs for the year	
Variable overhead	$10 per unit
Fixed overhead	$160,000
Units produced.............................	20,000 units

Refer to Vijay Company's data in QS 21-17. Compute its product cost per unit under variable costing.

QS 21-18[B]
Computing unit cost under variable costing   **P5**

Aces Inc., a manufacturer of tennis rackets, began operations this year. The company produced 6,000 rackets and sold 4,900. Each racket was sold at a price of $90. Fixed overhead costs are $78,000, and fixed selling and administrative costs are $65,200. The company also reports the following per unit costs for the year. Prepare an income statement under variable costing.

QS 21-19[B]
Variable costing income statement   **P5**

Variable production costs	$25
Variable selling and administrative expenses............	2

Aces Inc., a manufacturer of tennis rackets, began operations this year. The company produced 6,000 rackets and sold 4,900. Each racket was sold at a price of $90. Fixed overhead costs are $78,000, and fixed selling and administrative costs are $65,200. The company also reports the following per unit costs for the year. Prepare an income statement under absorption costing.

QS 21-20[B]
Absorption costing income statement
P5

Variable production costs	$25
Variable selling and administrative expenses............	2

A recent income statement for **BMW** reports the following (in € millions). Assume 75 percent of the cost of sales and 75 percent of the selling and administrative costs are variable costs, and the remaining 25 percent of each is fixed. Compute the contribution margin (in € millions). (Round computations using percentages to the nearest whole euro.)

QS 21-21
Contribution margin

A1

BMW Automotive Group	
Sales	€92,175
Cost of sales	74,043
Selling and administrative expenses..................	8,633

Connect

Following are five graphs representing various cost behaviors. (1) Identify whether the cost behavior in each graph is mixed, step-wise, fixed, variable, or curvilinear. (2) Identify the graph (by number) that best illustrates each cost behavior: (a) Factory policy requires one supervisor for every 30 factory workers; (b) real estate taxes on factory; (c) electricity charge that includes the standard monthly charge plus a charge for each kilowatt hour; (d) commissions to salespersons; and (e) costs of hourly paid workers that provide substantial gains in efficiency when a few workers are added but gradually smaller gains in efficiency when more workers are added.

EXERCISES

Exercise 21-1
Cost behavior in graphs

C1

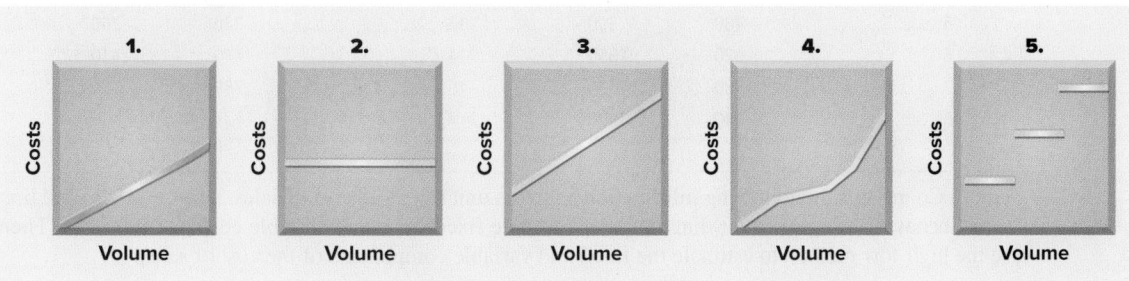

Exercise 21-2
Cost behavior defined
C1

The left column lists several cost classifications. The right column presents short definitions of those costs. In the blank space beside each of the numbers in the right column, write the letter of the cost best described by the definition.

A. Total cost
B. Mixed cost
C. Variable cost
D. Curvilinear cost
E. Step-wise cost
F. Fixed cost

_____ **1.** This cost is the combined amount of all the other costs.
_____ **2.** This cost remains constant over a limited range of volume; when it reaches the end of its limited range, it changes by a lump sum and remains at that level until it exceeds another limited range.
_____ **3.** This cost has a component that remains the same over all volume levels and another component that increases in direct proportion to increases in volume.
_____ **4.** This cost increases when volume increases, but the increase is not constant for each unit produced.
_____ **5.** This cost remains constant over all volume levels within the productive capacity for the planning period.
_____ **6.** This cost increases in direct proportion to increases in volume; its amount is constant for each unit produced.

Exercise 21-3
Cost behavior identification
C1

Following are five series of costs A through E measured at various volume levels. Identify each series as either fixed, variable, mixed, step-wise, or curvilinear.

	A	B	C	D	E	F
	Volume (Units)	Series A	Series B	Series C	Series D	Series E
1	0	$ 0	$2,500	$ 0	$1,000	$5,000
2	400	3,600	3,100	6,000	1,000	5,000
3	800	7,200	3,700	6,600	2,000	5,000
4	1,200	10,800	4,300	7,200	2,000	5,000
5	1,600	14,400	4,900	8,200	3,000	5,000
6	2,000	18,000	5,500	9,600	3,000	5,000
7	2,400	21,600	6,100	13,500	4,000	5,000

Exercise 21-4
Measurement of cost behavior using a scatter diagram
P1

A company reports the following information about its unit sales and its cost of sales. Each unit sells for $500. Use these data to prepare a scatter diagram. Draw an estimated line of cost behavior and determine whether the cost appears to be variable, fixed, or mixed.

Period	Unit Sales	Cost of Sales	Period	Unit Sales	Cost of Sales
1	22,500	$15,150	4	11,250	$ 8,250
2	17,250	11,250	5	13,500	9,000
3	15,750	10,500	6	18,750	14,250

Exercise 21-5
Scatter diagram and measurement of cost behavior
P1

Use the following information about unit sales and total cost of sales to prepare a scatter diagram. Draw a cost line that reflects the behavior displayed by this cost. Determine whether the cost is variable, step-wise, fixed, mixed, or curvilinear.

Period	Unit Sales	Cost of Sales	Period	Unit Sales	Cost of Sales
1	760	$590	9	580	$390
2	800	560	10	320	240
3	200	230	11	240	230
4	400	400	12	720	550
5	480	390	13	280	260
6	620	550	14	440	410
7	680	590	15	380	260
8	540	430			

Exercise 21-6
Cost behavior estimation—scatter diagram and high-low P1

Felix & Co. reports the following information about its unit sales and cost of sales. Draw an estimated line of cost behavior using a scatter diagram, and compute fixed costs and variable costs per unit sold. Then use the high-low method to estimate the fixed and variable components of the cost of sales.

Period	Unit Sales	Cost of Sales	Period	Unit Sales	Cost of Sales
1	0	$2,500	6	2,000	$5,500
2	400	3,100	7	2,400	6,100
3	800	3,700	8	2,800	6,700
4	1,200	4,300	9	3,200	7,300
5	1,600	4,900	10	3,600	7,900

Refer to the information from Exercise 21-6. Use spreadsheet software to use ordinary least-squares regression to estimate the cost equation, including fixed and variable cost amounts.

Exercise 21-7^A
Measurement of cost behavior using regression   P1

A jeans maker is designing a new line of jeans called Slims. The jeans will sell for $205 per pair and cost $164 per pair in variable costs to make.

1. Compute the contribution margin per pair.

2. Compute the contribution margin ratio.

3. Describe what the contribution margin ratio reveals about this new jeans line.

Exercise 21-8
Contribution margin

A1

Blanchard Company manufactures a single product that sells for $180 per unit and whose total variable costs are $135 per unit. The company's annual fixed costs are $562,500. Use this information to compute the company's (a) contribution margin, (b) contribution margin ratio, (c) break-even point in units, and (d) break-even point in dollars of sales.

Exercise 21-9
Contribution margin and break-even   P2

Blanchard Company manufactures a single product that sells for $180 per unit and whose total variable costs are $135 per unit. The company's annual fixed costs are $562,500. Prepare a CVP chart for the company.

Exercise 21-10
CVP chart   P3

Blanchard Company manufactures a single product that sells for $180 per unit and whose total variable costs are $135 per unit. The company's annual fixed costs are $562,500.

1. Prepare a contribution margin income statement for Blanchard Company showing sales, variable costs, and fixed costs at the break-even point.

2. If the company's fixed costs increase by $135,000, what amount of sales (in dollars) is needed to break even? Explain.

Exercise 21-11
Income reporting and break-even analysis

P2

Blanchard Company manufactures a single product that sells for $180 per unit and whose total variable costs are $135 per unit. The company's annual fixed costs are $562,500. Management targets an annual pretax income of $1,012,500. Assume that fixed costs remain at $562,500. Compute the (1) unit sales to earn the target income and (2) dollar sales to earn the target income.

Exercise 21-12
Computing sales to achieve target income   C2

Blanchard Company manufactures a single product that sells for $180 per unit and whose total variable costs are $135 per unit. The company's annual fixed costs are $562,500. The sales manager predicts that annual sales of the company's product will soon reach 40,000 units and its price will increase to $200 per unit. According to the production manager, variable costs are expected to increase to $140 per unit, but fixed costs will remain at $562,500. The income tax rate is 20%. What amounts of pretax and after-tax income can the company expect to earn from these predicted changes? (*Hint:* Prepare a forecasted contribution margin income statement as in Exhibit 21.21.)

Exercise 21-13
Forecasted income statement   C2

Check   Forecasted after-tax income, $1,470,000

Bloom Company management predicts that it will incur fixed costs of $160,000 and earn pretax income of $164,000 in the next period. Its expected contribution margin ratio is 25%. Use this information to compute the amounts of (1) total dollar sales and (2) total variable costs.

Exercise 21-14
Predicting sales and variable costs using contribution margin   C2

Harrison Co. expects to sell 200,000 units of its product next year, which would generate total sales of $17 million. Management predicts that pretax net income for next year will be $1,250,000 and that the contribution margin per unit will be $25. Use this information to compute next year's total expected (a) variable costs and (b) fixed costs.

Exercise 21-15
Computing variable and fixed costs   C2

Exercise 21-16
Break-even
P2

Hudson Co. reports the contribution margin income statement for 2017 below. Using this information, compute Hudson Co.'s (1) break-even point in units and (2) break-even point in sales dollars.

HUDSON CO.	
Contribution Margin Income Statement	
For Year Ended December 31, 2017	
Sales (9,600 units at $225 each)...................	$2,160,000
Variable costs (9,600 units at $180 each)	1,728,000
Contribution margin.............................	432,000
Fixed costs	324,000
Pretax income...................................	$ 108,000

Exercise 21-17
Target income and margin
of safety (in dollars)
C2

Refer to the information in Exercise 21-16.

1. Assume Hudson Co. has a target pretax income of $162,000 for 2018. What amount of sales (in dollars) is needed to produce this target income?

2. If Hudson achieves its target pretax income for 2018, what is its margin of safety (in percent)? (Round to one decimal place.)

Exercise 21-18
Evaluating strategies
C2

Refer to the information in Exercise 21-16. Assume the company is considering investing in a new machine that will increase its fixed costs by $40,500 per year and decrease its variable costs by $9 per unit. Prepare a forecasted contribution margin income statement for 2018 assuming the company purchases this machine.

Exercise 21-19
Evaluating strategies   **C2**

Refer to the information in Exercise 21-16. If the company raises its selling price to $240 per unit, compute its (1) contribution margin per unit, (2) contribution margin ratio, (3) break-even point in units, and (4) break-even point in sales dollars.

Exercise 21-20
Evaluating strategies   **C2**

Refer to the information in Exercise 21-16. The marketing manager believes that increasing advertising costs by $81,000 in 2018 will increase the company's sales volume to 11,000 units. Prepare a forecasted contribution margin income statement for 2018 assuming the company incurs the additional advertising costs.

Exercise 21-21
Predicting unit and dollar
sales   **C2**

Nombre Company management predicts $390,000 of variable costs, $430,000 of fixed costs, and a pretax income of $155,000 in the next period. Management also predicts that the contribution margin per unit will be $9. Use this information to compute the (1) total expected dollar sales for next period and (2) number of units expected to be sold next period.

Exercise 21-22
CVP analysis using
composite units   **P4**

Check   (3) 1,000 composite
units

Handy Home sells windows and doors in the ratio of 8:2 (windows:doors). The selling price of each window is $200 and of each door is $500. The variable cost of a window is $125 and of a door is $350. Fixed costs are $900,000. Use this information to determine the (1) selling price per composite unit, (2) variable costs per composite unit, (3) break-even point in composite units, and (4) number of units of each product that will be sold at the break-even point.

Exercise 21-23
CVP analysis using
composite units
P4

R&R Tax Service offers tax and consulting services to individuals and small businesses. Data for fees and costs of three types of tax returns follow. R&R provides services in the ratio of 5:3:2 (easy, moderate, business). Fixed costs total $18,000 for the tax season. Use this information to determine the (1) selling price per composite unit, (2) variable costs per composite unit, (3) break-even point in composite units, and (4) number of units of each product that will be sold at the break-even point.

Type of Return	Fee Charged	Variable Cost per Return
Easy (Form 1040EZ)	$ 50	$ 30
Moderate (Form 1040)	125	75
Business	275	100

Exercise 21-24
Operating leverage
computed and applied
A2

Company A is a manufacturer with current sales of $6,000,000 and a 60% contribution margin. Its fixed costs equal $2,600,000. Company B is a consulting firm with current service revenues of $4,500,000 and a 25% contribution margin. Its fixed costs equal $375,000. Compute the degree of operating leverage (DOL) for each company. Identify which company benefits more from a 20% increase in sales and explain why.

Refer to the information in Exercise 21-16.

1. Compute the company's degree of operating leverage for 2017.
2. If sales decrease by 5% in 2018, what will be the company's pretax income?
3. Assume sales for 2018 decrease by 5%. Prepare a contribution margin income statement for 2018.

Exercise 21-25
Degree of operating leverage

A2

A manufacturer reports the information below for three recent years. Compute income for each of the three years using absorption costing.

Exercise 21-26[B]
Computing absorption costing income

P5

	Year 1	Year 2	Year 3
Variable costing income	$110,000	$114,400	$118,950
Beginning finished goods inventory (units)	0	1,200	700
Ending finished goods inventory (units)	1,200	700	800
Fixed manufacturing overhead per unit	$2.50	$2.50	$2.50

Use the amounts shown on the contribution margin income statement below to compute the missing amounts denoted by letters *a* through *n*.

Exercise 21-27
Contribution margin income statement

A1

	Company A		Company B	
Number of units sold	*a*		1,975	
	Total	Per unit	Total	Per unit
Sales	$208,000	$65	*h*	*i*
Variable costs	150,400	*b*	$39,500	*j*
Contribution margin	*c*	*d*	43,450	*k*
Fixed costs	*e*	*f*	19,750	*l*
Net income	$ 46,400	*g*	*m*	*n*

---

connect

The following costs result from the production and sale of 1,000 drum sets manufactured by Tight Drums Company for the year ended December 31, 2017. The drum sets sell for $500 each. The company has a 25% income tax rate.

PROBLEM SET A

Problem 21-1A
Contribution margin income statement and contribution margin ratio

A1

Variable production costs		Fixed manufacturing costs	
Plastic for casing	$ 17,000	Taxes on factory	$ 5,000
Wages of assembly workers	82,000	Factory maintenance	10,000
Drum stands.........................	26,000	Factory machinery depreciation	40,000
Variable selling costs		Fixed selling and administrative costs	
Sales commissions....................	15,000	Lease of equipment for sales staff........	10,000
		Accounting staff salaries	35,000
		Administrative management salaries	125,000

Required

1. Prepare a contribution margin income statement for the company.
2. Compute its contribution margin per unit and its contribution margin ratio.

Check (1) Net income, $101,250

Analysis Component

3. Interpret the contribution margin and contribution margin ratio from part 2.

Alden Co.'s monthly unit sales and total cost data for its operating activities of the past year follow. Management wants to use these data to predict future fixed and variable costs.

Problem 21-2A
Scatter diagram and cost behavior estimation

P1

Month	Units Sold	Total Cost	Month	Units Sold	Total Cost
1	320,000	$160,000	7	340,000	$220,000
2	160,000	100,000	8	280,000	160,000
3	280,000	220,000	9	80,000	64,000
4	200,000	100,000	10	160,000	140,000
5	300,000	230,000	11	100,000	100,000
6	200,000	120,000	12	110,000	80,000

Required

1. Prepare a scatter diagram for these data with sales volume (in units) plotted on the horizontal axis and total cost plotted on the vertical axis.

2. Estimate both the variable costs per unit and the total monthly fixed costs using the high-low method. Draw the total costs line on the scatter diagram in part 1.

3. Use the estimated line of cost behavior and results from part 2 to predict future total costs when sales volume is (a) 200,000 units and (b) 300,000 units.

Problem 21-3A

CVP analysis and charting

P2   P3

Praveen Co. manufactures and markets a number of rope products. Management is considering the future of Product XT, a special rope for hang gliding, that has not been as profitable as planned. Since Product XT is manufactured and marketed independently of the other products, its total costs can be precisely measured. Next year's plans call for a $200 selling price per 100 yards of XT rope. Its fixed costs for the year are expected to be $270,000, up to a maximum capacity of 700,000 yards of rope. Forecasted variable costs are $140 per 100 yards of XT rope.

Required

1. Estimate Product XT's break-even point in terms of (a) sales units and (b) sales dollars.

2. Prepare a CVP chart for Product XT like that in Exhibit 21.14. Use 7,000 units (700,000 yards/100 yards) as the maximum number of sales units on the horizontal axis of the graph, and $1,400,000 as the maximum dollar amount on the vertical axis.

3. Prepare a contribution margin income statement showing sales, variable costs, and fixed costs for Product XT at the break-even point.

Problem 21-4A

Break-even analysis; income targeting and forecasting

C2   P2   A1

Astro Co. sold 20,000 units of its only product and incurred a $50,000 loss (ignoring taxes) for the current year, as shown here. During a planning session for year 2018's activities, the production manager notes that variable costs can be reduced 50% by installing a machine that automates several operations. To obtain these savings, the company must increase its annual fixed costs by $200,000. The maximum output capacity of the company is 40,000 units per year.

ASTRO COMPANY	
Contribution Margin Income Statement	
For Year Ended December 31, 2017	
Sales	$1,000,000
Variable costs	800,000
Contribution margin	200,000
Fixed costs	250,000
Net loss	$ (50,000)

Required

1. Compute the break-even point in dollar sales for year 2017.

2. Compute the predicted break-even point in dollar sales for year 2018 assuming the machine is installed and there is no change in the unit selling price.

3. Prepare a forecasted contribution margin income statement for 2018 that shows the expected results with the machine installed. Assume that the unit selling price and the number of units sold will not change, and no income taxes will be due.

4. Compute the sales level required in both dollars and units to earn $200,000 of target pretax income in 2018 with the machine installed and no change in unit sales price. Round answers to whole dollars and whole units.

5. Prepare a forecasted contribution margin income statement that shows the results at the sales level computed in part 4. Assume no income taxes will be due.

Problem 21-5A

Break-even analysis, different cost structures, and income calculations

C2   A1   P4

Henna Co. produces and sells two products, T and O. It manufactures these products in separate factories and markets them through different channels. They have no shared costs. This year, the company sold 50,000 units of each product. Sales and costs for each product follow.

	Product T	Product O
Sales	$2,000,000	$2,000,000
Variable costs	1,600,000	250,000
Contribution margin	400,000	1,750,000
Fixed costs	125,000	1,475,000
Income before taxes...............	275,000	275,000
Income taxes (32% rate).	88,000	88,000
Net income	$ 187,000	$ 187,000

Required

1. Compute the break-even point in dollar sales for each product. (Round the answer to whole dollars.)

2. Assume that the company expects sales of each product to decline to 30,000 units next year with no change in unit selling price. Prepare forecasted financial results for next year following the format of the contribution margin income statement as just shown with columns for each of the two products (assume a 32% tax rate). Also, assume that any loss before taxes yields a 32% tax benefit.

Check (2) After-tax income: T, $78,200; O, $(289,000)

3. Assume that the company expects sales of each product to increase to 60,000 units next year with no change in unit selling price. Prepare forecasted financial results for next year following the format of the contribution margin income statement shown with columns for each of the two products (assume a 32% tax rate).

(3) After-tax income: T, $241,400; O, $425,000

Analysis Component

4. If sales greatly decrease, which product would experience a greater loss? Explain.

5. Describe some factors that might have created the different cost structures for these two products.

This year Burchard Company sold 40,000 units of its only product for $25 per unit. Manufacturing and selling the product required $200,000 of fixed manufacturing costs and $325,000 of fixed selling and administrative costs. Its per unit variable costs follow.

Problem 21-6A
Analysis of price, cost, and volume changes for contribution margin and net income

P2 A1

Material...	$8.00
Direct labor (paid on the basis of completed units)	5.00
Variable overhead costs......................................	1.00
Variable selling and administrative costs	0.50

Next year the company will use new material, which will reduce material costs by 50% and direct labor costs by 60% and will not affect product quality or marketability. Management is considering an increase in the unit selling price to reduce the number of units sold because the factory's output is nearing its annual output capacity of 45,000 units. Two plans are being considered. Under plan 1, the company will keep the selling price at the current level and sell the same volume as last year. This plan will increase income because of the reduced costs from using the new material. Under plan 2, the company will increase the selling price by 20%. This plan will decrease unit sales volume by 10%. Under both plans 1 and 2, the total fixed costs and the variable costs per unit for overhead and for selling and administrative costs will remain the same.

Required

1. Compute the break-even point in dollar sales for both (a) plan 1 and (b) plan 2.

2. Prepare a forecasted contribution margin income statement with two columns showing the expected results of plan 1 and plan 2. The statements should report sales, total variable costs, contribution margin, total fixed costs, income before taxes, income taxes (30% rate), and net income.

Check (1) Break-even: Plan 1, $750,000; Plan 2, $700,000
(2) Net income: Plan 1, $122,500; Plan 2, $199,500

Patriot Co. manufactures and sells three products: red, white, and blue. Their unit selling prices are red, $20; white, $35; and blue, $65. The per unit variable costs to manufacture and sell these products are red, $12; white, $22; and blue, $50. Their sales mix is reflected in a ratio of 5:4:2 (red:white:blue). Annual fixed costs shared by all three products are $250,000. One type of raw material has been used to manufacture all three products. The company has developed a new material of equal quality for less cost. The new material would reduce variable costs per unit as follows: red, by $6; white, by $12; and blue, by $10. However, the new material requires new equipment, which will increase annual fixed costs by $50,000. (Round answers to whole composite units.)

Problem 21-7A
Break-even analysis with composite units

P4

Required

1. If the company continues to use the old material, determine its break-even point in both sales units and sales dollars of each individual product.

2. If the company uses the new material, determine its new break-even point in both sales units and sales dollars of each individual product.

Analysis Component

3. What insight does this analysis offer management for long-term planning?

PROBLEM SET B

Problem 21-1B

Contribution margin income statement and contribution margin ratio

A1

The following costs result from the production and sale of 12,000 CD sets manufactured by Gilmore Company for the year ended December 31, 2017. The CD sets sell for $18 each. The company has a 25% income tax rate.

Variable manufacturing costs	
Plastic for CD sets	$ 1,500
Wages of assembly workers	30,000
Labeling	3,000
Variable selling costs	
Sales commissions	6,000
Fixed manufacturing costs	
Rent on factory	6,750
Factory cleaning service	4,520
Factory machinery depreciation	20,000
Fixed selling and administrative costs	
Lease of office equipment	1,050
Systems staff salaries	15,000
Administrative management salaries	120,000

Required

1. Prepare a contribution margin income statement for the company.

2. Compute its contribution margin per unit and its contribution margin ratio.

Analysis Component

3. Interpret the contribution margin and contribution margin ratio from part 2.

Problem 21-2B

Scatter diagram and cost behavior estimation

P1

Sun Co.'s monthly unit sales and total cost data for its operating activities of the past year follow. Management wants to use these data to predict future fixed and variable costs. (Dollar and unit amounts are in thousands.)

Month	Units Sold	Total Cost	Month	Units Sold	Total Cost
1	195	$ 97	7	145	$ 93
2	125	87	8	185	105
3	105	73	9	135	85
4	155	89	10	85	58
5	95	81	11	175	95
6	215	110	12	115	79

Required

1. Prepare a scatter diagram for these data with sales volume (in units) plotted on the horizontal axis and total costs plotted on the vertical axis.

2. Estimate both the variable costs per unit and the total monthly fixed costs using the high-low method. Draw the total costs line on the scatter diagram in part 1.

3. Use the estimated line of cost behavior and results from part 2 to predict future total costs when sales volume is (a) 100 units and (b) 170 units.

Hip-Hop Co. manufactures and markets several products. Management is considering the future of one product, electronic keyboards, that has not been as profitable as planned. Since this product is manufactured and marketed independently of the other products, its total costs can be precisely measured. Next year's plans call for a $350 selling price per unit. The fixed costs for the year are expected to be $42,000, up to a maximum capacity of 700 units. Forecasted variable costs are $210 per unit.

Problem 21-3B
CVP analysis and charting
P2   P3

Required

1. Estimate the keyboards' break-even point in terms of (a) sales units and (b) sales dollars.
2. Prepare a CVP chart for keyboards like that in Exhibit 21.14. Use 700 keyboards as the maximum number of sales units on the horizontal axis of the graph, and $250,000 as the maximum dollar amount on the vertical axis.
3. Prepare a contribution margin income statement showing sales, variable costs, and fixed costs for keyboards at the break-even point.

Check (1) Break-even sales, 300 units

Rivera Co. sold 20,000 units of its only product and incurred a $50,000 loss (ignoring taxes) for the current year, as shown here. During a planning session for year 2018's activities, the production manager notes that variable costs can be reduced 50% by installing a machine that automates several operations. To obtain these savings, the company must increase its annual fixed costs by $150,000. The maximum output capacity of the company is 40,000 units per year.

Problem 21-4B
Break-even analysis; income targeting and forecasting
C2   P2   A1

RIVERA COMPANY	
Contribution Margin Income Statement	
For Year Ended December 31, 2017	
Sales	$750,000
Variable costs	600,000
Contribution margin	150,000
Fixed costs	200,000
Net loss	$ (50,000)

Required

1. Compute the break-even point in dollar sales for year 2017.
2. Compute the predicted break-even point in dollar sales for year 2018 assuming the machine is installed and no change occurs in the unit selling price. (Round the change in variable costs to a whole number.)
3. Prepare a forecasted contribution margin income statement for 2018 that shows the expected results with the machine installed. Assume that the unit selling price and the number of units sold will not change, and no income taxes will be due.
4. Compute the sales level required in both dollars and units to earn $200,000 of target pretax income in 2018 with the machine installed and no change in unit sales price. (Round answers to whole dollars and whole units.)
5. Prepare a forecasted contribution margin income statement that shows the results at the sales level computed in part 4. Assume no income taxes will be due.

Check (3) Net income, $100,000

(4) Required sales, $916,667 or 24,445 units (both rounded)

Stam Co. produces and sells two products, BB and TT. It manufactures these products in separate factories and markets them through different channels. They have no shared costs. This year, the company sold 50,000 units of each product. Sales and costs for each product follow.

Problem 21-5B
Break-even analysis, different cost structures, and income calculations
C2   P4   A1

	Product BB	Product TT
Sales	$800,000	$800,000
Variable costs	560,000	100,000
Contribution margin	240,000	700,000
Fixed costs	100,000	560,000
Income before taxes..............	140,000	140,000
Income taxes (32% rate).	44,800	44,800
Net income	$ 95,200	$ 95,200

Required

1. Compute the break-even point in dollar sales for each product. (Round the answer to the next whole dollar.)

2. Assume that the company expects sales of each product to decline to 33,000 units next year with no change in the unit selling price. Prepare forecasted financial results for next year following the format of the contribution margin income statement as shown here with columns for each of the two products (assume a 32% tax rate, and that any loss before taxes yields a 32% tax benefit).

3. Assume that the company expects sales of each product to increase to 64,000 units next year with no change in the unit selling prices. Prepare forecasted financial results for next year following the format of the contribution margin income statement as shown here with columns for each of the two products (assume a 32% tax rate).

Analysis Component

4. If sales greatly increase, which product would experience a greater increase in profit? Explain.

5. Describe some factors that might have created the different cost structures for these two products.

Problem 21-6B
Analysis of price, cost, and volume changes for contribution margin and net income

A1   P2

This year Best Company earned a disappointing 5.6% after-tax return on sales (net income/sales) from marketing 100,000 units of its only product. The company buys its product in bulk and repackages it for resale at the price of $20 per unit. Best incurred the following costs this year.

Total variable unit costs	$800,000
Total variable packaging costs.	$100,000
Fixed costs	$950,000
Income tax rate.	25%

The marketing manager claims that next year's results will be the same as this year's unless some changes are made. The manager predicts the company can increase the number of units sold by 80% if it reduces the selling price by 20% and upgrades the packaging. This change would increase variable packaging costs by 20%. Increased sales would allow the company to take advantage of a 25% quantity purchase discount on the cost of the bulk product. Neither the packaging change nor the volume discount would affect fixed costs, which provide an annual output capacity of 200,000 units.

Required

1. Compute the break-even point in dollar sales under the (a) existing business strategy and (b) new strategy that alters both unit selling price and variable costs. (Round answers to the next whole dollar.)

2. Prepare a forecasted contribution margin income statement with two columns showing the expected results of (a) the existing strategy and (b) changing to the new strategy. The statements should report sales, total variable costs (unit and packaging), contribution margin, fixed costs, income before taxes, income taxes, and net income. Also determine the after-tax return on sales for these two strategies.

Problem 21-7B
Break-even analysis with composite units

P4

Milano Co. manufactures and sells three products: product 1, product 2, and product 3. Their unit selling prices are product 1, $40; product 2, $30; and product 3, $20. The per unit variable costs to manufacture and sell these products are product 1, $30; product 2, $15; and product 3, $8. Their sales mix is reflected in a ratio of 6:4:2. Annual fixed costs shared by all three products are $270,000. One type of raw material has been used to manufacture products 1 and 2. The company has developed a new material of equal quality for less cost. The new material would reduce variable costs per unit as follows: product 1 by $10 and product 2 by $5. However, the new material requires new equipment, which will increase annual fixed costs by $50,000.

Required

1. If the company continues to use the old material, determine its break-even point in both sales units and sales dollars of each individual product.

2. If the company uses the new material, determine its new break-even point in both sales units and sales dollars of each individual product. (Round to the next whole unit.)

Analysis Component

3. What insight does this analysis offer management for long-term planning?

(This serial problem began in Chapter 1 and continues through most of the book. If previous chapter segments were not completed, the serial problem can begin at this point.)

SP 21   Business Solutions sells upscale modular desk units and office chairs in the ratio of 3:2 (desk unit:chair). The selling prices are $1,250 per desk unit and $500 per chair. The variable costs are $750 per desk unit and $250 per chair. Fixed costs are $120,000.

Required

1. Compute the selling price per composite unit.
2. Compute the variable costs per composite unit.
3. Compute the break-even point in composite units.
4. Compute the number of units of each product that would be sold at the break-even point.

Check   (3) 60 composite units

© Alexander Image/Shutterstock RF

Beyond the Numbers

BTN 21-1   Apple offers extended service contracts that provide repair coverage for its products. As you complete the following requirements, assume that Apple's repair services department uses many of the company's existing resources such as its facilities, repair machinery, and computer systems.

REPORTING IN ACTION

C1

APPLE

Required

1. Identify several of the variable, mixed, and fixed costs that Apple's repair services department is likely to incur in carrying out its services.
2. Assume that Apple's repair service revenues are expected to grow by 25% in the next year. How would we expect the costs identified in part 1 to change, if at all?
3. Based on the answer to part 2, can Apple use the contribution margin ratio to predict how income will change in response to increases in Apple's repair service revenues?

BTN 21-2   Both Apple and **Google** sell electronic devices, and each of these companies has a different product mix.

COMPARATIVE ANALYSIS

P2   A2

APPLE
GOOGLE

Required

1. Assume the following data are available for both companies. Compute each company's break-even point in unit sales. (Each company sells many devices at many different selling prices, and each has its own variable costs. This assignment assumes an *average* selling price per unit and an *average* cost per item.)

	Apple	Google
Average selling price per unit sold	$550 per unit	$470 per unit
Average variable cost per unit sold	$250 per unit	$270 per unit
Total fixed costs ($ in millions)	$36,000	$10,000

2. If unit sales were to decline, which company would experience the larger decline in operating profit? Explain.

BTN 21-3   Labor costs of an auto repair mechanic are seldom based on actual hours worked. Instead, this labor cost is based on an industry average of time estimated to complete a repair job. This means a customer can pay, for example, $120 for two hours of work on a car when the actual time worked was only one hour. Many experienced mechanics can complete repair jobs faster than the industry average. Assume that you are asked to complete such a survey for a repair center. The survey calls for objective input, and many questions require detailed cost data and analysis. The mechanics and owners know you

ETHICS CHALLENGE

C1

have the survey and encourage you to complete it in a way that increases the average billable hours for repair work.

Required

Write a one-page memorandum to the mechanics and owners that describes the direct labor analysis you will undertake in completing this survey.

COMMUNICATING IN PRACTICE

C2

BTN 21-4   Several important assumptions underlie CVP analysis. Assumptions often help simplify and focus our analysis of sales and costs. A common application of CVP analysis is as a tool to forecast sales, costs, and income.

Required

Assume that you are actively searching for a job. Prepare a half-page report identifying (1) three assumptions relating to your expected revenue (salary) and (2) three assumptions relating to your expected costs for the first year of your new job. Be prepared to discuss your assumptions in class.

TAKING IT TO THE NET

C1

BTN 21-5   Access and review the entrepreneurial information at **Business Owner's Toolkit** (**Toolkit.com**). Access and review its *New Business Cash Needs Checklist* (or similar worksheets related to controls of cash and costs) under the "**Starting Up**" link. (Look under the heading "Free Startup Downloads.")

Required

Write a half-page report that describes the information and resources available at the Business Owner's Toolkit to help the owner of a start-up business control and monitor its cash flows and costs.

TEAMWORK IN ACTION

C2

BTN 21-6   A local movie theater owner explains to you that ticket sales on weekends and evenings are strong, but attendance during the weekdays, Monday through Thursday, is poor. The owner proposes to offer a contract to the local grade school to show educational materials at the theater for a set charge per student during school hours. The owner asks your help to prepare a CVP analysis listing the cost and sales projections for the proposal. The owner must propose to the school's administration a charge per child. At a minimum, the charge per child needs to be sufficient for the theater to break even.

Required

Your team is to prepare two separate lists of questions that enable you to complete a reliable CVP analysis of this situation. One list is to be answered by the school's administration, the other by the owner of the movie theater.

ENTREPRENEURIAL DECISION

C1   A1

BTN 21-7   **Sweetgreen**, launched by entrepreneurs Nic Jammet, Jon Neman, and Nate Ru, is a fast-casual restaurant brand devoted to healthy salad choices. The company also sells T-shirts, hats, and other apparel.

Required

1. Identify at least two fixed costs that will not change regardless of how much salad Sweetgreen sells.
2. Sweetgreen is expanding. How could overly optimistic sales estimates potentially hurt its business?
3. Explain how cost-volume-profit analysis can help Nic, Jon, and Nate manage Sweetgreen.

HITTING THE ROAD

P4

BTN 21-8   Multiproduct break-even analysis is often viewed differently when actually applied in practice. You are to visit a local fast-food restaurant and count the number of items on the menu. To apply multiproduct break-even analysis to the restaurant, similar menu items must often be fit into groups. A reasonable approach is to classify menu items into approximately five groups. We then estimate average selling price and average variable cost to compute average contribution margin. (*Hint:* For fast-food restaurants, the highest contribution margin is with its beverages, at about 90%.)

Required

1. Prepare a one-year multiproduct break-even analysis for the restaurant you visit. Begin by establishing groups. Next, estimate each group's volume and contribution margin. These estimates are necessary to compute each group's contribution margin. Assume that annual fixed costs in total are $500,000 per year. (*Hint:* You must develop your own estimates on volume and contribution margin for each group to obtain the break-even point and sales.)

2. Prepare a one-page report on the results of your analysis. Comment on the volume of sales necessary to break even at a fast-food restaurant.

BTN 21-9   Access and review Samsung's website (Samsung.com) to answer the following questions.

GLOBAL DECISION

P4

Samsung

Required

1. Do you believe that Samsung's managers use single product CVP analysis or multiproduct break-even analysis? Explain.

2. How does the addition of a new product line affect Samsung's CVP analysis?

 **GLOBAL VIEW**

Survey evidence shows that many German companies have elaborate and detailed cost accounting systems. Over 90 percent of companies surveyed report their systems focus on *contribution margin*. This focus helps German companies like **BMW** control costs and plan production levels.

Recently, an auto analyst took apart a BMW i3 to determine its cost. With that cost estimate, and an estimated selling price of $50,000 per i3, the analyst estimates BMW can break even by selling 20,000 i3s per year. [Source: *Forbes.com,* "Unlocking the Secrets of BMW's Remarkable Car of the Future."]

 Global View Assignments

Discussion Question 21

Quick Study 21-21

BTN 21-9

22 chapter

Master Budgets and Planning

Chapter Preview

BUDGET PROCESS AND ADMINISTRATION

C1 Budgeting process

Benefits of budgeting

Human behavior

Reporting and timing

NTK 22-1

THE MASTER BUDGET AND ITS PREPARATION

C2 Master budget components

P1 Operating budgets

Capital expenditures budget

Investing budgets

Financing budgets

P2 Cash budget

NTK 22-2, 22-3, 22-4, 22-5

BUDGETED FINANCIAL STATEMENTS

P3 Budgeted income statement

Budgeted balance sheet

Using the master budget

Service companies

A1 Activity-based budgeting

P4 *Appendix:* Merchandiser budgeting

NTK 22-8

Learning Objectives

CONCEPTUAL

C1 Describe the benefits of budgeting.

C2 Describe a master budget and the process of preparing it.

ANALYTICAL

A1 Analyze expense planning using activity-based budgeting.

PROCEDURAL

P1 Prepare each component of a master budget—for a manufacturing company.

P2 Prepare a cash budget.

P3 Prepare budgeted financial statements.

P4 *Appendix 22A*—Prepare each component of a master budget—for a merchandising company.

Courtesy of TaTa Topper

Top This!

RICHMOND, VA—Breast Cancer Awareness Month, Coaches vs. Cancer basketball games, and student fund-raisers increase awareness and money to help cure cancer. Meanwhile, survivors struggle with basics such as being able to sleep comfortably. After a double mastectomy, Michelle Logan told her friend Marilyn Collins, a breast cancer survivor, that she could no longer sleep on her side or stomach. "I get it," insisted Marilyn, "I was you four years ago." Marilyn devised a solution. "I had a problem," recalls Michelle, "and Marilyn had a great idea!"

Marilyn's idea led to the **TaTa Topper (MarilynAndMichelle. com)**, a 4-inch-thick mattress cover with cutouts in the breast area. The design allowed the women to sleep comfortably. Although Marilyn and Michelle did not set out to start a business, they realized their product's potential. "Knowing that I can help other women, it's meaningful," explains Marilyn.

Michelle had worked in banking and had started and sold a successful business, but she and Marilyn had much to learn about making their venture viable. They began by attending a six-week class on starting a business. "I had no idea what a 'pitch' was," laughs Marilyn. They learned quickly and soon had

"Fix a problem"
—Marilyn Collins

developed product prototypes, designed packaging, and determined a price. They also found local businesses to make the foam toppers and fitted sheets.

The two learned to budget their cost of merchandise purchases, shipping, and other costs. "The manufacturer stores our inventory," explains Marilyn, "so we have very little overhead cost." Marilyn and Michelle are now developing more formal budget procedures. "If we don't plan for and make profits," admits Marilyn, "we can't help any women."

Michelle stresses that "sales forecasts are challenging because there are so many variables and unknowns." But a good sales forecast is the cornerstone of a good budget. All companies budget—manufacturers budget costs of materials, labor, and overhead, whereas service providers focus on labor budgets.

Both Marilyn and Michelle stress the importance of good mentors. Marilyn insists that "if you fix a problem and make people's lives better, you make a difference."

Sources: *Marilyn and Michelle website*, January 2017; *Richmond Times-Dispatch*, February 15, 2015; *WRIC News* interview, March 25, 2016; Author phone interview, April 9, 2016

BUDGET PROCESS AND ADMINISTRATION

Budgeting Process

C1
Describe the benefits of budgeting.

Managers must ensure that activities of employees and departments contribute to meeting the company's overall goals. This requires coordination and budgeting. **Budgeting,** the process of planning future business actions and expressing them as formal plans, helps to achieve this coordination.

A **budget** is a formal statement of a company's plans, expressed in monetary terms. Unlike long-term *strategic plans,* budgets typically cover shorter periods such as a month, quarter, or year. Budgets are useful in controlling operations. The **budgetary control** process, shown in Exhibit 22.1, refers to management's use of budgets to see that planned objectives are met.

EXHIBIT 22.1

Process of Budgetary Control

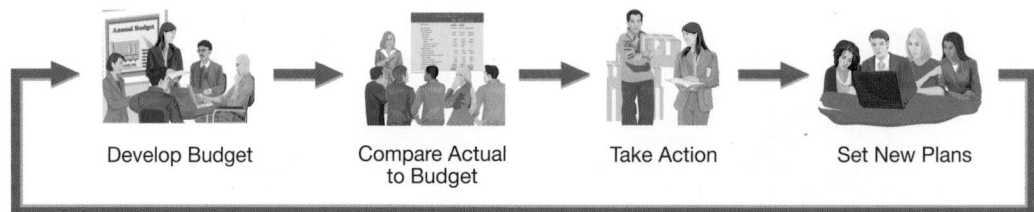

Develop Budget → Compare Actual to Budget → Take Action → Set New Plans

The budgetary control process involves at least four steps: (1) develop the budget from planned objectives, (2) compare actual results to budgeted amounts and analyze any differences, (3) take corrective and strategic actions, and (4) establish new planned objectives and prepare a new budget.

In this chapter we focus on the first step in the budgetary control process, developing a budget. In the next chapter we show how managers compare budgeted and actual amounts to guide corrective actions and make new plans.

Benefits of Budgeting

Budgets help fulfill the key managerial functions of planning and controlling. Benefits of written budgets include:

- **Planning**   A budget focuses on the future opportunities and threats to the organization. This focus on the future is important because the daily pressures of operating an organization can divert management's attention from planning. Budgeting makes managers devote time to *plan* for the future.

- **Control**   The *control* function requires management to evaluate (benchmark) operations against some norm. Since budgeted performance considers important company, industry, and economic factors, a comparison of actual to budgeted performance provides an effective monitoring and control system. This comparison assists management in identifying problems and taking corrective actions if necessary.

- **Coordination**   Budgeting helps to *coordinate* activities so that all employees and departments understand and work toward the company's overall goals.

- **Communication**   Written budgets effectively *communicate* management's specific action plans to all employees. When plans are not written down, conversations can lead to uncertainty and confusion among employees.

- **Motivation**   Budgets can be used to *motivate* employees. Budgeted performance levels can provide goals for employees to attain or even exceed. Many companies provide incentives, like cash bonuses, for employee performance that meets or exceeds budget goals.

Incentive Pay   Budgets are important in determining managers' pay. A recent survey shows that 82% of large companies tie managers' bonus payments to beating budget goals. For these companies, bonus payments are frequently more than 20% of total manager pay. ■

Budgeting and Human Behavior

Budgets provide standards for evaluating performance and can affect the attitudes of employees evaluated by them. Budgeted levels of performance must be realistic to avoid discouraging employees. Employees who will be evaluated should help prepare the budget to increase their commitment to it. For example, the sales department should be involved in developing sales estimates, while the production department should prepare its initial expense budget. This *bottom-up* process is usually more useful than a *top-down* approach in which top management passes down the budget without input. Performance evaluations must allow the affected employees to explain the reasons for apparent performance deficiencies, rather than assigning blame.

Budgeting has three important guidelines:

1. Employees affected by a budget should help prepare it (*participatory budgeting*).
2. Goals reflected in a budget should be challenging but attainable.
3. Evaluations offer opportunities to explain differences between actual and budgeted amounts.

Budgeting can be a positive motivating force when the guidelines are followed.

Potential Negative Outcomes of Budgeting   Managers must be aware of potential negative outcomes of budgeting. Under participatory budgeting, some employees might understate sales budgets and overstate expense budgets to allow themselves a cushion, or *budgetary slack,* to aid in meeting targets. Sometimes, pressure to meet budgeted results leads employees to engage in unethical behavior or commit fraud. Finally, some employees might always spend their budgeted amounts, even on unnecessary items, to ensure their budgets aren't reduced for the next period.

Example: Assume a company's sales force receives a bonus when sales exceed the budgeted amount. How would this arrangement affect the participatory sales forecasts? *Answer:* Sales reps may understate their budgeted sales.

Planning   Most companies allocate dollars based on budgets submitted by department managers. These managers verify the numbers and monitor the budget. Managers must remember, however, that a budget is judged by its success in helping achieve the company's mission. One analogy is that a hiker must know the route to properly plan a hike and monitor hiking progress. ■

© Pixland/AGE fotostock

Budget Reporting and Timing

The budget period usually coincides with the company's fiscal year. To provide specific guidance to help control operations, the annual budget usually is separated into quarterly or monthly budgets. These short-term budgets allow management to periodically evaluate performance and take corrective action.

The time required to prepare a budget can vary a lot. Large, complex organizations usually take longer to prepare their budgets than do smaller ones. This is because considerable effort is required to coordinate the different units (departments) within large organizations.

Companies Using Rolling Budgets

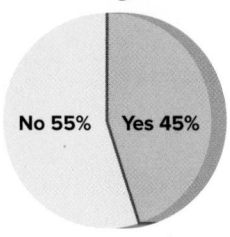

No 55%   Yes 45%

Many companies apply **continuous budgeting** by preparing **rolling budgets.** In continuous budgeting, a company continually revises its budgets as time passes. In a rolling budget, a company revises its entire set of budgets by adding a new quarterly budget to replace the quarter that just elapsed. Thus, at any point in time, monthly or quarterly budgets are available for the next 12 months or four quarters. The rolling budget below shows rolling budgets prepared at the end of five consecutive periods. The first set (at top) is prepared in December 2016 and covers the four calendar quarters of 2017. In March 2017, the company prepares another rolling budget for the next four quarters through March 2018. This same process is repeated every three months. As a result, management is continuously planning ahead.

The rolling budget below reflects an annual budget composed of four quarters, prepared four times per year using the most recent information available. When continuous budgeting is not used, the fourth-quarter budget is nine months old and perhaps out of date when applied.

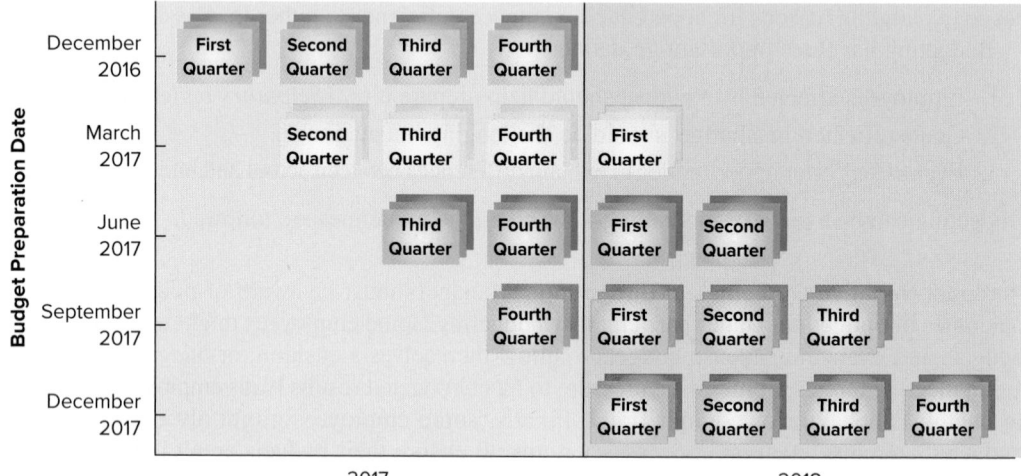

Rolling Budgets

Decision Insight

From Scratch   Many companies use **zero-based budgeting,** an approach that requires all expenses to be justified for each new budget. Rather than using last period's budgeted or actual amounts to determine this period's budgets, managers instead analyze each activity in the organization to see if it is necessary. Managers then build budgets around only those necessary activities. Made-from-scratch budgets can be useful in identifying waste and reducing costs. ∎

NEED-TO-KNOW 22-1

Budgeting Benefits

C1

Do More: QS 22-1, QS 22-2, E 22-1

Label each item below with *yes* if it describes a benefit of budgeting or *no* if it describes a potential negative outcome of budgeting.

_____ **1.** Budgets provide goals for employees to work toward.

_____ **2.** Written budgets help communicate plans to all employees.

_____ **3.** Some employees might understate sales targets in budgets.

_____ **4.** A budget forces managers to spend time planning for the future.

_____ **5.** Some employees might always spend budgeted amounts.

_____ **6.** With rolling budgets, managers can continuously plan ahead.

Solution

1. Yes   **2.** Yes   **3.** No   **4.** Yes   **5.** No   **6.** Yes

THE MASTER BUDGET

A **master budget** is a formal, comprehensive plan for a company's future. It contains several individual budgets that are linked with each other to form a coordinated plan.

C2

Describe a master budget and the process of preparing it.

Master Budget Components

Exhibit 22.2 summarizes the master budgeting process. The master budgeting process typically begins with the sales budget and ends with a cash budget and budgeted financial statements. The master budget includes individual budgets for sales, production (or purchases), various expenses, capital expenditures, and cash.

EXHIBIT 22.2

Master Budget Process for a Manufacturer

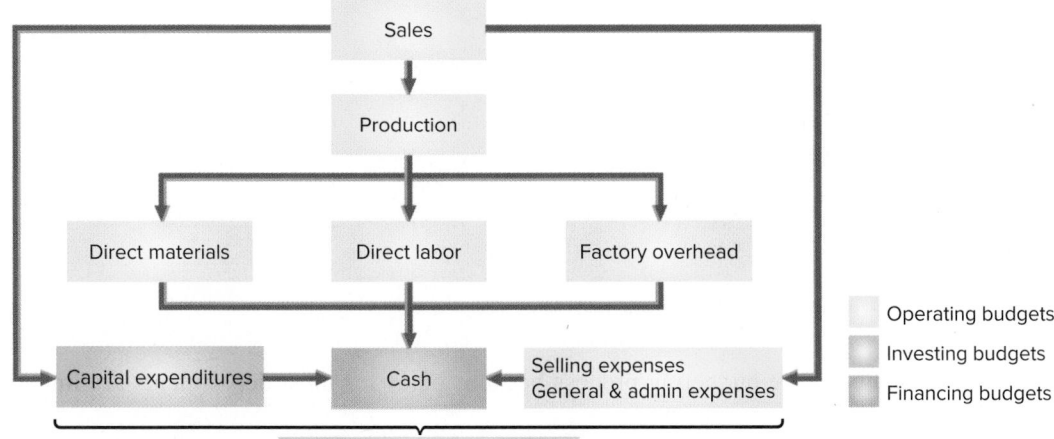

The number and types of budgets included in a master budget depend on the company's size and complexity. A manufacturer's master budget should include, at a minimum, several *operating* budgets (shown in yellow in Exhibit 22.2), a capital expenditures budget, and a cash budget. The capital expenditures budget summarizes the effects of *investing* activities on cash. The cash budget helps determine the company's need for *financing*.

Managers often express the expected financial results of these planned activities with a budgeted balance sheet and a budgeted income statement. Some budgets require the input of other budgets. For example, direct materials and direct labor budgets cannot be prepared until a production budget is prepared. A company cannot plan its production until it prepares a sales budget.

Point: Merchandisers prepare *merchandise purchase* budgets instead of the production and manufacturing budgets in Exhibit 22.2.

The rest of this chapter explains how Toronto Sticks Company (TSC), a manufacturer of youth hockey sticks, prepares its budgets. Its master budget includes operating, capital expenditures, and cash budgets for each month in each quarter. It also includes a budgeted income statement for each quarter and a budgeted balance sheet as of the last day of each quarter. We show how TSC prepares budgets for October, November, and December 2017. Exhibit 22.3 presents TSC's balance sheet at the start of this budgeting period, which we often refer to as we prepare the component budgets.

Courtesy JJW Images

Operating Budgets

This section explains TSC's preparation of operating budgets. Its operating budgets consist of the sales budget, production and manufacturing budgets, selling expense budget, and general and administrative expense budget. (The preparation of merchandising budgets is described in this chapter's appendix.)

P1

Prepare each component of a master budget—for a manufacturing company.

Sales Budget   The first step in preparing the master budget is the **sales budget,** which shows the planned sales units and the expected dollars from these sales. The sales budget is

EXHIBIT 22.3

Balance Sheet prior to the
Budgeting Periods

TORONTO STICKS COMPANY
Balance Sheet
September 30, 2017

Assets

Cash		$ 20,000
Accounts receivable		25,200
Raw materials inventory (178 pounds @ $20).............		3,560
Finished goods inventory (1,010 units @ $17)		17,170
Equipment*	$200,000	
Less: Accumulated depreciation	36,000	164,000
Total assets		$229,930

Liabilities and Equity

Liabilities		
Accounts payable	$ 7,060	
Income taxes payable (due 10/31/2017)	20,000	
Note payable	10,000	$ 37,060
Stockholders' equity		
Common stock	150,000	
Retained earnings	42,870	192,870
Total liabilities and equity		$229,930

* Equipment is depreciated on a straight-line basis over 10 years (salvage value is $20,000).

the starting point in the budgeting process because plans for most departments are linked to sales.

> **Operating Budgets**
>
> Sales
> Production
> Direct labor
> Direct materials
> Factory overhead
> Selling expenses
> General & administrative

The sales budget comes from a careful analysis of forecasted economic and market conditions, business capacity, and advertising plans. To illustrate, in September 2017, TSC sold 700 hockey sticks at $60 per unit. After considering sales predictions and market conditions, TSC prepares its sales budget for the next three months (see Exhibit 22.4). The sales budget in Exhibit 22.4 includes forecasts of both unit sales and unit prices. Some sales budgets are expressed only in total sales dollars, but most are more detailed and can include budgets for many different products, regions, departments, and sales representatives.

EXHIBIT 22.4

Sales Budget

	A	B	C	D	E
1	TORONTO STICKS COMPANY				
2	Sales Budget				
3	October 2017–December 2017				
4		October	November	December	Totals
5	Budgeted sales (units)	1,000	800	1,400	3,200
6	Selling price per unit	× $ 60	× $ 60	× $ 60	× $ 60
7	Total budgeted sales (dollars)	$60,000	$48,000	$84,000	$192,000

■ **Decision** Maker

Entrepreneur You run a start-up that manufactures designer clothes. Business is seasonal, and fashions and designs quickly change. How do you prepare reliable annual sales budgets? ■ [*Answer:* You must deal with two issues. First, because fashions and designs frequently change, you cannot heavily rely on previous budgets. As a result, you must carefully analyze the market to understand what designs are in vogue. This will help you plan the product mix and estimate demand. The second issue is the budgeting period. An annual sales budget may be unreliable because tastes can quickly change. Your best bet might be to prepare monthly and quarterly sales budgets that you continuously monitor and revise.]

Production Budget   A manufacturer prepares a **production budget,** which shows the number of units to be produced in a period. The production budget is based on the budgeted unit sales from the sales budget, along with inventory considerations. Manufacturers often determine a certain amount of **safety stock,** a quantity of inventory that provides protection against lost sales caused by unfulfilled demands from customers or delays in shipments from suppliers. Exhibit 22.5 shows how to compute the production required for a period. *A production budget does not show costs; it is always expressed in units of product.*

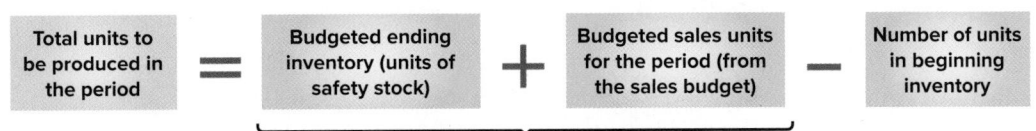

| Total units to be produced in the period | = | Budgeted ending inventory (units of safety stock) | + | Budgeted sales units for the period (from the sales budget) | − | Number of units in beginning inventory |

Required units for the period

EXHIBIT 22.5

Computing Production Requirements

After assessing the cost of keeping inventory along with the risk and cost of inventory short-ages, TSC decided that the number of units in its finished goods inventory at each month-end should equal 90% of next month's predicted sales. For example, inventory at the end of October should equal 90% of budgeted November sales, and so on. This information, along with knowl-edge of 1,010 units in inventory at September 30 (see Exhibit 22.3), allows the company to prepare the production budget shown in Exhibit 22.6. The actual number of units of ending in-ventory at September 30 is not consistent with TSC's policy. This is common, as sales forecasts are uncertain and production can sometimes be disrupted.

Example: Under a JIT system, how will sales in units differ from the number of units to produce? *Answer:* The two amounts are similar because future inventory should be near zero.

EXHIBIT 22.6

Production Budget

	A	B	C	D
1	**TORONTO STICKS COMPANY**			
2	**Production Budget**			
3	**October 2017–December 2017**			
4		**October**	**November**	**December**
5	Next month's budgeted sales (units) from sales budget*	800	1,400	900
6	Ratio of inventory to future sales	× 90%	× 90%	× 90%
7	Budgeted ending inventory (units)	720	1,260	810
8	Add: Budgeted sales (units)	1,000	800	1,400
9	Required units of available production	1,720	2,060	2,210
10	Deduct: Beginning inventory (units)	1,010**	720	1,260
11	Units to be produced	710	1,340	950

*From sales budget (Exhibit 22.4); January budgeted sales of 900 units from next quarter's sales budget.
**October's beginning inventory (1,010 units) is inconsistent with company policy.

Budgeted ending inventory
+ Budgeted sales
− Beginning inventory
= Units to produce

Use three steps to complete the production budget:

1. Compute budgeted ending inventory based on the company's inventory policy.
2. Add budgeted sales (from the sales budget).
3. Subtract beginning inventory.

The result is the required units to be produced for the period. The number of units to be produced provides the basis for *manufacturing budgets* for the production costs of those units—direct materials, direct labor, and overhead.

Courtesy JJW Images

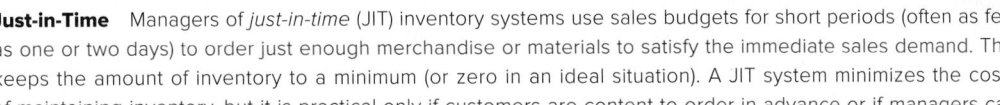

Decision Insight

Just-in-Time   Managers of *just-in-time* (JIT) inventory systems use sales budgets for short periods (often as few as one or two days) to order just enough merchandise or materials to satisfy the immediate sales demand. This keeps the amount of inventory to a minimum (or zero in an ideal situation). A JIT system minimizes the costs of maintaining inventory, but it is practical only if customers are content to order in advance or if managers can accurately determine short-term sales demand. Suppliers also must be able and willing to ship small quantities regularly and promptly. ■

Point: Accurate estimates of future sales are crucial in a JIT system.

NEED-TO-KNOW 22-2

Production Budget

P1

A manufacturing company predicts sales of 220 units for May and 250 units for June. The company wants each month's ending inventory to equal 30% of next month's predicted unit sales. Beginning inventory for May is 66 units. Compute the company's budgeted production in units for May.

Solution

	Units
Budgeted ending inventory for May (250 × 30%)	75
Plus: Budgeted sales for May	220
Required units of available production	295
Less: Beginning inventory	(66)
Total units to be produced during May	229

Do More: QS 22-12, QS 22-16, QS 22-17, E 22-3, E 22-10, E 22-11

Direct Materials Budget   The **direct materials budget** shows the budgeted costs for the direct materials that must be purchased to satisfy the budgeted production for the period. Whereas the production budget shows *units* to be produced, the direct materials budget translates the units to be produced into budgeted *costs*. (The same is true for the other two manufacturing budgets that we will discuss below—the direct labor budget and the factory overhead budget).

A direct materials budget requires the following inputs:

1. Number of units to produce (from the production budget).
2. Materials requirements per unit—How many units (pounds, gallons, etc.) of direct materials go into each unit of finished product?
3. Budgeted ending inventory (in units) of direct materials—As with finished goods, most companies maintain a safety stock of materials to ensure that production can continue.
4. Beginning inventory (in units) of direct materials.
5. Cost per unit of direct materials.

Materials (in pounds) to purchase are computed as:

$$\text{Materials to be purchased (pounds)} = \text{Budgeted production (units)} \times \text{Materials required for each unit (pounds)} + \text{Budgeted ending materials inventory (pounds)} - \text{Beginning materials inventory (pounds)}$$

Exhibit 22.7 shows the direct materials budget for TSC.

1. This budget begins with the budgeted production from the production budget.
2. Next, TSC needs to know the amount of direct materials needed for each of the units to be produced—in this case, half a pound (0.5) of wood. With these two inputs we can compute the amount of direct materials needed for production. For example, to produce 710 hockey sticks in October, TSC will need 355 pounds of wood (710 units × 0.5 lbs. = 355 lbs.).
3. TSC wants a safety stock of direct materials in inventory at the end of each month to complete 50% of the budgeted units to be produced in the next month. Since TSC expects to produce 1,340 units in November, requiring 670 pounds of materials, it needs ending inventory of direct materials of 335 pounds (50% × 670) in inventory at the end of October. TSC's total direct materials requirement for October is therefore 690 pounds (355 + 335).
4. TSC already has 178 pounds of direct materials in its beginning inventory (refer to Exhibit 22.3). TSC deducts this amount from the total materials requirements for the month. For October, the calculation is 690 pounds – 178 pounds = 512 pounds of direct materials to be purchased in October.

EXHIBIT 22.7

Direct Materials Budget

	A	B	C	D
1 2 3	**TORONTO STICKS COMPANY** **Direct Materials Budget** **October 2017–December 2017**			
4		**October**	**November**	**December**
5	Budgeted production units*	710	1,340	950
6	Materials requirements per unit	× 0.5	× 0.5	× 0.5
7	Materials needed for production (pounds)	355	×50% 670	×50% 475
8	Add: Budgeted ending inventory (pounds)	335	237.5	247.5**
9	Total materials requirements (pounds)	690	907.5	722.5
10	Deduct: Beginning inventory (pounds)	(178)	(335)	(237.5)
11	Materials to be purchased (pounds)	512	572.5	485.0
12				
13	Material price per pound	$ 20	$ 20	$ 20
14	Total cost of direct materials purchases	$10,240	$11,450	$9,700

Materials needed for production
+ Budgeted ending mtls. inventory
– Beginning mtls. inventory
= Materials to be purchased

*From production budget (Exhibit 22.6).
**Computed from January 2018 production requirements, assumed to be 990 units. 990 units × 0.5 lbs. per unit × 50% safety stock = 247.5 lbs.

5 The direct materials budget next translates the *pounds* of direct materials to be purchased into budgeted *costs*. TSC estimates that the cost of direct materials will be $20 per pound over the quarter. At $20 per pound, purchasing 512 pounds of direct materials for October production will cost $10,240 (computed as $20 × 512). Similar calculations yield the cost of direct materials purchases for November ($11,450) and December ($9,700). (For December, assume the budgeted ending inventory of direct materials, based on January's production requirements, is 247.5 pounds).

If the company expects direct materials costs to change in the future, it can easily include changes in the direct materials budget. For example, if the price of wood jumps to $25 per pound in December—say, because a long-term contract with the supplier was about to expire—TSC could simply change December's material price per pound in the direct materials budget.

Direct Labor Budget   The **direct labor budget** shows the budgeted costs for the direct labor that will be needed to satisfy the budgeted production for the period. Because there is no "inventory" of labor, the direct labor budget is easier to prepare than the direct materials budget.

A direct labor budget requires the following inputs:

1 Number of units to produce (from the production budget).

2 Labor requirements per unit—direct labor hours for each unit of finished product.

3 Cost per direct labor hour.

Budgeted amount of direct labor cost is computed as:

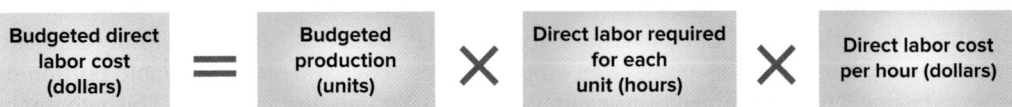

| **Budgeted direct labor cost (dollars)** | **=** | **Budgeted production (units)** | **×** | **Direct labor required for each unit (hours)** | **×** | **Direct labor cost per hour (dollars)** |

TSC's direct labor budget is shown in Exhibit 22.8.

1 The budgeted production line is taken from the production budget.

2 Fifteen minutes of labor time (a quarter of an hour) are required to produce one unit. Compute budgeted direct labor hours by multiplying the budgeted production for each month by one-quarter (0.25) of an hour.

3 Labor is paid $12 per hour. Compute the total cost of direct labor by multiplying budgeted labor hours by the labor rate of $12 per hour.

Estimated changes in direct labor costs can be easily included in the budgeting process. Companies thus can ensure the right amount of direct labor for periods in which production is expected to change or to take into account expected changes in direct labor rates.

Point: A quarter of an hour can be expressed as 0.25 hours (15 minutes/60 minutes = 0.25 hours).

EXHIBIT 22.8

Direct Labor Budget

Example: If TSC can reduce its direct labor requirements to 0.20 hours per unit by paying $14 per hour for more skilled workers, what is the total direct labor cost for December? *Answer:* $2,660.

	A	B	C	D
1	TORONTO STICKS COMPANY			
2	Direct Labor Budget			
3	October 2017–December 2017			
4		October	November	December
5	Budgeted production (units)*	710	1,340	950
6	Direct labor requirements per unit (hours)	× 0.25	× 0.25	× 0.25
7	Total direct labor hours needed	177.5	335	237.5
8				
9	Direct labor rate (per hour)	$ 12	$ 12	$ 12
10	Total cost of direct labor	$2,130	$4,020	$2,850

*From production budget (Exhibit 22.6).

NEED-TO-KNOW 22-3

Direct Materials and Direct Labor Budgets

P1

A manufacturing company budgets production of 800 units during June and 900 units during July. Each unit of finished goods requires 2 pounds of direct materials, at a cost of $8 per pound. The company maintains an inventory of direct materials equal to 10% of next month's budgeted production. Beginning direct materials inventory for June is 160 pounds. Each finished unit requires 1 hour of direct labor at the rate of $14 per hour. Compute the budgeted (a) cost of direct materials purchases for June and (b) direct labor cost for June.

Solution

a.

Direct Materials Budget (June)

Budgeted production (units)	800
Materials requirements per unit (lbs.)	× 2
Materials needed for production (lbs.)	1,600
Add: Budgeted ending inventory (lbs.)	180*
Total materials requirements (lbs.)	1,780
Less: Beginning inventory (lbs.)	(160)
Materials to be purchased (lbs.)	1,620
Material price per pound	$ 8
Total cost of direct materials purchases	$12,960

*900 units × 2 lbs. per unit × 10% = 180 lbs.

b.

Direct Labor Budget (June)

Budgeted production (units)	800
Labor requirements per unit (hours)	× 1
Total direct labor hours needed.	800
Labor rate (per hour)	$ 14
Direct labor cost (June)	$11,200

> Do More: QS 22-7, QS 22-8, QS 22-13, QS 22-14, E 22-4, E 22-5, E 22-8

Factory Overhead Budget   The **factory overhead budget** shows the budgeted costs for factory overhead that will be needed to complete the budgeted production for the period. TSC's factory overhead budget is shown in Exhibit 22.9. TSC separates variable and fixed overhead costs in its overhead budget, as do many companies.

Separating variable and fixed overhead costs enables companies to more closely estimate changes in overhead costs as production volume varies. TSC assigns the variable portion of overhead using a predetermined overhead rate of $2.50 per unit of production. This rate might

Point: Companies can use scatter diagrams, the high-low method, or regression analysis to classify overhead costs as fixed or variable.

EXHIBIT 22.9

Factory Overhead Budget

	A	B	C	D
1	TORONTO STICKS COMPANY			
2	Factory Overhead Budget			
3	October 2017–December 2017			
4		October	November	December
5	Budgeted production (units)*	710	1,340	950
6	Variable factory overhead rate	× $ 2.50	× $ 2.50	× $ 2.50
7	Budgeted variable overhead	1,775	3,350	2,375
8	Budgeted fixed overhead	1,500	1,500	1,500
9	Budgeted total overhead	$3,275	$4,850	$3,875

*From production budget (Exhibit 22.6).

be based on inputs such as direct materials costs, machine hours, direct labor hours, or other activity measures.

TSC's fixed overhead consists entirely of depreciation on manufacturing equipment. From Exhibit 22.3, this is computed as $18,000 per year [($200,000 – $20,000)/10 years], or $1,500 per month ($18,000/12 months). This fixed overhead cost stays constant at $1,500 per month.

The budget in Exhibit 22.9 is in condensed form; most overhead budgets are more detailed, listing each overhead cost item. Overhead budgets also commonly include supervisor salaries, indirect materials, indirect labor, utilities, and maintenance of manufacturing equipment. We explain these more detailed overhead budgets in the next chapter.

Product Cost per Unit   With the information from the three manufacturing budgets (direct materials, direct labor, and factory overhead), we can compute TSC's product cost per unit. This amount is useful in computing cost of goods sold and preparing a budgeted income statement, as we show later. For budgeting purposes, TSC assumes it will normally produce 3,000 units of product each quarter, yielding fixed overhead of $1.50 per unit (computed as $4,500/3,000). TSC's other product costs are all variable. Exhibit 22.10 summarizes the product cost per unit calculation.

Product Cost	Per Unit
Direct materials (½ pound of materials × $20 per pound of materials)	$10.00
Direct labor (0.25 hours of direct labor × $12 per hour of direct labor).	3.00
Variable overhead (from predetermined overhead rate).	2.50
Fixed overhead ($4,500 total fixed overhead per quarter/3,000 units of expected production per quarter).	1.50
Total product cost per unit*	$17.00

*At the normal production level of 3,000 units per quarter.

EXHIBIT 22.10

Product Cost per Unit

Selling Expense Budget   The **selling expense budget** is an estimate of the types and amounts of selling expenses expected during the budget period. It is usually prepared by the vice president of marketing or a sales manager. Budgeted selling expenses are based on the sales budget, plus a fixed amount of sales manager salaries.

TSC's selling expense budget is in Exhibit 22.11. The firm's selling expenses consist of commissions paid to sales personnel and a $2,000 monthly salary paid to the sales manager. Sales commissions equal 10% of total sales and are paid in the month sales occur. Sales commissions vary with sales volume, but the sales manager's salary is fixed. Other common selling expenses include advertising, delivery expenses, and marketing expenses.

	A	B	C	D	E
1		TORONTO STICKS COMPANY			
2		Selling Expense Budget			
3		October 2017–December 2017			
4		October	November	December	Totals
5	Budgeted sales*	$60,000	$48,000	$ 84,000	$192,000
6	Sales commission %	× 10%	× 10%	× 10%	× 10%
7	Sales commissions	6,000	4,800	8,400	19,200
8	Salary for sales manager	2,000	2,000	2,000	6,000
9	Total selling expenses	$ 8,000	$ 6,800	$ 10,400	$ 25,200

*From sales budget (Exhibit 22.4).

EXHIBIT 22.11

Selling Expense Budget

Example: If TSC expects a 12% sales commission will result in budgeted sales of $220,000 for the quarter, what is the total amount of selling expenses for the quarter? *Answer:* $32,400.

General and Administrative Expense Budget   The **general and administrative expense budget** plans the predicted operating expenses not included in the selling expenses or manufacturing budgets. The office manager responsible for general administration often is responsible for preparing the general and administrative expense budget.

Point: Some companies combine selling and general administrative expenses into a single budget.

Exhibit 22.12 shows TSC's general and administrative expense budget. It includes salaries of $54,000 per year, or $4,500 per month (paid each month when they are earned). Insurance, taxes, and depreciation on nonmanufacturing assets are other common examples of general and administrative expenses.

EXHIBIT 22.12

General and Administrative Expense Budget

	A	B	C	D	E
1	TORONTO STICKS COMPANY				
2	General and Administrative Expense Budget				
3	October 2017–December 2017				
4		October	November	December	Totals
5	Administrative salaries	$4,500	$4,500	$4,500	$13,500
6	Total general and administrative expenses	$4,500	$4,500	$4,500	$13,500

Example: In Exhibit 22.12, how would a rental agreement of $5,000 per month plus 1% of sales affect the general and administrative expense budget? (Budgeted sales are in Exhibit 22.4.) *Answer: Rent expense:* Oct. = $5,600; Nov. = $5,480; Dec. = $5,840; Total = $16,920; *Revised total general and administrative expenses:* Oct. = $10,100; Nov. = $9,980; Dec. = $10,340; Total = $30,420.

 **Decision** Insight

No Biz Like Snow Biz   Ski resorts' costs of making snow are in the millions of dollars for equipment alone. Snowmaking involves spraying droplets of water into the air, causing them to freeze and come down as snow. Making snow can cost more than $2,000 an hour. Snowmaking accounts for 40 to 50 percent of the budgeted costs for many ski resorts. ■

© Gail Shotlander/Getty Images

NEED-TO-KNOW 22-4

Selling and General and Administrative Expense Budgets

P1

Do More: QS 22-5, QS 22-11

A manufacturing company budgets sales of $70,000 during July. It pays sales commissions of 5% of sales and also pays a sales manager a salary of $3,000 per month. Other monthly costs include depreciation on office equipment ($500), insurance expense ($200), advertising ($1,000), and an office manager salary of $2,500 per month. For the month of July, compute the total (a) budgeted selling expense and (b) budgeted general and administrative expense.

Solution

a. Total budgeted selling expense = ($70,000 × 5%) + $3,000 + $1,000 = $7,500

b. Total budgeted general and administrative expense = $500 + $200 + $2,500 = $3,200

Investing Budgets

Information from operating budgets in the prior section is useful in preparing the capital expenditures budget—a key part of investing budgets.

Investing Budgets

Capital expenditures

Capital Expenditures Budget   The **capital expenditures budget** shows dollar amounts estimated to be spent to purchase additional plant assets and any cash expected to be received from plant asset disposals. This means the capital expenditures budget shows the company's expected investing activities in plant assets. It is usually prepared after the operating budgets. Since a company's plant assets determine its productive capacity, this budget is usually affected by long-range plans for the business. The process of preparing other budgets can reveal that the company requires more (or less) plant assets.

TSC does not anticipate disposal of any plant assets through December 2017, but it does plan to buy additional equipment for $25,000 cash near the end of December 2017. This is the only budgeted capital expenditure from October 2017 through December 2017. Thus, no separate budget is shown. TSC's cash budget will reflect this $25,000 planned expenditure.

Financing Budgets

Once we prepare operating and investing budgets, we normally proceed to financing budgets such as the cash budget, which is the focus of this section.

Cash Budget   A **cash budget** shows expected cash inflows and outflows during the budget period. Managing cash flows is vital for a firm's success. Most companies set an amount of cash they require. The cash budget is important because it helps the company meet this cash balance goal. If the cash budget indicates a potential cash shortfall, the company can prearrange loans to meet its obligations. If the cash budget indicates a potential cash windfall, the company can plan to pay off prior loans or make other investments. Exhibit 22.13 shows the general formula for the cash budget.

P2_____

Prepare a cash budget.

Financing Budgets

Cash budgets

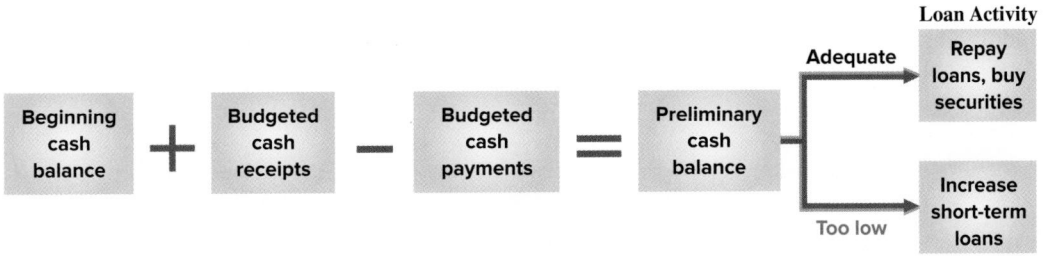

EXHIBIT 22.13

General Formula for Cash Budget

When preparing a cash budget, add budgeted cash receipts to the beginning cash balance and subtract budgeted cash payments. If the preliminary cash balance is too low, additional cash requirements appear in the budget as planned increases from short-term loans. If the preliminary cash balance exceeds the balance the company wants to maintain, the excess is used to repay loans (if any) or to acquire short-term investments.

Information for preparing the cash budget is mainly taken from the operating and capital expenditures budgets. Preparing the cash budget typically requires the preparation of other supporting schedules; we show the first of these, a schedule of cash receipts from sales, next.

Cash Receipts from Sales   Managers use the sales budget and knowledge about how frequently customers pay on credit sales to budget monthly cash receipts. To illustrate, Exhibit 22.14 presents TSC's schedule of budgeted cash receipts.

EXHIBIT 22.14

Computing Budgeted Cash Receipts from Sales

	A	B	C	D	E
1	TORONTO STICKS COMPANY				
2	Schedule of Cash Receipts from Sales				
3	October 2017–December 2017				
4		September	October	November	December
5	Sales*	$42,000	$60,000	$48,000	$84,000
6	Less: Ending accounts receivable (60%)	25,200**	36,000	28,800	50,400
7	Cash receipts from				
8	Cash sales (40% of sales)		24,000	19,200	33,600
9	Collections of prior month's receivables		25,200	36,000	28,800
10	Total cash receipts		$49,200	$55,200	$62,400

*From sales budget (Exhibit 22.4).
**Accounts receivable balance from September 30 balance sheet (Exhibit 22.3).

We begin with TSC's budgeted sales (Exhibit 22.4). Analysis of past sales indicates that 40% of the firm's sales are for cash. The remaining 60% are credit sales; these customers are expected to pay in full in the month following the sales. We now can compute the budgeted cash receipts from customers, as shown in Exhibit 22.14. October's budgeted cash receipts consist of $24,000 from expected October cash sales ($60,000 × 40%) plus the anticipated collection of $25,200 of accounts receivable from the end of September.

Alternative Collection Timing   The schedule above can be modified for alternative collection timing and/or uncollectible accounts. For example, if TSC collects 80% of credit sales in the

Point: Budgeted cash collections can be impacted by transaction fees for credit or debit cards. Companies like **Visa** and **American Express** charge different credit card fees, and banks charge fees to use debit cards.

first month after sale, 20% of credit sales in the second month after sale, and all other assumptions are unchanged, budgeted cash receipts for December are:

December budgeted cash receipts with alternative collection timing	
Cash receipts from December cash sales.....................................	$ 33,600
Collections of November's receivables ($48,000 × 60% × 80%)...................	23,040
Collections of October's receivables ($60,000 × 60% × 20%).....................	7,200
Total cash receipts	**$63,840**

Uncollectible Accounts   Some companies consider uncollectible accounts in their cash budgets. To do so, multiply credit sales by $(1 - \%$ of uncollectible receivables). For example, if in addition to the alternative collection timing above TSC estimates that 5% of all credit sales will not be collected, it computes its December cash receipts as:

December budgeted cash receipts with alternative collection timing and uncollectible accounts	
Cash receipts from December cash sales......................................	$ 33,600
Collections of November's receivables ($48,000 × 95% × 60% × 80%).............	21,888
Collections of October's receivables ($60,000 × 95% × 60% × 20%)...............	6,840
Total cash receipts	**$62,328**

Cash Payments for Materials   Managers use the beginning balance sheet (Exhibit 22.3) and the direct materials budget (Exhibit 22.7) to help prepare a schedule of cash payments for materials. Managers must also know *how* TSC purchases direct materials (pay cash or on account), and for credit purchases, how quickly TSC pays. TSC's materials purchases are entirely on account. It makes full payment during the month following its purchases. Using this information, the schedule of cash payments for materials is shown in Exhibit 22.15.

EXHIBIT 22.15

Computing Cash Payments for Materials Purchases

	A	B	C	D
1	**TORONTO STICKS COMPANY**			
2	**Schedule of Cash Payments for Direct Materials**			
3	**October 2017–December 2017**			
4		**October**	**November**	**December**
5	Materials purchases*	$10,240	$11,450	$ 9,700
6	Cash payments for			
7	Current month purchases (0%)	0	0	0
8	Prior month purchases (100%)	7,060**	10,240	11,450
9	Total cash payments for direct materials	$ 7,060	$10,240	$11,450

*From direct materials budget (Exhibit 22.7).

**Accounts Payable balance from September 30 balance sheet (Exhibit 22.3).

The schedule above can be modified for alternative payment timing. For example, if TSC paid for 20% of its purchases in the month of purchase and paid the remaining 80% of a month's purchases in the following month, its cash payments in December would equal $11,100, computed as (20% × $9,700) plus (80% × $11,450).

Preparing the Cash Budget   The cash budget summarizes many other budgets in terms of their effects on cash. To prepare the cash budget, TSC's managers use the budgets and other schedules listed below.

1. Cash receipts from sales (Exhibit 22.14).
2. Cash payments for direct materials (Exhibit 22.15).
3. Cash payments for direct labor (Exhibit 22.8).

4. Cash payments for overhead (Exhibit 22.9).
5. Cash payments for selling expenses (Exhibit 22.11).
6. Cash payments for general and administrative expenses (Exhibit 22.12).

The *fixed overhead* assigned to depreciation in the factory overhead budget (Exhibit 22.9) does not require a cash payment. Therefore, it is not included in the cash budget. Other types of fixed overhead—such as payments for property taxes and insurance—*are* included if they require cash payments.

   Additional information is typically needed to prepare the cash budget. For TSC, this additional information includes:

1. Income taxes payable (from the beginning balance sheet, Exhibit 22.3).
2. Expected dividend payments: TSC plans to pay $3,000 of cash dividends in the second month of each quarter.
3. Loan activity: TSC wants to maintain a minimum cash balance of $20,000 at each month-end. This is important, as it helps ensure TSC maintains enough cash to pay its bills as they come due. If TSC borrows cash, it must pay interest at the rate of 1% per month.

Exhibit 22.16 shows the full cash budget for TSC. The company begins October with $20,000 in cash. To this is added $49,200 in expected cash receipts from customers (from Exhibit 22.14). We next subtract expected cash payments for direct materials, direct labor, overhead, selling expenses, and general and administrative expenses. Income taxes of $20,000 were due as of the end of September 30, 2017, and payable in October. We next discuss TSC's loan activity, including any interest payments.

Courtesy JJW Images

EXHIBIT 22.16

Cash Budget

	A	B	C	D
1	**TORONTO STICKS COMPANY**			
2	**Cash Budget**			
3	**October 2017–December 2017**			
4		**October**	**November**	**December**
5	Beginning cash balance	$20,000	$20,000	$ 38,881
6	Add: Cash receipts from customers (Exhibit 22.14)	49,200	55,200	62,400
7	Total cash available	69,200	75,200	101,281
8	Less: Cash payments for			
9	Direct materials (Exhibit 22.15)	7,060	10,240	11,450
10	Direct labor (Exhibit 22.8)	2,130	4,020	2,850
11	Variable overhead (Exhibit 22.9)	1,775	3,350	2,375
12	Sales commissions (Exhibit 22.11)	6,000	4,800	8,400
13	Sales salaries (Exhibit 22.11)	2,000	2,000	2,000
14	General and administrative expenses (Exhibit 22.12)	4,500	4,500	4,500
15	Income taxes payable (Exhibit 22.3)	20,000		
16	Dividends		3,000	
17	Interest on bank loan			
18	October ($10,000 × 1%)*	100		
19	November ($4,365 × 1%)**		44	
20	Purchase of equipment			25,000
21	Total cash payments	43,565	31,954	56,575
22	Preliminary cash balance	$25,635	$43,246	$ 44,706
23	Loan activity			
24	Additional loan from bank			
25	Repayment of loan to bank	5,635	4,365	
26	Ending cash balance	$20,000	$38,881	$ 44,706
27	Loan balance, end of month†	$ 4,365	$ 0	$ 0

Cash			
Oct. 1	20,000		
Receipts	49,200		
		43,565	Payments
Prelim. bal.	25,635		
		5,635	Repay loan
Oct. 31	20,000		

* Beginning loan balance (note payable) from Exhibit 22.3.   ** Rounded to the nearest dollar.
† Beginning loan balance + New loans – Loan repayments. For October: $10,000 – $5,635 = $4,365.

Loan Activity   TSC has an agreement with its bank that promises additional loans at each month-end, if necessary, so that the company keeps a minimum cash balance of $20,000. If the cash balance exceeds $20,000 at month-end, TSC uses the excess to repay loans (if any) or buy short-term investments. If the cash balance is less than $20,000 at month-end, the bank loans TSC the difference.

At the end of each month, TSC pays the bank interest on any outstanding loan amount, at the monthly rate of 1% of the beginning balance of these loans. For October, this payment of $100 is 1% of the $10,000 note payable amount reported in the September 30 balance sheet of Exhibit 22.3. For November, TSC expects to pay interest of $44, computed as 1% of the $4,365 expected loan balance at October 31. No interest is budgeted for December because the company expects to repay the loans in full at the end of November. Exhibit 22.16 shows that the October 31 cash balance increases to $25,635 (before any loan-related activity). This amount is more than the $20,000 minimum. Thus, TSC will use the excess cash of $5,635 (computed as $25,635 − $20,000) to pay off a portion of its loan. At the end of November, TSC's preliminary cash balance is sufficient to pay off its remaining loan balance.

Had TSC's preliminary cash balance been below the $20,000 minimum in any month, TSC would have increased its loan from the bank so that the ending cash balance was $20,000. We show an example of this situation in **Need-To-Know 22-7** at the end of this chapter.

■ **Decision** Insight

Cash Cushion   Why do some companies maintain a minimum cash balance even when the budget shows extra cash is not needed? For example, **Apple's** cash and short-term investments balance is over $40 billion. According to Apple's CEO, Tim Cook, the cushion provides "flexibility and security," important in navigating uncertain economic times. A cash cushion enables companies to jump on new ventures or acquisitions that may present themselves. The **Boston Red Sox** keep a cash cushion for its trades involving players with "cash considerations." ■

© Adam Glanzman/Getty Images

NEED-TO-KNOW 22-5

Cash Budget

P2

Part 1

Diaz Co. predicts sales of $80,000 for January and $90,000 for February. Seventy percent of Diaz's sales are for cash, and the remaining 30% are credit sales. All credit sales are collected in the month after sale. January's beginning accounts receivable balance is $20,000. Compute budgeted cash receipts for January and February.

Solution

Budgeted Cash Receipts	January	February
Sales	$80,000	$90,000
Less: Ending accounts receivable (30%)	24,000 ⌐	27,000
Cash receipts from		
Cash sales (70% of sales)	56,000	63,000
Collections of prior month's receivables	20,000 └→	24,000
Total cash receipts	$76,000	$87,000

Do More: QS 22-6, QS 22-10, QS 22-19, E 22-18

Part 2

Use the following information to prepare a cash budget for the month ended January 31 for Garcia Company. The company requires a minimum $30,000 cash balance at the end of each month. Any preliminary cash balance above $30,000 is used to repay loans (if any). Garcia has a $2,000 loan outstanding at the beginning of January.

a. January 1 cash balance, $30,000

b. Cash receipts from sales, $132,000

c. Budgeted cash payments for materials, $63,500

d. Budgeted cash payments for labor, $33,400

e. Other budgeted cash expenses,* $8,200

f. Cash repayment of bank loan, $2,000

*Including loan interest for January.

Solution

GARCIA COMPANY		
Cash Budget		
For Month Ended January 31		
Beginning cash balance	$ 30,000	
Add: Cash receipts from sales...............	132,000	
Total cash available		$162,000
Less: Cash payments for		
Direct materials	63,500	
Direct labor	33,400	
Other cash expenses....................	8.200	
Total cash payments		105,100
Preliminary cash balance.................		$ 56,900
Loan activity:		
Repayment of loan to bank...............		2,000
Ending cash balance		$ 54,900
Loan balance, end of month		$ 0

Do More: QS 22-24, E 22-17, E 22-21, E 22-22

BUDGETED FINANCIAL STATEMENTS

One of the final steps in the budgeting process is summarizing the financial statement effects. We next illustrate TSC's budgeted income statement and budgeted balance sheet.

P3

Prepare budgeted financial statements.

Budgeted Income Statement

The **budgeted income statement** is a managerial accounting report showing predicted amounts of sales and expenses for the budget period. It summarizes the predicted income effects of the budgeted activities. Information needed to prepare a budgeted income statement is primarily taken from already-prepared budgets. The volume of information summarized in the budgeted income statement is so large for some companies that they often use spreadsheets to accumulate the budgeted transactions and classify them by their effects on income.

We condense TSC's budgeted income statement and show it in Exhibit 22.17. All information in this exhibit is taken from the component budgets we've examined in this chapter. Also, we now can predict the amount of income tax expense for the quarter, computed as 40% of the budgeted pretax income. For TSC, these taxes are not payable until January 31, 2018. Thus, these taxes are not shown on the October–December 2017 cash budget in Exhibit 22.16, but they are included on the December 31, 2017, balance sheet (shown next).

Budgeted Financial Statements
Income statement
Balance sheet

Point: Lenders often require potential borrowers to provide cash budgets, budgeted income statements, and budgeted balance sheets, as well as data on past performance.

EXHIBIT 22.17

Budgeted Income Statement

TORONTO STICKS COMPANY		
Budgeted Income Statement		
For Three Months Ended December 31, 2017		
Sales (Exhibit 22.4, 3,200 units @ $60)		$192,000
Cost of goods sold (3,200 units @ $17)*		54,400
Gross profit		137,600
Operating expenses		
Sales commissions (Exhibit 22.11)	$19,200	
Sales salaries (Exhibit 22.11)	6,000	
Administrative salaries (Exhibit 22.12)	13,500	
Interest expense (Exhibit 22.16).................	144	38,844
Income before income taxes		98,756
Income tax expense ($98,756 × 40%)**		39,502
Net income		$ 59,254

*$17 product cost per unit from Exhibit 22.10.   **Rounded to the nearest dollar.

Budgeted Balance Sheet

The final step in preparing the master budget is summarizing the company's predicted financial position. The **budgeted balance sheet** shows predicted amounts for the company's assets, liabilities, and equity as of the end of the budget period. TSC's budgeted balance sheet in Exhibit 22.18 is prepared using information from the other budgets. The sources of amounts are reported in the notes to the budgeted balance sheet.

EXHIBIT 22.18

Budgeted Balance Sheet

TORONTO STICKS COMPANY		
Budgeted Balance Sheet		
December 31, 2017		
Assets		
Cash[a]		$ 44,706
Accounts receivable[b]		50,400
Raw materials inventory[c]		4,950
Finished goods inventory[d]		13,770
Equipment[e]	$225,000	
Less: Accumulated depreciation[f]	40,500	184,500
Total assets		$298,326
Liabilities and Equity		
Liabilities		
Accounts payable[g]	$ 9,700	
Income taxes payable[h]	39,502	$ 49,202
Stockholders' equity		
Common stock[i]	150,000	
Retained earnings[j]	99,124	249,124
Total liabilities and equity		$298,326

Retained Earnings

		42,870	Sep. 30
		59,254	Net income
Dividends	3,000		
		99,124	Oct. 31

[a] Ending balance for December from the cash budget (in Exhibit 22.16).

[b] 60% of $84,000 sales budgeted for December from the sales budget (in Exhibit 22.4).

[c] 247.5 pounds of raw materials in budgeted ending inventory at the budgeted cost of $20 per pound (direct materials budget, Exhibit 22.7).

[d] 810 units in budgeted finished goods inventory (Exhibit 22.6) at the budgeted cost of $17 per unit (Exhibit 22.10).

[e] September 30 balance of $200,000 from the beginning balance sheet in Exhibit 22.3 plus $25,000 cost of new equipment from the cash budget in Exhibit 22.16.

[f] September 30 balance of $36,000 from the beginning balance sheet in Exhibit 22.3 plus $4,500 depreciation expense from the factory overhead budget in Exhibit 22.9.

[g] Budgeted cost of materials purchases for December from Exhibit 22.7, to be paid in January.

[h] Income tax expense from the budgeted income statement for the fourth quarter in Exhibit 22.17, to be paid in January.

[i] Unchanged from the beginning balance sheet in Exhibit 22.3.

[j] September 30 balance of $42,870 from the beginning balance sheet in Exhibit 22.3 plus budgeted net income of $59,254 from the budgeted income statement in Exhibit 22.17 minus budgeted cash dividends of $3,000 from the cash budget in Exhibit 22.16.

Using the Master Budget

For a master budget to be cost-beneficial, managers must use it to plan and control activities. The master budget is clearly a plan for future activities. In addition, any stage in the master budgeting process might reveal undesirable outcomes. The new information can cause management to change its decisions. For example, an early version of the cash budget could show an insufficient amount of cash unless cash outlays are reduced. This information could yield a reduction in planned equipment purchases. Likewise, a budgeted balance sheet might reveal too much debt from too many planned equipment purchases; the company could reduce its planned equipment purchases and thus reduce its need for borrowing.

In *controlling* operations, managers typically compare actual results to budgeted results. Differences between actual and budgeted results are called *variances*. Management examines variances, particularly large ones, to identify areas for improvement and take corrective action. We discuss variances in more detail in the next chapter.

Budgeting for Service Companies

Service providers also use master budgets. Since service providers do not manufacture goods and hold no inventory, they typically need fewer operating budgets than manufacturers do. Exhibit 22.19 shows the master budget process for a service provider.

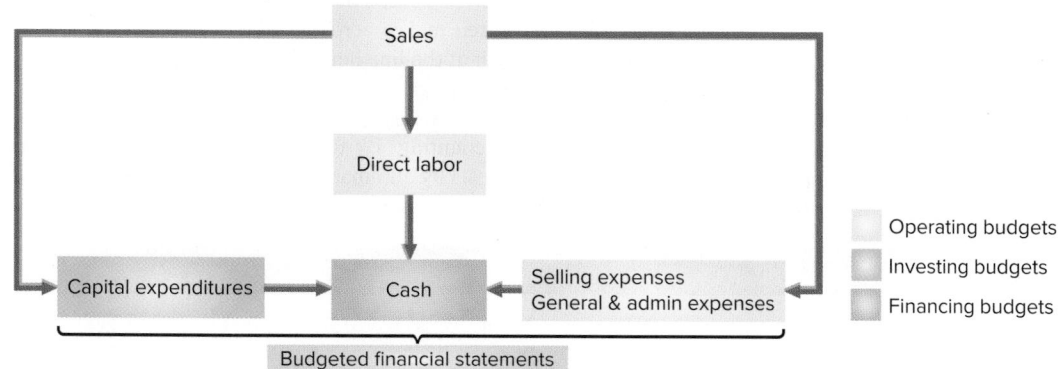

EXHIBIT 22.19

Master Budget Process for a Service Company

Exhibit 22.19 shows that service providers *do not prepare production, direct materials, or factory overhead budgets.* In addition, because many services such as accounting, banking, and landscaping are labor-intensive, the direct labor budget is important. If an accounting firm greatly underestimates the hours needed to complete an audit, it might charge too low a price. If the accounting firm greatly overestimates the hours needed, it might bid too high a price (and lose jobs) or incur excessive labor costs. Either way, the firm's profits can suffer if its direct labor budget is unrealistic.

 **SUSTAINABILITY AND ACCOUNTING**

Budgets translate an organization's strategic goals into dollar terms. When deciding on strategic goals, managers must consider their effects on budgets. **Johnson & Johnson**, a large manufacturer of pharmaceuticals, medical devices, and consumer health products, sets goals for both profits and sustainable practices. A recent company sustainability report discusses several sustainability goals and strategies, including some shown in Exhibit 22.20.

Sustainability Goal	Strategy to Achieve Goal
Reduce waste by 10%.	Purchase pulping machine to grind and recycle packaging.
Reduce CO_2 emissions by 20%.	Purchase hybrid vehicles.
Reduce water usage by 10%.	Update plumbing, install water recovery systems, employee training.

EXHIBIT 22.20

Sustainability Goals and Strategies

Several of the company's strategies involve asset purchases that will impact the capital expenditures budget. Additional employee training will impact the overhead budget. By reducing waste, increasing recycling, and reducing water usage, the company hopes to reduce some of the costs reflected in the direct materials and overhead budgets. Company managers periodically evaluate performance with respect to these goals and make any necessary adjustments to budgets.

TaTa Topper, this chapter's feature company, incorporates sustainability into its packaging. "We make our packaging as small as possible," says co-founder Marilyn Collins. "It reduces shelf space, which means our product is more likely to appear in stores, and it's good for the environment."

The owners discovered that by having the manufacturer hand roll rather than vacuum seal the toppers, they could use smaller boxes and avoid shipping problems due to their product bulging out of the boxes. These types of continuous improvements help companies both profit and reduce their environmental impact.

Courtesy of TaTa Topper

Decision Analysis    **Activity-Based Budgeting**

A1

Analyze expense planning using activity-based budgeting.

Activity-based budgeting (ABB) is a budget system based on expected *activities*. Knowledge of expected activities and their levels for the budget period enables management to plan for resources required to perform the activities.

Exhibit 22.21 contrasts a traditional budget with an activity-based budget for a company's accounting department. With a traditional budget, management often makes across-the-board budget cuts or increases. For example, management might decide that each of the line items in the traditional budget must be cut by 5%. This might not be a good strategic decision.

ABB requires management to list activities performed by, say, the accounting department such as auditing, tax reporting, financial reporting, and cost accounting. By focusing on the relation between activities and costs, management can attempt to reduce costs by eliminating nonvalue-added activities.

EXHIBIT 22.21

Activity-Based Budgeting versus Traditional Budgeting (for an accounting department)

Traditional Budget		Activity-Based Budget	
Salaries	$152,000	Auditing	$ 58,000
Supplies......................	22,000	Tax reporting	71,000
Depreciation..................	36,000	Financial reporting	63,000
Utilities	14,000	Cost accounting	32,000
Total........................	$224,000	Total	$224,000

 Decision Maker

Environmental Manager You hold the new position of environmental control manager for a chemical company. You are asked to develop a budget for your job and identify job responsibilities. How do you proceed? ■ [*Answer:* You are unlikely to have data on this new position to use in preparing your budget. In this situation, you can use activity-based budgeting. This requires developing a list of activities to conduct, the resources required to perform these activities, and the expenses associated with these resources. You should challenge yourself to be absolutely certain that the listed activities are necessary and that the listed resources are required.]

NEED-TO-KNOW 22-6

COMPREHENSIVE 1

Master Budget—Manufacturer

Payne Company's management asks you to prepare its master budget using the following information. The budget is to cover the months of April, May, and June of 2017.

PAYNE COMPANY
Balance Sheet
March 31, 2017

Assets			Liabilities and Equity		
Cash	$ 50,000		Accounts payable	$ 63,818	
Accounts receivable	175,000		Short-term notes payable	12,000	
Raw materials inventory	30,798*		Total current liabilities		$ 75,818
Finished goods inventory	96,600**		Long-term note payable		200,000
Total current assets		$352,398	Total liabilities		275,818
Equipment	480,000		Common stock	435,000	
Less: Accumulated depreciation	(90,000)		Retained earnings	31,580	
Equipment, net		390,000	Total stockholders' equity		466,580
Total assets		$742,398	Total liabilities and equity		$742,398

*2,425 pounds @ $12.70, rounded to nearest whole dollar   **8,400 units @ $11.50 per unit

Additional Information

a. Sales for March total 10,000 units. Expected sales (in units) are: 10,500 (April), 9,500 (May), 10,000 (June), and 10,500 (July). The product's selling price is $25 per unit.

b. Company policy calls for a given month's ending finished goods inventory to equal 80% of the next month's expected unit sales. The March 31 finished goods inventory is 8,400 units, which complies with the policy. The product's manufacturing cost is $11.50 per unit, including per unit costs of $6.35 for materials (0.5 lbs. at $12.70 per lb.), $3.75 for direct labor (0.25 hour × $15 direct labor rate per hour), $0.90 for variable overhead, and $0.50 for fixed overhead. Fixed overhead consists entirely of $5,000 of monthly depreciation expense. Company policy also calls for a given month's ending raw materials inventory to equal 50% of next month's expected materials needed for production. The March 31 inventory is 2,425 units of materials, which complies with the policy. The company expects to have 2,100 units of materials inventory on June 30.

c. Sales representatives' commissions are 12% of sales and are paid in the month of the sales. The sales manager's monthly salary will be $3,500 in April and $4,000 per month thereafter.

d. Monthly general and administrative expenses include $8,000 administrative salaries and 0.9% monthly interest on the long-term note payable.

e. The company expects 30% of sales to be for cash and the remaining 70% on credit. Receivables are collected in full in the month following the sale (none is collected in the month of the sale).

f. All direct materials purchases are on credit, and no payables arise from any other transactions. One month's purchases are fully paid in the next month. Materials cost $12.70 per pound.

g. The minimum ending cash balance for all months is $50,000. If necessary, the company borrows enough cash using a short-term note to reach the minimum. Short-term notes require an interest payment of 1% at each month-end (before any repayment). If the ending cash balance exceeds the minimum, the excess will be applied to repaying the short-term notes payable balance.

h. Dividends of $100,000 are to be declared and paid in May.

i. No cash payments for income taxes are to be made during the second calendar quarter. Income taxes will be assessed at 35% in the quarter.

j. Equipment purchases of $55,000 are scheduled for June.

Required

Prepare the following budgets and other financial information as required:

1. Sales budget, including budgeted sales for July.
2. Production budget.
3. Direct materials budget. Round costs of materials purchases to the nearest dollar.
4. Direct labor budget.
5. Factory overhead budget.
6. Selling expense budget.
7. General and administrative expense budget.
8. Expected cash receipts from customers and the expected June 30 balance of accounts receivable.
9. Expected cash payments for purchases and the expected June 30 balance of accounts payable.
10. Cash budget.
11. Budgeted income statement, budgeted statement of retained earnings, and budgeted balance sheet.

SOLUTION

1.

	A	B	C	D	E
1	**Sales Budget**	**April**	**May**	**June**	**Quarter**
2	Projected unit sales	10,500	9,500	10,000	
3	Selling price per unit	× $ 25	× $ 25	× $ 25	
4	Projected sales	$262,500	$237,500	$250,000	$750,000

2.

	A	B	C	D	E
1	**Production Budget**	**April**	**May**	**June**	**Quarter**
2	Next period's unit sales (part I)	9,500	10,000	10,500	
3	Ending inventory percent	× 80%	× 80%	× 80%	
4	Desired ending inventory	7,600	8,000	8,400	
5	Current period's unit sales (part I)	10,500	9,500	10,000	
6	Required units of available production	18,100	17,500	18,400	
7	Less: Beginning inventory	8,400	7,600	8,000	
8	Total units to be produced	9,700	9,900	10,400	

3.

	A	B	C	D
1	**Direct Materials Budget**	**April**	**May**	**June**
2	Budgeted production (units) (part 2)	9,700	9,900	10,400
3	Materials requirements per unit (pounds)	× 0.5	× 0.5	× 0.5
4	Materials needed for production (pounds)	4,850	4,950	5,200
5	Add: Budgeted ending inventory (pounds)	2,475	2,600	2,100
6	Total material requirements (pounds)	7,325	7,550	7,300
7	Deduct: Beginning inventory (pounds)	2,425	2,475	2,600
8	Materials to be purchased (pounds)	4,900	5,075	4,700
9				
10	Materials price per pound	$ 12.70	$ 12.70	$ 12.70
11	Total cost of direct materials purchases	$62,230	$64,453*	$59,690

*Rounded to nearest dollar.

4.

	A	B	C	D
1	**Direct Labor Budget**	**April**	**May**	**June**
2	Budgeted production (units) (part 2)	9,700	9,900	10,400
3	Labor requirements per unit (hours)	× 0.25	× 0.25	× 0.25
4	Total labor hours needed	2,425	2,475	2,600
5				
6	Labor rate (per hour)	$ 15	$ 15	$ 15
7	Total direct labor cost	$36,375	$37,125	$39,000

5.

	A	B	C	D
1	**Factory Overhead Budget**	**April**	**May**	**June**
2	Budgeted production (units) (part 2)	9,700	9,900	10,400
3	Variable factory overhead rate	× $ 0.90	× $ 0.90	× $ 0.90
4	Budgeted variable overhead	8,730	8,910	9,360
5	Budgeted fixed overhead	5,000	5,000	5,000
6	Budgeted total overhead	$13,730	$13,910	$14,360

6.

	A	B	C	D	E
1	**Selling Expense Budget**	**April**	**May**	**June**	**Quarter**
2	Budgeted sales (part 1)	$262,500	$237,500	$250,000	$750,000
3	Commission %	× 12%	× 12%	× 12%	× 12%
4	Sales commissions	31,500	28,500	30,000	90,000
5	Manager's salary	3,500	4,000	4,000	11,500
6	Budgeted selling expenses	$ 35,000	$ 32,500	$ 34,000	$101,500

7.

	A	B	C	D	E
1	**General and Administrative Expense Budget**	**April**	**May**	**June**	**Quarter**
2	Administrative salaries	$8,000	$8,000	$8,000	$24,000
3	Interest on long-term note				
4	payable (0.9% × $200,000)	1,800	1,800	1,800	5,400
5	Budgeted general and administrative expenses	$9,800	$9,800	$9,800	$29,400

8.

	A	B	C	D	E
1	**Schedule of Cash Receipts**	**April**	**May**	**June**	**Quarter**
2	Budgeted sales (part 1)	$262,500	$237,500	$250,000	
3	Ending accounts receivable (70%)	$183,750	$166,250	$175,000	
4	Cash receipts				
5	Cash sales (30% of budgeted sales)	$ 78,750	$ 71,250	$ 75,000	$225,000
6	Collections of prior month's receivables	175,000*	183,750	166,250	525,000
7	Total cash to be collected	$253,750	$255,000	$ 241,250	$750,000

*Accounts receivable balance from March 31 balance sheet.

9.

	A	B	C	D	E
1	**Schedule of Cash Payments for Materials**	**April**	**May**	**June**	**Quarter**
2	Cash payments (equal to prior month's				
3	materials purchases)	$63,818*	$62,230	$64,453	$190,501
4	Expected June 30 balance of accounts				
5	payable (June purchases)			$59,690	

*Accounts payable balance from March 31 balance sheet.

10.

	A	B	C	D
1	**Cash Budget**	**April**	**May**	**June**
2	Beginning cash balance	$ 50,000	$137,907	$142,342
3	Add: Cash receipts from customers (part 8)	253,750	255,000	241,250
4	Total cash available	303,750	392,907	383,592
5	Less: Cash payments for			
6	Direct materials (part 9)	63,818	62,230	64,453
7	Direct labor (part 4)	36,375	37,125	39,000
8	Variable overhead (part 5)	8,730	8,910	9,360
9	Sales commissions (part 6)	31,500	28,500	30,000
10	Salaries			
11	Sales (part 6)	3,500	4,000	4,000
12	Administrative (part 7)	8,000	8,000	8,000
13	Dividends		100,000	
14	Interest on long-term note (part 7)	1,800	1,800	1,800
15	Interest on bank loan			
16	October ($12,000 × 1%)	120		
17	Purchase of equipment			55,000
18	Total cash payments	153,843	250,565	211,613
19	**Loan activity:** Preliminary cash balance	$149,907	$142,342	$171,979
20	Additional loan from bank			
21	Repayment of loan to bank	12,000	0	0
22	Ending cash balance	$137,907	$142,342	$171,979
23	Loan balance, end of month	$ 0	$ 0	$ 0

11.

PAYNE COMPANY
Budgeted Income Statement
For Quarter Ended June 30, 2017

Sales (part 1)		$750,000
Cost of goods sold (30,000 units @ $11.50)		345,000
Gross profit		405,000
Operating expenses		
Sales commissions (part 6)	$90,000	
Sales salaries (part 6)	11,500	
Administrative salaries (part 7)	24,000	
Interest on long-term note (part 7)	5,400	
Interest on short-term notes (part 10)	120	
Total operating expenses		131,020
Income before income taxes		273,980
Income taxes ($273,980 × 35%)		95,893
Net income		$178,087

PAYNE COMPANY
Budgeted Statement of Retained Earnings
For Quarter Ended June 30, 2017

Retained earnings, March 31, 2017	$ 31,580
Net income	178,087
	209,667
Less: Cash dividends (part 10)	100,000
Retained earnings, June 30, 2017	$109,667

PAYNE COMPANY
Budgeted Balance Sheet
June 30, 2017

Assets

Cash (part 10)	$171,979	
Accounts receivable (part 8)	175,000	
Raw materials inventory (2,100 pounds @ $12.70)*	26,671	
Finished goods inventory (8,400 units @ $11.50)	96,600	
Total current assets		$470,250
Equipment (Mar. 31 bal. plus purchase)	535,000	
Less: Accumulated depreciation		
(Mar. 31 bal. plus depreciation expense)	105,000	430,000
Total assets		$900,250

Liabilities and Equity

Accounts payable (part 9)	$ 59,690	
Income taxes payable	95,893	
Total current liabilities		$155,583
Long-term note payable (Mar. 31 bal.)		200,000
Total liabilities		355,583
Common stock (Mar. 31 bal.)	435,000	
Retained earnings	109,667	
Total stockholders' equity		544,667
Total liabilities and equity		$900,250

*Plus $1 rounding difference.

NEED-TO-KNOW 22-7

COMPREHENSIVE 2

Master Budget—
Merchandiser

Wild Wood Company's management asks you to prepare its master budget using the following information. The budget is to cover the months of April, May, and June of 2017. Wild Wood is a merchandiser.

WILD WOOD COMPANY Balance Sheet March 31, 2017			
Assets		**Liabilities and Equity**	
Cash	$ 50,000	Accounts payable	$156,000
Accounts receivable	175,000	Short-term notes payable	12,000
Merchandise inventory (8,400 units × $15)......	126,000	Total current liabilities	168,000
Total current assets	351,000	Long-term note payable	200,000
Equipment	480,000	Total liabilities	368,000
Less: Accumulated depreciation	(90,000)	Common stock	235,000
Equipment, net	390,000	Retained earnings	138,000
		Total stockholders' equity	373,000
Total assets	$741,000	Total liabilities and equity	$741,000

Additional Information

a. Sales for March total 10,000 units. Each month's sales are expected to exceed the prior month's results
by 5%. The product's selling price is $25 per unit.

b. Company policy calls for a given month's ending inventory to equal 80% of the next month's expected
unit sales. The March 31 inventory is 8,400 units, which complies with the policy. The purchase price
is $15 per unit.

c. Sales representatives' commissions are 12.5% of sales and are paid in the month of the sales. The sales
manager's monthly salary will be $3,500 in April and $4,000 per month thereafter.

d. Monthly general and administrative expenses include $8,000 administrative salaries, $5,000 depreciation, and 0.9% monthly interest on the long-term note payable.

e. The company expects 30% of sales to be for cash and the remaining 70% on credit. Receivables are
collected in full in the month following the sale (none is collected in the month of the sale).

f. All merchandise purchases are on credit, and no payables arise from any other transactions. One
month's purchases are fully paid in the next month.

g. The minimum ending cash balance for all months is $50,000. If necessary, the company borrows
enough cash using a short-term note to reach the minimum. Short-term notes require an interest payment of 1% at each month-end (before any repayment). If the ending cash balance exceeds the minimum, the excess will be applied to repaying the short-term notes payable balance.

h. Dividends of $100,000 are to be declared and paid in May.

i. No cash payments for income taxes are to be made during the second calendar quarter. Income taxes
will be assessed at 35% in the quarter.

j. Equipment purchases of $55,000 are scheduled for June.

Required

Prepare the following budgets and other financial information as required:

1. Sales budget, including budgeted sales for July.

2. Purchases budget.

3. Selling expense budget.

4. General and administrative expense budget.

5. Expected cash receipts from customers and the expected June 30 balance of accounts receivable.

6. Expected cash payments for purchases and the expected June 30 balance of accounts payable.

7. Cash budget.

8. Budgeted income statement, budgeted statement of retained earnings, and budgeted balance sheet.

PLANNING THE SOLUTION

● The sales budget shows expected sales for each month in the quarter. Start by multiplying March sales
by 105% and then do the same for the remaining months. July's sales are needed for the purchases
budget. To complete the budget, multiply the expected unit sales by the selling price of $25 per unit.

- Use these results and the 80% inventory policy to budget the size of ending inventory for April, May, and June. Add the budgeted sales to these numbers and subtract the actual or expected beginning inventory for each month. The result is the number of units to be purchased each month. Multiply these numbers by the per unit cost of $15. Find the budgeted cost of goods sold by multiplying the unit sales in each month by the $15 cost per unit. Compute the cost of the June 30 ending inventory by multiplying the expected units available at that date by the $15 cost per unit.

- The selling expense budget has only two items. Find the amount of the sales representatives' commissions by multiplying the expected dollar sales in each month by the 12.5% commission rate. Then include the sales manager's salary of $3,500 in April and $4,000 in May and June.

- The general and administrative expense budget should show three items. Administrative salaries are fixed at $8,000 per month, and depreciation is $5,000 per month. Budget the monthly interest expense on the long-term note by multiplying its $200,000 balance by the 0.9% monthly interest rate.

- Determine the amounts of cash sales in each month by multiplying the budgeted sales by 30%. Add to this amount the credit sales of the prior month (computed as 70% of prior month's sales). April's cash receipts from collecting receivables equals the March 31 balance of $175,000. The expected June 30 accounts receivable balance equals 70% of June's total budgeted sales.

- Determine expected cash payments on accounts payable for each month by making them equal to the merchandise purchases in the prior month. The payments for April equal the March 31 balance of accounts payable shown on the beginning balance sheet. The June 30 balance of accounts payable equals merchandise purchases for June.

- Prepare the cash budget by combining the given information and the amounts of cash receipts and cash payments on account that you computed. Complete the cash budget for each month by either borrowing enough to raise the preliminary balance to the minimum or paying off short-term debt as much as the balance allows without falling below the minimum. Show the ending balance of the short-term note in the budget.

- Prepare the budgeted income statement by combining the budgeted items for all three months. Determine the income before income taxes and multiply it by the 35% rate to find the quarter's income tax expense.

- The budgeted statement of retained earnings should show the March 31 balance plus the quarter's net income minus the quarter's dividends.

- The budgeted balance sheet includes updated balances for all items that appear in the beginning balance sheet and an additional liability for unpaid income taxes. Amounts for all asset, liability, and equity accounts can be found either in the budgets, in other calculations, or by adding amounts found there to the beginning balances.

SOLUTION

1.

	A	B	C	D	E
1	**Calculation of Unit Sales**	**April**	**May**	**June**	**July**
2	Prior period's unit sales	10,000	10,500	11,025	11,576
3	Plus 5% growth*	500	525	551	579
4	Projected unit sales	10,500	11,025	11,576	12,155

*Rounded to nearest whole unit.

	A	B	C	D	E
1	**Sales Budget**	**April**	**May**	**June**	**Quarter**
2	Projected unit sales	10,500	11,025	11,576	
3	Selling price per unit	× $ 25	× $ 25	× $ 25	
4	Projected sales	$262,500	$275,625	$289,400	$827,525

2.

	A	B	C	D	E
1	**Purchases Budget**	**April**	**May**	**June**	**Quarter**
2	Next period's unit sales (part 1)	11,025	11,576	12,155	
3	Ending inventory percent	× 80%	× 80%	× 80%	
4	Desired ending inventory (units)	8,820	9,261	9,724	
5	Add: Current period's unit sales (part 1)	10,500	11,025	11,576	
6	Units to be available	19,320	20,286	21,300	
7	Less: Beginning inventory (units)	8,400	8,820	9,261	
8	Units to be purchased	10,920	11,466	12,039	
9	Budgeted cost per unit	× $ 15	× $ 15	× $ 15	
10	Budgeted purchases	$163,800	$171,990	$180,585	$516,375

3.

	A	B	C	D	E
1	**Selling Expense Budget**	**April**	**May**	**June**	**Quarter**
2	Budgeted sales (part 1)	$262,500	$275,625	$289,400	$827,525
3	Commission %	× 12.5%	× 12.5%	× 12.5%	× 12.5%
4	Sales commissions*	32,813	34,453	36,175	103,441
5	Manager's salary	3,500	4,000	4,000	11,500
6	Budgeted selling expenses*	$ 36,313	$ 38,453	$ 40,175	$114,941

*Rounded to the nearest dollar.

4.

	A	B	C	D	E
1	**General and Administrative Expense Budget**	**April**	**May**	**June**	**Quarter**
2	Administrative salaries	$ 8,000	$ 8,000	$ 8,000	$24,000
3	Depreciation	5,000	5,000	5,000	15,000
4	Interest on long-term note payable (0.9% × $200,000)	1,800	1,800	1,800	5,400
5	Budgeted expenses	$14,800	$14,800	$14,800	$44,400

5.

	A	B	C	D	E
1	**Schedule of Cash Receipts from Sales**	**April**	**May**	**June**	**Quarter**
2	Budgeted sales (part 1)	$262,500	$275,625	$289,400	
3	Ending accounts receivable (70% of sales)	$183,750	$192,938	$202,580	
4	Cash receipts				
5	Cash sales (30% of budgeted sales)	$ 78,750	$ 82,687	$ 86,820	$248,257
6	Collections of prior month's receivables	175,000*	183,750	192,938	551,688
7	Total cash to be collected	$253,750	$266,437	$ 279,758	$799,945

*March 31 Accounts Receivable balance (from balance sheet).

6.

	A	B	C	D	E
1	**Schedule of Cash Payments to Suppliers**	**April**	**May**	**June**	**Quarter**
2	Cash payments (equal to prior month's				
3	purchases)	$156,000*	$163,800	$171,990	$491,790
4	Expected June 30 balance of accounts				
5	payable (part 2, June purchases)			$180,585	

*March 31 Accounts Payable balance (from balance sheet).

7.

	A	B	C	D
1	**Cash Budget**	**April**	**May**	**June**
2	Beginning cash balance	$ 50,000	$ 89,517	$ 50,000
3	Add: Cash receipts (part 5)	253,750	266,437	279,758
4	Total cash available	303,750	355,954	329,758
5	Less: Cash payments for			
6	Merchandise (part 6)	156,000	163,800	171,990
7	Sales commissions (part 3)	32,813	34,453	36,175
8	Salaries			
9	Sales (part 3)	3,500	4,000	4,000
10	Administrative (part 4)	8,000	8,000	8,000
11	Interest on long-term note (part 4)	1,800	1,800	1,800
12	Dividends		100,000	
13	Equipment purchase			55,000
14	Interest on short-term notes			
15	April ($12,000 × 1%)	120		
16	June ($6,099 × 1%)			61
17	Total cash payments	202,233	312,053	277,026
18	Preliminary balance	101,517	43,901	52,732
19	Loan activity			
20	Additional loan		6,099	
21	Loan repayment	(12,000)		(2,732)
22	Ending cash balance	$ 89,517	$ 50,000	$ 50,000
23	Ending short-term notes payable balance	$ 0	$ 6,099	$ 3,367

8.

WILD WOOD COMPANY
Budgeted Income Statement
For Quarter Ended June 30, 2017

Sales (part 1)		$827,525
Cost of goods sold*		496,515
Gross profit		331,010
Operating expenses		
Sales commissions (part 3)	$103,441	
Sales salaries (part 3)	11,500	
Administrative salaries (part 4)	24,000	
Depreciation (part 4)	15,000	
Interest on long-term note (part 4)	5,400	
Interest on short-term note (part 7)	181	
Total operating expenses		159,522
Income before income taxes		171,488
Income taxes (35%)		60,021
Net income		$111,467

*33,101 units sold @ $15 per unit

WILD WOOD COMPANY
Budgeted Statement of Retained Earnings
For Quarter Ended June 30, 2017

Beginning retained earnings (Mar. 31 bal.)	$138,000
Net income	111,467
	249,467
Less: Cash dividends (part 7)	100,000
Ending retained earnings	$149,467

WILD WOOD COMPANY
Budgeted Balance Sheet
June 30, 2017

Assets			Liabilities and Equity		
Cash (part 7)	$ 50,000		Accounts payable (part 6)	$180,585	
Accounts receivable (part 5)	202,580		Short-term notes payable (part 7)	3,367	
Inventory (9,724 units @ $15 each)	145,860		Income taxes payable	60,021	
Total current assets		$398,440	Total current liabilities		$243,973
			Long-term note payable (Mar. 31 bal.)		200,000
			Total liabilities		443,973
Equipment (Mar. 31 bal. plus purchase)	535,000		Common stock (Mar. 31 bal.)	235,000	
Less: Accumulated depreciation			Retained earnings	149,467	
(Mar. 31 bal. plus depreciation expense)	105,000	430,000	Total stockholders' equity		384,467
Total assets		$828,440	Total liabilities and equity		$828,440

Merchandise Purchases Budget

22A

Exhibit 22A.1 shows the master budget sequence for a merchandiser. Unlike a manufacturing company, a merchandiser must prepare a merchandise purchases budget rather than a production budget. In addition, a merchandiser does not prepare direct materials, direct labor, or factory overhead budgets. In this appendix we show the merchandise purchases budget for Hockey Den (HD), a retailer of hockey sticks.

P4

Prepare each component of a master budget—for a merchandising company.

EXHIBIT 22A.1

Master Budget Sequence—Merchandiser

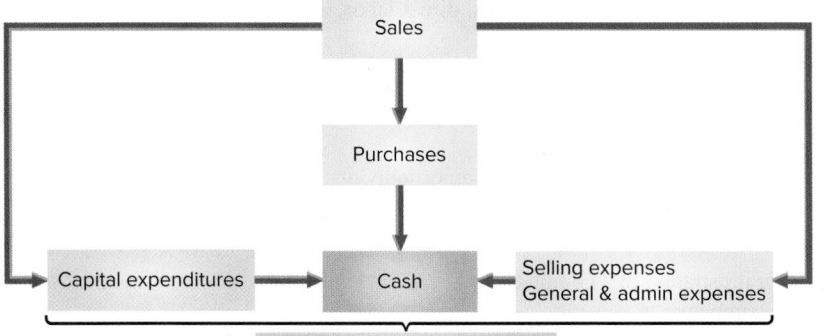

Preparing the Merchandise Purchases Budget   A merchandiser usually expresses a **merchandise purchases budget** in both units and dollars. Exhibit 22A.2 shows the general layout for this budget in equation form. If this formula is expressed in units and only one product is involved, we can compute the number of dollars of inventory to be purchased for the budget by multiplying the units to be purchased by the cost per unit.

EXHIBIT 22A.2

General Formula for Merchandise Purchases Budget

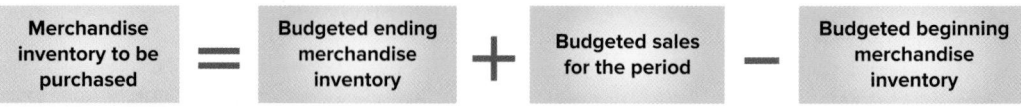

A merchandise purchases budget requires the following inputs:

1 Sales budget (in units).

2 Budgeted ending inventory (in units).

3 Cost per unit.

1   Toronto Sticks Company is an exclusive supplier of hockey sticks to HD, meaning that the companies use the same budgeted sales figures in preparing budgets. Thus, HD predicts unit sales as follows: October, 1,000; November, 800; December, 1,400; and January, 900.

2   After considering the costs of keeping inventory and inventory shortages, HD set a policy that ending inventory (in units) should equal 90% of next month's predicted sales. For example, inventory at the end of October should equal 90% of November's budgeted sales.

3   Finally, HD expects the per unit purchase cost of $60 to remain unchanged through the budgeting period. This information, along with knowledge of 1,010 units in inventory at September 30 (given), allows the company to prepare the merchandise purchases budget shown in Exhibit 22A.3.

EXHIBIT 22A.3

Merchandise Purchases Budget

Units to Purchase

Budgeted ending inventory
+ Budgeted sales
− Beginning inventory
= Units to be purchased

	A	B	C	D
1	**HOCKEY DEN**			
2	**Merchandise Purchases Budget**			
3	**October 2017–December 2017**			
4		**October**	**November**	**December**
5	Next month's budgeted sales (units)	800	1,400	900
6	Ratio of inventory to future sales	× 90%	× 90%	× 90%
7	Budgeted ending inventory (units)	720	1,260	810
8	Add: Budgeted sales (units)	1,000	800	1,400
9	Required units of available merchandise	1,720	2,060	2,210
10	Deduct: Beginning inventory (units)	1,010*	720	1,260
11	Total units to be purchased	710	1,340	950
12				
13	Budgeted cost per unit	$ 60	$ 60	$ 60
14	Budgeted cost of merchandise purchases	$42,600	$80,400	$57,000

*Does not comply with company policy.

The first three lines of HD's merchandise purchases budget determine the required ending inventories (in units). Budgeted unit sales are then added to the desired ending inventory to give the required units of available merchandise. We then subtract beginning inventory to determine the budgeted number of units to be purchased. The last line is the budgeted cost of the purchases, computed by multiplying the number of units to be purchased by the predicted cost per unit.

Other Master Budget Differences—Merchandiser vs. Manufacturer   In addition to preparing a purchases budget instead of production, direct materials, direct labor, and overhead budgets, other key differences in master budgets for merchandisers include:

● Depreciation expense is included in the general and administrative expense budget of the merchandiser. For the manufacturer, depreciation on manufacturing assets is included in the factory overhead budget and treated as a product cost.

● The budgeted balance sheet for the merchandiser will report only one asset for inventory. The balance sheet for the manufacturer will typically report three inventory assets: raw materials, work in process, and finished goods.

See Need-To-Know 22-7 for illustration of a complete master budget, including budgeted financial statements, for a merchandising company.

In preparing monthly budgets for the third quarter, a company budgeted sales of 120 units for July and 140 units for August. Management wants each month's ending inventory to be 60% of next month's sales. The June 30 inventory consists of 72 units. How many units should be purchased in July?

NEED-TO-KNOW 22-8

Merchandise Purchases Budget

P4

Solution

Merchandise Purchases Budget

	July
Next month's budgeted sales (units)................	140
Ratio of inventory to future sales..................	× 60%
Budgeted ending inventory (units)	84
Add: Budgeted sales (units)......................	+120
Required units of available merchandise	204
Deduct: Beginning inventory (units)	− 72
Units to be purchased	132

Do More: QS 22-28, QS 22-29, QS 22-30, E 22-24

Summary

C1 **Describe the benefits of budgeting.** Planning is a management responsibility of critical importance to business success. Budgeting is the process management uses to formalize its plans. Budgeting promotes management analysis and focuses its attention on the future. Budgeting also provides a basis for evaluating performance, serves as a source of motivation, is a means of coordinating activities, and communicates management's plans and instructions to employees.

C2 **Describe a master budget and the process of preparing it.** A master budget is a formal overall plan for a company. It consists of plans for business operations and capital expenditures, plus the financial results of those activities. The budgeting process begins with a sales budget. Based on expected sales volume, companies can budget production and manufacturing costs, selling expenses, and administrative expenses. Next, the capital expenditures budget is prepared, followed by the cash budget and budgeted financial statements.

A1 **Analyze expense planning using activity-based budgeting.** Activity-based budgeting requires management to identify activities performed by departments, plan necessary activity levels, identify resources required to perform these activities, and budget the resources.

P1 **Prepare each component of a master budget—for a manufacturing company.** A *master budget* is a collection of component budgets. From budgeted sales a manufacturer prepares a *production budget*. A *manufacturing budget* shows the budgeted production costs for direct materials, direct labor, and overhead. *Selling* and *general and administrative expense* budgets complete the operating budgets of the master budget. The *capital expenditures budget* reflects expected and asset purchases and disposals. The *cash budget* shows the impact of budgeted activities on cash.

P2 **Prepare a cash budget.** The cash budget shows expected cash inflows and outflows during a budgeting period. This budget helps management maintain the company's desired cash balance.

P3 **Prepare budgeted financial statements.** The operating budgets, capital expenditures budget, and cash budget contain much of the information to prepare a budgeted income statement for the budget period and a budgeted balance sheet at the end of the budget period. Budgeted financial statements show the expected financial consequences of the planned activities described in the budgets.

P4^A **Prepare each component of a master budget—for a merchandising company.** Merchandisers budget merchandise purchases instead of manufacturing costs. Merchandisers also prepare capital expenditure, selling expense, general and administrative expense, and cash budgets.

Key Terms

Activity-based budgeting (ABB)	Budgeted income statement	Continuous budgeting
Budget	Budgeting	Direct labor budget
Budgetary control	Capital expenditures budget	Direct materials budget
Budgeted balance sheet	Cash budget	Factory overhead budget

General and administrative expense budget	Production budget	Sales budget
Master budget	Rolling budget	Selling expense budget
Merchandise purchases budget	Safety stock	Zero-based budgeting

Multiple Choice Quiz

1. A plan that reports the units of merchandise to be produced by a manufacturing company during the budget period is called a

a. Capital expenditures budget.

b. Cash budget.

c. Production budget.

d. Manufacturing budget.

e. Sales budget.

2.^A A hardware store has budgeted sales of $36,000 for its power tool department in July. Management wants to have $7,000 in power tool inventory at the end of July. Its beginning inventory of power tools is expected to be $6,000. What is the budgeted dollar amount of merchandise purchases?

a. $36,000

b. $43,000

c. $42,000

d. $35,000

e. $37,000

3. A store has the following budgeted sales for the next five months.

May	$210,000
June	186,000
July	180,000
August	220,000
September	240,000

Cash sales are 25% of total sales and all credit sales are expected to be collected in the month following the sale. The total amount of cash expected to be received from customers in September is

a. $240,000.

b. $225,000.

c. $60,000.

d. $165,000.

e. $220,000.

4. A plan that shows the expected cash inflows and cash outflows during the budget period, including receipts from loans needed to maintain a minimum cash balance and repayments of such loans, is called

a. A rolling budget.

b. An income statement.

c. A balance sheet.

d. A cash budget.

e. An operating budget.

5. The following sales are predicted for a company's next four months.

	April	May	June	July
Unit sales	480	560	600	480

Each month's ending inventory of finished goods should be 30% of the next month's sales. At April 1, the finished goods inventory is 140 units. The budgeted production of units for May is

a. 572 units.

b. 560 units.

c. 548 units.

d. 600 units.

e. 180 units.

ANSWERS TO MULTIPLE CHOICE QUIZ

1. c

2. e; Budgeted purchases = $36,000 + $7,000 − $6,000 = $37,000

3. b; Cash collected = 25% of September sales + 75% of August sales = (0.25 × $240,000) + (0.75 × $220,000) = $225,000

4. d

5. a; 560 units + (0.30 × 600 units) − (0.30 × 560 units) = 572 units

---

^A *Superscript letter A denotes assignments based on Appendix 22A, which relates to budgets for merchandising companies.*

Ⓘ Icon denotes assignments that involve decision making.

Discussion Questions

1. Ⓘ Identify at least three benefits of budgeting in helping managers plan and control a business.

2. How does a budget benefit management in its control function?

3. Ⓘ What is the benefit of continuous budgeting?

4. Identify three usual time horizons for short-term planning and budgets.

5. Ⓘ Why should each department participate in preparing its own budget?

6. Ⓘ How does budgeting help management coordinate and plan business activities?

7. Ⓘ Why is the sales budget so important to the budgeting process?

8. What is a selling expense budget? What is a capital expenditures budget?

9. Identify at least two potential negative outcomes of budgeting.

10. **Google** prepares a cash budget. What is a cash budget? Why must operating budgets and the capital expenditures budget be prepared before the cash budget?   **GOOGLE**

11. **Apple** regularly uses budgets. What is the difference between a production budget and a manufacturing budget?   **APPLE**

12. 📱 Would a manager of an **Apple** retail store participate more in budgeting than a manager at the corporate offices? Explain.   **APPLE**

13. 📱 Does the manager of a **Samsung** distribution center participate in long-term budgeting? Explain.   **Samsung**

14. 📱 Assume that **Samsung's** consumer electronics division is charged with preparing a master budget. Identify the participants—for example, the sales manager for the sales budget—and describe the information each person provides in preparing the master budget.   **Samsung**

15. ♨ **Coca-Cola** recently redesigned its bottle to reduce its use of glass, thus lowering its bottle's weight and CO_2 emissions. Which budgets in the company's master budget will this redesign impact?

▨ connect

For each of the following items 1 through 5, indicate *yes* if the item is an important budgeting guideline or *no* if it is not.

_____ **1.** Employees should have the opportunity to explain differences from budgeted amounts.

_____ **2.** Budgets should include budgetary slack.

_____ **3.** Employees impacted by a budget should be consulted when it is prepared.

_____ **4.** Goals in a budget should be set low so targets can be reached.

_____ **5.** Budgetary goals should be attainable.

QUICK STUDY

QS 22-1
Budget motivation
C1

For each of the following items 1 through 6, indicate *yes* if it describes a potential benefit of budgeting or *no* if it describes a potential negative outcome of budgeting.

_____ **1.** Budgets help coordinate activities across departments.

_____ **2.** Budgets are useful in assigning blame for unexpected results.

_____ **3.** A budget forces managers to spend time planning for the future.

_____ **4.** Some employees might overstate expenses in budgets.

_____ **5.** Budgets can lead to excessive pressure to meet budgeted results.

_____ **6.** Budgets can provide incentives for good performance.

QS 22-2
Budgeting benefits
C1 📱

Identify which of the following sets of items are necessary components of the master budget.

_____ **1.** Operating budgets, historical income statement, and budgeted balance sheet.

_____ **2.** Prior sales reports, capital expenditures budget, and financial budgets.

_____ **3.** Sales budget, operating budgets, and historical financial budgets.

_____ **4.** Operating budgets, financial budgets, and capital expenditures budget.

QS 22-3
Components of a master budget
C2

Grace manufactures and sells miniature digital cameras for $250 each. 1,000 units were sold in May, and management forecasts 4% growth in unit sales each month. Determine (a) the number of units of camera sales and (b) the dollar amount of camera sales for the month of June.

QS 22-4
Sales budget   P1

Zilly Co. predicts sales of $400,000 for June. Zilly pays a sales manager a monthly salary of $6,000 and a commission of 8% of that month's sales dollars. Prepare a selling expense budget for the month of June.

QS 22-5
Selling expense budget   P1

Liza's predicts sales of $40,000 for May and $52,000 for June. Assume 60% of Liza's sales are for cash. The remaining 40% are credit sales; credit customers pay in the month following the sale. Compute the budgeted cash receipts for June.

QS 22-6
Cash budget   P2

QS 22-7
Manufacturing: Direct materials budget **P1**

Zortek Corp. budgets production of 400 units in January and 200 units in February. Each finished unit requires five pounds of raw material Z, which costs $2 per pound. Each month's ending inventory of raw materials should be 40% of the following month's budgeted production. The January 1 raw materials inventory has 130 pounds of Z. Prepare a direct materials budget for January.

QS 22-8
Manufacturing: Direct labor budget **P1**

Tora Co. plans to produce 1,020 units in July. Each unit requires two hours of direct labor. The direct labor rate is $20 per hour. Prepare a direct labor budget for July.

QS 22-9
Sales budget
P1

Scora, Inc., is preparing its master budget for the quarter ending March 31. It sells a single product for $50 per unit. Budgeted sales for the next three months follow. Prepare a sales budget for the months of January, February, and March.

	January	February	March
Sales in units	1,200	2,000	1,600

QS 22-10
Cash receipts budget **P2**

X-Tel budgets sales of $60,000 for April, $100,000 for May, and $80,000 for June. In addition, sales are 40% cash and 60% on credit. All credit sales are collected in the month following the sale. The April 1 balance in accounts receivable is $15,000. Prepare a schedule of budgeted cash receipts for April, May, and June.

QS 22-11
Selling expense budget
P1

X-Tel budgets sales of $60,000 for April, $100,000 for May, and $80,000 for June. In addition, sales commissions are 10% of sales dollars and the company pays a sales manager a salary of $6,000 per month. Sales commissions and salaries are paid in the month incurred. Prepare a selling expense budget for April, May, and June.

QS 22-12
Manufacturing:
Production budget
P1

Champ, Inc., predicts the following sales in units for the coming two months:

	May	June
Sales in units	180	200

Each month's ending inventory of finished units should be 60% of the next month's sales. The April 30 finished goods inventory is 108 units. Compute budgeted production (in units) for May.

QS 22-13
Manufacturing: Direct materials budget
P1

Miami Solar manufactures solar panels for industrial use. The company budgets production of 5,000 units (solar panels) in July and 5,300 units in August. Each unit requires 3 pounds of direct materials, which cost $6 per pound. The company's policy is to maintain direct materials inventory equal to 30% of the next month's direct materials requirement. As of June 30, the company has 4,500 pounds of direct materials in inventory, which complies with the policy. Prepare a direct materials budget for July.

QS 22-14
Manufacturing: Direct labor budget **P1**

Miami Solar budgets production of 5,000 solar panels in July. Each unit requires 4 hours of direct labor at a rate of $16 per hour. Prepare a direct labor budget for July.

QS 22-15
Manufacturing: Factory overhead budget **P1**

Miami Solar budgets production of 5,300 solar panels for August. Each unit requires 4 hours of direct labor at a rate of $16 per hour. Variable factory overhead is budgeted to be 70% of direct labor cost, and fixed factory overhead is $180,000 per month. Prepare a factory overhead budget for August.

QS 22-16
Manufacturing:
Production budget
P1

Atlantic Surf manufactures surfboards. The company's sales budget for the next three months is shown below. In addition, company policy is to maintain finished goods inventory equal (in units) to 40% of the next month's unit sales. As of June 30, the company has 1,600 finished surfboards in inventory, which complies with the policy. Prepare a production budget for the months of July and August.

	July	August	September
Sales (in units).........	4,000	6,500	3,500

Forrest Company manufactures phone chargers and has a JIT policy that ending inventory must equal 10% of the next month's sales. It estimates that October's actual ending inventory will consist of 40,000 units. November and December sales are estimated to be 400,000 and 350,000 units, respectively. Compute the number of units to be produced for the month of November.

QS 22-17
Manufacturing:
Production budget
P1

Hockey Pro budgets production of 3,900 hockey pucks during May. The company assigns variable overhead at the rate of $1.50 per unit. Fixed overhead equals $46,000 per month. Prepare a factory overhead budget for May.

QS 22-18
Manufacturing: Factory overhead budget   **P1**

Music World reports the following sales forecast: August, $150,000; and September, $170,000. Cash sales are normally 40% of total sales and all credit sales are expected to be collected in the month following the date of sale. Prepare a schedule of cash receipts for September.

QS 22-19
Cash receipts   **P2**

The Guitar Shoppe reports the following sales forecast: August, $150,000; September, $170,000. Cash sales are normally 40% of total sales, 55% of credit sales are collected in the month following sale, and the remaining 5% of credit sales are written off as uncollectible. Prepare a schedule of cash receipts for September.

QS 22-20
Cash receipts, with uncollectible accounts
P2

Wells Company reports the following sales forecast: September, $55,000; October, $66,000; and November, $80,000. All sales are on account. Collections of credit sales are received as follows: 25% in the month of sale, 60% in the first month after sale, and 10% in the second month after sale. 5% of all credit sales are written off as uncollectible. Prepare a schedule of cash receipts for November.

QS 22-21
Cash receipts, with uncollectible accounts   **P2**

Kingston anticipates total sales for June and July of $420,000 and $398,000, respectively. Cash sales are normally 60% of total sales. Of the credit sales, 20% are collected in the same month as the sale, 70% are collected during the first month after the sale, and the remaining 10% are collected in the second month after the sale. Determine the amount of accounts receivable reported on the company's budgeted balance sheet as of July 31.

QS 22-22
Computing budgeted accounts receivable
P2

Santos Co. is preparing a cash budget for February. The company has $20,000 cash at the beginning of February and anticipates $75,000 in cash receipts and $100,250 in cash payments during February. What amount, if any, must the company borrow during February to maintain a $5,000 cash balance? The company has no loans outstanding on February 1.

QS 22-23
Budgeted loan activity
P2

Use the following information to prepare a cash budget for the month ended on March 31 for Gado Company. The budget should show expected cash receipts and cash payments for the month of March and the balance expected on March 31.

a. Beginning cash balance on March 1, $72,000.
b. Cash receipts from sales, $300,000.
c. Budgeted cash payments for direct materials, $140,000.
d. Budgeted cash payments for direct labor, $80,000.
e. Other budgeted cash expenses, $45,000.
f. Cash repayment of bank loan, $20,000.

QS 22-24
Manufacturing:
Cash budget
P2

Following are selected accounts for a company. For each account, indicate whether it will appear on a budgeted income statement (BIS) or a budgeted balance sheet (BBS). If an item will not appear on either budgeted financial statement, label it NA.

QS 22-25
Budgeted financial statements
P3

Sales	_____	Interest expense on loan payable	_____
Office salaries expense	_____	Cash dividends paid	_____
Accumulated depreciation	_____	Bank loan owed	_____
Amortization expense	_____	Cost of goods sold	_____

QS 22-26ᴬ
Merchandising:
Cash payments for
merchandise   **P4**

Garda purchased $600,000 of merchandise in August and expects to purchase $720,000 in September. Merchandise purchases are paid as follows: 25% in the month of purchase and 75% in the following month. Compute cash payments for merchandise for September.

QS 22-27ᴬ
Merchandising:
Cash payments for
merchandise   **P4**

Torres Co. forecasts merchandise purchases of $15,800 in January, $18,600 in February, and $20,200 in March; 40% of purchases are paid in the month of purchase and 60% are paid in the following month. At December 31 of the prior year, the balance of accounts payable (for December purchases) is $22,000. Prepare a schedule of cash payments for merchandise for each of the months of January, February, and March.

QS 22-28ᴬ
Merchandising:
Computing purchases   **P4**

Raider-X Company forecasts sales of 18,000 units for April. Beginning inventory is 3,000 units. The desired ending inventory is 30% higher than the beginning inventory. How many units should Raider-X purchase in April?

QS 22-29ᴬ
Merchandising:
Computing purchases   **P4**

Lexi Company forecasts unit sales of 1,040,000 in April, 1,220,000 in May, 980,000 in June, and 1,020,000 in July. Beginning inventory on April 1 is 280,000 units, and the company wants to have 30% of next month's sales in inventory at the end of each month. Prepare a merchandise purchases budget for the months of April, May, and June.

QS 22-30ᴬ
Merchandising:
Purchases budget   **P4**

Montel Company's July sales budget calls for sales of $600,000. The store expects to begin July with $50,000 of inventory and to end the month with $40,000 of inventory. Gross margin is typically 40% of sales. Determine the budgeted cost of merchandise purchases for July.

QS 22-31
Activity-based budgeting

A1

Activity-based budgeting is a budget system based on *expected activities*. (1) Describe activity-based budgeting, and explain its preparation of budgets. (2) How does activity-based budgeting differ from traditional budgeting?

QS 22-32
Operating budgets

P1

Royal Philips Electronics of the Netherlands reports sales of €24,244 million for a recent year. Assume that the company expects sales growth of 3% for the next year. Also assume that selling expenses are typically 20% of sales, while general and administrative expenses are 4% of sales.

1. Compute budgeted sales for the next year.

2. Assume budgeted sales for next year is €25,000 million, and then compute budgeted selling expenses and budgeted general and administrative expenses for the next year.

QS 22-33
Sustainability and selling
expense budget

P1

MM Co. predicts sales of $30,000 for May. MM Co. pays a sales manager a monthly salary of $3,000 plus a commission of 6% of sales dollars. MM's production manager recently found a way to reduce the amount of packaging MM uses. As a result, MM's product will receive better placement on store shelves and thus May sales are predicted to increase by 8%. In addition, MM's shipping costs are predicted to decrease from 4% of sales to 3% of sales. Compute budgeted sales and budgeted selling expenses for May assuming MM switches to this more sustainable packaging.

EXERCISES

Exercise 22-1
Budget consequences

C1

Participatory budgeting can sometimes lead to negative consequences. From the following list of outcomes that can arise from participatory budgeting, identify those with potentially *negative* consequences.

_____ **a.** Budgetary slack will not be available to meet budgeted results.

_____ **b.** Employees might understate expense budgets.

_____ **c.** Employees might commit unethical or fraudulent acts to meet budgeted results.

_____ **d.** Employees set sales targets too high.

_____ **e.** Employees always spend budgeted amounts, even if on unnecessary items.

_____ **f.** Employees might understate sales budgets and overstate expense budgets.

Match the definitions 1 through 9 with the term or phrase *a* through *i*.

a. Budget

b. Cash budget

c. Merchandise purchases budget

d. Safety stock

e. Budgeted income statement

f. General and administrative expense budget

g. Sales budget

h. Master budget

i. Budgeted balance sheet

_____ **1.** A comprehensive business plan that includes specific plans for expected sales, the units of product to be produced, the merchandise or materials to be purchased, the expenses to be incurred, the long-term assets to be purchased, and the amounts of cash to be borrowed or loans to be repaid, as well as a budgeted income statement and balance sheet.

_____ **2.** A quantity of inventory or materials over the minimum to reduce the risk of running short.

_____ **3.** A plan showing the units of goods to be sold and the sales to be derived; the usual starting point in the budgeting process.

_____ **4.** An accounting report that presents predicted amounts of the company's revenues and expenses for the budgeting period.

_____ **5.** An accounting report that presents predicted amounts of the company's assets, liabilities, and equity balances at the end of the budget period.

_____ **6.** A plan that shows the units or costs of merchandise to be purchased by a merchandising company during the budget period.

_____ **7.** A formal statement of a company's future plans, usually expressed in monetary terms.

_____ **8.** A plan that shows predicted operating expenses not included in the selling expenses budget.

_____ **9.** A plan that shows the expected cash inflows and cash outflows during the budget period, including receipts from any loans needed to maintain a minimum cash balance and repayments of such loans.

Ruiz Co. provides the following sales forecast for the next four months:

	April	May	June	July
Sales (units).	500	580	540	620

The company wants to end each month with ending finished goods inventory equal to 25% of next month's forecasted sales. Finished goods inventory on April 1 is 190 units. Assume July's budgeted production is 540 units. Prepare a production budget for the months of April, May, and June.

Refer to the information in Exercise 22-3. In addition, each finished unit requires five pounds of raw materials and the company wants to end each month with raw materials inventory equal to 30% of next month's production needs. Beginning raw materials inventory for April was 663 pounds. Assume direct materials cost $4 per pound. Prepare a direct materials budget for April, May, and June.

The production budget for Manner Company shows units to be produced as follows: July, 620; August, 680; and September, 540. Each unit produced requires two hours of direct labor. The direct labor rate is currently $20 per hour but is predicted to be $21 per hour in September. Prepare a direct labor budget for the months July, August, and September.

Rida, Inc., a manufacturer in a seasonal industry, is preparing its direct materials budget for the second quarter. It plans production of 240,000 units in the second quarter and 52,500 units in the third quarter. Raw material inventory is 43,200 pounds at the beginning of the second quarter. Other information follows. Prepare a direct materials budget for the second quarter.

Direct materials . . . .   Each unit requires 0.60 pounds of a key raw material, priced at $175 per pound. The company plans to end each quarter with an ending inventory of materials equal to 30% of next quarter's budgeted materials requirements.

Exercise 22-7

Manufacturing: Direct labor and factory overhead budgets **P1**

Addison Co. budgets production of 2,400 units during the second quarter. In addition, information on its direct labor and its variable and fixed overhead is shown below. For the second quarter, prepare (1) a direct labor budget and (2) a factory overhead budget.

Direct labor	Each finished unit requires 4 direct labor hours, at a cost of $20 per hour.
Variable overhead	Applied at the rate of $11 per direct labor hour.
Fixed overhead	Budgeted at $450,000 per quarter.

Exercise 22-8

Manufacturing: Direct materials budget

P1

Ramos Co. provides the following sales forecast and production budget for the next four months:

	April	May	June	July
Sales (units)	500	580	530	600
Budgeted production (units)	442	570	544	540

The company plans for finished goods inventory of 120 units at the end of June. In addition, each finished unit requires 5 pounds of direct materials and the company wants to end each month with direct materials inventory equal to 30% of next month's production needs. Beginning direct materials inventory for April was 663 pounds. Direct materials cost $2 per pound. Each finished unit requires 0.50 hours of direct labor at the rate of $16 per hour. The company budgets variable overhead at the rate of $20 per direct labor hour and budgets fixed overhead of $8,000 per month. Prepare a direct materials budget for April, May, and June.

Exercise 22-9

Manufacturing: Direct labor and factory overhead budgets **P1**

Refer to Exercise 22-8. Prepare (1) a direct labor budget and (2) a factory overhead budget for April, May, and June.

Exercise 22-10

Manufacturing:

Production budget **P1**

Blue Wave Co. predicts the following unit sales for the coming four months: September, 4,000 units; October, 5,000 units; November, 7,000 units; and December, 7,600 units. The company's policy is to maintain finished goods inventory equal to 60% of the next month's sales. At the end of August, the company had 2,400 finished units on hand. Prepare a production budget for each of the months of September, October, and November.

Exercise 22-11

Manufacturing:

Production budget

P1

Tyler Co. predicts the following unit sales for the next four months: April, 3,000 units; May, 4,000 units; June, 6,000 units; and July, 2,000 units. The company's policy is to maintain finished goods inventory equal to 30% of the next month's sales. At the end of March, the company had 900 finished units on hand. Prepare a production budget for each of the months of April, May, and June.

Exercise 22-12

Manufacturing: Preparing production budgets (for two periods) **P1**

Check   Second-quarter production, 465,000 units

Electro Company manufactures an innovative automobile transmission for electric cars. Management predicts that ending finished goods inventory for the first quarter will be 90,000 units. The following unit sales of the transmissions are expected during the rest of the year: second quarter, 450,000 units; third quarter, 525,000 units; and fourth quarter, 475,000 units. Company policy calls for the ending finished goods inventory of a quarter to equal 20% of the next quarter's budgeted sales. Prepare a production budget for both the second and third quarters that shows the number of transmissions to manufacture.

Exercise 22-13

Manufacturing: Direct materials budget **P1**

Electro Company budgets production of 450,000 transmissions in the second quarter and 520,000 transmissions in the third quarter. Each transmission requires 0.80 pounds of a key raw material. The company aims to end each quarter with an ending inventory of direct materials equal to 20% of next quarter's budgeted materials requirements. Beginning inventory of this raw material is 72,000 pounds. Direct materials cost $1.70 per pound. Prepare a direct materials budget for the second quarter.

Exercise 22-14

Manufacturing: Direct labor budget **P1**

Branson Belts makes handcrafted belts. The company budgets production of 4,500 belts during the second quarter. Each belt requires 4 direct labor hours, at a cost of $17 per hour. Prepare a direct labor budget for the second quarter.

MCO Leather Goods manufactures leather purses. Each purse requires 2 pounds of direct materials at a cost of $4 per pound and 0.8 direct labor hours at a rate of $16 per hour. Variable manufacturing overhead is charged at a rate of $2 per direct labor hour. Fixed manufacturing overhead is $10,000 per month. The company's policy is to end each month with direct materials inventory equal to 40% of the next month's materials requirement. At the end of August the company had 3,680 pounds of direct materials in inventory. The company's production budget reports the following. Prepare budgets for September and October for (1) direct materials, (2) direct labor, and (3) factory overhead.

Exercise 22-15
Manufacturing: Direct materials, direct labor, and overhead budgets
P1

Production Budget	September	October	November
Units to be produced	4,600	6,200	5,800

Ornamental Sculptures Mfg. manufactures garden sculptures. Each sculpture requires 8 pounds of direct materials at a cost of $3 per pound and 0.5 direct labor hours at a rate of $18 per hour. Variable manufacturing overhead is charged at a rate of $3 per direct labor hour. Fixed manufacturing overhead is $4,000 per month. The company's policy is to maintain direct materials inventory equal to 20% of the next month's materials requirement. At the end of March the company had 5,280 pounds of direct materials in inventory. The company's production budget reports the following. Prepare budgets for March and April for (1) direct materials, (2) direct labor, and (3) factory overhead.

Exercise 22-16
Manufacturing: Direct materials, direct labor, and overhead budgets
P1

Production Budget	March	April	May
Units to be produced	3,300	4,600	4,800

Kayak Co. budgeted the following cash receipts (excluding cash receipts from loans received) and cash payments (excluding cash payments for loan principal and interest payments) for the first three months of next year.

Exercise 22-17
Preparation of cash budgets (for three periods)
P2

	Cash Receipts	Cash Payments
January	$525,000	$475,000
February	400,000	350,000
March	450,000	525,000

According to a credit agreement with the company's bank, Kayak promises to have a minimum cash balance of $30,000 at each month-end. In return, the bank has agreed that the company can borrow up to $150,000 at a monthly interest rate of 1%, paid on the last day of each month. The interest is computed based on the beginning balance of the loan for the month. The company repays loan principal with any cash in excess of $30,000 on the last day of each month. The company has a cash balance of $30,000 and a loan balance of $60,000 at January 1. Prepare monthly cash budgets for January, February, and March.

Check January ending cash balance, $30,000

Jasper Company has sales on account and for cash. Specifically, 70% of its sales are on account and 30% are for cash. Credit sales are collected in full in the month following the sale. The company forecasts sales of $525,000 for April, $535,000 for May, and $560,000 for June. The beginning balance of accounts receivable is $400,000 on April 1. Prepare a schedule of budgeted cash receipts for April, May, and June.

Exercise 22-18
Budgeted cash receipts
P2

Zisk Co. purchases raw materials on account. Budgeted purchase amounts are: April, $80,000; May, $110,000; and June, $120,000. Payments are made as follows: 70% in the month of purchase and 30% in the month after purchase. The March 31 balance of accounts payable is $22,000. Prepare a schedule of budgeted cash payments for April, May, and June.

Exercise 22-19
Budgeted cash payments
P2

Karim Corp. requires a minimum $8,000 cash balance. If necessary, loans are taken to meet this requirement at a cost of 1% interest per month (paid monthly). Any excess cash is used to repay loans at month-end. The cash balance on July 1 is $8,400, and the company has no outstanding loans. Forecasted cash receipts (other than for loans received) and forecasted cash payments (other than for loan or interest payments) follow. Prepare a cash budget for July, August, and September. (Round interest payments to the nearest whole dollar.)

Exercise 22-20
Cash budget
P2

	July	August	September
Cash receipts	$20,000	$26,000	$40,000
Cash payments	28,000	30,000	22,000

Exercise 22-21
Cash budget
P2

Foyert Corp. requires a minimum $30,000 cash balance. If necessary, loans are taken to meet this requirement at a cost of 1% interest per month (paid monthly). Any excess cash is used to repay loans at month-end. The cash balance on October 1 is $30,000, and the company has an outstanding loan of $10,000. Forecasted cash receipts (other than for loans received) and forecasted cash payments (other than for loan or interest payments) follow. Prepare a cash budget for October, November, and December. (Round interest payments to the nearest whole dollar.)

	October	November	December
Cash receipts	$110,000	$80,000	$100,000
Cash payments..............	120,000	75,000	80,000

Exercise 22-22
Manufacturing: Cash budget
P2

Use the following information to prepare the September cash budget for PTO Manufacturing Co. The following information relates to expected cash receipts and cash payments for the month ended September 30.

a. Beginning cash balance, September 1, $40,000.

b. Budgeted cash receipts from sales in September, $255,000.

c. Raw materials are purchased on account. Purchase amounts are: August (actual), $80,000; and September (budgeted), $110,000. Payments for direct materials are made as follows: 65% in the month of purchase and 35% in the month following purchase.

d. Budgeted cash payments for direct labor in September, $40,000.

e. Budgeted depreciation expense for September, $4,000.

f. Other cash expenses budgeted for September, $60,000.

g. Accrued income taxes payable in September, $10,000.

h. Bank loan interest payable in September, $1,000.

Exercise 22-23
Manufacturing: Cash budget
P2

Mike's Motors Corp. manufactures motors for dirt bikes. The company requires a minimum $30,000 cash balance at each month-end. If necessary, the company borrows to meet this requirement, at a cost of 2% interest per month (paid at the end of each month). Any cash balance above $30,000 at month-end is used to repay loans. The cash balance on July 1 is $34,000, and the company has no outstanding loans at that time. Forecasted cash receipts and forecasted cash payments (other than for loan activity) are as follows. Prepare a cash budget for July, August, and September.

	Cash Receipts	Cash Payments
July	$ 85,000	$113,000
August.....................	111,000	99,900
September	150,000	127,400

Exercise 22-24ᴬ
Merchandising:
Preparation of purchases budgets (for three periods)
P4

Walker Company prepares monthly budgets. The current budget plans for a September ending merchandise inventory of 30,000 units. Company policy is to end each month with merchandise inventory equal to 15% of budgeted sales for the following month. Budgeted sales and merchandise purchases for the next three months follow. The company budgets sales of 200,000 units in October.
  Prepare the merchandise purchases budgets for the months of July, August, and September.

	Sales (Units)	Purchases (Units)
July	180,000	200,250
August.............	315,000	308,250
September	270,000	259,500

Exercise 22-25ᴬ
Merchandising:
Preparing a cash budget
P4

Use the following information to prepare the July cash budget for Acco Co. It should show expected cash receipts and cash payments for the month and the cash balance expected on July 31.

a. Beginning cash balance on July 1: $50,000.

b. Cash receipts from sales: 30% is collected in the month of sale, 50% in the next month, and 20% in the second month after sale (uncollectible accounts are negligible and can be ignored). Sales amounts are: May (actual), $1,720,000; June (actual), $1,200,000; and July (budgeted), $1,400,000.

c. Payments on merchandise purchases: 60% in the month of purchase and 40% in the month following purchase. Purchases amounts are: June (actual), $700,000; and July (budgeted), $750,000.

d. Budgeted cash payments for salaries in July: $275,000.

e. Budgeted depreciation expense for July: $36,000.

f. Other cash expenses budgeted for July: $200,000.

g. Accrued income taxes due in July: $80,000.

h. Bank loan interest paid in July: $6,600.

Check   Ending cash balance, $122,400

Use the information in Exercise 22-25 and the following additional information to prepare a budgeted income statement for the month of July and a budgeted balance sheet for July 31.

a. Cost of goods sold is 55% of sales.

b. Inventory at the end of June is $80,000 and at the end of July is $60,000.

c. Salaries payable on June 30 are $50,000 and are expected to be $60,000 on July 31.

d. The equipment account balance is $1,600,000 on July 31. On June 30, the accumulated depreciation on equipment is $280,000.

e. The $6,600 cash payment of interest represents the 1% monthly expense on a bank loan of $660,000.

f. Income taxes payable on July 31 are $30,720, and the income tax rate is 30%.

g. The only other balance sheet accounts are: Common Stock, with a balance of $600,000 on June 30; and Retained Earnings, with a balance of $964,000 on June 30.

Exercise 22-26ᴬ
Merchandising: Preparing a budgeted income statement and balance sheet
P4

Check   Net income, $71,680; Total assets, $2,686,400

Hardy Company's cost of goods sold is consistently 60% of sales. The company plans ending merchandise inventory for each month equal to 20% of the next month's budgeted cost of goods sold. All merchandise is purchased on credit, and 50% of the purchases made during a month is paid for in that month. Another 35% is paid for during the first month after purchase, and the remaining 15% is paid for during the second month after purchase. Expected sales are: August (actual), $325,000; September (actual), $320,000; October (estimated), $250,000; and November (estimated), $310,000. Use this information to determine October's expected cash payments for purchases.

Exercise 22-27ᴬ
Merchandising: Computing budgeted cash payments for purchases   P4

Check   Budgeted purchases: August, $194,400; October, $157,200

Ahmed Company purchases all merchandise on credit. It recently budgeted the following month-end accounts payable balances and merchandise inventory balances. Cash payments on accounts payable during each month are expected to be: May, $1,600,000; June, $1,490,000; July, $1,425,000; and August, $1,495,000. Use the available information to compute the budgeted amounts of (1) merchandise purchases for June, July, and August and (2) cost of goods sold for June, July, and August.

Exercise 22-28ᴬ
Merchandising: Computing budgeted purchases and cost of goods sold
P4

	Accounts Payable	Merchandise Inventory
May 31	$150,000	$250,000
June 30	200,000	400,000
July 31	235,000	300,000
August 31	195,000	330,000

Check   June purchases, $1,540,000; June cost of goods sold, $1,390,000

Big Sound, a merchandising company specializing in home computer speakers, budgets its monthly cost of goods sold to equal 70% of sales. Its inventory policy calls for ending inventory at the end of each month to equal 20% of the next month's budgeted cost of goods sold. All purchases are on credit, and 25% of the purchases in a month is paid for in the same month. Another 60% is paid for during the first month after purchase, and the remaining 15% is paid for in the second month after purchase. The following sales budgets are set: July, $350,000; August, $290,000; September, $320,000; October, $275,000; and November, $265,000.

Compute the following: (1) budgeted merchandise purchases for July, August, September, and October; (2) budgeted payments on accounts payable for September and October; and (3) budgeted ending balances of accounts payable for September and October. (*Hint:* For part 1, refer to Exhibits 22A.2 and 22A.3 for guidance, but note that budgeted sales are in dollars for this assignment.)

Exercise 22-29ᴬ
Merchandising: Computing budgeted accounts payable and purchases—sales forecast in dollars
P4

Check   July purchases, $236,600; Sep. payments on accts. pay., $214,235

Exercise 22-30^A

Merchandising: Budgeted cash payments

P4

Hector Company reports the following sales and purchases data. Payments for purchases are made in the month after purchase. Selling expenses are 10% of sales, administrative expenses are 8% of sales, and both are paid in the month of sale. Rent expense of $7,400 is paid monthly. Depreciation expense is $2,300 per month. Prepare a schedule of budgeted cash payments for August and September.

	July	August	September
Sales	$50,000	$72,000	$66,000
Purchases	14,400	19,200	21,600

Exercise 22-31^A

Merchandising: Cash budget

P4

Castor, Inc., is preparing its master budget for the quarter ended June 30. Budgeted sales and cash payments for merchandise for the next three months follow:

Budgeted	April	May	June
Sales	$32,000	$40,000	$24,000
Cash payments for merchandise	20,200	16,800	17,200

Sales are 50% cash and 50% on credit. All credit sales are collected in the month following the sale. The March 31 balance sheet includes balances of $12,000 in cash, $12,000 in accounts receivable, $11,000 in accounts payable, and a $2,000 balance in loans payable. A minimum cash balance of $12,000 is required. Loans are obtained at the end of any month when a cash shortage occurs. Interest is 1% per month based on the beginning of the month loan balance and is paid at each month-end. If an excess balance of cash exists, loans are repaid at the end of the month. Operating expenses are paid in the month incurred and include sales commissions (10% of sales), shipping (2% of sales), office salaries ($5,000 per month), and rent ($3,000 per month). Prepare a cash budget for each of the months of April, May, and June (round all dollar amounts to the nearest whole dollar).

Exercise 22-32^A

Merchandising: Cash budget

P4

Kelsey is preparing its master budget for the quarter ended September 30. Budgeted sales and cash payments for merchandise for the next three months follow:

Budgeted	July	August	September
Sales	$64,000	$80,000	$48,000
Cash payments for merchandise	40,400	33,600	34,400

Sales are 20% cash and 80% on credit. All credit sales are collected in the month following the sale. The June 30 balance sheet includes balances of $15,000 in cash; $45,000 in accounts receivable; $4,500 in accounts payable; and a $5,000 balance in loans payable. A minimum cash balance of $15,000 is required. Loans are obtained at the end of any month when a cash shortage occurs. Interest is 1% per month based on the beginning-of-the-month loan balance and is paid at each month-end. If an excess balance of cash exists, loans are repaid at the end of the month. Operating expenses are paid in the month incurred and consist of sales commissions (10% of sales), office salaries ($4,000 per month), and rent ($6,500 per month). (1) Prepare a cash receipts budget for July, August, and September. (2) Prepare a cash budget for each of the months of July, August, and September. (Round all dollar amounts to the nearest whole dollar.)

Exercise 22-33^A

Merchandising: Budgeted balance sheet

P3

The following information is available for Zetrov Company:

a. The cash budget for March shows an ending bank loan of $10,000 and an ending cash balance of $50,000.

b. The sales budget for March indicates sales of $140,000. Accounts receivable are expected to be 70% of the current-month sales.

c. The merchandise purchases budget indicates that $89,000 in merchandise will be purchased on account in March. Purchases on account are paid 100% in the month following the purchase. Ending inventory for March is predicted to be 600 units at a cost of $35 each.

d. The budgeted income statement for March shows net income of $48,000. Depreciation expense of $1,000 and $26,000 in income tax expense were used in computing net income for March. Accrued taxes will be paid in April.

e. The balance sheet for February shows equipment of $84,000 with accumulated depreciation of $46,000, common stock of $25,000, and ending retained earnings of $8,000. There are no changes budgeted in the Equipment or Common Stock accounts.

Prepare a budgeted balance sheet at the end of March.

Fortune, Inc., is preparing its master budget for the first quarter. The company sells a single product at a price of $25 per unit. Sales (in units) are forecasted at 45,000 for January, 55,000 for February, and 50,000 for March. Cost of goods sold is $14 per unit. Other expense information for the first quarter follows. Prepare a budgeted income statement for this first quarter. (Round expense amounts to the nearest dollar.)

Exercise 22-34
Budgeted income statement
P3

Commissions	8% of sales dollars
Rent	$14,000 per month
Advertising	15% of sales dollars
Office salaries	$75,000 per month
Depreciation	$40,000 per month
Interest	5% annually on a $250,000 note payable
Tax rate	30%

Render Co. CPA is preparing activity-based budgets for 2017. The partners expect the firm to generate billable hours for the year as follows:

Exercise 22-35
Activity-based budgeting
A1

Data entry	2,200 hours
Auditing	4,800 hours
Tax	4,300 hours
Consulting	750 hours

The company pays $10 per hour to data-entry clerks, $40 per hour to audit personnel, $50 per hour to tax personnel, and $50 per hour to consulting personnel. Prepare a schedule of budgeted labor costs for 2017 using activity-based budgeting.

connect

Black Diamond Company produces snow skis. Each ski requires 2 pounds of carbon fiber. The company's management predicts that 5,000 skis and 6,000 pounds of carbon fiber will be in inventory on June 30 of the current year and that 150,000 skis will be sold during the next (third) quarter. A set of two skis sells for $300. Management wants to end the third quarter with 3,500 skis and 4,000 pounds of carbon fiber in inventory. Carbon fiber can be purchased for $15 per pound. Each ski requires 0.5 hours of direct labor at $20 per hour. Variable overhead is applied at the rate of $8 per direct labor hour. The company budgets fixed overhead of $1,782,000 for the quarter.

PROBLEM SET A

Problem 22-1A
Manufacturing:
Preparing production and manufacturing budgets

C2   P1

Required

1. Prepare the third-quarter production budget for skis.
2. Prepare the third-quarter direct materials (carbon fiber) budget; include the dollar cost of purchases.
3. Prepare the direct labor budget for the third quarter.
4. Prepare the factory overhead budget for the third quarter.

Check (1) Units manuf., 148,500
        (2) Cost of carbon fiber purchases, $4,425,000

Built-Tight is preparing its master budget for the quarter ended September 30, 2017. Budgeted sales and cash payments for product costs for the quarter follow:

Problem 22-2A
Manufacturing: Cash budget

P2

	A	B	C	D
1		July	August	September
2	Budgeted sales	$64,000	$80,000	$48,000
3	Budgeted cash payments for			
4	Direct materials	16,160	13,440	13,760
5	Direct labor	4,040	3,360	3,440
6	Factory overhead	20,200	16,800	17,200

Sales are 20% cash and 80% on credit. All credit sales are collected in the month following the sale. The June 30 balance sheet includes balances of $15,000 in cash; $45,000 in accounts receivable; $4,500 in accounts payable; and a $5,000 balance in loans payable. A minimum cash balance of $15,000 is required. Loans are obtained at the end of any month when a cash shortage occurs. Interest is 1% per month based on the beginning-of-the-month loan balance and is paid at each month-end. If an excess balance of cash exists, loans are repaid at the end of the month. Operating expenses are paid in the month incurred and consist of sales commissions (10% of sales), office salaries ($4,000 per month), and rent ($6,500 per month).

1. Prepare a cash receipts budget for July, August, and September.
2. Prepare a cash budget for each of the months of July, August, and September. (Round amounts to the dollar.)

Problem 22-3A

Manufacturing:

Preparation and analysis of budgeted income statements

P3

Merline Manufacturing makes its product for $75 per unit and sells it for $150 per unit. The sales staff receives a 10% commission on the sale of each unit. Its December income statement follows.

MERLINE MANUFACTURING	
Income Statement	
For Month Ended December 31, 2017	
Sales	$2,250,000
Cost of goods sold	1,125,000
Gross profit	1,125,000
Operating expenses	
Sales commissions (10%)	225,000
Advertising	250,000
Store rent	30,000
Administrative salaries	45,000
Depreciation—Office equipment	50,000
Other expenses	10,000
Total expenses	610,000
Net income	$ 515,000

Management expects December's results to be repeated in January, February, and March of 2018 without any changes in strategy. Management, however, has an alternative plan. It believes that unit sales will increase at a rate of 10% *each* month for the next three months (beginning with January) if the item's selling price is reduced to $125 per unit and advertising expenses are increased by 15% and remain at that level for all three months. The cost of its product will remain at $75 per unit, the sales staff will continue to earn a 10% commission, and the remaining expenses will stay the same.

Required

Check (1) Budgeted net income: January, $196,250; February, $258,125; March, $326,187

1. Prepare budgeted income statements for each of the months of January, February, and March that show the expected results from implementing the proposed changes. Use a three-column format, with one column for each month.

Analysis Component

2. Use the budgeted income statements from part 1 to recommend whether management should implement the proposed changes. Explain.

Problem 22-4A

Manufacturing:

Preparation of a complete master budget

P1 P2 P3

The management of Zigby Manufacturing prepared the following estimated balance sheet for March 2017:

ZIGBY MANUFACTURING				
Estimated Balance Sheet				
March 31, 2017				
Assets			**Liabilities and Equity**	
Cash	$ 40,000		Accounts payable	$ 200,500
Accounts receivable	342,248		Short-term notes payable	12,000
Raw materials inventory	98,500		Total current liabilities	212,500
Finished goods inventory	325,540		Long-term note payable	500,000
Total current assets	806,288		Total liabilities	712,500
Equipment	600,000		Common stock	335,000
Accumulated depreciation	(150,000)		Retained earnings	208,788
Equipment, net	450,000		Total stockholders' equity	543,788
Total assets	$1,256,288		Total liabilities and equity	$1,256,288

To prepare a master budget for April, May, and June of 2017, management gathers the following information:

a. Sales for March total 20,500 units. Forecasted sales in units are as follows: April, 20,500; May, 19,500; June, 20,000; and July, 20,500. Sales of 240,000 units are forecasted for the entire year. The product's selling price is $23.85 per unit and its total product cost is $19.85 per unit.

b. Company policy calls for a given month's ending raw materials inventory to equal 50% of the next month's materials requirements. The March 31 raw materials inventory is 4,925 units, which complies with the policy. The expected June 30 ending raw materials inventory is 4,000 units. Raw materials cost $20 per unit. Each finished unit requires 0.50 units of raw materials.

c. Company policy calls for a given month's ending finished goods inventory to equal 80% of the next month's expected unit sales. The March 31 finished goods inventory is 16,400 units, which complies with the policy.

d. Each finished unit requires 0.50 hours of direct labor at a rate of $15 per hour.

e. Overhead is allocated based on direct labor hours. The predetermined variable overhead rate is $2.70 per direct labor hour. Depreciation of $20,000 per month is treated as fixed factory overhead.

f. Sales representatives' commissions are 8% of sales and are paid in the month of the sales. The sales manager's monthly salary is $3,000.

g. Monthly general and administrative expenses include $12,000 administrative salaries and 0.9% monthly interest on the long-term note payable.

h. The company expects 30% of sales to be for cash and the remaining 70% on credit. Receivables are collected in full in the month following the sale (none are collected in the month of the sale).

i. All raw materials purchases are on credit, and no payables arise from any other transactions. One month's raw materials purchases are fully paid in the next month.

j. The minimum ending cash balance for all months is $40,000. If necessary, the company borrows enough cash using a short-term note to reach the minimum. Short-term notes require an interest payment of 1% at each month-end (before any repayment). If the ending cash balance exceeds the minimum, the excess will be applied to repaying the short-term notes payable balance.

k. Dividends of $10,000 are to be declared and paid in May.

l. No cash payments for income taxes are to be made during the second calendar quarter. Income tax will be assessed at 35% in the quarter and paid in the third calendar quarter.

m. Equipment purchases of $130,000 are budgeted for the last day of June.

Required

Prepare the following budgets and other financial information as required. All budgets and other financial information should be prepared for the second calendar quarter, except as otherwise noted below. Round calculations up to the nearest whole dollar, except for the amount of cash sales, which should be rounded down to the nearest whole dollar.

   1. Sales budget.
   2. Production budget.
   3. Raw materials budget.
   4. Direct labor budget.
   5. Factory overhead budget.
   6. Selling expense budget.
   7. General and administrative expense budget.
   8. Cash budget.
   9. Budgeted income statement for the entire second quarter (not for each month separately).
   10. Budgeted balance sheet as of the end of the second calendar quarter.

Check (2) Units to produce: April, 19,700; May, 19,900
(3) Cost of raw materials purchases: April, $198,000
(5) Total overhead cost: May, $46,865
(8) Ending cash balance: April, $83,346; May, $124,295
(10) Budgeted total assets: June 30, $1,299,440

Keggler's Supply is a merchandiser of three different products. The company's February 28 inventories are footwear, 20,000 units; sports equipment, 80,000 units; and apparel, 50,000 units. Management believes each of these inventories is too high. As a result, a new policy dictates that ending inventory in any month should equal 30% of the expected unit sales for the following month. Expected sales in units for March, April, May, and June follow.

Problem 22-5A[A]
Merchandising:
Preparation and analysis of purchases budgets

P4

	Budgeted Sales in Units			
	March	April	May	June
Footwear..............	15,000	25,000	32,000	35,000
Sports equipment	70,000	90,000	95,000	90,000
Apparel..............	40,000	38,000	37,000	25,000

Required

1. Prepare a merchandise purchases budget (in units) for each product for each of the months of March, April, and May.

Analysis Component

2. What business conditions might lead to inventory levels becoming too high?

Problem 22-6A^A

Merchandising:

Preparation of cash budgets (for three periods)

P4

During the last week of August, Oneida Company's owner approaches the bank for a $100,000 loan to be made on September 2 and repaid on November 30 with annual interest of 12%, for an interest cost of $3,000. The owner plans to increase the store's inventory by $80,000 during September and needs the loan to pay for inventory acquisitions. The bank's loan officer needs more information about Oneida's ability to repay the loan and asks the owner to forecast the store's November 30 cash position. On September 1, Oneida is expected to have a $5,000 cash balance, $159,100 of net accounts receivable, and $125,000 of accounts payable. Its budgeted sales, merchandise purchases, and various cash payments for the next three months follow.

	A	B	C	D
1	**Budgeted Figures***	**September**	**October**	**November**
2	Sales	$250,000	$375,000	$400,000
3	Merchandise purchases	240,000	225,000	200,000
4	Cash payments			
5	Payroll	20,000	22,000	24,000
6	Rent	10,000	10,000	10,000
7	Other cash expenses	35,000	30,000	20,000
8	Repayment of bank loan			100,000
9	Interest on the bank loan			3,000

*Operations began in August; August sales were $215,000 and purchases were $125,000.

The budgeted September merchandise purchases include the inventory increase. All sales are on account. The company predicts that 25% of credit sales is collected in the month of the sale, 45% in the month following the sale, 20% in the second month, 9% in the third, and the remainder is uncollectible. Applying these percents to the August credit sales, for example, shows that $96,750 of the $215,000 will be collected in September, $43,000 in October, and $19,350 in November. All merchandise is purchased on credit; 80% of the balance is paid in the month following a purchase, and the remaining 20% is paid in the second month. For example, of the $125,000 August purchases, $100,000 will be paid in September and $25,000 in October.

Required

Prepare a cash budget for September, October, and November. Show supporting calculations as needed.

Problem 22-7A^A

Merchandising:

Preparation and analysis of cash budgets with supporting inventory and purchases budgets

P4

Aztec Company sells its product for $180 per unit. Its actual and budgeted sales follow.

	Units	Dollars
April (actual)	4,000	$ 720,000
May (actual).	2,000	360,000
June (budgeted)	6,000	1,080,000
July (budgeted).	5,000	900,000
August (budgeted)	3,800	684,000

All sales are on credit. Recent experience shows that 20% of credit sales is collected in the month of the sale, 50% in the month after the sale, 28% in the second month after the sale, and 2% proves to be uncollectible. The product's purchase price is $110 per unit. 60% of purchases made in a month is paid in that month and the other 40% is paid in the next month. The company has a policy to maintain an ending monthly inventory of 20% of the next month's unit sales plus a safety stock of 100 units. The April 30 and May 31 actual inventory levels are consistent with this policy. Selling and administrative expenses for the year are $1,320,000 and are paid evenly throughout the year in cash. The company's minimum cash balance at month-end is $100,000. This minimum is maintained, if necessary, by borrowing cash from the bank. If the balance exceeds $100,000, the company repays as much of the loan as it can without going below the minimum. This type of loan carries an annual 12% interest rate. On May 31, the loan balance is $25,000, and the company's cash balance is $100,000. (Round amounts to the nearest dollar.)

Required

1. Prepare a schedule that shows the computation of cash collections of its credit sales (accounts receivable) in each of the months of June and July.

2. Prepare a schedule that shows the computation of budgeted ending inventories (in units) for April, May, June, and July.

3. Prepare the merchandise purchases budget for May, June, and July. Report calculations in units and then show the dollar amount of purchases for each month.

4. Prepare a schedule showing the computation of cash payments for product purchases for June and July.

5. Prepare a cash budget for June and July, including any loan activity and interest expense. Compute the loan balance at the end of each month.

Analysis Component

6. Refer to your answer to part 5. The cash budget indicates the company will need to borrow more than $18,000 in June. Suggest some reasons that knowing this information in May would be helpful to management.

Check (1) Cash collections: June, $597,600; July, $820,800

(3) Budgeted purchases: May, $308,000; June, $638,000

(5) Budgeted ending loan balance: June, $43,650; July, $0

Near the end of 2017, the management of Dimsdale Sports Co., a merchandising company, prepared the following estimated balance sheet for December 31, 2017.

Problem 22-8A[A]
Merchandising: Preparation of a complete master budget **P4**

DIMSDALE SPORTS COMPANY					
Estimated Balance Sheet					
December 31, 2017					
Assets			**Liabilities and Equity**		
Cash	$ 36,000		Accounts payable	$360,000	
Accounts receivable	525,000		Bank loan payable	15,000	
Inventory	150,000		Taxes payable (due 3/15/2018)	90,000	
Total current assets		$ 711,000	Total liabilities		$ 465,000
Equipment	540,000		Common stock	472,500	
Less: Accumulated depreciation	67,500		Retained earnings	246,000	
Equipment, net		472,500	Total stockholders' equity		718,500
Total assets		$1,183,500	Total liabilities and equity		$1,183,500

To prepare a master budget for January, February, and March of 2018, management gathers the following information.

a. The company's single product is purchased for $30 per unit and resold for $55 per unit. The expected inventory level of 5,000 units on December 31, 2017, is more than management's desired level, which is 20% of the next month's expected sales (in units). Expected sales are: January, 7,000 units; February, 9,000 units; March, 11,000 units; and April, 10,000 units.

b. Cash sales and credit sales represent 25% and 75%, respectively, of total sales. Of the credit sales, 60% is collected in the first month after the month of sale and 40% in the second month after the month of sale. For the December 31, 2017, accounts receivable balance, $125,000 is collected in January and the remaining $400,000 is collected in February.

c. Merchandise purchases are paid for as follows: 20% in the first month after the month of purchase and 80% in the second month after the month of purchase. For the December 31, 2017, accounts payable balance, $80,000 is paid in January 2018 and the remaining $280,000 is paid in February 2018.

d. Sales commissions equal to 20% of sales are paid each month. Sales salaries (excluding commissions) are $60,000 per year.

e. General and administrative salaries are $144,000 per year. Maintenance expense equals $2,000 per month and is paid in cash.

f. Equipment reported in the December 31, 2017, balance sheet was purchased in January 2017. It is being depreciated over eight years under the straight-line method with no salvage value. The following amounts for new equipment purchases are planned in the coming quarter: January, $36,000; February, $96,000; and March, $28,800. This equipment will be depreciated under the straight-line method over eight years with no salvage value. A full month's depreciation is taken for the month in which equipment is purchased.

g. The company plans to buy land at the end of March at a cost of $150,000, which will be paid with cash on the last day of the month.

h. The company has a working arrangement with its bank to obtain additional loans as needed. The interest rate is 12% per year, and interest is paid at each month-end based on the beginning balance. Partial or full payments on these loans can be made on the last day of the month. The company has agreed to maintain a minimum ending cash balance of $25,000 at the end of each month.

i. The income tax rate for the company is 40%. Income taxes on the first quarter's income will not be paid until April 15.

Required

Check   (2) Budgeted purchases: January, $114,000; February, $282,000

(3) Budgeted selling expenses: January, $82,000; February, $104,000

(6) Ending cash bal.: January, $30,100; February, $210,300

(8) Budgeted total assets at March 31, $1,568,650

Prepare a master budget for each of the first three months of 2018; include the following component budgets (show supporting calculations as needed, and round amounts to the nearest dollar):

1. Monthly sales budgets (showing both budgeted unit sales and dollar sales).
2. Monthly merchandise purchases budgets.
3. Monthly selling expense budgets.
4. Monthly general and administrative expense budgets.
5. Monthly capital expenditures budgets.
6. Monthly cash budgets.
7. Budgeted income statement for the entire first quarter (not for each month).
8. Budgeted balance sheet as of March 31, 2018.

PROBLEM SET B

Problem 22-1B
Manufacturing:
Preparing production and manufacturing budgets

C2   P1

NSA Company produces baseball bats. Each bat requires 3 pounds of aluminum alloy. Management predicts that 8,000 bats and 15,000 pounds of aluminum alloy will be in inventory on March 31 of the current year and that 250,000 bats will be sold during this year's second quarter. Bats sell for $80 each. Management wants to end the second quarter with 6,000 finished bats and 12,000 pounds of aluminum alloy in inventory. Aluminum alloy can be purchased for $4 per pound. Each bat requires 0.5 hours of direct labor at $18 per hour. Variable overhead is applied at the rate of $12 per direct labor hour. The company budgets fixed overhead of $1,776,000 for the quarter.

Required

Check   (1) Units manuf., 248,000

(2) Cost of materials purchases, $2,964,000

1. Prepare the second-quarter production budget for bats.
2. Prepare the second-quarter direct materials (aluminum alloy) budget; include the dollar cost of purchases.
3. Prepare the direct labor budget for the second quarter.
4. Prepare the factory overhead budget for the second quarter.

Problem 22-2B
Manufacturing:
Cash budget

P2

A1 Manufacturing is preparing its master budget for the quarter ended September 30, 2017. Budgeted sales and cash payments for product costs for the quarter follow.

	A	B	C	D
1		**July**	**August**	**September**
2	Budgeted sales	$63,400	$80,600	$48,600
3	Budgeted cash payments for			
4	Direct materials	12,480	9,900	10,140
5	Direct labor	10,400	8,250	8,450
6	Factory overhead	18,720	14,850	15,210

Sales are 20% cash and 80% on credit. All credit sales are collected in the month following the sale. The June 30 balance sheet includes balances of $12,900 in cash; $47,000 in accounts receivable; $5,100 in accounts payable; and a $2,600 balance in loans payable. A minimum cash balance of $12,600 is required. Loans are obtained at the end of any month when a cash shortage occurs. Interest is 1% per month based on the beginning-of-the-month loan balance and is paid at each month-end. If an excess balance of cash exists, loans are repaid at the end of the month. Operating expenses are paid in the month incurred and consist of sales commissions (10% of sales), office salaries ($4,600 per month), and rent ($7,100 per month).

1. Prepare a cash receipts budget for July, August, and September.
2. Prepare a cash budget for each of the months of July, August, and September. (Round amounts to the dollar.)

HCS MFG. makes its product for $60 per unit and sells it for $130 per unit. The sales staff receives a commission of 10% of dollar sales. Its June income statement follows.

Problem 22-3B
Manufacturing:
Preparation and analysis
of budgeted income
statements   **P3**

HCS MFG.	
Income Statement	
For Month Ended June 30, 2017	
Sales	$1,300,000
Cost of goods sold	600,000
Gross profit	700,000
Operating expenses	
Sales commissions (10%)	130,000
Advertising	200,000
Store rent	24,000
Administrative salaries	40,000
Depreciation—Office equipment	50,000
Other expenses	12,000
Total expenses	456,000
Net income	$ 244,000

Management expects June's results to be repeated in July, August, and September without any changes in strategy. Management, however, has another plan. It believes that unit sales will increase at a rate of 10% *each* month for the next three months (beginning with July) if the item's selling price is reduced to $115 per unit and advertising expenses are increased by 25% and remain at that level for all three months. The cost of its product will remain at $60 per unit, the sales staff will continue to earn a 10% commission, and the remaining expenses will stay the same.

Required

1. Prepare budgeted income statements for each of the months of July, August, and September that show the expected results from implementing the proposed changes. Use a three-column format, with one column for each month.

Check   Budgeted net
income: July, $102,500;
August, $150,350;
September, $202,985

Analysis Component

2. Use the budgeted income statements from part 1 to recommend whether management should implement the proposed plan. Explain.

The management of Nabar Manufacturing prepared the following estimated balance sheet for June 2017:

Problem 22-4B
Manufacturing:
Preparation of a complete
master budget

P1   P2   P3

NABAR MANUFACTURING			
Estimated Balance Sheet			
June 30, 2017			
Assets		**Liabilities and Equity**	
Cash	$ 40,000	Accounts payable	$ 51,400
Accounts receivable	249,900	Income taxes payable................	10,000
Raw materials inventory	35,000	Short-term notes payable	24,000
Finished goods inventory	241,080	Total current liabilities	85,400
Total current assets	565,980	Long-term note payable	300,000
Equipment	720,000	Total liabilities	385,400
Accumulated depreciation	(240,000)	Common stock	600,000
Equipment, net......................	480,000	Retained earnings	60,580
		Total stockholders' equity	660,580
Total assets........................	$1,045,980	Total liabilities and equity	$1,045,980

To prepare a master budget for July, August, and September of 2017, management gathers the following information:

a. Sales were 20,000 units in June. Forecasted sales in units are as follows: July, 21,000; August, 19,000; September, 20,000; and October, 24,000. The product's selling price is $17 per unit and its total product cost is $14.35 per unit.

b. Company policy calls for a given month's ending finished goods inventory to equal 70% of the next month's expected unit sales. The June 30 finished goods inventory is 16,800 units, which does not comply with the policy.

c. Company policy calls for a given month's ending raw materials inventory to equal 20% of the next month's materials requirements. The June 30 raw materials inventory is 4,375 units (which also fails to meet the policy). The budgeted September 30 raw materials inventory is 1,980 units. Raw materials cost $8 per unit. Each finished unit requires 0.50 units of raw materials.

d. Each finished unit requires 0.50 hours of direct labor at a rate of $16 per hour.

e. Overhead is allocated based on direct labor hours. The predetermined variable overhead rate is $2.70 per direct labor hour. Depreciation of $20,000 per month is treated as fixed factory overhead.

f. Monthly general and administrative expenses include $9,000 administrative salaries and 0.9% monthly interest on the long-term note payable.

g. Sales representatives' commissions are 10% of sales and are paid in the month of the sales. The sales manager's monthly salary is $3,500.

h. The company expects 30% of sales to be for cash and the remaining 70% on credit. Receivables are collected in full in the month following the sale (none are collected in the month of the sale).

i. All raw materials purchases are on credit, and no payables arise from any other transactions. One month's raw materials purchases are fully paid in the next month.

j. Dividends of $20,000 are to be declared and paid in August.

k. Income taxes payable at June 30 will be paid in July. Income tax expense will be assessed at 35% in the quarter and paid in October.

l. Equipment purchases of $100,000 are budgeted for the last day of September.

m. The minimum ending cash balance for all months is $40,000. If necessary, the company borrows enough cash using a short-term note to reach the minimum. Short-term notes require an interest payment of 1% at each month-end (before any repayment). If the ending cash balance exceeds the minimum, the excess will be applied to repaying the short-term notes payable balance.

Check   (2) Units to produce: July, 17,500; August, 19,700
(3) Cost of raw materials purchases: July, $50,760
(5) Total overhead cost: August, $46,595
(8) Ending cash balance: July, $96,835; August, $141,180
(10) Budgeted total assets: Sep. 30, $1,054,920

Required

Prepare the following budgets and other financial information as required. All budgets and other financial information should be prepared for the third calendar quarter, except as otherwise noted below. Round calculations to the nearest whole dollar.

1. Sales budget.
2. Production budget.
3. Raw materials budget.
4. Direct labor budget.
5. Factory overhead budget.
6. Selling expense budget.

7. General and administrative expense budget.
8. Cash budget.
9. Budgeted income statement for the entire quarter (not for each month separately).
10. Budgeted balance sheet as of September 30, 2017.

Problem 22-5B^A

Merchandising:

Preparation and analysis of purchases budgets

P4

H20 Sports is a merchandiser of three different products. The company's March 31 inventories are water skis, 40,000 units; tow ropes, 90,000 units; and life jackets, 150,000 units. Management believes inventory levels are too high for all three products. As a result, a new policy dictates that ending inventory in any month should equal 10% of the expected unit sales for the following month. Expected sales in units for April, May, June, and July follow.

	Budgeted Sales in Units			
	April	May	June	July
Water skis	70,000	90,000	130,000	100,000
Tow ropes	100,000	90,000	110,000	100,000
Life jackets	160,000	190,000	200,000	120,000

Required

Check   (1) April budgeted purchases: Water skis, 39,000; Tow ropes, 19,000; Life jackets, 29,000

1. Prepare a merchandise purchases budget (in units) for each product for each of the months of April, May, and June.

Analysis Component

2. What business conditions might lead to inventory levels becoming too high?

Problem 22-6B^A

Merchandising:

Preparation of cash budgets (for three periods)   **P4**

During the last week of March, Sony Stereo's owner approaches the bank for an $80,000 loan to be made on April 1 and repaid on June 30 with annual interest of 12%, for an interest cost of $2,400. The owner plans to increase the store's inventory by $60,000 in April and needs the loan to pay for inventory acquisitions. The bank's loan officer needs more information about Sony Stereo's ability to repay the loan and asks the owner to forecast the store's June 30 cash position. On April 1, Sony Stereo is expected to have a $3,000 cash balance, $135,000 of accounts receivable, and $100,000 of accounts payable. Its budgeted sales, merchandise purchases, and various cash payments for the next three months follow.

	A	B	C	D
1	**Budgeted Figures***	**April**	**May**	**June**
2	Sales	$220,000	$300,000	$380,000
3	Merchandise purchases	210,000	180,000	220,000
4	Cash payments			
5	Payroll	16,000	17,000	18,000
6	Rent	6,000	6,000	6,000
7	Other cash expenses	64,000	8,000	7,000
8	Repayment of bank loan			80,000
9	Interest on bank loan			2,400

*Operations began in March; March sales were $180,000 and purchases were $100,000.

The budgeted April merchandise purchases include the inventory increase. All sales are on account. The company predicts that 25% of credit sales is collected in the month of the sale, 45% in the month following the sale, 20% in the second month, 9% in the third, and the remainder is uncollectible. Applying these percents to the March credit sales, for example, shows that $81,000 of the $180,000 will be collected in April, $36,000 in May, and $16,200 in June. All merchandise is purchased on credit; 80% of the balance is paid in the month following a purchase and the remaining 20% is paid in the second month. For example, of the $100,000 March purchases, $80,000 will be paid in April and $20,000 in May.

Required

Prepare a cash budget for April, May, and June. Show supporting calculations as needed.

Check Budgeted cash balance: April, $53,000; May, $44,000; June, $34,800

Connick Company sells its product for $22 per unit. Its actual and budgeted sales follow.

	Units	Dollars
January (actual)	18,000	$396,000
February (actual)	22,500	495,000
March (budgeted)	19,000	418,000
April (budgeted)	18,750	412,500
May (budgeted)	21,000	462,000

Problem 22-7B[A]
Merchandising:
Preparation and analysis of cash budgets with supporting inventory and purchases budgets

P4

All sales are on credit. Recent experience shows that 40% of credit sales is collected in the month of the sale, 35% in the month after the sale, 23% in the second month after the sale, and 2% proves to be uncollectible. The product's purchase price is $12 per unit. Of purchases made in a month, 30% is paid in that month and the other 70% is paid in the next month. The company has a policy to maintain an ending monthly inventory of 20% of the next month's unit sales plus a safety stock of 100 units. The January 31 and February 28 actual inventory levels are consistent with this policy. Selling and administrative expenses for the year are $1,920,000 and are paid evenly throughout the year in cash. The company's minimum cash balance for month-end is $50,000. This minimum is maintained, if necessary, by borrowing cash from the bank. If the balance exceeds $50,000, the company repays as much of the loan as it can without going below the minimum. This type of loan carries an annual 12% interest rate. At February 28, the loan balance is $12,000, and the company's cash balance is $50,000.

Required

1. Prepare a schedule that shows the computation of cash collections of its credit sales (accounts receivable) in each of the months of March and April.

2. Prepare a schedule showing the computations of budgeted ending inventories (units) for January, February, March, and April.

3. Prepare the merchandise purchases budget for February, March, and April. Report calculations in units and then show the dollar amount of purchases for each month.

4. Prepare a schedule showing the computation of cash payments on product purchases for March and April.

5. Prepare a cash budget for March and April, including any loan activity and interest expense. Compute the loan balance at the end of each month.

Check (1) Cash collections: March, $431,530; April, $425,150

(3) Budgeted purchases: February, $261,600; March, $227,400

(5) Ending cash balance: March, $58,070; April, $94,920

Analysis Component

6. Refer to your answer to part 5. The cash budget indicates whether the company must borrow additional funds at the end of March. Suggest some reasons that knowing the loan needs in advance would be helpful to management.

Problem 22-8B[A]

Merchandising: Preparation of a complete master budget

P4

Near the end of 2017, the management of Isle Corp., a merchandising company, prepared the following estimated balance sheet for December 31, 2017.

ISLE CORPORATION Estimated Balance Sheet December 31, 2017					
Assets			**Liabilities and Equity**		
Cash	$ 36,000		Accounts payable	$360,000	
Accounts receivable	525,000		Bank loan payable	15,000	
Inventory	150,000		Taxes payable (due 3/15/2018)	90,000	
Total current assets		$ 711,000	Total liabilities		$ 465,000
Equipment	540,000		Common stock	472,500	
Less: Accumulated depreciation	67,500		Retained earnings	246,000	
Equipment, net...............		472,500	Total stockholders' equity		718,500
Total assets		$1,183,500	Total liabilities and equity		$1,183,500

To prepare a master budget for January, February, and March of 2018, management gathers the following information.

a. The company's single product is purchased for $30 per unit and resold for $45 per unit. The expected inventory level of 5,000 units on December 31, 2017, is more than management's desired level for 2018, which is 25% of the next month's expected sales (in units). Expected sales are: January, 6,000 units; February, 8,000 units; March, 10,000 units; and April, 9,000 units.

b. Cash sales and credit sales represent 25% and 75%, respectively, of total sales. Of the credit sales, 60% is collected in the first month after the month of sale and 40% in the second month after the month of sale. For the $525,000 accounts receivable balance at December 31, 2017, $315,000 is collected in January 2018 and the remaining $210,000 is collected in February 2018.

c. Merchandise purchases are paid for as follows: 20% in the first month after the month of purchase and 80% in the second month after the month of purchase. For the $360,000 accounts payable balance at December 31, 2017, $72,000 is paid in January 2018 and the remaining $288,000 is paid in February 2018.

d. Sales commissions equal to 20% of sales dollars are paid each month. Sales salaries (excluding commissions) are $90,000 per year.

e. General and administrative salaries are $144,000 per year. Maintenance expense equals $3,000 per month and is paid in cash.

f. Equipment reported in the December 31, 2017, balance sheet was purchased in January 2017. It is being depreciated over eight years under the straight-line method with no salvage value. The following amounts for new equipment purchases are planned in the coming quarter: January, $72,000; February, $96,000; and March, $28,800. This equipment will be depreciated using the straight-line method over eight years with no salvage value. A full month's depreciation is taken for the month in which equipment is purchased.

g. The company plans to buy land at the end of March at a cost of $150,000, which will be paid with cash on the last day of the month.

h. The company has a contract with its bank to obtain additional loans as needed. The interest rate is 12% per year, and interest is paid at each month-end based on the beginning balance. Partial or full payments on these loans are made on the last day of the month. The company has agreed to maintain a minimum ending cash balance of $36,000 at the end of each month.

i. The income tax rate for the company is 40%. Income taxes on the first quarter's income will not be paid until April 15.

Required

Prepare a master budget for each of the first three months of 2018; include the following component budgets (show supporting calculations as needed, and round amounts to the nearest dollar):

1. Monthly sales budgets (showing both budgeted unit sales and dollar sales).

2. Monthly merchandise purchases budgets.

3. Monthly selling expense budgets.

4. Monthly general and administrative expense budgets.

5. Monthly capital expenditures budgets.

6. Monthly cash budgets.

7. Budgeted income statement for the entire first quarter (not for each month).

8. Budgeted balance sheet as of March 31, 2018.

(6) Ending cash bal.: January, $182,850; February, $107,850

(8) Budgeted total assets at March 31, $1,346,875

(This serial problem began in Chapter 1 and continues through most of the book. If previous chapter segments were not completed, the serial problem can begin at this point.)

SERIAL PROBLEM
Business Solutions

P3

SP 22   Santana Rey expects second-quarter 2018 sales of **Business Solutions**'s line of computer furniture to be the same as the first quarter's sales (reported below) without any changes in strategy. Monthly sales averaged 40 desk units (sales price of $1,250) and 20 chairs (sales price of $500).

BUSINESS SOLUTIONS—Computer Furniture Segment Segment Income Statement* For Quarter Ended March 31, 2018	
Sales†	$180,000
Cost of goods sold‡	115,000
Gross profit	65,000
Expenses	
Sales commissions (10%)	18,000
Advertising expenses	9,000
Other fixed expenses	18,000
Total expenses	45,000
Net income	$ 20,000

© Alexander Image/Shutterstock RF

* Reflects revenue and expense activity only related to the computer furniture segment.
† Revenue: (120 desks × $1,250) + (60 chairs × $500) = $150,000 + $30,000 = $180,000
‡ Cost of goods sold: (120 desks × $750) + (60 chairs × $250) + $10,000 = $115,000

Santana Rey believes that sales will increase each month for the next three months (April, 48 desks, 32 chairs; May, 52 desks, 35 chairs; June, 56 desks, 38 chairs) *if* selling prices are reduced to $1,150 for desks and $450 for chairs, and advertising expenses are increased by 10% and remain at that level for all three months. The products' variable cost will remain at $750 for desks and $250 for chairs. The sales staff will continue to earn a 10% commission, the fixed manufacturing costs per month will remain at $10,000, and other fixed expenses will remain at $6,000 per month.

Required

1. Prepare budgeted income statements for the computer furniture segment for each of the months of April, May, and June that show the expected results from implementing the proposed changes. Use a three-column format, with one column for each month.

2. Use the budgeted income statements from part 1 to recommend whether Santana Rey should implement the proposed changes. Explain.

Check   (1) Budgeted income (loss): April, $(660); May, $945

Beyond the Numbers

BTN 22-1   Financial statements often serve as a starting point in formulating budgets. Review **Apple**'s financial statements in Appendix A to determine its cash paid for acquisitions of property, plant, and equipment in the current year and the budgeted cash needed for such acquisitions in the next year.

REPORTING IN ACTION

P3

APPLE

Required

1. Which financial statement reports the amount of cash paid for acquisitions of property, plant, and equipment? Explain where on the statement this information is reported.

2. Indicate the amount of cash (a) paid for acquisitions of property and equipment in the year ended September 26, 2015, and (b) to be paid (budgeted for) next year under the assumption that annual acquisitions of property and equipment equal 20% of the prior year's net income.

Fast Forward

3. Access Apple's financial statements for a year ending after September 26, 2015, from either its website [Apple.com] or the SEC's EDGAR database [SEC.gov]. Compare your answer for part 2 with actual cash paid for acquisitions of property and equipment for that fiscal year. Compute the error, if any, in your estimate. Speculate as to why cash paid for acquisitions of property and equipment was higher or lower than your estimate.

COMPARATIVE ANALYSIS

P2

APPLE
GOOGLE

BTN 22-2   Companies often budget selling expenses and general and administrative expenses (SGA) as a percentage of expected sales.

Required

1. For both **Apple** and **Google**, list the prior three years' sales (in dollars) and *total* selling expenses and general and administrative expenses (in dollars). Use the financial statements in Appendix A.

2. Compute the ratio of *total* selling expenses and general and administrative expenses to sales for each of the three years.

3. Using the data from part 2, predict both companies' *total* selling expenses and general and administrative expenses (in dollars) for the next two years. (If possible, compare your predictions to actual amounts for those years.)

ETHICS CHALLENGE

C1

BTN 22-3   Both the budget process and budgets themselves can impact management actions, both positively and negatively. For instance, a common practice among not-for-profit organizations and government agencies is for management to spend any amounts remaining in a budget at the end of the budget period, a practice often called "use it or lose it." The view is that if a department manager does not spend the budgeted amount, top management will reduce next year's budget by the amount not spent. To avoid losing budget dollars, department managers often spend all budgeted amounts regardless of the value added to products or services. All of us pay for the costs associated with this budget system.

Required

Write a half-page report to a local not-for-profit organization or government agency offering a solution to the "use it or lose it" budgeting problem.

COMMUNICATING IN PRACTICE

C2

BTN 22-4   The sales budget is usually the first and most crucial of the component budgets in a master budget because all other budgets usually rely on it for planning purposes.

Required

Assume that your company's sales staff provides information on expected sales and selling prices for items making up the sales budget. Prepare a one-page memorandum to your supervisor outlining concerns with the sales staff's input in the sales budget when its compensation is at least partly tied to these budgets. More generally, explain the importance of assessing any potential bias in information provided to the budget process.

TAKING IT TO THE NET

C1

BTN 22-5   Access information on e-budgets through **TheManageMentor** website (themanagementor.com/kuniverse/kmailers_universe/finance_kmailers/cfa/budgeting2.htm). Read the information provided.

Required

1. Assume the role of a senior manager in a large, multidivision company. What are the benefits of using e-budgets?

2. As a senior manager, what concerns do you have with the concept and application of e-budgets?

TEAMWORK IN ACTION

A1

BTN 22-6   Your team is to prepare a budget report outlining the costs of attending college (full-time) for the next two semesters (30 hours) or three quarters (45 hours). This budget's focus is solely on attending college; do not include personal items in the team's budget. Your budget must include tuition, books, supplies, club fees, food, housing, and all costs associated with travel to and from college. This budgeting exercise is similar to the initial phase in activity-based budgeting. Include a list of any assumptions you use in completing the budget. Be prepared to present your budget in class.

BTN 22-7   Marilyn and Michelle sells a foam mattress cover that allows patients to sleep better after surgery. Co-founders Marilyn Collins and Michelle Logan stress the importance of planning and budgeting for business success.

Required

1. How can budgeting help Marilyn and Michelle efficiently develop and operate their business?

2. Marilyn and Michelle hope to expand their business. How can a budget be useful in expanding a business's operations?

BTN 22-8   To help understand the factors impacting a sales budget, you are to visit three businesses with the same ownership or franchise membership. Record the selling prices of two identical products at each location, such as regular and premium gas sold at Chevron stations. You are likely to find a difference in prices for at least one of the three locations you visit.

Required

1. Identify at least three external factors that must be considered when setting the sales budget. (*Note:* There is a difference between internal and external factors that impact the sales budget.)

2. What factors might explain any differences identified in the prices of the businesses you visited?

BTN 22-9   Access Samsung's income statement (in Appendix A) for the business year 2015.

Required

1. Is Samsung's selling and administrative expenses budget likely to be an important budget in its master budgeting process? Explain.

2. Identify three examples of expenses that would be reported as selling and administrative expenses on Samsung's income statement.

3. Who likely has the initial responsibility for Samsung's selling and administrative expense budget? Explain.

 **GLOBAL VIEW**

Royal Philips Electronics of the Netherlands is a diversified company. Preparing budgets and evaluating progress help the company achieve its goals. In a recent annual report, the company reports that it budgets sales to grow at a faster pace than overall economic growth. Based on this sales target, company managers prepare detailed operating, capital expenditure, and financial budgets.

Budgeted and actual results of companies that do global business are impacted by changes in foreign currency exchange rates. While most of Royal Philips's cash payments are in euros, the company's sales are in euros, U.S. dollars, Chinese yuan, Brazilian real, and other currencies.

Forecasting future exchange rates and their impact on sales budgets is difficult. In addition, global economic and political uncertainties add to budgeting challenges.

 Global View Assignments

Discussion Question 13

Discussion Question 14

Quick Study 22-32

BTN 22-9

23

chapter

Flexible Budgets and Standard Costs

Learning Objectives

CONCEPTUAL

C1 Define *standard costs* and explain how standard cost information is useful for management by exception.

C2 Describe cost variances and what they reveal about performance.

ANALYTICAL

A1 Analyze changes in sales from expected amounts.

PROCEDURAL

P1 Prepare a flexible budget and interpret a flexible budget performance report.

P2 Compute materials and labor variances.

P3 Compute overhead controllable and volume variances.

P4 *Appendix 23A*—Compute overhead spending and efficiency variances.

P5 *Appendix 23A*—Prepare journal entries for standard costs and account for price and quantity variances.

Greg Powers/Courtesy of Riide

E-Z Riider

WASHINGTON, DC—Avid bikers Amber Wason and Jeff Stefanis believe electric bicycles are the solution to urban congestion and global energy needs. However, "we didn't see anything at an affordable price that people would want to ride," recalls Jeff. Amber adds, "no one in the U.S. had done it, so we decided to design and build our own."

Amber and Jeff spent a year and their own money to design and develop **Riide** (**Riide.com**), a lighter and cheaper e-bike. The duo set out to make their e-bike maintenance-free. "We obsessed over every detail," explains Jeff, "and we developed precise standards." They set standards for materials and labor. "We use only the highest quality components," says Amber, "and we reject any material that does not meet our requirements."

Amber and Jeff focus on *variances* between actual and expected costs. Materials price and quantity variances are used to control the costs of expensive raw materials. Unfavorable materials price variances can result from rising materials prices, which

"Have a vision"

—Amber Wason

can lead them to consider alternative suppliers or to raise selling price.

Each Riide bike is assembled by hand, so the company knows precisely how long each bike should take to assemble. If assembly takes longer than expected, Amber and Jeff investigate why and take corrective action.

Riide has sold out all of its production for many months in advance. "Our biggest challenge is keeping up with demand!" explains Amber. "We want to accelerate production."

When production accelerates, budgets quickly can become outdated. *Flexible budgets,* which reflect budgeted costs at different production levels, are useful in analyzing performance and controlling costs.

While attention to budgeting, standard costs, and variances is important, Amber and Jeff encourage others to have passion and give back. "We have a grand vision," claims Amber. "We have to."

Sources: *Riide website,* January 2017; *Pando,* January 9, 2014; *Urbanful,* January 13, 2015; *DCInno,* February 8, 2016; *Washington Post,* August 4, 2014

Section 1—Fixed and Flexible Budgets

Point: Budget reports are often used to determine bonuses of managers.

Managers use budgets to control operations and see that planned objectives are met. **Budget reports** compare budgeted results to actual results. Budget reports are progress reports, or *report cards,* on management's performance in achieving planned objectives. These reports can be prepared at any time and for any period. Three common periods for a budget report are a month, quarter, and year.

As we showed in the previous chapter, a *master budget* is based on a predicted level of activity, such as sales volume, for the budget period. In preparing a master budget, two alternative approaches can be used: *fixed budgeting* or *flexible budgeting.*

- A **fixed budget,** also called a *static budget,* is based on a single predicted amount of sales or other activity measure.
- A **flexible budget,** also called a *variable budget,* is based on several different amounts of sales or other activity measure.

Exhibit 23.1 shows the fixed and flexible budgets for a guitar manufacturer.

EXHIBIT 23.1

Fixed versus Flexible Budgets (condensed)

Fixed Budget (One activity level)		Flexible Budget (Several activity levels)			
Sales (in units)............	100	Sales (in units)	100	120	140
Sales (in dollars)	$80,000	Sales (in dollars)..........	$80,000	$96,000	$112,000
Costs...................	56,000	Costs...................	56,000	67,200	78,400
Net income..............	$24,000	Net income..............	$24,000	$28,800	$ 33,600

Exhibit 23.1 shows that the guitar maker forecasts $24,000 of net income if it sells 100 guitars. Only if the guitar maker sells exactly 100 guitars will the fixed budget be useful in evaluating how well the company controlled costs. A flexible budget can be prepared for any sales level (three are shown in Exhibit 23.1). It is more useful when the actual number of units sold differs from the expected level of unit sales predicted.

We next look at fixed budget reports. Knowing the limitations of such reports helps us see the benefits of flexible budgets.

FIXED BUDGET REPORTS

Fixed Budget Performance Report

One use of a budget is to compare actual results with planned activities. Information for this analysis is often presented in a *performance report* that shows budgeted amounts, actual amounts, and **variances** (differences between budgeted and actual amounts). In a fixed budget, the master budget is based on a *single prediction* for sales volume, and the budgeted amount for each cost essentially assumes this specific (or *fixed*) amount of sales will occur.

We illustrate fixed budget performance reports with SolCel, which manufactures portable solar cell phone chargers and related supplies. For January 2017, SolCel based its fixed budget on a prediction of 10,000 (composite) units of sales; costs also were budgeted based on 10,000 composite units of sales.

Exhibit 23.2 shows a **fixed budget performance report,** a report that compares actual results with the results expected under a fixed budget. SolCel's actual sales for the period were 12,000 composite units. In addition, SolCel produced 12,000 composite units during the period (meaning its inventory level did not change). The final column in the performance report shows the differences (variances) between the budgeted and actual dollar amounts for each budget item.

SOLCEL
Fixed Budget Performance Report
For Month Ended January 31, 2017

	Fixed Budget	Actual Results	Variances*
Sales (in units).............................	**10,000**	**12,000**	
Sales (in dollars)............................	$100,000	$125,000	$25,000 F
Cost of goods sold			
Direct materials	10,000	13,000	3,000 U
Direct labor............................	15,000	20,000	5,000 U
Overhead			
Factory supplies	2,000	2,100	100 U
Utilities...............................	3,000	4,000	1,000 U
Depreciation—Machinery	8,000	8,000	0
Supervisory salaries	11,000	11,000	0
Selling expenses			
Sales commissions......................	9,000	10,800	1,800 U
Shipping expenses......................	4,000	4,300	300 U
General and administrative expenses			
Office supplies	5,000	5,200	200 U
Insurance expenses......................	1,000	1,200	200 U
Depreciation—Office equipment..............	7,000	7,000	0
Administrative salaries....................	13,000	13,000	0
Total expenses..........................	88,000	99,600	11,600 U
Income from operations.....................	$ 12,000	$ 25,400	$13,400 F

* F = Favorable variance; U = Unfavorable variance.

EXHIBIT 23.2

Fixed Budget Performance Report

This type of performance report designates differences between budgeted and actual results as *variances*. We use the letters *F* and *U* to describe variances, with meanings as follows:

F = **Favorable variance**   When compared to budget, the actual cost or revenue contributes to a *higher* income. That is, actual revenue is higher than budgeted revenue, or actual cost is lower than budgeted cost.

U = **Unfavorable variance**   When compared to budget, the actual cost or revenue contributes to a *lower* income; actual revenue is lower than budgeted revenue, or actual cost is higher than budgeted cost.

Example: How is it that the favorable sales variance in Exhibit 23.2 is linked with so many unfavorable cost and expense variances? *Answer:* Costs have increased with the increase in sales.

Budget Reports for Evaluation

A primary use of budget reports is as a tool for management to monitor and control operations. From the fixed budget performance report in Exhibit 23.2, SolCel's management might raise questions such as:

- Why is actual income from operations $13,400 higher than budgeted?
- Is manufacturing using too much direct material?
- Is manufacturing using too much direct labor?
- Why are sales commissions higher than budgeted?
- Why are so many of the variances unfavorable?

The performance report in Exhibit 23.2 will not be very useful in answering these types of questions because it is not based on an "apples to apples" comparison. That is, the budgeted dollar amounts are based on 10,000 units of sales, but the actual dollar amounts are based on 12,000 units of sales. Clearly, the costs to

Point: The fixed budget report can be useful in evaluating the sales manager's performance because it shows both budgeted and actual sales.

make 12,000 units will be greater than the costs to make 10,000 units, so it is no surprise that SolCel's total expense variance is unfavorable. In addition, the costs in Exhibit 23.2 with the highest unfavorable variances (direct materials, direct labor, and sales commissions) are typically considered *variable* costs, which increase directly with sales activity. In general, the *fixed* budget performance report is not as useful in analyzing performance when actual sales differ from predicted sales. In the next section, we show how a *flexible* budget can be more useful in analyzing performance.

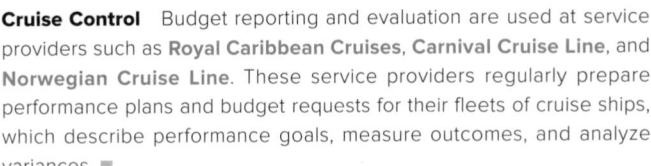 **Decision** Insight

Cruise Control   Budget reporting and evaluation are used at service providers such as **Royal Caribbean Cruises**, **Carnival Cruise Line**, and **Norwegian Cruise Line**. These service providers regularly prepare performance plans and budget requests for their fleets of cruise ships, which describe performance goals, measure outcomes, and analyze variances. ∎

© Melanie Stetson Freeman/The Christian Science Monitor/Getty Images

FLEXIBLE BUDGET REPORTS

Purpose of Flexible Budgets

To address limitations with the fixed budget performance report due to its lack of adjustment to changes in sales volume, management can use a flexible budget. A flexible budget is useful both before and after the period's activities are complete.

- A flexible budget prepared **before** the period is often based on several levels of activity. Budgets for those different levels can provide a "what-if" look at operations. The different levels often include both a best-case and worst-case scenario. This allows management to make adjustments to avoid or lessen the effects of the worst-case scenario.

- A flexible budget prepared **after** the period helps management evaluate past performance. It is especially useful for such an evaluation because it reflects budgeted revenues and costs based on the actual level of activity. The flexible budget gives an "apples to apples" comparison because the budgeted activity level is the same as the actual activity level. With a flexible budget, comparisons of actual results with budgeted performance are likely to reveal the real causes of any differences. Such information can help managers focus attention on real problem areas and implement corrective actions.

Preparation of Flexible Budgets

P1———

Prepare a flexible budget and interpret a flexible budget performance report.

To prepare a flexible budget, follow these steps:

1. Identify the activity level, such as units produced or sold.
2. Identify costs and classify them as fixed or variable within the relevant range of activity.
3. Compute budgeted *sales* (sales price per unit × number of units of activity). Then subtract the sum of budgeted *variable costs* (variable cost per unit × number of units of activity) plus budgeted *fixed* costs.

Point: The total amount of a variable cost changes in direct proportion to a change in activity level. The total amount of fixed cost remains unchanged regardless of changes in the level of activity within a relevant (normal) operating range.

In a flexible budget, we express each variable cost in one of two ways: either as (1) a constant dollar amount per unit of sales or as (2) a constant percentage of a sales dollar. In the case of a fixed cost, we express its budgeted amount as the total amount expected to occur at any sales volume within the relevant range.

Exhibit 23.3 shows a set of flexible budgets for SolCel for January 2017.

1. SolCel's management decides that the number of units sold is the relevant activity level. (For SolCel, the number of units sold equals the number of units produced.) For purposes of preparing the flexible budget, management decides it wants budgets at three different activity levels: 10,000 units, 12,000 units, and 14,000 units.

SOLCEL
Flexible Budgets
For Month Ended January 31, 2017

| | Flexible Budget | | Flexible Budget for Unit Sales of | | |
	Variable Amount per Unit	Total Fixed Cost	10,000	12,000	14,000
Sales	$10.00		$100,000	$120,000	$140,000
Variable costs					
Direct materials	1.00		10,000	12,000	14,000
Direct labor..............................	1.50		15,000	18,000	21,000
Factory supplies..........................	0.20		2,000	2,400	2,800
Utilities	0.30		3,000	3,600	4,200
Sales commissions........................	0.90		9,000	10,800	12,600
Shipping expenses........................	0.40		4,000	4,800	5,600
Office supplies	0.50		5,000	6,000	7,000
Total variable costs	4.80		48,000	57,600	67,200
Contribution margin.......................	$ 5.20		$ 52,000	$ 62,400	$ 72,800
Fixed costs					
Depreciation—Machinery		$ 8,000	8,000	8,000	8,000
Supervisory salaries.......................		11,000	11,000	11,000	11,000
Insurance expense.........................		1,000	1,000	1,000	1,000
Depreciation—Office equipment..............		7,000	7,000	7,000	7,000
Administrative salaries.....................		13,000	13,000	13,000	13,000
Total fixed costs		$40,000	40,000	40,000	40,000
Income from operations.....................			$ 12,000	$ 22,400	$ 32,800

EXHIBIT 23.3

Flexible Budgets (prepared Before the Period)

2 SolCel's management classifies its costs as variable (seven items listed under the "Variable costs" heading) or fixed (five costs listed under the "Fixed costs" heading). These classifications result from management's investigation of each expense using techniques such as the high-low or regression methods we showed in a previous chapter. Variable and fixed expense categories are *not* the same for every company, and we must avoid drawing conclusions from specific cases.

3 SolCel uses the sales price per unit, the variable cost per unit for each variable cost, and the three activity levels to compute sales and variable costs. For example, at the three different activity levels, sales are budgeted to equal $100,000 (computed as $10 × 10,000), $120,000 (computed as $10 × 12,000), and $140,000 (computed as $10 × 14,000), respectively. Likewise, budgeted direct labor equals $15,000 (computed as $1.50 × 10,000) if 10,000 units are sold and $21,000 (computed as $1.50 × 14,000) if 14,000 units are sold. SolCel then lists each of the fixed costs in total.

The flexible budgets in Exhibit 23.3 follow a *contribution margin format*—beginning with sales followed by variable costs and then fixed costs. The first column of numbers in Exhibit 23.3 shows the variable costs per unit for each of SolCel's variable costs. The second column of numbers shows SolCel's fixed costs, which won't change in total as sales volume changes. The third, fourth, and fifth number columns show the flexible budget amounts computed for three different sales volumes. For instance, the third number column's flexible budget is based on 10,000 units. In this column, total variable costs for each of SolCel's seven variable costs are computed as the variable cost per unit (from column 1) multiplied by 10,000 units. The fixed cost amounts in this column are the same as those in the second number column. Overall, the fixed cost amounts in the third number column of Exhibit 23.3 are the same as those in the fixed budget of Exhibit 23.2 because the expected sales volume (10,000 units) is the same for both budgets.

Point: The usefulness of a flexible budget depends on valid classification of variable and fixed costs. Some costs are mixed and must be analyzed to determine their variable and fixed portions.

Example: Using Exhibit 23.3, what is the budgeted income from operations for unit sales of (a) 11,000 and (b) 13,000? *Answers:* $17,200 for unit sales of 11,000; $27,600 for unit sales of 13,000.

Point: Flexible budgeting allows a budget to be prepared at any *actual* output level. Performance reports are then prepared comparing the flexible budget to actual revenues and costs.

The flexible budget in Exhibit 23.3 also reports budgeted costs for activity levels of 12,000 and 14,000 units. The total variable costs increase as the activity levels increase, but the total fixed costs stay unchanged as activity increases. A flexible budget like that in Exhibit 23.3 can be useful to management in planning operations. In addition, as we will show in the next section, a flexible budget prepared after period-end is particularly useful in analyzing performance when actual sales volume differs from that predicted by a fixed budget.

Formula for Total Budgeted Costs   For approximate "what-if" analyses, management can compute total budgeted costs at any activity level with this flexible budget formula.

> **Total budgeted costs = Total fixed costs + (Total variable cost per unit × Units of activity level)**

Using this formula, management can compute total budgeted costs for any number of activity levels, and then, at the end of the period, compare actual costs to budgeted costs at any activity level. For example, if 11,250 units are actually sold, total budgeted costs are computed as:

> $$\$94,000 = \$40,000 + (\$4.80 \times 11,250)$$

Flexible Budget Performance Report

SolCel's actual sales volume for January was 12,000 units. This sales volume is 2,000 units more than the 10,000 units originally predicted in the fixed budget. So, when management evaluates SolCel's performance, it needs a flexible budget showing actual and budgeted dollar amounts at 12,000 units.

A **flexible budget performance report** compares actual performance and budgeted performance based on actual sales volume (or other activity level). This report directs management's attention to those costs or revenues that differ substantially from budgeted amounts. In SolCel's

EXHIBIT 23.4

Flexible Budget
Performance Report
(prepared After the Period)

	Flexible Budget (12,000 units)	Actual Results (12,000 units)	Variances*
SOLCEL Flexible Budget Performance Report For Month Ended January 31, 2017			
Sales.....................................	$120,000	$125,000	$5,000 F
Variable costs			
Direct materials...........................	12,000	13,000	1,000 U
Direct labor..............................	18,000	20,000	2,000 U
Factory supplies	2,400	2,100	300 F
Utilities	3,600	4,000	400 U
Sales commissions	10,800	10,800	0
Shipping expenses.......................	4,800	4,300	500 F
Office supplies	6,000	5,200	800 F
Total variable costs......................	57,600	59,400	1,800 U
Contribution margin	62,400	65,600	3,200 F
Fixed costs			
Depreciation—Machinery..................	8,000	8,000	0
Supervisory salaries	11,000	11,000	0
Insurance expense.......................	1,000	1,200	200 U
Depreciation—Office equipment	7,000	7,000	0
Administrative salaries....................	13,000	13,000	0
Total fixed costs	40,000	40,200	200 U
Income from operations...................	$ 22,400	$ 25,400	$3,000 F

Point: Total budgeted costs = $97,600, computed as $40,000 + ($4.80 × 12,000).

* F = Favorable variance; U = Unfavorable variance.

case, we prepare this report after January's sales volume is known to be 12,000 units. Exhibit 23.4 shows SolCel's flexible budget performance report for January.

The flexible budget report shows a favorable income variance of $3,000. Management uses this report to investigate variances and evaluate SolCel's performance. Quite often management will focus on large variances. This report shows a $5,000 favorable variance in total dollar sales. Because actual and budgeted volumes are both 12,000 units, the $5,000 favorable sales variance must have resulted from a higher-than-expected selling price. Management would like to determine if the conditions that resulted in higher selling prices are likely to continue.

The other variances in Exhibit 23.4 also direct management's attention to areas where corrective actions can help control SolCel's operations. For example, both the direct materials and direct labor variances are relatively large and unfavorable. On the other hand, relatively large favorable variances are observed for shipping expenses and office supplies. Management will try to determine the causes for these variances, both favorable and unfavorable, and make changes to SolCel's operations if needed.

In addition to analyzing variances using a flexible budget performance report, management can also take a more detailed approach based on a *standard cost* system. We illustrate this analysis next in the Standard Costs section.

 Decision Maker

Entrepreneur The head of the strategic consulting division of your financial services firm complains to you about the unfavorable variances on the division's performance reports. "We worked on more consulting assignments than planned. It's not surprising our costs are higher than expected. To top it off, this report characterizes our work as *poor!*" How do you respond? ■ [*Answer:* From the complaints, this performance report appears to compare actual results with a fixed budget. This comparison is useful in determining whether the amount of work actually performed was more or less than planned, but it is not useful in determining whether the division was more or less efficient than planned. If the division worked on more assignments than expected, some costs will certainly increase. Therefore, you should prepare a flexible budget using the actual number of consulting assignments and then compare actual performance to the flexible budget.]

A manufacturing company reports the following fixed budget and actual results for the past year. The fixed budget assumes a selling price of $40 per unit. The fixed budget is based on 20,000 units of sales, and the actual results are based on 24,000 units of sales. Prepare a flexible budget performance report for the past year. Label variances as favorable (F) or unfavorable (U).

NEED-TO-KNOW 23-1

Flexible Budget

P1

	Fixed Budget (20,000 units)	Actual Results (24,000 units)
Sales	$800,000	$972,000
Variable costs*	160,000	240,000
Fixed costs	500,000	490,000

*Budgeted variable cost per unit = $160,000/20,000 = $8.00

Solution

Flexible Budget Performance Report			
	Flexible Budget (24,000 units)	Actual Results (24,000 units)	Variances
Sales	$960,000*	$972,000	$12,000 F
Variable costs	192,000**	240,000	48,000 U
Contribution margin	768,000	732,000	36,000 U
Fixed costs	500,000	490,000	10,000 F
Income from operations	$268,000	$242,000	$26,000 U

*24,000 × $40   **24,000 × $8

Do More: QS 23-1, QS 23-2, QS 23-3, QS 23-4, E 23-3, E 23-4

Section 2—Standard Costs

C1

Define *standard costs* and explain how standard cost information is useful for management by exception.

We show how *standard costs* can be used in a flexible budgeting system to enable management to better understand the reasons for variances. **Standard costs** are preset costs for delivering a product or service under normal conditions. These costs are established by personnel, engineering, and accounting studies using past experiences. Standard costs vary across companies, though manufacturing companies usually use standard costing for direct materials, direct labor, and overhead costs.

Management can use standard costs to assess the reasonableness of actual costs incurred for producing the product or providing the service. When actual costs vary from standard costs, management follows up to identify potential problems and take corrective actions. **Management by exception** means that managers focus attention on the most significant differences between actual costs and standard costs and give less attention to areas where performance is reasonably close to standard. Management by exception is especially useful when directed at controllable items, enabling top management to affect the actions of lower-level managers responsible for the company's revenues and costs.

Standard costs are often used in preparing budgets because they are the anticipated costs incurred under normal conditions. Terms such as *standard materials cost, standard labor cost,* and *standard overhead cost* are often used to refer to amounts budgeted for direct materials, direct labor, and overhead.

While many managers use standard costs to investigate manufacturing costs, standard costs can also help control *nonmanufacturing* costs. Companies providing services instead of products can also benefit from the use of standard costs. For example, while quality medical service is paramount, efficiency in providing that service is also important in controlling medical costs. The use of budgeting and standard costing is touted as an effective means to control and monitor medical costs, especially overhead.

MATERIALS AND LABOR STANDARDS

This section explains how to set direct materials and direct labor standards and how to prepare a standard cost card. Managerial accountants, engineers, personnel administrators, and other managers work together to set standard costs. To identify standards for direct labor costs, we can conduct time and motion studies for each labor operation in the process of providing a product or service. From these studies, management can learn the best way to perform the operation and then set the standard labor time required for the operation under normal conditions. Similarly, standards for direct materials are set by studying the quantity, grade, and cost of each material used. Standards should be challenging but attainable and should acknowledge machine breakdowns, material waste, and idle time.

Example: What factors might be considered when deciding whether to revise standard costs? *Answer:* Changes in the processes and/or resources needed to carry out the processes.

Regardless of the care used in setting standard costs and in revising them as conditions change, actual costs frequently differ from standard costs. For instance, the actual quantity of material or hours of direct labor used can differ from the standard, or the price paid per unit of material or hours of direct labor can differ from the standard.

    Decision Insight

Cruis'n Standards   The **Tesla** Model S consists of hundreds of parts for which engineers set standards. Various types of labor are also involved in its production, including machining, assembly, painting, and welding, and standards are set for each. Actual results are periodically compared with standards to assess performance. ∎

© Jasper Juinen/Bloomberg via Getty Images

Setting Standard Costs

To illustrate the setting of standard costs, we consider wooden baseball bats manufactured by ProBat. Its engineers have determined that manufacturing one bat requires 0.90 kilograms (kg) of high-grade wood. They also expect some loss of material as part of the process because of inefficiencies and waste. This results in adding an *allowance* of 0.10 kg, making the standard requirement 1.0 kg of wood for each bat.

The 0.90 kg portion is called an *ideal standard;* it is the quantity of material required if the process is 100% efficient without any loss or waste. Reality suggests that some loss of material usually occurs with any process. The standard of 1.0 kg is known as the *practical standard,* the quantity of material required under normal application of the process. The standard direct labor rate should include allowances for employee breaks, cleanup, and machine downtime. Most companies use practical rather than ideal standards.

Point: Companies promoting continuous improvement strive to achieve ideal standards by eliminating inefficiencies and waste.

ProBat needs to develop standard costs for direct materials, direct labor, and overhead. For direct materials and direct labor, ProBat must develop standard quantities and standard prices. For overhead, ProBat must consider the activities that drive overhead costs. ProBat's standard costs are:

Direct materials High-grade wood is purchased at a standard price of $25 per kg. The purchasing department sets this price as the expected price for the budget period. To determine this price, the purchasing department considers factors such as the quality of materials, economic conditions, supply factors (shortages and excesses), and available discounts.

Direct labor Two hours of labor time are required to manufacture a bat. The direct labor rate is $20 per hour (better-than-average skilled labor is required). This rate includes wages, taxes, and fringe benefits. When wage rates differ across employees due to seniority or skill level, the standard direct labor rate is based on the expected mix of workers.

Overhead ProBat assigns overhead at the rate of $10 per direct labor hour.

The standard costs of direct materials, direct labor, and overhead for one bat are shown in Exhibit 23.5 in a *standard cost card.* These standard cost amounts are then used to prepare manufacturing budgets for a budgeted level of production.

EXHIBIT 23.5

Standard Cost Card

STANDARD COST CARD			
Production Factor	**Standard Quantity**	**Standard Cost per Unit**	**Total Standard Cost**
Direct materials (wood)	1 kg	$25 per kg	$25
Direct labor	2 hours	$20 per hour	40
Overhead	2 labor hours	$10 per hour	20
		Total	**$85**

Cost Variance Analysis

Companies analyze differences between actual costs and standard costs to assess performance. A **cost variance,** also simply called a *variance,* is the difference between actual and standard costs. Cost variances can be favorable (F) or unfavorable (U).

Describe cost variances and what they reveal about performance.

- If actual cost is less than standard cost, the variance is considered favorable (F).
- If actual costs are greater than standard costs, the variance is unfavorable (U).[1]

This section discusses cost variance analysis. (In the Decision Analysis section of this chapter, we discuss sales variances.)

---

[1] Short-term favorable variances can sometimes lead to long-term unfavorable variances. For instance, if management spends less than the budgeted amount on maintenance or insurance, the performance report would show a favorable variance. Cutting these expenses can lead to major losses in the long run if machinery wears out prematurely or insurance coverage proves inadequate.

Exhibit 23.6 shows the flow of events in **variance analysis:** (1) preparing a standard cost performance report, (2) computing and analyzing variances, (3) identifying questions and their explanations, and (4) taking corrective and strategic actions (if needed). These variance analysis steps are interrelated and are frequently applied in good organizations.

EXHIBIT 23.6

Variance Analysis

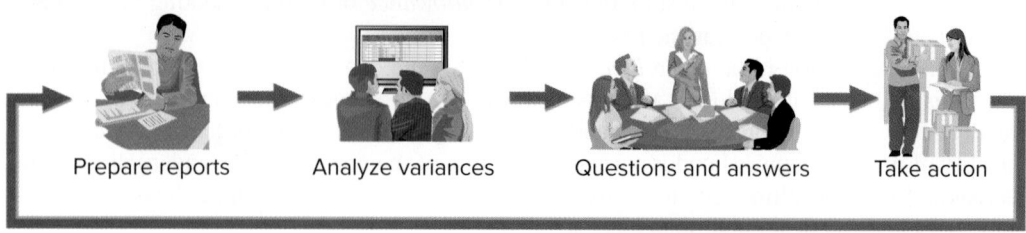

| Prepare reports | Analyze variances | Questions and answers | Take action |

Cost Variance Computation Exhibit 23.7 shows a general formula for computing any cost variance (CV).

EXHIBIT 23.7

Cost Variance Formulas*

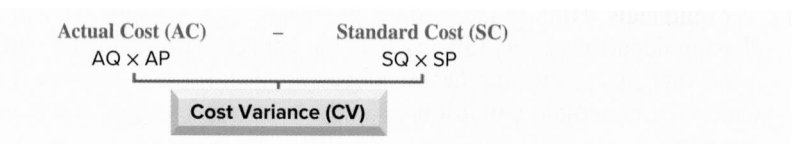

*AQ is actual quantity; AP is actual price; SP is standard price; SQ is standard quantity allowed for actual output.

Actual quantity (AQ) is the actual amount of material or labor used to manufacture the actual quantity of output for the period. Standard quantity (SQ) is the standard amount of input for the actual quantity of output for the period. For example, if ProBat's actual output is 500 bats, its standard quantity of direct labor is 1,000 hours (500 bats × 2 hours per bat). Actual price (AP) is the actual amount paid to acquire the actual direct material or direct labor used for the period. SP is the standard price.

Model of Price and Quantity Variances Two main factors cause a cost variance:

1. A difference between actual price per unit of input and standard price per unit of input results in a **price** (or rate) **variance.**
2. A difference between actual quantity of input used and standard quantity of input used results in a **quantity** (or usage or efficiency) **variance.**

Isolating these price and quantity factors in a cost variance leads to the formulas in Exhibit 23.8.

EXHIBIT 23.8

Price Variance and Quantity Variance Formulas

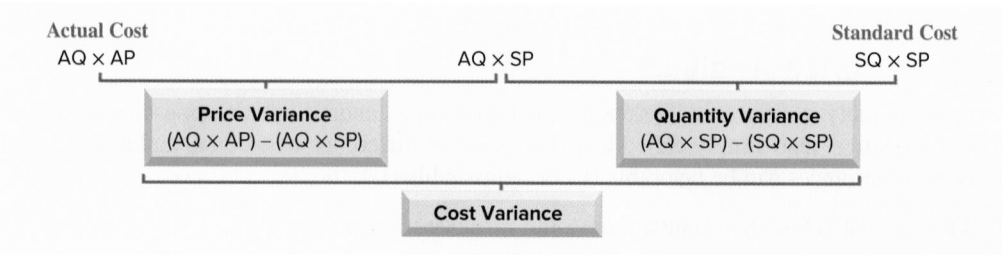

The model in Exhibit 23.8 separates total cost variance into separate price and quantity variances, which is useful in analyzing performance. Exhibit 23.8 illustrates three important rules in computing variances:

1. In computing a price variance, the quantity (actual) is held constant.
2. In computing a quantity variance, the price (standard) is held constant.
3. Cost variance, or total variance, is the sum of price and quantity variances.

Managers sometimes find it useful to use an alternative (but equivalent) computation for the price and quantity variances, as shown in Exhibit 23.9.

> **Price Variance (PV) = [Actual Price (AP) − Standard Price (SP)] × Actual Quantity (AQ)**
>
> **Quantity Variance (QV) = [Actual Quantity (AQ) − Standard Quantity (SQ)] × Standard Price (SP)**

EXHIBIT 23.9

Alternative Price Variance and Quantity Variance Formulas

The results from applying the formulas in Exhibits 23.8 and 23.9 are identical.

Computing Materials and Labor Variances

We show how to compute the direct materials and direct labor cost variances using data from G-Max, a manufacturer of specialty golf equipment and accessories. G-Max set the following standard quantities and costs for direct materials and direct labor per unit for one of its hand-crafted golf clubheads:

P2

Compute materials and labor variances.

Standard Quantities and Costs	
Direct materials (0.5 lb. per unit at $20 per lb.)	$10.00
Direct labor (1 hr. per unit at $16 per hr.)	16.00
Total standard direct cost per unit.	$26.00

Materials Cost Variances   During May 2017, G-Max budgeted to produce 4,000 clubheads (units). It actually produced only 3,500 units. It used 1,800 pounds of direct materials (titanium) costing $21 per pound, meaning its total direct materials cost was $37,800. To produce 3,500 units, G-Max should have used 1,750 pounds of direct materials (3,500 × 0.5 lb. per unit). This amount of 1,750 pounds is the standard quantity of direct materials that should have been used to produce 3,500 units. This information allows us to compute both actual and standard direct materials costs for G-Max's 3,500 units and its total direct materials cost variance as follows:

© Kristjan Maack/Getty Images/ Nordic Photos

Direct Materials	Quantity	Price per Unit	Cost
Actual cost	1,800 lbs. ×	$21 per lb.	= $37,800
Standard cost	1,750 lbs.* ×	$20 per lb.	= 35,000
Direct materials cost variance			= $ 2,800 U

*Standard quantity = 3,500 units × 0.5 lb. per unit

Management wishes to determine if this unfavorable cost variance is due to unfavorable quantity or price variances, or both. To better isolate the causes of this $2,800 unfavorable total direct materials cost variance, the materials price and quantity variances are computed and shown in Exhibit 23.10.

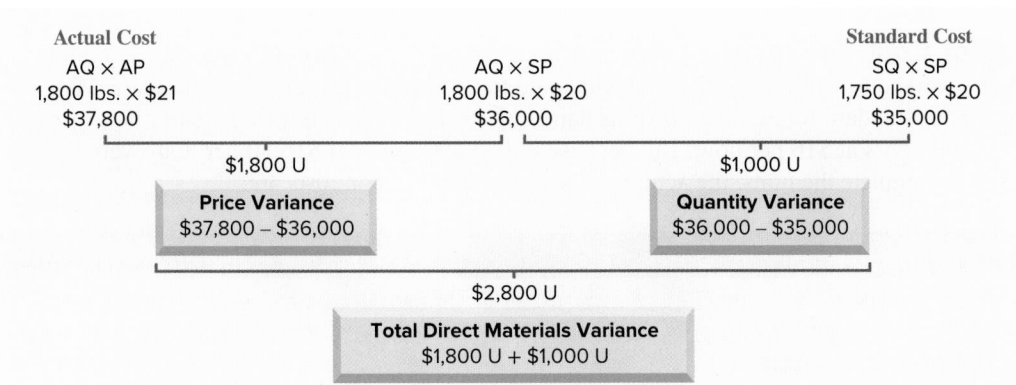

EXHIBIT 23.10

Materials Price and Quantity Variances*

*AQ is actual quantity; AP is actual price; SP is standard price; SQ is standard quantity allowed for actual output.

Point: The direct materials price variance can also be computed as ($21 − $20) × 18,000 = $1,800. The direct materials quantity variance can also be computed as (1,800 − 1,750) × $20 = $1,000.

We now can see the two components of the $2,800 unfavorable direct materials cost variance: The $1,800 unfavorable price variance results from paying $1 more per pound than the standard price, computed as 1,800 lbs. × $1. G-Max also used 50 pounds more of materials than the standard quantity (1,800 actual pounds −1,750 standard pounds). The $1,000 unfavorable quantity variance is computed as [(1,800 actual lbs. − 1,750 standard lbs.) × $20 standard price per lb.]. Detailed price and quantity variances allow management to ask the responsible individuals for explanations and corrective actions.

Evaluating Materials Variances

The purchasing department is usually responsible for the price paid for materials. Responsibility for explaining the price variance in this case rests with the purchasing manager as a price higher than standard caused the variance. The production department is usually responsible for the amount of material used. In this case, the production manager is responsible for explaining why the process used more than the standard amount of materials.

Variance analysis presents challenges. For instance, the production department could have used more than the standard amount of material because the materials' quality did not meet specifications and led to excessive waste. In this case, the purchasing manager is responsible for explaining why inferior materials were acquired. However, if analysis shows that waste was due to inefficiencies, not poor-quality material, the production manager is responsible for explaining what happened.

In evaluating price variances, managers must recognize that a favorable price variance can indicate a problem with poor product quality. **Redhook Ale**, a microbrewery in the Pacific Northwest, can probably save 10% to 15% in material prices by buying six-row barley malt instead of the better two-row from Washington's Yakima Valley. Attention to quality, however, has helped Redhook Ale increase its sales. Purchasing activities are judged on both the quality of the materials and the purchase price variance.

NEED-TO-KNOW 23-2

Direct Materials Price and Quantity Variances

P2

A manufacturing company reports the following for one of its products. Compute the direct materials (*a*) price variance and (*b*) quantity variance and classify each as favorable or unfavorable.

Direct materials standard.................	8 pounds @ $6 per pound
Actual direct materials used	83,000 pounds @ $5.80 per pound
Actual finished units produced	10,000

Solution

a. Price variance = (Actual quantity × Actual price) − (Actual quantity × Standard price)
= (83,000 × $5.80) − (83,000 × $6) = $16,600 Favorable

b. Quantity variance = (Actual quantity × Standard price) − (Standard quantity* × Standard price)
= (83,000 × $6) − (80,000 × $6) = $18,000 Unfavorable

*Standard quantity = 10,000 units × 8 standard pounds per unit = 80,000 pounds

Do More: QS 23-8, E 23-9, E 23-11, E 23-12, E 23-13

Labor Cost Variances

Labor cost for a product or service depends on the number of hours worked (quantity) and the wage rate paid to employees (price). To illustrate, G-Max's direct labor standard for 3,500 units of its handcrafted clubheads is one direct labor hour per unit, or 3,500 hours at $16 per hour. But because only 3,400 hours at $16.50 per hour were actually used to complete the units, the actual and standard direct labor costs are:

Direct Labor	Quantity	Rate per Hour	Cost
Actual cost	3,400 hrs.	× $16.50 per hr.	= $56,100
Standard cost	3,500 hrs.*	× $16.00 per hr.	= 56,000
Direct labor cost variance			= $ 100 U

*Standard quantity = 3,500 units × 1 standard direct labor hour per unit

Actual direct labor cost is merely $100 over the standard; that small difference might suggest no immediate concern. A closer look, however, might suggest problems. The direct labor cost variance can be divided into price and quantity variances, which are usually called *rate* and *efficiency* variances. Computing both the labor rate and efficiency variances reveals a more precise picture, as shown in Exhibit 23.11.

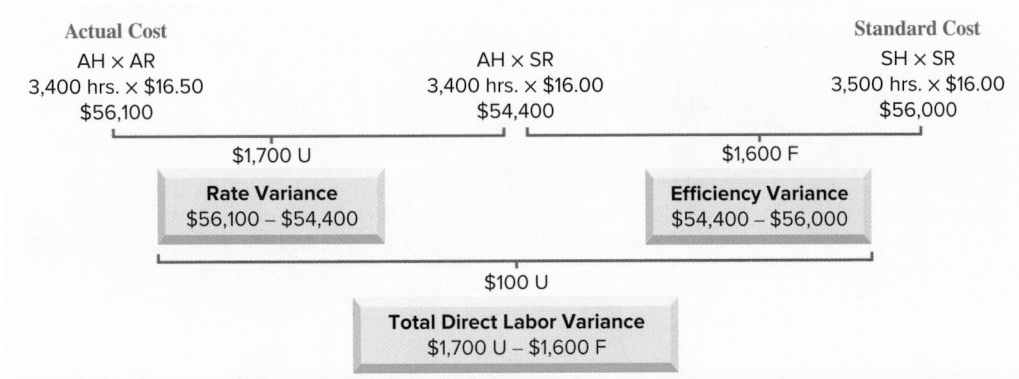

EXHIBIT 23.11

Labor Rate and Efficiency Variances*

Point: The direct labor efficiency variance can also be computed as $(3,400 - 3,500) \times \$16 = \$1,600$. The direct labor rate variance can also be computed as $(\$16.50 - \$16) \times 3,400 = \$1,700$.

* Here, we employ hours (H) for quantity (Q), and the wage rate (R) for price (P). Thus: AH is actual direct labor hours: AR is actual wage rate; SH is standard direct labor hours allowed for actual output; SR is standard wage rate.

Evaluating Labor Variances   Exhibit 23.11 shows that the $100 total unfavorable labor cost variance results from a $1,600 favorable efficiency variance and a $1,700 unfavorable rate variance. To produce 3,500 units, G-Max should use 3,500 direct labor hours (3,500 units × 1 direct labor hour per unit). The favorable efficiency variance results from using 100 fewer direct labor hours (3,400 actual DLH − 3,500 standard DLH) than standard for the units produced. The unfavorable rate variance results from paying a wage rate that is $0.50 per hour higher ($16.50 actual rate − $16.00 standard rate) than standard. The personnel administrator or the production manager needs to explain why the wage rate is higher than expected. The production manager should explain how the labor hours were reduced. If this experience can be repeated and transferred to other departments, more savings are possible.

Example: Compute the rate variance and the efficiency variance for Exhibit 23.11 if 3,700 actual hours are used at an actual price of $15.50 per hour. *Answer:* $1,700 favorable labor rate variance and $3,200 unfavorable labor efficiency variance.

One possible explanation of these labor rate and efficiency variances is the use of workers with different skill levels. If so, management must discuss the implications with the production manager who assigns workers to tasks. In this case, an investigation might show that higher-skilled workers were used to produce 3,500 units of handcrafted clubheads. As a result, fewer labor hours might be required for the work, but the wage rate paid these workers is higher than standard because of their greater skills. The effect of this strategy is a higher-than-standard total cost, which would require actions to remedy the situation or adjust the standard.

Other explanations for direct labor variances are possible. Lower-quality materials, poor employee training or supervision, equipment breakdowns, and idle workers due to reduced demand for the company's products could lead to unfavorable direct labor efficiency variances.

■ **Decision** Maker ━━━━━━━━━━━━━━━━━━━━━━━━━━━━

Production Manager   You receive the manufacturing variance report for June and discover a large unfavorable labor efficiency (quantity) variance. What factors do you investigate to identify its possible causes? ■   [*Answer:* An unfavorable labor efficiency variance occurs because more labor hours than standard were used during the period. Possible reasons for this include: (1) materials quality could be poor, resulting in more labor consumption due to rework; (2) unplanned interruptions (strike, breakdowns, accidents) could have occurred during the period; and (3) a different labor mix might have occurred for a strategic reason such as to expedite orders. This new labor mix could have consisted of a larger proportion of untrained labor, which resulted in more labor hours.]

NEED-TO-KNOW 23-3

Direct Labor Rate and Efficiency Variances

P2

The following information is available for a manufacturer. Compute the direct labor rate and efficiency variances and label them as favorable (F) or unfavorable (U).

Actual direct labor cost (6,250 hours @ $13.10 per hour)................	$81,875
Standard direct labor hours per unit....................................	2.0 hours
Standard direct labor rate per hour....................................	$13.00
Actual production (units)...	2,500 units
Budgeted production (units)...	3,000 units

Solution

Do More: QS 23-11, E 23-10, E 23-11, E 23-12, E 23-16

Total standard hours = 2,500 × 2.0 = 5,000
Rate variance   = ($13.10 − $13.00) × 6,250 = $625 U
Efficiency variance = (6,250 − 5,000) × $13.00 = $16,250 U

OVERHEAD STANDARDS AND VARIANCES

In previous chapters we showed how companies can use *predetermined overhead rates* to allocate overhead costs to products or services. In a standard costing system, this allocation is done using the *standard* amount of the overhead allocation base, such as standard labor hours or standard machine hours. We now show how to use standard costs to develop flexible overhead budgets.

Flexible Overhead Budgets

Standard overhead costs are the overhead amounts expected to occur at a certain activity level. Overhead includes fixed costs and variable costs. This requires management to classify overhead costs as fixed or variable (within a relevant range), and to develop a flexible budget for overhead costs.

To illustrate, the first two number columns of Exhibit 23.12 show the overhead cost structure to develop G-Max's flexible overhead budgets for May 2017. At the beginning of the year, G-Max predicted variable overhead costs of $1.00 per unit (clubhead), comprised of $0.40 per unit for indirect labor, $0.30 per unit for indirect materials, $0.20 per unit for power and lights, and $0.10 per unit for factory maintenance. In addition, G-Max predicts monthly fixed overhead of $4,000.

With these variable and fixed overhead cost amounts, G-Max can prepare flexible overhead budgets at various capacity levels (four rightmost number columns in Exhibit 23.12). At its maximum capacity (100% column), G-Max could produce 5,000 clubheads. At 70% of maximum capacity, G-Max could produce 3,500 (computed as 5,000 × 70%) clubheads. Recall that total variable costs will increase as production activity increases, but total fixed costs will not change as production activity changes. At 70% capacity, variable overhead costs are budgeted at $3,500 (3,500 × $1.00), while at 100% capacity variable costs are budgeted at $5,000 (5,000 × $1.00). At all capacity levels within the relevant range, fixed overhead costs are budgeted at $4,000 per month.

Point: With increased automation, machine hours are frequently used in applying overhead instead of labor hours.

Standard Overhead Rate

To apply overhead costs to products or services, management establishes the standard overhead cost rate, using the three-step process below.

Step 1: Determine an Allocation Base   The allocation base is a measure of input that management believes is related to overhead costs. Examples can include direct labor hours or machine hours. In this section, we assume that G-Max uses direct labor hours as an allocation base, and it has a standard of one direct labor hour per finished unit.

© Halfdark/Getty Images

EXHIBIT 23.12

Flexible Overhead Budgets

G-MAX
Flexible Overhead Budgets
For Month Ended May 31, 2017

	Flexible Budget		Flexible Budget at Capacity Level of			
	Variable Amount per Unit	Total Fixed Cost	70%	80%	90%	100%
Production (in units)	1 unit		3,500	4,000	4,500	5,000
Factory overhead						
Variable costs						
Indirect labor	$0.40/unit		$1,400	$1,600	$1,800	$2,000
Indirect materials.	0.30/unit		1,050	1,200	1,350	1,500
Power and lights	0.20/unit		700	800	900	1,000
Maintenance	0.10/unit		350	400	450	500
Total variable overhead costs	$1.00/unit		3,500	4,000	4,500	5,000
Fixed costs (per month)						
Building rent		$1,000	1,000	1,000	1,000	1,000
Depreciation—Machinery		1,200	1,200	1,200	1,200	1,200
Supervisory salaries		1,800	1,800	1,800	1,800	1,800
Total fixed overhead costs		$4,000	4,000	4,000	4,000	4,000
Total factory overhead.			$7,500	$8,000	$8,500	$9,000
Standard direct labor hours (1 DL hr./unit). . . .			3,500 hrs.	4,000 hrs.	4,500 hrs.	5,000 hrs.
Predetermined overhead rate per standard direct labor hour.				$ 2.00		

Step 2: Choose a Predicted Activity Level
When choosing the predicted activity level, management considers many factors. The level is rarely set at 100% of capacity. Difficulties in scheduling work, equipment breakdowns, and insufficient product demand typically cause the activity level to be less than full capacity. Also, good long-run management practices usually call for some excess plant capacity, to allow for special opportunities and demand changes. G-Max managers predicted an 80% activity level for May, or a production volume of 4,000 clubheads.

Step 3: Compute the Standard Overhead Rate
At the predicted activity level of 4,000 units, the flexible budget in Exhibit 23.12 predicts total overhead of $8,000. At this activity level of 4,000 units, G-Max's standard direct labor hours are 4,000 hours (4,000 units × 1 direct labor hour per unit). G-Max's standard overhead rate is then computed as:

$$\text{Standard overhead rate} = \frac{\text{Total overhead cost at predicted activity level}}{\text{Total direct labor hours at predicted activity level}}$$

$$= \frac{\$8,000}{4,000} = \$2 \text{ per direct labor hour}$$

This standard overhead rate is used in computing overhead cost variances, as we show next, and in recording journal entries in a standard cost system, which we show in the appendix to this chapter.

■ **Decision** Insight

Measuring Up   In the spirit of continuous improvement, competitors compare their processes and performance standards against benchmarks established by industry leaders. Companies that use **benchmarking** include **Jiffy Lube, All Tune and Lube,** and **SpeeDee Oil Change and Auto Service.** ■

P3

Compute overhead controllable and volume variances.

EXHIBIT 23.13

Applying Standard Overhead Cost

Computing Overhead Cost Variances

In a standard costing system, overhead is applied with the formula in Exhibit 23.13.

$$\text{Standard overhead applied} = \text{Actual production} \times \text{Standard amount of allocation base} \times \text{Standard overhead rate (at predicted activity level)}$$

The standard overhead applied is based on the standard amount of the allocation base that *should have been used,* based on the actual production. This standard activity amount is then multiplied by the predetermined standard overhead rate (at the predicted activity level). For G-Max, standard overhead applied is computed as:

$$3,500 \text{ units} \times 1 \text{ DLH per unit} \times \$2.00 \text{ per DLH} = \$7,000$$

G-Max produced 3,500 units during the month, which should have used 3,500 direct labor hours. At G-Max's predicted capacity level of 80%, the standard overhead rate was $2.00 per direct labor hour. The standard overhead applied is $7,000, as computed above.

Actual overhead incurred might differ from the standard overhead applied for the period, and management again will use *variance analysis*. The difference between the standard amount of overhead cost applied and the total actual overhead incurred is the **overhead cost variance** (total overhead variance), shown in Exhibit 23.14.

EXHIBIT 23.14

Overhead Cost Variance

$$\text{Overhead cost variance (OCV)} = \text{Actual overhead incurred (AOI)} - \text{Standard overhead applied (SOA)}$$

To illustrate, G-Max's actual overhead cost incurred in the month (found in other cost reports) is $7,650. Using the formula in Exhibit 23.14, G-Max's total overhead variance is $650, computed as:

Total Overhead Variance	
Actual total overhead (given)	$7,650
Standard overhead applied (3,500 units × 1 DLH per unit × $2.00 per DLH)	7,000
Total overhead variance	$ 650 U

This variance is unfavorable: G-Max's actual overhead was higher than the standard amount.

Overhead Controllable and Volume Variances   To help identify factors causing the total overhead cost variance, managers compute *overhead volume* and *overhead controllable variances,* as illustrated in Exhibit 23.15. The results are useful for taking strategic actions to improve company performance.

EXHIBIT 23.15

Framework for Understanding Total Overhead Variance

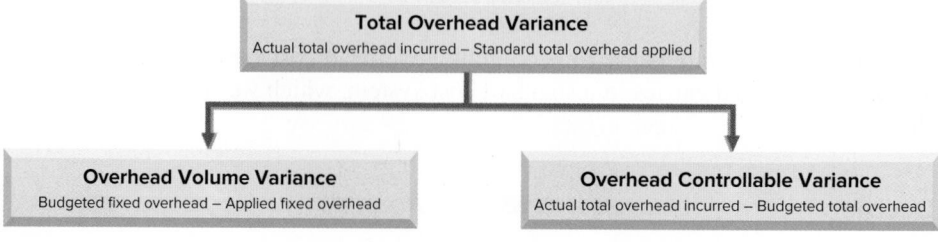

A **volume variance** occurs when the company operates at a different capacity level than was predicted. G-Max predicted it would manufacture 4,000 units, but it only manufactured

3,500 units. The volume variance is usually considered outside the control of the production manager, as it depends mainly on customer demand for the company's products.

The volume variance is based solely on *fixed* overhead. Recall that G-Max's standard *fixed* overhead rate at the predicted capacity level of 4,000 units was $1 per direct labor hour. The overhead volume variance is computed as:

Overhead Volume Variance	
Budgeted fixed overhead (at predicted capacity)	$4,000
Applied fixed overhead (3,500 units × 1 DLH per unit × $1.00 per DLH)	3,500
Volume variance	$ 500 U

The volume variance is unfavorable because G-Max made 500 fewer units than it expected. With a total overhead variance of $650 (unfavorable) and a volume variance of $500 (unfavorable), the controllable overhead variance is computed as:

Controllable variance = Total overhead variance − Overhead volume variance
$$\$150\ U = \$650 - \$500$$

More formally, the **controllable variance** is the difference between the actual overhead costs incurred and the budgeted overhead costs for the standard hours that should have been used for actual production. Controllable variance is the portion of total overhead variance that is considered to be under management's control. Since G-Max only produced 3,500 units during the month, we need to compare *actual* overhead costs to make 3,500 units to the *budgeted* cost to make 3,500 units. Budgeted total overhead cost to make 3,500 units is computed as:

Budgeted Total Overhead Cost	
Budgeted variable overhead cost	
(3,500 units × 1 DLH per unit × $1 VOH* rate per DLH)	$3,500
Budgeted fixed overhead cost	4,000
Budgeted total overhead cost	$7,500

*VOH is variable overhead

Controllable variance is then computed as:

Overhead Controllable Variance	
Actual total overhead (given)	$7,650
Budgeted total overhead (from above)	7,500
Controllable variance	$ 150 U

Analyzing Overhead Controllable and Volume Variances   How should management of G-Max interpret the unfavorable overhead controllable and volume variances? An unfavorable volume variance means that the company did not reach its predicted operating level. In this case, 80% of manufacturing capacity was budgeted, but only 70% was used. Management needs to know why the actual level of production differs from the expected level. The main purpose of the volume variance is to identify what portion of total overhead variance is caused by failing to meet the expected production level. Often the reasons for failing to meet this expected production level are due to factors, such as customer demand, that are beyond employees' control. This information permits management to focus on explanations for the controllable variance, as we discuss next.

Overhead Variance Reports　To help management isolate the reasons for the $150 unfavorable overhead controllable variance, an *overhead variance report* can be prepared. A complete overhead variance report provides managers information about specific overhead costs and how they differ from budgeted amounts. Exhibit 23.16 shows G-Max's overhead variance report for May. The overhead variance report shows the total overhead volume variance of $500 unfavorable (shown near the top of the report) and the $150 unfavorable overhead controllable variance (shown at the bottom right of the report). The detailed listing of individual overhead costs reveals the following: (1) Fixed overhead costs and variable factory maintenance costs were incurred as expected. (2) Costs for indirect labor and power and lights were higher than expected. (3) Indirect materials cost was less than expected. Management can use the variance overhead report to identify the individual overhead costs it wants to investigate.

Appendix 23A describes an expanded analysis of overhead variances.

EXHIBIT 23.16

Overhead Variance Report

Point: Both the flexible budget and actual results are based on 3,500 units produced.

G-MAX Overhead Variance Report For Month Ended May 31, 2017			
Overhead Volume Variance			
Expected production level	80% of capacity (4,000 units)		
Production level achieved	70% of capacity (3,500 units)		
Budgeted fixed overhead (4,000 DLH × $1.00).	$4,000		
Fixed overhead applied (3,500 DLH × $1.00)	$3,500		
Volume variance.	$ 500 U		
	Flexible Budget	**Actual Results**	**Variances***
Overhead Controllable Variance			
Variable overhead costs			
Indirect labor	$1,400	$1,525	$125 U
Indirect materials.	1,050	1,025	25 F
Power and lights	700	750	50 U
Maintenance.	350	350	0
Total variable overhead costs	3,500	3,650	150 U
Fixed overhead costs			
Building rent.	1,000	1,000	0
Depreciation—Machinery	1,200	1,200	0
Supervisory salaries.	1,800	1,800	0
Total fixed overhead costs.	4,000	4,000	0
Total overhead costs	$7,500	$7,650	$150 U

Total overhead variance = $650 unfavorable

* F = Favorable variance; U = Unfavorable variance.

NEED-TO-KNOW 23-4

Overhead Variances

P3

A manufacturing company uses standard costs and reports the information below for January. The company uses machine hours to apply overhead, and the standard is two machine hours per finished unit. Compute the total overhead cost variance, overhead controllable variance, and overhead volume variance for January. Indicate whether each variance is favorable or unfavorable.

Predicted activity level.	1,500 units
Variable overhead rate budgeted	$2.50 per machine hour
Fixed overhead budgeted	$6,000 per month ($2.00 per machine hour at predicted activity level)
Actual activity level.	1,800 units
Actual overhead costs	$15,800

Solution

Total overhead cost variance

Actual total overhead cost (given)	$15,800
Standard overhead applied (1,800 × 2 × $4.50)	16,200
Total overhead variance	$ 400 F

Do More: QS 23-13, QS 23-14, QS 23-15, E 23-17, E 23-19, E 23-20

Overhead controllable variance

Actual total overhead cost (given)	$15,800
Budgeted total overhead (1,800 × 2 × $2.50) + $6,000	15,000
Overhead controllable variance	$ 800 U

Overhead volume variance

Budgeted fixed overhead	$ 6,000
Applied fixed overhead (1,800 × 2 × $2)	7,200
Overhead volume variance	$1,200 F

Standard Costing—Management Considerations

Companies must consider many factors, both positive and negative, in deciding whether and how to use standard costing systems. Exhibit 23.17 summarizes some of these factors.

Standard Costing Considerations	
Positives	**Negatives**
Provides benchmarks for management by exception.	Standards are costly to develop and keep up to date.
Motivates employees to work toward goals.	Variances are not timely for adapting to rapidly changing business conditions.
Useful in the budgeting process.	
Isolates reasons for good or bad performance.	Employees might not try for continuous improvement.

EXHIBIT 23.17

Standard Costing Pros and Cons

 **SUSTAINABILITY AND ACCOUNTING**

As more companies report on their sustainability efforts, organizations provide structure for these reports. One group, the **International Integrated Reporting Council** (IIRC), is a global group of regulators, investors, and accountants that develops methods for integrated reporting. **Integrated reporting** is designed to concisely report how an organization's strategy, performance, sustainability efforts, and governance lead to value creation.

Intel, a maker of computer chips, follows many of the IIRC's recommendations. In its integrated report, Intel notes it links executive pay, in part, to corporate responsibility metrics. For example, 50% of top management's annual cash bonus is based on meeting operating performance targets, including those for corporate responsibility and environmental sustainability. For 2015, Intel's top five managers were paid nearly $10 million for meeting performance targets. By linking executive pay to sustainability targets, Intel motivates managers to integrate sustainability initiatives with their efforts to make financial profits and increase firm value.

Riide, this chapter's feature company, is built around environmental sustainability. Amber "hates traffic" and is focused on alternative energy solutions. At age three, Jeff ditched the training wheels on his Batman bike and never stopped riding.

The duo combined their passion for biking and energy conservation to design an e-bike that is environmentally friendly. They also give back to their community by working with the robotics club at a local high school. "We coach them on what it's like to bring a product to market," says Amber.

Kate Warren/Courtesy of Riide

  **Decision Analysis** ☐☐☐ **Sales Variances**

A1
_____
Analyze changes in sales
from expected amounts.

This chapter explained the computation and analysis of cost variances. A similar variance analysis can be applied to sales. For this analysis, the budgeted amount of unit sales is the predicted activity level, and the budgeted selling price can be treated as a "standard" price. To illustrate, consider the following sales data from G-Max for two of its golf products, Excel golf balls and Big Bert drivers.

	Budgeted	Actual
Sales of Excel golf balls (units)...............	1,000 units	1,100 units
Sales price per Excel golf ball	$10	$10.50
Sales of Big Bert drivers (units)	150 units	140 units
Sales price per Big Bert driver...............	$200	$190

Using this information, we compute both the _sales price variance_ and the _sales volume variance_, as shown in Exhibit 23.18. The sales price variance measures the impact of the actual sales price differing from the expected price. The sales volume variance measures the impact of operating at a different capacity level than predicted by the fixed budget. The total sales price variance is $850 unfavorable, and the total sales volume variance is $1,000 unfavorable. However, further analysis of these total sales variances reveals that both the sales price and sales volume variances for Excel golf balls are favorable, while both variances are unfavorable for the Big Bert driver.

EXHIBIT 23.18

Computing Sales Variances*

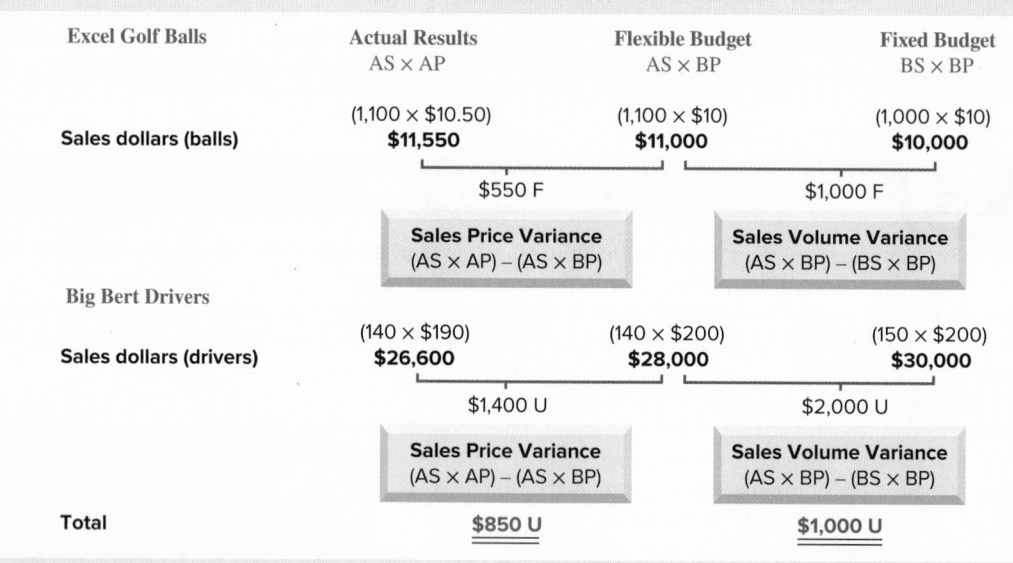

* AS = actual sales units; AP = actual sales price; BP = budgeted sales price; BS = budgeted sales units (fixed budget).

Managers use sales variances for planning and control purposes. G-Max sold 90 combined total units (both balls and drivers) more than budgeted, yet its total sales price and sales volume variances are unfavorable. The unfavorable sales price variance is due mainly to a decrease in the selling price of Big Bert drivers by $10 per unit. Management must assess whether this price decrease will continue. Likewise, the unfavorable sales volume variance is due to G-Max selling fewer Big Bert drivers (140) than were budgeted (150). Management must assess whether this decreased demand for Big Bert drivers will persist.

Overall, management can use the detailed sales variances to examine what caused the company to sell more golf balls and fewer drivers. Managers can also use this information to evaluate and even reward salespeople. Extra compensation is paid to salespeople who contribute to a higher profit margin.

■ **Decision** Maker

Sales Manager   The current performance report reveals a large favorable sales volume variance but an unfavorable sales price variance. You did not expect a large increase in sales volume. What steps do you take to analyze this situation? ■   [*Answer:* The unfavorable sales price variance suggests that actual prices were lower than budgeted prices. As the sales manager, you want to know the reasons for a lower-than-expected price. Perhaps your salespeople lowered the price of certain products by offering quantity discounts. You then might want to know what prompted them to offer the quantity discounts (perhaps competitors were offering discounts). You want to determine if the increased sales volume is due mainly to discounted prices or other factors (such as advertising).]

Pacific Company provides the following information about its budgeted and actual results for June 2017. Although the expected June volume was 25,000 units produced and sold, the company actually produced and sold 27,000 units, as detailed here:

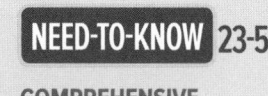

NEED-TO-KNOW 23-5

COMPREHENSIVE

	Budget (25,000 units)	Actual (27,000 units)
Selling price	$5.00 per unit	$141,210
Variable costs (per unit)		
Direct materials	1.24 per unit	$30,800
Direct labor.................................	1.50 per unit	37,800
Factory supplies*	0.25 per unit	9,990
Utilities*	0.50 per unit	16,200
Selling costs	0.40 per unit	9,180
Fixed costs (per month)		
Depreciation—Machinery*....................	$3,750	$3,710
Depreciation—Factory building*	2,500	2,500
General liability insurance....................	1,200	1,250
Property taxes on office equipment	500	485
Other administrative expense.................	750	900

* Indicates factory overhead item; $0.75 per unit or $3 per direct labor hour for variable overhead, and $0.25 per unit or $1 per direct labor hour for fixed overhead.

Standard costs based on expected output of 25,000 units:

	Standard Quantity	Total Cost
Direct materials, 4 oz. per unit @ $0.31 per oz..................	100,000 oz.	$31,000
Direct labor, 0.25 hrs. per unit @ $6.00 per hr.	6,250 hrs.	37,500
Overhead, 6,250 standard hours × $4.00 per DLH..............		25,000

Actual costs incurred to produce 27,000 units:

	Actual Quantity	Total Cost
Direct materials, 110,000 oz. @ $0.28 per oz..................	110,000 oz.	$30,800
Direct labor, 5,400 hrs. @ $7.00 per hr.	5,400 hrs.	37,800
Overhead ($9,990 + $16,200 + $3,710 + $2,500)		32,400

Required

1. Prepare June flexible budgets showing expected sales, costs, and net income assuming 20,000, 25,000, and 30,000 units of output produced and sold.
2. Prepare a flexible budget performance report that compares actual results with the amounts budgeted if the actual volume of 27,000 units had been expected.
3. Apply variance analysis for direct materials and direct labor.
4. Compute the total overhead variance and the overhead controllable and overhead volume variances.
5. Compute spending and efficiency variances for overhead. (Refer to Appendix 23A.)
6. Prepare journal entries to record standard costs, and price and quantity variances, for direct materials, direct labor, and factory overhead. (Refer to Appendix 23A.)

PLANNING THE SOLUTION

● Prepare a table showing the expected results at the three specified levels of output. Compute the variable costs by multiplying the per unit variable costs by the expected volumes. Include fixed costs at the given amounts. Combine the amounts in the table to show total variable costs, contribution margin, total fixed costs, and income from operations.

● Prepare a table showing the actual results and the amounts that should be incurred at 27,000 units. Show any differences in the third column and label them with an *F* for favorable if they increase income or a *U* for unfavorable if they decrease income.

● Using the chapter's format, compute these total variances and the individual variances requested:
  ● Total materials variance (including the direct materials quantity variance and the direct materials price variance).
  ● Total direct labor variance (including the direct labor efficiency variance and rate variance).
  ● Total overhead variance (including both controllable and volume overhead variances and their component variances). Variable overhead is applied at the rate of $3.00 per direct labor hour. Fixed overhead is applied at the rate of $1.00 per direct labor hour.

SOLUTION

1.

PACIFIC COMPANY
Flexible Budgets
For Month Ended June 30, 2017

	Flexible Budget		Flexible Budget for Unit Sales of		
	Variable Amount per Unit	Total Fixed Cost	20,000	25,000	30,000
Sales	$5.00		$100,000	$125,000	$150,000
Variable costs					
Direct materials	1.24		24,800	31,000	37,200
Direct labor............................	1.50		30,000	37,500	45,000
Factory supplies........................	0.25		5,000	6,250	7,500
Utilities	0.50		10,000	12,500	15,000
Selling costs............................	0.40		8,000	10,000	12,000
Total variable costs	3.89		77,800	97,250	116,700
Contribution margin........................	$1.11		22,200	27,750	33,300
Fixed costs					
Depreciation—Machinery		$3,750	3,750	3,750	3,750
Depreciation—Factory building.............		2,500	2,500	2,500	2,500
General liability insurance.................		1,200	1,200	1,200	1,200
Property taxes on office equipment		500	500	500	500
Other administrative expense..............		750	750	750	750
Total fixed costs		$8,700	8,700	8,700	8,700
Income from operations....................			$ 13,500	$ 19,050	$ 24,600

2.

PACIFIC COMPANY Flexible Budget Performance Report For Month Ended June 30, 2017	Flexible Budget	Actual Results	Variance**
Sales (27,000 units)	$135,000	$141,210	$6,210 F
Variable costs			
Direct materials	33,480	30,800	2,680 F
Direct labor.	40,500	37,800	2,700 F
Factory supplies*	6,750	9,990	3,240 U
Utilities*	13,500	16,200	2,700 U
Selling costs	10,800	9,180	1,620 F
Total variable costs	105,030	103,970	1,060 F
Contribution margin	29,970	37,240	7,270 F
Fixed costs			
Depreciation—Machinery*.	3,750	3,710	40 F
Depreciation—Factory building*	2,500	2,500	0
General liability insurance	1,200	1,250	50 U
Property taxes on office equipment	500	485	15 F
Other administrative expense.	750	900	150 U
Total fixed costs	8,700	8,845	145 U
Income from operations.	$ 21,270	$ 28,395	$7,125 F

* Indicates factory overhead item.   ** Abbreviations: F = Favorable variance; U = Unfavorable variance.

3. Variance analysis of materials and labor costs.

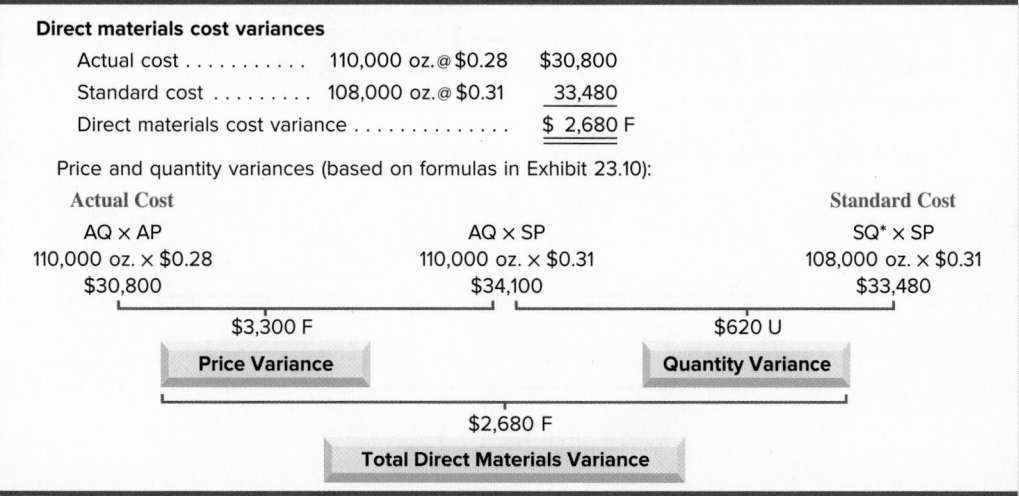

Direct materials cost variances

Actual cost	110,000 oz.@ $0.28	$30,800
Standard cost	108,000 oz.@ $0.31	33,480
Direct materials cost variance		$ 2,680 F

Price and quantity variances (based on formulas in Exhibit 23.10):

Actual Cost		**Standard Cost**
AQ × AP	AQ × SP	SQ* × SP
110,000 oz. × $0.28	110,000 oz. × $0.31	108,000 oz. × $0.31
$30,800	$34,100	$33,480

$3,300 F → **Price Variance** $620 U → **Quantity Variance**

$2,680 F → **Total Direct Materials Variance**

*SQ = 27,000 actual units of output × 4 oz. standard quantity per unit

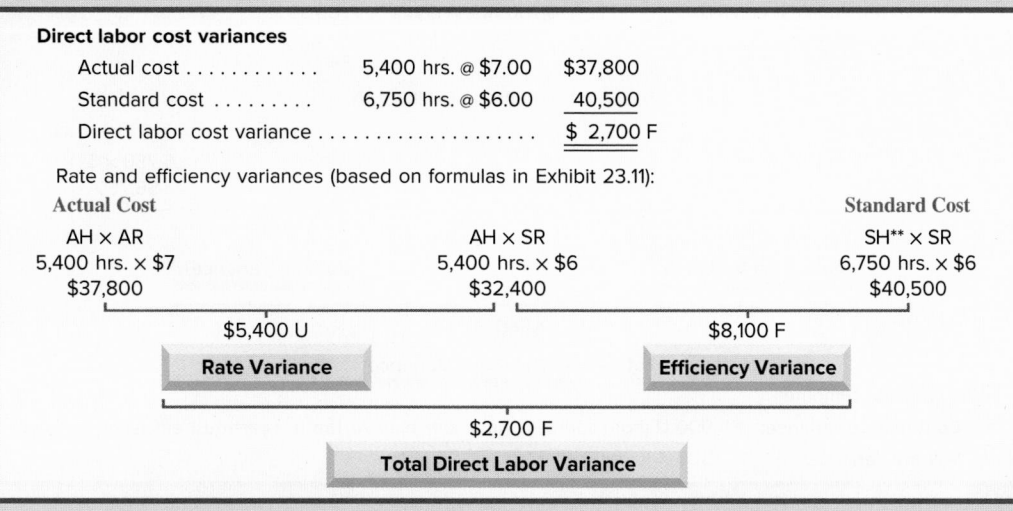

Direct labor cost variances

Actual cost	5,400 hrs. @ $7.00	$37,800
Standard cost	6,750 hrs. @ $6.00	40,500
Direct labor cost variance		$ 2,700 F

Rate and efficiency variances (based on formulas in Exhibit 23.11):

Actual Cost		**Standard Cost**
AH × AR	AH × SR	SH** × SR
5,400 hrs. × $7	5,400 hrs. × $6	6,750 hrs. × $6
$37,800	$32,400	$40,500

$5,400 U → **Rate Variance** $8,100 F → **Efficiency Variance**

$2,700 F → **Total Direct Labor Variance**

**SH = 27,000 actual units of output × 0.25 standard DLH per unit

4. Total, controllable, and volume variances for overhead.

Total overhead cost variance

Total overhead cost incurred . . . . (given)	$32,400
Total overhead applied . . . . (27,000 units × 0.25 DLH per unit × $4 per DLH)	27,000
Overhead cost variance	$ 5,400 U

Controllable variance

Total overhead cost incurred (given)	$32,400
Budgeted overhead (from flexible budget for 27,000 units)	26,500
Controllable variance	$ 5,900 U

Volume variance

Budgeted fixed overhead (at predicted capacity)	$ 6,250
Applied fixed overhead (6,750 standard DLH × $1.00 fixed overhead rate per DLH)	6,750
Volume variance	$ 500 F

5. Variable overhead spending variance, variable overhead efficiency variance, fixed overhead spending variance, and fixed overhead volume variance. (See Appendix 23A.)

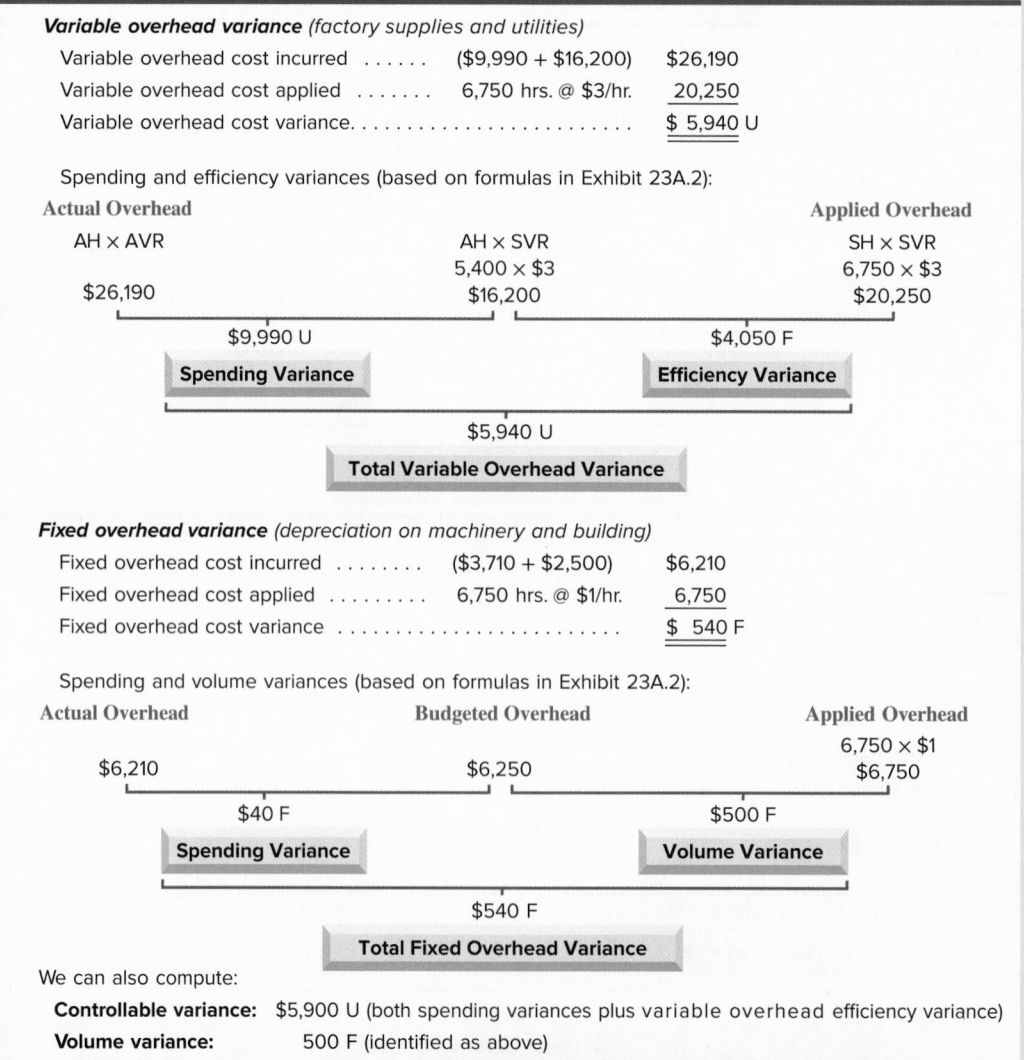

Variable overhead variance (factory supplies and utilities)

Variable overhead cost incurred	($9,990 + $16,200)	$26,190
Variable overhead cost applied	6,750 hrs. @ $3/hr.	20,250
Variable overhead cost variance.		$ 5,940 U

Spending and efficiency variances (based on formulas in Exhibit 23A.2):

Fixed overhead variance (depreciation on machinery and building)

Fixed overhead cost incurred	($3,710 + $2,500)	$6,210
Fixed overhead cost applied	6,750 hrs. @ $1/hr.	6,750
Fixed overhead cost variance		$ 540 F

Spending and volume variances (based on formulas in Exhibit 23A.2):

We can also compute:

Controllable variance: $5,900 U (both spending variances plus variable overhead efficiency variance)

Volume variance: 500 F (identified as above)

6. Journal entries under a standard cost system. (Refer to Appendix 23A.)

Work in Process Inventory	33,480	
Direct Materials Quantity Variance	620	
Direct Materials Price Variance		3,300
Raw Materials Inventory		30,800
Work in Process Inventory	40,500	
Direct Labor Rate Variance	5,400	
Direct Labor Efficiency Variance		8,100
Factory Wages Payable		37,800
Work in Process Inventory*	27,000	
Variable Overhead Spending Variance	9,990	
Variable Overhead Efficiency Variance		4,050
Fixed Overhead Spending Variance		40
Fixed Overhead Volume Variance		500
Factory Overhead**		32,400

  * Overhead applied = 6,750 standard DLH × \$4 per DLH
  ** Overhead incurred = \$9,990 + \$16,200 + \$3,710 + \$2,500

Expanded Overhead Variances and Standard Cost Accounting System

23A

EXPANDED OVERHEAD VARIANCES

Similar to analysis of direct materials and direct labor, overhead variances can be analyzed further. Exhibit 23A.1 shows an expanded framework for understanding these overhead variances.

This framework uses classifications of overhead costs as either variable or fixed. Within those two classifications are further types of variances—spending, efficiency, and volume variances. Volume variances were explained in the body of the chapter.

A **spending variance** occurs when management pays an amount different from the standard price to acquire an item. For instance, the actual wage rate paid to indirect labor might be higher than the standard rate. Similarly, actual supervisory salaries might be different than expected. Spending variances such as these cause management to investigate the reasons why the amount paid differs from the standard. Both variable and fixed overhead costs can yield their own spending variances.

Analyzing variable overhead includes computing an **efficiency variance,** which occurs when standard direct labor hours (the allocation base) expected for actual production differ from the actual direct labor hours used. This efficiency variance reflects on the cost-effectiveness in using the overhead allocation base (such as direct labor).

Exhibit 23A.1 shows that we can combine the variable overhead spending variance, the fixed overhead spending variance, and the variable overhead efficiency variance to get the controllable variance.

P4

Compute overhead spending and efficiency variances.

EXHIBIT 23A.1

Expanded Framework for Total Overhead Variance

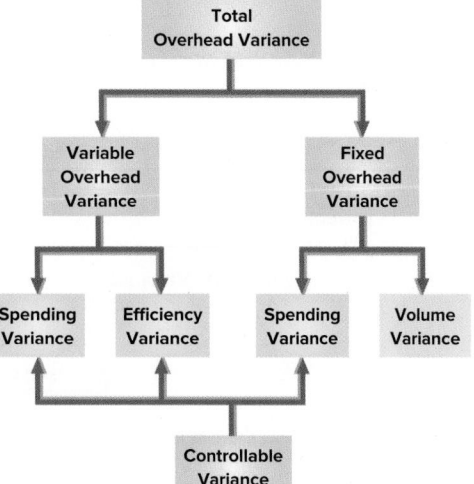

Computing Variable and Fixed Overhead Cost Variances To illustrate the computation of more detailed overhead cost variances, we return to G-Max. G-Max produced 3,500 units when 4,000 units were budgeted. Additional data from cost reports (from Exhibit 23.16) show that the actual overhead cost incurred is $7,650 (the variable portion of $3,650 and the fixed portion of $4,000). From Exhibit 23.12, each unit requires one hour of direct labor, variable overhead is applied at a rate of $1.00 per direct labor hour, and the predetermined fixed overhead rate is $1.00 per direct labor hour. With this information, we compute overhead variances for both variable and fixed overhead as follows:

Variable Overhead Variance	
Actual variable overhead (given)	$3,650
Applied variable overhead (3,500 units × 1 standard DLH × $1.00 VOH rate per DLH)	3,500
Variable overhead variance	$ 150 U

Fixed Overhead Variance	
Actual fixed overhead (given)	$4,000
Applied fixed overhead (3,500 units × 1 standard DLH × $1.00 FOH rate per DLH)	3,500
Fixed overhead variance	$ 500 U

Management should seek to determine the causes of these unfavorable variances and take corrective action. To help better isolate the causes of these variances, more detailed overhead variances can be used, as we show next.

Expanded Overhead Variance Formulas   Exhibit 23A.2 shows formulas to use in computing detailed overhead variances.

EXHIBIT 23A.2

Variable and Fixed Overhead Variances

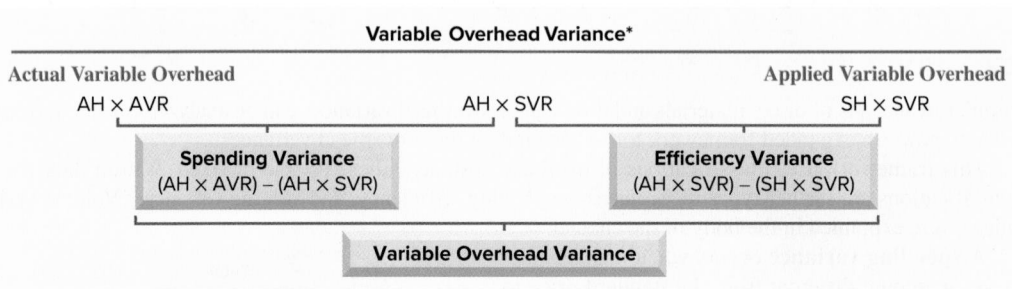

* AH = actual direct labor hours; AVR = actual variable overhead rate; SH = standard direct labor hours; SVR = standard variable overhead rate.

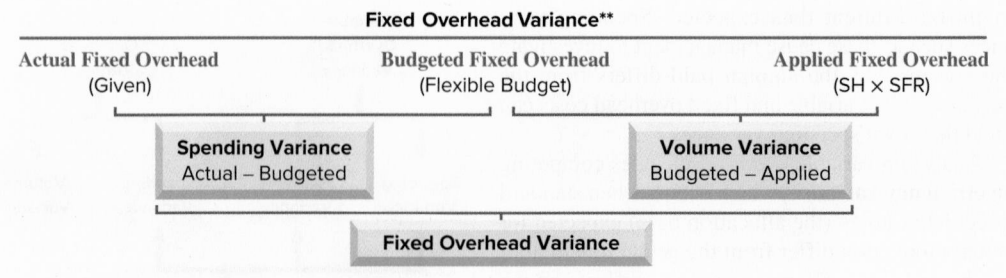

**SH = standard direct labor hours; SFR = standard fixed overhead rate.

Variable Overhead Cost Variances   Using these formulas, Exhibit 23A.3 offers insight into the causes of G-Max's $150 unfavorable variable overhead cost variance. G-Max applies overhead based on direct labor hours. It used 3,400 direct labor hours to produce 3,500 units. This compares favorably to the standard requirement of 3,500 direct labor hours at one labor hour per unit. At a standard variable overhead rate of $1.00 per direct labor hour, this should have resulted in variable overhead costs of $3,400 (middle column of Exhibit 23A.3).

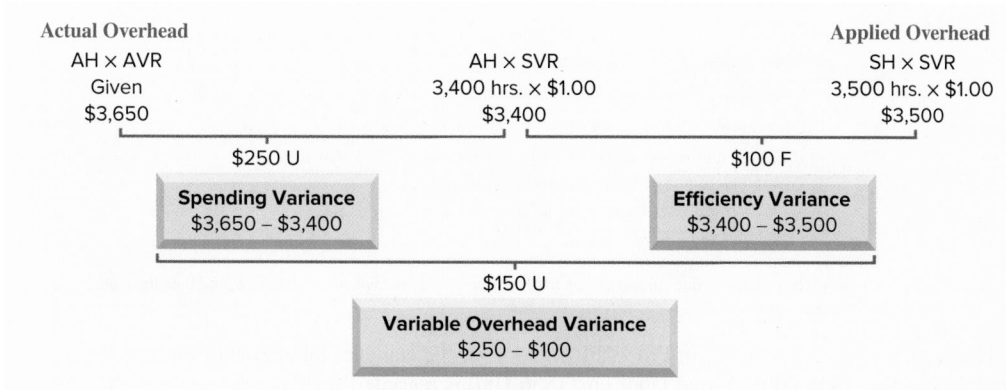

G-Max's cost records, however, report actual variable overhead of $3,650, or $250 higher than expected. This means G-Max has an unfavorable variable overhead spending variance of $250 ($3,650 − $3,400). On the other hand, G-Max used 100 fewer labor hours than expected to make 3,500 units, and its actual variable overhead is lower than its applied variable overhead. Thus, G-Max has a favorable variable overhead efficiency variance of $100 ($3,400 − $3,500).

Fixed Overhead Cost Variances Exhibit 23A.4 provides insight into the causes of G-Max's $500 unfavorable fixed overhead variance. G-Max reports that it incurred $4,000 in actual fixed overhead; this amount equals the budgeted fixed overhead for May at the expected production level of 4,000 units (see Exhibit 23.12). Thus, the fixed overhead spending variance is zero, suggesting good control of fixed overhead costs. G-Max's budgeted fixed overhead application rate is $1 per hour ($4,000/4,000 direct labor hours), but the actual production level is only 3,500 units.

With this information, we compute the fixed overhead volume variance shown in Exhibit 23A.4. The applied fixed overhead is computed by multiplying 3,500 standard hours allowed for the actual production by the $1 fixed overhead allocation rate. The volume variance of $500 occurs because 500 fewer units are produced than budgeted; namely, 80% of the manufacturing capacity is budgeted, but only 70% is used. Management needs to know why the actual level of production differs from the expected level.

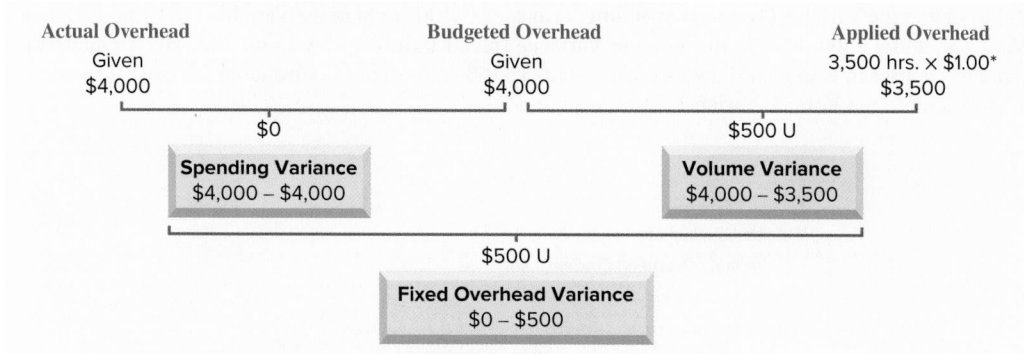

* 3,500 units × 1 DLH per unit × $1.00 FOH rate per DLH

STANDARD COST ACCOUNTING SYSTEM

We have shown how companies use standard costs in management reports. Most standard cost systems also record these costs and variances in accounts. This practice simplifies recordkeeping and helps in preparing reports. Although we do not need knowledge of standard cost accounting practices to understand standard costs and their use, we must know how to interpret the accounts in which standard costs and variances are recorded. The entries in this section briefly illustrate the important aspects of this process for G-Max's standard costs and variances for May.

The first of these entries records standard materials cost incurred in May in the Work in Process Inventory account. This part of the entry is similar to the usual accounting entry, but the amount of the debit equals the standard cost ($35,000) instead of the actual cost ($37,800). This entry credits Raw Materials Inventory for actual cost. The difference between standard and actual direct materials costs is recorded with debits to two separate materials variance accounts (recall Exhibit 23.10). Both the materials price and quantity variances are recorded as debits because they reflect additional costs higher than the standard cost (if actual costs were less than the standard, they are recorded as credits). This treatment (debit) reflects their unfavorable effect because they represent higher costs and lower income.

P5

Prepare journal entries
for standard costs and
account for price and
quantity variances.

May 31	Work in Process Inventory.	35,000	
	Direct Materials Price Variance*	1,800	
	Direct Materials Quantity Variance	1,000	
	Raw Materials Inventory.		37,800
	Charge production for standard quantity of materials used (1,750 lbs.) at the standard price ($20 per lb.), and record material price and material quantity variances.		

* Many companies record the materials price variance when materials are purchased. For simplicity, we record both the materials price and quantity variances when materials are issued to production.

The second entry debits Work in Process Inventory for the standard labor cost of the goods manufactured during May ($56,000). Actual labor cost ($56,100) is recorded with a credit to the Factory Wages Payable account. The difference between standard and actual labor costs is explained by two variances (see Exhibit 23.11). The direct labor rate variance is unfavorable and is debited to that account. The direct labor efficiency variance is favorable and that account is credited. The direct labor efficiency variance is favorable because it represents a lower cost and a higher net income.

May 31	Work in Process Inventory.	56,000	
	Direct Labor Rate Variance.	1,700	
	Direct Labor Efficiency Variance.		1,600
	Factory Wages Payable		56,100
	Charge production with 3,500 standard hours of direct labor at the standard $16 per hour rate, and record the labor rate and efficiency variances.		

The entry to assign standard predetermined overhead to the cost of goods manufactured must debit the $7,000 predetermined amount to the Work in Process Inventory account. Actual overhead costs of $7,650 were debited to Factory Overhead during the period (entries not shown here). Thus, when Factory Overhead is applied to Work in Process Inventory, the actual amount is credited to the Factory Overhead account. To account for the difference between actual and standard overhead costs, the entry includes a $250 debit to the Variable Overhead Spending Variance, a $100 credit to the Variable Overhead Efficiency Variance, and a $500 debit to the Volume Variance (recall Exhibits 23A.3 and 23A.4). (An alternative [simpler] approach is to record the difference with a $150 debit to the Controllable Variance account and a $500 debit to the Volume Variance account.)

May 31	Work in Process Inventory.	7,000	
	Volume Variance	500	
	Variable Overhead Spending Variance.	250	
	Variable Overhead Efficiency Variance		100
	Factory Overhead.		7,650
	Apply overhead at the standard rate of $2 per standard direct labor hour (3,500 hours), and record overhead variances.		

Point: If variances are material, they can be allocated between Work in Process Inventory, Finished Goods Inventory, and Cost of Goods Sold. This closing process is explained in advanced courses.

The balances of these different variance accounts accumulate until the end of the accounting period. As a result, the unfavorable variances of some months can offset the favorable variances of other months.

These ending variance account balances, which reflect results of the period's various transactions and events, are closed at period-end. If the amounts are *immaterial,* they are added to or subtracted from the balance of the Cost of Goods Sold account. This process is similar to that shown in the job order costing chapter for eliminating an underapplied or overapplied balance in the Factory Overhead account. (*Note:* These variance balances, which represent differences between actual and standard costs, must be added to or subtracted from the materials, labor, and overhead costs recorded. In this way, the recorded costs equal the actual costs incurred in the period; a company must use actual costs in external financial statements prepared in accordance with generally accepted accounting principles.)

Standard Costing Income Statement   In addition to the reports discussed in this chapter, management can use a **standard costing income statement** to summarize company performance for a period. This income statement reports sales and cost of goods sold at their *standard* amounts, and then lists the individual sales and cost variances to compute gross profit at actual cost. Exhibit 23A.5 provides an example. Unfavorable variances are *added* to cost of goods sold at standard cost; favorable variances are *subtracted* from cost of goods sold at standard cost.

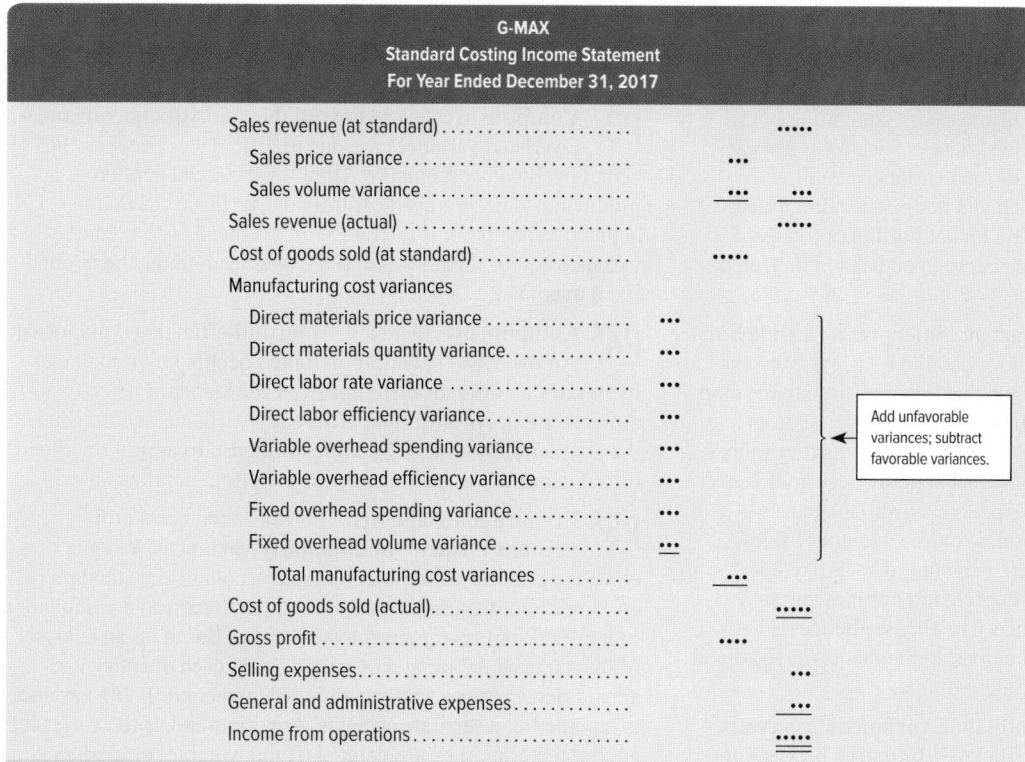

EXHIBIT 23A.5

Standard Costing Income Statement

G-MAX Standard Costing Income Statement For Year Ended December 31, 2017		
Sales revenue (at standard)		•••••
Sales price variance.	•••	
Sales volume variance.	••• •••	
Sales revenue (actual)	•••••	
Cost of goods sold (at standard)	•••••	
Manufacturing cost variances		
Direct materials price variance	•••	
Direct materials quantity variance.	•••	
Direct labor rate variance	•••	
Direct labor efficiency variance.	•••	
Variable overhead spending variance	•••	
Variable overhead efficiency variance	•••	
Fixed overhead spending variance.	•••	
Fixed overhead volume variance	•••	
Total manufacturing cost variances	•••	
Cost of goods sold (actual).	•••••	
Gross profit	••••	
Selling expenses.	•••	
General and administrative expenses.	•••	
Income from operations.	•••••	

Add unfavorable variances; subtract favorable variances.

Prepare the journal entry to record these direct materials variances:

Direct materials cost actually incurred.	$73,200
Direct materials quantity variance	3,800 F
Direct materials price variance.	1,300 U

Solution

Work in Process Inventory.	75,700	
Direct Materials Price Variance.	1,300	
Direct Materials Quantity Variance.		3,800
Raw Materials Inventory		73,200

NEED-TO-KNOW 23-6

Recording Variances

P4

Do More: QS 23-17, E 23-14

Summary

C1 **Define *standard costs* and explain how standard cost information is useful for management by exception.**
Standard costs are the normal costs that should be incurred to produce a product or perform a service. They should be based on a careful examination of the processes used to produce a product or perform a service as well as the quantities and prices that should be incurred in carrying out those processes. On a performance report, standard costs (which are flexible budget amounts) are compared to actual costs, and the differences are presented as variances. Standard cost accounting provides management information about costs that differ from budgeted (expected) amounts. Performance reports disclose the costs or areas of operations that have significant variances from budgeted amounts. This allows managers to focus more attention on the exceptions and less attention on areas proceeding normally.

C2 **Describe cost variances and what they reveal about performance.** Management can use variances to monitor and control activities. Total cost variances can be broken into price and quantity variances to direct management's attention to those responsible for quantities used and prices paid.

A1 **Analyze changes in sales from expected amounts.** Actual sales can differ from budgeted sales, and managers can investigate this difference by computing both the sales price and sales volume variances. The *sales price variance* refers to that portion of total variance resulting from a difference between actual and budgeted selling prices. The *sales volume variance* refers to that portion of total variance resulting from a difference between actual and budgeted sales quantities.

P1 **Prepare a flexible budget and interpret a flexible budget performance report.** A flexible budget expresses variable costs in per unit terms so that it can be used to develop budgeted amounts for any volume level within the relevant range. Thus, managers compute budgeted amounts for evaluation after a period for the volume that actually occurred. To prepare a flexible budget, we express each variable cost as a constant amount per unit of sales (or as a percent of sales dollars). In contrast, the budgeted amount of each fixed cost is expressed as a total amount expected to occur at any sales volume within the relevant range. The flexible budget is then determined using these computations and amounts for fixed and variable costs at the expected sales volume.

P2 **Compute materials and labor variances.** Materials and labor variances are due to differences between the actual costs incurred and the budgeted costs. The price (or rate) variance is computed by comparing the actual cost with the flexible budget amount that should have been incurred to acquire the actual quantity of resources. The quantity (or efficiency) variance is computed by comparing the flexible budget amount that should have been incurred to acquire the actual quantity of resources with the flexible budget amount that should have been incurred to acquire the standard quantity of resources.

P3 **Compute overhead controllable and volume variances.** Overhead variances are due to differences between the actual overhead costs incurred and the overhead applied to production. The overhead controllable variance equals the actual overhead minus the budgeted overhead. The volume variance equals the budgeted fixed overhead minus the applied fixed overhead.

P4ᴬ **Compute overhead spending and efficiency variances.** An overhead spending variance occurs when management pays an amount different from the standard price to acquire an item. An overhead efficiency variance occurs when the standard amount of the allocation base to assign overhead differs from the actual amount of the allocation base used.

P5ᴬ **Prepare journal entries for standard costs and account for price and quantity variances.** When a company records standard costs in its accounts, the standard costs of direct materials, direct labor, and overhead are debited to the Work in Process Inventory account. Based on an analysis of the material, labor, and overhead costs, each quantity variance, price variance, volume variance, and controllable variance is recorded in a separate account. At period-end, if the variances are not material, they are debited (if unfavorable) or credited (if favorable) to the Cost of Goods Sold account.

Key Terms

Benchmarking

Budget report

Controllable variance

Cost variance

Efficiency variance

Favorable variance

Fixed budget

Fixed budget performance report

Flexible budget

Flexible budget performance report

Integrated reporting

International Integrated Reporting Council

Management by exception

Overhead cost variance

Price variance

Quantity variance

Spending variance

Standard costing income statement

Standard costs

Unfavorable variance

Variance

Variance analysis

Volume variance

Multiple Choice Quiz

1. A company predicts its production and sales will be 24,000 units. At that level of activity, its fixed costs are budgeted at $300,000, and its variable costs are budgeted at $246,000. If its activity level declines to 20,000 units, what will be its budgeted fixed costs and its variable costs?

   a. Fixed, $300,000; variable, $246,000
   b. Fixed, $250,000; variable, $205,000
   c. Fixed, $300,000; variable, $205,000
   d. Fixed, $250,000; variable, $246,000
   e. Fixed, $300,000; variable, $300,000

2. Using the following information about a single product company, compute its total actual cost of direct materials used.
  - Direct materials standard cost: 5 lbs. × $2 per lb. = $10.
  - Total direct materials cost variance: $15,000 unfavorable.
  - Actual direct materials used: 300,000 lbs.
  - Actual units produced: 60,000 units.

a. $585,000	**c.** $300,000	**e.** $615,000
b. $600,000	**d.** $315,000	

3. A company uses four hours of direct labor to produce a product unit. The standard direct labor cost is $20 per hour. This period the company produced 20,000 units and used 84,160 hours of direct labor at a total cost of $1,599,040. What is its labor rate variance for the period?

a. $83,200 F	**c.** $84,160 F	**e.** $960 F
b. $84,160 U	**d.** $83,200 U	

4. A company's standard for a unit of its single product is $6 per unit in variable overhead (4 hours × $1.50 per hour). Actual data for the period show variable overhead costs of $150,000 and production of 24,000 units. Its total variable overhead cost variance is

a. $6,000 F.	**c.** $114,000 U.	**e.** $0.
b. $6,000 U.	**d.** $114,000 F.	

5. A company's standard for a unit of its single product is $4 per unit in fixed overhead ($24,000 total/6,000 units budgeted). Actual data for the period show total actual fixed overhead of $24,100 and production of 4,800 units. Its volume variance is

a. $4,800 U.	**c.** $100 U.	**e.** $4,900 U.
b. $4,800 F.	**d.** $100 F.	

ANSWERS TO MULTIPLE CHOICE QUIZ

1. c; Fixed costs remain at $300,000; Variable costs = ($246,000/24,000 units) × 20,000 units = $205,000

2. e; Budgeted direct materials + Unfavorable variance = Actual cost of direct materials used; or 60,000 units × $10 per unit = $600,000 + $15,000 U = $615,000

3. c; (AH × AR) − (AH × SR) = $1,599,040 − (84,160 hours × $20 per hour) = $84,160 F

4. b; Actual variable overhead − Variable overhead applied to production = Variable overhead cost variance; or $150,000 − (96,000 hours × $1.50 per hour) = $6,000 U

5. a; Budgeted fixed overhead − Fixed overhead applied to production = Volume variance; or $24,000 − (4,800 units × $4 per unit) = $4,800 U

---

^A *Superscript letter A denotes assignments based on Appendix 23A.*

[I] Icon denotes assignments that involve decision making.

Discussion Questions

1. [I] What limits the usefulness to managers of fixed budget performance reports?

2. [I] Identify the main purpose of a flexible budget for managers.

3. Prepare a flexible budget performance report title (in proper form) for Spalding Company for the calendar year 2017. Why is a proper title important for this or any report?

4. [I] What type of analysis does a flexible budget performance report help management perform?

5. In what sense can a variable cost be considered constant?

6. [I] What department is usually responsible for a direct labor rate variance? What department is usually responsible for a direct labor efficiency variance? Explain.

7. What is a price variance? What is a quantity variance?

8. [I] What is the purpose of using standard costs?

9. Google monitors its fixed overhead. In an analysis of fixed overhead cost variances, what is the volume variance? GOOGLE

10. What is the predetermined standard overhead rate? How is it computed?

11. In general, variance analysis is said to provide information about _____ and _____ variances.

12. [I] Samsung monitors its overhead. In an analysis of overhead cost variances, what is the controllable variance and what causes it? Samsung

13. What are the relations among standard costs, flexible budgets, variance analysis, and management by exception?

14. [I] How can the manager of advertising sales at Google use flexible budgets to enhance performance? GOOGLE

15. [I] Is it possible for a retail store such as Apple to use variances in analyzing its operating performance? Explain. APPLE

16. [I] Assume that Samsung is budgeted to operate at 80% of capacity but actually operates at 75% of capacity. What effect will the 5% deviation have on its controllable variance? Its volume variance? Samsung

17. List at least two positive and two negative features of standard costing systems.

18. Describe the concept of *management by exception* and explain how standard costs help managers apply this concept to control costs.

connect

QUICK STUDY

QS 23-1
Flexible budget
performance report
P1

Beech Company produced and sold 105,000 units of its product in May. For the level of production achieved in May, the budgeted amounts were: sales, $1,300,000; variable costs, $750,000; and fixed costs, $300,000. The following actual financial results are available for May. Prepare a flexible budget performance report for May.

	Actual
Sales (105,000 units)	$1,275,000
Variable costs	712,500
Fixed costs	300,000

QS 23-2
Flexible budget   **P1**

Based on predicted production of 24,000 units, a company anticipates $300,000 of fixed costs and $246,000 of variable costs. If the company actually produces 20,000 units, what are the flexible budget amounts of fixed and variable costs?

QS 23-3
Flexible budget
P1

Brodrick Company expects to produce 20,000 units for the year ending December 31. A flexible budget for 20,000 units of production reflects sales of $400,000; variable costs of $80,000; and fixed costs of $150,000. If the company instead expects to produce and sell 26,000 units for the year, calculate the expected level of income from operations.

QS 23-4
Flexible budget
performance report   **P1**

Refer to information in QS 23-3. Assume that actual sales for the year are $480,000 (26,000 units), actual variable costs for the year are $112,000, and actual fixed costs for the year are $145,000. Prepare a flexible budget performance report for the year.

QS 23-5
Standard cost card   **C1**

BatCo makes metal baseball bats. Each bat requires 1 kg of aluminum at $18 per kg and 0.25 direct labor hours at $20 per hour. Overhead is assigned at the rate of $40 per direct labor hour. What amounts would appear on a standard cost card for BatCo?

QS 23-6
Cost variances   **C2**

Refer to information in QS 23-5. Assume the actual cost to manufacture one metal bat is $40. Compute the cost variance and classify it as favorable or unfavorable.

QS 23-7
Materials variances
P2

Tercer reports the following for one of its products. Compute the total direct materials cost variance and classify it as favorable or unfavorable.

Direct materials standard (4 lbs. @ $2 per lb.)	$8 per finished unit
Actual finished units produced	60,000 units
Actual cost of direct materials used	$535,000

QS 23-8
Materials variances
P2

Tercer reports the following for one of its products. Compute the direct materials price and quantity variances and classify each as favorable or unfavorable.

Direct materials standard (4 lbs. @ $2 per lb.)	$8 per finished unit
Actual direct materials used	300,000 lbs.
Actual finished units produced	60,000 units
Actual cost of direct materials used	$535,000

QS 23-9
Materials cost variances   **P2**

For the current period, Kayenta Company's manufacturing operations yield a $4,000 unfavorable direct materials price variance. The actual price per pound of material is $78; the standard price is $77.50 per pound. How many pounds of material were used in the current period?

QS 23-10
Materials cost variances   **P2**

Juan Company's output for the current period was assigned a $150,000 standard direct materials cost. The direct materials variances included a $12,000 favorable price variance and a $2,000 favorable quantity variance. What is the actual total direct materials cost for the current period?

The following information describes a company's direct labor usage in a recent period. Compute the direct labor rate and efficiency variances for the period and classify each as favorable or unfavorable.

Actual direct labor hours used..	65,000
Actual direct labor rate per hour	$15
Standard direct labor rate per hour....................................	$14
Standard direct labor hours for units produced	67,000

QS 23-11
Direct labor variances
P2

Frontera Company's output for the current period results in a $20,000 unfavorable direct labor rate variance and a $10,000 unfavorable direct labor efficiency variance. Production for the current period was assigned a $400,000 standard direct labor cost. What is the actual total direct labor cost for the current period?

QS 23-12
Labor cost variances   P2

Fogel Co. expects to produce 116,000 units for the year. The company's flexible budget for 116,000 units of production shows variable overhead costs of $162,400 and fixed overhead costs of $124,000. For the year, the company incurred actual overhead costs of $262,800 while producing 110,000 units. Compute the controllable overhead variance and classify it as favorable or unfavorable.

QS 23-13
Controllable overhead variance   P3

AirPro Corp. reports the following for November. Compute the total overhead variance and controllable overhead variance for November and classify each as favorable or unfavorable.

Actual total factory overhead incurred	$28,175
Standard factory overhead:	
Variable overhead	$3.10 per unit produced
Fixed overhead	
($12,000/12,000 predicted units to be produced)	$1 per unit
Predicted units to produce.....................................	12,000 units
Actual units produced	9,800 units

QS 23-14
Controllable overhead variance
P3

Refer to information in QS 23-14. Compute the overhead volume variance for November and classify it as favorable or unfavorable.

QS 23-15
Volume variance   P3

Alvarez Company's output for the current period yields a $20,000 favorable overhead volume variance and a $60,400 unfavorable overhead controllable variance. Standard overhead applied to production for the period is $225,000. What is the actual total overhead cost incurred for the period?

QS 23-16
Overhead cost variances
P3

Refer to the information in QS 23-16. Alvarez records standard costs in its accounts. Prepare the journal entry to charge overhead costs to the Work in Process Inventory account and to record any variances.

QS 23-17^A
Preparing overhead entries
P5

Mosaic Company applies overhead using machine hours and reports the following information. Compute the total variable overhead cost variance and classify it as favorable or unfavorable.

Actual machine hours used	4,700 hours
Standard machine hours (for actual production)	5,000 hours
Actual variable overhead rate per hour	$4.15
Standard variable overhead rate per hour	$4.00

QS 23-18^A
Total variable overhead cost variance
P4

Refer to the information from QS 23-18. Compute the variable overhead spending variance and the variable overhead efficiency variance and classify each as favorable or unfavorable.

QS 23-19^A
Overhead spending and efficiency variances   P4

Farad, Inc., specializes in selling used trucks. During the month, Farad sold 50 trucks at an average price of $9,000 each. The budget for the month was to sell 45 trucks at an average price of $9,500 each. Compute the dealership's sales price variance and sales volume variance for the month and classify each as favorable or unfavorable.

QS 23-20
Computing sales price and volume variances   A1

In a recent year, **BMW** sold 182,158 of its 1 Series cars. Assume the company expected to sell 191,158 of these cars during the year. Also assume the budgeted sales price for each car was $30,000 and the actual sales price for each car was $30,200. Compute the sales price variance and the sales volume variance.

QS 23-21
Sales variances   A1

QS 23-22
Sustainability and standard costs

P1

MM Co. uses corrugated cardboard to ship its product to customers. Management believes it has found a more efficient way to package its products and use less cardboard. This new approach will reduce shipping costs from $10.00 per shipment to $9.25 per shipment. If the company forecasts 1,200 shipments this year, what amount of total direct materials costs would appear on the shipping department's flexible budget? How much is this sustainability improvement predicted to save in direct materials costs for this coming year?

QS 23-23
Sustainability and standard overhead rate

P3

HH Co. uses corrugated cardboard to ship its product to customers. Currently, the company's returns department incurs annual overhead costs of $72,000 and forecasts 2,000 returns per year. Management believes it has a found a better way to package its products. As a result, the company expects to reduce the number of shipments that are returned due to damage by 5%. In addition, the initiative is expected to reduce the department's annual overhead by $12,000. Compute the returns department's standard overhead rate per return (*a*) before the sustainability improvement and (*b*) after the sustainability improvement. (Round to the nearest cent.)

connect

EXERCISES

Exercise 23-1
Classification of costs as fixed or variable

P1

JPAK Company manufactures and sells mountain bikes. It normally operates eight hours a day, five days a week. Using this information, classify each of the following costs as fixed or variable with respect to the number of bikes made.

____ **a.** Bike frames   ____ **d.** Taxes on property   ____ **g.** Office supplies
____ **b.** Screws for assembly ____ **e.** Bike tires   ____ **h.** Depreciation on tools
____ **c.** Direct labor   ____ **f.** Gas used for heating   ____ **i.** Management salaries

Exercise 23-2
Preparing flexible budgets

P1

Tempo Company's fixed budget (based on sales of 7,000 units) for the first quarter of calendar year 2017 reveals the following. Prepare flexible budgets following the format of Exhibit 23.3 that show variable costs per unit, fixed costs, and three different flexible budgets for sales volumes of 6,000, 7,000, and 8,000 units.

		Fixed Budget
Sales (7,000 units)		$2,800,000
Cost of goods sold		
Direct materials	$280,000	
Direct labor	490,000	
Production supplies	175,000	
Plant manager salary	65,000	1,010,000
Gross profit		1,790,000
Selling expenses		
Sales commissions	140,000	
Packaging	154,000	
Advertising	125,000	419,000
Administrative expenses		
Administrative salaries	85,000	
Depreciation—Office equip.	35,000	
Insurance	20,000	
Office rent	36,000	176,000
Income from operations		$1,195,000

Check Income (at 6,000 units), $972,000

Exercise 23-3
Preparing a flexible budget performance report

P1

Solitaire Company's fixed budget performance report for June follows. The $315,000 budgeted expenses include $294,000 variable expenses and $21,000 fixed expenses. Actual expenses include $27,000 fixed expenses. Prepare a flexible budget performance report showing any variances between budgeted and actual results. List fixed and variable expenses separately.

	Fixed Budget	Actual Results	Variances
Sales (in units)	8,400	10,800	
Sales (in dollars)	$420,000	$540,000	$120,000 F
Total expenses	315,000	378,000	63,000 U
Income from operations	$105,000	$162,000	$ 57,000 F

Check Income variance, $21,000 F

Bay City Company's fixed budget performance report for July follows. The $647,500 budgeted total expenses include $487,500 variable expenses and $160,000 fixed expenses. Actual expenses include $158,000 fixed expenses. Prepare a flexible budget performance report that shows any variances between budgeted results and actual results. List fixed and variable expenses separately.

Exercise 23-4
Preparing a flexible budget performance report
P1

	Fixed Budget	Actual Results	Variances
Sales (in units)	7,500	7,200	
Sales (in dollars)	$750,000	$737,000	$13,000 U
Total expenses	647,500	641,000	6,500 F
Income from operations	$102,500	$ 96,000	$ 6,500 U

Check Income variance, $4,000 F

Match the terms *a* through *e* with their correct definition 1 through 5.

a. Standard cost card
b. Management by exception
c. Standard cost
d. Ideal standard
e. Practical standard

_____ **1.** Quantity of input required under normal conditions.
_____ **2.** Quantity of input required if a production process is 100% efficient.
_____ **3.** Managing by focusing on large differences from standard costs.
_____ **4.** Record that accumulates standard cost information.
_____ **5.** Preset cost for delivering a product or service under normal conditions.

Exercise 23-5
Standard costs
C1

Resset Co. provides the following results of April's operations: F indicates favorable and U indicates unfavorable. Applying the management by exception approach, which variances are of greatest concern? Why?

Exercise 23-6
Management by exception
C1

Direct materials price variance	$ 300 F
Direct materials quantity variance	3,000 U
Direct labor rate variance	100 U
Direct labor efficiency variance	2,200 F
Controllable overhead variance	400 U
Fixed overhead volume variance	500 F

Presented below are terms preceded by letters *a* through *j* and a list of definitions 1 through 10. Enter the letter of the term with the definition, using the space preceding the definition.

Exercise 23-7
Cost variances
C2

a. Fixed budget
b. Standard costs
c. Price variance
d. Quantity variance
e. Volume variance
f. Controllable variance
g. Cost variance
h. Flexible budget
i. Variance analysis
j. Management by exception

_____ **1.** The difference between actual and budgeted sales or cost caused by the difference between the actual price per unit and the budgeted price per unit.

_____ **2.** A planning budget based on a single predicted amount of sales or production volume; unsuitable for evaluations if the actual volume differs from the predicted volume.

_____ **3.** Preset costs for delivering a product, component, or service under normal conditions.

_____ **4.** A process of examining the differences between actual and budgeted sales or costs and describing them in terms of the amounts that resulted from price and quantity differences.

_____ **5.** The difference between the total budgeted overhead cost and the overhead cost that was allocated to products using the predetermined fixed overhead rate.

_____ **6.** A budget prepared based on predicted amounts of revenues and expenses corresponding to the actual level of output.

_____ **7.** The difference between actual and budgeted cost caused by the difference between the actual quantity and the budgeted quantity.

_____ **8.** The combination of both overhead spending variances (variable and fixed) and the variable overhead efficiency variance.

_____ **9.** A management process to focus on significant variances and give less attention to areas where performance is close to the standard.

_____ **10.** The difference between actual cost and standard cost, made up of a price variance and a quantity variance.

Exercise 23-8
Standard unit cost; total cost variance

C2

A manufactured product has the following information for June.

	Standard	Actual
Direct materials	6 lbs. @ $8 per lb.	48,500 lbs. @ $8.10 per lb.
Direct labor	2 hrs. @ $16 per hr.	15,700 hrs. @ $16.50 per hr.
Overhead	2 hrs. @ $12 per hr.	$198,000
Units manufactured		8,000

Compute the (1) standard cost per unit and (2) total cost variance for June. Indicate whether the cost variance is favorable or unfavorable.

Exercise 23-9
Direct materials variances   P2

Refer to the information in Exercise 23-8 and compute the (1) direct materials price and (2) direct materials quantity variances. Indicate whether each variance is favorable or unfavorable.

Exercise 23-10
Direct labor variances

P2

Refer to the information in Exercise 23-8 and compute the (1) direct labor rate and (2) direct labor efficiency variances. Indicate whether each variance is favorable or unfavorable.

Exercise 23-11
Direct materials and direct labor variances

P2

Hutto Corp. has set the following standard direct materials and direct labor costs per unit for the product it manufactures.

Direct materials (15 lbs. @ $4 per lb.)	$60
Direct labor (3 hrs. @ $15 per hr.)	45

During May the company incurred the following actual costs to produce 9,000 units.

Direct materials (138,000 lbs. @ $3.75 per lb.)	$517,500
Direct labor (31,000 hrs. @ $15.10 per hr.)	468,100

Compute the (1) direct materials price and quantity variances and (2) direct labor rate and efficiency variances. Indicate whether each variance is favorable or unfavorable.

Exercise 23-12
Direct materials and direct labor variances

P2

Reed Corp. has set the following standard direct materials and direct labor costs per unit for the product it manufactures.

Direct materials (10 lbs. @ $3 per lb.)	$30
Direct labor (2 hrs. @ $12 per hr.)	24

During June the company incurred the following actual costs to produce 9,000 units.

Direct materials (92,000 lbs. @ $2.95 per lb.)	$271,400
Direct labor (18,800 hrs. @ $12.05 per hr.)	226,540

Compute the (1) direct materials price and quantity variances and (2) direct labor rate and efficiency variances. Indicate whether each variance is favorable or unfavorable.

Exercise 23-13
Computation and interpretation of materials variances   P2

Check Price variance, $2,200 U

Hart Company made 3,000 bookshelves using 22,000 board feet of wood costing $266,200. The company's direct materials standards for one bookshelf are 8 board feet of wood at $12 per board foot.

1. Compute the direct materials price and quantity variances and classify each as favorable or unfavorable.

2. Interpret the direct materials variances.

Refer to Exercise 23-13. Hart Company records standard costs in its accounts and its materials variances in separate accounts when it assigns materials costs to the Work in Process Inventory account.

1. Show the journal entry that both charges the direct materials costs to the Work in Process Inventory account and records the materials variances in their proper accounts.

2. Assume that Hart's materials variances are the only variances accumulated in the accounting period and that they are immaterial. Prepare the adjusting journal entry to close the variance accounts at period-end.

3. Identify the variance that should be investigated according to the management by exception concept. Explain.

Exercise 23-14ᴬ

Materials variances recorded and closed

P5

Check   (2) Cr. to Cost of Goods Sold, $21,800

The following information describes production activities of Mercer Manufacturing for the year.

Actual direct materials used	16,000 lbs. at $4.05 per lb.
Actual direct labor used	5,545 hours for a total of $105,355
Actual units produced	30,000

Budgeted standards for each unit produced are 0.50 pounds of direct material at $4.00 per pound and 10 minutes of direct labor at $20 per hour.

1. Compute the direct materials price and quantity variances and classify each as favorable or unfavorable.

2. Compute the direct labor rate and efficiency variances and classify each as favorable or unfavorable.

Exercise 23-15

Direct materials and direct labor variances

P2

After evaluating Null Company's manufacturing process, management decides to establish standards of 3 hours of direct labor per unit of product and $15 per hour for the labor rate. During October, the company uses 16,250 hours of direct labor at a $247,000 total cost to produce 5,600 units of product. In November, the company uses 22,000 hours of direct labor at a $335,500 total cost to produce 6,000 units of product.

1. Compute the direct labor rate variance, the direct labor efficiency variance, and the total direct labor cost variance for each of these two months. Classify each variance as favorable or unfavorable.

2. Interpret the October direct labor variances.

Exercise 23-16

Computation and interpretation of labor variances   P2

Check   (1) October rate variance, $3,250 U

Sedona Company set the following standard costs for one unit of its product for 2017.

Direct material (20 lbs. @ $2.50 per lb.)	$ 50
Direct labor (10 hrs. @ $22.00 per hr.)	220
Factory variable overhead (10 hrs. @ $4.00 per hr.)	40
Factory fixed overhead (10 hrs. @ $1.60 per hr.)	16
Standard cost	$326

Exercise 23-17

Computation of total variable and fixed overhead variances

P3

The $5.60 ($4.00 + $1.60) total overhead rate per direct labor hour is based on an expected operating level equal to 75% of the factory's capacity of 50,000 units per month. The following monthly flexible budget information is also available.

	A	B	C	D
1		**Operating Levels (% of capacity)**		
2	**Flexible Budget**	**70%**	**75%**	**80%**
3	Budgeted output (units)	35,000	37,500	40,000
4	Budgeted labor (standard hours)	350,000	375,000	400,000
5	Budgeted overhead (dollars)			
6	Variable overhead	$1,400,000	$1,500,000	$1,600,000
7	Fixed overhead	600,000	600,000	600,000
8	Total overhead	$2,000,000	$2,100,000	$2,200,000

During the current month, the company operated at 70% of capacity, employees worked 340,000 hours, and the following actual overhead costs were incurred.

Variable overhead costs	$1,375,000
Fixed overhead costs	628,600
Total overhead costs	$2,003,600

Check (2) Variable overhead cost variance, $25,000 F

1. Show how the company computed its predetermined overhead application rate per hour for total overhead, variable overhead, and fixed overhead.

2. Compute the total variable and total fixed overhead variances and classify each as favorable or unfavorable.

Exercise 23-18^A

Computation and interpretation of overhead spending, efficiency, and volume variances   P4

Check (1) Variable overhead: Spending, $15,000 U; Efficiency, $40,000 F

Refer to the information from Exercise 23-17. Compute and interpret the following.

1. Variable overhead spending and efficiency variances.

2. Fixed overhead spending and volume variances.

3. Controllable variance.

Exercise 23-19

Computation of total overhead rate and total overhead variance

P3

Check (1) Overhead rate, $13.00 per hour

World Company expects to operate at 80% of its productive capacity of 50,000 units per month. At this planned level, the company expects to use 25,000 standard hours of direct labor. Overhead is allocated to products using a predetermined standard rate of 0.625 direct labor hours per unit. At the 80% capacity level, the total budgeted cost includes $50,000 fixed overhead cost and $275,000 variable overhead cost. In the current month, the company incurred $305,000 actual overhead and 22,000 actual labor hours while producing 35,000 units.

1. Compute the predetermined standard overhead rate for total overhead.

2. Compute and interpret the total overhead variance.

Exercise 23-20

Computation of volume and controllable overhead variances   P3

Check (2) $14,375 U

Refer to the information from Exercise 23-19. Compute the (1) overhead volume variance and (2) overhead controllable variance and classify each as favorable or unfavorable.

Exercise 23-21

Overhead controllable and volume variances; overhead variance report

P3

James Corp. applies overhead on the basis of direct labor hours. For the month of May, the company planned production of 8,000 units (80% of its production capacity of 10,000 units) and prepared the following overhead budget.

	Operating Level
Overhead Budget	**80%**
Production in units	8,000
Standard direct labor hours	24,000
Budgeted overhead	
Variable overhead costs	
Indirect materials...................	$15,000
Indirect labor	24,000
Power...........................	6,000
Maintenance	3,000
Total variable costs	48,000
Fixed overhead costs	
Rent of factory building	15,000
Depreciation—Machinery	10,000
Supervisory salaries	19,400
Total fixed costs	44,400
Total overhead costs	$92,400

During May, the company operated at 90% capacity (9,000 units) and incurred the following actual overhead costs.

Overhead costs (actual)	
Indirect materials	$15,000
Indirect labor	26,500
Power	6,750
Maintenance	4,000
Rent of factory building	15,000
Depreciation—Machinery	10,000
Supervisory salaries	22,000
Total actual overhead costs	$99,250

1. Compute the overhead controllable variance and classify it as favorable or unfavorable.

2. Compute the overhead volume variance and classify it as favorable or unfavorable.

3. Prepare an overhead variance report at the actual activity level of 9,000 units.

Blaze Corp. applies overhead on the basis of direct labor hours. For the month of March, the company planned production of 8,000 units (80% of its production capacity of 10,000 units) and prepared the following budget.

Exercise 23-22
Overhead controllable and volume variances; overhead variance report

P3

Overhead Budget	Operating Level 80%
Production in units	8,000
Standard direct labor hours	32,000
Budgeted overhead	
Variable overhead costs	
Indirect materials	$10,000
Indirect labor	16,000
Power	4,000
Maintenance	2,000
Total variable costs	32,000
Fixed overhead costs	
Rent of factory building	12,000
Depreciation—Machinery	20,000
Taxes and insurance	2,400
Supervisory salaries	13,600
Total fixed costs	48,000
Total overhead costs	$80,000

During March, the company operated at 90% capacity (9,000 units), and it incurred the following actual overhead costs.

Overhead costs (actual)	
Indirect materials	$10,000
Indirect labor	16,000
Power	4,500
Maintenance	3,000
Rent of factory building	12,000
Depreciation—Machinery	19,200
Taxes and insurance	3,000
Supervisory salaries	14,000
Total actual overhead costs	$81,700

1. Compute the overhead controllable variance.

2. Compute the overhead volume variance.

3. Prepare an overhead variance report at the actual activity level of 9,000 units.

Comp Wiz sells computers. During May 2017, it sold 350 computers at a $1,200 average price each. The May 2017 fixed budget included sales of 365 computers at an average price of $1,100 each.

Exercise 23-23
Computing and interpreting sales variances   A1

1. Compute the sales price variance and the sales volume variance for May 2017.

2. Interpret the findings.

PROBLEM SET A

Problem 23-1A

Preparation and analysis of a flexible budget

P1

Phoenix Company's 2017 master budget included the following fixed budget report. It is based on an expected production and sales volume of 15,000 units.

PHOENIX COMPANY Fixed Budget Report For Year Ended December 31, 2017		
Sales		$3,000,000
Cost of goods sold		
Direct materials	$975,000	
Direct labor.......................................	225,000	
Machinery repairs (variable cost)	60,000	
Depreciation—Plant equipment (straight-line).............	300,000	
Utilities ($45,000 is variable)	195,000	
Plant management salaries	200,000	1,955,000
Gross profit		1,045,000
Selling expenses		
Packaging..	75,000	
Shipping	105,000	
Sales salary (fixed annual amount)	250,000	430,000
General and administrative expenses		
Advertising expense	125,000	
Salaries...	241,000	
Entertainment expense	90,000	456,000
Income from operations		$ 159,000

Required

1. Classify all items listed in the fixed budget as variable or fixed. Also determine their amounts per unit or their amounts for the year, as appropriate.

2. Prepare flexible budgets (see Exhibit 23.3) for the company at sales volumes of 14,000 and 16,000 units.

3. The company's business conditions are improving. One possible result is a sales volume of 18,000 units. The company president is confident that this volume is within the relevant range of existing capacity. How much would operating income increase over the 2017 budgeted amount of $159,000 if this level is reached without increasing capacity?

4. An unfavorable change in business is remotely possible; in this case, production and sales volume for 2017 could fall to 12,000 units. How much income (or loss) from operations would occur if sales volume falls to this level?

Problem 23-2A

Preparation and analysis of a flexible budget performance report

P1   P2   A1

Refer to the information in Problem 23-1A. Phoenix Company's actual income statement for 2017 follows.

PHOENIX COMPANY Statement of Income from Operations For Year Ended December 31, 2017		
Sales (18,000 units)		$3,648,000
Cost of goods sold		
Direct materials	$1,185,000	
Direct labor.......................................	278,000	
Machinery repairs (variable cost)	63,000	
Depreciation—Plant equipment	300,000	
Utilities (fixed cost is $147,500)	200,500	
Plant management salaries............................	210,000	2,236,500
Gross profit		1,411,500
Selling expenses		
Packaging..	87,500	
Shipping	118,500	
Sales salary (annual)	268,000	474,000
General and administrative expenses		
Advertising expense	132,000	
Salaries...	241,000	
Entertainment expense	93,500	466,500
Income from operations		$ 471,000

Required

1. Prepare a flexible budget performance report for 2017.

Analysis Component

2. Analyze and interpret both the (a) sales variance and (b) direct materials cost variance.

Check (1) Variances: Fixed costs, $36,000 U; Income, $9,000 F

Antuan Company set the following standard costs for one unit of its product.

Direct materials (6 lbs. @ $5 per lb.)	$ 30
Direct labor (2 hrs. @ $17 per hr.)	34
Overhead (2 hrs. @ $18.50 per hr.)	37
Total standard cost	$101

Problem 23-3A
Flexible budget preparation; computation of materials, labor, and overhead variances; and overhead variance report

P1   P2   P3

The predetermined overhead rate ($18.50 per direct labor hour) is based on an expected volume of 75% of the factory's capacity of 20,000 units per month. Following are the company's budgeted overhead costs per month at the 75% capacity level.

Overhead Budget (75% Capacity)		
Variable overhead costs		
Indirect materials	$ 45,000	
Indirect labor	180,000	
Power	45,000	
Repairs and maintenance	90,000	
Total variable overhead costs		$360,000
Fixed overhead costs		
Depreciation—Building	24,000	
Depreciation—Machinery	80,000	
Taxes and insurance	12,000	
Supervision	79,000	
Total fixed overhead costs.		195,000
Total overhead costs		$555,000

The company incurred the following actual costs when it operated at 75% of capacity in October.

Direct materials (91,000 lbs. @ $5.10 per lb.)	$ 464,100	
Direct labor (30,500 hrs. @ $17.25 per hr.)	526,125	
Overhead costs		
Indirect materials	$ 44,250	
Indirect labor	177,750	
Power	43,000	
Repairs and maintenance	96,000	
Depreciation—Building	24,000	
Depreciation—Machinery	75,000	
Taxes and insurance	11,500	
Supervision	89,000	560,500
Total costs		$1,550,725

Required

1. Examine the monthly overhead budget to (a) determine the costs per unit for each variable overhead item and its total per unit costs and (b) identify the total fixed costs per month.

2. Prepare flexible overhead budgets (as in Exhibit 23.12) for October showing the amounts of each variable and fixed cost at the 65%, 75%, and 85% capacity levels.

3. Compute the direct materials cost variance, including its price and quantity variances.

Check (2) Budgeted total overhead at 13,000 units, $507,000

(3) Materials variances: Price, $9,100 U; Quantity, $5,000 U

4. Compute the direct labor cost variance, including its rate and efficiency variances.

5. Prepare a detailed overhead variance report (as in Exhibit 23.16) that shows the variances for individual items of overhead.

Problem 23-4A

Computation of materials, labor, and overhead variances

P2   P3

Trico Company set the following standard unit costs for its single product.

Direct materials (30 lbs. @ $4 per lb.)	$120
Direct labor (5 hrs. @ $14 per hr.)	70
Factory overhead—variable (5 hrs. @ $8 per hr.)	40
Factory overhead—fixed (5 hrs. @ $10 per hr.)	50
Total standard cost	$280

The predetermined overhead rate is based on a planned operating volume of 80% of the productive capacity of 60,000 units per quarter. The following flexible budget information is available.

	Operating Levels		
	70%	**80%**	**90%**
Production in units	42,000	48,000	54,000
Standard direct labor hours	210,000	240,000	270,000
Budgeted overhead			
Fixed factory overhead	$2,400,000	$2,400,000	$2,400,000
Variable factory overhead	$1,680,000	$1,920,000	$2,160,000

During the current quarter, the company operated at 90% of capacity and produced 54,000 units of product; actual direct labor totaled 265,000 hours. Units produced were assigned the following standard costs.

Direct materials (1,620,000 lbs. @ $4 per lb.)	$ 6,480,000
Direct labor (270,000 hrs. @ $14 per hr.)	3,780,000
Factory overhead (270,000 hrs. @ $18 per hr.)	4,860,000
Total standard cost	$15,120,000

Actual costs incurred during the current quarter follow.

Direct materials (1,615,000 lbs. @ $4.10 per lb.)	$ 6,621,500
Direct labor (265,000 hrs. @ $13.75 per hr.)	3,643,750
Fixed factory overhead costs	2,350,000
Variable factory overhead costs	2,200,000
Total actual costs	$14,815,250

Required

1. Compute the direct materials cost variance, including its price and quantity variances.

2. Compute the direct labor cost variance, including its rate and efficiency variances.

3. Compute the overhead controllable and volume variances.

Problem 23-5A[A]

Expanded overhead variances

P4

Refer to the information in Problem 23-4A.

Required

Compute these variances: (a) variable overhead spending and efficiency, (b) fixed overhead spending and volume, and (c) total overhead controllable.

Boss Company's standard cost accounting system recorded this information from its December operations.

Standard direct materials cost..	$100,000
Direct materials quantity variance (unfavorable)	3,000
Direct materials price variance (favorable)...............................	500
Actual direct labor cost	90,000
Direct labor efficiency variance (favorable)	7,000
Direct labor rate variance (unfavorable)...................................	1,200
Actual overhead cost	375,000
Volume variance (unfavorable)...	12,000
Controllable variance (unfavorable)	9,000

Problem 23-6A[A]

Materials, labor, and overhead variances recorded and analyzed

C1   P5

Required

1. Prepare December 31 journal entries to record the company's costs and variances for the month. (Do not prepare the journal entry to close the variances.)

Analysis Component

2. Identify the variances that would attract the attention of a manager who uses management by exception. Explain what action(s) the manager should consider.

Check   (1) Dr. Work in Process Inventory (for overhead), $354,000

Tohono Company's 2017 master budget included the following fixed budget report. It is based on an expected production and sales volume of 20,000 units.

PROBLEM SET B

Problem 23-1B
Preparation and analysis of a flexible budget

P1   A1

TOHONO COMPANY Fixed Budget Report For Year Ended December 31, 2017		
Sales		$3,000,000
Cost of goods sold		
Direct materials	$1,200,000	
Direct labor...	260,000	
Machinery repairs (variable cost)	57,000	
Depreciation—Machinery (straight-line)...................	250,000	
Utilities (25% is variable cost)	200,000	
Plant manager salaries	140,000	2,107,000
Gross profit...		893,000
Selling expenses		
Packaging...	80,000	
Shipping	116,000	
Sales salary (fixed annual amount)	160,000	356,000
General and administrative expenses		
Advertising	81,000	
Salaries...	241,000	
Entertainment expense	90,000	412,000
Income from operations................................		$ 125,000

Required

1. Classify all items listed in the fixed budget as variable or fixed. Also determine their amounts per unit or their amounts for the year, as appropriate.

2. Prepare flexible budgets (see Exhibit 23.3) for the company at sales volumes of 18,000 and 24,000 units.

3. The company's business conditions are improving. One possible result is a sales volume of 28,000 units. The company president is confident that this volume is within the relevant range of existing capacity. How much would operating income increase over the 2017 budgeted amount of $125,000 if this level is reached without increasing capacity?

4. An unfavorable change in business is remotely possible; in this case, production and sales volume for 2017 could fall to 14,000 units. How much income (or loss) from operations would occur if sales volume falls to this level?

Check   (2) Budgeted income at 24,000 units, $372,400

(4) Potential operating loss, $(246,100)

Problem 23-2B

Preparation and analysis of a flexible budget performance report

P1 A1

Refer to the information in Problem 23-1B. Tohono Company's actual income statement for 2017 follows.

TOHONO COMPANY		
Statement of Income from Operations		
For Year Ended December 31, 2017		
Sales (24,000 units)		$3,648,000
Cost of goods sold		
Direct materials	$1,400,000	
Direct labor.	360,000	
Machinery repairs (variable cost)	60,000	
Depreciation—Machinery	250,000	
Utilities (variable cost, $64,000).	218,000	
Plant manager salaries	155,000	2,443,000
Gross profit		1,205,000
Selling expenses		
Packaging.	90,000	
Shipping	124,000	
Sales salary (annual)	162,000	376,000
General and administrative expenses		
Advertising expense	104,000	
Salaries	232,000	
Entertainment expense	100,000	436,000
Income from operations		$ 393,000

Required

Check (1) Variances: Fixed costs, $45,000 U; Income, $20,600 F

1. Prepare a flexible budget performance report for 2017.

Analysis Component

2. Analyze and interpret both the (a) sales variance and (b) direct materials cost variance.

Problem 23-3B

Flexible budget preparation; computation of materials, labor, and overhead variances; and overhead variance report

P1 P2 P3

Suncoast Company set the following standard costs for one unit of its product.

Direct materials (4.5 lbs. @ $6 per lb.)	$27
Direct labor (1.5 hrs. @ $12 per hr.)	18
Overhead (1.5 hrs. @ $16 per hr.)	24
Total standard cost.	$69

The predetermined overhead rate ($16.00 per direct labor hour) is based on an expected volume of 75% of the factory's capacity of 20,000 units per month. Following are the company's budgeted overhead costs per month at the 75% capacity level.

Overhead Budget (75% Capacity)		
Variable overhead costs		
Indirect materials	$22,500	
Indirect labor	90,000	
Power	22,500	
Repairs and maintenance	45,000	
Total variable overhead costs		$180,000
Fixed overhead costs		
Depreciation—Building	24,000	
Depreciation—Machinery	72,000	
Taxes and insurance	18,000	
Supervision	66,000	
Total fixed overhead costs.		180,000
Total overhead costs		$360,000

The company incurred the following actual costs when it operated at 75% of capacity in December.

Direct materials (69,000 lbs. @ $6.10 per lb.)		$ 420,900
Direct labor (22,800 hrs. @ $12.30 per hr.)		280,440
Overhead costs		
Indirect materials	$21,600	
Indirect labor	82,260	
Power	23,100	
Repairs and maintenance	46,800	
Depreciation—Building	24,000	
Depreciation—Machinery	75,000	
Taxes and insurance	16,500	
Supervision	66,000	355,260
Total costs		$1,056,600

Required

1. Examine the monthly overhead budget to (a) determine the costs per unit for each variable overhead item and its total per unit costs and (b) identify the total fixed costs per month.
2. Prepare flexible overhead budgets (as in Exhibit 23.12) for December showing the amounts of each variable and fixed cost at the 65%, 75%, and 85% capacity levels.
3. Compute the direct materials cost variance, including its price and quantity variances.
4. Compute the direct labor cost variance, including its rate and efficiency variances.
5. Prepare a detailed overhead variance report (as in Exhibit 23.16) that shows the variances for individual items of overhead.

Check (2) Budgeted total overhead at 17,000 units, $384,000

(3) Materials variances: Price, $6,900 U; Quantity, $9,000 U

(4) Labor variances: Rate, $6,840 U; Efficiency, $3,600 U

Kryll Company set the following standard unit costs for its single product.

Problem 23-4B
Computation of materials, labor, and overhead variances

P2   P3

Direct materials (25 lbs. @ $4 per lb.).	$100
Direct labor (6 hrs. @ $8 per hr.)	48
Factory overhead—Variable (6 hrs. @ $5 per hr.)	30
Factory overhead—Fixed (6 hrs. @ $7 per hr.)	42
Total standard cost.	$220

The predetermined overhead rate is based on a planned operating volume of 80% of the productive capacity of 60,000 units per quarter. The following flexible budget information is available.

	Operating Levels		
	70%	80%	90%
Production in units	42,000	48,000	54,000
Standard direct labor hours	252,000	288,000	324,000
Budgeted overhead			
Fixed factory overhead	$2,016,000	$2,016,000	$2,016,000
Variable factory overhead	1,260,000	1,440,000	1,620,000

During the current quarter, the company operated at 70% of capacity and produced 42,000 units of product; direct labor hours worked were 250,000. Units produced were assigned the following standard costs:

Direct materials (1,050,000 lbs. @ $4 per lb.)	$4,200,000
Direct labor (252,000 hrs. @ $8 per hr.)	2,016,000
Factory overhead (252,000 hrs. @ $12 per hr.)	3,024,000
Total standard cost	$9,240,000

Actual costs incurred during the current quarter follow.

Direct materials (1,000,000 lbs. @ $4.25 per lb.)	$4,250,000
Direct labor (250,000 hrs. @ $7.75 per hr.)	1,937,500
Fixed factory overhead costs.	1,960,000
Variable factory overhead costs.	1,200,000
Total actual costs	$9,347,500

Required

1. Compute the direct materials cost variance, including its price and quantity variances.
2. Compute the direct labor cost variance, including its rate and efficiency variances.
3. Compute the total overhead controllable and volume variances.

Problem 23-5B[A]

Expanded overhead variances

P4

Refer to the information in Problem 23-4B.

Required

Compute these variances: (a) variable overhead spending and efficiency, (b) fixed overhead spending and volume, and (c) total overhead controllable.

Problem 23-6B[A]

Materials, labor, and overhead variances recorded and analyzed

C1   P5

Kenya Company's standard cost accounting system recorded this information from its June operations.

Standard direct materials cost.	$130,000
Direct materials quantity variance (favorable)	5,000
Direct materials price variance (favorable).	1,500
Actual direct labor cost	65,000
Direct labor efficiency variance (favorable)	3,000
Direct labor rate variance (unfavorable).	500
Actual overhead cost	250,000
Volume variance (unfavorable)	12,000
Controllable variance (unfavorable)	8,000

Required

1. Prepare journal entries dated June 30 to record the company's costs and variances for the month. (Do not prepare the journal entry to close the variances.)

Analysis Component

2. Identify the variances that would attract the attention of a manager who uses management by exception. Describe what action(s) the manager should consider.

SERIAL PROBLEM

Business Solutions

P1

© Alexander Image/Shutterstock RF

(This serial problem began in Chapter 1 and continues through most of the book. If previous chapter segments were not completed, the serial problem can begin at this point.)

SP 23   Business Solutions's second-quarter 2018 fixed budget performance report for its computer furniture operations follows. The $156,000 budgeted expenses include $108,000 in variable expenses for desks and $18,000 in variable expenses for chairs, as well as $30,000 fixed expenses. The actual expenses include $31,000 fixed expenses. Prepare a flexible budget performance report that shows any variances between budgeted results and actual results. List fixed and variable expenses separately.

	Fixed Budget	Actual Results	Variances
Desk sales (in units)	144	150	
Chair sales (in units)	72	80	
Desk sales.	$180,000	$186,000	$6,000 F
Chair sales	36,000	41,200	5,200 F
Total expenses	156,000	163,880	7,880 U
Income from operations.	$ 60,000	$ 63,320	$3,320 F

Beyond the Numbers

BTN 23-1   Analysis of flexible budgets and standard costs emphasizes the importance of a similar unit of measure for meaningful comparisons and evaluations. When **Apple** compiles its financial reports in compliance with GAAP, it applies the same unit of measurement, U.S. dollars, for most measures of business operations. One issue for Apple is how best to adjust account values for its subsidiaries that compile financial reports in currencies other than the U.S. dollar.

REPORTING IN ACTION

C1

APPLE

Required

1. Read Apple's Note 1 in Appendix A and identify the financial statement where it reports the annual adjustment for foreign currency translation for subsidiaries that do not use the U.S. dollar as their functional currency.
2. Translating financial statements requires the use of a currency exchange rate. For each of the following financial statement items, explain the exchange rate the company would apply to translate into U.S. dollars.
   a. Cash
   b. Sales revenue
   c. Property, plant and equipment

BTN 23-2   The usefulness of budgets, variances, and related analyses often depends on the accuracy of management's estimates of future sales activity.

COMPARATIVE ANALYSIS

A1

APPLE
GOOGLE

Required

1. Identify and record the prior three years' sales (in dollars) for **Apple** and **Google** using their financial statements in Appendix A.
2. Using the data in part 1, predict both companies' sales activity for the next two to three years. (If possible, compare your predictions to actual sales figures for those years.)

BTN 23-3   Setting materials, labor, and overhead standards is challenging. If standards are set too low, companies might purchase inferior products and employees might not work to their full potential. If standards are set too high, companies could be unable to offer a quality product at a profitable price and employees could be overworked. The ethical challenge is to set a high but reasonable standard. Assume that as a manager you are asked to set the standard materials price and quantity for the new 1,000 CKB Mega-Max chip, a technically advanced product. To properly set the price and quantity standards, you assemble a team of specialists to provide input.

ETHICS CHALLENGE

C1

Required

Identify four types of specialists that you would assemble to provide information to help set the materials price and quantity standards. Briefly explain why you chose each individual.

BTN 23-4   The reason we use the words *favorable* and *unfavorable* when evaluating variances is made clear when we look at the closing of accounts. To see this, consider that (1) all variance accounts are closed at the end of each period (temporary accounts), (2) a favorable variance is always a credit balance, and (3) an unfavorable variance is always a debit balance. Write a half-page memorandum to your instructor with three parts that answer the three following requirements. (Assume that variance accounts are closed to Cost of Goods Sold.)

COMMUNICATING IN PRACTICE

P5   C2

Required

1. Does Cost of Goods Sold increase or decrease when closing a favorable variance? Does gross margin increase or decrease when a favorable variance is closed to Cost of Goods Sold? Explain.
2. Does Cost of Goods Sold increase or decrease when closing an unfavorable variance? Does gross margin increase or decrease when an unfavorable variance is closed to Cost of Goods Sold? Explain.
3. Explain the meaning of a favorable variance and an unfavorable variance.

TAKING IT TO THE NET

C1

BTN 23-5 Access iSixSigma's website (iSixSigma.com) to search for and read information about the purpose and use of *benchmarking* to complete the following requirements. (*Hint:* Look in the "Methodology" link.)

Required

1. Write a one-paragraph explanation (in layperson's terms) of benchmarking.
2. How does standard costing relate to benchmarking?

TEAMWORK IN ACTION

C2

BTN 23-6 Many service industries link labor rate and time (quantity) standards with their processes. One example is the standard time to board an aircraft. The reason time plays such an important role in the service industry is that it is viewed as a competitive advantage: best service in the shortest amount of time. Although the labor rate component is difficult to observe, the time component of a service delivery standard is often readily apparent—for example, "Lunch will be served in less than five minutes, or it is free."

Required

Break into teams and select two service industries for your analysis. Identify and describe all the time elements each industry uses to create a competitive advantage.

ENTREPRENEURIAL DECISION

C1 C2

BTN 23-7 Riide, as discussed in the chapter opener, uses a costing system with standard costs for direct materials, direct labor, and overhead costs. Two comments frequently are mentioned in relation to standard costing and variance analysis: "Variances are not explanations" and "Management's goal is not to minimize variances."

Required

Write a short memo (no more than one page) to Amber Wason and Jeff Stefanis, Riide's co-founders, interpreting these two comments in the context of their electric bike business.

HITTING THE ROAD

C1

BTN 23-8 Training employees to use standard amounts of materials in production is common. Typically, large companies invest in this training but small organizations do not. One can observe these different practices in a trip to two different pizza businesses. Visit both a local pizza business and a national pizza chain business and then complete the following.

Required

1. Observe and record the number of raw material items used to make a typical cheese pizza. Also observe how the person making the pizza applies each item when preparing the pizza.
2. Record any differences in how items are applied between the two businesses.
3. Estimate which business is more profitable from your observations. Explain.

GLOBAL DECISION

A1

Samsung

BTN 23-9 Access the annual report of Samsung (at samsung.com) for the year ended December 31, 2015. The usefulness of its budgets, variances, and related analyses depends on the accuracy of management's estimates of future sales activity.

Required

1. Identify and record the prior two years' sales (in ₩ millions) for Samsung from its income statement.
2. Using the data in part 1, predict sales activity for Samsung for the next two years. Explain your prediction process.

GLOBAL VIEW

BMW, a German automobile manufacturer, uses standard costing and variance analysis. Production begins with huge rolls of steel and aluminum, which are then cut and pressed by large machines. Material must meet high quality standards, and the company sets standards for each of its machine operations.

In the assembly department, highly trained employees complete the assembly of the painted car chassis, often to customer specifications. BMW sets standards for how much labor should be used and monitors its employee performance. The company then computes and analyzes materials price and quantity variances and labor rate and efficiency variances and takes action as needed.

Like most manufacturers, BMW uses *practical standards* and thus must address waste of raw materials in its production process. In a recent year, BMW used over 3 million tons of steel, plastic, and aluminum to make over 1.8 million cars. Of the 665,000 tons of these raw materials wasted in production, over 98% are recyclable.

 Global View Assignments

Discussion Question 12

Discussion Question 16

Quick Study 23-31

BTN 23-9

24 chapter

Performance Measurement and Responsibility Accounting

Learning Objectives

CONCEPTUAL

C1 Distinguish between direct and indirect expenses and identify bases for allocating indirect expenses to departments.

C2 Explain transfer pricing and methods to set transfer prices.

C3 *Appendix 24C—*Describe allocation of joint costs across products.

ANALYTICAL

A1 Analyze investment centers using return on investment and residual income.

A2 Analyze investment centers using profit margin and investment turnover.

A3 Analyze investment centers using the balanced scorecard.

A4 Compute cycle time and cycle efficiency, and explain their importance to production management.

PROCEDURAL

P1 Prepare a responsibility accounting report using controllable costs.

P2 Allocate indirect expenses to departments.

P3 Prepare departmental income statements and contribution reports.

© Bryce Vickmark/
The New York Times/Redux

Sew Cool

BOSTON, MA—Aman Advani, Gihan Amarasiriwardena, and Kit Hickey wanted to design everyday clothes with performance features like those in athletic gear. Kit's work suits were stiff compared to her rock-climbing gear. Gihan couldn't find dress shirts to keep up with his bicycle commuting.

"Lines between work, play, and downtime are blurred," insists Aman. "We need clothes to keep up with our entire day." In response, the trio launched **Ministry of Supply** (**MinistryofSupply.com**).

"We design our products around real customers' daily activities," explains Aman. The company uses new materials, 3D printing, and thermal analysis to design better-fitting menswear that combats heat, moisture, and odor.

Their "frankensock" is a dress sock with an athletic sock sewn inside. The Mercury sweater has carbonized coffee in the fabric to absorb odors. One line of dress shirts uses a material engineered by NASA to adjust to changing temperatures. Gihan exclaims, "this is the next generation of clothing manufacturing and design."

The company carefully monitors its costs, including design, materials, labor, and overhead. The company is organized around product lines—shirts, pants, blazers, sweaters, and accessories—and the founders study income by product line to monitor performance and control costs. They apply cost concepts such as direct and indirect expenses and how to allocate expenses to product lines.

In addition to financial measures such as return on investment (ROI), residual income, and departmental income, the owners use nonfinancial information to guide their efforts. "We use customer feedback to continually improve our products," explains Kit, noting "we tried more than 20 iterations of our dress shirt."

Gihan, who ran a marathon in one of his company's suits, believes the "future of apparel will involve taking customer measurements by a scan and printing a garment for their unique body shape."

Ministry of Supply's high-tech approach has raised over $6 million in financing. Aman adds that "we work to triple total sales each year." Although accounting goals are important, the founders donate a portion of all sales to educational programs to fit their philosophy to *make a difference in the world.*

"Invent something new"

—Kit Hickey

Sources: *Ministry of Supply website,* January 2017; *Mashable.com,* April 14, 2016; *Esquire.com,* April 14, 2016; *Businessnewsdaily.com,* November 19, 2014; *New York Times,* May 19, 2013

RESPONSIBILITY ACCOUNTING

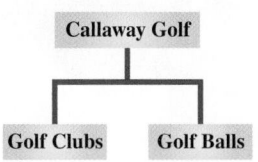

Performance Evaluation

Many large companies are easier to manage if they are divided into smaller units, called *divisions, segments,* or *departments.* For example, LinkedIn organizes its operations around three geographic segments: North America, Europe, and Asia-Pacific. Callaway Golf organizes its operations around two product lines, golf balls and golf clubs, while Kraft Heinz organizes its operations both geographically and around several product lines. In these **decentralized organizations,** decisions are made by unit managers rather than by top management. Top management then evaluates the performance of unit managers.

In **responsibility accounting,** unit managers are evaluated only on things for which they have control over. Methods of performance evaluation vary for cost centers, profit centers, and investment centers.

Point: Responsibility accounting does not place blame. Instead, it is used to identify opportunities for improving performance.

- A **cost center** incurs costs without directly generating revenues. The manufacturing departments of a manufacturer are cost centers. Also, its service departments, such as accounting, advertising, and purchasing, are cost centers. Kraft Heinz's Dover, Delaware, manufacturing plant is a cost center. *Cost center managers are evaluated on their success in controlling actual costs* compared to budgeted costs.

- A **profit center** generates revenues and incurs costs. Product lines are often evaluated as profit centers. Kraft Heinz's beverage and condiments product lines are profit centers. *Profit center managers are evaluated on their success in generating income.* A profit center manager would not have the authority to make major investing decisions, such as the decision to build a new manufacturing plant.

- An **investment center** generates revenues and incurs costs, and its manager is also responsible for the investments made in its operating assets. Kraft Heinz's chief operating officer for U.S. operations has the authority to make decisions such as building a new manufacturing plant. *Investment center managers are evaluated on their use of investment center assets to generate income.*

This chapter describes ways to measure performance for these three types of responsibility centers.

Controllable versus Uncontrollable Costs

P1

Prepare a responsibility accounting report using controllable costs.

We often evaluate a manager's performance using responsibility accounting reports that describe a department's activities in terms of whether a cost is controllable.

- **Controllable costs** are those for which a manager has the power to determine or at least significantly affect the amount incurred.

- **Uncontrollable costs** are not within the manager's control or influence.

Point: *Cost* refers to a monetary outlay to acquire some resource that has a future benefit. *Expense* usually refers to an expired cost.

For example, department managers often have little or no control over depreciation expense because they cannot affect the amount of equipment assigned to their departments. Also, department managers rarely control their own salaries. However, they can control or influence items such as the cost of supplies used in their department. When evaluating managers' performance, we should use data reflecting their departments' outputs along with their controllable costs and expenses.

A responsibility accounting system recognizes that control over costs and expenses belongs to several levels of management. We illustrate this in the partial organization chart in Exhibit 24.1. The lines in this chart connecting the managerial positions reflect channels of authority. For example, the three department managers (beverage, food, and service) in this company are responsible for controllable costs incurred in their departments. These department managers report to the vice president (VP) of the West region, who has overall control of the department costs. Similarly, the costs of the West region are reported to and controlled

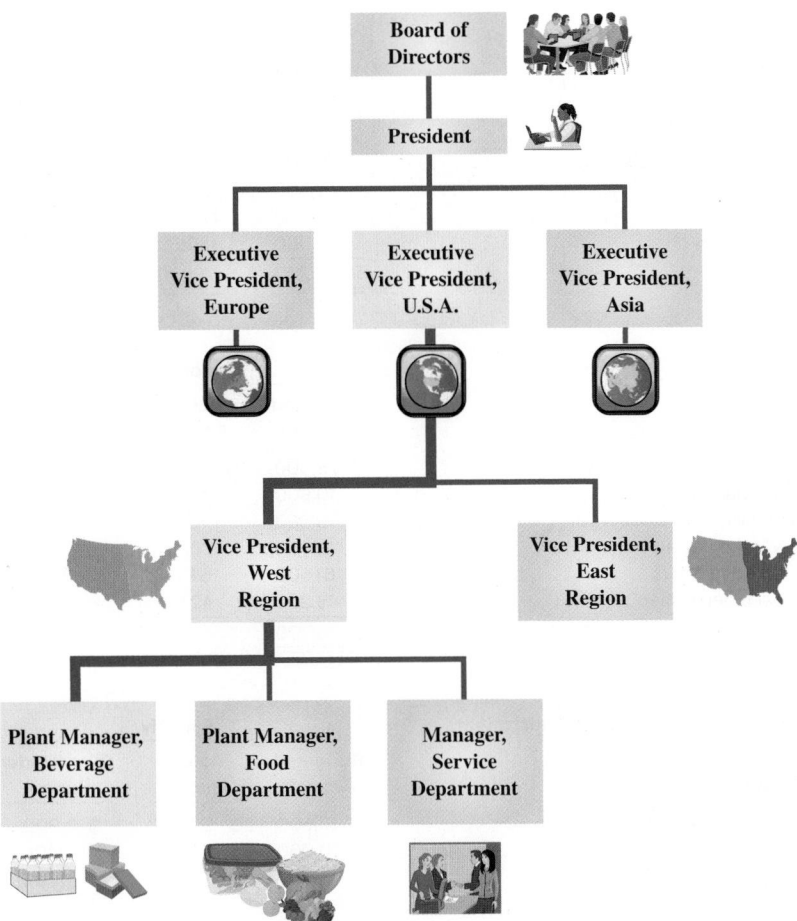

EXHIBIT 24.1

Responsibility Accounting
Chart (partial)

by the executive vice president (EVP) of U.S. operations, who in turn reports to the president, and, ultimately, the board of directors.

Responsibility Accounting for Cost Centers

A **responsibility accounting performance report** lists actual expenses that a manager is responsible for and their budgeted amounts. Management's analysis of differences between budgeted and actual amounts often results in corrective or strategic managerial actions. Upper-level management uses performance reports to evaluate the effectiveness of lower-level managers in keeping costs within budgeted amounts.

Point: Responsibility accounting typically uses *flexible* budgets.

Exhibit 24.2 shows summarized performance reports for the three management levels identified in Exhibit 24.1. The beverage department is a *cost center*, and its manager is responsible for controlling costs. Costs under the control of the beverage department plant manager are totaled and included among the controllable costs of the VP of the West region. Costs under the control of this VP are totaled and included among the controllable costs of the EVP of U.S. operations. In this way, responsibility accounting reports provide relevant information for each management level. (If the VP and EVP are responsible for more than just costs, the responsibility accounting system is expanded, as we show later in this chapter.)

The number of controllable costs reported varies across management levels. At lower levels, managers have limited responsibility and fewer controllable costs. Responsibility and control broaden for higher-level managers; their reports span a wider range of costs. However, reports to higher-level managers usually are summarized because: (1) lower-level managers are often responsible for detailed costs, and (2) detailed reports can obscure the broader issues facing top managers of an organization.

Point: Responsibility accounting divides a company into subunits, or *responsibility centers*.

EXHIBIT 24.2

Responsibility Accounting
Performance Reports

Executive Vice President, U.S. Operations	For July		
Controllable Costs	**Budgeted Amount**	**Actual Amount**	**Over (Under) Budget**
Salaries, VPs...............................	$ 80,000	$ 80,000	$ 0
Quality control costs........................	21,000	22,400	1,400
Office costs	29,500	28,800	(700)
West region...............................	276,700	279,500	2,800
East region...............................	390,000	380,600	(9,400)
Totals.....................................	$797,200	$ 791,300	$(5,900)

Vice President, West Region	For July		
Controllable Costs	**Budgeted Amount**	**Actual Amount**	**Over (Under) Budget**
Salaries, department managers	$ 75,000	$ 76,500	$ 1,500
Depreciation	10,600	10,600	0
Insurance	6,800	6,300	(500)
Beverage department......................	79,600	79,900	300
Food department..........................	61,500	64,200	2,700
Service department........................	43,200	42,000	(1,200)
Totals.....................................	$276,700	$279,500	$ 2,800

Plant Manager, Beverage Department	For July		
Controllable Costs	**Budgeted Amount**	**Actual Amount**	**Over (Under) Budget**
Direct materials	$ 51,600	$ 52,500	$ 900
Direct labor	20,000	19,600	(400)
Overhead	8,000	7,800	(200)
Totals.....................................	$ 79,600	$ 79,900	$ 300

NEED-TO-KNOW 24-1

Responsibility
Accounting

P1

Below are the annual budgeted and actual costs for the Western region's manufacturing plant of Rios Co. The plant has two operating departments: motorcycle and ATV. The plant manager is responsible for all of the plant's costs (other than her own salary). Each operating department has a manager who is responsible for that department's direct materials, direct labor, and overhead costs. Prepare responsibility accounting reports like those in Exhibit 24.2 for (1) the plant manager and (2) each operating department manager.

	Budgeted Amount		Actual Amount	
	Motorcycle	**ATV**	**Motorcycle**	**ATV**
Direct materials	$ 97,000	$138,000	$ 98,500	$133,800
Direct labor...............	52,000	105,000	56,100	101,300
Dept. mgr. salary...........	60,000	56,000	60,000	56,000
Rent and utilities...........	9,000	12,000	8,400	10,900
Overhead	45,000	81,000	47,000	78,000
Totals....................	$263,000	$392,000	$270,000	$380,000

Solution **1.**

Responsibility Accounting Performance Report
Plant Manager, Western Region

	Budgeted	Actual	Over (Under) Budget
Dept. mgr. salaries	$116,000	$116,000	$ 0
Rent and utilities...........	21,000	19,300	(1,700)
Motorcycle dept.*	194,000	201,600	7,600
ATV dept.**	324,000	313,100	(10,900)
Totals....................	$655,000	$650,000	$ (5,000)

 * Costs are from Motorcycle responsibility report, solution *2a*.
**Costs are from ATV responsibility report, solution *2b*.

2a.

Responsibility Accounting Performance Report
Department Manager, Motorcycle Department

	Budgeted	Actual	Over (Under) Budget
Direct materials	$ 97,000	$ 98,500	$1,500
Direct labor	52,000	56,100	4,100
Overhead	45,000	47,000	2,000
Totals	$194,000	$201,600	$7,600

2b.

Responsibility Accounting Performance Report
Department Manager, ATV Department

	Budgeted	Actual	Over (Under) Budget
Direct materials	$138,000	$133,800	$ (4,200)
Direct labor	105,000	101,300	(3,700)
Overhead	81,000	78,000	(3,000)
Totals	$324,000	$313,100	$(10,900)

Do More: QS 24-4, E 24-1, E 24-2, P 24-1

PROFIT CENTERS

When departments are organized as profit centers, responsibility accounting focuses on how well each department controlled costs *and* generated revenues. This leads to **departmental income statements** as a common way to report profit center performance. When computing departmental profits, we confront two accounting challenges that involve allocating expenses:

1. How to allocate *indirect expenses* such as rent and utilities, which benefit several departments.
2. How to allocate *service department expenses* such as payroll or purchasing, which perform services that benefit several departments.

We next explain these allocations and profit center income reporting.

Direct and Indirect Expenses

Direct expenses are costs readily traced to a department because they are incurred for that department's sole benefit. They are not allocated across departments. For example, the salary of an employee who works in only one department is a direct expense of that one department. Direct expenses are often, but not always, controllable costs.

    Indirect expenses are costs incurred for the joint benefit of more than one department; they cannot be readily traced to only one department. For example, if two or more departments share a single building, all enjoy the benefits of the expenses for rent, heat, and light. Likewise, the *operating departments* that perform an organization's main functions, for example, manufacturing and selling, benefit from the work of *service departments*. Service departments, like payroll and human resource management, do not generate revenues, but their support is crucial for the operating departments' success.

C1

Distinguish between direct and indirect expenses and identify bases for allocating indirect expenses to departments.

Point: Service department expenses can be viewed as a special case of indirect expenses.

Expense Allocations

General Model   Indirect and service department expenses are allocated across departments that benefit from them. Ideally, we allocate these expenses by using a cause-effect relation. Often such cause-effect relations are hard to identify. When we cannot identify cause-effect relations, we allocate each indirect or service department expense based on *approximating* the relative benefit each department receives. Exhibit 24.3 summarizes the general model for cost allocation.

EXHIBIT 24.3

General Model for Cost Allocation

Allocated cost = Total cost to allocate × Percentage of allocation base used

Allocating Indirect Expenses   Allocation bases vary across departments and organizations. No standard rule for the "best" allocation bases exists. Managers must use judgment in developing allocation bases because employee morale can suffer if allocations are perceived as unfair. Exhibit 24.4 shows some commonly used bases for allocating indirect expenses.

EXHIBIT 24.4

Bases for Allocating Indirect Expenses

Indirect Expense	Common Allocation Bases
Wages and salaries...............	Relative amount of hours worked in each department
Rent..........................	Square feet of space occupied
Utilities.......................	Square feet of space occupied
Advertising.....................	Percentage of total sales
Depreciation	Hours of depreciable asset used

© Purestock/SuperStock

Point: Some companies ask supervisors to estimate time spent supervising specific departments for purposes of expense allocation.

More complicated allocation schemes are possible. For example, some locations in a retail store (ground floor near the entrance, for example) are more valuable than others. Departments with better locations can be allocated more cost. Advertising campaigns can be analyzed to see the amount of advertising devoted to each department, or utilities costs can be allocated based on machine hours used in each department. Management must determine whether these more accurate cost allocations justify the effort and expense to compute them.

Allocating Service Department Expenses   To generate revenues, operating departments require services provided by departments such as personnel, payroll, and purchasing. Such service departments are typically evaluated as *cost centers* because they do not produce revenues. A departmental accounting system can accumulate and report costs incurred by each service department for this purpose. The system then allocates a service department's expenses to operating departments that benefit from them. Exhibit 24.5 shows some commonly used bases for allocating service department expenses to operating departments.

EXHIBIT 24.5

Bases for Allocating Service Department Expenses

Service Department	Common Allocation Bases
Office expenses	Number of employees or sales in each department
Personnel expenses...............	Number of employees in each department
Payroll expenses	Number of employees in each department
Purchasing costs	Dollar amounts of purchases or number of purchase orders processed
Maintenance expenses	Square feet of floor space occupied

Illustration of Cost Allocation   We illustrate the general approach to allocating costs by looking at cleaning services for a retail store (an indirect cost). An outside company cleans the retail store for a total cost of $800 per month. Management allocates this cost across the store's three departments based on floor space (in square feet) that each department occupies. Exhibit 24.6 shows this allocation.

EXHIBIT 24.6

Cost Allocation

Department	Department Square Feet	Percent of Total Square Feet		Cost Allocated to Department
Jewelry	2,400	60%	(2,400 sq ft/ 4,000 sq ft)	$480
Watch repair	600	15	(600 sq ft/ 4,000 sq ft)	120
China and silver..........	1,000	25	(1,000 sq ft/ 4,000 sq ft)	200
Totals	4,000	100%		$800

The total cost to allocate is $800. Since the jewelry department occupies 60% of the store's total floor space (2,400 square feet/4,000 square feet), it is allocated 60% of the total cleaning cost. This allocated cost of $480 is computed as $800 × 60%. When the allocation process is complete, these and other allocated costs are deducted in computing the net income for each department. The calculations are similar for other allocation bases and for service department costs.

Allocate a retailer's purchasing department's costs of $20,000 to its operating departments using each department's percentage of total purchase orders.

NEED-TO-KNOW 24-2

Cost Allocations

P2

Department	Number of Purchase Orders
Clothing...............	250
Health care.............	450
Sporting goods..........	300
Total.................	1,000

Solution

Clothing...............	$20,000 × 25% = $ 5,000
Health care.............	20,000 × 45% = 9,000
Sporting goods..........	20,000 × 30% = 6,000
Total.................	$20,000

Do More: QS 24-5, QS 24-6, QS 24-7, E 24-3, E 24-4, E 24-5

Departmental Income Statements

Departmental income is computed using the formula in Exhibit 24.7.

$$\begin{array}{c} \text{Departmental} \\ \text{income} \end{array} = \begin{array}{c} \text{Department} \\ \text{sales} \end{array} - \begin{array}{c} \text{Department direct} \\ \text{expenses} \end{array} - \begin{array}{c} \text{Allocated indirect} \\ \text{expenses} \end{array} - \begin{array}{c} \text{Allocated service} \\ \text{department expenses} \end{array}$$

EXHIBIT 24.7

Departmental Income

We prepare departmental income statements using **A-1 Hardware** and its five departments. Two of them (general office and purchasing) are service departments, and the other three (hardware, housewares, and appliances) are operating departments. Since the service departments do not generate sales, we do not prepare departmental income statements for them. Instead, we allocate their expenses to operating departments.

Preparing departmental income statements involves four steps.

P3

Prepare departmental income statements and contribution reports.

Step ①: Accumulating revenues, direct expenses, and indirect expenses by department.
Step ②: Allocating indirect expenses across both service and operating departments.
Step ③: Allocating service department expenses to operating departments.
Step ④: Preparing departmental income statements.

Exhibit 24.8 summarizes these steps in preparing departmental performance reports for cost centers and profit centers (links to the steps are coded with circled numbers *1* through *4*). A-1 Hardware's service departments (general office and purchasing) are cost centers, so their

Point: Operating departments generate revenues. Service departments do not.

EXHIBIT 24.8

Departmental Performance Reporting

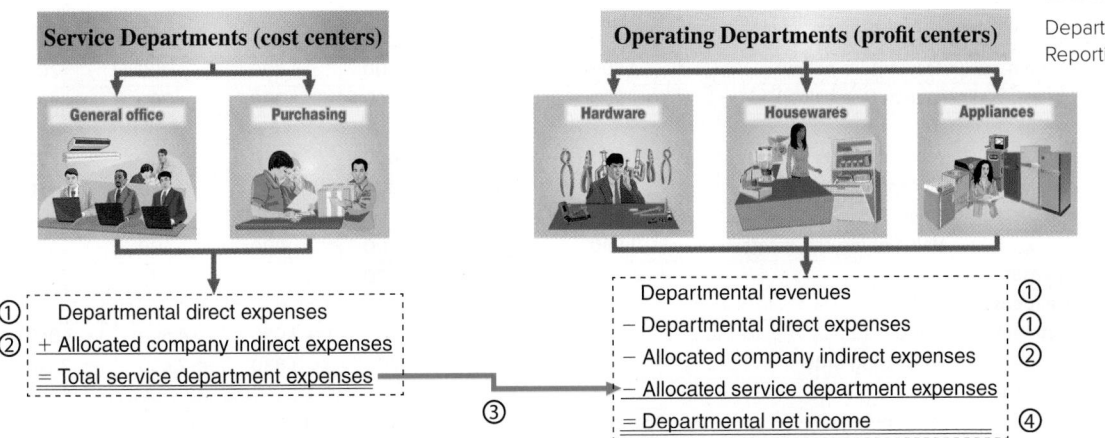

Point: We sometimes allocate service department costs across other service departments before allocating them to operating departments. This "step-wise" process is covered in advanced courses.

performance is based on how well they control their direct department expenses. The company's operating departments (hardware, housewares, and appliances) are **profit centers**, and their performance is based on how well they generate departmental net income.

Apply Step 1: We first collect the necessary data from general company and departmental accounts. Exhibit 24.9 shows these data.

EXHIBIT 24.9

Cost Data

	A	B	C	D	E	F	G
			A-1 HARDWARE Revenues and Expenses For Year Ended December 31, 2017				
4			Service Departments		Operating Departments		
		Expense Account Balance	General Office	Purchasing	Hardware	Housewares	Appliances
8	Sales............................		$ 0	$ 0	$119,500	$71,700	$47,800
9	**Direct expenses**						
10	Cost of goods sold...........	$ 147,800	0	0	73,800	43,800	30,200
11	Salaries.......................	51,900	13,300	8,200	15,600	7,000	7,800
12	Depreciation—Equip.......	1,500	500	300	400	100	200
13	Supplies......................	900	200	100	300	200	100
14	**Indirect expenses**						
15	Rent	12,000					
16	Utilities......................	2,400					
17	Advertising...................	1,000					
18	Insurance.....................	2,500					
19	**Total expenses.............**	**$220,000**					

Point: Sales and cost of goods sold data are from operating department records.

Exhibit 24.9 shows the direct and indirect expenses by department. Each department uses payroll records, fixed asset and depreciation records, and supplies requisitions to determine the amounts of its expenses for salaries, depreciation, and supplies. The total amount for each of these direct expenses is entered in the Expense Account Balance column. That column also lists the amount of each indirect expense.

EXHIBIT 24.10

Departmental Expense Allocation Spreadsheet

Apply Step 2: Using the general model, A-1 Hardware allocates indirect costs. We show this with the *departmental expense allocation spreadsheet* in Exhibit 24.10. After selecting allocation

	A	B	C	D	E	F	G
			A-1 HARDWARE Departmental Expense Allocations For Year Ended December 31, 2017				
4			Allocation of Expenses to Departments				
7	Allocation Base	Expense Account Balance	General Office Dept.	Purchasing Dept.	Hardware Dept.	Housewares Dept.	Appliances Dept.
8	**Direct expenses**						
9	Salaries expense..........................	(see note a below)	$ 51,900	$13,300	$8,200	$ 15,600	$ 7,000	$ 7,800
10	Depreciation—Equipment........	(see note a below)	1,500	500	300	400	100	200
11	Supplies expense..........................	(see note a below)	900	200	100	300	200	100
12	**Indirect expenses**						
13	Rent expense.................................	Amount and value of space....	12,000	600	600	4,860	3,240	2,700
14	Utilities expense...........................	Floor space..........................	2,400	300	300	810	540	450
15	Advertising expense....................	Sales...................................	1,000			500	300	200
16	Insurance expense.......................	Value of insured assets.............	2,500	400	200	900	600	400
17	Total department expenses.......		72,200	15,300	9,700	23,370	11,980	11,850
18	**Service department expenses**						
19	General office department.....	Sales...................................		(15,300)		→ 7,650	→ 4,590	→ 3,060
20	Purchasing department............	Purchasing orders........................			(9,700)	→ 3,880	→ 2,630	→ 3,190
21	Total expenses allocated to operating departments..........................		**$72,200**	**$ 0**	**$ 0**	**$34,900**	**$19,200**	**$18,100**

a The allocation base is not relevant as direct expenses are *not* allocated.

bases, indirect expenses are recorded in company accounts and allocated to both operating and service departments. **Detailed calculations for indirect expense allocations, which follow the general model of cost allocation, are in Appendix 24A** (see Exhibits 24A.1 thru 24A.6).

Apply Step 3: We then allocate service department expenses to operating departments. Service department expenses typically are not allocated to other service departments. After service department costs are allocated, no expenses remain in the service departments, as shown in row 21 of Exhibit 24.10. **Detailed calculations for service department expense allocations, which follow the general model of cost allocation, are in Appendix 24A** (see Exhibits 24A.7 and 24A.8).

Apply Step 4: The departmental expense allocation spreadsheet is now used to prepare departmental performance reports. The general office and purchasing departments are cost centers, and their managers are evaluated on their control of costs.

Exhibit 24.11 shows income statements for the three operating departments. This exhibit uses the spreadsheet (in Exhibit 24.10) for its operating expenses; information on sales and cost of goods sold comes from departmental records.

EXHIBIT 24.11

Departmental Income Statements (operating departments)

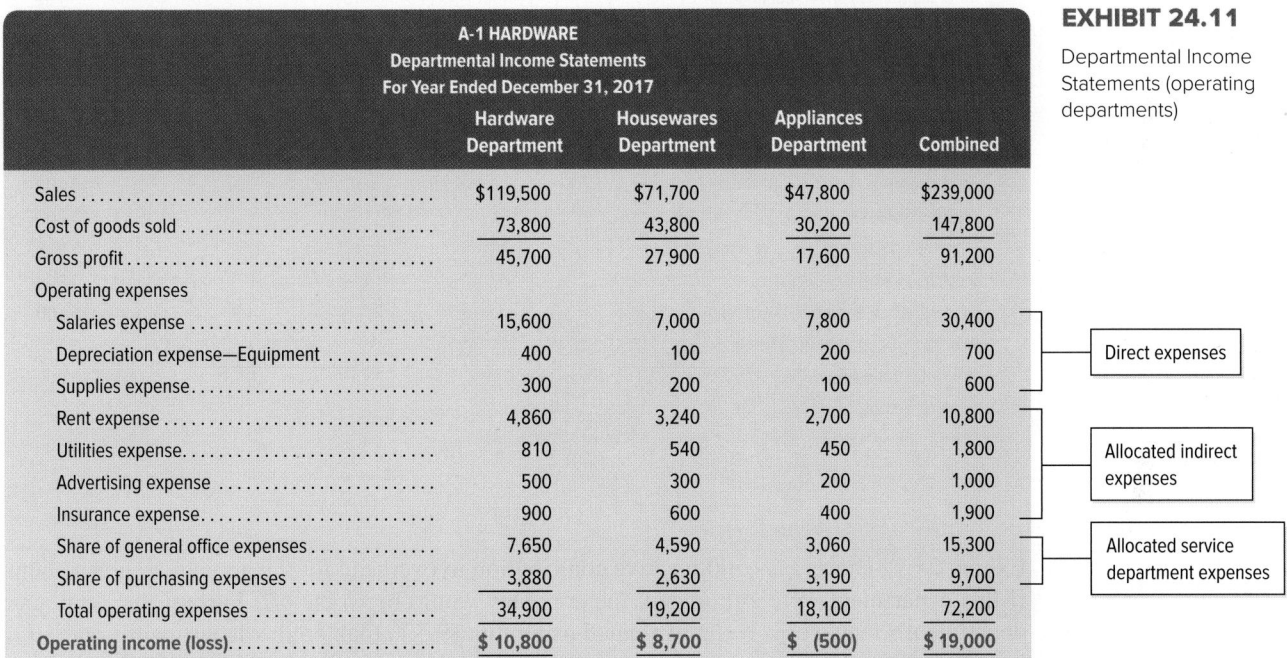

A-1 HARDWARE Departmental Income Statements For Year Ended December 31, 2017				
	Hardware Department	Housewares Department	Appliances Department	Combined
Sales	$119,500	$71,700	$47,800	$239,000
Cost of goods sold	73,800	43,800	30,200	147,800
Gross profit	45,700	27,900	17,600	91,200
Operating expenses				
Salaries expense	15,600	7,000	7,800	30,400
Depreciation expense—Equipment	400	100	200	700
Supplies expense	300	200	100	600
Rent expense	4,860	3,240	2,700	10,800
Utilities expense	810	540	450	1,800
Advertising expense	500	300	200	1,000
Insurance expense	900	600	400	1,900
Share of general office expenses	7,650	4,590	3,060	15,300
Share of purchasing expenses	3,880	2,630	3,190	9,700
Total operating expenses	34,900	19,200	18,100	72,200
Operating income (loss)	$ 10,800	$ 8,700	$ (500)	$ 19,000

Direct expenses → {Salaries expense, Depreciation expense—Equipment, Supplies expense}

Allocated indirect expenses → {Rent expense, Utilities expense, Advertising expense, Insurance expense}

Allocated service department expenses → {Share of general office expenses, Share of purchasing expenses}

Higher-level managers use departmental income statements to determine which of a company's departments are most profitable. After considering all costs, the hardware department is most profitable. The company might attempt to expand its hardware department.

Departmental Contribution to Overhead

Exhibit 24.11 shows that the appliances department reported an operating loss of $(500). Should this department be eliminated? We must be careful when indirect expenses are a large portion of total expenses and when weaknesses in assumptions and decisions in allocating indirect expenses can greatly affect income. Also, operating department managers might have no control over the level of service department services they use. In these and other cases, we might better evaluate profit center performance using the **departmental contribution to overhead,** a measure of the amount of sales less *direct* expenses. A department's contribution is said to be "to overhead" because of the practice of considering all indirect expenses as overhead. Thus, the excess of a department's sales over direct expenses is a contribution toward at least a portion of total overhead.

The upper half of Exhibit 24.12 shows a departmental contribution to overhead as part of an expanded income statement. Departmental contribution to overhead, because it focuses on the direct expenses that are under the profit center manager's control, is often a better way to assess that manager's performance.

EXHIBIT 24.12

Departmental Contribution to Overhead

A-1 HARDWARE Income Statement Showing Departmental Contribution to Overhead For Year Ended December 31, 2017	Hardware Department	Housewares Department	Appliances Department	Combined
Sales	$119,500	$ 71,700	$47,800	$239,000
Cost of goods sold	73,800	43,800	30,200	147,800
Gross profit	45,700	27,900	17,600	91,200
Direct expenses				
Salaries expense	15,600	7,000	7,800	30,400
Depreciation expense—Equipment	400	100	200	700
Supplies expense.	300	200	100	600
Total direct expenses.	16,300	7,300	8,100	31,700
Departmental contributions **to overhead**	**$ 29,400**	**$20,600**	**$ 9,500**	**$ 59,500**
Indirect expenses				
Rent expense				10,800
Utilities expense.				1,800
Advertising expense				1,000
Insurance expense.				1,900
General office department expense				15,300
Purchasing department expense				9,700
Total indirect expenses				40,500
Operating income				**$ 19,000**

Point: Operating income is the same in Exhibits 24.11 and 24.12. The method of reporting indirect expenses in Exhibit 24.12 does not change total income but does identify each operating department's contribution to overhead.

Exhibit 24.12 shows a $9,500 positive contribution to overhead for the appliances department. If this department were eliminated, the company would be worse off. Further, the appliance department's manager is better evaluated using this $9,500 than on the department's operating loss of $(500). The company also compares each department's contribution to overhead to budgeted amounts to assess each department's performance.

Behavioral Aspects of Departmental Performance Reports   An organization must consider potential effects on employee behavior from departmental income statements and contribution to overhead reports. These include:

- Indirect expenses are typically uncontrollable costs for department managers. Thus, departmental contribution to overhead might be a better way to evaluate department manager performance. Including uncontrollable costs in performance evaluation is inconsistent with responsibility accounting and can reduce manager morale.

- Alternatively, including indirect expenses in the department manager's performance evaluation can lead the manager to be more careful in using service departments, which can reduce the organization's costs.

- Some companies allocate *budgeted* service department costs rather than actual service costs. In this way, operating departments are not held responsible for excessive costs from service departments, and service departments are more likely to control their costs.

INVESTMENT CENTERS

We describe both financial and nonfinancial measures of investment center performance.

Financial Performance Evaluation Measures

Investment center managers are typically evaluated using performance measures that combine income and assets. These measures include:

- return on investment
- profit margin
- residual income
- investment turnover

A1_____

Analyze investment centers using return on investment and residual income.

To illustrate, let's consider ZTel Company, which operates two divisions as **investment centers**: LCD and S-Phone. The LCD division manufactures liquid crystal display (LCD) touch-screen monitors and sells them for use in computers, cellular phones, and other products. The S-Phone division sells smartphones. Exhibit 24.13 shows current-year income and assets for the divisions.

	LCD Division	S-Phone Division
Investment center income..........................	$ 526,500	$ 417,600
Investment center average invested assets............	2,500,000	1,850,000

EXHIBIT 24.13

Investment Center Income and Assets

Investment Center Return on Investment   One measure to evaluate division performance is the investment center **return on investment (ROI),** also called *return on assets* (ROA). This measure is computed as follows:

$$\text{Return on investment} = \frac{\text{Investment center income}}{\text{Investment center average invested assets}}$$

The return on investment for the LCD division is 21% (rounded), computed as $526,500/$2,500,000. The S-Phone division's return on investment is 23% (rounded), computed as $417,600/$1,850,000. ZTel's management can use ROI as part of its performance evaluation for its investment center managers. For example, actual ROI can be compared to targeted ROI or to the ROI for similar departments at competing businesses.

Investment Center Residual Income   Another way to evaluate division performance is to compute investment center **residual income,** which is computed as follows:

$$\text{Residual income} = \frac{\text{Investment center}}{\text{income}} - \frac{\text{Target investment center}}{\text{income}}$$

© princigalli/iStock/360/Getty Images

Assume ZTel's top management sets target income at 8% of investment center assets. For an investment center, this target percentage is typically the cost of obtaining financing. Applying this formula using data from Exhibit 24.13 yields the residual income for ZTel's divisions in Exhibit 24.14.

	LCD Division	S-Phone Division
Investment center income..........................	$526,500	$417,600
Less: Target investment center income		
$2,500,000 × 8%	200,000	
$1,850,000 × 8%		148,000
Investment center residual income..................	$326,500	$269,600

EXHIBIT 24.14

Investment Center Residual Income

Residual income is usually expressed in dollars. The LCD division produced more dollars of residual income than the S-Phone division. ZTel's management can use residual income, along with ROI, to evaluate investment center manager performance.

Using residual income to evaluate division performance encourages division managers to accept all opportunities that return more than the target income, thus increasing company value. For example, the S-Phone division might (mistakenly) not want to accept a new customer that will provide a 15% return on investment because that will reduce the S-Phone division's overall return on investment (23%, as shown above). However, the S-Phone division *should* accept this opportunity because the new customer would increase residual income by providing income above the target income of 8% of invested assets.

NEED-TO-KNOW 24-3

Return on Investment
and Residual income

A1

Do More: QS 24-9, QS 24-10,
E 24-9, E 24-10

The media division of a company reports income of $600,000, average invested assets of $7,500,000, and a target income of 6% of average invested assets. Compute the division's (a) return on investment and (b) residual income.

Solution

a. $600,000/$7,500,000 = 8%

b. $600,000 − ($7,500,000 × 6%) = $150,000

Issues in Computing Return on Investment and Residual Income   Evaluations of investment center performance using return on investment and residual income can be affected by how a company answers these questions:

1. How do you compute *average* invested assets? It is common to compute the average by adding the year's beginning amount of invested assets to the year's ending amount of invested assets, and dividing that sum by 2. Averages based on monthly or quarterly asset amounts are also acceptable. Seasonal variations in invested assets, if any, impact this average.

2. How do you measure invested assets? It is common to measure invested assets using their *net* book values. For example, depreciable assets would be measured at their cost minus accumulated depreciation. As net book value declines over a depreciable asset's useful life, the result is that return on investment and residual income would increase over that asset's life. This might cause managers not to invest in new assets. In addition, in measuring invested assets, companies commonly exclude assets that are not used in generating investment center income, such as land held for resale.

3. How do you measure investment center income? It is common to exclude both interest expense and tax expense from investment center income. Interest expense reflects a company's financing decisions, and tax expense is typically considered outside the control of an investment center manager. Excluding interest and taxes in these calculations enables more meaningful comparisons of return on investment and residual income across investment centers and companies.

Point: *Economic Value Added* (EVA®), developed and trademarked by Stern, Stewart, and Co., is an approach to address issues in computing residual income. This method uses a variety of adjustments to compute income, assets, and the target rate.

▇ **Decision** Insight ━━━━━━━━━━━━━━━━━━━━━━━━━━

In the Money   Executive pay is often linked to performance measures. Bonus payments are often based on exceeding a target return on investment or certain balanced scorecard indicators. Stock awards, such as stock options and restricted stock, reward executives when their company's stock price rises. The goal of bonus plans and stock awards is to encourage executives to make decisions that increase company performance and value. ▪

A2 _____

Analyze investment centers
using profit margin and
investment turnover.

Investment Center Profit Margin and Investment Turnover   We can further examine investment center (division) performance by splitting return on investment into two measures—profit margin and investment turnover—as follows.

Return on investment =	**Profit margin**	**×**	**Investment turnover**

$$\text{Return on investment} = \frac{\text{Investment center income}}{\text{Investment center sales}} \times \frac{\text{Investment center sales}}{\text{Investment center average assets}}$$

- **Profit margin** measures the income earned per dollar of sales. It equals investment center income divided by investment center sales. In analyzing investment center performance, we typically use a measure of income *before* tax.
- **Investment turnover** measures how efficiently an investment center generates sales from its invested assets. It equals investment center sales divided by investment center average assets.

Profit margin is expressed as a percent, while investment turnover is interpreted as the number of times assets were converted into sales. Higher profit margin and higher investment turnover indicate better performance.

Point: This partitioning of return on investment is sometimes called DuPont analysis.

To illustrate, consider **Walt Disney Co.**, which reports in Exhibit 24.15 results for two of its operating divisions: Media Networks and Parks and Resorts.

$ millions	Media Networks	Parks and Resorts
Sales	$23,264	$16,162
Income.	7,793	3,031
Average invested assets	30,262	23,335

EXHIBIT 24.15

Walt Disney Division Sales, Income, and Assets

Profit margin and investment turnover for these two divisions are computed and shown in Exhibit 24.16.

$ millions	Media Networks	Parks and Resorts
Profit margin		
$7,793/$23,264	33.50%	
$3,031/$16,162		18.75%
Investment turnover		
$23,264/$30,262	0.77	
$16,162/$23,335		0.69
Return on investment		
33.50% × 0.77	25.80%	
18.75% × 0.69		12.94

EXHIBIT 24.16

Walt Disney Division Profit Margin and Investment Turnover

Disney's Media Networks division makes 33.50 cents of profit for every dollar of sales, while its Parks and Resorts division makes 18.75 cents of profit per dollar of sales. The Media Networks division (0.77 investment turnover) is slightly more efficient than the Parks and Resorts division (0.69 investment turnover) in using assets. Top management can use profit margin and investment turnover to evaluate the performance of division managers. The measures can also aid management when considering further investment in its divisions. Because of both a much higher profit margin and higher investment turnover, the Media Networks division's return on investment (25.80%) is much greater than that of the Parks and Resorts division (12.94%).

■ **Decision** Maker

Division Manager   You manage a division in a highly competitive industry. You will receive a cash bonus if your division achieves an ROI above 12%. Your division's profit margin is 7%, equal to the industry average, and your division's investment turnover is 1.5. How can you increase your chance of receiving the bonus? ■   [*Answer:* Your division's ROI is 10.5% (7% × 1.5). In a competitive industry, it is difficult to increase profit margins by raising prices. Your division might be better able to control costs than increase profit margin. You might increase advertising to increase sales without increasing invested assets. Investment turnover and ROI increase if the advertising attracts customers.]

A division reports sales of $50,000, income of $2,000, and average invested assets of $10,000. Compute the division's (a) profit margin, (b) investment turnover, and (c) return on investment.

NEED-TO-KNOW 24-4

Margin, Turnover, and Return

A2

Solution

a. $2,000/$50,000 = 4%

b. $50,000/$10,000 = 5.0

c. $2,000/$10,000 = 20%

Do More: QS 24-12, E 24-10, E 24-11, E 24-12

Nonfinancial Performance Evaluation Measures

Evaluating performance solely on financial measures has limitations. For example, some investment center managers might forgo profitable opportunities to keep their return on investment high. Also, residual income is less useful when comparing investment centers of different size. And, both return on investment and residual income can encourage managers to focus too heavily on short-term financial goals.

In response to these limitations, companies consider *nonfinancial* measures. A delivery company such as **FedEx** might track the percentage of on-time deliveries. The percentage of defective tennis balls manufactured can be used to assess performance of **Penn**'s production managers. **Walmart**'s credit card screens commonly ask customers at checkout whether the cashier was friendly or the store was clean. **Coca-Cola** measures its water usage as part of an effort to enhance the sustainability of its production process. This kind of information can help division managers run their divisions and help top management evaluate division manager performance. A popular measure that includes nonfinancial indicators is the balanced scorecard.

Balanced Scorecard The **balanced scorecard** is a system of performance measures, including nonfinancial measures, used to assess company and division manager performance. The balanced scorecard requires managers to think of their company from four perspectives:

1. **Customer:** What do customers think of us?
2. **Internal processes:** Which of our operations are critical to meeting customer needs?
3. **Innovation and learning:** How can we improve?
4. **Financial:** What do our owners think of us?

The balanced scorecard collects information on several *key performance indicators* (KPIs) within each of the four perspectives. These key indicators vary across companies. Exhibit 24.17 lists common performance indicators used in the balanced scorecard.

  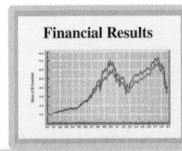

Customer	Internal Processes	Innovation/Learning	Financial
• Customer satisfaction rating	• Defect rates	• Employee satisfaction	• Net income
• # of new customers acquired	• Cycle time	• Employee turnover	• ROI
• % of on-time deliveries	• Product costs	• $ spent on training	• Sales growth
• % of sales from new products	• Labor hours per order	• # of new products	• Cash flow
• Time to fill orders	• Production days without an accident	• # of patents	• Residual income
• % of sales returned		• $ spent on research	• Stock price

After selecting key performance indicators, companies collect data on each indicator and compare actual amounts to target (goal) amounts to assess performance. For example, a company might have a goal of filling 98% of customer orders within two hours. Balanced scorecard reports are often presented in graphs or tables that can be updated frequently. Such timely information aids division managers in their decisions and can be used by top management to evaluate division manager performance.

Exhibit 24.18 is an example of balanced scorecard reporting on the customer perspective for an Internet retailer. This scorecard reports that the retailer is getting 62% of its potential customers successfully through the purchasing process, and that 2.2% of all orders are returned. The *color* of the circles in the Trend column reveals whether the company is exceeding its goal (green), roughly meeting the goal (gray), or not meeting the goal (red). The *direction* of the arrows reveals any trend in performance: an upward arrow indicates improvement, a downward arrow indicates declining performance, and an arrow pointing sideways indicates no change.

A review of this balanced scorecard suggests the retailer is meeting or exceeding its goals on orders returned and customer satisfaction. Further, purchasing success and customer satisfaction are improving. The company has received more customer complaints than was hoped for; *however,*

KPI: Customer Perspective	Actual	Goal	Trend
Potential customers purchasing	62%	80%	
Orders returned	2.2%	2%	
Customer satisfaction rating	9.5 of 10.0	9.5	
Number of customer complaints	142	100	

EXHIBIT 24.18

Balanced Scorecard Reporting: Internet Retailer

the number of customer complaints is declining. A manager would combine this information with similar information from the other three performance indicators (internal processes, innovation and learning, and financial perspectives) to get an overall view of division performance.

Classify each of the performance measures below into the most likely balanced scorecard perspective to which it relates: customer (C), internal processes (P), innovation and growth (I), or financial (F).

1. On-time delivery rate
2. Accident-free days
3. Sustainability training workshops held
4. Defective products made
5. Residual income
6. Patents applied for
7. Sales returns
8. Customer complaints

NEED-TO-KNOW 24-5

Balanced Scorecard

A3

Solution

1. C   **2.** P   **3.** I   **4.** P   **5.** F   **6.** I   **7.** C   **8.** C

Do More: QS 24-14, E 24-16, E 24-17

 **Decision Maker**

Center Manager   Your center's usual return on investment is 19%. You are considering two new investments. The first requires a $250,000 average investment and is expected to yield annual net income of $50,000. The second requires a $1 million average investment with an expected annual net income of $175,000. Do you pursue either? ∎   [*Answer:* The two investments are not comparable on the absolute dollars of income or on assets. For instance, the second provides a higher income in absolute dollars but requires a higher investment. We need return on investment for each: (1) $50,000 ÷ $250,000 = 20% and (2) $175,000 ÷ $1 million = 17.5%. Do you pursue one, both, or neither? Because alternative 1's return is higher than the center's usual return of 19%, it should be pursued, assuming its risks are acceptable. Alternative 2's return is lower than the usual 19% and is likely not acceptable.]

Transfer Pricing

Divisions in decentralized companies sometimes do business with one another. For example, a separate division of **Harley-Davidson** manufactures its plastic and fiberglass parts used in the company's motorcycles. **Anheuser-Busch InBev**'s metal container division makes cans used in its brewing operations, and also sells cans to soft-drink companies. A division of **Prince** produces strings used in tennis rackets made by Prince and other manufacturers.

The price used to record transfers of goods across divisions of the same company is called the **transfer price.** Transfer prices can be used in cost, profit, and investment centers.

In decentralized organizations, division managers have input on or decide transfer prices. Since these transfers are not with customers outside the company, the transfer price has no direct impact on the *company's* overall profits. However, transfer prices can impact *division* performance evaluations and, if set incorrectly, lead to bad decisions.

Transfer prices are set using one of three approaches:

1. Cost (for example, variable manufacturing cost per unit)
2. Market price
3. Negotiated price

To illustrate the impact of alternative transfer prices on divisional profits, consider ZTel, a smartphone manufacturer. ZTel's LCD division makes touch-screen monitors that are used in ZTel's smartphone division or sold to outside customers. LCD's variable manufacturing cost is

C2

Explain transfer pricing and methods to set transfer prices.

Point: Transfer pricing can impact company profits when divisions are located in countries with different tax rates; this is covered in advanced courses.

$40 per monitor, and the market price is $80 per monitor. There are two extreme positions one can take for the transfer price.

- **Low Transfer Price** The *smartphone division manager* wants to pay a *low* transfer price. The transfer price cannot be less than $40 per monitor, as any lower price would cause the LCD manager to lose money on each monitor sold.

- **High Transfer Price** The *LCD division manager* wants to receive a *high* transfer price. The transfer price cannot be more than $80 per monitor, as the smartphone division manager will not pay more than the market price.

This means the transfer price must be between $40 and $80 per monitor, and a negotiated price somewhere between these two extremes is reasonable. Appendix 24B expands on transfer pricing and details on the three approaches.

SUSTAINABILITY AND ACCOUNTING

This chapter focused on performance measurement and reporting. Companies report on their sustainability performance in a variety of ways. One approach integrates sustainability metrics in the four balanced scorecard perspectives (customer, internal process, innovation and learning, and financial). Many key performance indicators address the internal process and innovation and learning perspectives. For example, General Mills reports on its environmental targets and progress in its annual corporate sustainability report. Exhibit 24.19 captures how this information might appear as part of a balanced scorecard report.

EXHIBIT 24.19

Balanced Scorecard—
Sustainability

KPI: Internal Process Perspective	Actual Reduction	Target Reduction	Trend
Emissions	23%	20%	● ↑
Energy usage	10	20	● ↑
Solid waste	38	50	● ↑
Fuel	25	35	● ↑

Courtesy of Ministry of Supply

Some companies can report the direct effects on profits from a focus on sustainability. For example, Target recently started a *Made to Matter* department. To be sold in this department, brands must focus on consumer wellness and be committed to social responsibility. Target's *Made to Matter* department reported sales of over $1 billion in a recent year.

Ministry of Supply, this chapter's feature company, weaves sustainability into its production process. Instead of the traditional "cut-and-sew" approach, the company uses a "3D Robotic Knitting" process to make seamless garments with 3D printers. Not only do such seamless garments fit better, production is more sustainable as it wastes less fabric. According to Gihan Amarasiriwardena, one of the company's founders, "the traditional process wastes up to 30% of fabric. With our method, there is zero waste."

 **Decision Analysis** ■ ■ ■ **Cycle Time and Cycle Efficiency**

A4

Compute cycle time and cycle efficiency, and explain their importance to production management.

Manufacturing companies commonly use nonfinancial measures to evaluate the performance of their production processes. For example, as lean manufacturing practices help companies move toward just-in-time manufacturing, it is important for these companies to reduce the time to manufacture their products and to improve manufacturing efficiency. One metric that measures that time element is **cycle time (CT)**, which describes the time it takes to produce a product or service. It is defined in Exhibit 24.20.

EXHIBIT 24.20

Cycle Time

Cycle time = Process time + Inspection time + Move time + Wait time

Process time is the time spent producing the product. *Inspection time* is the time spent inspecting (1) raw materials when received, (2) work in process while in production, and (3) finished goods prior to shipment. *Move time* is the time spent moving (1) raw materials from storage to production and (2) work in process from one factory location to another factory location. *Wait time* is the time that an order or job sits with no production applied to it. Wait time can be due to order delays, bottlenecks in production, or poor scheduling.

Process time is considered **value-added time:** it is the only activity in cycle time that adds value to the product from the customer's perspective. The other three activities are considered **non-value-added time:** they add no value to the customer.

Companies strive to reduce non-value-added time to improve **cycle efficiency (CE),** which is a measure of production efficiency. Cycle efficiency is the ratio of value-added time to total cycle time, as shown in Exhibit 24.21.

$$\text{Cycle efficiency} = \frac{\text{Value-added time}}{\text{Cycle time}}$$

EXHIBIT 24.21

Cycle Efficiency

To illustrate, assume that Rocky Mountain Bikes receives and produces an order for 500 Tracker mountain bikes. Assume that it took the following times to produce this order.

 **Process time... 1.8 days**

 **Inspection time... 0.5 days**

 **Move time... 0.7 days**

 **Wait time... 3.0 days**

In this case, cycle time is 6.0 days (1.8 + 0.5 + 0.7 + 3.0 days). Cycle efficiency is 0.3, or 30%, computed as 1.8 days divided by 6.0 days. This means that Rocky Mountain Bikes's value-added time (its process time, or time spent working on the product) is 30%. The other 70% is spent on non-value-added activities.

If a company has a CE of 1, it means that its time is spent entirely on value-added activities. If the CE is low, the company should evaluate its production process to see if it can identify ways to reduce non-value-added activities. The 30% CE for Rocky Mountain Bikes is low, and its management should try to reduce non-value-added activities.

Management requests departmental income statements for Gamer's Haven, a computer store that has five departments. Three are operating departments (hardware, software, and repairs) and two are service departments (general office and purchasing).

NEED-TO-KNOW 24-6

COMPREHENSIVE

	General Office	Purchasing	Hardware	Software	Repairs
Sales	—	—	$960,000	$600,000	$840,000
Cost of goods sold	—	—	500,000	300,000	200,000
Direct expenses					
Payroll	$60,000	$45,000	80,000	25,000	325,000
Depreciation	6,000	7,200	33,000	4,200	9,600
Supplies	15,000	10,000	10,000	2,000	25,000

The departments incur several indirect expenses. To prepare departmental income statements, the indirect expenses must be allocated across the five departments. Then the expenses of the two service departments must be allocated to the three operating departments. Total cost amounts and the allocation bases for each indirect expense follow.

Indirect Expense	Total Cost	Allocation Basis
Rent	$150,000	Square footage occupied
Utilities	50,000	Square footage occupied
Advertising	125,000	Dollars of sales
Insurance	30,000	Value of assets insured
Service departments		
General office	?	Number of employees
Purchasing	?	Dollars of cost of goods sold

The following additional information is needed for indirect expense allocations.

Department	Square Feet	Sales	Insured Assets	Employees	Cost of Goods Sold
General office...........	500		$ 60,000		
Purchasing	500		72,000		
Hardware	4,000	$ 960,000	330,000	5	$ 500,000
Software	3,000	600,000	42,000	5	300,000
Repairs	2,000	840,000	96,000	10	200,000
Totals.................	10,000	$2,400,000	$600,000	20	$1,000,000

Required

1. Prepare a departmental expense allocation spreadsheet for Gamer's Haven.

2. Prepare a departmental income statement reporting net income for each operating department and for all operating departments combined.

PLANNING THE SOLUTION

- Set up and complete four tables to allocate the indirect expenses—one each for rent, utilities, advertising, and insurance.
- Allocate the departments' indirect expenses using a spreadsheet like the one in Exhibit 24.10. Enter the given amounts of the direct expenses for each department. Then enter the allocated amounts of the indirect expenses that you computed.
- Complete two tables for allocating the general office and purchasing department costs to the three operating departments. Enter these amounts on the spreadsheet and determine the total expenses allocated to the three operating departments.
- Prepare departmental income statements like the one in Exhibit 24.11. Show sales, cost of goods sold, gross profit, individual expenses, and net income for each of the three operating departments and for the combined company.

SOLUTION

Allocations of the four indirect expenses across the five departments.

Rent	Square Feet	Percent of Total	Allocated Cost
General office...........	500	5.0%	$ 7,500
Purchasing	500	5.0	7,500
Hardware	4,000	40.0	60,000
Software	3,000	30.0	45,000
Repairs	2,000	20.0	30,000
Totals.................	10,000	100.0%	$150,000

Utilities	Square Feet	Percent of Total	Allocated Cost
General office...........	500	5.0%	$ 2,500
Purchasing	500	5.0	2,500
Hardware	4,000	40.0	20,000
Software	3,000	30.0	15,000
Repairs	2,000	20.0	10,000
Totals.................	10,000	100.0%	$50,000

Advertising	Sales Dollars	Percent of Total	Allocated Cost
Hardware	$ 960,000	40.0%	$ 50,000
Software	600,000	25.0	31,250
Repairs	840,000	35.0	43,750
Totals...............	$2,400,000	100.0%	$125,000

Insurance	Assets Insured	Percent of Total	Allocated Cost
General office...........	$ 60,000	10.0%	$ 3,000
Purchasing	72,000	12.0	3,600
Hardware	330,000	55.0	16,500
Software	42,000	7.0	2,100
Repairs	96,000	16.0	4,800
Totals.................	$600,000	100.0%	$30,000

1. Allocations of service department expenses to the three operating departments.

General Office Allocations to	Employees	Percent of Total	Allocated Cost
Hardware	5	25.0%	$23,500
Software	5	25.0	23,500
Repairs	10	50.0	47,000
Totals.................	20	100.0%	$94,000

Purchasing Allocations to	Cost of Goods Sold	Percent of Total	Allocated Cost
Hardware	$ 500,000	50.0%	$37,900
Software	300,000	30.0	22,740
Repairs	200,000	20.0	15,160
Totals.................	$1,000,000	100.0%	$75,800

GAMER'S HAVEN
Departmental Expense Allocations
For Year Ended December 31, 2017

	Allocation Base	Expense Account Balance	General Office Dept.	Purchasing Dept.	Hardware Dept.	Software Dept.	Repairs Dept.
Direct Expenses							
Payroll....................................		$ 535,000	$ 60,000	$ 45,000	$ 80,000	$ 25,000	$ 325,000
Depreciation.............................		60,000	6,000	7,200	33,000	4,200	9,600
Supplies		62,000	15,000	10,000	10,000	2,000	25,000
Indirect Expenses							
Rent......................................	Square ft.	150,000	7,500	7,500	60,000	45,000	30,000
Utilities	Square ft.	50,000	2,500	2,500	20,000	15,000	10,000
Advertising	Sales	125,000	—	—	50,000	31,250	43,750
Insurance	Assets	30,000	3,000	3,600	16,500	2,100	4,800
Total expenses		1,012,000	94,000	75,800	269,500	124,550	448,150
Service Department Expenses							
General office............................	Employees		(94,000)		23,500	23,500	47,000
Purchasing	Goods sold			(75,800)	37,900	22,740	15,160
Total expenses allocated to operating departments		$1,012,000	$ 0	$ 0	$330,900	$170,790	$510,310

2. Departmental income statements.

GAMER'S HAVEN
Departmental Income Statements
For Year Ended December 31, 2017

	Hardware	Software	Repairs	Combined
Sales	$ 960,000	$ 600,000	$ 840,000	$2,400,000
Cost of goods sold	500,000	300,000	200,000	1,000,000
Gross profit........................	460,000	300,000	640,000	1,400,000
Expenses				
Payroll..........................	80,000	25,000	325,000	430,000
Depreciation.....................	33,000	4,200	9,600	46,800
Supplies	10,000	2,000	25,000	37,000
Rent............................	60,000	45,000	30,000	135,000
Utilities	20,000	15,000	10,000	45,000
Advertising	50,000	31,250	43,750	125,000
Insurance	16,500	2,100	4,800	23,400
Share of general office	23,500	23,500	47,000	94,000
Share of purchasing..............	37,900	22,740	15,160	75,800
Total expenses	330,900	170,790	510,310	1,012,000
Operating income................	$129,100	$129,210	$129,690	$ 388,000

24A

Cost Allocations

In this appendix we use our general model of cost allocation (see Exhibit 24.3) to show how the cost allocations in Exhibits 24.10 and 24.11 are computed. A-1 Hardware's departments use the allocation bases in Exhibit 24A.1: square feet of floor space, dollar value of insured assets, sales dollars, and number of purchase orders.

EXHIBIT 24A.1

Departments' Allocation Bases

Department	Floor Space (square feet)	Value of Insured Assets ($)	Sales ($)	Number of Purchase Orders*
General office	1,500	$ 38,000		—
Purchasing.............	1,500	19,000		—
Hardware.............	4,050	85,500	$119,500	394
Housewares	2,700	57,000	71,700	267
Appliances............	2,250	38,000	47,800	324
Total.................	12,000	$237,500	$239,000	985

*Purchasing department tracks purchase orders by department.

For each cost allocation that follows, we use the general formula here from Exhibit 24.3 to allocate indirect and service department costs.

> **Allocated cost = Total cost to allocate × Percentage of allocation base used**

From Exhibit 24.9, the company has these four indirect costs to allocate:

Rent expense.............	$12,000	Advertising expense	$1,000
Utilities expense	2,400	Insurance expense	2,500

Allocation of Rent The two service departments (general office and purchasing) occupy 25% of the total space (3,000 sq. feet/12,000 sq. feet). However, they are located near the back of the building, which is of lower value than space near the front that is occupied by operating departments. Management estimates that space near the back accounts for $1,200 (10%) of the total rent expense of $12,000. Exhibit 24A.2 shows how we allocate the $1,200 rent expense between these two service departments in proportion to their square footage.

EXHIBIT 24A.2

Allocating Indirect (Rent) Expense to Service Departments

Department	Square Feet	Percent of Total	Allocated Cost*
General office	1,500	50.0%	$ 600
Purchasing	1,500	50.0	600
Totals	3,000	100.0%	$1,200

*See row 13 of departmental expense allocation spreadsheet (Exhibit 24.10).

We then have the remaining amount of $10,800 ($12,000 − $1,200) of rent expense to allocate to the three operating departments, as shown in Exhibit 24A.3.

EXHIBIT 24A.3

Allocating Indirect (Rent) Expense to Operating Departments

Department	Square Feet	Percent of Total	Allocated Cost*
Hardware	4,050	45.0%	$ 4,860
Housewares.............	2,700	30.0	3,240
Appliances	2,250	25.0	2,700
Totals	9,000	100.0%	$10,800

*See row 13 of departmental expense allocation spreadsheet (Exhibit 24.10).

Allocation of Utilities We next allocate the $2,400 of utilities expense to all departments based on square footage occupied, as shown in Exhibit 24A.4.

Department	Square Feet	Percent of Total	Allocated Cost*
General office	1,500	12.50%	$ 300
Purchasing	1,500	12.50	300
Hardware	4,050	33.75	810
Housewares	2,700	22.50	540
Appliances	2,250	18.75	450
Totals.................	12,000	100.00%	$2,400

EXHIBIT 24A.4

Allocating Indirect (Utilities) Expense to All Departments

*See row 14 of departmental expense allocation spreadsheet (Exhibit 24.10).

Allocation of Advertising Exhibit 24A.5 shows the allocation of $1,000 of advertising expense to the three operating departments on the basis of sales dollars. We exclude the service departments from this allocation because they do not generate sales.

Department	Sales	Percent of Total	Allocated Cost*
Hardware	$119,500	50.0%	$ 500
Housewares	71,700	30.0	300
Appliances	47,800	20.0	200
Totals.................	$239,000	100.0%	$1,000

EXHIBIT 24A.5

Allocating Indirect (Advertising) Expense to Operating Departments

*See row 15 of departmental expense allocation spreadsheet (Exhibit 24.10).

Allocation of Insurance We allocate the $2,500 of insurance expense to each service and operating department, as shown in Exhibit 24A.6.

Department	Value of Insured Assets	Percent of Total	Allocated Cost*
General office............	$ 38,000	16.0%	$ 400
Purchasing	19,000	8.0	200
Hardware	85,500	36.0	900
Housewares	57,000	24.0	600
Appliances	38,000	16.0	400
Total.................	$237,500	100.0%	$2,500

EXHIBIT 24A.6

Allocating Indirect (Insurance) Expense to All Departments

*See row 16 of departmental expense allocation spreadsheet (Exhibit 24.10).

Allocation of Service Department Expenses Next we allocate the total expenses of the two service departments to the three operating departments. Exhibit 24A.7 shows the allocation of total general office expenses ($15,300) to operating departments. This amount of $15,300 includes the $14,000 of direct service department expenses, plus $1,300 of indirect expenses that were allocated to the general office department.

Department	Sales	Percent of Total	Allocated Cost*
Hardware	$119,500	50.0%	$ 7,650
Housewares	71,700	30.0	4,590
Appliances	47,800	20.0	3,060
Total.................	$239,000	100.0%	$15,300

EXHIBIT 24A.7

Allocating Service Department (General Office) Expenses to Operating Departments

*See row 19 of departmental expense allocation spreadsheet (Exhibit 24.10).

Exhibit 24A.8 shows the allocation of total purchasing department expenses ($9,700) to operating departments. This amount of $9,700 includes $8,600 of direct expenses plus $1,100 of indirect expenses that were allocated to the purchasing department.

EXHIBIT 24A.8

Allocating Service Department (Purchasing) Expenses to Operating Departments

Department	Number of Purchase Orders	Percent of Total	Allocated Cost*
Hardware	394	40.00%	$3,880
Housewares	267	27.11	2,630
Appliances	324	32.89	3,190
Total	985	100.00%	$9,700

*See row 20 of departmental expense allocation spreadsheet (Exhibit 24.10).

APPENDIX

24B

Transfer Pricing

In this appendix we show how to determine transfer prices and discuss issues in transfer pricing.

Alternative Transfer Prices The top portion of Exhibit 24B.1 reports data on the LCD division of ZTel. That division manufactures liquid crystal display (LCD) touch-screen monitors for use in ZTel's S-Phone division's smartphones. The monitors can also be used in other products. The LCD division can sell its monitors to the S-Phone division as well as to buyers other than S-Phone. Likewise, the S-Phone division can purchase monitors from suppliers other than LCD.

EXHIBIT 24B.1

LCD Division Manufacturing Information—Monitors

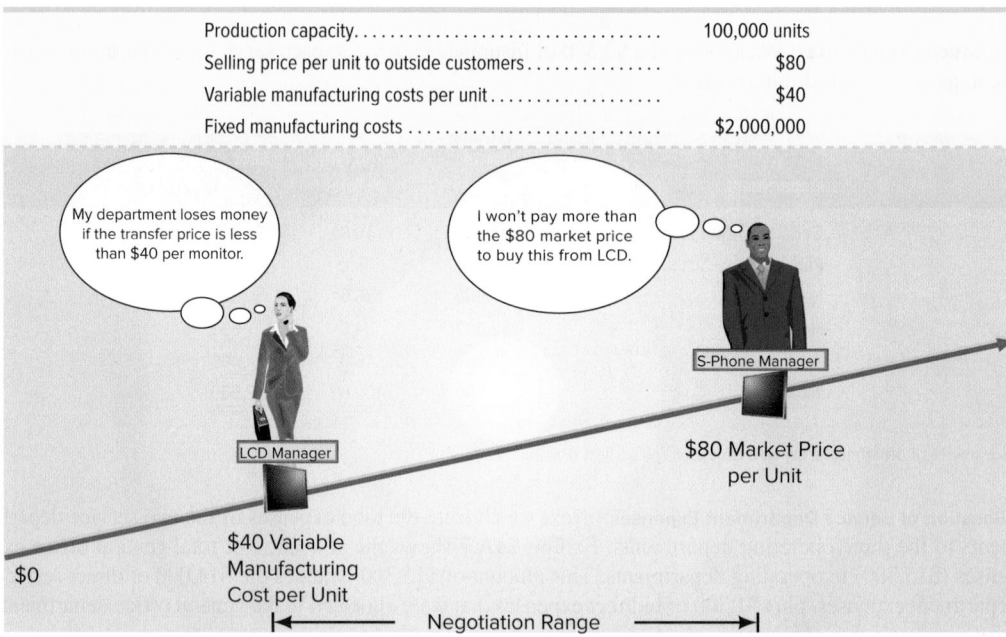

Production capacity	100,000 units
Selling price per unit to outside customers	$80
Variable manufacturing costs per unit	$40
Fixed manufacturing costs	$2,000,000

The bottom portion of Exhibit 24B.1 reveals the range of transfer prices for transfers of monitors from LCD to S-Phone. The transfer price can reasonably range from $40 (the variable manufacturing cost per unit) to $80 (the cost of buying the monitor from an outside supplier).

- The manager of LCD wants to report a divisional profit. Thus, this manager will not accept a transfer price less than $40; a price less than $40 would cause the division to lose money on each monitor transferred. The LCD manager will consider transfer prices of only $40 or more.

- The S-Phone division manager also wants to report a divisional profit. Thus, this manager will not pay more than $80 per monitor because similar monitors can be bought from outside suppliers at that price. The S-Phone manager will consider transfer prices of only $80 or less.

As any transfer price between $40 and $80 per monitor is possible, how does ZTel determine the transfer price? The answer depends in part on whether the LCD division has excess capacity to manufacture monitors.

No Excess Capacity   If the LCD division can sell every monitor it produces (100,000 units) at a market price of $80 per monitor, LCD managers would not accept any transfer price less than $80 per monitor. This is a **market-based transfer price**—one based on the market price of the good or service being transferred. Any transfer price less than $80 would cause the LCD division managers to incur an unnecessary *opportunity cost* that would lower the division's income and hurt its managers' performance evaluation.

Typically, a division operating at full capacity will sell to external customers rather than sell internally. Still, the market-based transfer price of $80 can be considered the maximum possible transfer price when there is excess capacity, which is the case we consider next.

Excess Capacity   Assume the LCD division is producing only 80,000 units. Because LCD has $2,000,000 of fixed manufacturing costs, both the LCD division and the top management of ZTel prefer that the S-Phone division purchases its monitors from LCD. For example, if S-Phone purchases its monitors from an outside supplier at the market price of $80 each, LCD manufactures no units. Then, LCD reports a division loss equal to its fixed costs, and ZTel overall reports a lower net income. With excess capacity, LCD should accept any transfer price of $40 per unit or greater, and S-Phone should purchase monitors from LCD. This will allow LCD to recover some (or all) of its fixed costs and increase ZTel's overall profits.

For example, if a transfer price of $50 per monitor is used, the S-Phone manager is pleased to buy from LCD since that price is below the market price of $80. For each monitor transferred from LCD to S-Phone at $50, the LCD division receives a *contribution margin* of $10 (computed as $50 transfer price less $40 variable cost) to contribute toward recovering its fixed costs. This form of transfer pricing is called **cost-based transfer pricing.** Under this approach the transfer price might be based on variable costs, total costs, or variable costs plus a markup.

With excess capacity, division managers will often negotiate a transfer price that lies between the variable cost per unit and the market price per unit. In this case, the **negotiated transfer price** and resulting departmental performance reports reflect, in part, the negotiating skills of the respective division managers. This might not be best for overall company performance. Determining the transfer price under excess capacity is complex and is covered in advanced courses.

Additional Issues in Transfer Pricing   Several additional issues arise in determining transfer prices that include the following:

- **No market price exists.** Sometimes there is no market price for the product being transferred. The product might be a key component that requires additional conversion costs at the next stage and is not easily replicated by an outside company. For example, there is no market for a console for a Nissan Maxima and there is no substitute console Nissan can use in assembling a Maxima. In this case, a market-based transfer price cannot be used.

- **Cost control.** To provide incentives for cost control, transfer prices might be based on standard, rather than actual, costs. For example, if a transfer price of actual variable costs plus a markup of $20 per unit is used in the case above, LCD has no incentive to control its costs.

- **Nonfinancial factors.** Factors such as quality control, reduced lead times, and impact on employee morale can be important factors in determining transfer prices.

Transfer Pricing Approaches Used by Companies

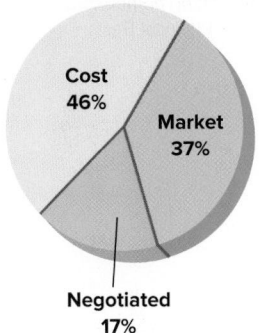

Cost 46%

Market 37%

Negotiated 17%

APPENDIX

Joint Costs and Their Allocation

24C

C3
Describe allocation of joint costs across products.

Most manufacturing processes involve **joint costs,** which refer to costs incurred to produce or purchase two or more products at the same time. For example, a sawmill company incurs joint costs when it buys logs that it cuts into lumber, as shown in Exhibit 24C.1. The joint costs include the logs (raw material) and their being cut (conversion) into boards classified as Clear, Select, No. 1 Common, No. 2 Common, No. 3 Common, and other types of lumber and by-products. After the logs are cut into boards, any further processing costs on the boards are not joint costs.

When a joint cost is incurred, a question arises as to whether to allocate it to different products resulting from it. The answer is that when management wishes to estimate the costs of individual products, joint costs are included and must be allocated to these joint products. However, when management needs information to help decide whether to sell a product at a certain point in the production process or to process it further,

EXHIBIT 24C.1

Joint Products from Logs

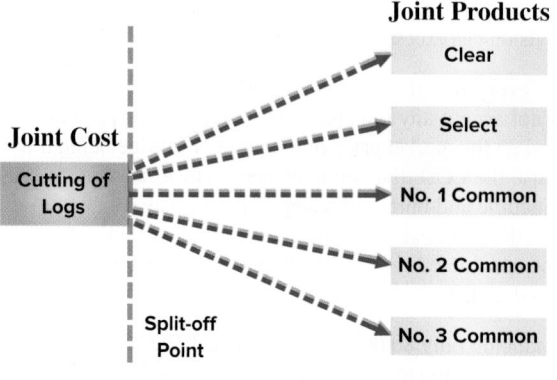

Joint Products

the joint costs are ignored. (We study this sell-or-process-further decision in a later chapter.)

Financial statements prepared according to GAAP must assign joint costs to products. To do this, management must decide how to allocate joint costs across products benefiting from these costs. If some products are sold and others remain in inventory, allocating joint costs involves assigning costs to both cost of goods sold and ending inventory.

The two usual methods to allocate joint costs are the (1) *physical basis* and (2) *value basis*. The physical basis typically involves allocating a joint cost using physical characteristics such as the ratio of pounds, cubic feet, or gallons of each joint product to the total pounds, cubic feet, or gallons of all joint products flowing from the cost. This method is not preferred because the resulting cost allocations do not reflect the relative market values the joint cost generates. The preferred approach is the value basis, which allocates a joint cost in proportion to the sales value of the output produced by the process at the "split-off point"; see Exhibit 24C.1. The split-off point is the point at which separate products can be identified.

Physical Basis Allocation of Joint Costs   To illustrate the physical basis of allocating a joint cost, we consider a sawmill that bought logs for $30,000. When cut, these logs produce 100,000 board feet of lumber in the grades and amounts shown in Exhibit 24C.2. The logs produce 20,000 board feet of No. 3 Common lumber, which is 20% of the total. With physical allocation, the No. 3 Common lumber is assigned 20% of the $30,000 cost of the logs, or $6,000 ($30,000 × 20%). Because this low-grade lumber sells for $4,000, this allocation gives a $2,000 loss from its production and sale. The physical basis for allocating joint costs does not reflect the extra value flowing into some products or the inferior value flowing into others. That is, the portion of a log that produces Clear and Select grade lumber is worth more than the portion used to produce the three grades of common lumber, but the physical basis fails to reflect this.

EXHIBIT 24C.2

Allocating Joint Costs on a Physical Basis

Grade of Lumber	Board Feet Produced	Percent of Total	Allocated Cost	Sales Value	Gross Profit
Clear and Select	10,000	10.0%	$ 3,000	$12,000	$ 9,000
No. 1 Common	30,000	30.0	9,000	18,000	9,000
No. 2 Common	40,000	40.0	12,000	16,000	4,000
No. 3 Common	20,000	20.0	6,000	4,000	(2,000)
Totals	100,000	100.0%	$30,000	$50,000	$20,000

Value Basis Allocation of Joint Costs   Exhibit 24C.3 illustrates the value basis method of allocation. It determines the percents of the total costs allocated to each grade by the ratio of each grade's sales value at the split-off point to the total sales value of $50,000 (sales value is the unit selling price multiplied by the number of units produced). The Clear and Select lumber grades receive 24% of the total cost ($12,000/$50,000) instead of the 10% portion using a physical basis. The No. 3 Common lumber receives only 8% of the total cost, or $2,400, which is much less than the $6,000 assigned to it using the physical basis.

EXHIBIT 24C.3

Allocating Joint Costs on a Value Basis

Grade of Lumber	Sales Value	Percent of Total	Allocated Cost	Gross Profit
Clear and Select	$12,000	24.0%	$ 7,200	$ 4,800
No. 1 Common	18,000	36.0	10,800	7,200
No. 2 Common	16,000	32.0	9,600	6,400
No. 3 Common	4,000	8.0	2,400	1,600
Totals	$50,000	100.0%	$30,000	$20,000

Example: Refer to Exhibit 24C.3. If the sales value of Clear and Select lumber is changed to $10,000, what is the revised ratio of the market value of No. 1 Common to the total? *Answer:* $18,000/$48,000 = 37.5%

An outcome of value basis allocation is that *each* grade produces exactly the same 40% gross profit at the split-off point. This 40% rate equals the gross profit rate from selling all the lumber made from the $30,000 logs for a combined price of $50,000. It is this closer matching of cost and revenues that makes the value basis allocation of joint costs the preferred method.

Summary

C1 **Distinguish between direct and indirect expenses and identify bases for allocating indirect expenses to departments.** Direct expenses are traced to a specific department and are incurred for the sole benefit of that department. Indirect expenses benefit more than one department. Indirect expenses are allocated to departments when computing departmental net income. Ideally, we allocate indirect expenses by using a cause-effect relation for the allocation base. When a cause-effect relation is not identifiable, each indirect expense is allocated on a basis reflecting the relative benefit received by each department.

C2 **Explain transfer pricing and methods to set transfer prices.** Transfer prices are used to record transfers of items between divisions of the same company. Transfer prices can be based on costs or market prices, or they can be negotiated by division managers.

C3[C] **Describe allocation of joint costs across products.** A joint cost refers to costs incurred to produce or purchase two or more products at the same time. When income statements are prepared, joint costs are usually allocated to the resulting joint products using either a physical or value basis.

A1 **Analyze investment centers using return on investment and residual income.** A financial measure often used to evaluate an investment center manager is the *return on investment,* also called *return on assets.* This measure is computed as the center's income divided by the center's average total assets. Residual income, computed as investment center income minus a target income, is an alternative financial measure of investment center performance.

A2 **Analyze investment centers using profit margin and investment turnover.** Return on investment can also be computed as profit margin times investment turnover. Profit margin (equal to income/sales) measures the income earned per dollar of sales, and investment turnover (equal to sales/assets) measures how efficiently a division uses its assets.

A3 **Analyze investment centers using the balanced scorecard.** A balanced scorecard uses a combination of financial and nonfinancial measures to evaluate performance. Customer, internal process, and innovation and learning are the three primary perspectives of nonfinancial measures used in balanced scorecards.

A4 **Compute cycle time and cycle efficiency, and explain their importance to production management.** It is important for companies to reduce the time to produce their products and to improve manufacturing efficiency. One measure of that time is cycle time (CT), defined as Process time + Inspection time + Move time + Wait time. Process time is value-added time; the others are non-value-added time. Cycle efficiency (CE) is the ratio of value-added time to total cycle time. If CE is low, management should evaluate its production process to see if it can reduce non-value-added activities.

P1 **Prepare a responsibility accounting report using controllable costs.** Responsibility accounting systems provide information for evaluating the performance of department managers. A responsibility accounting system's performance reports for evaluating department managers should include only the expenses (and revenues) that each manager controls.

P2 **Allocate indirect expenses to departments.** Indirect expenses include items like depreciation, rent, advertising, and other expenses that cannot be assigned directly to departments. Indirect expenses are recorded in company accounts, an allocation base is identified for each expense, and costs are allocated to departments. Departmental expense allocation spreadsheets are often used in allocating indirect expenses to departments.

P3 **Prepare departmental income statements and contribution reports.** Each profit center (department) is assigned its expenses to yield its own income statement. These costs include its direct expenses and its share of indirect expenses. The departmental income statement lists its revenues and costs of goods sold to determine gross profit. Its operating expenses (direct expenses and its indirect expenses allocated to the department) are deducted from gross profit to yield departmental net income. The departmental contribution report is similar to the departmental income statement in terms of computing the gross profit for each department. Then the direct operating expenses for each department are deducted from gross profit to determine the contribution generated by each department. Indirect operating expenses are deducted *in total* from the company's combined contribution.

Key Terms

Balanced scorecard	Direct expenses	Profit margin
Controllable costs	Indirect expenses	Residual income
Cost-based transfer pricing	Investment center	Responsibility accounting
Cost center	Investment turnover	Responsibility accounting performance report
Cycle efficiency (CE)	Joint cost	
Cycle time (CT)	Market-based transfer price	Return on investment
Decentralized organization	Negotiated transfer price	Transfer price
Departmental contribution to overhead	Non-value-added time	Uncontrollable costs
Departmental income statements	Profit center	Value-added time

Multiple Choice Quiz

1. A retailer has three departments—housewares, appliances, and clothing—and buys advertising that benefits all departments. Advertising expense is $150,000 for the year, and departmental sales for the year follow: housewares, $356,250; appliances, $641,250; and clothing, $427,500. How much advertising expense is allocated to appliances if allocation is based on departmental sales?

   a. $37,500   **c.** $45,000   **e.** $641,250

   b. $67,500   **d.** $150,000

2. Indirect expenses

   a. Cannot be readily traced to one department.

   b. Are allocated to departments based on the relative benefit each department receives.

   c. Are the same as uncontrollable expenses.

   d. *a*, *b*, and *c* above are all true.

   e. *a* and *b* above are true.

3. A division reports the information below. What is the division's investment turnover?

Sales	$500,000
Income	75,000
Average assets	200,000

   a. 37.5%   **c.** 2.5   **e.** 4

   b. 15   **d.** 2.67

4. A company operates three retail departments X, Y, and Z as profit centers. Which department has the largest dollar amount of departmental contribution to overhead, and what is the dollar amount contributed?

Department	Sales	Cost of Goods Sold	Direct Expenses	Allocated Indirect Expenses
X	$500,000	$350,000	$50,000	$40,000
Y	200,000	75,000	20,000	50,000
Z	350,000	150,000	75,000	10,000

   a. Department Y, $55,000   **d.** Department Z, $200,000

   b. Department Z, $125,000   **e.** Department X, $60,000

   c. Department X, $500,000

5. Using the data in question 4, Department X's contribution to overhead as a percentage of sales is

   a. 20%.   **c.** 12%.   **e.** 32%.

   b. 30%.   **d.** 48%.

ANSWERS TO MULTIPLE CHOICE QUIZ

1. b; [$641,250/($356,250 + $641,250 + $427,500)] × $150,000 = $67,500

2. d

3. c; $500,000/200,000 = 2.5

4. b;

	Department X	Department Y	Department Z
Sales	$500,000	$200,000	$350,000
Cost of goods sold	350,000	75,000	150,000
Gross profit	150,000	125,000	200,000
Direct expenses	50,000	20,000	75,000
Departmental contribution to overhead . . .	$100,000	$105,000	$125,000

5. a; $100,000/$500,000 = 20%

A,B,C   *Superscript letter A, B, or C denotes assignments based on Appendixes 24A, 24B, or 24C.*

🗆 Icon denotes assignments that involve decision making.

Discussion Questions

1. Why are many companies divided into departments?

2. What is the difference between operating departments and service departments?

3. 🗆 What are controllable costs?

4. _____ costs are not within the manager's control or influence.

5. 🗆 In responsibility accounting, why are reports to higher-level managers usually summarized?

6. 🗆 How are decisions made in decentralized organizations?

7. 🗆 Is it possible to evaluate a cost center's profitability? Explain.

8. What is the difference between direct and indirect expenses?

9. 🗆 Suggest a reasonable basis for allocating each of the following indirect expenses to departments: (a) salary of a supervisor who manages several departments, (b) rent, (c) heat, (d) electricity for lighting, (e) janitorial services,

(f) advertising, (g) expired insurance on equipment, and (h) property taxes on equipment.

10. **Samsung** has many departments. How is a department's contribution to overhead measured?   **Samsung**

11. [📱] **Google** aims to give its managers timely cost reports. In responsibility accounting, who receives timely cost reports and specific cost information? Explain.   **GOOGLE**

12. What is a transfer price? What are the three main approaches to setting transfer prices?

13.[B] Under what conditions is a market-based transfer price most likely to be used?

14.[C] What is a joint cost? How are joint costs usually allocated among the products produced from them?

15. [📱] Each **Apple** retail store has several departments. Why is it useful for its management   **APPLE**

to (a) collect accounting information about each department and (b) treat each department as a profit center?

16. [📱] **Apple** delivers its products to locations around the world. List three controllable and three uncontrollable costs for its delivery department.   **APPLE**

17. [📱] Define and describe *cycle time* and identify the components of cycle time.

18. [📱] Explain the difference between value-added time and non-value-added time.

19. Define and describe *cycle efficiency*.

20. [📱] Can management of a company such as **Samsung** use cycle time and cycle efficiency as useful measures of performance? Explain.   **Samsung**

▣ connect

In each blank next to the following terms, place the identifying letter of its best description.

_____ **1.** Cost center

_____ **2.** Investment center

_____ **3.** Departmental accounting system

_____ **4.** Operating department

_____ **5.** Profit center

_____ **6.** Responsibility accounting system

_____ **7.** Service department

A. Incurs costs without directly yielding revenues.

B. Provides information used to evaluate the performance of a department.

C. Holds manager responsible for revenues, costs, and investments.

D. Engages directly in manufacturing or in making sales directly to customers.

E. Does not directly manufacture products but contributes to profitability of the entire company.

F. Incurs costs and also generates revenues.

G. Provides information used to evaluate the performance of a department manager.

QUICK STUDY

QS 24-1
Allocation and measurement terms
C1

For each of the following types of indirect expenses and service department expenses, identify one allocation basis that could be used to distribute it to the departments indicated.

_____ **1.** Computer service expenses of production scheduling for operating departments.

_____ **2.** General office department expenses of the operating departments.

_____ **3.** Maintenance department expenses of the operating departments.

_____ **4.** Electric utility expenses of all departments.

QS 24-2
Basis for cost allocation
C1 [📱]

In each blank next to the following terms, place the identifying letter of its best description.

_____ **1.** Indirect expenses

_____ **2.** Controllable costs

_____ **3.** Direct expenses

_____ **4.** Uncontrollable costs

A. Costs not within a manager's control or influence.

B. Costs that can be readily traced to a department.

C. Costs that a manager has the ability to affect.

D. Costs incurred for the joint benefit of more than one department.

QS 24-3
Responsibility accounting terms
C1

Jose Ruiz manages a car dealer's service department. His department is organized as a cost center. Costs for a recent quarter are shown below. List the costs that would appear on a responsibility accounting report for the service department.

QS 24-4
Responsibility accounting report
P1

Cost of parts	$22,400	Shop supplies	$1,200
Mechanics' wages	14,300	Utilities (allocated)	800
Manager's salary	8,000	Administrative costs (allocated)............	2,200
Building depreciation (allocated).........	4,500		

QS 24-5
Allocating costs
to departments
P2

Macee Department Store has three departments, and it conducts advertising campaigns that benefit all departments. Advertising costs are $100,000 this year, and departmental sales for this year follow. How much advertising cost is allocated to each department if the allocation is based on departmental sales?

Department	Sales
1	$220,000
2	400,000
3	180,000

QS 24-6
Allocating costs
to departments   P2

Mervon Company has two operating departments: mixing and bottling. Mixing has 300 employees and bottling has 200 employees. Indirect factory costs include administrative costs of $160,000. Administrative costs are allocated to operating departments based on the number of workers. Determine the administrative costs allocated to each operating department.

QS 24-7
Allocating costs
to departments   P2

Mervon Company has two operating departments: mixing and bottling. Mixing occupies 22,000 square feet. Bottling occupies 18,000 square feet. Indirect factory costs include maintenance costs of $200,000. If maintenance costs are allocated to operating departments based on square footage occupied, determine the amount of maintenance costs allocated to each operating department.

QS 24-8
Rent expense allocated
to departments

P2

A retailer pays $130,000 rent each year for its two-story building. The space in this building is occupied by five departments as specified here.

Department	Square feet occupied
Jewelry	1,440 (first-floor)
Cosmetics	3,360 (first-floor)
Housewares	2,016 (second-floor)
Tools	960 (second-floor)
Shoes	1,824 (second-floor)

Check Allocated to jewelry
dept., $25,350

The company allocates 65% of total rent expense to the first floor and 35% to the second floor, and then allocates rent expense for each floor to the departments occupying that floor on the basis of space occupied. Determine the rent expense to be allocated to each department. (Round percents to the nearest one-tenth and dollar amounts to the nearest whole dollar.)

QS 24-9
Departmental contribution
to overhead
P3

Use the information in the following table to compute each department's contribution to overhead (both in dollars and as a percent). Which department contributes the largest dollar amount to total overhead? Which contributes the highest percent (as a percent of sales)? Round percents to one decimal.

	Dept. A	Dept. B	Dept. C
Sales	$53,000	$180,000	$84,000
Cost of goods sold	34,185	103,700	49,560
Gross profit	18,815	76,300	34,440
Total direct expenses	3,660	37,060	7,386
Contribution to overhead	$	$	$
Contribution percent (of sales)	%	%	%

QS 24-10
Computing return
on investment

A1

Compute return on investment for each of the divisions below (each is an investment center). Comment on the relative performance of each investment center.

Investment Center	Net Income	Average Assets	Return on Investment
Cameras and camcorders	$4,500,000	$20,000,000	_____ %
Phones and communications............	1,500,000	12,500,000	_____
Computers and accessories.............	800,000	10,000,000	_____

Refer to the information in QS 24-10. Assume a target income of 12% of average invested assets. Compute residual income for each division.

QS 24-11
Computing residual income **A1**

Fill in the blanks in the schedule below for two separate investment centers A and B. Round answers to the nearest whole percent.

QS 24-12
Performance measures
A1 **A2**

	Investment Center	
	A	B
Sales	$_____	$10,400,000
Net income	$ 352,000	$ _____
Average invested assets	$1,400,000	$ _____
Profit margin.	8.0%	_____%
Investment turnover.	_____	1.5
Return on investment.	_____%	12.0%

A company's shipping division (an investment center) has sales of $2,420,000, net income of $516,000, and average invested assets of $2,250,000. Compute the division's profit margin and investment turnover.

QS 24-13
Computing profit margin and investment turnover **A2**

Classify each of the performance measures below into the most likely balanced scorecard perspective it relates to. Label your answers using C (customer), P (internal process), I (innovation and growth), or F (financial).

QS 24-14
Performance measures—balanced scorecard
A3

_____ **1.** Customer wait time
_____ **2.** Number of days of employee absences
_____ **3.** Profit margin
_____ **4.** Number of new products introduced
_____ **5.** Change in market share
_____ **6.** Employee sustainability training sessions attended
_____ **7.** Length of time raw materials are in inventory
_____ **8.** Customer satisfaction index
_____ **9.** Gallons of water reused
_____ **10.** CO_2 emissions

Walt Disney reports the following information for its two Parks and Resorts divisions.

QS 24-15
Performance measures—balanced scorecard
A3

	U.S.		International	
	Current Year	Prior Year	Current Year	Prior Year
Hotel occupancy rates	87%	83%	79%	78%

Assume Walt Disney uses a balanced scorecard and sets a target of 85% occupancy in its resorts. Using Exhibit 24.18 as a guide, show how the company's performance on hotel occupancy would appear on a balanced scorecard report.

Compute and interpret (a) manufacturing cycle time and (b) manufacturing cycle efficiency using the following information from a manufacturing company.

QS 24-16
Manufacturing cycle time and efficiency
A4

Process time.	15.0 minutes
Inspection time.	2.0 minutes
Move time.	6.4 minutes
Wait time.	36.6 minutes

The windshield division of Fast Car Co. makes windshields for use in Fast Car's assembly division. The windshield division incurs variable costs of $200 per windshield and has capacity to make 500,000 windshields per year. The market price is $450 per windshield. The windshield division incurs total fixed costs of $3,000,000 per year. If the windshield division is operating at full capacity, what transfer price should be used on transfers between the windshield and assembly divisions? Explain.

QS 24-17[B]
Determining transfer prices without excess capacity
C2

QS 24-18ᴮ

Determining transfer prices with excess capacity **C2**

The windshield division of Fast Car Co. makes windshields for use in Fast Car's assembly division. The windshield division incurs variable costs of $200 per windshield and has capacity to make 500,000 windshields per year. The market price is $450 per windshield. The windshield division incurs total fixed costs of $3,000,000 per year. If the windshield division has excess capacity, what is the range of possible transfer prices that could be used on transfers between the windshield and assembly divisions? Explain.

QS 24-19ᶜ

Joint cost allocation

C3

A company purchases a 10,020-square-foot commercial building for $325,000 and spends an additional $50,000 to divide the space into two separate rental units and prepare it for rent. Unit A, which has the desirable location on the corner and contains 3,340 square feet, will be rented for $1.00 per square foot. Unit B contains 6,680 square feet and will be rented for $0.75 per square foot. How much of the joint cost should be assigned to Unit B using the value basis of allocation?

QS 24-20

Return on investment

A1

For a recent year L'Oréal reported operating profit of €3,385 (in millions) for its cosmetics division. Total assets were €12,888 (in millions) at the beginning of the year and €13,099 (in millions) at the end of the year. Compute return on investment for the year. State your answer as a percent, rounded to one decimal.

connect

EXERCISES

Exercise 24-1

Responsibility accounting report—cost center

P1

Arctica manufactures snowmobiles and ATVs. These products are made in different departments, and each department has its own manager. Each responsibility performance report only includes those costs that the particular department manager can control: raw materials, wages, supplies used, and equipment depreciation. Using the data below, prepare a responsibility accounting report for the snowmobile department.

	A	B	C	D	E	F	G
1		Budget			Actual		
2							
3		Snowmobile	ATV	Combined	Snowmobile	ATV	Combined
4	Raw materials	$ 19,500	$27,500	$ 47,000	$ 19,420	$28,820	$ 48,240
5	Employee wages	10,400	20,500	30,900	10,660	21,240	31,900
6	Dept. manager salary	4,300	5,200	9,500	4,400	4,400	8,800
7	Supplies used	3,300	900	4,200	3,170	920	4,090
8	Depreciation—Equip.	6,000	12,500	18,500	6,000	12,500	18,500
9	Utilities	360	540	900	330	500	830
10	Rent	5,700	6,300	12,000	5,300	6,300	11,600
11	**Totals**	$49,560	$73,440	$123,000	$49,280	$74,680	$123,960

Exercise 24-2

Responsibility accounting report—cost center **P1**

Refer to the information in Exercise 24-1 and prepare a responsibility accounting report for the ATV department.

Exercise 24-3

Service department expenses allocated to operating departments **P2**

The following is a partially completed lower section of a departmental expense allocation spreadsheet for Cozy Bookstore. It reports the total amounts of direct and indirect expenses allocated to its five departments. Complete the spreadsheet by allocating the expenses of the two service departments (advertising and purchasing) to the three operating departments.

	A	B	C	D	E	F	G
1			Allocation of Expenses to Departments				
2							
3		Allocation	Expense Account	Advertising	Purchasing	Books	Magazines	Newspapers
4		Base	Balance	Dept.	Dept.	Dept.	Dept.	Dept.
5	Total department expenses..........		$698,000	$24,000	$34,000	$425,000	$90,000	$125,000
6	**Service department expenses**							
7	Advertising department............. Sales			?		?	?	?
8	Purchasing department............. Purch. orders				?	?	?	?
9	Total expenses allocated to operating departments...............		?	$ 0	$ 0	?	?	?

Continued on next page . . .

Advertising and purchasing department expenses are allocated to operating departments on the basis of dollar sales and purchase orders, respectively. Information about the allocation bases for the three operating departments follows.

Department	Sales	Purchase Orders
Books	$495,000	516
Magazines	198,000	360
Newspapers	207,000	324
Total	$900,000	1,200

Check Total expenses allocated to books dept., $452,820

Exercise 24-4
Indirect payroll expense allocated to departments
P2

Jessica Porter works in both the jewelry department and the cosmetics department of a retail store. She assists customers in both departments and arranges and stocks merchandise in both departments. The store allocates her $30,000 annual wages between the two departments based on the time worked in the two departments. Jessica reported the following hours and activities spent in the two departments. Allocate Jessica's annual wages between the two departments.

Activities	Hours
Selling in jewelry department	51
Arranging and stocking merchandise in jewelry department	6
Selling in cosmetics department	12
Arranging and stocking merchandise in cosmetics department	7
Idle time spent waiting for a customer to enter one of the departments	4

Check Assign $7,500 to cosmetics

Exercise 24-5
Departmental expense allocations
P2

Woh Che Co. has four departments: materials, personnel, manufacturing, and packaging. In a recent month, the four departments incurred three shared indirect expenses. The amounts of these indirect expenses and the bases used to allocate them follow.

Indirect Expense	Cost	Allocation Base
Supervision	$ 82,500	Number of employees
Utilities	50,000	Square feet occupied
Insurance	22,500	Value of assets in use
Total	$155,000	

Departmental data for the company's recent reporting period follow.

Department	Employees	Square Feet	Asset Values
Materials	27	25,000	$ 6,000
Personnel	9	5,000	1,200
Manufacturing	63	55,000	37,800
Packaging	51	15,000	15,000
Total	150	100,000	$60,000

1. Use this information to allocate each of the three indirect expenses across the four departments.
2. Prepare a summary table that reports the indirect expenses assigned to each of the four departments.

Check (2) Total of $29,600 assigned to materials dept.

Exercise 24-6
Departmental expense allocation spreadsheet
P2

Marathon Running Shop has two service departments (advertising and administrative) and two operating departments (shoes and clothing). The table that follows shows the direct expenses incurred and square footage occupied by all four departments, as well as total sales for the two operating departments for the year 2017.

Department	Direct Expenses	Square Feet	Sales
Advertising	$ 18,000	1,120	—
Administrative	25,000	1,400	—
Shoes	103,000	7,140	$273,000
Clothing	15,000	4,340	77,000

The advertising department developed and distributed 120 advertisements during the year. Of these, 90 promoted shoes and 30 promoted clothing. Utilities expense of $64,000 is an indirect expense to all departments. Prepare a departmental expense allocation spreadsheet for Marathon Running Shop. The spreadsheet should assign (1) direct expenses to each of the four departments, (2) the $64,000 of utilities expense to the four departments on the basis of floor space occupied, (3) the advertising department's expenses to the two operating departments on the basis of the number of ads placed that promoted a department's products, and (4) the administrative department's expenses to the two operating departments based on the amount of sales. Provide supporting computations for the expense allocations.

Check Total expenses allocated to shoes dept., $177,472

Exercise 24-7
Departmental contribution report
P3

Below are departmental income statements for a guitar manufacturer. The manufacturer is considering eliminating its electric guitar department since it has a net loss. The company classifies advertising, rent, and utilities expenses as indirect.

WHOLESALE GUITARS
Departmental Income Statements
For Year Ended December 31, 2017

	Acoustic	Electric
Sales.	$112,500	$105,500
Cost of goods sold.	55,675	66,750
Gross profit	56,825	38,750
Operating expenses		
Advertising expense	8,075	6,250
Depreciation expense—Equipment	10,150	9,000
Salaries expense.	17,300	13,500
Supplies expense	2,030	1,700
Rent expense.	6,105	5,950
Utilities expense	3,045	2,550
Total operating expenses	46,705	38,950
Net income (loss)	$ 10,120	$ (200)

1. Prepare a departmental contribution report that shows each department's contribution to overhead.
2. Based on contribution to overhead, should the electric guitar department be eliminated?

Exercise 24-8
Departmental income statement and contribution to overhead
P3

Jansen Company reports the following for its ski department for the year 2017. All of its costs are direct, except as noted.

Sales	$605,000
Cost of goods sold	425,000
Salaries	112,000 ($15,000 is indirect)
Utilities	14,000 ($3,000 is indirect)
Depreciation	42,000 ($10,000 is indirect)
Office expenses	20,000 (all indirect)

Prepare a (1) departmental income statement for 2017 and (2) departmental contribution to overhead report for 2017. (3) Based on these two performance reports, should Jansen eliminate the ski department?

Exercise 24-9
Investment center analysis
A1

You must prepare a return on investment analysis for the regional manager of Fast & Great Burgers. This growing chain is trying to decide which outlet of two alternatives to open. The first location (A) requires a $1,000,000 investment and is expected to yield annual net income of $160,000. The second location (B) requires a $600,000 investment and is expected to yield annual net income of $108,000. Compute the return on investment for each Fast & Great Burgers alternative and then make your recommendation in a half-page memorandum to the regional manager. (The chain currently generates an 18% return on total assets.)

Megamart, a retailer of consumer goods, provides the following information on two of its departments (each considered an investment center).

Investment Center	Sales	Income	Average Invested Assets
Electronics....................	$40,000,000	$2,880,000	$16,000,000
Sporting goods................	20,000,000	2,040,000	12,000,000

1. Compute return on investment for each department. Using return on investment, which department is most efficient at using assets to generate returns for the company?

2. Assume a target income level of 12% of average invested assets. Compute residual income for each department. Which department generated the most residual income for the company?

3. Assume the electronics department is presented with a new investment opportunity that will yield a 15% return on investment. Should the new investment opportunity be accepted? Explain.

Refer to information in Exercise 24-10. Compute profit margin and investment turnover for each department. Which department generates the most net income per dollar of sales? Which department is most efficient at generating sales from average invested assets?

A food manufacturer reports the following for two of its divisions for a recent year.

$ millions	Beverage Division	Cheese Division
Invested assets, beginning	$2,662	$4,455
Invested assets, ending..............	2,593	4,400
Sales	2,681	3,925
Operating income..................	349	634

For each division, compute (1) return on investment, (2) profit margin, and (3) investment turnover for the year. Round answers to two decimal places.

Refer to the information in Exercise 24-12. Assume that each of the company's divisions has a required rate of return of 7%. Compute residual income for each division.

Apple Inc. reports the following for three of its geographic segments for a recent year.

$ millions	Americas	Europe	China
Operating income..................	$31,186	$16,527	$23,002
Sales	93,864	50,337	58,715

Compute profit margin for each division. Express answers as percentages, rounded to one decimal place.

ZNet Co. is a web-based retail company. The company reports the following for 2017.

Sales	$ 5,000,000
Operating income..	1,000,000
Average invested assets	12,500,000

The company's CEO believes that sales for 2018 will increase by 20% and both profit margin (%) and the level of average invested assets will be the same as for 2017.

1. Compute return on investment for 2017.

2. Compute profit margin for 2017.

3. If the CEO's forecast is correct, what will return on investment equal for 2018?

4. If the CEO's forecast is correct, what will investment turnover equal for 2018?

Exercise 24-16

Performance measures—
balanced scorecard

A3

USA Airlines uses the following performance measures. Classify each of the performance measures below into the most likely balanced scorecard perspective it relates to. Label your answers using C (customer), P (internal process), I (innovation and growth), or F (financial).

_____ **1.** Cash flow from operations

_____ **2.** Number of reports of mishandled or lost baggage

_____ **3.** Percentage of on-time departures

_____ **4.** On-time flight percentage

_____ **5.** Percentage of ground crew trained

_____ **6.** Return on investment

_____ **7.** Market value

_____ **8.** Accidents or safety incidents per mile flown

_____ **9.** Customer complaints

_____ **10.** Flight attendant training sessions attended

_____ **11.** Time airplane is on ground between flights

_____ **12.** Airplane miles per gallon of fuel

_____ **13.** Revenue per seat

_____ **14.** Cost of leasing airplanes

Exercise 24-17

Sustainability and the
balanced scorecard

A3

Midwest Mfg. uses a balanced scorecard as part of its performance evaluation. The company wants to include information on its sustainability efforts in its balanced scorecard. For each of the sustainability items below, indicate the most likely balanced scorecard perspective it relates to. Label your answers using C (customer), P (internal process), I (innovation and learning), or F (financial).

_____ **1.** CO_2 emissions

_____ **2.** Number of solar panels installed

_____ **3.** Gallons of water used

_____ **4.** Customer surveys of company's sustainability reputation

_____ **5.** Pounds of recyclable packaging used

_____ **6.** Pounds of trash diverted from landfill

_____ **7.** Dollar sales of green products

_____ **8.** Number of sustainability training workshops held

_____ **9.** Cubic feet of natural gas used

_____ **10.** Patents for green products applied for

Exercise 24-18

Manufacturing cycle time
and efficiency

A4

Oakwood Company produces maple bookcases. The following information is available for the production of a recent order of 500 bookcases.

Process time	6.0 days	Move time	3.2 days
Inspection time	0.8 days	Wait time	5.0 days

1. Compute the company's manufacturing cycle time.

Check (2) Manufacturing cycle efficiency, 0.40

2. Compute the company's manufacturing cycle efficiency. Interpret your answer.

3. Management believes it can reduce move time by 1.2 days and wait time by 2.8 days by adopting lean manufacturing techniques. Compute the company's manufacturing cycle efficiency assuming the company's predictions are correct.

Exercise 24-19

Manufacturing cycle time
and efficiency

A4

Best Ink produces printers for personal computers. The following information is available for production of a recent order of 500 printers.

Process time	16.0 hours	Move time	9.0 hours
Inspection time	3.5 hours	Wait time	21.5 hours

1. Compute the company's manufacturing cycle time.

2. Compute the company's manufacturing cycle efficiency. Interpret your answer.

3. Assume the company wishes to increase its manufacturing cycle efficiency to 0.80. What are some ways to accomplish this?

Exercise 24-20[B]

Determining transfer prices

C2

The trailer division of Baxter Bicycles makes bike trailers that attach to bicycles and can carry children or cargo. The trailers have a retail price of $200 each. Each trailer incurs $80 of variable manufacturing costs. The trailer division has capacity for 40,000 trailers per year and incurs fixed costs of $1,000,000 per year.

1. Assume the assembly division of Baxter Bicycles wants to buy 15,000 trailers per year from the trailer division. If the trailer division can sell all of the trailers it manufactures to outside customers, what price should be used on transfers between Baxter Bicycles's divisions? Explain.

Continued on next page . . .

2. Assume the trailer division currently only sells 20,000 trailers to outside customers, and the assembly division wants to buy 15,000 trailers per year from the trailer division. What is the range of acceptable prices that could be used on transfers between Baxter Bicycles's divisions? Explain.

3. Assume transfer prices of either $80 per trailer or $140 per trailer are being considered. Comment on the preferred transfer prices from the perspectives of the trailer division manager, the assembly division manager, and the top management of Baxter Bicycles.

Heart & Home Properties is developing a subdivision that includes 600 home lots. The 450 lots in the Canyon section are below a ridge and do not have views of the neighboring canyons and hills; the 150 lots in the Hilltop section offer unobstructed views. The expected selling price for each Canyon lot is $55,000 and for each Hilltop lot is $110,000. The developer acquired the land for $4,000,000 and spent another $3,500,000 on street and utilities improvements. Assign the joint land and improvement costs to the lots using the value basis of allocation and determine the average cost per lot.

Exercise 24-21^c

Assigning joint real estate costs   **C3**

Check   Total Hilltop cost, $3,000,000

Pirate Seafood Company purchases lobsters and processes them into tails and flakes. It sells the lobster tails for $21 per pound and the flakes for $14 per pound. On average, 100 pounds of lobster are processed into 52 pounds of tails and 22 pounds of flakes, with 26 pounds of waste. Assume that the company purchased 2,400 pounds of lobster for $4.50 per pound and processed the lobsters with an additional labor cost of $1,800. No materials or labor costs are assigned to the waste. If 1,096 pounds of tails and 324 pounds of flakes are sold, what is (1) the allocated cost of the sold items and (2) the allocated cost of the ending inventory? The company allocates joint costs on a value basis. (Round the dollar cost per pound to the nearest thousandth.)

Exercise 24-22^c

Assigning joint product costs

C3

Check   (2) Inventory cost, $2,268

L'Oréal reports the following for a recent year for the major divisions in its cosmetics branch.

Exercise 24-23

Profit margin and investment turnover

A2

€ millions	Sales	Income	Total Assets End of Year	Total Assets Beginning of Year
Professional products............	€ 2,717	€ 552	€ 2,624	€ 2,516
Consumer products	9,530	1,765	5,994	5,496
Luxury products	4,507	791	3,651	4,059
Active cosmetics................	1,386	278	830	817
Total.........................	€18,140	€3,386	€13,099	€12,888

1. Compute profit margin for each division. State your answers as percents, rounded to two decimal places. Which L'Oréal division has the highest profit margin?

2. Compute investment turnover for each division. Round your answers to two decimal places. Which L'Oréal division has the best investment turnover?

⊞ connect

Billie Whitehorse, the plant manager of Travel Free's Indiana plant, is responsible for all of that plant's costs other than her own salary. The plant has two operating departments and one service department. The camper and trailer operating departments manufacture different products and have their own managers. The office department, which Whitehorse also manages, provides services equally to the two operating departments. A budget is prepared for each operating department and the office department. The company's responsibility accounting system must assemble information to present budgeted and actual costs in performance reports for each operating department manager and the plant manager. Each performance report includes only those costs that a particular operating department manager can control: raw materials, wages, supplies used, and equipment depreciation. The plant manager is responsible for the department managers' salaries, utilities, building rent, office salaries other than her own, and other office costs plus all costs controlled by the two operating department managers. The annual departmental budgets and actual costs for the two operating departments follow.

PROBLEM SET A

Problem 24-1A

Responsibility accounting performance reports; controllable and budgeted costs

P1

	Budget			Actual		
	Campers	Trailers	Combined	Campers	Trailers	Combined
Raw materials..................	$195,000	$275,000	$ 470,000	$194,200	$273,200	$ 467,400
Employee wages	104,000	205,000	309,000	106,600	206,400	313,000
Dept. manager salary...........	43,000	52,000	95,000	44,000	53,500	97,500
Supplies used	33,000	90,000	123,000	31,700	91,600	123,300
Depreciation—Equip.	60,000	125,000	185,000	60,000	125,000	185,000
Utilities	3,600	5,400	9,000	3,300	5,000	8,300
Building rent	5,700	9,300	15,000	5,300	8,700	14,000
Office department costs.........	68,750	68,750	137,500	67,550	67,550	135,100
Totals......................	$513,050	$830,450	$1,343,500	$512,650	$830,950	$1,343,600

The office department's annual budget and its actual costs follow.

	Budget	Actual
Plant manager salary	$ 80,000	$ 82,000
Other office salaries	32,500	30,100
Other office costs	25,000	23,000
Totals........................	$137,500	$135,100

Required

1. Prepare responsibility accounting performance reports like those in Exhibit 24.2 that list costs controlled by the following:

   a. Manager of the camper department.

   b. Manager of the trailer department.

   c. Manager of the Indiana plant.

   In each report, include the budgeted and actual costs and show the amount that each actual cost is over or under the budgeted amount.

Check   (1a) $500 total over budget

          (1c) Indiana plant controllable costs, $1,900 total under budget

Analysis Component

2. Did the plant manager or the operating department managers better manage costs? Explain.

Problem 24-2A

Allocation of building occupancy costs to departments

P2

National Bank has several departments that occupy both floors of a two-story building. The departmental accounting system has a single account, Building Occupancy Cost, in its ledger. The types and amounts of occupancy costs recorded in this account for the current period follow.

Depreciation—Building	$18,000
Interest—Building mortgage	27,000
Taxes—Building and land...............	9,000
Gas (heating) expense	3,000
Lighting expense	3,000
Maintenance expense	6,000
Total occupancy cost	$66,000

The building has 4,000 square feet on each floor. In prior periods, the accounting manager merely divided the $66,000 occupancy cost by 8,000 square feet to find an average cost of $8.25 per square foot and then charged each department a building occupancy cost equal to this rate times the number of square feet that it occupied.

Diane Linder manages a first-floor department that occupies 1,000 square feet, and Juan Chiro manages a second-floor department that occupies 1,800 square feet of floor space. In discussing the departmental reports, the second-floor manager questions whether using the same rate per square foot for all departments makes sense because the first-floor space is more valuable. This manager also references a recent real estate study of average local rental costs for similar space that shows first-floor space worth $30 per square foot and second-floor space worth $20 per square foot (excluding costs for heating, lighting, and maintenance).

Required

1. Allocate occupancy costs to the Linder and Chiro departments using the current allocation method.
2. Allocate the depreciation, interest, and taxes occupancy costs to the Linder and Chiro departments in proportion to the relative market values of the floor space. Allocate the heating, lighting, and maintenance costs to the Linder and Chiro departments in proportion to the square feet occupied (ignoring floor space market values).

Check (1) Total allocated to Linder and Chiro, $23,100
(2) Total occupancy cost to Linder, $9,600

Analysis Component

3. Which allocation method would you prefer if you were a manager of a second-floor department? Explain.

Williams Company began operations in January 2017 with two operating (selling) departments and one service (office) department. Its departmental income statements follow.

Problem 24-3A
Departmental income statements; forecasts

P3

WILLIAMS COMPANY Departmental Income Statements For Year Ended December 31, 2017			
	Clock	**Mirror**	**Combined**
Sales	$130,000	$55,000	$185,000
Cost of goods sold	63,700	34,100	97,800
Gross profit	66,300	20,900	87,200
Direct expenses			
Sales salaries	20,000	7,000	27,000
Advertising	1,200	500	1,700
Store supplies used	900	400	1,300
Depreciation—Equipment	1,500	300	1,800
Total direct expenses	23,600	8,200	31,800
Allocated expenses			
Rent expense	7,020	3,780	10,800
Utilities expense	2,600	1,400	4,000
Share of office department expenses	10,500	4,500	15,000
Total allocated expenses	20,120	9,680	29,800
Total expenses	43,720	17,880	61,600
Net income	$ 22,580	$ 3,020	$ 25,600

Williams plans to open a third department in January 2018 that will sell paintings. Management predicts that the new department will generate $50,000 in sales with a 55% gross profit margin and will require the following direct expenses: sales salaries, $8,000; advertising, $800; store supplies, $500; and equipment depreciation, $200. It will fit the new department into the current rented space by taking some square footage from the other two departments. When opened, the new painting department will fill one-fifth of the space presently used by the clock department and one-fourth used by the mirror department. Management does not predict any increase in utilities costs, which are allocated to the departments in proportion to occupied space (or rent expense). The company allocates office department expenses to the operating departments in proportion to their sales. It expects the painting department to increase total office department expenses by $7,000. Since the painting department will bring new customers into the store, management expects sales in both the clock and mirror departments to increase by 8%. No changes for those departments' gross profit percents or their direct expenses are expected except for store supplies used, which will increase in proportion to sales.

Required

Prepare departmental income statements that show the company's predicted results of operations for calendar-year 2018 for the three operating (selling) departments and their combined totals. (Round percents to the nearest one-tenth and dollar amounts to the nearest whole dollar.)

Check 2018 forecasted combined net income (sales), $43,472 ($249,800)

Problem 24-4A

Departmental contribution
to income

P3

Vortex Company operates a retail store with two departments. Information about those departments follows.

	Department A	Department B
Sales	$800,000	$450,000
Cost of goods sold	497,000	291,000
Direct expenses		
Salaries......................	125,000	88,000
Insurance	20,000	10,000
Utilities	24,000	14,000
Depreciation..................	21,000	12,000
Maintenance.................	7,000	5,000

The company also incurred the following indirect costs.

Salaries	$36,000
Insurance	6,000
Depreciation	15,000
Office expenses	50,000

Indirect costs are allocated as follows: salaries on the basis of sales; insurance and depreciation on the basis of square footage; and office expenses on the basis of number of employees. Additional information about the departments follows.

Department	Square Footage	Number of Employees
A	28,000	75
B	12,000	50

Required

Check   (1) Dept. A net
income, $38,260

1. For each department, determine the departmental contribution to overhead and the departmental net income.

2. Should Department B be eliminated? Explain.

Problem 24-5A^C

Allocation of joint costs

C3

Georgia Orchards produced a good crop of peaches this year. After preparing the following income statement, the company is concerned about the net loss on its No. 3 peaches.

GEORGIA ORCHARDS Income Statement For Year Ended December 31, 2017				
	No. 1	No. 2	No. 3	Combined
Sales (by grade)				
No. 1: 300,000 lbs. @ $1.50/lb.....................	$450,000			
No. 2: 300,000 lbs. @ $1.00/lb.....................		$300,000		
No. 3: 750,000 lbs. @ $0.25/lb.....................			$ 187,500	
Total sales.....................				$937,500
Costs				
Tree pruning and care @ $0.30/lb	90,000	90,000	225,000	405,000
Picking, sorting, and grading @ $0.15/lb............	45,000	45,000	112,500	202,500
Delivery costs.....................	15,000	15,000	37,500	67,500
Total costs.....................	150,000	150,000	375,000	675,000
Net income (loss)	$300,000	$150,000	$(187,500)	$262,500

In preparing this statement, the company allocated joint costs among the grades on a physical basis as an equal amount per pound. The company's delivery cost records show that $30,000 of the $67,500 relates to crating the No. 1 and No. 2 peaches and hauling them to the buyer. The remaining $37,500 of delivery costs is for crating the No. 3 peaches and hauling them to the cannery.

Required

1. Prepare reports showing cost allocations on a sales value basis to the three grades of peaches. Separate the delivery costs into the amounts directly identifiable with each grade. Then allocate any shared delivery costs on the basis of the relative sales value of each grade. (Round percents to the nearest one-tenth and dollar amounts to the nearest whole dollar.)

2. Using your answers to part 1, prepare an income statement using the joint costs allocated on a sales value basis.

Analysis Component

3. Do you think delivery costs fit the definition of a joint cost? Explain.

Check (1) $129,600 tree pruning and care costs allocated to No. 2

(2) Net income from No. 1 & No. 2 peaches, $140,400 & $93,600

Britney Brown, the plant manager of LMN Co.'s Chicago plant, is responsible for all of that plant's costs other than her own salary. The plant has two operating departments and one service department. The refrigerator and dishwasher operating departments manufacture different products and have their own managers. The office department, which Brown also manages, provides services equally to the two operating departments. A monthly budget is prepared for each operating department and the office department. The company's responsibility accounting system must assemble information to present budgeted and actual costs in performance reports for each operating department manager and the plant manager. Each performance report includes only those costs that a particular operating department manager can control: raw materials, wages, supplies used, and equipment depreciation. The plant manager is responsible for the department managers' salaries, utilities, building rent, office salaries other than her own, and other office costs plus all costs controlled by the two operating department managers. The April departmental budgets and actual costs for the two operating departments follow.

PROBLEM SET B

Problem 24-1B
Responsibility accounting performance reports; controllable and budgeted costs

P1

	Budget			Actual		
	Refrigerators	Dishwashers	Combined	Refrigerators	Dishwashers	Combined
Raw materials...............	$400,000	$200,000	$ 600,000	$385,000	$202,000	$ 587,000
Employee wages	170,000	80,000	250,000	174,700	81,500	256,200
Dept. manager salary..........	55,000	49,000	104,000	55,000	46,500	101,500
Supplies used	15,000	9,000	24,000	14,000	9,700	23,700
Depreciation—Equip...........	53,000	37,000	90,000	53,000	37,000	90,000
Utilities	30,000	18,000	48,000	34,500	20,700	55,200
Building rent.................	63,000	17,000	80,000	65,800	16,500	82,300
Office department costs........	70,500	70,500	141,000	75,000	75,000	150,000
Totals.......................	$856,500	$480,500	$1,337,000	$857,000	$488,900	$1,345,900

The office department's budget and its actual costs for April follow.

	Budget	Actual
Plant manager salary	$ 80,000	$ 85,000
Other office salaries............	40,000	35,200
Other office costs	21,000	29,800
Totals.......................	$141,000	$150,000

Required

1. Prepare responsibility accounting performance reports like those in Exhibit 24.2 that list costs controlled by the following:
   a. Manager of the refrigerator department.
   b. Manager of the dishwasher department.
   c. Manager of the Chicago plant.
   In each report, include the budgeted and actual costs for the month and show the amount by which each actual cost is over or under the budgeted amount.

Check (1a) $11,300 total under budget

(1c) Chicago plant controllable costs, $3,900 total over budget

Analysis Component

2. Did the plant manager or the operating department managers better manage costs? Explain.

Problem 24-2B

Allocation of building occupancy costs to departments

P2

Harmon's has several departments that occupy all floors of a two-story building that includes a basement floor. Harmon rented this building under a long-term lease negotiated when rental rates were low. The departmental accounting system has a single account, Building Occupancy Cost, in its ledger. The types and amounts of occupancy costs recorded in this account for the current period follow.

Building rent	$400,000
Lighting expense	25,000
Cleaning expense.	40,000
Total occupancy cost	$465,000

The building has 7,500 square feet on each of the upper two floors but only 5,000 square feet in the basement. In prior periods, the accounting manager merely divided the $465,000 occupancy cost by 20,000 square feet to find an average cost of $23.25 per square foot and then charged each department a building occupancy cost equal to this rate times the number of square feet that it occupies.

Jordan Style manages a department that occupies 2,000 square feet of basement floor space. In discussing the departmental reports with other managers, she questions whether using the same rate per square foot for all departments makes sense because different floor space has different values. Style checked a recent real estate report of average local rental costs for similar space that shows first-floor space worth $40 per square foot, second-floor space worth $20 per square foot, and basement space worth $10 per square foot (excluding costs for lighting and cleaning).

Required

Check (1) Total costs allocated to Style's dept., $46,500

(2) Total occupancy cost to Style, $22,500

1. Allocate occupancy costs to Style's department using the current allocation method.
2. Allocate the building rent cost to Style's department in proportion to the relative market value of the floor space. Allocate to Style's department the lighting and cleaning costs in proportion to the square feet occupied (ignoring floor space market values). Then, compute the total occupancy cost allocated to Style's department.

Analysis Component

3. Which allocation method would you prefer if you were a manager of a basement department?

Problem 24-3B

Departmental income statements; forecasts

P3

Bonanza Entertainment began operations in January 2017 with two operating (selling) departments and one service (office) department. Its departmental income statements follow.

BONANZA ENTERTAINMENT Departmental Income Statements For Year Ended December 31, 2017			
	Movies	**Video Games**	**Combined**
Sales	$600,000	$200,000	$800,000
Cost of goods sold	420,000	154,000	574,000
Gross profit.	180,000	46,000	226,000
Direct expenses			
Sales salaries	37,000	15,000	52,000
Advertising	12,500	6,000	18,500
Store supplies used	4,000	1,000	5,000
Depreciation—Equipment	4,500	3,000	7,500
Total direct expenses.	58,000	25,000	83,000
Allocated expenses			
Rent expense	41,000	9,000	50,000
Utilities expense.	7,380	1,620	9,000
Share of office department expenses.	56,250	18,750	75,000
Total allocated expenses.	104,630	29,370	134,000
Total expenses	162,630	54,370	217,000
Net income (loss)	$ 17,370	$ (8,370)	$ 9,000

The company plans to open a third department in January 2018 that will sell compact discs. Management predicts that the new department will generate $300,000 in sales with a 35% gross profit margin and will require the following direct expenses: sales salaries, $18,000; advertising, $10,000; store supplies, $2,000; and equipment depreciation, $1,200. The company will fit the new department into the current rented space by taking some square footage from the other two departments. When opened, the new compact disc department will fill one-fourth of the space presently used by the movie department and one-third of the space used by the video game department. Management does not predict any increase in utilities costs, which are allocated to the departments in proportion to occupied space (or rent expense). The company allocates office department expenses to the operating departments in proportion to their sales. It expects the compact disc department to increase total office department expenses by $10,000. Since the compact disc department will bring new customers into the store, management expects sales in both the movie and video game departments to increase by 8%. No changes for those departments' gross profit percents or for their direct expenses are expected except for store supplies used, which will increase in proportion to sales.

Required

Prepare departmental income statements that show the company's predicted results of operations for calendar-year 2018 for the three operating (selling) departments and their combined totals. (Round percents to the nearest one-tenth and dollar amounts to the nearest whole dollar.)

Check   2018 forecasted Movies net income (sales), $52,450 ($648,000)

Sadar Company operates a store with two departments: guitar and piano. Information about those departments follows.

Problem 24-4B

Departmental contribution to income

P3

	Guitar Department	Piano Department
Sales	$370,500	$279,500
Cost of goods sold	320,000	175,000
Direct expenses		
Salaries....................	35,000	25,000
Maintenance................	12,000	10,000
Utilities	5,000	4,500
Insurance	4,200	3,700

The company also incurred the following indirect costs.

Advertising...............	$15,000
Salaries..................	27,000
Office expenses...........	3,200

Indirect costs are allocated as follows: advertising on the basis of sales; salaries on the basis of number of employees; and office expenses on the basis of square footage. Additional information about the departments follows.

Department	Square Footage	Number of Employees
Guitar...........	5,000	3
Piano...........	3,000	2

Required

1. For each department, determine the departmental contribution to overhead and the departmental net income.
2. Should the guitar department be eliminated? Explain.

Check   (1) Piano dept. net income, $42,850

Problem 24-5B^C

Allocation of joint costs

C3

Rita and Rick Redding own and operate a tomato grove. After preparing the following income statement, Rita and Rick are concerned about the loss on the No. 3 tomatoes.

RITA AND RICK REDDING Income Statement For Year Ended December 31, 2017	No. 1	No. 2	No. 3	Combined
Sales (by grade)				
No. 1: 500,000 lbs. @ $1.80/lb.	$900,000			
No. 2: 400,000 lbs. @ $1.25/lb.		$500,000		
No. 3: 100,000 lbs. @ $0.40/lb.			$ 40,000	
Total sales.				$1,440,000
Costs				
Land preparation, seeding, and cultivating @ $0.70/lb.	350,000	280,000	70,000	700,000
Harvesting, sorting, and grading @ $0.04/lb.	20,000	16,000	4,000	40,000
Delivery costs.	10,000	7,000	3,000	20,000
Total costs.	380,000	303,000	77,000	760,000
Net income (loss)	$520,000	$197,000	$(37,000)	$ 680,000

In preparing this statement, Rita and Rick allocated joint costs among the grades on a physical basis as an equal amount per pound. Also, their delivery cost records show that $17,000 of the $20,000 relates to crating the No. 1 and No. 2 tomatoes and hauling them to the buyer. The remaining $3,000 of delivery costs is for crating the No. 3 tomatoes and hauling them to the cannery.

Required

1. Prepare reports showing cost allocations on a sales value basis to the three grades of tomatoes. Separate the delivery costs into the amounts directly identifiable with each grade. Then allocate any shared delivery costs on the basis of the relative sales value of each grade. (Round percents to the nearest one-tenth and dollar amounts to the nearest whole dollar.)

2. Using your answers to part 1, prepare an income statement using the joint costs allocated on a sales value basis.

Analysis Component

3. Do you think delivery costs fit the definition of a joint cost? Explain.

SERIAL PROBLEM

Business Solutions A3

© Alexander Image/Shutterstock RF

(This serial problem began in Chapter 1 and continues through most of the book. If previous chapter segments were not completed, the serial problem can begin at this point.)

SP 24   Santana Rey's two departments, computer consulting services and computer workstation furniture manufacturing, have each been profitable for **Business Solutions**. Santana has heard of the balanced scorecard and wants you to provide details on how it could be used to measure performance of her departments.

Required

1. Explain the four performance perspectives included in a balanced scorecard.
2. For each of the four performance perspectives included in a balanced scorecard, provide examples of measures Santana could use to measure performance of her departments.

Beyond the Numbers

REPORTING IN ACTION

C1 **APPLE**

BTN 24-1   Review **Apple**'s income statement in Appendix A and identify its revenues for the year ended September 26, 2015, and each of the prior two years. For the year ended September 26, 2015, Apple reports the following product revenue mix. (Assume that its product revenue mix is the same for each of the three years reported when answering the requirements.)

iPhone	iPad	Mac	Services	Other
66%	10%	11%	9%	4%

Required

1. Compute the amount of revenue from each of its product lines for each of the three years reported.

2. If Apple wishes to evaluate each of its product lines, how can it allocate its operating expenses to each of them to determine each product line's profitability?

Fast Forward

3. Access Apple's annual report for a fiscal year ending after September 26, 2015, from its website (Apple.com) or the SEC's EDGAR database (SEC.gov). Locate its table of "Net Sales by Product" in the footnotes. How has its product mix changed from 2015?

BTN 24-2   Apple and Google compete in several product categories. Sales, income, and asset information are provided for fiscal year 2015 for each company below.

COMPARATIVE ANALYSIS

A2

APPLE

GOOGLE

$ millions	Apple	Google
Sales	$233,715	$ 74,989
Net income	53,394	16,348
Invested assets, beginning of year	231,839	129,187
Invested assets, end of year	290,479	147,461

Required

1. Compute profit margin for each company.

2. Compute investment turnover for each company.

Analysis Component

3. Using your answers to the questions above, compare the companies' performance for the year.

BTN 24-3   Super Security Co. offers a range of security services for athletes and entertainers. Each type of service is considered within a separate department. Marc Pincus, the overall manager, is compensated partly on the basis of departmental performance by staying within the quarterly cost budget. He often revises operations to make sure departments stay within budget. Says Pincus, "I will not go over budget even if it means slightly compromising the level and quality of service. These are minor compromises that don't significantly affect my clients, at least in the short term."

ETHICS CHALLENGE

P3

Required

1. Is there an ethical concern in this situation? If so, which parties are affected? Explain.

2. Can Pincus take action to eliminate or reduce any ethical concerns? Explain.

3. What is Super Security's ethical responsibility in offering professional services?

BTN 24-4   Improvement Station is a national home improvement chain with more than 100 stores throughout the country. The manager of each store receives a salary plus a bonus equal to a percent of the store's net income for the reporting period. The following net income calculation is on the Denver store manager's performance report for the recent monthly period.

COMMUNICATING IN PRACTICE

P2

Sales	$2,500,000
Cost of goods sold	800,000
Wages expense	500,000
Utilities expense	200,000
Home office expense	75,000
Net income	$ 925,000
Manager's bonus (0.5%)	$ 4,625

In previous periods, the bonus had also been 0.5%, but the performance report had not included any charges for the home office expense, which is now assigned to each store as a percent of its sales.

Required

Assume that you are the national office manager. Write a half-page memorandum to your store managers explaining why home office expense is in the new performance report.

TAKING IT TO THE NET

P2

BTN 24-5   This chapter described and used spreadsheets to prepare various managerial reports (see Exhibit 24.10). You can download from websites various tutorials showing how spreadsheets are used in managerial accounting and other business applications.

Required

1. Link to the website Lacher.com. Select "Table of Contents" under "Microsoft Excel Examples." Identify and list three tutorials for review.
2. Describe in a half-page memorandum to your instructor how the applications described in each tutorial are helpful in business and managerial decision making.

TEAMWORK IN ACTION

P1

APPLE

Samsung

BTN 24-6   Apple and Samsung compete across the world in several markets.

Required

1. Design a three-tier responsibility accounting organizational chart assuming that you have available internal information for both companies. Use Exhibit 24.1 as an example. The goal of this assignment is to design a reporting framework for the companies; numbers are not required. Limit your reporting framework to sales activity only.
2. Explain why it is important to have similar performance reports when comparing performance within a company (and across different companies). Be specific in your response.

ENTREPRENEURIAL DECISION

P3

BTN 24-7   Aman Advani, Gihan Amarasiriwardena, and Kit Hickey's company Ministry of Supply sells men's clothes and is organized by different product lines (departments).

Required

1. How can Ministry of Supply use departmental income statements to assist in understanding and controlling operations?
2. Are departmental income statements always the best measure of a department's performance? Explain.
3. Provide examples of nonfinancial performance indicators Ministry of Supply might use as part of a balanced scorecard system of performance evaluation.

HITTING THE ROAD

C1   P1

BTN 24-8   Visit a local movie theater and check out both its concession area and its viewing areas. The manager of a theater must confront questions such as:

- How much return do we earn on concessions?
- What types of movies generate the greatest sales?
- What types of movies generate the greatest net income?

Required

Assume that you are the new accounting manager for a 16-screen movie theater. You are to set up a responsibility accounting reporting framework for the theater.

1. Recommend how to segment the different departments of a movie theater for responsibility reporting.
2. Propose an expense allocation system for heat, rent, insurance, and maintenance costs of the theater.

BTN 24-9   Selected product data from **Samsung** (www.samsung.com) follow.

Product Segment for Year Ended (billions of Korean won)	Net Sales		Operating Income	
	Dec. 31, 2015	Dec. 31, 2014	Dec. 31, 2015	Dec. 31, 2014
Consumer electronics.................	₩ 46,895	₩ 50,183	₩ 1,254	₩ 1,184
IT and mobile communications	103,554	111,765	10,142	14,563

Required

1. Compute the percentage growth (or decline) in net sales for each product line from fiscal year 2014 to 2015. Round percents to one decimal.

2. Which product line's net sales grew (or declined) the most?

3. Which segment was the most profitable?

4. How can Samsung's managers use this information?

GLOBAL VIEW

L'Oréal is an international cosmetics company incorporated in France. With multiple brands and operations in over 100 countries, the company uses concepts of departmental accounting and controllable costs to evaluate performance. For example, for 2015 the company reports the following for the major divisions in its cosmetics branch:

Division (€ millions)	Operating Profit	
Consumer products	€2,386	
Professional products..................	679	
Luxury products	1,498	
Active cosmetics.....................	415	€4,978
Nonallocated costs...................		(644)
Cosmetics branch total................		€4,334

Similar to "Departmental contributions to overhead" in Exhibit 24.11

Similar to "Operating income" in Exhibit 24.11

For L'Oréal, nonallocated costs include costs that are not controllable by division managers, including fundamental research and development and costs of service operations like insurance and banking. Excluding noncontrollable costs enables L'Oréal to prepare more meaningful division performance evaluations.

 Global View Assignments

Discussion Question 10

Discussion Question 20

Quick Study 24-20

Exercise 24-14

Exercise 24-23

BTN 24-9

25 Capital Budgeting and Managerial Decisions

chapter

Learning Objectives

CONCEPTUAL

C1 Describe the importance of relevant costs for short-term decisions.

ANALYTICAL

A1 Evaluate short-term managerial decisions using relevant costs.

A2 Analyze a capital investment project using break-even time.

A3 *Appendix 25B*–Determine product selling price using cost data.

PROCEDURAL

P1 Compute payback period and describe its use.

P2 Compute accounting rate of return and explain its use.

P3 Compute net present value and describe its use.

P4 Compute internal rate of return and explain its use.

Courtesy of Simply Gum

Chew On This

NEW YORK—Caron Proschan finished lunch and reached for a piece of chewing gum. In contrast to the organic juice and salad she just finished, the gum was a mix of "alien" colors and chemicals. "I thought . . . there must be a natural gum," insists Caron. "After researching it, I found out there wasn't one." So, Caron launched her company, **Simply Gum** (**SimplyGum.com**).

Simply Gum is made using natural flavors, a natural chicle base, organic ingredients, and no synthetics. "We experimented with a lot of ingredients and flavors," explains Caron. Compared with its two main competitors, which have 95% of U.S. gum sales, Simply Gum can quickly change its manufacturing process, flavors, and distribution. "Our recipe is never done," exclaims Adeena Cohen, senior marketing manager. "We're constantly perfecting flavor and texture."

Caron uses contribution margins to decide whether adding new flavors would increase profits and whether to eliminate less profitable flavors. Unlike some peers that can rework standard materials, Caron explains that "raw materials that don't meet our standards never enter our production process."

"We want our gum to be everywhere"
—Caron Proschan

In addition to profits, Caron considers qualitative factors, including customer satisfaction. "We found out that people really want a better-for-you gum option," insists Caron.

In addition to short-term decisions involving sales mix, Simply Gum confronts long-run decisions on capital investments. "I assumed we'd find a contract manufacturer to make our gum, and we would figure out packaging, marketing, and sales," recalls Caron. "It turns out there was no manufacturer to make it, so we make it." This required Caron to consider the size of her manufacturing plant and the number and types of machines to use. Capital budgeting techniques—like payback period, net present value, and internal rate of return—help guide her.

Simply Gum now is sold in over 1,200 stores in the U.S. "We believe we've found a niche," proclaims Caron. She insists others can do the same if they "stay focused, work hard, and seek guidance."

Sources: *Simply Gum website,* January 2017; *The Wall Street Journal,* May 1, 2016; *Brandettes.com,* October 27, 2015; *Foodbusinessnews.net,* December 10, 2015; *Forbes.com,* January 11, 2016

Section 1—Capital Budgeting

Capital budgeting is the process of analyzing alternative long-term investments and deciding which assets to acquire or sell. Common examples of capital budgeting decisions include buying a machine or a building or acquiring an entire company. An objective for these decisions is to earn a satisfactory return on investment.

Exhibit 25.1 summarizes the capital budgeting process.

The process begins when department or plant managers submit proposals for new investments in property, plant, and equipment. A capital budget committee, usually made of members with accounting and finance expertise, evaluates the proposals and forms recommendations for approval or rejection. Finally, the board of directors approves the capital expenditures for the year.

Capital budgeting decisions require careful analysis because they are usually the most difficult and risky decisions that managers make. These decisions are difficult because they require predicting events that will not occur until well into the future. A capital budgeting decision is risky because (1) the outcome is uncertain, (2) large amounts of money are usually involved, (3) the investment involves a long-term commitment, and (4) the decision could be difficult or impossible to reverse, no matter how poor it turns out to be. Risk is especially high for investments in technology due to innovations and uncertainty.

Managers use several methods to evaluate capital budgeting decisions. Nearly all of these methods involve predicting future cash inflows and cash outflows of proposed investments, assessing the risk of and returns on those cash flows, and then choosing which investments to make. Exhibit 25.2 summarizes cash outflows (−) and cash inflows (+) over the life of a typical capital expenditure for a depreciable asset.

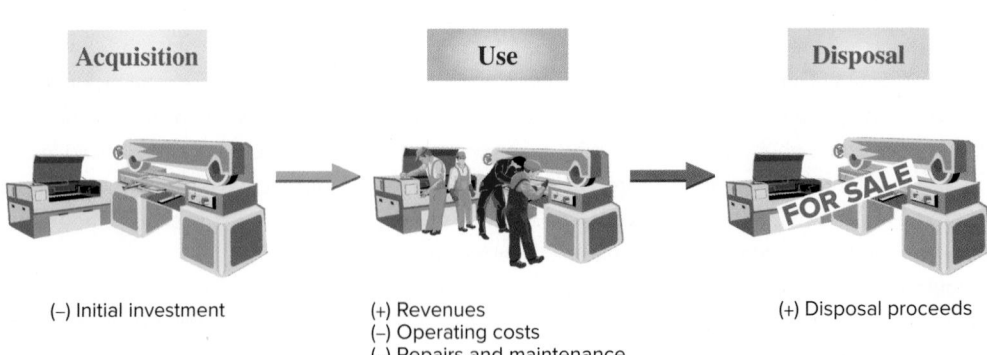

The investment begins with an initial cash outflow to acquire the depreciable asset. Over the asset's life it generates cash inflows from revenues. The asset also creates cash outflows for operating costs, repairs, and maintenance. Finally, the asset is disposed of, and its salvage value can provide another cash inflow.

Management often restates future cash flows in terms of their present value. This approach applies the time value of money: *A dollar today is worth more than a dollar tomorrow.* Similarly, a dollar tomorrow is worth less than a dollar today. Restating future cash flows in terms of their present value is called *discounting*. The time value of money is important when evaluating capital investments, but managers sometimes use methods that ignore it.

METHODS NOT USING TIME VALUE OF MONEY

All investments, whether they involve the purchase of a machine or another long-term asset, are expected to produce net cash flows. *Net cash flow* is cash inflows minus cash outflows. Sometimes managers perform simple analyses of the financial feasibility of an investment's net cash flow without using the time value of money. This section explains two common methods in this category: (1) payback period and (2) accounting rate of return.

Payback Period

An investment's **payback period (PBP)** is the expected amount of time to recover the initial investment amount. Managers prefer investing in assets with shorter payback periods to reduce the risk of an unprofitable investment over the long run. Acquiring assets with short payback periods reduces a company's risk from potentially inaccurate long-term predictions of future cash flows.

P1

Compute payback period and describe its use.

Payback Period with Even Cash Flows   To illustrate payback period for an investment with even cash flows, we look at data from FasTrac, a manufacturer of exercise equipment and supplies. (*Even cash flows* are cash flows that are the same amount each year; *uneven cash flows* are cash flows that are not all equal in amount.) FasTrac is considering several different capital investments, one of which is to purchase a machine to use in manufacturing a new product. The machine has these features:

Cost...	$16,000
Useful life	8 years
Salvage value	$0
Expected production per year...................	30,000 units
Product selling price per unit..................	$30

Exhibit 25.3 shows the expected annual net income and expected annual net cash flows for this asset over its life.

FASTRAC Cash Flow Analysis—Machinery Investment	Expected Net Income	Expected Net Cash Flow
Annual sales of new product	$30,000	$30,000
Less annual expenses		
Materials, labor, and overhead (except depreciation)	15,500	15,500
Depreciation—Machinery..	2,000	
Additional selling and administrative expenses	9,500	9,500
Annual pretax income...	3,000	
Income taxes (30% of pretax income)	900	900
Annual net income	$ 2,100	
Annual net cash flow...		$ 4,100

EXHIBIT 25.3

Cash Flow Analysis

Point: The payback method uses cash flows, not net income.

The amount of net cash flow from the machinery is computed by subtracting expected cash outflows from expected cash inflows. The Expected Net Cash Flow column of Exhibit 25.3 excludes all noncash revenues and expenses. Since depreciation does not impact cash flows, it is excluded. Alternatively, managers can adjust the projected net income for revenue and expense items that do not affect cash flows. For FasTrac, this means taking the $2,100 net income and adding back the $2,000 depreciation, to yield $4,100 of net cash flow.

The formula for computing the payback period of an investment that produces even net cash flows is in Exhibit 25.4.

EXHIBIT 25.4

Payback Period Formula with Even Cash Flows

$$\text{Payback period} = \frac{\textbf{Cost of investment}}{\textbf{Annual net cash flow}}$$

The payback period reflects the amount of time for the investment to generate enough net cash flow to return (or pay back) the cash initially invested to purchase it. FasTrac's payback period for this machine is just under four years.

$$\text{Payback period} = \frac{\$16,000}{\$4,100} = 3.9 \text{ years}$$

Point: Excel for payback.

	A	B
1	Investment	$16,000
2	Cash flow	$4,100
3	Payback period	

=B1/B2 = 3.9

The initial investment is fully recovered in 3.9 years, or just before reaching the halfway point of this machine's useful life of eight years.

Companies like short payback periods to increase return and reduce risk. The more quickly a company receives cash, the sooner it is available for other uses and the less time it is at risk of loss. A shorter payback period also improves the company's ability to respond to unanticipated changes and lowers its risk of having to keep an unprofitable investment.

■ **Decision** Insight

e-Payback   Health care providers are increasingly using electronic systems to improve their operations. With *e-charting*, doctors' orders and notes are saved electronically. Such systems allow for more personalized care plans, more efficient staffing, and reduced costs. Investments in such systems are evaluated on the basis of payback periods and other financial measures. ■

© Tetra Images/Getty Images

Payback Period with Uneven Cash Flows   What happens if the net cash flows are uneven? In this case, the payback period is computed using the *cumulative total of net cash flows*. The word *cumulative* refers to the addition of each period's net cash flows as we progress through time. To illustrate, consider data for another investment that FasTrac is considering. This machine is predicted to generate uneven net cash flows over the next eight years. The relevant data and payback period computation are shown in Exhibit 25.5.

Year 0 refers to the date of initial investment at which the $16,000 cash outflow occurs to acquire the machinery. By the end of year 1, the cumulative net cash flow is reduced to $(13,000), computed as the $(16,000) initial cash outflow plus year 1's $3,000 cash inflow. This process continues throughout the asset's life. The cumulative net cash flow amount changes from negative to positive in year 5. Specifically, at the end of year 4, the cumulative net cash flow is $(1,000). As soon as FasTrac receives net cash inflow of $1,000 during the fifth year, it has fully recovered the $16,000 initial investment. If we assume that cash flows are received uniformly *within* each year, receipt of the $1,000 occurs about one-fifth (0.20) of the way through the fifth year. This is computed as $1,000 divided by year 5's total net cash flow of $5,000, or 0.20. This yields a payback period of 4.2 years, computed as 4 years plus 0.20 of year 5.

EXHIBIT 25.5

Payback Period Calculation
with Uneven Cash Flows

Period*	Expected Net Cash Flows	Cumulative Net Cash Flows
Year 0	$(16,000)	$(16,000)
Year 1	3,000	(13,000)
Year 2	4,000	(9,000)
Year 3	4,000	(5,000)
Year 4	4,000	(1,000) ⎱ Payback occurs between years 4 and 5.
Year 5	5,000	4,000 ⎰
Year 6	3,000	7,000
Year 7	2,000	9,000
Year 8	2,000	11,000
Payback period = 4 years + $1,000/$5,000 of year 5 = 4.2 years		

Example: Find the payback period in Exhibit 25.5 if net cash flows for the first 4 years are: Year 1 = $6,000; Year 2 = $5,000; Year 3 = $4,000; Year 4 = $3,000. *Answer:* 3.33 years

* All cash inflows and outflows occur uniformly within each year 1 through 8.

Evaluating Payback Period

Payback period has two strengths.

- It uses cash flows, not income.
- It is easy to use.

Payback period has three main weaknesses:

- It does not reflect differences in the *timing* of net cash flows within the payback period.
- It ignores *all* cash flows after the point where an investment's costs are fully recovered.
- It ignores the time value of money.

To illustrate, if FasTrac had another investment with predicted cash inflows of $9,000, $3,000, $2,000, $1,800, and $1,000 in its first 5 years, its payback period would be 4.2 years. However, this alternative is more desirable because it returns cash more quickly. In addition, an investment with a 3-year payback period that stops producing cash after 4 years is likely not as good as an alternative with a 5-year payback period that generates net cash flows for 15 years. Because of these limitations, payback period should never be the only consideration in capital budgeting decisions.

A company is considering purchasing equipment costing $75,000. Future annual net cash flows from this equipment are $30,000, $25,000, $15,000, $10,000, and $5,000. Cash flows occur uniformly within each year. What is this investment's payback period?

NEED-TO-KNOW 25-1

Payback Period

P1

Solution

Period	Expected Net Cash Flows	Cumulative Net Cash Flows
Year 0	$(75,000)	$(75,000)
Year 1	30,000	(45,000)
Year 2	25,000	(20,000)
Year 3	15,000	(5,000) ⎱ Payback occurs between years 3 and 4.
Year 4	10,000	5,000 ⎰
Year 5	5,000	10,000
Payback period = 3.5 years, computed as 3 + $5,000/$10,000		

Do More: QS 25-1, QS 25-5, E 25-1, E 25-3, E 25-5

Accounting Rate of Return

The **accounting rate of return** is the percentage accounting return on annual average investment. It is called an "accounting" return because it is based on net income, rather than on cash flows. It is computed by dividing a project's after-tax net income by the average amount invested in it. To illustrate, we return to FasTrac's $16,000 machinery investment described in

P2 _____

Compute accounting rate of return and explain its use.

Exhibit 25.3. We first compute (1) the after-tax net income and (2) the average amount invested. The $2,100 after-tax net income is from Exhibit 25.3.

If a company uses straight-line depreciation, we find the average amount invested by using the formula in Exhibit 25.6. Because FasTrac uses straight-line depreciation, its average amount invested for the eight years equals the sum of the book value at the beginning of the asset's investment period and the book value at the end of its investment period, divided by 2, as shown in Exhibit 25.6.

EXHIBIT 25.6

Computing Average Amount Invested under Straight-Line Depreciation

$$\text{Annual average investment} \atop \text{(straight-line case only)} = \frac{\text{Beginning book value} + \text{Ending book value}}{2}$$

$$= \frac{\$16,000 + \$0}{2} = \$8,000$$

If an investment has a salvage value, the average amount invested when using straight-line depreciation is computed as (Beginning book value + Salvage value)/2.

If a company uses a depreciation method other than straight-line, for example, MACRS for tax purposes, the calculation of average book value is more complicated. In this case, the book value of the asset is computed for *each year* of its life. The general formula for the annual average investment is shown in Exhibit 25.7.

EXHIBIT 25.7

General Formula for Average Amount Invested

$$\text{Annual average investment} \atop \text{(general case)} = \frac{\text{Sum of individual years' average book values}}{\text{Number of years of the planned investment}}$$

Once we determine the annual after-tax net income and the annual average amount invested, the accounting rate of return is computed as shown in Exhibit 25.8. The numbers used are from FasTrac.

EXHIBIT 25.8

Accounting Rate of Return Formula

$$\text{Accounting rate of return} = \frac{\text{Annual after-tax net income}}{\text{Annual average investment}}$$

$$= \frac{\$2,100}{\$8,000} = 26.25\%$$

	A	B
1	Beg. book value	$16,000
2	End. book value	$0
3	Net income	$2,100
4	Attg. rate of return	◄

=B3/((B1+B2)/2) = 26.25%

FasTrac management must decide whether a 26.25% accounting rate of return is satisfactory. To make this decision, we must consider the investment's risk. We cannot say an investment with a 26.25% return is preferred over one with a lower return unless we consider any differences in risk. When comparing investments with similar lives and risk, a company will prefer the investment with the higher accounting rate of return.

Evaluating Accounting Rate of Return The accounting rate of return has three weaknesses:

- It ignores the time value of money.
- It focuses on income, not cash flows.
- If income (and thus the accounting rate of return) varies from year to year, the project might appear desirable in some years and not in others.

Because of these limitations, the accounting rate of return should never be the only consideration in capital budgeting decisions.

The following data relate to a company's decision on whether to purchase a machine:

Cost..................................	$180,000
Salvage value	15,000
Annual after-tax net income.............	40,000

Assume the company uses straight-line depreciation. What is the machine's accounting rate of return?

Solution

Annual average investment = ($180,000 + $15,000)/2 = $97,500
Accounting rate of return   = $40,000/$97,500 = 41% (rounded)

NEED-TO-KNOW 25-2

Accounting Rate
of Return

P2

Do More: QS 25-6, QS 25-7,
E 25-7, E 25-8

METHODS USING TIME VALUE OF MONEY

This section describes two capital budgeting methods that use the time value of money: (1) net present value and (2) internal rate of return. *(To apply these methods, you need a basic understanding of the concept of present value. An expanded explanation of present value concepts is in Appendix B near the end of the book. You can use the present value tables at the end of Appendix B to solve many of this chapter's assignments that use time value of money. Spreadsheet software like Excel and financial calculators can also be used.)*

Net Present Value

Net present value analysis applies the time value of money to future cash inflows and cash outflows so management can evaluate a project's benefits and costs at one point in time. Specifically, **net present value (NPV)** is computed by discounting the future net cash flows from the investment at the project's required rate of return and then subtracting the initial amount invested. A company's required return, often called its *hurdle rate,* is typically its **cost of capital,** which is an average of the rate the company must pay to its lenders.

   To illustrate, let's return to FasTrac's proposed machinery purchase described in Exhibit 25.3. Does this machine provide a satisfactory return while recovering the amount invested? Recall that the machine requires a $16,000 investment and is expected to provide $4,100 annual net cash inflows for the next eight years. If we assume that net cash inflows from this machine are received at each year-end and that FasTrac requires a 12% annual return, net present value can be computed as in Exhibit 25.9.

Methods Using Time Value of Money

P3

Compute net present value and describe its use.

Point: The assumption of end-of-year cash flows simplifies computations and is common in practice.

	Net Cash Flows*	Present Value of 1 at 12%**	Present Value of Net Cash Flows
Year 1	$ 4,100	0.8929	$ 3,661
Year 2	4,100	0.7972	3,269
Year 3	4,100	0.7118	2,918
Year 4	4,100	0.6355	2,606
Year 5	4,100	0.5674	2,326
Year 6	4,100	0.5066	2,077
Year 7	4,100	0.4523	1,854
Year 8	4,100	0.4039	1,656
Totals......................	$32,800		20,367
Initial investment..			(16,000)
Net present value..			**$ 4,367**

EXHIBIT 25.9

Net Present Value
Calculation with Equal
Cash Flows

*   Cash flows occur at the end of each year.
** Present value of 1 factors are taken from Table B.1 in Appendix B.

Example: What is the net present value in Exhibit 25.9 if a 10% return is applied? *Answer:* $5,873

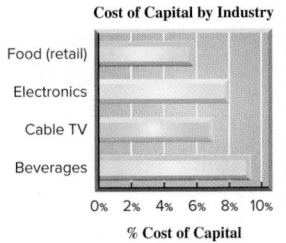

Cost of Capital by Industry

Source: stern.nyu.edu/adamordoran.

Point: Cost of capital computation is covered in advanced courses.

The first number column of Exhibit 25.9 shows annual net cash flows. Present value of 1 factors, also called *discount factors,* are shown in the second column. Taken from Table B.1 in Appendix B, they assume that net cash flows are received at each year-end. *(To simplify present value computations and for assignment material at the end of this chapter, we assume that net cash flows are received at year-end.)* Annual net cash flows from Exhibit 25.9 are multiplied by the discount factors to give present values of annual net cash flows in the far-right column. These annual amounts are summed to yield total present value of net cash flows of $20,367.

The last three lines of Exhibit 25.9 show the NPV computations. The asset's $16,000 initial cost is deducted from the $20,367 total present value of all future net cash flows to give this asset's NPV of $4,367. This means the present value of this machine's future net cash flows exceeds the initial $16,000 investment by $4,367. FasTrac should invest in this machine. **Rule:** If NPV > 0, invest.

Net Present Value Decision Rule

The decision rule in applying NPV is as follows: When an asset's expected future cash flows yield a *positive* net present value when discounted at the required rate of return, the asset should be acquired. This decision rule is reflected in the graphic below. When comparing several investment opportunities of similar cost and risk, we prefer the one with the highest positive net present value.

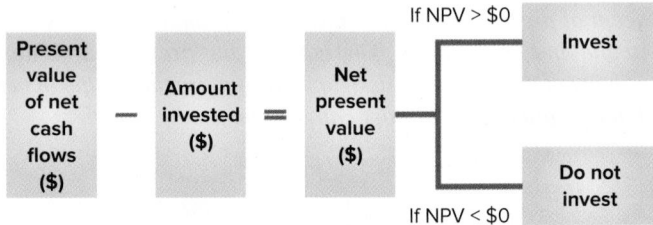

Simplifying Computations—Annuity

The computations in Exhibit 25.9 use separate present value of 1 factors for each of the eight years. Each year's net cash flow is multiplied by its present value of 1 factor to determine its present value; these are then added to give the asset's total present value. This computation can be simplified if annual net cash flows are equal in amount. A series of cash flows of equal dollar amount is called an **annuity.** In this case we use Table B.3, which gives the present value of 1 to be received periodically for a number of periods. To determine the present value of these eight annual receipts discounted at 12%, go down the 12% column of Table B.3 to the factor on the eighth line. This cumulative discount factor, also known as an *annuity* factor, is 4.9676. We then compute the $20,367 present value for these eight annual $4,100 receipts, computed as 4.9676 × $4,100. These calculations are summarized below.

Example: Why does the net present value of an investment increase when a lower discount rate is used? *Answer:* The present value of net cash flows increases.

Point: Excel for NPV.

	A	B
1	Investment	$16,000
2	Cash flow	$4,100
3	Periods	8
4	Interest rate	12%
5	Net present value	◄

=PV(B4,B3,−B2)−B1 = $4,367

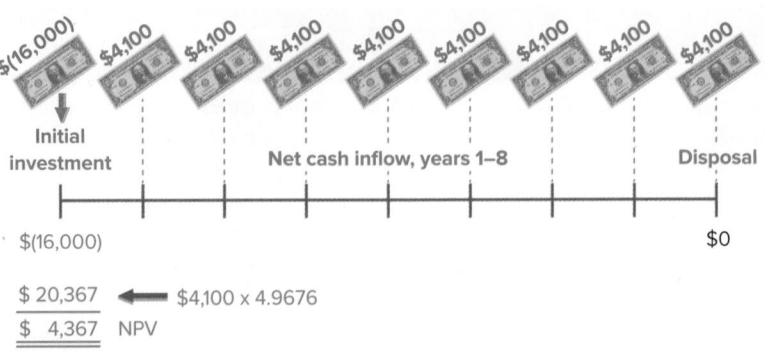

$ 20,367 ◄── $4,100 x 4.9676
$ 4,367 NPV

With a financial calculator:
N   8
I/Y   12
PMT   4100
CPT   PV
Multiply answer ($−20,367) by −1 since the company is receiving cash, and subtract initial investment ($16,000) to yield NPV of $4,367.

Simplifying Computations—Calculator or Excel

Another way to simplify present value calculations, whether net cash flows are equal in amount or not, is to use a calculator with compound interest functions or a spreadsheet program. Whatever procedure you use, it is important to understand the concepts behind these computations.

■ **Decision Ethics**

Systems Manager Management adopts a policy requiring purchases above $5,000 to be submitted with cash flow projections for capital budget approval. As systems manager, you want to upgrade your computers at a $25,000 cost. You consider submitting several orders each under $5,000 to avoid the approval process. You believe the computers will increase profits and wish to avoid a delay. What do you do? ■ [*Answer:* Your dilemma is whether to abide by rules designed to prevent abuse or to bend them to acquire an investment that you believe will benefit the firm. You should not pursue the latter action because breaking up the order into small components is dishonest and there are consequences. Develop a proposal for the entire package and then do all you can to expedite its processing, particularly by pointing out its benefits.]

Net Present Value Complications

The following factors can complicate NPV analysis. We discuss each of them.

- Unequal cash flows
- Salvage value
- Accelerated depreciation

- Comparing positive NPV projects
- Capital rationing
- Inflation

Uneven Cash Flows Net present value analysis can also be used when net cash flows are uneven (unequal). To illustrate, assume that FasTrac can choose only one capital investment from among Projects A, B, and C. Each project requires the same $12,000 initial investment. Future net cash flows for each project are shown in the first three number columns of Exhibit 25.10.

	Net Cash Flows			**Present Value of 1 at 10%**	**Present Value of Net Cash Flows**		
	A	**B**	**C**		**A**	**B**	**C**
Year 1	$ 5,000	$ 8,000	$ 1,000	0.9091	$ 4,546	$ 7,273	$ 909
Year 2	5,000	5,000	5,000	0.8264	4,132	4,132	4,132
Year 3	5,000	2,000	9,000	0.7513	3,757	1,503	6,762
Totals..................	$15,000	$15,000	$15,000		12,435	12,908	11,803
Initial investment					(12,000)	(12,000)	(12,000)
Net present value					$ 435	$ 908	$ (197)

EXHIBIT 25.10

Net Present Value Calculation with Uneven Cash Flows

The three projects in Exhibit 25.10 have the same expected total net cash flows of $15,000. Project A is expected to produce equal amounts of $5,000 each year. Project B is expected to produce a larger amount in the first year. Project C is expected to produce a larger amount in the third year. The fourth column of Exhibit 25.10 shows the present value of 1 factors from Table B.1 assuming 10% required return.

Computations in the three rightmost columns show that Project A has a $435 positive NPV. Project B has the largest NPV of $908 because it brings in cash more quickly. Project C has a $(197) *negative* NPV because its larger cash inflows are delayed. Projects with higher cash flows in earlier years generally yield higher net present values. If FasTrac requires a 10% return, it should reject Project C because its NPV implies a return *under* 10%. If only one project can be accepted, Project B appears best because it yields the highest NPV.

Example: If 12% is the required return in Exhibit 25.10, which project is preferred? *Answer:* Project B. Net present values are: A = $10; B = $553; C = $(715).

Example: Will the rankings of Projects A, B, and C change with the use of different discount rates, assuming the same rate is used for all projects? *Answer:* No; only the NPV amounts will change.

Salvage Value FasTrac predicted the $16,000 machine to have zero salvage value at the end of its useful life. In many cases, assets are expected to have salvage values. If so, this amount is an additional net cash inflow expected to be received at the end of the final year of the asset's life. All other computations remain the same. For example, the net present value of the $16,000 investment that yields $4,100 of net cash flows for eight years is $4,367, as shown in Exhibit 25.9. If that machine is expected to have a $1,500 salvage value at the end of its eight-year life, the present value of this salvage amount is $606 (computed as $1,500 × 0.4039). The net present value of the machine, including the present value of its expected salvage amount, is $4,973 (computed as $4,367 + $606).

Point: Excel for PV of salvage value.

	A	B
1	Salvage value	$1,500
2	Useful life	8
3	Interest rate	12%
4	Present value	

=PV(B3,B2,0,−B1) = $606

Accelerated Depreciation   Depreciation methods can affect net present value analysis. FasTrac computes depreciation using the straight-line method. Accelerated depreciation is commonly used for income tax purposes. Accelerated depreciation produces larger depreciation deductions in the early years of an asset's life and smaller deductions in later years. This pattern results in smaller income tax payments in early years and larger tax payments in later years. Accelerated depreciation does not change the basics of a present value analysis, but it can change the result. Using accelerated depreciation for tax reporting increases the NPV of an asset's cash flows because it produces larger net cash inflows in the early years of the asset's life. Using accelerated depreciation for tax reporting always makes an investment more desirable because early cash flows are more valuable than later ones.

Comparing Positive NPV Projects   When considering several projects of similar investment amounts and risk levels, we can compare the different projects' NPVs and rank them on the dollar amounts of their NPVs. However, if the amount invested differs substantially across projects, this is of limited value for comparison purposes. One way to compare projects, especially when a company cannot fund all positive net present value projects, is to use the **profitability index,** which is computed as

$$\text{Profitability index} = \frac{\text{Present value of net cash flows}}{\text{Initial investment}}$$

Exhibit 25.11 illustrates computation of the profitability index for three potential investments. A profitability index less than 1 indicates an investment with a *negative* net present value. Investment 3 shows an index of 0.9, meaning a negative NPV. This means we can drop #3 from consideration. Both Investments 1 and 2 have profitability indexes greater than 1, thus they have positive net present values. Investment 1's NPV equals $150,000 (computed as $900,000 − $750,000); Investment 2's NPV equals $125,000 (computed as $375,000 − $250,000). Ideally, the company would accept all positive NPV projects, but if forced to choose, it should select the project with the higher profitability index. Thus, Investment 2 is ranked ahead of Investment 1 based on its higher profitability index. **Rule:** Invest in the project with the highest profitability index.

EXHIBIT 25.11

Profitability Index

	Investment		
	1	**2**	**3**
Present value of net cash flows (a)	$900,000	$375,000	$270,000
Amount invested (b)	750,000	250,000	300,000
Profitability index (a)/(b)	**1.2**	**1.5**	**0.9**

Capital Rationing   Some firms face **capital rationing,** or financing constraints that limit them from accepting all positive NPV projects. This can be in two forms, hard rationing and soft rationing. *Hard rationing* is imposed by external forces, such as debt covenants that restrict the firm's ability to borrow more money. *Soft rationing* is internally imposed by management and the board of directors. For example, management might place spending limits on certain employees until they show they can make good decisions. Whether due to hard or soft capital rationing, the profitability index can be used to select the best of several competing projects.

Inflation   Large price-level increases should be considered in NPV analyses. Discount rates should already include inflation forecasts. Net cash flows can be adjusted for inflation by using *future value* computations. For example, if the expected net cash inflow in year 1 is $4,100 and 5% inflation is expected, then the expected net cash inflow in year 2 is $4,305, computed as $4,100 × 1.05 (1.05 is the future value of $1 [Table B.2] for 1 period with a 5% rate).

A company is considering two potential projects. Each project requires a $20,000 initial investment and is expected to generate end-of-year annual cash flows as shown below. Assuming a discount rate of 10%, compute the net present value of each project.

NEED-TO-KNOW 25-3

Net Present Value
P3

	Net Cash Inflows			
	Year 1	Year 2	Year 3	Total
Project A	$12,000	$8,500	$ 4,000	$24,500
Project B	4,500	8,500	13,000	26,000

Solution

Net present values are computed as follows.

		Project A		Project B	
Year	**Present Value of 1 at 10%**	**Net Cash Flows**	**Present Value of Net Cash Flows**	**Net Cash Flows**	**Present Value of Net Cash Flows**
1	0.9091	$12,000	$ 10,909	$ 4,500	$ 4,091
2	0.8264	8,500	7,024	8,500	7,024
3	0.7513	4,000	3,005	13,000	9,767
Totals		$24,500	$ 20,938	$26,000	$ 20,882
Initial investment			(20,000)		(20,000)
Net present value			$ 938		$ 882

Do More: QS 25-2, QS 25-8, QS 25-9, QS 25-11, E 25-2, E 25-6, E 25-9

Internal Rate of Return

Another means to evaluate capital investments is to use the **internal rate of return (IRR),** which equals the discount rate that yields an NPV of zero for an investment. This means that if we compute the total present value of a project's net cash flows using the IRR as the discount rate and then subtract the initial investment from this total present value, we get a zero NPV.

P4

Compute internal rate of return and explain its use.

To illustrate, we use the data for FasTrac's Project A from Exhibit 25.10 to compute its IRR. Below is the two-step process for computing IRR with even cash flows.

Step 1: Compute the present value factor for the investment project.

$$\text{Present value factor} = \frac{\text{Amount invested}}{\text{Annual net cash flows}} = \frac{\$12,000}{\$5,000} = 2.4000$$

Net Cash Flows Project A

Investment . . . . $(12,000)
Year 1   5,000
Year 2   5,000
Year 3   5,000
Hurdle rate = 10%

Step 2: Identify the discount rate (IRR) yielding the present value factor.
Search Table B.3 for a present value factor of 2.4000 in the 3-year row (equaling the 3-year project duration). The 12% discount rate yields a present value factor of 2.4018. This implies that the IRR is approximately 12%.

Point: Excel for IRR.

	A	B
1	Investment	-$12,000
2	Cash flow year 1	5,000
3	Cash flow year 2	5,000
4	Cash flow year 3	5,000
5	Internal rate of return	◄

=IRR(B1:B4) = 12%

When cash flows are equal, as with Project A, we compute the present value factor by dividing the initial investment by its annual net cash flows. We then use an annuity table to determine the discount rate equal to this present value factor. For FasTrac's Project A, we look across the 3-period row of Table B.3 and find that the discount rate corresponding to the present value

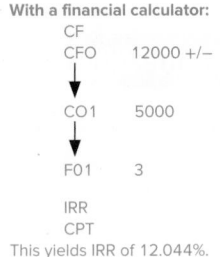

factor of 2.4000 roughly equals the 2.4018 value for the 12% rate. This row of Table B.3 is reproduced here:

| | Present Value of an Annuity of 1 for Three Periods | | | | |
| | Discount Rate | | | | |
Periods	1%	5%	10%	12%	15%
3	2.9410	2.7232	2.4869	**2.4018**	2.2832

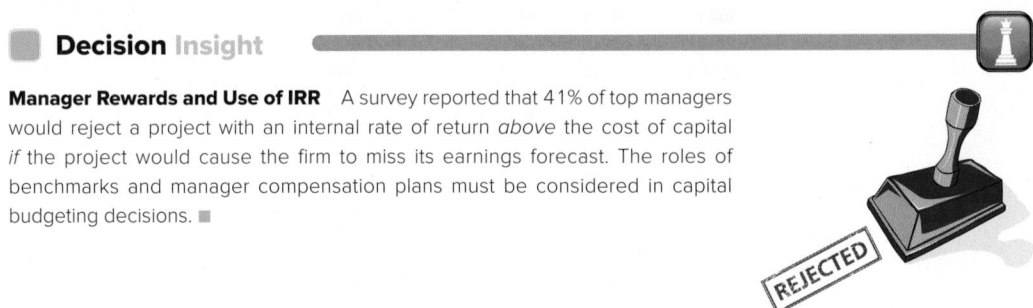

The 12% rate is the project's IRR. Because this project's IRR is greater than the hurdle rate of 10%, it should be accepted. **Rule:** If IRR > hurdle rate, invest.

Uneven Cash Flows   If net cash flows are uneven, it is best to use either a calculator or spreadsheet software to compute IRR. We can also use trial and error to compute IRR. We do this by selecting any reasonable discount rate and computing the NPV. If the amount is positive (negative), we recompute the NPV using a higher (lower) discount rate. We continue these steps until we reach a point where two consecutive computations result in NPVs having different signs (positive and negative). Because the NPV is zero using IRR, we know that the IRR lies between these two discount rates. We can then estimate its value.

■ Decision Insight

Manager Rewards and Use of IRR   A survey reported that 41% of top managers would reject a project with an internal rate of return *above* the cost of capital *if* the project would cause the firm to miss its earnings forecast. The roles of benchmarks and manager compensation plans must be considered in capital budgeting decisions. ■

Use of Internal Rate of Return   To use the IRR to evaluate a project, compare it to a predetermined **hurdle rate,** which is a minimum acceptable rate of return. The decision rule using IRR is applied as follows:

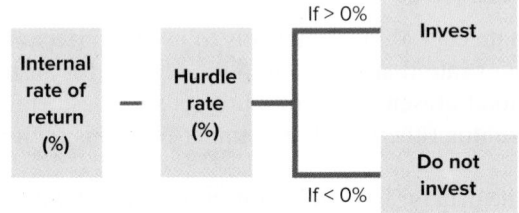

Management selects the hurdle rate to use in evaluating capital investments. If the IRR is higher than the hurdle rate, the investment should be made.

Comparing Projects Using IRR   Multiple projects are often ranked by the extent to which their IRR exceeds the hurdle rate. IRR can be used to compare projects with different amounts invested because the IRR is expressed as a percent rather than as a dollar value in NPV. The NPV approach is preferred to the IRR method when considering projects where the net annual cash flows change sign more than once over the project. This complication is explained in advanced courses.

■ Decision Maker

Entrepreneur   You are developing a new product and you use a 12% discount rate to compute its NPV. Your banker, from whom you hope to obtain a loan, expresses concern that your discount rate is too low. How do you respond? ■   [*Answer:* The banker is probably concerned because new products are risky and should therefore be evaluated using a higher rate of return. You should conduct a thorough technical analysis and obtain detailed market data and information about any similar products. These factors might support the use of a lower return. You must convince yourself that the risk level is consistent with the discount rate used. You should also be confident that your company has the capacity and the resources to handle the new product.]

NEED-TO-KNOW 25-4

A machine costing $58,880 is expected to generate net cash flows of $8,000 per year for each of the next 10 years.

1. Compute the machine's internal rate of return (IRR).

2. If a company's hurdle rate is 6.5%, use IRR to determine whether the company should purchase this machine.

Internal Rate of Return

P4

Solution

1. PV factor = Amount invested/Net cash flows = $58,880/$8,000 = 7.36. Scanning the "Periods equal 10" row in Table B.3 for a present value factor near 7.36 indicates the IRR is <u>6%</u>.

2. The machine should <u>not</u> be purchased because its IRR (6%) is less than the company's hurdle rate (6.5%).

Do More: QS 25-3, QS 25-13, E 25-13, E 25-14

Comparison of Capital Budgeting Methods

We explained four methods that managers use to evaluate capital investment projects. How do these methods compare with each other? Exhibit 25.12 addresses that question. Neither the payback period nor the accounting rate of return considers the time value of money. Both the net present value and the internal rate of return do.

EXHIBIT 25.12

Comparing Capital Budgeting Methods

	Payback Period	Accounting Rate of Return	Net Present Value	Internal Rate of Return
Measurement basis	• Cash flows	• Accrual income	• Cash flows	• Cash flows
Measurement unit	• Years	• Percent	• Dollars	• Percent
Strengths	• Easy to understand • Allows comparison of projects	• Easy to understand • Allows comparison of projects	• Reflects time value of money • Reflects varying risks over project's life	• Reflects time value of money • Allows comparisons of dissimilar projects
Limitations	• Ignores time value of money • Ignores cash flows after payback period	• Ignores time value of money • Ignores annual rates over life of project	• Difficult to compare dissimilar projects	• Ignores varying risks over life of project

● Payback period is probably the simplest method. It gives managers an estimate of how soon they will recover their initial investment. Managers sometimes use this method when they have limited cash to invest and a number of projects to choose from.

● Accounting rate of return yields a percent measure computed using accrual income instead of cash flows. The accounting rate of return is an average rate for the entire investment period.

● Net present value considers all estimated net cash flows for the project's expected life. It can be applied to even and uneven cash flows and can reflect changes in the level of risk over a project's life. Since NPV yields a dollar measure, comparing projects of unequal sizes is more difficult. The profitability index, based on each project's net present value, can be used in this case.

● Internal rate of return considers all cash flows from a project. It is readily computed when the cash flows are even but requires some trial and error or use of a financial calculator or computer when cash flows are uneven. Because the IRR is a percent measure, it is readily used to compare projects with different investment amounts. However, IRR does not reflect changes in risk over a project's life.

■ **Decision** Insight

And the Winner Is . . .   How do we choose among the methods for evaluating capital investments? Management surveys consistently show the internal rate of return (IRR) as the most popular method, followed by the payback period and net present value (NPV). Few companies use the accounting rate of return (ARR), but nearly all use more than one method. ■

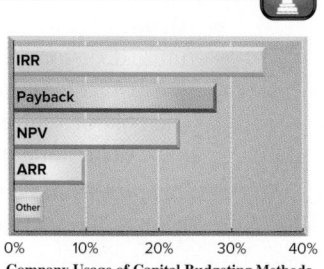

Company Usage of Capital Budgeting Methods

Section 2—Managerial Decisions

This section focuses on methods that use accounting information to make several important managerial decisions. Most of these involve short-term decisions. This differs from methods used for longer-term managerial decisions that are described in the first section of this chapter and in several other chapters of this book.

DECISIONS AND INFORMATION

This section explains how managers make decisions and the information relevant to those decisions.

Decision Making

Managerial decision making involves five steps: (1) define the decision task, (2) identify alternative courses of action, (3) collect relevant information and evaluate each alternative, (4) select the preferred course of action, and (5) analyze and assess decisions made. These five steps are illustrated in Exhibit 25.13.

EXHIBIT 25.13

Managerial Decision Making

| Define task and goal | Identify alternative actions | Collect relevant information | Select course of action | Analyze and assess decision |

Both managerial and financial accounting information play important roles in most management decisions. The accounting system is expected to provide primarily *financial* information such as performance reports and budget analyses for decision making. *Nonfinancial* information is also relevant, however; it includes information on environmental effects, political sensitivities, and social responsibility.

Relevant Costs and Benefits

C1

Describe the importance of relevant costs for short-term decisions.

In making short-term decisions, managers should focus on the relevant benefits and the relevant costs.

- **Incremental costs,** also called differential costs, are the relevant costs in making decisions. These are the additional costs incurred if a company pursues a certain course of action.
- **Relevant benefits,** the additional or *incremental* revenue generated by selecting a certain course of action over another, are the key rewards from that action.

Three types of costs are pertinent to our discussion of relevant costs: sunk costs, out-of-pocket costs, and opportunity costs.

- A *sunk cost* arises from a past decision and cannot be avoided or changed; it is irrelevant to future decisions. An example is the cost of computer equipment previously purchased by a company. This cost is not relevant to the decision of whether to replace the computer equipment. Likewise, depreciation of the original cost of plant (and intangible) assets is a sunk cost. Most of a company's allocated costs, including fixed overhead items such as depreciation and administrative expenses, are sunk costs.
  - An *out-of-pocket cost* requires a future outlay of cash and is relevant for current and future decisions. These costs are usually the direct result of management's decisions. For instance, future purchases of computer equipment involve out-of-pocket costs. The cost of future computer purchases is relevant to the decision of whether to replace the computer equipment.
  - An *opportunity cost* is the potential benefit lost by taking a specific action when two or more alternative choices are available. An example is a student giving up wages

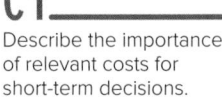

"Sunk costs are not relevant to my decision."   "I must consider out-of-pocket and opportunity costs."

from a job to attend summer school. The forgone wages should be considered as part of the total cost of attending summer school. Companies continually must choose from alternative courses of action. For instance, a company making standardized products might be approached by a customer to supply a special (nonstandard) product. A decision to accept or reject the special order must consider not only the profit to be made from the special order but also the profit given up by devoting time and resources to this order instead of pursuing an alternative project. The profit given up is an opportunity cost. Consideration of opportunity costs is important. Although opportunity costs are not entered in accounting records, they are relevant to many managerial decisions.

We show how to apply relevant costs and benefits to analyze common managerial decisions. Managers must also consider qualitative factors that are not easily expressed in terms of costs and benefits.

Match each of the terms below with its definition.

_____ **1.** Sunk cost

_____ **2.** Out-of-pocket cost

_____ **3.** Opportunity cost

_____ **4.** Incremental cost

_____ **5.** Relevant benefit

a. Additional costs incurred from a course of action

b. Incremental revenue from a course of action

c. A future outlay of cash

d. Potential benefit lost from taking a course of action

e. A cost that arises from a past decision and cannot be changed

NEED-TO-KNOW 25-5

Relevant Costs

C1

Solution

1. e   **2.** c   **3.** d   **4.** a   **5.** b

Do More: QS 25-17, E 25-16

MANAGERIAL DECISION SCENARIOS

Managers experience many different scenarios that require analyzing alternative actions and making decisions. We describe several different decision scenarios in this section. We set these tasks in the context of FasTrac, an exercise supplies and equipment manufacturer. *We treat each of these decision tasks as separate from each other.*

A1_____

Evaluate short-term managerial decisions using relevant costs.

Additional Business

FasTrac is operating at its normal level of 80% of full capacity. At this level, it produces and sells approximately 100,000 units of product annually. Its per unit and annual total sales and costs are shown in the contribution margin income statement in Exhibit 25.14. Its normal selling price is $10.00 per unit, and each unit sold generates $1.00 per unit of operating income.

EXHIBIT 25.14

Selected Operating Income Data

FasTrac Contribution Margin Income Statement For Year Ended December 31, 2017	Per Unit	Annual Total
Sales (100,000 units)	$10.00	$1,000,000
Variable costs		
Direct materials	(3.50)	(350,000)
Direct labor.	(2.20)	(220,000)
Variable overhead	(0.50)	(50,000)
Selling expenses	(1.40)	(140,000)
Contribution margin	2.40	240,000
Fixed costs		
Fixed overhead.	0.60	60,000
Administrative expenses	0.80	80,000
Operating income.	$ 1.00	$ 100,000

A current buyer of FasTrac's products wants to purchase additional units of its product and export them to another country. This buyer offers to buy 10,000 units of the product at $8.50 per unit, or $1.50 less than the current price. The offer price is low, but FasTrac is considering the proposal because this sale would be several times larger than any single previous sale and it would use idle capacity. Also, the units will be exported, so this new business will not affect current sales.

To determine whether to accept or reject this order, management needs to know whether accepting the offer will increase net income. If management relies incorrectly on per unit historical costs, it would mistakenly reject the sale because the selling price ($8.50) per unit is less than the total historical costs per unit ($9.00).

To correctly make its decision, FasTrac must analyze the costs of this potential new business differently. The $9.00 historical cost per unit is not necessarily the incremental cost of this order. The following information regarding the order is available:

- The variable manufacturing costs to produce this order will be the same as for FasTrac's normal business—$3.50 per unit for direct materials, $2.20 per unit for direct labor, and $0.50 per unit for variable overhead.

- Selling expenses for this order will be $0.20 per unit, which is less than the selling expenses of FasTrac's normal business.

- Fixed overhead expenses will not change regardless of whether this order is accepted.

- This order will incur *incremental* administrative expenses of $1,000 for clerical work. These are additional fixed costs due to this order.

We use this incremental cost information to determine whether FasTrac should accept this new business. The analysis of relevant benefits and costs in Exhibit 25.15 suggests that the additional business should be accepted. **The incremental revenue ($8.50 per unit) exceeds the incremental cost ($6.50 per unit), and the order would yield $20,000 of additional pretax income.** More generally, FasTrac would increase its income with any price that exceeds $6.50 per unit ($65,000 incremental cost/10,000 additional units). The key point is that *management must not blindly use historical costs, especially allocated overhead costs.* Instead, management must focus on the incremental costs to be incurred if the additional business is accepted.

EXHIBIT 25.15

Analysis of Additional Business Using Relevant Costs

FasTrac Contribution Margin Income Statement (for special order) For Year Ended December 31, 2017		
	Per Unit*	**Annual Total**
Sales (10,000 units).....................	$ 8.50	$ 85,000
Variable costs		
Direct materials......................	(3.50)	(35,000)
Direct labor	(2.20)	(22,000)
Variable overhead....................	(0.50)	(5,000)
Selling expenses.....................	(0.20)	(2,000)
Contribution margin	2.10	21,000
Fixed costs		
Fixed overhead	—	—
Administrative expenses	(0.10)	(1,000)
Operating income (incremental)...........	$ 2.00	$ 20,000

*Total cost per unit = $3.50 + $2.20 + $0.50 + $0.20 + $0.10 = $6.50

Point: Ignore allocated overhead costs. The analysis in Exhibit 25.15 uses only *incremental* fixed overhead costs.

Additional Factors   An analysis of the incremental costs pertaining to the additional volume is always relevant for this type of decision. We must be careful when the additional volume approaches or exceeds the factory's existing available capacity. If the additional volume requires the company to expand its capacity by obtaining more equipment, more space, or more personnel, the incremental costs could quickly exceed the incremental revenue.

Another cautionary note is the effect on existing sales. All new units of the extra business will be sold outside FasTrac's normal domestic sales channels. If accepting additional business would cause existing sales to decline, this information must be included in our analysis. The contribution margin lost from a decline in sales is an opportunity cost. The company must also consider whether this customer is really a one-time customer. If not, can the company continue to offer this low price in the long run?

Example: Exhibit 25.15 uses quantitative information. Suggest some qualitative factors to be considered when deciding whether to accept this project. *Answer:* (1) Impact on relationships with other customers and (2) improved relationship with customer buying additional units.

■ **Decision Maker**

Partner You are a partner in a small accounting firm that specializes in keeping the books and preparing taxes for clients. A local restaurant is interested in obtaining these services from your firm. Identify factors that are relevant in deciding whether to accept the engagement. ■ [*Answer:* You should identify the differences between existing clients and this potential client. A key difference is that the restaurant business has additional inventory components (groceries, vegetables, meats) and is likely to have a higher proportion of depreciable assets. These differences imply that the partner must spend more hours auditing the records and understanding the business, regulations, and standards that pertain. Such differences suggest that the partner must use a different "formula" for quoting a price to this potential client vis-à-vis current clients.]

A company receives a special order for 200 units that requires stamping the buyer's name on each unit, yielding an additional fixed cost of $400. Without the order, the company is operating at 75% of capacity and produces 7,500 units of product at the costs below. The company's normal selling price is $22 per unit.

NEED-TO-KNOW 25-6

Special Order

A1

Direct materials	$37,500
Direct labor	60,000
Overhead (30% variable)	20,000
Selling expenses (60% variable)	25,000

The sales price for the special order is $18 per unit. The special order will not affect normal unit sales and will not increase fixed overhead or fixed selling expenses. Variable selling expenses on the special order are reduced to one-half the normal amount. Should the company accept the special order?

Solution

Incremental variable costs per unit for this order of 200 units are computed as follows:

Direct materials ($37,500/7,500)	$ 5.00
Direct labor ($60,000/7,500)	8.00
Variable overhead [(0.30 × $20,000)/7,500]	0.80
Variable selling expenses [(0.60 × $25,000 × 0.5)/7,500]	1.00
Total incremental variable costs per unit	$14.80

The contribution margin from the special order is $640, computed as [($18.00 − $14.80) × 200]. This will cover the incremental fixed costs of $400 and yield incremental income of $240. **The offer should be accepted.**

Do More: QS 25-18, E 25-17, E 25-18

Make or Buy

The managerial decision to make or buy a component is common. For example, **Apple** buys the component parts for its electronic products, but it could consider making these components in its own manufacturing facilities. The process of buying goods or services from an external supplier is called **outsourcing.** This decision depends on incremental costs. We return to FasTrac to illustrate.

FasTrac currently buys part 417, a component of the main product it sells, for $1.20 per unit. FasTrac has excess productive capacity, and management is considering making part 417 instead of buying it. FasTrac estimates that making part 417 would incur variable costs of $0.45 for direct materials and $0.50 for direct labor. FasTrac's normal predetermined overhead rate is 100% of direct labor cost. If management *incorrectly* relies on this historical overhead rate, it would mistakenly believe that the cost to make the component part is $1.45 per unit ($0.45 + $0.50 + $0.50) and conclude the company is better off buying the part at $1.20 per unit. This analysis is flawed, however, because it uses the historical predetermined overhead rate.

Only *incremental* overhead costs are relevant to this decision. Incremental overhead costs might include, for example, additional power for operating machines, extra supplies, added cleanup costs, materials handling, and quality control. Assume that management computes an *incremental overhead rate* of $0.20 per unit if it makes the part. We can then prepare a per unit analysis, using relevant costs, as shown in Exhibit 25.16.

EXHIBIT 25.16

Make or Buy Analysis Using
Relevant Costs

$s per unit	Make	Buy
Direct materials	$0.45	—
Direct labor	0.50	—
Overhead costs (using incremental rate).	0.20	—
Purchase price.	—	$1.20
Total cost per unit	$1.15	$1.20

Exhibit 25.16 shows that the relevant cost to make part 417 is $1.15. It is cheaper to make the part than to buy it. We can see that if incremental overhead costs are less than $0.25 per unit, the total cost of making the part will be less than the purchase price of $1.20 per unit.

Additional Factors   While our analysis suggests it is cheaper to make part 417, FasTrac must consider several nonfinancial factors in the make or buy decision. These factors might include product quality, timeliness of delivery (especially in a just-in-time setting), reactions of customers and suppliers, and other intangibles like employee morale and workload. It must also consider whether making the part requires incremental fixed costs to expand plant capacity. When these additional factors are considered, small cost differences might not matter.

■ **Decision** Insight

Make or Buy IT   Companies apply make or buy decisions to their services. Many now outsource their information technology activities. Information technology companies provide infrastructure and services to enable businesses to focus on their key activities. It is argued that outsourcing saves money and streamlines operations, and without the headaches. ■

 **25-7**

Make or Buy

A1

A company currently pays $5 per unit to buy a key part for a product it manufactures. The company believes it can make the part for $1.50 per unit for direct materials and $2.50 per unit for direct labor. The company allocates overhead costs at the rate of 50% of direct labor. Incremental overhead costs to make this part are $0.75 per unit. Should the company make or buy the part?

Solution

$s per unit	Make	Buy
Direct materials	$1.50	—
Direct labor	2.50	—
Overhead	0.75	—
Cost to buy the part	—	$5.00
Total cost per unit	$4.75	$5.00

Do More: QS 25-19, QS 25-20,
E 25-19, E 25-20

The company should **make the part** because the cost to make it is less than the cost to buy it.

Scrap or Rework

Manufacturing processes sometimes yield defective products. In such cases, managers must make a decision on whether to scrap or rework products in process. Two points are important here. First, costs already incurred in manufacturing the defective units are sunk and not relevant. Second, we must consider opportunity costs—reworking the defective products uses productive capacity that could be devoted to normal operations.

To illustrate, assume that FasTrac has 10,000 defective units of a product that have already cost $1 per unit to manufacture. These units can be sold as is (as scrap) for $0.40 each, or they can be reworked for $0.80 per unit and then sold for their full price of $1.50 each. Should Fas-Trac sell the units as scrap or rework them?

The $1 per unit manufacturing cost already incurred is a sunk cost and irrelevant. Further, if FasTrac is operating near its maximum capacity, reworking the defects means that FasTrac is unable to manufacture 10,000 *new* units with an incremental cost of $1 per unit and a selling price of $1.50 per unit, meaning it incurs an *opportunity cost* of $0.50 per unit ($1.50 selling price − $1.00 incremental cost). Our analysis is reflected in Exhibit 25.17.

$s per unit	Scrap	Rework
Sale of scrapped/reworked units	$0.40	$ 1.50
Less out-of-pocket costs to rework defects		(0.80)
Less opportunity cost of not making new units		**(0.50)**
Incremental net income (per unit)	$0.40	$ 0.20

EXHIBIT 25.17

Scrap or Rework Analysis

Scrapping the 10,000 units would yield incremental income of $4,000, computed as 10,000 × $0.40; reworking the units would yield only $2,000 of income. Based on this analysis, the defective units should be scrapped and sold as is for $0.40 each. If we had failed to include the opportunity costs of $0.50 per unit, the rework option would mistakenly have seemed more favorable than scrapping.

Sell or Process Further

Some companies must decide whether to sell partially completed products as is or to process them further for sale as other products. For example, a peanut grower could sell its peanut harvest as is, or it could process peanuts into other products such as peanut butter, trail mix, and candy. The decision depends on the incremental costs and benefits of further processing.

To illustrate, suppose that FasTrac has 40,000 units of partially finished Product Q. It has already spent $30,000 to manufacture these 40,000 units. FasTrac can sell the 40,000 units to another manufacturer as raw material for $50,000. Alternatively, it can process them further and produce finished Products X, Y, and Z. Processing the units further will cost an additional $80,000 and will yield total revenues of $150,000. FasTrac must decide whether the added revenues from selling finished Products X, Y, and Z exceed the costs of finishing them.

Point: This $30,000 is a sunk cost. It won't change whether FasTrac sells now or processes further.

Exhibit 25.18 presents the analysis.

	Sell as Product Q	Process Further into Products X, Y, and Z
Incremental revenue	$50,000	$150,000
Incremental cost	—	(80,000)
Incremental income	$50,000	$ 70,000

EXHIBIT 25.18

Sell or Process Further Analysis

The analysis shows that the incremental income from processing further ($70,000) is greater than the incremental income ($50,000) from selling Product Q as is. Therefore, FasTrac should process further and earn an additional $20,000 of income ($70,000 − $50,000). The $30,000 of previously incurred manufacturing costs are *excluded* from the analysis. These costs are sunk, and they are not relevant to the decision. The incremental revenue from selling Product Q as is ($50,000) is properly included. It is the opportunity cost associated with processing further. The net benefit to processing further is $20,000.

Sell or Process Further

A1

For each of the two independent scenarios below, determine whether the company should sell the partially completed product as is or process it further into other saleable products.

1. $10,000 of manufacturing costs have been incurred to produce Product Alpha. Alpha can be sold as is for $30,000 or processed further into two separate products. The further processing will cost $15,000, and the resulting products can be sold for total revenues of $60,000.

2. $5,000 of manufacturing costs have been incurred to produce Product Delta. Delta can be sold as is for $150,000 or processed further into two separate products. The further processing will cost $75,000, and the resulting products can be sold for total revenues of $200,000.

Solution

1.

Alpha	Sell As Is	Process Further
Incremental revenue	$30,000	$ 60,000
Incremental cost.	—	(15,000)
Incremental income	$30,000	$ 45,000

Alpha should be **processed further**; doing so will yield an extra $15,000 ($45,000 − $30,000) of income.

2.

Delta	Sell As Is	Process Further
Incremental revenue	$150,000	$200,000
Incremental cost	—	(75,000)
Incremental income	$150,000	$125,000

Do More: QS 25-22, QS 25-23, E 25-23

Delta should be **sold as is**; doing so will yield an extra $25,000 ($150,000 − $125,000) of income.

Sales Mix Selection When Resources Are Constrained

Point: A method called *linear programming* is useful for finding the optimal sales mix for several products subject to many market and production constraints. This method is described in advanced courses.

When a company sells a mix of products, some are more profitable than others. Management concentrates sales efforts on more profitable products. If production facilities or other factors are limited, producing more of one product usually requires producing less of others. In this case, management must identify the most profitable combination, or *sales mix* of products. To identify the best sales mix, management focuses on the *contribution margin per unit of scarce resource.*

To illustrate, assume that FasTrac makes and sells two products, A and B. The same machines are used to produce both products. A and B have the following selling prices and variable costs per unit:

$s per unit	Product A	Product B
Selling price	$5.00	$7.50
Variable costs	3.50	5.50

FasTrac has an existing capacity of 100,000 machine hours per year. In addition, Product A uses 1 machine hour per unit while Product B uses 2 machine hours per unit. With limited resources, FasTrac should focus its productive capacity on the product that yields the highest contribution margin *per machine hour,* until market demand for that product is satisfied. Exhibit 25.19 shows the relevant analysis.

EXHIBIT 25.19

Sales Mix Analysis

	Product A	Product B
Selling price per unit.	$5.00	$7.50
Variable costs per unit	3.50	5.50
Contribution margin per unit (a).	$1.50	$2.00
Machine hours per unit (b)	1 hr.	2 hr.
Contribution margin per machine hour (a) ÷ (b).	**$1.50**	**$1.00**

Exhibit 25.19 shows that although Product B has a higher contribution margin per *unit,* Product A has a higher contribution margin per *machine hour.* In this case, FasTrac should produce as much of Product A as possible, up to the market demand. For example, if the market will buy all of Product A that FasTrac can produce, FasTrac should produce 100,000 units of Product A and none of Product B. This sales mix would yield a contribution margin of $150,000 per year, the maximum the company could make subject to its resource constraint.

Point: With such high demand, management should consider expanding its productive capacity.

If demand for Product A is limited—say, to 80,000 units—FasTrac will begin by producing those 80,000 units. This production level would leave 20,000 machine hours to devote to production of Product B. FasTrac would use these remaining machine hours to produce 10,000 units (20,000 machine hours/2 machine hours per unit) of Product B. This sales mix would yield the contribution margin shown in Exhibit 25.20.

Sales Mix	Contribution Margin	Machine Hours Used
Product A (80,000 × $1.50 per unit)...............	$120,000	80,000
Product B (10,000 × $2.00 per unit)...............	20,000	20,000
Total..	$140,000	100,000

EXHIBIT 25.20

Contribution Margin from Sales Mix, with Resource Constraint

With limited demand for Product A, the optimal sales mix yields a contribution margin of $140,000, the best the company can do subject to its resource constraint and market demand. In general, if demand for products is limited, management should produce its most profitable product (per unit of scarce resource) up to the point of total demand (or its capacity constraint). It then uses remaining capacity to produce its next most profitable product.

Point: FasTrac might consider buying more machines to reduce the constraint on production. A strategy designed to reduce the impact of constraints or bottlenecks on production is called the *theory of constraints.*

Decision Insight

Fashion Mix Companies such as **Gap, Abercrombie & Fitch,** and **American Eagle** must continuously monitor and manage the sales mix of their product lists. Selling their products worldwide further complicates their decision process. The contribution margin of each product is crucial to their product mix strategies. ■

© BananaStock/Punchstock

A company produces two products, Gamma and Omega. Gamma sells for $10 per unit and Omega sells for $12.50 per unit. Variable costs are $7 per unit of Gamma and $8 per unit of Omega. The company has a capacity of 5,000 machine hours per month. Gamma uses 1 machine hour per unit, and Omega uses 3 machine hours per unit.

NEED-TO-KNOW 25-9

Sales Mix with Constrained Resources

A1

1. Compute the contribution margin per machine hour for each product.
2. Assume demand for Gamma is limited to 3,800 units per month. How many units of Gamma and Omega should the company produce, and what will be the total contribution margin from this sales mix?

Solution

1.

	Gamma	Omega
Selling price per unit	$10.00	$12.50
Variable costs per unit	7.00	8.00
Contribution margin per unit (a).........................	$ 3.00	$ 4.50
Machine hours per unit (b)...............................	1 hr.	3 hr.
Contribution margin per machine hour [(a) ÷ (b)]	**$ 3.00**	**$ 1.50**

2. The company will begin by producing Gamma to meet the market demand of 3,800 units. This production level will consume 3,800 machine hours, leaving 1,200 machine hours to produce Omega. With 1,200 machine hours, the company can produce 400 units (1,200 machine hours/3 machine hours per unit) of Omega. The total contribution margin from this sales mix is:

Gamma............................	3,800 units × $3.00 per unit =	$ 11,400
Omega.............................	400 units × $4.50 per unit =	1,800
Total contribution margin		**$13,200**

Do More: QS 25-24, E 25-24

Segment Elimination

When a segment, division, or store is performing poorly, management must consider eliminating it. As we showed in a previous chapter, determining a segment's *contribution to overhead* is an important first step in this analysis. Segments with revenues less than direct costs are candidates for elimination. However, contribution to overhead is not sufficient for this decision. Instead, we must further classify the segment's expenses as avoidable or unavoidable.

- **Avoidable expenses** are amounts the company would not incur if it eliminated the segment.
- **Unavoidable expenses** are amounts that would continue even if the segment was eliminated.

Example: How can insurance be classified as either avoidable or unavoidable? *Answer:* It depends on whether the assets insured can be removed and the premiums canceled.

To illustrate, FasTrac is considering eliminating its treadmill division, which reported a $500 operating loss for the recent year, as shown in Exhibit 25.21. Exhibit 25.21 shows the treadmill division contributes $9,700 to recovery of overhead costs. The next step is to classify the division's costs as either avoidable or unavoidable. Variable costs, such as cost of goods sold and wages expense, are avoidable. In addition, some of the division's indirect expenses are avoidable; for example, if the treadmill division were eliminated, FasTrac could reduce its overall advertising expense by $400 and its overall insurance expense by $300. In addition, FasTrac could avoid office department expenses of $2,200 and purchasing expenses of $1,000 if the treadmill division were eliminated. These *avoidable* expenses would not be allocated to other divisions of the company; rather, these expenses would be eliminated. *Unavoidable* expenses, however, will be reallocated to other divisions if the treadmill division is eliminated.

EXHIBIT 25.21

Classification of Segment Operating Expenses for Analysis

Treadmill Division	Total	Avoidable Expenses	Unavoidable Expenses
Sales..	$47,800		
Cost of goods sold.................................	30,000	$30,000	
Gross profit	17,800		
Direct expenses			
Wages expense.....................................	7,900	7,900	
Depreciation expense—Equipment....................	200		$ 200
Total direct expenses	8,100		
Departmental contribution to overhead...................	$ 9,700		
Indirect expenses			
Rent and utilities expense	3,150		3,150
Advertising expense.................................	400	400	
Insurance expense	400	300	100
Share of office department expenses	3,060	2,200	860
Share of purchasing department expenses	3,190	1,000	2,190
Total indirect expenses.............................	10,200		
Operating income (loss)	$ (500)		
Total avoidable expenses		$41,800	
Total unavoidable expenses...........................			$6,500

Point: Analysis is summarized as:

Sales	$ 47,800
Avoidable expenses	(41,800)
Reduction in income	$ 6,000

Because sales > avoidable expenses, do *not* eliminate division.

FasTrac can avoid a total of $41,800 of expenses if it eliminates the treadmill division. However, because this division's sales are $47,800, eliminating the division would reduce FasTrac's income by $6,000 ($47,800 − $41,800). Based on this analysis, FasTrac should not eliminate its treadmill division. *Our decision rule is that a segment is a candidate for elimination if its revenues are less than its avoidable expenses.* Avoidable expenses can be viewed as the costs to generate this segment's revenues.

Additional Factors   When considering elimination of a segment, we must assess its impact on other segments. A segment could be unprofitable on its own, but it might still contribute to other segments' revenues and profits. It is possible then to continue a segment even when its revenues are less than its avoidable expenses. Similarly, a profitable segment might be discontinued if its space, assets, or staff can be more profitably used by expanding existing segments or by creating new ones. Our decision to keep or eliminate a segment requires a more complex analysis than simply looking at a segment's performance report.

Example: Give an example of a segment that a company might profitably use to attract customers even though it might incur a loss. *Answer:* Warranty and post-sales services.

A bike maker is considering eliminating its tandem bike division because it operates at a loss of $6,000 per year. Division sales for the year total $40,000, and the company reports the costs for this division as shown below. Should the tandem bike division be eliminated?

NEED-TO-KNOW 25-10

Segment Elimination

A1

	Avoidable Expenses	Unavoidable Expenses
Cost of goods sold	$30,000	$ —
Direct expenses	8,000	—
Indirect expenses.	2,500	3,000
Service department costs	250	2,250
Total.	$40,750	$5,250

Solution

Total avoidable costs of $40,750 are greater than the division's sales of $40,000, suggesting the division **should be eliminated**. Other factors might be relevant since the shortfall in sales ($750) is low. For example, are tandem bike sales expected to increase in the future? Does the sale of tandem bikes help sales of other types of products?

Do More: QS 25-25, QS 25-26, E 25-25

Keep or Replace Equipment

Businesses periodically must decide whether to keep using equipment or replace it. Advances in technology typically mean newer equipment can operate more efficiently and at lower cost than older equipment. If the reduction in *variable* manufacturing costs with the new equipment is greater than its net purchase price, the equipment should be replaced. In this setting, the net purchase price of the equipment is its total cost minus any trade-in allowance or cash receipt for the old equipment.

For example, FasTrac has a piece of manufacturing equipment with a book value (cost minus accumulated depreciation) of $20,000 and a remaining useful life of four years. At the end of four years the equipment will have a salvage value of zero. The market value of the equipment is currently $25,000.

FasTrac can purchase a new machine for $100,000 and receive $25,000 in return for trading in its old machine. The new machine will reduce FasTrac's variable manufacturing costs by $18,000 per year over the four-year life of the new machine. FasTrac's incremental analysis is shown in Exhibit 25.22.

Point: The book value of the old equipment is a sunk cost. It won't change regardless of FasTrac's decision.

	Increase or (Decrease) in Net Income
Cost to buy new machine.	$(100,000)
Cash received to trade in old machine	25,000
Reduction in variable manufacturing costs.	72,000*
Total increase (decrease) in net income	$ (3,000)

*18,000 × 4 years

EXHIBIT 25.22

Keep or Replace Analysis

Exhibit 25.22 shows that FasTrac should not replace the old equipment with this newer version as it will decrease income by $3,000. The book value of the old equipment ($20,000) is not relevant to this analysis. Book value is a sunk cost, and it cannot be changed regardless of whether FasTrac keeps or replaces this equipment.

SUSTAINABILITY AND ACCOUNTING

Net present value calculations extend to investments in sustainable energy sources like solar power. To illustrate, consider a potential investment of $11,000 in a solar panel system in Phoenix. The system is expected to last for 30 years and require $100 of maintenance costs per year. The typical home uses 14,000 kilowatt hours (kWh) of electricity per year, at a cost of $0.12 per kilowatt hour. According to the National Renewable Energy Laboratory (**pvwatts.nrel.gov**), a typical solar panel system in Phoenix could supply 8,642 kilowatts of electricity per year. The net present value of a potential investment in a solar panel system, using a 6% discount rate, is computed in Exhibit 25.23. The NPV is $1,898, indicating the investment should be accepted.

EXHIBIT 25.23

NPV of Solar Investment

Electricity cost savings (8,642 × $0.12)	$ 1,037
Annual maintenance costs.	(100)
Net annual cash inflows	$ 937
Present value of net cash inflows ($937 × 13.7648*)	$12,898
Initial investment	11,000
Net present value	**$ 1,898**

*From Table B.3: 30 periods, 6%

Predicting the future benefits of solar panel installations, however, in terms of reduced energy costs, is challenging for several reasons. First, the amount of solar energy that can be produced depends on geographic location, with locations nearer the equator typically better. Second, south-facing roofs are better able to capture solar energy than other orientations. Third, cost savings from solar energy require predictions of the future costs of other sources of power, which can be volatile. These factors must be considered when performing a net present value calculation on a potential investment in solar power.

Simply Gum, this chapter's feature company, uses only sustainable, natural ingredients. This means its gum is fully biodegradable, as opposed to gums that include chemicals, plastic, and other synthetics. (For the company's aims, see **Takepart.com/video/2014/11/12/her-company-caron-proschan-simply-gum**).

Simply Gum also uses recyclable materials for its packaging. Each piece of its gum includes a "post-chew" wrapper for convenient and clean disposal.

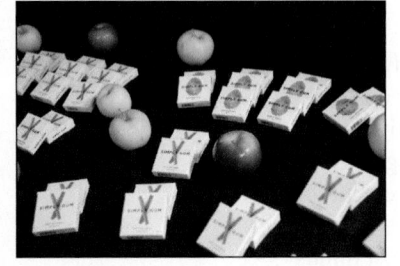

© Mike Coppola/Getty Images

Decision Analysis ▢▢▢   Break-Even Time

A2

Analyze a capital investment project using break-even time.

The first section of this chapter explained several methods to evaluate capital investments. Break-even time of an investment project is a variation of the payback period method that overcomes the limitation of not using the time value of money. **Break-even time (BET)** is a time-based measure used to evaluate a capital investment's acceptability. Its computation yields a measure of expected time, reflecting the time period until the *present value* of the net cash flows from an investment equals the initial cost of the investment. In basic terms, break-even time is computed by restating future cash flows in terms of present values and then determining the payback period using these present values.

To illustrate, we return to the FasTrac case involving a $16,000 investment in machinery. The annual net cash flows from this investment are projected at $4,100 for eight years. Exhibit 25.24 shows the computation of break-even time for this investment decision.

The rightmost column of this exhibit shows that break-even time is between 5 and 6 years, or about 5.2 years—also see margin graph (where the line crosses the zero point). This is the time the project takes to break

EXHIBIT 25.24

Break-Even Time Analysis*

Year	Cash Flows	Present Value of 1 at 10%	Present Value of Cash Flows	Cumulative Present Value of Cash Flows
0	$(16,000)	1.0000	$(16,000)	$(16,000)
1	4,100	0.9091	3,727	(12,273)
2	4,100	0.8264	3,388	(8,885)
3	4,100	0.7513	3,080	(5,805)
4	4,100	0.6830	2,800	(3,005)
5	4,100	0.6209	2,546	(459)
6	4,100	0.5645	2,314	1,855
7	4,100	0.5132	2,104	3,959
8	4,100	0.4665	1,913	5,872

Break-even time (pointing to years 5 and 6 cumulative values: (459) and 1,855)

* The time of analysis is the start of year 1 (same as end of year 0). All cash flows occur at the end of each year.

even after considering the time value of money (recall that the payback period computed without considering the time value of money was 3.9 years). We interpret this as cash flows earned after 5.2 years contribute to a positive net present value that, in this case, eventually amounts to $5,872.

Break-even time is a useful measure for managers because it identifies the point in time when they can expect the cash flows to begin to yield net positive returns. Managers expect a positive net present value from an investment if break-even time is less than the investment's estimated life. The method allows managers to compare and rank alternative investments, giving the project with the shortest break-even time the highest rank.

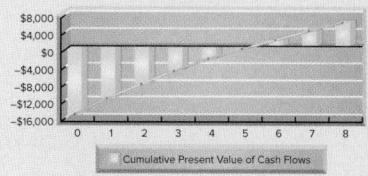

Cumulative Present Value of Cash Flows

▉ Decision Maker

Investment Manager Management asks you, the investment manager, to evaluate three alternative investments. Investment recovery time is crucial because cash is scarce. The time value of money is also important. Which capital budgeting method(s) do you use to assess the investments? ■ [*Answer:* You should probably focus on either the payback period or break-even time because both the time value of money and recovery time are important. The break-even time method is superior because it accounts for the time value of money, which is an important consideration in this decision.]

Determine the appropriate action in each of the following managerial decision situations.

NEED-TO-KNOW 25-11

COMPREHENSIVE

1. Packer Company is operating at 80% of its manufacturing capacity of 100,000 product units per year. A chain store has offered to buy an additional 10,000 units at $22 each and sell them to customers so as not to compete with Packer Company. The following data are available.

Costs at 80% Capacity	Per Unit	Total
Direct materials	$ 8.00	$ 640,000
Direct labor............................	7.00	560,000
Overhead (fixed and variable)	12.50	1,000,000
Totals..................................	$27.50	$2,200,000

In producing 10,000 additional units, fixed overhead costs would remain at their current level, but incremental variable overhead costs of $3 per unit would be incurred. Should the company accept or reject this order?

2. Green Company uses Part JR3 in manufacturing its products. It has always purchased this part from a supplier for $40 each. It recently upgraded its own manufacturing capabilities and has enough excess capacity (including trained workers) to begin manufacturing Part JR3 instead of buying it. The company prepares the following cost projections of making the part, assuming that overhead is allocated to the part at the normal predetermined rate of 200% of direct labor cost.

Direct materials	$11
Direct labor..	15
Overhead (fixed and variable) (200% of direct labor)...............	30
Total...	$56

The required volume of output to produce the part will not require any incremental fixed overhead. Incremental variable overhead cost will be $17 per unit. Should the company make or buy this part?

3. Gold Company's manufacturing process causes a relatively large number of defective parts to be produced. The defective parts can be (a) sold for scrap, (b) melted to recover the recycled metal for reuse, or (c) reworked to be good units. Reworking defective parts reduces the output of other good units because no excess capacity exists. Each unit reworked means that one new unit cannot be produced. The following information reflects 500 defective parts currently available.

Proceeds of selling as scrap	$2,500
Additional cost of melting down defective parts	400
Cost of purchases avoided by using recycled metal from defects	4,800
Cost to rework 500 defective parts	
Direct materials	0
Direct labor	1,500
Incremental overhead	1,750
Cost to produce 500 new parts	
Direct materials	6,000
Direct labor	5,000
Incremental overhead	3,200
Selling price per good unit	40

Should the company melt the parts, sell them as scrap, or rework them?

4. White Company can invest in one of two projects, TD1 or TD2. Each project requires an initial investment of $100,000 and produces the year-end cash inflows shown in the following table. Use net present values to determine which project, if any, should be chosen. Assume that the company requires a 10% return from its investments.

	Net Cash Flows	
	TD1	TD2
Year 1	$ 20,000	$ 40,000
Year 2	30,000	40,000
Year 3	70,000	40,000
Totals	$120,000	$120,000

PLANNING THE SOLUTION

- Determine whether Packer Company should accept the additional business by finding the incremental costs of materials, labor, and overhead that will be incurred if the order is accepted. Omit fixed costs that the order will not increase. If the incremental revenue exceeds the incremental cost, accept the order.

- Determine whether Green Company should make or buy the component by finding the incremental cost of making each unit. If the incremental cost exceeds the purchase price, the component should be purchased. If the incremental cost is less than the purchase price, make the component.

- Determine whether Gold Company should sell the defective parts, melt them down and recycle the metal, or rework them. To compare the three choices, examine all costs incurred and benefits received from the alternatives in working with the 500 defective units versus the production of 500 new units. For the scrapping alternative, include the costs of producing 500 new units and subtract the $2,500 proceeds from selling the old ones. For the melting alternative, include the costs of melting the defective units, add the net cost of new materials in excess over those obtained from recycling, and add the direct labor and overhead costs. For the reworking alternative, add the costs of direct labor and incremental overhead. Select the alternative that has the lowest cost. The cost assigned to the 500 defective units is sunk and not relevant in choosing among the three alternatives.

- Compute White Company's net present value of each investment using a 10% discount rate.

SOLUTION

1. This decision involves accepting additional business. Since current unit costs are $27.50, it appears initially as if the offer to sell for $22 should be rejected, but the $27.50 cost includes fixed costs. When the analysis includes only *incremental* costs, the per unit cost is as shown in the following table. The offer should be accepted because it will produce $4 of additional profit per unit (computed as $22 price less $18 incremental cost), which yields a total profit of $40,000 for the 10,000 additional units.

Direct materials	$ 8.00
Direct labor	7.00
Variable overhead (given)	3.00
Total incremental cost	$18.00

2. For this make or buy decision, the analysis must include only incremental overhead per unit ($30 − $17). When only the $17 incremental overhead is included, the relevant unit cost of manufacturing the part is shown in the following table. It would be better to continue buying the part for $40 instead of making it for $43.

Direct materials	$11.00
Direct labor	15.00
Variable overhead	17.00
Total incremental cost	$43.00

3. The goal of this scrap or rework decision is to identify the alternative that produces the greatest net benefit to the company. To compare the alternatives, we determine the net cost of obtaining 500 marketable units as follows:

Incremental Cost to Produce 500 Marketable Units	Sell As Is	Melt and Recycle	Rework Units
Direct materials			
New materials	$ 6,000	$6,000	
Recycled metal materials		(4,800)	
Net materials cost		1,200	
Melting costs		400	
Total direct materials cost	6,000	1,600	
Direct labor	5,000	5,000	$1,500
Incremental overhead	3,200	3,200	1,750
Cost to produce 500 marketable units	14,200	9,800	3,250
Less proceeds of selling defects as scrap	(2,500)		
Opportunity costs*			5,800
Incremental cost	$11,700	$9,800	$9,050

* The $5,800 opportunity cost is the lost contribution margin from not being able to produce and sell 500 units because of reworking, computed as ($40 − [$14,200/500 units]) × 500 units.

The incremental cost of 500 marketable parts is smallest if the defects are reworked.

4. TD1:

	Net Cash Flows	Present Value of 1 at 10%	Present Value of Net Cash Flows
Year 1	$ 20,000	0.9091	$ 18,182
Year 2	30,000	0.8264	24,792
Year 3	70,000	0.7513	52,591
Totals	$120,000		95,565
Amount invested			(100,000)
Net present value			**$ (4,435)**

TD2:

	Net Cash Flows	Present Value of 1 at 10%	Present Value of Net Cash Flows
Year 1	$ 40,000	0.9091	$ 36,364
Year 2	40,000	0.8264	33,056
Year 3	40,000	0.7513	30,052
Totals	$120,000		99,472
Amount invested			(100,000)
Net present value			**$ (528)**

White Company should not invest in either project. Both are expected to yield a negative net present value, and it should invest only in positive net present value projects.

25A

Using Excel to Compute Net Present Value and Internal Rate of Return

Computing present values and internal rates of return for projects with uneven cash flows is tedious and error prone. These calculations can be performed simply and accurately by using functions built into Excel. Many calculators and other types of spreadsheet software can perform them too. To illustrate, consider FasTrac, a company that is considering investing in a new machine with the expected cash flows shown in the following spreadsheet. Cash outflows are entered as negative numbers, and cash inflows are entered as positive numbers. Assume FasTrac requires a 12% annual return, entered as 0.12 in cell C1.

	A	B	C
1	Annual discount rate		0.12
2	Initial investment, made at beginning of period 1		–16000
3	Annual cash flows received at end of period:		
4		1	3000
5		2	4000
6		3	4000
7		4	4000
8		5	5000
9		6	3000
10		7	2000
11		8	2000
12			
13			=NPV(C1,C4:C11)+C2
14			
15			=IRR(C2:C11)

To compute the net present value of this project, the following is entered into cell C13:

$$=NPV(C1,C4:C11)+C2$$

This instructs Excel to use its NPV function to compute the present value of the cash flows in cells C4 through C11, using the discount rate in cell C1, and then add the amount of the (negative) initial investment. For this stream of cash flows and a discount rate of 12%, the net present value is $1,326.03.

To compute the internal rate of return for this project, the following is entered into cell C15:

$$=IRR(C2:C11)$$

This instructs Excel to use its IRR function to compute the internal rate of return of the cash flows in cells C2 through C11. By default, Excel starts with a guess of 10%, and then uses trial and error to find the IRR. The IRR equals 14% for this project.

25B

Product Pricing

A3
_____
Determine product selling price using cost data.

Managers use relevant costs in determining prices for special short-term decisions. But longer-run pricing decisions of management need to cover both variable and fixed costs, and yield a profit. There are several methods to help management in setting prices.

Cost-Plus Methods   _Cost-plus_ methods are common, where management adds a **markup** to cost to reach a target price. We will describe the **total cost method,** where management sets price equal to the product's total costs plus a desired profit on the product. This is a three-step process:

1. Determine total cost per unit.

$$\text{Total costs} = \frac{\text{Product (direct materials,}}{\text{direct labor, and overhead) costs}} + \frac{\text{Selling and}}{\text{administrative costs}}$$

Total cost per unit = Total costs ÷ Total units expected to be produced and sold

2. Determine the dollar markup per unit.

Markup per unit = Total cost per unit × Markup percentage

3. Determine selling price per unit.

Selling price per unit = Total cost per unit + Markup per unit

To illustrate, consider MpPro, a company that produces MP3 players. The company desires a 20% markup on the total cost of this product. It expects to produce and sell 10,000 players. The following additional information is available:

Variable costs (per unit)		Fixed costs (in dollars)	
Product costs	$44	Overhead	$140,000
Selling and administrative costs	6	Selling and administrative costs	60,000

We apply the three-step total cost method to determine price.

1. Total costs = Product costs + Selling and administrative costs
   = [($44 × 10,000 units) + $140,000] + [($6 × 10,000 units) + $60,000]
   = $700,000

   Total cost per unit = Total costs/Total units expected to be produced and sold
   = $700,000/10,000
   = $70

2. Markup per unit = Total cost per unit × Markup percentage
   = $70 × 20%
   = $14

3. Selling price per unit = Total cost per unit + Markup per unit
   = $70 + $14
   = $84

Companies often use cost-plus pricing as a starting point in determining selling prices. Many factors determine price, including consumer preferences and competition.

Target Costing When competition is high, companies might be "price takers," and have little control in setting prices. In such cases *target costing* can be useful. Target cost is defined as:

Target cost = Expected selling price − Desired profit

If the target cost is too high, lean techniques can be used to determine whether the cost can be reduced enough that the desired profit can be made. For example, if the market price for MP3 players is $80 each and MpPro still wants to make a profit of $14 per unit, it must find a way to reduce its total cost per unit to $66 (computed as $80 price − $14 desired profit).

Other Pricing Methods In addition to the total cost approach to cost-plus pricing, alternatives include approaches based on either product costs or variable costs. Since these alternative cost amounts are lower than total cost, companies that use these methods must adjust their desired markup percentage upward to ensure that the selling price covers all costs.

Sometimes companies compute the desired markup percentage using a target return on investment. For example, if MpPro targets a 14% return on invested assets of $1,000,000, its target profit is $140,000. This equals $14 per unit if 10,000 units are sold, as in this example. The markup percentage is then $14/$70 = 20%.

Variable Cost Method In addition to the total cost approach to cost-plus pricing, alternatives include approaches based on either product costs or variable costs. Because these alternative cost amounts are lower than total cost, companies that use these methods must increase their desired markup percentage to ensure that the selling price covers all costs. For the variable cost method, the markup percentage is determined as:

$$\text{Markup percentage} = \frac{\text{Target profit} + \text{Fixed overhead costs} + \text{Fixed selling and administrative costs}}{\text{Total variable costs}}$$

For MpPro, the markup percentage, using the variable cost approach, is computed as:

$$\text{Markup percentage} = \frac{\$140,000 + \$140,000 + \$60,000}{[(\$44 + \$6) \times 10,000]} = 68\%$$

With this markup percentage and total variable cost per unit of $50, the selling price is computed as:

$$\text{Selling price} = \$50 + (\$50 \times 68\%) = \$84$$

Summary

C1 Describe the importance of relevant costs for short-term decisions. A company must rely on relevant costs pertaining to alternative courses of action rather than historical costs. Out-of-pocket expenses and opportunity costs are relevant because these are avoidable; sunk costs are irrelevant because they result from past decisions and are therefore unavoidable. Managers must also consider the relevant benefits associated with alternative decisions.

A1 Evaluate short-term managerial decisions using relevant costs. Relevant costs are useful in making decisions such as to accept additional business, make or buy, and sell as is or process further. For example, the relevant factors in deciding whether to produce and sell additional units of product are incremental costs and incremental revenues from the additional volume.

A2 Analyze a capital investment project using break-even time. Break-even time (BET) is a method for evaluating capital investments by restating future cash flows in terms of their present values (discounting the cash flows) and then calculating the payback period using these present values of cash flows.

A3^B Determine product selling price using cost data. Product selling price can be estimated using total costs, plus a markup. Total costs include both product costs and selling and administrative expenses. A markup is added to yield management's desired profit.

P1 Compute payback period and describe its use. One way to compare potential investments is to compute and compare their payback periods. The payback period is an estimate of the expected time before the cumulative net cash inflow from the investment equals its initial cost. A payback period analysis fails to reflect risk of the cash flows, differences in the timing of cash flows within the payback period, and cash flows that occur after the payback period.

P2 Compute accounting rate of return and explain its use. A project's accounting rate of return is computed by dividing the expected annual after-tax net income by the average amount of investment in the project. When the net cash flows are received evenly throughout each period and straight-line depreciation is used, the average investment is computed as the average of the investment's initial book value and its salvage value.

P3 Compute net present value and describe its use. An investment's net present value is determined by predicting the future cash flows it is expected to generate, discounting them at a rate that represents an acceptable return, and then by subtracting the investment's initial cost from the sum of the present values. This technique can deal with any pattern of expected cash flows and applies a superior concept of return on investment.

P4 Compute internal rate of return and explain its use. The internal rate of return (IRR) is the discount rate that results in a zero net present value. When the cash flows are equal, we can compute the present value factor corresponding to the IRR by dividing the initial investment by the annual cash flows. We then use the annuity tables to determine the discount rate corresponding to this present value factor.

Key Terms

Accounting rate of return (ARR)	Cost of capital	Outsourcing
Annuity	Hurdle rate	Payback period (PBP)
Avoidable expense	Incremental cost	Profitability index
Break-even time (BET)	Internal rate of return (IRR)	Relevant benefits
Capital budgeting	Markup	Total cost method
Capital rationing	Net present value (NPV)	Unavoidable expense

Multiple Choice Quiz

1. A company inadvertently produced 3,000 defective MP3 players. The players cost $12 each to produce. A recycler offers to purchase the defective players as they are for $8 each. The production manager reports that the defects can be corrected for $10 each, enabling them to be sold at their regular market price of $19 each. The company should:

   a. Correct the defect and sell them at the regular price.

   b. Sell the players to the recycler for $8 each.

   c. Sell 2,000 to the recycler and repair the rest.

   d. Sell 1,000 to the recycler and repair the rest.

   e. Throw the players away.

2. A company's productive capacity is limited to 480,000 machine hours. Product X requires 10 machine hours to produce; Product Y requires 2 machine hours to produce. Product X sells for $32 per unit and has variable costs of $12 per unit; Product Y sells for $24 per unit and has variable costs of $10 per unit. Assuming that the company can sell as many of either product as it produces, it should:

   a. Produce X and Y in the ratio of 57% X and 43% Y.

   b. Produce X and Y in the ratio of 83% X and 17% Y.

   c. Produce equal amounts of Product X and Product Y.

   d. Produce only Product X.

   e. Produce only Product Y.

3. A company receives a special one-time order for 3,000 units of its product at $15 per unit. The company has excess capacity and it currently produces and sells the units at $20 each to its regular customers. Production costs are $13.50 per unit, which includes $9 of variable costs. To produce the special order, the company must incur additional fixed costs of $5,000. Should the company accept the special order?

   a. Yes, because incremental revenue exceeds incremental costs.

   b. No, because incremental costs exceed incremental revenue.

   c. No, because the units are being sold for $5 less than the regular price.

   d. Yes, because incremental costs exceed incremental revenue.

   e. No, because incremental costs exceed $15 per unit when total costs are considered.

4. A company is considering the purchase of equipment for $270,000. Projected annual cash inflow from this equipment is $61,200 per year. The payback period is:

   a. 0.2 years.   c. 4.4 years.   e. 3.9 years.

   b. 5.0 years.   d. 2.3 years.

5. A company buys a machine for $180,000 that has an expected life of nine years and no salvage value. The company expects an annual net income (after taxes of 30%) of $8,550. What is the accounting rate of return?

   a. 4.75%   c. 2.85%   e. 6.65%

   b. 42.75%   d. 9.50%

ANSWERS TO MULTIPLE CHOICE QUIZ

1. a; Reworking provides incremental revenue of $11 per unit ($19 − $8); it costs $10 to rework them. The company is better off by $1 per unit when it reworks these products and sells them at the regular price.

2. e; Product X has a $2 contribution margin per machine hour [($32 − $12)/10 MH]; Product Y has a $7 contribution margin per machine hour [($24 − $10)/2 MH]. It should produce as much of Product Y as possible.

3. a; Total revenue from the special order = 3,000 units × $15 per unit = $45,000; and Total costs for the special order = (3,000 units × $9 per unit) + $5,000 = $32,000. Net income from the special order = $45,000 − $32,000 = $13,000. Thus, yes, it should accept the order.

4. c; Payback = $270,000/$61,200 per year = 4.4 years.

5. d; Accounting rate of return = $8,550/[($180,000 + $0)/2] = 9.5%.

A,B   *Superscript letter A(B) denotes assignments based on Appendix 25A (25B).*

🛈 Icon denotes assignments that involve decision making.

Discussion Questions

1. Capital budgeting decisions require careful analysis because they are generally the most _____ and _____ decisions that management faces.

2. What is capital budgeting?

3. 🛈 Identify four reasons that capital budgeting decisions are risky.

4. Identify two disadvantages of using the payback period for comparing investments.

5. 🛈 Why is an investment more attractive to management if it has a shorter payback period?

6. What is the average amount invested in a machine during its predicted five-year life if it costs $200,000 and has a $20,000 salvage value? Assume that net income is received evenly throughout each year and straight-line depreciation is used.

7. If the present value of the expected net cash flows from a machine, discounted at 10%, exceeds the amount to be invested, what can you say about the investment's expected rate of return? What can you say about the expected rate of return if the present value of the net cash flows, discounted at 10%, is less than the investment amount?

8. Why is the present value of $100 that you expect to receive one year from today worth less than $100 received today? What is the present value of $100 that you expect to receive one year from today, discounted at 12%?

9. [I] If a potential investment's internal rate of return is above the company's hurdle rate, should the investment be made?

10. [I] Why does the use of the accelerated depreciation method (instead of straight-line) for income tax reporting increase an investment's value?

11. Google has many types of costs. What is an out-of-pocket cost? What is an opportunity cost? Are opportunity costs recorded in the accounting records? **GOOGLE**

12. [I] Samsung must confront sunk costs. Why are sunk costs irrelevant in deciding whether to sell a product in its present **Samsung**

condition or to make it into a new product through additional processing?

13. [I] Identify the incremental costs incurred by Apple for shipping one additional iPhone from a warehouse to a retail store along with the store's normal order of 75 iPhones. **APPLE**

14. [I] Apple is considering expanding a store. Identify three methods management can use to evaluate whether to expand. **APPLE**

15. [I] Assume that Samsung manufactures and sells 60,000 units of a product at $11,000 per unit in domestic markets. It costs $6,000 per unit to manufacture ($4,000 variable cost per unit, $2,000 fixed cost per unit). Can you describe a situation under which the company is willing to sell an additional 8,000 units of the product in an international market at $5,000 per unit? **Samsung**

---

connect

QUICK STUDY

QS 25-1
Payback period **P1**

Park Co. is considering an investment that requires immediate payment of $27,000 and provides expected cash inflows of $9,000 annually for four years. What is the investment's payback period?

QS 25-2
Net present value **P3**

Park Co. is considering an investment that requires immediate payment of $27,000 and provides expected cash inflows of $9,000 annually for four years. If Park Co. requires a 10% return on its investments, what is the net present value of this investment? (Round your calculations to the nearest dollar.)

QS 25-3
Internal rate of return **P4**

Park Co. is considering an investment that requires immediate payment of $27,000 and provides expected cash inflows of $9,000 annually for four years. Assume Park Co. requires a 10% return on its investments. Based on its internal rate of return, should Park Co. make the investment?

QS 25-4
Analyzing payback periods **P1**

Howard Co. is considering two alternative investments. The payback period is 3.5 years for Investment A and 4 years for Investment B.

1. If management relies on the payback period, which investment is preferred?

2. Why might Howard's analysis of these two alternatives lead to the selection of B over A?

QS 25-5
Payback period **P1**

Project A requires a $280,000 initial investment for new machinery with a five-year life and a salvage value of $30,000. The company uses straight-line depreciation. Project A is expected to yield annual net income of $20,000 per year for the next five years. Compute Project A's payback period.

QS 25-6
Accounting rate of return
P2

Project A requires a $280,000 initial investment for new machinery with a five-year life and a salvage value of $30,000. The company uses straight-line depreciation. Project A is expected to yield annual net income of $20,000 per year for the next five years. Compute Project A's accounting rate of return. Express your answer as a percentage, rounded to two decimal places.

QS 25-7
Computation of accounting rate of return **P2**

Peng Company is considering an investment expected to generate an average net income after taxes of $1,950 for three years. The investment costs $45,000 and has an estimated $6,000 salvage value. Compute the accounting rate of return for this investment; assume the company uses straight-line depreciation. Express your answer as a percentage, rounded to two decimal places.

QS 25-8
Net present value **P3**

Peng Company is considering an investment expected to generate an average net income after taxes of $1,950 for three years. The investment costs $45,000 and has an estimated $6,000 salvage value. Assume Peng requires a 15% return on its investments. Compute the net present value of this investment. (Round each present value calculation to the nearest dollar.)

If Quail Company invests $50,000 today, it can expect to receive $10,000 at the end of each year for the next seven years, plus an extra $6,000 at the end of the seventh year. What is the net present value of this investment assuming a required 10% return on investments? (Round present value calculations to the nearest dollar.)

QS 25-9
Compute net present value
P3

Yokam Company is considering two alternative projects. Project 1 requires an initial investment of $400,000 and has a present value of cash flows of $1,100,000. Project 2 requires an initial investment of $4 million and has a present value of cash flows of $6 million. Compute the profitability index for each project. Based on the profitability index, which project should the company prefer? Explain.

QS 25-10
Profitability index
P3

Following is information on an investment considered by Hudson Co. The investment has zero salvage value. The company requires a 12% return from its investments. Compute this investment's net present value.

QS 25-11
Net present value
P3

Investment A1	
Initial investment	$(200,000)
Expected net cash flows in year:	
1	100,000
2	90,000
3	75,000

Refer to the information in QS 25-11 and instead assume the investment has a salvage value of $20,000. Compute the investment's net present value.

QS 25-12
Net present value, with salvage value   P3

A company is considering investing in a new machine that requires a cash payment of $47,947 today. The machine will generate annual cash flows of $21,000 for the next three years. What is the internal rate of return if the company buys this machine?

QS 25-13
Internal rate of return   P4

A company is considering investing in a new machine that requires a cash payment of $47,947 today. The machine will generate annual cash flows of $21,000 for the next three years. Assume the company uses an 8% discount rate. Compute the net present value of this investment. (Round your answer to the nearest dollar.)

QS 25-14
Net present value   P3

A company is investing in a solar panel system to reduce its electricity costs. The system requires a cash payment of $125,374.60 today. The system is expected to generate net cash flows of $13,000 per year for the next 35 years. The investment has zero salvage value. The company requires an 8% return on its investments. Compute the net present value of this investment.

QS 25-15
Net present value
P3

A company is investing in a solar panel system to reduce its electricity costs. The system requires a cash payment of $125,374.60 today. The system is expected to generate net cash flows of $13,000 per year for the next 35 years. The investment has zero salvage value. Compute the internal rate of return on this investment.

QS 25-16
Internal rate of return
P4

Label each of the following statements as either true ("T") or false ("F").

_____ **1.** Relevant costs are also known as unavoidable costs.

_____ **2.** Incremental costs are also known as differential costs.

_____ **3.** An out-of-pocket cost requires a current and/or future outlay of cash.

_____ **4.** An opportunity cost is the potential benefit that is lost by taking a specific action when two or more alternative choices are available.

_____ **5.** A sunk cost will change with a future course of action.

QS 25-17
Relevant costs
C1

Radar Company sells bikes for $300 each. The company currently sells 3,750 bikes per year and could make as many as 5,000 bikes per year. The bikes cost $225 each to make; $150 in variable costs per bike and $75 of fixed costs per bike. Radar received an offer from a potential customer who wants to buy 750 bikes for $250 each. Incremental fixed costs to make this order are $50,000. No other costs will change if this order is accepted. Compute Radar's additional income (ignore taxes) if it accepts this order.

QS 25-18
Decision to accept additional business   A1

QS 25-19
Make or buy
A1

Kando Company incurs a $9 per unit cost for Product A, which it currently manufactures and sells for $13.50 per unit. Instead of manufacturing and selling this product, the company can purchase it for $5 per unit and sell it for $12 per unit. If it does so, unit sales would remain unchanged and $5 of the $9 per unit costs assigned to Product A would be eliminated. Should the company continue to manufacture Product A or purchase it for resale?

QS 25-20
Make or buy
A1

Xia Co. currently buys a component part for $5 per unit. Xia believes that making the part would require $2.25 per unit of direct materials and $1.00 per unit of direct labor. Xia allocates overhead using a predetermined overhead rate of 200% of direct labor cost. Xia estimates an incremental overhead rate of $0.75 per unit to make the part. Should Xia make or buy the part?

QS 25-21
Scrap or rework
A1

Signal mistakenly produced 1,000 defective cell phones. The phones cost $60 each to produce. A salvage company will buy the defective phones as they are for $30 each. It would cost Signal $80 per phone to rework the phones. If the phones are reworked, Signal could sell them for $120 each. Assume there is no opportunity cost associated with reworking the phones. Compute the incremental net income from reworking the phones.

QS 25-22
Sell or process further
A1

Holmes Company produces a product that can either be sold as is or processed further. Holmes has already spent $50,000 to produce 1,250 units that can be sold now for $67,500 to another manufacturer. Alternatively, Holmes can process the units further at an incremental cost of $250 per unit. If Holmes processes further, the units can be sold for $375 each. Compute the incremental income if Holmes processes further.

QS 25-23
Sell or process further   A1

A company has already incurred $5,000 of costs in producing 6,000 units of Product XY. Product XY can be sold as is for $15 per unit. Instead, the company could incur further processing costs of $8 per unit and sell the resulting product for $21 per unit. Should the company sell Product XY as is or process it further?

QS 25-24
Selection of sales mix
A1

Excel Memory Company can sell all units of computer memory X and Y that it can produce, but it has limited production capacity. It can produce two units of X per hour *or* three units of Y per hour, and it has 4,000 production hours available. Contribution margin is $5 for Product X and $4 for Product Y. What is the most profitable sales mix for this company?

QS 25-25
Segment elimination
A1

A guitar manufacturer is considering eliminating its electric guitar division because its $76,000 expenses are higher than its $72,000 sales. The company reports the following expenses for this division. Should the division be eliminated?

	Avoidable Expenses	Unavoidable Expenses
Cost of goods sold	$56,000	
Direct expenses	9,250	$1,250
Indirect expenses..................	470	1,600
Service department costs	6,000	1,430

QS 25-26
Segment elimination
A1

A division of a large company reports the information shown below for a recent year. Variable costs and direct fixed costs are avoidable, and 40% of the indirect fixed costs are avoidable. Based on this information, should the division be eliminated?

	Total
Sales	$200,000
Variable costs	145,000
Fixed costs	
Direct	30,000
Indirect	50,000
Operating loss...........	$ (25,000)

QS 25-27
Keep or replace decision
A1

Rory Company has a machine with a book value of $75,000 and a remaining five-year useful life. A new machine is available at a cost of $112,500, and Rory can also receive $60,000 for trading in its old machine. The new machine will reduce variable manufacturing costs by $13,000 per year over its five-year useful life. Should the machine be replaced?

Heels, a shoe manufacturer, is evaluating the costs and benefits of new equipment that would custom fit each pair of athletic shoes. The customer would have his or her foot scanned by digital computer equipment; this information would be used to cut the raw materials to provide the customer a perfect fit. The new equipment costs $90,000 and is expected to generate an additional $35,000 in cash flows for five years. A bank will make a $90,000 loan to the company at a 10% interest rate for this equipment's purchase. Use the following table to determine the break-even time for this equipment. (Round the present value of cash flows to the nearest dollar.)

QS 25-28
Computation of
break-even time
A2

Year	Cash Flows*	Present Value of 1 at 10%	Present Value of Cash Flows	Cumulative Present Value of Cash Flows
0	$(90,000)	1.0000	_____	_____
1	35,000	0.9091	_____	_____
2	35,000	0.8264	_____	_____
3	35,000	0.7513	_____	_____
4	35,000	0.6830	_____	_____
5	35,000	0.6209	_____	_____

* All cash flows occur at year-end.

Siemens AG invests €80 million to build a manufacturing plant to build wind turbines. The company predicts net cash flows of €16 million per year for the next eight years. Assume the company requires an 8% rate of return from its investments.

1. What is the payback period of this investment?

2. What is the net present value of this investment?

QS 25-29
Capital budgeting methods

P1   P3

Garcia Co. sells snowboards. Each snowboard requires direct materials of $100, direct labor of $30, and variable overhead of $45. The company expects fixed overhead costs of $635,000 and fixed selling and administrative costs of $115,000 for the next year. It expects to produce and sell 10,000 snowboards in the next year. What will be the selling price per unit if Garcia uses a markup of 15% of total cost?

QS 25-30ᴮ
Product pricing
A3

José Ruiz wants to start a company that makes snowboards. Competitors sell a similar snowboard for $240 each. José believes he can produce a snowboard for a total cost of $200 per unit, and he plans a 25% markup on his total cost. Compute José's planned selling price. Can Jose compete with his planned selling price?

QS 25-31ᴮ
Product pricing
A3

GoSnow sells snowboards. Each snowboard requires direct materials of $110, direct labor of $35, and variable overhead of $45. The company expects fixed overhead costs of $265,000 and fixed selling and administrative costs of $211,000 for the next year. The company has a target profit of $200,000. It expects to produce and sell 10,000 snowboards in the next year. Compute the selling price using the variable cost method.

QS 25-32ᴮ
Product pricing using
variable costs   A3

Mc Graw Hill connect

Beyer Company is considering the purchase of an asset for $180,000. It is expected to produce the following net cash flows. The cash flows occur evenly within each year. Compute the payback period for this investment (round years to two decimals).

EXERCISES

Exercise 25-1
Payback period computation;
uneven cash flows   P1

Check   3.08 years

	Year 1	Year 2	Year 3	Year 4	Year 5	Total
Net cash flows	$60,000	$40,000	$70,000	$125,000	$35,000	$330,000

Refer to the information in Exercise 25-1 and assume that Beyer requires a 10% return on its investments. Compute the net present value of this investment. (Round to the nearest dollar.) Should Beyer accept the investment?

Exercise 25-2
Net present value   P3

Exercise 25-3
Payback period computation; straight-line depreciation
P1

A machine can be purchased for $150,000 and used for five years, yielding the following net incomes. In projecting net incomes, straight-line depreciation is applied, using a five-year life and a zero salvage value. Compute the machine's payback period (ignore taxes). (Round the payback period to three decimals.)

	Year 1	Year 2	Year 3	Year 4	Year 5
Net income	$10,000	$25,000	$50,000	$37,500	$100,000

Exercise 25-4
Payback period; accelerated depreciation   P1

Check   2.265 years

Refer to the information in Exercise 25-3 and assume instead that double-declining depreciation is applied. Compute the machine's payback period (ignore taxes). (Round the payback period to three decimals.)

Exercise 25-5
Payback period computation; even cash flows
P1

Compute the payback period for each of these two separate investments (round the payback period to two decimals):

a. A new operating system for an existing machine is expected to cost $520,000 and have a useful life of six years. The system yields an incremental after-tax income of $150,000 each year after deducting its straight-line depreciation. The predicted salvage value of the system is $10,000.

b. A machine costs $380,000, has a $20,000 salvage value, is expected to last eight years, and will generate an after-tax income of $60,000 per year after straight-line depreciation.

Exercise 25-6
Net present value   P3

Refer to the information in Exercise 25-5. Assume the company requires a 10% rate of return on its investments. Compute the net present value of each potential investment. (Round to the nearest dollar.)

Exercise 25-7
Accounting rate of return
P2

A machine costs $700,000 and is expected to yield an after-tax net income of $52,000 each year. Management predicts this machine has a 10-year service life and a $100,000 salvage value, and it uses straight-line depreciation. Compute this machine's accounting rate of return.

Exercise 25-8
Payback period and accounting rate of return on investment
P1   P2

B2B Co. is considering the purchase of equipment that would allow the company to add a new product to its line. The equipment is expected to cost $360,000 with a 12-year life and no salvage value. It will be depreciated on a straight-line basis. The company expects to sell 144,000 units of the equipment's product each year. The expected annual income related to this equipment follows. Compute the (1) payback period and (2) accounting rate of return for this equipment.

Check   (1) 5.39 years
(2) 20.42%

Sales	$225,000
Costs	
Materials, labor, and overhead (except depreciation on new equipment)................	120,000
Depreciation on new equipment..	30,000
Selling and administrative expenses	22,500
Total costs and expenses...	172,500
Pretax income..	52,500
Income taxes (30%)	15,750
Net income	$ 36,750

Exercise 25-9
Computing net present value   P3

After evaluating the risk of the investment described in Exercise 25-8, B2B Co. concludes that it must earn at least an 8% return on this investment. Compute the net present value of this investment. (Round the net present value to the nearest dollar.)

Following is information on two alternative investments being considered by Jolee Company. The company requires a 10% return from its investments.

Exercise 25-10
NPV and profitability index
P3

	Project A	Project B
Initial investment	$(160,000)	$(105,000)
Expected net cash flows in year:		
1.........................	40,000	32,000
2.........................	56,000	50,000
3.........................	80,295	66,000
4.........................	90,400	72,000
5.........................	65,000	24,000

For each alternative project compute the (a) net present value and (b) profitability index. (Round your answers in part *b* to two decimal places.) If the company can only select one project, which should it choose? Explain.

Following is information on two alternative investments being considered by Tiger Co. The company requires a 4% return from its investments.

Exercise 25-11
Net present value,
profitability index
P3

	Project X1	Project X2
Initial investment	$(80,000)	$(120,000)
Expected net cash flows in year:		
1.........................	25,000	60,000
2.........................	35,500	50,000
3.........................	60,500	40,000

Compute each project's (a) net present value and (b) profitability index. (Round present value calculations to the nearest dollar and round the profitability index to two decimal places.) If the company can choose only one project, which should it choose? Explain.

Refer to the information in Exercise 25-11 and instead assume the company requires a 12% return on its investments. Compute each project's (a) net present value and (b) profitability index. (Round present value calculations to the nearest dollar.) Express the profitability index as a percentage (rounded to two decimal places). If the company can choose only one project, which should it choose? Explain.

Exercise 25-12
Net present value,
profitability index   P3

Refer to the information in Exercise 25-11. Create an Excel spreadsheet to compute the internal rate of return for each of the projects. Based on internal rate of return, determine whether the company should accept either of the two projects.

Exercise 25-13[A]
Internal rate of return   P4

Phoenix Company can invest in each of three cheese-making projects: C1, C2, and C3. Each project requires an initial investment of $228,000 and would yield the following annual cash flows.

Exercise 25-14
Computation and
interpretation of net
present value and
internal rate of return

P3   P4

	C1	C2	C3
Year 1	$ 12,000	$ 96,000	$180,000
Year 2	108,000	96,000	60,000
Year 3	168,000	96,000	48,000
Totals.........................	$288,000	$288,000	$288,000

1. Assuming that the company requires a 12% return from its investments, use net present value to determine which projects, if any, should be acquired.

2. Using the answer from part 1, explain whether the internal rate of return is higher or lower than 12% for Project C2.

Exercise 25-15ᴬ

Using Excel to
compute IRR   **P4**

Refer to the information in Exercise 25-10. Create an Excel spreadsheet to compute the internal rate of return for each of the projects. Round the percentage return to two decimals.

Exercise 25-16

Relevant costs

C1

Complete the following descriptions using the terms *a* through *e*.

    a. Opportunity cost   **b.** Avoidable costs   **c.** Sunk cost   **d.** Relevant benefits   **e.** Out-of-pocket cost

    1. A _____ arises from a past decision and cannot be avoided or changed; it is irrelevant to future decisions.

    2. _____ refer to the incremental revenue generated from taking one particular action over another.

    3. Relevant costs are also known as _____.

    4. An _____ requires a future outlay of cash and is relevant for current and future decision making.

    5. An _____ is the potential benefit lost by taking a specific action when two or more alternative choices are available.

Exercise 25-17

Accept new business or not

A1

Farrow Co. expects to sell 150,000 units of its product in the next period with the following results.

Sales (150,000 units)	$2,250,000
Costs and expenses	
Direct materials	300,000
Direct labor	600,000
Overhead	150,000
Selling expenses	225,000
Administrative expenses	385,500
Total costs and expenses	1,660,500
Net income	$ 589,500

The company has an opportunity to sell 15,000 additional units at $12 per unit. The additional sales would not affect its current expected sales. Direct materials and labor costs per unit would be the same for the additional units as they are for the regular units. However, the additional volume would create the following incremental costs: (1) total overhead would increase by 15% and (2) administrative expenses would increase by $64,500. Prepare an analysis to determine whether the company should accept or reject the offer to sell additional units at the reduced price of $12 per unit.

Check   Income increase, $3,000

Exercise 25-18

Accept new business or not

A1

Goshford Company produces a single product and has capacity to produce 100,000 units per month. Costs to produce its current sales of 80,000 units follow. The regular selling price of the product is $100 per unit. Management is approached by a new customer who wants to purchase 20,000 units of the product for $75 per unit. If the order is accepted, there will be no additional fixed manufacturing overhead, and no additional fixed selling and administrative expenses. The customer is not in the company's regular selling territory, so there will be a $5 per unit shipping expense in addition to the regular variable selling and administrative expenses.

	Per Unit	Costs at 80,000 Units
Direct materials	$12.50	$1,000,000
Direct labor	15.00	1,200,000
Variable manufacturing overhead	10.00	800,000
Fixed manufacturing overhead	17.50	1,400,000
Variable selling and administrative expenses	14.00	1,120,000
Fixed selling and administrative expenses	13.00	1,040,000
Totals	$82.00	$6,560,000

Check   (1) Additional volume effect on net income, $370,000

    1. Determine whether management should accept or reject the new business.

    2. What nonfinancial factors should management consider when deciding whether to take this order?

Gilberto Company currently manufactures 65,000 units per year of one of its crucial parts. Variable costs are $1.95 per unit, fixed costs related to making this part are $75,000 per year, and allocated fixed costs are $62,000 per year. Allocated fixed costs are unavoidable whether the company makes or buys the part. Gilberto is considering buying the part from a supplier for a quoted price of $3.25 per unit guaranteed for a three-year period. Should the company continue to manufacture the part, or should it buy the part from the outside supplier? Support your answer with analyses.

Exercise 25-19
Make or buy

A1

Check $9,500 increased costs to buy

Gelb Company currently manufactures 40,000 units per year of a key component for its manufacturing process. Variable costs are $1.95 per unit, fixed costs related to making this component are $65,000 per year, and allocated fixed costs are $58,500 per year. The allocated fixed costs are unavoidable whether the company makes or buys this component. The company is considering buying this component from a supplier for $3.50 per unit. Should it continue to manufacture the component, or should it buy this component from the outside supplier? Support your decision with analysis of the data provided.

Exercise 25-20
Make or buy

A1

Check Increased cost to make, $3,000

A company must decide between scrapping or reworking units that do not pass inspection. The company has 22,000 defective units that cost $6 per unit to manufacture. The units can be sold as is for $2.00 each, or they can be reworked for $4.50 each and then sold for the full price of $8.50 each. If the units are sold as is, the company will be able to build 22,000 replacement units at a cost of $6 each, and sell them at the full price of $8.50 each.

1. What is the incremental income from selling the units as scrap?
2. What is the incremental income from reworking and selling the units?
3. Should the company sell the units as scrap or rework them?

Exercise 25-21
Scrap or rework

A1

Varto Company has 7,000 units of its sole product in inventory that it produced last year at a cost of $22 each. This year's model is superior to last year's, and the 7,000 units cannot be sold at last year's regular selling price of $35 each. Varto has two alternatives for these items: (1) they can be sold to a wholesaler for $8 each or (2) they can be reworked at a cost of $125,000 and then sold for $25 each. Prepare an analysis to determine whether Varto should sell the products as is or rework them and then sell them.

Exercise 25-22
Scrap or rework A1

Check Incremental net income of reworking, $(6,000)

Cobe Company has already manufactured 28,000 units of Product A at a cost of $28 per unit. The 28,000 units can be sold at this stage for $700,000. Alternatively, the units can be further processed at a $420,000 total additional cost and be converted into 5,600 units of Product B and 11,200 units of Product C. Per unit selling price for Product B is $105 and for Product C is $70. Prepare an analysis that shows whether the 28,000 units of Product A should be processed further or not.

Exercise 25-23
Sell or process further

A1

Colt Company owns a machine that can produce two specialized products. Production time for Product TLX is two units per hour and for Product MTV is five units per hour. The machine's capacity is 2,750 hours per year. Both products are sold to a single customer who has agreed to buy all of the company's output up to a maximum of 4,700 units of Product TLX and 2,500 units of Product MTV. Selling prices and variable costs per unit to produce the products follow. Determine (1) the company's most profitable sales mix and (2) the contribution margin that results from that sales mix.

Exercise 25-24
Sales mix determination and analysis

A1

$s per unit	Product TLX	Product MTV
Selling price per unit	$15.00	$9.50
Variable costs per unit	4.80	5.50

Check (2) $55,940

Exercise 25-25

Analysis of income effects
from eliminating
departments

A1

Suresh Co. expects its five departments to yield the following income for next year.

	A	B	C	D	E	F	G
1		**Dept. M**	**Dept. N**	**Dept. O**	**Dept. P**	**Dept. T**	**Total**
2	Sales	$63,000	$ 35,000	$56,000	$42,000	$28,000	$224,000
3	Expenses						
4	Avoidable	9,800	36,400	22,400	14,000	37,800	120,400
5	Unavoidable	51,800	12,600	4,200	29,400	9,800	107,800
6	Total expenses	61,600	49,000	26,600	43,400	47,600	228,200
7	Net income (loss)	$ 1,400	$(14,000)	$29,400	$ (1,400)	$(19,600)	$ (4,200)

Check   Total income (loss)
(1) $(21,000), (2) $7,000

Recompute and prepare the departmental income statements (including a combined total column) for the company under each of the following separate scenarios: Management (1) eliminates departments with expected net losses and (2) eliminates departments with sales dollars that are less than avoidable expenses. Explain your answers to parts 1 and 2.

Exercise 25-26

Keep or replace

A1

Xinhong Company is considering replacing one of its manufacturing machines. The machine has a book value of $45,000 and a remaining useful life of five years, at which time its salvage value will be zero. It has a current market value of $52,000. Variable manufacturing costs are $36,000 per year for this machine. Information on two alternative replacement machines follows. Should Xinhong keep or replace its manufacturing machine? If the machine should be replaced, which alternative new machine should Xinhong purchase?

	Alternative A	Alternative B
Cost..	$115,000	$125,000
Variable manufacturing costs per year............	19,000	15,000

Exercise 25-27

Comparison of payback
and BET   P1   A2

This chapter explained two methods to evaluate investments using recovery time, the payback period and break-even time (BET). Refer to QS 25-28 and (1) compute the recovery time for both the payback period and break-even time, (2) discuss the advantage(s) of break-even time over the payback period, and (3) list two conditions under which payback period and break-even time are similar.

Exercise 25-28[B]

Product pricing using
total costs

A3

Steeze Co. makes snowboards and uses the total cost approach in setting product prices. Its costs for producing 10,000 units follow. The company targets a profit of $300,000 on this product.

Variable Costs per Unit		Fixed Costs (in total)	
Direct materials.............................	$100	Overhead..............................	$470,000
Direct labor	25	Selling	105,000
Overhead.................................	20	Administrative	325,000
Selling	5		

1. Compute the total cost per unit.
2. Compute the markup percentage on total cost.
3. Compute the product's selling price using the total cost method.

Exercise 25-29[B]

Product pricing using
variable costs

A3

Rios Co. makes drones and uses the variable cost approach in setting product prices. Its costs for producing 20,000 units follow. The company targets a profit of $300,000 on this product.

Variable Costs per Unit		Fixed Costs (in total)	
Direct materials.............................	$70	Overhead..............................	$670,000
Direct labor	40	Selling	305,000
Overhead.................................	25	Administrative	285,000
Selling	10		

1. Compute the variable cost per unit.
2. Compute the markup percentage on variable cost.
3. Compute the product's selling price using the variable cost method.

connect

Factor Company is planning to add a new product to its line. To manufacture this product, the company needs to buy a new machine at a $480,000 cost with an expected four-year life and a $20,000 salvage value. All sales are for cash, and all costs are out-of-pocket, except for depreciation on the new machine. Additional information includes the following.

Expected annual sales of new product......................................	$1,840,000
Expected annual costs of new product	
Direct materials	480,000
Direct labor...	672,000
Overhead (excluding straight-line depreciation on new machine)..............	336,000
Selling and administrative expenses	160,000
Income taxes	30%

Required

1. Compute straight-line depreciation for each year of this new machine's life. (Round depreciation amounts to the nearest dollar.)

2. Determine expected net income and net cash flow for each year of this machine's life. (Round answers to the nearest dollar.)

3. Compute this machine's payback period, assuming that cash flows occur evenly throughout each year. (Round the payback period to two decimals.)

4. Compute this machine's accounting rate of return, assuming that income is earned evenly throughout each year. (Round the percentage return to two decimals.)

5. Compute the net present value for this machine using a discount rate of 7% and assuming that cash flows occur at each year-end. (*Hint:* Salvage value is a cash inflow at the end of the asset's life. Round the net present value to the nearest dollar.)

PROBLEM SET A

Problem 25-1A
Computation of payback period, accounting rate of return, and net present value

P1   P2   P3

Check   (4) 21.56%

(5) $107,356

Most Company has an opportunity to invest in one of two new projects. Project Y requires a $350,000 investment for new machinery with a four-year life and no salvage value. Project Z requires a $350,000 investment for new machinery with a three-year life and no salvage value. The two projects yield the following predicted annual results. The company uses straight-line depreciation, and cash flows occur evenly throughout each year.

	Project Y	Project Z
Sales	$350,000	$280,000
Expenses		
Direct materials	49,000	35,000
Direct labor...............................	70,000	42,000
Overhead including depreciation	126,000	126,000
Selling and administrative expenses	25,000	25,000
Total expenses	270,000	228,000
Pretax income.............................	80,000	52,000
Income taxes (30%)	24,000	15,600
Net income................................	$ 56,000	$ 36,400

Required

1. Compute each project's annual expected net cash flows. (Round the net cash flows to the nearest dollar.)

2. Determine each project's payback period. (Round the payback period to two decimals.)

3. Compute each project's accounting rate of return. (Round the percentage return to one decimal.)

4. Determine each project's net present value using 8% as the discount rate. For part 4 only, assume that cash flows occur at each year-end. (Round the net present value to the nearest dollar.)

Analysis Component

5. Identify the project you would recommend to management and explain your choice.

Problem 25-2A
Analysis and computation of payback period, accounting rate of return, and net present value

P1   P2   P3

Check   For Project Y:
(2) 2.44 years, (3) 32%

(4) $125,286

Problem 25-3A
Computation of cash flows and net present values with alternative depreciation methods

P3

Manning Corporation is considering a new project requiring a $90,000 investment in test equipment with no salvage value. The project would produce $66,000 of pretax income before depreciation at the end of each of the next six years. The company's income tax rate is 40%. In compiling its tax return and computing its income tax payments, the company can choose between the two alternative depreciation schedules shown in the table.

	Straight-Line Depreciation	MACRS Depreciation*
Year 1	$ 9,000	$18,000
Year 2	18,000	28,800
Year 3	18,000	17,280
Year 4	18,000	10,368
Year 5	18,000	10,368
Year 6	9,000	5,184
Totals...........	$90,000	$90,000

* The modified accelerated cost recovery system (MACRS) for depreciation is discussed in Chapter 10.

Required

1. Prepare a five-column table that reports amounts (assuming use of straight-line depreciation) for each of the following for each of the six years: (a) pretax income before depreciation, (b) straight-line depreciation expense, (c) taxable income, (d) income taxes, and (e) net cash flow. Net cash flow equals the amount of income before depreciation minus the income taxes. (Round answers to the nearest dollar.)

2. Prepare a five-column table that reports amounts (assuming use of MACRS depreciation) for each of the following for each of the six years: (a) pretax income before depreciation, (b) MACRS depreciation expense, (c) taxable income, (d) income taxes, and (e) net cash flow. Net cash flow equals the income amount before depreciation minus the income taxes. (Round answers to the nearest dollar.)

Check Net present value: (3) $108,518

(4) $110,303

3. Compute the net present value of the investment if straight-line depreciation is used. Use 10% as the discount rate. (Round the net present value to the nearest dollar.)

4. Compute the net present value of the investment if MACRS depreciation is used. Use 10% as the discount rate. (Round the net present value to the nearest dollar.)

Analysis Component

5. Explain why the MACRS depreciation method increases this project's net present value.

Problem 25-4A
Analysis of income effects of additional business

A1

Jones Products manufactures and sells to wholesalers approximately 400,000 packages per year of underwater markers at $6 per package. Annual costs for the production and sale of this quantity are shown in the table.

Direct materials	$ 576,000
Direct labor......................	144,000
Overhead	320,000
Selling expenses.................	150,000
Administrative expenses	100,000
Total costs and expenses...........	$1,290,000

A new wholesaler has offered to buy 50,000 packages for $5.20 each. These markers would be marketed under the wholesaler's name and would not affect Jones Products's sales through its normal channels. A study of the costs of this additional business reveals the following:

● Direct materials costs are 100% variable.

● Per unit direct labor costs for the additional units would be 50% higher than normal because their production would require overtime pay at 1½ times the usual labor rate.

● Twenty-five percent of the normal annual overhead costs are fixed at any production level from 350,000 to 500,000 units. The remaining 75% of the annual overhead cost is variable with volume.

● Accepting the new business would involve no additional selling expenses.

● Accepting the new business would increase administrative expenses by a $5,000 fixed amount.

Required

Prepare a three-column comparative income statement that shows the following:

1. Annual operating income without the special order (column 1).
2. Annual operating income received from the new business only (column 2).
3. Combined annual operating income from normal business and the new business (column 3).

Check   Operating income:
(1) $1,110,000
         (2) $126,000

Edgerron Company is able to produce two products, G and B, with the same machine in its factory. The following information is available.

Problem 25-5A

Analysis of sales mix strategies

A1

	Product G	Product B
Selling price per unit	$120	$160
Variable costs per unit	40	90
Contribution margin per unit	$ 80	$ 70
Machine hours to produce 1 unit.............	0.4 hours	1.0 hours
Maximum unit sales per month	600 units	200 units

The company presently operates the machine for a single eight-hour shift for 22 working days each month. Management is thinking about operating the machine for two shifts, which will increase its productivity by another eight hours per day for 22 days per month. This change would require $15,000 additional fixed costs per month.

Required

1. Determine the contribution margin per machine hour that each product generates.
2. How many units of Product G and Product B should the company produce if it continues to operate with only one shift? How much total contribution margin does this mix produce each month?
3. If the company adds another shift, how many units of Product G and Product B should it produce? How much total contribution margin would this mix produce each month? Should the company add the new shift? Explain.
4. Suppose that the company determines that it can increase Product G's maximum sales to 700 units per month by spending $12,000 per month in marketing efforts. Should the company pursue this strategy and the double shift? Explain.

Check   Units of Product G:
(2) 440
(3) 600

Elegant Decor Company's management is trying to decide whether to eliminate Department 200, which has produced losses or low profits for several years. The company's 2017 departmental income statements show the following.

Problem 25-6A

Analysis of possible elimination of a department

A1

ELEGANT DECOR COMPANY Departmental Income Statements For Year Ended December 31, 2017	Dept. 100	Dept. 200	Combined
Sales	$436,000	$290,000	$726,000
Cost of goods sold	262,000	207,000	469,000
Gross profit................................	174,000	83,000	257,000
Operating expenses			
Direct expenses			
Advertising............................	17,000	12,000	29,000
Store supplies used.....................	4,000	3,800	7,800
Depreciation—Store equipment.............	5,000	3,300	8,300
Total direct expenses	26,000	19,100	45,100
Allocated expenses			
Sales salaries..........................	65,000	39,000	104,000
Rent expense...........................	9,440	4,720	14,160
Bad debts expense	9,900	8,100	18,000
Office salary............................	18,720	12,480	31,200
Insurance expense	2,000	1,100	3,100
Miscellaneous office expenses.............	2,400	1,600	4,000
Total allocated expenses...................	107,460	67,000	174,460
Total expenses	133,460	86,100	219,560
Net income (loss)	$ 40,540	$ (3,100)	$ 37,440

In analyzing whether to eliminate Department 200, management considers the following:

a. The company has one office worker who earns $600 per week, or $31,200 per year, and four sales-clerks who each earns $500 per week, or $26,000 per year for each salesclerk.

b. The full salaries of two salesclerks are charged to Department 100. The full salary of one salesclerk is charged to Department 200. The salary of the fourth clerk, who works half-time in both departments, is divided evenly between the two departments.

c. Eliminating Department 200 would avoid the sales salaries and the office salary currently allocated to it. However, management prefers another plan. Two salesclerks have indicated that they will be quit-ting soon. Management believes that their work can be done by the other two clerks if the one office worker works in sales half-time. Eliminating Department 200 will allow this shift of duties. If this change is implemented, half the office worker's salary would be reported as sales salaries and half would be reported as office salary.

d. The store building is rented under a long-term lease that cannot be changed. Therefore, Department 100 will use the space and equipment currently used by Department 200.

e. Closing Department 200 will eliminate its expenses for advertising, bad debts, and store supplies; 70% of the insurance expense allocated to it to cover its merchandise inventory; and 25% of the miscella-neous office expenses presently allocated to it.

Required

Check (1) Total expenses: (a) $688,560, (b) $284,070

1. Prepare a three-column report that lists items and amounts for (a) the company's total expenses (including cost of goods sold)—in column 1, (b) the expenses that would be eliminated by closing Department 200—in column 2, and (c) the expenses that will continue—in column 3.

(2) Forecasted net income without Department 200, $31,510

2. Prepare a forecasted annual income statement for the company reflecting the elimination of Department 200 assuming that it will not affect Department 100's sales and gross profit. The state-ment should reflect the reassignment of the office worker to one-half time as a salesclerk.

Analysis Component

3. Reconcile the company's combined net income with the forecasted net income assuming that Department 200 is eliminated (list both items and amounts). Analyze the reconciliation and explain why you think the department should or should not be eliminated.

PROBLEM SET B

Problem 25-1B
Computation of payback period, accounting rate of return, and net present value

P1 P2 P3

Cortino Company is planning to add a new product to its line. To manufacture this product, the company needs to buy a new machine at a $300,000 cost with an expected four-year life and a $20,000 salvage value. All sales are for cash and all costs are out-of-pocket, except for depreciation on the new machine. Additional information includes the following.

Expected annual sales of new product.....................................	$1,150,000
Expected annual costs of new product	
Direct materials	300,000
Direct labor...	420,000
Overhead (excluding straight-line depreciation on new machine)..............	210,000
Selling and administrative expenses	100,000
Income taxes	30%

Required

1. Compute straight-line depreciation for each year of this new machine's life. (Round depreciation amounts to the nearest dollar.)

2. Determine expected net income and net cash flow for each year of this machine's life. (Round answers to the nearest dollar.)

3. Compute this machine's payback period, assuming that cash flows occur evenly throughout each year. (Round the payback period to two decimals.)

Check (4) 21.88%

4. Compute this machine's accounting rate of return, assuming that income is earned evenly throughout each year. (Round the percentage return to two decimals.)

(5) $70,915

5. Compute the net present value for this machine using a discount rate of 7% and assuming that cash flows occur at each year-end. (*Hint:* Salvage value is a cash inflow at the end of the asset's life.)

Aikman Company has an opportunity to invest in one of two projects. Project A requires a $240,000 investment for new machinery with a four-year life and no salvage value. Project B also requires a $240,000 investment for new machinery with a three-year life and no salvage value. The two projects yield the following predicted annual results. The company uses straight-line depreciation, and cash flows occur evenly throughout each year.

Problem 25-2B

Analysis and computation of payback period, accounting rate of return, and net present value

P1   P2   P3

	Project A	Project B
Sales	$250,000	$200,000
Expenses		
Direct materials	35,000	25,000
Direct labor..........................	50,000	30,000
Overhead including depreciation	90,000	90,000
Selling and administrative expenses ...	18,000	18,000
Total expenses	193,000	163,000
Pretax income........................	57,000	37,000
Income taxes (30%)	17,100	11,100
Net income	$ 39,900	$ 25,900

Required

1. Compute each project's annual expected net cash flows. (Round net cash flows to the nearest dollar.)
2. Determine each project's payback period. (Round the payback period to two decimals.)
3. Compute each project's accounting rate of return. (Round the percentage return to one decimal.)
4. Determine each project's net present value using 8% as the discount rate. For part 4 only, assume that cash flows occur at each year-end. (Round net present values to the nearest dollar.)

Analysis Component

5. Identify the project you would recommend to management and explain your choice.

Check   For Project A:

(2) 2.4 years

(3) 33.3%

(4) $90,879

Grossman Corporation is considering a new project requiring a $30,000 investment in an asset having no salvage value. The project would produce $12,000 of pretax income before depreciation at the end of each of the next six years. The company's income tax rate is 40%. In compiling its tax return and computing its income tax payments, the company can choose between two alternative depreciation schedules as shown in the table.

Problem 25-3B

Computation of cash flows and net present values with alternative depreciation methods

P3

	Straight-Line Depreciation	MACRS Depreciation*
Year 1	$ 3,000	$ 6,000
Year 2	6,000	9,600
Year 3	6,000	5,760
Year 4	6,000	3,456
Year 5	6,000	3,456
Year 6	3,000	1,728
Totals.......	$30,000	$30,000

* The modified accelerated cost recovery system (MACRS) for depreciation is discussed in Chapter 10.

Required

1. Prepare a five-column table that reports amounts (assuming use of straight-line depreciation) for each of the following items for each of the six years: (a) pretax income before depreciation, (b) straight-line depreciation expense, (c) taxable income, (d) income taxes, and (e) net cash flow. Net cash flow equals the amount of income before depreciation minus the income taxes. (Round answers to the nearest dollar.)
2. Prepare a five-column table that reports amounts (assuming use of MACRS depreciation) for each of the following items for each of the six years: (a) pretax income before depreciation, (b) MACRS depreciation expense, (c) taxable income, (d) income taxes, and (e) net cash flow. Net cash flow equals the amount of income before depreciation minus the income taxes. (Round answers to the nearest dollar.)

3. Compute the net present value of the investment if straight-line depreciation is used. Use 10% as the discount rate. (Round the net present value to the nearest dollar.)

4. Compute the net present value of the investment if MACRS depreciation is used. Use 10% as the discount rate. (Round the net present value to the nearest dollar.)

Analysis Component

5. Explain why the MACRS depreciation method increases the net present value of this project.

Problem 25-4B
Analysis of income effects
of additional business

A1

Windmire Company manufactures and sells to local wholesalers approximately 300,000 units per month at a sales price of $4 per unit. Monthly costs for the production and sale of this quantity follow.

Direct materials	$384,000
Direct labor	96,000
Overhead	288,000
Selling expenses.	120,000
Administrative expenses	80,000
Total costs and expenses.	$968,000

A new out-of-state distributor has offered to buy 50,000 units next month for $3.44 each. These units would be marketed in other states and would not affect Windmire's sales through its normal channels. A study of the costs of this new business reveals the following:

● Direct materials costs are 100% variable.

● Per unit direct labor costs for the additional units would be 50% higher than normal because their production would require overtime pay at 1½ their normal rate to meet the distributor's deadline.

● Twenty-five percent of the normal annual overhead costs are fixed at any production level from 250,000 to 400,000 units. The remaining 75% is variable with volume.

● Accepting the new business would involve no additional selling expenses.

● Accepting the new business would increase administrative expenses by a $4,000 fixed amount.

Required

Prepare a three-column comparative income statement that shows the following:

1. Monthly operating income without the special order (column 1).

2. Monthly operating income received from the new business only (column 2).

3. Combined monthly operating income from normal business and the new business (column 3).

Problem 25-5B
Analysis of sales
mix strategies

A1

Sung Company is able to produce two products, R and T, with the same machine in its factory. The following information is available.

	Product R	Product T
Selling price per unit	$60	$80
Variable costs per unit	20	45
Contribution margin per unit	$40	$35
Machine hours to produce 1 unit	0.4 hours	1.0 hours
Maximum unit sales per month	550 units	175 units

The company presently operates the machine for a single eight-hour shift for 22 working days each month. Management is thinking about operating the machine for two shifts, which will increase its productivity by another eight hours per day for 22 days per month. This change would require $3,250 additional fixed costs per month.

Required

1. Determine the contribution margin per machine hour that each product generates.

2. How many units of Product R and Product T should the company produce if it continues to operate with only one shift? How much total contribution margin does this mix produce each month?

3. If the company adds another shift, how many units of Product R and Product T should it produce? How much total contribution margin would this mix produce each month? Should the company add the new shift? Explain.

4. Suppose that the company determines that it can increase Product R's maximum sales to 675 units per month by spending $4,500 per month in marketing efforts. Should the company pursue this strategy and the double shift? Explain.

Check   Units of Product R:

(2) 440

(3) 550

Esme Company's management is trying to decide whether to eliminate Department Z, which has produced low profits or losses for several years. The company's 2017 departmental income statements show the following.

Problem 25-6B
Analysis of possible elimination of a department

A1

ESME COMPANY Departmental Income Statements For Year Ended December 31, 2017	Dept. A	Dept. Z	Combined
Sales	$700,000	$175,000	$875,000
Cost of goods sold	461,300	125,100	586,400
Gross profit	238,700	49,900	288,600
Operating expenses			
Direct expenses			
Advertising	27,000	3,000	30,000
Store supplies used	5,600	1,400	7,000
Depreciation—Store equipment	14,000	7,000	21,000
Total direct expenses	46,600	11,400	58,000
Allocated expenses			
Sales salaries	70,200	23,400	93,600
Rent expense	22,080	5,520	27,600
Bad debts expense	21,000	4,000	25,000
Office salary	20,800	5,200	26,000
Insurance expense	4,200	1,400	5,600
Miscellaneous office expenses	1,700	2,500	4,200
Total allocated expenses	139,980	42,020	182,000
Total expenses	186,580	53,420	240,000
Net income (loss)	$ 52,120	$ (3,520)	$ 48,600

In analyzing whether to eliminate Department Z, management considers the following items:

a. The company has one office worker who earns $500 per week or $26,000 per year and four salesclerks who each earns $450 per week, or $23,400 per year for each salesclerk.

b. The full salaries of three salesclerks are charged to Department A. The full salary of one salesclerk is charged to Department Z.

c. Eliminating Department Z would avoid the sales salaries and the office salary currently allocated to it. However, management prefers another plan. Two salesclerks have indicated that they will be quitting soon. Management believes that their work can be done by the two remaining clerks if the one office worker works in sales half-time. Eliminating Department Z will allow this shift of duties. If this change is implemented, half the office worker's salary would be reported as sales salaries and half would be reported as office salary.

d. The store building is rented under a long-term lease that cannot be changed. Therefore, Department A will use the space and equipment currently used by Department Z.

e. Closing Department Z will eliminate its expenses for advertising, bad debts, and store supplies; 65% of the insurance expense allocated to it to cover its merchandise inventory; and 30% of the miscellaneous office expenses presently allocated to it.

Required

1. Prepare a three-column report that lists items and amounts for (a) the company's total expenses (including cost of goods sold)—in column 1, (b) the expenses that would be eliminated by closing Department Z—in column 2, and (c) the expenses that will continue—in column 3.

2. Prepare a forecasted annual income statement for the company reflecting the elimination of Department Z assuming that it will not affect Department A's sales and gross profit. The statement should reflect the reassignment of the office worker to one-half time as a salesclerk.

Analysis Component

3. Reconcile the company's combined net income with the forecasted net income assuming that Department Z is eliminated (list both items and amounts). Analyze the reconciliation and explain why you think the department should or should not be eliminated.

SERIAL PROBLEM

Business Solutions

P1   P2

© Alexander Image/Shutterstock RF

(This serial problem began in Chapter 1 and continues through most of the book. If previous chapter segments were not completed, the serial problem can begin at this point.)

SP 25   Santana Rey is considering the purchase of equipment for **Business Solutions** that would allow the company to add a new product to its computer furniture line. The equipment is expected to cost $300,000 and to have a six-year life and no salvage value. It will be depreciated on a straight-line basis. Business Solutions expects to sell 100 units of the equipment's product each year. The expected annual income related to this equipment follows.

Sales	$375,000
Costs	
Materials, labor, and overhead (except depreciation)	200,000
Depreciation on new equipment	50,000
Selling and administrative expenses	37,500
Total costs and expenses	287,500
Pretax income	87,500
Income taxes (30%)	26,250
Net income	$ 61,250

Required

Compute the (1) payback period and (2) accounting rate of return for this equipment. (Record ARR answers as percents, rounded to one decimal.)

Beyond the Numbers

REPORTING IN ACTION

P3

APPLE

BTN 25-1   Assume **Apple** invested $2.12 billion to expand its manufacturing capacity. Assume that these assets have a 10-year life, and that Apple requires a 10% internal rate of return on these assets.

Required

1. What is the amount of annual cash flows that Apple must earn from these projects to have a 10% internal rate of return? (*Hint:* Identify the 10-period, 10% factor from the present value of an annuity table, and then divide $2.12 billion by this factor to get the annual cash flows necessary.)

Fast Forward

2. Access Apple's financial statements for fiscal years ended after September 26, 2015, from its website (Apple.com) or the SEC's website (SEC.gov).

   a. Determine the amount that Apple invested in capital assets for the most recent year. (*Hint:* Refer to the statement of cash flows.)

   b. Assume a 10-year life and a 10% internal rate of return. What is the amount of cash flows that Apple must earn on these new projects?

BTN 25-2   Apple and Google sell a variety of products. Some products are more profitable than others. Teams of employees in each company make advertising, investment, and product mix decisions. A certain portion of advertising for both companies is on a local basis to a target audience.

COMPARATIVE ANALYSIS

A1

APPLE

GOOGLE

Required

1. Contact the local newspaper and ask the approximate cost of ad space (for example, cost of one page or one-half page of advertising) for a company's product or group of products (such as Apple iPads).
2. Estimate how many products this advertisement must sell to justify its cost. Begin by taking the product's sales price advertised for each company and assume a 20% contribution margin.
3. Prepare a half-page memorandum explaining the importance of effective advertising when making a product mix decision. Be prepared to present your ideas in class.

BTN 25-3   A consultant commented that "too often the numbers look good but feel bad." This comment often stems from *estimation error* common to capital budgeting proposals that relate to future cash flows. Three reasons for this error often exist. First, reliably predicting cash flows several years into the future is very difficult. Second, the present value of cash flows many years into the future (say, beyond 10 years) is often very small. Third, personal biases and expectations can influence present value computations.

ETHICS CHALLENGE

P3

Required

1. Compute the present value of $100 to be received in 10 years assuming a 12% discount rate.
2. Why is understanding the three reasons mentioned for estimation error important when evaluating investment projects? Link this response to your answer for part 1.

BTN 25-4   Payback period, accounting rate of return, net present value, and internal rate of return are common methods to evaluate capital investment opportunities. Assume that your manager asks you to identify the measurement basis and unit that each method offers and to list the advantages and disadvantages of each method. Present your response in memorandum format of less than one page.

COMMUNICATING IN PRACTICE

P1   P2   P3   P4

BTN 25-5   Many companies must determine whether to internally produce their component parts or to outsource them. Further, some companies now outsource key components or business processes to international providers. Access the website SourcingMag.com and review the available information on business process outsourcing (click on "What is BPO?").

TAKING IT TO THE NET

A1

Required

1. According to this website, what is business process outsourcing?
2. What types of processes are commonly outsourced, according to this website?
3. What are some of the benefits of business process outsourcing?

BTN 25-6   Break into teams and identify four reasons that an international airline such as Southwest or Delta would invest in a project when an analysis using both payback period and net present value indicate it to be a poor investment. (*Hint:* Think about qualitative factors.) Provide an example of an investment project that supports your answer.

TEAMWORK IN ACTION

P1   P3

BTN 25-7   Read the chapter opener about Caron Proschan and her company, Simply Gum. Suppose Caron's business continues to grow, and she builds a massive new manufacturing facility and warehousing center to make her business more efficient and reduce costs.

ENTREPRENEURIAL DECISION

P1   P2   P3   P4

Required

1. What are some of the management tools that Caron can use to evaluate whether the new manufacturing facility and warehousing center will be a good investment?
2. What information does Caron need to use the tools that you identified in your answer to part 1?
3. What are some of the advantages and disadvantages of each tool identified in your answer to part 1?

HITTING THE ROAD

P3

BTN 25-8   Visit or call a local auto dealership and inquire about leasing a car. Ask about the down payment and the required monthly payments. You will likely find the salesperson does not discuss the cost to purchase this car but focuses on the affordability of the monthly payments. This chapter gives you the tools to compute the cost of this car using the lease payment schedule in present dollars and to estimate the profit from leasing for an auto dealership.

Required

1. Compare the cost of leasing the car to buying it in present dollars using the information from the dealership you contact. (Assume you will make a final payment at the end of the lease and then own the car.)

2. Is it more costly to lease or buy the car? Support your answer with computations.

GLOBAL DECISION

C1

Samsung

BTN 25-9   Samsung's 2016 Corporate Sustainability Report notes that the company spent 523 billion Korean won in 2015 for programs devoted to better health and education for children.

Required

Explain why a company like Samsung would pursue such a costly program.

 **GLOBAL VIEW**

Siemens AG is a global electrical engineering and electronics company headquartered in Germany. Recently, the company invested £160 million to build a wind turbine plant in the United Kingdom. Net present value analyses support such decisions. In this case, Siemens foresees strong future cash flows based on increased demand for clean sources of energy, such as wind power.

 Global View Assignments

Discussion Question 12

Discussion Question 15

Quick Study 25-29

BTN 25-9

appendix A

Financial Statement Information

This appendix includes financial information for (1) **Apple**, (2) **Google**, and (3) **Samsung**. Apple states that it designs, manufactures, and markets mobile communication and media devices, personal computers, and portable digital music players, and sells a variety of related software, services, peripherals, networking solutions, and third-party digital content and applications; it competes with both Google and Samsung in the United States and globally. The information in this appendix is taken from their annual 10-K reports (or annual report for Samsung) filed with the SEC or other regulatory agency. An **annual report** is a summary of a company's financial results for the year along with its current financial condition and future plans. This report is directed to external users of financial information, but it also affects the actions and decisions of internal users.

A company often uses an annual report to showcase itself and its products. Many annual reports include photos, diagrams, and illustrations related to the company. The primary objective of annual reports, however, is the financial section, which communicates much information about a company, with most data drawn from the accounting information system. The layout of an annual report's financial section is fairly established and typically includes the following:

- Letter to Shareholders
- Financial History and Highlights
- Management Discussion and Analysis
- Management's Report on Financial Statements and on Internal Controls
- Report of Independent Accountants (Auditor's Report) and on Internal Controls
- Financial Statements
- Notes to Financial Statements
- List of Directors and Officers

This appendix provides the financial statements for Apple (plus selected notes), Google, and Samsung. The appendix is organized as follows:

- Apple **A-2** through **A-9**
- Google **A-10** through **A-13**
- Samsung **A-14** through **A-17**

Many assignments at the end of each chapter refer to information in this appendix. We encourage readers to spend time with these assignments; they are especially useful in showing the relevance and diversity of financial accounting and reporting.

APPLE
GOOGLE
Samsung

Special note: The SEC maintains the EDGAR (**E**lectronic **D**ata **G**athering, **A**nalysis, and **R**etrieval) database at **SEC.gov** for U.S. filers. The **Form 10-K** is the annual report form for most companies. It provides electronically accessible information. The **Form 10-KSB** is the annual report form filed by small businesses. It requires slightly less information than the Form 10-K. One of these forms must be filed within 90 days after the company's fiscal year-end. (Forms 10-K405, 10-KT, 10-KT405, and 10-KSB405 are slight variations of the usual form due to certain regulations or rules.)

APPLE

Apple Inc.
CONSOLIDATED BALANCE SHEETS
(In millions, except number of shares which are reflected in thousands and par value)

	September 26, 2015	September 27, 2014
ASSETS		
Current assets		
Cash and cash equivalents	$ 21,120	$ 13,844
Short-term marketable securities	20,481	11,233
Accounts receivable, less allowances of $82 and $86, respectively	16,849	17,460
Inventories	2,349	2,111
Deferred tax assets	5,546	4,318
Vendor non-trade receivables	13,494	9,759
Other current assets	9,539	9,806
Total current assets	89,378	68,531
Long-term marketable securities	164,065	130,162
Property, plant and equipment, net	22,471	20,624
Goodwill	5,116	4,616
Acquired intangible assets, net	3,893	4,142
Other assets	5,556	3,764
Total assets	$ 290,479	$ 231,839
LIABILITIES AND SHAREHOLDERS' EQUITY		
Current liabilities		
Accounts payable	$ 35,490	$ 30,196
Accrued expenses	25,181	18,453
Deferred revenue	8,940	8,491
Commercial paper	8,499	6,308
Current portion of long-term debt	2,500	0
Total current liabilities	80,610	63,448
Deferred revenue – non-current	3,624	3,031
Long-term debt	53,463	28,987
Other non-current liabilities	33,427	24,826
Total liabilities	171,124	120,292
Commitments and contingencies		
Shareholders' equity		
Common stock and additional paid-in capital, $0.00001 par value: 12,600,000 shares authorized; 5,578,753 and 5,866,161 shares issued and outstanding, respectively	27,416	23,313
Retained earnings	92,284	87,152
Accumulated other comprehensive income	(345)	1,082
Total shareholders' equity	119,355	111,547
Total liabilities and shareholders' equity	$ 290,479	$ 231,839

See accompanying Notes to Consolidated Financial Statements.

Apple Inc.
CONSOLIDATED STATEMENTS OF OPERATIONS
(In millions, except number of shares which are reflected in thousands and per share amounts)

Years ended	September 26, 2015	September 27, 2014	September 28, 2013
Net sales	$ 233,715	$ 182,795	$ 170,910
Cost of sales	140,089	112,258	106,606
Gross margin	93,626	70,537	64,304
Operating expenses			
Research and development	8,067	6,041	4,475
Selling, general and administrative	14,329	11,993	10,830
Total operating expenses	22,396	18,034	15,305
Operating income	71,230	52,503	48,999
Other income, net	1,285	980	1,156
Income before provision for income taxes	72,515	53,483	50,155
Provision for income taxes	19,121	13,973	13,118
Net income	$ 53,394	$ 39,510	$ 37,037
Earnings per share:			
Basic	$ 9.28	$ 6.49	$ 5.72
Diluted	$ 9.22	$ 6.45	$ 5.68
Shares used in computing earnings per share:			
Basic	5,753,421	6,085,572	6,477,320
Diluted	5,793,069	6,122,663	6,521,634
Cash dividends declared per common share	$ 1.98	$ 1.82	$ 1.64

See accompanying Notes to Consolidated Financial Statements.

Apple Inc.
CONSOLIDATED STATEMENTS OF COMPREHENSIVE INCOME
(In millions)

Years ended	September 26, 2015	September 27, 2014	September 28, 2013
Net income	$ 53,394	$ 39,510	$ 37,037
Other comprehensive income (loss):			
Change in foreign currency translation, net of tax effects of $201, $50 and $35, respectively	(411)	(137)	(112)
Change in unrealized gains/losses on derivative instruments:			
Change in fair value of derivatives, net of tax benefit (expense) of $(441), $(297) and $(351), respectively	2,905	1,390	522
Adjustment for net losses (gains) realized and included in net income, net of tax expense (benefit) of $630, $(36) and $255, respectively	(3,497)	149	(458)
Total change in unrecognized gains/losses on derivative instruments, net of tax	(592)	1,539	64
Change in unrealized gains/losses on marketable securities:			
Change in fair value of marketable securities, net of tax benefit (expense) of $264, $(153) and $458, respectively	(483)	285	(791)
Adjustment for net (gains) losses realized and included in net income, net of tax expense (benefit) of $(32), $71 and $82, respectively	59	(134)	(131)
Total change in unrealized gains/losses on marketable securities, net of tax	(424)	151	(922)
Total other comprehensive income (loss)	(1,427)	1,553	(970)
Total comprehensive income	$ 51,967	$ 41,063	$ 36,067

See accompanying Notes to Consolidated Financial Statements.

APPLE

Apple Inc.
CONSOLIDATED STATEMENTS OF SHAREHOLDERS' EQUITY
(In millions, except number of shares which are reflected in thousands)

	Common Stock and Additional Paid-In Capital		Retained Earnings	Accumulated Other Comprehensive Income (Loss)	Total Shareholders' Equity
	Shares	Amount			
Balances as of September 29, 2012	6,574,458	$ 16,422	$ 101,289	$ 499	$ 118,210
Net income	0	0	37,037	0	37,037
Other comprehensive income (loss)	0	0	0	(970)	(970)
Dividends and dividend equivalents declared	0	0	(10,676)	0	(10,676)
Repurchase of common stock	(328,837)	0	(22,950)	0	(22,950)
Share-based compensation	0	2,253	0	0	2,253
Common stock issued, net of shares withheld for employee taxes	48,873	(143)	(444)	0	(587)
Tax benefit from equity awards, including transfer pricing adjustments	0	1,232	0	0	1,232
Balances as of September 28, 2013	6,294,494	19,764	104,256	(471)	123,549
Net income	0	0	39,510	0	39,510
Other comprehensive income (loss)	0	0	0	1,553	1,553
Dividends and dividend equivalents declared	0	0	(11,215)	0	(11,215)
Repurchase of common stock	(488,677)	0	(45,000)	0	(45,000)
Share-based compensation	0	2,863	0	0	2,863
Common stock issued, net of shares withheld for employee taxes	60,344	(49)	(399)	0	(448)
Tax benefit from equity awards, including transfer pricing adjustments	0	735	0	0	735
Balances as of September 27, 2014	5,866,161	23,313	87,152	1,082	111,547
Net income	0	0	53,394	0	53,394
Other comprehensive income (loss)	0	0	0	(1,427)	(1,427)
Dividends and dividend equivalents declared	0	0	(11,627)	0	(11,627)
Repurchase of common stock	(325,032)	0	(36,026)	0	(36,026)
Share-based compensation	0	3,586	0	0	3,586
Common stock issued, net of shares withheld for employee taxes	37,624	(231)	(609)	0	(840)
Tax benefit from equity awards, including transfer pricing adjustments	0	748	0	0	748
Balances as of September 26, 2015	5,578,753	$ 27,416	$ 92,284	$ (345)	$ 119,355

See accompanying Notes to Consolidated Financial Statements.

Apple Inc.
CONSOLIDATED STATEMENTS OF CASH FLOWS
(In millions)

Years ended	September 26, 2015	September 27, 2014	September 28, 2013
Cash and cash equivalents, beginning of the year	$ 13,844	$ 14,259	$ 10,746
Operating activities:			
Net income	53,394	39,510	37,037
Adjustments to reconcile net income to cash generated by operating activities:			
Depreciation and amortization	11,257	7,946	6,757
Share-based compensation expense	3,586	2,863	2,253
Deferred income tax expense	1,382	2,347	1,141
Changes in operating assets and liabilities:			
Accounts receivable, net	611	(4,232)	(2,172)
Inventories	(238)	(76)	(973)
Vendor non-trade receivables	(3,735)	(2,220)	223
Other current and non-current assets	(179)	167	1,080
Accounts payable	5,400	5,938	2,340
Deferred revenue	1,042	1,460	1,459
Other current and non-current liabilities	8,746	6,010	4,521
Cash generated by operating activities	81,266	59,713	53,666
Investing activities:			
Purchases of marketable securities	(166,402)	(217,128)	(148,489)
Proceeds from maturities of marketable securities	14,538	18,810	20,317
Proceeds from sales of marketable securities	107,447	189,301	104,130
Payments made in connection with business acquisitions, net	(343)	(3,765)	(496)
Payments for acquisition of property, plant and equipment	(11,247)	(9,571)	(8,165)
Payments for acquisition of intangible assets	(241)	(242)	(911)
Other	(26)	16	(160)
Cash used in investing activities	(56,274)	(22,579)	(33,774)
Financing activities:			
Proceeds from issuance of common stock	543	730	530
Excess tax benefits from equity awards	749	739	701
Taxes paid related to net share settlement of equity awards	(1,499)	(1,158)	(1,082)
Dividends and dividend equivalents paid	(11,561)	(11,126)	(10,564)
Repurchase of common stock	(35,253)	(45,000)	(22,860)
Proceeds from issuance of term debt, net	27,114	11,960	16,896
Change in commercial paper, net	2,191	6,306	0
Cash used in financing activities	(17,716)	(37,549)	(16,379)
Increase (decrease) in cash and cash equivalents	7,276	(415)	3,513
Cash and cash equivalents, end of the year	$ 21,120	$ 13,844	$ 14,259
Supplemental cash flow disclosure:			
Cash paid for income taxes, net	$ 13,252	$ 10,026	$ 9,128
Cash paid for interest	$ 514	$ 339	$ 0

See accompanying Notes to Consolidated Financial Statements.

APPLE

APPLE

APPLE INC.
SELECTED NOTES TO CONSOLIDATED FINANCIAL STATEMENTS

Basis of Presentation and Preparation

The Company's fiscal year is the 52 or 53-week period that ends on the last Saturday of September. The Company's fiscal years 2015, 2014 and 2013 ended on September 26, 2015, September 27, 2014 and September 28, 2013, respectively. An additional week is included in the first fiscal quarter approximately every six years to realign fiscal quarters with calendar quarters. Fiscal years 2015, 2014 and 2013 each spanned 52 weeks. Unless otherwise stated, references to particular years, quarters, months and periods refer to the Company's fiscal years ended in September and the associated quarters, months and periods of those fiscal years.

Revenue Recognition

Net sales consist primarily of revenue from the sale of hardware, software, digital content and applications, accessories, and service and support contracts. The Company recognizes revenue when persuasive evidence of an arrangement exists, delivery has occurred, the sales price is fixed or determinable and collection is probable. Product is considered delivered to the customer once it has been shipped and title, risk of loss and rewards of ownership have been transferred. For most of the Company's product sales, these criteria are met at the time the product is shipped. For online sales to individuals, for some sales to education customers in the U.S., and for certain other sales, the Company defers revenue until the customer receives the product because the Company retains a portion of the risk of loss on these sales during transit. For payment terms in excess of the Company's standard payment terms, revenue is recognized as payments become due unless the Company has positive evidence that the sales price is fixed or determinable, such as a successful history of collection, without concession, on comparable arrangements. The Company recognizes revenue from the sale of hardware products, software bundled with hardware that is essential to the functionality of the hardware and third-party digital content sold on the iTunes Store in accordance with general revenue recognition accounting guidance. The Company recognizes revenue in accordance with industry specific software accounting guidance for the following types of sales transactions: (i) standalone sales of software products, (ii) sales of software upgrades and (iii) sales of software bundled with hardware not essential to the functionality of the hardware.

For the sale of most third-party products, the Company recognizes revenue based on the gross amount billed to customers because the Company establishes its own pricing for such products, retains related inventory risk for physical products, is the primary obligor to the customer and assumes the credit risk for amounts billed to its customers. For third-party applications sold through the App Store and Mac App Store and certain digital content sold through the iTunes Store, the Company does not determine the selling price of the products and is not the primary obligor to the customer. Therefore, the Company accounts for such sales on a net basis by recognizing in net sales only the commission it retains from each sale. The portion of the gross amount billed to customers that is remitted by the Company to third-party app developers and certain digital content owners is not reflected in the Company's Consolidated Statements of Operations.

The Company records deferred revenue when it receives payments in advance of the delivery of products or the performance of services. This includes amounts that have been deferred for unspecified and specified software upgrade rights and non-software services that are attached to hardware and software products. The Company sells gift cards redeemable at its retail and online stores, and also sells gift cards redeemable on iTunes Store, App Store, Mac App Store and iBooks Store for the purchase of digital content and software. The Company records deferred revenue upon the sale of the card, which is relieved upon redemption of the card by the customer. Revenue from AppleCare service and support contracts is deferred and recognized over the service coverage periods. AppleCare service and support contracts typically include extended phone support, repair services, web-based support resources and diagnostic tools offered under the Company's standard limited warranty.

The Company records reductions to revenue for estimated commitments related to price protection and other customer incentive programs. For transactions involving price protection, the Company recognizes revenue net of the estimated amount to be refunded. For the Company's other customer incentive programs, the estimated cost of these programs is recognized at the later of the date at which the Company has sold the product or the date at which the program is offered. The Company also records reductions to revenue for expected future product returns based on the Company's historical experience. Revenue is recorded net of taxes collected from customers that are remitted to governmental authorities, with the collected taxes recorded as current liabilities until remitted to the relevant government authority.

Shipping Costs

Amounts billed to customers related to shipping and handling are classified as revenue, and the Company's shipping and handling costs are classified as cost of sales.

Warranty Costs

The Company generally provides for the estimated cost of hardware and software warranties at the time the related revenue is recognized. The Company assesses the adequacy of its accrued warranty liabilities and adjusts the amounts as necessary based on actual experience and changes in future estimates.

Apple Inc. Notes—continued

Software Development Costs

Research and development ("R&D") costs are expensed as incurred. Development costs of computer software to be sold, leased, or otherwise marketed are subject to capitalization beginning when a product's technological feasibility has been established and ending when a product is available for general release to customers. In most instances, the Company's products are released soon after technological feasibility has been established and as a result software development costs were expensed as incurred.

Advertising Costs

Advertising costs are expensed as incurred and included in selling, general and administrative expenses. Advertising expense was $1.8 billion, $1.2 billion and $1.1 billion for 2015, 2014 and 2013, respectively.

Other Income and Expense

$ millions	2015	2014	2013
Interest and dividend income	$2,921	$1,795	$1,616
Interest expense	(733)	(384)	(136)
Other expense, net	(903)	(431)	(324)
Total other income (expense), net	$1,285	$ 980	$1,156

Earnings Per Share

Basic earnings per share is computed by dividing income available to common shareholders by the weighted-average number of shares of common stock outstanding during the period. Diluted earnings per share is computed by dividing income available to common shareholders by the weighted-average number of shares of common stock outstanding during the period increased to include the number of additional shares of common stock that would have been outstanding if the potentially dilutive securities had been issued.

Cash Equivalents and Marketable Securities

All highly liquid investments with maturities of three months or less at the date of purchase are classified as cash equivalents. The Company's marketable debt and equity securities have been classified and accounted for as available-for-sale. Management determines the appropriate classification of its investments at the time of purchase and reevaluates the classifications at each balance sheet date. The Company classifies its marketable debt securities as either short-term or long-term based on each instrument's underlying contractual maturity date. Marketable debt securities with maturities of 12 months or less are classified as short-term and marketable debt securities with maturities greater than 12 months are classified as long-term. Marketable equity securities, including mutual funds, are classified as either short-term or long-term based on the nature of each security and its availability for use in current operations. The Company's marketable debt and equity securities are carried at fair value, with unrealized gains and

losses, net of taxes, reported as a component of accumulated other comprehensive income ("AOCI") in shareholders' equity, with the exception of unrealized losses believed to be other-than-temporary which are reported in earnings in the current period. The cost of securities sold is based upon the specific identification method.

Accounts Receivable (Trade Receivables)

The Company has considerable trade receivables outstanding with its third-party cellular network carriers, wholesalers, retailers, value-added resellers, small and mid-sized businesses, and education, enterprise and government customers.

As of September 26, 2015, the Company had one customer that represented 10% or more of total trade receivables, which accounted for 12%. The Company's cellular network carriers accounted for 71% and 72% of trade receivables as of September 26, 2015 and September 27, 2014, respectively.

Allowance for Doubtful Accounts

The Company records its allowance for doubtful accounts based upon its assessment of various factors, including historical experience, age of the accounts receivable balances, credit quality of the Company's customers, current economic conditions and other factors that may affect the customers' ability to pay.

Inventories

Inventories are stated at the lower of cost, computed using the first-in, first-out method and net realizable value. Any adjustments to reduce the cost of inventories to their net realizable value are recognized in earnings in the current period. As of September 26, 2015 and September 27, 2014, the Company's inventories consist primarily of finished goods.

Property, Plant and Equipment

Property, plant and equipment are stated at cost. Depreciation is computed by use of the straight-line method over the estimated useful lives of the assets, which for buildings is the lesser of 30 years or the remaining life of the underlying building; between one to five years for machinery and equipment, including product tooling and manufacturing process equipment; and the shorter of lease terms or ten years for leasehold improvements. The Company capitalizes eligible costs to acquire or develop internal-use software that are incurred subsequent to the preliminary project stage. Capitalized costs related to internal-use software are amortized using the straight-line method over the estimated useful lives of the assets, which range from three to five years. Depreciation and amortization expense on property and equipment was

Apple Inc. Notes—continued

$9.2 billion, $6.9 billion and $5.8 billion during 2015, 2014 and 2013, respectively.

Property, Plant and Equipment, Net

$ millions	2015	2014
Land and buildings	$ 6,956	$ 4,863
Machinery, equipment and internal-use software	37,038	29,639
Leasehold improvements	5,263	4,513
Gross property, plant and equipment	49,257	39,015
Accumulated depreciation and amortization	(26,786)	(18,391)
Total property, plant and equipment, net	$ 22,471	$ 20,624

Long-Lived Assets Including Goodwill and Other Acquired Intangible Assets

The Company reviews property, plant and equipment, inventory component prepayments and certain identifiable intangibles, excluding goodwill, for impairment. Long-lived assets are reviewed for impairment whenever events or changes in circumstances indicate the carrying amount of an asset may not be recoverable. Recoverability of these assets is measured by comparison of their carrying amounts to future undiscounted cash flows the assets are expected to generate. If property, plant and equipment, inventory component prepayments and certain identifiable intangibles are considered to be impaired, the impairment to be recognized equals the amount by which the carrying value of the assets exceeds its fair value.

The Company does not amortize goodwill and intangible assets with indefinite useful lives, rather such assets are required to be tested for impairment at least annually or sooner whenever events or changes in circumstances indicate that the assets may be impaired. The Company performs its goodwill and intangible asset impairment tests in the fourth quarter of each year. The Company did not recognize any impairment charges related to goodwill or indefinite lived intangible assets during 2015, 2014 and 2013. The Company established reporting units based on its current reporting structure. For purposes of testing goodwill for impairment, goodwill has been allocated to these reporting units to the extent it relates to each reporting unit. In 2015 and 2014, the Company's goodwill was primarily allocated to the Americas and Europe reporting units.

The Company amortizes its intangible assets with definite useful lives over their estimated useful lives and reviews these assets for impairment. The Company typically amortizes its acquired intangible assets with definite useful lives over periods from three to seven years.

Goodwill and Other Intangible Assets

On July 31, 2014, the Company completed the acquisitions of Beats Music, LLC, which offers a subscription streaming music service, and Beats Electronics, LLC, which makes Beats® headphones, speakers and audio software (collectively, "Beats"). The total purchase price consideration for these acquisitions was $2.6 billion, which consisted primarily of cash, of which $2.2 billion was allocated to goodwill, $636 million to acquired intangible assets and $258 million to net liabilities assumed. The Company also completed various other business acquisitions during 2014 for an aggregate cash consideration, net of cash acquired, of $957 million, of which $828 million was allocated to goodwill, $257 million to acquired intangible assets and $128 million to net liabilities assumed. The Company's acquired intangible assets with definite useful lives primarily consist of patents and licenses and are amortized over periods typically from three to seven years. The following table summarizes the components of gross and net intangible asset balances as of September 26, 2015:

$ millions	2015 Gross Carrying Amount	Accumulated Amortization	Net Carrying Amount
Definite-lived and amortizable acquired intangible assets	$ 8,125	$ (4,332)	$ 3,793
Indefinite-lived and non-amortizable acquired intangible assets	100	0	100
Total acquired intangible assets	$ 8,225	$ (4,332)	$ 3,893

Fair Value Measurements

The Company applies fair value accounting for all financial assets and liabilities and non-financial assets and liabilities that are recognized or disclosed at fair value in the financial statements on a recurring basis. The Company defines fair value as the price that would be received from selling an asset or paid to transfer a liability in an orderly transaction between market participants at the measurement date. When determining the fair value measurements for assets and liabilities, which are required to be recorded at fair value, the Company considers the principal or most advantageous market in which the Company would transact and the market-based risk measurements or assumptions that market participants would use in pricing the asset or liability, such as risks inherent in valuation techniques, transfer restrictions and credit risk. Fair value is estimated by applying the following hierarchy, which prioritizes the inputs used to measure fair value into three levels and bases the categorization within the hierarchy upon the lowest level of input that is available and significant to the fair value measurement:

Level 1—Quoted prices in active markets for identical assets or liabilities.

Level 2—Observable inputs other than quoted prices in active markets for identical assets and liabilities, quoted prices for identical or similar assets or liabilities in inactive markets, or other inputs that are observable or can be corroborated by observable market data for substantially the full term of the assets or liabilities.

Apple Inc. Notes—continued

Level 3—Inputs that are generally unobservable and typically reflect management's estimate of assumptions that market participants would use in pricing the asset or liability.

The Company's valuation techniques used to measure the fair value of money market funds and certain marketable equity securities were derived from quoted prices in active markets for identical assets or liabilities. The valuation techniques used to measure the fair value of the Company's debt instruments and all other financial instruments, all of which have counterparties with high credit ratings, were valued based on quoted market prices or model driven valuations using significant inputs derived from or corroborated by observable market data.

In accordance with the fair value accounting requirements, companies may choose to measure eligible financial instruments and certain other items at fair value. The Company has not elected the fair value option for any eligible financial instruments.

Accrued Warranty and Indemnification

The following table shows changes in the Company's accrued warranties and related costs for 2015 and 2014 (in millions):

	2015	2014
Beginning accrued warranty and related costs	$ 4,159	$ 2,967
Cost of warranty claims	(4,401)	(3,760)
Accruals for product warranty	5,022	4,952
Ending accrued warranty and related costs	$ 4,780	$ 4,159

Long-Term Debt

As of September 26, 2015, the Company had outstanding floating- and fixed-rate notes with varying maturities for an aggregate principal amount of $55.7 billion (collectively the "Notes"). The Notes are senior unsecured obligations, and interest is payable in arrears. The Company recognized $722 million, $381 million and $136 million of interest expense on its term debt for 2015, 2014 and 2013, respectively. As of September 26, 2015 and September 27, 2014, the fair value of the Company's Notes, based on Level 2 inputs, was $54.9 billion and $28.5 billion, respectively.

Dividends

The Company declared and paid cash dividends per share during the periods presented as follows:

	2015		2014	
	Dividends Per Share	Amount (in millions)	Dividends Per Share	Amount (in millions)
Fourth quarter	$ 0.52	$ 2,950	$ 0.47	$ 2,807
Third quarter	0.52	2,997	0.47	2,830
Second quarter	0.47	2,734	0.44	2,655
First quarter	0.47	2,750	0.44	2,739
Total cash dividends declared and paid	$ 1.98	$ 11,431	$ 1.82	$ 11,031

Segment Information and Geographic Data

Net sales by product for 2015, 2014 and 2013 are as follows (in millions):

Net Sales by Product	2015	2014	2013
iPhone	$155,041	$101,991	$ 91,279
iPad	23,227	30,283	31,980
Mac	25,471	24,079	21,483
Services	19,909	18,063	16,051
Other Products	10,067	8,379	10,117
Total net sales	$233,715	$182,795	$170,910

The following table shows information by reportable operating segment for 2015, 2014 and 2013 (in millions):

	2015	2014	2013
Americas:			
Net sales	$93,864	$80,095	$77,093
Operating income	$31,186	$26,158	$24,829
Europe:			
Net sales	$50,337	$44,285	$40,980
Operating income	$16,527	$14,434	$12,767
Greater China:			
Net sales	$58,715	$31,853	$27,016
Operating income	$23,002	$11,039	$ 8,499
Japan:			
Net sales	$15,706	$15,314	$13,782
Operating income	$ 7,617	$ 6,904	$ 6,668
Rest of Asia Pacific:			
Net sales	$15,093	$11,248	$12,039
Operating income	$ 5,518	$ 3,674	$ 3,762

Google Inc.
CONSOLIDATED BALANCE SHEETS
(In millions, except share and par value amounts which are reflected in thousands, and par value per share amounts)

As of December 31	2014	2015
Assets		
Current assets		
Cash and cash equivalents	$ 18,347	$ 16,549
Marketable securities	46,048	56,517
Total cash, cash equivalents, and marketable securities (including securities loaned of $4,058 and $4,531)	64,395	73,066
Accounts receivable, net of allowance of $225 and $296	9,383	11,556
Receivable under reverse repurchase agreements	875	450
Income taxes receivable, net	591	1,903
Prepaid revenue share, expenses and other assets	3,412	3,139
Total current assets	78,656	90,114
Prepaid revenue share, expenses and other assets, non-current	3,187	3,181
Non-marketable investments	3,079	5,183
Deferred income taxes	176	251
Property and equipment, net	23,883	29,016
Intangible assets, net	4,607	3,847
Goodwill	15,599	15,869
Total assets	$ 129,187	$ 147,461
Liabilities and Stockholders' Equity		
Current liabilities		
Accounts payable	$ 1,715	$ 1,931
Short-term debt	2,009	3,225
Accrued compensation and benefits	3,069	3,539
Accrued expenses and other current liabilities	4,408	4,768
Accrued revenue share	1,952	2,329
Securities lending payable	2,778	2,428
Deferred revenue	752	788
Income taxes payable, net	96	302
Total current liabilities	16,779	19,310
Long-term debt	3,228	1,995
Deferred revenue, non-current	104	151
Income taxes payable, non-current	3,340	3,663
Deferred income taxes	758	189
Other long-term liabilities	1,118	1,822
Commitments and contingencies (Note 11)		
Stockholders' equity:		
Convertible preferred stock, $0.001 par value per share; 100,000 shares authorized, no shares issued and outstanding; 0.5 shares authorized, no shares issued and outstanding	0	0
Class A and Class B common stock, and Class C capital stock and additional paid-in capital, $0.001 par value per share: 15,000,000 shares authorized (Class A 9,000,000, Class B 3,000,000, Class C 3,000,000); 680,172 (Class A 286,560, Class B 53,213, Class C 340,399), and par value of $680 (Class A $287, Class B $53, Class C $340); and 1.5 shares authorized (Class A 0.5, Class B 0.5, Class C 0.5); 0.3 (Class A 0.1, Class B 0.1, Class C 0.1), and par value of $0, shares issued and outstanding	28,767	31,313
Accumulated other comprehensive income (loss)	27	(1,874)
Retained earnings	75,066	90,892
Total stockholders' equity	103,860	120,331
Total liabilities and stockholders' equity	$ 129,187	$ 147,461

See accompanying notes.

Google Inc.
CONSOLIDATED STATEMENTS OF INCOME
(In millions)

Year Ended December 31		2013		2014		2015
Revenues	$	55,519	$	66,001	$	74,989
Costs and expenses						
Cost of revenues		21,993		25,691		28,164
Research and development		7,137		9,832		12,282
Sales and marketing		6,554		8,131		9,047
General and administrative		4,432		5,851		6,136
Total costs and expenses		40,116		49,505		55,629
Income from operations		15,403		16,496		19,360
Other income (expense), net		496		763		291
Income from continuing operations before income taxes		15,899		17,259		19,651
Provision for income taxes		2,739		3,639		3,303
Net income from continuing operations	$	13,160	$	13,620	$	16,348
Net income (loss) from discontinued operations		(427)		516		0
Net income	$	12,733	$	14,136	$	16,348
Less: Adjustment Payment to Class C capital stockholders		0		0		522
Net income available to all stockholders	$	12,733	$	14,136	$	15,826

See accompanying notes.

Google Inc.
CONSOLIDATED STATEMENTS OF COMPREHENSIVE INCOME
(In millions)

Year Ended December 31		2013		2014		2015
Net income	$	12,733	$	14,136	$	16,348
Other comprehensive income (loss):						
Change in foreign currency translation adjustment		89		(996)		(1,067)
Available-for-sale investments:						
Change in net unrealized gains (losses)		(392)		505		(715)
Less: reclassification adjustment for net (gains) losses included in net income		(162)		(134)		208
Net change (net of tax effect of $212, $60, and $29)		(554)		371		(507)
Cash flow hedges:						
Change in net unrealized gains		112		651		676
Less: reclassification adjustment for net gains included in net income		(60)		(124)		(1,003)
Net change (net of tax effect of $30, $196, and $115)		52		527		(327)
Other comprehensive loss		(413)		(98)		(1,901)
Comprehensive income	$	12,320	$	14,038	$	14,447

See accompanying notes.

Google Inc.
CONSOLIDATED STATEMENTS OF STOCKHOLDERS' EQUITY
(In millions, except share amounts which are reflected in thousands)

	Class A and Class B Common Stock, Class C Capital Stock and Additional Paid-In Capital		Accumulated Other Comprehensive Income (Loss)	Retained Earnings	Total Stockholders' Equity
	Shares	Amount			
Balance as of December 31, 2012	659,958 $	22,835 $	538 $	48,197 $	71,570
Common stock issued	11,706	1,174	0	0	1,174
Stock-based compensation expense		3,343	0	0	3,343
Stock-based compensation tax benefits		449	0	0	449
Tax withholding related to vesting of restricted stock units		(1,879)	0	0	(1,879)
Net income		0	0	12,733	12,733
Other comprehensive loss		0	(413)	0	(413)
Balance as of December 31, 2013	671,664	25,922	125	60,930	86,977
Common and capital stock issued	8,508	465	0	0	465
Stock-based compensation expense		4,279	0	0	4,279
Stock-based compensation tax benefits		625	0	0	625
Tax withholding related to vesting of restricted stock units		(2,524)	0	0	(2,524)
Net income		0	0	14,136	14,136
Other comprehensive loss		0	(98)	0	(98)
Balance as of December 31, 2014	680,172	28,767	27	75,066	103,860
Common and capital stock issued	6,659	331	0	0	331
Stock-based compensation expense		5,151	0	0	5,151
Stock-based compensation tax benefits		815	0	0	815
Tax withholding related to vesting of restricted stock units		(1,954)	0	0	(1,954)
Alphabet share exchange	(687,684)	0	0	0	0
Capital transactions with Alphabet		(2,272)	0	0	(2,272)
Adjustment Payment to Class C capital stockholders	853	475	0	(522)	(47)
Net income		0	0	16,348	16,348
Other comprehensive loss		0	(1,901)	0	(1,901)
Balance as of December 31, 2015	0 $	31,313 $	(1,874) $	90,892 $	120,331

See accompanying notes.

Google Inc.
CONSOLIDATED STATEMENTS OF CASH FLOWS
(In millions)

Year Ended December 31	2013	2014	2015
Operating activities			
Net income	$ 12,733	$ 14,136	$ 16,348
Adjustments:			
Depreciation and impairment of property and equipment	2,781	3,523	4,132
Amortization and impairment of intangible assets	1,158	1,456	931
Stock-based compensation expense	3,343	4,279	5,203
Excess tax benefits from stock-based award activities	(481)	(648)	(548)
Deferred income taxes	(437)	(104)	(179)
Gain on divestiture of business	(700)	(740)	0
(Gain) loss on marketable and non-marketable investments, net	(166)	(390)	334
Other	272	192	212
Changes in assets and liabilities, net of effects of acquisitions:			
Accounts receivable	(1,307)	(1,641)	(2,094)
Income taxes, net	588	591	(179)
Prepaid revenue share, expenses and other assets	(930)	459	(318)
Accounts payable	605	436	203
Accrued expenses and other liabilities	713	757	1,597
Accrued revenue share	254	245	339
Deferred revenue	233	(175)	43
Net cash provided by operating activities	18,659	22,376	26,024
Investing activities			
Purchases of property and equipment	(7,358)	(10,959)	(9,915)
Purchases of marketable securities	(45,444)	(56,310)	(74,368)
Maturities and sales of marketable securities	38,314	51,315	62,905
Purchases of non-marketable investments	(569)	(1,227)	(2,172)
Cash collateral related to securities lending	(299)	1,403	(350)
Investments in reverse repurchase agreements	600	(775)	425
Proceeds from divestiture of business	2,525	386	0
Acquisitions, net of cash acquired, and purchases of intangibles and other assets	(1,448)	(4,888)	(236)
Net cash used in investing activities	(13,679)	(21,055)	(23,711)
Financing activities			
Net payments related to stock-based award activities	(781)	(2,069)	(1,612)
Excess tax benefits from stock-based award activities	481	648	548
Adjustment Payment to Class C capital stockholders	0	0	(47)
Capital transactions with Alphabet	0	0	(2,543)
Proceeds from issuance of debt, net of costs	10,768	11,625	13,705
Repayments of debt	(11,325)	(11,643)	(13,728)
Net cash used in financing activities	(857)	(1,439)	(3,677)
Effect of exchange rate changes on cash and cash equivalents	(3)	(433)	(434)
Net increase (decrease) in cash and cash equivalents	4,120	(551)	(1,798)
Cash and cash equivalents at beginning of period	14,778	18,898	18,347
Cash and cash equivalents at end of period	$ 18,898	$ 18,347	$ 16,549
Supplemental disclosures of cash flow information			
Cash paid for taxes	$ 1,932	$ 2,819	$ 3,338
Cash paid for interest	72	86	96

See accompanying notes.

Samsung Electronics Co., Ltd. and Subsidiaries
CONSOLIDATED STATEMENTS OF FINANCIAL POSITION

(In millions of Korean won)	December 31, 2015	December 31, 2014
	KRW	KRW
Assets		
Current assets		
Cash and cash equivalents	22,636,744	16,840,766
Short-term financial instruments	44,228,800	41,689,776
Short-term available-for-sale financial assets	4,627,530	3,286,798
Trade receivables	25,168,026	24,694,610
Non-trade receivables	3,352,663	3,539,875
Advances	1,706,003	1,989,470
Prepaid expenses	3,170,632	3,346,593
Inventories	18,811,794	17,317,504
Other current assets	1,035,460	1,795,143
Assets held-for-sale	77,073	645,491
Total current assets	124,814,725	115,146,026
Non-current assets		
Long-term available-for-sale financial assets	8,332,480	12,667,509
Investment in associates and joint ventures	5,276,348	5,232,461
Property, plant and equipment	86,477,110	80,872,950
Intangible assets	5,396,311	4,785,473
Long-term prepaid expenses	4,294,401	4,857,126
Deferred income tax assets	5,589,108	4,526,595
Other non-current assets	1,999,038	2,334,818
Total assets	242,179,521	230,422,958
Liabilities and Equity		
Current liabilities		
Trade and other payables	6,187,291	7,914,704
Short-term borrowings	11,155,425	8,029,299
Other payables	8,864,378	10,318,407
Advances received	1,343,432	1,427,230
Withholdings	992,733	1,161,635
Accrued expenses	11,628,739	12,876,777
Income tax payable	3,401,625	2,161,109
Current portion of long-term liabilities	221,548	1,778,667
Provisions	6,420,603	5,991,510
Other current liabilities	287,135	326,259
Liabilities held-for-sale	—	28,316
Total current liabilities	50,502,909	52,013,913
Non-current liabilities		
Debentures	1,230,448	1,355,882
Long-term borrowings	266,542	101,671
Long-term other payables	3,041,687	2,562,271
Net defined benefit liabilities	358,820	201,342
Deferred income tax liabilities	5,154,792	4,097,811
Provisions	522,378	499,290
Other non-current liabilities	2,042,140	1,502,590
Total liabilities	63,119,716	62,334,770
Equity attributable to owners of the parent		
Preferred stock	119,467	119,467
Common stock	778,047	778,047
Share premium	4,403,893	4,403,893
Retained earnings	185,132,014	169,529,604
Other components of equity	(17,580,451)	(12,729,387)
Accumulated other comprehensive income attributable to assets held-for-sale	23,797	80,101
	172,876,767	162,181,725
Non-controlling interests	6,183,038	5,906,463
Total equity	179,059,805	168,088,188
Total liabilities and equity	242,179,521	230,422,958

The accompanying notes are an integral part of these consolidated financial statements.

Samsung Electronics Co., Ltd. and Subsidiaries
CONSOLIDATED STATEMENTS OF INCOME

For the year ended December 31	2015	2014
(In millions of Korean won)	KRW	KRW
Revenue	200,653,482	206,205,987
Cost of sales	123,482,118	128,278,800
Gross profit	77,171,364	77,927,187
Selling and administrative expenses	50,757,922	52,902,116
Operating profit	26,413,442	25,025,071
Other non-operating income	1,685,947	3,801,357
Other non-operating expense	3,723,434	2,259,737
Share of profit of associates and joint ventures	1,101,932	342,516
Financial income	10,514,879	8,259,829
Financial expense	10,031,771	7,294,002
Profit before income tax	25,960,995	27,875,034
Income tax expense	6,900,851	4,480,676
Profit for the year	19,060,144	23,394,358
Profit attributable to owners of the parent	18,694,628	23,082,499
Profit attributable to non-controlling interests	365,516	311,859
Earnings per share for profit attributable to owners of the parent		
—Basic	126,305	153,105
—Diluted	126,303	153,096

Samsung Electronics Co., Ltd. and Subsidiaries
CONSOLIDATED STATEMENTS OF COMPREHENSIVE INCOME

For the year ended December 31	2015	2014
(In millions of Korean won)	KRW	KRW
Profit for the year	19,060,144	23,394,358
Other comprehensive loss		
Items not to be reclassified to profit or loss subsequently:		
Remeasurement of net defined benefit liabilities, net of tax	263,978	(710,318)
Items to be reclassified to profit or loss subsequently:		
Changes in value of available-for-sale financial assets, net of tax	(414,961)	(232,105)
Share of other comprehensive income (loss) of associates and joint ventures, net of tax	(41,261)	(128,932)
Foreign currency translation, net of tax	268,315	(922,059)
Other comprehensive income (loss) for the year, net of tax	76,071	(1,993,414)
Total comprehensive income for the year	19,136,215	21,400,944
Comprehensive income attributable to:		
Owners of the parent	18,804,189	20,990,732
Non-controlling interests	332,026	410,212

The accompanying notes are an integral part of these consolidated financial statements.

SAMSUNG

Samsung Electronics Co., Ltd. and Subsidiaries
CONSOLIDATED STATEMENTS OF CHANGES IN EQUITY

(In millions of Korean won)	Preferred stock	Common stock	Share premium	Retained earnings	Other components of equity	Accumulated other comprehensive income attributable to assets held-for-sale	Equity attributable to owners of the parent	Non-controlling interests	Total
Balance as at January 1, 2014	119,467	778,047	4,403,893	148,600,282	(9,459,073)	—	144,442,616	5,573,394	150,016,010
Profit for the year	—	—	—	23,082,499	—	—	23,082,499	311,859	23,394,358
Changes in value of available-for-sale financial assets, net of tax	—	—	—	—	(314,069)	—	(314,069)	81,964	(232,105)
Share of other comprehensive income (loss) of associates and joint ventures, net of tax	—	—	—	—	(128,495)	—	(128,495)	(437)	(128,932)
Foreign currency translation, net of tax	—	—	—	—	(954,999)	—	(954,999)	32,940	(922,059)
Remeasurement of net defined benefit liabilities, net of tax	—	—	—	—	(694,204)	—	(694,204)	(16,114)	(710,318)
Classified as held-for-sale	—	—	—	—	(80,101)	80,101	—	—	—
Total comprehensive income (loss)	—	—	—	23,082,499	(2,171,868)	80,101	20,990,732	410,212	21,400,944
Dividends	—	—	—	(2,157,011)	—	—	(2,157,011)	(74,216)	(2,231,227)
Capital transaction under common control	—	—	—	—	(158)	—	(158)	244	86
Changes in consolidated entities	—	—	—	—	—	—	—	569	569
Acquisition of treasury stock	—	—	—	—	(1,125,322)	—	(1,125,322)	—	(1,125,322)
Disposal of treasury stock	—	—	—	—	32,764	—	32,764	—	32,764
Stock option activities	—	—	—	—	(9,436)	—	(9,436)	—	(9,436)
Others	—	—	—	3,834	3,706	—	7,540	(3,740)	3,800
Total transactions with owners	—	—	—	(2,153,177)	(1,098,446)	—	(3,251,623)	(77,143)	(3,328,766)
Balance as at December 31, 2014	119,467	778,047	4,403,893	169,529,604	(12,729,387)	80,101	162,181,725	5,906,463	168,088,188
Profit for the year	—	—	—	18,694,628	—	—	18,694,628	365,516	19,060,144
Changes in value of available-for-sale financial assets, net of tax	—	—	—	—	(348,068)	(24,750)	(372,818)	(42,143)	(414,961)
Share of other comprehensive income (loss) of associates and joint ventures, net of tax	—	—	—	—	12,686	(54,118)	(41,432)	171	(41,261)
Foreign currency translation, net of tax	—	—	—	—	266,061	(1,233)	264,828	3,487	268,315
Remeasurement of net defined benefit liabilities, net of tax	—	—	—	—	258,983	—	258,983	4,995	263,978
Classified as held-for-sale	—	—	—	—	(23,797)	23,797	—	—	—
Total comprehensive income (loss)	—	—	—	18,694,628	165,865	(56,304)	18,804,189	332,026	19,136,215
Dividends	—	—	—	(3,073,481)	—	—	(3,073,481)	(54,603)	(3,128,084)
Capital transaction under common control	—	—	—	—	(5,314)	—	(5,314)	423	(4,891)
Changes in consolidated entities	—	—	—	—	—	—	—	(152)	(152)
Acquisition of treasury stock	—	—	—	—	(5,015,112)	—	(5,015,112)	—	(5,015,112)
Disposal of treasury stock	—	—	—	—	3,406	—	3,406	—	3,406
Stock option activities	—	—	—	—	(806)	—	(806)	—	(806)
Others	—	—	—	(18,737)	897	—	(17,840)	(1,119)	(18,959)
Total transactions with owners	—	—	—	(3,092,218)	(5,016,929)	—	(8,109,147)	(55,451)	(8,164,598)
Balance as at December 31, 2015	119,467	778,047	4,403,893	185,132,014	(17,580,451)	23,797	172,876,767	6,183,038	179,059,805

The accompanying notes are an integral part of these consolidated financial statements.

Samsung Electronics Co., Ltd. and Subsidiaries
CONSOLIDATED STATEMENTS OF CASH FLOWS

For the year ended December 31	2015	2014
(In millions of Korean Won)	KRW	KRW
Cash flows from operating activities		
Profit for the period	19,060,144	23,394,358
Adjustments	29,610,971	22,323,765
Changes in assets and liabilities arising from operating activities	(4,682,032)	(3,837,136)
Cash generated from operations	43,989,083	41,880,987
Interest received	2,151,741	1,555,373
Interest paid	(748,256)	(463,740)
Dividend received	266,369	1,495,658
Income tax paid	(5,597,176)	(7,492,889)
Net cash generated from operating activities	**40,061,761**	**36,975,389**
Cash flows from investing activities		
Net increase in short-term financial instruments	(5,762,783)	(1,110,842)
Proceeds from disposal of short-term available-for-sale financial assets	2,143,384	1,954,158
Acquisition of short-term available-for-sale financial assets	(509,349)	(2,667,610)
Proceeds from disposal of long-term financial instruments	3,999,710	94,089
Acquisition of long-term financial instruments	(132,733)	(3,248,374)
Proceeds from disposal of long-term available-for-sale financial assets	200,502	202,904
Acquisition of long-term available-for-sale financial assets	(232,530)	(6,212,102)
Proceeds from disposal of associates and joint ventures	278,009	2,014,430
Acquisition of associates and joint ventures	(137,917)	(719,800)
Disposal of property, plant and equipment	357,154	385,610
Purchases of property, plant and equipment	(25,880,222)	(22,042,943)
Disposal of intangible assets	1,083	31,731
Purchases of intangible assets	(1,501,881)	(1,324,307)
Cash outflows from business combinations	(411,445)	(176,625)
Others	421,231	13,273
Net cash used in investing activities	**(27,167,787)**	**(32,806,408)**
Cash flows from financing activities		
Net increase in short-term borrowings	3,202,416	1,833,419
Acquisition of treasury stock	(5,015,112)	(1,125,322)
Disposal of treasury stock	3,034	27,582
Proceeds from long-term borrowings and debentures	192,474	1,740,573
Repayment of long-term borrowings and debentures	(1,801,465)	(3,299,595)
Payment of dividends	(3,129,544)	(2,233,905)
Net increase in non-controlling interests	(25,312)	139
Net cash generated(used) in financing activities	**(6,573,509)**	**(3,057,109)**
Effect of exchange rate changes on cash and cash equivalents	(524,487)	(555,886)
Net increase(decrease) in cash and cash equivalents	**5,795,978**	**555,986**
Cash and cash equivalents		
Beginning of the period	16,840,766	16,284,780
End of the period	22,636,744	16,840,766

The accompanying notes are an integral part of these consolidated financial statements.

appendix

B

Time Value of Money

PRESENT AND FUTURE VALUE CONCEPTS

C1 Time is money

Concept of interest

VALUE OF A SINGLE AMOUNT

P1 Present value of a single amount

P2 Future value of a single amount

NTK B-1, B-2

VALUE OF AN ANNUITY

P3 Present value of an annuity

P4 Future value of an annuity

NTK B-3, B-4

Learning Objectives

CONCEPTUAL

C1 Describe the earning of interest and the concepts of present and future values.

PROCEDURAL

P1 Apply present value concepts to a single amount by using interest tables.

P2 Apply future value concepts to a single amount by using interest tables.

P3 Apply present value concepts to an annuity by using interest tables.

P4 Apply future value concepts to an annuity by using interest tables.

PRESENT AND FUTURE VALUE CONCEPTS

The old saying "Time is money" means that as time passes, the values of assets and liabilities change. This change is due to *interest,* which is a borrower's payment to the owner of an asset for its use. The most common example of interest is a savings account. Cash in the account earns interest paid by the financial institution. An example of a liability is a car loan. As we carry the balance of the loan, we accumulate interest costs on it. We must ultimately repay this loan with interest.

Present and future value computations enable us to measure or estimate the interest component of holding assets or liabilities over time. The present value computation is used to compute the value of future-day assets *today.* The future value computation is used to compute the value of present-day assets *at a future date.* The first section focuses on the present value of a single amount. The second section focuses on the future value of a single amount. Then both the present and future values of a series of amounts (called an *annuity*) are defined and explained.

C1_____

Describe the earning of interest and the concepts of present and future values.

▊ **Decision** Insight

What's Five Million Worth?   A maintenance worker duped out of a $5 million scratch-off ticket got his winnings seven years later. Robert Miles bought the ticket in 2006 at a convenience store where the owner and his two sons convinced Miles the ticket was worth $5,000 and paid him $4,000 for it. The brothers waited until 2012 to claim the jackpot, prompting an investigation, which uncovered the fraud. The $5 million will be paid to Miles as a $250,000 annuity from 2014 to 2033 or as a lump-sum payment of $3,210,000, which is about $2,124,378 after taxes. ■

PRESENT VALUE OF A SINGLE AMOUNT

Graph of PV of a Single Amount   We graphically express the present value, called *p*, of a single future amount, called *f*, that is received or paid at a future date in Exhibit B.1.

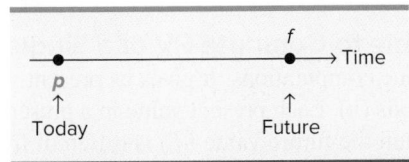

EXHIBIT B.1

Present Value of a Single Amount Diagram

Formula of PV of a Single Amount   The formula to compute the present value of a single amount is shown in Exhibit B.2, where *p* = present value (PV); *f* = future value (FV); *i* = rate of interest per period; and *n* = number of periods. (Interest is also called the *discount,* and an interest rate is also called the *discount rate.*)

P1_____

Apply present value concepts to a single amount by using interest tables.

EXHIBIT B.2

Present Value of a Single Amount Formula

$$p = \frac{f}{(1 + i)^n}$$

Illustration of PV of a Single Amount for One Period   To illustrate present value concepts, assume that we need $220 one period from today. We want to know how much we must invest now, for one period, at an interest rate of 10% to provide for this $220. For this illustration, the *p*, or present value, is the unknown amount—the specifics are shown graphically as follows:

(*i* = 0.10)   *f* = $220

p = ?

Conceptually, we know *p* must be less than $220. This is clear from the answer to: Would we rather have $220 today or $220 at some future date? If we had $220 today, we could invest it and see it grow to something more than $220 in the future. Therefore, we would prefer the $220 today. This means that if we were promised $220 in the future, we would take less than $220 today. But how much less? To answer that question, we compute an estimate of the present value of the $220 to be received one period from now using the formula in Exhibit B.2 as follows:

$$p = \frac{f}{(1+i)^n} = \frac{\$220}{(1+0.10)^1} = \$200$$

We interpret this result to say that given an interest rate of 10%, we are indifferent between $200 today or $220 at the end of one period.

Illustration of PV of a Single Amount for Multiple Periods

We can use this formula to compute the present value for *any number of periods*. To illustrate, consider a payment of $242 at the end of two periods at 10% interest. The present value of this $242 to be received two periods from now is computed as follows:

$$p = \frac{f}{(1+i)^n} = \frac{\$242}{(1+0.10)^2} = \$200$$

Together, these results tell us we are indifferent between $200 today, or $220 one period from today, or $242 two periods from today given a 10% interest rate per period.

The number of periods (n) in the present value formula does not have to be expressed in years. Any period of time such as a day, a month, a quarter, or a year can be used. Whatever period is used, the interest rate (i) must be compounded for the same period. This means that if a situation expresses n in months and i equals 12% per year, then i is transformed into interest earned per month (or 1%). In this case, interest is said to be *compounded monthly*. For example, the present value of $1 when n is 12 months and i is 12% compounded monthly follows:

$$p = \frac{1}{(1+0.01)^{12}} = \$0.8874$$

Using Present Value Table to Compute PV of a Single Amount

A present value table helps us with present value computations. It gives us present values (factors) for a variety of both interest rates (i) and periods (n). Each present value in a present value table assumes that the future value (f) equals 1. When the future value (f) is different from 1, we simply multiply the present value (p) from the table by that future value to give us the estimate. The formula used to construct a table of present values for a single future amount of 1 is shown in Exhibit B.3.

$$p = \frac{1}{(1+i)^n}$$

This formula is identical to that in Exhibit B.2 except that f equals 1. Table B.1 at the end of this appendix is such a present value table. It is often called a **present value of 1 table**. A present value table has three factors: p, i, and n. Knowing two of these three factors allows us to compute the third. (A fourth is f, but as already explained, we need only multiply the 1 used in the formula by f.) To illustrate the use of a present value table, consider three cases.

Case 1   Solve for p when knowing i and n. To show how we use a present value table, let's look again at how we estimate the present value of $220 (the f value) at the end of one period ($n = 1$) where the interest rate (i) is 10%. To solve this case, we go to the present value table (Table B.1) and look in the row for one period and in the column for 10% interest. Here we find a present value (p) of 0.9091 based on a future value of 1. This means, for instance, that $1 to be received one period from today at 10% interest is worth $0.9091 today. Because the future value in this case is not $1 but $220, we multiply the 0.9091 by $220 to get an answer of $200.

Case 2   Solve for n when knowing p and i. To illustrate, assume a $100,000 future value ($f$) that is worth $13,000 today ($p$) using an interest rate of 12% (i) but where n is unknown. In particular, we want to know how many periods (n) there are between the present value and the

---

Point: Excel for PV.

	A	B
1	Future value	$242
2	Periods	2
3	Period int. rate	10%
4	Present value	

=PV(B3,B2,0,−B1) = $200

I will pay your allowance at the end of the month. Do you want to wait or receive its present value today?

EXHIBIT B.3

Present Value of 1 Formula

future value. To put this in context, it would fit a situation in which we want to retire with $100,000 but currently have only $13,000 that is earning a 12% return and we are unable to save additional money. How long will it be before we can retire? To answer this, we go to Table B.1 and look in the 12% interest column. Here we find a column of present values (p) based on a future value of 1. To use the present value table for this solution, we must divide $13,000 (p) by $100,000 (f), which equals 0.1300. This is necessary because *a present value table defines* f *equal to 1, and* p *as a fraction of 1.* We look for a value nearest to 0.1300 (p), which we find in the row for 18 periods (n). This means that the present value of $100,000 at the end of 18 periods at 12% interest is $13,000; alternatively stated, we must work 18 more years.

Case 3   Solve for *i* when knowing *p* and *n*. In this case, we have, say, a $120,000 future value (f) worth $60,000 today (p) when there are nine periods (n) between the present and future values, but the interest rate is unknown. As an example, suppose we want to retire with $120,000 in nine years, but we have only $60,000 and we are unable to save additional money. What interest rate must we earn to retire with $120,000 in nine years? To answer this, we go to the present value table (Table B.1) and look in the row for nine periods. To use the present value table, we must divide $60,000 (p) by $120,000 (f), which equals 0.5000. Recall that this step is necessary because a present value table defines f equal to 1 and p as a fraction of 1. We look for a value in the row for nine periods that is nearest to 0.5000 (p), which we find in the column for 8% interest (i). This means that the present value of $120,000 at the end of nine periods at 8% interest is $60,000 or, in our example, we must earn 8% annual interest to retire in nine years.

A company is considering an investment expected to yield $70,000 after six years. If this company demands an 8% return, how much is it willing to pay for this investment today?

NEED-TO-KNOW B-1

Solution

Present Value of
a Single Amount

Today's value = $70,000 × 0.6302 = <u>$44,114</u> (using PV factor from Table B.1, i = 8%, n = 6)

P1

FUTURE VALUE OF A SINGLE AMOUNT

Formula of FV of a Single Amount   We must modify the formula for the present value of a single amount to obtain the formula for the future value of a single amount. In particular, we multiply both sides of the equation in Exhibit B.2 by $(1 + i)^n$ to get the result shown in Exhibit B.4.

P2

Apply future value concepts to a single amount by using interest tables.

$$f = p \times (1 + i)^n$$

EXHIBIT B.4

Future Value of a Single Amount Formula

Illustration of FV of a Single Amount for One Period   The future value (f) is defined in terms of p, i, and n. We can use this formula to determine that $200 (p) invested for one (n) period at an interest rate of 10% (i) yields a future value of $220 as follows:

$$\begin{aligned} f &= p \times (1 + i)^n \\ &= \$200 \times (1 + 0.10)^1 \\ &= \$220 \end{aligned}$$

Illustration of FV of a Single Amount for Multiple Periods   This formula can be used to compute the future value of an amount for *any number of periods* into the future. To illustrate, assume that $200 is invested for three periods at 10%. The future value of this $200 is $266.20, computed as follows:

Point: The FV factor in Table B.2 when n = 3 and i = 10% is 1.3310.

$$\begin{aligned} f &= p \times (1 + i)^n \\ &= \$200 \times (1 + 0.10)^3 \\ &= \$200 \times 1.3310 \\ &= \$266.20 \end{aligned}$$

Point: Excel for FV.

	A	B
1	Present value	$200
2	Periods	3
3	Period int. rate	10%
4	Future value	

=FV(B3,B2,0,−B1) = <u>$266.20</u>

Using Future Value Table to Compute FV of a Single Amount

A future value table makes it easier for us to compute future values (f) for many different combinations of interest rates (i) and time periods (n). Each future value in a future value table assumes the present value (p) is 1. If the future amount is something other than 1, we multiply our answer by that amount. The formula used to construct a table of future values (factors) for a single amount of 1 is in Exhibit B.5.

EXHIBIT B.5

Future Value of 1 Formula

$$f = (1 + i)^n$$

Table B.2 at the end of this appendix shows a table of future values for a current amount of 1. This type of table is called a **future value of 1 table**.

There are some important relations between Tables B.1 and B.2. In Table B.2, for the row where $n = 0$, the future value is 1 for each interest rate. This is so because no interest is earned when time does not pass. We also see that Tables B.1 and B.2 report the same information but in a different manner. In particular, one table is simply the *reciprocal* of the other. To illustrate this inverse relation, let's say we invest $100 for a period of five years at 12% per year. How much do we expect to have after five years? We can answer this question using Table B.2 by finding the future value (f) of 1, for five periods from now, compounded at 12%. From that table we find $f = 1.7623$. If we start with $100, the amount it accumulates to after five years is $176.23 ($100 × 1.7623). We can alternatively use Table B.1. Here we find that the present value (p) of 1, discounted five periods at 12%, is 0.5674. Recall the inverse relation between present value and future value. This means that $p = 1/f$ (or equivalently, $f = 1/p$). We can compute the future value of $100 invested for five periods at 12% as follows: $f = \$100 \times (1/0.5674) = \$176.24$ (which equals the $176.23 just computed, except for a 1 cent rounding difference).

A future value table has three factors: f, i, and n. Knowing two of these three factors allows us to compute the third. To illustrate, consider three possible cases.

Point:
1/PV factor = FV factor.
1/FV factor = PV factor.

Point: The FV factor when $n = 2$ and $i = 10\%$, is 1.2100. Its reciprocal, 0.8264, is the PV factor when $n = 2$ and $i = 10\%$.

Case 1　Solve for f when knowing i and n. Our preceding example fits this case. We found that $100 invested for five periods at 12% interest accumulates to $176.24.

Case 2　Solve for n when knowing f and i. In this case, we have, say, $2,000 ($p$) and we want to know how many periods (n) it will take to accumulate to $3,000 ($f$) at 7% interest ($i$). To answer this, we go to the future value table (Table B.2) and look in the 7% interest column. Here we find a column of future values (f) based on a present value of 1. To use a future value table, we must divide $3,000 ($f$) by $2,000 ($p$), which equals 1.500. This is necessary because *a future value table defines* p *equal to 1, and* f *as a multiple of 1.* We look for a value nearest to 1.50 (f), which we find in the row for six periods (n). This means that $2,000 invested for six periods at 7% interest accumulates to $3,000.

Case 3　Solve for i when knowing f and n. In this case, we have, say, $2,001 ($p$), and in nine years ($n$) we want to have $4,000 ($f$). What rate of interest must we earn to accomplish this? To answer that, we go to Table B.2 and search in the row for nine periods. To use a future value table, we must divide $4,000 ($f$) by $2,001 ($p$), which equals 1.9990. Recall that this is necessary because a future value table defines p equal to 1 and f as a multiple of 1. We look for a value nearest to 1.9990 (f), which we find in the column for 8% interest (i). This means that $2,001 invested for nine periods at 8% interest accumulates to $4,000.

NEED-TO-KNOW **B-2**

Future Value of a Single Amount

P2

Assume that you win a $150,000 cash sweepstakes today. You decide to deposit this cash in an account earning 8% annual interest, and you plan to quit your job when the account equals $555,000. How many years will it be before you can quit working?

Solution

Future value factor = $555,000/$150,000 = 3.7000

Searching for 3.7 in the 8% column of Table B.2 shows you cannot quit working for <u>17 years</u> if your deposit earns 8% interest.

PRESENT VALUE OF AN ANNUITY

Graph of PV of an Annuity   An *annuity* is a series of equal payments occurring at equal intervals. One example is a series of three annual payments of $100 each. An *ordinary annuity* is defined as equal end-of-period payments at equal intervals. An ordinary annuity of $100 for three periods and its present value (*p*) are illustrated in Exhibit B.6.

P3 _____

Apply present value concepts to an annuity by using interest tables.

EXHIBIT B.6

Present Value of an Ordinary Annuity Diagram

	$100	$100	$100	
				→ Time
p ↑	↑	↑	↑	
Today	Future (*n* = 1)	Future (*n* = 2)	Future (*n* = 3)	

Formula and Illustration of PV of an Annuity   One way to compute the present value of an ordinary annuity is to find the present value of each payment using our present value formula from Exhibit B.3. We then add each of the three present values. To illustrate, let's look at three $100 payments at the end of each of the next three periods with an interest rate of 15%. Our present value computations are

$$p = \frac{\$100}{(1 + 0.15)^1} + \frac{\$100}{(1 + 0.15)^2} + \frac{\$100}{(1 + 0.15)^3} = \$228.32$$

Using Present Value Table to Compute PV of an Annuity   This computation is identical to computing the present value of each payment (from Table B.1) and taking their sum or, alternatively, adding the values from Table B.1 for each of the three payments and multiplying their sum by the $100 annuity payment.

A more direct way is to use a present value of annuity table. Table B.3 at the end of this appendix is one such table. This table is called a **present value of an annuity of 1 table**. If we look at Table B.3 where *n* = 3 and *i* = 15%, we see the present value is 2.2832. This means that the present value of an annuity of 1 for three periods, with a 15% interest rate, equals 2.2832.

A present value of an annuity formula is used to construct Table B.3. It can also be constructed by adding the amounts in a present value of 1 table. To illustrate, we use Tables B.1 and B.3 to confirm this relation for the prior example.

From Table B.1		From Table B.3	
i = 15%, *n* = 1	0.8696		
i = 15%, *n* = 2	0.7561		
i = 15%, *n* = 3	0.6575		
Total.	2.2832	*i* = 15%, *n* = 3	2.2832

Point: Excel for PV annuity.

	A	B
1	Payment	$100
2	Periods	3
3	Period int. rate	15%
4	Present value	

=−PV(B3,B2,B1) = $228.32

We can also use business calculators or spreadsheet programs to find the present value of an annuity.

■ **Decision** Insight

Count Your Blessings   "I don't have good luck—I'm blessed," proclaimed Andrew "Jack" Whittaker, a sewage treatment contractor, after winning the largest ever undivided jackpot in a U.S. lottery. Whittaker had to choose between $315 million in 30 annual installments or $170 million in one lump sum ($112 million after-tax). ■

A company is considering an investment that would produce payments of $10,000 every six months for three years. The first payment would be received in six months. If this company requires an 8% annual return, what is the maximum amount it is willing to pay for this investment today?

NEED-TO-KNOW B-3

Present Value of an Annuity

P3

Solution

Maximum paid = $10,000 × 5.2421 = $52,421 (using PV of annuity factor from Table B.3, *i* = 4%, *n* = 6)

FUTURE VALUE OF AN ANNUITY

P4

Apply future value concepts to an annuity by using interest tables.

Graph of FV of an Annuity   The future value of an *ordinary annuity* is the accumulated value of each annuity payment with interest as of the date of the final payment. To illustrate, let's consider the earlier annuity of three annual payments of $100. Exhibit B.7 shows the point in time for the future value (f). The first payment is made two periods prior to the point when future value is determined, and the final payment occurs on the future value date.

EXHIBIT B.7

Future Value of an Ordinary Annuity Diagram

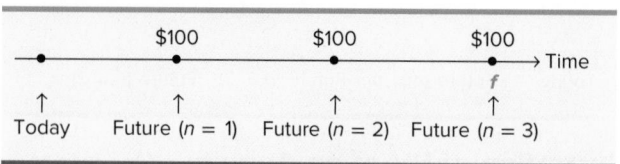

Point: An ordinary annuity is a series of equal cash flows, with the payment at the *end* of each period.

Formula and Illustration of FV of an Annuity   One way to compute the future value of an annuity is to use the formula to find the future value of *each* payment and add them. If we assume an interest rate of 15%, our calculation is

$$f = \$100 \times (1 + 0.15)^2 + \$100 \times (1 + 0.15)^1 + \$100 \times (1 + 0.15)^0 = \$347.25$$

This is identical to using Table B.2 and summing the future values of each payment, or adding the future values of the three payments of 1 and multiplying the sum by $100.

Using Future Value Table to Compute FV of an Annuity   A more direct way is to use a table showing future values of annuities. Such a table is called a **future value of an annuity of 1 table**. Table B.4 at the end of this appendix is one such table. Note that in Table B.4 when $n = 1$, the future values equal 1 ($f = 1$) for all rates of interest. This is because such an annuity consists of only one payment and the future value is determined on the date of that payment—no time passes between the payment and its future value. The future value of an annuity formula is used to construct Table B.4. We can also construct it by adding the amounts from a future value of 1 table. To illustrate, we use Tables B.2 and B.4 to confirm this relation for the prior example:

Point: Excel for FV annuity.

	A	B
1	Payment	$100
2	Periods	3
3	Period int. rate	15%
4	Future value	

=−FV(B3,B2,B1) = $347.25

From Table B.2		From Table B.4	
$i = 15\%, n = 0$	1.0000		
$i = 15\%, n = 1$	1.1500		
$i = 15\%, n = 2$	1.3225		
Total..................	3.4725	$i = 15\%, n = 3$...........	3.4725

Note that the future value in Table B.2 is 1.0000 when $n = 0$, but the future value in Table B.4 is 1.0000 when $n = 1$. Is this a contradiction? No. When $n = 0$ in Table B.2, the future value is determined on the date when a single payment occurs. This means that no interest is earned because no time has passed, and the future value equals the payment. Table B.4 describes annuities with equal payments occurring at the end of each period. When $n = 1$, the annuity has one payment, and its future value equals 1 on the date of its final and only payment. Again, no time passes between the payment and its future value date.

NEED-TO-KNOW B-4

Future Value of an Annuity

P4

A company invests $45,000 per year for five years at 12% annual interest. Compute the value of this annuity investment at the end of five years.

Solution

Future value = $45,000 × 6.3528 = $285,876 (using FV of annuity factor from Table B.4, $i = 12\%, n = 5$)

Summary

C1 **Describe the earning of interest and the concepts of present and future values.** Interest is payment by a borrower to the owner of an asset for its use. Present and future value computations are a way for us to estimate the interest component of holding assets or liabilities over a period of time.

P1 **Apply present value concepts to a single amount by using interest tables.** The present value of a single amount received at a future date is the amount that can be invested now at the specified interest rate to yield that future value.

P2 **Apply future value concepts to a single amount by using interest tables.** The future value of a single amount

invested at a specified rate of interest is the amount that would accumulate by the future date.

P3 **Apply present value concepts to an annuity by using interest tables.** The present value of an annuity is the amount that can be invested now at the specified interest rate to yield that series of equal periodic payments.

P4 **Apply future value concepts to an annuity by using interest tables.** The future value of an annuity invested at a specific rate of interest is the amount that would accumulate by the date of the final payment.

connect

Assume that you must estimate what the future value will be two years from today using the *future value of 1 table* (Table B.2). Which interest rate column *and* number-of-periods row do you use when working with the following rates?

1. 8% annual rate, compounded quarterly
2. 12% annual rate, compounded annually
3. 6% annual rate, compounded semiannually
4. 12% annual rate, compounded monthly (the answer for number-of-periods in part 4 is not shown in Table B.2)

QUICK STUDY

QS B-1
Identifying interest rates in tables

C1

Ken Francis is offered the possibility of investing $2,745 today; in return, he would receive $10,000 after 15 years. What is the annual rate of interest for this investment? (Use Table B.1.)

QS B-2
Interest rate on an investment   P1

Megan Brink is offered the possibility of investing $6,651 today at 6% interest per year in a desire to accumulate $10,000. How many years must Brink wait to accumulate $10,000? (Use Table B.1.)

QS B-3
Number of periods of an investment   P1

Flaherty is considering an investment that, if paid for immediately, is expected to return $140,000 five years from now. If Flaherty demands a 9% return, how much is she willing to pay for this investment?

QS B-4
Present value of an amount   P1

CII, Inc., invests $630,000 in a project expected to earn a 12% annual rate of return. The earnings will be reinvested in the project each year until the entire investment is liquidated 10 years later. What will the cash proceeds be when the project is liquidated?

QS B-5
Future value of an amount   P2

Beene Distributing is considering a project that will return $150,000 annually at the end of each year for the next six years. If Beene demands an annual return of 7% and pays for the project immediately, how much is it willing to pay for the project?

QS B-6
Present value of an annuity   P3

Claire Fitch is planning to begin an individual retirement program in which she will invest $1,500 at the end of each year. Fitch plans to retire after making 30 annual investments in the program earning a return of 10%. What is the value of the program on the date of the last payment (30 years from the present)?

QS B-7
Future value of an annuity   P4

EXERCISES

Exercise B-1
Present value of an amount   P1

Mike Derr Company expects to earn 10% per year on an investment that will pay $606,773 six years from now. Use Table B.1 to compute the present value of this investment. (Round the amount to the nearest dollar.)

Exercise B-2
Present value of an amount   P1

On January 1, 2016, a company agrees to pay $20,000 in three years. If the annual interest rate is 10%, determine how much cash the company can borrow with this agreement.

Exercise B-3
Number of periods of an investment   P2

Tom Thompson expects to invest $10,000 at 12% and, at the end of a certain period, receive $96,463. How many years will it be before Thompson receives the payment? (Use Table B.2.)

Exercise B-4
Interest rate on an investment   P2

Bill Padley expects to invest $10,000 for 25 years, after which he wants to receive $108,347. What rate of interest must Padley earn? (Use Table B.2.)

Exercise B-5
Future value of an amount   P2

Mark Welsch deposits $7,200 in an account that earns interest at an annual rate of 8%, compounded quarterly. The $7,200 plus earned interest must remain in the account 10 years before it can be withdrawn. How much money will be in the account at the end of 10 years?

Exercise B-6
Future value of an amount   P2

Catten, Inc., invests $163,170 today earning 7% per year for nine years. Use Table B.2 to compute the future value of the investment nine years from now. (Round the amount to the nearest dollar.)

Exercise B-7
Interest rate on an investment   P3

Jones expects an immediate investment of $57,466 to return $10,000 annually for eight years, with the first payment to be received one year from now. What rate of interest must Jones earn? (Use Table B.3.)

Exercise B-8
Number of periods of an investment   P3

Keith Riggins expects an investment of $82,014 to return $10,000 annually for several years. If Riggins earns a return of 10%, how many annual payments will he receive? (Use Table B.3.)

Exercise B-9
Present value of an annuity   P3

Dave Krug finances a new automobile by paying $6,500 cash and agreeing to make 40 monthly payments of $500 each, the first payment to be made one month after the purchase. The loan bears interest at an annual rate of 12%. What is the cost of the automobile?

Exercise B-10
Present values of annuities
P3

C&H Ski Club recently borrowed money and agreed to pay it back with a series of six annual payments of $5,000 each. C&H subsequently borrows more money and agrees to pay it back with a series of four annual payments of $7,500 each. The annual interest rate for both loans is 6%.

1. Use Table B.1 to find the present value of these two separate annuities. (Round amounts to the nearest dollar.)
2. Use Table B.3 to find the present value of these two separate annuities. (Round amounts to the nearest dollar.)

Exercise B-11
Present value with semiannual compounding
C1   P3

Otto Co. borrows money on April 30, 2016, by promising to make four payments of $13,000 each on November 1, 2016; May 1, 2017; November 1, 2017; and May 1, 2018.

1. How much money is Otto able to borrow if the interest rate is 8%, compounded semiannually?
2. How much money is Otto able to borrow if the interest rate is 12%, compounded semiannually?
3. How much money is Otto able to borrow if the interest rate is 16%, compounded semiannually?

Exercise B-12
Present value of bonds
P1   P3

Spiller Corp. plans to issue 10%, 15-year, $500,000 par value bonds payable that pay interest semiannually on June 30 and December 31. The bonds are dated December 31, 2016, and are issued on that date. If the market rate of interest for the bonds is 8% on the date of issue, what will be the total cash proceeds from the bond issue?

Compute the amount that can be borrowed under each of the following circumstances:

1. A promise to repay $90,000 seven years from now at an interest rate of 6%.

2. An agreement made on February 1, 2016, to make three separate payments of $20,000 on February 1 of 2017, 2018, and 2019. The annual interest rate is 10%.

Exercise B-13
Present value of an amount and of an annuity P1 P3

Algoe expects to invest $1,000 annually for 40 years to yield an accumulated value of $154,762 on the date of the last investment. For this to occur, what rate of interest must Algoe earn? (Use Table B.4.)

Exercise B-14
Interest rate on an investment P4

Steffi Derr expects to invest $10,000 annually that will earn 8%. How many annual investments must Derr make to accumulate $303,243 on the date of the last investment? (Use Table B.4.)

Exercise B-15
Number of periods of an investment P4

Kelly Malone plans to have $50 withheld from her monthly paycheck and deposited in a savings account that earns 12% annually, compounded monthly. If Malone continues with her plan for two and one-half years, how much will be accumulated in the account on the date of the last deposit?

Exercise B-16
Future value of an annuity P4

Starr Company decides to establish a fund that it will use 10 years from now to replace an aging production facility. The company will make a $100,000 initial contribution to the fund and plans to make quarterly contributions of $50,000 beginning in three months. The fund earns 12%, compounded quarterly. What will be the value of the fund 10 years from now?

Exercise B-17
Future value of an amount plus an annuity

P2   P4

---

a. How much would you have to deposit today if you wanted to have $60,000 in four years? Annual interest rate is 9%.

b. Assume that you are saving up for a trip around the world when you graduate in two years. If you can earn 8% on your investments, how much would you have to deposit today to have $15,000 when you graduate?

c. Would you rather have $463 now or $1,000 ten years from now? Assume that you can earn 9% on your investments.

d. Assume that a college parking sticker today costs $90. If the cost of parking is increasing at the rate of 5% per year, how much will the college parking sticker cost in eight years?

e. Assume that the average price of a new home is $158,500. If the cost of a new home is increasing at a rate of 10% per year, how much will a new home cost in eight years?

f. An investment will pay you $10,000 in 10 years *and* it will also pay you $400 at the end of *each* of the next 10 years (years 1 thru 10). If the annual interest rate is 6%, how much would you be willing to pay today for this type of investment?

g. A college student is reported in the newspaper as having won $10,000,000 in the Kansas State Lottery. However, as is often the custom with lotteries, she does *not* actually receive the entire $10 million now. Instead she will receive $500,000 at the end of the year for *each* of the next 20 years. If the annual interest rate is 6%, what is the present value (today's amount) that she won? (Ignore taxes.)

Exercise B-18
Practical applications of the time value of money

P1   P2   P3   P4

For each of the following situations, identify (1) the case as either (*a*) a present or a future value and (*b*) a single amount or an annuity, (2) the table you would use in your computations (but do not solve the problem), and (3) the interest rate and time periods you would use.

a. You need to accumulate $10,000 for a trip you wish to take in four years. You are able to earn 8% compounded semiannually on your savings. You plan to make only one deposit and let the money accumulate for four years. How would you determine the amount of the one-time deposit?

b. Assume the same facts as in part (*a*) except that you will make semiannual deposits to your savings account.

c. You want to retire after working 40 years with savings in excess of $1,000,000. You expect to save $4,000 a year for 40 years and earn an annual rate of interest of 8%. Will you be able to retire with more than $1,000,000 in 40 years? Explain.

d. A sweepstakes agency names you a grand prize winner. You can take $225,000 immediately or elect to receive annual installments of $30,000 for 20 years. You can earn 10% annually on any investments you make. Which prize do you choose to receive?

Exercise B-19
Using present and future value tables

C1   P1   P2   P3   P4

TABLE B.1*

Present Value of 1

$$p = 1/(1 + i)^n$$

Periods	1%	2%	3%	4%	5%	6%	7%	8%	9%	10%	12%	15%
						Rate						
1	0.9901	0.9804	0.9709	0.9615	0.9524	0.9434	0.9346	0.9259	0.9174	0.9091	0.8929	0.8696
2	0.9803	0.9612	0.9426	0.9246	0.9070	0.8900	0.8734	0.8573	0.8417	0.8264	0.7972	0.7561
3	0.9706	0.9423	0.9151	0.8890	0.8638	0.8396	0.8163	0.7938	0.7722	0.7513	0.7118	0.6575
4	0.9610	0.9238	0.8885	0.8548	0.8227	0.7921	0.7629	0.7350	0.7084	0.6830	0.6355	0.5718
5	0.9515	0.9057	0.8626	0.8219	0.7835	0.7473	0.7130	0.6806	0.6499	0.6209	0.5674	0.4972
6	0.9420	0.8880	0.8375	0.7903	0.7462	0.7050	0.6663	0.6302	0.5963	0.5645	0.5066	0.4323
7	0.9327	0.8706	0.8131	0.7599	0.7107	0.6651	0.6227	0.5835	0.5470	0.5132	0.4523	0.3759
8	0.9235	0.8535	0.7894	0.7307	0.6768	0.6274	0.5820	0.5403	0.5019	0.4665	0.4039	0.3269
9	0.9143	0.8368	0.7664	0.7026	0.6446	0.5919	0.5439	0.5002	0.4604	0.4241	0.3606	0.2843
10	0.9053	0.8203	0.7441	0.6756	0.6139	0.5584	0.5083	0.4632	0.4224	0.3855	0.3220	0.2472
11	0.8963	0.8043	0.7224	0.6496	0.5847	0.5268	0.4751	0.4289	0.3875	0.3505	0.2875	0.2149
12	0.8874	0.7885	0.7014	0.6246	0.5568	0.4970	0.4440	0.3971	0.3555	0.3186	0.2567	0.1869
13	0.8787	0.7730	0.6810	0.6006	0.5303	0.4688	0.4150	0.3677	0.3262	0.2897	0.2292	0.1625
14	0.8700	0.7579	0.6611	0.5775	0.5051	0.4423	0.3878	0.3405	0.2992	0.2633	0.2046	0.1413
15	0.8613	0.7430	0.6419	0.5553	0.4810	0.4173	0.3624	0.3152	0.2745	0.2394	0.1827	0.1229
16	0.8528	0.7284	0.6232	0.5339	0.4581	0.3936	0.3387	0.2919	0.2519	0.2176	0.1631	0.1069
17	0.8444	0.7142	0.6050	0.5134	0.4363	0.3714	0.3166	0.2703	0.2311	0.1978	0.1456	0.0929
18	0.8360	0.7002	0.5874	0.4936	0.4155	0.3503	0.2959	0.2502	0.2120	0.1799	0.1300	0.0808
19	0.8277	0.6864	0.5703	0.4746	0.3957	0.3305	0.2765	0.2317	0.1945	0.1635	0.1161	0.0703
20	0.8195	0.6730	0.5537	0.4564	0.3769	0.3118	0.2584	0.2145	0.1784	0.1486	0.1037	0.0611
25	0.7798	0.6095	0.4776	0.3751	0.2953	0.2330	0.1842	0.1460	0.1160	0.0923	0.0588	0.0304
30	0.7419	0.5521	0.4120	0.3083	0.2314	0.1741	0.1314	0.0994	0.0754	0.0573	0.0334	0.0151
35	0.7059	0.5000	0.3554	0.2534	0.1813	0.1301	0.0937	0.0676	0.0490	0.0356	0.0189	0.0075
40	0.6717	0.4529	0.3066	0.2083	0.1420	0.0972	0.0668	0.0460	0.0318	0.0221	0.0107	0.0037

* Used to compute the present value of a known future amount. For example: How much would you need to invest today at 10% compounded semiannually to accumulate $5,000 in 6 years from today? Using the factors of $n = 12$ and $i = 5\%$ (12 semiannual periods and a semiannual rate of 5%), the factor is 0.5568. You would need to invest $2,784 today ($5,000 × 0.5568).

TABLE B.2†

Future Value of 1

$$f = (1 + i)^n$$

Periods	1%	2%	3%	4%	5%	6%	7%	8%	9%	10%	12%	15%
						Rate						
0	1.0000	1.0000	1.0000	1.0000	1.0000	1.0000	1.0000	1.0000	1.0000	1.0000	1.0000	1.0000
1	1.0100	1.0200	1.0300	1.0400	1.0500	1.0600	1.0700	1.0800	1.0900	1.1000	1.1200	1.1500
2	1.0201	1.0404	1.0609	1.0816	1.1025	1.1236	1.1449	1.1664	1.1881	1.2100	1.2544	1.3225
3	1.0303	1.0612	1.0927	1.1249	1.1576	1.1910	1.2250	1.2597	1.2950	1.3310	1.4049	1.5209
4	1.0406	1.0824	1.1255	1.1699	1.2155	1.2625	1.3108	1.3605	1.4116	1.4641	1.5735	1.7490
5	1.0510	1.1041	1.1593	1.2167	1.2763	1.3382	1.4026	1.4693	1.5386	1.6105	1.7623	2.0114
6	1.0615	1.1262	1.1941	1.2653	1.3401	1.4185	1.5007	1.5869	1.6771	1.7716	1.9738	2.3131
7	1.0721	1.1487	1.2299	1.3159	1.4071	1.5036	1.6058	1.7138	1.8280	1.9487	2.2107	2.6600
8	1.0829	1.1717	1.2668	1.3686	1.4775	1.5938	1.7182	1.8509	1.9926	2.1436	2.4760	3.0590
9	1.0937	1.1951	1.3048	1.4233	1.5513	1.6895	1.8385	1.9990	2.1719	2.3579	2.7731	3.5179
10	1.1046	1.2190	1.3439	1.4802	1.6289	1.7908	1.9672	2.1589	2.3674	2.5937	3.1058	4.0456
11	1.1157	1.2434	1.3842	1.5395	1.7103	1.8983	2.1049	2.3316	2.5804	2.8531	3.4785	4.6524
12	1.1268	1.2682	1.4258	1.6010	1.7959	2.0122	2.2522	2.5182	2.8127	3.1384	3.8960	5.3503
13	1.1381	1.2936	1.4685	1.6651	1.8856	2.1329	2.4098	2.7196	3.0658	3.4523	4.3635	6.1528
14	1.1495	1.3195	1.5126	1.7317	1.9799	2.2609	2.5785	2.9372	3.3417	3.7975	4.8871	7.0757
15	1.1610	1.3459	1.5580	1.8009	2.0789	2.3966	2.7590	3.1722	3.6425	4.1772	5.4736	8.1371
16	1.1726	1.3728	1.6047	1.8730	2.1829	2.5404	2.9522	3.4259	3.9703	4.5950	6.1304	9.3576
17	1.1843	1.4002	1.6528	1.9479	2.2920	2.6928	3.1588	3.7000	4.3276	5.0545	6.8660	10.7613
18	1.1961	1.4282	1.7024	2.0258	2.4066	2.8543	3.3799	3.9960	4.7171	5.5599	7.6900	12.3755
19	1.2081	1.4568	1.7535	2.1068	2.5270	3.0256	3.6165	4.3157	5.1417	6.1159	8.6128	14.2318
20	1.2202	1.4859	1.8061	2.1911	2.6533	3.2071	3.8697	4.6610	5.6044	6.7275	9.6463	16.3665
25	1.2824	1.6406	2.0938	2.6658	3.3864	4.2919	5.4274	6.8485	8.6231	10.8347	17.0001	32.9190
30	1.3478	1.8114	2.4273	3.2434	4.3219	5.7435	7.6123	10.0627	13.2677	17.4494	29.9599	66.2118
35	1.4166	1.9999	2.8139	3.9461	5.5160	7.6861	10.6766	14.7853	20.4140	28.1024	52.7996	133.1755
40	1.4889	2.2080	3.2620	4.8010	7.0400	10.2857	14.9745	21.7245	31.4094	45.2593	93.0510	267.8635

† Used to compute the future value of a known present amount. For example: What is the accumulated value of $3,000 invested today at 8% compounded quarterly for 5 years? Using the factors of $n = 20$ and $i = 2\%$ (20 quarterly periods and a quarterly interest rate of 2%), the factor is 1.4859. The accumulated value is $4,457.70 ($3,000 × 1.4859).

$$p = \left[1 - \frac{1}{(1+i)^n}\right]/i$$

TABLE B.3‡

Present Value of an Annuity of 1

Periods	1%	2%	3%	4%	5%	6%	7%	8%	9%	10%	12%	15%
1	0.9901	0.9804	0.9709	0.9615	0.9524	0.9434	0.9346	0.9259	0.9174	0.9091	0.8929	0.8696
2	1.9704	1.9416	1.9135	1.8861	1.8594	1.8334	1.8080	1.7833	1.7591	1.7355	1.6901	1.6257
3	2.9410	2.8839	2.8286	2.7751	2.7232	2.6730	2.6243	2.5771	2.5313	2.4869	2.4018	2.2832
4	3.9020	3.8077	3.7171	3.6299	3.5460	3.4651	3.3872	3.3121	3.2397	3.1699	3.0373	2.8550
5	4.8534	4.7135	4.5797	4.4518	4.3295	4.2124	4.1002	3.9927	3.8897	3.7908	3.6048	3.3522
6	5.7955	5.6014	5.4172	5.2421	5.0757	4.9173	4.7665	4.6229	4.4859	4.3553	4.1114	3.7845
7	6.7282	6.4720	6.2303	6.0021	5.7864	5.5824	5.3893	5.2064	5.0330	4.8684	4.5638	4.1604
8	7.6517	7.3255	7.0197	6.7327	6.4632	6.2098	5.9713	5.7466	5.5348	5.3349	4.9676	4.4873
9	8.5660	8.1622	7.7861	7.4353	7.1078	6.8017	6.5152	6.2469	5.9952	5.7590	5.3282	4.7716
10	9.4713	8.9826	8.5302	8.1109	7.7217	7.3601	7.0236	6.7101	6.4177	6.1446	5.6502	5.0188
11	10.3676	9.7868	9.2526	8.7605	8.3064	7.8869	7.4987	7.1390	6.8052	6.4951	5.9377	5.2337
12	11.2551	10.5753	9.9540	9.3851	8.8633	8.3838	7.9427	7.5361	7.1607	6.8137	6.1944	5.4206
13	12.1337	11.3484	10.6350	9.9856	9.3936	8.8527	8.3577	7.9038	7.4869	7.1034	6.4235	5.5831
14	13.0037	12.1062	11.2961	10.5631	9.8986	9.2950	8.7455	8.2442	7.7862	7.3667	6.6282	5.7245
15	13.8651	12.8493	11.9379	11.1184	10.3797	9.7122	9.1079	8.5595	8.0607	7.6061	6.8109	5.8474
16	14.7179	13.5777	12.5611	11.6523	10.8378	10.1059	9.4466	8.8514	8.3126	7.8237	6.9740	5.9542
17	15.5623	14.2919	13.1661	12.1657	11.2741	10.4773	9.7632	9.1216	8.5436	8.0216	7.1196	6.0472
18	16.3983	14.9920	13.7535	12.6593	11.6896	10.8276	10.0591	9.3719	8.7556	8.2014	7.2497	6.1280
19	17.2260	15.6785	14.3238	13.1339	12.0853	11.1581	10.3356	9.6036	8.9501	8.3649	7.3658	6.1982
20	18.0456	16.3514	14.8775	13.5903	12.4622	11.4699	10.5940	9.8181	9.1285	8.5136	7.4694	6.2593
25	22.0232	19.5235	17.4131	15.6221	14.0939	12.7834	11.6536	10.6748	9.8226	9.0770	7.8431	6.4641
30	25.8077	22.3965	19.6004	17.2920	15.3725	13.7648	12.4090	11.2578	10.2737	9.4269	8.0552	6.5660
35	29.4086	24.9986	21.4872	18.6646	16.3742	14.4982	12.9477	11.6546	10.5668	9.6442	8.1755	6.6166
40	32.8347	27.3555	23.1148	19.7928	17.1591	15.0463	13.3317	11.9246	10.7574	9.7791	8.2438	6.6418

‡ Used to calculate the present value of a series of equal payments made at the end of each period. For example: What is the present value of $2,000 per year for 10 years assuming an annual interest rate of 9%. For (n = 10, i = 9%), the PV factor is 6.4177. $2,000 per year for 10 years is the equivalent of $12,835 today ($2,000 × 6.4177).

TABLE B.4§

Future Value of an Annuity of 1

$$f = [(1+i)^n - 1]/i$$

Periods	1%	2%	3%	4%	5%	6%	7%	8%	9%	10%	12%	15%
1	1.0000	1.0000	1.0000	1.0000	1.0000	1.0000	1.0000	1.0000	1.0000	1.0000	1.0000	1.0000
2	2.0100	2.0200	2.0300	2.0400	2.0500	2.0600	2.0700	2.0800	2.0900	2.1000	2.1200	2.1500
3	3.0301	3.0604	3.0909	3.1216	3.1525	3.1836	3.2149	3.2464	3.2781	3.3100	3.3744	3.4725
4	4.0604	4.1216	4.1836	4.2465	4.3101	4.3746	4.4399	4.5061	4.5731	4.6410	4.7793	4.9934
5	5.1010	5.2040	5.3091	5.4163	5.5256	5.6371	5.7507	5.8666	5.9847	6.1051	6.3528	6.7424
6	6.1520	6.3081	6.4684	6.6330	6.8019	6.9753	7.1533	7.3359	7.5233	7.7156	8.1152	8.7537
7	7.2135	7.4343	7.6625	7.8983	8.1420	8.3938	8.6540	8.9228	9.2004	9.4872	10.0890	11.0668
8	8.2857	8.5830	8.8923	9.2142	9.5491	9.8975	10.2598	10.6366	11.0285	11.4359	12.2997	13.7268
9	9.3685	9.7546	10.1591	10.5828	11.0266	11.4913	11.9780	12.4876	13.0210	13.5795	14.7757	16.7858
10	10.4622	10.9497	11.4639	12.0061	12.5779	13.1808	13.8164	14.4866	15.1929	15.9374	17.5487	20.3037
11	11.5668	12.1687	12.8078	13.4864	14.2068	14.9716	15.7836	16.6455	17.5603	18.5312	20.6546	24.3493
12	12.6825	13.4121	14.1920	15.0258	15.9171	16.8699	17.8885	18.9771	20.1407	21.3843	24.1331	29.0017
13	13.8093	14.6803	15.6178	16.6268	17.7130	18.8821	20.1406	21.4953	22.9534	24.5227	28.0291	34.3519
14	14.9474	15.9739	17.0863	18.2919	19.5986	21.0151	22.5505	24.2149	26.0192	27.9750	32.3926	40.5047
15	16.0969	17.2934	18.5989	20.0236	21.5786	23.2760	25.1290	27.1521	29.3609	31.7725	37.2797	47.5804
16	17.2579	18.6393	20.1569	21.8245	23.6575	25.6725	27.8881	30.3243	33.0034	35.9497	42.7533	55.7175
17	18.4304	20.0121	21.7616	23.6975	25.8404	28.2129	30.8402	33.7502	36.9737	40.5447	48.8837	65.0751
18	19.6147	21.4123	23.4144	25.6454	28.1324	30.9057	33.9990	37.4502	41.3013	45.5992	55.7497	75.8364
19	20.8109	22.8406	25.1169	27.6712	30.5390	33.7600	37.3790	41.4463	46.0185	51.1591	63.4397	88.2118
20	22.0190	24.2974	26.8704	29.7781	33.0660	36.7856	40.9955	45.7620	51.1601	57.2750	72.0524	102.4436
25	28.2432	32.0303	36.4593	41.6459	47.7271	54.8645	63.2490	73.1059	84.7009	98.3471	133.3339	212.7930
30	34.7849	40.5681	47.5754	56.0849	66.4388	79.0582	94.4608	113.2832	136.3075	164.4940	241.3327	434.7451
35	41.6603	49.9945	60.4621	73.6522	90.3203	111.4348	138.2369	172.3168	215.7108	271.0244	431.6635	881.1702
40	48.8864	60.4020	75.4013	95.0255	120.7998	154.7620	199.6351	259.0565	337.8824	442.5926	767.0914	1,779.0903

§ Used to calculate the future value of a series of equal payments made at the end of each period. For example: What is the future value of $4,000 per year for 6 years assuming an annual interest rate of 8%. For (n = 6, i = 8%), the FV factor is 7.3359. $4,000 per year for 6 years accumulates to $29,343.60 ($4,000 × 7.3359).

C
appendix

Activity-Based Costing

Learning Objectives

CONCEPTUAL

C1 Explain cost flows for activity-based costing.

ANALYTICAL

A1 Identify and assess advantages and disadvantages of activity-based costing.

PROCEDURAL

P1 Assign overhead costs using the plantwide overhead rate method.

P2 Assign overhead costs using activity-based costing.

PLANTWIDE OVERHEAD RATE METHOD

We previously explained how to assign overhead costs to jobs (and processes) by using a predetermined overhead rate per unit of an allocation base, such as direct labor cost. The use of a single plantwide overhead rate suggests that overhead allocation is simple. In reality, it can be complicated. This appendix reviews the traditional plantwide overhead rate method and then shows the activity-based costing method.

Cost Flows under Plantwide Overhead Rate Method

The *single plantwide overhead rate method,* or simply the *plantwide overhead rate method,* uses one overhead rate to allocate overhead costs to products. The target of the cost assignment, or **cost object,** is the unit of product—see Exhibit C.1. The rate is determined using volume-related measures such as direct labor hours or machine hours, which are readily available in most manufacturing settings. In some industries, overhead costs are closely related to these volume-related measures.

P1_____

Assign overhead costs using the plantwide overhead rate method.

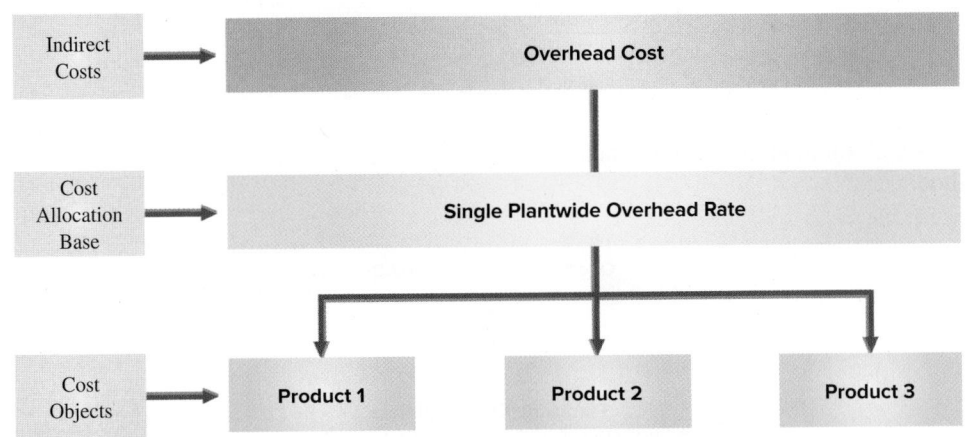

EXHIBIT C.1

Plantwide Overhead Rate Method

Applying the Plantwide Overhead Rate Method

Under the single plantwide overhead rate method, total budgeted overhead costs are divided by the allocation base, such as total direct labor hours, to arrive at a single plantwide overhead rate. This rate is used to assign overhead costs to *all products* based on the actual amount of allocation base used.

To illustrate, consider data from KartCo, a go-kart manufacturer that produces both standard and custom go-karts for amusement parks. The standard go-kart is a basic model sold primarily to amusement parks that service county and state fairs. Custom go-karts are produced for theme parks that need unique go-karts to fit their themes. KartCo applies overhead on the basis of direct labor hours and reports the budgeted production and direct labor hours for the coming year in Exhibit C.2.

EXHIBIT C.2

KartCo's Budgeted Production and Direct Labor Hours

	Number of Units	Direct Labor Hours per Unit	Total Direct Labor Hours
Standard go-kart..............	5,000	15	75,000
Custom go-kart................	1,000	25	25,000
Total........................			100,000

KartCo's budgeted overhead cost information for the year is shown below. Its overhead cost consists of indirect labor and factory utilities.

Total Budgeted Overhead Cost	Budgeted Cost
Indirect labor cost	$4,000,000
Factory utilities............................	800,000
Total budgeted overhead cost	$4,800,000

©Nick Daly/Getty Images/Digital Vision

The single plantwide overhead rate for KartCo is computed as follows.

$$\begin{aligned}\text{Plantwide overhead rate} &= \text{Total budgeted overhead cost} \div \text{Total budgeted direct labor hours} \\ &= \$4{,}800{,}000 \div 100{,}000 \text{ DLH} \\ &= \$48 \text{ per DLH}\end{aligned}$$

This plantwide overhead rate is then used to allocate overhead cost to products based on the number of direct labor hours required to produce each unit as follows.

Overhead allocated to each product unit = Plantwide overhead rate × DLH per unit

For KartCo, overhead cost is allocated to its two products as follows (on a per unit basis).

Overhead Cost per Unit
Standard go-kart: $48 per DLH × 15 DLH per unit = $ 720 per unit
Custom go-kart: $48 per DLH × 25 DLH per unit = $1,200 per unit

Exhibit C.3 summarizes the overhead allocation process for KartCo using the plantwide method.

EXHIBIT C.3

Plantwide Method—KartCo

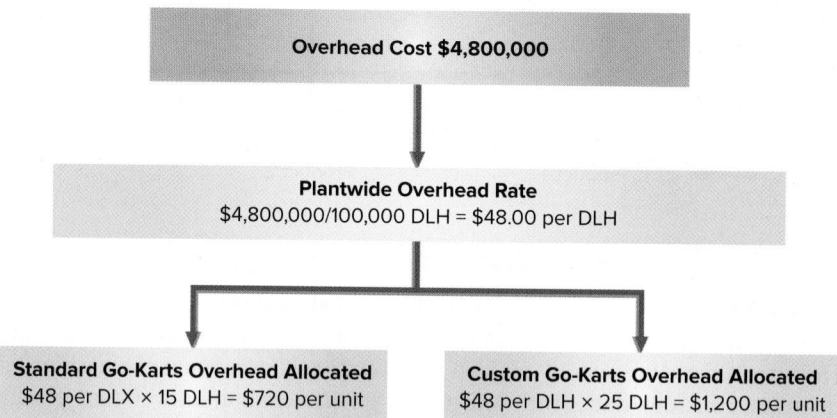

KartCo uses these per unit overhead costs to compute the product cost per unit as follows. Direct materials and direct labor costs per unit are from other cost records.

	Product Cost per Unit Using the Plantwide Rate Method			
	Direct Materials	Direct Labor	Overhead	Product Cost per Unit
Standard go-kart............	$400	$350	$ 720	$1,470
Custom go-kart.............	600	500	1,200	2,300

KartCo sells its standard model go-karts for $2,000 and its custom go-karts for $3,500 (per unit). A recent report from its marketing staff indicates that competitors are selling go-karts similar to KartCo's standard model for $1,200. Management is concerned that meeting this lower price would result in a loss of $270 ($1,200 − $1,470) on each standard go-kart sold.

KartCo has been swamped with orders for its custom go-kart and cannot meet demand. Accordingly, management is considering dropping the standard model and concentrating on the custom model. Yet management recognizes that its pricing and cost decisions are influenced by its cost allocations. Thus, before making any strategic decisions, management has directed its cost analysts to further review production costs for both the standard and custom go-kart models. To pursue this analysis, the cost analysts turned to the activity-based costing method.

NEED-TO-KNOW C-1

Plantwide Overhead
Rate Method

P1

HMS Mfg. predicts total overhead costs of $2,480,000 for the next year. HMS assigns overhead based on 125,000 budgeted direct labor hours.

1. Compute the single plantwide overhead rate based on budgeted direct labor hours.
2. Assume the deluxe model of the company's product required 25,000 direct labor hours during the year. How much overhead cost is assigned to the deluxe model?

Solution

1. Plantwide overhead rate = Total budgeted overhead cost/Total budgeted direct labor hours
     = $2,480,000/125,000 = $19.84 per direct labor hour
2. Overhead assigned to deluxe model = $19.84 × 25,000 = $496,000

Do More: QS C-2, E C-1

ACTIVITY-BASED COSTING

Cost Flows under Activity-Based Costing

For companies with only one product, or with multiple products that use about the same amount of overhead, using a single overhead cost rate based on volume is adequate. Multiple overhead rates can further improve on cost allocations. For example, a company might use direct labor hours to allocate overhead costs of its assembly department and machine hours to allocate costs of its machining department. This could result in more accurate overhead cost allocations, if different products use different amounts of direct labor and machine hours.

Yet, when a company has many products that consume different amounts of overhead, even the multiple overhead rate system based on volume is often inadequate. Such a system usually fails to reflect the products' different uses of overhead and often distorts product costs. *Specifically, low-volume complex products are usually undercosted, and high-volume simpler products are over-costed.* This can cause companies to believe that their complex products are more profitable than they really are, which can lead those companies to focus on them to the detriment of high-volume simpler products. This creates a demand for a better cost allocation system for overhead costs.

Activity-based costing (ABC) attempts to better allocate overhead costs to the proper users of overhead by focusing on *activities.* Activity-based costing follows three steps:

1. Identify activities and assign costs to activity cost pools.
2. Identify cost drivers and compute predetermined overhead rates (activity rates).
3. Assign overhead costs to cost objects.

We show this three-step activity-based costing method for KartCo.

Applying Activity-Based Costing

1. The first step identifies individual activities, which are pooled in a logical manner into homogenous groups, or *cost pools.* An **activity cost pool** is a collection of costs that are related to the same activity. An **activity cost driver,** or simply *cost driver,* is a factor that causes the cost of an activity to go up or down. For example, preparing an invoice, checking it, and sending it are activities of the "invoicing" process and can therefore be grouped in a single cost pool. Moreover, the number of invoices processed likely drives the costs of these activities.

KartCo applies step 1 below.

C1

Explain cost flows for activity-based costing.

Point: Activity-based costing is used in many settings. A study found that activity-based costing improves health care costing accuracy, enabling improved profitability analysis and decision making. However, identifying cost drivers in a health care setting is challenging.

P2

Assign overhead costs using activity-based costing.

Point: A cost driver is different from an allocation base. An allocation base is used as a basis for assigning overhead but need not have a cause-effect relation with the costs assigned. However, a cost driver has a cause-effect relation with the cost assigned.

Activity Cost Pool	Cost Assigned to Pool	Activity Cost Driver
Craftsmanship..............	$ 600,000	Direct labor hours
Setup......................	2,000,000	Number of batches
Design modification..........	1,200,000	Number of design modifications
Plant services..............	1,000,000	Square feet
Total.....................	$4,800,000	

2 In the second step, after all activity costs are accumulated in activity cost pools, **activity rates** are computed for each cost pool.

Activity rates, the predetermined overhead rates used in activity-based costing, are computed as follows:

$$\text{Activity rate} = \frac{\text{Total budgeted activity cost}}{\text{Budgeted activity-base usage}}$$

Costs are then allocated (assigned) to products using this formula:

$$\text{Allocated cost} = \text{Activity rate} \times \text{Actual amount of cost driver used}$$

KartCo collects this information to use in step 2.

Cost Driver	Activity Usage Standard Model	Activity Usage Custom Model	Total
Direct labor hours*............	25,000	5,000	30,000
Batches.....................	40	160	200
Design modifications	—	10	10
Square feet.................	12,000	8,000	20,000

* Standard model DLH = 5,000 units × 15 DLH per unit. Custom model DLH = 1,000 units × 25 DLH per unit.

Exhibit C.4 shows the 3-step activity-based costing method for KartCo.

For example, KartCo budgets $600,000 of costs in its craftsmanship pool. The cost driver for this cost pool is direct labor. The activity rate for the craftsmanship pool is computed as follows:

$$\text{Craftsmanship cost pool activity rate} = \$600,000 \div 30,000 \text{ DLH} = \$20 \text{ per DLH}$$

EXHIBIT C.4

Overhead Allocated to Go-Karts for KartCo

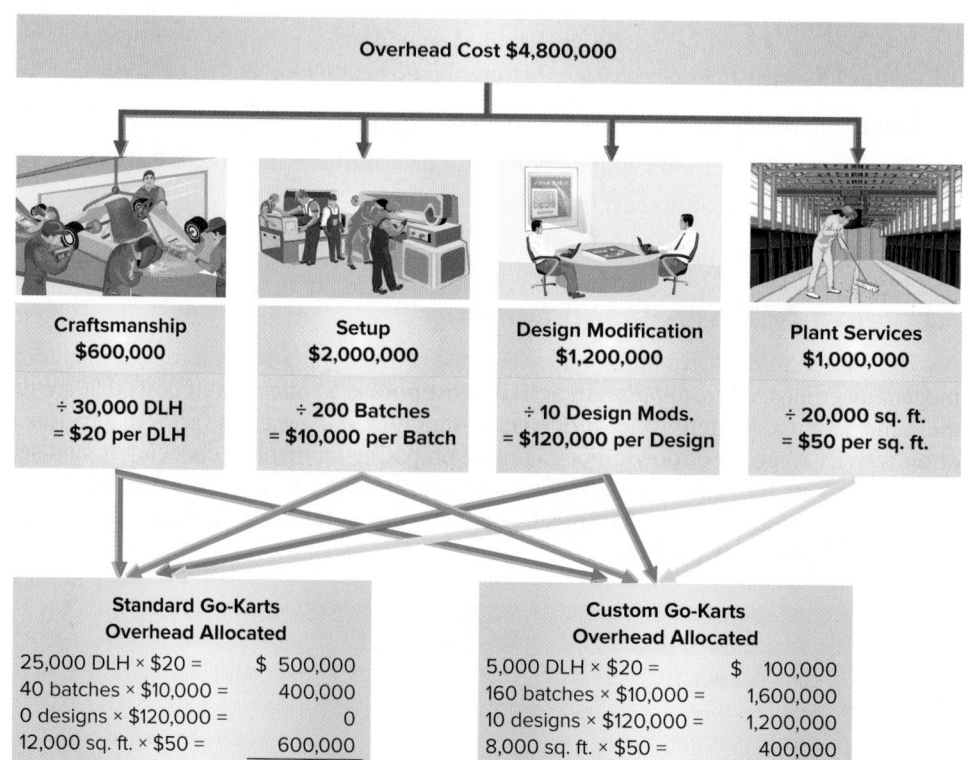

3 In the third step, overhead costs are allocated to products using activity rates and the *actual* amount of the cost driver used, as shown in Exhibit C.4. To illustrate, of the $600,000 of overhead costs in the craftsmanship cost pool, $500,000 is allocated to standard go-karts as follows:

$$
\begin{aligned}
\textbf{Overhead from craftsmanship pool} & \\
\textbf{allocated to standard go-kart} \quad &= \textbf{Cost driver used} \times \textbf{Activity rate} \\
&= \quad 25,000 \text{ DLH} \quad \times \$20 \text{ per DLH} \\
&= \quad \$500,000
\end{aligned}
$$

We know that standard go-karts used 25,000 direct labor hours and the activity rate for craftsmanship is $20 per direct labor hour. Multiplying the number of direct labor hours by the activity rate yields the craftsmanship costs assigned to standard go-karts ($500,000). Custom go-karts used 5,000 direct labor hours, so we assign $100,000 (5,000 DLH × $20 per DLH) of craftsmanship costs to that product line. We similarly allocate overhead of setup, design modification, and plant services pools to each type of go-kart. KartCo assigned no design-modification costs to standard go-karts because standard go-karts are sold as "off-the-shelf" items.

Using ABC, a total of $1,500,000 of overhead costs is allocated to standard go-karts and a total of $3,300,000 is allocated to custom go-karts. While the total overhead cost allocated ($4,800,000) is the same as under the plantwide method, the amounts allocated to the two product lines differ. Overhead cost per unit is computed by dividing total overhead cost allocated to each product line by the number of product units. KartCo's overhead cost per unit for its standard and custom go-karts is computed and shown in Exhibit C.5.

EXHIBIT C.5

Overhead Cost per Unit for Go-Karts Using ABC

	(A) Total Overhead Cost Allocated	(B) Units Produced	(A ÷ B) Overhead Cost per Unit
Standard go-kart..............	$1,500,000	5,000 units	$ 300 per unit
Custom go-kart..............	3,300,000	1,000 units	$3,300 per unit

Product cost per unit for KartCo using ABC for its two products follows. Direct materials and direct labor cost per unit are from other cost records.

	Direct Materials	Direct Labor	Overhead	Product Cost per Unit
Standard go-kart	$400	$350	$ 300	$1,050
Custom go-kart..............	600	500	3,300	4,400

Below we compare total product costs per unit for standard and custom go-karts, using either the plantwide or activity-based costing methods.

Product Cost per Unit	Standard	Custom
Plantwide cost allocation	$1,450	$2,400
Activity-based costing..	1,050	4,400

Assuming that ABC more accurately assigns costs, KartCo's management now sees how its competitors can sell their standard models at $1,200 and why KartCo is flooded with orders for custom go-karts. Specifically, if the cost to produce a standard go-kart is $1,050, as shown above (and not $1,470 as computed using the plantwide rate), a profit of $150 ($1,200 − $1,050) occurs on each standard unit sold at the competitive $1,200 market price. Further, selling its custom go-kart at $3,500 is a mistake because KartCo loses $900 ($3,500 − $4,400) on each custom go-kart sold. KartCo has underpriced its custom go-kart relative to its production costs and competitors' prices, which explains why the company has more custom orders than it can supply.

Activity Cost Pool	Cost Driver
Materials purchasing	Number of purchase orders
Materials handling	Number of materials requisitions
Personnel processing	Number of employees hired or laid off
Equipment depreciation	Number of products produced or hours of use
Quality inspection	Number of units inspected
Indirect labor in setting up equipment	Number of setups required
Engineering costs for product modifications	Number of modifications (engineering change orders)

Advantages and Disadvantages of Activity-Based Costing

While activity-based costing can improve the accuracy of overhead cost allocations, it has limitations. We next describe the major advantages and disadvantages of activity-based costing.

- ABC uses more allocation bases than a traditional cost system. For example, a Chicago-based manufacturer currently uses nearly 20 different activity cost drivers to assign overhead costs to its products. This can result in more accurate overhead cost allocation. However, it can be hard to identify so many different relevant activity cost drivers. Exhibit C.6 lists common examples of overhead cost pools and their usual cost drivers.

- ABC is especially effective when the same department or departments produce many different types of products. For instance, more complex products often require more help from service departments such as engineering, maintenance, and materials handling. With activity-based costing, the complex products are assigned a larger portion of overhead. The difference in overhead assigned can affect product pricing, make or buy, and other managerial decisions.

- ABC encourages managers to focus on *activities* and the use of those activities. ABC helps managers identify the activities that cause costs. This can help managers distinguish between costs from **value-added activities,** which add value to a product, and the costs of *non-value-added activities*, which do not. KartCo's value-added activities include the costs of machining, assembly, and design changes. One of its non-value-added activities is machine repair. Controlling costs requires changing how much of an activity is performed.

- ABC requires managers to look at each item and encourages them to manage each cost to increase the benefit from each dollar spent. It also encourages managers to cooperate because it shows how their efforts are interrelated. This results in *activity-based management.*

- ABC requires more effort to implement and maintain than a traditional cost system. Determining cost drivers for many activities can be challenging. ABC does not always conform to GAAP; thus it can't readily be used for external reporting. For these reasons, the costs of implementing an ABC system can be high.

NEED-TO-KNOW C-2

Activity-Based
Costing Method

P2

A company uses activity-based costing to determine the costs of its three products: A, B, and C. The budgeted cost and cost driver activity for each of the company's three activity cost pools follow.

Activity Cost Pool	Budgeted Cost	Budgeted Activity of Cost Driver		
		Product A	Product B	Product C
Activity 1	$70,000	6,000	9,000	20,000
Activity 2	45,000	7,000	15,000	8,000
Activity 3	82,000	2,500	1,000	1,625

1. Compute the overhead activity rates for each of the company's three activities.
2. Compute the total amount of overhead allocated to Product A. Assume the actual activity usage was the same as the budgeted activity for Product A.

Solution

1.

Activity Cost Pool	Budgeted Cost	÷	Activity Driver*	=	Activity Rate
Activity 1	$70,000		35,000		$ 2.00
Activity 2	45,000		30,000		1.50
Activity 3	82,000		5,125		16.00

*Computed as the sum of the budgeted cost driver activity of all three products.

2. Overhead allocated to Product A:

Activity Cost Pool	Activity Rate	×	Activity Usage	=	Overhead Allocated
Activity 1	$ 2.00	×	6,000	=	$12,000
Activity 2	1.50	×	7,000	=	10,500
Activity 3	16.00	×	2,500	=	40,000
Total.					$62,500

Do More: QS C-3, QS C-4, QS C-5, QS C-6, E C-2, E C-5

Summary

C1 **Explain cost flows for activity-based costing.** With ABC, overhead costs are first traced to the activities that cause them, and then cost pools are formed combining costs caused by the same activity. Overhead rates based on these activities are then used to assign overhead to products in proportion to the amount of activity required to produce them.

A1 **Identify and assess advantages and disadvantages of activity-based costing.** ABC improves product costing accuracy and draws management attention to relevant factors to control. The cost of constructing and maintaining an ABC system can sometimes outweigh its value.

P1 **Assign overhead costs using the plantwide overhead rate method.** The plantwide overhead rate equals total budgeted overhead divided by budgeted plant volume, the latter often measured in direct labor hours or machine hours. This rate multiplied by the number of direct labor hours (or machine hours) required for each product provides the overhead assigned to each product.

P2 **Assign overhead costs using activity-based costing.** In activity-based costing, the costs of related activities are collected and then pooled in some logical manner into activity cost pools. After all activity costs have been accumulated in an activity cost pool account, *cost objects* are assigned a portion of the total activity cost using a cost driver (allocation base).

Key Terms

Activity-based costing (ABC)	Activity cost pool	Cost object
Activity cost driver	Activity rate	Value-added activities

Icon denotes assignments that involve decision making.

Discussion Questions

1. Why are overhead costs allocated to products and not traced to products as direct materials and direct labor are?
2. Complete the following for a traditional two-stage allocation system: In the first stage, service department costs are assigned to _____ departments. In the second stage, a pre-determined overhead rate is computed for each operating department and used to assign overhead to _____.
3. What is the difference between operating departments and service departments?
4. What is activity-based costing? What is its goal?

5. What is a cost object?

6. What is an activity cost driver?

7. ⧗ What company circumstances especially encourage use of activity-based costing?

8. ⧗ Identify at least four typical cost pools for activity-based costing in most organizations.

9. In activity-based costing, costs in a cost pool are allocated to _____ using predetermined overhead rates.

10. **Samsung** must assign overhead costs to its products. Activity-based costing is generally considered more accurate than other methods of assigning overhead. If this is so, why do all manufacturers not use it?

Samsung

11. **Google** generates much of its revenue by providing online advertising. It is said that: "Activity-based costing is only useful for manufacturing companies." Is this a true statement? Explain.

GOOGLE

🅜 connect

QUICK STUDY

In the blank next to the following terms, place the letter A through D corresponding to the best description of that term.

QS C-1

Costing terminology

A1

_____ **1.** Activity

_____ **2.** Activity driver

_____ **3.** Cost pool

_____ **4.** Cost object

A. Measurement associated with an activity.

B. A group of costs that have the same activity drivers.

C. Anything to which costs will be assigned.

D. A task that causes a cost to be incurred.

QS C-2

Computing plantwide overhead rates

P1

Chan Company identified the following activities, costs, and activity drivers for 2017. The company manufactures two types of go-karts: fast and standard.

Activity	Expected Costs	Expected Activity
Handling materials	$625,000	100,000 parts
Inspecting product	900,000	1,500 batches
Processing purchase orders	105,000	700 orders
Paying suppliers	175,000	500 invoices
Insuring the factory	300,000	40,000 square feet
Designing packaging	75,000	2 models

1. Compute a single plantwide overhead rate assuming that the company assigns overhead based on 100,000 budgeted direct labor hours.

2. In January 2017, the fast model required 2,500 direct labor hours and the standard model required 6,000 direct labor hours. Assign overhead costs to each model using the single plantwide overhead rate.

QS C-3

Computing overhead rates under ABC   P2

Refer to the information in QS C-2. Compute the overhead activity rate for each activity, assuming the company uses activity-based costing.

QS C-4

Assigning costs using ABC

P2

Qinto Company sells two types of products, basic and deluxe. The company provides technical support for users of its products at an expected cost of $250,000 per year. The company expects to process 10,000 customer service calls per year.

1. Determine the company's cost of technical support per customer service call.

2. During the month of January, Qinto received 650 calls for customer service on its deluxe model and 150 calls for customer service on its basic model. Assign technical support costs to each model using activity-based costing (ABC).

A company has two products: standard and deluxe. The company expects to produce 34,300 standard units and 69,550 deluxe units. It uses activity-based costing and has prepared the following analysis showing budgeted cost and cost driver activity for each of its three activity cost pools.

Activity Cost Pool	Budgeted Cost	Budgeted Activity of Cost Driver	
		Standard	Deluxe
Activity 1	$87,000	3,000	2,800
Activity 2	62,000	4,500	5,500
Activity 3	93,000	2,500	5,250

QS C-5
Activity-based costing rates and allocations
P2

1. What is the overhead cost per unit for the standard units?

2. What is the overhead cost per unit for the deluxe units?

The following is taken from Mortan Co.'s internal records of its factory with two operating departments. The cost driver for indirect labor and supplies is direct labor costs, and the cost driver for the remaining overhead items is number of hours of machine use. Compute the total amount of overhead cost allocated to operating department 1 using activity-based costing.

QS C-6
Activity-based costing and overhead cost allocation
P2

	Direct Labor	Machine Use Hours
Operating department 1	$18,800	2,000
Operating department 2	13,200	1,200
Totals.	$32,000	3,200
Factory overhead costs		
Rent and utilities		$12,200
Indirect labor		5,400
General office expense		4,000
Depreciation—Equipment		3,000
Supplies		2,600
Total factory overhead.		$27,200

1. Which costing method tends to overstate the cost of high-volume products?

   a. Traditional volume-based costing

   b. Activity-based costing

   c. Job order costing

   d. Differential costing

2. If management wants the most accurate product cost, which of the following costing methods should be used?

   a. Volume-based costing using direct labor hours to allocate overhead

   b. Volume-based costing using a plantwide overhead rate

   c. Normal costing using a plantwide overhead rate

   d. Activity-based costing

3. Disadvantages of activity-based costing include which of the following?

   a. It is not acceptable under GAAP for external reporting.

   b. It can be costly to implement.

   c. It can be used in activity-based management.

   d. Both a. and b.

QS C-7
Multiple choice overhead questions
A1

Appendix C   Activity-Based Costing

EXERCISES

Exercise C-1
Using the plantwide overhead rate to assess prices

P1

Real Cool produces two different models of air conditioners. The company produces the mechanical systems in their components department. The mechanical systems are combined with the housing assembly in its finishing department. The activities, costs, and drivers associated with these two manufacturing processes and the production support process follow.

Process	Activity	Overhead Cost	Driver	Quantity
Components	Changeover	$ 500,000	Number of batches	800
	Machining	279,000	Machine hours	6,000
	Setups	225,000	Number of setups	120
		$1,004,000		
Finishing	Welding	$ 180,300	Welding hours	3,000
	Inspecting	210,000	Number of inspections	700
	Rework	75,000	Rework orders	300
		$ 465,300		
Support	Purchasing	$ 135,000	Purchase orders	450
	Providing space	32,000	Number of units	5,000
	Providing utilities	65,000	Number of units	5,000
		$ 232,000		

Additional production information concerning its two product lines follows.

	Model 145	Model 212
Units produced...................	1,500	3,500
Welding hours.....................	800	2,200
Batches	400	400
Number of inspections.............	400	300
Machine hours	1,800	4,200
Setups	60	60
Rework orders	160	140
Purchase orders..................	300	150

1. Using a plantwide overhead rate based on machine hours, compute the overhead cost per unit for each product line.

2. Determine the total cost per unit for each product line if the direct labor and direct materials costs per unit are $250 for Model 145 and $180 for Model 212.

Check   (3) Model 212, $(50.26) per unit loss

3. If the market price for Model 145 is $800 and the market price for Model 212 is $470, determine the profit or loss per unit for each model. Comment on the results.

Exercise C-2
Using ABC to assess prices

P2

Check   (3) Model 212, $24.88 per unit profit

Refer to the information in Exercise C-1 to answer the following requirements.

1. Using ABC, compute the overhead cost per unit for each product line.

2. Determine the total cost per unit for each product line if the direct labor and direct materials costs per unit are $250 for Model 145 and $180 for Model 212.

3. If the market price for Model 145 is $800 and the market price for Model 212 is $470, determine the profit or loss per unit for each model. Comment on the results.

Consider the following data for two products of Vigano Manufacturing.

Exercise C-3
Using ABC for strategic decisions

P1   P2

	Overhead Cost	Product A	Product B
Number of units produced.....................		10,000 units	2,000 units
Direct labor cost (@ $24 per DLH)...............		0.20 DLH per unit	0.25 DLH per unit
Direct materials cost.........................		$2 per unit	$3 per unit
Activity			
Machine setup	$121,000		
Parts handling	48,000		
Quality control inspections	80,000		
	$249,000		

1. Using direct labor hours as the basis for assigning overhead costs, determine the total production cost per unit for each product line.
2. If the market price for Product A is $20 and the market price for Product B is $60, determine the profit or loss per unit for each product. Comment on the results.
3. Consider the following additional information about these two product lines. If ABC is used for assigning overhead costs to products, what is the cost per unit for Product A and for Product B?

Check   (2) Product B, $26.10 per unit profit

Activity Drivers	Product A	Product B
Number of machine setups required for production	10 setups	12 setups
Number of parts required......................................	1 part/unit	3 parts/unit
Inspection hours required	40 hours	210 hours

4. Determine the profit or loss per unit for each product. Should this information influence company strategy? Explain.

(4) Product B, ($24.60) per unit loss

Singh and Smythe is an architectural firm that provides services for residential construction projects. The following data pertain to a recent reporting period.

Exercise C-4
Using ABC in a service company

P2

	Activities	Costs
Design department		
Client consultation	1,500 contact hours	$270,000
Drawings...	2,000 design hours	115,000
Modeling	40,000 square feet	30,000
Project management department		
Supervision	600 days	$120,000
Billings	8 jobs	10,000
Collections	8 jobs	12,000

1. Using ABC, compute the firm's activity overhead rates. Form activity cost pools where appropriate.
2. Assign costs to a 9,200-square-foot job that requires 450 contact hours, 340 design hours, and 200 days to complete.

Check   (2) $150,200

Health Co-op is an outpatient surgical clinic that wants to better understand its costs. It decides to prepare an activity-based cost analysis, including an estimate of the average cost of both general surgery and orthopedic surgery. The clinic's three cost centers and their cost drivers follow.

Exercise C-5
Activity-based costing

P2

Cost Center	Cost	Cost Driver	Driver Quantity
Professional salaries	$1,600,000	Professional hours	10,000
Patient services and supplies	27,000	Number of patients	600
Building cost	150,000	Square feet	1,500

The two main surgical units and their related data follow.

Service	Hours	Square Feet*	Patients
General surgery	2,500	600	400
Orthopedic surgery.	7,500	900	200

* Orthopedic surgery requires more space for patients, supplies, and equipment.

1. Assume costs are allocated based on number of patients. Compute the average cost per patient. (Round to the nearest whole dollar.)

Check   (3) Average cost of general surgery, $1,195 per patient

2. Compute the cost per cost driver for each of the three cost centers.

3. Use the results from part 1 to allocate costs from each of the three cost centers to the general surgery unit. Compute total cost and average cost per patient for the general surgery unit.

Exercise C-6

Activity-based costing

P2   A1

Northwest Company produces two types of glass shelving, rounded edge and squared edge, on the same production line. For the current period, the company reports the following data.

	Rounded Edge	Squared Edge	Total
Direct materials	$19,000	$ 43,200	$ 62,200
Direct labor.	12,200	23,800	36,000
Overhead (300% of direct labor cost)	36,600	71,400	108,000
Total cost.	$67,800	$138,400	$206,200
Quantity produced	10,500 ft.	14,100 ft.	
Average cost per ft. (rounded).	$ 6.46	$ 9.82	

Northwest's controller wishes to apply activity-based costing (ABC) to allocate the $108,000 of overhead costs incurred by the two product lines to see whether cost per foot would change markedly from that reported above. She has collected the following information.

Overhead Cost Category (Activity Cost Pool)	Cost
Supervision	$ 5,400
Depreciation of machinery.	56,600
Assembly line preparation	46,000
Total overhead	$108,000

She has also collected the following information about the cost drivers for each category (cost pool) and the amount of each driver used by the two product lines.

Overhead Cost Category (Activity Cost Pool)	Driver	Usage		
		Rounded Edge	Squared Edge	Total
Supervision	Direct labor cost ($)	$12,200	$23,800	$36,000
Depreciation of machinery	Machine hours	500 hours	1,500 hours	2,000 hours
Assembly line preparation	Setups (number)	40 times	210 times	250 times

Required

1. Assign these three overhead cost pools to each of the two products using ABC.

Check   (2) Rounded edge, $5.19; Squared edge, $10.76

2. Determine average cost per foot for each of the two products using ABC.

3. Compare the average cost per foot under ABC with the average cost per foot under the current method for each product. Explain why a difference between the two cost allocation methods exists.

connect

Craftmore Machining produces machine tools for the construction industry. The following details about overhead costs were taken from its company records.

PROBLEM SET A

Problem C-1A
Applying activity-based costing

P1   P2   A1

Production Activity	Indirect Labor	Indirect Materials	Other Overhead
Grinding..............................	$320,000		
Polishing		$135,000	
Product modification	600,000		
Providing power......................			$255,000
System calibration	500,000		

Additional information on the drivers for its production activities follows.

Grinding.....................	13,000 machine hours	Providing power	17,000 direct labor hours
Polishing	13,000 machine hours	System calibration...........	400 batches
Product modification	1,500 engineering hours		

Required

1. Compute the activity overhead rates using ABC. Form cost pools as appropriate.
2. Determine overhead costs to assign to the following jobs using ABC.

	Job 3175	Job 4286
Number of units	200 units	2,500 units
Machine hours	550 MH	5,500 MH
Engineering hours	26 eng. hours	32 eng. hours
Batches	30 batches	90 batches
Direct labor hours	500 DLH	4,375 DLH

3. What is the overhead cost per unit for Job 3175? What is the overhead cost per unit for Job 4286?
4. If the company used a plantwide overhead rate based on direct labor hours, what would be the overhead cost for each unit of Job 3175? Of Job 4286?
5. Compare the overhead costs per unit computed in requirements 3 and 4 for each job. Which method more accurately assigns overhead costs?

Check (3) Job 3175, $373.25 per unit

Tent Master produces two lines of tents sold to outdoor enthusiasts. The tents are cut to specifications in department A. In department B, the tents are sewn and folded. The activities, costs, and drivers associated with these two manufacturing processes and the company's production support activities follow.

Problem C-2A
Pricing analysis with ABC and a plantwide overhead rate

A1   P1   P2

Process	Activity	Overhead Cost	Driver	Quantity
Department A	Pattern alignment	$ 64,400	Batches	560
	Cutting	50,430	Machine hours	12,300
	Moving product	100,800	Moves	2,400
		$215,630		
Department B	Sewing	$327,600	Direct labor hours	4,200
	Inspecting	24,000	Inspections	600
	Folding	47,880	Units	22,800
		$399,480		
Support	Design	$280,000	Modification orders	280
	Providing space	51,600	Square feet	8,600
	Materials handling	184,000	Square yards	920,000
		$515,600		

Additional production information on the two lines of tents follows.

	Pup Tent	Pop-up Tent
Units produced..........................	15,200 units	7,600 units
Moves................................	800 moves	1,600 moves
Batches..............................	140 batches	420 batches
Number of inspections...................	240 inspections	360 inspections
Machine hours	7,000 MH	5,300 MH
Direct labor hours.......................	2,600 DLH	1,600 DLH
Modification orders	70 modification orders	210 modification orders
Space occupied	4,300 square feet	4,300 square feet
Material required	450,000 square yards	470,000 square yards

Required

1. Using a plantwide overhead rate based on direct labor hours, compute the overhead cost that is assigned to each pup tent and each pop-up tent.
2. Using the plantwide overhead rate, determine the total cost per unit for the two products if the direct materials and direct labor cost is $25 per pup tent and $32 per pop-up tent.
3. If the market price of the pup tent is $65 and the market price of the pop-up tent is $200, determine the gross profit per unit for each tent. What might management conclude about the pup tent?

Check   (4) Pup tent, $58.46 per unit cost

4. Using ABC, compute the total cost per unit for each tent if the direct labor and direct materials cost is $25 per pup tent and $32 per pop-up tent.
5. If the market price is $65 per pup tent and $200 per pop-up tent, determine the gross profit per unit for each tent. Comment on the results.
6. Would your pricing analysis be improved if the company used, instead of ABC, departmental rates determined using machine hours in department A and direct labor hours in department B? Explain.

Problem C-3A

Assessing impacts of using a plantwide overhead rate versus ABC

A1

Maxlon Company manufactures custom-made furniture for its local market and produces a line of home furnishings sold in retail stores across the country. The company uses traditional volume-based methods of assigning direct materials and direct labor to its product lines. Overhead has always been assigned by using a plantwide overhead rate based on direct labor hours. In the past few years, management has seen its line of retail products continue to sell at high volumes, but competition has forced it to lower prices on these items. The prices are declining to a level close to its cost of production.

Meanwhile, its custom-made furniture is in high demand, and customers have commented on its favorable (lower) prices compared to its competitors. Management is considering dropping its line of retail products and devoting all of its resources to custom-made furniture.

Required

1. What reasons could explain why competitors are forcing the company to lower prices on its high-volume retail products?
2. Why do you believe the company charges less for custom-order products than its competitors?
3. Does a company's costing method have any effect on its pricing decisions? Explain.
4. Aside from the differences in volume of output, what production differences do you believe exist between making custom-order furniture and mass-market furnishings?
5. What information might the company obtain from using ABC that it might not obtain using volume-based costing methods?

The following data are for the two products produced by Shakti Company.

Problem C-4A
Comparing costs using ABC with the plantwide overhead rate

P1 P2 A1

	Product A	Product B
Direct materials	$15 per unit	$24 per unit
Direct labor hours	0.3 DLH per unit	1.6 DLH per unit
Machine hours	0.1 MH per unit	1.2 MH per unit
Batches	125 batches	225 batches
Volume	10,000 units	2,000 units
Engineering modifications	12 modifications	58 modifications
Number of customers	500 customers	400 customers
Market price	$30 per unit	$120 per unit

The company's direct labor rate is $20 per direct labor hour (DLH). Additional information follows.

	Costs	Driver
Indirect manufacturing		
Engineering support	$24,500	Engineering modifications
Electricity	34,000	Machine hours
Setup costs	52,500	Batches
Nonmanufacturing		
Customer service	81,000	Number of customers

Required

1. Compute the manufacturing cost per unit using the plantwide overhead rate based on direct labor hours. What is the gross profit per unit?

2. How much gross profit is generated by each customer of Product A using the plantwide overhead rate? How much gross profit is generated by each customer of Product B using the plantwide overhead rate? What is the cost of providing customer service to each customer? What information is provided by this comparison?

3. Determine the manufacturing cost per unit of each product line using ABC. What is the gross profit per unit?

4. How much gross profit is generated by each customer of Product A using ABC? How much gross profit is generated by each customer of Product B using ABC? Is the gross profit per customer adequate?

5. Which method of product costing gives better information to managers of this company? Explain why.

Check   (1) Product A, $26.37 per unit manufacturing cost

(3) Product A, $24.30 per unit manufacturing cost

Healthy Day Company produces two beverages, PowerPunch and SlimLife. Data about these products follow.

Problem C-5A
Evaluating product line costs and prices using ABC

P2

	PowerPunch	SlimLife
Production volume	12,500 bottles	180,000 bottles
Liquid materials	1,400 gallons	37,000 gallons
Dry materials	620 pounds	12,000 pounds
Bottles	12,500 bottles	180,000 bottles
Labels	3 labels per bottle	1 label per bottle
Machine setups	500 setups	300 setups
Machine hours	200 MH	3,750 MH

Additional data from its two production departments follow.

Department	Driver	Cost
Mixing department		
Liquid materials	Gallons	$ 2,304
Dry materials	Pounds	6,941
Utilities	Machine hours	1,422
Bottling department		
Bottles.	Units	$77,000
Labeling	Labels per bottle	6,525
Machine setup	Setups	20,000

Required

1. Determine the cost of each product line using ABC.

2. What is the cost per bottle for PowerPunch? What is the cost per bottle of SlimLife? (*Hint:* Your answer should draw on the total cost for each product line computed in requirement 1.)

Check   (3) $2.22 profit per bottle

3. If PowerPunch sells for $3.75 per bottle, how much profit does the company earn per bottle of PowerPunch that it sells?

4. What is the minimum price that the company should set per bottle of SlimLife? Explain.

Problem C-6A
Activity-based costing

P2

Patient Health is an outpatient surgical clinic that was profitable for many years, but Medicare has cut its reimbursements by as much as 50%. As a result, the clinic wants to better understand its costs. It decides to prepare an activity-based cost analysis, including an estimate of the average cost of both general surgery and orthopedic surgery. The clinic's three cost centers and their cost drivers follow.

Cost Center	Cost	Cost Driver	Driver Quantity
Professional salaries	$2,000,000	Professional hours	10,000
Patient services and supplies	37,500	Number of patients	500
Building cost	300,000	Square feet	2,000

The two main surgical units and their related data follow.

Service	Hours	Square Feet*	Patients
General surgery	2,500	720	400
Orthopedic surgery.	7,500	1,280	100

* Orthopedic surgery requires more space for patients, supplies, and equipment.

Required

1. Compute the cost per cost driver for each of the three cost centers.

Check   (2) Average cost of general (orthopedic) surgery, $1,595 ($16,995) per patient

2. Use the results from part 1 to allocate costs from each of the three cost centers to both the general surgery and the orthopedic surgery units. Compute total cost and average cost per patient for both the general surgery and the orthopedic surgery units.

Analysis Component

3. Without providing computations, would the average cost of general surgery be higher or lower if all center costs were allocated based on the number of patients? Explain.

Fancy Foods produces gourmet gift baskets that it distributes online as well as from its small retail store. The following details about overhead costs are taken from its records.

PROBLEM SET B

Problem C-1B
Applying activity-based costing

P1   P2   A1

Production Activity	Indirect Labor	Indirect Materials	Other Overhead
Wrapping............................	$300,000	$200,000	
Assembling	400,000		
Product design	180,000		
Obtaining business licenses			$100,000
Cooking............................	150,000	120,000	

Additional information on the drivers for its production activities follows.

Wrapping.........................	100,000 units
Assembling.......................	20,000 direct labor hours
Product design....................	3,000 design hours
Obtaining business licenses	20,000 direct labor hours
Cooking...........................	1,000 batches

Required

1. Compute the activity overhead rates using ABC. Form cost pools as appropriate.
2. Determine the overhead costs to assign to the following jobs using ABC.

	Holiday Basket	Executive Basket
Number of units	8,000 units	1,000 units
Direct labor hours............	2,000 DLH	500 DLH
Design hours................	40 design hours	40 design hours
Batches....................	80 batches	200 batches

3. What is the overhead cost per unit for the Holiday Basket? What is the overhead cost per unit for the Executive Basket?

4. If the company used a plantwide overhead rate based on direct labor hours, what is the overhead cost for each Holiday Basket unit? What would be the overhead cost for each Executive Basket unit if a single plantwide overhead rate is used?

5. Compare the overhead costs per unit computed in requirements 3 and 4 for each job. Which cost assignment method provides the most accurate cost? Explain.

Check   (3) Holiday Basket, $14.25 per unit

(4) Holiday Basket, $18.13 per unit

Spicy Salsa Company produces its condiments in two types: Extra Fine for restaurant customers and Family Style for home use. Salsa is prepared in department 1 and packaged in department 2. The activities, overhead costs, and drivers associated with these two manufacturing processes and the company's production support activities follow.

Problem C-2B
Pricing analysis with ABC and a plantwide overhead rate

A1   P1   P2

Process	Activity	Overhead Cost	Driver	Quantity
Department 1	Mixing	$ 4,500	Machine hours	1,500
	Cooking	11,250	Machine hours	1,500
	Product testing	112,500	Batches	600
		$128,250		
Department 2	Machine calibration	$250,000	Production runs	400
	Labeling	12,000	Cases of output	120,000
	Defects	6,000	Cases of output	120,000
		$268,000		
Support	Recipe formulation	$ 90,000	Focus groups	45
	Heat, lights, and water	27,000	Machine hours	1,500
	Materials handling	65,000	Container types	8
		$182,000		

Additional production information about its two product lines follows.

	Extra Fine	Family Style
Units produced............................	20,000 cases	100,000 cases
Batches......................................	200 batches	400 batches
Machine hours	500 MH	1,000 MH
Focus groups	30 groups	15 groups
Container types	5 containers	3 containers
Production runs	200 runs	200 runs

Required

1. Using a plantwide overhead rate based on cases, compute the overhead cost that is assigned to each case of Extra Fine Salsa and each case of Family Style Salsa.

2. Using the plantwide overhead rate, determine the total cost per case for the two products if the direct materials and direct labor cost is $6 per case of Extra Fine and $5 per case of Family Style.

3. If the market price of Extra Fine Salsa is $18 per case and the market price of Family Style Salsa is $9 per case, determine the gross profit per case for each product. What might management conclude about each product line?

4. Using ABC, compute the total cost per case for each product type if the direct labor and direct materials cost is $6 per case of Extra Fine and $5 per case of Family Style.

5. If the market price is $18 per case of Extra Fine and $9 per case of Family Style, determine the gross profit per case for each product. How should management interpret the market prices given your computations?

6. Would your pricing analysis be improved if the company used departmental rates based on machine hours in department 1 and number of cases in department 2 instead of ABC? Explain.

Check (2) Cost per case: Extra Fine, $10.82; Family Style, $9.82

(4) Cost per case: Extra Fine, $20.02; Family Style, $7.98

Problem C-3B

Assessing impacts of using a plantwide overhead rate versus ABC

A1

Lakeside Paper produces cardboard boxes. The boxes require designing, cutting, and printing. (The boxes are shipped flat and customers fold them as necessary.) Lakeside has a reputation for providing high-quality products and excellent service to customers, who are major U.S. manufacturers. Costs are assigned to products based on the number of machine hours required to produce them.

Three years ago, a new marketing executive was hired. She suggested the company offer custom design and manufacturing services to small specialty manufacturers. These customers required boxes for their products and were eager to have Lakeside as a supplier. Within one year, Lakeside found that it was so busy with orders from small customers, it had trouble supplying boxes to all its customers on a timely basis. Large, long-time customers began to complain about slow service, and several took their business elsewhere. Within another 18 months, Lakeside was in financial distress with a backlog of orders to be filled.

Required

1. What do you believe are the major costs of making its boxes? How are those costs related to the volume of boxes produced?

2. How did Lakeside's new customers differ from its previous customers?

3. Would the unit cost to produce a box for new customers be different from the unit cost to produce a box for its previous customers? Explain.

4. Could Lakeside's fate have been different if it had used ABC for determining the cost of its boxes?

5. What information would have been available with ABC that might have been overlooked using a traditional volume-based costing method?

Problem C-4B

Comparing costs using ABC vs. the plantwide overhead rate

A1   P1   P2

Vargo Company makes two distinct products with the following information available for each.

	Standard	Deluxe
Direct materials	$4 per unit	$8 per unit
Direct labor hours	4 DLH per unit	5 DLH per unit
Machine hours	3 MH per unit	3 MH per unit
Batches	175 batches	75 batches
Volume	40,000 units	10,000 units
Engineering modifications...............	50 modifications	25 modifications
Number of customers....................	1,000 customers	1,000 customers
Market price	$92 per unit	$125 per unit

The company's direct labor rate is $20 per direct labor hour (DLH). Additional information follows.

	Costs	Driver
Indirect manufacturing		
Engineering support	$ 56,250	Engineering modifications
Electricity	112,500	Machine hours
Setup costs..................	41,250	Batches
Nonmanufacturing		
Customer service.............	250,000	Number of customers

Required

1. Compute the manufacturing cost per unit using the plantwide overhead rate based on machine hours. What is the gross profit per unit?

2. How much gross profit is generated by each customer of the standard product using the plantwide overhead rate? How much gross profit is generated by each customer of the deluxe product using the plantwide overhead rate? What is the cost of providing customer service to each customer? What information is provided by this comparison?

3. Determine the manufacturing cost per unit of each product line using ABC. What is the gross profit per unit?

4. How much gross profit is generated by each customer of the standard product using ABC? How much gross profit is generated by each customer of the deluxe product using ABC? Is the gross profit per customer adequate?

5. Which method of product costing gives better information to managers of this company? Explain.

Check (1) Gross profit per unit: Standard, $3.80; Deluxe, $12.80

(3) Gross profit per unit: Standard, $4.09; Deluxe, $11.64

MathGames produces two electronic, handheld educational games: *Fun with Fractions* and *Count Calculus*. Data on these products follow.

Problem C-5B
Evaluating product line costs and prices using ABC

P2

	Fun with Fractions	Count Calculus
Production volume	150,000 units	10,000 units
Components	450,000 parts	100,000 parts
Direct labor hours	15,000 DLH	2,000 DLH
Packaging materials...........	150,000 boxes	10,000 boxes
Shipping cartons	100 units per carton	25 units per carton
Machine setups	52 setups	52 setups
Machine hours	5,000 MH	2,000 MH

Additional data from its two production departments follow.

Department	Driver	Cost
Assembly department		
Component cost....................	Parts	$495,000
Assembly labor.....................	Direct labor hours	244,800
Maintenance	Machine hours	100,800
Wrapping department		
Packaging materials.................	Boxes	$460,800
Shipping	Cartons	27,360
Machine setup	Setups	187,200

Required

1. Using ABC, determine the cost of each product line.

2. What is the cost per unit for *Fun with Fractions*? What is the cost per unit of *Count Calculus*?

3. If *Count Calculus* sells for $59.95 per unit, how much profit does the company earn per unit of *Count Calculus* sold?

4. What is the minimum price that the company should set per unit of *Fun with Fractions*? Explain.

Check (3) $32.37 profit per unit

Problem C-6B

Activity-based costing

P2

Wooddale Landscaping has enjoyed profits for many years, but new competition has cut service revenue by as much as 30%. As a result, the company wants to better understand its costs. It decides to prepare an activity-based cost analysis, including an estimate of the average cost of both general landscaping services and custom-design landscaping services. The company's three cost centers and their cost drivers follow.

Cost Center	Cost	Cost Driver	Driver Quantity
Professional salaries	$600,000	Professional hours	10,000
Customer supplies	150,000	Number of customers	800
Building cost	240,000	Square feet	2,500

The two main landscaping units and their related data follow.

Service	Hours	Square Feet*	Customers
General landscaping	2,500	1,000	600
Custom-design landscaping	7,500	1,500	200

* Custom-design landscaping requires more space for equipment, supplies, and planning.

Required

1. Compute the cost per cost driver for each of the three cost centers.

Check   (2) Average cost of general (custom) landscaping, $597.50 ($3,157.50) per customer

2. Use the results from part 1 to allocate costs from each of the three cost centers to both the general landscaping and the custom-design landscaping units. Compute total cost and average cost per customer for both the general landscaping and the custom-design landscaping units.

Analysis Component

3. Without providing computations, would the average cost of general landscaping be higher or lower if all center costs were allocated based on the number of customers? Explain.

SERIAL PROBLEM

Business Solutions

P1   P2

© Alexander Image/Shutterstock RF

(This serial problem began in Chapter 1 and continues through most of the book. If previous chapter segments were not completed, the serial problem can begin at this point.)

SP C   After reading an article about activity-based costing in a trade journal for the furniture industry, Santana Rey wondered if it was time to critically analyze overhead costs at **Business Solutions**. In a recent month, Rey found that setup costs, inspection costs, and utility costs made up most of its overhead. Additional information about overhead follows.

Activity	Cost	Driver
Setting up machines..............	$20,000	25 batches
Inspecting components	7,500	5,000 parts
Providing utilities	10,000	5,000 machine hours

Overhead has been applied to output at a rate of 50% of direct labor costs. The following data pertain to Job 6.15.

Direct materials	$2,500	Number of parts	400 parts
Direct labor................	$3,500	Machine hours	600 machine hours
Batches...................	2 batches		

Required

1. What is the total cost of Job 6.15 if Business Solutions applies overhead at 50% of direct labor cost?

2. What is the total cost of Job 6.15 if Business Solutions uses activity-based costing?

3. Which approach to assigning overhead gives a better representation of the costs incurred to produce Job 6.15? Explain.

Index

Note: Page numbers followed by *n* indicate information found in footnotes. **Boldface** entries indicate defined terms.

Chart of Accounts

Following is a typical chart of accounts, which is used in several assignments. Each company has its own unique set of accounts and numbering system.
*An asterisk denotes a contra account.

Assets

Current Assets

101 Cash
102 Petty cash
103 Cash equivalents
104 Short-term investments
105 Fair value adjustment, _____ securities (S-T)
106 Accounts receivable
107 Allowance for doubtful accounts*
108 Allowance for sales discounts*
109 Interest receivable
110 Rent receivable
111 Notes receivable
112 Legal fees receivable
119 Merchandise inventory (or Inventory)
120 _____ inventory
121 Inventory returns estimated
124 Office supplies
125 Store supplies
126 _____ supplies
128 Prepaid insurance
129 Prepaid interest
131 Prepaid rent
132 Raw materials inventory
133 Work in process inventory, _____
134 Work in process inventory, _____
135 Finished goods inventory

Long-Term Investments

141 Long-term investments
142 Fair value adjustment, _____ securities (L-T)
144 Investment in _____
145 Bond sinking fund

Plant Assets

151 Automobiles
152 Accumulated depreciation—Automobiles*
153 Trucks
154 Accumulated depreciation—Trucks*
155 Boats
156 Accumulated depreciation—Boats*
157 Professional library
158 Accumulated depreciation—Professional library*
159 Law library
160 Accumulated depreciation—Law library*
161 Furniture
162 Accumulated depreciation—Furniture*
163 Office equipment

164 Accumulated depreciation—Office equipment*
165 Store equipment
166 Accumulated depreciation—Store equipment*
167 _____ equipment
168 Accumulated depreciation—_____ equipment*
169 Machinery
170 Accumulated depreciation—Machinery*
173 Building _____
174 Accumulated depreciation—Building _____*
175 Building _____
176 Accumulated depreciation—Building _____*
179 Land improvements _____
180 Accumulated depreciation—Land improvements _____*
181 Land improvements _____
182 Accumulated depreciation—Land improvements _____*
183 Land

Natural Resources

185 Mineral deposit
186 Accumulated depletion—Mineral deposit*

Intangible Assets

191 Patents
192 Leasehold
193 Franchise
194 Copyrights
195 Leasehold improvements
196 Licenses
197 Accumulated amortization—_____*
199 Goodwill

Liabilities

Current Liabilities

201 Accounts payable
202 Insurance payable
203 Interest payable
204 Legal fees payable
207 Office salaries payable
208 Rent payable
209 Salaries payable
210 Wages payable
211 Accrued payroll payable
212 Factory wages payable
214 Estimated warranty liability
215 Income taxes payable

216 Common dividend payable
217 Preferred dividend payable
218 State unemployment taxes payable
219 Employee federal income taxes payable
221 Employee medical insurance payable
222 Employee retirement program payable
223 Employee union dues payable
224 Federal unemployment taxes payable
225 FICA taxes payable
226 Estimated vacation pay liability
227 Sales refund payable

Unearned Revenues

230 Unearned consulting fees
231 Unearned legal fees
232 Unearned property management fees
233 Unearned _____ fees
234 Unearned _____ fees
235 Unearned janitorial revenue
236 Unearned _____ revenue
238 Unearned rent

Notes Payable

240 Short-term notes payable
241 Discount on short-term notes payable*
245 Notes payable
251 Long-term notes payable
252 Discount on long-term notes payable*

Long-Term Liabilities

253 Long-term lease liability
255 Bonds payable
256 Discount on bonds payable*
257 Premium on bonds payable
258 Deferred income tax liability

Equity

Owner's Equity

301 _____, Capital
302 _____, Withdrawals
303 _____, Capital
304 _____, Withdrawals
305 _____, Capital
306 _____, Withdrawals

Paid-In Capital

307 Common stock, $ _____ par value
308 Common stock, no-par value
309 Common stock, $ _____ stated value
310 Common stock dividend distributable
311 Paid-in capital in excess of par value, Common stock

312 Paid-in capital in excess of stated value, No-par common stock
313 Paid-in capital from retirement of common stock
314 Paid-in capital, Treasury stock
315 Preferred stock
316 Paid-in capital in excess of par value, Preferred stock

Retained Earnings

318 Retained earnings
319 Cash dividends (or Dividends)
320 Stock dividends

Other Equity Accounts

321 Treasury stock, Common*
322 Unrealized gain—Equity
323 Unrealized loss—Equity

Revenues

401 _____ fees earned
402 _____ fees earned
403 _____ revenues
404 Revenues
405 Commissions earned
406 Rent revenue (or Rent earned)
407 Dividends revenue (or Dividends earned)
408 Earnings from investment in _____
409 Interest revenue (or Interest earned)
410 Sinking fund earnings
413 Sales
414 Sales returns and allowances*
415 Sales discounts*

Cost of Sales

Cost of Goods Sold

502 Cost of goods sold
505 Purchases
506 Purchases returns and allowances*
507 Purchases discounts*
508 Transportation-in

Manufacturing

520 Raw materials purchases
521 Freight-in on raw materials
530 Direct labor
540 Factory overhead
541 Indirect materials
542 Indirect labor
543 Factory insurance expired
544 Factory supervision
545 Factory supplies used
546 Factory utilities
547 Miscellaneous production costs
548 Property taxes on factory building
549 Property taxes on factory equipment
550 Rent on factory building
551 Repairs, factory equipment
552 Small tools written off
560 Depreciation of factory equipment
561 Depreciation of factory building

Standard Cost Variances

580 Direct material quantity variance
581 Direct material price variance
582 Direct labor quantity variance
583 Direct labor price variance
584 Factory overhead volume variance
585 Factory overhead controllable variance

Expenses

Amortization, Depletion, and Depreciation

601 Amortization expense—_____
602 Amortization expense—_____
603 Depletion expense—_____
604 Depreciation expense—Boats
605 Depreciation expense—Automobiles
606 Depreciation expense—Building _____
607 Depreciation expense—Building _____
608 Depreciation expense—Land improvements _____
609 Depreciation expense—Land improvements _____
610 Depreciation expense—Law library
611 Depreciation expense—Trucks
612 Depreciation expense—_____ equipment
613 Depreciation expense—_____ equipment
614 Depreciation expense—_____
615 Depreciation expense—_____

Employee-Related Expenses

620 Office salaries expense
621 Sales salaries expense
622 Salaries expense
623 _____ wages expense
624 Employees' benefits expense
625 Payroll taxes expense

Financial Expenses

630 Cash over and short
631 Discounts lost
632 Factoring fee expense
633 Interest expense

Insurance Expenses

635 Insurance expense—Delivery equipment
636 Insurance expense—Office equipment
637 Insurance expense—_____

Rental Expenses

640 Rent expense
641 Rent expense—Office space
642 Rent expense—Selling space
643 Press rental expense
644 Truck rental expense
645 _____ rental expense

Supplies Expenses

650 Office supplies expense
651 Store supplies expense
652 _____ supplies expense
653 _____ supplies expense

Miscellaneous Expenses

655 Advertising expense
656 Bad debts expense
657 Blueprinting expense
658 Boat expense
659 Collection expense
661 Concessions expense
662 Credit card expense
663 Delivery expense
664 Dumping expense
667 Equipment expense
668 Food and drinks expense
671 Gas and oil expense
672 General and administrative expense
673 Janitorial expense
674 Legal fees expense
676 Mileage expense
677 Miscellaneous expenses
678 Mower and tools expense
679 Operating expense
680 Organization expense
681 Permits expense
682 Postage expense
683 Property taxes expense
684 Repairs expense—_____
685 Repairs expense—_____
687 Selling expense
688 Telephone expense
689 Travel and entertainment expense
690 Utilities expense
691 Warranty expense
692 _____ expense
695 Income taxes expense

Gains and Losses

701 Gain on retirement of bonds
702 Gain on sale of machinery
703 Gain on sale of investments
704 Gain on sale of trucks
705 Gain on _____
706 Foreign exchange gain or loss
801 Loss on disposal of machinery
802 Loss on exchange of equipment
803 Loss on exchange of _____
804 Loss on sale of notes
805 Loss on retirement of bonds
806 Loss on sale of investments
807 Loss on sale of machinery
808 Loss on _____
809 Unrealized gain—Income
810 Unrealized loss—Income
811 Impairment gain
812 Impairment loss

Clearing Accounts

901 Income summary
902 Manufacturing summary

① Cost Types

Variable costs: Total cost changes in proportion to volume of activity.

Fixed costs: Total cost does not change in proportion to volume of activity.

Mixed costs: Cost consists of both a variable and a fixed element.

② Product Costs

Direct materials: Raw materials costs directly linked to finished product.

Direct labor: Employee costs directly linked to finished product.

Overhead: Production costs indirectly linked to finished product.

③ Costing Systems

Job order costing: Costs assigned to each unique unit or batch of units.

Process costing: Costs assigned to similar products that are mass-produced in a continuous manner.

④ Costing Ratios

Contribution margin ratio = (Net sales − Variable costs)/Net sales

Predetermined overhead rate = Estimated overhead costs/Estimated activity base

Break-even point in units = Total fixed costs/Contribution margin per unit

⑤ Planning and Control Metrics

Cost variance = Actual cost − Standard (budgeted) cost

Sales (revenue) variance = Actual sales − Standard (budgeted) sales

⑥ Capital Budgeting

Payback period = Time expected to recover investment cost

Accounting rate of return = Expected annual net income/Average annual investment

Net present value (NPV) = Present value of future cash flows − Investment cost

NPV rule: 1. Compute net present value (NPV in $)
2. If NPV > 0, then accept project; If NPV < 0, then reject project

Internal rate 1. Compute internal rate of return (IRR in %)
of return rule: 2. If IRR > hurdle rate, accept project; If IRR < hurdle rate, reject project

⑦ Costing Terminology

Relevant range: Organization's normal range of operating activity.

Direct cost: Cost incurred for the benefit of one cost object.

Indirect cost: Cost incurred for the benefit of more than one cost object.

Product cost: Cost that is necessary and integral to finished products.

Period cost: Cost identified more with a time period than with finished products.

Overhead cost: Cost not separately or directly traceable to a cost object.

Relevant cost: Cost that is pertinent to a decision.

Opportunity cost: Benefit lost by choosing an action from two or more alternatives.

Sunk cost: Cost already incurred that cannot be avoided or changed.

Standard cost: Cost computed using standard price and standard quantity.

Budget: Formal statement of an organization's future plans.

Break-even point: Sales level at which an organization earns zero profit.

Incremental cost: Cost incurred only if the organization undertakes a certain action.

Transfer price: Price on transactions between divisions within a company.

⑧ Standard Cost Variances

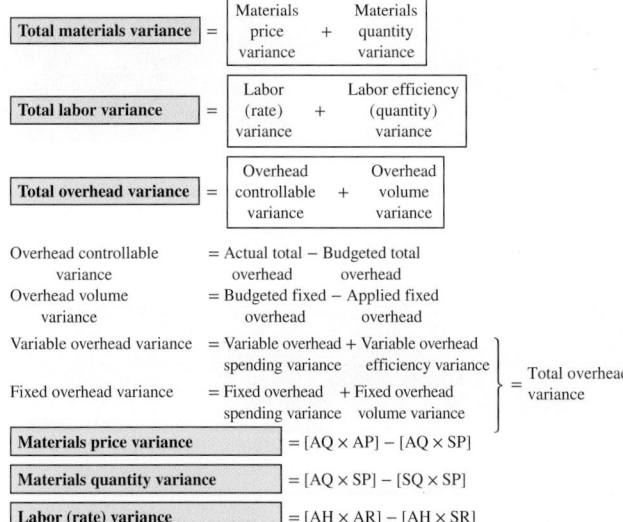

| Total materials variance | = | Materials price variance + Materials quantity variance |

| Total labor variance | = | Labor (rate) variance + Labor efficiency (quantity) variance |

| Total overhead variance | = | Overhead controllable variance + Overhead volume variance |

Overhead controllable variance = Actual total overhead − Budgeted total overhead

Overhead volume variance = Budgeted fixed overhead − Applied fixed overhead

Variable overhead variance = Variable overhead spending variance + Variable overhead efficiency variance

Fixed overhead variance = Fixed overhead spending variance + Fixed overhead volume variance

} = Total overhead variance

| Materials price variance | = [AQ × AP] − [AQ × SP] |

| Materials quantity variance | = [AQ × SP] − [SQ × SP] |

| Labor (rate) variance | = [AH × AR] − [AH × SR] |

| Labor efficiency (quantity) variance | = [AH × SR] − [SH × SR] |

Variable overhead spending variance = [AH × AVR] − [AH × SVR]

Variable overhead efficiency variance = [AH × SVR] − [SH × SVR]

Fixed overhead spending variance = Actual fixed overhead − Budgeted fixed overhead

where AQ is Actual Quantity of materials; AP is Actual Price of materials; AH is Actual Hours of labor; AR is Actual Rate of wages; AVR is Actual Variable Rate of overhead; SQ is Standard Quantity of materials; SP is Standard Price of materials; SH is Standard Hours of labor; SR is Standard Rate of wages; SVR is Standard Variable Rate of overhead.

⑨ Sales Variances

| Sales price variance | = [AS × AP] − [AS × BP] |

| Sales volume variance | = [AS × BP] − [BS × BP] |

where AS = Actual Sales units; AP = Actual sales Price; BP = Budgeted sales Price; BS = Budgeted Sales units (fixed budget).

Schedule of Cost of Goods Manufactured
For *period* Ended *date*

Direct materials		
Raw materials inventory, Beginning	$	#
Raw materials purchases		#
Raw materials available for use		#
Less raw materials inventory, Ending		(#)
Direct materials used		#
Direct labor		#
Overhead costs		
Total overhead costs		#
Total manufacturing costs		#
Add work in process inventory, Beginning		#
Total cost of work in process		#
Less work in process inventory, Ending		(#)
Cost of goods manufactured	$	#

Contribution Margin Income Statement
For *period* Ended *date*

Net sales (revenues)	$	#
Total variable costs		#
Contribution margin		#
Total fixed costs		#
Net income (pretax)	$	#

Flexible Budget
For *period* Ended *date*

	Flexible Budget		Flexible Budget for Unit Sales of #
	Variable Amount per Unit	Fixed Cost	
Sales (revenues)	$ #		$ #
Variable costs			
Examples: Direct materials, Direct labor, Other variable costs	#		#
Total variable costs	#		#
Contribution margin	$ #		#
Fixed costs			
Examples: Depreciation, Manager salaries, Administrative salaries		$ #	#
Total fixed costs		$ #	#
Income from operations			$ #

Budget Performance Report*
For *period* Ended *date*

	Budget	Actual Performance	Variances†
Sales: In units	#	#	
In dollars	$ #	$ #	$ # F or U
Cost of sales			
Direct costs	#	#	# F or U
Indirect costs	#	#	# F or U
Selling expenses			
Examples: Commissions	#	#	# F or U
Shipping expenses	#	#	# F or U
General and administrative expenses			
Examples: Administrative salaries	#	#	# F or U
Total expenses	$ #	$ #	$ # F or U
Income from operations	$ #	$ #	$ # F or U

* Applies to both flexible and fixed budgets. † F = Favorable variance; U = Unfavorable variance.

Master Budget Sequence

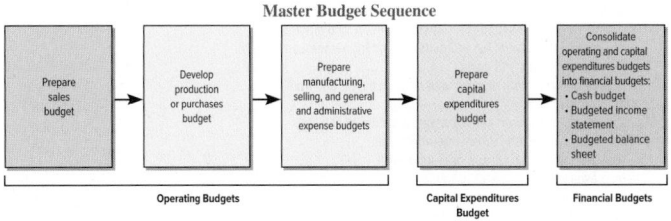

Income Statement*
For *period* Ended *date*

Net sales (revenues).	$	#
Cost of goods sold (cost of sales)		#
Gross margin (gross profit).		#
Operating expenses		
Examples: depreciation, salaries, wages, rent, utilities, ...	$ #	
interest, amortization, advertising, insurance, ...	#	
taxes, selling, general and administrative	#	
Total operating expenses.		#
Nonoperating gains and losses (unusual and/or infrequent).		#
Net income (net profit or earnings)	$	#

* A typical chart of accounts is at the end of the book and classifies all accounts by financial statement categories.

Balance Sheet
Date

ASSETS

Current assets
Examples: cash, cash equivalents, short-term investments, ...	$ #	
accounts receivable, current portion of notes receivable, ...	#	
inventory, inventory returns estimated, prepaid expenses.	#	
Total current assets	$	#

Long-term investments
Examples: investment in stock, investment in bonds, ...	#	
land for expansion.	#	
Total long-term investments		#

Plant assets
Examples: equipment, machinery, buildings, land.	#	
Total plant assets, net of depreciation		#

Intangible assets
Examples: patent, trademark, copyright, license, goodwill	#	
Total intangible assets, net of amortization		#
Total assets	$	#

LIABILITIES AND EQUITY

Current liabilities
Examples: accounts payable, wages payable, salaries payable, ...	$ #	
current notes payable, taxes payable, interest payable, ...	#	
unearned revenues, current portion of debt, sales refund payable	#	
Total current liabilities	$	#

Long-term liabilities
Examples: notes payable, bonds payable, lease liability	#	
Total long-term liabilities		#
Total liabilities		#

Equity*
Owner, capital.		#
Total liabilities and equity.	$	#

* A corporation's equity consists of: paid-in capital and retained earnings (less any treasury stock).

Statement of Cash Flows
For *period* Ended *date*

Cash flows from operating activities		
[Prepared using the indirect (see below)† or direct method]		
Net cash provided (used) by operating activities.	$	#
Cash flows from investing activities		
[List of individual investing inflows and outflows]		
Net cash provided (used) by investing activities		#
Cash flows from financing activities		
[List of individual financing inflows and outflows]		
Net cash provided (used) by financing activities		#
Net increase (decrease) in cash	$	#
Cash (and equivalents) balance at beginning of period		#
Cash (and equivalents) balance at end of period.	$	#

Attach separate schedule or note disclosure of "Noncash investing and financing transactions."

†Indirect Method: Cash Flows from Operating Activities

Cash flows from operating activities		
Net income	$	#
Adjustments for operating items not providing or using cash		
+Noncash expenses and losses.	$ #	
Examples: Expenses for depreciation, depletion, and amortization;		
losses from disposal of long-term assets and from retirement of debt		
−Noncash revenues and gains.	#	
Examples: Gains from disposal of long-term assets and from		
retirement of debt		
Adjustments for changes in current assets and current liabilities		
+Decrease in noncash current operating asset.	#	
−Increase in noncash current operating asset	#	
+Increase in current operating liability	#	
−Decrease in current operating liability.	#	
Net cash provided (used) by operating activities	$	#

Statement of Owner's Equity
For *period* Ended *date*

Owner, Capital, beginning	$	#
Add: Investments by owner	$ #	
Net income	#	#
		#
Less: Withdrawals by owner.		#
Net loss (if exists)		#
Owner, Capital, ending.	$	#

Statement of Retained Earnings (CORPORATION only)
For *period* Ended *date*

Retained earnings, beginning.	$	#
Add: Net income		#
		#
Less: Dividends declared		#
Net loss (if exists)		#
Retained earnings, ending.	$	#

Premium Bond Amortization (Straight-Line) Table†

Semiannual Period-End	Unamortized Bond Premium*	Bond Carrying Value**
Bond life-start	$ #	$ #
. . . .	:	:
Bond life-end.	0	par

† Bond carrying value is adjusted downward to par and its amortized premium downward to zero over the bond life (note: carrying value less unamortized bond premium equals par).
* Equals total bond premium less its accumulated amortization.
** Equals bond par value plus its unamortized bond premium.

Discount Bond Amortization (Straight-Line) Table†

Semiannual Period-End	Unamortized Bond Discount*	Bond Carrying Value**
Bond life-start	$ #	$ #
. . . .	:	:
Bond life-end	0	par

† Bond carrying value is adjusted upward to par and its amortized discount downward to zero over the bond life (note: unamortized bond discount plus carrying value equals par).
* Equals total bond discount less its accumulated amortization.
** Equals bond par value less its unamortized bond discount.

Effective Interest Amortization Table for Bonds with Semiannual Interest Payment

Semiannual Interest Period-End	Cash Interest Paid[A]	Bond Interest Expense[B]	Discount or Premium Amortization[C]	Unamortized Discount or Premium[D]	Carrying Value[E]
#	#	#	#	#	#
:	:	:	:	:	:

[A]Par value multiplied by the semiannual contract rate.
[B]Prior period's carrying value multiplied by the semiannual market rate.
[C]The difference between interest paid and bond interest expense.
[D]Prior period's unamortized discount or premium less the current period's discount or premium amortization.
[E]Par value less unamortized discount or plus unamortized premium.

Installment Notes Payment Table

| Period Ending Date | Beginning Balance | Payments | | | Ending Balance |
		Debit Interest Expense	Debit Notes Payable	Credit Cash	
			+	=	
#	#	#	#	#	#
:	:	:	:	:	:

Bank Reconciliation
Date

Bank statement balance	$#	Book balance.		$#
Add: Unrecorded deposits	#	Add: Unrecorded bank credits		#
Bank errors understating		Book errors understating		
the balance.	#	the balance		#
Less: Outstanding checks	#	Less: Unrecorded bank debits		#
Bank errors overstating		Book errors overstating		
the balance.	#	the balance		#
Adjusted bank balance	**$#**	**Adjusted book balance**.		**$#**

Balances are equal (reconciled)

BRIEF REVIEW: SELECTED TRANSACTIONS AND RELATIONS

① Merchandising Transactions Summary—Perpetual Inventory System

	Merchandising Transactions	Merchandising Entries	Dr.	Cr.
Purchases	Purchasing merchandise for resale.	Merchandise Inventory . . . . Cash or Accounts Payable	#	#
	Paying freight costs on purchases; FOB shipping point.	Merchandise Inventory . . . . Cash	#	#
	Paying within discount period.	Accounts Payable . . . . Merchandise Inventory . . . . Cash	#	# #
	Paying outside discount period.	Accounts Payable . . . . Cash	#	#
	Recording purchases returns or allowances.	Cash or Accounts Payable . . . . Merchandise Inventory	#	#
Sales	Selling merchandise.	Cash or Accounts Receivable . . . . Sales . . . . Cost of Goods Sold . . . . Merchandise Inventory	# #	# #
	Receiving payment within discount period.	Cash . . . . Sales Discounts . . . . Accounts Receivable	# #	#
	Receiving payment outside discount period.	Cash . . . . Accounts Receivable	#	#
	Receiving sales returns of nondefective inventory.	Sales Returns and Allowances . . . . Cash or Accounts Receivable . . . . Merchandise Inventory . . . . Cost of Goods Sold	# #	# #
	Recognizing sales allowances.	Sales Returns and Allowances . . . . Cash or Accounts Receivable	#	#
	Paying freight costs on sales; FOB destination.	Delivery Expense . . . . Cash	#	#

	Merchandising Events	Adjusting and Closing Entries	Dr.	Cr.
Adjusting	Adjustment for shrinkage (occurs when recorded amount larger than physical inventory).	Cost of Goods Sold . . . . Merchandise Inventory	#	#
	Period-end adjustment for expected sales discounts.*	Sales Discounts . . . . Allowance for Sales Discounts	#	#
	Period-end adjustment for expected returns—both revenue side and cost side.*	Sales Returns and Allowances . . . . Sales Refund Payable . . . . Inventory Returns Estimated . . . . Cost of Goods Sold	# #	# #
Closing	Closing temporary accounts with credit balances.	Sales . . . . Income Summary	#	#
	Closing temporary accounts with debit balances.	Income Summary . . . . Sales Returns and Allowances . . . . Sales Discounts . . . . Cost of Goods Sold . . . . Delivery Expense . . . . "Other Expenses"	#	# # # # #

* Period-end adjustments depend on unadjusted balances, which can reverse the debit and credit in the adjusting entries shown; the entries in gray are covered in Appendix 5C.

② Merchandising Cash Flows

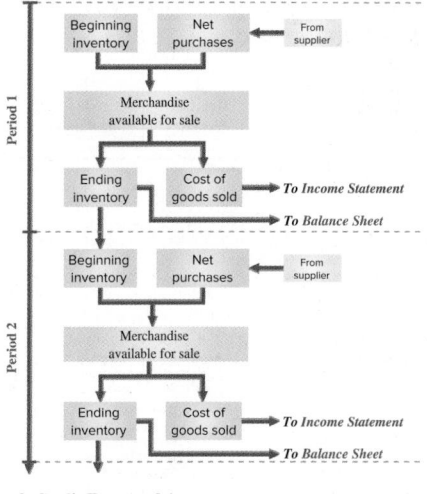

③ Credit Terms and Amounts

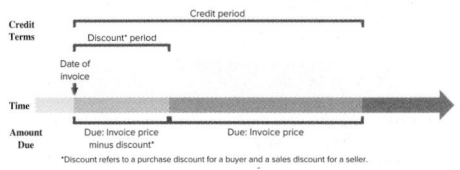

*Discount refers to a purchase discount for a buyer and a sales discount for a seller.

④ Bad Debts Estimation

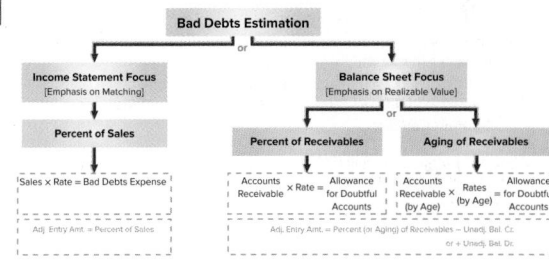

⑤ Bond Valuation

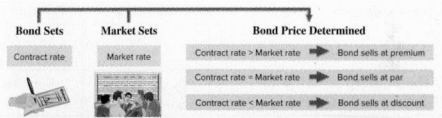

Bond Sets	Market Sets	Bond Price Determined
Contract rate	Market rate	Contract rate > Market rate ➡ Bond sells at premium
		Contract rate = Market rate ➡ Bond sells at par
		Contract rate < Market rate ➡ Bond sells at discount

⑥ Stock Transactions Summary

	Stock Transactions	Stock Entries	Dr.	Cr.
Issue Common Stock	Issue par value common stock at par (par stock recorded at par).	Cash . . . . Common Stock	#	#
	Issue par value common stock at premium (par stock recorded at par).	Cash . . . . Common Stock . . . . Paid-In Capital in Excess of Par Value, Common Stock	#	# #
	Issue no-par value common stock (no-par stock recorded at amount received).	Cash . . . . Common Stock	#	#
	Issue stated value common stock at stated value (stated stock recorded at stated value).	Cash . . . . Common Stock	#	#
	Issue stated value common stock at premium (stated stock recorded at stated value).	Cash . . . . Common Stock . . . . Paid-In Capital in Excess of Stated Value, Common Stock	#	# #
Issue Preferred Stock	Issue par value preferred stock at par (par stock recorded at par).	Cash . . . . Preferred Stock	#	#
	Issue par value preferred stock at premium (par stock recorded at par).	Cash . . . . Preferred Stock . . . . Paid-In Capital in Excess of Par Value, Preferred Stock	#	# #
Reacquire Common Stock	Reacquire its own common stock (treasury stock recorded at cost).	Treasury Stock, Common . . . . Cash	#	#
Reissue Common Stock	Reissue its treasury stock at cost (treasury stock removed at cost).	Cash . . . . Treasury Stock, Common	#	#
	Reissue its treasury stock above cost (treasury stock removed at cost).	Cash . . . . Treasury Stock, Common . . . . Paid-In Capital, Treasury	#	# #
	Reissue its treasury stock below cost (treasury stock removed at cost; if paid-in capital is insufficient to cover amount below cost, retained earnings is debited for remainder).	Cash . . . . Paid-In Capital, Treasury . . . . Retained Earnings (if necessary) . . . . Treasury Stock, Common	# # #	#

⑦ Dividend Transactions

Account Affected	Type of Dividend		
	Cash Dividend	Stock Dividend	Stock Split
Cash	Decrease	—	—
Common Stock	—	Increase	—
Retained Earnings	Decrease	Decrease	—

⑧ A Rose by Any Other Name

The same financial statement sometimes receives different titles. Following are some of the more common aliases.*

Balance Sheet	Statement of Financial Position Statement of Financial Condition
Income Statement	Statement of Income Operating Statement Statement of Operations Statement of Operating Activity Earnings Statement Statement of Earnings Profit and Loss (P&L) Statement
Statement of Cash Flows	Statement of Cash Flow Cash Flows Statement Statement of Changes in Cash Position Statement of Changes in Financial Position
Statement of Owner's Equity	Statement of Changes in Owner's Equity Statement of Changes in Owner's Capital Statement of Shareholders' Equity† Statement of Changes in Shareholders' Equity† Statement of Stockholders' Equity and Comprehensive Income† Statement of Changes in Capital Accounts†

*The term **Consolidated** often precedes or follows these statement titles to reflect the combination of different entities, such as a parent company and its subsidiaries.
† Corporation only.

FUNDAMENTALS

① Accounting Equation

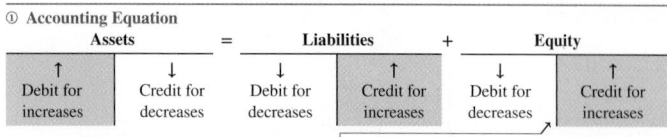

	Assets	=	Liabilities	+	Equity
	↑ Debit for increases / ↓ Credit for decreases		↓ Debit for decreases / ↑ Credit for increases		↓ Debit for decreases / ↑ Credit for increases

Owner's Capital*	−	Owner's Withdrawals*	+	Revenues	−	Expenses
↓ Dr. for decreases / ↑ Cr. for increases		↑ Dr. for increases / ↓ Cr. for decreases		↓ Dr. for decreases / ↑ Cr. for increases		↑ Dr. for increases / ↓ Cr. for decreases

▨ Indicates normal balance.

*Comparable corporate accounts are Common Stock (Paid-In Capital) and Dividends.

② Accounting Cycle

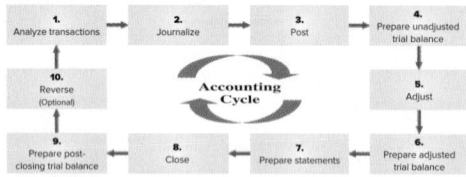

1. Analyze transactions
2. Journalize
3. Post
4. Prepare unadjusted trial balance
5. Adjust
6. Prepare adjusted trial balance
7. Prepare statements
8. Close
9. Prepare post-closing trial balance
10. Reverse (Optional)

Accounting Cycle

③ Adjustments and Entries

Type	Adjusting Entry	
Prepaid Expenses	Dr. Expense	Cr. Asset*
Unearned Revenues	Dr. Liability	Cr. Revenue
Accrued Expenses	Dr. Expense	Cr. Liability
Accrued Revenues	Dr. Asset	Cr. Revenue

* For depreciation, credit Accumulated Depreciation (contra asset).

④ Four-Step Closing Process

1. Transfer revenue and gain account balances to Income Summary.
2. Transfer expense and loss account balances to Income Summary.
3. Transfer Income Summary balance to Owner's Capital (or Retained Earnings if corp.).
4. Transfer Withdrawals balance to Owner's Capital (or Dividends to Retained Earnings if corp.).

⑤ Accounting Concepts

Characteristics	Assumptions	Principles	Constraints
Relevance	Business entity	Measurement (historical cost)	Cost-benefit
Reliability	Going concern	Revenue recognition	Materiality
Comparability	Monetary unit	Expense recognition	Industry practice
Consistency	Periodicity	Full disclosure	Conservatism

⑥ Ownership of Inventory

Shipping Terms	Ownership Transfers at	Goods in Transit Owned by	Transportation Costs Paid by
FOB shipping point	Shipping point	Buyer	Buyer — Merchandise Inventory... # / Cash... #
FOB destination	Destination	Seller	Seller — Delivery Expense... # / Cash... #

⑦ Inventory Costing Methods

- Specific identification (SI)
- First-in, first-out (FIFO)
- Weighted-average (WA)
- Last-in, first-out (LIFO)

⑧ Depreciation and Depletion

Straight-line:
$$\frac{\text{Cost} - \text{Salvage value}}{\text{Useful life in periods}}$$

Units-of-production:
$$\frac{\text{Cost} - \text{Salvage value}}{\text{Useful life in units}} \times \text{Units produced in current period}$$

Declining-balance: Rate* × Beginning-of-period book value
* Rate is often double the straight-line rate, or 2 × (1/Useful life)

Depletion:
$$\frac{\text{Cost} - \text{Salvage value}}{\text{Total capacity in units}} \times \text{Units extracted in current period}$$

⑨ Interest Computation

Interest = Principal (face) × Rate × Time

⑩ Accounting for Investment Securities

Classification*	Accounting
Short-Term Investment in Securities	
Held-to-maturity (debt) securities	**Cost** (without any discount or premium amortization)
Trading (debt and equity) securities	**Fair value** (with fair value adjustment to income)
Available-for-sale (debt and equity) securities	**Fair value** (with fair value adjustment to equity)
Long-Term Investment in Securities	
Held-to-maturity (debt) securities	**Cost** (with any discount or premium amortization)
Available-for-sale (debt and equity) securities	**Fair value** (with fair value adjustment to equity)
Equity securities with significant influence	Equity method
Equity securities with controlling influence	Equity method (with consolidation)

* A *fair value option* allows companies to report HTM and AFS securities much like trading securities.

ANALYSES

① Liquidity and Efficiency

$$\text{Current ratio} = \frac{\text{Current assets}}{\text{Current liabilities}}$$ — pp. 163 & 729

Working capital = Current assets − Current liabilities — p. 729

$$\text{Acid-test ratio} = \frac{\text{Cash} + \text{Short-term investments} + \text{Current receivables}}{\text{Current liabilities}}$$ — pp. 213 & 730

$$\text{Accounts receivable turnover} = \frac{\text{Net sales}}{\text{Average accounts receivable, net}}$$ — pp. 402 & 730

$$\text{Credit risk ratio} = \frac{\text{Allowance for doubtful accounts}}{\text{Accounts receivable, net}}$$ — p. 402

$$\text{Inventory turnover} = \frac{\text{Cost of goods sold}}{\text{Average inventory}}$$ — pp. 266 & 730

$$\text{Days' sales uncollected} = \frac{\text{Accounts receivable, net}}{\text{Net sales}} \times 365*$$ — pp. 266 & 362 & 731

$$\text{Days' sales in inventory} = \frac{\text{Ending inventory}}{\text{Cost of goods sold}} \times 365*$$ — pp. 266 & 731 & 781

$$\text{Total asset turnover} = \frac{\text{Net sales}}{\text{Average total assets}}$$ — pp. 443 & 731

$$\text{Plant asset useful life} = \frac{\text{Plant asset cost}}{\text{Depreciation expense}}$$ — p. 443

$$\text{Plant asset age} = \frac{\text{Accumulated depreciation}}{\text{Depreciation expense}}$$ — p. 444

$$\text{Days' cash expense coverage} = \frac{\text{Cash and cash equivalents}}{\text{Average daily cash expenses}}$$ — p. 348

* 360 days is also commonly used.

② Solvency

$$\text{Debt ratio} = \frac{\text{Total liabilities}}{\text{Total assets}} \qquad \text{Equity ratio} = \frac{\text{Total equity}}{\text{Total assets}}$$ — pp. 74 & 732

$$\text{Debt-to-equity} = \frac{\text{Total liabilities}}{\text{Total equity}}$$ — pp. 603 & 732

$$\text{Times interest earned} = \frac{\text{Income before interest expense and income taxes}}{\text{Interest expense}}$$ — pp. 481 & 733

$$\text{Cash coverage of growth} = \frac{\text{Cash flow from operations}}{\text{Cash outflow for plant assets}}$$ — p. 682

$$\text{Cash coverage of debt} = \frac{\text{Cash flow from operations}}{\text{Total noncurrent liabilities}}$$ — p. 682

③ Profitability

$$\text{Profit margin ratio} = \frac{\text{Net income}}{\text{Net sales}}$$ — pp. 118 & 733

$$\text{Gross margin ratio} = \frac{\text{Net sales} - \text{Cost of goods sold}}{\text{Net sales}}$$ — p. 214

$$\text{Return on total assets} = \frac{\text{Net income}}{\text{Average total assets}}$$ — pp. 22 & 642

$$= \text{Profit margin ratio} \times \text{Total asset turnover}$$ — p. 734

$$\text{Return on common stockholders' equity} = \frac{\text{Net income} - \text{Preferred dividends}}{\text{Average common stockholders' equity}}$$ — p. 734

$$\text{Book value per common share} = \frac{\text{Stockholders' equity applicable to common shares}}{\text{Number of common shares outstanding}}$$ — p. 564

$$\text{Basic earnings per share} = \frac{\text{Net income} - \text{Preferred dividends}}{\text{Weighted-average common shares outstanding}}$$ — p. 563

$$\text{Cash flow on total assets} = \frac{\text{Cash flow from operations}}{\text{Average total assets}}$$ — p. 682

$$\text{Payout ratio} = \frac{\text{Cash dividends declared on common stock}}{\text{Net income}}$$ — p. 564

④ Market

$$\text{Price-earnings ratio} = \frac{\text{Market value (price) per share}}{\text{Earnings per share}}$$ — pp. 563 & 735

$$\text{Dividend yield} = \frac{\text{Annual cash dividends per share}}{\text{Market price per share}}$$ — pp. 564 & 735

Residual income = Net income − Target net income — p. 1051